Mechanical Costs with RSMeans data

Brian Adams, Senior Editor

2023
46th annual edition

Chief Technology Officer
Chris Gaudreau

Chief Product Officer
Ted Kail

Director, Data Operations
Sam Giffin

Principal Engineer
Bob Mewis

Engineering and Research
Matthew Doheny, Sr. Manager

Engineers: Architectural Divisions
1, 3, 4, 5, 6, 7, 8, 9, 10, 11, 12, 13, 41
Sam Babbitt
Stephen Bell
Sergeleen Edouard
Richard Goldin
Scott Keller
Thomas Lane

Engineers: Civil Divisions and Wages
2, 31, 32, 33, 34, 35, 44, 46
Derrick Hale, PE
Christopher Babbitt
Michael Lynch
Elisa Mello
Giles Munyard
David Yazbek

Engineers: Mechanical, Electrical, Plumbing & Conveying Divisions
14, 21, 22, 23, 25, 26, 27, 28, 48
Joseph Kelble
Brian Adams
Michelle Curran
Antonio D'Aulerio
Thomas Lyons
Jake MacDonald

Contributing Engineers
John Melin, PE, Manager
Paul Cowan
Barry Hutchinson
Gerard Lafond, PE
Matthew Sorrentino

Production
Debra Panarelli, Manager
Jonathan Forgit
Sheryl Rose
Janice Thalin

Data Quality
Patrice Bruesch, QA Lead and Testing Strategist, Technology
David Byars
Ellen D'Amico

Cover Design
Blaire Collins

Data Management Ecosystem
Audrey Considine
Kedar Gaikwad
Todd Glowac
Srini Narla

RSMeans data from Gordian
Construction Publishers & Consultants
30 Patewood Dr., Suite 350
Greenville, SC 29615
United States of America
1.800.448.8182
rsmeans.com

Copyright 2022 by The Gordian Group Inc.
All rights reserved.
Cover photo © iStock.com/Freezingtime

Printed in the United States of America
ISSN 1524-3702
ISBN 978-1-955341-63-9

Gordian's authors, editors, and engineers apply diligence and judgment in locating and using reliable sources for the information published. However, Gordian makes no express or implied warranty or guarantee in connection with the content of the information contained herein, including the accuracy, correctness, value, sufficiency, or completeness of the data, methods, and other information contained herein. Gordian makes no express or implied warranty of merchantability or fitness for a particular purpose. Gordian shall have no liability to any customer or third party for any loss, expense, or damage, including consequential, incidental, special, or punitive damage, including lost profits or lost revenue, caused directly or indirectly by any error or omission, or arising out of, or in connection with, the information contained herein. For the purposes of this paragraph, "Gordian" shall include The Gordian Group, Inc., and its divisions, subsidiaries, successors, parent companies, and their employees, partners, principals, agents and representatives, and any third-party providers or sources of information or data. Gordian grants the purchaser of this publication limited license to use the cost data contained herein for purchaser's internal business purposes in connection with construction estimating and related work. The publication, and all cost data contained herein, may not be reproduced, integrated into any software or computer program, developed into a database or other electronic compilation, stored in an information storage or retrieval system, or transmitted or distributed to anyone in any form or by any means, electronic or mechanical, including photocopying or scanning, without prior written permission of Gordian. This publication is subject to protection under copyright law, trade secret law and other intellectual property laws of the United States, Canada and other jurisdictions. Gordian and its affiliates exclusively own and retain all rights, title and interest in and to this publication and the cost data contained herein including, without limitation, all copyright, patent, trademark and trade secret rights. Except for the limited license contained herein, your purchase of this publication does not grant you any intellectual property rights in the publication or the cost data.

 $362.00 per copy (in United States)
Price is subject to change without prior notice.

Related Data and Services

Our engineers recommend the following products and services to complement *Mechanical Costs with RSMeans data*:

Annual Cost Data Books
2023 Assemblies Costs with RSMeans data
2023 Square Foot Costs with RSMeans data

Reference Books
Estimating Building Costs
RSMeans Estimating Handbook
Green Building: Project Planning & Estimating
How to Estimate with RSMeans data
Plan Reading & Material Takeoff
Project Scheduling & Management for Construction
Universal Design Ideas for Style, Comfort & Safety

Virtual, Instructor-led & On-site Training Offerings
Unit Price Estimating
Training for Our Online Estimating Solution
Practical Project Management for Construction Professionals
Mechanical & Electrical Estimating
Square Foot & Assemblies Estimating

RSMeans data
For access to the latest cost data, an intuitive search, and an easy-to-use estimate builder, take advantage of the time savings available from our online application.

To learn more visit: **RSMeans.com/online**

Enterprise Solutions
Building owners, facility managers, building product manufacturers and attorneys across the public and private sectors engage with RSMeans data Enterprise to solve unique challenges where trusted construction cost data is critical.

To learn more visit: **RSMeans.com/Enterprise**

Custom Built Data Sets
Building and Space Models: Quickly plan construction costs across multiple locations based on geography, project size, building system component, product options and other variables for precise budgeting and cost control.

Predictive Analytics: Accurately plan future builds with custom graphical interactive dashboards, negotiate future costs of tenant build-outs and identify and compare national account pricing.

Consulting
Building Product Manufacturing Analytics: Validate your claims and assist with new product launches.

Third-Party Legal Resources: Used in cases of construction cost or estimate disputes, construction product failure vs. installation failure, eminent domain, class action construction product liability and more.

API
For resellers or internal application integration, RSMeans data is offered via API. Deliver Unit, Assembly and Square Foot Model data within your interface. To learn more about how you can provide your customers with the latest in localized construction cost data visit:
RSMeans.com/API

Table of Contents

Foreword	iv
How the Cost Data Is Built: An Overview	v
Estimating with RSMeans data: Unit Prices	vii
How to Use the Cost Data: The Details	ix
Unit Price Section	1
RSMeans data: Unit Prices—How They Work	2
Assemblies Section	495
RSMeans data: Assemblies—How They Work	498
Reference Section	607
Construction Equipment Rental Costs	609
Crew Listings	621
Historical Cost Indexes	658
City Cost Indexes	659
Location Factors	702
Reference Tables	708
Change Orders	745
Project Costs	749
Abbreviations	754
Index	758
Training Class Options	786
Labor Trade Rates including Overhead & Profit	Inside Back Cover

Foreword

The Value of RSMeans data from Gordian
Since 1942, RSMeans data has been the industry-standard materials, labor, and equipment cost information database for contractors, facility owners and managers, architects, engineers and anyone else that requires the latest localized construction cost information. More than 75 years later, the objective remains the same: to provide facility and construction professionals with the most current and comprehensive construction cost database possible.

With the constant influx of new construction methods and materials, in addition to ever-changing labor and material costs, last year's cost data is not reliable for today's designs, estimates or budgets. Gordian's cost engineers apply real-world construction experience to identify and quantify new building products and methodologies, adjust productivity rates and adjust costs to local market conditions across the nation. This adds up to more than 30,000 hours in cost research annually. This unparalleled construction cost expertise is why so many facility and construction professionals rely on RSMeans data year over year.

About Gordian
Gordian is the leading provider of facility and construction cost data, software, and services for all phases of the building lifecycle. From planning to design, procurement, construction, and operations, Gordian delivers groundbreaking solutions to contractors, architects, engineers, business and financial officers, and facility owners in local, state, and federal governments, education, healthcare, and other industries. A pioneer of Job Order Contracting (JOC), Gordian's offerings also include our proprietary RSMeans data and Facility Intelligence solutions. We develop and maintain the largest collection of labor, material, and equipment data and associated costs for all areas of construction. Gordian's solutions are accessed through our innovative software platforms and supported by a team of industry experts proven to help clients maximize efficiency, optimize cost savings, and increase building quality.

Our Commitment
At Gordian, we do more than talk about the quality of our data and the usefulness of its application. We stand behind all of our RSMeans data — from historical cost indexes to construction materials and techniques — to craft current costs and predict future trends. If you have any questions about our products or services, please call us toll-free at 800.448.8182 or visit our website at gordian.com.

How the Cost Data Is Built: An Overview

Unit Prices*
All cost data have been divided into 50 divisions according to the MasterFormat® system of classification and numbering.

Assemblies*
The cost data in this section have been organized in an "Assemblies" format. These assemblies are the functional elements of a building and are arranged according to the seven elements of the UNIFORMAT II classification system. For a complete explanation of a typical "Assembly," see "RSMeans data: Assemblies—How They Work."

Residential Models*
Model buildings for four classes of construction — economy, average, custom, and luxury — are developed and shown with complete costs per square foot.

Commercial/Industrial/Institutional Models*
This section contains complete costs for 77 typical model buildings expressed as costs per square foot.

Green Commercial/Industrial/Institutional Models*
This section contains complete costs for 25 green model buildings expressed as costs per square foot.

References*
This section includes information on Equipment Rental Costs, Crew Listings, Historical Cost Indexes, City Cost Indexes, Location Factors, Reference Tables and Change Orders, as well as a listing of abbreviations.

- **Equipment Rental Costs:** Included are the average costs to rent and operate hundreds of pieces of construction equipment.
- **Crew Listings:** This section lists all the crews referenced in the cost data. A crew is composed of more than one trade classification and/or the addition of power equipment to any trade classification. Power equipment is included in the cost of the crew. Costs are shown both with bare labor rates and with the installing contractor's overhead and profit added. For each, the total crew cost per eight-hour day and the composite cost per labor-hour are listed.

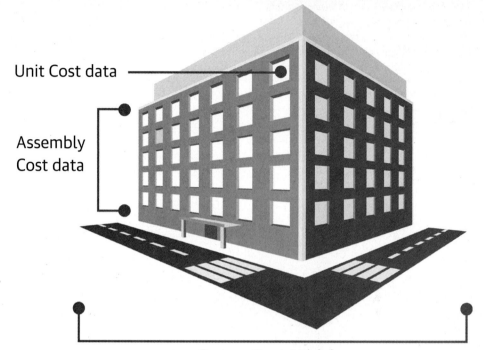

Square Foot Models

- **Historical Cost Indexes:** These indexes provide you with data to adjust construction costs over time.
- **City Cost Indexes:** All costs in this data set are U.S. national averages. Costs vary by region. You can adjust for this by CSI Division to over 730 cities in 900+ 3-digit zip codes throughout the U.S. and Canada by using this data.
- **Location Factors:** You can adjust total project costs to over 730 cities in 900+ 3-digit zip codes throughout the U.S. and Canada by using the weighted number, which applies across all divisions.
- **Reference Tables:** At the beginning of selected major classifications in the Unit Prices are reference numbers indicators. These numbers refer you to related information in the Reference Section. In this section, you'll find reference tables, explanations and estimating information that support how we develop the unit price data, technical data and estimating procedures.
- **Change Orders:** This section includes information on the factors that influence the pricing of change orders.
- **Abbreviations:** A listing of abbreviations used throughout this information, along with the terms they represent, is included.

Index (printed versions only)
A comprehensive listing of all terms and subjects will help you quickly find what you need when you are not sure where it occurs in MasterFormat®.

Conclusion
This information is designed to be as comprehensive and easy to use as possible.

The Construction Specifications Institute (CSI) and Construction Specifications Canada (CSC) have produced the 2018 edition of MasterFormat®, a system of titles and numbers used extensively to organize construction information.

All unit prices in the RSMeans cost data are now arranged in the 50-division MasterFormat® 2018 system.

---

* Not all information is available in all data sets

Note: The material prices in RSMeans cost data are "contractor's prices." They are the prices that contractors can expect to pay at the lumberyards, suppliers'/distributors' warehouses, etc. Small orders of specialty items would be higher than the costs shown, while very large orders, such as truckload lots, would be less. The variation would depend on the size, timing, and negotiating power of the contractor. The labor costs are primarily for new construction or major renovation rather than repairs or minor alterations. With reasonable exercise of judgment, the figures can be used for any building work.

Estimating with RSMeans data: Unit Prices

Following these steps will allow you to complete an accurate estimate using RSMeans data: Unit Prices.

1. Scope Out the Project
- Think through the project and identify the CSI divisions needed in your estimate.
- Identify the individual work tasks that will need to be covered in your estimate.
- The Unit Price data have been divided into 50 divisions according to CSI MasterFormat® 2018.
- In printed versions, the Unit Price Section Table of Contents on page 1 may also be helpful when scoping out your project.
- Experienced estimators find it helpful to begin with Division 2 and continue through completion. Division 1 can be estimated after the full project scope is known.

2. Quantify
- Determine the number of units required for each work task that you identified.
- Experienced estimators include an allowance for waste in their quantities. (Waste is not included in our Unit Price line items unless otherwise stated.)

3. Price the Quantities
- Use the search tools available to locate individual Unit Price line items for your estimate.
- Reference Numbers indicated within a Unit Price section refer to additional information that you may find useful.
- The crew indicates who is performing the work for that task. Crew codes are expanded in the Crew Listings in the Reference Section to include all trades and equipment that comprise the crew.
- The Daily Output is the amount of work the crew is expected to complete in one day.
- The Labor-Hours value is the amount of time it will take for the crew to install one unit of work.
- The abbreviated Unit designation indicates the unit of measure upon which the crew, productivity, and prices are based.
- Bare Costs are shown for materials, labor and equipment needed to complete the Unit Price line item. Bare costs do not include waste, project overhead, payroll insurance, payroll taxes, main office overhead or profit.
- The Total Incl O&P cost is the billing rate or invoice amount of the installing contractor or subcontractor who performs the work for the Unit Price line item.

4. Multiply
- Multiply the total number of units needed for your project by the Total Incl O&P cost for each Unit Price line item.
- Be careful that your take off unit of measure matches the unit of measure in the Unit column.
- The price you calculate is an estimate for a completed item of work.
- Keep scoping individual tasks, determining the number of units required for those tasks, matching each task with individual Unit Price line items and multiplying quantities by Total Incl O&P costs.
- An estimate completed in this manner is priced as if a subcontractor, or set of subcontractors, is performing the work. The estimate does not yet include Project Overhead or Estimate Summary components such as general contractor markups on subcontracted work, general contractor office overhead and profit, contingency and location factors.

5. Project Overhead
- Include project overhead items from Division 1-General Requirements.
- These items are needed to make the job run. They are typically, but not always, provided by the general contractor. Items include, but are not limited to, field personnel, insurance, performance bond, permits, testing, temporary utilities, field office and storage facilities, temporary scaffolding and platforms, equipment mobilization and demobilization, temporary roads and sidewalks, winter protection, temporary barricades and fencing, temporary security, temporary signs, field engineering and layout, final cleaning and commissioning.
- Each item should be quantified and matched to individual Unit Price line items in Division 1, then priced and added to your estimate.
- An alternate method of estimating project overhead costs is to apply a percentage of the total project cost — usually 5% to 15% with an average of 10% (see General Conditions).
- Include other project related expenses in your estimate such as:
  - Rented equipment not itemized in the Crew Listings
  - Rubbish handling throughout the project (see section 02 41 19.19)

6. Estimate Summary
- Include sales tax as required by laws of your state or county.
- Include the general contractor's markup on self-performed work, usually 5% to 15% with an average of 10%.
- Include the general contractor's markup on subcontracted work, usually 5% to 15% with an average of 10%.
- Include the general contractor's main office overhead and profit:
  - RSMeans data provides general guidelines on the general contractor's main office overhead (see section 01 31 13.60 and Reference Number R013113-50).
  - Markups will depend on the size of the general contractor's operations, projected annual revenue, the level of risk and the level of competition in the local area and for this project in particular.
- Include a contingency, usually 3% to 5%, if appropriate.
- Adjust your estimate to the project's location by using the City Cost Indexes or the Location Factors in the Reference Section:
  - Look at the rules in "How to Use the City Cost Indexes" to see how to apply the Indexes for your location.
  - When the proper Index or Factor has been identified for the project's location, convert it to a multiplier by dividing it by 100, then multiply that multiplier by your estimated total cost. The original estimated total cost will now be adjusted up or down from the national average to a total that is appropriate for your location.

Editors' Note:
We urge you to spend time reading and understanding the supporting material. An accurate estimate requires experience, knowledge, and careful calculation. The more you know about how we at RSMeans developed the data, the more accurate your estimate will be. In addition, it is important to take into consideration the reference material such as Equipment Listings, Crew Listings, City Cost Indexes, Location Factors, and Reference Tables.

How to Use the Cost Data: The Details

What's Behind the Numbers? The Development of Cost Data

RSMeans data engineers continually monitor developments in the construction industry to ensure reliable, thorough and up-to-date cost information. While overall construction costs may vary relative to general economic conditions, price fluctuations within the industry are dependent upon many factors. Individual price variations may, in fact, be opposite to overall economic trends. Therefore, costs are constantly tracked and complete updates are performed yearly. Also, new items are frequently added in response to changes in materials and methods.

Costs in U.S. Dollars

All costs represent U.S. national averages and are given in U.S. dollars. The City Cost Index (CCI) with RSMeans data can be used to adjust costs to a particular location. The CCI for Canada can be used to adjust U.S. national averages to local costs in Canadian dollars. No exchange rate conversion is necessary because it has already been factored in.

G The processes or products identified by the green symbol in our publications have been determined to be environmentally responsible and/or resource-efficient solely by RSMeans data engineering staff. The inclusion of the green symbol does not represent compliance with any specific industry association or standard.

Material Costs

RSMeans data engineers contact manufacturers, dealers, distributors and contractors all across the U.S. and Canada to determine national average material costs. If you have access to current material costs for your specific location, you may wish to make adjustments to reflect differences from the national average. Included within material costs are fasteners for a normal installation. RSMeans data engineers use manufacturers' recommendations, written specifications and/or standard construction practices for the sizing and spacing of fasteners. Adjustments to material costs may be required for your specific application or location. The manufacturer's warranty is assumed. Extended warranties are not included in the material costs.
Material costs do not include sales tax.

Labor Costs

Labor costs are based upon a mathematical average of trade-specific wages in 30 major U.S. cities. The type of wage (union, open shop or residential) is identified on the inside back cover of printed publications or selected by the estimator when using the electronic products. Markups for the wages can also be found on the inside back cover of printed publications and/or under the labor references found in the electronic products.

- If wage rates in your area vary from those used, or if rate increases are expected within a given year, labor costs should be adjusted accordingly.

Labor costs reflect productivity based on actual working conditions. In addition to actual installation, these figures include time spent during a normal weekday on tasks, such as material receiving and handling, mobilization at the site, site movement, breaks and cleanup.

Productivity data is developed over an extended period so as not to be influenced by abnormal variations and reflects a typical average.

Equipment Costs

Equipment costs include not only rental but also operating costs for equipment under normal use. The operating costs include parts and labor for routine servicing, such as the repair and replacement of pumps, filters and worn lines. Normal operating expendables, such as fuel, lubricants, tires and electricity (where applicable) are also included. Extraordinary operating expendables with highly variable wear patterns, such as diamond bits and blades, are excluded. These costs are included under materials. Equipment rental rates are obtained from industry sources throughout North America — contractors, suppliers, dealers, manufacturers and distributors.

Rental rates can also be treated as reimbursement costs for contractor-owned equipment. Owned equipment costs include depreciation, loan payments, interest, taxes, insurance, storage and major repairs.

Equipment costs do not include operators' wages.

Equipment Cost/Day—The cost of equipment required for each crew is included in the Crew Listings in the Reference Section (small tools that are considered essential everyday tools are not listed out separately). The Crew Listings itemize specialized tools and heavy equipment along with labor trades. The daily cost of itemized equipment included in a crew is based on dividing the weekly bare rental rate by five (5) (number of working days per week), then adding the hourly operating cost times eight (8) (the number of hours per day). This Equipment Cost/Day is shown in the last column of the Equipment Rental Costs in the Reference Section.

Mobilization, Demobilization—The cost to move construction equipment from an equipment yard or rental company to the job site and back again is not included in equipment costs. Mobilization (to the site) and demobilization (from the site) costs can be found in the Unit Price Section. If a piece of equipment is already at the job site, it is not appropriate to utilize mobilization or demobilization costs again in an estimate.

Overhead and Profit

Total Cost including O&P for the installing contractor is shown in the last column of the Unit Price and/or Assemblies. This figure is the sum of the bare material cost plus 10% for profit, the bare labor cost plus total overhead and profit, and the bare equipment cost plus 10% for profit. Details for the calculation of overhead and profit on labor are shown on the inside back cover of the printed product and in the Reference Section of the electronic product.

General Conditions

Cost data in this dataset are presented in two ways: Bare Costs and Total Cost including O&P (Overhead and Profit). General Conditions, or General Requirements, of the contract should also be added to the Total Cost including O&P when applicable. Costs for General Conditions are listed in Division 1 of the Unit Price Section and in the Reference Section.

General Conditions for the installing contractor may range from 0% to 10% of the Total Cost including O&P. For the general or prime contractor, costs for General Conditions may range from 5% to 15% of the Total Cost including O&P, with a figure of 10% as the most typical allowance. If applicable, the Assemblies and Models sections use costs that include the installing contractor's overhead and profit (O&P).

Factors Affecting Costs

Costs can vary depending upon a number of variables. Here's a listing of some factors that affect costs and points to consider.

Quality: The prices for materials and the workmanship upon which productivity is based represent sound construction work. They are also in line with industry standard and manufacturer specifications and are frequently used by federal, state and local governments.

Overtime: We have made no allowance for overtime. If you anticipate premium time or work beyond normal working hours, be sure to make an appropriate adjustment to your labor costs.

Productivity: The productivity, daily output and labor-hour figures for each line item are based on an eight-hour work day in daylight hours in moderate temperatures and up to a 14' working height unless otherwise indicated. For work that extends beyond normal work hours or is performed under adverse conditions, productivity may decrease.

Size of Project: The size, scope of work and type of construction project will have a significant impact on cost. Economies of scale can reduce costs for large projects. Unit costs can often run higher for small projects.

Location: Material prices are for metropolitan areas. However, in dense urban areas, traffic and site storage limitations may increase costs. Beyond a 20-mile radius of metropolitan areas, extra trucking or transportation charges may also increase the material costs slightly. On the other hand, lower wage rates may be in effect. Be sure to consider both of these factors when preparing an estimate, particularly if the job site is located in a central city or remote rural location. In addition, highly specialized subcontract items may require travel and per-diem expenses for mechanics.

Other Factors

- Season of year
- Contractor management
- Weather conditions
- Local union restrictions
- Building code requirements
- Availability of:
  - adequate energy
  - skilled labor
  - building materials
- Owner's special requirements/restrictions
- Safety requirements
- Environmental considerations
- Access

Unpredictable Factors: General business conditions influence "in-place" costs of all items. Substitute materials and construction methods may have to be employed. These may affect the installed cost and/or life cycle costs. Such factors may be difficult to evaluate and cannot necessarily be predicted on the basis of the job's location in a particular section of the country. Thus, where these factors apply, you may find significant but unavoidable cost variations for which you will have to apply a measure of judgment to your estimate.

Rounding of Costs

In printed publications only, all unit prices in excess of $5.00 have been rounded to make them easier to use and still maintain adequate precision of the results.

How Subcontracted Items Affect Costs

A considerable portion of all large construction jobs is usually subcontracted. In fact, the percentage done by subcontractors is constantly increasing and may run over 90%. Since the workers employed by these companies do nothing else but install their particular products, they soon become experts in that line. As a result, installation by these firms is accomplished so efficiently that the total in-place cost, even with the general contractor's overhead and profit, is no more, and often less, than if the principal contractor had handled the installation. Companies that deal with construction specialties are anxious to have their products perform well and, consequently, the installation will be the best possible.

Contingencies

The allowance for contingencies generally provides for unforeseen construction difficulties. On alterations or repair jobs, 20% is not too much. If drawings are final and only field contingencies are being considered, 2% or 3% is probably sufficient and often nothing needs to be added. Contractually, changes in plans will be covered by extras. The contractor should consider inflationary price trends and possible material shortages during the course of the job. These escalation factors are dependent upon both economic conditions and the anticipated time between the estimate and actual construction. If drawings are not complete or approved, or a budget cost is wanted, it is wise to add 5% to 10%. Contingencies, then, are a matter of judgment.

Important Estimating Considerations

The productivity, or daily output, of each craftsman or crew assumes a well-managed job where tradesmen with the proper tools and equipment, along with the appropriate construction materials, are present. Included are daily set-up and cleanup time, break time and plan layout time. Unless otherwise indicated, time for material movement on site (for items that can be transported by hand) of up to 200' into the building and to the first or second floor is also included. If material has to be transported by other means, over greater distances or to higher floors, an additional allowance should be considered by the estimator.

While horizontal movement is typically a sole function of distances, vertical transport introduces other variables that can significantly impact productivity. In an occupied building, the use of elevators (assuming access, size and required protective measures are acceptable) must be understood at the time of the estimate. For new construction, hoist wait and cycle times can easily be 15 minutes and may result in scheduled access extending beyond the normal work day. Finally, all vertical transport will impose strict weight limits likely to preclude the use of any motorized material handling.

The productivity, or daily output, also assumes installation that meets manufacturer/designer/ standard specifications. A time allowance for quality control checks, minor adjustments and any task required to ensure proper function or operation is also included. For items that require connections to services, time is included for positioning, leveling, securing the unit and making all the necessary connections (and start up where applicable) to ensure a complete installation. Estimating of the services themselves (electrical, plumbing, water, steam, hydraulics, dust collection, etc.) is separate.

In some cases, the estimator must consider the use of a crane and an appropriate crew for the installation of large or heavy items. For those situations where a crane is not included in the assigned crew and as part of the line item cost, then equipment rental costs, mobilization and demobilization costs, and operator and support personnel costs must be considered.

Labor-Hours

The labor-hours expressed in this publication are derived by dividing the total daily labor-hours for the crew by the daily output. Based on average installation time and the assumptions listed above, the labor-hours include: direct labor, indirect labor and nonproductive time. A typical day for a craftsman might include but is not limited to:

- Direct Work
  - Measuring and layout
  - Preparing materials
  - Actual installation
  - Quality assurance/quality control
- Indirect Work
  - Reading plans or specifications
  - Preparing space
  - Receiving materials
  - Material movement
  - Giving or receiving instruction
  - Miscellaneous
- Non-Work
  - Chatting
  - Personal issues
  - Breaks
  - Interruptions (i.e., sickness, weather, material or equipment shortages, etc.)

If any of the items for a typical day do not apply to the particular work or project situation, the estimator should make any necessary adjustments.

Final Checklist

Estimating can be a straightforward process provided you remember the basics. Here's a checklist of some of the steps you should remember to complete before finalizing your estimate.

Did you remember to:

- Factor in the City Cost Index for your locale?
- Take into consideration which items have been marked up and by how much?
- Mark up the entire estimate sufficiently for your purposes?
- Read the background information on techniques and technical matters that could impact your project time span and cost?
- Include all components of your project in the final estimate?
- Double check your figures for accuracy?
- Call RSMeans data engineers if you have any questions about your estimate or the data you've used? Remember, Gordian stands behind all of our products, including our extensive RSMeans data solutions. If you have any questions about your estimate, about the costs you've used from our data or even about the technical aspects of the job that may affect your estimate, feel free to call the Gordian RSMeans editors at 800.448.8182.

Save Time. Go Online.

For access to the latest cost data, an intuitive search and pre-calculated location costs, take advantage of the time savings available from our online application.

rsmeans.com/online

Unit Price Section

Table of Contents

Sect. No.		Page
	General Requirements	
01 11	Summary of Work	8
01 21	Allowances	8
01 31	Project Management and Coordination	10
01 32	Construction Progress Documentation	12
01 41	Regulatory Requirements	12
01 45	Quality Control	12
01 51	Temporary Utilities	12
01 52	Construction Facilities	13
01 54	Construction Aids	13
01 55	Vehicular Access and Parking	16
01 56	Temporary Barriers and Enclosures	16
01 58	Project Identification	18
01 66	Product Storage and Handling Requirements	18
01 74	Cleaning and Waste Management	18
01 91	Commissioning	19
01 93	Facility Maintenance	19
	Existing Conditions	
02 41	Demolition	22
02 65	Underground Storage Tank Removal	24
02 81	Transportation and Disposal of Hazardous Materials	24
02 82	Asbestos Remediation	25
02 87	Biohazard Remediation	28
	Concrete	
03 01	Maintenance of Concrete	32
03 11	Concrete Forming	32
03 15	Concrete Accessories	32
03 21	Reinforcement Bars	36
03 22	Fabric and Grid Reinforcing	36
03 30	Cast-In-Place Concrete	36
03 31	Structural Concrete	37
03 35	Concrete Finishing	38
03 54	Cast Underlayment	39
03 63	Epoxy Grouting	39
03 82	Concrete Boring	39
	Masonry	
04 05	Common Work Results for Masonry	42
04 21	Clay Unit Masonry	42
	Metals	
05 05	Common Work Results for Metals	44
05 12	Structural Steel Framing	47
	Wood, Plastics & Composites	
06 16	Sheathing	50
	Thermal & Moisture Protection	
07 65	Flexible Flashing	52
07 71	Roof Specialties	53
07 72	Roof Accessories	53
07 76	Roof Pavers	53
07 84	Firestopping	54
07 91	Preformed Joint Seals	55
07 92	Joint Sealants	56
	Openings	
08 34	Special Function Doors	60
08 91	Louvers	60
08 95	Vents	62
	Finishes	
09 22	Supports for Plaster and Gypsum Board	64
09 69	Access Flooring	64
09 91	Painting	65
	Specialties	
10 31	Manufactured Fireplaces	68
10 35	Stoves	68

Sect. No.		Page
	Equipment	
11 11	Vehicle Service Equipment	70
11 21	Retail and Service Equipment	70
11 30	Residential Equipment	71
11 32	Unit Kitchens	72
11 41	Foodservice Storage Equipment	72
11 44	Food Cooking Equipment	73
11 46	Food Dispensing Equipment	73
11 48	Foodservice Cleaning and Disposal Equipment	73
11 53	Laboratory Equipment	73
11 71	Medical Sterilizing Equipment	74
11 73	Patient Care Equipment	75
11 74	Dental Equipment	75
11 78	Mortuary Equipment	75
11 81	Facility Maintenance Equipment	76
11 82	Facility Solid Waste Handling Equipment	76
	Special Construction	
13 11	Swimming Pools	78
13 18	Ice Rinks	79
13 21	Controlled Environment Rooms	79
13 24	Special Activity Rooms	80
13 34	Fabricated Engineered Structures	81
13 47	Facility Protection	81
	Conveying Equipment	
14 91	Facility Chutes	84
14 92	Pneumatic Tube Systems	84
	Plumbing	
22 01	Operation and Maintenance of Plumbing	86
22 05	Common Work Results for Plumbing	87
22 07	Plumbing Insulation	107
22 11	Facility Water Distribution	126
22 12	Facility Potable-Water Storage Tanks	239
22 13	Facility Sanitary Sewerage	240
22 14	Facility Storm Drainage	244
22 15	General Service Compressed-Air Systems	245
22 31	Domestic Water Softeners	247
22 35	Domestic Water Heat Exchangers	247
22 41	Residential Plumbing Fixtures	247
22 51	Swimming Pool Plumbing Systems	248
22 52	Fountain Plumbing Systems	248
22 62	Vacuum Systems for Laboratory and Healthcare Facilities	248
22 63	Gas Systems for Laboratory and Healthcare Facilities	249
	Heating Ventilation Air Conditioning	
23 05	Common Work Results for HVAC	252
23 07	HVAC Insulation	266
23 09	Instrumentation and Control for HVAC	268
23 11	Facility Fuel Piping	278
23 12	Facility Fuel Pumps	281
23 13	Facility Fuel-Storage Tanks	281
23 21	Hydronic Piping and Pumps	284
23 22	Steam and Condensate Piping and Pumps	302
23 23	Refrigerant Piping	303
23 31	HVAC Ducts and Casings	306
23 33	Air Duct Accessories	321
23 34	HVAC Fans	330
23 35	Special Exhaust Systems	337
23 36	Air Terminal Units	340
23 37	Air Outlets and Inlets	341
23 38	Ventilation Hoods	350
23 41	Particulate Air Filtration	351
23 42	Gas-Phase Air Filtration	353
23 43	Electronic Air Cleaners	353
23 51	Breechings, Chimneys, and Stacks	353
23 52	Heating Boilers	361

Sect. No.		Page
23 53	Heating Boiler Feedwater Equipment	369
23 54	Furnaces	370
23 55	Fuel-Fired Heaters	373
23 56	Solar Energy Heating Equipment	376
23 57	Heat Exchangers for HVAC	378
23 61	Refrigerant Compressors	379
23 62	Packaged Compressor and Condenser Units	381
23 63	Refrigerant Condensers	381
23 64	Packaged Water Chillers	383
23 65	Cooling Towers	387
23 72	Air-to-Air Energy Recovery Equipment	389
23 73	Indoor Central-Station Air-Handling Units	389
23 74	Packaged Outdoor HVAC Equipment	391
23 76	Evaporative Air-Cooling Equipment	394
23 81	Decentralized Unitary HVAC Equipment	396
23 82	Convection Heating and Cooling Units	401
23 83	Radiant Heating Units	413
23 84	Humidity Control Equipment	419
23 91	Prefabricated Equipment Supports	420
	Electrical	
26 01	Operation and Maintenance of Electrical Systems	422
26 05	Common Work Results for Electrical	423
26 24	Switchboards and Panelboards	431
26 29	Low-Voltage Controllers	432
	Electronic Safety & Security	
28 18	Security Access Detection Equipment	436
28 23	Video Management System	436
28 31	Intrusion Detection	436
28 42	Gas Detection and Alarm	437
28 46	Fire Detection and Alarm	437
	Earthwork	
31 05	Common Work Results for Earthwork	440
31 23	Excavation and Fill	440
31 41	Shoring	454
31 52	Cofferdams	455
	Exterior Improvements	
32 12	Flexible Paving	458
32 84	Planting Irrigation	459
	Utilities	
33 01	Operation and Maintenance of Utilities	462
33 05	Common Work Results for Utilities	466
33 11	Groundwater Sources	468
33 14	Water Utility Transmission and Distribution	469
33 16	Water Utility Storage Tanks	476
33 31	Sanitary Sewerage Piping	477
33 41	Subdrainage	478
33 42	Stormwater Conveyance	479
33 52	Hydrocarbon Transmission and Distribution	482
33 61	Hydronic Energy Distribution	483
33 63	Steam Energy Distribution	485
	Pollution Control Equipment	
44 11	Particulate Control Equipment	490
	Water and Wastewater Equipment	
46 23	Grit Removal And Handling Equipment	494
46 25	Oil and Grease Separation and Removal Equipment	494

RSMeans data: Unit Prices— How They Work

All RSMeans data: Unit Prices are organized in the same way.

03 30 Cast-In-Place Concrete

03 30 53 – Miscellaneous Cast-In-Place Concrete

03 30 53.40 Concrete In Place		Crew	Daily Output	Labor-Hours	Unit	Material	2023 Bare Costs Labor	Equipment	Total	Total Incl O&P
0010	**CONCRETE IN PLACE**									
0020	Including forms (4 uses), Grade 60 rebar, concrete (Portland cement									
0050	Type I), placement and finishing unless otherwise indicated									
0500	Chimney foundations (5000 psi), over 5 C.Y.	C-14C	32.22	3.476	C.Y.	232	195	.94	427.94	545
0510	(3500 psi), under 5 C.Y.	"	23.71	4.724	"	279	265	1.28	545.28	700
3540	Equipment pad (3000 psi), 3' x 3' x 6" thick	C-14H	45	1.067	Ea.	83	61.50	.66	145.16	183
3550	4' x 4' x 6" thick		30	1.600		120	92	.99	212.99	270
3560	5' x 5' x 8" thick		18	2.667		216	153	1.65	370.65	470
3570	6' x 6' x 8" thick		14	3.429		284	197	2.13	483.13	610
3580	8' x 8' x 10" thick		8	6		590	345	3.72	938.72	1,175
3590	10' x 10' x 12" thick		5	9.600		980	550	5.95	1,535.95	1,900
3800	Footings (3000 psi), spread under 1 C.Y.	C-14C	28	4	C.Y.	257	224	1.08	482.08	620
3825	1 C.Y. to 5 C.Y.		43	2.605		330	146	.70	476.70	580
3850	Over 5 C.Y.		75	1.493		315	84	.40	399.40	470

It is important to understand the structure of RSMeans data: Unit Prices so that you can find information easily and use it correctly.

---

❶ Line Numbers

Line Numbers consist of 12 characters, which identify a unique location in the database for each task. The first six (6) or eight (8) digits conform to the Construction Specifications Institute MasterFormat® 2018. The remainder of the digits are a further breakdown in order to arrange items in understandable groups of similar tasks. Line numbers are consistent across all of our publications, so a line number in any of our products will always refer to the same item of work.

❷ Descriptions

Descriptions are shown in a hierarchical structure to make them readable. In order to read a complete description, read up through the indents to the top of the section. Include everything that is above and to the left that is not contradicted by information below. For instance, the complete description for line 03 30 53.40 3550 is "Concrete in place, including forms (4 uses), Grade 60 rebar, concrete (Portland cement Type 1), placement and finishing unless otherwise indicated; Equipment pad (3,000 psi), 4' × 4' × 6" thick."

❸ RSMeans data

When using **RSMeans data**, it is important to read through an entire section to ensure that you use the data that most closely matches your work. Note that sometimes there is additional information shown in the section that may improve your price. There are frequently lines that further describe, add to or adjust data for specific situations.

❹ Reference Information

Gordian's engineers have created **reference** information to assist you in your estimate. **If** there is information that applies to a section, it will be indicated at the start of the section. The Reference Section is located in the back of the data set.

❺ Crews

Crews include labor and/or equipment necessary to accomplish each task. In this case, Crew C-14H is used. Gordian's staff selects a crew to represent the workers and equipment that are typically used for that task. In this case, Crew C-14H consists of one carpenter foreperson (outside), two carpenters, one rodman, one laborer, one cement finisher and one gas engine vibrator. Details of all crews can be found in the Reference Section.

Crews - Standard

Crew No.	Bare Costs		Incl. Subs O&P		Cost Per Labor-Hour	
Crew C-14H	Hr.	Daily	Hr.	Daily	Bare Costs	Incl. O&P
1 Carpenter Foreman (outside)	$60.60	$484.80	$90.20	$721.60	$57.43	$85.32
2 Carpenters	58.60	937.60	87.25	1396.00		
1 Rodman (reinf.)	64.55	516.40	96.40	771.20		
1 Laborer	47.25	378.00	70.35	562.80		
1 Cement Finisher	55.00	440.00	80.45	643.60		
1 Gas Engine Vibrator		29.68		32.65	.62	.68
48 L.H., Daily Totals		$2786.48		$4127.85	$58.05	$86.00

⑥ Daily Output

The **Daily Output** is the amount of work that the crew can do in a normal 8-hour workday, including mobilization, layout, movement of materials and cleanup. In this case, crew C-14H can install thirty 4' × 4' × 6" thick concrete pads in a day. Daily output is variable and based on many factors, including the size of the job, location and environmental conditions. RSMeans data represents work done in daylight (or adequate lighting) and temperate conditions.

⑦ Labor-Hours

The figure in the **Labor-Hours** column is the amount of labor required to perform one unit of work—in this case the amount of labor required to construct one 4' × 4' equipment pad. This figure is calculated by dividing the number of hours of labor in the crew by the daily output (48 labor-hours divided by 30 pads = 1.6 hours of labor per pad). Multiply 1.6 times 60 to see the value in minutes: 60 × 1.6 = 96 minutes. Note: The labor-hour figure is not dependent on the crew size. A change in crew size will result in a corresponding change in daily output, but the labor-hours per unit of work will not change.

⑧ Unit of Measure

Unit Prices include the typical **Unit of Measure** used for estimating that item. For concrete-in-place the typical unit is cubic yards (C.Y.) or each (Ea.). For installing broadloom carpet it is square yard and for gypsum board it is square foot. The estimator needs to take special care that the unit in the data matches the unit in the take-off. Unit conversions may be found in the Reference Section.

⑨ Bare Costs

Bare Costs are the costs of materials, labor, and equipment that the installing contractor pays. They represent the cost, in U.S. dollars, for one unit of work. They do not include any markups for profit or labor burden.

⑩ Bare Total

The **Total column** represents the total bare cost for the installing contractor in U.S. dollars. In this case, the sum of $120 for material + $92 for labor + $.99 for equipment is $212.99.

⑪ Total Incl O&P

The **Total Incl O&P column** is the total cost, including overhead and profit, that the installing contractor will charge the customer. This represents the cost of materials plus 10% profit, the cost of labor plus labor burden and 10% profit, and the cost of equipment plus 10% profit. It does not include the general contractor's overhead and profit. Note: See the inside back cover of the printed product or the Reference Section of the electronic product for details on how the labor burden is calculated.

National Average

The RSMeans data in our print publications represent a "national average" cost. This data should be modified to the project location using the **City Cost Indexes** *or* **Location Factors** *tables found in the Reference Section. Use the Location Factors to adjust estimate totals if the project covers multiple trades. Use the City Cost Indexes (CCI) for single trade projects or projects where a more detailed analysis is required. All figures in the two tables are derived from the same research. The last row of data in the CCI — the weighted average — is the same as the numbers reported for each location in the location factor table.*

RSMeans data: Unit Prices— How They Work (Continued)

Project Name: Pre-Engineered Steel Building		Architect: As Shown						
Location:	Anywhere, USA						01/01/23	STD
Line Number	Description	Qty	Unit	Material	Labor	Equipment	SubContract	Estimate Total
03 30 53.40 3940	Strip footing, 12" x 24", reinforced	15	C.Y.	$3,345.00	$1,965.00	$9.45	$0.00	
03 30 53.40 3950	Strip footing, 12" x 36", reinforced	34	C.Y.	$7,140.00	$3,570.00	$17.00	$0.00	
03 11 13.65 3000	Concrete slab edge forms	500	L.F.	$415.00	$1,485.00	$0.00	$0.00	
03 22 11.10 0200	Welded wire fabric reinforcing	150	C.S.F.	$9,225.00	$5,025.00	$0.00	$0.00	
03 31 13.35 0300	Ready mix concrete, 4000 psi for slab on grade	278	C.Y.	$45,036.00	$0.00	$0.00	$0.00	
03 31 13.70 4300	Place, strike off & consolidate concrete slab	278	C.Y.	$0.00	$5,977.00	$150.12	$0.00	
03 35 13.30 0250	Machine float & trowel concrete slab	15,000	S.F.	$0.00	$10,950.00	$750.00	$0.00	
03 15 16.20 0140	Cut control joints in concrete slab	950	L.F.	$38.00	$465.50	$95.00	$0.00	
03 39 23.13 0300	Sprayed concrete curing membrane	150	C.S.F.	$2,400.00	$1,192.50	$0.00	$0.00	
Division 03	Subtotal			$67,599.00	$30,630.00	$1,021.57	$0.00	$99,250.57
08 36 13.10 2650	Manual 10' x 10' steel sectional overhead door	8	Ea.	$14,200.00	$4,160.00	$0.00	$0.00	
08 36 13.10 2860	Insulation and steel back panel for OH door	800	S.F.	$5,360.00	$0.00	$0.00	$0.00	
Division 08	Subtotal			$19,560.00	$4,160.00	$0.00	$0.00	$23,720.00
13 34 19.50 1100	Pre-Engineered Steel Building, 100' x 150' x 24'	15,000	SF Flr.	$0.00	$0.00	$0.00	$420,000.00	
13 34 19.50 6050	Framing for PESB door opening, 3' x 7'	4	Opng.	$0.00	$0.00	$0.00	$2,600.00	
13 34 19.50 6100	Framing for PESB door opening, 10' x 10'	8	Opng.	$0.00	$0.00	$0.00	$10,800.00	
13 34 19.50 6200	Framing for PESB window opening, 4' x 3'	6	Opng.	$0.00	$0.00	$0.00	$3,870.00	
13 34 19.50 5750	PESB door, 3' x 7', single leaf	4	Opng.	$3,320.00	$828.00	$0.00	$0.00	
13 34 19.50 7750	PESB sliding window, 4' x 3' with screen	6	Opng.	$3,120.00	$702.00	$67.80	$0.00	
13 34 19.50 6550	PESB gutter, eave type, 26 ga., painted	300	L.F.	$2,670.00	$969.00	$0.00	$0.00	
13 34 19.50 8650	PESB roof vent, 12" wide x 10' long	15	Ea.	$750.00	$3,870.00	$0.00	$0.00	
13 34 19.50 6900	PESB insulation, vinyl faced, 4" thick	27,400	S.F.	$42,470.00	$11,234.00	$0.00	$0.00	
Division 13	Subtotal			$52,330.00	$17,603.00	$67.80	$437,270.00	$507,270.80
			Subtotal	$139,489.00	$52,393.00	$1,089.37	$437,270.00	$630,241.37
Division 01	General Requirements @ 7%			9,764.23	3,667.51	76.26	30,608.90	
			Estimate Subtotal	$149,253.23	$56,060.51	$1,165.63	$467,878.90	$630,241.37
			Sales Tax @ 5%	7,462.66		58.28	11,696.97	
			Subtotal A	156,715.89	56,060.51	1,223.91	479,575.87	
			GC O & P	15,671.59	28,142.38	122.39	47,957.59	
			Subtotal B	172,387.48	84,202.89	1,346.30	527,533.46	$785,470.12
			Contingency @ 5%					39,273.51
			Subtotal C					$824,743.63
			Bond @ $12/1000 +10% O&P					10,886.62
			Subtotal D					$835,630.25
			Location Adjustment Factor		112.50			104,453.78
			Grand Total					$940,084.03

This estimate is based on an interactive spreadsheet. You are free to download it and adjust it to your methodology. A copy of this spreadsheet is available at **RSMeans.com/2023books**.

Sample Estimate

This sample demonstrates the elements of an estimate, including a tally of the RSMeans data lines and a summary of the markups on a contractor's work to arrive at a total cost to the owner. The Location Factor with RSMeans data is added at the bottom of the estimate to adjust the cost of the work to a specific location.

❶ Work Performed

The body of the estimate shows the RSMeans data selected, including the line number, a brief description of each item, its take-off unit and quantity, and the bare costs of materials, labor and equipment. This estimate also includes a column titled "SubContract." This data is taken from the column "Total Incl O&P" and represents the total that a subcontractor would charge a general contractor for the work, including the sub's markup for overhead and profit.

❷ Division 1, General Requirements

This is the first division numerically but the last division estimated. Division 1 includes project-wide needs provided by the general contractor. These requirements vary by project but may include temporary facilities and utilities, security, testing, project cleanup, etc. For small projects a percentage can be used — typically between 5% and 15% of project cost. For large projects the costs may be itemized and priced individually.

❸ Sales Tax

If the work is subject to state or local sales taxes, the amount must be added to the estimate. Sales tax may be added to material costs, equipment costs and subcontracted work. In this case, sales tax was added in all three categories. It was assumed that approximately half the subcontracted work would be material cost, so the tax was applied to 50% of the subcontract total.

❹ GC O&P

This entry represents the general contractor's markup on material, labor, equipment and subcontractor costs. Our standard markup on materials, equipment and subcontracted work is 10%. In this estimate, the markup on the labor performed by the GC's workers uses "Skilled Workers Average" shown in Column F on the table "Installing Contractor's Overhead & Profit," which can be found on the inside back cover of the printed product or in the Reference Section of the electronic product.

❺ Contingency

A factor for contingency may be added to any estimate to represent the cost of unknowns that may occur between the time that the estimate is performed and the time the project is constructed. The amount of the allowance will depend on the stage of design at which the estimate is done and the contractor's assessment of the risk involved. Refer to section 01 21 16.50 for contingency allowances.

❻ Bonds

Bond costs should be added to the estimate. The figures here represent a typical performance bond, ensuring the owner that if the general contractor does not complete the obligations in the construction contract the bonding company will pay the cost for completion of the work.

❼ Location Adjustment

Published prices are based on national average costs. If necessary, adjust the total cost of the project using a location factor from the "Location Factor" table or the "City Cost Index" table. Use location factors if the work is general, covering multiple trades. If the work is by a single trade (e.g., masonry) use the more specific data found in the "City Cost Indexes."

Division 1 — General Requirements

Estimating Tips

01 20 00 Price and Payment Procedures

- Allowances that should be added to estimates to cover contingencies and job conditions that are not included in the national average material and labor costs are shown in Section 01 21.
- When estimating historic preservation projects (depending on the condition of the existing structure and the owner's requirements), a 15–20% contingency or allowance is recommended, regardless of the stage of the drawings.

01 30 00 Administrative Requirements

- Before determining a final cost estimate, it is good practice to review all the items listed in Subdivisions 01 31 and 01 32 to make final adjustments for items that may need customizing to specific job conditions.
- Requirements for initial and periodic submittals can represent a significant cost to the General Requirements of a job. Thoroughly check the submittal specifications when estimating a project to determine any costs that should be included.

01 40 00 Quality Requirements

- All projects will require some degree of quality control. This cost is not included in the unit cost of construction listed in each division. Depending upon the terms of the contract, the various costs of inspection and testing can be the responsibility of either the owner or the contractor. Be sure to include the required costs in your estimate.

01 50 00 Temporary Facilities and Controls

- Barricades, access roads, safety nets, scaffolding, security, and many more requirements for the execution of a safe project are elements of direct cost. These costs can easily be overlooked when preparing an estimate. When looking through the major classifications of this subdivision, determine which items apply to each division in your estimate.
- Construction equipment rental costs can be found in the Reference Section in Section 01 54 33. Operators' wages are not included in equipment rental costs.
- Equipment mobilization and demobilization costs are not included in equipment rental costs and must be considered separately.
- The cost of small tools provided by the installing contractor for his workers is covered in the "Overhead" column on the "Installing Contractor's Overhead and Profit" table that lists labor trades, base rates, and markups. Therefore, it is included in the "Total Incl. O&P" cost of any unit price line item.

01 70 00 Execution and Closeout Requirements

- When preparing an estimate, thoroughly read the specifications to determine the requirements for Contract Closeout. Final cleaning, record documentation, operation and maintenance data, warranties and bonds, and spare parts and maintenance materials can all be elements of cost for the completion of a contract. Do not overlook these in your estimate.

Reference Numbers

Reference numbers are shown at the beginning of some major classifications. These numbers refer to related items in the Reference Section. The reference information may be an estimating procedure, an alternate pricing method, or technical information.

Note: Not all subdivisions listed here necessarily appear. ■

Same Data. Simplified.

Enjoy the convenience and efficiency of accessing your costs anywhere:

- **Skip the multiplier** by setting your location
- **Quickly search,** edit, favorite and share costs
- **Stay on top of price changes** with automatic updates

Discover more at rsmeans.com/online

No part of this cost data may be reproduced, stored in a retrieval system, or transmitted in any form or by any means without prior written permission of Gordian.

01 11 Summary of Work

01 11 31 – Professional Consultants

01 11 31.10 Architectural Fees

		Crew	Daily Output	Labor-Hours	Unit	Material	2023 Bare Costs Labor	Equipment	Total	Total Incl O&P
0010	**ARCHITECTURAL FEES** R011110-10									
2000	For "Greening" of building [G]				Project				3%	3%

01 11 31.30 Engineering Fees

		Crew	Daily Output	Labor-Hours	Unit	Material	2023 Bare Costs Labor	Equipment	Total	Total Incl O&P
0010	**ENGINEERING FEES** R011110-30									
0020	Educational planning consultant, minimum				Project				.50%	.50%
0100	Maximum				"				2.50%	2.50%
0200	Electrical, minimum				Contrct				4.10%	4.10%
0300	Maximum								10.10%	10.10%
0400	Elevator & conveying systems, minimum								2.50%	2.50%
0500	Maximum								5%	5%
0600	Food service & kitchen equipment, minimum								8%	8%
0700	Maximum								12%	12%
1000	Mechanical (plumbing & HVAC), minimum								4.10%	4.10%
1100	Maximum								10.10%	10.10%

01 21 Allowances

01 21 16 – Contingency Allowances

01 21 16.50 Contingencies

		Crew	Daily Output	Labor-Hours	Unit	Material	2023 Bare Costs Labor	Equipment	Total	Total Incl O&P
0010	**CONTINGENCIES**, Add to estimate									
0020	Conceptual stage				Project				20%	20%
0050	Schematic stage								15%	15%
0100	Preliminary working drawing stage (Design Dev.)								10%	10%
0150	Final working drawing stage								3%	3%

01 21 53 – Factors Allowance

01 21 53.50 Factors

		Crew	Daily Output	Labor-Hours	Unit	Material	2023 Bare Costs Labor	Equipment	Total	Total Incl O&P
0010	**FACTORS** Cost adjustments R012153-10									
0100	Add to construction costs for particular job requirements									
0500	Cut & patch to match existing construction, add, minimum				Costs	2%	3%			
0550	Maximum					5%	9%			
0800	Dust protection, add, minimum					1%	2%			
0850	Maximum					4%	11%			
1100	Equipment usage curtailment, add, minimum					1%	1%			
1150	Maximum					3%	10%			
1400	Material handling & storage limitation, add, minimum					1%	1%			
1450	Maximum					6%	7%			
1700	Protection of existing work, add, minimum					2%	2%			
1750	Maximum					5%	7%			
2000	Shift work requirements, add, minimum						5%			
2050	Maximum						30%			
2300	Temporary shoring and bracing, add, minimum					2%	5%			
2350	Maximum					5%	12%			

01 21 53.60 Security Factors

		Crew	Daily Output	Labor-Hours	Unit	Material	2023 Bare Costs Labor	Equipment	Total	Total Incl O&P
0010	**SECURITY FACTORS** R012153-60									
0100	Additional costs due to security requirements									
0110	Daily search of personnel, supplies, equipment and vehicles									
0120	Physical search, inventory and doc of assets, at entry				Costs		30%			
0130	At entry and exit						50%			
0140	Physical search, at entry						6.25%			
0150	At entry and exit						12.50%			
0160	Electronic scan search, at entry						2%			

01 21 Allowances

01 21 53 – Factors Allowance

01 21 53.60 Security Factors	Crew	Daily Output	Labor-Hours	Unit	Material	2023 Bare Costs Labor	Equipment	Total	Total Incl O&P
0170 At entry and exit				Costs		4%			
0180 Visual inspection only, at entry						.25%			
0190 At entry and exit						.50%			
0200 ID card or display sticker only, at entry						.12%			
0210 At entry and exit				↓		.25%			
0220 Day 1 as described below, then visual only for up to 5 day job duration									
0230 Physical search, inventory and doc of assets, at entry				Costs		5%			
0240 At entry and exit						10%			
0250 Physical search, at entry						1.25%			
0260 At entry and exit						2.50%			
0270 Electronic scan search, at entry						.42%			
0280 At entry and exit				↓		.83%			
0290 Day 1 as described below, then visual only for 6-10 day job duration									
0300 Physical search, inventory and doc of assets, at entry				Costs		2.50%			
0310 At entry and exit						5%			
0320 Physical search, at entry						.63%			
0330 At entry and exit						1.25%			
0340 Electronic scan search, at entry						.21%			
0350 At entry and exit				↓		.42%			
0360 Day 1 as described below, then visual only for 11-20 day job duration									
0370 Physical search, inventory and doc of assets, at entry				Costs		1.25%			
0380 At entry and exit						2.50%			
0390 Physical search, at entry						.31%			
0400 At entry and exit						.63%			
0410 Electronic scan search, at entry						.10%			
0420 At entry and exit				↓		.21%			
0430 Beyond 20 days, costs are negligible									
0440 Escort required to be with tradesperson during work effort				Costs		6.25%			

01 21 53.65 Infectious Disease Precautions

	Crew	Daily Output	Labor-Hours	Unit	Material	Labor	Equipment	Total	Total Incl O&P
0010 **INFECTIOUS DISEASE PRECAUTIONS** R012153-65									
0100 Additional costs due to infectious disease precautions									
0120 Daily temperature checks				Costs		1%			
0130 Donning & doffing masks and gloves						1%			
0140 Washing hands						1%			
0150 Informational meetings						2%			
0160 Maintaining social distance						1%			
0170 Disinfecting tools or equipment				↓		3%			
0200 N95 rated masks				Ea.	2.33			2.33	2.56
0210 Surgical masks				"	.74			.74	.82
0220 Black nitrile disposable gloves				Pair	.70			.70	.77
0250 Hand washing station & 2 x weekly service				Week				158	174

01 21 55 – Job Conditions Allowance

01 21 55.50 Job Conditions

	Crew	Daily Output	Labor-Hours	Unit	Material	Labor	Equipment	Total	Total Incl O&P
0010 **JOB CONDITIONS** Modifications to applicable									
0020 cost summaries									
0100 Economic conditions, favorable, deduct				Project				2%	2%
0200 Unfavorable, add								5%	5%
0300 Hoisting conditions, favorable, deduct								2%	2%
0400 Unfavorable, add								5%	5%
0700 Labor availability, surplus, deduct								1%	1%
0800 Shortage, add								10%	10%
0900 Material storage area, available, deduct				↓				1%	1%

01 21 Allowances

01 21 55 – Job Conditions Allowance

01 21 55.50 Job Conditions

		Crew	Daily Output	Labor-Hours	Unit	Material	2023 Bare Costs Labor	Equipment	Total	Total Incl O&P
1000	Not available, add				Project				2%	2%
1100	Subcontractor availability, surplus, deduct								5%	5%
1200	Shortage, add								12%	12%
1300	Work space, available, deduct								2%	2%
1400	Not available, add				▼				5%	5%

01 21 57 – Overtime Allowance

01 21 57.50 Overtime

0010	**OVERTIME** for early completion of projects or where	R012909-90								
0020	labor shortages exist, add to usual labor, up to					Costs		100%			

01 21 63 – Taxes

01 21 63.10 Taxes

0010	**TAXES**	R012909-80								
0020	Sales tax, State, average					%	5.08%			
0050	Maximum	R012909-85					7.50%			
0200	Social Security, on first $118,500 of wages							7.65%			
0300	Unemployment, combined Federal and State, minimum	R012909-86						.60%			
0350	Average							9.60%			
0400	Maximum					▼		12%			

01 31 Project Management and Coordination

01 31 13 – Project Coordination

01 31 13.20 Field Personnel

		Crew	Daily Output	Labor-Hours	Unit	Material	Labor	Equipment	Total	Total Incl O&P
0010	**FIELD PERSONNEL**									
0020	Clerk, average				Week		500		500	750
0100	Field engineer, junior engineer						1,700		1,700	2,549
0120	Engineer						2,180		2,180	3,269
0140	Senior engineer						2,660		2,660	3,989
0160	General purpose laborer, average	1 Clab	.20	40			1,900		1,900	2,825
0180	Project manager, minimum						2,175		2,175	3,262
0200	Average						2,500		2,500	3,749
0220	Maximum						2,850		2,850	4,274
0240	Superintendent, minimum						2,150		2,150	3,224
0260	Average						2,325		2,325	3,525
0280	Maximum						2,650		2,650	4,025
0290	Timekeeper, average				▼		1,350		1,350	2,050

01 31 13.30 Insurance

0010	**INSURANCE**	R013113-40								
0020	Builders risk, standard, minimum					Job				.24%	.24%
0050	Maximum	R013113-50								.80%	.80%
0200	All-risk type, minimum									.25%	.25%
0250	Maximum	R013113-60				▼				.62%	.62%
0400	Contractor's equipment floater, minimum					Value				.50%	.50%
0450	Maximum					"				1.50%	1.50%
0600	Public liability, average					Job				2.02%	2.02%
0800	Workers' compensation & employer's liability, average										
0850	by trade, carpentry, general					Payroll		8.92%			
1000	Electrical							3.92%			
1150	Insulation							8.13%			
1450	Plumbing							4.42%			
1550	Sheet metal work (HVAC)					▼		5.86%			

01 31 Project Management and Coordination

01 31 13 – Project Coordination

01 31 13.50 General Contractor's Mark-Up	Crew	Daily Output	Labor-Hours	Unit	Material	2023 Bare Costs Labor	Equipment	Total	Total Incl O&P
0010	**GENERAL CONTRACTOR'S MARK-UP** on Change Orders									
0200	Extra work, by subcontractors, add				%				10%	10%
0250	By General Contractor, add								15%	15%
0400	Omitted work, by subcontractors, deduct all but								5%	5%
0450	By General Contractor, deduct all but								7.50%	7.50%
0600	Overtime work, by subcontractors, add								15%	15%
0650	By General Contractor, add								10%	10%

01 31 13.80 Overhead and Profit									
0010	**OVERHEAD & PROFIT** Allowance to add to items in this									
0020	book that do not include Subs O&P, average				%				25%	
0100	Allowance to add to items in this book that	R013113-55								
0110	do include Subs O&P, minimum				%				5%	5%
0150	Average								10%	10%
0200	Maximum								15%	15%
0300	Typical, by size of project, under $100,000								30%	
0350	$500,000 project								25%	
0400	$2,000,000 project								20%	
0450	Over $10,000,000 project								15%	

01 31 13.90 Performance Bond									
0010	**PERFORMANCE BOND**	R013113-80								
0020	For buildings, minimum				Job				.60%	.60%
0100	Maximum				"				2.50%	2.50%

01 31 14 – Facilities Services Coordination

01 31 14.20 Lock Out/Tag Out

		Crew	Daily Output	Labor-Hours	Unit	Material	Labor	Equipment	Total	Total Incl O&P
0010	**LOCK OUT/TAG OUT**									
0020	Miniature circuit breaker lock out device	1 Elec	220	.036	Ea.	38	2.45		40.45	45
0030	Miniature pin circuit breaker lock out device		220	.036		33	2.45		35.45	40
0040	Single circuit breaker lock out device		220	.036		36	2.45		38.45	43
0050	Multi-pole circuit breaker lock out device (15 to 225 Amp)		210	.038		32.50	2.57		35.07	39.50
0060	Large 3 pole circuit breaker lock out device (over 225 Amp)		210	.038		37	2.57		39.57	44.50
0080	Square D I-Line circuit breaker lock out device		210	.038		112	2.57		114.57	127
0090	Lock out disconnect switch, 30 to 100 Amp		330	.024		23	1.63		24.63	28
0100	100 to 400 Amp		330	.024		23	1.63		24.63	28
0110	Over 400 Amp		330	.024		23	1.63		24.63	28
0120	Lock out hasp for multiple lockout tags		200	.040		7.40	2.69		10.09	12.10
0130	Electrical cord plug lock out device		220	.036		11.90	2.45		14.35	16.75
0140	Electrical plug prong lock out device (3-wire grounding plug)		220	.036		7.90	2.45		10.35	12.30
0150	Wall switch lock out		200	.040		34.50	2.69		37.19	41.50
0160	Fire alarm pull station lock out	1 Stpi	200	.040		32	2.90		34.90	39.50
0170	Sprinkler valve tamper and flow switch lock out device	1 Skwk	220	.036		30.50	2.23		32.73	37
0180	Lock out sign		330	.024		18.80	1.48		20.28	22.50
0190	Lock out tag		440	.018		5.70	1.11		6.81	7.90

01 32 Construction Progress Documentation

01 32 33 – Photographic Documentation

01 32 33.50 Photographs

		Crew	Daily Output	Labor-Hours	Unit	Material	2023 Bare Costs Labor	Equipment	Total	Total Incl O&P
0010	**PHOTOGRAPHS**									
0020	8" x 10", 4 shots, 2 prints ea., std. mounting				Set	570			570	625
0100	Hinged linen mounts					580			580	635
0200	8" x 10", 4 shots, 2 prints each, in color					600			600	660
0300	For I.D. slugs, add to all above				↓	5.35			5.35	5.85
1500	Time lapse equipment, camera and projector, buy				Ea.	2,725			2,725	2,975
1550	Rent per month				"	1,375			1,375	1,525
1700	Cameraman and processing, black & white				Day	1,350			1,350	1,500
1720	Color				"	1,600			1,600	1,750

01 41 Regulatory Requirements

01 41 26 – Permit Requirements

01 41 26.50 Permits

		Crew	Daily Output	Labor-Hours	Unit	Material	2023 Bare Costs Labor	Equipment	Total	Total Incl O&P
0010	**PERMITS**									
0020	Rule of thumb, most cities, minimum				Job				.50%	.50%
0100	Maximum				"				2%	2%

01 45 Quality Control

01 45 23 – Testing and Inspecting Services

01 45 23.50 Testing

		Crew	Daily Output	Labor-Hours	Unit	Material	2023 Bare Costs Labor	Equipment	Total	Total Incl O&P
0010	**TESTING** and Inspecting Services									
5820	Non-destructive metal testing, dye penetrant				Day				556	612
5840	Magnetic particle								556	612
5860	Radiography								556	612
5880	Ultrasonic				↓				556	612
9000	Thermographic testing, for bldg envelope heat loss, average 2,000 S.F. G				Ea.				500	500

01 51 Temporary Utilities

01 51 13 – Temporary Electricity

01 51 13.80 Temporary Utilities

		Crew	Daily Output	Labor-Hours	Unit	Material	2023 Bare Costs Labor	Equipment	Total	Total Incl O&P
0010	**TEMPORARY UTILITIES**									
0350	Lighting, lamps, wiring, outlets, 40,000 S.F. building, 8 strings	1 Elec	34	.235	CSF Flr	3.58	15.85		19.43	27.50
0360	16 strings	"	17	.471		7.15	31.50		38.65	55
0400	Power for temp lighting only, 6.6 KWH, per month								.92	1.01
0430	11.8 KWH, per month								1.65	1.82
0450	23.6 KWH, per month								3.30	3.63
0600	Power for job duration incl. elevator, etc., minimum								53	58
0650	Maximum				↓				110	121
0675	Temporary cooling				Ea.	1,100			1,100	1,225

01 52 Construction Facilities

01 52 13 – Field Offices and Sheds

01 52 13.20 Office and Storage Space

		Crew	Daily Output	Labor-Hours	Unit	Material	2023 Bare Costs Labor	Equipment	Total	Total Incl O&P
0010	OFFICE AND STORAGE SPACE									
0020	Office trailer, furnished, no hookups, 20' x 8', buy	2 Skwk	1	16	Ea.	10,500	980		11,480	13,000
0250	Rent per month					201			201	221
0300	32' x 8', buy	2 Skwk	.70	22.857		15,800	1,400		17,200	19,400
0350	Rent per month					255			255	280
0400	50' x 10', buy	2 Skwk	.60	26.667		31,900	1,625		33,525	37,600
0450	Rent per month					370			370	405
0500	50' x 12', buy	2 Skwk	.50	32		27,100	1,950		29,050	32,800
0550	Rent per month					475			475	520
0700	For air conditioning, rent per month, add					55.50			55.50	61
0800	For delivery, add per mile				Mile	12.55			12.55	13.80
0900	Bunk house trailer, 8' x 40' duplex dorm with kitchen, no hookups, buy	2 Carp	1	16	Ea.	93,500	940		94,440	104,500
0910	9 man with kitchen and bath, no hookups, buy		1	16		95,500	940		96,440	106,500
0920	18 man sleeper with bath, no hookups, buy		1	16		103,000	940		103,940	115,000
1000	Portable buildings, prefab, on skids, economy, 8' x 8'		265	.060	S.F.	105	3.54		108.54	121
1100	Deluxe, 8' x 12'		150	.107	"	90.50	6.25		96.75	109
1200	Storage boxes, 20' x 8', buy	2 Skwk	1.80	8.889	Ea.	5,025	545		5,570	6,350
1250	Rent per month					126			126	138
1300	40' x 8', buy	2 Skwk	1.40	11.429		7,925	700		8,625	9,775
1350	Rent per month					155			155	170

01 52 13.40 Field Office Expense

		Crew	Daily Output	Labor-Hours	Unit	Material	Labor	Equipment	Total	Total Incl O&P
0010	FIELD OFFICE EXPENSE									
0100	Office equipment rental average				Month	239			239	263
0120	Office supplies, average				"	94.50			94.50	104
0125	Office trailer rental, see Section 01 52 13.20									
0140	Telephone bill; avg. bill/month incl. long dist.				Month	91.50			91.50	100
0160	Lights & HVAC				"	171			171	188

01 54 Construction Aids

01 54 16 – Temporary Hoists

01 54 16.50 Weekly Forklift Crew

		Crew	Daily Output	Labor-Hours	Unit	Material	Labor	Equipment	Total	Total Incl O&P
0010	WEEKLY FORKLIFT CREW									
0100	All-terrain forklift, 45' lift, 35' reach, 9000 lb. capacity	A-3P	.20	40	Week		2,400	3,375	5,775	7,250

01 54 19 – Temporary Cranes

01 54 19.50 Daily Crane Crews

		Crew	Daily Output	Labor-Hours	Unit	Material	Labor	Equipment	Total	Total Incl O&P
0010	DAILY CRANE CREWS for small jobs, portal to portal R015433-15									
0100	12-ton truck-mounted hydraulic crane	A-3H	1	8	Day		530	2,150	2,680	3,175
0200	25-ton	A-3I	1	8			530	2,275	2,805	3,300
0300	40-ton	A-3J	1	8			530	2,450	2,980	3,500
0400	55-ton	A-3K	1	16			980	2,625	3,605	4,325
0500	80-ton	A-3L	1	16			980	2,800	3,780	4,525
0900	If crane is needed on a Saturday, Sunday or Holiday									
0910	At time-and-a-half, add				Day		50%			
0920	At double time, add				"		100%			

01 54 19.60 Monthly Tower Crane Crew

		Crew	Daily Output	Labor-Hours	Unit	Material	Labor	Equipment	Total	Total Incl O&P
0010	MONTHLY TOWER CRANE CREW, excludes concrete footing									
0100	Static tower crane, 130' high, 106' jib, 6200 lb. capacity	A-3N	.05	176	Month		11,700	41,600	53,300	63,000

01 54 Construction Aids

01 54 23 – Temporary Scaffolding and Platforms

01 54 23.70 Scaffolding		Crew	Daily Output	Labor-Hours	Unit	Material	2023 Bare Costs Labor	2023 Bare Costs Equipment	Total	Total Incl O&P
0010	**SCAFFOLDING** R015423-10									
0015	Steel tube, regular, no plank, labor only to erect & dismantle									
0090	Building exterior, wall face, 1 to 5 stories, 6'-4" x 5' frames	3 Carp	8	3	C.S.F.		176		176	262
0200	6 to 12 stories	4 Carp	8	4			234		234	350
0301	13 to 20 stories	5 Clab	8	5			236		236	350
0460	Building interior, wall face area, up to 16' high	3 Carp	12	2			117		117	175
0560	16' to 40' high		10	2.400	↓		141		141	209
0800	Building interior floor area, up to 30' high		150	.160	C.C.F.		9.40		9.40	13.95
0900	Over 30' high	4 Carp	160	.200	"		11.70		11.70	17.45
0906	Complete system for face of walls, no plank, material only rent/mo				C.S.F.	95.50			95.50	105
0908	Interior spaces, no plank, material only rent/mo				C.C.F.	6.30			6.30	6.95
0910	Steel tubular, heavy duty shoring, buy									
0920	Frames 5' high 2' wide				Ea.	83			83	91.50
0925	5' high 4' wide					99.50			99.50	110
0930	6' high 2' wide					100			100	110
0935	6' high 4' wide				↓	124			124	136
0940	Accessories									
0945	Cross braces				Ea.	21			21	23
0950	U-head, 8" x 8"					18.40			18.40	20.50
0955	J-head, 4" x 8"					17.05			17.05	18.75
0960	Base plate, 7" x 7"					15.45			15.45	17
0965	Leveling jack				↓	19.25			19.25	21
1000	Steel tubular, regular, buy									
1100	Frames 3' high 5' wide				Ea.	92			92	101
1150	5' high 5' wide					111			111	122
1200	6'-4" high 5' wide					119			119	131
1350	7'-6" high 6' wide					98.50			98.50	108
1500	Accessories, cross braces					17.20			17.20	18.95
1550	Guardrail post					17.05			17.05	18.75
1600	Guardrail 7' section					10.75			10.75	11.80
1650	Screw jacks & plates					20.50			20.50	22.50
1700	Sidearm brackets					14.50			14.50	15.95
1750	8" casters					34			34	37.50
1800	Plank 2" x 10" x 16'-0"					77.50			77.50	85.50
1900	Stairway section					360			360	395
1910	Stairway starter bar					18.15			18.15	20
1920	Stairway inside handrail					102			102	112
1930	Stairway outside handrail					112			112	123
1940	Walk-thru frame guardrail				↓	51.50			51.50	56.50
2000	Steel tubular, regular, rent/mo.									
2100	Frames 3' high 5' wide				Ea.	10.70			10.70	11.75
2150	5' high 5' wide					10.70			10.70	11.75
2200	6'-4" high 5' wide					7			7	7.70
2250	7'-6" high 6' wide					12.10			12.10	13.30
2500	Accessories, cross braces					3			3	3.30
2550	Guardrail post					3.60			3.60	3.96
2600	Guardrail 7' section					13.55			13.55	14.90
2650	Screw jacks & plates					4.50			4.50	4.95
2700	Sidearm brackets					12			12	13.20
2750	8" casters					10			10	11
2800	Outrigger for rolling tower					12.75			12.75	14.05
2850	Plank 2" x 10" x 16'-0"					12.10			12.10	13.30

01 54 Construction Aids

01 54 23 – Temporary Scaffolding and Platforms

01 54 23.70 Scaffolding

		Crew	Daily Output	Labor-Hours	Unit	Material	2023 Bare Costs Labor	2023 Bare Costs Equipment	Total	Total Incl O&P
2900	Stairway section				Ea.	39			39	43
2940	Walk-thru frame guardrail				↓	10.80			10.80	11.90
3000	Steel tubular, heavy duty shoring, rent/mo.									
3250	5' high 2' & 4' wide				Ea.	10.30			10.30	11.30
3300	6' high 2' & 4' wide					10.30			10.30	11.30
3500	Accessories, cross braces					1.11			1.11	1.22
3600	U-head, 8" x 8"					3.03			3.03	3.33
3650	J-head, 4" x 8"					3.03			3.03	3.33
3700	Base plate, 8" x 8"					1.11			1.11	1.22
3750	Leveling jack					3.01			3.01	3.31
5700	Planks, 2" x 10" x 16'-0", labor only to erect & remove to 50' H	3 Carp	72	.333			19.55		19.55	29
5800	Over 50' high	4 Carp	80	.400	↓		23.50		23.50	35
6000	Heavy duty shoring for elevated slab forms to 8'-2" high, floor area									
6100	Labor only to erect & dismantle	4 Carp	16	2	C.S.F.		117		117	175
6110	Materials only, rent/mo.				"	53			53	58.50
6500	To 14'-8" high									
6600	Labor only to erect & dismantle	4 Carp	10	3.200	C.S.F.		188		188	279
6610	Materials only, rent/mo				"	77.50			77.50	85.50

01 54 23.75 Scaffolding Specialties

		Crew	Daily Output	Labor-Hours	Unit	Material	Labor	Equipment	Total	Total Incl O&P
0010	**SCAFFOLDING SPECIALTIES**									
1200	Sidewalk bridge, heavy duty steel posts & beams, including									
1210	parapet protection & waterproofing (material cost is rent/month)									
1220	8' to 10' wide, 2 posts	3 Carp	15	1.600	L.F.	69.50	94		163.50	216
1230	3 posts	"	10	2.400	"	101	141		242	320
1500	Sidewalk bridge using tubular steel scaffold frames including									
1510	planking (material cost is rent/month)	3 Carp	45	.533	L.F.	11.40	31.50		42.90	59
1600	For 2 uses per month, deduct from all above					50%				
1700	For 1 use every 2 months, add to all above					100%				
1900	Catwalks, 20" wide, no guardrails, 7' span, buy				Ea.	229			229	252
2000	10' span, buy					291			291	320
3720	Putlog, standard, 8' span, with hangers, buy					49			49	54
3730	Rent per month					17.15			17.15	18.85
3750	12' span, buy					106			106	116
3755	Rent per month					21.50			21.50	23.50
3760	Trussed type, 16' span, buy					545			545	600
3770	Rent per month					25.50			25.50	28
3790	22' span, buy					550			550	605
3795	Rent per month					34			34	37.50
3800	Rolling ladders with handrails, 30" wide, buy, 2 step					296			296	325
4000	7 step					900			900	990
4050	10 step					1,275			1,275	1,400
4100	Rolling towers, buy, 5' wide, 7' long, 10' high					1,425			1,425	1,550
4200	For additional 5' high sections, to buy				↓	257			257	283
4300	Complete incl. wheels, railings, outriggers,									
4350	21' high, to buy				Ea.	2,175			2,175	2,400
4400	Rent/month = 5% of purchase cost				"	109			109	119

01 54 36 – Equipment Mobilization

01 54 36.50 Mobilization

		Crew	Daily Output	Labor-Hours	Unit	Material	Labor	Equipment	Total	Total Incl O&P
0010	**MOBILIZATION** (Use line item again for demobilization) R015436-50									
0015	Up to 25 mi. haul dist. (50 mi. RT for mob/demob crew)									
1200	Small equipment, placed in rear of, or towed by pickup truck	A-3A	4	2	Ea.		119	48	167	231
1300	Equipment hauled on 3-ton capacity towed trailer	A-3Q	2.67	3	↓		179	101	280	380

01 54 Construction Aids

01 54 36 – Equipment Mobilization

01 54 36.50 Mobilization

		Crew	Daily Output	Labor-Hours	Unit	Material	2023 Bare Costs Labor	2023 Bare Costs Equipment	Total	Total Incl O&P
1400	20-ton capacity	B-34U	2	8	Ea.		460	245	705	955
1500	40-ton capacity	B-34N	2	8			475	375	850	1,125
1600	50-ton capacity	B-34V	1	24			1,450	1,200	2,650	3,500
1700	Crane, truck-mounted, up to 75 ton (driver only)	1 Eqhv	4	2			133		133	197
1800	Over 75 ton (with chase vehicle)	A-3E	2.50	6.400			390	76.50	466.50	665
2400	Crane, large lattice boom, requiring assembly	B-34W	.50	144	↓		8,375	8,450	16,825	21,800
2500	For each additional 5 miles haul distance, add						10%	10%		
3000	For large pieces of equipment, allow for assembly/knockdown									
3100	For mob/demob of micro-tunneling equip, see Section 33 05 07.36									

01 55 Vehicular Access and Parking

01 55 23 – Temporary Roads

01 55 23.50 Roads and Sidewalks

		Crew	Daily Output	Labor-Hours	Unit	Material	Labor	Equipment	Total	Total Incl O&P
0010	**ROADS AND SIDEWALKS** Temporary									
0050	Roads, gravel fill, no surfacing, 4" gravel depth	B-14	715	.067	S.Y.	8.25	3.33	.39	11.97	14.45
0100	8" gravel depth	"	615	.078	"	16.45	3.88	.45	20.78	24.50
1000	Ramp, 3/4" plywood on 2" x 6" joists, 16" OC	2 Carp	300	.053	S.F.	3.56	3.13		6.69	8.55
1100	On 2" x 10" joists, 16" OC	"	275	.058	"	5.25	3.41		8.66	10.85

01 56 Temporary Barriers and Enclosures

01 56 13 – Temporary Air Barriers

01 56 13.60 Tarpaulins

		Crew	Daily Output	Labor-Hours	Unit	Material	Labor	Equipment	Total	Total Incl O&P
0010	**TARPAULINS**									
0020	Cotton duck, 10-13.13 oz./S.Y., 6' x 8'				S.F.	.81			.81	.89
0050	30' x 30'					.60			.60	.66
0100	Polyvinyl coated nylon, 14-18 oz., minimum					1.14			1.14	1.25
0150	Maximum					1.38			1.38	1.52
0200	Reinforced polyethylene 3 mils thick, white					.25			.25	.28
0300	4 mils thick, white, clear or black					.11			.11	.12
0400	5.5 mils thick, clear					.11			.11	.12
0500	White, fire retardant					.50			.50	.55
0600	12 mils, oil resistant, fire retardant					.49			.49	.54
0700	8.5 mils, black					.41			.41	.45
0710	Woven polyethylene, 6 mils thick					.07			.07	.08
0730	Polyester reinforced w/integral fastening system, 11 mils thick					.16			.16	.18
0740	Polyethylene, reflective, 23 mils thick				↓	1.30			1.30	1.43

01 56 13.90 Winter Protection

		Crew	Daily Output	Labor-Hours	Unit	Material	Labor	Equipment	Total	Total Incl O&P
0010	**WINTER PROTECTION**									
0100	Framing to close openings	2 Clab	500	.032	S.F.	1.19	1.51		2.70	3.56
0200	Tarpaulins hung over scaffolding, 8 uses, not incl. scaffolding		1500	.011		.24	.50		.74	1.01
0250	Tarpaulin polyester reinf. w/integral fastening system, 11 mils thick		1600	.010		.20	.47		.67	.92
0300	Prefab fiberglass panels, steel frame, 8 uses	↓	1200	.013	↓	3.19	.63		3.82	4.45

01 56 16 – Temporary Dust Barriers

01 56 16.10 Dust Barriers, Temporary

		Crew	Daily Output	Labor-Hours	Unit	Material	Labor	Equipment	Total	Total Incl O&P
0010	**DUST BARRIERS, TEMPORARY**, erect and dismantle									
0020	Spring loaded telescoping pole & head, to 12', erect and dismantle	1 Clab	240	.033	Ea.		1.58		1.58	2.35
0025	Cost per day (based upon 250 days)				Day	.61			.61	.67
0030	To 21', erect and dismantle	1 Clab	240	.033	Ea.		1.58		1.58	2.35

01 56 Temporary Barriers and Enclosures

01 56 16 – Temporary Dust Barriers

01 56 16.10 Dust Barriers, Temporary

		Crew	Daily Output	Labor-Hours	Unit	Material	2023 Bare Costs Labor	Equipment	Total	Total Incl O&P
0035	Cost per day (based upon 250 days)				Day	1.21			1.21	1.33
0040	Accessories, caution tape reel, erect and dismantle	1 Clab	480	.017	Ea.		.79		.79	1.17
0045	Cost per day (based upon 250 days)				Day	.31			.31	.34
0060	Foam rail and connector, erect and dismantle	1 Clab	240	.033	Ea.		1.58		1.58	2.35
0065	Cost per day (based upon 250 days)				Day	.26			.26	.29
0070	Caution tape	1 Clab	384	.021	C.L.F.	1.99	.98		2.97	3.66
0080	Zipper, standard duty		60	.133	Ea.	16.15	6.30		22.45	27
0090	Heavy duty		48	.167	"	23.50	7.90		31.40	38
0100	Polyethylene sheet, 4 mil		37	.216	Sq.	5.35	10.20		15.55	21
0110	6 mil		37	.216	"	6.85	10.20		17.05	22.50
1000	Dust partition, 6 mil polyethylene, 1" x 3" frame	2 Carp	2000	.008	S.F.	.39	.47		.86	1.13
1080	2" x 4" frame	"	2000	.008	"	.91	.47		1.38	1.70
1085	Negative air machine, 1800 CFM				Ea.	990			990	1,100
1090	Adhesive strip application, 2" width	1 Clab	192	.042	C.L.F.	13.50	1.97		15.47	17.80
4000	Dust & infectious control partition, adj. to 10' high, obscured, 4' panel	2 Carp	90	.178	Ea.	595	10.40		605.40	670
4010	3' panel		90	.178		560	10.40		570.40	635
4020	2' panel		90	.178		440	10.40		450.40	500
4030	1' panel	1 Carp	90	.089		292	5.20		297.20	330
4040	6" panel	"	90	.089		270	5.20		275.20	305
4050	2' panel with HEPA filtered discharge port	2 Carp	90	.178		510	10.40		520.40	575
4060	3' panel with 32" door		90	.178		920	10.40		930.40	1,025
4070	4' panel with 36" door		90	.178		1,025	10.40		1,035.40	1,150
4080	4'-6" panel with 44" door		90	.178		1,225	10.40		1,235.40	1,375
4090	Hinged corner		80	.200		188	11.70		199.70	223
4100	Outside corner		80	.200		156	11.70		167.70	188
4110	T post		80	.200		166	11.70		177.70	199
4120	Accessories, ceiling grid clip		360	.044		7.25	2.60		9.85	11.90
4130	Panel locking clip		360	.044		5	2.60		7.60	9.40
4140	Panel joint closure strip		360	.044		8.30	2.60		10.90	13
4150	Screw jack		360	.044		7.15	2.60		9.75	11.80
4160	Digital pressure difference gauge					290			290	320
4180	Combination lockset	1 Carp	13	.615		205	36		241	279
4185	Sealant tape, 2" wide	1 Clab	192	.042	C.L.F.	13.50	1.97		15.47	17.80
4190	System in place, including door and accessories									
4200	Based upon 25 uses	2 Carp	51	.314	L.F.	10.05	18.40		28.45	38.50
4210	Based upon 50 uses		51	.314		5.05	18.40		23.45	33
4230	Based upon 100 uses		51	.314		2.51	18.40		20.91	30.50

01 56 23 – Temporary Barricades

01 56 23.10 Barricades

		Crew	Daily Output	Labor-Hours	Unit	Material	2023 Bare Costs Labor	Equipment	Total	Total Incl O&P
0010	**BARRICADES**									
0020	5' high, 3 rail @ 2" x 8", fixed	2 Carp	20	.800	L.F.	13.45	47		60.45	85
0150	Movable		30	.533		12.15	31.50		43.65	60
1000	Guardrail, wooden, 3' high, 1" x 6" on 2" x 4" posts		200	.080		2.48	4.69		7.17	9.75
1100	2" x 6" on 4" x 4" posts		165	.097		4.26	5.70		9.96	13.15
1200	Portable metal with base pads, buy					17.25			17.25	18.95
1250	Typical installation, assume 10 reuses	2 Carp	600	.027		2.87	1.56		4.43	5.50
1300	Barricade tape, polyethylene, 7 mil, 3" wide x 300' long roll	1 Clab	128	.063	Ea.	5.95	2.95		8.90	10.95
3000	Detour signs, set up and remove									
3010	Reflective aluminum, MUTCD, 24" x 24", post mounted	1 Clab	20	.400	Ea.	4.26	18.90		23.16	32.50
4000	Roof edge portable barrier stands and warning flags, 50 uses	1 Rohe	9100	.001	L.F.	.10	.03		.13	.17
4010	100 uses	"	9100	.001	"	.05	.03		.08	.12

01 56 Temporary Barriers and Enclosures

01 56 26 – Temporary Fencing

01 56 26.50 Temporary Fencing

		Crew	Daily Output	Labor-Hours	Unit	Material	2023 Bare Costs Labor	Equipment	Total	Total Incl O&P
0010	**TEMPORARY FENCING**									
0020	Chain link, 11 ga., 4' high	2 Clab	400	.040	L.F.	2.20	1.89		4.09	5.25
0100	6' high		300	.053		5.35	2.52		7.87	9.65
0200	Rented chain link, 6' high, to 1000' (up to 12 mo.)		400	.040		3.16	1.89		5.05	6.30
0250	Over 1000' (up to 12 mo.)		300	.053		3.73	2.52		6.25	7.85
0350	Plywood, painted, 2" x 4" frame, 4' high	A-4	135	.178		9.60	9.90		19.50	25.50
0400	4" x 4" frame, 8' high	"	110	.218		18.30	12.15		30.45	38
0500	Wire mesh on 4" x 4" posts, 4' high	2 Carp	100	.160		13.05	9.40		22.45	28.50
0550	8' high	"	80	.200		19.65	11.70		31.35	39

01 56 29 – Temporary Protective Walkways

01 56 29.50 Protection

		Crew	Daily Output	Labor-Hours	Unit	Material	2023 Bare Costs Labor	Equipment	Total	Total Incl O&P
0010	**PROTECTION**									
0020	Stair tread, 2" x 12" planks, 1 use	1 Carp	75	.107	Tread	12.75	6.25		19	23.50
0100	Exterior plywood, 1/2" thick, 1 use		65	.123		3.47	7.20		10.67	14.55
0200	3/4" thick, 1 use		60	.133		5.15	7.80		12.95	17.30
2200	Sidewalks, 2" x 12" planks, 2 uses		350	.023	S.F.	2.12	1.34		3.46	4.33
2300	Exterior plywood, 2 uses, 1/2" thick		750	.011		.58	.63		1.21	1.57
2400	5/8" thick		650	.012		.69	.72		1.41	1.82
2500	3/4" thick		600	.013		.86	.78		1.64	2.10

01 58 Project Identification

01 58 13 – Temporary Project Signage

01 58 13.50 Signs

		Crew	Daily Output	Labor-Hours	Unit	Material	2023 Bare Costs Labor	Equipment	Total	Total Incl O&P
0010	**SIGNS**									
0020	High intensity reflectorized, no posts, buy				Ea.	16.35			16.35	17.95

01 66 Product Storage and Handling Requirements

01 66 19 – Material Handling

01 66 19.10 Material Handling

		Crew	Daily Output	Labor-Hours	Unit	Material	2023 Bare Costs Labor	Equipment	Total	Total Incl O&P
0010	**MATERIAL HANDLING**									
0020	Above 2nd story, via stairs, per C.Y. of material per floor	2 Clab	145	.110	C.Y.		5.20		5.20	7.75
0030	Via elevator, per C.Y. of material		240	.067			3.15		3.15	4.69
0050	Distances greater than 200', per C.Y. of material per each addl 200'		300	.053			2.52		2.52	3.75

01 74 Cleaning and Waste Management

01 74 13 – Progress Cleaning

01 74 13.20 Cleaning Up

		Crew	Daily Output	Labor-Hours	Unit	Material	2023 Bare Costs Labor	Equipment	Total	Total Incl O&P
0010	**CLEANING UP**									
0020	After job completion, allow, minimum				Job				.30%	.30%
0040	Maximum				"				1%	1%
0050	Cleanup of floor area, continuous, per day, during const.	A-5	24	.750	M.S.F.	4.56	36	3.77	44.33	62.50
0100	Final by GC at end of job	"	11.50	1.565	"	4.82	75	7.85	87.67	126

01 91 Commissioning

01 91 13 – General Commissioning Requirements

01 91 13.50 Building Commissioning	Crew	Daily Output	Labor-Hours	Unit	Material	2023 Bare Costs Labor	Equipment	Total	Total Incl O&P
0010 **BUILDING COMMISSIONING**									
0100 Systems operation and verification during turnover				%				.25%	.25%
0150 Including all systems subcontractors								.50%	.50%
0200 Systems design assistance, operation, verification and training								.50%	.50%
0250 Including all systems subcontractors				▼				1%	1%

01 93 Facility Maintenance

01 93 13 – Facility Maintenance Procedures

01 93 13.15 Mechanical Facilities Maintenance

		Crew	Daily Output	Labor-Hours	Unit	Material	Labor	Equipment	Total	Total Incl O&P
0010	**MECHANICAL FACILITIES MAINTENANCE**									
0100	Air conditioning system maintenance									
0130	Belt, replace	1 Stpi	15	.533	Ea.		38.50		38.50	57.50
0170	Fan, clean		16	.500			36.50		36.50	54
0180	Filter, remove, clean, replace		12	.667			48.50		48.50	72
0190	Flexible coupling alignment, inspect		40	.200			14.50		14.50	21.50
0200	Gas leak, locate and repair		4	2			145		145	216
0250	Pump packing gland, remove and replace		11	.727			53		53	78.50
0270	Tighten		32	.250			18.15		18.15	27
0290	Pump, disassemble and assemble		4	2			145		145	216
0300	Air pressure regulator, disassemble, clean, assemble	1 Skwk	4	2			123		123	184
0310	Repair or replace part	"	6	1.333			81.50		81.50	123
0320	Purging system	1 Stpi	16	.500			36.50		36.50	54
0400	Compressor, air, remove or install fan wheel	1 Skwk	20	.400			24.50		24.50	37
0410	Disassemble or assemble 2 cylinder, 2 stage		4	2			123		123	184
0420	4 cylinder, 4 stage		1	8			490		490	735
0430	Repair or replace part	▼	2	4	▼		245		245	370
0700	Demolition, for mech. demolition see Section 23 05 05.10 or 22 05 05.10									
0800	Ductwork, clean									
0810	Rectangular									
0820	6" G	1 Shee	187.50	.043	L.F.		2.99		2.99	4.51
0830	8" G		140.63	.057			3.99		3.99	6
0840	10" G		112.50	.071			4.99		4.99	7.50
0850	12" G		93.75	.085			6		6	9
0860	14" G		80.36	.100			7		7	10.50
0870	16" G	▼	70.31	.114	▼		8		8	12.05
0900	Round									
0910	4" G	1 Shee	358.10	.022	L.F.		1.57		1.57	2.36
0920	6" G		238.73	.034			2.35		2.35	3.54
0930	8" G		179.05	.045			3.13		3.13	4.72
0940	10" G		143.24	.056			3.92		3.92	5.90
0950	12" G		119.37	.067			4.70		4.70	7.10
0960	16" G	▼	89.52	.089	▼		6.25		6.25	9.45
1000	Expansion joint, not screwed, install or remove	1 Stpi	3	2.667	Ea.		193		193	289
1010	Repack	"	6	1.333	"		96.50		96.50	144
1200	Fire protection equipment									
1220	Fire hydrant, replace	Q-1	3	5.333	Ea.		345		345	515
1230	Service, lubricate, inspect, flush, clean	1 Plum	7	1.143			82.50		82.50	123
1240	Test	"	11	.727	▼		52.50		52.50	78
1310	Inspect valves, pressure, nozzle	1 Spri	4	2	System		142		142	211
1800	Plumbing fixtures, for installation see Section 22 41 00									
1801	Plumbing fixtures									

01 93 Facility Maintenance

01 93 13 – Facility Maintenance Procedures

01 93 13.15 Mechanical Facilities Maintenance		Crew	Daily Output	Labor-Hours	Unit	Material	2023 Bare Costs Labor	2023 Bare Costs Equipment	Total	Total Incl O&P
1850	Open drain with toilet auger	1 Plum	16	.500	Ea.		36		36	53.50
1870	Plaster trap, clean	"	6	1.333			96		96	143
1881	Clean commode	1 Clab	20	.400		.27	18.90		19.17	28.50
1882	Clean commode seat		48	.167		.13	7.90		8.03	11.90
1884	Clean double sink		20	.400		.27	18.90		19.17	28.50
1886	Clean bathtub		12	.667		.53	31.50		32.03	47.50
1888	Clean fiberglass tub/shower		8	1		.67	47.50		48.17	71
1889	Clean faucet set		32	.250		.11	11.80		11.91	17.70
1891	Clean shower head		80	.100		.01	4.73		4.74	7.05
1893	Clean water heater		16	.500		.93	23.50		24.43	36
1900	Relief valve, test and adjust	1 Stpi	20	.400			29		29	43.50
1910	Clean pump, heater, or motor for whirlpool	1 Clab	16	.500		.13	23.50		23.63	35
1920	Clean thermal cover for whirlpool	"	16	.500		1.33	23.50		24.83	36.50
2000	Repair or replace, steam trap	1 Stpi	8	1			72.50		72.50	108
2020	Y-type or bell strainer		6	1.333			96.50		96.50	144
2040	Water trap or vacuum breaker, screwed joints		13	.615			44.50		44.50	66.50
2100	Steam specialties, clean									
2120	Air separator with automatic trap, 1" fittings	1 Stpi	12	.667	Ea.		48.50		48.50	72
2130	Bucket trap, 2" pipe		7	1.143			83		83	124
2150	Drip leg, 2" fitting		45	.178			12.90		12.90	19.25
2200	Thermodynamic trap, 1" fittings		50	.160			11.60		11.60	17.30
2210	Thermostatic		65	.123			8.95		8.95	13.30
2240	Screen and seat in Y-type strainer, plug type		25	.320			23		23	34.50
2242	Screen and seat in Y-type strainer, flange type		12	.667			48.50		48.50	72
2500	Valve, replace broken handwheel		24	.333			24		24	36
3000	Valve, overhaul, regulator, relief, flushometer, mixing									
3040	Cold water, gas	1 Stpi	5	1.600	Ea.		116		116	173
3050	Hot water, steam		3	2.667			193		193	289
3080	Globe, gate, check up to 4" cold water, gas		10	.800			58		58	86.50
3090	Hot water, steam		5	1.600			116		116	173
3100	Over 4" ID hot or cold line		1.40	5.714			415		415	620
3120	Remove and replace, gate, globe or check up to 4"	Q-5	6	2.667			174		174	260
3130	Over 4"	"	2	8			520		520	780
3150	Repack up to 4"	1 Stpi	13	.615			44.50		44.50	66.50
3160	Over 4"	"	4	2			145		145	216

Division 2 Existing Conditions

Estimating Tips
02 30 00 Subsurface Investigation
In preparing estimates on structures involving earthwork or foundations, all information concerning soil characteristics should be obtained. Look particularly for hazardous waste, evidence of prior dumping of debris, and previous stream beds.

02 40 00 Demolition and Structure Moving
The costs shown for selective demolition do not include rubbish handling or disposal. These items should be estimated separately using RSMeans data or other sources.

- Historic preservation often requires that the contractor remove materials from the existing structure, rehab them, and replace them. The estimator must be aware of any related measures and precautions that must be taken when doing selective demolition and cutting and patching. Requirements may include special handling and storage, as well as security.
- In addition to Subdivision 02 41 00, you can find selective demolition items in each division. Example: Roofing demolition is in Division 7.
- Absent of any other specific reference, an approximate demolish-in-place cost can be obtained by halving the new-install labor cost. To remove for reuse, allow the entire new-install labor figure.

02 40 00 Building Deconstruction
This section provides costs for the careful dismantling and recycling of most low-rise building materials.

02 50 00 Containment of Hazardous Waste
This section addresses on-site hazardous waste disposal costs.

02 80 00 Hazardous Material Disposal/Remediation
This subdivision includes information on hazardous waste handling, asbestos remediation, lead remediation, and mold remediation. See reference numbers R028213-20 and R028319-60 for further guidance in using these unit price lines.

02 90 00 Monitoring Chemical Sampling, Testing Analysis
This section provides costs for on-site sampling and testing hazardous waste.

Reference Numbers
Reference numbers are shown at the beginning of some major classifications. These numbers refer to related items in the Reference Section. The reference information may be an estimating procedure, an alternate pricing method, or technical information.

Note: Not all subdivisions listed here necessarily appear. ∎

Same Data. Simplified.
Enjoy the convenience and efficiency of accessing your costs anywhere:
- **Skip the multiplier** by setting your location
- **Quickly search,** edit, favorite and share costs
- **Stay on top of price changes** with automatic updates

Discover more at rsmeans.com/online

No part of this cost data may be reproduced, stored in a retrieval system, or transmitted in any form or by any means without prior written permission of Gordian.

02 41 Demolition

02 41 13 – Selective Site Demolition

02 41 13.17 Demolish, Remove Pavement and Curb

		Crew	Daily Output	Labor-Hours	Unit	Material	2023 Bare Costs Labor	2023 Bare Costs Equipment	Total	Total Incl O&P
0010	**DEMOLISH, REMOVE PAVEMENT AND CURB** R024119-10									
5010	Pavement removal, bituminous roads, up to 3" thick	B-38	690	.058	S.Y.		3.09	1.93	5.02	6.70
5050	4"-6" thick		420	.095			5.10	3.17	8.27	11.05
5100	Bituminous driveways		640	.063			3.33	2.08	5.41	7.25
5200	Concrete to 6" thick, hydraulic hammer, mesh reinforced		255	.157			8.35	5.20	13.55	18.20
5300	Rod reinforced		200	.200	↓		10.65	6.65	17.30	23
5400	Concrete, 7"-24" thick, plain		33	1.212	C.Y.		64.50	40.50	105	141
5500	Reinforced		24	1.667	"		89	55.50	144.50	193
5600	With hand held air equipment, bituminous, to 6" thick	B-39	1900	.025	S.F.		1.25	.16	1.41	2.05
5700	Concrete to 6" thick, no reinforcing		1600	.030			1.49	.20	1.69	2.43
5800	Mesh reinforced		1400	.034			1.70	.22	1.92	2.78
5900	Rod reinforced	↓	765	.063	↓		3.12	.41	3.53	5.10

02 41 13.23 Utility Line Removal

		Crew	Daily Output	Labor-Hours	Unit	Material	Labor	Equipment	Total	Total Incl O&P
0010	**UTILITY LINE REMOVAL**									
0015	No hauling, abandon catch basin or manhole	B-6	7	3.429	Ea.		176	39.50	215.50	305
0020	Remove existing catch basin or manhole, masonry		4	6			310	69.50	379.50	535
0030	Catch basin or manhole frames and covers, stored		13	1.846			95	21.50	116.50	165
0040	Remove and reset	↓	7	3.429			176	39.50	215.50	305
0900	Hydrants, fire, remove only	B-21A	5	8			470	128	598	835
0950	Remove and reset	"	2	20	↓		1,175	320	1,495	2,100

02 41 13.30 Minor Site Demolition

		Crew	Daily Output	Labor-Hours	Unit	Material	Labor	Equipment	Total	Total Incl O&P
0010	**MINOR SITE DEMOLITION** R024119-10									
4000	Sidewalk removal, bituminous, 2" thick	B-6	350	.069	S.Y.		3.52	.79	4.31	6.10
4010	2-1/2" thick		325	.074			3.80	.85	4.65	6.60
4050	Brick, set in mortar		185	.130			6.65	1.50	8.15	11.60
4100	Concrete, plain, 4"		160	.150			7.70	1.73	9.43	13.40
4110	Plain, 5"		140	.171			8.80	1.98	10.78	15.30
4120	Plain, 6"		120	.200			10.30	2.31	12.61	17.85
4200	Mesh reinforced, concrete, 4"		150	.160			8.20	1.85	10.05	14.30
4210	5" thick		131	.183			9.40	2.12	11.52	16.35
4220	6" thick	↓	112	.214	↓		11	2.48	13.48	19.10

02 41 19 – Selective Demolition

02 41 19.13 Selective Building Demolition

0010	**SELECTIVE BUILDING DEMOLITION**
0020	Costs related to selective demolition of specific building components
0025	are included under Common Work Results (XX 05)
0030	in the component's appropriate division.

02 41 19.19 Selective Demolition

		Crew	Daily Output	Labor-Hours	Unit	Material	Labor	Equipment	Total	Total Incl O&P
0010	**SELECTIVE DEMOLITION**, Rubbish Handling R024119-10									
0020	The following are to be added to the demolition prices									
0600	Dumpster, weekly rental, 1 dump/week, 6 C.Y. capacity (2 tons)				Week	415			415	455
0700	10 C.Y. capacity (3 tons)					480			480	530
0725	20 C.Y. capacity (5 tons) R024119-20					565			565	625
0800	30 C.Y. capacity (7 tons)					730			730	800
0840	40 C.Y. capacity (10 tons)				↓	775			775	850
2000	Load, haul, dump and return, 0'-50' haul, hand carried	2 Clab	24	.667	C.Y.		31.50		31.50	47
2005	Wheeled		37	.432			20.50		20.50	30.50
2040	0'-100' haul, hand carried		16.50	.970			46		46	68
2045	Wheeled		25	.640			30		30	45
2050	Forklift	A-3R	25	.320			19.10	12.45	31.55	42
2080	Haul and return, add per each extra 100' haul, hand carried	2 Clab	35.50	.451	↓		21.50		21.50	31.50

02 41 Demolition

02 41 19 – Selective Demolition

02 41 19.19 Selective Demolition

		Crew	Daily Output	Labor-Hours	Unit	Material	2023 Bare Costs Labor	Equipment	Total	Total Incl O&P
2085	Wheeled	2 Clab	54	.296	C.Y.		14		14	21
2120	For travel in elevators, up to 10 floors, add		140	.114			5.40		5.40	8.05
2130	0'-50' haul, incl. up to 5 riser stairs, hand carried		23	.696			33		33	49
2135	Wheeled		35	.457			21.50		21.50	32
2140	6-10 riser stairs, hand carried		22	.727			34.50		34.50	51
2145	Wheeled		34	.471			22		22	33
2150	11-20 riser stairs, hand carried		20	.800			38		38	56.50
2155	Wheeled		31	.516			24.50		24.50	36.50
2160	21-40 riser stairs, hand carried		16	1			47.50		47.50	70.50
2165	Wheeled		24	.667			31.50		31.50	47
2170	0'-100' haul, incl. 5 riser stairs, hand carried		15	1.067			50.50		50.50	75
2175	Wheeled		23	.696			33		33	49
2180	6-10 riser stairs, hand carried		14	1.143			54		54	80.50
2185	Wheeled		21	.762			36		36	53.50
2190	11-20 riser stairs, hand carried		12	1.333			63		63	94
2195	Wheeled		18	.889			42		42	62.50
2200	21-40 riser stairs, hand carried		8	2			94.50		94.50	141
2205	Wheeled		12	1.333			63		63	94
2210	Haul and return, add per each extra 100' haul, hand carried		35.50	.451			21.50		21.50	31.50
2215	Wheeled		54	.296			14		14	21
2220	For each additional flight of stairs, up to 5 risers, add		550	.029	Flight		1.37		1.37	2.05
2225	6-10 risers, add		275	.058			2.75		2.75	4.09
2230	11-20 risers, add		138	.116			5.50		5.50	8.15
2235	21-40 risers, add		69	.232			10.95		10.95	16.30
3000	Loading & trucking, including 2 mile haul, chute loaded	B-16	45	.711	C.Y.		35.50	17.60	53.10	72.50
3040	Hand loading truck, 50' haul	"	48	.667			33	16.50	49.50	67.50
3080	Machine loading truck	B-17	120	.267			14	5.80	19.80	27.50
5000	Haul, per mile, up to 8 C.Y. truck	B-34B	1165	.007			.38	.68	1.06	1.32
5100	Over 8 C.Y. truck	"	1550	.005			.29	.51	.80	.99

02 41 19.20 Selective Demolition, Dump Charges

		Crew	Daily Output	Labor-Hours	Unit	Material	Labor	Equipment	Total	Total Incl O&P
0010	**SELECTIVE DEMOLITION, DUMP CHARGES** R024119-10									
0020	Dump charges, typical urban city, tipping fees only									
0100	Building construction materials				Ton	74			74	81
0200	Trees, brush, lumber					63			63	69.50
0300	Rubbish only					63			63	69.50
0500	Reclamation station, usual charge					74			74	81

02 41 19.27 Selective Demolition, Torch Cutting

		Crew	Daily Output	Labor-Hours	Unit	Material	Labor	Equipment	Total	Total Incl O&P
0010	**SELECTIVE DEMOLITION, TORCH CUTTING** R024119-10									
0020	Steel, 1" thick plate	E-25	333	.024	L.F.	2.91	1.60	.04	4.55	5.70
0040	1" diameter bar	"	600	.013	Ea.	.48	.89	.02	1.39	1.93
1000	Oxygen lance cutting, reinforced concrete walls									
1040	12"-16" thick walls	1 Clab	10	.800	L.F.		38		38	56.50
1080	24" thick walls	"	6	1.333	"		63		63	94

02 65 Underground Storage Tank Removal

02 65 10 – Underground Tank and Contaminated Soil Removal

02 65 10.30 Removal of Underground Storage Tanks		Crew	Daily Output	Labor-Hours	Unit	Material	2023 Bare Costs Labor	2023 Bare Costs Equipment	Total	Total Incl O&P
0010	**REMOVAL OF UNDERGROUND STORAGE TANKS** R026510-20									
0011	Petroleum storage tanks, non-leaking									
0100	Excavate & load onto trailer									
0110	3,000 gal. to 5,000 gal. tank	G	B-14	4	12	Ea.		595	69	664	960
0120	6,000 gal. to 8,000 gal. tank	G	B-3A	3	13.333			670	395	1,065	1,425
0130	9,000 gal. to 12,000 gal. tank	G	"	2	20	↓		1,000	595	1,595	2,150
0190	Known leaking tank, add					%				100%	100%
0200	Remove sludge, water and remaining product from bottom										
0201	of tank with vacuum truck										
0300	3,000 gal. to 5,000 gal. tank	G	A-13	5	1.600	Ea.		95.50	164	259.50	320
0310	6,000 gal. to 8,000 gal. tank	G		4	2			119	205	324	405
0320	9,000 gal. to 12,000 gal. tank	G	↓	3	2.667	↓		159	273	432	535
0390	Dispose of sludge off-site, average					Gal.				6.25	6.80
0400	Insert inert solid CO_2 "dry ice" into tank										
0401	For cleaning/transporting tanks (1.5 lb./100 gal. cap)	G	1 Clab	500	.016	Lb.	1.35	.76		2.11	2.62
1020	Haul tank to certified salvage dump, 100 miles round trip										
1023	3,000 gal. to 5,000 gal. tank					Ea.				760	830
1026	6,000 gal. to 8,000 gal. tank									880	960
1029	9,000 gal. to 12,000 gal. tank					↓				1,050	1,150
1100	Disposal of contaminated soil to landfill										
1110	Minimum					C.Y.				145	160
1111	Maximum					"				400	440
1120	Disposal of contaminated soil to										
1121	bituminous concrete batch plant										
1130	Minimum					C.Y.				80	88
1131	Maximum					"				115	125
2010	Decontamination of soil on site incl poly tarp on top/bottom										
2011	Soil containment berm and chemical treatment										
2020	Minimum	G	B-11C	100	.160	C.Y.	8.45	8.80	2.77	20.02	25.50
2021	Maximum	G	"	100	.160		10.95	8.80	2.77	22.52	28.50
2050	Disposal of decontaminated soil, minimum									135	150
2055	Maximum					↓				400	440

02 81 Transportation and Disposal of Hazardous Materials

02 81 20 – Hazardous Waste Handling

02 81 20.10 Hazardous Waste Cleanup/Pickup/Disposal

		Crew	Daily Output	Labor-Hours	Unit	Material	Labor	Equipment	Total	Total Incl O&P
0010	**HAZARDOUS WASTE CLEANUP/PICKUP/DISPOSAL**									
0100	For contractor rental equipment, i.e., dozer,									
0110	Front end loader, dump truck, etc., see 01 54 33 Reference Section									
1000	Solid pickup									
1100	55 gal. drums					Ea.				240	265
1120	Bulk material, minimum					Ton				190	210
1130	Maximum					"				595	655
1200	Transportation to disposal site										
1220	Truckload = 80 drums or 25 C.Y. or 18 tons										
1260	Minimum					Mile				3.95	4.45
1270	Maximum					"				7.25	7.98
3000	Liquid pickup, vacuum truck, stainless steel tank										
3100	Minimum charge, 4 hours										
3110	1 compartment, 2200 gallon					Hr.				140	155
3120	2 compartment, 5000 gallon					"				200	225

02 81 Transportation and Disposal of Hazardous Materials

02 81 20 – Hazardous Waste Handling

02 81 20.10 Hazardous Waste Cleanup/Pickup/Disposal	Crew	Daily Output	Labor-Hours	Unit	Material	2023 Bare Costs Labor	Equipment	Total	Total Incl O&P
3400 Transportation in 6900 gallon bulk truck				Mile				7.95	8.75
3410 In teflon lined truck				"				10.20	11.25
5000 Heavy sludge or dry vacuumable material				Hr.				140	155
6000 Dumpsite disposal charge, minimum				Ton				140	155
6020 Maximum				"				415	455

02 82 Asbestos Remediation

02 82 13 – Asbestos Abatement

02 82 13.39 Asbestos Remediation Plans and Methods

	Crew	Daily Output	Labor-Hours	Unit	Material	2023 Bare Costs Labor	Equipment	Total	Total Incl O&P
0010 **ASBESTOS REMEDIATION PLANS AND METHODS**									
0100 Building Survey-Commercial Building				Ea.				2,200	2,400
0200 Asbestos Abatement Remediation Plan				"				1,350	1,475

02 82 13.41 Asbestos Abatement Equipment

	Crew	Daily Output	Labor-Hours	Unit	Material	2023 Bare Costs Labor	Equipment	Total	Total Incl O&P
0010 **ASBESTOS ABATEMENT EQUIPMENT** R028213-20									
0011 Equipment and supplies, buy									
0200 Air filtration device, 2000 CFM				Ea.	1,050			1,050	1,150
0250 Large volume air sampling pump, minimum					291			291	320
0260 Maximum					1,450			1,450	1,600
0300 Airless sprayer unit, 2 gun					2,600			2,600	2,850
0350 Light stand, 500 watt					31.50			31.50	34.50
0400 Personal respirators									
0410 Negative pressure, 1/2 face, dual operation, minimum				Ea.	28			28	31
0420 Maximum					28.50			28.50	31.50
0450 P.A.P.R., full face, minimum					840			840	925
0460 Maximum					1,075			1,075	1,175
0470 Supplied air, full face, including air line, minimum					254			254	279
0480 Maximum					1,025			1,025	1,125
0500 Personnel sampling pump					310			310	340
1500 Power panel, 20 unit, including GFI					675			675	745
1600 Shower unit, including pump and filters					965			965	1,050
1700 Supplied air system (type C)					3,925			3,925	4,325
1750 Vacuum cleaner, HEPA, 16 gal., stainless steel, wet/dry					1,450			1,450	1,600
1760 55 gallon					1,850			1,850	2,050
1800 Vacuum loader, 9-18 ton/hr.					135,500			135,500	149,000
1900 Water atomizer unit, including 55 gal. drum					283			283	310
2000 Worker protection, whole body, foot, head cover & gloves, plastic					10.60			10.60	11.65
2500 Respirator, single use					2			2	2.20
2550 Cartridge for respirator					14.50			14.50	15.95
2570 Glove bag, 7 mil, 50" x 64"					12.50			12.50	13.75
2580 10 mil, 44" x 60"					12.65			12.65	13.90
2590 6 mil, 44" x 60"					7.75			7.75	8.55
6000 Disposable polyethylene bags, 6 mil, 3 C.F.					1.20			1.20	1.32
6300 Disposable fiber drums, 55gal					29			29	31.50
6400 Pressure sensitive caution labels, 3" x 5"					3.26			3.26	3.59
6450 11" x 17"					17.60			17.60	19.35
6500 Negative air machine, 1800 CFM					990			990	1,100

02 82 13.42 Preparation of Asbestos Containment Area

	Crew	Daily Output	Labor-Hours	Unit	Material	2023 Bare Costs Labor	Equipment	Total	Total Incl O&P
0010 **PREPARATION OF ASBESTOS CONTAINMENT AREA** R028213-20									
0100 Pre-cleaning, HEPA vacuum and wet wipe, flat surfaces	A-9	12000	.005	S.F.	.02	.35		.37	.56
0200 Protect carpeted area, 2 layers 6 mil poly on 3/4" plywood	"	1000	.064		2.82	4.18		7	9.50

02 82 Asbestos Remediation

02 82 13 – Asbestos Abatement

02 82 13.42 Preparation of Asbestos Containment Area

		Crew	Daily Output	Labor-Hours	Unit	Material	2023 Bare Costs Labor	Equipment	Total	Total Incl O&P
0300	Separation barrier, 2" x 4" @ 16", 1/2" plywood ea. side, 8' high	2 Carp	400	.040	S.F.	4.99	2.34		7.33	9
0310	12' high		320	.050		4.85	2.93		7.78	9.70
0320	16' high		200	.080		4.78	4.69		9.47	12.25
0400	Personnel decontam. chamber, 2" x 4" @ 16", 3/4" ply ea. side		280	.057		5.95	3.35		9.30	11.55
0450	Waste decontam. chamber, 2" x 4" studs @ 16", 3/4" ply ea. side	↓	360	.044	↓	5.95	2.60		8.55	10.45
0500	Cover surfaces with polyethylene sheeting									
0501	Including glue and tape									
0550	Floors, each layer, 6 mil	A-9	8000	.008	S.F.	.07	.52		.59	.88
0551	4 mil		9000	.007		.06	.46		.52	.77
0560	Walls, each layer, 6 mil		6000	.011		.07	.70		.77	1.15
0561	4 mil	↓	7000	.009	↓	.06	.60		.66	.97
0570	For heights above 14', add						20%			
0575	For heights above 20', add						30%			
0580	For fire retardant poly, add					100%				
0590	For large open areas, deduct					10%	20%			
0600	Seal floor penetrations with foam firestop to 36 sq. in.	2 Carp	200	.080	Ea.	20.50	4.69		25.19	29.50
0610	36 sq. in. to 72 sq. in.		125	.128		41	7.50		48.50	56
0615	72 sq. in. to 144 sq. in.		80	.200		82	11.70		93.70	107
0620	Wall penetrations, to 36 sq. in.		180	.089		20.50	5.20		25.70	30.50
0630	36 sq. in. to 72 sq. in.		100	.160		41	9.40		50.40	59
0640	72 sq. in. to 144 sq. in.	↓	60	.267		82	15.65		97.65	114
0800	Caulk seams with latex	1 Carp	230	.035	L.F.	.21	2.04		2.25	3.26
0900	Set up neg. air machine, 1-2k CFM/25 M.C.F. volume	1 Asbe	4.30	1.860	Ea.		121		121	186
0950	Set up and remove portable shower unit	2 Asbe	4	4	"		261		261	400

02 82 13.43 Bulk Asbestos Removal

		Crew	Daily Output	Labor-Hours	Unit	Material	Labor	Equipment	Total	Total Incl O&P
0010	**BULK ASBESTOS REMOVAL**									
0020	Includes disposable tools and 2 suits and 1 respirator filter/day/worker									
0200	Boiler insulation	A-9	480	.133	S.F.	.75	8.70		9.45	14.15
0210	With metal lath, add				%				50%	50%
0300	Boiler breeching or flue insulation	A-9	520	.123	S.F.	.55	8.05		8.60	12.90
0310	For active boiler, add				%				100%	100%
0400	Duct or AHU insulation	A-10B	440	.073	S.F.	.32	4.75		5.07	7.60
0500	Duct vibration isolation joints, up to 24 sq. in. duct	A-9	56	1.143	Ea.	5.10	74.50		79.60	120
0520	25 sq. in. to 48 sq. in. duct		48	1.333		5.95	87		92.95	140
0530	49 sq. in. to 76 sq. in. duct		40	1.600	↓	7.15	105		112.15	168
0600	Pipe insulation, air cell type, up to 4" diameter pipe		900	.071	L.F.	.32	4.64		4.96	7.45
0610	4" to 8" diameter pipe		800	.080		.36	5.20		5.56	8.40
0620	10" to 12" diameter pipe		700	.091		.41	5.95		6.36	9.60
0630	14" to 16" diameter pipe		550	.116	↓	.52	7.60		8.12	12.15
0650	Over 16" diameter pipe		650	.098	S.F.	.44	6.45		6.89	10.35
0700	With glove bag up to 3" diameter pipe		200	.320	L.F.	.79	21		21.79	33
1000	Pipe fitting insulation up to 4" diameter pipe		320	.200	Ea.	.89	13.05		13.94	21
1100	6" to 8" diameter pipe		304	.211		.94	13.75		14.69	22
1110	10" to 12" diameter pipe		192	.333		1.49	22		23.49	35
1120	14" to 16" diameter pipe		128	.500	↓	2.23	32.50		34.73	52.50
1130	Over 16" diameter pipe		176	.364	S.F.	1.62	24		25.62	38.50
1200	With glove bag, up to 8" diameter pipe		75	.853	L.F.	9.15	55.50		64.65	95.50
2000	Scrape foam fireproofing from flat surface		2400	.027	S.F.	.12	1.74		1.86	2.79
2100	Irregular surfaces		1200	.053		.24	3.48		3.72	5.60
3000	Remove cementitious material from flat surface		1800	.036		.16	2.32		2.48	3.72
3100	Irregular surface		1000	.064		.20	4.18		4.38	6.60
6000	Remove contaminated soil from crawl space by hand	↓	400	.160	C.F.	.71	10.45		11.16	16.80

02 82 Asbestos Remediation

02 82 13 – Asbestos Abatement

02 82 13.43 Bulk Asbestos Removal	Crew	Daily Output	Labor-Hours	Unit	Material	2023 Bare Costs Labor	Equipment	Total	Total Incl O&P
6100 With large production vacuum loader	A-12	700	.091	C.F.	.41	5.95	1.17	7.53	10.90
7000 Radiator backing, not including radiator removal	A-9	1200	.053	S.F.	.24	3.48		3.72	5.60
9000 For type B (supplied air) respirator equipment, add				%				10%	10%
02 82 13.44 Demolition In Asbestos Contaminated Area									
0010 **DEMOLITION IN ASBESTOS CONTAMINATED AREA**									
0200 Ceiling, including suspension system, plaster and lath	A-9	2100	.030	S.F.	.14	1.99		2.13	3.19
0210 Finished plaster, leaving wire lath		585	.109		.49	7.15		7.64	11.50
0220 Suspended acoustical tile		3500	.018		.08	1.19		1.27	1.92
0230 Concealed tile grid system		3000	.021		.10	1.39		1.49	2.23
0240 Metal pan grid system		1500	.043		.19	2.79		2.98	4.47
0250 Gypsum board		2500	.026		.11	1.67		1.78	2.69
0260 Lighting fixtures up to 2' x 4'		72	.889	Ea.	3.97	58		61.97	93.50
0400 Partitions, non load bearing									
0410 Plaster, lath, and studs	A-9	690	.093	S.F.	.91	6.05		6.96	10.25
0450 Gypsum board and studs	"	1390	.046	"	.21	3.01		3.22	4.83
9000 For type B (supplied air) respirator equipment, add				%				10%	10%
02 82 13.45 OSHA Testing									
0010 **OSHA TESTING**									
0100 Certified technician, minimum				Day		340		340	340
0110 Maximum						670		670	670
0121 Industrial hygienist, minimum						385		385	385
0130 Maximum						755		755	755
0200 Asbestos sampling and PCM analysis, NIOSH 7400, minimum	1 Asbe	8	1	Ea.	20.50	65.50		86	123
0210 Maximum		4	2		27.50	131		158.50	230
1000 Cleaned area samples		8	1		20.50	65.50		86	123
1100 PCM air sample analysis, NIOSH 7400, minimum		8	1		20.50	65.50		86	123
1110 Maximum		4	2		27.50	131		158.50	230
1200 TEM air sample analysis, NIOSH 7402, minimum								80	106
1210 Maximum								360	450
02 82 13.46 Decontamination of Asbestos Containment Area									
0010 **DECONTAMINATION OF ASBESTOS CONTAINMENT AREA**									
0100 Spray exposed substrate with surfactant (bridging)									
0200 Flat surfaces	A-9	6000	.011	S.F.	.45	.70		1.15	1.57
0250 Irregular surfaces		4000	.016	"	.50	1.04		1.54	2.15
0300 Pipes, beams, and columns		2000	.032	L.F.	.50	2.09		2.59	3.75
1000 Spray encapsulate polyethylene sheeting		8000	.008	S.F.	.50	.52		1.02	1.35
1100 Roll down polyethylene sheeting		8000	.008	"		.52		.52	.80
1500 Bag polyethylene sheeting		400	.160	Ea.	1.42	10.45		11.87	17.55
2000 Fine clean exposed substrate, with nylon brush		2400	.027	S.F.		1.74		1.74	2.66
2500 Wet wipe substrate		4800	.013			.87		.87	1.33
2600 Vacuum surfaces, fine brush		6400	.010			.65		.65	1
3000 Structural demolition									
3100 Wood stud walls	A-9	2800	.023	S.F.		1.49		1.49	2.28
3500 Window manifolds, not incl. window replacement		4200	.015			1		1	1.52
3600 Plywood carpet protection		2000	.032			2.09		2.09	3.20
4000 Remove custom decontamination facility	A-10A	8	3	Ea.	18.55	196		214.55	320
4100 Remove portable decontamination facility	3 Asbe	12	2	"	17.05	131		148.05	219
5000 HEPA vacuum, shampoo carpeting	A-9	4800	.013	S.F.	.14	.87		1.01	1.48
9000 Final cleaning of protected surfaces	A-10A	8000	.003	"		.20		.20	.30

02 82 Asbestos Remediation

02 82 13 – Asbestos Abatement

02 82 13.47 Asbestos Waste Pkg., Handling, and Disp.

	Crew	Daily Output	Labor-Hours	Unit	Material	2023 Bare Costs Labor	Equipment	Total	Total Incl O&P
0010 **ASBESTOS WASTE PACKAGING, HANDLING, AND DISPOSAL**									
0100 Collect and bag bulk material, 3 C.F. bags, by hand	A-9	400	.160	Ea.	1.20	10.45		11.65	17.30
0200 Large production vacuum loader	A-12	880	.073		1.75	4.75	.93	7.43	10.20
1000 Double bag and decontaminate	A-9	960	.067		1.20	4.35		5.55	7.95
2000 Containerize bagged material in drums, per 55gal drum	"	800	.080		29	5.20		34.20	39.50
3000 Cart bags 50' to dumpster	2 Asbe	400	.040			2.61		2.61	3.99
5000 Disposal charges, not including haul, minimum				C.Y.				61	67
5020 Maximum				"				355	395
9000 For type B (supplied air) respirator equipment, add				%				10%	10%

02 82 13.48 Asbestos Encapsulation With Sealants

	Crew	Daily Output	Labor-Hours	Unit	Material	Labor	Equipment	Total	Total Incl O&P
0010 **ASBESTOS ENCAPSULATION WITH SEALANTS**									
0100 Ceilings and walls, minimum	A-9	21000	.003	S.F.	.61	.20		.81	.97
0110 Maximum		10600	.006	"	.66	.39		1.05	1.33
0300 Pipes to 12" diameter including minor repairs, minimum		800	.080	L.F.	.74	5.20		5.94	8.80
0310 Maximum		400	.160	"	1.44	10.45		11.89	17.60

02 87 Biohazard Remediation

02 87 13 – Mold Remediation

02 87 13.16 Mold Remediation Preparation and Containment

	Crew	Daily Output	Labor-Hours	Unit	Material	Labor	Equipment	Total	Total Incl O&P
0010 **MOLD REMEDIATION PREPARATION AND CONTAINMENT**									
6010 Preparation of mold containment area R028213-20									
6100 Pre-cleaning, HEPA vacuum and wet wipe, flat surfaces	A-9	12000	.005	S.F.	.02	.35		.37	.56
6300 Separation barrier, 2" x 4" @ 16", 1/2" plywood ea. side, 8' high	2 Carp	333	.048		5.80	2.82		8.62	10.60
6310 12' high		320	.050		6.55	2.93		9.48	11.55
6320 16' high		200	.080		2.69	4.69		7.38	9.95
6400 Personnel decontam. chamber, 2" x 4" @ 16", 3/4" ply ea. side		280	.057		5.45	3.35		8.80	11
6450 Waste decontam. chamber, 2" x 4" studs @ 16", 3/4" ply each side		360	.044		22	2.60		24.60	28
6500 Cover surfaces with polyethylene sheeting									
6501 Including glue and tape									
6550 Floors, each layer, 6 mil	A-9	8000	.008	S.F.	.07	.52		.59	.88
6551 4 mil		9000	.007		.06	.46		.52	.77
6560 Walls, each layer, 6 mil		6000	.011		.07	.70		.77	1.15
6561 4 mil		7000	.009		.06	.60		.66	.97
6570 For heights above 14', add						20%			
6575 For heights above 20', add						30%			
6580 For fire retardant poly, add					100%				
6590 For large open areas, deduct					10%	20%			
6600 Seal floor penetrations with foam firestop to 36 sq. in.	2 Carp	200	.080	Ea.	20.50	4.69		25.19	29.50
6610 36 sq. in. to 72 sq. in.		125	.128		41	7.50		48.50	56
6615 72 sq. in. to 144 sq. in.		80	.200		82	11.70		93.70	107
6620 Wall penetrations, to 36 sq. in.		180	.089		20.50	5.20		25.70	30.50
6630 36 sq. in. to 72 sq. in.		100	.160		41	9.40		50.40	59
6640 72 sq. in. to 144 sq. in.		60	.267		82	15.65		97.65	114
6800 Caulk seams with latex caulk	1 Carp	230	.035	L.F.	.21	2.04		2.25	3.26
6900 Set up neg. air machine, 1-2k CFM/25 M.C.F. volume	1 Asbe	4.30	1.860	Ea.		121		121	186

02 87 13.33 Removal and Disposal of Materials With Mold

	Crew	Daily Output	Labor-Hours	Unit	Material	Labor	Equipment	Total	Total Incl O&P
0010 **REMOVAL AND DISPOSAL OF MATERIALS WITH MOLD**									
0015 Demolition in mold contaminated area									
0200 Ceiling, including suspension system, plaster and lath	A-9	2100	.030	S.F.	.14	1.99		2.13	3.19
0210 Finished plaster, leaving wire lath		585	.109			.49	7.15	7.64	11.50

02 87 Biohazard Remediation

02 87 13 – Mold Remediation

02 87 13.33 Removal and Disposal of Materials With Mold

		Crew	Daily Output	Labor-Hours	Unit	Material	2023 Bare Costs Labor	Equipment	Total	Total Incl O&P
0220	Suspended acoustical tile	A-9	3500	.018	S.F.	.08	1.19		1.27	1.92
0230	Concealed tile grid system		3000	.021		.10	1.39		1.49	2.23
0240	Metal pan grid system		1500	.043		.19	2.79		2.98	4.47
0250	Gypsum board		2500	.026		.11	1.67		1.78	2.69
0255	Plywood		2500	.026		.11	1.67		1.78	2.69
0260	Lighting fixtures up to 2' x 4'		72	.889	Ea.	3.97	58		61.97	93.50
0400	Partitions, non load bearing									
0410	Plaster, lath, and studs	A-9	690	.093	S.F.	.91	6.05		6.96	10.25
0450	Gypsum board and studs		1390	.046		.21	3.01		3.22	4.83
0465	Carpet & pad		1390	.046		.21	3.01		3.22	4.83
0600	Pipe insulation, air cell type, up to 4" diameter pipe		900	.071	L.F.	.32	4.64		4.96	7.45
0610	4" to 8" diameter pipe		800	.080		.36	5.20		5.56	8.40
0620	10" to 12" diameter pipe		700	.091		.41	5.95		6.36	9.60
0630	14" to 16" diameter pipe		550	.116		.52	7.60		8.12	12.15
0650	Over 16" diameter pipe		650	.098	S.F.	.44	6.45		6.89	10.35
9000	For type B (supplied air) respirator equipment, add				%		10%		10%	

02 87 19 – Bio-Hazard and Infectious Disease Control Remediation

02 87 19.10 Temporary Barriers, Including Ppe

		Crew	Daily Output	Labor-Hours	Unit	Material	Labor	Equipment	Total	Total Incl O&P
0010	**TEMPORARY BARRIERS, including PPE**									
0100	Infectious control partition, adjustable to 10' high, obscured, 4' panel	2 Carp	75	.213	Ea.	595	12.50		607.50	675
0110	3' panel		75	.213		565	12.50		577.50	640
0120	2' panel		75	.213		440	12.50		452.50	505
0130	1' panel	1 Carp	75	.107		293	6.25		299.25	330
0140	6" panel	"	75	.107		271	6.25		277.25	305
0150	2' panel with HEPA filtered discharge port	2 Carp	75	.213		515	12.50		527.50	585
0160	3' panel with 32" door		75	.213		920	12.50		932.50	1,050
0170	4' panel with 36" door		75	.213		1,025	12.50		1,037.50	1,150
0180	4'-6" panel with 44" door		75	.213		1,225	12.50		1,237.50	1,375
0190	Hinged corner		68	.235		189	13.80		202.80	229
0200	Outside corner		68	.235		157	13.80		170.80	194
0210	T post		68	.235		167	13.80		180.80	205
0220	Accessories, ceiling grid clip		300	.053		7.60	3.13		10.73	13
0230	Panel locking clip		300	.053		5.35	3.13		8.48	10.55
0240	Panel joint closure strip		300	.053		8.60	3.13		11.73	14.15
0250	Screw jack		300	.053		7.50	3.13		10.63	12.90
0260	Digital pressure difference gauge					290			290	320
0280	Combination lockset	1 Carp	11	.727		209	42.50		251.50	294
0285	Sealant tape, 2" wide	1 Clab	165	.048	C.L.F.	13.80	2.29		16.09	18.55
0290	System in place, including door and accessories									
0300	Based upon 25 uses	2 Carp	43	.372	L.F.	12.40	22		34.40	46
0310	Based upon 50 uses		43	.372		7.35	22		29.35	40.50
0330	Based upon 100 uses		43	.372		4.85	22		26.85	38
0400	Separation barrier, 2" x 4" @ 16" O.C., 1/2" plywood each side, 8' high		340	.047	S.F.	5.30	2.76		8.06	9.90
0410	12' high		275	.058		5.20	3.41		8.61	10.85
0420	16' high		170	.094		5.35	5.50		10.85	14.10
0430	5/8" FR GWB each side, 8' high		290	.055		3.51	3.23		6.74	8.65
0440	12' high		235	.068		3.37	3.99		7.36	9.65
0450	16' high		144	.111		3.30	6.50		9.80	13.35

02 87 19.20 Temporary Protection, Including Ppe

		Crew	Daily Output	Labor-Hours	Unit	Material	Labor	Equipment	Total	Total Incl O&P
0010	**TEMPORARY PROTECTION, including PPE**									
0100	Infectious control protection, 6 mil plastic sheeting, applied to floors	1 Skwk	1900	.004	S.F.	.07	.26		.33	.47
0110	Applied to walls		1400	.006		.07	.35		.42	.61

02 87 Biohazard Remediation

02 87 19 – Bio-Hazard and Infectious Disease Control Remediation

02 87 19.20 Temporary Protection, Including Ppe		Crew	Daily Output	Labor-Hours	Unit	Material	2023 Bare Costs Labor	2023 Bare Costs Equipment	Total	Total Incl O&P
0120	Applied to ceilings	1 Skwk	1000	.008	S.F.	.07	.49		.56	.82
0130	Sealant tape, 2" wide	1 Clab	165	.048	C.L.F.	13.80	2.29		16.09	18.55
0140	Floor covering, 1/8" tempered hardboard	2 Carp	878	.018	S.F.	.73	1.07		1.80	2.39
0150	1/2" CDX		878	.018		1.42	1.07		2.49	3.15
0160	3/4" CDX		755	.021		1.98	1.24		3.22	4.02

02 87 19.30 Infectious Control Equipment and Supplies

		Crew	Daily Output	Labor-Hours	Unit	Material	Labor	Equipment	Total	Total Incl O&P
0010	**INFECTIOUS CONTROL EQUIPMENT AND SUPPLIES**									
0100	Entry/exit decontamination chamber, portable, 10 uses	A-10C	12	2	Ea.	259	131	30	420	520
0105	Negative air machine, 1800 CFM					990			990	1,100
0110	Disposable polyethylene bags, 6 mil, 3 C.F.					1.20			1.20	1.32
0130	Paper towels, carton of 12, 350' rolls					77			77	85
0140	Heavy duty wipes, 160 per box					38.50			38.50	42
0200	Tent, including frame, weights, roof, walls, 5' x 5'	2 Skwk	32	.500		2,150	30.50		2,180.50	2,425
0205	5' x 10'		24	.667		2,500	41		2,541	2,800
0210	10' x 10'		24	.667		3,125	41		3,166	3,475
0220	13' x 26'		12	1.333		7,475	81.50		7,556.50	8,350
0230	13' x 26', flat roof infirmary		12	1.333		7,600	81.50		7,681.50	8,475
0240	13' x 26', drive through screening		12	1.333		8,800	81.50		8,881.50	9,800
0242	LED light kit for tents, 15 watt	1 Elec	48	.167		199	11.25		210.25	236
0244	Halogen heating kit, 1500 watt	"	48	.167		500	11.25		511.25	565
0250	Medical partition system, including frame, drapes, 5' x 5'	2 Skwk	48	.333		1,300	20.50		1,320.50	1,450

02 87 19.40 Infectious Control Cleaning, Includes Ppe

		Crew	Daily Output	Labor-Hours	Unit	Material	Labor	Equipment	Total	Total Incl O&P
0010	**INFECTIOUS CONTROL CLEANING, Includes PPE**									
0100	Infectious control cleaning, including PPE and antimicrobial spray, floors	1 Skwk	3600	.002	S.F.	.06	.14		.20	.27
0110	Walls		3000	.003		.06	.16		.22	.32
0120	Ceilings		2700	.003		.07	.18		.25	.34
0130	Countertops		3300	.002		.06	.15		.21	.29
0140	Other surfaces		2600	.003		.07	.19		.26	.35
0150	Plumbing fixtures		14	.571	Ea.	4.07	35		39.07	57
0160	Bathroom accessories		30	.267		1.87	16.35		18.22	26.50
0170	Kitchen appliance		9	.889		7	54.50		61.50	89.50
0180	Electrical switches and receptacles		140	.057		.41	3.50		3.91	5.70
0190	Work station		9	.889		7.50	54.50		62	90.50
0200	Door and window hardware		88	.091		.62	5.55		6.17	9.05
0250	Supply / return ductwork, up to 2 S.F. cross section		240	.033	L.F.	.50	2.04		2.54	3.62
0260	2 to 4 S.F. cross section		192	.042		.74	2.55		3.29	4.65
0270	4 to 8 S.F. cross section		144	.056		.92	3.40		4.32	6.10
0280	8 SF cross section		102	.078		1.40	4.80		6.20	8.75
0300	Duct coil		5	1.600	Ea.	11.95	98		109.95	160
0310	Duct damper and vane set		77	.104		1.61	6.35		7.96	11.30
0320	Fan coil unit or VAV box		8	1		7.25	61.50		68.75	100
0330	Air handling unit and coil		2	4		29	245		274	400
0340	Grill / diffuser or register		32	.250		2.14	15.30		17.44	25.50

Estimating Tips
General
- Carefully check all the plans and specifications. Concrete often appears on drawings other than structural drawings, including mechanical and electrical drawings for equipment pads. The cost of cutting and patching is often difficult to estimate. See Subdivision 03 81 for Concrete Cutting, Subdivision 02 41 19.16 for Cutout Demolition, Subdivision 03 05 05.10 for Concrete Demolition, and Subdivision 02 41 19.19 for Rubbish Handling (handling, loading, and hauling of debris).
- Always obtain concrete prices from suppliers near the job site. A volume discount can often be negotiated, depending upon competition in the area. Remember to add for waste, particularly for slabs and footings on grade.

03 10 00 Concrete Forming and Accessories
- A primary cost for concrete construction is forming. Most jobs today are constructed with prefabricated forms. The selection of the forms best suited for the job and the total square feet of forms required for efficient concrete forming and placing are key elements in estimating concrete construction. Enough forms must be available for erection to make efficient use of the concrete placing equipment and crew.
- Concrete accessories for forming and placing depend upon the systems used. Study the plans and specifications to ensure that all special accessory requirements have been included in the cost estimate, such as anchor bolts, inserts, and hangers.
- Included within costs for forms-in-place are all necessary bracing and shoring.

03 20 00 Concrete Reinforcing
- Ascertain that the reinforcing steel supplier has included all accessories, cutting, bending, and an allowance for lapping, splicing, and waste. A good rule of thumb is 10% for lapping, splicing, and waste. Also, 10% waste should be allowed for welded wire fabric.
- The unit price items in the subdivisions for Reinforcing In Place, Glass Fiber Reinforcing, and Welded Wire Fabric include the labor to install accessories such as beam and slab bolsters, high chairs, and bar ties and tie wire. The material cost for these accessories is not included; they may be obtained from the Accessories Subdivisions.

03 30 00 Cast-In-Place Concrete
- When estimating structural concrete, pay particular attention to requirements for concrete additives, curing methods, and surface treatments. Special consideration for climate, hot or cold, must be included in your estimate. Be sure to include requirements for concrete placing equipment and concrete finishing.
- For accurate concrete estimating, the estimator must consider each of the following major components individually: forms, reinforcing steel, ready-mix concrete, placement of the concrete, and finishing of the top surface. For faster estimating, Subdivision 03 30 53.40 for Concrete-In-Place can be used; here, various items of concrete work are presented that include the costs of all five major components (unless specifically stated otherwise).

03 40 00 Precast Concrete
03 50 00 Cast Decks and Underlayment
- The cost of hauling precast concrete structural members is often an important factor. For this reason, it is important to get a quote from the nearest supplier. It may become economically feasible to set up precasting beds on the site if the hauling costs are prohibitive.

Reference Numbers
Reference numbers are shown at the beginning of some major classifications. These numbers refer to related items in the Reference Section. The reference information may be an estimating procedure, an alternate pricing method, or technical information.

Note: Not all subdivisions listed here necessarily appear. ■

Same Data. Simplified.

Enjoy the convenience and efficiency of accessing your costs anywhere:
- **Skip the multiplier** by setting your location
- **Quickly search,** edit, favorite and share costs
- **Stay on top of price changes** with automatic updates

Discover more at rsmeans.com/online

No part of this cost data may be reproduced, stored in a retrieval system, or transmitted in any form or by any means without prior written permission of Gordian.

03 01 Maintenance of Concrete

03 01 30 – Maintenance of Cast-In-Place Concrete

03 01 30.62 Concrete Patching

		Crew	Daily Output	Labor-Hours	Unit	Material	2023 Bare Costs Labor	Equipment	Total	Total Incl O&P
0010	**CONCRETE PATCHING**									
0100	Floors, 1/4" thick, small areas, regular grout	1 Cefi	170	.047	S.F.	1.24	2.59		3.83	5.15
0150	Epoxy grout	"	100	.080	"	16.80	4.40		21.20	25
2000	Walls, including chipping, cleaning and epoxy grout									
2100	1/4" deep	1 Cefi	65	.123	S.F.	6	6.75		12.75	16.50
2150	1/2" deep		50	.160		12	8.80		20.80	26
2200	3/4" deep	↓	40	.200	↓	18	11		29	36

03 11 Concrete Forming

03 11 13 – Structural Cast-In-Place Concrete Forming

03 11 13.40 Forms In Place, Equipment Foundations

		Crew	Daily Output	Labor-Hours	Unit	Material	Labor	Equipment	Total	Total Incl O&P
0010	**FORMS IN PLACE, EQUIPMENT FOUNDATIONS**									
0020	1 use	C-2	160	.300	SFCA	8.05	17.10		25.15	34.50
0050	2 use		190	.253		4.43	14.40		18.83	26.50
0100	3 use		200	.240		3.22	13.70		16.92	24
0150	4 use	↓	205	.234	↓	2.63	13.35		15.98	23

03 11 13.45 Forms In Place, Footings

		Crew	Daily Output	Labor-Hours	Unit	Material	Labor	Equipment	Total	Total Incl O&P
0010	**FORMS IN PLACE, FOOTINGS**									
0020	Continuous wall, plywood, 1 use	C-1	375	.085	SFCA	14.35	4.76		19.11	23
0050	2 use		440	.073		7.90	4.06		11.96	14.75
0100	3 use		470	.068		5.75	3.80		9.55	11.95
0150	4 use		485	.066		4.67	3.68		8.35	10.65
5000	Spread footings, job-built lumber, 1 use		305	.105		5.85	5.85		11.70	15.15
5050	2 use		371	.086		3.24	4.81		8.05	10.70
5100	3 use		401	.080		2.34	4.45		6.79	9.20
5150	4 use	↓	414	.077	↓	1.90	4.31		6.21	8.50

03 11 13.65 Forms In Place, Slab On Grade

		Crew	Daily Output	Labor-Hours	Unit	Material	Labor	Equipment	Total	Total Incl O&P
0010	**FORMS IN PLACE, SLAB ON GRADE**									
3000	Edge forms, wood, 4 use, on grade, to 6" high	C-1	600	.053	L.F.	.83	2.97		3.80	5.35
6000	Trench forms in floor, wood, 1 use		160	.200	SFCA	5.40	11.15		16.55	22.50
6050	2 use		175	.183		2.96	10.20		13.16	18.45
6100	3 use		180	.178		2.15	9.90		12.05	17.10
6150	4 use	↓	185	.173	↓	1.75	9.65		11.40	16.25

03 15 Concrete Accessories

03 15 05 – Concrete Forming Accessories

03 15 05.75 Sleeves and Chases

			Crew	Daily Output	Labor-Hours	Unit	Material	Labor	Equipment	Total	Total Incl O&P
0010	**SLEEVES AND CHASES**										
0100	Plastic, 1 use, 12" long, 2" diameter		1 Carp	100	.080	Ea.	3.41	4.69		8.10	10.75
0150	4" diameter			90	.089		.91	5.20		6.11	8.75
0200	6" diameter			75	.107		17.45	6.25		23.70	28.50
0250	12" diameter			60	.133		50.50	7.80		58.30	67.50
5000	Sheet metal, 2" diameter	G		100	.080		3.30	4.69		7.99	10.65
5100	4" diameter	G		90	.089		4.12	5.20		9.32	12.30
5150	6" diameter	G		75	.107		5.20	6.25		11.45	15
5200	12" diameter	G		60	.133		9.80	7.80		17.60	22.50
6000	Steel pipe, 2" diameter	G		100	.080		17.45	4.69		22.14	26
6100	4" diameter	G		90	.089		49	5.20		54.20	62
6150	6" diameter	G	↓	75	.107	↓	90	6.25		96.25	108

03 15 Concrete Accessories

03 15 05 – Concrete Forming Accessories

03 15 05.75 Sleeves and Chases		Crew	Daily Output	Labor-Hours	Unit	Material	2023 Bare Costs Labor	Equipment	Total	Total Incl O&P
6200	12" diameter	G 1 Carp	60	.133	Ea.	136	7.80		143.80	162

03 15 16 – Concrete Construction Joints

03 15 16.20 Control Joints, Saw Cut

		Crew	Daily Output	Labor-Hours	Unit	Material	Labor	Equipment	Total	Total Incl O&P
0010	**CONTROL JOINTS, SAW CUT**									
0100	Sawcut control joints in green concrete									
0120	1" depth	C-27	2000	.008	L.F.	.03	.44	.09	.56	.77
0140	1-1/2" depth		1800	.009		.04	.49	.10	.63	.88
0160	2" depth	↓	1600	.010	↓	.06	.55	.11	.72	.98
0180	Sawcut joint reservoir in cured concrete									
0182	3/8" wide x 3/4" deep, with single saw blade	C-27	1000	.016	L.F.	.04	.88	.18	1.10	1.53
0184	1/2" wide x 1" deep, with double saw blades		900	.018		.08	.98	.20	1.26	1.74
0186	3/4" wide x 1-1/2" deep, with double saw blades	↓	800	.020		.17	1.10	.22	1.49	2.04
0190	Water blast joint to wash away laitance, 2 passes	C-29	2500	.003			.15	.04	.19	.28
0200	Air blast joint to blow out debris and air dry, 2 passes	C-28	2000	.004	↓		.22	.02	.24	.34
0300	For backer rod, see Section 07 91 23.10									
0342	For joint sealant, see Section 07 92 13.20									

03 15 19 – Cast-In Concrete Anchors

03 15 19.10 Anchor Bolts

		Crew	Daily Output	Labor-Hours	Unit	Material	Labor	Equipment	Total	Total Incl O&P
0010	**ANCHOR BOLTS**									
0015	Made from recycled materials									
0025	Single bolts installed in fresh concrete, no templates									
0030	Hooked w/nut and washer, 1/2" diameter, 8" long G	1 Carp	132	.061	Ea.	2.23	3.55		5.78	7.75
0040	12" long G		131	.061		2.48	3.58		6.06	8.10
0050	5/8" diameter, 8" long G		129	.062		4.02	3.63		7.65	9.85
0060	12" long G		127	.063		4.95	3.69		8.64	10.95
0070	3/4" diameter, 8" long G		127	.063		4.95	3.69		8.64	10.95
0080	12" long G	↓	125	.064	↓	6.20	3.75		9.95	12.40
0090	2-bolt pattern, including job-built 2-hole template, per set									
0100	J-type, incl. hex nut & washer, 1/2" diameter x 6" long G	1 Carp	21	.381	Set	8	22.50		30.50	42
0110	12" long G		21	.381		9	22.50		31.50	43
0120	18" long G		21	.381		10.50	22.50		33	44.50
0130	3/4" diameter x 8" long G		20	.400		13.95	23.50		37.45	50.50
0140	12" long G		20	.400		16.40	23.50		39.90	53
0150	18" long G		20	.400		20	23.50		43.50	57
0160	1" diameter x 12" long G		19	.421		41	24.50		65.50	81.50
0170	18" long G		19	.421		48.50	24.50		73	90
0180	24" long G		19	.421		58	24.50		82.50	101
0190	36" long G		18	.444		78	26		104	125
0200	1-1/2" diameter x 18" long G		17	.471		54.50	27.50		82	101
0210	24" long G		16	.500		64	29.50		93.50	114
0300	L-type, incl. hex nut & washer, 3/4" diameter x 12" long G		20	.400		19.05	23.50		42.55	56
0310	18" long G		20	.400		23.50	23.50		47	60.50
0320	24" long G		20	.400		27.50	23.50		51	65
0330	30" long G		20	.400		34	23.50		57.50	72
0340	36" long G		20	.400		38	23.50		61.50	77
0350	1" diameter x 12" long G		19	.421		31.50	24.50		56	71
0360	18" long G		19	.421		38	24.50		62.50	78.50
0370	24" long G		19	.421		46	24.50		70.50	87
0380	30" long G		19	.421		53.50	24.50		78	95.50
0390	36" long G		18	.444		61	26		87	106
0400	42" long G		18	.444		73	26		99	120
0410	48" long G	↓	18	.444		81.50	26		107.50	129

03 15 Concrete Accessories

03 15 19 – Cast-In Concrete Anchors

03 15 19.10 Anchor Bolts		Crew	Daily Output	Labor-Hours	Unit	Material	2023 Bare Costs Labor	Equipment	Total	Total Incl O&P
0420	1-1/4" diameter x 18" long	G 1 Carp	18	.444	Set	57	26		83	102
0430	24" long	G	18	.444		67	26		93	113
0440	30" long	G	17	.471		77	27.50		104.50	126
0450	36" long	G	17	.471		87	27.50		114.50	137
0460	42" long	G 2 Carp	32	.500		97.50	29.50		127	152
0470	48" long	G	32	.500		111	29.50		140.50	166
0480	54" long	G	31	.516		130	30.50		160.50	188
0490	60" long	G	31	.516		143	30.50		173.50	202
0500	1-1/2" diameter x 18" long	G	33	.485		82.50	28.50		111	134
0510	24" long	G	32	.500		95.50	29.50		125	149
0520	30" long	G	31	.516		108	30.50		138.50	163
0530	36" long	G	30	.533		123	31.50		154.50	182
0540	42" long	G	30	.533		140	31.50		171.50	201
0550	48" long	G	29	.552		156	32.50		188.50	220
0560	54" long	G	28	.571		190	33.50		223.50	259
0570	60" long	G	28	.571		208	33.50		241.50	278
0580	1-3/4" diameter x 18" long	G	31	.516		113	30.50		143.50	170
0590	24" long	G	30	.533		132	31.50		163.50	193
0600	30" long	G	29	.552		153	32.50		185.50	217
0610	36" long	G	28	.571		175	33.50		208.50	242
0620	42" long	G	27	.593		196	34.50		230.50	267
0630	48" long	G	26	.615		215	36		251	290
0640	54" long	G	26	.615		265	36		301	345
0650	60" long	G	25	.640		286	37.50		323.50	370
0660	2" diameter x 24" long	G	27	.593		159	34.50		193.50	226
0670	30" long	G	27	.593		178	34.50		212.50	248
0680	36" long	G	26	.615		195	36		231	269
0690	42" long	G	25	.640		218	37.50		255.50	295
0700	48" long	G	24	.667		249	39		288	330
0710	54" long	G	23	.696		296	41		337	385
0720	60" long	G	23	.696		320	41		361	410
0730	66" long	G	22	.727		340	42.50		382.50	440
0740	72" long	G	21	.762		370	44.50		414.50	475
1000	4-bolt pattern, including job-built 4-hole template, per set									
1100	J-type, incl. hex nut & washer, 1/2" diameter x 6" long	G 1 Carp	19	.421	Set	11.95	24.50		36.45	49.50
1110	12" long	G	19	.421		13.95	24.50		38.45	52
1120	18" long	G	18	.444		16.95	26		42.95	57.50
1130	3/4" diameter x 8" long	G	17	.471		24	27.50		51.50	67
1140	12" long	G	17	.471		29	27.50		56.50	72.50
1150	18" long	G	17	.471		36	27.50		63.50	81
1160	1" diameter x 12" long	G	16	.500		77.50	29.50		107	129
1170	18" long	G	15	.533		93	31.50		124.50	149
1180	24" long	G	15	.533		112	31.50		143.50	171
1190	36" long	G	15	.533		152	31.50		183.50	215
1200	1-1/2" diameter x 18" long	G	13	.615		105	36		141	169
1210	24" long	G	12	.667		124	39		163	194
1300	L-type, incl. hex nut & washer, 3/4" diameter x 12" long	G	17	.471		34	27.50		61.50	78.50
1310	18" long	G	17	.471		42.50	27.50		70	87.50
1320	24" long	G	17	.471		51	27.50		78.50	97
1330	30" long	G	16	.500		63.50	29.50		93	114
1340	36" long	G	16	.500		72	29.50		101.50	123
1350	1" diameter x 12" long	G	16	.500		58.50	29.50		88	108
1360	18" long	G	15	.533		72	31.50		103.50	126

03 15 Concrete Accessories

03 15 19 – Cast-In Concrete Anchors

03 15 19.10 Anchor Bolts

			Crew	Daily Output	Labor-Hours	Unit	Material	2023 Bare Costs Labor	Equipment	Total	Total Incl O&P
1370	24" long	G	1 Carp	15	.533	Set	88	31.50		119.50	144
1380	30" long	G		15	.533		103	31.50		134.50	161
1390	36" long	G		15	.533		118	31.50		149.50	176
1400	42" long	G		14	.571		142	33.50		175.50	206
1410	48" long	G		14	.571		159	33.50		192.50	225
1420	1-1/4" diameter x 18" long	G		14	.571		110	33.50		143.50	171
1430	24" long	G		14	.571		130	33.50		163.50	193
1440	30" long	G		13	.615		150	36		186	219
1450	36" long	G		13	.615		170	36		206	241
1460	42" long	G	2 Carp	25	.640		191	37.50		228.50	267
1470	48" long	G		24	.667		218	39		257	298
1480	54" long	G		23	.696		256	41		297	345
1490	60" long	G		23	.696		281	41		322	370
1500	1-1/2" diameter x 18" long	G		25	.640		161	37.50		198.50	233
1510	24" long	G		24	.667		187	39		226	264
1520	30" long	G		23	.696		211	41		252	293
1530	36" long	G		22	.727		242	42.50		284.50	330
1540	42" long	G		22	.727		275	42.50		317.50	370
1550	48" long	G		21	.762		310	44.50		354.50	405
1560	54" long	G		20	.800		375	47		422	485
1570	60" long	G		20	.800		410	47		457	520
1580	1-3/4" diameter x 18" long	G		22	.727		223	42.50		265.50	310
1590	24" long	G		21	.762		261	44.50		305.50	355
1600	30" long	G		21	.762		305	44.50		349.50	400
1610	36" long	G		20	.800		345	47		392	450
1620	42" long	G		19	.842		385	49.50		434.50	500
1630	48" long	G		18	.889		425	52		477	550
1640	54" long	G		18	.889		525	52		577	660
1650	60" long	G		17	.941		570	55		625	705
1660	2" diameter x 24" long	G		19	.842		315	49.50		364.50	420
1670	30" long	G		18	.889		350	52		402	470
1680	36" long	G		18	.889		385	52		437	505
1690	42" long	G		17	.941		430	55		485	555
1700	48" long	G		16	1		495	58.50		553.50	635
1710	54" long	G		15	1.067		590	62.50		652.50	740
1720	60" long	G		15	1.067		630	62.50		692.50	790
1730	66" long	G		14	1.143		675	67		742	845
1740	72" long	G		14	1.143		740	67		807	915
1990	For galvanized, add					Ea.	75%				

03 15 19.45 Machinery Anchors

0010	**MACHINERY ANCHORS**, heavy duty, incl. sleeve, floating base nut,										
0020	lower stud & coupling nut, fiber plug, connecting stud, washer & nut.										
0030	For flush mounted embedment in poured concrete heavy equip. pads.										
0200	Stud & bolt, 1/2" diameter	G	E-16	40	.400	Ea.	89	26	3.68	118.68	142
0300	5/8" diameter	G		35	.457		104	30	4.20	138.20	165
0500	3/4" diameter	G		30	.533		126	35	4.90	165.90	197
0600	7/8" diameter	G		25	.640		141	42	5.90	188.90	226
0800	1" diameter	G		20	.800		154	52.50	7.35	213.85	258
0900	1-1/4" diameter	G		15	1.067		204	70	9.80	283.80	345

03 21 Reinforcement Bars

03 21 11 – Plain Steel Reinforcement Bars

03 21 11.60 Reinforcing In Place		Crew	Daily Output	Labor-Hours	Unit	Material	2023 Bare Costs Labor	Equipment	Total	Total Incl O&P
0010	**REINFORCING IN PLACE**, 50-60 ton lots, A615 Grade 60									
0020	Includes labor, but not material cost, to install accessories									
0030	Made from recycled materials									
0502	Footings, #4 to #7	G	4 Rodm	4200	.008	Lb.	.71	.49		1.20	1.51
0552	#8 to #18	G		7200	.004		.71	.29		1	1.21
0602	Slab on grade, #3 to #7	G		4200	.008		.71	.49		1.20	1.51
0900	For other than 50-60 ton lots										
1000	Under 10 ton job, #3 to #7, add						25%	10%			
1010	#8 to #18, add						20%	10%			
1050	10-50 ton job, #3 to #7, add						10%				
1060	#8 to #18, add						5%				
1100	60-100 ton job, #3 to #7, deduct						5%				
1110	#8 to #18, deduct						10%				
1150	Over 100 ton job, #3 to #7, deduct						10%				
1160	#8 to #18, deduct						15%				

03 22 Fabric and Grid Reinforcing

03 22 11 – Plain Welded Wire Fabric Reinforcing

03 22 11.10 Plain Welded Wire Fabric

			Crew	Daily Output	Labor-Hours	Unit	Material	Labor	Equipment	Total	Total Incl O&P
0010	**PLAIN WELDED WIRE FABRIC** ASTM A185										
0020	Includes labor, but not material cost, to install accessories										
0030	Made from recycled materials										
0050	Sheets										
0100	6 x 6 - W1.4 x W1.4 (10 x 10) 21 lb./C.S.F.	G	2 Rodm	35	.457	C.S.F.	37.50	29.50		67	85.50

03 22 13 – Galvanized Welded Wire Fabric Reinforcing

03 22 13.10 Galvanized Welded Wire Fabric

		Unit	Material			Total	Total Incl O&P
0010	**GALVANIZED WELDED WIRE FABRIC**						
0100	Add to plain welded wire pricing for galvanized welded wire	Lb.	.28			.28	.31

03 22 16 – Epoxy-Coated Welded Wire Fabric Reinforcing

03 22 16.10 Epoxy-Coated Welded Wire Fabric

		Unit	Material			Total	Total Incl O&P
0010	**EPOXY-COATED WELDED WIRE FABRIC**						
0100	Add to plain welded wire pricing for epoxy-coated welded wire	Lb.	.56			.56	.61

03 30 Cast-In-Place Concrete

03 30 53 – Miscellaneous Cast-In-Place Concrete

03 30 53.40 Concrete In Place

		Crew	Daily Output	Labor-Hours	Unit	Material	Labor	Equipment	Total	Total Incl O&P
0010	**CONCRETE IN PLACE**									
0020	Including forms (4 uses), Grade 60 rebar, concrete (Portland cement									
0050	Type I), placement and finishing unless otherwise indicated									
0500	Chimney foundations (5000 psi), over 5 C.Y.	C-14C	32.22	3.476	C.Y.	232	195	.94	427.94	545
0510	(3500 psi), under 5 C.Y.	"	23.71	4.724	"	279	265	1.28	545.28	700
3540	Equipment pad (3000 psi), 3' x 3' x 6" thick	C-14H	45	1.067	Ea.	83	61.50	.66	145.16	183
3550	4' x 4' x 6" thick		30	1.600		120	92	.99	212.99	270
3560	5' x 5' x 8" thick		18	2.667		216	153	1.65	370.65	470
3570	6' x 6' x 8" thick		14	3.429		284	197	2.13	483.13	610
3580	8' x 8' x 10" thick		8	6		590	345	3.72	938.72	1,175
3590	10' x 10' x 12" thick		5	9.600		980	550	5.95	1,535.95	1,900
3800	Footings (3000 psi), spread under 1 C.Y.	C-14C	28	4	C.Y.	257	224	1.08	482.08	620

03 30 Cast-In-Place Concrete

03 30 53 – Miscellaneous Cast-In-Place Concrete

03 30 53.40 Concrete In Place

		Crew	Daily Output	Labor-Hours	Unit	Material	2023 Bare Costs Labor	Equipment	Total	Total Incl O&P
3825	1 C.Y. to 5 C.Y.	C-14C	43	2.605	C.Y.	330	146	.70	476.70	580
3850	Over 5 C.Y.	"	75	1.493		315	84	.40	399.40	470
3900	Footings, strip (3000 psi), 18" x 9", unreinforced	C-14L	40	2.400		211	131	.74	342.74	430
3920	18" x 9", reinforced	C-14C	35	3.200		245	179	.86	424.86	540
3925	20" x 10", unreinforced	C-14L	45	2.133		202	117	.66	319.66	395
3930	20" x 10", reinforced	C-14C	40	2.800		229	157	.76	386.76	485
3935	24" x 12", unreinforced	C-14L	55	1.745		194	95.50	.54	290.04	355
3940	24" x 12", reinforced	C-14C	48	2.333		223	131	.63	354.63	440
3945	36" x 12", unreinforced	C-14L	70	1.371		184	75	.43	259.43	315
3950	36" x 12", reinforced	C-14C	60	1.867		210	105	.50	315.50	390
4000	Foundation mat (3000 psi), under 10 C.Y.	"	38.67	2.896		310	162	.78	472.78	585
4650	Slab on grade (3500 psi), not including finish, 4" thick	C-14E	60.75	1.449		204	83.50	.49	287.99	350
4700	6" thick	"	92	.957		191	55	.33	246.33	292
4701	Thickened slab edge (3500 psi), for slab on grade poured									
4702	monolithically with slab; depth is in addition to slab thickness;									
4703	formed vertical outside edge, earthen bottom and inside slope									
4705	8" deep x 8" wide bottom, unreinforced	C-14L	2190	.044	L.F.	6.10	2.40	.01	8.51	10.25
4710	8" x 8", reinforced	C-14C	1670	.067		9.45	3.76	.02	13.23	16
4715	12" deep x 12" wide bottom, unreinforced	C-14L	1800	.053		11.80	2.92	.02	14.74	17.35
4720	12" x 12", reinforced	C-14C	1310	.086		17.95	4.80	.02	22.77	27
4725	16" deep x 16" wide bottom, unreinforced	C-14L	1440	.067		19.30	3.65	.02	22.97	26.50
4730	16" x 16", reinforced	C-14C	1120	.100		26.50	5.60	.03	32.13	38
4735	20" deep x 20" wide bottom, unreinforced	C-14L	1150	.083		28.50	4.56	.03	33.09	38.50
4740	20" x 20", reinforced	C-14C	920	.122		38	6.85	.03	44.88	52
4745	24" deep x 24" wide bottom, unreinforced	C-14L	930	.103		40	5.65	.03	45.68	52.50
4750	24" x 24", reinforced	C-14C	740	.151		52	8.50	.04	60.54	70
4751	Slab on grade (3500 psi), incl. troweled finish, not incl. forms									
4760	or reinforcing, over 10,000 S.F., 4" thick	C-14F	3425	.021	S.F.	2.05	1.11	.01	3.17	3.90
4820	6" thick		3350	.021		3	1.13	.01	4.14	4.97
4840	8" thick		3184	.023		4.11	1.19	.01	5.31	6.30
4900	12" thick		2734	.026		6.15	1.39	.01	7.55	8.85
4950	15" thick		2505	.029		7.75	1.51	.01	9.27	10.75

03 31 Structural Concrete

03 31 13 – Heavyweight Structural Concrete

03 31 13.35 Heavyweight Concrete, Ready Mix

		Crew	Daily Output	Labor-Hours	Unit	Material	2023 Bare Costs Labor	Equipment	Total	Total Incl O&P
0010	**HEAVYWEIGHT CONCRETE, READY MIX**, delivered									
0012	Includes local aggregate, sand, Portland cement (Type I) and water									
0015	Excludes all additives and treatments									
0020	2000 psi				C.Y.	148			148	163
0100	2500 psi					151			151	166
0150	3000 psi					154			154	170
0200	3500 psi					158			158	174
0300	4000 psi					162			162	178
1000	For high early strength (Portland cement Type III), add					10%				
1300	For winter concrete (hot water), add					8.50			8.50	9.35
1410	For mid-range water reducer, add					6.40			6.40	7.05
1420	For high-range water reducer/superplasticizer, add					8.50			8.50	9.35
1430	For retarder, add					6.05			6.05	6.65
1440	For non-Chloride accelerator, add					9.50			9.50	10.45
1450	For Chloride accelerator, per 1%, add					5			5	5.50

03 31 Structural Concrete

03 31 13 – Heavyweight Structural Concrete

03 31 13.35 Heavyweight Concrete, Ready Mix

		Crew	Daily Output	Labor-Hours	Unit	Material	2023 Bare Costs Labor	2023 Bare Costs Equipment	Total	Total Incl O&P
1460	For fiber reinforcing, synthetic (1 lb./C.Y.), add				C.Y.	10.40			10.40	11.45
1500	For Saturday delivery, add				▼	15			15	16.50
1510	For truck holding/waiting time past 1st hour per load, add				Hr.	143			143	157
1520	For short load (less than 4 C.Y.), add per load				Ea.	125			125	138
2000	For all lightweight aggregate, add				C.Y.	45%				

03 31 13.70 Placing Concrete

		Crew	Daily Output	Labor-Hours	Unit	Material	2023 Bare Costs Labor	2023 Bare Costs Equipment	Total	Total Incl O&P
0010	**PLACING CONCRETE**									
0020	Includes labor and equipment to place, level (strike off) and consolidate									
1200	Duct bank, direct chute	C-6	155	.310	C.Y.		15.15	.38	15.53	23
1900	Footings, continuous, shallow, direct chute	"	120	.400			19.55	.50	20.05	29.50
1950	Pumped	C-20	150	.427			21.50	5.90	27.40	38.50
2000	With crane and bucket	C-7	90	.800			41	28.50	69.50	92
2100	Footings, continuous, deep, direct chute	C-6	140	.343			16.75	.43	17.18	25.50
2150	Pumped	C-20	160	.400			20	5.55	25.55	36
2200	With crane and bucket	C-7	110	.655			33.50	23.50	57	75
2400	Footings, spread, under 1 C.Y., direct chute	C-6	55	.873			42.50	1.08	43.58	64.50
2450	Pumped	C-20	65	.985			49.50	13.65	63.15	89
2500	With crane and bucket	C-7	45	1.600			82	57	139	184
2600	Over 5 C.Y., direct chute	C-6	120	.400			19.55	.50	20.05	29.50
2650	Pumped	C-20	150	.427			21.50	5.90	27.40	38.50
2700	With crane and bucket	C-7	100	.720			37	25.50	62.50	83
2900	Foundation mats, over 20 C.Y., direct chute	C-6	350	.137			6.70	.17	6.87	10.15
2950	Pumped	C-20	400	.160			8.05	2.22	10.27	14.45
3000	With crane and bucket	C-7	300	.240	▼		12.25	8.55	20.80	27.50

03 35 Concrete Finishing

03 35 13 – High-Tolerance Concrete Floor Finishing

03 35 13.30 Finishing Floors, High Tolerance

		Crew	Daily Output	Labor-Hours	Unit	Material	2023 Bare Costs Labor	2023 Bare Costs Equipment	Total	Total Incl O&P
0010	**FINISHING FLOORS, HIGH TOLERANCE**									
0012	Finishing of fresh concrete flatwork requires that concrete									
0013	first be placed, struck off & consolidated									
0015	Basic finishing for various unspecified flatwork									
0100	Bull float only	C-10	4000	.006	S.F.		.31		.31	.46
0125	Bull float & manual float		2000	.012			.63		.63	.92
0150	Bull float, manual float & broom finish, w/edging & joints		1850	.013			.68		.68	1
0200	Bull float, manual float & manual steel trowel	▼	1265	.019	▼		.99		.99	1.46
0210	For specified Random Access Floors in ACI Classes 1, 2, 3 and 4 to achieve									
0215	Composite Overall Floor Flatness and Levelness values up to FF35/FL25									
0250	Bull float, machine float & machine trowel (walk-behind)	C-10C	1715	.014	S.F.		.73	.05	.78	1.13
0300	Power screed, bull float, machine float & trowel (walk-behind)	C-10D	2400	.010			.52	.07	.59	.85
0350	Power screed, bull float, machine float & trowel (ride-on)	C-10E	4000	.006	▼		.31	.08	.39	.55
0352	For specified Random Access Floors in ACI Classes 5, 6, 7 and 8 to achieve									
0354	Composite Overall Floor Flatness and Levelness values up to FF50/FL50									
0356	Add for two-dimensional restraightening after power float	C-10	6000	.004	S.F.		.21		.21	.31
0358	For specified Random or Defined Access Floors in ACI Class 9 to achieve									
0360	Composite Overall Floor Flatness and Levelness values up to FF100/FL100									
0362	Add for two-dimensional restraightening after bull float & power float	C-10	3000	.008	S.F.		.42		.42	.62
0364	For specified Superflat Defined Access Floors in ACI Class 9 to achieve									
0366	Minimum Floor Flatness and Levelness values of FF100/FL100									
0368	Add for 2-dim'l restraightening after bull float, power float, power trowel	C-10	2000	.012	S.F.		.63		.63	.92

03 54 Cast Underlayment

03 54 16 – Hydraulic Cement Underlayment

03 54 16.50 Cement Underlayment

		Crew	Daily Output	Labor-Hours	Unit	Material	2023 Bare Costs Labor	Equipment	Total	Total Incl O&P
0010	**CEMENT UNDERLAYMENT**									
2510	Underlayment, P.C. based, self-leveling, 4100 psi, pumped, 1/4" thick	C-8	20000	.003	S.F.	2.37	.15	.04	2.56	2.88
2520	1/2" thick		19000	.003		4.74	.15	.04	4.93	5.50
2530	3/4" thick		18000	.003		7.10	.16	.05	7.31	8.10
2540	1" thick		17000	.003		9.50	.17	.05	9.72	10.75
2550	1-1/2" thick		15000	.004		14.20	.19	.06	14.45	16
2560	Hand placed, 1/2" thick	C-18	450	.020		4.74	.95	.33	6.02	7
2610	Topping, P.C. based, self-leveling, 6100 psi, pumped, 1/4" thick	C-8	20000	.003		2.45	.15	.04	2.64	2.96
2620	1/2" thick		19000	.003		4.89	.15	.04	5.08	5.70
2630	3/4" thick		18000	.003		7.35	.16	.05	7.56	8.35
2660	1" thick		17000	.003		9.80	.17	.05	10.02	11.05
2670	1-1/2" thick		15000	.004		14.70	.19	.06	14.95	16.50
2680	Hand placed, 1/2" thick	C-18	450	.020		4.89	.95	.33	6.17	7.20

03 63 Epoxy Grouting

03 63 05 – Grouting of Dowels and Fasteners

03 63 05.10 Epoxy Only

		Crew	Daily Output	Labor-Hours	Unit	Material	2023 Bare Costs Labor	Equipment	Total	Total Incl O&P
0010	**EPOXY ONLY**									
1500	Chemical anchoring, epoxy cartridge, excludes layout, drilling, fastener									
1530	For fastener 3/4" diam. x 6" embedment	2 Skwk	72	.222	Ea.	4.69	13.60		18.29	25.50
1535	1" diam. x 8" embedment		66	.242		7.05	14.85		21.90	30.50
1540	1-1/4" diam. x 10" embedment		60	.267		14.05	16.35		30.40	40
1545	1-3/4" diam. x 12" embedment		54	.296		23.50	18.15		41.65	53.50
1550	14" embedment		48	.333		28	20.50		48.50	61.50
1555	2" diam. x 12" embedment		42	.381		37.50	23.50		61	76.50
1560	18" embedment		32	.500		47	30.50		77.50	97.50

03 82 Concrete Boring

03 82 13 – Concrete Core Drilling

03 82 13.10 Core Drilling

		Crew	Daily Output	Labor-Hours	Unit	Material	2023 Bare Costs Labor	Equipment	Total	Total Incl O&P
0010	**CORE DRILLING**									
0015	Includes bit cost, layout and set-up time									
0020	Reinforced concrete slab, up to 6" thick									
0100	1" diameter core	B-89A	17	.941	Ea.	.22	51	6.95	58.17	84.50
0150	For each additional inch of slab thickness in same hole, add		1440	.011		.04	.60	.08	.72	1.03
0200	2" diameter core		16.50	.970		.30	52.50	7.15	59.95	86.50
0250	For each additional inch of slab thickness in same hole, add		1080	.015		.05	.80	.11	.96	1.38
0300	3" diameter core		16	1		.43	54.50	7.40	62.33	89.50
0350	For each additional inch of slab thickness in same hole, add		720	.022		.07	1.21	.16	1.44	2.06
0500	4" diameter core		15	1.067		.57	58	7.85	66.42	96
0550	For each additional inch of slab thickness in same hole, add		480	.033		.10	1.81	.25	2.16	3.08
0700	6" diameter core		14	1.143		.91	62	8.45	71.36	103
0750	For each additional inch of slab thickness in same hole, add		360	.044		.15	2.41	.33	2.89	4.14
0900	8" diameter core		13	1.231		1.32	67	9.10	77.42	111
0950	For each additional inch of slab thickness in same hole, add		288	.056		.22	3.01	.41	3.64	5.20
1100	10" diameter core		12	1.333		1.62	72.50	9.85	83.97	121
1150	For each additional inch of slab thickness in same hole, add		240	.067		.27	3.62	.49	4.38	6.25
1300	12" diameter core		11	1.455		1.85	79	10.75	91.60	132
1350	For each additional inch of slab thickness in same hole, add		206	.078		.31	4.21	.57	5.09	7.25

For customer support on your Mechanical Costs with RSMeans data, call 800.448.8182.

03 82 Concrete Boring

03 82 13 – Concrete Core Drilling

03 82 13.10 Core Drilling

		Crew	Daily Output	Labor-Hours	Unit	Material	2023 Bare Costs Labor	2023 Bare Costs Equipment	Total	Total Incl O&P
1500	14" diameter core	B-89A	10	1.600	Ea.	2.29	87	11.80	101.09	146
1550	For each additional inch of slab thickness in same hole, add		180	.089		.38	4.82	.66	5.86	8.35
1700	18" diameter core		9	1.778		2.98	96.50	13.10	112.58	162
1750	For each additional inch of slab thickness in same hole, add		144	.111		.50	6.05	.82	7.37	10.45
1754	24" diameter core		8	2		4.73	109	14.75	128.48	183
1756	For each additional inch of slab thickness in same hole, add		120	.133		.79	7.25	.98	9.02	12.75
1760	For horizontal holes, add to above						20%	20%		
1770	Prestressed hollow core plank, 8" thick									
1780	1" diameter core	B-89A	17.50	.914	Ea.	.30	49.50	6.75	56.55	81.50
1790	For each additional inch of plank thickness in same hole, add		3840	.004		.04	.23	.03	.30	.41
1794	2" diameter core		17.25	.928		.40	50.50	6.85	57.75	83.50
1796	For each additional inch of plank thickness in same hole, add		2880	.006		.05	.30	.04	.39	.56
1800	3" diameter core		17	.941		.57	51	6.95	58.52	85
1810	For each additional inch of plank thickness in same hole, add		1920	.008		.07	.45	.06	.58	.83
1820	4" diameter core		16.50	.970		.76	52.50	7.15	60.41	87
1830	For each additional inch of plank thickness in same hole, add		1280	.013		.10	.68	.09	.87	1.21
1840	6" diameter core		15.50	1.032		1.21	56	7.60	64.81	93.50
1850	For each additional inch of plank thickness in same hole, add		960	.017		.15	.90	.12	1.17	1.66
1860	8" diameter core		15	1.067		1.76	58	7.85	67.61	97
1870	For each additional inch of plank thickness in same hole, add		768	.021		.22	1.13	.15	1.50	2.10
1880	10" diameter core		14	1.143		2.16	62	8.45	72.61	105
1890	For each additional inch of plank thickness in same hole, add		640	.025		.27	1.36	.18	1.81	2.53
1900	12" diameter core		13.50	1.185		2.47	64.50	8.75	75.72	108
1910	For each additional inch of plank thickness in same hole, add		548	.029		.31	1.58	.22	2.11	2.95

03 82 16 – Concrete Drilling

03 82 16.10 Concrete Impact Drilling

		Crew	Daily Output	Labor-Hours	Unit	Material	2023 Bare Costs Labor	2023 Bare Costs Equipment	Total	Total Incl O&P
0010	**CONCRETE IMPACT DRILLING**									
0020	Includes bit cost, layout and set-up time, no anchors									
0050	Up to 4" deep in concrete/brick floors/walls									
0100	Holes, 1/4" diameter	1 Carp	75	.107	Ea.	.04	6.25		6.29	9.35
0150	For each additional inch of depth in same hole, add		430	.019		.01	1.09		1.10	1.63
0200	3/8" diameter		63	.127		.03	7.45		7.48	11.15
0250	For each additional inch of depth in same hole, add		340	.024		.01	1.38		1.39	2.06
0300	1/2" diameter		50	.160		.04	9.40		9.44	14
0350	For each additional inch of depth in same hole, add		250	.032		.01	1.88		1.89	2.80
0400	5/8" diameter		48	.167		.05	9.75		9.80	14.60
0450	For each additional inch of depth in same hole, add		240	.033		.01	1.95		1.96	2.92
0500	3/4" diameter		45	.178		.08	10.40		10.48	15.60
0550	For each additional inch of depth in same hole, add		220	.036		.02	2.13		2.15	3.19
0600	7/8" diameter		43	.186		.07	10.90		10.97	16.35
0650	For each additional inch of depth in same hole, add		210	.038		.02	2.23		2.25	3.34
0700	1" diameter		40	.200		.16	11.70		11.86	17.65
0750	For each additional inch of depth in same hole, add		190	.042		.04	2.47		2.51	3.72
0800	1-1/4" diameter		38	.211		.23	12.35		12.58	18.60
0850	For each additional inch of depth in same hole, add		180	.044		.06	2.60		2.66	3.94
0900	1-1/2" diameter		35	.229		.35	13.40		13.75	20.50
0950	For each additional inch of depth in same hole, add		165	.048		.09	2.84		2.93	4.33
1000	For ceiling installations, add						40%			

Estimating Tips
04 05 00 Common Work Results for Masonry

- The terms mortar and grout are often used interchangeably—and incorrectly. Mortar is used to bed masonry units, seal the entry of air and moisture, provide architectural appearance, and allow for size variations in the units. Grout is used primarily in reinforced masonry construction and to bond the masonry to the reinforcing steel. Common mortar types are M (2500 psi), S (1800 psi), N (750 psi), and O (350 psi), and they conform to ASTM C270. Grout is either fine or coarse and conforms to ASTM C476, and in-place strengths generally exceed 2500 psi. Mortar and grout are different components of masonry construction and are placed by entirely different methods. An estimator should be aware of their unique uses and costs.
- Mortar is included in all assembled masonry line items. The mortar cost, part of the assembled masonry material cost, includes all ingredients, all labor, and all equipment required. Please see reference number R040513-10.
- Waste, specifically the loss/droppings of mortar and the breakage of brick and block, is included in all unit cost lines that include mortar and masonry units in this division. A factor of 25% is added for mortar and 3% for brick and concrete masonry units.
- Scaffolding or staging is not included in any of the Division 4 costs. Refer to Subdivision 01 54 23 for scaffolding and staging costs.

04 20 00 Unit Masonry

- The most common types of unit masonry are brick and concrete masonry. The major classifications of brick are building brick (ASTM C62), facing brick (ASTM C216), glazed brick, fire brick, and pavers. Many varieties of texture and appearance can exist within these classifications, and the estimator would be wise to check local custom and availability within the project area. For repair and remodeling jobs, matching the existing brick may be the most important criteria.
- Brick and concrete block are priced by the piece and then converted into a price per square foot of wall. Openings less than two square feet are generally ignored by the estimator because any savings in units used are offset by the cutting and trimming required.
- It is often difficult and expensive to find and purchase small lots of historic brick. Costs can vary widely. Many design issues affect costs, selection of mortar mix, and repairs or replacement of masonry materials. Cleaning techniques must be reflected in the estimate.
- All masonry walls, whether interior or exterior, require bracing. The cost of bracing walls during construction should be included by the estimator, and this bracing must remain in place until permanent bracing is complete. Permanent bracing of masonry walls is accomplished by masonry itself, in the form of pilasters or abutting wall corners, or by anchoring the walls to the structural frame. Accessories in the form of anchors, anchor slots, and ties are used, but their supply and installation can be by different trades. For instance, anchor slots on spandrel beams and columns are supplied and welded in place by the steel fabricator, but the ties from the slots into the masonry are installed by the bricklayer. Regardless of the installation method, the estimator must be certain that these accessories are accounted for in pricing.

Reference Numbers

Reference numbers are shown at the beginning of some major classifications. These numbers refer to related items in the Reference Section. The reference information may be an estimating procedure, an alternate pricing method, or technical information.

Note: Not all subdivisions listed here necessarily appear. ∎

Same Data. Simplified.

Enjoy the convenience and efficiency of accessing your costs anywhere:
- **Skip the multiplier** by setting your location
- **Quickly search,** edit, favorite and share costs
- **Stay on top of price changes** with automatic updates

Discover more at rsmeans.com/online

No part of this cost data may be reproduced, stored in a retrieval system, or transmitted in any form or by any means without prior written permission of Gordian.

04 05 Common Work Results for Masonry

04 05 23 – Masonry Accessories

04 05 23.19 Masonry Cavity Drainage, Weepholes, and Vents	Crew	Daily Output	Labor-Hours	Unit	Material	2023 Bare Costs Labor	Equipment	Total	Total Incl O&P
0010 **MASONRY CAVITY DRAINAGE, WEEPHOLES, AND VENTS**									
0020 Extruded aluminum, 4" deep, 2-3/8" x 8-1/8"	1 Bric	30	.267	Ea.	16.50	15.35		31.85	41
0050 5" x 8-1/8"		25	.320		23.50	18.40		41.90	53
0100 2-1/4" x 25"		25	.320		163	18.40		181.40	207
0150 5" x 16-1/2"		22	.364		87	21		108	128
0175 5" x 24"		22	.364		77.50	21		98.50	117
0200 6" x 16-1/2"		22	.364		83.50	21		104.50	124
0250 7-3/4" x 16-1/2"		20	.400		12.60	23		35.60	48.50
0400 For baked enamel finish, add					35%				
0500 For cast aluminum, painted, add					60%				
1000 Stainless steel ventilators, 6" x 6"	1 Bric	25	.320		187	18.40		205.40	234
1050 8" x 8"		24	.333		144	19.15		163.15	187
1100 12" x 12"		23	.348		161	20		181	207
1150 12" x 6"		24	.333		86	19.15		105.15	124
1200 Foundation block vent, galv., 1-1/4" thk, 8" high, 16" long, no damper		30	.267		22	15.35		37.35	47
1250 For damper, add					3.49			3.49	3.84
1450 Drainage and ventilation fabric	2 Bric	1450	.011	S.F.	.82	.63		1.45	1.85

04 21 Clay Unit Masonry

04 21 13 – Brick Masonry

04 21 13.15 Chimney

	Crew	Daily Output	Labor-Hours	Unit	Material	Labor	Equipment	Total	Total Incl O&P
0010 **CHIMNEY**, excludes foundation, scaffolding, grout and reinforcing									
0100 Brick, 16" x 16", 8" flue	D-1	18.20	.879	V.L.F.	62.50	46		108.50	138
0150 16" x 20" with one 8" x 12" flue		16	1		75	52		127	161
0200 16" x 24" with two 8" x 8" flues		14	1.143		112	59.50		171.50	213
0250 20" x 20" with one 12" x 12" flue		13.70	1.168		86.50	61		147.50	187
0300 20" x 24" with two 8" x 12" flues		12	1.333		130	69.50		199.50	247
0350 20" x 32" with two 12" x 12" flues		10	1.600		165	83.50		248.50	305

Estimating Tips

05 05 00 Common Work Results for Metals

- Nuts, bolts, washers, connection angles, and plates can add a significant amount to both the tonnage of a structural steel job and the estimated cost. As a rule of thumb, add 10% to the total weight to account for these accessories.
- Type 2 steel construction, commonly referred to as "simple construction," consists generally of field-bolted connections with lateral bracing supplied by other elements of the building, such as masonry walls or x-bracing. The estimator should be aware, however, that shop connections may be accomplished by welding or bolting. The method may be particular to the fabrication shop and may have an impact on the estimated cost.

05 10 00 Structural Steel

- Steel items can be obtained from two sources: a fabrication shop or a metals service center. Fabrication shops can fabricate items under more controlled conditions than crews in the field can. They are also more efficient and can produce items more economically. Metal service centers serve as a source of long mill shapes to both fabrication shops and contractors.
- Most line items in this structural steel subdivision, and most items in 05 50 00 Metal Fabrications, are indicated as being shop fabricated. The bare material cost for these shop fabricated items is the "Invoice Cost" from the shop and includes the mill base price of steel plus mill extras, transportation to the shop, shop drawings and detailing where warranted, shop fabrication and handling, sandblasting and a shop coat of primer paint, all necessary structural bolts, and delivery to the job site. The bare labor cost and bare equipment cost for these shop fabricated items are for field installation or erection.
- Line items in Subdivision 05 12 23.40 Lightweight Framing, and other items scattered in Division 5, are indicated as being field fabricated. The bare material cost for these field fabricated items is the "Invoice Cost" from the metals service center and includes the mill base price of steel plus mill extras, transportation to the metals service center, material handling, and delivery of long lengths of mill shapes to the job site. Material costs for structural bolts and welding rods should be added to the estimate. The bare labor cost and bare equipment cost for these items are for both field fabrication and field installation or erection, and include time for cutting, welding, and drilling in the fabricated metal items. Drilling into concrete and fasteners to fasten field fabricated items to other work is not included and should be added to the estimate.

05 20 00 Steel Joist Framing

- In any given project the total weight of open web steel joists is determined by the loads to be supported and the design. However, economies can be realized in minimizing the amount of labor used to place the joists. This is done by maximizing the joist spacing and therefore minimizing the number of joists required to be installed on the job. Certain spacings and locations may be required by the design, but in other cases maximizing the spacing and keeping it as uniform as possible will keep the costs down.

05 30 00 Steel Decking

- The takeoff and estimating of a metal deck involve more than the area of the floor or roof and the type of deck specified or shown on the drawings. Many different sizes and types of openings may exist. Small openings for individual pipes or conduits may be drilled after the floor/roof is installed, but larger openings may require special deck lengths as well as reinforcing or structural support. The estimator should determine who will be supplying this reinforcing. Additionally, some deck terminations are part of the deck package, such as screed angles and pour stops, and others will be part of the steel contract, such as angles attached to structural members and cast-in-place angles and plates. The estimator must ensure that all pieces are accounted for in the complete estimate.

05 50 00 Metal Fabrications

- The most economical steel stairs are those that use common materials, standard details, and most importantly, a uniform and relatively simple method of field assembly. Commonly available A36/A992 channels and plates are very good choices for the main stringers of the stairs, as are angles and tees for the carrier members. Risers and treads are usually made by specialty shops, and it is most economical to use a typical detail in as many places as possible. The stairs should be pre-assembled and shipped directly to the site. The field connections should be simple and straightforward enough to be accomplished efficiently, and with minimum equipment and labor.

Reference Numbers

Reference numbers are shown at the beginning of some major classifications. These numbers refer to related items in the Reference Section. The reference information may be an estimating procedure, an alternate pricing method, or technical information.

Note: Not all subdivisions listed here necessarily appear. ∎

Same Data. Simplified.

Enjoy the convenience and efficiency of accessing your costs anywhere:
- **Skip the multiplier** by setting your location
- **Quickly search,** edit, favorite and share costs
- **Stay on top of price changes** with automatic updates

Discover more at rsmeans.com/online

No part of this cost data may be reproduced, stored in a retrieval system, or transmitted in any form or by any means without prior written permission of Gordian.

05 05 Common Work Results for Metals

05 05 19 – Post-Installed Concrete Anchors

05 05 19.10 Chemical Anchors		Crew	Daily Output	Labor-Hours	Unit	Material	2023 Bare Costs Labor	Equipment	Total	Total Incl O&P
0010	**CHEMICAL ANCHORS**									
0020	Includes layout & drilling									
1430	Chemical anchor, w/rod & epoxy cartridge, 3/4" diameter x 9-1/2" long	B-89A	27	.593	Ea.	9.55	32	4.37	45.92	63.50
1435	1" diameter x 11-3/4" long		24	.667		17.10	36	4.92	58.02	78
1440	1-1/4" diameter x 14" long		21	.762		33.50	41.50	5.60	80.60	105
1445	1-3/4" diameter x 15" long		20	.800		67.50	43.50	5.90	116.90	146
1450	18" long		17	.941		81	51	6.95	138.95	174
1455	2" diameter x 18" long		16	1		123	54.50	7.40	184.90	224
1460	24" long	▼	15	1.067	▼	160	58	7.85	225.85	271

05 05 19.20 Expansion Anchors			Crew	Daily Output	Labor-Hours	Unit	Material	Labor	Equipment	Total	Total Incl O&P
0010	**EXPANSION ANCHORS**										
0100	Anchors for concrete, brick or stone, no layout and drilling										
0200	Expansion shields, zinc, 1/4" diameter, 1-5/16" long, single	G	1 Carp	90	.089	Ea.	.57	5.20		5.77	8.40
0300	1-3/8" long, double	G		85	.094		.75	5.50		6.25	9.05
0400	3/8" diameter, 1-1/2" long, single	G		85	.094		.92	5.50		6.42	9.20
0500	2" long, double	G		80	.100		1.60	5.85		7.45	10.50
0600	1/2" diameter, 2-1/16" long, single	G		80	.100		1.60	5.85		7.45	10.50
0700	2-1/2" long, double	G		75	.107		1.98	6.25		8.23	11.50
0800	5/8" diameter, 2-5/8" long, single	G		75	.107		2.56	6.25		8.81	12.10
0900	2-3/4" long, double	G		70	.114		3.57	6.70		10.27	13.90
1000	3/4" diameter, 2-3/4" long, single	G		70	.114		4.07	6.70		10.77	14.45
1100	3-15/16" long, double	G	▼	65	.123	▼	6.20	7.20		13.40	17.60
2100	Hollow wall anchors for gypsum wall board, plaster or tile										
2300	1/8" diameter, short	G	1 Carp	160	.050	Ea.	.43	2.93		3.36	4.83
2400	Long	G		150	.053		.37	3.13		3.50	5.05
2500	3/16" diameter, short	G		150	.053		.85	3.13		3.98	5.60
2600	Long	G		140	.057		.97	3.35		4.32	6.05
2700	1/4" diameter, short	G		140	.057		1.18	3.35		4.53	6.30
2800	Long	G		130	.062		.97	3.61		4.58	6.40
3000	Toggle bolts, bright steel, 1/8" diameter, 2" long	G		85	.094		.30	5.50		5.80	8.55
3100	4" long	G		80	.100		.29	5.85		6.14	9.05
3200	3/16" diameter, 3" long	G		80	.100		.34	5.85		6.19	9.10
3300	6" long	G		75	.107		.57	6.25		6.82	9.95
3400	1/4" diameter, 3" long	G		75	.107		.46	6.25		6.71	9.80
3500	6" long	G		70	.114		.69	6.70		7.39	10.70
3600	3/8" diameter, 3" long	G		70	.114		1.18	6.70		7.88	11.25
3700	6" long	G		60	.133		1.91	7.80		9.71	13.75
3800	1/2" diameter, 4" long	G		60	.133		2.70	7.80		10.50	14.60
3900	6" long	G	▼	50	.160	▼	3.29	9.40		12.69	17.55
5000	Screw anchors for concrete, masonry,										
5100	stone & tile, no layout or drilling included										
5700	Lag screw shields, 1/4" diameter, short	G	1 Carp	90	.089	Ea.	.31	5.20		5.51	8.10
5800	Long	G		85	.094		.40	5.50		5.90	8.65
5900	3/8" diameter, short	G		85	.094		.68	5.50		6.18	8.95
6000	Long	G		80	.100		.83	5.85		6.68	9.65
6100	1/2" diameter, short	G		80	.100		.84	5.85		6.69	9.65
6200	Long	G		75	.107		1.30	6.25		7.55	10.75
6300	5/8" diameter, short	G		70	.114		1.25	6.70		7.95	11.35
6400	Long	G		65	.123		1.95	7.20		9.15	12.90
6600	Lead, #6 & #8, 3/4" long	G		260	.031		.32	1.80		2.12	3.03
6700	#10 - #14, 1-1/2" long	G		200	.040		.69	2.34		3.03	4.25
6800	#16 & #18, 1-1/2" long	G		160	.050		.99	2.93		3.92	5.45

05 05 Common Work Results for Metals

05 05 19 – Post-Installed Concrete Anchors

05 05 19.20 Expansion Anchors

		Crew	Daily Output	Labor-Hours	Unit	Material	2023 Bare Costs Labor	Equipment	Total	Total Incl O&P
6900	Plastic, #6 & #8, 3/4" long	1 Carp	260	.031	Ea.	.03	1.80		1.83	2.71
7000	#8 & #10, 7/8" long		240	.033		.03	1.95		1.98	2.94
7100	#10 & #12, 1" long		220	.036		.05	2.13		2.18	3.23
7200	#14 & #16, 1-1/2" long		160	.050		.08	2.93		3.01	4.45
8000	Wedge anchors, not including layout or drilling									
8050	Carbon steel, 1/4" diameter, 1-3/4" long G	1 Carp	150	.053	Ea.	.86	3.13		3.99	5.60
8100	3-1/4" long G		140	.057		1.14	3.35		4.49	6.25
8150	3/8" diameter, 2-1/4" long G		145	.055		.46	3.23		3.69	5.30
8200	5" long G		140	.057		.81	3.35		4.16	5.90
8250	1/2" diameter, 2-3/4" long G		140	.057		1	3.35		4.35	6.10
8300	7" long G		125	.064		1.71	3.75		5.46	7.50
8350	5/8" diameter, 3-1/2" long G		130	.062		2.45	3.61		6.06	8.05
8400	8-1/2" long G		115	.070		5.20	4.08		9.28	11.80
8450	3/4" diameter, 4-1/4" long G		115	.070		3.97	4.08		8.05	10.40
8500	10" long G		95	.084		9	4.93		13.93	17.30
8550	1" diameter, 6" long G		100	.080		9.05	4.69		13.74	16.95
8575	9" long G		85	.094		11.75	5.50		17.25	21
8600	12" long G		75	.107		12.70	6.25		18.95	23.50
8650	1-1/4" diameter, 9" long G		70	.114		55	6.70		61.70	70.50
8700	12" long G		60	.133		70.50	7.80		78.30	89
8750	For type 303 stainless steel, add					350%				
8800	For type 316 stainless steel, add					450%				
8950	Self-drilling concrete screw, hex washer head, 3/16" diam. x 1-3/4" long G	1 Carp	300	.027	Ea.	.25	1.56		1.81	2.61
8960	2-1/4" long G		250	.032		.26	1.88		2.14	3.08
8970	Phillips flat head, 3/16" diam. x 1-3/4" long G		300	.027		.20	1.56		1.76	2.55
8980	2-1/4" long G		250	.032		.21	1.88		2.09	3.02

05 05 21 – Fastening Methods for Metal

05 05 21.15 Drilling Steel

		Crew	Daily Output	Labor-Hours	Unit	Material	2023 Bare Costs Labor	Equipment	Total	Total Incl O&P
0010	**DRILLING STEEL**									
1910	Drilling & layout for steel, up to 1/4" deep, no anchor									
1920	Holes, 1/4" diameter	1 Sswk	112	.071	Ea.	.06	4.61		4.67	7.15
1925	For each additional 1/4" depth, add		336	.024		.06	1.54		1.60	2.43
1930	3/8" diameter		104	.077		.04	4.97		5.01	7.70
1935	For each additional 1/4" depth, add		312	.026		.04	1.66		1.70	2.60
1940	1/2" diameter		96	.083		.07	5.40		5.47	8.40
1945	For each additional 1/4" depth, add		288	.028		.07	1.79		1.86	2.84
1950	5/8" diameter		88	.091		.07	5.85		5.92	9.15
1955	For each additional 1/4" depth, add		264	.030		.07	1.96		2.03	3.09
1960	3/4" diameter		80	.100		.13	6.45		6.58	10.10
1965	For each additional 1/4" depth, add		240	.033		.13	2.15		2.28	3.45
1970	7/8" diameter		72	.111		.11	7.15		7.26	11.15
1975	For each additional 1/4" depth, add		216	.037		.11	2.39		2.50	3.80
1980	1" diameter		64	.125		.24	8.05		8.29	12.70
1985	For each additional 1/4" depth, add		192	.042		.24	2.69		2.93	4.40
1990	For drilling up, add					40%				

05 05 21.90 Welding Steel

		Crew	Daily Output	Labor-Hours	Unit	Material	2023 Bare Costs Labor	Equipment	Total	Total Incl O&P
0010	**WELDING STEEL**, Structural									
0020	Field welding, 1/8" E6011, cost per welder, no operating engineer	E-14	8	1	Hr.	8	66.50	18.40	92.90	132
0200	With 1/2 operating engineer	E-13	8	1.500		8	96.50	18.40	122.90	176
0300	With 1 operating engineer	E-12	8	2		8	126	18.40	152.40	220
0500	With no operating engineer, 2# weld rod per ton	E-14	8	1	Ton	8	66.50	18.40	92.90	132
0600	8# E6011 per ton	"	2	4		32	266	73.50	371.50	525

05 05 Common Work Results for Metals

05 05 21 – Fastening Methods for Metal

05 05 21.90 Welding Steel

		Crew	Daily Output	Labor-Hours	Unit	Material	2023 Bare Costs Labor	Equipment	Total	Total Incl O&P
0800	With one operating engineer per welder, 2# E6011 per ton	E-12	8	2	Ton	8	126	18.40	152.40	220
0900	8# E6011 per ton	"	2	8	↓	32	505	73.50	610.50	880
1200	Continuous fillet, down welding									
1300	Single pass, 1/8" thick, 0.1#/L.F.	E-14	150	.053	L.F.	.40	3.55	.98	4.93	6.95
1400	3/16" thick, 0.2#/L.F.		75	.107		.80	7.10	1.96	9.86	14
1500	1/4" thick, 0.3#/L.F.		50	.160		1.20	10.65	2.94	14.79	21
1610	5/16" thick, 0.4#/L.F.		38	.211		1.60	14	3.87	19.47	27.50
1800	3 passes, 3/8" thick, 0.5#/L.F.		30	.267		2	17.75	4.90	24.65	35
2010	4 passes, 1/2" thick, 0.7#/L.F.		22	.364		2.80	24	6.70	33.50	48
2200	5 to 6 passes, 3/4" thick, 1.3#/L.F.		12	.667		5.20	44.50	12.25	61.95	87.50
2400	8 to 11 passes, 1" thick, 2.4#/L.F.	↓	6	1.333		9.60	88.50	24.50	122.60	175
2600	For vertical joint welding, add						20%			
2700	Overhead joint welding, add						300%			
2900	For semi-automatic welding, obstructed joints, deduct						5%			
3000	Exposed joints, deduct				↓		15%			
4000	Cleaning and welding plates, bars, or rods									
4010	to existing beams, columns, or trusses	E-14	12	.667	L.F.	2	44.50	12.25	58.75	84

05 05 23 – Metal Fastenings

05 05 23.30 Lag Screws

			Crew	Daily Output	Labor-Hours	Unit	Material	Labor	Equipment	Total	Total Incl O&P
0010	**LAG SCREWS**										
0020	Steel, 1/4" diameter, 2" long	G	1 Carp	200	.040	Ea.	.15	2.34		2.49	3.66
0100	3/8" diameter, 3" long	G		150	.053		.51	3.13		3.64	5.20
0200	1/2" diameter, 3" long	G		130	.062		1.15	3.61		4.76	6.60
0300	5/8" diameter, 3" long	G	↓	120	.067	↓	1.83	3.91		5.74	7.80

05 05 23.35 Machine Screws

			Crew	Daily Output	Labor-Hours	Unit	Material	Labor	Equipment	Total	Total Incl O&P
0010	**MACHINE SCREWS**										
0020	Steel, round head, #8 x 1" long	G	1 Carp	4.80	1.667	C	5.05	97.50		102.55	151
0110	#8 x 2" long	G		2.40	3.333		8.40	195		203.40	300
0200	#10 x 1" long	G		4	2		7.10	117		124.10	183
0300	#10 x 2" long	G	↓	2	4	↓	12	234		246	365

05 05 23.50 Powder Actuated Tools and Fasteners

			Crew	Daily Output	Labor-Hours	Unit	Material	Labor	Equipment	Total	Total Incl O&P
0010	**POWDER ACTUATED TOOLS & FASTENERS**										
0020	Stud driver, .22 caliber, single shot					Ea.	95.50			95.50	105
0100	.27 caliber, semi automatic, strip					"	575			575	635
0300	Powder load, single shot, .22 cal, power level 2, brown					C	7.25			7.25	8
0400	Strip, .27 cal, power level 4, red						15.05			15.05	16.60
0600	Drive pin, .300 x 3/4" long	G	1 Carp	4.80	1.667		5.40	97.50		102.90	151
0700	.300 x 3" long with washer	G	"	4	2	↓	13.85	117		130.85	190

05 05 23.55 Rivets

			Crew	Daily Output	Labor-Hours	Unit	Material	Labor	Equipment	Total	Total Incl O&P
0010	**RIVETS**										
0100	Aluminum rivet & mandrel, 1/2" grip length x 1/8" diameter	G	1 Carp	4.80	1.667	C	3.78	97.50		101.28	149
0200	3/16" diameter	G		4	2		6.95	117		123.95	183
0300	Aluminum rivet, steel mandrel, 1/8" diameter	G		4.80	1.667		3.62	97.50		101.12	149
0400	3/16" diameter	G		4	2		6.65	117		123.65	182
0500	Copper rivet, steel mandrel, 1/8" diameter	G		4.80	1.667		9.20	97.50		106.70	155
1200	Steel rivet and mandrel, 1/8" diameter	G		4.80	1.667		5.45	97.50		102.95	151
1300	3/16" diameter	G		4	2		8.75	117		125.75	185
1400	Hand riveting tool, standard					Ea.	13.25			13.25	14.60
1500	Deluxe						465			465	515
1600	Power riveting tool, standard						615			615	680
1700	Deluxe						1,625			1,625	1,800

05 05 Common Work Results for Metals

05 05 23 – Metal Fastenings

05 05 23.70 Structural Blind Bolts

		Crew	Daily Output	Labor-Hours	Unit	Material	2023 Bare Costs Labor	Equipment	Total	Total Incl O&P
0010	**STRUCTURAL BLIND BOLTS**									
0100	1/4" diameter x 1/4" grip	G 1 Sswk	240	.033	Ea.	.98	2.15		3.13	4.39
0150	1/2" grip	G	216	.037		.93	2.39		3.32	4.70
0200	3/8" diameter x 1/2" grip	G	232	.034		1.91	2.23		4.14	5.55
0250	3/4" grip	G	208	.038		2	2.48		4.48	6
0300	1/2" diameter x 1/2" grip	G	224	.036		4.14	2.31		6.45	8.10
0350	3/4" grip	G	200	.040		4.14	2.58		6.72	8.55
0400	5/8" diameter x 3/4" grip	G	216	.037		6.50	2.39		8.89	10.85
0450	1" grip	G	192	.042		6.50	2.69		9.19	11.30

05 12 Structural Steel Framing

05 12 23 – Structural Steel for Buildings

05 12 23.40 Lightweight Framing

		Crew	Daily Output	Labor-Hours	Unit	Material	2023 Bare Costs Labor	Equipment	Total	Total Incl O&P
0010	**LIGHTWEIGHT FRAMING**									
0015	Made from recycled materials									
0400	Angle framing, field fabricated, 4" and larger	G E-3	440	.055	Lb.	.95	3.56	.33	4.84	6.90
0450	Less than 4" angles	G	265	.091		.99	5.90	.56	7.45	10.80
0600	Channel framing, field fabricated, 8" and larger	G	500	.048		.99	3.13	.29	4.41	6.25
0650	Less than 8" channels	G	335	.072		.99	4.67	.44	6.10	8.75
1000	Continuous slotted channel framing system, shop fab, simple framing	G 2 Sswk	2400	.007		5.10	.43		5.53	6.25
1200	Complex framing	G "	1600	.010		5.75	.65		6.40	7.35
1250	Plate & bar stock for reinforcing beams and trusses	G				1.81			1.81	1.99
1300	Cross bracing, rods, shop fabricated, 3/4" diameter	G E-3	700	.034		1.97	2.24	.21	4.42	5.85
1310	7/8" diameter	G	850	.028		1.97	1.84	.17	3.98	5.20
1320	1" diameter	G	1000	.024		1.97	1.57	.15	3.69	4.74
1330	Angle, 5" x 5" x 3/8"	G	2800	.009		1.97	.56	.05	2.58	3.09
1350	Hanging lintels, shop fabricated	G	850	.028		1.97	1.84	.17	3.98	5.20
1380	Roof frames, shop fabricated, 3'-0" square, 5' span	G E-2	4200	.013		1.97	.85	.64	3.46	4.17
1400	Tie rod, not upset, 1-1/2" to 4" diameter, with turnbuckle	G 2 Sswk	800	.020		2.14	1.29		3.43	4.34
1420	No turnbuckle	G	700	.023		2.06	1.48		3.54	4.53
1500	Upset, 1-3/4" to 4" diameter, with turnbuckle	G	800	.020		2.14	1.29		3.43	4.34
1520	No turnbuckle	G	700	.023		2.06	1.48		3.54	4.53

05 12 23.60 Pipe Support Framing

		Crew	Daily Output	Labor-Hours	Unit	Material	2023 Bare Costs Labor	Equipment	Total	Total Incl O&P
0010	**PIPE SUPPORT FRAMING**									
0020	Under 10#/L.F., shop fabricated	G E-4	3900	.008	Lb.	2.21	.53	.04	2.78	3.29
0200	10.1 to 15#/L.F.	G	4300	.007		2.17	.48	.03	2.68	3.18
0400	15.1 to 20#/L.F.	G	4800	.007		2.14	.43	.03	2.60	3.05
0600	Over 20#/L.F.	G	5400	.006		2.11	.39	.03	2.53	2.94

Division Notes

	CREW	DAILY OUTPUT	LABOR-HOURS	UNIT	BARE COSTS				TOTAL INCL O&P
					MAT.	LABOR	EQUIP.	TOTAL	

Estimating Tips
06 05 00 Common Work Results for Wood, Plastics, and Composites

- Common to any wood-framed structure are the accessory connector items such as screws, nails, adhesives, hangers, connector plates, straps, angles, and hold-downs. For typical wood-framed buildings, such as residential projects, the aggregate total for these items can be significant, especially in areas where seismic loading is a concern. For floor and wall framing, the material cost is based on 10 to 25 lbs. of accessory connectors per MBF. Hold-downs, hangers, and other connectors should be taken off by the piece.

  Included with material costs are fasteners for a normal installation. Gordian's RSMeans engineers use manufacturers' recommendations, written specifications, and/or standard construction practice for the sizing and spacing of fasteners. Prices for various fasteners are shown for informational purposes only. Adjustments should be made if unusual fastening conditions exist.

06 10 00 Carpentry

- Lumber is a traded commodity and therefore sensitive to supply and demand in the marketplace. Even with "budgetary" estimating of wood-framed projects, it is advisable to call local suppliers for the latest market pricing.

- The common quantity unit for wood-framed projects is "thousand board feet" (MBF). A board foot is a volume of wood—1" x 1' x 1' or 144 cubic inches. Board-foot quantities are generally calculated using nominal material dimensions—dressed sizes are ignored. Board foot per lineal foot of any stick of lumber can be calculated by dividing the nominal cross-sectional area by 12. As an example, 2,000 lineal feet of 2 x 12 equates to 4 MBF by dividing the nominal area, 2 x 12, by 12, which equals 2, and multiplying that by 2,000 to give 4,000 board feet. This simple rule applies to all nominal dimensioned lumber.

- Waste is an issue of concern at the quantity takeoff for any area of construction. Framing lumber is sold in even foot lengths, i.e., 8', 10', 12', 14', 16', and depending on spans, wall heights, and the grade of lumber, waste is inevitable. A rule of thumb for lumber waste is 5–10% depending on material quality and the complexity of the framing.

- Wood in various forms and shapes is used in many projects, even where the main structural framing is steel, concrete, or masonry. Plywood as a back-up partition material and 2x boards used as blocking and cant strips around roof edges are two common examples. The estimator should ensure that the costs of all wood materials are included in the final estimate.

06 20 00 Finish Carpentry

- It is necessary to consider the grade of workmanship when estimating labor costs for erecting millwork and an interior finish. In practice, there are three grades: premium, custom, and economy. The RSMeans daily output for base and case moldings is in the range of 200 to 250 L.F. per carpenter per day. This is appropriate for most average custom-grade projects. For premium projects, an adjustment to productivity of 25–50% should be made, depending on the complexity of the job.

Reference Numbers

Reference numbers are shown at the beginning of some major classifications. These numbers refer to related items in the Reference Section. The reference information may be an estimating procedure, an alternate pricing method, or technical information.

Note: Not all subdivisions listed here necessarily appear. ■

Same Data. Simplified.

Enjoy the convenience and efficiency of accessing your costs anywhere:

- **Skip the multiplier** by setting your location
- **Quickly search,** edit, favorite and share costs
- **Stay on top of price changes** with automatic updates

Discover more at rsmeans.com/online

No part of this cost data may be reproduced, stored in a retrieval system, or transmitted in any form or by any means without prior written permission of Gordian.

06 16 Sheathing

06 16 36 – Wood Panel Product Sheathing

06 16 36.10 Sheathing		Crew	Daily Output	Labor-Hours	Unit	Material	2023 Bare Costs Labor	Equipment	Total	Total Incl O&P
0010	**SHEATHING**									
0012	Plywood on roofs, CDX									
0030	5/16" thick	2 Carp	1600	.010	S.F.	.99	.59		1.58	1.96
0035	Pneumatic nailed		1952	.008		.99	.48		1.47	1.81
0050	3/8" thick		1525	.010		1.08	.61		1.69	2.11
0055	Pneumatic nailed		1860	.009		1.08	.50		1.58	1.94
0100	1/2" thick		1400	.011		1.16	.67		1.83	2.27
0105	Pneumatic nailed		1708	.009		1.16	.55		1.71	2.09
0200	5/8" thick		1300	.012		1.37	.72		2.09	2.58
0205	Pneumatic nailed		1586	.010		1.37	.59		1.96	2.39
0300	3/4" thick		1200	.013		1.71	.78		2.49	3.04
0305	Pneumatic nailed		1464	.011		1.71	.64		2.35	2.83
0500	Plywood on walls, with exterior CDX, 3/8" thick		1200	.013		1.08	.78		1.86	2.35
0505	Pneumatic nailed		1488	.011		1.08	.63		1.71	2.13
0600	1/2" thick		1125	.014		1.16	.83		1.99	2.51
0605	Pneumatic nailed		1395	.011		1.16	.67		1.83	2.27
0700	5/8" thick		1050	.015		1.37	.89		2.26	2.84
0705	Pneumatic nailed		1302	.012		1.37	.72		2.09	2.58
0800	3/4" thick		975	.016		1.71	.96		2.67	3.31
0805	Pneumatic nailed		1209	.013		1.71	.78		2.49	3.03

Division 7 Thermal & Moisture Protection

Estimating Tips
07 10 00 Dampproofing and Waterproofing
- Be sure of the job specifications before pricing this subdivision. The difference in cost between waterproofing and dampproofing can be great. Waterproofing will hold back standing water. Dampproofing prevents the transmission of water vapor. Also included in this section are vapor retarding membranes.

07 20 00 Thermal Protection
- Insulation and fireproofing products are measured by area, thickness, volume, or R-value. Specifications may give only what the specific R-value should be in a certain situation. The estimator may need to choose the type of insulation to meet that R-value.

07 30 00 Steep Slope Roofing
07 40 00 Roofing and Siding Panels
- Many roofing and siding products are bought and sold by the square. One square is equal to an area that measures 100 square feet.

  This simple change in unit of measure could create a large error if the estimator is not observant. Accessories necessary for a complete installation must be figured into any calculations for both material and labor.

07 50 00 Membrane Roofing
07 60 00 Flashing and Sheet Metal
07 70 00 Roofing and Wall Specialties and Accessories
- The items in these subdivisions compose a roofing system. No one component completes the installation, and all must be estimated. Built-up or single-ply membrane roofing systems are made up of many products and installation trades. Wood blocking at roof perimeters or penetrations, parapet coverings, reglets, roof drains, gutters, downspouts, sheet metal flashing, skylights, smoke vents, and roof hatches all need to be considered along with the roofing material. Several different installation trades will need to work together on the roofing system. Inherent difficulties in the scheduling and coordination of various trades must be accounted for when estimating labor costs.

07 90 00 Joint Protection
- To complete the weather-tight shell, the sealants and caulkings must be estimated. Where different materials meet—at expansion joints, at flashing penetrations, and at hundreds of other locations throughout a construction project—caulking and sealants provide another line of defense against water penetration. Often, an entire system is based on the proper location and placement of caulking or sealants. The detailed drawings that are included as part of a set of architectural plans show typical locations for these materials. When caulking or sealants are shown at typical locations, this means the estimator must include them for all the locations where this detail is applicable. Be careful to keep different types of sealants separate, and remember to consider backer rods and primers if necessary.

Reference Numbers
Reference numbers are shown at the beginning of some major classifications. These numbers refer to related items in the Reference Section. The reference information may be an estimating procedure, an alternate pricing method, or technical information.

Note: Not all subdivisions listed here necessarily appear. ■

Same Data. Simplified.
Enjoy the convenience and efficiency of accessing your costs anywhere:
- **Skip the multiplier** by setting your location
- **Quickly search,** edit, favorite and share costs
- **Stay on top of price changes** with automatic updates

Discover more at rsmeans.com/online

No part of this cost data may be reproduced, stored in a retrieval system, or transmitted in any form or by any means without prior written permission of Gordian.

07 65 Flexible Flashing

07 65 10 – Sheet Metal Flashing

07 65 10.10 Sheet Metal Flashing and Counter Flashing		Crew	Daily Output	Labor-Hours	Unit	Material	2023 Bare Costs Labor	Equipment	Total	Total Incl O&P
0010	**SHEET METAL FLASHING AND COUNTER FLASHING**									
0011	Including up to 4 bends									
0020	Aluminum, mill finish, .013" thick	1 Rofc	145	.055	S.F.	1.68	2.86		4.54	6.50
0030	.016" thick		145	.055		.95	2.86		3.81	5.70
0060	.019" thick		145	.055		6.70	2.86		9.56	12
0100	.032" thick		145	.055		6.70	2.86		9.56	12
0200	.040" thick		145	.055		5.70	2.86		8.56	10.95
0300	.050" thick		145	.055		8	2.86		10.86	13.45
0400	Painted finish, add					.40			.40	.44
1600	Copper, 16 oz. sheets, under 1000 lb.	1 Rofc	115	.070		20	3.60		23.60	28
1700	Over 4000 lb.		155	.052		20	2.67		22.67	26.50
1900	20 oz. sheets, under 1000 lb.		110	.073		17.50	3.77		21.27	25.50
2000	Over 4000 lb.		145	.055		16.65	2.86		19.51	23
2200	24 oz. sheets, under 1000 lb.		105	.076		20.50	3.95		24.45	29
2300	Over 4000 lb.		135	.059		19.55	3.07		22.62	26.50
2500	32 oz. sheets, under 1000 lb.		100	.080		27.50	4.14		31.64	37
2600	Over 4000 lb.		130	.062		26.50	3.19		29.69	34
5800	Lead, 2.5 lb./S.F., up to 12" wide		135	.059		8.45	3.07		11.52	14.25
5900	Over 12" wide		135	.059		8.45	3.07		11.52	14.25
8900	Stainless steel sheets, 32 ga.		155	.052		4.58	2.67		7.25	9.40
9000	28 ga.		155	.052		12.45	2.67		15.12	18.05
9100	26 ga.		155	.052		9.70	2.67		12.37	15
9200	24 ga.		155	.052		11.60	2.67		14.27	17.10
9400	Terne coated stainless steel, .015" thick, 28 ga.		155	.052		10.50	2.67		13.17	15.90
9500	.018" thick, 26 ga.		155	.052		10	2.67		12.67	15.35
9600	Zinc and copper alloy (brass), .020" thick		155	.052		11.65	2.67		14.32	17.20
9700	.027" thick		155	.052		13.75	2.67		16.42	19.45
9800	.032" thick		155	.052		16	2.67		18.67	22
9900	.040" thick		155	.052		22	2.67		24.67	28.50

07 65 13 – Laminated Sheet Flashing

07 65 13.10 Laminated Sheet Flashing		Crew	Daily Output	Labor-Hours	Unit	Material	Labor	Equipment	Total	Total Incl O&P
0010	**LAMINATED SHEET FLASHING**, Including up to 4 bends									
4300	Copper-clad stainless steel, .015" thick, under 500 lb.	1 Rofc	115	.070	S.F.	8.90	3.60		12.50	15.65
4400	Over 2000 lb.		155	.052		8.75	2.67		11.42	14
4600	.018" thick, under 500 lb.		100	.080		10.20	4.14		14.34	17.95
4700	Over 2000 lb.		145	.055		10.50	2.86		13.36	16.20
8550	Shower pan, 3 ply copper and fabric, 3 oz.		155	.052		5.30	2.67		7.97	10.20
8600	7 oz.		155	.052		6.45	2.67		9.12	11.40
9300	Stainless steel, paperbacked 2 sides, .005" thick		330	.024		5.20	1.26		6.46	7.80

07 65 19 – Plastic Sheet Flashing

07 65 19.10 Plastic Sheet Flashing and Counter Flashing		Crew	Daily Output	Labor-Hours	Unit	Material	Labor	Equipment	Total	Total Incl O&P
0010	**PLASTIC SHEET FLASHING AND COUNTER FLASHING**									
7300	Polyvinyl chloride, black, 10 mil	1 Rofc	285	.028	S.F.	.35	1.45		1.80	2.75
7400	20 mil		285	.028		.34	1.45		1.79	2.73
7600	30 mil		285	.028		.43	1.45		1.88	2.83
7700	60 mil		285	.028		1.14	1.45		2.59	3.61
7900	Black or white for exposed roofs, 60 mil		285	.028		5.30	1.45		6.75	8.15
8060	PVC tape, 5" x 45 mils, for joint covers, 100 L.F./roll				Ea.	150			150	165
8850	Polyvinyl chloride, 30 mil	1 Rofc	160	.050	S.F.	1.07	2.59		3.66	5.40

07 71 Roof Specialties

07 71 16 – Manufactured Counterflashing Systems

07 71 16.20 Pitch Pockets, Variable Sizes		Crew	Daily Output	Labor-Hours	Unit	Material	2023 Bare Costs Labor	Equipment	Total	Total Incl O&P
0010	PITCH POCKETS, VARIABLE SIZES									
0100	Adjustable, 4" to 7", welded corners, 4" deep	1 Rofc	48	.167	Ea.	46	8.65		54.65	64.50
0200	Side extenders, 6"	"	240	.033	"	4.27	1.73		6	7.50

07 71 23 – Manufactured Gutters and Downspouts

07 71 23.10 Downspouts

0010	DOWNSPOUTS									
0020	Aluminum, embossed, .020" thick, 2" x 3"	1 Shee	190	.042	L.F.	1.85	2.95		4.80	6.50
0100	Enameled		190	.042		1.85	2.95		4.80	6.50
4800	Steel, galvanized, round, corrugated, 2" or 3" diameter, 28 ga.		190	.042		4.18	2.95		7.13	9.05
4900	4" diameter, 28 ga.		145	.055		5.70	3.87		9.57	12.10
5100	5" diameter, 26 ga.		130	.062		6.25	4.32		10.57	13.35
5400	6" diameter, 28 ga.		105	.076		7.20	5.35		12.55	15.95
5500	26 ga.		105	.076		7.20	5.35		12.55	15.95

07 72 Roof Accessories

07 72 26 – Ridge Vents

07 72 26.10 Ridge Vents and Accessories

0010	RIDGE VENTS AND ACCESSORIES									
2300	Ridge vent strip, mill finish	1 Shee	155	.052	L.F.	3.79	3.62		7.41	9.60

07 72 53 – Snow Guards

07 72 53.10 Snow Guard Options

0010	SNOW GUARD OPTIONS									
0100	Slate & asphalt shingle roofs, fastened with nails	1 Rofc	160	.050	Ea.	15.50	2.59		18.09	21.50
0200	Standing seam metal roofs, fastened with set screws		48	.167		22	8.65		30.65	38.50
0300	Surface mount for metal roofs, fastened with solder		48	.167		9.65	8.65		18.30	24.50
0400	Double rail pipe type, including pipe		130	.062	L.F.	44.50	3.19		47.69	54

07 76 Roof Pavers

07 76 16 – Roof Decking Pavers

07 76 16.10 Roof Pavers and Supports

0010	ROOF PAVERS AND SUPPORTS									
1000	Roof decking pavers, concrete blocks, 2" thick, natural	1 Clab	115	.070	S.F.	1.88	3.29		5.17	6.95
1100	Colors		115	.070	"	1.88	3.29		5.17	6.95
1200	Support pedestal, bottom cap		960	.008	Ea.	3.60	.39		3.99	4.55
1300	Top cap		960	.008		6.60	.39		6.99	7.85
1400	Leveling shims, 1/16"		1920	.004		1.63	.20		1.83	2.08
1500	1/8"		1920	.004		1.99	.20		2.19	2.48
1600	Buffer pad		960	.008		7.70	.39		8.09	9.05
1700	PVC legs (4" SDR 35)		2880	.003	Inch	.29	.13		.42	.52
2000	Alternate pricing method, system in place		101	.079	S.F.	8.15	3.74		11.89	14.50

07 84 Firestopping

07 84 13 – Penetration Firestopping

07 84 13.10 Firestopping

		Crew	Daily Output	Labor-Hours	Unit	Material	2023 Bare Costs Labor	Equipment	Total	Total Incl O&P
0010	**FIRESTOPPING** R078413-30									
0100	Metallic piping, non insulated									
0110	Through walls, 2" diameter	1 Carp	16	.500	Ea.	11.75	29.50		41.25	56.50
0120	4" diameter		14	.571		20.50	33.50		54	72.50
0130	6" diameter		12	.667		30	39		69	91
0140	12" diameter		10	.800		25.50	47		72.50	98.50
0150	Through floors, 2" diameter		32	.250		5.90	14.65		20.55	28.50
0160	4" diameter		28	.286		10.30	16.75		27.05	36.50
0170	6" diameter		24	.333		15.05	19.55		34.60	45.50
0180	12" diameter		20	.400		13.25	23.50		36.75	49.50
0190	Metallic piping, insulated									
0200	Through walls, 2" diameter	1 Carp	16	.500	Ea.	20.50	29.50		50	66
0210	4" diameter		14	.571		30	33.50		63.50	83
0220	6" diameter		12	.667		40.50	39		79.50	103
0230	12" diameter		10	.800		69	47		116	146
0240	Through floors, 2" diameter		32	.250		10.30	14.65		24.95	33.50
0250	4" diameter		28	.286		15.05	16.75		31.80	41.50
0260	6" diameter		24	.333		20	19.55		39.55	51
0270	12" diameter		20	.400		34.50	23.50		58	73
0280	Non metallic piping, non insulated									
0290	Through walls, 2" diameter	1 Carp	12	.667	Ea.	71.50	39		110.50	137
0300	4" diameter		10	.800		132	47		179	215
0310	6" diameter		8	1		252	58.50		310.50	365
0330	Through floors, 2" diameter		16	.500		45	29.50		74.50	93
0340	4" diameter		6	1.333		82.50	78		160.50	207
0350	6" diameter		6	1.333		150	78		228	280
0370	Ductwork, insulated & non insulated, round									
0380	Through walls, 6" diameter	1 Carp	12	.667	Ea.	40.50	39		79.50	103
0390	12" diameter		10	.800		69	47		116	146
0400	18" diameter		8	1		84	58.50		142.50	180
0410	Through floors, 6" diameter		16	.500		20	29.50		49.50	65.50
0420	12" diameter		14	.571		15.05	33.50		48.55	66.50
0430	18" diameter		12	.667		18.20	39		57.20	78
0440	Ductwork, insulated & non insulated, rectangular									
0450	With stiffener/closure angle, through walls, 6" x 12"	1 Carp	8	1	Ea.	53	58.50		111.50	146
0460	12" x 24"		6	1.333		106	78		184	232
0470	24" x 48"		4	2		212	117		329	410
0480	With stiffener/closure angle, through floors, 6" x 12"		10	.800		10.75	47		57.75	82
0490	12" x 24"		8	1		53	58.50		111.50	146
0500	24" x 48"		6	1.333		106	78		184	232
0510	Multi trade openings									
0520	Through walls, 6" x 12"	1 Carp	2	4	Ea.	80.50	234		314.50	440
0530	12" x 24"	"	1	8		217	470		687	940
0540	24" x 48"	2 Carp	1	16		655	940		1,595	2,125
0550	48" x 96"	"	.75	21.333		2,625	1,250		3,875	4,725
0560	Through floors, 6" x 12"	1 Carp	2	4		49.50	234		283.50	405
0570	12" x 24"	"	1	8		65.50	470		535.50	770
0580	24" x 48"	2 Carp	.75	21.333		142	1,250		1,392	2,000
0590	48" x 96"	"	.50	32		335	1,875		2,210	3,175
0600	Structural penetrations, through walls									
0610	Steel beams, W8 x 10	1 Carp	8	1	Ea.	76	58.50		134.50	171
0620	W12 x 14		6	1.333		110	78		188	237
0630	W21 x 44		5	1.600		169	94		263	325

07 84 Firestopping

07 84 13 – Penetration Firestopping

07 84 13.10 Firestopping

		Crew	Daily Output	Labor-Hours	Unit	Material	2023 Bare Costs Labor	Equipment	Total	Total Incl O&P
0640	W36 x 135	1 Carp	3	2.667	Ea.	240	156		396	495
0650	Bar joists, 18" deep		6	1.333		44	78		122	165
0660	24" deep		6	1.333		62.50	78		140.50	185
0670	36" deep		5	1.600		93.50	94		187.50	243
0680	48" deep	↓	4	2	↓	135	117		252	325
0690	Construction joints, floor slab at exterior wall									
0700	Precast, brick, block or drywall exterior									
0710	2" wide joint	1 Carp	125	.064	L.F.	11.30	3.75		15.05	18.05
0720	4" wide joint	"	75	.107	"	17.45	6.25		23.70	28.50
0730	Metal panel, glass or curtain wall exterior									
0740	2" wide joint	1 Carp	40	.200	L.F.	12.85	11.70		24.55	31.50
0750	4" wide joint	"	25	.320	"	14.60	18.75		33.35	44
0760	Floor slab to drywall partition									
0770	Flat joint	1 Carp	100	.080	L.F.	14.80	4.69		19.49	23.50
0780	Fluted joint		50	.160		17.20	9.40		26.60	33
0790	Etched fluted joint	↓	75	.107	↓	20.50	6.25		26.75	32
0800	Floor slab to concrete/masonry partition									
0810	Flat joint	1 Carp	75	.107	L.F.	17.25	6.25		23.50	28.50
0820	Fluted joint	"	50	.160	"	18.80	9.40		28.20	34.50
0830	Concrete/CMU wall joints									
0840	1" wide	1 Carp	100	.080	L.F.	21	4.69		25.69	30
0850	2" wide		75	.107		32.50	6.25		38.75	45.50
0860	4" wide	↓	50	.160	↓	37	9.40		46.40	54.50
0870	Concrete/CMU floor joints									
0880	1" wide	1 Carp	200	.040	L.F.	22	2.34		24.34	27.50
0890	2" wide		150	.053		25.50	3.13		28.63	32.50
0900	4" wide	↓	100	.080	↓	37	4.69		41.69	47.50

07 91 Preformed Joint Seals

07 91 13 – Compression Seals

07 91 13.10 Compression Seals

		Crew	Daily Output	Labor-Hours	Unit	Material	2023 Bare Costs Labor	Equipment	Total	Total Incl O&P
0010	**COMPRESSION SEALS**									
4900	O-ring type cord, 1/4"	1 Bric	472	.017	L.F.	.54	.97		1.51	2.05
4910	1/2"		440	.018		1.44	1.05		2.49	3.15
4920	3/4"		424	.019		2.88	1.08		3.96	4.80
4930	1"		408	.020		5.80	1.13		6.93	8.05
4940	1-1/4"		384	.021		13.90	1.20		15.10	17.10
4950	1-1/2"		368	.022		17.10	1.25		18.35	20.50
4960	1-3/4"		352	.023		19.95	1.31		21.26	24
4970	2"	↓	344	.023		35	1.34		36.34	40

07 91 16 – Joint Gaskets

07 91 16.10 Joint Gaskets

		Crew	Daily Output	Labor-Hours	Unit	Material	2023 Bare Costs Labor	Equipment	Total	Total Incl O&P
0010	**JOINT GASKETS**									
4400	Joint gaskets, neoprene, closed cell w/adh, 1/8" x 3/8"	1 Bric	240	.033	L.F.	.22	1.92		2.14	3.12
4500	1/4" x 3/4"		215	.037		.68	2.14		2.82	3.96
4700	1/2" x 1"		200	.040		.78	2.30		3.08	4.31
4800	3/4" x 1-1/2"	↓	165	.048	↓	1.72	2.79		4.51	6.10

07 91 Preformed Joint Seals

07 91 23 – Backer Rods

07 91 23.10 Backer Rods

		Crew	Daily Output	Labor-Hours	Unit	Material	2023 Bare Costs Labor	Equipment	Total	Total Incl O&P
0010	**BACKER RODS**									
0030	Backer rod, polyethylene, 1/4" diameter	1 Bric	4.60	1.739	C.L.F.	7	100		107	158
0050	1/2" diameter		4.60	1.739		16	100		116	168
0070	3/4" diameter		4.60	1.739		17	100		117	169
0090	1" diameter		4.60	1.739		30	100		130	183

07 91 26 – Joint Fillers

07 91 26.10 Joint Fillers

		Crew	Daily Output	Labor-Hours	Unit	Material	Labor	Equipment	Total	Total Incl O&P
0010	**JOINT FILLERS**									
4360	Butyl rubber filler, 1/4" x 1/4"	1 Bric	290	.028	L.F.	.36	1.59		1.95	2.78
4365	1/2" x 1/2"		250	.032		1.44	1.84		3.28	4.34
4370	1/2" x 3/4"		210	.038		2.16	2.19		4.35	5.65
4375	3/4" x 3/4"		230	.035		3.24	2		5.24	6.55
4380	1" x 1"		180	.044		4.31	2.56		6.87	8.60
4390	For coloring, add					12%				
4980	Polyethylene joint backing, 1/4" x 2"	1 Bric	2.08	3.846	C.L.F.	14	221		235	345
4990	1/4" x 6"		1.28	6.250	"	150	360		510	705
5600	Silicone, room temp vulcanizing foam seal, 1/4" x 1/2"		1312	.006	L.F.	.37	.35		.72	.94
5610	1/2" x 1/2"		656	.012		.74	.70		1.44	1.86
5620	1/2" x 3/4"		442	.018		1.11	1.04		2.15	2.78
5630	3/4" x 3/4"		328	.024		1.67	1.40		3.07	3.94
5640	1/8" x 1"		1312	.006		.37	.35		.72	.94
5650	1/8" x 3"		442	.018		1.11	1.04		2.15	2.78
5670	1/4" x 3"		295	.027		2.22	1.56		3.78	4.78
5680	1/4" x 6"		148	.054		4.44	3.11		7.55	9.55
5690	1/2" x 6"		82	.098		8.90	5.60		14.50	18.15
5700	1/2" x 9"		52.50	.152		13.30	8.75		22.05	28
5710	1/2" x 12"		33	.242		17.75	13.95		31.70	40.50

07 92 Joint Sealants

07 92 13 – Elastomeric Joint Sealants

07 92 13.20 Caulking and Sealant Options

		Crew	Daily Output	Labor-Hours	Unit	Material	Labor	Equipment	Total	Total Incl O&P
0010	**CAULKING AND SEALANT OPTIONS**									
0050	Latex acrylic based, bulk				Gal.	39			39	43
0055	Bulk in place 1/4" x 1/4" bead	1 Bric	300	.027	L.F.	.12	1.53		1.65	2.44
0060	1/4" x 3/8"		294	.027		.21	1.56		1.77	2.58
0065	1/4" x 1/2"		288	.028		.27	1.60		1.87	2.70
0075	3/8" x 3/8"		284	.028		.31	1.62		1.93	2.77
0080	3/8" x 1/2"		280	.029		.41	1.64		2.05	2.92
0085	3/8" x 5/8"		276	.029		.51	1.67		2.18	3.07
0095	3/8" x 3/4"		272	.029		.61	1.69		2.30	3.22
0100	1/2" x 1/2"		275	.029		.55	1.67		2.22	3.11
0105	1/2" x 5/8"		269	.030		.69	1.71		2.40	3.32
0110	1/2" x 3/4"		263	.030		.82	1.75		2.57	3.54
0115	1/2" x 7/8"		256	.031		.96	1.80		2.76	3.76
0120	1/2" x 1"		250	.032		1.10	1.84		2.94	3.97
0125	3/4" x 3/4"		244	.033		1.24	1.89		3.13	4.19
0130	3/4" x 1"		225	.036		1.65	2.04		3.69	4.88
0135	1" x 1"		200	.040		2.19	2.30		4.49	5.85
0190	Cartridges				Gal.	47			47	52
0200	11 fl. oz. cartridge				Ea.	4.06			4.06	4.47

07 92 Joint Sealants

07 92 13 – Elastomeric Joint Sealants

07 92 13.20 Caulking and Sealant Options	Crew	Daily Output	Labor-Hours	Unit	Material	2023 Bare Costs Labor	Equipment	Total	Total Incl O&P
0500	1/4" x 1/2"	1 Bric	288	.028	L.F.	.33	1.60		1.93	2.76
0600	1/2" x 1/2"		275	.029		.66	1.67		2.33	3.24
0800	3/4" x 3/4"		244	.033		1.49	1.89		3.38	4.47
0900	3/4" x 1"		225	.036		1.99	2.04		4.03	5.25
1000	1" x 1"		200	.040		2.49	2.30		4.79	6.20
1400	Butyl based, bulk				Gal.	53			53	58.50
1500	Cartridges				"	53			53	58.50
1700	1/4" x 1/2", 154 L.F./gal.	1 Bric	288	.028	L.F.	.35	1.60		1.95	2.78
1800	1/2" x 1/2", 77 L.F./gal.	"	275	.029	"	.69	1.67		2.36	3.27
2300	Polysulfide compounds, 1 component, bulk				Gal.	108			108	119
2600	1 or 2 component, in place, 1/4" x 1/4", 308 L.F./gal.	1 Bric	300	.027	L.F.	.35	1.53		1.88	2.69
2700	1/2" x 1/4", 154 L.F./gal.		288	.028		.70	1.60		2.30	3.17
2900	3/4" x 3/8", 68 L.F./gal.		272	.029		1.59	1.69		3.28	4.29
3000	1" x 1/2", 38 L.F./gal.		250	.032		2.85	1.84		4.69	5.90
3200	Polyurethane, 1 or 2 component				Gal.	70.50			70.50	77.50
3300	Cartridges				"	84			84	92.50
3500	Bulk, in place, 1/4" x 1/4"	1 Bric	300	.027	L.F.	.23	1.53		1.76	2.55
3655	1/2" x 1/4"		288	.028		.46	1.60		2.06	2.90
3800	3/4" x 3/8"		272	.029		1.04	1.69		2.73	3.68
3900	1" x 1/2"		250	.032		1.83	1.84		3.67	4.77
4100	Silicone rubber, bulk				Gal.	85			85	93.50
4200	Cartridges				"	57.50			57.50	63.50

07 92 16 – Rigid Joint Sealants

07 92 16.10 Rigid Joint Sealants

		Crew	Daily Output	Labor-Hours	Unit	Material	Labor	Equipment	Total	Total Incl O&P
0010	**RIGID JOINT SEALANTS**									
5800	Tapes, sealant, PVC foam adhesive, 1/16" x 1/4"				C.L.F.	4.83			4.83	5.30
5900	1/16" x 1/2"					8.25			8.25	9.10
5950	1/16" x 1"					15.35			15.35	16.90
6000	1/8" x 1/2"					11.65			11.65	12.80

07 92 19 – Acoustical Joint Sealants

07 92 19.10 Acoustical Sealant

		Crew	Daily Output	Labor-Hours	Unit	Material	Labor	Equipment	Total	Total Incl O&P
0010	**ACOUSTICAL SEALANT**									
0020	Acoustical sealant, elastomeric, cartridges				Ea.	5.45			5.45	5.95
0025	In place, 1/4" x 1/4"	1 Bric	300	.027	L.F.	.22	1.53		1.75	2.54
0030	1/4" x 1/2"		288	.028		.44	1.60		2.04	2.89
0035	1/2" x 1/2"		275	.029		.89	1.67		2.56	3.49
0040	1/2" x 3/4"		263	.030		1.33	1.75		3.08	4.09
0045	3/4" x 3/4"		244	.033		2	1.89		3.89	5.05
0050	1" x 1"		200	.040		3.55	2.30		5.85	7.35

Division Notes

		CREW	DAILY OUTPUT	LABOR-HOURS	UNIT	BARE COSTS				TOTAL INCL O&P
						MAT.	LABOR	EQUIP.	TOTAL	

Division Notes

Division 8 Openings

Estimating Tips
08 10 00 Doors and Frames
All exterior doors should be addressed for their energy conservation (insulation and seals).
- Most metal doors and frames look alike, but there may be significant differences among them. When estimating these items, be sure to choose the line item that most closely compares to the specification or door schedule requirements regarding:
  - type of metal
  - metal gauge
  - door core material
  - fire rating
  - finish
- Wood and plastic doors vary considerably in price. The primary determinant is the veneer material. Lauan, birch, and oak are the most common veneers. Other variables include the following:
  - hollow or solid core
  - fire rating
  - flush or raised panel
  - finish
- Door pricing includes bore for cylindrical locksets and mortise for hinges.

08 30 00 Specialty Doors and Frames
- There are many varieties of special doors, and they are usually priced per each. Add frames, hardware, or operators required for a complete installation.

08 40 00 Entrances, Storefronts, and Curtain Walls
- Glazed curtain walls consist of the metal tube framing and the glazing material. The cost data in this subdivision is presented for the metal tube framing alone or the composite wall. If your estimate requires a detailed takeoff of the framing, be sure to add the glazing cost and any tints.

08 50 00 Windows
- Steel windows are unglazed and aluminum can be glazed or unglazed. Some metal windows are priced without glass. Refer to 08 80 00 Glazing for glass pricing. The grade C indicates commercial grade windows, usually ASTM C-35.
- All wood windows and vinyl are priced preglazed. The glazing is insulating glass. Add the cost of screens and grills if required and not already included.

08 70 00 Hardware
- Hardware costs add considerably to the cost of a door. The most efficient method to determine the hardware requirements for a project is to review the door and hardware schedule together. One type of door may have different hardware, depending on the door usage.
- Door hinges are priced by the pair, with most doors requiring 1-1/2 pairs per door. The hinge prices do not include installation labor because it is included in door installation. Hinges are classified according to the frequency of use, base material, and finish.

08 80 00 Glazing
- Different openings require different types of glass. The most common types are:
  - float
  - tempered
  - insulating
  - impact-resistant
  - ballistic-resistant
- Most exterior windows are glazed with insulating glass. Entrance doors and window walls, where the glass is less than 18" from the floor, are generally glazed with tempered glass. Interior windows and some residential windows are glazed with float glass.
- Coastal communities require the use of impact-resistant glass, dependent on wind speed.
- The insulation or 'u' value is a strong consideration, along with solar heat gain, to determine total energy efficiency.

Reference Numbers
Reference numbers are shown at the beginning of some major classifications. These numbers refer to related items in the Reference Section. The reference information may be an estimating procedure, an alternate pricing method, or technical information.

Note: Not all subdivisions listed here necessarily appear. ■

Same Data. Simplified.
Enjoy the convenience and efficiency of accessing your costs anywhere:
- **Skip the multiplier** by setting your location
- **Quickly search,** edit, favorite and share costs
- **Stay on top of price changes** with automatic updates

Discover more at rsmeans.com/online

No part of this cost data may be reproduced, stored in a retrieval system, or transmitted in any form or by any means without prior written permission of Gordian.

08 34 Special Function Doors

08 34 13 – Cold Storage Doors

08 34 13.10 Doors for Cold Area Storage

		Crew	Daily Output	Labor-Hours	Unit	Material	2023 Bare Costs Labor	Equipment	Total	Total Incl O&P
0010	**DOORS FOR COLD AREA STORAGE**									
0020	Single, 20 ga. galvanized steel									
0300	Horizontal sliding, 5' x 7', manual operation, 3.5" thick	2 Carp	2	8	Ea.	3,950	470		4,420	5,050
0400	4" thick		2	8		4,075	470		4,545	5,175
0500	6" thick		2	8		4,025	470		4,495	5,125
0800	5' x 7', power operation, 2" thick		1.90	8.421		3,775	495		4,270	4,875
0900	4" thick		1.90	8.421		6,675	495		7,170	8,075
1000	6" thick		1.90	8.421		7,600	495		8,095	9,075
1300	9' x 10', manual operation, 2" insulation		1.70	9.412		5,050	550		5,600	6,375
1400	4" insulation		1.70	9.412		5,725	550		6,275	7,125
1500	6" insulation		1.70	9.412		5,775	550		6,325	7,175
1800	Power operation, 2" insulation		1.60	10		7,950	585		8,535	9,625
1900	4" insulation		1.60	10		9,075	585		9,660	10,900
2000	6" insulation		1.70	9.412		9,600	550		10,150	11,400
2300	For stainless steel face, add					25%				
3000	Hinged, lightweight, 3' x 7'-0", 2" thick	2 Carp	2	8	Ea.	1,900	470		2,370	2,800
3050	4" thick		1.90	8.421		1,875	495		2,370	2,775
3300	Polymer doors, 3' x 7'-0"		1.90	8.421		1,900	495		2,395	2,825
3350	6" thick		1.40	11.429		1,900	670		2,570	3,100
3600	Stainless steel, 3' x 7'-0", 4" thick		1.90	8.421		1,950	495		2,445	2,875
3650	6" thick		1.40	11.429		1,900	670		2,570	3,100
3900	Painted, 3' x 7'-0", 4" thick		1.90	8.421		1,550	495		2,045	2,425
3950	6" thick		1.40	11.429		2,750	670		3,420	4,025
5000	Bi-parting, electric operated									
5010	6' x 8' opening, galv. faces, 4" thick for cooler	2 Carp	.80	20	Opng.	8,450	1,175		9,625	11,100
5050	For freezer, 4" thick		.80	20		9,300	1,175		10,475	12,000
5300	For door buck framing and door protection, add		2.50	6.400		750	375		1,125	1,375
6000	Galvanized batten door, galvanized hinges, 4' x 7'		2	8		2,225	470		2,695	3,150
6050	6' x 8'		1.80	8.889		2,900	520		3,420	3,975
6500	Fire door, 3 hr., 6' x 8', single slide		.80	20		10,000	1,175		11,175	12,800
6550	Double, bi-parting		.70	22.857		12,800	1,350		14,150	16,100

08 91 Louvers

08 91 16 – Operable Wall Louvers

08 91 16.10 Movable Blade Louvers

		Crew	Daily Output	Labor-Hours	Unit	Material	2023 Bare Costs Labor	Equipment	Total	Total Incl O&P
0010	**MOVABLE BLADE LOUVERS**									
0100	PVC, commercial grade, 12" x 12"	1 Shee	20	.400	Ea.	104	28		132	158
0110	16" x 16"		14	.571		122	40		162	195
0120	18" x 18"		14	.571		125	40		165	199
0130	24" x 24"		14	.571		179	40		219	258
0140	30" x 30"		12	.667		215	47		262	305
0150	36" x 36"		12	.667		310	47		357	410
0300	Stainless steel, commercial grade, 12" x 12"		20	.400		246	28		274	315
0310	16" x 16"		14	.571		395	40		435	495
0320	18" x 18"		14	.571		335	40		375	430
0330	20" x 20"		14	.571		385	40		425	485
0340	24" x 24"		14	.571		460	40		500	565
0350	30" x 30"		12	.667		515	47		562	635
0360	36" x 36"		12	.667		625	47		672	755

08 91 Louvers

08 91 19 – Fixed Louvers

08 91 19.10 Aluminum Louvers

		Crew	Daily Output	Labor-Hours	Unit	Material	2023 Bare Costs Labor	2023 Bare Costs Equipment	Total	Total Incl O&P
0010	**ALUMINUM LOUVERS**									
0020	Aluminum with screen, residential, 8" x 8"	1 Carp	38	.211	Ea.	79.50	12.35		91.85	105
0100	12" x 12"		38	.211		130	12.35		142.35	161
0200	12" x 18"		35	.229		148	13.40		161.40	182
0250	14" x 24"		30	.267		212	15.65		227.65	257
0300	18" x 24"		27	.296		221	17.35		238.35	270
0500	24" x 30"		24	.333		221	19.55		240.55	273
0700	Triangle, adjustable, small		20	.400		142	23.50		165.50	191
0800	Large		15	.533		193	31.50		224.50	259
1200	Extruded aluminum, see Section 23 37 15.40									
2100	Round, aluminum, 3/4" deep, 1" diameter	1 Carp	85	.094	Ea.	.86	5.50		6.36	9.15
2150	3" diameter		60	.133		1.65	7.80		9.45	13.45
2200	4" diameter		50	.160		2.21	9.40		11.61	16.40
2250	6" diameter		30	.267		5.60	15.65		21.25	29.50
3000	PVC, commercial grade, 12" x 12"	1 Shee	20	.400		14.80	28		42.80	59
3010	12" x 18"		20	.400		114	28		142	169
3020	12" x 24"		20	.400		228	28		256	294
3030	14" x 24"		20	.400		234	28		262	300
3100	Aluminum, commercial grade, 12" x 12"		20	.400		189	28		217	251
3110	24" x 24"		16	.500		335	35		370	425
3120	24" x 36"		16	.500		495	35		530	600
3130	36" x 24"		16	.500		495	35		530	600
3140	36" x 36"		14	.571		680	40		720	810
3150	36" x 48"		10	.800		590	56		646	735
3160	48" x 36"		10	.800		585	56		641	730
3170	48" x 48"		10	.800		735	56		791	895
3180	60" x 48"		8	1		1,200	70		1,270	1,400
3190	60" x 60"		8	1		1,500	70		1,570	1,750

08 91 19.20 Steel Louvers

		Crew	Daily Output	Labor-Hours	Unit	Material	2023 Bare Costs Labor	2023 Bare Costs Equipment	Total	Total Incl O&P
0010	**STEEL LOUVERS**									
3300	Galvanized steel, fixed blades, commercial grade, 18" x 18"	1 Shee	20	.400	Ea.	244	28		272	310
3310	24" x 24"		20	.400		350	28		378	430
3320	24" x 36"		16	.500		400	35		435	495
3330	36" x 24"		16	.500		385	35		420	480
3340	36" x 36"		14	.571		470	40		510	575
3350	36" x 48"		10	.800		565	56		621	705
3360	48" x 36"		10	.800		545	56		601	685
3370	48" x 48"		10	.800		630	56		686	780
3380	60" x 48"		10	.800		775	56		831	940
3390	60" x 60"		10	.800		925	56		981	1,100

08 95 Vents

08 95 13 – Soffit Vents

08 95 13.10 Wall Louvers		Crew	Daily Output	Labor-Hours	Unit	Material	2023 Bare Costs Labor	Equipment	Total	Total Incl O&P
0010	**WALL LOUVERS**									
2340	Baked enamel finish	1 Carp	200	.040	L.F.	.88	2.34		3.22	4.46
2400	Under eaves vent, aluminum, mill finish, 16" x 4"		48	.167	Ea.	2.48	9.75		12.23	17.30
2500	16" x 8"		48	.167	"	3.32	9.75		13.07	18.20

Estimating Tips
General
- Room Finish Schedule: A complete set of plans should contain a room finish schedule. If one is not available, it would be well worth the time and effort to obtain one.

09 20 00 Plaster and Gypsum Board
- Lath is estimated by the square yard plus a 5% allowance for waste. Furring, channels, and accessories are measured by the linear foot. An extra foot should be allowed for each accessory miter or stop.
- Plaster is also estimated by the square yard. Deductions for openings vary by preference, from zero deduction to 50% of all openings over 2 feet in width. The estimator should allow one extra square foot for each linear foot of horizontal interior or exterior angle located below the ceiling level. Also, double the areas of small radius work.
- Drywall accessories, studs, track, and acoustical caulking are all measured by the linear foot. Drywall taping is figured by the square foot. Gypsum wallboard is estimated by the square foot. No material deductions should be made for door or window openings under 32 S.F.

09 60 00 Flooring
- Tile and terrazzo areas are taken off on a square foot basis. Trim and base materials are measured by the linear foot. Accent tiles are listed per each. Two basic methods of installation are used. Mud set is approximately 30% more expensive than thin set. The cost of grout is included with tile unit price lines unless otherwise noted. In terrazzo work, be sure to include the linear footage of embedded decorative strips, grounds, machine rubbing, and power cleanup.
- Wood flooring is available in strip, parquet, or block configuration. The latter two types are set in adhesives with quantities estimated by the square foot. The laying pattern will influence labor costs and material waste. In addition to the material and labor for laying wood floors, the estimator must make allowances for sanding and finishing these areas, unless the flooring is prefinished.
- Sheet flooring is measured by the square yard. Roll widths vary, so consideration should be given to use the most economical width, as waste must be figured into the total quantity. Consider also the installation methods available—direct glue down or stretched. Direct glue-down installation is assumed with sheet carpet unit price lines unless otherwise noted.

09 70 00 Wall Finishes
- Wall coverings are estimated by the square foot. The area to be covered is measured—length by height of the wall above the baseboards—to calculate the square footage of each wall. This figure is divided by the number of square feet in the single roll which is being used. Deduct, in full, the areas of openings such as doors and windows. Where a pattern match is required allow 25–30% waste.

09 80 00 Acoustic Treatment
- Acoustical systems fall into several categories. The takeoff of these materials should be by the square foot of area with a 5% allowance for waste. Do not forget about scaffolding, if applicable, when estimating these systems.

09 90 00 Painting and Coating
- New line items created for cut-ins with reference diagram.
- A major portion of the work in painting involves surface preparation. Be sure to include cleaning, sanding, filling, and masking costs in the estimate.
- Protection of adjacent surfaces is not included in painting costs. When considering the method of paint application, an important factor is the amount of protection and masking required. These must be estimated separately and may be the determining factor in choosing the method of application.

Reference Numbers
Reference numbers are shown at the beginning of some major classifications. These numbers refer to related items in the Reference Section. The reference information may be an estimating procedure, an alternate pricing method, or technical information.

Note: Not all subdivisions listed here necessarily appear. ■

Same Data. Simplified.
Enjoy the convenience and efficiency of accessing your costs anywhere:
- **Skip the multiplier** by setting your location
- **Quickly search**, edit, favorite and share costs
- **Stay on top of price changes** with automatic updates

Discover more at rsmeans.com/online

No part of this cost data may be reproduced, stored in a retrieval system, or transmitted in any form or by any means without prior written permission of Gordian.

09 22 Supports for Plaster and Gypsum Board

09 22 03 – Fastening Methods for Finishes

09 22 03.20 Drilling Plaster/Drywall

		Crew	Daily Output	Labor-Hours	Unit	Material	2023 Bare Costs Labor	Equipment	Total	Total Incl O&P
0010	**DRILLING PLASTER/DRYWALL**									
1100	Drilling & layout for drywall/plaster walls, up to 1" deep, no anchor									
1200	Holes, 1/4" diameter	1 Carp	150	.053	Ea.	.01	3.13		3.14	4.66
1300	3/8" diameter		140	.057			3.35		3.35	4.99
1400	1/2" diameter		130	.062			3.61		3.61	5.35
1500	3/4" diameter		120	.067		.01	3.91		3.92	5.80
1600	1" diameter		110	.073		.02	4.26		4.28	6.35
1700	1-1/4" diameter		100	.080		.03	4.69		4.72	7.05
1800	1-1/2" diameter	↓	90	.089	↓	.04	5.20		5.24	7.80
1900	For ceiling installations, add						40%			

09 69 Access Flooring

09 69 13 – Rigid-Grid Access Flooring

09 69 13.10 Access Floors

		Crew	Daily Output	Labor-Hours	Unit	Material	2023 Bare Costs Labor	Equipment	Total	Total Incl O&P
0010	**ACCESS FLOORS**									
0015	Access floor pkg. including panel, pedestal, & stringers 1500 lbs. load									
0100	Package pricing, conc. fill panels, no fin., 6" ht.	4 Carp	750	.043	S.F.	4.48	2.50		6.98	8.65
0105	12" ht.		750	.043		4.56	2.50		7.06	8.70
0110	18" ht.		750	.043		4.63	2.50		7.13	8.80
0115	24" ht.		750	.043		4.71	2.50		7.21	8.90
0120	Package pricing, steel panels, no fin., 6" ht.		750	.043		7.50	2.50		10	11.95
0125	12" ht.		750	.043		7.50	2.50		10	11.95
0130	18" ht.		750	.043		7.50	2.50		10	11.95
0135	24" ht.		750	.043		7.55	2.50		10.05	12
0140	Package pricing, wood core panels, no fin., 6" ht.		750	.043		5.45	2.50		7.95	9.70
0145	12" ht.		750	.043		5.50	2.50		8	9.75
0150	18" ht.		750	.043		5.50	2.50		8	9.75
0155	24" ht.		750	.043		5.55	2.50		8.05	9.80
0160	Pkg. pricing, conc. fill pnls, no stringers, no fin., 6" ht, 1250 lbs. load		700	.046		17.35	2.68		20.03	23
0165	12" ht.		700	.046		17.60	2.68		20.28	23.50
0170	18" ht.		700	.046		17.75	2.68		20.43	23.50
0175	24" ht.	↓	700	.046		18	2.68		20.68	24
0250	Panels, 2' x 2' conc. fill, no fin.	2 Carp	500	.032		22	1.88		23.88	27.50
0255	With 1/8" high pressure laminate		500	.032		54.50	1.88		56.38	63
0260	Metal panels with 1/8" high pressure laminate		500	.032		65	1.88		66.88	74.50
0265	Wood core panels with 1/8" high pressure laminate		500	.032		42.50	1.88		44.38	50
0400	Aluminum panels, no fin.	↓	500	.032		34	1.88		35.88	40.50
0600	For carpet covering, add					8.95			8.95	9.85
0700	For vinyl floor covering, add					9.50			9.50	10.45
0900	For high pressure laminate covering, add					7.90			7.90	8.65
0910	For snap on stringer system, add	2 Carp	1000	.016		1.41	.94		2.35	2.95
1000	Machine cutouts after initial installation	1 Carp	50	.160	Ea.	19.15	9.40		28.55	35
1050	Pedestals, 6" to 12"	2 Carp	85	.188		8.95	11.05		20	26.50
1100	Air conditioning grilles, 4" x 12"	1 Carp	17	.471		70.50	27.50		98	119
1150	4" x 18"	"	14	.571	↓	96.50	33.50		130	156
1200	Approach ramps, steel	2 Carp	60	.267	S.F.	29	15.65		44.65	55
1300	Aluminum	"	40	.400	"	34	23.50		57.50	72.50
1500	Handrail, 2 rail, aluminum	1 Carp	15	.533	L.F.	122	31.50		153.50	182

09 91 Painting

09 91 23 – Interior Painting

09 91 23.52 Miscellaneous, Interior		Crew	Daily Output	Labor-Hours	Unit	Material	2023 Bare Costs Labor	Equipment	Total	Total Incl O&P
0010	MISCELLANEOUS, INTERIOR R099100-10									
3800	Grilles, per side, oil base, primer coat, brushwork	1 Pord	520	.015	S.F.	.20	.76		.96	1.34
3850	Spray		1140	.007		.20	.35		.55	.74
3880	Paint 1 coat, brushwork		520	.015		.36	.76		1.12	1.52
3900	Spray		1140	.007		.40	.35		.75	.96
3920	Paint 2 coats, brushwork		325	.025		.69	1.22		1.91	2.57
3940	Spray		650	.012		.79	.61		1.40	1.78
3950	Prime & paint 1 coat		325	.025		.55	1.22		1.77	2.42
3960	Prime & paint 2 coats		270	.030		.54	1.47		2.01	2.78
4500	Louvers, 1 side, primer, brushwork		524	.015		.10	.76		.86	1.23
4520	Paint 1 coat, brushwork		520	.015		.16	.76		.92	1.31
4530	Spray		1140	.007		.18	.35		.53	.72
4540	Paint 2 coats, brushwork		325	.025		.31	1.22		1.53	2.15
4550	Spray		650	.012		.35	.61		.96	1.29
4560	Paint 3 coats, brushwork		270	.030		.46	1.47		1.93	2.69
4570	Spray		500	.016		.52	.79		1.31	1.75
5000	Pipe, 1"-4" diameter, primer or sealer coat, oil base, brushwork	2 Pord	1250	.013	L.F.	.10	.64		.74	1.05
5100	Spray		2165	.007		.09	.37		.46	.64
5200	Paint 1 coat, brushwork		1250	.013		.19	.64		.83	1.15
5300	Spray		2165	.007		.16	.37		.53	.72
5350	Paint 2 coats, brushwork		775	.021		.33	1.03		1.36	1.88
5400	Spray		1240	.013		.36	.64		1	1.35
5420	Paint 3 coats, brushwork		775	.021		.49	1.03		1.52	2.06
5450	5"-8" diameter, primer or sealer coat, brushwork		620	.026		.20	1.28		1.48	2.12
5500	Spray		1085	.015		.33	.73		1.06	1.44
5550	Paint 1 coat, brushwork		620	.026		.50	1.28		1.78	2.45
5600	Spray		1085	.015		.55	.73		1.28	1.69
5650	Paint 2 coats, brushwork		385	.042		.66	2.06		2.72	3.78
5700	Spray		620	.026		.73	1.28		2.01	2.70
5720	Paint 3 coats, brushwork		385	.042		.97	2.06		3.03	4.13
5750	9"-12" diameter, primer or sealer coat, brushwork		415	.039		.30	1.91		2.21	3.17
5800	Spray		725	.022		.60	1.10		1.70	2.28
5850	Paint 1 coat, brushwork		415	.039		.51	1.91		2.42	3.40
6000	Spray		725	.022		.56	1.10		1.66	2.24
6200	Paint 2 coats, brushwork		260	.062		.98	3.06		4.04	5.60
6250	Spray		415	.039		1.09	1.91		3	4.04
6270	Paint 3 coats, brushwork		260	.062		1.46	3.06		4.52	6.15
6300	13"-16" diameter, primer or sealer coat, brushwork		310	.052		.40	2.56		2.96	4.24
6350	Spray		540	.030		.45	1.47		1.92	2.67
6400	Paint 1 coat, brushwork		310	.052		.68	2.56		3.24	4.54
6450	Spray		540	.030		.75	1.47		2.22	3.01
6500	Paint 2 coats, brushwork		195	.082		1.31	4.07		5.38	7.50
6550	Spray		310	.052		1.46	2.56		4.02	5.40
6600	Radiators, per side, primer, brushwork	1 Pord	520	.015	S.F.	.10	.76		.86	1.24
6620	Paint, 1 coat		520	.015		.09	.76		.85	1.23
6640	2 coats		340	.024		.31	1.17		1.48	2.07
6660	3 coats		283	.028		.46	1.40		1.86	2.59

For customer support on your Mechanical Costs with RSMeans data, call 800.448.8182.

Division Notes

	CREW	DAILY OUTPUT	LABOR-HOURS	UNIT	BARE COSTS				TOTAL INCL O&P
					MAT.	LABOR	EQUIP.	TOTAL	

Division 10 Specialties

Estimating Tips
General
- The items in this division are usually priced per square foot or each.
- Many items in Division 10 require some type of support system or special anchors that are not usually furnished with the item. The required anchors must be added to the estimate in the appropriate division.
- Some items in Division 10, such as lockers, may require assembly before installation. Verify the amount of assembly required. Assembly can often exceed installation time.

10 20 00 Interior Specialties
- Support angles and blocking are not included in the installation of toilet compartments, shower/dressing compartments, or cubicles. Appropriate line items from Division 5 or 6 may need to be added to support the installations.
- Toilet partitions are priced by the stall. A stall consists of a side wall, pilaster, and door with hardware. Toilet tissue holders and grab bars are extra.
- The required acoustical rating of a folding partition can have a significant impact on costs. Verify the sound transmission coefficient rating of the panel priced against the specification requirements.
- Grab bar installation does not include supplemental blocking or backing to support the required load. When grab bars are installed at an existing facility, provisions must be made to attach the grab bars to a solid structure.

Reference Numbers
Reference numbers are shown at the beginning of some major classifications. These numbers refer to related items in the Reference Section. The reference information may be an estimating procedure, an alternate pricing method, or technical information.

Note: Not all subdivisions listed here necessarily appear. ■

Same Data. Simplified.

Enjoy the convenience and efficiency of accessing your costs anywhere:
- **Skip the multiplier** by setting your location
- **Quickly search,** edit, favorite and share costs
- **Stay on top of price changes** with automatic updates

Discover more at rsmeans.com/online

No part of this cost data may be reproduced, stored in a retrieval system, or transmitted in any form or by any means without prior written permission of Gordian.

10 31 Manufactured Fireplaces

10 31 13 – Manufactured Fireplace Chimneys

10 31 13.10 Fireplace Chimneys

		Crew	Daily Output	Labor-Hours	Unit	Material	2023 Bare Costs Labor	2023 Bare Costs Equipment	Total	Total Incl O&P
0010	**FIREPLACE CHIMNEYS**									
0500	Chimney dbl. wall, all stainless, over 8'-6", 7" diam., add to fireplace	1 Carp	33	.242	V.L.F.	116	14.20		130.20	148
0600	10" diameter, add to fireplace		32	.250		116	14.65		130.65	150
0700	12" diameter, add to fireplace		31	.258		277	15.10		292.10	330
0800	14" diameter, add to fireplace		30	.267		289	15.65		304.65	340
1000	Simulated brick chimney top, 4' high, 16" x 16"		10	.800	Ea.	335	47		382	435
1100	24" x 24"		7	1.143	"	785	67		852	965

10 31 23 – Prefabricated Fireplaces

10 31 23.10 Fireplace, Prefabricated

		Crew	Daily Output	Labor-Hours	Unit	Material	2023 Bare Costs Labor	2023 Bare Costs Equipment	Total	Total Incl O&P
0010	**FIREPLACE, PREFABRICATED,** free standing or wall hung									
0100	With hood & screen, painted	1 Carp	1.30	6.154	Ea.	4,550	360		4,910	5,525
0150	Average		1	8		2,075	470		2,545	3,000
0200	Stainless steel		.90	8.889		2,525	520		3,045	3,575
1500	Simulated logs, gas fired, 40,000 BTU, 2' long, manual safety pilot		7	1.143	Set	1,050	67		1,117	1,250
1600	Adjustable flame remote pilot		6	1.333		3,175	78		3,253	3,600
1700	Electric, 1,500 BTU, 1'-6" long, incandescent flame		7	1.143		570	67		637	725
1800	1,500 BTU, LED flame		6	1.333		570	78		648	740

10 35 Stoves

10 35 13 – Heating Stoves

10 35 13.10 Wood Burning Stoves

		Crew	Daily Output	Labor-Hours	Unit	Material	2023 Bare Costs Labor	2023 Bare Costs Equipment	Total	Total Incl O&P
0010	**WOOD BURNING STOVES**									
0015	Cast iron, less than 1,500 S.F.	2 Carp	1.30	12.308	Ea.	1,600	720		2,320	2,850
0020	1,500 to 2,000 S.F.		1	16		3,250	940		4,190	4,975
0030	greater than 2,000 S.F.		.80	20		3,550	1,175		4,725	5,650
0050	For gas log lighter, add					26			26	29

Division 11 Equipment

Estimating Tips
General
- The items in this division are usually priced per square foot or each. Many of these items are purchased by the owner for installation by the contractor. Check the specifications for responsibilities and include time for receiving, storage, installation, and mechanical and electrical hookups in the appropriate divisions.
- Many items in Division 11 require some type of support system that is not usually furnished with the item. Examples of these systems include blocking for the attachment of casework and support angles/blocking for ceiling-hung projection screens. The required blocking or supports must be added to the estimate in the appropriate division.
- Some items in Division 11 may require assembly or electrical hookups. Verify the amount of assembly required or the need for a hard electrical connection and add the appropriate costs.

Reference Numbers
Reference numbers are shown at the beginning of some major classifications. These numbers refer to related items in the Reference Section. The reference information may be an estimating procedure, an alternate pricing method, or technical information.

Same Data. Simplified.
Enjoy the convenience and efficiency of accessing your costs anywhere:
- **Skip the multiplier** by setting your location
- **Quickly search,** edit, favorite and share costs
- **Stay on top of price changes** with automatic updates

Discover more at rsmeans.com/online

No part of this cost data may be reproduced, stored in a retrieval system, or transmitted in any form or by any means without prior written permission of Gordian.

11 11 Vehicle Service Equipment

11 11 13 – Compressed-Air Vehicle Service Equipment

11 11 13.10 Compressed Air Equipment		Crew	Daily Output	Labor-Hours	Unit	Material	2023 Bare Costs Labor	Equipment	Total	Total Incl O&P
0010	COMPRESSED AIR EQUIPMENT									
0030	Compressors, electric, 1-1/2 HP, standard controls	L-4	1.50	16	Ea.	1,100	895		1,995	2,575
0550	Dual controls		1.50	16		1,050	895		1,945	2,525
0600	5 HP, 115/230 volt, standard controls		1	24		1,600	1,350		2,950	3,800
0650	Dual controls	↓	1	24	↓	1,600	1,350		2,950	3,800

11 11 19 – Vehicle Lubrication Equipment

11 11 19.10 Lubrication Equipment		Crew	Daily Output	Labor-Hours	Unit	Material	Labor	Equipment	Total	Total Incl O&P
0010	LUBRICATION EQUIPMENT									
3000	Lube equipment, 3 reel type, with pumps, not including piping	L-4	.50	48	Set	11,700	2,675		14,375	16,900
3700	Pump lubrication, pneumatic, not incl. air compressor									
3710	Oil/gear lube	Q-1	9.60	1.667	Ea.	1,100	108		1,208	1,350
3720	Grease	"	9.60	1.667	"	194	108		302	375

11 11 33 – Vehicle Spray Painting Equipment

11 11 33.10 Spray Painting Equipment		Crew	Daily Output	Labor-Hours	Unit	Material	Labor	Equipment	Total	Total Incl O&P
0010	SPRAY PAINTING EQUIPMENT									
4000	Spray painting booth, 26' long, complete	L-4	.40	60	Ea.	24,600	3,350		27,950	32,200

11 21 Retail and Service Equipment

11 21 73 – Commercial Laundry and Dry Cleaning Equipment

11 21 73.16 Drying and Conditioning Equipment		Crew	Daily Output	Labor-Hours	Unit	Material	Labor	Equipment	Total	Total Incl O&P
0010	DRYING AND CONDITIONING EQUIPMENT									
0100	Dryers, not including rough-in									
1500	Industrial, 30 lb. capacity	1 Plum	2	4	Ea.	1,650	288		1,938	2,250
1600	50 lb. capacity	"	1.70	4.706	"	5,275	340		5,615	6,325

11 21 73.26 Commercial Washers and Extractors		Crew	Daily Output	Labor-Hours	Unit	Material	Labor	Equipment	Total	Total Incl O&P
0010	COMMERCIAL WASHERS AND EXTRACTORS, not including rough-in									
6000	Combination washer/extractor, 20 lb. capacity	L-6	1.50	8	Ea.	5,950	565		6,515	7,400
6100	30 lb. capacity		.80	15		12,700	1,050		13,750	15,500
6200	50 lb. capacity		.68	17.647		16,000	1,250		17,250	19,500
6300	75 lb. capacity		.30	40		15,800	2,825		18,625	21,600
6350	125 lb. capacity	↓	.16	75		34,800	5,275		40,075	46,200

11 21 73.33 Coin-Operated Laundry Equipment		Crew	Daily Output	Labor-Hours	Unit	Material	Labor	Equipment	Total	Total Incl O&P
0010	COIN-OPERATED LAUNDRY EQUIPMENT									
0990	Dryer, gas fired									
1000	Commercial, 30 lb. capacity, coin operated, single	1 Plum	3	2.667	Ea.	1,750	192		1,942	2,200
1100	Double stacked	"	2	4	"	2,125	288		2,413	2,750
5290	Clothes washer									
5300	Commercial, coin operated, average	1 Plum	3	2.667	Ea.	1,575	192		1,767	2,000

11 21 83 – Photo Processing Equipment

11 21 83.13 Darkroom Equipment		Crew	Daily Output	Labor-Hours	Unit	Material	Labor	Equipment	Total	Total Incl O&P
0010	DARKROOM EQUIPMENT									
0020	Developing sink, 5" deep, 24" x 48"	Q-1	2	8	Ea.	405	520		925	1,225
0050	48" x 52"		1.70	9.412		970	610		1,580	1,975
0200	10" deep, 24" x 48"		1.70	9.412		1,775	610		2,385	2,875
0250	24" x 108"	↓	1.50	10.667	↓	5,175	690		5,865	6,725

11 30 Residential Equipment

11 30 13 – Residential Appliances

11 30 13.15 Cooking Equipment

		Crew	Daily Output	Labor-Hours	Unit	Material	2023 Bare Costs Labor	2023 Bare Costs Equipment	Total	Total Incl O&P
0010	**COOKING EQUIPMENT**									
0020	Cooking range, 30" free standing, 1 oven, minimum	2 Clab	10	1.600	Ea.	700	75.50		775.50	885
0050	Maximum		4	4		935	189		1,124	1,300
0150	2 oven, minimum		10	1.600		3,500	75.50		3,575.50	3,975
0200	Maximum	↓	10	1.600	↓	4,475	75.50		4,550.50	5,050

11 30 13.16 Refrigeration Equipment

		Crew	Daily Output	Labor-Hours	Unit	Material	Labor	Equipment	Total	Total Incl O&P
0010	**REFRIGERATION EQUIPMENT**									
5200	Icemaker, automatic, 20 lbs./day	1 Plum	7	1.143	Ea.	1,400	82.50		1,482.50	1,675
5350	51 lbs./day	"	2	4	"	2,650	288		2,938	3,350

11 30 13.17 Kitchen Cleaning Equipment

		Crew	Daily Output	Labor-Hours	Unit	Material	Labor	Equipment	Total	Total Incl O&P
0010	**KITCHEN CLEANING EQUIPMENT**									
2750	Dishwasher, built-in, 2 cycles, minimum	L-1	4	4	Ea.	500	279		779	965
2800	Maximum		2	8		980	560		1,540	1,900
2950	4 or more cycles, minimum		4	4		680	279		959	1,150
2960	Average		4	4		905	279		1,184	1,400
3000	Maximum	↓	2	8	↓	790	560		1,350	1,700

11 30 13.18 Waste Disposal Equipment

		Crew	Daily Output	Labor-Hours	Unit	Material	Labor	Equipment	Total	Total Incl O&P
0010	**WASTE DISPOSAL EQUIPMENT**									
3300	Garbage disposal, sink type, minimum	L-1	10	1.600	Ea.	124	112		236	300
3350	Maximum	"	10	1.600	"	256	112		368	445

11 30 13.19 Kitchen Ventilation Equipment

		Crew	Daily Output	Labor-Hours	Unit	Material	Labor	Equipment	Total	Total Incl O&P
0010	**KITCHEN VENTILATION EQUIPMENT**									
4150	Hood for range, 2 speed, vented, 30" wide, minimum	L-3	5	3.200	Ea.	110	204		314	425
4200	Maximum		3	5.333		1,150	340		1,490	1,750
4300	42" wide, minimum		5	3.200		175	204		379	495
4330	Custom		5	3.200		167	204		371	490
4350	Maximum	↓	3	5.333		204	340		544	730
4500	For ventless hood, 2 speed, add					70			70	77
4650	For vented 1 speed, deduct from maximum				↓	130			130	143

11 30 13.24 Washers

		Crew	Daily Output	Labor-Hours	Unit	Material	Labor	Equipment	Total	Total Incl O&P
0010	**WASHERS**									
5000	Residential, 4 cycle, average	1 Plum	3	2.667	Ea.	1,150	192		1,342	1,550
6650	Washing machine, automatic, minimum		3	2.667		665	192		857	1,025
6700	Maximum	↓	1	8	↓	700	575		1,275	1,625

11 30 13.25 Dryers

		Crew	Daily Output	Labor-Hours	Unit	Material	Labor	Equipment	Total	Total Incl O&P
0010	**DRYERS**									
0500	Gas fired residential, 16 lb. capacity, average	1 Plum	3	2.667	Ea.	1,300	192		1,492	1,725
7450	Vent kits for dryers	1 Carp	10	.800	"	64	47		111	141

11 30 15 – Miscellaneous Residential Appliances

11 30 15.13 Sump Pumps

		Crew	Daily Output	Labor-Hours	Unit	Material	Labor	Equipment	Total	Total Incl O&P
0010	**SUMP PUMPS**									
6400	Cellar drainer, pedestal, 1/3 HP, molded PVC base	1 Plum	3	2.667	Ea.	138	192		330	440
6450	Solid brass	"	2	4	"	251	288		539	705
6460	Sump pump, see also Section 22 14 29.16									

11 30 15.23 Water Heaters

		Crew	Daily Output	Labor-Hours	Unit	Material	Labor	Equipment	Total	Total Incl O&P
0010	**WATER HEATERS**									
6900	Electric, glass lined, 30 gallon, minimum	L-1	5	3.200	Ea.	750	223		973	1,150
6950	Maximum		3	5.333		1,050	370		1,420	1,700
7100	80 gallon, minimum		2	8		2,100	560		2,660	3,125
7150	Maximum	↓	1	16		2,900	1,125		4,025	4,850

11 30 Residential Equipment

11 30 15 – Miscellaneous Residential Appliances

11 30 15.23 Water Heaters

		Crew	Daily Output	Labor-Hours	Unit	Material	2023 Bare Costs Labor	2023 Bare Costs Equipment	Total	Total Incl O&P
7180	Gas, glass lined, 30 gallon, minimum	2 Plum	5	3.200	Ea.	1,900	231		2,131	2,450
7220	Maximum		3	5.333		2,650	385		3,035	3,475
7260	50 gallon, minimum		2.50	6.400		740	460		1,200	1,500
7300	Maximum		1.50	10.667		1,025	770		1,795	2,275

11 30 15.43 Air Quality

		Crew	Daily Output	Labor-Hours	Unit	Material	Labor	Equipment	Total	Total Incl O&P
0010	**AIR QUALITY**									
2450	Dehumidifier, portable, automatic, 15 pint	1 Elec	4	2	Ea.	184	135		319	400
2550	40 pint		3.75	2.133		330	144		474	580
3550	Heater, electric, built-in, 1250 watt, ceiling type, minimum		4	2		136	135		271	350
3600	Maximum		3	2.667		258	180		438	550
3700	Wall type, minimum		4	2		117	135		252	330
3750	Maximum		3	2.667		135	180		315	415
3900	1500 watt wall type, with blower		4	2		227	135		362	450
3950	3000 watt		3	2.667		224	180		404	515
4850	Humidifier, portable, 8 gallons/day					170			170	187
5000	15 gallons/day					276			276	305

11 32 Unit Kitchens

11 32 13 – Metal Unit Kitchens

11 32 13.10 Commercial Unit Kitchens

		Crew	Daily Output	Labor-Hours	Unit	Material	Labor	Equipment	Total	Total Incl O&P
0010	**COMMERCIAL UNIT KITCHENS**									
1500	Combination range, refrigerator and sink, 30" wide, minimum	L-1	2	8	Ea.	1,300	560		1,860	2,250
1550	Maximum		1	16		1,525	1,125		2,650	3,325
1570	60" wide, average		1.40	11.429		2,075	795		2,870	3,450
1590	72" wide, average		1.20	13.333		2,075	930		3,005	3,650
1600	Office model, 48" wide		2	8		3,300	560		3,860	4,450
1620	Refrigerator and sink only		2.40	6.667		3,425	465		3,890	4,475
1640	Combination range, refrigerator, sink, microwave									
1660	Oven and ice maker	L-1	.80	20	Ea.	5,925	1,400		7,325	8,600

11 41 Foodservice Storage Equipment

11 41 13 – Refrigerated Food Storage Cases

11 41 13.10 Refrigerated Food Cases

		Crew	Daily Output	Labor-Hours	Unit	Material	Labor	Equipment	Total	Total Incl O&P
0010	**REFRIGERATED FOOD CASES**									
0030	Dairy, multi-deck, 12' long	Q-5	3	5.333	Ea.	18,300	350		18,650	20,600
0100	For rear sliding doors, add					1,975			1,975	2,175
0200	Delicatessen case, service deli, 12' long, single deck	Q-5	3.90	4.103		14,100	268		14,368	15,900
0300	Multi-deck, 18 S.F. shelf display		3	5.333		8,350	350		8,700	9,700
0400	Freezer, self-contained, chest-type, 30 C.F.		3.90	4.103		2,350	268		2,618	3,000
0500	Glass door, upright, 78 C.F.		3.30	4.848		9,300	315		9,615	10,700
0600	Frozen food, chest type, 12' long		3.30	4.848		6,850	315		7,165	8,025
0700	Glass door, reach-in, 5 door		3	5.333		10,600	350		10,950	12,200
0800	Island case, 12' long, single deck		3.30	4.848		8,775	315		9,090	10,100
0900	Multi-deck		3	5.333		10,600	350		10,950	12,200
1000	Meat case, 12' long, single deck		3.30	4.848		7,450	315		7,765	8,675
1050	Multi-deck		3.10	5.161		10,200	335		10,535	11,700
1100	Produce, 12' long, single deck		3.30	4.848		6,600	315		6,915	7,725
1200	Multi-deck		3.10	5.161		8,525	335		8,860	9,875

11 41 Foodservice Storage Equipment

11 41 13 – Refrigerated Food Storage Cases

11 41 13.20 Refrigerated Food Storage Equipment

		Crew	Daily Output	Labor-Hours	Unit	Material	2023 Bare Costs Labor	2023 Bare Costs Equipment	Total	Total Incl O&P
0010	**REFRIGERATED FOOD STORAGE EQUIPMENT**									
2350	Cooler, reach-in, beverage, 6' long	Q-1	6	2.667	Ea.	3,875	173		4,048	4,525
4300	Freezers, reach-in, 44 C.F.		4	4		2,950	259		3,209	3,600
4500	68 C.F.		3	5.333		8,525	345		8,870	9,900

11 44 Food Cooking Equipment

11 44 13 – Commercial Ranges

11 44 13.10 Cooking Equipment

		Crew	Daily Output	Labor-Hours	Unit	Material	2023 Bare Costs Labor	2023 Bare Costs Equipment	Total	Total Incl O&P
0010	**COOKING EQUIPMENT**									
0020	Bake oven, gas, one section	Q-1	8	2	Ea.	4,400	130		4,530	5,050
0300	Two sections		7	2.286		9,875	148		10,023	11,100
0600	Three sections		6	2.667		13,600	173		13,773	15,200
0900	Electric convection, single deck	L-7	4	7		15,300	395		15,695	17,500
6350	Kettle, w/steam jacket, tilting, w/positive lock, SS, 20 gallons		7	4		16,500	226		16,726	18,400
6600	60 gallons		6	4.667		23,000	264		23,264	25,700

11 46 Food Dispensing Equipment

11 46 83 – Ice Machines

11 46 83.10 Commercial Ice Equipment

		Crew	Daily Output	Labor-Hours	Unit	Material	2023 Bare Costs Labor	2023 Bare Costs Equipment	Total	Total Incl O&P
0010	**COMMERCIAL ICE EQUIPMENT**									
5800	Ice cube maker, 50 lbs./day	Q-1	6	2.667	Ea.	2,075	173		2,248	2,525
6050	500 lbs./day	"	4	4	"	2,975	259		3,234	3,650

11 48 Foodservice Cleaning and Disposal Equipment

11 48 13 – Commercial Dishwashers

11 48 13.10 Dishwashers

		Crew	Daily Output	Labor-Hours	Unit	Material	2023 Bare Costs Labor	2023 Bare Costs Equipment	Total	Total Incl O&P
0010	**DISHWASHERS**									
2700	Dishwasher, commercial, rack type									
2720	10 to 12 racks/hour	Q-1	3.20	5	Ea.	38,500	325		38,825	42,900
2730	Energy star rated, 35 to 40 racks/hour [G]		1.30	12.308		6,350	800		7,150	8,175
2740	50 to 60 racks/hour [G]		1.30	12.308		9,050	800		9,850	11,200
2800	Automatic, 190 to 230 racks/hour	L-6	.35	34.286		31,600	2,425		34,025	38,300
2820	235 to 275 racks/hour		.25	48		31,600	3,375		34,975	39,800
2840	8,750 to 12,500 dishes/hour		.10	120		51,500	8,450		59,950	69,000

11 53 Laboratory Equipment

11 53 13 – Laboratory Fume Hoods

11 53 13.13 Recirculating Laboratory Fume Hoods

		Crew	Daily Output	Labor-Hours	Unit	Material	2023 Bare Costs Labor	2023 Bare Costs Equipment	Total	Total Incl O&P
0010	**RECIRCULATING LABORATORY FUME HOODS**									
0600	Fume hood, with countertop & base, not including HVAC									
0610	Simple, minimum	2 Carp	5.40	2.963	L.F.	895	174		1,069	1,250
0620	Complex, including fixtures		2.40	6.667		11,400	390		11,790	13,100
0630	Special, maximum		1.70	9.412		2,025	550		2,575	3,050
0670	Service fixtures, average				Ea.	1,950			1,950	2,150
0680	For sink assembly with hot and cold water, add	1 Plum	1.40	5.714	"	685	410		1,095	1,375

11 53 Laboratory Equipment

11 53 19 – Laboratory Sterilizers

11 53 19.13 Sterilizers

		Crew	Daily Output	Labor-Hours	Unit	Material	2023 Bare Costs Labor	2023 Bare Costs Equipment	Total	Total Incl O&P
0010	**STERILIZERS**									
0700	Glassware washer, undercounter, minimum	L-1	1.80	8.889	Ea.	8,325	620		8,945	10,100
0710	Maximum	"	1	16		18,300	1,125		19,425	21,800
1850	Utensil washer-sanitizer	1 Plum	2	4		7,475	288		7,763	8,650

11 53 33 – Emergency Safety Appliances

11 53 33.13 Emergency Equipment

		Crew	Daily Output	Labor-Hours	Unit	Material	Labor	Equipment	Total	Total Incl O&P
0010	**EMERGENCY EQUIPMENT**									
1400	Safety equipment, eye wash, hand held				Ea.	420			420	460
1450	Deluge shower				"	294			294	325

11 53 43 – Service Fittings and Accessories

11 53 43.13 Fittings

		Crew	Daily Output	Labor-Hours	Unit	Material	Labor	Equipment	Total	Total Incl O&P
0010	**FITTINGS**									
1600	Sink, one piece plastic, flask wash, hose, free standing	1 Plum	1.60	5	Ea.	345	360		705	915
1610	Epoxy resin sink, 25" x 16" x 10"	"	2	4	"	1,775	288		2,063	2,375
8000	Alternate pricing method: as percent of lab furniture									
8050	Installation, not incl. plumbing & duct work				% Furn.				22%	22%
8100	Plumbing, final connections, simple system								10%	10%
8110	Moderately complex system								15%	15%
8120	Complex system								20%	20%
8150	Electrical, simple system								10%	10%
8160	Moderately complex system								20%	20%
8170	Complex system								35%	35%

11 71 Medical Sterilizing Equipment

11 71 10 – Medical Sterilizers & Distillers

11 71 10.10 Sterilizers and Distillers

		Crew	Daily Output	Labor-Hours	Unit	Material	Labor	Equipment	Total	Total Incl O&P
0010	**STERILIZERS AND DISTILLERS**									
0700	Distiller, water, steam heated, 50 gal. capacity	1 Plum	1.40	5.714	Ea.	45,200	410		45,610	50,500
5600	Sterilizers, floor loading, 26" x 62" x 42", single door, steam					61,000			61,000	67,000
5650	Double door, steam					61,000			61,000	67,000
5800	General purpose, 20" x 20" x 38", single door					29,300			29,300	32,200
6000	Portable, counter top, steam, minimum					4,100			4,100	4,500
6020	Maximum					2,200			2,200	2,425
6050	Portable, counter top, gas, 17" x 15" x 32-1/2"					3,650			3,650	4,000
6150	Manual washer/sterilizer, 16" x 16" x 26"	1 Plum	2	4		3,200	288		3,488	3,950
6200	Steam generators, electric 10 kW to 180 kW, freestanding									
6250	Minimum	1 Elec	3	2.667	Ea.	6,450	180		6,630	7,375
6300	Maximum	"	.70	11.429		3,400	770		4,170	4,900
8200	Bed pan washer-sanitizer	1 Plum	2	4		7,675	288		7,963	8,875

11 73 Patient Care Equipment

11 73 10 – Patient Treatment Equipment

11 73 10.10 Treatment Equipment		Crew	Daily Output	Labor-Hours	Unit	Material	2023 Bare Costs Labor	2023 Bare Costs Equipment	Total	Total Incl O&P
0010	**TREATMENT EQUIPMENT**									
1800	Heat therapy unit, humidified, 26" x 78" x 28"				Ea.	360			360	395
8400	Whirlpool bath, mobile, sst, 18" x 24" x 60"					5,350			5,350	5,900
8450	Fixed, incl. mixing valves	1 Plum	2	4	↓	8,650	288		8,938	9,950

11 74 Dental Equipment

11 74 10 – Dental Office Equipment

11 74 10.10 Diagnostic and Treatment Equipment		Crew	Daily Output	Labor-Hours	Unit	Material	2023 Bare Costs Labor	2023 Bare Costs Equipment	Total	Total Incl O&P
0010	**DIAGNOSTIC AND TREATMENT EQUIPMENT**									
0020	Central suction system, minimum	1 Plum	1.20	6.667	Ea.	1,975	480		2,455	2,900
0100	Maximum	"	.90	8.889		4,725	640		5,365	6,125
0600	Chair, electric or hydraulic, minimum	1 Skwk	.50	16		4,175	980		5,155	6,075
0700	Maximum		.25	32		6,775	1,950		8,725	10,400
2000	Light, ceiling mounted, minimum		8	1		940	61.50		1,001.50	1,125
2100	Maximum	↓	8	1		3,175	61.50		3,236.50	3,600
2200	Unit light, minimum	2 Skwk	5.33	3.002		1,175	184		1,359	1,575
2210	Maximum		5.33	3.002		2,450	184		2,634	2,950
2220	Track light, minimum		3.20	5		2,700	305		3,005	3,425
2230	Maximum	↓	3.20	5		4,200	305		4,505	5,075
2300	Sterilizers, steam portable, minimum					3,675			3,675	4,050
2350	Maximum					8,325			8,325	9,150
2600	Steam, institutional					4,225			4,225	4,650
2650	Dry heat, electric, portable, 3 trays				↓	2,150			2,150	2,375

11 78 Mortuary Equipment

11 78 13 – Mortuary Refrigerators

11 78 13.10 Mortuary and Autopsy Equipment		Crew	Daily Output	Labor-Hours	Unit	Material	2023 Bare Costs Labor	2023 Bare Costs Equipment	Total	Total Incl O&P
0010	**MORTUARY AND AUTOPSY EQUIPMENT**									
0015	Autopsy table, standard	1 Plum	1	8	Ea.	8,550	575		9,125	10,300
0020	Deluxe	"	.60	13.333		3,175	960		4,135	4,925
3200	Mortuary refrigerator, end operated, 2 capacity					6,125			6,125	6,750
3300	6 capacity				↓	13,500			13,500	14,900

11 78 16 – Crematorium Equipment

11 78 16.10 Crematory		Crew	Daily Output	Labor-Hours	Unit	Material	2023 Bare Costs Labor	2023 Bare Costs Equipment	Total	Total Incl O&P
0010	**CREMATORY**									
1500	Crematory, not including building, 1 place	Q-3	.20	160	Ea.	77,500	11,000		88,500	102,000
1750	2 place	"	.10	320	"	111,000	21,900		132,900	154,500

11 81 Facility Maintenance Equipment

11 81 19 – Vacuum Cleaning Systems

11 81 19.10 Vacuum Cleaning

		Crew	Daily Output	Labor-Hours	Unit	Material	2023 Bare Costs Labor	Equipment	Total	Total Incl O&P
0010	**VACUUM CLEANING**									
0020	Central, 3 inlet, residential	1 Skwk	.90	8.889	Total	1,200	545		1,745	2,150
0200	Commercial		.70	11.429		1,425	700		2,125	2,625
0400	5 inlet system, residential		.50	16		1,925	980		2,905	3,575
0600	7 inlet system, commercial		.40	20		1,250	1,225		2,475	3,225
0800	9 inlet system, residential	↓	.30	26.667	↓	4,400	1,625		6,025	7,300

11 82 Facility Solid Waste Handling Equipment

11 82 19 – Packaged Incinerators

11 82 19.10 Packaged Gas Fired Incinerators

		Crew	Daily Output	Labor-Hours	Unit	Material	2023 Bare Costs Labor	Equipment	Total	Total Incl O&P
0010	**PACKAGED GAS FIRED INCINERATORS**									
4400	Incinerator, gas, not incl. chimney, elec. or pipe, 50 lbs./hr., minimum	Q-3	.80	40	Ea.	45,000	2,750		47,750	53,500
4420	Maximum		.70	45.714		41,200	3,125		44,325	50,000
4440	200 lbs./hr., minimum (batch type)		.60	53.333		68,000	3,650		71,650	80,000
4460	Maximum (with feeder)		.50	64		78,000	4,400		82,400	92,500
4480	400 lbs./hr., minimum (batch type)		.30	107		91,500	7,325		98,825	111,500
4500	Maximum (with feeder)		.25	128		84,000	8,775		92,775	105,500
4520	800 lbs./hr., with feeder, minimum		.20	160		112,500	11,000		123,500	140,000
4540	Maximum		.17	188		201,500	12,900		214,400	241,000
4560	1,200 lbs./hr., with feeder, minimum		.15	213		141,000	14,600		155,600	177,000
4580	Maximum		.11	291		198,000	20,000		218,000	247,000
4600	2,000 lbs./hr., with feeder, minimum		.10	320		375,000	21,900		396,900	445,000
4620	Maximum		.05	640		633,000	43,900		676,900	762,000
4700	For heat recovery system, add, minimum		.25	128		95,000	8,775		103,775	117,500
4710	Add, maximum		.11	291		263,500	20,000		283,500	319,500
4720	For automatic ash conveyer, add	↓	.50	64	↓	37,000	4,400		41,400	47,300

11 82 26 – Facility Waste Compactors

11 82 26.10 Compactors

		Crew	Daily Output	Labor-Hours	Unit	Material	2023 Bare Costs Labor	Equipment	Total	Total Incl O&P
0010	**COMPACTORS**									
0020	Compactors, 115 volt, 250 lbs./hr., chute fed	L-4	1	24	Ea.	11,900	1,350		13,250	15,100
0100	Hand fed		2.40	10		16,000	560		16,560	18,400
0300	Multi-bag, 230 volt, 600 lbs./hr., chute fed		1	24		16,000	1,350		17,350	19,600
0400	Hand fed		1	24		16,000	1,350		17,350	19,600
0500	Containerized, hand fed, 2 to 6 C.Y. containers, 250 lbs./hr.		1	24		15,900	1,350		17,250	19,500
0550	For chute fed, add per floor		1	24		1,425	1,350		2,775	3,600
1000	Heavy duty industrial compactor, 0.5 C.Y. capacity		1	24		10,600	1,350		11,950	13,700
1050	1.0 C.Y. capacity		1	24		16,200	1,350		17,550	19,800
1100	3.0 C.Y. capacity		.50	48		27,700	2,675		30,375	34,500
1150	5.0 C.Y. capacity		.50	48		35,000	2,675		37,675	42,500
1200	Combination shredder/compactor (5,000 lbs./hr.)		.50	48		68,000	2,675		70,675	78,500
1400	For handling hazardous waste materials, 55 gallon drum packer, std.					20,800			20,800	22,900
1410	55 gallon drum packer w/HEPA filter					25,000			25,000	27,600
1420	55 gallon drum packer w/charcoal & HEPA filter					33,400			33,400	36,700
1430	All of the above made explosion proof, add					1,950			1,950	2,150
5800	Shredder, industrial, minimum					28,000			28,000	30,800
5850	Maximum					141,000			141,000	155,000
5900	Baler, industrial, minimum					10,600			10,600	11,600
5950	Maximum				↓	615,500			615,500	677,000

Division 13 — Special Construction

Estimating Tips
General
- The items and systems in this division are usually estimated, purchased, supplied, and installed as a unit by one or more subcontractors. The estimator must ensure that all parties are operating from the same set of specifications and assumptions, and that all necessary items are estimated and will be provided. Many times the complex items and systems are covered, but the more common ones, such as excavation or a crane, are overlooked for the very reason that everyone assumes nobody could miss them. The estimator should be the central focus and be able to ensure that all systems are complete.
- It is important to consider factors such as site conditions, weather, shape and size of building, as well as labor availability as they may impact the overall cost of erecting special structures and systems included in this division.
- Another area where problems can develop in this division is at the interface between systems. The estimator must ensure, for instance, that anchor bolts, nuts, and washers are estimated and included for the air-supported structures and pre-engineered buildings to be bolted to their foundations. Utility supply is a common area where essential items or pieces of equipment can be missed or overlooked because each subcontractor may feel it is another's responsibility. The estimator should also be aware of certain items which may be supplied as part of a package but installed by others, and ensure that the installing contractor's estimate includes the cost of installation. Conversely, the estimator must also ensure that items are not costed by two different subcontractors, resulting in an inflated overall estimate.

13 30 00 Special Structures
- The foundations and floor slab, as well as rough mechanical and electrical, should be estimated, as this work is required for the assembly and erection of the structure. Generally, as noted in the data set, the pre-engineered building comes as a shell. Pricing is based on the size and structural design parameters stated in the reference section. Additional features, such as windows and doors with their related structural framing, must also be included by the estimator. Here again, the estimator must have a clear understanding of the scope of each portion of the work and all the necessary interfaces.

Reference Numbers
Reference numbers are shown at the beginning of some major classifications. These numbers refer to related items in the Reference Section. The reference information may be an estimating procedure, an alternate pricing method, or technical information.

Note: Not all subdivisions listed here necessarily appear. ∎

Same Data. Simplified.

Enjoy the convenience and efficiency of accessing your costs anywhere:
- **Skip the multiplier** by setting your location
- **Quickly search,** edit, favorite and share costs
- **Stay on top of price changes** with automatic updates

Discover more at rsmeans.com/online

No part of this cost data may be reproduced, stored in a retrieval system, or transmitted in any form or by any means without prior written permission of Gordian.

13 11 Swimming Pools

13 11 13 – Below-Grade Swimming Pools

13 11 13.50 Swimming Pools

		Crew	Daily Output	Labor-Hours	Unit	Material	2023 Bare Costs Labor	2023 Bare Costs Equipment	Total	Total Incl O&P
0010	**SWIMMING POOLS** Residential in-ground, vinyl lined									
0020	Concrete sides, w/equip, sand bottom	B-52	300	.187	SF Surf	43	10.15	2.10	55.25	65
0100	Metal or polystyrene sides	B-14	410	.117		81	5.80	.68	87.48	98.50
0200	Add for vermiculite bottom					4.09			4.09	4.50
0500	Gunite bottom and sides, white plaster finish									
0600	12' x 30' pool	B-52	145	.386	SF Surf	60.50	21	4.34	85.84	102
0720	16' x 32' pool		155	.361		54.50	19.60	4.06	78.16	93.50
0750	20' x 40' pool		250	.224		48.50	12.15	2.52	63.17	74.50
0810	Concrete bottom and sides, tile finish									
0820	12' x 30' pool	B-52	80	.700	SF Surf	61	38	7.85	106.85	132
0830	16' x 32' pool		95	.589		50.50	32	6.60	89.10	110
0840	20' x 40' pool		130	.431		40	23.50	4.84	68.34	84
1100	Motel, gunite with plaster finish, incl. medium									
1150	capacity filtration & chlorination	B-52	115	.487	SF Surf	74.50	26.50	5.45	106.45	127
1200	Municipal, gunite with plaster finish, incl. high									
1250	capacity filtration & chlorination	B-52	100	.560	SF Surf	96.50	30.50	6.30	133.30	158
1350	Add for formed gutters				L.F.	142			142	156
1360	Add for stainless steel gutters				"	420			420	460
1700	Filtration and deck equipment only, as % of total				Total				20%	20%
1800	Automatic vacuum, hand tools, etc., 20' x 40' pool				SF Pool				.56	.62
1900	5,000 S.F. pool				"				.11	.12
3000	Painting pools, preparation + 3 coats, 20' x 40' pool, epoxy	2 Pord	.33	48.485	Total	2,350	2,400		4,750	6,150
3100	Rubber base paint, 18 gallons	"	.33	48.485		1,250	2,400		3,650	4,950
3500	42' x 82' pool, 75 gallons, epoxy paint	3 Pord	.14	171		9,925	8,500		18,425	23,500
3600	Rubber base paint	"	.14	171		5,225	8,500		13,725	18,300

13 11 23 – On-Grade Swimming Pools

13 11 23.50 Swimming Pools

		Crew	Daily Output	Labor-Hours	Unit	Material	Labor	Equipment	Total	Total Incl O&P
0010	**SWIMMING POOLS** Residential above ground, steel construction									
0100	Round, 15' diam.	B-80A	3	8	Ea.	975	380	130	1,485	1,775
0120	18' diam.		2.50	9.600		1,025	455	156	1,636	2,000
0140	21' diam.		2	12		1,150	565	195	1,910	2,325
0160	24' diam.		1.80	13.333		1,325	630	217	2,172	2,625
0180	27' diam.		1.50	16		1,650	755	261	2,666	3,225
0200	30' diam.		1	24		1,925	1,125	390	3,440	4,225
0220	Oval, 12' x 24'		2.30	10.435		1,675	495	170	2,340	2,775
0240	15' x 30'		1.80	13.333		4,875	630	217	5,722	6,525
0260	18' x 33'		1	24		2,650	1,125	390	4,165	5,050

13 11 46 – Swimming Pool Accessories

13 11 46.50 Swimming Pool Equipment

		Crew	Daily Output	Labor-Hours	Unit	Material	Labor	Equipment	Total	Total Incl O&P
0010	**SWIMMING POOL EQUIPMENT**									
0020	Diving stand, stainless steel, 3 meter	2 Carp	.40	40	Ea.	20,300	2,350		22,650	25,800
0300	1 meter	"	2.70	5.926		17,000	345		17,345	19,200
2100	Lights, underwater, 12 volt, with transformer, 300 watt	1 Elec	1	8		291	540		831	1,125
2200	110 volt, 500 watt, standard		1	8		320	540		860	1,150
2400	Low water cutoff type		1	8		345	540		885	1,175
2800	Heaters, see Section 23 52 28.10									

13 18 Ice Rinks

13 18 13 – Ice Rink Floor Systems

13 18 13.50 Ice Skating

		Crew	Daily Output	Labor-Hours	Unit	Material	2023 Bare Costs Labor	Equipment	Total	Total Incl O&P
0010	**ICE SKATING** Equipment incl. refrigeration, plumbing & cooling									
0020	coils & concrete slab, 85' x 200' rink									
0300	55° system, 5 mos., 100 ton				Total	602,000			602,000	662,500
0700	90° system, 12 mos., 135 ton				"	685,000			685,000	753,500
1200	Subsoil heating system (recycled from compressor), 85' x 200'	Q-7	.27	119	Ea.	44,200	8,175		52,375	61,000
1300	Subsoil insulation, 2 lb. polystyrene with vapor barrier, 85' x 200'	2 Carp	.14	114	"	32,000	6,700		38,700	45,200

13 18 16 – Ice Rink Dasher Boards

13 18 16.50 Ice Rink Dasher Boards

		Crew	Daily Output	Labor-Hours	Unit	Material	Labor	Equipment	Total	Total Incl O&P
0010	**ICE RINK DASHER BOARDS**									
1000	Dasher boards, 1/2" H.D. polyethylene faced steel frame, 3' acrylic									
1020	screen at sides, 5' acrylic ends, 85' x 200'	F-5	.06	533	Ea.	138,000	31,500		169,500	199,000
1100	Fiberglass & aluminum construction, same sides and ends	"	.06	533	"	154,000	31,500		185,500	216,500

13 21 Controlled Environment Rooms

13 21 13 – Clean Rooms

13 21 13.50 Clean Room Components

		Crew	Daily Output	Labor-Hours	Unit	Material	Labor	Equipment	Total	Total Incl O&P
0010	**CLEAN ROOM COMPONENTS**									
1100	Clean room, soft wall, 12' x 12', Class 100	1 Carp	.18	44.444	Ea.	16,500	2,600		19,100	22,100
1110	Class 1,000		.18	44.444		17,400	2,600		20,000	23,000
1120	Class 10,000		.21	38.095		15,500	2,225		17,725	20,300
1130	Class 100,000		.21	38.095		12,700	2,225		14,925	17,200
2800	Ceiling grid support, slotted channel struts 4'-0" OC, ea. way				S.F.				5.90	6.50
3000	Ceiling panel, vinyl coated foil on mineral substrate									
3020	Sealed, non-perforated				S.F.				3.72	4.13
4000	Ceiling panel seal, silicone sealant, 150 L.F./gal.	1 Carp	150	.053	L.F.	.28	3.13		3.41	4.96
4100	Two sided adhesive tape	"	240	.033	"	.13	1.95		2.08	3.05
4200	Clips, one per panel				Ea.	1			1	1.10
6000	HEPA filter, 2' x 4', 99.97% eff., 3" dp beveled frame (silicone seal)					380			380	415
6040	6" deep skirted frame (channel seal)					515			515	570
6100	99.99% efficient, 3" deep beveled frame (silicone seal)					480			480	530
6140	6" deep skirted frame (channel seal)					560			560	615
6200	99.999% efficient, 3" deep beveled frame (silicone seal)					635			635	695
6240	6" deep skirted frame (channel seal)					670			670	735
7000	Wall panel systems, including channel strut framing									
7020	Polyester coated aluminum, particle board				S.F.				18.20	18.20
7100	Porcelain coated aluminum, particle board								32	32
7400	Wall panel support, slotted channel struts, to 12' high								16.35	16.35

13 21 26 – Cold Storage Rooms

13 21 26.50 Refrigeration

		Crew	Daily Output	Labor-Hours	Unit	Material	Labor	Equipment	Total	Total Incl O&P
0010	**REFRIGERATION**									
0020	Curbs, 12" high, 4" thick, concrete	2 Carp	58	.276	L.F.	3.29	16.15		19.44	27.50
1000	Doors, see Section 08 34 13.10									
2400	Finishes, 2 coat Portland cement plaster, 1/2" thick	1 Plas	48	.167	S.F.	.80	8.90		9.70	14.10
2500	For galvanized reinforcing mesh, add	1 Lath	335	.024		.61	1.40		2.01	2.71
2700	3/16" thick latex cement	1 Plas	88	.091		1.49	4.85		6.34	8.85
2900	For glass cloth reinforced ceilings, add	"	450	.018		.64	.95		1.59	2.11
3100	Fiberglass panels, 1/8" thick	1 Carp	149.45	.054		2.37	3.14		5.51	7.30
3200	Polystyrene, plastic finish ceiling, 1" thick		274	.029		2.82	1.71		4.53	5.65
3400	2" thick		274	.029		3.17	1.71		4.88	6.05
3500	4" thick		219	.037		4.03	2.14		6.17	7.60

13 21 Controlled Environment Rooms

13 21 26 – Cold Storage Rooms

13 21 26.50 Refrigeration		Crew	Daily Output	Labor-Hours	Unit	Material	2023 Bare Costs Labor	Equipment	Total	Total Incl O&P
3800	Floors, concrete, 4" thick	1 Cefi	93	.086	S.F.	2	4.73		6.73	9.10
3900	6" thick	"	85	.094	↓	3.14	5.20		8.34	11
4000	Insulation, 1" to 6" thick, cork				B.F.	1.49			1.49	1.64
4100	Urethane					.83			.83	.91
4300	Polystyrene, regular					1.26			1.26	1.39
4400	Bead board				↓	.34			.34	.37
4600	Installation of above, add per layer	2 Carp	657.60	.024	S.F.	.44	1.43		1.87	2.60
4700	Wall and ceiling juncture		298.90	.054	L.F.	1.40	3.14		4.54	6.20
4900	Partitions, galvanized sandwich panels, 4" thick, stock		219.20	.073	S.F.	10.05	4.28		14.33	17.40
5000	Aluminum or fiberglass	↓	219.20	.073	"	6.40	4.28		10.68	13.40
5200	Prefab walk-in, 7'-6" high, aluminum, incl. refrigeration, door & floor									
5210	not incl. partitions, 6' x 6'	2 Carp	54.80	.292	SF Flr.	105	17.10		122.10	141
5500	10' x 10'		82.20	.195		84.50	11.40		95.90	110
5700	12' x 14'		109.60	.146		75.50	8.55		84.05	96
5800	12' x 20'	↓	109.60	.146		115	8.55		123.55	139
6100	For 8'-6" high, add					5%				
6300	Rule of thumb for complete units, w/o doors & refrigeration, cooler	2 Carp	146	.110		175	6.40		181.40	202
6400	Freezer		109.60	.146	↓	112	8.55		120.55	136
6600	Shelving, plated or galvanized, steel wire type		360	.044	SF Hor.	8.30	2.60		10.90	13.05
6700	Slat shelf type	↓	375	.043		17.55	2.50		20.05	23
6900	For stainless steel shelving, add					300%				
7000	Vapor barrier, on wood walls	2 Carp	1644	.010	S.F.	.19	.57		.76	1.06
7200	On masonry walls	"	1315	.012	"	.33	.71		1.04	1.42
7500	For air curtain doors, see Section 23 34 33.10									

13 24 Special Activity Rooms

13 24 16 – Saunas

13 24 16.50 Saunas and Heaters		Crew	Daily Output	Labor-Hours	Unit	Material	2023 Bare Costs Labor	Equipment	Total	Total Incl O&P
0010	**SAUNAS AND HEATERS**									
0020	Prefabricated, incl. heater & controls, 7' high, 6' x 4', C/C	L-7	2.20	12.727	Ea.	5,825	720		6,545	7,500
0050	6' x 4', C/P		2	14		4,750	795		5,545	6,400
0400	6' x 5', C/C		2	14		5,900	795		6,695	7,650
0450	6' x 5', C/P		2	14		5,675	795		6,470	7,425
0600	6' x 6', C/C		1.80	15.556		15,600	880		16,480	18,400
0650	6' x 6', C/P		1.80	15.556		6,325	880		7,205	8,275
0800	6' x 9', C/C		1.60	17.500		8,175	990		9,165	10,500
0850	6' x 9', C/P		1.60	17.500		6,425	990		7,415	8,550
1000	8' x 12', C/C		1.10	25.455		19,800	1,450		21,250	24,000
1050	8' x 12', C/P		1.10	25.455		23,300	1,450		24,750	27,800
1200	8' x 8', C/C		1.40	20		10,800	1,125		11,925	13,500
1250	8' x 8', C/P		1.40	20		7,850	1,125		8,975	10,300
1400	8' x 10', C/C		1.20	23.333		9,975	1,325		11,300	13,000
1450	8' x 10', C/P		1.20	23.333		9,100	1,325		10,425	12,000
1600	10' x 12', C/C		1	28		15,700	1,575		17,275	19,700
1650	10' x 12', C/P		1	28		15,700	1,575		17,275	19,700
2500	Heaters only (incl. above), wall mounted, to 200 C.F.					1,125			1,125	1,250
2750	To 300 C.F.					1,275			1,275	1,400
3000	Floor standing, to 720 C.F., 10,000 watts, w/controls	1 Elec	3	2.667		3,250	180		3,430	3,850
3250	To 1,000 C.F., 16,000 watts	"	3	2.667	↓	4,475	180		4,655	5,175

13 24 Special Activity Rooms

13 24 26 – Steam Baths

13 24 26.50 Steam Baths and Components

		Crew	Daily Output	Labor-Hours	Unit	Material	2023 Bare Costs Labor	Equipment	Total	Total Incl O&P
0010	**STEAM BATHS AND COMPONENTS**									
0020	Heater, timer & head, single, to 140 C.F.	1 Plum	1.20	6.667	Ea.	2,375	480		2,855	3,325
0500	To 300 C.F.		1.10	7.273		6,500	525		7,025	7,900
1000	Commercial size, with blow-down assembly, to 800 C.F.		.90	8.889		6,750	640		7,390	8,375
1500	To 2,500 C.F.	↓	.80	10		7,975	720		8,695	9,850
2000	Multiple, motels, apts., 2 baths, w/blow-down assm., 500 C.F.	Q-1	1.30	12.308		7,450	800		8,250	9,400
2500	4 baths	"	.70	22.857		11,200	1,475		12,675	14,600
2700	Conversion unit for residential tub, including door				↓	4,575			4,575	5,025

13 34 Fabricated Engineered Structures

13 34 23 – Fabricated Structures

13 34 23.10 Comfort Stations

		Crew	Daily Output	Labor-Hours	Unit	Material	Labor	Equipment	Total	Total Incl O&P
0010	**COMFORT STATIONS** Prefab., stock, w/doors, windows & fixt.									
0100	Not incl. interior finish or electrical									
0300	Mobile, on steel frame, 2 unit				S.F.	201			201	221
0350	7 unit					320			320	350
0400	Permanent, including concrete slab, 2 unit	B-12J	50	.320		259	18.15	17.60	294.75	330
0500	6 unit	"	43	.372	↓	221	21	20.50	262.50	297
0600	Alternate pricing method, mobile, 2 fixture				fixture	6,900			6,900	7,575
0650	7 fixture					12,000			12,000	13,200
0700	Permanent, 2 unit	B-12J	.70	22.857		21,400	1,300	1,250	23,950	26,800
0750	6 unit	"	.50	32	↓	18,400	1,825	1,750	21,975	24,900

13 34 23.16 Fabricated Control Booths

		Crew	Daily Output	Labor-Hours	Unit	Material	Labor	Equipment	Total	Total Incl O&P
0010	**FABRICATED CONTROL BOOTHS**									
0100	Guard House, prefab conc. w/bullet resistant doors & windows, roof & wiring									
0110	8' x 8', Level III	L-10	1	24	Ea.	61,500	1,575	2,150	65,225	72,500
0120	8' x 8', Level IV	"	1	24	"	79,000	1,575	2,150	82,725	92,000

13 47 Facility Protection

13 47 13 – Cathodic Protection

13 47 13.16 Cathodic Prot. for Underground Storage Tanks

		Crew	Daily Output	Labor-Hours	Unit	Material	Labor	Equipment	Total	Total Incl O&P
0010	**CATHODIC PROTECTION FOR UNDERGROUND STORAGE TANKS**									
1000	Anodes, magnesium type, 9 #	R-15	18.50	2.595	Ea.	45	172	18.70	235.70	325
1010	17 #		13	3.692		92.50	244	26.50	363	495
1020	32 #		10	4.800		136	320	34.50	490.50	655
1030	48 #	↓	7.20	6.667		174	440	48	662	900
1100	Graphite type w/epoxy cap, 3" x 60" (32 #)	R-22	8.40	4.438		160	274		434	580
1110	4" x 80" (68 #)		6	6.213		278	385		663	875
1120	6" x 72" (80 #)		5.20	7.169		1,675	440		2,115	2,500
1130	6" x 36" (45 #)	↓	9.60	3.883		850	239		1,089	1,300
2000	Rectifiers, silicon type, air cooled, 28 V/10 A	R-19	3.50	5.714		2,675	385		3,060	3,500
2010	20 V/20 A		3.50	5.714		2,675	385		3,060	3,525
2100	Oil immersed, 28 V/10 A		3	6.667		2,725	450		3,175	3,675
2110	20 V/20 A	↓	3	6.667	↓	3,600	450		4,050	4,625
3000	Anode backfill, coke breeze	R-22	3850	.010	Lb.	.31	.60		.91	1.23
4000	Cable, HMWPE, No. 8		2.40	15.533	M.L.F.	975	960		1,935	2,500
4010	No. 6		2.40	15.533		1,275	960		2,235	2,850
4020	No. 4		2.40	15.533		2,075	960		3,035	3,700

13 47 Facility Protection

13 47 13 – Cathodic Protection

13 47 13.16 Cathodic Prot. for Underground Storage Tanks		Crew	Daily Output	Labor-Hours	Unit	Material	2023 Bare Costs Labor	Equipment	Total	Total Incl O&P
4030	No. 2	R-22	2.40	15.533	M.L.F.	3,000	960		3,960	4,725
4040	No. 1		2.20	16.945		2,250	1,050		3,300	4,050
4050	No. 1/0		2.20	16.945		4,700	1,050		5,750	6,725
4060	No. 2/0		2.20	16.945		6,000	1,050		7,050	8,150
4070	No. 4/0	↓	2	18.640	↓	9,600	1,150		10,750	12,300
5000	Test station, 7 terminal box, flush curb type w/lockable cover	R-19	12	1.667	Ea.	90	112		202	266
5010	Reference cell, 2" diam. PVC conduit, cplg., plug, set flush	"	4.80	4.167	"	179	281		460	615

Division 14 Conveying Equipment

Estimating Tips
General
- Many products in Division 14 will require some type of support or blocking for installation not included with the item itself. Examples are supports for conveyors or tube systems, attachment points for lifts, and footings for hoists or cranes. Add these supports in the appropriate division.

14 10 00 Dumbwaiters
14 20 00 Elevators
- Dumbwaiters and elevators are estimated and purchased in a method similar to buying a car. The manufacturer has a base unit with standard features. Added to this base unit price will be whatever options the owner or specifications require. Increased load capacity, additional vertical travel, additional stops, higher speed, and cab finish options are items to be considered. When developing an estimate for dumbwaiters and elevators, remember that some items needed by the installers may have to be included as part of the general contract.

Examples are:
- ☐ shaftway
- ☐ rail support brackets
- ☐ machine room
- ☐ electrical supply
- ☐ sill angles
- ☐ electrical connections
- ☐ pits
- ☐ roof penthouses
- ☐ pit ladders

Check the job specifications and drawings before pricing.
- Installation of elevators and handicapped lifts in historic structures can require significant additional costs. The associated structural requirements may involve cutting into and repairing finishes, moldings, flooring, etc. The estimator must account for these special conditions.

14 30 00 Escalators and Moving Walks
- Escalators and moving walks are specialty items installed by specialty contractors. There are numerous options associated with these items. For specific options, contact a manufacturer or contractor. In a method similar to estimating dumbwaiters and elevators, you should verify the extent of general contract work and add items as necessary.

14 40 00 Lifts
14 90 00 Other Conveying Equipment
- Products such as correspondence lifts, chutes, and pneumatic tube systems, as well as other items specified in this subdivision, may require trained installers. The general contractor might not have any choice as to who will perform the installation or when it will be performed. Long lead times are often required for these products, making early decisions in scheduling necessary.

Reference Numbers
Reference numbers are shown at the beginning of some major classifications. These numbers refer to related items in the Reference Section. The reference information may be an estimating procedure, an alternate pricing method, or technical information.

Note: Not all subdivisions listed here necessarily appear. ■

Same Data. Simplified.
Enjoy the convenience and efficiency of accessing your costs anywhere:
- **Skip the multiplier** by setting your location
- **Quickly search,** edit, favorite and share costs
- **Stay on top of price changes** with automatic updates

Discover more at rsmeans.com/online

No part of this cost data may be reproduced, stored in a retrieval system, or transmitted in any form or by any means without prior written permission of Gordian.

14 91 Facility Chutes

14 91 33 – Laundry and Linen Chutes

14 91 33.10 Chutes		Crew	Daily Output	Labor-Hours	Unit	Material	2023 Bare Costs Labor	2023 Bare Costs Equipment	Total	Total Incl O&P
0011	**CHUTES**, linen, trash or refuse									
0050	Aluminized steel, 16 ga., 18" diameter	2 Shee	3.50	4.571	Floor	2,100	320		2,420	2,800
0100	24" diameter		3.20	5		2,325	350		2,675	3,075
0200	30" diameter		3	5.333		2,700	375		3,075	3,525
0300	36" diameter		2.80	5.714		3,075	400		3,475	4,000
0400	Galvanized steel, 16 ga., 18" diameter		3.50	4.571		1,250	320		1,570	1,850
0500	24" diameter		3.20	5		1,400	350		1,750	2,075
0600	30" diameter		3	5.333		1,575	375		1,950	2,325
0700	36" diameter		2.80	5.714		1,875	400		2,275	2,675
0800	Stainless steel, 18" diameter		3.50	4.571		4,050	320		4,370	4,925
0900	24" diameter		3.20	5		3,525	350		3,875	4,400
1000	30" diameter		3	5.333		4,625	375		5,000	5,650
1005	36" diameter		2.80	5.714		4,875	400		5,275	5,975
1200	Linen chute bottom collector, aluminized steel		4	4	Ea.	1,775	281		2,056	2,375
1300	Stainless steel		4	4		2,250	281		2,531	2,900
1500	Refuse, bottom hopper, aluminized steel, 18" diameter		3	5.333		950	375		1,325	1,625
1600	24" diameter		3	5.333		1,050	375		1,425	1,725
1800	36" diameter		3	5.333		1,275	375		1,650	1,975

14 91 82 – Trash Chutes

14 91 82.10 Trash Chutes and Accessories		Crew	Daily Output	Labor-Hours	Unit	Material	Labor	Equipment	Total	Total Incl O&P
0010	**TRASH CHUTES AND ACCESSORIES**									
2900	Package chutes, spiral type, minimum	2 Shee	4.50	3.556	Floor	3,000	249		3,249	3,675
3000	Maximum	"	1.50	10.667	"	7,825	750		8,575	9,725

14 92 Pneumatic Tube Systems

14 92 10 – Conventional, Automatic and Computer Controlled Pneumatic Tube Systems

14 92 10.10 Pneumatic Tube Systems		Crew	Daily Output	Labor-Hours	Unit	Material	Labor	Equipment	Total	Total Incl O&P
0010	**PNEUMATIC TUBE SYSTEMS**									
0020	100' long, single tube, 2 stations, stock									
0100	3" diameter	2 Stpi	.12	133	Total	5,625	9,675		15,300	20,600
0300	4" diameter	"	.09	178	"	6,675	12,900		19,575	26,600
0400	Twin tube, two stations or more, conventional system									
0600	2-1/2" round	2 Stpi	62.50	.256	L.F.	37	18.55		55.55	68.50
0700	3" round		46	.348		56.50	25		81.50	99.50
0900	4" round		49.60	.323		67	23.50		90.50	109
1000	4" x 7" oval		37.60	.426		85	31		116	139
1050	Add for blower		2	8	System	6,025	580		6,605	7,500
1110	Plus for each round station, add		7.50	2.133	Ea.	1,850	155		2,005	2,250
1150	Plus for each oval station, add		7.50	2.133	"	1,850	155		2,005	2,250
1200	Alternate pricing method: base cost, economy model		.75	21.333	Total	5,625	1,550		7,175	8,500
1300	Custom model		.25	64	"	12,600	4,650		17,250	20,800
1500	Plus total system length, add, for economy model		93.40	.171	L.F.	8.15	12.45		20.60	27.50
1600	For custom model		37.60	.426	"	17.90	31		48.90	65.50
1800	Completely automatic system, 4" round, 15 to 50 stations		.29	55.172	Station	19,700	4,000		23,700	27,700
2200	51 to 144 stations		.32	50		13,200	3,625		16,825	19,900
2400	6" round or 4" x 7" oval, 15 to 50 stations		.24	66.667		24,100	4,825		28,925	33,700
2800	51 to 144 stations		.23	69.565		17,900	5,050		22,950	27,200

Estimating Tips
22 10 00 Plumbing Piping and Pumps

This subdivision is primarily basic pipe and related materials. The pipe may be used by any of the mechanical disciplines, i.e., plumbing, fire protection, heating, and air conditioning.

Note: CPVC plastic piping approved for fire protection is located in 21 11 13.

- The labor adjustment factors listed in Subdivision 22 01 02.20 apply throughout Divisions 21, 22, and 23. CAUTION: the correct percentage may vary for the same items. For example, the percentage add for the basic pipe installation should be based on the maximum height that the installer must install for that particular section. If the pipe is to be located 14' above the floor but it is suspended on threaded rod from beams, the bottom flange of which is 18' high (4' rods), then the height is actually 18' and the add is 20%. The pipe cover, however, does not have to go above the 14' and so the add should be 10%.
- Most pipe is priced first as straight pipe with a joint (coupling, weld, etc.) every 10' and a hanger usually every 10'. There are exceptions with hanger spacing such as for cast iron pipe (5') and plastic pipe (3 per 10'). Following each type of pipe there are several lines listing sizes and the amount to be subtracted to delete couplings and hangers. This is for pipe that is to be buried or supported together on trapeze hangers. The reason that the couplings are deleted is that these runs are usually long, and frequently longer lengths of pipe are used. By deleting the couplings, the estimator is expected to look up and add back the correct reduced number of couplings.
- When preparing an estimate, it may be necessary to approximate the fittings. Fittings usually run between 25% and 50% of the cost of the pipe. The lower percentage is for simpler runs, and the higher number is for complex areas, such as mechanical rooms.
- For historic restoration projects, the systems must be as invisible as possible, and pathways must be sought for pipes, conduit, and ductwork. While installations in accessible spaces (such as basements and attics) are relatively straightforward to estimate, labor costs may be more difficult to determine when delivery systems must be concealed.

22 40 00 Plumbing Fixtures

- Plumbing fixture costs usually require two lines: the fixture itself and its "rough-in, supply, and waste."
- In the Assemblies Section (Plumbing D2010) for the desired fixture, the System Components Group at the center of the page shows the fixture on the first line. The rest of the list (fittings, pipe, tubing, etc.) will total up to what we refer to in the Unit Price section as "Rough-in, supply, waste, and vent." Note that for most fixtures we allow a nominal 5' of tubing to reach from the fixture to a main or riser.
- Remember that gas- and oil-fired units need venting.

Reference Numbers

Reference numbers are shown at the beginning of some major classifications. These numbers refer to related items in the Reference Section. The reference information may be an estimating procedure, an alternate pricing method, or technical information.

Note: Not all subdivisions listed here necessarily appear. ■

Same Data. Simplified.

Enjoy the convenience and efficiency of accessing your costs anywhere:

- **Skip the multiplier** by setting your location
- **Quickly search,** edit, favorite and share costs
- **Stay on top of price changes** with automatic updates

Discover more at rsmeans.com/online

No part of this cost data may be reproduced, stored in a retrieval system, or transmitted in any form or by any means without prior written permission of Gordian.

Note: "Powered in part by CINX™, based on licensed proprietary information of Harrison Publishing House, Inc."

Note: Trade Service, in part, has been used as a reference source for some of the material prices used in Division 22.

22 01 Operation and Maintenance of Plumbing

22 01 02 – Labor Adjustments

22 01 02.10 Boilers, General

		Crew	Daily Output	Labor-Hours	Unit	Material	2023 Bare Costs Labor	Equipment	Total	Total Incl O&P
0010	**BOILERS, GENERAL**, Prices do not include flue piping, elec. wiring,									
0020	gas or oil piping, boiler base, pad, or tankless unless noted									
0100	Boiler H.P.: 10 KW = 34 lb./steam/hr. = 33,475 BTU/hr.									
0150	To convert SFR to BTU rating: Hot water, 150 x SFR;									
0160	Forced hot water, 180 x SFR; steam, 240 x SFR									

22 01 02.20 Labor Adjustment Factors

0010	**LABOR ADJUSTMENT FACTORS** (For Div. 21, 22 and 23) R220102-20									
0100	Labor factors: The below are reasonable suggestions, but									
0110	each project must be evaluated for its own peculiarities, and									
0120	the adjustments be increased or decreased depending on the									
0130	severity of the special conditions.									
1000	Add to labor for elevated installation (Above floor level)									
1080	10' to 14.5' high R221113-70						10%			
1100	15' to 19.5' high						20%			
1120	20' to 24.5' high						25%			
1140	25' to 29.5' high						35%			
1160	30' to 34.5' high						40%			
1180	35' to 39.5' high						50%			
1200	40' and higher						55%			
2000	Add to labor for crawl space									
2100	3' high						40%			
2140	4' high						30%			
3000	Add to labor for multi-story building									
3010	For new construction (No elevator available)									
3100	Add for floors 3 thru 10						5%			
3110	Add for floors 11 thru 15						10%			
3120	Add for floors 16 thru 20						15%			
3130	Add for floors 21 thru 30						20%			
3140	Add for floors 31 and up						30%			
3170	For existing structure (Elevator available)									
3180	Add for work on floor 3 and above						2%			
4000	Add to labor for working in existing occupied buildings									
4100	Hospital						35%			
4140	Office building						25%			
4180	School						20%			
4220	Factory or warehouse						15%			
4260	Multi dwelling						15%			
5000	Add to labor, miscellaneous									
5100	Cramped shaft						35%			
5140	Congested area						15%			
5180	Excessive heat or cold						30%			
9000	Labor factors: The above are reasonable suggestions, but									
9010	each project should be evaluated for its own peculiarities.									
9100	Other factors to be considered are:									
9140	Movement of material and equipment through finished areas									
9180	Equipment room									
9220	Attic space									
9260	No service road									
9300	Poor unloading/storage area									
9340	Congested site area/heavy traffic									

22 05 Common Work Results for Plumbing

22 05 05 – Selective Demolition for Plumbing

22 05 05.10 Plumbing Demolition

		Crew	Daily Output	Labor-Hours	Unit	Material	2023 Bare Costs Labor	2023 Bare Costs Equipment	Total	Total Incl O&P
0010	**PLUMBING DEMOLITION** R220105-10									
0400	Air compressor, up thru 2 HP	Q-1	10	1.600	Ea.		104		104	155
0410	3 HP thru 7-1/2 HP R024119-10		5.60	2.857			185		185	276
0420	10 HP thru 15 HP		1.40	11.429			740		740	1,100
0430	20 HP thru 30 HP	Q-2	1.30	18.462			1,250		1,250	1,850
0500	Backflow preventer, up thru 2" diameter	1 Plum	17	.471			34		34	50.50
0510	2-1/2" thru 3" diameter	Q-1	10	1.600			104		104	155
0520	4" thru 6" diameter	"	5	3.200			208		208	310
0530	8" thru 10" diameter	Q-2	3	8			540		540	800
1900	Piping fittings, single connection, up thru 1-1/2" diameter	1 Plum	30	.267			19.20		19.20	28.50
1910	2" thru 4" diameter		14	.571			41		41	61.50
1980	Pipe hanger/support removal		80	.100			7.20		7.20	10.75
2000	Piping, metal, up thru 1-1/2" diameter		200	.040	L.F.		2.88		2.88	4.30
2050	2" thru 3-1/2" diameter		150	.053			3.84		3.84	5.75
2100	4" thru 6" diameter	2 Plum	100	.160			11.55		11.55	17.20
2150	8" thru 14" diameter	"	60	.267			19.20		19.20	28.50
2153	16" thru 20" diameter	Q-18	70	.343			23	.92	23.92	35.50
2155	24" thru 26" diameter		55	.436			29.50	1.17	30.67	45.50
2156	30" thru 36" diameter		40	.600			40.50	1.60	42.10	62.50
2160	Plastic pipe with fittings, up thru 1-1/2" diameter	1 Plum	250	.032			2.31		2.31	3.44
2162	2" thru 3" diameter	"	200	.040			2.88		2.88	4.30
2164	4" thru 6" diameter	Q-1	200	.080			5.20		5.20	7.75
2166	8" thru 14" diameter		150	.107			6.90		6.90	10.30
2168	16" diameter		100	.160			10.40		10.40	15.45
2180	Pumps, all fractional horse-power		12	1.333	Ea.		86.50		86.50	129
2184	1 HP thru 5 HP		6	2.667			173		173	258
2186	7-1/2 HP thru 15 HP		2.50	6.400			415		415	620
2188	20 HP thru 25 HP	Q-2	4	6			405		405	600
2190	30 HP thru 60 HP		.80	30			2,025		2,025	3,000
2192	75 HP thru 100 HP		.60	40			2,700		2,700	4,000
2194	150 HP		.50	48			3,225		3,225	4,825
2230	Temperature maintenance cable	1 Plum	1200	.007	L.F.		.48		.48	.72
3100	Tanks, water heaters and liquid containers									
3110	Up thru 45 gallons	Q-1	22	.727	Ea.		47		47	70.50
3120	50 thru 120 gallons		14	1.143			74		74	111
3130	130 thru 240 gallons		7.60	2.105			137		137	204
3140	250 thru 500 gallons		5.40	2.963			192		192	287
3150	600 thru 1,000 gallons	Q-2	1.60	15			1,000		1,000	1,500
3160	1,100 thru 2,000 gallons		.70	34.286			2,300		2,300	3,450
3170	2,100 thru 4,000 gallons		.50	48			3,225		3,225	4,825
9100	Valve, metal valves or strainers and similar, up thru 1-1/2" diameter	1 Stpi	28	.286			20.50		20.50	31
9110	2" thru 3" diameter	Q-1	11	1.455			94.50		94.50	141
9120	4" thru 6" diameter	"	8	2			130		130	193
9130	8" thru 14" diameter	Q-2	8	3			202		202	300
9140	16" thru 20" diameter		2	12			805		805	1,200
9150	24" diameter		1.20	20			1,350		1,350	2,000
9200	Valve, plastic, up thru 1-1/2" diameter	1 Plum	42	.190			13.70		13.70	20.50
9210	2" thru 3" diameter		15	.533			38.50		38.50	57.50
9220	4" thru 6" diameter		12	.667			48		48	71.50
9300	Vent flashing and caps		55	.145			10.50		10.50	15.65
9350	Water filter, commercial, 1" thru 1-1/2"	Q-1	2	8			520		520	775
9360	2" thru 2-1/2"	"	1.60	10			650		650	965
9400	Water heaters									

22 05 Common Work Results for Plumbing

22 05 05 – Selective Demolition for Plumbing

22 05 05.10 Plumbing Demolition		Crew	Daily Output	Labor-Hours	Unit	Material	2023 Bare Costs Labor	Equipment	Total	Total Incl O&P
9410	Up thru 245 GPH	Q-1	2.40	6.667	Ea.		430		430	645
9420	250 thru 756 GPH		1.60	10			650		650	965
9430	775 thru 1,640 GPH		.80	20			1,300		1,300	1,925
9440	1,650 thru 4,000 GPH	Q-2	.50	48			3,225		3,225	4,825
9470	Water softener	Q-1	2	8			520		520	775

22 05 23 – General-Duty Valves for Plumbing Piping

22 05 23.10 Valves, Brass

0010	**VALVES, BRASS**									
0032	For motorized valves, see Section 23 09 53.10									
0500	Gas cocks, threaded									
0510	1/4"	1 Plum	26	.308	Ea.	31	22		53	67.50
0520	3/8"		24	.333		31	24		55	70.50
0530	1/2"		24	.333		40	24		64	80
0540	3/4"		22	.364		37	26		63	80
0550	1"		19	.421		57.50	30.50		88	109
0560	1-1/4"		15	.533		71	38.50		109.50	136
0570	1-1/2"		13	.615		112	44.50		156.50	189
0580	2"		11	.727		180	52.50		232.50	276
0672	For larger sizes use lubricated plug valve, Section 23 05 23.70									

22 05 23.20 Valves, Bronze

0010	**VALVES, BRONZE** R220523-90									
1020	Angle, 150 lb., rising stem, threaded									
1030	1/8"	1 Plum	24	.333	Ea.	231	24		255	290
1040	1/4"		24	.333		231	24		255	290
1050	3/8"		24	.333		229	24		253	288
1060	1/2"		22	.364		229	26		255	291
1070	3/4"		20	.400		315	29		344	390
1080	1"		19	.421		435	30.50		465.50	525
1090	1-1/4"		15	.533		500	38.50		538.50	610
1100	1-1/2"		13	.615		810	44.50		854.50	955
1102	Soldered same price as threaded									
1110	2"	1 Plum	11	.727	Ea.	1,275	52.50		1,327.50	1,475
1300	Ball									
1304	Soldered									
1312	3/8"	1 Plum	21	.381	Ea.	24.50	27.50		52	68
1316	1/2"		18	.444		21.50	32		53.50	71.50
1320	3/4"		17	.471		40.50	34		74.50	95
1324	1"		15	.533		54.50	38.50		93	118
1328	1-1/4"		13	.615		84.50	44.50		129	159
1332	1-1/2"		11	.727		108	52.50		160.50	197
1336	2"		9	.889		175	64		239	288
1340	2-1/2"		7	1.143		605	82.50		687.50	790
1344	3"		5	1.600		710	115		825	950
1350	Single union end									
1358	3/8"	1 Plum	21	.381	Ea.	37.50	27.50		65	82
1362	1/2"		18	.444		39	32		71	91
1366	3/4"		17	.471		71	34		105	129
1370	1"		15	.533		94	38.50		132.50	161
1374	1-1/4"		13	.615		112	44.50		156.50	189
1378	1-1/2"		11	.727		100	52.50		152.50	188
1382	2"		9	.889		274	64		338	395
1398	Threaded, 150 psi									

22 05 Common Work Results for Plumbing

22 05 23 – General-Duty Valves for Plumbing Piping

22 05 23.20 Valves, Bronze		Crew	Daily Output	Labor-Hours	Unit	Material	2023 Bare Costs Labor	Equipment	Total	Total Incl O&P
1400	1/4"	1 Plum	24	.333	Ea.	22	24		46	60
1430	3/8"		24	.333		23	24		47	61
1450	1/2"		22	.364		21.50	26		47.50	63
1460	3/4"		20	.400		35	29		64	81.50
1470	1"		19	.421		58	30.50		88.50	109
1480	1-1/4"		15	.533		69.50	38.50		108	134
1490	1-1/2"		13	.615		88	44.50		132.50	163
1500	2"		11	.727		134	52.50		186.50	226
1510	2-1/2"		9	.889		108	64		172	215
1520	3"		8	1		700	72		772	875
1522	Solder the same price as threaded									
1600	Butterfly, 175 psi, full port, solder or threaded ends									
1610	Stainless steel disc and stem									
1620	1/4"	1 Plum	24	.333	Ea.	32	24		56	71
1630	3/8"		24	.333		33.50	24		57.50	72.50
1640	1/2"		22	.364		37.50	26		63.50	80
1650	3/4"		20	.400		60.50	29		89.50	110
1660	1"		19	.421		78	30.50		108.50	131
1670	1-1/4"		15	.533		119	38.50		157.50	189
1680	1-1/2"		13	.615		162	44.50		206.50	244
1690	2"		11	.727		193	52.50		245.50	290
1750	Check, swing, class 150, regrinding disc, threaded									
1800	1/8"	1 Plum	24	.333	Ea.	101	24		125	148
1830	1/4"		24	.333		109	24		133	156
1840	3/8"		24	.333		160	24		184	212
1850	1/2"		24	.333		132	24		156	182
1860	3/4"		20	.400		186	29		215	248
1870	1"		19	.421		246	30.50		276.50	315
1880	1-1/4"		15	.533		395	38.50		433.50	495
1890	1-1/2"		13	.615		355	44.50		399.50	455
1900	2"		11	.727		600	52.50		652.50	740
1910	2-1/2"	Q-1	15	1.067		1,575	69		1,644	1,825
1920	3"	"	13	1.231		1,750	80		1,830	2,050
2000	For 200 lb., add					5%	10%			
2040	For 300 lb., add					15%	15%			
2060	Check swing, 300 lb., lead free unless noted, sweat, 3/8" size	1 Plum	24	.333	Ea.	217	24		241	275
2070	1/2"		24	.333		239	24		263	299
2080	3/4"		20	.400		320	29		349	395
2090	1"		19	.421		395	30.50		425.50	480
2100	1-1/4"		15	.533		530	38.50		568.50	645
2110	1-1/2"		13	.615		575	44.50		619.50	695
2120	2"		11	.727		1,025	52.50		1,077.50	1,225
2130	2-1/2", not lead free	Q-1	15	1.067		435	69		504	585
2140	3", not lead free	"	13	1.231		3,825	80		3,905	4,350
2350	Check, lift, class 150, horizontal composition disc, threaded									
2430	1/4"	1 Plum	24	.333	Ea.	274	24		298	335
2440	3/8"		24	.333		355	24		379	425
2450	1/2"		24	.333		310	24		334	375
2460	3/4"		20	.400		365	29		394	450
2470	1"		19	.421		540	30.50		570.50	640
2480	1-1/4"		15	.533		720	38.50		758.50	850
2490	1-1/2"		13	.615		860	44.50		904.50	1,000
2500	2"		11	.727		1,375	52.50		1,427.50	1,575

For customer support on your Mechanical Costs with RSMeans data, call 800.448.8182.

22 05 Common Work Results for Plumbing

22 05 23 – General-Duty Valves for Plumbing Piping

22 05 23.20 Valves, Bronze		Crew	Daily Output	Labor-Hours	Unit	Material	2023 Bare Costs Labor	Equipment	Total	Total Incl O&P
2850	Gate, N.R.S., soldered, 125 psi									
2900	3/8"	1 Plum	24	.333	Ea.	107	24		131	153
2920	1/2"		24	.333		115	24		139	163
2940	3/4"		20	.400		127	29		156	182
2950	1"		19	.421		181	30.50		211.50	245
2960	1-1/4"		15	.533		277	38.50		315.50	365
2970	1-1/2"		13	.615		310	44.50		354.50	405
2980	2"		11	.727		435	52.50		487.50	560
2990	2-1/2"	Q-1	15	1.067		1,125	69		1,194	1,325
3000	3"	"	13	1.231		1,325	80		1,405	1,575
3350	Threaded, class 150									
3410	1/4"	1 Plum	24	.333	Ea.	164	24		188	217
3420	3/8"		24	.333		164	24		188	217
3430	1/2"		24	.333		168	24		192	221
3440	3/4"		20	.400		171	29		200	231
3450	1"		19	.421		235	30.50		265.50	305
3460	1-1/4"		15	.533		289	38.50		327.50	380
3470	1-1/2"		13	.615		435	44.50		479.50	540
3480	2"		11	.727		495	52.50		547.50	620
3490	2-1/2"	Q-1	15	1.067		1,150	69		1,219	1,375
3500	3"	"	13	1.231		1,775	80		1,855	2,075
3600	Gate, flanged, 150 lb.									
3610	1"	1 Plum	7	1.143	Ea.	1,775	82.50		1,857.50	2,075
3620	1-1/2"		6	1.333		2,200	96		2,296	2,575
3630	2"		5	1.600		3,250	115		3,365	3,750
3634	2-1/2"	Q-1	5	3.200		5,000	208		5,208	5,800
3640	3"	"	4.50	3.556		5,850	231		6,081	6,775
3850	Rising stem, soldered, 300 psi									
3900	3/8"	1 Plum	24	.333	Ea.	242	24		266	300
3920	1/2"		24	.333		236	24		260	296
3940	3/4"		20	.400		270	29		299	340
3950	1"		19	.421		365	30.50		395.50	445
3960	1-1/4"		15	.533		505	38.50		543.50	615
3970	1-1/2"		13	.615		615	44.50		659.50	740
3980	2"		11	.727		985	52.50		1,037.50	1,150
3990	2-1/2"	Q-1	15	1.067		2,100	69		2,169	2,400
4000	3"	"	13	1.231		3,250	80		3,330	3,700
4250	Threaded, class 150									
4310	1/4"	1 Plum	24	.333	Ea.	150	24		174	201
4320	3/8"		24	.333		150	24		174	201
4330	1/2"		24	.333		147	24		171	198
4340	3/4"		20	.400		159	29		188	218
4350	1"		19	.421		206	30.50		236.50	271
4360	1-1/4"		15	.533		279	38.50		317.50	365
4370	1-1/2"		13	.615		350	44.50		394.50	455
4380	2"		11	.727		475	52.50		527.50	600
4390	2-1/2"	Q-1	15	1.067		955	69		1,024	1,150
4400	3"	"	13	1.231		1,550	80		1,630	1,825
4500	For 300 psi, threaded, add					100%	15%			
4540	For chain operated type, add					15%				
4850	Globe, class 150, rising stem, threaded									
4920	1/4"	1 Plum	24	.333	Ea.	201	24		225	257
4940	3/8"		24	.333		198	24		222	254

22 05 Common Work Results for Plumbing

22 05 23 – General-Duty Valves for Plumbing Piping

22 05 23.20 Valves, Bronze		Crew	Daily Output	Labor-Hours	Unit	Material	2023 Bare Costs Labor	Equipment	Total	Total Incl O&P
4950	1/2"	1 Plum	24	.333	Ea.	180	24		204	234
4960	3/4"		20	.400		240	29		269	305
4970	1"		19	.421		415	30.50		445.50	500
4980	1-1/4"		15	.533		585	38.50		623.50	705
4990	1-1/2"		13	.615		700	44.50		744.50	835
5000	2"		11	.727		1,200	52.50		1,252.50	1,400
5010	2-1/2"	Q-1	15	1.067		2,400	69		2,469	2,750
5020	3"	"	13	1.231		3,425	80		3,505	3,900
5120	For 300 lb. threaded, add					50%	15%			
5130	Globe, 300 lb., sweat, 3/8" size	1 Plum	24	.333	Ea.	223	24		247	282
5140	1/2"		24	.333		225	24		249	283
5150	3/4"		20	.400		305	29		334	380
5160	1"		19	.421		420	30.50		450.50	510
5170	1-1/4"		15	.533		665	38.50		703.50	790
5180	1-1/2"		13	.615		805	44.50		849.50	955
5190	2"		11	.727		1,225	52.50		1,277.50	1,400
5200	2-1/2"	Q-1	15	1.067		2,325	69		2,394	2,650
5210	3"	"	13	1.231		2,975	80		3,055	3,400
5600	Relief, pressure & temperature, self-closing, ASME, threaded									
5640	3/4"	1 Plum	28	.286	Ea.	305	20.50		325.50	365
5650	1"		24	.333		455	24		479	535
5660	1-1/4"		20	.400		805	29		834	930
5670	1-1/2"		18	.444		1,450	32		1,482	1,650
5680	2"		16	.500		1,850	36		1,886	2,100
5950	Pressure, poppet type, threaded									
6000	1/2"	1 Plum	30	.267	Ea.	45	19.20		64.20	78
6040	3/4"	"	28	.286	"	111	20.50		131.50	153
6400	Pressure, water, ASME, threaded									
6440	3/4"	1 Plum	28	.286	Ea.	101	20.50		121.50	142
6450	1"		24	.333		183	24		207	237
6460	1-1/4"		20	.400		505	29		534	600
6470	1-1/2"		18	.444		1,050	32		1,082	1,225
6480	2"		16	.500		1,525	36		1,561	1,750
6490	2-1/2"		15	.533		6,275	38.50		6,313.50	6,950
6900	Reducing, water pressure									
6920	300 psi to 25-75 psi, threaded or sweat									
6940	1/2"	1 Plum	24	.333	Ea.	254	24		278	315
6950	3/4"		20	.400		830	29		859	960
6960	1"		19	.421		1,275	30.50		1,305.50	1,475
6970	1-1/4"		15	.533		2,200	38.50		2,238.50	2,450
6980	1-1/2"		13	.615		1,100	44.50		1,144.50	1,275
6990	2"		11	.727		5,000	52.50		5,052.50	5,575
7100	For built-in by-pass or 10-35 psi, add					69.50			69.50	76.50
7700	High capacity, 250 psi to 25-75 psi, threaded									
7740	1/2"	1 Plum	24	.333	Ea.	1,325	24		1,349	1,475
7780	3/4"		20	.400		1,075	29		1,104	1,225
7790	1"		19	.421		1,550	30.50		1,580.50	1,750
7800	1-1/4"		15	.533		2,675	38.50		2,713.50	3,000
7810	1-1/2"		13	.615		3,900	44.50		3,944.50	4,375
7820	2"		11	.727		5,700	52.50		5,752.50	6,350
7830	2-1/2"		9	.889		8,150	64		8,214	9,075
7840	3"		8	1		9,775	72		9,847	10,800
7850	3" flanged (iron body)	Q-1	10	1.600		8,675	104		8,779	9,675

22 05 Common Work Results for Plumbing

22 05 23 – General-Duty Valves for Plumbing Piping

22 05 23.20 Valves, Bronze		Crew	Daily Output	Labor-Hours	Unit	Material	2023 Bare Costs Labor	Equipment	Total	Total Incl O&P
7860	4" flanged (iron body)	Q-1	8	2	Ea.	12,500	130		12,630	14,000
7920	For higher pressure, add					25%				
8000	Silent check, bronze trim									
8010	Compact wafer type, for 125 or 150 lb. flanges									
8020	1-1/2"	1 Plum	11	.727	Ea.	585	52.50		637.50	725
8021	2"	"	9	.889		620	64		684	775
8022	2-1/2"	Q-1	9	1.778		670	115		785	905
8023	3"		8	2		750	130		880	1,025
8024	4"	↓	5	3.200		1,250	208		1,458	1,675
8025	5"	Q-2	6	4		1,325	269		1,594	1,850
8026	6"		5	4.800		1,450	325		1,775	2,075
8027	8"		4.50	5.333		2,100	360		2,460	2,850
8028	10"		4	6		3,725	405		4,130	4,700
8029	12"	↓	3	8	↓	8,725	540		9,265	10,400
8050	For 250 or 300 lb. flanges, thru 6" no change									
8051	For 8" and 10", add				Ea.	40%	10%			
8060	Full flange wafer type, 150 lb.									
8061	1"	1 Plum	14	.571	Ea.	70.50	41		111.50	139
8062	1-1/4"		12	.667		70.50	48		118.50	149
8063	1-1/2"		11	.727		70.50	52.50		123	156
8064	2"	↓	9	.889		805	64		869	980
8065	2-1/2"	Q-1	9	1.778		104	115		219	287
8066	3"		8	2		155	130		285	365
8067	4"	↓	5	3.200		224	208		432	555
8068	5"	Q-2	6	4		375	269		644	810
8069	6"	"	5	4.800		510	325		835	1,050
8080	For 300 lb., add				↓	40%	10%			
8100	Globe type, 150 lb.									
8110	2"	1 Plum	9	.889	Ea.	795	64		859	965
8111	2-1/2"	Q-1	9	1.778		990	115		1,105	1,275
8112	3"		8	2		1,175	130		1,305	1,500
8113	4"	↓	5	3.200		1,650	208		1,858	2,100
8114	5"	Q-2	6	4		2,000	269		2,269	2,600
8115	6"	"	5	4.800	↓	2,800	325		3,125	3,550
8130	For 300 lb., add					20%	10%			
8140	Screwed end type, 250 lb.									
8141	1/2"	1 Plum	24	.333	Ea.	72	24		96	116
8142	3/4"		20	.400		72	29		101	123
8143	1"		19	.421		82.50	30.50		113	136
8144	1-1/4"		15	.533		114	38.50		152.50	183
8145	1-1/2"		13	.615		128	44.50		172.50	206
8146	2"	↓	11	.727	↓	172	52.50		224.50	267
8350	Tempering, water, sweat connections									
8400	1/2"	1 Plum	24	.333	Ea.	150	24		174	202
8440	3/4"	"	20	.400	"	248	29		277	315
8650	Threaded connections									
8700	1/2"	1 Plum	24	.333	Ea.	236	24		260	296
8740	3/4"		20	.400		1,675	29		1,704	1,875
8750	1"		19	.421		1,875	30.50		1,905.50	2,125
8760	1-1/4"		15	.533		2,900	38.50		2,938.50	3,225
8770	1-1/2"		13	.615		3,175	44.50		3,219.50	3,550
8780	2"	↓	11	.727	↓	4,750	52.50		4,802.50	5,300

22 05 Common Work Results for Plumbing

22 05 23 – General-Duty Valves for Plumbing Piping

22 05 23.60 Valves, Plastic		Crew	Daily Output	Labor-Hours	Unit	Material	2023 Bare Costs Labor	Equipment	Total	Total Incl O&P
0010	**VALVES, PLASTIC** R220523-90									
1100	Angle, PVC, threaded									
1110	1/4"	1 Plum	26	.308	Ea.	65.50	22		87.50	105
1120	1/2"		26	.308		93.50	22		115.50	136
1130	3/4"		25	.320		111	23		134	157
1140	1"	↓	23	.348	↓	135	25		160	186
1150	Ball, PVC, socket or threaded, true union									
1230	1/2"	1 Plum	26	.308	Ea.	42	22		64	79.50
1240	3/4"		25	.320		50	23		73	89.50
1250	1"		23	.348		60	25		85	104
1260	1-1/4"		21	.381		96	27.50		123.50	146
1270	1-1/2"		20	.400		95.50	29		124.50	148
1280	2"	↓	17	.471		195	34		229	266
1290	2-1/2"	Q-1	26	.615		247	40		287	330
1300	3"		24	.667		305	43		348	400
1310	4"	↓	20	.800		515	52		567	650
1360	For PVC, flanged, add					100%	15%			
1450	Double union 1/2"	1 Plum	26	.308		65	22		87	105
1460	3/4"		25	.320		77	23		100	119
1470	1"		23	.348		94.50	25		119.50	142
1480	1-1/4"		21	.381		127	27.50		154.50	180
1490	1-1/2"		20	.400		167	29		196	226
1500	2"	↓	17	.471	↓	201	34		235	273
1650	CPVC, socket or threaded, single union									
1700	1/2"	1 Plum	26	.308	Ea.	66.50	22		88.50	106
1720	3/4"		25	.320		83.50	23		106.50	127
1730	1"		23	.348		99	25		124	147
1750	1-1/4"		21	.381		196	27.50		223.50	256
1760	1-1/2"		20	.400		160	29		189	219
1770	2"		17	.471		220	34		254	293
1780	3"	Q-1	24	.667		640	43		683	770
1840	For CPVC, flanged, add					65%	15%			
1880	For true union, socket or threaded, add				↓	50%	5%			
2050	Polypropylene, threaded									
2100	1/4"	1 Plum	26	.308	Ea.	57.50	22		79.50	96.50
2120	3/8"		26	.308		59.50	22		81.50	98.50
2130	1/2"		26	.308		49	22		71	87
2140	3/4"		25	.320		59	23		82	99.50
2150	1"		23	.348		69	25		94	114
2160	1-1/4"		21	.381		91.50	27.50		119	142
2170	1-1/2"		20	.400		114	29		143	168
2180	2"	↓	17	.471		152	34		186	218
2190	3"	Q-1	24	.667		345	43		388	445
2200	4"	"	20	.800	↓	610	52		662	750
2550	PVC, three way, socket or threaded									
2600	1/2"	1 Plum	26	.308	Ea.	81	22		103	123
2640	3/4"		25	.320		98	23		121	143
2650	1"		23	.348		117	25		142	167
2660	1-1/2"		20	.400		164	29		193	224
2670	2"		17	.471		216	34		250	289
2680	3"	Q-1	24	.667		665	43		708	795
2740	For flanged, add				↓	60%	15%			

22 05 Common Work Results for Plumbing

22 05 23 – General-Duty Valves for Plumbing Piping

22 05 23.60 Valves, Plastic		Crew	Daily Output	Labor-Hours	Unit	Material	2023 Bare Costs Labor	Equipment	Total	Total Incl O&P
3150	Ball check, PVC, socket or threaded									
3200	1/4"	1 Plum	26	.308	Ea.	62.50	22		84.50	102
3220	3/8"		26	.308		62.50	22		84.50	102
3240	1/2"		26	.308		64	22		86	104
3250	3/4"		25	.320		71.50	23		94.50	113
3260	1"		23	.348		89.50	25		114.50	136
3270	1-1/4"		21	.381		150	27.50		177.50	206
3280	1-1/2"		20	.400		150	29		179	208
3290	2"		17	.471		204	34		238	276
3310	3"	Q-1	24	.667		570	43		613	690
3320	4"	"	20	.800		805	52		857	965
3360	For PVC, flanged, add					50%	15%			
3750	CPVC, socket or threaded									
3800	1/2"	1 Plum	26	.308	Ea.	118	22		140	163
3840	3/4"		25	.320		117	23		140	164
3850	1"		23	.348		139	25		164	191
3860	1-1/2"		20	.400		239	29		268	305
3870	2"		17	.471		263	34		297	340
3880	3"	Q-1	24	.667		870	43		913	1,025
3920	4"	"	20	.800		1,175	52		1,227	1,375
3930	For CPVC, flanged, add					40%	15%			
4340	Polypropylene, threaded									
4360	1/2"	1 Plum	26	.308	Ea.	106	22		128	149
4400	3/4"		25	.320		100	23		123	145
4440	1"		23	.348		134	25		159	185
4450	1-1/2"		20	.400		178	29		207	239
4460	2"		17	.471		320	34		354	400
4500	For polypropylene flanged, add					200%	15%			
4850	Foot valve, PVC, socket or threaded									
4900	1/2"	1 Plum	34	.235	Ea.	73	16.95		89.95	106
4930	3/4"		32	.250		83	18		101	119
4940	1"		28	.286		109	20.50		129.50	150
4950	1-1/4"		27	.296		235	21.50		256.50	290
4960	1-1/2"		26	.308		209	22		231	263
4970	2"		24	.333		242	24		266	305
4980	3"		20	.400		580	29		609	680
4990	4"		18	.444		1,025	32		1,057	1,175
5000	For flanged, add					25%	10%			
5050	CPVC, socket or threaded									
5060	1/2"	1 Plum	34	.235	Ea.	98	16.95		114.95	134
5070	3/4"		32	.250		137	18		155	177
5080	1"		28	.286		168	20.50		188.50	215
5090	1-1/4"		27	.296		255	21.50		276.50	310
5100	1-1/2"		26	.308		255	22		277	315
5110	2"		24	.333		320	24		344	385
5120	3"		20	.400		650	29		679	760
5130	4"		18	.444		1,175	32		1,207	1,350
5140	For flanged, add					25%	10%			
5280	Needle valve, PVC, threaded									
5300	1/4"	1 Plum	26	.308	Ea.	91	22		113	133
5340	3/8"		26	.308		104	22		126	147
5360	1/2"		26	.308		103	22		125	147
5380	For polypropylene, add					10%				

22 05 Common Work Results for Plumbing

22 05 23 – General-Duty Valves for Plumbing Piping

22 05 23.60 Valves, Plastic		Crew	Daily Output	Labor-Hours	Unit	Material	2023 Bare Costs Labor	Equipment	Total	Total Incl O&P
5800	Y check, PVC, socket or threaded									
5820	1/2"	1 Plum	26	.308	Ea.	93	22		115	135
5840	3/4"		25	.320		101	23		124	146
5850	1"		23	.348		109	25		134	158
5860	1-1/4"		21	.381		171	27.50		198.50	230
5870	1-1/2"		20	.400		187	29		216	249
5880	2"		17	.471		232	34		266	305
5890	2-1/2"		15	.533		495	38.50		533.50	605
5900	3"	Q-1	24	.667		495	43		538	610
5910	4"	"	20	.800		810	52		862	970
5960	For PVC flanged, add					45%	15%			
6350	Y sediment strainer, PVC, socket or threaded									
6400	1/2"	1 Plum	26	.308	Ea.	64.50	22		86.50	104
6440	3/4"		24	.333		69.50	24		93.50	113
6450	1"		23	.348		82.50	25		107.50	128
6460	1-1/4"		21	.381		256	27.50		283.50	325
6470	1-1/2"		20	.400		170	29		199	230
6480	2"		17	.471		170	34		204	238
6490	2-1/2"		15	.533		475	38.50		513.50	580
6500	3"	Q-1	24	.667		410	43		453	520
6510	4"	"	20	.800		685	52		737	835
6560	For PVC, flanged, add					55%	15%			

22 05 29 – Hangers and Supports for Plumbing Piping and Equipment

22 05 29.10 Hangers & Supp. for Plumb'g/HVAC Pipe/Equip.		Crew	Daily Output	Labor-Hours	Unit	Material	2023 Bare Costs Labor	Equipment	Total	Total Incl O&P
0010	**HANGERS AND SUPPORTS FOR PLUMB'G/HVAC PIPE/EQUIP.**									
0011	TYPE numbers per MSS-SP58									
0050	Brackets									
0060	Beam side or wall, malleable iron, TYPE 34									
0070	3/8" threaded rod size	1 Plum	48	.167	Ea.	8.40	12		20.40	27
0080	1/2" threaded rod size		48	.167		15	12		27	34.50
0090	5/8" threaded rod size		48	.167		25.50	12		37.50	46
0100	3/4" threaded rod size		48	.167		23	12		35	43
0110	7/8" threaded rod size		48	.167		25	12		37	45.50
0120	For concrete installation, add						30%			
0150	Wall, welded steel, medium, TYPE 32									
0160	0 size, 12" wide, 18" deep	1 Plum	34	.235	Ea.	695	16.95		711.95	790
0170	1 size, 18" wide, 24" deep		34	.235		825	16.95		841.95	930
0180	2 size, 24" wide, 30" deep		34	.235		1,100	16.95		1,116.95	1,225
0200	Beam attachment, welded, TYPE 22									
0202	3/8"	Q-15	80	.200	Ea.	34.50	12.95	.80	48.25	58
0203	1/2"		76	.211		21	13.65	.84	35.49	44.50
0204	5/8"		72	.222		22	14.40	.89	37.29	47
0205	3/4"		68	.235		30	15.25	.94	46.19	57
0206	7/8"		64	.250		62.50	16.20	1	79.70	94
0207	1"		56	.286		102	18.55	1.15	121.70	141
0300	Clamps									
0310	C-clamp, for mounting on steel beam flange, w/locknut, TYPE 23									
0320	3/8" threaded rod size	1 Plum	160	.050	Ea.	6.15	3.60		9.75	12.15
0330	1/2" threaded rod size		160	.050		7.65	3.60		11.25	13.80
0340	5/8" threaded rod size		160	.050		10.30	3.60		13.90	16.65
0350	3/4" threaded rod size		160	.050		6.85	3.60		10.45	12.85
0352	7/8" threaded rod size		140	.057		23.50	4.12		27.62	31.50

22 05 Common Work Results for Plumbing

22 05 29 – Hangers and Supports for Plumbing Piping and Equipment

22 05 29.10 Hangers & Supp. for Plumb'g/HVAC Pipe/Equip.

		Crew	Daily Output	Labor-Hours	Unit	Material	2023 Bare Costs Labor	2023 Bare Costs Equipment	Total	Total Incl O&P
0400	High temperature to 1050°F, alloy steel									
0410	4" pipe size	Q-1	106	.151	Ea.	59	9.80		68.80	79.50
0420	6" pipe size		106	.151		86	9.80		95.80	109
0430	8" pipe size		97	.165		98	10.70		108.70	124
0440	10" pipe size		84	.190		125	12.35		137.35	156
0450	12" pipe size		72	.222		165	14.40		179.40	204
0460	14" pipe size		64	.250		289	16.20		305.20	345
0470	16" pipe size		56	.286		325	18.55		343.55	385
0480	Beam clamp, flange type, TYPE 25									
0482	For 3/8" bolt	1 Plum	48	.167	Ea.	18.05	12		30.05	38
0483	For 1/2" bolt		44	.182		14.30	13.10		27.40	35.50
0484	For 5/8" bolt		40	.200		14.30	14.40		28.70	37
0485	For 3/4" bolt		36	.222		14.30	16		30.30	39.50
0486	For 1" bolt		32	.250		9.60	18		27.60	37.50
0500	I-beam, for mounting on bottom flange, strap iron, TYPE 21									
0530	4" flange size	1 Plum	93	.086	Ea.	24	6.20		30.20	36
0540	5" flange size		92	.087		36.50	6.25		42.75	49.50
0550	6" flange size		90	.089		29.50	6.40		35.90	42
0560	7" flange size		88	.091		33	6.55		39.55	46.50
0570	8" flange size		86	.093		35	6.70		41.70	48.50
0600	One hole, vertical mounting, malleable iron									
0610	1/2" pipe size	1 Plum	160	.050	Ea.	3.38	3.60		6.98	9.05
0620	3/4" pipe size		145	.055		4.32	3.98		8.30	10.70
0630	1" pipe size		136	.059		4.60	4.24		8.84	11.35
0640	1-1/4" pipe size		128	.063		6.80	4.50		11.30	14.15
0650	1-1/2" pipe size		120	.067		7.95	4.80		12.75	15.85
0660	2" pipe size		112	.071		10.40	5.15		15.55	19.15
0670	2-1/2" pipe size		104	.077		20.50	5.55		26.05	31
0680	3" pipe size		96	.083		27.50	6		33.50	39
0690	3-1/2" pipe size		90	.089		14.65	6.40		21.05	25.50
0700	4" pipe size		84	.095		24	6.85		30.85	37
0750	Riser or extension pipe, carbon steel, TYPE 8									
0756	1/2" pipe size	1 Plum	52	.154	Ea.	6.35	11.10		17.45	23.50
0760	3/4" pipe size		48	.167		4.40	12		16.40	22.50
0770	1" pipe size		47	.170		4.54	12.25		16.79	23.50
0780	1-1/4" pipe size		46	.174		8.10	12.55		20.65	27.50
0790	1-1/2" pipe size		45	.178		6	12.80		18.80	25.50
0800	2" pipe size		43	.186		6.15	13.40		19.55	27
0810	2-1/2" pipe size		41	.195		6.40	14.05		20.45	28
0820	3" pipe size		40	.200		7.20	14.40		21.60	29.50
0830	3-1/2" pipe size		39	.205		21	14.80		35.80	45
0840	4" pipe size		38	.211		8.85	15.15		24	32.50
0850	5" pipe size		37	.216		29	15.60		44.60	54.50
0860	6" pipe size		36	.222		35.50	16		51.50	63
0870	8" pipe size		34	.235		84.50	16.95		101.45	118
0880	10" pipe size		32	.250		87.50	18		105.50	123
0890	12" pipe size		28	.286		124	20.50		144.50	167
0900	For plastic coating 3/4" to 4", add					190%				
0910	For copper plating 3/4" to 4", add					58%				
0950	Two piece, complete, carbon steel, medium weight, TYPE 4									
0960	1/2" pipe size	Q-1	137	.117	Ea.	10.50	7.55		18.05	23
0970	3/4" pipe size		134	.119		4.54	7.75		12.29	16.55
0980	1" pipe size		132	.121		4.64	7.85		12.49	16.80

22 05 Common Work Results for Plumbing

22 05 29 – Hangers and Supports for Plumbing Piping and Equipment

22 05 29.10 Hangers & Supp. for Plumb'g/HVAC Pipe/Equip.		Crew	Daily Output	Labor-Hours	Unit	Material	2023 Bare Costs Labor	Equipment	Total	Total Incl O&P
0990	1-1/4" pipe size	Q-1	130	.123	Ea.	5.20	8		13.20	17.60
1000	1-1/2" pipe size		126	.127		5.15	8.25		13.40	17.95
1010	2" pipe size		124	.129		8.75	8.35		17.10	22
1020	2-1/2" pipe size		120	.133		17.70	8.65		26.35	32.50
1030	3" pipe size		117	.137		19.45	8.85		28.30	34.50
1040	3-1/2" pipe size		114	.140		32.50	9.10		41.60	49
1050	4" pipe size		110	.145		31.50	9.45		40.95	48.50
1060	5" pipe size		106	.151		61	9.80		70.80	81.50
1070	6" pipe size		104	.154		68	10		78	90
1080	8" pipe size		100	.160		81	10.40		91.40	104
1090	10" pipe size		96	.167		154	10.80		164.80	185
1100	12" pipe size		89	.180		187	11.65		198.65	223
1110	14" pipe size		82	.195		305	12.65		317.65	360
1120	16" pipe size	↓	68	.235		330	15.25		345.25	390
1130	For galvanized, add				↓	45%				
1150	Insert, concrete									
1160	Wedge type, carbon steel body, malleable iron nut, galvanized									
1170	1/4" threaded rod size	1 Plum	96	.083	Ea.	24	6		30	35
1180	3/8" threaded rod size		96	.083		2.17	6		8.17	11.35
1190	1/2" threaded rod size		96	.083		2.37	6		8.37	11.55
1200	5/8" threaded rod size		96	.083		3.24	6		9.24	12.50
1210	3/4" threaded rod size		96	.083		3.56	6		9.56	12.85
1220	7/8" threaded rod size	↓	96	.083	↓	52.50	6		58.50	67
1250	Pipe guide sized for insulation									
1260	No. 1, 1" pipe size, 1" thick insulation	1 Stpi	26	.308	Ea.	500	22.50		522.50	585
1270	No. 2, 1-1/4"-2" pipe size, 1" thick insulation		23	.348		500	25		525	590
1280	No. 3, 1-1/4"-2" pipe size, 1-1/2" thick insulation		21	.381		305	27.50		332.50	380
1290	No. 4, 2-1/2"-3-1/2" pipe size, 1-1/2" thick insulation		18	.444		345	32		377	430
1300	No. 5, 4"-5" pipe size, 1-1/2" thick insulation	↓	16	.500		360	36.50		396.50	455
1310	No. 6, 5"-6" pipe size, 2" thick insulation	Q-5	21	.762		415	50		465	535
1320	No. 7, 8" pipe size, 2" thick insulation		16	1		545	65.50		610.50	695
1330	No. 8, 10" pipe size, 2" thick insulation	↓	12	1.333		810	87		897	1,025
1340	No. 9, 12" pipe size, 2" thick insulation	Q-6	17	1.412		810	95.50		905.50	1,025
1350	No. 10, 12"-14" pipe size, 2-1/2" thick insulation		16	1.500		975	102		1,077	1,225
1360	No. 11, 16" pipe size, 2-1/2" thick insulation		10.50	2.286		975	155		1,130	1,300
1370	No. 12, 16"-18" pipe size, 3" thick insulation		9	2.667		1,375	181		1,556	1,775
1380	No. 13, 20" pipe size, 3" thick insulation		7.50	3.200		1,375	217		1,592	1,825
1390	No. 14, 24" pipe size, 3" thick insulation	↓	7	3.429	↓	1,950	232		2,182	2,500
1400	Bands									
1410	Adjustable band, carbon steel, for non-insulated pipe, TYPE 7									
1420	1/2" pipe size	Q-1	142	.113	Ea.	1.27	7.30		8.57	12.30
1430	3/4" pipe size		140	.114		1.26	7.40		8.66	12.45
1440	1" pipe size		137	.117		1.26	7.55		8.81	12.70
1450	1-1/4" pipe size		134	.119		1.13	7.75		8.88	12.80
1460	1-1/2" pipe size		131	.122		1.39	7.90		9.29	13.35
1470	2" pipe size		129	.124		1.39	8.05		9.44	13.55
1480	2-1/2" pipe size		125	.128		2.01	8.30		10.31	14.60
1490	3" pipe size		122	.131		2.65	8.50		11.15	15.60
1500	3-1/2" pipe size		119	.134		1.51	8.70		10.21	14.65
1510	4" pipe size		114	.140		4.30	9.10		13.40	18.30
1520	5" pipe size		110	.145		5.45	9.45		14.90	20
1530	6" pipe size		108	.148		6.40	9.60		16	21.50
1540	8" pipe size	↓	104	.154	↓	10.55	10		20.55	26.50

22 05 Common Work Results for Plumbing

22 05 29 – Hangers and Supports for Plumbing Piping and Equipment

22 05 29.10 Hangers & Supp. for Plumb'g/HVAC Pipe/Equip.		Crew	Daily Output	Labor-Hours	Unit	Material	2023 Bare Costs Labor	Equipment	Total	Total Incl O&P
1550	For copper plated, add					50%				
1560	For galvanized, add					30%				
1570	For plastic coating, add					30%				
1600	Adjusting nut malleable iron, steel band, TYPE 9									
1610	1/2" pipe size, galvanized band	Q-1	137	.117	Ea.	9.90	7.55		17.45	22
1620	3/4" pipe size, galvanized band		135	.119		6.20	7.70		13.90	18.30
1630	1" pipe size, galvanized band		132	.121		10.20	7.85		18.05	23
1640	1-1/4" pipe size, galvanized band		129	.124		10.25	8.05		18.30	23.50
1650	1-1/2" pipe size, galvanized band		126	.127		10.60	8.25		18.85	24
1660	2" pipe size, galvanized band		124	.129		11.05	8.35		19.40	24.50
1670	2-1/2" pipe size, galvanized band		120	.133		17.45	8.65		26.10	32
1680	3" pipe size, galvanized band		117	.137		18.25	8.85		27.10	33
1690	3-1/2" pipe size, galvanized band		114	.140		8.10	9.10		17.20	22.50
1700	4" pipe size, cadmium plated band		110	.145		46.50	9.45		55.95	65
1740	For plastic coated band, add					35%				
1750	For completely copper coated, add					45%				
1800	Clevis, adjustable, carbon steel, for non-insulated pipe, TYPE 1									
1810	1/2" pipe size	Q-1	137	.117	Ea.	2.37	7.55		9.92	13.90
1820	3/4" pipe size		135	.119		1.85	7.70		9.55	13.50
1830	1" pipe size		132	.121		1.87	7.85		9.72	13.75
1840	1-1/4" pipe size		129	.124		1.86	8.05		9.91	14.05
1850	1-1/2" pipe size		126	.127		2.18	8.25		10.43	14.70
1860	2" pipe size		124	.129		2.66	8.35		11.01	15.45
1870	2-1/2" pipe size		120	.133		4.08	8.65		12.73	17.40
1880	3" pipe size		117	.137		4.90	8.85		13.75	18.60
1890	3-1/2" pipe size		114	.140		4.89	9.10		13.99	18.95
1900	4" pipe size		110	.145		5.60	9.45		15.05	20
1910	5" pipe size		106	.151		7.20	9.80		17	22.50
1920	6" pipe size		104	.154		8.20	10		18.20	24
1930	8" pipe size		100	.160		14.70	10.40		25.10	31.50
1940	10" pipe size		96	.167		30	10.80		40.80	49.50
1950	12" pipe size		89	.180		79.50	11.65		91.15	105
1960	14" pipe size		82	.195		116	12.65		128.65	147
1970	16" pipe size		68	.235		128	15.25		143.25	164
1971	18" pipe size		54	.296		211	19.20		230.20	261
1972	20" pipe size		38	.421		410	27.50		437.50	495
1980	For galvanized, add					66%				
1990	For copper plated 1/2" to 4", add					77%				
2000	For light weight 1/2" to 4", deduct					13%				
2010	Insulated pipe type, 3/4" to 12" pipe, add					180%				
2020	Insulated pipe type, chrome-moly U-strap, add					530%				
2250	Split ring, malleable iron, for non-insulated pipe, TYPE 11									
2260	1/2" pipe size	Q-1	137	.117	Ea.	17.80	7.55		25.35	31
2270	3/4" pipe size		135	.119		17.95	7.70		25.65	31
2280	1" pipe size		132	.121		19	7.85		26.85	32.50
2290	1-1/4" pipe size		129	.124		23.50	8.05		31.55	38
2300	1-1/2" pipe size		126	.127		28.50	8.25		36.75	44
2310	2" pipe size		124	.129		32.50	8.35		40.85	48
2320	2-1/2" pipe size		120	.133		47	8.65		55.65	64.50
2330	3" pipe size		117	.137		58.50	8.85		67.35	77.50
2340	3-1/2" pipe size		114	.140		25.50	9.10		34.60	41.50
2350	4" pipe size		110	.145		61	9.45		70.45	81
2360	5" pipe size		106	.151		81	9.80		90.80	104

22 05 Common Work Results for Plumbing

22 05 29 – Hangers and Supports for Plumbing Piping and Equipment

22 05 29.10 Hangers & Supp. for Plumb'g/HVAC Pipe/Equip.		Crew	Daily Output	Labor-Hours	Unit	Material	2023 Bare Costs Labor	Equipment	Total	Total Incl O&P
2370	6" pipe size	Q-1	104	.154	Ea.	181	10		191	214
2380	8" pipe size	▼	100	.160	▼	266	10.40		276.40	305
2390	For copper plated, add					8%				
2400	Channels, steel, 3/4" x 1-1/2"	1 Plum	80	.100	L.F.	7.20	7.20		14.40	18.65
2404	1-1/2" x 1-1/2"		70	.114		8.15	8.25		16.40	21.50
2408	1-7/8" x 1-1/2"		60	.133		51	9.60		60.60	70.50
2412	3" x 1-1/2"		50	.160	▼	43	11.55		54.55	64.50
2416	Hangers, trapeze channel support, 12 ga. 1-1/2" x 1-1/2", 12" wide, steel		8.80	.909	Ea.	57.50	65.50		123	161
2418	18" wide, steel		8.30	.964		61.50	69.50		131	172
2430	Spring nuts, long, 1/4"		120	.067		.73	4.80		5.53	7.95
2432	3/8"		100	.080		1.16	5.75		6.91	9.90
2434	1/2"		80	.100		1.04	7.20		8.24	11.90
2436	5/8"		80	.100		6.45	7.20		13.65	17.85
2438	3/4"		75	.107		8.60	7.70		16.30	21
2440	Spring nuts, short, 1/4"		120	.067		1.99	4.80		6.79	9.35
2442	3/8"		100	.080		2.08	5.75		7.83	10.90
2444	1/2"	▼	80	.100	▼	3.04	7.20		10.24	14.10
2500	Washer, flat steel									
2502	3/8"	1 Plum	240	.033	Ea.	.07	2.40		2.47	3.66
2503	1/2"		220	.036		.22	2.62		2.84	4.15
2504	5/8"		200	.040		.10	2.88		2.98	4.41
2505	3/4"		180	.044		.21	3.20		3.41	5
2506	7/8"		160	.050		.96	3.60		4.56	6.40
2507	1"		140	.057		1.03	4.12		5.15	7.30
2508	1-1/4"	▼	120	.067	▼	1.60	4.80		6.40	8.90
2520	Nut, steel, hex									
2522	3/8"	1 Plum	200	.040	Ea.	.22	2.88		3.10	4.54
2523	1/2"		180	.044		.53	3.20		3.73	5.35
2524	5/8"		160	.050		.85	3.60		4.45	6.30
2525	3/4"		140	.057		1.42	4.12		5.54	7.70
2526	7/8"		120	.067		2.28	4.80		7.08	9.65
2527	1"		100	.080		3.15	5.75		8.90	12.05
2528	1-1/4"	▼	80	.100	▼	7.85	7.20		15.05	19.40
2532	Turnbuckle, TYPE 13									
2534	3/8"	1 Plum	80	.100	Ea.	24.50	7.20		31.70	38
2535	1/2"		72	.111		31	8		39	46
2536	5/8"		64	.125		32.50	9		41.50	49
2537	3/4"		56	.143		44	10.30		54.30	64
2538	7/8"		48	.167		60	12		72	84
2539	1"		40	.200		73.50	14.40		87.90	102
2540	1-1/4"	▼	32	.250	▼	131	18		149	171
2650	Rods, carbon steel									
2660	Continuous thread									
2670	1/4" thread size	1 Plum	144	.056	L.F.	.43	4		4.43	6.40
2680	3/8" thread size		144	.056		.46	4		4.46	6.45
2690	1/2" thread size		144	.056		.72	4		4.72	6.75
2700	5/8" thread size		144	.056		1.03	4		5.03	7.10
2710	3/4" thread size		144	.056		1.81	4		5.81	7.95
2720	7/8" thread size		144	.056		2.27	4		6.27	8.45
2721	1" thread size	Q-1	160	.100		3.86	6.50		10.36	13.90
2722	1-1/8" thread size	"	120	.133		32.50	8.65		41.15	49
2725	1/4" thread size, bright finish	1 Plum	144	.056		1.94	4		5.94	8.10
2726	1/2" thread size, bright finish	"	144	.056	▼	9.95	4		13.95	16.90

For customer support on your Mechanical Costs with RSMeans data, call 800.448.8182.

22 05 Common Work Results for Plumbing

22 05 29 – Hangers and Supports for Plumbing Piping and Equipment

22 05 29.10 Hangers & Supp. for Plumb'g/HVAC Pipe/Equip.		Crew	Daily Output	Labor-Hours	Unit	Material	2023 Bare Costs Labor	2023 Bare Costs Equipment	Total	Total Incl O&P
2730	For galvanized, add					40%				
2820	Rod couplings									
2821	3/8"	1 Plum	60	.133	Ea.	1.57	9.60		11.17	16.10
2822	1/2"		54	.148		8.60	10.65		19.25	25.50
2823	5/8"		48	.167		10.55	12		22.55	29.50
2824	3/4"		44	.182		13.65	13.10		26.75	34.50
2825	7/8"		40	.200		23	14.40		37.40	46.50
2826	1"		34	.235		32.50	16.95		49.45	61
2827	1-1/8"	▼	30	.267	▼	77.50	19.20		96.70	114
2860	Pipe hanger assy, adj. clevis, saddle, rod, clamp, insul. allowance									
2864	1/2" pipe size	Q-5	35	.457	Ea.	72	30		102	124
2866	3/4" pipe size		34.80	.460		70.50	30		100.50	123
2868	1" pipe size		34.60	.462		60.50	30		90.50	112
2869	1-1/4" pipe size		34.30	.466		60.50	30.50		91	113
2870	1-1/2" pipe size		33.90	.472		69	31		100	122
2872	2" pipe size		33.30	.480		75	31.50		106.50	130
2874	2-1/2" pipe size		32.30	.495		95.50	32.50		128	153
2876	3" pipe size		31.20	.513		101	33.50		134.50	161
2880	4" pipe size		30.70	.521		105	34		139	166
2884	6" pipe size		29.80	.537		153	35		188	222
2888	8" pipe size		28	.571		170	37.50		207.50	243
2892	10" pipe size		25.20	.635		299	41.50		340.50	390
2896	12" pipe size	▼	23.20	.690	▼	360	45		405	465
2900	Rolls									
2910	Adjustable yoke, carbon steel with CI roll, TYPE 43									
2918	2" pipe size	Q-1	140	.114	Ea.	17.40	7.40		24.80	30
2920	2-1/2" pipe size		137	.117		15.60	7.55		23.15	28.50
2930	3" pipe size		131	.122		40	7.90		47.90	56
2940	3-1/2" pipe size		124	.129		51	8.35		59.35	68.50
2950	4" pipe size		117	.137		50	8.85		58.85	68
2960	5" pipe size		110	.145		58.50	9.45		67.95	78
2970	6" pipe size		104	.154		24.50	10		34.50	41.50
2980	8" pipe size		96	.167		34	10.80		44.80	53
2990	10" pipe size		80	.200		60	12.95		72.95	85.50
3000	12" pipe size		68	.235		110	15.25		125.25	144
3010	14" pipe size		56	.286		495	18.55		513.55	570
3020	16" pipe size	▼	48	.333	▼	605	21.50		626.50	695
3050	Chair, carbon steel with CI roll									
3060	2" pipe size	1 Plum	68	.118	Ea.	43	8.50		51.50	59.50
3070	2-1/2" pipe size		65	.123		46.50	8.85		55.35	64
3080	3" pipe size		62	.129		47.50	9.30		56.80	66.50
3090	3-1/2" pipe size		60	.133		36	9.60		45.60	54.50
3100	4" pipe size		58	.138		61	9.95		70.95	82
3110	5" pipe size		56	.143		67	10.30		77.30	89.50
3120	6" pipe size		53	.151		93.50	10.90		104.40	119
3130	8" pipe size		50	.160		126	11.55		137.55	156
3140	10" pipe size		48	.167		159	12		171	192
3150	12" pipe size	▼	46	.174		238	12.55		250.55	280
3170	Single pipe roll (see line 2650 for rods), TYPE 41, 1" pipe size	Q-1	137	.117		29.50	7.55		37.05	44
3180	1-1/4" pipe size		131	.122		16.25	7.90		24.15	29.50
3190	1-1/2" pipe size		129	.124		31	8.05		39.05	46
3200	2" pipe size		124	.129		32	8.35		40.35	48
3210	2-1/2" pipe size	▼	118	.136	▼	34.50	8.80		43.30	51

22 05 Common Work Results for Plumbing

22 05 29 – Hangers and Supports for Plumbing Piping and Equipment

22 05 29.10 Hangers & Supp. for Plumb'g/HVAC Pipe/Equip.		Crew	Daily Output	Labor-Hours	Unit	Material	2023 Bare Costs Labor	Equipment	Total	Total Incl O&P
3220	3" pipe size	Q-1	115	.139	Ea.	36.50	9		45.50	53.50
3230	3-1/2" pipe size		113	.142		38.50	9.20		47.70	56
3240	4" pipe size		112	.143		45	9.25		54.25	63.50
3250	5" pipe size		110	.145		46	9.45		55.45	64.50
3260	6" pipe size		101	.158		76.50	10.25		86.75	99.50
3270	8" pipe size		90	.178		102	11.55		113.55	129
3280	10" pipe size		80	.200		125	12.95		137.95	156
3290	12" pipe size		68	.235		187	15.25		202.25	228
3291	14" pipe size		56	.286		290	18.55		308.55	350
3292	16" pipe size		48	.333		395	21.50		416.50	465
3293	18" pipe size		40	.400		435	26		461	515
3294	20" pipe size		35	.457		520	29.50		549.50	615
3296	24" pipe size		30	.533		915	34.50		949.50	1,050
3297	30" pipe size		25	.640		1,650	41.50		1,691.50	1,875
3298	36" pipe size		20	.800		965	52		1,017	1,125
3300	Saddles (add vertical pipe riser, usually 3" diameter)									
3310	Pipe support, complete, adjust., CI saddle, TYPE 36									
3320	2-1/2" pipe size	1 Plum	96	.083	Ea.	288	6		294	325
3330	3" pipe size		88	.091		238	6.55		244.55	272
3340	3-1/2" pipe size		79	.101		310	7.30		317.30	350
3350	4" pipe size		68	.118		345	8.50		353.50	390
3360	5" pipe size		64	.125		265	9		274	305
3370	6" pipe size		59	.136		370	9.75		379.75	420
3380	8" pipe size		53	.151		400	10.90		410.90	455
3390	10" pipe size		50	.160		425	11.55		436.55	485
3400	12" pipe size		48	.167		445	12		457	510
3450	For standard pipe support, one piece, CI, deduct					34%				
3460	For stanchion support, CI with steel yoke, deduct					60%				
3550	Insulation shield 1" thick, 1/2" pipe size, TYPE 40	1 Asbe	100	.080	Ea.	15.90	5.20		21.10	25.50
3560	3/4" pipe size		100	.080		16.90	5.20		22.10	26.50
3570	1" pipe size		98	.082		18.40	5.35		23.75	28
3580	1-1/4" pipe size		98	.082		19.35	5.35		24.70	29.50
3590	1-1/2" pipe size		96	.083		24	5.45		29.45	35
3600	2" pipe size		96	.083		20.50	5.45		25.95	31
3610	2-1/2" pipe size		94	.085		32	5.55		37.55	43.50
3620	3" pipe size		94	.085		30	5.55		35.55	41.50
3630	2" thick, 3-1/2" pipe size		92	.087		38.50	5.65		44.15	50.50
3640	4" pipe size		92	.087		43.50	5.65		49.15	56.50
3650	5" pipe size		90	.089		62.50	5.80		68.30	77.50
3660	6" pipe size		90	.089		64.50	5.80		70.30	80
3670	8" pipe size		88	.091		107	5.95		112.95	127
3680	10" pipe size		88	.091		114	5.95		119.95	134
3690	12" pipe size		86	.093		199	6.05		205.05	228
3700	14" pipe size		86	.093		225	6.05		231.05	256
3710	16" pipe size		84	.095		239	6.20		245.20	273
3720	18" pipe size		84	.095		284	6.20		290.20	320
3730	20" pipe size		82	.098		298	6.35		304.35	340
3732	24" pipe size		80	.100		325	6.55		331.55	370
3750	Covering protection saddle, TYPE 39									
3760	1" covering size									
3770	3/4" pipe size	1 Plum	68	.118	Ea.	22.50	8.50		31	37
3780	1" pipe size		68	.118		22.50	8.50		31	37
3790	1-1/4" pipe size		68	.118		19	8.50		27.50	33.50

For customer support on your Mechanical Costs with RSMeans data, call 800.448.8182.

22 05 Common Work Results for Plumbing

22 05 29 – Hangers and Supports for Plumbing Piping and Equipment

22 05 29.10 Hangers & Supp. for Plumb'g/HVAC Pipe/Equip.		Crew	Daily Output	Labor-Hours	Unit	Material	2023 Bare Costs Labor	Equipment	Total	Total Incl O&P
3800	1-1/2" pipe size	1 Plum	66	.121	Ea.	24	8.75		32.75	39.50
3810	2" pipe size		66	.121		19.95	8.75		28.70	35
3820	2-1/2" pipe size		64	.125		24	9		33	40
3830	3" pipe size		64	.125		28	9		37	44
3840	3-1/2" pipe size		62	.129		30.50	9.30		39.80	47.50
3850	4" pipe size		62	.129		27	9.30		36.30	44
3860	5" pipe size		60	.133		37	9.60		46.60	55
3870	6" pipe size		60	.133		44	9.60		53.60	63
3900	1-1/2" covering size									
3910	3/4" pipe size	1 Plum	68	.118	Ea.	17.35	8.50		25.85	32
3920	1" pipe size		68	.118		29	8.50		37.50	44.50
3930	1-1/4" pipe size		68	.118		11.50	8.50		20	25.50
3940	1-1/2" pipe size		66	.121		29	8.75		37.75	45
3950	2" pipe size		66	.121		16.30	8.75		25.05	31
3960	2-1/2" pipe size		64	.125		37.50	9		46.50	54.50
3970	3" pipe size		64	.125		37.50	9		46.50	54.50
3980	3-1/2" pipe size		62	.129		52.50	9.30		61.80	72
3990	4" pipe size		62	.129		38.50	9.30		47.80	56
4000	5" pipe size		60	.133		38.50	9.60		48.10	56.50
4010	6" pipe size		60	.133		54	9.60		63.60	74
4020	8" pipe size		58	.138		71	9.95		80.95	93
4022	10" pipe size		56	.143		71	10.30		81.30	93.50
4024	12" pipe size		54	.148		120	10.65		130.65	148
4028	2" covering size									
4029	2-1/2" pipe size	1 Plum	62	.129	Ea.	36	9.30		45.30	53.50
4032	3" pipe size		60	.133		38	9.60		47.60	56.50
4033	4" pipe size		58	.138		26.50	9.95		36.45	44
4034	6" pipe size		56	.143		63.50	10.30		73.80	85.50
4035	8" pipe size		54	.148		75	10.65		85.65	98.50
4080	10" pipe size		58	.138		79.50	9.95		89.45	102
4090	12" pipe size		56	.143		134	10.30		144.30	163
4100	14" pipe size		56	.143		134	10.30		144.30	163
4110	16" pipe size		54	.148		182	10.65		192.65	216
4120	18" pipe size		54	.148		182	10.65		192.65	216
4130	20" pipe size		52	.154		164	11.10		175.10	197
4150	24" pipe size		50	.160		236	11.55		247.55	277
4160	30" pipe size		48	.167		260	12		272	305
4180	36" pipe size		45	.178		280	12.80		292.80	330
4186	2-1/2" covering size									
4187	3" pipe size	1 Plum	58	.138	Ea.	42.50	9.95		52.45	62
4188	4" pipe size		56	.143		44	10.30		54.30	64
4189	6" pipe size		52	.154		70.50	11.10		81.60	94
4190	8" pipe size		48	.167		83	12		95	109
4191	10" pipe size		44	.182		91	13.10		104.10	120
4192	12" pipe size		40	.200		140	14.40		154.40	176
4193	14" pipe size		36	.222		80.50	16		96.50	113
4194	16" pipe size		32	.250		155	18		173	197
4195	18" pipe size		28	.286		173	20.50		193.50	221
4200	Sockets									
4210	Rod end, malleable iron, TYPE 16									
4220	1/4" thread size	1 Plum	240	.033	Ea.	5.80	2.40		8.20	9.95
4230	3/8" thread size		240	.033		2.64	2.40		5.04	6.50
4240	1/2" thread size		230	.035		3.40	2.51		5.91	7.50

22 05 Common Work Results for Plumbing

22 05 29 – Hangers and Supports for Plumbing Piping and Equipment

22 05 29.10 Hangers & Supp. for Plumb'g/HVAC Pipe/Equip.		Crew	Daily Output	Labor-Hours	Unit	Material	2023 Bare Costs Labor	Equipment	Total	Total Incl O&P
4250	5/8" thread size	1 Plum	225	.036	Ea.	14.30	2.56		16.86	19.55
4260	3/4" thread size		220	.036		20	2.62		22.62	26
4270	7/8" thread size	↓	210	.038		28	2.74		30.74	35
4290	Strap, 1/2" pipe size, TYPE 26	Q-1	142	.113		4.61	7.30		11.91	15.95
4300	3/4" pipe size		140	.114		5.70	7.40		13.10	17.35
4310	1" pipe size		137	.117		7.15	7.55		14.70	19.15
4320	1-1/4" pipe size		134	.119		7.20	7.75		14.95	19.50
4330	1-1/2" pipe size		131	.122		7.70	7.90		15.60	20.50
4340	2" pipe size		129	.124		8.50	8.05		16.55	21.50
4350	2-1/2" pipe size		125	.128		13.25	8.30		21.55	27
4360	3" pipe size		122	.131		17.20	8.50		25.70	31.50
4370	3-1/2" pipe size		119	.134		19	8.70		27.70	34
4380	4" pipe size	↓	114	.140	↓	17.95	9.10		27.05	33.50
4400	U-bolt, carbon steel									
4410	Standard, with nuts, TYPE 42									
4420	1/2" pipe size	1 Plum	160	.050	Ea.	2.56	3.60		6.16	8.15
4430	3/4" pipe size		158	.051		3.32	3.65		6.97	9.10
4450	1" pipe size		152	.053		3.52	3.79		7.31	9.50
4460	1-1/4" pipe size		148	.054		4.01	3.89		7.90	10.20
4470	1-1/2" pipe size		143	.056		4.33	4.03		8.36	10.75
4480	2" pipe size		139	.058		4.66	4.15		8.81	11.35
4490	2-1/2" pipe size		134	.060		7.80	4.30		12.10	14.95
4500	3" pipe size		128	.063		8.20	4.50		12.70	15.70
4510	3-1/2" pipe size		122	.066		8.55	4.72		13.27	16.50
4520	4" pipe size		117	.068		8.80	4.93		13.73	17.05
4530	5" pipe size		114	.070		7.20	5.05		12.25	15.50
4540	6" pipe size		111	.072		14.95	5.20		20.15	24
4550	8" pipe size		109	.073		17.75	5.30		23.05	27.50
4560	10" pipe size		107	.075		32	5.40		37.40	43
4570	12" pipe size	↓	104	.077	↓	42.50	5.55		48.05	55.50
4580	For plastic coating on 1/2" thru 6" size, add					150%				
4700	U-hook, carbon steel, requires mounting screws or bolts									
4710	3/4" thru 2" pipe size									
4720	6" long	1 Plum	96	.083	Ea.	1.77	6		7.77	10.90
4730	8" long		96	.083		1.92	6		7.92	11.05
4740	10" long		96	.083		2.26	6		8.26	11.45
4750	12" long	↓	96	.083		2.98	6		8.98	12.25
4760	For copper plated, add					50%				
7000	Roof supports									
7006	Duct									
7010	Rectangular, open, 12" off roof									
7020	To 18" wide	Q-9	26	.615	Ea.	263	39		302	350
7030	To 24" wide	"	22	.727		305	46		351	410
7040	To 36" wide	Q-10	30	.800		350	52.50		402.50	465
7050	To 48" wide		28	.857		395	56		451	520
7060	To 60" wide	↓	24	1	↓	440	65.50		505.50	580
7100	Equipment									
7120	Equipment support	Q-5	20	.800	Ea.	115	52		167	205
7300	Pipe									
7310	Roller type									
7320	Up to 2-1/2" diam. pipe									
7324	3-1/2" off roof	Q-5	24	.667	Ea.	19.75	43.50		63.25	87
7326	Up to 10" off roof	"	20	.800	"	45	52		97	128

22 05 Common Work Results for Plumbing

22 05 29 – Hangers and Supports for Plumbing Piping and Equipment

22 05 29.10 Hangers & Supp. for Plumb'g/HVAC Pipe/Equip.		Crew	Daily Output	Labor-Hours	Unit	Material	2023 Bare Costs Labor	Equipment	Total	Total Incl O&P
7340	2-1/2" to 3-1/2" diam. pipe									
7342	Up to 16" off roof	Q-5	18	.889	Ea.	80	58		138	175
7360	4" to 5" diam. pipe									
7362	Up to 12" off roof	Q-5	16	1	Ea.	114	65.50		179.50	223
7400	Strut/channel type									
7410	Up to 2-1/2" diam. pipe									
7424	3-1/2" off roof	Q-5	24	.667	Ea.	18.95	43.50		62.45	86
7426	Up to 10" off roof	"	20	.800	"	49.50	52		101.50	133
7440	Strut and roller type									
7452	2-1/2" to 3-1/2" diam. pipe									
7454	Up to 16" off roof	Q-5	18	.889	Ea.	115	58		173	214
7460	Strut and hanger type									
7470	Up to 3" diam. pipe									
7474	Up to 8" off roof	Q-5	19	.842	Ea.	73	55		128	163
8000	Pipe clamp, plastic, 1/2" CTS	1 Plum	80	.100		.27	7.20		7.47	11.05
8010	3/4" CTS		73	.110		.28	7.90		8.18	12.10
8020	1" CTS		68	.118		.69	8.50		9.19	13.40
8080	Economy clamp, 1/4" CTS		175	.046		.08	3.29		3.37	5
8090	3/8" CTS		168	.048		.08	3.43		3.51	5.20
8100	1/2" CTS		160	.050		.08	3.60		3.68	5.45
8110	3/4" CTS		145	.055		.08	3.98		4.06	6.05
8200	Half clamp, 1/2" CTS		80	.100		.09	7.20		7.29	10.85
8210	3/4" CTS		73	.110		.15	7.90		8.05	11.95
8300	Suspension clamp, 1/2" CTS		80	.100		.27	7.20		7.47	11.05
8310	3/4" CTS		73	.110		.28	7.90		8.18	12.10
8320	1" CTS		68	.118		.61	8.50		9.11	13.30
8400	Insulator, 1/2" CTS		80	.100		.40	7.20		7.60	11.20
8410	3/4" CTS		73	.110		.41	7.90		8.31	12.25
8420	1" CTS		68	.118		.43	8.50		8.93	13.10
8500	J hook clamp with nail, 1/2" CTS		240	.033		.13	2.40		2.53	3.72
8501	3/4" CTS		240	.033		.14	2.40		2.54	3.73
8800	Wire cable support system									
8810	Cable with hook terminal and locking device									
8830	2 mm (.079") diam. cable (100 lb. cap.)									
8840	1 m (3.3') length, with hook	1 Shee	96	.083	Ea.	5.90	5.85		11.75	15.30
8850	2 m (6.6') length, with hook		84	.095		7	6.70		13.70	17.75
8860	3 m (9.9') length, with hook		72	.111		7.80	7.80		15.60	20.50
8870	5 m (16.4') length, with hook	Q-9	60	.267		9.55	16.85		26.40	36
8880	10 m (32.8') length, with hook	"	30	.533		13.70	33.50		47.20	65.50
8900	3 mm (.118") diam. cable (200 lb. cap.)									
8910	1 m (3.3') length, with hook	1 Shee	96	.083	Ea.	17.15	5.85		23	27.50
8920	2 m (6.6') length, with hook		84	.095		.85	6.70		7.55	11
8930	3 m (9.9') length, with hook		72	.111		21	7.80		28.80	35
8940	5 m (16.4') length, with hook	Q-9	60	.267		18.20	16.85		35.05	45.50
8950	10 m (32.8') length, with hook	"	30	.533		16.30	33.50		49.80	68.50
9000	Cable system accessories									
9010	Anchor bolt, 3/8", with nut	1 Shee	140	.057	Ea.	3.85	4.01		7.86	10.30
9020	Air duct corner protector		160	.050		1.70	3.51		5.21	7.15
9030	Air duct support attachment		140	.057		3.56	4.01		7.57	9.95
9040	Flange clip, hammer-on style									
9044	For flange thickness 3/32"-9/64", 160 lb. cap.	1 Shee	180	.044	Ea.	.88	3.12		4	5.65
9048	For flange thickness 1/8"-1/4", 200 lb. cap.		160	.050		.98	3.51		4.49	6.40
9052	For flange thickness 5/16"-1/2", 200 lb. cap.		150	.053		2.10	3.74		5.84	7.95

22 05 Common Work Results for Plumbing

22 05 29 – Hangers and Supports for Plumbing Piping and Equipment

22 05 29.10 Hangers & Supp. for Plumb'g/HVAC Pipe/Equip.		Crew	Daily Output	Labor-Hours	Unit	Material	2023 Bare Costs Labor	Equipment	Total	Total Incl O&P
9056	For flange thickness 9/16"-3/4", 200 lb. cap.	1 Shee	140	.057	Ea.	2.62	4.01		6.63	8.95
9060	Wire insulation protection tube	↓	180	.044	L.F.	.89	3.12		4.01	5.70
9070	Wire cutter				Ea.	140			140	154

22 05 33 – Heat Tracing for Plumbing Piping

22 05 33.20 Temperature Maintenance Cable

0010	**TEMPERATURE MAINTENANCE CABLE**									
0040	Components									
0080	Heating cable									
0100	208 V									
0150	140°F	Q-1	1060.80	.015	L.F.	15.90	.98		16.88	18.95
0200	120 V									
0220	125°F	Q-1	1060.80	.015	L.F.	7.10	.98		8.08	9.25
0300	Power kit w/1 end seal	1 Elec	48.80	.164	Ea.	253	11.05		264.05	295
0310	Splice kit		35.50	.225		262	15.20		277.20	310
0320	End seal		160	.050		19.80	3.37		23.17	27
0330	Tee kit w/1 end seal		26.80	.299		272	20		292	330
0340	Powered splice w/2 end seals		20	.400		225	27		252	288
0350	Powered tee kit w/3 end seals		18	.444		289	30		319	365
0360	Cross kit w/2 end seals	↓	18.60	.430	↓	298	29		327	375
0500	Recommended thickness of fiberglass insulation									
0510	Pipe size									
0520	1/2" to 1" use 1" insulation									
0530	1-1/4" to 2" use 1-1/2" insulation									
0540	2-1/2" to 6" use 2" insulation									
0560	NOTE: For pipe sizes 1-1/4" and smaller use 1/4" larger diameter									
0570	insulation to allow room for installation over cable.									

22 05 48 – Vibration and Seismic Controls for Plumbing Piping and Equipment

22 05 48.40 Vibration Absorbers

0010	**VIBRATION ABSORBERS**									
0100	Hangers, neoprene flex									
0200	10-120 lb. capacity				Ea.	26.50			26.50	29
0220	75-550 lb. capacity					44			44	48.50
0240	250-1,100 lb. capacity					92.50			92.50	102
0260	1,000-4,000 lb. capacity					144			144	158
0500	Spring flex, 60 lb. capacity					41			41	45
0520	450 lb. capacity					63.50			63.50	69.50
0540	900 lb. capacity					92.50			92.50	102
0560	1,100-1,300 lb. capacity				↓	92.50			92.50	102
0600	Rubber in shear									
0610	45-340 lb., up to 1/2" rod size	1 Stpi	22	.364	Ea.	25	26.50		51.50	67
0620	130-700 lb., up to 3/4" rod size		20	.400		53.50	29		82.50	102
0630	50-1,000 lb., up to 3/4" rod size	↓	18	.444		70.50	32		102.50	126
1000	Mounts, neoprene, 45-380 lb. capacity					18.90			18.90	21
1020	250-1,100 lb. capacity					60			60	66
1040	1,000-4,000 lb. capacity					117			117	129
1100	Spring flex, 60 lb. capacity					76			76	84
1120	165 lb. capacity					78.50			78.50	86
1140	260 lb. capacity					93.50			93.50	103
1160	450 lb. capacity					96			96	105
1180	600 lb. capacity					99.50			99.50	109
1200	750 lb. capacity					161			161	177
1220	900 lb. capacity				↓	158			158	174

22 05 Common Work Results for Plumbing

22 05 48 – Vibration and Seismic Controls for Plumbing Piping and Equipment

22 05 48.40 Vibration Absorbers

		Crew	Daily Output	Labor-Hours	Unit	Material	2023 Bare Costs Labor	2023 Bare Costs Equipment	Total	Total Incl O&P
1240	1,100 lb. capacity				Ea.	194			194	213
1260	1,300 lb. capacity					194			194	213
1280	1,500 lb. capacity					211			211	232
1300	1,800 lb. capacity					262			262	289
1320	2,200 lb. capacity					330			330	360
1340	2,600 lb. capacity				↓	330			330	360
1399	Spring type									
1400	2 piece									
1410	50-1,000 lb.	1 Stpi	12	.667	Ea.	225	48.50		273.50	320
1420	1,100-1,600 lb.	"	12	.667	"	267	48.50		315.50	365
1500	Double spring open									
1510	150-450 lb.	1 Stpi	24	.333	Ea.	154	24		178	205
1520	500-1,000 lb.		24	.333		171	24		195	224
1530	1,100-1,600 lb.		24	.333		171	24		195	224
1540	1,700-2,400 lb.		24	.333		167	24		191	220
1550	2,500-3,400 lb.	↓	24	.333		285	24		309	350
2000	Pads, cork rib, 18" x 18" x 1", 10-50 psi					174			174	192
2020	18" x 36" x 1", 10-50 psi					330			330	365
2100	Shear flexible pads, 18" x 18" x 3/8", 20-70 psi					70.50			70.50	77.50
2120	18" x 36" x 3/8", 20-70 psi				↓	165			165	182
2150	Laminated neoprene and cork									
2160	1" thick	1 Stpi	16	.500	S.F.	89.50	36.50		126	153
2200	Neoprene elastomer isolation bearing pad									
2230	464 psi, 5/8" x 19-11/16" x 39-3/8"	1 Stpi	16	.500	Ea.	68	36.50		104.50	129
3000	Note overlap in capacities due to deflections									

22 05 53 – Identification for Plumbing Piping and Equipment

22 05 53.10 Piping System Identification Labels

		Crew	Daily Output	Labor-Hours	Unit	Material	2023 Bare Costs Labor	2023 Bare Costs Equipment	Total	Total Incl O&P
0010	**PIPING SYSTEM IDENTIFICATION LABELS**									
0100	Indicate contents and flow direction									
0106	Pipe markers									
0110	Plastic snap around									
0114	1/2" pipe	1 Plum	80	.100	Ea.	3.98	7.20		11.18	15.15
0116	3/4" pipe		80	.100		5.05	7.20		12.25	16.35
0118	1" pipe		80	.100		4.93	7.20		12.13	16.15
0120	2" pipe		75	.107		6.10	7.70		13.80	18.20
0122	3" pipe		70	.114		11.45	8.25		19.70	25
0124	4" pipe		60	.133		11.45	9.60		21.05	27
0126	6" pipe		60	.133		12.75	9.60		22.35	28.50
0128	8" pipe		56	.143		17.40	10.30		27.70	34.50
0130	10" pipe		56	.143		17.40	10.30		27.70	34.50
0200	Over 10" pipe size	↓	50	.160	↓	19.80	11.55		31.35	39
1110	Self adhesive									
1114	1" pipe	1 Plum	80	.100	Ea.	3	7.20		10.20	14.05
1116	2" pipe		75	.107		3	7.70		10.70	14.75
1118	3" pipe		70	.114		4.17	8.25		12.42	16.90
1120	4" pipe		60	.133		4.17	9.60		13.77	18.95
1122	6" pipe		60	.133		5.10	9.60		14.70	19.95
1124	8" pipe		56	.143		6.35	10.30		16.65	22.50
1126	10" pipe		56	.143		10.20	10.30		20.50	26.50
1200	Over 10" pipe size	↓	50	.160	↓	10.20	11.55		21.75	28.50
2000	Valve tags									
2010	Numbered plus identifying legend									

22 05 Common Work Results for Plumbing

22 05 53 – Identification for Plumbing Piping and Equipment

22 05 53.10 Piping System Identification Labels		Crew	Daily Output	Labor-Hours	Unit	Material	2023 Bare Costs Labor	Equipment	Total	Total Incl O&P
2100	Brass, 2" diameter	1 Plum	40	.200	Ea.	5	14.40		19.40	27
2200	Plastic, 1-1/2" diameter	"	40	.200	"	3.93	14.40		18.33	26

22 07 Plumbing Insulation

22 07 16 – Plumbing Equipment Insulation

22 07 16.10 Insulation for Plumbing Equipment

			Crew	Daily Output	Labor-Hours	Unit	Material	Labor	Equipment	Total	Total Incl O&P
0010	**INSULATION FOR PLUMBING EQUIPMENT**										
2900	Domestic water heater wrap kit										
2920	1-1/2" with vinyl jacket, 20 to 60 gal.	G	1 Plum	8	1	Ea.	26.50	72		98.50	136

22 07 19 – Plumbing Piping Insulation

22 07 19.10 Piping Insulation

			Crew	Daily Output	Labor-Hours	Unit	Material	Labor	Equipment	Total	Total Incl O&P
0010	**PIPING INSULATION**										
0110	Insulation req'd. is based on the surface size/area to be covered										
0230	Insulated protectors (ADA)										
0235	For exposed piping under sinks or lavatories										
0240	Vinyl coated foam, velcro tabs										
0245	P Trap, 1-1/4" or 1-1/2"		1 Plum	32	.250	Ea.	18.80	18		36.80	47.50
0260	Valve and supply cover										
0265	1/2", 3/8", and 7/16" pipe size		1 Plum	32	.250	Ea.	18.50	18		36.50	47.50
0280	Tailpiece offset (wheelchair)										
0285	1-1/4" pipe size		1 Plum	32	.250	Ea.	15.35	18		33.35	44
0600	Pipe covering (price copper tube one size less than IPS)										
1000	Mineral wool										
1010	Preformed, 1200°F, plain										
1014	1" wall										
1016	1/2" iron pipe size	G	Q-14	230	.070	L.F.	2.60	4.09		6.69	9.10
1018	3/4" iron pipe size	G		220	.073		8.35	4.27		12.62	15.75
1022	1" iron pipe size	G		210	.076		2.78	4.47		7.25	9.90
1024	1-1/4" iron pipe size	G		205	.078		2.85	4.58		7.43	10.15
1026	1-1/2" iron pipe size	G		205	.078		2.70	4.58		7.28	9.95
1028	2" iron pipe size	G		200	.080		3.66	4.70		8.36	11.25
1030	2-1/2" iron pipe size	G		190	.084		3.75	4.95		8.70	11.70
1032	3" iron pipe size	G		180	.089		4	5.20		9.20	12.40
1034	4" iron pipe size	G		150	.107		4.93	6.25		11.18	15
1036	5" iron pipe size	G		140	.114		5.60	6.70		12.30	16.40
1038	6" iron pipe size	G		120	.133		5.95	7.85		13.80	18.55
1040	7" iron pipe size	G		110	.145		6.95	8.55		15.50	20.50
1042	8" iron pipe size	G		100	.160		9.60	9.40		19	25
1044	9" iron pipe size	G		90	.178		10.15	10.45		20.60	27
1046	10" iron pipe size	G		90	.178		11.45	10.45		21.90	28.50
1050	1-1/2" wall										
1052	1/2" iron pipe size	G	Q-14	225	.071	L.F.	4.43	4.18		8.61	11.25
1054	3/4" iron pipe size	G		215	.074		13.05	4.37		17.42	21
1056	1" iron pipe size	G		205	.078		4.61	4.58		9.19	12.05
1058	1-1/4" iron pipe size	G		200	.080		4.70	4.70		9.40	12.35
1060	1-1/2" iron pipe size	G		200	.080		4.93	4.70		9.63	12.60
1062	2" iron pipe size	G		190	.084		5.25	4.95		10.20	13.30
1064	2-1/2" iron pipe size	G		180	.089		5.70	5.20		10.90	14.25
1066	3" iron pipe size	G		165	.097		5.95	5.70		11.65	15.25
1068	4" iron pipe size	G		140	.114		7.10	6.70		13.80	18.10

22 07 Plumbing Insulation

22 07 19 – Plumbing Piping Insulation

22 07 19.10 Piping Insulation		Crew	Daily Output	Labor-Hours	Unit	Material	2023 Bare Costs Labor	Equipment	Total	Total Incl O&P
1070	5" iron pipe size	Q-14	130	.123	L.F.	7.60	7.25		14.85	19.40
1072	6" iron pipe size		110	.145		7.85	8.55		16.40	21.50
1074	7" iron pipe size		100	.160		9.25	9.40		18.65	24.50
1076	8" iron pipe size		90	.178		10.30	10.45		20.75	27.50
1078	9" iron pipe size		85	.188		11.85	11.05		22.90	30
1080	10" iron pipe size		80	.200		13	11.75		24.75	32.50
1082	12" iron pipe size		75	.213		14.85	12.55		27.40	35.50
1084	14" iron pipe size		70	.229		17	13.40		30.40	39
1086	16" iron pipe size		65	.246		18.75	14.45		33.20	42.50
1088	18" iron pipe size		60	.267		22	15.65		37.65	48
1090	20" iron pipe size		55	.291		23	17.10		40.10	51.50
1092	22" iron pipe size		50	.320		26.50	18.80		45.30	58
1094	24" iron pipe size		45	.356		28.50	21		49.50	63
1100	2" wall									
1102	1/2" iron pipe size	Q-14	220	.073	L.F.	5.75	4.27		10.02	12.85
1104	3/4" iron pipe size		210	.076		5.95	4.47		10.42	13.40
1106	1" iron pipe size		200	.080		6.30	4.70		11	14.15
1108	1-1/4" iron pipe size		190	.084		6.75	4.95		11.70	15
1110	1-1/2" iron pipe size		190	.084		7.05	4.95		12	15.30
1112	2" iron pipe size		180	.089		7.40	5.20		12.60	16.15
1114	2-1/2" iron pipe size		170	.094		8.35	5.55		13.90	17.65
1116	3" iron pipe size		160	.100		8.95	5.85		14.80	18.80
1118	4" iron pipe size		130	.123		10.40	7.25		17.65	22.50
1120	5" iron pipe size		120	.133		11.55	7.85		19.40	24.50
1122	6" iron pipe size		100	.160		12	9.40		21.40	27.50
1124	8" iron pipe size		80	.200		14.60	11.75		26.35	34
1126	10" iron pipe size		70	.229		17.80	13.40		31.20	40
1128	12" iron pipe size		65	.246		19.75	14.45		34.20	43.50
1130	14" iron pipe size		60	.267		22	15.65		37.65	48.50
1132	16" iron pipe size		55	.291		25	17.10		42.10	53.50
1134	18" iron pipe size		50	.320		27	18.80		45.80	59
1136	20" iron pipe size		45	.356		31	21		52	66
1138	22" iron pipe size		45	.356		34	21		55	69
1140	24" iron pipe size		40	.400		35.50	23.50		59	75
1150	4" wall									
1152	1-1/4" iron pipe size	Q-14	170	.094	L.F.	18.20	5.55		23.75	28.50
1154	1-1/2" iron pipe size		165	.097		18.95	5.70		24.65	29.50
1156	2" iron pipe size		155	.103		19.30	6.05		25.35	30.50
1158	4" iron pipe size		105	.152		24.50	8.95		33.45	40.50
1160	6" iron pipe size		75	.213		29	12.55		41.55	50.50
1162	8" iron pipe size		60	.267		32.50	15.65		48.15	60
1164	10" iron pipe size		50	.320		39.50	18.80		58.30	72.50
1166	12" iron pipe size		45	.356		43	21		64	79.50
1168	14" iron pipe size		40	.400		46.50	23.50		70	87
1170	16" iron pipe size		35	.457		52	27		79	98.50
1172	18" iron pipe size		32	.500		56.50	29.50		86	107
1174	20" iron pipe size		30	.533		60.50	31.50		92	115
1176	22" iron pipe size		28	.571		68	33.50		101.50	126
1178	24" iron pipe size		26	.615		72	36		108	135
4280	Cellular glass, closed cell foam, all service jacket, sealant,									
4281	working temp. (-450°F to +900°F), 0 water vapor transmission									
4284	1" wall									
4286	1/2" iron pipe size	Q-14	120	.133	L.F.	8.80	7.85		16.65	21.50

22 07 Plumbing Insulation

22 07 19 – Plumbing Piping Insulation

22 07 19.10 Piping Insulation		Crew	Daily Output	Labor-Hours	Unit	Material	2023 Bare Costs Labor	Equipment	Total	Total Incl O&P
4300	1-1/2" wall									
4301	1" iron pipe size	Q-14 G	105	.152	L.F.	16.80	8.95		25.75	32
4304	2-1/2" iron pipe size	G	90	.178		29	10.45		39.45	47.50
4306	3" iron pipe size	G	85	.188		28	11.05		39.05	48
4308	4" iron pipe size	G	70	.229		31.50	13.40		44.90	55
4310	5" iron pipe size	G	65	.246		37	14.45		51.45	62.50
4320	2" wall									
4322	1" iron pipe size	Q-14 G	100	.160	L.F.	24	9.40		33.40	41
4324	2-1/2" iron pipe size	G	85	.188		35.50	11.05		46.55	56
4326	3" iron pipe size	G	80	.200		37.50	11.75		49.25	59
4328	4" iron pipe size	G	65	.246		40.50	14.45		54.95	66.50
4330	5" iron pipe size	G	60	.267		52.50	15.65		68.15	81.50
4332	6" iron pipe size	G	50	.320		49	18.80		67.80	83
4336	8" iron pipe size	G	40	.400		56	23.50		79.50	97.50
4338	10" iron pipe size	G	35	.457		64.50	27		91.50	112
4350	2-1/2" wall									
4360	12" iron pipe size	Q-14 G	32	.500	L.F.	98	29.50		127.50	153
4362	14" iron pipe size	G	28	.571	"	96	33.50		129.50	158
4370	3" wall									
4378	6" iron pipe size	Q-14 G	48	.333	L.F.	68.50	19.60		88.10	106
4380	8" iron pipe size	G	38	.421		84	24.50		108.50	131
4382	10" iron pipe size	G	33	.485		99	28.50		127.50	153
4384	16" iron pipe size	G	25	.640		139	37.50		176.50	211
4386	18" iron pipe size	G	22	.727		157	42.50		199.50	239
4388	20" iron pipe size	G	20	.800		158	47		205	246
4400	3-1/2" wall									
4412	12" iron pipe size	Q-14 G	27	.593	L.F.	93	35		128	155
4414	14" iron pipe size	G	" 25	.640	"	119	37.50		156.50	189
4430	4" wall									
4446	16" iron pipe size	Q-14 G	22	.727	L.F.	137	42.50		179.50	217
4448	18" iron pipe size	G	20	.800		136	47		183	221
4450	20" iron pipe size	G	18	.889		197	52		249	297
4480	Fittings, average with fabric and mastic									
4484	1" wall									
4486	1/2" iron pipe size	1 Asbe G	40	.200	Ea.	15.05	13.05		28.10	36.50
4500	1-1/2" wall									
4502	1" iron pipe size	1 Asbe G	38	.211	Ea.	23.50	13.75		37.25	46.50
4504	2-1/2" iron pipe size	G	32	.250		43.50	16.30		59.80	73
4506	3" iron pipe size	G	30	.267		45.50	17.40		62.90	76.50
4508	4" iron pipe size	G	28	.286		58.50	18.65		77.15	93
4510	5" iron pipe size	G	24	.333		76	22		98	117
4520	2" wall									
4522	1" iron pipe size	1 Asbe G	36	.222	Ea.	28.50	14.50		43	53.50
4524	2-1/2" iron pipe size	G	30	.267		56.50	17.40		73.90	89
4526	3" iron pipe size	G	28	.286		53.50	18.65		72.15	87
4528	4" iron pipe size	G	24	.333		68	22		90	109
4530	5" iron pipe size	G	22	.364		92	23.50		115.50	138
4532	6" iron pipe size	G	20	.400		117	26		143	169
4536	8" iron pipe size	G	12	.667		169	43.50		212.50	253
4538	10" iron pipe size	G	8	1		238	65.50		303.50	360
4550	2-1/2" wall									
4560	12" iron pipe size	1 Asbe G	6	1.333	Ea.	280	87		367	445
4562	14" iron pipe size	G	" 4	2	"	315	131		446	545

22 07 Plumbing Insulation

22 07 19 – Plumbing Piping Insulation

22 07 19.10 Piping Insulation		Crew	Daily Output	Labor-Hours	Unit	Material	2023 Bare Costs Labor	Equipment	Total	Total Incl O&P
4570	3" wall									
4578	6" iron pipe size	G 1 Asbe	16	.500	Ea.	124	32.50		156.50	187
4580	8" iron pipe size	G	10	.800		143	52		195	238
4582	10" iron pipe size	G	6	1.333		192	87		279	345
4900	Calcium silicate, with 8 oz. canvas cover									
5100	1" wall, 1/2" iron pipe size	G Q-14	170	.094	L.F.	6.30	5.55		11.85	15.40
5130	3/4" iron pipe size	G	170	.094		3.12	5.55		8.67	11.90
5140	1" iron pipe size	G	170	.094		6.05	5.55		11.60	15.10
5150	1-1/4" iron pipe size	G	165	.097		6.15	5.70		11.85	15.45
5160	1-1/2" iron pipe size	G	165	.097		6.20	5.70		11.90	15.55
5170	2" iron pipe size	G	160	.100		3.55	5.85		9.40	12.90
5180	2-1/2" iron pipe size	G	160	.100		3.74	5.85		9.59	13.10
5190	3" iron pipe size	G	150	.107		8.10	6.25		14.35	18.55
5200	4" iron pipe size	G	140	.114		10.15	6.70		16.85	21.50
5210	5" iron pipe size	G	135	.119		11.15	6.95		18.10	23
5220	6" iron pipe size	G	130	.123		11.80	7.25		19.05	24
5280	1-1/2" wall, 1/2" iron pipe size	G	150	.107		6.90	6.25		13.15	17.15
5310	3/4" iron pipe size	G	150	.107		3.34	6.25		9.59	13.25
5320	1" iron pipe size	G	150	.107		7.60	6.25		13.85	18
5330	1-1/4" iron pipe size	G	145	.110		8.20	6.50		14.70	18.90
5340	1-1/2" iron pipe size	G	145	.110		4.23	6.50		10.73	14.55
5350	2" iron pipe size	G	140	.114		9.70	6.70		16.40	21
5360	2-1/2" iron pipe size	G	140	.114		10.55	6.70		17.25	22
5370	3" iron pipe size	G	135	.119		11.10	6.95		18.05	23
5380	4" iron pipe size	G	125	.128		12.85	7.50		20.35	25.50
5390	5" iron pipe size	G	120	.133		14.50	7.85		22.35	28
5400	6" iron pipe size	G	110	.145		14.95	8.55		23.50	29.50
5402	8" iron pipe size	G	95	.168		19.60	9.90		29.50	36.50
5404	10" iron pipe size	G	85	.188		25.50	11.05		36.55	45
5406	12" iron pipe size	G	80	.200		31	11.75		42.75	52
5408	14" iron pipe size	G	75	.213		34	12.55		46.55	56.50
5410	16" iron pipe size	G	70	.229		38	13.40		51.40	62.50
5412	18" iron pipe size	G	65	.246		42	14.45		56.45	68.50
5460	2" wall, 1/2" iron pipe size	G	135	.119		10.65	6.95		17.60	22.50
5490	3/4" iron pipe size	G	135	.119		11.15	6.95		18.10	23
5500	1" iron pipe size	G	135	.119		11.75	6.95		18.70	23.50
5510	1-1/4" iron pipe size	G	130	.123		12.60	7.25		19.85	25
5520	1-1/2" iron pipe size	G	130	.123		13.15	7.25		20.40	25.50
5530	2" iron pipe size	G	125	.128		13.90	7.50		21.40	27
5540	2-1/2" iron pipe size	G	125	.128		16.45	7.50		23.95	29.50
5550	3" iron pipe size	G	120	.133		8.20	7.85		16.05	21
5560	4" iron pipe size	G	115	.139		19.20	8.15		27.35	33.50
5570	5" iron pipe size	G	110	.145		22	8.55		30.55	37
5580	6" iron pipe size	G	105	.152		11.80	8.95		20.75	26.50
5581	8" iron pipe size	G	95	.168		28.50	9.90		38.40	46.50
5582	10" iron pipe size	G	85	.188		35.50	11.05		46.55	56
5583	12" iron pipe size	G	80	.200		39.50	11.75		51.25	61.50
5584	14" iron pipe size	G	75	.213		43.50	12.55		56.05	67
5585	16" iron pipe size	G	70	.229		48	13.40		61.40	73
5586	18" iron pipe size	G	65	.246		52.50	14.45		66.95	79.50
5587	3" wall, 1-1/4" iron pipe size	G	100	.160		19.45	9.40		28.85	36
5588	1-1/2" iron pipe size	G	100	.160		19.60	9.40		29	36
5589	2" iron pipe size	G	95	.168		20.50	9.90		30.40	37.50

22 07 Plumbing Insulation

22 07 19 – Plumbing Piping Insulation

22 07 19.10 Piping Insulation			Crew	Daily Output	Labor-Hours	Unit	Material	2023 Bare Costs Labor	Equipment	Total	Total Incl O&P
5590	2-1/2" iron pipe size	G	Q-14	95	.168	L.F.	23.50	9.90		33.40	41
5591	3" iron pipe size	G		90	.178		24	10.45		34.45	42.50
5592	4" iron pipe size	G		85	.188		30.50	11.05		41.55	50.50
5593	6" iron pipe size	G		80	.200		37	11.75		48.75	58.50
5594	8" iron pipe size	G		75	.213		44	12.55		56.55	67.50
5595	10" iron pipe size	G		65	.246		53	14.45		67.45	80
5596	12" iron pipe size	G		60	.267		58.50	15.65		74.15	88.50
5597	14" iron pipe size	G		55	.291		65.50	17.10		82.60	98
5598	16" iron pipe size	G		50	.320		72.50	18.80		91.30	109
5599	18" iron pipe size	G		45	.356		79.50	21		100.50	119
5600	Calcium silicate, no cover										
5720	1" wall, 1/2" iron pipe size	G	Q-14	180	.089	L.F.	6.30	5.20		11.50	14.95
5740	3/4" iron pipe size	G		180	.089		6.30	5.20		11.50	14.95
5750	1" iron pipe size	G		180	.089		6.05	5.20		11.25	14.65
5760	1-1/4" iron pipe size	G		175	.091		6.15	5.35		11.50	14.95
5770	1-1/2" iron pipe size	G		175	.091		6.35	5.35		11.70	15.15
5780	2" iron pipe size	G		170	.094		7.15	5.55		12.70	16.30
5790	2-1/2" iron pipe size	G		170	.094		7.55	5.55		13.10	16.75
5800	3" iron pipe size	G		160	.100		8.10	5.85		13.95	17.95
5810	4" iron pipe size	G		150	.107		10.15	6.25		16.40	21
5820	5" iron pipe size	G		145	.110		10.55	6.50		17.05	21.50
5830	6" iron pipe size	G		140	.114		11.10	6.70		17.80	22.50
5900	1-1/2" wall, 1/2" iron pipe size	G		160	.100		6.65	5.85		12.50	16.30
5920	3/4" iron pipe size	G		160	.100		6.75	5.85		12.60	16.45
5930	1" iron pipe size	G		160	.100		7.40	5.85		13.25	17.15
5940	1-1/4" iron pipe size	G		155	.103		7.95	6.05		14	18
5950	1-1/2" iron pipe size	G		155	.103		8.55	6.05		14.60	18.65
5960	2" iron pipe size	G		150	.107		9.40	6.25		15.65	19.95
5970	2-1/2" iron pipe size	G		150	.107		10.30	6.25		16.55	21
5980	3" iron pipe size	G		145	.110		10.75	6.50		17.25	22
5990	4" iron pipe size	G		135	.119		12.45	6.95		19.40	24.50
6000	5" iron pipe size	G		130	.123		14	7.25		21.25	26.50
6010	6" iron pipe size	G		120	.133		14.30	7.85		22.15	28
6020	7" iron pipe size	G		115	.139		16.80	8.15		24.95	31
6030	8" iron pipe size	G		105	.152		18.95	8.95		27.90	34.50
6040	9" iron pipe size	G		100	.160		23	9.40		32.40	39.50
6050	10" iron pipe size	G		95	.168		25	9.90		34.90	42.50
6060	12" iron pipe size	G		90	.178		28	10.45		38.45	47
6070	14" iron pipe size	G		85	.188		33.50	11.05		44.55	54
6080	16" iron pipe size	G		80	.200		37.50	11.75		49.25	59.50
6090	18" iron pipe size	G		75	.213		41.50	12.55		54.05	65
6120	2" wall, 1/2" iron pipe size	G		145	.110		9.65	6.50		16.15	20.50
6140	3/4" iron pipe size	G		145	.110		10.20	6.50		16.70	21
6150	1" iron pipe size	G		145	.110		10.75	6.50		17.25	21.50
6160	1-1/4" iron pipe size	G		140	.114		11.50	6.70		18.20	23
6170	1-1/2" iron pipe size	G		140	.114		6.45	6.70		13.15	17.35
6180	2" iron pipe size	G		135	.119		6.80	6.95		13.75	18.10
6190	2-1/2" iron pipe size	G		135	.119		8.15	6.95		15.10	19.65
6200	3" iron pipe size	G		130	.123		16.55	7.25		23.80	29.50
6210	4" iron pipe size	G		125	.128		19.15	7.50		26.65	32.50
6220	5" iron pipe size	G		120	.133		10.80	7.85		18.65	24
6230	6" iron pipe size	G		115	.139		24	8.15		32.15	39
6240	7" iron pipe size	G		110	.145		24	8.55		32.55	39

22 07 Plumbing Insulation

22 07 19 – Plumbing Piping Insulation

22 07 19.10 Piping Insulation		Crew	Daily Output	Labor-Hours	Unit	Material	2023 Bare Costs Labor	Equipment	Total	Total Incl O&P
6250	8" iron pipe size	Q-14 G	105	.152	L.F.	14.10	8.95		23.05	29
6260	9" iron pipe size	G	100	.160		29.50	9.40		38.90	47
6270	10" iron pipe size	G	95	.168		33	9.90		42.90	51
6280	12" iron pipe size	G	90	.178		36.50	10.45		46.95	56
6290	14" iron pipe size	G	85	.188		40	11.05		51.05	61
6300	16" iron pipe size	G	80	.200		44	11.75		55.75	66.50
6310	18" iron pipe size	G	75	.213		48	12.55		60.55	72
6320	20" iron pipe size	G	65	.246		59.50	14.45		73.95	87.50
6330	22" iron pipe size	G	60	.267		65.50	15.65		81.15	96.50
6340	24" iron pipe size	G	55	.291		67	17.10		84.10	100
6360	3" wall, 1/2" iron pipe size	G	115	.139		17.50	8.15		25.65	32
6380	3/4" iron pipe size	G	115	.139		17.60	8.15		25.75	32
6390	1" iron pipe size	G	115	.139		17.75	8.15		25.90	32
6400	1-1/4" iron pipe size	G	110	.145		18	8.55		26.55	33
6410	1-1/2" iron pipe size	G	110	.145		18.05	8.55		26.60	33
6420	2" iron pipe size	G	105	.152		18.70	8.95		27.65	34
6430	2-1/2" iron pipe size	G	105	.152		22	8.95		30.95	37.50
6440	3" iron pipe size	G	100	.160		22	9.40		31.40	39
6450	4" iron pipe size	G	95	.168		28.50	9.90		38.40	46
6460	5" iron pipe size	G	90	.178		30.50	10.45		40.95	50
6470	6" iron pipe size	G	90	.178		34.50	10.45		44.95	54
6480	7" iron pipe size	G	85	.188		38.50	11.05		49.55	59.50
6490	8" iron pipe size	G	85	.188		7.50	11.05		18.55	25
6500	9" iron pipe size	G	80	.200		46.50	11.75		58.25	69.50
6510	10" iron pipe size	G	75	.213		49.50	12.55		62.05	73.50
6520	12" iron pipe size	G	70	.229		55	13.40		68.40	81
6530	14" iron pipe size	G	65	.246		61.50	14.45		75.95	90
6540	16" iron pipe size	G	60	.267		68	15.65		83.65	99
6550	18" iron pipe size	G	55	.291		75	17.10		92.10	109
6560	20" iron pipe size	G	50	.320		89	18.80		107.80	127
6570	22" iron pipe size	G	45	.356		96.50	21		117.50	138
6580	24" iron pipe size	G	40	.400		104	23.50		127.50	150
6600	Fiberglass, with all service jacket									
6640	1/2" wall, 1/2" iron pipe size	Q-14 G	250	.064	L.F.	1.50	3.76		5.26	7.40
6660	3/4" iron pipe size	G	240	.067		1.74	3.92		5.66	7.90
6670	1" iron pipe size	G	230	.070		2	4.09		6.09	8.45
6680	1-1/4" iron pipe size	G	220	.073		1.90	4.27		6.17	8.65
6690	1-1/2" iron pipe size	G	220	.073		2.20	4.27		6.47	8.95
6700	2" iron pipe size	G	210	.076		2.36	4.47		6.83	9.45
6710	2-1/2" iron pipe size	G	200	.080		2.57	4.70		7.27	10.05
6840	1" wall, 1/2" iron pipe size	G	240	.067		1.86	3.92		5.78	8.05
6860	3/4" iron pipe size	G	230	.070		2.04	4.09		6.13	8.50
6870	1" iron pipe size	G	220	.073		2.18	4.27		6.45	8.95
6880	1-1/4" iron pipe size	G	210	.076		2.36	4.47		6.83	9.45
6890	1-1/2" iron pipe size	G	210	.076		2.82	4.47		7.29	9.95
6900	2" iron pipe size	G	200	.080		2.75	4.70		7.45	10.25
6910	2-1/2" iron pipe size	G	190	.084		3.13	4.95		8.08	11
6920	3" iron pipe size	G	180	.089		3.36	5.20		8.56	11.70
6930	3-1/2" iron pipe size	G	170	.094		3.45	5.55		9	12.25
6940	4" iron pipe size	G	150	.107		4.44	6.25		10.69	14.50
6950	5" iron pipe size	G	140	.114		5	6.70		11.70	15.75
6960	6" iron pipe size	G	120	.133		5.30	7.85		13.15	17.85
6970	7" iron pipe size	G	110	.145		7.60	8.55		16.15	21.50

22 07 Plumbing Insulation

22 07 19 – Plumbing Piping Insulation

22 07 19.10 Piping Insulation		Crew	Daily Output	Labor-Hours	Unit	Material	2023 Bare Costs Labor	Equipment	Total	Total Incl O&P
6980	8" iron pipe size	G Q-14	100	.160	L.F.	8.65	9.40		18.05	24
6990	9" iron pipe size	G	90	.178		9.45	10.45		19.90	26.50
7000	10" iron pipe size	G	90	.178		9.45	10.45		19.90	26.50
7010	12" iron pipe size	G	80	.200		10.40	11.75		22.15	29.50
7020	14" iron pipe size	G	80	.200		11.20	11.75		22.95	30.50
7030	16" iron pipe size	G	70	.229		21	13.40		34.40	44
7040	18" iron pipe size	G	70	.229		16.75	13.40		30.15	39
7050	20" iron pipe size	G	60	.267		18.75	15.65		34.40	44.50
7060	24" iron pipe size	G	60	.267		23	15.65		38.65	49
7080	1-1/2" wall, 1/2" iron pipe size	G	230	.070		3.52	4.09		7.61	10.10
7100	3/4" iron pipe size	G	220	.073		3.52	4.27		7.79	10.40
7110	1" iron pipe size	G	210	.076		3.77	4.47		8.24	11
7120	1-1/4" iron pipe size	G	200	.080		4.24	4.70		8.94	11.85
7130	1-1/2" iron pipe size	G	200	.080		4.42	4.70		9.12	12.05
7140	2" iron pipe size	G	190	.084		4.84	4.95		9.79	12.85
7150	2-1/2" iron pipe size	G	180	.089		5.25	5.20		10.45	13.75
7160	3" iron pipe size	G	170	.094		5.45	5.55		11	14.45
7170	3-1/2" iron pipe size	G	160	.100		5.45	5.85		11.30	15
7180	4" iron pipe size	G	140	.114		6.25	6.70		12.95	17.10
7190	5" iron pipe size	G	130	.123		9.25	7.25		16.50	21.50
7200	6" iron pipe size	G	110	.145		7.35	8.55		15.90	21
7210	7" iron pipe size	G	100	.160		10.30	9.40		19.70	25.50
7220	8" iron pipe size	G	90	.178		10.30	10.45		20.75	27.50
7230	9" iron pipe size	G	85	.188		11.10	11.05		22.15	29
7240	10" iron pipe size	G	80	.200		11.10	11.75		22.85	30
7250	12" iron pipe size	G	75	.213		12.75	12.55		25.30	33
7260	14" iron pipe size	G	70	.229		15.30	13.40		28.70	37.50
7270	16" iron pipe size	G	65	.246		18.90	14.45		33.35	43
7280	18" iron pipe size	G	60	.267		28.50	15.65		44.15	55.50
7290	20" iron pipe size	G	55	.291		21.50	17.10		38.60	50
7300	24" iron pipe size	G	50	.320		52	18.80		70.80	86
7320	2" wall, 1/2" iron pipe size	G	220	.073		5.60	4.27		9.87	12.70
7340	3/4" iron pipe size	G	210	.076		5.80	4.47		10.27	13.20
7350	1" iron pipe size	G	200	.080		6.15	4.70		10.85	13.95
7360	1-1/4" iron pipe size	G	190	.084		6.50	4.95		11.45	14.70
7370	1-1/2" iron pipe size	G	190	.084		6.80	4.95		11.75	15.05
7380	2" iron pipe size	G	180	.089		7.15	5.20		12.35	15.90
7390	2-1/2" iron pipe size	G	170	.094		7.70	5.55		13.25	16.95
7400	3" iron pipe size	G	160	.100		8.15	5.85		14	18
7410	3-1/2" iron pipe size	G	150	.107		8.15	6.25		14.40	18.60
7420	4" iron pipe size	G	130	.123		9.55	7.25		16.80	21.50
7430	5" iron pipe size	G	120	.133		10.90	7.85		18.75	24
7440	6" iron pipe size	G	100	.160		9.30	9.40		18.70	24.50
7450	7" iron pipe size	G	90	.178		13.70	10.45		24.15	31
7460	8" iron pipe size	G	80	.200		13.70	11.75		25.45	33
7470	9" iron pipe size	G	75	.213		14.30	12.55		26.85	35
7480	10" iron pipe size	G	70	.229		16.40	13.40		29.80	38.50
7490	12" iron pipe size	G	65	.246		18.70	14.45		33.15	42.50
7500	14" iron pipe size	G	60	.267		24	15.65		39.65	50.50
7510	16" iron pipe size	G	55	.291		35	17.10		52.10	64.50
7520	18" iron pipe size	G	50	.320		58	18.80		76.80	92.50
7530	20" iron pipe size	G	45	.356		42.50	21		63.50	78.50
7540	24" iron pipe size	G	40	.400		47.50	23.50		71	88.50

For customer support on your Mechanical Costs with RSMeans data, call 800.448.8182.

22 07 Plumbing Insulation

22 07 19 – Plumbing Piping Insulation

22 07 19.10 Piping Insulation		Crew	Daily Output	Labor-Hours	Unit	Material	2023 Bare Costs Labor	Equipment	Total	Total Incl O&P
7560	2-1/2" wall, 1/2" iron pipe size	G Q-14	210	.076	L.F.	6.35	4.47		10.82	13.80
7562	3/4" iron pipe size	G	200	.080		9.20	4.70		13.90	17.35
7564	1" iron pipe size	G	190	.084		9.60	4.95		14.55	18.15
7566	1-1/4" iron pipe size	G	185	.086		12.60	5.10		17.70	21.50
7568	1-1/2" iron pipe size	G	180	.089		15.45	5.20		20.65	25
7570	2" iron pipe size	G	170	.094		8.30	5.55		13.85	17.55
7572	2-1/2" iron pipe size	G	160	.100		9.50	5.85		15.35	19.45
7574	3" iron pipe size	G	150	.107		13.30	6.25		19.55	24
7576	3-1/2" iron pipe size	G	140	.114		10.40	6.70		17.10	21.50
7578	4" iron pipe size	G	120	.133		11.50	7.85		19.35	24.50
7580	5" iron pipe size	G	110	.145		7.60	8.55		16.15	21.50
7582	6" iron pipe size	G	90	.178		16.50	10.45		26.95	34
7584	7" iron pipe size	G	80	.200		22	11.75		33.75	42
7586	8" iron pipe size	G	70	.229		23.50	13.40		36.90	46
7588	9" iron pipe size	G	65	.246		18.45	14.45		32.90	42.50
7590	10" iron pipe size	G	60	.267		20	15.65		35.65	46
7592	12" iron pipe size	G	55	.291		24.50	17.10		41.60	53
7594	14" iron pipe size	G	50	.320		29	18.80		47.80	60.50
7596	16" iron pipe size	G	45	.356		33	21		54	68.50
7598	18" iron pipe size	G	40	.400		36	23.50		59.50	75.50
7602	24" iron pipe size	G	30	.533		47.50	31.50		79	100
7620	3" wall, 1/2" iron pipe size	G	200	.080		11.30	4.70		16	19.60
7622	3/4" iron pipe size	G	190	.084		11.90	4.95		16.85	20.50
7624	1" iron pipe size	G	180	.089		13.25	5.20		18.45	22.50
7626	1-1/4" iron pipe size	G	175	.091		15.60	5.35		20.95	25.50
7628	1-1/2" iron pipe size	G	170	.094		13.45	5.55		19	23.50
7630	2" iron pipe size	G	160	.100		14.40	5.85		20.25	25
7632	2-1/2" iron pipe size	G	150	.107		14.95	6.25		21.20	26
7634	3" iron pipe size	G	140	.114		12.15	6.70		18.85	23.50
7636	3-1/2" iron pipe size	G	130	.123		18.65	7.25		25.90	31.50
7638	4" iron pipe size	G	110	.145		14.40	8.55		22.95	29
7640	5" iron pipe size	G	100	.160		16.30	9.40		25.70	32.50
7642	6" iron pipe size	G	80	.200		17.45	11.75		29.20	37
7644	7" iron pipe size	G	70	.229		19.05	13.40		32.45	41.50
7646	8" iron pipe size	G	60	.267		22	15.65		37.65	48
7648	9" iron pipe size	G	55	.291		22.50	17.10		39.60	50.50
7650	10" iron pipe size	G	50	.320		25.50	18.80		44.30	57
7652	12" iron pipe size	G	45	.356		32	21		53	67
7654	14" iron pipe size	G	40	.400		72	23.50		95.50	115
7656	16" iron pipe size	G	35	.457		55	27		82	102
7658	18" iron pipe size	G	32	.500		59	29.50		88.50	110
7660	20" iron pipe size	G	30	.533		46	31.50		77.50	98.50
7662	24" iron pipe size	G	28	.571		98	33.50		131.50	160
7664	26" iron pipe size	G	26	.615		64.50	36		100.50	127
7666	30" iron pipe size	G	24	.667		67	39		106	134
7800	For fiberglass with standard canvas jacket, deduct					5%				
7802	For fittings, add 3 L.F. for each fitting									
7804	plus 4 L.F. for each flange of the fitting									
7820	Polyethylene tubing flexible closed cell foam, UV resistant									
7828	Standard temperature (-90°F to +212°F)									
7830	3/8" wall, 1/8" iron pipe size	G 1 Asbe	130	.062	L.F.	.47	4.02		4.49	6.65
7831	1/4" iron pipe size	G	130	.062		.48	4.02		4.50	6.70
7832	3/8" iron pipe size	G	130	.062		.45	4.02		4.47	6.65

22 07 Plumbing Insulation

22 07 19 – Plumbing Piping Insulation

22 07 19.10 Piping Insulation		Crew	Daily Output	Labor-Hours	Unit	Material	2023 Bare Costs Labor	Equipment	Total	Total Incl O&P
7833	1/2" iron pipe size	G 1 Asbe	126	.063	L.F.	.62	4.14		4.76	7.05
7834	3/4" iron pipe size	G	122	.066		.61	4.28		4.89	7.20
7835	1" iron pipe size	G	120	.067		.78	4.35		5.13	7.50
7836	1-1/4" iron pipe size	G	118	.068		.99	4.42		5.41	7.85
7837	1-1/2" iron pipe size	G	118	.068		1.03	4.42		5.45	7.90
7838	2" iron pipe size	G	116	.069		1.64	4.50		6.14	8.70
7839	2-1/2" iron pipe size	G	114	.070		1.58	4.58		6.16	8.75
7840	3" iron pipe size	G	112	.071		3.22	4.66		7.88	10.70
7842	1/2" wall, 1/8" iron pipe size	G	120	.067		.56	4.35		4.91	7.25
7843	1/4" iron pipe size	G	120	.067		.74	4.35		5.09	7.45
7844	3/8" iron pipe size	G	120	.067		.78	4.35		5.13	7.50
7845	1/2" iron pipe size	G	118	.068		.90	4.42		5.32	7.75
7846	3/4" iron pipe size	G	116	.069		.92	4.50		5.42	7.90
7847	1" iron pipe size	G	114	.070		.96	4.58		5.54	8.05
7848	1-1/4" iron pipe size	G	112	.071		1.11	4.66		5.77	8.35
7849	1-1/2" iron pipe size	G	110	.073		1.22	4.75		5.97	8.60
7850	2" iron pipe size	G	108	.074		2.31	4.83		7.14	9.95
7851	2-1/2" iron pipe size	G	106	.075		2.98	4.92		7.90	10.85
7852	3" iron pipe size	G	104	.077		3.89	5		8.89	12
7853	3-1/2" iron pipe size	G	102	.078		4.35	5.10		9.45	12.65
7854	4" iron pipe size	G	100	.080		5.15	5.20		10.35	13.70
7855	3/4" wall, 1/8" iron pipe size	G	110	.073		.85	4.75		5.60	8.20
7856	1/4" iron pipe size	G	110	.073		.92	4.75		5.67	8.25
7857	3/8" iron pipe size	G	108	.074		1.29	4.83		6.12	8.80
7858	1/2" iron pipe size	G	106	.075		1.53	4.92		6.45	9.25
7859	3/4" iron pipe size	G	104	.077		1.81	5		6.81	9.70
7860	1" iron pipe size	G	102	.078		2.13	5.10		7.23	10.20
7861	1-1/4" iron pipe size	G	100	.080		2.36	5.20		7.56	10.60
7862	1-1/2" iron pipe size	G	100	.080		2.99	5.20		8.19	11.30
7863	2" iron pipe size	G	98	.082		4.10	5.35		9.45	12.65
7864	2-1/2" iron pipe size	G	96	.083		5.15	5.45		10.60	14
7865	3" iron pipe size	G	94	.085		5.10	5.55		10.65	14.10
7866	3-1/2" iron pipe size	G	92	.087		7.30	5.65		12.95	16.75
7867	4" iron pipe size	G	90	.089		8.15	5.80		13.95	17.80
7868	1" wall, 1/4" iron pipe size	G	100	.080		2.23	5.20		7.43	10.45
7869	3/8" iron pipe size	G	98	.082		2.10	5.35		7.45	10.45
7870	1/2" iron pipe size	G	96	.083		2.82	5.45		8.27	11.40
7871	3/4" iron pipe size	G	94	.085		3.22	5.55		8.77	12.05
7872	1" iron pipe size	G	92	.087		3.94	5.65		9.59	13.05
7873	1-1/4" iron pipe size	G	90	.089		4.46	5.80		10.26	13.75
7874	1-1/2" iron pipe size	G	90	.089		5.50	5.80		11.30	14.90
7875	2" iron pipe size	G	88	.091		6.60	5.95		12.55	16.30
7876	2-1/2" iron pipe size	G	86	.093		9.15	6.05		15.20	19.40
7877	3" iron pipe size	G	84	.095		9.90	6.20		16.10	20.50
7878	Contact cement, quart can	G			Ea.	16.50			16.50	18.15
7879	Rubber tubing, flexible closed cell foam									
7880	3/8" wall, 1/4" iron pipe size	G 1 Asbe	120	.067	L.F.	.70	4.35		5.05	7.40
7900	3/8" iron pipe size	G	120	.067		.75	4.35		5.10	7.50
7910	1/2" iron pipe size	G	115	.070		.87	4.54		5.41	7.90
7920	3/4" iron pipe size	G	115	.070		.96	4.54		5.50	8
7930	1" iron pipe size	G	110	.073		1.09	4.75		5.84	8.45
7940	1-1/4" iron pipe size	G	110	.073		1.24	4.75		5.99	8.60
7950	1-1/2" iron pipe size	G	110	.073		1.53	4.75		6.28	8.95

22 07 Plumbing Insulation

22 07 19 – Plumbing Piping Insulation

22 07 19.10 Piping Insulation		Crew	Daily Output	Labor-Hours	Unit	Material	2023 Bare Costs Labor	Equipment	Total	Total Incl O&P
8100	1/2" wall, 1/4" iron pipe size G	1 Asbe	90	.089	L.F.	1.14	5.80		6.94	10.10
8120	3/8" iron pipe size G		90	.089		1.13	5.80		6.93	10.10
8130	1/2" iron pipe size G		89	.090		1.25	5.85		7.10	10.35
8140	3/4" iron pipe size G		89	.090		1.30	5.85		7.15	10.40
8150	1" iron pipe size G		88	.091		2.48	5.95		8.43	11.80
8160	1-1/4" iron pipe size G		87	.092		1.72	6		7.72	11.10
8170	1-1/2" iron pipe size G		87	.092		1.97	6		7.97	11.35
8180	2" iron pipe size G		86	.093		2.52	6.05		8.57	12.05
8190	2-1/2" iron pipe size G		86	.093		4.37	6.05		10.42	14.10
8200	3" iron pipe size G		85	.094		5.15	6.15		11.30	15.05
8210	3-1/2" iron pipe size G		85	.094		6.50	6.15		12.65	16.55
8220	4" iron pipe size G		80	.100		7.10	6.55		13.65	17.80
8230	5" iron pipe size G		80	.100		9.05	6.55		15.60	19.95
8240	6" iron pipe size G		75	.107		9.05	6.95		16	20.50
8300	3/4" wall, 1/4" iron pipe size G		90	.089		1.60	5.80		7.40	10.60
8320	3/8" iron pipe size G		90	.089		1.74	5.80		7.54	10.75
8330	1/2" iron pipe size G		89	.090		1.90	5.85		7.75	11.05
8340	3/4" iron pipe size G		89	.090		2.28	5.85		8.13	11.45
8350	1" iron pipe size G		88	.091		2.77	5.95		8.72	12.10
8360	1-1/4" iron pipe size G		87	.092		3.17	6		9.17	12.70
8370	1-1/2" iron pipe size G		87	.092		4.21	6		10.21	13.85
8380	2" iron pipe size G		86	.093		5.10	6.05		11.15	14.95
8390	2-1/2" iron pipe size G		86	.093		5.70	6.05		11.75	15.55
8400	3" iron pipe size G		85	.094		6.35	6.15		12.50	16.35
8410	3-1/2" iron pipe size G		85	.094		7.05	6.15		13.20	17.15
8420	4" iron pipe size G		80	.100		8.10	6.55		14.65	18.90
8430	5" iron pipe size G		80	.100		13.85	6.55		20.40	25.50
8440	6" iron pipe size G		80	.100		19	6.55		25.55	31
8444	1" wall, 1/2" iron pipe size G		86	.093		3.40	6.05		9.45	13.05
8445	3/4" iron pipe size G		84	.095		4.19	6.20		10.39	14.10
8446	1" iron pipe size G		84	.095		5.10	6.20		11.30	15.10
8447	1-1/4" iron pipe size G		82	.098		5.90	6.35		12.25	16.25
8448	1-1/2" iron pipe size G		82	.098		6.55	6.35		12.90	16.95
8449	2" iron pipe size G		80	.100		7.85	6.55		14.40	18.65
8450	2-1/2" iron pipe size G	▼	80	.100	▼	7.70	6.55		14.25	18.50
8456	Rubber insulation tape, 1/8" x 2" x 30' G				Ea.	25			25	27.50
8460	Polyolefin tubing, flexible closed cell foam, UV stabilized, work									
8462	temp. -165°F to +210°F, 0 water vapor transmission									
8464	3/8" wall, 1/8" iron pipe size G	1 Asbe	140	.057	L.F.	.48	3.73		4.21	6.25
8466	1/4" iron pipe size G		140	.057		.50	3.73		4.23	6.25
8468	3/8" iron pipe size G		140	.057		.56	3.73		4.29	6.30
8470	1/2" iron pipe size G		136	.059		.62	3.84		4.46	6.55
8472	3/4" iron pipe size G		132	.061		.62	3.95		4.57	6.75
8474	1" iron pipe size G		130	.062		.83	4.02		4.85	7.05
8476	1-1/4" iron pipe size G		128	.063		1.02	4.08		5.10	7.35
8478	1-1/2" iron pipe size G		128	.063		1.24	4.08		5.32	7.60
8480	2" iron pipe size G		126	.063		1.50	4.14		5.64	8
8482	2-1/2" iron pipe size G		123	.065		2.18	4.24		6.42	8.90
8484	3" iron pipe size G		121	.066		2.42	4.31		6.73	9.25
8486	4" iron pipe size G		118	.068		5.80	4.42		10.22	13.15
8500	1/2" wall, 1/8" iron pipe size G		130	.062		.70	4.02		4.72	6.90
8502	1/4" iron pipe size G		130	.062		.76	4.02		4.78	7
8504	3/8" iron pipe size G		130	.062		.82	4.02		4.84	7.05

For customer support on your Mechanical Costs with RSMeans data, call 800.448.8182.

22 07 Plumbing Insulation

22 07 19 – Plumbing Piping Insulation

22 07 19.10 Piping Insulation

			Crew	Daily Output	Labor-Hours	Unit	Material	2023 Bare Costs Labor	Equipment	Total	Total Incl O&P
8506		1/2" iron pipe size	G	1 Asbe	128	.063	L.F.	.88	4.08		4.96	7.20
8508		3/4" iron pipe size	G		126	.063		1.03	4.14		5.17	7.50
8510		1" iron pipe size	G		123	.065		1.18	4.24		5.42	7.80
8512		1-1/4" iron pipe size	G		121	.066		1.39	4.31		5.70	8.15
8514		1-1/2" iron pipe size	G		119	.067		1.67	4.39		6.06	8.55
8516		2" iron pipe size	G		117	.068		2.11	4.46		6.57	9.10
8518		2-1/2" iron pipe size	G		114	.070		2.86	4.58		7.44	10.15
8520		3" iron pipe size	G		112	.071		3.72	4.66		8.38	11.25
8522		4" iron pipe size	G		110	.073		5.15	4.75		9.90	12.90
8534	3/4" wall, 1/8" iron pipe size		G		120	.067		1.08	4.35		5.43	7.85
8536		1/4" iron pipe size	G		120	.067		1.14	4.35		5.49	7.90
8538		3/8" iron pipe size	G		117	.068		1.31	4.46		5.77	8.25
8540		1/2" iron pipe size	G		114	.070		1.45	4.58		6.03	8.60
8542		3/4" iron pipe size	G		112	.071		1.57	4.66		6.23	8.90
8544		1" iron pipe size	G		110	.073		2.20	4.75		6.95	9.65
8546		1-1/4" iron pipe size	G		108	.074		2.94	4.83		7.77	10.65
8548		1-1/2" iron pipe size	G		108	.074		3.44	4.83		8.27	11.20
8550		2" iron pipe size	G		106	.075		4.35	4.92		9.27	12.35
8552		2-1/2" iron pipe size	G		104	.077		5.50	5		10.50	13.75
8554		3" iron pipe size	G		102	.078		6.85	5.10		11.95	15.35
8556		4" iron pipe size	G		100	.080		9	5.20		14.20	17.90
8570	1" wall, 1/8" iron pipe size		G		110	.073		1.95	4.75		6.70	9.40
8572		1/4" iron pipe size	G		108	.074		3.54	4.83		8.37	11.30
8574		3/8" iron pipe size	G		106	.075		2.04	4.92		6.96	9.80
8576		1/2" iron pipe size	G		104	.077		2.16	5		7.16	10.10
8578		3/4" iron pipe size	G		102	.078		2.75	5.10		7.85	10.90
8580		1" iron pipe size	G		100	.080		3.27	5.20		8.47	11.60
8582		1-1/4" iron pipe size	G		97	.082		3.72	5.40		9.12	12.35
8584		1-1/2" iron pipe size	G		97	.082		4.25	5.40		9.65	12.95
8586		2" iron pipe size	G		95	.084		6	5.50		11.50	15
8588		2-1/2" iron pipe size	G		93	.086		7.85	5.60		13.45	17.20
8590		3" iron pipe size	G		91	.088		9.55	5.75		15.30	19.25
8606	Contact adhesive (R-320)		G				Qt.	26			26	28.50
8608	Contact adhesive (R-320)		G				Gal.	104			104	114
8610	NOTE: Preslit/preglued vs. unslit, same price											

22 07 19.30 Piping Insulation Protective Jacketing, PVC

			Crew	Daily Output	Labor-Hours	Unit	Material	Labor	Equipment	Total	Total Incl O&P
0010	**PIPING INSULATION PROTECTIVE JACKETING, PVC**										
0100	PVC, white, 48" lengths cut from roll goods										
0120	20 mil thick										
0140	Size based on OD of insulation										
0150	1-1/2" ID		Q-14	270	.059	L.F.	3.47	3.48		6.95	9.10
0152	2" ID			260	.062		2.17	3.61		5.78	7.95
0154	2-1/2" ID			250	.064		.61	3.76		4.37	6.40
0156	3" ID			240	.067		4.24	3.92		8.16	10.65
0158	3-1/2" ID			230	.070		2.65	4.09		6.74	9.15
0160	4" ID			220	.073		2.83	4.27		7.10	9.65
0162	4-1/2" ID			210	.076		3.17	4.47		7.64	10.35
0164	5" ID			200	.080		5.45	4.70		10.15	13.15
0166	5-1/2" ID			190	.084		1.23	4.95		6.18	8.90
0168	6" ID			180	.089		6.30	5.20		11.50	14.95
0170	6-1/2" ID			175	.091		1.28	5.35		6.63	9.60
0172	7" ID			170	.094		6.85	5.55		12.40	16

22 07 Plumbing Insulation

22 07 19 – Plumbing Piping Insulation

22 07 19.30 Piping Insulation Protective Jacketing, PVC		Crew	Daily Output	Labor-Hours	Unit	Material	2023 Bare Costs Labor	Equipment	Total	Total Incl O&P
0174	7-1/2" ID	Q-14	164	.098	L.F.	1.48	5.75		7.23	10.40
0176	8" ID		161	.099		3.90	5.85		9.75	13.25
0178	8-1/2" ID		158	.101		1.87	5.95		7.82	11.15
0180	9" ID		155	.103		1.97	6.05		8.02	11.40
0182	9-1/2" ID		152	.105		1.85	6.20		8.05	11.50
0184	10" ID		149	.107		2.17	6.30		8.47	12.05
0186	10-1/2" ID		146	.110		2.30	6.45		8.75	12.40
0188	11" ID		143	.112		2.40	6.55		8.95	12.70
0190	11-1/2" ID		140	.114		2.20	6.70		8.90	12.65
0192	12" ID		137	.117		2.61	6.85		9.46	13.35
0194	12-1/2" ID		134	.119		2.68	7		9.68	13.70
0195	13" ID		132	.121		2.82	7.10		9.92	14
0196	13-1/2" ID		132	.121		2.91	7.10		10.01	14.10
0198	14" ID		130	.123		3.02	7.25		10.27	14.35
0200	15" ID		128	.125		3.20	7.35		10.55	14.75
0202	16" ID		126	.127		3.43	7.45		10.88	15.15
0204	17" ID		124	.129		3.62	7.60		11.22	15.60
0206	18" ID		122	.131		3.84	7.70		11.54	16
0208	19" ID		120	.133		4.05	7.85		11.90	16.45
0210	20" ID		118	.136		4.33	7.95		12.28	16.95
0212	21" ID		116	.138		4.49	8.10		12.59	17.35
0214	22" ID		114	.140		4.73	8.25		12.98	17.80
0216	23" ID		112	.143		4.94	8.40		13.34	18.30
0218	24" ID		110	.145		5.15	8.55		13.70	18.70
0220	25" ID		108	.148		5.35	8.70		14.05	19.20
0222	26" ID		106	.151		5.60	8.85		14.45	19.70
0224	27" ID		104	.154		5.80	9.05		14.85	20
0226	28" ID		102	.157		6	9.20		15.20	20.50
0228	29" ID		100	.160		6.20	9.40		15.60	21
0230	30" ID	▼	98	.163	▼	6.45	9.60		16.05	22
0300	For colors, add				Ea.	10%				
1000	30 mil thick									
1010	Size based on OD of insulation									
1020	2" ID	Q-14	260	.062	L.F.	.74	3.61		4.35	6.35
1022	2-1/2" ID		250	.064		3.72	3.76		7.48	9.85
1024	3" ID		240	.067		2.63	3.92		6.55	8.90
1026	3-1/2" ID		230	.070		1.23	4.09		5.32	7.60
1028	4" ID		220	.073		4.09	4.27		8.36	11.05
1030	4-1/2" ID		210	.076		1.54	4.47		6.01	8.55
1032	5" ID		200	.080		1.69	4.70		6.39	9.05
1034	5-1/2" ID		190	.084		1.87	4.95		6.82	9.60
1036	6" ID		180	.089		1.99	5.20		7.19	10.20
1038	6-1/2" ID		175	.091		2.18	5.35		7.53	10.60
1040	7" ID		170	.094		2.33	5.55		7.88	11
1042	7-1/2" ID		164	.098		2.51	5.75		8.26	11.50
1044	8" ID		161	.099		2.64	5.85		8.49	11.85
1046	8-1/2" ID		158	.101		2.82	5.95		8.77	12.20
1048	9" ID		155	.103		2.97	6.05		9.02	12.50
1050	9-1/2" ID		152	.105		3.14	6.20		9.34	12.90
1052	10" ID		149	.107		5.05	6.30		11.35	15.25
1054	10-1/2" ID		146	.110		3.45	6.45		9.90	13.65
1056	11" ID		143	.112		3.63	6.55		10.18	14.05
1058	11-1/2" ID	▼	140	.114	▼	3.78	6.70		10.48	14.40

22 07 Plumbing Insulation

22 07 19 – Plumbing Piping Insulation

22 07 19.30 Piping Insulation Protective Jacketing, PVC		Crew	Daily Output	Labor-Hours	Unit	Material	2023 Bare Costs Labor	Equipment	Total	Total Incl O&P
1060	12" ID	Q-14	137	.117	L.F.	3.93	6.85		10.78	14.80
1062	12-1/2" ID		134	.119		4.09	7		11.09	15.25
1063	13" ID		132	.121		4.24	7.10		11.34	15.55
1064	13-1/2" ID		132	.121		4.43	7.10		11.53	15.75
1066	14" ID		130	.123		4.55	7.25		11.80	16.05
1068	15" ID		128	.125		4.88	7.35		12.23	16.60
1070	16" ID		126	.127		5.20	7.45		12.65	17.15
1072	17" ID		124	.129		5.55	7.60		13.15	17.70
1074	18" ID		122	.131		5.85	7.70		13.55	18.20
1076	19" ID		120	.133		6.15	7.85		14	18.75
1078	20" ID		118	.136		6.45	7.95		14.40	19.30
1080	21" ID		116	.138		6.80	8.10		14.90	19.85
1082	22" ID		114	.140		7.10	8.25		15.35	20.50
1084	23" ID		112	.143		7.45	8.40		15.85	21
1086	24" ID		110	.145		7.75	8.55		16.30	21.50
1088	25" ID		108	.148		8.10	8.70		16.80	22
1090	26" ID		106	.151		8.40	8.85		17.25	23
1092	27" ID		104	.154		8.75	9.05		17.80	23.50
1094	28" ID		102	.157		9.05	9.20		18.25	24
1096	29" ID		100	.160		9.35	9.40		18.75	24.50
1098	30" ID		98	.163		9.70	9.60		19.30	25.50
1300	For colors, add				Ea.	10%				
2000	PVC, white, fitting covers									
2020	Fiberglass insulation inserts included with sizes 1-3/4" thru 9-3/4"									
2030	Size is based on OD of insulation									
2040	90° elbow fitting									
2060	1-3/4"	Q-14	135	.119	Ea.	.61	6.95		7.56	11.30
2062	2"		130	.123		.76	7.25		8.01	11.90
2064	2-1/4"		128	.125		.88	7.35		8.23	12.20
2068	2-1/2"		126	.127		.93	7.45		8.38	12.40
2070	2-3/4"		123	.130		1.10	7.65		8.75	12.90
2072	3"		120	.133		5.60	7.85		13.45	18.20
2074	3-3/8"		116	.138		1.26	8.10		9.36	13.80
2076	3-3/4"		113	.142		1.34	8.30		9.64	14.15
2078	4-1/8"		110	.145		1.77	8.55		10.32	15
2080	4-3/4"		105	.152		2.14	8.95		11.09	16.05
2082	5-1/4"		100	.160		2.50	9.40		11.90	17.10
2084	5-3/4"		95	.168		3.16	9.90		13.06	18.65
2086	6-1/4"		90	.178		5.25	10.45		15.70	22
2088	6-3/4"		87	.184		5.55	10.80		16.35	22.50
2090	7-1/4"		85	.188		6.90	11.05		17.95	24.50
2092	7-3/4"		83	.193		7.30	11.30		18.60	25.50
2094	8-3/4"		80	.200		9.35	11.75		21.10	28.50
2096	9-3/4"		77	.208		12.50	12.20		24.70	32.50
2098	10-7/8"		74	.216		13.95	12.70		26.65	35
2100	11-7/8"		71	.225		16	13.25		29.25	37.50
2102	12-7/8"		68	.235		22	13.80		35.80	45.50
2104	14-1/8"		66	.242		23	14.25		37.25	47.50
2106	15-1/8"		64	.250		25	14.70		39.70	50
2108	16-1/8"		63	.254		27	14.90		41.90	53
2110	17-1/8"		62	.258		30	15.15		45.15	56
2112	18-1/8"		61	.262		40.50	15.40		55.90	68
2114	19-1/8"		60	.267		52.50	15.65		68.15	82

22 07 Plumbing Insulation

22 07 19 – Plumbing Piping Insulation

22 07 19.30 Piping Insulation Protective Jacketing, PVC		Crew	Daily Output	Labor-Hours	Unit	Material	2023 Bare Costs Labor	Equipment	Total	Total Incl O&P
2116	20-1/8"	Q-14	59	.271	Ea.	67.50	15.95		83.45	99
2200	45° elbow fitting									
2220	1-3/4" thru 9-3/4" same price as 90° elbow fitting									
2320	10-7/8"	Q-14	74	.216	Ea.	13.95	12.70		26.65	35
2322	11-7/8"		71	.225		15.40	13.25		28.65	37
2324	12-7/8"		68	.235		17.15	13.80		30.95	40
2326	14-1/8"		66	.242		19.60	14.25		33.85	43.50
2328	15-1/8"		64	.250		21	14.70		35.70	45.50
2330	16-1/8"		63	.254		24	14.90		38.90	49.50
2332	17-1/8"		62	.258		27	15.15		42.15	53
2334	18-1/8"		61	.262		33	15.40		48.40	60
2336	19-1/8"		60	.267		45	15.65		60.65	73.50
2338	20-1/8"		59	.271		51	15.95		66.95	80.50
2400	Tee fitting									
2410	1-3/4"	Q-14	96	.167	Ea.	1.15	9.80		10.95	16.20
2412	2"		94	.170		1.31	10		11.31	16.75
2414	2-1/4"		91	.176		1.41	10.35		11.76	17.35
2416	2-1/2"		88	.182		1.54	10.70		12.24	18.05
2418	2-3/4"		85	.188		1.70	11.05		12.75	18.75
2420	3"		82	.195		10.10	11.45		21.55	28.50
2422	3-3/8"		79	.203		2.12	11.90		14.02	20.50
2424	3-3/4"		76	.211		2.63	12.35		14.98	22
2426	4-1/8"		73	.219		2.85	12.85		15.70	23
2428	4-3/4"		70	.229		3.54	13.40		16.94	24.50
2430	5-1/4"		67	.239		4.26	14.05		18.31	26
2432	5-3/4"		63	.254		5.65	14.90		20.55	29.50
2434	6-1/4"		60	.267		7.45	15.65		23.10	32
2436	6-3/4"		59	.271		9.20	15.95		25.15	34.50
2438	7-1/4"		57	.281		14.85	16.50		31.35	41.50
2440	7-3/4"		54	.296		16.30	17.40		33.70	44.50
2442	8-3/4"		52	.308		19.80	18.05		37.85	49.50
2444	9-3/4"		50	.320		23.50	18.80		42.30	54.50
2446	10-7/8"		48	.333		23.50	19.60		43.10	56
2448	11-7/8"		47	.340		26.50	20		46.50	59.50
2450	12-7/8"		46	.348		29	20.50		49.50	63.50
2452	14-1/8"		45	.356		31.50	21		52.50	66.50
2454	15-1/8"		44	.364		34	21.50		55.50	70
2456	16-1/8"		43	.372		37	22		59	74
2458	17-1/8"		42	.381		39.50	22.50		62	77.50
2460	18-1/8"		41	.390		43.50	23		66.50	82.50
2462	19-1/8"		40	.400		47.50	23.50		71	88
2464	20-1/8"		39	.410		52.50	24		76.50	94.50
4000	Mechanical grooved fitting cover, including insert									
4020	90° elbow fitting									
4030	3/4" & 1"	Q-14	140	.114	Ea.	5.95	6.70		12.65	16.80
4040	1-1/4" & 1-1/2"		135	.119		7.50	6.95		14.45	18.90
4042	2"		130	.123		9.55	7.25		16.80	21.50
4044	2-1/2"		125	.128		10.65	7.50		18.15	23
4046	3"		120	.133		11.90	7.85		19.75	25
4048	3-1/2"		115	.139		13.80	8.15		21.95	27.50
4050	4"		110	.145		15.35	8.55		23.90	30
4052	5"		100	.160		19.10	9.40		28.50	35.50
4054	6"		90	.178		28.50	10.45		38.95	47.50

22 07 Plumbing Insulation

22 07 19 – Plumbing Piping Insulation

22 07 19.30 Piping Insulation Protective Jacketing, PVC

		Crew	Daily Output	Labor-Hours	Unit	Material	2023 Bare Costs Labor	Equipment	Total	Total Incl O&P
4056	8"	Q-14	80	.200	Ea.	30.50	11.75		42.25	52
4058	10"		75	.213		39.50	12.55		52.05	62.50
4060	12"		68	.235		56.50	13.80		70.30	83
4062	14"		65	.246		84	14.45		98.45	114
4064	16"		63	.254		114	14.90		128.90	148
4066	18"	▼	61	.262	▼	157	15.40		172.40	196
4100	45° elbow fitting									
4120	3/4" & 1"	Q-14	140	.114	Ea.	5.35	6.70		12.05	16.15
4130	1-1/4" & 1-1/2"		135	.119		6.85	6.95		13.80	18.15
4140	2"		130	.123		9.35	7.25		16.60	21.50
4142	2-1/2"		125	.128		10.40	7.50		17.90	23
4144	3"		120	.133		10.65	7.85		18.50	23.50
4146	3-1/2"		115	.139		14.25	8.15		22.40	28
4148	4"		110	.145		17.50	8.55		26.05	32.50
4150	5"		100	.160		18.60	9.40		28	35
4152	6"		90	.178		26	10.45		36.45	44.50
4154	8"		80	.200		27.50	11.75		39.25	48
4156	10"		75	.213		35	12.55		47.55	57.50
4158	12"		68	.235		52.50	13.80		66.30	79
4160	14"		65	.246		72	14.45		86.45	101
4162	16"		63	.254		87	14.90		101.90	119
4164	18"	▼	61	.262	▼	139	15.40		154.40	176
4200	Tee fitting									
4220	3/4" & 1"	Q-14	93	.172	Ea.	7.80	10.10		17.90	24
4230	1-1/4" & 1-1/2"		90	.178		9.90	10.45		20.35	27
4240	2"		87	.184		15.95	10.80		26.75	34
4242	2-1/2"		84	.190		17.75	11.20		28.95	36.50
4244	3"		80	.200		19.05	11.75		30.80	39
4246	3-1/2"		77	.208		20.50	12.20		32.70	41
4248	4"		73	.219		25.50	12.85		38.35	47.50
4250	5"		67	.239		31.50	14.05		45.55	56
4252	6"		60	.267		42	15.65		57.65	70
4254	8"		54	.296		45.50	17.40		62.90	76.50
4256	10"		50	.320		51.50	18.80		70.30	85.50
4258	12"		46	.348		78.50	20.50		99	118
4260	14"		43	.372		114	22		136	159
4262	16"		42	.381		117	22.50		139.50	163
4264	18"	▼	41	.390	▼	174	23		197	226

22 07 19.40 Pipe Insulation Protective Jacketing, Aluminum

		Crew	Daily Output	Labor-Hours	Unit	Material	2023 Bare Costs Labor	Equipment	Total	Total Incl O&P
0010	**PIPE INSULATION PROTECTIVE JACKETING, ALUMINUM**									
0100	Metal roll jacketing									
0120	Aluminum with polykraft moisture barrier									
0140	Smooth, based on OD of insulation, .016" thick									
0180	1/2" ID	Q-14	220	.073	L.F.	.36	4.27		4.63	6.95
0190	3/4" ID		215	.074		.46	4.37		4.83	7.20
0200	1" ID		210	.076		.56	4.47		5.03	7.45
0210	1-1/4" ID		205	.078		2.74	4.58		7.32	10
0220	1-1/2" ID		202	.079		2.74	4.65		7.39	10.10
0230	1-3/4" ID		199	.080		.98	4.72		5.70	8.30
0240	2" ID		195	.082		1.47	4.82		6.29	8.95
0250	2-1/4" ID		191	.084		1.22	4.92		6.14	8.90
0260	2-1/2" ID	▼	187	.086		1.21	5.05		6.26	9.05

22 07 Plumbing Insulation

22 07 19 – Plumbing Piping Insulation

22 07 19.40 Pipe Insulation Protective Jacketing, Aluminum	Crew	Daily Output	Labor-Hours	Unit	Material	2023 Bare Costs Labor	Equipment	Total	Total Incl O&P
0270	2-3/4" ID	Q-14	184	.087	L.F.	1.47	5.10		6.57	9.40
0280	3" ID		180	.089		1.64	5.20		6.84	9.80
0290	3-1/4" ID		176	.091		1.64	5.35		6.99	9.95
0300	3-1/2" ID		172	.093		1.80	5.45		7.25	10.35
0310	3-3/4" ID		169	.095		1.75	5.55		7.30	10.45
0320	4" ID		165	.097		1.97	5.70		7.67	10.85
0330	4-1/4" ID		161	.099		2.16	5.85		8.01	11.35
0340	4-1/2" ID		157	.102		4.32	6		10.32	13.90
0350	4-3/4" ID		154	.104		2.39	6.10		8.49	12
0360	5" ID		150	.107		4.99	6.25		11.24	15.10
0370	5-1/4" ID		146	.110		2.63	6.45		9.08	12.75
0380	5-1/2" ID		143	.112		2.51	6.55		9.06	12.80
0390	5-3/4" ID		139	.115		2.88	6.75		9.63	13.50
0400	6" ID		135	.119		2.77	6.95		9.72	13.70
0410	6-1/4" ID		133	.120		3.11	7.05		10.16	14.20
0420	6-1/2" ID		131	.122		5.65	7.15		12.80	17.20
0430	7" ID		128	.125		3.13	7.35		10.48	14.70
0440	7-1/4" ID		125	.128		3.24	7.50		10.74	15.05
0450	7-1/2" ID		123	.130		3.34	7.65		10.99	15.35
0460	8" ID		121	.132		3.52	7.75		11.27	15.75
0470	8-1/2" ID		119	.134		3.75	7.90		11.65	16.25
0480	9" ID		116	.138		3.96	8.10		12.06	16.75
0490	9-1/2" ID		114	.140		4.20	8.25		12.45	17.20
0500	10" ID		112	.143		4.28	8.40		12.68	17.55
0510	10-1/2" ID		110	.145		5.05	8.55		13.60	18.65
0520	11" ID		107	.150		4.81	8.80		13.61	18.75
0530	11-1/2" ID		105	.152		5.05	8.95		14	19.25
0540	12" ID		103	.155		5	9.10		14.10	19.45
0550	12-1/2" ID		100	.160		5.45	9.40		14.85	20.50
0560	13" ID		99	.162		5.65	9.50		15.15	21
0570	14" ID		98	.163		6.10	9.60		15.70	21.50
0580	15" ID		96	.167		6.55	9.80		16.35	22
0590	16" ID		95	.168		6.95	9.90		16.85	23
0600	17" ID		93	.172		7.35	10.10		17.45	23.50
0610	18" ID		92	.174		7.65	10.20		17.85	24
0620	19" ID		90	.178		8.25	10.45		18.70	25
0630	20" ID		89	.180		8.65	10.55		19.20	25.50
0640	21" ID		87	.184		9.10	10.80		19.90	26.50
0650	22" ID		86	.186		9.50	10.95		20.45	27
0660	23" ID		84	.190		9.95	11.20		21.15	28
0670	24" ID	▼	83	.193		10.35	11.30		21.65	28.50
0710	For smooth .020" thick, add					27%	10%			
0720	For smooth .024" thick, add					52%	20%			
0730	For smooth .032" thick, add					104%	33%			
0800	For stucco embossed, add					1%				
0820	For corrugated, add					2.50%				
0900	White aluminum with polysurlyn moisture barrier				▼					
0910	Smooth, % is an add to polykraft lines of same thickness									
0940	For smooth .016" thick, add				L.F.	35%				
0960	For smooth .024" thick, add				"	22%				
1000	Aluminum fitting covers									
1010	Size is based on OD of insulation									
1020	90° LR elbow, 2 piece									

22 07 Plumbing Insulation

22 07 19 – Plumbing Piping Insulation

22 07 19.40 Pipe Insulation Protective Jacketing, Aluminum		Crew	Daily Output	Labor-Hours	Unit	Material	2023 Bare Costs Labor	Equipment	Total	Total Incl O&P
1100	1-1/2"	Q-14	140	.114	Ea.	5.45	6.70		12.15	16.25
1110	1-3/4"		135	.119		5.45	6.95		12.40	16.65
1120	2"		130	.123		6.90	7.25		14.15	18.65
1130	2-1/4"		128	.125		6.90	7.35		14.25	18.85
1140	2-1/2"		126	.127		4.90	7.45		12.35	16.80
1150	2-3/4"		123	.130		6.90	7.65		14.55	19.30
1160	3"		120	.133		7.50	7.85		15.35	20.50
1170	3-1/4"		117	.137		7.50	8.05		15.55	20.50
1180	3-1/2"		115	.139		8.85	8.15		17	22
1190	3-3/4"		113	.142		9.05	8.30		17.35	22.50
1200	4"		110	.145		6.75	8.55		15.30	20.50
1210	4-1/4"		108	.148		9.75	8.70		18.45	24
1220	4-1/2"		106	.151		9.75	8.85		18.60	24.50
1230	4-3/4"		104	.154		9.75	9.05		18.80	24.50
1240	5"		102	.157		11	9.20		20.20	26
1250	5-1/4"		100	.160		12.70	9.40		22.10	28.50
1260	5-1/2"		97	.165		15.80	9.70		25.50	32
1270	5-3/4"		95	.168		15.80	9.90		25.70	32.50
1280	6"		92	.174		13.45	10.20		23.65	30.50
1290	6-1/4"		90	.178		13.45	10.45		23.90	31
1300	6-1/2"		87	.184		16.20	10.80		27	34.50
1310	7"		85	.188		19.70	11.05		30.75	38.50
1320	7-1/4"		84	.190		19.70	11.20		30.90	38.50
1330	7-1/2"		83	.193		29	11.30		40.30	49.50
1340	8"		82	.195		23	11.45		34.45	42.50
1350	8-1/2"		80	.200		40	11.75		51.75	62
1360	9"		78	.205		40	12.05		52.05	62.50
1370	9-1/2"		77	.208		29.50	12.20		41.70	51
1380	10"		76	.211		31	12.35		43.35	53.50
1390	10-1/2"		75	.213		30	12.55		42.55	52
1400	11"		74	.216		30	12.70		42.70	52.50
1410	11-1/2"		72	.222		34	13.05		47.05	57.50
1420	12"		71	.225		34	13.25		47.25	57.50
1430	12-1/2"		69	.232		60.50	13.60		74.10	88
1440	13"		68	.235		60.50	13.80		74.30	88
1450	14"		66	.242		81.50	14.25		95.75	112
1460	15"		64	.250		85	14.70		99.70	116
1470	16"		63	.254		93	14.90		107.90	125
2000	45° elbow, 2 piece									
2010	2-1/2"	Q-14	126	.127	Ea.	5.70	7.45		13.15	17.65
2020	2-3/4"		123	.130		5.70	7.65		13.35	17.95
2030	3"		120	.133		6.45	7.85		14.30	19.10
2040	3-1/4"		117	.137		6.45	8.05		14.50	19.40
2050	3-1/2"		115	.139		7.35	8.15		15.50	20.50
2060	3-3/4"		113	.142		7.35	8.30		15.65	21
2070	4"		110	.145		7.45	8.55		16	21.50
2080	4-1/4"		108	.148		8.50	8.70		17.20	22.50
2090	4-1/2"		106	.151		8.50	8.85		17.35	23
2100	4-3/4"		104	.154		8.50	9.05		17.55	23
2110	5"		102	.157		10	9.20		19.20	25
2120	5-1/4"		100	.160		10	9.40		19.40	25.50
2130	5-1/2"		97	.165		10.50	9.70		20.20	26.50
2140	6"		92	.174		10.50	10.20		20.70	27

22 07 Plumbing Insulation

22 07 19 – Plumbing Piping Insulation

22 07 19.40 Pipe Insulation Protective Jacketing, Aluminum		Crew	Daily Output	Labor-Hours	Unit	Material	2023 Bare Costs Labor	Equipment	Total	Total Incl O&P
2150	6-1/2"	Q-14	87	.184	Ea.	14.45	10.80		25.25	32.50
2160	7"		85	.188		14.45	11.05		25.50	33
2170	7-1/2"		83	.193		14.65	11.30		25.95	33.50
2180	8"		82	.195		14.65	11.45		26.10	33.50
2190	8-1/2"		80	.200		18.20	11.75		29.95	38
2200	9"		78	.205		18.20	12.05		30.25	38.50
2210	9-1/2"		77	.208		25	12.20		37.20	46
2220	10"		76	.211		25	12.35		37.35	46.50
2230	10-1/2"		75	.213		23.50	12.55		36.05	45
2240	11"		74	.216		23.50	12.70		36.20	45.50
2250	11-1/2"		72	.222		28.50	13.05		41.55	51
2260	12"		71	.225		28.50	13.25		41.75	51
2270	13"		68	.235		33.50	13.80		47.30	57.50
2280	14"		66	.242		41	14.25		55.25	67
2290	15"		64	.250		63	14.70		77.70	91.50
2300	16"		63	.254		68	14.90		82.90	98
2310	17"		62	.258		66.50	15.15		81.65	96.50
2320	18"		61	.262		76	15.40		91.40	107
2330	19"		60	.267		93	15.65		108.65	126
2340	20"		59	.271		89.50	15.95		105.45	123
2350	21"		58	.276		97	16.20		113.20	132
3000	Tee, 4 piece									
3010	2-1/2"	Q-14	88	.182	Ea.	36	10.70		46.70	56
3020	2-3/4"		86	.186		36	10.95		46.95	56
3030	3"		84	.190		40.50	11.20		51.70	61.50
3040	3-1/4"		82	.195		40.50	11.45		51.95	62
3050	3-1/2"		80	.200		42.50	11.75		54.25	64.50
3060	4"		78	.205		43	12.05		55.05	65.50
3070	4-1/4"		76	.211		45	12.35		57.35	68.50
3080	4-1/2"		74	.216		45	12.70		57.70	69
3090	4-3/4"		72	.222		45	13.05		58.05	69.50
3100	5"		70	.229		46.50	13.40		59.90	72
3110	5-1/4"		68	.235		46.50	13.80		60.30	72.50
3120	5-1/2"		66	.242		48.50	14.25		62.75	75.50
3130	6"		64	.250		48.50	14.70		63.20	76
3140	6-1/2"		60	.267		53.50	15.65		69.15	83
3150	7"		58	.276		53.50	16.20		69.70	84
3160	7-1/2"		56	.286		59.50	16.80		76.30	91
3170	8"		54	.296		59.50	17.40		76.90	92
3180	8-1/2"		52	.308		61	18.05		79.05	94.50
3190	9"		50	.320		61	18.80		79.80	96
3200	9-1/2"		49	.327		45.50	19.20		64.70	79.50
3210	10"		48	.333		45.50	19.60		65.10	80
3220	10-1/2"		47	.340		48.50	20		68.50	83.50
3230	11"		46	.348		48.50	20.50		69	84.50
3240	11-1/2"		45	.356		51	21		72	88
3250	12"		44	.364		51	21.50		72.50	88.50
3260	13"		43	.372		53.50	22		75.50	92.50
3270	14"		42	.381		56	22.50		78.50	95.50
3280	15"		41	.390		60.50	23		83.50	102
3290	16"		40	.400		62	23.50		85.50	105
3300	17"		39	.410		71.50	24		95.50	116
3310	18"		38	.421		74	24.50		98.50	120

22 07 Plumbing Insulation

22 07 19 – Plumbing Piping Insulation

22 07 19.40 Pipe Insulation Protective Jacketing, Aluminum		Crew	Daily Output	Labor-Hours	Unit	Material	2023 Bare Costs Labor	Equipment	Total	Total Incl O&P
3320	19"	Q-14	37	.432	Ea.	82	25.50		107.50	130
3330	20"		36	.444		84	26		110	133
3340	22"		35	.457		107	27		134	158
3350	23"		34	.471		110	27.50		137.50	164
3360	24"	▼	31	.516	▼	113	30.50		143.50	171
22 07 19.50 Pipe Insulation Protective Jacketing, St. Stl.										
0010	**PIPE INSULATION PROTECTIVE JACKETING, STAINLESS STEEL**									
0100	Metal roll jacketing									
0120	Type 304 with moisture barrier									
0140	Smooth, based on OD of insulation, .010" thick									
0260	2-1/2" ID	Q-14	250	.064	L.F.	4.74	3.76		8.50	10.95
0270	2-3/4" ID		245	.065		3.73	3.84		7.57	9.95
0280	3" ID		240	.067		4.03	3.92		7.95	10.45
0290	3-1/4" ID		235	.068		4.38	4		8.38	10.90
0300	3-1/2" ID		230	.070		4.64	4.09		8.73	11.35
0310	3-3/4" ID		225	.071		4.99	4.18		9.17	11.90
0320	4" ID		220	.073		5.25	4.27		9.52	12.35
0330	4-1/4" ID		215	.074		5.55	4.37		9.92	12.80
0340	4-1/2" ID		210	.076		5.85	4.47		10.32	13.30
0350	5" ID		200	.080		6.50	4.70		11.20	14.35
0360	5-1/2" ID		190	.084		7.10	4.95		12.05	15.35
0370	6" ID		180	.089		7.70	5.20		12.90	16.45
0380	6-1/2" ID		175	.091		8.30	5.35		13.65	17.35
0390	7" ID		170	.094		8.95	5.55		14.50	18.25
0400	7-1/2" ID		164	.098		9.50	5.75		15.25	19.20
0410	8" ID		161	.099		10.10	5.85		15.95	20
0420	8-1/2" ID		158	.101		10.75	5.95		16.70	21
0430	9" ID		155	.103		11.35	6.05		17.40	22
0440	9-1/2" ID		152	.105		11.95	6.20		18.15	22.50
0450	10" ID		149	.107		12.55	6.30		18.85	23.50
0460	10-1/2" ID		146	.110		13.20	6.45		19.65	24.50
0470	11" ID		143	.112		13.80	6.55		20.35	25
0480	12" ID		137	.117		15	6.85		21.85	27
0490	13" ID		132	.121		16.20	7.10		23.30	29
0500	14" ID	▼	130	.123		17.40	7.25		24.65	30
0700	For smooth .016" thick, add				▼	45%	33%			
1000	Stainless steel, Type 316, fitting covers									
1010	Size is based on OD of insulation									
1020	90° LR elbow, 2 piece									
1100	1-1/2"	Q-14	126	.127	Ea.	14.30	7.45		21.75	27
1110	2-3/4"		123	.130		14.95	7.65		22.60	28
1120	3"		120	.133		15.60	7.85		23.45	29
1130	3-1/4"		117	.137		15.60	8.05		23.65	29.50
1140	3-1/2"		115	.139		16.40	8.15		24.55	30.50
1150	3-3/4"		113	.142		17.35	8.30		25.65	32
1160	4"		110	.145		19.05	8.55		27.60	34
1170	4-1/4"		108	.148		25.50	8.70		34.20	41.50
1180	4-1/2"		106	.151		25.50	8.85		34.35	41.50
1190	5"		102	.157		26	9.20		35.20	42.50
1200	5-1/2"		97	.165		38.50	9.70		48.20	57.50
1210	6"		92	.174		42.50	10.20		52.70	62
1220	6-1/2"	▼	87	.184	▼	58.50	10.80		69.30	80.50

For customer support on your Mechanical Costs with RSMeans data, call 800.448.8182.

22 07 Plumbing Insulation

22 07 19 – Plumbing Piping Insulation

22 07 19.50 Pipe Insulation Protective Jacketing, St. Stl.		Crew	Daily Output	Labor-Hours	Unit	Material	2023 Bare Costs Labor	2023 Bare Costs Equipment	Total	Total Incl O&P
1230	7"	Q-14	85	.188	Ea.	58.50	11.05		69.55	81
1240	7-1/2"		83	.193		68	11.30		79.30	92.50
1250	8"		80	.200		68	11.75		79.75	93
1260	8-1/2"		80	.200		70.50	11.75		82.25	95.50
1270	9"		78	.205		107	12.05		119.05	136
1280	9-1/2"		77	.208		105	12.20		117.20	135
1290	10"		76	.211		105	12.35		117.35	135
1300	10-1/2"		75	.213		126	12.55		138.55	158
1310	11"		74	.216		120	12.70		132.70	151
1320	12"		71	.225		136	13.25		149.25	170
1330	13"		68	.235		189	13.80		202.80	229
1340	14"	▼	66	.242	▼	190	14.25		204.25	231
2000	45° elbow, 2 piece									
2010	2-1/2"	Q-14	126	.127	Ea.	12.45	7.45		19.90	25
2020	2-3/4"		123	.130		12.45	7.65		20.10	25.50
2030	3"		120	.133		13.35	7.85		21.20	26.50
2040	3-1/4"		117	.137		13.35	8.05		21.40	27
2050	3-1/2"		115	.139		13.55	8.15		21.70	27.50
2060	3-3/4"		113	.142		13.55	8.30		21.85	27.50
2070	4"		110	.145		17.40	8.55		25.95	32
2080	4-1/4"		108	.148		24.50	8.70		33.20	40.50
2090	4-1/2"		106	.151		24.50	8.85		33.35	40.50
2100	4-3/4"		104	.154		24.50	9.05		33.55	41
2110	5"		102	.157		25	9.20		34.20	41.50
2120	5-1/2"		97	.165		25	9.70		34.70	42.50
2130	6"		92	.174		29.50	10.20		39.70	48
2140	6-1/2"		87	.184		29.50	10.80		40.30	49
2150	7"		85	.188		50	11.05		61.05	72
2160	7-1/2"		83	.193		51	11.30		62.30	73.50
2170	8"		82	.195		51	11.45		62.45	73.50
2180	8-1/2"		80	.200		59.50	11.75		71.25	83.50
2190	9"		78	.205		59.50	12.05		71.55	84
2200	9-1/2"		77	.208		70	12.20		82.20	95.50
2210	10"		76	.211		70	12.35		82.35	96
2220	10-1/2"		75	.213		84	12.55		96.55	112
2230	11"		74	.216		84	12.70		96.70	112
2240	12"		71	.225		91.50	13.25		104.75	121
2250	13"	▼	68	.235	▼	108	13.80		121.80	139

22 11 Facility Water Distribution

22 11 13 – Facility Water Distribution Piping

22 11 13.14 Pipe, Brass

		Crew	Daily Output	Labor-Hours	Unit	Material	2023 Bare Costs Labor	2023 Bare Costs Equipment	Total	Total Incl O&P
0010	**PIPE, BRASS**, Plain end									
0900	Field threaded, coupling & clevis hanger assembly 10' OC									
0920	Regular weight									
1120	1/2" diameter	1 Plum	48	.167	L.F.	12.70	12		24.70	32
1140	3/4" diameter		46	.174		14.60	12.55		27.15	35
1160	1" diameter	▼	43	.186		8	13.40		21.40	29
1180	1-1/4" diameter	Q-1	72	.222		24.50	14.40		38.90	48.50
1200	1-1/2" diameter		65	.246		32	15.95		47.95	59
1220	2" diameter	▼	53	.302		39.50	19.60		59.10	72.50

22 11 Facility Water Distribution

22 11 13 – Facility Water Distribution Piping

22 11 13.14 Pipe, Brass

		Crew	Daily Output	Labor-Hours	Unit	Material	2023 Bare Costs Labor	Equipment	Total	Total Incl O&P
1240	2-1/2" diameter	Q-1	41	.390	L.F.	61.50	25.50		87	105
1260	3" diameter	↓	31	.516		64	33.50		97.50	121
1300	4" diameter	Q-2	37	.649	↓	198	43.50		241.50	283
1930	To delete coupling & hanger, subtract									
1940	1/2" diam.					40%	46%			
1950	3/4" diam. to 1-1/2" diam.					39%	39%			
1960	2" diam. to 4" diam.					48%	35%			

22 11 13.16 Pipe Fittings, Brass

		Crew	Daily Output	Labor-Hours	Unit	Material	2023 Bare Costs Labor	Equipment	Total	Total Incl O&P
0010	**PIPE FITTINGS, BRASS**, Rough bronze, threaded, lead free.									
1000	Standard wt., 90° elbow									
1040	1/8"	1 Plum	13	.615	Ea.	37	44.50		81.50	107
1060	1/4"		13	.615		37	44.50		81.50	107
1080	3/8"		13	.615		37	44.50		81.50	107
1100	1/2"		12	.667		37	48		85	112
1120	3/4"		11	.727		49.50	52.50		102	133
1140	1"	↓	10	.800		80.50	57.50		138	175
1160	1-1/4"	Q-1	17	.941		130	61		191	234
1180	1-1/2"		16	1		189	65		254	305
1200	2"		14	1.143		282	74		356	420
1220	2-1/2"		11	1.455		625	94.50		719.50	830
1240	3"	↓	8	2		955	130		1,085	1,250
1260	4"	Q-2	11	2.182		1,950	147		2,097	2,350
1280	5"		8	3		4,225	202		4,427	4,950
1300	6"	↓	7	3.429		7,900	231		8,131	9,050
1500	45° elbow, 1/8"	1 Plum	13	.615		45.50	44.50		90	116
1540	1/4"		13	.615		45.50	44.50		90	116
1560	3/8"		13	.615		45.50	44.50		90	116
1580	1/2"		12	.667		45.50	48		93.50	122
1600	3/4"		11	.727		64.50	52.50		117	149
1620	1"	↓	10	.800		110	57.50		167.50	207
1640	1-1/4"	Q-1	17	.941		174	61		235	283
1660	1-1/2"		16	1		220	65		285	340
1680	2"		14	1.143		355	74		429	500
1700	2-1/2"		11	1.455		680	94.50		774.50	885
1720	3"	↓	8	2		830	130		960	1,100
1740	4"	Q-2	11	2.182		1,850	147		1,997	2,250
1760	5"		8	3		3,450	202		3,652	4,100
1780	6"	↓	7	3.429		4,775	231		5,006	5,600
2000	Tee, 1/8"	1 Plum	9	.889		43.50	64		107.50	143
2040	1/4"		9	.889		43.50	64		107.50	143
2060	3/8"		9	.889		52	64		116	153
2080	1/2"		8	1		45	72		117	157
2100	3/4"		7	1.143		61.50	82.50		144	191
2120	1"	↓	6	1.333		128	96		224	284
2140	1-1/4"	Q-1	10	1.600		191	104		295	365
2160	1-1/2"		9	1.778		216	115		331	410
2180	2"		8	2		360	130		490	590
2200	2-1/2"		7	2.286		855	148		1,003	1,150
2220	3"	↓	5	3.200		1,300	208		1,508	1,725
2240	4"	Q-2	7	3.429		3,225	231		3,456	3,900
2260	5"		5	4.800		5,075	325		5,400	6,050
2280	6"	↓	4	6		8,350	405		8,755	9,775

For customer support on your Mechanical Costs with RSMeans data, call 800.448.8182.

22 11 Facility Water Distribution

22 11 13 – Facility Water Distribution Piping

22 11 13.16 Pipe Fittings, Brass

		Crew	Daily Output	Labor-Hours	Unit	Material	2023 Bare Costs Labor	2023 Bare Costs Equipment	Total	Total Incl O&P
2500	Coupling, 1/8"	1 Plum	26	.308	Ea.	31	22		53	67
2540	1/4"		22	.364		31	26		57	73
2560	3/8"		18	.444		31	32		63	82
2580	1/2"		15	.533		31	38.50		69.50	91.50
2600	3/4"		14	.571		43.50	41		84.50	109
2620	1"		13	.615		74	44.50		118.50	148
2640	1-1/4"	Q-1	22	.727		123	47		170	207
2660	1-1/2"		20	.800		161	52		213	255
2680	2"		18	.889		265	57.50		322.50	380
2700	2-1/2"		14	1.143		450	74		524	605
2720	3"		10	1.600		625	104		729	845
2740	4"	Q-2	12	2		1,300	135		1,435	1,625
2760	5"		10	2.400		2,375	161		2,536	2,850
2780	6"		9	2.667		3,400	179		3,579	4,025
3000	Union, 125 lb.									
3020	1/8"	1 Plum	12	.667	Ea.	50.50	48		98.50	127
3040	1/4"		12	.667		61.50	48		109.50	139
3060	3/8"		12	.667		61.50	48		109.50	139
3080	1/2"		11	.727		61.50	52.50		114	146
3100	3/4"		10	.800		84.50	57.50		142	179
3120	1"		9	.889		127	64		191	236
3140	1-1/4"	Q-1	16	1		184	65		249	300
3160	1-1/2"		15	1.067		220	69		289	345
3180	2"		13	1.231		296	80		376	445
3200	2-1/2"		10	1.600		1,100	104		1,204	1,350
3220	3"		7	2.286		1,375	148		1,523	1,750
3240	4"	Q-2	10	2.400		4,100	161		4,261	4,750
3320	For 250 lb. (navy pattern), add					100%				

22 11 13.23 Pipe/Tube, Copper

		Crew	Daily Output	Labor-Hours	Unit	Material	2023 Bare Costs Labor	2023 Bare Costs Equipment	Total	Total Incl O&P
0010	**PIPE/TUBE, COPPER**, Solder joints R221113-50									
0100	Solder									
0120	Solder, lead free, roll				Lb.	45			45	49.50
1000	Type K tubing, couplings & clevis hanger assemblies 10' OC									
1100	1/4" diameter	1 Plum	84	.095	L.F.	7.10	6.85		13.95	18.10
1120	3/8" diameter		82	.098		5.15	7.05		12.20	16.20
1140	1/2" diameter		78	.103		5.45	7.40		12.85	17
1160	5/8" diameter		77	.104		8.10	7.50		15.60	20
1180	3/4" diameter		74	.108		7.75	7.80		15.55	20
1200	1" diameter		66	.121		7.65	8.75		16.40	21.50
1220	1-1/4" diameter		56	.143		10.10	10.30		20.40	26.50
1240	1-1/2" diameter		50	.160		13.05	11.55		24.60	31.50
1260	2" diameter		40	.200		20	14.40		34.40	43.50
1280	2-1/2" diameter	Q-1	60	.267		57.50	17.30		74.80	89.50
1300	3" diameter		54	.296		45	19.20		64.20	78
1320	3-1/2" diameter		42	.381		66.50	24.50		91	110
1330	4" diameter		38	.421		85	27.50		112.50	134
1340	5" diameter		32	.500		158	32.50		190.50	222
1360	6" diameter	Q-2	38	.632		246	42.50		288.50	335
1380	8" diameter	"	34	.706		365	47.50		412.50	470
1390	For other than full hard temper, add					13%				
1440	For silver solder, add						15%			
1800	For medical clean (oxygen class), add					12%				

22 11 Facility Water Distribution

22 11 13 – Facility Water Distribution Piping

22 11 13.23 Pipe/Tube, Copper

		Crew	Daily Output	Labor-Hours	Unit	Material	2023 Bare Costs Labor	Equipment	Total	Total Incl O&P
1950	To delete cplgs. & hngrs., 1/4"-1" pipe, subtract					27%	60%			
1960	1-1/4"-3" pipe, subtract					14%	52%			
1970	3-1/2"-5" pipe, subtract					10%	60%			
1980	6"-8" pipe, subtract					19%	53%			
2000	Type L tubing, couplings & clevis hanger assemblies 10' OC									
2100	1/4" diameter	1 Plum	88	.091	L.F.	4.02	6.55		10.57	14.15
2120	3/8" diameter		84	.095		4.59	6.85		11.44	15.30
2140	1/2" diameter		81	.099		4.92	7.10		12.02	16
2160	5/8" diameter		79	.101		6.15	7.30		13.45	17.70
2180	3/4" diameter		76	.105		6.40	7.60		14	18.35
2200	1" diameter		68	.118		6.25	8.50		14.75	19.55
2220	1-1/4" diameter		58	.138		8.85	9.95		18.80	24.50
2240	1-1/2" diameter		52	.154		11.40	11.10		22.50	29
2260	2" diameter	↓	42	.190		24	13.70		37.70	47
2280	2-1/2" diameter	Q-1	62	.258		29	16.75		45.75	57
2300	3" diameter		56	.286		40	18.55		58.55	71.50
2320	3-1/2" diameter		43	.372		60.50	24		84.50	103
2340	4" diameter		39	.410		75	26.50		101.50	122
2360	5" diameter	↓	34	.471		136	30.50		166.50	196
2380	6" diameter	Q-2	40	.600		206	40.50		246.50	287
2400	8" diameter	"	36	.667		292	45		337	385
2410	For other than full hard temper, add				↓	21%				
2590	For silver solder, add						15%			
2900	For medical clean (oxygen class), add					12%				
2940	To delete cplgs. & hngrs., 1/4"-1" pipe, subtract					37%	63%			
2960	1-1/4"-3" pipe, subtract					12%	53%			
2970	3-1/2"-5" pipe, subtract					12%	63%			
2980	6"-8" pipe, subtract					24%	55%			
3000	Type M tubing, couplings & clevis hanger assemblies 10' OC									
3100	1/4" diameter	1 Plum	90	.089	L.F.	5.40	6.40		11.80	15.45
3120	3/8" diameter		87	.092		5.95	6.65		12.60	16.45
3140	1/2" diameter		84	.095		4.42	6.85		11.27	15.10
3160	5/8" diameter		81	.099		4.60	7.10		11.70	15.65
3180	3/4" diameter		78	.103		5.55	7.40		12.95	17.15
3200	1" diameter		70	.114		5.25	8.25		13.50	18.10
3220	1-1/4" diameter		60	.133		7.90	9.60		17.50	23
3240	1-1/2" diameter		54	.148		10.60	10.65		21.25	27.50
3260	2" diameter	↓	44	.182		16.60	13.10		29.70	38
3280	2-1/2" diameter	Q-1	64	.250		27	16.20		43.20	54
3300	3" diameter		58	.276		36.50	17.90		54.40	66.50
3320	3-1/2" diameter		45	.356		57	23		80	97
3340	4" diameter		40	.400		72	26		98	118
3360	5" diameter		36	.444		137	29		166	194
3370	6" diameter	Q-2	42	.571		208	38.50		246.50	286
3380	8" diameter	"	38	.632	↓	293	42.50		335.50	390
3440	For silver solder, add						15%			
3960	To delete cplgs. & hngrs., 1/4"-1" pipe, subtract					35%	65%			
3970	1-1/4"-3" pipe, subtract					19%	56%			
3980	3-1/2"-5" pipe, subtract					13%	65%			
3990	6"-8" pipe, subtract					28%	58%			
4000	Type DWV tubing, couplings & clevis hanger assemblies 10' OC									
4100	1-1/4" diameter	1 Plum	60	.133	L.F.	9.45	9.60		19.05	25
4120	1-1/2" diameter	↓	54	.148	↓	11.90	10.65		22.55	29

22 11 Facility Water Distribution

22 11 13 – Facility Water Distribution Piping

22 11 13.23 Pipe/Tube, Copper		Crew	Daily Output	Labor-Hours	Unit	Material	2023 Bare Costs Labor	2023 Bare Costs Equipment	Total	Total Incl O&P
4140	2" diameter	1 Plum	44	.182	L.F.	16.80	13.10		29.90	38
4160	3" diameter	Q-1	58	.276		35	17.90		52.90	65
4180	4" diameter	"	40	.400		92.50	26		118.50	141
4200	5" diameter	"	36	.444		161	29		190	220
4220	6" diameter	Q-2	42	.571		245	38.50		283.50	330
4240	8" diameter	"	38	.632		785	42.50		827.50	925
4730	To delete cplgs. & hngrs., 1-1/4"-2" pipe, subtract					16%	53%			
4740	3"-4" pipe, subtract					13%	60%			
4750	5"-8" pipe, subtract					23%	58%			
5200	ACR tubing, type L, hard temper, cleaned and									
5220	capped, no couplings or hangers									
5240	3/8" OD				L.F.	.90			.90	.99
5250	1/2" OD					1.36			1.36	1.50
5260	5/8" OD					1.75			1.75	1.93
5270	3/4" OD					2.35			2.35	2.59
5280	7/8" OD					2.80			2.80	3.08
5290	1-1/8" OD					4.02			4.02	4.42
5300	1-3/8" OD					5.30			5.30	5.85
5310	1-5/8" OD					6.90			6.90	7.60
5320	2-1/8" OD					10.50			10.50	11.55
5330	2-5/8" OD					15.10			15.10	16.60
5340	3-1/8" OD					20.50			20.50	22.50
5350	3-5/8" OD					41.50			41.50	46
5360	4-1/8" OD					36			36	40
5380	ACR tubing, type L, hard, cleaned and capped									
5381	No couplings or hangers									
5384	3/8"	1 Stpi	160	.050	L.F.	.90	3.63		4.53	6.40
5385	1/2"		160	.050		1.36	3.63		4.99	6.90
5386	5/8"		160	.050		1.75	3.63		5.38	7.35
5387	3/4"		130	.062		2.35	4.46		6.81	9.25
5388	7/8"		130	.062		2.80	4.46		7.26	9.75
5389	1-1/8"		115	.070		4.02	5.05		9.07	11.95
5390	1-3/8"		100	.080		5.30	5.80		11.10	14.50
5391	1-5/8"		90	.089		6.90	6.45		13.35	17.20
5392	2-1/8"	"	80	.100		10.50	7.25		17.75	22.50
5393	2-5/8"	Q-5	125	.128		15.10	8.35		23.45	29
5394	3-1/8"		105	.152		20.50	9.95		30.45	37.50
5395	4-1/8"	"	95	.168		36	11		47	56.50
5800	Refrigeration tubing, dryseal, 50' coils									
5840	1/8" OD				Coil	21.50			21.50	24
5850	3/16" OD					52.50			52.50	57.50
5860	1/4" OD					29			29	32
5870	5/16" OD					88			88	97
5880	3/8" OD					41			41	45
5890	1/2" OD					58.50			58.50	64.50
5900	5/8" OD					78			78	86
5910	3/4" OD					93.50			93.50	103
5920	7/8" OD					139			139	152
5930	1-1/8" OD					202			202	222
5940	1-3/8" OD					350			350	385
5950	1-5/8" OD					440			440	485
9400	Sub assemblies used in assembly systems									
9410	Chilled water unit, coil connections per unit under 10 ton	Q-5	.80	20	System	2,400	1,300		3,700	4,600

22 11 Facility Water Distribution

22 11 13 – Facility Water Distribution Piping

22 11 13.23 Pipe/Tube, Copper

		Crew	Daily Output	Labor-Hours	Unit	Material	2023 Bare Costs Labor	Equipment	Total	Total Incl O&P
9420	Chilled water unit, coil connections per unit 10 ton and up	Q-5	1	16	System	3,450	1,050		4,500	5,350
9430	Chilled water dist. piping per ton, less than 61 ton systems	▼	26	.615		56.50	40		96.50	122
9440	Chilled water dist. piping per ton, 61 through 120 ton systems	Q-6	31	.774		45	52.50		97.50	128
9450	Chilled water dist. piping/ton, 135 ton systems and up	Q-8	25.40	1.260		145	87	2.53	234.53	292
9510	Refrigerant piping/ton of cooling for remote condensers	Q-5	2	8		480	520		1,000	1,300
9520	Refrigerant piping per ton up to 10 ton w/remote condensing unit		2.40	6.667		179	435		614	845
9530	Refrigerant piping per ton, 20 ton w/remote condensing unit		2	8		228	520		748	1,025
9540	Refrigerant piping per ton, 40 ton w/remote condensing unit	▼	1.90	8.421		380	550		930	1,225
9550	Refrigerant piping per ton, 75-80 ton w/remote condensing unit	Q-6	2.40	10		485	675		1,160	1,525
9560	Refrigerant piping per ton, 100 ton w/remote condensing unit	"	2.20	10.909	▼	640	740		1,380	1,800

22 11 13.25 Pipe/Tube Fittings, Copper

		Crew	Daily Output	Labor-Hours	Unit	Material	2023 Bare Costs Labor	Equipment	Total	Total Incl O&P
0010	**PIPE/TUBE FITTINGS, COPPER**, Wrought unless otherwise noted									
0020	For silver solder, add						15%			
0040	Solder joints, copper x copper									
0070	90° elbow, 1/4"	1 Plum	22	.364	Ea.	8.50	26		34.50	48.50
0090	3/8"		22	.364		8.20	26		34.20	48
0100	1/2"		20	.400		2.95	29		31.95	46.50
0110	5/8"		19	.421		4.65	30.50		35.15	50
0120	3/4"		19	.421		6.50	30.50		37	52
0130	1"		16	.500		16	36		52	71
0140	1-1/4"		15	.533		23.50	38.50		62	83.50
0150	1-1/2"		13	.615		37	44.50		81.50	107
0160	2"	▼	11	.727		66	52.50		118.50	151
0170	2-1/2"	Q-1	13	1.231		121	80		201	252
0180	3"		11	1.455		174	94.50		268.50	335
0190	3-1/2"		10	1.600		585	104		689	800
0200	4"		9	1.778		375	115		490	585
0210	5"	▼	6	2.667		1,625	173		1,798	2,050
0220	6"	Q-2	9	2.667		2,000	179		2,179	2,475
0230	8"	"	8	3		8,000	202		8,202	9,100
0250	45° elbow, 1/4"	1 Plum	22	.364		15.05	26		41.05	55.50
0270	3/8"		22	.364		12.95	26		38.95	53.50
0280	1/2"		20	.400		2.03	29		31.03	45
0290	5/8"		19	.421		22.50	30.50		53	70
0300	3/4"		19	.421		9.05	30.50		39.55	55
0310	1"		16	.500		23	36		59	78.50
0320	1-1/4"		15	.533		30.50	38.50		69	91
0330	1-1/2"		13	.615		37.50	44.50		82	107
0340	2"	▼	11	.727		62.50	52.50		115	147
0350	2-1/2"	Q-1	13	1.231		121	80		201	252
0360	3"		13	1.231		170	80		250	305
0370	3-1/2"		10	1.600		315	104		419	500
0380	4"		9	1.778		345	115		460	550
0390	5"	▼	6	2.667		1,375	173		1,548	1,750
0400	6"	Q-2	9	2.667		2,000	179		2,179	2,475
0410	8"	"	8	3		9,450	202		9,652	10,700
0450	Tee, 1/4"	1 Plum	14	.571		16.90	41		57.90	80
0470	3/8"		14	.571		13.55	41		54.55	76.50
0480	1/2"		13	.615		1.89	44.50		46.39	68
0490	5/8"		12	.667		31	48		79	106
0500	3/4"		12	.667		11.95	48		59.95	84.50
0510	1"		10	.800	▼	14.05	57.50		71.55	101

22 11 Facility Water Distribution

22 11 13 – Facility Water Distribution Piping

22 11 13.25	Pipe/Tube Fittings, Copper	Crew	Daily Output	Labor-Hours	Unit	Material	2023 Bare Costs Labor	Equipment	Total	Total Incl O&P
0520	1-1/4"	1 Plum	9	.889	Ea.	49.50	64		113.50	150
0530	1-1/2"		8	1		74.50	72		146.50	189
0540	2"	▼	7	1.143		118	82.50		200.50	253
0550	2-1/2"	Q-1	8	2		217	130		347	430
0560	3"		7	2.286		315	148		463	565
0570	3-1/2"		6	2.667		990	173		1,163	1,325
0580	4"		5	3.200		735	208		943	1,125
0590	5"	▼	4	4		2,450	259		2,709	3,050
0600	6"	Q-2	6	4		3,325	269		3,594	4,075
0610	8"	"	5	4.800		12,900	325		13,225	14,700
0612	Tee, reducing on the outlet, 1/4"	1 Plum	15	.533		51	38.50		89.50	114
0613	3/8"		15	.533		43.50	38.50		82	105
0614	1/2"		14	.571		40	41		81	106
0615	5/8"		13	.615		81	44.50		125.50	155
0616	3/4"		12	.667		18.45	48		66.45	92
0617	1"		11	.727		87.50	52.50		140	175
0618	1-1/4"		10	.800		86.50	57.50		144	181
0619	1-1/2"		9	.889		92	64		156	197
0620	2"	▼	8	1		150	72		222	272
0621	2-1/2"	Q-1	9	1.778		415	115		530	625
0622	3"		8	2		470	130		600	710
0623	4"		6	2.667		845	173		1,018	1,200
0624	5"	▼	5	3.200		3,650	208		3,858	4,300
0625	6"	Q-2	7	3.429		6,425	231		6,656	7,400
0626	8"	"	6	4		24,800	269		25,069	27,600
0630	Tee, reducing on the run, 1/4"	1 Plum	15	.533		58	38.50		96.50	121
0631	3/8"		15	.533		65.50	38.50		104	130
0632	1/2"		14	.571		55	41		96	122
0633	5/8"		13	.615		22.50	44.50		67	91
0634	3/4"		12	.667		44.50	48		92.50	121
0635	1"		11	.727		70.50	52.50		123	156
0636	1-1/4"		10	.800		114	57.50		171.50	211
0637	1-1/2"		9	.889		196	64		260	310
0638	2"	▼	8	1		250	72		322	385
0639	2-1/2"	Q-1	9	1.778		535	115		650	760
0640	3"		8	2		740	130		870	1,000
0641	4"		6	2.667		1,600	173		1,773	2,000
0642	5"	▼	5	3.200		4,450	208		4,658	5,200
0643	6"	Q-2	7	3.429		6,775	231		7,006	7,800
0644	8"	"	6	4		17,200	269		17,469	19,400
0650	Coupling, 1/4"	1 Plum	24	.333		3.29	24		27.29	39.50
0670	3/8"		24	.333		4.29	24		28.29	40.50
0680	1/2"		22	.364		3.54	26		29.54	43
0690	5/8"		21	.381		9.35	27.50		36.85	51.50
0700	3/4"		21	.381		7.10	27.50		34.60	49
0710	1"		18	.444		14.20	32		46.20	63.50
0715	1-1/4"		17	.471		25	34		59	78
0716	1-1/2"		15	.533		33	38.50		71.50	93.50
0718	2"	▼	13	.615		55	44.50		99.50	127
0721	2-1/2"	Q-1	15	1.067		112	69		181	227
0722	3"		13	1.231		153	80		233	287
0724	3-1/2"		8	2		287	130		417	510
0726	4"	▼	7	2.286		335	148		483	590

22 11 Facility Water Distribution

22 11 13 – Facility Water Distribution Piping

22 11 13.25 Pipe/Tube Fittings, Copper

		Crew	Daily Output	Labor-Hours	Unit	Material	2023 Bare Costs Labor	Equipment	Total	Total Incl O&P
0728	5"	Q-1	6	2.667	Ea.	700	173		873	1,025
0731	6"	Q-2	8	3		1,175	202		1,377	1,575
0732	8"	"	7	3.429		3,775	231		4,006	4,500
0741	Coupling, reducing, concentric									
0743	1/2"	1 Plum	23	.348	Ea.	8.20	25		33.20	46.50
0745	3/4"		21.50	.372		12.40	27		39.40	53.50
0747	1"		19.50	.410		19.40	29.50		48.90	65.50
0748	1-1/4"		18	.444		35.50	32		67.50	87
0749	1-1/2"		16	.500		45	36		81	103
0751	2"		14	.571		85	41		126	155
0752	2-1/2"		13	.615		157	44.50		201.50	239
0753	3"	Q-1	14	1.143		190	74		264	320
0755	4"	"	8	2		385	130		515	620
0757	5"	Q-2	7.50	3.200		2,100	215		2,315	2,625
0759	6"		7	3.429		3,350	231		3,581	4,025
0761	8"		6.50	3.692		8,900	248		9,148	10,200
0771	Cap, sweat									
0773	1/2"	1 Plum	40	.200	Ea.	3.45	14.40		17.85	25.50
0775	3/4"		38	.211		6.40	15.15		21.55	29.50
0777	1"		32	.250		14.95	18		32.95	43.50
0778	1-1/4"		29	.276		19.80	19.90		39.70	51.50
0779	1-1/2"		26	.308		29	22		51	65
0781	2"		22	.364		53.50	26		79.50	98
0791	Flange, sweat									
0793	3"	Q-1	22	.727	Ea.	725	47		772	865
0795	4"		18	.889		1,000	57.50		1,057.50	1,175
0797	5"		12	1.333		1,900	86.50		1,986.50	2,200
0799	6"	Q-2	18	1.333		1,975	89.50		2,064.50	2,300
0801	8"	"	16	1.500		3,775	101		3,876	4,300
0850	Unions, 1/4"	1 Plum	21	.381		109	27.50		136.50	161
0870	3/8"		21	.381		110	27.50		137.50	162
0880	1/2"		19	.421		64.50	30.50		95	116
0890	5/8"		18	.444		250	32		282	325
0900	3/4"		18	.444		80.50	32		112.50	137
0910	1"		15	.533		126	38.50		164.50	197
0920	1-1/4"		14	.571		207	41		248	290
0930	1-1/2"		12	.667		273	48		321	370
0940	2"		10	.800		465	57.50		522.50	595
0950	2-1/2"	Q-1	12	1.333		1,025	86.50		1,111.50	1,250
0960	3"	"	10	1.600		2,650	104		2,754	3,050
0980	Adapter, copper x male IPS, 1/4"	1 Plum	20	.400		46	29		75	93.50
0990	3/8"		20	.400		23	29		52	68
1000	1/2"		18	.444		9.85	32		41.85	59
1010	3/4"		17	.471		16.50	34		50.50	68.50
1020	1"		15	.533		42	38.50		80.50	104
1030	1-1/4"		13	.615		60.50	44.50		105	133
1040	1-1/2"		12	.667		71	48		119	150
1050	2"		11	.727		120	52.50		172.50	210
1060	2-1/2"	Q-1	10.50	1.524		420	99		519	605
1070	3"		10	1.600		525	104		629	730
1080	3-1/2"		9	1.778		360	115		475	565
1090	4"		8	2		685	130		815	945
1200	5", cast		6	2.667		3,000	173		3,173	3,550

For customer support on your Mechanical Costs with RSMeans data, call 800.448.8182.

22 11 Facility Water Distribution

22 11 13 – Facility Water Distribution Piping

22 11 13.25 Pipe/Tube Fittings, Copper

		Crew	Daily Output	Labor-Hours	Unit	Material	2023 Bare Costs Labor	Equipment	Total	Total Incl O&P
1210	6", cast	Q-2	8.50	2.824	Ea.	3,400	190		3,590	4,000
1214	Adapter, copper x female IPS									
1216	1/2"	1 Plum	18	.444	Ea.	15.65	32		47.65	65
1218	3/4"		17	.471		21.50	34		55.50	74
1220	1"		15	.533		49	38.50		87.50	112
1221	1-1/4"		13	.615		71	44.50		115.50	144
1222	1-1/2"		12	.667		111	48		159	194
1224	2"		11	.727		151	52.50		203.50	244
1250	Cross, 1/2"		10	.800		75	57.50		132.50	169
1260	3/4"		9.50	.842		146	60.50		206.50	251
1270	1"		8	1		248	72		320	380
1280	1-1/4"		7.50	1.067		355	77		432	505
1290	1-1/2"		6.50	1.231		505	88.50		593.50	690
1300	2"	▼	5.50	1.455		960	105		1,065	1,200
1310	2-1/2"	Q-1	6.50	2.462		2,225	160		2,385	2,675
1320	3"	"	5.50	2.909	▼	1,225	189		1,414	1,625
1500	Tee fitting, mechanically formed (Type 1, 'branch sizes up to 2 in.')									
1520	1/2" run size, 3/8" to 1/2" branch size	1 Plum	80	.100	Ea.		7.20		7.20	10.75
1530	3/4" run size, 3/8" to 3/4" branch size		60	.133			9.60		9.60	14.35
1540	1" run size, 3/8" to 1" branch size		54	.148			10.65		10.65	15.90
1550	1-1/4" run size, 3/8" to 1-1/4" branch size		48	.167			12		12	17.90
1560	1-1/2" run size, 3/8" to 1-1/2" branch size		40	.200			14.40		14.40	21.50
1570	2" run size, 3/8" to 2" branch size		35	.229			16.45		16.45	24.50
1580	2-1/2" run size, 1/2" to 2" branch size		32	.250			18		18	27
1590	3" run size, 1" to 2" branch size		26	.308			22		22	33
1600	4" run size, 1" to 2" branch size	▼	24	.333	▼		24		24	36
1640	Tee fitting, mechanically formed (Type 2, branches 2-1/2" thru 4")									
1650	2-1/2" run size, 2-1/2" branch size	1 Plum	12.50	.640	Ea.		46		46	69
1660	3" run size, 2-1/2" to 3" branch size		12	.667			48		48	71.50
1670	3-1/2" run size, 2-1/2" to 3-1/2" branch size		11	.727			52.50		52.50	78
1680	4" run size, 2-1/2" to 4" branch size		10.50	.762			55		55	82
1698	5" run size, 2" to 4" branch size		9.50	.842			60.50		60.50	90.50
1700	6" run size, 2" to 4" branch size		8.50	.941			68		68	101
1710	8" run size, 2" to 4" branch size	▼	7	1.143	▼		82.50		82.50	123
1800	ACR fittings, OD size									
1802	Tee, straight									
1808	5/8"	1 Stpi	12	.667	Ea.	2.08	48.50		50.58	74.50
1810	3/4"		12	.667		12.95	48.50		61.45	86
1812	7/8"		10	.800		5	58		63	92
1813	1"		10	.800		138	58		196	238
1814	1-1/8"		10	.800		58	58		116	151
1816	1-3/8"		9	.889		20.50	64.50		85	119
1818	1-5/8"		8	1		89.50	72.50		162	207
1820	2-1/8"		7	1.143		49.50	83		132.50	179
1822	2-5/8"	Q-5	8	2		91.50	131		222.50	295
1824	3-1/8"		7	2.286		131	149		280	370
1826	4-1/8"	▼	5	3.200	▼	305	209		514	650
1830	90° elbow									
1836	5/8"	1 Stpi	19	.421	Ea.	17.10	30.50		47.60	64.50
1838	3/4"		19	.421		2.27	30.50		32.77	48
1840	7/8"		16	.500		12.45	36.50		48.95	67.50
1842	1-1/8"		16	.500		8.35	36.50		44.85	63
1844	1-3/8"	▼	15	.533	▼	44.50	38.50		83	106

22 11 Facility Water Distribution

22 11 13 – Facility Water Distribution Piping

22 11 13.25 Pipe/Tube Fittings, Copper		Crew	Daily Output	Labor-Hours	Unit	Material	2023 Bare Costs Labor	2023 Bare Costs Equipment	Total	Total Incl O&P
1846	1-5/8"	1 Stpi	13	.615	Ea.	37.50	44.50		82	108
1848	2-1/8"		11	.727		28	53		81	110
1850	2-5/8"	Q-5	13	1.231		51.50	80.50		132	177
1852	3-1/8"		11	1.455		73	95		168	222
1854	4-1/8"	▼	9	1.778	▼	160	116		276	350
1860	Coupling									
1866	5/8"	1 Stpi	21	.381	Ea.	.91	27.50		28.41	42
1868	3/4"		21	.381		2.41	27.50		29.91	43.50
1870	7/8"		18	.444		1.84	32		33.84	50
1871	1"		18	.444		24.50	32		56.50	75
1872	1-1/8"		18	.444		3.66	32		35.66	52
1874	1-3/8"		17	.471		6.40	34		40.40	58
1876	1-5/8"		15	.533		8.45	38.50		46.95	67
1878	2-1/8"	▼	13	.615		14.15	44.50		58.65	82
1880	2-5/8"	Q-5	15	1.067		29	69.50		98.50	136
1882	3-1/8"		13	1.231		39.50	80.50		120	164
1884	4-1/8"	▼	7	2.286	▼	250	149		399	500
2000	DWV, solder joints, copper x copper									
2030	90° elbow, 1-1/4"	1 Plum	13	.615	Ea.	50	44.50		94.50	121
2050	1-1/2"		12	.667		66.50	48		114.50	145
2070	2"	▼	10	.800		107	57.50		164.50	203
2090	3"	Q-1	10	1.600		258	104		362	440
2100	4"	"	9	1.778		1,250	115		1,365	1,550
2150	45° elbow, 1-1/4"	1 Plum	13	.615		41	44.50		85.50	111
2170	1-1/2"		12	.667		38.50	48		86.50	114
2180	2"	▼	10	.800		78	57.50		135.50	172
2190	3"	Q-1	10	1.600		175	104		279	350
2200	4"	"	9	1.778		158	115		273	345
2250	Tee, sanitary, 1-1/4"	1 Plum	9	.889		88	64		152	193
2270	1-1/2"		8	1		109	72		181	227
2290	2"	▼	7	1.143		150	82.50		232.50	288
2310	3"	Q-1	7	2.286		630	148		778	915
2330	4"	"	6	2.667		1,400	173		1,573	1,775
2400	Coupling, 1-1/4"	1 Plum	14	.571		21	41		62	84.50
2420	1-1/2"		13	.615		26	44.50		70.50	94.50
2440	2"	▼	11	.727		36	52.50		88.50	118
2460	3"	Q-1	11	1.455		83.50	94.50		178	233
2480	4"	"	10	1.600	▼	184	104		288	355
2602	Traps, see Section 22 13 16.60									
3500	Compression joint fittings									
3510	As used for plumbing and oil burner work									
3520	Fitting price includes nuts and sleeves									
3540	Sleeve, 1/8"				Ea.	.33			.33	.36
3550	3/16"					.33			.33	.36
3560	1/4"					.07			.07	.08
3570	5/16"					.19			.19	.21
3580	3/8"					.68			.68	.75
3600	1/2"					.90			.90	.99
3620	Nut, 1/8"					.29			.29	.32
3630	3/16"					.51			.51	.56
3640	1/4"					.50			.50	.55
3650	5/16"					.50			.50	.55
3660	3/8"				▼	.81			.81	.89

22 11 Facility Water Distribution

22 11 13 – Facility Water Distribution Piping

	22 11 13.25 Pipe/Tube Fittings, Copper	Crew	Daily Output	Labor-Hours	Unit	Material	2023 Bare Costs Labor	Equipment	Total	Total Incl O&P
3670	1/2"				Ea.	1.41			1.41	1.55
3710	Union, 1/8"	1 Plum	26	.308		2.02	22		24.02	35
3720	3/16"		24	.333		1.92	24		25.92	38
3730	1/4"		24	.333		3.88	24		27.88	40.50
3740	5/16"		23	.348		4.52	25		29.52	42.50
3750	3/8"		22	.364		2.75	26		28.75	42
3760	1/2"		22	.364		7.70	26		33.70	47.50
3780	5/8"		21	.381		4.69	27.50		32.19	46
3820	Union tee, 1/8"		17	.471		7.65	34		41.65	59
3830	3/16"		16	.500		4.40	36		40.40	58.50
3840	1/4"		15	.533		7.70	38.50		46.20	66
3850	5/16"		15	.533		5.60	38.50		44.10	63.50
3860	3/8"		15	.533		11.05	38.50		49.55	69.50
3870	1/2"		15	.533		16.90	38.50		55.40	76
3910	Union elbow, 1/4"		24	.333		2.61	24		26.61	39
3920	5/16"		23	.348		4	25		29	42
3930	3/8"		22	.364		8.10	26		34.10	48
3940	1/2"		22	.364		12	26		38	52
3980	Female connector, 1/8"		26	.308		1.64	22		23.64	35
4000	3/16" x 1/8"		24	.333		1.97	24		25.97	38
4010	1/4" x 1/8"		24	.333		3.07	24		27.07	39.50
4020	1/4"		24	.333		4.55	24		28.55	41
4030	3/8" x 1/4"		22	.364		4.12	26		30.12	43.50
4040	1/2" x 3/8"		22	.364		6.55	26		32.55	46
4050	5/8" x 1/2"		21	.381		9.25	27.50		36.75	51
4090	Male connector, 1/8"		26	.308		1.16	22		23.16	34.50
4100	3/16" x 1/8"		24	.333		1.29	24		25.29	37.50
4110	1/4" x 1/8"		24	.333		1.37	24		25.37	37.50
4120	1/4"		24	.333		1.37	24		25.37	37.50
4130	5/16" x 1/8"		23	.348		3.05	25		28.05	41
4140	5/16" x 1/4"		23	.348		1.79	25		26.79	39.50
4150	3/8" x 1/8"		22	.364		3.29	26		29.29	42.50
4160	3/8" x 1/4"		22	.364		4.16	26		30.16	43.50
4170	3/8"		22	.364		4.16	26		30.16	43.50
4180	3/8" x 1/2"		22	.364		5.70	26		31.70	45.50
4190	1/2" x 3/8"		22	.364		5.50	26		31.50	45
4200	1/2"		22	.364		6.20	26		32.20	46
4210	5/8" x 1/2"		21	.381		7.15	27.50		34.65	49
4240	Male elbow, 1/8"		26	.308		4.98	22		26.98	38.50
4250	3/16" x 1/8"		24	.333		2.83	24		26.83	39
4260	1/4" x 1/8"		24	.333		2.91	24		26.91	39
4270	1/4"		24	.333		3.45	24		27.45	40
4280	3/8" x 1/4"		22	.364		6	26		32	45.50
4290	3/8"		22	.364		10.30	26		36.30	50.50
4300	1/2" x 1/4"		22	.364		9.95	26		35.95	50
4310	1/2" x 3/8"		22	.364		15.65	26		41.65	56
4340	Female elbow, 1/8"		26	.308		5.55	22		27.55	39
4350	1/4" x 1/8"		24	.333		6.05	24		30.05	42.50
4360	1/4"		24	.333		7.25	24		31.25	44
4370	3/8" x 1/4"		22	.364		7.15	26		33.15	47
4380	1/2" x 3/8"		22	.364		6.95	26		32.95	46.50
4390	1/2"		22	.364		9.40	26		35.40	49.50
4420	Male run tee, 1/4" x 1/8"		15	.533		7.45	38.50		45.95	65.50

22 11 Facility Water Distribution

22 11 13 – Facility Water Distribution Piping

22 11 13.25 Pipe/Tube Fittings, Copper		Crew	Daily Output	Labor-Hours	Unit	Material	2023 Bare Costs Labor	Equipment	Total	Total Incl O&P
4430	5/16" x 1/8"	1 Plum	15	.533	Ea.	7.40	38.50		45.90	65.50
4440	3/8" x 1/4"		15	.533		11.50	38.50		50	70
4480	Male branch tee, 1/4" x 1/8"		15	.533		8.60	38.50		47.10	67
4490	1/4"		15	.533		8.40	38.50		46.90	67
4500	3/8" x 1/4"		15	.533		5.60	38.50		44.10	63.50
4510	1/2" x 3/8"		15	.533		8.70	38.50		47.20	67
4520	1/2"	▼	15	.533	▼	13.95	38.50		52.45	73
4800	Flare joint fittings									
4810	Refrigeration fittings									
4820	Flare joint nuts and labor not incl. in price. Add 1 nut per jnt.									
4830	90° elbow, 1/4"				Ea.	3.44			3.44	3.78
4840	3/8"					2.97			2.97	3.27
4850	1/2"					3.82			3.82	4.20
4860	5/8"					5.60			5.60	6.20
4870	3/4"					9.85			9.85	10.85
5030	Tee, 1/4"					4.04			4.04	4.44
5040	5/16"					5.30			5.30	5.85
5050	3/8"					4.06			4.06	4.47
5060	1/2"					7.40			7.40	8.15
5070	5/8"					7.50			7.50	8.25
5080	3/4"					9.85			9.85	10.85
5140	Union, 3/16"					2.03			2.03	2.23
5150	1/4"					1.27			1.27	1.40
5160	5/16"					1.90			1.90	2.09
5170	3/8"					1.11			1.11	1.22
5180	1/2"					1.64			1.64	1.80
5190	5/8"					3.81			3.81	4.19
5200	3/4"					15.65			15.65	17.20
5260	Long flare nut, 3/16"	1 Stpi	42	.190		.44	13.80		14.24	21
5270	1/4"		41	.195		1.42	14.15		15.57	22.50
5280	5/16"		40	.200		2.59	14.50		17.09	24.50
5290	3/8"		39	.205		2.42	14.90		17.32	24.50
5300	1/2"		38	.211		2.95	15.25		18.20	26.50
5310	5/8"		37	.216		9	15.70		24.70	33.50
5320	3/4"		34	.235		18.90	17.05		35.95	46.50
5380	Short flare nut, 3/16"		42	.190		6.25	13.80		20.05	27.50
5390	1/4"		41	.195		1	14.15		15.15	22
5400	5/16"		40	.200		1.20	14.50		15.70	23
5410	3/8"		39	.205		.68	14.90		15.58	23
5420	1/2"		38	.211		2.89	15.25		18.14	26
5430	5/8"		36	.222		3.66	16.10		19.76	28
5440	3/4"	▼	34	.235		9.90	17.05		26.95	36.50
5500	90° elbow flare by MIPS, 1/4"					3.79			3.79	4.17
5510	3/8"					4.62			4.62	5.10
5520	1/2"					7.40			7.40	8.10
5530	5/8"					9.40			9.40	10.30
5540	3/4"					13.60			13.60	14.95
5600	Flare by FIPS, 1/4"					7			7	7.70
5610	3/8"					6.90			6.90	7.60
5620	1/2"					9.90			9.90	10.90
5670	Flare by sweat, 1/4"					3.01			3.01	3.31
5680	3/8"				▼	5.90			5.90	6.50
5690	1/2"					6.75			6.75	7.40

22 11 Facility Water Distribution

22 11 13 – Facility Water Distribution Piping

22 11 13.25 Pipe/Tube Fittings, Copper		Crew	Daily Output	Labor-Hours	Unit	Material	2023 Bare Costs Labor	Equipment	Total	Total Incl O&P
5700	5/8"				Ea.	17.90			17.90	19.70
5760	Tee flare by IPS, 1/4"					3.94			3.94	4.33
5770	3/8"					8.90			8.90	9.80
5780	1/2"					14.95			14.95	16.45
5790	5/8"					11.80			11.80	13
5850	Connector, 1/4"					1.52			1.52	1.67
5860	3/8"					2.26			2.26	2.49
5870	1/2"					2.76			2.76	3.04
5880	5/8"					5.50			5.50	6.05
5890	3/4"					7.55			7.55	8.35
5950	Seal cap, 1/4"					.39			.39	.43
5960	3/8"					.31			.31	.34
5970	1/2"					.93			.93	1.02
5980	5/8"					2.63			2.63	2.89
5990	3/4"					8.55			8.55	9.45
6000	Water service fittings									
6010	Flare joints nut and labor are included in the fitting price.									
6020	90° elbow, C x C, 3/8"	1 Plum	19	.421	Ea.	97	30.50		127.50	152
6030	1/2"		18	.444		186	32		218	253
6040	3/4"		16	.500		237	36		273	315
6050	1"		15	.533		251	38.50		289.50	335
6080	2"		10	.800		1,625	57.50		1,682.50	1,875
6090	90° elbow, C x MPT, 3/8"		19	.421		73.50	30.50		104	126
6100	1/2"		18	.444		141	32		173	203
6110	3/4"		16	.500		164	36		200	234
6120	1"		15	.533		445	38.50		483.50	550
6130	1-1/4"		13	.615		620	44.50		664.50	745
6140	1-1/2"		12	.667		920	48		968	1,100
6150	2"		10	.800		525	57.50		582.50	665
6160	90° elbow, C x FPT, 3/8"		19	.421		79	30.50		109.50	132
6170	1/2"		18	.444		152	32		184	215
6180	3/4"		16	.500		188	36		224	261
6190	1"		15	.533		435	38.50		473.50	540
6200	1-1/4"		13	.615		213	44.50		257.50	300
6210	1-1/2"		12	.667		820	48		868	970
6220	2"		10	.800		1,175	57.50		1,232.50	1,375
6230	Tee, C x C x C, 3/8"		13	.615		156	44.50		200.50	238
6240	1/2"		12	.667		272	48		320	370
6250	3/4"		11	.727		211	52.50		263.50	310
6260	1"		10	.800		320	57.50		377.50	435
6330	Tube nut, C x nut seat, 3/8"		40	.200		28.50	14.40		42.90	52.50
6340	1/2"		38	.211		28.50	15.15		43.65	53.50
6350	3/4"		34	.235		55	16.95		71.95	86
6360	1"		32	.250		100	18		118	137
6380	Coupling, C x C, 3/8"		19	.421		95.50	30.50		126	150
6390	1/2"		18	.444		167	32		199	232
6400	3/4"		16	.500		212	36		248	287
6410	1"		15	.533		390	38.50		428.50	490
6420	1-1/4"		12	.667		630	48		678	765
6430	1-1/2"		12	.667		960	48		1,008	1,125
6440	2"		10	.800		1,450	57.50		1,507.50	1,650
6450	Adapter, C x FPT, 3/8"		19	.421		72	30.50		102.50	124
6460	1/2"		18	.444		126	32		158	187

22 11 Facility Water Distribution

22 11 13 – Facility Water Distribution Piping

22 11 13.25 Pipe/Tube Fittings, Copper

		Crew	Daily Output	Labor-Hours	Unit	Material	2023 Bare Costs Labor	Equipment	Total	Total Incl O&P
6470	3/4"	1 Plum	16	.500	Ea.	153	36		189	222
6480	1"		15	.533		325	38.50		363.50	420
6490	1-1/4"		13	.615		188	44.50		232.50	273
6500	1-1/2"		12	.667		690	48		738	830
6510	2"		10	.800		500	57.50		557.50	635
6520	Adapter, C x MPT, 3/8"		19	.421		59	30.50		89.50	110
6530	1/2"		18	.444		113	32		145	172
6540	3/4"		16	.500		155	36		191	225
6550	1"		15	.533		275	38.50		313.50	360
6560	1-1/4"		13	.615		395	44.50		439.50	500
6570	1-1/2"		12	.667		690	48		738	825
6580	2"		10	.800		930	57.50		987.50	1,100
6992	Tube connector fittings, See Section 22 11 13.76 for plastic ftng.									
7000	Insert type brass/copper, 100 psi @ 180°F, CTS									
7010	Adapter MPT 3/8" x 1/2" CTS	1 Plum	29	.276	Ea.	4.16	19.90		24.06	34
7020	1/2" x 1/2"		26	.308		4.35	22		26.35	38
7030	3/4" x 1/2"		26	.308		7.75	22		29.75	41.50
7040	3/4" x 3/4"		25	.320		3.55	23		26.55	38.50
7050	Adapter CTS 1/2" x 1/2" sweat		24	.333		3.03	24		27.03	39.50
7060	3/4" x 3/4" sweat		22	.364		.97	26		26.97	40
7070	Coupler center set 3/8" CTS		25	.320		1.98	23		24.98	36.50
7080	1/2" CTS		23	.348		1.58	25		26.58	39
7090	3/4" CTS		22	.364		1.98	26		27.98	41
7100	Elbow 90°, copper 3/8"		25	.320		3.94	23		26.94	39
7110	1/2" CTS		23	.348		2.76	25		27.76	40.50
7120	3/4" CTS		22	.364		7.65	26		33.65	47.50
7130	Tee copper 3/8" CTS		17	.471		5.10	34		39.10	56
7140	1/2" CTS		15	.533		3.62	38.50		42.12	61.50
7150	3/4" CTS		14	.571		5.55	41		46.55	67.50
7160	3/8" x 3/8" x 1/2"		16	.500		6.55	36		42.55	60.50
7170	1/2" x 3/8" x 1/2"		15	.533		4.22	38.50		42.72	62
7180	3/4" x 1/2" x 3/4"		14	.571		5.30	41		46.30	67.50

22 11 13.27 Pipe/Tube, Grooved Joint for Copper

		Crew	Daily Output	Labor-Hours	Unit	Material	2023 Bare Costs Labor	Equipment	Total	Total Incl O&P
0010	**PIPE/TUBE, GROOVED JOINT FOR COPPER**									
4000	Fittings: coupling material required at joints not incl. in fitting price.									
4001	Add 1 selected coupling, material only, per joint for installed price.									
4010	Coupling, rigid style									
4018	2" diameter	1 Plum	50	.160	Ea.	46	11.55		57.55	67.50
4020	2-1/2" diameter	Q-1	80	.200		51	12.95		63.95	75.50
4022	3" diameter		67	.239		57	15.50		72.50	86
4024	4" diameter		50	.320		85.50	21		106.50	125
4026	5" diameter		40	.400		143	26		169	196
4028	6" diameter	Q-2	50	.480		188	32.50		220.50	255
4100	Elbow, 90° or 45°									
4108	2" diameter	1 Plum	25	.320	Ea.	78	23		101	121
4110	2-1/2" diameter	Q-1	40	.400		84.50	26		110.50	132
4112	3" diameter		33	.485		118	31.50		149.50	176
4114	4" diameter		25	.640		269	41.50		310.50	360
4116	5" diameter		20	.800		760	52		812	915
4118	6" diameter	Q-2	25	.960		1,225	64.50		1,289.50	1,425
4200	Tee									
4208	2" diameter	1 Plum	17	.471	Ea.	127	34		161	190

22 11 Facility Water Distribution

22 11 13 – Facility Water Distribution Piping

22 11 13.27 Pipe/Tube, Grooved Joint for Copper

		Crew	Daily Output	Labor-Hours	Unit	Material	2023 Bare Costs Labor	Equipment	Total	Total Incl O&P
4210	2-1/2" diameter	Q-1	27	.593	Ea.	135	38.50		173.50	207
4212	3" diameter		22	.727		201	47		248	292
4214	4" diameter		17	.941		440	61		501	570
4216	5" diameter		13	1.231		1,225	80		1,305	1,475
4218	6" diameter	Q-2	17	1.412		1,525	95		1,620	1,825
4300	Reducer, concentric									
4310	3" x 2-1/2" diameter	Q-1	35	.457	Ea.	112	29.50		141.50	167
4312	4" x 2-1/2" diameter		32	.500		227	32.50		259.50	299
4314	4" x 3" diameter		29	.552		227	36		263	305
4316	5" x 3" diameter		25	.640		635	41.50		676.50	760
4318	5" x 4" diameter		22	.727		635	47		682	770
4320	6" x 3" diameter	Q-2	28	.857		690	57.50		747.50	845
4322	6" x 4" diameter		26	.923		690	62		752	855
4324	6" x 5" diameter		24	1		690	67.50		757.50	860
4350	Flange, w/groove gasket									
4351	ANSI class 125 and 150									
4355	2" diameter	1 Plum	23	.348	Ea.	350	25		375	425
4356	2-1/2" diameter	Q-1	37	.432		365	28		393	445
4358	3" diameter		31	.516		385	33.50		418.50	475
4360	4" diameter		23	.696		420	45		465	535
4362	5" diameter		19	.842		565	54.50		619.50	700
4364	6" diameter	Q-2	23	1.043		615	70		685	780

22 11 13.29 Pipe, Fittings and Valves, Copper, Pressed-Joint

		Crew	Daily Output	Labor-Hours	Unit	Material	2023 Bare Costs Labor	Equipment	Total	Total Incl O&P
0010	**PIPE, FITTINGS AND VALVES, COPPER, PRESSED-JOINT**									
0040	Pipe/tube includes coupling & clevis type hanger assy's, 10' OC									
0120	Type K									
0130	1/2" diameter	1 Plum	78	.103	L.F.	5.55	7.40		12.95	17.10
0134	3/4" diameter		74	.108		7.70	7.80		15.50	20
0138	1" diameter		66	.121		7.55	8.75		16.30	21.50
0142	1-1/4" diameter		56	.143		9.30	10.30		19.60	25.50
0146	1-1/2" diameter		50	.160		12.85	11.55		24.40	31.50
0150	2" diameter		40	.200		18.55	14.40		32.95	42
0154	2-1/2" diameter	Q-1	60	.267		58.50	17.30		75.80	90
0158	3" diameter		54	.296		44.50	19.20		63.70	77.50
0162	4" diameter		38	.421		72.50	27.50		100	120
0180	To delete cplgs. & hngrs., 1/2" pipe, subtract					19%	48%			
0184	3/4"-2" pipe, subtract					14%	46%			
0186	2-1/2"-4" pipe, subtract					24%	34%			
0220	Type L									
0230	1/2" diameter	1 Plum	81	.099	L.F.	5	7.10		12.10	16.10
0234	3/4" diameter		76	.105		6.35	7.60		13.95	18.30
0238	1" diameter		68	.118		6.20	8.50		14.70	19.45
0242	1-1/4" diameter		58	.138		8.10	9.95		18.05	23.50
0246	1-1/2" diameter		52	.154		11.20	11.10		22.30	29
0250	2" diameter		42	.190		22.50	13.70		36.20	45.50
0254	2-1/2" diameter	Q-1	62	.258		30	16.75		46.75	58
0258	3" diameter		56	.286		40	18.55		58.55	71.50
0262	4" diameter		39	.410		62.50	26.50		89	109
0280	To delete cplgs. & hngrs., 1/2" pipe, subtract					21%	52%			
0284	3/4"-2" pipe, subtract					17%	46%			
0286	2-1/2"-4" pipe, subtract					23%	35%			
0320	Type M									

22 11 Facility Water Distribution

22 11 13 – Facility Water Distribution Piping

22 11 13.29 Pipe, Fittings and Valves, Copper, Pressed-Joint		Crew	Daily Output	Labor-Hours	Unit	Material	2023 Bare Costs Labor	Equipment	Total	Total Incl O&P
0330	1/2" diameter	1 Plum	84	.095	L.F.	4.50	6.85		11.35	15.20
0334	3/4" diameter		78	.103		5.50	7.40		12.90	17.05
0338	1" diameter		70	.114		5.15	8.25		13.40	17.95
0342	1-1/4" diameter		60	.133		7.15	9.60		16.75	22
0346	1-1/2" diameter		54	.148		10.45	10.65		21.10	27.50
0350	2" diameter		44	.182		15.10	13.10		28.20	36
0354	2-1/2" diameter	Q-1	64	.250		28	16.20		44.20	54.50
0358	3" diameter		58	.276		36	17.90		53.90	66
0362	4" diameter		40	.400		59.50	26		85.50	104
0380	To delete cplgs. & hngrs., 1/2" pipe, subtract					32%	49%			
0384	3/4"-2" pipe, subtract					21%	46%			
0386	2-1/2"-4" pipe, subtract					25%	36%			
1600	Fittings									
1610	Press joints, copper x copper									
1620	Note: Reducing fittings show most expensive size combination.									
1800	90° elbow, 1/2"	1 Plum	36.60	.219	Ea.	5.85	15.75		21.60	30
1810	3/4"		27.50	.291		5.70	21		26.70	38
1820	1"		25.90	.309		15.60	22.50		38.10	50
1830	1-1/4"		20.90	.383		24.50	27.50		52	68
1840	1-1/2"		18.30	.437		59.50	31.50		91	113
1850	2"		15.70	.510		57.50	36.50		94	118
1860	2-1/2"	Q-1	25.90	.618		238	40		278	320
1870	3"		22	.727		300	47		347	400
1880	4"		16.30	.982		355	63.50		418.50	485
2000	45° elbow, 1/2"	1 Plum	36.60	.219		5.45	15.75		21.20	29.50
2010	3/4"		27.50	.291		6.90	21		27.90	39
2020	1"		25.90	.309		22	22.50		44.50	57
2030	1-1/4"		20.90	.383		29.50	27.50		57	73.50
2040	1-1/2"		18.30	.437		51	31.50		82.50	103
2050	2"		15.70	.510		70.50	36.50		107	133
2060	2-1/2"	Q-1	25.90	.618		153	40		193	228
2070	3"		22	.727		214	47		261	305
2080	4"		16.30	.982		305	63.50		368.50	430
2200	Tee, 1/2"	1 Plum	27.50	.291		7.40	21		28.40	39.50
2210	3/4"		20.70	.386		12.95	28		40.95	56
2220	1"		19.40	.412		23.50	29.50		53	70.50
2230	1-1/4"		15.70	.510		41	36.50		77.50	100
2240	1-1/2"		13.80	.580		78	42		120	148
2250	2"		11.80	.678		96	49		145	179
2260	2-1/2"	Q-1	19.40	.825		286	53.50		339.50	395
2270	3"		16.50	.970		350	63		413	480
2280	4"		12.20	1.311		500	85		585	675
2400	Tee, reducing on the outlet									
2410	3/4"	1 Plum	20.70	.386	Ea.	10.55	28		38.55	53
2420	1"		19.40	.412		26	29.50		55.50	73
2430	1-1/4"		15.70	.510		37.50	36.50		74	96.50
2440	1-1/2"		13.80	.580		79	42		121	149
2450	2"		11.80	.678		123	49		172	209
2460	2-1/2"	Q-1	19.40	.825		370	53.50		423.50	485
2470	3"		16.50	.970		460	63		523	600
2480	4"		12.20	1.311		555	85		640	735
2600	Tee, reducing on the run									
2610	3/4"	1 Plum	20.70	.386	Ea.	21	28		49	64.50

22 11 Facility Water Distribution

22 11 13 – Facility Water Distribution Piping

22 11 13.29 Pipe, Fittings and Valves, Copper, Pressed-Joint

		Crew	Daily Output	Labor-Hours	Unit	Material	2023 Bare Costs Labor	Equipment	Total	Total Incl O&P
2620	1"	1 Plum	19.40	.412	Ea.	40	29.50		69.50	88.50
2630	1-1/4"		15.70	.510		79.50	36.50		116	143
2640	1-1/2"		13.80	.580		121	42		163	197
2650	2"		11.80	.678		134	49		183	220
2660	2-1/2"	Q-1	19.40	.825		430	53.50		483.50	555
2670	3"		16.50	.970		515	63		578	665
2680	4"		12.20	1.311		645	85		730	835
2800	Coupling, 1/2"	1 Plum	36.60	.219		4.37	15.75		20.12	28.50
2810	3/4"		27.50	.291		6.60	21		27.60	39
2820	1"		25.90	.309		13.25	22.50		35.75	47.50
2830	1-1/4"		20.90	.383		17.10	27.50		44.60	60
2840	1-1/2"		18.30	.437		31	31.50		62.50	81.50
2850	2"		15.70	.510		40	36.50		76.50	99
2860	2-1/2"	Q-1	25.90	.618		119	40		159	191
2870	3"		22	.727		151	47		198	237
2880	4"		16.30	.982		214	63.50		277.50	330
3000	Union, 1/2"	1 Plum	36.60	.219		27.50	15.75		43.25	53.50
3010	3/4"		27.50	.291		34.50	21		55.50	69.50
3020	1"		25.90	.309		55.50	22.50		78	94
3030	1-1/4"		20.90	.383		106	27.50		133.50	158
3040	1-1/2"		18.30	.437		139	31.50		170.50	200
3050	2"		15.70	.510		223	36.50		259.50	300
3200	Adapter, tube to MPT									
3210	1/2"	1 Plum	15.10	.530	Ea.	5.35	38		43.35	63
3220	3/4"		13.60	.588		9.65	42.50		52.15	73.50
3230	1"		11.60	.690		20.50	49.50		70	96.50
3240	1-1/4"		9.90	.808		38.50	58		96.50	129
3250	1-1/2"		9	.889		41.50	64		105.50	141
3260	2"		7.90	1.013		109	73		182	228
3270	2-1/2"	Q-1	13.40	1.194		231	77.50		308.50	370
3280	3"		10.60	1.509		291	98		389	465
3290	4"		7.70	2.078		355	135		490	590
3400	Adapter, tube to FPT									
3410	1/2"	1 Plum	15.10	.530	Ea.	6.65	38		44.65	64.50
3420	3/4"		13.60	.588		10.35	42.50		52.85	74.50
3430	1"		11.60	.690		19.80	49.50		69.30	96
3440	1-1/4"		9.90	.808		45.50	58		103.50	137
3450	1-1/2"		9	.889		63.50	64		127.50	166
3460	2"		7.90	1.013		106	73		179	226
3470	2-1/2"	Q-1	13.40	1.194		261	77.50		338.50	400
3480	3"		10.60	1.509		430	98		528	615
3490	4"		7.70	2.078		550	135		685	805
3600	Flange									
3620	1"	1 Plum	36.20	.221	Ea.	195	15.90		210.90	239
3630	1-1/4"		29.30	.273		278	19.65		297.65	335
3640	1-1/2"		25.60	.313		305	22.50		327.50	375
3650	2"		22	.364		345	26		371	420
3660	2-1/2"	Q-1	36.20	.442		345	28.50		373.50	425
3670	3"		30.80	.519		420	33.50		453.50	515
3680	4"		22.80	.702		470	45.50		515.50	590
3800	Cap, 1/2"	1 Plum	53.10	.151		9.25	10.85		20.10	26.50
3810	3/4"		39.80	.201		14.85	14.50		29.35	38
3820	1"		37.50	.213		24.50	15.35		39.85	50

22 11 Facility Water Distribution

22 11 13 – Facility Water Distribution Piping

22 11 13.29 Pipe, Fittings and Valves, Copper, Pressed-Joint		Crew	Daily Output	Labor-Hours	Unit	Material	2023 Bare Costs Labor	Equipment	Total	Total Incl O&P
3830	1-1/4"	1 Plum	30.40	.263	Ea.	27.50	18.95		46.45	58.50
3840	1-1/2"		26.60	.301		42.50	21.50		64	79
3850	2"		22.80	.351		51.50	25.50		77	94.50
3860	2-1/2"	Q-1	37.50	.427		160	27.50		187.50	218
3870	3"		31.90	.502		202	32.50		234.50	271
3880	4"	▼	23.60	.678	▼	236	44		280	325
4000	Reducer									
4010	3/4"	1 Plum	27.50	.291	Ea.	20	21		41	53.50
4020	1"		25.90	.309		37	22.50		59.50	73.50
4030	1-1/4"		20.90	.383		51	27.50		78.50	97
4040	1-1/2"		18.30	.437		65	31.50		96.50	119
4050	2"	▼	15.70	.510		90.50	36.50		127	155
4060	2-1/2"	Q-1	25.90	.618		228	40		268	310
4070	3"		22	.727		310	47		357	410
4080	4"	▼	16.30	.982		400	63.50		463.50	535
4100	Stub out, 1/2"	1 Plum	50	.160		13.55	11.55		25.10	32
4110	3/4"		35	.229		24.50	16.45		40.95	51.50
4120	1"	▼	30	.267	▼	26.50	19.20		45.70	57.50
6000	Valves									
6200	Ball valve									
6210	1/2"	1 Plum	25.60	.313	Ea.	41.50	22.50		64	79
6220	3/4"		19.20	.417		48.50	30		78.50	98.50
6230	1"		18.10	.442		67.50	32		99.50	122
6240	1-1/4"		14.70	.544		127	39		166	199
6250	1-1/2"		12.80	.625		146	45		191	227
6260	2"	▼	11	.727	▼	269	52.50		321.50	375
6400	Check valve									
6410	1/2"	1 Plum	30	.267	Ea.	42	19.20		61.20	74.50
6420	3/4"		22.50	.356		53.50	25.50		79	97
6430	1"		21.20	.377		34.50	27		61.50	78.50
6440	1-1/4"		17.20	.465		89.50	33.50		123	149
6450	1-1/2"		15	.533		127	38.50		165.50	198
6460	2"	▼	12.90	.620	▼	133	44.50		177.50	213
6600	Butterfly valve, lug type									
6660	2-1/2"	Q-1	9	1.778	Ea.	197	115		312	390
6670	3"		8	2		242	130		372	460
6680	4"	▼	5	3.200	▼	300	208		508	640

22 11 13.44 Pipe, Steel

0010	**PIPE, STEEL**	R221113-50								
0020	All pipe sizes are to Spec. A-53 unless noted otherwise	R221113-70								
0032	Schedule 10, see Line 22 11 13.48 0500									
0050	Schedule 40, threaded, with couplings, and clevis hanger									
0060	assemblies sized for covering, 10' OC									
0540	Black, 1/4" diameter	1 Plum	66	.121	L.F.	9.70	8.75		18.45	23.50
0550	3/8" diameter		65	.123		12.75	8.85		21.60	27.50
0560	1/2" diameter		63	.127		5.60	9.15		14.75	19.80
0570	3/4" diameter		61	.131		7.05	9.45		16.50	22
0580	1" diameter	▼	53	.151		9.70	10.90		20.60	27
0590	1-1/4" diameter	Q-1	89	.180		12.80	11.65		24.45	31.50
0600	1-1/2" diameter		80	.200		15.25	12.95		28.20	36
0610	2" diameter		64	.250		20.50	16.20		36.70	46.50
0620	2-1/2" diameter	▼	50	.320	▼	34	21		55	68

22 11 Facility Water Distribution
22 11 13 – Facility Water Distribution Piping

22 11 13.44 Pipe, Steel		Crew	Daily Output	Labor-Hours	Unit	Material	2023 Bare Costs Labor	Equipment	Total	Total Incl O&P
0630	3" diameter	Q-1	43	.372	L.F.	44	24		68	84.50
0640	3-1/2" diameter		40	.400		63	26		89	108
0650	4" diameter		36	.444		64.50	29		93.50	114
0809	A-106, gr. A/B, seamless w/cplgs. & clevis hanger assemblies									
0811	1/4" diameter	1 Plum	66	.121	L.F.	5.95	8.75		14.70	19.55
0812	3/8" diameter		65	.123		5.95	8.85		14.80	19.70
0813	1/2" diameter		63	.127		4.89	9.15		14.04	19.05
0814	3/4" diameter		61	.131		5.70	9.45		15.15	20.50
0815	1" diameter		53	.151		6.85	10.90		17.75	24
0816	1-1/4" diameter	Q-1	89	.180		8.80	11.65		20.45	27
0817	1-1/2" diameter		80	.200		10.40	12.95		23.35	31
0819	2" diameter		64	.250		12.25	16.20		28.45	37.50
0821	2-1/2" diameter		50	.320		10.10	21		31.10	42
0822	3" diameter		43	.372		23	24		47	61.50
0823	4" diameter		36	.444		37.50	29		66.50	84.50
1220	To delete coupling & hanger, subtract									
1230	1/4" diam. to 3/4" diam.					31%	56%			
1240	1" diam. to 1-1/2" diam.					23%	51%			
1250	2" diam. to 4" diam.					23%	41%			
1280	All pipe sizes are to Spec. A-53 unless noted otherwise									
1281	Schedule 40, threaded, with couplings and clevis hanger									
1282	assemblies sized for covering, 10' OC									
1290	Galvanized, 1/4" diameter	1 Plum	66	.121	L.F.	13.50	8.75		22.25	28
1300	3/8" diameter		65	.123		17.80	8.85		26.65	33
1310	1/2" diameter		63	.127		6.60	9.15		15.75	21
1320	3/4" diameter		61	.131		8.30	9.45		17.75	23.50
1330	1" diameter		53	.151		11.35	10.90		22.25	28.50
1340	1-1/4" diameter	Q-1	89	.180		15.05	11.65		26.70	34
1350	1-1/2" diameter		80	.200		17.90	12.95		30.85	39
1360	2" diameter		64	.250		24	16.20		40.20	50.50
1370	2-1/2" diameter		50	.320		39	21		60	74
1380	3" diameter		43	.372		51	24		75	92
1390	3-1/2" diameter		40	.400		41.50	26		67.50	84.50
1400	4" diameter		36	.444		76	29		105	127
1750	To delete coupling & hanger, subtract									
1760	1/4" diam. to 3/4" diam.					31%	56%			
1770	1" diam. to 1-1/2" diam.					23%	51%			
1780	2" diam. to 4" diam.					23%	41%			
2000	Welded, sch. 40, on yoke & roll hanger assy's, sized for covering, 10' OC									
2040	Black, 1" diameter	Q-15	93	.172	L.F.	12.40	11.15	.69	24.24	31
2050	1-1/4" diameter		84	.190		16.30	12.35	.76	29.41	37
2060	1-1/2" diameter		76	.211		18.45	13.65	.84	32.94	42
2070	2" diameter		61	.262		23	17	1.05	41.05	51.50
2080	2-1/2" diameter		47	.340		32.50	22	1.37	55.87	70.50
2090	3" diameter		43	.372		41	24	1.49	66.49	82.50
2100	3-1/2" diameter		39	.410		44.50	26.50	1.65	72.65	90.50
2110	4" diameter		37	.432		52	28	1.73	81.73	101
2120	5" diameter		32	.500		27	32.50	2.01	61.51	80
2130	6" diameter	Q-16	36	.667		94	45	1.78	140.78	172
2140	8" diameter		29	.828		109	55.50	2.21	166.71	205
2150	10" diameter		24	1		139	67.50	2.67	209.17	256
2160	12" diameter		19	1.263		191	85	3.37	279.37	340
2170	14" diameter (two rod roll type hanger for 14" diam. and up)		15	1.600		192	108	4.27	304.27	375

22 11 Facility Water Distribution

22 11 13 – Facility Water Distribution Piping

22 11 13.44 Pipe, Steel

		Crew	Daily Output	Labor-Hours	Unit	Material	2023 Bare Costs Labor	2023 Bare Costs Equipment	Total	Total Incl O&P
2180	16" diameter (two rod roll type hanger)	Q-16	13	1.846	L.F.	277	124	4.93	405.93	495
2190	18" diameter (two rod roll type hanger)		11	2.182		264	147	5.85	416.85	515
2200	20" diameter (two rod roll type hanger)		9	2.667		297	179	7.10	483.10	600
2220	24" diameter (two rod roll type hanger)		8	3		395	202	8	605	745
2345	Sch. 40, A-53, gr. A/B, ERW, welded w/hngrs.									
2346	2" diameter	Q-15	61	.262	L.F.	11	17	1.05	29.05	39
2347	2-1/2" diameter		47	.340		14.70	22	1.37	38.07	50.50
2348	3" diameter		43	.372		17.60	24	1.49	43.09	57
2349	4" diameter		38	.421		21.50	27.50	1.69	50.69	66.50
2350	6" diameter	Q-16	37	.649		36	43.50	1.73	81.23	106
2351	8" diameter		29	.828		105	55.50	2.21	162.71	200
2352	10" diameter		24	1		148	67.50	2.67	218.17	266
2560	To delete hanger, subtract									
2570	1" diam. to 1-1/2" diam.					15%	34%			
2580	2" diam. to 3-1/2" diam.					9%	21%			
2590	4" diam. to 12" diam.					5%	12%			
2596	14" diam. to 24" diam.					3%	10%			
2640	Galvanized, 1" diameter	Q-15	93	.172	L.F.	13.95	11.15	.69	25.79	33
2650	1-1/4" diameter		84	.190		18.40	12.35	.76	31.51	39.50
2660	1-1/2" diameter		76	.211		21	13.65	.84	35.49	44.50
2670	2" diameter		61	.262		26.50	17	1.05	44.55	55.50
2680	2-1/2" diameter		47	.340		19.75	22	1.37	43.12	56.50
2690	3" diameter		43	.372		25	24	1.49	50.49	65
2700	3-1/2" diameter		39	.410		22	26.50	1.65	50.15	65.50
2710	4" diameter		37	.432		29.50	28	1.73	59.23	76.50
2720	5" diameter		32	.500		27	32.50	2.01	61.51	80
2730	6" diameter	Q-16	36	.667		36.50	45	1.78	83.28	109
2740	8" diameter		29	.828		59	55.50	2.21	116.71	150
2750	10" diameter		24	1		137	67.50	2.67	207.17	253
2760	12" diameter		19	1.263		205	85	3.37	293.37	355
3160	To delete hanger, subtract									
3170	1" diam. to 1-1/2" diam.					30%	34%			
3180	2" diam. to 3-1/2" diam.					19%	21%			
3190	4" diam. to 12" diam.					10%	12%			
3250	Flanged, 150 lb. weld neck, on yoke & roll hangers									
3260	sized for covering, 10' OC									
3290	Black, 1" diameter	Q-15	70	.229	L.F.	21	14.80	.92	36.72	46.50
3300	1-1/4" diameter		64	.250		27	16.20	1	44.20	54.50
3310	1-1/2" diameter		58	.276		25	17.90	1.11	44.01	55
3320	2" diameter		45	.356		30	23	1.43	54.43	69
3330	2-1/2" diameter		36	.444		40.50	29	1.78	71.28	89.50
3340	3" diameter		32	.500		49.50	32.50	2.01	84.01	105
3350	3-1/2" diameter		29	.552		55.50	36	2.21	93.71	117
3360	4" diameter		26	.615		63	40	2.47	105.47	131
3370	5" diameter		21	.762		47	49.50	3.06	99.56	129
3380	6" diameter	Q-16	25	.960		117	64.50	2.56	184.06	227
3390	8" diameter		19	1.263		135	85	3.37	223.37	280
3400	10" diameter		16	1.500		221	101	4.01	326.01	395
3410	12" diameter		14	1.714		264	115	4.58	383.58	470
3470	For 300 lb. flanges, add					63%				
3480	For 600 lb. flanges, add					310%				
3960	To delete flanges & hanger, subtract									
3970	1" diam. to 2" diam.					76%	65%			

22 11 Facility Water Distribution

22 11 13 – Facility Water Distribution Piping

22 11 13.44 Pipe, Steel		Crew	Daily Output	Labor-Hours	Unit	Material	2023 Bare Costs Labor	Equipment	Total	Total Incl O&P
3980	2-1/2" diam. to 4" diam.					62%	59%			
3990	5" diam. to 12" diam.					60%	46%			
4040	Galvanized, 1" diameter	Q-15	70	.229	L.F.	23	14.80	.92	38.72	48
4050	1-1/4" diameter		64	.250		27	16.20	1	44.20	55
4060	1-1/2" diameter		58	.276		31.50	17.90	1.11	50.51	62.50
4070	2" diameter		45	.356		34	23	1.43	58.43	73.50
4080	2-1/2" diameter		36	.444		27.50	29	1.78	58.28	75.50
4090	3" diameter		32	.500		32.50	32.50	2.01	67.01	86.50
4100	3-1/2" diameter		29	.552		31.50	36	2.21	69.71	90.50
4110	4" diameter		26	.615		40.50	40	2.47	82.97	107
4120	5" diameter	▼	21	.762		47	49.50	3.06	99.56	129
4130	6" diameter	Q-16	25	.960		63	64.50	2.56	130.06	169
4140	8" diameter		19	1.263		75.50	85	3.37	163.87	214
4150	10" diameter		16	1.500		205	101	4.01	310.01	380
4160	12" diameter	▼	14	1.714		248	115	4.58	367.58	450
4220	For 300 lb. flanges, add					65%				
4240	For 600 lb. flanges, add				▼	350%				
4660	To delete flanges & hanger, subtract									
4670	1" diam. to 2" diam.					73%	65%			
4680	2-1/2" diam. to 4" diam.					58%	59%			
4690	5" diam. to 12" diam.					43%	46%			
4750	Schedule 80, threaded, with couplings, and clevis hanger assemblies									
4760	sized for covering, 10' OC									
4790	Black, 1/4" diameter	1 Plum	54	.148	L.F.	10.60	10.65		21.25	27.50
4800	3/8" diameter		53	.151		13.35	10.90		24.25	31
4810	1/2" diameter		52	.154		7.75	11.10		18.85	25
4820	3/4" diameter		50	.160		9.60	11.55		21.15	28
4830	1" diameter	▼	45	.178		13.05	12.80		25.85	33.50
4840	1-1/4" diameter	Q-1	75	.213		18.10	13.85		31.95	40.50
4850	1-1/2" diameter		69	.232		21	15.05		36.05	46
4860	2" diameter		56	.286		28.50	18.55		47.05	59
4870	2-1/2" diameter		44	.364		40	23.50		63.50	79
4880	3" diameter		38	.421		52.50	27.50		80	98
4890	3-1/2" diameter		35	.457		39.50	29.50		69	87.50
4900	4" diameter		32	.500		47	32.50		79.50	100
5061	A-106, gr. A/B seamless with cplgs. & clevis hanger assemblies, 1/4" diam.	1 Plum	63	.127		9.55	9.15		18.70	24
5062	3/8" diameter		62	.129		10.80	9.30		20.10	25.50
5063	1/2" diameter		61	.131		7.70	9.45		17.15	22.50
5064	3/4" diameter		57	.140		8.45	10.10		18.55	24.50
5065	1" diameter	▼	51	.157		9.70	11.30		21	27.50
5066	1-1/4" diameter	Q-1	85	.188		12.85	12.20		25.05	32.50
5067	1-1/2" diameter		77	.208		13.70	13.50		27.20	35
5071	2" diameter		61	.262		18	17		35	45.50
5072	2-1/2" diameter		48	.333		20.50	21.50		42	55
5073	3" diameter		41	.390		24.50	25.50		50	64.50
5074	4" diameter	▼	35	.457	▼	32.50	29.50		62	79.50
5430	To delete coupling & hanger, subtract									
5440	1/4" diam. to 1/2" diam.					31%	54%			
5450	3/4" diam. to 1-1/2" diam.					28%	49%			
5460	2" diam. to 4" diam.					21%	40%			
5510	Galvanized, 1/4" diameter	1 Plum	54	.148	L.F.	17.05	10.65		27.70	34.50
5520	3/8" diameter		53	.151		18.45	10.90		29.35	36.50
5530	1/2" diameter	▼	52	.154	▼	5.45	11.10		16.55	22.50

22 11 Facility Water Distribution

22 11 13 – Facility Water Distribution Piping

22 11 13.44 Pipe, Steel

		Crew	Daily Output	Labor-Hours	Unit	Material	2023 Bare Costs Labor	Equipment	Total	Total Incl O&P
5540	3/4" diameter	1 Plum	50	.160	L.F.	6.60	11.55		18.15	24.50
5550	1" diameter	↓	45	.178		7.95	12.80		20.75	28
5560	1-1/4" diameter	Q-1	75	.213		11.05	13.85		24.90	32.50
5570	1-1/2" diameter		69	.232		12.65	15.05		27.70	36.50
5580	2" diameter		56	.286		17.60	18.55		36.15	47
5590	2-1/2" diameter		44	.364		28	23.50		51.50	66
5600	3" diameter		38	.421		36	27.50		63.50	80.50
5610	3-1/2" diameter		35	.457		42	29.50		71.50	90.50
5620	4" diameter	↓	32	.500	↓	53.50	32.50		86	108
5930	To delete coupling & hanger, subtract									
5940	1/4" diam. to 1/2" diam.					31%	54%			
5950	3/4" diam. to 1-1/2" diam.					28%	49%			
5960	2" diam. to 4" diam.					21%	40%			
6000	Welded, on yoke & roller hangers									
6010	sized for covering, 10' OC									
6040	Black, 1" diameter	Q-15	85	.188	L.F.	14.85	12.20	.75	27.80	35.50
6050	1-1/4" diameter		79	.203		19.95	13.15	.81	33.91	42.50
6060	1-1/2" diameter		72	.222		23	14.40	.89	38.29	48
6070	2" diameter		57	.281		29	18.20	1.13	48.33	60
6080	2-1/2" diameter		44	.364		39	23.50	1.46	63.96	79.50
6090	3" diameter		40	.400		50	26	1.60	77.60	95.50
6100	3-1/2" diameter		34	.471		31	30.50	1.89	63.39	81.50
6110	4" diameter		33	.485		37	31.50	1.94	70.44	89.50
6120	5" diameter, A-106B	↓	26	.615		66.50	40	2.47	108.97	135
6130	6" diameter, A-106B	Q-16	30	.800		135	54	2.14	191.14	231
6140	8" diameter, A-106B		25	.960		159	64.50	2.56	226.06	274
6150	10" diameter, A-106B		20	1.200		415	80.50	3.20	498.70	580
6160	12" diameter, A-106B	↓	15	1.600	↓	640	108	4.27	752.27	865
6540	To delete hanger, subtract									
6550	1" diam. to 1-1/2" diam.					30%	14%			
6560	2" diam. to 3" diam.					23%	9%			
6570	3-1/2" diam. to 5" diam.					12%	6%			
6580	6" diam. to 12" diam.					10%	4%			
6610	Galvanized, 1" diameter	Q-15	85	.188	L.F.	9.75	12.20	.75	22.70	29.50
6650	1-1/4" diameter		79	.203		12.90	13.15	.81	26.86	34.50
6660	1-1/2" diameter		72	.222		14.45	14.40	.89	29.74	38.50
6670	2" diameter		57	.281		17.85	18.20	1.13	37.18	48
6680	2-1/2" diameter		44	.364		27	23.50	1.46	51.96	66
6690	3" diameter		40	.400		34	26	1.60	61.60	77.50
6700	3-1/2" diameter		34	.471		34	30.50	1.89	66.39	84.50
6710	4" diameter		33	.485		43.50	31.50	1.94	76.94	96.50
6720	5" diameter, A-106B	↓	26	.615		47	40	2.47	89.47	114
6730	6" diameter, A-106B	Q-16	30	.800		68	54	2.14	124.14	157
6740	8" diameter, A-106B		25	.960		192	64.50	2.56	259.06	310
6750	10" diameter, A-106B		20	1.200		355	80.50	3.20	438.70	515
6760	12" diameter, A-106B	↓	15	1.600	↓	1,000	108	4.27	1,112.27	1,275
7150	To delete hanger, subtract									
7160	1" diam. to 1-1/2" diam.					26%	14%			
7170	2" diam. to 3" diam.					16%	9%			
7180	3-1/2" diam. to 5" diam.					10%	6%			
7190	6" diam. to 12" diam.					7%	4%			
7250	Flanged, 300 lb. weld neck, on yoke & roll hangers									
7260	sized for covering, 10' OC									

22 11 Facility Water Distribution

22 11 13 – Facility Water Distribution Piping

22 11 13.44 Pipe, Steel

		Crew	Daily Output	Labor-Hours	Unit	Material	2023 Bare Costs Labor	Equipment	Total	Total Incl O&P
7290	Black, 1" diameter	Q-15	66	.242	L.F.	24	15.70	.97	40.67	51
7300	1-1/4" diameter		61	.262		29	17	1.05	47.05	58.50
7310	1-1/2" diameter		54	.296		32.50	19.20	1.19	52.89	65.50
7320	2" diameter		42	.381		38	24.50	1.53	64.03	80.50
7330	2-1/2" diameter		33	.485		51.50	31.50	1.94	84.94	106
7340	3" diameter		29	.552		62.50	36	2.21	100.71	125
7350	3-1/2" diameter		24	.667		48.50	43	2.67	94.17	120
7360	4" diameter		23	.696		54	45	2.79	101.79	130
7370	5" diameter		19	.842		99	54.50	3.38	156.88	194
7380	6" diameter	Q-16	23	1.043		170	70	2.79	242.79	295
7390	8" diameter		17	1.412		210	95	3.77	308.77	380
7400	10" diameter		14	1.714		510	115	4.58	629.58	735
7410	12" diameter		12	2		760	135	5.35	900.35	1,050
7470	For 600 lb. flanges, add					100%				
7940	To delete flanges & hanger, subtract									
7950	1" diam. to 1-1/2" diam.					75%	66%			
7960	2" diam. to 3" diam.					62%	60%			
7970	3-1/2" diam. to 5" diam.					54%	66%			
7980	6" diam. to 12" diam.					55%	62%			
8040	Galvanized, 1" diameter	Q-15	66	.242	L.F.	19	15.70	.97	35.67	45.50
8050	1-1/4" diameter		61	.262		22	17	1.05	40.05	51
8060	1-1/2" diameter		54	.296		23.50	19.20	1.19	43.89	56
8070	2" diameter		42	.381		27	24.50	1.53	53.03	68.50
8080	2-1/2" diameter		33	.485		39.50	31.50	1.94	72.94	92.50
8090	3" diameter		29	.552		46.50	36	2.21	84.71	107
8100	3-1/2" diameter		24	.667		51	43	2.67	96.67	123
8110	4" diameter		23	.696		60.50	45	2.79	108.29	137
8120	5" diameter, A-106B		19	.842		79.50	54.50	3.38	137.38	173
8130	6" diameter, A-106B	Q-16	23	1.043		102	70	2.79	174.79	221
8140	8" diameter, A-106B		17	1.412		243	95	3.77	341.77	415
8150	10" diameter, A-106B		14	1.714		450	115	4.58	569.58	675
8160	12" diameter, A-106B		12	2		1,125	135	5.35	1,265.35	1,425
8240	For 600 lb. flanges, add					100%				
8300	To delete flanges & hangers, subtract									
8310	1" diam. to 1-1/2" diam.					72%	66%			
8320	2" diam. to 3" diam.					59%	60%			
8330	3-1/2" diam. to 5" diam.					51%	66%			
8340	6" diam. to 12" diam.					49%	62%			
9000	Threading pipe labor, one end, all schedules through 80									
9010	1/4" through 3/4" pipe size	1 Plum	80	.100	Ea.		7.20		7.20	10.75
9020	1" through 2" pipe size		73	.110			7.90		7.90	11.80
9030	2-1/2" pipe size		53	.151			10.90		10.90	16.20
9040	3" pipe size		50	.160			11.55		11.55	17.20
9050	3-1/2" pipe size	Q-1	89	.180			11.65		11.65	17.40
9060	4" pipe size		73	.219			14.20		14.20	21
9070	5" pipe size		53	.302			19.60		19.60	29
9080	6" pipe size		46	.348			22.50		22.50	33.50
9090	8" pipe size		29	.552			36		36	53.50
9100	10" pipe size		21	.762			49.50		49.50	73.50
9110	12" pipe size		13	1.231			80		80	119
9120	Cutting pipe labor, one cut									
9124	Shop fabrication, machine cut									
9126	Schedule 40, straight pipe									

22 11 Facility Water Distribution

22 11 13 – Facility Water Distribution Piping

22 11 13.44 Pipe, Steel		Crew	Daily Output	Labor-Hours	Unit	Material	2023 Bare Costs Labor	2023 Bare Costs Equipment	Total	Total Incl O&P
9128	2" pipe size or less	1 Stpi	62	.129	Ea.		9.35		9.35	13.95
9130	2-1/2" pipe size		56	.143			10.35		10.35	15.45
9132	3" pipe size		42	.190			13.80		13.80	20.50
9134	4" pipe size		31	.258			18.70		18.70	28
9136	5" pipe size		26	.308			22.50		22.50	33.50
9138	6" pipe size		19	.421			30.50		30.50	45.50
9140	8" pipe size		14	.571			41.50		41.50	62
9142	10" pipe size		10	.800			58		58	86.50
9144	12" pipe size	▼	7	1.143			83		83	124
9146	14" pipe size	Q-5	10.50	1.524			99.50		99.50	148
9148	16" pipe size		8.60	1.860			121		121	181
9150	18" pipe size		7	2.286			149		149	223
9152	20" pipe size		5.80	2.759			180		180	269
9154	24" pipe size	▼	4	4	▼		261		261	390
9160	Schedule 80, straight pipe									
9164	2" pipe size or less	1 Stpi	42	.190	Ea.		13.80		13.80	20.50
9166	2-1/2" pipe size		37	.216			15.70		15.70	23.50
9168	3" pipe size		31	.258			18.70		18.70	28
9170	4" pipe size		23	.348			25		25	37.50
9172	5" pipe size		18	.444			32		32	48
9174	6" pipe size		14.60	.548			40		40	59.50
9176	8" pipe size	▼	10	.800			58		58	86.50
9178	10" pipe size	Q-5	14	1.143			74.50		74.50	111
9180	12" pipe size	"	10	1.600	▼		104		104	156
9200	Welding labor per joint									
9210	Schedule 40									
9230	1/2" pipe size	Q-15	32	.500	Ea.		32.50	2.01	34.51	50.50
9240	3/4" pipe size		27	.593			38.50	2.38	40.88	60
9250	1" pipe size		23	.696			45	2.79	47.79	70.50
9260	1-1/4" pipe size		20	.800			52	3.21	55.21	81
9270	1-1/2" pipe size		19	.842			54.50	3.38	57.88	85
9280	2" pipe size		16	1			65	4.01	69.01	101
9290	2-1/2" pipe size		13	1.231			80	4.94	84.94	124
9300	3" pipe size		12	1.333			86.50	5.35	91.85	135
9310	4" pipe size		10	1.600			104	6.40	110.40	162
9320	5" pipe size		9	1.778			115	7.15	122.15	180
9330	6" pipe size		8	2			130	8	138	202
9340	8" pipe size		5	3.200			208	12.85	220.85	325
9350	10" pipe size		4	4			259	16.05	275.05	405
9360	12" pipe size		3	5.333			345	21.50	366.50	540
9370	14" pipe size		2.60	6.154			400	24.50	424.50	620
9380	16" pipe size		2.20	7.273			470	29	499	735
9390	18" pipe size		2	8			520	32	552	810
9400	20" pipe size		1.80	8.889			575	35.50	610.50	900
9410	22" pipe size		1.70	9.412			610	37.50	647.50	950
9420	24" pipe size	▼	1.50	10.667	▼		690	43	733	1,075
9450	Schedule 80									
9460	1/2" pipe size	Q-15	27	.593	Ea.		38.50	2.38	40.88	60
9470	3/4" pipe size		23	.696			45	2.79	47.79	70.50
9480	1" pipe size		20	.800			52	3.21	55.21	81
9490	1-1/4" pipe size		19	.842			54.50	3.38	57.88	85
9500	1-1/2" pipe size		18	.889			57.50	3.56	61.06	90
9510	2" pipe size		15	1.067			69	4.28	73.28	108

22 11 Facility Water Distribution

22 11 13 – Facility Water Distribution Piping

22 11 13.44 Pipe, Steel

		Crew	Daily Output	Labor-Hours	Unit	Material	2023 Bare Costs Labor	Equipment	Total	Total Incl O&P
9520	2-1/2" pipe size	Q-15	12	1.333	Ea.		86.50	5.35	91.85	135
9530	3" pipe size		11	1.455			94.50	5.85	100.35	147
9540	4" pipe size		8	2			130	8	138	202
9550	5" pipe size		6	2.667			173	10.70	183.70	270
9560	6" pipe size		5	3.200			208	12.85	220.85	325
9570	8" pipe size		4	4			259	16.05	275.05	405
9580	10" pipe size		3	5.333			345	21.50	366.50	540
9590	12" pipe size	↓	2	8			520	32	552	810
9600	14" pipe size	Q-16	2.60	9.231			620	24.50	644.50	950
9610	16" pipe size		2.30	10.435			700	28	728	1,075
9620	18" pipe size		2	12			805	32	837	1,225
9630	20" pipe size		1.80	13.333			895	35.50	930.50	1,375
9640	22" pipe size		1.60	15			1,000	40	1,040	1,550
9650	24" pipe size	↓	1.50	16			1,075	42.50	1,117.50	1,650

22 11 13.45 Pipe Fittings, Steel, Threaded

		Crew	Daily Output	Labor-Hours	Unit	Material	2023 Bare Costs Labor	Equipment	Total	Total Incl O&P
0010	**PIPE FITTINGS, STEEL, THREADED**									
0020	Cast iron									
0040	Standard weight, black									
0060	90° elbow, straight									
0070	1/4"	1 Plum	16	.500	Ea.	17.05	36		53.05	72.50
0080	3/8"		16	.500		24.50	36		60.50	80.50
0090	1/2"		15	.533		10.80	38.50		49.30	69.50
0100	3/4"		14	.571		11.25	41		52.25	74
0110	1"	↓	13	.615		13.35	44.50		57.85	80.50
0120	1-1/4"	Q-1	22	.727		18.95	47		65.95	91.50
0130	1-1/2"		20	.800		26	52		78	107
0140	2"		18	.889		41	57.50		98.50	131
0150	2-1/2"		14	1.143		98	74		172	219
0160	3"		10	1.600		161	104		265	330
0170	3-1/2"		8	2		435	130		565	675
0180	4"	↓	6	2.667	↓	298	173		471	590
0250	45° elbow, straight									
0260	1/4"	1 Plum	16	.500	Ea.	22	36		58	78
0270	3/8"		16	.500		23.50	36		59.50	79.50
0280	1/2"		15	.533		16.55	38.50		55.05	76
0300	3/4"		14	.571		16.65	41		57.65	80
0320	1"	↓	13	.615		19.55	44.50		64.05	87.50
0330	1-1/4"	Q-1	22	.727		26.50	47		73.50	99.50
0340	1-1/2"		20	.800		43.50	52		95.50	126
0350	2"		18	.889		50	57.50		107.50	141
0360	2-1/2"		14	1.143		131	74		205	255
0370	3"		10	1.600		207	104		311	385
0380	3-1/2"		8	2		510	130		640	755
0400	4"	↓	6	2.667	↓	430	173		603	735
0500	Tee, straight									
0510	1/4"	1 Plum	10	.800	Ea.	28	57.50		85.50	117
0520	3/8"		10	.800		26	57.50		83.50	115
0530	1/2"		9	.889		16.85	64		80.85	114
0540	3/4"		9	.889		19.65	64		83.65	117
0550	1"	↓	8	1		17.50	72		89.50	126
0560	1-1/4"	Q-1	14	1.143		32	74		106	146
0570	1-1/2"		13	1.231		41.50	80		121.50	165

22 11 Facility Water Distribution

22 11 13 – Facility Water Distribution Piping

22 11 13.45 Pipe Fittings, Steel, Threaded		Crew	Daily Output	Labor-Hours	Unit	Material	2023 Bare Costs Labor	2023 Bare Costs Equipment	Total	Total Incl O&P
0580	2"	Q-1	11	1.455	Ea.	58	94.50		152.50	205
0590	2-1/2"		9	1.778		150	115		265	335
0600	3"		6	2.667		231	173		404	510
0610	3-1/2"		5	3.200		465	208		673	820
0620	4"		4	4		450	259		709	880
0660	Tee, reducing, run or outlet									
0661	1/2"	1 Plum	9	.889	Ea.	43.50	64		107.50	144
0662	3/4"		9	.889		27.50	64		91.50	126
0663	1"		8	1		23.50	72		95.50	133
0664	1-1/4"	Q-1	14	1.143		31.50	74		105.50	146
0665	1-1/2"		13	1.231		58.50	80		138.50	184
0666	2"		11	1.455		69	94.50		163.50	217
0667	2-1/2"		9	1.778		170	115		285	360
0668	3"		6	2.667		297	173		470	585
0669	3-1/2"		5	3.200		750	208		958	1,125
0670	4"		4	4		580	259		839	1,025
0674	Reducer, concentric									
0675	3/4"	1 Plum	18	.444	Ea.	30.50	32		62.50	81.50
0676	1"	"	15	.533		20.50	38.50		59	80
0677	1-1/4"	Q-1	26	.615		53	40		93	118
0678	1-1/2"		24	.667		75	43		118	147
0679	2"		21	.762		98.50	49.50		148	182
0680	2-1/2"		18	.889		140	57.50		197.50	240
0681	3"		14	1.143		232	74		306	365
0682	3-1/2"		12	1.333		475	86.50		561.50	655
0683	4"		10	1.600		475	104		579	680
0687	Reducer, eccentric									
0688	3/4"	1 Plum	16	.500	Ea.	63.50	36		99.50	124
0689	1"	"	14	.571		68.50	41		109.50	137
0690	1-1/4"	Q-1	25	.640		102	41.50		143.50	175
0691	1-1/2"		22	.727		139	47		186	224
0692	2"		20	.800		184	52		236	280
0693	2-1/2"		16	1		281	65		346	405
0694	3"		12	1.333		440	86.50		526.50	615
0695	3-1/2"		10	1.600		675	104		779	900
0696	4"		9	1.778		885	115		1,000	1,150
0700	Standard weight, galvanized cast iron									
0720	90° elbow, straight									
0730	1/4"	1 Plum	16	.500	Ea.	23.50	36		59.50	79.50
0740	3/8"		16	.500		23.50	36		59.50	79.50
0750	1/2"		15	.533		29.50	38.50		68	90
0760	3/4"		14	.571		23	41		64	86.50
0770	1"		13	.615		30.50	44.50		75	99.50
0780	1-1/4"	Q-1	22	.727		41	47		88	116
0790	1-1/2"		20	.800		64.50	52		116.50	149
0800	2"		18	.889		82.50	57.50		140	177
0810	2-1/2"		14	1.143		170	74		244	298
0820	3"		10	1.600		258	104		362	440
0830	3-1/2"		8	2		410	130		540	650
0840	4"		6	2.667		475	173		648	780
0900	45° elbow, straight									
0910	1/4"	1 Plum	16	.500	Ea.	32	36		68	89
0920	3/8"		16	.500		28	36		64	84.50

22 11 Facility Water Distribution

22 11 13 – Facility Water Distribution Piping

22 11 13.45 Pipe Fittings, Steel, Threaded

		Crew	Daily Output	Labor-Hours	Unit	Material	2023 Bare Costs Labor	Equipment	Total	Total Incl O&P
0930	1/2"	1 Plum	15	.533	Ea.	23	38.50		61.50	83
0940	3/4"		14	.571		26.50	41		67.50	90.50
0950	1"	↓	13	.615		52	44.50		96.50	123
0960	1-1/4"	Q-1	22	.727		76.50	47		123.50	155
0970	1-1/2"		20	.800		90	52		142	177
0980	2"		18	.889		126	57.50		183.50	225
0990	2-1/2"		14	1.143		190	74		264	320
1000	3"		10	1.600		395	104		499	590
1010	3-1/2"		8	2		735	130		865	1,000
1020	4"	↓	6	2.667		690	173		863	1,025
1100	Tee, straight									
1110	1/4"	1 Plum	10	.800	Ea.	28.50	57.50		86	117
1120	3/8"		10	.800		24.50	57.50		82	113
1130	1/2"		9	.889		39.50	64		103.50	139
1140	3/4"		9	.889		37.50	64		101.50	137
1150	1"	↓	8	1		35.50	72		107.50	146
1160	1-1/4"	Q-1	14	1.143		62	74		136	179
1170	1-1/2"		13	1.231		82	80		162	209
1180	2"		11	1.455		102	94.50		196.50	254
1190	2-1/2"		9	1.778		210	115		325	405
1200	3"		6	2.667		690	173		863	1,025
1210	3-1/2"		5	3.200		585	208		793	955
1220	4"	↓	4	4	↓	810	259		1,069	1,275
1300	Extra heavy weight, black									
1310	Couplings, steel straight									
1320	1/4"	1 Plum	19	.421	Ea.	8.60	30.50		39.10	54.50
1330	3/8"		19	.421		9.35	30.50		39.85	55.50
1340	1/2"		19	.421		12.65	30.50		43.15	59
1350	3/4"		18	.444		13.55	32		45.55	63
1360	1"	↓	15	.533		17.20	38.50		55.70	76.50
1370	1-1/4"	Q-1	26	.615		27.50	40		67.50	90
1380	1-1/2"		24	.667		27.50	43		70.50	95
1390	2"		21	.762		42	49.50		91.50	120
1400	2-1/2"		18	.889		62.50	57.50		120	155
1410	3"		14	1.143		74.50	74		148.50	193
1420	3-1/2"		12	1.333		100	86.50		186.50	239
1430	4"	↓	10	1.600		117	104		221	284
1510	90° elbow, straight									
1520	1/2"	1 Plum	15	.533	Ea.	58.50	38.50		97	122
1530	3/4"		14	.571		59.50	41		100.50	127
1540	1"	↓	13	.615		72	44.50		116.50	145
1550	1-1/4"	Q-1	22	.727		107	47		154	189
1560	1-1/2"		20	.800		133	52		185	224
1580	2"		18	.889		164	57.50		221.50	266
1590	2-1/2"		14	1.143		380	74		454	525
1600	3"		10	1.600		535	104		639	745
1610	4"	↓	6	2.667		1,175	173		1,348	1,525
1650	45° elbow, straight									
1660	1/2"	1 Plum	15	.533	Ea.	79.50	38.50		118	145
1670	3/4"		14	.571		80.50	41		121.50	150
1680	1"	↓	13	.615		96.50	44.50		141	172
1690	1-1/4"	Q-1	22	.727		159	47		206	246
1700	1-1/2"	↓	20	.800		175	52		227	270

22 11 Facility Water Distribution

22 11 13 – Facility Water Distribution Piping

22 11 13.45 Pipe Fittings, Steel, Threaded

		Crew	Daily Output	Labor-Hours	Unit	Material	2023 Bare Costs Labor	Equipment	Total	Total Incl O&P
1710	2"	Q-1	18	.889	Ea.	249	57.50		306.50	360
1720	2-1/2"		14	1.143		405	74		479	555
1800	Tee, straight									
1810	1/2"	1 Plum	9	.889	Ea.	91	64		155	196
1820	3/4"		9	.889		91	64		155	196
1830	1"		8	1		110	72		182	228
1840	1-1/4"	Q-1	14	1.143		164	74		238	291
1850	1-1/2"		13	1.231		211	80		291	350
1860	2"		11	1.455		262	94.50		356.50	430
1870	2-1/2"		9	1.778		575	115		690	805
1880	3"		6	2.667		780	173		953	1,125
1890	4"		4	4		1,525	259		1,784	2,050
4000	Standard weight, black									
4010	Couplings, steel straight, merchants									
4030	1/4"	1 Plum	19	.421	Ea.	2.31	30.50		32.81	47.50
4040	3/8"		19	.421		2.78	30.50		33.28	48
4050	1/2"		19	.421		2.95	30.50		33.45	48.50
4060	3/4"		18	.444		3.77	32		35.77	52
4070	1"		15	.533		5.25	38.50		43.75	63.50
4080	1-1/4"	Q-1	26	.615		6.75	40		46.75	67
4090	1-1/2"		24	.667		8.50	43		51.50	74
4100	2"		21	.762		12.20	49.50		61.70	87
4110	2-1/2"		18	.889		37	57.50		94.50	127
4120	3"		14	1.143		52	74		126	169
4130	3-1/2"		12	1.333		92.50	86.50		179	231
4140	4"		10	1.600		92.50	104		196.50	257
4166	Plug, 1/4"	1 Plum	38	.211		5	15.15		20.15	28
4167	3/8"		38	.211		4.16	15.15		19.31	27
4168	1/2"		38	.211		4.81	15.15		19.96	28
4169	3/4"		32	.250		12.90	18		30.90	41
4170	1"		30	.267		13.75	19.20		32.95	43.50
4171	1-1/4"	Q-1	52	.308		15.80	19.95		35.75	47.50
4172	1-1/2"		48	.333		22.50	21.50		44	56.50
4173	2"		42	.381		29	24.50		53.50	69
4176	2-1/2"		36	.444		43	29		72	90
4180	4"		20	.800		93	52		145	180
4200	Standard weight, galvanized									
4210	Couplings, steel straight, merchants									
4230	1/4"	1 Plum	19	.421	Ea.	2.66	30.50		33.16	48
4240	3/8"		19	.421		3.40	30.50		33.90	48.50
4250	1/2"		19	.421		3.61	30.50		34.11	49
4260	3/4"		18	.444		4.53	32		36.53	53
4270	1"		15	.533		6.35	38.50		44.85	64.50
4280	1-1/4"	Q-1	26	.615		8.10	40		48.10	68.50
4290	1-1/2"		24	.667		10.05	43		53.05	75.50
4300	2"		21	.762		15.05	49.50		64.55	90
4310	2-1/2"		18	.889		34.50	57.50		92	124
4320	3"		14	1.143		49.50	74		123.50	166
4330	3-1/2"		12	1.333		107	86.50		193.50	247
4340	4"		10	1.600		107	104		211	273
4370	Plug, galvanized, square head									
4374	1/2"	1 Plum	38	.211	Ea.	13	15.15		28.15	37
4375	3/4"		32	.250		11.65	18		29.65	40

22 11 Facility Water Distribution

22 11 13 – Facility Water Distribution Piping

22 11 13.45 Pipe Fittings, Steel, Threaded

		Crew	Daily Output	Labor-Hours	Unit	Material	2023 Bare Costs Labor	Equipment	Total	Total Incl O&P
4376	1"	1 Plum	30	.267	Ea.	11.65	19.20		30.85	41.50
4377	1-1/4"	Q-1	52	.308		19.40	19.95		39.35	51.50
4378	1-1/2"		48	.333		26	21.50		47.50	61
4379	2"		42	.381		32.50	24.50		57	73
4380	2-1/2"		36	.444		68.50	29		97.50	119
4381	3"		28	.571		88	37		125	153
4382	4"		20	.800		242	52		294	345
4385	8"		20	.800		178	52		230	274
4700	Nipple, black									
4710	1/2" x 4" long	1 Plum	19	.421	Ea.	5.90	30.50		36.40	51.50
4712	3/4" x 4" long		18	.444		7.10	32		39.10	56
4714	1" x 4" long		15	.533		9.90	38.50		48.40	68.50
4716	1-1/4" x 4" long	Q-1	26	.615		12.35	40		52.35	73
4718	1-1/2" x 4" long		24	.667		14.55	43		57.55	80.50
4720	2" x 4" long		21	.762		20.50	49.50		70	96
4722	2-1/2" x 4" long		18	.889		55	57.50		112.50	147
4724	3" x 4" long		14	1.143		70	74		144	188
4726	4" x 4" long		10	1.600		94.50	104		198.50	259
4800	Nipple, galvanized									
4810	1/2" x 4" long	1 Plum	19	.421	Ea.	7.20	30.50		37.70	53
4812	3/4" x 4" long		18	.444		8.95	32		40.95	58
4814	1" x 4" long		15	.533		12	38.50		50.50	70.50
4816	1-1/4" x 4" long	Q-1	26	.615		14.70	40		54.70	75.50
4818	1-1/2" x 4" long		24	.667		18.60	43		61.60	85
4820	2" x 4" long		21	.762		23.50	49.50		73	99.50
4822	2-1/2" x 4" long		18	.889		62	57.50		119.50	155
4824	3" x 4" long		14	1.143		82.50	74		156.50	202
4826	4" x 4" long		10	1.600		111	104		215	277
5000	Malleable iron, 150 lb.									
5020	Black									
5040	90° elbow, straight									
5060	1/4"	1 Plum	16	.500	Ea.	8.40	36		44.40	63
5070	3/8"		16	.500		8.40	36		44.40	63
5080	1/2"		15	.533		5.80	38.50		44.30	64
5090	3/4"		14	.571		7	41		48	69
5100	1"		13	.615		12.20	44.50		56.70	79.50
5110	1-1/4"	Q-1	22	.727		20	47		67	92.50
5120	1-1/2"		20	.800		26.50	52		78.50	107
5130	2"		18	.889		45.50	57.50		103	136
5140	2-1/2"		14	1.143		102	74		176	223
5150	3"		10	1.600		149	104		253	320
5160	3-1/2"		8	2		430	130		560	665
5170	4"		6	2.667		283	173		456	570
5250	45° elbow, straight									
5270	1/4"	1 Plum	16	.500	Ea.	12.65	36		48.65	67.50
5280	3/8"		16	.500		12.65	36		48.65	67.50
5290	1/2"		15	.533		9.60	38.50		48.10	68
5300	3/4"		14	.571		11.90	41		52.90	74.50
5310	1"		13	.615		14.95	44.50		59.45	82.50
5320	1-1/4"	Q-1	22	.727		26.50	47		73.50	99.50
5330	1-1/2"		20	.800		33	52		85	114
5340	2"		18	.889		49.50	57.50		107	141
5350	2-1/2"		14	1.143		143	74		217	269

22 11 Facility Water Distribution

22 11 13 – Facility Water Distribution Piping

22 11 13.45 Pipe Fittings, Steel, Threaded		Crew	Daily Output	Labor-Hours	Unit	Material	2023 Bare Costs Labor	Equipment	Total	Total Incl O&P
5360	3"	Q-1	10	1.600	Ea.	186	104		290	360
5370	3-1/2"		8	2		340	130		470	570
5380	4"	▼	6	2.667	▼	365	173		538	660
5450	Tee, straight									
5470	1/4"	1 Plum	10	.800	Ea.	12.20	57.50		69.70	99.50
5480	3/8"		10	.800		12.20	57.50		69.70	99.50
5490	1/2"		9	.889		7.80	64		71.80	104
5500	3/4"		9	.889		11.20	64		75.20	108
5510	1"	▼	8	1		19.10	72		91.10	128
5520	1-1/4"	Q-1	14	1.143		31	74		105	145
5530	1-1/2"		13	1.231		38.50	80		118.50	162
5540	2"		11	1.455		65.50	94.50		160	213
5550	2-1/2"		9	1.778		142	115		257	330
5560	3"		6	2.667		209	173		382	485
5570	3-1/2"		5	3.200		505	208		713	865
5580	4"	▼	4	4	▼	505	259		764	940
5601	Tee, reducing, on outlet									
5602	1/2"	1 Plum	9	.889	Ea.	13.25	64		77.25	110
5603	3/4"		9	.889		17.25	64		81.25	115
5604	1"	▼	8	1		22	72		94	131
5605	1-1/4"	Q-1	14	1.143		38	74		112	153
5606	1-1/2"		13	1.231		54.50	80		134.50	179
5607	2"		11	1.455		115	94.50		209.50	267
5608	2-1/2"		9	1.778		184	115		299	375
5609	3"		6	2.667		292	173		465	580
5610	3-1/2"		5	3.200		650	208		858	1,025
5611	4"	▼	4	4	▼	595	259		854	1,050
5650	Coupling									
5670	1/4"	1 Plum	19	.421	Ea.	10.45	30.50		40.95	56.50
5680	3/8"		19	.421		10.45	30.50		40.95	56.50
5690	1/2"		19	.421		8.05	30.50		38.55	54
5700	3/4"		18	.444		9.45	32		41.45	58.50
5710	1"	▼	15	.533		14.10	38.50		52.60	73
5720	1-1/4"	Q-1	26	.615		16.20	40		56.20	77.50
5730	1-1/2"		24	.667		22	43		65	88.50
5740	2"		21	.762		32.50	49.50		82	109
5750	2-1/2"		18	.889		89.50	57.50		147	185
5760	3"		14	1.143		121	74		195	244
5770	3-1/2"		12	1.333		239	86.50		325.50	390
5780	4"	▼	10	1.600		244	104		348	425
5840	Reducer, concentric, 1/4"	1 Plum	19	.421		11	30.50		41.50	57
5850	3/8"		19	.421		11	30.50		41.50	57
5860	1/2"		19	.421		9.45	30.50		39.95	55.50
5870	3/4"		16	.500		10.60	36		46.60	65
5880	1"	▼	15	.533		16.45	38.50		54.95	75.50
5890	1-1/4"	Q-1	26	.615		21	40		61	83
5900	1-1/2"		24	.667		27	43		70	94
5910	2"		21	.762		39	49.50		88.50	116
5911	2-1/2"		18	.889		89	57.50		146.50	184
5912	3"		14	1.143		135	74		209	259
5913	3-1/2"		12	1.333		460	86.50		546.50	640
5914	4"	▼	10	1.600		440	104		544	640
5981	Bushing, 1/4"	1 Plum	19	.421		1.63	30.50		32.13	47

22 11 Facility Water Distribution

22 11 13 − Facility Water Distribution Piping

22 11 13.45 Pipe Fittings, Steel, Threaded

		Crew	Daily Output	Labor-Hours	Unit	Material	2023 Bare Costs Labor	2023 Bare Costs Equipment	Total	Total Incl O&P
5982	3/8"	1 Plum	19	.421	Ea.	1.94	30.50		32.44	47
5983	1/2"		19	.421		8.65	30.50		39.15	54.50
5984	3/4"		16	.500		9.45	36		45.45	64
5985	1"		15	.533		9.95	38.50		48.45	68.50
5986	1-1/4"	Q-1	26	.615		12.95	40		52.95	74
5987	1-1/2"		24	.667		16.45	43		59.45	82.50
5988	2"		21	.762		20.50	49.50		70	96.50
5989	Cap, 1/4"	1 Plum	38	.211		9.75	15.15		24.90	33
5991	3/8"		38	.211		9.25	15.15		24.40	32.50
5992	1/2"		38	.211		5.85	15.15		21	29
5993	3/4"		32	.250		7.95	18		25.95	36
5994	1"		30	.267		9.65	19.20		28.85	39
5995	1-1/4"	Q-1	52	.308		12.70	19.95		32.65	44
5996	1-1/2"		48	.333		17.45	21.50		38.95	51
5997	2"		42	.381		25.50	24.50		50	65
6000	For galvanized elbows, tees, and couplings, add					20%				
6058	For galvanized reducers, caps and bushings, add					20%				
6100	90° elbow, galvanized, 150 lb., reducing									
6110	3/4" x 1/2"	1 Plum	15.40	.519	Ea.	16.75	37.50		54.25	74.50
6112	1" x 3/4"		14	.571		21.50	41		62.50	85
6114	1" x 1/2"		14.50	.552		23	40		63	84.50
6116	1-1/4" x 1"	Q-1	24.20	.661		36	43		79	104
6118	1-1/4" x 3/4"		25.40	.630		43	41		84	109
6120	1-1/4" x 1/2"		26.20	.611		46	39.50		85.50	110
6122	1-1/2" x 1-1/4"		21.60	.741		57.50	48		105.50	135
6124	1-1/2" x 1"		23.50	.681		57.50	44		101.50	130
6126	1-1/2" x 3/4"		24.60	.650		57.50	42		99.50	127
6128	2" x 1-1/2"		20.50	.780		67	50.50		117.50	150
6130	2" x 1-1/4"		21	.762		77	49.50		126.50	158
6132	2" x 1"		22.80	.702		80	45.50		125.50	156
6134	2" x 3/4"		23.90	.669		81.50	43.50		125	154
6136	2-1/2" x 2"		12.30	1.301		228	84.50		312.50	375
6138	2-1/2" x 1-1/2"		12.50	1.280		254	83		337	405
6140	3" x 2-1/2"		8.60	1.860		415	121		536	635
6142	3" x 2"		11.80	1.356		360	88		448	525
6144	4" x 3"		8.20	1.951		935	127		1,062	1,225
6160	90° elbow, black, 150 lb., reducing									
6170	1" x 3/4"	1 Plum	14	.571	Ea.	14.65	41		55.65	77.50
6174	1-1/2" x 1"	Q-1	23.50	.681		35	44		79	104
6178	1-1/2" x 3/4"		24.60	.650		40	42		82	107
6182	2" x 1-1/2"		20.50	.780		50.50	50.50		101	131
6186	2" x 1"		22.80	.702		57	45.50		102.50	131
6190	2" x 3/4"		23.90	.669		60.50	43.50		104	131
6194	2-1/2" x 2"		12.30	1.301		138	84.50		222.50	278
7000	Union, with brass seat									
7010	1/4"	1 Plum	15	.533	Ea.	43.50	38.50		82	106
7020	3/8"		15	.533		30	38.50		68.50	90.50
7030	1/2"		14	.571		27	41		68	91.50
7040	3/4"		13	.615		31.50	44.50		76	101
7050	1"		12	.667		40.50	48		88.50	117
7060	1-1/4"	Q-1	21	.762		58.50	49.50		108	138
7070	1-1/2"		19	.842		73	54.50		127.50	162
7080	2"		17	.941		84.50	61		145.50	184

22 11 Facility Water Distribution

22 11 13 – Facility Water Distribution Piping

22 11 13.45 Pipe Fittings, Steel, Threaded

		Crew	Daily Output	Labor-Hours	Unit	Material	2023 Bare Costs Labor	2023 Bare Costs Equipment	Total	Total Incl O&P
7090	2-1/2"	Q-1	13	1.231	Ea.	252	80		332	395
7100	3"		9	1.778		305	115		420	505
7120	Union, galvanized									
7124	1/2"	1 Plum	14	.571	Ea.	36	41		77	101
7125	3/4"		13	.615		41.50	44.50		86	112
7126	1"		12	.667		54.50	48		102.50	131
7127	1-1/4"	Q-1	21	.762		78.50	49.50		128	160
7128	1-1/2"		19	.842		95	54.50		149.50	187
7129	2"		17	.941		109	61		170	211
7130	2-1/2"		13	1.231		380	80		460	540
7131	3"		9	1.778		530	115		645	755
7500	Malleable iron, 300 lb.									
7520	Black									
7540	90° elbow, straight, 1/4"	1 Plum	16	.500	Ea.	29.50	36		65.50	86
7560	3/8"		16	.500		26	36		62	82.50
7570	1/2"		15	.533		35.50	38.50		74	96.50
7580	3/4"		14	.571		38.50	41		79.50	104
7590	1"		13	.615		49	44.50		93.50	120
7600	1-1/4"	Q-1	22	.727		71.50	47		118.50	149
7610	1-1/2"		20	.800		84.50	52		136.50	171
7620	2"		18	.889		121	57.50		178.50	219
7630	2-1/2"		14	1.143		315	74		389	455
7640	3"		10	1.600		360	104		464	550
7650	4"		6	2.667		935	173		1,108	1,275
7700	45° elbow, straight, 1/4"	1 Plum	16	.500		44	36		80	102
7720	3/8"		16	.500		44	36		80	102
7730	1/2"		15	.533		49	38.50		87.50	111
7740	3/4"		14	.571		54.50	41		95.50	122
7750	1"		13	.615		60	44.50		104.50	132
7760	1-1/4"	Q-1	22	.727		96.50	47		143.50	177
7770	1-1/2"		20	.800		126	52		178	216
7780	2"		18	.889		190	57.50		247.50	295
7790	2-1/2"		14	1.143		445	74		519	600
7800	3"		10	1.600		585	104		689	795
7810	4"		6	2.667		1,325	173		1,498	1,700
7850	Tee, straight, 1/4"	1 Plum	10	.800		37	57.50		94.50	127
7870	3/8"		10	.800		39.50	57.50		97	129
7880	1/2"		9	.889		50	64		114	151
7890	3/4"		9	.889		54	64		118	155
7900	1"		8	1		65	72		137	179
7910	1-1/4"	Q-1	14	1.143		93	74		167	213
7920	1-1/2"		13	1.231		109	80		189	239
7930	2"		11	1.455		160	94.50		254.50	315
7940	2-1/2"		9	1.778		410	115		525	620
7950	3"		6	2.667		555	173		728	870
7960	4"		4	4		1,650	259		1,909	2,200
8050	Couplings, straight, 1/4"	1 Plum	19	.421		26.50	30.50		57	74.50
8070	3/8"		19	.421		26.50	30.50		57	74.50
8080	1/2"		19	.421		29.50	30.50		60	77.50
8090	3/4"		18	.444		34	32		66	85.50
8100	1"		15	.533		39	38.50		77.50	101
8110	1-1/4"	Q-1	26	.615		46.50	40		86.50	111
8120	1-1/2"		24	.667		69.50	43		112.50	141

22 11 Facility Water Distribution

22 11 13 – Facility Water Distribution Piping

22 11 13.45 Pipe Fittings, Steel, Threaded		Crew	Daily Output	Labor-Hours	Unit	Material	2023 Bare Costs Labor	Equipment	Total	Total Incl O&P
8130	2"	Q-1	21	.762	Ea.	100	49.50		149.50	184
8140	2-1/2"		18	.889		193	57.50		250.50	298
8150	3"		14	1.143		278	74		352	415
8160	4"		10	1.600		525	104		629	730
8162	6"	▼	10	1.600	▼	525	104		629	730
8200	Galvanized									
8220	90° elbow, straight, 1/4"	1 Plum	16	.500	Ea.	53	36		89	112
8222	3/8"		16	.500		54	36		90	113
8224	1/2"		15	.533		64	38.50		102.50	128
8226	3/4"		14	.571		72	41		113	141
8228	1"	▼	13	.615		92.50	44.50		137	168
8230	1-1/4"	Q-1	22	.727		145	47		192	230
8232	1-1/2"		20	.800		157	52		209	251
8234	2"		18	.889		264	57.50		321.50	375
8236	2-1/2"		14	1.143		590	74		664	755
8238	3"		10	1.600		695	104		799	915
8240	4"	▼	6	2.667	▼	2,175	173		2,348	2,625
8280	45° elbow, straight									
8282	1/2"	1 Plum	15	.533	Ea.	103	38.50		141.50	172
8284	3/4"		14	.571		110	41		151	183
8286	1"	▼	13	.615		120	44.50		164.50	198
8288	1-1/4"	Q-1	22	.727		187	47		234	276
8290	1-1/2"		20	.800		242	52		294	345
8292	2"	▼	18	.889		335	57.50		392.50	455
8310	Tee, straight, 1/4"	1 Plum	10	.800		75	57.50		132.50	169
8312	3/8"		10	.800		76.50	57.50		134	170
8314	1/2"		9	.889		96	64		160	201
8316	3/4"		9	.889		105	64		169	212
8318	1"		8	1		130	72		202	250
8320	1-1/4"	Q-1	14	1.143		186	74		260	315
8322	1-1/2"		13	1.231		193	80		273	330
8324	2"		11	1.455		310	94.50		404.50	480
8326	2-1/2"		9	1.778		975	115		1,090	1,250
8328	3"		6	2.667		1,100	173		1,273	1,475
8330	4"	▼	4	4		2,975	259		3,234	3,650
8380	Couplings, straight, 1/4"	1 Plum	19	.421		34.50	30.50		65	83
8382	3/8"		19	.421		50	30.50		80.50	100
8384	1/2"		19	.421		51	30.50		81.50	101
8386	3/4"		18	.444		57.50	32		89.50	112
8388	1"	▼	15	.533		76.50	38.50		115	142
8390	1-1/4"	Q-1	26	.615		99.50	40		139.50	170
8392	1-1/2"		24	.667		141	43		184	220
8394	2"		21	.762		170	49.50		219.50	261
8396	2-1/2"		18	.889		470	57.50		527.50	600
8398	3"		14	1.143		560	74		634	725
8399	4"	▼	10	1.600	▼	920	104		1,024	1,175
8529	Black									
8530	Reducer, concentric, 1/4"	1 Plum	19	.421	Ea.	36.50	30.50		67	85.50
8531	3/8"		19	.421		35	30.50		65.50	83.50
8532	1/2"		17	.471		42.50	34		76.50	97
8533	3/4"		16	.500		43.50	36		79.50	101
8534	1"	▼	15	.533		51.50	38.50		90	115
8535	1-1/4"	Q-1	26	.615		68	40		108	135

22 11 Facility Water Distribution

22 11 13 – Facility Water Distribution Piping

22 11 13.45 Pipe Fittings, Steel, Threaded

		Crew	Daily Output	Labor-Hours	Unit	Material	2023 Bare Costs Labor	Equipment	Total	Total Incl O&P
8536	1-1/2"	Q-1	24	.667	Ea.	106	43		149	182
8537	2"	↓	21	.762		134	49.50		183.50	221
8550	Cap, 1/4"	1 Plum	38	.211		27.50	15.15		42.65	52.50
8551	3/8"		38	.211		27.50	15.15		42.65	52.50
8552	1/2"		34	.235		27	16.95		43.95	55
8553	3/4"		32	.250		34	18		52	64.50
8554	1"	↓	30	.267		45	19.20		64.20	78
8555	1-1/4"	Q-1	52	.308		49.50	19.95		69.45	84.50
8556	1-1/2"		48	.333		72.50	21.50		94	112
8557	2"	↓	42	.381		101	24.50		125.50	148
8570	Plug, 1/4"	1 Plum	38	.211		5.50	15.15		20.65	28.50
8571	3/8"		38	.211		5.75	15.15		20.90	29
8572	1/2"		34	.235		6	16.95		22.95	32
8573	3/4"		32	.250		7.50	18		25.50	35.50
8574	1"	↓	30	.267		11.50	19.20		30.70	41
8575	1-1/4"	Q-1	52	.308		23.50	19.95		43.45	56
8576	1-1/2"		48	.333		27	21.50		48.50	61.50
8577	2"	↓	42	.381		42.50	24.50		67	84
9500	Union with brass seat, 1/4"	1 Plum	15	.533		63.50	38.50		102	128
9530	3/8"		15	.533		64.50	38.50		103	129
9540	1/2"		14	.571		52	41		93	119
9550	3/4"		13	.615		57.50	44.50		102	130
9560	1"	↓	12	.667		75.50	48		123.50	155
9570	1-1/4"	Q-1	21	.762		123	49.50		172.50	209
9580	1-1/2"		19	.842		129	54.50		183.50	224
9590	2"		17	.941		159	61		220	266
9600	2-1/2"		13	1.231		515	80		595	685
9610	3"		9	1.778		665	115		780	900
9620	4"		5	3.200		2,325	208		2,533	2,850
9630	Union, all iron, 1/4"	1 Plum	15	.533		98.50	38.50		137	166
9650	3/8"		15	.533		98.50	38.50		137	166
9660	1/2"		14	.571		104	41		145	176
9670	3/4"		13	.615		111	44.50		155.50	189
9680	1"	↓	12	.667		137	48		185	222
9690	1-1/4"	Q-1	21	.762		210	49.50		259.50	305
9700	1-1/2"		19	.842		128	54.50		182.50	223
9710	2"		17	.941		108	61		169	210
9720	2-1/2"		13	1.231		144	80		224	277
9730	3"		9	1.778		218	115		333	410
9750	For galvanized unions, add				↓	15%				
9757	Forged steel, 3000 lb.									
9758	Black									
9760	90° elbow, 1/4"	1 Plum	16	.500	Ea.	32.50	36		68.50	89
9761	3/8"		16	.500		32.50	36		68.50	89
9762	1/2"		15	.533		25	38.50		63.50	84.50
9763	3/4"		14	.571		31	41		72	95.50
9764	1"	↓	13	.615		46	44.50		90.50	117
9765	1-1/4"	Q-1	22	.727		88	47		135	167
9766	1-1/2"		20	.800		113	52		165	203
9767	2"	↓	18	.889		137	57.50		194.50	237
9780	45° elbow, 1/4"	1 Plum	16	.500		41	36		77	98.50
9781	3/8"		16	.500		41	36		77	98.50
9782	1/2"		15	.533		40.50	38.50		79	102

22 11 Facility Water Distribution

22 11 13 – Facility Water Distribution Piping

22 11 13.45 Pipe Fittings, Steel, Threaded		Crew	Daily Output	Labor-Hours	Unit	Material	2023 Bare Costs Labor	Equipment	Total	Total Incl O&P
9783	3/4"	1 Plum	14	.571	Ea.	46.50	41		87.50	113
9784	1"	↓	13	.615		63.50	44.50		108	136
9785	1-1/4"	Q-1	22	.727		88	47		135	168
9786	1-1/2"		20	.800		126	52		178	217
9787	2"	↓	18	.889		174	57.50		231.50	278
9800	Tee, 1/4"	1 Plum	10	.800		39.50	57.50		97	129
9801	3/8"		10	.800		39.50	57.50		97	129
9802	1/2"		9	.889		35.50	64		99.50	135
9803	3/4"		9	.889		47.50	64		111.50	148
9804	1"		8	1		63	72		135	176
9805	1-1/4"	Q-1	14	1.143		122	74		196	245
9806	1-1/2"		13	1.231		142	80		222	276
9807	2"	↓	11	1.455		184	94.50		278.50	345
9820	Reducer, concentric, 1/4"	1 Plum	19	.421		19.75	30.50		50.25	66.50
9821	3/8"		19	.421		20.50	30.50		51	67.50
9822	1/2"		17	.471		20.50	34		54.50	73
9823	3/4"		16	.500		24.50	36		60.50	80.50
9824	1"	↓	15	.533		32	38.50		70.50	92.50
9825	1-1/4"	Q-1	26	.615		56	40		96	121
9826	1-1/2"		24	.667		60.50	43		103.50	131
9827	2"	↓	21	.762		88	49.50		137.50	170
9840	Cap, 1/4"	1 Plum	38	.211		12.15	15.15		27.30	36
9841	3/8"		38	.211		12.15	15.15		27.30	36
9842	1/2"		34	.235		11.80	16.95		28.75	38.50
9843	3/4"		32	.250		16.45	18		34.45	45
9844	1"	↓	30	.267		25.50	19.20		44.70	56.50
9845	1-1/4"	Q-1	52	.308		40.50	19.95		60.45	74.50
9846	1-1/2"		48	.333		48.50	21.50		70	85.50
9847	2"	↓	42	.381		70	24.50		94.50	114
9860	Plug, 1/4"	1 Plum	38	.211		4.53	15.15		19.68	27.50
9861	3/8"		38	.211		5.90	15.15		21.05	29
9862	1/2"		34	.235		4.90	16.95		21.85	31
9863	3/4"		32	.250		6.20	18		24.20	34
9864	1"	↓	30	.267		9.50	19.20		28.70	39
9865	1-1/4"	Q-1	52	.308		22.50	19.95		42.45	54.50
9866	1-1/2"		48	.333		29.50	21.50		51	64.50
9867	2"	↓	42	.381		47	24.50		71.50	88.50
9880	Union, bronze seat, 1/4"	1 Plum	15	.533		89.50	38.50		128	156
9881	3/8"		15	.533		89.50	38.50		128	156
9882	1/2"		14	.571		86	41		127	156
9883	3/4"		13	.615		115	44.50		159.50	192
9884	1"	↓	12	.667		130	48		178	215
9885	1-1/4"	Q-1	21	.762		252	49.50		301.50	350
9886	1-1/2"		19	.842		260	54.50		314.50	370
9887	2"	↓	17	.941		355	61		416	480
9900	Coupling, 1/4"	1 Plum	19	.421		12.55	30.50		43.05	59
9901	3/8"		19	.421		12.55	30.50		43.05	59
9902	1/2"		17	.471		10.35	34		44.35	62
9903	3/4"		16	.500		13.45	36		49.45	68.50
9904	1"	↓	15	.533		23.50	38.50		62	83.50
9905	1-1/4"	Q-1	26	.615		39	40		79	103
9906	1-1/2"		24	.667		50.50	43		93.50	120
9907	2"	↓	21	.762		63	49.50		112.50	143

22 11 Facility Water Distribution

22 11 13 – Facility Water Distribution Piping

22 11 13.47 Pipe Fittings, Steel	Crew	Daily Output	Labor-Hours	Unit	Material	2023 Bare Costs Labor	Equipment	Total	Total Incl O&P
0010 **PIPE FITTINGS, STEEL**, flanged, welded & special									
0020 Flanged joints, CI, standard weight, black. One gasket & bolt									
0040 set, mat'l only, required at each joint, not included (see line 0620)									
0060 90° elbow, straight, 1-1/2" pipe size	Q-1	14	1.143	Ea.	1,025	74		1,099	1,225
0080 2" pipe size		13	1.231		570	80		650	745
0090 2-1/2" pipe size		12	1.333		615	86.50		701.50	805
0100 3" pipe size		11	1.455		515	94.50		609.50	705
0110 4" pipe size		8	2		635	130		765	895
0120 5" pipe size		7	2.286		1,500	148		1,648	1,875
0130 6" pipe size	Q-2	9	2.667		995	179		1,174	1,375
0140 8" pipe size		8	3		1,725	202		1,927	2,200
0150 10" pipe size		7	3.429		3,775	231		4,006	4,500
0160 12" pipe size		6	4		7,575	269		7,844	8,725
0171 90° elbow, reducing									
0172 2-1/2" by 2" pipe size	Q-1	12	1.333	Ea.	2,000	86.50		2,086.50	2,325
0173 3" by 2-1/2" pipe size		11	1.455		1,900	94.50		1,994.50	2,250
0174 4" by 3" pipe size		8	2		1,400	130		1,530	1,750
0175 5" by 3" pipe size		7	2.286		3,775	148		3,923	4,375
0176 6" by 4" pipe size	Q-2	9	2.667		1,750	179		1,929	2,200
0177 8" by 6" pipe size		8	3		2,550	202		2,752	3,100
0178 10" by 8" pipe size		7	3.429		4,850	231		5,081	5,700
0179 12" by 10" pipe size		6	4		9,300	269		9,569	10,600
0200 45° elbow, straight, 1-1/2" pipe size	Q-1	14	1.143		1,450	74		1,524	1,700
0220 2" pipe size		13	1.231		825	80		905	1,025
0230 2-1/2" pipe size		12	1.333		880	86.50		966.50	1,100
0240 3" pipe size		11	1.455		855	94.50		949.50	1,075
0250 4" pipe size		8	2		965	130		1,095	1,250
0260 5" pipe size		7	2.286		2,300	148		2,448	2,750
0270 6" pipe size	Q-2	9	2.667		1,575	179		1,754	2,000
0280 8" pipe size		8	3		2,300	202		2,502	2,825
0290 10" pipe size		7	3.429		4,875	231		5,106	5,700
0300 12" pipe size		6	4		7,425	269		7,694	8,575
0310 Cross, straight									
0311 2-1/2" pipe size	Q-1	6	2.667	Ea.	2,225	173		2,398	2,675
0312 3" pipe size		5	3.200		1,900	208		2,108	2,400
0313 4" pipe size		4	4		2,475	259		2,734	3,100
0314 5" pipe size		3	5.333		6,550	345		6,895	7,750
0315 6" pipe size	Q-2	5	4.800		5,200	325		5,525	6,200
0316 8" pipe size		4	6		955	405		1,360	1,650
0317 10" pipe size		3	8		1,875	540		2,415	2,875
0318 12" pipe size		2	12		2,125	805		2,930	3,550
0350 Tee, straight, 1-1/2" pipe size	Q-1	10	1.600		1,200	104		1,304	1,450
0370 2" pipe size		9	1.778		625	115		740	855
0380 2-1/2" pipe size		8	2		910	130		1,040	1,200
0390 3" pipe size		7	2.286		635	148		783	920
0400 4" pipe size		5	3.200		970	208		1,178	1,375
0410 5" pipe size		4	4		2,600	259		2,859	3,225
0420 6" pipe size	Q-2	6	4		1,400	269		1,669	1,950
0430 8" pipe size		5	4.800		2,400	325		2,725	3,125
0440 10" pipe size		4	6		6,450	405		6,855	7,700
0450 12" pipe size		3	8		10,100	540		10,640	12,000
0459 Tee, reducing on outlet									

22 11 Facility Water Distribution

22 11 13 – Facility Water Distribution Piping

22 11 13.47 Pipe Fittings, Steel		Crew	Daily Output	Labor-Hours	Unit	Material	2023 Bare Costs Labor	2023 Bare Costs Equipment	Total	Total Incl O&P
0460	2-1/2" by 2" pipe size	Q-1	8	2	Ea.	520	130		650	765
0461	3" by 2-1/2" pipe size		7	2.286		266	148		414	515
0462	4" by 3" pipe size		5	3.200		2,000	208		2,208	2,500
0463	5" by 4" pipe size		4	4		850	259		1,109	1,325
0464	6" by 4" pipe size	Q-2	6	4		1,925	269		2,194	2,500
0465	8" by 6" pipe size		5	4.800		3,000	325		3,325	3,775
0466	10" by 8" pipe size		4	6		6,850	405		7,255	8,125
0467	12" by 10" pipe size		3	8		1,700	540		2,240	2,675
0476	Reducer, concentric									
0477	3" by 2-1/2"	Q-1	12	1.333	Ea.	1,150	86.50		1,236.50	1,375
0478	4" by 3"		9	1.778		1,275	115		1,390	1,575
0479	5" by 4"		8	2		1,975	130		2,105	2,375
0480	6" by 4"	Q-2	10	2.400		1,725	161		1,886	2,125
0481	8" by 6"		9	2.667		2,150	179		2,329	2,650
0482	10" by 8"		8	3		4,450	202		4,652	5,200
0483	12" by 10"		7	3.429		7,675	231		7,906	8,800
0492	Reducer, eccentric									
0493	4" by 3"	Q-1	8	2	Ea.	2,075	130		2,205	2,475
0494	5" by 4"	"	7	2.286		3,400	148		3,548	3,975
0495	6" by 4"	Q-2	9	2.667		1,975	179		2,154	2,425
0496	8" by 6"		8	3		2,500	202		2,702	3,025
0497	10" by 8"		7	3.429		6,350	231		6,581	7,325
0498	12" by 10"		6	4		975	269		1,244	1,475
0500	For galvanized elbows and tees, add					100%				
0520	For extra heavy weight elbows and tees, add					140%				
0620	Gasket and bolt set, 150 lb., 1/2" pipe size	1 Plum	20	.400		5.95	29		34.95	49.50
0622	3/4" pipe size		19	.421		5.05	30.50		35.55	50.50
0624	1" pipe size		18	.444		7.90	32		39.90	56.50
0626	1-1/4" pipe size		17	.471		9.55	34		43.55	61
0628	1-1/2" pipe size		15	.533		8	38.50		46.50	66.50
0630	2" pipe size		13	.615		14.95	44.50		59.45	82.50
0640	2-1/2" pipe size		12	.667		14.25	48		62.25	87
0650	3" pipe size		11	.727		13.50	52.50		66	93
0660	3-1/2" pipe size		9	.889		24.50	64		88.50	123
0670	4" pipe size		8	1		22	72		94	131
0680	5" pipe size		7	1.143		37.50	82.50		120	165
0690	6" pipe size		6	1.333		73.50	96		169.50	224
0700	8" pipe size		5	1.600		39.50	115		154.50	215
0710	10" pipe size		4.50	1.778		77	128		205	276
0720	12" pipe size		4.20	1.905		98	137		235	315
0730	14" pipe size		4	2		114	144		258	340
0740	16" pipe size		3	2.667		141	192		333	440
0750	18" pipe size		2.70	2.963		147	213		360	480
0760	20" pipe size		2.30	3.478		340	251		591	750
0780	24" pipe size		1.90	4.211		425	305		730	920
0790	26" pipe size		1.60	5		580	360		940	1,175
0810	30" pipe size		1.40	5.714		1,125	410		1,535	1,875
0830	36" pipe size		1.10	7.273		2,100	525		2,625	3,100
0850	For 300 lb. gasket set, add					40%				
2000	Flanged unions, 125 lb., black, 1/2" pipe size	1 Plum	17	.471	Ea.	169	34		203	237
2040	3/4" pipe size		17	.471		202	34		236	274
2050	1" pipe size		16	.500		196	36		232	270
2060	1-1/4" pipe size	Q-1	28	.571		232	37		269	310

22 11 Facility Water Distribution

22 11 13 – Facility Water Distribution Piping

22 11 13.47 Pipe Fittings, Steel		Crew	Daily Output	Labor-Hours	Unit	Material	2023 Bare Costs Labor	2023 Bare Costs Equipment	Total	Total Incl O&P
2070	1-1/2" pipe size	Q-1	27	.593	Ea.	214	38.50		252.50	293
2080	2" pipe size		26	.615		252	40		292	335
2090	2-1/2" pipe size		24	.667		340	43		383	440
2100	3" pipe size		22	.727		385	47		432	495
2110	3-1/2" pipe size		18	.889		655	57.50		712.50	805
2120	4" pipe size		16	1		525	65		590	670
2130	5" pipe size		14	1.143		1,225	74		1,299	1,450
2140	6" pipe size	Q-2	19	1.263		1,150	85		1,235	1,375
2150	8" pipe size	"	16	1.500		2,775	101		2,876	3,200
2200	For galvanized unions, add					150%				
2290	Threaded flange									
2300	Cast iron									
2310	Black, 125 lb., per flange									
2320	1" pipe size	1 Plum	27	.296	Ea.	73.50	21.50		95	113
2330	1-1/4" pipe size	Q-1	44	.364		99.50	23.50		123	144
2340	1-1/2" pipe size		40	.400		81.50	26		107.50	128
2350	2" pipe size		36	.444		91.50	29		120.50	144
2360	2-1/2" pipe size		28	.571		107	37		144	174
2370	3" pipe size		20	.800		138	52		190	230
2380	3-1/2" pipe size		16	1		207	65		272	325
2390	4" pipe size		12	1.333		165	86.50		251.50	310
2400	5" pipe size		10	1.600		263	104		367	445
2410	6" pipe size	Q-2	14	1.714		297	115		412	495
2420	8" pipe size		12	2		470	135		605	715
2430	10" pipe size		10	2.400		830	161		991	1,150
2440	12" pipe size		8	3		1,975	202		2,177	2,475
2460	For galvanized flanges, add					95%				
2490	Blind flange									
2492	Cast iron									
2494	Black, 125 lb., per flange									
2496	1" pipe size	1 Plum	27	.296	Ea.	132	21.50		153.50	177
2500	1-1/2" pipe size	Q-1	40	.400		148	26		174	202
2502	2" pipe size		36	.444		167	29		196	227
2504	2-1/2" pipe size		28	.571		184	37		221	258
2506	3" pipe size		20	.800		221	52		273	320
2508	4" pipe size		12	1.333		283	86.50		369.50	440
2510	5" pipe size		10	1.600		460	104		564	660
2512	6" pipe size	Q-2	14	1.714		500	115		615	720
2514	8" pipe size		12	2		785	135		920	1,050
2516	10" pipe size		10	2.400		1,150	161		1,311	1,525
2518	12" pipe size		8	3		2,350	202		2,552	2,875
2520	For galvanized flanges, add					80%				
2570	Threaded flange									
2580	Forged steel									
2590	Black, 150 lb., per flange									
2600	1/2" pipe size	1 Plum	30	.267	Ea.	37	19.20		56.20	69
2610	3/4" pipe size		28	.286		37	20.50		57.50	71
2620	1" pipe size		27	.296		37	21.50		58.50	72.50
2630	1-1/4" pipe size	Q-1	44	.364		37	23.50		60.50	75.50
2640	1-1/2" pipe size		40	.400		37	26		63	79
2650	2" pipe size		36	.444		37	29		66	84
2660	2-1/2" pipe size		28	.571		60.50	37		97.50	122
2670	3" pipe size		20	.800		45	52		97	127

22 11 Facility Water Distribution

22 11 13 – Facility Water Distribution Piping

22 11 13.47 Pipe Fittings, Steel		Crew	Daily Output	Labor-Hours	Unit	Material	2023 Bare Costs Labor	Equipment	Total	Total Incl O&P
2690	4" pipe size	Q-1	12	1.333	Ea.	59.50	86.50		146	195
2700	5" pipe size	↓	10	1.600		111	104		215	277
2710	6" pipe size	Q-2	14	1.714		124	115		239	310
2720	8" pipe size		12	2		209	135		344	430
2730	10" pipe size	↓	10	2.400	↓	380	161		541	660
2860	Black, 300 lb., per flange									
2870	1/2" pipe size	1 Plum	30	.267	Ea.	41	19.20		60.20	73.50
2880	3/4" pipe size		28	.286		42	20.50		62.50	77
2890	1" pipe size	↓	27	.296		42	21.50		63.50	78.50
2900	1-1/4" pipe size	Q-1	44	.364		42	23.50		65.50	81.50
2910	1-1/2" pipe size		40	.400		42	26		68	85
2920	2" pipe size		36	.444		47.50	29		76.50	95.50
2930	2-1/2" pipe size		28	.571		79.50	37		116.50	143
2940	3" pipe size		20	.800		71.50	52		123.50	156
2960	4" pipe size	↓	12	1.333		103	86.50		189.50	242
2970	6" pipe size	Q-2	14	1.714	↓	192	115		307	385
3000	Weld joint, butt, carbon steel, standard weight									
3040	90° elbow, long radius									
3050	1/2" pipe size	Q-15	16	1	Ea.	15	65	4.01	84.01	117
3060	3/4" pipe size		16	1		15	65	4.01	84.01	117
3070	1" pipe size		16	1		15	65	4.01	84.01	117
3080	1-1/4" pipe size		14	1.143		15	74	4.58	93.58	133
3090	1-1/2" pipe size		13	1.231		15	80	4.94	99.94	141
3100	2" pipe size		10	1.600		28	104	6.40	138.40	193
3110	2-1/2" pipe size		8	2		23.50	130	8	161.50	227
3120	3" pipe size		7	2.286		55	148	9.15	212.15	292
3130	4" pipe size		5	3.200		48.50	208	12.85	269.35	375
3136	5" pipe size	↓	4	4		147	259	16.05	422.05	565
3140	6" pipe size	Q-16	5	4.800		102	325	12.80	439.80	605
3150	8" pipe size		3.75	6.400		198	430	17.10	645.10	875
3160	10" pipe size		3	8		380	540	21.50	941.50	1,250
3170	12" pipe size		2.50	9.600		565	645	25.50	1,235.50	1,625
3180	14" pipe size		2	12		1,200	805	32	2,037	2,550
3190	16" pipe size		1.50	16		1,100	1,075	42.50	2,217.50	2,875
3191	18" pipe size		1.25	19.200		1,475	1,300	51.50	2,826.50	3,575
3192	20" pipe size		1.15	20.870		2,025	1,400	55.50	3,480.50	4,375
3194	24" pipe size	↓	1.02	23.529	↓	2,900	1,575	63	4,538	5,600
3200	45° elbow, long									
3210	1/2" pipe size	Q-15	16	1	Ea.	95	65	4.01	164.01	206
3220	3/4" pipe size		16	1		95	65	4.01	164.01	206
3230	1" pipe size		16	1		20	65	4.01	89.01	123
3240	1-1/4" pipe size		14	1.143		20	74	4.58	98.58	138
3250	1-1/2" pipe size		13	1.231		20	80	4.94	104.94	146
3260	2" pipe size		10	1.600		27	104	6.40	137.40	192
3270	2-1/2" pipe size		8	2		24.50	130	8	162.50	229
3280	3" pipe size		7	2.286		24.50	148	9.15	181.65	258
3290	4" pipe size		5	3.200		42	208	12.85	262.85	370
3296	5" pipe size	↓	4	4		92.50	259	16.05	367.55	505
3300	6" pipe size	Q-16	5	4.800		120	325	12.80	457.80	625
3310	8" pipe size		3.75	6.400		200	430	17.10	647.10	880
3320	10" pipe size		3	8		400	540	21.50	961.50	1,275
3330	12" pipe size		2.50	9.600		565	645	25.50	1,235.50	1,625
3340	14" pipe size	↓	2	12		760	805	32	1,597	2,075

22 11 Facility Water Distribution

22 11 13 – Facility Water Distribution Piping

22 11 13.47 Pipe Fittings, Steel		Crew	Daily Output	Labor-Hours	Unit	Material	2023 Bare Costs Labor	Equipment	Total	Total Incl O&P
3341	16" pipe size	Q-16	1.50	16	Ea.	1,350	1,075	42.50	2,467.50	3,150
3342	18" pipe size		1.25	19.200		1,925	1,300	51.50	3,276.50	4,075
3343	20" pipe size		1.15	20.870		2,000	1,400	55.50	3,455.50	4,325
3345	24" pipe size		1.05	22.857		3,025	1,525	61	4,611	5,700
3346	26" pipe size		.85	28.235		4,125	1,900	75.50	6,100.50	7,425
3347	30" pipe size		.45	53.333		4,525	3,575	142	8,242	10,500
3349	36" pipe size		.38	63.158		4,975	4,250	169	9,394	12,000
3350	Tee, straight									
3352	For reducing tees and concentrics see starting line 4600									
3360	1/2" pipe size	Q-15	10	1.600	Ea.	47.50	104	6.40	157.90	215
3370	3/4" pipe size		10	1.600		47.50	104	6.40	157.90	215
3380	1" pipe size		10	1.600		62.50	104	6.40	172.90	231
3390	1-1/4" pipe size		9	1.778		62.50	115	7.15	184.65	249
3400	1-1/2" pipe size		8	2		62.50	130	8	200.50	271
3410	2" pipe size		6	2.667		59.50	173	10.70	243.20	335
3420	2-1/2" pipe size		5	3.200		62.50	208	12.85	283.35	395
3430	3" pipe size		4	4		69.50	259	16.05	344.55	480
3440	4" pipe size		3	5.333		98	345	21.50	464.50	645
3446	5" pipe size		2.50	6.400		239	415	25.50	679.50	910
3450	6" pipe size	Q-16	3	8		168	540	21.50	729.50	1,000
3460	8" pipe size		2.50	9.600		435	645	25.50	1,105.50	1,475
3470	10" pipe size		2	12		855	805	32	1,692	2,175
3480	12" pipe size		1.60	15		805	1,000	40	1,845	2,425
3481	14" pipe size		1.30	18.462		2,100	1,250	49.50	3,399.50	4,200
3482	16" pipe size		1	24		1,575	1,625	64	3,264	4,200
3483	18" pipe size		.80	30		3,750	2,025	80	5,855	7,225
3484	20" pipe size		.75	32		5,850	2,150	85.50	8,085.50	9,725
3486	24" pipe size		.70	34.286		7,550	2,300	91.50	9,941.50	11,900
3487	26" pipe size		.55	43.636		10,300	2,925	117	13,342	15,800
3488	30" pipe size		.30	80		11,300	5,375	214	16,889	20,700
3490	36" pipe size		.25	96		12,500	6,450	256	19,206	23,600
3491	Eccentric reducer, 1-1/2" pipe size	Q-15	14	1.143		69.50	74	4.58	148.08	193
3492	2" pipe size		11	1.455		80.50	94.50	5.85	180.85	236
3493	2-1/2" pipe size		9	1.778		88.50	115	7.15	210.65	277
3494	3" pipe size		8	2		116	130	8	254	330
3495	4" pipe size		6	2.667		234	173	10.70	417.70	525
3496	6" pipe size	Q-16	5	4.800		350	325	12.80	687.80	880
3497	8" pipe size		4	6		405	405	16	826	1,075
3498	10" pipe size		3	8		695	540	21.50	1,256.50	1,575
3499	12" pipe size		2.50	9.600		1,025	645	25.50	1,695.50	2,125
3501	Cap, 1-1/2" pipe size	Q-15	28	.571		23.50	37	2.29	62.79	83.50
3502	2" pipe size		22	.727		29	47	2.92	78.92	106
3503	2-1/2" pipe size		18	.889		30.50	57.50	3.56	91.56	123
3504	3" pipe size		16	1		30.50	65	4.01	99.51	134
3505	4" pipe size		12	1.333		38	86.50	5.35	129.85	176
3506	6" pipe size	Q-16	10	2.400		76	161	6.40	243.40	330
3507	8" pipe size		8	3		107	202	8	317	425
3508	10" pipe size		6	4		208	269	10.70	487.70	640
3509	12" pipe size		5	4.800		315	325	12.80	652.80	840
3511	14" pipe size		4	6		385	405	16	806	1,050
3512	16" pipe size		4	6		445	405	16	866	1,100
3513	18" pipe size		3	8		665	540	21.50	1,226.50	1,550
3517	Weld joint, butt, carbon steel, extra strong									

22 11 Facility Water Distribution

22 11 13 – Facility Water Distribution Piping

22 11 13.47 Pipe Fittings, Steel		Crew	Daily Output	Labor-Hours	Unit	Material	2023 Bare Costs Labor	Equipment	Total	Total Incl O&P
3519	90° elbow, long									
3520	1/2" pipe size	Q-15	13	1.231	Ea.	132	80	4.94	216.94	269
3530	3/4" pipe size		12	1.333		132	86.50	5.35	223.85	280
3540	1" pipe size		11	1.455		132	94.50	5.85	232.35	292
3550	1-1/4" pipe size		10	1.600		132	104	6.40	242.40	305
3560	1-1/2" pipe size		9	1.778		132	115	7.15	254.15	325
3570	2" pipe size		8	2		33.50	130	8	171.50	239
3580	2-1/2" pipe size		7	2.286		47	148	9.15	204.15	283
3590	3" pipe size		6	2.667		60.50	173	10.70	244.20	335
3600	4" pipe size		4	4		99	259	16.05	374.05	510
3606	5" pipe size	▼	3.50	4.571		237	296	18.35	551.35	720
3610	6" pipe size	Q-16	4.50	5.333		251	360	14.25	625.25	825
3620	8" pipe size		3.50	6.857		475	460	18.30	953.30	1,225
3630	10" pipe size		2.50	9.600		1,000	645	25.50	1,670.50	2,100
3640	12" pipe size	▼	2.25	10.667	▼	1,225	715	28.50	1,968.50	2,450
3650	45° elbow, long									
3660	1/2" pipe size	Q-15	13	1.231	Ea.	94	80	4.94	178.94	228
3670	3/4" pipe size		12	1.333		94	86.50	5.35	185.85	239
3680	1" pipe size		11	1.455		26.50	94.50	5.85	126.85	176
3690	1-1/4" pipe size		10	1.600		26.50	104	6.40	136.90	191
3700	1-1/2" pipe size		9	1.778		26.50	115	7.15	148.65	209
3710	2" pipe size		8	2		35	130	8	173	240
3720	2-1/2" pipe size		7	2.286		78	148	9.15	235.15	315
3730	3" pipe size		6	2.667		45	173	10.70	228.70	320
3740	4" pipe size		4	4		71	259	16.05	346.05	480
3746	5" pipe size	▼	3.50	4.571		169	296	18.35	483.35	645
3750	6" pipe size	Q-16	4.50	5.333		195	360	14.25	569.25	765
3760	8" pipe size		3.50	6.857		335	460	18.30	813.30	1,075
3770	10" pipe size		2.50	9.600		650	645	25.50	1,320.50	1,700
3780	12" pipe size	▼	2.25	10.667	▼	965	715	28.50	1,708.50	2,150
3800	Tee, straight									
3810	1/2" pipe size	Q-15	9	1.778	Ea.	207	115	7.15	329.15	410
3820	3/4" pipe size		8.50	1.882		35	122	7.55	164.55	229
3830	1" pipe size		8	2		105	130	8	243	315
3840	1-1/4" pipe size		7	2.286		62.50	148	9.15	219.65	300
3850	1-1/2" pipe size		6	2.667		35	173	10.70	218.70	310
3860	2" pipe size		5	3.200		74	208	12.85	294.85	405
3870	2-1/2" pipe size		4	4		123	259	16.05	398.05	540
3880	3" pipe size		3.50	4.571		195	296	18.35	509.35	675
3890	4" pipe size		2.50	6.400		185	415	25.50	625.50	850
3896	5" pipe size	▼	2.25	7.111		405	460	28.50	893.50	1,175
3900	6" pipe size	Q-16	2.25	10.667		355	715	28.50	1,098.50	1,500
3910	8" pipe size		2	12		700	805	32	1,537	2,000
3920	10" pipe size		1.75	13.714		1,050	920	36.50	2,006.50	2,575
3930	12" pipe size	▼	1.50	16		1,525	1,075	42.50	2,642.50	3,325
4000	Eccentric reducer, 1-1/2" pipe size	Q-15	10	1.600		46.50	104	6.40	156.90	213
4010	2" pipe size		9	1.778		60	115	7.15	182.15	246
4020	2-1/2" pipe size		8	2		90	130	8	228	300
4030	3" pipe size		7	2.286		74.50	148	9.15	231.65	315
4040	4" pipe size		5	3.200		116	208	12.85	336.85	450
4046	5" pipe size	▼	4.70	3.404		500	221	13.65	734.65	895
4050	6" pipe size	Q-16	4.50	5.333		480	360	14.25	854.25	1,075
4060	8" pipe size	▼	3.50	6.857	▼	495	460	18.30	973.30	1,250

22 11 Facility Water Distribution

22 11 13 – Facility Water Distribution Piping

22 11 13.47	Pipe Fittings, Steel	Crew	Daily Output	Labor-Hours	Unit	Material	2023 Bare Costs Labor	Equipment	Total	Total Incl O&P
4070	10" pipe size	Q-16	2.50	9.600	Ea.	840	645	25.50	1,510.50	1,925
4080	12" pipe size		2.25	10.667		1,075	715	28.50	1,818.50	2,275
4090	14" pipe size		2.10	11.429		1,875	770	30.50	2,675.50	3,225
4100	16" pipe size		1.90	12.632		2,325	850	33.50	3,208.50	3,875
4151	Cap, 1-1/2" pipe size	Q-15	24	.667		29	43	2.67	74.67	99.50
4152	2" pipe size		18	.889		29	57.50	3.56	90.06	122
4153	2-1/2" pipe size		16	1		40	65	4.01	109.01	145
4154	3" pipe size		14	1.143		44.50	74	4.58	123.08	165
4155	4" pipe size		10	1.600		60.50	104	6.40	170.90	229
4156	6" pipe size	Q-16	9	2.667		123	179	7.10	309.10	410
4157	8" pipe size		7	3.429		184	231	9.15	424.15	560
4158	10" pipe size		5	4.800		283	325	12.80	620.80	805
4159	12" pipe size		4	6		380	405	16	801	1,025
4190	Weld fittings, reducing, standard weight									
4200	Welding ring w/spacer pins, 2" pipe size				Ea.	4.33			4.33	4.76
4210	2-1/2" pipe size					3.63			3.63	3.99
4220	3" pipe size					4.59			4.59	5.05
4230	4" pipe size					5.10			5.10	5.65
4236	5" pipe size					6.35			6.35	7
4240	6" pipe size					6.65			6.65	7.35
4250	8" pipe size					7.35			7.35	8.10
4260	10" pipe size					8.55			8.55	9.40
4270	12" pipe size					9.95			9.95	10.90
4280	14" pipe size					10.10			10.10	11.10
4290	16" pipe size					11.80			11.80	12.95
4300	18" pipe size					13.20			13.20	14.50
4310	20" pipe size					15			15	16.50
4330	24" pipe size					21			21	23.50
4340	26" pipe size					25.50			25.50	28
4350	30" pipe size					29			29	32
4370	36" pipe size					35.50			35.50	39
4600	Tee, reducing on outlet									
4601	2-1/2" x 2" pipe size	Q-15	5	3.200	Ea.	75.50	208	12.85	296.35	405
4602	3" x 2-1/2" pipe size		4	4		73.50	259	16.05	348.55	485
4604	4" x 3" pipe size		3	5.333		93.50	345	21.50	460	640
4605	5" x 4" pipe size		2.50	6.400		202	415	25.50	642.50	870
4606	6" x 5" pipe size	Q-16	3	8		182	540	21.50	743.50	1,025
4607	8" x 6" pipe size		2.50	9.600		345	645	25.50	1,015.50	1,375
4608	10" x 8" pipe size		2	12		640	805	32	1,477	1,950
4609	12" x 10" pipe size		1.60	15		800	1,000	40	1,840	2,425
4610	16" x 12" pipe size		1.50	16		3,625	1,075	42.50	4,742.50	5,650
4611	14" x 12" pipe size		1.52	15.789		1,425	1,050	42	2,517	3,200
4618	Reducer, concentric									
4619	2-1/2" by 2" pipe size	Q-15	10	1.600	Ea.	61	104	6.40	171.40	229
4620	3" by 2-1/2" pipe size		9	1.778		26.50	115	7.15	148.65	209
4621	3-1/2" by 3" pipe size		8	2		76	130	8	214	285
4622	4" by 2-1/2" pipe size		7	2.286		41.50	148	9.15	198.65	277
4623	5" by 3" pipe size		7	2.286		209	148	9.15	366.15	460
4624	6" by 4" pipe size	Q-16	6	4		71	269	10.70	350.70	490
4625	8" by 6" pipe size		5	4.800		93	325	12.80	430.80	595
4626	10" by 8" pipe size		4	6		180	405	16	601	815
4627	12" by 10" pipe size		3	8		425	540	21.50	986.50	1,300
4660	Reducer, eccentric									

For customer support on your Mechanical Costs with RSMeans data, call 800.448.8182.

167

22 11 Facility Water Distribution

22 11 13 – Facility Water Distribution Piping

22 11 13.47 Pipe Fittings, Steel		Crew	Daily Output	Labor-Hours	Unit	Material	2023 Bare Costs Labor	Equipment	Total	Total Incl O&P
4662	3" x 2" pipe size	Q-15	8	2	Ea.	44.50	130	8	182.50	251
4664	4" x 3" pipe size		6	2.667		132	173	10.70	315.70	415
4666	4" x 2" pipe size	▼	6	2.667		66	173	10.70	249.70	345
4670	6" x 4" pipe size	Q-16	5	4.800		111	325	12.80	448.80	615
4672	6" x 3" pipe size		5	4.800		175	325	12.80	512.80	685
4676	8" x 6" pipe size		4	6		350	405	16	771	1,000
4678	8" x 4" pipe size		4	6		260	405	16	681	905
4682	10" x 8" pipe size		3	8		310	540	21.50	871.50	1,175
4684	10" x 6" pipe size		3	8		550	540	21.50	1,111.50	1,425
4688	12" x 10" pipe size		2.50	9.600		485	645	25.50	1,155.50	1,525
4690	12" x 8" pipe size		2.50	9.600		765	645	25.50	1,435.50	1,825
4691	14" x 12" pipe size		2.20	10.909		855	735	29	1,619	2,075
4693	16" x 14" pipe size		1.80	13.333		1,300	895	35.50	2,230.50	2,800
4694	16" x 12" pipe size		2	12		1,725	805	32	2,562	3,125
4696	18" x 16" pipe size	▼	1.60	15	▼	2,350	1,000	40	3,390	4,150
5000	Weld joint, socket, forged steel, 3000 lb., schedule 40 pipe									
5010	90° elbow, straight									
5020	1/4" pipe size	Q-15	22	.727	Ea.	40	47	2.92	89.92	118
5030	3/8" pipe size		22	.727		40	47	2.92	89.92	118
5040	1/2" pipe size		20	.800		19.35	52	3.21	74.56	103
5050	3/4" pipe size		20	.800		23	52	3.21	78.21	107
5060	1" pipe size		20	.800		32	52	3.21	87.21	117
5070	1-1/4" pipe size		18	.889		57	57.50	3.56	118.06	152
5080	1-1/2" pipe size		16	1		66.50	65	4.01	135.51	174
5090	2" pipe size		12	1.333		97.50	86.50	5.35	189.35	242
5100	2-1/2" pipe size		10	1.600		305	104	6.40	415.40	495
5110	3" pipe size		8	2		495	130	8	633	745
5120	4" pipe size	▼	6	2.667	▼	1,275	173	10.70	1,458.70	1,675
5130	45° elbow, straight									
5134	1/4" pipe size	Q-15	22	.727	Ea.	40	47	2.92	89.92	118
5135	3/8" pipe size		22	.727		40	47	2.92	89.92	118
5136	1/2" pipe size		20	.800		29.50	52	3.21	84.71	114
5137	3/4" pipe size		20	.800		34.50	52	3.21	89.71	119
5140	1" pipe size		20	.800		34.50	52	3.21	89.71	119
5150	1-1/4" pipe size		18	.889		61.50	57.50	3.56	122.56	158
5160	1-1/2" pipe size		16	1		75.50	65	4.01	144.51	184
5170	2" pipe size		12	1.333		122	86.50	5.35	213.85	269
5180	2-1/2" pipe size		10	1.600		320	104	6.40	430.40	510
5190	3" pipe size		8	2		540	130	8	678	795
5200	4" pipe size	▼	6	2.667	▼	1,100	173	10.70	1,283.70	1,475
5250	Tee, straight									
5254	1/4" pipe size	Q-15	15	1.067	Ea.	44	69	4.28	117.28	156
5255	3/8" pipe size		15	1.067		44	69	4.28	117.28	156
5256	1/2" pipe size		13	1.231		27.50	80	4.94	112.44	155
5257	3/4" pipe size		13	1.231		33.50	80	4.94	118.44	161
5260	1" pipe size		13	1.231		45.50	80	4.94	130.44	175
5270	1-1/4" pipe size		12	1.333		70	86.50	5.35	161.85	212
5280	1-1/2" pipe size		11	1.455		93	94.50	5.85	193.35	249
5290	2" pipe size		8	2		134	130	8	272	350
5300	2-1/2" pipe size		6	2.667		385	173	10.70	568.70	695
5310	3" pipe size		5	3.200		920	208	12.85	1,140.85	1,350
5320	4" pipe size	▼	4	4	▼	1,475	259	16.05	1,750.05	2,025
5350	For reducing sizes, add					60%				

22 11 Facility Water Distribution

22 11 13 – Facility Water Distribution Piping

22 11 13.47 Pipe Fittings, Steel

		Crew	Daily Output	Labor-Hours	Unit	Material	2023 Bare Costs Labor	2023 Bare Costs Equipment	Total	Total Incl O&P
5450	Couplings									
5451	1/4" pipe size	Q-15	23	.696	Ea.	25.50	45	2.79	73.29	98.50
5452	3/8" pipe size		23	.696		4.42	45	2.79	52.21	75.50
5453	1/2" pipe size		21	.762		6	49.50	3.06	58.56	83.50
5454	3/4" pipe size		21	.762		10.65	49.50	3.06	63.21	88.50
5460	1" pipe size		20	.800		7.10	52	3.21	62.31	89
5470	1-1/4" pipe size		20	.800		14.90	52	3.21	70.11	97.50
5480	1-1/2" pipe size		18	.889		15.50	57.50	3.56	76.56	107
5490	2" pipe size		14	1.143		20	74	4.58	98.58	138
5500	2-1/2" pipe size		12	1.333		50	86.50	5.35	141.85	190
5510	3" pipe size		9	1.778		170	115	7.15	292.15	365
5520	4" pipe size		7	2.286		154	148	9.15	311.15	400
5570	Union, 1/4" pipe size		21	.762		87	49.50	3.06	139.56	172
5571	3/8" pipe size		21	.762		87	49.50	3.06	139.56	172
5572	1/2" pipe size		19	.842		79.50	54.50	3.38	137.38	173
5573	3/4" pipe size		19	.842		127	54.50	3.38	184.88	225
5574	1" pipe size		19	.842		28.50	54.50	3.38	86.38	117
5575	1-1/4" pipe size		17	.941		221	61	3.77	285.77	340
5576	1-1/2" pipe size		15	1.067		249	69	4.28	322.28	380
5577	2" pipe size		11	1.455		315	94.50	5.85	415.35	490
5600	Reducer, 1/4" pipe size		23	.696		64.50	45	2.79	112.29	142
5601	3/8" pipe size		23	.696		68	45	2.79	115.79	146
5602	1/2" pipe size		21	.762		41.50	49.50	3.06	94.06	122
5603	3/4" pipe size		21	.762		41.50	49.50	3.06	94.06	122
5604	1" pipe size		21	.762		58	49.50	3.06	110.56	141
5605	1-1/4" pipe size		19	.842		74	54.50	3.38	131.88	167
5607	1-1/2" pipe size		17	.941		79.50	61	3.77	144.27	183
5608	2" pipe size		13	1.231		87.50	80	4.94	172.44	221
5612	Cap, 1/4" pipe size		46	.348		24	22.50	1.39	47.89	61.50
5613	3/8" pipe size		46	.348		24	22.50	1.39	47.89	61.50
5614	1/2" pipe size		42	.381		14.70	24.50	1.53	40.73	55
5615	3/4" pipe size		42	.381		17.75	24.50	1.53	43.78	58
5616	1" pipe size		42	.381		26	24.50	1.53	52.03	67
5617	1-1/4" pipe size		38	.421		30.50	27.50	1.69	59.69	76
5618	1-1/2" pipe size		34	.471		15.55	30.50	1.89	47.94	64.50
5619	2" pipe size		26	.615		68	40	2.47	110.47	137
5630	T-O-L, 1/4" pipe size, nozzle		23	.696		12.75	45	2.79	60.54	84.50
5631	3/8" pipe size, nozzle		23	.696		13.15	45	2.79	60.94	85
5632	1/2" pipe size, nozzle		22	.727		5.30	47	2.92	55.22	79.50
5633	3/4" pipe size, nozzle		21	.762		6.10	49.50	3.06	58.66	83.50
5634	1" pipe size, nozzle		20	.800		7.10	52	3.21	62.31	89
5635	1-1/4" pipe size, nozzle		18	.889		11.30	57.50	3.56	72.36	102
5636	1-1/2" pipe size, nozzle		16	1		11.30	65	4.01	80.31	113
5637	2" pipe size, nozzle		12	1.333		12.85	86.50	5.35	104.70	149
5638	2-1/2" pipe size, nozzle		10	1.600		104	104	6.40	214.40	276
5639	4" pipe size, nozzle		6	2.667		97	173	10.70	280.70	375
5640	W-O-L, 1/4" pipe size, nozzle		23	.696		32	45	2.79	79.79	106
5641	3/8" pipe size, nozzle		23	.696		26.50	45	2.79	74.29	99.50
5642	1/2" pipe size, nozzle		22	.727		26.50	47	2.92	76.42	103
5643	3/4" pipe size, nozzle		21	.762		13.85	49.50	3.06	66.41	92
5644	1" pipe size, nozzle		20	.800		14.50	52	3.21	69.71	97
5645	1-1/4" pipe size, nozzle		18	.889		33.50	57.50	3.56	94.56	127
5646	1-1/2" pipe size, nozzle		16	1		34.50	65	4.01	103.51	139

For customer support on your Mechanical Costs with RSMeans data, call 800.448.8182.

22 11 Facility Water Distribution

22 11 13 – Facility Water Distribution Piping

22 11 13.47 Pipe Fittings, Steel

		Crew	Daily Output	Labor-Hours	Unit	Material	2023 Bare Costs Labor	Equipment	Total	Total Incl O&P
5647	2" pipe size, nozzle	Q-15	12	1.333	Ea.	35	86.50	5.35	126.85	173
5648	2-1/2" pipe size, nozzle		10	1.600		80	104	6.40	190.40	250
5649	3" pipe size, nozzle		8	2		43.50	130	8	181.50	250
5650	4" pipe size, nozzle		6	2.667		111	173	10.70	294.70	390
5651	5" pipe size, nozzle		5	3.200		273	208	12.85	493.85	625
5652	6" pipe size, nozzle		4	4		305	259	16.05	580.05	740
5653	8" pipe size, nozzle		3	5.333		880	345	21.50	1,246.50	1,500
5654	10" pipe size, nozzle		2.60	6.154		825	400	24.50	1,249.50	1,525
5655	12" pipe size, nozzle		2.20	7.273		1,575	470	29	2,074	2,450
5674	S-O-L, 1/4" pipe size, outlet		23	.696		15.80	45	2.79	63.59	88
5675	3/8" pipe size, outlet		23	.696		15.80	45	2.79	63.59	88
5676	1/2" pipe size, outlet		22	.727		15.85	47	2.92	65.77	91
5677	3/4" pipe size, outlet		21	.762		8.45	49.50	3.06	61.01	86
5678	1" pipe size, outlet		20	.800		9.40	52	3.21	64.61	91.50
5679	1-1/4" pipe size, outlet		18	.889		29.50	57.50	3.56	90.56	122
5680	1-1/2" pipe size, outlet		16	1		29.50	65	4.01	98.51	133
5681	2" pipe size, outlet	↓	12	1.333	↓	31	86.50	5.35	122.85	169
6000	Weld-on flange, forged steel									
6020	Slip-on, 150 lb. flange (welded front and back)									
6050	1/2" pipe size	Q-15	18	.889	Ea.	24.50	57.50	3.56	85.56	117
6060	3/4" pipe size		18	.889		24.50	57.50	3.56	85.56	117
6070	1" pipe size		17	.941		24.50	61	3.77	89.27	122
6080	1-1/4" pipe size		16	1		24.50	65	4.01	93.51	128
6090	1-1/2" pipe size		15	1.067		24.50	69	4.28	97.78	135
6100	2" pipe size		12	1.333		19.85	86.50	5.35	111.70	157
6110	2-1/2" pipe size		10	1.600		34.50	104	6.40	144.90	200
6120	3" pipe size		9	1.778		33	115	7.15	155.15	216
6130	3-1/2" pipe size		7	2.286		42	148	9.15	199.15	277
6140	4" pipe size		6	2.667		42	173	10.70	225.70	315
6150	5" pipe size		5	3.200		76	208	12.85	296.85	410
6160	6" pipe size	Q-16	6	4		69.50	269	10.70	349.20	490
6170	8" pipe size		5	4.800		105	325	12.80	442.80	610
6180	10" pipe size		4	6		178	405	16	599	815
6190	12" pipe size		3	8		215	540	21.50	776.50	1,050
6191	14" pipe size		2.50	9.600		350	645	25.50	1,020.50	1,375
6192	16" pipe size	↓	1.80	13.333	↓	560	895	35.50	1,490.50	1,975
6200	300 lb. flange									
6210	1/2" pipe size	Q-15	17	.941	Ea.	33	61	3.77	97.77	131
6220	3/4" pipe size		17	.941		33	61	3.77	97.77	131
6230	1" pipe size		16	1		33	65	4.01	102.01	137
6240	1-1/4" pipe size		13	1.231		33	80	4.94	117.94	160
6250	1-1/2" pipe size		12	1.333		33	86.50	5.35	124.85	171
6260	2" pipe size		11	1.455		39	94.50	5.85	139.35	190
6270	2-1/2" pipe size		9	1.778		44	115	7.15	166.15	228
6280	3" pipe size		7	2.286		50	148	9.15	207.15	287
6290	4" pipe size		6	2.667		71	173	10.70	254.70	350
6300	5" pipe size		4	4		116	259	16.05	391.05	530
6310	6" pipe size	Q-16	5	4.800		121	325	12.80	458.80	625
6320	8" pipe size		4	6		203	405	16	624	840
6330	10" pipe size		3.40	7.059		345	475	18.85	838.85	1,100
6340	12" pipe size	↓	2.80	8.571		435	575	23	1,033	1,375
6400	Welding neck, 150 lb. flange									
6410	1/2" pipe size	Q-15	40	.400	Ea.	36	26	1.60	63.60	80

22 11 Facility Water Distribution

22 11 13 – Facility Water Distribution Piping

22 11 13.47 Pipe Fittings, Steel		Crew	Daily Output	Labor-Hours	Unit	Material	2023 Bare Costs Labor	Equipment	Total	Total Incl O&P
6420	3/4" pipe size	Q-15	36	.444	Ea.	36	29	1.78	66.78	84.50
6430	1" pipe size		32	.500		41.50	32.50	2.01	76.01	96
6440	1-1/4" pipe size		29	.552		50.50	36	2.21	88.71	111
6450	1-1/2" pipe size		26	.615		31	40	2.47	73.47	96.50
6460	2" pipe size		20	.800		29	52	3.21	84.21	113
6470	2-1/2" pipe size		16	1		31.50	65	4.01	100.51	135
6480	3" pipe size		14	1.143		36	74	4.58	114.58	156
6500	4" pipe size		10	1.600		43.50	104	6.40	153.90	210
6510	5" pipe size		8	2		83	130	8	221	293
6520	6" pipe size	Q-16	10	2.400		63	161	6.40	230.40	320
6530	8" pipe size		7	3.429		111	231	9.15	351.15	475
6540	10" pipe size		6	4		179	269	10.70	458.70	610
6550	12" pipe size		5	4.800		260	325	12.80	597.80	780
6551	14" pipe size		4.50	5.333		470	360	14.25	844.25	1,075
6552	16" pipe size		3	8		740	540	21.50	1,301.50	1,650
6553	18" pipe size		2.50	9.600		1,000	645	25.50	1,670.50	2,100
6554	20" pipe size		2.30	10.435		1,225	700	28	1,953	2,425
6556	24" pipe size		2	12		1,625	805	32	2,462	3,025
6557	26" pipe size		1.70	14.118		2,150	950	37.50	3,137.50	3,850
6558	30" pipe size		.90	26.667		2,475	1,800	71	4,346	5,475
6559	36" pipe size		.75	32		2,850	2,150	85.50	5,085.50	6,425
6560	300 lb. flange									
6570	1/2" pipe size	Q-15	36	.444	Ea.	43.50	29	1.78	74.28	92.50
6580	3/4" pipe size		34	.471		43.50	30.50	1.89	75.89	95
6590	1" pipe size		30	.533		43.50	34.50	2.14	80.14	101
6600	1-1/4" pipe size		28	.571		43.50	37	2.29	82.79	106
6610	1-1/2" pipe size		24	.667		43.50	43	2.67	89.17	115
6620	2" pipe size		18	.889		39.50	57.50	3.56	100.56	133
6630	2-1/2" pipe size		14	1.143		55.50	74	4.58	134.08	177
6640	3" pipe size		12	1.333		56.50	86.50	5.35	148.35	197
6650	4" pipe size		8	2		74	130	8	212	283
6660	5" pipe size		7	2.286		144	148	9.15	301.15	390
6670	6" pipe size	Q-16	9	2.667		148	179	7.10	334.10	440
6680	8" pipe size		6	4		248	269	10.70	527.70	685
6690	10" pipe size		5	4.800		440	325	12.80	777.80	980
6700	12" pipe size		4	6		565	405	16	986	1,250
6710	14" pipe size		3.50	6.857		1,250	460	18.30	1,728.30	2,075
6720	16" pipe size		2	12		1,475	805	32	2,312	2,850
7740	Plain ends for plain end pipe, mechanically coupled									
7750	Cplg. & labor required at joints not included, add 1 per									
7760	joint for installed price, see line 9180									
7770	Malleable iron, painted, unless noted otherwise									
7800	90° elbow, 1"				Ea.	221			221	243
7810	1-1/2"					261			261	287
7820	2"					390			390	430
7830	2-1/2"					455			455	500
7840	3"					470			470	520
7860	4"					535			535	590
7870	5" welded steel					615			615	675
7880	6"					775			775	855
7890	8" welded steel					1,450			1,450	1,600
7900	10" welded steel					1,850			1,850	2,025
7910	12" welded steel					2,050			2,050	2,275

22 11 Facility Water Distribution

22 11 13 – Facility Water Distribution Piping

22 11 13.47 Pipe Fittings, Steel		Crew	Daily Output	Labor-Hours	Unit	Material	2023 Bare Costs Labor	Equipment	Total	Total Incl O&P
7970	45° elbow, 1"				Ea.	133			133	146
7980	1-1/2"					197			197	217
7990	2"					410			410	455
8000	2-1/2"					410			410	455
8010	3"					470			470	520
8030	4"					490			490	540
8040	5" welded steel					615			615	675
8050	6"					705			705	775
8060	8"					825			825	905
8070	10" welded steel					850			850	935
8080	12" welded steel					1,525			1,525	1,700
8140	Tee, straight 1"					247			247	271
8150	1-1/2"					320			320	350
8160	2"					320			320	350
8170	2-1/2"					415			415	455
8180	3"					635			635	700
8200	4"					910			910	1,000
8210	5" welded steel					1,250			1,250	1,375
8220	6"					1,075			1,075	1,200
8230	8" welded steel					1,550			1,550	1,725
8240	10" welded steel					3,050			3,050	3,350
8250	12" welded steel					2,850			2,850	3,150
8340	Segmentally welded steel, painted									
8390	Wye 2"				Ea.	450			450	495
8400	2-1/2"					450			450	495
8410	3"					540			540	595
8430	4"					585			585	640
8440	5"					1,025			1,025	1,125
8450	6"					1,250			1,250	1,375
8460	8"					1,825			1,825	2,000
8470	10"					2,825			2,825	3,100
8480	12"					2,550			2,550	2,825
8540	Wye, lateral 2"					430			430	470
8550	2-1/2"					495			495	540
8560	3"					585			585	645
8580	4"					805			805	885
8590	5"					1,375			1,375	1,500
8600	6"					1,400			1,400	1,550
8610	8"					2,350			2,350	2,600
8620	10"					2,350			2,350	2,600
8630	12"					4,325			4,325	4,775
8690	Cross, 2"					273			273	300
8700	2-1/2"					273			273	300
8710	3"					325			325	360
8730	4"					685			685	755
8740	5"					1,025			1,025	1,125
8750	6"					1,075			1,075	1,175
8760	8"					1,550			1,550	1,700
8770	10"					2,650			2,650	2,900
8780	12"					2,775			2,775	3,075
8800	Tees, reducing 2" x 1"					365			365	405
8810	2" x 1-1/2"					365			365	405
8820	3" x 1"					365			365	400

22 11 Facility Water Distribution

22 11 13 – Facility Water Distribution Piping

22 11 13.47 Pipe Fittings, Steel

		Crew	Daily Output	Labor-Hours	Unit	Material	2023 Bare Costs Labor	2023 Bare Costs Equipment	Total	Total Incl O&P
8830	3" x 1-1/2"				Ea.	272			272	299
8840	3" x 2"					365			365	405
8850	4" x 1"					540			540	595
8860	4" x 1-1/2"					540			540	595
8870	4" x 2"					395			395	435
8880	4" x 2-1/2"					245			245	270
8890	4" x 3"					405			405	445
8900	6" x 2"					560			560	620
8910	6" x 3"					690			690	755
8920	6" x 4"					575			575	630
8930	8" x 2"					1,000			1,000	1,100
8940	8" x 3"					890			890	980
8950	8" x 4"					1,225			1,225	1,350
8960	8" x 5"					705			705	780
8970	8" x 6"					915			915	1,000
8980	10" x 4"					795			795	875
8990	10" x 6"					820			820	900
9000	10" x 8"					1,275			1,275	1,400
9010	12" x 6"					2,125			2,125	2,325
9020	12" x 8"					1,575			1,575	1,750
9030	12" x 10"					1,575			1,575	1,725
9080	Adapter nipples 3" long									
9090	1"				Ea.	30			30	33
9100	1-1/2"					39.50			39.50	43.50
9110	2"					39.50			39.50	43.50
9120	2-1/2"					45			45	49.50
9130	3"					55			55	60.50
9140	4"					88.50			88.50	97
9150	6"					231			231	254
9180	Coupling, mechanical, plain end pipe to plain end pipe or fitting									
9190	1"	Q-1	29	.552	Ea.	134	36		170	201
9200	1-1/2"		28	.571		134	37		171	203
9210	2"		27	.593		134	38.50		172.50	205
9220	2-1/2"		26	.615		134	40		174	207
9230	3"		25	.640		195	41.50		236.50	277
9240	3-1/2"		24	.667		226	43		269	315
9250	4"		22	.727		226	47		273	320
9260	5"	Q-2	28	.857		320	57.50		377.50	435
9270	6"		24	1		390	67.50		457.50	530
9280	8"		19	1.263		690	85		775	880
9290	10"		16	1.500		890	101		991	1,125
9300	12"		12	2		1,125	135		1,260	1,425
9310	Outlets for precut holes through pipe wall									
9331	Strapless type, with gasket									
9332	4" to 8" pipe x 1/2"	1 Plum	13	.615	Ea.	147	44.50		191.50	227
9333	4" to 8" pipe x 3/4"		13	.615		156	44.50		200.50	238
9334	10" pipe and larger x 1/2"		11	.727		147	52.50		199.50	239
9335	10" pipe and larger x 3/4"		11	.727		156	52.50		208.50	250
9341	Thermometer wells with gasket									
9342	4" to 8" pipe, 6" stem	1 Plum	14	.571	Ea.	219	41		260	305
9343	8" pipe and larger, 6" stem	"	13	.615	"	219	44.50		263.50	305
9800	Mech. tee, cast iron, grooved or threaded, w/nuts and bolts									
9940	For galvanized fittings for plain end pipe, add					20%				

22 11 Facility Water Distribution

22 11 13 – Facility Water Distribution Piping

22 11 13.48 Pipe, Fittings and Valves, Steel, Grooved-Joint

		Crew	Daily Output	Labor-Hours	Unit	Material	2023 Bare Costs Labor	Equipment	Total	Total Incl O&P
0010	**PIPE, FITTINGS AND VALVES, STEEL, GROOVED-JOINT**									
0012	Fittings are ductile iron. Steel fittings noted.									
0020	Pipe includes coupling & clevis type hanger assemblies, 10' OC									
0500	Schedule 10, black									
0550	2" diameter	1 Plum	43	.186	L.F.	9.75	13.40		23.15	31
0560	2-1/2" diameter	Q-1	61	.262		12.10	17		29.10	39
0570	3" diameter		55	.291		13.95	18.85		32.80	43.50
0580	3-1/2" diameter		53	.302		20	19.60		39.60	51
0590	4" diameter		49	.327		19.05	21		40.05	52.50
0600	5" diameter		40	.400		24	26		50	65
0610	6" diameter	Q-2	46	.522		30.50	35		65.50	86
0620	8" diameter	"	41	.585		44	39.50		83.50	107
0700	To delete couplings & hangers, subtract									
0710	2" diam. to 5" diam.					25%	20%			
0720	6" diam. to 8" diam.					27%	15%			
1000	Schedule 40, black									
1040	3/4" diameter	1 Plum	71	.113	L.F.	10.25	8.10		18.35	23.50
1050	1" diameter		63	.127		12.15	9.15		21.30	27
1060	1-1/4" diameter		58	.138		16.05	9.95		26	32.50
1070	1-1/2" diameter		51	.157		18.65	11.30		29.95	37.50
1080	2" diameter		40	.200		23.50	14.40		37.90	47.50
1090	2-1/2" diameter	Q-1	57	.281		33.50	18.20		51.70	64
1100	3" diameter		50	.320		42.50	21		63.50	77.50
1110	4" diameter		45	.356		60.50	23		83.50	101
1120	5" diameter		37	.432		39	28		67	85
1130	6" diameter	Q-2	42	.571		109	38.50		147.50	178
1140	8" diameter		37	.649		129	43.50		172.50	206
1150	10" diameter		31	.774		178	52		230	274
1160	12" diameter		27	.889		203	60		263	315
1170	14" diameter		20	1.200		222	80.50		302.50	365
1180	16" diameter		17	1.412		320	95		415	495
1190	18" diameter		14	1.714		325	115		440	530
1200	20" diameter		12	2		410	135		545	650
1210	24" diameter		10	2.400		445	161		606	730
1740	To delete coupling & hanger, subtract									
1750	3/4" diam. to 2" diam.					65%	27%			
1760	2-1/2" diam. to 5" diam.					41%	18%			
1770	6" diam. to 12" diam.					31%	13%			
1780	14" diam. to 24" diam.					35%	10%			
1800	Galvanized									
1840	3/4" diameter	1 Plum	71	.113	L.F.	11.45	8.10		19.55	24.50
1850	1" diameter		63	.127		13.75	9.15		22.90	29
1860	1-1/4" diameter		58	.138		18.15	9.95		28.10	35
1870	1-1/2" diameter		51	.157		21	11.30		32.30	40.50
1880	2" diameter		40	.200		27	14.40		41.40	51
1890	2-1/2" diameter	Q-1	57	.281		21.50	18.20		39.70	50.50
1900	3" diameter		50	.320		26.50	21		47.50	60
1910	4" diameter		45	.356		38	23		61	76
1920	5" diameter		37	.432		39.50	28		67.50	85
1930	6" diameter	Q-2	42	.571		51.50	38.50		90	115
1940	8" diameter		37	.649		78	43.50		121.50	151
1950	10" diameter		31	.774		176	52		228	271

22 11 Facility Water Distribution

22 11 13 – Facility Water Distribution Piping

22 11 13.48 Pipe, Fittings and Valves, Steel, Grooved-Joint

		Crew	Daily Output	Labor-Hours	Unit	Material	2023 Bare Costs Labor	Equipment	Total	Total Incl O&P
1960	12" diameter	Q-2	27	.889	L.F.	217	60		277	325
2540	To delete coupling & hanger, subtract									
2550	3/4" diam. to 2" diam.					36%	27%			
2560	2-1/2" diam. to 5" diam.					19%	18%			
2570	6" diam. to 12" diam.					14%	13%			
2600	Schedule 80, black									
2610	3/4" diameter	1 Plum	65	.123	L.F.	11.80	8.85		20.65	26
2650	1" diameter		61	.131		14.70	9.45		24.15	30.50
2660	1-1/4" diameter		55	.145		19.75	10.50		30.25	37
2670	1-1/2" diameter		49	.163		23.50	11.75		35.25	43
2680	2" diameter		38	.211		29.50	15.15		44.65	55
2690	2-1/2" diameter	Q-1	54	.296		40	19.20		59.20	72.50
2700	3" diameter		48	.333		51.50	21.50		73	89
2710	4" diameter		44	.364		45	23.50		68.50	84.50
2720	5" diameter		35	.457		79	29.50		108.50	131
2730	6" diameter	Q-2	40	.600		146	40.50		186.50	220
2740	8" diameter		35	.686		176	46		222	263
2750	10" diameter		29	.828		415	55.50		470.50	540
2760	12" diameter		24	1		640	67.50		707.50	800
3240	To delete coupling & hanger, subtract									
3250	3/4" diam. to 2" diam.					30%	25%			
3260	2-1/2" diam. to 5" diam.					14%	17%			
3270	6" diam. to 12" diam.					12%	12%			
3300	Galvanized									
3310	3/4" diameter	1 Plum	65	.123	L.F.	8.85	8.85		17.70	23
3350	1" diameter		61	.131		9.55	9.45		19	24.50
3360	1-1/4" diameter		55	.145		12.70	10.50		23.20	29.50
3370	1-1/2" diameter		46	.174		14.70	12.55		27.25	35
3380	2" diameter		38	.211		19.45	15.15		34.60	44
3390	2-1/2" diameter	Q-1	54	.296		28.50	19.20		47.70	60
3400	3" diameter		48	.333		37	21.50		58.50	72.50
3410	4" diameter		44	.364		53	23.50		76.50	93
3420	5" diameter		35	.457		59	29.50		88.50	109
3430	6" diameter	Q-2	40	.600		80	40.50		120.50	148
3440	8" diameter		35	.686		210	46		256	300
3450	10" diameter		29	.828		370	55.50		425.50	490
3460	12" diameter		24	1		1,025	67.50		1,092.50	1,225
3920	To delete coupling & hanger, subtract									
3930	3/4" diam. to 2" diam.					30%	25%			
3940	2-1/2" diam. to 5" diam.					15%	17%			
3950	6" diam. to 12" diam.					11%	12%			
3990	Fittings: coupling material required at joints not incl. in fitting price.									
3994	Add 1 selected coupling, material only, per joint for installed price.									
4000	Elbow, 90° or 45°, painted									
4030	3/4" diameter	1 Plum	50	.160	Ea.	119	11.55		130.55	148
4040	1" diameter		50	.160		64	11.55		75.55	87.50
4050	1-1/4" diameter		40	.200		64	14.40		78.40	92
4060	1-1/2" diameter		33	.242		64	17.45		81.45	96.50
4070	2" diameter		25	.320		64	23		87	105
4080	2-1/2" diameter	Q-1	40	.400		64	26		90	109
4090	3" diameter		33	.485		112	31.50		143.50	170
4100	4" diameter		25	.640		122	41.50		163.50	196
4110	5" diameter		20	.800		288	52		340	395

22.11 Facility Water Distribution

22 11 13 – Facility Water Distribution Piping

	22 11 13.48 Pipe, Fittings and Valves, Steel, Grooved-Joint	Crew	Daily Output	Labor-Hours	Unit	Material	2023 Bare Costs Labor	2023 Bare Costs Equipment	Total	Total Incl O&P
4120	6" diameter	Q-2	25	.960	Ea.	340	64.50		404.50	465
4130	8" diameter		21	1.143		700	77		777	885
4140	10" diameter		18	1.333		1,300	89.50		1,389.50	1,550
4150	12" diameter		15	1.600		1,425	108		1,533	1,725
4170	14" diameter		12	2		1,300	135		1,435	1,650
4180	16" diameter		11	2.182		1,700	147		1,847	2,100
4190	18" diameter	Q-3	14	2.286		2,150	157		2,307	2,600
4200	20" diameter		12	2.667		2,850	183		3,033	3,400
4210	24" diameter		10	3.200		4,125	219		4,344	4,850
4250	For galvanized elbows, add					26%				
4690	Tee, painted									
4700	3/4" diameter	1 Plum	38	.211	Ea.	127	15.15		142.15	163
4740	1" diameter		33	.242		98.50	17.45		115.95	134
4750	1-1/4" diameter		27	.296		98.50	21.50		120	140
4760	1-1/2" diameter		22	.364		98.50	26		124.50	147
4770	2" diameter		17	.471		98.50	34		132.50	159
4780	2-1/2" diameter	Q-1	27	.593		98.50	38.50		137	166
4790	3" diameter		22	.727		134	47		181	219
4800	4" diameter		17	.941		204	61		265	315
4810	5" diameter		13	1.231		475	80		555	640
4820	6" diameter	Q-2	17	1.412		545	95		640	740
4830	8" diameter		14	1.714		1,200	115		1,315	1,500
4840	10" diameter		12	2		1,550	135		1,685	1,900
4850	12" diameter		10	2.400		2,025	161		2,186	2,475
4851	14" diameter		9	2.667		1,650	179		1,829	2,100
4852	16" diameter		8	3		1,875	202		2,077	2,350
4853	18" diameter	Q-3	10	3.200		2,350	219		2,569	2,900
4854	20" diameter		9	3.556		3,350	244		3,594	4,050
4855	24" diameter		8	4		5,100	274		5,374	6,025
4900	For galvanized tees, add					24%				
4906	Couplings, rigid style, painted									
4908	1" diameter	1 Plum	100	.080	Ea.	49.50	5.75		55.25	63
4909	1-1/4" diameter		100	.080		46.50	5.75		52.25	59.50
4910	1-1/2" diameter		67	.119		49.50	8.60		58.10	67.50
4912	2" diameter		50	.160		63.50	11.55		75.05	86.50
4914	2-1/2" diameter	Q-1	80	.200		71.50	12.95		84.45	98.50
4916	3" diameter		67	.239		83	15.50		98.50	115
4918	4" diameter		50	.320		115	21		136	157
4920	5" diameter		40	.400		148	26		174	201
4922	6" diameter	Q-2	50	.480		195	32.50		227.50	263
4924	8" diameter		42	.571		305	38.50		343.50	395
4926	10" diameter		35	.686		595	46		641	725
4928	12" diameter		32	.750		665	50.50		715.50	805
4930	14" diameter		24	1		580	67.50		647.50	740
4931	16" diameter		20	1.200		620	80.50		700.50	805
4932	18" diameter		18	1.333		720	89.50		809.50	925
4933	20" diameter		16	1.500		980	101		1,081	1,225
4934	24" diameter		13	1.846		1,250	124		1,374	1,550
4940	Flexible, standard, painted									
4950	3/4" diameter	1 Plum	100	.080	Ea.	36.50	5.75		42.25	49
4960	1" diameter		100	.080		36.50	5.75		42.25	49
4970	1-1/4" diameter		80	.100		47	7.20		54.20	62.50
4980	1-1/2" diameter		67	.119		51	8.60		59.60	69.50

22 11 Facility Water Distribution

22 11 13 – Facility Water Distribution Piping

22 11 13.48 Pipe, Fittings and Valves, Steel, Grooved-Joint		Crew	Daily Output	Labor-Hours	Unit	Material	2023 Bare Costs Labor	Equipment	Total	Total Incl O&P
4990	2" diameter	1 Plum	50	.160	Ea.	55	11.55		66.55	77.50
5000	2-1/2" diameter	Q-1	80	.200		63.50	12.95		76.45	89.50
5010	3" diameter		67	.239		70	15.50		85.50	100
5020	3-1/2" diameter		57	.281		100	18.20		118.20	137
5030	4" diameter		50	.320		101	21		122	142
5040	5" diameter		40	.400		151	26		177	205
5050	6" diameter	Q-2	50	.480		179	32.50		211.50	244
5070	8" diameter		42	.571		289	38.50		327.50	380
5090	10" diameter		35	.686		470	46		516	585
5110	12" diameter		32	.750		535	50.50		585.50	665
5120	14" diameter		24	1		765	67.50		832.50	940
5130	16" diameter		20	1.200		1,000	80.50		1,080.50	1,225
5140	18" diameter		18	1.333		1,175	89.50		1,264.50	1,425
5150	20" diameter		16	1.500		1,850	101		1,951	2,175
5160	24" diameter		13	1.846		2,025	124		2,149	2,400
5176	Lightweight style, painted									
5178	1-1/2" diameter	1 Plum	67	.119	Ea.	45	8.60		53.60	62.50
5180	2" diameter	"	50	.160		55	11.55		66.55	77.50
5182	2-1/2" diameter	Q-1	80	.200		63.50	12.95		76.45	89.50
5184	3" diameter		67	.239		70	15.50		85.50	100
5186	3-1/2" diameter		57	.281		84	18.20		102.20	120
5188	4" diameter		50	.320		101	21		122	142
5190	5" diameter		40	.400		151	26		177	205
5192	6" diameter	Q-2	50	.480		179	32.50		211.50	244
5194	8" diameter		42	.571		289	38.50		327.50	380
5196	10" diameter		35	.686		590	46		636	720
5198	12" diameter		32	.750		655	50.50		705.50	795
5200	For galvanized couplings, add					33%				
5220	Tee, reducing, painted									
5225	2" x 1-1/2" diameter	Q-1	38	.421	Ea.	206	27.50		233.50	268
5226	2-1/2" x 2" diameter		28	.571		206	37		243	283
5227	3" x 2-1/2" diameter		23	.696		182	45		227	268
5228	4" x 3" diameter		18	.889		245	57.50		302.50	355
5229	5" x 4" diameter		15	1.067		520	69		589	680
5230	6" x 4" diameter	Q-2	18	1.333		575	89.50		664.50	765
5231	8" x 6" diameter		15	1.600		1,200	108		1,308	1,475
5232	10" x 8" diameter		13	1.846		1,325	124		1,449	1,650
5233	12" x 10" diameter		11	2.182		1,675	147		1,822	2,050
5234	14" x 12" diameter		10	2.400		1,750	161		1,911	2,150
5235	16" x 12" diameter		9	2.667		1,500	179		1,679	1,925
5236	18" x 12" diameter	Q-3	12	2.667		1,800	183		1,983	2,250
5237	18" x 16" diameter		11	2.909		2,275	200		2,475	2,800
5238	20" x 16" diameter		10	3.200		2,950	219		3,169	3,575
5239	24" x 20" diameter		9	3.556		4,675	244		4,919	5,500
5240	Reducer, concentric, painted									
5241	2-1/2" x 2" diameter	Q-1	43	.372	Ea.	74.50	24		98.50	118
5242	3" x 2-1/2" diameter		35	.457		89.50	29.50		119	143
5243	4" x 3" diameter		29	.552		108	36		144	173
5244	5" x 4" diameter		22	.727		148	47		195	234
5245	6" x 4" diameter	Q-2	26	.923		172	62		234	282
5246	8" x 6" diameter		23	1.043		440	70		510	590
5247	10" x 8" diameter		20	1.200		865	80.50		945.50	1,075
5248	12" x 10" diameter		16	1.500		1,550	101		1,651	1,850

22 11 Facility Water Distribution

22 11 13 – Facility Water Distribution Piping

22 11 13.48 Pipe, Fittings and Valves, Steel, Grooved-Joint

		Crew	Daily Output	Labor-Hours	Unit	Material	2023 Bare Costs Labor	Equipment	Total	Total Incl O&P
5255	Eccentric, painted									
5256	2-1/2" x 2" diameter	Q-1	42	.381	Ea.	154	24.50		178.50	206
5257	3" x 2-1/2" diameter		34	.471		176	30.50		206.50	239
5258	4" x 3" diameter		28	.571		214	37		251	291
5259	5" x 4" diameter		21	.762		290	49.50		339.50	395
5260	6" x 4" diameter	Q-2	25	.960		335	64.50		399.50	465
5261	8" x 6" diameter		22	1.091		680	73.50		753.50	855
5262	10" x 8" diameter		19	1.263		1,775	85		1,860	2,100
5263	12" x 10" diameter		15	1.600		2,450	108		2,558	2,850
5270	Coupling, reducing, painted									
5272	2" x 1-1/2" diameter	1 Plum	52	.154	Ea.	72	11.10		83.10	95.50
5274	2-1/2" x 2" diameter	Q-1	82	.195		93	12.65		105.65	121
5276	3" x 2" diameter		69	.232		105	15.05		120.05	139
5278	4" x 2" diameter		52	.308		166	19.95		185.95	212
5280	5" x 4" diameter		42	.381		186	24.50		210.50	242
5282	6" x 4" diameter	Q-2	52	.462		280	31		311	355
5284	8" x 6" diameter	"	44	.545		420	36.50		456.50	515
5290	Outlet coupling, painted									
5294	1-1/2" x 1" pipe size	1 Plum	65	.123	Ea.	95	8.85		103.85	118
5296	2" x 1" pipe size	"	48	.167		96.50	12		108.50	124
5298	2-1/2" x 1" pipe size	Q-1	78	.205		148	13.30		161.30	182
5300	2-1/2" x 1-1/4" pipe size		70	.229		166	14.80		180.80	205
5302	3" x 1" pipe size		65	.246		188	15.95		203.95	231
5304	4" x 3/4" pipe size		48	.333		208	21.50		229.50	261
5306	4" x 1-1/2" pipe size		46	.348		294	22.50		316.50	360
5308	6" x 1-1/2" pipe size	Q-2	44	.545		415	36.50		451.50	510
5320	Outlet, strap-on T, painted									
5324	Threaded female branch									
5330	2" pipe x 1-1/2" branch size	1 Plum	50	.160	Ea.	68.50	11.55		80.05	92.50
5334	2-1/2" pipe x 1-1/2" branch size	Q-1	80	.200		83	12.95		95.95	111
5338	3" pipe x 1-1/2" branch size		67	.239		86	15.50		101.50	118
5342	3" pipe x 2" branch size		59	.271		99	17.60		116.60	135
5346	4" pipe x 2" branch size		50	.320		104	21		125	145
5350	4" pipe x 2-1/2" branch size		47	.340		108	22		130	152
5354	4" pipe x 3" branch size		43	.372		115	24		139	163
5358	5" pipe x 3" branch size		40	.400		142	26		168	195
5362	6" pipe x 2" branch size	Q-2	50	.480		130	32.50		162.50	191
5366	6" pipe x 3" branch size		47	.511		148	34.50		182.50	214
5370	6" pipe x 4" branch size		44	.545		164	36.50		200.50	236
5374	8" pipe x 2-1/2" branch size		42	.571		226	38.50		264.50	305
5378	8" pipe x 4" branch size		38	.632		245	42.50		287.50	335
5390	Grooved branch									
5394	2" pipe x 1-1/4" branch size	1 Plum	78	.103	Ea.	68.50	7.40		75.90	86.50
5398	2" pipe x 1-1/2" branch size	"	50	.160		68.50	11.55		80.05	92.50
5402	2-1/2" pipe x 1-1/2" branch size	Q-1	80	.200		83	12.95		95.95	111
5406	3" pipe x 1-1/2" branch size		67	.239		86	15.50		101.50	118
5410	3" pipe x 2" branch size		59	.271		99	17.60		116.60	135
5414	4" pipe x 2" branch size		50	.320		104	21		125	145
5418	4" pipe x 2-1/2" branch size		47	.340		108	22		130	152
5422	4" pipe x 3" branch size		43	.372		115	24		139	163
5426	5" pipe x 3" branch size		40	.400		142	26		168	195
5430	6" pipe x 2" branch size	Q-2	50	.480		130	32.50		162.50	191
5434	6" pipe x 3" branch size		47	.511		148	34.50		182.50	214

22 11 Facility Water Distribution

22 11 13 – Facility Water Distribution Piping

22 11 13.48 Pipe, Fittings and Valves, Steel, Grooved-Joint		Crew	Daily Output	Labor-Hours	Unit	Material	2023 Bare Costs Labor	2023 Bare Costs Equipment	Total	Total Incl O&P
5438	6" pipe x 4" branch size	Q-2	44	.545	Ea.	164	36.50		200.50	236
5442	8" pipe x 2-1/2" branch size		42	.571		226	38.50		264.50	305
5446	8" pipe x 4" branch size		38	.632		245	42.50		287.50	335
5750	Flange, w/groove gasket, black steel									
5754	See Line 22 11 13.47 0620 for gasket & bolt set									
5760	ANSI class 125 and 150, painted									
5780	2" pipe size	1 Plum	23	.348	Ea.	209	25		234	267
5790	2-1/2" pipe size	Q-1	37	.432		259	28		287	325
5800	3" pipe size		31	.516		279	33.50		312.50	355
5820	4" pipe size		23	.696		370	45		415	480
5830	5" pipe size		19	.842		430	54.50		484.50	555
5840	6" pipe size	Q-2	23	1.043		470	70		540	625
5850	8" pipe size		17	1.412		530	95		625	725
5860	10" pipe size		14	1.714		840	115		955	1,100
5870	12" pipe size		12	2		1,100	135		1,235	1,400
5880	14" pipe size		10	2.400		1,900	161		2,061	2,350
5890	16" pipe size		9	2.667		2,200	179		2,379	2,700
5900	18" pipe size		6	4		2,725	269		2,994	3,400
5910	20" pipe size		5	4.800		3,275	325		3,600	4,075
5920	24" pipe size		4.50	5.333		4,200	360		4,560	5,125
5940	ANSI class 350, painted									
5946	2" pipe size	1 Plum	23	.348	Ea.	261	25		286	325
5948	2-1/2" pipe size	Q-1	37	.432		300	28		328	370
5950	3" pipe size		31	.516		410	33.50		443.50	500
5952	4" pipe size		23	.696		545	45		590	670
5954	5" pipe size		19	.842		620	54.50		674.50	765
5956	6" pipe size	Q-2	23	1.043		720	70		790	900
5958	8" pipe size		17	1.412		830	95		925	1,050
5960	10" pipe size		14	1.714		1,325	115		1,440	1,625
5962	12" pipe size		12	2		1,400	135		1,535	1,750
6100	Cross, painted									
6110	2" diameter	1 Plum	12.50	.640	Ea.	174	46		220	261
6112	2-1/2" diameter	Q-1	20	.800		174	52		226	270
6114	3" diameter		15.50	1.032		310	67		377	440
6116	4" diameter		12.50	1.280		510	83		593	690
6118	6" diameter	Q-2	12.50	1.920		1,325	129		1,454	1,675
6120	8" diameter		10.50	2.286		1,750	154		1,904	2,150
6122	10" diameter		9	2.667		2,875	179		3,054	3,450
6124	12" diameter		7.50	3.200		4,175	215		4,390	4,900
7400	Suction diffuser									
7402	Grooved end inlet x flanged outlet									
7410	3" x 3"	Q-1	27	.593	Ea.	1,675	38.50		1,713.50	1,900
7412	4" x 4"		19	.842		2,275	54.50		2,329.50	2,575
7414	5" x 5"		14	1.143		2,675	74		2,749	3,025
7416	6" x 6"	Q-2	20	1.200		3,350	80.50		3,430.50	3,825
7418	8" x 8"		15	1.600		6,250	108		6,358	7,025
7420	10" x 10"		12	2		8,500	135		8,635	9,550
7422	12" x 12"		9	2.667		14,000	179		14,179	15,700
7424	14" x 14"		7	3.429		13,000	231		13,231	14,600
7426	16" x 14"		6	4		13,300	269		13,569	15,100
7500	Strainer, tee type, painted									
7506	2" pipe size	1 Plum	21	.381	Ea.	1,125	27.50		1,152.50	1,275
7508	2-1/2" pipe size	Q-1	30	.533		1,175	34.50		1,209.50	1,350

22 11 Facility Water Distribution

22 11 13 – Facility Water Distribution Piping

22 11 13.48 Pipe, Fittings and Valves, Steel, Grooved-Joint		Crew	Daily Output	Labor-Hours	Unit	Material	2023 Bare Costs Labor	Equipment	Total	Total Incl O&P
7510	3" pipe size	Q-1	28	.571	Ea.	1,325	37		1,362	1,500
7512	4" pipe size		20	.800		1,500	52		1,552	1,725
7514	5" pipe size		15	1.067		2,175	69		2,244	2,475
7516	6" pipe size	Q-2	23	1.043		2,350	70		2,420	2,675
7518	8" pipe size		16	1.500		3,600	101		3,701	4,125
7520	10" pipe size		13	1.846		5,300	124		5,424	6,000
7522	12" pipe size		10	2.400		6,800	161		6,961	7,750
7524	14" pipe size		8	3		17,500	202		17,702	19,500
7526	16" pipe size		7	3.429		21,700	231		21,931	24,200
7570	Expansion joint, max. 3" travel									
7572	2" diameter	1 Plum	24	.333	Ea.	1,425	24		1,449	1,575
7574	3" diameter	Q-1	31	.516		1,625	33.50		1,658.50	1,825
7576	4" diameter	"	23	.696		2,150	45		2,195	2,425
7578	6" diameter	Q-2	38	.632		3,325	42.50		3,367.50	3,725
7790	Valves: coupling material required at joints not incl. in valve price.									
7794	Add 1 selected coupling, material only, per joint for installed price.									
7800	Ball valve w/handle, carbon steel trim									
7810	1-1/2" pipe size	1 Plum	31	.258	Ea.	252	18.60		270.60	305
7812	2" pipe size	"	24	.333		280	24		304	345
7814	2-1/2" pipe size	Q-1	38	.421		610	27.50		637.50	710
7816	3" pipe size		31	.516		985	33.50		1,018.50	1,125
7818	4" pipe size		23	.696		1,525	45		1,570	1,750
7820	6" pipe size	Q-2	24	1		4,650	67.50		4,717.50	5,225
7830	With gear operator									
7834	2-1/2" pipe size	Q-1	38	.421	Ea.	1,225	27.50		1,252.50	1,400
7836	3" pipe size		31	.516		1,750	33.50		1,783.50	1,975
7838	4" pipe size		23	.696		2,225	45		2,270	2,525
7840	6" pipe size	Q-2	24	1		5,225	67.50		5,292.50	5,850
7870	Check valve									
7874	2-1/2" pipe size	Q-1	38	.421	Ea.	540	27.50		567.50	630
7876	3" pipe size		31	.516		635	33.50		668.50	745
7878	4" pipe size		23	.696		670	45		715	805
7880	5" pipe size		18	.889		1,125	57.50		1,182.50	1,300
7882	6" pipe size	Q-2	24	1		1,325	67.50		1,392.50	1,550
7884	8" pipe size		19	1.263		1,800	85		1,885	2,100
7886	10" pipe size		16	1.500		4,825	101		4,926	5,450
7888	12" pipe size		13	1.846		5,700	124		5,824	6,450
7900	Plug valve, balancing, w/lever operator									
7906	3" pipe size	Q-1	31	.516	Ea.	1,100	33.50		1,133.50	1,250
7908	4" pipe size	"	23	.696		1,350	45		1,395	1,575
7909	6" pipe size	Q-2	24	1		2,075	67.50		2,142.50	2,375
7916	With gear operator									
7920	3" pipe size	Q-1	31	.516	Ea.	2,075	33.50		2,108.50	2,350
7922	4" pipe size	"	23	.696		2,150	45		2,195	2,450
7924	6" pipe size	Q-2	24	1		2,925	67.50		2,992.50	3,300
7926	8" pipe size		19	1.263		4,475	85		4,560	5,050
7928	10" pipe size		16	1.500		5,650	101		5,751	6,375
7930	12" pipe size		13	1.846		8,625	124		8,749	9,650
8000	Butterfly valve, 2 position handle, with standard trim									
8010	1-1/2" pipe size	1 Plum	30	.267	Ea.	505	19.20		524.20	585
8020	2" pipe size	"	23	.348		505	25		530	595
8030	3" pipe size	Q-1	30	.533		725	34.50		759.50	845
8050	4" pipe size	"	22	.727		795	47		842	945

22 11 Facility Water Distribution

22 11 13 – Facility Water Distribution Piping

22 11 13.48 Pipe, Fittings and Valves, Steel, Grooved-Joint		Crew	Daily Output	Labor-Hours	Unit	Material	2023 Bare Costs Labor	Equipment	Total	Total Incl O&P
8070	6" pipe size	Q-2	23	1.043	Ea.	1,600	70		1,670	1,875
8080	8" pipe size		18	1.333		2,150	89.50		2,239.50	2,500
8090	10" pipe size	↓	15	1.600	↓	3,550	108		3,658	4,050
8200	With stainless steel trim									
8240	1-1/2" pipe size	1 Plum	30	.267	Ea.	640	19.20		659.20	735
8250	2" pipe size	"	23	.348		640	25		665	745
8270	3" pipe size	Q-1	30	.533		860	34.50		894.50	995
8280	4" pipe size	"	22	.727		935	47		982	1,100
8300	6" pipe size	Q-2	23	1.043		1,750	70		1,820	2,025
8310	8" pipe size		18	1.333		4,300	89.50		4,389.50	4,850
8320	10" pipe size		15	1.600		7,175	108		7,283	8,050
8322	12" pipe size		12	2		8,250	135		8,385	9,275
8324	14" pipe size		10	2.400		10,600	161		10,761	11,800
8326	16" pipe size	↓	9	2.667		17,600	179		17,779	19,600
8328	18" pipe size	Q-3	12	2.667		18,800	183		18,983	21,000
8330	20" pipe size		10	3.200		23,100	219		23,319	25,700
8332	24" pipe size	↓	9	3.556	↓	30,900	244		31,144	34,400
8336	Note: sizes 8" up w/manual gear operator									
9000	Cut one groove, labor									
9010	3/4" pipe size	Q-1	152	.105	Ea.		6.85		6.85	10.20
9020	1" pipe size		140	.114			7.40		7.40	11.05
9030	1-1/4" pipe size		124	.129			8.35		8.35	12.50
9040	1-1/2" pipe size		114	.140			9.10		9.10	13.55
9050	2" pipe size		104	.154			10		10	14.90
9060	2-1/2" pipe size		96	.167			10.80		10.80	16.10
9070	3" pipe size		88	.182			11.80		11.80	17.60
9080	3-1/2" pipe size		83	.193			12.50		12.50	18.65
9090	4" pipe size		78	.205			13.30		13.30	19.85
9100	5" pipe size		72	.222			14.40		14.40	21.50
9110	6" pipe size		70	.229			14.80		14.80	22
9120	8" pipe size		54	.296			19.20		19.20	28.50
9130	10" pipe size		38	.421			27.50		27.50	40.50
9140	12" pipe size		30	.533			34.50		34.50	51.50
9150	14" pipe size		20	.800			52		52	77.50
9160	16" pipe size		19	.842			54.50		54.50	81.50
9170	18" pipe size		18	.889			57.50		57.50	86
9180	20" pipe size		17	.941			61		61	91
9190	24" pipe size	↓	15	1.067	↓		69		69	103
9210	Roll one groove									
9220	3/4" pipe size	Q-1	266	.060	Ea.		3.90		3.90	5.80
9230	1" pipe size		228	.070			4.55		4.55	6.80
9240	1-1/4" pipe size		200	.080			5.20		5.20	7.75
9250	1-1/2" pipe size		178	.090			5.85		5.85	8.70
9260	2" pipe size		116	.138			8.95		8.95	13.35
9270	2-1/2" pipe size		110	.145			9.45		9.45	14.05
9280	3" pipe size		100	.160			10.40		10.40	15.45
9290	3-1/2" pipe size		94	.170			11.05		11.05	16.45
9300	4" pipe size		86	.186			12.05		12.05	18
9310	5" pipe size		84	.190			12.35		12.35	18.40
9320	6" pipe size		80	.200			12.95		12.95	19.35
9330	8" pipe size		66	.242			15.70		15.70	23.50
9340	10" pipe size		58	.276			17.90		17.90	26.50
9350	12" pipe size	↓	46	.348			22.50		22.50	33.50

22 11 Facility Water Distribution

22 11 13 – Facility Water Distribution Piping

22 11 13.48 Pipe, Fittings and Valves, Steel, Grooved-Joint		Crew	Daily Output	Labor-Hours	Unit	Material	2023 Bare Costs Labor	Equipment	Total	Total Incl O&P
9360	14" pipe size	Q-1	30	.533	Ea.		34.50		34.50	51.50
9370	16" pipe size		28	.571			37		37	55.50
9380	18" pipe size		27	.593			38.50		38.50	57.50
9390	20" pipe size		25	.640			41.50		41.50	62
9400	24" pipe size		23	.696			45		45	67.50
22 11 13.60 Tubing, Stainless Steel										
0010	**TUBING, STAINLESS STEEL**									
5000	Tubing									
5010	Type 304, no joints, no hangers									
5020	.035 wall									
5021	1/4"	1 Plum	160	.050	L.F.	11.10	3.60		14.70	17.55
5022	3/8"		160	.050		4.61	3.60		8.21	10.40
5023	1/2"		160	.050		11.90	3.60		15.50	18.40
5024	5/8"		160	.050		7.30	3.60		10.90	13.35
5025	3/4"		133	.060		8.75	4.33		13.08	16.10
5026	7/8"		133	.060		9.25	4.33		13.58	16.65
5027	1"		114	.070		10.20	5.05		15.25	18.75
5040	.049 wall									
5041	1/4"	1 Plum	160	.050	L.F.	4.29	3.60		7.89	10.05
5042	3/8"		160	.050		5.95	3.60		9.55	11.90
5043	1/2"		160	.050		6.60	3.60		10.20	12.60
5044	5/8"		160	.050		8.90	3.60		12.50	15.15
5045	3/4"		133	.060		9.45	4.33		13.78	16.85
5046	7/8"		133	.060		14.30	4.33		18.63	22
5047	1"		114	.070		10.50	5.05		15.55	19.10
5060	.065 wall									
5061	1/4"	1 Plum	160	.050	L.F.	4.81	3.60		8.41	10.65
5062	3/8"		160	.050		6.65	3.60		10.25	12.65
5063	1/2"		160	.050		8.05	3.60		11.65	14.20
5064	5/8"		160	.050		9.75	3.60		13.35	16.10
5065	3/4"		133	.060		10.35	4.33		14.68	17.85
5066	7/8"		133	.060		11.90	4.33		16.23	19.50
5067	1"		114	.070		11.60	5.05		16.65	20.50
5210	Type 316									
5220	.035 wall									
5221	1/4"	1 Plum	160	.050	L.F.	5.30	3.60		8.90	11.15
5222	3/8"		160	.050		6.90	3.60		10.50	12.95
5223	1/2"		160	.050		10.95	3.60		14.55	17.40
5224	5/8"		160	.050		8.35	3.60		11.95	14.50
5225	3/4"		133	.060		19.50	4.33		23.83	28
5226	7/8"		133	.060		17.55	4.33		21.88	26
5227	1"		114	.070		13.95	5.05		19	23
5240	.049 wall									
5241	1/4"	1 Plum	160	.050	L.F.	6.30	3.60		9.90	12.30
5242	3/8"		160	.050		10.40	3.60		14	16.80
5243	1/2"		160	.050		10.80	3.60		14.40	17.20
5244	5/8"		160	.050		13.30	3.60		16.90	19.95
5245	3/4"		133	.060		17.15	4.33		21.48	25.50
5246	7/8"		133	.060		15.80	4.33		20.13	24
5247	1"		114	.070		14.30	5.05		19.35	23.50
5260	.065 wall									
5261	1/4"	1 Plum	160	.050	L.F.	6.40	3.60		10	12.40

22 11 Facility Water Distribution

22 11 13 – Facility Water Distribution Piping

22 11 13.60 Tubing, Stainless Steel		Crew	Daily Output	Labor-Hours	Unit	Material	2023 Bare Costs Labor	Equipment	Total	Total Incl O&P
5262	3/8"	1 Plum	160	.050	L.F.	10.65	3.60		14.25	17.05
5263	1/2"		160	.050		9.25	3.60		12.85	15.55
5264	5/8"		160	.050		10.75	3.60		14.35	17.15
5265	3/4"		133	.060		11.25	4.33		15.58	18.85
5266	7/8"		133	.060		18.50	4.33		22.83	27
5267	1"		114	.070		17.60	5.05		22.65	27

22 11 13.61 Tubing Fittings, Stainless Steel

		Crew	Daily Output	Labor-Hours	Unit	Material	Labor	Equipment	Total	Total Incl O&P
0010	**TUBING FITTINGS, STAINLESS STEEL**									
8200	Tube fittings, compression type									
8202	Type 316									
8204	90° elbow									
8206	1/4"	1 Plum	24	.333	Ea.	27.50	24		51.50	66.50
8207	3/8"		22	.364		34	26		60	76.50
8208	1/2"		22	.364		55.50	26		81.50	101
8209	5/8"		21	.381		62.50	27.50		90	110
8210	3/4"		21	.381		98.50	27.50		126	149
8211	7/8"		20	.400		152	29		181	210
8212	1"		20	.400		188	29		217	250
8220	Union tee									
8222	1/4"	1 Plum	15	.533	Ea.	39	38.50		77.50	101
8224	3/8"		15	.533		50.50	38.50		89	113
8225	1/2"		15	.533		77.50	38.50		116	143
8226	5/8"		14	.571		87	41		128	158
8227	3/4"		14	.571		116	41		157	190
8228	7/8"		13	.615		227	44.50		271.50	315
8229	1"		13	.615		249	44.50		293.50	340
8234	Union									
8236	1/4"	1 Plum	24	.333	Ea.	19.15	24		43.15	57
8237	3/8"		22	.364		27	26		53	69
8238	1/2"		22	.364		40.50	26		66.50	83.50
8239	5/8"		21	.381		53	27.50		80.50	99
8240	3/4"		21	.381		66	27.50		93.50	114
8241	7/8"		20	.400		108	29		137	162
8242	1"		20	.400		114	29		143	168
8250	Male connector									
8252	1/4" x 1/4"	1 Plum	24	.333	Ea.	12.25	24		36.25	49.50
8253	3/8" x 3/8"		22	.364		19.15	26		45.15	60
8254	1/2" x 1/2"		22	.364		28.50	26		54.50	70
8256	3/4" x 3/4"		21	.381		43.50	27.50		71	88.50
8258	1" x 1"		20	.400		75.50	29		104.50	126

22 11 13.64 Pipe, Stainless Steel

		Crew	Daily Output	Labor-Hours	Unit	Material	Labor	Equipment	Total	Total Incl O&P
0010	**PIPE, STAINLESS STEEL**									
0020	Welded, with clevis type hanger assemblies, 10' OC									
0500	Schedule 5, type 304									
0540	1/2" diameter	Q-15	128	.125	L.F.	8.55	8.10	.50	17.15	22
0550	3/4" diameter		116	.138		10.45	8.95	.55	19.95	25.50
0560	1" diameter		103	.155		10.90	10.05	.62	21.57	27.50
0570	1-1/4" diameter		93	.172		16.90	11.15	.69	28.74	36
0580	1-1/2" diameter		85	.188		20.50	12.20	.75	33.45	41.50
0590	2" diameter		69	.232		35	15.05	.93	50.98	62
0600	2-1/2" diameter		53	.302		31	19.60	1.21	51.81	65
0610	3" diameter		48	.333		97	21.50	1.34	119.84	140

For customer support on your Mechanical Costs with RSMeans data, call 800.448.8182.

22 11 Facility Water Distribution

22 11 13 – Facility Water Distribution Piping

22 11 13.64 Pipe, Stainless Steel

		Crew	Daily Output	Labor-Hours	Unit	Material	2023 Bare Costs Labor	Equipment	Total	Total Incl O&P
0620	4" diameter	Q-15	44	.364	L.F.	167	23.50	1.46	191.96	220
0630	5" diameter	▼	36	.444		73.50	29	1.78	104.28	125
0640	6" diameter	Q-16	42	.571		440	38.50	1.53	480.03	540
0650	8" diameter		34	.706		675	47.50	1.88	724.38	820
0660	10" diameter		26	.923		86.50	62	2.46	150.96	190
0670	12" diameter	▼	21	1.143	▼	530	77	3.05	610.05	705
0700	To delete hangers, subtract									
0710	1/2" diam. to 1-1/2" diam.					8%	19%			
0720	2" diam. to 5" diam.					4%	9%			
0730	6" diam. to 12" diam.					3%	4%			
0750	For small quantities, add				L.F.	10%				
1250	Schedule 5, type 316									
1290	1/2" diameter	Q-15	128	.125	L.F.	9.80	8.10	.50	18.40	23.50
1300	3/4" diameter		116	.138		11.75	8.95	.55	21.25	27
1310	1" diameter		103	.155		18.05	10.05	.62	28.72	35.50
1320	1-1/4" diameter		93	.172		22.50	11.15	.69	34.34	42.50
1330	1-1/2" diameter		85	.188		31	12.20	.75	43.95	53
1340	2" diameter		69	.232		43	15.05	.93	58.98	70.50
1350	2-1/2" diameter		53	.302		114	19.60	1.21	134.81	156
1360	3" diameter		48	.333		146	21.50	1.34	168.84	193
1370	4" diameter		44	.364		181	23.50	1.46	205.96	236
1380	5" diameter	▼	36	.444		207	29	1.78	237.78	273
1390	6" diameter	Q-16	42	.571		246	38.50	1.53	286.03	330
1400	8" diameter		34	.706		370	47.50	1.88	419.38	485
1410	10" diameter		26	.923		440	62	2.46	504.46	580
1420	12" diameter	▼	21	1.143		156	77	3.05	236.05	290
1490	For small quantities, add				▼	10%				
1940	To delete hanger, subtract									
1950	1/2" diam. to 1-1/2" diam.					5%	19%			
1960	2" diam. to 5" diam.					3%	9%			
1970	6" diam. to 12" diam.					2%	4%			
2000	Schedule 10, type 304									
2040	1/4" diameter	Q-15	131	.122	L.F.	13.60	7.90	.49	21.99	27.50
2050	3/8" diameter		128	.125		11.40	8.10	.50	20	25
2060	1/2" diameter		125	.128		8.80	8.30	.51	17.61	22.50
2070	3/4" diameter		113	.142		10.45	9.20	.57	20.22	26
2080	1" diameter		100	.160		11.90	10.40	.64	22.94	29.50
2090	1-1/4" diameter		91	.176		18.10	11.40	.71	30.21	37.50
2100	1-1/2" diameter		83	.193		20.50	12.50	.77	33.77	42
2110	2" diameter		67	.239		18.85	15.50	.96	35.31	45
2120	2-1/2" diameter		51	.314		35	20.50	1.26	56.76	71
2130	3" diameter		46	.348		41.50	22.50	1.39	65.39	80.50
2140	4" diameter		42	.381		52.50	24.50	1.53	78.53	96.50
2150	5" diameter	▼	35	.457		118	29.50	1.83	149.33	176
2160	6" diameter	Q-16	40	.600		83	40.50	1.60	125.10	153
2170	8" diameter		33	.727		91.50	49	1.94	142.44	175
2180	10" diameter		25	.960		137	64.50	2.56	204.06	250
2190	12" diameter	▼	21	1.143		107	77	3.05	187.05	236
2250	For small quantities, add				▼	10%				
2650	To delete hanger, subtract									
2660	1/4" diam. to 3/4" diam.					9%	22%			
2670	1" diam. to 2" diam.					4%	15%			
2680	2-1/2" diam. to 5" diam.					3%	8%			

22 11 Facility Water Distribution

22 11 13 – Facility Water Distribution Piping

22 11 13.64 Pipe, Stainless Steel

		Crew	Daily Output	Labor-Hours	Unit	Material	2023 Bare Costs Labor	Equipment	Total	Total Incl O&P
2690	6" diam. to 12" diam.					3%	4%			
2750	Schedule 10, type 316									
2790	1/4" diameter	Q-15	131	.122	L.F.	10.10	7.90	.49	18.49	23.50
2800	3/8" diameter		128	.125		12.05	8.10	.50	20.65	26
2810	1/2" diameter		125	.128		7.80	8.30	.51	16.61	21.50
2820	3/4" diameter		113	.142		9.20	9.20	.57	18.97	24.50
2830	1" diameter		100	.160		13.80	10.40	.64	24.84	31.50
2840	1-1/4" diameter		91	.176		16.70	11.40	.71	28.81	36
2850	1-1/2" diameter		83	.193		21	12.50	.77	34.27	42.50
2860	2" diameter		67	.239		24	15.50	.96	40.46	50.50
2870	2-1/2" diameter		51	.314		35.50	20.50	1.26	57.26	71
2880	3" diameter		46	.348		41	22.50	1.39	64.89	80
2890	4" diameter		42	.381		55.50	24.50	1.53	81.53	99.50
2900	5" diameter		35	.457		74	29.50	1.83	105.33	127
2910	6" diameter	Q-16	40	.600		84	40.50	1.60	126.10	154
2920	8" diameter		33	.727		84.50	49	1.94	135.44	168
2930	10" diameter		25	.960		112	64.50	2.56	179.06	223
2940	12" diameter		21	1.143		127	77	3.05	207.05	257
2990	For small quantities, add					10%				
3430	To delete hanger, subtract									
3440	1/4" diam. to 3/4" diam.					6%	22%			
3450	1" diam. to 2" diam.					3%	15%			
3460	2-1/2" diam. to 5" diam.					2%	8%			
3470	6" diam. to 12" diam.					2%	4%			
3500	Threaded, couplings and clevis hanger assemblies, 10' OC									
3520	Schedule 40, type 304									
3540	1/4" diameter	1 Plum	54	.148	L.F.	7	10.65		17.65	23.50
3550	3/8" diameter		53	.151		7.85	10.90		18.75	25
3560	1/2" diameter		52	.154		8.90	11.10		20	26.50
3570	3/4" diameter		51	.157		12.05	11.30		23.35	30
3580	1" diameter		45	.178		18.20	12.80		31	39
3590	1-1/4" diameter	Q-1	76	.211		24	13.65		37.65	47
3600	1-1/2" diameter		69	.232		30	15.05		45.05	55.50
3610	2" diameter		57	.281		43	18.20		61.20	74
3620	2-1/2" diameter		44	.364		71	23.50		94.50	113
3630	3" diameter		38	.421		92	27.50		119.50	142
3640	4" diameter	Q-2	51	.471		131	31.50		162.50	191
3740	For small quantities, add					10%				
4200	To delete couplings & hangers, subtract									
4210	1/4" diam. to 3/4" diam.					15%	56%			
4220	1" diam. to 2" diam.					18%	49%			
4230	2-1/2" diam. to 4" diam.					34%	40%			
4250	Schedule 40, type 316									
4290	1/4" diameter	1 Plum	54	.148	L.F.	15.25	10.65		25.90	32.50
4300	3/8" diameter		53	.151		15.95	10.90		26.85	34
4310	1/2" diameter		52	.154		17.50	11.10		28.60	36
4320	3/4" diameter		51	.157		22	11.30		33.30	41
4330	1" diameter		45	.178		32	12.80		44.80	54
4340	1-1/4" diameter	Q-1	76	.211		43.50	13.65		57.15	68.50
4350	1-1/2" diameter		69	.232		44	15.05		59.05	71
4360	2" diameter		57	.281		68.50	18.20		86.70	103
4370	2-1/2" diameter		44	.364		122	23.50		145.50	169
4380	3" diameter		38	.421		162	27.50		189.50	219

22 11 Facility Water Distribution

22 11 13 – Facility Water Distribution Piping

22 11 13.64 Pipe, Stainless Steel

		Crew	Daily Output	Labor-Hours	Unit	Material	2023 Bare Costs Labor	Equipment	Total	Total Incl O&P
4390	4" diameter	Q-2	51	.471	L.F.	215	31.50		246.50	283
4490	For small quantities, add					10%				
4900	To delete couplings & hangers, subtract									
4910	1/4" diam. to 3/4" diam.					12%	56%			
4920	1" diam. to 2" diam.					14%	49%			
4930	2-1/2" diam. to 4" diam.					27%	40%			
5000	Schedule 80, type 304									
5040	1/4" diameter	1 Plum	53	.151	L.F.	22	10.90		32.90	40
5050	3/8" diameter		52	.154		27	11.10		38.10	46
5060	1/2" diameter		51	.157		27.50	11.30		38.80	47.50
5070	3/4" diameter		48	.167		26.50	12		38.50	47
5080	1" diameter		43	.186		34.50	13.40		47.90	57.50
5090	1-1/4" diameter	Q-1	73	.219		72	14.20		86.20	100
5100	1-1/2" diameter		67	.239		56.50	15.50		72	85.50
5110	2" diameter		54	.296		74	19.20		93.20	110
5190	For small quantities, add					10%				
5700	To delete couplings & hangers, subtract									
5710	1/4" diam. to 3/4" diam.					10%	53%			
5720	1" diam. to 2" diam.					14%	47%			
5750	Schedule 80, type 316									
5790	1/4" diameter	1 Plum	53	.151	L.F.	26.50	10.90		37.40	45.50
5800	3/8" diameter		52	.154		32	11.10		43.10	52
5810	1/2" diameter		51	.157		29	11.30		40.30	49
5820	3/4" diameter		48	.167		32.50	12		44.50	54
5830	1" diameter		43	.186		48.50	13.40		61.90	73
5840	1-1/4" diameter	Q-1	73	.219		45	14.20		59.20	71
5850	1-1/2" diameter		67	.239		64.50	15.50		80	94
5860	2" diameter		54	.296		84.50	19.20		103.70	122
5950	For small quantities, add					10%				
7000	To delete couplings & hangers, subtract									
7010	1/4" diam. to 3/4" diam.					9%	53%			
7020	1" diam. to 2" diam.					14%	47%			
8000	Weld joints with clevis type hanger assemblies, 10' OC									
8010	Schedule 40, type 304									
8050	1/8" pipe size	Q-15	126	.127	L.F.	5.30	8.25	.51	14.06	18.65
8060	1/4" pipe size		125	.128		5.65	8.30	.51	14.46	19.20
8070	3/8" pipe size		122	.131		6.25	8.50	.53	15.28	20
8080	1/2" pipe size		118	.136		6.70	8.80	.54	16.04	21
8090	3/4" pipe size		109	.147		9.10	9.50	.59	19.19	25
8100	1" pipe size		95	.168		13.55	10.90	.68	25.13	32
8110	1-1/4" pipe size		86	.186		16.70	12.05	.75	29.50	37
8120	1-1/2" pipe size		78	.205		22	13.30	.82	36.12	45
8130	2" pipe size		62	.258		29.50	16.75	1.03	47.28	58.50
8140	2-1/2" pipe size		49	.327		40.50	21	1.31	62.81	77.50
8150	3" pipe size		44	.364		50.50	23.50	1.46	75.46	92
8160	3-1/2" pipe size		44	.364		119	23.50	1.46	143.96	168
8170	4" pipe size		39	.410		71	26.50	1.65	99.15	119
8180	5" pipe size		32	.500		118	32.50	2.01	152.51	180
8190	6" pipe size	Q-16	37	.649		115	43.50	1.73	160.23	194
8191	6" pipe size		37	.649		114	43.50	1.73	159.23	192
8200	8" pipe size		29	.828		164	55.50	2.21	221.71	266
8210	10" pipe size		24	1		495	67.50	2.67	565.17	650
8220	12" pipe size		20	1.200		680	80.50	3.20	763.70	875

22 11 Facility Water Distribution

22 11 13 – Facility Water Distribution Piping

22 11 13.64 Pipe, Stainless Steel

		Crew	Daily Output	Labor-Hours	Unit	Material	2023 Bare Costs Labor	Equipment	Total	Total Incl O&P
8300	Schedule 40, type 316									
8310	1/8" pipe size	Q-15	126	.127	L.F.	20.50	8.25	.51	29.26	35.50
8320	1/4" pipe size		125	.128		13.65	8.30	.51	22.46	28
8330	3/8" pipe size		122	.131		14	8.50	.53	23.03	28.50
8340	1/2" pipe size		118	.136		14.90	8.80	.54	24.24	30
8350	3/4" pipe size		109	.147		18.40	9.50	.59	28.49	35
8360	1" pipe size		95	.168		26.50	10.90	.68	38.08	46
8370	1-1/4" pipe size		86	.186		34.50	12.05	.75	47.30	57
8380	1-1/2" pipe size		78	.205		34	13.30	.82	48.12	58.50
8390	2" pipe size		62	.258		52.50	16.75	1.03	70.28	84
8400	2-1/2" pipe size		49	.327		85.50	21	1.31	107.81	127
8410	3" pipe size		44	.364		112	23.50	1.46	136.96	160
8420	3-1/2" pipe size		44	.364		146	23.50	1.46	170.96	197
8430	4" pipe size		39	.410		143	26.50	1.65	171.15	199
8440	5" pipe size	▼	32	.500		275	32.50	2.01	309.51	355
8450	6" pipe size	Q-16	37	.649		160	43.50	1.73	205.23	243
8460	8" pipe size		29	.828		282	55.50	2.21	339.71	395
8470	10" pipe size		24	1		795	67.50	2.67	865.17	980
8480	12" pipe size	▼	20	1.200	▼	690	80.50	3.20	773.70	885
8500	Schedule 80, type 304									
8510	1/4" pipe size	Q-15	110	.145	L.F.	18.70	9.45	.58	28.73	35
8520	3/8" pipe size		109	.147		23.50	9.50	.59	33.59	41
8530	1/2" pipe size		106	.151		24.50	9.80	.61	34.91	42.50
8540	3/4" pipe size		96	.167		22	10.80	.67	33.47	41.50
8550	1" pipe size		87	.184		28.50	11.95	.74	41.19	49.50
8560	1-1/4" pipe size		81	.198		58.50	12.80	.79	72.09	84.50
8570	1-1/2" pipe size		74	.216		44.50	14	.87	59.37	71
8580	2" pipe size		58	.276		56	17.90	1.11	75.01	89.50
8590	2-1/2" pipe size		46	.348		130	22.50	1.39	153.89	178
8600	3" pipe size		41	.390		91	25.50	1.56	118.06	139
8610	4" pipe size	▼	33	.485		111	31.50	1.94	144.44	172
8630	6" pipe size	Q-16	30	.800	▼	198	54	2.14	254.14	300
8640	Schedule 80, type 316									
8650	1/4" pipe size	Q-15	110	.145	L.F.	24.50	9.45	.58	34.53	41.50
8660	3/8" pipe size		109	.147		30	9.50	.59	40.09	48
8670	1/2" pipe size		106	.151		26.50	9.80	.61	36.91	44.50
8680	3/4" pipe size		96	.167		29	10.80	.67	40.47	49
8690	1" pipe size		87	.184		43	11.95	.74	55.69	66
8700	1-1/4" pipe size		81	.198		34.50	12.80	.79	48.09	58
8710	1-1/2" pipe size		74	.216		54.50	14	.87	69.37	82
8720	2" pipe size		58	.276		68	17.90	1.11	87.01	102
8730	2-1/2" pipe size		46	.348		89.50	22.50	1.39	113.39	133
8740	3" pipe size		41	.390		107	25.50	1.56	134.06	156
8760	4" pipe size	▼	33	.485		141	31.50	1.94	174.44	204
8770	6" pipe size	Q-16	30	.800	▼	255	54	2.14	311.14	360
9100	Threading pipe labor, sst, one end, schedules 40 & 80									
9110	1/4" through 3/4" pipe size	1 Plum	61.50	.130	Ea.		9.35		9.35	14
9120	1" through 2" pipe size		55.90	.143			10.30		10.30	15.40
9130	2-1/2" pipe size		41.50	.193			13.90		13.90	20.50
9140	3" pipe size		38.50	.208			14.95		14.95	22.50
9150	3-1/2" pipe size	Q-1	68.40	.234			15.15		15.15	22.50
9160	4" pipe size		73	.219			14.20		14.20	21
9170	5" pipe size	▼	40.70	.393	▼		25.50		25.50	38

22 11 Facility Water Distribution

22 11 13 – Facility Water Distribution Piping

22 11 13.64 Pipe, Stainless Steel

		Crew	Daily Output	Labor-Hours	Unit	Material	2023 Bare Costs Labor	Equipment	Total	Total Incl O&P
9180	6" pipe size	Q-1	35.40	.452	Ea.		29.50		29.50	43.50
9190	8" pipe size		22.30	.717			46.50		46.50	69.50
9200	10" pipe size		16.10	.994			64.50		64.50	96
9210	12" pipe size	▼	12.30	1.301	▼		84.50		84.50	126
9250	Welding labor per joint for stainless steel									
9260	Schedule 5 and 10									
9270	1/4" pipe size	Q-15	36	.444	Ea.		29	1.78	30.78	45
9280	3/8" pipe size		35	.457			29.50	1.83	31.33	46
9290	1/2" pipe size		35	.457			29.50	1.83	31.33	46
9300	3/4" pipe size		28	.571			37	2.29	39.29	58
9310	1" pipe size		25	.640			41.50	2.57	44.07	65
9320	1-1/4" pipe size		22	.727			47	2.92	49.92	73.50
9330	1-1/2" pipe size		21	.762			49.50	3.06	52.56	77
9340	2" pipe size		18	.889			57.50	3.56	61.06	90
9350	2-1/2" pipe size		12	1.333			86.50	5.35	91.85	135
9360	3" pipe size		9.73	1.644			107	6.60	113.60	166
9370	4" pipe size		7.37	2.171			141	8.70	149.70	220
9380	5" pipe size		6.15	2.602			169	10.45	179.45	263
9390	6" pipe size		5.71	2.802			182	11.25	193.25	283
9400	8" pipe size		3.69	4.336			281	17.40	298.40	440
9410	10" pipe size		2.91	5.498			355	22	377	555
9420	12" pipe size	▼	2.31	6.926	▼		450	28	478	700
9500	Schedule 40									
9510	1/4" pipe size	Q-15	28	.571	Ea.		37	2.29	39.29	58
9520	3/8" pipe size		27	.593			38.50	2.38	40.88	60
9530	1/2" pipe size		25.40	.630			41	2.53	43.53	64
9540	3/4" pipe size		22.22	.720			46.50	2.89	49.39	72.50
9550	1" pipe size		20.25	.790			51	3.17	54.17	80
9560	1-1/4" pipe size		18.82	.850			55	3.41	58.41	86
9570	1-1/2" pipe size		17.78	.900			58.50	3.61	62.11	91
9580	2" pipe size		15.09	1.060			69	4.25	73.25	108
9590	2-1/2" pipe size		7.96	2.010			130	8.05	138.05	203
9600	3" pipe size		6.43	2.488			161	10	171	252
9610	4" pipe size		4.88	3.279			213	13.15	226.15	330
9620	5" pipe size		4.26	3.756			244	15.05	259.05	380
9630	6" pipe size		3.77	4.244			275	17	292	430
9640	8" pipe size		2.44	6.557			425	26.50	451.50	665
9650	10" pipe size		1.92	8.333			540	33.50	573.50	840
9660	12" pipe size	▼	1.52	10.526	▼		685	42	727	1,075
9750	Schedule 80									
9760	1/4" pipe size	Q-15	21.55	.742	Ea.		48	2.98	50.98	75.50
9770	3/8" pipe size		20.75	.771			50	3.09	53.09	78
9780	1/2" pipe size		19.54	.819			53	3.28	56.28	82.50
9790	3/4" pipe size		17.09	.936			60.50	3.75	64.25	94.50
9800	1" pipe size		15.58	1.027			66.50	4.12	70.62	104
9810	1-1/4" pipe size		14.48	1.105			71.50	4.43	75.93	112
9820	1-1/2" pipe size		13.68	1.170			76	4.69	80.69	118
9830	2" pipe size		11.61	1.378			89.50	5.55	95.05	139
9840	2-1/2" pipe size		6.12	2.614			170	10.50	180.50	265
9850	3" pipe size		4.94	3.239			210	13	223	330
9860	4" pipe size		3.75	4.267			277	17.10	294.10	435
9870	5" pipe size		3.27	4.893			315	19.60	334.60	495
9880	6" pipe size	▼	2.90	5.517			360	22	382	560

22 11 Facility Water Distribution

22 11 13 – Facility Water Distribution Piping

22 11 13.64 Pipe, Stainless Steel

		Crew	Daily Output	Labor-Hours	Unit	Material	2023 Bare Costs Labor	2023 Bare Costs Equipment	Total	Total Incl O&P
9890	8" pipe size	Q-15	1.87	8.556	Ea.		555	34.50	589.50	865
9900	10" pipe size		1.48	10.811			700	43.50	743.50	1,100
9910	12" pipe size		1.17	13.675			885	55	940	1,375
9920	Schedule 160, 1/2" pipe size		17	.941			61	3.77	64.77	95
9930	3/4" pipe size		14.81	1.080			70	4.33	74.33	109
9940	1" pipe size		13.50	1.185			77	4.75	81.75	120
9950	1-1/4" pipe size		12.55	1.275			82.50	5.10	87.60	129
9960	1-1/2" pipe size		11.85	1.350			87.50	5.40	92.90	137
9970	2" pipe size		10	1.600			104	6.40	110.40	162
9980	3" pipe size		4.28	3.738			242	15	257	375
9990	4" pipe size	↓	3.25	4.923	↓		320	19.75	339.75	495

22 11 13.66 Pipe Fittings, Stainless Steel

		Crew	Daily Output	Labor-Hours	Unit	Material	2023 Bare Costs Labor	2023 Bare Costs Equipment	Total	Total Incl O&P
0010	**PIPE FITTINGS, STAINLESS STEEL**									
0100	Butt weld joint, schedule 5, type 304									
0120	90° elbow, long									
0140	1/2"	Q-15	17.50	.914	Ea.	28	59.50	3.67	91.17	123
0150	3/4"		14	1.143		28	74	4.58	106.58	147
0160	1"		12.50	1.280		29.50	83	5.15	117.65	162
0170	1-1/4"		11	1.455		40	94.50	5.85	140.35	192
0180	1-1/2"		10.50	1.524		34	99	6.10	139.10	191
0190	2"		9	1.778		40	115	7.15	162.15	224
0200	2-1/2"		6	2.667		93	173	10.70	276.70	370
0210	3"		4.86	3.292		86.50	214	13.20	313.70	430
0220	3-1/2"		4.27	3.747		255	243	15.05	513.05	660
0230	4"		3.69	4.336		145	281	17.40	443.40	600
0240	5"	↓	3.08	5.195		540	335	21	896	1,125
0250	6"	Q-16	4.29	5.594		420	375	14.95	809.95	1,025
0260	8"		2.76	8.696		880	585	23	1,488	1,875
0270	10"		2.18	11.009		1,350	740	29.50	2,119.50	2,625
0280	12"	↓	1.73	13.873		1,925	935	37	2,897	3,575
0320	For schedule 5, type 316, add				↓	30%				
0600	45° elbow, long									
0620	1/2"	Q-15	17.50	.914	Ea.	28	59.50	3.67	91.17	123
0630	3/4"		14	1.143		28	74	4.58	106.58	147
0640	1"		12.50	1.280		29.50	83	5.15	117.65	162
0650	1-1/4"		11	1.455		40	94.50	5.85	140.35	192
0660	1-1/2"		10.50	1.524		34	99	6.10	139.10	191
0670	2"		9	1.778		40	115	7.15	162.15	224
0680	2-1/2"		6	2.667		93	173	10.70	276.70	370
0690	3"		4.86	3.292		69.50	214	13.20	296.70	410
0700	3-1/2"		4.27	3.747		255	243	15.05	513.05	660
0710	4"		3.69	4.336		118	281	17.40	416.40	570
0720	5"	↓	3.08	5.195		435	335	21	791	1,000
0730	6"	Q-16	4.29	5.594		294	375	14.95	683.95	900
0740	8"		2.76	8.696		620	585	23	1,228	1,575
0750	10"		2.18	11.009		1,075	740	29.50	1,844.50	2,325
0760	12"	↓	1.73	13.873		1,350	935	37	2,322	2,950
0800	For schedule 5, type 316, add				↓	25%				
1100	Tee, straight									
1130	1/2"	Q-15	11.66	1.372	Ea.	83.50	89	5.50	178	231
1140	3/4"		9.33	1.715		83.50	111	6.90	201.40	266
1150	1"	↓	8.33	1.921	↓	88	125	7.70	220.70	291

22 11 Facility Water Distribution

22 11 13 – Facility Water Distribution Piping

22 11 13.66 Pipe Fittings, Stainless Steel

		Crew	Daily Output	Labor-Hours	Unit	Material	2023 Bare Costs Labor	Equipment	Total	Total Incl O&P
1160	1-1/4"	Q-15	7.33	2.183	Ea.	71	142	8.75	221.75	299
1170	1-1/2"		7	2.286		69.50	148	9.15	226.65	310
1180	2"		6	2.667		73	173	10.70	256.70	350
1190	2-1/2"		4	4		175	259	16.05	450.05	595
1200	3"		3.24	4.938		128	320	19.80	467.80	640
1210	3-1/2"		2.85	5.614		365	365	22.50	752.50	970
1220	4"		2.46	6.504		198	420	26	644	875
1230	5"		2	8		630	520	32	1,182	1,500
1240	6"	Q-16	2.85	8.421		495	565	22.50	1,082.50	1,425
1250	8"		1.84	13.043		1,050	875	35	1,960	2,500
1260	10"		1.45	16.552		1,700	1,125	44	2,869	3,575
1270	12"		1.15	20.870		2,375	1,400	55.50	3,830.50	4,750
1320	For schedule 5, type 316, add					25%				
2000	Butt weld joint, schedule 10, type 304									
2020	90° elbow, long									
2040	1/2"	Q-15	17	.941	Ea.	7.45	61	3.77	72.22	103
2050	3/4"		14	1.143		7.60	74	4.58	86.18	124
2060	1"		12.50	1.280		8.50	83	5.15	96.65	139
2070	1-1/4"		11	1.455		13	94.50	5.85	113.35	162
2080	1-1/2"		10.50	1.524		10.60	99	6.10	115.70	165
2090	2"		9	1.778		12.75	115	7.15	134.90	194
2100	2-1/2"		6	2.667		23	173	10.70	206.70	295
2110	3"		4.86	3.292		27.50	214	13.20	254.70	365
2120	3-1/2"		4.27	3.747		253	243	15.05	511.05	655
2130	4"		3.69	4.336		45.50	281	17.40	343.90	490
2140	5"		3.08	5.195		535	335	21	891	1,125
2150	6"	Q-16	4.29	5.594		121	375	14.95	510.95	710
2160	8"		2.76	8.696		201	585	23	809	1,125
2170	10"		2.18	11.009		500	740	29.50	1,269.50	1,675
2180	12"		1.73	13.873		770	935	37	1,742	2,300
2500	45° elbow, long									
2520	1/2"	Q-15	17.50	.914	Ea.	9.45	59.50	3.67	72.62	103
2530	3/4"		14	1.143		9.65	74	4.58	88.23	127
2540	1"		12.50	1.280		10.70	83	5.15	98.85	141
2550	1-1/4"		11	1.455		17.90	94.50	5.85	118.25	167
2560	1-1/2"		10.50	1.524		10.90	99	6.10	116	166
2570	2"		9	1.778		13	115	7.15	135.15	194
2580	2-1/2"		6	2.667		20.50	173	10.70	204.20	292
2590	3"		4.86	3.292		23.50	214	13.20	250.70	360
2600	3-1/2"		4.27	3.747		253	243	15.05	511.05	655
2610	4"		3.69	4.336		38	281	17.40	336.40	480
2620	5"		3.08	5.195		248	335	21	604	795
2630	6"	Q-16	4.29	5.594		82	375	14.95	471.95	665
2640	8"		2.76	8.696		146	585	23	754	1,050
2650	10"		2.18	11.009		360	740	29.50	1,129.50	1,525
2660	12"		1.73	13.873		550	935	37	1,522	2,050
2670	Reducer, concentric									
2674	1" x 3/4"	Q-15	13.25	1.208	Ea.	20	78.50	4.84	103.34	144
2676	2" x 1-1/2"	"	9.75	1.641		14.55	106	6.60	127.15	182
2678	6" x 4"	Q-16	4.91	4.888		36.50	330	13.05	379.55	545
2680	Caps									
2682	1"	Q-15	25	.640	Ea.	22.50	41.50	2.57	66.57	89.50
2684	1-1/2"		21	.762		24.50	49.50	3.06	77.06	103

22 11 Facility Water Distribution

22 11 13 – Facility Water Distribution Piping

22 11 13.66 Pipe Fittings, Stainless Steel		Crew	Daily Output	Labor-Hours	Unit	Material	2023 Bare Costs Labor	Equipment	Total	Total Incl O&P
2685	2"	Q-15	18	.889	Ea.	21	57.50	3.56	82.06	113
2686	4"	↓	7.38	2.168		33.50	141	8.70	183.20	256
2687	6"	Q-16	8.58	2.797	↓	54.50	188	7.45	249.95	350
3000	Tee, straight									
3030	1/2"	Q-15	11.66	1.372	Ea.	26.50	89	5.50	121	168
3040	3/4"		9.33	1.715		26.50	111	6.90	144.40	203
3050	1"		8.33	1.921		27	125	7.70	159.70	224
3060	1-1/4"		7.33	2.183		41.50	142	8.75	192.25	266
3070	1-1/2"		7	2.286		27	148	9.15	184.15	261
3080	2"		6	2.667		29	173	10.70	212.70	300
3090	2-1/2"		4	4		76	259	16.05	351.05	485
3100	3"		3.24	4.938		53.50	320	19.80	393.30	560
3110	3-1/2"		2.85	5.614		201	365	22.50	588.50	790
3120	4"		2.46	6.504		80	420	26	526	745
3130	5"	↓	2	8		620	520	32	1,172	1,500
3140	6"	Q-16	2.85	8.421		183	565	22.50	770.50	1,075
3150	8"		1.84	13.043		375	875	35	1,285	1,750
3151	10"		1.45	16.552		470	1,125	44	1,639	2,225
3152	12"	↓	1.15	20.870		1,075	1,400	55.50	2,530.50	3,325
3154	For schedule 10, type 316, add					25%				
3281	Butt weld joint, schedule 40, type 304									
3284	90° elbow, long, 1/2"	Q-15	12.70	1.260	Ea.	8.30	81.50	5.05	94.85	137
3288	3/4"		11.10	1.441		8.45	93.50	5.80	107.75	155
3289	1"		10.13	1.579		9.60	102	6.35	117.95	171
3290	1-1/4"		9.40	1.702		14.30	110	6.85	131.15	188
3300	1-1/2"		8.89	1.800		11.35	117	7.20	135.55	194
3310	2"		7.55	2.119		15.75	137	8.50	161.25	232
3320	2-1/2"		3.98	4.020		33.50	261	16.10	310.60	445
3330	3"		3.21	4.984		42.50	325	20	387.50	550
3340	3-1/2"		2.83	5.654		460	365	22.50	847.50	1,075
3350	4"		2.44	6.557		79	425	26.50	530.50	750
3360	5"	↓	2.13	7.512		720	485	30	1,235	1,550
3370	6"	Q-16	2.83	8.481		215	570	22.50	807.50	1,100
3380	8"		1.83	13.115		390	880	35	1,305	1,800
3390	10"		1.44	16.667		1,500	1,125	44.50	2,669.50	3,375
3400	12"	↓	1.14	21.053	↓	2,750	1,425	56	4,231	5,175
3410	For schedule 40, type 316, add					25%				
3460	45° elbow, long, 1/2"	Q-15	12.70	1.260	Ea.	11.45	81.50	5.05	98	140
3470	3/4"		11.10	1.441		11.55	93.50	5.80	110.85	158
3480	1"		10.13	1.579		11.65	102	6.35	120	173
3490	1-1/4"		9.40	1.702		16.90	110	6.85	133.75	191
3500	1-1/2"		8.89	1.800		13.15	117	7.20	137.35	196
3510	2"		7.55	2.119		16.35	137	8.50	161.85	232
3520	2-1/2"		3.98	4.020		33.50	261	16.10	310.60	445
3530	3"		3.21	4.984		30.50	325	20	375.50	535
3540	3-1/2"		2.83	5.654		460	365	22.50	847.50	1,075
3550	4"		2.44	6.557		55	425	26.50	506.50	725
3560	5"	↓	2.13	7.512		505	485	30	1,020	1,325
3570	6"	Q-16	2.83	8.481		138	570	22.50	730.50	1,025
3580	8"		1.83	13.115		272	880	35	1,187	1,675
3590	10"		1.44	16.667		1,500	1,125	44.50	2,669.50	3,375
3600	12"		1.14	21.053		855	1,425	56	2,336	3,100
3610	For schedule 40, type 316, add					25%				

22 11 Facility Water Distribution

22 11 13 – Facility Water Distribution Piping

22 11 13.66 Pipe Fittings, Stainless Steel		Crew	Daily Output	Labor-Hours	Unit	Material	2023 Bare Costs Labor	Equipment	Total	Total Incl O&P
3660	Tee, straight 1/2"	Q-15	8.46	1.891	Ea.	27.50	123	7.60	158.10	221
3670	3/4"		7.40	2.162		27.50	140	8.65	176.15	249
3680	1"		6.74	2.374		28	154	9.50	191.50	271
3690	1-1/4"		6.27	2.552		46.50	165	10.25	221.75	310
3700	1-1/2"		5.92	2.703		28.50	175	10.85	214.35	305
3710	2"		5.03	3.181		30.50	206	12.75	249.25	360
3720	2-1/2"		2.65	6.038		76	390	24	490	695
3730	3"		2.14	7.477		61.50	485	30	576.50	825
3740	3-1/2"		1.88	8.511		335	550	34	919	1,225
3750	4"		1.62	9.877		87.50	640	39.50	767	1,100
3760	5"	↓	1.42	11.268		775	730	45	1,550	2,000
3770	6"	Q-16	1.88	12.766		197	860	34	1,091	1,525
3780	8"		1.22	19.672		575	1,325	52.50	1,952.50	2,675
3790	10"		.96	25		2,375	1,675	67	4,117	5,200
3800	12"	↓	.76	31.579	↓	2,575	2,125	84.50	4,784.50	6,125
3810	For schedule 40, type 316, add					25%				
3820	Tee, reducing on outlet, 3/4" x 1/2"	Q-15	7.73	2.070	Ea.	95.50	134	8.30	237.80	315
3822	1" x 1/2"		7.24	2.210		120	143	8.85	271.85	355
3824	1" x 3/4"		6.96	2.299		110	149	9.20	268.20	355
3826	1-1/4" x 1"		6.43	2.488		270	161	10	441	550
3828	1-1/2" x 1/2"		6.58	2.432		162	158	9.75	329.75	425
3830	1-1/2" x 3/4"		6.35	2.520		152	163	10.10	325.10	420
3832	1-1/2" x 1"		6.18	2.589		116	168	10.40	294.40	390
3834	2" x 1"		5.50	2.909		208	189	11.65	408.65	525
3836	2" x 1-1/2"		5.30	3.019		175	196	12.10	383.10	495
3838	2-1/2" x 2"		3.15	5.079		264	330	20.50	614.50	805
3840	3" x 1-1/2"		2.72	5.882		267	380	23.50	670.50	890
3842	3" x 2"		2.65	6.038		222	390	24	636	855
3844	4" x 2"		2.10	7.619		131	495	30.50	656.50	915
3846	4" x 3"		1.77	9.040		405	585	36.50	1,026.50	1,350
3848	5" x 4"	↓	1.48	10.811		930	700	43.50	1,673.50	2,125
3850	6" x 3"	Q-16	2.19	10.959		1,025	735	29.50	1,789.50	2,250
3852	6" x 4"		2.04	11.765		890	790	31.50	1,711.50	2,200
3854	8" x 4"		1.46	16.438		2,075	1,100	44	3,219	3,975
3856	10" x 8"		.69	34.783		3,500	2,350	93	5,943	7,450
3858	12" x 10"	↓	.55	43.636		4,675	2,925	117	7,717	9,650
3950	Reducer, concentric, 3/4" x 1/2"	Q-15	11.85	1.350		18.65	87.50	5.40	111.55	157
3952	1" x 3/4"		10.60	1.509		21.50	98	6.05	125.55	177
3954	1-1/4" x 3/4"		10.19	1.570		64	102	6.30	172.30	229
3956	1-1/4" x 1"		9.76	1.639		31	106	6.55	143.55	200
3958	1-1/2" x 3/4"		9.88	1.619		54.50	105	6.50	166	224
3960	1-1/2" x 1"		9.47	1.690		107	110	6.80	223.80	288
3962	2" x 1"		8.65	1.850		20.50	120	7.40	147.90	210
3964	2" x 1-1/2"		8.16	1.961		16.35	127	7.85	151.20	217
3966	2-1/2" x 1"		5.71	2.802		93.50	182	11.25	286.75	385
3968	2-1/2" x 2"		5.21	3.071		73	199	12.30	284.30	390
3970	3" x 1"		4.88	3.279		64	213	13.15	290.15	400
3972	3" x 1-1/2"		4.72	3.390		29	220	13.60	262.60	375
3974	3" x 2"		4.51	3.548		26.50	230	14.25	270.75	390
3976	4" x 2"		3.69	4.336		38	281	17.40	336.40	480
3978	4" x 3"		2.77	5.776		29	375	23	427	620
3980	5" x 3"		2.56	6.250		485	405	25	915	1,175
3982	5" x 4"	↓	2.27	7.048		390	455	28.50	873.50	1,150

22 11 Facility Water Distribution

22 11 13 – Facility Water Distribution Piping

22 11 13.66 Pipe Fittings, Stainless Steel

		Crew	Daily Output	Labor-Hours	Unit	Material	2023 Bare Costs Labor	Equipment	Total	Total Incl O&P
3984	6" x 3"	Q-16	3.57	6.723	Ea.	112	450	17.95	579.95	820
3986	6" x 4"		3.19	7.524		76	505	20	601	860
3988	8" x 4"		2.44	9.836		246	660	26.50	932.50	1,275
3990	8" x 6"		2.22	10.811		172	725	29	926	1,300
3992	10" x 6"		1.91	12.565		730	845	33.50	1,608.50	2,100
3994	10" x 8"		1.61	14.907		605	1,000	40	1,645	2,200
3995	12" x 6"		1.63	14.724		1,375	990	39.50	2,404.50	3,050
3996	12" x 8"		1.41	17.021		1,025	1,150	45.50	2,220.50	2,875
3997	12" x 10"		1.27	18.898		725	1,275	50.50	2,050.50	2,750
4000	Socket weld joint, 3,000 lb., type 304									
4100	90° elbow									
4140	1/4"	Q-15	13.47	1.188	Ea.	41	77	4.76	122.76	165
4150	3/8"		12.97	1.234		53	80	4.95	137.95	183
4160	1/2"		12.21	1.310		56	85	5.25	146.25	194
4170	3/4"		10.68	1.498		68	97	6	171	226
4180	1"		9.74	1.643		102	107	6.60	215.60	279
4190	1-1/4"		9.05	1.768		305	115	7.10	427.10	515
4200	1-1/2"		8.55	1.871		218	121	7.50	346.50	430
4210	2"		7.26	2.204		345	143	8.85	496.85	605
4300	45° elbow									
4340	1/4"	Q-15	13.47	1.188	Ea.	74	77	4.76	155.76	202
4350	3/8"		12.97	1.234		74.50	80	4.95	159.45	206
4360	1/2"		12.21	1.310		74.50	85	5.25	164.75	215
4370	3/4"		10.68	1.498		84.50	97	6	187.50	245
4380	1"		9.74	1.643		122	107	6.60	235.60	300
4390	1-1/4"		9.05	1.768		360	115	7.10	482.10	575
4400	1-1/2"		8.55	1.871		207	121	7.50	335.50	415
4410	2"		7.26	2.204		370	143	8.85	521.85	635
4500	Tee									
4540	1/4"	Q-15	8.97	1.784	Ea.	93	116	7.15	216.15	282
4550	3/8"		8.64	1.852		111	120	7.45	238.45	310
4560	1/2"		8.13	1.968		90.50	128	7.90	226.40	298
4570	3/4"		7.12	2.247		104	146	9	259	340
4580	1"		6.48	2.469		141	160	9.90	310.90	405
4590	1-1/4"		6.03	2.653		375	172	10.65	557.65	685
4600	1-1/2"		5.69	2.812		415	182	11.30	608.30	740
4610	2"		4.83	3.313		595	215	13.30	823.30	990
5000	Socket weld joint, 3,000 lb., type 316									
5100	90° elbow									
5140	1/4"	Q-15	13.47	1.188	Ea.	86.50	77	4.76	168.26	215
5150	3/8"		12.97	1.234		101	80	4.95	185.95	235
5160	1/2"		12.21	1.310		80.50	85	5.25	170.75	222
5170	3/4"		10.68	1.498		106	97	6	209	269
5180	1"		9.74	1.643		151	107	6.60	264.60	330
5190	1-1/4"		9.05	1.768		405	115	7.10	527.10	625
5200	1-1/2"		8.55	1.871		355	121	7.50	483.50	580
5210	2"		7.26	2.204		570	143	8.85	721.85	850
5300	45° elbow									
5340	1/4"	Q-15	13.47	1.188	Ea.	174	77	4.76	255.76	310
5350	3/8"		12.97	1.234		174	80	4.95	258.95	315
5360	1/2"		12.21	1.310		116	85	5.25	206.25	260
5370	3/4"		10.68	1.498		128	97	6	231	293
5380	1"		9.74	1.643		230	107	6.60	343.60	420

22 11 Facility Water Distribution

22 11 13 – Facility Water Distribution Piping

22 11 13.66 Pipe Fittings, Stainless Steel

		Crew	Daily Output	Labor-Hours	Unit	Material	2023 Bare Costs Labor	Equipment	Total	Total Incl O&P
5390	1-1/4"	Q-15	9.05	1.768	Ea.	415	115	7.10	537.10	640
5400	1-1/2"		8.55	1.871		360	121	7.50	488.50	590
5410	2"	↓	7.26	2.204	↓	540	143	8.85	691.85	820
5500	Tee									
5540	1/4"	Q-15	8.97	1.784	Ea.	117	116	7.15	240.15	310
5550	3/8"		8.64	1.852		143	120	7.45	270.45	345
5560	1/2"		8.13	1.968		106	128	7.90	241.90	315
5570	3/4"		7.12	2.247		131	146	9	286	370
5580	1"		6.48	2.469		237	160	9.90	406.90	510
5590	1-1/4"		6.03	2.653		480	172	10.65	662.65	795
5600	1-1/2"		5.69	2.812		505	182	11.30	698.30	840
5610	2"	↓	4.83	3.313		790	215	13.30	1,018.30	1,200
5700	For socket weld joint, 6,000 lb., type 304 and 316, add				↓	100%				
6000	Threaded companion flange									
6010	Stainless steel, 150 lb., type 304									
6020	1/2" diam.	1 Plum	30	.267	Ea.	30	19.20		49.20	61
6030	3/4" diam.		28	.286		34.50	20.50		55	68
6040	1" diam.	↓	27	.296		37.50	21.50		59	73.50
6050	1-1/4" diam.	Q-1	44	.364		48.50	23.50		72	88.50
6060	1-1/2" diam.		40	.400		49	26		75	92.50
6070	2" diam.		36	.444		64	29		93	114
6080	2-1/2" diam.		28	.571		96	37		133	162
6090	3" diam.		20	.800		96.50	52		148.50	184
6110	4" diam.	↓	12	1.333		133	86.50		219.50	275
6130	6" diam.	Q-2	14	1.714		231	115		346	425
6140	8" diam.	"	12	2	↓	430	135		565	675
6150	For type 316, add					40%				
6260	Weld flanges, stainless steel, type 304									
6270	Slip on, 150 lb. (welded, front and back)									
6280	1/2" diam.	Q-15	12.70	1.260	Ea.	28	81.50	5.05	114.55	159
6290	3/4" diam.		11.11	1.440		29	93.50	5.75	128.25	177
6300	1" diam.		10.13	1.579		31.50	102	6.35	139.85	195
6310	1-1/4" diam.		9.41	1.700		44	110	6.80	160.80	220
6320	1-1/2" diam.		8.89	1.800		44	117	7.20	168.20	230
6330	2" diam.		7.55	2.119		53.50	137	8.50	199	273
6340	2-1/2" diam.		3.98	4.020		77	261	16.10	354.10	490
6350	3" diam.		3.21	4.984		85	325	20	430	595
6370	4" diam.	↓	2.44	6.557		114	425	26.50	565.50	790
6390	6" diam.	Q-16	1.89	12.698		174	855	34	1,063	1,500
6400	8" diam.	"	1.22	19.672	↓	315	1,325	52.50	1,692.50	2,375
6410	For type 316, add					40%				
6530	Weld neck 150 lb.									
6540	1/2" diam.	Q-15	25.40	.630	Ea.	30.50	41	2.53	74.03	97.50
6550	3/4" diam.		22.22	.720		36	46.50	2.89	85.39	112
6560	1" diam.		20.25	.790		39.50	51	3.17	93.67	123
6570	1-1/4" diam.		18.82	.850		62.50	55	3.41	120.91	154
6580	1-1/2" diam.		17.78	.900		56	58.50	3.61	118.11	152
6590	2" diam.		15.09	1.060		59	69	4.25	132.25	172
6600	2-1/2" diam.		7.96	2.010		95.50	130	8.05	233.55	310
6610	3" diam.		6.43	2.488		96.50	161	10	267.50	360
6630	4" diam.		4.88	3.279		145	213	13.15	371.15	490
6640	5" diam.	↓	4.26	3.756		207	244	15.05	466.05	610
6650	6" diam.	Q-16	5.66	4.240		211	285	11.30	507.30	670

22 11 Facility Water Distribution

22 11 13 – Facility Water Distribution Piping

22 11 13.66 Pipe Fittings, Stainless Steel		Crew	Daily Output	Labor-Hours	Unit	Material	2023 Bare Costs Labor	Equipment	Total	Total Incl O&P
6652	8" diam.	Q-16	3.65	6.575	Ea.	375	440	17.55	832.55	1,100
6654	10" diam.		2.88	8.333		430	560	22.50	1,012.50	1,325
6656	12" diam.		2.28	10.526		530	710	28	1,268	1,650
6670	For type 316, add					23%				
7000	Threaded joint, 150 lb., type 304									
7030	90° elbow									
7040	1/8"	1 Plum	13	.615	Ea.	27.50	44.50		72	96.50
7050	1/4"		13	.615		27.50	44.50		72	96.50
7070	3/8"		13	.615		32.50	44.50		77	102
7080	1/2"		12	.667		30	48		78	105
7090	3/4"		11	.727		37	52.50		89.50	119
7100	1"		10	.800		51.50	57.50		109	143
7110	1-1/4"	Q-1	17	.941		83	61		144	182
7120	1-1/2"		16	1		98	65		163	205
7130	2"		14	1.143		137	74		211	261
7140	2-1/2"		11	1.455		320	94.50		414.50	490
7150	3"		8	2		450	130		580	690
7160	4"	Q-2	11	2.182		765	147		912	1,075
7180	45° elbow									
7190	1/8"	1 Plum	13	.615	Ea.	40	44.50		84.50	110
7200	1/4"		13	.615		40	44.50		84.50	110
7210	3/8"		13	.615		41	44.50		85.50	111
7220	1/2"		12	.667		42	48		90	118
7230	3/4"		11	.727		48.50	52.50		101	132
7240	1"		10	.800		57	57.50		114.50	149
7250	1-1/4"	Q-1	17	.941		82	61		143	181
7260	1-1/2"		16	1		104	65		169	211
7270	2"		14	1.143		147	74		221	273
7280	2-1/2"		11	1.455		435	94.50		529.50	620
7290	3"		8	2		630	130		760	890
7300	4"	Q-2	11	2.182		1,075	147		1,222	1,425
7320	Tee, straight									
7330	1/8"	1 Plum	9	.889	Ea.	42	64		106	142
7340	1/4"		9	.889		42	64		106	142
7350	3/8"		9	.889		46	64		110	147
7360	1/2"		8	1		44.50	72		116.50	156
7370	3/4"		7	1.143		52	82.50		134.50	180
7380	1"		6.50	1.231		66.50	88.50		155	205
7390	1-1/4"	Q-1	11	1.455		117	94.50		211.50	269
7400	1-1/2"		10	1.600		148	104		252	320
7410	2"		9	1.778		186	115		301	375
7420	2-1/2"		7	2.286		455	148		603	720
7430	3"		5	3.200		685	208		893	1,050
7440	4"	Q-2	7	3.429		1,525	231		1,756	2,050
7460	Coupling, straight									
7470	1/8"	1 Plum	19	.421	Ea.	11.50	30.50		42	57.50
7480	1/4"		19	.421		13.65	30.50		44.15	60
7490	3/8"		19	.421		16.20	30.50		46.70	63
7500	1/2"		19	.421		22	30.50		52.50	69
7510	3/4"		18	.444		29.50	32		61.50	80.50
7520	1"		15	.533		46.50	38.50		85	109
7530	1-1/4"	Q-1	26	.615		75	40		115	142
7540	1-1/2"		24	.667		83	43		126	156

22 11 Facility Water Distribution

22 11 13 – Facility Water Distribution Piping

22 11 13.66 Pipe Fittings, Stainless Steel		Crew	Daily Output	Labor-Hours	Unit	Material	2023 Bare Costs Labor	Equipment	Total	Total Incl O&P
7550	2"	Q-1	21	.762	Ea.	133	49.50		182.50	220
7560	2-1/2"		18	.889		305	57.50		362.50	420
7570	3"	↓	14	1.143		415	74		489	570
7580	4"	Q-2	16	1.500		595	101		696	805
7600	Reducer, concentric, 1/2"	1 Plum	12	.667		36.50	48		84.50	112
7610	3/4"		11	.727		47	52.50		99.50	130
7612	1"	↓	10	.800		78	57.50		135.50	172
7614	1-1/4"	Q-1	17	.941		165	61		226	273
7616	1-1/2"		16	1		181	65		246	296
7618	2"		14	1.143		282	74		356	420
7620	2-1/2"		11	1.455		740	94.50		834.50	955
7622	3"	↓	8	2		825	130		955	1,100
7624	4"	Q-2	11	2.182	↓	1,375	147		1,522	1,725
7710	Union									
7720	1/8"	1 Plum	12	.667	Ea.	54.50	48		102.50	132
7730	1/4"		12	.667		56.50	48		104.50	134
7740	3/8"		12	.667		63	48		111	141
7750	1/2"		11	.727		75.50	52.50		128	161
7760	3/4"		10	.800		102	57.50		159.50	198
7770	1"	↓	9	.889		149	64		213	260
7780	1-1/4"	Q-1	16	1		350	65		415	480
7790	1-1/2"		15	1.067		380	69		449	525
7800	2"		13	1.231		480	80		560	650
7810	2-1/2"		10	1.600		935	104		1,039	1,175
7820	3"	↓	7	2.286		1,225	148		1,373	1,575
7830	4"	Q-2	10	2.400	↓	1,700	161		1,861	2,125
7838	Caps									
7840	1/2"	1 Plum	24	.333	Ea.	10.05	24		34.05	47
7841	3/4"		22	.364		26	26		52	67.50
7842	1"	↓	20	.400		23.50	29		52.50	69
7843	1-1/2"	Q-1	32	.500		97	32.50		129.50	156
7844	2"	"	28	.571		115	37		152	183
7845	4"	Q-2	22	1.091		660	73.50		733.50	840
7850	For 150 lb., type 316, add				↓	25%				
8750	Threaded joint, 2,000 lb., type 304									
8770	90° elbow									
8780	1/8"	1 Plum	13	.615	Ea.	14.45	44.50		58.95	82
8790	1/4"		13	.615		37.50	44.50		82	108
8800	3/8"		13	.615		20.50	44.50		65	88.50
8810	1/2"		12	.667		61	48		109	139
8820	3/4"		11	.727		31.50	52.50		84	113
8830	1"	↓	10	.800		48	57.50		105.50	139
8840	1-1/4"	Q-1	17	.941		156	61		217	262
8850	1-1/2"		16	1		243	65		308	365
8860	2"	↓	14	1.143	↓	340	74		414	485
8880	45° elbow									
8890	1/8"	1 Plum	13	.615	Ea.	23.50	44.50		68	92
8900	1/4"		13	.615		71.50	44.50		116	145
8910	3/8"		13	.615		85	44.50		129.50	160
8920	1/2"		12	.667		85	48		133	165
8930	3/4"		11	.727		98.50	52.50		151	186
8940	1"	↓	10	.800		122	57.50		179.50	220
8950	1-1/4"	Q-1	17	.941		203	61		264	315

22 11 Facility Water Distribution

22 11 13 – Facility Water Distribution Piping

22 11 13.66 Pipe Fittings, Stainless Steel

		Crew	Daily Output	Labor-Hours	Unit	Material	2023 Bare Costs Labor	2023 Bare Costs Equipment	Total	Total Incl O&P
8960	1-1/2"	Q-1	16	1	Ea.	272	65		337	395
8970	2"	↓	14	1.143	↓	310	74		384	455
8990	Tee, straight									
9000	1/8"	1 Plum	9	.889	Ea.	12.90	64		76.90	110
9010	1/4"		9	.889		49.50	64		113.50	150
9020	3/8"		9	.889		64.50	64		128.50	167
9030	1/2"		8	1		79.50	72		151.50	195
9040	3/4"		7	1.143		106	82.50		188.50	240
9050	1"	↓	6.50	1.231		130	88.50		218.50	274
9060	1-1/4"	Q-1	11	1.455		217	94.50		311.50	380
9070	1-1/2"		10	1.600		290	104		394	475
9080	2"	↓	9	1.778	↓	335	115		450	540
9100	For couplings and unions use 3,000 lb., type 304									
9120	2,000 lb., type 316									
9130	90° elbow									
9140	1/8"	1 Plum	13	.615	Ea.	16.90	44.50		61.40	84.50
9150	1/4"		13	.615		47	44.50		91.50	118
9160	3/8"		13	.615		54	44.50		98.50	126
9170	1/2"		12	.667		70	48		118	148
9180	3/4"		11	.727		38	52.50		90.50	120
9190	1"	↓	10	.800		80	57.50		137.50	174
9200	1-1/4"	Q-1	17	.941		239	61		300	355
9210	1-1/2"		16	1		139	65		204	250
9220	2"	↓	14	1.143		240	74		314	375
9240	45° elbow									
9250	1/8"	1 Plum	13	.615	Ea.	32.50	44.50		77	102
9260	1/4"		13	.615		89	44.50		133.50	164
9270	3/8"		13	.615		89	44.50		133.50	164
9280	1/2"		12	.667		90	48		138	171
9300	3/4"		11	.727		105	52.50		157.50	194
9310	1"	↓	10	.800		161	57.50		218.50	263
9320	1-1/4"	Q-1	17	.941		215	61		276	325
9330	1-1/2"		16	1		305	65		370	430
9340	2"	↓	14	1.143	↓	405	74		479	560
9360	Tee, straight									
9370	1/8"	1 Plum	9	.889	Ea.	19.95	64		83.95	118
9380	1/4"		9	.889		58.50	64		122.50	160
9390	3/8"		9	.889		72.50	64		136.50	175
9400	1/2"		8	1		89	72		161	205
9410	3/4"		7	1.143		50	82.50		132.50	178
9420	1"	↓	6.50	1.231		176	88.50		264.50	325
9430	1-1/4"	Q-1	11	1.455		268	94.50		362.50	435
9440	1-1/2"		10	1.600		161	104		265	330
9450	2"	↓	9	1.778	↓	615	115		730	845
9470	For couplings and unions use 3,000 lb., type 316									
9490	3,000 lb., type 304									
9510	Coupling									
9520	1/8"	1 Plum	19	.421	Ea.	26	30.50		56.50	74
9530	1/4"		19	.421		32.50	30.50		63	81
9540	3/8"		19	.421		35.50	30.50		66	84
9550	1/2"		19	.421		30.50	30.50		61	79
9560	3/4"		18	.444		43	32		75	95.50
9570	1"	↓	15	.533	↓	59.50	38.50		98	123

For customer support on your Mechanical Costs with RSMeans data, call 800.448.8182.

22 11 Facility Water Distribution

22 11 13 – Facility Water Distribution Piping

22 11 13.66 Pipe Fittings, Stainless Steel		Crew	Daily Output	Labor-Hours	Unit	Material	2023 Bare Costs Labor	Equipment	Total	Total Incl O&P
9580	1-1/4"	Q-1	26	.615	Ea.	132	40		172	205
9590	1-1/2"		24	.667		123	43		166	200
9600	2"	▼	21	.762	▼	177	49.50		226.50	269
9620	Union									
9630	1/8"	1 Plum	12	.667	Ea.	201	48		249	293
9640	1/4"		12	.667		179	48		227	269
9650	3/8"		12	.667		179	48		227	269
9660	1/2"		11	.727		179	52.50		231.50	275
9670	3/4"		10	.800		219	57.50		276.50	325
9680	1"	▼	9	.889		335	64		399	465
9690	1-1/4"	Q-1	16	1		625	65		690	780
9700	1-1/2"		15	1.067		705	69		774	880
9710	2"	▼	13	1.231	▼	940	80		1,020	1,150
9730	3,000 lb., type 316									
9750	Coupling									
9770	1/8"	1 Plum	19	.421	Ea.	9.40	30.50		39.90	55.50
9780	1/4"		19	.421		21.50	30.50		52	68.50
9790	3/8"		19	.421		23	30.50		53.50	70.50
9800	1/2"		19	.421		25	30.50		55.50	72.50
9810	3/4"		18	.444		35.50	32		67.50	87
9820	1"	▼	15	.533		52.50	38.50		91	115
9830	1-1/4"	Q-1	26	.615		105	40		145	175
9840	1-1/2"		24	.667		99.50	43		142.50	175
9850	2"	▼	21	.762	▼	167	49.50		216.50	257
9870	Union									
9880	1/8"	1 Plum	12	.667	Ea.	184	48		232	274
9890	1/4"		12	.667		184	48		232	274
9900	3/8"		12	.667		213	48		261	305
9910	1/2"		11	.727		213	52.50		265.50	310
9920	3/4"		10	.800		278	57.50		335.50	390
9930	1"	▼	9	.889		440	64		504	575
9940	1-1/4"	Q-1	16	1		765	65		830	935
9950	1-1/2"		15	1.067		945	69		1,014	1,150
9960	2"	▼	13	1.231	▼	1,200	80		1,280	1,450

22 11 13.74 Pipe, Plastic

		Crew	Daily Output	Labor-Hours	Unit	Material	Labor	Equipment	Total	Total Incl O&P
0010	**PIPE, PLASTIC**									
0020	Fiberglass reinforced, couplings 10' OC, clevis hanger assy's, 3 per 10'									
0080	General service									
0120	2" diameter	Q-1	59	.271	L.F.	22	17.60		39.60	50.50
0140	3" diameter		52	.308		30.50	19.95		50.45	63.50
0150	4" diameter		48	.333		39.50	21.50		61	75.50
0160	6" diameter	▼	39	.410		47	26.50		73.50	91.50
0170	8" diameter	Q-2	49	.490		79.50	33		112.50	137
0180	10" diameter		41	.585		123	39.50		162.50	194
0190	12" diameter	▼	36	.667	▼	170	45		215	254
0600	PVC, high impact/pressure, cplgs. 10' OC, clevis hanger assy's, 3 per 10'									
1020	Schedule 80									
1070	1/2" diameter	1 Plum	50	.160	L.F.	10.20	11.55		21.75	28.50
1080	3/4" diameter		47	.170		10.85	12.25		23.10	30
1090	1" diameter		43	.186		5.20	13.40		18.60	25.50
1100	1-1/4" diameter		39	.205		6.70	14.80		21.50	29.50
1110	1-1/2" diameter	▼	34	.235		8.05	16.95		25	34.50

22 11 Facility Water Distribution

22 11 13 – Facility Water Distribution Piping

22 11 13.74 Pipe, Plastic		Crew	Daily Output	Labor-Hours	Unit	Material	2023 Bare Costs Labor	2023 Bare Costs Equipment	Total	Total Incl O&P
1120	2" diameter	Q-1	55	.291	L.F.	10	18.85		28.85	39
1140	3" diameter		50	.320		19.30	21		40.30	52
1150	4" diameter		46	.348		26	22.50		48.50	62.50
1170	6" diameter	↓	38	.421	↓	57	27.50		84.50	103
1730	To delete coupling & hangers, subtract									
1740	1/2" diam.					62%	80%			
1750	3/4" diam. to 1-1/4" diam.					58%	73%			
1760	1-1/2" diam. to 6" diam.					40%	57%			
1800	PVC, couplings 10' OC, clevis hanger assemblies, 3 per 10'									
1820	Schedule 40									
1860	1/2" diameter	1 Plum	54	.148	L.F.	9.90	10.65		20.55	27
1870	3/4" diameter		51	.157		10.25	11.30		21.55	28
1880	1" diameter		46	.174		4.44	12.55		16.99	23.50
1890	1-1/4" diameter		42	.190		5.35	13.70		19.05	26.50
1900	1-1/2" diameter	↓	36	.222		6.75	16		22.75	31.50
1910	2" diameter	Q-1	59	.271		8.05	17.60		25.65	35
1920	2-1/2" diameter		56	.286		12.20	18.55		30.75	41
1930	3" diameter		53	.302		15.15	19.60		34.75	45.50
1940	4" diameter		48	.333		11.30	21.50		32.80	44.50
1950	5" diameter		43	.372		31.50	24		55.50	70.50
1960	6" diameter	↓	39	.410		37.50	26.50		64	80.50
1970	8" diameter	Q-2	48	.500		69.50	33.50		103	127
1980	10" diameter		43	.558		104	37.50		141.50	171
1990	12" diameter		42	.571		162	38.50		200.50	236
2000	14" diameter		31	.774		270	52		322	375
2010	16" diameter	↓	23	1.043	↓	365	70		435	505
2340	To delete coupling & hangers, subtract									
2360	1/2" diam. to 1-1/4" diam.					65%	74%			
2370	1-1/2" diam. to 6" diam.					44%	57%			
2380	8" diam. to 12" diam.					41%	53%			
2390	14" diam. to 16" diam.					48%	45%			
2420	Schedule 80									
2440	1/4" diameter	1 Plum	58	.138	L.F.	8.95	9.95		18.90	24.50
2450	3/8" diameter		55	.145		8.95	10.50		19.45	25.50
2460	1/2" diameter		50	.160		9.95	11.55		21.50	28
2470	3/4" diameter		47	.170		10.60	12.25		22.85	30
2480	1" diameter		43	.186		4.80	13.40		18.20	25.50
2490	1-1/4" diameter		39	.205		6.15	14.80		20.95	29
2500	1-1/2" diameter	↓	34	.235		8.15	16.95		25.10	34.50
2510	2" diameter	Q-1	55	.291		9.05	18.85		27.90	38
2520	2-1/2" diameter		52	.308		12.55	19.95		32.50	44
2530	3" diameter		50	.320		20.50	21		41.50	53.50
2540	4" diameter		46	.348		27.50	22.50		50	63.50
2550	5" diameter		42	.381		32.50	24.50		57	72.50
2560	6" diameter	↓	38	.421		53	27.50		80.50	99
2570	8" diameter	Q-2	47	.511		93	34.50		127.50	153
2580	10" diameter		42	.571		114	38.50		152.50	184
2590	12" diameter		38	.632	↓	177	42.50		219.50	258
2830	To delete coupling & hangers, subtract									
2840	1/4" diam. to 1/2" diam.					66%	80%			
2850	3/4" diam. to 1-1/4" diam.					61%	73%			
2860	1-1/2" diam. to 6" diam.					41%	57%			
2870	8" diam. to 12" diam.					31%	50%			

22 11 Facility Water Distribution

22 11 13 – Facility Water Distribution Piping

22 11 13.74 Pipe, Plastic		Crew	Daily Output	Labor-Hours	Unit	Material	2023 Bare Costs Labor	Equipment	Total	Total Incl O&P
2900	Schedule 120									
2910	1/2" diameter	1 Plum	50	.160	L.F.	10.85	11.55		22.40	29
2950	3/4" diameter		47	.170		11.80	12.25		24.05	31.50
2960	1" diameter		43	.186		6.60	13.40		20	27.50
2970	1-1/4" diameter		39	.205		8.75	14.80		23.55	31.50
2980	1-1/2" diameter		33	.242		10.50	17.45		27.95	37.50
2990	2" diameter	Q-1	54	.296		13.90	19.20		33.10	44
3000	2-1/2" diameter		52	.308		21.50	19.95		41.45	53.50
3010	3" diameter		49	.327		42	21		63	77.50
3020	4" diameter		45	.356		38.50	23		61.50	77
3030	6" diameter		37	.432		102	28		130	154
3240	To delete coupling & hangers, subtract									
3250	1/2" diam. to 1-1/4" diam.					52%	74%			
3260	1-1/2" diam. to 4" diam.					30%	57%			
3270	6" diam.					17%	50%			
3300	PVC, pressure, couplings 10' OC, clevis hanger assy's, 3 per 10'									
3310	SDR 26, 160 psi									
3350	1-1/4" diameter	1 Plum	42	.190	L.F.	5.10	13.70		18.80	26
3360	1-1/2" diameter	"	36	.222		6.55	16		22.55	31
3370	2" diameter	Q-1	59	.271		7.85	17.60		25.45	34.50
3380	2-1/2" diameter		56	.286		11.75	18.55		30.30	40.50
3390	3" diameter		53	.302		15.60	19.60		35.20	46
3400	4" diameter		48	.333		22.50	21.50		44	57
3420	6" diameter		39	.410		43.50	26.50		70	87.50
3430	8" diameter	Q-2	48	.500		77	33.50		110.50	135
3660	To delete coupling & clevis hanger assy's, subtract									
3670	1-1/4" diam.					63%	68%			
3680	1-1/2" diam. to 4" diam.					48%	57%			
3690	6" diam. to 8" diam.					60%	54%			
3720	SDR 21, 200 psi, 1/2" diameter	1 Plum	54	.148	L.F.	9.80	10.65		20.45	26.50
3740	3/4" diameter		51	.157		9.85	11.30		21.15	27.50
3750	1" diameter		46	.174		3.63	12.55		16.18	22.50
3760	1-1/4" diameter		42	.190		5.35	13.70		19.05	26.50
3770	1-1/2" diameter		36	.222		4.99	16		20.99	29.50
3780	2" diameter	Q-1	59	.271		6.80	17.60		24.40	33.50
3790	2-1/2" diameter		56	.286		9.85	18.55		28.40	38.50
3800	3" diameter		53	.302		10.95	19.60		30.55	41
3810	4" diameter		48	.333		14.70	21.50		36.20	48
3830	6" diameter		39	.410		29.50	26.50		56	72
3840	8" diameter	Q-2	48	.500		58.50	33.50		92	114
4000	To delete coupling & hangers, subtract									
4010	1/2" diam. to 3/4" diam.					71%	77%			
4020	1" diam. to 1-1/4" diam.					63%	70%			
4030	1-1/2" diam. to 6" diam.					44%	57%			
4040	8" diam.					46%	54%			
4100	DWV type, schedule 40, couplings 10' OC, clevis hanger assy's, 3 per 10'									
4210	ABS, schedule 40, foam core type									
4212	Plain end black									
4214	1-1/2" diameter	1 Plum	39	.205	L.F.	5.55	14.80		20.35	28
4216	2" diameter	Q-1	62	.258		7	16.75		23.75	32.50
4218	3" diameter		56	.286		14.60	18.55		33.15	43.50
4220	4" diameter		51	.314		22	20.50		42.50	54.50
4222	6" diameter		42	.381		65	24.50		89.50	109

22 11 Facility Water Distribution

22 11 13 – Facility Water Distribution Piping

22 11 13.74 Pipe, Plastic

		Crew	Daily Output	Labor-Hours	Unit	Material	2023 Bare Costs Labor	2023 Bare Costs Equipment	Total	Total Incl O&P
4240	To delete coupling & hangers, subtract									
4244	1-1/2" diam. to 6" diam.					43%	48%			
4400	PVC									
4410	1-1/4" diameter	1 Plum	42	.190	L.F.	8.50	13.70		22.20	30
4420	1-1/2" diameter	"	36	.222		4.77	16		20.77	29.50
4460	2" diameter	Q-1	59	.271		6.10	17.60		23.70	32.50
4470	3" diameter		53	.302		12.85	19.60		32.45	43
4480	4" diameter		48	.333		18	21.50		39.50	52
4490	6" diameter		39	.410		48	26.50		74.50	92
4500	8" diameter	Q-2	48	.500		76	33.50		109.50	134
4510	To delete coupling & hangers, subtract									
4520	1-1/4" diam. to 1-1/2" diam.					48%	60%			
4530	2" diam. to 8" diam.					42%	54%			
4532	to delete hangers, 2" diam. to 8" diam.	Q-1	50	.320	L.F.	3.12	21		24.12	34.50
4550	PVC, schedule 40, foam core type									
4552	Plain end, white									
4554	1-1/2" diameter	1 Plum	39	.205	L.F.	3.27	14.80		18.07	25.50
4556	2" diameter	Q-1	62	.258		5.65	16.75		22.40	31
4558	3" diameter		56	.286		11.55	18.55		30.10	40
4560	4" diameter		51	.314		16.80	20.50		37.30	49
4562	6" diameter		42	.381		38.50	24.50		63	79.50
4564	8" diameter	Q-2	51	.471		61	31.50		92.50	114
4568	10" diameter		48	.500		78.50	33.50		112	137
4570	12" diameter		46	.522		93	35		128	155
4580	To delete coupling & hangers, subtract									
4582	1-1/2" diam. to 2" diam.					58%	54%			
4584	3" diam. to 12" diam.					46%	42%			
4800	PVC, clear pipe, cplgs. 10' OC, clevis hanger assy's 3 per 10', Sched. 40									
4840	1/4" diameter	1 Plum	59	.136	L.F.	9.30	9.75		19.05	25
4850	3/8" diameter		56	.143		9.70	10.30		20	26
4860	1/2" diameter		54	.148		10.45	10.65		21.10	27.50
4870	3/4" diameter		51	.157		11.20	11.30		22.50	29
4880	1" diameter		46	.174		6.30	12.55		18.85	25.50
4890	1-1/4" diameter		42	.190		8	13.70		21.70	29.50
4900	1-1/2" diameter		36	.222		9.40	16		25.40	34.50
4910	2" diameter	Q-1	59	.271		12.35	17.60		29.95	39.50
4920	2-1/2" diameter		56	.286		18.35	18.55		36.90	47.50
4930	3" diameter		53	.302		25	19.60		44.60	56.50
4940	3-1/2" diameter		50	.320		38.50	21		59.50	73
4950	4" diameter		48	.333		37	21.50		58.50	72.50
5250	To delete coupling & hangers, subtract									
5260	1/4" diam. to 3/8" diam.					60%	81%			
5270	1/2" diam. to 3/4" diam.					41%	77%			
5280	1" diam. to 1-1/2" diam.					26%	67%			
5290	2" diam. to 4" diam.					16%	58%			
5300	CPVC, socket joint, couplings 10' OC, clevis hanger assemblies, 3 per 10'									
5302	Schedule 40									
5304	1/2" diameter	1 Plum	54	.148	L.F.	10.75	10.65		21.40	28
5305	3/4" diameter		51	.157		12	11.30		23.30	30
5306	1" diameter		46	.174		13.35	12.55		25.90	33.50
5307	1-1/4" diameter		42	.190		9.50	13.70		23.20	31
5308	1-1/2" diameter		36	.222		11.45	16		27.45	36.50
5309	2" diameter	Q-1	59	.271		17.95	17.60		35.55	46

22 11 Facility Water Distribution

22 11 13 – Facility Water Distribution Piping

22 11 13.74 Pipe, Plastic

		Crew	Daily Output	Labor-Hours	Unit	Material	2023 Bare Costs Labor	Equipment	Total	Total Incl O&P
5310	2-1/2" diameter	Q-1	56	.286	L.F.	22.50	18.55		41.05	52
5311	3" diameter		53	.302		40	19.60		59.60	73
5312	4" diameter		48	.333		54	21.50		75.50	91.50
5314	6" diameter		43	.372		97.50	24		121.50	143
5318	To delete coupling & hangers, subtract									
5319	1/2" diam. to 3/4" diam.					37%	77%			
5320	1" diam. to 1-1/4" diam.					27%	70%			
5321	1-1/2" diam. to 3" diam.					21%	57%			
5322	4" diam. to 6" diam.					16%	57%			
5324	Schedule 80									
5325	1/2" diameter	1 Plum	50	.160	L.F.	19.25	11.55		30.80	38
5326	3/4" diameter		47	.170		20.50	12.25		32.75	41
5327	1" diameter		43	.186		14.30	13.40		27.70	36
5328	1-1/4" diameter		39	.205		9.70	14.80		24.50	32.50
5329	1-1/2" diameter		34	.235		17.75	16.95		34.70	45
5330	2" diameter	Q-1	55	.291		19.95	18.85		38.80	50
5331	2-1/2" diameter		52	.308		26.50	19.95		46.45	59.50
5332	3" diameter		50	.320		45	21		66	80.50
5333	4" diameter		46	.348		62	22.50		84.50	102
5334	6" diameter		38	.421		122	27.50		149.50	175
5335	8" diameter	Q-2	47	.511		234	34.50		268.50	310
5339	To delete couplings & hangers, subtract									
5340	1/2" diam. to 3/4" diam.					44%	77%			
5341	1" diam. to 1-1/4" diam.					32%	71%			
5342	1-1/2" diam. to 4" diam.					25%	58%			
5343	6" diam. to 8" diam.					20%	53%			
5360	CPVC, threaded, couplings 10' OC, clevis hanger assemblies, 3 per 10'									
5380	Schedule 40									
5460	1/2" diameter	1 Plum	54	.148	L.F.	12.30	10.65		22.95	29.50
5470	3/4" diameter		51	.157		14.70	11.30		26	33
5480	1" diameter		46	.174		16.15	12.55		28.70	36.50
5490	1-1/4" diameter		42	.190		11.75	13.70		25.45	33.50
5500	1-1/2" diameter		36	.222		13.35	16		29.35	38.50
5510	2" diameter	Q-1	59	.271		20	17.60		37.60	48
5520	2-1/2" diameter		56	.286		25	18.55		43.55	55
5530	3" diameter		53	.302		40.50	19.60		60.10	73.50
5540	4" diameter		48	.333		61.50	21.50		83	100
5550	6" diameter		43	.372		102	24		126	148
5730	To delete coupling & hangers, subtract									
5740	1/2" diam. to 3/4" diam.					37%	77%			
5750	1" diam. to 1-1/4" diam.					27%	70%			
5760	1-1/2" diam. to 3" diam.					21%	57%			
5770	4" diam. to 6" diam.					16%	57%			
5800	Schedule 80									
5860	1/2" diameter	1 Plum	50	.160	L.F.	21	11.55		32.55	40
5870	3/4" diameter		47	.170		23	12.25		35.25	44
5880	1" diameter		43	.186		17.10	13.40		30.50	39
5890	1-1/4" diameter		39	.205		11.90	14.80		26.70	35
5900	1-1/2" diameter		34	.235		19.65	16.95		36.60	47
5910	2" diameter	Q-1	55	.291		22	18.85		40.85	52.50
5920	2-1/2" diameter		52	.308		29	19.95		48.95	62
5930	3" diameter		50	.320		45.50	21		66.50	81
5940	4" diameter		46	.348		69.50	22.50		92	110

22 11 Facility Water Distribution

22 11 13 – Facility Water Distribution Piping

22 11 13.74 Pipe, Plastic

		Crew	Daily Output	Labor-Hours	Unit	Material	2023 Bare Costs Labor	2023 Bare Costs Equipment	Total	Total Incl O&P
5950	6" diameter	Q-1	38	.421	L.F.	126	27.50		153.50	180
5960	8" diameter	Q-2	47	.511		226	34.50		260.50	299
6060	To delete couplings & hangers, subtract									
6070	1/2" diam. to 3/4" diam.					44%	77%			
6080	1" diam. to 1-1/4" diam.					32%	71%			
6090	1-1/2" diam. to 4" diam.					25%	58%			
6100	6" diam. to 8" diam.					20%	53%			
6240	CTS, 1/2" diameter	1 Plum	54	.148	L.F.	8.75	10.65		19.40	25.50
6250	3/4" diameter		51	.157		5.75	11.30		17.05	23
6260	1" diameter		46	.174		11.50	12.55		24.05	31.50
6270	1-1/4" diameter		42	.190		18.90	13.70		32.60	41.50
6280	1-1/2" diameter		36	.222		25	16		41	51.50
6290	2" diameter	Q-1	59	.271		41	17.60		58.60	71
6370	To delete coupling & hangers, subtract									
6380	1/2" diam.					51%	79%			
6390	3/4" diam.					40%	76%			
6392	1" thru 2" diam.					72%	68%			
7280	PEX, flexible, no couplings or hangers									
7282	Note: For labor costs add 25% to the couplings and fittings labor total.									
7285	For fittings see section 23 83 16.10 7000									
7300	Non-barrier type, hot/cold tubing rolls									
7310	1/4" diameter x 100'				L.F.	.49			.49	.54
7350	3/8" diameter x 100'					.63			.63	.69
7360	1/2" diameter x 100'					.52			.52	.57
7370	1/2" diameter x 500'					.70			.70	.77
7380	1/2" diameter x 1000'					.52			.52	.57
7400	3/4" diameter x 100'					.88			.88	.97
7410	3/4" diameter x 500'					.87			.87	.96
7420	3/4" diameter x 1000'					1.90			1.90	2.09
7460	1" diameter x 100'					1.56			1.56	1.72
7470	1" diameter x 300'					1.54			1.54	1.69
7480	1" diameter x 500'					1.90			1.90	2.09
7500	1-1/4" diameter x 100'					4.13			4.13	4.54
7510	1-1/4" diameter x 300'					3.76			3.76	4.14
7540	1-1/2" diameter x 100'					4.29			4.29	4.72
7550	1-1/2" diameter x 300'					4.10			4.10	4.51
7596	Most sizes available in red or blue									
7700	Non-barrier type, hot/cold tubing straight lengths									
7710	1/2" diameter x 20'				L.F.	.73			.73	.80
7750	3/4" diameter x 20'					2.15			2.15	2.37
7760	1" diameter x 20'					2.24			2.24	2.46
7770	1-1/4" diameter x 20'					5.20			5.20	5.70
7780	1-1/2" diameter x 20'					5.80			5.80	6.40
7790	2" diameter					14.75			14.75	16.25
7796	Most sizes available in red or blue									
9000	Polypropylene pipe									
9002	For fusion weld fittings and accessories see line 22 11 13.76 9400									
9004	Note: sizes 1/2" thru 4" use socket fusion									
9005	Sizes 6" thru 10" use butt fusion									
9010	SDR 7.4 (domestic hot water piping)									
9011	Enhanced to minimize thermal expansion and high temperature life									
9016	13' lengths, size is ID, includes joints 13' OC and hangers 3 per 10'									
9020	3/8" diameter	1 Plum	53	.151	L.F.	3.87	10.90		14.77	20.50

22 11 Facility Water Distribution

22 11 13 – Facility Water Distribution Piping

22 11 13.74 Pipe, Plastic

		Crew	Daily Output	Labor-Hours	Unit	Material	2023 Bare Costs Labor	Equipment	Total	Total Incl O&P
9022	1/2" diameter	1 Plum	52	.154	L.F.	4.65	11.10		15.75	21.50
9024	3/4" diameter		50	.160		5.65	11.55		17.20	23.50
9026	1" diameter		45	.178		7.15	12.80		19.95	27
9028	1-1/4" diameter		40	.200		10.65	14.40		25.05	33
9030	1-1/2" diameter	↓	35	.229		15.55	16.45		32	41.50
9032	2" diameter	Q-1	58	.276		20.50	17.90		38.40	49
9034	2-1/2" diameter		55	.291		28.50	18.85		47.35	59.50
9036	3" diameter		52	.308		38	19.95		57.95	71.50
9038	3-1/2" diameter		49	.327		57.50	21		78.50	94.50
9040	4" diameter		46	.348		58.50	22.50		81	98
9042	6" diameter	↓	39	.410		87	26.50		113.50	135
9044	8" diameter	Q-2	48	.500		133	33.50		166.50	196
9046	10" diameter	"	43	.558	↓	211	37.50		248.50	288
9050	To delete joint & hangers, subtract									
9052	3/8" diam. to 1" diam.					45%	65%			
9054	1-1/4" diam. to 4" diam.					15%	45%			
9056	6" diam. to 10" diam.					5%	24%			
9060	SDR 11 (domestic cold water piping)									
9062	13' lengths, size is ID, includes joints 13' OC and hangers 3 per 10'									
9064	1/2" diameter	1 Plum	57	.140	L.F.	4.22	10.10		14.32	19.75
9066	3/4" diameter		54	.148		4.67	10.65		15.32	21
9068	1" diameter		49	.163		5.80	11.75		17.55	24
9070	1-1/4" diameter		45	.178		8	12.80		20.80	28
9072	1-1/2" diameter	↓	40	.200		11	14.40		25.40	33.50
9074	2" diameter	Q-1	62	.258		15.90	16.75		32.65	42.50
9076	2-1/2" diameter		59	.271		21	17.60		38.60	49.50
9078	3" diameter		56	.286		28.50	18.55		47.05	59
9080	3-1/2" diameter		53	.302		41.50	19.60		61.10	75
9082	4" diameter		50	.320		46	21		67	81.50
9084	6" diameter	↓	47	.340		58.50	22		80.50	97.50
9086	8" diameter	Q-2	51	.471		91	31.50		122.50	147
9088	10" diameter	"	46	.522	↓	139	35		174	205
9090	To delete joint & hangers, subtract									
9092	1/2" diam. to 1" diam.					45%	65%			
9094	1-1/4" diam. to 4" diam.					15%	45%			
9096	6" diam. to 10" diam.					5%	24%			

22 11 13.76 Pipe Fittings, Plastic

		Crew	Daily Output	Labor-Hours	Unit	Material	2023 Bare Costs Labor	Equipment	Total	Total Incl O&P
0010	**PIPE FITTINGS, PLASTIC**									
0030	Epoxy resin, fiberglass reinforced, general service									
0100	3"	Q-1	20.80	.769	Ea.	179	50		229	272
0110	4"		16.50	.970		192	63		255	305
0120	6"	↓	10.10	1.584		355	103		458	545
0130	8"	Q-2	9.30	2.581		655	174		829	980
0140	10"		8.50	2.824		825	190		1,015	1,200
0150	12"	↓	7.60	3.158	↓	1,175	212		1,387	1,625
0170	Elbow, 90°, flanged									
0172	2"	Q-1	23	.696	Ea.	410	45		455	520
0173	3"		16	1		470	65		535	610
0174	4"		13	1.231		610	80		690	790
0176	6"	↓	8	2		1,100	130		1,230	1,425
0177	8"	Q-2	9	2.667		2,000	179		2,179	2,475
0178	10"	↓	7	3.429	↓	2,725	231		2,956	3,350

22 11 Facility Water Distribution

22 11 13 – Facility Water Distribution Piping

22 11 13.76	Pipe Fittings, Plastic	Crew	Daily Output	Labor-Hours	Unit	Material	2023 Bare Costs Labor	2023 Bare Costs Equipment	Total	Total Incl O&P
0179	12"	Q-2	5	4.800	Ea.	3,675	325		4,000	4,525
0186	Elbow, 45°, flanged									
0188	2"	Q-1	23	.696	Ea.	410	45		455	520
0189	3"		16	1		470	65		535	610
0190	4"		13	1.231		610	80		690	790
0192	6"	↓	8	2		1,100	130		1,230	1,425
0193	8"	Q-2	9	2.667		2,025	179		2,204	2,500
0194	10"		7	3.429		2,825	231		3,056	3,450
0195	12"	↓	5	4.800	↓	3,825	325		4,150	4,700
0352	Tee, flanged									
0354	2"	Q-1	17	.941	Ea.	555	61		616	700
0355	3"		10	1.600		730	104		834	960
0356	4"		8	2		820	130		950	1,100
0358	6"	↓	5	3.200		1,400	208		1,608	1,850
0359	8"	Q-2	6	4		2,675	269		2,944	3,325
0360	10"		5	4.800		3,875	325		4,200	4,750
0361	12"	↓	4	6	↓	5,350	405		5,755	6,475
0365	Wye, flanged									
0367	2"	Q-1	17	.941	Ea.	1,100	61		1,161	1,300
0368	3"		10	1.600		1,500	104		1,604	1,800
0369	4"		8	2		2,000	130		2,130	2,400
0371	6"	↓	5	3.200		2,850	208		3,058	3,425
0372	8"	Q-2	6	4		4,625	269		4,894	5,500
0373	10"		5	4.800		7,200	325		7,525	8,400
0374	12"	↓	4	6	↓	10,500	405		10,905	12,100
0380	Couplings									
0410	2"	Q-1	33.10	.483	Ea.	27	31.50		58.50	76
0420	3"		20.80	.769		35.50	50		85.50	114
0430	4"		16.50	.970		50	63		113	149
0440	6"	↓	10.10	1.584		63.50	103		166.50	223
0450	8"	Q-2	9.30	2.581		107	174		281	375
0460	10"		8.50	2.824		380	190		570	700
0470	12"	↓	7.60	3.158	↓	540	212		752	910
0473	High corrosion resistant couplings, add					30%				
0474	Reducer, concentric, flanged									
0475	2" x 1-1/2"	Q-1	30	.533	Ea.	1,050	34.50		1,084.50	1,225
0476	3" x 2"		24	.667		1,150	43		1,193	1,350
0477	4" x 3"		19	.842		1,300	54.50		1,354.50	1,500
0479	6" x 4"	↓	15	1.067		1,300	69		1,369	1,525
0480	8" x 6"	Q-2	16	1.500		2,125	101		2,226	2,500
0481	10" x 8"		13	1.846		1,975	124		2,099	2,350
0482	12" x 10"	↓	11	2.182	↓	3,050	147		3,197	3,600
0486	Adapter, bell x male or female									
0488	2"	Q-1	28	.571	Ea.	54	37		91	115
0489	3"		20	.800		81.50	52		133.50	167
0491	4"		17	.941		96.50	61		157.50	197
0492	6"	↓	12	1.333		222	86.50		308.50	375
0493	8"	Q-2	15	1.600		320	108		428	510
0494	10"	"	11	2.182	↓	460	147		607	725
0528	Flange									
0532	2"	Q-1	46	.348	Ea.	71	22.50		93.50	112
0533	3"		32	.500		98.50	32.50		131	158
0534	4"		26	.615	↓	125	40		165	197

22 11 Facility Water Distribution

22 11 13 – Facility Water Distribution Piping

22 11 13.76 Pipe Fittings, Plastic

		Crew	Daily Output	Labor-Hours	Unit	Material	2023 Bare Costs Labor	Equipment	Total	Total Incl O&P
0536	6"	Q-1	16	1	Ea.	148	65		213	260
0537	8"	Q-2	18	1.333		365	89.50		454.50	535
0538	10"		14	1.714		515	115		630	735
0539	12"		10	2.400		645	161		806	950
2100	PVC schedule 80, socket joint									
2110	90° elbow, 1/2"	1 Plum	30.30	.264	Ea.	4.74	19		23.74	33.50
2130	3/4"		26	.308		6.10	22		28.10	39.50
2140	1"		22.70	.352		9.80	25.50		35.30	49
2150	1-1/4"		20.20	.396		12.75	28.50		41.25	56.50
2160	1-1/2"		18.20	.440		14.05	31.50		45.55	62.50
2170	2"	Q-1	33.10	.483		16.95	31.50		48.45	65
2180	3"		20.80	.769		43.50	50		93.50	122
2190	4"		16.50	.970		68	63		131	169
2200	6"		10.10	1.584		193	103		296	365
2210	8"	Q-2	9.30	2.581		530	174		704	845
2250	45° elbow, 1/2"	1 Plum	30.30	.264		8.95	19		27.95	38.50
2270	3/4"		26	.308		13.65	22		35.65	48
2280	1"		22.70	.352		20.50	25.50		46	60.50
2290	1-1/4"		20.20	.396		25.50	28.50		54	70.50
2300	1-1/2"		18.20	.440		31	31.50		62.50	81
2310	2"	Q-1	33.10	.483		40	31.50		71.50	90.50
2320	3"		20.80	.769		99.50	50		149.50	184
2330	4"		16.50	.970		184	63		247	297
2340	6"		10.10	1.584		232	103		335	410
2350	8"	Q-2	9.30	2.581		505	174		679	815
2400	Tee, 1/2"	1 Plum	20.20	.396		13.40	28.50		41.90	57.50
2420	3/4"		17.30	.462		14.05	33.50		47.55	65
2430	1"		15.20	.526		17.60	38		55.60	76
2440	1-1/4"		13.50	.593		47	42.50		89.50	115
2450	1-1/2"		12.10	.661		48.50	47.50		96	124
2460	2"	Q-1	20	.800		60.50	52		112.50	144
2470	3"		13.90	1.151		80	74.50		154.50	199
2480	4"		11	1.455		95	94.50		189.50	246
2490	6"		6.70	2.388		325	155		480	585
2500	8"	Q-2	6.20	3.871		755	260		1,015	1,225
2510	Flange, socket, 150 lb., 1/2"	1 Plum	55.60	.144		35	10.35		45.35	54
2514	3/4"		47.60	.168		37	12.10		49.10	59
2518	1"		41.70	.192		41.50	13.80		55.30	66
2522	1-1/2"		33.30	.240		43.50	17.30		60.80	74
2526	2"	Q-1	60.60	.264		62.50	17.10		79.60	94.50
2530	4"		30.30	.528		135	34		169	200
2534	6"		18.50	.865		213	56		269	320
2538	8"	Q-2	17.10	1.404		350	94.50		444.50	525
2550	Coupling, 1/2"	1 Plum	30.30	.264		8.95	19		27.95	38.50
2570	3/4"		26	.308		12.40	22		34.40	46.50
2580	1"		22.70	.352		12.95	25.50		38.45	52.50
2590	1-1/4"		20.20	.396		17.75	28.50		46.25	62
2600	1-1/2"		18.20	.440		27	31.50		58.50	76.50
2610	2"	Q-1	33.10	.483		28.50	31.50		60	78
2620	3"		20.80	.769		58	50		108	139
2630	4"		16.50	.970		72.50	63		135.50	174
2640	6"		10.10	1.584		156	103		259	325
2650	8"	Q-2	9.30	2.581		212	174		386	495

22 11 Facility Water Distribution

22 11 13 – Facility Water Distribution Piping

22 11 13.76 Pipe Fittings, Plastic		Crew	Daily Output	Labor-Hours	Unit	Material	2023 Bare Costs Labor	Equipment	Total	Total Incl O&P
2660	10"	Q-2	8.50	2.824	Ea.	400	190		590	725
2670	12"		7.60	3.158		700	212		912	1,075
2700	PVC (white), schedule 40, socket joints									
2760	90° elbow, 1/2"	1 Plum	33.30	.240	Ea.	.90	17.30		18.20	27
2770	3/4"		28.60	.280		1.02	20		21.02	31
2780	1"		25	.320		1.84	23		24.84	36.50
2790	1-1/4"		22.20	.360		3.04	26		29.04	42
2800	1-1/2"		20	.400		3.56	29		32.56	47
2810	2"	Q-1	36.40	.440		5.40	28.50		33.90	48.50
2820	2-1/2"		26.70	.599		18.10	39		57.10	78
2830	3"		22.90	.699		21.50	45.50		67	91.50
2840	4"		18.20	.879		38.50	57		95.50	128
2850	5"		12.10	1.322		79	86		165	215
2860	6"		11.10	1.441		123	93.50		216.50	274
2870	8"	Q-2	10.30	2.330		315	157		472	585
2980	45° elbow, 1/2"	1 Plum	33.30	.240		1.64	17.30		18.94	28
2990	3/4"		28.60	.280		2.55	20		22.55	33
3000	1"		25	.320		3.04	23		26.04	38
3010	1-1/4"		22.20	.360		4.33	26		30.33	43.50
3020	1-1/2"		20	.400		5.30	29		34.30	49
3030	2"	Q-1	36.40	.440		6.95	28.50		35.45	50
3040	2-1/2"		26.70	.599		18.15	39		57.15	78
3050	3"		22.90	.699		28.50	45.50		74	99
3060	4"		18.20	.879		50.50	57		107.50	141
3070	5"		12.10	1.322		102	86		188	240
3080	6"		11.10	1.441		125	93.50		218.50	276
3090	8"	Q-2	10.30	2.330		300	157		457	565
3180	Tee, 1/2"	1 Plum	22.20	.360		1.22	26		27.22	40
3190	3/4"		19	.421		1.28	30.50		31.78	46.50
3200	1"		16.70	.479		2.24	34.50		36.74	54
3210	1-1/4"		14.80	.541		3.57	39		42.57	62
3220	1-1/2"		13.30	.602		4.58	43.50		48.08	69.50
3230	2"	Q-1	24.20	.661		6.70	43		49.70	71.50
3240	2-1/2"		17.80	.899		19.90	58.50		78.40	109
3250	3"		15.20	1.053		32.50	68.50		101	138
3260	4"		12.10	1.322		51	86		137	184
3270	5"		8.10	1.975		141	128		269	345
3280	6"		7.40	2.162		170	140		310	395
3290	8"	Q-2	6.80	3.529		450	237		687	850
3380	Coupling, 1/2"	1 Plum	33.30	.240		.65	17.30		17.95	26.50
3390	3/4"		28.60	.280		.90	20		20.90	31
3400	1"		25	.320		1.57	23		24.57	36
3410	1-1/4"		22.20	.360		1.88	26		27.88	40.50
3420	1-1/2"		20	.400		2.32	29		31.32	45.50
3430	2"	Q-1	36.40	.440		3.56	28.50		32.06	46.50
3440	2-1/2"		26.70	.599		7.85	39		46.85	66.50
3450	3"		22.90	.699		12.25	45.50		57.75	81
3460	4"		18.20	.879		17.75	57		74.75	105
3470	5"		12.10	1.322		33	86		119	165
3480	6"		11.10	1.441		56	93.50		149.50	201
3490	8"	Q-2	10.30	2.330		107	157		264	350
3600	Cap, schedule 40, PVC socket 1/2"	1 Plum	60.60	.132		.90	9.50		10.40	15.20
3610	3/4"		51.90	.154		1.04	11.10		12.14	17.70

22 11 Facility Water Distribution

22 11 13 – Facility Water Distribution Piping

22 11 13.76 Pipe Fittings, Plastic

		Crew	Daily Output	Labor-Hours	Unit	Material	2023 Bare Costs Labor	Equipment	Total	Total Incl O&P
3620	1"	1 Plum	45.50	.176	Ea.	1.64	12.65		14.29	20.50
3630	1-1/4"		40.40	.198		2.36	14.25		16.61	24
3640	1-1/2"	↓	36.40	.220		2.55	15.85		18.40	26.50
3650	2"	Q-1	66.10	.242		3.04	15.70		18.74	27
3660	2-1/2"		48.50	.330		9.90	21.50		31.40	43
3670	3"		41.60	.385		10.80	25		35.80	49
3680	4"	↓	33.10	.483		24	31.50		55.50	73
3690	6"	↓	20.20	.792		58	51.50		109.50	141
3700	8"	Q-2	18.60	1.290	↓	146	87		233	289
3710	Reducing insert, schedule 40, socket weld									
3712	3/4"	1 Plum	31.50	.254	Ea.	1.04	18.30		19.34	28.50
3713	1"		27.50	.291		1.88	21		22.88	33.50
3715	1-1/2"	↓	22	.364		2.68	26		28.68	42
3716	2"	Q-1	40	.400		4.44	26		30.44	43.50
3717	4"		20	.800		23.50	52		75.50	104
3718	6"	↓	12.20	1.311		58	85		143	191
3719	8"	Q-2	11.30	2.124	↓	216	143		359	450
3730	Reducing insert, socket weld x female/male thread									
3732	1/2"	1 Plum	38.30	.209	Ea.	4.78	15.05		19.83	28
3733	3/4"		32.90	.243		2.95	17.50		20.45	29.50
3734	1"		28.80	.278		4.13	20		24.13	34.50
3736	1-1/2"	↓	23	.348		7.45	25		32.45	45.50
3737	2"	Q-1	41.90	.382		7.95	25		32.95	46
3738	4"	"	20.90	.766	↓	76	49.50		125.50	158
3742	Male adapter, socket weld x male thread									
3744	1/2"	1 Plum	38.30	.209	Ea.	.90	15.05		15.95	23.50
3745	3/4"		32.90	.243		.99	17.50		18.49	27
3746	1"		28.80	.278		1.78	20		21.78	32
3748	1-1/2"	↓	23	.348		2.66	25		27.66	40.50
3749	2"	Q-1	41.90	.382		3.81	25		28.81	41
3750	4"	"	20.90	.766	↓	21	49.50		70.50	97
3754	Female adapter, socket weld x female thread									
3756	1/2"	1 Plum	38.30	.209	Ea.	1.12	15.05		16.17	23.50
3757	3/4"		32.90	.243		1.41	17.50		18.91	27.50
3758	1"		28.80	.278		1.64	20		21.64	32
3760	1-1/2"	↓	23	.348		2.91	25		27.91	40.50
3761	2"	Q-1	41.90	.382		3.89	25		28.89	41.50
3762	4"	"	20.90	.766	↓	22	49.50		71.50	98
3800	PVC, schedule 80, socket joints									
3810	Reducing insert									
3812	3/4"	1 Plum	28.60	.280	Ea.	3.02	20		23.02	33.50
3813	1"		25	.320		8.65	23		31.65	44
3815	1-1/2"	↓	20	.400		18.45	29		47.45	63.50
3816	2"	Q-1	36.40	.440		26.50	28.50		55	71.50
3817	4"		18.20	.879		100	57		157	196
3818	6"	↓	11.10	1.441		140	93.50		233.50	293
3819	8"	Q-2	10.20	2.353	↓	805	158		963	1,125
3830	Reducing insert, socket weld x female/male thread									
3832	1/2"	1 Plum	34.80	.230	Ea.	18.90	16.55		35.45	45.50
3833	3/4"		29.90	.268		11.60	19.30		30.90	42
3834	1"		26.10	.307		18.15	22		40.15	53
3836	1-1/2"	↓	20.90	.383		23	27.50		50.50	66
3837	2"	Q-1	38	.421		33.50	27.50		61	77.50

22 11 Facility Water Distribution

22 11 13 – Facility Water Distribution Piping

22 11 13.76 Pipe Fittings, Plastic

		Crew	Daily Output	Labor-Hours	Unit	Material	2023 Bare Costs Labor	2023 Bare Costs Equipment	Total	Total Incl O&P
3838	4"	Q-1	19	.842	Ea.	162	54.50		216.50	260
3844	Adapter, male socket x male thread									
3846	1/2"	1 Plum	34.80	.230	Ea.	7.30	16.55		23.85	32.50
3847	3/4"		29.90	.268		8.05	19.30		27.35	38
3848	1"		26.10	.307		13.95	22		35.95	48.50
3850	1-1/2"		20.90	.383		23.50	27.50		51	67
3851	2"	Q-1	38	.421		34	27.50		61.50	78
3852	4"	"	19	.842		76	54.50		130.50	165
3860	Adapter, female socket x female thread									
3862	1/2"	1 Plum	34.80	.230	Ea.	8.75	16.55		25.30	34
3863	3/4"		29.90	.268		13.05	19.30		32.35	43.50
3864	1"		26.10	.307		19.20	22		41.20	54
3866	1-1/2"		20.90	.383		38	27.50		65.50	83
3867	2"	Q-1	38	.421		66.50	27.50		94	114
3868	4"	"	19	.842		203	54.50		257.50	305
3872	Union, socket joints									
3874	1/2"	1 Plum	25.80	.310	Ea.	19.20	22.50		41.70	54.50
3875	3/4"		22.10	.362		24.50	26		50.50	66
3876	1"		19.30	.415		28	30		58	75
3878	1-1/2"		15.50	.516		62.50	37		99.50	125
3879	2"	Q-1	28.10	.569		85	37		122	149
3888	Cap									
3890	1/2"	1 Plum	54.50	.147	Ea.	9.15	10.60		19.75	26
3891	3/4"		46.70	.171		9.70	12.35		22.05	29
3892	1"		41	.195		17.20	14.05		31.25	40
3894	1-1/2"		32.80	.244		20.50	17.55		38.05	49
3895	2"	Q-1	59.50	.269		54.50	17.45		71.95	86
3896	4"		30	.533		165	34.50		199.50	233
3897	6"		18.20	.879		410	57		467	535
3898	8"	Q-2	16.70	1.437		525	96.50		621.50	725
4500	DWV, ABS, non pressure, socket joints									
4540	1/4 bend, 1-1/4"	1 Plum	20.20	.396	Ea.	25.50	28.50		54	70.50
4560	1-1/2"	"	18.20	.440		19.90	31.50		51.40	69
4570	2"	Q-1	33.10	.483		18.75	31.50		50.25	67
4580	3"		20.80	.769		77	50		127	159
4590	4"		16.50	.970		158	63		221	268
4600	6"		10.10	1.584		675	103		778	895
4650	1/8 bend, same as 1/4 bend									
4800	Tee, sanitary									
4820	1-1/4"	1 Plum	13.50	.593	Ea.	34	42.50		76.50	101
4830	1-1/2"	"	12.10	.661		29.50	47.50		77	104
4840	2"	Q-1	20	.800		45.50	52		97.50	128
4850	3"		13.90	1.151		123	74.50		197.50	246
4860	4"		11	1.455		219	94.50		313.50	380
4862	Tee, sanitary, reducing, 2" x 1-1/2"		22	.727		39.50	47		86.50	114
4864	3" x 2"		15.30	1.046		98	68		166	209
4868	4" x 3"		12.10	1.322		220	86		306	370
4870	Combination Y and 1/8 bend									
4872	1-1/2"	1 Plum	12.10	.661	Ea.	76.50	47.50		124	155
4874	2"	Q-1	20	.800		77.50	52		129.50	163
4876	3"		13.90	1.151		185	74.50		259.50	315
4878	4"		11	1.455		385	94.50		479.50	565
4880	3" x 1-1/2"		15.50	1.032		209	67		276	330

22 11 Facility Water Distribution

22 11 13 – Facility Water Distribution Piping

22 11 13.76 Pipe Fittings, Plastic

		Crew	Daily Output	Labor-Hours	Unit	Material	2023 Bare Costs Labor	Equipment	Total	Total Incl O&P
4882	4" x 3"	Q-1	12.10	1.322	Ea.	277	86		363	435
4900	Wye, 1-1/4"	1 Plum	13.50	.593		39	42.50		81.50	107
4902	1-1/2"	"	12.10	.661		48.50	47.50		96	125
4904	2"	Q-1	20	.800		63.50	52		115.50	148
4906	3"		13.90	1.151		137	74.50		211.50	262
4908	4"		11	1.455		278	94.50		372.50	445
4910	6"		6.70	2.388		835	155		990	1,150
4918	3" x 1-1/2"		15.50	1.032		121	67		188	233
4920	4" x 3"		12.10	1.322		240	86		326	390
4922	6" x 4"		6.90	2.319		760	150		910	1,050
4930	Double wye, 1-1/2"	1 Plum	9.10	.879		150	63.50		213.50	260
4932	2"	Q-1	16.60	.964		179	62.50		241.50	290
4934	3"		10.40	1.538		400	100		500	590
4936	4"		8.25	1.939		785	126		911	1,050
4940	2" x 1-1/2"		16.80	.952		170	62		232	279
4942	3" x 2"		10.60	1.509		279	98		377	450
4944	4" x 3"		8.45	1.893		650	123		773	900
4946	6" x 4"		7.25	2.207		890	143		1,033	1,200
4950	Reducer bushing, 2" x 1-1/2"		36.40	.440		15.65	28.50		44.15	59.50
4952	3" x 1-1/2"		27.30	.586		68.50	38		106.50	132
4954	4" x 2"		18.20	.879		127	57		184	225
4956	6" x 4"		11.10	1.441		355	93.50		448.50	530
4960	Couplings, 1-1/2"	1 Plum	18.20	.440		10.20	31.50		41.70	58
4962	2"	Q-1	33.10	.483		12.80	31.50		44.30	60.50
4963	3"		20.80	.769		38.50	50		88.50	117
4964	4"		16.50	.970		64.50	63		127.50	165
4966	6"		10.10	1.584		269	103		372	450
4970	2" x 1-1/2"		33.30	.480		27.50	31		58.50	76.50
4972	3" x 1-1/2"		21	.762		81	49.50		130.50	163
4974	4" x 3"		16.70	.958		121	62		183	226
4978	Closet flange, 4"	1 Plum	32	.250		73	18		91	108
4980	4" x 3"	"	34	.235		80	16.95		96.95	113
5000	DWV, PVC, schedule 40, socket joints									
5040	1/4 bend, 1-1/4"	1 Plum	20.20	.396	Ea.	53.50	28.50		82	101
5060	1-1/2"	"	18.20	.440		15.30	31.50		46.80	64
5070	2"	Q-1	33.10	.483		24	31.50		55.50	73
5080	3"		20.80	.769		71	50		121	153
5090	4"		16.50	.970		140	63		203	248
5100	6"		10.10	1.584		490	103		593	695
5105	8"	Q-2	9.30	2.581		635	174		809	960
5106	10"	"	8.50	2.824		775	190		965	1,150
5110	1/4 bend, long sweep, 1-1/2"	1 Plum	18.20	.440		35.50	31.50		67	86
5112	2"	Q-1	33.10	.483		39.50	31.50		71	90
5114	3"		20.80	.769		91	50		141	175
5116	4"		16.50	.970		172	63		235	283
5150	1/8 bend, 1-1/4"	1 Plum	20.20	.396		36.50	28.50		65	82.50
5170	1-1/2"	"	18.20	.440		14.95	31.50		46.45	63.50
5180	2"	Q-1	33.10	.483		22.50	31.50		54	71
5190	3"		20.80	.769		63.50	50		113.50	144
5200	4"		16.50	.970		116	63		179	222
5210	6"		10.10	1.584		430	103		533	630
5215	8"	Q-2	9.30	2.581		146	174		320	420
5216	10"	"	8.50	2.824		725	190		915	1,075

22 11 Facility Water Distribution

22 11 13 – Facility Water Distribution Piping

22 11 13.76 Pipe Fittings, Plastic

		Crew	Daily Output	Labor-Hours	Unit	Material	2023 Bare Costs Labor	Equipment	Total	Total Incl O&P
5217	12"	Q-2	7.60	3.158	Ea.	895	212		1,107	1,300
5250	Tee, sanitary 1-1/4"	1 Plum	13.50	.593		57	42.50		99.50	127
5254	1-1/2"	"	12.10	.661		26.50	47.50		74	101
5255	2"	Q-1	20	.800		39.50	52		91.50	121
5256	3"		13.90	1.151		104	74.50		178.50	225
5257	4"		11	1.455		189	94.50		283.50	350
5259	6"		6.70	2.388		760	155		915	1,075
5261	8"	Q-2	6.20	3.871		1,675	260		1,935	2,250
5276	Tee, sanitary, reducing									
5281	2" x 1-1/2" x 1-1/2"	Q-1	23	.696	Ea.	34.50	45		79.50	106
5282	2" x 1-1/2" x 2"		22	.727		41.50	47		88.50	117
5283	2" x 2" x 1-1/2"		22	.727		16.80	47		63.80	89
5284	3" x 3" x 1-1/2"		15.50	1.032		36.50	67		103.50	140
5285	3" x 3" x 2"		15.30	1.046		78	68		146	187
5286	4" x 4" x 1-1/2"		12.30	1.301		198	84.50		282.50	345
5287	4" x 4" x 2"		12.20	1.311		163	85		248	305
5288	4" x 4" x 3"		12.10	1.322		107	86		193	246
5291	6" x 6" x 4"		6.90	2.319		355	150		505	615
5294	Tee, double sanitary									
5295	1-1/2"	1 Plum	9.10	.879	Ea.	59	63.50		122.50	159
5296	2"	Q-1	16.60	.964		79.50	62.50		142	181
5297	3"		10.40	1.538		222	100		322	395
5298	4"		8.25	1.939		355	126		481	585
5303	Wye, reducing									
5304	2" x 1-1/2" x 1-1/2"	Q-1	23	.696	Ea.	67	45		112	141
5305	2" x 2" x 1-1/2"		22	.727		58.50	47		105.50	135
5306	3" x 3" x 2"		15.30	1.046		191	68		259	310
5307	4" x 4" x 2"		12.20	1.311		141	85		226	282
5309	4" x 4" x 3"		12.10	1.322		191	86		277	340
5314	Combination Y & 1/8 bend, 1-1/2"	1 Plum	12.10	.661		64.50	47.50		112	142
5315	2"	Q-1	20	.800		81	52		133	167
5317	3"		13.90	1.151		178	74.50		252.50	305
5318	4"		11	1.455		350	94.50		444.50	525
5319	6"		6.70	2.388		1,325	155		1,480	1,700
5320	8"	Q-2	6.20	3.871		2,025	260		2,285	2,625
5321	10"		5.70	4.211		3,200	283		3,483	3,950
5322	12"		5.10	4.706		3,775	315		4,090	4,625
5324	Combination Y & 1/8 bend, reducing									
5325	2" x 2" x 1-1/2"	Q-1	22	.727	Ea.	91	47		138	171
5327	3" x 3" x 1-1/2"		15.50	1.032		162	67		229	278
5328	3" x 3" x 2"		15.30	1.046		122	68		190	235
5329	4" x 4" x 2"		12.20	1.311		183	85		268	330
5331	Wye, 1-1/4"	1 Plum	13.50	.593		73	42.50		115.50	144
5332	1-1/2"	"	12.10	.661		48.50	47.50		96	125
5333	2"	Q-1	20	.800		48	52		100	130
5334	3"		13.90	1.151		129	74.50		203.50	253
5335	4"		11	1.455		235	94.50		329.50	400
5336	6"		6.70	2.388		680	155		835	975
5337	8"	Q-2	6.20	3.871		1,200	260		1,460	1,700
5338	10"		5.70	4.211		1,500	283		1,783	2,075
5339	12"		5.10	4.706		2,450	315		2,765	3,150
5341	2" x 1-1/2"	Q-1	22	.727		16.80	47		63.80	89
5342	3" x 1-1/2"		15.50	1.032		25	67		92	128

22 11 Facility Water Distribution

22 11 13 – Facility Water Distribution Piping

22 11 13.76 Pipe Fittings, Plastic

		Crew	Daily Output	Labor-Hours	Unit	Material	2023 Bare Costs Labor	Equipment	Total	Total Incl O&P
5343	4" x 3"	Q-1	12.10	1.322	Ea.	54.50	86		140.50	188
5344	6" x 4"	↓	6.90	2.319		148	150		298	385
5345	8" x 6"	Q-2	6.40	3.750		260	252		512	660
5347	Double wye, 1-1/2"	1 Plum	9.10	.879		109	63.50		172.50	215
5348	2"	Q-1	16.60	.964		130	62.50		192.50	236
5349	3"	↓	10.40	1.538		254	100		354	430
5350	4"	↓	8.25	1.939	↓	545	126		671	790
5353	Double wye, reducing									
5354	2" x 2" x 1-1/2" x 1-1/2"	Q-1	16.80	.952	Ea.	111	62		173	215
5355	3" x 3" x 2" x 2"		10.60	1.509		189	98		287	355
5356	4" x 4" x 3" x 3"		8.45	1.893		405	123		528	635
5357	6" x 6" x 4" x 4"	↓	7.25	2.207		1,425	143		1,568	1,800
5374	Coupling, 1-1/4"	1 Plum	20.20	.396		34.50	28.50		63	80.50
5376	1-1/2"	"	18.20	.440		7.20	31.50		38.70	55
5378	2"	Q-1	33.10	.483		9.85	31.50		41.35	57.50
5380	3"		20.80	.769		34.50	50		84.50	113
5390	4"		16.50	.970		58.50	63		121.50	158
5400	6"	↓	10.10	1.584		191	103		294	365
5402	8"	Q-2	9.30	2.581		320	174		494	610
5404	2" x 1-1/2"	Q-1	33.30	.480		22	31		53	70.50
5406	3" x 1-1/2"		21	.762		64	49.50		113.50	144
5408	4" x 3"		16.70	.958		104	62		166	208
5410	Reducer bushing, 2" x 1-1/4"		36.50	.438		6.85	28.50		35.35	50
5411	2" x 1-1/2"		36.40	.440		12.45	28.50		40.95	56
5412	3" x 1-1/2"		27.30	.586		17.20	38		55.20	75.50
5413	3" x 2"		27.10	.590		31.50	38.50		70	91.50
5414	4" x 2"		18.20	.879		104	57		161	200
5415	4" x 3"		16.70	.958		54	62		116	152
5416	6" x 4"	↓	11.10	1.441		268	93.50		361.50	435
5418	8" x 6"	Q-2	10.20	2.353		525	158		683	810
5425	Closet flange 4"	Q-1	32	.500		90	32.50		122.50	148
5426	4" x 3"	"	34	.471	↓	96	30.50		126.50	151
5450	Solvent cement for PVC, industrial grade, per quart				Qt.	33			33	36.50
5500	CPVC, Schedule 80, threaded joints									
5540	90° elbow, 1/4"	1 Plum	32	.250	Ea.	24	18		42	53
5560	1/2"		30.30	.264		13.85	19		32.85	44
5570	3/4"		26	.308		20.50	22		42.50	56
5580	1"		22.70	.352		29	25.50		54.50	70
5590	1-1/4"		20.20	.396		56	28.50		84.50	104
5600	1-1/2"	↓	18.20	.440		60	31.50		91.50	114
5610	2"	Q-1	33.10	.483		80.50	31.50		112	136
5620	2-1/2"		24.20	.661		251	43		294	340
5630	3"		20.80	.769		269	50		319	370
5640	4"		16.50	.970		420	63		483	560
5650	6"	↓	10.10	1.584	↓	455	103		558	655
5660	45° elbow same as 90° elbow									
5700	Tee, 1/4"	1 Plum	22	.364	Ea.	46.50	26		72.50	90
5702	1/2"		20.20	.396		46.50	28.50		75	93.50
5704	3/4"		17.30	.462		67	33.50		100.50	123
5706	1"		15.20	.526		72	38		110	136
5708	1-1/4"		13.50	.593		72.50	42.50		115	143
5710	1-1/2"	↓	12.10	.661		76	47.50		123.50	155
5712	2"	Q-1	20	.800		84.50	52		136.50	171

22 11 Facility Water Distribution

22 11 13 – Facility Water Distribution Piping

22 11 13.76 Pipe Fittings, Plastic		Crew	Daily Output	Labor-Hours	Unit	Material	2023 Bare Costs Labor	Equipment	Total	Total Incl O&P
5714	2-1/2"	Q-1	16.20	.988	Ea.	415	64		479	550
5716	3"		13.90	1.151		480	74.50		554.50	640
5718	4"		11	1.455		1,150	94.50		1,244.50	1,400
5720	6"	▼	6.70	2.388		1,200	155		1,355	1,525
5730	Coupling, 1/4"	1 Plum	32	.250		30.50	18		48.50	60.50
5732	1/2"		30.30	.264		25	19		44	56
5734	3/4"		26	.308		40.50	22		62.50	77.50
5736	1"		22.70	.352		46	25.50		71.50	88.50
5738	1-1/4"		20.20	.396		48.50	28.50		77	96
5740	1-1/2"	▼	18.20	.440		52.50	31.50		84	105
5742	2"	Q-1	33.10	.483		61.50	31.50		93	115
5744	2-1/2"		24.20	.661		111	43		154	186
5746	3"		20.80	.769		97.50	50		147.50	183
5748	4"		16.50	.970		199	63		262	315
5750	6"	▼	10.10	1.584		335	103		438	525
5752	8"	Q-2	9.30	2.581	▼	700	174		874	1,025
5900	CPVC, Schedule 80, socket joints									
5904	90° elbow, 1/4"	1 Plum	32	.250	Ea.	22.50	18		40.50	52
5906	1/2"		30.30	.264		8.90	19		27.90	38.50
5908	3/4"		26	.308		11.35	22		33.35	45.50
5910	1"		22.70	.352		18	25.50		43.50	58
5912	1-1/4"		20.20	.396		39	28.50		67.50	85.50
5914	1-1/2"	▼	18.20	.440		43.50	31.50		75	95
5916	2"	Q-1	33.10	.483		52.50	31.50		84	105
5918	2-1/2"		24.20	.661		121	43		164	197
5920	3"		20.80	.769		137	50		187	226
5922	4"		16.50	.970		247	63		310	365
5924	6"		10.10	1.584		495	103		598	700
5926	8"	▼	9.30	1.720		1,225	112		1,337	1,500
5930	45° elbow, 1/4"	1 Plum	32	.250		34	18		52	64
5932	1/2"		30.30	.264		10.90	19		29.90	40.50
5934	3/4"		26	.308		15.70	22		37.70	50.50
5936	1"		22.70	.352		25	25.50		50.50	65.50
5938	1-1/4"		20.20	.396		49	28.50		77.50	96.50
5940	1-1/2"	▼	18.20	.440		50.50	31.50		82	103
5942	2"	Q-1	33.10	.483		56.50	31.50		88	109
5944	2-1/2"		24.20	.661		116	43		159	191
5946	3"		20.80	.769		148	50		198	238
5948	4"		16.50	.970		204	63		267	320
5950	6"		10.10	1.584		630	103		733	845
5952	8"	▼	9.30	1.720		1,300	112		1,412	1,600
5960	Tee, 1/4"	1 Plum	22	.364		21	26		47	62
5962	1/2"		20.20	.396		21	28.50		49.50	65.50
5964	3/4"		17.30	.462		21	33.50		54.50	73
5966	1"		15.20	.526		26	38		64	85
5968	1-1/4"		13.50	.593		55	42.50		97.50	124
5970	1-1/2"	▼	12.10	.661		63	47.50		110.50	140
5972	2"	Q-1	20	.800		70	52		122	155
5974	2-1/2"		16.20	.988		178	64		242	292
5976	3"		13.90	1.151		178	74.50		252.50	305
5978	4"		11	1.455		237	94.50		331.50	400
5980	6"	▼	6.70	2.388		615	155		770	910
5982	8"	Q-2	6.20	3.871		1,775	260		2,035	2,350

22 11 Facility Water Distribution

22 11 13 – Facility Water Distribution Piping

22 11 13.76 Pipe Fittings, Plastic		Crew	Daily Output	Labor-Hours	Unit	Material	2023 Bare Costs Labor	Equipment	Total	Total Incl O&P
5990	Coupling, 1/4"	1 Plum	32	.250	Ea.	24	18		42	53.50
5992	1/2"		30.30	.264		9.40	19		28.40	39
5994	3/4"		26	.308		13.15	22		35.15	47.50
5996	1"		22.70	.352		17.70	25.50		43.20	57.50
5998	1-1/4"		20.20	.396		26.50	28.50		55	71.50
6000	1-1/2"	▼	18.20	.440		33.50	31.50		65	83.50
6002	2"	Q-1	33.10	.483		39	31.50		70.50	89
6004	2-1/2"		24.20	.661		86.50	43		129.50	159
6006	3"		20.80	.769		94	50		144	178
6008	4"		16.50	.970		123	63		186	229
6010	6"	▼	10.10	1.584		289	103		392	475
6012	8"	Q-2	9.30	2.581	▼	780	174		954	1,125
6200	CTS, 100 psi at 180°F, hot and cold water									
6230	90° elbow, 1/2"	1 Plum	20	.400	Ea.	.59	29		29.59	43.50
6250	3/4"		19	.421		.97	30.50		31.47	46
6251	1"		16	.500		2.84	36		38.84	56.50
6252	1-1/4"		15	.533		5.65	38.50		44.15	64
6253	1-1/2"	▼	14	.571		10.20	41		51.20	73
6254	2"	Q-1	23	.696		19.60	45		64.60	89
6260	45° elbow, 1/2"	1 Plum	20	.400		.74	29		29.74	44
6280	3/4"		19	.421		1.30	30.50		31.80	46.50
6281	1"		16	.500		3.28	36		39.28	57
6282	1-1/4"		15	.533		6.95	38.50		45.45	65
6283	1-1/2"	▼	14	.571		10.10	41		51.10	72.50
6284	2"	Q-1	23	.696		21	45		66	91
6290	Tee, 1/2"	1 Plum	13	.615		.76	44.50		45.26	67
6310	3/4"		12	.667		1.42	48		49.42	73
6311	1"		11	.727		7.10	52.50		59.60	86
6312	1-1/4"		10	.800		10.95	57.50		68.45	98
6313	1-1/2"	▼	10	.800		14.20	57.50		71.70	102
6314	2"	Q-1	17	.941		23	61		84	117
6320	Coupling, 1/2"	1 Plum	22	.364		.48	26		26.48	39.50
6340	3/4"		21	.381		.77	27.50		28.27	42
6341	1"		18	.444		2.88	32		34.88	51
6342	1-1/4"		17	.471		3.71	34		37.71	54.50
6343	1-1/2"	▼	16	.500		5.25	36		41.25	59.50
6344	2"	Q-1	28	.571	▼	10	37		47	66.50
6360	Solvent cement for CPVC, commercial grade, per quart				Qt.	50.50			50.50	55.50
7340	PVC flange, slip-on, Sch 80 std., 1/2"	1 Plum	22	.364	Ea.	11.85	26		37.85	52
7350	3/4"		21	.381		12.70	27.50		40.20	55
7360	1"		18	.444		14.20	32		46.20	63.50
7370	1-1/4"		17	.471		14.65	34		48.65	66.50
7380	1-1/2"	▼	16	.500		14.95	36		50.95	70
7390	2"	Q-1	26	.615		19.85	40		59.85	81.50
7400	2-1/2"		24	.667		29	43		72	96
7410	3"		18	.889		32	57.50		89.50	121
7420	4"		15	1.067		40	69		109	148
7430	6"	▼	10	1.600		63.50	104		167.50	225
7440	8"	Q-2	11	2.182		189	147		336	425
7550	Union, schedule 40, socket joints, 1/2"	1 Plum	19	.421		9.75	30.50		40.25	55.50
7560	3/4"		18	.444		11.05	32		43.05	60
7570	1"		15	.533		11.40	38.50		49.90	70
7580	1-1/4"		14	.571		35	41		76	100

22 11 Facility Water Distribution

22 11 13 – Facility Water Distribution Piping

22 11 13.76 Pipe Fittings, Plastic		Crew	Daily Output	Labor-Hours	Unit	Material	2023 Bare Costs Labor	2023 Bare Costs Equipment	Total	Total Incl O&P
7590	1-1/2"	1 Plum	13	.615	Ea.	38.50	44.50		83	108
7600	2"	Q-1	20	.800	▼	51.50	52		103.50	134
7992	Polybutyl/polyethyl pipe, for copper fittings see Line 22 11 13.25 7000									
8000	Compression type, PVC, 160 psi cold water									
8010	Coupling, 3/4" CTS	1 Plum	21	.381	Ea.	4.06	27.50		31.56	45.50
8020	1" CTS		18	.444		5.05	32		37.05	53.50
8030	1-1/4" CTS		17	.471		7.10	34		41.10	58.50
8040	1-1/2" CTS		16	.500		9.75	36		45.75	64
8050	2" CTS		15	.533		13.50	38.50		52	72.50
8060	Female adapter, 3/4" FPT x 3/4" CTS		23	.348		9.60	25		34.60	48
8070	3/4" FPT x 1" CTS		21	.381		12.75	27.50		40.25	55
8080	1" FPT x 1" CTS		20	.400		11.20	29		40.20	55.50
8090	1-1/4" FPT x 1-1/4" CTS		18	.444		11.45	32		43.45	60.50
8100	1-1/2" FPT x 1-1/2" CTS		16	.500		13.05	36		49.05	68
8110	2" FPT x 2" CTS		13	.615		24.50	44.50		69	92.50
8130	Male adapter, 3/4" MPT x 3/4" CTS		23	.348		8	25		33	46.50
8140	3/4" MPT x 1" CTS		21	.381		10.85	27.50		38.35	53
8150	1" MPT x 1" CTS		20	.400		9.55	29		38.55	53.50
8160	1-1/4" MPT x 1-1/4" CTS		18	.444		12.85	32		44.85	62
8170	1-1/2" MPT x 1-1/2" CTS		16	.500		15.45	36		51.45	70.50
8180	2" MPT x 2" CTS		13	.615		20	44.50		64.50	88
8200	Spigot adapter, 3/4" IPS x 3/4" CTS		23	.348		2.73	25		27.73	40.50
8210	3/4" IPS x 1" CTS		21	.381		4.17	27.50		31.67	45.50
8220	1" IPS x 1" CTS		20	.400		3.34	29		32.34	46.50
8230	1-1/4" IPS x 1-1/4" CTS		18	.444		5.05	32		37.05	53.50
8240	1-1/2" IPS x 1-1/2" CTS		16	.500		5.30	36		41.30	59.50
8250	2" IPS x 2" CTS	▼	13	.615	▼	6.55	44.50		51.05	73
8270	Price includes insert stiffeners									
8280	250 psi is same price as 160 psi									
8300	Insert type, nylon, 160 & 250 psi, cold water									
8310	Clamp ring stainless steel, 3/4" IPS	1 Plum	115	.070	Ea.	4.47	5		9.47	12.35
8320	1" IPS		107	.075		5.40	5.40		10.80	14
8330	1-1/4" IPS		101	.079		4.60	5.70		10.30	13.55
8340	1-1/2" IPS		95	.084		6.40	6.05		12.45	16.10
8350	2" IPS		85	.094		8.35	6.80		15.15	19.25
8370	Coupling, 3/4" IPS		22	.364		1.85	26		27.85	41
8380	1" IPS		19	.421		1.94	30.50		32.44	47
8390	1-1/4" IPS		18	.444		2.87	32		34.87	51
8400	1-1/2" IPS		17	.471		3.38	34		37.38	54
8410	2" IPS		16	.500		6.40	36		42.40	60.50
8430	Elbow, 90°, 3/4" IPS		22	.364		3.70	26		29.70	43
8440	1" IPS		19	.421		4.08	30.50		34.58	49.50
8450	1-1/4" IPS		18	.444		4.58	32		36.58	53
8460	1-1/2" IPS		17	.471		5.40	34		39.40	56.50
8470	2" IPS		16	.500		7.50	36		43.50	62
8490	Male adapter, 3/4" IPS x 3/4" MPT		25	.320		1.85	23		24.85	36.50
8500	1" IPS x 1" MPT		21	.381		1.90	27.50		29.40	43
8510	1-1/4" IPS x 1-1/4" MPT		20	.400		3.02	29		32.02	46.50
8520	1-1/2" IPS x 1-1/2" MPT		18	.444		3.38	32		35.38	51.50
8530	2" IPS x 2" MPT		15	.533		6.50	38.50		45	64.50
8550	Tee, 3/4" IPS		14	.571		3.59	41		44.59	65.50
8560	1" IPS		13	.615		4.64	44.50		49.14	71
8570	1-1/4" IPS	▼	12	.667	▼	7.25	48		55.25	79.50

22 11 Facility Water Distribution

22 11 13 – Facility Water Distribution Piping

22 11 13.76 Pipe Fittings, Plastic		Crew	Daily Output	Labor-Hours	Unit	Material	2023 Bare Costs Labor	Equipment	Total	Total Incl O&P
8580	1-1/2" IPS	1 Plum	11	.727	Ea.	8.25	52.50		60.75	87
8590	2" IPS	↓	10	.800	↓	16.30	57.50		73.80	104
8610	Insert type, PVC, 100 psi @ 180°F, hot & cold water									
8620	Coupler, male, 3/8" CTS x 3/8" MPT	1 Plum	29	.276	Ea.	1.21	19.90		21.11	31
8630	3/8" CTS x 1/2" MPT		28	.286		1.21	20.50		21.71	32
8640	1/2" CTS x 1/2" MPT		27	.296		1.23	21.50		22.73	33.50
8650	1/2" CTS x 3/4" MPT		26	.308		4.79	22		26.79	38.50
8660	3/4" CTS x 1/2" MPT		25	.320		4.33	23		27.33	39.50
8670	3/4" CTS x 3/4" MPT		25	.320		1.65	23		24.65	36.50
8700	Coupling, 3/8" CTS x 1/2" CTS		25	.320		6.60	23		29.60	42
8710	1/2" CTS		23	.348		8.75	25		33.75	47
8730	3/4" CTS		22	.364		20	26		46	61
8750	Elbow 90°, 3/8" CTS		25	.320		6.45	23		29.45	41.50
8760	1/2" CTS		23	.348		8.70	25		33.70	47
8770	3/4" CTS		22	.364		11.85	26		37.85	52
8800	Rings, crimp, copper, 3/8" CTS		120	.067		.33	4.80		5.13	7.50
8810	1/2" CTS		117	.068		.34	4.93		5.27	7.70
8820	3/4" CTS		115	.070		.45	5		5.45	7.95
8850	Reducer tee, bronze, 3/8" x 3/8" x 1/2" CTS		17	.471		7.60	34		41.60	59
8860	1/2" x 1/2" x 3/4" CTS		15	.533		16.55	38.50		55.05	75.50
8870	3/4" x 1/2" x 1/2" CTS		14	.571		16.35	41		57.35	79.50
8890	3/4" x 3/4" x 1/2" CTS		14	.571		16.35	41		57.35	79.50
8900	1" x 1/2" x 1/2" CTS		14	.571		27.50	41		68.50	92
8930	Tee, 3/8" CTS		17	.471		4.81	34		38.81	56
8940	1/2" CTS		15	.533		4.45	38.50		42.95	62.50
8950	3/4" CTS	↓	14	.571	↓	5.60	41		46.60	67.50
8960	Copper rings included in fitting price									
9000	Flare type, assembled, acetal, hot & cold water									
9010	Coupling, 1/4" & 3/8" CTS	1 Plum	24	.333	Ea.	5.50	24		29.50	42
9020	1/2" CTS		22	.364		6.30	26		32.30	46
9030	3/4" CTS		21	.381		9.30	27.50		36.80	51.50
9040	1" CTS		18	.444		11.85	32		43.85	61
9050	Elbow 90°, 1/4" CTS		26	.308		6.10	22		28.10	39.50
9060	3/8" CTS		24	.333		6.55	24		30.55	43
9070	1/2" CTS		22	.364		7.75	26		33.75	47.50
9080	3/4" CTS		21	.381		11.85	27.50		39.35	54
9090	1" CTS		18	.444		17.15	32		49.15	67
9110	Tee, 1/4" CTS		16	.500		6.45	36		42.45	60.50
9114	3/8" CTS		15	.533		7.25	38.50		45.75	65.50
9120	1/2" CTS		14	.571		8.65	41		49.65	71
9130	3/4" CTS		13	.615		13.50	44.50		58	81
9140	1" CTS	↓	12	.667	↓	18.10	48		66.10	91.50
9400	Polypropylene, fittings and accessories									
9404	Fittings fusion welded, sizes are ID									
9408	Note: sizes 1/2" thru 4" use socket fusion									
9410	Sizes 6" thru 10" use butt fusion									
9416	Coupling									
9420	3/8"	1 Plum	39	.205	Ea.	1.48	14.80		16.28	23.50
9422	1/2"		37.40	.214		1.61	15.40		17.01	25
9424	3/4"		35.40	.226		1.79	16.30		18.09	26.50
9426	1"		29.70	.269		2.36	19.40		21.76	31.50
9428	1-1/4"		27.60	.290		2.83	21		23.83	34
9430	1-1/2"	↓	24.80	.323		5.95	23		28.95	41

22 11 Facility Water Distribution

22 11 13 – Facility Water Distribution Piping

22 11 13.76 Pipe Fittings, Plastic

		Crew	Daily Output	Labor-Hours	Unit	Material	2023 Bare Costs Labor	2023 Bare Costs Equipment	Total	Total Incl O&P
9432	2"	Q-1	43	.372	Ea.	11.90	24		35.90	49
9434	2-1/2"		35.60	.449		13.30	29		42.30	58
9436	3"		30.90	.518		29	33.50		62.50	82
9438	3-1/2"		27.80	.576		47.50	37.50		85	108
9440	4"		25	.640		62.50	41.50		104	131
9442	Reducing coupling, female to female									
9446	2" to 1-1/2"	Q-1	49	.327	Ea.	23.50	21		44.50	57.50
9448	2-1/2" to 2"		41.20	.388		26	25		51	66
9450	3" to 2-1/2"		33.10	.483		25.50	31.50		57	74.50
9470	Reducing bushing, female to female									
9472	1/2" to 3/8"	1 Plum	38.20	.209	Ea.	1.97	15.10		17.07	24.50
9474	3/4" to 3/8" or 1/2"		36.50	.219		2.47	15.80		18.27	26
9476	1" to 3/4" or 1/2"		33.10	.242		3.30	17.40		20.70	29.50
9478	1-1/4" to 3/4" or 1"		28.70	.279		5.10	20		25.10	35.50
9480	1-1/2" to 1/2" thru 1-1/4"		26.20	.305		8.40	22		30.40	42.50
9482	2" to 1/2" thru 1-1/2"	Q-1	43	.372		16.85	24		40.85	54.50
9484	2-1/2" to 1/2" thru 2"		41.20	.388		18.85	25		43.85	58
9486	3" to 1-1/2" thru 2-1/2"		33.10	.483		30.50	31.50		62	80
9488	3-1/2" to 2" thru 3"		29.20	.548		67	35.50		102.50	127
9490	4" to 2-1/2" thru 3-1/2"		26.20	.611		76	39.50		115.50	143
9491	6" to 4" SDR 7.4		16.50	.970		125	63		188	232
9492	6" to 4" SDR 11		16.50	.970		105	63		168	209
9493	8" to 6" SDR 7.4		10.10	1.584		185	103		288	355
9494	8" to 6" SDR 11		10.10	1.584		118	103		221	283
9495	10" to 8" SDR 7.4		7.80	2.051		253	133		386	475
9496	10" to 8" SDR 11		7.80	2.051		174	133		307	390
9500	90° elbow									
9504	3/8"	1 Plum	39	.205	Ea.	1.98	14.80		16.78	24
9506	1/2"		37.40	.214		2.37	15.40		17.77	25.50
9508	3/4"		35.40	.226		3.05	16.30		19.35	28
9510	1"		29.70	.269		3.19	19.40		22.59	32.50
9512	1-1/4"		27.60	.290		6.80	21		27.80	38.50
9514	1-1/2"		24.80	.323		14.60	23		37.60	50.50
9516	2"	Q-1	43	.372		22.50	24		46.50	60.50
9518	2-1/2"		35.60	.449		50	29		79	98
9520	3"		30.90	.518		82.50	33.50		116	141
9522	3-1/2"		27.80	.576		117	37.50		154.50	185
9524	4"		25	.640		131	41.50		172.50	206
9526	6" SDR 7.4		5.55	2.883		261	187		448	565
9528	6" SDR 11		5.55	2.883		217	187		404	515
9530	8" SDR 7.4	Q-2	8.10	2.963		500	199		699	845
9532	8" SDR 11		8.10	2.963		360	199		559	695
9534	10" SDR 7.4		7.50	3.200		670	215		885	1,050
9536	10" SDR 11		7.50	3.200		485	215		700	855
9551	45° elbow									
9554	3/8"	1 Plum	39	.205	Ea.	1.98	14.80		16.78	24
9556	1/2"		37.40	.214		2.37	15.40		17.77	25.50
9558	3/4"		35.40	.226		3.05	16.30		19.35	28
9564	1"		29.70	.269		4.41	19.40		23.81	34
9566	1-1/4"		27.60	.290		6.80	21		27.80	38.50
9568	1-1/2"		24.80	.323		14.60	23		37.60	50.50
9570	2"	Q-1	43	.372		22	24		46	60.50
9572	2-1/2"		35.60	.449		49	29		78	97.50

For customer support on your Mechanical Costs with RSMeans data, call 800.448.8182.

22 11 Facility Water Distribution

22 11 13 – Facility Water Distribution Piping

22 11 13.76 Pipe Fittings, Plastic

		Crew	Daily Output	Labor-Hours	Unit	Material	2023 Bare Costs Labor	Equipment	Total	Total Incl O&P
9574	3"	Q-1	30.90	.518	Ea.	90.50	33.50		124	150
9576	3-1/2"		27.80	.576		129	37.50		166.50	198
9578	4"		25	.640		199	41.50		240.50	281
9580	6" SDR 7.4		5.55	2.883		223	187		410	525
9582	6" SDR 11		5.55	2.883		212	187		399	515
9584	8" SDR 7.4	Q-2	8.10	2.963		450	199		649	790
9586	8" SDR 11		8.10	2.963		340	199		539	670
9588	10" SDR 7.4		7.50	3.200		725	215		940	1,125
9590	10" SDR 11		7.50	3.200		450	215		665	815
9600	Tee									
9604	3/8"	1 Plum	26	.308	Ea.	2.64	22		24.64	36
9606	1/2"		24.90	.321		3.20	23		26.20	38
9608	3/4"		23.70	.338		4.41	24.50		28.91	41.50
9610	1"		19.90	.402		4.05	29		33.05	47.50
9612	1-1/4"		18.50	.432		8.55	31		39.55	56
9614	1-1/2"		16.60	.482		24.50	34.50		59	79
9616	2"	Q-1	26.80	.597		25.50	38.50		64	85.50
9618	2-1/2"		23.80	.672		42.50	43.50		86	112
9620	3"		20.60	.777		70	50.50		120.50	152
9622	3-1/2"		18.40	.870		151	56.50		207.50	250
9624	4"		16.70	.958		200	62		262	315
9626	6" SDR 7.4		3.70	4.324		276	280		556	725
9628	6" SDR 11		3.70	4.324		221	280		501	665
9630	8" SDR 7.4	Q-2	5.40	4.444		605	299		904	1,100
9632	8" SDR 11		5.40	4.444		450	299		749	940
9634	10" SDR 7.4		5	4.800		1,050	325		1,375	1,625
9636	10" SDR 11		5	4.800		700	325		1,025	1,250
9638	For reducing tee use same tee price									
9660	End cap									
9662	3/8"	1 Plum	78	.103	Ea.	2.81	7.40		10.21	14.10
9664	1/2"		74.60	.107		3.48	7.75		11.23	15.35
9666	3/4"		71.40	.112		4.41	8.05		12.46	16.90
9668	1"		59.50	.134		5.35	9.70		15.05	20.50
9670	1-1/4"		55.60	.144		8.40	10.35		18.75	24.50
9672	1-1/2"		49.50	.162		8.40	11.65		20.05	26.50
9674	2"	Q-1	80	.200		14.05	12.95		27	35
9676	2-1/2"		71.40	.224		28	14.55		42.55	52.50
9678	3"		61.70	.259		63.50	16.80		80.30	95
9680	3-1/2"		55.20	.290		76.50	18.80		95.30	112
9682	4"		50	.320		117	21		138	159
9684	6" SDR 7.4		26.50	.604		160	39		199	235
9686	6" SDR 11		26.50	.604		124	39		163	195
9688	8" SDR 7.4	Q-2	16.30	1.472		160	99		259	325
9690	8" SDR 11		16.30	1.472		134	99		233	295
9692	10" SDR 7.4		14.90	1.611		240	108		348	425
9694	10" SDR 11		14.90	1.611		164	108		272	345
9800	Accessories and tools									
9802	Pipe clamps for suspension, not including rod or beam clamp									
9804	3/8"	1 Plum	74	.108	Ea.	3.63	7.80		11.43	15.60
9805	1/2"		70	.114		4.55	8.25		12.80	17.30
9806	3/4"		68	.118		4.61	8.50		13.11	17.70
9807	1"		66	.121		5.70	8.75		14.45	19.30
9808	1-1/4"		64	.125		5.85	9		14.85	19.90

22 11 Facility Water Distribution

22 11 13 – Facility Water Distribution Piping

22 11 13.76 Pipe Fittings, Plastic

		Crew	Daily Output	Labor-Hours	Unit	Material	2023 Bare Costs Labor	2023 Bare Costs Equipment	Total	Total Incl O&P
9809	1-1/2"	1 Plum	62	.129	Ea.	5.55	9.30		14.85	19.95
9810	2"	Q-1	110	.145		7.95	9.45		17.40	23
9811	2-1/2"		104	.154		10.20	10		20.20	26
9812	3"		98	.163		11.90	10.60		22.50	29
9813	3-1/2"		92	.174		12.05	11.30		23.35	30
9814	4"		86	.186		21.50	12.05		33.55	42
9815	6"		70	.229		16.45	14.80		31.25	40
9816	8"	Q-2	100	.240		59	16.15		75.15	89
9817	10"	"	94	.255		67.50	17.15		84.65	99.50
9820	Pipe cutter									
9822	For 3/8" thru 1-1/4"				Ea.	182			182	200
9824	For 1-1/2" thru 4"				"	174			174	191
9826	Note: Pipes may be cut with standard									
9827	iron saw with blades for plastic.									
9982	For plastic hangers see Line 22 05 29.10 8000									
9986	For copper/brass fittings see Line 22 11 13.25 7000									

22 11 13.78 Pipe, High Density Polyethylene Plastic (HDPE)

		Crew	Daily Output	Labor-Hours	Unit	Material	2023 Bare Costs Labor	2023 Bare Costs Equipment	Total	Total Incl O&P
0010	**PIPE, HIGH DENSITY POLYETHYLENE PLASTIC (HDPE)**									
0020	Not incl. hangers, trenching, backfill, hoisting or digging equipment.									
0030	Standard length is 40', add a weld for each joint									
0035	For HDPE weld machine see 015433401685 in equipment rental									
0040	Single wall									
0050	Straight									
0054	1" diameter DR 11				L.F.	.89			.89	.98
0058	1-1/2" diameter DR 11					1.75			1.75	1.93
0062	2" diameter DR 11					2			2	2.20
0066	3" diameter DR 11					3.66			3.66	4.03
0070	3" diameter DR 17					2.59			2.59	2.85
0074	4" diameter DR 11					5.35			5.35	5.90
0078	4" diameter DR 17					3.62			3.62	3.98
0082	6" diameter DR 11					10.50			10.50	11.55
0086	6" diameter DR 17					7.20			7.20	7.90
0090	8" diameter DR 11					18.40			18.40	20
0094	8" diameter DR 26					6.30			6.30	6.90
0098	10" diameter DR 11					27.50			27.50	30.50
0102	10" diameter DR 26					18.30			18.30	20
0106	12" diameter DR 11					39			39	43
0110	12" diameter DR 26					27.50			27.50	30
0114	16" diameter DR 11					88.50			88.50	97
0118	16" diameter DR 26					39.50			39.50	43.50
0122	18" diameter DR 11					113			113	124
0126	18" diameter DR 26					52			52	57
0130	20" diameter DR 11					137			137	151
0134	20" diameter DR 26					61			61	67
0138	22" diameter DR 11					167			167	184
0142	22" diameter DR 26					76			76	83.50
0146	24" diameter DR 11					198			198	218
0150	24" diameter DR 26					88.50			88.50	97
0154	28" diameter DR 17					183			183	201
0158	28" diameter DR 26					122			122	134
0162	30" diameter DR 21					171			171	188
0166	30" diameter DR 26					140			140	154

22 11 Facility Water Distribution

22 11 13 – Facility Water Distribution Piping

22 11 13.78 Pipe, High Density Polyethylene Plastic (HDPE)	Crew	Daily Output	Labor-Hours	Unit	Material	2023 Bare Costs Labor	Equipment	Total	Total Incl O&P
0170 36" diameter DR 26				L.F.	140			140	154
0174 42" diameter DR 26					271			271	298
0178 48" diameter DR 26					355			355	390
0182 54" diameter DR 26				▼	450			450	490
0300 90° elbow									
0304 1" diameter DR 11				Ea.	8.80			8.80	9.65
0308 1-1/2" diameter DR 11					11.05			11.05	12.15
0312 2" diameter DR 11					9.60			9.60	10.55
0316 3" diameter DR 11					22			22	24.50
0320 3" diameter DR 17					22			22	24.50
0324 4" diameter DR 11					32.50			32.50	36
0328 4" diameter DR 17					31			31	34
0332 6" diameter DR 11					70			70	77
0336 6" diameter DR 17					70			70	77
0340 8" diameter DR 11					170			170	187
0344 8" diameter DR 26					154			154	170
0348 10" diameter DR 11					159			159	175
0352 10" diameter DR 26					600			600	660
0356 12" diameter DR 11					211			211	232
0360 12" diameter DR 26					620			620	685
0364 16" diameter DR 11					815			815	895
0368 16" diameter DR 26					800			800	880
0372 18" diameter DR 11					1,025			1,025	1,125
0376 18" diameter DR 26					965			965	1,050
0380 20" diameter DR 11					1,200			1,200	1,325
0384 20" diameter DR 26					1,175			1,175	1,275
0388 22" diameter DR 11					1,250			1,250	1,375
0392 22" diameter DR 26					1,200			1,200	1,325
0396 24" diameter DR 11					1,400			1,400	1,550
0400 24" diameter DR 26					1,375			1,375	1,500
0404 28" diameter DR 17					1,700			1,700	1,875
0408 28" diameter DR 26					1,600			1,600	1,775
0412 30" diameter DR 17					2,400			2,400	2,650
0416 30" diameter DR 26					2,200			2,200	2,425
0420 36" diameter DR 26					2,800			2,800	3,100
0424 42" diameter DR 26					3,600			3,600	3,975
0428 48" diameter DR 26					4,200			4,200	4,625
0432 54" diameter DR 26				▼	10,000			10,000	11,000
0500 45° elbow									
0512 2" diameter DR 11				Ea.	8.85			8.85	9.70
0516 3" diameter DR 11					22			22	24.50
0520 3" diameter DR 17					22			22	24.50
0524 4" diameter DR 11					31			31	34
0528 4" diameter DR 17					31			31	34
0532 6" diameter DR 11					70.50			70.50	77.50
0536 6" diameter DR 17					70.50			70.50	77.50
0540 8" diameter DR 11					174			174	192
0544 8" diameter DR 26					101			101	112
0548 10" diameter DR 11					650			650	715
0552 10" diameter DR 26					600			600	660
0556 12" diameter DR 11					690			690	755
0560 12" diameter DR 26					620			620	685
0564 16" diameter DR 11				▼	360			360	395

22 11 Facility Water Distribution

22 11 13 – Facility Water Distribution Piping

22 11 13.78 Pipe, High Density Polyethylene Plastic (HDPE)

		Crew	Daily Output	Labor-Hours	Unit	Material	2023 Bare Costs Labor	Equipment	Total	Total Incl O&P
0568	16" diameter DR 26				Ea.	340			340	375
0572	18" diameter DR 11					385			385	420
0576	18" diameter DR 26					350			350	385
0580	20" diameter DR 11					580			580	640
0584	20" diameter DR 26					550			550	605
0588	22" diameter DR 11					800			800	880
0592	22" diameter DR 26					760			760	840
0596	24" diameter DR 11					985			985	1,075
0600	24" diameter DR 26					945			945	1,025
0604	28" diameter DR 17					1,125			1,125	1,225
0608	28" diameter DR 26					1,075			1,075	1,200
0612	30" diameter DR 17					1,375			1,375	1,525
0616	30" diameter DR 26					1,350			1,350	1,475
0620	36" diameter DR 26					1,700			1,700	1,875
0624	42" diameter DR 26					2,200			2,200	2,400
0628	48" diameter DR 26					2,375			2,375	2,625
0632	54" diameter DR 26					3,200			3,200	3,500
0700	Tee									
0704	1" diameter DR 11				Ea.	11.50			11.50	12.65
0708	1-1/2" diameter DR 11					16.15			16.15	17.75
0712	2" diameter DR 11					13.85			13.85	15.20
0716	3" diameter DR 11					25.50			25.50	28
0720	3" diameter DR 17					25.50			25.50	28
0724	4" diameter DR 11					37			37	40.50
0728	4" diameter DR 17					37			37	40.50
0732	6" diameter DR 11					92			92	101
0736	6" diameter DR 17					92			92	101
0740	8" diameter DR 11					228			228	251
0744	8" diameter DR 17					228			228	251
0748	10" diameter DR 11					680			680	750
0752	10" diameter DR 17					680			680	750
0756	12" diameter DR 11					910			910	1,000
0760	12" diameter DR 17					910			910	1,000
0764	16" diameter DR 11					480			480	525
0768	16" diameter DR 17					395			395	435
0772	18" diameter DR 11					675			675	745
0776	18" diameter DR 17					555			555	610
0780	20" diameter DR 11					825			825	910
0784	20" diameter DR 17					675			675	745
0788	22" diameter DR 11					1,050			1,050	1,175
0792	22" diameter DR 17					835			835	920
0796	24" diameter DR 11					1,300			1,300	1,450
0800	24" diameter DR 17					1,100			1,100	1,225
0804	28" diameter DR 17					2,150			2,150	2,350
0812	30" diameter DR 17					2,450			2,450	2,700
0820	36" diameter DR 17					4,050			4,050	4,450
0824	42" diameter DR 26					4,500			4,500	4,975
0828	48" diameter DR 26					4,850			4,850	5,325
1000	Flange adptr, w/back-up ring and 1/2 cost of plated bolt set									
1004	1" diameter DR 11				Ea.	44			44	48
1008	1-1/2" diameter DR 11					44			44	48
1012	2" diameter DR 11					18.85			18.85	20.50
1016	3" diameter DR 11					32.50			32.50	35.50

22 11 Facility Water Distribution

22 11 13 – Facility Water Distribution Piping

22 11 13.78 Pipe, High Density Polyethylene Plastic (HDPE)		Crew	Daily Output	Labor-Hours	Unit	Material	2023 Bare Costs Labor	Equipment	Total	Total Incl O&P
1020	3" diameter DR 17				Ea.	32.50			32.50	35.50
1024	4" diameter DR 11					44			44	48
1028	4" diameter DR 17					44			44	48
1032	6" diameter DR 11					62.50			62.50	68.50
1036	6" diameter DR 17					62.50			62.50	68.50
1040	8" diameter DR 11					90			90	99
1044	8" diameter DR 26					90			90	99
1048	10" diameter DR 11					88.50			88.50	97.50
1052	10" diameter DR 26					143			143	157
1056	12" diameter DR 11					210			210	231
1060	12" diameter DR 26					210			210	231
1064	16" diameter DR 11					450			450	495
1068	16" diameter DR 26					450			450	495
1072	18" diameter DR 11					585			585	640
1076	18" diameter DR 26					585			585	640
1080	20" diameter DR 11					810			810	890
1084	20" diameter DR 26					810			810	890
1088	22" diameter DR 11					880			880	965
1092	22" diameter DR 26					875			875	965
1096	24" diameter DR 17					955			955	1,050
1100	24" diameter DR 32.5					955			955	1,050
1104	28" diameter DR 15.5					1,300			1,300	1,425
1108	28" diameter DR 32.5					1,300			1,300	1,425
1112	30" diameter DR 11					1,500			1,500	1,650
1116	30" diameter DR 21					1,500			1,500	1,650
1120	36" diameter DR 26					1,650			1,650	1,800
1124	42" diameter DR 26					1,875			1,875	2,050
1128	48" diameter DR 26					2,275			2,275	2,500
1132	54" diameter DR 26					2,775			2,775	3,050
1200	Reducer									
1208	2" x 1-1/2" diameter DR 11				Ea.	13.25			13.25	14.60
1212	3" x 2" diameter DR 11					13.25			13.25	14.60
1216	4" x 2" diameter DR 11					15.45			15.45	17
1220	4" x 3" diameter DR 11					19.85			19.85	22
1224	6" x 4" diameter DR 11					46.50			46.50	51
1228	8" x 6" diameter DR 11					70.50			70.50	77.50
1232	10" x 8" diameter DR 11					121			121	133
1236	12" x 8" diameter DR 11					199			199	218
1240	12" x 10" diameter DR 11					159			159	175
1244	14" x 12" diameter DR 11					176			176	194
1248	16" x 14" diameter DR 11					225			225	248
1252	18" x 16" diameter DR 11					274			274	300
1256	20" x 18" diameter DR 11					545			545	595
1260	22" x 20" diameter DR 11					665			665	735
1264	24" x 22" diameter DR 11					750			750	825
1268	26" x 24" diameter DR 11					880			880	970
1272	28" x 24" diameter DR 11					1,125			1,125	1,250
1276	32" x 28" diameter DR 17					1,450			1,450	1,600
1280	36" x 32" diameter DR 17					1,975			1,975	2,175
4000	Welding labor per joint, not including welding machine									
4010	Pipe joint size (cost based on thickest wall for each diam.)									
4030	1" pipe size	4 Skwk	273	.117	Ea.		7.20		7.20	10.80
4040	1-1/2" pipe size		175	.183			11.20		11.20	16.80

22 11 Facility Water Distribution

22 11 13 – Facility Water Distribution Piping

22 11 13.78 Pipe, High Density Polyethylene Plastic (HDPE)

		Crew	Daily Output	Labor-Hours	Unit	Material	2023 Bare Costs Labor	Equipment	Total	Total Incl O&P
4050	2" pipe size	4 Skwk	128	.250	Ea.		15.30		15.30	23
4060	3" pipe size		100	.320			19.60		19.60	29.50
4070	4" pipe size	▼	77	.416			25.50		25.50	38
4080	6" pipe size	5 Skwk	63	.635			39		39	58.50
4090	8" pipe size		48	.833			51		51	76.50
4100	10" pipe size	▼	40	1			61.50		61.50	92
4110	12" pipe size	6 Skwk	41	1.171			71.50		71.50	108
4120	16" pipe size		34	1.412			86.50		86.50	130
4130	18" pipe size	▼	32	1.500			92		92	138
4140	20" pipe size	8 Skwk	37	1.730			106		106	159
4150	22" pipe size		35	1.829			112		112	168
4160	24" pipe size		34	1.882			115		115	173
4170	28" pipe size		33	1.939			119		119	178
4180	30" pipe size		32	2			123		123	184
4190	36" pipe size		31	2.065			126		126	190
4200	42" pipe size	▼	30	2.133			131		131	196
4210	48" pipe size	9 Skwk	33	2.182			134		134	201
4220	54" pipe size	"	31	2.323	▼		142		142	214
5000	Dual wall contained pipe									
5040	Straight									
5054	1" DR 11 x 3" DR 11				L.F.	8.35			8.35	9.15
5058	1" DR 11 x 4" DR 11					8.80			8.80	9.65
5062	1-1/2" DR 11 x 4" DR 17					9.70			9.70	10.65
5066	2" DR 11 x 4" DR 17					10.20			10.20	11.25
5070	2" DR 11 x 6" DR 17					15.45			15.45	17
5074	3" DR 11 x 6" DR 17					17.35			17.35	19.10
5078	3" DR 11 x 6" DR 26					14.80			14.80	16.30
5086	3" DR 17 x 8" DR 17					18.85			18.85	20.50
5090	4" DR 11 x 8" DR 17					26			26	29
5094	4" DR 17 x 8" DR 26					20.50			20.50	22.50
5098	6" DR 11 x 10" DR 17					40.50			40.50	44.50
5102	6" DR 17 x 10" DR 26					27.50			27.50	30.50
5106	6" DR 26 x 10" DR 26					26			26	28.50
5110	8" DR 17 x 12" DR 26					40			40	44
5114	8" DR 26 x 12" DR 32.5					36.50			36.50	40
5118	10" DR 17 x 14" DR 26					59.50			59.50	65.50
5122	10" DR 17 x 16" DR 26					42.50			42.50	47
5126	10" DR 26 x 16" DR 26					56.50			56.50	62.50
5130	12" DR 26 x 16" DR 26					59.50			59.50	65.50
5134	12" DR 17 x 18" DR 26					83			83	91
5138	12" DR 26 x 18" DR 26					78.50			78.50	86.50
5142	14" DR 26 x 20" DR 32.5					80			80	88
5146	16" DR 26 x 22" DR 32.5					88.50			88.50	97.50
5150	18" DR 26 x 24" DR 32.5					110			110	121
5154	20" DR 32.5 x 28" DR 32.5					125			125	137
5158	22" DR 32.5 x 30" DR 32.5					125			125	137
5162	24" DR 32.5 x 32" DR 32.5					130			130	143
5166	36" DR 32.5 x 42" DR 32.5				▼	151			151	166
5300	Force transfer coupling									
5354	1" DR 11 x 3" DR 11				Ea.	288			288	315
5358	1" DR 11 x 4" DR 17					340			340	375
5362	1-1/2" DR 11 x 4" DR 17					325			325	355
5366	2" DR 11 x 4" DR 17				▼	325			325	355

22 11 Facility Water Distribution

22 11 13 – Facility Water Distribution Piping

22 11 13.78	Pipe, High Density Polyethylene Plastic (HDPE)	Crew	Daily Output	Labor-Hours	Unit	Material	2023 Bare Costs Labor	Equipment	Total	Total Incl O&P
5370	2" DR 11 x 6" DR 17				Ea.	555			555	610
5374	3" DR 11 x 6" DR 17					595			595	655
5378	3" DR 11 x 6" DR 26					595			595	655
5382	3" DR 11 x 8" DR 11					595			595	655
5386	3" DR 11 x 8" DR 17					650			650	715
5390	4" DR 11 x 8" DR 17					665			665	730
5394	4" DR 17 x 8" DR 26					670			670	740
5398	6" DR 11 x 10" DR 17					795			795	875
5402	6" DR 17 x 10" DR 26					760			760	835
5406	6" DR 26 x 10" DR 26					1,025			1,025	1,150
5410	8" DR 17 x 12" DR 26					1,100			1,100	1,225
5414	8" DR 26 x 12" DR 32.5					1,275			1,275	1,400
5418	10" DR 17 x 14" DR 26					1,500			1,500	1,650
5422	10" DR 17 x 16" DR 26					1,525			1,525	1,675
5426	10" DR 26 x 16" DR 26					1,700			1,700	1,850
5430	12" DR 26 x 16" DR 26					2,050			2,050	2,250
5434	12" DR 17 x 18" DR 26					2,075			2,075	2,275
5438	12" DR 26 x 18" DR 26					2,275			2,275	2,500
5442	14" DR 26 x 20" DR 32.5					2,525			2,525	2,775
5446	16" DR 26 x 22" DR 32.5					2,775			2,775	3,050
5450	18" DR 26 x 24" DR 32.5					3,075			3,075	3,375
5454	20" DR 32.5 x 28" DR 32.5					3,375			3,375	3,700
5458	22" DR 32.5 x 30" DR 32.5					3,725			3,725	4,100
5462	24" DR 32.5 x 32" DR 32.5					4,100			4,100	4,525
5466	36" DR 32.5 x 42" DR 32.5					4,400			4,400	4,850
5600	90° elbow									
5654	1" DR 11 x 3" DR 11				Ea.	315			315	345
5658	1" DR 11 x 4" DR 17					375			375	410
5662	1-1/2" DR 11 x 4" DR 17					385			385	420
5666	2" DR 11 x 4" DR 17					375			375	410
5670	2" DR 11 x 6" DR 17					540			540	595
5674	3" DR 11 x 6" DR 17					585			585	645
5678	3" DR 17 x 6" DR 26					595			595	655
5682	3" DR 17 x 8" DR 11					800			800	880
5686	3" DR 17 x 8" DR 17					850			850	935
5690	4" DR 11 x 8" DR 17					720			720	795
5694	4" DR 17 x 8" DR 26					695			695	765
5698	6" DR 11 x 10" DR 17					1,250			1,250	1,375
5702	6" DR 17 x 10" DR 26					1,275			1,275	1,400
5706	6" DR 26 x 10" DR 26					1,250			1,250	1,375
5710	8" DR 17 x 12" DR 26					1,675			1,675	1,825
5714	8" DR 26 x 12" DR 32.5					1,375			1,375	1,525
5718	10" DR 17 x 14" DR 26					1,650			1,650	1,800
5722	10" DR 17 x 16" DR 26					1,600			1,600	1,750
5726	10" DR 26 x 16" DR 26					1,575			1,575	1,750
5730	12" DR 26 x 16" DR 26					1,625			1,625	1,800
5734	12" DR 17 x 18" DR 26					1,775			1,775	1,950
5738	12" DR 26 x 18" DR 26					1,800			1,800	1,975
5742	14" DR 26 x 20" DR 32.5					1,925			1,925	2,125
5746	16" DR 26 x 22" DR 32.5					2,025			2,025	2,225
5750	18" DR 26 x 24" DR 32.5					2,100			2,100	2,300
5754	20" DR 32.5 x 28" DR 32.5					2,175			2,175	2,375
5758	22" DR 32.5 x 30" DR 32.5					2,250			2,250	2,475

22 11 Facility Water Distribution

22 11 13 – Facility Water Distribution Piping

22 11 13.78 Pipe, High Density Polyethylene Plastic (HDPE)

		Crew	Daily Output	Labor-Hours	Unit	Material	2023 Bare Costs Labor	Equipment	Total	Total Incl O&P
5762	24" DR 32.5 x 32" DR 32.5				Ea.	2,325			2,325	2,550
5766	36" DR 32.5 x 42" DR 32.5				↓	2,400			2,400	2,650
5800	45° elbow									
5804	1" DR 11 x 3" DR 11				Ea.	365			365	405
5808	1" DR 11 x 4" DR 17					300			300	330
5812	1-1/2" DR 11 x 4" DR 17					305			305	335
5816	2" DR 11 x 4" DR 17					291			291	320
5820	2" DR 11 x 6" DR 17					415			415	460
5824	3" DR 11 x 6" DR 17					450			450	490
5828	3" DR 17 x 6" DR 26					450			450	495
5832	3" DR 17 x 8" DR 11					575			575	630
5836	3" DR 17 x 8" DR 17					645			645	710
5840	4" DR 11 x 8" DR 17					530			530	585
5844	4" DR 17 x 8" DR 26					540			540	590
5848	6" DR 11 x 10" DR 17					840			840	925
5852	6" DR 17 x 10" DR 26					850			850	935
5856	6" DR 26 x 10" DR 26					955			955	1,050
5860	8" DR 17 x 12" DR 26					1,125			1,125	1,250
5864	8" DR 26 x 12" DR 32.5					1,075			1,075	1,175
5868	10" DR 17 x 14" DR 26					1,200			1,200	1,325
5872	10" DR 17 x 16" DR 26					1,150			1,150	1,275
5876	10" DR 26 x 16" DR 26					1,225			1,225	1,350
5880	12" DR 26 x 16" DR 26					1,100			1,100	1,225
5884	12" DR 17 x 18" DR 26					1,575			1,575	1,725
5888	12" DR 26 x 18" DR 26					1,400			1,400	1,525
5892	14" DR 26 x 20" DR 32.5					1,525			1,525	1,675
5896	16" DR 26 x 22" DR 32.5					1,575			1,575	1,725
5900	18" DR 26 x 24" DR 32.5					1,675			1,675	1,825
5904	20" DR 32.5 x 28" DR 32.5					1,650			1,650	1,825
5908	22" DR 32.5 x 30" DR 32.5					1,725			1,725	1,900
5912	24" DR 32.5 x 32" DR 32.5					1,775			1,775	1,950
5916	36" DR 32.5 x 42" DR 32.5				↓	1,850			1,850	2,025
6000	Access port with 4" riser									
6050	1" DR 11 x 4" DR 17				Ea.	435			435	480
6054	1-1/2" DR 11 x 4" DR 17					440			440	485
6058	2" DR 11 x 6" DR 17					535			535	590
6062	3" DR 11 x 6" DR 17					545			545	595
6066	3" DR 17 x 6" DR 26					525			525	580
6070	3" DR 17 x 8" DR 11					545			545	595
6074	3" DR 17 x 8" DR 17					565			565	620
6078	4" DR 11 x 8" DR 17					580			580	640
6082	4" DR 17 x 8" DR 26					555			555	610
6086	6" DR 11 x 10" DR 17					680			680	745
6090	6" DR 17 x 10" DR 26					620			620	680
6094	6" DR 26 x 10" DR 26					650			650	715
6098	8" DR 17 x 12" DR 26					695			695	765
6102	8" DR 26 x 12" DR 32.5				↓	685			685	750
6200	End termination with vent plug									
6204	1" DR 11 x 3" DR 11				Ea.	148			148	163
6208	1" DR 11 x 4" DR 17					216			216	238
6212	1-1/2" DR 11 x 4" DR 17					216			216	238
6216	2" DR 11 x 4" DR 17					216			216	238
6220	2" DR 11 x 6" DR 17				↓	440			440	480

22 11 Facility Water Distribution

22 11 13 – Facility Water Distribution Piping

22 11 13.78 Pipe, High Density Polyethylene Plastic (HDPE)	Crew	Daily Output	Labor-Hours	Unit	Material	2023 Bare Costs Labor	Equipment	Total	Total Incl O&P
6224	3" DR 11 x 6" DR 17				Ea.	440			440	480
6228	3" DR 17 x 6" DR 26					440			440	480
6232	3" DR 17 x 8" DR 11					425			425	465
6236	3" DR 17 x 8" DR 17					475			475	520
6240	4" DR 11 x 8" DR 17					565			565	620
6244	4" DR 17 x 8" DR 26					530			530	585
6248	6" DR 11 x 10" DR 17					615			615	675
6252	6" DR 17 x 10" DR 26					570			570	625
6256	6" DR 26 x 10" DR 26					830			830	910
6260	8" DR 17 x 12" DR 26					870			870	955
6264	8" DR 26 x 12" DR 32.5					1,050			1,050	1,150
6268	10" DR 17 x 14" DR 26					1,375			1,375	1,525
6272	10" DR 17 x 16" DR 26					1,300			1,300	1,425
6276	10" DR 26 x 16" DR 26					1,475			1,475	1,625
6280	12" DR 26 x 16" DR 26					1,625			1,625	1,775
6284	12" DR 17 x 18" DR 26					1,900			1,900	2,075
6288	12" DR 26 x 18" DR 26					2,075			2,075	2,275
6292	14" DR 26 x 20" DR 32.5					2,325			2,325	2,550
6296	16" DR 26 x 22" DR 32.5					2,600			2,600	2,850
6300	18" DR 26 x 24" DR 32.5					2,925			2,925	3,200
6304	20" DR 32.5 x 28" DR 32.5					3,250			3,250	3,575
6308	22" DR 32.5 x 30" DR 32.5					3,625			3,625	4,000
6312	24" DR 32.5 x 32" DR 32.5					4,075			4,075	4,475
6316	36" DR 32.5 x 42" DR 32.5					4,500			4,500	4,950
6600	Tee									
6604	1" DR 11 x 3" DR 11				Ea.	365			365	405
6608	1" DR 11 x 4" DR 17					400			400	440
6612	1-1/2" DR 11 x 4" DR 17					410			410	455
6616	2" DR 11 x 4" DR 17					375			375	410
6620	2" DR 11 x 6" DR 17					600			600	660
6624	3" DR 11 x 6" DR 17					705			705	775
6628	3" DR 17 x 6" DR 26					670			670	735
6632	3" DR 17 x 8" DR 11					820			820	905
6636	3" DR 17 x 8" DR 17					890			890	980
6640	4" DR 11 x 8" DR 17					1,075			1,075	1,175
6644	4" DR 17 x 8" DR 26					1,075			1,075	1,175
6648	6" DR 11 x 10" DR 17					1,400			1,400	1,525
6652	6" DR 17 x 10" DR 26					1,400			1,400	1,550
6656	6" DR 26 x 10" DR 26					1,725			1,725	1,900
6660	8" DR 17 x 12" DR 26					1,725			1,725	1,900
6664	8" DR 26 x 12" DR 32.5					2,225			2,225	2,450
6668	10" DR 17 x 14" DR 26					2,575			2,575	2,850
6672	10" DR 17 x 16" DR 26					2,875			2,875	3,150
6676	10" DR 26 x 16" DR 26					2,875			2,875	3,150
6680	12" DR 26 x 16" DR 26					3,250			3,250	3,600
6684	12" DR 17 x 18" DR 26					3,250			3,250	3,600
6688	12" DR 26 x 18" DR 26					3,700			3,700	4,075
6692	14" DR 26 x 20" DR 32.5					4,175			4,175	4,600
6696	16" DR 26 x 22" DR 32.5					4,725			4,725	5,200
6700	18" DR 26 x 24" DR 32.5					5,375			5,375	5,925
6704	20" DR 32.5 x 28" DR 32.5					6,075			6,075	6,675
6708	22" DR 32.5 x 30" DR 32.5					6,875			6,875	7,550
6712	24" DR 32.5 x 32" DR 32.5					7,775			7,775	8,550

22 11 Facility Water Distribution

22 11 13 – Facility Water Distribution Piping

22 11 13.78 Pipe, High Density Polyethylene Plastic (HDPE)

		Crew	Daily Output	Labor-Hours	Unit	Material	2023 Bare Costs Labor	Equipment	Total	Total Incl O&P
6716	36" DR 32.5 x 42" DR 32.5				Ea.	8,925			8,925	9,825
6800	Wye									
6816	2" DR 11 x 4" DR 17				Ea.	910			910	1,000
6820	2" DR 11 x 6" DR 17					1,125			1,125	1,250
6824	3" DR 11 x 6" DR 17					1,200			1,200	1,300
6828	3" DR 17 x 6" DR 26					320			320	355
6832	3" DR 17 x 8" DR 11					1,275			1,275	1,400
6836	3" DR 17 x 8" DR 17					1,375			1,375	1,525
6840	4" DR 11 x 8" DR 17					1,525			1,525	1,675
6844	4" DR 17 x 8" DR 26					955			955	1,050
6848	6" DR 11 x 10" DR 17					595			595	655
6852	6" DR 17 x 10" DR 26					1,450			1,450	1,600
6856	6" DR 26 x 10" DR 26					2,025			2,025	2,225
6860	8" DR 17 x 12" DR 26					2,825			2,825	3,125
6864	8" DR 26 x 12" DR 32.5					2,350			2,350	2,575
6868	10" DR 17 x 14" DR 26					2,500			2,500	2,750
6872	10" DR 17 x 16" DR 26					2,700			2,700	2,975
6876	10" DR 26 x 16" DR 26					2,925			2,925	3,225
6880	12" DR 26 x 16" DR 26					3,150			3,150	3,475
6884	12" DR 17 x 18" DR 26					3,400			3,400	3,725
6888	12" DR 26 x 18" DR 26					3,675			3,675	4,025
6892	14" DR 26 x 20" DR 32.5					3,925			3,925	4,325
6896	16" DR 26 x 22" DR 32.5					4,150			4,150	4,550
6900	18" DR 26 x 24" DR 32.5					4,750			4,750	5,225
6904	20" DR 32.5 x 28" DR 32.5					4,975			4,975	5,450
6908	22" DR 32.5 x 30" DR 32.5					5,350			5,350	5,900
6912	24" DR 32.5 x 32" DR 32.5					5,775			5,775	6,350
9000	Welding labor per joint, not including welding machine									
9010	Pipe joint size, outer pipe (cost based on the thickest walls)									
9020	Straight pipe									
9050	3" pipe size	4 Skwk	96	.333	Ea.		20.50		20.50	30.50
9060	4" pipe size	"	77	.416			25.50		25.50	38
9070	6" pipe size	5 Skwk	60	.667			41		41	61.50
9080	8" pipe size	"	40	1			61.50		61.50	92
9090	10" pipe size	6 Skwk	41	1.171			71.50		71.50	108
9100	12" pipe size		39	1.231			75.50		75.50	113
9110	14" pipe size		38	1.263			77.50		77.50	116
9120	16" pipe size		35	1.371			84		84	126
9130	18" pipe size	8 Skwk	45	1.422			87		87	131
9140	20" pipe size		42	1.524			93.50		93.50	140
9150	22" pipe size		40	1.600			98		98	147
9160	24" pipe size		38	1.684			103		103	155
9170	28" pipe size		37	1.730			106		106	159
9180	30" pipe size		36	1.778			109		109	164
9190	32" pipe size		35	1.829			112		112	168
9200	42" pipe size		32	2			123		123	184

22 11 19 – Domestic Water Piping Specialties

22 11 19.10 Flexible Connectors

		Crew	Daily Output	Labor-Hours	Unit	Material	2023 Bare Costs Labor	Equipment	Total	Total Incl O&P
0010	**FLEXIBLE CONNECTORS**, Corrugated, 5/8" OD, 3/4" ID									
0050	Gas, seamless brass, steel fittings									
0200	12" long	1 Plum	36	.222	Ea.	26	16		42	52.50
0220	18" long		36	.222		32	16		48	59.50

22 11 Facility Water Distribution

22 11 19 – Domestic Water Piping Specialties

22 11 19.10 Flexible Connectors

		Crew	Daily Output	Labor-Hours	Unit	Material	2023 Bare Costs Labor	2023 Bare Costs Equipment	Total	Total Incl O&P
0240	24" long	1 Plum	34	.235	Ea.	38	16.95		54.95	67.50
0260	30" long		34	.235		41	16.95		57.95	70.50
0280	36" long		32	.250		45.50	18		63.50	77
0320	48" long		30	.267		57.50	19.20		76.70	92
0340	60" long		30	.267		68.50	19.20		87.70	104
0360	72" long		30	.267		79.50	19.20		98.70	116
2000	Water, copper tubing, dielectric separators									
2100	12" long	1 Plum	36	.222	Ea.	12.85	16		28.85	38
2220	15" long		36	.222		14.30	16		30.30	39.50
2240	18" long		36	.222		13.15	16		29.15	38.50
2260	24" long		34	.235		19.10	16.95		36.05	46.50

22 11 19.14 Flexible Metal Hose

		Crew	Daily Output	Labor-Hours	Unit	Material	Labor	Equipment	Total	Total Incl O&P
0010	**FLEXIBLE METAL HOSE**, Connectors, standard lengths									
0100	Bronze braided, bronze ends									
0120	3/8" diameter x 12"	1 Stpi	26	.308	Ea.	31.50	22.50		54	68
0140	1/2" diameter x 12"		24	.333		38	24		62	78
0160	3/4" diameter x 12"		20	.400		61	29		90	111
0180	1" diameter x 18"		19	.421		77.50	30.50		108	131
0200	1-1/2" diameter x 18"		13	.615		117	44.50		161.50	196
0220	2" diameter x 18"		11	.727		150	53		203	244
1000	Carbon steel ends									
1020	1/4" diameter x 12"	1 Stpi	28	.286	Ea.	59.50	20.50		80	96.50
1040	3/8" diameter x 12"		26	.308		39.50	22.50		62	77
1060	1/2" diameter x 12"		24	.333		53.50	24		77.50	95
1080	1/2" diameter x 24"		24	.333		74.50	24		98.50	118
1120	3/4" diameter x 12"		20	.400		73	29		102	124
1140	3/4" diameter x 24"		20	.400		87.50	29		116.50	140
1160	3/4" diameter x 36"		20	.400		99	29		128	153
1180	1" diameter x 18"		19	.421		88	30.50		118.50	143
1200	1" diameter x 30"		19	.421		101	30.50		131.50	157
1220	1" diameter x 36"		19	.421		116	30.50		146.50	174
1240	1-1/4" diameter x 18"		15	.533		310	38.50		348.50	400
1260	1-1/4" diameter x 36"		15	.533		138	38.50		176.50	210
1280	1-1/2" diameter x 18"		13	.615		157	44.50		201.50	240
1300	1-1/2" diameter x 36"		13	.615		157	44.50		201.50	240
1320	2" diameter x 24"		11	.727		177	53		230	273
1340	2" diameter x 36"		11	.727		196	53		249	294
1360	2-1/2" diameter x 24"		9	.889		340	64.50		404.50	470
1380	2-1/2" diameter x 36"		9	.889		199	64.50		263.50	315
1400	3" diameter x 24"		7	1.143		705	83		788	900
1420	3" diameter x 36"		7	1.143		1,600	83		1,683	1,900
2000	Carbon steel braid, carbon steel solid ends									
2100	1/2" diameter x 12"	1 Stpi	24	.333	Ea.	64.50	24		88.50	107
2120	3/4" diameter x 12"		20	.400		72	29		101	123
2140	1" diameter x 12"		19	.421		117	30.50		147.50	174
2160	1-1/4" diameter x 12"		15	.533		91.50	38.50		130	158
2180	1-1/2" diameter x 12"		13	.615		101	44.50		145.50	178
3000	Stainless steel braid, welded on carbon steel ends									
3100	1/2" diameter x 12"	1 Stpi	24	.333	Ea.	82	24		106	127
3120	3/4" diameter x 12"		20	.400		96	29		125	150
3140	3/4" diameter x 24"		20	.400		107	29		136	162
3160	3/4" diameter x 36"		20	.400		120	29		149	176

22 11 Facility Water Distribution

22 11 19 – Domestic Water Piping Specialties

22 11 19.14 Flexible Metal Hose

		Crew	Daily Output	Labor-Hours	Unit	Material	2023 Bare Costs Labor	2023 Bare Costs Equipment	Total	Total Incl O&P
3180	1" diameter x 12"	1 Stpi	19	.421	Ea.	144	30.50		174.50	204
3200	1" diameter x 24"		19	.421		147	30.50		177.50	207
3220	1" diameter x 36"		19	.421		145	30.50		175.50	206
3240	1-1/4" diameter x 12"		15	.533		163	38.50		201.50	237
3260	1-1/4" diameter x 24"		15	.533		174	38.50		212.50	249
3280	1-1/4" diameter x 36"		15	.533		196	38.50		234.50	273
3300	1-1/2" diameter x 12"		13	.615		105	44.50		149.50	183
3320	1-1/2" diameter x 24"		13	.615		204	44.50		248.50	292
3340	1-1/2" diameter x 36"		13	.615		120	44.50		164.50	199
3400	Metal stainless steel braid, over corrugated stainless steel, flanged ends									
3410	150 psi									
3420	1/2" diameter x 12"	1 Stpi	24	.333	Ea.	100	24		124	146
3430	1" diameter x 12"		20	.400		154	29		183	213
3440	1-1/2" diameter x 12"		15	.533		100	38.50		138.50	168
3450	2-1/2" diameter x 9"		12	.667		168	48.50		216.50	257
3460	3" diameter x 9"		9	.889		168	64.50		232.50	281
3470	4" diameter x 9"		7	1.143		219	83		302	365
3480	4" diameter x 30"		5	1.600		450	116		566	670
3490	4" diameter x 36"		4.80	1.667		450	121		571	675
3500	6" diameter x 11"		5	1.600		390	116		506	605
3510	6" diameter x 36"		3.80	2.105		695	153		848	990
3520	8" diameter x 12"		4	2		605	145		750	880
3530	10" diameter x 13"		3	2.667		815	193		1,008	1,200
3540	12" diameter x 14"	Q-5	4	4		1,375	261		1,636	1,900
6000	Molded rubber with helical wire reinforcement									
6010	150 psi									
6020	1-1/2" diameter x 12"	1 Stpi	15	.533	Ea.	48	38.50		86.50	111
6030	2" diameter x 12"		12	.667		156	48.50		204.50	244
6040	3" diameter x 12"		8	1		163	72.50		235.50	287
6050	4" diameter x 12"		6	1.333		207	96.50		303.50	370
6060	6" diameter x 18"		4	2		310	145		455	555
6070	8" diameter x 24"		3	2.667		435	193		628	765
6080	10" diameter x 24"		2	4		525	290		815	1,025
6090	12" diameter x 24"	Q-5	3	5.333		600	350		950	1,175
7000	Molded teflon with stainless steel flanges									
7010	150 psi									
7020	2-1/2" diameter x 3-3/16"	Q-1	7.80	2.051	Ea.	920	133		1,053	1,225
7030	3" diameter x 3-5/8"		6.50	2.462		860	160		1,020	1,175
7040	4" diameter x 3-5/8"		5	3.200		1,100	208		1,308	1,500
7050	6" diameter x 4"		4.30	3.721		1,525	241		1,766	2,025
7060	8" diameter x 6"		3.80	4.211		2,425	273		2,698	3,050

22 11 19.18 Mixing Valve

		Crew	Daily Output	Labor-Hours	Unit	Material	2023 Bare Costs Labor	2023 Bare Costs Equipment	Total	Total Incl O&P
0010	**MIXING VALVE**, Automatic, water tempering.									
0040	1/2" size	1 Stpi	19	.421	Ea.	625	30.50		655.50	730
0050	3/4" size		18	.444		535	32		567	635
0100	1" size		16	.500		995	36.50		1,031.50	1,150
0120	1-1/4" size		13	.615		1,350	44.50		1,394.50	1,550
0140	1-1/2" size		10	.800		1,325	58		1,383	1,550
0160	2" size		8	1		1,725	72.50		1,797.50	1,975
0170	2-1/2" size		6	1.333		1,725	96.50		1,821.50	2,025
0180	3" size		4	2		3,925	145		4,070	4,550
0190	4" size		3	2.667		3,925	193		4,118	4,625

22 11 Facility Water Distribution

22 11 19 – Domestic Water Piping Specialties

22 11 19.22 Pressure Reducing Valve

		Crew	Daily Output	Labor-Hours	Unit	Material	2023 Bare Costs Labor	2023 Bare Costs Equipment	Total	Total Incl O&P
0010	**PRESSURE REDUCING VALVE**, Steam, pilot operated.									
0100	Threaded, iron body									
0200	1-1/2" size	1 Stpi	8	1	Ea.	2,650	72.50		2,722.50	3,000
0220	2" size	"	5	1.600	"	3,800	116		3,916	4,375
1000	Flanged, iron body, 125 lb. flanges									
1020	2" size	1 Stpi	8	1	Ea.	5,175	72.50		5,247.50	5,800
1040	2-1/2" size	"	4	2		4,050	145		4,195	4,675
1060	3" size	Q-5	4.50	3.556		4,525	232		4,757	5,325
1080	4" size	"	3	5.333		5,425	350		5,775	6,500
1500	For 250 lb. flanges, add					5%				

22 11 19.26 Pressure Regulators

		Crew	Daily Output	Labor-Hours	Unit	Material	2023 Bare Costs Labor	2023 Bare Costs Equipment	Total	Total Incl O&P
0010	**PRESSURE REGULATORS**									
0100	Gas appliance regulators									
0106	Main burner and pilot applications									
0108	Rubber seat poppet type									
0109	1/8" pipe size	1 Stpi	24	.333	Ea.	29.50	24		53.50	68.50
0110	1/4" pipe size		24	.333		29.50	24		53.50	68.50
0112	3/8" pipe size		24	.333		25	24		49	63
0113	1/2" pipe size		24	.333		30	24		54	69
0114	3/4" pipe size		20	.400		30	29		59	76.50
0122	Lever action type									
0123	3/8" pipe size	1 Stpi	24	.333	Ea.	46	24		70	86.50
0124	1/2" pipe size		24	.333		24	24		48	62
0125	3/4" pipe size		20	.400		60	29		89	110
0126	1" pipe size		19	.421		60.50	30.50		91	113
0132	Double diaphragm type									
0133	3/8" pipe size	1 Stpi	24	.333	Ea.	71.50	24		95.50	115
0134	1/2" pipe size		24	.333		89.50	24		113.50	135
0135	3/4" pipe size		20	.400		148	29		177	207
0136	1" pipe size		19	.421		141	30.50		171.50	201
0137	1-1/4" pipe size		15	.533		445	38.50		483.50	550
0138	1-1/2" pipe size		13	.615		1,100	44.50		1,144.50	1,275
0139	2" pipe size		11	.727		790	53		843	950
0140	2-1/2" pipe size	Q-5	15	1.067		2,125	69.50		2,194.50	2,425
0141	3" pipe size		13	1.231		1,650	80.50		1,730.50	1,950
0142	4" pipe size (flanged)		8	2		3,200	131		3,331	3,700
0160	Main burner only									
0162	Straight-thru-flow design									
0163	1/2" pipe size	1 Stpi	24	.333	Ea.	63	24		87	106
0164	3/4" pipe size		20	.400		63	29		92	113
0165	1" pipe size		19	.421		114	30.50		144.50	171
0166	1-1/4" pipe size		15	.533		98	38.50		136.50	166
0200	Oil, light, hot water, ordinary steam, threaded									
0220	Bronze body, 1/4" size	1 Stpi	24	.333	Ea.	345	24		369	415
0230	3/8" size		24	.333		355	24		379	425
0240	1/2" size		24	.333		460	24		484	540
0250	3/4" size		20	.400		510	29		539	605
0260	1" size		19	.421		900	30.50		930.50	1,025
0270	1-1/4" size		15	.533		1,025	38.50		1,063.50	1,175
0280	1-1/2" size		13	.615		1,125	44.50		1,169.50	1,325
0290	2" size		11	.727		1,800	53		1,853	2,050
0320	Iron body, 1/4" size		24	.333		201	24		225	257

22 11 Facility Water Distribution

22 11 19 – Domestic Water Piping Specialties

22 11 19.26 Pressure Regulators		Crew	Daily Output	Labor-Hours	Unit	Material	2023 Bare Costs Labor	Equipment	Total	Total Incl O&P
0330	3/8" size	1 Stpi	24	.333	Ea.	370	24		394	440
0340	1/2" size		24	.333		390	24		414	460
0350	3/4" size		20	.400		470	29		499	565
0360	1" size		19	.421		610	30.50		640.50	715
0370	1-1/4" size		15	.533		530	38.50		568.50	645
0380	1-1/2" size		13	.615		590	44.50		634.50	715
0390	2" size		11	.727		855	53		908	1,025
0500	Oil, heavy, viscous fluids, threaded									
0520	Bronze body, 3/8" size	1 Stpi	24	.333	Ea.	425	24		449	505
0530	1/2" size		24	.333		570	24		594	665
0540	3/4" size		20	.400		610	29		639	715
0550	1" size		19	.421		795	30.50		825.50	920
0560	1-1/4" size		15	.533		1,075	38.50		1,113.50	1,225
0570	1-1/2" size		13	.615		1,225	44.50		1,269.50	1,425
0600	Iron body, 3/8" size		24	.333		340	24		364	410
0620	1/2" size		24	.333		410	24		434	490
0630	3/4" size		20	.400		465	29		494	560
0640	1" size		19	.421		575	30.50		605.50	675
0650	1-1/4" size		15	.533		795	38.50		833.50	935
0660	1-1/2" size		13	.615		890	44.50		934.50	1,050
0800	Process steam, wet or super heated, monel trim, threaded									
0820	Bronze body, 1/4" size	1 Stpi	24	.333	Ea.	975	24		999	1,100
0830	3/8" size		24	.333		975	24		999	1,100
0840	1/2" size		24	.333		1,125	24		1,149	1,250
0850	3/4" size		20	.400		1,325	29		1,354	1,500
0860	1" size		19	.421		1,700	30.50		1,730.50	1,925
0870	1-1/4" size		15	.533		2,125	38.50		2,163.50	2,375
0880	1-1/2" size		13	.615		2,550	44.50		2,594.50	2,875
0920	Iron body, max 125 PSIG press out, 1/4" size		24	.333		1,375	24		1,399	1,525
0930	3/8" size		24	.333		1,400	24		1,424	1,550
0940	1/2" size		24	.333		1,750	24		1,774	1,950
0950	3/4" size		20	.400		2,125	29		2,154	2,375
0960	1" size		19	.421		2,700	30.50		2,730.50	3,000
0970	1-1/4" size		15	.533		3,225	38.50		3,263.50	3,600
0980	1-1/2" size		13	.615		3,875	44.50		3,919.50	4,350
3000	Steam, high capacity, bronze body, stainless steel trim									
3020	Threaded, 1/2" diameter	1 Stpi	24	.333	Ea.	9,600	24		9,624	10,600
3030	3/4" diameter		24	.333		10,600	24		10,624	11,700
3040	1" diameter		19	.421		2,250	30.50		2,280.50	2,525
3060	1-1/4" diameter		15	.533		1,900	38.50		1,938.50	2,150
3080	1-1/2" diameter		13	.615		6,950	44.50		6,994.50	7,725
3100	2" diameter		11	.727		8,500	53		8,553	9,425
3120	2-1/2" diameter	Q-5	12	1.333		10,600	87		10,687	11,700
3140	3" diameter	"	11	1.455		12,000	95		12,095	13,200
3500	Flanged connection, iron body, 125 lb. W.S.P.									
3520	3" diameter	Q-5	11	1.455	Ea.	13,300	95		13,395	14,700
3540	4" diameter	"	5	3.200	"	16,800	209		17,009	18,700
9002	For water pressure regulators, see Section 22 05 23.20									

22 11 Facility Water Distribution

22 11 19 – Domestic Water Piping Specialties

22 11 19.30 Pressure and Temperature Safety Plug

		Crew	Daily Output	Labor-Hours	Unit	Material	2023 Bare Costs Labor	2023 Bare Costs Equipment	Total	Total Incl O&P
0010	**PRESSURE & TEMPERATURE SAFETY PLUG**									
1000	3/4" external thread, 3/8" diam. element									
1020	Carbon steel									
1050	7-1/2" insertion	1 Stpi	32	.250	Ea.	78	18.15		96.15	113
1120	304 stainless steel									
1150	7-1/2" insertion	1 Stpi	32	.250	Ea.	61.50	18.15		79.65	94.50
1220	316 stainless steel									
1250	7-1/2" insertion	1 Stpi	32	.250	Ea.	110	18.15		128.15	148

22 11 19.32 Pressure and Temperature Measurement Plug

		Crew	Daily Output	Labor-Hours	Unit	Material	2023 Bare Costs Labor	2023 Bare Costs Equipment	Total	Total Incl O&P
0010	**PRESSURE & TEMPERATURE MEASUREMENT PLUG**									
0020	A permanent access port for insertion of									
0030	a pressure or temperature measuring probe									
0100	Plug, brass									
0110	1/4" MNPT, 1-1/2" long	1 Stpi	32	.250	Ea.	24.50	18.15		42.65	54
0120	3" long		31	.258		19.65	18.70		38.35	49.50
0140	1/2" MNPT, 1-1/2" long		30	.267		17.45	19.35		36.80	48
0150	3" long		29	.276		24	20		44	56
0200	Pressure gauge probe adapter									
0210	1/8" diameter, 1-1/2" probe				Ea.	25.50			25.50	28
0220	3" probe				"	32.50			32.50	36
0300	Temperature gauge, 5" stem									
0310	Analog				Ea.	17.55			17.55	19.30
0330	Digital				"	48			48	52.50
0400	Pressure gauge, compound									
0410	1/4" MNPT				Ea.	31.50			31.50	34.50
0500	Pressure and temperature test kit									
0510	Contains 2 thermometers and 2 pressure gauges									
0520	Kit				Ea.	570			570	630

22 11 19.34 Sleeves and Escutcheons

		Crew	Daily Output	Labor-Hours	Unit	Material	2023 Bare Costs Labor	2023 Bare Costs Equipment	Total	Total Incl O&P
0010	**SLEEVES & ESCUTCHEONS**									
0100	Pipe sleeve									
0110	Steel, w/water stop, 12" long, with link seal									
0120	2" diam. for 1/2" carrier pipe	1 Plum	8.40	.952	Ea.	116	68.50		184.50	229
0130	2-1/2" diam. for 3/4" carrier pipe		8	1		130	72		202	250
0140	2-1/2" diam. for 1" carrier pipe		8	1		123	72		195	243
0150	3" diam. for 1-1/4" carrier pipe		7.20	1.111		157	80		237	292
0160	3-1/2" diam. for 1-1/2" carrier pipe		6.80	1.176		185	85		270	330
0170	4" diam. for 2" carrier pipe		6	1.333		176	96		272	335
0180	4" diam. for 2-1/2" carrier pipe		6	1.333		174	96		270	335
0190	5" diam. for 3" carrier pipe		5.40	1.481		201	107		308	380
0200	6" diam. for 4" carrier pipe		4.80	1.667		220	120		340	420
0210	10" diam. for 6" carrier pipe	Q-1	8	2		435	130		565	675
0220	12" diam. for 8" carrier pipe		7.20	2.222		605	144		749	880
0230	14" diam. for 10" carrier pipe		6.40	2.500		615	162		777	920
0240	16" diam. for 12" carrier pipe		5.80	2.759		685	179		864	1,025
0250	18" diam. for 14" carrier pipe		5.20	3.077		1,200	200		1,400	1,625
0260	24" diam. for 18" carrier pipe		4	4		1,800	259		2,059	2,350
0270	24" diam. for 20" carrier pipe		4	4		1,575	259		1,834	2,100
0280	30" diam. for 24" carrier pipe		3.20	5		2,050	325		2,375	2,725
0500	Wall sleeve									
0510	Ductile iron with rubber gasket seal									
0520	3"	1 Plum	8.40	.952	Ea.	330	68.50		398.50	460

22 11 Facility Water Distribution

22 11 19 – Domestic Water Piping Specialties

22 11 19.34 Sleeves and Escutcheons		Crew	Daily Output	Labor-Hours	Unit	Material	2023 Bare Costs Labor	Equipment	Total	Total Incl O&P
0530	4"	1 Plum	7.20	1.111	Ea.	350	80		430	505
0540	6"		6	1.333		425	96		521	615
0550	8"		4	2		1,900	144		2,044	2,300
0560	10"		3	2.667		2,300	192		2,492	2,800
0570	12"		2.40	3.333		2,725	240		2,965	3,325
5000	Escutcheon									
5100	Split ring, pipe									
5110	Chrome plated									
5120	1/2"	1 Plum	160	.050	Ea.	1.35	3.60		4.95	6.85
5130	3/4"		160	.050		1.48	3.60		5.08	7
5140	1"		135	.059		1.58	4.27		5.85	8.10
5150	1-1/2"		115	.070		2.23	5		7.23	9.90
5160	2"		100	.080		2.48	5.75		8.23	11.35
5170	4"		80	.100		8.10	7.20		15.30	19.65
5180	6"		68	.118		12.70	8.50		21.20	26.50
5400	Shallow flange type									
5410	Chrome plated steel									
5420	1/2" CTS	1 Plum	180	.044	Ea.	.53	3.20		3.73	5.35
5430	3/4" CTS		180	.044		.57	3.20		3.77	5.40
5440	1/2" IPS		180	.044		.53	3.20		3.73	5.35
5450	3/4" IPS		180	.044		.65	3.20		3.85	5.50
5460	1" IPS		175	.046		.76	3.29		4.05	5.75
5470	1-1/2" IPS		170	.047		1.24	3.39		4.63	6.40
5480	2" IPS		160	.050		1.51	3.60		5.11	7

22 11 19.38 Water Supply Meters		Crew	Daily Output	Labor-Hours	Unit	Material	Labor	Equipment	Total	Total Incl O&P
0010	**WATER SUPPLY METERS**									
1000	Detector, serves dual systems such as fire and domestic or									
1020	process water, wide range cap., UL and FM approved									
1100	3" mainline x 2" by-pass, 400 GPM	Q-1	3.60	4.444	Ea.	13,100	288		13,388	14,800
1140	4" mainline x 2" by-pass, 700 GPM	"	2.50	6.400		13,100	415		13,515	15,000
1180	6" mainline x 3" by-pass, 1,600 GPM	Q-2	2.60	9.231		20,000	620		20,620	22,900
1220	8" mainline x 4" by-pass, 2,800 GPM		2.10	11.429		29,600	770		30,370	33,800
1260	10" mainline x 6" by-pass, 4,400 GPM		2	12		42,400	805		43,205	47,800
1300	10" x 12" mainlines x 6" by-pass, 5,400 GPM		1.70	14.118		57,500	950		58,450	64,500
2000	Domestic/commercial, bronze									
2020	Threaded									
2060	5/8" diameter, to 20 GPM	1 Plum	16	.500	Ea.	185	36		221	258
2080	3/4" diameter, to 30 GPM		14	.571		465	41		506	570
2100	1" diameter, to 50 GPM		12	.667		625	48		673	760
2300	Threaded/flanged									
2340	1-1/2" diameter, to 100 GPM	1 Plum	8	1	Ea.	1,425	72		1,497	1,675
2360	2" diameter, to 160 GPM	"	6	1.333	"	2,075	96		2,171	2,425
2600	Flanged, compound									
2640	3" diameter, 320 GPM	Q-1	3	5.333	Ea.	2,200	345		2,545	2,950
2660	4" diameter, to 500 GPM		1.50	10.667		3,275	690		3,965	4,625
2680	6" diameter, to 1,000 GPM		1	16		8,225	1,050		9,275	10,600
2700	8" diameter, to 1,800 GPM		.80	20		9,575	1,300		10,875	12,400
7000	Turbine									
7260	Flanged									
7300	2" diameter, to 160 GPM	1 Plum	7	1.143	Ea.	1,000	82.50		1,082.50	1,225
7320	3" diameter, to 450 GPM	Q-1	3.60	4.444		1,700	288		1,988	2,300
7340	4" diameter, to 650 GPM	"	2.50	6.400		2,850	415		3,265	3,750

22 11 Facility Water Distribution

22 11 19 – Domestic Water Piping Specialties

22 11 19.38 Water Supply Meters

		Crew	Daily Output	Labor-Hours	Unit	Material	2023 Bare Costs Labor	Equipment	Total	Total Incl O&P
7360	6" diameter, to 1,800 GPM	Q-2	2.60	9.231	Ea.	4,675	620		5,295	6,075
7380	8" diameter, to 2,500 GPM		2.10	11.429		8,025	770		8,795	9,975
7400	10" diameter, to 5,500 GPM		1.70	14.118		10,800	950		11,750	13,300

22 11 19.42 Backflow Preventers

		Crew	Daily Output	Labor-Hours	Unit	Material	Labor	Equipment	Total	Total Incl O&P
0010	**BACKFLOW PREVENTERS**, Includes valves									
0020	and four test cocks, corrosion resistant, automatic operation									
1000	Double check principle									
1010	Threaded, with ball valves									
1020	3/4" pipe size	1 Plum	16	.500	Ea.	254	36		290	335
1030	1" pipe size		14	.571		435	41		476	535
1040	1-1/2" pipe size		10	.800		820	57.50		877.50	985
1050	2" pipe size		7	1.143		1,225	82.50		1,307.50	1,475
1080	Threaded, with gate valves									
1100	3/4" pipe size	1 Plum	16	.500	Ea.	1,975	36		2,011	2,225
1120	1" pipe size		14	.571		2,000	41		2,041	2,250
1140	1-1/2" pipe size		10	.800		1,775	57.50		1,832.50	2,025
1160	2" pipe size		7	1.143		3,175	82.50		3,257.50	3,600
1200	Flanged, valves are gate									
1210	3" pipe size	Q-1	4.50	3.556	Ea.	2,175	231		2,406	2,725
1220	4" pipe size	"	3	5.333		2,675	345		3,020	3,475
1230	6" pipe size	Q-2	3	8		4,150	540		4,690	5,350
1240	8" pipe size		2	12		7,375	805		8,180	9,300
1250	10" pipe size		1	24		10,400	1,625		12,025	13,800
1300	Flanged, valves are OS&Y									
1370	1" pipe size	1 Plum	5	1.600	Ea.	2,175	115		2,290	2,550
1374	1-1/2" pipe size		5	1.600		1,975	115		2,090	2,325
1378	2" pipe size		4.80	1.667		3,375	120		3,495	3,875
1380	3" pipe size	Q-1	4.50	3.556		3,625	231		3,856	4,325
1400	4" pipe size	"	3	5.333		3,750	345		4,095	4,625
1420	6" pipe size	Q-2	3	8		5,675	540		6,215	7,050
1430	8" pipe size	"	2	12		17,100	805		17,905	20,000
4000	Reduced pressure principle									
4100	Threaded, bronze, valves are ball									
4120	3/4" pipe size	1 Plum	16	.500	Ea.	245	36		281	325
4140	1" pipe size		14	.571		395	41		436	495
4150	1-1/4" pipe size		12	.667		1,825	48		1,873	2,075
4160	1-1/2" pipe size		10	.800		1,500	57.50		1,557.50	1,725
4180	2" pipe size		7	1.143		620	82.50		702.50	810
5000	Flanged, bronze, valves are OS&Y									
5060	2-1/2" pipe size	Q-1	5	3.200	Ea.	5,050	208		5,258	5,850
5080	3" pipe size		4.50	3.556		5,175	231		5,406	6,050
5100	4" pipe size		3	5.333		6,700	345		7,045	7,900
5120	6" pipe size	Q-2	3	8		10,200	540		10,740	12,000
5200	Flanged, iron, valves are gate									
5210	2-1/2" pipe size	Q-1	5	3.200	Ea.	4,050	208		4,258	4,750
5220	3" pipe size		4.50	3.556		4,150	231		4,381	4,925
5230	4" pipe size		3	5.333		5,375	345		5,720	6,450
5240	6" pipe size	Q-2	3	8		7,950	540		8,490	9,550
5250	8" pipe size		2	12		11,800	805		12,605	14,200
5260	10" pipe size		1	24		16,200	1,625		17,825	20,300
5600	Flanged, iron, valves are OS&Y									
5660	2-1/2" pipe size	Q-1	5	3.200	Ea.	5,050	208		5,258	5,850

22 11 Facility Water Distribution

22 11 19 – Domestic Water Piping Specialties

22 11 19.42 Backflow Preventers

		Crew	Daily Output	Labor-Hours	Unit	Material	2023 Bare Costs Labor	2023 Bare Costs Equipment	Total	Total Incl O&P
5680	3" pipe size	Q-1	4.50	3.556	Ea.	5,175	231		5,406	6,050
5700	4" pipe size	↓	3	5.333		6,700	345		7,045	7,900
5720	6" pipe size	Q-2	3	8		10,200	540		10,740	12,000
5740	8" pipe size		2	12		18,000	805		18,805	21,000
5760	10" pipe size	↓	1	24	↓	19,600	1,625		21,225	23,900

22 11 19.50 Vacuum Breakers

		Crew	Daily Output	Labor-Hours	Unit	Material	Labor	Equipment	Total	Total Incl O&P
0010	**VACUUM BREAKERS**									
0013	See also backflow preventers Section 22 11 19.42									
1000	Anti-siphon continuous pressure type									
1010	Max. 150 psi - 210°F									
1020	Bronze body									
1030	1/2" size	1 Stpi	24	.333	Ea.	345	24		369	410
1040	3/4" size		20	.400		345	29		374	420
1050	1" size		19	.421		350	30.50		380.50	430
1060	1-1/4" size		15	.533		700	38.50		738.50	830
1070	1-1/2" size		13	.615		845	44.50		889.50	990
1080	2" size	↓	11	.727	↓	550	53		603	685
1200	Max. 125 psi with atmospheric vent									
1210	Brass, in-line construction									
1220	1/4" size	1 Stpi	24	.333	Ea.	234	24		258	293
1230	3/8" size	"	24	.333		234	24		258	293
1260	For polished chrome finish, add				↓	13%				
2000	Anti-siphon, non-continuous pressure type									
2010	Hot or cold water 125 psi - 210°F									
2020	Bronze body									
2030	1/4" size	1 Stpi	24	.333	Ea.	143	24		167	193
2040	3/8" size		24	.333		143	24		167	193
2050	1/2" size		24	.333		160	24		184	212
2060	3/4" size		20	.400		192	29		221	255
2070	1" size		19	.421		296	30.50		326.50	370
2080	1-1/4" size		15	.533		520	38.50		558.50	630
2090	1-1/2" size		13	.615		575	44.50		619.50	695
2100	2" size		11	.727		945	53		998	1,125
2110	2-1/2" size		8	1		2,725	72.50		2,797.50	3,100
2120	3" size	↓	6	1.333	↓	3,600	96.50		3,696.50	4,125
2150	For polished chrome finish, add					50%				
3000	Air gap fitting									
3020	1/2" NPT size	1 Plum	19	.421	Ea.	104	30.50		134.50	160
3030	1" NPT size	"	15	.533		104	38.50		142.50	173
3040	2" NPT size	Q-1	21	.762		132	49.50		181.50	219
3050	3" NPT size		14	1.143		425	74		499	580
3060	4" NPT size	↓	10	1.600	↓	279	104		383	460

22 11 19.54 Water Hammer Arresters/Shock Absorbers

		Crew	Daily Output	Labor-Hours	Unit	Material	Labor	Equipment	Total	Total Incl O&P
0010	**WATER HAMMER ARRESTERS/SHOCK ABSORBERS**									
0490	Copper									
0500	3/4" male IPS for 1 to 11 fixtures	1 Plum	12	.667	Ea.	44.50	48		92.50	121
0600	1" male IPS for 12 to 32 fixtures		8	1		74.50	72		146.50	189
0700	1-1/4" male IPS for 33 to 60 fixtures		8	1		72.50	72		144.50	187
0800	1-1/2" male IPS for 61 to 113 fixtures		8	1		105	72		177	223
0900	2" male IPS for 114 to 154 fixtures		8	1		155	72		227	278
1000	2-1/2" male IPS for 155 to 330 fixtures	↓	4	2		445	144		589	705
4000	Bellows type									

22 11 Facility Water Distribution

22 11 19 – Domestic Water Piping Specialties

22 11 19.54 Water Hammer Arresters/Shock Absorbers

		Crew	Daily Output	Labor-Hours	Unit	Material	2023 Bare Costs Labor	Equipment	Total	Total Incl O&P
4010	3/4" FNPT, to 11 fixture units	1 Plum	10	.800	Ea.	495	57.50		552.50	630
4020	1" FNPT, to 32 fixture units		8.80	.909		1,000	65.50		1,065.50	1,200
4030	1" FNPT, to 60 fixture units		8.80	.909		1,500	65.50		1,565.50	1,750
4040	1" FNPT, to 113 fixture units		8.80	.909		3,775	65.50		3,840.50	4,250
4050	1" FNPT, to 154 fixture units		6.60	1.212		4,250	87.50		4,337.50	4,800
4060	1-1/2" FNPT, to 300 fixture units		5	1.600		5,225	115		5,340	5,925

22 11 19.64 Hydrants

		Crew	Daily Output	Labor-Hours	Unit	Material	Labor	Equipment	Total	Total Incl O&P
0010	**HYDRANTS**									
0050	Wall type, moderate climate, bronze, encased									
0200	3/4" IPS connection	1 Plum	16	.500	Ea.	1,725	36		1,761	1,950
0300	1" IPS connection		14	.571		3,625	41		3,666	4,025
0500	Anti-siphon type, 3/4" connection		16	.500		1,350	36		1,386	1,525
1000	Non-freeze, bronze, exposed									
1100	3/4" IPS connection, 4" to 9" thick wall	1 Plum	14	.571	Ea.	820	41		861	965
1120	10" to 14" thick wall		12	.667		720	48		768	860
1140	15" to 19" thick wall		12	.667		915	48		963	1,075
1160	20" to 24" thick wall		10	.800		1,250	57.50		1,307.50	1,450
1200	For 1" IPS connection, add					15%	10%			
1240	For 3/4" adapter type vacuum breaker, add				Ea.	145			145	160
1280	For anti-siphon type, add				"	310			310	340
2000	Non-freeze bronze, encased, anti-siphon type									
2100	3/4" IPS connection, 5" to 9" thick wall	1 Plum	14	.571	Ea.	2,050	41		2,091	2,325
2120	10" to 14" thick wall		12	.667		2,675	48		2,723	3,025
2140	15" to 19" thick wall		12	.667		2,850	48		2,898	3,225
2160	20" to 24" thick wall		10	.800		2,950	57.50		3,007.50	3,325
2200	For 1" IPS connection, add					10%	10%			
3000	Ground box type, bronze frame, 3/4" IPS connection									
3080	Non-freeze, all bronze, polished face, set flush									
3100	2' depth of bury	1 Plum	8	1	Ea.	1,875	72		1,947	2,175
3120	3' depth of bury		8	1		1,150	72		1,222	1,350
3140	4' depth of bury		8	1		1,275	72		1,347	1,500
3160	5' depth of bury		7	1.143		1,375	82.50		1,457.50	1,625
3180	6' depth of bury		7	1.143		1,450	82.50		1,532.50	1,725
3200	7' depth of bury		6	1.333		2,775	96		2,871	3,200
3220	8' depth of bury		5	1.600		1,625	115		1,740	1,950
3240	9' depth of bury		4	2		3,100	144		3,244	3,625
3260	10' depth of bury		4	2		1,800	144		1,944	2,200
3400	For 1" IPS connection, add					15%	10%			
3450	For 1-1/4" IPS connection, add					325%	14%			
3500	For 1-1/2" IPS connection, add					370%	18%			
3550	For 2" IPS connection, add					445%	24%			
3600	For tapped drain port in box, add					177			177	194
4000	Non-freeze, CI body, bronze frame & scoriated cover									
4010	with hose storage									
4100	2' depth of bury	1 Plum	7	1.143	Ea.	3,625	82.50		3,707.50	4,125
4120	3' depth of bury		7	1.143		3,800	82.50		3,882.50	4,300
4140	4' depth of bury		7	1.143		3,900	82.50		3,982.50	4,425
4160	5' depth of bury		6.50	1.231		2,725	88.50		2,813.50	3,125
4180	6' depth of bury		6	1.333		2,425	96		2,521	2,825
4200	7' depth of bury		5.50	1.455		4,200	105		4,305	4,775
4220	8' depth of bury		5	1.600		4,300	115		4,415	4,925
4240	9' depth of bury		4.50	1.778		4,025	128		4,153	4,625

22 11 Facility Water Distribution

22 11 19 – Domestic Water Piping Specialties

22 11 19.64 Hydrants

		Crew	Daily Output	Labor-Hours	Unit	Material	2023 Bare Costs Labor	Equipment	Total	Total Incl O&P
4260	10' depth of bury	1 Plum	4	2	Ea.	4,625	144		4,769	5,325
4280	For 1" IPS connection, add					885			885	970
4300	For tapped drain port in box, add				↓	177			177	194
5000	Moderate climate, all bronze, polished face									
5020	and scoriated cover, set flush									
5100	3/4" IPS connection	1 Plum	16	.500	Ea.	1,375	36		1,411	1,550
5120	1" IPS connection	"	14	.571		3,125	41		3,166	3,475
5200	For tapped drain port in box, add				↓	196			196	216
6000	Ground post type, all non-freeze, all bronze, aluminum casing									
6010	guard, exposed head, 3/4" IPS connection									
6100	2' depth of bury	1 Plum	8	1	Ea.	1,850	72		1,922	2,150
6120	3' depth of bury		8	1		1,250	72		1,322	1,475
6140	4' depth of bury		8	1		2,175	72		2,247	2,475
6160	5' depth of bury		7	1.143		1,450	82.50		1,532.50	1,700
6180	6' depth of bury		7	1.143		2,475	82.50		2,557.50	2,850
6200	7' depth of bury		6	1.333		1,650	96		1,746	1,950
6220	8' depth of bury		5	1.600		1,750	115		1,865	2,100
6240	9' depth of bury		4	2		3,100	144		3,244	3,625
6260	10' depth of bury	↓	4	2	↓	3,275	144		3,419	3,825
6300	For 1" IPS connection, add					40%	10%			
6350	For 1-1/4" IPS connection, add					140%	14%			
6400	For 1-1/2" IPS connection, add					225%	18%			
6450	For 2" IPS connection, add					315%	24%			

22 11 23 – Domestic Water Pumps

22 11 23.10 General Utility Pumps

		Crew	Daily Output	Labor-Hours	Unit	Material	Labor	Equipment	Total	Total Incl O&P
0010	**GENERAL UTILITY PUMPS**									
2000	Single stage									
3000	Double suction,									
3140	50 HP, 5" D x 6" S	Q-2	.33	72.727	Ea.	11,300	4,900		16,200	19,700
3180	60 HP, 6" D x 8" S	Q-3	.30	107		27,300	7,325		34,625	40,900
3190	75 HP, to 2,500 GPM		.28	114		33,100	7,850		40,950	48,200
3220	100 HP, to 3,000 GPM		.26	123		42,600	8,450		51,050	59,500
3240	150 HP, to 4,000 GPM	↓	.24	133	↓	44,500	9,150		53,650	62,500
4000	Centrifugal, end suction, mounted on base									
4010	Horizontal mounted, with drip proof motor, rated @ 100' head									
4020	Vertical split case, single stage									
4040	100 GPM, 5 HP, 1-1/2" discharge	Q-1	1.70	9.412	Ea.	7,250	610		7,860	8,875
4050	200 GPM, 10 HP, 2" discharge		1.30	12.308		7,925	800		8,725	9,925
4060	250 GPM, 10 HP, 3" discharge	↓	1.28	12.500		8,700	810		9,510	10,800
4070	300 GPM, 15 HP, 2" discharge	Q-2	1.56	15.385		9,800	1,025		10,825	12,400
4080	500 GPM, 20 HP, 4" discharge		1.44	16.667		12,300	1,125		13,425	15,200
4090	750 GPM, 30 HP, 4" discharge		1.20	20		13,000	1,350		14,350	16,300
4100	1,050 GPM, 40 HP, 5" discharge		1	24		11,300	1,625		12,925	14,800
4110	1,500 GPM, 60 HP, 6" discharge		.60	40		27,300	2,700		30,000	34,000
4120	2,000 GPM, 75 HP, 6" discharge		.50	48		19,500	3,225		22,725	26,200
4130	3,000 GPM, 100 HP, 8" discharge	↓	.40	60	↓	37,100	4,025		41,125	46,900
4200	Horizontal split case, single stage									
4210	100 GPM, 7.5 HP, 1-1/2" discharge	Q-1	1.70	9.412	Ea.	8,325	610		8,935	10,100
4220	250 GPM, 15 HP, 2-1/2" discharge	"	1.30	12.308		9,750	800		10,550	11,900
4230	500 GPM, 20 HP, 4" discharge	Q-2	1.60	15		12,000	1,000		13,000	14,700
4240	750 GPM, 25 HP, 5" discharge		1.54	15.584		14,500	1,050		15,550	17,600
4250	1,000 GPM, 40 HP, 5" discharge		1.20	20		14,500	1,350		15,850	18,000

22 11 Facility Water Distribution

22 11 23 – Domestic Water Pumps

22 11 23.10 General Utility Pumps		Crew	Daily Output	Labor-Hours	Unit	Material	2023 Bare Costs Labor	Equipment	Total	Total Incl O&P
4260	1,500 GPM, 50 HP, 6" discharge	Q-3	1.42	22.535	Ea.	19,600	1,550		21,150	23,900
4270	2,000 GPM, 75 HP, 8" discharge		1.14	28.070		25,500	1,925		27,425	31,000
4280	3,000 GPM, 100 HP, 10" discharge		.96	33.333		35,800	2,275		38,075	42,800
4290	3,500 GPM, 150 HP, 10" discharge		.86	37.209		44,500	2,550		47,050	53,000
4300	4,000 GPM, 200 HP, 10" discharge		.66	48.485		38,400	3,325		41,725	47,200
4330	Horizontal split case, two stage, 500' head									
4340	100 GPM, 40 HP, 1-1/2" discharge	Q-2	1.70	14.118	Ea.	29,400	950		30,350	33,700
4350	200 GPM, 50 HP, 1-1/2" discharge	"	1.44	16.667		31,600	1,125		32,725	36,500
4360	300 GPM, 75 HP, 2" discharge	Q-3	1.57	20.382		42,200	1,400		43,600	48,600
4370	400 GPM, 100 HP, 3" discharge		1.14	28.070		48,900	1,925		50,825	57,000
4380	800 GPM, 200 HP, 4" discharge		.86	37.209		68,000	2,550		70,550	78,500
5000	Centrifugal, in-line									
5006	Vertical mount, iron body, 125 lb. flgd, 1,800 RPM TEFC mtr									
5010	Single stage									
5012	.5 HP, 1-1/2" suction & discharge	Q-1	3.20	5	Ea.	2,425	325		2,750	3,150
5014	.75 HP, 2" suction & discharge		2.80	5.714		4,800	370		5,170	5,825
5015	1 HP, 3" suction & discharge		2.50	6.400		2,675	415		3,090	3,575
5016	1.5 HP, 3" suction & discharge		2.30	6.957		5,450	450		5,900	6,675
5018	2 HP, 4" suction & discharge		2.10	7.619		7,325	495		7,820	8,775
5020	3 HP, 5" suction & discharge		1.90	8.421		5,375	545		5,920	6,750
5030	5 HP, 6" suction & discharge		1.60	10		5,875	650		6,525	7,425
5040	7.5 HP, 6" suction & discharge		1.30	12.308		6,800	800		7,600	8,700
5050	10 HP, 8" suction & discharge	Q-2	1.80	13.333		8,000	895		8,895	10,100
5060	15 HP, 8" suction & discharge		1.70	14.118		9,425	950		10,375	11,800
5064	20 HP, 8" suction & discharge		1.60	15		11,300	1,000		12,300	13,900
5070	30 HP, 8" suction & discharge		1.50	16		22,500	1,075		23,575	26,300
5080	40 HP, 8" suction & discharge		1.40	17.143		27,000	1,150		28,150	31,400
5090	50 HP, 8" suction & discharge		1.30	18.462		27,500	1,250		28,750	32,100
5094	60 HP, 8" suction & discharge		.90	26.667		33,000	1,800		34,800	39,000
5100	75 HP, 8" suction & discharge	Q-3	.60	53.333		33,000	3,650		36,650	41,800
5110	100 HP, 8" suction & discharge	"	.50	64		23,400	4,400		27,800	32,300

22 11 23.11 Miscellaneous Pumps

		Crew	Daily Output	Labor-Hours	Unit	Material	Labor	Equipment	Total	Total Incl O&P
0010	**MISCELLANEOUS PUMPS**									
0020	Water pump, portable, gasoline powered									
0100	170 GPH, 2" discharge	Q-1	11	1.455	Ea.	1,225	94.50		1,319.50	1,500
0110	343 GPH, 3" discharge		10.50	1.524		1,125	99		1,224	1,400
0120	608 GPH, 4" discharge		10	1.600		2,550	104		2,654	2,950
0500	Pump, propylene body, housing and impeller									
0510	22 GPM, 1/3 HP, 40' HD	1 Plum	5	1.600	Ea.	810	115		925	1,050
0520	33 GPM, 1/2 HP, 40' HD	Q-1	5	3.200		645	208		853	1,025
0530	53 GPM, 3/4 HP, 40' HD	"	4	4		1,275	259		1,534	1,775
0600	Rotary pump, CI									
0614	282 GPH, 3/4 HP, 1" discharge	Q-1	4.50	3.556	Ea.	1,850	231		2,081	2,400
0618	277 GPH, 1 HP, 1" discharge		4	4		1,850	259		2,109	2,400
0624	1,100 GPH, 1.5 HP, 1-1/4" discharge		3.60	4.444		5,100	288		5,388	6,025
0628	1,900 GPH, 2 HP, 1-1/4" discharge		3.20	5		6,850	325		7,175	8,000
1000	Turbine pump, CI									
1010	50 GPM, 2 HP, 3" discharge	Q-1	.80	20	Ea.	5,900	1,300		7,200	8,400
1020	100 GPM, 3 HP, 4" discharge	Q-2	.96	25		11,100	1,675		12,775	14,700
1030	250 GPM, 15 HP, 6" discharge	"	.94	25.532		13,800	1,725		15,525	17,800
1040	500 GPM, 25 HP, 6" discharge	Q-3	1.22	26.230		13,900	1,800		15,700	18,000
1050	1,000 GPM, 50 HP, 8" discharge		1.14	28.070		19,200	1,925		21,125	24,000

22 11 Facility Water Distribution

22 11 23 – Domestic Water Pumps

22 11 23.11 Miscellaneous Pumps

		Crew	Daily Output	Labor-Hours	Unit	Material	2023 Bare Costs Labor	2023 Bare Costs Equipment	Total	Total Incl O&P
1060	2,000 GPM, 100 HP, 10" discharge	Q-3	1	32	Ea.	22,800	2,200		25,000	28,300
1070	3,000 GPM, 150 HP, 10" discharge		.80	40		36,600	2,750		39,350	44,400
1080	4,000 GPM, 200 HP, 12" discharge		.70	45.714		40,100	3,125		43,225	48,800
1090	6,000 GPM, 300 HP, 14" discharge		.60	53.333		61,000	3,650		64,650	72,500
1100	10,000 GPM, 300 HP, 18" discharge		.58	55.172		70,500	3,775		74,275	83,000
2000	Centrifugal stainless steel pumps									
2100	100 GPM, 100' TDH, 3 HP	Q-1	1.80	8.889	Ea.	19,900	575		20,475	22,800
2130	250 GPM, 100' TDH, 10 HP	"	1.28	12.500		27,900	810		28,710	31,900
2160	500 GPM, 100' TDH, 20 HP	Q-2	1.44	16.667		31,900	1,125		33,025	36,800
2200	Vertical turbine stainless steel pumps									
2220	100 GPM, 100' TDH, 7.5 HP	Q-2	.95	25.263	Ea.	111,500	1,700		113,200	125,500
2240	250 GPM, 100' TDH, 15 HP		.94	25.532		123,500	1,725		125,225	138,500
2260	500 GPM, 100' TDH, 20 HP		.93	25.806		135,500	1,725		137,225	151,500
2280	750 GPM, 100' TDH, 30 HP	Q-3	1.19	26.891		147,500	1,850		149,350	165,000
2300	1,000 GPM, 100' TDH, 40 HP	"	1.16	27.586		159,500	1,900		161,400	178,500
2320	100 GPM, 200' TDH, 15 HP	Q-2	.94	25.532		171,500	1,725		173,225	191,000
2340	250 GPM, 200' TDH, 25 HP	Q-3	1.22	26.230		183,500	1,800		185,300	204,000
2360	500 GPM, 200' TDH, 40 HP		1.16	27.586		195,500	1,900		197,400	218,000
2380	750 GPM, 200' TDH, 60 HP		1.13	28.319		185,000	1,950		186,950	206,500
2400	1,000 GPM, 200' TDH, 75 HP		1.12	28.571		203,000	1,950		204,950	226,500

22 11 23.13 Domestic-Water Packaged Booster Pumps

		Crew	Daily Output	Labor-Hours	Unit	Material	Labor	Equipment	Total	Total Incl O&P
0010	**DOMESTIC-WATER PACKAGED BOOSTER PUMPS**									
0200	Pump system, with diaphragm tank, control, press. switch									
0300	1 HP pump	Q-1	1.30	12.308	Ea.	11,800	800		12,600	14,200
0400	1-1/2 HP pump		1.25	12.800		11,900	830		12,730	14,400
0420	2 HP pump		1.20	13.333		11,200	865		12,065	13,600
0440	3 HP pump		1.10	14.545		12,400	945		13,345	15,000
0460	5 HP pump	Q-2	1.50	16		12,600	1,075		13,675	15,500
0480	7-1/2 HP pump		1.42	16.901		15,200	1,125		16,325	18,500
0500	10 HP pump		1.34	17.910		15,900	1,200		17,100	19,300
2000	Pump system, variable speed, base, controls, starter									
2010	Duplex, 100' head									
2020	400 GPM, 7-1/2 HP, 4" discharge	Q-2	.70	34.286	Ea.	71,500	2,300		73,800	82,000
2025	Triplex, 100' head									
2030	1,000 GPM, 15 HP, 6" discharge	Q-2	.50	48	Ea.	76,500	3,225		79,725	89,000
2040	1,700 GPM, 30 HP, 6" discharge	"	.30	80		114,500	5,375		119,875	133,500
0020	Chlorinator Injector, sewer, gas injected w/booster pump	Q-1	1.30	12.308		2,450	800		3,250	3,900

22 12 Facility Potable-Water Storage Tanks

22 12 21 – Facility Underground Potable-Water Storage Tanks

22 12 21.13 Fiberglass, Undrgrnd Pot.-Water Storage Tanks

		Crew	Daily Output	Labor-Hours	Unit	Material	Labor	Equipment	Total	Total Incl O&P
0010	**FIBERGLASS, UNDERGROUND POTABLE-WATER STORAGE TANKS**									
0020	Excludes excavation, backfill & piping									
0030	Single wall									
2000	600 gallon capacity	B-21B	3.75	10.667	Ea.	1,400	550	575	2,525	2,975
2010	1,000 gallon capacity		3.50	11.429		2,650	590	615	3,855	4,450
2020	2,000 gallon capacity		3.25	12.308		4,425	635	660	5,720	6,525
2030	4,000 gallon capacity		3	13.333		8,025	685	715	9,425	10,600
2040	6,000 gallon capacity		2.65	15.094		27,300	775	810	28,885	32,000
2050	8,000 gallon capacity		2.30	17.391		15,300	895	935	17,130	19,200
2060	10,000 gallon capacity		2	20		22,600	1,025	1,075	24,700	27,500

22 12 Facility Potable-Water Storage Tanks

22 12 21 – Facility Underground Potable-Water Storage Tanks

22 12 21.13 Fiberglass, Undrgrnd Pot.-Water Storage Tanks		Crew	Daily Output	Labor-Hours	Unit	Material	2023 Bare Costs Labor	Equipment	Total	Total Incl O&P
2070	12,000 gallon capacity	B-21B	1.50	26.667	Ea.	21,100	1,375	1,425	23,900	26,800
2080	15,000 gallon capacity		1	40		26,800	2,050	2,150	31,000	35,000
2090	20,000 gallon capacity		.75	53.333		37,700	2,750	2,875	43,325	48,700
2100	25,000 gallon capacity		.50	80		52,000	4,125	4,300	60,425	68,000
2110	30,000 gallon capacity		.35	114		63,000	5,875	6,150	75,025	84,500
2120	40,000 gallon capacity		.30	133		85,500	6,850	7,175	99,525	112,000

22 12 23 – Facility Indoor Potable-Water Storage Tanks

22 12 23.13 Facility Steel, Indoor Pot.-Water Storage Tanks

		Crew	Daily Output	Labor-Hours	Unit	Material	Labor	Equipment	Total	Total Incl O&P
0010	**FACILITY STEEL, INDOOR POT.-WATER STORAGE TANKS**									
2000	Galvanized steel, 15 gal., 14" diam. x 26" LOA	1 Plum	12	.667	Ea.	1,025	48		1,073	1,200
2060	30 gal., 14" diam. x 49" LOA		11	.727		1,150	52.50		1,202.50	1,325
2080	80 gal., 20" diam. x 64" LOA		9	.889		1,700	64		1,764	1,975
2100	135 gal., 24" diam. x 75" LOA		6	1.333		2,525	96		2,621	2,925
2120	240 gal., 30" diam. x 86" LOA		4	2		4,675	144		4,819	5,375
2140	300 gal., 36" diam. x 76" LOA		3	2.667		6,575	192		6,767	7,500
2160	400 gal., 36" diam. x 100" LOA	Q-1	4	4		8,000	259		8,259	9,175
2180	500 gal., 36" diam. x 126" LOA	"	3	5.333		9,975	345		10,320	11,500
3000	Glass lined, P.E., 80 gal., 20" diam. x 60" LOA	1 Plum	9	.889		4,175	64		4,239	4,700
3060	140 gal., 24" diam. x 75" LOA		6	1.333		5,750	96		5,846	6,475
3080	200 gal., 30" diam. x 71" LOA		4	2		7,825	144		7,969	8,825
3100	350 gal., 36" diam. x 86" LOA		3	2.667		9,450	192		9,642	10,700
3120	450 gal., 42" diam. x 79" LOA	Q-1	4	4		12,900	259		13,159	14,500
3140	600 gal., 48" diam. x 81" LOA		3	5.333		15,700	345		16,045	17,800
3160	750 gal., 48" diam. x 105" LOA		3	5.333		17,600	345		17,945	19,900
3180	900 gal., 54" diam. x 95" LOA		2.50	6.400		24,500	415		24,915	27,600
3200	1,500 gal., 54" diam. x 153" LOA		2	8		31,500	520		32,020	35,500
3220	1,800 gal., 54" diam. x 181" LOA		1.50	10.667		35,300	690		35,990	39,800
3240	2,000 gal., 60" diam. x 165" LOA		1	16		40,400	1,050		41,450	46,100
3260	3,500 gal., 72" diam. x 201" LOA	Q-2	1.50	16		51,000	1,075		52,075	58,000

22 13 Facility Sanitary Sewerage

22 13 16 – Sanitary Waste and Vent Piping

22 13 16.40 Pipe Fittings, Cast Iron for Drainage

		Crew	Daily Output	Labor-Hours	Unit	Material	Labor	Equipment	Total	Total Incl O&P
0010	**PIPE FITTINGS, CAST IRON FOR DRAINAGE**, Special									
1000	Drip pan elbow (safety valve discharge elbow)									
1010	Cast iron, threaded inlet									
1014	2-1/2"	Q-1	8	2	Ea.	2,450	130		2,580	2,900
1015	3"		6.40	2.500		2,625	162		2,787	3,150
1017	4"		4.80	3.333		3,550	216		3,766	4,225
1018	Cast iron, flanged inlet									
1019	6"	Q-2	3.60	6.667	Ea.	2,975	450		3,425	3,950
1020	8"	"	2.60	9.231	"	3,700	620		4,320	5,000

22 13 16.60 Traps

		Crew	Daily Output	Labor-Hours	Unit	Material	Labor	Equipment	Total	Total Incl O&P
0010	**TRAPS**									
4700	Copper, drainage, drum trap									
4800	3" x 5" solid, 1-1/2" pipe size	1 Plum	16	.500	Ea.	660	36		696	780
4840	3" x 6" swivel, 1-1/2" pipe size	"	16	.500	"	1,450	36		1,486	1,650
5100	P trap, standard pattern									
5200	1-1/4" pipe size	1 Plum	18	.444	Ea.	435	32		467	525
5240	1-1/2" pipe size		17	.471		330	34		364	415

22 13 Facility Sanitary Sewerage

22 13 16 – Sanitary Waste and Vent Piping

22 13 16.60 Traps		Crew	Daily Output	Labor-Hours	Unit	Material	2023 Bare Costs Labor	Equipment	Total	Total Incl O&P
5260	2" pipe size	1 Plum	15	.533	Ea.	510	38.50		548.50	620
5280	3" pipe size	↓	11	.727	↓	1,450	52.50		1,502.50	1,675
5340	With cleanout, swivel joint and slip joint									
5360	1-1/4" pipe size	1 Plum	18	.444	Ea.	197	32		229	265
5400	1-1/2" pipe size		17	.471		860	34		894	995
5420	2" pipe size	↓	15	.533	↓	740	38.50		778.50	870
6710	ABS DWV P trap, solvent weld joint									
6720	1-1/2" pipe size	1 Plum	18	.444	Ea.	70	32		102	125
6722	2" pipe size		17	.471		85	34		119	144
6724	3" pipe size		15	.533		365	38.50		403.50	460
6726	4" pipe size	↓	14	.571	↓	670	41		711	795
6732	PVC DWV P trap, solvent weld joint									
6733	1-1/2" pipe size	1 Plum	18	.444	Ea.	57	32		89	111
6734	2" pipe size		17	.471		69	34		103	127
6735	3" pipe size		15	.533		233	38.50		271.50	315
6736	4" pipe size		14	.571		560	41		601	675
6760	PP DWV, dilution trap, 1-1/2" pipe size		16	.500		360	36		396	450
6770	P trap, 1-1/2" pipe size		17	.471		90	34		124	150
6780	2" pipe size		16	.500		133	36		169	200
6790	3" pipe size		14	.571		244	41		285	330
6800	4" pipe size		13	.615		410	44.50		454.50	515
6830	S trap, 1-1/2" pipe size		16	.500		74	36		110	135
6840	2" pipe size		15	.533		111	38.50		149.50	180
6850	Universal trap, 1-1/2" pipe size		14	.571		148	41		189	224
6860	PVC DWV hub x hub, basin trap, 1-1/4" pipe size		18	.444		57	32		89	111
6870	Sink P trap, 1-1/2" pipe size		18	.444		15.90	32		47.90	65.50
6880	Tubular S trap, 1-1/2" pipe size	↓	17	.471	↓	41	34		75	95.50
6890	PVC sch. 40 DWV, drum trap									
6900	1-1/2" pipe size	1 Plum	16	.500	Ea.	57.50	36		93.50	117
6910	P trap, 1-1/2" pipe size		18	.444		13.35	32		45.35	62.50
6920	2" pipe size		17	.471		17.95	34		51.95	70.50
6930	3" pipe size		15	.533		47	38.50		85.50	109
6940	4" pipe size		14	.571		139	41		180	214
6950	P trap w/clean out, 1-1/2" pipe size		18	.444		22.50	32		54.50	73
6960	2" pipe size		17	.471		27	34		61	80
6970	P trap adjustable, 1-1/2" pipe size		17	.471		15.25	34		49.25	67.50
6980	P trap adj. w/union & cleanout, 1-1/2" pipe size	↓	16	.500	↓	58.50	36		94.50	118

22 13 16.80 Vent Flashing and Caps

		Crew	Daily Output	Labor-Hours	Unit	Material	Labor	Equipment	Total	Total Incl O&P
0010	**VENT FLASHING AND CAPS**									
0120	Vent caps									
0140	Cast iron									
0180	2-1/2" to 3-5/8" pipe	1 Plum	21	.381	Ea.	59	27.50		86.50	106
0190	4" to 4-1/8" pipe	"	19	.421	"	85	30.50		115.50	139
0900	Vent flashing									
1000	Aluminum with lead ring									
1020	1-1/4" pipe	1 Plum	20	.400	Ea.	6.40	29		35.40	50
1030	1-1/2" pipe		20	.400		6.10	29		35.10	49.50
1040	2" pipe		18	.444		6.05	32		38.05	54.50
1050	3" pipe		17	.471		6.75	34		40.75	58
1060	4" pipe	↓	16	.500	↓	8.15	36		44.15	62.50
1350	Copper with neoprene ring									
1400	1-1/4" pipe	1 Plum	20	.400	Ea.	83.50	29		112.50	135

22 13 Facility Sanitary Sewerage

22 13 16 – Sanitary Waste and Vent Piping

22 13 16.80 Vent Flashing and Caps

		Crew	Daily Output	Labor-Hours	Unit	Material	2023 Bare Costs Labor	Equipment	Total	Total Incl O&P
1430	1-1/2" pipe	1 Plum	20	.400	Ea.	83.50	29		112.50	135
1440	2" pipe		18	.444		83.50	32		115.50	140
1450	3" pipe		17	.471		101	34		135	162
1460	4" pipe		16	.500		101	36		137	165
2000	Galvanized with neoprene ring									
2020	1-1/4" pipe	1 Plum	20	.400	Ea.	16.20	29		45.20	61
2030	1-1/2" pipe		20	.400		21.50	29		50.50	66.50
2040	2" pipe		18	.444		22	32		54	72
2050	3" pipe		17	.471		24	34		58	77
2060	4" pipe		16	.500		28	36		64	84
2980	Neoprene, one piece									
3000	1-1/4" pipe	1 Plum	24	.333	Ea.	3.64	24		27.64	40
3030	1-1/2" pipe		24	.333		3.61	24		27.61	40
3040	2" pipe		23	.348		5.60	25		30.60	43.50
3050	3" pipe		21	.381		7.55	27.50		35.05	49.50
3060	4" pipe		20	.400		11.25	29		40.25	55.50
4000	Lead, 4#, 8" skirt, vent through roof									
4100	2" pipe	1 Plum	18	.444	Ea.	49.50	32		81.50	103
4110	3" pipe		17	.471		56.50	34		90.50	113
4120	4" pipe		16	.500		64	36		100	124
4130	6" pipe		14	.571		96	41		137	167

22 13 26 – Sanitary Waste Separators

22 13 26.10 Separators

		Crew	Daily Output	Labor-Hours	Unit	Material	2023 Bare Costs Labor	Equipment	Total	Total Incl O&P
0010	**SEPARATORS**, Entrainment eliminator, steel body, 150 PSIG									
0100	1/4" size	1 Stpi	24	.333	Ea.	335	24		359	405
0120	1/2" size		24	.333		276	24		300	340
0140	3/4" size		20	.400		282	29		311	355
0160	1" size		19	.421		360	30.50		390.50	440
0180	1-1/4" size		15	.533		380	38.50		418.50	480
0200	1-1/2" size		13	.615		420	44.50		464.50	530
0220	2" size		11	.727		470	53		523	595
0240	2-1/2" size	Q-5	15	1.067		2,050	69.50		2,119.50	2,375
0260	3" size		13	1.231		1,900	80.50		1,980.50	2,225
0280	4" size		10	1.600		2,600	104		2,704	3,000
0300	5" size		6	2.667		3,075	174		3,249	3,625
0320	6" size		3	5.333		3,350	350		3,700	4,200
0340	8" size	Q-6	4.40	5.455		3,875	370		4,245	4,825
0360	10" size	"	4	6		7,200	405		7,605	8,525
1000	For 300 PSIG, add					15%				

22 13 29 – Sanitary Sewerage Pumps

22 13 29.13 Wet-Pit-Mounted, Vertical Sewerage Pumps

		Crew	Daily Output	Labor-Hours	Unit	Material	2023 Bare Costs Labor	Equipment	Total	Total Incl O&P
0010	**WET-PIT-MOUNTED, VERTICAL SEWERAGE PUMPS**									
0020	Controls incl. alarm/disconnect panel w/wire. Excavation not included									
0260	Simplex, 9 GPM at 60 PSIG, 91 gal. tank				Ea.	4,300			4,300	4,725
0300	Unit with manway, 26" ID, 18" high					4,775			4,775	5,250
0340	26" ID, 36" high					4,675			4,675	5,150
0380	43" ID, 4' high					4,975			4,975	5,475
0600	Simplex, 9 GPM at 60 PSIG, 150 gal. tank, indoor					5,000			5,000	5,500
0700	Unit with manway, 26" ID, 36" high					5,725			5,725	6,275
0740	26" ID, 4' high					5,875			5,875	6,475
2000	Duplex, 18 GPM at 60 PSIG, 150 gal. tank, indoor					9,250			9,250	10,200
2060	Unit with manway, 43" ID, 4' high					11,000			11,000	12,100

22 13 Facility Sanitary Sewerage

22 13 29 – Sanitary Sewerage Pumps

22 13 29.13 Wet-Pit-Mounted, Vertical Sewerage Pumps		Crew	Daily Output	Labor-Hours	Unit	Material	2023 Bare Costs Labor	Equipment	Total	Total Incl O&P
2400	For core only				Ea.	2,325			2,325	2,550
3000	Indoor residential type installation									
3020	Simplex, 9 GPM at 60 PSIG, 91 gal. HDPE tank				Ea.	4,325			4,325	4,750
22 13 29.14 Sewage Ejector Pumps										
0010	**SEWAGE EJECTOR PUMPS**, With operating and level controls									
0100	Simplex system incl. tank, cover, pump 15' head									
0500	37 gal. PE tank, 12 GPM, 1/2 HP, 2" discharge	Q-1	3.20	5	Ea.	595	325		920	1,125
0510	3" discharge		3.10	5.161		630	335		965	1,200
0530	87 GPM, .7 HP, 2" discharge		3.20	5		910	325		1,235	1,475
0540	3" discharge		3.10	5.161		990	335		1,325	1,600
0600	45 gal. coated stl. tank, 12 GPM, 1/2 HP, 2" discharge		3	5.333		1,050	345		1,395	1,700
0610	3" discharge		2.90	5.517		1,100	360		1,460	1,750
0630	87 GPM, .7 HP, 2" discharge		3	5.333		1,375	345		1,720	2,025
0640	3" discharge		2.90	5.517		1,450	360		1,810	2,100
0660	134 GPM, 1 HP, 2" discharge		2.80	5.714		1,475	370		1,845	2,175
0680	3" discharge		2.70	5.926		1,550	385		1,935	2,275
0700	70 gal. PE tank, 12 GPM, 1/2 HP, 2" discharge		2.60	6.154		1,150	400		1,550	1,850
0710	3" discharge		2.40	6.667		1,225	430		1,655	2,000
0730	87 GPM, .7 HP, 2" discharge		2.50	6.400		1,525	415		1,940	2,300
0740	3" discharge		2.30	6.957		1,575	450		2,025	2,400
0760	134 GPM, 1 HP, 2" discharge		2.20	7.273		1,600	470		2,070	2,475
0770	3" discharge		2	8		1,725	520		2,245	2,650
0800	75 gal. coated stl. tank, 12 GPM, 1/2 HP, 2" discharge		2.40	6.667		1,275	430		1,705	2,050
0810	3" discharge		2.20	7.273		1,325	470		1,795	2,150
0830	87 GPM, .7 HP, 2" discharge		2.30	6.957		1,600	450		2,050	2,425
0840	3" discharge		2.10	7.619		1,675	495		2,170	2,575
0860	134 GPM, 1 HP, 2" discharge		2	8		1,725	520		2,245	2,675
0880	3" discharge		1.80	8.889		1,800	575		2,375	2,825
1040	Duplex system incl. tank, covers, pumps									
1060	110 gal. fiberglass tank, 24 GPM, 1/2 HP, 2" discharge	Q-1	1.60	10	Ea.	2,300	650		2,950	3,500
1080	3" discharge		1.40	11.429		2,400	740		3,140	3,750
1100	174 GPM, .7 HP, 2" discharge		1.50	10.667		2,975	690		3,665	4,300
1120	3" discharge		1.30	12.308		3,100	800		3,900	4,600
1140	268 GPM, 1 HP, 2" discharge		1.20	13.333		3,225	865		4,090	4,850
1160	3" discharge		1	16		3,350	1,050		4,400	5,225
1260	135 gal. coated stl. tank, 24 GPM, 1/2 HP, 2" discharge	Q-2	1.70	14.118		2,375	950		3,325	4,025
2000	3" discharge		1.60	15		2,525	1,000		3,525	4,275
2640	174 GPM, .7 HP, 2" discharge		1.60	15		3,100	1,000		4,100	4,925
2660	3" discharge		1.50	16		3,275	1,075		4,350	5,200
2700	268 GPM, 1 HP, 2" discharge		1.30	18.462		3,375	1,250		4,625	5,550
3040	3" discharge		1.10	21.818		3,600	1,475		5,075	6,150
3060	275 gal. coated stl. tank, 24 GPM, 1/2 HP, 2" discharge		1.50	16		2,975	1,075		4,050	4,875
3080	3" discharge		1.40	17.143		3,000	1,150		4,150	5,025
3100	174 GPM, .7 HP, 2" discharge		1.40	17.143		3,825	1,150		4,975	5,925
3120	3" discharge		1.30	18.462		4,125	1,250		5,375	6,375
3140	268 GPM, 1 HP, 2" discharge		1.10	21.818		4,200	1,475		5,675	6,825
3160	3" discharge		.90	26.667		4,425	1,800		6,225	7,550
3260	Pump system accessories, add									
3300	Alarm horn and lights, 115 V mercury switch	Q-1	8	2	Ea.	117	130		247	320
3340	Switch, mag. contactor, alarm bell, light, 3 level control		5	3.200		600	208		808	965
3380	Alternator, mercury switch activated		4	4		1,075	259		1,334	1,550

22 14 Facility Storm Drainage

22 14 29 – Sump Pumps

22 14 29.13 Wet-Pit-Mounted, Vertical Sump Pumps

		Crew	Daily Output	Labor-Hours	Unit	Material	2023 Bare Costs Labor	Equipment	Total	Total Incl O&P
0010	**WET-PIT-MOUNTED, VERTICAL SUMP PUMPS**									
0400	Molded PVC base, 21 GPM at 15' head, 1/3 HP	1 Plum	5	1.600	Ea.	138	115		253	325
0800	Iron base, 21 GPM at 15' head, 1/3 HP		5	1.600		155	115		270	345
1200	Solid brass, 21 GPM at 15' head, 1/3 HP	↓	5	1.600	↓	251	115		366	450
2000	Sump pump, single stage									
2010	25 GPM, 1 HP, 1-1/2" discharge	Q-1	1.80	8.889	Ea.	4,000	575		4,575	5,250
2020	75 GPM, 1-1/2 HP, 2" discharge		1.50	10.667		4,225	690		4,915	5,675
2030	100 GPM, 2 HP, 2-1/2" discharge		1.30	12.308		1,575	800		2,375	2,950
2040	150 GPM, 3 HP, 3" discharge		1.10	14.545		4,300	945		5,245	6,150
2050	200 GPM, 3 HP, 3" discharge	↓	1	16		4,575	1,050		5,625	6,575
2060	300 GPM, 10 HP, 4" discharge	Q-2	1.20	20		4,925	1,350		6,275	7,425
2070	500 GPM, 15 HP, 5" discharge		1.10	21.818		4,975	1,475		6,450	7,650
2080	800 GPM, 20 HP, 6" discharge		1	24		6,625	1,625		8,250	9,700
2090	1,000 GPM, 30 HP, 6" discharge		.85	28.235		7,275	1,900		9,175	10,800
2100	1,600 GPM, 50 HP, 8" discharge	↓	.72	33.333		11,300	2,250		13,550	15,900
2110	2,000 GPM, 60 HP, 8" discharge	Q-3	.85	37.647		11,600	2,575		14,175	16,700
2202	For general purpose float switch, copper coated float, add	Q-1	5	3.200	↓	120	208		328	440

22 14 29.16 Submersible Sump Pumps

		Crew	Daily Output	Labor-Hours	Unit	Material	Labor	Equipment	Total	Total Incl O&P
0010	**SUBMERSIBLE SUMP PUMPS**									
1000	Elevator sump pumps, automatic									
1010	Complete systems, pump, oil detector, controls and alarm									
1020	1-1/2" discharge, does not include the sump pit/tank									
1040	1/3 HP, 115 V	1 Plum	4.40	1.818	Ea.	1,650	131		1,781	2,000
1050	1/2 HP, 115 V		4	2		1,725	144		1,869	2,125
1060	1/2 HP, 230 V		4	2		1,725	144		1,869	2,125
1070	3/4 HP, 115 V		3.60	2.222		1,825	160		1,985	2,250
1080	3/4 HP, 230 V	↓	3.60	2.222	↓	1,800	160		1,960	2,225
1100	Sump pump only									
1110	1/3 HP, 115 V	1 Plum	6.40	1.250	Ea.	152	90		242	300
1120	1/2 HP, 115 V		5.80	1.379		218	99.50		317.50	390
1130	1/2 HP, 230 V		5.80	1.379		253	99.50		352.50	425
1140	3/4 HP, 115 V		5.40	1.481		289	107		396	480
1150	3/4 HP, 230 V	↓	5.40	1.481	↓	330	107		437	520
1200	Oil detector, control and alarm only									
1210	115 V	1 Plum	8	1	Ea.	1,925	72		1,997	2,225
1220	230 V	"	8	1	"	2,025	72		2,097	2,325
7000	Sump pump, automatic									
7100	Plastic, 1-1/4" discharge, 1/4 HP	1 Plum	6.40	1.250	Ea.	149	90		239	298
7140	1/3 HP		6	1.333		197	96		293	360
7160	1/2 HP		5.40	1.481		214	107		321	395
7180	1-1/2" discharge, 1/2 HP		5.20	1.538		136	111		247	315
7500	Cast iron, 1-1/4" discharge, 1/4 HP		6	1.333		245	96		341	415
7540	1/3 HP		6	1.333		221	96		317	385
7560	1/2 HP	↓	5	1.600	↓	340	115		455	545

22 14 53 – Rainwater Storage Tanks

22 14 53.13 Fiberglass, Rainwater Storage Tank

		Crew	Daily Output	Labor-Hours	Unit	Material	Labor	Equipment	Total	Total Incl O&P
0010	**FIBERGLASS, RAINWATER STORAGE TANK**									
2000	600 gallon	B-21B	3.75	10.667	Ea.	1,400	550	575	2,525	2,975
2010	1,000 gallon		3.50	11.429		2,650	590	615	3,855	4,450
2020	2,000 gallon		3.25	12.308		4,425	635	660	5,720	6,525
2030	4,000 gallon		3	13.333		8,025	685	715	9,425	10,600
2040	6,000 gallon	↓	2.65	15.094	↓	27,300	775	810	28,885	32,000

22 14 Facility Storm Drainage

22 14 53 – Rainwater Storage Tanks

22 14 53.13 Fiberglass, Rainwater Storage Tank		Crew	Daily Output	Labor-Hours	Unit	Material	2023 Bare Costs Labor	Equipment	Total	Total Incl O&P
2050	8,000 gallon	B-21B	2.30	17.391	Ea.	15,300	895	935	17,130	19,200
2060	10,000 gallon		2	20		22,600	1,025	1,075	24,700	27,500
2070	12,000 gallon		1.50	26.667		21,100	1,375	1,425	23,900	26,800
2080	15,000 gallon		1	40		26,800	2,050	2,150	31,000	35,000
2090	20,000 gallon		.75	53.333		37,700	2,750	2,875	43,325	48,700
2100	25,000 gallon		.50	80		52,000	4,125	4,300	60,425	68,000
2110	30,000 gallon		.35	114		63,000	5,875	6,150	75,025	84,500
2120	40,000 gallon	↓	.30	133	↓	85,500	6,850	7,175	99,525	112,000

22 15 General Service Compressed-Air Systems

22 15 13 – General Service Compressed-Air Piping

22 15 13.10 Compressor Accessories

		Crew	Daily Output	Labor-Hours	Unit	Material	2023 Bare Costs Labor	Equipment	Total	Total Incl O&P
0010	**COMPRESSOR ACCESSORIES**									
1700	Refrigerated air dryers with ambient air filters									
1710	10 CFM	Q-5	8	2	Ea.	915	131		1,046	1,200
1715	15 CFM		7.30	2.192		1,025	143		1,168	1,350
1716	20 CFM		6.90	2.319		2,650	151		2,801	3,125
1720	25 CFM		6.60	2.424		1,675	158		1,833	2,075
1730	50 CFM		6.20	2.581		2,475	169		2,644	2,975
1740	75 CFM		5.80	2.759		3,050	180		3,230	3,650
1750	100 CFM		5.60	2.857		4,125	187		4,312	4,825
1751	125 CFM		5.40	2.963		4,075	193		4,268	4,800
1752	175 CFM		5	3.200		4,350	209		4,559	5,075
1753	200 CFM		4.80	3.333		5,100	218		5,318	5,925
1754	300 CFM		4.40	3.636		6,775	237		7,012	7,800
1755	400 CFM		4	4		11,000	261		11,261	12,500
1756	500 CFM		3.80	4.211		12,400	275		12,675	14,000
1757	600 CFM		3.40	4.706		17,900	305		18,205	20,200
1758	800 CFM		3	5.333		24,500	350		24,850	27,500
1759	1,000 CFM	↓	2.60	6.154	↓	26,500	400		26,900	29,800
3460	Air filter, regulator, lubricator combination									
3470	Flush mount									
3480	Adjustable range 0-140 psi									
3500	1/8" NPT, 34 SCFM	1 Stpi	17	.471	Ea.	126	34		160	190
3510	1/4" NPT, 61 SCFM		17	.471		228	34		262	300
3520	3/8" NPT, 85 SCFM		16	.500		233	36.50		269.50	310
3530	1/2" NPT, 150 SCFM		15	.533		250	38.50		288.50	335
3540	3/4" NPT, 171 SCFM		14	.571		305	41.50		346.50	400
3550	1" NPT, 150 SCFM	↓	13	.615	↓	490	44.50		534.50	605
4000	Couplers, air line, sleeve type									
4010	Female, connection size NPT									
4020	1/4"	1 Stpi	38	.211	Ea.	10.35	15.25		25.60	34.50
4030	3/8"		36	.222		9.20	16.10		25.30	34
4040	1/2"		35	.229		19.75	16.60		36.35	46
4050	3/4"	↓	34	.235	↓	24.50	17.05		41.55	52.50
4100	Male									
4110	1/4"	1 Stpi	38	.211	Ea.	7.25	15.25		22.50	31
4120	3/8"		36	.222		11.50	16.10		27.60	36.50
4130	1/2"		35	.229		20.50	16.60		37.10	47
4140	3/4"	↓	34	.235	↓	18.05	17.05		35.10	45.50
4150	Coupler, combined male and female halves									

22 15 General Service Compressed-Air Systems

22 15 13 – General Service Compressed-Air Piping

22 15 13.10 Compressor Accessories		Crew	Daily Output	Labor-Hours	Unit	Material	2023 Bare Costs Labor	Equipment	Total	Total Incl O&P
4160	1/2"	1 Stpi	17	.471	Ea.	40.50	34		74.50	95.50
4170	3/4"	"	15	.533	"	42.50	38.50		81	105

22 15 19 – General Service Packaged Air Compressors and Receivers

22 15 19.10 Air Compressors

0010	**AIR COMPRESSORS**									
5250	Air, reciprocating air cooled, splash lubricated, tank mounted									
5300	Single stage, 1 phase, 140 psi									
5303	1/2 HP, 17 gal. tank	1 Stpi	3	2.667	Ea.	2,200	193		2,393	2,725
5305	3/4 HP, 30 gal. tank		2.60	3.077		1,800	223		2,023	2,325
5307	1 HP, 30 gal. tank		2.20	3.636		2,650	264		2,914	3,325
5309	2 HP, 30 gal. tank	Q-5	4	4		3,175	261		3,436	3,900
5310	3 HP, 30 gal. tank		3.60	4.444		3,500	290		3,790	4,275
5314	3 HP, 60 gal. tank		3.50	4.571		4,475	299		4,774	5,375
5320	5 HP, 60 gal. tank		3.20	5		3,875	325		4,200	4,725
5330	5 HP, 80 gal. tank		3	5.333		7,200	350		7,550	8,450
5340	7.5 HP, 80 gal. tank		2.60	6.154		5,800	400		6,200	7,000
5600	2 stage pkg., 3 phase									
5650	6 CFM at 125 psi, 1-1/2 HP, 60 gal. tank	Q-5	3	5.333	Ea.	3,100	350		3,450	3,925
5670	10.9 CFM at 125 psi, 3 HP, 80 gal. tank		1.50	10.667		6,275	695		6,970	7,950
5680	38.7 CFM at 125 psi, 10 HP, 120 gal. tank		.60	26.667		10,900	1,750		12,650	14,600
5690	105 CFM at 125 psi, 25 HP, 250 gal. tank	Q-6	.60	40		19,600	2,700		22,300	25,700
5800	With single stage pump									
5850	8.3 CFM at 125 psi, 2 HP, 80 gal. tank	Q-6	3.50	6.857	Ea.	3,325	465		3,790	4,375
5860	38.7 CFM at 125 psi, 10 HP, 120 gal. tank	"	.90	26.667	"	6,250	1,800		8,050	9,575
6000	Reciprocating, 2 stage, tank mtd, 3 ph, cap rated @ 175 PSIG									
6050	Pressure lubricated, hvy. duty, 9.7 CFM, 3 HP, 120 gal. tank	Q-5	1.30	12.308	Ea.	5,625	805		6,430	7,375
6054	5 CFM, 1-1/2 HP, 80 gal. tank		2.80	5.714		3,175	375		3,550	4,050
6056	6.4 CFM, 2 HP, 80 gal. tank		2	8		3,325	520		3,845	4,450
6058	8.1 CFM, 3 HP, 80 gal. tank		1.70	9.412		3,875	615		4,490	5,200
6059	14.8 CFM, 5 HP, 80 gal. tank		1	16		3,875	1,050		4,925	5,800
6060	16.5 CFM, 5 HP, 120 gal. tank		1	16		5,375	1,050		6,425	7,450
6063	13 CFM, 6 HP, 80 gal. tank		.90	17.778		5,900	1,150		7,050	8,200
6066	19.8 CFM, 7.5 HP, 80 gal. tank		.80	20		6,925	1,300		8,225	9,575
6070	25.8 CFM, 7-1/2 HP, 120 gal. tank		.80	20		5,525	1,300		6,825	8,025
6078	34.8 CFM, 10 HP, 80 gal. tank		.70	22.857		8,075	1,500		9,575	11,100
6080	34.8 CFM, 10 HP, 120 gal. tank		.60	26.667		9,050	1,750		10,800	12,600
6090	53.7 CFM, 15 HP, 120 gal. tank	Q-6	.80	30		8,250	2,025		10,275	12,100
6100	76.7 CFM, 20 HP, 120 gal. tank		.70	34.286		11,100	2,325		13,425	15,700
6104	76.7 CFM, 20 HP, 240 gal. tank		.68	35.294		13,900	2,400		16,300	18,900
6110	90.1 CFM, 25 HP, 120 gal. tank		.63	38.095		13,900	2,575		16,475	19,200
6120	101 CFM, 30 HP, 120 gal. tank		.57	42.105		12,100	2,850		14,950	17,600
6130	101 CFM, 30 HP, 250 gal. tank		.52	46.154		14,400	3,125		17,525	20,500
6200	Oil-less, 13.6 CFM, 5 HP, 120 gal. tank	Q-5	.88	18.182		15,300	1,175		16,475	18,600
6210	13.6 CFM, 5 HP, 250 gal. tank		.80	20		16,300	1,300		17,600	20,000
6220	18.2 CFM, 7.5 HP, 120 gal. tank		.73	21.918		15,200	1,425		16,625	18,800
6230	18.2 CFM, 7.5 HP, 250 gal. tank		.67	23.881		16,300	1,550		17,850	20,300
6250	30.5 CFM, 10 HP, 120 gal. tank		.57	28.070		17,900	1,825		19,725	22,400
6260	30.5 CFM, 10 HP, 250 gal. tank		.53	30.189		19,100	1,975		21,075	24,000
6270	41.3 CFM, 15 HP, 120 gal. tank	Q-6	.70	34.286		19,500	2,325		21,825	24,900
6280	41.3 CFM, 15 HP, 250 gal. tank	"	.67	35.821		20,600	2,425		23,025	26,300

22 31 Domestic Water Softeners

22 31 13 – Residential Domestic Water Softeners

22 31 13.10 Residential Water Softeners

		Crew	Daily Output	Labor-Hours	Unit	Material	2023 Bare Costs Labor	2023 Bare Costs Equipment	Total	Total Incl O&P
0010	**RESIDENTIAL WATER SOFTENERS**									
7350	Water softener, automatic, to 30 grains per gallon	2 Plum	5	3.200	Ea.	590	231		821	995
7400	To 100 grains per gallon	"	4	4	"	530	288		818	1,025

22 35 Domestic Water Heat Exchangers

22 35 30 – Water Heating by Steam

22 35 30.10 Water Heating Transfer Package

		Crew	Daily Output	Labor-Hours	Unit	Material	2023 Bare Costs Labor	2023 Bare Costs Equipment	Total	Total Incl O&P
0010	**WATER HEATING TRANSFER PACKAGE**, Complete controls,									
0020	expansion tank, converter, air separator									
1000	Hot water, 180°F enter, 200°F exit, 15# steam									
1010	One pump system, 28 GPM	Q-6	.75	32	Ea.	24,000	2,175		26,175	29,600
1020	35 GPM		.70	34.286		27,400	2,325		29,725	33,600
1040	55 GPM		.65	36.923		30,700	2,500		33,200	37,500
1060	130 GPM		.55	43.636		39,000	2,950		41,950	47,300
1080	255 GPM		.40	60		51,000	4,075		55,075	62,000
1100	550 GPM		.30	80		78,000	5,425		83,425	94,000
1120	800 GPM		.25	96		79,500	6,500		86,000	97,000
1220	Two pump system, 28 GPM		.70	34.286		32,500	2,325		34,825	39,300
1240	35 GPM		.65	36.923		40,000	2,500		42,500	47,800
1260	55 GPM		.60	40		41,200	2,700		43,900	49,500
1280	130 GPM		.50	48		54,500	3,250		57,750	64,500
1300	255 GPM		.35	68.571		71,500	4,650		76,150	85,500
1320	550 GPM		.25	96		87,000	6,500		93,500	105,000
1340	800 GPM		.20	120		105,000	8,125		113,125	127,500

22 41 Residential Plumbing Fixtures

22 41 39 – Residential Faucets, Supplies and Trim

22 41 39.10 Faucets and Fittings

		Crew	Daily Output	Labor-Hours	Unit	Material	2023 Bare Costs Labor	2023 Bare Costs Equipment	Total	Total Incl O&P
0010	**FAUCETS AND FITTINGS**									
5000	Sillcock, compact, brass, IPS or copper to hose	1 Plum	24	.333	Ea.	19.40	24		43.40	57.50
6000	Stop and waste valves, bronze									
6100	Angle, solder end 1/2"	1 Plum	24	.333	Ea.	59	24		83	101
6110	3/4"		20	.400		68.50	29		97.50	118
6300	Straightway, solder end 3/8"		24	.333		21	24		45	59
6310	1/2"		24	.333		33	24		57	72.50
6320	3/4"		20	.400		37.50	29		66.50	84.50
6410	Straightway, threaded 1/2"		24	.333		39	24		63	79
6420	3/4"		20	.400		44	29		73	91.50
6430	1"		19	.421		23.50	30.50		54	71

22 51 Swimming Pool Plumbing Systems

22 51 19 – Swimming Pool Water Treatment Equipment

22 51 19.50 Swimming Pool Filtration Equipment	Crew	Daily Output	Labor-Hours	Unit	Material	2023 Bare Costs Labor	Equipment	Total	Total Incl O&P
0010 **SWIMMING POOL FILTRATION EQUIPMENT**									
0900 Filter system, sand or diatomite type, incl. pump, 6,000 gal./hr.	2 Plum	1.80	8.889	Total	1,250	640		1,890	2,325
1020 Add for chlorination system, 800 S.F. pool		3	5.333	Ea.	143	385		528	730
1040 5,000 S.F. pool		3	5.333	"	2,875	385		3,260	3,725

22 52 Fountain Plumbing Systems

22 52 16 – Fountain Pumps

22 52 16.10 Fountain Water Pumps

	Crew	Daily Output	Labor-Hours	Unit	Material	2023 Bare Costs Labor	Equipment	Total	Total Incl O&P
0010 **FOUNTAIN WATER PUMPS**									
0100 Pump w/controls									
0200 Single phase, 100' cord, 1/2 HP pump	2 Skwk	4.40	3.636	Ea.	1,675	223		1,898	2,175
0300 3/4 HP pump		4.30	3.721		1,775	228		2,003	2,300
0400 1 HP pump		4.20	3.810		2,075	233		2,308	2,625
0500 1-1/2 HP pump		4.10	3.902		2,350	239		2,589	2,925
0600 2 HP pump		4	4		5,625	245		5,870	6,550
0700 Three phase, 200' cord, 5 HP pump		3.90	4.103		8,125	251		8,376	9,300
0800 7-1/2 HP pump		3.80	4.211		15,200	258		15,458	17,100
0900 10 HP pump		3.70	4.324		17,000	265		17,265	19,100
1000 15 HP pump		3.60	4.444		23,700	272		23,972	26,500
2000 DESIGN NOTE: Use two horsepower per surface acre.									

22 52 33 – Fountain Ancillary

22 52 33.10 Fountain Miscellaneous

	Crew	Daily Output	Labor-Hours	Unit	Material	2023 Bare Costs Labor	Equipment	Total	Total Incl O&P
0010 **FOUNTAIN MISCELLANEOUS**									
1300 Lights w/mounting kits, 200 watt	2 Skwk	18	.889	Ea.	1,200	54.50		1,254.50	1,400
1400 300 watt		18	.889		1,375	54.50		1,429.50	1,600
1500 500 watt		18	.889		1,600	54.50		1,654.50	1,850
1600 Color blender		12	1.333		610	81.50		691.50	800

22 62 Vacuum Systems for Laboratory and Healthcare Facilities

22 62 19 – Vacuum Equipment for Laboratory and Healthcare Facilities

22 62 19.70 Healthcare Vacuum Equipment

	Crew	Daily Output	Labor-Hours	Unit	Material	2023 Bare Costs Labor	Equipment	Total	Total Incl O&P
0010 **HEALTHCARE VACUUM EQUIPMENT**									
0300 Dental oral									
0310 Duplex									
0330 165 SCFM with 77 gal. separator	Q-2	1.30	18.462	Ea.	55,500	1,250		56,750	63,000
1100 Vacuum system									
1110 Vacuum outlet alarm panel	1 Plum	3.20	2.500	Ea.	1,100	180		1,280	1,475
2000 Medical, with receiver									
2100 Rotary vane type, lubricated, with controls									
2110 Simplex									
2120 1.5 HP, 80 gal. tank	Q-1	8	2	Ea.	7,125	130		7,255	8,050
2130 2 HP, 80 gal. tank		7	2.286		7,375	148		7,523	8,350
2140 3 HP, 80 gal. tank		6.60	2.424		7,775	157		7,932	8,775
2150 5 HP, 80 gal. tank		6	2.667		8,475	173		8,648	9,575
2200 Duplex									
2210 1 HP, 80 gal. tank	Q-1	8.40	1.905	Ea.	11,400	124		11,524	12,700
2220 1.5 HP, 80 gal. tank		7.80	2.051		11,700	133		11,833	13,100
2230 2 HP, 80 gal. tank		6.80	2.353		12,600	153		12,753	14,100
2240 3 HP, 120 gal. tank		6	2.667		13,700	173		13,873	15,400

22 62 Vacuum Systems for Laboratory and Healthcare Facilities

22 62 19 – Vacuum Equipment for Laboratory and Healthcare Facilities

22 62 19.70 Healthcare Vacuum Equipment

		Crew	Daily Output	Labor-Hours	Unit	Material	2023 Bare Costs Labor	2023 Bare Costs Equipment	Total	Total Incl O&P
2250	5 HP, 120 gal. tank	Q-1	5.40	2.963	Ea.	15,600	192		15,792	17,500
2260	7.5 HP, 200 gal. tank	Q-2	7	3.429		22,300	231		22,531	24,900
2270	10 HP, 200 gal. tank		6.40	3.750		25,800	252		26,052	28,800
2280	15 HP, 200 gal. tank		5.80	4.138		46,100	278		46,378	51,500
2290	20 HP, 200 gal. tank		5	4.800		52,500	325		52,825	58,500
2300	25 HP, 200 gal. tank		4	6		61,000	405		61,405	68,000
2400	Triplex									
2410	7.5 HP, 200 gal. tank	Q-2	6.40	3.750	Ea.	35,400	252		35,652	39,400
2420	10 HP, 200 gal. tank		5.70	4.211		41,300	283		41,583	45,800
2430	15 HP, 200 gal. tank		4.90	4.898		69,500	330		69,830	77,000
2440	20 HP, 200 gal. tank		4	6		79,500	405		79,905	88,000
2450	25 HP, 200 gal. tank		3.70	6.486		92,000	435		92,435	101,500
2500	Quadruplex									
2510	7.5 HP, 200 gal. tank	Q-2	5.30	4.528	Ea.	44,100	305		44,405	49,100
2520	10 HP, 200 gal. tank		4.70	5.106		51,000	345		51,345	56,500
2530	15 HP, 200 gal. tank		4	6		92,000	405		92,405	101,500
2540	20 HP, 200 gal. tank		3.60	6.667		104,500	450		104,950	115,500
2550	25 HP, 200 gal. tank		3.20	7.500		121,500	505		122,005	135,000
4000	Liquid ring type, water sealed, with controls									
4200	Duplex									
4210	1.5 HP, 120 gal. tank	Q-1	6	2.667	Ea.	22,500	173		22,673	25,100
4220	3 HP, 120 gal. tank	"	5.50	2.909		23,500	189		23,689	26,100
4230	4 HP, 120 gal. tank	Q-2	6.80	3.529		25,000	237		25,237	27,900
4240	5 HP, 120 gal. tank		6.50	3.692		26,400	248		26,648	29,500
4250	7.5 HP, 200 gal. tank		6.20	3.871		32,200	260		32,460	35,800
4260	10 HP, 200 gal. tank		5.80	4.138		40,100	278		40,378	44,500
4270	15 HP, 200 gal. tank		5.10	4.706		48,600	315		48,915	54,000
4280	20 HP, 200 gal. tank		4.60	5.217		63,000	350		63,350	69,500
4290	30 HP, 200 gal. tank		4	6		75,000	405		75,405	83,000

22 63 Gas Systems for Laboratory and Healthcare Facilities

22 63 13 – Gas Piping for Laboratory and Healthcare Facilities

22 63 13.70 Healthcare Gas Piping

		Crew	Daily Output	Labor-Hours	Unit	Material	2023 Bare Costs Labor	2023 Bare Costs Equipment	Total	Total Incl O&P
0010	**HEALTHCARE GAS PIPING**									
1000	Nitrogen or oxygen system									
1010	Cylinder manifold									
1020	5 cylinder	1 Plum	.80	10	Ea.	5,900	720		6,620	7,550
1026	10 cylinder	"	.40	20		7,100	1,450		8,550	9,950
1050	Nitrogen generator, 30 LPM	Q-5	.40	40		31,700	2,600		34,300	38,800
3000	Outlets and valves									
3010	Recessed, wall mounted									
3012	Single outlet	1 Plum	3.20	2.500	Ea.	44.50	180		224.50	320
3100	Ceiling outlet									
3190	Zone valve with box									
3210	2" valve size	1 Plum	3.20	2.500	Ea.	410	180		590	725
4000	Alarm panel, medical gases and vacuum									
4010	Alarm panel	1 Plum	3.20	2.500	Ea.	1,100	180		1,280	1,475

Division Notes

		CREW	DAILY OUTPUT	LABOR-HOURS	UNIT	BARE COSTS				TOTAL INCL O&P
						MAT.	LABOR	EQUIP.	TOTAL	

Estimating Tips
The labor adjustment factors listed in Subdivision 22 01 02.20 also apply to Division 23.

23 10 00 Facility Fuel Systems
- The prices in this subdivision for above- and below-ground storage tanks do not include foundations or hold-down slabs, unless noted. The estimator should refer to Divisions 3 and 31 for foundation system pricing. In addition to the foundations, required tank accessories, such as tank gauges, leak detection devices, and additional manholes and piping, must be added to the tank prices.

23 50 00 Central Heating Equipment
- When estimating the cost of an HVAC system, check to see who is responsible for providing and installing the temperature control system. It is possible to overlook controls, assuming that they would be included in the electrical estimate.
- When looking up a boiler, be careful on specified capacity. Some manufacturers rate their products on output while others use input.
- Include HVAC insulation for pipe, boiler, and duct (wrap and liner).
- Be careful when looking up mechanical items to get the correct pressure rating and connection type (thread, weld, flange).

23 70 00 Central HVAC Equipment
- Combination heating and cooling units are sized by the air conditioning requirements. (See Reference No. R236000-20 for the preliminary sizing guide.)
- A ton of air conditioning is nominally 400 CFM.
- Rectangular duct is taken off by the linear foot for each size, but its cost is usually estimated by the pound. Remember that SMACNA standards now base duct on internal pressure.
- Prefabricated duct is estimated and purchased like pipe: straight sections and fittings.
- Note that cranes or other lifting equipment are not included on any lines in Division 23. For example, if a crane is required to lift a heavy piece of pipe into place high above a gym floor, or to put a rooftop unit on the roof of a four-story building, etc., it must be added. Due to the potential for extreme variation—from nothing additional required to a major crane or helicopter—we feel that including a nominal amount for "lifting contingency" would be useless and detract from the accuracy of the estimate. When using equipment rental cost data from RSMeans, do not forget to include the cost of the operator(s).

Reference Numbers
Reference numbers are shown at the beginning of some major classifications. These numbers refer to related items in the Reference Section. The reference information may be an estimating procedure, an alternate pricing method, or technical information.

Note: Not all subdivisions listed here necessarily appear. ■

Same Data. Simplified.
Enjoy the convenience and efficiency of accessing your costs anywhere:
- **Skip the multiplier** by setting your location
- **Quickly search,** edit, favorite and share costs
- **Stay on top of price changes** with automatic updates

Discover more at rsmeans.com/online

No part of this cost data may be reproduced, stored in a retrieval system, or transmitted in any form or by any means without prior written permission of Gordian.

Note: "Powered in part by CINX™, based on licensed proprietary information of Harrison Publishing House, Inc."

Note: Trade Service, in part, has been used as a reference source for some of the material prices used in Division 23.

23 05 Common Work Results for HVAC

23 05 02 – HVAC General

23 05 02.10 Air Conditioning, General		Crew	Daily Output	Labor-Hours	Unit	Material	2023 Bare Costs Labor	2023 Bare Costs Equipment	Total	Total Incl O&P
0010	**AIR CONDITIONING, GENERAL** Prices are for standard efficiencies (SEER 13)									
0020	for upgrade to SEER 14 add					10%				

23 05 05 – Selective Demolition for HVAC

23 05 05.10 HVAC Demolition

			Crew	Daily Output	Labor-Hours	Unit	Material	Labor	Equipment	Total	Total Incl O&P
0010	**HVAC DEMOLITION**	R220105-10									
0100	Air conditioner, split unit, 3 ton		Q-5	2	8	Ea.		520		520	780
0150	Package unit, 3 ton	R024119-10	Q-6	3	8			540		540	810
0190	Rooftop, self contained, up to 5 ton		1 Plum	1.20	6.667	↓		480		480	715
0250	Air curtain		Q-9	20	.800	L.F.		50.50		50.50	76
0254	Air filters, up thru 16,000 CFM			20	.800	Ea.		50.50		50.50	76
0256	20,000 thru 60,000 CFM		↓	16	1	↓		63		63	95
0297	Boiler blowdown		Q-5	8	2			131		131	195
0298	Boilers										
0300	Electric, up thru 148 kW		Q-19	2	12	Ea.		790		790	1,175
0310	150 thru 518 kW		"	1	24			1,575		1,575	2,350
0320	550 thru 2,000 kW		Q-21	.40	80			5,400		5,400	8,050
0330	2,070 kW and up		"	.30	107			7,225		7,225	10,700
0340	Gas and/or oil, up thru 150 MBH		Q-7	2.20	14.545			1,000		1,000	1,500
0350	160 thru 2,000 MBH			.80	40			2,750		2,750	4,125
0360	2,100 thru 4,500 MBH			.50	64			4,425		4,425	6,600
0370	4,600 thru 7,000 MBH			.30	107			7,375		7,375	11,000
0380	7,100 thru 12,000 MBH			.16	200			13,800		13,800	20,600
0390	12,200 thru 25,000 MBH		↓	.12	267			18,400		18,400	27,500
0400	Central station air handler unit, up thru 15 ton		Q-5	1.60	10			655		655	975
0410	17.5 thru 30 ton		"	.80	20	↓		1,300		1,300	1,950
0430	Computer room unit										
0434	Air cooled split, up thru 10 ton		Q-5	.67	23.881	Ea.		1,550		1,550	2,325
0436	12 thru 23 ton			.53	30.189			1,975		1,975	2,950
0440	Chilled water, up thru 10 ton			1.30	12.308			805		805	1,200
0444	12 thru 23 ton			1	16			1,050		1,050	1,550
0450	Glycol system, up thru 10 ton			.53	30.189			1,975		1,975	2,950
0454	12 thru 23 ton			.40	40			2,600		2,600	3,900
0460	Water cooled, not including condenser, up thru 10 ton			.80	20			1,300		1,300	1,950
0464	12 thru 23 ton			.60	26.667			1,750		1,750	2,600
0600	Condenser, up thru 50 ton		↓	1	16			1,050		1,050	1,550
0610	51 thru 100 ton		Q-6	.90	26.667			1,800		1,800	2,700
0620	101 thru 1,000 ton		"	.70	34.286			2,325		2,325	3,450
0660	Condensing unit, up thru 10 ton		Q-5	1.25	12.800			835		835	1,250
0670	11 thru 50 ton		"	.40	40			2,600		2,600	3,900
0680	60 thru 100 ton		Q-6	.30	80			5,425		5,425	8,075
0700	Cooling tower, up thru 400 ton			.80	30			2,025		2,025	3,025
0710	450 thru 600 ton			.53	45.283			3,075		3,075	4,575
0720	700 thru 1,300 ton		↓	.40	60			4,075		4,075	6,050
0780	Dehumidifier, up thru 155 lb./hr.		Q-1	8	2			130		130	193
0790	240 lb./hr. and up		"	2	8	↓		520		520	775
1560	Ductwork										
1570	Metal, steel, sst, fabricated		Q-9	1000	.016	Lb.		1.01		1.01	1.52
1580	Aluminum, fabricated			485	.033	"		2.08		2.08	3.14
1590	Spiral, prefabricated			400	.040	L.F.		2.53		2.53	3.80
1600	Fiberglass, prefabricated			400	.040			2.53		2.53	3.80
1610	Flex, prefabricated			500	.032			2.02		2.02	3.04
1620	Glass fiber reinforced plastic, prefabricated		↓	280	.057	↓		3.61		3.61	5.45

23 05 Common Work Results for HVAC

23 05 05 – Selective Demolition for HVAC

23 05 05.10 HVAC Demolition		Crew	Daily Output	Labor-Hours	Unit	Material	2023 Bare Costs Labor	2023 Bare Costs Equipment	Total	Total Incl O&P
1630	Diffusers, registers or grills, up thru 20" max dimension	1 Shee	50	.160	Ea.		11.20		11.20	16.90
1640	21 thru 36" max dimension		36	.222			15.60		15.60	23.50
1650	Above 36" max dimension		30	.267			18.70		18.70	28
1700	Evaporator, up thru 12,000 BTUH	Q-5	5.30	3.019			197		197	294
1710	12,500 thru 30,000 BTUH	"	2.70	5.926			385		385	575
1720	31,000 BTUH and up	Q-6	1.50	16			1,075		1,075	1,625
1730	Evaporative cooler, up thru 5 HP	Q-9	2.70	5.926			375		375	565
1740	10 thru 30 HP	"	.67	23.881			1,500		1,500	2,275
1750	Exhaust systems									
1760	Exhaust components	1 Shee	8	1	System		70		70	106
1770	Weld fume hoods	"	20	.400	Ea.		28		28	42.50
2120	Fans, up thru 1 HP or 2,000 CFM	Q-9	8	2			126		126	190
2124	1-1/2 thru 10 HP or 20,000 CFM		5.30	3.019			191		191	287
2128	15 thru 30 HP or above 20,000 CFM		4	4			253		253	380
2150	Fan coil air conditioner, chilled water, up thru 7.5 ton	Q-5	14	1.143			74.50		74.50	111
2154	Direct expansion, up thru 10 ton		8	2			131		131	195
2158	11 thru 30 ton		2	8			520		520	780
2170	Flue shutter damper	Q-9	8	2			126		126	190
2200	Furnace, electric	Q-20	2	10			640		640	960
2300	Gas or oil, under 120 MBH	Q-9	4	4			253		253	380
2340	Over 120 MBH	"	3	5.333			335		335	505
2730	Heating and ventilating unit	Q-5	2.70	5.926			385		385	575
2740	Heater, electric, wall, baseboard and quartz	1 Elec	10	.800			54		54	80
2750	Heater, electric, unit, cabinet, fan and convector	"	8	1			67.50		67.50	100
2760	Heat exchanger, shell and tube type	Q-5	1.60	10			655		655	975
2770	Plate type	Q-6	.60	40			2,700		2,700	4,050
2810	Heat pump									
2820	Air source, split, 4 thru 10 ton	Q-5	.90	17.778	Ea.		1,150		1,150	1,725
2830	15 thru 25 ton	Q-6	.80	30			2,025		2,025	3,025
2850	Single package, up thru 12 ton	Q-5	1	16			1,050		1,050	1,550
2860	Water source, up thru 15 ton	"	.90	17.778			1,150		1,150	1,725
2870	20 thru 50 ton	Q-6	.80	30			2,025		2,025	3,025
2910	Heat recovery package, up thru 20,000 CFM	Q-5	2	8			520		520	780
2920	25,000 CFM and up		1.20	13.333			870		870	1,300
2930	Heat transfer package, up thru 130 GPM		.80	20			1,300		1,300	1,950
2934	255 thru 800 GPM		.42	38.095			2,500		2,500	3,700
2940	Humidifier		10.60	1.509			98.50		98.50	147
2961	Hydronic unit heaters, up thru 200 MBH		14	1.143			74.50		74.50	111
2962	Above 200 MBH		8	2			131		131	195
2964	Valance units		32	.500			32.50		32.50	48.50
2966	Radiant floor heating									
2967	System valves, controls, manifolds	Q-5	16	1	Ea.		65.50		65.50	97.50
2968	Per room distribution		8	2			131		131	195
2970	Hydronic heating, baseboard radiation		16	1			65.50		65.50	97.50
2976	Convectors and free standing radiators		18	.889			58		58	86.50
2980	Induced draft fan, up thru 1 HP	Q-9	4.60	3.478			220		220	330
2984	1-1/2 HP thru 7-1/2 HP	"	2.20	7.273			460		460	690
2988	Infrared unit	Q-5	16	1			65.50		65.50	97.50
2992	Louvers	1 Shee	46	.174	S.F.		12.20		12.20	18.40
3000	Mechanical equipment, light items. Unit is weight, not cooling.	Q-5	.90	17.778	Ton		1,150		1,150	1,725
3600	Heavy items		1.10	14.545	"		950		950	1,425
3720	Make-up air unit, up thru 6,000 CFM		3	5.333	Ea.		350		350	520
3730	6,500 thru 30,000 CFM		1.60	10			655		655	975

23 05 Common Work Results for HVAC

23 05 05 – Selective Demolition for HVAC

23 05 05.10 HVAC Demolition

		Crew	Daily Output	Labor-Hours	Unit	Material	2023 Bare Costs Labor	Equipment	Total	Total Incl O&P
3740	35,000 thru 75,000 CFM	Q-6	1	24	Ea.		1,625		1,625	2,425
3800	Mixing boxes, constant and VAV	Q-9	18	.889			56		56	84.50
4000	Packaged terminal air conditioner, up thru 18,000 BTUH	Q-5	8	2			131		131	195
4010	24,000 thru 48,000 BTUH	"	2.80	5.714	▼		375		375	555
5000	Refrigerant compressor, reciprocating or scroll									
5010	Up thru 5 ton	1 Stpi	6	1.333	Ea.		96.50		96.50	144
5020	5.08 thru 10 ton	Q-5	6	2.667			174		174	260
5030	15 thru 50 ton	"	3	5.333			350		350	520
5040	60 thru 130 ton	Q-6	2.80	8.571	▼		580		580	865
5090	Remove refrigerant from system	1 Stpi	40	.200	Lb.		14.50		14.50	21.50
5100	Rooftop air conditioner, up thru 10 ton	Q-5	1.40	11.429	Ea.		745		745	1,125
5110	12 thru 40 ton	Q-6	1	24			1,625		1,625	2,425
5120	50 thru 140 ton		.50	48			3,250		3,250	4,850
5130	150 thru 300 ton		.30	80			5,425		5,425	8,075
6000	Self contained single package air conditioner, up thru 10 ton	Q-5	1.60	10			655		655	975
6010	15 thru 60 ton	Q-6	1.20	20			1,350		1,350	2,025
6100	Space heaters, up thru 200 MBH	Q-5	10	1.600			104		104	156
6110	Over 200 MBH		5	3.200			209		209	310
6200	Split ductless, both sections	▼	8	2			131		131	195
6300	Steam condensate meter	1 Stpi	11	.727			53		53	78.50
6600	Thru-the-wall air conditioner	L-2	8	2	▼		104		104	155
7000	Vent chimney, prefabricated, up thru 12" diameter	Q-9	94	.170	V.L.F.		10.75		10.75	16.20
7010	14" thru 36" diameter		40	.400			25.50		25.50	38
7020	38" thru 48" diameter	▼	32	.500			31.50		31.50	47.50
7030	54" thru 60" diameter	Q-10	14	1.714	▼		112		112	169
7400	Ventilators, up thru 14" neck diameter	Q-9	58	.276	Ea.		17.40		17.40	26
7410	16" thru 50" neck diameter		40	.400			25.50		25.50	38
7450	Relief vent, up thru 24" x 96"		22	.727			46		46	69
7460	48" x 60" thru 96" x 144"	▼	10	1.600			101		101	152
8000	Water chiller up thru 10 ton	Q-5	2.50	6.400			420		420	625
8010	15 thru 100 ton	Q-6	.48	50			3,375		3,375	5,050
8020	110 thru 500 ton	Q-7	.29	110			7,625		7,625	11,400
8030	600 thru 1000 ton		.23	139			9,600		9,600	14,300
8040	1100 ton and up		.20	160			11,000		11,000	16,500
8041	Absorption Chiller		.02	1600			110,500		110,500	165,000
8042	HVAC demo, water chiller plant	▼	.01	4571			315,500		315,500	471,000
8400	Window air conditioner	1 Carp	16	.500			29.50		29.50	43.50
8401	HVAC demo, water chiller, 1100 ton and up	"	12	.667	Ton		39		39	58

23 05 23 – General-Duty Valves for HVAC Piping

23 05 23.20 Valves, Bronze/Brass

		Crew	Daily Output	Labor-Hours	Unit	Material	Labor	Equipment	Total	Total Incl O&P
0010	**VALVES, BRONZE/BRASS**									
0020	Brass									
1300	Ball combination valves, shut-off and union									
1310	Solder, with strainer, drain and PT ports									
1320	1/2"	1 Stpi	17	.471	Ea.	118	34		152	181
1330	3/4"		16	.500		129	36.50		165.50	196
1340	1"		14	.571		174	41.50		215.50	253
1350	1-1/4"		12	.667		224	48.50		272.50	320
1360	1-1/2"		10	.800		330	58		388	445
1370	2"		8	1		415	72.50		487.50	565
1410	Threaded, with strainer, drain and PT ports									
1420	1/2"	1 Stpi	20	.400	Ea.	118	29		147	174

23 05 Common Work Results for HVAC

23 05 23 – General-Duty Valves for HVAC Piping

23 05 23.20 Valves, Bronze/Brass

		Crew	Daily Output	Labor-Hours	Unit	Material	2023 Bare Costs Labor	2023 Bare Costs Equipment	Total	Total Incl O&P
1430	3/4"	1 Stpi	18	.444	Ea.	129	32		161	190
1440	1"		17	.471		174	34		208	242
1450	1-1/4"		12	.667		224	48.50		272.50	320
1460	1-1/2"		11	.727		330	53		383	440
1470	2"		9	.889		415	64.50		479.50	550

23 05 23.30 Valves, Iron Body

		Crew	Daily Output	Labor-Hours	Unit	Material	Labor	Equipment	Total	Total Incl O&P
0010	**VALVES, IRON BODY** R220523-90									
0022	For grooved joint, see Section 22 11 13.48									
0100	Angle, 125 lb.									
0110	Flanged									
0116	2"	1 Plum	5	1.600	Ea.	2,700	115		2,815	3,150
0118	4"	Q-1	3	5.333		4,475	345		4,820	5,450
0120	6"	Q-2	3	8		8,900	540		9,440	10,600
0122	8"	"	2.50	9.600		15,700	645		16,345	18,200
0560	Butterfly, lug type, pneumatic operator, 2" size	1 Stpi	14	.571		630	41.50		671.50	755
0570	3"	Q-1	8	2		655	130		785	915
0580	4"	"	5	3.200		770	208		978	1,150
0590	6"	Q-2	5	4.800		1,050	325		1,375	1,625
0600	8"		4.50	5.333		1,475	360		1,835	2,125
0610	10"		4	6		1,825	405		2,230	2,625
0620	12"		3	8		2,525	540		3,065	3,575
0630	14"		2.30	10.435		3,675	700		4,375	5,075
0640	18"		1.50	16		6,650	1,075		7,725	8,900
0650	20"		1	24		8,450	1,625		10,075	11,700
0790	Butterfly, lug type, gear operated, 2" size, 200 lb. except noted	1 Plum	14	.571		775	41		816	910
0800	2-1/2"	Q-1	9	1.778		775	115		890	1,025
0810	3"		8	2		705	130		835	970
0820	4"		5	3.200		925	208		1,133	1,325
0830	5"	Q-2	5	4.800		1,150	325		1,475	1,750
0840	6"		5	4.800		1,275	325		1,600	1,875
0850	8"		4.50	5.333		1,650	360		2,010	2,325
0860	10"		4	6		2,000	405		2,405	2,775
0870	12"		3	8		3,150	540		3,690	4,275
0880	14", 150 lb.		2.30	10.435		5,675	700		6,375	7,300
0890	16", 150 lb.		1.75	13.714		9,250	920		10,170	11,600
0900	18", 150 lb.		1.50	16		11,600	1,075		12,675	14,400
0910	20", 150 lb.		1	24		15,500	1,625		17,125	19,400
0930	24", 150 lb.		.75	32		26,300	2,150		28,450	32,100
1020	Butterfly, wafer type, gear actuator, 200 lb.									
1030	2"	1 Plum	14	.571	Ea.	118	41		159	192
1040	2-1/2"	Q-1	9	1.778		120	115		235	305
1050	3"		8	2		124	130		254	330
1060	4"		5	3.200		138	208		346	460
1070	5"	Q-2	5	4.800		155	325		480	650
1080	6"		5	4.800		176	325		501	675
1090	8"		4.50	5.333		219	360		579	775
1100	10"		4	6		294	405		699	925
1110	12"		3	8		725	540		1,265	1,600
1200	Wafer type, lever actuator, 200 lb.									
1220	2"	1 Plum	14	.571	Ea.	330	41		371	425
1230	2-1/2"	Q-1	9	1.778		292	115		407	490
1240	3"		8	2		310	130		440	535

23 05 Common Work Results for HVAC

23 05 23 – General-Duty Valves for HVAC Piping

	23 05 23.30 Valves, Iron Body	Crew	Daily Output	Labor-Hours	Unit	Material	2023 Bare Costs Labor	Equipment	Total	Total Incl O&P
1250	4"	Q-1	5	3.200	Ea.	375	208		583	720
1260	5"	Q-2	5	4.800		780	325		1,105	1,325
1270	6"		5	4.800		630	325		955	1,175
1280	8"		4.50	5.333		1,125	360		1,485	1,775
1290	10"		4	6		715	405		1,120	1,375
1300	12"		3	8		1,575	540		2,115	2,550
1650	Gate, 125 lb., N.R.S.									
2150	Flanged									
2200	2"	1 Plum	5	1.600	Ea.	1,225	115		1,340	1,500
2240	2-1/2"	Q-1	5	3.200		1,250	208		1,458	1,675
2260	3"		4.50	3.556		1,400	231		1,631	1,875
2280	4"		3	5.333		2,150	345		2,495	2,900
2290	5"	Q-2	3.40	7.059		3,400	475		3,875	4,450
2300	6"		3	8		2,300	540		2,840	3,325
2320	8"		2.50	9.600		5,400	645		6,045	6,925
2340	10"		2.20	10.909		8,150	735		8,885	10,100
2360	12"		1.70	14.118		13,100	950		14,050	15,800
2370	14"		1.30	18.462		24,400	1,250		25,650	28,700
2380	16"		1	24		33,900	1,625		35,525	39,700
2420	For 250 lb. flanged, add					200%	10%			
3550	OS&Y, 125 lb., flanged									
3600	2"	1 Plum	5	1.600	Ea.	1,025	115		1,140	1,325
3640	2-1/2"	Q-1	5	3.200		935	208		1,143	1,325
3660	3"		4.50	3.556		1,025	231		1,256	1,475
3670	3-1/2"		3	5.333		1,125	345		1,470	1,775
3680	4"		3	5.333		1,500	345		1,845	2,175
3690	5"	Q-2	3.40	7.059		2,375	475		2,850	3,325
3700	6"		3	8		2,375	540		2,915	3,425
3720	8"		2.50	9.600		4,900	645		5,545	6,350
3740	10"		2.20	10.909		8,950	735		9,685	11,000
3760	12"		1.70	14.118		12,200	950		13,150	14,800
3770	14"		1.30	18.462		24,900	1,250		26,150	29,300
3780	16"		1	24		35,400	1,625		37,025	41,300
3790	18"		.80	30		42,900	2,025		44,925	50,000
3800	20"		.60	40		60,000	2,700		62,700	70,000
3830	24"		.50	48		89,000	3,225		92,225	102,500
3900	For 175 lb., flanged, add					200%	10%			
4350	Globe, OS&Y									
4540	Class 125, flanged									
4550	2"	1 Plum	5	1.600	Ea.	2,075	115		2,190	2,450
4560	2-1/2"	Q-1	5	3.200		2,075	208		2,283	2,600
4570	3"		4.50	3.556		2,200	231		2,431	2,750
4580	4"		3	5.333		3,625	345		3,970	4,525
4590	5"	Q-2	3.40	7.059		6,600	475		7,075	7,975
4600	6"		3	8		6,600	540		7,140	8,075
4610	8"		2.50	9.600		12,900	645		13,545	15,200
4612	10"		2.20	10.909		20,200	735		20,935	23,300
4614	12"		1.70	14.118		11,200	950		12,150	13,800
5040	Class 250, flanged									
5050	2"	1 Plum	4.50	1.778	Ea.	3,300	128		3,428	3,850
5060	2-1/2"	Q-1	4.50	3.556		3,900	231		4,131	4,650
5070	3"		4	4		4,450	259		4,709	5,275
5080	4"		2.70	5.926		6,525	385		6,910	7,750

23 05 Common Work Results for HVAC

23 05 23 – General-Duty Valves for HVAC Piping

23 05 23.30 Valves, Iron Body		Crew	Daily Output	Labor-Hours	Unit	Material	2023 Bare Costs Labor	Equipment	Total	Total Incl O&P
5090	5"	Q-2	3	8	Ea.	11,700	540		12,240	13,700
5100	6"		2.70	8.889		11,700	600		12,300	13,800
5110	8"		2.20	10.909		19,800	735		20,535	22,900
5120	10"		2	12		17,500	805		18,305	20,400
5130	12"	↓	1.60	15		26,200	1,000		27,200	30,400
5240	Valve sprocket rim w/chain, for 2" valve	1 Stpi	30	.267		289	19.35		308.35	350
5250	2-1/2" valve		27	.296		217	21.50		238.50	270
5260	3-1/2" valve		25	.320		455	23		478	535
5270	6" valve		20	.400		217	29		246	282
5280	8" valve		18	.444		605	32		637	715
5290	12" valve		16	.500		405	36.50		441.50	500
5300	16" valve		12	.667		900	48.50		948.50	1,075
5310	20" valve		10	.800		900	58		958	1,075
5320	36" valve	↓	8	1	↓	585	72.50		657.50	755
5450	Swing check, 125 lb., threaded									
5500	2"	1 Plum	11	.727	Ea.	285	52.50		337.50	395
5540	2-1/2"	Q-1	15	1.067		355	69		424	495
5550	3"		13	1.231		380	80		460	540
5560	4"	↓	10	1.600	↓	520	104		624	730
5950	Flanged									
5994	1"	1 Plum	7	1.143	Ea.	455	82.50		537.50	625
5998	1-1/2"		6	1.333		760	96		856	980
6000	2"	↓	5	1.600		900	115		1,015	1,175
6040	2-1/2"	Q-1	5	3.200		725	208		933	1,100
6050	3"		4.50	3.556		750	231		981	1,175
6060	4"	↓	3	5.333		1,175	345		1,520	1,825
6070	6"	Q-2	3	8		2,350	540		2,890	3,400
6080	8"		2.50	9.600		3,975	645		4,620	5,325
6090	10"		2.20	10.909		7,575	735		8,310	9,425
6100	12"		1.70	14.118		12,600	950		13,550	15,300
6102	14"		1.55	15.484		16,600	1,050		17,650	19,900
6104	16"		1.40	17.143		29,400	1,150		30,550	34,100
6110	18"		1.30	18.462		33,600	1,250		34,850	38,900
6112	20"		1	24		53,500	1,625		55,125	61,500
6114	24"	↓	.75	32	↓	60,000	2,150		62,150	69,000
6160	For 250 lb. flanged, add					200%	20%			
6600	Silent check, bronze trim									
6610	Compact wafer type, for 125 or 150 lb. flanges									
6630	1-1/2"	1 Plum	11	.727	Ea.	163	52.50		215.50	258
6640	2"	"	9	.889		199	64		263	315
6650	2-1/2"	Q-1	9	1.778		217	115		332	410
6660	3"		8	2		231	130		361	445
6670	4"	↓	5	3.200		295	208		503	635
6680	5"	Q-2	6	4		390	269		659	830
6690	6"		6	4		520	269		789	970
6700	8"		4.50	5.333		880	360		1,240	1,500
6710	10"		4	6		1,525	405		1,930	2,275
6720	12"	↓	3	8	↓	2,900	540		3,440	4,000
6740	For 250 or 300 lb. flanges, thru 6" no change									
6741	For 8" and 10", add				Ea.	11%	10%			
6750	Twin disc									
6752	2"	1 Plum	9	.889	Ea.	790	64		854	965
6754	4"	Q-1	5	3.200	↓	1,300	208		1,508	1,725

23 05 Common Work Results for HVAC

23 05 23 – General-Duty Valves for HVAC Piping

23 05 23.30 Valves, Iron Body

		Crew	Daily Output	Labor-Hours	Unit	Material	2023 Bare Costs Labor	Equipment	Total	Total Incl O&P
6756	6"	Q-2	5	4.800	Ea.	1,925	325		2,250	2,575
6758	8"		4.50	5.333		2,950	360		3,310	3,750
6760	10"		4	6		4,700	405		5,105	5,750
6762	12"		3	8		6,100	540		6,640	7,500
6764	18"		1.50	16		26,300	1,075		27,375	30,500
6766	24"	↓	.75	32	↓	37,000	2,150		39,150	43,900
6800	Full flange type, 150 lb.									
6810	1"	1 Plum	14	.571	Ea.	184	41		225	264
6811	1-1/4"		12	.667		194	48		242	285
6812	1-1/2"		11	.727		225	52.50		277.50	325
6813	2"	↓	9	.889		258	64		322	380
6814	2-1/2"	Q-1	9	1.778		310	115		425	515
6815	3"		8	2		325	130		455	550
6816	4"	↓	5	3.200		400	208		608	750
6817	5"	Q-2	6	4		630	269		899	1,100
6818	6"		5	4.800		830	325		1,155	1,400
6819	8"		4.50	5.333		1,400	360		1,760	2,075
6820	10"	↓	4	6		1,775	405		2,180	2,550
6840	For 250 lb., add				↓	30%	10%			
6900	Globe type, 125 lb.									
6910	2"	1 Plum	9	.889	Ea.	360	64		424	495
6911	2-1/2"	Q-1	9	1.778		485	115		600	705
6912	3"		8	2		430	130		560	670
6913	4"	↓	5	3.200		770	208		978	1,150
6914	5"	Q-2	6	4		1,075	269		1,344	1,575
6915	6"		5	4.800		1,350	325		1,675	1,950
6916	8"		4.50	5.333		2,450	360		2,810	3,225
6917	10"		4	6		3,100	405		3,505	4,000
6918	12"		3	8		5,350	540		5,890	6,675
6919	14"		2.30	10.435		7,025	700		7,725	8,775
6920	16"		1.75	13.714		7,775	920		8,695	9,925
6921	18"		1.50	16		11,200	1,075		12,275	14,000
6922	20"		1	24		13,600	1,625		15,225	17,400
6923	24"	↓	.75	32		21,300	2,150		23,450	26,600
6940	For 250 lb., add				↓	40%	10%			
6980	Screwed end type, 125 lb.									
6981	1"	1 Plum	19	.421	Ea.	174	30.50		204.50	236
6982	1-1/4"		15	.533		229	38.50		267.50	310
6983	1-1/2"		13	.615		278	44.50		322.50	370
6984	2"	↓	11	.727		380	52.50		432.50	500

23 05 23.50 Valves, Multipurpose

		Crew	Daily Output	Labor-Hours	Unit	Material	Labor	Equipment	Total	Total Incl O&P
0010	**VALVES, MULTIPURPOSE**									
0100	Functions as a shut off, balancing, check & metering valve									
1000	Cast iron body									
1010	Threaded									
1020	1-1/2" size	1 Stpi	11	.727	Ea.	505	53		558	635
1030	2" size	"	8	1		615	72.50		687.50	785
1040	2-1/2" size	Q-5	5	3.200	↓	665	209		874	1,050
1200	Flanged									
1210	3" size	Q-5	4.20	3.810	Ea.	765	249		1,014	1,200
1220	4" size	"	3	5.333		1,550	350		1,900	2,225
1230	5" size	Q-6	3.80	6.316		1,825	430		2,255	2,675

23 05 Common Work Results for HVAC

23 05 23 – General-Duty Valves for HVAC Piping

23 05 23.50 Valves, Multipurpose

		Crew	Daily Output	Labor-Hours	Unit	Material	2023 Bare Costs Labor	Equipment	Total	Total Incl O&P
1240	6" size	Q-6	3	8	Ea.	2,200	540		2,740	3,225
1250	8" size		2.50	9.600		3,950	650		4,600	5,325
1260	10" size		2.20	10.909		5,675	740		6,415	7,325
1270	12" size		2.10	11.429		10,200	775		10,975	12,400
1280	14" size	↓	2	12		15,900	815		16,715	18,700

23 05 23.70 Valves, Semi-Steel

		Crew	Daily Output	Labor-Hours	Unit	Material	Labor	Equipment	Total	Total Incl O&P
0010	**VALVES, SEMI-STEEL** R220523-90									
1020	Lubricated plug valve, threaded, 200 psi									
1030	1/2"	1 Plum	18	.444	Ea.	134	32		166	196
1040	3/4"		16	.500		169	36		205	240
1050	1"		14	.571		193	41		234	274
1060	1-1/4"		12	.667		169	48		217	258
1070	1-1/2"		11	.727		201	52.50		253.50	299
1080	2"	↓	8	1		615	72		687	785
1090	2-1/2"	Q-1	5	3.200		675	208		883	1,050
1100	3"	"	4.50	3.556		315	231		546	690
6990	Flanged, 200 psi									
7000	2"	1 Plum	8	1	Ea.	605	72		677	770
7010	2-1/2"	Q-1	5	3.200		905	208		1,113	1,300
7020	3"		4.50	3.556		1,125	231		1,356	1,600
7030	4"		3	5.333		1,550	345		1,895	2,225
7036	5"	↓	2.50	6.400		970	415		1,385	1,700
7040	6"	Q-2	3	8		1,275	540		1,815	2,200
7050	8"		2.50	9.600		2,275	645		2,920	3,475
7060	10"		2.20	10.909		3,800	735		4,535	5,275
7070	12"	↓	1.70	14.118		6,175	950		7,125	8,200

23 05 23.80 Valves, Steel

		Crew	Daily Output	Labor-Hours	Unit	Material	Labor	Equipment	Total	Total Incl O&P
0010	**VALVES, STEEL** R220523-90									
0800	Cast									
1350	Check valve, swing type, 150 lb., flanged									
1370	1"	1 Plum	10	.800	Ea.	970	57.50		1,027.50	1,150
1400	2"	"	8	1		955	72		1,027	1,150
1440	2-1/2"	Q-1	5	3.200		1,100	208		1,308	1,500
1450	3"		4.50	3.556		1,175	231		1,406	1,625
1460	4"	↓	3	5.333		1,900	345		2,245	2,625
1470	6"	Q-2	3	8		2,925	540		3,465	4,025
1480	8"		2.50	9.600		4,325	645		4,970	5,750
1490	10"		2.20	10.909		6,650	735		7,385	8,425
1500	12"		1.70	14.118		11,900	950		12,850	14,500
1510	14"		1.30	18.462		15,500	1,250		16,750	18,900
1520	16"	↓	1	24		17,300	1,625		18,925	21,500
1540	For 300 lb., flanged, add					50%	15%			
1548	For 600 lb., flanged, add					110%	20%			
1571	300 lb., 2"	1 Plum	7.40	1.081		1,200	78		1,278	1,425
1572	2-1/2"	Q-1	4.20	3.810		1,800	247		2,047	2,350
1573	3"		4	4		1,800	259		2,059	2,350
1574	4"	↓	2.80	5.714		2,450	370		2,820	3,250
1575	6"	Q-2	2.90	8.276		4,750	555		5,305	6,050
1576	8"		2.40	10		6,975	675		7,650	8,675
1577	10"		2.10	11.429		10,500	770		11,270	12,800
1578	12"		1.60	15		15,200	1,000		16,200	18,200
1579	14"	↓	1.20	20		22,200	1,350		23,550	26,400

23 05 Common Work Results for HVAC

23 05 23 – General-Duty Valves for HVAC Piping

23 05 23.80 Valves, Steel

		Crew	Daily Output	Labor-Hours	Unit	Material	2023 Bare Costs Labor	Equipment	Total	Total Incl O&P
1581	16"	Q-2	.90	26.667	Ea.	28,300	1,800		30,100	33,800
1950	Gate valve, 150 lb., flanged									
2000	2"	1 Plum	8	1	Ea.	975	72		1,047	1,175
2040	2-1/2"	Q-1	5	3.200		1,300	208		1,508	1,750
2050	3"		4.50	3.556		1,400	231		1,631	1,900
2060	4"	↓	3	5.333		1,950	345		2,295	2,675
2070	6"	Q-2	3	8		3,025	540		3,565	4,125
2080	8"		2.50	9.600		4,750	645		5,395	6,200
2090	10"		2.20	10.909		6,550	735		7,285	8,300
2100	12"		1.70	14.118		9,100	950		10,050	11,400
2110	14"		1.30	18.462		14,500	1,250		15,750	17,800
2120	16"		1	24		18,700	1,625		20,325	23,000
2130	18"		.80	30		24,500	2,025		26,525	29,900
2140	20"	↓	.60	40	↓	28,300	2,700		31,000	35,100
2650	300 lb., flanged									
2700	2"	1 Plum	7.40	1.081	Ea.	1,300	78		1,378	1,550
2740	2-1/2"	Q-1	4.20	3.810		1,775	247		2,022	2,325
2750	3"		4	4		1,900	259		2,159	2,450
2760	4"	↓	2.80	5.714		2,650	370		3,020	3,450
2770	6"	Q-2	2.90	8.276		4,475	555		5,030	5,750
2780	8"		2.40	10		7,200	675		7,875	8,925
2790	10"		2.10	11.429		10,100	770		10,870	12,300
2800	12"		1.60	15		15,400	1,000		16,400	18,400
2810	14"		1.20	20		27,300	1,350		28,650	32,100
2820	16"		.90	26.667		34,300	1,800		36,100	40,400
2830	18"		.70	34.286		48,400	2,300		50,700	57,000
2840	20"	↓	.50	48	↓	53,500	3,225		56,725	64,000
3650	Globe valve, 150 lb., flanged									
3700	2"	1 Plum	8	1	Ea.	1,200	72		1,272	1,400
3740	2-1/2"	Q-1	5	3.200		1,500	208		1,708	1,950
3750	3"		4.50	3.556		1,675	231		1,906	2,200
3760	4"	↓	3	5.333		2,200	345		2,545	2,950
3770	6"	Q-2	3	8		3,450	540		3,990	4,600
3780	8"		2.50	9.600		6,475	645		7,120	8,100
3790	10"		2.20	10.909		11,900	735		12,635	14,200
3800	12"	↓	1.70	14.118	↓	16,300	950		17,250	19,300
4080	300 lb., flanged									
4100	2"	1 Plum	7.40	1.081	Ea.	1,600	78		1,678	1,875
4140	2-1/2"	Q-1	4.20	3.810		2,175	247		2,422	2,750
4150	3"		4	4		2,175	259		2,434	2,750
4160	4"	↓	2.80	5.714		3,000	370		3,370	3,850
4170	6"	Q-2	2.90	8.276		5,400	555		5,955	6,775
4180	8"		2.40	10		10,600	675		11,275	12,600
4190	10"		2.10	11.429		17,600	770		18,370	20,600
4200	12"	↓	1.60	15		21,100	1,000		22,100	24,800
4680	600 lb., flanged									
4700	2"	1 Plum	7	1.143	Ea.	2,225	82.50		2,307.50	2,575
4740	2-1/2"	Q-1	4	4		3,575	259		3,834	4,300
4750	3"		3.60	4.444		3,575	288		3,863	4,350
4760	4"	↓	2.50	6.400		5,500	415		5,915	6,675
4770	6"	Q-2	2.60	9.231		11,600	620		12,220	13,700
4780	8"	"	2.10	11.429	↓	25,100	770		25,870	28,800
4800	Silent check, 316 S.S. trim									

23 05 Common Work Results for HVAC

23 05 23 – General-Duty Valves for HVAC Piping

23 05 23.80 Valves, Steel

		Crew	Daily Output	Labor-Hours	Unit	Material	2023 Bare Costs Labor	2023 Bare Costs Equipment	Total	Total Incl O&P
4810	Full flange type, 150 lb.									
4811	1"	1 Plum	14	.571	Ea.	915	41		956	1,050
4812	1-1/4"		12	.667		745	48		793	885
4813	1-1/2"		11	.727		1,000	52.50		1,052.50	1,175
4814	2"	▼	9	.889		1,200	64		1,264	1,425
4815	2-1/2"	Q-1	9	1.778		1,450	115		1,565	1,775
4816	3"		8	2		1,700	130		1,830	2,050
4817	4"	▼	5	3.200		2,300	208		2,508	2,850
4818	5"	Q-2	6	4		2,900	269		3,169	3,575
4819	6"		5	4.800		3,750	325		4,075	4,600
4820	8"		4.50	5.333		5,425	360		5,785	6,475
4821	10"	▼	4	6		7,625	405		8,030	9,000
4840	For 300 lb., add					20%	10%			
4860	For 600 lb., add				▼	50%	15%			
4900	Globe type, 150 lb.									
4910	2"	1 Plum	9	.889	Ea.	1,425	64		1,489	1,675
4911	2-1/2"	Q-1	9	1.778		1,725	115		1,840	2,075
4912	3"		8	2		1,925	130		2,055	2,325
4913	4"	▼	5	3.200		2,550	208		2,758	3,100
4914	5"	Q-2	6	4		3,200	269		3,469	3,925
4915	6"		5	4.800		3,950	325		4,275	4,825
4916	8"		4.50	5.333		5,525	360		5,885	6,600
4917	10"		4	6		9,575	405		9,980	11,100
4918	12"		3	8		11,800	540		12,340	13,700
4919	14"		2.30	10.435		12,400	700		13,100	14,700
4920	16"		1.75	13.714		17,300	920		18,220	20,400
4921	18"	▼	1.50	16		18,100	1,075		19,175	21,600
4940	For 300 lb., add					30%	10%			
4960	For 600 lb., add				▼	60%	15%			
5150	Forged									
5340	Ball valve, 1,500 psi, threaded, 1/4" size	1 Plum	24	.333	Ea.	77.50	24		101.50	121
5350	3/8"		24	.333		77.50	24		101.50	121
5360	1/2"		24	.333		127	24		151	176
5370	3/4"		20	.400		127	29		156	183
5380	1"		19	.421		193	30.50		223.50	257
5390	1-1/4"		15	.533		212	38.50		250.50	291
5400	1-1/2"		13	.615		370	44.50		414.50	475
5410	2"	▼	11	.727		400	52.50		452.50	520
5460	Ball valve, 800 lb., socket weld, 1/4" size	Q-15	19	.842		77.50	54.50	3.38	135.38	170
5470	3/8"		19	.842		77.50	54.50	3.38	135.38	170
5480	1/2"		19	.842		94	54.50	3.38	151.88	189
5490	3/4"		19	.842		125	54.50	3.38	182.88	223
5500	1"		15	1.067		156	69	4.28	229.28	280
5510	1-1/4"		13	1.231		212	80	4.94	296.94	355
5520	1-1/2"		11	1.455		271	94.50	5.85	371.35	445
5530	2"	▼	8.50	1.882	▼	360	122	7.55	489.55	585
5550	Ball valve, 150 lb., flanged									
5560	4"	Q-1	3	5.333	Ea.	2,475	345		2,820	3,250
5570	6"	Q-2	3	8	▼	5,500	540		6,040	6,850
5580	8"	"	2.50	9.600		9,900	645		10,545	11,900
5650	Check valve, class 800, horizontal									
5651	Socket									
5652	1/4"	Q-15	19	.842	Ea.	90	54.50	3.38	147.88	184

23 05 Common Work Results for HVAC

23 05 23 – General-Duty Valves for HVAC Piping

23 05 23.80 Valves, Steel

		Crew	Daily Output	Labor-Hours	Unit	Material	2023 Bare Costs Labor	Equipment	Total	Total Incl O&P
5654	3/8"	Q-15	19	.842	Ea.	90	54.50	3.38	147.88	184
5656	1/2"		19	.842		90	54.50	3.38	147.88	184
5658	3/4"		19	.842		96.50	54.50	3.38	154.38	191
5660	1"		15	1.067		114	69	4.28	187.28	233
5662	1-1/4"		13	1.231		222	80	4.94	306.94	370
5664	1-1/2"		11	1.455		222	94.50	5.85	322.35	390
5666	2"	▼	8.50	1.882	▼	310	122	7.55	439.55	530
5698	Threaded									
5700	1/4"	1 Plum	24	.333	Ea.	85	24		109	130
5720	3/8"		24	.333		85	24		109	130
5730	1/2"		24	.333		50	24		74	91
5740	3/4"		20	.400		59.50	29		88.50	109
5750	1"		19	.421		79	30.50		109.50	132
5760	1-1/4"		15	.533		152	38.50		190.50	225
5770	1-1/2"		13	.615		161	44.50		205.50	243
5780	2"	▼	11	.727		223	52.50		275.50	325
5840	For class 150, flanged, add					100%	15%			
5860	For class 300, flanged, add				▼	120%	20%			
6100	Gate, class 800, OS&Y, socket									
6102	3/8"	Q-15	19	.842	Ea.	58	54.50	3.38	115.88	149
6103	1/2"		19	.842		58	54.50	3.38	115.88	149
6104	3/4"		19	.842		63.50	54.50	3.38	121.38	155
6105	1"		15	1.067		77	69	4.28	150.28	192
6106	1-1/4"		13	1.231		145	80	4.94	229.94	284
6107	1-1/2"		11	1.455		145	94.50	5.85	245.35	305
6108	2"	▼	8.50	1.882	▼	188	122	7.55	317.55	395
6118	Threaded									
6120	3/8"	1 Plum	24	.333	Ea.	58	24		82	100
6130	1/2"		24	.333		58	24		82	100
6140	3/4"		20	.400		63.50	29		92.50	113
6150	1"		19	.421		77	30.50		107.50	130
6160	1-1/4"		15	.533		96	38.50		134.50	163
6170	1-1/2"		13	.615		145	44.50		189.50	226
6180	2"	▼	11	.727		188	52.50		240.50	285
6260	For OS&Y, flanged, add				▼	100%	20%			
6700	Globe, OS&Y, class 800, socket									
6710	1/4"	Q-15	19	.842	Ea.	89	54.50	3.38	146.88	183
6720	3/8"		19	.842		89	54.50	3.38	146.88	183
6730	1/2"		19	.842		89	54.50	3.38	146.88	183
6740	3/4"		19	.842		102	54.50	3.38	159.88	197
6750	1"		15	1.067		133	69	4.28	206.28	254
6760	1-1/4"		13	1.231		260	80	4.94	344.94	410
6770	1-1/2"		11	1.455		260	94.50	5.85	360.35	435
6780	2"	▼	8.50	1.882		335	122	7.55	464.55	555
6860	For OS&Y, flanged, add				▼	300%	20%			
6880	Threaded									
6882	1/4"	1 Plum	24	.333	Ea.	89	24		113	134
6884	3/8"		24	.333		89	24		113	134
6886	1/2"		24	.333		89	24		113	134
6888	3/4"		20	.400		102	29		131	155
6890	1"		19	.421		133	30.50		163.50	191
6892	1-1/4"		15	.533		260	38.50		298.50	345
6894	1-1/2"		13	.615		260	44.50		304.50	350

23 05 Common Work Results for HVAC

23 05 23 – General-Duty Valves for HVAC Piping

23 05 23.80 Valves, Steel

		Crew	Daily Output	Labor-Hours	Unit	Material	2023 Bare Costs Labor	Equipment	Total	Total Incl O&P
6896	2"	1 Plum	11	.727	Ea.	335	52.50		387.50	445

23 05 23.90 Valves, Stainless Steel

		Crew	Daily Output	Labor-Hours	Unit	Material	2023 Bare Costs Labor	Equipment	Total	Total Incl O&P
0010	**VALVES, STAINLESS STEEL** R220523-90									
1610	Ball, threaded 1/4"	1 Stpi	24	.333	Ea.	51.50	24		75.50	92.50
1620	3/8"		24	.333		51.50	24		75.50	92.50
1630	1/2"		22	.364		52.50	26.50		79	97
1640	3/4"		20	.400		85	29		114	137
1650	1"		19	.421		105	30.50		135.50	162
1660	1-1/4"		15	.533		197	38.50		235.50	275
1670	1-1/2"		13	.615		206	44.50		250.50	293
1680	2"		11	.727		272	53		325	380
1700	Check, 200 lb., threaded									
1710	1/4"	1 Plum	24	.333	Ea.	144	24		168	195
1720	1/2"		22	.364		69.50	26		95.50	116
1730	3/4"		20	.400		143	29		172	201
1750	1"		19	.421		163	30.50		193.50	224
1760	1-1/2"		13	.615		360	44.50		404.50	465
1770	2"		11	.727		615	52.50		667.50	755
1800	150 lb., flanged									
1810	2-1/2"	Q-1	5	3.200	Ea.	1,375	208		1,583	1,800
1820	3"		4.50	3.556		2,000	231		2,231	2,550
1830	4"		3	5.333		3,000	345		3,345	3,825
1840	6"	Q-2	3	8		5,300	540		5,840	6,625
1850	8"	"	2.50	9.600		10,800	645		11,445	12,900
2100	Gate, OS&Y, 150 lb., flanged									
2120	1/2"	1 Plum	18	.444	Ea.	510	32		542	610
2140	3/4"		16	.500		490	36		526	595
2150	1"		14	.571		615	41		656	740
2160	1-1/2"		11	.727		1,200	52.50		1,252.50	1,375
2170	2"		8	1		1,425	72		1,497	1,650
2180	2-1/2"	Q-1	5	3.200		1,825	208		2,033	2,300
2190	3"		4.50	3.556		1,825	231		2,056	2,350
2200	4"		3	5.333		2,700	345		3,045	3,500
2205	5"		2.80	5.714		5,550	370		5,920	6,650
2210	6"	Q-2	3	8		5,050	540		5,590	6,350
2220	8"		2.50	9.600		8,775	645		9,420	10,600
2230	10"		2.30	10.435		15,200	700		15,900	17,800
2240	12"		1.90	12.632		20,300	850		21,150	23,700
2260	For 300 lb., flanged, add					120%	15%			
2600	600 lb., flanged									
2620	1/2"	1 Plum	16	.500	Ea.	188	36		224	261
2640	3/4"		14	.571		203	41		244	285
2650	1"		12	.667		244	48		292	340
2660	1-1/2"		10	.800		390	57.50		447.50	515
2670	2"		7	1.143		535	82.50		617.50	715
2680	2-1/2"	Q-1	4	4		6,675	259		6,934	7,700
2690	3"	"	3.60	4.444		6,675	288		6,963	7,750
3100	Globe, OS&Y, 150 lb., flanged									
3120	1/2"	1 Plum	18	.444	Ea.	485	32		517	585
3140	3/4"		16	.500		525	36		561	635
3150	1"		14	.571		690	41		731	815
3160	1-1/2"		11	.727		1,075	52.50		1,127.50	1,250

23 05 Common Work Results for HVAC

23 05 23 – General-Duty Valves for HVAC Piping

23 05 23.90 Valves, Stainless Steel

		Crew	Daily Output	Labor-Hours	Unit	Material	2023 Bare Costs Labor	Equipment	Total	Total Incl O&P
3170	2"	1 Plum	8	1	Ea.	1,425	72		1,497	1,650
3180	2-1/2"	Q-1	5	3.200		3,100	208		3,308	3,700
3190	3"		4.50	3.556		3,100	231		3,331	3,750
3200	4"		3	5.333		4,950	345		5,295	5,975
3210	6"	Q-2	3	8		8,325	540		8,865	9,975
5000	Silent check, 316 S.S. body and trim									
5010	Compact wafer type, 300 lb.									
5020	1"	1 Plum	14	.571	Ea.	1,675	41		1,716	1,900
5021	1-1/4"		12	.667		1,675	48		1,723	1,925
5022	1-1/2"		11	.727		1,875	52.50		1,927.50	2,150
5023	2"		9	.889		2,150	64		2,214	2,475
5024	2-1/2"	Q-1	9	1.778		2,725	115		2,840	3,175
5025	3"	"	8	2		3,400	130		3,530	3,925
5100	Full flange wafer type, 150 lb.									
5110	1"	1 Plum	14	.571	Ea.	1,100	41		1,141	1,250
5111	1-1/4"		12	.667		1,175	48		1,223	1,375
5112	1-1/2"		11	.727		1,350	52.50		1,402.50	1,550
5113	2"		9	.889		1,750	64		1,814	2,025
5114	2-1/2"	Q-1	9	1.778		2,075	115		2,190	2,450
5115	3"		8	2		2,350	130		2,480	2,800
5116	4"		5	3.200		3,525	208		3,733	4,175
5117	5"	Q-2	6	4		4,075	269		4,344	4,900
5118	6"		5	4.800		5,125	325		5,450	6,100
5119	8"		4.50	5.333		5,550	360		5,910	6,625
5120	10"		4	6		14,000	405		14,405	16,000
5200	Globe type, 300 lb.									
5210	2"	1 Plum	9	.889	Ea.	2,100	64		2,164	2,400
5211	2-1/2"	Q-1	9	1.778		2,575	115		2,690	3,025
5212	3"		8	2		3,175	130		3,305	3,700
5213	4"		5	3.200		4,425	208		4,633	5,175
5214	5"	Q-2	6	4		5,750	269		6,019	6,725
5215	6"		5	4.800		7,000	325		7,325	8,175
5216	8"		4.50	5.333		9,900	360		10,260	11,400
5217	10"		4	6		9,725	405		10,130	11,300
5300	Screwed end type, 300 lb.									
5310	1/2"	1 Plum	24	.333	Ea.	91	24		115	136
5311	3/4"		20	.400		108	29		137	162
5312	1"		19	.421		125	30.50		155.50	182
5313	1-1/4"		15	.533		167	38.50		205.50	242
5314	1-1/2"		13	.615		180	44.50		224.50	264
5315	2"		11	.727		222	52.50		274.50	320

23 05 93 – Testing, Adjusting, and Balancing for HVAC

23 05 93.10 Balancing, Air

		Crew	Daily Output	Labor-Hours	Unit	Material	2023 Bare Costs Labor	Equipment	Total	Total Incl O&P
0010	**BALANCING, AIR** (Subcontractor's quote incl. material and labor)									
0900	Heating and ventilating equipment									
1000	Centrifugal fans, utility sets				Ea.				420	420
1100	Heating and ventilating unit								630	630
1200	In-line fan								630	630
1300	Propeller and wall fan								119	119
1400	Roof exhaust fan								280	280
2000	Air conditioning equipment, central station								910	910
2100	Built-up low pressure unit								840	840

23 05 Common Work Results for HVAC

23 05 93 – Testing, Adjusting, and Balancing for HVAC

23 05 93.10 Balancing, Air

		Crew	Daily Output	Labor-Hours	Unit	Material	2023 Bare Costs Labor	2023 Bare Costs Equipment	Total	Total Incl O&P
2200	Built-up high pressure unit				Ea.				980	980
2300	Built-up high pressure dual duct								1,550	1,550
2400	Built-up variable volume								1,825	1,825
2500	Multi-zone A.C. and heating unit								630	630
2600	For each zone over one, add								140	140
2700	Package A.C. unit								350	350
2800	Rooftop heating and cooling unit								490	490
3000	Supply, return, exhaust, registers & diffusers, avg. height ceiling								84	84
3100	High ceiling								126	126
3200	Floor height								70	70
3300	Off mixing box								56	56
3500	Induction unit								91	91
3600	Lab fume hood								420	420
3700	Linear supply								210	210
3800	Linear supply high								245	245
4000	Linear return								70	70
4100	Light troffers								84	84
4200	Moduline - master								84	84
4300	Moduline - slaves								42	42
4400	Regenerators								560	560
4500	Taps into ceiling plenums								105	105
4600	Variable volume boxes								84	84

23 05 93.20 Balancing, Water

		Crew	Daily Output	Labor-Hours	Unit	Material	Labor	Equipment	Total	Total Incl O&P
0010	**BALANCING, WATER** (Subcontractor's quote incl. material and labor)									
0050	Air cooled condenser				Ea.				256	256
0080	Boiler								515	515
0100	Cabinet unit heater								88	88
0200	Chiller								620	620
0300	Convector								73	73
0400	Converter								365	365
0500	Cooling tower								475	475
0600	Fan coil unit, unit ventilator								132	132
0700	Fin tube and radiant panels								146	146
0800	Main and duct re-heat coils								135	135
0810	Heat exchanger								135	135
0900	Main balancing cocks								110	110
1000	Pumps								320	320
1100	Unit heater								102	102

23 05 93.50 Piping, Testing

		Crew	Daily Output	Labor-Hours	Unit	Material	Labor	Equipment	Total	Total Incl O&P
0010	**PIPING, TESTING**									
0100	Nondestructive testing									
0110	Nondestructive hydraulic pressure test, isolate & 1 hr. hold									
0120	1" - 4" pipe									
0140	0-250 L.F.	1 Stpi	1.33	6.015	Ea.		435		435	650
0160	250-500 L.F.	"	.80	10			725		725	1,075
0180	500-1000 L.F.	Q-5	1.14	14.035			915		915	1,375
0200	1000-2000 L.F.		.80	20			1,300		1,300	1,950
0320	0-250 L.F.		1	16			1,050		1,050	1,550
0340	250-500 L.F.		.73	21.918			1,425		1,425	2,125
0360	500-1000 L.F.		.53	30.189			1,975		1,975	2,950
0380	1000-2000 L.F.		.38	42.105			2,750		2,750	4,100
1000	Pneumatic pressure test, includes soaping joints									

23 05 Common Work Results for HVAC

23 05 93 – Testing, Adjusting, and Balancing for HVAC

23 05 93.50 Piping, Testing

		Crew	Daily Output	Labor-Hours	Unit	Material	2023 Bare Costs Labor	Equipment	Total	Total Incl O&P
1120	1" - 4" pipe									
1140	0-250 L.F.	Q-5	2.67	5.993	Ea.	14.40	390		404.40	600
1160	250-500 L.F.		1.33	12.030		29	785		814	1,200
1180	500-1000 L.F.		.80	20		43	1,300		1,343	2,000
1200	1000-2000 L.F.		.50	32		57.50	2,100		2,157.50	3,200
1300	6" - 10" pipe									
1320	0-250 L.F.	Q-5	1.33	12.030	Ea.	14.40	785		799.40	1,200
1340	250-500 L.F.		.67	23.881		29	1,550		1,579	2,350
1360	500-1000 L.F.		.40	40		57.50	2,600		2,657.50	3,975
1380	1000-2000 L.F.		.25	64		72	4,175		4,247	6,300
2000	X-Ray of welds									
2110	2" diam.	1 Stpi	8	1	Ea.	22.50	72.50		95	133
2120	3" diam.		8	1		22.50	72.50		95	133
2130	4" diam.		8	1		34	72.50		106.50	146
2140	6" diam.		8	1		34	72.50		106.50	146
2150	8" diam.		6.60	1.212		34	88		122	169
2160	10" diam.		6	1.333		45.50	96.50		142	194
3000	Liquid penetration of welds									
3110	2" diam.	1 Stpi	14	.571	Ea.	15.50	41.50		57	79
3120	3" diam.		13.60	.588		15.50	42.50		58	80.50
3130	4" diam.		13.40	.597		15.50	43.50		59	81.50
3140	6" diam.		13.20	.606		15.50	44		59.50	82.50
3150	8" diam.		13	.615		23.50	44.50		68	92
3160	10" diam.		12.80	.625		23.50	45.50		69	93

23 07 HVAC Insulation

23 07 13 – Duct Insulation

23 07 13.10 Duct Thermal Insulation

			Crew	Daily Output	Labor-Hours	Unit	Material	2023 Bare Costs Labor	Equipment	Total	Total Incl O&P
0010	**DUCT THERMAL INSULATION**										
0110	Insulation req'd. is based on the surface size/area to be covered										
3000	Ductwork										
3020	Blanket type, fiberglass, flexible										
3030	Fire rated for grease and hazardous exhaust ducts										
3060	1-1/2" thick		Q-14	84	.190	S.F.	5	11.20		16.20	22.50
3090	Fire rated for plenums										
3100	1/2" x 24" x 25'		Q-14	1.94	8.247	Roll	5.10	485		490.10	745
3110	1/2" x 24" x 25'			98	.163	S.F.	.10	9.60		9.70	14.75
3120	1/2" x 48" x 25'			1.04	15.385	Roll	345	905		1,250	1,750
3126	1/2" x 48" x 25'			104	.154	S.F.	3.47	9.05		12.52	17.60
3140	FSK vapor barrier wrap, .75 lb. density										
3160	1" thick	G	Q-14	350	.046	S.F.	.61	2.68		3.29	4.78
3170	1-1/2" thick	G		320	.050		.59	2.94		3.53	5.15
3180	2" thick	G		300	.053		1.38	3.13		4.51	6.30
3190	3" thick	G		260	.062		1.23	3.61		4.84	6.90
3200	4" thick	G		242	.066		.89	3.88		4.77	6.95
3210	Vinyl jacket, same as FSK										
3280	Unfaced, 1 lb. density										
3310	1" thick	G	Q-14	360	.044	S.F.	.34	2.61		2.95	4.36
3320	1-1/2" thick	G		330	.048		.47	2.85		3.32	4.88
3330	2" thick	G		310	.052		.63	3.03		3.66	5.35
3400	FSK facing, 1 lb. density										

23 07 HVAC Insulation

23 07 13 – Duct Insulation

23 07 13.10 Duct Thermal Insulation

			Crew	Daily Output	Labor-Hours	Unit	Material	2023 Bare Costs Labor	Equipment	Total	Total Incl O&P
3420		1-1/2" thick	G Q-14	310	.052	S.F.	1.11	3.03		4.14	5.85
3430		2" thick	G "	300	.053	"	.90	3.13		4.03	5.80
3450	FSK facing, 1.5 lb. density										
3470		1-1/2" thick	G Q-14	300	.053	S.F.	1.31	3.13		4.44	6.25
3480		2" thick	G "	290	.055	"	1.75	3.24		4.99	6.90
3730	Sheet insulation										
3760	Polyethylene foam, closed cell, UV resistant										
3770	Standard temperature (-90°F to +212°F)										
3771		1/4" thick	G Q-14	450	.036	S.F.	2.54	2.09		4.63	6
3772		3/8" thick	G	440	.036		3.63	2.14		5.77	7.25
3773		1/2" thick	G	420	.038		4.44	2.24		6.68	8.30
3774		3/4" thick	G	400	.040		6.35	2.35		8.70	10.60
3775		1" thick	G	380	.042		8.60	2.47		11.07	13.25
3776		1-1/2" thick	G	360	.044		13.55	2.61		16.16	18.95
3777		2" thick	G	340	.047		17.95	2.76		20.71	24
3778		2-1/2" thick	G	320	.050		23	2.94		25.94	30
3779	Adhesive (see line 7878)										
3780	Foam, rubber										
3782		1" thick	G 1 Stpi	50	.160	S.F.	5.90	11.60		17.50	24
3795	Finishes										
3800		Stainless steel woven mesh	Q-14	100	.160	S.F.	.79	9.40		10.19	15.20
3810		For .010" stainless steel, add		160	.100		6.85	5.85		12.70	16.50
3820		18 oz. fiberglass cloth, pasted on		170	.094		1.54	5.55		7.09	10.15
3900		8 oz. canvas, pasted on		180	.089		.27	5.20		5.47	8.30
3940		For .016" aluminum jacket, add		200	.080		2.13	4.70		6.83	9.55
7000	Board insulation										
7020	Mineral wool, 1200° F										
7022	6 lb. density, plain										
7024		1" thick	G Q-14	370	.043	S.F.	1.05	2.54		3.59	5.05
7026		1-1/2" thick	G	350	.046		.48	2.68		3.16	4.64
7028		2" thick	G	330	.048		.63	2.85		3.48	5.05
7030		3" thick	G	300	.053		.78	3.13		3.91	5.65
7032		4" thick	G	280	.057		1.28	3.36		4.64	6.55
7038	8 lb. density, plain										
7040		1" thick	G Q-14	360	.044	S.F.	.39	2.61		3	4.42
7042		1-1/2" thick	G	340	.047		.57	2.76		3.33	4.86
7044		2" thick	G	320	.050		.77	2.94		3.71	5.35
7046		3" thick	G	290	.055		1.16	3.24		4.40	6.25
7048		4" thick	G	270	.059		1.52	3.48		5	6.95
7060	10 lb. density, plain										
7062		1" thick	G Q-14	350	.046	S.F.	.54	2.68		3.22	4.70
7064		1-1/2" thick	G	330	.048		.81	2.85		3.66	5.25
7066		2" thick	G	310	.052		1.08	3.03		4.11	5.85
7068		3" thick	G	280	.057		1.63	3.36		4.99	6.95
7070		4" thick	G	260	.062		2.07	3.61		5.68	7.85
7878	Contact cement, quart can					Ea.	16.50			16.50	18.15

23 07 16 – HVAC Equipment Insulation

23 07 16.10 HVAC Equipment Thermal Insulation

			Crew	Daily Output	Labor-Hours	Unit	Material	Labor	Equipment	Total	Total Incl O&P
0010	**HVAC EQUIPMENT THERMAL INSULATION**										
0110	Insulation req'd. is based on the surface size/area to be covered										
1000	Boiler, 1-1/2" calcium silicate only		G Q-14	110	.145	S.F.	8.95	8.55		17.50	23
1020		Plus 2" fiberglass	G "	80	.200	"	14.55	11.75		26.30	34

23 07 HVAC Insulation

23 07 16 – HVAC Equipment Insulation

23 07 16.10 HVAC Equipment Thermal Insulation

		Crew	Daily Output	Labor-Hours	Unit	Material	2023 Bare Costs Labor	Equipment	Total	Total Incl O&P
2000	Breeching, 2" calcium silicate									
2020	Rectangular G	Q-14	42	.381	S.F.	10.15	22.50		32.65	45
2040	Round G	"	38.70	.413	"	10.15	24.50		34.65	48
2300	Calcium silicate block, +200°F to +1,200°F									
2310	On irregular surfaces, valves and fittings									
2340	1" thick G	Q-14	30	.533	S.F.	5.65	31.50		37.15	54.50
2360	1-1/2" thick G		25	.640		6.25	37.50		43.75	64.50
2380	2" thick G		22	.727		7.95	42.50		50.45	74
2400	3" thick G	↓	18	.889	↓	12.60	52		64.60	94
2410	On plane surfaces									
2420	1" thick G	Q-14	126	.127	S.F.	5.65	7.45		13.10	17.65
2430	1-1/2" thick G		120	.133		6.25	7.85		14.10	18.90
2440	2" thick G		100	.160		7.95	9.40		17.35	23
2450	3" thick G	↓	70	.229	↓	12.60	13.40		26	34.50

23 09 Instrumentation and Control for HVAC

23 09 13 – Instrumentation and Control Devices for HVAC

23 09 13.60 Water Level Controls

		Crew	Daily Output	Labor-Hours	Unit	Material	2023 Bare Costs Labor	Equipment	Total	Total Incl O&P
0010	**WATER LEVEL CONTROLS**									
1000	Electric water feeder	1 Stpi	12	.667	Ea.	585	48.50		633.50	710
2000	Feeder cut-off combination									
2100	Steam system up to 5,000 sq. ft.	1 Stpi	12	.667	Ea.	1,300	48.50		1,348.50	1,500
2200	Steam system above 5,000 sq. ft.		12	.667		1,600	48.50		1,648.50	1,825
2300	Steam and hot water, high pressure	↓	10	.800	↓	1,875	58		1,933	2,125
3000	Low water cut-off for hot water boiler, 50 psi maximum									
3100	1" top & bottom equalizing pipes, manual reset	1 Stpi	14	.571	Ea.	705	41.50		746.50	835
3200	1" top & bottom equalizing pipes		14	.571		560	41.50		601.50	675
3300	2-1/2" side connection for nipple-to-boiler		14	.571		630	41.50		671.50	755
4000	Low water cut-off for low pressure steam with quick hook-up ftgs.									
4100	For installation in gauge glass tappings	1 Stpi	16	.500	Ea.	540	36.50		576.50	650
4200	Built-in type, 2-1/2" tap, 3-1/8" insertion		16	.500		430	36.50		466.50	530
4300	Built-in type, 2-1/2" tap, 1-3/4" insertion		16	.500		465	36.50		501.50	565
4400	Side connection to 2-1/2" tapping		16	.500		500	36.50		536.50	605
5000	Pump control, low water cut-off and alarm switch	↓	14	.571	↓	1,400	41.50		1,441.50	1,575
9000	Water gauges, complete									
9010	Rough brass, wheel type									
9020	125 psi at 350°F									
9030	3/8" pipe size	1 Stpi	11	.727	Ea.	79.50	53		132.50	166
9040	1/2" pipe size	"	10	.800	"	97	58		155	194
9060	200 psi at 400°F									
9070	3/8" pipe size	1 Stpi	11	.727	Ea.	113	53		166	203
9080	1/2" pipe size		10	.800		110	58		168	209
9090	3/4" pipe size	↓	9	.889	↓	126	64.50		190.50	235
9130	Rough brass, chain lever type									
9140	250 psi at 400°F									
9200	Polished brass, wheel type									
9210	200 psi at 400°F									
9220	3/8" pipe size	1 Stpi	11	.727	Ea.	212	53		265	310
9230	1/2" pipe size		10	.800		215	58		273	325
9240	3/4" pipe size	↓	9	.889	↓	227	64.50		291.50	345
9260	Polished brass, chain lever type									

23 09 Instrumentation and Control for HVAC

23 09 13 – Instrumentation and Control Devices for HVAC

23 09 13.60 Water Level Controls		Crew	Daily Output	Labor-Hours	Unit	Material	2023 Bare Costs Labor	2023 Bare Costs Equipment	Total	Total Incl O&P
9270	250 psi at 400°F									
9280	1/2" pipe size	1 Stpi	10	.800	Ea.	310	58		368	425
9290	3/4" pipe size	"	9	.889	"	340	64.50		404.50	465
9400	Bronze, high pressure, ASME									
9410	1/2" pipe size	1 Stpi	10	.800	Ea.	390	58		448	515
9420	3/4" pipe size	"	9	.889	"	415	64.50		479.50	550
9460	Chain lever type									
9470	1/2" pipe size	1 Stpi	10	.800	Ea.	495	58		553	630
9480	3/4" pipe size	"	9	.889	"	520	64.50		584.50	670
9500	316 stainless steel, high pressure, ASME									
9510	500 psi at 450°F									
9520	1/2" pipe size	1 Stpi	10	.800	Ea.	1,075	58		1,133	1,275
9530	3/4" pipe size	"	9	.889	"	1,050	64.50		1,114.50	1,250

23 09 23 – Direct-Digital Control System for HVAC

23 09 23.10 Control Components/DDC Systems

		Crew	Daily Output	Labor-Hours	Unit	Material	2023 Bare Costs Labor	2023 Bare Costs Equipment	Total	Total Incl O&P
0010	**CONTROL COMPONENTS/DDC SYSTEMS** (Sub's quote incl. M & L)									
0100	Analog inputs									
0110	Sensors (avg. 50' run in 1/2" EMT)									
0120	Duct temperature				Ea.				465	465
0130	Space temperature								665	665
0140	Duct humidity, +/- 3%								595	595
0150	Space humidity, +/- 2%								1,150	1,150
0160	Duct static pressure								680	680
0170	CFM/transducer								920	920
0172	Water temperature								940	940
0174	Water flow								3,450	3,450
0176	Water pressure differential								975	975
0177	Steam flow								2,400	2,400
0178	Steam pressure								1,025	1,025
0180	KW/transducer								1,350	1,350
0182	KWH totalization (not incl. elec. meter pulse xmtr.)								625	625
0190	Space static pressure								1,075	1,075
1000	Analog outputs (avg. 50' run in 1/2" EMT)									
1010	P/I transducer				Ea.				635	635
1020	Analog output, matl. in MUX								305	305
1030	Pneumatic (not incl. control device)								645	645
1040	Electric (not incl. control device)								380	380
2000	Status (alarms)									
2100	Digital inputs (avg. 50' run in 1/2" EMT)									
2110	Freeze				Ea.				435	435
2120	Fire								395	395
2130	Differential pressure (air)	2 Elec	3	5.333		385	360		745	960
2140	Differential pressure (water)								975	975
2150	Current sensor								435	435
2160	Duct high temperature thermostat								570	570
2170	Duct smoke detector								705	705
2200	Digital output (avg. 50' run in 1/2" EMT)									
2210	Start/stop				Ea.				340	340
2220	On/off (maintained contact)				"				585	585
3000	Controller MUX panel, incl. function boards									
3100	48 point				Ea.				5,275	5,275
3110	128 point				"				7,225	7,225

23 09 Instrumentation and Control for HVAC

23 09 23 – Direct-Digital Control System for HVAC

23 09 23.10 Control Components/DDC Systems

		Crew	Daily Output	Labor-Hours	Unit	Material	2023 Bare Costs Labor	Equipment	Total	Total Incl O&P
3200	DDC controller (avg. 50' run in conduit)									
3210	Mechanical room									
3214	16 point controller (incl. 120 volt/1 phase power supply)				Ea.				3,275	3,275
3229	32 point controller (incl. 120 volt/1 phase power supply)				"				5,425	5,425
3230	Includes software programming and checkout									
3260	Space									
3266	VAV terminal box (incl. space temp. sensor)				Ea.				840	840
3280	Host computer (avg. 50' run in conduit)									
3281	Package complete with PC, keyboard,									
3282	printer, monitor, basic software				Ea.				3,150	3,150
4000	Front end costs									
4100	Computer (P.C.) with software program				Ea.				6,350	6,350
4200	Color graphics software									3,925	3,925
4300	Color graphics slides									490	490
4350	Additional printer									980	980
4400	Communications trunk cable				L.F.				3.80	3.80
4500	Engineering labor (not incl. dftg.)				Point				94	94
4600	Calibration labor									120	120
4700	Start-up, checkout labor									120	120
4800	Programming labor, as req'd										
5000	Communications bus (data transmission cable)									
5010	#18 twisted shielded pair in 1/2" EMT conduit				C.L.F.				380	380
8000	Applications software										
8050	Basic maintenance manager software (not incl. data base entry)				Ea.				1,950	1,950
8100	Time program				Point				6.85	6.85
8120	Duty cycle									13.65	13.65
8140	Optimum start/stop									41.50	41.50
8160	Demand limiting									20.50	20.50
8180	Enthalpy program									41.50	41.50
8200	Boiler optimization				Ea.				1,225	1,225
8220	Chiller optimization				"				1,625	1,625
8240	Custom applications										
8260	Cost varies with complexity										

23 09 43 – Pneumatic Control System for HVAC

23 09 43.10 Pneumatic Control Systems

		Crew	Daily Output	Labor-Hours	Unit	Material	2023 Bare Costs Labor	Equipment	Total	Total Incl O&P
0010	**PNEUMATIC CONTROL SYSTEMS** R230500-10									
0011	Including a nominal 50' of tubing. Add control panelboard if req'd.									
0100	Heating and ventilating, split system									
0200	Mixed air control, economizer cycle, panel readout, tubing									
0220	Up to 10 tons [G]	Q-19	.68	35.294	Ea.	6,600	2,325		8,925	10,700
0240	For 10 to 20 tons [G]		.63	37.915		7,425	2,500		9,925	11,900
0260	For over 20 tons [G]		.58	41.096		8,050	2,700		10,750	12,900
0270	Enthalpy cycle, up to 10 tons		.50	48.387		7,625	3,200		10,825	13,200
0280	For 10 to 20 tons		.46	52.174		8,250	3,450		11,700	14,200
0290	For over 20 tons		.42	56.604		8,225	3,725		11,950	14,600
0300	Heating coil, hot water, 3 way valve,									
0320	Freezestat, limit control on discharge, readout	Q-5	.69	23.088	Ea.	4,900	1,500		6,400	7,625
0500	Cooling coil, chilled water, room									
0520	Thermostat, 3 way valve	Q-5	2	8	Ea.	2,100	520		2,620	3,100
0600	Cooling tower, fan cycle, damper control,									
0620	Control system including water readout in/out at panel	Q-19	.67	35.821		8,675	2,375		11,050	13,100
1000	Unit ventilator, day/night operation,									

23 09 Instrumentation and Control for HVAC

23 09 43 – Pneumatic Control System for HVAC

23 09 43.10 Pneumatic Control Systems

		Crew	Daily Output	Labor-Hours	Unit	Material	2023 Bare Costs Labor	Equipment	Total	Total Incl O&P
1100	freezestat, ASHRAE, cycle 2	Q-19	.91	26.374	Ea.	4,650	1,750		6,400	7,700
2000	Compensated hot water from boiler, valve control,									
2100	readout and reset at panel, up to 60 GPM	Q-19	.55	43.956	Ea.	9,425	2,900		12,325	14,700
2120	For 120 GPM		.51	47.059		9,275	3,100		12,375	14,800
2140	For 240 GPM		.49	49.180		10,500	3,250		13,750	16,400
3000	Boiler room combustion air, damper to 5 S.F., controls		1.37	17.582		4,325	1,150		5,475	6,500
3500	Fan coil, heating and cooling valves, 4 pipe control system		3	8		2,050	530		2,580	3,025
3600	Heat exchanger system controls		.86	27.907		4,075	1,850		5,925	7,225
3900	Multizone control (one per zone), includes thermostat, damper									
3910	motor and reset of discharge temperature	Q-5	.51	31.373	Ea.	4,175	2,050		6,225	7,650
4000	Pneumatic thermostat, including controlling room radiator valve	"	2.43	6.593		1,250	430		1,680	2,025
4040	Program energy saving optimizer G	Q-19	1.21	19.786		10,800	1,300		12,100	13,900
4060	Pump control system	"	3	8		1,925	530		2,455	2,900
4080	Reheat coil control system, not incl. coil	Q-5	2.43	6.593		1,625	430		2,055	2,450
4500	Air supply for pneumatic control system									
4600	Tank mounted duplex compressor, starter, alternator,									
4620	piping, dryer, PRV station and filter									
4630	1/2 HP	Q-19	.68	35.139	Ea.	16,900	2,325		19,225	22,100
4640	3/4 HP		.64	37.383		16,300	2,475		18,775	21,600
4650	1 HP		.61	39.539		18,500	2,600		21,100	24,200
4660	1-1/2 HP		.58	41.739		19,000	2,750		21,750	25,000
4680	3 HP		.55	43.956		25,900	2,900		28,800	32,800
4690	5 HP		.42	57.143		49,200	3,775		52,975	59,500
4800	Main air supply, includes 3/8" copper main and labor	Q-5	1.82	8.791	C.L.F.	570	575		1,145	1,475
7000	Static pressure control for air handling unit, includes pressure									
7010	sensor, receiver controller, readout and damper motors	Q-19	.64	37.383	Ea.	13,500	2,475		15,975	18,500
8600	VAV boxes, incl. thermostat, damper motor, reheat coil & tubing	Q-5	1.46	10.989	"	1,950	720		2,670	3,200

23 09 53 – Pneumatic and Electric Control System for HVAC

23 09 53.10 Control Components

		Crew	Daily Output	Labor-Hours	Unit	Material	Labor	Equipment	Total	Total Incl O&P
0010	**CONTROL COMPONENTS**									
0500	Aquastats									
0508	Immersion type									
0510	High/low limit, breaks contact w/temp rise	1 Stpi	4	2	Ea.	410	145		555	665
0514	Sequencing, break 2 switches w/temp rise		4	2		228	145		373	465
0518	Circulating, makes contact w/temp rise		4	2		305	145		450	550
0600	Carbon monoxide detector system									
0606	Panel	1 Stpi	4	2	Ea.	1,550	145		1,695	1,925
0610	Sensor		7.30	1.096		905	79.50		984.50	1,125
0680	Controller for VAV box, includes actuator		7.30	1.096		535	79.50		614.50	710
0700	Controller, receiver									
0730	Pneumatic, panel mount, single input	1 Plum	8	1	Ea.	285	72		357	420
0740	With conversion mounting bracket		8	1		1,325	72		1,397	1,550
0750	Dual input, with control point adjustment		7	1.143		1,325	82.50		1,407.50	1,600
0850	Electric, single snap switch	1 Elec	4	2		720	135		855	995
0860	Dual snap switches		3	2.667		970	180		1,150	1,350
0870	Humidity controller		8	1		400	67.50		467.50	540
0880	Load limiting controller		8	1		695	67.50		762.50	865
0890	Temperature controller		8	1		300	67.50		367.50	430
0900	Control panel readout									
0910	Panel up to 12 indicators	1 Stpi	1.20	6.667	Ea.	450	485		935	1,225
0914	Panel up to 24 indicators		.86	9.302		415	675		1,090	1,450
0918	Panel up to 48 indicators		.50	16		1,075	1,150		2,225	2,925

23 09 Instrumentation and Control for HVAC

23 09 53 – Pneumatic and Electric Control System for HVAC

23 09 53.10 Control Components		Crew	Daily Output	Labor-Hours	Unit	Material	2023 Bare Costs Labor	2023 Bare Costs Equipment	Total	Total Incl O&P
1000	Enthalpy control, boiler water temperature control									
1010	governed by outdoor temperature, with timer	1 Elec	3	2.667	Ea.	590	180		770	915
1300	Energy control/monitor									
1320	BTU computer meter and controller	1 Stpi	1	8	Ea.	965	580		1,545	1,950
1600	Flow meters									
1610	Gas	1 Stpi	4	2	Ea.	125	145		270	355
1620	Liquid	"	4	2	"	126	145		271	355
1640	Freezestat									
1644	20' sensing element, adjustable	1 Stpi	3.50	2.286	Ea.	96	166		262	355
2000	Gauges, pressure or vacuum									
2100	2" diameter dial	1 Stpi	32	.250	Ea.	12.40	18.15		30.55	40.50
2200	2-1/2" diameter dial		32	.250		15.35	18.15		33.50	44
2300	3-1/2" diameter dial		32	.250		33	18.15		51.15	63
2400	4-1/2" diameter dial	▼	32	.250	▼	37.50	18.15		55.65	68
2700	Flanged iron case, black ring									
2800	3-1/2" diameter dial	1 Stpi	32	.250	Ea.	175	18.15		193.15	220
2900	4-1/2" diameter dial		32	.250		158	18.15		176.15	200
3000	6" diameter dial	▼	32	.250		250	18.15		268.15	300
3010	Steel case, 0-300 psi									
3012	2" diameter dial	1 Stpi	16	.500	Ea.	8.80	36.50		45.30	63.50
3014	4" diameter dial	"	16	.500	"	24	36.50		60.50	80.50
3020	Aluminum case, 0-300 psi									
3022	3-1/2" diameter dial	1 Stpi	16	.500	Ea.	21	36.50		57.50	77.50
3024	4-1/2" diameter dial		16	.500		35	36.50		71.50	92.50
3026	6" diameter dial		16	.500		284	36.50		320.50	365
3028	8-1/2" diameter dial	▼	16	.500		495	36.50		531.50	600
3030	Brass case, 0-300 psi									
3032	2" diameter dial	1 Stpi	16	.500	Ea.	27	36.50		63.50	84
3034	4-1/2" diameter dial	"	16	.500	"	128	36.50		164.50	195
3040	Steel case, high pressure, 0-10,000 psi									
3042	4-1/2" diameter dial	1 Stpi	16	.500	Ea.	300	36.50		336.50	385
3044	6-1/2" diameter dial		16	.500		228	36.50		264.50	305
3046	8-1/2" diameter dial	▼	16	.500	▼	590	36.50		626.50	705
3080	Pressure gauge, differential, magnehelic									
3084	0-2" W.C., with air filter kit	1 Stpi	6	1.333	Ea.	42.50	96.50		139	191
3300	For compound pressure-vacuum, add					18%				
3350	Humidistat									
3360	Pneumatic operation									
3361	Room humidistat, direct acting	1 Stpi	12	.667	Ea.	550	48.50		598.50	675
3362	Room humidistat, reverse acting		12	.667		173	48.50		221.50	262
3363	Room humidity transmitter		17	.471		670	34		704	790
3364	Duct mounted controller		12	.667		395	48.50		443.50	500
3365	Duct mounted transmitter		12	.667		670	48.50		718.50	805
3366	Humidity indicator, 3-1/2"	▼	28	.286		320	20.50		340.50	380
3390	Electric operated	1 Shee	8	1	▼	69	70		139	182
3400	Relays									
3430	Pneumatic/electric	1 Plum	16	.500	Ea.	560	36		596	670
3440	Pneumatic proportioning		8	1		490	72		562	645
3450	Pneumatic switching		12	.667		400	48		448	510
3460	Selector, 3 point		6	1.333		315	96		411	490
3470	Pneumatic time delay	▼	8	1		575	72		647	735
3500	Sensor, air operated									
3520	Humidity	1 Plum	16	.500	Ea.	395	36		431	485

23 09 Instrumentation and Control for HVAC

23 09 53 – Pneumatic and Electric Control System for HVAC

23 09 53.10 Control Components		Crew	Daily Output	Labor-Hours	Unit	Material	2023 Bare Costs Labor	2023 Bare Costs Equipment	Total	Total Incl O&P
3540	Pressure	1 Plum	16	.500	Ea.	167	36		203	238
3560	Temperature	↓	12	.667	↓	700	48		748	840
3600	Electric operated									
3620	Humidity	1 Elec	8	1	Ea.	215	67.50		282.50	335
3650	Pressure		8	1		375	67.50		442.50	510
3680	Temperature	↓	10	.800	↓	167	54		221	264
3700	Switches									
3710	Minimum position									
3720	Electrical	1 Stpi	4	2	Ea.	77.50	145		222.50	300
3730	Pneumatic	"	4	2	"	360	145		505	610
4000	Thermometers									
4100	Dial type, 3-1/2" diameter, vapor type, union connection	1 Stpi	32	.250	Ea.	226	18.15		244.15	276
4120	Liquid type, union connection		32	.250		435	18.15		453.15	505
4130	Remote reading, 15' capillary		32	.250		470	18.15		488.15	540
4500	Stem type, 6-1/2" case, 2" stem, 1/2" NPT		32	.250		60	18.15		78.15	93
4520	4" stem, 1/2" NPT		32	.250		73.50	18.15		91.65	108
4600	9" case, 3-1/2" stem, 3/4" NPT		28	.286		48	20.50		68.50	84
4620	6" stem, 3/4" NPT		28	.286		57.50	20.50		78	94.50
4640	8" stem, 3/4" NPT		28	.286		192	20.50		212.50	242
4660	12" stem, 1" NPT	↓	26	.308	↓	188	22.50		210.50	241
4670	Bi-metal, dial type, steel case brass stem									
4672	2" dial, 4" - 9" stem	1 Stpi	16	.500	Ea.	45.50	36.50		82	105
4673	2-1/2" dial, 4" - 9" stem		16	.500		45.50	36.50		82	105
4674	3-1/2" dial, 4" - 9" stem		16	.500		56.50	36.50		93	116
4680	Mercury filled, industrial, union connection type									
4682	Angle stem, 7" scale	1 Stpi	16	.500	Ea.	61.50	36.50		98	122
4683	9" scale		16	.500		170	36.50		206.50	241
4684	12" scale		16	.500		218	36.50		254.50	293
4686	Straight stem, 7" scale		16	.500		166	36.50		202.50	237
4687	9" scale		16	.500		217	36.50		253.50	292
4688	12" scale	↓	16	.500		261	36.50		297.50	340
4690	Mercury filled, industrial, separable socket type, with well									
4692	Angle stem, with socket, 7" scale	1 Stpi	16	.500	Ea.	200	36.50		236.50	274
4693	9" scale		16	.500		200	36.50		236.50	274
4694	12" scale		16	.500		237	36.50		273.50	315
4696	Straight stem, with socket, 7" scale		16	.500		156	36.50		192.50	226
4697	9" scale		16	.500		156	36.50		192.50	226
4698	12" scale	↓	16	.500		192	36.50		228.50	265
5000	Thermostats									
5030	Manual	1 Stpi	8	1	Ea.	51.50	72.50		124	165
5040	1 set back, electric, timed [G]		8	1		101	72.50		173.50	219
5050	2 set back, electric, timed [G]		8	1		251	72.50		323.50	385
5100	Locking cover	↓	20	.400		27	29		56	73
5200	24 hour, automatic, clock [G]	1 Shee	8	1		226	70		296	355
5220	Electric, low voltage, 2 wire	1 Elec	13	.615		39	41.50		80.50	105
5230	3 wire		10	.800		44.50	54		98.50	129
5236	Heating/cooling, low voltage, with clock	↓	8	1		227	67.50		294.50	350
5240	Pneumatic									
5250	Single temp., single pressure	1 Stpi	8	1	Ea.	545	72.50		617.50	710
5251	Dual pressure		8	1		760	72.50		832.50	950
5252	Dual temp., dual pressure		8	1		900	72.50		972.50	1,100
5253	Reverse acting w/averaging element		8	1		233	72.50		305.50	365
5254	Heating-cooling w/deadband	↓	8	1		1,225	72.50		1,297.50	1,425

23 09 Instrumentation and Control for HVAC

23 09 53 – Pneumatic and Electric Control System for HVAC

23 09 53.10 Control Components		Crew	Daily Output	Labor-Hours	Unit	Material	2023 Bare Costs Labor	Equipment	Total	Total Incl O&P
5255	Integral w/piston top valve actuator	1 Stpi	8	1	Ea.	385	72.50		457.50	535
5256	Dual temp., dual pressure		8	1		395	72.50		467.50	540
5257	Low limit, 8' averaging element		8	1		430	72.50		502.50	585
5258	Room single temp. proportional		8	1		138	72.50		210.50	260
5260	Dual temp, direct acting for VAV fan		8	1		275	72.50		347.50	415
5262	Capillary tube type, 20', 30°F to 100°F	↓	8	1	↓	315	72.50		387.50	460
5300	Transmitter, pneumatic									
5320	Temperature averaging element	Q-1	8	2	Ea.	251	130		381	470
5350	Pressure differential	1 Plum	7	1.143		2,100	82.50		2,182.50	2,425
5370	Humidity, duct		8	1		670	72		742	840
5380	Room		12	.667		670	48		718	810
5390	Temperature, with averaging element	↓	6	1.333	↓	400	96		496	585
5500	Timer/time clocks									
5510	7 day, 12 hr. battery	1 Stpi	2.60	3.077	Ea.	320	223		543	685
5600	Recorders									
5610	Hydrograph humidity, wall mtd., aluminum case, grad. chart									
5612	8"	1 Stpi	1.60	5	Ea.	485	365		850	1,075
5614	10"	"	1.60	5	"	1,850	365		2,215	2,600
5620	Thermo-hydrograph, wall mtd., grad. chart, 5' SS probe									
5622	8"	1 Stpi	1.60	5	Ea.	1,100	365		1,465	1,750
5624	10"	"	1.60	5	"	2,050	365		2,415	2,800
5630	Time of operation, wall mtd., 1 pen cap, 24 hr. clock									
5632	6"	1 Stpi	1.60	5	Ea.	645	365		1,010	1,250
5634	8"	"	1.60	5	"	1,225	365		1,590	1,900
5640	Pressure & vacuum, bourdon tube type									
5642	Flush mount, 1 pen									
5644	4"	1 Stpi	1.60	5	Ea.	880	365		1,245	1,500
5645	6"		1.60	5		405	365		770	985
5646	8"		1.60	5		995	365		1,360	1,650
5648	10"	↓	1.60	5	↓	1,875	365		2,240	2,600
6000	Valves, motorized zone									
6100	Sweat connections, 1/2" C x C	1 Stpi	20	.400	Ea.	107	29		136	162
6110	3/4" C x C		20	.400		107	29		136	162
6120	1" C x C		19	.421		140	30.50		170.50	200
6140	1/2" C x C, with end switch, 2 wire		20	.400		106	29		135	160
6150	3/4" C x C, with end switch, 2 wire		20	.400		106	29		135	160
6160	1" C x C, with end switch, 2 wire	↓	19	.421	↓	130	30.50		160.50	190
7090	Valves, motor controlled, including actuator									
7100	Electric motor actuated									
7200	Brass, two way, screwed									
7210	1/2" pipe size	L-6	36	.333	Ea.	395	23.50		418.50	470
7220	3/4" pipe size		30	.400		670	28		698	775
7230	1" pipe size		28	.429		775	30		805	900
7240	1-1/2" pipe size		19	.632		870	44.50		914.50	1,025
7250	2" pipe size	↓	16	.750	↓	1,225	53		1,278	1,425
7350	Brass, three way, screwed									
7360	1/2" pipe size	L-6	33	.364	Ea.	400	25.50		425.50	480
7370	3/4" pipe size		27	.444		485	31.50		516.50	575
7380	1" pipe size		25.50	.471		605	33		638	720
7384	1-1/4" pipe size		21	.571		820	40.50		860.50	960
7390	1-1/2" pipe size		17	.706		460	50		510	580
7400	2" pipe size	↓	14	.857	↓	615	60.50		675.50	765
7550	Iron body, two way, flanged									

23 09 Instrumentation and Control for HVAC

23 09 53 – Pneumatic and Electric Control System for HVAC

23 09 53.10 Control Components		Crew	Daily Output	Labor-Hours	Unit	Material	2023 Bare Costs Labor	2023 Bare Costs Equipment	Total	Total Incl O&P
7560	2-1/2" pipe size	L-6	4	3	Ea.	545	211		756	915
7570	3" pipe size		3	4		1,025	282		1,307	1,550
7580	4" pipe size		2	6		1,475	425		1,900	2,225
7850	Iron body, three way, flanged									
7860	2-1/2" pipe size	L-6	3	4	Ea.	1,000	282		1,282	1,525
7870	3" pipe size		2.50	4.800		1,175	340		1,515	1,800
7880	4" pipe size		2	6		1,850	425		2,275	2,650
8000	Pneumatic, air operated									
8050	Brass, two way, screwed									
8060	1/2" pipe size, class 250	1 Plum	24	.333	Ea.	117	24		141	165
8070	3/4" pipe size, class 250		20	.400		165	29		194	225
8080	1" pipe size, class 250		19	.421		214	30.50		244.50	280
8090	1-1/4" pipe size, class 125		15	.533		296	38.50		334.50	385
8100	1-1/2" pipe size, class 125		13	.615		390	44.50		434.50	495
8110	2" pipe size, class 125		11	.727		470	52.50		522.50	600
8180	Brass, three way, screwed									
8190	1/2" pipe size, class 250	1 Plum	22	.364	Ea.	141	26		167	195
8200	3/4" pipe size, class 250		18	.444		205	32		237	273
8210	1" pipe size, class 250		17	.471		205	34		239	276
8214	1-1/4" pipe size, class 250		14	.571		415	41		456	520
8220	1-1/2" pipe size, class 125		11	.727		460	52.50		512.50	585
8230	2" pipe size, class 125		9	.889		615	64		679	770
8450	Iron body, two way, flanged									
8510	2-1/2" pipe size, class 125	Q-1	5	3.200	Ea.	890	208		1,098	1,300
8520	3" pipe size, class 125		4.50	3.556		1,025	231		1,256	1,475
8530	4" pipe size, class 125		3	5.333		1,475	345		1,820	2,125
8540	5" pipe size, class 125	Q-2	3.40	7.059		2,575	475		3,050	3,550
8550	6" pipe size, class 125	"	3	8		4,025	540		4,565	5,225
8560	Iron body, three way, flanged									
8570	2-1/2" pipe size, class 125	Q-1	4.50	3.556	Ea.	1,000	231		1,231	1,450
8580	3" pipe size, class 125		4	4		1,175	259		1,434	1,675
8590	4" pipe size, class 125		2.50	6.400		4,175	415		4,590	5,225
8600	6" pipe size, class 125	Q-2	3	8		3,600	540		4,140	4,775
9005	Pneumatic system misc. components									
9010	Adding/subtracting repeater	1 Stpi	20	.400	Ea.	480	29		509	575
9020	Adjustable ratio network		16	.500		345	36.50		381.50	435
9030	Comparator		20	.400		455	29		484	545
9040	Cumulator									
9041	Air switching	1 Stpi	20	.400	Ea.	370	29		399	450
9042	Averaging		20	.400		545	29		574	645
9043	2:1 ratio		20	.400		625	29		654	730
9044	Sequencing		20	.400		212	29		241	277
9045	Two-position		16	.500		545	36.50		581.50	655
9046	Two-position pilot		16	.500		730	36.50		766.50	860
9050	Damper actuator									
9051	For smoke control	1 Stpi	8	1	Ea.	550	72.50		622.50	715
9052	For ventilation	"	8	1	"	420	72.50		492.50	570
9053	Series duplex pedestal mounted									
9054	For inlet vanes on fans, compressors	1 Stpi	6	1.333	Ea.	4,200	96.50		4,296.50	4,775
9060	Enthalpy logic center		16	.500		625	36.50		661.50	740
9070	High/low pressure selector		22	.364		152	26.50		178.50	207
9080	Signal limiter		20	.400		266	29		295	335
9081	Transmitter		28	.286		89	20.50		109.50	129

23 09 Instrumentation and Control for HVAC

23 09 53 – Pneumatic and Electric Control System for HVAC

23 09 53.10 Control Components		Crew	Daily Output	Labor-Hours	Unit	Material	2023 Bare Costs Labor	2023 Bare Costs Equipment	Total	Total Incl O&P
9090	Optimal start									
9092	Mass temperature transmitter	1 Stpi	18	.444	Ea.	415	32		447	505
9100	Step controller with positioner, time delay restrictor									
9110	recycler air valve, switches and cam settings									
9112	With cabinet									
9113	6 points	1 Stpi	4	2	Ea.	1,225	145		1,370	1,575
9114	6 points, 6 manual sequences		2	4		1,675	290		1,965	2,275
9115	8 points	↓	3	2.667	↓	1,475	193		1,668	1,925
9200	Pressure controller and switches									
9210	High static pressure limit	1 Stpi	8	1	Ea.	605	72.50		677.50	775
9220	Pressure transmitter		8	1		640	72.50		712.50	815
9230	Differential pressure transmitter		8	1		2,275	72.50		2,347.50	2,625
9240	Static pressure transmitter		8	1		1,325	72.50		1,397.50	1,575
9250	Proportional-only control, single input		6	1.333		1,325	96.50		1,421.50	1,600
9260	Proportional plus integral, single input		6	1.333		1,625	96.50		1,721.50	1,950
9270	Proportional-only, dual input		6	1.333		1,825	96.50		1,921.50	2,150
9280	Proportional plus integral, dual input		6	1.333		2,500	96.50		2,596.50	2,900
9281	Time delay for above proportional units		16	.500		310	36.50		346.50	400
9290	Proportional/2 position controller units		6	1.333		915	96.50		1,011.50	1,150
9300	Differential pressure control direct/reverse	↓	6	1.333	↓	795	96.50		891.50	1,025
9310	Air pressure reducing valve									
9311	1/8" size	1 Stpi	18	.444	Ea.	84.50	32		116.50	141
9315	Precision valve, 1/4" size		17	.471		550	34		584	655
9320	Air flow controller		12	.667		445	48.50		493.50	560
9330	Booster relay volume amplifier		18	.444		292	32		324	370
9340	Series restrictor, straight		60	.133		10.30	9.65		19.95	26
9341	T-fitting		40	.200		13.20	14.50		27.70	36
9342	In-line adjustable		48	.167		101	12.10		113.10	129
9350	Diode tee		40	.200		39	14.50		53.50	64.50
9351	Restrictor tee		40	.200		43.50	14.50		58	69
9360	Pneumatic gradual switch		8	1		910	72.50		982.50	1,100
9361	Selector switch		8	1		315	72.50		387.50	455
9370	Electro-pneumatic motor driven servo		10	.800		1,925	58		1,983	2,175
9390	Fan control switch and mounting base		16	.500		178	36.50		214.50	250
9400	Circulating pump sequencer	↓	14	.571	↓	2,075	41.50		2,116.50	2,325
9410	Pneumatic tubing, fittings and accessories									
9414	Tubing, urethane									
9415	1/8" OD x 1/16" ID	1 Stpi	120	.067	L.F.	1.64	4.84		6.48	9
9416	1/4" OD x 1/8" ID		115	.070		3.53	5.05		8.58	11.45
9417	5/32" OD x 3/32" ID	↓	110	.073	↓	2.06	5.30		7.36	10.10
9420	Coupling, straight									
9422	Barb x barb									
9423	1/4" x 5/32"	1 Stpi	160	.050	Ea.	2.72	3.63		6.35	8.40
9424	1/4" x 1/4"		158	.051		2.35	3.67		6.02	8.10
9425	3/8" x 3/8"		154	.052		3.99	3.77		7.76	10
9426	3/8" x 1/4"		150	.053		1.88	3.87		5.75	7.80
9427	1/2" x 1/4"		148	.054		1.67	3.92		5.59	7.70
9428	1/2" x 3/8"		144	.056		1.87	4.03		5.90	8.05
9429	1/2" x 1/2"		140	.057		4.33	4.15		8.48	10.95
9440	Tube x tube									
9441	1/4" x 1/4"	1 Stpi	100	.080	Ea.	3.91	5.80		9.71	12.95
9442	3/8" x 1/4"		96	.083		7.90	6.05		13.95	17.70
9443	3/8" x 3/8"	↓	92	.087		4.87	6.30		11.17	14.75

23 09 Instrumentation and Control for HVAC

23 09 53 – Pneumatic and Electric Control System for HVAC

23 09 53.10 Control Components		Crew	Daily Output	Labor-Hours	Unit	Material	2023 Bare Costs Labor	Equipment	Total	Total Incl O&P
9444	1/2" x 3/8"	1 Stpi	88	.091	Ea.	8.05	6.60		14.65	18.70
9445	1/2" x 1/2"	↓	84	.095	↓	8.90	6.90		15.80	20
9450	Elbow coupling									
9452	Barb x barb									
9454	1/4" x 1/4"	1 Stpi	158	.051	Ea.	3.19	3.67		6.86	9
9455	3/8" x 3/8"		154	.052		11.55	3.77		15.32	18.30
9456	1/2" x 1/2"	↓	140	.057	↓	16.45	4.15		20.60	24.50
9460	Tube x tube									
9462	1/2" x 1/2"	1 Stpi	84	.095	Ea.	24	6.90		30.90	36.50
9470	Tee coupling									
9472	Barb x barb x barb									
9474	1/4" x 1/4" x 5/32"	1 Stpi	108	.074	Ea.	3.66	5.35		9.01	12.05
9475	1/4" x 1/4" x 1/4"		104	.077		1.97	5.60		7.57	10.45
9476	3/8" x 3/8" x 5/32"		102	.078		9.05	5.70		14.75	18.45
9477	3/8" x 3/8" x 1/4"		99	.081		3.67	5.85		9.52	12.80
9478	3/8" x 3/8" x 3/8"		98	.082		3.72	5.90		9.62	12.95
9479	1/2" x 1/2" x 1/4"		96	.083		11.75	6.05		17.80	22
9480	1/2" x 1/2" x 3/8"		95	.084		14.80	6.10		20.90	25.50
9481	1/2" x 1/2" x 1/2"	↓	92	.087	↓	5.35	6.30		11.65	15.30
9484	Tube x tube x tube									
9485	1/4" x 1/4" x 1/4"	1 Stpi	66	.121	Ea.	7.75	8.80		16.55	21.50
9486	3/8" x 1/4" x 1/4"		64	.125		1.97	9.05		11.02	15.70
9487	3/8" x 3/8" x 1/4"		61	.131		18.55	9.50		28.05	34.50
9488	3/8" x 3/8" x 3/8"		60	.133		24	9.65		33.65	41
9489	1/2" x 1/2" x 3/8"		58	.138		34.50	10		44.50	53
9490	1/2" x 1/2" x 1/2"	↓	56	.143	↓	9.05	10.35		19.40	25.50
9492	Needle valve									
9494	Tube x tube									
9495	1/4" x 1/4"	1 Stpi	86	.093	Ea.	19.25	6.75		26	31
9496	3/8" x 3/8"	"	82	.098	"	33	7.10		40.10	47
9600	Electronic system misc. components									
9610	Electric motor damper actuator	1 Elec	8	1	Ea.	815	67.50		882.50	995
9620	Damper position indicator		10	.800		268	54		322	375
9630	Pneumatic-electronic transducer	↓	12	.667	↓	152	45		197	234
9700	Modulating step controller									
9701	For 2-5 steps	1 Elec	5.30	1.509	Ea.	955	102		1,057	1,200
9702	6-10 steps		3.20	2.500		256	168		424	530
9703	11-15 steps		2.70	2.963		570	200		770	920
9704	16-20 steps	↓	1.60	5	↓	845	335		1,180	1,425
9710	Staging network									
9740	Accessory unit regulator									
9750	Accessory power supply	1 Elec	18	.444	Ea.	156	30		186	217
9760	Step down transformer	"	16	.500	"	345	33.50		378.50	430

23 11 Facility Fuel Piping

23 11 13 – Facility Fuel-Oil Piping

23 11 13.10 Fuel Oil Specialties

		Crew	Daily Output	Labor-Hours	Unit	Material	2023 Bare Costs Labor	2023 Bare Costs Equipment	Total	Total Incl O&P
0010	**FUEL OIL SPECIALTIES**									
0020	Foot valve, single poppet, metal to metal construction									
0040	Bevel seat, 1/2" diameter	1 Stpi	20	.400	Ea.	151	29		180	210
0060	3/4" diameter		18	.444		77.50	32		109.50	134
0080	1" diameter		16	.500		87	36.50		123.50	150
0100	1-1/4" diameter		15	.533		216	38.50		254.50	295
0120	1-1/2" diameter		13	.615		120	44.50		164.50	199
0140	2" diameter		11	.727		159	53		212	254
0160	Foot valve, double poppet, metal to metal construction									
0164	1" diameter	1 Stpi	15	.533	Ea.	192	38.50		230.50	270
0166	1-1/2" diameter	"	12	.667	"	365	48.50		413.50	470
0400	Fuel fill box, flush type									
0408	Nonlocking, watertight									
0410	1-1/2" diameter	1 Stpi	12	.667	Ea.	30	48.50		78.50	105
0440	2" diameter		10	.800		48	58		106	140
0450	2-1/2" diameter		9	.889		87	64.50		151.50	192
0460	3" diameter		7	1.143		101	83		184	235
0470	4" diameter		5	1.600		202	116		318	395
0500	Locking inner cover									
0510	2" diameter	1 Stpi	8	1	Ea.	24	72.50		96.50	135
0520	2-1/2" diameter		7	1.143		134	83		217	271
0530	3" diameter		5	1.600		54	116		170	232
0540	4" diameter		4	2		74	145		219	298
0600	Fuel system components									
0620	Spill container	1 Stpi	4	2	Ea.	1,300	145		1,445	1,650
0640	Fill adapter, 4", straight drop		8	1		101	72.50		173.50	219
0680	Fill cap, 4"		30	.267		49	19.35		68.35	83
0700	Extractor fitting, 4" x 1-1/2"		8	1		695	72.50		767.50	875
0740	Vapor hose adapter, 4"		8	1		163	72.50		235.50	288
0760	Wood gage stick, 10'					14.95			14.95	16.45
1000	Oil filters, 3/8" IPT, 20 gal. per hour	1 Stpi	20	.400		27.50	29		56.50	73.50
1020	32 gal. per hour		18	.444		77	32		109	133
1040	40 gal. per hour		16	.500		72.50	36.50		109	134
1060	50 gal. per hour		14	.571		74	41.50		115.50	144
2000	Remote tank gauging system, self contained									
2100	Single tank kit/8 sensors inputs w/printer	1 Stpi	2.50	3.200	Ea.	5,350	232		5,582	6,225
2120	Two tank kit/8 sensors inputs w/printer		2	4		7,150	290		7,440	8,300
3000	Valve, ball check, globe type, 3/8" diameter		24	.333		16.25	24		40.25	54
3500	Fusible, 3/8" diameter		24	.333		33.50	24		57.50	72.50
3600	1/2" diameter		24	.333		80	24		104	124
3610	3/4" diameter		20	.400		183	29		212	245
3620	1" diameter		19	.421		495	30.50		525.50	585
4000	Nonfusible, 3/8" diameter		24	.333		33	24		57	72.50
4500	Shutoff, gate type, lever handle, spring-fusible kit									
4520	1/4" diameter	1 Stpi	14	.571	Ea.	34.50	41.50		76	100
4540	3/8" diameter		12	.667		83.50	48.50		132	164
4560	1/2" diameter		10	.800		122	58		180	222
4570	3/4" diameter		8	1		142	72.50		214.50	264
4580	Lever handle, requires weight and fusible kit									
4600	1" diameter	1 Stpi	9	.889	Ea.	445	64.50		509.50	585
4620	1-1/4" diameter		8	1		750	72.50		822.50	935
4640	1-1/2" diameter		7	1.143		565	83		648	750
4660	2" diameter		6	1.333		1,150	96.50		1,246.50	1,425

23 11 Facility Fuel Piping

23 11 13 – Facility Fuel-Oil Piping

23 11 13.10 Fuel Oil Specialties

		Crew	Daily Output	Labor-Hours	Unit	Material	2023 Bare Costs Labor	2023 Bare Costs Equipment	Total	Total Incl O&P
4680	For fusible link, weight and braided wire, add				Ea.	5%				
5000	Vent alarm, whistling signal					45.50			45.50	50
5500	Vent protector/breather, 1-1/4" diameter	1 Stpi	32	.250		27.50	18.15		45.65	57.50
5520	1-1/2" diameter		32	.250		32.50	18.15		50.65	62.50
5540	2" diameter		32	.250		67	18.15		85.15	101
5560	3" diameter		28	.286		93.50	20.50		114	134
5580	4" diameter		24	.333		121	24		145	169
5600	Dust cap, breather, 2"	↓	40	.200	↓	13.55	14.50		28.05	36.50
8000	Fuel oil and tank heaters									
8020	Electric, capacity rated at 230 volts									
8040	Immersion element in steel manifold									
8060	96 GPH at 50°F rise	Q-5	6.40	2.500	Ea.	1,625	163		1,788	2,050
8070	128 GPH at 50°F rise		6.20	2.581		1,625	169		1,794	2,050
8080	160 GPH at 50°F rise		5.90	2.712		1,875	177		2,052	2,325
8090	192 GPH at 50°F rise		5.50	2.909		2,050	190		2,240	2,525
8100	240 GPH at 50°F rise		5.10	3.137		2,350	205		2,555	2,900
8110	288 GPH at 50°F rise		4.60	3.478		2,575	227		2,802	3,175
8120	384 GPH at 50°F rise		3.10	5.161		3,000	335		3,335	3,800
8130	480 GPH at 50°F rise		2.30	6.957		3,775	455		4,230	4,825
8140	576 GPH at 50°F rise	↓	2.10	7.619	↓	3,775	500		4,275	4,900
8300	Suction stub, immersion type									
8320	75" long, 750 watts	1 Stpi	14	.571	Ea.	1,075	41.50		1,116.50	1,225
8330	99" long, 2000 watts		12	.667		1,550	48.50		1,598.50	1,775
8340	123" long, 3000 watts	↓	10	.800	↓	1,675	58		1,733	1,925
8660	Steam, cross flow, rated at 5 PSIG									
8680	42 GPH	Q-5	7	2.286	Ea.	2,475	149		2,624	2,950
8690	73 GPH		6.70	2.388		2,975	156		3,131	3,500
8700	112 GPH		6.20	2.581		3,000	169		3,169	3,550
8710	158 GPH		5.80	2.759		3,275	180		3,455	3,875
8720	187 GPH		4	4		4,625	261		4,886	5,500
8730	270 GPH	↓	3.60	4.444		4,825	290		5,115	5,750
8740	365 GPH	Q-6	4.90	4.898		5,850	330		6,180	6,950
8750	635 GPH		3.70	6.486		7,175	440		7,615	8,525
8760	845 GPH		2.50	9.600		10,800	650		11,450	12,900
8770	1420 GPH		1.60	15		17,700	1,025		18,725	20,900
8780	2100 GPH	↓	1.10	21.818	↓	24,200	1,475		25,675	28,900

23 11 23 – Facility Natural-Gas Piping

23 11 23.10 Gas Meters

		Crew	Daily Output	Labor-Hours	Unit	Material	Labor	Equipment	Total	Total Incl O&P
0010	**GAS METERS**									
4000	Residential									
4010	Gas meter, residential, 3/4" pipe size	1 Plum	14	.571	Ea.	365	41		406	465
4020	Gas meter, residential, 1" pipe size		12	.667		370	48		418	480
4030	Gas meter, residential, 1-1/4" pipe size	↓	10	.800	↓	335	57.50		392.50	455

23 11 23.20 Gas Piping, Flexible (Csst)

		Crew	Daily Output	Labor-Hours	Unit	Material	Labor	Equipment	Total	Total Incl O&P
0010	**GAS PIPING, FLEXIBLE (CSST)**									
0100	Tubing with lightning protection									
0110	3/8"	1 Stpi	65	.123	L.F.	4.25	8.95		13.20	18
0120	1/2"		62	.129		4.77	9.35		14.12	19.20
0130	3/4"		60	.133		6.20	9.65		15.85	21.50
0140	1"		55	.145		8.85	10.55		19.40	25.50
0150	1-1/4"		50	.160		11.05	11.60		22.65	29.50
0160	1-1/2"	↓	45	.178		19.50	12.90		32.40	41

23 11 Facility Fuel Piping

23 11 23 – Facility Natural-Gas Piping

23 11 23.20 Gas Piping, Flexible (Csst)

		Crew	Daily Output	Labor-Hours	Unit	Material	2023 Bare Costs Labor	2023 Bare Costs Equipment	Total	Total Incl O&P
0170	2"	1 Stpi	40	.200	L.F.	28	14.50		42.50	52
0200	Tubing for underground/underslab burial									
0210	3/8"	1 Stpi	65	.123	L.F.	5.90	8.95		14.85	19.80
0220	1/2"		62	.129		6.70	9.35		16.05	21.50
0230	3/4"		60	.133		10.05	9.65		19.70	25.50
0240	1"		55	.145		11.50	10.55		22.05	28.50
0250	1-1/4"		50	.160		15.45	11.60		27.05	34.50
0260	1-1/2"		45	.178		29	12.90		41.90	51.50
0270	2"	↓	40	.200	↓	34.50	14.50		49	59.50
3000	Fittings									
3010	Straight									
3100	Tube to NPT									
3110	3/8"	1 Stpi	29	.276	Ea.	17.40	20		37.40	49
3120	1/2"		27	.296		19.45	21.50		40.95	53.50
3130	3/4"		25	.320		26.50	23		49.50	63.50
3140	1"		23	.348		41	25		66	82.50
3150	1-1/4"		20	.400		91	29		120	144
3160	1-1/2"		17	.471		187	34		221	257
3170	2"	↓	15	.533		320	38.50		358.50	410
3200	Coupling									
3210	3/8"	1 Stpi	29	.276	Ea.	34	20		54	67.50
3220	1/2"		27	.296		36	21.50		57.50	71.50
3230	3/4"		25	.320		49	23		72	88.50
3240	1"		23	.348		84	25		109	130
3250	1-1/4"		20	.400		186	29		215	249
3260	1-1/2"		17	.471		355	34		389	440
3270	2"	↓	15	.533	↓	605	38.50		643.50	725
3300	Flange fitting									
3310	3/8"	1 Stpi	25	.320	Ea.	23.50	23		46.50	60.50
3320	1/2"		22	.364		24.50	26.50		51	66.50
3330	3/4"		19	.421		31	30.50		61.50	80
3340	1"		16	.500		45.50	36.50		82	104
3350	1-1/4"	↓	12	.667		101	48.50		149.50	183
3400	90° flange valve									
3410	3/8"	1 Stpi	25	.320	Ea.	39	23		62	77
3420	1/2"		22	.364		46	26.50		72.50	90
3430	3/4"	↓	19	.421	↓	65	30.50		95.50	117
4000	Tee									
4120	1/2"	1 Stpi	20.50	.390	Ea.	62	28.50		90.50	111
4130	3/4"		19	.421		67.50	30.50		98	120
4140	1"	↓	17.50	.457	↓	130	33		163	193
5000	Reducing									
5110	Tube to NPT									
5120	3/4" to 1/2" NPT	1 Stpi	26	.308	Ea.	28.50	22.50		51	65
5130	1" to 3/4" NPT	"	24	.333	"	44	24		68	84.50
5200	Reducing tee									
5210	1/2" x 3/8" x 3/8"	1 Stpi	21	.381	Ea.	74.50	27.50		102	123
5220	3/4" x 1/2" x 1/2"		20	.400		70	29		99	121
5230	1" x 3/4" x 1/2"		18	.444		116	32		148	175
5240	1-1/4" x 1-1/4" x 1"		15.60	.513		310	37		347	395
5250	1-1/2" x 1-1/2" x 1-1/4"		13.30	.602		470	43.50		513.50	585
5260	2" x 2" x 1-1/2"	↓	11.80	.678		710	49		759	855
5300	Manifold with four ports and mounting bracket									

23 11 Facility Fuel Piping

23 11 23 – Facility Natural-Gas Piping

23 11 23.20 Gas Piping, Flexible (Csst)

		Crew	Daily Output	Labor-Hours	Unit	Material	2023 Bare Costs Labor	Equipment	Total	Total Incl O&P
5302	Labor to mount manifold does not include making pipe									
5304	connections which are included in fitting labor.									
5310	3/4" x 1/2" x 1/2" (4)	1 Stpi	76	.105	Ea.	54.50	7.65		62.15	71.50
5330	1-1/4" x 1" x 3/4" (4)		72	.111		78.50	8.05		86.55	98.50
5350	2" x 1-1/2" x 1" (4)	↓	68	.118	↓	98.50	8.55		107.05	121
5600	Protective striker plate									
5610	Quarter plate, 3" x 2"	1 Stpi	88	.091	Ea.	1.26	6.60		7.86	11.25
5620	Half plate, 3" x 7"		82	.098		2.71	7.10		9.81	13.55
5630	Full plate, 3" x 12"	↓	78	.103	↓	5.10	7.45		12.55	16.70

23 12 Facility Fuel Pumps

23 12 13 – Facility Fuel-Oil Pumps

23 12 13.10 Pump and Motor Sets

		Crew	Daily Output	Labor-Hours	Unit	Material	2023 Bare Costs Labor	Equipment	Total	Total Incl O&P
0010	**PUMP AND MOTOR SETS**									
1810	Light fuel and diesel oils									
1820	20 GPH, 1/3 HP	Q-5	6	2.667	Ea.	2,000	174		2,174	2,450
1830	27 GPH, 1/3 HP		6	2.667		2,000	174		2,174	2,450
1840	80 GPH, 1/3 HP		5	3.200		2,000	209		2,209	2,500
1850	145 GPH, 1/2 HP		4	4		2,100	261		2,361	2,725
1860	277 GPH, 1 HP		4	4		2,350	261		2,611	2,975
1870	700 GPH, 1-1/2 HP		3	5.333		6,125	350		6,475	7,250
1880	1000 GPH, 2 HP		3	5.333		6,200	350		6,550	7,350
1890	1800 GPH, 5 HP	↓	1.80	8.889	↓	10,100	580		10,680	12,000

23 13 Facility Fuel-Storage Tanks

23 13 13 – Facility Underground Fuel-Oil, Storage Tanks

23 13 13.09 Single-Wall Steel Fuel-Oil Tanks

		Crew	Daily Output	Labor-Hours	Unit	Material	2023 Bare Costs Labor	Equipment	Total	Total Incl O&P
0010	**SINGLE-WALL STEEL FUEL-OIL TANKS**									
5000	Tanks, steel ugnd., sti-p3, not incl. hold-down bars									
5500	Excavation, pad, pumps and piping not included									
5510	Single wall, 500 gallon capacity, 7 ga. shell	Q-5	2.70	5.926	Ea.	2,475	385		2,860	3,300
5520	1,000 gallon capacity, 7 ga. shell	"	2.50	6.400		3,575	420		3,995	4,550
5530	2,000 gallon capacity, 1/4" thick shell	Q-7	4.60	6.957		5,150	480		5,630	6,400
5535	2,500 gallon capacity, 7 ga. shell	Q-5	3	5.333		6,950	350		7,300	8,150
5540	5,000 gallon capacity, 1/4" thick shell	Q-7	3.20	10		16,300	690		16,990	18,900
5560	10,000 gallon capacity, 1/4" thick shell		2	16		13,300	1,100		14,400	16,300
5580	15,000 gallon capacity, 5/16" thick shell		1.70	18.824		13,700	1,300		15,000	17,000
5600	20,000 gallon capacity, 5/16" thick shell		1.50	21.333		33,300	1,475		34,775	38,800
5610	25,000 gallon capacity, 3/8" thick shell		1.30	24.615		38,200	1,700		39,900	44,500
5620	30,000 gallon capacity, 3/8" thick shell		1.10	29.091		42,900	2,000		44,900	50,000
5630	40,000 gallon capacity, 3/8" thick shell		.90	35.556		56,000	2,450		58,450	65,000
5640	50,000 gallon capacity, 3/8" thick shell	↓	.80	40	↓	63,500	2,750		66,250	74,000

23 13 Facility Fuel-Storage Tanks

23 13 13 – Facility Underground Fuel-Oil, Storage Tanks

23 13 13.13 Dbl-Wall Steel, Undrgrnd Fuel-Oil, Stor. Tanks	Crew	Daily Output	Labor-Hours	Unit	Material	2023 Bare Costs Labor	Equipment	Total	Total Incl O&P
0010 **DOUBLE-WALL STEEL, UNDERGROUND FUEL-OIL, STORAGE TANKS**									
6200 Steel, underground, 360°, double wall, UL listed,									
6210 with sti-P3 corrosion protection,									
6220 (dielectric coating, cathodic protection, electrical									
6230 isolation) 30 year warranty,									
6240 not incl. manholes or hold-downs.									
6250 500 gallon capacity	Q-5	2.40	6.667	Ea.	4,400	435		4,835	5,475
6260 1,000 gallon capacity	"	2.25	7.111		4,775	465		5,240	5,975
6270 2,000 gallon capacity	Q-7	4.16	7.692		6,325	530		6,855	7,750
6280 3,000 gallon capacity		3.90	8.205		9,100	565		9,665	10,800
6290 4,000 gallon capacity		3.64	8.791		10,700	605		11,305	12,700
6300 5,000 gallon capacity		2.91	10.997		11,500	760		12,260	13,800
6310 6,000 gallon capacity		2.42	13.223		14,800	915		15,715	17,700
6320 8,000 gallon capacity		2.08	15.385		14,600	1,050		15,650	17,700
6330 10,000 gallon capacity		1.82	17.582		18,200	1,225		19,425	21,800
6340 12,000 gallon capacity		1.70	18.824		20,300	1,300		21,600	24,300
6350 15,000 gallon capacity		1.33	24.060		27,200	1,650		28,850	32,400
6360 20,000 gallon capacity		1.33	24.060		44,900	1,650		46,550	52,000
6370 25,000 gallon capacity		1.16	27.586		53,500	1,900		55,400	62,000
6380 30,000 gallon capacity		1.03	31.068		49,600	2,150		51,750	57,500
6390 40,000 gallon capacity		.80	40		167,000	2,750		169,750	187,500
6395 50,000 gallon capacity		.73	43.836		203,000	3,025		206,025	227,500
6400 For hold-downs 500-2,000 gal., add		16	2	Set	265	138		403	500
6410 For hold-downs 3,000-6,000 gal., add		12	2.667		460	184		644	780
6420 For hold-downs 8,000-12,000 gal., add		11	2.909		655	201		856	1,025
6430 For hold-downs 15,000 gal., add		9	3.556		895	246		1,141	1,350
6440 For hold-downs 20,000 gal., add		8	4		1,025	276		1,301	1,525
6450 For hold-downs 20,000 gal. plus, add		6	5.333		1,250	370		1,620	1,925
6500 For manways, add				Ea.	1,475			1,475	1,625
6600 In place with hold-downs									
6652 550 gallon capacity	Q-5	1.84	8.696	Ea.	4,650	570		5,220	5,975

23 13 13.23 Glass-Fiber-Reinfcd-Plastic, Fuel-Oil, Storage

	Crew	Daily Output	Labor-Hours	Unit	Material	2023 Bare Costs Labor	Equipment	Total	Total Incl O&P
0010 **GLASS-FIBER-REINFCD-PLASTIC, UNDERGRND. FUEL-OIL, STORAGE**									
0210 Fiberglass, underground, single wall, UL listed, not including									
0220 manway or hold-down strap									
0225 550 gallon capacity	Q-5	2.67	5.993	Ea.	5,225	390		5,615	6,325
0230 1,000 gallon capacity	"	2.46	6.504		6,725	425		7,150	8,025
0240 2,000 gallon capacity	Q-7	4.57	7.002		10,800	485		11,285	12,600
0245 3,000 gallon capacity		3.90	8.205		10,900	565		11,465	12,800
0250 4,000 gallon capacity		3.55	9.014		14,600	620		15,220	16,900
0255 5,000 gallon capacity		3.20	10		13,300	690		13,990	15,600
0260 6,000 gallon capacity		2.67	11.985		12,500	830		13,330	14,900
0270 8,000 gallon capacity		2.29	13.974		19,500	965		20,465	22,900
0280 10,000 gallon capacity		2	16		19,600	1,100		20,700	23,300
0282 12,000 gallon capacity		1.88	17.021		20,800	1,175		21,975	24,700
0284 15,000 gallon capacity		1.68	19.048		30,000	1,325		31,325	35,000
0290 20,000 gallon capacity		1.45	22.069		41,800	1,525		43,325	48,300
0300 25,000 gallon capacity		1.28	25		72,000	1,725		73,725	81,500
0320 30,000 gallon capacity		1.14	28.070		108,500	1,950		110,450	122,000
0340 40,000 gallon capacity		.89	35.955		154,000	2,475		156,475	173,000
0360 48,000 gallon capacity		.81	39.506		228,500	2,725		231,225	255,500
0500 For manway, fittings and hold-downs, add					20%	15%			

23 13 Facility Fuel-Storage Tanks

23 13 13 – Facility Underground Fuel-Oil, Storage Tanks

23 13 13.23 Glass-Fiber-Reinfcd-Plastic, Fuel-Oil, Storage		Crew	Daily Output	Labor-Hours	Unit	Material	2023 Bare Costs Labor	Equipment	Total	Total Incl O&P
0600	For manways, add				Ea.	3,525			3,525	3,875
1000	For helical heating coil, add	Q-5	2.50	6.400		6,950	420		7,370	8,275
1020	Fiberglass, underground, double wall, UL listed									
1030	includes manways, not incl. hold-down straps									
1040	600 gallon capacity	Q-5	2.42	6.612	Ea.	11,500	430		11,930	13,200
1050	1,000 gallon capacity	"	2.25	7.111		15,700	465		16,165	18,000
1060	2,500 gallon capacity	Q-7	4.16	7.692		21,700	530		22,230	24,700
1070	3,000 gallon capacity		3.90	8.205		24,300	565		24,865	27,500
1080	4,000 gallon capacity		3.64	8.791		25,400	605		26,005	28,800
1090	6,000 gallon capacity		2.42	13.223		31,500	915		32,415	36,100
1100	8,000 gallon capacity		2.08	15.385		40,100	1,050		41,150	45,700
1110	10,000 gallon capacity		1.82	17.582		48,500	1,225		49,725	55,500
1120	12,000 gallon capacity		1.70	18.824		50,500	1,300		51,800	57,500
1122	15,000 gallon capacity		1.52	21.053		90,000	1,450		91,450	101,000
1124	20,000 gallon capacity		1.33	24.060		97,000	1,650		98,650	109,000
1126	25,000 gallon capacity		1.16	27.586		112,000	1,900		113,900	126,500
1128	30,000 gallon capacity		1.03	31.068		134,500	2,150		136,650	151,000
1140	For hold-down straps, add					2%	10%			
1150	For hold-downs 500-4,000 gal., add	Q-7	16	2	Set	560	138		698	820
1160	For hold-downs 5,000-15,000 gal., add		8	4		1,125	276		1,401	1,625
1170	For hold-downs 20,000 gal., add		5.33	6.004		1,675	415		2,090	2,475
1180	For hold-downs 25,000 gal., add		4	8		2,225	550		2,775	3,275
1190	For hold-downs 30,000 gal., add		2.60	12.308		3,350	850		4,200	4,950
2210	Fiberglass, underground, single wall, UL listed, including									
2220	hold-down straps, no manways									
2225	550 gallon capacity	Q-5	2	8	Ea.	5,775	520		6,295	7,125
2230	1,000 gallon capacity	"	1.88	8.511		7,275	555		7,830	8,825
2240	2,000 gallon capacity	Q-7	3.55	9.014		11,300	620		11,920	13,400
2250	4,000 gallon capacity		2.90	11.034		15,100	760		15,860	17,700
2260	6,000 gallon capacity		2	16		13,600	1,100		14,700	16,600
2270	8,000 gallon capacity		1.78	17.978		20,600	1,250		21,850	24,500
2280	10,000 gallon capacity		1.60	20		20,800	1,375		22,175	24,900
2282	12,000 gallon capacity		1.52	21.053		21,900	1,450		23,350	26,300
2284	15,000 gallon capacity		1.39	23.022		31,100	1,600		32,700	36,600
2290	20,000 gallon capacity		1.14	28.070		43,500	1,950		45,450	50,500
2300	25,000 gallon capacity		.96	33.333		74,000	2,300		76,300	85,000
2320	30,000 gallon capacity		.80	40		111,500	2,750		114,250	127,000
3020	Fiberglass, underground, double wall, UL listed									
3030	includes manways and hold-down straps									
3040	600 gallon capacity	Q-5	1.86	8.602	Ea.	12,000	560		12,560	14,000
3050	1,000 gallon capacity	"	1.70	9.412		16,300	615		16,915	18,800
3060	2,500 gallon capacity	Q-7	3.29	9.726		22,200	670		22,870	25,500
3070	3,000 gallon capacity		3.13	10.224		24,800	705		25,505	28,400
3080	4,000 gallon capacity		2.93	10.922		25,900	755		26,655	29,600
3090	6,000 gallon capacity		1.86	17.204		32,600	1,200		33,800	37,700
3100	8,000 gallon capacity		1.65	19.394		41,200	1,350		42,550	47,300
3110	10,000 gallon capacity		1.48	21.622		49,700	1,500		51,200	56,500
3120	12,000 gallon capacity		1.40	22.857		51,500	1,575		53,075	59,000
3122	15,000 gallon capacity		1.28	25		91,000	1,725		92,725	102,500
3124	20,000 gallon capacity		1.06	30.189		98,500	2,075		100,575	111,500
3126	25,000 gallon capacity		.90	35.556		114,500	2,450		116,950	129,500
3128	30,000 gallon capacity		.74	43.243		138,000	2,975		140,975	156,500

23 13 Facility Fuel-Storage Tanks

23 13 23 – Facility Aboveground Fuel-Oil, Storage Tanks

23 13 23.16 Horizontal, Stl, Abvgrd Fuel-Oil, Storage Tanks

		Crew	Daily Output	Labor-Hours	Unit	Material	2023 Bare Costs Labor	Equipment	Total	Total Incl O&P
0010	**HORIZONTAL, STEEL, ABOVEGROUND FUEL-OIL, STORAGE TANKS**									
3000	Steel, storage, aboveground, including cradles, coating,									
3020	fittings, not including foundation, pumps or piping									
3040	Single wall, 275 gallon	Q-5	5	3.200	Ea.	1,875	209		2,084	2,375
3060	550 gallon	"	2.70	5.926		7,150	385		7,535	8,450
3080	1,000 gallon	Q-7	5	6.400		12,000	440		12,440	13,900
3100	1,500 gallon		4.75	6.737		18,400	465		18,865	20,900
3120	2,000 gallon		4.60	6.957		17,700	480		18,180	20,200
3140	5,000 gallon		3.20	10		26,200	690		26,890	29,900
3150	10,000 gallon		2	16		39,300	1,100		40,400	45,000
3160	15,000 gallon		1.70	18.824		53,500	1,300		54,800	60,500
3170	20,000 gallon		1.45	22.069		64,000	1,525		65,525	73,000
3180	25,000 gallon		1.30	24.615		116,500	1,700		118,200	131,000
3190	30,000 gallon		1.10	29.091		87,000	2,000		89,000	99,000
3320	Double wall, 500 gallon capacity	Q-5	2.40	6.667		3,925	435		4,360	4,950
3330	2,000 gallon capacity	Q-7	4.15	7.711		6,925	530		7,455	8,400
3340	4,000 gallon capacity		3.60	8.889		14,800	615		15,415	17,100
3350	6,000 gallon capacity		2.40	13.333		41,600	920		42,520	47,200
3360	8,000 gallon capacity		2	16		48,800	1,100		49,900	55,000
3370	10,000 gallon capacity		1.80	17.778		57,000	1,225		58,225	65,000
3380	15,000 gallon capacity		1.50	21.333		79,000	1,475		80,475	89,000
3390	20,000 gallon capacity		1.30	24.615		95,500	1,700		97,200	107,500
3400	25,000 gallon capacity		1.15	27.826		90,500	1,925		92,425	102,500
3410	30,000 gallon capacity		1	32		122,500	2,200		124,700	138,500

23 13 23.26 Horizontal, Conc., Abvgrd Fuel-Oil, Stor. Tanks

		Crew	Daily Output	Labor-Hours	Unit	Material	Labor	Equipment	Total	Total Incl O&P
0010	**HORIZONTAL, CONCRETE, ABOVEGROUND FUEL-OIL, STORAGE TANKS**									
0050	Concrete, storage, aboveground, including pad & pump									
0100	500 gallon	F-3	2	20	Ea.	13,700	1,200	1,075	15,975	18,100
0200	1,000 gallon	"	2	20		19,200	1,200	1,075	21,475	24,200
0300	2,000 gallon	F-4	2	24		24,700	1,425	1,225	27,350	30,700
0400	4,000 gallon		2	24		31,600	1,425	1,225	34,250	38,300
0500	8,000 gallon		2	24		49,500	1,425	1,225	52,150	58,000
0600	12,000 gallon		2	24		66,000	1,425	1,225	68,650	76,000

23 21 Hydronic Piping and Pumps

23 21 20 – Hydronic HVAC Piping Specialties

23 21 20.10 Air Control

		Crew	Daily Output	Labor-Hours	Unit	Material	Labor	Equipment	Total	Total Incl O&P
0010	**AIR CONTROL**									
0030	Air separator, with strainer									
0040	2" diameter	Q-5	6	2.667	Ea.	1,775	174		1,949	2,200
0080	2-1/2" diameter		5	3.200		1,975	209		2,184	2,475
0100	3" diameter		4	4		3,050	261		3,311	3,750
0120	4" diameter		3	5.333		4,300	350		4,650	5,250
0130	5" diameter	Q-6	3.60	6.667		5,475	450		5,925	6,700
0140	6" diameter		3.40	7.059		6,550	480		7,030	7,950
0160	8" diameter		3	8		9,775	540		10,315	11,600
0180	10" diameter		2.20	10.909		15,200	740		15,940	17,800
0200	12" diameter		1.70	14.118		25,200	955		26,155	29,100
0210	14" diameter		1.30	18.462		30,000	1,250		31,250	34,900
0220	16" diameter		1	24		44,800	1,625		46,425	51,500

23 21 Hydronic Piping and Pumps

23 21 20 – Hydronic HVAC Piping Specialties

23 21 20.10 Air Control		Crew	Daily Output	Labor-Hours	Unit	Material	2023 Bare Costs Labor	Equipment	Total	Total Incl O&P
0230	18" diameter	Q-6	.80	30	Ea.	59,000	2,025		61,025	68,000
0240	20" diameter	↓	.60	40	↓	66,000	2,700		68,700	76,500
0300	Without strainer									
0310	2" diameter	Q-5	6	2.667	Ea.	1,100	174		1,274	1,450
0320	2-1/2" diameter		5	3.200		1,300	209		1,509	1,725
0330	3" diameter		4	4		1,825	261		2,086	2,425
0340	4" diameter		3	5.333		2,825	350		3,175	3,625
0350	5" diameter	↓	2.40	6.667		3,800	435		4,235	4,850
0360	6" diameter	Q-6	3.40	7.059		4,375	480		4,855	5,525
0370	8" diameter		3	8		5,825	540		6,365	7,225
0380	10" diameter		2.20	10.909		8,850	740		9,590	10,900
0390	12" diameter		1.70	14.118		13,600	955		14,555	16,400
0400	14" diameter		1.30	18.462		20,400	1,250		21,650	24,300
0410	16" diameter		1	24		28,500	1,625		30,125	33,700
0420	18" diameter		.80	30		37,100	2,025		39,125	43,800
0430	20" diameter	↓	.60	40	↓	44,500	2,700		47,200	53,000
1000	Micro-bubble separator for total air removal, closed loop system									
1010	Requires bladder type tank in system.									
1020	Water (hot or chilled) or glycol system									
1030	Threaded									
1040	3/4" diameter	1 Stpi	20	.400	Ea.	95.50	29		124.50	149
1050	1" diameter		19	.421		111	30.50		141.50	168
1060	1-1/4" diameter		16	.500		147	36.50		183.50	215
1070	1-1/2" diameter		13	.615		195	44.50		239.50	281
1080	2" diameter	↓	11	.727		1,325	53		1,378	1,525
1090	2-1/2" diameter	Q-5	15	1.067		1,575	69.50		1,644.50	1,825
1100	3" diameter		13	1.231		2,125	80.50		2,205.50	2,450
1110	4" diameter	↓	10	1.600	↓	2,350	104		2,454	2,750
1230	Flanged									
1250	2" diameter	1 Stpi	8	1	Ea.	2,075	72.50		2,147.50	2,375
1260	2-1/2" diameter	Q-5	5	3.200		2,250	209		2,459	2,775
1270	3" diameter		4.50	3.556		3,050	232		3,282	3,700
1280	4" diameter	↓	3	5.333		3,300	350		3,650	4,150
1290	5" diameter	Q-6	3.40	7.059		4,650	480		5,130	5,825
1300	6" diameter	"	3	8	↓	6,075	540		6,615	7,500
1400	Larger sizes available									
1590	With extended tank dirt catcher									
1600	Flanged									
1620	2" diameter	1 Stpi	7.40	1.081	Ea.	5,050	78.50		5,128.50	5,675
1630	2-1/2" diameter	Q-5	4.20	3.810		3,875	249		4,124	4,625
1640	3" diameter		4	4		7,400	261		7,661	8,525
1650	4" diameter	↓	2.80	5.714		8,250	375		8,625	9,625
1660	5" diameter	Q-6	3.10	7.742		11,800	525		12,325	13,800
1670	6" diameter	"	2.90	8.276	↓	14,600	560		15,160	16,800
1800	With drain/dismantle/cleaning access flange									
1810	Flanged									
1820	2" diameter	Q-5	4.60	3.478	Ea.	3,750	227		3,977	4,450
1830	2-1/2" diameter		4	4		4,050	261		4,311	4,850
1840	3" diameter		3.60	4.444		4,950	290		5,240	5,875
1850	4" diameter	↓	2.50	6.400		5,650	420		6,070	6,850
1860	5" diameter	Q-6	2.80	8.571		10,400	580		10,980	12,300
1870	6" diameter	"	2.60	9.231	↓	13,400	625		14,025	15,600
2000	Boiler air fitting, separator									

23 21 Hydronic Piping and Pumps

23 21 20 – Hydronic HVAC Piping Specialties

23 21 20.10 Air Control

		Crew	Daily Output	Labor-Hours	Unit	Material	2023 Bare Costs Labor	2023 Bare Costs Equipment	Total	Total Incl O&P
2010	1-1/4"	Q-5	22	.727	Ea.	320	47.50		367.50	425
2020	1-1/2"		20	.800		610	52		662	750
2021	2"	↓	18	.889	↓	1,075	58		1,133	1,250
2400	Compression tank air fitting									
2410	For tanks 9" to 24" diameter	1 Stpi	15	.533	Ea.	200	38.50		238.50	278
2420	For tanks 100 gallon or larger	"	12	.667	"	565	48.50		613.50	690

23 21 20.14 Air Purging Scoop

		Crew	Daily Output	Labor-Hours	Unit	Material	Labor	Equipment	Total	Total Incl O&P
0010	**AIR PURGING SCOOP**, With tappings.									
0020	For air vent and expansion tank connection									
0100	1" pipe size, threaded	1 Stpi	19	.421	Ea.	26	30.50		56.50	74
0110	1-1/4" pipe size, threaded		15	.533		36.50	38.50		75	98
0120	1-1/2" pipe size, threaded		13	.615		80.50	44.50		125	155
0130	2" pipe size, threaded	↓	11	.727		91.50	53		144.50	180
0140	2-1/2" pipe size, threaded	Q-5	15	1.067		197	69.50		266.50	320
0150	3" pipe size, threaded		13	1.231		256	80.50		336.50	400
0160	4" 150 lb. flanges	↓	3	5.333	↓	575	350		925	1,150

23 21 20.18 Automatic Air Vent

		Crew	Daily Output	Labor-Hours	Unit	Material	Labor	Equipment	Total	Total Incl O&P
0010	**AUTOMATIC AIR VENT**									
0020	Cast iron body, stainless steel internals, float type									
0060	1/2" NPT inlet, 300 psi	1 Stpi	12	.667	Ea.	181	48.50		229.50	271
0140	3/4" NPT inlet, 300 psi		12	.667		181	48.50		229.50	271
0180	1/2" NPT inlet, 250 psi		10	.800		370	58		428	490
0220	3/4" NPT inlet, 250 psi		10	.800		370	58		428	490
0260	1" NPT inlet, 250 psi	↓	10	.800		540	58		598	675
0340	1-1/2" NPT inlet, 250 psi	Q-5	12	1.333		1,150	87		1,237	1,375
0380	2" NPT inlet, 250 psi	"	12	1.333	↓	1,150	87		1,237	1,375
0600	Forged steel body, stainless steel internals, float type									
0640	1/2" NPT inlet, 750 psi	1 Stpi	12	.667	Ea.	1,225	48.50		1,273.50	1,425
0680	3/4" NPT inlet, 750 psi		12	.667		1,225	48.50		1,273.50	1,425
0760	3/4" NPT inlet, 1,000 psi	↓	10	.800		1,825	58		1,883	2,100
0800	1" NPT inlet, 1,000 psi	Q-5	12	1.333		1,825	87		1,912	2,150
0880	1-1/2" NPT inlet, 1,000 psi		10	1.600		5,175	104		5,279	5,850
0920	2" NPT inlet, 1,000 psi	↓	10	1.600		5,175	104		5,279	5,850
1100	Formed steel body, noncorrosive									
1110	1/8" NPT inlet, 150 psi	1 Stpi	32	.250	Ea.	19.35	18.15		37.50	48.50
1120	1/4" NPT inlet, 150 psi		32	.250		65	18.15		83.15	98.50
1130	3/4" NPT inlet, 150 psi	↓	32	.250		65	18.15		83.15	98.50
1300	Chrome plated brass, automatic/manual, for radiators									
1310	1/8" NPT inlet, nickel plated brass	1 Stpi	32	.250	Ea.	11.30	18.15		29.45	39.50

23 21 20.22 Circuit Sensor

		Crew	Daily Output	Labor-Hours	Unit	Material	Labor	Equipment	Total	Total Incl O&P
0010	**CIRCUIT SENSOR**, Flow meter									
0020	Metering stations									
0040	Wafer orifice insert type									
0060	2-1/2" pipe size	Q-5	12	1.333	Ea.	450	87		537	625
0100	3" pipe size		11	1.455		525	95		620	715
0140	4" pipe size		8	2		575	131		706	830
0180	5" pipe size		7.30	2.192		750	143		893	1,050
0220	6" pipe size	↓	6.40	2.500		880	163		1,043	1,225
0260	8" pipe size	Q-6	5.30	4.528		1,225	305		1,530	1,800
0280	10" pipe size		4.60	5.217		1,275	355		1,630	1,925
0360	12" pipe size	↓	4.20	5.714		2,325	385		2,710	3,150

23 21 Hydronic Piping and Pumps

23 21 20 – Hydronic HVAC Piping Specialties

23 21 20.26 Circuit Setter

		Crew	Daily Output	Labor-Hours	Unit	Material	2023 Bare Costs Labor	Equipment	Total	Total Incl O&P
0010	**CIRCUIT SETTER**, Balance valve									
0012	Bronze body, soldered									
0013	1/2" size	1 Stpi	24	.333	Ea.	100	24		124	147
0014	3/4" size	"	20	.400	"	107	29		136	161
0018	Threaded									
0019	1/2" pipe size	1 Stpi	22	.364	Ea.	104	26.50		130.50	155
0020	3/4" pipe size		20	.400		111	29		140	167
0040	1" pipe size		18	.444		144	32		176	207
0050	1-1/4" pipe size		15	.533		212	38.50		250.50	291
0060	1-1/2" pipe size		12	.667		250	48.50		298.50	345
0080	2" pipe size		10	.800		360	58		418	480
0100	2-1/2" pipe size	Q-5	15	1.067		810	69.50		879.50	995
0120	3" pipe size	"	10	1.600		1,150	104		1,254	1,400
0130	Cast iron body, flanged									
0136	3" pipe size, flanged	Q-5	4	4	Ea.	1,100	261		1,361	1,600
0140	4" pipe size	"	3	5.333		1,700	350		2,050	2,400
0200	For differential meter, accurate to 1%, add					870			870	955
0300	For differential meter 400 psi/200°F continuous, add					2,925			2,925	3,200

23 21 20.30 Cocks, Drains and Specialties

		Crew	Daily Output	Labor-Hours	Unit	Material	Labor	Equipment	Total	Total Incl O&P
0010	**COCKS, DRAINS AND SPECIALTIES**									
1000	Boiler drain									
1010	Pipe thread to hose									
1020	Bronze									
1030	1/2" size	1 Stpi	36	.222	Ea.	23	16.10		39.10	49.50
1040	3/4" size	"	34	.235	"	28	17.05		45.05	56.50
1100	Solder to hose									
1110	Bronze									
1120	1/2" size	1 Stpi	46	.174	Ea.	23.50	12.60		36.10	45
1130	3/4" size	"	44	.182	"	25.50	13.20		38.70	47.50
1600	With built-in vacuum breaker									
1610	1/2" I.P. or solder	1 Stpi	36	.222	Ea.	34.50	16.10		50.60	62
1630	With tamper proof vacuum breaker									
1640	1/2" I.P. or solder	1 Stpi	36	.222	Ea.	76	16.10		92.10	108
1650	3/4" I.P. or solder	"	34	.235	"	73	17.05		90.05	106
3000	Cocks									
3010	Air, lever or tee handle									
3020	Bronze, single thread									
3030	1/8" size	1 Stpi	52	.154	Ea.	15.65	11.15		26.80	34
3040	1/4" size		46	.174		13.80	12.60		26.40	34
3050	3/8" size		40	.200		17.05	14.50		31.55	40.50
3060	1/2" size		36	.222		20	16.10		36.10	46
3100	Bronze, double thread									
3110	1/8" size	1 Stpi	26	.308	Ea.	20	22.50		42.50	55.50
3120	1/4" size		22	.364		17.45	26.50		43.95	58.50
3130	3/8" size		18	.444		22	32		54	72
3140	1/2" size		15	.533		26.50	38.50		65	87
4000	Steam									
4010	Bronze									
4020	1/8" size	1 Stpi	26	.308	Ea.	28	22.50		50.50	64
4030	1/4" size		22	.364		37	26.50		63.50	80.50
4040	3/8" size		18	.444		32.50	32		64.50	84
4050	1/2" size		15	.533		32.50	38.50		71	93.50

23 21 Hydronic Piping and Pumps

23 21 20 – Hydronic HVAC Piping Specialties

23 21 20.30 Cocks, Drains and Specialties

		Crew	Daily Output	Labor-Hours	Unit	Material	2023 Bare Costs Labor	Equipment	Total	Total Incl O&P
4060	3/4" size	1 Stpi	14	.571	Ea.	40.50	41.50		82	107
4070	1" size		13	.615		59	44.50		103.50	132
4080	1-1/4" size		11	.727		80.50	53		133.50	167
4090	1-1/2" size		10	.800		124	58		182	224
4100	2" size	↓	9	.889	↓	177	64.50		241.50	290
4300	Bronze, 3 way									
4320	1/4" size	1 Stpi	15	.533	Ea.	53.50	38.50		92	117
4330	3/8" size		12	.667		53.50	48.50		102	131
4340	1/2" size		10	.800		56.50	58		114.50	149
4350	3/4" size		9.50	.842		97	61		158	198
4360	1" size		8.50	.941		117	68.50		185.50	231
4370	1-1/4" size		7.50	1.067		148	77.50		225.50	278
4380	1-1/2" size		6.50	1.231		204	89.50		293.50	355
4390	2" size	↓	6	1.333	↓	300	96.50		396.50	475
4500	Gauge cock, brass									
4510	1/4" FPT	1 Stpi	24	.333	Ea.	13.80	24		37.80	51
4512	1/4" MPT	"	24	.333	"	17.70	24		41.70	55.50
4600	Pigtail, steam syphon									
4604	1/4"	1 Stpi	24	.333	Ea.	30	24		54	69
4650	Snubber valve									
4654	1/4"	1 Stpi	22	.364	Ea.	5.75	26.50		32.25	46
4660	Nipple, black steel									
4664	1/4" x 3"	1 Stpi	37	.216	Ea.	6.10	15.70		21.80	30

23 21 20.34 Dielectric Unions

		Crew	Daily Output	Labor-Hours	Unit	Material	2023 Bare Costs Labor	Equipment	Total	Total Incl O&P
0010	**DIELECTRIC UNIONS**, Standard gaskets for water and air									
0020	250 psi maximum pressure									
0280	Female IPT to sweat, straight									
0300	1/2" pipe size	1 Plum	24	.333	Ea.	9.95	24		33.95	47
0340	3/4" pipe size		20	.400		11.05	29		40.05	55
0360	1" pipe size		19	.421		14.90	30.50		45.40	61.50
0380	1-1/4" pipe size		15	.533		17.95	38.50		56.45	77
0400	1-1/2" pipe size		13	.615		34.50	44.50		79	104
0420	2" pipe size	↓	11	.727	↓	47	52.50		99.50	130
0580	Female IPT to brass pipe thread, straight									
0600	1/2" pipe size	1 Plum	24	.333	Ea.	21.50	24		45.50	59.50
0640	3/4" pipe size		20	.400		23.50	29		52.50	68.50
0660	1" pipe size		19	.421		43.50	30.50		74	92.50
0680	1-1/4" pipe size		15	.533		43	38.50		81.50	105
0700	1-1/2" pipe size		13	.615		62.50	44.50		107	135
0720	2" pipe size	↓	11	.727		113	52.50		165.50	202
0780	Female IPT to female IPT, straight									
0800	1/2" pipe size	1 Plum	24	.333	Ea.	25	24		49	63.50
0840	3/4" pipe size		20	.400		29	29		58	75
0860	1" pipe size		19	.421		38	30.50		68.50	86.50
0880	1-1/4" pipe size		15	.533		51	38.50		89.50	114
0900	1-1/2" pipe size		13	.615		77	44.50		121.50	151
0920	2" pipe size	↓	11	.727	↓	115	52.50		167.50	205
2000	175 psi maximum pressure									
2180	Female IPT to sweat									
2240	2" pipe size	1 Plum	9	.889	Ea.	231	64		295	350
2260	2-1/2" pipe size	Q-1	15	1.067		279	69		348	410
2280	3" pipe size	↓	14	1.143		385	74		459	535

23 21 Hydronic Piping and Pumps

23 21 20 – Hydronic HVAC Piping Specialties

23 21 20.34 Dielectric Unions

		Crew	Daily Output	Labor-Hours	Unit	Material	2023 Bare Costs Labor	2023 Bare Costs Equipment	Total	Total Incl O&P
2300	4" pipe size	Q-1	11	1.455	Ea.	1,000	94.50		1,094.50	1,275
2480	Female IPT to brass pipe									
2500	1-1/2" pipe size	1 Plum	11	.727	Ea.	310	52.50		362.50	420
2540	2" pipe size	"	9	.889		325	64		389	450
2560	2-1/2" pipe size	Q-1	15	1.067		360	69		429	500
2580	3" pipe size		14	1.143		360	74		434	505
2600	4" pipe size	↓	11	1.455	↓	510	94.50		604.50	705

23 21 20.38 Expansion Couplings

		Crew	Daily Output	Labor-Hours	Unit	Material	Labor	Equipment	Total	Total Incl O&P
0010	**EXPANSION COUPLINGS**, Hydronic									
0100	Copper to copper, sweat									
1000	Baseboard riser fitting, 5" stub by coupling 12" long									
1020	1/2" diameter	1 Stpi	24	.333	Ea.	29	24		53	68
1040	3/4" diameter		20	.400		33	29		62	80
1060	1" diameter		19	.421		57.50	30.50		88	109
1080	1-1/4" diameter	↓	15	.533	↓	75	38.50		113.50	140
1180	9" stub by tubing 8" long									
1200	1/2" diameter	1 Stpi	24	.333	Ea.	26	24		50	64.50
1220	3/4" diameter		20	.400		34.50	29		63.50	81.50
1240	1" diameter		19	.421		48	30.50		78.50	98
1260	1-1/4" diameter	↓	15	.533	↓	68	38.50		106.50	132

23 21 20.42 Expansion Joints

		Crew	Daily Output	Labor-Hours	Unit	Material	Labor	Equipment	Total	Total Incl O&P
0010	**EXPANSION JOINTS**									
0100	Bellows type, neoprene cover, flanged spool									
0140	6" face to face, 1-1/4" diameter	1 Stpi	11	.727	Ea.	390	53		443	510
0160	1-1/2" diameter	"	10.60	.755		390	55		445	510
0180	2" diameter	Q-5	13.30	1.203		395	78.50		473.50	550
0190	2-1/2" diameter		12.40	1.290		410	84.50		494.50	575
0200	3" diameter		11.40	1.404		460	91.50		551.50	640
0210	4" diameter		8.40	1.905		495	124		619	730
0220	5" diameter		7.60	2.105		605	137		742	870
0230	6" diameter		6.80	2.353		625	154		779	915
0240	8" diameter		5.40	2.963		725	193		918	1,075
0250	10" diameter		5	3.200		1,000	209		1,209	1,400
0260	12" diameter		4.60	3.478		1,150	227		1,377	1,600
0480	10" face to face, 2" diameter		13	1.231		570	80.50		650.50	745
0500	2-1/2" diameter		12	1.333		600	87		687	790
0520	3" diameter		11	1.455		610	95		705	810
0540	4" diameter		8	2		695	131		826	960
0560	5" diameter		7	2.286		830	149		979	1,125
0580	6" diameter		6	2.667		855	174		1,029	1,200
0600	8" diameter		5	3.200		1,025	209		1,234	1,425
0620	10" diameter		4.60	3.478		1,125	227		1,352	1,600
0640	12" diameter		4	4		1,400	261		1,661	1,950
0660	14" diameter		3.80	4.211		1,725	275		2,000	2,300
0680	16" diameter		2.90	5.517		2,000	360		2,360	2,725
0700	18" diameter		2.50	6.400		2,250	420		2,670	3,100
0720	20" diameter		2.10	7.619		2,350	500		2,850	3,350
0740	24" diameter		1.80	8.889		2,775	580		3,355	3,925
0760	26" diameter		1.40	11.429		3,075	745		3,820	4,525
0780	30" diameter		1.20	13.333		3,450	870		4,320	5,100
0800	36" diameter	↓	1	16	↓	3,950	1,050		5,000	5,900
1000	Bellows with internal sleeves and external covers									

23 21 Hydronic Piping and Pumps

23 21 20 – Hydronic HVAC Piping Specialties

23 21 20.42 Expansion Joints

		Crew	Daily Output	Labor-Hours	Unit	Material	2023 Bare Costs Labor	2023 Bare Costs Equipment	Total	Total Incl O&P
1010	Stainless steel, 150 lb.									
1020	With male threads									
1040	3/4" diameter	1 Stpi	20	.400	Ea.	109	29		138	164
1050	1" diameter		19	.421		118	30.50		148.50	176
1060	1-1/4" diameter		16	.500		121	36.50		157.50	188
1070	1-1/2" diameter		13	.615		144	44.50		188.50	226
1080	2" diameter	▼	11	.727	▼	164	53		217	259
1110	With flanged ends									
1120	1-1/4" diameter	1 Stpi	12	.667	Ea.	160	48.50		208.50	248
1130	1-1/2" diameter		11	.727		182	53		235	279
1140	2" diameter	▼	9	.889		248	64.50		312.50	370
1150	3" diameter	Q-5	8	2		345	131		476	575
1160	4" diameter	"	5	3.200		1,225	209		1,434	1,650
1170	5" diameter	Q-6	6	4		1,450	271		1,721	2,000
1180	6" diameter		5	4.800		1,650	325		1,975	2,275
1190	8" diameter		4.50	5.333		2,375	360		2,735	3,175
1200	10" diameter		4	6		4,075	405		4,480	5,075
1210	12" diameter	▼	3.60	6.667	▼	4,025	450		4,475	5,100

23 21 20.46 Expansion Tanks

		Crew	Daily Output	Labor-Hours	Unit	Material	2023 Bare Costs Labor	2023 Bare Costs Equipment	Total	Total Incl O&P
0010	**EXPANSION TANKS**									
1400	Plastic, corrosion resistant, see Plumbing Costs									
1507	Underground fuel-oil storage tanks, see Section 23 13 13									
1512	Tank leak detection systems, see Section 28 33 33.50									
2000	Steel, liquid expansion, ASME, painted, 15 gallon capacity	Q-5	17	.941	Ea.	935	61.50		996.50	1,125
2020	24 gallon capacity		14	1.143		780	74.50		854.50	965
2040	30 gallon capacity		12	1.333		1,125	87		1,212	1,350
2060	40 gallon capacity		10	1.600		1,300	104		1,404	1,575
2080	60 gallon capacity		8	2		1,550	131		1,681	1,925
2100	80 gallon capacity		7	2.286		1,675	149		1,824	2,075
2120	100 gallon capacity		6	2.667		2,275	174		2,449	2,750
2130	120 gallon capacity		5	3.200		2,425	209		2,634	2,975
2140	135 gallon capacity		4.50	3.556		2,525	232		2,757	3,125
2150	175 gallon capacity		4	4		3,975	261		4,236	4,775
2160	220 gallon capacity		3.60	4.444		4,500	290		4,790	5,375
2170	240 gallon capacity		3.30	4.848		4,700	315		5,015	5,625
2180	305 gallon capacity		3	5.333		6,625	350		6,975	7,800
2190	400 gallon capacity	▼	2.80	5.714	▼	8,125	375		8,500	9,475
2360	Galvanized									
2370	15 gallon capacity	Q-5	17	.941	Ea.	1,500	61.50		1,561.50	1,750
2380	24 gallon capacity		14	1.143		1,625	74.50		1,699.50	1,900
2390	30 gallon capacity		12	1.333		1,675	87		1,762	1,975
2400	40 gallon capacity		10	1.600		2,075	104		2,179	2,425
2410	60 gallon capacity		8	2		2,375	131		2,506	2,800
2420	80 gallon capacity		7	2.286		2,450	149		2,599	2,925
2430	100 gallon capacity		6	2.667		3,550	174		3,724	4,150
2440	120 gallon capacity		5	3.200		3,225	209		3,434	3,850
2450	135 gallon capacity		4.50	3.556		4,000	232		4,232	4,750
2460	175 gallon capacity		4	4		5,050	261		5,311	5,950
2470	220 gallon capacity		3.60	4.444		6,475	290		6,765	7,550
2480	240 gallon capacity		3.30	4.848		6,775	315		7,090	7,925
2490	305 gallon capacity		3	5.333		8,650	350		9,000	10,000
2500	400 gallon capacity	▼	2.80	5.714	▼	12,100	375		12,475	13,900

23 21 Hydronic Piping and Pumps

23 21 20 – Hydronic HVAC Piping Specialties

23 21 20.46 Expansion Tanks

		Crew	Daily Output	Labor-Hours	Unit	Material	2023 Bare Costs Labor	Equipment	Total	Total Incl O&P
3000	Steel ASME expansion, rubber diaphragm, 19 gal. cap. accept.	Q-5	12	1.333	Ea.	3,550	87		3,637	4,025
3020	31 gallon capacity		8	2		3,950	131		4,081	4,550
3040	61 gallon capacity		6	2.667		5,925	174		6,099	6,775
3060	79 gallon capacity		5	3.200		5,650	209		5,859	6,525
3080	119 gallon capacity		4	4		5,975	261		6,236	6,975
3100	158 gallon capacity		3.80	4.211		8,325	275		8,600	9,550
3120	211 gallon capacity		3.30	4.848		9,600	315		9,915	11,100
3140	317 gallon capacity		2.80	5.714		12,500	375		12,875	14,400
3160	422 gallon capacity		2.60	6.154		18,600	400		19,000	21,100
3180	528 gallon capacity		2.40	6.667		20,400	435		20,835	23,100

23 21 20.50 Float Valves

		Crew	Daily Output	Labor-Hours	Unit	Material	Labor	Equipment	Total	Total Incl O&P
0010	**FLOAT VALVES**									
0020	With ball and bracket									
0030	Single seat, threaded									
0040	Brass body									
0050	1/2"	1 Stpi	11	.727	Ea.	101	53		154	190
0060	3/4"		9	.889		114	64.50		178.50	222
0070	1"		7	1.143		203	83		286	345
0080	1-1/2"		4.50	1.778		278	129		407	495
0090	2"		3.60	2.222		297	161		458	565
0300	For condensate receivers, CI, in-line mount									
0320	1" inlet	1 Stpi	7	1.143	Ea.	185	83		268	325
0360	For condensate receiver, CI, external float, flanged tank mount									
0370	3/4" inlet	1 Stpi	5	1.600	Ea.	114	116		230	299

23 21 20.54 Flow Check Control

		Crew	Daily Output	Labor-Hours	Unit	Material	Labor	Equipment	Total	Total Incl O&P
0010	**FLOW CHECK CONTROL**									
0100	Bronze body, soldered									
0110	3/4" size	1 Stpi	20	.400	Ea.	90	29		119	143
0120	1" size	"	19	.421	"	109	30.50		139.50	165
0200	Cast iron body, threaded									
0210	3/4" size	1 Stpi	20	.400	Ea.	47	29		76	95
0220	1" size		19	.421		48	30.50		78.50	98.50
0230	1-1/4" size		15	.533		74	38.50		112.50	139
0240	1-1/2" size		13	.615		144	44.50		188.50	225
0250	2" size		11	.727		206	53		259	305
0300	Flanged inlet, threaded outlet									
0310	2-1/2" size	1 Stpi	8	1	Ea.	420	72.50		492.50	570
0320	3" size	Q-5	9	1.778		520	116		636	745
0330	4" size	"	7	2.286		970	149		1,119	1,300

23 21 20.58 Hydronic Heating Control Valves

		Crew	Daily Output	Labor-Hours	Unit	Material	Labor	Equipment	Total	Total Incl O&P
0010	**HYDRONIC HEATING CONTROL VALVES**									
0050	Hot water, nonelectric, thermostatic									
0100	Radiator supply, 1/2" diameter	1 Stpi	24	.333	Ea.	42	24		66	82
0120	3/4" diameter		20	.400		48	29		77	96
0140	1" diameter		19	.421		136	30.50		166.50	196
0160	1-1/4" diameter		15	.533		117	38.50		155.50	186
0500	For low pressure steam, add					25%				
1000	Manual, radiator supply									
1010	1/2" pipe size, angle union	1 Stpi	24	.333	Ea.	106	24		130	153
1020	3/4" pipe size, angle union		20	.400		133	29		162	191
1030	1" pipe size, angle union		19	.421		172	30.50		202.50	235
1100	Radiator, balancing, straight, sweat connections									

23 21 Hydronic Piping and Pumps

23 21 20 – Hydronic HVAC Piping Specialties

23 21 20.58 Hydronic Heating Control Valves

		Crew	Daily Output	Labor-Hours	Unit	Material	2023 Bare Costs Labor	Equipment	Total	Total Incl O&P
1110	1/2" pipe size	1 Stpi	24	.333	Ea.	35	24		59	74.50
1120	3/4" pipe size		20	.400		48.50	29		77.50	97
1130	1" pipe size	↓	19	.421	↓	79.50	30.50		110	133
1200	Steam, radiator, supply									
1210	1/2" pipe size, angle union	1 Stpi	24	.333	Ea.	108	24		132	154
1220	3/4" pipe size, angle union		20	.400		117	29		146	172
1230	1" pipe size, angle union		19	.421		135	30.50		165.50	194
1240	1-1/4" pipe size, angle union	↓	15	.533		173	38.50		211.50	248
8000	System balancing and shut-off									
8020	Butterfly, quarter turn, calibrated, threaded or solder									
8040	Bronze, -30°F to +350°F, pressure to 175 psi									
8060	1/2" size	1 Stpi	22	.364	Ea.	37.50	26.50		64	80.50
8070	3/4" size		20	.400		60.50	29		89.50	110
8080	1" size		19	.421		78	30.50		108.50	131
8090	1-1/4" size		15	.533		119	38.50		157.50	189
8100	1-1/2" size		13	.615		162	44.50		206.50	245
8110	2" size	↓	11	.727	↓	193	53		246	291

23 21 20.62 Liquid Drainers

		Crew	Daily Output	Labor-Hours	Unit	Material	2023 Bare Costs Labor	Equipment	Total	Total Incl O&P
0010	**LIQUID DRAINERS**									
0100	Guided lever type									
0110	Cast iron body, threaded									
0120	1/2" pipe size	1 Stpi	22	.364	Ea.	137	26.50		163.50	190
0130	3/4" pipe size		20	.400		360	29		389	440
0140	1" pipe size		19	.421		575	30.50		605.50	675
0150	1-1/2" pipe size		11	.727		1,075	53		1,128	1,250
0160	2" pipe size	↓	8	1	↓	1,075	72.50		1,147.50	1,275
0200	Forged steel body, threaded									
0210	1/2" pipe size	1 Stpi	18	.444	Ea.	1,150	32		1,182	1,325
0220	3/4" pipe size		16	.500		1,150	36.50		1,186.50	1,325
0230	1" pipe size	↓	14	.571		1,750	41.50		1,791.50	1,975
0240	1-1/2" pipe size	Q-5	10	1.600		5,975	104		6,079	6,725
0250	2" pipe size	"	8	2	↓	5,975	131		6,106	6,775
0300	Socket weld									
0310	1/2" pipe size	Q-17	16	1	Ea.	1,575	65.50	4.01	1,644.51	1,825
0320	3/4" pipe size		14	1.143		1,575	74.50	4.58	1,654.08	1,850
0330	1" pipe size		12	1.333		2,275	87	5.35	2,367.35	2,625
0340	1-1/2" pipe size		9	1.778		6,175	116	7.15	6,298.15	6,975
0350	2" pipe size	↓	7	2.286	↓	6,175	149	9.15	6,333.15	7,025
0400	Flanged									
0410	1/2" pipe size	1 Stpi	12	.667	Ea.	3,250	48.50		3,298.50	3,650
0420	3/4" pipe size		10	.800		3,250	58		3,308	3,650
0430	1" pipe size	↓	7	1.143		4,075	83		4,158	4,625
0440	1-1/2" pipe size	Q-5	9	1.778		8,300	116		8,416	9,300
0450	2" pipe size	"	7	2.286	↓	8,300	149		8,449	9,350
1000	Fixed lever and snap action type									
1100	Cast iron body, threaded									
1110	1/2" pipe size	1 Stpi	22	.364	Ea.	212	26.50		238.50	273
1120	3/4" pipe size		20	.400		560	29		589	660
1130	1" pipe size	↓	19	.421	↓	560	30.50		590.50	660
1200	Forged steel body, threaded									
1210	1/2" pipe size	1 Stpi	18	.444	Ea.	1,475	32		1,507	1,675
1220	3/4" pipe size	↓	16	.500		1,475	36.50		1,511.50	1,675

23 21 Hydronic Piping and Pumps

23 21 20 – Hydronic HVAC Piping Specialties

23 21 20.62 Liquid Drainers		Crew	Daily Output	Labor-Hours	Unit	Material	2023 Bare Costs Labor	Equipment	Total	Total Incl O&P
1230	1" pipe size	1 Stpi	14	.571	Ea.	3,650	41.50		3,691.50	4,050
1240	1-1/4" pipe size	↓	12	.667	↓	3,650	48.50		3,698.50	4,075
2000	High pressure high leverage type									
2100	Forged steel body, threaded									
2110	1/2" pipe size	1 Stpi	18	.444	Ea.	2,900	32		2,932	3,225
2120	3/4" pipe size		16	.500		2,900	36.50		2,936.50	3,225
2130	1" pipe size		14	.571		4,850	41.50		4,891.50	5,375
2140	1-1/4" pipe size	↓	12	.667		4,850	48.50		4,898.50	5,400
2150	1-1/2" pipe size	Q-5	10	1.600		7,300	104		7,404	8,175
2160	2" pipe size	"	8	2	↓	7,300	131		7,431	8,225
2200	Socket weld									
2210	1/2" pipe size	Q-17	16	1	Ea.	3,125	65.50	4.01	3,194.51	3,550
2220	3/4" pipe size		14	1.143		3,125	74.50	4.58	3,204.08	3,575
2230	1" pipe size		12	1.333		5,100	87	5.35	5,192.35	5,725
2240	1-1/4" pipe size		11	1.455		5,100	95	5.85	5,200.85	5,750
2250	1-1/2" pipe size		9	1.778		7,525	116	7.15	7,648.15	8,475
2260	2" pipe size	↓	7	2.286	↓	7,525	149	9.15	7,683.15	8,525
2300	Flanged									
2310	1/2" pipe size	1 Stpi	12	.667	Ea.	4,200	48.50		4,248.50	4,700
2320	3/4" pipe size		10	.800		4,200	58		4,258	4,700
2330	1" pipe size		7	1.143		6,625	83		6,708	7,400
2340	1-1/4" pipe size	↓	6	1.333		6,625	96.50		6,721.50	7,425
2350	1-1/2" pipe size	Q-5	9	1.778		9,050	116		9,166	10,100
2360	2" pipe size	"	7	2.286		9,050	149		9,199	10,200
3000	Guided lever dual gravity type									
3100	Cast iron body, threaded									
3110	1/2" pipe size	1 Stpi	22	.364	Ea.	530	26.50		556.50	620
3120	3/4" pipe size		20	.400		530	29		559	625
3130	1" pipe size		19	.421		765	30.50		795.50	890
3140	1-1/2" pipe size		11	.727		1,475	53		1,528	1,700
3150	2" pipe size	↓	8	1		1,475	72.50		1,547.50	1,725
3200	Forged steel body, threaded									
3210	1/2" pipe size	1 Stpi	18	.444	Ea.	1,575	32		1,607	1,800
3220	3/4" pipe size		16	.500		1,575	36.50		1,611.50	1,800
3230	1" pipe size	↓	14	.571		2,350	41.50		2,391.50	2,625
3240	1-1/2" pipe size	Q-5	10	1.600		6,250	104		6,354	7,025
3250	2" pipe size	"	8	2		6,250	131		6,381	7,075
3300	Socket weld									
3310	1/2" pipe size	Q-17	16	1	Ea.	1,775	65.50	4.01	1,844.51	2,075
3320	3/4" pipe size		14	1.143		1,775	74.50	4.58	1,854.08	2,100
3330	1" pipe size		12	1.333		2,575	87	5.35	2,667.35	2,975
3340	1-1/2" pipe size		9	1.778		6,475	116	7.15	6,598.15	7,300
3350	2" pipe size	↓	7	2.286	↓	6,475	149	9.15	6,633.15	7,350
3400	Flanged									
3410	1/2" pipe size	1 Stpi	12	.667	Ea.	2,875	48.50		2,923.50	3,250
3420	3/4" pipe size		10	.800		2,875	58		2,933	3,250
3430	1" pipe size	↓	7	1.143		3,775	83		3,858	4,275
3440	1-1/2" pipe size	Q-5	9	1.778		8,000	116		8,116	8,975
3450	2" pipe size	"	7	2.286		8,000	149		8,149	9,025

23 21 Hydronic Piping and Pumps

23 21 20 – Hydronic HVAC Piping Specialties

23 21 20.66 Monoflow Tee Fitting

		Crew	Daily Output	Labor-Hours	Unit	Material	2023 Bare Costs Labor	2023 Bare Costs Equipment	Total	Total Incl O&P
0010	**MONOFLOW TEE FITTING**									
1100	For one pipe hydronic, supply and return									
1110	Copper, soldered									
1120	3/4" x 1/2" size	1 Stpi	13	.615	Ea.	27	44.50		71.50	96
1130	1" x 1/2" size		12	.667		30	48.50		78.50	105
1140	1" x 3/4" size		11	.727		30	53		83	112
1150	1-1/4" x 1/2" size		11	.727		30.50	53		83.50	112
1160	1-1/4" x 3/4" size		10	.800		30.50	58		88.50	120
1170	1-1/2" x 3/4" size		10	.800		45	58		103	136
1180	1-1/2" x 1" size		9	.889		45	64.50		109.50	146
1190	2" x 3/4" size		9	.889		68.50	64.50		133	171
1200	2" x 1" size	▼	8	1	▼	68.50	72.50		141	183

23 21 20.70 Steam Traps

		Crew	Daily Output	Labor-Hours	Unit	Material	2023 Bare Costs Labor	2023 Bare Costs Equipment	Total	Total Incl O&P
0010	**STEAM TRAPS**									
0030	Cast iron body, threaded									
0040	Inverted bucket									
0050	1/2" pipe size	1 Stpi	12	.667	Ea.	170	48.50		218.50	259
0070	3/4" pipe size		10	.800		296	58		354	410
0100	1" pipe size		9	.889		455	64.50		519.50	595
0120	1-1/4" pipe size		8	1		690	72.50		762.50	870
0130	1-1/2" pipe size		7	1.143		865	83		948	1,075
0140	2" pipe size	▼	6	1.333	▼	1,350	96.50		1,446.50	1,650
0200	With thermic vent & check valve									
0202	1/2" pipe size	1 Stpi	12	.667	Ea.	201	48.50		249.50	293
0204	3/4" pipe size		10	.800		340	58		398	460
0206	1" pipe size		9	.889		495	64.50		559.50	640
0208	1-1/4" pipe size		8	1		750	72.50		822.50	935
0210	1-1/2" pipe size		7	1.143		960	83		1,043	1,175
0212	2" pipe size	▼	6	1.333		1,475	96.50		1,571.50	1,750
1000	Float & thermostatic, 15 psi									
1010	3/4" pipe size	1 Stpi	16	.500	Ea.	202	36.50		238.50	276
1020	1" pipe size		15	.533		194	38.50		232.50	272
1030	1-1/4" pipe size		13	.615		235	44.50		279.50	325
1040	1-1/2" pipe size		9	.889		340	64.50		404.50	470
1060	2" pipe size	▼	6	1.333		975	96.50		1,071.50	1,225
1100	For vacuum breaker, add				▼	74.50			74.50	82
1110	Differential condensate controller									
1120	With union and manual metering valve									
1130	1/2" pipe size	1 Stpi	24	.333	Ea.	745	24		769	855
1140	3/4" pipe size		20	.400		865	29		894	995
1150	1" pipe size		19	.421		1,150	30.50		1,180.50	1,325
1160	1-1/4" pipe size		15	.533		1,575	38.50		1,613.50	1,775
1170	1-1/2" pipe size		13	.615		1,900	44.50		1,944.50	2,150
1180	2" pipe size	▼	11	.727	▼	2,450	53		2,503	2,775
1290	Brass body, threaded									
1300	Thermostatic, angle union, 25 psi									
1310	1/2" pipe size	1 Stpi	24	.333	Ea.	99.50	24		123.50	145
1320	3/4" pipe size		20	.400		192	29		221	255
1330	1" pipe size	▼	19	.421		272	30.50		302.50	345
1990	Carbon steel body, threaded									
2000	Controlled disc, integral strainer & blow down									
2010	Threaded									

23 21 Hydronic Piping and Pumps
23 21 20 – Hydronic HVAC Piping Specialties

23 21 20.70 Steam Traps		Crew	Daily Output	Labor-Hours	Unit	Material	2023 Bare Costs Labor	Equipment	Total	Total Incl O&P
2020	3/8" pipe size	1 Stpi	24	.333	Ea.	330	24		354	400
2030	1/2" pipe size		24	.333		330	24		354	400
2040	3/4" pipe size		20	.400		445	29		474	535
2050	1" pipe size	↓	19	.421	↓	570	30.50		600.50	670
2100	Socket weld									
2110	3/8" pipe size	Q-17	17	.941	Ea.	395	61.50	3.77	460.27	530
2120	1/2" pipe size		16	1		395	65.50	4.01	464.51	535
2130	3/4" pipe size		14	1.143		515	74.50	4.58	594.08	680
2140	1" pipe size	↓	12	1.333		645	87	5.35	737.35	845
2170	Flanged, 600 lb. ASA									
2180	3/8" pipe size	1 Stpi	12	.667	Ea.	890	48.50		938.50	1,050
2190	1/2" pipe size		12	.667		890	48.50		938.50	1,050
2200	3/4" pipe size		10	.800		1,075	58		1,133	1,250
2210	1" pipe size	↓	7	1.143	↓	1,250	83		1,333	1,500
5000	Forged steel body									
5010	Inverted bucket									
5020	Threaded									
5030	1/2" pipe size	1 Stpi	12	.667	Ea.	600	48.50		648.50	735
5040	3/4" pipe size		10	.800		1,050	58		1,108	1,225
5050	1" pipe size		9	.889		1,575	64.50		1,639.50	1,825
5060	1-1/4" pipe size		8	1		2,275	72.50		2,347.50	2,600
5070	1-1/2" pipe size		7	1.143		3,225	83		3,308	3,675
5080	2" pipe size	↓	6	1.333	↓	5,650	96.50		5,746.50	6,375
5100	Socket weld									
5110	1/2" pipe size	Q-17	16	1	Ea.	725	65.50	4.01	794.51	895
5120	3/4" pipe size		14	1.143		1,175	74.50	4.58	1,254.08	1,400
5130	1" pipe size		12	1.333		1,675	87	5.35	1,767.35	1,975
5140	1-1/4" pipe size		10	1.600		2,400	104	6.40	2,510.40	2,800
5150	1-1/2" pipe size		9	1.778		3,350	116	7.15	3,473.15	3,850
5160	2" pipe size	↓	7	2.286	↓	5,800	149	9.15	5,958.15	6,600
5200	Flanged									
5210	1/2" pipe size	1 Stpi	12	.667	Ea.	1,125	48.50		1,173.50	1,300
5220	3/4" pipe size		10	.800		1,825	58		1,883	2,075
5230	1" pipe size		7	1.143		2,500	83		2,583	2,875
5240	1-1/4" pipe size		6	1.333		3,375	96.50		3,471.50	3,850
5250	1-1/2" pipe size	Q-5	9	1.778		4,300	116		4,416	4,925
5260	2" pipe size	"	7	2.286	↓	6,775	149		6,924	7,675
6000	Stainless steel body									
6010	Inverted bucket									
6020	Threaded									
6030	1/2" pipe size	1 Stpi	12	.667	Ea.	199	48.50		247.50	291
6040	3/4" pipe size		10	.800		262	58		320	375
6050	1" pipe size	↓	9	.889	↓	930	64.50		994.50	1,125
6100	Threaded with thermic vent									
6110	1/2" pipe size	1 Stpi	12	.667	Ea.	239	48.50		287.50	335
6120	3/4" pipe size		10	.800		310	58		368	425
6130	1" pipe size	↓	9	.889	↓	930	64.50		994.50	1,125
6200	Threaded with check valve									
6210	1/2" pipe size	1 Stpi	12	.667	Ea.	285	48.50		333.50	385
6220	3/4" pipe size	"	10	.800	"	390	58		448	515
6300	Socket weld									
6310	1/2" pipe size	Q-17	16	1	Ea.	231	65.50	4.01	300.51	355
6320	3/4" pipe size	"	14	1.143	"	299	74.50	4.58	378.08	445

23 21 Hydronic Piping and Pumps

23 21 20 – Hydronic HVAC Piping Specialties

23 21 20.74 Strainers, Basket Type		Crew	Daily Output	Labor-Hours	Unit	Material	2023 Bare Costs Labor	2023 Bare Costs Equipment	Total	Total Incl O&P
0010	**STRAINERS, BASKET TYPE**, Perforated stainless steel basket									
0100	Brass or monel available									
2000	Simplex style									
2300	Bronze body									
2320	Screwed, 3/8" pipe size	1 Stpi	22	.364	Ea.	246	26.50		272.50	310
2340	1/2" pipe size		20	.400		275	29		304	345
2360	3/4" pipe size		17	.471		315	34		349	400
2380	1" pipe size		15	.533		350	38.50		388.50	445
2400	1-1/4" pipe size		13	.615		530	44.50		574.50	645
2420	1-1/2" pipe size		12	.667		495	48.50		543.50	615
2440	2" pipe size		10	.800		605	58		663	750
2460	2-1/2" pipe size	Q-5	15	1.067		1,350	69.50		1,419.50	1,575
2480	3" pipe size	"	14	1.143		2,000	74.50		2,074.50	2,300
2600	Flanged, 2" pipe size	1 Stpi	6	1.333		1,175	96.50		1,271.50	1,450
2620	2-1/2" pipe size	Q-5	4.50	3.556		2,050	232		2,282	2,600
2640	3" pipe size		3.50	4.571		2,300	299		2,599	2,975
2660	4" pipe size		3	5.333		3,525	350		3,875	4,400
2680	5" pipe size	Q-6	3.40	7.059		5,625	480		6,105	6,925
2700	6" pipe size		3	8		6,875	540		7,415	8,350
2710	8" pipe size		2.50	9.600		11,200	650		11,850	13,300
3600	Iron body									
3700	Screwed, 3/8" pipe size	1 Stpi	22	.364	Ea.	214	26.50		240.50	275
3720	1/2" pipe size		20	.400		238	29		267	305
3740	3/4" pipe size		17	.471		300	34		334	380
3760	1" pipe size		15	.533		310	38.50		348.50	400
3780	1-1/4" pipe size		13	.615		405	44.50		449.50	510
3800	1-1/2" pipe size		12	.667		445	48.50		493.50	560
3820	2" pipe size		10	.800		530	58		588	670
3840	2-1/2" pipe size	Q-5	15	1.067		710	69.50		779.50	885
3860	3" pipe size	"	14	1.143		860	74.50		934.50	1,050
4000	Flanged, 2" pipe size	1 Stpi	6	1.333		820	96.50		916.50	1,050
4020	2-1/2" pipe size	Q-5	4.50	3.556		1,100	232		1,332	1,575
4040	3" pipe size		3.50	4.571		1,150	299		1,449	1,725
4060	4" pipe size		3	5.333		1,775	350		2,125	2,475
4080	5" pipe size	Q-6	3.40	7.059		2,675	480		3,155	3,675
4100	6" pipe size		3	8		3,425	540		3,965	4,575
4120	8" pipe size		2.50	9.600		6,200	650		6,850	7,800
4140	10" pipe size		2.20	10.909		13,600	740		14,340	16,100
6000	Cast steel body									
6400	Screwed, 1" pipe size	1 Stpi	15	.533	Ea.	520	38.50		558.50	635
6410	1-1/4" pipe size		13	.615		775	44.50		819.50	920
6420	1-1/2" pipe size		12	.667		775	48.50		823.50	925
6440	2" pipe size		10	.800		1,075	58		1,133	1,275
6460	2-1/2" pipe size	Q-5	15	1.067		1,550	69.50		1,619.50	1,800
6480	3" pipe size	"	14	1.143		2,000	74.50		2,074.50	2,300
6560	Flanged, 2" pipe size	1 Stpi	6	1.333		2,000	96.50		2,096.50	2,350
6580	2-1/2" pipe size	Q-5	4.50	3.556		1,550	232		1,782	2,050
6600	3" pipe size		3.50	4.571		3,200	299		3,499	3,975
6620	4" pipe size		3	5.333		4,550	350		4,900	5,525
6640	6" pipe size	Q-6	3	8		8,300	540		8,840	9,925
6660	8" pipe size	"	2.50	9.600		13,300	650		13,950	15,600
7000	Stainless steel body									

23 21 Hydronic Piping and Pumps

23 21 20 – Hydronic HVAC Piping Specialties

23 21 20.74 Strainers, Basket Type

		Crew	Daily Output	Labor-Hours	Unit	Material	2023 Bare Costs Labor	Equipment	Total	Total Incl O&P
7200	Screwed, 1" pipe size	1 Stpi	15	.533	Ea.	660	38.50		698.50	785
7210	1-1/4" pipe size		13	.615		1,025	44.50		1,069.50	1,200
7220	1-1/2" pipe size		12	.667		1,025	48.50		1,073.50	1,200
7240	2" pipe size		10	.800		1,525	58		1,583	1,750
7260	2-1/2" pipe size	Q-5	15	1.067		2,150	69.50		2,219.50	2,475
7280	3" pipe size	"	14	1.143		2,975	74.50		3,049.50	3,375
7400	Flanged, 2" pipe size	1 Stpi	6	1.333		4,825	96.50		4,921.50	5,475
7420	2-1/2" pipe size	Q-5	4.50	3.556		4,725	232		4,957	5,550
7440	3" pipe size		3.50	4.571		4,825	299		5,124	5,775
7460	4" pipe size		3	5.333		7,600	350		7,950	8,875
7480	6" pipe size	Q-6	3	8		15,200	540		15,740	17,500
7500	8" pipe size	"	2.50	9.600		22,100	650		22,750	25,300
8100	Duplex style									
8200	Bronze body									
8240	Screwed, 3/4" pipe size	1 Stpi	16	.500	Ea.	1,825	36.50		1,861.50	2,050
8260	1" pipe size		14	.571		1,825	41.50		1,866.50	2,050
8280	1-1/4" pipe size		12	.667		3,075	48.50		3,123.50	3,475
8300	1-1/2" pipe size		11	.727		3,075	53		3,128	3,475
8320	2" pipe size		9	.889		5,800	64.50		5,864.50	6,475
8340	2-1/2" pipe size	Q-5	14	1.143		7,475	74.50		7,549.50	8,325
8420	Flanged, 2" pipe size	1 Stpi	6	1.333		7,125	96.50		7,221.50	8,000
8440	2-1/2" pipe size	Q-5	4.50	3.556		9,850	232		10,082	11,100
8460	3" pipe size		3.50	4.571		10,700	299		10,999	12,200
8480	4" pipe size		3	5.333		14,600	350		14,950	16,500
8500	5" pipe size	Q-6	3.40	7.059		35,300	480		35,780	39,500
8520	6" pipe size	"	3	8		34,300	540		34,840	38,500
8700	Iron body									
8740	Screwed, 3/4" pipe size	1 Stpi	16	.500	Ea.	2,425	36.50		2,461.50	2,725
8760	1" pipe size		14	.571		2,425	41.50		2,466.50	2,725
8780	1-1/4" pipe size		12	.667		2,700	48.50		2,748.50	3,050
8800	1-1/2" pipe size		11	.727		2,700	53		2,753	3,050
8820	2" pipe size		9	.889		4,575	64.50		4,639.50	5,125
8840	2-1/2" pipe size	Q-5	14	1.143		5,050	74.50		5,124.50	5,650
9000	Flanged, 2" pipe size	1 Stpi	6	1.333		4,875	96.50		4,971.50	5,525
9020	2-1/2" pipe size	Q-5	4.50	3.556		5,225	232		5,457	6,100
9040	3" pipe size		3.50	4.571		5,675	299		5,974	6,700
9060	4" pipe size		3	5.333		9,600	350		9,950	11,100
9080	5" pipe size	Q-6	3.40	7.059		20,900	480		21,380	23,700
9100	6" pipe size		3	8		20,900	540		21,440	23,800
9120	8" pipe size		2.50	9.600		41,500	650		42,150	46,600
9140	10" pipe size		2.20	10.909		59,000	740		59,740	66,000
9160	12" pipe size		1.70	14.118		65,500	955		66,455	73,500
9170	14" pipe size		1.40	17.143		77,000	1,150		78,150	86,000
9180	16" pipe size		1	24		94,500	1,625		96,125	106,500
9300	Cast steel body									
9340	Screwed, 1" pipe size	1 Stpi	14	.571	Ea.	3,125	41.50		3,166.50	3,500
9360	1-1/2" pipe size		11	.727		5,050	53		5,103	5,625
9380	2" pipe size		9	.889		6,700	64.50		6,764.50	7,450
9460	Flanged, 2" pipe size		6	1.333		5,225	96.50		5,321.50	5,900
9480	2-1/2" pipe size	Q-5	4.50	3.556		7,050	232		7,282	8,100
9500	3" pipe size		3.50	4.571		7,675	299		7,974	8,900
9520	4" pipe size		3	5.333		9,450	350		9,800	10,900
9540	6" pipe size	Q-6	3	8		17,700	540		18,240	20,300

23 21 Hydronic Piping and Pumps

23 21 20 – Hydronic HVAC Piping Specialties

23 21 20.74 Strainers, Basket Type

		Crew	Daily Output	Labor-Hours	Unit	Material	2023 Bare Costs Labor	Equipment	Total	Total Incl O&P
9560	8" pipe size	Q-6	2.50	9.600	Ea.	44,600	650		45,250	50,000
9700	Stainless steel body									
9740	Screwed, 1" pipe size	1 Stpi	14	.571	Ea.	4,425	41.50		4,466.50	4,925
9760	1-1/2" pipe size		11	.727		6,650	53		6,703	7,375
9780	2" pipe size		9	.889		9,375	64.50		9,439.50	10,400
9860	Flanged, 2" pipe size	↓	6	1.333		10,100	96.50		10,196.50	11,200
9880	2-1/2" pipe size	Q-5	4.50	3.556		16,900	232		17,132	18,900
9900	3" pipe size		3.50	4.571		18,500	299		18,799	20,700
9920	4" pipe size	↓	3	5.333		24,000	350		24,350	26,900
9940	6" pipe size	Q-6	3	8		36,700	540		37,240	41,200
9960	8" pipe size	"	2.50	9.600	↓	91,500	650		92,150	102,000

23 21 20.76 Strainers, Y Type, Bronze Body

		Crew	Daily Output	Labor-Hours	Unit	Material	2023 Bare Costs Labor	Equipment	Total	Total Incl O&P
0010	**STRAINERS, Y TYPE, BRONZE BODY**									
0050	Screwed, 125 lb., 1/4" pipe size	1 Stpi	24	.333	Ea.	63	24		87	105
0070	3/8" pipe size		24	.333		63	24		87	105
0100	1/2" pipe size		20	.400		52	29		81	101
0120	3/4" pipe size		19	.421		77.50	30.50		108	131
0140	1" pipe size		17	.471		115	34		149	177
0150	1-1/4" pipe size		15	.533		182	38.50		220.50	258
0160	1-1/2" pipe size		14	.571		246	41.50		287.50	330
0180	2" pipe size		13	.615		320	44.50		364.50	420
0182	3" pipe size	↓	12	.667		2,150	48.50		2,198.50	2,450
0200	300 lb., 2-1/2" pipe size	Q-5	17	.941		1,225	61.50		1,286.50	1,450
0220	3" pipe size		16	1		1,525	65.50		1,590.50	1,775
0240	4" pipe size	↓	15	1.067	↓	2,800	69.50		2,869.50	3,175
0500	For 300 lb. rating 1/4" thru 2", add					15%				
1000	Flanged, 150 lb., 1-1/2" pipe size	1 Stpi	11	.727	Ea.	650	53		703	795
1020	2" pipe size	"	8	1		795	72.50		867.50	985
1030	2-1/2" pipe size	Q-5	5	3.200		1,325	209		1,534	1,775
1040	3" pipe size		4.50	3.556		1,650	232		1,882	2,150
1060	4" pipe size		3	5.333		2,525	350		2,875	3,300
1080	5" pipe size	Q-6	3.40	7.059		3,625	480		4,105	4,700
1100	6" pipe size		3	8		4,850	540		5,390	6,150
1106	8" pipe size	↓	2.60	9.231	↓	5,275	625		5,900	6,725
1500	For 300 lb. rating, add					40%				

23 21 20.78 Strainers, Y Type, Iron Body

		Crew	Daily Output	Labor-Hours	Unit	Material	2023 Bare Costs Labor	Equipment	Total	Total Incl O&P
0010	**STRAINERS, Y TYPE, IRON BODY**									
0050	Screwed, 250 lb., 1/4" pipe size	1 Stpi	20	.400	Ea.	26.50	29		55.50	72.50
0070	3/8" pipe size		20	.400		26.50	29		55.50	72.50
0100	1/2" pipe size		20	.400		26.50	29		55.50	72.50
0120	3/4" pipe size		18	.444		30.50	32		62.50	82
0140	1" pipe size		16	.500		40	36.50		76.50	98
0150	1-1/4" pipe size		15	.533		56.50	38.50		95	120
0160	1-1/2" pipe size		12	.667		76.50	48.50		125	157
0180	2" pipe size		8	1		115	72.50		187.50	234
0200	2-1/2" pipe size	Q-5	12	1.333		475	87		562	650
0220	3" pipe size		11	1.455		510	95		605	700
0240	4" pipe size	↓	5	3.200	↓	865	209		1,074	1,275
0500	For galvanized body, add					50%				
1000	Flanged, 125 lb., 1-1/2" pipe size	1 Stpi	11	.727	Ea.	360	53		413	475
1020	2" pipe size	"	8	1	↓	253	72.50		325.50	385
1030	2-1/2" pipe size	Q-5	5	3.200		228	209		437	560

23 21 Hydronic Piping and Pumps

23 21 20 – Hydronic HVAC Piping Specialties

23 21 20.78 Strainers, Y Type, Iron Body

		Crew	Daily Output	Labor-Hours	Unit	Material	2023 Bare Costs Labor	Equipment	Total	Total Incl O&P
1040	3" pipe size	Q-5	4.50	3.556	Ea.	335	232		567	710
1060	4" pipe size		3	5.333		550	350		900	1,125
1080	5" pipe size	Q-6	3.40	7.059		660	480		1,140	1,450
1100	6" pipe size		3	8		1,100	540		1,640	2,025
1120	8" pipe size		2.50	9.600		1,850	650		2,500	3,025
1140	10" pipe size		2	12		3,375	815		4,190	4,925
1160	12" pipe size		1.70	14.118		5,075	955		6,030	7,000
1170	14" pipe size		1.30	18.462		9,350	1,250		10,600	12,200
1180	16" pipe size		1	24		13,300	1,625		14,925	17,000
1500	For 250 lb. rating, add					20%				
2000	For galvanized body, add					50%				
2500	For steel body, add					40%				

23 21 20.80 Suction Diffusers

		Crew	Daily Output	Labor-Hours	Unit	Material	Labor	Equipment	Total	Total Incl O&P
0010	**SUCTION DIFFUSERS**									
0100	Cast iron body with integral straightening vanes, strainer									
1000	Flanged									
1010	2" inlet, 1-1/2" pump side	1 Stpi	6	1.333	Ea.	350	96.50		446.50	530
1020	2" pump side	"	5	1.600		475	116		591	700
1030	3" inlet, 2" pump side	Q-5	6.50	2.462		440	161		601	725
1040	2-1/2" pump side		5.30	3.019		645	197		842	1,000
1050	3" pump side		4.50	3.556		655	232		887	1,075
1060	4" inlet, 3" pump side		3.50	4.571		745	299		1,044	1,275
1070	4" pump side		3	5.333		865	350		1,215	1,475
1080	5" inlet, 4" pump side	Q-6	3.80	6.316		980	430		1,410	1,725
1090	5" pump side		3.40	7.059		1,175	480		1,655	2,025
1100	6" inlet, 4" pump side		3.30	7.273		1,025	495		1,520	1,850
1110	5" pump side		3.10	7.742		1,225	525		1,750	2,125
1120	6" pump side		3	8		1,300	540		1,840	2,225
1130	8" inlet, 6" pump side		2.70	8.889		1,500	600		2,100	2,550
1140	8" pump side		2.50	9.600		2,525	650		3,175	3,750
1150	10" inlet, 6" pump side		2.40	10		2,900	675		3,575	4,200
1160	8" pump side		2.30	10.435		3,000	705		3,705	4,350
1170	10" pump side		2.20	10.909		4,200	740		4,940	5,725
1180	12" inlet, 8" pump side		2	12		4,425	815		5,240	6,075
1190	10" pump side		1.80	13.333		5,125	905		6,030	6,975
1200	12" pump side		1.70	14.118		5,525	955		6,480	7,500
1210	14" inlet, 12" pump side		1.50	16		7,150	1,075		8,225	9,500
1220	14" pump side		1.30	18.462		8,175	1,250		9,425	10,900

23 21 20.84 Thermoflo Indicator

		Crew	Daily Output	Labor-Hours	Unit	Material	Labor	Equipment	Total	Total Incl O&P
0010	**THERMOFLO INDICATOR**, For balancing									
1000	Sweat connections, 1-1/4" pipe size	1 Stpi	12	.667	Ea.	955	48.50		1,003.50	1,125
1020	1-1/2" pipe size		10	.800		970	58		1,028	1,150
1040	2" pipe size		8	1		1,025	72.50		1,097.50	1,225
1060	2-1/2" pipe size		7	1.143		1,550	83		1,633	1,825
2000	Flange connections, 3" pipe size	Q-5	5	3.200		1,850	209		2,059	2,350
2020	4" pipe size		4	4		2,225	261		2,486	2,850
2030	5" pipe size		3.50	4.571		2,800	299		3,099	3,525
2040	6" pipe size		3	5.333		3,000	350		3,350	3,825
2060	8" pipe size		2	8		3,650	520		4,170	4,775

23 21 Hydronic Piping and Pumps

23 21 20 – Hydronic HVAC Piping Specialties

23 21 20.88 Venturi Flow

		Crew	Daily Output	Labor-Hours	Unit	Material	2023 Bare Costs Labor	Equipment	Total	Total Incl O&P
0010	**VENTURI FLOW**, Measuring device									
0050	1/2" diameter	1 Stpi	24	.333	Ea.	335	24		359	405
0100	3/4" diameter		20	.400		305	29		334	385
0120	1" diameter		19	.421		330	30.50		360.50	405
0140	1-1/4" diameter		15	.533		410	38.50		448.50	510
0160	1-1/2" diameter		13	.615		410	44.50		454.50	515
0180	2" diameter		11	.727		440	53		493	560
0200	2-1/2" diameter	Q-5	16	1		600	65.50		665.50	760
0220	3" diameter		14	1.143		620	74.50		694.50	790
0240	4" diameter		11	1.455		925	95		1,020	1,175
0260	5" diameter	Q-6	4	6		1,225	405		1,630	1,925
0280	6" diameter		3.50	6.857		1,350	465		1,815	2,175
0300	8" diameter		3	8		1,725	540		2,265	2,700
0320	10" diameter		2	12		4,100	815		4,915	5,700
0330	12" diameter		1.80	13.333		5,800	905		6,705	7,725
0340	14" diameter		1.60	15		6,575	1,025		7,600	8,775
0350	16" diameter		1.40	17.143		7,550	1,150		8,700	10,000
0500	For meter, add					2,800			2,800	3,075

23 21 20.94 Weld End Ball Joints

		Crew	Daily Output	Labor-Hours	Unit	Material	2023 Bare Costs Labor	Equipment	Total	Total Incl O&P
0010	**WELD END BALL JOINTS**, Steel									
0050	2-1/2" diameter	Q-17	13	1.231	Ea.	945	80.50	4.94	1,030.44	1,175
0100	3" diameter		12	1.333		1,150	87	5.35	1,242.35	1,400
0120	4" diameter		11	1.455		1,700	95	5.85	1,800.85	2,025
0140	5" diameter	Q-18	14	1.714		1,800	116	4.58	1,920.58	2,175
0160	6" diameter		12	2		2,475	135	5.35	2,615.35	2,925
0180	8" diameter		9	2.667		3,900	181	7.10	4,088.10	4,550
0200	10" diameter		8	3		6,175	203	8	6,386	7,125
0220	12" diameter		6	4		7,250	271	10.70	7,531.70	8,375

23 21 20.98 Zone Valves

		Crew	Daily Output	Labor-Hours	Unit	Material	2023 Bare Costs Labor	Equipment	Total	Total Incl O&P
0010	**ZONE VALVES**									
1000	Bronze body									
1010	2 way, 125 psi									
1020	Standard, 65' pump head									
1030	1/2" soldered	1 Stpi	24	.333	Ea.	178	24		202	232
1040	3/4" soldered		20	.400		178	29		207	240
1050	1" soldered		19	.421		191	30.50		221.50	256
1060	1-1/4" soldered		15	.533		224	38.50		262.50	305
1200	High head, 125' pump head									
1210	1/2" soldered	1 Stpi	24	.333	Ea.	231	24		255	290
1220	3/4" soldered		20	.400		219	29		248	285
1230	1" soldered		19	.421		239	30.50		269.50	310
1300	Geothermal, 150' pump head									
1310	3/4" soldered	1 Stpi	20	.400	Ea.	215	29		244	280
1320	1" soldered		19	.421		320	30.50		350.50	400
1330	3/4" threaded		20	.400		221	29		250	287
3000	3 way, 125 psi									
3200	Bypass, 65' pump head									
3210	1/2" soldered	1 Stpi	24	.333	Ea.	221	24		245	279
3220	3/4" soldered		20	.400		228	29		257	295
3230	1" soldered		19	.421		260	30.50		290.50	330
9000	Transformer, for up to 3 zone valves		20	.400		38	29		67	85.50

23 21 Hydronic Piping and Pumps

23 21 23 – Hydronic Pumps

23 21 23.13 In-Line Centrifugal Hydronic Pumps	Crew	Daily Output	Labor-Hours	Unit	Material	2023 Bare Costs Labor	2023 Bare Costs Equipment	Total	Total Incl O&P
0010 **IN-LINE CENTRIFUGAL HYDRONIC PUMPS**									
0600 Bronze, sweat connections, 1/40 HP, in line									
0640 3/4" size	Q-1	16	1	Ea.	335	65		400	465
1000 Flange connection, 3/4" to 1-1/2" size									
1040 1/12 HP	Q-1	6	2.667	Ea.	770	173		943	1,100
1060 1/8 HP		6	2.667		1,550	173		1,723	1,975
1100 1/3 HP		6	2.667		1,750	173		1,923	2,175
1140 2" size, 1/6 HP		5	3.200		2,250	208		2,458	2,775
1180 2-1/2" size, 1/4 HP		5	3.200		2,425	208		2,633	2,950
1220 3" size, 1/4 HP		4	4		2,675	259		2,934	3,325
1260 1/3 HP		4	4		3,100	259		3,359	3,775
1300 1/2 HP		4	4		3,175	259		3,434	3,850
1340 3/4 HP		4	4		2,925	259		3,184	3,600
1380 1 HP		4	4		4,575	259		4,834	5,400
2000 Cast iron, flange connection									
2040 3/4" to 1-1/2" size, in line, 1/12 HP	Q-1	6	2.667	Ea.	615	173		788	940
2060 1/8 HP		6	2.667		980	173		1,153	1,325
2100 1/3 HP		6	2.667		1,100	173		1,273	1,450
2140 2" size, 1/6 HP		5	3.200		1,200	208		1,408	1,625
2180 2-1/2" size, 1/4 HP		5	3.200		1,150	208		1,358	1,550
2220 3" size, 1/4 HP		4	4		1,125	259		1,384	1,600
2260 1/3 HP		4	4		1,425	259		1,684	1,950
2300 1/2 HP		4	4		1,475	259		1,734	2,000
2340 3/4 HP		4	4		1,725	259		1,984	2,250
2380 1 HP		4	4		2,475	259		2,734	3,100
2600 For nonferrous impeller, add					3%				
3000 High head, bronze impeller									
3030 1-1/2" size, 1/2 HP	Q-1	5	3.200	Ea.	1,300	208		1,508	1,725
3040 1-1/2" size, 3/4 HP		5	3.200		1,800	208		2,008	2,275
3050 2" size, 1 HP		4	4		2,175	259		2,434	2,775
3090 2" size, 1-1/2 HP		4	4		2,550	259		2,809	3,175
4000 Close coupled, end suction, bronze impeller									
4040 1-1/2" size, 1-1/2 HP, to 40 GPM	Q-1	3	5.333	Ea.	3,100	345		3,445	3,925
4090 2" size, 2 HP, to 50 GPM		3	5.333		3,400	345		3,745	4,250
4100 2" size, 3 HP, to 90 GPM		2.30	6.957		3,000	450		3,450	3,975
4190 2-1/2" size, 3 HP, to 150 GPM		2	8		4,375	520		4,895	5,575
4300 3" size, 5 HP, to 225 GPM		1.80	8.889		4,575	575		5,150	5,900
4410 3" size, 10 HP, to 350 GPM		1.60	10		7,925	650		8,575	9,700
4420 4" size, 7-1/2 HP, to 350 GPM		1.60	10		5,475	650		6,125	7,000
4520 4" size, 10 HP, to 600 GPM	Q-2	1.70	14.118		8,450	950		9,400	10,700
4530 5" size, 15 HP, to 1,000 GPM		1.70	14.118		5,975	950		6,925	7,975
4610 5" size, 20 HP, to 1,350 GPM		1.50	16		6,750	1,075		7,825	9,025
4620 5" size, 25 HP, to 1,550 GPM		1.50	16		10,800	1,075		11,875	13,500
5000 Base mounted, bronze impeller, coupling guard									
5040 1-1/2" size, 1-1/2 HP, to 40 GPM	Q-1	2.30	6.957	Ea.	8,650	450		9,100	10,200
5090 2" size, 2 HP, to 50 GPM		2.30	6.957		9,700	450		10,150	11,400
5100 2" size, 3 HP, to 90 GPM		2	8		9,600	520		10,120	11,400
5190 2-1/2" size, 3 HP, to 150 GPM		1.80	8.889		11,400	575		11,975	13,400
5300 3" size, 5 HP, to 225 GPM		1.60	10		14,000	650		14,650	16,400
5410 4" size, 5 HP, to 350 GPM		1.50	10.667		14,300	690		14,990	16,700
5420 4" size, 7-1/2 HP, to 350 GPM		1.50	10.667		13,500	690		14,190	15,900
5520 5" size, 10 HP, to 600 GPM	Q-2	1.60	15		17,100	1,000		18,100	20,300

23 21 Hydronic Piping and Pumps

23 21 23 – Hydronic Pumps

23 21 23.13 In-Line Centrifugal Hydronic Pumps

		Crew	Daily Output	Labor-Hours	Unit	Material	2023 Bare Costs Labor	Equipment	Total	Total Incl O&P
5530	5" size, 15 HP, to 1,000 GPM	Q-2	1.60	15	Ea.	18,300	1,000		19,300	21,700
5610	6" size, 20 HP, to 1,350 GPM		1.40	17.143		29,100	1,150		30,250	33,700
5620	6" size, 25 HP, to 1,550 GPM	↓	1.40	17.143	↓	23,400	1,150		24,550	27,500
5800	The above pump capacities are based on 1,800 RPM,									
5810	at a 60' head. Increasing the RPM									
5820	or decreasing the head will increase the GPM.									

23 21 29 – Automatic Condensate Pump Units

23 21 29.10 Condensate Removal Pump System

			Crew	Daily Output	Labor-Hours	Unit	Material	Labor	Equipment	Total	Total Incl O&P
0010	**CONDENSATE REMOVAL PUMP SYSTEM**										
0020	Pump with 1 gal. ABS tank										
0100	115 V										
0120	1/50 HP, 200 GPH	G	1 Stpi	12	.667	Ea.	233	48.50		281.50	330
0140	1/18 HP, 270 GPH	G		10	.800		232	58		290	345
0160	1/5 HP, 450 GPH	G	↓	8	1	↓	243	72.50		315.50	375
0200	230 V										
0240	1/18 HP, 270 GPH		1 Stpi	10	.800	Ea.	258	58		316	370
0260	1/5 HP, 450 GPH	G	"	8	1	"	625	72.50		697.50	795

23 22 Steam and Condensate Piping and Pumps

23 22 13 – Steam and Condensate Heating Piping

23 22 13.23 Aboveground Steam and Condensate Piping

		Crew	Daily Output	Labor-Hours	Unit	Material	Labor	Equipment	Total	Total Incl O&P
0010	**ABOVEGROUND STEAM AND CONDENSATE HEATING PIPING**									
0020	Condensate meter									
0100	500 lb. per hour	1 Stpi	14	.571	Ea.	4,850	41.50		4,891.50	5,400
0140	1500 lb. per hour	↓	7	1.143		5,600	83		5,683	6,275
0160	3000 lb. per hour	↓	5	1.600		6,125	116		6,241	6,925
0200	12,000 lb. per hour	Q-5	3.50	4.571	↓	7,625	299		7,924	8,825

23 22 23 – Steam Condensate Pumps

23 22 23.10 Condensate Return System

		Crew	Daily Output	Labor-Hours	Unit	Material	Labor	Equipment	Total	Total Incl O&P
0010	**CONDENSATE RETURN SYSTEM**									
2000	Simplex									
2010	With pump, motor, CI receiver, float switch									
2020	3/4 HP, 15 GPM	Q-1	1.80	8.889	Ea.	3,075	575		3,650	4,250
2100	Duplex									
2110	With 2 pumps and motors, CI receiver, float switch, alternator									
2120	3/4 HP, 15 GPM, 15 gal. CI receiver	Q-1	1.40	11.429	Ea.	7,575	740		8,315	9,425
2130	1 HP, 25 GPM		1.20	13.333		9,100	865		9,965	11,300
2140	1-1/2 HP, 45 GPM		1	16		10,600	1,050		11,650	13,300
2150	1-1/2 HP, 60 GPM	↓	1	16	↓	11,800	1,050		12,850	14,600

23 23 Refrigerant Piping

23 23 13 – Refrigerant Piping Valves

23 23 13.10 Valves		Crew	Daily Output	Labor-Hours	Unit	Material	2023 Bare Costs Labor	2023 Bare Costs Equipment	Total	Total Incl O&P
0010	**VALVES**									
8100	Check valve, soldered									
8110	5/8"	1 Stpi	36	.222	Ea.	93	16.10		109.10	126
8114	7/8"		26	.308		113	22.50		135.50	158
8118	1-1/8"		18	.444		124	32		156	184
8122	1-3/8"		14	.571		199	41.50		240.50	281
8126	1-5/8"		13	.615		297	44.50		341.50	390
8130	2-1/8"		12	.667		284	48.50		332.50	380
8134	2-5/8"	Q-5	22	.727		405	47.50		452.50	515
8138	3-1/8"	"	20	.800		540	52		592	670
8500	Refrigeration valve, packless, soldered									
8510	1/2"	1 Stpi	38	.211	Ea.	33.50	15.25		48.75	59.50
8514	5/8"		36	.222		35	16.10		51.10	62
8518	7/8"		26	.308		263	22.50		285.50	325
8520	Packed, soldered									
8522	1-1/8"	1 Stpi	18	.444	Ea.	315	32		347	395
8526	1-3/8"		14	.571		490	41.50		531.50	600
8530	1-5/8"		13	.615		440	44.50		484.50	550
8534	2-1/8"		12	.667		1,050	48.50		1,098.50	1,250
8538	2-5/8"	Q-5	22	.727		1,550	47.50		1,597.50	1,775
8542	3-1/8"		20	.800		1,550	52		1,602	1,800
8546	4-1/8"		18	.889		2,525	58		2,583	2,850
8600	Solenoid valve, flange/solder									
8610	1/2"	1 Stpi	38	.211	Ea.	315	15.25		330.25	375
8614	5/8"		36	.222		450	16.10		466.10	520
8618	3/4"		30	.267		620	19.35		639.35	715
8622	7/8"		26	.308		675	22.50		697.50	775
8626	1-1/8"		18	.444		785	32		817	915
8630	1-3/8"		14	.571		945	41.50		986.50	1,100
8634	1-5/8"		13	.615		1,325	44.50		1,369.50	1,525
8638	2-1/8"		12	.667		1,450	48.50		1,498.50	1,675
8800	Thermostatic valve, flange/solder									
8810	1/2-3 ton, 3/8" x 5/8"	1 Stpi	9	.889	Ea.	147	64.50		211.50	258
8814	4-5 ton, 1/2" x 7/8"		7	1.143		150	83		233	289
8818	6-8 ton, 5/8" x 7/8"		5	1.600		299	116		415	505
8822	7-12 ton, 7/8" x 1-1/8"		4	2		350	145		495	600
8826	15-20 ton, 7/8" x 1-3/8"		3.20	2.500		350	181		531	655

23 23 16 – Refrigerant Piping Specialties

23 23 16.10 Refrigerant Piping Component Specialties

		Crew	Daily Output	Labor-Hours	Unit	Material	Labor	Equipment	Total	Total Incl O&P
0010	**REFRIGERANT PIPING COMPONENT SPECIALTIES**									
0600	Accumulator									
0610	3/4"	1 Stpi	8.80	.909	Ea.	52.50	66		118.50	156
0614	7/8"		6.40	1.250		67	90.50		157.50	209
0618	1-1/8"		4.80	1.667		116	121		237	310
0622	1-3/8"		4	2		122	145		267	350
0626	1-5/8"		3.20	2.500		129	181		310	415
0630	2-1/8"		2.40	3.333		410	242		652	810
0700	Condensate drip/drain pan, electric, 10" x 9" x 2-3/4"		24	.333		107	24		131	153
1000	Filter dryer									
1010	Replaceable core type, solder									
1020	1/2"	1 Stpi	20	.400	Ea.	36.50	29		65.50	84
1030	5/8"		19	.421		38	30.50		68.50	87.50

23 23 Refrigerant Piping

23 23 16 – Refrigerant Piping Specialties

23 23 16.10 Refrigerant Piping Component Specialties		Crew	Daily Output	Labor-Hours	Unit	Material	2023 Bare Costs Labor	Equipment	Total	Total Incl O&P
1040	7/8"	1 Stpi	18	.444	Ea.	38	32		70	90
1050	1-1/8"		15	.533		127	38.50		165.50	197
1060	1-3/8"		14	.571		113	41.50		154.50	186
1070	1-5/8"		12	.667		203	48.50		251.50	296
1080	2-1/8"		10	.800		435	58		493	565
1090	2-5/8"		9	.889		685	64.50		749.50	850
1100	3-1/8"		8	1		840	72.50		912.50	1,025
1200	Sealed in-line, solder									
1210	1/4"	1 Stpi	22	.364	Ea.	30.50	26.50		57	73
1220	3/8"		21	.381		25.50	27.50		53	69
1230	1/2"		20	.400		30.50	29		59.50	77
1260	5/8"		19	.421		41.50	30.50		72	91
1270	7/8"		18	.444		45	32		77	97.50
1290	1-1/8"		15	.533		68.50	38.50		107	133
4000	P-trap, suction line, solder									
4010	5/8"	1 Stpi	19	.421	Ea.	115	30.50		145.50	173
4020	3/4"		19	.421		288	30.50		318.50	360
4030	7/8"		18	.444		134	32		166	195
4040	1-1/8"		15	.533		325	38.50		363.50	420
4050	1-3/8"		14	.571		365	41.50		406.50	460
4060	1-5/8"		12	.667		555	48.50		603.50	680
4070	2-1/8"		10	.800		1,150	58		1,208	1,325
5000	Sightglass									
5010	Moisture and liquid indicator, solder									
5020	1/4"	1 Stpi	22	.364	Ea.	18	26.50		44.50	59.50
5030	3/8"		21	.381		18.15	27.50		45.65	61
5040	1/2"		20	.400		23	29		52	68.50
5050	5/8"		19	.421		23.50	30.50		54	71.50
5060	7/8"		18	.444		35	32		67	86.50
5070	1-1/8"		15	.533		38	38.50		76.50	99
5080	1-3/8"		14	.571		75.50	41.50		117	145
5090	1-5/8"		12	.667		85	48.50		133.50	166
5100	2-1/8"		10	.800		88.50	58		146.50	184
7400	Vacuum pump set									
7410	Two stage, high vacuum continuous duty	1 Stpi	8	1	Ea.	4,000	72.50		4,072.50	4,500

23 23 16.16 Refrigerant Line Sets

23 23 16.16 Refrigerant Line Sets		Crew	Daily Output	Labor-Hours	Unit	Material	2023 Bare Costs Labor	Equipment	Total	Total Incl O&P
0010	**REFRIGERANT LINE SETS**, Standard									
0100	Copper tube									
0110	1/2" insulation, both tubes									
0120	Combination 1/4" and 1/2" tubes									
0130	10' set	Q-5	42	.381	Ea.	185	25		210	241
0135	15' set		42	.381		80.50	25		105.50	126
0140	20' set		40	.400		294	26		320	365
0150	30' set		37	.432		395	28		423	475
0160	40' set		35	.457		490	30		520	585
0170	50' set		32	.500		635	32.50		667.50	745
0180	100' set		22	.727		1,125	47.50		1,172.50	1,325
0300	Combination 1/4" and 3/4" tubes									
0310	10' set	Q-5	40	.400	Ea.	62.50	26		88.50	108
0320	20' set		38	.421		110	27.50		137.50	162
0330	30' set		35	.457		165	30		195	226
0340	40' set		33	.485		216	31.50		247.50	284

23 23 Refrigerant Piping

23 23 16 – Refrigerant Piping Specialties

23 23 16.16 Refrigerant Line Sets		Crew	Daily Output	Labor-Hours	Unit	Material	2023 Bare Costs Labor	Equipment	Total	Total Incl O&P
0350	50' set	Q-5	30	.533	Ea.	271	35		306	350
0380	100' set	↓	20	.800	↓	620	52		672	760
0500	Combination 3/8" & 3/4" tubes									
0510	10' set	Q-5	28	.571	Ea.	170	37.50		207.50	243
0520	20' set		36	.444		274	29		303	345
0530	30' set		34	.471		315	30.50		345.50	390
0540	40' set		31	.516		400	33.50		433.50	490
0550	50' set		28	.571		585	37.50		622.50	695
0580	100' set	↓	18	.889	↓	1,075	58		1,133	1,250
0700	Combination 3/8" & 1-1/8" tubes									
0710	10' set	Q-5	36	.444	Ea.	125	29		154	182
0720	20' set		33	.485		365	31.50		396.50	450
0730	30' set		31	.516		480	33.50		513.50	575
0740	40' set		28	.571		630	37.50		667.50	750
0750	50' set	↓	26	.615	↓	850	40		890	995
0900	Combination 1/2" & 3/4" tubes									
0910	10' set	Q-5	37	.432	Ea.	75.50	28		103.50	125
0920	20' set		35	.457		134	30		164	193
0930	30' set		33	.485		202	31.50		233.50	269
0940	40' set		30	.533		265	35		300	345
0950	50' set		27	.593		570	38.50		608.50	685
0980	100' set	↓	17	.941	↓	670	61.50		731.50	825
2100	Combination 1/2" & 1-1/8" tubes									
2110	10' set	Q-5	35	.457	Ea.	129	30		159	187
2120	20' set		31	.516		221	33.50		254.50	294
2130	30' set		29	.552		335	36		371	420
2140	40' set		25	.640		445	42		487	555
2150	50' set	↓	14	1.143	↓	925	74.50		999.50	1,125
2300	For 1" thick insulation add					30%	15%			
3000	Refrigerant line sets, min-split, flared									
3100	Combination 1/4" & 3/8" tubes									
3120	15' set	Q-5	41	.390	Ea.	80	25.50		105.50	126
3140	25' set		38.50	.416		113	27		140	165
3160	35' set		37	.432		142	28		170	199
3180	50' set	↓	30	.533	↓	194	35		229	265
3200	Combination 1/4" & 1/2" tubes									
3220	15' set	Q-5	41	.390	Ea.	85.50	25.50		111	132
3240	25' set		38.50	.416		116	27		143	168
3260	35' set		37	.432		149	28		177	206
3280	50' set	↓	30	.533	↓	201	35		236	274

23 23 23 – Refrigerants

23 23 23.10 Anti-Freeze

		Crew	Daily Output	Labor-Hours	Unit	Material	Labor	Equipment	Total	Total Incl O&P
0010	**ANTI-FREEZE**, Inhibited									
0900	Ethylene glycol concentrated									
1000	55 gallon drums, small quantities				Gal.	15.20			15.20	16.70
1200	Large quantities					11.85			11.85	13
2000	Propylene glycol, for solar heat, small quantities					25.50			25.50	28
2100	Large quantities				↓	13.20			13.20	14.50

23 23 23.20 Refrigerant

		Crew	Daily Output	Labor-Hours	Unit	Material	Labor	Equipment	Total	Total Incl O&P
0010	**REFRIGERANT**									
4420	R-22, 30 lb. disposable cylinder				Lb.	26.50			26.50	29
4428	R-134A, 30 lb. disposable cylinder				↓	6.75			6.75	7.45

23 23 Refrigerant Piping

23 23 23 – Refrigerants

23 23 23.20 Refrigerant		Crew	Daily Output	Labor-Hours	Unit	Material	2023 Bare Costs Labor	Equipment	Total	Total Incl O&P
4434	R-407C, 30 lb. disposable cylinder				Lb.	12			12	13.20
4440	R-408A, 25 lb. disposable cylinder					27.50			27.50	30
4450	R-410A, 25 lb. disposable cylinder					11.75			11.75	12.90
4470	R-507, 25 lb. disposable cylinder					7.45			7.45	8.20

23 31 HVAC Ducts and Casings

23 31 13 – Metal Ducts

23 31 13.13 Rectangular Metal Ducts

		Crew	Daily Output	Labor-Hours	Unit	Material	2023 Bare Costs Labor	Equipment	Total	Total Incl O&P
0010	**RECTANGULAR METAL DUCTS**									
0020	Fabricated rectangular, includes fittings, joints, supports,									
0021	allowance for flexible connections and field sketches.									
0030	Does not include "as-built dwgs." or insulation. R233100-30									
0031	NOTE: Fabrication and installation are combined									
0040	as LABOR cost. Approx. 25% fittings assumed. R233100-40									
0042	Fabrication/Inst. is to commercial quality standards									
0043	(SMACNA or equiv.) for structure, sealing, leak testing, etc. R233100-50									
0050	Add to labor for elevated installation									
0051	of fabricated ductwork									
0052	10' to 15' high						6%			
0053	15' to 20' high						12%			
0054	20' to 25' high						15%			
0055	25' to 30' high						21%			
0056	30' to 35' high						24%			
0057	35' to 40' high						30%			
0058	Over 40' high						33%			
0072	For duct insulation see Line 23 07 13.10 3000									
0100	Aluminum, alloy 3003-H14, under 100 lb.	Q-10	75	.320	Lb.	3.39	21		24.39	35
0110	100 to 500 lb.		80	.300		1.92	19.65		21.57	31.50
0120	500 to 1,000 lb.		95	.253		2.18	16.55		18.73	27.50
0140	1,000 to 2,000 lb.		120	.200		2.11	13.10		15.21	22
0150	2,000 to 5,000 lb.		130	.185		2.05	12.10		14.15	20.50
0160	Over 5,000 lb.		145	.166		2.11	10.85		12.96	18.60
0500	Galvanized steel, under 200 lb.		235	.102		.67	6.70		7.37	10.80
0520	200 to 500 lb.		245	.098		.75	6.40		7.15	10.50
0540	500 to 1,000 lb.		255	.094		.70	6.15		6.85	10.05
0560	1,000 to 2,000 lb.		265	.091		.73	5.95		6.68	9.75
0570	2,000 to 5,000 lb.		275	.087		.60	5.70		6.30	9.25
0580	Over 5,000 lb.		285	.084		.73	5.50		6.23	9.10
0600	For large quantities special prices available from supplier									
1000	Stainless steel, type 304, under 100 lb.	Q-10	165	.145	Lb.	5.55	9.50		15.05	20.50
1020	100 to 500 lb.		175	.137		4.45	9		13.45	18.45
1030	500 to 1,000 lb.		190	.126		3.23	8.25		11.48	16
1040	1,000 to 2,000 lb.		200	.120		2.88	7.85		10.73	15
1050	2,000 to 5,000 lb.		225	.107		2.49	7		9.49	13.25
1060	Over 5,000 lb.		235	.102		3.13	6.70		9.83	13.50
1080	Note: Minimum order cost exceeds per lb. cost for min. wt.									
1100	For medium pressure ductwork, add				Lb.		15%			
1200	For high pressure ductwork, add						40%			
1210	For welded ductwork, add						85%			
1220	For 30% fittings, add						11%			
1224	For 40% fittings, add						34%			

23 31 HVAC Ducts and Casings

23 31 13 – Metal Ducts

23 31 13.13 Rectangular Metal Ducts		Crew	Daily Output	Labor-Hours	Unit	Material	2023 Bare Costs Labor	Equipment	Total	Total Incl O&P
1228	For 50% fittings, add				Lb.		56%			
1232	For 60% fittings, add						79%			
1236	For 70% fittings, add						101%			
1240	For 80% fittings, add						124%			
1244	For 90% fittings, add						147%			
1248	For 100% fittings, add						169%			
1252	Note: Fittings add includes time for detailing and installation.									
1276	Duct tape, 2" x 60 yd roll				Ea.	13.50			13.50	14.85
1277	Duct sealer		1 Shee	304.72	.026	L.F.	13.50	1.84		15.34	17.65

23 31 13.16 Round and Flat-Oval Spiral Ducts

		Crew	Daily Output	Labor-Hours	Unit	Material	Labor	Equipment	Total	Total Incl O&P
0010	**ROUND AND FLAT-OVAL SPIRAL DUCTS**									
0020	Fabricated round and flat oval spiral, includes hangers,									
0021	supports and field sketches.									
1280	Add to labor for elevated installation									
1282	of prefabricated (purchased) ductwork									
1283	10' to 15' high						10%			
1284	15' to 20' high						20%			
1285	20' to 25' high						25%			
1286	25' to 30' high						35%			
1287	30' to 35' high						40%			
1288	35' to 40' high						50%			
1289	Over 40' high						55%			
5400	Spiral preformed, steel, galv., straight lengths, max 10" spwg.									
5410	4" diameter, 26 ga.	Q-9	360	.044	L.F.	4.12	2.81		6.93	8.75
5416	5" diameter, 26 ga.		320	.050		4.63	3.16		7.79	9.85
5420	6" diameter, 26 ga.		280	.057		5.20	3.61		8.81	11.15
5425	7" diameter, 26 ga.		240	.067		5.85	4.21		10.06	12.75
5430	8" diameter, 26 ga.		200	.080		6.55	5.05		11.60	14.80
5440	10" diameter, 26 ga.		160	.100		8.15	6.30		14.45	18.50
5450	12" diameter, 26 ga.		120	.133		9.80	8.40		18.20	23.50
5460	14" diameter, 26 ga.		80	.200		11.15	12.65		23.80	31.50
5480	16" diameter, 24 ga.		60	.267		15.95	16.85		32.80	43
5490	18" diameter, 24 ga.		50	.320		19.30	20		39.30	51.50
5500	20" diameter, 24 ga.	Q-10	65	.369		19.95	24		43.95	58.50
5510	22" diameter, 24 ga.		60	.400		22	26		48	63.50
5520	24" diameter, 24 ga.		55	.436		24	28.50		52.50	69.50
5540	30" diameter, 22 ga.		45	.533		37	35		72	93
5600	36" diameter, 22 ga.		40	.600		54	39.50		93.50	119
5800	Connector, 4" diameter	Q-9	100	.160	Ea.	24	10.10		34.10	41.50
5810	5" diameter		94	.170		24	10.75		34.75	42.50
5820	6" diameter		88	.182		22.50	11.50		34	42
5840	8" diameter		78	.205		25.50	12.95		38.45	47.50
5860	10" diameter		70	.229		25.50	14.45		39.95	49.50
5880	12" diameter		50	.320		25.50	20		45.50	58.50
5900	14" diameter		44	.364		27	23		50	64
5920	16" diameter		40	.400		27	25.50		52.50	67.50
5930	18" diameter		37	.432		27	27.50		54.50	70.50
5940	20" diameter		34	.471		28.50	29.50		58	76.50
5950	22" diameter		31	.516		30	32.50		62.50	82
5960	24" diameter		28	.571		31.50	36		67.50	89
5980	30" diameter		22	.727		18.65	46		64.65	89.50
6000	36" diameter		18	.889		23	56		79	110

23 31 HVAC Ducts and Casings

23 31 13 – Metal Ducts

23 31 13.16 Round and Flat-Oval Spiral Ducts		Crew	Daily Output	Labor-Hours	Unit	Material	2023 Bare Costs Labor	Equipment	Total	Total Incl O&P
6300	Elbow, 45°, 4" diameter	Q-9	60	.267	Ea.	22	16.85		38.85	49.50
6310	5" diameter		52	.308		7.70	19.40		27.10	38
6320	6" diameter		44	.364		33	23		56	70.50
6340	8" diameter		28	.571		37.50	36		73.50	95.50
6360	10" diameter		18	.889		43.50	56		99.50	133
6380	12" diameter		13	1.231		63	77.50		140.50	186
6400	14" diameter		11	1.455		91.50	92		183.50	239
6420	16" diameter		10	1.600		106	101		207	269
6430	18" diameter		9.60	1.667		148	105		253	320
6440	20" diameter	Q-10	14	1.714		166	112		278	350
6450	22" diameter		13	1.846		199	121		320	400
6460	24" diameter		12	2		91.50	131		222.50	298
6480	30" diameter		9	2.667		144	175		319	420
6500	36" diameter		7	3.429		178	224		402	535
6600	Elbow, 90°, 4" diameter	Q-9	60	.267		4.62	16.85		21.47	30.50
6610	5" diameter		52	.308		5.40	19.40		24.80	35.50
6620	6" diameter		44	.364		5.75	23		28.75	41
6625	7" diameter		36	.444		6.55	28		34.55	50
6630	8" diameter		28	.571		8.95	36		44.95	64.50
6640	10" diameter		18	.889		11.05	56		67.05	96.50
6650	12" diameter		13	1.231		14	77.50		91.50	132
6660	14" diameter		11	1.455		18.55	92		110.55	159
6670	16" diameter		10	1.600		25.50	101		126.50	180
6676	18" diameter		9.60	1.667		77.50	105		182.50	244
6680	20" diameter	Q-10	14	1.714		94.50	112		206.50	273
6684	22" diameter		13	1.846		88	121		209	279
6690	24" diameter		12	2		148	131		279	360
6700	30" diameter		9	2.667		200	175		375	485
6710	36" diameter		7	3.429		266	224		490	630
6720	End cap									
6722	4"	Q-9	110	.145	Ea.	28.50	9.20		37.70	45.50
6724	6"		94	.170		39	10.75		49.75	59
6725	8"		88	.182		40.50	11.50		52	62
6726	10"		78	.205		40.50	12.95		53.45	64
6727	12"		70	.229		42	14.45		56.45	67.50
6728	14"		50	.320		54	20		74	90
6729	16"		44	.364		54	23		77	94
6730	18"		40	.400		55.50	25.50		81	99
6731	20"		37	.432		60	27.50		87.50	107
6732	22"		34	.471		84	29.50		113.50	138
6733	24"		30	.533		91.50	33.50		125	152
6800	Reducing coupling, 6" x 4"		46	.348		33	22		55	69
6820	8" x 6"		40	.400		20.50	25.50		46	60.50
6840	10" x 8"		32	.500		60	31.50		91.50	114
6860	12" x 10"		24	.667		70.50	42		112.50	141
6880	14" x 12"		20	.800		76.50	50.50		127	160
6900	16" x 14"		18	.889		139	56		195	238
6920	18" x 16"		16	1		154	63		217	265
6940	20" x 18"	Q-10	24	1		65.50	65.50		131	171
6950	22" x 20"		23	1.043		123	68.50		191.50	238
6960	24" x 22"		22	1.091		189	71.50		260.50	315
6980	30" x 28"		18	1.333		128	87.50		215.50	273
7000	36" x 34"		16	1.500		142	98		240	305

For customer support on your Mechanical Costs with RSMeans data, call 800.448.8182.

23 31 HVAC Ducts and Casings

23 31 13 – Metal Ducts

23 31 13.16 Round and Flat-Oval Spiral Ducts		Crew	Daily Output	Labor-Hours	Unit	Material	2023 Bare Costs Labor	2023 Bare Costs Equipment	Total	Total Incl O&P
7100	Tee, 90°, 4" diameter	Q-9	40	.400	Ea.	16.40	25.50		41.90	56
7110	5" diameter		34.60	.462		16.80	29		45.80	62.50
7120	6" diameter		30	.533		55	33.50		88.50	111
7130	8" diameter		19	.842		63.50	53		116.50	150
7140	10" diameter		12	1.333		92.50	84		176.50	229
7150	12" diameter		9	1.778		116	112		228	296
7160	14" diameter		7	2.286		90	144		234	315
7170	16" diameter		6.70	2.388		77	151		228	310
7176	18" diameter		6	2.667		112	168		280	380
7180	20" diameter	Q-10	8.70	2.759		144	181		325	430
7190	24" diameter		7	3.429		194	224		418	555
7200	30" diameter		6	4		285	262		547	710
7210	36" diameter		5	4.800		365	315		680	875
7250	Saddle tap									
7254	4" diameter on 6" diameter	Q-9	36	.444	Ea.	33	28		61	79
7256	5" diameter on 7" diameter		35.80	.447		23.50	28		51.50	68.50
7258	6" diameter on 8" diameter		35.40	.452		36.50	28.50		65	83
7260	6" diameter on 10" diameter		35.20	.455		36.50	28.50		65	83
7262	6" diameter on 12" diameter		35	.457		36.50	29		65.50	83.50
7264	7" diameter on 9" diameter		35.20	.455		27	28.50		55.50	72.50
7266	8" diameter on 10" diameter		35	.457		29	29		58	75.50
7268	8" diameter on 12" diameter		34.80	.460		41.50	29		70.50	89
7270	8" diameter on 14" diameter		34.50	.464		41.50	29.50		71	89.50
7272	10" diameter on 12" diameter		34.20	.468		51.50	29.50		81	102
7274	10" diameter on 14" diameter		33.80	.473		51.50	30		81.50	102
7276	10" diameter on 16" diameter		33.40	.479		33	30		63	82
7278	10" diameter on 18" diameter		33	.485		41.50	30.50		72	91.50
7280	12" diameter on 14" diameter		32.60	.491		56	31		87	108
7282	12" diameter on 18" diameter		32.20	.497		38.50	31.50		70	90
7284	14" diameter on 16" diameter		31.60	.506		51	32		83	105
7286	14" diameter on 20" diameter		31	.516		59	32.50		91.50	114
7288	16" diameter on 20" diameter		30	.533		79.50	33.50		113	138
7290	18" diameter on 20" diameter		28	.571		98	36		134	163
7292	20" diameter on 22" diameter		26	.615		126	39		165	198
7294	22" diameter on 24" diameter		24	.667		140	42		182	218
7400	Steel, PVC coated both sides, straight lengths									
7410	4" diameter, 26 ga.	Q-9	360	.044	L.F.	17.15	2.81		19.96	23
7416	5" diameter, 26 ga.		240	.067		5.50	4.21		9.71	12.40
7420	6" diameter, 26 ga.		280	.057		4.50	3.61		8.11	10.40
7440	8" diameter, 26 ga.		200	.080		6.15	5.05		11.20	14.35
7460	10" diameter, 26 ga.		160	.100		7.75	6.30		14.05	18
7480	12" diameter, 26 ga.		120	.133		8.75	8.40		17.15	22.50
7500	14" diameter, 26 ga.		80	.200		11.75	12.65		24.40	32
7520	16" diameter, 24 ga.		60	.267		15.70	16.85		32.55	43
7540	18" diameter, 24 ga.		45	.356		17.50	22.50		40	53.50
7560	20" diameter, 24 ga.	Q-10	65	.369		18.50	24		42.50	57
7580	24" diameter, 24 ga.		55	.436		22.50	28.50		51	67.50
7600	30" diameter, 22 ga.		45	.533		28.50	35		63.50	84
7620	36" diameter, 22 ga.		40	.600		34	39.50		73.50	96.50
7890	Connector, 4" diameter	Q-9	100	.160	Ea.	2.98	10.10		13.08	18.50
7896	5" diameter		83	.193		3.32	12.15		15.47	22
7900	6" diameter		88	.182		3.78	11.50		15.28	21.50
7920	8" diameter		78	.205		4.46	12.95		17.41	24.50

23 31 HVAC Ducts and Casings

23 31 13 – Metal Ducts

23 31 13.16 Round and Flat-Oval Spiral Ducts		Crew	Daily Output	Labor-Hours	Unit	Material	2023 Bare Costs Labor	Equipment	Total	Total Incl O&P
7940	10" diameter	Q-9	70	.229	Ea.	47.50	14.45		61.95	74
7960	12" diameter		50	.320		6.05	20		26.05	37
7980	14" diameter		44	.364		6.40	23		29.40	41.50
8000	16" diameter		40	.400		8.45	25.50		33.95	47.50
8020	18" diameter		37	.432		9.50	27.50		37	51.50
8040	20" diameter		34	.471		10.15	29.50		39.65	56
8060	24" diameter		28	.571		12.55	36		48.55	68.50
8080	30" diameter		22	.727		16.80	46		62.80	87.50
8100	36" diameter		18	.889		20.50	56		76.50	107
8390	Elbow, 45°, 4" diameter		60	.267		51.50	16.85		68.35	82.50
8396	5" diameter		36	.444		30.50	28		58.50	76
8400	6" diameter		44	.364		64.50	23		87.50	106
8420	8" diameter		28	.571		88	36		124	151
8440	10" diameter		18	.889		26.50	56		82.50	114
8460	12" diameter		13	1.231		35	77.50		112.50	156
8480	14" diameter		11	1.455		36	92		128	178
8500	16" diameter		10	1.600		33.50	101		134.50	189
8520	18" diameter		9	1.778		28.50	112		140.50	201
8540	20" diameter	Q-10	13	1.846		110	121		231	305
8560	24" diameter		11	2.182		136	143		279	365
8580	30" diameter		9	2.667		203	175		378	485
8600	36" diameter		7	3.429		238	224		462	600
8800	Elbow, 90°, 4" diameter	Q-9	60	.267		83.50	16.85		100.35	118
8804	5" diameter		52	.308		104	19.40		123.40	144
8806	6" diameter		44	.364		113	23		136	159
8808	8" diameter		28	.571		29.50	36		65.50	87
8810	10" diameter		18	.889		179	56		235	282
8812	12" diameter		13	1.231		36.50	77.50		114	157
8814	14" diameter		11	1.455		41.50	92		133.50	184
8816	16" diameter		10	1.600		33	101		134	189
8818	18" diameter		9.60	1.667		40.50	105		145.50	204
8820	20" diameter	Q-10	14	1.714		51	112		163	226
8822	24" diameter		12	2		119	131		250	330
8824	30" diameter		9	2.667		244	175		419	530
8826	36" diameter		7	3.429		350	224		574	725
9000	Reducing coupling									
9040	6" x 4"	Q-9	46	.348	Ea.	68.50	22		90.50	109
9060	8" x 6"		40	.400		85	25.50		110.50	132
9080	10" x 8"		32	.500		103	31.50		134.50	161
9100	12" x 10"		24	.667		22	42		64	87.50
9120	14" x 12"		20	.800		40	50.50		90.50	120
9140	16" x 14"		18	.889		36.50	56		92.50	125
9160	18" x 16"		16	1		45	63		108	145
9180	20" x 18"	Q-10	24	1		51.50	65.50		117	155
9200	24" x 22"		22	1.091		68	71.50		139.50	183
9220	30" x 28"		18	1.333		164	87.50		251.50	310
9240	36" x 34"		16	1.500		162	98		260	325
9800	Steel, stainless, straight lengths									
9810	3" diameter, 26 ga.	Q-9	400	.040	L.F.	17.30	2.53		19.83	23
9820	4" diameter, 26 ga.		360	.044		22	2.81		24.81	28.50
9830	5" diameter, 26 ga.		320	.050		30.50	3.16		33.66	39
9840	6" diameter, 26 ga.		280	.057		36	3.61		39.61	45
9850	7" diameter, 26 ga.		240	.067		42	4.21		46.21	52.50

23 31 HVAC Ducts and Casings

23 31 13 – Metal Ducts

23 31 13.16 Round and Flat-Oval Spiral Ducts		Crew	Daily Output	Labor-Hours	Unit	Material	2023 Bare Costs Labor	Equipment	Total	Total Incl O&P
9860	8" diameter, 26 ga.	Q-9	200	.080	L.F.	42.50	5.05		47.55	54
9870	9" diameter, 26 ga.		180	.089		39.50	5.60		45.10	52
9880	10" diameter, 26 ga.		160	.100		54	6.30		60.30	69
9890	12" diameter, 26 ga.		120	.133		64	8.40		72.40	83
9900	14" diameter, 26 ga.	↓	80	.200		84	12.65		96.65	111

23 31 13.17 Round Grease Duct

		Crew	Daily Output	Labor-Hours	Unit	Material	2023 Bare Costs Labor	Equipment	Total	Total Incl O&P
0010	**ROUND GREASE DUCT**									
1280	Add to labor for elevated installation									
1282	of prefabricated (purchased) ductwork									
1283	10' to 15' high						10%			
1284	15' to 20' high						20%			
1285	20' to 25' high						25%			
1286	25' to 30' high						35%			
1287	30' to 35' high						40%			
1288	35' to 40' high						50%			
1289	Over 40' high						55%			
4020	Zero clearance, 2 hr. fire rated, UL listed, 3" double wall									
4030	304 interior, aluminized exterior, all sizes are ID									
4032	For 316 interior and aluminized exterior, add					6%				
4034	For 304 interior and 304 exterior, add					21%				
4036	For 316 interior and 316 exterior, add					40%				
4040	Straight									
4052	6"	Q-9	34.20	.468	L.F.	88.50	29.50		118	142
4054	8"		29.64	.540		102	34		136	164
4056	10"		27.36	.585		114	37		151	181
4058	12"		25.10	.637		130	40		170	204
4060	14"		23.94	.668		147	42		189	226
4062	16"		22.80	.702		160	44.50		204.50	242
4064	18"	↓	21.66	.739		188	46.50		234.50	277
4066	20"	Q-10	20.52	1.170		214	76.50		290.50	350
4068	22"		19.38	1.238		242	81		323	390
4070	24"		18.24	1.316		274	86		360	430
4072	26"		17.67	1.358		294	89		383	460
4074	28"		17.10	1.404		310	92		402	485
4076	30"		15.96	1.504		330	98.50		428.50	515
4078	32"		15.39	1.559		355	102		457	550
4080	36"	↓	14.25	1.684	↓	395	110		505	600
4100	Adjustable section, 30" long									
4104	6"	Q-9	17.10	.936	Ea.	269	59		328	385
4106	8"		14.82	1.080		325	68		393	465
4108	10"		13.68	1.170		370	74		444	520
4110	12"		12.54	1.276		420	80.50		500.50	585
4112	14"		11.97	1.337		465	84.50		549.50	635
4114	16"		11.40	1.404		530	88.50		618.50	720
4116	18"	↓	10.83	1.477		590	93.50		683.50	790
4118	20"	Q-10	10.26	2.339		695	153		848	995
4120	22"		9.69	2.477		785	162		947	1,100
4122	24"		9.12	2.632		890	172		1,062	1,250
4124	26"		8.83	2.718		950	178		1,128	1,325
4126	28"		8.55	2.807		990	184		1,174	1,350
4128	30"		8.26	2.906		1,075	190		1,265	1,475
4130	32"	↓	7.98	3.008		1,150	197		1,347	1,575

23 31 HVAC Ducts and Casings
23 31 13 – Metal Ducts

23 31 13.17 Round Grease Duct		Crew	Daily Output	Labor-Hours	Unit	Material	2023 Bare Costs Labor	2023 Bare Costs Equipment	Total	Total Incl O&P
4132	36"	Q-10	6.84	3.509	Ea.	1,275	230		1,505	1,750
4140	Tee, 90°, grease									
4144	6"	Q-9	13.68	1.170	Ea.	485	74		559	640
4146	8"		12.54	1.276		535	80.50		615.50	705
4148	10"		11.97	1.337		595	84.50		679.50	775
4150	12"		11.40	1.404		685	88.50		773.50	890
4152	14"		10.26	1.559		785	98.50		883.50	1,000
4154	16"		9.12	1.754		865	111		976	1,125
4156	18"		7.98	2.005		1,025	127		1,152	1,325
4158	20"		9.69	1.651		1,175	104		1,279	1,450
4160	22"		8.26	1.937		1,300	122		1,422	1,625
4162	24"		6.84	2.339		1,450	148		1,598	1,825
4164	26"		6.55	2.443		1,600	154		1,754	1,975
4166	28"	Q-10	6.27	3.828		1,750	251		2,001	2,300
4168	30"		5.98	4.013		2,100	263		2,363	2,700
4170	32"		5.70	4.211		2,450	276		2,726	3,125
4172	36"		5.13	4.678		2,725	305		3,030	3,450
4180	Cleanout tee cap									
4184	6"	Q-9	21.09	.759	Ea.	100	48		148	182
4186	8"		19.38	.826		105	52		157	195
4188	10"		18.24	.877		113	55.50		168.50	209
4190	12"		17.10	.936		121	59		180	222
4192	14"		15.96	1.003		129	63.50		192.50	237
4194	16"		14.25	1.123		142	71		213	263
4196	18"		13.68	1.170		151	74		225	277
4198	20"	Q-10	15.39	1.559		167	102		269	335
4200	22"		12.54	1.914		181	125		306	390
4202	24"		11.97	2.005		197	131		328	415
4204	26"		11.40	2.105		215	138		353	445
4206	28"		10.83	2.216		234	145		379	475
4208	30"		10.26	2.339		255	153		408	510
4210	32"		9.69	2.477		278	162		440	550
4212	36"		8.55	2.807		325	184		509	635
4220	Elbow, 45°									
4224	6"	Q-9	17.10	.936	Ea.	335	59		394	455
4226	8"		14.82	1.080		375	68		443	520
4228	10"		13.68	1.170		425	74		499	580
4230	12"		12.54	1.276		485	80.50		565.50	655
4232	14"		11.97	1.337		545	84.50		629.50	725
4234	16"		11.40	1.404		620	88.50		708.50	815
4236	18"		10.83	1.477		700	93.50		793.50	910
4238	20"	Q-10	10.26	2.339		790	153		943	1,100
4240	22"		9.69	2.477		885	162		1,047	1,225
4242	24"		9.12	2.632		1,025	172		1,197	1,375
4244	26"		8.83	2.718		1,075	178		1,253	1,450
4246	28"		8.55	2.807		1,275	184		1,459	1,675
4248	30"		8.26	2.906		1,300	190		1,490	1,700
4250	32"		7.98	3.008		1,525	197		1,722	2,000
4252	36"		6.84	3.509		2,075	230		2,305	2,625
4260	Elbow, 90°									
4264	6"	Q-9	17.10	.936	Ea.	645	59		704	800
4266	8"		14.82	1.080		725	68		793	905
4268	10"		13.68	1.170		885	74		959	1,075

23 31 HVAC Ducts and Casings

23 31 13 – Metal Ducts

23 31 13.17 Round Grease Duct		Crew	Daily Output	Labor-Hours	Unit	Material	2023 Bare Costs Labor	Equipment	Total	Total Incl O&P
4270	12"	Q-9	12.54	1.276	Ea.	1,000	80.50		1,080.50	1,225
4272	14"		11.97	1.337		1,075	84.50		1,159.50	1,300
4274	16"		11.40	1.404		1,225	88.50		1,313.50	1,450
4276	18"		10.83	1.477		1,450	93.50		1,543.50	1,750
4278	20"	Q-10	10.26	2.339		1,550	153		1,703	1,925
4280	22"		9.69	2.477		1,725	162		1,887	2,150
4282	24"		9.12	2.632		1,950	172		2,122	2,400
4284	26"		8.83	2.718		2,100	178		2,278	2,600
4286	28"		8.55	2.807		2,200	184		2,384	2,700
4288	30"		8.26	2.906		2,550	190		2,740	3,100
4290	32"		7.98	3.008		3,050	197		3,247	3,650
4292	36"		6.84	3.509		3,975	230		4,205	4,725
4300	Support strap									
4304	6"	Q-9	25.50	.627	Ea.	110	39.50		149.50	181
4306	8"		22	.727		139	46		185	221
4308	10"		20.50	.780		143	49.50		192.50	231
4310	12"		18.80	.851		154	53.50		207.50	250
4312	14"		17.90	.894		167	56.50		223.50	268
4314	16"		17	.941		168	59.50		227.50	275
4316	18"		16.20	.988		170	62.50		232.50	281
4318	20"	Q-10	15.40	1.558		190	102		292	365
4320	22"	"	14.50	1.655		211	108		319	395
4340	Plate support assembly									
4344	6"	Q-9	14.82	1.080	Ea.	161	68		229	280
4346	8"		12.54	1.276		188	80.50		268.50	330
4348	10"		11.40	1.404		202	88.50		290.50	355
4350	12"		10.26	1.559		215	98.50		313.50	385
4352	14"		9.69	1.651		254	104		358	435
4354	16"		9.12	1.754		265	111		376	460
4356	18"		8.55	1.871		282	118		400	490
4358	20"	Q-10	9.12	2.632		296	172		468	585
4360	22"		8.55	2.807		300	184		484	605
4362	24"		7.98	3.008		315	197		512	640
4364	26"		7.69	3.121		345	204		549	690
4366	28"		7.41	3.239		385	212		597	740
4368	30"		7.12	3.371		415	221		636	790
4370	32"		6.84	3.509		465	230		695	855
4372	36"		5.70	4.211		560	276		836	1,025
4380	Wall guide assembly									
4384	6"	Q-9	19.10	.838	Ea.	206	53		259	305
4386	8"		16.50	.970		233	61		294	350
4388	10"		15.30	1.046		246	66		312	370
4390	12"		14.10	1.135		257	71.50		328.50	390
4392	14"		13.40	1.194		278	75.50		353.50	420
4394	16"		12.75	1.255		282	79		361	430
4396	18"		12.10	1.322		286	83.50		369.50	440
4398	20"	Q-10	11.50	2.087		305	137		442	545
4400	22"		10.90	2.202		330	144		474	575
4402	24"		10.20	2.353		360	154		514	625
4404	26"		9.90	2.424		390	159		549	670
4406	28"		9.60	2.500		405	164		569	690
4408	30"		9.30	2.581		450	169		619	750
4410	32"		9	2.667		475	175		650	790

23 31 HVAC Ducts and Casings

23 31 13 – Metal Ducts

	23 31 13.17 Round Grease Duct	Crew	Daily Output	Labor-Hours	Unit	Material	2023 Bare Costs Labor	Equipment	Total	Total Incl O&P
4412	36"	Q-10	7.60	3.158	Ea.	525	207		732	885
4420	Hood transition, flanged or unflanged									
4424	6"	Q-9	15.60	1.026	Ea.	84	65		149	190
4426	8"		13.50	1.185		95.50	75		170.50	218
4428	10"		12.50	1.280		106	81		187	239
4430	12"		11.40	1.404		127	88.50		215.50	272
4432	14"		10.90	1.468		143	92.50		235.50	297
4434	16"		10.40	1.538		154	97		251	315
4436	18"		9.80	1.633		177	103		280	350
4438	20"	Q-10	9.40	2.553		188	167		355	460
4440	22"		8.80	2.727		205	179		384	495
4442	24"		8.30	2.892		230	189		419	540
4444	26"		8.10	2.963		236	194		430	550
4446	28"		7.80	3.077		251	201		452	580
4448	30"		7.50	3.200		273	210		483	615
4450	32"		7.30	3.288		286	215		501	640
4452	36"		6.20	3.871		320	253		573	730
4460	Fan adapter									
4464	6"	Q-9	15	1.067	Ea.	264	67.50		331.50	390
4466	8"		13	1.231		299	77.50		376.50	445
4468	10"		12	1.333		325	84		409	485
4470	12"		11	1.455		365	92		457	545
4472	14"		10.50	1.524		400	96		496	585
4474	16"		10	1.600		435	101		536	630
4476	18"		9.50	1.684		475	106		581	680
4478	20"	Q-10	9	2.667		505	175		680	820
4480	22"		8.50	2.824		540	185		725	875
4482	24"		8	3		570	196		766	925
4484	26"		7.70	3.117		605	204		809	970
4486	28"		7.50	3.200		635	210		845	1,025
4488	30"		7.20	3.333		670	218		888	1,075
4490	32"		7	3.429		705	224		929	1,125
4492	36"		6	4		780	262		1,042	1,250
4500	Tapered increaser/reducer									
4530	6" x 10" diam.	Q-9	13.40	1.194	Ea.	340	75.50		415.50	490
4540	6" x 20" diam.		10.10	1.584		350	100		450	535
4550	8" x 10" diam.		13.20	1.212		405	76.50		481.50	565
4560	8" x 20" diam.		9.90	1.616		415	102		517	615
4570	10" x 20" diam.		10.60	1.509		480	95.50		575.50	675
4580	10" x 28" diam.	Q-10	8.60	2.791		490	183		673	815
4590	12" x 20" diam.		8.80	2.727		555	179		734	880
4600	14" x 28" diam.		8.40	2.857		635	187		822	980
4610	16" x 20" diam.		8.60	2.791		695	183		878	1,050
4620	16" x 30" diam.		8.30	2.892		700	189		889	1,050
4630	18" x 24" diam.		8.80	2.727		760	179		939	1,100
4640	18" x 30" diam.		8.10	2.963		770	194		964	1,125
4650	20" x 24" diam.		8.30	2.892		825	189		1,014	1,200
4660	20" x 32" diam.		8	3		835	196		1,031	1,225
4670	24" x 26" diam.		8	3		950	196		1,146	1,350
4680	24" x 36" diam.		7.30	3.288		980	215		1,195	1,400
4690	28" x 30" diam.		7.90	3.038		1,100	199		1,299	1,500
4700	28" x 36" diam.		7.10	3.380		1,125	221		1,346	1,550
4710	30" x 36" diam.		6.90	3.478		1,175	228		1,403	1,650

23 31 HVAC Ducts and Casings

23 31 13 – Metal Ducts

23 31 13.17 Round Grease Duct

		Crew	Daily Output	Labor-Hours	Unit	Material	2023 Bare Costs Labor	2023 Bare Costs Equipment	Total	Total Incl O&P
4730	Many intermediate standard sizes of tapered fittings are available									

23 31 13.19 Metal Duct Fittings

		Crew	Daily Output	Labor-Hours	Unit	Material	Labor	Equipment	Total	Total Incl O&P
0010	**METAL DUCT FITTINGS**									
0350	Duct collar, spin-in type									
0352	Without damper									
0354	Round									
0356	4"	1 Shee	32	.250	Ea.	6.45	17.55		24	33.50
0357	5"		30	.267		7.50	18.70		26.20	36.50
0358	6"		28	.286		9.20	20		29.20	40
0359	7"		26	.308		10.55	21.50		32.05	44
0360	8"		24	.333		12.10	23.50		35.60	48.50
0361	9"		22	.364		13.50	25.50		39	53.50
0362	10"		20	.400		14.80	28		42.80	59
0363	12"		17	.471		17.75	33		50.75	69
2000	Fabrics for flexible connections, with metal edge		100	.080	L.F.	5.20	5.60		10.80	14.15
2100	Without metal edge		160	.050	"	4.21	3.51		7.72	9.95

23 31 16 – Nonmetal Ducts

23 31 16.13 Fibrous-Glass Ducts

		Crew	Daily Output	Labor-Hours	Unit	Material	Labor	Equipment	Total	Total Incl O&P
0010	**FIBROUS-GLASS DUCTS**									
1280	Add to labor for elevated installation									
1282	of prefabricated (purchased) ductwork									
1283	10' to 15' high						10%			
1284	15' to 20' high						20%			
1285	20' to 25' high						25%			
1286	25' to 30' high						35%			
1287	30' to 35' high						40%			
1288	35' to 40' high						50%			
1289	Over 40' high						55%			
3490	Rigid fiberglass duct board, foil reinf. kraft facing									
3500	Rectangular, 1" thick, alum. faced, (FRK), std. weight	Q-10	350	.069	SF Surf	.99	4.49		5.48	7.85

23 31 16.16 Thermoset Fiberglass-Reinforced Plastic Ducts

		Crew	Daily Output	Labor-Hours	Unit	Material	Labor	Equipment	Total	Total Incl O&P
0010	**THERMOSET FIBERGLASS-REINFORCED PLASTIC DUCTS**									
1280	Add to labor for elevated installation									
1282	of prefabricated (purchased) ductwork									
1283	10' to 15' high						10%			
1284	15' to 20' high						20%			
1285	20' to 25' high						25%			
1286	25' to 30' high						35%			
1287	30' to 35' high						40%			
1288	35' to 40' high						50%			
1289	Over 40' high						55%			
3550	Rigid fiberglass reinforced plastic, FM approved									
3552	for acid fume and smoke exhaust system, nonflammable									
3554	Straight, 4" diameter	Q-9	200	.080	L.F.	11.60	5.05		16.65	20.50
3555	6" diameter		146	.110		4.08	6.90		10.98	14.90
3556	8" diameter		106	.151		18.40	9.55		27.95	34.50
3557	10" diameter		85	.188		4.80	11.90		16.70	23
3558	12" diameter		68	.235		26	14.85		40.85	51
3559	14" diameter		50	.320		38	20		58	72.50
3560	16" diameter		40	.400		42.50	25.50		68	85
3561	18" diameter		31	.516		47.50	32.50		80	101
3562	20" diameter	Q-10	44	.545		52	35.50		87.50	112

23 31 HVAC Ducts and Casings

23 31 16 – Nonmetal Ducts

23 31 16.16 Thermoset Fiberglass-Reinforced Plastic Ducts		Crew	Daily Output	Labor-Hours	Unit	Material	2023 Bare Costs Labor	Equipment	Total	Total Incl O&P
3563	22" diameter	Q-10	40	.600	L.F.	56.50	39.50		96	121
3564	24" diameter		37	.649		61	42.50		103.50	131
3565	26" diameter		34	.706		65.50	46		111.50	142
3566	28" diameter		28	.857		70.50	56		126.50	162
3567	30" diameter		24	1		75	65.50		140.50	181
3568	32" diameter		22.60	1.062		79.50	69.50		149	193
3569	34" diameter		21.60	1.111		84	72.50		156.50	203
3570	36" diameter		20.60	1.165		89	76.50		165.50	213
3571	38" diameter		19.80	1.212		137	79.50		216.50	270
3572	42" diameter		18.30	1.311		153	86		239	297
3573	46" diameter		17	1.412		169	92.50		261.50	325
3574	50" diameter		15.90	1.509		184	99		283	350
3575	54" diameter		14.90	1.611		202	105		307	380
3576	60" diameter		13.60	1.765		231	116		347	430
3577	64" diameter		12.80	1.875		340	123		463	560
3578	68" diameter		12.20	1.967		360	129		489	590
3579	72" diameter		11.90	2.017		390	132		522	625
3584	Note: joints are cemented with									
3586	fiberglass resin, included in material cost.									
3590	Elbow, 90°, 4" diameter	Q-9	20.30	.788	Ea.	56	50		106	137
3591	6" diameter		13.80	1.159		78	73		151	196
3592	8" diameter		10	1.600		86	101		187	247
3593	10" diameter		7.80	2.051		113	130		243	320
3594	12" diameter		6.50	2.462		143	155		298	390
3595	14" diameter		5.50	2.909		176	184		360	470
3596	16" diameter		4.80	3.333		209	210		419	545
3597	18" diameter		4.40	3.636		299	230		529	675
3598	20" diameter	Q-10	5.90	4.068		315	266		581	745
3599	22" diameter		5.40	4.444		390	291		681	865
3600	24" diameter		4.90	4.898		445	320		765	975
3601	26" diameter		4.60	5.217		450	340		790	1,000
3602	28" diameter		4.20	5.714		565	375		940	1,175
3603	30" diameter		3.90	6.154		630	405		1,035	1,300
3604	32" diameter		3.70	6.486		700	425		1,125	1,400
3605	34" diameter		3.45	6.957		825	455		1,280	1,600
3606	36" diameter		3.20	7.500		945	490		1,435	1,800
3607	38" diameter		3.07	7.818		1,350	510		1,860	2,250
3608	42" diameter		2.70	8.889		1,625	580		2,205	2,650
3609	46" diameter		2.54	9.449		1,875	620		2,495	3,000
3610	50" diameter		2.33	10.300		2,175	675		2,850	3,425
3611	54" diameter		2.14	11.215		2,500	735		3,235	3,850
3612	60" diameter		1.94	12.371		3,325	810		4,135	4,900
3613	64" diameter		1.82	13.187		4,850	865		5,715	6,625
3614	68" diameter		1.71	14.035		5,375	920		6,295	7,300
3615	72" diameter		1.62	14.815		5,950	970		6,920	8,000
3626	Elbow, 45°, 4" diameter	Q-9	22.30	.717		54	45.50		99.50	127
3627	6" diameter		15.20	1.053		74.50	66.50		141	182
3628	8" diameter		11	1.455		79	92		171	225
3629	10" diameter		8.60	1.860		83.50	117		200.50	269
3630	12" diameter		7.20	2.222		91.50	140		231.50	310
3631	14" diameter		6.10	2.623		112	166		278	370
3632	16" diameter		5.28	3.030		134	191		325	435
3633	18" diameter		4.84	3.306		156	209		365	485

23 31 HVAC Ducts and Casings

23 31 16 – Nonmetal Ducts

23 31 16.16 Thermoset Fiberglass-Reinforced Plastic Ducts		Crew	Daily Output	Labor-Hours	Unit	Material	2023 Bare Costs Labor	Equipment	Total	Total Incl O&P
3634	20" diameter	Q-10	6.50	3.692	Ea.	181	242		423	565
3635	22" diameter		5.94	4.040		247	265		512	670
3636	24" diameter		5.40	4.444		281	291		572	750
3637	26" diameter		5.06	4.743		320	310		630	820
3638	28" diameter		4.62	5.195		345	340		685	890
3639	30" diameter		4.30	5.581		400	365		765	990
3640	32" diameter		4.07	5.897		440	385		825	1,075
3641	34" diameter		3.80	6.316		520	415		935	1,200
3642	36" diameter		3.52	6.818		605	445		1,050	1,325
3643	38" diameter		3.38	7.101		845	465		1,310	1,625
3644	42" diameter		2.97	8.081		1,000	530		1,530	1,925
3645	46" diameter		2.80	8.571		1,175	560		1,735	2,150
3646	50" diameter		2.56	9.375		1,375	615		1,990	2,425
3647	54" diameter		2.35	10.213		1,550	670		2,220	2,725
3648	60" diameter		2.13	11.268		2,100	740		2,840	3,400
3649	64" diameter		2	12		3,050	785		3,835	4,525
3650	68" diameter		1.88	12.766		3,375	835		4,210	4,950
3651	72" diameter		1.78	13.483		3,725	885		4,610	5,400
3660	Tee, 90°, 4" diameter	Q-9	14.06	1.138		30.50	72		102.50	142
3661	6" diameter		9.52	1.681		47	106		153	212
3662	8" diameter		6.98	2.292		64	145		209	289
3663	10" diameter		5.45	2.936		83.50	185		268.50	370
3664	12" diameter		4.60	3.478		104	220		324	445
3665	14" diameter		3.86	4.145		152	262		414	560
3666	16" diameter		3.40	4.706		181	297		478	650
3667	18" diameter		3.05	5.246		214	330		544	735
3668	20" diameter	Q-10	4.12	5.825		251	380		631	850
3669	22" diameter		3.78	6.349		286	415		701	940
3670	24" diameter		3.46	6.936		325	455		780	1,050
3671	26" diameter		3.20	7.500		365	490		855	1,150
3672	28" diameter		2.96	8.108		410	530		940	1,250
3673	30" diameter		2.75	8.727		460	570		1,030	1,375
3674	32" diameter		2.54	9.449		505	620		1,125	1,475
3675	34" diameter		2.40	10		555	655		1,210	1,600
3676	36" diameter		2.27	10.573		610	690		1,300	1,725
3677	38" diameter		2.15	11.163		915	730		1,645	2,100
3678	42" diameter		1.91	12.565		1,100	825		1,925	2,475
3679	46" diameter		1.78	13.483		1,300	885		2,185	2,750
3680	50" diameter		1.63	14.724		1,500	965		2,465	3,100
3681	54" diameter		1.50	16		1,750	1,050		2,800	3,500
3682	60" diameter		1.35	17.778		2,175	1,175		3,350	4,150
3683	64" diameter		1.27	18.898		3,275	1,225		4,500	5,475
3684	68" diameter		1.20	20		3,650	1,300		4,950	6,000
3685	72" diameter		1.13	21.239		4,100	1,400		5,500	6,600
3690	For Y @ 45°, add					22%				
3700	Blast gate, 4" diameter	Q-9	22.30	.717		149	45.50		194.50	231
3701	6" diameter		15.20	1.053		168	66.50		234.50	285
3702	8" diameter		11	1.455		226	92		318	385
3703	10" diameter		8.60	1.860		258	117		375	460
3704	12" diameter		7.20	2.222		315	140		455	555
3705	14" diameter		6.10	2.623		350	166		516	635
3706	16" diameter		5.28	3.030		390	191		581	715
3707	18" diameter		4.84	3.306		390	209		599	745

23 31 HVAC Ducts and Casings

23 31 16 – Nonmetal Ducts

23 31 16.16 Thermoset Fiberglass-Reinforced Plastic Ducts		Crew	Daily Output	Labor-Hours	Unit	Material	2023 Bare Costs Labor	Equipment	Total	Total Incl O&P
3708	20" diameter	Q-10	6.50	3.692	Ea.	460	242		702	870
3709	22" diameter		5.94	4.040		495	265		760	945
3710	24" diameter		5.40	4.444		535	291		826	1,025
3711	26" diameter		5.06	4.743		570	310		880	1,100
3712	28" diameter		4.62	5.195		615	340		955	1,175
3713	30" diameter		4.30	5.581		650	365		1,015	1,275
3714	32" diameter		4.07	5.897		710	385		1,095	1,350
3715	34" diameter		3.80	6.316		775	415		1,190	1,475
3716	36" diameter		3.52	6.818		835	445		1,280	1,600
3717	38" diameter		3.38	7.101		1,125	465		1,590	1,950
3718	42" diameter		2.97	8.081		1,300	530		1,830	2,225
3719	46" diameter		2.80	8.571		1,475	560		2,035	2,475
3720	50" diameter		2.56	9.375		1,700	615		2,315	2,800
3721	54" diameter		2.35	10.213		1,900	670		2,570	3,100
3722	60" diameter		2.13	11.268		2,225	740		2,965	3,550
3723	64" diameter		2	12		2,475	785		3,260	3,900
3724	68" diameter		1.88	12.766		2,750	835		3,585	4,275
3725	72" diameter		1.78	13.483		3,025	885		3,910	4,650
3740	Reducers, 4" diameter	Q-9	24.50	.653		37	41		78	103
3741	6" diameter		16.70	.958		55.50	60.50		116	152
3742	8" diameter		12	1.333		75	84		159	210
3743	10" diameter		9.50	1.684		92.50	106		198.50	262
3744	12" diameter		7.90	2.025		111	128		239	315
3745	14" diameter		6.70	2.388		129	151		280	370
3746	16" diameter		5.80	2.759		147	174		321	425
3747	18" diameter		5.30	3.019		167	191		358	470
3748	20" diameter	Q-10	7.20	3.333		185	218		403	535
3749	22" diameter		6.50	3.692		298	242		540	695
3750	24" diameter		5.90	4.068		325	266		591	755
3751	26" diameter		5.60	4.286		350	281		631	810
3752	28" diameter		5.10	4.706		380	310		690	885
3753	30" diameter		4.70	5.106		410	335		745	955
3754	32" diameter		4.50	5.333		435	350		785	1,000
3755	34" diameter		4.20	5.714		465	375		840	1,075
3756	36" diameter		3.90	6.154		490	405		895	1,150
3757	38" diameter		3.70	6.486		745	425		1,170	1,450
3758	42" diameter		3.30	7.273		820	475		1,295	1,625
3759	46" diameter		3.10	7.742		900	505		1,405	1,750
3760	50" diameter		2.80	8.571		975	560		1,535	1,925
3761	54" diameter		2.60	9.231		1,050	605		1,655	2,050
3762	60" diameter		2.34	10.256		1,175	670		1,845	2,300
3763	64" diameter		2.20	10.909		1,825	715		2,540	3,100
3764	68" diameter		2.06	11.650		1,950	765		2,715	3,275
3765	72" diameter		1.96	12.245		2,075	800		2,875	3,475
3780	Flange, per each, 4" diameter	Q-9	40.60	.394		90	25		115	137
3781	6" diameter		27.70	.578		105	36.50		141.50	170
3782	8" diameter		20.50	.780		131	49.50		180.50	218
3783	10" diameter		16.30	.982		157	62		219	267
3784	12" diameter		13.90	1.151		181	72.50		253.50	310
3785	14" diameter		11.30	1.416		209	89.50		298.50	365
3786	16" diameter		9.70	1.649		235	104		339	415
3787	18" diameter		8.30	1.928		261	122		383	470
3788	20" diameter	Q-10	11.30	2.124		286	139		425	525

For customer support on your Mechanical Costs with RSMeans data, call 800.448.8182.

23 31 HVAC Ducts and Casings

23 31 16 – Nonmetal Ducts

23 31 16.16 Thermoset Fiberglass-Reinforced Plastic Ducts		Crew	Daily Output	Labor-Hours	Unit	Material	2023 Bare Costs Labor	Equipment	Total	Total Incl O&P
3789	22" diameter	Q-10	10.40	2.308	Ea.	310	151		461	575
3790	24" diameter		9.50	2.526		340	165		505	625
3791	26" diameter		8.80	2.727		365	179		544	675
3792	28" diameter		8.20	2.927		395	192		587	720
3793	30" diameter		7.60	3.158		415	207		622	765
3794	32" diameter		7.20	3.333		440	218		658	815
3795	34" diameter		6.80	3.529		470	231		701	865
3796	36" diameter		6.40	3.750		495	246		741	915
3797	38" diameter		6.10	3.934		520	258		778	965
3798	42" diameter		5.50	4.364		570	286		856	1,050
3799	46" diameter		5	4.800		625	315		940	1,150
3800	50" diameter		4.60	5.217		680	340		1,020	1,250
3801	54" diameter		4.20	5.714		725	375		1,100	1,375
3802	60" diameter		3.80	6.316		805	415		1,220	1,525
3803	64" diameter		3.60	6.667		855	435		1,290	1,600
3804	68" diameter		3.40	7.059		910	460		1,370	1,700
3805	72" diameter	↓	3.20	7.500	↓	965	490		1,455	1,800
23 31 16.19 PVC Ducts										
0010	**PVC DUCTS**									
4000	Rigid plastic, corrosive fume resistant PVC									
4020	Straight, 6" diameter	Q-9	220	.073	L.F.	24.50	4.59		29.09	34
4040	8" diameter		160	.100		34.50	6.30		40.80	47.50
4060	10" diameter		120	.133		43.50	8.40		51.90	60.50
4070	12" diameter		100	.160		50	10.10		60.10	70
4080	14" diameter		70	.229		62	14.45		76.45	90
4090	16" diameter		62	.258		71.50	16.30		87.80	103
4100	18" diameter	↓	58	.276		97.50	17.40		114.90	133
4110	20" diameter	Q-10	75	.320		90.50	21		111.50	131
4130	24" diameter	"	55	.436	↓	122	28.50		150.50	177
4250	Coupling, 6" diameter	Q-9	88	.182	Ea.	43	11.50		54.50	65
4270	8" diameter		78	.205		56	12.95		68.95	81
4290	10" diameter		70	.229		64.50	14.45		78.95	92.50
4300	12" diameter		55	.291		70	18.35		88.35	105
4310	14" diameter		44	.364		90.50	23		113.50	134
4320	16" diameter		40	.400		95.50	25.50		121	143
4330	18" diameter	↓	38	.421		124	26.50		150.50	176
4340	20" diameter	Q-10	55	.436		148	28.50		176.50	206
4360	24" diameter	"	45	.533		186	35		221	258
4470	Elbow, 90°, 6" diameter	Q-9	44	.364		195	23		218	250
4490	8" diameter		28	.571		219	36		255	296
4510	10" diameter		18	.889		266	56		322	375
4520	12" diameter		15	1.067		300	67.50		367.50	430
4530	14" diameter		11	1.455		350	92		442	525
4540	16" diameter	↓	10	1.600		455	101		556	650
4550	18" diameter	Q-10	15	1.600		630	105		735	855
4560	20" diameter		14	1.714		940	112		1,052	1,200
4580	24" diameter	↓	12	2	↓	1,150	131		1,281	1,475
4750	Elbow 45°, use 90° and deduct					25%				

23 31 HVAC Ducts and Casings

23 31 16 – Nonmetal Ducts

23 31 16.21 Polypropylene Ducts		Crew	Daily Output	Labor-Hours	Unit	Material	2023 Bare Costs Labor	Equipment	Total	Total Incl O&P
0010	**POLYPROPYLENE DUCTS**									
0020	Rigid plastic, corrosive fume resistant, flame retardant, PP									
0110	Straight, 4" diameter	Q-9	200	.080	L.F.	9.35	5.05		14.40	17.90
0120	6" diameter		146	.110		16.20	6.90		23.10	28
0140	8" diameter		106	.151		23.50	9.55		33.05	40.50
0160	10" diameter		85	.188		30	11.90		41.90	50.50
0170	12" diameter		68	.235		34.50	14.85		49.35	60.50
0180	14" diameter		50	.320		43.50	20		63.50	78
0190	16" diameter		40	.400		63	25.50		88.50	107
0200	18" diameter		31	.516		86	32.50		118.50	144
0210	20" diameter	Q-10	44	.545		104	35.50		139.50	168
0220	22" diameter		40	.600		95	39.50		134.50	164
0230	24" diameter		37	.649		207	42.50		249.50	291
0250	28" diameter		28	.857		279	56		335	390
0270	32" diameter		24	1		315	65.50		380.50	445
0400	Coupling									
0410	4" diameter	Q-9	23	.696	Ea.	28	44		72	97
0420	6" diameter		16	1		36	63		99	135
0430	8" diameter		11.40	1.404		39	88.50		127.50	176
0440	10" diameter		9	1.778		53	112		165	227
0450	12" diameter		8	2		61	126		187	257
0460	14" diameter		6.60	2.424		93	153		246	335
0470	16" diameter		5.70	2.807		98.50	177		275.50	375
0480	18" diameter		5.20	3.077		141	194		335	450
0490	20" diameter	Q-10	6.80	3.529		158	231		389	525
0500	22" diameter		6.20	3.871		202	253		455	600
0510	24" diameter		5.80	4.138		330	271		601	770
0520	28" diameter		5.50	4.364		460	286		746	935
0530	32" diameter		5.20	4.615		500	300		800	1,000
0800	Elbow, 90°									
0810	4" diameter	Q-9	22	.727	Ea.	42.50	46		88.50	116
0820	6" diameter		15.40	1.039		59	65.50		124.50	164
0830	8" diameter		11	1.455		69	92		161	214
0840	10" diameter		8.60	1.860		98.50	117		215.50	285
0850	12" diameter		7.70	2.078		240	131		371	460
0860	14" diameter		6.40	2.500		278	158		436	545
0870	16" diameter		5.40	2.963		296	187		483	605
0880	18" diameter	Q-10	7.50	3.200		920	210		1,130	1,325
0890	20" diameter		6.60	3.636		1,025	238		1,263	1,475
0896	22" diameter		6.10	3.934		1,125	258		1,383	1,625
0900	24" diameter		5.60	4.286		1,600	281		1,881	2,175
0910	28" diameter		5.40	4.444		3,350	291		3,641	4,150
0920	32" diameter		5.20	4.615		3,500	300		3,800	4,300
1000	Elbow, 45°									
1020	4" diameter	Q-9	22	.727	Ea.	31	46		77	104
1030	6" diameter		15.40	1.039		49	65.50		114.50	153
1040	8" diameter		11	1.455		57	92		149	201
1050	10" diameter		8.60	1.860		78.50	117		195.50	263
1060	12" diameter		7.70	2.078		196	131		327	415
1070	14" diameter		6.40	2.500		221	158		379	480
1080	16" diameter		5.40	2.963		235	187		422	540
1090	18" diameter	Q-10	7.50	3.200		575	210		785	950

23 31 HVAC Ducts and Casings

23 31 16 – Nonmetal Ducts

23 31 16.21 Polypropylene Ducts

		Crew	Daily Output	Labor-Hours	Unit	Material	2023 Bare Costs Labor	Equipment	Total	Total Incl O&P
1100	20" diameter	Q-10	6.60	3.636	Ea.	730	238		968	1,150
1106	22" diameter		6.10	3.934		765	258		1,023	1,225
1110	24" diameter		5.60	4.286		1,200	281		1,481	1,725
1120	28" diameter		5.40	4.444		1,800	291		2,091	2,425
1130	32" diameter		5.20	4.615		2,200	300		2,500	2,850
1200	Tee									
1210	4" diameter	Q-9	16.50	.970	Ea.	137	61		198	242
1220	6" diameter		11.60	1.379		178	87		265	325
1230	8" diameter		8.30	1.928		222	122		344	430
1240	10" diameter		6.50	2.462		310	155		465	575
1250	12" diameter		5.80	2.759		535	174		709	850
1260	14" diameter		4.80	3.333		530	210		740	900
1270	16" diameter		4.05	3.951		620	249		869	1,050
1280	18" diameter	Q-10	5.60	4.286		770	281		1,051	1,275
1290	20" diameter		4.90	4.898		845	320		1,165	1,425
1300	22" diameter		4.40	5.455		1,050	355		1,405	1,700
1310	24" diameter		4.20	5.714		2,225	375		2,600	3,025
1320	28" diameter		4.10	5.854		2,750	385		3,135	3,625
1330	32" diameter		4	6		3,425	395		3,820	4,375

23 31 16.22 Duct Board

		Crew	Daily Output	Labor-Hours	Unit	Material	Labor	Equipment	Total	Total Incl O&P
0010	**DUCT BOARD**									
3800	Rigid, resin bonded fibrous glass, FSK									
3810	Temperature, bacteria and fungi resistant									
3820	1" thick	Q-14	150	.107	S.F.	2.25	6.25		8.50	12.10
3830	1-1/2" thick		130	.123		2.63	7.25		9.88	13.95
3840	2" thick		120	.133		3.63	7.85		11.48	16

23 33 Air Duct Accessories

23 33 13 – Dampers

23 33 13.13 Volume-Control Dampers

		Crew	Daily Output	Labor-Hours	Unit	Material	Labor	Equipment	Total	Total Incl O&P
0010	**VOLUME-CONTROL DAMPERS**									
5990	Multi-blade dampers, opposed blade, 8" x 6"	1 Shee	24	.333	Ea.	14.25	23.50		37.75	50.50
5994	8" x 8"		22	.364		14.25	25.50		39.75	54
5996	10" x 10"		21	.381		133	26.50		159.50	187
6000	12" x 12"		21	.381		133	26.50		159.50	187
6020	12" x 18"		18	.444		203	31		234	270
6030	14" x 10"		20	.400		138	28		166	195
6031	14" x 14"		17	.471		158	33		191	224
6032	16" x 10"		18	.444		138	31		169	199
6033	16" x 12"		17	.471		199	33		232	269
6035	16" x 16"		16	.500		158	35		193	227
6036	18" x 14"		16	.500		166	35		201	236
6037	18" x 16"		15	.533		166	37.50		203.50	240
6038	18" x 18"		15	.533		199	37.50		236.50	276
6040	18" x 24"		12	.667		305	47		352	405
6060	18" x 28"		10	.800		160	56		216	261
6068	20" x 6"		18	.444		58	31		89	111
6069	20" x 8"		16	.500		69.50	35		104.50	129
6070	20" x 16"		14	.571		240	40		280	325
6071	20" x 18"		13	.615		199	43		242	284
6072	20" x 20"		13	.615		199	43		242	284

23 33 Air Duct Accessories

23 33 13 – Dampers

23 33 13.13	Volume-Control Dampers	Crew	Daily Output	Labor-Hours	Unit	Material	2023 Bare Costs Labor	Equipment	Total	Total Incl O&P
6073	22" x 6"	1 Shee	20	.400	Ea.	59.50	28		87.50	108
6074	22" x 18"		14	.571		52	40		92	118
6075	22" x 20"		12	.667		139	47		186	224
6076	24" x 16"		11	.727		249	51		300	350
6077	22" x 22"		10	.800		229	56		285	335
6078	24" x 20"		8	1		211	70		281	340
6080	24" x 24"		8	1		229	70		299	360
6100	24" x 28"		6	1.333		175	93.50		268.50	335
6110	26" x 26"		6	1.333		265	93.50		358.50	435
6120	28" x 28"	Q-9	11	1.455		265	92		357	430
6130	30" x 18"		10	1.600		320	101		421	500
6132	30" x 24"		7	2.286		355	144		499	605
6133	30" x 30"		6.60	2.424		305	153		458	565
6135	32" x 32"		6.40	2.500		305	158		463	575
6150	34" x 34"		6	2.667		375	168		543	665
6151	36" x 12"		10	1.600		243	101		344	420
6152	36" x 16"		8	2		259	126		385	475
6156	36" x 32"		6.30	2.540		375	160		535	650
6157	36" x 34"		6.20	2.581		395	163		558	680
6158	36" x 36"		6	2.667		355	168		523	645
6160	44" x 28"		5.80	2.759		420	174		594	725
6180	48" x 36"		5.60	2.857		570	180		750	895
6200	56" x 36"		5.40	2.963		645	187		832	985
6220	60" x 36"		5.20	3.077		690	194		884	1,050
6240	60" x 44"		5	3.200		800	202		1,002	1,175
7500	Variable volume modulating motorized damper, incl. elect. mtr.									
7504	8" x 6"	1 Shee	15	.533	Ea.	242	37.50		279.50	325
7506	10" x 6"		14	.571		242	40		282	325
7510	10" x 10"		13	.615		252	43		295	340
7520	12" x 12"		12	.667		260	47		307	355
7522	12" x 16"		11	.727		261	51		312	365
7524	16" x 10"		12	.667		257	47		304	355
7526	16" x 14"		10	.800		269	56		325	380
7528	16" x 18"		9	.889		277	62.50		339.50	400
7540	18" x 12"		10	.800		270	56		326	380
7542	18" x 18"		8	1		282	70		352	415
7544	20" x 14"		8	1		292	70		362	425
7546	20" x 18"		7	1.143		300	80		380	450
7560	24" x 12"		8	1		294	70		364	430
7562	24" x 18"		7	1.143		315	80		395	470
7568	28" x 10"		7	1.143		294	80		374	445
7580	28" x 16"		6	1.333		297	93.50		390.50	465
7590	30" x 14"		5	1.600		300	112		412	505
7600	30" x 18"		4	2		390	140		530	640
7610	30" x 24"		3.80	2.105		520	148		668	800
7690	48" x 48"	Q-9	6	2.667		1,525	168		1,693	1,925
7694	6' x 14' w/2 motors	"	3	5.333		5,350	335		5,685	6,375
7700	For thermostat, add	1 Shee	8	1		57.50	70		127.50	170
7800	For transformer 40 VA capacity, add	"	16	.500		40	35		75	97
8000	Multi-blade dampers, parallel blade									
8100	8" x 8"	1 Shee	24	.333	Ea.	144	23.50		167.50	194
8120	12" x 8"		22	.364		144	25.50		169.50	198
8140	16" x 10"		20	.400		151	28		179	209

23 33 Air Duct Accessories

23 33 13 – Dampers

23 33 13.13 Volume-Control Dampers

		Crew	Daily Output	Labor-Hours	Unit	Material	2023 Bare Costs Labor	Equipment	Total	Total Incl O&P
8160	18" x 12"	1 Shee	18	.444	Ea.	155	31		186	217
8180	22" x 12"		15	.533		164	37.50		201.50	237
8200	24" x 16"		11	.727		194	51		245	290
8220	28" x 16"		10	.800		258	56		314	370
8240	30" x 16"		8	1		203	70		273	330
8260	30" x 18"	↓	7	1.143	↓	256	80		336	400
8400	Round damper, butterfly, vol. control w/lever lock reg.									
8410	6" diam.	1 Shee	22	.364	Ea.	182	25.50		207.50	239
8412	7" diam.		21	.381		55.50	26.50		82	102
8414	8" diam.		20	.400		190	28		218	252
8416	9" diam.		19	.421		55.50	29.50		85	106
8418	10" diam.		18	.444		61	31		92	115
8420	12" diam.		16	.500		210	35		245	284
8422	14" diam.		14	.571		80.50	40		120.50	149
8424	16" diam.		13	.615		131	43		174	209
8426	18" diam.		12	.667		99	47		146	180
8428	20" diam.		11	.727		136	51		187	226
8430	24" diam.		10	.800		168	56		224	270
8432	30" diam.		9	.889		235	62.50		297.50	355
8434	36" diam.	↓	8	1	↓	315	70		385	450
8500	Round motor operated damper									
8510	6" diam.	1 Shee	22	.364	Ea.	137	25.50		162.50	190
8512	7" diam.		21	.381		134	26.50		160.50	189
8514	8" diam.		20	.400		141	28		169	198
8516	10" diam.		18	.444		154	31		185	216
8518	12" diam.		16	.500		150	35		185	219
8520	14" diam.	↓	14	.571	↓	184	40		224	263

23 33 13.16 Fire Dampers

		Crew	Daily Output	Labor-Hours	Unit	Material	2023 Bare Costs Labor	Equipment	Total	Total Incl O&P
0010	**FIRE DAMPERS**									
3000	Fire damper, curtain type, 1-1/2 hr. rated, vertical, 6" x 6"	1 Shee	24	.333	Ea.	27.50	23.50		51	65.50
3020	8" x 6"		22	.364		27.50	25.50		53	69
3021	8" x 8"		22	.364		45	25.50		70.50	88
3030	10" x 10"		22	.364		57.50	25.50		83	102
3040	12" x 6"		22	.364		34.50	25.50		60	76.50
3044	12" x 12"		20	.400		52.50	28		80.50	101
3060	20" x 6"		18	.444		45.50	31		76.50	97
3080	12" x 8"		22	.364		40	25.50		65.50	82.50
3100	24" x 8"		16	.500		55	35		90	114
3120	12" x 10"		21	.381		52	26.50		78.50	97.50
3140	24" x 10"		15	.533		78	37.50		115.50	143
3160	36" x 10"		12	.667		96	47		143	177
3180	16" x 12"		20	.400		72	28		100	122
3200	24" x 12"		13	.615		71.50	43		114.50	144
3220	48" x 12"		10	.800		95.50	56		151.50	190
3238	14" x 14"		19	.421		78	29.50		107.50	131
3240	16" x 14"		18	.444		78	31		109	133
3260	24" x 14"		12	.667		82.50	47		129.50	161
3280	30" x 14"		11	.727		103	51		154	190
3298	16" x 16"		18	.444		68	31		99	122
3300	18" x 16"		17	.471		83	33		116	141
3320	24" x 16"		11	.727		72	51		123	157
3340	36" x 16"	↓	10	.800	↓	100	56		156	195

23 33 Air Duct Accessories

23 33 13 – Dampers

23 33 13.16	Fire Dampers	Crew	Daily Output	Labor-Hours	Unit	Material	2023 Bare Costs Labor	Equipment	Total	Total Incl O&P
3356	18" x 18"	1 Shee	16	.500	Ea.	96	35		131	159
3360	24" x 18"		10	.800		91	56		147	185
3380	48" x 18"		8	1		131	70		201	251
3398	20" x 20"		10	.800		83	56		139	176
3400	24" x 20"		8	1		78	70		148	192
3420	36" x 20"		7	1.143		102	80		182	233
3440	24" x 22"		7	1.143		106	80		186	238
3460	30" x 22"		6	1.333		117	93.50		210.50	269
3478	24" x 24"		8	1		81	70		151	195
3480	26" x 24"	↓	7	1.143		96	80		176	226
3484	32" x 24"	Q-9	13	1.231		102	77.50		179.50	229
3500	48" x 24"		12	1.333		136	84		220	276
3520	28" x 26"		13	1.231		107	77.50		184.50	235
3540	30" x 28"		12	1.333		119	84		203	258
3560	48" x 30"		11	1.455		173	92		265	330
3580	48" x 36"		10	1.600		176	101		277	345
3590	32" x 40"		10	1.600		144	101		245	310
3600	44" x 44"		10	1.600		192	101		293	365
3620	48" x 48"	↓	8	2	↓	216	126		342	430
3700	UL label included in above									
3800	For horizontal operation, add				Ea.	20%				
3900	For cap for blades out of air stream, add					20%				
4000	For 10" 22 ga., UL approved sleeve, add					35%				
4100	For 10" 22 ga., UL sleeve, 100% free area, add				↓	65%				
4200	For oversize openings group dampers									
4210	Fire damper, round, Type A, 1-1/2 hour									
4214	4" diam.	1 Shee	20	.400	Ea.	78	28		106	129
4216	5" diam.		16	.500		93	35		128	155
4218	6" diam.		14.30	.559		93.50	39		132.50	162
4220	7" diam.		13.30	.602		108	42		150	183
4222	8" diam.		11.40	.702		113	49		162	199
4224	9" diam.		10.80	.741		119	52		171	209
4226	10" diam.		10	.800		141	56		197	240
4228	12" diam.		9.50	.842		184	59		243	291
4230	14" diam.		8.20	.976		125	68.50		193.50	240
4232	16" diam.		7.60	1.053		114	74		188	237
4234	18" diam.		7.20	1.111		127	78		205	257
4236	20" diam.		6.40	1.250		172	87.50		259.50	320
4238	22" diam.		6.10	1.311		200	92		292	360
4240	24" diam.		5.70	1.404		209	98.50		307.50	380
4242	26" diam.		5.50	1.455		235	102		337	415
4244	28" diam.		5.40	1.481		231	104		335	410
4246	30" diam.	↓	5.30	1.509	↓	258	106		364	445
4502	Power open-spring close, sleeve and actuator motor mounted, 1-1/2 hour									
4506	6" x 6"	1 Shee	24	.333	Ea.	98	23.50		121.50	143
4510	8" x 8"		22	.364		455	25.50		480.50	540
4520	16" x 8"		20	.400		560	28		588	665
4540	18" x 8"		18	.444		565	31		596	665
4560	20" x 8"		16	.500		570	35		605	680
4580	10" x 10"		21	.381		570	26.50		596.50	665
4600	24" x 10"		15	.533		590	37.50		627.50	705
4620	30" x 10"		12	.667		605	47		652	735
4640	12" x 12"	↓	20	.400	↓	580	28		608	685

23 33 Air Duct Accessories

23 33 13 – Dampers

23 33 13.16 Fire Dampers

		Crew	Daily Output	Labor-Hours	Unit	Material	2023 Bare Costs Labor	Equipment	Total	Total Incl O&P
4660	18" x 12"	1 Shee	18	.444	Ea.	595	31		626	700
4680	24" x 12"		13	.615		610	43		653	735
4700	30" x 12"		11	.727		620	51		671	760
4720	14" x 14"		17	.471		600	33		633	710
4740	16" x 14"		18	.444		605	31		636	710
4760	20" x 14"		14	.571		615	40		655	735
4780	24" x 14"		12	.667		625	47		672	760
4800	30" x 14"		10	.800		640	56		696	790
4820	16" x 16"		16	.500		620	35		655	735
4840	20" x 16"		14	.571		635	40		675	755
4860	24" x 16"		11	.727		645	51		696	785
4880	30" x 16"		8	1		660	70		730	835
4900	18" x 18"		15	.533		640	37.50		677.50	760
5000	24" x 18"		10	.800		660	56		716	815
5020	36" x 18"		7	1.143		700	80		780	890
5040	20" x 20"		13	.615		665	43		708	795
5060	24" x 20"		8	1		680	70		750	850
5080	30" x 20"		8	1		700	70		770	875
5100	36" x 20"		7	1.143		720	80		800	910
5120	24" x 24"		8	1		715	70		785	890
5130	30" x 24"		7.60	1.053		740	74		814	920
5140	36" x 24"	Q-9	12	1.333		760	84		844	960
5141	36" x 30"		10	1.600		820	101		921	1,050
5142	40" x 36"		8	2		1,450	126		1,576	1,775
5143	48" x 48"		4	4		2,850	253		3,103	3,525
5150	Damper operator motor, 24 or 120 volt	1 Shee	16	.500		580	35		615	690

23 33 13.25 Exhaust Vent Damper

		Crew	Daily Output	Labor-Hours	Unit	Material	Labor	Equipment	Total	Total Incl O&P
0010	**EXHAUST VENT DAMPER**, Auto, OB with elect. actuator.									
1110	6" x 6"	1 Shee	24	.333	Ea.	127	23.50		150.50	175
1114	8" x 6"		23	.348		131	24.50		155.50	181
1116	8" x 8"		22	.364		135	25.50		160.50	188
1118	10" x 6"		23	.348		135	24.50		159.50	186
1120	10" x 10"		22	.364		144	25.50		169.50	197
1122	12" x 6"		22	.364		136	25.50		161.50	189
1124	12" x 10"		21	.381		151	26.50		177.50	207
1126	12" x 12"		20	.400		138	28		166	195
1128	14" x 6"		21	.381		140	26.50		166.50	195
1130	14" x 10"		19	.421		159	29.50		188.50	220
1132	16" x 6"		21	.381		156	26.50		182.50	213
1134	16" x 8"		20	.400		158	28		186	217
1136	18" x 6"		20	.400		150	28		178	208
1138	18" x 8"		19	.421		159	29.50		188.50	220

23 33 13.28 Splitter Damper Assembly

		Crew	Daily Output	Labor-Hours	Unit	Material	Labor	Equipment	Total	Total Incl O&P
0010	**SPLITTER DAMPER ASSEMBLY**									
7000	Self locking, 1' rod	1 Shee	24	.333	Ea.	35.50	23.50		59	74.50
7020	3' rod		22	.364		48.50	25.50		74	91.50
7040	4' rod		20	.400		54	28		82	102
7060	6' rod		18	.444		65.50	31		96.50	119

23 33 13.32 Relief Damper

		Crew	Daily Output	Labor-Hours	Unit	Material	Labor	Equipment	Total	Total Incl O&P
0010	**RELIEF DAMPER**, Electronic bypass with tight seal									
8310	8" x 6"	1 Shee	22	.364	Ea.	365	25.50		390.50	440
8314	10" x 6"		22	.364		365	25.50		390.50	440

23 33 Air Duct Accessories

23 33 13 – Dampers

23 33 13.32	Relief Damper	Crew	Daily Output	Labor-Hours	Unit	Material	2023 Bare Costs Labor	Equipment	Total	Total Incl O&P
8318	10" x 10"	1 Shee	21	.381	Ea.	400	26.50		426.50	480
8322	12" x 12"		20	.400		390	28		418	470
8326	12" x 16"		19	.421		400	29.50		429.50	485
8330	16" x 10"		20	.400		420	28		448	505
8334	16" x 14"		18	.444		425	31		456	515
8338	16" x 18"		17	.471		470	33		503	565
8342	18" x 12"		18	.444		470	31		501	560
8346	18" x 18"		15	.533		370	37.50		407.50	460
8350	20" x 14"		14	.571		440	40		480	545
8354	20" x 18"		13	.615		480	43		523	595
8358	24" x 12"		13	.615		450	43		493	560
8362	24" x 18"		10	.800		315	56		371	435
8363	24" x 24"		10	.800		485	56		541	620
8364	24" x 36"		9	.889		575	62.50		637.50	730
8365	24" x 48"		6	1.333		645	93.50		738.50	850
8366	28" x 10"		13	.615		315	43		358	415
8370	28" x 16"		10	.800		495	56		551	630
8374	30" x 14"		11	.727		355	51		406	470
8378	30" x 18"		8	1		505	70		575	660
8382	30" x 24"		6	1.333		530	93.50		623.50	725
8390	46" x 36"		4	2		710	140		850	995
8394	48" x 48"		3	2.667		780	187		967	1,150
8396	54" x 36"	▼	2	4	▼	825	281		1,106	1,325

23 33 19 – Duct Silencers

23 33 19.10 Duct Silencers

		Crew	Daily Output	Labor-Hours	Unit	Material	Labor	Equipment	Total	Total Incl O&P
0010	**DUCT SILENCERS**									
9000	Silencers, noise control for air flow, duct				MCFM	101			101	111
9004	Duct sound trap, packaged									
9010	12" x 18" x 36", 2,000 CFM	1 Shee	12	.667	Ea.	860	47		907	1,025
9011	24" x 18" x 36", 9,000 CFM	Q-9	80	.200		970	12.65		982.65	1,100
9012	24" x 24" x 36", 9,000 CFM		60	.267		1,450	16.85		1,466.85	1,625
9013	24" x 30" x 36", 9,000 CFM		50	.320		1,550	20		1,570	1,725
9014	24" x 36" x 36", 9,000 CFM		40	.400		1,950	25.50		1,975.50	2,175
9015	24" x 48" x 36", 9,000 CFM		28	.571		2,525	36		2,561	2,825
9018	36" x 18" x 36", 6,300 CFM		42	.381		1,950	24		1,974	2,150
9019	36" x 36" x 36", 6,300 CFM		21	.762		3,875	48		3,923	4,350
9020	36" x 48" x 36", 6,300 CFM		14	1.143		5,050	72		5,122	5,650
9021	36" x 60" x 36", 6,300 CFM		13	1.231		6,400	77.50		6,477.50	7,175
9022	48" x 48" x 36", 6,300 CFM		12	1.333		6,800	84		6,884	7,600
9023	24" x 24" x 60", 6,000 CFM		3.60	4.444		2,225	281		2,506	2,875
9026	24" x 30" x 60", 7,000 CFM		3.50	4.571		2,475	289		2,764	3,150
9030	24" x 36" x 60", 8,000 CFM		3.40	4.706		2,700	297		2,997	3,425
9034	24" x 48" x 60", 11,000 CFM		3.30	4.848		2,375	305		2,680	3,050
9038	36" x 18" x 60", 6,300 CFM		3.50	4.571		1,900	289		2,189	2,500
9042	36" x 36" x 60", 12,000 CFM		3.30	4.848		2,925	305		3,230	3,650
9046	36" x 48" x 60", 17,000 CFM		3.10	5.161		3,925	325		4,250	4,800
9050	36" x 60" x 60", 20,000 CFM		2.80	5.714		4,875	360		5,235	5,900
9054	48" x 48" x 60", 23,000 CFM		2.60	6.154		5,525	390		5,915	6,650
9056	48" x 60" x 60", 23,000 CFM	▼	2.10	7.619	▼	6,900	480		7,380	8,300

23 33 Air Duct Accessories

23 33 23 – Turning Vanes

23 33 23.13 Air Turning Vanes

		Crew	Daily Output	Labor-Hours	Unit	Material	2023 Bare Costs Labor	2023 Bare Costs Equipment	Total	Total Incl O&P
0010	**AIR TURNING VANES**									
9400	Turning vane components									
9410	Turning vane rail	1 Shee	160	.050	L.F.	1.03	3.51		4.54	6.45
9420	Double thick, factory fab. vane		300	.027		1.51	1.87		3.38	4.48
9428	12" high set		170	.047		2.28	3.30		5.58	7.50
9432	14" high set		160	.050		2.66	3.51		6.17	8.25
9434	16" high set		150	.053		3.04	3.74		6.78	9
9436	18" high set		144	.056		3.42	3.90		7.32	9.60
9438	20" high set		138	.058		3.80	4.07		7.87	10.35
9440	22" high set		130	.062		4.18	4.32		8.50	11.10
9442	24" high set		124	.065		4.56	4.53		9.09	11.80
9444	26" high set		116	.069		4.94	4.84		9.78	12.75
9446	30" high set	↓	112	.071	↓	5.70	5		10.70	13.80

23 33 33 – Duct-Mounting Access Doors

23 33 33.13 Duct Access Doors

		Crew	Daily Output	Labor-Hours	Unit	Material	2023 Bare Costs Labor	2023 Bare Costs Equipment	Total	Total Incl O&P
0010	**DUCT ACCESS DOORS**									
1000	Duct access door, insulated, 6" x 6"	1 Shee	14	.571	Ea.	29.50	40		69.50	93
1020	10" x 10"		11	.727		38	51		89	119
1040	12" x 12"		10	.800		41.50	56		97.50	130
1050	12" x 18"		9	.889		43.50	62.50		106	142
1060	16" x 12"		9	.889		38.50	62.50		101	136
1070	18" x 18"		8	1		76	70		146	190
1074	24" x 18"		8	1		70.50	70		140.50	184
1080	24" x 24"	↓	8	1	↓	124	70		194	242

23 33 46 – Flexible Ducts

23 33 46.10 Flexible Air Ducts

		Crew	Daily Output	Labor-Hours	Unit	Material	2023 Bare Costs Labor	2023 Bare Costs Equipment	Total	Total Incl O&P
0010	**FLEXIBLE AIR DUCTS**									
1280	Add to labor for elevated installation									
1282	of prefabricated (purchased) ductwork									
1283	10' to 15' high						10%			
1284	15' to 20' high						20%			
1285	20' to 25' high						25%			
1286	25' to 30' high						35%			
1287	30' to 35' high						40%			
1288	35' to 40' high						50%			
1289	Over 40' high						55%			
1300	Flexible, coated fiberglass fabric on corr. resist. metal helix									
1400	pressure to 12" (WG) UL-181									
1500	Noninsulated, 3" diameter	Q-9	400	.040	L.F.	2.34	2.53		4.87	6.35
1520	4" diameter		360	.044		2.72	2.81		5.53	7.20
1540	5" diameter		320	.050		3.22	3.16		6.38	8.30
1560	6" diameter		280	.057		3.71	3.61		7.32	9.55
1580	7" diameter		240	.067		4.29	4.21		8.50	11.05
1600	8" diameter		200	.080		4.87	5.05		9.92	12.95
1620	9" diameter		180	.089		5.40	5.60		11	14.40
1640	10" diameter		160	.100		6	6.30		12.30	16.10
1660	12" diameter		120	.133		7.55	8.40		15.95	21
1680	14" diameter		80	.200		8.75	12.65		21.40	28.50
1700	16" diameter	↓	60	.267	↓	11.55	16.85		28.40	38
1800	For plastic cable tie, add				Ea.	.53			.53	.58
1900	Insulated, 1" thick, PE jacket, 3" diameter [G]	Q-9	380	.042	L.F.	3.13	2.66		5.79	7.45

23 33 Air Duct Accessories

23 33 46 – Flexible Ducts

23 33 46.10 Flexible Air Ducts		Crew	Daily Output	Labor-Hours	Unit	Material	2023 Bare Costs Labor	Equipment	Total	Total Incl O&P
1910	4" diameter G	Q-9	340	.047	L.F.	4.64	2.97		7.61	9.60
1920	5" diameter G		300	.053		5.50	3.37		8.87	11.10
1940	6" diameter G		260	.062		5.50	3.88		9.38	11.90
1960	7" diameter G		220	.073		6.70	4.59		11.29	14.30
1980	8" diameter G		180	.089		6.70	5.60		12.30	15.85
2000	9" diameter G		160	.100		8.35	6.30		14.65	18.65
2020	10" diameter G		140	.114		8.35	7.20		15.55	20
2040	12" diameter G		100	.160		9.90	10.10		20	26
2060	14" diameter G		80	.200		11.90	12.65		24.55	32
2080	16" diameter G		60	.267		16.20	16.85		33.05	43.50
2100	18" diameter G		45	.356		17.75	22.50		40.25	53.50
2120	20" diameter G	Q-10	65	.369		12.65	24		36.65	50.50
2500	Insulated, heavy duty, coated fiberglass fabric									
2520	4" diameter G	Q-9	340	.047	L.F.	4.95	2.97		7.92	9.95
2540	5" diameter G		300	.053		6.90	3.37		10.27	12.65
2560	6" diameter G		260	.062		6.90	3.88		10.78	13.45
2580	7" diameter G		220	.073		8.40	4.59		12.99	16.15
2600	8" diameter G		180	.089		9.45	5.60		15.05	18.85
2620	9" diameter G		160	.100		10.40	6.30		16.70	21
2640	10" diameter G		140	.114		10.40	7.20		17.60	22.50
2660	12" diameter G		100	.160		14.05	10.10		24.15	30.50
2680	14" diameter G		80	.200		14.90	12.65		27.55	35.50
2700	16" diameter G		60	.267		17.30	16.85		34.15	44.50
2720	18" diameter G		45	.356		18.90	22.50		41.40	55
2800	Flexible, aluminum, pressure to 12" (WG) UL-181									
2820	Non-insulated									
2830	3" diameter	Q-9	400	.040	L.F.	1.60	2.53		4.13	5.55
2831	4" diameter		360	.044		2.04	2.81		4.85	6.45
2832	5" diameter		320	.050		2.53	3.16		5.69	7.55
2833	6" diameter		280	.057		3.25	3.61		6.86	9.05
2834	7" diameter		240	.067		3.91	4.21		8.12	10.65
2835	8" diameter		200	.080		4.40	5.05		9.45	12.45
2836	9" diameter		180	.089		5.25	5.60		10.85	14.20
2837	10" diameter		160	.100		6.20	6.30		12.50	16.35
2838	12" diameter		120	.133		8.10	8.40		16.50	21.50
2839	14" diameter		80	.200		9.15	12.65		21.80	29
2840	15" diameter		70	.229		8.95	14.45		23.40	31.50
2841	16" diameter		60	.267		14.25	16.85		31.10	41
2842	18" diameter		45	.356		16.15	22.50		38.65	52
2843	20" diameter	Q-10	65	.369		18.05	24		42.05	56.50
2880	Insulated, 1" thick with 3/4 lb., PE jacket									
2890	3" diameter G	Q-9	380	.042	L.F.	3.34	2.66		6	7.65
2891	4" diameter G		340	.047		5.05	2.97		8.02	10.05
2892	5" diameter G		300	.053		5.65	3.37		9.02	11.30
2893	6" diameter G		260	.062		6.75	3.88		10.63	13.30
2894	7" diameter G		220	.073		8.05	4.59		12.64	15.75
2895	8" diameter G		180	.089		8.15	5.60		13.75	17.40
2896	9" diameter G		160	.100		9.55	6.30		15.85	20
2897	10" diameter G		140	.114		11.40	7.20		18.60	23.50
2898	12" diameter G		100	.160		13.40	10.10		23.50	30
2899	14" diameter G		80	.200		15.05	12.65		27.70	35.50
2900	15" diameter G		70	.229		15.30	14.45		29.75	38.50
2901	16" diameter G		60	.267		21.50	16.85		38.35	49

23 33 Air Duct Accessories

23 33 46 - Flexible Ducts

23 33 46.10 Flexible Air Ducts		Crew	Daily Output	Labor-Hours	Unit	Material	2023 Bare Costs Labor	Equipment	Total	Total Incl O&P
2902	18" diameter	Q-9	45	.356	L.F.	24.50	22.50		47	61
3000	Transitions, 3" deep, square to round									
3010	6" x 6" to round	Q-9	44	.364	Ea.	17.60	23		40.60	54
3014	6" x 12" to round		42	.381		22.50	24		46.50	61
3018	8" x 8" to round		40	.400		22	25.50		47.50	62
3022	9" x 9" to round		38	.421		22.50	26.50		49	65
3026	9" x 12" to round		37	.432		29	27.50		56.50	73
3030	9" x 15" to round		36	.444		33.50	28		61.50	79.50
3034	10" x 10" to round		34	.471		26.50	29.50		56	74
3038	10" x 22" to round		32	.500		42	31.50		73.50	93.50
3042	12" x 12" to round		30	.533		30.50	33.50		64	84
3046	12" x 18" to round		28	.571		42	36		78	101
3050	12" x 24" to round		26	.615		42	39		81	105
3054	15" x 15" to round		25	.640		39	40.50		79.50	104
3058	15" x 18" to round		24	.667		48	42		90	117
3062	18" x 18" to round		22	.727		49.50	46		95.50	124
3066	21" x 21" to round		21	.762		49.50	48		97.50	127
3070	22" x 22" to round		20	.800		52.50	50.50		103	134
3074	24" x 24" to round	▼	18	.889	▼	55	56		111	145
5000	Flexible, aluminum, acoustical, pressure to 2" (WG), NFPA-90A									
5010	Fiberglass insulation 1-1/2" thick, 1/2 lb. density									
5020	Polyethylene jacket, UL approved									
5026	5" diameter	G Q-9	300	.053	L.F.	6.40	3.37		9.77	12.05
5030	6" diameter	G	260	.062		7.65	3.88		11.53	14.25
5034	7" diameter	G	220	.073		9.15	4.59		13.74	16.95
5038	8" diameter	G	180	.089		9.35	5.60		14.95	18.75
5042	9" diameter	G	160	.100		10.95	6.30		17.25	21.50
5046	10" diameter	G	140	.114		12.95	7.20		20.15	25
5050	12" diameter	G	100	.160		15.50	10.10		25.60	32.50
5054	14" diameter	G	80	.200		17.40	12.65		30.05	38
5058	16" diameter	G ▼	60	.267	▼	24.50	16.85		41.35	52.50
5072	Hospital grade, PE jacket, UL approved									
5076	5" diameter	G Q-9	300	.053	L.F.	6.20	3.37		9.57	11.90
5080	6" diameter	G	260	.062		8	3.88		11.88	14.65
5084	7" diameter	G	220	.073		9.45	4.59		14.04	17.30
5088	8" diameter	G	180	.089		9.70	5.60		15.30	19.10
5092	9" diameter	G	160	.100		11.30	6.30		17.60	22
5096	10" diameter	G	140	.114		13.50	7.20		20.70	25.50
5100	12" diameter	G	100	.160		15.95	10.10		26.05	33
5104	14" diameter	G	80	.200		17.90	12.65		30.55	38.50
5108	16" diameter	G ▼	60	.267	▼	21	16.85		37.85	48.50
5140	Flexible, aluminum, silencer, pressure to 12" (WG), NFPA-90A									
5144	Fiberglass insulation 1-1/2" thick, 1/2 lb. density									
5148	Aluminum outer shell, UL approved									
5152	5" diameter	G Q-9	290	.055	L.F.	22.50	3.48		25.98	30.50
5156	6" diameter	G	250	.064		20.50	4.04		24.54	29
5160	7" diameter	G	210	.076		29	4.81		33.81	39.50
5164	8" diameter	G	170	.094		26	5.95		31.95	37.50
5168	9" diameter	G	150	.107		35.50	6.75		42.25	49
5172	10" diameter	G	130	.123		31.50	7.75		39.25	46.50
5176	12" diameter	G	90	.178		36	11.20		47.20	56.50
5180	14" diameter	G	70	.229		40.50	14.45		54.95	66
5184	16" diameter	G ▼	50	.320	▼	57.50	20		77.50	93.50

23 33 Air Duct Accessories

23 33 46 – Flexible Ducts

23 33 46.10 Flexible Air Ducts

	23 33 46.10 Flexible Air Ducts		Crew	Daily Output	Labor-Hours	Unit	Material	2023 Bare Costs Labor	Equipment	Total	Total Incl O&P
5200	Hospital grade, aluminum shell, UL approved										
5204	5" diameter	G	Q-9	280	.057	L.F.	23.50	3.61		27.11	31
5208	6" diameter	G		240	.067		21.50	4.21		25.71	30
5212	7" diameter	G		200	.080		30	5.05		35.05	40.50
5216	8" diameter	G		160	.100		26.50	6.30		32.80	38.50
5220	9" diameter	G		140	.114		36.50	7.20		43.70	51
5224	10" diameter	G		130	.123		32.50	7.75		40.25	47.50
5228	12" diameter	G		80	.200		34.50	12.65		47.15	56.50
5232	14" diameter	G		60	.267		39	16.85		55.85	68.50
5236	16" diameter	G		40	.400		52	25.50		77.50	95

23 33 53 – Duct Liners

23 33 53.10 Duct Liner Board

0010	**DUCT LINER BOARD**										
3340	Board type fiberglass liner, FSK, 1-1/2 lb. density										
3344	1" thick	G	Q-14	150	.107	S.F.	1.38	6.25		7.63	11.10
3345	1-1/2" thick	G		130	.123		1.52	7.25		8.77	12.70
3346	2" thick	G		120	.133		2.08	7.85		9.93	14.30
3348	3" thick	G		110	.145		2.27	8.55		10.82	15.55
3350	4" thick	G		100	.160		2.77	9.40		12.17	17.40
3356	3 lb. density, 1" thick	G		150	.107		3.80	6.25		10.05	13.80
3358	1-1/2" thick	G		130	.123		2.34	7.25		9.59	13.60
3360	2" thick	G		120	.133		2.29	7.85		10.14	14.50
3362	2-1/2" thick	G		110	.145		3.17	8.55		11.72	16.55
3364	3" thick	G		100	.160		3.63	9.40		13.03	18.35
3366	4" thick	G		90	.178		4.55	10.45		15	21
3370	6 lb. density, 1" thick	G		140	.114		2.47	6.70		9.17	12.95
3374	1-1/2" thick	G		120	.133		3.29	7.85		11.14	15.60
3378	2" thick	G		100	.160		4.15	9.40		13.55	18.90
3490	Board type, fiberglass liner, 3 lb. density										
3680	No finish										
3700	1" thick	G	Q-14	170	.094	S.F.	.98	5.55		6.53	9.55
3710	1-1/2" thick	G		140	.114		3.95	6.70		10.65	14.60
3720	2" thick	G		130	.123		4.81	7.25		12.06	16.35
3940	Board type, non-fibrous foam										
3950	Temperature, bacteria and fungi resistant										
3960	1" thick	G	Q-14	150	.107	S.F.	3.89	6.25		10.14	13.90
3970	1-1/2" thick	G		130	.123		6.75	7.25		14	18.50
3980	2" thick	G		120	.133		5.40	7.85		13.25	17.95

23 34 HVAC Fans

23 34 13 – Axial HVAC Fans

23 34 13.10 Axial Flow HVAC Fans

0010	**AXIAL FLOW HVAC FANS**										
0020	Air conditioning and process air handling										
0500	Axial flow, constant speed										
0505	Direct drive, 1/8" S.P.										
0510	12", 1,060 CFM, 1/6 HP		Q-20	3	6.667	Ea.	940	425		1,365	1,675
0514	12", 2,095 CFM, 1/2 HP			3	6.667		1,550	425		1,975	2,350
0518	16", 2,490 CFM, 1/3 HP			2.80	7.143		785	455		1,240	1,550
0522	20", 4,130 CFM, 3/4 HP			2.60	7.692		1,325	490		1,815	2,200

23 34 HVAC Fans

23 34 13 – Axial HVAC Fans

23 34 13.10 Axial Flow HVAC Fans

		Crew	Daily Output	Labor-Hours	Unit	Material	2023 Bare Costs Labor	2023 Bare Costs Equipment	Total	Total Incl O&P
0526	22", 4,700 CFM, 3/4 HP	Q-20	2.60	7.692	Ea.	1,950	490		2,440	2,900
0530	24", 5,850 CFM, 1 HP		2.50	8		2,000	510		2,510	2,975
0534	24", 7,925 CFM, 1-1/2 HP		2.40	8.333		1,900	535		2,435	2,875
0538	30", 10,640 CFM, 2 HP		2.20	9.091		3,225	580		3,805	4,425
0542	30", 14,765 CFM, 2-1/2 HP		2.10	9.524		3,550	610		4,160	4,825
0546	36", 16,780 CFM, 2 HP		2.10	9.524		3,850	610		4,460	5,175
0550	36", 22,920 CFM, 5 HP		1.80	11.111		4,300	710		5,010	5,800
0560	Belt drive, 1/8" S.P.									
0562	15", 2,800 CFM, 1/3 HP	Q-20	3.20	6.250	Ea.	1,400	400		1,800	2,125
0564	15", 3,400 CFM, 1/2 HP		3	6.667		1,300	425		1,725	2,100
0568	18", 3,280 CFM, 1/3 HP		2.80	7.143		1,475	455		1,930	2,300
0572	18", 3,900 CFM, 1/2 HP		2.80	7.143		1,400	455		1,855	2,200
0576	18", 5,250 CFM, 1 HP		2.70	7.407		1,450	475		1,925	2,300
0584	24", 6,430 CFM, 1 HP		2.50	8		2,050	510		2,560	3,025
0588	24", 8,860 CFM, 2 HP		2.40	8.333		2,000	535		2,535	3,000
0592	30", 9,250 CFM, 1 HP		2.20	9.091		2,675	580		3,255	3,800
0596	30", 16,900 CFM, 5 HP		2	10		2,725	640		3,365	3,950
0604	36", 14,475 CFM, 2 HP		2.30	8.696		3,175	555		3,730	4,325
0608	36", 20,080 CFM, 5 HP		1.80	11.111		3,275	710		3,985	4,675
0616	42", 29,000 CFM, 7-1/2 HP		1.40	14.286		4,375	915		5,290	6,200
1500	Vaneaxial, low pressure, 2,000 CFM, 1/2 HP		3.60	5.556		2,625	355		2,980	3,400
1520	4,000 CFM, 1 HP		3.20	6.250		2,725	400		3,125	3,600
1540	8,000 CFM, 2 HP		2.80	7.143		3,675	455		4,130	4,725
1560	16,000 CFM, 5 HP		2.40	8.333		5,650	535		6,185	7,025

23 34 14 – Blower HVAC Fans

23 34 14.10 Blower Type HVAC Fans

		Crew	Daily Output	Labor-Hours	Unit	Material	2023 Bare Costs Labor	2023 Bare Costs Equipment	Total	Total Incl O&P
0010	**BLOWER TYPE HVAC FANS**									
2000	Blowers, direct drive with motor, complete									
2020	1,045 CFM @ 0.5" S.P., 1/5 HP	Q-20	18	1.111	Ea.	360	71		431	505
2040	1,385 CFM @ 0.5" S.P., 1/4 HP		18	1.111		335	71		406	475
2060	1,640 CFM @ 0.5" S.P., 1/3 HP		18	1.111		340	71		411	480
2080	1,760 CFM @ 0.5" S.P., 1/2 HP		18	1.111		325	71		396	460
2090	4 speed									
2100	1,164 to 1,739 CFM @ 0.5" S.P., 1/3 HP	Q-20	16	1.250	Ea.	360	80		440	515
2120	1,467 to 2,218 CFM @ 1.0" S.P., 3/4 HP	"	14	1.429	"	355	91.50		446.50	525
2500	Ceiling fan, right angle, extra quiet, 0.10" S.P.									
2520	95 CFM	Q-20	20	1	Ea.	300	64		364	425
2540	210 CFM		19	1.053		355	67.50		422.50	490
2560	385 CFM		18	1.111		455	71		526	605
2580	885 CFM		16	1.250		890	80		970	1,100
2600	1,650 CFM		13	1.538		1,225	98.50		1,323.50	1,500
2620	2,960 CFM		11	1.818		1,650	116		1,766	1,975
2640	For wall or roof cap, add	1 Shee	16	.500		300	35		335	385
2660	For straight thru fan, add					10%				
2680	For speed control switch, add	1 Elec	16	.500		165	33.50		198.50	231
7500	Utility set, steel construction, pedestal, 1/4" S.P.									
7520	Direct drive, 150 CFM, 1/8 HP	Q-20	6.40	3.125	Ea.	1,000	200		1,200	1,400
7540	485 CFM, 1/6 HP		5.80	3.448		1,225	221		1,446	1,675
7560	1,950 CFM, 1/2 HP		4.80	4.167		1,475	267		1,742	2,025
7580	2,410 CFM, 3/4 HP		4.40	4.545		2,975	291		3,266	3,700
7600	3,328 CFM, 1-1/2 HP		3	6.667		2,950	425		3,375	3,875
7680	V-belt drive, drive cover, 3 phase									

23 34 HVAC Fans

23 34 14 – Blower HVAC Fans

23 34 14.10 Blower Type HVAC Fans

		Crew	Daily Output	Labor-Hours	Unit	Material	2023 Bare Costs Labor	2023 Bare Costs Equipment	Total	Total Incl O&P
7700	800 CFM, 1/4 HP	Q-20	6	3.333	Ea.	1,275	213		1,488	1,725
7720	1,300 CFM, 1/3 HP		5	4		1,325	256		1,581	1,825
7740	2,000 CFM, 1 HP		4.60	4.348		1,575	278		1,853	2,150
7760	2,900 CFM, 3/4 HP		4.20	4.762		2,125	305		2,430	2,775
7780	3,600 CFM, 3/4 HP		4	5		2,600	320		2,920	3,350
7800	4,800 CFM, 1 HP		3.50	5.714		3,075	365		3,440	3,925
7820	6,700 CFM, 1-1/2 HP		3	6.667		3,800	425		4,225	4,825
7830	7,500 CFM, 2 HP		2.50	8		5,150	510		5,660	6,450
7840	11,000 CFM, 3 HP		2	10		6,875	640		7,515	8,525
7860	13,000 CFM, 3 HP		1.60	12.500		7,000	800		7,800	8,900
7880	15,000 CFM, 5 HP		1	20		7,250	1,275		8,525	9,900
7900	17,000 CFM, 7-1/2 HP		.80	25		7,750	1,600		9,350	10,900
7920	20,000 CFM, 7-1/2 HP		.80	25		9,225	1,600		10,825	12,600

23 34 16 – Centrifugal HVAC Fans

23 34 16.10 Centrifugal Type HVAC Fans

		Crew	Daily Output	Labor-Hours	Unit	Material	Labor	Equipment	Total	Total Incl O&P
0010	**CENTRIFUGAL TYPE HVAC FANS**									
0200	In-line centrifugal, supply/exhaust booster									
0220	aluminum wheel/hub, disconnect switch, 1/4" S.P.									
0240	500 CFM, 10" diameter connection	Q-20	3	6.667	Ea.	1,725	425		2,150	2,550
0260	1,380 CFM, 12" diameter connection		2	10		2,025	640		2,665	3,175
0280	1,520 CFM, 16" diameter connection		2	10		1,875	640		2,515	3,025
0300	2,560 CFM, 18" diameter connection		1	20		2,075	1,275		3,350	4,225
0320	3,480 CFM, 20" diameter connection		.80	25		2,400	1,600		4,000	5,025
0326	5,080 CFM, 20" diameter connection		.75	26.667		2,575	1,700		4,275	5,425
0340	7,500 CFM, 22" diameter connection		.70	28.571		3,225	1,825		5,050	6,275
0350	10,000 CFM, 27" diameter connection		.65	30.769		3,750	1,975		5,725	7,075
3500	Centrifugal, airfoil, motor and drive, complete									
3520	1,000 CFM, 1/2 HP	Q-20	2.50	8	Ea.	2,275	510		2,785	3,275
3540	2,000 CFM, 1 HP		2	10		2,475	640		3,115	3,675
3560	4,000 CFM, 3 HP		1.80	11.111		3,250	710		3,960	4,625
3580	8,000 CFM, 7-1/2 HP		1.40	14.286		4,900	915		5,815	6,775
3600	12,000 CFM, 10 HP		1	20		6,675	1,275		7,950	9,275
4000	Single width, belt drive, not incl. motor, capacities									
4020	at 2,000 fpm, 2.5" S.P. for indicated motor									
4040	6,900 CFM, 5 HP	Q-9	2.40	6.667	Ea.	4,750	420		5,170	5,850
4060	10,340 CFM, 7-1/2 HP		2.20	7.273		6,075	460		6,535	7,375
4080	15,320 CFM, 10 HP		2	8		6,625	505		7,130	8,025
4100	22,780 CFM, 15 HP		1.80	8.889		11,600	560		12,160	13,600
4120	33,840 CFM, 20 HP		1.60	10		15,400	630		16,030	17,900
4140	41,400 CFM, 25 HP		1.40	11.429		18,100	720		18,820	21,000
4160	50,100 CFM, 30 HP		.80	20		25,100	1,275		26,375	29,500
4200	Double width wheel, 12,420 CFM, 7-1/2 HP		2.20	7.273		5,775	460		6,235	7,050
4220	18,620 CFM, 15 HP		2	8		9,725	505		10,230	11,500
4240	27,580 CFM, 20 HP		1.80	8.889		10,100	560		10,660	11,900
4260	40,980 CFM, 25 HP		1.50	10.667		15,800	675		16,475	18,400
4280	60,920 CFM, 40 HP		1	16		25,100	1,000		26,100	29,100
4300	74,520 CFM, 50 HP		.80	20		25,300	1,275		26,575	29,700
4320	90,160 CFM, 50 HP		.70	22.857		37,300	1,450		38,750	43,200
4340	110,300 CFM, 60 HP		.50	32		55,000	2,025		57,025	63,500
4360	134,960 CFM, 75 HP		.40	40		67,000	2,525		69,525	78,000
5000	Utility set, centrifugal, V belt drive, motor									
5020	1/4" S.P., 1,200 CFM, 1/4 HP	Q-20	6	3.333	Ea.	2,500	213		2,713	3,075

23 34 HVAC Fans

23 34 16 – Centrifugal HVAC Fans

23 34 16.10 Centrifugal Type HVAC Fans		Crew	Daily Output	Labor-Hours	Unit	Material	2023 Bare Costs Labor	Equipment	Total	Total Incl O&P
5040	1,520 CFM, 1/3 HP	Q-20	5	4	Ea.	3,025	256		3,281	3,700
5060	1,850 CFM, 1/2 HP		4	5		3,025	320		3,345	3,800
5080	2,180 CFM, 3/4 HP		3	6.667		3,425	425		3,850	4,425
5100	1/2" S.P., 3,600 CFM, 1 HP		2	10		3,500	640		4,140	4,800
5120	4,250 CFM, 1-1/2 HP		1.60	12.500		5,050	800		5,850	6,750
5140	4,800 CFM, 2 HP		1.40	14.286		6,325	915		7,240	8,325
5160	6,920 CFM, 5 HP		1.30	15.385		6,900	985		7,885	9,050
5180	7,700 CFM, 7-1/2 HP	▼	1.20	16.667	▼	7,500	1,075		8,575	9,850
5200	For explosion proof motor, add					15%				
5300	Fume exhauster without hose and intake nozzle									
5310	630 CFM, 1-1/2 HP	Q-20	2	10	Ea.	995	640		1,635	2,050
5320	Hose extension kit 5'	"	20	1	"	47.50	64		111.50	148
5500	Fans, industrial exhauster, for air which may contain granular matl.									
5520	1,000 CFM, 1-1/2 HP	Q-20	2.50	8	Ea.	3,825	510		4,335	5,000
5540	2,000 CFM, 3 HP		2	10		4,500	640		5,140	5,900
5560	4,000 CFM, 7-1/2 HP		1.80	11.111		6,200	710		6,910	7,900
5580	8,000 CFM, 15 HP		1.40	14.286		8,025	915		8,940	10,200
5600	12,000 CFM, 30 HP	▼	1	20	▼	12,500	1,275		13,775	15,600
7000	Roof exhauster, centrifugal, aluminum housing, 12" galvanized									
7020	curb, bird screen, back draft damper, 1/4" S.P.									
7100	Direct drive, 320 CFM, 11" sq. damper	Q-20	7	2.857	Ea.	815	183		998	1,175
7120	600 CFM, 11" sq. damper		6	3.333		1,050	213		1,263	1,475
7140	815 CFM, 13" sq. damper		5	4		1,050	256		1,306	1,525
7160	1,450 CFM, 13" sq. damper		4.20	4.762		1,450	305		1,755	2,050
7180	2,050 CFM, 16" sq. damper		4	5		2,175	320		2,495	2,875
7200	V-belt drive, 1,650 CFM, 12" sq. damper		6	3.333		1,350	213		1,563	1,825
7220	2,750 CFM, 21" sq. damper		5	4		162	256		418	565
7230	3,500 CFM, 21" sq. damper		4.50	4.444		1,950	284		2,234	2,575
7240	4,910 CFM, 23" sq. damper		4	5		2,200	320		2,520	2,900
7260	8,525 CFM, 28" sq. damper		3	6.667		3,050	425		3,475	4,000
7280	13,760 CFM, 35" sq. damper		2	10		4,050	640		4,690	5,400
7300	20,558 CFM, 43" sq. damper	▼	1	20		8,625	1,275		9,900	11,400
7320	For 2 speed winding, add					15%				
7340	For explosion proof motor, add					825			825	905
7360	For belt driven, top discharge, add				▼	15%				
7400	Roof mounted kitchen exhaust, aluminum, centrifugal									
7410	Direct drive, 1/4" S.P., 2 speed, temp to 200°F									
7414	1/3 HP, 2,038 CFM	Q-20	7	2.857	Ea.	1,275	183		1,458	1,700
7416	1/2 HP, 2,393 CFM		6	3.333		1,225	213		1,438	1,675
7418	3/4 HP, 4,329 CFM	▼	5	4	▼	1,925	256		2,181	2,475
7424	Belt drive, 1/4" S.P., temp to 250°F									
7426	3/4 HP, 2,757 CFM	Q-20	5	4	Ea.	1,800	256		2,056	2,375
7428	1-1/2 HP, 4,913 CFM		4	5		2,325	320		2,645	3,050
7430	1-1/2 HP, 5,798 CFM	▼	4	5	▼	2,375	320		2,695	3,075
7450	Upblast, propeller, w/backdraft damper, bird screen & curb									
7454	30,300 CFM @ 3/8" S.P., 5 HP	Q-20	1.60	12.500	Ea.	5,550	800		6,350	7,300
7458	36,000 CFM @ 1/2" S.P., 15 HP	"	1.60	12.500	"	7,900	800		8,700	9,875
8500	Wall exhausters, centrifugal, auto damper, 1/8" S.P.									
8520	Direct drive, 610 CFM, 1/20 HP	Q-20	14	1.429	Ea.	1,350	91.50		1,441.50	1,600
8540	796 CFM, 1/12 HP		13	1.538		1,650	98.50		1,748.50	1,950
8560	822 CFM, 1/6 HP		12	1.667		1,275	107		1,382	1,550
8580	1,320 CFM, 1/4 HP		12	1.667		1,225	107		1,332	1,500
8600	1,756 CFM, 1/4 HP	▼	11	1.818	▼	1,500	116		1,616	1,825

23 34 HVAC Fans

23 34 16 – Centrifugal HVAC Fans

23 34 16.10 Centrifugal Type HVAC Fans

		Crew	Daily Output	Labor-Hours	Unit	Material	2023 Bare Costs Labor	Equipment	Total	Total Incl O&P
8620	1,983 CFM, 1/4 HP	Q-20	10	2	Ea.	1,525	128		1,653	1,900
8640	2,900 CFM, 1/2 HP		9	2.222		4,125	142		4,267	4,750
8660	3,307 CFM, 3/4 HP		8	2.500		1,775	160		1,935	2,200
8670	5,940 CFM, 1 HP	↓	7	2.857	↓	1,550	183		1,733	2,000
9500	V-belt drive, 3 phase									
9520	2,800 CFM, 1/4 HP	Q-20	9	2.222	Ea.	2,275	142		2,417	2,750
9540	3,740 CFM, 1/2 HP		8	2.500		2,375	160		2,535	2,850
9560	4,400 CFM, 3/4 HP		7	2.857		2,400	183		2,583	2,925
9580	5,700 CFM, 1-1/2 HP	↓	6	3.333	↓	2,500	213		2,713	3,075

23 34 23 – HVAC Power Ventilators

23 34 23.10 HVAC Power Circulators and Ventilators

			Crew	Daily Output	Labor-Hours	Unit	Material	Labor	Equipment	Total	Total Incl O&P
0010	**HVAC POWER CIRCULATORS AND VENTILATORS**										
3000	Paddle blade air circulator, 3 speed switch										
3020	42", 5,000 CFM high, 3,000 CFM low	G	1 Elec	2.40	3.333	Ea.	179	225		404	530
3040	52", 6,500 CFM high, 4,000 CFM low	G	"	2.20	3.636	"	154	245		399	535
3100	For antique white motor, same cost										
3200	For brass plated motor, same cost										
3300	For light adaptor kit, add	G				Ea.	43.50			43.50	48
3310	Industrial grade, reversible, 4 blade										
3312	5,500 CFM		Q-20	5	4	Ea.	136	256		392	535
3314	7,600 CFM			5	4		197	256		453	600
3316	21,015 CFM		↓	4	5	↓	244	320		564	750
4000	High volume, low speed (HVLS), paddle blade air circulator										
4010	Variable speed, reversible, 1 HP motor, motor control panel,										
4020	motor drive cable, control cable with remote, and safety cable.										
4140	8' diameter		Q-5	1.50	10.667	Ea.	8,250	695		8,945	10,100
4150	10' diameter			1.45	11.034		5,500	720		6,220	7,125
4160	12' diameter			1.40	11.429		9,025	745		9,770	11,100
4170	14' diameter			1.35	11.852		5,825	775		6,600	7,575
4180	16' diameter			1.30	12.308		8,850	805		9,655	11,000
4190	18' diameter			1.25	12.800		5,925	835		6,760	7,775
4200	20' diameter			1.20	13.333		7,850	870		8,720	9,925
4210	24' diameter		↓	1	16	↓	6,475	1,050		7,525	8,675
6000	Propeller exhaust, wall shutter										
6020	Direct drive, one speed, 0.075" S.P.										
6100	653 CFM, 1/30 HP		Q-20	10	2	Ea.	320	128		448	545
6120	1,033 CFM, 1/20 HP			9	2.222		277	142		419	520
6140	1,323 CFM, 1/15 HP			8	2.500		525	160		685	820
6160	2,444 CFM, 1/4 HP		↓	7	2.857		365	183		548	675
6300	V-belt drive, 3 phase										
6320	6,175 CFM, 3/4 HP		Q-20	5	4	Ea.	1,300	256		1,556	1,800
6340	7,500 CFM, 3/4 HP			5	4		1,350	256		1,606	1,850
6360	10,100 CFM, 1 HP			4.50	4.444		1,550	284		1,834	2,150
6380	14,300 CFM, 1-1/2 HP			4	5		1,875	320		2,195	2,550
6400	19,800 CFM, 2 HP			3	6.667		2,150	425		2,575	3,025
6420	26,250 CFM, 3 HP			2.60	7.692		2,650	490		3,140	3,650
6440	38,500 CFM, 5 HP			2.20	9.091		3,325	580		3,905	4,550
6460	46,000 CFM, 7-1/2 HP			2	10		3,425	640		4,065	4,725
6480	51,500 CFM, 10 HP		↓	1.80	11.111	↓	3,475	710		4,185	4,900
6490	V-belt drive, 115 V, residential, whole house										
6500	Ceiling-wall, 5,200 CFM, 1/4 HP, 30" x 30"		1 Shee	6	1.333	Ea.	665	93.50		758.50	870
6510	7,500 CFM, 1/3 HP, 36" x 36"			5	1.600		695	112		807	935

23 34 HVAC Fans

23 34 23 – HVAC Power Ventilators

23 34 23.10 HVAC Power Circulators and Ventilators	Crew	Daily Output	Labor-Hours	Unit	Material	2023 Bare Costs Labor	Equipment	Total	Total Incl O&P
6520 10,500 CFM, 1/3 HP, 42" x 42"	1 Shee	5	1.600	Ea.	725	112		837	970
6530 13,200 CFM, 1/3 HP, 48" x 48"		4	2		805	140		945	1,100
6540 15,445 CFM, 1/2 HP, 48" x 48"		4	2		835	140		975	1,125
6550 17,025 CFM, 1/2 HP, 54" x 54"	▼	4	2	▼	1,600	140		1,740	1,975
6560 For two speed motor, add					20%				
6570 Shutter, automatic, ceiling/wall									
6580 30" x 30"	1 Shee	8	1	Ea.	217	70		287	345
6590 36" x 36"		8	1		248	70		318	380
6600 42" x 42"		8	1		310	70		380	445
6610 48" x 48"		7	1.143		335	80		415	490
6620 54" x 54"		6	1.333		445	93.50		538.50	625
6630 Timer, shut off, to 12 hour	▼	20	.400	▼	71	28		99	121
6650 Residential, bath exhaust, grille, back draft damper									
6660 50 CFM	Q-20	24	.833	Ea.	50	53.50		103.50	135
6670 110 CFM		22	.909		111	58		169	210
6672 180 CFM		22	.909		168	58		226	273
6673 210 CFM		22	.909		206	58		264	315
6674 260 CFM		22	.909		245	58		303	360
6675 300 CFM		22	.909		188	58		246	295
6680 Light combination, squirrel cage, 100 watt, 70 CFM	▼	24	.833	▼	153	53.50		206.50	248
6700 Light/heater combination, ceiling mounted									
6710 70 CFM, 1,450 watt	Q-20	24	.833	Ea.	189	53.50		242.50	288
6800 Heater combination, recessed, 70 CFM		24	.833		85.50	53.50		139	174
6820 With 2 infrared bulbs		23	.870		101	55.50		156.50	195
6840 Wall mount, 170 CFM		22	.909		298	58		356	420
6846 Ceiling mount, 180 CFM		22	.909		249	58		307	360
6900 Kitchen exhaust, grille, complete, 160 CFM		22	.909		146	58		204	248
6910 180 CFM		20	1		110	64		174	217
6920 270 CFM		18	1.111		215	71		286	345
6930 350 CFM	▼	16	1.250	▼	173	80		253	310
6940 Residential roof jacks and wall caps									
6944 Wall cap with back draft damper									
6946 3" & 4" diam. round duct	1 Shee	11	.727	Ea.	25	51		76	105
6948 6" diam. round duct	"	11	.727	"	60	51		111	143
6958 Roof jack with bird screen and back draft damper									
6960 3" & 4" diam. round duct	1 Shee	11	.727	Ea.	31	51		82	112
6962 3-1/4" x 10" rectangular duct	"	10	.800	"	39.50	56		95.50	128
6980 Transition									
6982 3-1/4" x 10" to 6" diam. round	1 Shee	20	.400	Ea.	26.50	28		54.50	72
8020 Attic, roof type									
8030 Aluminum dome, damper & curb									
8080 12" diameter, 1,000 CFM (gravity)	1 Elec	10	.800	Ea.	700	54		754	855
8090 16" diameter, 1,500 CFM (gravity)		9	.889		850	60		910	1,025
8100 20" diameter, 2,500 CFM (gravity)		8	1		1,050	67.50		1,117.50	1,250
8110 26" diameter, 4,000 CFM (gravity)		7	1.143		1,250	77		1,327	1,500
8120 32" diameter, 6,500 CFM (gravity)		6	1.333		1,725	90		1,815	2,025
8130 38" diameter, 8,000 CFM (gravity)		5	1.600		2,550	108		2,658	2,975
8140 50" diameter, 13,000 CFM (gravity)	▼	4	2	▼	3,725	135		3,860	4,275
8160 Plastic, ABS dome									
8180 1,050 CFM	1 Elec	14	.571	Ea.	207	38.50		245.50	284
8200 1,600 CFM	"	12	.667	"	310	45		355	405
8240 Attic, wall type, with shutter, one speed									
8250 12" diameter, 1,000 CFM	1 Elec	14	.571	Ea.	515	38.50		553.50	620

23 34 HVAC Fans

23 34 23 – HVAC Power Ventilators

23 34 23.10 HVAC Power Circulators and Ventilators

		Crew	Daily Output	Labor-Hours	Unit	Material	2023 Bare Costs Labor	2023 Bare Costs Equipment	Total	Total Incl O&P
8260	14" diameter, 1,500 CFM	1 Elec	12	.667	Ea.	555	45		600	675
8270	16" diameter, 2,000 CFM	↓	9	.889	↓	630	60		690	780
8290	Whole house, wall type, with shutter, one speed									
8300	30" diameter, 4,800 CFM	1 Elec	7	1.143	Ea.	1,350	77		1,427	1,600
8310	36" diameter, 7,000 CFM		6	1.333		1,475	90		1,565	1,725
8320	42" diameter, 10,000 CFM		5	1.600		1,650	108		1,758	1,950
8330	48" diameter, 16,000 CFM	↓	4	2		2,050	135		2,185	2,450
8340	For two speed, add				↓	123			123	135
8350	Whole house, lay-down type, with shutter, one speed									
8360	30" diameter, 4,500 CFM	1 Elec	8	1	Ea.	1,425	67.50		1,492.50	1,675
8370	36" diameter, 6,500 CFM		7	1.143		1,550	77		1,627	1,825
8380	42" diameter, 9,000 CFM		6	1.333		1,700	90		1,790	1,975
8390	48" diameter, 12,000 CFM	↓	5	1.600		1,925	108		2,033	2,275
8440	For two speed, add					92			92	101
8450	For 12 hour timer switch, add	1 Elec	32	.250	↓	92	16.85		108.85	126

23 34 33 – Air Curtains

23 34 33.10 Air Barrier Curtains

		Crew	Daily Output	Labor-Hours	Unit	Material	Labor	Equipment	Total	Total Incl O&P
0010	**AIR BARRIER CURTAINS**, Incl. motor starters, transformers,									
0050	and door switches									
2450	Conveyor openings or service windows									
3000	Service window, 5' high x 25" wide	2 Shee	5	3.200	Ea.	385	224		609	760
3100	Environmental separation									
3110	Door heights up to 8', low profile, super quiet									
3120	Unheated, variable speed									
3130	36" wide	2 Shee	4	4	Ea.	830	281		1,111	1,350
3134	42" wide		3.80	4.211		865	295		1,160	1,400
3138	48" wide		3.60	4.444		885	310		1,195	1,450
3142	60" wide	↓	3.40	4.706		920	330		1,250	1,500
3146	72" wide	Q-3	4.60	6.957		1,100	475		1,575	1,900
3150	96" wide		4.40	7.273		1,600	500		2,100	2,500
3154	120" wide		4.20	7.619		1,675	525		2,200	2,625
3158	144" wide	↓	4	8	↓	2,075	550		2,625	3,100
3200	Door heights up to 10'									
3210	Unheated									
3230	36" wide	2 Shee	3.80	4.211	Ea.	940	295		1,235	1,475
3234	42" wide		3.60	4.444		965	310		1,275	1,525
3238	48" wide		3.40	4.706		1,050	330		1,380	1,650
3242	60" wide	↓	3.20	5		1,250	350		1,600	1,900
3246	72" wide	Q-3	4.40	7.273		1,675	500		2,175	2,575
3250	96" wide		4.20	7.619		2,050	525		2,575	3,025
3254	120" wide		4	8		2,500	550		3,050	3,575
3258	144" wide	↓	3.80	8.421	↓	3,225	580		3,805	4,400
3300	Door heights up to 12'									
3310	Unheated									
3334	42" wide	2 Shee	3.40	4.706	Ea.	1,275	330		1,605	1,900
3338	48" wide		3.20	5		1,350	350		1,700	2,000
3342	60" wide	↓	3	5.333		1,300	375		1,675	2,025
3346	72" wide	Q-3	4.20	7.619		2,425	525		2,950	3,450
3350	96" wide		4	8		2,475	550		3,025	3,550
3354	120" wide		3.80	8.421		2,875	580		3,455	4,000
3358	144" wide	↓	3.60	8.889	↓	3,275	610		3,885	4,525
3400	Door heights up to 16'									

23 34 HVAC Fans

23 34 33 – Air Curtains

23 34 33.10 Air Barrier Curtains

		Crew	Daily Output	Labor-Hours	Unit	Material	2023 Bare Costs Labor	2023 Bare Costs Equipment	Total	Total Incl O&P
3410	Unheated									
3438	48" wide	2 Shee	3	5.333	Ea.	1,600	375		1,975	2,325
3442	60" wide	"	2.80	5.714		1,675	400		2,075	2,450
3446	72" wide	Q-3	3.80	8.421		3,075	580		3,655	4,225
3450	96" wide		3.60	8.889		2,925	610		3,535	4,100
3454	120" wide		3.40	9.412		4,050	645		4,695	5,400
3458	144" wide		3.20	10		4,100	685		4,785	5,550
3470	Heated, electric									
3474	48" wide	2 Shee	2.90	5.517	Ea.	2,800	385		3,185	3,650
3478	60" wide	"	2.70	5.926		2,850	415		3,265	3,775
3482	72" wide	Q-3	3.70	8.649		4,750	595		5,345	6,100
3486	96" wide		3.50	9.143		4,750	625		5,375	6,150
3490	120" wide		3.30	9.697		5,400	665		6,065	6,925
3474	144" wide		3.10	10.323		6,325	710		7,035	8,000

23 34 39.10 Powerfoil

		Crew	Daily Output	Labor-Hours	Unit	Material	2023 Bare Costs Labor	2023 Bare Costs Equipment	Total	Total Incl O&P
0010	**POWERFOIL**									
2301	Powerfoil, 8' diameter	R-1A	2.40	6.667	Ea.	9,475	405		9,880	11,000
2302	10'		2.40	6.667		9,575	405		9,980	11,100
2303	12'		2.40	6.667		9,700	405		10,105	11,300
2304	14'		2.40	6.667		9,800	405		10,205	11,400
2305	16'		2	8		9,900	485		10,385	11,600
2306	18'		2	8		10,000	485		10,485	11,700
2307	20'		2	8		10,100	485		10,585	11,800
2308	24'		2	8		10,400	485		10,885	12,100
2400	Powerfoil with Hybrid Airfoil									
2401	12'	R-1A	2	8	Ea.	10,200	485		10,685	12,000
2402	14'		2	8		10,400	485		10,885	12,100
2403	16'		1.75	9.143		10,500	555		11,055	12,300
2404	18'		1.75	9.143		10,600	555		11,155	12,400
2405	20'		1.75	9.143		10,700	555		11,255	12,500
2406	24'		1.75	9.143		10,900	555		11,455	12,800

23 35 Special Exhaust Systems

23 35 16 – Engine Exhaust Systems

23 35 16.10 Engine Exhaust Removal Systems

		Crew	Daily Output	Labor-Hours	Unit	Material	2023 Bare Costs Labor	2023 Bare Costs Equipment	Total	Total Incl O&P
0010	**ENGINE EXHAUST REMOVAL SYSTEMS**	D3090-320								
0500	Engine exhaust, garage, in-floor system									
0510	Single tube outlet assemblies									
0520	For transite pipe ducting, self-storing tube									
0530	3" tubing adapter plate	1 Shee	16	.500	Ea.	310	35		345	395
0540	4" tubing adapter plate		16	.500		315	35		350	400
0550	5" tubing adapter plate		16	.500		310	35		345	400
0600	For vitrified tile ducting									
0610	3" tubing adapter plate, self-storing tube	1 Shee	16	.500	Ea.	305	35		340	395
0620	4" tubing adapter plate, self-storing tube		16	.500		315	35		350	400
0660	5" tubing adapter plate, self-storing tube		16	.500		315	35		350	400
0800	Two tube outlet assemblies									
0810	For transite pipe ducting, self-storing tube									
0820	3" tubing, dual exhaust adapter plate	1 Shee	16	.500	Ea.	315	35		350	405
0850	For vitrified tile ducting									
0860	3" tubing, dual exhaust, self-storing tube	1 Shee	16	.500	Ea.	345	35		380	435

23 35 Special Exhaust Systems

23 35 16 – Engine Exhaust Systems

23 35 16.10 Engine Exhaust Removal Systems		Crew	Daily Output	Labor-Hours	Unit	Material	2023 Bare Costs Labor	Equipment	Total	Total Incl O&P
0870	3" tubing, double outlet, non-storing tubes	1 Shee	16	.500	Ea.	345	35		380	435
0900	Accessories for metal tubing (overhead systems also)									
0910	Adapters, for metal tubing end									
0920	3" tail pipe type				Ea.	60			60	66
0930	4" tail pipe type					66.50			66.50	73
0940	5" tail pipe type					67.50			67.50	74.50
0990	5" diesel stack type					355			355	390
1000	6" diesel stack type					420			420	465
1100	Bullnose (guide) required for in-floor assemblies									
1110	3" tubing size				Ea.	36			36	39.50
1120	4" tubing size					37			37	41
1130	5" tubing size					39.50			39.50	43.50
1150	Plain rings, for tubing end									
1160	3" tubing size				Ea.	25.50			25.50	28
1170	4" tubing size				"	42.50			42.50	47
1200	Tubing, galvanized, flexible (for overhead systems also)									
1210	3" ID				L.F.	12.15			12.15	13.35
1220	4" ID					14.85			14.85	16.35
1230	5" ID					17.50			17.50	19.25
1240	6" ID					20.50			20.50	22.50
1250	Stainless steel, flexible (for overhead system also)									
1260	3" ID				L.F.	24.50			24.50	27
1270	4" ID					33.50			33.50	37
1280	5" ID					38			38	42
1290	6" ID					44.50			44.50	48.50
1500	Engine exhaust, garage, overhead components, for neoprene tubing									
1510	Alternate metal tubing & accessories see above									
1550	Adapters, for neoprene tubing end									
1560	3" tail pipe, adjustable, neoprene				Ea.	71			71	78
1570	3" tail pipe, heavy wall neoprene					80			80	88
1580	4" tail pipe, heavy wall neoprene					118			118	130
1590	5" tail pipe, heavy wall neoprene					140			140	154
1650	Connectors, tubing									
1660	3" interior, aluminum				Ea.	25.50			25.50	28.50
1670	4" interior, aluminum					42.50			42.50	47
1710	5" interior, neoprene					67			67	73.50
1750	3" spiralock, neoprene					25.50			25.50	28
1760	4" spiralock, neoprene					42.50			42.50	47
1780	Y for 3" ID tubing, neoprene, dual exhaust					240			240	264
1790	Y for 4" ID tubing, aluminum, dual exhaust					190			190	208
1850	Elbows, aluminum, splice into tubing for strap									
1860	3" neoprene tubing size				Ea.	64.50			64.50	71
1870	4" neoprene tubing size					45.50			45.50	50
1900	Flange assemblies, connect tubing to overhead duct					81			81	89
2000	Hardware and accessories									
2020	Cable, galvanized, 1/8" diameter				L.F.	.60			.60	.66
2040	Cleat, tie down cable or rope				Ea.	6.20			6.20	6.80
2060	Pulley					8.55			8.55	9.40
2080	Pulley hook, universal					6.20			6.20	6.80
2100	Rope, nylon, 1/4" diameter				L.F.	.43			.43	.47
2120	Winch, 1" diameter				Ea.	125			125	138
2150	Lifting strap, mounts on neoprene									
2160	3" tubing size				Ea.	31			31	34

23 35 Special Exhaust Systems

23 35 16 – Engine Exhaust Systems

23 35 16.10 Engine Exhaust Removal Systems

		Crew	Daily Output	Labor-Hours	Unit	Material	2023 Bare Costs Labor	2023 Bare Costs Equipment	Total	Total Incl O&P
2170	4" tubing size				Ea.	31			31	34
2180	5" tubing size					31			31	34
2190	6" tubing size					31			31	34
2200	Tubing, neoprene, 11' lengths									
2210	3" ID				L.F.	14.55			14.55	16
2220	4" ID					19			19	21
2230	5" ID					34.50			34.50	38
2500	Engine exhaust, thru-door outlet									
2510	3" tube size	1 Carp	16	.500	Ea.	75.50	29.50		105	127
2530	4" tube size	"	16	.500	"	66	29.50		95.50	116
3000	Tubing, exhaust, flex hose, with									
3010	coupler, damper and tail pipe adapter									
3020	Neoprene									
3040	3" x 20'	1 Shee	6	1.333	Ea.	430	93.50		523.50	610
3050	4" x 15'		5.40	1.481		480	104		584	680
3060	4" x 20'		5	1.600		575	112		687	800
3070	5" x 15'		4.40	1.818		760	128		888	1,025
3100	Galvanized									
3110	3" x 20'	1 Shee	6	1.333	Ea.	360	93.50		453.50	535
3120	4" x 17'		5.60	1.429		395	100		495	585
3130	4" x 20'		5	1.600		440	112		552	655
3140	5" x 17'		4.60	1.739		470	122		592	700
8000	Blower, for tailpipe exhaust system									
8010	Direct drive									
8012	495 CFM, 1/3 HP	Q-9	5	3.200	Ea.	3,125	202		3,327	3,725
8014	1,445 CFM, 3/4 HP		4	4		3,900	253		4,153	4,675
8016	1,840 CFM, 1-1/2 HP		3	5.333		4,675	335		5,010	5,625
8030	Beltdrive									
8032	1,400 CFM, 1 HP	Q-9	4	4	Ea.	3,900	253		4,153	4,675
8034	2,023 CFM, 1-1/2 HP		3	5.333		5,450	335		5,785	6,500
8036	2,750 CFM, 2 HP		2	8		6,425	505		6,930	7,825
8038	4,400 CFM, 3 HP		1.80	8.889		9,475	560		10,035	11,200
8040	7,060 CFM, 5 HP		1.40	11.429		13,500	720		14,220	16,000

23 35 43 – Welding Fume Elimination Systems

23 35 43.10 Welding Fume Elimination System Components

		Crew	Daily Output	Labor-Hours	Unit	Material	2023 Bare Costs Labor	2023 Bare Costs Equipment	Total	Total Incl O&P
0010	**WELDING FUME ELIMINATION SYSTEM COMPONENTS**									
7500	Welding fume elimination accessories for garage exhaust systems									
7600	Cut off (blast gate)									
7610	3" tubing size, 3" x 6" opening	1 Shee	24	.333	Ea.	32.50	23.50		56	71
7620	4" tubing size, 4" x 8" opening		24	.333		33.50	23.50		57	71.50
7630	5" tubing size, 5" x 10" opening		24	.333		37.50	23.50		61	76.50
7640	6" tubing size		24	.333		41.50	23.50		65	81
7650	8" tubing size		24	.333		54	23.50		77.50	94
7700	Hoods, magnetic, with handle & screen									
7710	3" tubing size, 3" x 6" opening	1 Shee	24	.333	Ea.	121	23.50		144.50	168
7720	4" tubing size, 4" x 8" opening		24	.333		107	23.50		130.50	152
7730	5" tubing size, 5" x 10" opening		24	.333		107	23.50		130.50	152

23 36 Air Terminal Units

23 36 13 – Constant-Air-Volume Units

23 36 13.10 Constant Volume Mixing Boxes

		Crew	Daily Output	Labor-Hours	Unit	Material	2023 Bare Costs Labor	Equipment	Total	Total Incl O&P
0010	**CONSTANT VOLUME MIXING BOXES**									
5180	Mixing box, includes electric or pneumatic motor									
5192	Recommend use with silencer, see Line 23 33 19.10 0010									
5200	Constant volume, 150 to 270 CFM	Q-9	12	1.333	Ea.	1,350	84		1,434	1,625
5210	270 to 600 CFM		11	1.455		1,225	92		1,317	1,500
5230	550 to 1,000 CFM		9	1.778		1,225	112		1,337	1,525
5240	1,000 to 1,600 CFM		8	2		1,425	126		1,551	1,775
5250	1,300 to 1,900 CFM		6	2.667		1,450	168		1,618	1,850
5260	550 to 2,640 CFM		5.60	2.857		1,600	180		1,780	2,050
5270	650 to 3,120 CFM	↓	5.20	3.077	↓	1,525	194		1,719	1,975

23 36 16 – Variable-Air-Volume Units

23 36 16.10 Variable Volume Mixing Boxes

		Crew	Daily Output	Labor-Hours	Unit	Material	2023 Bare Costs Labor	Equipment	Total	Total Incl O&P
0010	**VARIABLE VOLUME MIXING BOXES**									
5180	Mixing box, includes electric or pneumatic motor									
5192	Recommend use with attenuator, see Line 23 33 19.10 0010									
5500	VAV cool only, pneumatic, pressure independent 300 to 600 CFM	Q-9	11	1.455	Ea.	985	92		1,077	1,225
5510	500 to 1,000 CFM		9	1.778		1,000	112		1,112	1,275
5520	800 to 1,600 CFM		9	1.778		1,050	112		1,162	1,325
5530	1,100 to 2,000 CFM		8	2		1,075	126		1,201	1,375
5540	1,500 to 3,000 CFM		7	2.286		1,125	144		1,269	1,475
5550	2,000 to 4,000 CFM	↓	6	2.667	↓	1,150	168		1,318	1,525
5600	VAV, HW coils, damper, actuator and thermostat									
5610	200 CFM	Q-9	11	1.455	Ea.	1,350	92		1,442	1,625
5620	400 CFM		10	1.600		1,375	101		1,476	1,650
5630	600 CFM		10	1.600		1,375	101		1,476	1,650
5640	800 CFM		8	2		1,400	126		1,526	1,750
5650	1,000 CFM		8	2		1,400	126		1,526	1,750
5660	1,250 CFM		6	2.667		1,550	168		1,718	1,950
5670	1,500 CFM		6	2.667		1,550	168		1,718	1,950
5680	2,000 CFM		4	4		1,875	253		2,128	2,450
5684	3,000 CFM	↓	3.80	4.211	↓	2,050	266		2,316	2,650
5700	VAV cool only, fan powered, damper, actuator, thermostat									
5710	200 CFM	Q-9	10	1.600	Ea.	1,850	101		1,951	2,200
5720	400 CFM		9	1.778		2,275	112		2,387	2,700
5730	600 CFM		9	1.778		2,275	112		2,387	2,700
5740	800 CFM		7	2.286		2,450	144		2,594	2,925
5750	1,000 CFM		7	2.286		2,450	144		2,594	2,925
5760	1,250 CFM		5	3.200		2,650	202		2,852	3,200
5770	1,500 CFM		5	3.200		2,650	202		2,852	3,200
5780	2,000 CFM	↓	4	4	↓	2,925	253		3,178	3,575
5800	VAV fan powr'd, with HW coils, dampers, actuators, thermostat									
5810	200 CFM	Q-9	10	1.600	Ea.	2,650	101		2,751	3,075
5820	400 CFM		9	1.778		2,725	112		2,837	3,175
5830	600 CFM		9	1.778		2,725	112		2,837	3,175
5840	800 CFM		7	2.286		2,900	144		3,044	3,400
5850	1,000 CFM		7	2.286		2,900	144		3,044	3,400
5860	1,250 CFM		5	3.200		3,300	202		3,502	3,925
5870	1,500 CFM		5	3.200		3,300	202		3,502	3,925
5880	2,000 CFM	↓	3.50	4.571	↓	3,550	289		3,839	4,325
5900	Variable volume, fan powered, single duct with direct digital control									
5910	225 CFM	Q-9	12	1.333	Ea.	325	84		409	485
5912	350 CFM	↓	12	1.333		255	84		339	405

23 36 Air Terminal Units

23 36 16 – Variable-Air-Volume Units

23 36 16.10 Variable Volume Mixing Boxes

		Crew	Daily Output	Labor-Hours	Unit	Material	2023 Bare Costs Labor	Equipment	Total	Total Incl O&P
5914	500 CFM	Q-9	12	1.333	Ea.	380	84		464	545
5916	650 CFM		12	1.333		320	84		404	475
5918	900 CFM		12	1.333		241	84		325	390
5920	1050 CFM		11	1.455		282	92		374	450
5922	1400 CFM		10	1.600		245	101		346	420
5924	2000 CFM		9	1.778		286	112		398	485
5926	3000 CFM		8	2		305	126		431	525
5928	4000 CFM		7	2.286		325	144		469	575

23 37 Air Outlets and Inlets

23 37 13 – Diffusers, Registers, and Grilles

23 37 13.10 Diffusers

			Crew	Daily Output	Labor-Hours	Unit	Material	2023 Bare Costs Labor	Equipment	Total	Total Incl O&P
0010	**DIFFUSERS**, Aluminum, opposed blade damper unless noted										
0100	Ceiling, linear, also for sidewall										
0120	2" wide	R233100-30	1 Shee	32	.250	L.F.	31.50	17.55		49.05	61
0140	3" wide			30	.267		36	18.70		54.70	67.50
0160	4" wide	R233700-60		26	.308		27	21.50		48.50	62
0180	6" wide			24	.333		33.50	23.50		57	71.50
0200	8" wide			22	.364		60.50	25.50		86	106
0220	10" wide			20	.400		44.50	28		72.50	91.50
0240	12" wide			18	.444		60	31		91	113
0260	For floor or sill application, add						15%				
0500	Perforated, 24" x 24" lay-in panel size, 6" x 6"		1 Shee	16	.500	Ea.	220	35		255	295
0520	8" x 8"			15	.533		223	37.50		260.50	300
0530	9" x 9"			14	.571		234	40		274	320
0540	10" x 10"			14	.571		234	40		274	320
0560	12" x 12"			12	.667		244	47		291	340
0580	15" x 15"			11	.727		266	51		317	370
0590	16" x 16"			11	.727		260	51		311	365
0600	18" x 18"			10	.800		279	56		335	390
0610	20" x 20"			10	.800		299	56		355	415
0620	24" x 24"			9	.889		350	62.50		412.50	480
1000	Rectangular, 1 to 4 way blow, 6" x 6"			16	.500		52.50	35		87.50	111
1010	8" x 8"			15	.533		73.50	37.50		111	137
1014	9" x 9"			15	.533		64	37.50		101.50	127
1016	10" x 10"			15	.533		108	37.50		145.50	176
1020	12" x 6"			15	.533		90.50	37.50		128	156
1040	12" x 9"			14	.571		96.50	40		136.50	167
1060	12" x 12"			12	.667		85.50	47		132.50	165
1070	14" x 6"			13	.615		98.50	43		141.50	173
1074	14" x 14"			12	.667		160	47		207	247
1080	18" x 12"			11	.727		174	51		225	268
1120	15" x 15"			10	.800		112	56		168	208
1140	18" x 15"			9	.889		205	62.50		267.50	320
1150	18" x 18"			9	.889		155	62.50		217.50	264
1160	21" x 21"			8	1		284	70		354	420
1170	24" x 12"			10	.800		214	56		270	320
1180	24" x 24"			7	1.143		355	80		435	510
1500	Round, butterfly damper, steel, diffuser size, 6" diameter			18	.444		21	31		52	70
1520	8" diameter			16	.500		22.50	35		57.50	78
1540	10" diameter			14	.571		28	40		68	91.50

23 37 Air Outlets and Inlets

23 37 13 – Diffusers, Registers, and Grilles

23 37 13.10 Diffusers		Crew	Daily Output	Labor-Hours	Unit	Material	2023 Bare Costs Labor	Equipment	Total	Total Incl O&P
1560	12" diameter	1 Shee	12	.667	Ea.	38	47		85	113
1580	14" diameter		10	.800		49	56		105	138
1600	18" diameter	▼	9	.889	▼	121	62.50		183.50	227
1700	Round, steel, adjustable core, annular segmented damper, diffuser size									
1704	6" diameter	1 Shee	18	.444	Ea.	87	31		118	143
1708	8" diameter		16	.500		120	35		155	185
1712	10" diameter		14	.571		143	40		183	218
1716	12" diameter		12	.667		176	47		223	265
1720	14" diameter		10	.800		207	56		263	315
1724	18" diameter		9	.889		435	62.50		497.50	570
1728	20" diameter		9	.889		500	62.50		562.50	645
1732	24" diameter		8	1		430	70		500	580
1736	30" diameter		7	1.143		1,075	80		1,155	1,300
1740	36" diameter		6	1.333		1,325	93.50		1,418.50	1,600
2000	T-bar mounting, 24" x 24" lay-in frame, 6" x 6"		16	.500		72	35		107	133
2020	8" x 8"		14	.571		72.50	40		112.50	140
2040	12" x 12"		12	.667		88.50	47		135.50	168
2060	16" x 16"		11	.727		134	51		185	224
2080	18" x 18"	▼	10	.800	▼	131	56		187	230
2500	Combination supply and return									
2520	21" x 21" supply, 15" x 15" return	Q-9	10	1.600	Ea.	194	101		295	365
2540	24" x 24" supply, 18" x 18" return		9.50	1.684		224	106		330	405
2560	27" x 27" supply, 18" x 18" return		9	1.778		254	112		366	450
2580	30" x 30" supply, 21" x 21" return		8.50	1.882		345	119		464	560
2600	33" x 33" supply, 21" x 21" return		8	2		375	126		501	600
2620	36" x 36" supply, 24" x 24" return	▼	7.50	2.133	▼	440	135		575	690
3000	Baseboard, white enameled steel									
3100	18" long	1 Shee	20	.400	Ea.	11.75	28		39.75	55.50
3120	24" long		18	.444		24	31		55	73.50
3140	48" long	▼	16	.500	▼	44.50	35		79.50	102
3400	For matching return, deduct					10%				
4000	Floor, steel, adjustable pattern									
4100	2" x 10"	1 Shee	34	.235	Ea.	16.65	16.50		33.15	43.50
4120	2" x 12"		32	.250		18.30	17.55		35.85	46.50
4140	2" x 14"		30	.267		21	18.70		39.70	51
4200	4" x 10"		28	.286		18.35	20		38.35	50
4220	4" x 12"		26	.308		20.50	21.50		42	55
4240	4" x 14"		25	.320		24	22.50		46.50	60.50
4260	6" x 10"		26	.308		29	21.50		50.50	64.50
4280	6" x 12"		24	.333		29	23.50		52.50	67
4300	6" x 14"	▼	22	.364	▼	31.50	25.50		57	73.50
4500	Linear bar diffuser in wall, sill or ceiling									
4510	2" wide	1 Shee	32	.250	L.F.	80.50	17.55		98.05	115
4512	3" wide		30	.267		87	18.70		105.70	124
4514	4" wide		26	.308		107	21.50		128.50	151
4516	6" wide		24	.333		133	23.50		156.50	181
4520	10" wide		20	.400		177	28		205	238
4522	12" wide	▼	18	.444	▼	199	31		230	266
5000	Sidewall, aluminum, 3 way dispersion									
5100	8" x 4"	1 Shee	24	.333	Ea.	10.25	23.50		33.75	46.50
5110	8" x 6"		24	.333		11	23.50		34.50	47
5120	10" x 4"		22	.364		10.30	25.50		35.80	50
5130	10" x 6"	▼	22	.364		11	25.50		36.50	50.50

23 37 Air Outlets and Inlets

23 37 13 – Diffusers, Registers, and Grilles

23 37 13.10 Diffusers

		Crew	Daily Output	Labor-Hours	Unit	Material	2023 Bare Costs Labor	Equipment	Total	Total Incl O&P
5140	10" x 8"	1 Shee	20	.400	Ea.	15.80	28		43.80	60
5160	12" x 4"		18	.444		11.65	31		42.65	60
5170	12" x 6"		17	.471		12.25	33		45.25	63
5180	12" x 8"		16	.500		16.65	35		51.65	71.50
5200	14" x 4"		15	.533		13	37.50		50.50	71
5220	14" x 6"		14	.571		14.30	40		54.30	76.50
5240	14" x 8"		13	.615		18.60	43		61.60	85.50
5260	16" x 6"		12.50	.640		20.50	45		65.50	90
6000	For steel diffusers instead of aluminum, deduct					10%				

23 37 13.30 Grilles

		Crew	Daily Output	Labor-Hours	Unit	Material	2023 Bare Costs Labor	Equipment	Total	Total Incl O&P
0010	**GRILLES**									
0020	Aluminum, unless noted otherwise									
0100	Air supply, single deflection, adjustable									
0120	8" x 4"	1 Shee	30	.267	Ea.	14.35	18.70		33.05	44
0140	8" x 8"		28	.286		21.50	20		41.50	53.50
0160	10" x 4"		24	.333		20.50	23.50		44	57.50
0180	10" x 10"		23	.348		20	24.50		44.50	59
0200	12" x 6"		23	.348		24.50	24.50		49	64
0220	12" x 12"		22	.364		32	25.50		57.50	73.50
0230	14" x 6"		23	.348		27	24.50		51.50	67
0240	14" x 8"		23	.348		29	24.50		53.50	69
0260	14" x 14"		22	.364		39	25.50		64.50	81.50
0270	18" x 8"		23	.348		22.50	24.50		47	61.50
0280	18" x 10"		23	.348		26	24.50		50.50	65.50
0300	18" x 18"		21	.381		60	26.50		86.50	107
0320	20" x 12"		22	.364		43.50	25.50		69	86.50
0340	20" x 20"		21	.381		72.50	26.50		99	120
0350	24" x 8"		20	.400		28	28		56	73.50
0360	24" x 14"		18	.444		38	31		69	89
0380	24" x 24"		15	.533		79	37.50		116.50	143
0400	30" x 8"		20	.400		36	28		64	82.50
0420	30" x 10"		19	.421		59.50	29.50		89	110
0440	30" x 12"		18	.444		44	31		75	95.50
0460	30" x 16"		17	.471		57	33		90	112
0480	30" x 18"		17	.471		73	33		106	130
0500	30" x 30"		14	.571		114	40		154	186
0520	36" x 12"		17	.471		81	33		114	139
0540	36" x 16"		16	.500		69.50	35		104.50	130
0560	36" x 18"		15	.533		77	37.50		114.50	141
0570	36" x 20"		15	.533		84.50	37.50		122	150
0580	36" x 24"		14	.571		109	40		149	181
0600	36" x 28"		13	.615		134	43		177	213
0620	36" x 30"		12	.667		219	47		266	310
0640	36" x 32"		12	.667		162	47		209	249
0660	36" x 34"		11	.727		176	51		227	271
0680	36" x 36"		11	.727		191	51		242	287
0700	For double deflecting, add					70%				
1000	Air return, steel, 6" x 6"	1 Shee	26	.308		27	21.50		48.50	62
1020	10" x 6"		24	.333		27	23.50		50.50	64.50
1040	14" x 6"		23	.348		32	24.50		56.50	72
1060	10" x 8"		23	.348		32	24.50		56.50	72
1080	16" x 8"		22	.364		38.50	25.50		64	81

23 37 Air Outlets and Inlets

23 37 13 – Diffusers, Registers, and Grilles

23 37 13.30 Grilles		Crew	Daily Output	Labor-Hours	Unit	Material	2023 Bare Costs Labor	Equipment	Total	Total Incl O&P
1100	12" x 12"	1 Shee	22	.364	Ea.	38.50	25.50		64	81
1120	24" x 12"		18	.444		50	31		81	102
1140	30" x 12"		16	.500		65.50	35		100.50	125
1160	14" x 14"		22	.364		43.50	25.50		69	86.50
1180	16" x 16"		22	.364		48.50	25.50		74	91.50
1200	18" x 18"		21	.381		55	26.50		81.50	101
1220	24" x 18"		16	.500		62	35		97	122
1240	36" x 18"		15	.533		97	37.50		134.50	163
1260	24" x 24"		15	.533		75.50	37.50		113	140
1280	36" x 24"		14	.571		107	40		147	179
1300	48" x 24"		12	.667		180	47		227	269
1320	48" x 30"		11	.727		249	51		300	350
1340	36" x 36"		13	.615		142	43		185	222
1360	48" x 36"		11	.727		315	51		366	420
1380	48" x 48"		8	1		310	70		380	450
2000	Door grilles, 12" x 12"		22	.364		144	25.50		169.50	198
2020	18" x 12"		22	.364		159	25.50		184.50	214
2040	24" x 12"		18	.444		105	31		136	162
2060	18" x 18"		18	.444		214	31		245	282
2080	24" x 18"		16	.500		146	35		181	214
2100	24" x 24"		15	.533		340	37.50		377.50	425
3000	Filter grille with filter, 12" x 12"		24	.333		75.50	23.50		99	118
3020	18" x 12"		20	.400		100	28		128	153
3040	24" x 18"		18	.444		129	31		160	189
3060	24" x 24"		16	.500		137	35		172	204
3080	30" x 24"		14	.571		168	40		208	246
3100	30" x 30"		13	.615		199	43		242	284
3950	Eggcrate, framed, 6" x 6" opening		26	.308		21	21.50		42.50	55.50
3954	8" x 8" opening		24	.333		26	23.50		49.50	63.50
3960	10" x 10" opening		23	.348		32.50	24.50		57	72.50
3970	12" x 12" opening		22	.364		37.50	25.50		63	79.50
3980	14" x 14" opening		22	.364		47.50	25.50		73	90.50
3984	16" x 16" opening		21	.381		54	26.50		80.50	100
3990	18" x 18" opening		21	.381		63.50	26.50		90	110
4020	22" x 22" opening		17	.471		71.50	33		104.50	128
4040	24" x 24" opening		15	.533		95.50	37.50		133	162
4044	28" x 28" opening		14	.571		135	40		175	209
4048	36" x 36" opening		12	.667		154	47		201	241
4050	48" x 24" opening		12	.667		196	47		243	286
4060	Eggcrate, lay-in, T-bar system									
4070	48" x 24" sheet	1 Shee	40	.200	Ea.	102	14.05		116.05	133
5000	Transfer grille, vision proof, 8" x 4"		30	.267		23	18.70		41.70	53
5020	8" x 6"		28	.286		20.50	20		40.50	52.50
5040	8" x 8"		26	.308		22.50	21.50		44	57.50
5060	10" x 6"		24	.333		21	23.50		44.50	58.50
5080	10" x 10"		23	.348		27	24.50		51.50	66.50
5090	12" x 6"		23	.348		22.50	24.50		47	62
5100	12" x 10"		22	.364		29.50	25.50		55	70.50
5110	12" x 12"		22	.364		31.50	25.50		57	73.50
5120	14" x 10"		22	.364		31.50	25.50		57	73.50
5140	16" x 8"		21	.381		31.50	26.50		58	75.50
5160	18" x 12"		20	.400		41.50	28		69.50	88
5170	18" x 18"		21	.381		58.50	26.50		85	105

23 37 Air Outlets and Inlets

23 37 13 – Diffusers, Registers, and Grilles

23 37 13.30 Grilles

		Crew	Daily Output	Labor-Hours	Unit	Material	2023 Bare Costs Labor	2023 Bare Costs Equipment	Total	Total Incl O&P
5180	20" x 12"	1 Shee	20	.400	Ea.	44.50	28		72.50	91.50
5200	20" x 20"		19	.421		70.50	29.50		100	122
5220	24" x 12"		17	.471		50.50	33		83.50	105
5240	24" x 24"		16	.500		96.50	35		131.50	159
5260	30" x 6"		15	.533		44.50	37.50		82	106
5280	30" x 8"		15	.533		52	37.50		89.50	114
5300	30" x 12"		14	.571		65	40		105	132
5320	30" x 16"		13	.615		77	43		120	150
5340	30" x 20"		12	.667		97.50	47		144.50	178
5360	30" x 24"		11	.727		120	51		171	209
5380	30" x 30"		10	.800		158	56		214	259
6000	For steel grilles instead of aluminum in above, deduct					10%				
6200	Plastic, eggcrate, lay-in, T-bar system									
6210	48" x 24" sheet	1 Shee	50	.160	Ea.	21.50	11.20		32.70	40.50
6250	Steel door louver									
6270	With fire link, steel only									
6350	12" x 18"	1 Shee	22	.364	Ea.	263	25.50		288.50	330
6410	12" x 24"		21	.381		292	26.50		318.50	360
6470	18" x 18"		20	.400		292	28		320	365
6530	18" x 24"		19	.421		335	29.50		364.50	415
6660	24" x 24"		15	.533		340	37.50		377.50	430

23 37 13.60 Registers

		Crew	Daily Output	Labor-Hours	Unit	Material	2023 Bare Costs Labor	2023 Bare Costs Equipment	Total	Total Incl O&P
0010	**REGISTERS**									
0980	Air supply									
1000	Ceiling/wall, O.B. damper, anodized aluminum									
1010	One or two way deflection, adj. curved face bars									
1014	6" x 6"	1 Shee	24	.333	Ea.	43.50	23.50		67	83
1020	8" x 4"		26	.308		36.50	21.50		58	72.50
1040	8" x 8"		24	.333		54.50	23.50		78	95
1060	10" x 6"		20	.400		33.50	28		61.50	79.50
1080	10" x 10"		19	.421		67.50	29.50		97	119
1100	12" x 6"		19	.421		34	29.50		63.50	82
1120	12" x 12"		18	.444		80	31		111	135
1140	14" x 8"		17	.471		32	33		65	85
1160	14" x 14"		18	.444		62.50	31		93.50	116
1170	16" x 16"		17	.471		69.50	33		102.50	126
1180	18" x 8"		18	.444		52	31		83	105
1200	18" x 18"		17	.471		95	33		128	155
1220	20" x 4"		19	.421		28.50	29.50		58	76
1240	20" x 6"		18	.444		48	31		79	99.50
1260	20" x 8"		18	.444		52.50	31		83.50	105
1280	20" x 20"		17	.471		116	33		149	177
1290	22" x 22"		15	.533		133	37.50		170.50	203
1300	24" x 4"		17	.471		35.50	33		68.50	88.50
1320	24" x 6"		16	.500		59	35		94	118
1340	24" x 8"		13	.615		64.50	43		107.50	136
1350	24" x 18"		12	.667		119	47		166	202
1360	24" x 24"		11	.727		163	51		214	257
1380	30" x 4"		16	.500		44.50	35		79.50	102
1400	30" x 6"		15	.533		74	37.50		111.50	138
1420	30" x 8"		14	.571		85	40		125	154
1440	30" x 24"		12	.667		211	47		258	305

23 37 Air Outlets and Inlets
23 37 13 – Diffusers, Registers, and Grilles

23 37 13.60 Registers		Crew	Daily Output	Labor-Hours	Unit	Material	2023 Bare Costs Labor	Equipment	Total	Total Incl O&P
1460	30" x 30"	1 Shee	10	.800	Ea.	270	56		326	380
1504	4 way deflection, adjustable curved face bars									
1510	6" x 6"	1 Shee	26	.308	Ea.	52.50	21.50		74	90
1514	8" x 8"		24	.333		65.50	23.50		89	107
1518	10" x 10"		19	.421		81	29.50		110.50	134
1522	12" x 6"		19	.421		41	29.50		70.50	89.50
1526	12" x 12"		18	.444		95.50	31		126.50	152
1530	14" x 14"		18	.444		75	31		106	130
1534	16" x 16"		17	.471		83.50	33		116.50	141
1538	18" x 18"		17	.471		114	33		147	176
1542	22" x 22"		16	.500		160	35		195	229
1980	One way deflection, adj. vert. or horiz. face bars									
1990	6" x 6"	1 Shee	26	.308	Ea.	36.50	21.50		58	73
2000	8" x 4"		26	.308		45	21.50		66.50	82
2020	8" x 8"		24	.333		53	23.50		76.50	93.50
2040	10" x 6"		20	.400		53.50	28		81.50	102
2060	10" x 10"		19	.421		62.50	29.50		92	114
2080	12" x 6"		19	.421		58	29.50		87.50	108
2100	12" x 12"		18	.444		75.50	31		106.50	130
2120	14" x 8"		17	.471		53.50	33		86.50	108
2140	14" x 12"		18	.444		55.50	31		86.50	109
2160	14" x 14"		18	.444		72	31		103	126
2180	16" x 6"		18	.444		46.50	31		77.50	98
2200	16" x 12"		18	.444		61.50	31		92.50	115
2220	16" x 16"		17	.471		92.50	33		125.50	152
2240	18" x 8"		18	.444		54	31		85	107
2260	18" x 12"		17	.471		75.50	33		108.50	133
2280	18" x 18"		16	.500		95.50	35		130.50	158
2300	20" x 10"		18	.444		64	31		95	118
2320	20" x 16"		16	.500		89	35		124	151
2340	20" x 20"		16	.500		117	35		152	182
2360	24" x 12"		15	.533		81	37.50		118.50	146
2380	24" x 16"		14	.571		108	40		148	180
2400	24" x 20"		12	.667		135	47		182	219
2420	24" x 24"		10	.800		165	56		221	266
2440	30" x 12"		13	.615		105	43		148	180
2460	30" x 16"		13	.615		136	43		179	215
2480	30" x 24"		11	.727		213	51		264	310
2500	30" x 30"		9	.889		272	62.50		334.50	395
2520	36" x 12"		11	.727		130	51		181	220
2540	36" x 24"		10	.800		300	56		356	415
2560	36" x 36"		8	1		440	70		510	585
2600	For 2 way deflect., adj. vert. or horiz. face bars, add					40%				
2700	Above registers in steel instead of aluminum, deduct					10%				
3000	Baseboard, hand adj. damper, enameled steel									
3012	8" x 6"	1 Shee	26	.308	Ea.	15.30	21.50		36.80	49.50
3020	10" x 6"		24	.333		16.65	23.50		40.15	53.50
3040	12" x 5"		23	.348		11	24.50		35.50	49
3060	12" x 6"		23	.348		18.10	24.50		42.60	57
3080	12" x 8"		22	.364		26	25.50		51.50	67.50
3100	14" x 6"		20	.400		19.65	28		47.65	64
4000	Floor, toe operated damper, enameled steel									
4020	4" x 8"	1 Shee	32	.250	Ea.	28.50	17.55		46.05	57.50

23 37 Air Outlets and Inlets
23 37 13 – Diffusers, Registers, and Grilles

23 37 13.60 Registers		Crew	Daily Output	Labor-Hours	Unit	Material	2023 Bare Costs Labor	Equipment	Total	Total Incl O&P
4040	4" x 12"	1 Shee	26	.308	Ea.	33.50	21.50		55	69
4060	6" x 8"		28	.286		30.50	20		50.50	63.50
4080	6" x 14"		22	.364		38.50	25.50		64	81
4100	8" x 10"		22	.364		34.50	25.50		60	76.50
4120	8" x 16"		20	.400		23	28		51	68
4140	10" x 10"		20	.400		41.50	28		69.50	88
4160	10" x 16"		18	.444		38	31		69	88.50
4180	12" x 12"		18	.444		51	31		82	103
4200	12" x 24"		16	.500		38	35		73	95
4220	14" x 14"		16	.500		82	35		117	143
4240	14" x 20"	↓	15	.533	↓	77	37.50		114.50	142
4300	Spiral pipe supply register									
4310	Steel, with air scoop									
4320	4" x 12", for 8" thru 13" diameter duct	1 Shee	25	.320	Ea.	107	22.50		129.50	151
4330	4" x 18", for 8" thru 13" diameter duct		18	.444		125	31		156	184
4340	6" x 12", for 14" thru 21" diameter duct		19	.421		114	29.50		143.50	170
4350	6" x 16", for 14" thru 21" diameter duct		18	.444		130	31		161	190
4360	6" x 20", for 14" thru 21" diameter duct		17	.471		142	33		175	206
4370	6" x 24", for 14" thru 21" diameter duct		16	.500		168	35		203	238
4380	8" x 16", for 22" thru 31" diameter duct		19	.421		136	29.50		165.50	194
4390	8" x 18", for 22" thru 31" diameter duct		18	.444		114	31		145	173
4400	8" x 24", for 22" thru 31" diameter duct	↓	15	.533	↓	175	37.50		212.50	249
4980	Air return									
5000	Ceiling or wall, fixed 45° face blades									
5010	Adjustable O.B. damper, anodized aluminum									
5020	4" x 8"	1 Shee	26	.308	Ea.	30	21.50		51.50	65.50
5040	6" x 8"		24	.333		33	23.50		56.50	71.50
5060	6" x 10"		19	.421		36	29.50		65.50	84
5070	6" x 12"		19	.421		39	29.50		68.50	87.50
5080	6" x 16"		18	.444		46.50	31		77.50	98
5100	8" x 10"		19	.421		39	29.50		68.50	87.50
5120	8" x 12"		16	.500		43.50	35		78.50	101
5140	10" x 10"		18	.444		42	31		73	93.50
5160	10" x 16"		17	.471		55.50	33		88.50	111
5170	12" x 12"		18	.444		50.50	31		81.50	103
5180	12" x 18"		18	.444		66	31		97	120
5184	12" x 24"		14	.571		81	40		121	150
5200	12" x 30"		12	.667		105	47		152	186
5210	12" x 36"		10	.800		130	56		186	228
5220	16" x 16"		17	.471		81	33		114	139
5240	18" x 18"		16	.500		95.50	35		130.50	158
5250	18" x 24"		13	.615		121	43		164	198
5254	18" x 30"		11	.727		153	51		204	245
5260	18" x 36"		10	.800		184	56		240	287
5270	20" x 20"		10	.800		117	56		173	214
5274	20" x 24"		12	.667		135	47		182	219
5280	24" x 24"		11	.727		165	51		216	258
5290	24" x 30"		10	.800		213	56		269	320
5300	24" x 36"		8	1		262	70		332	395
5320	24" x 48"		6	1.333		355	93.50		448.50	530
5340	30" x 30"	↓	6.50	1.231		272	86.50		358.50	430
5344	30" x 120"	Q-9	6	2.667		1,175	168		1,343	1,550
5360	36" x 36"	1 Shee	6	1.333	↓	440	93.50		533.50	620

23 37 Air Outlets and Inlets

23 37 13 – Diffusers, Registers, and Grilles

23 37 13.60 Registers

		Crew	Daily Output	Labor-Hours	Unit	Material	2023 Bare Costs Labor	Equipment	Total	Total Incl O&P
5370	40" x 32"	1 Shee	6	1.333	Ea.	405	93.50		498.50	585
5400	Ceiling or wall, removable-reversible core, single deflection									
5402	Adjustable O.B. damper, radiused frame with border, aluminum									
5410	8" x 4"	1 Shee	26	.308	Ea.	25.50	21.50		47	60.50
5414	8" x 6"		24	.333		25.50	23.50		49	63
5418	10" x 6"		19	.421		28.50	29.50		58	76
5422	10" x 10"		18	.444		35	31		66	85.50
5426	12" x 6"		19	.421		75.50	29.50		105	128
5430	12" x 12"		18	.444		39.50	31		70.50	90.50
5434	16" x 16"		16	.500		42.50	35		77.50	100
5438	18" x 18"		17	.471		67	33		100	123
5442	20" x 20"		16	.500		104	35		139	167
5446	24" x 12"		15	.533		63	37.50		100.50	126
5450	24" x 18"		13	.615		104	43		147	179
5454	24" x 24"		11	.727		106	51		157	193
5458	30" x 12"		13	.615		67	43		110	139
5462	30" x 18"		12.50	.640		96.50	45		141.50	174
5466	30" x 24"		11	.727		241	51		292	340
5470	30" x 30"		9	.889		257	62.50		319.50	375
5474	36" x 12"		11	.727		82.50	51		133.50	168
5478	36" x 18"		10.50	.762		116	53.50		169.50	208
5482	36" x 24"		10	.800		249	56		305	360
5486	36" x 30"		9	.889		264	62.50		326.50	385
5490	36" x 36"		8	1		282	70		352	415
6000	For steel construction instead of aluminum, deduct					10%				

23 37 15 – Air Outlets and Inlets, HVAC Louvers

23 37 15.40 HVAC Louvers

		Crew	Daily Output	Labor-Hours	Unit	Material	2023 Bare Costs Labor	Equipment	Total	Total Incl O&P
0010	**HVAC LOUVERS**									
0100	Aluminum, extruded, with screen, mill finish									
1002	Brick vent, see also Section 04 05 23.19									
1100	Standard, 4" deep, 8" wide, 5" high	1 Shee	24	.333	Ea.	50.50	23.50		74	90.50
1200	Modular, 4" deep, 7-3/4" wide, 5" high		24	.333		52.50	23.50		76	92.50
1300	Speed brick, 4" deep, 11-5/8" wide, 3-7/8" high		24	.333		52.50	23.50		76	92.50
1400	Fuel oil brick, 4" deep, 8" wide, 5" high		24	.333		90.50	23.50		114	135
2000	Cooling tower and mechanical equip., screens, light weight		40	.200	S.F.	22.50	14.05		36.55	46
2020	Standard weight		35	.229		60	16.05		76.05	90
2500	Dual combination, automatic, intake or exhaust		20	.400		82	28		110	133
2520	Manual operation		20	.400		61	28		89	110
2540	Electric or pneumatic operation		20	.400		61	28		89	110
2560	Motor, for electric or pneumatic		14	.571	Ea.	705	40		745	835
3000	Fixed blade, continuous line									
3100	Mullion type, stormproof	1 Shee	28	.286	S.F.	61	20		81	97
3200	Stormproof		28	.286		61	20		81	97
3300	Vertical line		28	.286		72	20		92	110
3500	For damper to use with above, add					50%	30%			
3520	Motor, for damper, electric or pneumatic	1 Shee	14	.571	Ea.	705	40		745	835
4000	Operating, 45°, manual, electric or pneumatic		24	.333	S.F.	81.50	23.50		105	125
4100	Motor, for electric or pneumatic		14	.571	Ea.	705	40		745	835
4200	Penthouse, roof		56	.143	S.F.	36	10		46	54.50
4300	Walls		40	.200		85	14.05		99.05	115
5000	Thinline, under 4" thick, fixed blade		40	.200		35	14.05		49.05	59.50
5010	Finishes, applied by mfr. at additional cost, available in colors									

23 37 Air Outlets and Inlets

23 37 15 – Air Outlets and Inlets, HVAC Louvers

23 37 15.40 HVAC Louvers		Crew	Daily Output	Labor-Hours	Unit	Material	2023 Bare Costs Labor	Equipment	Total	Total Incl O&P
5020	Prime coat only, add				S.F.	4.84			4.84	5.30
5040	Baked enamel finish coating, add					8.90			8.90	9.80
5060	Anodized finish, add					9.65			9.65	10.65
5080	Duranodic finish, add					17.55			17.55	19.35
5100	Fluoropolymer finish coating, add					27.50			27.50	30.50
9000	Stainless steel, fixed blade, continuous line									
9010	Hospital grade									
9110	20 ga.		1 Shee	22	.364	S.F.	60	25.50		85.50	105
9980	For small orders (under 10 pieces), add					"	25%				

23 37 23 – HVAC Gravity Ventilators

23 37 23.10 HVAC Gravity Air Ventilators

		Crew	Daily Output	Labor-Hours	Unit	Material	Labor	Equipment	Total	Total Incl O&P
0010	**HVAC GRAVITY AIR VENTILATORS**, Includes base									
1280	Rotary ventilators, wind driven, galvanized									
1300	4" neck diameter	Q-9	20	.800	Ea.	108	50.50		158.50	195
1320	5" neck diameter		18	.889		75.50	56		131.50	168
1340	6" neck diameter		16	1		109	63		172	215
1360	8" neck diameter		14	1.143		119	72		191	240
1380	10" neck diameter		12	1.333		139	84		223	280
1400	12" neck diameter		10	1.600		164	101		265	330
1420	14" neck diameter		10	1.600		249	101		350	425
1440	16" neck diameter		9	1.778		295	112		407	495
1460	18" neck diameter		9	1.778		350	112		462	555
1480	20" neck diameter		8	2		360	126		486	585
1500	24" neck diameter		8	2		570	126		696	815
1520	30" neck diameter		7	2.286		505	144		649	770
1540	36" neck diameter		6	2.667		805	168		973	1,150
1600	For aluminum, add					30%				
2000	Stationary, gravity, syphon, galvanized									
2100	3" neck diameter, 40 CFM	Q-9	24	.667	Ea.	82	42		124	154
2120	4" neck diameter, 50 CFM		20	.800		87	50.50		137.50	172
2140	5" neck diameter, 58 CFM		18	.889		92	56		148	186
2160	6" neck diameter, 66 CFM		16	1		96	63		159	201
2180	7" neck diameter, 86 CFM		15	1.067		109	67.50		176.50	221
2200	8" neck diameter, 110 CFM		14	1.143		124	72		196	245
2220	10" neck diameter, 140 CFM		12	1.333		157	84		241	300
2240	12" neck diameter, 160 CFM		10	1.600		198	101		299	370
2260	14" neck diameter, 250 CFM		10	1.600		320	101		421	500
2280	16" neck diameter, 380 CFM		9	1.778		360	112		472	565
2300	18" neck diameter, 500 CFM		9	1.778		400	112		512	610
2320	20" neck diameter, 625 CFM		8	2		490	126		616	725
2340	24" neck diameter, 900 CFM		8	2		640	126		766	890
2360	30" neck diameter, 1,375 CFM		7	2.286		450	144		594	710
2380	36" neck diameter, 2,000 CFM		6	2.667		650	168		818	970
2400	42" neck diameter, 3,000 CFM		4	4		955	253		1,208	1,425
2410	48" neck diameter, 4,000 CFM		3	5.333		1,575	335		1,910	2,225
2500	For aluminum, add					30%				
2520	For stainless steel, add					60%				
2530	For copper, add					100%				
3000	Rotating chimney cap, galvanized, 4" neck diameter	Q-9	20	.800		65	50.50		115.50	148
3020	5" neck diameter		18	.889		66	56		122	157
3040	6" neck diameter		16	1		69	63		132	171
3060	7" neck diameter		15	1.067		85	67.50		152.50	195

23 37 Air Outlets and Inlets

23 37 23 – HVAC Gravity Ventilators

23 37 23.10 HVAC Gravity Air Ventilators

		Crew	Daily Output	Labor-Hours	Unit	Material	2023 Bare Costs Labor	Equipment	Total	Total Incl O&P
3080	8" neck diameter	Q-9	14	1.143	Ea.	89	72		161	207
3100	10" neck diameter		12	1.333		175	84		259	320
3600	Stationary chimney rain cap, galvanized, 3" neck diameter		24	.667		22	42		64	87.50
3620	4" neck diameter		20	.800		24	50.50		74.50	103
3640	6" neck diameter		16	1		28	63		91	126
3680	8" neck diameter		14	1.143		35	72		107	148
3700	10" neck diameter		12	1.333		42	84		126	173
3720	12" neck diameter		10	1.600		49	101		150	206
3740	14" neck diameter		10	1.600		28	101		129	183
3760	16" neck diameter		9	1.778		29.50	112		141.50	202
3770	18" neck diameter		9	1.778		46.50	112		158.50	221
3780	20" neck diameter		8	2		62.50	126		188.50	259
3790	24" neck diameter		8	2		79.50	126		205.50	277
4200	Stationary mushroom, aluminum, 16" orifice diameter		10	1.600		1,000	101		1,101	1,250
4220	26" orifice diameter		6.15	2.602		1,500	164		1,664	1,900
4230	30" orifice diameter		5.71	2.802		2,175	177		2,352	2,675
4240	38" orifice diameter		5	3.200		3,125	202		3,327	3,725
4250	42" orifice diameter		4.70	3.404		4,150	215		4,365	4,875
4260	50" orifice diameter		4.44	3.604		4,925	228		5,153	5,775
5000	Relief vent									
5500	Rectangular, aluminum, galvanized curb									
5510	intake/exhaust, 0.033" SP									
5580	500 CFM, 12" x 12"	Q-9	8.60	1.860	Ea.	1,125	117		1,242	1,400
5600	600 CFM, 12" x 16"		8	2		1,250	126		1,376	1,575
5620	750 CFM, 12" x 20"		7.20	2.222		1,325	140		1,465	1,650
5640	1,000 CFM, 12" x 24"		6.60	2.424		1,400	153		1,553	1,750
5660	1,500 CFM, 12" x 36"		5.80	2.759		1,900	174		2,074	2,325
5680	3,000 CFM, 20" x 42"		4	4		2,450	253		2,703	3,075
5700	5,000 CFM, 20" x 72"		3	5.333		3,525	335		3,860	4,375
5720	6,000 CFM, 24" x 72"		2.30	6.957		3,825	440		4,265	4,850
5740	10,000 CFM, 48" x 60"		1.80	8.889		4,800	560		5,360	6,150
5760	12,000 CFM, 48" x 72"		1.60	10		5,300	630		5,930	6,775
5780	13,750 CFM, 60" x 66"		1.40	11.429		5,850	720		6,570	7,525
5800	15,000 CFM, 60" x 72"		1.30	12.308		6,275	775		7,050	8,075
5820	18,000 CFM, 72" x 72"		1.20	13.333		7,100	840		7,940	9,075
5880	Size is throat area, volume is at 500 fpm									
7000	Note: sizes based on exhaust. Intake, with 0.125" SP									
7100	loss, approximately twice listed capacity.									

23 38 Ventilation Hoods

23 38 13 – Commercial-Kitchen Hoods

23 38 13.10 Hood and Ventilation Equipment

		Crew	Daily Output	Labor-Hours	Unit	Material	2023 Bare Costs Labor	Equipment	Total	Total Incl O&P
0010	**HOOD AND VENTILATION EQUIPMENT**									
2970	Exhaust hood, sst, gutter on all sides, 4' x 4' x 2'	1 Carp	1.80	4.444	Ea.	2,825	260		3,085	3,525
2980	4' x 4' x 7'	"	1.60	5		2,450	293		2,743	3,125
7800	Vent hood, wall canopy with fire protection, 30"	L-3A	9	1.333		112	85		197	250
7810	Without fire protection, 36"		10	1.200		98.50	76.50		175	222
7820	Island canopy with fire protection, 30"		7	1.714		780	109		889	1,025
7830	Without fire protection, 36"		8	1.500		800	95.50		895.50	1,025
7840	Back shelf with fire protection, 30"		11	1.091		415	69.50		484.50	560
7850	Without fire protection, black, 36"		12	1		475	64		539	620

23 38 Ventilation Hoods

23 38 13 – Commercial-Kitchen Hoods

23 38 13.10 Hood and Ventilation Equipment

		Crew	Daily Output	Labor-Hours	Unit	Material	2023 Bare Costs Labor	2023 Bare Costs Equipment	Total	Total Incl O&P
7852	Without fire protection, stainless steel, 36"	L-3A	12	1	Ea.	480	64		544	625
7860	Range hood & CO_2 system, 30"	1 Carp	2.50	3.200		4,875	188		5,063	5,625
7950	Hood fire protection system, electric stove	Q-1	3	5.333		2,000	345		2,345	2,725
7952	Hood fire protection system, gas stove	"	3	5.333		2,400	345		2,745	3,175

23 38 13.20 Kitchen Ventilation

		Crew	Daily Output	Labor-Hours	Unit	Material	Labor	Equipment	Total	Total Incl O&P
0010	**KITCHEN VENTILATION**, Commercial									
6000	Exhaust hoods and fans									
6100	Centrifugal grease extraction									
6110	Water wash type									
6120	Per foot of length	Q-10	7.10	3.380	L.F.	1,975	221		2,196	2,500
6200	Non water wash type									
6210	Per foot of length	Q-10	13.40	1.791	L.F.	1,450	117		1,567	1,775
6400	Island style ventilator									
6410	Water wash type									
6420	Per foot of length	Q-10	7.10	3.380	L.F.	2,625	221		2,846	3,225
6460	Non water wash type									
6470	Per foot of length	Q-10	13.40	1.791	L.F.	885	117		1,002	1,150

23 41 Particulate Air Filtration

23 41 13 – Panel Air Filters

23 41 13.10 Panel Type Air Filters

			Crew	Daily Output	Labor-Hours	Unit	Material	Labor	Equipment	Total	Total Incl O&P
0010	**PANEL TYPE AIR FILTERS**										
2950	Mechanical media filtration units										
3000	High efficiency type, with frame, non-supported	G				MCFM	33			33	36
3100	Supported type	G				"	47.50			47.50	52
5500	Throwaway glass or paper media type, 12" x 36" x 1"					Ea.	2.30			2.30	2.53

23 41 16 – Renewable-Media Air Filters

23 41 16.10 Disposable Media Air Filters

		Crew	Daily Output	Labor-Hours	Unit	Material	Labor	Equipment	Total	Total Incl O&P
0010	**DISPOSABLE MEDIA AIR FILTERS**									
5000	Renewable disposable roll				C.S.F.	5.10			5.10	5.60
5800	Filter, bag type									
5810	90-95% efficiency									
5820	24" x 12" x 29", 0.75-1.25 MCFM	1 Shee	1.90	4.211	Ea.	61	295		356	510
5830	24" x 24" x 29", 1.5-2.5 MCFM	"	1.90	4.211	"	98	295		393	555
5850	80-85% efficiency									
5860	24" x 12" x 29", 0.75-1.25 MCFM	1 Shee	1.90	4.211	Ea.	54	295		349	505
5870	24" x 24" x 29", 1.5-2.5 MCFM	"	1.90	4.211	"	94	295		389	550

23 41 19 – Washable Air Filters

23 41 19.10 Permanent Air Filters

			Crew	Daily Output	Labor-Hours	Unit	Material	Labor	Equipment	Total	Total Incl O&P
0010	**PERMANENT AIR FILTERS**										
4500	Permanent washable	G				MCFM	24.50			24.50	27

23 41 23 – Extended Surface Filters

23 41 23.10 Expanded Surface Filters

			Crew	Daily Output	Labor-Hours	Unit	Material	Labor	Equipment	Total	Total Incl O&P
0010	**EXPANDED SURFACE FILTERS**										
4000	Medium efficiency, extended surface	G				MCFM	5.75			5.75	6.30

23 41 Particulate Air Filtration

23 41 33 – High-Efficiency Particulate Filtration

23 41 33.10 HEPA Filters

		Crew	Daily Output	Labor-Hours	Unit	Material	2023 Bare Costs Labor	2023 Bare Costs Equipment	Total	Total Incl O&P
0010	**HEPA FILTERS**									
6000	HEPA filter complete w/particle board,									
6010	kraft paper frame, separator material									
6020	95% DOP efficiency									
6030	12" x 12" x 6", 150 CFM	1 Shee	3.70	2.162	Ea.	44	152		196	277
6034	24" x 12" x 6", 375 CFM		1.90	4.211		73	295		368	525
6038	24" x 18" x 6", 450 CFM		1.90	4.211		89.50	295		384.50	545
6042	24" x 24" x 6", 700 CFM		1.90	4.211		101	295		396	555
6046	12" x 12" x 12", 250 CFM		3.70	2.162		74	152		226	310
6050	24" x 12" x 12", 500 CFM		1.90	4.211		104	295		399	560
6054	24" x 18" x 12", 875 CFM		1.90	4.211		146	295		441	605
6058	24" x 24" x 12", 1,000 CFM		1.90	4.211		157	295		452	615
6100	99% DOP efficiency									
6110	12" x 12" x 6", 150 CFM	1 Shee	3.70	2.162	Ea.	45.50	152		197.50	279
6114	24" x 12" x 6", 325 CFM		1.90	4.211		76	295		371	530
6118	24" x 18" x 6", 550 CFM		1.90	4.211		92.50	295		387.50	545
6122	24" x 24" x 6", 775 CFM		1.90	4.211		105	295		400	560
6124	24" x 48" x 6", 775 CFM		1.30	6.154		205	430		635	875
6126	12" x 12" x 12", 250 CFM		3.60	2.222		76.50	156		232.50	320
6130	24" x 12" x 12", 500 CFM		1.90	4.211		108	295		403	565
6134	24" x 18" x 12", 775 CFM		1.90	4.211		151	295		446	610
6138	24" x 24" x 12", 1,100 CFM		1.90	4.211		163	295		458	625
6500	HEPA filter housing, 14 ga. galv. sheet metal									
6510	12" x 12" x 6"	1 Shee	2.50	3.200	Ea.	655	224		879	1,075
6514	24" x 12" x 6"		2	4		735	281		1,016	1,225
6518	12" x 12" x 12"		2.40	3.333		655	234		889	1,075
6522	14" x 12" x 12"		2.30	3.478		655	244		899	1,100
6526	24" x 18" x 6"		1.90	4.211		935	295		1,230	1,475
6530	24" x 24" x 6"		1.80	4.444		850	310		1,160	1,400
6534	24" x 48" x 6"		1.70	4.706		1,150	330		1,480	1,750
6538	24" x 72" x 6"		1.60	5		1,450	350		1,800	2,125
6542	24" x 18" x 12"		1.80	4.444		935	310		1,245	1,500
6546	24" x 24" x 12"		1.70	4.706		1,050	330		1,380	1,650
6550	24" x 48" x 12"		1.60	5		1,225	350		1,575	1,875
6554	24" x 72" x 12"		1.50	5.333		1,525	375		1,900	2,250
6558	48" x 48" x 6"	Q-9	2.80	5.714		1,675	360		2,035	2,400
6562	48" x 72" x 6"		2.60	6.154		2,025	390		2,415	2,800
6566	48" x 96" x 6"		2.40	6.667		2,550	420		2,970	3,425
6570	48" x 48" x 12"		2.70	5.926		1,675	375		2,050	2,425
6574	48" x 72" x 12"		2.50	6.400		2,025	405		2,430	2,825
6578	48" x 96" x 12"		2.30	6.957		2,550	440		2,990	3,450
6582	114" x 72" x 12"		2	8		3,525	505		4,030	4,625

23 42 Gas-Phase Air Filtration

23 42 13 – Activated-Carbon Air Filtration

23 42 13.10 Charcoal Type Air Filtration

		Crew	Daily Output	Labor-Hours	Unit	Material	2023 Bare Costs Labor	2023 Bare Costs Equipment	Total	Total Incl O&P
0010	**CHARCOAL TYPE AIR FILTRATION**									
0050	Activated charcoal type, full flow				MCFM	640			640	700
0060	Full flow, impregnated media 12" deep					220			220	242
0070	HEPA filter & frame for field erection					495			495	545
0080	HEPA filter-diffuser, ceiling install.				▼	325			325	355

23 43 Electronic Air Cleaners

23 43 13 – Washable Electronic Air Cleaners

23 43 13.10 Electronic Air Cleaners

		Crew	Daily Output	Labor-Hours	Unit	Material	Labor	Equipment	Total	Total Incl O&P
0010	**ELECTRONIC AIR CLEANERS**									
2000	Electronic air cleaner, duct mounted									
2150	1,000 CFM	1 Shee	4	2	Ea.	430	140		570	685
2200	1,200 CFM		3.80	2.105		595	148		743	880
2250	1,400 CFM		3.60	2.222		600	156		756	895
2260	2,000 CFM	▼	3.20	2.500	▼	570	175		745	890

23 51 Breechings, Chimneys, and Stacks

23 51 13 – Draft Control Devices

23 51 13.13 Draft-Induction Fans

		Crew	Daily Output	Labor-Hours	Unit	Material	Labor	Equipment	Total	Total Incl O&P
0010	**DRAFT-INDUCTION FANS**									
1000	Breeching installation									
1800	Hot gas, 600°F, variable pitch pulley and motor									
1840	6" diam. inlet, 1/4 HP, 1 phase, 400 CFM	Q-9	6	2.667	Ea.	2,550	168		2,718	3,050
1860	8" diam. inlet, 1/4 HP, 1 phase, 1,120 CFM		4	4		3,350	253		3,603	4,050
1870	9" diam. inlet, 3/4 HP, 1 phase, 1,440 CFM		3.60	4.444		4,100	281		4,381	4,925
1880	10" diam. inlet, 3/4 HP, 1 phase, 2,000 CFM		3.30	4.848		4,150	305		4,455	5,000
1900	12" diam. inlet, 3/4 HP, 3 phase, 2,960 CFM		3	5.333		4,550	335		4,885	5,525
1910	14" diam. inlet, 1 HP, 3 phase, 4,160 CFM		2.60	6.154		3,775	390		4,165	4,725
1920	16" diam. inlet, 2 HP, 3 phase, 5,500 CFM		2.30	6.957		5,100	440		5,540	6,275
1950	20" diam. inlet, 3 HP, 3 phase, 9,760 CFM		1.50	10.667		7,350	675		8,025	9,125
1960	22" diam. inlet, 5 HP, 3 phase, 13,360 CFM		1	16		10,900	1,000		11,900	13,500
1980	24" diam. inlet, 7-1/2 HP, 3 phase, 17,760 CFM	▼	.80	20	▼	13,300	1,275		14,575	16,500
2300	For multi-blade damper at fan inlet, add					20%				
3600	Chimney-top installation									
3700	6" size	1 Shee	8	1	Ea.	1,800	70		1,870	2,075
3740	8" size		7	1.143		1,975	80		2,055	2,300
3750	10" size		6.50	1.231		2,575	86.50		2,661.50	2,950
3780	13" size	▼	6	1.333		2,650	93.50		2,743.50	3,050
3880	For speed control switch, add					150			150	165
3920	For thermal fan control, add				▼	183			183	201
5500	Flue blade style damper for draft control,									
5510	locking quadrant blade									
5550	8" size	Q-9	8	2	Ea.	625	126		751	880
5560	9" size		7.50	2.133		705	135		840	980
5570	10" size		7	2.286		685	144		829	970
5580	12" size		6.50	2.462		710	155		865	1,025
5590	14" size		6	2.667		700	168		868	1,025
5600	16" size		5.50	2.909		725	184		909	1,075
5610	18" size		5	3.200		755	202		957	1,150

23 51 Breechings, Chimneys, and Stacks

23 51 13 – Draft Control Devices

23 51 13.13 Draft-Induction Fans

		Crew	Daily Output	Labor-Hours	Unit	Material	2023 Bare Costs Labor	Equipment	Total	Total Incl O&P
5620	20" size	Q-9	4.50	3.556	Ea.	805	224		1,029	1,225
5630	22" size		4	4		815	253		1,068	1,275
5640	24" size		3.50	4.571		865	289		1,154	1,375
5650	27" size		3	5.333		905	335		1,240	1,500
5660	30" size		2.50	6.400		1,025	405		1,430	1,725
5670	32" size		2	8		1,075	505		1,580	1,925
5680	36" size	↓	1.50	10.667	↓	1,175	675		1,850	2,325

23 51 13.16 Vent Dampers

		Crew	Daily Output	Labor-Hours	Unit	Material	Labor	Equipment	Total	Total Incl O&P
0010	**VENT DAMPERS**									
5000	Vent damper, bi-metal, gas, 3" diameter	Q-9	24	.667	Ea.	97.50	42		139.50	171
5010	4" diameter		24	.667		73.50	42		115.50	145
5020	5" diameter		23	.696		97.50	44		141.50	173
5030	6" diameter		22	.727		73.50	46		119.50	150
5040	7" diameter		21	.762		75.50	48		123.50	156
5050	8" diameter	↓	20	.800	↓	81.50	50.50		132	166

23 51 13.19 Barometric Dampers

		Crew	Daily Output	Labor-Hours	Unit	Material	Labor	Equipment	Total	Total Incl O&P
0010	**BAROMETRIC DAMPERS**									
1000	Barometric, gas fired system only, 6" size for 5" and 6" pipes	1 Shee	20	.400	Ea.	148	28		176	206
1020	7" size, for 6" and 7" pipes		19	.421		158	29.50		187.50	219
1040	8" size, for 7" and 8" pipes		18	.444		205	31		236	272
1060	9" size, for 8" and 9" pipes	↓	16	.500	↓	230	35		265	305
2000	All fuel, oil, oil/gas, coal									
2020	10" for 9" and 10" pipes	1 Shee	15	.533	Ea.	345	37.50		382.50	430
2040	12" for 11" and 12" pipes		15	.533		450	37.50		487.50	545
2060	14" for 13" and 14" pipes		14	.571		580	40		620	700
2080	16" for 15" and 16" pipes		13	.615		815	43		858	960
2100	18" for 17" and 18" pipes		12	.667		1,075	47		1,122	1,275
2120	20" for 19" and 21" pipes	↓	10	.800		1,300	56		1,356	1,500
2140	24" for 22" and 25" pipes	Q-9	12	1.333		1,575	84		1,659	1,875
2160	28" for 26" and 30" pipes		10	1.600		1,975	101		2,076	2,300
2180	32" for 31" and 34" pipes	↓	8	2		2,525	126		2,651	2,975
3260	For thermal switch for above, add	1 Shee	24	.333	↓	134	23.50		157.50	183

23 51 23 – Gas Vents

23 51 23.10 Gas Chimney Vents

		Crew	Daily Output	Labor-Hours	Unit	Material	Labor	Equipment	Total	Total Incl O&P
0010	**GAS CHIMNEY VENTS**, Prefab metal, UL listed									
0020	Gas, double wall, galvanized steel									
0080	3" diameter	Q-9	72	.222	V.L.F.	10.90	14.05		24.95	33
0100	4" diameter		68	.235		13.50	14.85		28.35	37.50
0120	5" diameter		64	.250		15.30	15.80		31.10	41
0140	6" diameter		60	.267		18.25	16.85		35.10	45.50
0160	7" diameter		56	.286		35	18.05		53.05	65.50
0180	8" diameter		52	.308		37	19.40		56.40	70.50
0200	10" diameter		48	.333		71	21		92	110
0220	12" diameter		44	.364		84.50	23		107.50	128
0240	14" diameter		42	.381		141	24		165	191
0260	16" diameter		40	.400		203	25.50		228.50	261
0280	18" diameter	↓	38	.421		250	26.50		276.50	315
0300	20" diameter	Q-10	36	.667		295	43.50		338.50	390
0320	22" diameter		34	.706		375	46		421	480
0340	24" diameter	↓	32	.750	↓	465	49		514	585
0600	For 4", 5" and 6" oval, add					50%				
0650	Gas, double wall, galvanized steel, fittings									

23 51 Breechings, Chimneys, and Stacks

23 51 23 – Gas Vents

23 51 23.10 Gas Chimney Vents		Crew	Daily Output	Labor-Hours	Unit	Material	2023 Bare Costs Labor	Equipment	Total	Total Incl O&P
0660	Elbow 45°, 3" diameter	Q-9	36	.444	Ea.	19.25	28		47.25	63.50
0670	4" diameter		34	.471		23	29.50		52.50	70.50
0680	5" diameter		32	.500		27	31.50		58.50	77.50
0690	6" diameter		30	.533		33.50	33.50		67	87.50
0700	7" diameter		28	.571		53.50	36		89.50	114
0710	8" diameter		26	.615		71.50	39		110.50	137
0720	10" diameter		24	.667		152	42		194	231
0730	12" diameter		22	.727		162	46		208	247
0740	14" diameter		21	.762		254	48		302	355
0750	16" diameter		20	.800		330	50.50		380.50	440
0760	18" diameter		19	.842		435	53		488	555
0770	20" diameter	Q-10	18	1.333		485	87.50		572.50	660
0780	22" diameter		17	1.412		775	92.50		867.50	990
0790	24" diameter		16	1.500		985	98		1,083	1,225
0916	Adjustable length									
0918	3" diameter, to 12"	Q-9	36	.444	Ea.	24.50	28		52.50	69.50
0920	4" diameter, to 12"		34	.471		28.50	29.50		58	76.50
0924	6" diameter, to 12"		30	.533		36.50	33.50		70	91
0928	8" diameter, to 12"		26	.615		69	39		108	134
0930	10" diameter, to 18"		24	.667		212	42		254	297
0932	12" diameter, to 18"		22	.727		215	46		261	305
0936	16" diameter, to 18"		20	.800		435	50.50		485.50	555
0938	18" diameter, to 18"		19	.842		500	53		553	630
0944	24" diameter, to 18"	Q-10	16	1.500		950	98		1,048	1,200
0950	Elbow 90°, adjustable, 3" diameter	Q-9	36	.444		32.50	28		60.50	78.50
0960	4" diameter		34	.471		38.50	29.50		68	87
0970	5" diameter		32	.500		45.50	31.50		77	98
0980	6" diameter		30	.533		55.50	33.50		89	112
0990	7" diameter		28	.571		95.50	36		131.50	160
1010	8" diameter		26	.615		97	39		136	166
1020	Wall thimble, 4 to 7" adjustable, 3" diameter		36	.444		20.50	28		48.50	65
1022	4" diameter		34	.471		23	29.50		52.50	70.50
1024	5" diameter		32	.500		28	31.50		59.50	78.50
1026	6" diameter		30	.533		29	33.50		62.50	82
1028	7" diameter		28	.571		59.50	36		95.50	120
1030	8" diameter		26	.615		73.50	39		112.50	140
1040	Roof flashing, 3" diameter		36	.444		11.30	28		39.30	55
1050	4" diameter		34	.471		13.10	29.50		42.60	59.50
1060	5" diameter		32	.500		32.50	31.50		64	83
1070	6" diameter		30	.533		31	33.50		64.50	85
1080	7" diameter		28	.571		41.50	36		77.50	100
1090	8" diameter		26	.615		44	39		83	107
1100	10" diameter		24	.667		59.50	42		101.50	129
1110	12" diameter		22	.727		83.50	46		129.50	161
1120	14" diameter		20	.800		189	50.50		239.50	284
1130	16" diameter		18	.889		220	56		276	325
1140	18" diameter		16	1		310	63		373	440
1150	20" diameter	Q-10	18	1.333		415	87.50		502.50	585
1160	22" diameter		14	1.714		515	112		627	735
1170	24" diameter		12	2		600	131		731	850
1200	Tee, 3" diameter	Q-9	27	.593		50	37.50		87.50	112
1210	4" diameter		26	.615		54	39		93	118
1220	5" diameter		25	.640		57	40.50		97.50	124

23 51 Breechings, Chimneys, and Stacks

23 51 23 – Gas Vents

23 51 23.10 Gas Chimney Vents		Crew	Daily Output	Labor-Hours	Unit	Material	2023 Bare Costs Labor	Equipment	Total	Total Incl O&P
1230	6" diameter	Q-9	24	.667	Ea.	65	42		107	135
1240	7" diameter		23	.696		93	44		137	168
1250	8" diameter		22	.727		102	46		148	181
1260	10" diameter		21	.762		271	48		319	370
1270	12" diameter		20	.800		278	50.50		328.50	380
1280	14" diameter		18	.889		495	56		551	630
1290	16" diameter		16	1		735	63		798	905
1300	18" diameter		14	1.143		885	72		957	1,075
1310	20" diameter	Q-10	17	1.412		1,225	92.50		1,317.50	1,475
1320	22" diameter		13	1.846		1,550	121		1,671	1,900
1330	24" diameter		12	2		1,800	131		1,931	2,175
1460	Tee cap, 3" diameter	Q-9	45	.356		3.36	22.50		25.86	37.50
1470	4" diameter		42	.381		3.61	24		27.61	40
1480	5" diameter		40	.400		4.63	25.50		30.13	43
1490	6" diameter		37	.432		6.75	27.50		34.25	48.50
1500	7" diameter		35	.457		11.30	29		40.30	56
1510	8" diameter		34	.471		12.35	29.50		41.85	58.50
1520	10" diameter		32	.500		99.50	31.50		131	158
1530	12" diameter		30	.533		99.50	33.50		133	160
1540	14" diameter		28	.571		104	36		140	169
1550	16" diameter		25	.640		106	40.50		146.50	177
1560	18" diameter		24	.667		125	42		167	202
1570	20" diameter	Q-10	27	.889		141	58		199	244
1580	22" diameter		22	1.091		136	71.50		207.50	257
1590	24" diameter		21	1.143		160	75		235	289
1750	Top, 3" diameter	Q-9	46	.348		25.50	22		47.50	61
1760	4" diameter		44	.364		27	23		50	64
1770	5" diameter		42	.381		25	24		49	63.50
1780	6" diameter		40	.400		33.50	25.50		59	74.50
1790	7" diameter		38	.421		74	26.50		100.50	121
1800	8" diameter		36	.444		91	28		119	143
1810	10" diameter		34	.471		149	29.50		178.50	209
1820	12" diameter		32	.500		182	31.50		213.50	248
1830	14" diameter		30	.533		291	33.50		324.50	370
1840	16" diameter		28	.571		375	36		411	465
1850	18" diameter		26	.615		515	39		554	625
1860	20" diameter	Q-10	28	.857		780	56		836	945
1870	22" diameter		22	1.091		1,200	71.50		1,271.50	1,425
1880	24" diameter		20	1.200		1,500	78.50		1,578.50	1,775
1900	Gas, double wall, galvanized steel, oval									
1904	4" x 1'	Q-9	68	.235	V.L.F.	22	14.85		36.85	46.50
1906	5" x 1'		64	.250		138	15.80		153.80	176
1908	5"/6" x 1'		60	.267		53.50	16.85		70.35	84.50
1910	Oval fittings									
1912	Adjustable length									
1914	4" diameter to 12" long	Q-9	34	.471	Ea.	22.50	29.50		52	69.50
1916	5" diameter to 12" long		32	.500		29.50	31.50		61	80
1918	5"/6" diameter to 12" long		30	.533		33	33.50		66.50	86.50
1920	Elbow 45°									
1922	4"	Q-9	34	.471	Ea.	46.50	29.50		76	96
1924	5"		32	.500		93.50	31.50		125	151
1926	5"/6"		30	.533		95.50	33.50		129	156
1930	Elbow 45°, flat									

23 51 Breechings, Chimneys, and Stacks

23 51 23 – Gas Vents

23 51 23.10 Gas Chimney Vents

		Crew	Daily Output	Labor-Hours	Unit	Material	2023 Bare Costs Labor	2023 Bare Costs Equipment	Total	Total Incl O&P
1932	4"	Q-9	34	.471	Ea.	46.50	29.50		76	96
1934	5"		32	.500		93.50	31.50		125	151
1936	5"/6"	↓	30	.533	↓	95.50	33.50		129	156
1940	Top									
1942	4"	Q-9	44	.364	Ea.	41	23		64	79.50
1944	5"		42	.381		36.50	24		60.50	76
1946	5"/6"	↓	40	.400	↓	47	25.50		72.50	90
1950	Adjustable flashing									
1952	4"	Q-9	34	.471	Ea.	19.65	29.50		49.15	66.50
1954	5"		32	.500		57.50	31.50		89	111
1956	5"/6"	↓	30	.533	↓	62	33.50		95.50	119
1960	Tee									
1962	4"	Q-9	26	.615	Ea.	69	39		108	135
1964	5"		25	.640		141	40.50		181.50	216
1966	5"/6"	↓	24	.667	↓	144	42		186	222
1970	Tee with short snout									
1972	4"	Q-9	26	.615	Ea.	57.50	39		96.50	122

23 51 26 – All-Fuel Vent Chimneys

23 51 26.10 All-Fuel Vent Chimneys, Press. Tight, Dbl. Wall

		Crew	Daily Output	Labor-Hours	Unit	Material	Labor	Equipment	Total	Total Incl O&P
0010	**ALL-FUEL VENT CHIMNEYS, PRESSURE TIGHT, DOUBLE WALL**									
3200	All fuel, pressure tight, double wall, 1" insulation, UL listed, 1,400°F.									
3210	304 stainless steel liner, aluminized steel outer jacket									
3220	6" diameter	Q-9	60	.267	L.F.	86	16.85		102.85	121
3221	8" diameter		52	.308		106	19.40		125.40	147
3222	10" diameter		48	.333		145	21		166	192
3223	12" diameter		44	.364		90	23		113	134
3224	14" diameter		42	.381		274	24		298	335
3225	16" diameter		40	.400		123	25.50		148.50	173
3226	18" diameter	↓	38	.421		109	26.50		135.50	160
3227	20" diameter	Q-10	36	.667		158	43.50		201.50	239
3228	24" diameter		32	.750		196	49		245	290
3229	28" diameter		30	.800		225	52.50		277.50	325
3230	32" diameter		27	.889		262	58		320	375
3231	36" diameter		25	.960		274	63		337	395
3232	42" diameter		22	1.091		315	71.50		386.50	460
3233	48" diameter	↓	19	1.263	↓	365	82.50		447.50	525
3260	For 316 stainless steel liner, add					30%				
3280	All fuel, pressure tight, double wall fittings									
3284	304 stainless steel inner, aluminized steel jacket									
3288	Adjustable 20"/29" section									
3292	6" diameter	Q-9	30	.533	Ea.	225	33.50		258.50	298
3293	8" diameter		26	.615		254	39		293	340
3294	10" diameter		24	.667		290	42		332	385
3295	12" diameter		22	.727		325	46		371	425
3296	14" diameter		21	.762		280	48		328	385
3297	16" diameter		20	.800		375	50.50		425.50	485
3298	18" diameter	↓	19	.842		455	53		508	580
3299	20" diameter	Q-10	18	1.333		480	87.50		567.50	655
3300	24" diameter		16	1.500		615	98		713	825
3301	28" diameter		15	1.600		670	105		775	895
3302	32" diameter		14	1.714		800	112		912	1,050
3303	36" diameter		12	2		980	131		1,111	1,275

23 51 Breechings, Chimneys, and Stacks

23 51 26 – All-Fuel Vent Chimneys

	23 51 26.10 All-Fuel Vent Chimneys, Press. Tight, Dbl. Wall	Crew	Daily Output	Labor-Hours	Unit	Material	2023 Bare Costs Labor	Equipment	Total	Total Incl O&P
3304	42" diameter	Q-10	11	2.182	Ea.	1,050	143		1,193	1,375
3305	48" diameter	↓	10	2.400	↓	1,250	157		1,407	1,600
3350	Elbow 90° fixed									
3354	6" diameter	Q-9	30	.533	Ea.	460	33.50		493.50	555
3355	8" diameter		26	.615		520	39		559	630
3356	10" diameter		24	.667		590	42		632	710
3357	12" diameter		22	.727		665	46		711	805
3358	14" diameter		21	.762		755	48		803	905
3359	16" diameter		20	.800		855	50.50		905.50	1,025
3360	18" diameter	↓	19	.842		965	53		1,018	1,125
3361	20" diameter	Q-10	18	1.333		1,100	87.50		1,187.50	1,325
3362	24" diameter		16	1.500		1,400	98		1,498	1,675
3363	28" diameter		15	1.600		1,600	105		1,705	1,925
3364	32" diameter		14	1.714		2,175	112		2,287	2,550
3365	36" diameter		12	2		2,825	131		2,956	3,325
3366	42" diameter		11	2.182		3,375	143		3,518	3,950
3367	48" diameter	↓	10	2.400		3,975	157		4,132	4,575
3380	For 316 stainless steel liner, add				↓	30%				
3400	Elbow 45°									
3404	6" diameter	Q-9	30	.533	Ea.	231	33.50		264.50	305
3405	8" diameter		26	.615		276	39		315	365
3406	10" diameter		24	.667		296	42		338	390
3407	12" diameter		22	.727		335	46		381	440
3408	14" diameter		21	.762		405	48		453	520
3409	16" diameter		20	.800		455	50.50		505.50	575
3410	18" diameter	↓	19	.842		515	53		568	645
3411	20" diameter	Q-10	18	1.333		605	87.50		692.50	795
3412	24" diameter		16	1.500		775	98		873	1,000
3413	28" diameter		15	1.600		860	105		965	1,100
3414	32" diameter		14	1.714		1,150	112		1,262	1,450
3415	36" diameter		12	2		1,550	131		1,681	1,900
3416	42" diameter		11	2.182		1,825	143		1,968	2,225
3417	48" diameter	↓	10	2.400		2,000	157		2,157	2,425
3430	For 316 stainless steel liner, add				↓	30%				
3450	Tee 90°									
3454	6" diameter	Q-9	24	.667	Ea.	278	42		320	370
3455	8" diameter		22	.727		300	46		346	400
3456	10" diameter		21	.762		335	48		383	445
3457	12" diameter		20	.800		390	50.50		440.50	500
3458	14" diameter		18	.889		470	56		526	600
3459	16" diameter		16	1		535	63		598	680
3460	18" diameter	↓	14	1.143		625	72		697	800
3461	20" diameter	Q-10	17	1.412		705	92.50		797.50	915
3462	24" diameter		12	2		830	131		961	1,100
3463	28" diameter		11	2.182		1,100	143		1,243	1,425
3464	32" diameter		10	2.400		1,500	157		1,657	1,875
3465	36" diameter		9	2.667		1,275	175		1,450	1,675
3466	42" diameter		6	4		1,900	262		2,162	2,475
3467	48" diameter	↓	5	4.800		2,200	315		2,515	2,875
3480	For tee cap, add					35%	20%			
3500	For 316 stainless steel liner, add				↓	30%				
3520	Plate support, galvanized									
3524	6" diameter	Q-9	26	.615	Ea.	138	39		177	210

23 51 Breechings, Chimneys, and Stacks

23 51 26 – All-Fuel Vent Chimneys

	23 51 26.10 All-Fuel Vent Chimneys, Press. Tight, Dbl. Wall	Crew	Daily Output	Labor-Hours	Unit	Material	2023 Bare Costs Labor	Equipment	Total	Total Incl O&P
3525	8" diameter	Q-9	22	.727	Ea.	162	46		208	247
3526	10" diameter		20	.800		176	50.50		226.50	270
3527	12" diameter		18	.889		185	56		241	289
3528	14" diameter		17	.941		219	59.50		278.50	330
3529	16" diameter		16	1		232	63		295	350
3530	18" diameter		15	1.067		244	67.50		311.50	370
3531	20" diameter	Q-10	16	1.500		253	98		351	425
3532	24" diameter		14	1.714		264	112		376	460
3533	28" diameter		13	1.846		325	121		446	535
3534	32" diameter		12	2		390	131		521	625
3535	36" diameter		10	2.400		520	157		677	805
3536	42" diameter		9	2.667		585	175		760	905
3537	48" diameter		8	3		670	196		866	1,025
3570	Bellows, lined									
3574	6" diameter	Q-9	30	.533	Ea.	1,700	33.50		1,733.50	1,925
3575	8" diameter		26	.615		1,750	39		1,789	1,975
3576	10" diameter		24	.667		1,775	42		1,817	2,025
3577	12" diameter		22	.727		1,800	46		1,846	2,075
3578	14" diameter		21	.762		1,450	48		1,498	1,675
3579	16" diameter		20	.800		1,900	50.50		1,950.50	2,150
3580	18" diameter		19	.842		1,950	53		2,003	2,225
3581	20" diameter	Q-10	18	1.333		1,975	87.50		2,062.50	2,300
3582	24" diameter		16	1.500		2,125	98		2,223	2,500
3583	28" diameter		15	1.600		2,275	105		2,380	2,650
3584	32" diameter		14	1.714		2,550	112		2,662	2,975
3585	36" diameter		12	2		2,825	131		2,956	3,300
3586	42" diameter		11	2.182		3,175	143		3,318	3,700
3587	48" diameter		10	2.400		3,650	157		3,807	4,225
3590	For all 316 stainless steel construction, add					55%				
3600	Ventilated roof thimble, 304 stainless steel									
3620	6" diameter	Q-9	26	.615	Ea.	297	39		336	385
3624	8" diameter		22	.727		288	46		334	385
3625	10" diameter		20	.800		287	50.50		337.50	390
3626	12" diameter		18	.889		330	56		386	445
3627	14" diameter		17	.941		345	59.50		404.50	465
3628	16" diameter		16	1		380	63		443	515
3629	18" diameter		15	1.067		410	67.50		477.50	550
3630	20" diameter	Q-10	16	1.500		420	98		518	610
3631	24" diameter		14	1.714		465	112		577	680
3632	28" diameter		13	1.846		495	121		616	720
3633	32" diameter		12	2		535	131		666	785
3634	36" diameter		10	2.400		575	157		732	870
3635	42" diameter		9	2.667		650	175		825	980
3636	48" diameter		8	3		720	196		916	1,075
3650	For 316 stainless steel, add					30%				
3670	Exit cone, 316 stainless steel only									
3674	6" diameter	Q-9	46	.348	Ea.	218	22		240	273
3675	8" diameter		42	.381		223	24		247	281
3676	10" diameter		40	.400		221	25.50		246.50	281
3677	12" diameter		38	.421		251	26.50		277.50	315
3678	14" diameter		37	.432		248	27.50		275.50	315
3679	16" diameter		36	.444		275	28		303	350
3680	18" diameter		35	.457		335	29		364	410

23 51 Breechings, Chimneys, and Stacks

23 51 26 – All-Fuel Vent Chimneys

	23 51 26.10 All-Fuel Vent Chimneys, Press. Tight, Dbl. Wall	Crew	Daily Output	Labor-Hours	Unit	Material	2023 Bare Costs Labor	Equipment	Total	Total Incl O&P
3681	20" diameter	Q-10	28	.857	Ea.	400	56		456	525
3682	24" diameter		26	.923		535	60.50		595.50	680
3683	28" diameter		25	.960		705	63		768	870
3684	32" diameter		24	1		875	65.50		940.50	1,050
3685	36" diameter		22	1.091		1,050	71.50		1,121.50	1,250
3686	42" diameter		21	1.143		1,175	75		1,250	1,425
3687	48" diameter	▼	20	1.200	▼	1,375	78.50		1,453.50	1,625
3720	Roof guide, 304 stainless steel									
3724	6" diameter	Q-9	25	.640	Ea.	109	40.50		149.50	181
3725	8" diameter		21	.762		127	48		175	212
3726	10" diameter		19	.842		138	53		191	232
3727	12" diameter		17	.941		143	59.50		202.50	248
3728	14" diameter		16	1		167	63		230	279
3729	16" diameter		15	1.067		177	67.50		244.50	295
3730	18" diameter	▼	14	1.143		187	72		259	315
3731	20" diameter	Q-10	15	1.600		197	105		302	375
3732	24" diameter		13	1.846		206	121		327	410
3733	28" diameter		12	2		251	131		382	475
3734	32" diameter		11	2.182		310	143		453	555
3735	36" diameter		9	2.667		370	175		545	670
3736	42" diameter		8	3		435	196		631	770
3737	48" diameter	▼	7	3.429		495	224		719	885
3750	For 316 stainless steel, add				▼	30%				
3770	Rain cap with bird screen									
3774	6" diameter	Q-9	46	.348	Ea.	330	22		352	400
3775	8" diameter		42	.381		385	24		409	460
3776	10" diameter		40	.400		450	25.50		475.50	535
3777	12" diameter		38	.421		520	26.50		546.50	610
3778	14" diameter		37	.432		600	27.50		627.50	700
3779	16" diameter		36	.444		680	28		708	795
3780	18" diameter	▼	35	.457		775	29		804	895
3781	20" diameter	Q-10	28	.857		880	56		936	1,050
3782	24" diameter		26	.923		1,050	60.50		1,110.50	1,275
3783	28" diameter		25	.960		1,250	63		1,313	1,475
3784	32" diameter		24	1		1,425	65.50		1,490.50	1,650
3785	36" diameter		22	1.091		1,675	71.50		1,746.50	1,950
3786	42" diameter		21	1.143		2,025	75		2,100	2,350
3787	48" diameter	▼	20	1.200		2,300	78.50		2,378.50	2,650

	23 51 26.30 All-Fuel Vent Chimneys, Double Wall, St. Stl.	Crew	Daily Output	Labor-Hours	Unit	Material	2023 Bare Costs Labor	Equipment	Total	Total Incl O&P
0010	**ALL-FUEL VENT CHIMNEYS, DOUBLE WALL, STAINLESS STEEL**									
7780	All fuel, pressure tight, double wall, 4" insulation, UL listed, 1,400°F.									
7790	304 stainless steel liner, aluminized steel outer jacket									
7800	6" diameter	Q-9	60	.267	V.L.F.	60.50	16.85		77.35	92
7804	8" diameter		52	.308		88	19.40		107.40	126
7806	10" diameter		48	.333		100	21		121	142
7808	12" diameter		44	.364		117	23		140	164
7810	14" diameter	▼	42	.381		131	24		155	180
7880	For 316 stainless steel liner, add				L.F.	30%				
8000	All fuel, double wall, stainless steel fittings									
8010	Roof support, 6" diameter	Q-9	30	.533	Ea.	135	33.50		168.50	200
8030	8" diameter		26	.615		142	39		181	216
8040	10" diameter	▼	24	.667		170	42		212	251

23 51 Breechings, Chimneys, and Stacks

23 51 26 – All-Fuel Vent Chimneys

23 51 26.30 All-Fuel Vent Chimneys, Double Wall, St. Stl.

		Crew	Daily Output	Labor-Hours	Unit	Material	2023 Bare Costs Labor	Equipment	Total	Total Incl O&P
8050	12" diameter	Q-9	22	.727	Ea.	178	46		224	265
8060	14" diameter		21	.762		191	48		239	284
8100	Elbow 45°, 6" diameter		30	.533		276	33.50		309.50	355
8140	8" diameter		26	.615		315	39		354	405
8160	10" diameter		24	.667		380	42		422	485
8180	12" diameter		22	.727		410	46		456	520
8200	14" diameter		21	.762		475	48		523	595
8300	Insulated tee, 6" diameter		30	.533		350	33.50		383.50	430
8360	8" diameter		26	.615		365	39		404	460
8380	10" diameter		24	.667		390	42		432	495
8400	12" diameter		22	.727		475	46		521	595
8420	14" diameter		20	.800		560	50.50		610.50	690
8500	Boot tee, 6" diameter		28	.571		790	36		826	925
8520	8" diameter		24	.667		845	42		887	990
8530	10" diameter		22	.727		955	46		1,001	1,125
8540	12" diameter		20	.800		1,125	50.50		1,175.50	1,300
8550	14" diameter		18	.889		1,150	56		1,206	1,350
8600	Rain cap with bird screen, 6" diameter		30	.533		355	33.50		388.50	440
8640	8" diameter		26	.615		385	39		424	485
8660	10" diameter		24	.667		395	42		437	500
8680	12" diameter		22	.727		555	46		601	680
8700	14" diameter		21	.762		585	48		633	720
8800	Flat roof flashing, 6" diameter		30	.533		130	33.50		163.50	194
8840	8" diameter		26	.615		132	39		171	205
8860	10" diameter		24	.667		142	42		184	220
8880	12" diameter		22	.727		159	46		205	244
8900	14" diameter		21	.762		167	48		215	257

23 52 Heating Boilers

23 52 13 – Electric Boilers

23 52 13.10 Electric Boilers, ASME

			Crew	Daily Output	Labor-Hours	Unit	Material	Labor	Equipment	Total	Total Incl O&P
0010	**ELECTRIC BOILERS, ASME**, Standard controls and trim	R235000-30									
1000	Steam, 6 KW, 20.5 MBH		Q-19	1.20	20	Ea.	4,525	1,325		5,850	6,950
1040	9 KW, 30.7 MBH	D3020-102		1.20	20		4,350	1,325		5,675	6,750
1060	18 KW, 61.4 MBH			1.20	20		4,475	1,325		5,800	6,900
1080	24 KW, 81.8 MBH	D3020-104		1.10	21.818		5,175	1,450		6,625	7,850
1120	36 KW, 123 MBH			1.10	21.818		5,725	1,450		7,175	8,450
1160	60 KW, 205 MBH			1	24		7,175	1,575		8,750	10,200
1220	112 KW, 382 MBH			.75	32		9,950	2,100		12,050	14,100
1240	148 KW, 505 MBH			.65	36.923		10,300	2,425		12,725	15,000
1260	168 KW, 573 MBH			.60	40		21,400	2,650		24,050	27,500
1280	222 KW, 758 MBH			.55	43.636		25,000	2,875		27,875	31,800
1300	296 KW, 1,010 MBH			.45	53.333		26,500	3,525		30,025	34,400
1320	300 KW, 1,023 MBH			.40	60		26,400	3,950		30,350	34,900
1340	370 KW, 1,263 MBH			.35	68.571		29,200	4,525		33,725	38,900
1360	444 KW, 1,515 MBH			.30	80		31,300	5,275		36,575	42,300
1380	518 KW, 1,768 MBH		Q-21	.36	88.889		32,700	6,000		38,700	44,900
1400	592 KW, 2,020 MBH			.34	94.118		35,900	6,375		42,275	48,900
1420	666 KW, 2,273 MBH			.32	100		37,300	6,775		44,075	51,000
1460	740 KW, 2,526 MBH			.28	114		38,800	7,725		46,525	54,000
1480	814 KW, 2,778 MBH			.25	128		45,900	8,650		54,550	63,500

23 52 Heating Boilers

23 52 13 – Electric Boilers

23 52 13.10 Electric Boilers, ASME

		Crew	Daily Output	Labor-Hours	Unit	Material	2023 Bare Costs Labor	Equipment	Total	Total Incl O&P
1500	962 KW, 3,283 MBH	Q-21	.22	145	Ea.	45,500	9,825		55,325	64,500
1520	1,036 KW, 3,536 MBH		.20	160		47,600	10,800		58,400	68,500
1540	1,110 KW, 3,788 MBH		.19	168		50,500	11,400		61,900	72,500
1560	2,070 KW, 7,063 MBH		.18	178		69,000	12,000		81,000	94,000
1580	2,250 KW, 7,677 MBH		.17	188		81,000	12,700		93,700	108,000
1600	2,340 KW, 7,984 MBH		.16	200		103,500	13,500		117,000	133,500
2000	Hot water, 7.5 KW, 25.6 MBH	Q-19	1.30	18.462		5,150	1,225		6,375	7,500
2020	15 KW, 51.2 MBH		1.30	18.462		5,450	1,225		6,675	7,825
2040	30 KW, 102 MBH		1.20	20		5,550	1,325		6,875	8,075
2060	45 KW, 164 MBH		1.20	20		5,425	1,325		6,750	7,925
2070	60 KW, 205 MBH		1.20	20		5,800	1,325		7,125	8,350
2080	75 KW, 256 MBH		1.10	21.818		6,125	1,450		7,575	8,900
2100	90 KW, 307 MBH		1.10	21.818		6,175	1,450		7,625	8,925
2120	105 KW, 358 MBH		1	24		7,150	1,575		8,725	10,200
2140	120 KW, 410 MBH		.90	26.667		6,825	1,750		8,575	10,100
2160	135 KW, 461 MBH		.75	32		7,575	2,100		9,675	11,500
2180	150 KW, 512 MBH		.65	36.923		7,975	2,425		10,400	12,400
2200	165 KW, 563 MBH		.60	40		8,200	2,650		10,850	13,000
2220	296 KW, 1,010 MBH		.55	43.636		16,300	2,875		19,175	22,200
2280	370 KW, 1,263 MBH		.40	60		18,000	3,950		21,950	25,800
2300	444 KW, 1,515 MBH		.35	68.571		21,700	4,525		26,225	30,700
2340	518 KW, 1,768 MBH	Q-21	.44	72.727		24,000	4,925		28,925	33,700
2360	592 KW, 2,020 MBH		.43	74.419		26,300	5,025		31,325	36,500
2400	666 KW, 2,273 MBH		.40	80		28,500	5,400		33,900	39,500
2420	740 KW, 2,526 MBH		.39	82.051		28,700	5,550		34,250	39,900
2440	814 KW, 2,778 MBH		.38	84.211		30,900	5,700		36,600	42,500
2460	888 KW, 3,031 MBH		.37	86.486		33,400	5,850		39,250	45,500
2480	962 KW, 3,283 MBH		.36	88.889		35,400	6,000		41,400	47,900
2500	1,036 KW, 3,536 MBH		.34	94.118		36,600	6,375		42,975	49,700
2520	1,110 KW, 3,788 MBH		.33	96.970		39,900	6,550		46,450	53,500
2540	1,440 KW, 4,915 MBH		.32	100		44,300	6,775		51,075	59,000
2560	1,560 KW, 5,323 MBH		.31	103		50,500	6,975		57,475	66,000
2580	1,680 KW, 5,733 MBH		.30	107		54,000	7,225		61,225	70,000
2600	1,800 KW, 6,143 MBH		.29	110		57,500	7,475		64,975	74,500
2620	1,980 KW, 6,757 MBH		.28	114		60,500	7,725		68,225	78,000
2640	2,100 KW, 7,167 MBH		.27	119		69,000	8,025		77,025	88,000
2660	2,220 KW, 7,576 MBH		.26	123		70,000	8,325		78,325	89,500
2680	2,400 KW, 8,191 MBH		.25	128		73,000	8,650		81,650	93,000
2700	2,610 KW, 8,905 MBH		.24	133		77,000	9,025		86,025	98,000
2720	2,790 KW, 9,519 MBH		.23	139		81,000	9,400		90,400	103,000
2740	2,970 KW, 10,133 MBH		.21	152		83,000	10,300		93,300	106,500
2760	3,150 KW, 10,748 MBH		.19	168		80,000	11,400		91,400	105,000
2780	3,240 KW, 11,055 MBH		.18	178		82,000	12,000		94,000	108,000
2800	3,420 KW, 11,669 MBH		.17	188		95,500	12,700		108,200	124,000
2820	3,600 KW, 12,283 MBH		.16	200		100,500	13,500		114,000	130,500

23 52 16 – Condensing Boilers

23 52 16.24 Condensing Boilers

			Crew	Daily Output	Labor-Hours	Unit	Material	Labor	Equipment	Total	Total Incl O&P
0010	**CONDENSING BOILERS**, Cast iron, high efficiency										
0020	Packaged with standard controls, circulator and trim										
0030	Intermittent (spark) pilot, natural or LP gas										
0040	Hot water, DOE MBH output (AFUE %)										
0100	42 MBH (84.0%)	G	Q-5	1.80	8.889	Ea.	2,075	580		2,655	3,150

23 52 Heating Boilers

23 52 16 – Condensing Boilers

23 52 16.24 Condensing Boilers

			Crew	Daily Output	Labor-Hours	Unit	Material	2023 Bare Costs Labor	Equipment	Total	Total Incl O&P
0120	57 MBH (84.3%)	G	Q-5	1.60	10	Ea.	2,250	655		2,905	3,450
0140	85 MBH (84.0%)	G		1.40	11.429		2,525	745		3,270	3,900
0160	112 MBH (83.7%)	G		1.20	13.333		2,850	870		3,720	4,425
0180	140 MBH (83.3%)	G	Q-6	1.60	15		3,175	1,025		4,200	5,025
0200	167 MBH (83.0%)	G		1.40	17.143		3,900	1,150		5,050	6,025
0220	194 MBH (82.7%)	G		1.20	20		3,975	1,350		5,325	6,375

23 52 19 – Pulse Combustion Boilers

23 52 19.20 Pulse Type Combustion Boilers

			Crew	Daily Output	Labor-Hours	Unit	Material	Labor	Equipment	Total	Total Incl O&P
0010	**PULSE TYPE COMBUSTION BOILERS**, High efficiency										
7990	Special feature gas fired boilers										
8000	Pulse combustion, standard controls/trim										
8010	Hot water, DOE MBH output (AFUE %)										
8030	71 MBH (95.2%)		Q-5	1.60	10	Ea.	4,050	655		4,705	5,425
8050	94 MBH (95.3%)	G		1.40	11.429		4,475	745		5,220	6,050
8080	139 MBH (95.6%)	G		1.20	13.333		5,025	870		5,895	6,825
8090	207 MBH (95.4%)			1.16	13.793		5,675	900		6,575	7,600
8120	270 MBH (96.4%)			1.12	14.286		7,850	935		8,785	10,100
8130	365 MBH (91.7%)			1.07	14.953		8,875	975		9,850	11,200

23 52 23 – Cast-Iron Boilers

23 52 23.20 Gas-Fired Boilers

			Crew	Daily Output	Labor-Hours	Unit	Material	Labor	Equipment	Total	Total Incl O&P
0010	**GAS-FIRED BOILERS**, Natural or propane, standard controls, packaged R235000-10										
1000	Cast iron, with insulated jacket										
2000	Steam, gross output, 81 MBH R235000-20		Q-7	1.40	22.857	Ea.	3,150	1,575		4,725	5,825
2020	102 MBH			1.30	24.615		2,600	1,700		4,300	5,400
2040	122 MBH R235000-30			1	32		3,450	2,200		5,650	7,100
2060	163 MBH			.90	35.556		3,450	2,450		5,900	7,425
2080	203 MBH			.90	35.556		4,150	2,450		6,600	8,200
2100	240 MBH			.85	37.647		4,225	2,600		6,825	8,525
2120	280 MBH			.80	40		4,500	2,750		7,250	9,075
2140	320 MBH			.70	45.714		4,825	3,150		7,975	10,000
2160	360 MBH			.63	51.200		5,500	3,525		9,025	11,300
2180	400 MBH			.56	56.838		5,825	3,925		9,750	12,300
2200	440 MBH			.51	62.500		6,275	4,325		10,600	13,300
2220	544 MBH			.45	71.588		9,150	4,950		14,100	17,500
2240	765 MBH			.43	74.419		11,700	5,150		16,850	20,600
2260	892 MBH			.38	84.211		14,000	5,825		19,825	24,100
2280	1,275 MBH			.34	94.118		17,800	6,500		24,300	29,300
2300	1,530 MBH			.32	100		20,900	6,900		27,800	33,200
2320	1,875 MBH			.30	107		29,100	7,375		36,475	43,000
2340	2,170 MBH			.26	122		30,900	8,425		39,325	46,500
2360	2675 MBH			.20	163		26,700	11,300		38,000	46,200
2380	3,060 MBH			.19	172		28,400	11,900		40,300	48,900
2400	3,570 MBH			.18	182		40,400	12,600		53,000	63,000
2420	4,207 MBH			.16	205		44,200	14,200		58,400	69,500
2440	4,720 MBH			.15	208		61,500	14,300		75,800	89,500
2460	5,660 MBH			.15	221		72,000	15,200		87,200	102,000
2480	6,100 MBH			.13	246		87,000	17,000		104,000	121,500
2500	6,390 MBH			.12	267		90,500	18,400		108,900	127,500
2520	6,680 MBH			.11	291		93,000	20,100		113,100	132,500
2540	6,970 MBH			.10	320		97,000	22,100		119,100	139,500
3000	Hot water, gross output, 80 MBH			1.46	21.918		2,875	1,525		4,400	5,400
3020	100 MBH			1.35	23.704		2,800	1,625		4,425	5,550

23 52 Heating Boilers

23 52 23 – Cast-Iron Boilers

23 52 23.20 Gas-Fired Boilers

		Crew	Daily Output	Labor-Hours	Unit	Material	2023 Bare Costs Labor	Equipment	Total	Total Incl O&P
3040	122 MBH	Q-7	1.10	29.091	Ea.	3,050	2,000		5,050	6,350
3060	163 MBH		1	32		3,575	2,200		5,775	7,225
3080	203 MBH		1	32		4,175	2,200		6,375	7,875
3100	240 MBH		.95	33.684		4,275	2,325		6,600	8,200
3120	280 MBH		.90	35.556		3,875	2,450		6,325	7,925
3140	320 MBH		.80	40		4,250	2,750		7,000	8,800
3160	360 MBH		.71	45.070		4,825	3,100		7,925	9,975
3180	400 MBH		.64	50		5,175	3,450		8,625	10,800
3200	440 MBH		.58	54.983		5,550	3,800		9,350	11,800
3220	544 MBH		.51	62.992		8,725	4,350		13,075	16,100
3240	765 MBH		.46	70.022		11,200	4,825		16,025	19,500
3260	1,088 MBH		.40	80		14,700	5,525		20,225	24,500
3280	1,275 MBH		.36	89.888		17,300	6,200		23,500	28,300
3300	1,530 MBH		.31	105		20,500	7,250		27,750	33,300
3320	2,000 MBH		.26	125		25,300	8,625		33,925	40,700
3340	2,312 MBH		.22	148		29,300	10,200		39,500	47,500
3360	2,856 MBH		.20	160		30,800	11,000		41,800	50,500
3380	3,264 MBH		.18	180		32,700	12,400		45,100	54,500
3400	3,996 MBH		.16	195		35,800	13,500		49,300	59,500
3420	4,488 MBH		.15	211		35,000	14,500		49,500	60,000
3440	4,720 MBH		.15	221		69,500	15,200		84,700	99,000
3460	5,520 MBH		.14	229		113,000	15,800		128,800	148,000
3480	6,100 MBH		.13	250		119,500	17,300		136,800	157,000
3500	6,390 MBH		.11	286		99,500	19,700		119,200	139,000
3520	6,680 MBH		.10	311		118,000	21,500		139,500	161,500
3540	6,970 MBH		.09	360		129,500	24,800		154,300	179,000
7000	For tankless water heater, add					10%				
7050	For additional zone valves up to 312 MBH, add					200			200	220

23 52 23.30 Gas/Oil Fired Boilers

		Crew	Daily Output	Labor-Hours	Unit	Material	2023 Bare Costs Labor	Equipment	Total	Total Incl O&P
0010	**GAS/OIL FIRED BOILERS**, Combination with burners and controls, packaged									
1000	Cast iron with insulated jacket									
2000	Steam, gross output, 720 MBH	Q-7	.43	74.074	Ea.	16,200	5,125		21,325	25,400
2020	810 MBH		.38	83.990		16,200	5,800		22,000	26,500
2040	1,084 MBH		.34	93.023		18,600	6,425		25,025	30,000
2060	1,360 MBH		.33	98.160		21,100	6,775		27,875	33,300
2080	1,600 MBH		.30	107		20,000	7,400		27,400	33,100
2100	2,040 MBH		.25	130		23,600	8,975		32,575	39,400
2120	2,450 MBH		.21	156		24,800	10,800		35,600	43,400
2140	2,700 MBH		.19	166		26,300	11,400		37,700	46,000
2160	3,000 MBH		.18	176		28,500	12,100		40,600	49,500
2180	3,270 MBH		.17	184		36,100	12,700		48,800	58,500
2200	3,770 MBH		.17	192		74,000	13,200		87,200	101,000
2220	4,070 MBH		.16	200		78,000	13,800		91,800	106,000
2240	4,650 MBH		.15	211		82,000	14,500		96,500	112,000
2260	5,230 MBH		.14	224		91,000	15,500		106,500	123,000
2280	5,520 MBH		.14	235		99,000	16,200		115,200	133,000
2300	5,810 MBH		.13	248		101,000	17,100		118,100	136,500
2320	6,100 MBH		.12	260		102,500	18,000		120,500	139,500
2340	6,390 MBH		.11	296		106,000	20,500		126,500	147,500
2360	6,680 MBH		.10	320		104,500	22,100		126,600	148,000
2380	6,970 MBH		.09	372		112,500	25,700		138,200	162,500
2900	Hot water, gross output									

23 52 Heating Boilers

23 52 23 – Cast-Iron Boilers

23 52 23.30 Gas/Oil Fired Boilers

		Crew	Daily Output	Labor-Hours	Unit	Material	2023 Bare Costs Labor	Equipment	Total	Total Incl O&P
2910	200 MBH	Q-6	.62	39.024	Ea.	11,800	2,650		14,450	17,000
2920	300 MBH		.49	49.080		11,800	3,325		15,125	18,000
2930	400 MBH		.41	57.971		13,800	3,925		17,725	21,100
2940	500 MBH		.36	67.039		14,800	4,550		19,350	23,100
3000	584 MBH	Q-7	.44	72.072		14,900	4,975		19,875	23,800
3020	876 MBH		.41	79.012		21,700	5,450		27,150	32,000
3040	1,168 MBH		.31	104		28,700	7,175		35,875	42,300
3060	1,460 MBH		.28	113		30,900	7,800		38,700	45,600
3080	2,044 MBH		.26	122		41,900	8,425		50,325	58,500
3100	2,628 MBH		.21	150		49,100	10,400		59,500	69,500
3120	3,210 MBH		.18	175		54,000	12,100		66,100	77,500
3140	3,796 MBH		.17	186		60,500	12,800		73,300	85,500
3160	4,088 MBH		.16	195		69,000	13,500		82,500	96,000
3180	4,672 MBH		.16	204		75,000	14,100		89,100	103,500
3200	5,256 MBH		.15	218		85,500	15,000		100,500	116,500
3220	6,000 MBH, 179 BHP		.13	256		120,500	17,700		138,200	159,500
3240	7,130 MBH, 213 BHP		.08	386		126,500	26,600		153,100	178,500
3260	9,800 MBH, 286 BHP		.06	533		145,500	36,800		182,300	215,000
3280	10,900 MBH, 325.6 BHP		.05	593		176,500	40,900		217,400	255,000
3290	12,200 MBH, 364.5 BHP		.05	667		192,500	46,000		238,500	280,000
3300	13,500 MBH, 403.3 BHP		.04	727		213,000	50,000		263,000	309,500

23 52 23.40 Oil-Fired Boilers

		Crew	Daily Output	Labor-Hours	Unit	Material	2023 Bare Costs Labor	Equipment	Total	Total Incl O&P
0010	**OIL-FIRED BOILERS**, Standard controls, flame retention burner, packaged									
1000	Cast iron, with insulated flush jacket									
2000	Steam, gross output, 109 MBH	Q-7	1.20	26.667	Ea.	2,500	1,850		4,350	5,500
2020	144 MBH		1.10	29.091		2,800	2,000		4,800	6,075
2040	173 MBH		1	32		3,175	2,200		5,375	6,800
2060	207 MBH		.90	35.556		3,400	2,450		5,850	7,375
2080	236 MBH		.85	37.647		3,725	2,600		6,325	7,975
2100	300 MBH		.70	45.714		4,525	3,150		7,675	9,675
2120	480 MBH		.50	64		6,450	4,425		10,875	13,700
2140	665 MBH		.45	71.111		8,325	4,900		13,225	16,500
2160	794 MBH		.41	78.049		9,975	5,400		15,375	19,000
2180	1,084 MBH		.38	85.106		11,800	5,875		17,675	21,700
2200	1,360 MBH		.33	98.160		14,400	6,775		21,175	25,900
2220	1,600 MBH		.26	122		19,000	8,425		27,425	33,500
2240	2,175 MBH		.24	134		17,500	9,250		26,750	33,000
2260	2,480 MBH		.21	156		21,000	10,800		31,800	39,200
2280	3,000 MBH		.19	170		24,200	11,800		36,000	44,100
2300	3,550 MBH		.17	187		29,500	12,900		42,400	52,000
2320	3,820 MBH		.16	200		36,000	13,800		49,800	60,000
2340	4,360 MBH		.15	215		39,500	14,800		54,300	65,500
2360	4,940 MBH		.14	225		72,000	15,600		87,600	102,500
2380	5,520 MBH		.14	235		85,000	16,200		101,200	117,500
2400	6,100 MBH		.13	256		97,000	17,700		114,700	133,500
2420	6,390 MBH		.11	291		102,500	20,100		122,600	142,500
2440	6,680 MBH		.10	314		105,000	21,700		126,700	148,000
2460	6,970 MBH		.09	364		109,000	25,100		134,100	157,500
3000	Hot water, same price as steam									
4000	For tankless coil in smaller sizes, add				Ea.	15%				

23 52 Heating Boilers

23 52 23 – Cast-Iron Boilers

23 52 23.60 Solid-Fuel Boilers

		Crew	Daily Output	Labor-Hours	Unit	Material	2023 Bare Costs Labor	Equipment	Total	Total Incl O&P
0010	**SOLID-FUEL BOILERS**									
3000	Stoker fired (coal/wood/biomass) cast iron with flush jacket and									
3400	insulation, steam or water, gross output, 1,280 MBH	Q-6	.36	66.667	Ea.	174,000	4,525		178,525	198,000
3420	1,460 MBH		.30	80		180,500	5,425		185,925	206,500
3440	1,640 MBH		.28	85.714		193,500	5,800		199,300	221,500
3460	1,820 MBH		.26	92.308		209,500	6,250		215,750	239,500
3480	2,000 MBH		.25	96		226,000	6,500		232,500	258,000
3500	2,360 MBH		.23	104		221,000	7,075		228,075	253,500
3540	2,725 MBH	▼	.20	120		229,000	8,125		237,125	264,000
3800	2,950 MBH	Q-7	.16	200		246,000	13,800		259,800	291,000
3820	3,210 MBH		.15	213		259,500	14,700		274,200	307,000
3840	3,480 MBH		.14	229		261,500	15,800		277,300	311,000
3841	3,550 MBH		.14	229		261,500	15,800		277,300	311,000
3860	3,745 MBH		.14	229		259,500	15,800		275,300	309,000
3880	4,000 MBH		.13	246		262,000	17,000		279,000	313,500
3900	4,200 MBH		.13	246		264,500	17,000		281,500	316,500
3920	4,400 MBH		.12	267		266,500	18,400		284,900	321,000
3940	4,600 MBH	▼	.12	267		270,500	18,400		288,900	325,000

23 52 26 – Steel Boilers

23 52 26.40 Oil-Fired Boilers

		Crew	Daily Output	Labor-Hours	Unit	Material	Labor	Equipment	Total	Total Incl O&P
0010	**OIL-FIRED BOILERS**, Standard controls, flame retention burner									
5000	Steel, with insulated flush jacket									
7000	Hot water, gross output, 103 MBH	Q-6	1.60	15	Ea.	2,225	1,025		3,250	3,975
7020	122 MBH		1.45	16.506		2,125	1,125		3,250	4,000
7040	137 MBH		1.36	17.595		2,875	1,200		4,075	4,925
7060	168 MBH		1.30	18.405		2,800	1,250		4,050	4,950
7080	225 MBH		1.22	19.704		4,300	1,325		5,625	6,750
7100	315 MBH		.96	25.105		5,650	1,700		7,350	8,750
7120	420 MBH		.70	34.483		5,325	2,325		7,650	9,350
7140	525 MBH		.57	42.403		8,525	2,875		11,400	13,700
7180	735 MBH		.48	50.104		8,600	3,400		12,000	14,500
7220	1,050 MBH		.37	65.753		21,400	4,450		25,850	30,300
7280	2,310 MBH	▼	.21	115		35,900	7,775		43,675	51,000
7320	3,150 MBH		.13	185		43,100	12,500		55,600	66,000
7340	For tankless coil in steam or hot water, add					7%				

23 52 26.70 Packaged Water Tube Boilers

		Crew	Daily Output	Labor-Hours	Unit	Material	Labor	Equipment	Total	Total Incl O&P
0010	**PACKAGED WATER TUBE BOILERS**									
2000	Packaged water tube, #2 oil, steam or hot water, gross output									
2010	200 MBH	Q-6	1.50	16	Ea.	4,550	1,075		5,625	6,625
2014	275 MBH		1.40	17.143		5,075	1,150		6,225	7,300
2018	360 MBH		1.10	21.818		7,050	1,475		8,525	9,950
2022	520 MBH		.65	36.923		6,775	2,500		9,275	11,200
2026	600 MBH		.60	40		9,475	2,700		12,175	14,500
2030	720 MBH		.55	43.636		12,000	2,950		14,950	17,600
2034	960 MBH	▼	.48	50		14,800	3,375		18,175	21,400
2040	1,200 MBH	Q-7	.50	64		27,600	4,425		32,025	37,000
2044	1,440 MBH		.45	71.111		34,000	4,900		38,900	44,700
2060	1,600 MBH		.40	80		40,000	5,525		45,525	52,500
2068	1,920 MBH		.35	91.429		43,400	6,325		49,725	57,000
2072	2,160 MBH		.33	96.970		48,100	6,700		54,800	63,000
2080	2,400 MBH	▼	.30	107		54,000	7,375		61,375	70,500

23 52 Heating Boilers

23 52 26 – Steel Boilers

23 52 26.70 Packaged Water Tube Boilers

		Crew	Daily Output	Labor-Hours	Unit	Material	2023 Bare Costs Labor	Equipment	Total	Total Incl O&P
2100	3,200 MBH	Q-7	.25	128	Ea.	61,500	8,850		70,350	80,500
2120	4,800 MBH	▼	.20	160	▼	80,500	11,000		91,500	105,000
2200	Gas fired									
2204	200 MBH	Q-6	1.50	16	Ea.	8,200	1,075		9,275	10,700
2208	275 MBH		1.40	17.143		8,600	1,150		9,750	11,200
2212	360 MBH		1.10	21.818		8,900	1,475		10,375	12,000
2216	520 MBH		.65	36.923		9,300	2,500		11,800	13,900
2220	600 MBH		.60	40		11,900	2,700		14,600	17,200
2224	720 MBH		.55	43.636		11,100	2,950		14,050	16,600
2228	960 MBH	▼	.48	50		20,300	3,375		23,675	27,500
2232	1,220 MBH	Q-7	.50	64		18,700	4,425		23,125	27,100
2236	1,440 MBH		.45	71.111		22,300	4,900		27,200	31,900
2240	1,680 MBH		.40	80		37,200	5,525		42,725	49,200
2244	1,920 MBH		.35	91.429		33,000	6,325		39,325	45,700
2248	2,160 MBH		.33	96.970		38,100	6,700		44,800	52,000
2252	2,400 MBH	▼	.30	107	▼	42,800	7,375		50,175	58,000

23 52 28 – Swimming Pool Boilers

23 52 28.10 Swimming Pool Heaters

		Crew	Daily Output	Labor-Hours	Unit	Material	2023 Bare Costs Labor	Equipment	Total	Total Incl O&P
0010	**SWIMMING POOL HEATERS**, Not including wiring, external									
0020	piping, base or pad									
0160	Gas fired, input, 155 MBH	Q-6	1.50	16	Ea.	1,875	1,075		2,950	3,675
0200	199 MBH		1	24		2,025	1,625		3,650	4,650
0220	250 MBH		.70	34.286		2,200	2,325		4,525	5,850
0240	300 MBH		.60	40		2,300	2,700		5,000	6,575
0260	399 MBH		.50	48		2,575	3,250		5,825	7,675
0280	500 MBH		.40	60		7,375	4,075		11,450	14,200
0300	650 MBH		.35	68.571		7,850	4,650		12,500	15,600
0320	750 MBH		.33	72.727		8,575	4,925		13,500	16,800
0360	990 MBH		.22	109		11,500	7,400		18,900	23,700
0370	1,260 MBH		.21	114		17,600	7,750		25,350	30,900
0380	1,440 MBH		.19	126		19,500	8,550		28,050	34,300
0400	1,800 MBH		.14	171		20,900	11,600		32,500	40,300
0410	2,070 MBH	▼	.13	185		24,600	12,500		37,100	45,700
2000	Electric, 12 KW, 4,800 gallon pool	Q-19	3	8		2,450	530		2,980	3,475
2020	15 KW, 7,200 gallon pool		2.80	8.571		2,575	565		3,140	3,700
2040	24 KW, 9,600 gallon pool		2.40	10		3,300	660		3,960	4,625
2060	30 KW, 12,000 gallon pool		2	12		3,375	790		4,165	4,875
2080	36 KW, 14,400 gallon pool		1.60	15		3,925	990		4,915	5,800
2100	57 KW, 24,000 gallon pool	▼	1.20	20	▼	4,375	1,325		5,700	6,800
9000	To select pool heater: 12 BTUH x S.F. pool area									
9010	X temperature differential = required output									
9050	For electric, KW = gallons x 2.5 divided by 1,000									
9100	For family home type pool, double the									
9110	Rated gallon capacity = 1/2°F rise per hour									

23 52 39 – Fire-Tube Boilers

23 52 39.13 Scotch Marine Boilers

		Crew	Daily Output	Labor-Hours	Unit	Material	2023 Bare Costs Labor	Equipment	Total	Total Incl O&P
0010	**SCOTCH MARINE BOILERS**									
1000	Packaged fire tube, #2 oil, gross output									
1006	15 psi steam									
1010	1,005 MBH, 30 HP	Q-6	.33	72.072	Ea.	63,000	4,875		67,875	77,000
1014	1,675 MBH, 50 HP	"	.26	93.023		70,500	6,300		76,800	87,000
1020	3,348 MBH, 100 HP	Q-7	.21	152	▼	118,500	10,500		129,000	145,500

23 52 Heating Boilers

23 52 39 – Fire-Tube Boilers

23 52 39.13 Scotch Marine Boilers		Crew	Daily Output	Labor-Hours	Unit	Material	2023 Bare Costs Labor	Equipment	Total	Total Incl O&P
1030	5,025 MBH, 150 HP	Q-7	.17	193	Ea.	149,000	13,300		162,300	184,000
1040	6,696 MBH, 200 HP		.14	224		172,500	15,500		188,000	213,000
1050	8,375 MBH, 250 HP		.14	232		171,000	16,000		187,000	212,500
1060	10,044 MBH, 300 HP		.13	252		181,000	17,400		198,400	225,000
1080	16,740 MBH, 500 HP		.08	381		246,000	26,300		272,300	310,000
1100	23,435 MBH, 700 HP		.07	485		301,500	33,500		335,000	382,000
1102	26,780 MBH, 800 HP		.07	485		332,500	33,500		366,000	416,000
1104	30,125 MBH, 900 HP		.06	500		606,500	34,500		641,000	719,000
1106	33,475 MBH, 1,000 HP		.06	525		642,000	36,200		678,200	760,500
1107	36,825 MBH, 1,100 HP		.06	552		689,500	38,100		727,600	815,000
1108	40,170 MBH, 1,200 HP		.06	582		722,500	40,200		762,700	855,000
1110	46,865 MBH, 1,400 HP		.05	604		761,500	41,700		803,200	899,500
1112	53,560 MBH, 1,600 HP		.05	627		827,500	43,300		870,800	974,500
1114	60,250 MBH, 1,800 HP		.05	667		854,500	46,000		900,500	1,008,500
1116	66,950 MBH, 2,000 HP		.05	696		905,000	48,000		953,000	1,067,000
1118	73,650 MBH, 2,200 HP		.04	744		978,000	51,500		1,029,500	1,152,000
1120	To fire #6, add		.83	38.554		18,200	2,650		20,850	24,100
1140	To fire #6, and gas, add		.42	76.190		26,800	5,250		32,050	37,400
1141	1,675 MBH, 50 HP	Q-6	.26	93.023		95,000	6,300		101,300	114,000
1142	6,696 MBH, 200 HP	Q-7	.14	224		165,000	15,500		180,500	204,500
1143	10,044 MBH, 300 HP		.13	252		203,000	17,400		220,400	249,000
1144	16,740 MBH, 500 HP		.08	381		266,500	26,300		292,800	332,000
1145	23,435 MBH, 700 HP		.07	485		320,500	33,500		354,000	403,000
1146	30,125 MBH, 900 HP		.06	500		563,500	34,500		598,000	671,000
1160	For high pressure, add					29,800			29,800	32,800
1180	For duplex package feed system									
1200	To 3,348 MBH boiler, add	Q-7	.54	59.259	Ea.	14,400	4,100		18,500	22,000
1220	To 6,696 MBH boiler, add		.41	78.049		17,100	5,400		22,500	26,800
1240	To 10,044 MBH boiler, add		.38	84.211		19,600	5,825		25,425	30,300
1260	To 16,740 MBH boiler, add		.28	114		22,400	7,900		30,300	36,400
1280	To 23,435 MBH boiler, add		.25	128		26,400	8,850		35,250	42,300
1300	150 psi steam									
1310	1,005 MBH, 30 HP	Q-6	.33	72.072	Ea.	67,000	4,875		71,875	81,000
1320	1,675 MBH, 50 HP	"	.26	93.023		79,500	6,300		85,800	97,000
1330	3,350 MBH, 100 HP	Q-7	.21	152		142,000	10,500		152,500	171,500
1340	5,025 MBH, 150 HP		.17	193		181,000	13,300		194,300	219,000
1350	6,700 MBH, 200 HP		.14	224		167,000	15,500		182,500	207,000
1360	10,050 MBH, 300 HP		.13	252		227,000	17,400		244,400	275,500
1400	Packaged Scotch Marine, #6 oil									
1410	15 psi steam									
1420	1,675 MBH, 50 HP	Q-6	.25	97.166	Ea.	97,000	6,575		103,575	117,000
1430	3,350 MBH, 100 HP	Q-7	.20	159		113,000	11,000		124,000	141,000
1440	5,025 MBH, 150 HP		.16	203		138,000	14,000		152,000	173,000
1450	6,700 MBH, 200 HP		.14	234		158,000	16,100		174,100	197,500
1460	8,375 MBH, 250 HP		.13	244		196,500	16,900		213,400	241,000
1470	10,050 MBH, 300 HP		.12	262		220,500	18,100		238,600	269,500
1480	13,400 MBH, 400 HP		.09	352		280,000	24,300		304,300	344,000
1500	150 psi steam									
1510	1,675 MBH, 50 HP	Q-6	.25	97.166	Ea.	115,000	6,575		121,575	136,500
1520	3,350 MBH, 100 HP	Q-7	.20	159		162,500	11,000		173,500	195,000
1530	5,025 MBH, 150 HP		.16	203		171,000	14,000		185,000	209,500
1540	6,700 MBH, 200 HP		.14	234		220,500	16,100		236,600	266,500
1550	8,375 MBH, 250 HP		.13	244		214,500	16,900		231,400	261,000

23 52 Heating Boilers

23 52 39 – Fire-Tube Boilers

23 52 39.13 Scotch Marine Boilers

		Crew	Daily Output	Labor-Hours	Unit	Material	2023 Bare Costs Labor	Equipment	Total	Total Incl O&P
1560	10,050 MBH, 300 HP	Q-7	.12	262	Ea.	238,500	18,100		256,600	289,500
1570	13,400 MBH, 400 HP	↓	.09	352	↓	276,500	24,300		300,800	340,000

23 52 84 – Boiler Blowdown

23 52 84.10 Boiler Blowdown Systems

		Crew	Daily Output	Labor-Hours	Unit	Material	Labor	Equipment	Total	Incl O&P
0010	**BOILER BLOWDOWN SYSTEMS**									
1010	Boiler blowdown, auto/manual to 2,000 MBH	Q-5	3.75	4.267	Ea.	7,125	279		7,404	8,250
1020	7,300 MBH	"	3	5.333	"	7,525	350		7,875	8,800

23 52 88 – Burners

23 52 88.10 Replacement Type Burners

		Crew	Daily Output	Labor-Hours	Unit	Material	Labor	Equipment	Total	Incl O&P
0010	**REPLACEMENT TYPE BURNERS**									
0990	Residential, conversion, gas fired, LP or natural									
1000	Gun type, atmospheric input 50 to 225 MBH	Q-1	2.50	6.400	Ea.	1,725	415		2,140	2,525
1020	100 to 400 MBH		2	8		2,875	520		3,395	3,950
1040	300 to 1,000 MBH	↓	1.70	9.412	↓	8,725	610		9,335	10,500
2000	Commercial and industrial, gas/oil, input									
2050	400 MBH	Q-1	1.50	10.667	Ea.	4,350	690		5,040	5,825
2090	670 MBH		1.40	11.429		4,375	740		5,115	5,925
2140	1,155 MBH		1.30	12.308		4,875	800		5,675	6,575
2200	1,800 MBH		1.20	13.333		4,900	865		5,765	6,700
2260	3,000 MBH		1.10	14.545		4,350	945		5,295	6,200
2320	4,100 MBH	↓	1	16	↓	6,750	1,050		7,800	8,975
3000	Flame retention oil fired assembly, input									
3020	.50 to 2.25 GPH	Q-1	2.40	6.667	Ea.	365	430		795	1,050
3040	2.0 to 5.0 GPH		2	8		340	520		860	1,150
3060	3.0 to 7.0 GPH		1.80	8.889		630	575		1,205	1,550
3080	6.0 to 12.0 GPH	↓	1.60	10		1,025	650		1,675	2,100
4600	Gas safety, shut off valve, 3/4" threaded	1 Stpi	20	.400		193	29		222	256
4610	1" threaded		19	.421		186	30.50		216.50	251
4620	1-1/4" threaded		15	.533		210	38.50		248.50	289
4630	1-1/2" threaded		13	.615		227	44.50		271.50	315
4640	2" threaded	↓	11	.727		254	53		307	360
4650	2-1/2" threaded	Q-1	15	1.067		291	69		360	425
4660	3" threaded		13	1.231		580	80		660	755
4670	4" flanged	↓	3	5.333		2,850	345		3,195	3,650
4680	6" flanged	Q-2	3	8	↓	6,375	540		6,915	7,800

23 53 Heating Boiler Feedwater Equipment

23 53 24 – Shot Chemical Feeder

23 53 24.10 Chemical Feeder

		Crew	Daily Output	Labor-Hours	Unit	Material	Labor	Equipment	Total	Incl O&P
0010	**CHEMICAL FEEDER**									
0200	Shot chem feeder, by pass, in line mount, 300 PSIG, 1.7 gallon	2 Stpi	1.80	8.889	Ea.	305	645		950	1,300
0230	12 gallon		.93	17.204		485	1,250		1,735	2,375
0400	300 lb., ASME, 5 gallon		1.24	12.903		296	935		1,231	1,725
0420	10 gallon		.93	17.204		450	1,250		1,700	2,350
0020	Corrosion coupon rack, PVC, 4 station		2	8		345	580		925	1,250
0030	Corrosion coupon rack, PVC, 5 station		1.80	8.889		450	645		1,095	1,450
0040	Corrosion coupon rack, PVC, 6 station	↓	1.60	10	↓	760	725		1,485	1,900

23 54 Furnaces

23 54 13 – Electric-Resistance Furnaces

23 54 13.10 Electric Furnaces

		Crew	Daily Output	Labor-Hours	Unit	Material	2023 Bare Costs Labor	Equipment	Total	Total Incl O&P
0010	**ELECTRIC FURNACES**, Hot air, blowers, std. controls									
0011	not including gas, oil or flue piping									
1000	Electric, UL listed									
1070	10.2 MBH	Q-20	4.40	4.545	Ea.	365	291		656	835
1080	17.1 MBH		4.60	4.348		450	278		728	915
1100	34.1 MBH		4.40	4.545		560	291		851	1,050
1120	51.6 MBH		4.20	4.762		620	305		925	1,150
1140	68.3 MBH		4	5		615	320		935	1,150
1160	85.3 MBH		3.80	5.263		650	335		985	1,225

23 54 16 – Fuel-Fired Furnaces

23 54 16.13 Gas-Fired Furnaces

		Crew	Daily Output	Labor-Hours	Unit	Material	2023 Bare Costs Labor	Equipment	Total	Total Incl O&P
0010	**GAS-FIRED FURNACES**									
3000	Gas, AGA certified, upflow, direct drive models									
3020	45 MBH input	Q-9	4	4	Ea.	760	253		1,013	1,225
3040	60 MBH input		3.80	4.211		685	266		951	1,150
3060	75 MBH input		3.60	4.444		935	281		1,216	1,450
3100	100 MBH input		3.20	5		890	315		1,205	1,450
3120	125 MBH input		3	5.333		925	335		1,260	1,525
3130	150 MBH input		2.80	5.714		1,850	360		2,210	2,600
3140	200 MBH input		2.60	6.154		3,625	390		4,015	4,550
3160	300 MBH input		2.30	6.957		4,300	440		4,740	5,375
3180	400 MBH input		2	8		5,950	505		6,455	7,275
3200	Gas fired wall furnace									
3204	Horizontal flow									
3208	7.7 MBH	Q-9	7	2.286	Ea.	1,375	144		1,519	1,725
3212	14 MBH		6.50	2.462		880	155		1,035	1,200
3216	24 MBH		5	3.200		855	202		1,057	1,250
3220	49 MBH		4	4		1,175	253		1,428	1,675
3224	65 MBH		3.60	4.444		1,225	281		1,506	1,775
3240	Up-flow									
3244	7.7 MBH	Q-9	7	2.286	Ea.	820	144		964	1,125
3248	14 MBH		6.50	2.462		825	155		980	1,150
3252	24 MBH		5	3.200		860	202		1,062	1,250
3254	35 MBH		4.50	3.556		915	224		1,139	1,350
3256	49 MBH		4	4		1,775	253		2,028	2,325
3260	65 MBH		3.60	4.444		1,575	281		1,856	2,175
3500	Gas furnace									
3510	Up-flow									
3514	1,200 CFM, 45 MBH	Q-9	4	4	Ea.	1,200	253		1,453	1,700
3518	75 MBH		3.60	4.444		1,300	281		1,581	1,850
3522	100 MBH		3.20	5		1,450	315		1,765	2,075
3526	125 MBH		3	5.333		1,475	335		1,810	2,125
3530	150 MBH		2.80	5.714		1,650	360		2,010	2,375
3540	2,000 CFM, 75 MBH		3.60	4.444		1,450	281		1,731	2,025
3544	100 MBH		3.20	5		1,625	315		1,940	2,275
3548	120 MBH		3	5.333		1,725	335		2,060	2,400
3560	Horizontal flow									
3564	1,200 CFM, 45 MBH	Q-9	4	4	Ea.	1,400	253		1,653	1,900
3568	60 MBH		3.80	4.211		1,450	266		1,716	2,000
3572	70 MBH		3.60	4.444		1,500	281		1,781	2,075
3576	2,000 CFM, 90 MBH		3.30	4.848		1,650	305		1,955	2,275
3580	110 MBH		3.10	5.161		1,900	325		2,225	2,600

23 54 Furnaces

23 54 16 – Fuel-Fired Furnaces

23 54 16.14 Condensing Furnaces

		Crew	Daily Output	Labor-Hours	Unit	Material	2023 Bare Costs Labor	Equipment	Total	Total Incl O&P
0010	**CONDENSING FURNACES**, High efficiency									
0020	Oil fired, packaged, complete									
0030	Upflow									
0040	Output @ 95% A.F.U.E.									
0100	49 MBH @ 1,000 CFM	Q-9	3.70	4.324	Ea.	8,350	273		8,623	9,575
0110	73.5 MBH @ 2,000 CFM		3.60	4.444		8,725	281		9,006	10,000
0120	96 MBH @ 2,000 CFM		3.40	4.706		8,725	297		9,022	10,100
0130	115.6 MBH @ 2,000 CFM		3.40	4.706		8,725	297		9,022	10,100
0140	147 MBH @ 2,000 CFM		3.30	4.848		20,000	305		20,305	22,400
0150	192 MBH @ 4,000 CFM		2.60	6.154		20,700	390		21,090	23,400
0170	231.5 MBH @ 4,000 CFM		2.30	6.957		20,700	440		21,140	23,500
0260	For variable speed motor, add					810			810	895
0270	Note: Also available in horizontal, counterflow and lowboy configurations.									

23 54 16.16 Oil-Fired Furnaces

		Crew	Daily Output	Labor-Hours	Unit	Material	Labor	Equipment	Total	Total Incl O&P
0010	**OIL-FIRED FURNACES**									
6000	Oil, UL listed, atomizing gun type burner									
6020	56 MBH output	Q-9	3.60	4.444	Ea.	3,600	281		3,881	4,375
6030	84 MBH output		3.50	4.571		3,800	289		4,089	4,600
6040	95 MBH output		3.40	4.706		3,825	297		4,122	4,650
6060	134 MBH output		3.20	5		3,725	315		4,040	4,575
6080	151 MBH output		3	5.333		4,125	335		4,460	5,050
6100	200 MBH input		2.60	6.154		5,100	390		5,490	6,175
6120	300 MBH input		2.30	6.957		4,525	440		4,965	5,625
6140	400 MBH input		2	8		5,275	505		5,780	6,550
6200	Up flow									
6210	105 MBH	Q-9	3.40	4.706	Ea.	3,650	297		3,947	4,475
6220	140 MBH		3.30	4.848		4,000	305		4,305	4,850
6230	168 MBH		2.90	5.517		5,825	350		6,175	6,925
6260	Lo-boy style									
6270	105 MBH	Q-9	3.40	4.706	Ea.	3,825	297		4,122	4,650
6280	140 MBH		3.30	4.848		4,125	305		4,430	5,000
6290	189 MBH		2.80	5.714		5,825	360		6,185	6,950
6320	Down flow									
6330	105 MBH	Q-9	3.40	4.706	Ea.	3,825	297		4,122	4,650
6340	140 MBH		3.30	4.848		4,125	305		4,430	5,000
6350	168 MBH		2.90	5.517		6,625	350		6,975	7,825
6380	Horizontal									
6390	105 MBH	Q-9	3.40	4.706	Ea.	3,825	297		4,122	4,650
6400	140 MBH		3.30	4.848		4,125	305		4,430	5,000
6410	189 MBH		2.80	5.714		5,825	360		6,185	6,950

23 54 16.21 Solid Fuel-Fired Furnaces

			Crew	Daily Output	Labor-Hours	Unit	Material	Labor	Equipment	Total	Total Incl O&P
0010	**SOLID FUEL-FIRED FURNACES**										
6020	Wood fired furnaces										
6030	Includes hot water coil, thermostat, and auto draft control										
6040	24" long firebox	G	Q-9	4	4	Ea.	6,375	253		6,628	7,375
6050	30" long firebox	G		3.60	4.444		6,750	281		7,031	7,850
6060	With fireplace glass doors	G		3.20	5		9,150	315		9,465	10,600
6200	Wood/oil fired furnaces, includes two thermostats										
6210	Includes hot water coil and auto draft control										
6240	24" long firebox	G	Q-9	3.40	4.706	Ea.	7,825	297		8,122	9,075
6250	30" long firebox	G		3	5.333		8,700	335		9,035	10,100
6260	With fireplace glass doors	G		2.80	5.714		10,500	360		10,860	12,000

For customer support on your Mechanical Costs with RSMeans data, call 800.448.8182.

23 54 Furnaces

23 54 16 – Fuel-Fired Furnaces

23 54 16.21 Solid Fuel-Fired Furnaces

		Crew	Daily Output	Labor-Hours	Unit	Material	2023 Bare Costs Labor	Equipment	Total	Total Incl O&P
6400	Wood/gas fired furnaces, includes two thermostats									
6410	Includes hot water coil and auto draft control									
6440	24" long firebox	G Q-9	2.80	5.714	Ea.	8,700	360		9,060	10,100
6450	30" long firebox	G	2.40	6.667		9,450	420		9,870	11,000
6460	With fireplace glass doors	G	2	8		11,800	505		12,305	13,700
6600	Wood/oil/gas fired furnaces, optional accessories									
6610	Hot air plenum	Q-9	16	1	Ea.	194	63		257	310
6620	Safety heat dump		24	.667		180	42		222	262
6630	Auto air intake		18	.889		268	56		324	380
6640	Cold air return package		14	1.143		298	72		370	440
6650	Wood fork					97.50			97.50	107
6700	Wood fired outdoor furnace									
6740	24" long firebox	G Q-9	3.80	4.211	Ea.	5,750	266		6,016	6,725
6760	Wood fired outdoor furnace, optional accessories									
6770	Chimney section, stainless steel, 6" ID x 3' long	G Q-9	36	.444	Ea.	291	28		319	365
6780	Chimney cap, stainless steel	G "	40	.400	"	140	25.50		165.50	192
6800	Wood fired hot water furnace									
6820	Includes 200 gal. hot water storage, thermostat, and auto draft control									
6840	30" long firebox	G Q-9	2.10	7.619	Ea.	13,100	480		13,580	15,100
6850	Water to air heat exchanger									
6870	Includes mounting kit and blower relay									
6880	140 MBH, 18.75" W x 18.75" L	Q-9	7.50	2.133	Ea.	525	135		660	785
6890	200 MBH, 24" W x 24" L	"	7	2.286	"	745	144		889	1,025
6900	Water to water heat exchanger									
6940	100 MBH	Q-9	6.50	2.462	Ea.	530	155		685	815
6960	290 MBH	"	6	2.667	"	760	168		928	1,100
7000	Optional accessories									
7010	Large volume circulation pump (2 included)	Q-9	14	1.143	Ea.	345	72		417	490
7020	Air bleed fittings (package)		24	.667		74	42		116	145
7030	Domestic water preheater		6	2.667		310	168		478	595
7040	Smoke pipe kit		4	4		131	253		384	525

23 54 24 – Furnace Components for Cooling

23 54 24.10 Furnace Components and Combinations

		Crew	Daily Output	Labor-Hours	Unit	Material	2023 Bare Costs Labor	Equipment	Total	Total Incl O&P
0010	**FURNACE COMPONENTS AND COMBINATIONS**									
0080	Coils, A.C. evaporator, for gas or oil furnaces									
0090	Add-on, with holding charge									
0100	Upflow									
0120	1-1/2 ton cooling	Q-5	4	4	Ea.	258	261		519	675
0130	2 ton cooling		3.70	4.324		270	282		552	715
0140	3 ton cooling		3.30	4.848		420	315		735	930
0150	4 ton cooling		3	5.333		525	350		875	1,100
0160	5 ton cooling		2.70	5.926		590	385		975	1,225
0300	Downflow									
0330	2-1/2 ton cooling	Q-5	3	5.333	Ea.	330	350		680	885
0340	3-1/2 ton cooling		2.60	6.154		485	400		885	1,125
0350	5 ton cooling		2.20	7.273		590	475		1,065	1,350
0600	Horizontal									
0630	2 ton cooling	Q-5	3.90	4.103	Ea.	360	268		628	795
0640	3 ton cooling		3.50	4.571		445	299		744	935
0650	4 ton cooling		3.20	5		575	325		900	1,125
0660	5 ton cooling		2.90	5.517		630	360		990	1,225
2000	Cased evaporator coils for air handlers									

23 54 Furnaces

23 54 24 – Furnace Components for Cooling

23 54 24.10 Furnace Components and Combinations

		Crew	Daily Output	Labor-Hours	Unit	Material	2023 Bare Costs Labor	Equipment	Total	Total Incl O&P
2100	1-1/2 ton cooling	Q-5	4.40	3.636	Ea.	293	237		530	675
2110	2 ton cooling		4.10	3.902		279	255		534	685
2120	2-1/2 ton cooling		3.90	4.103		330	268		598	760
2130	3 ton cooling		3.70	4.324		400	282		682	860
2140	3-1/2 ton cooling		3.50	4.571		545	299		844	1,050
2150	4 ton cooling		3.20	5		575	325		900	1,125
2160	5 ton cooling		2.90	5.517		570	360		930	1,175
3010	Air handler, modular									
3100	With cased evaporator cooling coil									
3120	1-1/2 ton cooling	Q-5	3.80	4.211	Ea.	675	275		950	1,150
3130	2 ton cooling		3.50	4.571		685	299		984	1,200
3140	2-1/2 ton cooling		3.30	4.848		800	315		1,115	1,350
3150	3 ton cooling		3.10	5.161		895	335		1,230	1,500
3160	3-1/2 ton cooling		2.90	5.517		1,000	360		1,360	1,625
3170	4 ton cooling		2.50	6.400		1,150	420		1,570	1,900
3180	5 ton cooling		2.10	7.619		1,225	500		1,725	2,100
3500	With no cooling coil									
3520	1-1/2 ton coil size	Q-5	12	1.333	Ea.	955	87		1,042	1,175
3530	2 ton coil size		10	1.600		670	104		774	890
3540	2-1/2 ton coil size		10	1.600		755	104		859	985
3554	3 ton coil size		9	1.778		960	116		1,076	1,225
3560	3-1/2 ton coil size		9	1.778		1,075	116		1,191	1,350
3570	4 ton coil size		8.50	1.882		940	123		1,063	1,200
3580	5 ton coil size		8	2		1,225	131		1,356	1,550
4000	With heater									
4120	5 kW, 17.1 MBH	Q-5	16	1	Ea.	1,025	65.50		1,090.50	1,225
4130	7.5 kW, 25.6 MBH		15.60	1.026		905	67		972	1,100
4140	10 kW, 34.2 MBH		15.20	1.053		1,100	68.50		1,168.50	1,300
4150	12.5 kW, 42.7 MBH		14.80	1.081		1,300	70.50		1,370.50	1,550
4160	15 kW, 51.2 MBH		14.40	1.111		1,425	72.50		1,497.50	1,675
4170	25 kW, 85.4 MBH		14	1.143		2,300	74.50		2,374.50	2,625
4180	30 kW, 102 MBH		13	1.231		2,650	80.50		2,730.50	3,050

23 55 Fuel-Fired Heaters

23 55 13 – Fuel-Fired Duct Heaters

23 55 13.16 Gas-Fired Duct Heaters

		Crew	Daily Output	Labor-Hours	Unit	Material	2023 Bare Costs Labor	Equipment	Total	Total Incl O&P
0010	**GAS-FIRED DUCT HEATERS**, Includes burner, controls, stainless steel									
0020	heat exchanger. Gas fired, electric ignition									
0030	Indoor installation									
0080	100 MBH output	Q-5	5	3.200	Ea.	2,825	209		3,034	3,425
0100	120 MBH output		4	4		3,125	261		3,386	3,825
0130	200 MBH output		2.70	5.926		4,025	385		4,410	5,000
0140	240 MBH output		2.30	6.957		4,900	455		5,355	6,075
0160	280 MBH output		2	8		5,550	520		6,070	6,875
0180	320 MBH output		1.60	10		3,800	655		4,455	5,175
0300	For powered venter and adapter, add					505			505	555
0502	For required flue pipe, see Section 23 51 23.10									
1000	Outdoor installation, with power venter									
1020	75 MBH output	Q-5	4	4	Ea.	3,350	261		3,611	4,075
1040	94 MBH output		4	4		3,825	261		4,086	4,600
1060	120 MBH output		4	4		4,125	261		4,386	4,950

23 55 Fuel-Fired Heaters

23 55 13 – Fuel-Fired Duct Heaters

23 55 13.16 Gas-Fired Duct Heaters

		Crew	Daily Output	Labor-Hours	Unit	Material	2023 Bare Costs Labor	Equipment	Total	Total Incl O&P
1080	157 MBH output	Q-5	3.50	4.571	Ea.	3,800	299		4,099	4,625
1100	187 MBH output		3	5.333		5,450	350		5,800	6,525
1120	225 MBH output		2.50	6.400		5,675	420		6,095	6,875
1140	300 MBH output		1.80	8.889		6,275	580		6,855	7,775
1160	375 MBH output		1.60	10		6,475	655		7,130	8,100
1180	450 MBH output		1.40	11.429		7,350	745		8,095	9,200
1200	600 MBH output		1	16		9,950	1,050		11,000	12,500
1300	Aluminized exchanger, subtract					15%				
1500	For two stage gas valve, add					785			785	865

23 55 23 – Gas-Fired Radiant Heaters

23 55 23.10 Infrared Type Heating Units

		Crew	Daily Output	Labor-Hours	Unit	Material	2023 Bare Costs Labor	Equipment	Total	Total Incl O&P
0010	**INFRARED TYPE HEATING UNITS**									
0020	Gas fired, unvented, electric ignition, 100% shutoff.									
0030	Piping and wiring not included									
0100	Input, 30 MBH	Q-5	6	2.667	Ea.	1,050	174		1,224	1,400
0120	45 MBH		5	3.200		1,375	209		1,584	1,800
0140	50 MBH		4.50	3.556		1,400	232		1,632	1,900
0160	60 MBH		4	4		2,050	261		2,311	2,650
0180	75 MBH		3	5.333		1,400	350		1,750	2,075
0200	90 MBH		2.50	6.400		2,150	420		2,570	2,975
0220	105 MBH		2	8		1,650	520		2,170	2,575
0240	120 MBH		2	8		2,450	520		2,970	3,475
1000	Gas fired, vented, electric ignition, tubular									
1020	Piping and wiring not included, 20' to 80' lengths									
1030	Single stage, input, 60 MBH	Q-6	4.50	5.333	Ea.	1,950	360		2,310	2,700
1040	80 MBH		3.90	6.154		1,750	415		2,165	2,550
1050	100 MBH		3.40	7.059		1,975	480		2,455	2,900
1060	125 MBH		2.90	8.276		1,850	560		2,410	2,850
1070	150 MBH		2.70	8.889		2,425	600		3,025	3,575
1080	170 MBH		2.50	9.600		1,725	650		2,375	2,875
1090	200 MBH		2.20	10.909		2,525	740		3,265	3,875
1100	Note: Final pricing may vary due to									
1110	tube length and configuration package selected									
1130	Two stage, input, 60 MBH high, 45 MBH low	Q-6	4.50	5.333	Ea.	2,150	360		2,510	2,900
1140	80 MBH high, 60 MBH low		3.90	6.154		2,150	415		2,565	2,975
1150	100 MBH high, 65 MBH low		3.40	7.059		2,150	480		2,630	3,075
1160	125 MBH high, 95 MBH low		2.90	8.276		2,175	560		2,735	3,200
1170	150 MBH high, 100 MBH low		2.70	8.889		2,175	600		2,775	3,275
1180	170 MBH high, 125 MBH low		2.50	9.600		2,400	650		3,050	3,625
1190	200 MBH high, 150 MBH low		2.20	10.909		3,225	740		3,965	4,625
1220	Note: Final pricing may vary due to									
1230	tube length and configuration package selected									

23 55 33 – Fuel-Fired Unit Heaters

23 55 33.13 Oil-Fired Unit Heaters

		Crew	Daily Output	Labor-Hours	Unit	Material	2023 Bare Costs Labor	Equipment	Total	Total Incl O&P
0010	**OIL-FIRED UNIT HEATERS**, Cabinet, grilles, fan, ctrl., burner, no piping									
6000	Oil fired, suspension mounted, 94 MBH output	Q-5	4	4	Ea.	4,575	261		4,836	5,450
6040	140 MBH output		3	5.333		4,875	350		5,225	5,900
6060	184 MBH output		3	5.333		5,275	350		5,625	6,325

23 55 Fuel-Fired Heaters

23 55 33 – Fuel-Fired Unit Heaters

23 55 33.16 Gas-Fired Unit Heaters

		Crew	Daily Output	Labor-Hours	Unit	Material	2023 Bare Costs Labor	Equipment	Total	Total Incl O&P
0010	**GAS-FIRED UNIT HEATERS**, Cabinet, grilles, fan, ctrls., burner, no piping									
0022	thermostat, no piping. For flue see Section 23 51 23.10									
1000	Gas fired, floor mounted									
1100	60 MBH output	Q-5	10	1.600	Ea.	730	104		834	960
1120	80 MBH output		9	1.778		740	116		856	990
1140	100 MBH output		8	2		810	131		941	1,075
1160	120 MBH output		7	2.286		925	149		1,074	1,250
1180	180 MBH output		6	2.667		1,150	174		1,324	1,525
1500	Rooftop mounted, power vent, stainless steel exchanger									
1520	75 MBH input	Q-6	4	6	Ea.	3,375	405		3,780	4,325
1540	100 MBH input		3.60	6.667		3,475	450		3,925	4,500
1560	125 MBH input		3.30	7.273		3,575	495		4,070	4,650
1580	150 MBH input		3	8		3,775	540		4,315	4,950
1600	175 MBH input		2.60	9.231		3,900	625		4,525	5,200
1620	225 MBH input		2.30	10.435		4,600	705		5,305	6,100
1640	300 MBH input		1.90	12.632		5,350	855		6,205	7,150
1660	350 MBH input		1.40	17.143		5,975	1,150		7,125	8,300
1680	450 MBH input		1.20	20		6,200	1,350		7,550	8,850
1720	700 MBH input		.80	30		13,500	2,025		15,525	17,800
1760	1,200 MBH input		.30	80		6,125	5,425		11,550	14,800
1900	For aluminized steel exchanger, subtract					10%				
2000	Suspension mounted, propeller fan, 20 MBH output	Q-5	8.50	1.882		755	123		878	1,025
2020	40 MBH output		7.50	2.133		830	139		969	1,125
2040	60 MBH output		7	2.286		1,800	149		1,949	2,200
2060	80 MBH output		6	2.667		1,000	174		1,174	1,350
2080	100 MBH output		5.50	2.909		1,150	190		1,340	1,550
2100	130 MBH output		5	3.200		1,275	209		1,484	1,700
2120	140 MBH output		4.50	3.556		2,450	232		2,682	3,050
2140	160 MBH output		4	4		1,400	261		1,661	1,925
2160	180 MBH output		3.50	4.571		3,650	299		3,949	4,475
2180	200 MBH output		3	5.333		1,625	350		1,975	2,300
2200	240 MBH output		2.70	5.926		1,875	385		2,260	2,650
2220	280 MBH output		2.30	6.957		3,600	455		4,055	4,625
2240	320 MBH output		2	8		2,475	520		2,995	3,500
2500	For powered venter and adapter, add					390			390	430
3000	Suspension mounted, blower type, 40 MBH output	Q-5	6.80	2.353		755	154		909	1,050
3020	60 MBH output		6.60	2.424		915	158		1,073	1,225
3040	84 MBH output		5.80	2.759		880	180		1,060	1,225
3060	104 MBH output		5.20	3.077		970	201		1,171	1,375
3080	140 MBH output		4.30	3.721		1,150	243		1,393	1,625
3100	180 MBH output		3.30	4.848		1,450	315		1,765	2,075
3120	240 MBH output		2.50	6.400		1,675	420		2,095	2,475
3140	280 MBH output		2	8		1,450	520		1,970	2,350
4000	Suspension mounted, sealed combustion system,									
4020	Aluminized steel exchanger, powered vent									
4040	100 MBH output	Q-5	5	3.200	Ea.	2,150	209		2,359	2,675
4060	120 MBH output		4.70	3.404		2,400	222		2,622	2,975
4080	160 MBH output		3.70	4.324		2,650	282		2,932	3,350
4100	200 MBH output		2.90	5.517		3,150	360		3,510	4,000
4120	240 MBH output		2.50	6.400		3,425	420		3,845	4,375
4140	320 MBH output		1.70	9.412		4,025	615		4,640	5,375
5000	Wall furnace, 17.5 MBH output		6	2.667		620	174		794	945

23 55 Fuel-Fired Heaters

23 55 33 – Fuel-Fired Unit Heaters

23 55 33.16 Gas-Fired Unit Heaters		Crew	Daily Output	Labor-Hours	Unit	Material	2023 Bare Costs Labor	2023 Bare Costs Equipment	Total	Total Incl O&P
5020	24 MBH output	Q-5	5	3.200	Ea.	620	209		829	995
5040	35 MBH output	↓	4	4	↓	660	261		921	1,125

23 56 Solar Energy Heating Equipment

23 56 16 – Packaged Solar Heating Equipment

23 56 16.40 Solar Heating Systems

0010	**SOLAR HEATING SYSTEMS** R235616-60									
0020	System/package prices, not including connecting									
0030	pipe, insulation, or special heating/plumbing fixtures									
0152	For solar ultraviolet pipe insulation see Section 22 07 19.10									
0500	Hot water, standard package, low temperature									
0540	1 collector, circulator, fittings, 65 gal. tank	G	Q-1	.50	32	Ea.	5,525	2,075		7,600	9,175
0580	2 collectors, circulator, fittings, 120 gal. tank	G		.40	40		5,500	2,600		8,100	9,925
0620	3 collectors, circulator, fittings, 120 gal. tank	G	↓	.34	47.059	↓	8,850	3,050		11,900	14,300
0700	Medium temperature package									
0720	1 collector, circulator, fittings, 80 gal. tank	G	Q-1	.50	32	Ea.	5,175	2,075		7,250	8,800
0740	2 collectors, circulator, fittings, 120 gal. tank	G		.40	40		8,250	2,600		10,850	13,000
0780	3 collectors, circulator, fittings, 120 gal. tank	G	↓	.30	53.333		8,975	3,450		12,425	15,000
0980	For each additional 120 gal. tank, add	G				↓	1,825			1,825	2,000

23 56 19 – Solar Heating Components

23 56 19.50 Solar Heating Ancillary

0010	**SOLAR HEATING ANCILLARY**									
2300	Circulators, air									
2310	Blowers									
2330	100-300 S.F. system, 1/10 HP	G	Q-9	16	1	Ea.	272	63		335	395
2340	300-500 S.F. system, 1/5 HP	G		15	1.067		365	67.50		432.50	500
2350	Two speed, 100-300 S.F., 1/10 HP	G		14	1.143		149	72		221	273
2400	Reversible fan, 20" diameter, 2 speed	G		18	.889		117	56		173	214
2550	Booster fan 6" diameter, 120 CFM	G		16	1		38	63		101	137
2570	6" diameter, 225 CFM	G		16	1		47	63		110	147
2580	8" diameter, 150 CFM	G		16	1		43	63		106	143
2590	8" diameter, 310 CFM	G		14	1.143		66	72		138	182
2600	8" diameter, 425 CFM	G		14	1.143		74	72		146	191
2650	Rheostat	G		32	.500		16.10	31.50		47.60	65
2660	Shutter/damper	G		12	1.333		59.50	84		143.50	193
2670	Shutter motor	G	↓	16	1		148	63		211	258
2800	Circulators, liquid, 1/25 HP, 5.3 GPM	G	Q-1	14	1.143		210	74		284	340
2820	1/20 HP, 17 GPM	G		12	1.333		310	86.50		396.50	470
2850	1/20 HP, 17 GPM, stainless steel	G		12	1.333		264	86.50		350.50	420
2870	1/12 HP, 30 GPM	G	↓	10	1.600	↓	360	104		464	550
3000	Collector panels, air with aluminum absorber plate									
3010	Wall or roof mount									
3040	Flat black, plastic glazing									
3080	4' x 8'	G	Q-9	6	2.667	Ea.	690	168		858	1,025
3100	4' x 10'	G		5	3.200	"	850	202		1,052	1,250
3200	Flush roof mount, 10' to 16' x 22" wide	G		96	.167	L.F.	183	10.50		193.50	218
3210	Manifold, by L.F. width of collectors	G		160	.100	"	152	6.30		158.30	177
3300	Collector panels, liquid with copper absorber plate									
3320	Black chrome, tempered glass glazing									
3330	Alum. frame, 4' x 8', 5/32" single glazing	G	Q-1	9.50	1.684	Ea.	1,050	109		1,159	1,350

23 56 Solar Energy Heating Equipment

23 56 19 – Solar Heating Components

23 56 19.50 Solar Heating Ancillary		Crew	Daily Output	Labor-Hours	Unit	Material	2023 Bare Costs Labor	Equipment	Total	Total Incl O&P
3390	Alum. frame, 4' x 10', 5/32" single glazing	G Q-1	6	2.667	Ea.	1,225	173		1,398	1,575
3450	Flat black, alum. frame, 3.5' x 7.5'	G	9	1.778		770	115		885	1,025
3500	4' x 8'	G	5.50	2.909		935	189		1,124	1,300
3520	4' x 10'	G	10	1.600		1,150	104		1,254	1,425
3540	4' x 12.5'	G	5	3.200		1,250	208		1,458	1,675
3550	Liquid with fin tube absorber plate									
3560	Alum. frame 4' x 8' tempered glass	G Q-1	10	1.600	Ea.	585	104		689	800
3580	Liquid with vacuum tubes, 4' x 6'-10"	G	9	1.778		960	115		1,075	1,225
3600	Liquid, full wetted, plastic, alum. frame, 4' x 10'	G	5	3.200		330	208		538	675
3650	Collector panel mounting, flat roof or ground rack	G	7	2.286		268	148		416	515
3670	Roof clamps	G	70	.229	Set	3.59	14.80		18.39	26
3700	Roof strap, teflon	G 1 Plum	205	.039	L.F.	25	2.81		27.81	31.50
3900	Differential controller with two sensors									
3930	Thermostat, hard wired	G 1 Plum	8	1	Ea.	116	72		188	234
3950	Line cord and receptacle	G	12	.667		234	48		282	330
4050	Pool valve system	G	2.50	3.200		188	231		419	550
4070	With 12 VAC actuator	G	2	4		335	288		623	795
4080	Pool pump system, 2" pipe size	G	6	1.333		202	96		298	365
4100	Five station with digital read-out	G	3	2.667		280	192		472	595
4150	Sensors									
4200	Brass plug, 1/2" MPT	G 1 Plum	32	.250	Ea.	15.50	18		33.50	44
4210	Brass plug, reversed	G	32	.250		30	18		48	60
4220	Freeze prevention	G	32	.250		26	18		44	56
4240	Screw attached	G	32	.250		18	18		36	47
4250	Brass, immersion	G	32	.250		18	18		36	47
4300	Heat exchanger									
4315	includes coil, blower, circulator									
4316	and controller for DHW and space hot air									
4330	Fluid to air coil, up flow, 45 MBH	G Q-1	4	4	Ea.	335	259		594	755
4380	70 MBH	G	3.50	4.571		380	296		676	860
4400	80 MBH	G	3	5.333		505	345		850	1,075
4580	Fluid to fluid package includes two circulating pumps									
4590	expansion tank, check valve, relief valve									
4600	controller, high temperature cutoff and sensors	G Q-1	2.50	6.400	Ea.	790	415		1,205	1,500
4650	Heat transfer fluid									
4700	Propylene glycol, inhibited anti-freeze	G 1 Plum	28	.286	Gal.	25.50	20.50		46	58.50
4800	Solar storage tanks, knocked down									
4810	Air, galvanized steel clad, double wall, 4" fiberglass insulation									
5120	45 mil reinforced polypropylene lining,									
5140	4' high, 4' x 4' = 64 C.F./450 gallons	G Q-9	2	8	Ea.	3,000	505		3,505	4,050
5150	4' x 8' = 128 C.F./900 gallons	G	1.50	10.667		4,800	675		5,475	6,300
5160	4' x 12' = 190 C.F./1,300 gallons	G	1.30	12.308		6,000	775		6,775	7,775
5170	8' x 8' = 250 C.F./1,700 gallons	G	1	16		7,625	1,000		8,625	9,900
5190	6'-3" high, 7' x 7' = 306 C.F./2,000 gallons	G Q-10	1.20	20		14,100	1,300		15,400	17,500
5200	7' x 10'-6" = 459 C.F./3,000 gallons	G	.80	30		17,500	1,975		19,475	22,200
5210	7' x 14' = 613 C.F./4,000 gallons	G	.60	40		22,200	2,625		24,825	28,500
5220	10'-6" x 10'-6" = 689 C.F./4,500 gallons	G	.50	48		21,000	3,150		24,150	27,700
5230	10'-6" x 14' = 919 C.F./6,000 gallons	G	.40	60		24,400	3,925		28,325	32,800
5240	14' x 14' = 1,225 C.F./8,000 gallons	G Q-11	.40	80		29,300	5,350		34,650	40,300
5250	14' x 17'-6" = 1,531 C.F./10,000 gallons	G	.30	107		31,700	7,125		38,825	45,500
5260	17'-6" x 17'-6" = 1,914 C.F./12,500 gallons	G	.25	128		43,500	8,550		52,050	60,500
5270	17'-6" x 21' = 2,297 C.F./15,000 gallons	G	.20	160		40,700	10,700		51,400	61,000
5280	21' x 21' = 2,756 C.F./18,000 gallons	G	.18	178		43,100	11,900		55,000	65,500

23 56 Solar Energy Heating Equipment

23 56 19 – Solar Heating Components

23 56 19.50 Solar Heating Ancillary

			Crew	Daily Output	Labor-Hours	Unit	Material	2023 Bare Costs Labor	Equipment	Total	Total Incl O&P
5290		30 mil reinforced Hypalon lining, add					.02%				
7000	Solar control valves and vents										
7050		Air purger, 1" pipe size	G	1 Plum	12	.667	Ea.	53	48		101	130
7070		Air eliminator, automatic 3/4" size	G		32	.250		31	18		49	61
7090		Air vent, automatic, 1/8" fitting	G		32	.250		16.05	18		34.05	44.50
7100		Manual, 1/8" NPT	G		32	.250		3.33	18		21.33	30.50
7120		Backflow preventer, 1/2" pipe size	G		16	.500		89.50	36		125.50	152
7130		3/4" pipe size	G		16	.500		74.50	36		110.50	136
7150		Balancing valve, 3/4" pipe size	G		20	.400		56.50	29		85.50	105
7180		Draindown valve, 1/2" copper tube	G		9	.889		221	64		285	340
7200		Flow control valve, 1/2" pipe size	G		22	.364		144	26		170	197
7220		Expansion tank, up to 5 gal.	G		32	.250		66	18		84	99.50
7250		Hydronic controller (aquastat)	G		8	1		155	72		227	278
7400		Pressure gauge, 2" dial	G		32	.250		25.50	18		43.50	55
7450		Relief valve, temp. and pressure 3/4" pipe size	G		30	.267		27	19.20		46.20	58
7500	Solenoid valve, normally closed										
7520		Brass, 3/4" NPT, 24V	G	1 Plum	9	.889	Ea.	174	64		238	288
7530		1" NPT, 24V	G		9	.889		274	64		338	395
7750		Vacuum relief valve, 3/4" pipe size	G		32	.250		31.50	18		49.50	61.50
7800	Thermometers										
7820		Digital temperature monitoring, 4 locations	G	1 Plum	2.50	3.200	Ea.	168	231		399	530
7900		Upright, 1/2" NPT	G		8	1		59	72		131	172
7970		Remote probe, 2" dial	G		8	1		35	72		107	146
7990		Stem, 2" dial, 9" stem	G		16	.500		23	36		59	78.50
8250	Water storage tank with heat exchanger and electric element										
8270		66 gal. with 2" x 2 lb. density insulation	G	1 Plum	1.60	5	Ea.	2,100	360		2,460	2,825
8300		80 gal. with 2" x 2 lb. density insulation	G		1.60	5		1,800	360		2,160	2,525
8380		120 gal. with 2" x 2 lb. density insulation	G		1.40	5.714		1,750	410		2,160	2,550
8400		120 gal. with 2" x 2 lb. density insul., 40 S.F. heat coil	G		1.40	5.714		2,600	410		3,010	3,500
8500	Water storage module, plastic										
8600		Tubular, 12" diameter, 4' high	G	1 Carp	48	.167	Ea.	102	9.75		111.75	127
8610		12" diameter, 8' high	G		40	.200		160	11.70		171.70	193
8620		18" diameter, 5' high	G		38	.211		180	12.35		192.35	216
8630		18" diameter, 10' high	G		32	.250		264	14.65		278.65	310
8640		58" diameter, 5' high	G	2 Carp	32	.500		860	29.50		889.50	995
8650		Cap, 12" diameter	G					20.50			20.50	22.50
8660		18" diameter	G					26			26	28.50

23 57 Heat Exchangers for HVAC

23 57 16 – Steam-to-Water Heat Exchangers

23 57 16.10 Shell/Tube Type Steam-to-Water Heat Exch.

			Crew	Daily Output	Labor-Hours	Unit	Material	2023 Bare Costs Labor	Equipment	Total	Total Incl O&P
0010	**SHELL AND TUBE TYPE STEAM-TO-WATER HEAT EXCHANGERS**										
0016	Shell & tube type, 2 or 4 pass, 3/4" OD copper tubes,										
0020	C.I. heads, C.I. tube sheet, steel shell										
0100	Hot water 40°F to 180°F, by steam at 10 psi										
0120		8 GPM		Q-5	6	2.667	Ea.	3,050	174		3,224	3,600
0140		10 GPM			5	3.200		4,575	209		4,784	5,325
0160		40 GPM			4	4		7,050	261		7,311	8,175
0180		64 GPM			2	8		28,600	520		29,120	32,200
0200		96 GPM			1	16		51,500	1,050		52,550	58,500
0220		120 GPM		Q-6	1.50	16		69,000	1,075		70,075	77,500

23 57 Heat Exchangers for HVAC

23 57 16 – Steam-to-Water Heat Exchangers

23 57 16.10 Shell/Tube Type Steam-to-Water Heat Exch.		Crew	Daily Output	Labor-Hours	Unit	Material	2023 Bare Costs Labor	Equipment	Total	Total Incl O&P
0240	168 GPM	Q-6	1	24	Ea.	84,500	1,625		86,125	95,500
0260	240 GPM		.80	30		132,000	2,025		134,025	148,500
0300	600 GPM		.70	34.286		78,000	2,325		80,325	89,500
0500	For bronze head and tube sheet, add					50%				

23 57 19 – Liquid-to-Liquid Heat Exchangers

23 57 19.13 Plate-Type, Liquid-to-Liquid Heat Exchangers

		Crew	Daily Output	Labor-Hours	Unit	Material	Labor	Equipment	Total	Total Incl O&P
0010	**PLATE-TYPE, LIQUID-TO-LIQUID HEAT EXCHANGERS**									
3000	Plate type,									
3100	400 GPM	Q-6	.80	30	Ea.	52,000	2,025		54,025	60,500
3120	800 GPM	"	.50	48		90,000	3,250		93,250	104,000
3140	1,200 GPM	Q-7	.34	94.118		133,500	6,500		140,000	156,500
3160	1,800 GPM	"	.24	133		177,000	9,200		186,200	208,500

23 57 19.16 Shell-Type, Liquid-to-Liquid Heat Exchangers

		Crew	Daily Output	Labor-Hours	Unit	Material	Labor	Equipment	Total	Total Incl O&P
0010	**SHELL-TYPE, LIQUID-TO-LIQUID HEAT EXCHANGERS**									
1000	Hot water 40°F to 140°F, by water at 200°F									
1020	7 GPM	Q-5	6	2.667	Ea.	13,500	174		13,674	15,200
1040	16 GPM		5	3.200		20,000	209		20,209	22,200
1060	34 GPM		4	4		29,500	261		29,761	32,900
1080	55 GPM		3	5.333		41,900	350		42,250	46,600
1100	74 GPM		1.50	10.667		54,000	695		54,695	60,500
1120	86 GPM		1.40	11.429		71,000	745		71,745	79,000
1140	112 GPM	Q-6	2	12		88,000	815		88,815	98,000
1160	126 GPM		1.80	13.333		110,000	905		110,905	122,500
1180	152 GPM		1	24		87,000	1,625		88,625	98,000

23 61 Refrigerant Compressors

23 61 13 – Centrifugal Refrigerant Compressors

23 61 13.10 Centrifugal Compressors

		Crew	Daily Output	Labor-Hours	Unit	Material	Labor	Equipment	Total	Total Incl O&P
0010	**CENTRIFUGAL COMPRESSORS**									
0100	Refrigeration, centrifugal including switches & protective devices									
0210	200 ton	Q-7	.23	137	Ea.	40,000	9,475		49,475	58,000
0220	300 ton		.17	187		42,000	12,900		54,900	65,500
0230	400 ton		.14	227		48,900	15,700		64,600	77,500
0240	500 ton		.14	237		49,200	16,400		65,600	78,500
0250	600 ton		.13	248		56,500	17,100		73,600	88,000
0260	700 ton		.12	260		58,500	18,000		76,500	91,500
0270	800 ton		.12	271		71,000	18,700		89,700	106,000
0280	900 ton		.11	288		82,000	19,900		101,900	120,000
0290	1,000 ton		.11	296		93,000	20,500		113,500	132,500
0300	1,100 ton		.10	308		95,500	21,200		116,700	137,000
0310	1,200 ton		.10	317		99,000	21,900		120,900	141,500
0320	1,300 ton		.10	327		97,500	22,500		120,000	140,500
0330	1,400 ton		.09	340		103,000	23,500		126,500	148,500
0340	1,500 ton		.09	352		108,500	24,300		132,800	155,500

23 61 15 – Rotary Refrigerant Compressors

23 61 15.10 Rotary Compressors

		Crew	Daily Output	Labor-Hours	Unit	Material	Labor	Equipment	Total	Total Incl O&P
0010	**ROTARY COMPRESSORS**									
0100	Refrigeration, hermetic, switches and protective devices									
0210	1.25 ton	1 Stpi	3	2.667	Ea.	291	193		484	610
0220	1.42 ton		3	2.667		294	193		487	615

23 61 Refrigerant Compressors

23 61 15 – Rotary Refrigerant Compressors

	23 61 15.10 Rotary Compressors	Crew	Daily Output	Labor-Hours	Unit	Material	2023 Bare Costs Labor	Equipment	Total	Total Incl O&P
0230	1.68 ton	1 Stpi	2.80	2.857	Ea.	320	207		527	660
0240	2.00 ton		2.60	3.077		330	223		553	695
0250	2.37 ton		2.50	3.200		370	232		602	755
0260	2.67 ton		2.40	3.333		390	242		632	790
0270	3.53 ton		2.30	3.478		425	252		677	845
0280	4.43 ton		2.20	3.636		545	264		809	995
0290	5.08 ton		2.10	3.810		600	276		876	1,075
0300	5.22 ton		2	4		845	290		1,135	1,375
0310	7.31 ton	Q-5	3	5.333		1,350	350		1,700	2,000
0320	9.95 ton		2.60	6.154		1,600	400		2,000	2,350
0330	11.6 ton		2.50	6.400		2,025	420		2,445	2,875
0340	15.25 ton		2.30	6.957		2,800	455		3,255	3,750
0350	17.7 ton		2.10	7.619		3,000	500		3,500	4,050

23 61 16 – Reciprocating Refrigerant Compressors

	23 61 16.10 Reciprocating Compressors	Crew	Daily Output	Labor-Hours	Unit	Material	2023 Bare Costs Labor	Equipment	Total	Total Incl O&P
0010	**RECIPROCATING COMPRESSORS**									
0990	Refrigeration, recip. hermetic, switches & protective devices									
1000	10 ton	Q-5	1	16	Ea.	20,000	1,050		21,050	23,600
1100	20 ton	Q-6	.72	33.333		26,600	2,250		28,850	32,600
1200	30 ton		.64	37.500		32,800	2,550		35,350	39,900
1300	40 ton		.44	54.545		37,800	3,700		41,500	47,100
1400	50 ton		.20	120		39,300	8,125		47,425	55,500
1500	75 ton	Q-7	.27	119		43,500	8,175		51,675	60,000
1600	130 ton	"	.21	152		49,700	10,500		60,200	70,000

23 61 19 – Scroll Refrigerant Compressors

	23 61 19.10 Scroll Compressors	Crew	Daily Output	Labor-Hours	Unit	Material	2023 Bare Costs Labor	Equipment	Total	Total Incl O&P
0010	**SCROLL COMPRESSORS**									
1800	Refrigeration, scroll type									
1810	1.5 ton	1 Stpi	2.70	2.963	Ea.	970	215		1,185	1,400
1820	2.5 ton		2.50	3.200		1,025	232		1,257	1,475
1830	2.75 ton		2.35	3.404		810	247		1,057	1,250
1840	3 ton		2.30	3.478		1,025	252		1,277	1,500
1850	3.5 ton		2.25	3.556		980	258		1,238	1,450
1860	4 ton		2.20	3.636		1,075	264		1,339	1,575
1870	5 ton		2.10	3.810		1,275	276		1,551	1,800
1880	6 ton	Q-5	3.70	4.324		1,325	282		1,607	1,900
1900	7.5 ton		3.20	5		3,000	325		3,325	3,775
1910	10 ton		3.10	5.161		3,025	335		3,360	3,825
1920	13 ton		2.90	5.517		2,825	360		3,185	3,625
1960	25 ton		2.20	7.273		7,400	475		7,875	8,825

23 62 Packaged Compressor and Condenser Units

23 62 13 – Packaged Air-Cooled Refrigerant Compressor and Condenser Units

23 62 13.10 Packaged Air-Cooled Refrig. Condensing Units

		Crew	Daily Output	Labor-Hours	Unit	Material	2023 Bare Costs Labor	Equipment	Total	Total Incl O&P
0010	**PACKAGED AIR-COOLED REFRIGERANT CONDENSING UNITS**									
0020	Condensing unit									
0030	Air cooled, compressor, standard controls									
0050	1.5 ton	Q-5	2.50	6.400	Ea.	1,350	420		1,770	2,100
0100	2 ton		2.10	7.619		1,375	500		1,875	2,275
0200	2.5 ton		1.70	9.412		1,475	615		2,090	2,550
0300	3 ton		1.30	12.308		1,650	805		2,455	3,025
0350	3.5 ton		1.10	14.545		1,850	950		2,800	3,475
0400	4 ton		.90	17.778		2,050	1,150		3,200	3,975
0500	5 ton		.60	26.667		2,375	1,750		4,125	5,225
0550	7.5 ton		.55	29.091		3,600	1,900		5,500	6,775
0560	8.5 ton		.53	30.189		3,475	1,975		5,450	6,775
0600	10 ton		.50	32		3,525	2,100		5,625	7,000
0620	12.5 ton		.48	33.333		4,625	2,175		6,800	8,325
0650	15 ton		.40	40		8,525	2,600		11,125	13,300
0700	20 ton	Q-6	.40	60		9,775	4,075		13,850	16,900
0720	25 ton		.35	68.571		18,800	4,650		23,450	27,600
0750	30 ton		.30	80		16,600	5,425		22,025	26,400
0800	40 ton		.20	120		25,000	8,125		33,125	39,600
0840	50 ton		.18	133		21,600	9,025		30,625	37,200
0860	60 ton		.16	150		24,100	10,200		34,300	41,600
0900	70 ton		.14	171		28,600	11,600		40,200	48,700
1000	80 ton		.12	200		31,800	13,500		45,300	55,000
1010	90 ton		.09	267		38,300	18,100		56,400	69,000
1100	100 ton		.09	267		44,400	18,100		62,500	75,500

23 62 23 – Packaged Water-Cooled Refrigerant Compressor and Condenser Units

23 62 23.10 Pckgd. Water-Cooled Refrigerant Condns. Units

		Crew	Daily Output	Labor-Hours	Unit	Material	2023 Bare Costs Labor	Equipment	Total	Total Incl O&P
0010	**PACKAGED WATER-COOLED REFRIGERANT CONDENSING UNITS**									
2000	Water cooled, compressor, heat exchanger, controls									
2100	5 ton	Q-5	.70	22.857	Ea.	16,200	1,500		17,700	20,000
2110	10 ton		.60	26.667		18,400	1,750		20,150	22,900
2200	15 ton		.50	32		24,600	2,100		26,700	30,200
2300	20 ton	Q-6	.40	60		34,400	4,075		38,475	44,000
2310	30 ton		.30	80		35,200	5,425		40,625	46,800
2400	40 ton		.20	120		37,900	8,125		46,025	54,000

23 63 Refrigerant Condensers

23 63 13 – Air-Cooled Refrigerant Condensers

23 63 13.10 Air-Cooled Refrig. Condensers

		Crew	Daily Output	Labor-Hours	Unit	Material	2023 Bare Costs Labor	Equipment	Total	Total Incl O&P
0010	**AIR-COOLED REFRIG. CONDENSERS**									
0080	Air cooled, belt drive, propeller fan									
0220	45 ton	Q-6	.70	34.286	Ea.	20,300	2,325		22,625	25,800
0240	50 ton		.69	34.985		21,900	2,375		24,275	27,500
0260	54 ton		.64	37.795		23,900	2,550		26,450	30,000
0280	59 ton		.58	41.308		26,200	2,800		29,000	33,100
0300	65 ton		.53	45.541		31,300	3,075		34,375	39,000
0320	73 ton		.47	51.173		34,300	3,475		37,775	42,900
0340	81 ton		.42	56.738		37,800	3,850		41,650	47,300
0360	86 ton		.40	60.302		39,700	4,075		43,775	49,800
0380	88 ton		.39	61.697		42,600	4,175		46,775	53,000

23 63 Refrigerant Condensers

23 63 13 – Air-Cooled Refrigerant Condensers

23 63 13.10 Air-Cooled Refrig. Condensers

		Crew	Daily Output	Labor-Hours	Unit	Material	2023 Bare Costs Labor	Equipment	Total	Total Incl O&P
0400	101 ton	Q-7	.45	70.640	Ea.	54,500	4,875		59,375	67,000
0500	159 ton		.31	103		75,000	7,100		82,100	92,500
0600	228 ton		.22	148		58,000	10,200		68,200	79,000
0650	320 ton		.16	206		149,500	14,300		163,800	186,000
0660	475 ton		.11	296		120,500	20,500		141,000	163,000
1500	May be specified single or multi-circuit									
1550	Air cooled, direct drive, propeller fan									
1590	1 ton	Q-5	3.80	4.211	Ea.	1,925	275		2,200	2,500
1600	1-1/2 ton		3.60	4.444		2,350	290		2,640	3,000
1620	2 ton		3.20	5		2,525	325		2,850	3,250
1630	3 ton		2.40	6.667		2,800	435		3,235	3,725
1640	5 ton		2	8		5,125	520		5,645	6,400
1650	8 ton		1.80	8.889		6,450	580		7,030	7,975
1660	10 ton		1.40	11.429		7,900	745		8,645	9,800
1670	12 ton		1.30	12.308		8,875	805		9,680	11,000
1680	14 ton		1.20	13.333		10,100	870		10,970	12,500
1690	16 ton		1.10	14.545		11,100	950		12,050	13,600
1700	21 ton		1	16		12,800	1,050		13,850	15,700
1720	26 ton		.84	19.002		14,400	1,250		15,650	17,700
1740	30 ton		.70	22.792		17,900	1,500		19,400	21,900
1760	41 ton	Q-6	.77	31.008		19,700	2,100		21,800	24,700
1780	52 ton		.66	36.419		28,000	2,475		30,475	34,600
1800	63 ton		.55	44.037		31,000	2,975		33,975	38,600
1820	76 ton		.45	52.980		35,100	3,600		38,700	44,100
1840	86 ton		.40	60		43,400	4,075		47,475	54,000
1860	97 ton		.35	67.989		49,400	4,600		54,000	61,500
1880	105 ton	Q-7	.44	73.563		57,000	5,075		62,075	70,000
1890	118 ton		.39	82.687		61,500	5,700		67,200	76,000
1900	126 ton		.36	88.154		71,500	6,075		77,575	87,500
1910	136 ton		.34	95.238		80,000	6,575		86,575	98,000
1920	142 ton		.32	99.379		82,000	6,850		88,850	100,000

23 63 30 – Lubricants

23 63 30.10 Lubricant Oils

		Crew	Daily Output	Labor-Hours	Unit	Material	2023 Bare Costs Labor	Equipment	Total	Total Incl O&P
0010	**LUBRICANT OILS**									
8000	Oils									
8100	Lubricating									
8120	Oil, lubricating				Oz.	.30			.30	.33
8500	Refrigeration									
8520	Oil, refrigeration				Gal.	48			48	53
8525	Oil, refrigeration				Qt.	12.05			12.05	13.25

23 63 33 – Evaporative Refrigerant Condensers

23 63 33.10 Evaporative Condensers

		Crew	Daily Output	Labor-Hours	Unit	Material	2023 Bare Costs Labor	Equipment	Total	Total Incl O&P
0010	**EVAPORATIVE CONDENSERS**									
3400	Evaporative, copper coil, pump, fan motor									
3440	10 ton	Q-5	.54	29.630	Ea.	13,100	1,925		15,025	17,300
3460	15 ton		.50	32		13,200	2,100		15,300	17,600
3480	20 ton		.47	34.043		13,500	2,225		15,725	18,100
3500	25 ton		.45	35.556		10,600	2,325		12,925	15,100
3520	30 ton		.42	38.095		11,100	2,500		13,600	15,900
3540	40 ton	Q-6	.49	48.980		11,700	3,325		15,025	17,800
3560	50 ton		.39	61.538		16,000	4,175		20,175	23,800
3580	65 ton		.35	68.571		16,400	4,650		21,050	24,900

23 63 Refrigerant Condensers

23 63 33 – Evaporative Refrigerant Condensers

23 63 33.10 Evaporative Condensers		Crew	Daily Output	Labor-Hours	Unit	Material	2023 Bare Costs Labor	Equipment	Total	Total Incl O&P
3600	80 ton	Q-6	.33	72.727	Ea.	18,200	4,925		23,125	27,400
3620	90 ton		.29	82.759		19,900	5,600		25,500	30,300
3640	100 ton	Q-7	.36	88.889		22,600	6,150		28,750	34,000
3660	110 ton		.33	96.970		27,000	6,700		33,700	39,700
3680	125 ton		.30	107		29,200	7,375		36,575	43,200
3700	135 ton		.28	114		31,000	7,900		38,900	45,900
3720	150 ton		.25	128		33,500	8,850		42,350	50,000
3740	165 ton		.23	139		34,600	9,600		44,200	52,500
3760	185 ton		.22	145		40,000	10,000		50,000	59,000
3860	For fan damper control, add	Q-5	2	8		925	520		1,445	1,800

23 64 Packaged Water Chillers

23 64 13 – Absorption Water Chillers

23 64 13.13 Direct-Fired Absorption Water Chillers

		Crew	Daily Output	Labor-Hours	Unit	Material	Labor	Equipment	Total	Total Incl O&P
0010	**DIRECT-FIRED ABSORPTION WATER CHILLERS**									
3000	Gas fired, air cooled									
3220	5 ton	Q-5	.60	26.667	Ea.	9,200	1,750		10,950	12,700
3270	10 ton	"	.40	40	"	23,800	2,600		26,400	30,100
4000	Water cooled, duplex									
4130	100 ton	Q-7	.13	246	Ea.	153,500	17,000		170,500	194,500
4140	200 ton		.11	283		192,000	19,600		211,600	240,500
4150	300 ton		.11	299		248,500	20,700		269,200	304,000
4160	400 ton		.10	317		323,000	21,900		344,900	387,500
4170	500 ton		.10	330		406,500	22,800		429,300	481,500
4180	600 ton		.09	340		480,000	23,500		503,500	563,000
4190	700 ton		.09	360		532,500	24,800		557,300	622,500
4200	800 ton		.08	381		643,000	26,300		669,300	746,000
4210	900 ton		.08	400		745,000	27,600		772,600	860,500
4220	1,000 ton		.08	421		827,500	29,100		856,600	954,000

23 64 13.16 Indirect-Fired Absorption Water Chillers

		Crew	Daily Output	Labor-Hours	Unit	Material	Labor	Equipment	Total	Total Incl O&P
0010	**INDIRECT-FIRED ABSORPTION WATER CHILLERS**									
0020	Steam or hot water, water cooled									
0050	100 ton	Q-7	.13	240	Ea.	141,500	16,600		158,100	180,500
0100	148 ton		.12	258		270,500	17,800		288,300	324,500
0200	200 ton		.12	276		301,500	19,000		320,500	360,000
0240	250 ton		.11	291		330,000	20,100		350,100	393,500
0300	354 ton		.11	305		414,000	21,000		435,000	487,000
0400	420 ton		.10	323		450,500	22,300		472,800	529,000
0500	665 ton		.09	340		566,500	23,500		590,000	658,000
0600	750 ton		.09	364		739,000	25,100		764,100	850,500
0700	850 ton		.08	386		792,500	26,600		819,100	911,500
0800	955 ton		.08	410		755,500	28,300		783,800	873,000
0900	1,125 ton		.08	421		872,000	29,100		901,100	1,003,000
1000	1,250 ton		.07	444		1,047,500	30,700		1,078,200	1,198,000
1100	1,465 ton		.07	464		1,247,500	32,000		1,279,500	1,420,000
1200	1,660 ton		.07	478		1,467,500	33,000		1,500,500	1,663,500
2000	For two stage unit, add					80%	25%			

23 64 Packaged Water Chillers

23 64 16 – Centrifugal Water Chillers

23 64 16.10 Centrifugal Type Water Chillers

		Crew	Daily Output	Labor-Hours	Unit	Material	2023 Bare Costs Labor	Equipment	Total	Total Incl O&P
0010	**CENTRIFUGAL TYPE WATER CHILLERS**, With standard controls									
0020	Centrifugal liquid chiller, water cooled									
0030	not including water tower									
0100	2,000 ton (twin 1,000 ton units)	Q-7	.07	478	Ea.	916,500	33,000		949,500	1,057,000
0274	Centrifugal, packaged unit, water cooled, not incl. tower									
0278	200 ton	Q-7	.19	172	Ea.	145,000	11,900		156,900	176,500
0279	300 ton		.14	234		165,000	16,100		181,100	205,500
0280	400 ton		.11	283		159,500	19,600		179,100	204,000
0282	450 ton		.11	291		206,000	20,100		226,100	256,500
0290	500 ton		.11	296		211,500	20,500		232,000	263,000
0292	550 ton		.11	305		258,500	21,000		279,500	315,500
0300	600 ton		.10	311		279,000	21,500		300,500	339,000
0302	650 ton		.10	320		297,500	22,100		319,600	360,500
0304	700 ton		.10	327		320,500	22,500		343,000	386,000
0306	750 ton		.10	333		343,000	23,000		366,000	412,000
0310	800 ton		.09	340		366,000	23,500		389,500	437,500
0312	850 ton		.09	352		389,000	24,300		413,300	464,000
0316	900 ton		.09	360		412,500	24,800		437,300	490,500
0318	950 ton		.09	364		435,000	25,100		460,100	516,500
0320	1,000 ton		.09	372		458,000	25,700		483,700	542,500
0324	1,100 ton		.08	386		420,000	26,600		446,600	501,500
0330	1,200 ton		.08	395		506,500	27,300		533,800	598,000
0340	1,300 ton		.08	410		484,000	28,300		512,300	574,000
0350	1,400 ton		.08	421		590,500	29,100		619,600	693,500
0360	1,500 ton		.08	427		626,000	29,500		655,500	732,500
0370	1,600 ton		.07	438		666,500	30,300		696,800	778,500
0380	1,700 ton		.07	451		709,500	31,100		740,600	826,500
0390	1,800 ton		.07	457		751,500	31,600		783,100	873,500
0400	1,900 ton		.07	471		792,000	32,500		824,500	919,500
0430	2,000 ton		.07	492		835,500	34,000		869,500	969,500
0440	2,500 ton		.06	525		1,047,000	36,200		1,083,200	1,205,500

23 64 19 – Reciprocating Water Chillers

23 64 19.10 Reciprocating Type Water Chillers

		Crew	Daily Output	Labor-Hours	Unit	Material	Labor	Equipment	Total	Total Incl O&P
0010	**RECIPROCATING TYPE WATER CHILLERS**, With standard controls									
0494	Water chillers, integral air cooled condenser									
0538	60 ton cooling	Q-7	.28	115	Ea.	48,100	7,950		56,050	65,000
0552	80 ton cooling		.26	123		63,000	8,500		71,500	81,500
0554	90 ton cooling		.25	126		67,000	8,700		75,700	86,500
0640	150 ton cooling		.23	138		109,500	9,525		119,025	134,500
0654	190 ton cooling		.22	144		128,000	9,950		137,950	155,500
0660	210 ton cooling		.22	148		134,500	10,200		144,700	163,500
0664	275 ton cooling		.21	156		172,000	10,800		182,800	205,000
0666	300 ton cooling		.20	160		175,500	11,000		186,500	209,500
0668	330 ton cooling		.20	164		209,500	11,300		220,800	247,500
0670	360 ton cooling		.19	168		232,000	11,600		243,600	272,500
0672	390 ton cooling		.19	173		240,500	11,900		252,400	282,500
0980	Water cooled, multiple compressor, semi-hermetic, tower not incl.									
1090	45 ton cooling	Q-7	.29	111	Ea.	30,000	7,675		37,675	44,400
1130	75 ton cooling		.23	139		46,300	9,600		55,900	65,500
1140	85 ton cooling		.21	152		52,500	10,500		63,000	73,500
1150	95 ton cooling		.19	165		52,000	11,400		63,400	74,500
1160	100 ton cooling		.18	180		51,000	12,400		63,400	74,500

23 64 Packaged Water Chillers

23 64 19 – Reciprocating Water Chillers

	23 64 19.10 Reciprocating Type Water Chillers	Crew	Daily Output	Labor-Hours	Unit	Material	2023 Bare Costs Labor	Equipment	Total	Total Incl O&P
1170	115 ton cooling	Q-7	.17	190	Ea.	58,000	13,200		71,200	83,500
1180	125 ton cooling		.16	196		65,000	13,600		78,600	91,500
1200	145 ton cooling		.16	203		64,000	14,000		78,000	91,000
1210	155 ton cooling		.15	211		67,500	14,500		82,000	95,500
1300	Water cooled, single compressor, semi-hermetic, tower not incl.									
1320	40 ton cooling	Q-7	.30	108	Ea.	20,800	7,475		28,275	33,900
1340	50 ton cooling		.28	114		25,800	7,875		33,675	40,000
1360	60 ton cooling		.25	126		28,600	8,700		37,300	44,500
4000	Packaged chiller, remote air cooled condensers not incl.									
4020	15 ton cooling	Q-7	.30	108	Ea.	22,000	7,475		29,475	35,300
4030	20 ton cooling		.28	116		22,100	8,000		30,100	36,200
4040	25 ton cooling		.25	126		28,600	8,700		37,300	44,500
4050	35 ton cooling		.24	134		35,100	9,250		44,350	52,500
4060	40 ton cooling		.22	144		36,400	9,950		46,350	55,000
4066	45 ton cooling		.21	150		29,000	10,300		39,300	47,300
4070	50 ton cooling		.21	154		37,900	10,600		48,500	57,500
4080	60 ton cooling		.20	164		38,400	11,300		49,700	59,000
4090	75 ton cooling		.18	174		58,000	12,000		70,000	81,500
4100	85 ton cooling		.17	184		59,500	12,700		72,200	84,500
4110	95 ton cooling		.17	194		50,500	13,400		63,900	76,000
4120	105 ton cooling		.16	204		65,500	14,100		79,600	93,000
4130	115 ton cooling		.15	213		57,500	14,700		72,200	85,500
4140	125 ton cooling		.14	224		60,000	15,500		75,500	89,500
4150	145 ton cooling		.14	234		93,500	16,100		109,600	127,000

23 64 23 – Scroll Water Chillers

23 64 23.10 Scroll Water Chillers

		Crew	Daily Output	Labor-Hours	Unit	Material	Labor	Equipment	Total	Total Incl O&P
0010	**SCROLL WATER CHILLERS**, With standard controls									
0480	Packaged w/integral air cooled condenser									
0482	10 ton cooling	Q-7	.34	94.118	Ea.	16,400	6,500		22,900	27,700
0490	15 ton cooling		.37	86.486		19,700	5,975		25,675	30,600
0500	20 ton cooling		.34	94.118		25,000	6,500		31,500	37,200
0510	25 ton cooling		.34	94.118		34,000	6,500		40,500	47,100
0515	30 ton cooling		.31	102		35,700	7,025		42,725	49,700
0517	35 ton cooling		.31	105		38,300	7,250		45,550	53,000
0520	40 ton cooling		.30	108		40,500	7,475		47,975	55,500
0528	45 ton cooling		.29	110		37,800	7,600		45,400	53,000
0536	50 ton cooling		.28	113		46,800	7,800		54,600	63,000
0540	70 ton cooling		.27	119		62,000	8,175		70,175	80,000
0590	100 ton cooling		.25	128		76,000	8,850		84,850	96,500
0600	110 ton cooling		.24	133		78,500	9,200		87,700	99,500
0630	130 ton cooling		.24	133		95,000	9,200		104,200	118,000
0670	170 ton cooling		.23	139		117,500	9,600		127,100	143,500
0671	210 ton cooling		.22	145		134,500	10,000		144,500	163,000
0675	250 ton cooling		.21	152		150,000	10,500		160,500	180,500
0676	275 ton cooling		.21	152		172,000	10,500		182,500	204,500
0677	300 ton cooling		.20	160		175,500	11,000		186,500	209,500
0678	330 ton cooling		.20	160		209,500	11,000		220,500	247,000
0679	390 ton cooling		.19	168		240,500	11,600		252,100	282,000
0680	Scroll water cooled, single compressor, hermetic, tower not incl.									
0700	2 ton cooling	Q-5	.57	28.070	Ea.	4,175	1,825		6,000	7,325
0710	5 ton cooling		.57	28.070		5,000	1,825		6,825	8,225
0720	6 ton cooling		.42	38.005		6,325	2,475		8,800	10,700

23 64 Packaged Water Chillers

23 64 23 – Scroll Water Chillers

23 64 23.10 Scroll Water Chillers

		Crew	Daily Output	Labor-Hours	Unit	Material	2023 Bare Costs Labor	Equipment	Total	Total Incl O&P
0740	8 ton cooling	Q-5	.31	52.117	Ea.	6,900	3,400		10,300	12,700
0760	10 ton cooling	Q-6	.36	67.039		7,950	4,550		12,500	15,500
0780	15 ton cooling	"	.36	66.667		12,400	4,525		16,925	20,400
0800	20 ton cooling	Q-7	.38	83.990		14,200	5,800		20,000	24,300
0820	30 ton cooling	"	.33	96.096	↓	15,900	6,625		22,525	27,400
0900	Scroll water cooled, multiple compressor, hermetic, tower not incl.									
0910	15 ton cooling	Q-6	.36	66.667	Ea.	22,000	4,525		26,525	30,900
0930	30 ton cooling	Q-7	.36	88.889		28,600	6,150		34,750	40,700
0935	35 ton cooling		.31	103		35,100	7,125		42,225	49,200
0940	40 ton cooling		.30	107		36,400	7,375		43,775	51,000
0950	50 ton cooling		.28	114		37,900	7,900		45,800	53,500
0960	60 ton cooling		.25	128		38,400	8,850		47,250	55,500
0962	75 ton cooling		.23	139		58,000	9,600		67,600	78,000
0964	85 ton cooling		.23	139		59,500	9,600		69,100	80,000
0970	100 ton cooling		.18	178		65,500	12,300		77,800	90,500
0980	115 ton cooling		.17	188		57,500	13,000		70,500	83,000
0990	125 ton cooling		.16	200		60,000	13,800		73,800	87,000
0995	145 ton cooling	↓	.16	200	↓	93,500	13,800		107,300	123,500

23 64 26 – Rotary-Screw Water Chillers

23 64 26.10 Rotary-Screw Type Water Chillers

		Crew	Daily Output	Labor-Hours	Unit	Material	2023 Bare Costs Labor	Equipment	Total	Total Incl O&P
0010	**ROTARY-SCREW TYPE WATER CHILLERS**, With standard controls									
0110	Screw, liquid chiller, air cooled, insulated evaporator									
0120	130 ton	Q-7	.14	229	Ea.	107,000	15,800		122,800	141,500
0124	160 ton		.13	246		138,000	17,000		155,000	177,000
0128	180 ton		.13	250		155,000	17,300		172,300	196,000
0132	210 ton		.12	258		160,000	17,800		177,800	202,500
0136	270 ton		.12	267		195,500	18,400		213,900	242,500
0140	320 ton	↓	.12	276	↓	217,500	19,000		236,500	268,000
0200	Packaged unit, water cooled, not incl. tower									
0210	80 ton	Q-7	.14	224	Ea.	56,500	15,500		72,000	85,000
0220	100 ton		.14	230		69,000	15,900		84,900	99,500
0230	150 ton		.13	241		85,000	16,600		101,600	118,500
0240	200 ton		.13	252		89,500	17,400		106,900	124,000
0250	250 ton		.12	260		117,000	18,000		135,000	155,500
0260	300 ton		.12	267		138,500	18,400		156,900	180,000
0270	350 ton	↓	.12	276	↓	172,500	19,000		191,500	218,500
1450	Water cooled, tower not included									
1560	135 ton cooling, screw compressors	Q-7	.14	235	Ea.	71,500	16,200		87,700	102,500
1580	150 ton cooling, screw compressors		.13	241		82,500	16,600		99,100	116,000
1620	200 ton cooling, screw compressors		.13	250		114,000	17,300		131,300	151,000
1660	291 ton cooling, screw compressors	↓	.12	260	↓	119,000	18,000		137,000	158,000

23 64 33 – Modular Water Chillers

23 64 33.10 Direct Expansion Type Water Chillers

		Crew	Daily Output	Labor-Hours	Unit	Material	2023 Bare Costs Labor	Equipment	Total	Total Incl O&P
0010	**DIRECT EXPANSION TYPE WATER CHILLERS**, With standard controls									
8000	Direct expansion, shell and tube type, for built up systems									
8020	1 ton	Q-5	2	8	Ea.	8,950	520		9,470	10,600
8030	5 ton		1.90	8.421		14,900	550		15,450	17,100
8040	10 ton		1.70	9.412		18,400	615		19,015	21,200
8050	20 ton		1.50	10.667		21,100	695		21,795	24,300
8060	30 ton		1	16		26,800	1,050		27,850	31,100
8070	50 ton	↓	.90	17.778		43,100	1,150		44,250	49,100
8080	100 ton	Q-6	.90	26.667		68,000	1,800		69,800	77,500

23 65 Cooling Towers

23 65 13 – Forced-Draft Cooling Towers

23 65 13.10 Forced-Draft Type Cooling Towers

		Crew	Daily Output	Labor-Hours	Unit	Material	2023 Bare Costs Labor	Equipment	Total	Total Incl O&P
0010	**FORCED-DRAFT TYPE COOLING TOWERS**, Packaged units D3030-310									
0070	Galvanized steel									
0080	Induced draft, crossflow									
0100	Vertical, belt drive, 61 tons	Q-6	90	.267	TonAC	229	18.05		247.05	279
0150	100 ton		100	.240		221	16.25		237.25	267
0200	115 ton		109	.220		192	14.90		206.90	233
0250	131 ton		120	.200		231	13.55		244.55	274
0260	162 ton	▼	132	.182	▼	186	12.30		198.30	223
1000	For higher capacities, use multiples									
1500	Induced air, double flow									
1900	Vertical, gear drive, 167 ton	Q-6	126	.190	TonAC	181	12.90		193.90	218
2000	297 ton		129	.186		111	12.60		123.60	142
2100	582 ton		132	.182		62	12.30		74.30	87
2150	849 ton		142	.169		83.50	11.45		94.95	109
2200	1,016 ton	▼	150	.160	▼	84.50	10.85		95.35	109
2500	Blow through, centrifugal type									
2510	50 ton	Q-6	2.28	10.526	Ea.	15,000	715		15,715	17,600
2520	75 ton		1.52	15.789		19,400	1,075		20,475	22,900
2524	100 ton	▼	1.22	19.672		24,300	1,325		25,625	28,700
2528	125 ton	Q-7	1.31	24.427		26,600	1,675		28,275	31,700
2532	200 ton		.82	39.216		37,200	2,700		39,900	45,000
2536	250 ton		.65	49.231		44,300	3,400		47,700	54,000
2540	300 ton		.54	59.259		51,000	4,100		55,100	62,000
2544	350 ton		.47	68.085		57,500	4,700		62,200	70,500
2548	400 ton		.41	78.049		60,000	5,400		65,400	74,000
2552	450 ton		.36	88.154		72,000	6,075		78,075	88,500
2556	500 ton		.32	100		77,000	6,900		83,900	95,000
2560	550 ton		.30	108		83,000	7,450		90,450	102,000
2564	600 ton		.27	118		87,000	8,125		95,125	107,500
2568	650 ton		.25	127		96,500	8,800		105,300	119,000
2572	700 ton		.23	137		113,500	9,475		122,975	138,500
2576	750 ton		.22	147		121,500	10,100		131,600	148,500
2580	800 ton		.21	152		131,500	10,500		142,000	160,500
2584	850 ton		.20	157		140,000	10,800		150,800	170,000
2588	900 ton		.20	162		148,000	11,200		159,200	179,500
2592	950 ton		.19	170		156,500	11,800		168,300	189,500
2596	1,000 ton	▼	.18	181	▼	161,000	12,500		173,500	196,000
2700	Axial fan, induced draft									
2710	50 ton	Q-6	2.28	10.526	Ea.	13,200	715		13,915	15,600
2720	75 ton		1.52	15.789		15,500	1,075		16,575	18,600
2724	100 ton	▼	1.22	19.672		16,400	1,325		17,725	20,000
2728	125 ton	Q-7	1.31	24.427		20,200	1,675		21,875	24,700
2732	200 ton		.82	39.216		34,200	2,700		36,900	41,800
2736	250 ton		.65	49.231		38,600	3,400		42,000	47,600
2740	300 ton		.54	59.259		45,100	4,100		49,200	55,500
2744	350 ton		.47	68.085		48,100	4,700		52,800	60,000
2748	400 ton		.41	78.049		55,500	5,400		60,900	69,000
2752	450 ton		.36	88.154		61,500	6,075		67,575	76,500
2756	500 ton		.32	100		65,000	6,900		71,900	82,500
2760	550 ton		.30	108		73,000	7,450		80,450	91,000
2764	600 ton		.27	118		77,000	8,125		85,125	96,500
2768	650 ton		.25	127		84,000	8,800		92,800	105,500
2772	700 ton	▼	.23	137	▼	95,500	9,475		104,975	119,000

23 65 Cooling Towers

23 65 13 – Forced-Draft Cooling Towers

23 65 13.10 Forced-Draft Type Cooling Towers		Crew	Daily Output	Labor-Hours	Unit	Material	2023 Bare Costs Labor	Equipment	Total	Total Incl O&P
2776	750 ton	Q-7	.22	147	Ea.	99,500	10,100		109,600	124,000
2780	800 ton		.21	152		103,500	10,500		114,000	129,500
2784	850 ton		.20	157		104,500	10,800		115,300	130,500
2788	900 ton		.20	162		108,000	11,200		119,200	135,000
2792	950 ton		.19	170		114,000	11,800		125,800	142,500
2796	1,000 ton		.18	181		120,500	12,500		133,000	151,000
3000	For higher capacities, use multiples									
3500	For pumps and piping, add	Q-6	38	.632	TonAC	114	43		157	190
4000	For absorption systems, add				"	75%	75%			
4100	Cooling water chemical feeder	Q-5	3	5.333	Ea.	480	350		830	1,050
5000	Fiberglass tower on galvanized steel support structure									
5010	Draw thru									
5100	100 ton	Q-6	1.40	17.143	Ea.	15,300	1,150		16,450	18,500
5120	120 ton		1.20	20		18,300	1,350		19,650	22,200
5140	140 ton		1	24		18,700	1,625		20,325	23,000
5160	160 ton		.80	30		20,200	2,025		22,225	25,200
5180	180 ton		.65	36.923		23,600	2,500		26,100	29,700
5251	600 ton		.16	150		86,500	10,200		96,700	110,000
5252	1,000 ton		.10	250		144,000	16,900		160,900	183,500
5300	For stainless steel support structure, add					30%				
5360	For higher capacities, use multiples of each size									
6000	Stainless steel									
6010	Induced draft, crossflow, horizontal, belt drive									
6100	57 ton	Q-6	1.50	16	Ea.	30,400	1,075		31,475	35,100
6120	91 ton		.99	24.242		37,400	1,650		39,050	43,600
6140	111 ton		.43	55.814		56,500	3,775		60,275	67,500
6160	126 ton		.22	109		58,000	7,400		65,400	75,000
6170	Induced draft, crossflow, vertical, gear drive									
6172	167 ton	Q-6	.75	32	Ea.	68,000	2,175		70,175	78,000
6174	297 ton		.43	55.814		75,500	3,775		79,275	88,500
6176	582 ton		.23	104		121,000	7,075		128,075	143,500
6178	849 ton		.17	141		168,000	9,550		177,550	199,000
6180	1,016 ton		.15	160		213,000	10,800		223,800	250,500

23 65 33 – Liquid Coolers

23 65 33.10 Liquid Cooler, Closed Circuit Type Cooling Towers

		Crew	Daily Output	Labor-Hours	Unit	Material	Labor	Equipment	Total	Total Incl O&P
0010	**LIQUID COOLER, CLOSED CIRCUIT TYPE COOLING TOWERS**									
0070	Packaged options include: vibration switch, sump sweeper piping,									
0076	grooved coil connections, fan motor inverter capable,									
0080	304 st. stl. cold water basin, external platform w/ladder.									
0100	50 ton	Q-6	2	12	Ea.	40,900	815		41,715	46,100
0150	100 ton	"	1.13	21.239		81,500	1,450		82,950	92,000
0200	150 ton	Q-7	.98	32.653		122,500	2,250		124,750	138,500
0250	200 ton		.78	41.026		163,500	2,825		166,325	184,000
0300	250 ton		.63	50.794		204,500	3,500		208,000	229,500

23 72 Air-to-Air Energy Recovery Equipment

23 72 13 – Heat-Wheel Air-to-Air Energy-Recovery Equipment

23 72 13.10 Heat-Wheel Air-to-Air Energy Recovery Equip.		Crew	Daily Output	Labor-Hours	Unit	Material	2023 Bare Costs Labor	2023 Bare Costs Equipment	Total	Total Incl O&P
0010	**HEAT-WHEEL AIR-TO-AIR ENERGY RECOVERY EQUIPMENT**									
0100	Air to air									
4000	Enthalpy recovery wheel									
4010	1,000 max CFM	G	Q-9	1.20	13.333	Ea.	7,650	840		8,490	9,700
4020	2,000 max CFM	G		1	16		9,025	1,000		10,025	11,500
4030	4,000 max CFM	G		.80	20		10,500	1,275		11,775	13,400
4040	6,000 max CFM	G		.70	22.857		12,200	1,450		13,650	15,600
4050	8,000 max CFM	G	Q-10	1	24		13,400	1,575		14,975	17,100
4060	10,000 max CFM	G		.90	26.667		16,000	1,750		17,750	20,200
4070	20,000 max CFM	G		.80	30		29,300	1,975		31,275	35,200
4080	25,000 max CFM	G		.70	34.286		35,500	2,250		37,750	42,400
4090	30,000 max CFM	G		.50	48		39,300	3,150		42,450	48,000
4100	40,000 max CFM	G		.45	53.333		54,500	3,500		58,000	65,500
4110	50,000 max CFM	G		.40	60		63,500	3,925		67,425	76,000

23 72 16 – Heat-Pipe Air-To-Air Energy-Recovery Equipment

23 72 16.10 Heat Pipes

		Crew	Daily Output	Labor-Hours	Unit	Material	Labor	Equipment	Total	Total Incl O&P
0010	**HEAT PIPES**									
8000	Heat pipe type, glycol, 50% efficient									
8010	100 MBH, 1,700 CFM	1 Stpi	.80	10	Ea.	5,275	725		6,000	6,900
8020	160 MBH, 2,700 CFM		.60	13.333		7,100	965		8,065	9,250
8030	620 MBH, 4,000 CFM		.40	20		10,700	1,450		12,150	14,000

23 73 Indoor Central-Station Air-Handling Units

23 73 13 – Modular Indoor Central-Station Air-Handling Units

23 73 13.10 Air-Handling Units

		Crew	Daily Output	Labor-Hours	Unit	Material	Labor	Equipment	Total	Total Incl O&P
0010	**AIR-HANDLING UNITS**, Built-Up									
0100	With cooling/heating coil section, filters, mixing box									
0880	Single zone, horizontal/vertical									
0890	Constant volume									
0900	1,600 CFM	Q-5	1.20	13.333	Ea.	5,975	870		6,845	7,875
0906	2,000 CFM		1.10	14.545		10,500	950		11,450	12,900
0910	3,000 CFM		1	16		10,900	1,050		11,950	13,600
0916	4,000 CFM		.95	16.842		14,200	1,100		15,300	17,300
0920	5,000 CFM	Q-6	1.40	17.143		17,300	1,150		18,450	20,800
0926	6,500 CFM		1.30	18.462		21,700	1,250		22,950	25,800
0930	7,500 CFM		1.20	20		33,700	1,350		35,050	39,100
0936	9,200 CFM		1.10	21.818		36,800	1,475		38,275	42,600
0940	11,500 CFM		1	24		43,300	1,625		44,925	50,000
0946	13,200 CFM		.90	26.667		37,200	1,800		39,000	43,700
0950	16,500 CFM		.80	30		66,500	2,025		68,525	76,000
0960	19,500 CFM		.70	34.286		77,000	2,325		79,325	88,500
0970	22,000 CFM		.60	40		87,000	2,700		89,700	100,000
0980	27,000 CFM		.50	48		73,000	3,250		76,250	85,500
0990	34,000 CFM		.40	60		93,000	4,075		97,075	108,000
1000	40,000 CFM		.30	80		111,000	5,425		116,425	130,500
1010	47,000 CFM		.20	120		122,000	8,125		130,125	146,500
2300	Multi-zone, horizontal or vertical, blow-thru fan									
2310	3,000 CFM	Q-5	1	16	Ea.	8,625	1,050		9,675	11,000
2314	4,000 CFM	"	.95	16.842		12,000	1,100		13,100	14,800
2318	5,000 CFM	Q-6	1.40	17.143		14,900	1,150		16,050	18,100

For customer support on your Mechanical Costs with RSMeans data, call 800.448.8182.

23 73 Indoor Central-Station Air-Handling Units

23 73 13 – Modular Indoor Central-Station Air-Handling Units

23 73 13.10 Air-Handling Units		Crew	Daily Output	Labor-Hours	Unit	Material	2023 Bare Costs Labor	Equipment	Total	Total Incl O&P
2322	6,500 CFM	Q-6	1.30	18.462	Ea.	19,300	1,250		20,550	23,200
2326	7,500 CFM		1.20	20		21,200	1,350		22,550	25,300
2330	9,200 CFM		1.10	21.818		27,500	1,475		28,975	32,400
2334	11,500 CFM		1	24		30,300	1,625		31,925	35,700
2336	13,200 CFM		.90	26.667		34,700	1,800		36,500	40,800
2340	16,500 CFM		.80	30		43,200	2,025		45,225	50,500
2344	19,500 CFM		.70	34.286		51,000	2,325		53,325	59,500
2348	22,000 CFM		.60	40		57,500	2,700		60,200	67,500
2350	22,500 CFM		.55	43.636		58,000	2,950		60,950	68,500
2352	27,000 CFM		.50	48		61,000	3,250		64,250	72,500
2356	34,000 CFM		.40	60		77,000	4,075		81,075	91,000
2360	40,000 CFM		.30	80		83,500	5,425		88,925	100,000
2364	47,000 CFM		.20	120		106,500	8,125		114,625	129,000

23 73 13.20 Air-Handling Units, Packaged Indoor Type

0010	**AIR-HANDLING UNITS, PACKAGED INDOOR TYPE**									
0040	Cooling coils may be chilled water or DX									
0050	Heating coils may be hot water, steam or electric									
1090	Constant volume									
1200	2,000 CFM	Q-5	1.10	14.545	Ea.	12,100	950		13,050	14,700
1400	5,000 CFM	Q-6	.80	30		19,500	2,025		21,525	24,500
1550	10,000 CFM		.54	44.444		28,800	3,000		31,800	36,100
1670	15,000 CFM		.38	63.158		59,000	4,275		63,275	71,000
1700	20,000 CFM		.31	77.419		74,500	5,250		79,750	90,000
1710	30,000 CFM		.27	88.889		101,500	6,025		107,525	120,500
2300	Variable air volume									
2330	2,000 CFM	Q-5	1	16	Ea.	17,300	1,050		18,350	20,600
2340	5,000 CFM	Q-6	.70	34.286		23,800	2,325		26,125	29,700
2350	10,000 CFM		.50	48		46,300	3,250		49,550	56,000
2360	15,000 CFM		.40	60		67,500	4,075		71,575	80,500
2370	20,000 CFM		.29	82.759		86,500	5,600		92,100	103,500
2380	30,000 CFM		.20	120		104,500	8,125		112,625	127,000

23 73 39 – Indoor, Direct Gas-Fired Heating and Ventilating Units

23 73 39.10 Make-Up Air Unit

0010	**MAKE-UP AIR UNIT**									
0020	Indoor suspension, natural/LP gas, direct fired,									
0032	standard control. For flue see Section 23 51 23.10									
0040	70°F temperature rise, MBH is input									
0100	75 MBH input	Q-6	3.60	6.667	Ea.	4,925	450		5,375	6,100
0120	100 MBH input		3.40	7.059		5,650	480		6,130	6,950
0140	125 MBH input		3.20	7.500		5,275	510		5,785	6,550
0160	150 MBH input		3	8		5,825	540		6,365	7,200
0180	175 MBH input		2.80	8.571		5,950	580		6,530	7,425
0200	200 MBH input		2.60	9.231		7,100	625		7,725	8,725
0220	225 MBH input		2.40	10		6,550	675		7,225	8,200
0240	250 MBH input		2	12		7,625	815		8,440	9,600
0260	300 MBH input		1.90	12.632		7,850	855		8,705	9,900
0280	350 MBH input		1.75	13.714		9,625	930		10,555	12,000
0300	400 MBH input		1.60	15		16,200	1,025		17,225	19,300
0320	840 MBH input		1.20	20		33,100	1,350		34,450	38,500
0340	1,200 MBH input		.88	27.273		42,700	1,850		44,550	49,800
0600	For discharge louver assembly, add					5%				
0700	For filters, add					10%				

23 73 Indoor Central-Station Air-Handling Units

23 73 39 – Indoor, Direct Gas-Fired Heating and Ventilating Units

23 73 39.10 Make-Up Air Unit

		Crew	Daily Output	Labor-Hours	Unit	Material	2023 Bare Costs Labor	Equipment	Total	Total Incl O&P
0800	For air shut-off damper section, add				Ea.	30%				

23 74 Packaged Outdoor HVAC Equipment

23 74 13 – Packaged, Outdoor, Central-Station Air-Handling Units

23 74 13.10 Packaged, Outdoor Type, Central-Station AHU

		Crew	Daily Output	Labor-Hours	Unit	Material	Labor	Equipment	Total	Total Incl O&P
0010	**PACKAGED, OUTDOOR TYPE, CENTRAL-STATION AIR-HANDLING UNITS**									
2900	Cooling coils may be chilled water or DX									
2910	Heating coils may be hot water, steam or electric									
3000	Weathertight, ground or rooftop									
3010	Constant volume									
3100	2,000 CFM	Q-6	1	24	Ea.	25,400	1,625		27,025	30,400
3140	5,000 CFM		.79	30.380		29,600	2,050		31,650	35,700
3150	10,000 CFM		.52	46.154		69,500	3,125		72,625	81,000
3160	15,000 CFM		.41	58.537		101,000	3,975		104,975	117,000
3170	20,000 CFM		.30	80		139,000	5,425		144,425	161,000
3180	30,000 CFM		.24	100		161,000	6,775		167,775	187,000
3200	Variable air volume									
3210	2,000 CFM	Q-6	.96	25	Ea.	16,800	1,700		18,500	21,000
3240	5,000 CFM		.73	32.877		33,900	2,225		36,125	40,500
3250	10,000 CFM		.50	48		72,000	3,250		75,250	84,000
3260	15,000 CFM		.40	60		110,500	4,075		114,575	127,500
3270	20,000 CFM		.29	82.759		143,500	5,600		149,100	166,000
3280	30,000 CFM		.20	120		169,000	8,125		177,125	198,000

23 74 23 – Packaged, Outdoor, Heating-Only Makeup-Air Units

23 74 23.16 Packaged, Ind.-Fired, In/Outdoor

		Crew	Daily Output	Labor-Hours	Unit	Material	Labor	Equipment	Total	Total Incl O&P
0010	**PACKAGED, IND.-FIRED, IN/OUTDOOR**, Heat-Only Makeup-Air Units									
1000	Rooftop unit, natural gas, gravity vent, S.S. exchanger									
1010	70°F temperature rise, MBH is input									
1020	250 MBH	Q-6	4	6	Ea.	18,500	405		18,905	20,900
1040	400 MBH		3.60	6.667		21,100	450		21,550	23,900
1060	550 MBH		3.30	7.273		23,000	495		23,495	26,000
1080	750 MBH		3	8		27,200	540		27,740	30,800
1100	1,000 MBH		2.60	9.231		30,500	625		31,125	34,500
1120	1,750 MBH		2.30	10.435		34,400	705		35,105	38,900
1140	2,500 MBH		1.90	12.632		51,000	855		51,855	57,500
1160	3,250 MBH		1.40	17.143		43,700	1,150		44,850	49,700
1180	4,000 MBH		1.20	20		75,500	1,350		76,850	85,000
1200	6,000 MBH		1	24		95,500	1,625		97,125	107,500
1600	For cleanable filters, add					5%				
1700	For electric modulating gas control, add					10%				

23 74 33 – Dedicated Outdoor-Air Units

23 74 33.10 Rooftop Air Conditioners

			Crew	Daily Output	Labor-Hours	Unit	Material	Labor	Equipment	Total	Total Incl O&P
0010	**ROOFTOP AIR CONDITIONERS**, Standard controls, curb, economizer										
1000	Single zone, electric cool, gas heat										
1100	3 ton cooling, 60 MBH heating	D3050-150	Q-5	.70	22.857	Ea.	1,825	1,500		3,325	4,250
1120	4 ton cooling, 95 MBH heating	D3050-155		.61	26.403		3,475	1,725		5,200	6,400
1140	5 ton cooling, 112 MBH heating	R236000-10		.56	28.521		4,275	1,850		6,125	7,475
1145	6 ton cooling, 140 MBH heating	R236000-20		.52	30.769		5,325	2,000		7,325	8,875
1150	7.5 ton cooling, 170 MBH heating			.50	32.258		6,525	2,100		8,625	10,300
1156	8.5 ton cooling, 170 MBH heating			.46	34.783		7,375	2,275		9,650	11,500

23 74 Packaged Outdoor HVAC Equipment

23 74 33 – Dedicated Outdoor-Air Units

23 74 33.10 Rooftop Air Conditioners		Crew	Daily Output	Labor-Hours	Unit	Material	2023 Bare Costs Labor	Equipment	Total	Total Incl O&P
1160	10 ton cooling, 200 MBH heating	Q-6	.67	35.982	Ea.	8,050	2,425		10,475	12,500
1170	12.5 ton cooling, 230 MBH heating		.63	37.975		9,100	2,575		11,675	13,800
1180	15 ton cooling, 270 MBH heating		.57	42.032		12,200	2,850		15,050	17,700
1190	17.5 ton cooling, 330 MBH heating		.52	45.889		13,100	3,100		16,200	19,100
1200	20 ton cooling, 360 MBH heating	Q-7	.67	47.976		15,700	3,325		19,025	22,300
1210	25 ton cooling, 450 MBH heating		.56	57.554		36,900	3,975		40,875	46,500
1220	30 ton cooling, 540 MBH heating		.47	68.376		37,200	4,725		41,925	48,000
1240	40 ton cooling, 675 MBH heating		.35	91.168		45,400	6,300		51,700	59,500
1260	50 ton cooling, 810 MBH heating		.28	114		51,500	7,875		59,375	68,500
1265	60 ton cooling, 900 MBH heating		.23	137		61,500	9,450		70,950	82,000
1270	80 ton cooling, 1,000 MBH heating		.20	160		80,500	11,000		91,500	105,000
1275	90 ton cooling, 1,200 MBH heating		.17	188		113,000	13,000		126,000	144,000
1280	100 ton cooling, 1,350 MBH heating		.14	229		125,500	15,800		141,300	161,500
1300	Electric cool, electric heat									
1310	5 ton	Q-5	.63	25.600	Ea.	6,250	1,675		7,925	9,375
1314	10 ton	Q-6	.74	32.432		7,325	2,200		9,525	11,300
1318	15 ton	"	.64	37.795		10,400	2,550		12,950	15,300
1322	20 ton	Q-7	.74	43.185		12,900	2,975		15,875	18,700
1326	25 ton		.62	51.696		14,600	3,575		18,175	21,400
1330	30 ton		.52	61.657		25,200	4,250		29,450	34,200
1334	40 ton		.39	82.051		33,600	5,675		39,275	45,400
1338	50 ton		.31	103		42,400	7,075		49,475	57,000
1342	60 ton		.26	123		51,000	8,500		59,500	69,000
1346	75 ton		.21	154		64,000	10,600		74,600	86,000
2000	Multizone, electric cool, gas heat, economizer									
2100	15 ton cooling, 360 MBH heating	Q-7	.61	52.545	Ea.	71,000	3,625		74,625	83,500
2120	20 ton cooling, 360 MBH heating		.53	60.038		64,000	4,150		68,150	76,500
2140	25 ton cooling, 450 MBH heating		.45	71.910		77,000	4,975		81,975	92,000
2160	28 ton cooling, 450 MBH heating		.41	79.012		86,500	5,450		91,950	103,000
2180	30 ton cooling, 540 MBH heating		.37	85.562		97,500	5,900		103,400	116,000
2200	40 ton cooling, 540 MBH heating		.28	114		111,000	7,875		118,875	134,000
2210	50 ton cooling, 540 MBH heating		.23	142		142,000	9,825		151,825	171,000
2220	70 ton cooling, 1,500 MBH heating		.16	199		151,500	13,700		165,200	187,000
2240	80 ton cooling, 1,500 MBH heating		.14	229		173,000	15,800		188,800	213,500
2260	90 ton cooling, 1,500 MBH heating		.13	256		205,000	17,700		222,700	251,500
2280	105 ton cooling, 1,500 MBH heating		.11	291		228,000	20,100		248,100	280,500
2400	For hot water heat coil, deduct					5%				
2500	For steam heat coil, deduct					2%				
2600	For electric heat, deduct					3%	5%			
4000	Single zone, electric cool, gas heat, variable air volume									
4100	12.5 ton cooling, 230 MBH heating	Q-6	.55	43.716	Ea.	11,700	2,950		14,650	17,300
4120	18 ton cooling, 330 MBH heating	"	.46	52.747		16,500	3,575		20,075	23,500
4140	25 ton cooling, 450 MBH heating	Q-7	.48	66.116		41,100	4,575		45,675	52,000
4160	40 ton cooling, 675 MBH heating		.31	105		52,500	7,250		59,750	69,000
4180	60 ton cooling, 900 MBH heating		.20	158		75,000	10,900		85,900	98,500
4200	80 ton cooling, 1,000 MBH heating		.15	209		97,000	14,400		111,400	128,000
5000	Single zone, electric cool only									
5050	3 ton cooling	Q-5	.88	18.203	Ea.	4,000	1,200		5,200	6,175
5060	4 ton cooling		.76	21.108		3,925	1,375		5,300	6,375
5070	5 ton cooling		.70	22.792		2,700	1,500		4,200	5,200
5080	6 ton cooling		.65	24.502		4,375	1,600		5,975	7,175
5090	7.5 ton cooling		.62	25.806		6,450	1,675		8,125	9,600
5100	8.5 ton cooling		.59	26.981		7,550	1,750		9,300	10,900

23 74 Packaged Outdoor HVAC Equipment

23 74 33 – Dedicated Outdoor-Air Units

23 74 33.10 Rooftop Air Conditioners		Crew	Daily Output	Labor-Hours	Unit	Material	2023 Bare Costs Labor	Equipment	Total	Total Incl O&P
5110	10 ton cooling	Q-6	.83	28.812	Ea.	8,525	1,950		10,475	12,300
5120	12.5 ton cooling		.80	30		11,500	2,025		13,525	15,600
5130	15 ton cooling		.71	33.613		15,600	2,275		17,875	20,600
5140	17.5 ton cooling		.65	36.697		16,200	2,475		18,675	21,500
5150	20 ton cooling	Q-7	.83	38.415		22,800	2,650		25,450	29,100
5160	25 ton cooling		.70	45.977		21,900	3,175		25,075	28,700
5170	30 ton cooling		.59	54.701		24,500	3,775		28,275	32,600
5180	40 ton cooling		.44	73.059		33,000	5,050		38,050	43,800
5190	50 ton cooling		.38	84.211		39,100	5,825		44,925	51,500
5200	60 ton cooling		.28	114		50,000	7,900		57,900	67,000
5400	For low heat, add					7%				
5410	For high heat, add					10%				
6000	Single zone electric cooling with variable volume distribution									
6020	20 ton cooling	Q-7	.72	44.199	Ea.	22,700	3,050		25,750	29,500
6030	25 ton cooling		.61	52.893		27,500	3,650		31,150	35,800
6040	30 ton cooling		.51	62.868		30,700	4,350		35,050	40,300
6050	40 ton cooling		.38	83.990		38,100	5,800		43,900	50,500
6060	50 ton cooling		.31	105		39,500	7,250		46,750	54,500
6070	60 ton cooling		.25	126		52,500	8,700		61,200	71,000
6200	For low heat, add					7%				
6210	For high heat, add					10%				
7000	Multizone, cool/heat, variable volume distribution									
7100	50 ton cooling	Q-7	.20	164	Ea.	103,500	11,300		114,800	130,500
7110	70 ton cooling		.14	229		144,500	15,800		160,300	182,500
7120	90 ton cooling		.11	296		158,500	20,500		179,000	205,000
7130	105 ton cooling		.10	333		189,000	23,000		212,000	242,500
7140	120 ton cooling		.08	381		216,000	26,300		242,300	276,500
7150	140 ton cooling		.07	444		227,500	30,700		258,200	296,500
7300	Penthouse unit, cool/heat, variable volume distribution									
7400	150 ton cooling	Q-7	.10	311	Ea.	361,000	21,500		382,500	429,500
7410	170 ton cooling		.10	320		396,000	22,100		418,100	468,500
7420	200 ton cooling		.10	327		466,000	22,500		488,500	546,000
7430	225 ton cooling		.09	340		593,500	23,500		617,000	688,000
7440	250 ton cooling		.09	360		520,500	24,800		545,300	609,500
7450	270 ton cooling		.09	364		562,000	25,100		587,100	655,500
7460	300 ton cooling		.09	372		624,500	25,700		650,200	725,500
9400	Sub assemblies for assembly systems									
9410	Ductwork, per ton, rooftop 1 zone units	Q-9	.96	16.667	Ton	385	1,050		1,435	2,000
9420	Ductwork, per ton, rooftop multizone units		.50	32		545	2,025		2,570	3,650
9430	Ductwork, VAV cooling/ton, rooftop multizone, 1 zone/ton		.32	50		810	3,150		3,960	5,650
9440	Ductwork per ton, packaged water & air cooled units		1.26	12.698		81	800		881	1,300
9450	Ductwork per ton, split system remote condensing units		1.32	12.121		76	765		841	1,225
9500	Ductwork package for residential units, 1 ton		.80	20	Ea.	640	1,275		1,915	2,600
9520	2 ton		.40	40		1,275	2,525		3,800	5,200
9530	3 ton		.27	59.259		1,925	3,750		5,675	7,750
9540	4 ton	Q-10	.30	80		2,550	5,250		7,800	10,700
9550	5 ton		.23	104		3,200	6,825		10,025	13,800
9560	6 ton		.20	120		3,850	7,850		11,700	16,000
9570	7 ton		.17	141		4,475	9,250		13,725	18,800
9580	8 ton		.15	160		5,125	10,500		15,625	21,400

23 76 Evaporative Air-Cooling Equipment

23 76 13 – Direct Evaporative Air Coolers

23 76 13.10 Evaporative Coolers

			Crew	Daily Output	Labor-Hours	Unit	Material	2023 Bare Costs Labor	Equipment	Total	Total Incl O&P
0010	**EVAPORATIVE COOLERS** (Swamp Coolers) ducted, not incl. duct.										
0100	Side discharge style, capacities at 0.25" S.P.										
0120	1,785 CFM, 1/3 HP, 115 V	G	Q-9	5	3.200	Ea.	705	202		907	1,075
0140	2,740 CFM, 1/3 HP, 115 V	G		4.50	3.556		850	224		1,074	1,275
0160	3,235 CFM, 1/2 HP, 115 V	G		4	4		845	253		1,098	1,300
0180	3,615 CFM, 1/2 HP, 230 V	G		3.60	4.444		1,025	281		1,306	1,550
0200	4,215 CFM, 3/4 HP, 230 V	G		3.20	5		1,125	315		1,440	1,725
0220	5,255 CFM, 1 HP, 115/230 V	G		3	5.333		2,550	335		2,885	3,325
0240	6,090 CFM, 1 HP, 230/460 V	G		2.80	5.714		2,900	360		3,260	3,750
0260	8,300 CFM, 1-1/2 HP, 230/460 V	G		2.60	6.154		3,700	390		4,090	4,650
0280	8,360 CFM, 1-1/2 HP, 230/460 V	G		2.20	7.273		2,825	460		3,285	3,800
0300	9,725 CFM, 2 HP, 230/460 V	G		1.80	8.889		3,175	560		3,735	4,350
0320	11,715 CFM, 3 HP, 230/460 V	G		1.40	11.429		4,400	720		5,120	5,925
0340	14,410 CFM, 5 HP, 230/460 V	G		1	16		5,225	1,000		6,225	7,275
0400	For two-speed motor, add						5%				
0500	For down discharge style, add						10%				

23 76 26 – Fan Coil Evaporators for Coolers/Freezers

23 76 26.10 Evaporators

		Crew	Daily Output	Labor-Hours	Unit	Material	Labor	Equipment	Total	Total Incl O&P
0010	**EVAPORATORS**, DX coils, remote compressors not included.									
1000	Coolers, reach-in type, above freezing temperatures									
1300	Shallow depth, wall mount, 7 fins per inch, air defrost									
1310	600 BTUH, 8" fan, rust-proof core	Q-5	3.80	4.211	Ea.	800	275		1,075	1,300
1320	900 BTUH, 8" fan, rust-proof core		3.30	4.848		1,000	315		1,315	1,575
1330	1,200 BTUH, 8" fan, rust-proof core		3	5.333		1,325	350		1,675	1,975
1340	1,800 BTUH, 8" fan, rust-proof core		2.40	6.667		1,375	435		1,810	2,175
1350	2,500 BTUH, 10" fan, rust-proof core		2.20	7.273		1,450	475		1,925	2,300
1360	3,500 BTUH, 10" fan		2	8		1,575	520		2,095	2,500
1370	4,500 BTUH, 10" fan		1.90	8.421		1,775	550		2,325	2,775
1390	For pan drain, add					84.50			84.50	93
1600	Undercounter refrigerators, ceiling or wall mount,									
1610	8 fins per inch, air defrost, rust-proof core									
1630	800 BTUH, one 6" fan	Q-5	5	3.200	Ea.	460	209		669	815
1640	1,300 BTUH, two 6" fans		4	4		590	261		851	1,050
1650	1,700 BTUH, two 6" fans		3.60	4.444		660	290		950	1,150
2000	Coolers, reach-in and walk-in types, above freezing temperatures									
2600	Two-way discharge, ceiling mount, 150 to 4,100 CFM,									
2610	above 34°F applications, air defrost									
2630	900 BTUH, 7 fins per inch, 8" fan	Q-5	4	4	Ea.	510	261		771	950
2660	2,500 BTUH, 7 fins per inch, 10" fan		2.60	6.154		940	400		1,340	1,625
2690	5,500 BTUH, 7 fins per inch, 12" fan		1.70	9.412		1,875	615		2,490	2,975
2720	8,500 BTUH, 8 fins per inch, 16" fan		1.20	13.333		2,525	870		3,395	4,075
2750	15,000 BTUH, 7 fins per inch, 18" fan		1.10	14.545		3,125	950		4,075	4,850
2770	24,000 BTUH, 7 fins per inch, two 16" fans		1	16		4,675	1,050		5,725	6,675
2790	30,000 BTUH, 7 fins per inch, two 18" fans		.90	17.778		5,800	1,150		6,950	8,100
2850	Two-way discharge, low profile, ceiling mount,									
2860	8 fins per inch, 200 to 570 CFM, air defrost									
2880	800 BTUH, one 6" fan	Q-5	4	4	Ea.	560	261		821	1,000
2890	1,300 BTUH, two 6" fans		3.50	4.571		675	299		974	1,200
2900	1,800 BTUH, two 6" fans		3.30	4.848		835	315		1,150	1,400
2910	2,700 BTUH, three 6" fans		2.70	5.926		1,025	385		1,410	1,700
3000	Coolers, walk-in type, above freezing temperatures									
3300	General use, ceiling mount, 108 to 2,080 CFM									

23 76 Evaporative Air-Cooling Equipment

23 76 26 – Fan Coil Evaporators for Coolers/Freezers

23 76 26.10 Evaporators

		Crew	Daily Output	Labor-Hours	Unit	Material	2023 Bare Costs Labor	Equipment	Total	Total Incl O&P
3320	600 BTUH, 7 fins per inch, 6" fan	Q-5	5.20	3.077	Ea.	415	201		616	760
3340	1,200 BTUH, 7 fins per inch, 8" fan		3.70	4.324		575	282		857	1,050
3360	1,800 BTUH, 7 fins per inch, 10" fan		2.70	5.926		805	385		1,190	1,450
3380	3,500 BTUH, 7 fins per inch, 12" fan		2.40	6.667		1,175	435		1,610	1,950
3400	5,500 BTUH, 8 fins per inch, 12" fan		2	8		1,325	520		1,845	2,225
3430	8,500 BTUH, 8 fins per inch, 16" fan		1.40	11.429		1,975	745		2,720	3,300
3460	15,000 BTUH, 7 fins per inch, two 16" fans		1.10	14.545		3,150	950		4,100	4,900
3640	Low velocity, high latent load, ceiling mount,									
3650	1,050 to 2,420 CFM, air defrost, 6 fins per inch									
3670	6,700 BTUH, two 10" fans	Q-5	1.30	12.308	Ea.	4,050	805		4,855	5,650
3680	10,000 BTUH, three 10" fans		1	16		5,100	1,050		6,150	7,150
3690	13,500 BTUH, three 10" fans		1	16		6,475	1,050		7,525	8,675
3700	18,000 BTUH, four 10" fans		1	16		8,075	1,050		9,125	10,400
3710	26,500 BTUH, four 10" fans		.80	20		10,200	1,300		11,500	13,300
3730	For electric defrost, add					17%				
5000	Freezers and coolers, reach-in type, above 34°F									
5030	to sub-freezing temperature range, low latent load,									
5050	air defrost, 7 fins per inch									
5070	1,200 BTUH, 8" fan, rustproof core	Q-5	4.40	3.636	Ea.	565	237		802	975
5080	1,500 BTUH, 8" fan, rustproof core		4.20	3.810		590	249		839	1,025
5090	1,800 BTUH, 8" fan, rustproof core		3.70	4.324		600	282		882	1,075
5100	2,500 BTUH, 10" fan, rustproof core		2.90	5.517		690	360		1,050	1,300
5110	3,500 BTUH, 10" fan, rustproof core		2.50	6.400		950	420		1,370	1,675
5120	4,500 BTUH, 12" fan, rustproof core		2.10	7.619		1,225	500		1,725	2,100
6000	Freezers and coolers, walk-in type									
6050	1,960 to 18,000 CFM, medium profile									
6060	Standard motor, 6 fins per inch, to -30°F, all aluminum									
6080	10,500 BTUH, air defrost, one 18" fan	Q-5	1.40	11.429	Ea.	4,525	745		5,270	6,100
6090	12,500 BTUH, air defrost, one 18" fan		1.40	11.429		5,925	745		6,670	7,625
6100	16,400 BTUH, air defrost, one 18" fan		1.30	12.308		6,150	805		6,955	7,975
6110	20,900 BTUH, air defrost, one 18" fan		1	16		7,500	1,050		8,550	9,800
6120	27,000 BTUH, air defrost, two 18" fans		1	16		9,575	1,050		10,625	12,100
6130	32,900 BTUH, air defrost, two 20" fans	Q-6	1.30	18.462		7,725	1,250		8,975	10,400
6140	39,000 BTUH, air defrost, two 20" fans		1.25	19.200		9,975	1,300		11,275	13,000
6150	44,100 BTUH, air defrost, three 20" fans		1	24		11,400	1,625		13,025	15,000
6155	53,000 BTUH, air defrost, three 20" fans		1	24		12,500	1,625		14,125	16,200
6160	66,200 BTUH, air defrost, four 20" fans		1	24		12,100	1,625		13,725	15,700
6170	78,000 BTUH, air defrost, four 20" fans		.80	30		14,000	2,025		16,025	18,400
6180	88,200 BTUH, air defrost, four 24" fans		.60	40		15,100	2,700		17,800	20,700
6190	110,000 BTUH, air defrost, four 24" fans		.50	48		18,200	3,250		21,450	24,900
6330	Hot gas defrost, standard motor units, add					35%				
6370	Electric defrost, 230V, standard motor, add					16%				
6410	460V, standard or high capacity motor, add					25%				
6800	Eight fins per inch, increases BTUH 75%									
6810	Standard capacity, add				Ea.	5%				
6830	Hot gas & electric defrost not recommended									
7000	800 to 4,150 CFM, 12" fans									
7010	Four fins per inch									
7030	3,400 BTUH, 1 fan	Q-5	2.80	5.714	Ea.	1,075	375		1,450	1,725
7040	4,200 BTUH, 1 fan		2.40	6.667		1,100	435		1,535	1,850
7050	5,300 BTUH, 1 fan		1.90	8.421		1,275	550		1,825	2,225
7060	6,800 BTUH, 1 fan		1.70	9.412		1,675	615		2,290	2,750
7070	8,400 BTUH, 2 fans		1.60	10		1,900	655		2,555	3,050

For customer support on your Mechanical Costs with RSMeans data, call 800.448.8182.

23 76 Evaporative Air-Cooling Equipment

23 76 26 – Fan Coil Evaporators for Coolers/Freezers

23 76 26.10 Evaporators		Crew	Daily Output	Labor-Hours	Unit	Material	2023 Bare Costs Labor	2023 Bare Costs Equipment	Total	Total Incl O&P
7080	10,500 BTUH, 2 fans	Q-5	1.40	11.429	Ea.	1,975	745		2,720	3,300
7090	13,000 BTUH, 3 fans		1.30	12.308		2,125	805		2,930	3,525
7100	17,000 BTUH, 4 fans		1.20	13.333		3,100	870		3,970	4,725
7110	21,500 BTUH, 5 fans		1	16		4,050	1,050		5,100	6,025
7160	Six fins per inch increases BTUH 35%, add					5%				
7180	Eight fins per inch increases BTUH 53%,									
7190	not recommended for below 35°F, add				Ea.	8%				
7210	For 12°F temperature differential, add					20%				
7230	For adjustable thermostat control, add					555			555	610
7240	For hot gas defrost, except 8 fin models									
7250	on applications below 35°F, add				Ea.	58%				
7260	For electric defrost, except 8 fin models									
7270	on applications below 35°F, add				Ea.	36%				
8000	Freezers, pass-thru door uprights, walk-in storage									
8300	Low temperature, thin profile, electric defrost									
8310	138 to 1,800 CFM, 5 fins per inch									
8320	900 BTUH, one 6" fan	Q-5	3.30	4.848	Ea.	720	315		1,035	1,275
8340	1,500 BTUH, two 6" fans		2.20	7.273		1,075	475		1,550	1,900
8360	2,600 BTUH, three 6" fans		1.90	8.421		1,500	550		2,050	2,475
8370	3,300 BTUH, four 6" fans		1.70	9.412		1,700	615		2,315	2,800
8380	4,400 BTUH, five 6" fans		1.40	11.429		2,350	745		3,095	3,725
8400	7,000 BTUH, three 10" fans		1.30	12.308		2,975	805		3,780	4,450
8410	8,700 BTUH, four 10" fans		1.10	14.545		2,625	950		3,575	4,300
8450	For air defrost, deduct					325			325	360

23 81 Decentralized Unitary HVAC Equipment

23 81 13 – Packaged Terminal Air-Conditioners

23 81 13.10 Packaged Cabinet Type Air-Conditioners

		Crew	Daily Output	Labor-Hours	Unit	Material	Labor	Equipment	Total	Total Incl O&P
0010	**PACKAGED CABINET TYPE AIR-CONDITIONERS**, Cabinet, wall sleeve,									
0100	louver, electric heat, thermostat, manual changeover, 208 V									
0200	6,000 BTUH cooling, 8,800 BTU heat	Q-5	6	2.667	Ea.	1,200	174		1,374	1,550
0220	9,000 BTUH cooling, 13,900 BTU heat		5	3.200		3,475	209		3,684	4,125
0240	12,000 BTUH cooling, 13,900 BTU heat		4	4		3,800	261		4,061	4,575
0260	15,000 BTUH cooling, 13,900 BTU heat		3	5.333		1,950	350		2,300	2,675
0280	18,000 BTUH cooling, 10 KW heat		2.40	6.667		4,725	435		5,160	5,825
0300	24,000 BTUH cooling, 10 KW heat		1.90	8.421		4,750	550		5,300	6,025
0320	30,000 BTUH cooling, 10 KW heat		1.40	11.429		6,125	745		6,870	7,850
0340	36,000 BTUH cooling, 10 KW heat		1.25	12.800		5,275	835		6,110	7,075
0360	42,000 BTUH cooling, 10 KW heat		1	16		6,150	1,050		7,200	8,300
0380	48,000 BTUH cooling, 10 KW heat		.90	17.778		7,750	1,150		8,900	10,300
0500	For hot water coil, increase heat by 10%, add					5%	10%			
1000	For steam, increase heat output by 30%, add					8%	10%			

23 81 19 – Self-Contained Air-Conditioners

23 81 19.10 Window Unit Air Conditioners

		Crew	Daily Output	Labor-Hours	Unit	Material	Labor	Equipment	Total	Total Incl O&P
0010	**WINDOW UNIT AIR CONDITIONERS**									
4000	Portable/window, 15 amp, 125 V grounded receptacle required									
4060	5,000 BTUH	1 Carp	8	1	Ea.	330	58.50		388.50	455
4340	6,000 BTUH		8	1		370	58.50		428.50	500
4480	8,000 BTUH		6	1.333		410	78		488	565
4500	10,000 BTUH		6	1.333		540	78		618	710

23 81 Decentralized Unitary HVAC Equipment

23 81 19 – Self-Contained Air-Conditioners

23 81 19.10 Window Unit Air Conditioners		Crew	Daily Output	Labor-Hours	Unit	Material	2023 Bare Costs Labor	Equipment	Total	Total Incl O&P
4520	12,000 BTUH	L-2	8	2	Ea.	2,300	104		2,404	2,675
4600	Window/thru-the-wall, 15 amp, 230 V grounded receptacle required									
4780	18,000 BTUH	L-2	6	2.667	Ea.	1,150	138		1,288	1,475
4940	25,000 BTUH		4	4		2,475	207		2,682	3,025
4960	29,000 BTUH	↓	4	4		1,475	207		1,682	1,925

23 81 19.20 Self-Contained Single Package		Crew	Daily Output	Labor-Hours	Unit	Material	Labor	Equipment	Total	Total Incl O&P
0010	**SELF-CONTAINED SINGLE PACKAGE**									
0100	Air cooled, for free blow or duct, not incl. remote condenser									
0110	Constant volume									
0200	3 ton cooling	Q-5	1	16	Ea.	4,275	1,050		5,325	6,250
0210	4 ton cooling	"	.80	20		4,650	1,300		5,950	7,075
0220	5 ton cooling	Q-6	1.20	20		5,000	1,350		6,350	7,525
0230	7.5 ton cooling	"	.90	26.667		5,975	1,800		7,775	9,275
0240	10 ton cooling	Q-7	1	32		8,800	2,200		11,000	13,000
0250	15 ton cooling		.95	33.684		10,900	2,325		13,225	15,500
0260	20 ton cooling		.90	35.556		14,200	2,450		16,650	19,300
0270	25 ton cooling		.85	37.647		21,600	2,600		24,200	27,700
0280	30 ton cooling		.80	40		28,600	2,750		31,350	35,600
0300	40 ton cooling		.60	53.333		41,500	3,675		45,175	51,000
0320	50 ton cooling	↓	.50	64		55,000	4,425		59,425	67,000
0340	60 ton cooling	Q-8	.40	80	↓	63,500	5,525	161	69,186	78,000
0380	With hot water heat, variable air volume									
0390	10 ton cooling	Q-7	.96	33.333	Ea.	12,100	2,300		14,400	16,700
0400	20 ton cooling		.86	37.209		19,900	2,575		22,475	25,700
0410	30 ton cooling		.76	42.105		37,700	2,900		40,600	45,700
0420	40 ton cooling		.58	55.172		52,500	3,800		56,300	63,500
0430	50 ton cooling	↓	.48	66.667		70,000	4,600		74,600	84,000
0440	60 ton cooling	Q-8	.38	84.211	↓	83,000	5,825	169	88,994	100,500
0490	For duct mounting, no price change									
0500	For steam heating coils, add				Ea.	10%	10%			
0550	Packaged, with electric heat									
0552	Constant volume									
0560	5 ton cooling	Q-6	1.20	20	Ea.	9,300	1,350		10,650	12,200
0570	10 ton cooling	Q-7	1	32		15,400	2,200		17,600	20,200
0580	20 ton cooling		.90	35.556		23,600	2,450		26,050	29,700
0590	30 ton cooling		.80	40		44,400	2,750		47,150	53,000
0600	40 ton cooling		.60	53.333		58,500	3,675		62,175	70,000
0610	50 ton cooling	↓	.50	64	↓	78,500	4,425		82,925	93,000
0700	Variable air volume									
0710	10 ton cooling	Q-7	1	32	Ea.	17,800	2,200		20,000	22,900
0720	20 ton cooling		.90	35.556		27,900	2,450		30,350	34,300
0730	30 ton cooling		.80	40		50,500	2,750		53,250	59,500
0740	40 ton cooling		.60	53.333		65,500	3,675		69,175	77,500
0750	50 ton cooling	↓	.50	64		88,000	4,425		92,425	103,500
0760	60 ton cooling	Q-8	.40	80	↓	98,000	5,525	161	103,686	116,500
1000	Water cooled for free blow or duct, not including tower									
1010	Constant volume									
1100	3 ton cooling	Q-6	1	24	Ea.	3,950	1,625		5,575	6,775
1120	5 ton cooling		1	24		5,200	1,625		6,825	8,125
1130	7.5 ton cooling	↓	.80	30		7,175	2,025		9,200	10,900
1140	10 ton cooling	Q-7	.90	35.556		9,225	2,450		11,675	13,800
1150	15 ton cooling	↓	.85	37.647	↓	13,300	2,600		15,900	18,500

23 81 Decentralized Unitary HVAC Equipment

23 81 19 – Self-Contained Air-Conditioners

23 81 19.20 Self-Contained Single Package

		Crew	Daily Output	Labor-Hours	Unit	Material	2023 Bare Costs Labor	2023 Bare Costs Equipment	Total	Total Incl O&P
1160	20 ton cooling	Q-7	.80	40	Ea.	28,300	2,750		31,050	35,200
1170	25 ton cooling		.75	42.667		33,300	2,950		36,250	41,000
1180	30 ton cooling		.70	45.714		37,500	3,150		40,650	45,900
1200	40 ton cooling		.40	80		45,600	5,525		51,125	58,500
1220	50 ton cooling		.30	107		53,000	7,375		60,375	69,500
1240	60 ton cooling	Q-8	.30	107		59,500	7,375	214	67,089	76,500
1300	For hot water or steam heat coils, add					12%	10%			
2000	Water cooled with electric heat, not including tower									
2010	Constant volume									
2100	5 ton cooling	Q-6	1.20	20	Ea.	9,475	1,350		10,825	12,400
2120	10 ton cooling	Q-7	1	32		15,800	2,200		18,000	20,700
2130	15 ton cooling	"	.90	35.556		22,700	2,450		25,150	28,600
2400	Variable air volume									
2440	10 ton cooling	Q-7	1	32	Ea.	18,200	2,200		20,400	23,300
2450	15 ton cooling	"	.90	35.556	"	26,900	2,450		29,350	33,300
2600	Water cooled, hot water coils, not including tower									
2610	Variable air volume									
2640	10 ton cooling	Q-7	1	32	Ea.	12,500	2,200		14,700	17,100
2650	15 ton cooling	"	.80	40	"	18,900	2,750		21,650	24,900

23 81 23 – Computer-Room Air-Conditioners

23 81 23.10 Computer Room Units

		Crew	Daily Output	Labor-Hours	Unit	Material	2023 Bare Costs Labor	2023 Bare Costs Equipment	Total	Total Incl O&P
0010	**COMPUTER ROOM UNITS** D3050-185									
1000	Air cooled, includes remote condenser but not									
1020	interconnecting tubing or refrigerant									
1080	3 ton	Q-5	.50	32	Ea.	31,200	2,100		33,300	37,400
1120	5 ton		.45	35.556		33,300	2,325		35,625	40,200
1160	6 ton		.30	53.333		60,000	3,475		63,475	71,000
1200	8 ton		.27	59.259		62,500	3,875		66,375	74,500
1240	10 ton		.25	64		65,000	4,175		69,175	77,500
1280	15 ton		.22	72.727		71,500	4,750		76,250	86,000
1290	18 ton		.20	80		79,000	5,225		84,225	95,000
1300	20 ton	Q-6	.26	92.308		86,000	6,250		92,250	104,000
1320	22 ton		.24	100		87,000	6,775		93,775	105,500
1360	30 ton		.21	114		107,000	7,750		114,750	129,000
2200	Chilled water, for connection to									
2220	existing chiller system of adequate capacity									
2260	5 ton	Q-5	.74	21.622	Ea.	22,600	1,400		24,000	27,000
2280	6 ton		.52	30.769		21,900	2,000		23,900	27,100
2300	8 ton		.50	32		22,800	2,100		24,900	28,200
2320	10 ton		.49	32.653		23,000	2,125		25,125	28,500
2330	12 ton		.49	32.990		24,100	2,150		26,250	29,700
2360	15 ton		.48	33.333		25,600	2,175		27,775	31,500
2400	20 ton		.46	34.783		27,200	2,275		29,475	33,300
2440	25 ton	Q-6	.63	38.095		29,000	2,575		31,575	35,800
2460	30 ton		.57	42.105		31,400	2,850		34,250	38,900
2480	35 ton		.52	46.154		31,800	3,125		34,925	39,700
2500	45 ton		.46	52.174		33,600	3,525		37,125	42,200
2520	50 ton		.42	57.143		38,500	3,875		42,375	48,100
2540	60 ton		.38	63.158		41,000	4,275		45,275	51,500
2560	77 ton		.35	68.571		63,500	4,650		68,150	76,500
2580	95 ton		.32	75		74,000	5,075		79,075	88,500
4000	Glycol system, complete except for interconnecting tubing									

23 81 Decentralized Unitary HVAC Equipment

23 81 23 – Computer-Room Air-Conditioners

23 81 23.10 Computer Room Units

		Crew	Daily Output	Labor-Hours	Unit	Material	2023 Bare Costs Labor	Equipment	Total	Total Incl O&P
4060	3 ton	Q-5	.40	40	Ea.	39,200	2,600		41,800	47,000
4100	5 ton		.38	42.105		42,900	2,750		45,650	51,500
4120	6 ton		.25	64		59,500	4,175		63,675	71,500
4140	8 ton		.23	69.565		69,000	4,550		73,550	82,500
4160	10 ton		.21	76.190		73,500	4,975		78,475	88,000
4180	12 ton	▼	.19	84.211		72,500	5,500		78,000	88,000
4200	15 ton	Q-6	.26	92.308		90,500	6,250		96,750	109,500
4240	20 ton		.24	100		99,500	6,775		106,275	119,500
4280	22 ton		.23	104		105,000	7,075		112,075	126,000
4430	30 ton	▼	.22	109	▼	130,000	7,400		137,400	154,000
8000	Water cooled system, not including condenser,									
8020	water supply or cooling tower									
8060	3 ton	Q-5	.62	25.806	Ea.	31,800	1,675		33,475	37,500
8100	5 ton		.54	29.630		35,900	1,925		37,825	42,300
8120	6 ton		.35	45.714		34,500	2,975		37,475	42,500
8140	8 ton		.33	48.485		56,500	3,175		59,675	67,000
8160	10 ton		.31	51.613		58,500	3,375		61,875	69,500
8180	12 ton		.29	55.172		58,000	3,600		61,600	69,500
8200	15 ton	▼	.27	59.259		68,500	3,875		72,375	81,500
8240	20 ton	Q-6	.38	63.158		74,000	4,275		78,275	87,500
8280	22 ton		.35	68.571		77,500	4,650		82,150	92,000
8300	30 ton	▼	.30	80	▼	96,500	5,425		101,925	114,000

23 81 26 – Split-System Air-Conditioners

23 81 26.10 Split Ductless Systems

		Crew	Daily Output	Labor-Hours	Unit	Material	Labor	Equipment	Total	Total Incl O&P
0010	**SPLIT DUCTLESS SYSTEMS**									
0100	Cooling only, single zone									
0110	Wall mount									
0120	3/4 ton cooling	Q-5	2	8	Ea.	1,150	520		1,670	2,050
0130	1 ton cooling		1.80	8.889		1,325	580		1,905	2,325
0140	1-1/2 ton cooling		1.60	10		2,050	655		2,705	3,225
0150	2 ton cooling		1.40	11.429		2,350	745		3,095	3,700
0160	3 ton cooling	▼	1.20	13.333	▼	2,350	870		3,220	3,875
1000	Ceiling mount									
1020	2 ton cooling	Q-5	1.40	11.429	Ea.	2,075	745		2,820	3,400
1030	3 ton cooling	"	1.20	13.333	"	2,650	870		3,520	4,225
3000	Multizone									
3010	Wall mount									
3020	2 @ 3/4 ton cooling	Q-5	1.80	8.889	Ea.	3,500	580		4,080	4,725
5000	Cooling/Heating									
5010	Wall mount									
5110	1 ton cooling	Q-5	1.70	9.412	Ea.	1,350	615		1,965	2,400
5120	1-1/2 ton cooling	"	1.50	10.667		2,050	695		2,745	3,300
7000	Accessories for all split ductless systems									
7010	Add for ambient frost control	Q-5	8	2	Ea.	270	131		401	490
7020	Add for tube/wiring kit (line sets)									
7030	15' kit	Q-5	32	.500	Ea.	76.50	32.50		109	133
7036	25' kit		28	.571		55.50	37.50		93	117
7040	35' kit		24	.667		133	43.50		176.50	211
7050	50' kit	▼	20	.800	▼	175	52		227	271

23 81 Decentralized Unitary HVAC Equipment

23 81 29 – Variable Refrigerant Flow HVAC Systems

23 81 29.10 Heat Pump, Gas Driven

		Crew	Daily Output	Labor-Hours	Unit	Material	2023 Bare Costs Labor	2023 Bare Costs Equipment	Total	Total Incl O&P
0010	**HEAT PUMP, GAS DRIVEN**, Variable refrigerant volume (VRV) type									
0020	Not including interconnecting tubing or multi-zone controls									
1000	For indoor fan VRV type AHU see 23 82 19.40									
1010	Multi-zone split									
1020	Outdoor unit									
1100	8 tons cooling, for up to 17 zones	Q-5	1.30	12.308	Ea.	32,600	805		33,405	37,000
1110	Isolation rails		2.60	6.154	Pair	1,150	400		1,550	1,850
1160	15 tons cooling, for up to 33 zones		1	16	Ea.	42,900	1,050		43,950	48,800
1170	Isolation rails		2.60	6.154	Pair	1,350	400		1,750	2,100
2000	Packaged unit									
2020	Outdoor unit									
2200	11 tons cooling	Q-5	1.30	12.308	Ea.	42,000	805		42,805	47,300
2210	Roof curb adapter	"	2.60	6.154		725	400		1,125	1,400
2220	Thermostat	1 Stpi	1.30	6.154		435	445		880	1,150

23 81 43 – Air-Source Unitary Heat Pumps

23 81 43.10 Air-Source Heat Pumps

		Crew	Daily Output	Labor-Hours	Unit	Material	2023 Bare Costs Labor	2023 Bare Costs Equipment	Total	Total Incl O&P
0010	**AIR-SOURCE HEAT PUMPS**, Not including interconnecting tubing									
1000	Air to air, split system, not including curbs, pads, fan coil and ductwork									
1010	For curbs/pads see Section 23 91 10									
1012	Outside condensing unit only, for fan coil see Section 23 82 19.10									
1015	1.5 ton cooling, 7 MBH heat @ 0°F	Q-5	2.40	6.667	Ea.	1,575	435		2,010	2,375
1020	2 ton cooling, 8.5 MBH heat @ 0°F		2	8		1,700	520		2,220	2,650
1030	2.5 ton cooling, 10 MBH heat @ 0°F		1.60	10		1,875	655		2,530	3,050
1040	3 ton cooling, 13 MBH heat @ 0°F		1.20	13.333		2,075	870		2,945	3,575
1050	3.5 ton cooling, 18 MBH heat @ 0°F		1	16		2,225	1,050		3,275	3,975
1054	4 ton cooling, 24 MBH heat @ 0°F		.80	20		2,400	1,300		3,700	4,600
1060	5 ton cooling, 27 MBH heat @ 0°F		.50	32		2,625	2,100		4,725	6,000
1080	7.5 ton cooling, 33 MBH heat @ 0°F		.45	35.556		3,875	2,325		6,200	7,725
1100	10 ton cooling, 50 MBH heat @ 0°F	Q-6	.64	37.500		6,400	2,550		8,950	10,800
1120	15 ton cooling, 64 MBH heat @ 0°F		.50	48		11,100	3,250		14,350	17,100
1130	20 ton cooling, 85 MBH heat @ 0°F		.35	68.571		20,300	4,650		24,950	29,300
1140	25 ton cooling, 119 MBH heat @ 0°F		.25	96		23,300	6,500		29,800	35,300
1500	Single package, not including curbs, pads, or plenums									
1502	0.5 ton cooling, supplementary heat included	Q-5	8	2	Ea.	2,925	131		3,056	3,425
1504	0.75 ton cooling, supplementary heat included		6	2.667		3,100	174		3,274	3,650
1506	1 ton cooling, supplementary heat included		4	4		4,000	261		4,261	4,800
1510	1.5 ton cooling, 5 MBH heat @ 0°F		1.55	10.323		3,500	675		4,175	4,850
1520	2 ton cooling, 6.5 MBH heat @ 0°F		1.50	10.667		3,550	695		4,245	4,950
1540	2.5 ton cooling, 8 MBH heat @ 0°F		1.40	11.429		3,450	745		4,195	4,900
1560	3 ton cooling, 10 MBH heat @ 0°F		1.20	13.333		3,950	870		4,820	5,650
1570	3.5 ton cooling, 11 MBH heat @ 0°F		1	16		4,400	1,050		5,450	6,375
1580	4 ton cooling, 13 MBH heat @ 0°F		.96	16.667		4,725	1,100		5,825	6,825
1620	5 ton cooling, 27 MBH heat @ 0°F		.65	24.615		5,350	1,600		6,950	8,275
1640	7.5 ton cooling, 35 MBH heat @ 0°F		.40	40		8,200	2,600		10,800	12,900
1648	10 ton cooling, 45 MBH heat @ 0°F	Q-6	.40	60		10,700	4,075		14,775	17,900
1652	12 ton cooling, 50 MBH heat @ 0°F	"	.36	66.667		12,300	4,525		16,825	20,200
1696	Supplementary electric heat coil incl., unless noted otherwise									
6000	Air to water, single package, excluding storage tank and ductwork									
6010	Includes circulating water pump, air duct connections, digital temperature									
6020	controller with remote tank temp. probe and sensor for storage tank.									
6040	Water heating - air cooling capacity									
6110	35.5 MBH heat water, 2.3 ton cool air	Q-5	1.60	10	Ea.	17,800	655		18,455	20,600

23 81 Decentralized Unitary HVAC Equipment

23 81 43 – Air-Source Unitary Heat Pumps

23 81 43.10 Air-Source Heat Pumps

		Crew	Daily Output	Labor-Hours	Unit	Material	2023 Bare Costs Labor	Equipment	Total	Total Incl O&P
6120	58 MBH heat water, 3.8 ton cool air	Q-5	1.10	14.545	Ea.	20,300	950		21,250	23,800
6130	76 MBH heat water, 4.9 ton cool air		.87	18.391		24,300	1,200		25,500	28,500
6140	98 MBH heat water, 6.5 ton cool air		.62	25.806		31,400	1,675		33,075	37,000
6150	113 MBH heat water, 7.4 ton cool air		.59	27.119		34,400	1,775		36,175	40,500
6160	142 MBH heat water, 9.2 ton cool air		.52	30.769		41,700	2,000		43,700	48,900
6170	171 MBH heat water, 11.1 ton cool air		.49	32.653		49,000	2,125		51,125	57,000

23 81 46 – Water-Source Unitary Heat Pumps

23 81 46.10 Water Source Heat Pumps

		Crew	Daily Output	Labor-Hours	Unit	Material	2023 Bare Costs Labor	Equipment	Total	Total Incl O&P
0010	**WATER SOURCE HEAT PUMPS**, Not incl. connecting tubing or water source									
2000	Water source to air, single package									
2100	1 ton cooling, 13 MBH heat @ 75°F	Q-5	2	8	Ea.	2,225	520		2,745	3,200
2120	1.5 ton cooling, 17 MBH heat @ 75°F		1.80	8.889		2,050	580		2,630	3,125
2140	2 ton cooling, 19 MBH heat @ 75°F		1.70	9.412		2,450	615		3,065	3,600
2160	2.5 ton cooling, 25 MBH heat @ 75°F		1.60	10		6,600	655		7,255	8,225
2180	3 ton cooling, 27 MBH heat @ 75°F		1.40	11.429		6,900	745		7,645	8,725
2190	3.5 ton cooling, 29 MBH heat @ 75°F		1.30	12.308		2,950	805		3,755	4,450
2200	4 ton cooling, 31 MBH heat @ 75°F		1.20	13.333		3,400	870		4,270	5,050
2220	5 ton cooling, 29 MBH heat @ 75°F		.90	17.778		3,575	1,150		4,725	5,650
2240	7.5 ton cooling, 35 MBH heat @ 75°F		.60	26.667		7,075	1,750		8,825	10,400
2250	8 ton cooling, 40 MBH heat @ 75°F		.58	27.586		6,950	1,800		8,750	10,300
2260	10 ton cooling, 50 MBH heat @ 75°F		.53	30.189		7,625	1,975		9,600	11,400
2280	15 ton cooling, 64 MBH heat @ 75°F	Q-6	.47	51.064		15,800	3,450		19,250	22,600
2300	20 ton cooling, 100 MBH heat @ 75°F		.41	58.537		17,200	3,975		21,175	24,800
2310	25 ton cooling, 100 MBH heat @ 75°F		.32	75		23,400	5,075		28,475	33,400
2320	30 ton cooling, 128 MBH heat @ 75°F		.24	102		25,700	6,925		32,625	38,600
2340	40 ton cooling, 200 MBH heat @ 75°F		.21	117		36,300	7,925		44,225	52,000
2360	50 ton cooling, 200 MBH heat @ 75°F		.15	160		41,000	10,800		51,800	61,500
3960	For supplementary heat coil, add					10%				
4000	For increase in capacity thru use									
4020	of solar collector, size boiler at 60%									

23 82 Convection Heating and Cooling Units

23 82 13 – Valance Heating and Cooling Units

23 82 13.16 Valance Units

		Crew	Daily Output	Labor-Hours	Unit	Material	2023 Bare Costs Labor	Equipment	Total	Total Incl O&P
0010	**VALANCE UNITS**									
6000	Valance units, complete with 1/2" cooling coil, enclosure									
6020	2 tube	Q-5	18	.889	L.F.	39.50	58		97.50	130
6040	3 tube		16	1		47	65.50		112.50	149
6060	4 tube		16	1		52.50	65.50		118	155
6080	5 tube		15	1.067		61	69.50		130.50	171
6100	6 tube		15	1.067		63.50	69.50		133	174
6120	8 tube		14	1.143		92	74.50		166.50	212
6200	For 3/4" cooling coil, add					10%				

23 82 Convection Heating and Cooling Units

23 82 16 – Air Coils

23 82 16.10 Flanged Coils

		Crew	Daily Output	Labor-Hours	Unit	Material	2023 Bare Costs Labor	Equipment	Total	Total Incl O&P
0010	**FLANGED COILS**									
0100	Basic water, DX, or condenser coils									
0110	Copper tubes, alum. fins, galv. end sheets									
0112	H is finned height, L is finned length									
0120	3/8" x 0.016" tubing, 0.0065 aluminum fins									
0130	2 row, 8 fins per inch									
0140	4" H x 12" L	Q-5	48	.333	Ea.	1,375	22		1,397	1,550
0150	4" H x 24" L		38.38	.417		1,450	27		1,477	1,650
0160	4" H x 48" L		19.25	.831		1,500	54.50		1,554.50	1,725
0170	4" H x 72" L		12.80	1.250		1,625	81.50		1,706.50	1,925
0180	6" H x 12" L		48	.333		1,375	22		1,397	1,525
0190	6" H x 24" L		25.60	.625		1,425	41		1,466	1,625
0200	6" H x 48" L		12.80	1.250		1,550	81.50		1,631.50	1,825
0210	6" H x 72" L		8.53	1.876		2,250	122		2,372	2,625
0220	10" H x 12" L		30.73	.521		1,475	34		1,509	1,675
0230	10" H x 24" L		15.33	1.044		1,575	68		1,643	1,825
0240	10" H x 48" L		7.69	2.081		1,700	136		1,836	2,050
0250	10" H x 72" L		5.12	3.125		1,850	204		2,054	2,350
0260	12" H x 12" L		25.60	.625		1,550	41		1,591	1,775
0270	12" H x 24" L		12.80	1.250		1,625	81.50		1,706.50	1,900
0280	12" H x 48" L		6.40	2.500		1,750	163		1,913	2,175
0290	12" H x 72" L		4.27	3.747		1,975	245		2,220	2,550
0300	16" H x 16" L		14.38	1.113		1,600	72.50		1,672.50	1,875
0310	16" H x 24" L		9.59	1.668		1,725	109		1,834	2,050
0320	16" H x 48" L		4.80	3.333		1,875	218		2,093	2,400
0330	16" H x 72" L		3.20	5		2,125	325		2,450	2,825
0340	20" H x 24" L		7.69	2.081		1,825	136		1,961	2,200
0350	20" H x 48" L		3.84	4.167		2,000	272		2,272	2,625
0360	20" H x 72" L		2.56	6.250		2,675	410		3,085	3,525
0370	24" H x 24" L		6.40	2.500		1,925	163		2,088	2,350
0380	24" H x 48" L		3.20	5		2,125	325		2,450	2,825
0390	24" H x 72" L		2.13	7.512		2,850	490		3,340	3,850
0400	30" H x 28" L		4.39	3.645		2,100	238		2,338	2,675
0410	30" H x 48" L		2.56	6.250		2,725	410		3,135	3,600
0420	30" H x 72" L		1.71	9.357		3,025	610		3,635	4,225
0430	30" H x 84" L		1.46	10.959		3,225	715		3,940	4,625
0440	34" H x 32" L		3.39	4.720		2,225	310		2,535	2,875
0450	34" H x 48" L		2.26	7.080		2,825	460		3,285	3,800
0460	34" H x 72" L		1.51	10.596		3,125	690		3,815	4,475
0470	34" H x 84" L		1.29	12.403		3,400	810		4,210	4,950
0600	For 10 fins per inch, add					1%				
0610	For 12 fins per inch, add					3%				
0620	For 4 row, add				Ea.	30%	50%			
0630	For 6 row, add					60%	100%			
0640	For 8 row, add					80%	150%			
1100	1/2" x 0.017" tubing, 0.0065 aluminum fins									
1110	2 row, 8 fins per inch									
1120	5" H x 6" L	Q-5	40	.400	Ea.	1,375	26		1,401	1,575
1130	5" H x 20" L		37.10	.431		1,450	28		1,478	1,650
1140	5" H x 45" L		16.41	.975		1,500	63.50		1,563.50	1,750
1150	5" H x 90" L		8.21	1.949		2,175	127		2,302	2,600
1160	7.5" H x 5" L		38.50	.416		1,350	27		1,377	1,525

23 82 Convection Heating and Cooling Units

23 82 16 – Air Coils

23 82 16.10 Flanged Coils		Crew	Daily Output	Labor-Hours	Unit	Material	2023 Bare Costs Labor	2023 Bare Costs Equipment	Total	Total Incl O&P
1170	7.5" H x 20" L	Q-5	24.62	.650	Ea.	1,450	42.50		1,492.50	1,650
1180	7.5" H x 45" L		10.94	1.463		1,575	95.50		1,670.50	1,875
1190	7.5" H x 90" L		5.46	2.930		2,400	191		2,591	2,900
1200	12.5" H x 10" L		29.49	.543		1,475	35.50		1,510.50	1,650
1210	12.5" H x 20" L		14.75	1.085		1,575	71		1,646	1,825
1220	12.5" H x 45" L		6.55	2.443		1,775	160		1,935	2,200
1230	12.5" H x 90" L		3.28	4.878		2,500	320		2,820	3,250
1240	15" H x 15" L		16.41	.975		1,500	63.50		1,563.50	1,750
1250	15" H x 30" L		8.21	1.949		1,750	127		1,877	2,125
1260	15" H x 45" L		5.46	2.930		1,875	191		2,066	2,325
1270	15" H x 90" L		2.73	5.861		2,575	385		2,960	3,400
1280	20" H x 20" L		9.22	1.735		1,875	113		1,988	2,225
1290	20" H x 45" L		4.10	3.902		2,350	255		2,605	2,950
1300	20" H x 90" L		2.05	7.805		2,875	510		3,385	3,925
1310	25" H x 25" L		5.90	2.712		1,925	177		2,102	2,400
1320	25" H x 45" L		3.28	4.878		2,400	320		2,720	3,100
1330	25" H x 90" L		1.64	9.756		2,975	635		3,610	4,225
1340	30" H x 30" L		4.10	3.902		2,475	255		2,730	3,100
1350	30" H x 45" L		2.73	5.861		2,475	385		2,860	3,300
1360	30" H x 90" L		1.37	11.679		3,400	765		4,165	4,875
1370	35" H x 35" L		3.01	5.316		3,700	345		4,045	4,600
1380	35" H x 45" L		2.34	6.838		2,650	445		3,095	3,575
1390	35" H x 90" L		1.17	13.675		3,650	895		4,545	5,350
1400	42.5" H x 45" L		1.93	8.290		2,875	540		3,415	3,950
1410	42.5" H x 75" L		1.16	13.793		3,675	900		4,575	5,400
1420	42.5" H x 105" L	▼	.83	19.277		4,400	1,250		5,650	6,700
1600	For 10 fins per inch, add					2%				
1610	For 12 fins per inch, add					5%				
1620	For 4 row, add					35%	50%			
1630	For 6 row, add					65%	100%			
1640	For 8 row, add				▼	90%	150%			
2010	5/8" x 0.020" tubing, 0.0065 aluminum fins									
2020	2 row, 8 fins per inch									
2030	6" H x 6" L	Q-5	38	.421	Ea.	1,375	27.50		1,402.50	1,550
2040	6" H x 24" L		24.96	.641		1,450	42		1,492	1,675
2050	6" H x 48" L		12.48	1.282		1,525	83.50		1,608.50	1,800
2060	6" H x 96" L		6.24	2.564		2,000	167		2,167	2,450
2070	12" H x 12" L		24.96	.641		1,525	42		1,567	1,775
2080	12" H x 24" L		12.48	1.282		1,775	83.50		1,858.50	2,075
2090	12" H x 48" L		6.24	2.564		1,925	167		2,092	2,375
2100	12" H x 96" L		3.12	5.128		3,100	335		3,435	3,900
2110	18" H x 24" L		8.32	1.923		1,950	126		2,076	2,325
2120	18" H x 48" L		4.16	3.846		1,875	251		2,126	2,425
2130	18" H x 96" L		2.08	7.692		2,500	500		3,000	3,500
2140	24" H x 24" L		6.24	2.564		2,050	167		2,217	2,500
2150	24" H x 48" L		3.12	5.128		2,075	335		2,410	2,775
2160	24" H x 96" L		1.56	10.256		2,925	670		3,595	4,200
2170	30" H x 30" L		3.99	4.010		2,175	262		2,437	2,775
2180	30" H x 48" L		2.50	6.400		2,350	420		2,770	3,200
2190	30" H x 96" L		1.25	12.800		2,975	835		3,810	4,525
2200	30" 120" L		1	16		3,000	1,050		4,050	4,850
2210	36" H x 36" L		2.77	5.776		2,350	375		2,725	3,150
2220	36" H x 48" L	▼	2.08	7.692	▼	2,500	500		3,000	3,500

23 82 Convection Heating and Cooling Units

23 82 16 – Air Coils

23 82 16.10 Flanged Coils		Crew	Daily Output	Labor-Hours	Unit	Material	2023 Bare Costs Labor	Equipment	Total	Total Incl O&P
2230	36" H x 90" L	Q-5	1.11	14.414	Ea.	2,875	940		3,815	4,550
2240	36" H x 120" L		.83	19.277		3,275	1,250		4,525	5,475
2250	42" H x 48" L		1.78	8.989		2,825	585		3,410	4,000
2260	42" H x 90" L		.95	16.842		3,175	1,100		4,275	5,150
2270	42" H x 120" L		.71	22.535		4,325	1,475		5,800	6,975
2280	51" H x 48" L		1.47	10.884		3,125	710		3,835	4,500
2290	51" H x 96" L		.73	21.918		4,850	1,425		6,275	7,450
2300	51" H x 120" L		.59	27.119		4,925	1,775		6,700	8,075
2500	For 10 fins per inch, add					3%				
2510	For 12 fins per inch, add					6%				
2520	For 4 row, add				Ea.	40%	50%			
2530	For 6 row, add					80%	100%			
2540	For 8 row, add					110%	150%			
3000	Hot water booster coils									
3010	Copper tubes, alum. fins, galv. end sheets									
3012	H is finned height, L is finned length									
3020	1/2" x 0.017" tubing, 0.0065 aluminum fins									
3030	1 row, 10 fins per inch									
3040	5" H x 10" L	Q-5	40	.400	Ea.	985	26		1,011	1,125
3050	5" H x 25" L		33.18	.482		1,075	31.50		1,106.50	1,225
3060	10" H x 10" L		39	.410		1,025	27		1,052	1,175
3070	10" H x 20" L		20.73	.772		1,100	50.50		1,150.50	1,300
3080	10" H x 30" L		13.83	1.157		1,150	75.50		1,225.50	1,400
3090	15" H x 15" L		18.44	.868		1,050	56.50		1,106.50	1,225
3110	15" H x 20" L		13.83	1.157		1,150	75.50		1,225.50	1,400
3120	15" H x 30" L		9.22	1.735		1,225	113		1,338	1,525
3130	20" H x 20" L		10.37	1.543		1,225	101		1,326	1,475
3140	20" H x 30" L		6.91	2.315		1,275	151		1,426	1,625
3150	20" H x 40" L		5.18	3.089		1,325	202		1,527	1,775
3160	25" H x 25" L		6.64	2.410		1,325	157		1,482	1,675
3170	25" H x 35" L		4.74	3.376		1,375	220		1,595	1,825
3180	25" H x 45" L		3.69	4.336		1,650	283		1,933	2,250
3190	30" H x 30" L		4.61	3.471		1,400	227		1,627	1,875
3200	30" H x 40" L		3.46	4.624		1,450	300		1,750	2,050
3210	30" H x 50" L		2.76	5.797		1,500	380		1,880	2,225
3300	For 2 row, add					20%	50%			
3400	1/2" x 0.020" tubing, 0.008 aluminum fins									
3410	2 row, 10 fins per inch									
3420	20" H x 27" L	Q-5	7.27	2.201	Ea.	1,450	144		1,594	1,825
3430	20" H x 36" L		5.44	2.941		1,525	192		1,717	1,950
3440	20" H x 45" L		4.35	3.678		1,475	240		1,715	1,975
3450	25" H x 45" L		3.49	4.585		2,025	299		2,324	2,700
3460	25" H x 54" L		2.90	5.517		2,250	360		2,610	3,000
3470	30" H x 54" L		2.42	6.612		2,400	430		2,830	3,300
3480	35" H x 54" L		2.07	7.729		2,550	505		3,055	3,575
3490	35" H x 63" L		1.78	8.989		2,550	585		3,135	3,700
3500	40" H x 72" L		1.36	11.765		3,225	770		3,995	4,675
3510	55" H x 63" L		1.13	14.159		3,575	925		4,500	5,300
3520	55" H x 72" L		.99	16.162		3,950	1,050		5,000	5,925
3530	55" H x 81" L		.88	18.182		4,350	1,175		5,525	6,550
3540	75" H x 81" L		.64	25		5,325	1,625		6,950	8,275
3550	75" H x 90" L		.58	27.586		5,450	1,800		7,250	8,650
3560	75" H x 108" L		.48	33.333		6,100	2,175		8,275	9,975

23 82 Convection Heating and Cooling Units

23 82 16 – Air Coils

23 82 16.10 Flanged Coils		Crew	Daily Output	Labor-Hours	Unit	Material	2023 Bare Costs Labor	Equipment	Total	Total Incl O&P
3800	5/8" x 0.020" tubing, 0.0065 aluminum fins									
3810	1 row, 10 fins per inch									
3820	6" H x 12" L	Q-5	38	.421	Ea.	1,075	27.50		1,102.50	1,225
3830	6" H x 24" L		28.80	.556		1,150	36.50		1,186.50	1,300
3840	6" H x 30" L		23.04	.694		895	45.50		940.50	1,050
3850	12" H x 12" L		28.80	.556		1,175	36.50		1,211.50	1,350
3860	12" H x 24" L		14.40	1.111		880	72.50		952.50	1,075
3870	12" H x 30" L		11.52	1.389		1,225	90.50		1,315.50	1,475
3880	18" H x 18" L		12.80	1.250		1,425	81.50		1,506.50	1,675
3890	18" H x 24" L		9.60	1.667		1,450	109		1,559	1,750
3900	18" H x 36" L		6.40	2.500		1,500	163		1,663	1,900
3910	24" H x 24" L		7.20	2.222		1,500	145		1,645	1,875
3920	24" H x 30" L		4.80	3.333		1,400	218		1,618	1,875
3930	24" H x 36" L		5.05	3.168		1,425	207		1,632	1,850
3940	30" H x 30" L		4.61	3.471		1,450	227		1,677	1,950
3950	30" H x 36" L		3.85	4.159		1,500	272		1,772	2,050
3960	30" H x 42" L		3.29	4.863		1,625	320		1,945	2,275
3970	36" H x 36" L		3.20	5		1,650	325		1,975	2,300
3980	36" H x 42" L		2.74	5.839		1,700	380		2,080	2,450
4100	For 2 row, add					30%	50%			
4400	Steam and hot water heating coils									
4410	Copper tubes, alum. fins. galv. end sheets									
4412	H is finned height, L is finned length									
4420	5/8" tubing, to 175 PSIG working pressure									
4430	1 row, 8 fins per inch									
4440	6" H x 6" L	Q-5	38	.421	Ea.	1,600	27.50		1,627.50	1,800
4450	6" H x 12" L		37	.432		1,600	28		1,628	1,825
4460	6" H x 24" L		24.48	.654		1,700	42.50		1,742.50	1,950
4470	6" H x 36" L		16.32	.980		1,475	64		1,539	1,725
4480	6" H x 48" L		12.24	1.307		1,550	85.50		1,635.50	1,825
4490	6" H x 84" L		6.99	2.289		2,550	149		2,699	3,025
4500	6" H x 108" L		5.44	2.941		2,800	192		2,992	3,350
4510	12" H x 12" L		24.48	.654		1,550	42.50		1,592.50	1,800
4520	12" H x 24" L		12.24	1.307		1,625	85.50		1,710.50	1,925
4530	12" H x 36" L		8.16	1.961		1,775	128		1,903	2,150
4540	12" H x 48" L		6.12	2.614		1,800	171		1,971	2,225
4550	12" H x 84" L		3.50	4.571		2,200	299		2,499	2,875
4560	12" H x 108" L		2.72	5.882		2,750	385		3,135	3,600
4570	18" H x 18" L		10.88	1.471		1,725	96		1,821	2,050
4580	18" H x 24" L		8.16	1.961		1,800	128		1,928	2,175
4590	18" H x 48" L		4.08	3.922		2,125	256		2,381	2,700
4600	18" H x 84" L		2.33	6.867		2,850	450		3,300	3,800
4610	18" H x 108" L		1.81	8.840		3,875	575		4,450	5,125
4620	24" H x 24" L		6.12	2.614		2,125	171		2,296	2,575
4630	24" H x 48" L		3.06	5.229		2,475	340		2,815	3,225
4640	24" H x 84" L		1.75	9.143		3,925	595		4,520	5,225
4650	24" H x 108" L		1.36	11.765		4,725	770		5,495	6,350
4660	36" H x 36" L		2.72	5.882		2,750	385		3,135	3,600
4670	36" H x 48" L		2.04	7.843		3,000	510		3,510	4,050
4680	36" H x 84" L		1.17	13.675		4,300	895		5,195	6,050
4690	36" H x 108" L		.91	17.582		6,300	1,150		7,450	8,650
4700	48" H x 48" L		1.53	10.458		4,175	685		4,860	5,625
4710	48" H x 84" L		.87	18.391		6,275	1,200		7,475	8,700

23 82 Convection Heating and Cooling Units

23 82 16 – Air Coils

23 82 16.10 Flanged Coils		Crew	Daily Output	Labor-Hours	Unit	Material	2023 Bare Costs Labor	2023 Bare Costs Equipment	Total	Total Incl O&P
4720	48" H x 108" L	Q-5	.68	23.529	Ea.	7,475	1,525		9,000	10,500
4730	48" H x 126" L	↓	.58	27.586	↓	7,900	1,800		9,700	11,400
4910	For 10 fins per inch, add					2%				
4920	For 12 fins per inch, add					5%				
4930	For 2 row, add					30%	50%			
4940	For 3 row, add					50%	100%			
4950	For 4 row, add					80%	123%			
4960	For 230 PSIG heavy duty, add					20%	30%			
6000	**Steam, heavy duty, 200 PSIG**									
6010	Copper tubes, alum. fins, galv. end sheets									
6012	H is finned height, L is finned length									
6020	1" x 0.035" tubing, 0.010 aluminum fins									
6030	1 row, 8 fins per inch									
6040	12" H x 12" L	Q-5	24.48	.654	Ea.	1,775	42.50		1,817.50	2,025
6050	12" H x 24" L		12.24	1.307		2,100	85.50		2,185.50	2,450
6060	12" H x 36" L		8.16	1.961		2,225	128		2,353	2,650
6070	12" H x 48" L		6.12	2.614		2,275	171		2,446	2,775
6080	12" H x 84" L		3.50	4.571		2,300	299		2,599	2,975
6090	12" H x 108" L		2.72	5.882		3,000	385		3,385	3,850
6100	18" H x 24" L		8.16	1.961		2,150	128		2,278	2,550
6110	18" H x 36" L		5.44	2.941		1,900	192		2,092	2,375
6120	18" H x 48" L		4.08	3.922		2,475	256		2,731	3,100
6130	18" H x 84" L		2.33	6.867		3,475	450		3,925	4,500
6140	18" H x 108" L		1.81	8.840		4,950	575		5,525	6,300
6150	24" H x 24" L		6.12	2.614		1,975	171		2,146	2,425
6160	24" H x 36" L		4.08	3.922		2,200	256		2,456	2,800
6170	24" H x 48" L		3.06	5.229		2,500	340		2,840	3,250
6180	24" H x 84" L		1.75	9.143		4,725	595		5,320	6,100
6190	24" H x 108" L		1.36	11.765		5,850	770		6,620	7,600
6200	30" H x 36" L		3.26	4.908		3,100	320		3,420	3,875
6210	30" H x 48" L		2.45	6.531		4,225	425		4,650	5,275
6220	30" H x 84" L		1.40	11.429		5,750	745		6,495	7,450
6230	30" H x 108" L		1.09	14.679		6,825	960		7,785	8,925
6240	36" H x 36" L		2.72	5.882		4,250	385		4,635	5,250
6250	36" H x 48" L		2.04	7.843		4,450	510		4,960	5,675
6260	36" H x 84" L		1.17	13.675		6,500	895		7,395	8,475
6270	36" H x 108" L		.91	17.582		7,725	1,150		8,875	10,200
6280	36" H x 120" L		.82	19.512		8,225	1,275		9,500	11,000
6290	48" H x 48" L		1.53	10.458		6,150	685		6,835	7,775
6300	48" H x 84" L		.87	18.391		6,525	1,200		7,725	8,975
6310	48" H x 108" L		.68	23.529		9,625	1,525		11,150	12,900
6320	48" H x 120" L	↓	.61	26.230	↓	10,300	1,725		12,025	13,900
6400	For 10 fins per inch, add					4%				
6410	For 12 fins per inch, add					10%				

23 82 16.20 Duct Heaters

		Crew	Daily Output	Labor-Hours	Unit	Material	Labor	Equipment	Total	Total Incl O&P
0010	**DUCT HEATERS**, Electric, 480 V, 3 Ph.									
0020	Finned tubular insert, 500°F									
0100	8" wide x 6" high, 4.0 kW	Q-20	16	1.250	Ea.	940	80		1,020	1,150
0120	12" high, 8.0 kW		15	1.333		1,550	85.50		1,635.50	1,825
0140	18" high, 12.0 kW		14	1.429		2,175	91.50		2,266.50	2,525
0160	24" high, 16.0 kW		13	1.538		2,800	98.50		2,898.50	3,225
0180	30" high, 20.0 kW	↓	12	1.667		3,425	107		3,532	3,925

23 82 Convection Heating and Cooling Units

23 82 16 – Air Coils

23 82 16.20 Duct Heaters		Crew	Daily Output	Labor-Hours	Unit	Material	2023 Bare Costs Labor	Equipment	Total	Total Incl O&P
0300	12" wide x 6" high, 6.7 kW	Q-20	15	1.333	Ea.	995	85.50		1,080.50	1,225
0320	12" high, 13.3 kW		14	1.429		1,600	91.50		1,691.50	1,900
0340	18" high, 20.0 kW		13	1.538		2,250	98.50		2,348.50	2,625
0360	24" high, 26.7 kW		12	1.667		2,900	107		3,007	3,350
0380	30" high, 33.3 kW		11	1.818		3,550	116		3,666	4,075
0500	18" wide x 6" high, 13.3 kW		14	1.429		1,075	91.50		1,166.50	1,325
0520	12" high, 26.7 kW		13	1.538		1,850	98.50		1,948.50	2,175
0540	18" high, 40.0 kW		12	1.667		2,450	107		2,557	2,850
0560	24" high, 53.3 kW		11	1.818		3,250	116		3,366	3,750
0580	30" high, 66.7 kW		10	2		4,075	128		4,203	4,675
0700	24" wide x 6" high, 17.8 kW		13	1.538		1,200	98.50		1,298.50	1,475
0720	12" high, 35.6 kW		12	1.667		2,000	107		2,107	2,350
0740	18" high, 53.3 kW		11	1.818		2,825	116		2,941	3,300
0760	24" high, 71.1 kW		10	2		3,625	128		3,753	4,175
0780	30" high, 88.9 kW		9	2.222		4,425	142		4,567	5,100
0900	30" wide x 6" high, 22.2 kW		12	1.667		1,275	107		1,382	1,550
0920	12" high, 44.4 kW		11	1.818		2,100	116		2,216	2,500
0940	18" high, 66.7 kW		10	2		3,000	128		3,128	3,500
0960	24" high, 88.9 kW		9	2.222		4,300	142		4,442	4,975
0980	30" high, 111.0 kW		8	2.500		4,700	160		4,860	5,400
1400	Note decreased kW available for									
1410	each duct size at same cost									
1420	See line 5000 for modifications and accessories									
2000	Finned tubular flange with insulated									
2020	terminal box, 500°F									
2100	12" wide x 36" high, 54 kW	Q-20	10	2	Ea.	4,625	128		4,753	5,275
2120	40" high, 60 kW		9	2.222		5,325	142		5,467	6,075
2200	24" wide x 36" high, 118.8 kW		9	2.222		5,625	142		5,767	6,400
2220	40" high, 132 kW		8	2.500		5,850	160		6,010	6,675
2400	36" wide x 8" high, 40 kW		11	1.818		2,375	116		2,491	2,775
2420	16" high, 80 kW		10	2		3,125	128		3,253	3,650
2440	24" high, 120 kW		9	2.222		4,100	142		4,242	4,750
2460	32" high, 160 kW		8	2.500		5,250	160		5,410	6,025
2480	36" high, 180 kW		7	2.857		6,475	183		6,658	7,400
2500	40" high, 200 kW		6	3.333		7,175	213		7,388	8,225
2600	40" wide x 8" high, 45 kW		11	1.818		2,450	116		2,566	2,875
2620	16" high, 90 kW		10	2		3,375	128		3,503	3,925
2640	24" high, 135 kW		9	2.222		4,300	142		4,442	4,950
2660	32" high, 180 kW		8	2.500		5,725	160		5,885	6,525
2680	36" high, 202.5 kW		7	2.857		6,575	183		6,758	7,525
2700	40" high, 225 kW		6	3.333		7,500	213		7,713	8,575
2800	48" wide x 8" high, 54.8 kW		10	2		2,575	128		2,703	3,025
2820	16" high, 109.8 kW		9	2.222		3,575	142		3,717	4,150
2840	24" high, 164.4 kW		8	2.500		4,550	160		4,710	5,250
2860	32" high, 219.2 kW		7	2.857		6,050	183		6,233	6,925
2880	36" high, 246.6 kW		6	3.333		6,975	213		7,188	8,000
2900	40" high, 274 kW		5	4		7,875	256		8,131	9,050
3000	56" wide x 8" high, 64 kW		9	2.222		2,925	142		3,067	3,450
3020	16" high, 128 kW		8	2.500		4,050	160		4,210	4,725
3040	24" high, 192 kW		7	2.857		4,925	183		5,108	5,700
3060	32" high, 256 kW		6	3.333		6,875	213		7,088	7,900
3080	36" high, 288 kW		5	4		7,900	256		8,156	9,050
3100	40" high, 320 kW		4	5		8,725	320		9,045	10,100

23 82 Convection Heating and Cooling Units

23 82 16 – Air Coils

23 82 16.20 Duct Heaters		Crew	Daily Output	Labor-Hours	Unit	Material	2023 Bare Costs Labor	Equipment	Total	Total Incl O&P
3200	64" wide x 8" high, 74 kW	Q-20	8	2.500	Ea.	3,025	160		3,185	3,575
3220	16" high, 148 kW		7	2.857		4,175	183		4,358	4,875
3240	24" high, 222 kW		6	3.333		5,325	213		5,538	6,175
3260	32" high, 296 kW		5	4		7,125	256		7,381	8,225
3280	36" high, 333 kW		4	5		8,500	320		8,820	9,825
3300	40" high, 370 kW		3	6.667		9,375	425		9,800	10,900
3800	Note decreased kW available for									
3820	each duct size at same cost									
5000	Duct heater modifications and accessories									
5120	T.C.O. limit auto or manual reset	Q-20	42	.476	Ea.	154	30.50		184.50	215
5140	Thermostat		28	.714		655	45.50		700.50	790
5160	Overheat thermocouple (removable)		7	2.857		930	183		1,113	1,300
5180	Fan interlock relay		18	1.111		224	71		295	355
5200	Air flow switch		20	1		194	64		258	310
5220	Split terminal box cover		100	.200		64	12.80		76.80	89.50
8000	To obtain BTU multiply kW by 3413									

23 82 19 – Fan Coil Units

23 82 19.10 Fan Coil Air Conditioning

		Crew	Daily Output	Labor-Hours	Unit	Material	Labor	Equipment	Total	Total Incl O&P
0010	**FAN COIL AIR CONDITIONING**									
0030	Fan coil AC, cabinet mounted, filters and controls									
0100	Chilled water, 1/2 ton cooling	Q-5	8	2	Ea.	765	131		896	1,025
0110	3/4 ton cooling		7	2.286		745	149		894	1,050
0120	1 ton cooling		6	2.667		880	174		1,054	1,225
0140	1-1/2 ton cooling		5.50	2.909		920	190		1,110	1,300
0150	2 ton cooling		5.25	3.048		1,250	199		1,449	1,675
0160	2-1/2 ton cooling		5	3.200		2,450	209		2,659	2,975
0180	3 ton cooling		4	4		2,675	261		2,936	3,350
0262	For hot water coil, add					40%	10%			
0300	Console, 2 pipe with electric heat									
0310	1/2 ton cooling	Q-5	8	2	Ea.	1,725	131		1,856	2,100
0315	3/4 ton cooling		7	2.286		1,875	149		2,024	2,300
0320	1 ton cooling		6	2.667		2,025	174		2,199	2,475
0330	1-1/2 ton cooling		5.50	2.909		2,450	190		2,640	2,975
0340	2 ton cooling		4.70	3.404		3,250	222		3,472	3,900
0345	2-1/2 ton cooling		4.70	3.404		4,700	222		4,922	5,500
0350	3 ton cooling		4	4		6,250	261		6,511	7,275
0360	4 ton cooling		4	4		6,525	261		6,786	7,575
0940	Direct expansion, for use w/air cooled condensing unit, 1-1/2 ton cooling		5	3.200		785	209		994	1,175
0950	2 ton cooling		4.80	3.333		770	218		988	1,175
0960	2-1/2 ton cooling		4.40	3.636		900	237		1,137	1,350
0970	3 ton cooling		3.80	4.211		1,100	275		1,375	1,600
0980	3-1/2 ton cooling		3.60	4.444		1,125	290		1,415	1,675
0990	4 ton cooling		3.40	4.706		1,075	305		1,380	1,650
1000	5 ton cooling		3	5.333		1,425	350		1,775	2,075
1020	7-1/2 ton cooling		3	5.333		2,100	350		2,450	2,850
1040	10 ton cooling	Q-6	2.60	9.231		2,450	625		3,075	3,625
1042	12-1/2 ton cooling		2.30	10.435		3,100	705		3,805	4,450
1050	15 ton cooling		1.60	15		3,225	1,025		4,250	5,050
1060	20 ton cooling		.70	34.286		4,850	2,325		7,175	8,775
1070	25 ton cooling		.65	36.923		5,850	2,500		8,350	10,200
1080	30 ton cooling		.60	40		6,175	2,700		8,875	10,900
1500	For hot water coil, add					40%	10%			

23 82 Convection Heating and Cooling Units

23 82 19 – Fan Coil Units

23 82 19.10 Fan Coil Air Conditioning

		Crew	Daily Output	Labor-Hours	Unit	Material	2023 Bare Costs Labor	2023 Bare Costs Equipment	Total	Total Incl O&P
1512	For condensing unit add see Section 23 62									
3000	Chilled water, horizontal unit, housing, 2 pipe, fan control, no valves									
3100	1/2 ton cooling	Q-5	8	2	Ea.	1,650	131		1,781	2,000
3110	1 ton cooling		6	2.667		1,900	174		2,074	2,350
3120	1-1/2 ton cooling		5.50	2.909		2,175	190		2,365	2,650
3130	2 ton cooling		5.25	3.048		2,550	199		2,749	3,100
3140	3 ton cooling		4	4		3,150	261		3,411	3,875
3150	3-1/2 ton cooling		3.80	4.211		3,550	275		3,825	4,300
3160	4 ton cooling		3.80	4.211		3,550	275		3,825	4,300
3170	5 ton cooling		3.40	4.706		4,050	305		4,355	4,900
3180	6 ton cooling		3.40	4.706		4,050	305		4,355	4,900
3190	7 ton cooling		2.90	5.517		4,500	360		4,860	5,450
3200	8 ton cooling		2.90	5.517		4,500	360		4,860	5,450
3210	10 ton cooling	Q-6	2.80	8.571		4,675	580		5,255	6,000
3212	12-1/2 ton cooling		2.50	9.600		3,825	650		4,475	5,175
3214	15 ton cooling		2.30	10.435		5,475	705		6,180	7,075
3216	20 ton cooling		2.10	11.429		6,250	775		7,025	8,025
3218	25 ton cooling		1.80	13.333		7,700	905		8,605	9,825
3220	30 ton cooling		1.60	15		11,400	1,025		12,425	14,100
3240	For hot water coil, add					40%	10%			
4000	With electric heat, 2 pipe									
4100	1/2 ton cooling	Q-5	8	2	Ea.	1,925	131		2,056	2,300
4105	3/4 ton cooling		7	2.286		2,125	149		2,274	2,550
4110	1 ton cooling		6	2.667		2,375	174		2,549	2,875
4120	1-1/2 ton cooling		5.50	2.909		2,650	190		2,840	3,175
4130	2 ton cooling		5.25	3.048		3,250	199		3,449	3,900
4135	2-1/2 ton cooling		4.80	3.333		4,600	218		4,818	5,375
4140	3 ton cooling		4	4		6,000	261		6,261	7,000
4150	3-1/2 ton cooling		3.80	4.211		7,175	275		7,450	8,275
4160	4 ton cooling		3.60	4.444		8,250	290		8,540	9,500
4170	5 ton cooling		3.40	4.706		9,650	305		9,955	11,100
4180	6 ton cooling		3.20	5		9,650	325		9,975	11,100
4190	7 ton cooling		2.90	5.517		10,300	360		10,660	11,800
4200	8 ton cooling		2.20	7.273		11,000	475		11,475	12,800
4210	10 ton cooling	Q-6	2.80	8.571		11,800	580		12,380	13,900

23 82 19.20 Heating and Ventilating Units

		Crew	Daily Output	Labor-Hours	Unit	Material	Labor	Equipment	Total	Total Incl O&P
0010	**HEATING AND VENTILATING UNITS**, Classroom units									
0020	Includes filter, heating/cooling coils, standard controls									
0080	750 CFM, 2 tons cooling	Q-6	2	12	Ea.	5,525	815		6,340	7,275
0100	1,000 CFM, 2-1/2 tons cooling		1.60	15		6,375	1,025		7,400	8,525
0120	1,250 CFM, 3 tons cooling		1.40	17.143		6,575	1,150		7,725	8,950
0140	1,500 CFM, 4 tons cooling		.80	30		7,025	2,025		9,050	10,800
0160	2,000 CFM, 5 tons cooling		.50	48		8,275	3,250		11,525	14,000
0500	For electric heat, add					35%				
1000	For no cooling, deduct					25%	10%			

23 82 19.40 Fan Coil Air Conditioning

		Crew	Daily Output	Labor-Hours	Unit	Material	Labor	Equipment	Total	Total Incl O&P
0010	**FAN COIL AIR CONDITIONING**, Variable refrigerant volume (VRV) type									
0020	Not including interconnecting tubing or multi-zone controls									
0030	For VRV condensing unit see section 23 81 29.10									
0050	Indoor type, ducted									
0100	Vertical concealed									
0130	1 ton cooling	G Q-5	2.97	5.387	Ea.	3,000	350		3,350	3,825

23 82 Convection Heating and Cooling Units

23 82 19 – Fan Coil Units

23 82 19.40 Fan Coil Air Conditioning		Crew	Daily Output	Labor-Hours	Unit	Material	2023 Bare Costs Labor	Equipment	Total	Total Incl O&P
0140	1.5 ton cooling	Q-5 G	2.77	5.776	Ea.	3,050	375		3,425	3,900
0150	2 ton cooling	G	2.70	5.926		3,425	385		3,810	4,350
0160	2.5 ton cooling	G	2.60	6.154		3,475	400		3,875	4,425
0170	3 ton cooling	G	2.50	6.400		3,650	420		4,070	4,650
0180	3.5 ton cooling	G	2.30	6.957		4,225	455		4,680	5,325
0190	4 ton cooling	G	2.19	7.306		3,875	475		4,350	4,950
0200	4.5 ton cooling	G	2.08	7.692		4,250	500		4,750	5,425
0230	Outside air connection possible									
1100	Ceiling concealed									
1130	0.6 ton cooling	Q-5 G	2.60	6.154	Ea.	2,225	400		2,625	3,050
1140	0.75 ton cooling	G	2.60	6.154		2,200	400		2,600	3,000
1150	1 ton cooling	G	2.60	6.154		2,225	400		2,625	3,050
1152	Screening door	1 Stpi G	5.20	1.538		123	112		235	300
1160	1.5 ton cooling	Q-5 G	2.60	6.154		2,300	400		2,700	3,150
1162	Screening door	1 Stpi G	5.20	1.538		143	112		255	325
1170	2 ton cooling	Q-5 G	2.60	6.154		2,825	400		3,225	3,700
1172	Screening door	1 Stpi G	5.20	1.538		123	112		235	300
1180	2.5 ton cooling	Q-5 G	2.60	6.154		3,150	400		3,550	4,050
1182	Screening door	1 Stpi G	5.20	1.538		214	112		326	400
1190	3 ton cooling	Q-5 G	2.60	6.154		3,450	400		3,850	4,400
1192	Screening door	1 Stpi G	5.20	1.538		214	112		326	400
1200	4 ton cooling	Q-5 G	2.30	6.957		3,550	455		4,005	4,575
1202	Screening door	1 Stpi G	5.20	1.538		214	112		326	400
1220	6 ton cooling	Q-5 G	2.08	7.692		5,800	500		6,300	7,125
1230	8 ton cooling	" G	1.89	8.466		6,525	555		7,080	8,000
1260	Outside air connection possible									
4050	Indoor type, duct-free									
4100	Ceiling mounted cassette									
4130	0.75 ton cooling	Q-5 G	3.46	4.624	Ea.	2,275	300		2,575	2,975
4140	1 ton cooling	G	2.97	5.387		2,475	350		2,825	3,250
4150	1.5 ton cooling	G	2.77	5.776		2,400	375		2,775	3,200
4160	2 ton cooling	G	2.60	6.154		2,750	400		3,150	3,625
4170	2.5 ton cooling	G	2.50	6.400		2,900	420		3,320	3,800
4180	3 ton cooling	G	2.30	6.957		3,200	455		3,655	4,175
4190	4 ton cooling	G	2.08	7.692		3,475	500		3,975	4,575
4198	For ceiling cassette decoration panel, add	1 Stpi G	5.20	1.538		370	112		482	570
4230	Outside air connection possible									
4500	Wall mounted									
4530	0.6 ton cooling	Q-5 G	5.20	3.077	Ea.	1,250	201		1,451	1,675
4540	0.75 ton cooling	G	5.20	3.077		1,300	201		1,501	1,725
4550	1 ton cooling	G	4.16	3.846		1,500	251		1,751	2,025
4560	1.5 ton cooling	G	3.77	4.244		1,650	277		1,927	2,225
4570	2 ton cooling	G	3.46	4.624		2,025	300		2,325	2,675
4590	Condensate pump for the above air handlers	1 Stpi G	6.46	1.238		266	90		356	425
4700	Floor standing unit									
4730	1 ton cooling	Q-5 G	2.60	6.154	Ea.	2,100	400		2,500	2,900
4740	1.5 ton cooling	G	2.60	6.154		2,375	400		2,775	3,225
4750	2 ton cooling	G	2.60	6.154		2,550	400		2,950	3,400
4800	Floor standing unit, concealed									
4830	1 ton cooling	Q-5 G	2.60	6.154	Ea.	2,025	400		2,425	2,825
4840	1.5 ton cooling	G	2.60	6.154		2,275	400		2,675	3,100
4850	2 ton cooling	G	2.60	6.154		2,475	400		2,875	3,325
4880	Outside air connection possible									

23 82 Convection Heating and Cooling Units

23 82 19 – Fan Coil Units

23 82 19.40 Fan Coil Air Conditioning		Crew	Daily Output	Labor-Hours	Unit	Material	2023 Bare Costs Labor	Equipment	Total	Total Incl O&P
8000	Accessories									
8100	Branch divergence pipe fitting									
8110	Capacity under 76 MBH	1 Stpi	2.50	3.200	Ea.	191	232		423	555
8120	76 MBH to 112 MBH		2.50	3.200		223	232		455	590
8130	112 MBH to 234 MBH	↓	2.50	3.200	↓	625	232		857	1,025
8200	Header pipe fitting									
8210	Max 4 branches									
8220	Capacity under 76 MBH	1 Stpi	1.70	4.706	Ea.	300	340		640	840
8260	Max 8 branches									
8270	76 MBH to 112 MBH	1 Stpi	1.70	4.706	Ea.	560	340		900	1,125
8280	112 MBH to 234 MBH	"	1.30	6.154	"	895	445		1,340	1,650

23 82 29 – Radiators

23 82 29.10 Hydronic Heating

	23 82 29.10 Hydronic Heating	Crew	Daily Output	Labor-Hours	Unit	Material	2023 Bare Costs Labor	Equipment	Total	Total Incl O&P
0010	**HYDRONIC HEATING**, Terminal units, not incl. main supply pipe									
1000	Radiation									
1100	Panel, baseboard, C.I., including supports, no covers	Q-5	46	.348	L.F.	54.50	22.50		77	94
3000	Radiators, cast iron									
3100	Free standing or wall hung, 6 tube, 25" high	Q-5	96	.167	Section	72	10.90		82.90	95.50
3150	4 tube, 25" high		96	.167		53.50	10.90		64.40	75.50
3200	4 tube, 19" high	↓	96	.167	↓	50	10.90		60.90	71.50
3250	Adj. brackets, 2 per wall radiator up to 30 sections	1 Stpi	32	.250	Ea.	52	18.15		70.15	84.50
3500	Recessed, 20" high x 5" deep, without grille	Q-5	60	.267	Section	59.50	17.40		76.90	91.50
3525	Free standing or wall hung, 30" high	"	60	.267	↓	47	17.40		64.40	77.50
3600	For inlet grille, add					6.55			6.55	7.20
9500	To convert SFR to BTU rating: Hot water, 150 x SFR									
9510	Forced hot water, 180 x SFR; steam, 240 x SFR									

23 82 33 – Convectors

23 82 33.10 Convector Units

	23 82 33.10 Convector Units	Crew	Daily Output	Labor-Hours	Unit	Material	2023 Bare Costs Labor	Equipment	Total	Total Incl O&P
0010	**CONVECTOR UNITS**, Terminal units, not incl. main supply pipe									
2204	Convector, multifin, 2 pipe w/cabinet									
2210	17" H x 24" L	Q-5	10	1.600	Ea.	111	104		215	278
2214	17" H x 36" L		8.60	1.860		167	121		288	365
2218	17" H x 48" L		7.40	2.162		222	141		363	455
2222	21" H x 24" L		9	1.778		124	116		240	310
2226	21" H x 36" L		8.20	1.951		186	127		313	395
2228	21" H x 48" L	↓	6.80	2.353	↓	248	154		402	500
2240	For knob operated damper, add					140%				
2241	For metal trim strips, add	Q-5	64	.250	Ea.	6.70	16.35		23.05	32
2243	For snap-on inlet grille, add					10%	10%			
2245	For hinged access door, add	Q-5	64	.250	Ea.	40	16.35		56.35	68
2246	For air chamber, auto-venting, add	"	58	.276	"	8.65	18		26.65	36.50

23 82 36 – Finned-Tube Radiation Heaters

23 82 36.10 Finned Tube Radiation

	23 82 36.10 Finned Tube Radiation	Crew	Daily Output	Labor-Hours	Unit	Material	2023 Bare Costs Labor	Equipment	Total	Total Incl O&P
0010	**FINNED TUBE RADIATION**, Terminal units, not incl. main supply pipe									
1150	Fin tube, wall hung, 14" slope top cover, with damper									
1200	1-1/4" copper tube, 4-1/4" alum. fin	Q-5	38	.421	L.F.	49.50	27.50		77	95
1250	1-1/4" steel tube, 4-1/4" steel fin		36	.444		43	29		72	91
1255	2" steel tube, 4-1/4" steel fin	↓	32	.500		47.50	32.50		80	101
1260	21", two tier, slope top, w/damper									
1262	1-1/4" copper tube, 4-1/4" alum. fin	Q-5	30	.533	L.F.	62	35		97	121
1264	1-1/4" steel tube, 4-1/4" steel fin	↓	28	.571		51.50	37.50		89	112

23 82 Convection Heating and Cooling Units

23 82 36 – Finned-Tube Radiation Heaters

23 82 36.10 Finned Tube Radiation

		Crew	Daily Output	Labor-Hours	Unit	Material	2023 Bare Costs Labor	Equipment	Total	Total Incl O&P
1266	2" steel tube, 4-1/4" steel fin	Q-5	25	.640	L.F.	56	42		98	124
1270	10", flat top, with damper									
1272	1-1/4" copper tube, 4-1/4" alum. fin	Q-5	38	.421	L.F.	26	27.50		53.50	70
1274	1-1/4" steel tube, 4-1/4" steel fin		36	.444		43	29		72	90.50
1276	2" steel tube, 4-1/4" steel fin	↓	32	.500	↓	45.50	32.50		78	98.50
1280	17", two tier, flat top, w/damper									
1282	1-1/4" copper tube, 4-1/4" alum. fin	Q-5	30	.533	L.F.	55.50	35		90.50	113
1284	1-1/4" steel tube, 4-1/4" steel fin		28	.571		51.50	37.50		89	113
1286	2" steel tube, 4-1/4" steel fin	↓	25	.640	↓	56	42		98	124
1301	Rough in wall hung, steel fin w/supply & balance valves	1 Stpi	.91	8.791	Ea.	405	640		1,045	1,400
1310	Baseboard, pkgd, 1/2" copper tube, alum. fin, 7" high	Q-5	60	.267	L.F.	11.80	17.40		29.20	39
1320	3/4" copper tube, alum. fin, 7" high		58	.276		7.85	18		25.85	35.50
1340	1" copper tube, alum. fin, 8-7/8" high		56	.286		20	18.65		38.65	50
1360	1-1/4" copper tube, alum. fin, 8-7/8" high		54	.296		30.50	19.35		49.85	62.50
1380	1-1/4" IPS steel tube with steel fins	↓	52	.308	↓	32.50	20		52.50	65.50
1381	Rough in baseboard panel & fin tube, supply & balance valves	1 Stpi	1.06	7.547	Ea.	445	550		995	1,300
1500	Note: fin tube may also require corners, caps, etc.									

23 82 39 – Unit Heaters

23 82 39.13 Cabinet Unit Heaters

		Crew	Daily Output	Labor-Hours	Unit	Material	Labor	Equipment	Total	Total Incl O&P
0010	**CABINET UNIT HEATERS**									
5400	Cabinet, horizontal, hot water, blower type									
5420	20 MBH	Q-5	10	1.600	Ea.	1,950	104		2,054	2,300
5430	60 MBH		7	2.286		2,575	149		2,724	3,075
5440	100 MBH		5	3.200		3,700	209		3,909	4,375
5450	120 MBH	↓	4	4	↓	2,125	261		2,386	2,750

23 82 39.16 Propeller Unit Heaters

		Crew	Daily Output	Labor-Hours	Unit	Material	Labor	Equipment	Total	Total Incl O&P
0010	**PROPELLER UNIT HEATERS**									
3950	Unit heaters, propeller, 115 V 2 psi steam, 60°F entering air									
4000	Horizontal, 12 MBH	Q-5	12	1.333	Ea.	535	87		622	720
4020	28.2 MBH		10	1.600		765	104		869	995
4040	36.5 MBH		8	2		695	131		826	960
4060	43.9 MBH		8	2		695	131		826	960
4080	56.5 MBH		7.50	2.133		715	139		854	995
4100	65.6 MBH		7	2.286		735	149		884	1,025
4120	87.6 MBH		6.50	2.462		985	161		1,146	1,325
4140	96.8 MBH		6	2.667		1,550	174		1,724	1,950
4160	133.3 MBH		5	3.200		1,650	209		1,859	2,125
4180	157.6 MBH		4	4		1,800	261		2,061	2,375
4200	197.7 MBH		3	5.333		1,925	350		2,275	2,650
4220	257.2 MBH		2.50	6.400		2,125	420		2,545	2,950
4240	286.9 MBH		2	8		1,850	520		2,370	2,800
4260	364 MBH		1.80	8.889		2,975	580		3,555	4,150
4270	404 MBH	↓	1.60	10	↓	3,850	655		4,505	5,200
4300	Vertical diffuser same price									
4310	Vertical flow, 40 MBH	Q-5	11	1.455	Ea.	895	95		990	1,125
4314	58.5 MBH		8	2		1,075	131		1,206	1,375
4318	92 MBH		7	2.286		880	149		1,029	1,200
4322	109.7 MBH		6	2.667		1,650	174		1,824	2,075
4326	131 MBH		4	4		1,650	261		1,911	2,225
4330	160 MBH		3	5.333		1,750	350		2,100	2,450
4334	194 MBH		2.20	7.273		1,200	475		1,675	2,025
4338	212 MBH		2.10	7.619		2,375	500		2,875	3,375

23 82 Convection Heating and Cooling Units

23 82 39 – Unit Heaters

23 82 39.16 Propeller Unit Heaters		Crew	Daily Output	Labor-Hours	Unit	Material	2023 Bare Costs Labor	Equipment	Total	Total Incl O&P
4342	247 MBH	Q-5	1.96	8.163	Ea.	1,875	535		2,410	2,850
4346	297 MBH		1.80	8.889		3,200	580		3,780	4,375
4350	333 MBH	Q-6	1.90	12.632		2,050	855		2,905	3,525
4354	420 MBH (460 V)		1.80	13.333		2,625	905		3,530	4,225
4358	500 MBH (460 V)		1.71	14.035		3,325	950		4,275	5,100
4362	570 MBH (460 V)		1.40	17.143		4,150	1,150		5,300	6,300
4366	620 MBH (460 V)		1.30	18.462		6,575	1,250		7,825	9,100
4370	960 MBH (460 V)		1.10	21.818		8,450	1,475		9,925	11,500
4400	Unit heaters, propeller, hot water, 115 V, 60 degree F entering air									
4404	Horizontal									
4408	6 MBH	Q-5	11	1.455	Ea.	535	95		630	730
4412	12 MBH		11	1.455		535	95		630	730
4416	16 MBH		10	1.600		590	104		694	800
4420	24 MBH		9	1.778		765	116		881	1,025
4424	29 MBH		8	2		695	131		826	960
4428	47 MBH		7	2.286		720	149		869	1,025
4432	63 MBH		6	2.667		990	174		1,164	1,350
4436	81 MBH		5.50	2.909		1,550	190		1,740	1,975
4440	90 MBH		5	3.200		1,650	209		1,859	2,125
4460	133 MBH		4	4		1,800	261		2,061	2,375
4464	139 MBH		3.50	4.571		1,925	299		2,224	2,575
4468	198 MBH		2.50	6.400		2,125	420		2,545	2,950
4472	224 MBH		2	8		2,350	520		2,870	3,350
4476	273 MBH		1.50	10.667		1,375	695		2,070	2,575
4500	Vertical									
4504	8 MBH	Q-5	13	1.231	Ea.	1,025	80.50		1,105.50	1,250
4508	12 MBH		13	1.231		1,025	80.50		1,105.50	1,250
4512	16 MBH		13	1.231		1,025	80.50		1,105.50	1,250
4516	30 MBH		12	1.333		1,025	87		1,112	1,250
4520	43 MBH		11	1.455		1,075	95		1,170	1,325
4524	57 MBH		8	2		1,275	131		1,406	1,600
4528	68 MBH		7	2.286		1,325	149		1,474	1,675
4540	105 MBH		6	2.667		1,525	174		1,699	1,925
4544	123 MBH		5	3.200		1,625	209		1,834	2,100
4550	140 MBH		5	3.200		1,875	209		2,084	2,350
4554	156 MBH		4	4		2,325	261		2,586	2,950
4560	210 MBH		4	4		2,875	261		3,136	3,575
4564	223 MBH		3	5.333		3,175	350		3,525	4,000
4568	257 MBH		2	8		3,175	520		3,695	4,250

23 83 Radiant Heating Units

23 83 16 – Radiant-Heating Hydronic Piping

23 83 16.10 Radiant Floor Heating		Crew	Daily Output	Labor-Hours	Unit	Material	2023 Bare Costs Labor	Equipment	Total	Total Incl O&P
0010	**RADIANT FLOOR HEATING**									
0100	Tubing, PEX (cross-linked polyethylene)									
0110	Oxygen barrier type for systems with ferrous materials									
0120	1/2"	Q-5	800	.020	L.F.	1.14	1.31		2.45	3.20
0130	3/4"		535	.030		1.61	1.95		3.56	4.68
0140	1"		400	.040		2.52	2.61		5.13	6.65
0200	Non barrier type for ferrous free systems									
0210	1/2"	Q-5	800	.020	L.F.	.63	1.31		1.94	2.64

23 83 Radiant Heating Units

23 83 16 – Radiant-Heating Hydronic Piping

23 83 16.10 Radiant Floor Heating		Crew	Daily Output	Labor-Hours	Unit	Material	2023 Bare Costs Labor	Equipment	Total	Total Incl O&P
0220	3/4"	Q-5	535	.030	L.F.	1.15	1.95		3.10	4.18
0230	1"	↓	400	.040	↓	1.97	2.61		4.58	6.05
1000	Manifolds									
1110	Brass									
1120	With supply and return valves, flow meter, thermometer,									
1122	auto air vent and drain/fill valve.									
1130	1", 2 circuit	Q-5	14	1.143	Ea.	370	74.50		444.50	515
1140	1", 3 circuit		13.50	1.185		420	77.50		497.50	580
1150	1", 4 circuit		13	1.231		460	80.50		540.50	625
1154	1", 5 circuit		12.50	1.280		545	83.50		628.50	725
1158	1", 6 circuit		12	1.333		595	87		682	785
1162	1", 7 circuit		11.50	1.391		650	91		741	850
1166	1", 8 circuit		11	1.455		720	95		815	930
1172	1", 9 circuit		10.50	1.524		775	99.50		874.50	1,000
1174	1", 10 circuit		10	1.600		830	104		934	1,075
1178	1", 11 circuit		9.50	1.684		865	110		975	1,125
1182	1", 12 circuit	↓	9	1.778	↓	955	116		1,071	1,225
1610	Copper manifold header (cut to size)									
1620	1" header, 12 circuit 1/2" sweat outlets	Q-5	3.33	4.805	Ea.	134	315		449	615
1630	1-1/4" header, 12 circuit 1/2" sweat outlets		3.20	5		155	325		480	655
1640	1-1/4" header, 12 circuit 3/4" sweat outlets		3	5.333		167	350		517	705
1650	1-1/2" header, 12 circuit 3/4" sweat outlets		3.10	5.161		201	335		536	725
1660	2" header, 12 circuit 3/4" sweat outlets	↓	2.90	5.517	↓	295	360		655	860
3000	Valves									
3110	Thermostatic zone valve actuator with end switch	Q-5	40	.400	Ea.	55.50	26		81.50	100
3114	Thermostatic zone valve actuator	"	36	.444	"	105	29		134	159
3120	Motorized straight zone valve with operator complete									
3130	3/4"	Q-5	35	.457	Ea.	171	30		201	233
3140	1"		32	.500		185	32.50		217.50	253
3150	1-1/4"	↓	29.60	.541	↓	236	35.50		271.50	315
3500	4 way mixing valve, manual, brass									
3530	1"	Q-5	13.30	1.203	Ea.	245	78.50		323.50	385
3540	1-1/4"		11.40	1.404		265	91.50		356.50	430
3550	1-1/2"		11	1.455		340	95		435	515
3560	2"		10.60	1.509		480	98.50		578.50	675
3800	Mixing valve motor, 4 way for valves, 1" and 1-1/4"		34	.471		405	30.50		435.50	490
3810	Mixing valve motor, 4 way for valves, 1-1/2" and 2"	↓	30	.533	↓	465	35		500	565
5000	Radiant floor heating, zone control panel									
5120	4 zone actuator valve control, expandable	Q-5	20	.800	Ea.	157	52		209	251
5130	6 zone actuator valve control, expandable		18	.889		292	58		350	405
6070	Thermal track, straight panel for long continuous runs, 5.333 S.F.		40	.400		38.50	26		64.50	81
6080	Thermal track, utility panel, for direction reverse at run end, 5.333 S.F.		40	.400		38.50	26		64.50	81
6090	Combination panel, for direction reverse plus straight run, 5.333 S.F.	↓	40	.400	↓	38.50	26		64.50	81
7000	PEX tubing fittings									
7100	Compression type									
7116	Coupling									
7120	1/2" x 1/2"	1 Stpi	27	.296	Ea.	7.30	21.50		28.80	40
7124	3/4" x 3/4"	"	23	.348	"	17.60	25		42.60	57
7130	Adapter									
7132	1/2" x female sweat 1/2"	1 Stpi	27	.296	Ea.	4.75	21.50		26.25	37.50
7134	1/2" x female sweat 3/4"		26	.308		5.30	22.50		27.80	39.50
7136	5/8" x female sweat 3/4"		24	.333		7.60	24		31.60	44.50
7140	Elbow									

23 83 Radiant Heating Units

23 83 16 – Radiant-Heating Hydronic Piping

23 83 16.10 Radiant Floor Heating

		Crew	Daily Output	Labor-Hours	Unit	Material	2023 Bare Costs Labor	2023 Bare Costs Equipment	Total	Total Incl O&P
7142	1/2" x female sweat 1/2"	1 Stpi	27	.296	Ea.	7.25	21.50		28.75	40
7144	1/2" x female sweat 3/4"		26	.308		8.50	22.50		31	43
7146	5/8" x female sweat 3/4"		24	.333		9.50	24		33.50	46.50
7200	Insert type									
7206	PEX x male NPT									
7210	1/2" x 1/2"	1 Stpi	29	.276	Ea.	3.38	20		23.38	33.50
7220	3/4" x 3/4"		27	.296		4.98	21.50		26.48	37.50
7230	1" x 1"		26	.308		8.40	22.50		30.90	43
7300	PEX coupling									
7310	1/2" x 1/2"	1 Stpi	30	.267	Ea.	1.28	19.35		20.63	30.50
7320	3/4" x 3/4"		29	.276		1.93	20		21.93	32
7330	1" x 1"		28	.286		2.99	20.50		23.49	34.50
7400	PEX stainless crimp ring									
7410	1/2" x 1/2"	1 Stpi	86	.093	Ea.	.61	6.75		7.36	10.70
7420	3/4" x 3/4"		84	.095		.83	6.90		7.73	11.20
7430	1" x 1"		82	.098		1.19	7.10		8.29	11.85

23 83 33 – Electric Radiant Heaters

23 83 33.10 Electric Heating

		Crew	Daily Output	Labor-Hours	Unit	Material	2023 Bare Costs Labor	2023 Bare Costs Equipment	Total	Total Incl O&P
0010	**ELECTRIC HEATING**, not incl. conduit or feed wiring									
1100	Rule of thumb: Baseboard units, including control	1 Elec	4.40	1.818	KW	138	122		260	335
1300	Baseboard heaters, 2' long, 350 watt		8	1	Ea.	41.50	67.50		109	146
1400	3' long, 750 watt		8	1		44.50	67.50		112	149
1600	4' long, 1,000 watt		6.70	1.194		54	80.50		134.50	179
1800	5' long, 935 watt		5.70	1.404		64.50	94.50		159	211
2000	6' long, 1,500 watt		5	1.600		72.50	108		180.50	240
2200	7' long, 1,310 watt		4.40	1.818		74	122		196	264
2400	8' long, 2,000 watt		4	2		89.50	135		224.50	299
2600	9' long, 1,680 watt		3.60	2.222		99.50	150		249.50	330
2800	10' long, 1,875 watt		3.30	2.424		97.50	163		260.50	350
2950	Wall heaters with fan, 120 to 277 volt									
3160	Recessed, residential, 750 watt	1 Elec	6	1.333	Ea.	96.50	90		186.50	239
3170	1,000 watt		6	1.333		385	90		475	560
3180	1,250 watt		5	1.600		132	108		240	305
3190	1,500 watt		4	2		415	135		550	660
3210	2,000 watt		4	2		122	135		257	335
3230	2,500 watt		3.50	2.286		425	154		579	695
3240	3,000 watt		3	2.667		380	180		560	680
3250	4,000 watt		2.70	2.963		380	200		580	715
3260	Commercial, 750 watt		6	1.333		264	90		354	425
3270	1,000 watt		6	1.333		252	90		342	410
3280	1,250 watt		5	1.600		252	108		360	435
3290	1,500 watt		4	2		251	135		386	475
3300	2,000 watt		4	2		252	135		387	475
3310	2,500 watt		3.50	2.286		252	154		406	505
3320	3,000 watt		3	2.667		425	180		605	730
3330	4,000 watt		2.70	2.963		580	200		780	930
3600	Thermostats, integral		16	.500		34	33.50		67.50	87.50
3800	Line voltage, 1 pole		8	1		34.50	67.50		102	138
3810	2 pole		8	1		27	67.50		94.50	130
4000	Heat trace system, 400 degree									
4020	115 V, 2.5 watts/L.F.	1 Elec	530	.015	L.F.	11.70	1.02		12.72	14.35
4030	5 watts/L.F.		530	.015		11.70	1.02		12.72	14.35

23 83 Radiant Heating Units

23 83 33 – Electric Radiant Heaters

23 83 33.10 Electric Heating		Crew	Daily Output	Labor-Hours	Unit	Material	2023 Bare Costs Labor	Equipment	Total	Total Incl O&P
4050	10 watts/L.F.	1 Elec	530	.015	L.F.	8.60	1.02		9.62	11
4060	208 V, 5 watts/L.F.		530	.015		11.70	1.02		12.72	14.35
4080	480 V, 8 watts/L.F.		530	.015		11.70	1.02		12.72	14.35
4200	Heater raceway									
4260	Heat transfer cement									
4280	1 gallon				Ea.	96.50			96.50	106
4300	5 gallon				"	283			283	310
4320	Cable tie									
4340	3/4" pipe size	1 Elec	470	.017	Ea.	.03	1.15		1.18	1.73
4360	1" pipe size		444	.018		.03	1.21		1.24	1.83
4380	1-1/4" pipe size		400	.020		.03	1.35		1.38	2.03
4400	1-1/2" pipe size		355	.023		.03	1.52		1.55	2.29
4420	2" pipe size		320	.025		.02	1.68		1.70	2.52
4440	3" pipe size		160	.050		.02	3.37		3.39	5
4460	4" pipe size		100	.080		.07	5.40		5.47	8.10
4480	Thermostat NEMA 3R, 22 amp, 0-150 degree, 10' cap.		8	1		210	67.50		277.50	330
4500	Thermostat NEMA 4X, 25 amp, 40 degree, 5-1/2' cap.		7	1.143		210	77		287	345
4520	Thermostat NEMA 4X, 22 amp, 25-325 degree, 10' cap.		7	1.143		575	77		652	750
4540	Thermostat NEMA 4X, 22 amp, 15-140 degree		6	1.333		470	90		560	655
4580	Thermostat NEMA 4, 7, 9, 22 amp, 25-325 degree, 10' cap.		3.60	2.222		690	150		840	980
4600	Thermostat NEMA 4, 7, 9, 22 amp, 15-140 degree		3	2.667		645	180		825	975
4720	Fiberglass application tape, 36 yard roll		11	.727		58	49		107	137
5000	Radiant heating ceiling panels, 2' x 4', 500 watt		16	.500		325	33.50		358.50	405
5050	750 watt		16	.500		320	33.50		353.50	400
5200	For recessed plaster frame, add		32	.250		138	16.85		154.85	176
5300	Infrared quartz heaters, 120 volts, 1,000 watt		6.70	1.194		300	80.50		380.50	450
5350	1,500 watt		5	1.600		315	108		423	510
5400	240 volts, 1,500 watt		5	1.600		282	108		390	470
5450	2,000 watt		4	2		320	135		455	555
5500	3,000 watt		3	2.667		345	180		525	645
5550	4,000 watt		2.60	3.077		370	207		577	715
5570	Modulating control		.80	10		156	675		831	1,175
5600	Unit heaters, heavy duty, with fan & mounting bracket									
5650	Single phase, 208-240-277 volt, 3 kW	1 Elec	6	1.333	Ea.	610	90		700	805
5750	5 kW		5.50	1.455		640	98		738	845
5800	7 kW		5	1.600		855	108		963	1,100
5850	10 kW		4	2		1,200	135		1,335	1,525
5950	15 kW		3.80	2.105		2,025	142		2,167	2,425
6000	480 volt, 3 kW		6	1.333		525	90		615	715
6020	4 kW		5.80	1.379		365	93		458	545
6040	5 kW		5.50	1.455		375	98		473	560
6060	7 kW		5	1.600		580	108		688	800
6080	10 kW		4	2		1,200	135		1,335	1,525
6100	13 kW		3.80	2.105		2,150	142		2,292	2,575
6120	15 kW		3.70	2.162		1,075	146		1,221	1,400
6140	20 kW		3.50	2.286		2,925	154		3,079	3,450
6300	3 phase, 208-240 volt, 5 kW		5.50	1.455		535	98		633	735
6320	7 kW		5	1.600		860	108		968	1,100
6340	10 kW		4	2		885	135		1,020	1,175
6360	15 kW		3.70	2.162		1,675	146		1,821	2,075
6380	20 kW		3.50	2.286		2,975	154		3,129	3,500
6400	25 kW		3.30	2.424		3,150	163		3,313	3,700
6500	480 volt, 5 kW		5.50	1.455		760	98		858	980

23 83 Radiant Heating Units

23 83 33 – Electric Radiant Heaters

23 83 33.10 Electric Heating		Crew	Daily Output	Labor-Hours	Unit	Material	2023 Bare Costs Labor	Equipment	Total	Total Incl O&P
6520	7 kW	1 Elec	5	1.600	Ea.	1,075	108		1,183	1,325
6540	10 kW		4	2		1,025	135		1,160	1,350
6560	13 kW		3.80	2.105		1,775	142		1,917	2,150
6580	15 kW		3.70	2.162		1,675	146		1,821	2,050
6600	20 kW		3.50	2.286		2,475	154		2,629	2,950
6620	25 kW		3.30	2.424		3,775	163		3,938	4,400
6630	30 kW		3	2.667		4,275	180		4,455	4,975
6640	40 kW		2	4		5,175	269		5,444	6,100
6650	50 kW		1.60	5		5,975	335		6,310	7,075
6800	Vertical discharge heaters, with fan									
6820	Single phase, 208-240-277 volt, 10 kW	1 Elec	4	2	Ea.	1,050	135		1,185	1,350
6840	15 kW		3.70	2.162		1,750	146		1,896	2,175
6900	3 phase, 208-240 volt, 10 kW		4	2		1,125	135		1,260	1,450
6920	15 kW		3.70	2.162		1,750	146		1,896	2,150
6940	20 kW		3.50	2.286		3,225	154		3,379	3,775
6960	25 kW		3.30	2.424		3,550	163		3,713	4,150
6980	30 kW		3	2.667		3,350	180		3,530	3,950
7000	40 kW		2	4		4,800	269		5,069	5,675
7020	50 kW		1.60	5		5,500	335		5,835	6,550
7100	480 volt, 10 kW		4	2		1,325	135		1,460	1,650
7120	15 kW		3.70	2.162		2,150	146		2,296	2,600
7140	20 kW		3.50	2.286		2,950	154		3,104	3,475
7160	25 kW		3.30	2.424		3,875	163		4,038	4,500
7180	30 kW		3	2.667		4,225	180		4,405	4,925
7200	40 kW		2	4		4,375	269		4,644	5,225
7900	Cabinet convector heaters, 240 volt, three phase,									
7920	3' long, 2,000 watt	1 Elec	5.30	1.509	Ea.		102		102	151
7940	3,000 watt		5.30	1.509		1,925	102		2,027	2,250
7960	4,000 watt		5.30	1.509		1,975	102		2,077	2,325
7980	6,000 watt		4.60	1.739		2,050	117		2,167	2,425
8000	8,000 watt		4.60	1.739		2,125	117		2,242	2,500
8020	4' long, 4,000 watt		4.60	1.739		1,850	117		1,967	2,200
8040	6,000 watt		4	2		1,925	135		2,060	2,300
8060	8,000 watt		4	2		2,025	135		2,160	2,425
8080	10,000 watt		4	2		2,050	135		2,185	2,450
8100	Available also in 208 or 277 volt									
8200	Cabinet unit heaters, 120 to 277 volt, 1 pole,									
8220	wall mounted, 2 kW	1 Elec	4.60	1.739	Ea.	1,850	117		1,967	2,200
8230	3 kW		4.60	1.739		1,925	117		2,042	2,275
8240	4 kW		4.40	1.818		1,975	122		2,097	2,350
8250	5 kW		4.40	1.818		2,025	122		2,147	2,400
8260	6 kW		4.20	1.905		2,050	128		2,178	2,450
8270	8 kW		4	2		2,125	135		2,260	2,525
8280	10 kW		3.80	2.105		2,050	142		2,192	2,450
8290	12 kW		3.50	2.286		1,950	154		2,104	2,375
8300	13.5 kW		2.90	2.759		2,125	186		2,311	2,600
8310	16 kW		2.70	2.963		2,175	200		2,375	2,675
8320	20 kW		2.30	3.478		3,300	234		3,534	3,975
8330	24 kW		1.90	4.211		3,350	284		3,634	4,100
8350	Recessed, 2 kW		4.40	1.818		2,050	122		2,172	2,425
8370	3 kW		4.40	1.818		2,125	122		2,247	2,500
8380	4 kW		4.20	1.905		2,175	128		2,303	2,575
8390	5 kW		4.20	1.905		2,225	128		2,353	2,650

23 83 Radiant Heating Units

23 83 33 – Electric Radiant Heaters

23 83 33.10 Electric Heating		Crew	Daily Output	Labor-Hours	Unit	Material	2023 Bare Costs Labor	Equipment	Total	Total Incl O&P
8400	6 kW	1 Elec	4	2	Ea.	2,025	135		2,160	2,425
8410	8 kW		3.80	2.105		2,125	142		2,267	2,550
8420	10 kW		3.50	2.286		2,650	154		2,804	3,150
8430	12 kW		2.90	2.759		2,675	186		2,861	3,225
8440	13.5 kW		2.70	2.963		2,700	200		2,900	3,250
8450	16 kW		2.30	3.478		2,700	234		2,934	3,325
8460	20 kW		1.90	4.211		3,225	284		3,509	3,975
8470	24 kW		1.60	5		3,275	335		3,610	4,100
8490	Ceiling mounted, 2 kW		3.20	2.500		2,050	168		2,218	2,500
8510	3 kW		3.20	2.500		2,125	168		2,293	2,575
8520	4 kW		3	2.667		2,175	180		2,355	2,650
8530	5 kW		3	2.667		2,225	180		2,405	2,725
8540	6 kW		2.80	2.857		2,250	192		2,442	2,750
8550	8 kW		2.40	3.333		2,325	225		2,550	2,875
8560	10 kW		2.20	3.636		2,150	245		2,395	2,725
8570	12 kW		2	4		2,175	269		2,444	2,800
8580	13.5 kW		1.50	5.333		2,225	360		2,585	2,975
8590	16 kW		1.30	6.154		2,275	415		2,690	3,125
8600	20 kW		.90	8.889		3,225	600		3,825	4,450
8610	24 kW		.60	13.333		3,275	900		4,175	4,925
8630	208 to 480 V, 3 pole									
8650	Wall mounted, 2 kW	1 Elec	4.60	1.739	Ea.	2,050	117		2,167	2,425
8670	3 kW		4.60	1.739		1,925	117		2,042	2,275
8680	4 kW		4.40	1.818		1,975	122		2,097	2,350
8690	5 kW		4.40	1.818		2,025	122		2,147	2,400
8700	6 kW		4.20	1.905		2,050	128		2,178	2,450
8710	8 kW		4	2		2,125	135		2,260	2,525
8720	10 kW		3.80	2.105		2,050	142		2,192	2,450
8730	12 kW		3.50	2.286		2,075	154		2,229	2,525
8740	13.5 kW		2.90	2.759		2,125	186		2,311	2,600
8750	16 kW		2.70	2.963		2,175	200		2,375	2,675
8760	20 kW		2.30	3.478		3,100	234		3,334	3,750
8770	24 kW		1.90	4.211		3,350	284		3,634	4,100
8790	Recessed, 2 kW		4.40	1.818		2,050	122		2,172	2,425
8810	3 kW		4.40	1.818		2,125	122		2,247	2,500
8820	4 kW		4.20	1.905		2,175	128		2,303	2,575
8830	5 kW		4.20	1.905		2,225	128		2,353	2,650
8840	6 kW		4	2		2,250	135		2,385	2,675
8850	8 kW		3.80	2.105		2,325	142		2,467	2,750
8860	10 kW		3.50	2.286		2,150	154		2,304	2,575
8870	12 kW		2.90	2.759		2,175	186		2,361	2,675
8880	13.5 kW		2.70	2.963		2,225	200		2,425	2,750
8890	16 kW		2.30	3.478		3,400	234		3,634	4,075
8900	20 kW		1.90	4.211		3,450	284		3,734	4,225
8920	24 kW		1.60	5		3,500	335		3,835	4,350
8940	Ceiling mount, 2 kW		3.20	2.500		2,050	168		2,218	2,500
8950	3 kW		3.20	2.500		2,125	168		2,293	2,575
8960	4 kW		3	2.667		2,175	180		2,355	2,650
8970	5 kW		3	2.667		2,225	180		2,405	2,725
8980	6 kW		2.80	2.857		2,250	192		2,442	2,750
8990	8 kW		2.40	3.333		2,125	225		2,350	2,675
9000	10 kW		2.20	3.636		2,650	245		2,895	3,300
9020	13.5 kW		1.50	5.333		2,700	360		3,060	3,475

23 83 Radiant Heating Units

23 83 33 – Electric Radiant Heaters

23 83 33.10 Electric Heating		Crew	Daily Output	Labor-Hours	Unit	Material	2023 Bare Costs Labor	Equipment	Total	Total Incl O&P
9030	16 kW	1 Elec	1.30	6.154	Ea.	3,400	415		3,815	4,350
9040	20 kW		.90	8.889		3,450	600		4,050	4,700
9060	24 kW		.60	13.333		3,275	900		4,175	4,925
9230	13.5 kW, 40,956 BTU		2.20	3.636		2,150	245		2,395	2,725
9250	24 kW, 81,912 BTU		2	4		2,375	269		2,644	3,000

23 84 Humidity Control Equipment

23 84 13 – Humidifiers

23 84 13.10 Humidifier Units

		Crew	Daily Output	Labor-Hours	Unit	Material	Labor	Equipment	Total	Total Incl O&P
0010	**HUMIDIFIER UNITS**									
0520	Steam, room or duct, filter, regulators, auto. controls, 220 V									
0540	11 lb./hr.	Q-5	6	2.667	Ea.	2,925	174		3,099	3,475
0560	22 lb./hr.		5	3.200		3,225	209		3,434	3,850
0580	33 lb./hr.		4	4		3,300	261		3,561	4,050
0600	50 lb./hr.		4	4		3,675	261		3,936	4,450
0620	100 lb./hr.		3	5.333		5,450	350		5,800	6,500
0640	150 lb./hr.		2.50	6.400		6,975	420		7,395	8,300
0660	200 lb./hr.		2	8		8,775	520		9,295	10,500
0700	With blower									
0720	11 lb./hr.	Q-5	5.50	2.909	Ea.	4,050	190		4,240	4,725
0740	22 lb./hr.		4.75	3.368		5,550	220		5,770	6,425
0760	33 lb./hr.		3.75	4.267		4,500	279		4,779	5,375
0780	50 lb./hr.		3.50	4.571		5,800	299		6,099	6,825
0800	100 lb./hr.		2.75	5.818		6,475	380		6,855	7,700
0820	150 lb./hr.		2	8		9,325	520		9,845	11,100
0840	200 lb./hr.		1.50	10.667		12,400	695		13,095	14,700
1000	Steam for duct installation, manifold with pneum. controls									
1010	3-191 lb./hr., 24" x 24"	Q-5	5	3.200	Ea.	2,675	209		2,884	3,225
1020	3-191 lb./hr., 48" x 48"		4.60	3.478		4,375	227		4,602	5,150
1030	65-334 lb./hr., 36" x 36"		4.80	3.333		3,900	218		4,118	4,625
1040	65-334 lb./hr., 72" x 72"		4	4		4,225	261		4,486	5,050
1050	100-690 lb./hr., 48" x 48"		4	4		5,475	261		5,736	6,425
1060	100-690 lb./hr., 84" x 84"		3.60	4.444		6,450	290		6,740	7,525
1070	220-2000 lb./hr., 72" x 72"		3.80	4.211		6,275	275		6,550	7,300
1080	220-2000 lb./hr., 144" x 144"		3.40	4.706		7,350	305		7,655	8,525
1090	For electrically controlled unit, add					805			805	885
1092	For additional manifold, add					25%	15%			
1200	Electric steam, self generating, with manifold									
1210	1-96 lb./hr., 12" x 72"	Q-5	3.60	4.444	Ea.	11,500	290		11,790	13,000
1220	20-168 lb./hr., 12" x 72"		3.60	4.444		18,300	290		18,590	20,600
1290	For room mounting, add		16	1		277	65.50		342.50	405
5000	Furnace type, wheel bypass									
5020	10 GPD	1 Stpi	4	2	Ea.	305	145		450	550
5040	14 GPD		3.80	2.105		284	153		437	540
5060	19 GPD		3.60	2.222		380	161		541	660

23 84 Humidity Control Equipment

23 84 16 – Mechanical Dehumidification Units

23 84 16.10 Dehumidifier Units

		Crew	Daily Output	Labor-Hours	Unit	Material	2023 Bare Costs Labor	2023 Bare Costs Equipment	Total	Total Incl O&P
0010	**DEHUMIDIFIER UNITS**									
6000	Self contained with filters and standard controls									
6040	1.5 lb./hr., 50 CFM	1 Plum	8	1	Ea.	9,075	72		9,147	10,100
6060	3 lb./hr., 150 CFM	Q-1	12	1.333		7,600	86.50		7,686.50	8,500
6065	6 lb./hr., 150 CFM		9	1.778		15,800	115		15,915	17,500
6070	16 to 20 lb./hr., 600 CFM		5	3.200		26,800	208		27,008	29,700
6080	30 to 40 lb./hr., 1,125 CFM		4	4		46,300	259		46,559	51,500
6090	60 to 75 lb./hr., 2,250 CFM		3	5.333		60,500	345		60,845	67,000
6100	120 to 155 lb./hr., 4,500 CFM		2	8		107,000	520		107,520	118,500
6110	240 to 310 lb./hr., 9,000 CFM		1.50	10.667		153,500	690		154,190	169,500
6120	400 to 515 lb./hr., 15,000 CFM	Q-2	1.60	15		164,000	1,000		165,000	182,000
6130	530 to 690 lb./hr., 20,000 CFM		1.40	17.143		178,000	1,150		179,150	197,000
6140	800 to 1030 lb./hr., 30,000 CFM		1.20	20		202,500	1,350		203,850	224,500
6150	1060 to 1375 lb./hr., 40,000 CFM		1	24		281,500	1,625		283,125	312,500

23 91 Prefabricated Equipment Supports

23 91 10 – Prefabricated Curbs, Pads and Stands

23 91 10.10 Prefabricated Pads and Stands

		Crew	Daily Output	Labor-Hours	Unit	Material	2023 Bare Costs Labor	2023 Bare Costs Equipment	Total	Total Incl O&P
0010	**PREFABRICATED PADS AND STANDS**									
6000	Pad, fiberglass reinforced concrete with polystyrene foam core									
6070	24" x 24"	1 Shee	16	.500	Ea.	42.50	35		77.50	99.50
6090	24" x 36"		12	.667		65	47		112	142
6110	24" x 42"		8	1		79	70		149	193
6150	26" x 36"	Q-9	8	2		60	126		186	256
6170	28" x 38"	1 Shee	8	1		70.50	70		140.50	184
6190	30" x 30"		12	.667		69	47		116	147
6220	30" x 36"		8	1		78	70		148	192
6240	30" x 40"	Q-9	8	2		92	126		218	291
6260	32" x 32"		7	2.286		80	144		224	305
6280	36" x 36"		8	2		83	126		209	282
6300	36" x 40"		7	2.286		120	144		264	350
6320	36" x 48"		7	2.286		140	144		284	370
6340	36" x 54"		6	2.667		141	168		309	410
6360	36" x 60" x 3"		7	2.286		188	144		332	425
6400	41" x 47" x 3"		6	2.667		187	168		355	460
6490	26" round		10	1.600		37.50	101		138.50	193
6550	30" round		9	1.778		49	112		161	223
6600	36" round		8	2		63.50	126		189.50	260
6700	For 3" thick pad, add					20%	5%			
8800	Stand, corrosion-resistant plastic									
8850	Heat pump, 6" high	1 Shee	32	.250	Ea.	5.70	17.55		23.25	33
8870	12" high	"	32	.250	"	5.95	17.55		23.50	33

Estimating Tips
26 05 00 Common Work Results for Electrical
- Conduit should be taken off in three main categories—power distribution, branch power, and branch lighting—so the estimator can concentrate on systems and components, therefore making it easier to ensure all items have been accounted for.
- For cost modifications for elevated conduit installation, add the percentages to labor according to the height of installation and only to the quantities exceeding the different height levels, not to the total conduit quantities. Refer to subdivision 26 01 02.20 for labor adjustment factors.
- Remember that aluminum wiring of equal ampacity is larger in diameter than copper and may require larger conduit.
- If more than three wires at a time are being pulled, deduct percentages from the labor hours of that grouping of wires.
- When taking off grounding systems, identify separately the type and size of wire, and list each unique type of ground connection.
- The estimator should take the weights of materials into consideration when completing a takeoff. Topics to consider include: How will the materials be supported? What methods of support are available? How high will the support structure have to reach? Will the final support structure be able to withstand the total burden? Is the support material included or separate from the fixture, equipment, and material specified?
- Do not overlook the costs for equipment used in the installation. If scaffolding or highlifts are available in the field, contractors may use them in lieu of the proposed ladders and rolling staging.

26 20 00 Low-Voltage Electrical Transmission
- Supports and concrete pads may be shown on drawings for the larger equipment, or the support system may be only a piece of plywood for the back of a panelboard. In either case, they must be included in the costs.

26 40 00 Electrical and Cathodic Protection
- When taking off cathodic protection systems, identify the type and size of cable, and list each unique type of anode connection.

26 50 00 Lighting
- Fixtures should be taken off room by room using the fixture schedule, specifications, and the ceiling plan. For large concentrations of lighting fixtures in the same area, deduct the percentages from labor hours.

Reference Numbers
Reference numbers are shown at the beginning of some major classifications. These numbers refer to related items in the Reference Section. The reference information may be an estimating procedure, an alternate pricing method, or technical information.

Note: Not all subdivisions listed here necessarily appear. ■

Same Data. Simplified.
Enjoy the convenience and efficiency of accessing your costs anywhere:
- **Skip the multiplier** by setting your location
- **Quickly search,** edit, favorite and share costs
- **Stay on top of price changes** with automatic updates

Discover more at rsmeans.com/online

No part of this cost data may be reproduced, stored in a retrieval system, or transmitted in any form or by any means without prior written permission of Gordian.

Note: "Powered in part by CINX™, based on licensed proprietary information of Harrison Publishing House, Inc."

Note: The following companies, in part, have been used as a reference source for some of the material prices used in Division 26:

Electriflex

Trade Service

26 01 Operation and Maintenance of Electrical Systems

26 01 02 – Labor Adjustment

26 01 02.20 Labor Adjustment Factors

		Crew	Daily Output	Labor-Hours	Unit	Material	2023 Bare Costs Labor	Equipment	Total	Total Incl O&P
0010	**LABOR ADJUSTMENT FACTORS** (For Div. 26, 27 and 28) R260519-90									
0100	Subtract from labor for Economy of Scale for Wire									
0110	4-5 wires						25%			
0120	6-10 wires						30%			
0130	11-15 wires						35%			
0140	over 15 wires						40%			
0150	Labor adjustment factors (For Div. 26, 27, 28 and 48)									
0200	Labor factors: The below are reasonable suggestions, but									
0210	each project must be evaluated for its own peculiarities, and									
0220	the adjustments be increased or decreased depending on the									
0230	severity of the special conditions.									
1000	Add to labor for elevated installation (above floor level)									
1010	10' to 14.5' high						10%			
1020	15' to 19.5' high						20%			
1030	20' to 24.5' high						25%			
1040	25' to 29.5' high						35%			
1050	30' to 34.5' high						40%			
1060	35' to 39.5' high						50%			
1070	40' and higher						55%			
2000	Add to labor for crawl space									
2010	3' high						40%			
2020	4' high						30%			
3000	Add to labor for multi-story building									
3100	For new construction (No elevator available)									
3110	Add for floors 3 thru 10						5%			
3120	Add for floors 11 thru 15						10%			
3130	Add for floors 16 thru 20						15%			
3140	Add for floors 21 thru 30						20%			
3150	Add for floors 31 and up						30%			
3200	For existing structure (Elevator available)									
3210	Add for work on floor 3 and above						2%			
4000	Add to labor for working in existing occupied buildings									
4010	Hospital						35%			
4020	Office building						25%			
4030	School						20%			
4040	Factory or warehouse						15%			
4050	Multi-dwelling						15%			
5000	Add to labor, miscellaneous									
5010	Cramped shaft						35%			
5020	Congested area						15%			
5030	Excessive heat or cold						30%			
6000	Labor factors: the above are reasonable suggestions, but									
6100	each project should be evaluated for its own peculiarities									
6200	Other factors to be considered are:									
6210	Movement of material and equipment through finished areas						10%			
6220	Equipment room min security direct access w/authorization						15%			
6230	Attic space						25%			
6240	No service road						25%			
6250	Poor unloading/storage area, no hydraulic lifts or jacks						20%			
6260	Congested site area/heavy traffic						20%			
7000	Correctional facilities (no compounding division 1 adjustment factors)									
7010	Minimum security w/facilities escort						30%			
7020	Medium security w/facilities and correctional officer escort						40%			

26 01 Operation and Maintenance of Electrical Systems

26 01 02 – Labor Adjustment

26 01 02.20 Labor Adjustment Factors		Crew	Daily Output	Labor-Hours	Unit	Material	2023 Bare Costs Labor	Equipment	Total	Total Incl O&P
7030	Max security w/facilities & correctional officer escort (no inmate contact)						50%			

26 05 Common Work Results for Electrical

26 05 33 – Raceway and Boxes for Electrical Systems

26 05 33.95 Cutting and Drilling

		Crew	Daily Output	Labor-Hours	Unit	Material	Labor	Equipment	Total	Total Incl O&P
0010	**CUTTING AND DRILLING**									
0100	Hole drilling to 10' high, concrete wall									
0110	8" thick, 1/2" pipe size	R-31	12	.667	Ea.	.30	45	5.10	50.40	72.50
0120	3/4" pipe size		12	.667		.30	45	5.10	50.40	72.50
0130	1" pipe size		9.50	.842		.40	56.50	6.45	63.35	92
0140	1-1/4" pipe size		9.50	.842		.40	56.50	6.45	63.35	92
0150	1-1/2" pipe size		9.50	.842		.40	56.50	6.45	63.35	92
0160	2" pipe size		4.40	1.818		.57	122	13.95	136.52	198
0170	2-1/2" pipe size		4.40	1.818		.57	122	13.95	136.52	198
0180	3" pipe size		4.40	1.818		.57	122	13.95	136.52	198
0190	3-1/2" pipe size		3.30	2.424		.76	163	18.60	182.36	264
0200	4" pipe size		3.30	2.424		.76	163	18.60	182.36	264
0500	12" thick, 1/2" pipe size		9.40	.851		.44	57.50	6.55	64.49	92.50
0520	3/4" pipe size		9.40	.851		.44	57.50	6.55	64.49	92.50
0540	1" pipe size		7.30	1.096		.61	74	8.40	83.01	120
0560	1-1/4" pipe size		7.30	1.096		.61	74	8.40	83.01	120
0570	1-1/2" pipe size		7.30	1.096		.61	74	8.40	83.01	120
0580	2" pipe size		3.60	2.222		.86	150	17.05	167.91	242
0590	2-1/2" pipe size		3.60	2.222		.86	150	17.05	167.91	242
0600	3" pipe size		3.60	2.222		.86	150	17.05	167.91	242
0610	3-1/2" pipe size		2.80	2.857		1.15	192	22	215.15	310
0630	4" pipe size		2.50	3.200		1.15	216	24.50	241.65	350
0650	16" thick, 1/2" pipe size		7.60	1.053		.59	71	8.10	79.69	115
0670	3/4" pipe size		7	1.143		.59	77	8.80	86.39	124
0690	1" pipe size		6	1.333		.81	90	10.25	101.06	145
0710	1-1/4" pipe size		5.50	1.455		.81	98	11.15	109.96	159
0730	1-1/2" pipe size		5.50	1.455		.81	98	11.15	109.96	159
0750	2" pipe size		3	2.667		1.15	180	20.50	201.65	291
0770	2-1/2" pipe size		2.70	2.963		1.15	200	23	224.15	325
0790	3" pipe size		2.50	3.200		1.15	216	24.50	241.65	350
0810	3-1/2" pipe size		2.30	3.478		1.53	234	26.50	262.03	380
0830	4" pipe size		2	4		1.53	269	30.50	301.03	435
0850	20" thick, 1/2" pipe size		6.40	1.250		.74	84	9.60	94.34	136
0870	3/4" pipe size		6	1.333		.74	90	10.25	100.99	145
0890	1" pipe size		5	1.600		1.01	108	12.30	121.31	175
0910	1-1/4" pipe size		4.80	1.667		1.01	112	12.80	125.81	182
0930	1-1/2" pipe size		4.60	1.739		1.01	117	13.35	131.36	190
0950	2" pipe size		2.70	2.963		1.43	200	23	224.43	325
0970	2-1/2" pipe size		2.40	3.333		1.43	225	25.50	251.93	365
0990	3" pipe size		2.20	3.636		1.43	245	28	274.43	395
1010	3-1/2" pipe size		2	4		1.91	269	30.50	301.41	435
1030	4" pipe size		1.70	4.706		1.91	315	36	352.91	510
1050	24" thick, 1/2" pipe size		5.50	1.455		.89	98	11.15	110.04	159
1070	3/4" pipe size		5.10	1.569		.89	106	12.05	118.94	171
1090	1" pipe size		4.30	1.860		1.21	125	14.30	140.51	203
1110	1-1/4" pipe size		4	2		1.21	135	15.35	151.56	218

26 05 Common Work Results for Electrical

26 05 33 – Raceway and Boxes for Electrical Systems

26 05 33.95 Cutting and Drilling		Crew	Daily Output	Labor-Hours	Unit	Material	2023 Bare Costs Labor	Equipment	Total	Total Incl O&P
1130	1-1/2" pipe size	R-31	4	2	Ea.	1.21	135	15.35	151.56	218
1150	2" pipe size		2.40	3.333		1.72	225	25.50	252.22	365
1170	2-1/2" pipe size		2.20	3.636		1.72	245	28	274.72	395
1190	3" pipe size		2	4		1.72	269	30.50	301.22	435
1210	3-1/2" pipe size		1.80	4.444		2.29	299	34	335.29	485
1230	4" pipe size		1.50	5.333		2.29	360	41	403.29	585
1500	Brick wall, 8" thick, 1/2" pipe size		18	.444		.30	30	3.41	33.71	48.50
1520	3/4" pipe size		18	.444		.30	30	3.41	33.71	48.50
1540	1" pipe size		13.30	.602		.40	40.50	4.62	45.52	65.50
1560	1-1/4" pipe size		13.30	.602		.40	40.50	4.62	45.52	65.50
1580	1-1/2" pipe size		13.30	.602		.40	40.50	4.62	45.52	65.50
1600	2" pipe size		5.70	1.404		.57	94.50	10.80	105.87	152
1620	2-1/2" pipe size		5.70	1.404		.57	94.50	10.80	105.87	152
1640	3" pipe size		5.70	1.404		.57	94.50	10.80	105.87	152
1660	3-1/2" pipe size		4.40	1.818		.76	122	13.95	136.71	198
1680	4" pipe size		4	2		.76	135	15.35	151.11	218
1700	12" thick, 1/2" pipe size		14.50	.552		.44	37	4.24	41.68	60
1720	3/4" pipe size		14.50	.552		.44	37	4.24	41.68	60
1740	1" pipe size		11	.727		.61	49	5.60	55.21	80
1760	1-1/4" pipe size		11	.727		.61	49	5.60	55.21	80
1780	1-1/2" pipe size		11	.727		.61	49	5.60	55.21	80
1800	2" pipe size		5	1.600		.86	108	12.30	121.16	174
1820	2-1/2" pipe size		5	1.600		.86	108	12.30	121.16	174
1840	3" pipe size		5	1.600		.86	108	12.30	121.16	174
1860	3-1/2" pipe size		3.80	2.105		1.15	142	16.15	159.30	230
1880	4" pipe size		3.30	2.424		1.15	163	18.60	182.75	265
1900	16" thick, 1/2" pipe size		12.30	.650		.59	44	5	49.59	71
1920	3/4" pipe size		12.30	.650		.59	44	5	49.59	71
1940	1" pipe size		9.30	.860		.81	58	6.60	65.41	94
1960	1-1/4" pipe size		9.30	.860		.81	58	6.60	65.41	94
1980	1-1/2" pipe size		9.30	.860		.81	58	6.60	65.41	94
2000	2" pipe size		4.40	1.818		1.15	122	13.95	137.10	199
2010	2-1/2" pipe size		4.40	1.818		1.15	122	13.95	137.10	199
2030	3" pipe size		4.40	1.818		1.15	122	13.95	137.10	199
2050	3-1/2" pipe size		3.30	2.424		1.53	163	18.60	183.13	265
2070	4" pipe size		3	2.667		1.53	180	20.50	202.03	291
2090	20" thick, 1/2" pipe size		10.70	.748		.74	50.50	5.75	56.99	82
2110	3/4" pipe size		10.70	.748		.74	50.50	5.75	56.99	82
2130	1" pipe size		8	1		1.01	67.50	7.70	76.21	110
2150	1-1/4" pipe size		8	1		1.01	67.50	7.70	76.21	110
2170	1-1/2" pipe size		8	1		1.01	67.50	7.70	76.21	110
2190	2" pipe size		4	2		1.43	135	15.35	151.78	218
2210	2-1/2" pipe size		4	2		1.43	135	15.35	151.78	218
2230	3" pipe size		4	2		1.43	135	15.35	151.78	218
2250	3-1/2" pipe size		3	2.667		1.91	180	20.50	202.41	292
2270	4" pipe size		2.70	2.963		1.91	200	23	224.91	325
2290	24" thick, 1/2" pipe size		9.40	.851		.89	57.50	6.55	64.94	93
2310	3/4" pipe size		9.40	.851		.89	57.50	6.55	64.94	93
2330	1" pipe size		7.10	1.127		1.21	76	8.65	85.86	124
2350	1-1/4" pipe size		7.10	1.127		1.21	76	8.65	85.86	124
2370	1-1/2" pipe size		7.10	1.127		1.21	76	8.65	85.86	124
2390	2" pipe size		3.60	2.222		1.72	150	17.05	168.77	243
2410	2-1/2" pipe size		3.60	2.222		1.72	150	17.05	168.77	243

26 05 Common Work Results for Electrical

26 05 33 – Raceway and Boxes for Electrical Systems

26 05 33.95 Cutting and Drilling

		Crew	Daily Output	Labor-Hours	Unit	Material	2023 Bare Costs Labor	2023 Bare Costs Equipment	Total	Total Incl O&P
2430	3" pipe size	R-31	3.60	2.222	Ea.	1.72	150	17.05	168.77	243
2450	3-1/2" pipe size	↓	2.80	2.857		2.29	192	22	216.29	315
2470	4" pipe size	↓	2.50	3.200	↓	2.29	216	24.50	242.79	350
3000	Knockouts to 8' high, metal boxes & enclosures									
3020	With hole saw, 1/2" pipe size	1 Elec	53	.151	Ea.		10.15		10.15	15.10
3040	3/4" pipe size		47	.170			11.45		11.45	17.05
3050	1" pipe size		40	.200			13.45		13.45	20
3060	1-1/4" pipe size		36	.222			14.95		14.95	22
3070	1-1/2" pipe size		32	.250			16.85		16.85	25
3080	2" pipe size		27	.296			19.95		19.95	29.50
3090	2-1/2" pipe size		20	.400			27		27	40
4010	3" pipe size		16	.500			33.50		33.50	50
4030	3-1/2" pipe size		13	.615			41.50		41.50	61.50
4050	4" pipe size	↓	11	.727	↓		49		49	73

26 05 83 – Wiring Connections

26 05 83.10 Motor Connections

		Crew	Daily Output	Labor-Hours	Unit	Material	Labor	Equipment	Total	Total Incl O&P
0010	**MOTOR CONNECTIONS**									
0020	Flexible conduit and fittings, 115 volt, 1 phase, up to 1 HP motor	1 Elec	8	1	Ea.	6.60	67.50		74.10	107
0050	2 HP motor		6.50	1.231		13.85	83		96.85	138
0100	3 HP motor		5.50	1.455		12.10	98		110.10	159
0110	230 volt, 3 phase, 3 HP motor		6.78	1.180		8	79.50		87.50	127
0112	5 HP motor		5.47	1.463		6.85	98.50		105.35	154
0114	7-1/2 HP motor		4.61	1.735		12.05	117		129.05	187
0120	10 HP motor		4.20	1.905		21.50	128		149.50	215
0150	15 HP motor		3.30	2.424		21.50	163		184.50	267
0200	25 HP motor		2.70	2.963		32	200		232	330
0400	50 HP motor		2.20	3.636		66.50	245		311.50	440
0600	100 HP motor		1.50	5.333		151	360		511	700
1500	460 volt, 5 HP motor, 3 phase		8	1		7.25	67.50		74.75	108
1520	10 HP motor		8	1		7.25	67.50		74.75	108
1530	25 HP motor		6	1.333		15.10	90		105.10	150
1540	30 HP motor		6	1.333		15.10	90		105.10	150
1550	40 HP motor		5	1.600		20	108		128	182
1560	50 HP motor		5	1.600		24	108		132	187
1570	60 HP motor		3.80	2.105		27.50	142		169.50	241
1580	75 HP motor		3.50	2.286		40.50	154		194.50	274
1590	100 HP motor		2.50	3.200		58	216		274	385
1600	125 HP motor		2	4		74.50	269		343.50	480
1610	150 HP motor		1.80	4.444		77.50	299		376.50	530
1620	200 HP motor		1.50	5.333		130	360		490	680
2005	460 volt, 5 HP motor, 3 phase, w/sealtite		8	1		14.90	67.50		82.40	116
2010	10 HP motor		8	1		14.90	67.50		82.40	116
2015	25 HP motor		6	1.333		26	90		116	162
2020	30 HP motor		6	1.333		26	90		116	162
2025	40 HP motor		5	1.600		39	108		147	203
2030	50 HP motor		5	1.600		40.50	108		148.50	205
2035	60 HP motor		3.80	2.105		64	142		206	282
2040	75 HP motor		3.50	2.286		71	154		225	305
2045	100 HP motor		2.50	3.200		93	216		309	425
2055	150 HP motor		1.80	4.444		101	299		400	555
2060	200 HP motor	↓	1.50	5.333		385	360		745	960

26 05 Common Work Results for Electrical

26 05 90 – Residential Applications

26 05 90.10 Residential Wiring		Crew	Daily Output	Labor-Hours	Unit	Material	2023 Bare Costs Labor	Equipment	Total	Total Incl O&P
0010	**RESIDENTIAL WIRING**									
0020	20' avg. runs and #14/2 wiring incl. unless otherwise noted									
1000	Service & panel, includes 24' SE-AL cable, service eye, meter,									
1010	Socket, panel board, main bkr., ground rod, 15 or 20 amp									
1020	1-pole circuit breakers, and misc. hardware									
1100	100 amp, with 10 branch breakers	1 Elec	1.19	6.723	Ea.	605	455		1,060	1,350
1110	With PVC conduit and wire		.92	8.696		695	585		1,280	1,625
1120	With RGS conduit and wire		.73	10.959		975	740		1,715	2,175
1150	150 amp, with 14 branch breakers		1.03	7.767		915	525		1,440	1,775
1170	With PVC conduit and wire		.82	9.756		1,075	655		1,730	2,175
1180	With RGS conduit and wire	↓	.67	11.940		1,650	805		2,455	3,025
1200	200 amp, with 18 branch breakers	2 Elec	1.80	8.889		1,550	600		2,150	2,600
1220	With PVC conduit and wire		1.46	10.959		1,725	740		2,465	2,975
1230	With RGS conduit and wire	↓	1.24	12.903		2,400	870		3,270	3,925
1800	Lightning surge suppressor	1 Elec	32	.250	↓	93	16.85		109.85	128
2000	Switch devices									
2100	Single pole, 15 amp, ivory, with a 1-gang box, cover plate,									
2110	Type NM (Romex) cable	1 Elec	17.10	.468	Ea.	12.90	31.50		44.40	61
2120	Type MC cable		14.30	.559		23	37.50		60.50	81
2130	EMT & wire		5.71	1.401		54.50	94.50		149	200
2150	3-way, #14/3, type NM cable		14.55	.550		15.70	37		52.70	72.50
2170	Type MC cable		12.31	.650		30.50	44		74.50	98.50
2180	EMT & wire		5	1.600		59.50	108		167.50	225
2200	4-way, #14/3, type NM cable		14.55	.550		24	37		61	81.50
2220	Type MC cable		12.31	.650		38.50	44		82.50	108
2230	EMT & wire		5	1.600		67.50	108		175.50	234
2250	S.P., 20 amp, #12/2, type NM cable		13.33	.600		19.25	40.50		59.75	81
2270	Type MC cable		11.43	.700		27.50	47		74.50	100
2280	EMT & wire		4.85	1.649		59	111		170	230
2290	S.P. rotary dimmer, 600 W, no wiring		17	.471		30.50	31.50		62	80.50
2300	S.P. rotary dimmer, 600 W, type NM cable		14.55	.550		40	37		77	99
2320	Type MC cable		12.31	.650		50	44		94	120
2330	EMT & wire		5	1.600		86	108		194	255
2350	3-way rotary dimmer, type NM cable		13.33	.600		42.50	40.50		83	107
2370	Type MC cable		11.43	.700		52.50	47		99.50	128
2380	EMT & wire	↓	4.85	1.649	↓	88.50	111		199.50	262
2400	Interval timer wall switch, 20 amp, 1-30 min., #12/2									
2410	Type NM cable	1 Elec	14.55	.550	Ea.	91	37		128	155
2420	Type MC cable		12.31	.650		92	44		136	166
2430	EMT & wire	↓	5	1.600	↓	131	108		239	305
2500	Decorator style									
2510	S.P., 15 amp, type NM cable	1 Elec	17.10	.468	Ea.	19.40	31.50		50.90	68.50
2520	Type MC cable		14.30	.559		29.50	37.50		67	88.50
2530	EMT & wire		5.71	1.401		61	94.50		155.50	207
2550	3-way, #14/3, type NM cable		14.55	.550		22	37		59	79.50
2570	Type MC cable		12.31	.650		37	44		81	106
2580	EMT & wire		5	1.600		66	108		174	233
2600	4-way, #14/3, type NM cable		14.55	.550		30.50	37		67.50	88.50
2620	Type MC cable		12.31	.650		45	44		89	115
2630	EMT & wire		5	1.600		74	108		182	242
2650	S.P., 20 amp, #12/2, type NM cable		13.33	.600		26	40.50		66.50	88.50
2670	Type MC cable		11.43	.700		34	47		81	107

26 05 Common Work Results for Electrical

26 05 90 – Residential Applications

26 05 90.10 Residential Wiring		Crew	Daily Output	Labor-Hours	Unit	Material	2023 Bare Costs Labor	Equipment	Total	Total Incl O&P
2680	EMT & wire	1 Elec	4.85	1.649	Ea.	65.50	111		176.50	237
2700	S.P., slide dimmer, type NM cable		17.10	.468		44	31.50		75.50	95.50
2720	Type MC cable		14.30	.559		54.50	37.50		92	116
2730	EMT & wire		5.71	1.401		90	94.50		184.50	239
2750	S.P., touch dimmer, type NM cable		17.10	.468		38	31.50		69.50	88.50
2770	Type MC cable		14.30	.559		48	37.50		85.50	109
2780	EMT & wire		5.71	1.401		84	94.50		178.50	232
2800	3-way touch dimmer, type NM cable		13.33	.600		40	40.50		80.50	104
2820	Type MC cable		11.43	.700		50	47		97	125
2830	EMT & wire	▼	4.85	1.649	▼	86	111		197	260
3000	Combination devices									
3100	S.P. switch/15 amp recpt., ivory, 1-gang box, plate									
3110	Type NM cable	1 Elec	11.43	.700	Ea.	28	47		75	101
3120	Type MC cable		10	.800		38	54		92	122
3130	EMT & wire		4.40	1.818		74	122		196	263
3150	S.P. switch/pilot light, type NM cable		11.43	.700		29.50	47		76.50	103
3170	Type MC cable		10	.800		39.50	54		93.50	124
3180	EMT & wire		4.43	1.806		75.50	122		197.50	264
3190	2-S.P. switches, 2-#14/2, no wiring		14	.571		5.35	38.50		43.85	63
3200	2-S.P. switches, 2-#14/2, type NM cables		10	.800		34.50	54		88.50	118
3220	Type MC cable		8.89	.900		43	60.50		103.50	138
3230	EMT & wire		4.10	1.951		84	131		215	288
3250	3-way switch/15 amp recpt., #14/3, type NM cable		10	.800		37.50	54		91.50	122
3270	Type MC cable		8.89	.900		52.50	60.50		113	148
3280	EMT & wire		4.10	1.951		81.50	131		212.50	285
3300	2-3 way switches, 2-#14/3, type NM cables		8.89	.900		49	60.50		109.50	144
3320	Type MC cable		8	1		67	67.50		134.50	174
3330	EMT & wire		4	2		94	135		229	305
3350	S.P. switch/20 amp recpt., #12/2, type NM cable		10	.800		41.50	54		95.50	126
3370	Type MC cable		8.89	.900		42.50	60.50		103	137
3380	EMT & wire	▼	4.10	1.951	▼	81.50	131		212.50	285
3400	Decorator style									
3410	S.P. switch/15 amp recpt., type NM cable	1 Elec	11.43	.700	Ea.	34.50	47		81.50	108
3420	Type MC cable		10	.800		44.50	54		98.50	129
3430	EMT & wire		4.40	1.818		80.50	122		202.50	271
3450	S.P. switch/pilot light, type NM cable		11.43	.700		36	47		83	110
3470	Type MC cable		10	.800		46	54		100	131
3480	EMT & wire		4.40	1.818		82	122		204	273
3500	2-S.P. switches, 2-#14/2, type NM cables		10	.800		41	54		95	125
3520	Type MC cable		8.89	.900		49.50	60.50		110	145
3530	EMT & wire		4.10	1.951		90.50	131		221.50	295
3550	3-way/15 amp recpt., #14/3, type NM cable		10	.800		44.50	54		98.50	129
3570	Type MC cable		8.89	.900		59	60.50		119.50	155
3580	EMT & wire		4.10	1.951		88	131		219	292
3650	2-3 way switches, 2-#14/3, type NM cables		8.89	.900		55.50	60.50		116	151
3670	Type MC cable		8	1		73.50	67.50		141	181
3680	EMT & wire		4	2		101	135		236	310
3700	S.P. switch/20 amp recpt., #12/2, type NM cable		10	.800		48	54		102	133
3720	Type MC cable		8.89	.900		49	60.50		109.50	144
3730	EMT & wire	▼	4.10	1.951	▼	88	131		219	292
4000	Receptacle devices									
4010	Duplex outlet, 15 amp recpt., ivory, 1-gang box, plate									
4015	Type NM cable	1 Elec	14.55	.550	Ea.	13.45	37		50.45	70

26 05 Common Work Results for Electrical

26 05 90 – Residential Applications

26 05 90.10 Residential Wiring

		Crew	Daily Output	Labor-Hours	Unit	Material	2023 Bare Costs Labor	Equipment	Total	Total Incl O&P
4020	Type MC cable	1 Elec	12.31	.650	Ea.	23.50	44		67.50	91
4030	EMT & wire		5.33	1.501		55	101		156	211
4050	With #12/2, type NM cable		12.31	.650		16.55	44		60.55	83
4070	Type MC cable		10.67	.750		24.50	50.50		75	102
4080	EMT & wire		4.71	1.699		56.50	114		170.50	232
4100	20 amp recpt., #12/2, type NM cable		12.31	.650		28	44		72	95.50
4120	Type MC cable		10.67	.750		36	50.50		86.50	115
4130	EMT & wire		4.71	1.699		68	114		182	245
4140	For GFI see Section 26 05 90.10 line 4300 below									
4150	Decorator style, 15 amp recpt., type NM cable	1 Elec	14.55	.550	Ea.	19.95	37		56.95	77
4170	Type MC cable		12.31	.650		30	44		74	98
4180	EMT & wire		5.33	1.501		61.50	101		162.50	218
4200	With #12/2, type NM cable		12.31	.650		23	44		67	90.50
4220	Type MC cable		10.67	.750		31	50.50		81.50	109
4230	EMT & wire		4.71	1.699		63	114		177	239
4250	20 amp recpt., #12/2, type NM cable		12.31	.650		34.50	44		78.50	103
4270	Type MC cable		10.67	.750		42.50	50.50		93	122
4280	EMT & wire		4.71	1.699		74.50	114		188.50	252
4300	GFI, 15 amp recpt., type NM cable		12.31	.650		32.50	44		76.50	101
4320	Type MC cable		10.67	.750		43	50.50		93.50	122
4330	EMT & wire		4.71	1.699		74.50	114		188.50	252
4350	GFI with #12/2, type NM cable		10.67	.750		36	50.50		86.50	115
4370	Type MC cable		9.20	.870		44	58.50		102.50	135
4380	EMT & wire		4.21	1.900		75.50	128		203.50	273
4400	20 amp recpt., #12/2, type NM cable		10.67	.750		53.50	50.50		104	134
4420	Type MC cable		9.20	.870		61.50	58.50		120	155
4430	EMT & wire		4.21	1.900		93.50	128		221.50	293
4500	Weather-proof cover for above receptacles, add		32	.250		4.48	16.85		21.33	30
4550	Air conditioner outlet, 20 amp-240 volt recpt.									
4560	30' of #12/2, 2 pole circuit breaker									
4570	Type NM cable	1 Elec	10	.800	Ea.	94.50	54		148.50	184
4580	Type MC cable		9	.889		101	60		161	200
4590	EMT & wire		4	2		133	135		268	345
4600	Decorator style, type NM cable		10	.800		101	54		155	191
4620	Type MC cable		9	.889		108	60		168	207
4630	EMT & wire		4	2		140	135		275	355
4650	Dryer outlet, 30 amp-240 volt recpt., 20' of #10/3									
4660	2 pole circuit breaker									
4670	Type NM cable	1 Elec	6.41	1.248	Ea.	90.50	84		174.50	225
4680	Type MC cable		5.71	1.401		79.50	94.50		174	228
4690	EMT & wire		3.48	2.299		128	155		283	370
4700	Range outlet, 50 amp-240 volt recpt., 30' of #8/3									
4710	Type NM cable	1 Elec	4.21	1.900	Ea.	163	128		291	370
4720	Type MC cable		4	2		141	135		276	355
4730	EMT & wire		2.96	2.703		174	182		356	460
4750	Central vacuum outlet, type NM cable		6.40	1.250		93	84		177	227
4770	Type MC cable		5.71	1.401		90	94.50		184.50	240
4780	EMT & wire		3.48	2.299		145	155		300	390
4800	30 amp-110 volt locking recpt., #10/2 circ. bkr.									
4810	Type NM cable	1 Elec	6.20	1.290	Ea.	114	87		201	255
4820	Type MC cable		5.40	1.481		103	100		203	261
4830	EMT & wire		3.20	2.500		173	168		341	440
4900	Low voltage outlets									

26 05 Common Work Results for Electrical

26 05 90 – Residential Applications

26 05 90.10 Residential Wiring

		Crew	Daily Output	Labor-Hours	Unit	Material	2023 Bare Costs Labor	Equipment	Total	Total Incl O&P
4910	Telephone recpt., 20' of 4/C phone wire	1 Elec	26	.308	Ea.	10.55	20.50		31.05	42.50
4920	TV recpt., 20' of RG59U coax wire, F type connector	"	16	.500	"	18.75	33.50		52.25	70.50
4950	Door bell chime, transformer, 2 buttons, 60' of bellwire									
4970	Economy model	1 Elec	11.50	.696	Ea.	72	47		119	149
4980	Custom model		11.50	.696		120	47		167	202
4990	Luxury model, 3 buttons		9.50	.842		208	56.50		264.50	315
6000	Lighting outlets									
6050	Wire only (for fixture), type NM cable	1 Elec	32	.250	Ea.	13.45	16.85		30.30	40
6070	Type MC cable		24	.333		13	22.50		35.50	48
6080	EMT & wire		10	.800		43.50	54		97.50	128
6100	Box (4") and wire (for fixture), type NM cable		25	.320		23	21.50		44.50	57
6120	Type MC cable		20	.400		22.50	27		49.50	64.50
6130	EMT & wire		11	.727		53	49		102	132
6200	Fixtures (use with line 6050 or 6100 above)									
6210	Canopy style, economy grade	1 Elec	40	.200	Ea.	24.50	13.45		37.95	47
6220	Custom grade		40	.200		63.50	13.45		76.95	89.50
6250	Dining room chandelier, economy grade		19	.421		101	28.50		129.50	153
6260	Custom grade		19	.421		385	28.50		413.50	460
6270	Luxury grade		15	.533		3,200	36		3,236	3,575
6310	Kitchen fixture (fluorescent), economy grade		30	.267		90.50	17.95		108.45	126
6320	Custom grade		25	.320		220	21.50		241.50	274
6350	Outdoor, wall mounted, economy grade		30	.267		45	17.95		62.95	75.50
6360	Custom grade		30	.267		139	17.95		156.95	180
6370	Luxury grade		25	.320		248	21.50		269.50	305
6410	Outdoor PAR floodlights, 1 lamp, 150 watt		20	.400		17.85	27		44.85	59.50
6420	2 lamp, 150 watt each		20	.400		28.50	27		55.50	71.50
6430	For infrared security sensor, add		32	.250		114	16.85		130.85	150
6450	Outdoor, quartz-halogen, 300 watt flood		20	.400		48	27		75	93
6600	Recessed downlight, round, pre-wired, 50 or 75 watt trim		30	.267		56.50	17.95		74.45	89
6610	With shower light trim		30	.267		86.50	17.95		104.45	122
6620	With wall washer trim		28	.286		87	19.25		106.25	124
6630	With eye-ball trim		28	.286		36	19.25		55.25	68.50
6700	Porcelain lamp holder		40	.200		3.12	13.45		16.57	23.50
6710	With pull switch		40	.200		13.55	13.45		27	35
6750	Fluorescent strip, 2-20 watt tube, wrap around diffuser, 24"		24	.333		52	22.50		74.50	90.50
6770	2-34 watt tubes, 48"		20	.400		149	27		176	204
6800	Bathroom heat lamp, 1-250 watt		28	.286		41	19.25		60.25	73.50
6810	2-250 watt lamps		28	.286		72	19.25		91.25	108
6820	For timer switch, see Section 26 05 90.10 line 2400									
6900	Outdoor post lamp, incl. post, fixture, 35' of #14/2									
6910	Type NM cable	1 Elec	3.50	2.286	Ea.	405	154		559	675
6920	Photo-eye, add		27	.296		15.20	19.95		35.15	46
6950	Clock dial time switch, 24 hr., w/enclosure, type NM cable		11.43	.700		93	47		140	173
6970	Type MC cable		11	.727		103	49		152	187
6980	EMT & wire		4.85	1.649		135	111		246	315
7000	Alarm systems									
7050	Smoke detectors, box, #14/3, type NM cable	1 Elec	14.55	.550	Ea.	40.50	37		77.50	99.50
7070	Type MC cable		12.31	.650		47.50	44		91.50	118
7080	EMT & wire		5	1.600		76.50	108		184.50	244
7090	For relay output to security system, add					10.70			10.70	11.75
8000	Residential equipment									
8050	Disposal hook-up, incl. switch, outlet box, 3' of flex									
8060	20 amp-1 pole circ. bkr., and 25' of #12/2									

26 05 Common Work Results for Electrical

26 05 90 – Residential Applications

26 05 90.10 Residential Wiring	Crew	Daily Output	Labor-Hours	Unit	Material	2023 Bare Costs Labor	Equipment	Total	Total Incl O&P
8070 Type NM cable	1 Elec	10	.800	Ea.	40	54		94	124
8080 Type MC cable		8	1		47.50	67.50		115	152
8090 EMT & wire		5	1.600		86	108		194	255
8100 Trash compactor or dishwasher hook-up, incl. outlet box,									
8110 3' of flex, 15 amp-1 pole circ. bkr., and 25' of #14/2									
8120 Type NM cable	1 Elec	10	.800	Ea.	34	54		88	117
8130 Type MC cable		8	1		45	67.50		112.50	150
8140 EMT & wire		5	1.600		79.50	108		187.50	248
8150 Hot water sink dispenser hook-up, use line 8100									
8200 Vent/exhaust fan hook-up, type NM cable	1 Elec	32	.250	Ea.	13.45	16.85		30.30	40
8220 Type MC cable		24	.333		13	22.50		35.50	48
8230 EMT & wire		10	.800		43.50	54		97.50	128
8250 Bathroom vent fan, 50 CFM (use with above hook-up)									
8260 Economy model	1 Elec	15	.533	Ea.	23.50	36		59.50	79
8270 Low noise model		15	.533		60	36		96	120
8280 Custom model		12	.667		120	45		165	199
8300 Bathroom or kitchen vent fan, 110 CFM									
8310 Economy model	1 Elec	15	.533	Ea.	75	36		111	136
8320 Low noise model	"	15	.533	"	121	36		157	187
8350 Paddle fan, variable speed (w/o lights)									
8360 Economy model (AC motor)	1 Elec	10	.800	Ea.	157	54		211	253
8362 With light kit		10	.800		201	54		255	300
8370 Custom model (AC motor)		10	.800		385	54		439	500
8372 With light kit		10	.800		425	54		479	550
8380 Luxury model (DC motor)		8	1		299	67.50		366.50	430
8382 With light kit		8	1		340	67.50		407.50	475
8390 Remote speed switch for above, add		12	.667		48.50	45		93.50	120
8500 Whole house exhaust fan, ceiling mount, 36", variable speed									
8510 Remote switch, incl. shutters, 20 amp-1 pole circ. bkr.									
8520 30' of #12/2, type NM cable	1 Elec	4	2	Ea.	1,675	135		1,810	2,025
8530 Type MC cable		3.50	2.286		1,675	154		1,829	2,075
8540 EMT & wire		3	2.667		1,725	180		1,905	2,175
8600 Whirlpool tub hook-up, incl. timer switch, outlet box									
8610 3' of flex, 20 amp-1 pole GFI circ. bkr.									
8620 30' of #12/2, type NM cable	1 Elec	5	1.600	Ea.	266	108		374	455
8630 Type MC cable		4.20	1.905		268	128		396	485
8640 EMT & wire		3.40	2.353		300	158		458	565
8650 Hot water heater hook-up, incl. 1-2 pole circ. bkr., box;									
8660 3' of flex, 20' of #10/2, type NM cable	1 Elec	5	1.600	Ea.	48.50	108		156.50	213
8670 Type MC cable		4.20	1.905		51	128		179	247
8680 EMT & wire		3.40	2.353		78.50	158		236.50	320
9000 Heating/air conditioning									
9050 Furnace/boiler hook-up, incl. firestat, local on-off switch									
9060 Emergency switch, and 40' of type NM cable	1 Elec	4	2	Ea.	82	135		217	290
9070 Type MC cable		3.50	2.286		90.50	154		244.50	330
9080 EMT & wire		1.50	5.333		155	360		515	705
9100 Air conditioner hook-up, incl. local 60 amp disc. switch									
9110 3' sealtite, 40 amp, 2 pole circuit breaker									
9130 40' of #8/2, type NM cable	1 Elec	3.50	2.286	Ea.	239	154		393	490
9140 Type MC cable		3	2.667		224	180		404	515
9150 EMT & wire		1.30	6.154		285	415		700	930
9200 Heat pump hook-up, 1-40 & 1-100 amp 2 pole circ. bkr.									
9210 Local disconnect switch, 3' sealtite									

26 05 Common Work Results for Electrical

26 05 90 – Residential Applications

26 05 90.10 Residential Wiring

		Crew	Daily Output	Labor-Hours	Unit	Material	2023 Bare Costs Labor	Equipment	Total	Total Incl O&P
9220	40' of #8/2 & 30' of #3/2									
9230	Type NM cable	1 Elec	1.30	6.154	Ea.	810	415		1,225	1,500
9240	Type MC cable	↓	1.08	7.407	↓	525	500		1,025	1,325
9250	EMT & wire		.94	8.511		765	575		1,340	1,700
9500	Thermostat hook-up, using low voltage wire									
9520	Heating only, 25' of #18-3	1 Elec	24	.333	Ea.	14	22.50		36.50	49
9530	Heating/cooling, 25' of #18-4	"	20	.400	"	15.05	27		42.05	56.50

26 24 Switchboards and Panelboards

26 24 19 – Motor-Control Centers

26 24 19.40 Motor Starters and Controls

		Crew	Daily Output	Labor-Hours	Unit	Material	2023 Bare Costs Labor	Equipment	Total	Total Incl O&P
0010	**MOTOR STARTERS AND CONTROLS**									
0050	Magnetic, FVNR, with enclosure and heaters, 480 volt									
0080	2 HP, size 00	1 Elec	3.50	2.286	Ea.	151	154		305	395
0100	5 HP, size 0		2.30	3.478		460	234		694	855
0200	10 HP, size 1	↓	1.60	5		214	335		549	735
0300	25 HP, size 2	2 Elec	2.20	7.273		425	490		915	1,200
0400	50 HP, size 3		1.80	8.889		705	600		1,305	1,675
0500	100 HP, size 4		1.20	13.333		1,600	900		2,500	3,075
0600	200 HP, size 5		.90	17.778		3,650	1,200		4,850	5,800
0610	400 HP, size 6	↓	.80	20		10,600	1,350		11,950	13,600
0620	NEMA 7, 5 HP, size 0	1 Elec	1.60	5		2,575	335		2,910	3,350
0630	10 HP, size 1	"	1.10	7.273		2,700	490		3,190	3,700
0640	25 HP, size 2	2 Elec	1.80	8.889		4,350	600		4,950	5,700
0650	50 HP, size 3		1.20	13.333		6,550	900		7,450	8,525
0660	100 HP, size 4		.90	17.778		8,450	1,200		9,650	11,100
0670	200 HP, size 5	↓	.50	32		13,700	2,150		15,850	18,300
0700	Combination, with motor circuit protectors, 5 HP, size 0	1 Elec	1.80	4.444		1,475	299		1,774	2,075
0800	10 HP, size 1	"	1.30	6.154		1,550	415		1,965	2,325
0900	25 HP, size 2	2 Elec	2	8		2,150	540		2,690	3,150
1000	50 HP, size 3		1.32	12.121		3,125	815		3,940	4,650
1200	100 HP, size 4	↓	.80	20		6,850	1,350		8,200	9,525
1220	NEMA 7, 5 HP, size 0	1 Elec	1.30	6.154		3,450	415		3,865	4,425
1230	10 HP, size 1	"	1	8		3,550	540		4,090	4,700
1240	25 HP, size 2	2 Elec	1.32	12.121		4,725	815		5,540	6,425
1250	50 HP, size 3		.80	20		7,800	1,350		9,150	10,600
1260	100 HP, size 4		.60	26.667		12,200	1,800		14,000	16,100
1270	200 HP, size 5	↓	.40	40		26,400	2,700		29,100	33,000
1400	Combination, with fused switch, 5 HP, size 0	1 Elec	1.80	4.444		1,400	299		1,699	1,975
1600	10 HP, size 1	"	1.30	6.154		1,400	415		1,815	2,150
1800	25 HP, size 2	2 Elec	2	8		2,300	540		2,840	3,325
2000	50 HP, size 3		1.32	12.121		3,725	815		4,540	5,325
2200	100 HP, size 4	↓	.80	20		7,400	1,350		8,750	10,200
3500	Magnetic FVNR with NEMA 12, enclosure & heaters, 480 volt									
3600	5 HP, size 0	1 Elec	2.20	3.636	Ea.	260	245		505	650
3700	10 HP, size 1	"	1.50	5.333		390	360		750	965
3800	25 HP, size 2	2 Elec	2	8		735	540		1,275	1,600
3900	50 HP, size 3		1.60	10		1,125	675		1,800	2,250
4000	100 HP, size 4		1	16		2,700	1,075		3,775	4,575
4100	200 HP, size 5	↓	.80	20		6,475	1,350		7,825	9,125
4200	Combination, with motor circuit protectors, 5 HP, size 0	1 Elec	1.70	4.706		860	315		1,175	1,425

26 24 Switchboards and Panelboards

26 24 19 – Motor-Control Centers

26 24 19.40 Motor Starters and Controls		Crew	Daily Output	Labor-Hours	Unit	Material	2023 Bare Costs Labor	Equipment	Total	Total Incl O&P
4300	10 HP, size 1	1 Elec	1.20	6.667	Ea.	895	450		1,345	1,650
4400	25 HP, size 2	2 Elec	1.80	8.889		1,350	600		1,950	2,375
4500	50 HP, size 3		1.20	13.333		2,175	900		3,075	3,725
4600	100 HP, size 4		.74	21.622		4,925	1,450		6,375	7,600
4700	Combination, with fused switch, 5 HP, size 0	1 Elec	1.70	4.706		710	315		1,025	1,250
4800	10 HP, size 1	"	1.20	6.667		735	450		1,185	1,475
4900	25 HP, size 2	2 Elec	1.80	8.889		1,125	600		1,725	2,125
5000	50 HP, size 3		1.20	13.333		1,800	900		2,700	3,300
5100	100 HP, size 4		.74	21.622		3,650	1,450		5,100	6,200
5200	Factory installed controls, adders to size 0 thru 5									
5300	Start-stop push button	1 Elec	32	.250	Ea.	54.50	16.85		71.35	85
5400	Hand-off-auto-selector switch		32	.250		54.50	16.85		71.35	85
5500	Pilot light		32	.250		102	16.85		118.85	137
5600	Start-stop-pilot		32	.250		157	16.85		173.85	197
5700	Auxiliary contact, NO or NC		32	.250		75	16.85		91.85	108
5800	NO-NC		32	.250		150	16.85		166.85	190

26 29 Low-Voltage Controllers

26 29 13 – Enclosed Controllers

26 29 13.20 Control Stations

		Crew	Daily Output	Labor-Hours	Unit	Material	2023 Bare Costs Labor	Equipment	Total	Total Incl O&P
0010	**CONTROL STATIONS**									
0050	NEMA 1, heavy duty, stop/start	1 Elec	8	1	Ea.	335	67.50		402.50	470
0100	Stop/start, pilot light		6.20	1.290		370	87		457	540
0200	Hand/off/automatic		6.20	1.290		375	87		462	540
0400	Stop/start/reverse		5.30	1.509		485	102		587	685
0500	NEMA 7, heavy duty, stop/start		6	1.333		470	90		560	650
0600	Stop/start, pilot light		4	2		680	135		815	950

26 29 23 – Variable-Frequency Motor Controllers

26 29 23.10 Variable Frequency Drives/Adj. Frequency Drives

			Crew	Daily Output	Labor-Hours	Unit	Material	2023 Bare Costs Labor	Equipment	Total	Total Incl O&P
0010	**VARIABLE FREQUENCY DRIVES/ADJ. FREQUENCY DRIVES**										
0100	Enclosed (NEMA 1), 460 volt, for 3 HP motor size	G	1 Elec	.80	10	Ea.	1,750	675		2,425	2,925
0110	5 HP motor size	G		.80	10		1,975	675		2,650	3,175
0120	7.5 HP motor size	G		.67	11.940		2,400	805		3,205	3,850
0130	10 HP motor size	G		.67	11.940		2,650	805		3,455	4,100
0140	15 HP motor size	G	2 Elec	.89	17.978		3,400	1,200		4,600	5,525
0150	20 HP motor size	G		.89	17.978		4,275	1,200		5,475	6,500
0160	25 HP motor size	G		.67	23.881		5,075	1,600		6,675	7,975
0170	30 HP motor size	G		.67	23.881		6,150	1,600		7,750	9,175
0180	40 HP motor size	G		.67	23.881		7,125	1,600		8,725	10,200
0190	50 HP motor size	G		.53	30.189		9,375	2,025		11,400	13,300
0200	60 HP motor size	G	R-3	.56	35.714		11,800	2,400	345	14,545	16,900
0210	75 HP motor size	G		.56	35.714		13,600	2,400	345	16,345	18,900
0220	100 HP motor size	G		.50	40		16,400	2,700	385	19,485	22,500
0230	125 HP motor size	G		.50	40		17,800	2,700	385	20,885	24,000
0240	150 HP motor size	G		.50	40		23,300	2,700	385	26,385	30,000
0250	200 HP motor size	G		.42	47.619		32,900	3,200	460	36,560	41,500
1100	Custom-engineered, 460 volt, for 3 HP motor size	G	1 Elec	.56	14.286		4,325	960		5,285	6,200
1110	5 HP motor size	G		.56	14.286		4,400	960		5,360	6,250
1120	7.5 HP motor size	G		.47	17.021		3,725	1,150		4,875	5,800
1130	10 HP motor size	G		.47	17.021		3,950	1,150		5,100	6,050

26 29 Low-Voltage Controllers

26 29 23 – Variable-Frequency Motor Controllers

26 29 23.10 Variable Frequency Drives/Adj. Frequency Drives		Crew	Daily Output	Labor-Hours	Unit	Material	2023 Bare Costs Labor	Equipment	Total	Total Incl O&P
1140	15 HP motor size [G]	2 Elec	.62	25.806	Ea.	5,975	1,750		7,725	9,125
1150	20 HP motor size [G]		.62	25.806		3,675	1,750		5,425	6,625
1160	25 HP motor size [G]		.47	34.043		6,875	2,300		9,175	11,000
1170	30 HP motor size [G]		.47	34.043		7,975	2,300		10,275	12,200
1180	40 HP motor size [G]		.47	34.043		9,000	2,300		11,300	13,300
1190	50 HP motor size [G]		.37	43.243		13,300	2,900		16,200	18,900
1200	60 HP motor size [G]	R-3	.39	51.282		20,000	3,450	495	23,945	27,600
1210	75 HP motor size [G]		.39	51.282		16,700	3,450	495	20,645	24,100
1220	100 HP motor size [G]		.35	57.143		23,400	3,850	550	27,800	32,100
1230	125 HP motor size [G]		.35	57.143		25,100	3,850	550	29,500	33,900
1240	150 HP motor size [G]		.35	57.143		28,400	3,850	550	32,800	37,600
1250	200 HP motor size [G]		.29	68.966		32,700	4,650	665	38,015	43,500
2000	For complex & special design systems to meet specific									
2010	requirements, obtain quote from vendor.									

Division Notes

		CREW	DAILY OUTPUT	LABOR-HOURS	UNIT	BARE COSTS				TOTAL INCL O&P
						MAT.	LABOR	EQUIP.	TOTAL	

Division Notes

		CREW	DAILY OUTPUT	LABOR-HOURS	UNIT	BARE COSTS				TOTAL INCL O&P
						MAT.	LABOR	EQUIP.	TOTAL	

Estimating Tips

- When estimating material costs for electronic safety and security systems, it is always prudent to obtain manufacturers' quotations for equipment prices and special installation requirements that may affect the total cost.
- Fire alarm systems consist of control panels, annunciator panels, batteries with rack, charger, and fire alarm actuating and indicating devices. Some fire alarm systems include speakers, telephone lines, door closer controls, and other components. Be careful not to overlook the costs related to installation for these items. Also be aware of costs for integrated automation instrumentation and terminal devices, control equipment, control wiring, and programming. Insurance underwriters may have specific requirements for the type of materials to be installed or design requirements based on the hazard to be protected. Local jurisdictions may have requirements not covered by code. It is advisable to be aware of any special conditions.
- Security equipment includes items such as CCTV, access control, and other detection and identification systems to perform alert and alarm functions. Be sure to consider the costs related to installation for this security equipment, such as for integrated automation instrumentation and terminal devices, control equipment, control wiring, and programming.

Reference Numbers

Reference numbers are shown at the beginning of some major classifications. These numbers refer to related items in the Reference Section. The reference information may be an estimating procedure, an alternate pricing method, or technical information.

Division 28
Electronic Safety & Security

Same Data. Simplified.

Enjoy the convenience and efficiency of accessing your costs anywhere:

- **Skip the multiplier** by setting your location
- **Quickly search,** edit, favorite and share costs
- **Stay on top of price changes** with automatic updates

Discover more at rsmeans.com/online

No part of this cost data may be reproduced, stored in a retrieval system, or transmitted in any form or by any means without prior written permission of Gordian.

Note: Trade Service, in part, has been used as a reference source for some of the material prices used in Division 28.

28 18 Security Access Detection Equipment

28 18 11 – Security Access Metal Detectors

28 18 11.13 Security Access Metal Detectors		Crew	Daily Output	Labor-Hours	Unit	Material	2023 Bare Costs Labor	Equipment	Total	Total Incl O&P
0010	SECURITY ACCESS METAL DETECTORS									
0240	Metal detector, hand-held, wand type, unit only				Ea.	129			129	138
0250	Metal detector, walk through portal type, single zone	1 Elec	2	4		1,275	269		1,544	1,800
0260	Multi-zone	"	2	4		2,475	269		2,744	3,125

28 18 13 – Security Access X-Ray Equipment

28 18 13.16 Security Access X-Ray Equipment

		Crew	Daily Output	Labor-Hours	Unit	Material	Labor	Equipment	Total	Total Incl O&P
0010	SECURITY ACCESS X-RAY EQUIPMENT									
0290	X-ray machine, desk top, for mail/small packages/letters	1 Elec	4	2	Ea.	3,425	135		3,560	3,975
0300	Conveyor type, incl. monitor		2	4		19,600	269		19,869	21,900
0310	Includes additional features		2	4		34,800	269		35,069	38,700
0320	X-ray machine, large unit, for airports, incl. monitor	2 Elec	1	16		48,900	1,075		49,975	55,500
0330	Full console	"	.50	32		84,000	2,150		86,150	95,000

28 18 15 – Security Access Explosive Detection Equipment

28 18 15.23 Security Access Explosive Detection Equipment

		Crew	Daily Output	Labor-Hours	Unit	Material	Labor	Equipment	Total	Total Incl O&P
0010	SECURITY ACCESS EXPLOSIVE DETECTION EQUIPMENT									
0270	Explosives detector, walk through portal type	1 Elec	2	4	Ea.	175,000	269		175,269	193,000
0280	Hand-held, battery operated				"				25,500	28,100

28 23 Video Management System

28 23 23 – Video Surveillance Systems Infrastructure

28 23 23.50 Video Surveillance Equipments

		Crew	Daily Output	Labor-Hours	Unit	Material	Labor	Equipment	Total	Total Incl O&P
0010	VIDEO SURVEILLANCE EQUIPMENTS									
0200	Video cameras, wireless, hidden in exit signs, clocks, etc., incl. receiver	1 Elec	3	2.667	Ea.	205	180		385	490
0210	Accessories for video recorder, single camera		3	2.667		178	180		358	465
0220	For multiple cameras		3	2.667		1,500	180		1,680	1,925
0230	Video cameras, wireless, for under vehicle searching, complete		2	4		13,300	269		13,569	15,000
0234	Master monitor station, 3 doors x 5 color monitor with tilt feature		2	4		960	269		1,229	1,450

28 31 Intrusion Detection

28 31 16 – Intrusion Detection Systems Infrastructure

28 31 16.50 Intrusion Detection

		Crew	Daily Output	Labor-Hours	Unit	Material	Labor	Equipment	Total	Total Incl O&P
0010	INTRUSION DETECTION, not including wires & conduits									
0100	Burglar alarm, battery operated, mechanical trigger	1 Elec	4	2	Ea.	283	135		418	510
0200	Electrical trigger		4	2		340	135		475	570
0400	For outside key control, add		8	1		87	67.50		154.50	196
0600	For remote signaling circuitry, add		8	1		144	67.50		211.50	259
0800	Card reader, flush type, standard		2.70	2.963		680	200		880	1,050
1000	Multi-code		2.70	2.963		620	200		820	975

28 42 Gas Detection and Alarm

28 42 15 – Gas Detection Sensors

28 42 15.50 Tank Leak Detection Systems	Crew	Daily Output	Labor-Hours	Unit	Material	2023 Bare Costs Labor	Equipment	Total	Total Incl O&P
0010 **TANK LEAK DETECTION SYSTEMS** Liquid and vapor									
0100 For hydrocarbons and hazardous liquids/vapors									
0120 Controller, data acquisition, incl. printer, modem, RS232 port									
0140 24 channel, for use with all probes				Ea.	6,325			6,325	6,975
0160 9 channel, for external monitoring				"	2,125			2,125	2,325
0200 Probes									
0210 Well monitoring									
0220 Liquid phase detection				Ea.	845			845	930
0230 Hydrocarbon vapor, fixed position					1,025			1,025	1,125
0240 Hydrocarbon vapor, float mounted					775			775	855
0250 Both liquid and vapor hydrocarbon					1,025			1,025	1,125
0300 Secondary containment, liquid phase									
0310 Pipe trench/manway sump				Ea.	875			875	965
0320 Double wall pipe and manual sump					735			735	810
0330 Double wall fiberglass annular space					525			525	580
0340 Double wall steel tank annular space					320			320	350
0500 Accessories									
0510 Modem, non-dedicated phone line				Ea.	405			405	445
0600 Monitoring, internal									
0610 Automatic tank gauge, incl. overfill				Ea.	1,575			1,575	1,750
0620 Product line				"	1,650			1,650	1,800
0700 Monitoring, special									
0710 Cathodic protection				Ea.	895			895	985
0720 Annular space chemical monitor				"	1,225			1,225	1,350

28 46 Fire Detection and Alarm

28 46 11 – Fire Sensors and Detectors

28 46 11.21 Carbon-Monoxide Detection Sensors

	Crew	Daily Output	Labor-Hours	Unit	Material	Labor	Equipment	Total	Total Incl O&P
0010 **CARBON-MONOXIDE DETECTION SENSORS**									
8400 Smoke and carbon monoxide alarm battery operated photoelectric low profile	1 Elec	24	.333	Ea.	98	22.50		120.50	142
8410 low profile photoelectric battery powered		24	.333		48	22.50		70.50	86
8420 photoelectric low profile sealed lithium		24	.333		84	22.50		106.50	126
8430 Photoelectric low profile sealed lithium smoke and CO with voice combo		24	.333		58.50	22.50		81	97.50
8500 Carbon monoxide sensor, wall mount 1Mod 1 relay output smoke & heat		24	.333		470	22.50		492.50	550
8700 Carbon monoxide detector, battery operated, wall mounted		16	.500		45	33.50		78.50	99.50
8710 Hardwired, wall and ceiling mounted		8	1		80	67.50		147.50	188
8720 Duct mounted		8	1		360	67.50		427.50	500

28 46 11.27 Other Sensors

	Crew	Daily Output	Labor-Hours	Unit	Material	Labor	Equipment	Total	Total Incl O&P
0010 **OTHER SENSORS**									
5200 Smoke detector, ceiling type	1 Elec	6.20	1.290	Ea.	155	87		242	300
5240 Smoke detector, addressable type		6	1.333		241	90		331	400
5400 Duct type		3.20	2.500		330	168		498	615
5420 Duct addressable type		3.20	2.500		202	168		370	470

28 46 11.50 Fire and Heat Detectors

	Crew	Daily Output	Labor-Hours	Unit	Material	Labor	Equipment	Total	Total Incl O&P
0010 **FIRE & HEAT DETECTORS**									
5000 Detector, rate of rise	1 Elec	8	1	Ea.	33	67.50		100.50	137
5100 Fixed temp fire alarm	"	7	1.143	"	44	77		121	162

28 46 Fire Detection and Alarm

28 46 20 – Fire Alarm

28 46 20.50 Alarm Panels and Devices		Crew	Daily Output	Labor-Hours	Unit	Material	2023 Bare Costs Labor	Equipment	Total	Total Incl O&P
0010	**ALARM PANELS AND DEVICES**, not including wires & conduits									
3600	4 zone	2 Elec	2	8	Ea.	490	540		1,030	1,350
3700	5 zone		1.50	10.667		645	720		1,365	1,775
3800	8 zone		1	16		660	1,075		1,735	2,325
3900	10 zone		1.25	12.800		1,050	860		1,910	2,425
4000	12 zone	▼	.67	23.988		2,875	1,625		4,500	5,550
4020	Alarm device, tamper, flow	1 Elec	8	1		227	67.50		294.50	350
4050	Actuating device		8	1		370	67.50		437.50	505
4200	Battery and rack		4	2		520	135		655	770
4400	Automatic charger		8	1		590	67.50		657.50	750
4600	Signal bell		8	1		56.50	67.50		124	163
4610	Fire alarm signal bell 10" red 20-24 V P		8	1		205	67.50		272.50	325
4800	Trouble buzzer or manual station		8	1		85	67.50		152.50	194
5425	Duct smoke and heat detector 2 wire		8	1		179	67.50		246.50	296
5430	Fire alarm duct detector controller		3	2.667		222	180		402	510
5435	Fire alarm duct detector sensor kit		8	1		86	67.50		153.50	195
5440	Remote test station for smoke detector duct type		5.30	1.509		59	102		161	216
5460	Remote fire alarm indicator light		5.30	1.509		30.50	102		132.50	185
5600	Strobe and horn		5.30	1.509		105	102		207	267
5610	Strobe and horn (ADA type)		5.30	1.509		132	102		234	296
5620	Visual alarm (ADA type)		6.70	1.194		116	80.50		196.50	247
5800	electric bell		6.70	1.194		56.50	80.50		137	182
6000	Door holder, electro-magnetic		4	2		106	135		241	315
6200	Combination holder and closer		3.20	2.500		176	168		344	445
6600	Drill switch		8	1		545	67.50		612.50	700
6800	Master box		2.70	2.963		6,575	200		6,775	7,550
7000	Break glass station		8	1		65	67.50		132.50	172
7800	Remote annunciator, 8 zone lamp		1.80	4.444		345	299		644	825
8000	12 zone lamp	2 Elec	2.60	6.154		455	415		870	1,125
8200	16 zone lamp	"	2.20	7.273	▼	440	490		930	1,225

Estimating Tips
31 05 00 Common Work Results for Earthwork

- Estimating the actual cost of performing earthwork requires careful consideration of the variables involved. This includes items such as type of soil, whether water will be encountered, dewatering, whether banks need bracing, disposal of excavated earth, and length of haul to fill or spoil sites, etc. If the project has large quantities of cut or fill, consider raising or lowering the site to reduce costs, while paying close attention to the effect on site drainage and utilities.
- If the project has large quantities of fill, creating a borrow pit on the site can significantly lower the costs.
- It is very important to consider what time of year the project is scheduled for completion. Bad weather can create large cost overruns from dewatering, site repair, and lost productivity from cold weather.

Reference Numbers
Reference numbers are shown at the beginning of some major classifications. These numbers refer to related items in the Reference Section. The reference information may be an estimating procedure, an alternate pricing method, or technical information.

Note: Not all subdivisions listed here necessarily appear. ■

Same Data. Simplified.

Enjoy the convenience and efficiency of accessing your costs anywhere:
- **Skip the multiplier** by setting your location
- **Quickly search,** edit, favorite and share costs
- **Stay on top of price changes** with automatic updates

Discover more at rsmeans.com/online

No part of this cost data may be reproduced, stored in a retrieval system, or transmitted in any form or by any means without prior written permission of Gordian.

31 05 Common Work Results for Earthwork

31 05 23 – Cement and Concrete for Earthwork

31 05 23.30 Plant Mixed Bituminous Concrete	Crew	Daily Output	Labor-Hours	Unit	Material	2023 Bare Costs Labor	Equipment	Total	Total Incl O&P
0010 **PLANT MIXED BITUMINOUS CONCRETE**									
0020 Asphaltic concrete plant mix (145 lb./C.F.)				Ton	71.50			71.50	78.50
0040 Asphaltic concrete less than 300 tons add trucking costs									
0200 All weather patching mix, hot				Ton	73			73	80
0250 Cold patch					107			107	118
0300 Berm mix				↓	71.50			71.50	78.50

31 23 Excavation and Fill

31 23 16 – Excavation

31 23 16.13 Excavating, Trench

		Crew	Daily Output	Labor-Hours	Unit	Material	Labor	Equipment	Total	Total Incl O&P
0010	**EXCAVATING, TRENCH** G1030-805									
0011	Or continuous footing									
0020	Common earth with no sheeting or dewatering included									
0050	1' to 4' deep, 3/8 C.Y. excavator	B-11C	150	.107	B.C.Y.		5.90	1.85	7.75	10.80
0060	1/2 C.Y. excavator	B-11M	200	.080			4.41	1.79	6.20	8.50
0090	4' to 6' deep, 1/2 C.Y. excavator	"	200	.080			4.41	1.79	6.20	8.50
0100	5/8 C.Y. excavator	B-12Q	250	.064			3.63	3.25	6.88	9
0110	3/4 C.Y. excavator	B-12F	300	.053			3.03	3.05	6.08	7.85
0300	1/2 C.Y. excavator, truck mounted	B-12J	200	.080			4.54	4.40	8.94	11.60
0500	6' to 10' deep, 3/4 C.Y. excavator	B-12F	225	.071			4.04	4.07	8.11	10.50
0600	1 C.Y. excavator, truck mounted	B-12K	400	.040			2.27	3.80	6.07	7.55
0900	10' to 14' deep, 3/4 C.Y. excavator	B-12F	200	.080			4.54	4.58	9.12	11.80
1000	1-1/2 C.Y. excavator	B-12B	540	.030			1.68	2.19	3.87	4.91
1300	14' to 20' deep, 1 C.Y. excavator	B-12A	320	.050			2.84	3.08	5.92	7.60
1340	20' to 24' deep, 1 C.Y. excavator	"	288	.056			3.15	3.43	6.58	8.45
1352	4' to 6' deep, 1/2 C.Y. excavator w/trench box	B-13H	188	.085			4.83	5.40	10.23	13.10
1354	5/8 C.Y. excavator	"	235	.068			3.87	4.31	8.18	10.50
1356	3/4 C.Y. excavator	B-13G	282	.057			3.22	3.71	6.93	8.85
1362	6' to 10' deep, 3/4 C.Y. excavator w/trench box		212	.075			4.29	4.94	9.23	11.85
1374	10' to 14' deep, 3/4 C.Y. excavator w/trench box	↓	188	.085			4.83	5.55	10.38	13.35
1376	1-1/2 C.Y. excavator	B-13E	508	.032			1.79	2.59	4.38	5.50
1381	14' to 20' deep, 1 C.Y. excavator w/trench box	B-13D	301	.053			3.02	3.71	6.73	8.60
1386	20' to 24' deep, 1 C.Y. excavator w/trench box	"	271	.059			3.35	4.13	7.48	9.55
1400	By hand with pick and shovel 2' to 6' deep, light soil	1 Clab	8	1			47.50		47.50	70.50
1500	Heavy soil	"	4	2			94.50		94.50	141
1700	For tamping backfilled trenches, air tamp, add	A-1G	100	.080			3.78	.88	4.66	6.60
1900	Vibrating plate, add	B-18	180	.133	↓		6.40	.81	7.21	10.40
2100	Trim sides and bottom for concrete pours, common earth		1500	.016	S.F.		.77	.10	.87	1.25
2300	Hardpan	↓	600	.040	"		1.92	.24	2.16	3.12
5020	Loam & sandy clay with no sheeting or dewatering included									
5050	1' to 4' deep, 3/8 C.Y. tractor loader/backhoe	B-11C	162	.099	B.C.Y.		5.45	1.71	7.16	10
5060	1/2 C.Y. excavator	B-11M	216	.074			4.09	1.66	5.75	7.90
5080	4' to 6' deep, 1/2 C.Y. excavator	"	216	.074			4.09	1.66	5.75	7.90
5090	5/8 C.Y. excavator	B-12Q	276	.058			3.29	2.95	6.24	8.15
5100	3/4 C.Y. excavator	B-12F	324	.049			2.80	2.83	5.63	7.30
5130	1/2 C.Y. excavator, truck mounted	B-12J	216	.074			4.21	4.08	8.29	10.75
5140	6' to 10' deep, 3/4 C.Y. excavator	B-12F	243	.066			3.74	3.77	7.51	9.70
5160	1 C.Y. excavator, truck mounted	B-12K	432	.037			2.10	3.52	5.62	7
5190	10' to 14' deep, 3/4 C.Y. excavator	B-12F	216	.074			4.21	4.24	8.45	10.90
5210	1-1/2 C.Y. excavator	B-12B	583	.027			1.56	2.03	3.59	4.56
5250	14' to 20' deep, 1 C.Y. excavator	B-12A	346	.046			2.63	2.85	5.48	7.05

31 23 Excavation and Fill

31 23 16 – Excavation

31 23 16.13 Excavating, Trench

		Crew	Daily Output	Labor-Hours	Unit	Material	2023 Bare Costs Labor	2023 Bare Costs Equipment	Total	Total Incl O&P
5300	20' to 24' deep, 1 C.Y. excavator	B-12A	311	.051	B.C.Y.		2.92	3.17	6.09	7.85
5352	4' to 6' deep, 1/2 C.Y. excavator w/trench box	B-13H	205	.078			4.43	4.94	9.37	12.05
5354	5/8 C.Y. excavator	"	257	.062			3.53	3.94	7.47	9.60
5356	3/4 C.Y. excavator	B-13G	308	.052			2.95	3.40	6.35	8.15
5362	6' to 10' deep, 3/4 C.Y. excavator w/trench box		231	.069			3.93	4.53	8.46	10.85
5370	10' to 14' deep, 3/4 C.Y. excavator w/trench box		205	.078			4.43	5.10	9.53	12.20
5374	1-1/2 C.Y. excavator	B-13E	554	.029			1.64	2.38	4.02	5.05
5382	14' to 20' deep, 1 C.Y. excavator w/trench box	B-13D	329	.049			2.76	3.40	6.16	7.85
5392	20' to 24' deep, 1 C.Y. excavator w/trench box	"	295	.054			3.08	3.79	6.87	8.75
6020	Sand & gravel with no sheeting or dewatering included									
6050	1' to 4' deep, 3/8 C.Y. excavator	B-11C	165	.097	B.C.Y.		5.35	1.68	7.03	9.80
6060	1/2 C.Y. excavator	B-11M	220	.073			4.01	1.63	5.64	7.75
6080	4' to 6' deep, 1/2 C.Y. excavator	"	220	.073			4.01	1.63	5.64	7.75
6090	5/8 C.Y. excavator	B-12Q	275	.058			3.30	2.96	6.26	8.15
6100	3/4 C.Y. excavator	B-12F	330	.048			2.75	2.77	5.52	7.15
6130	1/2 C.Y. excavator, truck mounted	B-12J	220	.073			4.13	4	8.13	10.55
6140	6' to 10' deep, 3/4 C.Y. excavator	B-12F	248	.065			3.66	3.69	7.35	9.50
6160	1 C.Y. excavator, truck mounted	B-12K	440	.036			2.06	3.46	5.52	6.85
6190	10' to 14' deep, 3/4 C.Y. excavator	B-12F	220	.073			4.13	4.16	8.29	10.75
6210	1-1/2 C.Y. excavator	B-12B	594	.027			1.53	2	3.53	4.48
6250	14' to 20' deep, 1 C.Y. excavator	B-12A	352	.045			2.58	2.80	5.38	6.90
6300	20' to 24' deep, 1 C.Y. excavator	"	317	.050			2.87	3.11	5.98	7.70
6352	4' to 6' deep, 1/2 C.Y. excavator w/trench box	B-13H	209	.077			4.35	4.84	9.19	11.80
6362	6' to 10' deep, 3/4 C.Y. excavator w/trench box	B-13G	236	.068			3.85	4.44	8.29	10.65
6370	10' to 14' deep, 3/4 C.Y. excavator w/trench box	"	209	.077			4.35	5	9.35	11.95
6374	1-1/2 C.Y. excavator	B-13E	564	.028			1.61	2.33	3.94	4.97
6382	14' to 20' deep, 1 C.Y. excavator w/trench box	B-13D	334	.048			2.72	3.35	6.07	7.75
6392	20' to 24' deep, 1 C.Y. excavator w/trench box	"	301	.053			3.02	3.71	6.73	8.60
7020	Dense hard clay with no sheeting or dewatering included									
7050	1' to 4' deep, 3/8 C.Y. excavator	B-11C	132	.121	B.C.Y.		6.70	2.10	8.80	12.25
7060	1/2 C.Y. excavator	B-11M	176	.091			5	2.03	7.03	9.70
7080	4' to 6' deep, 1/2 C.Y. excavator	"	176	.091			5	2.03	7.03	9.70
7090	5/8 C.Y. excavator	B-12Q	220	.073			4.13	3.70	7.83	10.20
7100	3/4 C.Y. excavator	B-12F	264	.061			3.44	3.47	6.91	8.90
7130	1/2 C.Y. excavator, truck mounted	B-12J	176	.091			5.15	5	10.15	13.20
7140	6' to 10' deep, 3/4 C.Y. excavator	B-12F	198	.081			4.59	4.62	9.21	11.95
7160	1 C.Y. excavator, truck mounted	B-12K	352	.045			2.58	4.32	6.90	8.60
7190	10' to 14' deep, 3/4 C.Y. excavator	B-12F	176	.091			5.15	5.20	10.35	13.40
7210	1-1/2 C.Y. excavator	B-12B	475	.034			1.91	2.50	4.41	5.60
7250	14' to 20' deep, 1 C.Y. excavator	B-12A	282	.057			3.22	3.50	6.72	8.65
7300	20' to 24' deep, 1 C.Y. excavator	"	254	.063			3.58	3.88	7.46	9.55

31 23 16.14 Excavating, Utility Trench

		Crew	Daily Output	Labor-Hours	Unit	Material	Labor	Equipment	Total	Total Incl O&P
0010	**EXCAVATING, UTILITY TRENCH**									
0011	Common earth									
0050	Trenching with chain trencher, 12 HP, operator walking									
0100	4" wide trench, 12" deep	B-53	800	.010	L.F.		.60	.25	.85	1.17
0150	18" deep		750	.011			.64	.27	.91	1.25
0200	24" deep		700	.011			.68	.29	.97	1.34
0300	6" wide trench, 12" deep		650	.012			.73	.31	1.04	1.43
0350	18" deep		600	.013			.80	.34	1.14	1.55
0400	24" deep		550	.015			.87	.37	1.24	1.69
0450	36" deep		450	.018			1.06	.45	1.51	2.07

31 23 Excavation and Fill

31 23 16 – Excavation

31 23 16.14 Excavating, Utility Trench

		Crew	Daily Output	Labor-Hours	Unit	Material	2023 Bare Costs Labor	Equipment	Total	Total Incl O&P
0600	8" wide trench, 12" deep	B-53	475	.017	L.F.		1.01	.43	1.44	1.97
0650	18" deep		400	.020			1.19	.51	1.70	2.34
0700	24" deep		350	.023			1.36	.58	1.94	2.67
0750	36" deep	▼	300	.027	▼		1.59	.67	2.26	3.11
1000	Backfill by hand including compaction, add									
1050	4" wide trench, 12" deep	A-1G	800	.010	L.F.		.47	.11	.58	.82
1100	18" deep		530	.015			.71	.17	.88	1.24
1150	24" deep		400	.020			.95	.22	1.17	1.65
1300	6" wide trench, 12" deep		540	.015			.70	.16	.86	1.22
1350	18" deep		405	.020			.93	.22	1.15	1.63
1400	24" deep		270	.030			1.40	.33	1.73	2.44
1450	36" deep		180	.044			2.10	.49	2.59	3.67
1600	8" wide trench, 12" deep		400	.020			.95	.22	1.17	1.65
1650	18" deep		265	.030			1.43	.33	1.76	2.49
1700	24" deep		200	.040			1.89	.44	2.33	3.29
1750	36" deep	▼	135	.059	▼		2.80	.65	3.45	4.89
2000	Chain trencher, 40 HP operator riding									
2050	6" wide trench and backfill, 12" deep	B-54	1200	.007	L.F.		.40	.32	.72	.94
2100	18" deep		1000	.008			.48	.39	.87	1.14
2150	24" deep		975	.008			.49	.40	.89	1.17
2200	36" deep		900	.009			.53	.43	.96	1.26
2250	48" deep		750	.011			.64	.52	1.16	1.52
2300	60" deep		650	.012			.73	.59	1.32	1.74
2400	8" wide trench and backfill, 12" deep		1000	.008			.48	.39	.87	1.14
2450	18" deep		950	.008			.50	.41	.91	1.20
2500	24" deep		900	.009			.53	.43	.96	1.26
2550	36" deep		800	.010			.60	.48	1.08	1.42
2600	48" deep		650	.012			.73	.59	1.32	1.74
2700	12" wide trench and backfill, 12" deep		975	.008			.49	.40	.89	1.17
2750	18" deep		860	.009			.56	.45	1.01	1.32
2800	24" deep		800	.010			.60	.48	1.08	1.42
2850	36" deep		725	.011			.66	.53	1.19	1.57
3000	16" wide trench and backfill, 12" deep		835	.010			.57	.46	1.03	1.36
3050	18" deep		750	.011			.64	.52	1.16	1.52
3100	24" deep	▼	700	.011	▼		.68	.55	1.23	1.63
3200	Compaction with vibratory plate, add								35%	35%
5100	Hand excavate and trim for pipe bells after trench excavation									
5200	8" pipe	1 Clab	155	.052	L.F.		2.44		2.44	3.63
5300	18" pipe	"	130	.062	"		2.91		2.91	4.33

31 23 16.16 Structural Excavation for Minor Structures

		Crew	Daily Output	Labor-Hours	Unit	Material	Labor	Equipment	Total	Total Incl O&P
0010	**STRUCTURAL EXCAVATION FOR MINOR STRUCTURES**									
0015	Hand, pits to 6' deep, sandy soil	1 Clab	8	1	B.C.Y.		47.50		47.50	70.50
0100	Heavy soil or clay		4	2			94.50		94.50	141
0300	Pits 6' to 12' deep, sandy soil		5	1.600			75.50		75.50	113
0500	Heavy soil or clay		3	2.667			126		126	188
0700	Pits 12' to 18' deep, sandy soil		4	2			94.50		94.50	141
0900	Heavy soil or clay	▼	2	4	▼		189		189	281
1500	For wet or muck hand excavation, add to above								50%	50%

31 23 16.30 Drilling and Blasting Rock

		Crew	Daily Output	Labor-Hours	Unit	Material	Labor	Equipment	Total	Total Incl O&P
0010	**DRILLING AND BLASTING ROCK**									
0020	Rock, open face, under 1,500 C.Y.	B-47	225	.107	B.C.Y.	4.51	5.55	7.80	17.86	22
0100	Over 1,500 C.Y.	▼	300	.080	▼	4.51	4.17	5.85	14.53	17.55

31 23 Excavation and Fill

31 23 16 – Excavation

31 23 16.30 Drilling and Blasting Rock

		Crew	Daily Output	Labor-Hours	Unit	Material	2023 Bare Costs Labor	Equipment	Total	Total Incl O&P
0200	Areas where blasting mats are required, under 1,500 C.Y.	B-47	175	.137	B.C.Y.	4.51	7.15	10	21.66	26.50
0250	Over 1,500 C.Y.		250	.096		4.51	5	7	16.51	20
2200	Trenches, up to 1,500 C.Y.		22	1.091		13.10	57	79.50	149.60	186
2300	Over 1,500 C.Y.		26	.923		13.10	48	67.50	128.60	160

31 23 19 – Dewatering

31 23 19.20 Dewatering Systems

		Crew	Daily Output	Labor-Hours	Unit	Material	Labor	Equipment	Total	Incl O&P
0010	**DEWATERING SYSTEMS**									
0020	Excavate drainage trench, 2' wide, 2' deep	B-11C	90	.178	C.Y.		9.80	3.08	12.88	18
0100	2' wide, 3' deep, with backhoe loader	"	135	.119			6.55	2.05	8.60	12
0200	Excavate sump pits by hand, light soil	1 Clab	7.10	1.127			53		53	79.50
0300	Heavy soil	"	3.50	2.286			108		108	161
0500	Pumping 8 hrs., attended 2 hrs./day, incl. 20 L.F.									
0550	of suction hose & 100 L.F. discharge hose									
0600	2" diaphragm pump used for 8 hrs.	B-10H	4	3	Day		173	18.65	191.65	279
0650	4" diaphragm pump used for 8 hrs.	B-10I	4	3			173	49.50	222.50	315
0800	8 hrs. attended, 2" diaphragm pump	B-10H	1	12			695	74.50	769.50	1,100
0900	3" centrifugal pump	B-10J	1	12			695	101	796	1,125
1000	4" diaphragm pump	B-10I	1	12			695	198	893	1,250
1100	6" centrifugal pump	B-10K	1	12			695	455	1,150	1,525
1300	CMP, incl. excavation 3' deep, 12" diameter	B-6	115	.209	L.F.	13.90	10.75	2.41	27.06	34
1400	18" diameter		100	.240	"	21.50	12.35	2.77	36.62	45.50
1600	Sump hole construction, incl. excavation and gravel, pit		1250	.019	C.F.	1.08	.99	.22	2.29	2.90
1700	With 12" gravel collar, 12" pipe, corrugated, 16 ga.		70	.343	L.F.	22.50	17.60	3.96	44.06	55.50
1800	15" pipe, corrugated, 16 ga.		55	.436		29.50	22.50	5.05	57.05	71.50
1900	18" pipe, corrugated, 16 ga.		50	.480		34.50	24.50	5.55	64.55	80
2000	24" pipe, corrugated, 14 ga.		40	.600		41	31	6.95	78.95	99
2200	Wood lining, up to 4' x 4', add		300	.080	SFCA	15.30	4.11	.92	20.33	24
9950	See Section 31 23 19.40 for wellpoints									
9960	See Section 31 23 19.30 for deep well systems									

31 23 19.30 Wells

		Crew	Daily Output	Labor-Hours	Unit	Material	Labor	Equipment	Total	Incl O&P
0010	**WELLS**									
0011	For dewatering 10' to 20' deep, 2' diameter									
0020	with steel casing, minimum	B-6	165	.145	V.L.F.	36	7.50	1.68	45.18	53
0050	Average		98	.245		44	12.60	2.83	59.43	70.50
0100	Maximum		49	.490		50	25	5.65	80.65	98.50
0300	For dewatering pumps see 01 54 33 in Reference Section									
0500	For domestic water wells, see Section 33 21 13.10									

31 23 19.40 Wellpoints

		Crew	Daily Output	Labor-Hours	Unit	Material	Labor	Equipment	Total	Incl O&P
0010	**WELLPOINTS** R312319-90									
0011	For equipment rental, see 01 54 33 in Reference Section									
0100	Installation and removal of single stage system									
0110	Labor only, 0.75 labor-hours per L.F.	1 Clab	10.70	.748	LF Hdr		35.50		35.50	52.50
0200	2.0 labor-hours per L.F.	"	4	2	"		94.50		94.50	141
0400	Pump operation, 4 @ 6 hr. shifts									
0410	Per 24 hr. day	4 Eqlt	1.27	25.197	Day		1,500		1,500	2,250
0500	Per 168 hr. week, 160 hr. straight, 8 hr. double time		.18	178	Week		10,600		10,600	15,800
0550	Per 4.3 week month		.04	800	Month		47,800		47,800	71,000
0600	Complete installation, operation, equipment rental, fuel &									
0610	removal of system with 2" wellpoints 5' OC									
0700	100' long header, 6" diameter, first month	4 Eqlt	3.23	9.907	LF Hdr	154	590		744	1,050
0800	Thereafter, per month		4.13	7.748		123	465		588	825
1000	200' long header, 8" diameter, first month		6	5.333		147	320		467	635

31 23 Excavation and Fill

31 23 19 – Dewatering

31 23 19.40 Wellpoints

		Crew	Daily Output	Labor-Hours	Unit	Material	2023 Bare Costs Labor	2023 Bare Costs Equipment	Total	Total Incl O&P
1100	Thereafter, per month	4 Eqlt	8.39	3.814	LF Hdr		69	228	297	415
1300	500' long header, 8" diameter, first month		10.63	3.010			54	180	234	325
1400	Thereafter, per month		20.91	1.530			38.50	91.50	130	179
1600	1,000' long header, 10" diameter, first month		11.62	2.754			46	164	210	296
1700	Thereafter, per month		41.81	.765			23	45.50	68.50	93.50
1900	Note: above figures include pumping 168 hrs. per week,									
1910	the pump operator, and one stand-by pump.									

31 23 23 – Fill

31 23 23.13 Backfill

		Crew	Daily Output	Labor-Hours	Unit	Material	Labor	Equipment	Total	Total Incl O&P
0010	**BACKFILL**				G1030–805					
0015	By hand, no compaction, light soil	1 Clab	14	.571	L.C.Y.		27		27	40
0100	Heavy soil		11	.727	"		34.50		34.50	51
0300	Compaction in 6" layers, hand tamp, add to above		20.60	.388	B.C.Y.		18.35		18.35	27.50
0400	Roller compaction operator walking, add	B-10A	100	.120			6.95	1.58	8.53	12.05
0500	Air tamp, add	B-9D	190	.211			10.05	1.88	11.93	17
0600	Vibrating plate, add	A-1D	60	.133			6.30	2.40	8.70	12.05
0800	Compaction in 12" layers, hand tamp, add to above	1 Clab	34	.235			11.10		11.10	16.55
0900	Roller compaction operator walking, add	B-10A	150	.080			4.62	1.05	5.67	8.05
1000	Air tamp, add	B-9	285	.140			6.70	1.10	7.80	11.15
1100	Vibrating plate, add	A-1E	90	.089			4.20	1.62	5.82	8.05
1300	Dozer backfilling, bulk, up to 300' haul, no compaction	B-10B	1200	.010	L.C.Y.		.58	1.15	1.73	2.13
1400	Air tamped, add	B-11B	80	.200	B.C.Y.		10.70	6.20	16.90	22.50
1600	Compacting backfill, 6" to 12" lifts, vibrating roller	B-10C	800	.015			.87	2.58	3.45	4.13
1700	Sheepsfoot roller	B-10D	750	.016			.92	2.44	3.36	4.06
1900	Dozer backfilling, trench, up to 300' haul, no compaction	B-10B	900	.013	L.C.Y.		.77	1.54	2.31	2.84
2000	Air tamped, add	B-11B	80	.200	B.C.Y.		10.70	6.20	16.90	22.50
2200	Compacting backfill, 6" to 12" lifts, vibrating roller	B-10C	700	.017			.99	2.95	3.94	4.71
2300	Sheepsfoot roller	B-10D	650	.018			1.07	2.81	3.88	4.68

31 23 23.16 Fill By Borrow and Utility Bedding

		Crew	Daily Output	Labor-Hours	Unit	Material	Labor	Equipment	Total	Total Incl O&P
0010	**FILL BY BORROW AND UTILITY BEDDING**									
0049	Utility bedding, for pipe & conduit, not incl. compaction									
0050	Crushed or screened bank run gravel	B-6	150	.160	L.C.Y.	51.50	8.20	1.85	61.55	71
0100	Crushed stone 3/4" to 1/2"		150	.160		38.50	8.20	1.85	48.55	57
0200	Sand, dead or bank		150	.160		13.85	8.20	1.85	23.90	29.50
0500	Compacting bedding in trench	A-1D	90	.089	B.C.Y.		4.20	1.60	5.80	8
0600	If material source exceeds 2 miles, add for extra mileage.									
0610	See Section 31 23 23.20 for hauling mileage add.									

31 23 23.17 General Fill

		Crew	Daily Output	Labor-Hours	Unit	Material	Labor	Equipment	Total	Total Incl O&P
0010	**GENERAL FILL**									
0011	Spread dumped material, no compaction									
0020	By dozer	B-10B	1000	.012	L.C.Y.		.69	1.38	2.07	2.55
0100	By hand	1 Clab	12	.667	"		31.50		31.50	47
0500	Gravel fill, compacted, under floor slabs, 4" deep	B-37	10000	.005	S.F.	.52	.24	.03	.79	.95
0600	6" deep		8600	.006		.77	.28	.03	1.08	1.30
0700	9" deep		7200	.007		1.29	.33	.04	1.66	1.95
0800	12" deep		6000	.008		1.81	.40	.05	2.26	2.63
1000	Alternate pricing method, 4" deep		120	.400	B.C.Y.	38.50	19.85	2.40	60.75	74.50
1100	6" deep		160	.300		38.50	14.90	1.80	55.20	66.50
1200	9" deep		200	.240		38.50	11.90	1.44	51.84	62
1300	12" deep		220	.218		38.50	10.85	1.31	50.66	60
1400	Granular fill				L.C.Y.	26			26	28.50

31 23 Excavation and Fill

31 23 23 – Fill

31 23 23.20 Hauling

		Crew	Daily Output	Labor-Hours	Unit	Material	2023 Bare Costs Labor	2023 Bare Costs Equipment	Total	Total Incl O&P
0010	**HAULING**									
0011	Excavated or borrow, loose cubic yards									
0012	no loading equipment, including hauling, waiting, loading/dumping									
0013	time per cycle (wait, load, travel, unload or dump & return)									
0014	8 C.Y. truck, 15 MPH avg., cycle 0.5 miles, 10 min. wait/ld./uld.	B-34A	320	.025	L.C.Y.		1.39	1.30	2.69	3.51
0016	cycle 1 mile		272	.029			1.63	1.54	3.17	4.13
0018	cycle 2 miles		208	.038			2.13	2.01	4.14	5.40
0020	cycle 4 miles		144	.056			3.08	2.90	5.98	7.80
0022	cycle 6 miles		112	.071			3.96	3.73	7.69	10
0024	cycle 8 miles		88	.091			5.05	4.74	9.79	12.75
0026	20 MPH avg., cycle 0.5 mile		336	.024			1.32	1.24	2.56	3.34
0028	cycle 1 mile		296	.027			1.50	1.41	2.91	3.79
0030	cycle 2 miles		240	.033			1.85	1.74	3.59	4.67
0032	cycle 4 miles		176	.045			2.52	2.37	4.89	6.40
0034	cycle 6 miles		136	.059			3.26	3.07	6.33	8.25
0036	cycle 8 miles		112	.071			3.96	3.73	7.69	10
0044	25 MPH avg., cycle 4 miles		192	.042			2.31	2.17	4.48	5.85
0046	cycle 6 miles		160	.050			2.77	2.61	5.38	7
0048	cycle 8 miles		128	.063			3.47	3.26	6.73	8.80
0050	30 MPH avg., cycle 4 miles		216	.037			2.05	1.93	3.98	5.20
0052	cycle 6 miles		176	.045			2.52	2.37	4.89	6.40
0054	cycle 8 miles		144	.056			3.08	2.90	5.98	7.80
0114	15 MPH avg., cycle 0.5 mile, 15 min. wait/ld./uld.		224	.036			1.98	1.86	3.84	5
0116	cycle 1 mile		200	.040			2.22	2.09	4.31	5.60
0118	cycle 2 miles		168	.048			2.64	2.49	5.13	6.70
0120	cycle 4 miles		120	.067			3.70	3.48	7.18	9.35
0122	cycle 6 miles		96	.083			4.62	4.35	8.97	11.70
0124	cycle 8 miles		80	.100			5.55	5.20	10.75	14.05
0126	20 MPH avg., cycle 0.5 mile		232	.034			1.91	1.80	3.71	4.84
0128	cycle 1 mile		208	.038			2.13	2.01	4.14	5.40
0130	cycle 2 miles		184	.043			2.41	2.27	4.68	6.10
0132	cycle 4 miles		144	.056			3.08	2.90	5.98	7.80
0134	cycle 6 miles		112	.071			3.96	3.73	7.69	10
0136	cycle 8 miles		96	.083			4.62	4.35	8.97	11.70
0144	25 MPH avg., cycle 4 miles		152	.053			2.92	2.75	5.67	7.40
0146	cycle 6 miles		128	.063			3.47	3.26	6.73	8.80
0148	cycle 8 miles		112	.071			3.96	3.73	7.69	10
0150	30 MPH avg., cycle 4 miles		168	.048			2.64	2.49	5.13	6.70
0152	cycle 6 miles		144	.056			3.08	2.90	5.98	7.80
0154	cycle 8 miles		120	.067			3.70	3.48	7.18	9.35
0214	15 MPH avg., cycle 0.5 mile, 20 min. wait/ld./uld.		176	.045			2.52	2.37	4.89	6.40
0216	cycle 1 mile		160	.050			2.77	2.61	5.38	7
0218	cycle 2 miles		136	.059			3.26	3.07	6.33	8.25
0220	cycle 4 miles		104	.077			4.27	4.01	8.28	10.75
0222	cycle 6 miles		88	.091			5.05	4.74	9.79	12.75
0224	cycle 8 miles		72	.111			6.15	5.80	11.95	15.60
0226	20 MPH avg., cycle 0.5 mile		176	.045			2.52	2.37	4.89	6.40
0228	cycle 1 mile		168	.048			2.64	2.49	5.13	6.70
0230	cycle 2 miles		144	.056			3.08	2.90	5.98	7.80
0232	cycle 4 miles		120	.067			3.70	3.48	7.18	9.35
0234	cycle 6 miles		96	.083			4.62	4.35	8.97	11.70
0236	cycle 8 miles		88	.091			5.05	4.74	9.79	12.75

31 23 Excavation and Fill

31 23 23 – Fill

31 23 23.20 Hauling

		Crew	Daily Output	Labor-Hours	Unit	Material	2023 Bare Costs Labor	Equipment	Total	Total Incl O&P
0244	25 MPH avg., cycle 4 miles	B-34A	128	.063	L.C.Y.		3.47	3.26	6.73	8.80
0246	cycle 6 miles		112	.071			3.96	3.73	7.69	10
0248	cycle 8 miles		96	.083			4.62	4.35	8.97	11.70
0250	30 MPH avg., cycle 4 miles		136	.059			3.26	3.07	6.33	8.25
0252	cycle 6 miles		120	.067			3.70	3.48	7.18	9.35
0254	cycle 8 miles		104	.077			4.27	4.01	8.28	10.75
0314	15 MPH avg., cycle 0.5 mile, 25 min. wait/ld./uld.		144	.056			3.08	2.90	5.98	7.80
0316	cycle 1 mile		128	.063			3.47	3.26	6.73	8.80
0318	cycle 2 miles		112	.071			3.96	3.73	7.69	10
0320	cycle 4 miles		96	.083			4.62	4.35	8.97	11.70
0322	cycle 6 miles		80	.100			5.55	5.20	10.75	14.05
0324	cycle 8 miles		64	.125			6.95	6.50	13.45	17.55
0326	20 MPH avg., cycle 0.5 mile		144	.056			3.08	2.90	5.98	7.80
0328	cycle 1 mile		136	.059			3.26	3.07	6.33	8.25
0330	cycle 2 miles		120	.067			3.70	3.48	7.18	9.35
0332	cycle 4 miles		104	.077			4.27	4.01	8.28	10.75
0334	cycle 6 miles		88	.091			5.05	4.74	9.79	12.75
0336	cycle 8 miles		80	.100			5.55	5.20	10.75	14.05
0344	25 MPH avg., cycle 4 miles		112	.071			3.96	3.73	7.69	10
0346	cycle 6 miles		96	.083			4.62	4.35	8.97	11.70
0348	cycle 8 miles		88	.091			5.05	4.74	9.79	12.75
0350	30 MPH avg., cycle 4 miles		112	.071			3.96	3.73	7.69	10
0352	cycle 6 miles		104	.077			4.27	4.01	8.28	10.75
0354	cycle 8 miles		96	.083			4.62	4.35	8.97	11.70
0414	15 MPH avg., cycle 0.5 mile, 30 min. wait/ld./uld.		120	.067			3.70	3.48	7.18	9.35
0416	cycle 1 mile		112	.071			3.96	3.73	7.69	10
0418	cycle 2 miles		96	.083			4.62	4.35	8.97	11.70
0420	cycle 4 miles		80	.100			5.55	5.20	10.75	14.05
0422	cycle 6 miles		72	.111			6.15	5.80	11.95	15.60
0424	cycle 8 miles		64	.125			6.95	6.50	13.45	17.55
0426	20 MPH avg., cycle 0.5 mile		120	.067			3.70	3.48	7.18	9.35
0428	cycle 1 mile		112	.071			3.96	3.73	7.69	10
0430	cycle 2 miles		104	.077			4.27	4.01	8.28	10.75
0432	cycle 4 miles		88	.091			5.05	4.74	9.79	12.75
0434	cycle 6 miles		80	.100			5.55	5.20	10.75	14.05
0436	cycle 8 miles		72	.111			6.15	5.80	11.95	15.60
0444	25 MPH avg., cycle 4 miles		96	.083			4.62	4.35	8.97	11.70
0446	cycle 6 miles		88	.091			5.05	4.74	9.79	12.75
0448	cycle 8 miles		80	.100			5.55	5.20	10.75	14.05
0450	30 MPH avg., cycle 4 miles		96	.083			4.62	4.35	8.97	11.70
0452	cycle 6 miles		88	.091			5.05	4.74	9.79	12.75
0454	cycle 8 miles		80	.100			5.55	5.20	10.75	14.05
0514	15 MPH avg., cycle 0.5 mile, 35 min. wait/ld./uld.		104	.077			4.27	4.01	8.28	10.75
0516	cycle 1 mile		96	.083			4.62	4.35	8.97	11.70
0518	cycle 2 miles		88	.091			5.05	4.74	9.79	12.75
0520	cycle 4 miles		72	.111			6.15	5.80	11.95	15.60
0522	cycle 6 miles		64	.125			6.95	6.50	13.45	17.55
0524	cycle 8 miles		56	.143			7.90	7.45	15.35	20
0526	20 MPH avg., cycle 0.5 mile		104	.077			4.27	4.01	8.28	10.75
0528	cycle 1 mile		96	.083			4.62	4.35	8.97	11.70
0530	cycle 2 miles		96	.083			4.62	4.35	8.97	11.70
0532	cycle 4 miles		80	.100			5.55	5.20	10.75	14.05
0534	cycle 6 miles		72	.111			6.15	5.80	11.95	15.60

31 23 Excavation and Fill

31 23 23 – Fill

31 23 23.20 Hauling

		Crew	Daily Output	Labor-Hours	Unit	Material	2023 Bare Costs Labor	Equipment	Total	Total Incl O&P
0536	cycle 8 miles	B-34A	64	.125	L.C.Y.		6.95	6.50	13.45	17.55
0544	25 MPH avg., cycle 4 miles		88	.091			5.05	4.74	9.79	12.75
0546	cycle 6 miles		80	.100			5.55	5.20	10.75	14.05
0548	cycle 8 miles		72	.111			6.15	5.80	11.95	15.60
0550	30 MPH avg., cycle 4 miles		88	.091			5.05	4.74	9.79	12.75
0552	cycle 6 miles		80	.100			5.55	5.20	10.75	14.05
0554	cycle 8 miles		72	.111			6.15	5.80	11.95	15.60
1014	12 C.Y. truck, cycle 0.5 mile, 15 MPH avg., 15 min. wait/ld./uld.	B-34B	336	.024			1.32	2.36	3.68	4.56
1016	cycle 1 mile		300	.027			1.48	2.64	4.12	5.10
1018	cycle 2 miles		252	.032			1.76	3.14	4.90	6.10
1020	cycle 4 miles		180	.044			2.46	4.40	6.86	8.50
1022	cycle 6 miles		144	.056			3.08	5.50	8.58	10.65
1024	cycle 8 miles		120	.067			3.70	6.60	10.30	12.75
1025	cycle 10 miles		96	.083			4.62	8.25	12.87	15.95
1026	20 MPH avg., cycle 0.5 mile		348	.023			1.27	2.27	3.54	4.40
1028	cycle 1 mile		312	.026			1.42	2.54	3.96	4.91
1030	cycle 2 miles		276	.029			1.61	2.87	4.48	5.55
1032	cycle 4 miles		216	.037			2.05	3.66	5.71	7.10
1034	cycle 6 miles		168	.048			2.64	4.71	7.35	9.15
1036	cycle 8 miles		144	.056			3.08	5.50	8.58	10.65
1038	cycle 10 miles		120	.067			3.70	6.60	10.30	12.75
1040	25 MPH avg., cycle 4 miles		228	.035			1.95	3.47	5.42	6.75
1042	cycle 6 miles		192	.042			2.31	4.12	6.43	8
1044	cycle 8 miles		168	.048			2.64	4.71	7.35	9.15
1046	cycle 10 miles		144	.056			3.08	5.50	8.58	10.65
1050	30 MPH avg., cycle 4 miles		252	.032			1.76	3.14	4.90	6.10
1052	cycle 6 miles		216	.037			2.05	3.66	5.71	7.10
1054	cycle 8 miles		180	.044			2.46	4.40	6.86	8.50
1056	cycle 10 miles		156	.051			2.84	5.05	7.89	9.85
1060	35 MPH avg., cycle 4 miles		264	.030			1.68	3	4.68	5.80
1062	cycle 6 miles		228	.035			1.95	3.47	5.42	6.75
1064	cycle 8 miles		204	.039			2.17	3.88	6.05	7.50
1066	cycle 10 miles		180	.044			2.46	4.40	6.86	8.50
1068	cycle 20 miles		120	.067			3.70	6.60	10.30	12.75
1069	cycle 30 miles		84	.095			5.30	9.40	14.70	18.25
1070	cycle 40 miles		72	.111			6.15	11	17.15	21.50
1072	40 MPH avg., cycle 6 miles		240	.033			1.85	3.30	5.15	6.40
1074	cycle 8 miles		216	.037			2.05	3.66	5.71	7.10
1076	cycle 10 miles		192	.042			2.31	4.12	6.43	8
1078	cycle 20 miles		120	.067			3.70	6.60	10.30	12.75
1080	cycle 30 miles		96	.083			4.62	8.25	12.87	15.95
1082	cycle 40 miles		72	.111			6.15	11	17.15	21.50
1084	cycle 50 miles		60	.133			7.40	13.20	20.60	25.50
1094	45 MPH avg., cycle 8 miles		216	.037			2.05	3.66	5.71	7.10
1096	cycle 10 miles		204	.039			2.17	3.88	6.05	7.50
1098	cycle 20 miles		132	.061			3.36	6	9.36	11.60
1100	cycle 30 miles		108	.074			4.11	7.35	11.46	14.20
1102	cycle 40 miles		84	.095			5.30	9.40	14.70	18.25
1104	cycle 50 miles		72	.111			6.15	11	17.15	21.50
1106	50 MPH avg., cycle 10 miles		216	.037			2.05	3.66	5.71	7.10
1108	cycle 20 miles		144	.056			3.08	5.50	8.58	10.65
1110	cycle 30 miles		108	.074			4.11	7.35	11.46	14.20
1112	cycle 40 miles		84	.095			5.30	9.40	14.70	18.25

31 23 Excavation and Fill

31 23 23 – Fill

31 23 23.20 Hauling		Crew	Daily Output	Labor-Hours	Unit	Material	2023 Bare Costs Labor	2023 Bare Costs Equipment	Total	Total Incl O&P
1114	cycle 50 miles	B-34B	72	.111	L.C.Y.		6.15	11	17.15	21.50
1214	15 MPH avg., cycle 0.5 mile, 20 min. wait/ld./uld.		264	.030			1.68	3	4.68	5.80
1216	cycle 1 mile		240	.033			1.85	3.30	5.15	6.40
1218	cycle 2 miles		204	.039			2.17	3.88	6.05	7.50
1220	cycle 4 miles		156	.051			2.84	5.05	7.89	9.85
1222	cycle 6 miles		132	.061			3.36	6	9.36	11.60
1224	cycle 8 miles		108	.074			4.11	7.35	11.46	14.20
1225	cycle 10 miles		96	.083			4.62	8.25	12.87	15.95
1226	20 MPH avg., cycle 0.5 mile		264	.030			1.68	3	4.68	5.80
1228	cycle 1 mile		252	.032			1.76	3.14	4.90	6.10
1230	cycle 2 miles		216	.037			2.05	3.66	5.71	7.10
1232	cycle 4 miles		180	.044			2.46	4.40	6.86	8.50
1234	cycle 6 miles		144	.056			3.08	5.50	8.58	10.65
1236	cycle 8 miles		132	.061			3.36	6	9.36	11.60
1238	cycle 10 miles		108	.074			4.11	7.35	11.46	14.20
1240	25 MPH avg., cycle 4 miles		192	.042			2.31	4.12	6.43	8
1242	cycle 6 miles		168	.048			2.64	4.71	7.35	9.15
1244	cycle 8 miles		144	.056			3.08	5.50	8.58	10.65
1246	cycle 10 miles		132	.061			3.36	6	9.36	11.60
1250	30 MPH avg., cycle 4 miles		204	.039			2.17	3.88	6.05	7.50
1252	cycle 6 miles		180	.044			2.46	4.40	6.86	8.50
1254	cycle 8 miles		156	.051			2.84	5.05	7.89	9.85
1256	cycle 10 miles		144	.056			3.08	5.50	8.58	10.65
1260	35 MPH avg., cycle 4 miles		216	.037			2.05	3.66	5.71	7.10
1262	cycle 6 miles		192	.042			2.31	4.12	6.43	8
1264	cycle 8 miles		168	.048			2.64	4.71	7.35	9.15
1266	cycle 10 miles		156	.051			2.84	5.05	7.89	9.85
1268	cycle 20 miles		108	.074			4.11	7.35	11.46	14.20
1269	cycle 30 miles		72	.111			6.15	11	17.15	21.50
1270	cycle 40 miles		60	.133			7.40	13.20	20.60	25.50
1272	40 MPH avg., cycle 6 miles		192	.042			2.31	4.12	6.43	8
1274	cycle 8 miles		180	.044			2.46	4.40	6.86	8.50
1276	cycle 10 miles		156	.051			2.84	5.05	7.89	9.85
1278	cycle 20 miles		108	.074			4.11	7.35	11.46	14.20
1280	cycle 30 miles		84	.095			5.30	9.40	14.70	18.25
1282	cycle 40 miles		72	.111			6.15	11	17.15	21.50
1284	cycle 50 miles		60	.133			7.40	13.20	20.60	25.50
1294	45 MPH avg., cycle 8 miles		180	.044			2.46	4.40	6.86	8.50
1296	cycle 10 miles		168	.048			2.64	4.71	7.35	9.15
1298	cycle 20 miles		120	.067			3.70	6.60	10.30	12.75
1300	cycle 30 miles		96	.083			4.62	8.25	12.87	15.95
1302	cycle 40 miles		72	.111			6.15	11	17.15	21.50
1304	cycle 50 miles		60	.133			7.40	13.20	20.60	25.50
1306	50 MPH avg., cycle 10 miles		180	.044			2.46	4.40	6.86	8.50
1308	cycle 20 miles		132	.061			3.36	6	9.36	11.60
1310	cycle 30 miles		96	.083			4.62	8.25	12.87	15.95
1312	cycle 40 miles		84	.095			5.30	9.40	14.70	18.25
1314	cycle 50 miles		72	.111			6.15	11	17.15	21.50
1414	15 MPH avg., cycle 0.5 mile, 25 min. wait/ld./uld.		204	.039			2.17	3.88	6.05	7.50
1416	cycle 1 mile		192	.042			2.31	4.12	6.43	8
1418	cycle 2 miles		168	.048			2.64	4.71	7.35	9.15
1420	cycle 4 miles		132	.061			3.36	6	9.36	11.60
1422	cycle 6 miles		120	.067			3.70	6.60	10.30	12.75

31 23 Excavation and Fill

31 23 23 – Fill

31 23 23.20 Hauling

		Crew	Daily Output	Labor-Hours	Unit	Material	2023 Bare Costs Labor	2023 Bare Costs Equipment	Total	Total Incl O&P
1424	cycle 8 miles	B-34B	96	.083	L.C.Y.		4.62	8.25	12.87	15.95
1425	cycle 10 miles		84	.095			5.30	9.40	14.70	18.25
1426	20 MPH avg., cycle 0.5 mile		216	.037			2.05	3.66	5.71	7.10
1428	cycle 1 mile		204	.039			2.17	3.88	6.05	7.50
1430	cycle 2 miles		180	.044			2.46	4.40	6.86	8.50
1432	cycle 4 miles		156	.051			2.84	5.05	7.89	9.85
1434	cycle 6 miles		132	.061			3.36	6	9.36	11.60
1436	cycle 8 miles		120	.067			3.70	6.60	10.30	12.75
1438	cycle 10 miles		96	.083			4.62	8.25	12.87	15.95
1440	25 MPH avg., cycle 4 miles		168	.048			2.64	4.71	7.35	9.15
1442	cycle 6 miles		144	.056			3.08	5.50	8.58	10.65
1444	cycle 8 miles		132	.061			3.36	6	9.36	11.60
1446	cycle 10 miles		108	.074			4.11	7.35	11.46	14.20
1450	30 MPH avg., cycle 4 miles		168	.048			2.64	4.71	7.35	9.15
1452	cycle 6 miles		156	.051			2.84	5.05	7.89	9.85
1454	cycle 8 miles		132	.061			3.36	6	9.36	11.60
1456	cycle 10 miles		120	.067			3.70	6.60	10.30	12.75
1460	35 MPH avg., cycle 4 miles		180	.044			2.46	4.40	6.86	8.50
1462	cycle 6 miles		156	.051			2.84	5.05	7.89	9.85
1464	cycle 8 miles		144	.056			3.08	5.50	8.58	10.65
1466	cycle 10 miles		132	.061			3.36	6	9.36	11.60
1468	cycle 20 miles		96	.083			4.62	8.25	12.87	15.95
1469	cycle 30 miles		72	.111			6.15	11	17.15	21.50
1470	cycle 40 miles		60	.133			7.40	13.20	20.60	25.50
1472	40 MPH avg., cycle 6 miles		168	.048			2.64	4.71	7.35	9.15
1474	cycle 8 miles		156	.051			2.84	5.05	7.89	9.85
1476	cycle 10 miles		144	.056			3.08	5.50	8.58	10.65
1478	cycle 20 miles		96	.083			4.62	8.25	12.87	15.95
1480	cycle 30 miles		84	.095			5.30	9.40	14.70	18.25
1482	cycle 40 miles		60	.133			7.40	13.20	20.60	25.50
1484	cycle 50 miles		60	.133			7.40	13.20	20.60	25.50
1494	45 MPH avg., cycle 8 miles		156	.051			2.84	5.05	7.89	9.85
1496	cycle 10 miles		144	.056			3.08	5.50	8.58	10.65
1498	cycle 20 miles		108	.074			4.11	7.35	11.46	14.20
1500	cycle 30 miles		84	.095			5.30	9.40	14.70	18.25
1502	cycle 40 miles		72	.111			6.15	11	17.15	21.50
1504	cycle 50 miles		60	.133			7.40	13.20	20.60	25.50
1506	50 MPH avg., cycle 10 miles		156	.051			2.84	5.05	7.89	9.85
1508	cycle 20 miles		120	.067			3.70	6.60	10.30	12.75
1510	cycle 30 miles		96	.083			4.62	8.25	12.87	15.95
1512	cycle 40 miles		72	.111			6.15	11	17.15	21.50
1514	cycle 50 miles		60	.133			7.40	13.20	20.60	25.50
1614	15 MPH avg., cycle 0.5 mile, 30 min. wait/ld./uld.		180	.044			2.46	4.40	6.86	8.50
1616	cycle 1 mile		168	.048			2.64	4.71	7.35	9.15
1618	cycle 2 miles		144	.056			3.08	5.50	8.58	10.65
1620	cycle 4 miles		120	.067			3.70	6.60	10.30	12.75
1622	cycle 6 miles		108	.074			4.11	7.35	11.46	14.20
1624	cycle 8 miles		84	.095			5.30	9.40	14.70	18.25
1625	cycle 10 miles		84	.095			5.30	9.40	14.70	18.25
1626	20 MPH avg., cycle 0.5 mile		180	.044			2.46	4.40	6.86	8.50
1628	cycle 1 mile		168	.048			2.64	4.71	7.35	9.15
1630	cycle 2 miles		156	.051			2.84	5.05	7.89	9.85
1632	cycle 4 miles		132	.061			3.36	6	9.36	11.60

31 23 Excavation and Fill

31 23 23 – Fill

31 23 23.20 Hauling		Crew	Daily Output	Labor-Hours	Unit	Material	2023 Bare Costs Labor	Equipment	Total	Total Incl O&P
1634	cycle 6 miles	B-34B	120	.067	L.C.Y.		3.70	6.60	10.30	12.75
1636	cycle 8 miles		108	.074			4.11	7.35	11.46	14.20
1638	cycle 10 miles		96	.083			4.62	8.25	12.87	15.95
1640	25 MPH avg., cycle 4 miles		144	.056			3.08	5.50	8.58	10.65
1642	cycle 6 miles		132	.061			3.36	6	9.36	11.60
1644	cycle 8 miles		108	.074			4.11	7.35	11.46	14.20
1646	cycle 10 miles		108	.074			4.11	7.35	11.46	14.20
1650	30 MPH avg., cycle 4 miles		144	.056			3.08	5.50	8.58	10.65
1652	cycle 6 miles		132	.061			3.36	6	9.36	11.60
1654	cycle 8 miles		120	.067			3.70	6.60	10.30	12.75
1656	cycle 10 miles		108	.074			4.11	7.35	11.46	14.20
1660	35 MPH avg., cycle 4 miles		156	.051			2.84	5.05	7.89	9.85
1662	cycle 6 miles		144	.056			3.08	5.50	8.58	10.65
1664	cycle 8 miles		132	.061			3.36	6	9.36	11.60
1666	cycle 10 miles		120	.067			3.70	6.60	10.30	12.75
1668	cycle 20 miles		84	.095			5.30	9.40	14.70	18.25
1669	cycle 30 miles		72	.111			6.15	11	17.15	21.50
1670	cycle 40 miles		60	.133			7.40	13.20	20.60	25.50
1672	40 MPH avg., cycle 6 miles		144	.056			3.08	5.50	8.58	10.65
1674	cycle 8 miles		132	.061			3.36	6	9.36	11.60
1676	cycle 10 miles		120	.067			3.70	6.60	10.30	12.75
1678	cycle 20 miles		96	.083			4.62	8.25	12.87	15.95
1680	cycle 30 miles		72	.111			6.15	11	17.15	21.50
1682	cycle 40 miles		60	.133			7.40	13.20	20.60	25.50
1684	cycle 50 miles		48	.167			9.25	16.50	25.75	32
1694	45 MPH avg., cycle 8 miles		144	.056			3.08	5.50	8.58	10.65
1696	cycle 10 miles		132	.061			3.36	6	9.36	11.60
1698	cycle 20 miles		96	.083			4.62	8.25	12.87	15.95
1700	cycle 30 miles		84	.095			5.30	9.40	14.70	18.25
1702	cycle 40 miles		60	.133			7.40	13.20	20.60	25.50
1704	cycle 50 miles		60	.133			7.40	13.20	20.60	25.50
1706	50 MPH avg., cycle 10 miles		132	.061			3.36	6	9.36	11.60
1708	cycle 20 miles		108	.074			4.11	7.35	11.46	14.20
1710	cycle 30 miles		84	.095			5.30	9.40	14.70	18.25
1712	cycle 40 miles		72	.111			6.15	11	17.15	21.50
1714	cycle 50 miles		60	.133			7.40	13.20	20.60	25.50
2000	Hauling, 8 C.Y. truck, small project cost per hour	B-34A	8	1	Hr.		55.50	52	107.50	141
2100	12 C.Y. truck	B-34B	8	1			55.50	99	154.50	192
2150	16.5 C.Y. truck	B-34C	8	1			55.50	87	142.50	179
2175	18 C.Y. 8 wheel truck	B-34I	8	1			55.50	98.50	154	191
2200	20 C.Y. truck	B-34D	8	1			55.50	89.50	145	182
2300	Grading at dump, or embankment if required, by dozer	B-10B	1000	.012	L.C.Y.		.69	1.38	2.07	2.55
2310	Spotter at fill or cut, if required	1 Clab	8	1	Hr.		47.50		47.50	70.50
9014	18 C.Y. truck, 8 wheels,15 min. wait/ld./uld.,15 MPH, cycle 0.5 mi.	B-34I	504	.016	L.C.Y.		.88	1.56	2.44	3.04
9016	cycle 1 mile		450	.018			.99	1.75	2.74	3.40
9018	cycle 2 miles		378	.021			1.17	2.09	3.26	4.04
9020	cycle 4 miles		270	.030			1.64	2.92	4.56	5.65
9022	cycle 6 miles		216	.037			2.05	3.65	5.70	7.10
9024	cycle 8 miles		180	.044			2.46	4.38	6.84	8.50
9025	cycle 10 miles		144	.056			3.08	5.50	8.58	10.60
9026	20 MPH avg., cycle 0.5 mile		522	.015			.85	1.51	2.36	2.93
9028	cycle 1 mile		468	.017			.95	1.68	2.63	3.27
9030	cycle 2 miles		414	.019			1.07	1.90	2.97	3.69

31 23 Excavation and Fill

31 23 23 – Fill

31 23 23.20 Hauling		Crew	Daily Output	Labor-Hours	Unit	Material	2023 Bare Costs Labor	Equipment	Total	Total Incl O&P
9032	cycle 4 miles	B-34I	324	.025	L.C.Y.		1.37	2.43	3.80	4.73
9034	cycle 6 miles		252	.032			1.76	3.13	4.89	6.05
9036	cycle 8 miles		216	.037			2.05	3.65	5.70	7.10
9038	cycle 10 miles		180	.044			2.46	4.38	6.84	8.50
9040	25 MPH avg., cycle 4 miles		342	.023			1.30	2.31	3.61	4.48
9042	cycle 6 miles		288	.028			1.54	2.74	4.28	5.30
9044	cycle 8 miles		252	.032			1.76	3.13	4.89	6.05
9046	cycle 10 miles		216	.037			2.05	3.65	5.70	7.10
9050	30 MPH avg., cycle 4 miles		378	.021			1.17	2.09	3.26	4.04
9052	cycle 6 miles		324	.025			1.37	2.43	3.80	4.73
9054	cycle 8 miles		270	.030			1.64	2.92	4.56	5.65
9056	cycle 10 miles		234	.034			1.90	3.37	5.27	6.55
9060	35 MPH avg., cycle 4 miles		396	.020			1.12	1.99	3.11	3.86
9062	cycle 6 miles		342	.023			1.30	2.31	3.61	4.48
9064	cycle 8 miles		288	.028			1.54	2.74	4.28	5.30
9066	cycle 10 miles		270	.030			1.64	2.92	4.56	5.65
9068	cycle 20 miles		162	.049			2.74	4.87	7.61	9.45
9070	cycle 30 miles		126	.063			3.52	6.25	9.77	12.15
9072	cycle 40 miles		90	.089			4.93	8.75	13.68	17
9074	40 MPH avg., cycle 6 miles		360	.022			1.23	2.19	3.42	4.25
9076	cycle 8 miles		324	.025			1.37	2.43	3.80	4.73
9078	cycle 10 miles		288	.028			1.54	2.74	4.28	5.30
9080	cycle 20 miles		180	.044			2.46	4.38	6.84	8.50
9082	cycle 30 miles		144	.056			3.08	5.50	8.58	10.60
9084	cycle 40 miles		108	.074			4.11	7.30	11.41	14.20
9086	cycle 50 miles		90	.089			4.93	8.75	13.68	17
9094	45 MPH avg., cycle 8 miles		324	.025			1.37	2.43	3.80	4.73
9096	cycle 10 miles		306	.026			1.45	2.58	4.03	5
9098	cycle 20 miles		198	.040			2.24	3.98	6.22	7.75
9100	cycle 30 miles		144	.056			3.08	5.50	8.58	10.60
9102	cycle 40 miles		126	.063			3.52	6.25	9.77	12.15
9104	cycle 50 miles		108	.074			4.11	7.30	11.41	14.20
9106	50 MPH avg., cycle 10 miles		324	.025			1.37	2.43	3.80	4.73
9108	cycle 20 miles		216	.037			2.05	3.65	5.70	7.10
9110	cycle 30 miles		162	.049			2.74	4.87	7.61	9.45
9112	cycle 40 miles		126	.063			3.52	6.25	9.77	12.15
9114	cycle 50 miles		108	.074			4.11	7.30	11.41	14.20
9214	20 min. wait/ld./uld.,15 MPH, cycle 0.5 mi.		396	.020			1.12	1.99	3.11	3.86
9216	cycle 1 mile		360	.022			1.23	2.19	3.42	4.25
9218	cycle 2 miles		306	.026			1.45	2.58	4.03	5
9220	cycle 4 miles		234	.034			1.90	3.37	5.27	6.55
9222	cycle 6 miles		198	.040			2.24	3.98	6.22	7.75
9224	cycle 8 miles		162	.049			2.74	4.87	7.61	9.45
9225	cycle 10 miles		144	.056			3.08	5.50	8.58	10.60
9226	20 MPH avg., cycle 0.5 mile		396	.020			1.12	1.99	3.11	3.86
9228	cycle 1 mile		378	.021			1.17	2.09	3.26	4.04
9230	cycle 2 miles		324	.025			1.37	2.43	3.80	4.73
9232	cycle 4 miles		270	.030			1.64	2.92	4.56	5.65
9234	cycle 6 miles		216	.037			2.05	3.65	5.70	7.10
9236	cycle 8 miles		198	.040			2.24	3.98	6.22	7.75
9238	cycle 10 miles		162	.049			2.74	4.87	7.61	9.45
9240	25 MPH avg., cycle 4 miles		288	.028			1.54	2.74	4.28	5.30
9242	cycle 6 miles		252	.032			1.76	3.13	4.89	6.05

31 23 Excavation and Fill

31 23 23 – Fill

31 23 23.20 Hauling

		Crew	Daily Output	Labor-Hours	Unit	Material	2023 Bare Costs Labor	Equipment	Total	Total Incl O&P
9244	cycle 8 miles	B-34I	216	.037	L.C.Y.		2.05	3.65	5.70	7.10
9246	cycle 10 miles		198	.040			2.24	3.98	6.22	7.75
9250	30 MPH avg., cycle 4 miles		306	.026			1.45	2.58	4.03	5
9252	cycle 6 miles		270	.030			1.64	2.92	4.56	5.65
9254	cycle 8 miles		234	.034			1.90	3.37	5.27	6.55
9256	cycle 10 miles		216	.037			2.05	3.65	5.70	7.10
9260	35 MPH avg., cycle 4 miles		324	.025			1.37	2.43	3.80	4.73
9262	cycle 6 miles		288	.028			1.54	2.74	4.28	5.30
9264	cycle 8 miles		252	.032			1.76	3.13	4.89	6.05
9266	cycle 10 miles		234	.034			1.90	3.37	5.27	6.55
9268	cycle 20 miles		162	.049			2.74	4.87	7.61	9.45
9270	cycle 30 miles		108	.074			4.11	7.30	11.41	14.20
9272	cycle 40 miles		90	.089			4.93	8.75	13.68	17
9274	40 MPH avg., cycle 6 miles		288	.028			1.54	2.74	4.28	5.30
9276	cycle 8 miles		270	.030			1.64	2.92	4.56	5.65
9278	cycle 10 miles		234	.034			1.90	3.37	5.27	6.55
9280	cycle 20 miles		162	.049			2.74	4.87	7.61	9.45
9282	cycle 30 miles		126	.063			3.52	6.25	9.77	12.15
9284	cycle 40 miles		108	.074			4.11	7.30	11.41	14.20
9286	cycle 50 miles		90	.089			4.93	8.75	13.68	17
9294	45 MPH avg., cycle 8 miles		270	.030			1.64	2.92	4.56	5.65
9296	cycle 10 miles		252	.032			1.76	3.13	4.89	6.05
9298	cycle 20 miles		180	.044			2.46	4.38	6.84	8.50
9300	cycle 30 miles		144	.056			3.08	5.50	8.58	10.60
9302	cycle 40 miles		108	.074			4.11	7.30	11.41	14.20
9304	cycle 50 miles		90	.089			4.93	8.75	13.68	17
9306	50 MPH avg., cycle 10 miles		270	.030			1.64	2.92	4.56	5.65
9308	cycle 20 miles		198	.040			2.24	3.98	6.22	7.75
9310	cycle 30 miles		144	.056			3.08	5.50	8.58	10.60
9312	cycle 40 miles		126	.063			3.52	6.25	9.77	12.15
9314	cycle 50 miles		108	.074			4.11	7.30	11.41	14.20
9414	25 min. wait/ld./uld.,15 MPH, cycle 0.5 mi.		306	.026			1.45	2.58	4.03	5
9416	cycle 1 mile		288	.028			1.54	2.74	4.28	5.30
9418	cycle 2 miles		252	.032			1.76	3.13	4.89	6.05
9420	cycle 4 miles		198	.040			2.24	3.98	6.22	7.75
9422	cycle 6 miles		180	.044			2.46	4.38	6.84	8.50
9424	cycle 8 miles		144	.056			3.08	5.50	8.58	10.60
9425	cycle 10 miles		126	.063			3.52	6.25	9.77	12.15
9426	20 MPH avg., cycle 0.5 mile		324	.025			1.37	2.43	3.80	4.73
9428	cycle 1 mile		306	.026			1.45	2.58	4.03	5
9430	cycle 2 miles		270	.030			1.64	2.92	4.56	5.65
9432	cycle 4 miles		234	.034			1.90	3.37	5.27	6.55
9434	cycle 6 miles		198	.040			2.24	3.98	6.22	7.75
9436	cycle 8 miles		180	.044			2.46	4.38	6.84	8.50
9438	cycle 10 miles		144	.056			3.08	5.50	8.58	10.60
9440	25 MPH avg., cycle 4 miles		252	.032			1.76	3.13	4.89	6.05
9442	cycle 6 miles		216	.037			2.05	3.65	5.70	7.10
9444	cycle 8 miles		198	.040			2.24	3.98	6.22	7.75
9446	cycle 10 miles		180	.044			2.46	4.38	6.84	8.50
9450	30 MPH avg., cycle 4 miles		252	.032			1.76	3.13	4.89	6.05
9452	cycle 6 miles		234	.034			1.90	3.37	5.27	6.55
9454	cycle 8 miles		198	.040			2.24	3.98	6.22	7.75
9456	cycle 10 miles		180	.044			2.46	4.38	6.84	8.50

31 23 Excavation and Fill

31 23 23 – Fill

31 23 23.20 Hauling

		Crew	Daily Output	Labor-Hours	Unit	Material	2023 Bare Costs Labor	Equipment	Total	Total Incl O&P
9460	35 MPH avg., cycle 4 miles	B-34I	270	.030	L.C.Y.		1.64	2.92	4.56	5.65
9462	cycle 6 miles		234	.034			1.90	3.37	5.27	6.55
9464	cycle 8 miles		216	.037			2.05	3.65	5.70	7.10
9466	cycle 10 miles		198	.040			2.24	3.98	6.22	7.75
9468	cycle 20 miles		144	.056			3.08	5.50	8.58	10.60
9470	cycle 30 miles		108	.074			4.11	7.30	11.41	14.20
9472	cycle 40 miles		90	.089			4.93	8.75	13.68	17
9474	40 MPH avg., cycle 6 miles		252	.032			1.76	3.13	4.89	6.05
9476	cycle 8 miles		234	.034			1.90	3.37	5.27	6.55
9478	cycle 10 miles		216	.037			2.05	3.65	5.70	7.10
9480	cycle 20 miles		144	.056			3.08	5.50	8.58	10.60
9482	cycle 30 miles		126	.063			3.52	6.25	9.77	12.15
9484	cycle 40 miles		90	.089			4.93	8.75	13.68	17
9486	cycle 50 miles		90	.089			4.93	8.75	13.68	17
9494	45 MPH avg., cycle 8 miles		234	.034			1.90	3.37	5.27	6.55
9496	cycle 10 miles		216	.037			2.05	3.65	5.70	7.10
9498	cycle 20 miles		162	.049			2.74	4.87	7.61	9.45
9500	cycle 30 miles		126	.063			3.52	6.25	9.77	12.15
9502	cycle 40 miles		108	.074			4.11	7.30	11.41	14.20
9504	cycle 50 miles		90	.089			4.93	8.75	13.68	17
9506	50 MPH avg., cycle 10 miles		234	.034			1.90	3.37	5.27	6.55
9508	cycle 20 miles		180	.044			2.46	4.38	6.84	8.50
9510	cycle 30 miles		144	.056			3.08	5.50	8.58	10.60
9512	cycle 40 miles		108	.074			4.11	7.30	11.41	14.20
9514	cycle 50 miles		90	.089			4.93	8.75	13.68	17
9614	30 min. wait/ld./uld.,15 MPH, cycle 0.5 mi.		270	.030			1.64	2.92	4.56	5.65
9616	cycle 1 mile		252	.032			1.76	3.13	4.89	6.05
9618	cycle 2 miles		216	.037			2.05	3.65	5.70	7.10
9620	cycle 4 miles		180	.044			2.46	4.38	6.84	8.50
9622	cycle 6 miles		162	.049			2.74	4.87	7.61	9.45
9624	cycle 8 miles		126	.063			3.52	6.25	9.77	12.15
9625	cycle 10 miles		126	.063			3.52	6.25	9.77	12.15
9626	20 MPH avg., cycle 0.5 mile		270	.030			1.64	2.92	4.56	5.65
9628	cycle 1 mile		252	.032			1.76	3.13	4.89	6.05
9630	cycle 2 miles		234	.034			1.90	3.37	5.27	6.55
9632	cycle 4 miles		198	.040			2.24	3.98	6.22	7.75
9634	cycle 6 miles		180	.044			2.46	4.38	6.84	8.50
9636	cycle 8 miles		162	.049			2.74	4.87	7.61	9.45
9638	cycle 10 miles		144	.056			3.08	5.50	8.58	10.60
9640	25 MPH avg., cycle 4 miles		216	.037			2.05	3.65	5.70	7.10
9642	cycle 6 miles		198	.040			2.24	3.98	6.22	7.75
9644	cycle 8 miles		180	.044			2.46	4.38	6.84	8.50
9646	cycle 10 miles		162	.049			2.74	4.87	7.61	9.45
9650	30 MPH avg., cycle 4 miles		216	.037			2.05	3.65	5.70	7.10
9652	cycle 6 miles		198	.040			2.24	3.98	6.22	7.75
9654	cycle 8 miles		180	.044			2.46	4.38	6.84	8.50
9656	cycle 10 miles		162	.049			2.74	4.87	7.61	9.45
9660	35 MPH avg., cycle 4 miles		234	.034			1.90	3.37	5.27	6.55
9662	cycle 6 miles		216	.037			2.05	3.65	5.70	7.10
9664	cycle 8 miles		198	.040			2.24	3.98	6.22	7.75
9666	cycle 10 miles		180	.044			2.46	4.38	6.84	8.50
9668	cycle 20 miles		126	.063			3.52	6.25	9.77	12.15
9670	cycle 30 miles		108	.074			4.11	7.30	11.41	14.20

31 23 Excavation and Fill

31 23 23 – Fill

31 23 23.20 Hauling

		Crew	Daily Output	Labor-Hours	Unit	Material	2023 Bare Costs Labor	Equipment	Total	Total Incl O&P
9672	cycle 40 miles	B-34I	90	.089	L.C.Y.		4.93	8.75	13.68	17
9674	40 MPH avg., cycle 6 miles		216	.037			2.05	3.65	5.70	7.10
9676	cycle 8 miles		198	.040			2.24	3.98	6.22	7.75
9678	cycle 10 miles		180	.044			2.46	4.38	6.84	8.50
9680	cycle 20 miles		144	.056			3.08	5.50	8.58	10.60
9682	cycle 30 miles		108	.074			4.11	7.30	11.41	14.20
9684	cycle 40 miles		90	.089			4.93	8.75	13.68	17
9686	cycle 50 miles		72	.111			6.15	10.95	17.10	21.50
9694	45 MPH avg., cycle 8 miles		216	.037			2.05	3.65	5.70	7.10
9696	cycle 10 miles		198	.040			2.24	3.98	6.22	7.75
9698	cycle 20 miles		144	.056			3.08	5.50	8.58	10.60
9700	cycle 30 miles		126	.063			3.52	6.25	9.77	12.15
9702	cycle 40 miles		108	.074			4.11	7.30	11.41	14.20
9704	cycle 50 miles		90	.089			4.93	8.75	13.68	17
9706	50 MPH avg., cycle 10 miles		198	.040			2.24	3.98	6.22	7.75
9708	cycle 20 miles		162	.049			2.74	4.87	7.61	9.45
9710	cycle 30 miles		126	.063			3.52	6.25	9.77	12.15
9712	cycle 40 miles		108	.074			4.11	7.30	11.41	14.20
9714	cycle 50 miles		90	.089			4.93	8.75	13.68	17

31 41 Shoring

31 41 16 – Sheet Piling

31 41 16.10 Sheet Piling Systems

			Crew	Daily Output	Labor-Hours	Unit	Material	Labor	Equipment	Total	Total Incl O&P
0010	**SHEET PILING SYSTEMS**										
0020	Sheet piling, 50,000 psi steel, not incl. wales, 22 psf, left in place		B-40	10.81	5.920	Ton	2,575	365	360	3,300	3,800
0100	Drive, extract & salvage	R314116-45		6	10.667		510	660	645	1,815	2,275
0300	20' deep excavation, 27 psf, left in place			12.95	4.942		2,575	305	300	3,180	3,650
0400	Drive, extract & salvage			6.55	9.771		510	605	595	1,710	2,125
1200	15' deep excavation, 22 psf, left in place			983	.065	S.F.	30	4.02	3.95	37.97	43.50
1300	Drive, extract & salvage			545	.117		5.75	7.25	7.10	20.10	25
1500	20' deep excavation, 27 psf, left in place			960	.067		37.50	4.11	4.04	45.65	52
1600	Drive, extract & salvage			485	.132		7.45	8.15	8	23.60	29.50
2100	Rent steel sheet piling and wales, first month					Ton	320			320	350
2200	Per added month						32			32	35
2300	Rental piling left in place, add to rental						1,175			1,175	1,300
2500	Wales, connections & struts, 2/3 salvage						510			510	565
3900	Wood, solid sheeting, incl. wales, braces and spacers,	R314116-40									
3910	drive, extract & salvage, 8' deep excavation		B-31	330	.121	S.F.	5.55	6.05	.76	12.36	15.95
4000	10' deep, 50 S.F./hr. in & 150 S.F./hr. out			300	.133		5.70	6.65	.84	13.19	17.05
4100	12' deep, 45 S.F./hr. in & 135 S.F./hr. out			270	.148		5.85	7.40	.93	14.18	18.50
4200	14' deep, 42 S.F./hr. in & 126 S.F./hr. out			250	.160		6.05	8	1.01	15.06	19.65
4300	16' deep, 40 S.F./hr. in & 120 S.F./hr. out			240	.167		6.25	8.30	1.05	15.60	20.50
4400	18' deep, 38 S.F./hr. in & 114 S.F./hr. out			230	.174		6.45	8.70	1.09	16.24	21.50
4520	Left in place, 8' deep, 55 S.F./hr.			440	.091		10	4.54	.57	15.11	18.40
4540	10' deep, 50 S.F./hr.			400	.100		10.50	4.99	.63	16.12	19.70
4560	12' deep, 45 S.F./hr.			360	.111		11.10	5.55	.70	17.35	21
4565	14' deep, 42 S.F./hr.			335	.119		11.75	5.95	.75	18.45	22.50
4570	16' deep, 40 S.F./hr.			320	.125		12.50	6.25	.79	19.54	24
4700	Alternate pricing, left in place, 8' deep			1.76	22.727	M.B.F.	2,250	1,125	143	3,518	4,325
4800	Drive, extract and salvage, 8' deep			1.32	30.303	"	2,000	1,525	191	3,716	4,650

31 52 Cofferdams

31 52 16 – Timber Cofferdams

31 52 16.10 Cofferdams		Crew	Daily Output	Labor-Hours	Unit	Material	2023 Bare Costs Labor	Equipment	Total	Total Incl O&P
0010	**COFFERDAMS**									
0011	Incl. mobilization and temporary sheeting									
0080	Soldier beams & lagging H-piles with 3" wood sheeting									
0090	horizontal between piles, including removal of wales & braces									
0100	No hydrostatic head, 15' deep, 1 line of braces, minimum	B-50	545	.206	S.F.	21	12	5.30	38.30	47.50
0200	Maximum		495	.226		23.50	13.25	5.85	42.60	52.50
1300	No hydrostatic head, left in place, 15' deep, 1 line of braces, min.		635	.176		28.50	10.30	4.56	43.36	51.50
1400	Maximum		575	.195		30.50	11.40	5.05	46.95	56.50
2350	Lagging only, 3" thick wood between piles 8' OC, minimum	B-46	400	.120		4.72	6.50	.13	11.35	15.25
2370	Maximum		250	.192		7.10	10.40	.22	17.72	24
2400	Open sheeting no bracing, for trenches to 10' deep, min.		1736	.028		2.12	1.50	.03	3.65	4.65
2450	Maximum		1510	.032		2.36	1.72	.04	4.12	5.25
2500	Tie-back method, add to open sheeting, add, minimum								20%	20%
2550	Maximum								60%	60%
2700	Tie-backs only, based on tie-backs total length, minimum	B-46	86.80	.553	L.F.	19.60	30	.62	50.22	67.50
2750	Maximum		38.50	1.247	"	34.50	67.50	1.40	103.40	143
3500	Tie-backs only, typical average, 25' long		2	24	Ea.	860	1,300	27	2,187	2,950
3600	35' long		1.58	30.380	"	1,150	1,650	34	2,834	3,825
6000	See also Section 31 41 16.10									

Division Notes

		CREW	DAILY OUTPUT	LABOR-HOURS	UNIT	BARE COSTS				TOTAL INCL O&P
						MAT.	LABOR	EQUIP.	TOTAL	

Division 32 — Exterior Improvements

Estimating Tips

32 01 00 Operations and Maintenance of Exterior Improvements

- Recycling of asphalt pavement is becoming very popular and is an alternative to removal and replacement. It can be a good value engineering proposal if removed pavement can be recycled, either at the project site or at another site that is reasonably close to the project site. Sections on repair of flexible and rigid pavement are included.

32 10 00 Bases, Ballasts, and Paving

- When estimating paving, keep in mind the project schedule. Also note that prices for asphalt and concrete are generally higher in the cold seasons. Lines for pavement markings, including tactile warning systems and fence lines, are included.

32 90 00 Planting

- The timing of planting and guarantee specifications often dictate the costs for establishing tree and shrub growth and a stand of grass or ground cover. Establish the work performance schedule to coincide with the local planting season. Maintenance and growth guarantees can add 20–100% to the total landscaping cost and can be contractually cumbersome. The cost to replace trees and shrubs can be as high as 5% of the total cost, depending on the planting zone, soil conditions, and time of year.

Reference Numbers

Reference numbers are shown at the beginning of some major classifications. These numbers refer to related items in the Reference Section. The reference information may be an estimating procedure, an alternate pricing method, or technical information.

Note: Not all subdivisions listed here necessarily appear. ■

Same Data. Simplified.

Enjoy the convenience and efficiency of accessing your costs anywhere:

- **Skip the multiplier** by setting your location
- **Quickly search,** edit, favorite and share costs
- **Stay on top of price changes** with automatic updates

Discover more at rsmeans.com/online

No part of this cost data may be reproduced, stored in a retrieval system, or transmitted in any form or by any means without prior written permission of Gordian.

32 12 Flexible Paving

32 12 16 – Asphalt Paving

32 12 16.13 Plant-Mix Asphalt Paving

		Crew	Daily Output	Labor-Hours	Unit	Material	2023 Bare Costs Labor	Equipment	Total	Total Incl O&P
0010	**PLANT-MIX ASPHALT PAVING**									
0020	For highways and large paved areas, excludes hauling									
0025	See Section 31 23 23.20 for hauling costs									
0080	Binder course, 1-1/2" thick	B-25	7725	.011	S.Y.	5.85	.59	.40	6.84	7.70
0120	2" thick		6345	.014		7.75	.72	.49	8.96	10.15
0130	2-1/2" thick		5620	.016		9.70	.81	.55	11.06	12.50
0160	3" thick		4905	.018		11.65	.93	.64	13.22	14.90
0170	3-1/2" thick		4520	.019		13.60	1.01	.69	15.30	17.20
0200	4" thick	▼	4140	.021		15.55	1.10	.75	17.40	19.55
0300	Wearing course, 1" thick	B-25B	10575	.009		3.85	.48	.33	4.66	5.30
0340	1-1/2" thick		7725	.012		6.45	.65	.45	7.55	8.55
0380	2" thick		6345	.015		8.70	.80	.55	10.05	11.35
0420	2-1/2" thick		5480	.018		10.70	.92	.64	12.26	13.85
0460	3" thick		4900	.020		12.80	1.03	.71	14.54	16.35
0470	3-1/2" thick		4520	.021		15	1.12	.77	16.89	19
0480	4" thick	▼	4140	.023		17.15	1.22	.84	19.21	21.50
0600	Porous pavement, 1-1/2" open graded friction course	B-25	7725	.011	▼	19.75	.59	.40	20.74	23
0800	Alternate method of figuring paving costs									
0810	Binder course, 1-1/2" thick	B-25	630	.140	Ton	71.50	7.25	4.95	83.70	94.50
0811	2" thick		690	.128		71.50	6.60	4.52	82.62	93.50
0812	3" thick		800	.110		71.50	5.70	3.90	81.10	91
0813	4" thick	▼	900	.098		71.50	5.05	3.46	80.01	90
0850	Wearing course, 1" thick	B-25B	575	.167		76	8.80	6.10	90.90	104
0851	1-1/2" thick		630	.152		76	8.05	5.55	89.60	102
0852	2" thick		690	.139		76	7.35	5.05	88.40	100
0853	2-1/2" thick		765	.125		76	6.60	4.57	87.17	99
0854	3" thick	▼	800	.120	▼	76	6.30	4.37	86.67	98
1000	Pavement replacement over trench, 2" thick	B-17C	90	.533	S.Y.	8	28	22.50	58.50	75.50
1050	4" thick		70	.686		15.85	36	29	80.85	102
1080	6" thick	▼	55	.873		25	45.50	37	107.50	137

32 12 16.14 Asphaltic Concrete Paving

		Crew	Daily Output	Labor-Hours	Unit	Material	Labor	Equipment	Total	Total Incl O&P
0011	**ASPHALTIC CONCRETE PAVING**, parking lots & driveways									
0015	No asphalt hauling included									
0018	Use 6.05 C.Y. per inch per M.S.F. for hauling									
0020	6" stone base, 2" binder course, 1" topping	B-25C	9000	.005	S.F.	2.21	.28	.30	2.79	3.18
0025	2" binder course, 2" topping		9000	.005		2.67	.28	.30	3.25	3.69
0030	3" binder course, 2" topping		9000	.005		3.11	.28	.30	3.69	4.17
0035	4" binder course, 2" topping		9000	.005		3.54	.28	.30	4.12	4.64
0040	1-1/2" binder course, 1" topping		9000	.005		2	.28	.30	2.58	2.95
0042	3" binder course, 1" topping		9000	.005		2.65	.28	.30	3.23	3.66
0045	3" binder course, 3" topping		9000	.005		3.57	.28	.30	4.15	4.68
0050	4" binder course, 3" topping		9000	.005		4	.28	.30	4.58	5.15
0055	4" binder course, 4" topping		9000	.005		4.46	.28	.30	5.04	5.65
0300	Binder course, 1-1/2" thick		35000	.001		.65	.07	.08	.80	.91
0400	2" thick		25000	.002		.84	.10	.11	1.05	1.19
0500	3" thick		15000	.003		1.30	.17	.18	1.65	1.88
0600	4" thick		10800	.004		1.70	.23	.25	2.18	2.50
0800	Sand finish course, 3/4" thick		41000	.001		.37	.06	.07	.50	.57
0900	1" thick		34000	.001		.46	.07	.08	.61	.70
1000	Fill pot holes, hot mix, 2" thick	B-16	4200	.008		.90	.38	.19	1.47	1.77
1100	4" thick		3500	.009		1.31	.46	.23	2	2.38
1120	6" thick	▼	3100	.010		1.77	.51	.26	2.54	2.99

32 12 Flexible Paving

32 12 16 – Asphalt Paving

32 12 16.14 Asphaltic Concrete Paving		Crew	Daily Output	Labor-Hours	Unit	Material	2023 Bare Costs Labor	Equipment	Total	Total Incl O&P
1140	Cold patch, 2" thick	B-51	3000	.016	S.F.	1.34	.78	.12	2.24	2.77
1160	4" thick		2700	.018		2.56	.86	.13	3.55	4.24
1180	6" thick		1900	.025		3.97	1.23	.19	5.39	6.40

32 84 Planting Irrigation

32 84 23 – Underground Sprinklers

32 84 23.10 Sprinkler Irrigation System		Crew	Daily Output	Labor-Hours	Unit	Material	2023 Bare Costs Labor	Equipment	Total	Total Incl O&P
0010	**SPRINKLER IRRIGATION SYSTEM**									
0011	For lawns									
0800	Residential system, custom, 1" supply	B-20	2000	.012	S.F.	.32	.63		.95	1.29
0900	1-1/2" supply	"	1800	.013	"	.48	.70		1.18	1.58

Division Notes

		CREW	DAILY OUTPUT	LABOR-HOURS	UNIT	BARE COSTS				TOTAL INCL O&P
						MAT.	LABOR	EQUIP.	TOTAL	

Division 33 Utilities

Estimating Tips
33 10 00 Water Utilities
33 30 00 Sanitary Sewerage Utilities
33 40 00 Storm Drainage Utilities

- Never assume that the water, sewer, and drainage lines will go in at the early stages of the project — both site and project specific conditions must be taken into consideration when assessing the cost implications for utility work, with particular attention paid to the scheduling of works. Consider the site access needs before dividing the site in half with open trenches, loose pipe, and machinery obstructions. Always inspect the site to establish that the site drawings are complete. Check off all existing utilities on your drawings as you locate them. Be especially careful with underground utilities because appurtenances are sometimes buried during regrading or repaving operations. If you find any discrepancies, mark up the site plan for further research. Differing site conditions can be very costly if discovered later in the project.

- See also Section 33 01 00 for restoration of pipe where removal/replacement may be undesirable. Use of new types of piping materials can reduce the overall project cost.

Owners/design engineers should consider the installing contractor as a valuable source of current information on utility products and local conditions that could lead to significant cost savings.

Reference Numbers
Reference numbers are shown at the beginning of some major classifications. These numbers refer to related items in the Reference Section. The reference information may be an estimating procedure, an alternate pricing method, or technical information.

Note: Not all subdivisions listed here necessarily appear. ∎

Same Data. Simplified.

Enjoy the convenience and efficiency of accessing your costs anywhere:

- **Skip the multiplier** by setting your location
- **Quickly search,** edit, favorite and share costs
- **Stay on top of price changes** with automatic updates

Discover more at rsmeans.com/online

No part of this cost data may be reproduced, stored in a retrieval system, or transmitted in any form or by any means without prior written permission of Gordian.

Note: "Powered in part by CINX™, based on licensed proprietary information of Harrison Publishing House, Inc."

Note: Trade Service, in part, has been used as a reference source for some of the material prices used in Division 33

33 01 Operation and Maintenance of Utilities

33 01 10 – Operation and Maintenance of Water Utilities

33 01 10.10 Corrosion Resistance

		Crew	Daily Output	Labor-Hours	Unit	Material	2023 Bare Costs Labor	2023 Bare Costs Equipment	Total	Total Incl O&P
0010	**CORROSION RESISTANCE**									
0012	Wrap & coat, add to pipe, 4" diameter				L.F.	4.02			4.02	4.42
0020	5" diameter					4.96			4.96	5.45
0040	6" diameter					5.90			5.90	6.50
0060	8" diameter					7.80			7.80	8.55
0080	10" diameter					9.50			9.50	10.45
0100	12" diameter					10.70			10.70	11.75
0120	14" diameter					12.70			12.70	13.95
0140	16" diameter					14.25			14.25	15.70
0160	18" diameter					16.30			16.30	17.95
0180	20" diameter					18			18	19.80
0200	24" diameter					21.50			21.50	23.50
0220	Small diameter pipe, 1" diameter, add					1.18			1.18	1.30
0240	2" diameter					2.12			2.12	2.33
0260	2-1/2" diameter					2.24			2.24	2.46
0280	3" diameter				▼	3.14			3.14	3.45
0300	Fittings, field covered, add				S.F.	14.40			14.40	15.85
0500	Coating, bituminous, per diameter inch, 1 coat, add				L.F.	.27			.27	.30
0540	3 coat					.91			.91	1
0560	Coal tar epoxy, per diameter inch, 1 coat, add					.37			.37	.41
0600	3 coat					1.02			1.02	1.12
1000	Polyethylene H.D. extruded, 0.025" thk., 1/2" diameter, add					.15			.15	.17
1020	3/4" diameter					.25			.25	.28
1040	1" diameter					.29			.29	.32
1060	1-1/4" diameter					.38			.38	.42
1080	1-1/2" diameter					.43			.43	.47
1100	0.030" thk., 2" diameter					.59			.59	.65
1120	2-1/2" diameter					.75			.75	.83
1140	0.035" thk., 3" diameter					.81			.81	.89
1160	3-1/2" diameter					.93			.93	1.02
1180	4" diameter					1.10			1.10	1.21
1200	0.040" thk., 5" diameter					1.35			1.35	1.49
1220	6" diameter					1.61			1.61	1.77
1240	8" diameter					2.05			2.05	2.26
1260	10" diameter					2.64			2.64	2.90
1280	12" diameter					3.16			3.16	3.48
1300	0.060" thk., 14" diameter					4.17			4.17	4.59
1320	16" diameter					4.78			4.78	5.25
1340	18" diameter					4.75			4.75	5.25
1360	20" diameter				▼	5.30			5.30	5.85
1380	Fittings, field wrapped, add				S.F.	3.24			3.24	3.56

33 01 10.20 Pipe Repair

		Crew	Daily Output	Labor-Hours	Unit	Material	2023 Bare Costs Labor	2023 Bare Costs Equipment	Total	Total Incl O&P
0010	**PIPE REPAIR**									
0020	Not including excavation or backfill									
0100	Clamp, stainless steel, lightweight, for steel pipe									
0110	3" long, 1/2" diameter pipe	1 Plum	34	.235	Ea.	20	16.95		36.95	47.50
0120	3/4" diameter pipe		32	.250		21.50	18		39.50	50.50
0130	1" diameter pipe		30	.267		23.50	19.20		42.70	54
0140	1-1/4" diameter pipe		28	.286		26.50	20.50		47	59.50
0150	1-1/2" diameter pipe		26	.308		27.50	22		49.50	63.50
0160	2" diameter pipe		24	.333		30	24		54	69
0170	2-1/2" diameter pipe	▼	23	.348		32	25		57	72.50

33 01 Operation and Maintenance of Utilities

33 01 10 – Operation and Maintenance of Water Utilities

33 01 10.20 Pipe Repair		Crew	Daily Output	Labor-Hours	Unit	Material	2023 Bare Costs Labor	Equipment	Total	Total Incl O&P
0180	3" diameter pipe	1 Plum	22	.364	Ea.	33.50	26		59.50	75.50
0190	3-1/2" diameter pipe		21	.381		33.50	27.50		61	77.50
0200	4" diameter pipe	B-20	44	.545		36	28.50		64.50	82.50
0210	5" diameter pipe		42	.571		44.50	30		74.50	93.50
0220	6" diameter pipe		38	.632		47	33		80	102
0230	8" diameter pipe		30	.800		56	42		98	125
0240	10" diameter pipe		28	.857		385	45		430	495
0250	12" diameter pipe		24	1		405	52.50		457.50	525
0260	14" diameter pipe		22	1.091		445	57.50		502.50	575
0270	16" diameter pipe		20	1.200		480	63		543	625
0280	18" diameter pipe		18	1.333		505	70		575	660
0290	20" diameter pipe		16	1.500		535	79		614	710
0300	24" diameter pipe		14	1.714		595	90		685	790
0360	For 6" long, add					100%	40%			
0370	For 9" long, add					200%	100%			
0380	For 12" long, add					300%	150%			
0390	For 18" long, add					500%	200%			
0400	Pipe freezing for live repairs of systems 3/8" to 6"									
0410	Note: Pipe freezing can also be used to install a valve into a live system									
0420	Pipe freezing each side 3/8"	2 Skwk	8	2	Ea.	585	123		708	825
0425	Pipe freezing each side 3/8", second location same kit		8	2		35	123		158	223
0430	Pipe freezing each side 3/4"		8	2		585	123		708	825
0435	Pipe freezing each side 3/4", second location same kit		8	2		35	123		158	223
0440	Pipe freezing each side 1-1/2"		6	2.667		585	163		748	885
0445	Pipe freezing each side 1-1/2", second location same kit		6	2.667		35	163		198	284
0450	Pipe freezing each side 2"		6	2.667		585	163		748	885
0455	Pipe freezing each side 2", second location same kit		6	2.667		35	163		198	284
0460	Pipe freezing each side 2-1/2" to 3"		6	2.667		895	163		1,058	1,225
0465	Pipe freezing each side 2-1/2" to 3", second location same kit		6	2.667		70	163		233	320
0470	Pipe freezing each side 4"		4	4		1,600	245		1,845	2,125
0475	Pipe freezing each side 4", second location same kit		4	4		103	245		348	485
0480	Pipe freezing each side 5" to 6"		4	4		5,050	245		5,295	5,950
0485	Pipe freezing each side 5" to 6", second location same kit		4	4		310	245		555	710
0490	Pipe freezing extra 20 lb. CO_2 cylinders (3/8" to 2" - 1 ea, 3" - 2 ea)					271			271	298
0500	Pipe freezing extra 50 lb. CO_2 cylinders (4" - 2 ea, 5"-6" - 6 ea)					785			785	865
1000	Clamp, stainless steel, with threaded service tap									
1040	Full seal for iron, steel, PVC pipe									
1100	6" long, 2" diameter pipe	1 Plum	17	.471	Ea.	138	34		172	203
1110	2-1/2" diameter pipe		16	.500		158	36		194	227
1120	3" diameter pipe		15.60	.513		165	37		202	236
1130	3-1/2" diameter pipe		15	.533		192	38.50		230.50	269
1140	4" diameter pipe	B-20	32	.750		190	39.50		229.50	268
1150	6" diameter pipe		28	.857		232	45		277	325
1160	8" diameter pipe		21	1.143		274	60		334	390
1170	10" diameter pipe		20	1.200		350	63		413	480
1180	12" diameter pipe		17	1.412		400	74		474	550
1200	8" long, 2" diameter pipe	1 Plum	11.72	.683		205	49		254	300
1210	2-1/2" diameter pipe		11	.727		216	52.50		268.50	315
1220	3" diameter pipe		10.75	.744		227	53.50		280.50	330
1230	3-1/2" diameter pipe		10.34	.774		237	55.50		292.50	345
1240	4" diameter pipe	B-20	22	1.091		250	57.50		307.50	360
1250	6" diameter pipe		19.31	1.243		297	65.50		362.50	425
1260	8" diameter pipe		14.48	1.657		345	87		432	510

33 01 Operation and Maintenance of Utilities

33 01 10 – Operation and Maintenance of Water Utilities

33 01 10.20 Pipe Repair

		Crew	Daily Output	Labor-Hours	Unit	Material	2023 Bare Costs Labor	Equipment	Total	Total Incl O&P
1270	10" diameter pipe	B-20	13.80	1.739	Ea.	445	91.50		536.50	620
1280	12" diameter pipe	▼	11.72	2.048		495	108		603	705
1300	12" long, 2" diameter pipe	1 Plum	9.44	.847		292	61		353	410
1310	2-1/2" diameter pipe		8.89	.900		300	65		365	430
1320	3" diameter pipe		8.67	.923		315	66.50		381.50	445
1330	3-1/2" diameter pipe	▼	8.33	.960		330	69		399	465
1340	4" diameter pipe	B-20	17.78	1.350		350	71		421	490
1350	6" diameter pipe		15.56	1.542		415	81		496	575
1360	8" diameter pipe		11.67	2.057		485	108		593	695
1370	10" diameter pipe		11.11	2.160		610	114		724	845
1380	12" diameter pipe	▼	9.44	2.542		710	134		844	980
1400	20" long, 2" diameter pipe	1 Plum	8.10	.988		420	71		491	565
1410	2-1/2" diameter pipe		7.62	1.050		460	75.50		535.50	625
1420	3" diameter pipe		7.43	1.077		530	77.50		607.50	695
1430	3-1/2" diameter pipe	▼	7.14	1.120		560	80.50		640.50	735
1440	4" diameter pipe	B-20	15.24	1.575		585	83		668	765
1450	6" diameter pipe		13.33	1.800		690	94.50		784.50	900
1460	8" diameter pipe		10	2.400		800	126		926	1,075
1470	10" diameter pipe		9.52	2.521		980	133		1,113	1,275
1480	12" diameter pipe	▼	8.10	2.963	▼	1,125	156		1,281	1,475
1600	Clamp, stainless steel, single section									
1640	Full seal for iron, steel, PVC pipe									
1700	6" long, 2" diameter pipe	1 Plum	17	.471	Ea.	143	34		177	209
1710	2-1/2" diameter pipe		16	.500		152	36		188	221
1720	3" diameter pipe		15.60	.513		172	37		209	244
1730	3-1/2" diameter pipe	▼	15	.533		181	38.50		219.50	257
1740	4" diameter pipe	B-20	32	.750		190	39.50		229.50	268
1750	6" diameter pipe		27	.889		232	46.50		278.50	325
1760	8" diameter pipe		21	1.143		274	60		334	390
1770	10" diameter pipe		20	1.200		350	63		413	480
1780	12" diameter pipe		17	1.412		400	74		474	550
1800	8" long, 2" diameter pipe	1 Plum	11.72	.683		205	49		254	300
1805	2-1/2" diameter pipe		11.03	.725		219	52.50		271.50	320
1810	3" diameter pipe		10.76	.743		226	53.50		279.50	330
1815	3-1/2" diameter pipe	▼	10.34	.774		241	55.50		296.50	350
1820	4" diameter pipe	B-20	22.07	1.087		251	57		308	360
1825	6" diameter pipe		19.31	1.243		296	65.50		361.50	425
1830	8" diameter pipe		14.48	1.657		340	87		427	505
1835	10" diameter pipe		13.79	1.740		445	91.50		536.50	620
1840	12" diameter pipe	▼	11.72	2.048		495	108		603	705
1850	12" long, 2" diameter pipe	1 Plum	9.44	.847		292	61		353	410
1855	2-1/2" diameter pipe		8.89	.900		305	65		370	430
1860	3" diameter pipe		8.67	.923		315	66.50		381.50	445
1865	3-1/2" diameter pipe	▼	8.33	.960		335	69		404	475
1870	4" diameter pipe	B-20	17.78	1.350		350	71		421	490
1875	6" diameter pipe		15.56	1.542		410	81		491	570
1880	8" diameter pipe		11.67	2.057		475	108		583	685
1885	10" diameter pipe		11.11	2.160		610	114		724	845
1890	12" diameter pipe	▼	9.44	2.542		715	134		849	985
1900	20" long, 2" diameter pipe	1 Plum	8.10	.988		375	71		446	515
1905	2-1/2" diameter pipe		7.62	1.050		415	75.50		490.50	570
1910	3" diameter pipe		7.43	1.077		475	77.50		552.50	635
1915	3-1/2" diameter pipe	▼	7.14	1.120		490	80.50		570.50	655

33 01 Operation and Maintenance of Utilities

33 01 10 – Operation and Maintenance of Water Utilities

33 01 10.20 Pipe Repair		Crew	Daily Output	Labor-Hours	Unit	Material	2023 Bare Costs Labor	Equipment	Total	Total Incl O&P
1920	4" diameter pipe	B-20	15.24	1.575	Ea.	585	83		668	765
1925	6" diameter pipe		13.33	1.800		695	94.50		789.50	905
1930	8" diameter pipe		10	2.400		785	126		911	1,050
1935	10" diameter pipe		9.52	2.521		980	133		1,113	1,275
1940	12" diameter pipe	▼	8.10	2.963	▼	1,125	156		1,281	1,475
2000	Clamp, stainless steel, two section									
2040	Full seal, for iron, steel, PVC pipe									
2100	8" long, 4" diameter pipe	B-20	24	1	Ea.	360	52.50		412.50	475
2110	6" diameter pipe		20	1.200		415	63		478	550
2120	8" diameter pipe		13	1.846		475	97		572	670
2130	10" diameter pipe		12	2		420	105		525	615
2140	12" diameter pipe		10	2.400		685	126		811	945
2200	10" long, 4" diameter pipe		16	1.500		475	79		554	640
2210	6" diameter pipe		13	1.846		535	97		632	730
2220	8" diameter pipe		9	2.667		590	140		730	860
2230	10" diameter pipe		8	3		775	158		933	1,100
2240	12" diameter pipe	▼	7	3.429	▼	890	180		1,070	1,250
2242	Clamp, stainless steel, three section									
2244	Full seal, for iron, steel, PVC pipe									
2250	10" long, 14" diameter pipe	B-20	6.40	3.750	Ea.	1,350	197		1,547	1,800
2260	16" diameter pipe		6	4		1,250	210		1,460	1,700
2270	18" diameter pipe		5	4.800		1,675	252		1,927	2,225
2280	20" diameter pipe		4.60	5.217		1,925	274		2,199	2,525
2290	24" diameter pipe	▼	4	6		2,175	315		2,490	2,875
2320	For 12" long, add to 10"					15%	25%			
2330	For 20" long, add to 10"				▼	70%	55%			
8000	For internal cleaning and inspection, see Section 33 01 30.11									
8100	For pipe testing, see Section 23 05 93.50									

33 01 30 – Operation and Maintenance of Sewer Utilities

33 01 30.11 Television Inspection of Sewers

		Crew	Daily Output	Labor-Hours	Unit	Material	Labor	Equipment	Total	Total Incl O&P
0010	**TELEVISION INSPECTION OF SEWERS**									
0100	Pipe internal cleaning & inspection, cleaning, pressure pipe systems									
0120	Pig method, lengths 1000' to 10,000'									
0140	4" diameter thru 24" diameter, minimum				L.F.				3.60	4.14
0160	Maximum				"				18	21
6000	Sewage/sanitary systems									
6100	Power rodder with header & cutters									
6110	Mobilization charge, minimum				Total				695	800
6120	Mobilization charge, maximum				"				9,125	10,600
6140	Cleaning 4"-12" diameter				L.F.				6	6.60
6190	14"-24" diameter								8	8.80
6240	30" diameter								9.60	10.50
6250	36" diameter								12	13.20
6260	48" diameter								16	17.60
6270	60" diameter								24	26.50
6280	72" diameter				▼				48	53
9000	Inspection, television camera with video									
9060	up to 500 linear feet				Total				715	820
9220	up to 500 linear feet				"					

33 01 Operation and Maintenance of Utilities

33 01 30 – Operation and Maintenance of Sewer Utilities

33 01 30.23 Pipe Bursting

		Crew	Daily Output	Labor-Hours	Unit	Material	2023 Bare Costs Labor	Equipment	Total	Total Incl O&P
0010	**PIPE BURSTING**									
0011	300' runs, replace with HDPE pipe									
0020	Not including excavation, backfill, shoring, or dewatering									
0100	6" to 15" diameter, minimum				L.F.				200	220
0200	Maximum								550	605
0300	18" to 36" diameter, minimum								650	715
0400	Maximum								1,050	1,150
0500	Mobilize and demobilize, minimum				Job				3,000	3,300
0600	Maximum				"				32,100	35,400

33 01 30.74 Sliplining, Excludes Cleaning

		Crew	Daily Output	Labor-Hours	Unit	Material	Labor	Equipment	Total	Total Incl O&P
0010	**SLIPLINING, excludes cleaning** and video inspection									
0020	Pipe relined with one pipe size smaller than original (4" for 6")									
0100	6" diameter, original size	B-6B	600	.080	L.F.	1.97	3.83	1.80	7.60	9.85
0150	8" diameter, original size		600	.080		3.35	3.83	1.80	8.98	11.35
0200	10" diameter, original size		600	.080		10.50	3.83	1.80	16.13	19.25
0250	12" diameter, original size		400	.120		6.85	5.75	2.70	15.30	19.05
0300	14" diameter, original size		400	.120		14.30	5.75	2.70	22.75	27.50
0350	16" diameter, original size	B-6C	300	.160		10.80	7.65	6.05	24.50	30
0400	18" diameter, original size	"	300	.160		13.70	7.65	6.05	27.40	33
1000	Pipe HDPE lining, make service line taps	B-6	4	6	Ea.	104	310	69.50	483.50	650

33 05 Common Work Results for Utilities

33 05 07 – Trenchless Installation of Utility Piping

33 05 07.23 Utility Boring and Jacking

		Crew	Daily Output	Labor-Hours	Unit	Material	Labor	Equipment	Total	Total Incl O&P
0010	**UTILITY BORING AND JACKING**									
0011	Casing only, 100' minimum,									
0020	not incl. jacking pits or dewatering									
0100	Roadwork, 1/2" thick wall, 24" diameter casing	B-42	20	3.200	L.F.	163	170	143	476	590
0200	36" diameter		16	4		252	213	179	644	795
0300	48" diameter		15	4.267		350	227	191	768	935
0500	Railroad work, 24" diameter		15	4.267		163	227	191	581	730
0600	36" diameter		14	4.571		252	243	204	699	865
0700	48" diameter		12	5.333		350	284	238	872	1,075
0900	For ledge, add								20%	20%
1000	Small diameter boring, 3", sandy soil	B-82	900	.018		44.50	.95	.13	45.58	50.50
1040	Rocky soil	"	500	.032		44.50	1.71	.23	46.44	52
1100	Prepare jacking pits, incl. mobilization & demobilization, minimum				Ea.				3,225	3,700
1101	Maximum				"				22,000	25,500

33 05 07.36 Microtunneling

		Crew	Daily Output	Labor-Hours	Unit	Material	Labor	Equipment	Total	Total Incl O&P
0010	**MICROTUNNELING**									
0011	Not including excavation, backfill, shoring,									
0020	or dewatering, average 50'/day, slurry method									
0100	24" to 48" outside diameter, minimum				L.F.				965	965
0110	Adverse conditions, add				"				500	500
1000	Rent microtunneling machine, average monthly lease				Month				97,500	107,000
1010	Operating technician				Day				630	705
1100	Mobilization and demobilization, minimum				Job				41,200	45,900
1110	Maximum				"				445,500	490,500

33 05 Common Work Results for Utilities

33 05 61 – Concrete Manholes

33 05 61.10 Storm Drainage Manholes, Frames and Covers

	33 05 61.10 Storm Drainage Manholes, Frames and Covers	Crew	Daily Output	Labor-Hours	Unit	Material	2023 Bare Costs Labor	Equipment	Total	Total Incl O&P
0010	**STORM DRAINAGE MANHOLES, FRAMES & COVERS**									
0020	Excludes footing, excavation, backfill (See line items for frame & cover)									
0050	Brick, 4' inside diameter, 4' deep	D-1	1	16	Ea.	1,475	835		2,310	2,875
0100	6' deep		.70	22.857		2,175	1,200		3,375	4,150
0150	8' deep		.50	32		2,825	1,675		4,500	5,625
0200	Add for 1' depth increase		4	4	V.L.F.	370	208		578	725
0400	Concrete blocks (radial), 4' ID, 4' deep		1.50	10.667	Ea.	480	555		1,035	1,350
0500	6' deep		1	16		625	835		1,460	1,925
0600	8' deep		.70	22.857		770	1,200		1,970	2,625
0700	For depths over 8', add		5.50	2.909	V.L.F.	76	152		228	310
0800	Concrete, cast in place, 4' x 4', 8" thick, 4' deep	C-14H	2	24	Ea.	785	1,375	14.90	2,174.90	2,925
0900	6' deep		1.50	32		1,150	1,850	19.85	3,019.85	4,000
1000	8' deep		1	48		1,625	2,750	30	4,405	5,925
1100	For depths over 8', add		8	6	V.L.F.	199	345	3.72	547.72	735
1110	Precast, 4' ID, 4' deep	B-22	4.10	7.317	Ea.	1,225	405	70.50	1,700.50	2,000
1120	6' deep		3	10		1,475	555	96.50	2,126.50	2,550
1130	8' deep		2	15		1,875	830	145	2,850	3,475
1140	For depths over 8', add		16	1.875	V.L.F.	167	104	18.10	289.10	360
1150	5' ID, 4' deep	B-6	3	8	Ea.	2,325	410	92.50	2,827.50	3,250
1160	6' deep		2	12		2,850	615	139	3,604	4,200
1170	8' deep		1.50	16		3,375	820	185	4,380	5,150
1180	For depths over 8', add		12	2	V.L.F.	340	103	23	466	555
1190	6' ID, 4' deep		2	12	Ea.	4,100	615	139	4,854	5,600
1200	6' deep		1.50	16		4,100	820	185	5,105	5,925
1210	8' deep		1	24		4,800	1,225	277	6,302	7,400
1220	For depths over 8', add		8	3	V.L.F.	440	154	34.50	628.50	755
1250	Slab tops, precast, 8" thick									
1300	4' diameter manhole	B-6	8	3	Ea.	285	154	34.50	473.50	585
1400	5' diameter manhole		7.50	3.200		540	164	37	741	880
1500	6' diameter manhole		7	3.429		925	176	39.50	1,140.50	1,325
3800	Steps, heavyweight cast iron, 7" x 9"	1 Bric	40	.200		21	11.50		32.50	40.50
3900	8" x 9"		40	.200		25	11.50		36.50	45
3928	12" x 10-1/2"		40	.200		86	11.50		97.50	112
4000	Standard sizes, galvanized steel		40	.200		29	11.50		40.50	49.50
4100	Aluminum		40	.200		37	11.50		48.50	58.50
4150	Polyethylene		40	.200		36	11.50		47.50	57
0300	Cleanout Access Housing, X-Hvy Dty, Ductile Iron	B-20	10	2.400		1,600	126		1,726	1,950
0306	Vandal Proof, Add					111			111	122
0313	Galvanized, Add					890			890	980

33 05 97 – Identification and Signage for Utilities

33 05 97.05 Utility Connection

		Crew	Daily Output	Labor-Hours	Unit	Material	Labor	Equipment	Total	Total Incl O&P
0010	**UTILITY CONNECTION**									
0020	Water, sanitary, stormwater, gas, single connection	B-14	1	48	Ea.	4,425	2,375	277	7,077	8,700
0030	Telecommunication	"	3	16	"	450	795	92.50	1,337.50	1,775

33 05 97.10 Utility Accessories

		Crew	Daily Output	Labor-Hours	Unit	Material	Labor	Equipment	Total	Total Incl O&P
0010	**UTILITY ACCESSORIES** G1030-805									
0400	Underground tape, detectable, reinforced, alum. foil core, 2"	1 Clab	150	.053	C.L.F.	2	2.52		4.52	5.95

33 11 Groundwater Sources

33 11 13 – Potable Water Supply Wells

33 11 13.10 Wells and Accessories		Crew	Daily Output	Labor-Hours	Unit	Material	2023 Bare Costs Labor	Equipment	Total	Total Incl O&P
0010	**WELLS & ACCESSORIES**									
0011	Domestic									
0100	Drilled, 4" to 6" diameter	B-23	120	.333	L.F.		15.90	10.40	26.30	35
0200	8" diameter	"	95.20	.420	"		20	13.10	33.10	44.50
0400	Gravel pack well, 40' deep, incl. gravel & casing, complete									
0500	24" diameter casing x 18" diameter screen	B-23	.13	308	Total	51,000	14,700	9,600	75,300	89,000
0600	36" diameter casing x 18" diameter screen		.12	333	"	52,500	15,900	10,400	78,800	93,000
0800	Observation wells, 1-1/4" riser pipe	↓	163	.245	V.L.F.	24	11.70	7.65	43.35	52.50
0900	For flush Buffalo roadway box, add	1 Skwk	16.60	.482	Ea.	69	29.50		98.50	121
1200	Test well, 2-1/2" diameter, up to 50' deep (15 to 50 GPM)	B-23	1.51	26.490	"	1,175	1,250	825	3,250	4,075
1300	Over 50' deep, add	"	121.80	.328	L.F.	31.50	15.65	10.25	57.40	69.50
1500	Pumps, installed in wells to 100' deep, 4" submersible									
1510	1/2 HP	Q-1	3.22	4.969	Ea.	965	320		1,285	1,525
1520	3/4 HP		2.66	6.015		1,000	390		1,390	1,675
1600	1 HP	↓	2.29	6.987		1,250	455		1,705	2,050
1700	1-1/2 HP	Q-22	1.60	10		1,600	650	1,350	3,600	4,200
1800	2 HP		1.33	12.030		2,200	780	1,625	4,605	5,375
1900	3 HP		1.14	14.035		2,725	910	1,875	5,510	6,400
2000	5 HP		1.14	14.035		3,025	910	1,875	5,810	6,750
2050	Remove and install motor only, 4 HP		1.14	14.035		2,000	910	1,875	4,785	5,625
3000	Pump, 6" submersible, 25' to 150' deep, 25 HP, 103 to 400 GPM		.89	17.978		12,300	1,175	2,425	15,900	18,000
3100	25' to 500' deep, 30 HP, 104 to 400 GPM	↓	.73	21.918	↓	14,500	1,425	2,950	18,875	21,300
8110	Well screen assembly, stainless steel, 2" diameter	B-23A	273	.088	L.F.	126	4.68	3.59	134.27	150
8120	3" diameter		253	.095		186	5.05	3.87	194.92	216
8130	4" diameter		200	.120		240	6.40	4.89	251.29	279
8140	5" diameter		168	.143		224	7.60	5.85	237.45	265
8150	6" diameter		126	.190		252	10.15	7.75	269.90	300
8160	8" diameter		98.50	.244		335	12.95	9.95	357.90	400
8170	10" diameter		73	.329		420	17.50	13.40	450.90	500
8180	12" diameter		62.50	.384		490	20.50	15.65	526.15	590
8190	14" diameter		54.30	.442		550	23.50	18	591.50	660
8200	16" diameter		48.30	.497		605	26.50	20.50	652	725
8210	18" diameter		39.20	.612		765	32.50	25	822.50	920
8220	20" diameter		31.20	.769		870	41	31.50	942.50	1,050
8230	24" diameter		23.80	1.008		1,075	53.50	41	1,169.50	1,300
8240	26" diameter		21	1.143		1,350	61	46.50	1,457.50	1,650
8244	Well casing or drop pipe, PVC, 1/2" diameter		550	.044		1.72	2.32	1.78	5.82	7.30
8245	3/4" diameter		550	.044		1.74	2.32	1.78	5.84	7.30
8246	1" diameter		550	.044		1.79	2.32	1.78	5.89	7.40
8247	1-1/4" diameter		520	.046		2.24	2.45	1.88	6.57	8.20
8248	1-1/2" diameter		490	.049		2.38	2.60	2	6.98	8.70
8249	1-3/4" diameter		380	.063		2.43	3.36	2.58	8.37	10.50
8250	2" diameter		280	.086		2.79	4.56	3.50	10.85	13.70
8252	3" diameter		260	.092		5.50	4.91	3.76	14.17	17.50
8254	4" diameter		205	.117		5.85	6.25	4.77	16.87	21
8255	5" diameter		170	.141		5.90	7.50	5.75	19.15	24
8256	6" diameter		130	.185		11.25	9.80	7.55	28.60	35.50
8258	8" diameter		100	.240		17.15	12.75	9.80	39.70	48.50
8260	10" diameter		73	.329		27.50	17.50	13.40	58.40	71.50
8262	12" diameter		62	.387		31.50	20.50	15.80	67.80	82.50
8300	Slotted PVC, 1-1/4" diameter		521	.046		3.80	2.45	1.88	8.13	9.90
8310	1-1/2" diameter		488	.049		3.94	2.62	2.01	8.57	10.45
8320	2" diameter	↓	273	.088	↓	5.10	4.68	3.59	13.37	16.50

33 11 Groundwater Sources

33 11 13 – Potable Water Supply Wells

33 11 13.10 Wells and Accessories

		Crew	Daily Output	Labor-Hours	Unit	Material	2023 Bare Costs Labor	Equipment	Total	Total Incl O&P
8330	3" diameter	B-23A	253	.095	L.F.	8.95	5.05	3.87	17.87	21.50
8340	4" diameter		200	.120		9.55	6.40	4.89	20.84	25.50
8350	5" diameter		168	.143		20.50	7.60	5.85	33.95	40.50
8360	6" diameter		126	.190		22	10.15	7.75	39.90	48
8370	8" diameter		98.50	.244		32.50	12.95	9.95	55.40	66.50
8400	Artificial gravel pack, 2" screen, 6" casing	B-23B	174	.138		5.95	7.35	7.85	21.15	26
8405	8" casing		111	.216		8.15	11.50	12.30	31.95	39.50
8410	10" casing		74.50	.322		11.25	17.15	18.35	46.75	58
8415	12" casing		60	.400		17.95	21.50	23	62.45	76.50
8420	14" casing		50.20	.478		18.35	25.50	27	70.85	88
8425	16" casing		40.70	.590		24	31.50	33.50	89	110
8430	18" casing		36	.667		29.50	35.50	38	103	127
8435	20" casing		29.50	.814		32.50	43.50	46.50	122.50	152
8440	24" casing		25.70	.934		37.50	49.50	53	140	174
8445	26" casing		24.60	.976		41.50	52	55.50	149	184
8450	30" casing		20	1.200		47.50	64	68.50	180	223
8455	36" casing		16.40	1.463		52	78	83.50	213.50	265
8500	Develop well		8	3	Hr.	400	160	171	731	870
8550	Pump test well		8	3		127	160	171	458	565
8560	Standby well	B-23A	8	3		131	160	122	413	515
8570	Standby, drill rig		8	3			160	122	282	370
8580	Surface seal well, concrete filled		1	24	Ea.	1,425	1,275	980	3,680	4,550
8590	Well test pump, install & remove	B-23	1	40			1,900	1,250	3,150	4,225
8600	Well sterilization, chlorine	2 Clab	1	16		82	755		837	1,225
8610	Well water pressure switch	1 Clab	12	.667		129	31.50		160.50	189
8630	Well water pressure switch with manual reset	"	12	.667		171	31.50		202.50	235
9950	See Section 31 23 19.40 for wellpoints									
9960	See Section 31 23 19.30 for drainage wells									

33 11 13.20 Water Supply Wells, Pumps

		Crew	Daily Output	Labor-Hours	Unit	Material	Labor	Equipment	Total	Total Incl O&P
0010	**WATER SUPPLY WELLS, PUMPS**									
0011	With pressure control									
1000	Deep well, jet, 42 gal. galvanized tank									
1040	3/4 HP	1 Plum	.80	10	Ea.	1,500	720		2,220	2,700
3000	Shallow well, jet, 30 gal. galvanized tank									
3040	1/2 HP	1 Plum	2	4	Ea.	1,200	288		1,488	1,750

33 14 Water Utility Transmission and Distribution

33 14 13 – Public Water Utility Distribution Piping

33 14 13.15 Water Supply, Ductile Iron Pipe

		Crew	Daily Output	Labor-Hours	Unit	Material	Labor	Equipment	Total	Total Incl O&P
0010	**WATER SUPPLY, DUCTILE IRON PIPE** R331113-80									
0020	Not including excavation or backfill									
2000	Pipe, class 50 water piping, 18' lengths									
2020	Mechanical joint, 4" diameter	B-21	200	.140	L.F.	101	7.65	.96	109.61	123
2040	6" diameter		160	.175		120	9.55	1.21	130.76	148
2060	8" diameter		133.33	.210		169	11.45	1.45	181.90	204
2080	10" diameter		114.29	.245		220	13.35	1.69	235.04	264
2100	12" diameter		105.26	.266		272	14.50	1.83	288.33	325
2120	14" diameter		100	.280		141	15.25	1.93	158.18	180
2140	16" diameter		72.73	.385		143	21	2.65	166.65	192
2160	18" diameter		68.97	.406		192	22	2.80	216.80	247
2170	20" diameter		57.14	.490		194	26.50	3.38	223.88	257

33 14 Water Utility Transmission and Distribution

33 14 13 – Public Water Utility Distribution Piping

33 14 13.15 Water Supply, Ductile Iron Pipe

		Crew	Daily Output	Labor-Hours	Unit	Material	2023 Bare Costs Labor	Equipment	Total	Total Incl O&P
2180	24" diameter	B-21	47.06	.595	L.F.	213	32.50	4.10	249.60	288
3000	Push-on joint, 4" diameter		400	.070		24	3.82	.48	28.30	32.50
3020	6" diameter		333.33	.084		23.50	4.58	.58	28.66	33.50
3040	8" diameter		200	.140		33	7.65	.96	41.61	49
3060	10" diameter		181.82	.154		51	8.40	1.06	60.46	70
3080	12" diameter		160	.175		54	9.55	1.21	64.76	75
3100	14" diameter		133.33	.210		54	11.45	1.45	66.90	78
3120	16" diameter		114.29	.245		57.50	13.35	1.69	72.54	85
3140	18" diameter		100	.280		64	15.25	1.93	81.18	95
3160	20" diameter		88.89	.315		66.50	17.20	2.17	85.87	101
3180	24" diameter		76.92	.364		92.50	19.85	2.51	114.86	134
8000	Piping, fittings, mechanical joint, AWWA C110									
8006	90° bend, 4" diameter	B-20	16	1.500	Ea.	258	79		337	400
8020	6" diameter	"	12.80	1.875		410	98.50		508.50	600
8040	8" diameter	B-21	10.67	2.624		670	143	18.10	831.10	975
8060	10" diameter		11.43	2.450		1,075	134	16.90	1,225.90	1,425
8080	12" diameter		10.53	2.659		1,525	145	18.30	1,688.30	1,900
8100	14" diameter		10	2.800		2,350	153	19.30	2,522.30	2,825
8120	16" diameter		7.27	3.851		2,850	210	26.50	3,086.50	3,475
8140	18" diameter		6.90	4.058		4,075	221	28	4,324	4,825
8160	20" diameter		5.71	4.904		4,950	267	34	5,251	5,850
8180	24" diameter		4.70	5.957		7,250	325	41	7,616	8,500
8200	Wye or tee, 4" diameter	B-20	10.67	2.249		555	118		673	785
8220	6" diameter	"	8.53	2.814		965	148		1,113	1,300
8240	8" diameter	B-21	7.11	3.938		1,350	215	27	1,592	1,825
8260	10" diameter		7.62	3.675		1,725	200	25.50	1,950.50	2,225
8280	12" diameter		7.02	3.989		3,225	218	27.50	3,470.50	3,875
8300	14" diameter		6.67	4.198		4,775	229	29	5,033	5,625
8320	16" diameter		4.85	5.773		5,050	315	40	5,405	6,075
8340	18" diameter		4.60	6.087		8,325	330	42	8,697	9,700
8360	20" diameter		3.81	7.349		9,825	400	50.50	10,275.50	11,500
8380	24" diameter		3.14	8.917		14,600	485	61.50	15,146.50	16,900
8398	45° bend, 4" diameter	B-20	16	1.500		255	79		334	400
8400	6" diameter	"	12.80	1.875		390	98.50		488.50	575
8405	8" diameter	B-21	10.67	2.624		570	143	18.10	731.10	865
8410	12" diameter		10.53	2.659		1,200	145	18.30	1,363.30	1,550
8420	16" diameter		7.27	3.851		2,425	210	26.50	2,661.50	3,000
8430	20" diameter		5.71	4.904		3,525	267	34	3,826	4,300
8440	24" diameter		4.70	5.957		4,925	325	41	5,291	5,950
8450	Decreaser, 6" x 4" diameter	B-20	14.22	1.688		355	88.50		443.50	525
8460	8" x 6" diameter	B-21	11.64	2.406		545	131	16.55	692.55	810
8470	10" x 6" diameter		13.33	2.101		725	115	14.45	854.45	985
8480	12" x 6" diameter		12.70	2.205		1,025	120	15.20	1,160.20	1,325
8490	16" x 6" diameter		10	2.800		1,275	153	19.30	1,447.30	1,650
8500	20" x 6" diameter		8.42	3.325		5,550	181	23	5,754	6,400
8552	For water utility valves see Section 33 14 19									
8700	Joint restraint, ductile iron mechanical joints									
8710	4" diameter	B-20	32	.750	Ea.	45	39.50		84.50	109
8720	6" diameter	"	25.60	.938		54	49.50		103.50	133
8730	8" diameter	B-21	21.33	1.313		82	71.50	9.05	162.55	207
8740	10" diameter		18.28	1.532		132	83.50	10.55	226.05	282
8750	12" diameter		16.84	1.663		171	90.50	11.45	272.95	335
8760	14" diameter		16	1.750		236	95.50	12.05	343.55	415

33 14 Water Utility Transmission and Distribution

33 14 13 – Public Water Utility Distribution Piping

33 14 13.15 Water Supply, Ductile Iron Pipe

		Crew	Daily Output	Labor-Hours	Unit	Material	2023 Bare Costs Labor	Equipment	Total	Total Incl O&P
8770	16" diameter	B-21	11.64	2.406	Ea.	299	131	16.55	446.55	545
8780	18" diameter		11.03	2.539		425	138	17.50	580.50	690
8785	20" diameter		9.14	3.063		525	167	21	713	850
8790	24" diameter		7.53	3.718		725	203	25.50	953.50	1,125
9600	Steel sleeve with tap, 4" diameter	B-20	3	8		550	420		970	1,225
9620	6" diameter		2	12		590	630		1,220	1,600
9630	8" diameter		2	12		750	630		1,380	1,775

33 14 13.25 Water Supply, Polyvinyl Chloride Pipe

		Crew	Daily Output	Labor-Hours	Unit	Material	2023 Bare Costs Labor	Equipment	Total	Total Incl O&P
0010	**WATER SUPPLY, POLYVINYL CHLORIDE PIPE** R331113-80									
0020	Not including excavation or backfill, unless specified									
2100	PVC pipe, Class 150, 1-1/2" diameter	Q-1A	750	.013	L.F.	1.43	.97		2.40	3.01
2120	2" diameter		686	.015		1.40	1.06		2.46	3.11
2140	2-1/2" diameter		500	.020		2.37	1.45		3.82	4.77
2160	3" diameter	B-20	430	.056		3.04	2.93		5.97	7.70
3010	AWWA C905, PR 100, DR 25									
3030	14" diameter	B-21	213	.131	L.F.	18.80	7.15	.91	26.86	32
3040	16" diameter		200	.140		25.50	7.65	.96	34.11	40.50
3050	18" diameter		160	.175		31	9.55	1.21	41.76	49.50
3060	20" diameter		133	.211		38.50	11.50	1.45	51.45	61.50
3070	24" diameter		107	.262		57.50	14.25	1.80	73.55	86.50
3080	30" diameter		80	.350		96.50	19.10	2.41	118.01	137
3090	36" diameter		80	.350		149	19.10	2.41	170.51	195
3100	42" diameter		60	.467		202	25.50	3.22	230.72	264
3200	48" diameter		60	.467		257	25.50	3.22	285.72	325
4520	Pressure pipe Class 150, SDR 18, AWWA C900, 4" diameter	B-20	380	.063		5.20	3.32		8.52	10.65
4530	6" diameter	"	316	.076		7.50	3.99		11.49	14.20
4540	8" diameter	B-21	264	.106		9.60	5.80	.73	16.13	20
4550	10" diameter		220	.127		13.05	6.95	.88	20.88	25.50
4560	12" diameter		186	.151		17.75	8.20	1.04	26.99	33
8000	Fittings with rubber gasket									
8003	Class 150, DR 18									
8006	90° bend, 4" diameter	B-20	100	.240	Ea.	57	12.60		69.60	82
8020	6" diameter	"	90	.267		102	14		116	133
8040	8" diameter	B-21	80	.350		197	19.10	2.41	218.51	247
8060	10" diameter		50	.560		385	30.50	3.86	419.36	470
8080	12" diameter		30	.933		570	51	6.45	627.45	710
8100	Tee, 4" diameter		90	.311		165	16.95	2.14	184.09	210
8120	6" diameter		80	.350		269	19.10	2.41	290.51	325
8140	8" diameter		70	.400		490	22	2.76	514.76	575
8160	10" diameter		40	.700		1,450	38	4.82	1,492.82	1,650
8180	12" diameter		20	1.400		2,075	76.50	9.65	2,161.15	2,400
8200	45° bend, 4" diameter	B-20	100	.240		73	12.60		85.60	99.50
8220	6" diameter	"	90	.267		134	14		148	168
8240	8" diameter	B-21	50	.560		335	30.50	3.86	369.36	415
8260	10" diameter		50	.560		655	30.50	3.86	689.36	770
8280	12" diameter		30	.933		1,025	51	6.45	1,082.45	1,200
8300	Reducing tee 6" x 4"		100	.280		171	15.25	1.93	188.18	213
8320	8" x 6"		90	.311		305	16.95	2.14	324.09	365
8330	10" x 6"		90	.311		267	16.95	2.14	286.09	320
8340	10" x 8"		90	.311		286	16.95	2.14	305.09	345
8350	12" x 6"		90	.311		360	16.95	2.14	379.09	425
8360	12" x 8"		90	.311		395	16.95	2.14	414.09	465

33 14 Water Utility Transmission and Distribution

33 14 13 – Public Water Utility Distribution Piping

	33 14 13.25 Water Supply, Polyvinyl Chloride Pipe	Crew	Daily Output	Labor-Hours	Unit	Material	2023 Bare Costs Labor	Equipment	Total	Total Incl O&P
8400	Tapped service tee (threaded type) 6" x 6" x 3/4"	B-21	100	.280	Ea.	130	15.25	1.93	147.18	168
8430	6" x 6" x 1"		90	.311		130	16.95	2.14	149.09	171
8440	6" x 6" x 1-1/2"		90	.311		130	16.95	2.14	149.09	171
8450	6" x 6" x 2"		90	.311		130	16.95	2.14	149.09	171
8460	8" x 8" x 3/4"		90	.311		191	16.95	2.14	210.09	238
8470	8" x 8" x 1"		90	.311		191	16.95	2.14	210.09	238
8480	8" x 8" x 1-1/2"		90	.311		191	16.95	2.14	210.09	238
8490	8" x 8" x 2"		90	.311		191	16.95	2.14	210.09	238
8500	Repair coupling 4"	B-20	100	.240		35.50	12.60		48.10	58
8520	6" diameter		90	.267		54.50	14		68.50	80.50
8540	8" diameter		50	.480		131	25		156	182
8560	10" diameter		50	.480		276	25		301	345
8580	12" diameter		50	.480		350	25		375	425
8600	Plug end 4"		100	.240		30.50	12.60		43.10	53
8620	6" diameter		90	.267		55.50	14		69.50	82
8640	8" diameter		50	.480		94	25		119	141
8660	10" diameter		50	.480		150	25		175	203
8680	12" diameter		50	.480		202	25		227	260
8700	PVC pipe, joint restraint									
8710	4" diameter	B-20	32	.750	Ea.	46.50	39.50		86	111
8720	6" diameter		25.60	.938		57.50	49.50		107	137
8730	8" diameter		21.33	1.125		83.50	59		142.50	181
8740	10" diameter		18.28	1.313		133	69		202	249
8750	12" diameter		16.84	1.425		140	75		215	266
8760	14" diameter		16	1.500		190	79		269	325
8770	16" diameter		11.64	2.062		256	108		364	445
8780	18" diameter		11.03	2.176		315	114		429	515
8785	20" diameter		9.14	2.626		445	138		583	695
8790	24" diameter		7.53	3.187		515	168		683	815
	33 14 13.35 Water Supply, HDPE									
0010	**WATER SUPPLY, HDPE**									
0011	Butt fusion joints, SDR 21 40' lengths not including excavation or backfill									
0100	4" diameter	B-22A	400	.100	L.F.	.91	5.45	1.80	8.16	11.10
0200	6" diameter		380	.105		1.97	5.70	1.89	9.56	12.75
0300	8" diameter		320	.125		3.35	6.80	2.24	12.39	16.25
0400	10" diameter		300	.133		10.50	7.25	2.39	20.14	25
0500	12" diameter		260	.154		6.85	8.35	2.76	17.96	23
0600	14" diameter	B-22B	220	.182		14.30	9.85	5.35	29.50	36.50
0700	16" diameter		180	.222		10.80	12.05	6.50	29.35	37
0800	18" diameter		140	.286		13.70	15.50	8.40	37.60	47.50
0850	20" diameter		130	.308		27	16.70	9	52.70	64.50
0900	24" diameter		100	.400		24.50	21.50	11.75	57.75	72.50
1000	Fittings									
1100	Elbows, 90 degrees									
1200	4" diameter	B-22A	32	1.250	Ea.	43	68	22.50	133.50	173
1300	6" diameter		28	1.429		37.50	77.50	25.50	140.50	185
1400	8" diameter		24	1.667		75	90.50	30	195.50	251
1500	10" diameter		18	2.222		112	121	40	273	345
1600	12" diameter		12	3.333		149	181	60	390	500
1700	14" diameter	B-22B	9	4.444		233	241	130	604	760
1800	16" diameter		6	6.667		730	360	196	1,286	1,550
1900	18" diameter		4	10		450	545	293	1,288	1,625

33 14 Water Utility Transmission and Distribution

33 14 13 – Public Water Utility Distribution Piping

33 14 13.35 Water Supply, HDPE

		Crew	Daily Output	Labor-Hours	Unit	Material	2023 Bare Costs Labor	2023 Bare Costs Equipment	Total	Total Incl O&P
2000	24" diameter	B-22B	3	13.333	Ea.	940	725	390	2,055	2,525
2100	Tees									
2200	4" diameter	B-22A	30	1.333	Ea.	25	72.50	24	121.50	162
2300	6" diameter		26	1.538		43	83.50	27.50	154	203
2400	8" diameter		22	1.818		64.50	98.50	32.50	195.50	254
2500	10" diameter		15	2.667		85	145	48	278	360
2600	12" diameter		10	4		355	217	72	644	795
2700	14" diameter	B-22B	8	5		420	271	147	838	1,025
2800	16" diameter		6	6.667		495	360	196	1,051	1,300
2900	18" diameter		4	10		605	545	293	1,443	1,800
3000	24" diameter		2	20		740	1,075	585	2,400	3,075
4100	Caps									
4110	4" diameter	B-22A	34	1.176	Ea.	23	64	21	108	144
4120	6" diameter		30	1.333		28	72.50	24	124.50	165
4130	8" diameter		26	1.538		46.50	83.50	27.50	157.50	207
4150	10" diameter		20	2		115	109	36	260	330
4160	12" diameter		14	2.857		139	155	51.50	345.50	440

33 14 17 – Site Water Utility Service Laterals

33 14 17.15 Tapping, Crosses and Sleeves

		Crew	Daily Output	Labor-Hours	Unit	Material	2023 Bare Costs Labor	2023 Bare Costs Equipment	Total	Total Incl O&P
0010	**TAPPING, CROSSES AND SLEEVES**									
4000	Drill and tap pressurized main (labor only)									
4100	6" main, 1" to 2" service	Q-1	3	5.333	Ea.		345		345	515
4150	8" main, 1" to 2" service	"	2.75	5.818	"		375		375	565
4500	Tap and insert gate valve									
4600	8" main, 4" branch	B-21	3.20	8.750	Ea.		475	60.50	535.50	775
4650	6" branch		2.70	10.370			565	71.50	636.50	925
4700	10" main, 4" branch		2.70	10.370			565	71.50	636.50	925
4750	6" branch		2.35	11.915			650	82	732	1,050
4800	12" main, 6" branch		2.35	11.915			650	82	732	1,050
4850	8" branch		2.35	11.915			650	82	732	1,050
7020	Crosses, 4" x 4"		37	.757		1,400	41.50	5.20	1,446.70	1,625
7030	6" x 4"		25	1.120		1,675	61	7.70	1,743.70	1,950
7040	6" x 6"		25	1.120		1,675	61	7.70	1,743.70	1,950
7060	8" x 6"		21	1.333		2,050	72.50	9.20	2,131.70	2,375
7080	8" x 8"		21	1.333		2,225	72.50	9.20	2,306.70	2,575
7100	10" x 6"		21	1.333		4,050	72.50	9.20	4,131.70	4,600
7120	10" x 10"		21	1.333		4,400	72.50	9.20	4,481.70	4,950
7140	12" x 6"		18	1.556		4,050	85	10.70	4,145.70	4,625
7160	12" x 12"		18	1.556		5,125	85	10.70	5,220.70	5,800
7180	14" x 6"		16	1.750		10,100	95.50	12.05	10,207.55	11,300
7200	14" x 14"		16	1.750		10,700	95.50	12.05	10,807.55	12,000
7220	16" x 6"		14	2		10,900	109	13.80	11,022.80	12,100
7240	16" x 10"		14	2		11,000	109	13.80	11,122.80	12,300
7260	16" x 16"		14	2		11,600	109	13.80	11,722.80	12,900
7280	18" x 6"		10	2.800		16,200	153	19.30	16,372.30	18,100
7300	18" x 12"		10	2.800		16,400	153	19.30	16,572.30	18,200
7320	18" x 18"		10	2.800		16,800	153	19.30	16,972.30	18,700
7340	20" x 6"		8	3.500		13,100	191	24	13,315	14,800
7360	20" x 12"		8	3.500		14,100	191	24	14,315	15,800
7380	20" x 20"		8	3.500		20,600	191	24	20,815	22,900
7400	24" x 6"		6	4.667		17,000	255	32	17,287	19,100
7420	24" x 12"		6	4.667		17,200	255	32	17,487	19,300

33 14 Water Utility Transmission and Distribution

33 14 17 – Site Water Utility Service Laterals

33 14 17.15 Tapping, Crosses and Sleeves		Crew	Daily Output	Labor-Hours	Unit	Material	2023 Bare Costs Labor	2023 Bare Costs Equipment	Total	Total Incl O&P
7440	24" x 18"	B-21	6	4.667	Ea.	26,100	255	32	26,387	29,100
7460	24" x 24"		6	4.667		26,700	255	32	26,987	29,800
7600	Cut-in sleeves with rubber gaskets, 4"		18	1.556		735	85	10.70	830.70	950
7620	6"		12	2.333		910	127	16.10	1,053.10	1,200
7640	8"		10	2.800		1,075	153	19.30	1,247.30	1,450
7660	10"		10	2.800		1,525	153	19.30	1,697.30	1,925
7680	12"		9	3.111		2,100	170	21.50	2,291.50	2,575
7800	Cut-in valves with rubber gaskets, 4"		18	1.556		510	85	10.70	605.70	700
7820	6"		12	2.333		660	127	16.10	803.10	935
7840	8"		10	2.800		910	153	19.30	1,082.30	1,250
7860	10"		10	2.800		1,375	153	19.30	1,547.30	1,750
7880	12"		9	3.111		1,725	170	21.50	1,916.50	2,150
7900	Tapping valve 4", MJ, ductile iron		18	1.556		645	85	10.70	740.70	845
7920	6", MJ, ductile iron		12	2.333		890	127	16.10	1,033.10	1,200
8000	Sleeves with rubber gaskets, 4" x 4"		37	.757		1,125	41.50	5.20	1,171.70	1,300
8010	6" x 4"		25	1.120		1,325	61	7.70	1,393.70	1,575
8020	6" x 6"		25	1.120		1,325	61	7.70	1,393.70	1,575
8030	8" x 4"		21	1.333		1,525	72.50	9.20	1,606.70	1,800
8040	8" x 6"		21	1.333		1,575	72.50	9.20	1,656.70	1,850
8060	8" x 8"		21	1.333		1,950	72.50	9.20	2,031.70	2,250
8070	10" x 4"		21	1.333		1,425	72.50	9.20	1,506.70	1,700
8080	10" x 6"		21	1.333		1,525	72.50	9.20	1,606.70	1,800
8090	10" x 8"		21	1.333		1,925	72.50	9.20	2,006.70	2,250
8100	10" x 10"		21	1.333		2,600	72.50	9.20	2,681.70	3,000
8110	12" x 4"		18	1.556		1,500	85	10.70	1,595.70	1,800
8120	12" x 6"		18	1.556		1,650	85	10.70	1,745.70	1,950
8130	12" x 8"		18	1.556		2,100	85	10.70	2,195.70	2,450
8135	12" x 10"		18	1.556		2,800	85	10.70	2,895.70	3,225
8140	12" x 12"		18	1.556		3,100	85	10.70	3,195.70	3,550
8160	14" x 6"		16	1.750		2,275	95.50	12.05	2,382.55	2,675
8180	14" x 14"		16	1.750		5,025	95.50	12.05	5,132.55	5,675
8200	16" x 6"		14	2		2,725	109	13.80	2,847.80	3,175
8220	16" x 10"		14	2		3,150	109	13.80	3,272.80	3,625
8240	16" x 16"		14	2		5,425	109	13.80	5,547.80	6,150
8260	18" x 6"		10	2.800		2,000	153	19.30	2,172.30	2,450
8280	18" x 12"		10	2.800		3,825	153	19.30	3,997.30	4,450
8300	18" x 18"		10	2.800		6,000	153	19.30	6,172.30	6,850
8320	20" x 6"		8	3.500		2,075	191	24	2,290	2,575
8340	20" x 12"		8	3.500		3,725	191	24	3,940	4,400
8360	20" x 20"		8	3.500		6,500	191	24	6,715	7,450
8380	24" x 6"		6	4.667		2,350	255	32	2,637	3,025
8400	24" x 12"		6	4.667		4,200	255	32	4,487	5,050
8420	24" x 18"		6	4.667		6,875	255	32	7,162	7,975
8440	24" x 24"	▼	6	4.667		10,500	255	32	10,787	11,900
8800	Hydrant valve box, 6' long	B-20	20	1.200		360	63		423	495
8820	8' long		18	1.333		415	70		485	565
8830	Valve box w/lid 4' deep		14	1.714		117	90		207	264
8840	Valve box and large base w/lid	▼	14	1.714	▼	360	90		450	530

33 14 Water Utility Transmission and Distribution

33 14 19 – Valves and Hydrants for Water Utility Service

33 14 19.10 Valves

		Crew	Daily Output	Labor-Hours	Unit	Material	2023 Bare Costs Labor	2023 Bare Costs Equipment	Total	Total Incl O&P
0010	**VALVES**, water distribution									
0011	See Sections 22 05 23.20 and 22 05 23.60									
3000	Butterfly valves with boxes, cast iron, mechanical joint									
3100	4" diameter	B-6	6	4	Ea.	1,050	206	46	1,302	1,500
3140	6" diameter		6	4		1,375	206	46	1,627	1,875
3180	8" diameter		6	4		1,750	206	46	2,002	2,300
3300	10" diameter		6	4		2,100	206	46	2,352	2,675
3340	12" diameter		6	4		3,275	206	46	3,527	3,950
3400	14" diameter		4	6		6,050	310	69.50	6,429.50	7,175
3440	16" diameter		4	6		9,600	310	69.50	9,979.50	11,100
3460	18" diameter		4	6		12,000	310	69.50	12,379.50	13,600
3480	20" diameter		4	6		15,800	310	69.50	16,179.50	17,900
3500	24" diameter		4	6		26,700	310	69.50	27,079.50	29,800
3510	30" diameter		4	6		16,900	310	69.50	17,279.50	19,100
3520	36" diameter		4	6		21,000	310	69.50	21,379.50	23,600
3530	42" diameter		4	6		26,600	310	69.50	26,979.50	29,800
3540	48" diameter		4	6		34,300	310	69.50	34,679.50	38,200
3600	With lever operator									
3610	4" diameter	B-6	6	4	Ea.	925	206	46	1,177	1,375
3614	6" diameter		6	4		1,275	206	46	1,527	1,750
3616	8" diameter		6	4		1,650	206	46	1,902	2,150
3618	10" diameter		6	4		2,000	206	46	2,252	2,525
3620	12" diameter		6	4		3,150	206	46	3,402	3,825
3622	14" diameter		4	6		5,675	310	69.50	6,054.50	6,775
3624	16" diameter		4	6		9,250	310	69.50	9,629.50	10,700
3626	18" diameter		4	6		11,600	310	69.50	11,979.50	13,300
3628	20" diameter		4	6		15,500	310	69.50	15,879.50	17,500
3630	24" diameter		4	6		26,300	310	69.50	26,679.50	29,400
3700	Check valves, flanged									
3710	4" diameter	B-6	6	4	Ea.	1,175	206	46	1,427	1,650
3714	6" diameter		6	4		2,350	206	46	2,602	2,950
3716	8" diameter		6	4		3,975	206	46	4,227	4,700
3718	10" diameter		6	4		7,575	206	46	7,827	8,675
3720	12" diameter		6	4		12,600	206	46	12,852	14,300
3726	18" diameter		4	6		33,600	310	69.50	33,979.50	37,500
3730	24" diameter		4	6		60,000	310	69.50	60,379.50	66,500
3800	Gate valves, C.I., 125 psi, mechanical joint, w/boxes									
3810	4" diameter	B-6	6	4	Ea.	1,600	206	46	1,852	2,125
3814	6" diameter		6	4		2,500	206	46	2,752	3,100
3816	8" diameter		6	4		5,025	206	46	5,277	5,875
3818	10" diameter		6	4		9,050	206	46	9,302	10,300
3820	12" diameter		6	4		12,300	206	46	12,552	13,900
3822	14" diameter		4	6		25,300	310	69.50	25,679.50	28,300
3824	16" diameter		4	6		35,700	310	69.50	36,079.50	39,800
3826	18" diameter		4	6		43,300	310	69.50	43,679.50	48,100
3828	20" diameter		4	6		60,000	310	69.50	60,379.50	66,500
3830	24" diameter		4	6		89,000	310	69.50	89,379.50	98,500
3831	30" diameter		4	6		58,500	310	69.50	58,879.50	65,000
3832	36" diameter		4	6		91,500	310	69.50	91,879.50	101,000

33 14 Water Utility Transmission and Distribution

33 14 19 – Valves and Hydrants for Water Utility Service

33 14 19.20 Valves

		Crew	Daily Output	Labor-Hours	Unit	Material	2023 Bare Costs Labor	Equipment	Total	Total Incl O&P
0010	**VALVES**									
0011	Special trim or use									
9000	Valves, gate valve, N.R.S. PIV with post, 4" diameter	B-6	6	4	Ea.	3,375	206	46	3,627	4,050
9020	6" diameter		6	4		4,275	206	46	4,527	5,050
9040	8" diameter		6	4		6,775	206	46	7,027	7,800
9060	10" diameter		6	4		10,800	206	46	11,052	12,300
9080	12" diameter		6	4		14,100	206	46	14,352	15,900
9100	14" diameter		6	4		26,800	206	46	27,052	29,900
9120	OS&Y, 4" diameter		6	4		1,050	206	46	1,302	1,525
9140	6" diameter		6	4		1,475	206	46	1,727	1,975
9160	8" diameter		6	4		1,625	206	46	1,877	2,125
9180	10" diameter		6	4		5,125	206	46	5,377	5,975
9200	12" diameter		6	4		3,675	206	46	3,927	4,400
9220	14" diameter		4	6		5,400	310	69.50	5,779.50	6,450
9400	Check valves, rubber disc, 2-1/2" diameter		6	4		545	206	46	797	955
9420	3" diameter		6	4		670	206	46	922	1,100
9440	4" diameter		6	4		1,175	206	46	1,427	1,650
9480	6" diameter		6	4		2,350	206	46	2,602	2,950
9500	8" diameter		6	4		3,975	206	46	4,227	4,700
9520	10" diameter		6	4		7,575	206	46	7,827	8,675
9540	12" diameter		6	4		12,600	206	46	12,852	14,300
9542	14" diameter		4	6		8,675	310	69.50	9,054.50	10,100
9700	Detector check valves, reducing, 4" diameter		6	4		2,525	206	46	2,777	3,125
9720	6" diameter		6	4		4,050	206	46	4,302	4,800
9740	8" diameter		6	4		5,550	206	46	5,802	6,450
9760	10" diameter		6	4		8,275	206	46	8,527	9,450
9800	Galvanized, 4" diameter		6	4		2,450	206	46	2,702	3,050
9820	6" diameter		6	4		3,575	206	46	3,827	4,300
9840	8" diameter		6	4		6,225	206	46	6,477	7,200
9860	10" diameter		6	4		11,200	206	46	11,452	12,700

33 16 Water Utility Storage Tanks

33 16 11 – Elevated Composite Water Storage Tanks

33 16 11.50 Elevated Water Storage Tanks

		Crew	Daily Output	Labor-Hours	Unit	Material	2023 Bare Costs Labor	Equipment	Total	Total Incl O&P
0010	**ELEVATED WATER STORAGE TANKS**									
0011	Not incl. pipe, pumps or foundation									
3000	Elevated water tanks, 100' to bottom capacity line, incl. painting									
3010	50,000 gallons				Ea.				185,000	204,000
3300	100,000 gallons								280,000	307,500
3400	250,000 gallons								751,500	826,500
3600	500,000 gallons								1,336,000	1,470,000
3700	750,000 gallons								1,622,000	1,783,500
3900	1,000,000 gallons								2,322,000	2,556,000

33 16 23 – Ground-Level Steel Water Storage Tanks

33 16 23.13 Steel Water Storage Tanks

		Crew	Daily Output	Labor-Hours	Unit	Material	2023 Bare Costs Labor	Equipment	Total	Total Incl O&P
0010	**STEEL WATER STORAGE TANKS**									
0910	Steel, ground level, ht./diam. less than 1, not incl. fdn., 100,000 gallons				Ea.				202,000	244,500
1000	250,000 gallons								295,500	324,000
1200	500,000 gallons								417,000	458,500
1250	750,000 gallons								538,000	591,500

33 16 Water Utility Storage Tanks

33 16 23 – Ground-Level Steel Water Storage Tanks

33 16 23.13 Steel Water Storage Tanks

		Crew	Daily Output	Labor-Hours	Unit	Material	2023 Bare Costs Labor	Equipment	Total	Total Incl O&P
1300	1,000,000 gallons				Ea.				558,000	725,500
1500	2,000,000 gallons								1,043,000	1,148,000
1600	4,000,000 gallons								2,121,000	2,333,000
1800	6,000,000 gallons								3,095,000	3,405,000
1850	8,000,000 gallons								4,068,000	4,475,000
1910	10,000,000 gallons								5,050,000	5,554,500
2100	Steel standpipes, ht./diam. more than 1,100' to overflow, no fdn.									
2200	500,000 gallons				Ea.				546,500	600,500
2400	750,000 gallons								722,500	794,500
2500	1,000,000 gallons								1,060,500	1,167,000
2700	1,500,000 gallons								1,749,000	1,923,000
2800	2,000,000 gallons								2,327,000	2,559,000

33 16 36 – Ground-Level Reinforced Concrete Water Storage Tanks

33 16 36.16 Prestressed Conc. Water Storage Tanks

		Crew	Daily Output	Labor-Hours	Unit	Material	Labor	Equipment	Total	Total Incl O&P
0010	**PRESTRESSED CONC. WATER STORAGE TANKS**									
0020	Not including fdn., pipe or pumps, 250,000 gallons				Ea.				299,000	329,500
0100	500,000 gallons								487,000	536,000
0300	1,000,000 gallons								707,000	807,500
0400	2,000,000 gallons								1,072,000	1,179,000
0600	4,000,000 gallons								1,706,000	1,877,000
0700	6,000,000 gallons								2,266,000	2,493,000
0750	8,000,000 gallons								2,924,000	3,216,000
0800	10,000,000 gallons								3,533,000	3,886,000

33 16 56 – Ground-Level Plastic Water Storage Cisterns

33 16 56.23 Plastic-Coated Fabric Pillow Water Tanks

		Crew	Daily Output	Labor-Hours	Unit	Material	Labor	Equipment	Total	Total Incl O&P
0010	**PLASTIC-COATED FABRIC PILLOW WATER TANKS**									
7000	Water tanks, vinyl coated fabric pillow tanks, freestanding, 5,000 gallons	4 Clab	4	8	Ea.	3,325	380		3,705	4,250
7100	Supporting embankment not included, 25,000 gallons	6 Clab	2	24		9,925	1,125		11,050	12,600
7200	50,000 gallons	8 Clab	1.50	42.667		15,200	2,025		17,225	19,700
7300	100,000 gallons	9 Clab	.90	80		107,000	3,775		110,775	123,500
7400	150,000 gallons		.50	144		119,500	6,800		126,300	141,500
7500	200,000 gallons		.40	180		131,500	8,500		140,000	157,000
7600	250,000 gallons		.30	240		159,000	11,300		170,300	192,000

33 31 Sanitary Sewerage Piping

33 31 11 – Public Sanitary Sewerage Gravity Piping

33 31 11.25 Sewage Collection, Polyvinyl Chloride Pipe

		Crew	Daily Output	Labor-Hours	Unit	Material	Labor	Equipment	Total	Total Incl O&P
0010	**SEWAGE COLLECTION, POLYVINYL CHLORIDE PIPE**									
0020	Not including excavation or backfill									
2000	20' lengths, SDR 35, B&S, 4" diameter	B-20	375	.064	L.F.	3.44	3.37		6.81	8.85
2040	6" diameter		350	.069		8.15	3.61		11.76	14.35
2080	13' lengths, SDR 35, B&S, 8" diameter		335	.072		9.90	3.77		13.67	16.50
2120	10" diameter	B-21	330	.085		12.05	4.63	.58	17.26	21
2160	12" diameter		320	.088		16.95	4.77	.60	22.32	26.50
2170	14" diameter		280	.100		33.50	5.45	.69	39.64	45.50
2200	15" diameter		240	.117		57	6.35	.80	64.15	73
2250	16" diameter		220	.127		49.50	6.95	.88	57.33	66
4000	Piping, DWV PVC, no exc./bkfill., 10' L, Sch 40, 4" diameter	B-20	375	.064		14.70	3.37		18.07	21
4010	6" diameter		350	.069		42.50	3.61		46.11	52
4020	8" diameter		335	.072		68	3.77		71.77	80.50

33 31 Sanitary Sewerage Piping

33 31 11 – Public Sanitary Sewerage Gravity Piping

33 31 11.37 Centrif. Cst. Fbgs-Reinf. Polymer Mort. Util. Pipe	Crew	Daily Output	Labor-Hours	Unit	Material	2023 Bare Costs Labor	Equipment	Total	Total Incl O&P
0010 **CENTRIF. CST. FBGS-REINF. POLYMER MORT. UTIL. PIPE**									
0020 Not including excavation or backfill									
3348 48" diameter, SN 46, 25psi	B-13B	40	1.400	L.F.	208	72	61.50	341.50	405
3354 54" diameter		40	1.400		340	72	61.50	473.50	550
3363 63" diameter		20	2.800		420	144	123	687	810
3418 18" diameter, 100psi		60	.933		147	48	41	236	279
3424 24" diameter		60	.933		162	48	41	251	295
3436 36" diameter		40	1.400		183	72	61.50	316.50	375
3444 44" diameter		40	1.400		201	72	61.50	334.50	395
3448 48" diameter		40	1.400		224	72	61.50	357.50	420

33 41 Subdrainage

33 41 16 – Subdrainage Piping

33 41 16.25 Piping, Subdrainage, Corrugated Metal

	Crew	Daily Output	Labor-Hours	Unit	Material	Labor	Equipment	Total	Total Incl O&P
0010 **PIPING, SUBDRAINAGE, CORRUGATED METAL**									
0021 Not including excavation and backfill									
2010 Aluminum, perforated									
2020 6" diameter, 18 ga.	B-20	380	.063	L.F.	8.05	3.32		11.37	13.80
2200 8" diameter, 16 ga.	"	370	.065		13.20	3.41		16.61	19.60
2220 10" diameter, 16 ga.	B-21	360	.078		16.50	4.24	.54	21.28	25
2240 12" diameter, 16 ga.		285	.098		18.50	5.35	.68	24.53	29
2260 18" diameter, 16 ga.		205	.137		27.50	7.45	.94	35.89	42.50
3000 Uncoated galvanized, perforated									
3020 6" diameter, 18 ga.	B-20	380	.063	L.F.	8.55	3.32		11.87	14.35
3200 8" diameter, 16 ga.	"	370	.065		10.25	3.41		13.66	16.40
3220 10" diameter, 16 ga.	B-21	360	.078		10.90	4.24	.54	15.68	18.90
3240 12" diameter, 16 ga.		285	.098		12.10	5.35	.68	18.13	22
3260 18" diameter, 16 ga.		205	.137		18.55	7.45	.94	26.94	32.50
4000 Steel, perforated, asphalt coated									
4020 6" diameter, 18 ga.	B-20	380	.063	L.F.	7.60	3.32		10.92	13.30
4030 8" diameter, 18 ga.	"	370	.065		11.75	3.41		15.16	18.05
4040 10" diameter, 16 ga.	B-21	360	.078		11.90	4.24	.54	16.68	20
4050 12" diameter, 16 ga.		285	.098		11.90	5.35	.68	17.93	22
4060 18" diameter, 16 ga.		205	.137		21.50	7.45	.94	29.89	35.50

33 41 16.30 Piping, Subdrainage, Plastic

	Crew	Daily Output	Labor-Hours	Unit	Material	Labor	Equipment	Total	Total Incl O&P
0010 **PIPING, SUBDRAINAGE, PLASTIC**									
0020 Not including excavation and backfill									
2100 Perforated PVC, 4" diameter	B-14	314	.153	L.F.	3.44	7.60	.88	11.92	16.05
2110 6" diameter		300	.160		8.15	7.95	.92	17.02	22
2120 8" diameter		290	.166		9	8.20	.96	18.16	23
2130 10" diameter		280	.171		11.15	8.50	.99	20.64	26
2140 12" diameter		270	.178		15.70	8.85	1.03	25.58	31.50

33 42 Stormwater Conveyance

33 42 11 – Stormwater Gravity Piping

33 42 11.40 Piping, Storm Drainage, Corrugated Metal		Crew	Daily Output	Labor-Hours	Unit	Material	2023 Bare Costs Labor	Equipment	Total	Total Incl O&P
0010	**PIPING, STORM DRAINAGE, CORRUGATED METAL**									
0020	Not including excavation or backfill									
2000	Corrugated metal pipe, galvanized									
2040	8" diameter, 16 ga.	B-14	330	.145	L.F.	8.40	7.20	.84	16.44	21
2060	10" diameter, 16 ga.		260	.185		8.75	9.15	1.07	18.97	24.50
2080	12" diameter, 16 ga.		210	.229		13.90	11.35	1.32	26.57	33.50
2100	15" diameter, 16 ga.		200	.240		14.70	11.90	1.38	27.98	35.50
2120	18" diameter, 16 ga.		190	.253		21.50	12.55	1.46	35.51	44.50
2140	24" diameter, 14 ga.		160	.300		24	14.90	1.73	40.63	50.50
2160	30" diameter, 14 ga.	B-13	120	.467		30.50	24	18.95	73.45	90.50
2180	36" diameter, 12 ga.		120	.467		34	24	18.95	76.95	94.50
2200	48" diameter, 12 ga.		100	.560		46	29	22.50	97.50	119
2220	60" diameter, 10 ga.	B-13B	75	.747		81	38.50	33	152.50	183
2240	72" diameter, 8 ga.	"	45	1.244		84	64	54.50	202.50	248
2500	Galvanized, uncoated, 20' lengths									
2520	8" diameter, 16 ga.	B-14	355	.135	L.F.	9.45	6.70	.78	16.93	21.50
2540	10" diameter, 16 ga.		280	.171		9.45	8.50	.99	18.94	24
2560	12" diameter, 16 ga.		220	.218		31.50	10.85	1.26	43.61	52
2580	15" diameter, 16 ga.		220	.218		30	10.85	1.26	42.11	50.50
2600	18" diameter, 16 ga.		205	.234		35.50	11.65	1.35	48.50	58
2620	24" diameter, 14 ga.		175	.274		40	13.60	1.58	55.18	66
2640	30" diameter, 14 ga.	B-13	130	.431		32.50	22	17.50	72	88
2660	36" diameter, 12 ga.		130	.431		37	22	17.50	76.50	93
2680	48" diameter, 12 ga.		110	.509		54.50	26.50	20.50	101.50	122
2690	60" diameter, 10 ga.	B-13B	78	.718		90	37	31.50	158.50	189
2780	End sections, 8" diameter	B-14	35	1.371	Ea.	95	68	7.90	170.90	215
2785	10" diameter		35	1.371		93	68	7.90	168.90	213
2790	12" diameter		35	1.371		111	68	7.90	186.90	232
2800	18" diameter		30	1.600		129	79.50	9.25	217.75	270
2810	24" diameter	B-13	25	2.240		218	115	91	424	510
2820	30" diameter		25	2.240		395	115	91	601	705
2825	36" diameter		20	2.800		525	144	114	783	915
2830	48" diameter		10	5.600		1,150	289	227	1,666	1,925
2835	60" diameter	B-13B	5	11.200		2,250	575	490	3,315	3,875
2840	72" diameter	"	4	14		2,600	720	615	3,935	4,600

33 42 11.60 Sewage/Drainage Collection, Concrete Pipe

		Crew	Daily Output	Labor-Hours	Unit	Material	Labor	Equipment	Total	Total Incl O&P
0010	**SEWAGE/DRAINAGE COLLECTION, CONCRETE PIPE**									
0020	Not including excavation or backfill									
1000	Non-reinforced pipe, extra strength, B&S or T&G joints									
1010	6" diameter	B-14	265.04	.181	L.F.	11.95	9	1.04	21.99	27.50
1020	8" diameter		224	.214		13.15	10.65	1.24	25.04	31.50
1030	10" diameter		216	.222		14.55	11.05	1.28	26.88	34
1040	12" diameter		200	.240		15.15	11.90	1.38	28.43	36
1050	15" diameter		180	.267		22	13.25	1.54	36.79	45.50
1060	18" diameter		144	.333		27.50	16.55	1.92	45.97	56.50
1070	21" diameter		112	.429		28.50	21.50	2.47	52.47	65.50
1080	24" diameter		100	.480		33	24	2.77	59.77	75
2000	Reinforced culvert, class 3, no gaskets									
2010	12" diameter	B-14	150	.320	L.F.	22	15.90	1.85	39.75	50
2020	15" diameter		150	.320		26.50	15.90	1.85	44.25	54.50
2030	18" diameter		132	.364		30.50	18.05	2.10	50.65	63
2035	21" diameter		120	.400		35.50	19.85	2.31	57.66	71.50

33 42 Stormwater Conveyance

33 42 11 – Stormwater Gravity Piping

33 42 11.60 Sewage/Drainage Collection, Concrete Pipe

		Crew	Daily Output	Labor-Hours	Unit	Material	2023 Bare Costs Labor	Equipment	Total	Total Incl O&P
2040	24" diameter	B-14	100	.480	L.F.	44	24	2.77	70.77	87
2045	27" diameter	B-13	92	.609		50.50	31.50	24.50	106.50	129
2050	30" diameter		88	.636		61	33	26	120	145
2060	36" diameter	↓	72	.778		104	40	31.50	175.50	208
2070	42" diameter	B-13B	68	.824		147	42.50	36	225.50	265
2080	48" diameter		64	.875		198	45	38.50	281.50	325
2085	54" diameter		56	1		201	51.50	44	296.50	345
2090	60" diameter		48	1.167		236	60	51.50	347.50	405
2100	72" diameter		40	1.400		340	72	61.50	473.50	550
2120	84" diameter		32	1.750		550	90	77	717	825
2140	96" diameter	↓	24	2.333		660	120	103	883	1,025
2200	With gaskets, class 3, 12" diameter	B-21	168	.167		24.50	9.10	1.15	34.75	41.50
2220	15" diameter		160	.175		29	9.55	1.21	39.76	47.50
2230	18" diameter		152	.184		33.50	10.05	1.27	44.82	53.50
2235	21" diameter		152	.184		39.50	10.05	1.27	50.82	59.50
2240	24" diameter	↓	136	.206		54	11.25	1.42	66.67	78
2260	30" diameter	B-13	88	.636		73	33	26	132	158
2270	36" diameter	"	72	.778		118	40	31.50	189.50	224
2290	48" diameter	B-13B	64	.875		217	45	38.50	300.50	350
2310	72" diameter	"	40	1.400		370	72	61.50	503.50	580
2330	Flared ends, 12" diameter	B-21	31	.903	Ea.	66	49.50	6.20	121.70	153
2340	15" diameter		25	1.120		71	61	7.70	139.70	178
2400	18" diameter		20	1.400		78.50	76.50	9.65	164.65	211
2420	24" diameter	↓	14	2		93.50	109	13.80	216.30	281
2440	36" diameter	B-13	10	5.600	↓	164	289	227	680	860
3080	Radius pipe, add to pipe prices, 12" to 60" diameter				L.F.	50%				
3090	Over 60" diameter, add				"	20%				
3500	Reinforced elliptical, 8' lengths, C507 class 3									
3520	14" x 23" inside, round equivalent 18" diameter	B-21	82	.341	L.F.	43.50	18.60	2.35	64.45	78.50
3524	18" x 29" inside, round equivalent 30" diameter	B-13	58	.966		61.50	50	39	150.50	185
3525	22" x 36" inside, round equivalent 30" diameter		58	.966		81	50	39	170	206
3530	24" x 38" inside, round equivalent 30" diameter		58	.966		81	50	39	170	206
3540	29" x 45" inside, round equivalent 36" diameter		52	1.077		111	55.50	43.50	210	253
3550	38" x 60" inside, round equivalent 48" diameter		38	1.474		228	76	60	364	430
3560	48" x 76" inside, round equivalent 60" diameter		26	2.154		297	111	87.50	495.50	585
3570	58" x 91" inside, round equivalent 72" diameter	↓	22	2.545	↓	415	131	103	649	770
3780	Concrete slotted pipe, class 4 mortar joint									
3800	12" diameter	B-21	168	.167	L.F.	36.50	9.10	1.15	46.75	55
3840	18" diameter	"	152	.184	"	45.50	10.05	1.27	56.82	66.50
3900	Concrete slotted pipe, Class 4 O-ring joint									
3940	12" diameter	B-21	168	.167	L.F.	29.50	9.10	1.15	39.75	47.50
3960	18" diameter	"	152	.184	"	47	10.05	1.27	58.32	68.50

33 42 13 – Stormwater Culverts

33 42 13.15 Oval Arch Culverts

		Crew	Daily Output	Labor-Hours	Unit	Material	2023 Bare Costs Labor	Equipment	Total	Total Incl O&P
0010	**OVAL ARCH CULVERTS**									
3000	Corrugated galvanized or aluminum, coated & paved									
3020	17" x 13", 16 ga., 15" equivalent	B-14	200	.240	L.F.	14.20	11.90	1.38	27.48	35
3040	21" x 15", 16 ga., 18" equivalent		150	.320		14.55	15.90	1.85	32.30	41.50
3060	28" x 20", 14 ga., 24" equivalent		125	.384		22	19.05	2.22	43.27	55.50
3080	35" x 24", 14 ga., 30" equivalent	↓	100	.480		27.50	24	2.77	54.27	68.50
3100	42" x 29", 12 ga., 36" equivalent	B-13	100	.560		25.50	29	22.50	77	96
3120	49" x 33", 12 ga., 42" equivalent	↓	90	.622		32.50	32	25.50	90	112

33 42 Stormwater Conveyance

33 42 13 – Stormwater Culverts

33 42 13.15 Oval Arch Culverts

		Crew	Daily Output	Labor-Hours	Unit	Material	2023 Bare Costs Labor	Equipment	Total	Total Incl O&P
3140	57" x 38", 12 ga., 48" equivalent	B-13	75	.747	L.F.	43	38.50	30.50	112	139
3160	Steel, plain oval arch culverts, plain									
3180	17" x 13", 16 ga., 15" equivalent	B-14	225	.213	L.F.	23	10.60	1.23	34.83	42
3200	21" x 15", 16 ga., 18" equivalent		175	.274		37.50	13.60	1.58	52.68	63.50
3220	28" x 20", 14 ga., 24" equivalent	↓	150	.320		16.95	15.90	1.85	34.70	44
3240	35" x 24", 14 ga., 30" equivalent	B-13	108	.519		22	26.50	21	69.50	87
3260	42" x 29", 12 ga., 36" equivalent		108	.519		39	26.50	21	86.50	106
3280	49" x 33", 12 ga., 42" equivalent		92	.609		47.50	31.50	24.50	103.50	126
3300	57" x 38", 12 ga., 48" equivalent		75	.747	↓	47.50	38.50	30.50	116.50	143
3320	End sections, 17" x 13"		22	2.545	Ea.	345	131	103	579	690
3340	42" x 29"	↓	17	3.294	"	460	170	134	764	905
3360	Multi-plate arch, steel	B-20	1690	.014	Lb.	1.08	.75		1.83	2.31

33 42 33 – Stormwater Curbside Drains and Inlets

33 42 33.13 Catch Basins

		Crew	Daily Output	Labor-Hours	Unit	Material	Labor	Equipment	Total	Total Incl O&P
0010	**CATCH BASINS**									
0011	Not including footing & excavation									
1600	Frames & grates, C.I., 24" square, 500 lb.	B-6	7.80	3.077	Ea.	1,050	158	35.50	1,243.50	1,425
1700	26" D shape, 600 lb.		7	3.429		1,950	176	39.50	2,165.50	2,450
1800	Light traffic, 18" diameter, 100 lb.		10	2.400		895	123	27.50	1,045.50	1,200
1900	24" diameter, 300 lb.		8.70	2.759		1,000	142	32	1,174	1,350
2000	36" diameter, 900 lb.		5.80	4.138		1,425	213	48	1,686	1,950
2100	Heavy traffic, 24" diameter, 400 lb.		7.80	3.077		945	158	35.50	1,138.50	1,325
2200	36" diameter, 1,150 lb.		3	8		2,900	410	92.50	3,402.50	3,875
2300	Mass. State standard, 26" diameter, 475 lb.		7	3.429		1,225	176	39.50	1,440.50	1,650
2400	30" diameter, 620 lb.		7	3.429		455	176	39.50	670.50	805
2500	Watertight, 24" diameter, 350 lb.		7.80	3.077		2,000	158	35.50	2,193.50	2,475
2600	26" diameter, 500 lb.		7	3.429		1,600	176	39.50	1,815.50	2,050
2700	32" diameter, 575 lb.	↓	6	4		1,100	206	46	1,352	1,550
2800	3 piece cover & frame, 10" deep,									
2900	1,200 lb., for heavy equipment	B-6	3	8	Ea.	1,300	410	92.50	1,802.50	2,150
3000	Raised for paving 1-1/4" to 2" high									
3100	4 piece expansion ring									
3200	20" to 26" diameter	1 Clab	3	2.667	Ea.	269	126		395	485
3300	30" to 36" diameter	"	3	2.667	"	430	126		556	665
3320	Frames and covers, existing, raised for paving, 2", including									
3340	row of brick, concrete collar, up to 12" wide frame	B-6	18	1.333	Ea.	63	68.50	15.40	146.90	188
3360	20" to 26" wide frame		11	2.182		95	112	25	232	300
3380	30" to 36" wide frame	↓	9	2.667		118	137	31	286	370
3400	Inverts, single channel brick	D-1	3	5.333		136	278		414	565
3500	Concrete		5	3.200		165	167		332	430
3600	Triple channel, brick		2	8		224	415		639	870
3700	Concrete	↓	3	5.333	↓	187	278		465	620

33 52 Hydrocarbon Transmission and Distribution

33 52 13 – Liquid Hydrocarbon Piping

33 52 13.16 Gasoline Piping		Crew	Daily Output	Labor-Hours	Unit	Material	2023 Bare Costs Labor	Equipment	Total	Total Incl O&P
0010	**GASOLINE PIPING**									
0020	Primary containment pipe, fiberglass-reinforced									
0030	Plastic pipe 15' & 30' lengths									
0040	2" diameter	Q-6	425	.056	L.F.	6.55	3.82		10.37	12.90
0050	3" diameter		400	.060		8.90	4.06		12.96	15.85
0060	4" diameter	↓	375	.064	↓	11.55	4.33		15.88	19.15
0100	Fittings									
0110	Elbows, 90° & 45°, bell ends, 2"	Q-6	24	1	Ea.	39.50	67.50		107	145
0120	3" diameter		22	1.091		51.50	74		125.50	167
0130	4" diameter		20	1.200		64.50	81.50		146	192
0200	Tees, bell ends, 2"		21	1.143		52	77.50		129.50	172
0210	3" diameter		18	1.333		59.50	90.50		150	200
0220	4" diameter		15	1.600		73	108		181	243
0230	Flanges bell ends, 2"		24	1		28	67.50		95.50	132
0240	3" diameter		22	1.091		35	74		109	149
0250	4" diameter		20	1.200		39	81.50		120.50	164
0260	Sleeve couplings, 2"		21	1.143		10.80	77.50		88.30	127
0270	3" diameter		18	1.333		17.05	90.50		107.55	154
0280	4" diameter		15	1.600		18.95	108		126.95	183
0290	Threaded adapters, 2"		21	1.143		17.70	77.50		95.20	134
0300	3" diameter		18	1.333		23	90.50		113.50	161
0310	4" diameter		15	1.600		33	108		141	198
0320	Reducers, 2"		27	.889		24	60		84	117
0330	3" diameter		22	1.091		24	74		98	137
0340	4" diameter	↓	20	1.200	↓	32	81.50		113.50	157
1010	Gas station product line for secondary containment (double wall)									
1100	Fiberglass reinforced plastic pipe 25' lengths									
1120	Pipe, plain end, 3" diameter	Q-6	375	.064	L.F.	32.50	4.33		36.83	42
1130	4" diameter		350	.069		26.50	4.64		31.14	36
1140	5" diameter		325	.074		29.50	5		34.50	40
1150	6" diameter	↓	300	.080	↓	33	5.40		38.40	44
1200	Fittings									
1230	Elbows, 90° & 45°, 3" diameter	Q-6	18	1.333	Ea.	137	90.50		227.50	286
1240	4" diameter		16	1.500		165	102		267	335
1250	5" diameter		14	1.714		159	116		275	345
1260	6" diameter		12	2		197	135		332	420
1270	Tees, 3" diameter		15	1.600		171	108		279	350
1280	4" diameter		12	2		163	135		298	380
1290	5" diameter		9	2.667		213	181		394	505
1300	6" diameter		6	4		300	271		571	735
1310	Couplings, 3" diameter		18	1.333		48.50	90.50		139	189
1320	4" diameter		16	1.500		110	102		212	272
1330	5" diameter		14	1.714		197	116		313	390
1340	6" diameter		12	2		310	135		445	540
1350	Cross-over nipples, 3" diameter		18	1.333		9.20	90.50		99.70	145
1360	4" diameter		16	1.500		11.25	102		113.25	163
1370	5" diameter		14	1.714		15.60	116		131.60	190
1380	6" diameter		12	2		16.30	135		151.30	220
1400	Telescoping, reducers, concentric 4" x 3"		18	1.333		39	90.50		129.50	178
1410	5" x 4"		17	1.412		84	95.50		179.50	236
1420	6" x 5"	↓	16	1.500		236	102		338	410

33 52 Hydrocarbon Transmission and Distribution

33 52 16 – Gas Hydrocarbon Piping

33 52 16.20 Piping, Gas Service and Distribution, P.E.	Crew	Daily Output	Labor-Hours	Unit	Material	2023 Bare Costs Labor	Equipment	Total	Total Incl O&P
0010 **PIPING, GAS SERVICE AND DISTRIBUTION, POLYETHYLENE**									
0020 Not including excavation or backfill									
1000 60 psi coils, compression coupling @ 100′, 1/2″ diameter, SDR 11	B-20A	608	.053	L.F.	.64	2.98		3.62	5.15
1010 1″ diameter, SDR 11		544	.059		1.73	3.33		5.06	6.85
1040 1-1/4″ diameter, SDR 11		544	.059		2.78	3.33		6.11	8
1100 2″ diameter, SDR 11		488	.066		4.68	3.71		8.39	10.70
1160 3″ diameter, SDR 11		408	.078		10.15	4.44		14.59	17.80
1500 60 psi 40′ joints with coupling, 3″ diameter, SDR 11	B-21A	408	.098		10.65	5.75	1.56	17.96	22
1540 4″ diameter, SDR 11		352	.114		10.85	6.65	1.81	19.31	24
1600 6″ diameter, SDR 11		328	.122		52.50	7.15	1.95	61.60	70.50
1640 8″ diameter, SDR 11		272	.147		87.50	8.60	2.35	98.45	112

33 61 Hydronic Energy Distribution

33 61 13 – Underground Hydronic Energy Distribution

33 61 13.20 Pipe Conduit, Prefabricated/Preinsulated	Crew	Daily Output	Labor-Hours	Unit	Material	2023 Bare Costs Labor	Equipment	Total	Total Incl O&P
0010 **PIPE CONDUIT, PREFABRICATED/PREINSULATED**									
0020 Does not include trenching, fittings or crane.									
0300 For cathodic protection, add 12 to 14%									
0310 of total built-up price (casing plus service pipe)									
0580 Polyurethane insulated system, 250°F max. temp.									
0620 Black steel service pipe, standard wt., 1/2″ insulation									
0660 3/4″ diam. pipe size	Q-17	54	.296	L.F.	121	19.35	1.19	141.54	163
0670 1″ diam. pipe size		50	.320		133	21	1.28	155.28	179
0680 1-1/4″ diam. pipe size		47	.340		149	22	1.37	172.37	199
0690 1-1/2″ diam. pipe size		45	.356		161	23	1.43	185.43	213
0700 2″ diam. pipe size		42	.381		167	25	1.53	193.53	223
0710 2-1/2″ diam. pipe size		34	.471		170	30.50	1.89	202.39	235
0720 3″ diam. pipe size		28	.571		197	37.50	2.29	236.79	275
0730 4″ diam. pipe size		22	.727		248	47.50	2.92	298.42	345
0740 5″ diam. pipe size		18	.889		315	58	3.56	376.56	440
0750 6″ diam. pipe size	Q-18	23	1.043		370	70.50	2.79	443.29	515
0760 8″ diam. pipe size		19	1.263		540	85.50	3.37	628.87	725
0770 10″ diam. pipe size		16	1.500		680	102	4.01	786.01	905
0780 12″ diam. pipe size		13	1.846		845	125	4.93	974.93	1,125
0790 14″ diam. pipe size		11	2.182		945	148	5.85	1,098.85	1,275
0800 16″ diam. pipe size		10	2.400		1,075	163	6.40	1,244.40	1,450
0810 18″ diam. pipe size		8	3		1,250	203	8	1,461	1,700
0820 20″ diam. pipe size		7	3.429		1,375	232	9.15	1,616.15	1,875
0830 24″ diam. pipe size		6	4		1,700	271	10.70	1,981.70	2,300
0900 For 1″ thick insulation, add					10%				
0940 For 1-1/2″ thick insulation, add					13%				
0980 For 2″ thick insulation, add					20%				
1500 Gland seal for system, 3/4″ diam. pipe size	Q-17	32	.500	Ea.	1,400	32.50	2.01	1,434.51	1,600
1510 1″ diam. pipe size		32	.500		1,400	32.50	2.01	1,434.51	1,600
1540 1-1/4″ diam. pipe size		30	.533		1,500	35	2.14	1,537.14	1,700
1550 1-1/2″ diam. pipe size		30	.533		1,500	35	2.14	1,537.14	1,700
1560 2″ diam. pipe size		28	.571		1,775	37.50	2.29	1,814.79	2,000
1570 2-1/2″ diam. pipe size		26	.615		1,925	40	2.47	1,967.47	2,175
1580 3″ diam. pipe size		24	.667		2,050	43.50	2.67	2,096.17	2,325
1590 4″ diam. pipe size		22	.727		2,425	47.50	2.92	2,475.42	2,750

33 61 Hydronic Energy Distribution

33 61 13 – Underground Hydronic Energy Distribution

33 61 13.20 Pipe Conduit, Prefabricated/Preinsulated		Crew	Daily Output	Labor-Hours	Unit	Material	2023 Bare Costs Labor	Equipment	Total	Total Incl O&P
1600	5" diam. pipe size	Q-17	19	.842	Ea.	3,000	55	3.38	3,058.38	3,375
1610	6" diam. pipe size	Q-18	26	.923		3,175	62.50	2.46	3,239.96	3,600
1620	8" diam. pipe size		25	.960		3,700	65	2.56	3,767.56	4,150
1630	10" diam. pipe size		23	1.043		4,300	70.50	2.79	4,373.29	4,825
1640	12" diam. pipe size		21	1.143		4,750	77.50	3.05	4,830.55	5,350
1650	14" diam. pipe size		19	1.263		5,325	85.50	3.37	5,413.87	6,000
1660	16" diam. pipe size		18	1.333		6,300	90.50	3.56	6,394.06	7,075
1670	18" diam. pipe size		16	1.500		6,675	102	4.01	6,781.01	7,500
1680	20" diam. pipe size		14	1.714		7,600	116	4.58	7,720.58	8,525
1690	24" diam. pipe size	↓	12	2	↓	8,425	135	5.35	8,565.35	9,475
2000	Elbow, 45° for system									
2020	3/4" diam. pipe size	Q-17	14	1.143	Ea.	920	74.50	4.58	999.08	1,125
2040	1" diam. pipe size		13	1.231		945	80.50	4.94	1,030.44	1,175
2050	1-1/4" diam. pipe size		11	1.455		1,075	95	5.85	1,175.85	1,325
2060	1-1/2" diam. pipe size		9	1.778		1,075	116	7.15	1,198.15	1,350
2070	2" diam. pipe size		6	2.667		1,150	174	10.70	1,334.70	1,550
2080	2-1/2" diam. pipe size		4	4		1,275	261	16.05	1,552.05	1,800
2090	3" diam. pipe size		3.50	4.571		1,475	299	18.35	1,792.35	2,075
2100	4" diam. pipe size		3	5.333		1,700	350	21.50	2,071.50	2,425
2110	5" diam. pipe size	↓	2.80	5.714		2,200	375	23	2,598	3,000
2120	6" diam. pipe size	Q-18	4	6		2,475	405	16	2,896	3,350
2130	8" diam. pipe size		3	8		3,600	540	21.50	4,161.50	4,800
2140	10" diam. pipe size		2.40	10		4,400	675	26.50	5,101.50	5,875
2150	12" diam. pipe size		2	12		5,800	815	32	6,647	7,625
2160	14" diam. pipe size		1.80	13.333		7,200	905	35.50	8,140.50	9,325
2170	16" diam. pipe size		1.60	15		8,575	1,025	40	9,640	11,000
2180	18" diam. pipe size		1.30	18.462		10,800	1,250	49.50	12,099.50	13,700
2190	20" diam. pipe size		1	24		13,600	1,625	64	15,289	17,400
2200	24" diam. pipe size	↓	.70	34.286	↓	17,000	2,325	91.50	19,416.50	22,300
2260	For elbow, 90°, add					25%				
2300	For tee, straight, add					85%	30%			
2340	For tee, reducing, add					170%	30%			
2380	For weldolet, straight, add					50%				
2400	Polyurethane insulation, 1"									
2410	FRP carrier and casing									
2420	4"	Q-5	18	.889	L.F.	71	58		129	165
2422	6"	Q-6	23	1.043		123	70.50		193.50	241
2424	8"		19	1.263		201	85.50		286.50	350
2426	10"		16	1.500		271	102		373	450
2428	12"	↓	13	1.846	↓	355	125		480	575
2430	FRP carrier and PVC casing									
2440	4"	Q-5	18	.889	L.F.	29.50	58		87.50	119
2444	8"	Q-6	19	1.263		63.50	85.50		149	198
2446	10"		16	1.500		91.50	102		193.50	252
2448	12"	↓	13	1.846	↓	125	125		250	325
2450	PVC carrier and casing									
2460	4"	Q-1	36	.444	L.F.	15.15	29		44.15	59.50
2462	6"	"	29	.552		21.50	36		57.50	77.50
2464	8"	Q-2	36	.667		30.50	45		75.50	101
2466	10"		32	.750		40	50.50		90.50	119
2468	12"	↓	31	.774	↓	48	52		100	131

33 63 Steam Energy Distribution

33 63 13 – Underground Steam and Condensate Distribution Piping

33 63 13.10 Calcium Silicate Insulated System	Crew	Daily Output	Labor-Hours	Unit	Material	2023 Bare Costs Labor	Equipment	Total	Total Incl O&P
0010 **CALCIUM SILICATE INSULATED SYSTEM**									
0011 High temp. (1200 degrees F)									
2840 Steel casing with protective exterior coating									
2850 6-5/8" diameter	Q-18	52	.462	L.F.	176	31.50	1.23	208.73	241
2860 8-5/8" diameter		50	.480		191	32.50	1.28	224.78	260
2870 10-3/4" diameter		47	.511		224	34.50	1.36	259.86	299
2880 12-3/4" diameter		44	.545		244	37	1.46	282.46	325
2890 14" diameter		41	.585		275	39.50	1.56	316.06	365
2900 16" diameter		39	.615		295	41.50	1.64	338.14	390
2910 18" diameter		36	.667		325	45	1.78	371.78	425
2920 20" diameter		34	.706		365	48	1.88	414.88	480
2930 22" diameter		32	.750		505	51	2	558	635
2940 24" diameter		29	.828		580	56	2.21	638.21	725
2950 26" diameter		26	.923		665	62.50	2.46	729.96	825
2960 28" diameter		23	1.043		820	70.50	2.79	893.29	1,025
2970 30" diameter		21	1.143		880	77.50	3.05	960.55	1,075
2980 32" diameter		19	1.263		985	85.50	3.37	1,073.87	1,200
2990 34" diameter		18	1.333		995	90.50	3.56	1,089.06	1,250
3000 36" diameter		16	1.500		1,075	102	4.01	1,181.01	1,325
3040 For multi-pipe casings, add					10%				
3060 For oversize casings, add					2%				
3400 Steel casing gland seal, single pipe									
3420 6-5/8" diameter	Q-18	25	.960	Ea.	2,675	65	2.56	2,742.56	3,050
3440 8-5/8" diameter		23	1.043		3,125	70.50	2.79	3,198.29	3,550
3450 10-3/4" diameter		21	1.143		3,500	77.50	3.05	3,580.55	3,975
3460 12-3/4" diameter		19	1.263		4,125	85.50	3.37	4,213.87	4,650
3470 14" diameter		17	1.412		4,575	95.50	3.77	4,674.27	5,200
3480 16" diameter		16	1.500		5,350	102	4.01	5,456.01	6,050
3490 18" diameter		15	1.600		5,950	108	4.27	6,062.27	6,725
3500 20" diameter		13	1.846		6,575	125	4.93	6,704.93	7,450
3510 22" diameter		12	2		7,400	135	5.35	7,540.35	8,325
3520 24" diameter		11	2.182		8,300	148	5.85	8,453.85	9,350
3530 26" diameter		10	2.400		9,475	163	6.40	9,644.40	10,600
3540 28" diameter		9.50	2.526		10,700	171	6.75	10,877.75	12,100
3550 30" diameter		9	2.667		10,900	181	7.10	11,088.10	12,300
3560 32" diameter		8.50	2.824		12,300	191	7.55	12,498.55	13,800
3570 34" diameter		8	3		13,300	203	8	13,511	15,000
3580 36" diameter		7	3.429		14,200	232	9.15	14,441.15	16,000
3620 For multi-pipe casings, add					5%				
4000 Steel casing anchors, single pipe									
4020 6-5/8" diameter	Q-18	8	3	Ea.	2,400	203	8	2,611	2,975
4040 8-5/8" diameter		7.50	3.200		2,500	217	8.55	2,725.55	3,075
4050 10-3/4" diameter		7	3.429		3,275	232	9.15	3,516.15	3,950
4060 12-3/4" diameter		6.50	3.692		3,500	250	9.85	3,759.85	4,225
4070 14" diameter		6	4		4,125	271	10.70	4,406.70	4,975
4080 16" diameter		5.50	4.364		4,775	296	11.65	5,082.65	5,700
4090 18" diameter		5	4.800		5,400	325	12.80	5,737.80	6,450
4100 20" diameter		4.50	5.333		5,950	360	14.25	6,324.25	7,100
4110 22" diameter		4	6		6,625	405	16	7,046	7,925
4120 24" diameter		3.50	6.857		7,225	465	18.30	7,708.30	8,625
4130 26" diameter		3	8		8,175	540	21.50	8,736.50	9,800
4140 28" diameter		2.50	9.600		9,000	650	25.50	9,675.50	10,900
4150 30" diameter		2	12		9,525	815	32	10,372	11,700

33 63 Steam Energy Distribution

33 63 13 – Underground Steam and Condensate Distribution Piping

33 63 13.10 Calcium Silicate Insulated System		Crew	Daily Output	Labor-Hours	Unit	Material	2023 Bare Costs Labor	Equipment	Total	Total Incl O&P
4160	32" diameter	Q-18	1.50	16	Ea.	11,400	1,075	42.50	12,517.50	14,200
4170	34" diameter		1	24		12,800	1,625	64	14,489	16,600
4180	36" diameter	↓	1	24	↓	13,900	1,625	64	15,589	17,800
4220	For multi-pipe, add					5%	20%			
4800	Steel casing elbow									
4820	6-5/8" diameter	Q-18	15	1.600	Ea.	3,400	108	4.27	3,512.27	3,925
4830	8-5/8" diameter		15	1.600		3,650	108	4.27	3,762.27	4,175
4850	10-3/4" diameter		14	1.714		4,400	116	4.58	4,520.58	5,025
4860	12-3/4" diameter		13	1.846		5,200	125	4.93	5,329.93	5,925
4870	14" diameter		12	2		5,600	135	5.35	5,740.35	6,350
4880	16" diameter		11	2.182		6,100	148	5.85	6,253.85	6,950
4890	18" diameter		10	2.400		6,950	163	6.40	7,119.40	7,900
4900	20" diameter		9	2.667		7,425	181	7.10	7,613.10	8,450
4910	22" diameter		8	3		8,000	203	8	8,211	9,125
4920	24" diameter		7	3.429		8,800	232	9.15	9,041.15	10,000
4930	26" diameter		6	4		9,650	271	10.70	9,931.70	11,000
4940	28" diameter		5	4.800		10,400	325	12.80	10,737.80	12,000
4950	30" diameter		4	6		10,500	405	16	10,921	12,100
4960	32" diameter		3	8		11,900	540	21.50	12,461.50	13,900
4970	34" diameter		2	12		13,100	815	32	13,947	15,600
4980	36" diameter	↓	2	12	↓	13,900	815	32	14,747	16,500
5500	Black steel service pipe, std. wt., 1" thick insulation									
5510	3/4" diameter pipe size	Q-17	54	.296	L.F.	110	19.35	1.19	130.54	150
5540	1" diameter pipe size		50	.320		113	21	1.28	135.28	156
5550	1-1/4" diameter pipe size		47	.340		142	22	1.37	165.37	192
5560	1-1/2" diameter pipe size		45	.356		149	23	1.43	173.43	200
5570	2" diameter pipe size		42	.381		162	25	1.53	188.53	217
5580	2-1/2" diameter pipe size		34	.471		169	30.50	1.89	201.39	234
5590	3" diameter pipe size		28	.571		148	37.50	2.29	187.79	221
5600	4" diameter pipe size		22	.727		155	47.50	2.92	205.42	245
5610	5" diameter pipe size	↓	18	.889		213	58	3.56	274.56	325
5620	6" diameter pipe size	Q-18	23	1.043	↓	229	70.50	2.79	302.29	360
6000	Black steel service pipe, std. wt., 1-1/2" thick insul.									
6010	3/4" diameter pipe size	Q-17	54	.296	L.F.	130	19.35	1.19	150.54	173
6040	1" diameter pipe size		50	.320		136	21	1.28	158.28	181
6050	1-1/4" diameter pipe size		47	.340		146	22	1.37	169.37	196
6060	1-1/2" diameter pipe size		45	.356		144	23	1.43	168.43	195
6070	2" diameter pipe size		42	.381		155	25	1.53	181.53	210
6080	2-1/2" diameter pipe size		34	.471		141	30.50	1.89	173.39	204
6090	3" diameter pipe size		28	.571		157	37.50	2.29	196.79	231
6100	4" diameter pipe size		22	.727		180	47.50	2.92	230.42	272
6110	5" diameter pipe size	↓	18	.889		241	58	3.56	302.56	355
6120	6" diameter pipe size	Q-18	23	1.043		252	70.50	2.79	325.29	385
6130	8" diameter pipe size		19	1.263		325	85.50	3.37	413.87	485
6140	10" diameter pipe size		16	1.500		420	102	4.01	526.01	615
6150	12" diameter pipe size	↓	13	1.846		480	125	4.93	609.93	715
6190	For 2" thick insulation, add					15%				
6220	For 2-1/2" thick insulation, add					25%				
6260	For 3" thick insulation, add				↓	30%				
6800	Black steel service pipe, ex. hvy. wt., 1" thick insul.									
6820	3/4" diameter pipe size	Q-17	50	.320	L.F.	131	21	1.28	153.28	176
6840	1" diameter pipe size		47	.340		139	22	1.37	162.37	188
6850	1-1/4" diameter pipe size		44	.364		154	24	1.46	179.46	206

33 63 Steam Energy Distribution

33 63 13 – Underground Steam and Condensate Distribution Piping

33 63 13.10 Calcium Silicate Insulated System		Crew	Daily Output	Labor-Hours	Unit	Material	2023 Bare Costs Labor	Equipment	Total	Total Incl O&P
6860	1-1/2" diameter pipe size	Q-17	42	.381	L.F.	155	25	1.53	181.53	210
6870	2" diameter pipe size		40	.400		171	26	1.60	198.60	229
6880	2-1/2" diameter pipe size		31	.516		140	33.50	2.07	175.57	207
6890	3" diameter pipe size		27	.593		161	38.50	2.38	201.88	237
6900	4" diameter pipe size		21	.762		199	50	3.06	252.06	296
6910	5" diameter pipe size		17	.941		187	61.50	3.77	252.27	300
6920	6" diameter pipe size	Q-18	22	1.091		181	74	2.91	257.91	310
7400	Black steel service pipe, ex. hvy. wt., 1-1/2" thick insul.									
7420	3/4" diameter pipe size	Q-17	50	.320	L.F.	97	21	1.28	119.28	139
7440	1" diameter pipe size		47	.340		122	22	1.37	145.37	169
7450	1-1/4" diameter pipe size		44	.364		134	24	1.46	159.46	184
7460	1-1/2" diameter pipe size		42	.381		131	25	1.53	157.53	183
7470	2" diameter pipe size		40	.400		140	26	1.60	167.60	195
7480	2-1/2" diameter pipe size		31	.516		130	33.50	2.07	165.57	196
7490	3" diameter pipe size		27	.593		144	38.50	2.38	184.88	218
7500	4" diameter pipe size		21	.762		183	50	3.06	236.06	278
7510	5" diameter pipe size		17	.941		252	61.50	3.77	317.27	375
7520	6" diameter pipe size	Q-18	22	1.091		253	74	2.91	329.91	390
7530	8" diameter pipe size		18	1.333		415	90.50	3.56	509.06	595
7540	10" diameter pipe size		15	1.600		390	108	4.27	502.27	590
7550	12" diameter pipe size		13	1.846		465	125	4.93	594.93	700
7590	For 2" thick insulation, add					13%				
7640	For 2-1/2" thick insulation, add					18%				
7680	For 3" thick insulation, add					24%				

33 63 13.20 Combined Steam Pipe With Condensate Return

		Crew	Daily Output	Labor-Hours	Unit	Material	Labor	Equipment	Total	Total Incl O&P
0010	**COMBINED STEAM PIPE WITH CONDENSATE RETURN**									
9010	8" and 4" in 24" case	Q-18	100	.240	L.F.	595	16.25	.64	611.89	675
9020	6" and 3" in 20" case		104	.231		500	15.65	.62	516.27	575
9030	3" and 1-1/2" in 16" case		110	.218		375	14.80	.58	390.38	435
9040	2" and 1-1/4" in 12-3/4" case		114	.211		315	14.25	.56	329.81	365
9050	1-1/2" and 1-1/4" in 10-3/4" case		116	.207		370	14	.55	384.55	430
9100	Steam pipe only (no return)									
9110	6" in 18" case	Q-18	108	.222	L.F.	405	15.05	.59	420.64	475
9120	4" in 14" case		112	.214		315	14.50	.57	330.07	365
9130	3" in 14" case		114	.211		299	14.25	.56	313.81	350
9140	2-1/2" in 12-3/4" case		118	.203		278	13.75	.54	292.29	325
9150	2" in 12-3/4" case		122	.197		263	13.30	.53	276.83	310

Division Notes

		CREW	DAILY OUTPUT	LABOR-HOURS	UNIT	BARE COSTS				TOTAL INCL O&P
						MAT.	LABOR	EQUIP.	TOTAL	

Estimating Tips

This section involves equipment and construction costs for air, noise, and odor pollution control systems. These systems may be interrelated and care must be taken that the complete systems are estimated. For example, air pollution equipment may include dust and air-entrained particles that have to be collected. The vacuum systems could be noisy, requiring silencers to reduce noise pollution, and the collected solids have to be disposed of to prevent solid pollution.

Reference Numbers

Reference numbers are shown at the beginning of some major classifications. These numbers refer to related items in the Reference Section. The reference information may be an estimating procedure, an alternate pricing method, or technical information.

Division 44

Pollution & Waste Control Equipment

Same Data. Simplified.

Enjoy the convenience and efficiency of accessing your costs anywhere:

- **Skip the multiplier** by setting your location
- **Quickly search,** edit, favorite and share costs
- **Stay on top of price changes** with automatic updates

Discover more at rsmeans.com/online

No part of this cost data may be reproduced, stored in a retrieval system, or transmitted in any form or by any means without prior written permission of Gordian.

44 11 Particulate Control Equipment

44 11 16 – Fugitive Dust Barrier Systems

44 11 16.10 Dust Collection Systems		Crew	Daily Output	Labor-Hours	Unit	Material	2023 Bare Costs Labor	Equipment	Total	Total Incl O&P
0010	**DUST COLLECTION SYSTEMS** Commercial/Industrial									
0120	Central vacuum units									
0130	Includes stand, filters and motorized shaker									
0200	500 CFM, 10" inlet, 2 HP	Q-20	2.40	8.333	Ea.	4,200	535		4,735	5,425
0220	1,000 CFM, 10" inlet, 3 HP		2.20	9.091		4,475	580		5,055	5,800
0240	1,500 CFM, 10" inlet, 5 HP		2	10		4,450	640		5,090	5,825
0260	3,000 CFM, 13" inlet, 10 HP		1.50	13.333		6,700	855		7,555	8,650
0280	5,000 CFM, 16" inlet, 2 @ 10 HP		1	20		15,500	1,275		16,775	18,900
1000	Vacuum tubing, galvanized									
1100	2-1/8" OD, 16 ga.	Q-9	440	.036	L.F.	3.76	2.30		6.06	7.60
1110	2-1/2" OD, 16 ga.		420	.038		4.07	2.40		6.47	8.10
1120	3" OD, 16 ga.		400	.040		4.15	2.53		6.68	8.35
1130	3-1/2" OD, 16 ga.		380	.042		6.35	2.66		9.01	11
1140	4" OD, 16 ga.		360	.044		7.30	2.81		10.11	12.25
1150	5" OD, 14 ga.		320	.050		10.35	3.16		13.51	16.10
1160	6" OD, 14 ga.		280	.057		12.50	3.61		16.11	19.20
1170	8" OD, 14 ga.		200	.080		19.35	5.05		24.40	29
1180	10" OD, 12 ga.		160	.100		56.50	6.30		62.80	71.50
1190	12" OD, 12 ga.		120	.133		53	8.40		61.40	71
1200	14" OD, 12 ga.		80	.200		60	12.65		72.65	85
1940	Hose, flexible wire reinforced rubber									
1956	3" diam.	Q-9	400	.040	L.F.	8.05	2.53		10.58	12.65
1960	4" diam.		360	.044		9.80	2.81		12.61	15.05
1970	5" diam.		320	.050		12.25	3.16		15.41	18.25
1980	6" diam.		280	.057		12.50	3.61		16.11	19.20
2000	90° elbow, slip fit									
2110	2-1/8" diam.	Q-9	70	.229	Ea.	16.75	14.45		31.20	40
2120	2-1/2" diam.		65	.246		23.50	15.55		39.05	49.50
2130	3" diam.		60	.267		32	16.85		48.85	60.50
2140	3-1/2" diam.		55	.291		39	18.35		57.35	70.50
2150	4" diam.		50	.320		48.50	20		68.50	84
2160	5" diam.		45	.356		92	22.50		114.50	135
2170	6" diam.		40	.400		127	25.50		152.50	178
2180	8" diam.		30	.533		242	33.50		275.50	315
2400	45° elbow, slip fit									
2410	2-1/8" diam.	Q-9	70	.229	Ea.	14.65	14.45		29.10	37.50
2420	2-1/2" diam.		65	.246		21.50	15.55		37.05	47.50
2430	3" diam.		60	.267		26	16.85		42.85	54
2440	3-1/2" diam.		55	.291		33	18.35		51.35	63.50
2450	4" diam.		50	.320		42.50	20		62.50	77.50
2460	5" diam.		45	.356		71.50	22.50		94	113
2470	6" diam.		40	.400		97	25.50		122.50	145
2480	8" diam.		35	.457		190	29		219	253
2800	90° TY, slip fit thru 6" diam.									
2810	2-1/8" diam.	Q-9	42	.381	Ea.	32.50	24		56.50	72
2820	2-1/2" diam.		39	.410		42.50	26		68.50	86
2830	3" diam.		36	.444		56.50	28		84.50	105
2840	3-1/2" diam.		33	.485		71.50	30.50		102	125
2850	4" diam.		30	.533		154	33.50		187.50	221
2860	5" diam.		27	.593		196	37.50		233.50	272
2870	6" diam.		24	.667		267	42		309	355
2880	8" diam., butt end					565			565	625
2890	10" diam., butt end					655			655	720

44 11 Particulate Control Equipment

44 11 16 – Fugitive Dust Barrier Systems

44 11 16.10 Dust Collection Systems

		Crew	Daily Output	Labor-Hours	Unit	Material	2023 Bare Costs Labor	Equipment	Total	Total Incl O&P
2900	12" diam., butt end				Ea.	655			655	720
2910	14" diam., butt end					2,325			2,325	2,550
2920	6" x 4" diam., butt end					163			163	179
2930	8" x 4" diam., butt end					310			310	340
2940	10" x 4" diam., butt end					405			405	445
2950	12" x 4" diam., butt end					465			465	510
3100	90° elbow, butt end, segmented									
3110	8" diam., butt end, segmented				Ea.	635			635	695
3120	10" diam., butt end, segmented					605			605	665
3130	12" diam., butt end, segmented					207			207	228
3140	14" diam., butt end, segmented					264			264	290
3200	45° elbow, butt end, segmented									
3210	8" diam., butt end, segmented				Ea.	106			106	117
3220	10" diam., butt end, segmented					218			218	239
3230	12" diam., butt end, segmented					119			119	131
3240	14" diam., butt end, segmented					810			810	890
3400	All butt end fittings require one coupling per joint.									
3410	Labor for fitting included with couplings.									
3460	Compression coupling, galvanized, neoprene gasket									
3470	2-1/8" diam.	Q-9	44	.364	Ea.	15.90	23		38.90	52
3480	2-1/2" diam.		44	.364		15.90	23		38.90	52
3490	3" diam.		38	.421		18.45	26.50		44.95	60.50
3500	3-1/2" diam.		35	.457		19.30	29		48.30	64.50
3510	4" diam.		33	.485		21	30.50		51.50	69
3520	5" diam.		29	.552		25.50	35		60.50	80.50
3530	6" diam.		26	.615		29.50	39		68.50	91
3540	8" diam.		22	.727		53	46		99	128
3550	10" diam.		20	.800		67.50	50.50		118	150
3560	12" diam.		18	.889		75	56		131	168
3570	14" diam.		16	1		113	63		176	219
3800	Air gate valves, galvanized									
3810	2-1/8" diam.	Q-9	30	.533	Ea.	110	33.50		143.50	172
3820	2-1/2" diam.		28	.571		119	36		155	186
3830	3" diam.		26	.615		127	39		166	199
3840	4" diam.		23	.696		147	44		191	228
3850	6" diam.		18	.889		205	56		261	310

44 11 96 – Dry Plate Electrostatic Precipitator Equipment

44 11 96.10 Electrostatic Precipitators

		Crew	Daily Output	Labor-Hours	Unit	Material	2023 Bare Costs Labor	Equipment	Total	Total Incl O&P
0010	**ELECTROSTATIC PRECIPITATORS**									
4100	Smoke pollution control									
4110	Exhaust air volume									
4120	1 to 2.4 MCFM	Q-10	2.15	11.163	MCFM	28,800	730		29,530	32,800
4130	2.4 to 4.8 MCFM		2.70	8.889		58,500	580		59,080	65,500
4140	4.8 to 7.2 MCFM		3.60	6.667		80,000	435		80,435	88,500
4150	7.2 to 12 MCFM		5.40	4.444		139,000	291		139,291	153,000

Division Notes

	CREW	DAILY OUTPUT	LABOR-HOURS	UNIT	BARE COSTS				TOTAL INCL O&P
					MAT.	LABOR	EQUIP.	TOTAL	

Estimating Tips
This division contains information about water and wastewater equipment and systems, which was formerly located in Division 44. The main areas of focus are total wastewater treatment plants and components of wastewater treatment plants. Also included in this section are oil/water separators for wastewater treatment.

Reference Numbers
Reference numbers are shown at the beginning of some major classifications. These numbers refer to related items in the Reference Section. The reference information may be an estimating procedure, an alternate pricing method, or technical information.

Same Data. Simplified.
Enjoy the convenience and efficiency of accessing your costs anywhere:
- **Skip the multiplier** by setting your location
- **Quickly search**, edit, favorite and share costs
- **Stay on top of price changes** with automatic updates

Discover more at rsmeans.com/online

No part of this cost data may be reproduced, stored in a retrieval system, or transmitted in any form or by any means without prior written permission of Gordian.

46 23 Grit Removal And Handling Equipment

46 23 23 – Vortex Grit Removal Equipment

46 23 23.10 Rainwater Filters

		Crew	Daily Output	Labor-Hours	Unit	Material	2023 Bare Costs Labor	2023 Bare Costs Equipment	Total	Total Incl O&P
0010	**RAINWATER FILTERS**									
0100	42 gal./min	B-21	3.50	8	Ea.	60,000	435	55	60,490	66,500
0200	65 gal./min		3.50	8		60,000	435	55	60,490	66,500
0300	208 gal./min		3.50	8		60,000	435	55	60,490	66,500

46 25 Oil and Grease Separation and Removal Equipment

46 25 13 – Coalescing Oil-Water Separators

46 25 13.20 Oil/Water Separators

		Crew	Daily Output	Labor-Hours	Unit	Material	Labor	Equipment	Total	Total Incl O&P
0010	**OIL/WATER SEPARATORS**									
0020	Underground, tank only									
0030	Excludes excavation, backfill & piping									
0100	200 GPM	B-21	3.50	8	Ea.	60,000	435	55	60,490	66,500
0110	400 GPM		3.25	8.615		74,000	470	59.50	74,529.50	82,000
0120	600 GPM		2.75	10.182		107,500	555	70	108,125	119,500
0130	800 GPM		2.50	11.200		132,500	610	77	133,187	146,500
0140	1,000 GPM		2	14		138,500	765	96.50	139,361.50	154,000
0150	1,200 GPM		1.50	18.667		164,000	1,025	129	165,154	182,000
0160	1,500 GPM		1	28		199,500	1,525	193	201,218	222,000

46 25 16 – API Oil-Water Separators

46 25 16.10 Oil/Water Separators

		Crew	Daily Output	Labor-Hours	Unit	Material	Labor	Equipment	Total	Total Incl O&P
0010	**OIL/WATER SEPARATORS**									
0020	Complete system, not including excavation and backfill									
0100	Treated capacity 0.2 C.F./second	B-22	1	30	Ea.	11,700	1,650	290	13,640	15,700
0200	0.5 C.F./second	B-13	.75	74.667		15,500	3,850	3,025	22,375	26,200
0300	1.0 C.F./second		.60	93.333		20,700	4,800	3,800	29,300	34,100
0400	2.4 to 3.0 C.F./second		.30	187		34,700	9,625	7,575	51,900	61,000
0500	11 C.F./second		.17	329		28,800	17,000	13,400	59,200	71,500
0600	22 C.F./second	B-13	.10	560		47,900	28,900	22,700	99,500	120,500

Assemblies Section

Table of Contents

Table No.	Page
A SUBSTRUCTURE	
A2020 Basement Walls	
A2020 220 Subdrainage Piping	504
D SERVICES	
D2020 Domestic Water Distribution	
D2020 265 Solar, Closed Loop, Add-On Hot Water Systems	507
D2020 270 Solar, Drainback, Hot Water Systems	509
D2020 275 Solar, Draindown, Hot Water Systems	511
D2020 280 Solar, Recirculation, Domestic Hot Water Systems	513
D2020 285 Thermosyphon, Hot Water	515
D2020 290 Solar, Hot Water, Air To Water Heat Exchange	517
D2020 295 Solar, Closed Loop, Hot Water Systems	519
D3010 Energy Supply	
D3010 510 Apartment Building Heating - Fin Tube Radiation	520
D3010 520 Commercial Building Heating - Fin Tube Radiation	521
D3010 530 Commercial Bldg. Heating - Terminal Unit Heaters	522
D3010 650 Solar, Closed Loop, Space/Hot Water Systems	525
D3010 660 Solar Swimming Pool Heater Systems	527
D3010 675 Air To Water Heat Exchange	529
D3020 Heat Generating Systems	
D3020 102 Small Heating Systems, Hydronic, Electric Boilers	530
D3020 104 Large Heating Systems, Hydronic, Electric Boilers	531
D3020 108 Heating Systems, Unit Heaters	532
D3020 110 Heating System, Fin Tube Radiation	533
D3020 126 Electric Boiler, Hot Water	534
D3020 128 Electric Boiler, Steam	535
D3020 130 Boiler, Cast Iron, Hot Water, Gas	536
D3020 134 Boiler, Cast Iron, Steam, Gas	537
D3020 136 Boiler, Cast Iron, Hot Water, Gas/Oil	537
D3020 138 Boiler, Cast Iron, Steam, Gas/Oil	537
D3020 330 Circulating Pump Systems, End Suction	538
D3020 340 Circulating Pump Systems, Double Suction	538
D3030 Cooling Generating Systems	
D3030 110 Chilled Water, Air Cooled Condenser Systems	539
D3030 115 Chilled Water, Cooling Tower Systems	541
D3030 130 Reciprocating Chiller, Water Cooled	543
D3030 135 Reciprocating Chiller, Air Cooled	543
D3030 140 Centrifugal Chiller, Water Cooled	544
D3030 145 Gas Absorption Chiller, Water Cooled	545
D3030 150 Steam Absorption Chiller, Water Cooled	545
D3030 310 Galvanized Draw Through Cooling Tower	546
D3030 320 Fiberglass Draw Through Cooling Tower	546
D3030 330 Stainless Steel Draw Through Cooling Tower	546
D3040 Distribution Systems	
D3040 106 Field Fabricated Air Handling Unit	547
D3040 108 Field Fabricated VAV Air Handling Unit	548
D3040 110 Central Station Air Handling Unit	549
D3040 112 Central Station Air Handling Unit, VAV	550
D3040 114 Rooftop Air Handling Unit	551
D3040 116 Rooftop Air Handling Unit, VAV	552
D3040 118 Fan Coil A/C Unit, Two Pipe	553
D3040 120 Fan Coil A/C Unit, Two Pipe, Electric Heat	553
D3040 122 Fan Coil A/C Unit, Four Pipe	554
D3040 124 Fan Coil A/C, Horizontal, Duct Mount, 2 Pipe	554
D3040 126 Fan Coil A/C, Horiz., Duct Mount, 2 Pipe, Elec. Ht.	554
D3040 128 Fan Coil A/C, Horizontal, Duct Mount, 4 Pipe	554
D3040 132 VAV Terminal, Cooling Only	555
D3040 134 VAV Terminal, Hot Water Reheat	555
D3040 136 Fan Powered VAV Terminal, Cooling Only	555
D3040 138 Fan Powered VAV Terminal, Hot Water Reheat	556
D3040 220 Centrifugal In Line Fan Systems	557
D3040 230 Utility Set Fan Systems	557
D3040 240 Roof Exhaust Fan Systems	558
D3040 250 Commercial/Industrial Vacuum Dust Collection	559
D3040 260 Kitchen Exhaust/Make-Up Air	560
D3040 610 Heat Exchanger, Plate Type	561
D3040 620 Heat Exchanger, Shell & Tube	561
D3050 Terminal & Package Units	
D3050 120 Unit Heaters, Gas	562
D3050 130 Unit Heaters, Hydronic	562
D3050 140 Cabinet Unit Heaters, Hydronic	563
D3050 150 Rooftop Single Zone Unit Systems	564
D3050 155 Rooftop Multizone Unit Systems	566
D3050 160 Self-contained, Water Cooled Unit Systems	568
D3050 165 Self-contained, Air Cooled Unit Systems	570
D3050 170 Split Systems With Air Cooled Condensing Units	572
D3050 175 Rooftop Air Conditioner, Const. Volume	574
D3050 180 Rooftop Air Conditioner, Variable Air Volume	574
D3050 185 Computer Room Cooling Units	575
D3050 201 Packaged A/C, Elec. Ht., Const. Volume	575
D3050 202 Packaged Air Conditioner, Elect. Heat, VAV	576
D3050 203 Packaged A/C, Hot Wtr. Heat, Const. Volume	576
D3050 204 Packaged A/C, Hot Wtr. Heat, VAV	576
D3050 210 AC Unit, Package, Elec. Ht., Water Cooled	577
D3050 215 AC Unit, Package, Elec. Ht., Water Cooled, VAV	577
D3050 220 AC Unit, Package, Hot Water Coil, Water Cooled	578
D3050 225 AC Unit, Package, HW Coil, Water Cooled, VAV	578
D3050 230 Heat Pump, Water Source, Central Station	579
D3050 235 Heat Pump, Water Source, Console	579
D3050 240 Heat Pump, Horizontal, Duct Mounted	579
D3050 245 Heat Pump, Rooftop, Air/Air	580
D3050 255 Thru-Wall A/C Unit	581
D3050 260 Thru-Wall Heat Pump	581
D3090 Other HVAC Systems/Equip	
D3090 310 Fume Hood Exhaust Systems	582
D3090 320 Garage Exhaust Systems	583
D3090 750 Seismic Concrete Equipment Pads	584

Table of Contents

Table No.	Page
G BUILDING SITEWORK	
G1030 Site Earthwork	
G1030 805 Trenching Common Earth	588
G1030 806 Trenching Loam & Sandy Clay	590
G1030 807 Trenching Sand & Gravel	592
G1030 815 Pipe Bedding	594
G3010 Water Supply	
G3010 110 Water Distribution Piping	596
G3020 Sanitary Sewer	
G3020 110 Drainage & Sewage Piping	597
G3030 Storm Sewer	
G3030 210 Manholes & Catch Basins	599
G3060 Fuel Distribution	
G3060 110 Gas Service Piping	601
G3060 310 Fiberglass Fuel Tank, Double Wall	602
G3060 320 Steel Fuel Tank, Double Wall	604
G3060 325 Steel Tank, Above Ground, Single Wall	605
G3060 330 Steel Tank, Above Ground, Double Wall	605

RSMeans data: Assemblies— How They Work

Assemblies estimating provides a fast and reasonably accurate way to develop construction costs. An assembly is the grouping of individual work items — with appropriate quantities — to provide a cost for a major construction component in a convenient unit of measure.

An assemblies estimate is often used during early stages of design development to compare the cost impact of various design alternatives on total building cost.

Assemblies estimates are also used as an efficient tool to verify construction estimates.

Assemblies estimates do not require a completed design or detailed drawings. Instead, they are based on the general size of the structure and other known parameters of the project. The degree of accuracy of an assemblies estimate is generally within +/- 15%.

Most assemblies consist of three major elements: a graphic, the system components, and the cost data itself. The **graphic** is a visual representation showing the typical appearance of the assembly

❶ Unique 12-Character Identifier

Our assemblies are identified by a **unique 12-character identifier**. The assemblies are numbered using UNIFORMAT II, ASTM Standard E1557. The first five characters represent this system to level three. The last seven characters represent further breakdown in order to arrange items in understandable groups of similar tasks. Line numbers are consistent across all of our publications, so a line number in any assemblies data set will always refer to the same item.

❷ Reference Box

Information is available in the Reference Section to assist the estimator with estimating procedures, alternate pricing methods, and additional technical information.

The **Reference Box** indicates the exact location of this information in the Reference Section. The "R" stands for "reference," and the remaining characters are the line numbers.

❸ Narrative Descriptions

Our assemblies descriptions appear in two formats: narrative and table. **Narrative descriptions** are shown in a hierarchical structure to make them readable. In order to read a complete description, read up through the indents to the top of the section. Include everything that is above and to the left that is not contradicted by information below.

D30 HVAC
D3010 Energy Supply

Basis for Heat Loss Estimate, Apartment Type Structures:

1. Masonry walls and flat roof are insulated. U factor is assumed at .08.
2. Window glass area taken as BOCA minimum, 1/10th of floor area. Double insulating glass with 1/4" air space, U = .65.
3. Infiltration = 0.3 C.F. per hour per S.F. of net wall.
4. Concrete floor loss is 2 BTUH per S.F.
5. Temperature difference taken as 70°F.
6. Ventilating or makeup air has not been included and must be added if desired. Air shafts are not used.

System Components	QUANTITY	UNIT	COST EACH		
			MAT.	INST.	TOTAL
❶ SYSTEM D3010 510 1760 HEATING SYSTEM, FIN TUBE RADIATION, FORCED HOT WATER 1,000 S.F. AREA, 10,000 C.F. VOLUME					
Boiler, oil fired, CI, burner, ctrls/insul/breech/pipe/fttng/valves, 109 MBH	1.000	Ea.	4,812.50	4,812.50	9,625
Circulating pump, CI flange connection, 1/12 HP	1.000	Ea.	680	258	938
Expansion tank, painted steel, ASME 18 Gal capacity	1.000	Ea.	855	111	966
Storage tank, steel, above ground, 275 Gal capacity w/supports	1.000	Ea.	2,075	310	2,385
Copper tubing type L, solder joint, hanger 10' OC, 3/4" diam	100.000	L.F.	705	1,130	1,835
Radiation, 3/4" copper tube w/alum fin baseboard pkg, 7" high	30.000	L.F.	259.50	810	1,069.50
Pipe covering, calcium silicate w/cover, 1' wall, 3/4' diam	100.000	L.F.	695	845	1,540
TOTAL			10,082	8,276.50	18,358.50
COST PER S.F.			10.08	8.28	18.36

D3010 510	Apartment Building Heating - Fin Tube Radiation		COST PER S.F.		
			MAT.	INST.	TOTAL
1740	Heating systems, fin tube radiation, forced hot water				
1760	1,000 S.F. area, 10,000 C.F. volume		10.10	8.28	18.38
1800	10,000 S.F. area, 100,000 C.F. volume	❷ R235000-10	4.32	4.98	9.30
1840	20,000 S.F. area, 200,000 C.F. volume		4.20	5.60	9.80
1880	30,000 S.F. area, 300,000 C.F. volume	R235000-20	4.10	5.40	9.50
1890					

For supplemental customizable square foot estimating forms, visit: RSMeans.com/2023books

498

in question. It is frequently accompanied by additional explanatory technical information describing the class of items. The **System Components** is a listing of the individual tasks that make up the assembly, including the quantity and unit of measure for each item, along with the cost of material and installation. The **Assemblies data** below lists prices for other similar systems with dimensional and/or size variations.

All of our assemblies costs represent the cost for the installing contractor. An allowance for profit has been added to all material, labor, and equipment rental costs. A markup for labor burdens, including workers' compensation, fixed overhead, and business overhead, is included with installation costs.

The information in RSMeans cost data represents a "national average" cost. This data should be modified to the project location using the **City Cost Indexes** or **Location Factors** tables found in the Reference Section.

④ Unit of Measure

All RSMeans data: Assemblies include a typical **Unit of Measure** used for estimating that item. For instance, for continuous footings or foundation walls the unit is linear feet (L.F.). For spread footings the unit is each (Ea.). The estimator needs to take special care that the unit in the data matches the unit in the takeoff. Abbreviations and unit conversions can be found in the Reference Section.

⑤ System Components

System Components are listed separately to detail what is included in the development of the total system price.

D30 HVAC
D3010 Energy Supply

Basis for Heat Loss Estimate, Apartment Type Structures:
1. Masonry walls and flat roof are insulated. U factor is assumed at .08.
2. Window glass area taken as BOCA minimum, 1/10th of floor area. Double insulating glass with 1/4" air space, U = .65.
3. Infiltration = 0.3 C.F. per hour per S.F. of net wall.
4. Concrete floor loss is 2 BTUH per S.F.
5. Temperature difference taken as 70°F.
6. Ventilating or makeup air has not been included and must be added if desired. Air shafts are not used.

System Components	QUANTITY	UNIT	COST EACH		
			MAT.	INST.	TOTAL
SYSTEM D3010 510 1760 HEATING SYSTEM, FIN TUBE RADIATION, FORCED HOT WATER 1,000 S.F. AREA, 10,000 C.F. VOLUME					
Boiler, oil fired, CI, burner, ctrls/insul/breech/pipe/ftng/valves, 109 MBH	1.000	Ea.	4,812.50	4,812.50	9,625
Circulating pump, CI flange connection, 1/12 HP	1.000	Ea.	680	258	938
Expansion tank, painted steel, ASME 18 Gal capacity	1.000	Ea.	855	111	966
Storage tank, steel, above ground, 275 Gal capacity w/supports	1.000	Ea.	2,075	310	2,385
Copper tubing type L, solder joint, hanger 10' OC, 3/4" diam	100.000	L.F.	705	1,130	1,835
Radiation, 3/4" copper tube w/alum fin baseboard pkg, 7" high	30.000	L.F.	259.50	810	1,069.50
Pipe covering, calcium silicate w/cover, 1' wall, 3/4" diam	100.000	L.F.	695	845	1,540
TOTAL			10,082	8,276.50	18,358.50
COST PER S.F.			10.08	8.28	18.36

D3010 510	Apartment Building Heating - Fin Tube Radiation		COST PER S.F.		
			MAT.	INST.	TOTAL
1740	Heating systems, fin tube radiation, forced hot water				
1760	1,000 S.F. area, 10,000 C.F. volume		10.10	8.28	18.38
1800	10,000 S.F. area, 100,000 C.F. volume	R235000 -10	4.32	4.98	9.30
1840	20,000 S.F. area, 200,000 C.F. volume		4.20	5.60	9.80
1880	30,000 S.F. area, 300,000 C.F. volume	R235000 -20	4.10	5.40	9.50
1890					

RSMeans data: Assemblies—How They Work (Continued)

Sample Estimate

This sample demonstrates the elements of an estimate, including a tally of the RSMeans data lines. Published assemblies costs include all markups for labor burden and profit for the installing contractor. This estimate adds a summary of the markups applied by a general contractor on the installing contractor's work. These figures represent the total cost to the owner. The location factor with RSMeans data is applied at the bottom of the estimate to adjust the cost of the work to a specific location.

Project Name:	Interior Fit-out, ABC Office			
Location:	Anywhere, USA		Date: 1/1/2023	STD
Assembly Number	Description	Qty.	Unit	Subtotal
❶ C1010 124 1200	Wood partition, 2 x 4 @ 16" OC w/5/8" FR gypsum board	560	S.F.	$3,656.80
C1020 114 1800	Metal door & frame, flush hollow core, 3'-0" x 7'-0"	2	Ea.	$2,370.00
C3010 230 0080	Painting, brushwork, primer & 2 coats	1,120	S.F.	$1,556.80
C3020 410 0140	Carpet, tufted, nylon, roll goods, 12' wide, 26 oz	240	S.F.	$703.20
C3030 210 6000	Acoustic ceilings, 24" x 48" tile, tee grid suspension	200	S.F.	$1,896.00
D5020 125 0560	Receptacles incl plate, box, conduit, wire, 20 A duplex	8	Ea.	$2,844.00
D5020 125 0720	Light switch incl plate, box, conduit, wire, 20 A single pole	2	Ea.	$692.00
D5020 210 0560	Fluorescent fixtures, recess mounted, 20 per 1000 SF	200	S.F.	$3,310.00
	Assembly Subtotal			$17,028.80
	Sales Tax @ ❷	5 %		$ 425.72
	General Requirements @ ❸	7 %		$ 1,192.02
	Subtotal A			$18,646.54
	GC Overhead @ ❹	5 %		$ 932.33
	Subtotal B			$19,578.86
	GC Profit @ ❺	5 %		$ 978.94
	Subtotal C			$20,557.81
	Adjusted by Location Factor ❻	112.5		$ 23,127.53
	Architects Fee @ ❼	8 %		$ 1,850.20
	Contingency @ ❽	15 %		$ 3,469.13
	Project Total Cost			$ 28,446.86

This estimate is based on an interactive spreadsheet. You are free to download it and adjust it to your methodology. A copy of this spreadsheet is available at **RSMeans.com/2023books**.

❶ Work Performed
The body of the estimate shows the RSMeans data selected, including line numbers, a brief description of each item, its takeoff quantity and unit, and the total installed cost, including the installing contractor's overhead and profit.

❷ Sales Tax
If the work is subject to state or local sales taxes, the amount must be added to the estimate. In a conceptual estimate, it can be assumed that one half of the total represents material costs. Therefore, apply the sales tax rate to 50% of the assembly subtotal.

❸ General Requirements
This item covers project-wide needs provided by the general contractor. These items vary by project but may include temporary facilities and utilities, security, testing, project cleanup, etc. In assemblies estimates a percentage is used—typically between 5% and 15% of project cost.

❹ General Contractor Overhead
This entry represents the general contractor's markup on all work to cover project administration costs.

❺ General Contractor Profit
This entry represents the General Contractor's profit on all work performed. The value included here can vary widely by project and is influenced by the General Contractor's perception of the project's financial risk and market conditions.

❻ Location Factor
RSMeans published data are based on national average costs. If necessary, adjust the total cost of the project using a location factor from the "Location Factor" table or the "City Cost Indexes" table found in the Reference Section. Use location factors if the work is general, covering the work of multiple trades. If the work is by a single trade (e.g., masonry), use the more specific data found in the City Cost Indexes.

To adjust costs by location factors, multiply the base cost by the factor and divide by 100.

❼ Architect's Fee
If appropriate, add the design cost to the project estimate. These fees vary based on project complexity and size. Typical design and engineering fees can be found in the Reference Section.

❽ Contingency
A factor for contingency may be added to any estimate to represent the cost of unknowns that may occur between the time that the estimate is performed and the time the project is constructed. The amount of the allowance will depend on the stage of design at which the estimate is done, as well as the contractor's assessment of the risk involved.

A Substructure

Same Data. Simplified.

Enjoy the convenience and efficiency of accessing your costs anywhere:
- **Skip the multiplier** by setting your location
- **Quickly search,** edit, favorite and share costs
- **Stay on top of price changes** with automatic updates

Discover more at rsmeans.com/online

No part of this cost data may be reproduced, stored in a retrieval system, or transmitted in any form or by any means without prior written permission of Gordian.

A20 Basement Construction

A2020 Basement Walls

A2020 220	Subdrainage Piping	COST PER L.F.		
		MAT.	INST.	TOTAL
2000	Piping, excavation & backfill excluded, PVC, perforated			
2110	3" diameter	3.78	5.05	8.83
2130	4" diameter	3.78	5.05	8.83
2140	5" diameter	8.95	5.40	14.35
2150	6" diameter	8.95	5.40	14.35
3000	Metal alum. or steel, perforated asphalt coated			
3150	6" diameter	8.85	4.96	13.81
3160	8" diameter	14.50	5.10	19.60
3170	10" diameter	18.15	6.95	25.10
3180	12" diameter	20.50	8.75	29.25
3220	18" diameter	30.50	12.15	42.65
4000	Corrugated HDPE tubing			
4130	4" diameter	1.60	.94	2.54
4150	6" diameter	4.14	1.25	5.39
4160	8" diameter	15.20	1.61	16.81
4180	12" diameter	8.95	5.55	14.50
4200	15" diameter	11.25	6.30	17.55
4220	18" diameter	18.60	9.05	27.65

Same Data. Simplified.

Enjoy the convenience and efficiency of accessing your costs anywhere:
- **Skip the multiplier** by setting your location
- **Quickly search,** edit, favorite and share costs
- **Stay on top of price changes** with automatic updates

Discover more at rsmeans.com/online

No part of this cost data may be reproduced, stored in a retrieval system, or transmitted in any form or by any means without prior written permission of Gordian.

D20 Plumbing

D2020 Domestic Water Distribution

In this closed-loop indirect collection system, fluid with a low freezing temperature, such as propylene glycol, transports heat from the collectors to water storage. The transfer fluid is contained in a closed-loop consisting of collectors, supply and return piping, and a remote heat exchanger. The heat exchanger transfers heat energy from the fluid in the collector loop to potable water circulated in a storage loop. A typical two-or-three panel system contains 5 to 6 gallons of heat transfer fluid.

When the collectors become approximately 20°F warmer than the storage temperature, a controller activates the circulator on the collector and storage loops. The circulators will move the fluid and potable water through the heat exchanger until heat collection no longer occurs. At that point, the system shuts down. Since the heat transfer medium is a fluid with a very low freezing temperature, there is no need for it to be drained from the system between periods of collection.

D20 Plumbing

D2020 Domestic Water Distribution

System Components		QUANTITY	UNIT	COST EACH		
				MAT.	INST.	TOTAL
SYSTEM D2020 265 2760						
SOLAR, CLOSED LOOP, ADD-ON HOT WATER SYS., EXTERNAL HEAT EXCHANGER						
3/4" TUBING, TWO 3'X7' BLACK CHROME COLLECTORS						
A,B,G,L,K,M	Heat exchanger fluid-fluid pkg incl 2 circulators, expansion tank, Check valve, relief valve, controller, hi temp cutoff, & 2 sensors	1.000	Ea.	870	620	1,490
C	Thermometer, 2" dial	3.000	Ea.	75	160.50	235.50
D, T	Fill & drain valve, brass, 3/4" connection	1.000	Ea.	21.50	36	57.50
E	Air vent, manual, 1/8" fitting	2.000	Ea.	7.32	54	61.32
F	Air purger	1.000	Ea.	58	71.50	129.50
H	Strainer, Y type, bronze body, 3/4" IPS	1.000	Ea.	85	45.50	130.50
I	Valve, gate, bronze, NRS, soldered 3/4" diam	6.000	Ea.	834	258	1,092
J	Neoprene vent flashing	2.000	Ea.	24.80	86	110.80
N, N-1	Relief valve temp & press, 150 psi 210°F self-closing 3/4" IPS	1.000	Ea.	29.50	28.50	58
O	Pipe covering, urethane, ultraviolet cover, 1" wall 3/4" diam	20.000	L.F.	60.60	157	217.60
P	Pipe covering, fiberglass, all service jacket, 1" wall, 3/4" diam	50.000	L.F.	112	312.50	424.50
Q	Collector panel solar energy blk chrome on copper, 1/8" temp glass 3'x7'	2.000	Ea.	2,350	326	2,676
	Roof clamps for solar energy collector panels	2.000	Set	7.90	44	51.90
R	Valve, swing check, bronze, regrinding disc, 3/4" diam	2.000	Ea.	410	86	496
S	Pressure gauge, 60 psi, 2" dial	1.000	Ea.	28	27	55
U	Valve, water tempering, bronze, sweat connections, 3/4" diam	1.000	Ea.	273	43	316
W-2, V	Tank water storage w/heating element, drain, relief valve, existing	1.000	Ea.			
	Copper tubing type L, solder joint, hanger 10' OC 3/4" diam	20.000	L.F.	141	226	367
	Copper tubing, type M, solder joint, hanger 10' OC 3/4" diam	70.000	L.F.	430.50	770	1,200.50
	Sensor wire, #22-2 conductor multistranded	.500	C.L.F.	10.75	40	50.75
	Solar energy heat transfer fluid, propylene glycol anti-freeze	6.000	Gal.	168	183	351
	Wrought copper fittings & solder, 3/4" diam	76.000	Ea.	543.40	3,420	3,963.40
	TOTAL			6,540.27	6,994.50	13,534.77

D2020 265	Solar, Closed Loop, Add-On Hot Water Systems	COST EACH		
		MAT.	INST.	TOTAL
2550	Solar, closed loop, add-on hot water system, external heat exchanger			
2570	3/8" tubing, 3 ea. 4' x 4'-4" vacuum tube collectors	7,125	6,575	13,700
2580	1/2" tubing, 4 ea. 4 x 4'-4" vacuum tube collectors	7,625	7,100	14,725
2600	2 ea. 3'x7' black chrome collectors	5,775	6,700	12,475
2620	3 ea. 3'x7' black chrome collectors	6,950	6,875	13,825
2640	2 ea. 3'x7' flat black collectors	5,125	6,725	11,850
2660	3 ea. 3'x7' flat black collectors	5,975	6,900	12,875
2700	3/4" tubing, 3 ea. 3'x7' black chrome collectors	7,725	7,175	14,900
2720	3 ea. 3'x7' flat black absorber plate collectors	6,725	7,200	13,925
2740	2 ea. 4'x9' flat black w/plastic glazing collectors	6,250	7,225	13,475
2760	2 ea. 3'x7' black chrome collectors	6,550	7,000	13,550
2780	1" tubing, 4 ea 2'x9' plastic absorber & glazing collectors	8,100	8,125	16,225
2800	4 ea. 3'x7' black chrome absorber collectors	10,200	8,175	18,375
2820	4 ea. 3'x7' flat black absorber collectors	8,900	8,200	17,100

(R235616-60)

D20 Plumbing

D2020 Domestic Water Distribution

In the drainback indirect-collection system, the heat transfer fluid is distilled water contained in a loop consisting of collectors, supply and return piping, and an unpressurized holding tank. A large heat exchanger containing incoming potable water is immersed in the holding tank. When a controller activates solar collection, the distilled water is pumped through the collectors and heated and pumped back down to the holding tank. When the temperature differential between the water in the collectors and water in storage is such that collection no longer occurs, the pump turns off and gravity causes the distilled water in the collector loop to drain back to the holding tank. All the loop piping is pitched so that the water can drain out of the collectors and piping and not freeze there. As hot water is needed in the home, incoming water first flows through the holding tank with the immersed heat exchanger and is warmed and then flows through a conventional heater for any supplemental heating that is necessary.

D20 Plumbing

D2020 Domestic Water Distribution

System Components		QUANTITY	UNIT	COST EACH		
				MAT.	INST.	TOTAL
SYSTEM D2020 270 2760						
SOLAR, DRAINBACK, ADD ON, HOT WATER, IMMERSED HEAT EXCHANGER						
3/4" TUBING, THREE EA 3'X7' BLACK CHROME COLLECTOR						
A, B	Differential controller 2 sensors, thermostat, solar energy system	1.000	Ea.	258	71.50	329.50
C	Thermometer 2" dial	3.000	Ea.	75	160.50	235.50
D, T	Fill & drain valve, brass, 3/4" connection	1.000	Ea.	21.50	36	57.50
E-1	Automatic air vent 1/8" fitting	1.000	Ea.	17.70	27	44.70
H	Strainer, Y type, bronze body, 3/4" IPS	1.000	Ea.	85	45.50	130.50
I	Valve, gate, bronze, NRS, soldered 3/4" diam	2.000	Ea.	278	86	364
J	Neoprene vent flashing	2.000	Ea.	24.80	86	110.80
L	Circulator, solar heated liquid, 1/20 HP	1.000	Ea.	340	129	469
N	Relief valve temp. & press. 150 psi 210°F self-closing 3/4" IPS	1.000	Ea.	29.50	28.50	58
O	Pipe covering, urethane, ultraviolet cover, 1" wall, 3/4" diam	20.000	L.F.	60.60	157	217.60
P	Pipe covering, fiberglass, all service jacket, 1" wall, 3/4" diam	50.000	L.F.	112	312.50	424.50
Q	Collector panel solar energy blk chrome on copper, 1/8" temp glas 3'x7'	3.000	Ea.	3,525	489	4,014
	Roof clamps for solar energy collector panels	3.000	Set	11.85	66	77.85
R	Valve, swing check, bronze, regrinding disc, 3/4" diam	1.000	Ea.	205	43	248
U	Valve, water tempering, bronze sweat connections, 3/4" diam	1.000	Ea.	273	43	316
V	Tank, water storage w/heating element, drain, relief valve, existing	1.000	Ea.			
W	Tank, water storage immersed heat exchr elec 2"x1/2# insul 120 gal	1.000	Ea.	1,925	615	2,540
X	Valve, globe, bronze, rising stem, 3/4" diam, soldered	3.000	Ea.	792	129	921
Y	Flow control valve	1.000	Ea.	158	39	197
Z	Valve, ball, bronze, solder 3/4" diam, solar loop flow control	1.000	Ea.	38.50	43	81.50
	Copper tubing, type L, solder joint, hanger 10' OC 3/4" diam	20.000	L.F.	141	226	367
	Copper tubing, type M, solder joint, hanger 10' OC 3/4" diam	70.000	L.F.	430.50	770	1,200.50
	Sensor wire, #22-2 conductor, multistranded	.500	C.L.F.	10.75	40	50.75
	Wrought copper fittings & solder, 3/4" diam	76.000	Ea.	543.40	3,420	3,963.40
	TOTAL			9,356.10	7,062.50	16,418.60

D2020 270	Solar, Drainback, Hot Water Systems		COST EACH		
			MAT.	INST.	TOTAL
2550	Solar, drainback, hot water, immersed heat exchanger				
2560	3/8" tubing, 3 ea. 4' x 4'-4" vacuum tube collectors	R235616-60	8,825	6,375	15,200
2580	1/2" tubing, 4 ea 4' x 4'-4" vacuum tube collectors, 80 gal tank		9,250	6,925	16,175
2600	120 gal tank		9,175	7,000	16,175
2640	2 ea. 3'x7' blk chrome collectors, 80 gal tank		7,375	6,500	13,875
2660	3 ea. 3'x7' blk chrome collectors, 120 gal tank		8,475	6,775	15,250
2700	2 ea. 3'x7' flat blk collectors, 120 gal tank		6,650	6,600	13,250
2720	3 ea. 3'x7' flat blk collectors, 120 gal tank		7,500	6,800	14,300
2760	3/4" tubing, 3 ea 3'x7' black chrome collectors, 120 gal tank		9,350	7,075	16,425
2780	3 ea. 3'x7' flat black absorber collectors, 120 gal tank		8,375	7,100	15,475
2800	2 ea. 4'x9' flat blk w/plastic glazing collectors 120 gal tank		7,875	7,125	15,000
2840	1" tubing, 4 ea. 2'x9' plastic absorber & glazing collectors, 120 gal tank		10,000	8,025	18,025
2860	4 ea. 3'x7' black chrome absorber collectors, 120 gal tank		12,100	8,050	20,150
2880	4 ea. 3'x7' flat black absorber collectors, 120 gal tank		10,800	8,075	18,875

D20 Plumbing

D2020 Domestic Water Distribution

In the draindown direct-collection system, incoming domestic water is heated in the collectors. When the controller activates solar collection, domestic water is first heated as it flows through the collectors and is then pumped to storage. When conditions are no longer suitable for heat collection, the pump shuts off and the water in the loop drains down and out of the system by means of solenoid valves and properly pitched piping.

D20 Plumbing

D2020 Domestic Water Distribution

System Components	QUANTITY	UNIT	COST EACH		
			MAT.	INST.	TOTAL
SYSTEM D2020 275 2760					
SOLAR, DRAINDOWN, HOT WATER, DIRECT COLLECTION					
3/4" TUBING, THREE 3'X7' BLACK CHROME COLLECTORS					
A, B Differential controller, 2 sensors, thermostat, solar energy system	1.000	Ea.	258	71.50	329.50
A-1 Solenoid valve, solar heating loop, brass, 3/4" diam, 24 volts	3.000	Ea.	576	286.50	862.50
B-1 Solar energy sensor, freeze prevention	1.000	Ea.	29	27	56
C Thermometer, 2" dial	3.000	Ea.	75	160.50	235.50
E-1 Vacuum relief valve, 3/4" diam	1.000	Ea.	34.50	27	61.50
F-1 Air vent, automatic, 1/8" fitting	1.000	Ea.	17.70	27	44.70
H Strainer, Y type, bronze body, 3/4" IPS	1.000	Ea.	85	45.50	130.50
I Valve, gate, bronze, NRS, soldered, 3/4" diam	2.000	Ea.	278	86	364
J Vent flashing neoprene	2.000	Ea.	24.80	86	110.80
K Circulator, solar heated liquid, 1/25 HP	1.000	Ea.	231	111	342
N Relief valve temp & press 150 psi 210°F self-closing 3/4" IPS	1.000	Ea.	29.50	28.50	58
O Pipe covering, urethane, ultraviolet cover, 1" wall, 3/4" diam	20.000	L.F.	60.60	157	217.60
P Pipe covering, fiberglass, all service jacket, 1" wall, 3/4" diam	50.000	L.F.	112	312.50	424.50
Roof clamps for solar energy collector panels	3.000	Set	11.85	66	77.85
Q Collector panel solar energy blk chrome on copper, 1/8" temp glass 3'x7'	3.000	Ea.	3,525	489	4,014
R Valve, swing check, bronze, regrinding disc, 3/4" diam, soldered	2.000	Ea.	410	86	496
T Drain valve, brass, 3/4" connection	2.000	Ea.	43	72	115
U Valve, water tempering, bronze, sweat connections, 3/4" diam	1.000	Ea.	273	43	316
W, W-2 Tank, water storage elec elem 2"x1/2# insul 120 gal	1.000	Ea.	1,925	615	2,540
X Valve, globe, bronze, rising stem, 3/4" diam, soldered	1.000	Ea.	264	43	307
Copper tubing, type L, solder joints, hangers 10' OC 3/4" diam	20.000	L.F.	141	226	367
Copper tubing, type M, solder joints, hangers 10' OC 3/4" diam	70.000	L.F.	430.50	770	1,200.50
Sensor wire, #22-2 conductor, multistranded	.500	C.L.F.	10.75	40	50.75
Wrought copper fittings & solder, 3/4" diam	76.000	Ea.	543.40	3,420	3,963.40
TOTAL			**9,388.60**	**7,296**	**16,684.60**

D2020 275	Solar, Draindown, Hot Water Systems	COST EACH		
		MAT.	INST.	TOTAL
2550	Solar, draindown, hot water			
2560	3/8" tubing, 3 ea. 4' x 4'-4" vacuum tube collectors, 80 gal tank	8,300	6,975	15,275
2580	1/2" tubing, 4 ea. 4' x 4'-4" vacuum tube collectors, 80 gal tank	9,350	7,150	16,500
2600	120 gal tank	9,275	7,250	16,525
2640	2 ea. 3'x7' black chrome collectors, 80 gal tank	7,500	6,750	14,250
2660	3 ea. 3'x7' black chrome collectors, 120 gal tank	8,600	7,025	15,625
2700	2 ea. 3'x7' flat black collectors, 120 gal tank	6,775	6,850	13,625
2720	3 ea. 3'x7' flat black collectors, 120 gal tank	7,475	7,000	14,475
2760	3/4" tubing, 3 ea. 3'x7' black chrome collectors, 120 gal tank	9,400	7,300	16,700
2780	3 ea. 3'x7' flat collectors, 120 gal tank	8,400	7,325	15,725
2800	2 ea. 4'x9' flat black & plastic glazing collectors, 120 gal tank	7,900	7,350	15,250
2840	1" tubing, 4 ea. 2'x9' plastic absorber & glazing collectors, 120 gal tank	13,700	9,700	23,400
2860	4 ea. 3'x7' black chrome absorber collectors, 120 gal tank	13,300	9,175	22,475
2880	4 ea. 3'x7' flat black absorber collectors, 120 gal tank	10,800	8,325	19,125

Note: R235616-60

D20 Plumbing

D2020 Domestic Water Distribution

In the recirculation system, (a direct-collection system), incoming domestic water is heated in the collectors. When the controller activates solar collection, domestic water is heated as it flows through the collectors and then it flows back to storage. When conditions are not suitable for heat collection, the pump shuts off and the flow of the water stops. In this type of system, water remains in the collector loop at all times. A "frost sensor" at the collector activates the circulation of warm water from storage through the collectors when protection from freezing is required.

D20 Plumbing

D2020 Domestic Water Distribution

System Components	QUANTITY	UNIT	COST EACH		
			MAT.	INST.	TOTAL
SYSTEM D2020 280 2820					
SOLAR, RECIRCULATION, HOT WATER					
3/4" TUBING, TWO 3'X7' BLACK CHROME COLLECTORS					
A, B Differential controller 2 sensors, thermostat, for solar energy system	1.000	Ea.	258	71.50	329.50
A-1 Solenoid valve, solar heating loop, brass, 3/4" IPS, 24 volts	2.000	Ea.	384	191	575
B-1 Solar energy sensor freeze prevention	1.000	Ea.	29	27	56
C Thermometer, 2" dial	3.000	Ea.	75	160.50	235.50
D Drain valve, brass, 3/4" connection	1.000	Ea.	21.50	36	57.50
F-1 Air vent, automatic, 1/8" fitting	1.000	Ea.	17.70	27	44.70
H Strainer, Y type, bronze body, 3/4" IPS	1.000	Ea.	85	45.50	130.50
I Valve, gate, bronze, 125 lb, soldered 3/4" diam	3.000	Ea.	417	129	546
J Vent flashing, neoprene	2.000	Ea.	24.80	86	110.80
L Circulator, solar heated liquid, 1/20 HP	1.000	Ea.	340	129	469
N Relief valve, temp & press 150 psi 210° F self-closing 3/4" IPS	2.000	Ea.	59	57	116
O Pipe covering, urethane, ultraviolet cover, 1" wall, 3/4" diam	20.000	L.F.	60.60	157	217.60
P Pipe covering, fiberglass, all service jacket, 1" wall 3/4" diam	50.000	L.F.	112	312.50	424.50
Q Collector panel solar energy blk chrome on copper, 1/8" temp glass 3'x7'	2.000	Ea.	2,350	326	2,676
Roof clamps for solar energy collector panels	2.000	Set	7.90	44	51.90
R Valve, swing check, bronze, 125 lb, regrinding disc, soldered 3/4" diam	2.000	Ea.	410	86	496
U Valve, water tempering, bronze, sweat connections, 3/4" diam	1.000	Ea.	273	43	316
V Tank, water storage, w/heating element, drain, relief valve, existing	1.000	Ea.			
X Valve, globe, bronze, 125 lb, 3/4" diam	2.000	Ea.	528	86	614
Copper tubing, type L, solder joints, hangers 10' OC 3/4" diam	20.000	L.F.	141	226	367
Copper tubing, type M, solder joints, hangers 10' OC 3/4" diam	70.000	L.F.	430.50	770	1,200.50
Wrought copper fittings & solder, 3/4" diam	76.000	Ea.	543.40	3,420	3,963.40
Sensor wire, #22-2 conductor, multistranded	.500	C.L.F.	10.75	40	50.75
TOTAL			6,578.15	6,470	13,048.15

D2020 280	Solar, Recirculation, Domestic Hot Water Systems		COST EACH		
			MAT.	INST.	TOTAL
2550	Solar, recirculation, hot water				
2560	3/8" tubing, 3 ea. 4' x 4'-4" vacuum tube collectors		7,150	6,050	13,200
2580	1/2" tubing, 4 ea. 4' x 4'-4" vacuum tube collectors		7,575	6,575	14,150
2640	2 ea. 3'x7' black chrome collectors	R235616-60	5,725	6,175	11,900
2660	3 ea. 3'x7' black chrome collectors		6,900	6,375	13,275
2700	2 ea. 3'x7' flat black collectors		5,050	6,200	11,250
2720	3 ea. 3'x7' flat black collectors		5,900	6,400	12,300
2760	3/4" tubing, 3 ea. 3'x7' black chrome collectors		7,750	6,650	14,400
2780	3 ea. 3'x7' flat black absorber plate collectors		6,775	6,675	13,450
2800	2 ea. 4'x9' flat black w/plastic glazing collectors		6,275	6,700	12,975
2820	2 ea. 3'x7' black chrome collectors		6,575	6,475	13,050
2840	1" tubing, 4 ea. 2'x9' black plastic absorber & glazing collectors		8,550	7,600	16,150
2860	4 ea. 3'x7' black chrome absorber collectors		10,700	7,650	18,350
2880	4 ea. 3'x7' flat black absorber collectors		9,350	7,675	17,025

D20 Plumbing

D2020 Domestic Water Distribution

The thermosyphon domestic hot water system, a direct collection system, operates under city water pressure and does not require pumps for system operation. An insulated water storage tank is located above the collectors. As the sun heats the collectors, warm water in them rises by means of natural convection; the colder water in the storage tank flows into the collectors by means of gravity. As long as the sun is shining the water continues to flow through the collectors and to become warmer.

To prevent freezing, the system must be drained or the collectors covered with an insulated lid when the temperature drops below 32°F.

D20 Plumbing

D2020 Domestic Water Distribution

System Components	QUANTITY	UNIT	COST EACH		
			MAT.	INST.	TOTAL
SYSTEM D2020 285 0960 SOLAR, THERMOSYPHON, WATER HEATER 3/4" TUBING, TWO 3'X7' BLACK CHROME COLLECTORS					
D-1 Framing lumber, fir, 2" x 6" x 8', tank cradle	.008	M.B.F.	16.40	9	25.40
F-1 Framing lumber, fir, 2" x 4" x 24', sleepers	.016	M.B.F.	30	26.80	56.80
I Valve, gate, bronze, 125 lb, soldered 1/2" diam	2.000	Ea.	254	72	326
J Vent flashing, neoprene	4.000	Ea.	49.60	172	221.60
O Pipe covering, urethane, ultraviolet cover, 1" wall, 1/2"diam	40.000	L.F.	95.20	308	403.20
P Pipe covering fiberglass all service jacket 1" wall 1/2" diam	160.000	L.F.	328	960	1,288
Q Collector panel solar, blk chrome on copper, 3/16" temp glass 3'-6" x 7.5'	2.000	Ea.	1,690	344	2,034
Y Flow control valve, globe, bronze, 125#, soldered, 1/2" diam	1.000	Ea.	198	36	234
U Valve, water tempering, bronze, sweat connections, 1/2" diam	1.000	Ea.	166	36	202
W Tank, water storage, solar energy system, 80 Gal, 2" x 1/2 lb insul	1.000	Ea.	2,000	535	2,535
Copper tubing type L, solder joints, hangers 10' OC 1/2" diam	150.000	L.F.	810	1,590	2,400
Copper tubing type M, solder joints, hangers 10' OC 1/2" diam	50.000	L.F.	243	512.50	755.50
Sensor wire, #22-2 gauge multistranded	.500	C.L.F.	10.75	40	50.75
Wrought copper fittings & solder, 1/2" diam	75.000	Ea.	243.75	3,225	3,468.75
TOTAL			6,134.70	7,866.30	14,001

D2020 285	Thermosyphon, Hot Water		COST EACH		
			MAT.	INST.	TOTAL
0960 0970	Solar, thermosyphon, hot water, two collector system	R235616 -60	6,125	7,875	14,000

D20 Plumbing

D2020 Domestic Water Distribution

This domestic hot water pre-heat system includes heat exchanger with a circulating pump, blower, air-to-water, coil and controls, mounted in the upper collector manifold. Heat from the hot air coming out of the collectors is transferred through the heat exchanger. For each degree of DHW preheating gained, one degree less heating is needed from the fuel fired water heater. The system is simple, inexpensive to operate and can provide a substantial portion of DHW requirements for modest additional cost.

D20 Plumbing

D2020 Domestic Water Distribution

System Components	QUANTITY	UNIT	COST EACH MAT.	COST EACH INST.	COST EACH TOTAL
SYSTEM D2020 290 2560					
SOLAR, HOT WATER, AIR TO WATER HEAT EXCHANGE					
THREE COLLECTORS, OPTICAL BLACK ON ALUM., 7.5' x 3.5', 80 GAL TANK					
A, B Differential controller, 2 sensors, thermostat, solar energy system	1.000	Ea.	258	71.50	329.50
C Thermometer, 2" dial	2.000	Ea.	50	107	157
C-1 Heat exchanger, air to fluid, up flow 70 MBH	1.000	Ea.	420	440	860
E Air vent, manual, for solar energy system 1/8" fitting	1.000	Ea.	3.66	27	30.66
F Air purger	1.000	Ea.	58	71.50	129.50
G Expansion tank	1.000	Ea.	72.50	27	99.50
H Strainer, Y type, bronze body, 1/2" IPS	1.000	Ea.	57.50	43.50	101
I Valve, gate, bronze, 125 lb, NRS, soldered 1/2" diam	5.000	Ea.	635	180	815
N Relief valve, temp & pressure solar 150 psi 210°F self-closing	1.000	Ea.	29.50	28.50	58
P Pipe covering, fiberglass, all service jacket, 1" wall, 1/2" diam	60.000	L.F.	123	360	483
Q Collector panel solar energy, air, black on alum plate, 7.5' x 3.5'	3.000	Ea.	2,535	516	3,051
B-1, R-1 Shutter damper for solar heater circulator	1.000	Ea.	65.50	127	192.50
B-1, R-1 Shutter motor for solar heater circulator	1.000	Ea.	163	95	258
R Backflow preventer, 1/2" pipe size	2.000	Ea.	197	107	304
T Drain valve, brass, 3/4" connection	1.000	Ea.	21.50	36	57.50
U Valve, water tempering, bronze, sweat connections, 1/2" diam	1.000	Ea.	166	36	202
W Tank, water storage, solar energy system, 80 Gal, 2" x 2 lb insul	1.000	Ea.	2,000	535	2,535
V Tank, water storage, w/heating element, drain, relief valve, existing	1.000	System			
X Valve, globe, bronze, 125 lb, rising stem, 1/2" diam	1.000	Ea.	198	36	234
Copper tubing type M, solder joints, hangers 10' OC, 1/2" diam	50.000	L.F.	243	512.50	755.50
Copper tubing type L, solder joints, hangers 10' OC 1/2" diam	10.000	L.F.	54	106	160
Wrought copper fittings & solder, 1/2" diam	10.000	Ea.	32.50	430	462.50
Sensor wire, #22-2 conductor multistranded	.500	C.L.F.	10.75	40	50.75
Q-1, Q-2 Ductwork, fiberglass, aluminized jacket, 1-1/2" thick, 8" diam	32.000	S.F.	332.80	270.40	603.20
Q-3 Manifold for flush mount solar energy collector panels, air	6.000	L.F.	1,002	57	1,059
TOTAL			8,728.21	4,259.90	12,988.11

D2020 290	Solar, Hot Water, Air To Water Heat Exchange		MAT.	INST.	TOTAL
2550	Solar, hot water, air to water heat exchange				
2560	Three collectors, optical black on aluminum, 7.5' x 3.5', 80 Gal tank		8,725	4,250	12,975
2580	Four collectors, optical black on aluminum, 7.5' x 3.5', 80 Gal tank	R235616 -60	9,975	4,500	14,475
2600	Four collectors, optical black on aluminum, 7.5' x 3.5', 120 Gal tank		9,900	4,600	14,500

D20 Plumbing

D2020 Domestic Water Distribution

In this closed-loop indirect collection system, fluid with a low freezing temperature, such as propylene glycol, transports heat from the collectors to water storage. The transfer fluid is contained in a closed-loop consisting of collectors, supply and return piping, and a heat exchanger immersed in the storage tank. A typical two-or-three panel system contains 5 to 6 gallons of heat transfer fluid.

When the collectors become approximately 20°F warmer than the storage temperature, a controller activates the circulator. The circulator moves the fluid continuously through the collectors until the temperature difference between the collectors and storage is such that heat collection no longer occurs; at that point, the circulator shuts off. Since the heat transfer fluid has a very low freezing temperature, there is no need for it to be drained from the collectors between periods of collection.

D20 Plumbing

D2020 Domestic Water Distribution

System Components	QUANTITY	UNIT	COST EACH MAT.	COST EACH INST.	COST EACH TOTAL
SYSTEM D2020 295 2760					
SOLAR, CLOSED LOOP, HOT WATER SYSTEM, IMMERSED HEAT EXCHANGER					
3/4" TUBING, THREE 3' X 7' BLACK CHROME COLLECTORS					
A, B Differential controller, 2 sensors, thermostat, solar energy system	1.000	Ea.	258	71.50	329.50
C Thermometer 2" dial	3.000	Ea.	75	160.50	235.50
A, D, T Fill & drain valves, brass, 3/4" connection	3.000	Ea.	64.50	108	172.50
E Air vent, manual, 1/8" fitting	1.000	Ea.	3.66	27	30.66
F Air purger	1.000	Ea.	58	71.50	129.50
G Expansion tank	1.000	Ea.	72.50	27	99.50
I Valve, gate, bronze, NRS, soldered 3/4" diam	3.000	Ea.	417	129	546
J Neoprene vent flashing	2.000	Ea.	24.80	86	110.80
K Circulator, solar heated liquid, 1/25 HP	1.000	Ea.	231	111	342
N, N-1 Relief valve, temp & press 150 psi 210°F self-closing 3/4" IPS	2.000	Ea.	59	57	116
O Pipe covering, urethane ultraviolet cover, 1" wall, 3/4" diam	20.000	L.F.	60.60	157	217.60
P Pipe covering, fiberglass, all service jacket, 1" wall, 3/4" diam	50.000	L.F.	112	312.50	424.50
Roof clamps for solar energy collector panel	3.000	Set	11.85	66	77.85
Q Collector panel solar blk chrome on copper, 1/8" temp glass, 3'x7'	3.000	Ea.	3,525	489	4,014
R-1 Valve, swing check, bronze, regrinding disc, 3/4" diam, soldered	1.000	Ea.	205	43	248
S Pressure gauge, 60 psi, 2-1/2" dial	1.000	Ea.	28	27	55
U Valve, water tempering, bronze, sweat connections, 3/4" diam	1.000	Ea.	273	43	316
W, W-2 Tank, water storage immersed heat exchr elec elem 2"x2# insul 120 Gal	1.000	Ea.	1,925	615	2,540
X Valve, globe, bronze, rising stem, 3/4" diam, soldered	1.000	Ea.	264	43	307
Copper tubing type L, solder joint, hanger 10' OC 3/4" diam	20.000	L.F.	141	226	367
Copper tubing, type M, solder joint, hanger 10' OC 3/4" diam	70.000	L.F.	430.50	770	1,200.50
Sensor wire, #22-2 conductor multistranded	.500	C.L.F.	10.75	40	50.75
Solar energy heat transfer fluid, propylene glycol, anti-freeze	6.000	Gal.	168	183	351
Wrought copper fittings & solder, 3/4" diam	76.000	Ea.	543.40	3,420	3,963.40
TOTAL			**8,961.56**	**7,283**	**16,244.56**

D2020 295	Solar, Closed Loop, Hot Water Systems		MAT.	INST.	TOTAL
2550	Solar, closed loop, hot water system, immersed heat exchanger				
2560	3/8" tubing, 3 ea. 4' x 4'-4" vacuum tube collectors, 80 gal. tank		8,525	6,625	15,150
2580	1/2" tubing, 4 ea. 4' x 4'-4" vacuum tube collectors, 80 gal. tank		9,000	7,150	16,150
2600	120 gal. tank		8,925	7,225	16,150
2640	2 ea. 3'x7' black chrome collectors, 80 gal. tank	R235616 -60	7,175	6,825	14,000
2660	120 gal. tank		7,075	6,825	13,900
2700	2 ea. 3'x7' flat black collectors, 120 gal. tank		6,400	6,850	13,250
2720	3 ea. 3'x7' flat black collectors, 120 gal. tank		7,250	7,025	14,275
2760	3/4" tubing, 3 ea. 3'x7' black chrome collectors, 120 gal. tank		8,950	7,275	16,225
2780	3 ea. 3'x7' flat black collectors, 120 gal. tank		7,975	7,300	15,275
2800	2 ea. 4'x9' flat black w/plastic glazing collectors 120 gal. tank		7,475	7,325	14,800
2840	1" tubing, 4 ea. 2'x9' plastic absorber & glazing collectors 120 gal. tank		9,250	8,200	17,450
2860	4 ea. 3'x7' black chrome collectors, 120 gal. tank		11,400	8,225	19,625
2880	4 ea. 3'x7' flat black absorber collectors, 120 gal. tank		10,000	8,275	18,275

D30 HVAC

D3010 Energy Supply

Basis for Heat Loss Estimate, Apartment Type Structures:

1. Masonry walls and flat roof are insulated. U factor is assumed at .08.
2. Window glass area taken as BOCA minimum, 1/10th of floor area. Double insulating glass with 1/4" air space, U = .65.
3. Infiltration = 0.3 C.F. per hour per S.F. of net wall.
4. Concrete floor loss is 2 BTUH per S.F.
5. Temperature difference taken as 70°F.
6. Ventilating or makeup air has not been included and must be added if desired. Air shafts are not used.

System Components	QUANTITY	UNIT	COST EACH MAT.	COST EACH INST.	COST EACH TOTAL
SYSTEM D3010 510 1760					
HEATING SYSTEM, FIN TUBE RADIATION, FORCED HOT WATER					
1,000 S.F. AREA, 10,000 C.F. VOLUME					
Boiler, oil fired, CI, burner, ctrls/insul/breech/pipe/ftng/valves, 109 MBH	1.000	Ea.	4,812.50	4,812.50	9,625
Circulating pump, CI flange connection, 1/12 HP	1.000	Ea.	680	258	938
Expansion tank, painted steel, ASME 18 Gal capacity	1.000	Ea.	855	111	966
Storage tank, steel, above ground, 275 Gal capacity w/supports	1.000	Ea.	2,075	310	2,385
Copper tubing type L, solder joint, hanger 10' OC, 3/4" diam	100.000	L.F.	705	1,130	1,835
Radiation, 3/4" copper tube w/alum fin baseboard pkg, 7" high	30.000	L.F.	259.50	810	1,069.50
Pipe covering, calcium silicate w/cover, 1' wall, 3/4' diam	100.000	L.F.	695	845	1,540
TOTAL			10,082	8,276.50	18,358.50
COST PER S.F.			10.08	8.28	18.36

D3010 510	Apartment Building Heating - Fin Tube Radiation		COST PER S.F. MAT.	COST PER S.F. INST.	COST PER S.F. TOTAL
1740	Heating systems, fin tube radiation, forced hot water				
1760	1,000 S.F. area, 10,000 C.F. volume		10.10	8.28	18.38
1800	10,000 S.F. area, 100,000 C.F. volume	R235000-10	4.32	4.98	9.30
1840	20,000 S.F. area, 200,000 C.F. volume		4.20	5.60	9.80
1880	30,000 S.F. area, 300,000 C.F. volume	R235000-20	4.10	5.40	9.50
1890					

D30 HVAC

D3010 Energy Supply

Fin Tube Radiator

Basis for Heat Loss Estimate, Factory or Commercial Type Structures:

1. Walls and flat roof are of lightly insulated concrete block or metal. U factor is assumed at .17.
2. Windows and doors are figured at 1-1/2 S.F. per linear foot of building perimeter. The U factor for flat single glass is 1.13.
3. Infiltration is approximately 5 C.F. per hour per S.F. of wall.
4. Concrete floor loss is 2 BTUH per S.F. of floor.
5. Temperature difference is assumed at 70°F.
6. Ventilation or makeup air has not been included and must be added if desired.

System Components	QUANTITY	UNIT	COST EACH		
			MAT.	INST.	TOTAL
SYSTEM D3010 520 1960					
HEATING SYSTEM, FIN TUBE RADIATION, FORCED HOT WATER					
1,000 S.F. BLDG., ONE FLOOR					
Boiler, oil fired, CI, burner/ctrls/insul/breech/pipe/ftngs/valves, 109 MBH	1.000	Ea.	4,812.50	4,812.50	9,625
Expansion tank, painted steel, ASME 18 Gal capacity	1.000	Ea.	3,900	130	4,030
Storage tank, steel, above ground, 550 Gal capacity w/supports	1.000	Ea.	7,875	575	8,450
Circulating pump, CI flanged, 1/8 HP	1.000	Ea.	1,075	258	1,333
Pipe, steel, black, sch. 40, threaded, cplg & hngr 10'OC, 1-1/2" diam.	260.000	L.F.	4,355	5,031	9,386
Pipe covering, calcium silicate w/cover , 1" wall, 1-1/2" diam	260.000	L.F.	1,781	2,262	4,043
Radiation, steel 1-1/4" tube & 4-1/4" fin w/cover & damper, wall hung	42.000	L.F.	1,995	1,827	3,822
Rough in, steel fin tube radiation w/supply & balance valves	4.000	Set	1,780	3,800	5,580
TOTAL			27,573.50	18,695.50	46,269
COST PER S.F.			27.57	18.70	46.27

D3010 520	Commercial Building Heating - Fin Tube Radiation		COST PER S.F.		
			MAT.	INST.	TOTAL
1940	Heating systems, fin tube radiation, forced hot water				
1960	1,000 S.F. bldg, one floor		27.60	18.70	46.30
2000	10,000 S.F., 100,000 C.F., total two floors	R235000 -10	7.15	7.10	14.25
2040	**100,000 S.F., 1,000,000 C.F., total three floors**		2.98	3.18	6.16
2080	1,000,000 S.F., 10,000,000 C.F., total five floors	R235000 -20	1.68	1.69	3.37
2090					

D30 HVAC

D3010 Energy Supply

Unit Heater

Basis for Heat Loss Estimate, Factory or Commercial Type Structures:

1. Walls and flat roof are of lightly insulated concrete block or metal. U factor is assumed at .17.
2. Windows and doors are figured at 1-1/2 S.F. per linear foot of building perimeter. The U factor for flat single glass is 1.13.
3. Infiltration is approximately 5 C.F. per hour per S.F. of wall.
4. Concrete floor loss is 2 BTUH per S.F. of floor.
5. Temperature difference is assumed at 70°F.
6. Ventilation or makeup air has not been included and must be added if desired.

System Components	QUANTITY	UNIT	COST EACH		
			MAT.	INST.	TOTAL
SYSTEM D3010 530 1880					
HEATING SYSTEM, TERMINAL UNIT HEATERS, FORCED HOT WATER					
1,000 S.F. BLDG., ONE FLOOR					
Boiler oil fired, CI, burner/ctrls/insul/breech/pipe/ftngs/valves, 109 MBH	1.000	Ea.	4,812.50	4,812.50	9,625
Expansion tank, painted steel, ASME 18 Gal capacity	1.000	Ea.	3,900	130	4,030
Storage tank, steel, above ground, 550 Gal capacity w/supports	1.000	Ea.	7,875	575	8,450
Circulating pump, CI, flanged, 1/8 HP	1.000	Ea.	1,075	258	1,333
Pipe, steel, black, schedule 40, threaded, cplg & hngr 10' OC 1-1/2" diam	260.000	L.F.	4,355	5,031	9,386
Pipe covering, calcium silicate w/cover, 1" wall, 1-1/2" diam	260.000	L.F.	1,781	2,262	4,043
Unit heater, 1 speed propeller, horizontal, 200° EWT, 26.9 MBH	2.000	Ea.	1,530	390	1,920
Unit heater piping hookup with controls	2.000	Set	2,800	3,700	6,500
TOTAL			28,128.50	17,158.50	45,287
COST PER S.F.			28.13	17.16	45.29

D3010 530	Commercial Bldg. Heating - Terminal Unit Heaters		COST PER S.F.		
			MAT.	INST.	TOTAL
1860	Heating systems, terminal unit heaters, forced hot water				
1880	1,000 S.F. bldg., one floor		28.10	17.20	45.30
1920	10,000 S.F. bldg., 100,000 C.F. total two floors	R235000 -10	7.05	5.90	12.95
1960	100,000 S.F. bldg., 1,000,000 C.F. total three floors		3.39	2.91	6.30
2000	1,000,000 S.F. bldg., 10,000,000 C.F. total five floors	R235000 -20	2.41	1.90	4.31
2010					

D30 HVAC

D3010 Energy Supply

Many styles of active solar energy systems exist. Those shown on the following page represent the majority of systems now being installed in different regions of the country.

The five active domestic hot water (DHW) systems which follow are typically specified as two or three panel systems with additional variations being the type of glazing and size of the storage tanks. Various combinations have been costed for the user's evaluation and comparison. The basic specifications from which the following systems were developed satisfy the construction detail requirements specified in the HUD Intermediate Minimum Property Standards (IMPS). If these standards are not complied with, the renewable energy system's costs could be significantly lower than shown.

To develop the system's specifications and costs it was necessary to make a number of assumptions about the systems. Certain systems are more appropriate to one climatic region than another or the systems may require modifications to be usable in particular locations. Specific instances in which the systems are not appropriate throughout the country as specified, or in which modification will be needed include the following:

- The freeze protection mechanisms provided in the DHW systems vary greatly. In harsh climates, where freeze is a major concern, a closed-loop indirect collection system may be more appropriate than a direct collection system.
- The thermosyphon water heater system described cannot be used when temperatures drop below 32°F.
- In warm climates it may be necessary to modify the systems installed to prevent overheating.

For each renewable resource (solar) system a schematic diagram and descriptive summary of the system is provided along with a list of all the components priced as part of the system. The costs were developed based on these specifications.

Considerations affecting costs which may increase or decrease beyond the estimates presented here include the following:

- Special structural qualities (allowance for earthquake, future expansion, high winds, and unusual spans or shapes);
- Isolated building site or rough terrain that would affect the transportation of personnel, material, or equipment;
- Unusual climatic conditions during the construction process;
- Substitution of other materials or system components for those used in the system specifications.

D30 HVAC

D3010 Energy Supply

In this closed-loop indirect collection system, fluid with a low freezing temperature, propylene glycol, transports heat from the collectors to water storage. The transfer fluid is contained in a closed loop consisting of collectors, supply and return piping, and a heat exchanger immersed in the storage tank.

When the collectors become approximately 20°F warmer than the storage temperature, the controller activates the circulator. The circulator moves the fluid continuously until the temperature difference between fluid in the collectors and storage is such that the collection will no longer occur and then the circulator turns off. Since the heat transfer fluid has a very low freezing temperature, there is no need for it to be drained from the collectors between periods of collection.

D30 HVAC

D3010 Energy Supply

System Components	QUANTITY	UNIT	COST EACH MAT.	COST EACH INST.	COST EACH TOTAL
SYSTEM D3010 650 2750					
SOLAR, CLOSED LOOP, SPACE/HOT WATER					
1" TUBING, TEN 3'X7' BLK CHROME ON COPPER ABSORBER COLLECTORS					
A, B Differential controller 2 sensors, thermostat, solar energy system	2.000	Ea.	516	143	659
C Thermometer, 2" dial	10.000	Ea.	250	535	785
C-1 Heat exchanger, solar energy system, fluid to air, up flow, 80 MBH	1.000	Ea.	555	515	1,070
D, T Fill & drain valves, brass, 3/4" connection	5.000	Ea.	107.50	180	287.50
D-1 Fan center	1.000	Ea.	212	178	390
E Air vent, manual, 1/8" fitting	1.000	Ea.	3.66	27	30.66
E-2 Thermostat, 2 stage for sensing room temperature	1.000	Ea.	276	108	384
F Air purger	2.000	Ea.	116	143	259
F-1 Controller, liquid temperature, solar energy system	1.000	Ea.	131	172	303
G Expansion tank	2.000	Ea.	145	54	199
I Valve, gate, bronze, 125 lb, soldered, 1" diam	5.000	Ea.	1,000	225	1,225
J Vent flashing, neoprene	2.000	Ea.	24.80	86	110.80
K Circulator, solar heated liquid, 1/25 HP	2.000	Ea.	462	222	684
L Circulator, solar heated liquid, 1/20 HP	1.000	Ea.	340	129	469
N Relief valve, temp & pressure 150 psi 210°F self-closing	4.000	Ea.	118	114	232
N-1 Relief valve, pressure poppet, bronze, 30 psi, 3/4" IPS	3.000	Ea.	366	91.50	457.50
O Pipe covering, urethane, ultraviolet cover, 1" wall, 1" diam	50.000	L.F.	151.50	392.50	544
P Pipe covering, fiberglass, all service jacket, 1" wall, 1" diam	60.000	L.F.	134.40	375	509.40
Q Collector panel solar energy blk chrome on copper 1/8" temp glass 3'x7'	10.000	Ea.	11,750	1,630	13,380
Roof clamps for solar energy collector panel	10.000	Set	39.50	220	259.50
R Valve, swing check, bronze, 125 lb, regrinding disc, 3/4" & 1" diam	4.000	Ea.	1,084	180	1,264
S Pressure gage, 0-60 psi, for solar energy system	2.000	Ea.	56	54	110
U Valve, water tempering, bronze, sweat connections, 3/4" diam	1.000	Ea.	273	43	316
W, W-1, W-2 Tank, water storage immersed heat xchr elec elem 2"x1/2# ins 120 gal	4.000	Ea.	7,700	2,460	10,160
X Valve, globe, bronze, 125 lb, rising stem, 1" diam	3.000	Ea.	1,365	135	1,500
Y Valve, flow control	1.000	Ea.	158	39	197
Copper tubing, type M, solder joint, hanger 10' OC 1" diam	110.000	L.F.	638	1,353	1,991
Copper tubing, type L, solder joint, hanger 10' OC 3/4" diam	20.000	L.F.	141	226	367
Wrought copper fittings & solder, 3/4" & 1" diam	121.000	Ea.	2,129.60	6,473.50	8,603.10
Sensor, wire, #22-2 conductor, multistranded	.700	C.L.F.	15.05	56	71.05
Ductwork, galvanized steel, for heat exchanger	8.000	Lb.	5.92	80.40	86.32
Solar energy heat transfer fluid propylene glycol, anti-freeze	25.000	Gal.	700	762.50	1,462.50
TOTAL			30,963.93	17,402.40	48,366.33

D3010 650	Solar, Closed Loop, Space/Hot Water Systems		COST EACH MAT.	COST EACH INST.	COST EACH TOTAL
2540	Solar, closed loop, space/hot water				
2550	1/2" tubing, 12 ea. 4'x4'4" vacuum tube collectors		28,100	16,300	44,400
2600	3/4" tubing, 12 ea. 4'x4'4" vacuum tube collectors	R235616 -60	30,200	16,700	46,900
2650	10 ea. 3' x 7' black chrome absorber collectors		29,400	16,200	45,600
2700	10 ea. 3' x 7' flat black absorber collectors		26,100	16,300	42,400
2750	1" tubing, 10 ea. 3' x 7' black chrome absorber collectors		31,000	17,400	48,400
2800	10 ea. 3' x 7' flat black absorber collectors		27,900	17,500	45,400
2850	6 ea. 4' x 9' flat black w/plastic glazing collectors		25,600	17,400	43,000
2900	12 ea. 2' x 9' plastic absorber and glazing collectors		27,200	17,700	44,900

D30 HVAC

D3010 Energy Supply

This draindown pool system uses a differential thermostat similar to those used in solar domestic hot water and space heating applications. To heat the pool, the pool water passes through the conventional pump-filter loop and then flows through the collectors. When collection is not possible, or when the pool temperature is reached, all water drains from the solar loop back to the pool through the existing piping. The modes are controlled by solenoid valves or other automatic valves in conjunction with a vacuum breaker relief valve, which facilitates draindown.

D30 HVAC

D3010 Energy Supply

System Components

System Components	QUANTITY	UNIT	COST EACH		
			MAT.	INST.	TOTAL
SYSTEM D3010 660 2640					
SOLAR SWIMMING POOL HEATER, ROOF MOUNTED COLLECTORS					
TEN 4' X 10' FULLY WETTED UNGLAZED PLASTIC ABSORBERS					
A Differential thermostat/controller, 110V, adj pool pump system	1.000	Ea.	365	430	795
A-1 Solenoid valve, PVC, normally 1 open 1 closed (included)	2.000	Ea.			
B Sensor, thermistor type (included)	2.000	Ea.			
E-1 Valve, vacuum relief	1.000	Ea.	34.50	27	61.50
Q Collector panel, solar energy, plastic, liquid full wetted, 4' x 10'	10.000	Ea.	3,650	3,100	6,750
R Valve, ball check, PVC, socket, 1-1/2" diam	1.000	Ea.	165	43	208
Z Valve, ball, PVC, socket, 1-1/2" diam	3.000	Ea.	315	129	444
Pipe, PVC, sch 40, 1-1/2" diam	80.000	L.F.	596	1,920	2,516
Pipe fittings, PVC sch 40, socket joint, 1-1/2" diam	10.000	Ea.	39.20	430	469.20
Sensor wire, #22-2 conductor, multistranded	.500	C.L.F.	10.75	40	50.75
Roof clamps for solar energy collector panels	10.000	Set	39.50	220	259.50
Roof strap, teflon for solar energy collector panels	26.000	L.F.	715	108.94	823.94
TOTAL			5,929.95	6,447.94	12,377.89

D3010 660	Solar Swimming Pool Heater Systems		COST EACH		
			MAT.	INST.	TOTAL
2530	Solar swimming pool heater systems, roof mounted collectors				
2540	10 ea. 3'x7' black chrome absorber, 1/8" temp. glass		14,000	4,975	18,975
2560	10 ea. 4'x8' black chrome absorber, 3/16" temp. glass	R235616	15,500	5,925	21,425
2580	10 ea. 3'8"x6' flat black absorber, 3/16" temp. glass	-60	10,700	5,075	15,775
2600	10 ea. 4'x9' flat black absorber, plastic glazing		12,500	6,150	18,650
2620	10 ea. 2'x9' rubber absorber, plastic glazing		15,200	6,675	21,875
2640	10 ea. 4'x10' fully wetted unglazed plastic absorber		5,925	6,450	12,375
2660	Ground mounted collectors				
2680	10 ea. 3'x7' black chrome absorber, 1/8" temp. glass		14,300	5,550	19,850
2700	10 ea. 4'x8' black chrome absorber, 3/16" temp. glass		15,800	6,500	22,300
2720	10 ea. 3'8"x6' flat blk absorber, 3/16" temp. glass		11,000	5,650	16,650
2740	10 ea. 4'x9' flat blk absorber, plastic glazing		12,800	6,750	19,550
2760	10 ea. 2'x9' rubber absorber, plastic glazing		15,400	7,025	22,425
2780	10 ea. 4'x10' fully wetted unglazed plastic absorber		6,175	7,025	13,200

D30 HVAC

D3010 Energy Supply

The complete Solar Air Heating System provides maximum savings of conventional fuel with both space heating and year-round domestic hot water heating. It allows for the home air conditioning to operate simultaneously and independently from the solar domestic water heating in summer. The system's modes of operation are:

Mode 1: The building is heated directly from the collectors with air circulated by the Solar Air Mover.

Mode 2: When heat is not needed in the building, the dampers change within the air mover to circulate the air from the collectors to the rock storage bin.

Mode 3: When heat is not available from the collector array and is available in rock storage, the air mover draws heated air from rock storage and directs it into the building. When heat is not available from the collectors or the rock storage bin, the auxiliary heating unit will provide heat for the building. The size of the collector array is typically 25% the size of the main floor area.

D30 HVAC

D3010 Energy Supply

System Components				COST EACH		
		QUANTITY	UNIT	MAT.	INST.	TOTAL
SYSTEM D3010 675 1210						
SOLAR, SPACE/HOT WATER, AIR TO WATER HEAT EXCHANGE						
A, B	Differential controller 2 sensors thermos., solar energy sys liquid loop	1.000	Ea.	258	71.50	329.50
A-1, B	Differential controller 2 sensors 6 station solar energy sys air loop	1.000	Ea.	310	287	597
B-1	Solar energy sensor, freeze prevention	1.000	Ea.	29	27	56
C	Thermometer for solar energy system, 2" dial	2.000	Ea.	50	107	157
C-1	Heat exchanger, solar energy system, air to fluid, up flow, 70 MBH	1.000	Ea.	420	440	860
D	Drain valve, brass, 3/4" connection	2.000	Ea.	43	72	115
E	Air vent, manual, for solar energy system 1/8" fitting	1.000	Ea.	3.66	27	30.66
E-1	Thermostat, 2 stage for sensing room temperature	1.000	Ea.	276	108	384
F	Air purger	1.000	Ea.	58	71.50	129.50
G	Expansion tank, for solar energy system	1.000	Ea.	72.50	27	99.50
I	Valve, gate, bronze, 125 lb, NRS, soldered 3/4" diam	2.000	Ea.	278	86	364
K	Circulator, solar heated liquid, 1/25 HP	1.000	Ea.	231	111	342
N	Relief valve temp & press 150 psi 210°F self-closing, 3/4" IPS	1.000	Ea.	29.50	28.50	58
N-1	Relief valve, pressure, poppet, bronze, 30 psi, 3/4" IPS	1.000	Ea.	122	30.50	152.50
P	Pipe covering, fiberglass, all service jacket, 1" wall, 3/4" diam	60.000	L.F.	134.40	375	509.40
Q-3	Manifold for flush mount solar energy collector panels	20.000	L.F.	3,340	190	3,530
Q	Collector panel solar energy, air, black on alum. plate, 7.5' x 3.5'	10.000	Ea.	8,450	1,720	10,170
R	Valve, swing check, bronze, 125 lb, regrinding disc, 3/4" diam	2.000	Ea.	410	86	496
S	Pressure gage, 2" dial, for solar energy system	1.000	Ea.	28	27	55
U	Valve, water tempering, bronze, sweat connections, 3/4" diam	1.000	Ea.	273	43	316
W, W-2	Tank, water storage, solar, elec element 2"x1/2# insul, 80 Gal	1.000	Ea.	2,000	535	2,535
X	Valve, globe, bronze, 125 lb, soldered, 3/4" diam	1.000	Ea.	264	43	307
	Copper tubing type L, solder joints, hangers 10' OC 3/4" diam	10.000	L.F.	70.50	113	183.50
	Copper tubing type M, solder joints, hangers 10' OC 3/4" diam	60.000	L.F.	369	660	1,029
	Wrought copper fittings & solder, 3/4" diam	26.000	Ea.	185.90	1,170	1,355.90
	Sensor wire, #22-2 conductor multistranded	1.200	C.L.F.	25.80	96	121.80
Q-1	Duct work, rigid fiberglass, rectangular	400.000	S.F.	436	2,700	3,136
	Duct work, spiral preformed, steel, PVC coated both sides, 12" x 10"	8.000	Ea.	192	508	700
R-2	Shutter/damper for solar heater circulator	9.000	Ea.	589.50	1,143	1,732.50
K-1	Shutter motor for solar heater circulator blower	9.000	Ea.	1,467	855	2,322
K-1	Fan, solar energy heated air circulator, space & DHW system	1.000	Ea.	1,775	3,050	4,825
R-3, R-4, V	Tank, solar energy air storage, 6'-3"H 7'x7' = 306 CF/2000 Gal	1.000	Ea.	15,500	1,975	17,475
Z-2	Crushed stone 1-1/2"	11.000	C.Y.	357.50	103.18	460.68
C-2	Thermometer, remote probe, 2" dial	1.000	Ea.	38.50	107	145.50
R-1	Solenoid valve	1.000	Ea.	192	95.50	287.50
Z-1	Furnace, supply diffusers, return grilles, existing	1.000	Ea.	15,500	1,975	17,475
	TOTAL			53,778.76	19,063.68	72,842.44

D3010 675	Air To Water Heat Exchange		COST EACH		
			MAT.	INST.	TOTAL
1210	Solar, air to water heat exchange, for space/hot water heating	R235616 -60	54,000	19,100	73,100
1220					

D30 HVAC

D3020 Heat Generating Systems

Boiler   Baseboard Radiation

Small Electric Boiler
System Considerations:
1. Terminal units are fin tube baseboard radiation rated at 720 BTU/hr with 200° water temperature or 820 BTU/hr steam.
2. Primary use being for residential or smaller supplementary areas, the floor levels are based on 7-1/2' ceiling heights.
3. All distribution piping is copper for boilers through 205 MBH. All piping for larger systems is steel pipe.

System Components	QUANTITY	UNIT	COST EACH MAT.	COST EACH INST.	COST EACH TOTAL
SYSTEM D3020 102 1120					
SMALL HEATING SYSTEM, HYDRONIC, ELECTRIC BOILER					
1,480 S.F., 61 MBH, STEAM, 1 FLOOR					
Boiler, electric steam, std cntrls, trim, ftngs and valves, 18 KW, 61.4 MBH	1.000	Ea.	5,417.50	2,172.50	7,590
Copper tubing type L, solder joint, hanger 10'OC, 1-1/4" diam	160.000	L.F.	1,560	2,368	3,928
Radiation, 3/4" copper tube w/alum fin baseboard pkg 7" high	60.000	L.F.	519	1,620	2,139
Rough in baseboard panel or fin tube with valves & traps	10.000	Set	4,900	8,150	13,050
Pipe covering, calcium silicate w/cover, 1" wall 1-1/4" diam	160.000	L.F.	1,080	1,392	2,472
Low water cut-off, quick hookup, in gage glass tappings	1.000	Ea.	595	54	649
TOTAL			14,071.50	15,756.50	29,828
COST PER S.F.			9.85	11.03	20.88

D3020 102	Small Heating Systems, Hydronic, Electric Boilers		COST PER S.F. MAT.	COST PER S.F. INST.	COST PER S.F. TOTAL
1100	Small heating systems, hydronic, electric boilers				
1120	Steam, 1 floor, 1480 S.F., 61 M.B.H.		9.87	11.06	20.93
1160	3,000 S.F., 123 M.B.H.	R235000 -10	7.55	9.35	16.90
1200	5,000 S.F., 205 M.B.H.		6.65	8.60	15.25
1240	2 floors, 12,400 S.F., 512 M.B.H.	R235000 -20	6.25	8.55	14.80
1280	3 floors, 24,800 S.F., 1023 M.B.H.		6.50	8.45	14.95
1320	34,750 S.F., 1,433 M.B.H.	R235000 -30	6.05	8.20	14.25
1360	Hot water, 1 floor, 1,000 S.F., 41 M.B.H.		14.50	5.95	20.45
1400	2,500 S.F., 103 M.B.H.		11.15	10.65	21.80
1440	2 floors, 4,850 S.F., 205 M.B.H.		11.05	12.75	23.80
1480	3 floors, 9,700 S.F., 410 M.B.H.		11.95	13.25	25.20

D30 HVAC

D3020 Heat Generating Systems

Boiler

Unit Heater

Large Electric Boiler System Considerations:
1. Terminal units are all unit heaters of the same size. Quantities are varied to accommodate total requirements.
2. All air is circulated through the heaters a minimum of three times per hour.
3. As the capacities are adequate for commercial use, floor levels are based on 10′ ceiling heights.
4. All distribution piping is black steel pipe.

System Components	QUANTITY	UNIT	COST EACH MAT.	COST EACH INST.	COST EACH TOTAL
SYSTEM D3020 104 1240					
LARGE HEATING SYSTEM, HYDRONIC, ELECTRIC BOILER					
9,280 S.F., 135 KW, 461 MBH, 1 FLOOR					
Boiler, electric hot water, std ctrls, trim, ftngs, valves, 135 KW, 461 MBH	1.000	Ea.	12,487.50	4,725	17,212.50
Expansion tank, painted steel, 60 Gal capacity ASME	1.000	Ea.	6,525	260	6,785
Circulating pump, CI, close cpld, 50 GPM, 2 HP, 2″ pipe conn	1.000	Ea.	3,725	515	4,240
Unit heater, 1 speed propeller, horizontal, 200° EWT, 72.7 MBH	7.000	Ea.	11,900	1,981	13,881
Unit heater piping hookup with controls	7.000	Set	9,800	12,950	22,750
Pipe, steel, black, schedule 40, welded, 2-1/2″ diam	380.000	L.F.	13,680	13,110	26,790
Pipe covering, calcium silicate w/cover, 1″ wall, 2-1/2″ diam	380.000	L.F.	1,561.80	3,420	4,981.80
TOTAL			59,679.30	36,961	96,640.30
COST PER S.F.			5.97	3.70	9.67

D3020 104	Large Heating Systems, Hydronic, Electric Boilers		COST PER S.F. MAT.	COST PER S.F. INST.	COST PER S.F. TOTAL
1230	Large heating systems, hydronic, electric boilers				
1240	9,280 S.F., 135 K.W., 461 M.B.H., 1 floor		5.95	3.70	9.65
1280	14,900 S.F., 240 K.W., 820 M.B.H., 2 floors		8.90	6.45	15.35
1320	18,600 S.F., 296 K.W., 1,010 M.B.H., 3 floors	R235000 -10	9.10	7	16.10
1360	26,100 S.F., 420 K.W., 1,432 M.B.H., 4 floors		8.95	6.85	15.80
1400	39,100 S.F., 666 K.W., 2,273 M.B.H., 4 floors	R235000 -20	7.65	5.75	13.40
1440	57,700 S.F., 900 K.W., 3,071 M.B.H., 5 floors		8	5.65	13.65
1480	111,700 S.F., 1,800 K.W., 6,148 M.B.H., 6 floors	R235000 -30	7.15	4.86	12.01
1520	149,000 S.F., 2,400 K.W., 8,191 M.B.H., 8 floors		7.10	4.85	11.95
1560	223,300 S.F., 3,600 K.W., 12,283 M.B.H., 14 floors		7.75	5.50	13.25

D30 HVAC

D3020 Heat Generating Systems

Unit Heater

Fossil Fuel Boiler System Considerations:

1. Terminal units are horizontal unit heaters. Quantities are varied to accommodate total heat loss per building.
2. Unit heater selection was determined by their capacity to circulate the building volume a minimum of three times per hour in addition to the BTU output.
3. Systems shown are forced hot water. Steam boilers cost slightly more than hot water boilers. However, this is compensated for by the smaller size or fewer terminal units required with steam.
4. Floor levels are based on 10' story heights.
5. MBH requirements are gross boiler output.

System Components	QUANTITY	UNIT	COST EACH		
			MAT.	INST.	TOTAL
SYSTEM D3020 108 1280					
HEATING SYSTEM, HYDRONIC, FOSSIL FUEL, TERMINAL UNIT HEATERS					
CAST IRON BOILER, GAS, 80 MBH, 1,070 S.F. BUILDING					
Boiler, gas, hot water, CI, burner, controls, insulation, breeching, 80 MBH	1.000	Ea.	3,307.50	2,362.50	5,670
Pipe, steel, black, schedule 40, threaded, cplg & hngr 10'OC, 2" diam	200.000	L.F.	4,500	4,800	9,300
Unit heater, 1 speed propeller, horizontal, 200° EWT, 72.7 MBH	2.000	Ea.	3,400	566	3,966
Unit heater piping hookup with controls	2.000	Set	2,800	3,700	6,500
Expansion tank, painted steel, ASME, 18 Gal capacity	1.000	Ea.	3,900	130	4,030
Circulating pump, CI, flange connection, 1/12 HP	1.000	Ea.	680	258	938
Pipe covering, calcium silicate w/cover, 1" wall, 2" diam	200.000	L.F.	782	1,800	2,582
TOTAL			19,369.50	13,616.50	32,986
COST PER S.F.			17.43	12.25	29.68

D3020 108	Heating Systems, Unit Heaters		COST PER S.F.		
			MAT.	INST.	TOTAL
1260	Heating systems, hydronic, fossil fuel, terminal unit heaters,				
1280	Cast iron boiler, gas, 80 M.B.H., 1,070 S.F. bldg.		17.46	12.24	29.70
1320	163 M.B.H., 2,140 S.F. bldg.	R235000 -10	11.70	8.65	20.35
1360	544 M.B.H., 7,250 S.F. bldg.		8.55	6.10	14.65
1400	1,088 M.B.H., 14,500 S.F. bldg.	R235000 -20	7.75	5.80	13.55
1440	3,264 M.B.H., 43,500 S.F. bldg.		6.50	4.37	10.87
1480	5,032 M.B.H., 67,100 S.F. bldg.	R235000 -30	7.20	4.49	11.69
1520	Oil, 109 M.B.H., 1,420 S.F. bldg.		19.75	11.35	31.10
1560	235 M.B.H., 3,150 S.F. bldg.		11.45	8.05	19.50
1600	940 M.B.H., 12,500 S.F. bldg.		9.05	5.30	14.35
1640	1,600 M.B.H., 21,300 S.F. bldg.		8	5.10	13.10
1680	2,480 M.B.H., 33,100 S.F. bldg.		7.35	4.58	11.93
1720	3,350 M.B.H., 44,500 S.F. bldg.		7.55	4.68	12.23
1760	Coal, 148 M.B.H., 1,975 S.F. bldg.		102	7.40	109.40
1800	300 M.B.H., 4,000 S.F. bldg.		53	5.80	58.80
1840	2,360 M.B.H., 31,500 S.F. bldg.		14.30	4.66	18.96

D30 HVAC

D3020 Heat Generating Systems

Fin Tube Radiator

Fossil Fuel Boiler System Considerations:

1. Terminal units are commercial steel fin tube radiation. Quantities are varied to accommodate total heat loss per building.
2. Systems shown are forced hot water. Steam boilers cost slightly more than hot water boilers. However, this is compensated for by the smaller size or fewer terminal units required with steam.
3. Floor levels are based on 10' story heights.
4. MBH requirements are gross boiler output.

System Components	QUANTITY	UNIT	COST EACH MAT.	COST EACH INST.	COST EACH TOTAL
SYSTEM D3020 110 3240 HEATING SYSTEM, HYDRONIC, FOSSIL FUEL, FIN TUBE RADIATION CAST IRON BOILER, GAS, 80 MBH, 1,070 S.F. BLDG.					
Boiler, gas, hot water, CI, burner, controls, insulation, breeching, 80 MBH	1.000	Ea.	3,150	2,250	5,400
Pipe, steel, black, schedule 40, threaded, 2" diam	200.000	L.F.	4,500	4,800	9,300
Radiation, steel 1-1/4" tube & 4-1/4" fin w/cover & damper, wall hung	80.000	L.F.	3,800	3,480	7,280
Rough-in, wall hung steel fin radiation with supply & balance valves	8.000	Set	3,560	7,600	11,160
Expansion tank, painted steel, ASME, 18 Gal capacity	1.000	Ea.	3,900	130	4,030
Circulating pump, CI flanged, 1/12 HP	1.000	Ea.	680	258	938
Pipe covering, calcium silicate w/cover, 1" wall, 2" diam	200.000	L.F.	782	1,800	2,582
TOTAL			20,372	20,318	40,690
COST PER S.F.			18.33	18.29	36.62

D3020 110	Heating System, Fin Tube Radiation		COST PER S.F. MAT.	COST PER S.F. INST.	COST PER S.F. TOTAL
3230	Heating systems, hydronic, fossil fuel, fin tube radiation				
3240	Cast iron boiler, gas, 80 MBH, 1,070 S.F. bldg.		18.36	18.27	36.63
3280	169 M.B.H., 2,140 S.F. bldg.	R235000 -10	11.60	12.10	23.70
3320	544 M.B.H., 7,250 S.F. bldg.		9.75	10.35	20.10
3360	1,088 M.B.H., 14,500 S.F. bldg.	R235000 -20	9.15	10.15	19.30
3400	3,264 M.B.H., 43,500 S.F. bldg.		8.20	8.95	17.15
3440	5,032 M.B.H., 67,100 S.F. bldg.	R235000 -30	8.95	9.10	18.05
3480	Oil, 109 M.B.H., 1,420 S.F. bldg.		23.50	21	44.50
3520	235 M.B.H., 3,150 S.F. bldg.		12.65	12.25	24.90
3560	940 M.B.H., 12,500 S.F. bldg.		10.50	9.75	20.25
3600	1,600 M.B.H., 21,300 S.F. bldg.		9.70	9.70	19.40
3640	2,480 M.B.H., 33,100 S.F. bldg.		9.05	9.20	18.25
3680	3,350 M.B.H., 44,500 S.F. bldg.		9.20	9.25	18.45
3720	Coal, 148 M.B.H., 1,975 S.F. bldg.		103	11.55	114.55
3760	300 M.B.H., 4,000 S.F. bldg.		54	9.90	63.90
3800	2,360 M.B.H., 31,500 S.F. bldg.		15.95	9.20	25.15
4080	Steel boiler, oil, 97 M.B.H., 1,300 S.F. bldg.		17.45	17.15	34.60
4120	315 M.B.H., 4,550 S.F. bldg.		8.55	8.70	17.25
4160	525 M.B.H., 7,000 S.F. bldg.		12.30	10	22.30
4200	1,050 M.B.H., 14,000 S.F. bldg.		11.25	10	21.25
4240	2,310 M.B.H., 30,800 S.F. bldg.		10	9.25	19.25
4280	3,150 M.B.H., 42,000 S.F. bldg.		9.75	9.35	19.10

D30 HVAC

D3020 Heat Generating Systems

Electric Boiler, Hot Water

System Components	QUANTITY	UNIT	MAT.	INST.	TOTAL
SYSTEM D3020 126 1010					
BOILER, ELECTRIC, HOT WATER, 15 kW, 52 MBH					
Boilers, electric, ASME, hot water, 15 KW, 52 MBH	1.000	Ea.	6,000	1,825	7,825
Pipe, black steel, Sch 40, threaded, W/coupling & hangers, 10' OC, 3/4" dia	11.500	L.F.	89.13	162.15	251.28
Pipe, black steel, Sch 40, threaded, W/coupling & hangers, 10' OC, 1" dia	21.500	L.F.	228.98	348.30	577.28
Elbow, 90°, black, straight, 3/4" dia.	6.000	Ea.	46.20	369	415.20
Elbow, 90°, black, straight, 1" dia.	6.000	Ea.	80.70	396	476.70
Tee, black, straight, 3/4" dia.	1.000	Ea.	12.30	95.50	107.80
Tee, black, straight, 1" dia.	2.000	Ea.	42	214	256
Tee, black, reducing, 1" dia.	2.000	Ea.	48	214	262
Union, black with brass seat, 3/4" dia.	1.000	Ea.	34.50	66	100.50
Union, black with brass seat, 1" dia.	2.000	Ea.	90	143	233
Pipe nipples, 3/4" diam.	3.000	Ea.	11.63	21.15	32.78
Pipe nipples, 1" diam.	3.000	Ea.	15.98	24.30	40.28
Valves, bronze, gate, N.R.S., threaded, class 150, 3/4" size	2.000	Ea.	376	86	462
Valves, bronze, gate, N.R.S., threaded, class 150, 1" size	2.000	Ea.	516	90	606
Thermometer, stem type, 9" case, 8" stem, 3/4" NPT	1.000	Ea.	422	62	484
Tank, steel, liquid expansion, ASME, painted, 15 gallon capacity	1.000	Ea.	1,025	91.50	1,116.50
Pump, circulating, bronze, flange connection, 3/4" to 1-1/2" size, 1/8 HP	1.000	Ea.	1,725	258	1,983
Insulation, fiberglass pipe covering, 1" wall, 1" IPS	20.000	L.F.	48	131	179
TOTAL			10,811.42	4,596.90	15,408.32

D3020 126	Electric Boiler, Hot Water	MAT.	INST.	TOTAL
1010	Boiler, electric, hot water, 15 kW, 52 MBH	10,800	4,600	15,400
1020	30 kW, 103 MBH	11,100	4,850	15,950
1030	60 kW, 205 MBH	11,600	5,000	16,600
1040	120 kW, 410 MBH	14,500	6,000	20,500
1050	150 kW, 510 MBH	22,300	11,500	33,800
1060	210 kW, 716 MBH	26,000	12,600	38,600
1070	296 kW, 1010 MBH	34,700	13,000	47,700
1080	444 kW, 1515 MBH	42,800	17,500	60,300
1090	666 kW, 2273 MBH	51,000	19,000	70,000
1100	900 kW, 3071 MBH	64,000	22,100	86,100
1110	1320 kW, 4505 MBH	71,000	23,200	94,200
1120	2100 kW, 7167 MBH	102,500	28,100	130,600

D30 HVAC

D3020 Heat Generating Systems

D3020 126		Electric Boiler, Hot Water	COST EACH		
			MAT.	INST.	TOTAL
1130		2610 kW, 8905 MBH	127,000	33,900	160,900
1140		3600 kW, 12,283 MBH	153,000	40,700	193,700

D3020 128		Electric Boiler, Steam	COST EACH		
			MAT.	INST.	TOTAL
1010	Boiler, electric, steam, 18 kW, 61.4 MBH		7,000	4,400	11,400
1020		36 kW, 123 MBH	8,700	4,675	13,375
1030		60 kW, 205 MBH	21,800	9,500	31,300
1040		120 kW, 409 MBH	24,800	10,500	35,300
1050		150 kW, 512 MBH	29,200	15,700	44,900
1060		210 kW, 716 MBH	47,000	16,900	63,900
1070		300 kW, 1023 MBH	48,500	18,500	67,000
1080		510 kW, 1740 MBH	58,500	24,000	82,500
1090		720 kW, 2456 MBH	64,000	25,200	89,200
1100		1080 kW, 3685 MBH	77,000	30,000	107,000
1110		1260 kW, 4300 MBH	78,500	31,900	110,400
1120		1620 kW, 5527 MBH	83,000	36,000	119,000
1130		2070 kW, 7063 MBH	106,500	37,800	144,300
1140		2340 kW, 7984 MBH	157,500	43,000	200,500

D30 HVAC

D3020 Heat Generating Systems

Cast Iron Boiler, Hot Water, Gas Fired

System Components	QUANTITY	UNIT	COST EACH		
			MAT.	INST.	TOTAL
SYSTEM D3020 130 1010					
BOILER, CAST IRON, GAS, HOT WATER, 100 MBH					
Boilers, gas fired, std controls, CI, insulated, HW, gross output 100 MBH	1.000	Ea.	3,100	2,450	5,550
Pipe, black steel, Sch 40, threaded, W/coupling & hangers, 10' OC, 3/4" dia	22.500	L.F.	174.38	317.25	491.63
Pipe, black steel, Sch 40, threaded, W/coupling & hangers, 10' OC, 1" dia.	21.500	L.F.	228.98	348.30	577.28
Elbow, 90°, black, straight, 3/4" dia.	9.000	Ea.	69.30	553.50	622.80
Elbow, 90°, black, straight, 1" dia.	6.000	Ea.	80.70	396	476.70
Tee, black, straight, 3/4" dia.	2.000	Ea.	24.60	191	215.60
Tee, black, straight, 1" dia.	2.000	Ea.	42	214	256
Tee, black, reducing, 1" dia.	2.000	Ea.	48	214	262
Pipe cap, black, 3/4" dia.	1.000	Ea.	8.75	27	35.75
Union, black with brass seat, 3/4" dia.	2.000	Ea.	69	132	201
Union, black with brass seat, 1" dia.	2.000	Ea.	90	143	233
Pipe nipples, black, 3/4" dia.	5.000	Ea.	19.38	35.25	54.63
Pipe nipples, black, 1" dia.	3.000	Ea.	15.98	24.30	40.28
Valves, bronze, gate, N.R.S., threaded, class 150, 3/4" size	2.000	Ea.	376	86	462
Valves, bronze, gate, N.R.S., threaded, class 150, 1" size	2.000	Ea.	516	90	606
Gas cock, brass, 3/4" size	1.000	Ea.	41	39	80
Thermometer, stem type, 9" case, 8" stem, 3/4" NPT	2.000	Ea.	422	62	484
Tank, steel, liquid expansion, ASME, painted, 15 gallon capacity	1.000	Ea.	1,025	91.50	1,116.50
Pump, circulating, bronze, flange connection, 3/4" to 1-1/2" size, 1/8 HP	1.000	Ea.	1,725	258	1,983
Vent chimney, all fuel, pressure tight, double wall, SS, 6" dia.	20.000	L.F.	1,900	510	2,410
Vent chimney, elbow, 90° fixed, 6" dia.	2.000	Ea.	1,010	101	1,111
Vent chimney, Tee, 6" dia.	2.000	Ea.	610	127	737
Vent chimney, ventilated roof thimble, 6" dia.	1.000	Ea.	325	58.50	383.50
Vent chimney, flat roof flashing, 6" dia.	1.000	Ea.	143	50.50	193.50
Vent chimney, stack cap, 6" diameter	1.000	Ea.	365	33	398
Insulation, fiberglass pipe covering, 1" wall, 1" IPS	20.000	L.F.	48	131	179
TOTAL			12,477.07	6,683.10	19,160.17

D3020 130	Boiler, Cast Iron, Hot Water, Gas	COST EACH		
		MAT.	INST.	TOTAL
1010	Boiler, cast iron, gas, hot water, 100 MBH	12,500	6,675	19,175
1020	200 MBH	14,300	7,650	21,950
1030	320 MBH	12,700	8,325	21,025
1040	440 MBH	18,500	10,700	29,200
1050	544 MBH	29,200	16,700	45,900
1060	765 MBH	36,000	17,900	53,900

D30 HVAC

D3020 Heat Generating Systems

D3020 130 Boiler, Cast Iron, Hot Water, Gas

		MAT.	INST.	TOTAL
1070	1088 MBH	40,200	19,200	59,400
1080	1530 MBH	49,100	25,400	74,500
1090	2312 MBH	59,000	29,900	88,900
1100	2856 MBH	67,500	32,200	99,700
1110	3808 MBH	79,000	37,600	116,600
1120	4720 MBH	115,000	42,300	157,300
1130	6100 MBH	171,500	47,000	218,500
1140	6970 MBH	182,000	58,000	240,000

D3020 134 Boiler, Cast Iron, Steam, Gas

		MAT.	INST.	TOTAL
1010	Boiler, cast iron, gas, steam, 100 MBH	9,700	6,450	16,150
1020	200 MBH	22,900	12,200	35,100
1030	320 MBH	24,500	13,700	38,200
1040	544 MBH	33,400	21,300	54,700
1050	765 MBH	39,100	22,200	61,300
1060	1275 MBH	46,100	24,400	70,500
1070	2675 MBH	59,500	35,500	95,000
1080	3570 MBH	83,000	39,800	122,800
1090	4720 MBH	107,000	42,500	149,500
1100	6100 MBH	139,500	49,400	188,900
1110	6970 MBH	150,000	58,000	208,000

D3020 136 Boiler, Cast Iron, Hot Water, Gas/Oil

		MAT.	INST.	TOTAL
1010	Boiler, cast iron, gas & oil, hot water, 584 MBH	36,500	18,600	55,100
1020	876 MBH	48,300	19,900	68,200
1030	1168 MBH	56,000	22,500	78,500
1040	1460 MBH	61,000	27,000	88,000
1050	2044 MBH	73,000	28,000	101,000
1060	2628 MBH	94,000	33,900	127,900
1070	3210 MBH	99,500	36,400	135,900
1080	3796 MBH	106,500	37,600	144,100
1090	4672 MBH	122,500	39,400	161,900
1100	5256 MBH	147,500	47,700	195,200
1110	6000 MBH	173,000	48,600	221,600
1120	9800 MBH	214,500	83,000	297,500
1130	12,200 MBH	266,000	96,500	362,500
1140	13,500 MBH	289,000	103,000	392,000

D3020 138 Boiler, Cast Iron, Steam, Gas/Oil

		MAT.	INST.	TOTAL
1010	Boiler, cast iron, gas & oil, steam, 810 MBH	44,600	24,100	68,700
1020	1360 MBH	50,000	25,700	75,700
1030	2040 MBH	56,500	33,000	89,500
1040	2700 MBH	59,500	36,700	96,200
1050	3270 MBH	79,000	40,900	119,900
1060	3770 MBH	121,000	41,700	162,700
1070	4650 MBH	134,500	47,500	182,000
1080	5520 MBH	153,000	50,000	203,000
1090	6100 MBH	156,500	52,500	209,000
1100	6970 MBH	168,000	64,000	232,000

D30 HVAC

D3020 Heat Generating Systems

Base Mounted End-Suction Pump

System Components	QUANTITY	UNIT	MAT.	INST.	TOTAL
SYSTEM D3020 330 1010					
PUMP, BASE MTD. WITH MOTOR, END-SUCTION, 2-1/2" SIZE, 3 HP, TO 150 GPM					
Pump, circulating, CI, base mounted, 2-1/2" size, 3 HP, to 150 GPM	1.000	Ea.	12,500	860	13,360
Pipe, black steel, Sch. 40, on yoke & roll hangers, 10' O.C., 2-1/2" dia	12.000	L.F.	432	414	846
Elbow, 90°, weld joint, steel, 2-1/2" pipe size	1.000	Ea.	25.50	201.80	227.30
Flange, weld neck, 150 LB, 2-1/2" pipe size	8.000	Ea.	276	807.28	1,083.28
Valve, iron body, gate, 125 lb., N.R.S., flanged, 2-1/2" size	1.000	Ea.	1,375	310	1,685
Strainer, Y type, iron body, flanged, 125 lb., 2-1/2" pipe size	1.000	Ea.	251	310	561
Multipurpose valve, CI body, 2" size	1.000	Ea.	675	108	783
Expansion joint, flanged spool, 6" F to F, 2-1/2" dia	2.000	Ea.	900	252	1,152
T-O-L, weld joint, socket, 1/4" pipe size, nozzle	2.000	Ea.	28.10	141.14	169.24
T-O-L, weld joint, socket, 1/2" pipe size, nozzle	2.000	Ea.	11.70	147.42	159.12
Control gauges, pressure or vacuum, 3-1/2" diameter dial	2.000	Ea.	72	54	126
Pressure/temperature relief plug, 316 SS, 3/4" OD, 7-1/2" insertion	2.000	Ea.	242	54	296
Insulation, fiberglass pipe covering, 1-1/2" wall, 2-1/2" IPS	12.000	L.F.	69	96	165
Water flow	1.000	Ea.	2,075	1,300	3,375
Pump balancing	1.000	Ea.		380	380
TOTAL			18,932.30	5,435.64	24,367.94

D3020 330	Circulating Pump Systems, End Suction	MAT.	INST.	TOTAL
1010	Pump, base mtd with motor, end-suction, 2-1/2" size, 3 HP, to 150 GPM	18,900	5,425	24,325
1020	3" size, 5 HP, to 225 GPM	22,900	6,150	29,050
1030	4" size, 7-1/2 HP, to 350 GPM	24,300	7,300	31,600
1040	5" size, 15 HP, to 1000 GPM	33,000	10,800	43,800
1050	6" size, 25 HP, to 1550 GPM	45,800	13,000	58,800

D3020 340	Circulating Pump Systems, Double Suction	MAT.	INST.	TOTAL
1010	Pump, base mtd w/motor, double suction, 6" size, 50 HP, to 1200 GPM	32,400	18,600	51,000
1020	8" size, 75 HP, to 2500 GPM	65,500	24,900	90,400
1030	8" size, 100 HP, to 3000 GPM	90,500	27,800	118,300
1040	10" size, 150 HP, to 4000 GPM	121,500	31,400	152,900
1010	9,000 BTUH cooling, 13,900 BTU heat	2,925	310	3,235

D30 HVAC

D3030 Cooling Generating Systems

Design Assumptions: The chilled water, air cooled systems priced, utilize reciprocating hermetic compressors and propeller-type condenser fans. Piping with pumps and expansion tanks is included based on a two pipe system. No ducting is included and the fan-coil units are cooling only. Water treatment and balancing are not included. Chilled water piping is insulated. Area distribution is through the use of multiple fan coil units. Fewer but larger fan coil units with duct distribution would be approximately the same S.F. cost.

System Components	QUANTITY	UNIT	COST EACH MAT.	COST EACH INST.	COST EACH TOTAL
SYSTEM D3030 110 1200 PACKAGED CHILLER, AIR COOLED, WITH FAN COIL UNIT APARTMENT CORRIDORS, 3,000 S.F., 5.50 TON					
Fan coil air conditioning unit, cabinet mounted & filters chilled water	1.000	Ea.	5,407.35	714.87	6,122.22
Water chiller, air conditioning unit, air cooled	1.000	Ea.	7,562.50	2,667.50	10,230
Chilled water unit coil connections	1.000	Ea.	2,650	1,950	4,600
Chilled water distribution piping	440.000	L.F.	27,280	26,400	53,680
TOTAL			42,899.85	31,732.37	74,632.22
COST PER S.F.			12.87	9.52	22.39

*Cooling requirements would lead to choosing a water cooled unit.

D3030 110	Chilled Water, Air Cooled Condenser Systems	COST PER S.F. MAT.	COST PER S.F. INST.	COST PER S.F. TOTAL
1180	Packaged chiller, air cooled, with fan coil unit			
1200	Apartment corridors, 3,000 S.F., 5.50 ton	12.87	9.51	22.38
1240	6,000 S.F., 11.00 ton	11.35	8.40	19.75
1280	10,000 S.F., 18.33 ton	9.15	6.35	15.50
1320	20,000 S.F., 36.66 ton	7.15	4.59	11.74
1360	40,000 S.F., 73.33 ton	5.55	4.59	10.14
1440	Banks and libraries, 3,000 S.F., 12.50 ton	18.65	12.30	30.95
1480	6,000 S.F., 25.00 ton	16.15	9.95	26.10
1520	10,000 S.F., 41.66 ton	12.70	6.90	19.60
1560	20,000 S.F., 83.33 ton	9.75	6.20	15.95
1600	40,000 S.F., 167 ton*			
1680	Bars and taverns, 3,000 S.F., 33.25 ton	29.50	14.35	43.85
1720	6,000 S.F., 66.50 ton	25	10.85	35.85
1760	10,000 S.F., 110.83 ton	15.80	3.25	19.05
1800	20,000 S.F., 220 ton*			
1840	40,000 S.F., 440 ton*			
1920	Bowling alleys, 3,000 S.F., 17.00 ton	22	13.75	35.75
1960	6,000 S.F., 34.00 ton	17.35	9.60	26.95
2000	10,000 S.F., 56.66 ton	14.15	6.85	21
2040	20,000 S.F., 113.33 ton	10.65	6.25	16.90
2080	40,000 S.F., 227 ton*			
2160	Department stores, 3,000 S.F., 8.75 ton	18.15	11.75	29.90
2200	6,000 S.F., 17.50 ton	13.30	9	22.30
2240	10,000 S.F., 29.17 ton	10.80	6.45	17.25
2280	20,000 S.F., 58.33 ton	8.60	4.72	13.32
2320	40,000 S.F., 116.66 ton	6.80	4.72	11.52

D30 HVAC

D3030 Cooling Generating Systems

D3030 110	Chilled Water, Air Cooled Condenser Systems	COST PER S.F.		
		MAT.	INST.	TOTAL
2400	Drug stores, 3,000 S.F., 20.00 ton	24.50	14.20	38.70
2440	6,000 S.F., 40.00 ton	19.80	10.35	30.15
2480	10,000 S.F., 66.66 ton	15.30	8.85	24.15
2520	20,000 S.F., 133.33 ton	12.90	6.55	19.45
2560	40,000 S.F., 267 ton*			
2640	Factories, 2,000 S.F., 10.00 ton	17.15	11.80	28.95
2680	6,000 S.F., 20.00 ton	14.65	9.50	24.15
2720	10,000 S.F., 33.33 ton	11.40	6.60	18
2760	20,000 S.F., 66.66 ton	8.45	5.90	14.35
2800	40,000 S.F., 133.33 ton	7.45	4.83	12.28
2880	Food supermarkets, 3,000 S.F., 8.50 ton	17.90	11.70	29.60
2920	6,000 S.F., 17.00 ton	13.15	8.95	22.10
2960	10,000 S.F., 28.33 ton	10.30	6.30	16.60
3000	20,000 S.F., 56.66 ton	8.30	4.62	12.92
3040	40,000 S.F., 113.33 ton	6.45	4.73	11.18
3120	Medical centers, 3,000 S.F., 7.00 ton	16.75	11.40	28.15
3160	6,000 S.F., 14.00 ton	12.25	8.70	20.95
3200	10,000 S.F., 23.33 ton	10.15	6.60	16.75
3240	20,000 S.F., 46.66 ton	8.15	4.82	12.97
3280	40,000 S.F., 93.33 ton	6	4.65	10.65
3360	Offices, 3,000 S.F., 9.50 ton	16.55	11.65	28.20
3400	6,000 S.F., 19.00 ton	14.35	9.40	23.75
3440	10,000 S.F., 31.66 ton	11.15	6.55	17.70
3480	20,000 S.F., 63.33 ton	8.60	6	14.60
3520	40,000 S.F., 126.66 ton	7.40	4.88	12.28
3600	Restaurants, 3,000 S.F., 15.00 ton	20	12.75	32.75
3640	6,000 S.F., 30.00 ton	16.95	9.65	26.60
3680	10,000 S.F., 50.00 ton	14	7	21
3720	20,000 S.F., 100.00 ton	11.20	6.55	17.75
3760	40,000 S.F., 200 ton*			
3840	Schools and colleges, 3,000 S.F., 11.50 ton	18.05	12.10	30.15
3880	6,000 S.F., 23.00 ton	15.55	9.75	25.30
3920	10,000 S.F., 38.33 ton	12.20	6.80	19
3960	20,000 S.F., 76.66 ton	9.70	6.25	15.95
4000	40,000 S.F., 153 ton*			

D30 HVAC

D3030 Cooling Generating Systems

General: Water cooled chillers are available in the same sizes as air cooled units. They are also available in larger capacities.

Design Assumptions: The chilled water systems with water cooled condenser include reciprocating hermetic compressors, water cooling tower, pumps, piping and expansion tanks and are based on a two pipe system. Chilled water piping is insulated. No ducts are included and fan-coil units are cooling only. Area distribution is through use of multiple fan coil units. Fewer but larger fan coil units with duct distribution would be approximately the same S.F. cost. Water treatment and balancing are not included.

System Components	QUANTITY	UNIT	COST EACH MAT.	COST EACH INST.	COST EACH TOTAL
SYSTEM D3030 115 1320					
PACKAGED CHILLER, WATER COOLED, WITH FAN COIL UNIT					
APARTMENT CORRIDORS, 4,000 S.F., 7.33 TON					
Fan coil air conditioner unit, cabinet mounted & filters, chilled water	2.000	Ea.	7,206.85	952.77	8,159.62
Water chiller, water cooled, 1 compressor, hermetic scroll,	1.000	Ea.	6,961.60	4,648.70	11,610.30
Cooling tower, draw thru single flow, belt drive	1.000	Ea.	1,847.16	197.91	2,045.07
Cooling tower pumps & piping	1.000	System	923.58	469.12	1,392.70
Chilled water unit coil connections	2.000	Ea.	5,300	3,900	9,200
Chilled water distribution piping	520.000	L.F.	32,240	31,200	63,440
TOTAL			54,479.19	41,368.50	95,847.69
COST PER S.F.			16.34	12.41	28.75

*Cooling requirements would lead to choosing a water cooled unit.

D3030 115	Chilled Water, Cooling Tower Systems	COST PER S.F. MAT.	COST PER S.F. INST.	COST PER S.F. TOTAL
1300	Packaged chiller, water cooled, with fan coil unit			
1320	Apartment corridors, 4,000 S.F., 7.33 ton	16.35	12.42	28.77
1360	6,000 S.F., 11.00 ton	11.30	8.85	20.15
1400	10,000 S.F., 18.33 ton	9.90	6.65	16.55
1440	20,000 S.F., 26.66 ton	7.80	4.78	12.58
1480	40,000 S.F., 73.33 ton	5.95	4.77	10.72
1520	60,000 S.F., 110.00 ton	5.60	5.05	10.65
1600	Banks and libraries, 4,000 S.F., 16.66 ton	19.65	11.20	30.85
1640	6,000 S.F., 25.00 ton	17.25	9.85	27.10
1680	10,000 S.F., 41.66 ton	13.80	7.30	21.10
1720	20,000 S.F., 83.33 ton	10.50	6.50	17
1760	40,000 S.F., 166.66 ton	14.75	8.45	23.20
1800	60,000 S.F., 250.00 ton	15.45	8.90	24.35
1880	Bars and taverns, 4,000 S.F., 44.33 ton	30.50	13.90	44.40
1920	6,000 S.F., 66.50 ton	25	14.40	39.40
1960	10,000 S.F., 110.83 ton	21.50	11	32.50
2000	20,000 S.F., 221.66 ton	28.50	11.45	39.95
2040	40,000 S.F., 440 ton*			
2080	60,000 S.F., 660 ton*			
2160	Bowling alleys, 4,000 S.F., 22.66 ton	22	12.55	34.55
2200	6,000 S.F., 34.00 ton	19.75	10.55	30.30
2240	10,000 S.F., 56.66 ton	15.90	7.85	23.75
2280	20,000 S.F., 113.33 ton	11.80	7.15	18.95
2320	40,000 S.F., 226.66 ton	17.55	8.40	25.95

Note: Row 1400 shows reference code R236000-20.

D30 HVAC

D3030 Cooling Generating Systems

D3030 115	Chilled Water, Cooling Tower Systems	COST PER S.F.		
		MAT.	INST.	TOTAL
2360	60,000 S.F., 340 ton			
2440	Department stores, 4,000 S.F., 11.66 ton	14.50	11.10	25.60
2480	6,000 S.F., 17.50 ton	15.10	9.15	24.25
2520	10,000 S.F., 29.17 ton	11.30	6.65	17.95
2560	20,000 S.F., 58.33 ton	8.75	5.05	13.80
2600	40,000 S.F., 116.66 ton	6.90	5.10	12
2640	60,000 S.F., 175.00 ton	13.60	8.20	21.80
2720	Drug stores, 4,000 S.F., 26.66 ton	24	12.60	36.60
2760	6,000 S.F., 40.00 ton	21.50	10.75	32.25
2800	10,000 S.F., 66.66 ton	16	9.75	25.75
2840	20,000 S.F., 133.33 ton	13.50	7.60	21.10
2880	40,000 S.F., 266.67 ton	19.15	9.50	28.65
2920	60,000 S.F., 400 ton*			
3000	Factories, 4,000 S.F., 13.33 ton	17.65	10.70	28.35
3040	6,000 S.F., 20.00 ton	14.95	9.40	24.35
3080	10,000 S.F., 33.33 ton	12.10	6.85	18.95
3120	20,000 S.F., 66.66 ton	8.60	6.30	14.90
3160	40,000 S.F., 133.33 ton	7.75	5.35	13.10
3200	60,000 S.F., 200.00 ton	14.25	8.60	22.85
3280	Food supermarkets, 4,000 S.F., 11.33 ton	14.35	11.05	25.40
3320	6,000 S.F., 17.00 ton	13.75	9.15	22.90
3360	10,000 S.F., 28.33 ton	11.15	6.60	17.75
3400	20,000 S.F., 56.66 ton	9	5.05	14.05
3440	40,000 S.F., 113.33 ton	6.90	5.10	12
3480	60,000 S.F., 170.00 ton	13.55	8.20	21.75
3560	Medical centers, 4,000 S.F., 9.33 ton	12.85	10.15	23
3600	6,000 S.F., 14.00 ton	13.70	8.80	22.50
3640	10,000 S.F., 23.33 ton	10.75	6.55	17.30
3680	20,000 S.F., 46.66 ton	8.35	4.93	13.28
3720	40,000 S.F., 93.33 ton	6.60	4.98	11.58
3760	60,000 S.F., 140.00 ton	12.45	8.30	20.75
3840	Offices, 4,000 S.F., 12.66 ton	17.25	10.60	27.85
3880	6,000 S.F., 19.00 ton	15.05	9.60	24.65
3920	10,000 S.F., 31.66 ton	12.15	6.95	19.10
3960	20,000 S.F., 63.33 ton	8.55	6.30	14.85
4000	40,000 S.F., 126.66 ton	12.90	8	20.90
4040	60,000 S.F., 190.00 ton	13.90	8.50	22.40
4120	Restaurants, 4,000 S.F., 20.00 ton	19.95	11.65	31.60
4160	6,000 S.F., 30.00 ton	18.10	9.90	28
4200	10,000 S.F., 50.00 ton	14.90	7.55	22.45
4240	20,000 S.F., 100.00 ton	12	7	19
4280	40,000 S.F., 200.00 ton	15.05	8.15	23.20
4320	60,000 S.F., 300.00 ton	16.75	9.20	25.95
4400	Schools and colleges, 4,000 S.F., 15.33 ton	18.85	11	29.85
4440	6,000 S.F., 23.00 ton	16.55	9.65	26.20
4480	10,000 S.F., 38.33 ton	13.20	7.15	20.35
4520	20,000 S.F., 76.66 ton	10.20	6.45	16.65
4560	40,000 S.F., 153.33 ton	14.10	8.25	22.35
4600	60,000 S.F., 230.00 ton	14.45	8.60	23.05

D30 HVAC

D3030 Cooling Generating Systems

Chilled Water Piping

Reciprocating Chiller, Water Cooled

Condenser Water Piping

System Components	QUANTITY	UNIT	COST EACH		
			MAT.	INST.	TOTAL
SYSTEM D3030 130 1010					
CHILLER, RECIPROCATING, WATER COOLED, STD. CONTROLS, 60 TON					
Water chiller, water cooled, 60 ton cooling	1.000	Ea.	42,200	13,200	55,400
Pipe, black steel, welded, Sch. 40, on yoke & roll hgrs, 10' O.C., 4" dia	40.000	L.F.	2,300	1,756.40	4,056.40
Elbow, 90°, weld joint, butt, 4" pipe size	8.000	Ea.	424	2,592.80	3,016.80
Flange, welding neck, 150 lb., 4" pipe size	16.000	Ea.	760	2,592.80	3,352.80
Valves, iron body, butterfly, lug type, lever actuator, 4" size	4.000	Ea.	1,640	1,240	2,880
Expansion joints, bellows type, flange spool, 6" F to F, 4" dia	4.000	Ea.	2,180	740	2,920
T-O-L socket, weld joint, 1/4" pipe size, nozzle	4.000	Ea.	56.20	282.28	338.48
T-O-L socket, weld joint, 3/4" pipe size, nozzle	4.000	Ea.	26.80	307.44	334.24
Thermometers, stem type, 9" case, 8" stem, 3/4" NPT	4.000	Ea.	844	124	968
Gauges, pressure or vacuum, 3-1/2" diameter dial	4.000	Ea.	144	108	252
Insulation, fiberglass pipe covering, 1-1/2" wall, 4" IPS	20.000	L.F.	137	205	342
Chiller balancing	1.000	Ea.		735	735
TOTAL			50,712	23,883.72	74,595.72

D3030 130	Reciprocating Chiller, Water Cooled	COST EACH		
		MAT.	INST.	TOTAL
1010	Chiller, reciprocating, water cooled, std. controls, 60 Ton	50,500	23,900	74,400
1020	100 Ton	82,000	30,300	112,300
1030	150 Ton	103,500	39,200	142,700
1040	200 Ton	138,500	41,300	179,800

D3030 135	Reciprocating Chiller, Air Cooled	COST EACH		
		MAT.	INST.	TOTAL
1010	Chiller, reciprocating, air cooled, std. controls, 20 Ton	30,800	13,900	44,700
1020	30 Ton	42,500	14,700	57,200
1030	40 Ton	48,400	15,700	64,100

D30 HVAC

D3030 Cooling Generating Systems

Chilled Water Piping

Centrifugal Chiller, Water Cooled, Hermetic

Condenser Water Piping

System Components	QUANTITY	UNIT	COST EACH MAT.	COST EACH INST.	COST EACH TOTAL
SYSTEM D3030 140 1010					
CHILLER, CENTRIF., WATER COOLED, PKGD. HERMETIC, STD. CONTROLS, 200 TON					
Water chiller, cntfgl, water cooled, not incl. tower, 200 ton	1.000	Ea.	159,000	17,700	176,700
Pipe, black steel, welded, Sch. 40, on yoke & roll hgrs, 10' OC, 6" dia	40.000	L.F.	4,120	2,758.40	6,878.40
Elbow, 90°, weld joint, 6" pipe size	8.000	Ea.	896	3,952.80	4,848.80
Flange, welding neck, 150 lb., 6" pipe size	16.000	Ea.	1,112	3,968.80	5,080.80
Valves, iron body, butterfly, lug type, lever actuator, 6" size	4.000	Ea.	2,760	1,920	4,680
Expansion joints, bellows type, flange spool, 6" F to F, 6" dia	4.000	Ea.	2,740	916	3,656
T-O-L socket, weld jiont, 1/4" pipe size, nozzle	4.000	Ea.	56.20	282.28	338.48
T-O-L socket, weld jiont, 3/4" pipe size, nozzle	4.000	Ea.	26.80	307.44	334.24
Thermometers, stem type, 9" case, 8" stem, 3/4" NPT	4.000	Ea.	844	124	968
Gauges, pressure or vacuum, 3-1/2" diameter dial	4.000	Ea.	144	108	252
Insulation, fiberglass pipe covering, 1-1/2" wall, 6" IPS	40.000	L.F.	324	522	846
Chiller balancing	1.000	Ea.		735	735
TOTAL			172,023	33,294.72	205,317.72

D3030 140	Centrifugal Chiller, Water Cooled		MAT.	INST.	TOTAL
1010	Chiller, centrif., water cooled, pkgd. hermetic, std controls, 200 Ton		172,000	33,300	205,300
1020		400 Ton	198,500	50,500	249,000
1030		1,000 Ton	567,500	74,500	642,000
1040		1,500 Ton	787,000	92,000	879,000

D30 HVAC

D3030 Cooling Generating Systems

Chilled Water Piping (Condenser Water Piping Similar)   **Gas Absorption Chiller, Water Cooled**   **Gas Piping**

System Components	QUANTITY	UNIT	COST EACH		
			MAT.	INST.	TOTAL
SYSTEM D3030 145 1010					
CHILLER, GAS FIRED ABSORPTION, WATER COOLED, STD. CONTROLS, 800 TON					
Absorption water chiller, gas fired, water cooled, 800 ton	1.000	Ea.	707,000	39,200	746,200
Pipe, black steel, weld, Sch. 40, on yoke & roll hangers, 10' O.C., 10" dia	20.000	L.F.	3,060	2,058.80	5,118.80
Pipe, black steel, welded, Sch. 40, 14" dia., (two rod roll type hanger)	44.000	L.F.	9,328	7,246.80	16,574.80
Pipe, black steel, weld, Sch. 40, on yoke & roll hangers, 10' O.C., 4" dia	20.000	L.F.	1,150	878.20	2,028.20
Elbow, 90°, weld joint, 10" pipe size	4.000	Ea.	1,680	3,294	4,974
Elbow, 90°, weld joint, 14" pipe size	6.000	Ea.	7,950	7,413	15,363
Elbow, 90°, weld joint, 4" pipe size	3.000	Ea.	159	972.30	1,131.30
Flange, welding neck, 150 lb., 10" pipe size	8.000	Ea.	1,576	3,294	4,870
Flange, welding neck, 150 lb., 14" pipe size	14.000	Ea.	7,210	7,709.80	14,919.80
Flange, welding neck, 150 lb., 4" pipe size	3.000	Ea.	142.50	486.15	628.65
Valves, iron body, butterfly, lug type, gear operated, 10" size	2.000	Ea.	4,350	1,200	5,550
Valves, iron body, butterfly, lug type, gear operated, 14" size	5.000	Ea.	31,250	5,250	36,500
Valves, semi-steel, lubricated plug valve, flanged, 4" pipe size	1.000	Ea.	1,700	515	2,215
Expansion joints, bellows type, flange spool, 6" F to F, 10" dia	2.000	Ea.	2,200	620	2,820
Expansion joints, bellows type, flange spool, 10" F to F, 14" dia	2.000	Ea.	3,800	820	4,620
T-O-L socket, weld joint, 1/4" pipe size, nozzle	4.000	Ea.	56.20	282.28	338.48
T-O-L socket, weld joint, 3/4" pipe size, nozzle	4.000	Ea.	26.80	307.44	334.24
Thermometers, stem type, 9" case, 8" stem, 3/4" NPT	4.000	Ea.	844	124	968
Gauges, pressure or vacuum, 3-1/2" diameter dial	4.000	Ea.	144	108	252
Insulation, fiberglass pipe covering, 2" wall, 10" IPS	20.000	L.F.	361	410	771
Vent chimney, all fuel, pressure tight, double wall, SS, 12" dia	20.000	L.F.	1,980	690	2,670
Chiller balancing	1.000	Ea.		735	735
TOTAL			**785,967.50**	**83,614.77**	**869,582.27**

D3030 145	Gas Absorption Chiller, Water Cooled	COST EACH		
		MAT.	INST.	TOTAL
1010	Chiller, gas fired absorption, water cooled, std. ctrls, 800 Ton	786,000	83,500	869,500
1020	1000 Ton	1,046,500	107,500	1,154,000

D3030 150	Steam Absorption Chiller, Water Cooled	COST EACH		
		MAT.	INST.	TOTAL
1010	Chiller, steam absorption, water cooled, std. ctrls, 750 Ton	920,500	99,000	1,019,500
1020	955 Ton	989,000	118,500	1,107,500
1030	1465 Ton	1,571,500	136,000	1,707,500
1040	1660 Ton	1,916,000	154,000	2,070,000

D30 HVAC

D3030 Cooling Generating Systems

Cold Water Fill

Drain To Waste Piping

Cooling Tower

Condenser Water Piping

System Components	QUANTITY	UNIT	COST EACH MAT.	COST EACH INST.	COST EACH TOTAL
SYSTEM D3030 310 1010					
COOLING TOWER, GALVANIZED STEEL, PACKAGED UNIT, DRAW THRU, 60 TON					
Cooling towers, draw thru, single flow, belt drive, 60 tons	1.000	Ea.	15,120	1,620	16,740
Pipe, black steel, welded, Sch. 40, on yoke & roll hangers, 10' OC, 4" dia.	40.000	L.F.	2,300	1,756.40	4,056.40
Tubing, copper, Type L, couplings & hangers 10' OC, 1-1/2" dia.	20.000	L.F.	251	331	582
Elbow, 90°, copper, cu x cu, 1-1/2" dia.	3.000	Ea.	121.50	198	319.50
Elbow, 90°, weld joint, 4" pipe size	6.000	Ea.	318	1,944.60	2,262.60
Flange, welding neck, 150 lb., 4" pipe size	6.000	Ea.	285	972.30	1,257.30
Valves, bronze, gate, N.R.S., soldered, 125 psi, 1-1/2" size	1.000	Ea.	340	66	406
Valves, iron body, butterfly, lug type, lever actuator, 4" size	2.000	Ea.	820	620	1,440
Electric heat trace system, 400 degree, 115v, 5 watts/L.F.	160.000	L.F.	2,056	241.60	2,297.60
Insulation, fiberglass pipe covering, , 1-1/2" wall, 4" IPS	40.000	L.F.	274	410	684
Insulation, fiberglass pipe covering, 1" wall, 1-1/2" IPS	20.000	L.F.	62	137	199
Cooling tower condenser control system	1.000	Ea.	9,550	3,525	13,075
Cooling tower balancing	1.000	Ea.		565	565
TOTAL			31,497.50	12,386.90	43,884.40

D3030 310	Galvanized Draw Through Cooling Tower	COST EACH MAT.	COST EACH INST.	COST EACH TOTAL
1010	Cooling tower, galvanized steel, packaged unit, draw thru, 60 Ton	31,500	12,400	43,900
1020	110 Ton	40,400	14,500	54,900
1030	300 Ton	59,000	22,000	81,000
1040	600 Ton	75,000	32,800	107,800
1050	1000 Ton	152,500	48,300	200,800

D3030 320	Fiberglass Draw Through Cooling Tower	COST EACH MAT.	COST EACH INST.	COST EACH TOTAL
1010	Cooling tower, fiberglass, packaged unit, draw thru, 100 Ton	33,200	12,500	45,700
1020	120 Ton	37,400	14,100	51,500
1030	140 Ton	42,900	18,800	61,700
1040	160 Ton	56,500	24,800	81,300
1050	180 Ton	86,000	35,900	121,900

D3030 330	Stainless Steel Draw Through Cooling Tower	COST EACH MAT.	COST EACH INST.	COST EACH TOTAL
1010	Cooling tower, stainless steel, packaged unit, draw thru, 60 Ton	49,900	12,400	62,300
1020	110 Ton	58,500	14,600	73,100
1030	300 Ton	105,500	22,000	127,500
1040	600 Ton	167,000	32,300	199,300
1050	1000 Ton	294,500	48,400	342,900

D30 HVAC

D3040 Distribution Systems

Built-Up Air Handling Unit

System Components	QUANTITY	UNIT	COST EACH		
			MAT.	INST.	TOTAL
SYSTEM D3040 106 1010					
AHU, FIELD FAB., BLT. UP, COOL/HEAT COILS, FLTRS., CONST. VOL., 40,000 CFM					
AHU, Built-up, cool/heat coils, filters, mix box, constant volume	1.000	Ea.	122,500	8,075	130,575
Pipe, black steel, welded, Sch. 40, on yoke & roll hgrs, 10' OC, 3" dia.	26.000	L.F.	1,170	978.64	2,148.64
Pipe, black steel, welded, Sch. 40, on yoke & roll hgrs, 10' OC, 4" dia	20.000	L.F.	1,150	878.20	2,028.20
Elbow, 90°, weld joint, 3" pipe size	5.000	Ea.	302.50	1,155.50	1,458
Elbow, 90°, weld joint, 4" pipe size	4.000	Ea.	212	1,296.40	1,508.40
Tee, welded, reducing on outlet, 3" by 2-1/2" pipe	3.000	Ea.	243	1,207.95	1,450.95
Tee, welded, reducing on outlet, 4" by 3" pipe	2.000	Ea.	206	1,077	1,283
Reducer, eccentric, weld joint, 3" pipe size	4.000	Ea.	508	807.20	1,315.20
Reducer, eccentric, weld joint, 4" pipe size	4.000	Ea.	1,028	1,079	2,107
Flange, weld neck, 150 LB, 2-1/2" pipe size	3.000	Ea.	103.50	302.73	406.23
Flange, weld neck, 150 lb., 3" pipe size	14.000	Ea.	553	1,624.70	2,177.70
Flange, weld neck, 150 lb., 4" pipe size	10.000	Ea.	475	1,620.50	2,095.50
Valves, iron body, butterfly, lug type, lever actuator, 3" size	2.000	Ea.	680	386	1,066
Valves, iron body, butterfly, lug type, lever actuator, 4" size	2.000	Ea.	820	620	1,440
Strainer, Y type, iron body, flanged, 125 lb., 3" pipe size	1.000	Ea.	365	345	710
Strainer, Y type, iron body, flanged, 125 lb., 4" pipe size	1.000	Ea.	605	520	1,125
Valve, electric motor actuated, iron body, 3 way, flanged, 2-1/2" pipe	1.000	Ea.	1,100	420	1,520
Valve, electric motor actuated, iron body, two way, flanged, 3" pipe size	1.000	Ea.	1,125	420	1,545
Expansion joints, bellows type, flange spool, 6" F to F, 3" dia	2.000	Ea.	1,010	274	1,284
Expansion joints, bellows type, flange spool, 6" F to F, 4" dia	2.000	Ea.	1,090	370	1,460
T-O-L socket, weld joint, 1/4" pipe size, nozzle	4.000	Ea.	56.20	282.28	338.48
T-O-L socket, weld joint, 1/2" pipe size, nozzle	12.000	Ea.	70.20	884.52	954.72
Thermometers, stem type, 9" case, 8" stem, 3/4" NPT	4.000	Ea.	844	124	968
Pressure/temperature relief plug, 316 SS, 3/4"OD, 7-1/2" insertion	4.000	Ea.	484	108	592
Insulation, fiberglass pipe covering, 1-1/2" wall, 3" IPS	26.000	L.F.	156	219.70	375.70
Insulation, fiberglass pipe covering, 1-1/2" wall, 4" IPS	20.000	L.F.	137	205	342
Fan coil control system	1.000	Ea.	2,250	785	3,035
Re-heat coil balancing	2.000	Ea.		320	320
Air conditioner balancing	1.000	Ea.		1,025	1,025
TOTAL			139,243.40	27,411.32	166,654.72

D3040 106	Field Fabricated Air Handling Unit	COST EACH		
		MAT.	INST.	TOTAL
1010	AHU, field fab, blt up, cool/heat coils, fltrs, const vol, 40,000 CFM	139,000	27,400	166,400
1020	60,000 CFM	171,000	42,400	213,400
1030	75,000 CFM	150,000	44,700	194,700

D30 HVAC

D3040 Distribution Systems

D3040 108	Field Fabricated VAV Air Handling Unit	COST EACH		
		MAT.	INST.	TOTAL
1010	AHU, field fab, blt up, cool/heat coils, fltrs, VAV, 75,000 CFM	152,000	51,500	203,500
1020	100,000 CFM	238,000	68,000	306,000
1030	150,000 CFM	396,500	109,000	505,500

D30 HVAC

D3040 Distribution Systems

Chilled Water Piping   Central Station Air Handling Unit   Hot Water Piping

System Components	QUANTITY	UNIT	COST EACH MAT.	COST EACH INST.	COST EACH TOTAL
SYSTEM D3040 110 1010					
AHU, CENTRAL STATION, COOL/HEAT COILS, CONST. VOL., FLTRS., 2,000 CFM					
Central station air handling unit, chilled water, 2,000 CFM	1.000	Ea.	13,300	1,425	14,725
Pipe, black steel, Sch 40, threaded, W/cplgs & hangers, 10' OC, 1" dia.	32.500	L.F.	346.13	526.50	872.63
Pipe, black steel, Sch 40, threaded, W/cplg & hangers, 10' OC, 1-1/4" dia.	26.000	L.F.	366.60	452.40	819
Elbow, 90°, black, straight, 1" dia.	4.000	Ea.	53.80	264	317.80
Elbow, 90°, black, straight, 1-1/4" dia.	4.000	Ea.	88	282	370
Tee, black, reducing, 1" dia.	8.000	Ea.	192	856	1,048
Tee, black, reducing, 1-1/4" dia.	8.000	Ea.	332	888	1,220
Reducer, concentric, black, 1" dia.	4.000	Ea.	72.40	230	302.40
Reducer, concentric, black, 1-1/4" dia.	4.000	Ea.	94	238	332
Union, black with brass seat, 1" dia.	4.000	Ea.	180	286	466
Union, black with brass seat, 1-1/4" dia.	2.000	Ea.	128	147	275
Pipe nipple, black, 1" dia	13.000	Ea.	69.23	105.30	174.53
Pipe nipple, black, 1-1/4" dia	12.000	Ea.	84.60	104.40	189
Valves, bronze, gate, N.R.S., threaded, class 150, 1" size	2.000	Ea.	516	90	606
Valves, bronze, gate, N.R.S., threaded, class 150, 1-1/4" size	2.000	Ea.	640	115	755
Strainer, Y type, bronze body, screwed, 150 lb., 1" pipe size	1.000	Ea.	126	51	177
Strainer, Y type, bronze body, screwed, 150 lb., 1-1/4" pipe size	1.000	Ea.	200	57.50	257.50
Valve, electric motor actuated, brass, 3 way, screwed, 3/4" pipe	1.000	Ea.	530	46.50	576.50
Valve, electric motor actuated, brass, 2 way, screwed, 1" pipe size	1.000	Ea.	855	45	900
Thermometers, stem type, 9" case, 8" stem, 3/4" NPT	4.000	Ea.	844	124	968
Pressure/temperature relief plug, 316 SS, 3/4"OD, 7-1/2" insertion	4.000	Ea.	484	108	592
Insulation, fiberglass pipe covering, 1" wall, 1" IPS	26.000	L.F.	62.40	170.30	232.70
Insulation, fiberglass pipe covering, 1" wall, 1-1/4" IPS	20.000	L.F.	52	137	189
Fan coil control system	1.000	Ea.	2,250	785	3,035
Re-heat coil balancing	2.000	Ea.		320	320
Multizone A/C balancing	1.000	Ea.		760	760
TOTAL			21,866.16	8,613.90	30,480.06

D3040 110	Central Station Air Handling Unit	COST EACH MAT.	COST EACH INST.	COST EACH TOTAL
1010	AHU, Central station, cool/heat coils, constant vol, fltrs, 2,000 CFM	21,900	8,625	30,525
1020	5,000 CFM	33,100	11,100	44,200
1030	10,000 CFM	47,200	15,400	62,600
1040	15,000 CFM	82,000	20,900	102,900
1050	20,000 CFM	99,500	24,400	123,900

D30 HVAC

D3040 Distribution Systems

D3040 112	Central Station Air Handling Unit, VAV	COST EACH		
		MAT.	INST.	TOTAL
1010	AHU, central station, cool/heat coils, VAV, fltrs, 5,000 CFM	37,800	11,500	49,300
1020	10,000 CFM	66,500	15,800	82,300
1030	15,000 CFM	92,000	20,600	112,600
1040	20,000 CFM	112,500	24,900	137,400
1050	30,000 CFM	132,500	28,600	161,100

D30 HVAC

D3040 Distribution Systems

Rooftop Air Handling Unit

System Components	QUANTITY	UNIT	COST EACH MAT.	COST EACH INST.	COST EACH TOTAL
SYSTEM D3040 114 1010					
AHU, ROOFTOP, COOL/HEAT COILS, FLTRS., CONST. VOL., 2,000 CFM					
AHU, Built-up, cool/heat coils, filter, mix box, rooftop, constant volume	1.000	Ea.	28,000	2,425	30,425
Pipe, black steel, Sch 40, threaded, W/cplgs & hangers, 10′ OC, 1″ dia.	32.500	L.F.	346.13	526.50	872.63
Pipe, black steel, Sch 40, threaded, W/cplg & hangers, 10′ OC, 1-1/4″ dia.	26.000	L.F.	366.60	452.40	819
Elbow, 90°, black, straight, 1″ dia.	4.000	Ea.	53.80	264	317.80
Elbow, 90°, black, straight, 1-1/4″ dia.	4.000	Ea.	88	282	370
Tee, black, reducing, 1″ dia.	8.000	Ea.	192	856	1,048
Tee, black, reducing, 1-1/4″ dia.	8.000	Ea.	332	888	1,220
Reducer, black, concentric, 1″ dia.	4.000	Ea.	72.40	230	302.40
Reducer, black, concentric, 1-1/4″ dia.	4.000	Ea.	94	238	332
Union, black with brass seat, 1″ dia.	4.000	Ea.	180	286	466
Union, black with brass seat, 1-1/4″ dia.	2.000	Ea.	128	147	275
Pipe nipples, 1″ dia	13.000	Ea.	69.23	105.30	174.53
Pipe nipples, 1-1/4″ dia	12.000	Ea.	84.60	104.40	189
Valves, bronze, gate, N.R.S., threaded, class 150, 1″ size	2.000	Ea.	516	90	606
Valves, bronze, gate, N.R.S., threaded, class 150, 1-1/4″ size	2.000	Ea.	640	115	755
Strainer, Y type, bronze body, screwed, 150 lb., 1″ pipe size	1.000	Ea.	126	51	177
Strainer, Y type, bronze body, screwed, 150 lb., 1-1/4″ pipe size	1.000	Ea.	200	57.50	257.50
Valve, electric motor actuated, brass, 3 way, screwed, 3/4″ pipe	1.000	Ea.	530	46.50	576.50
Valve, electric motor actuated, brass, 2 way, screwed, 1″ pipe size	1.000	Ea.	855	45	900
Thermometers, stem type, 9″ case, 8″ stem, 3/4″ NPT	4.000	Ea.	844	124	968
Pressure/temperature relief plug, 316 SS, 3/4″OD, 7-1/2″ insertion	4.000	Ea.	484	108	592
Insulation, fiberglass pipe covering, 1″ wall, 1″ IPS	26.000	L.F.	62.40	170.30	232.70
Insulation, fiberglass pipe covering, 1″ wall, 1-1/4″ IPS	20.000	L.F.	52	137	189
Insulation pipe covering .016″ aluminum jacket finish, add	45.000	S.F.	105.30	324	429.30
Fan coil control system	1.000	Ea.	2,250	785	3,035
Re-heat coil balancing	2.000	Ea.		320	320
Rooftop unit heat/cool balancing	1.000	Ea.		590	590
TOTAL			36,671.46	9,767.90	46,439.36

D3040 114	Rooftop Air Handling Unit	COST EACH MAT.	COST EACH INST.	COST EACH TOTAL
1010	AHU, rooftop, cool/heat coils, constant vol., fltrs, 2,000 CFM	36,700	9,775	46,475
1020	5,000 CFM	44,300	11,400	55,700

D30 HVAC

D3040 Distribution Systems

D3040 114	Rooftop Air Handling Unit	COST EACH		
		MAT.	INST.	TOTAL
1030	10,000 CFM	92,000	15,700	107,700
1040	15,000 CFM	128,500	20,800	149,300
1050	20,000 CFM	171,000	25,100	196,100

D3040 116	Rooftop Air Handling Unit, VAV	COST EACH		
		MAT.	INST.	TOTAL
1010	AHU, rooftop, cool/heat coils, VAV, fltrs, 5,000 CFM	48,900	11,600	60,500
1020	10,000 CFM	94,500	15,900	110,400
1030	15,000 CFM	139,000	21,000	160,000
1040	20,000 CFM	175,500	25,400	200,900
1050	30,000 CFM	204,000	29,100	233,100

D30 HVAC

D3040 Distribution Systems

Horizontal Fan Coil Air Conditioning System

System Components	QUANTITY	UNIT	COST EACH MAT.	INST.	TOTAL
SYSTEM D3040 124 1010					
FAN COIL A/C SYSTEM, HORIZONTAL, W/HOUSING, CONTROLS; 2 PIPE, 1/2 TON					
Fan coil A/C, horizontal housing, filters, chilled water, 1/2 ton cooling	1.000	Ea.	1,800	195	1,995
Pipe, black steel, Sch 40, threaded, W/cplgs & hangers, 10' OC, 3/4" dia.	21.500	L.F.	166.63	303.15	469.78
Elbow, 90°, black, straight, 3/4" dia.	6.000	Ea.	46.20	369	415.20
Tee, black, straight, 3/4" dia.	2.000	Ea.	24.60	191	215.60
Union, black with brass seat, 3/4" dia.	2.000	Ea.	69	132	201
Pipe nipples, 3/4" diam	3.000	Ea.	11.63	21.15	32.78
Valves, bronze, gate, N.R.S., threaded, class 150, 3/4" size	2.000	Ea.	376	86	462
Circuit setter, balance valve, bronze body, threaded, 3/4" pipe size	1.000	Ea.	123	43.50	166.50
Insulation, fiberglass pipe covering, 1" wall, 3/4" IPS	20.000	L.F.	44.80	125	169.80
Ductwork, 12" x 8" fabricated, galvanized steel, 12 LF	55.000	Lb.	40.70	552.75	593.45
Insulation, ductwork, blanket type, fiberglass, 1" thk, 1-1/2 LB density	40.000	S.F.	220	684	904
Diffusers, aluminum, OB damper, ceiling, perf, 24"x24" panel size, 6"x6"	2.000	Ea.	484	106	590
Ductwork, flexible, fiberglass fabric, insulated, 1"thk, PE jacket, 6" dia	16.000	L.F.	96.80	93.60	190.40
Round volume control damper 6" dia.	2.000	Ea.	400	77	477
Fan coil unit balancing	1.000	Ea.		110	110
Re-heat coil balancing	1.000	Ea.		160	160
Diffuser/register, high, balancing	2.000	Ea.		304	304
TOTAL			3,903.36	3,553.15	7,456.51

D3040 118	Fan Coil A/C Unit, Two Pipe	COST EACH		
		MAT.	INST.	TOTAL
1010	Fan coil A/C system, cabinet mounted, controls, 2 pipe, 1/2 Ton	1,700	1,625	3,325
1020	1 Ton	2,150	1,800	3,950
1030	1-1/2 Ton	2,200	1,825	4,025
1040	2 Ton	3,450	2,250	5,700
1050	3 Ton	5,025	2,325	7,350

D3040 120	Fan Coil A/C Unit, Two Pipe, Electric Heat	COST EACH		
		MAT.	INST.	TOTAL
1010	Fan coil A/C system, cabinet mntd, elect. ht, controls, 2 pipe, 1/2 Ton	2,750	1,625	4,375
1020	1 Ton	3,400	1,800	5,200
1030	1-1/2 Ton	3,875	1,825	5,700
1040	2 Ton	5,650	2,275	7,925
1050	3 Ton	8,950	2,325	11,275

D30 HVAC

D3040 Distribution Systems

D3040 122	Fan Coil A/C Unit, Four Pipe	COST EACH		
		MAT.	INST.	TOTAL
1010	Fan coil A/C system, cabinet mounted, controls, 4 pipe, 1/2 Ton	2,950	3,150	6,100
1020	1 Ton	3,400	3,350	6,750
1030	1-1/2 Ton	3,475	3,375	6,850
1040	2 Ton	4,350	3,500	7,850
1050	3 Ton	6,900	3,750	10,650

D3040 124	Fan Coil A/C, Horizontal, Duct Mount, 2 Pipe	COST EACH		
		MAT.	INST.	TOTAL
1010	Fan coil A/C system, horizontal w/housing, controls, 2 pipe, 1/2 Ton	3,900	3,550	7,450
1020	1 Ton	5,175	5,650	10,825
1030	1-1/2 Ton	6,550	7,600	14,150
1040	2 Ton	8,225	9,450	17,675
1050	3 Ton	10,600	13,100	23,700
1060	3-1/2 Ton	11,100	13,400	24,500
1070	4 Ton	11,600	15,700	27,300
1080	5 Ton	13,900	20,100	34,000
1090	6 Ton	14,200	21,500	35,700
1100	7 Ton	14,600	22,000	36,600
1110	8 Ton	14,600	22,300	36,900
1120	10 Ton	15,400	22,900	38,300

D3040 126	Fan Coil A/C, Horiz., Duct Mount, 2 Pipe, Elec. Ht.	COST EACH		
		MAT.	INST.	TOTAL
1010	Fan coil A/C system, horiz. hsng, elect. ht, ctrls, 2 pipe, 1/2 Ton	4,200	3,550	7,750
1020	1 Ton	5,700	5,650	11,350
1030	1-1/2 Ton	7,075	7,600	14,675
1040	2 Ton	9,025	9,450	18,475
1050	3 Ton	13,800	13,400	27,200
1060	3-1/2 Ton	15,000	13,400	28,400
1070	4 Ton	16,700	15,700	32,400
1080	5 Ton	20,100	20,100	40,200
1090	6 Ton	20,300	21,500	41,800
1100	7 Ton	21,500	22,300	43,800
1110	8 Ton	21,900	23,000	44,900
1120	10 Ton	23,300	22,000	45,300

D3040 128	Fan Coil A/C, Horizontal, Duct Mount, 4 Pipe	COST EACH		
		MAT.	INST.	TOTAL
1010	Fan coil A/C system, horiz. w/cabinet, controls, 4 pipe, 1/2 Ton	5,475	5,050	10,525
1020	1 Ton	6,875	7,350	14,225
1030	1-1/2 Ton	8,350	9,150	17,500
1040	2 Ton	9,700	10,700	20,400
1050	3 Ton	12,700	14,800	27,500
1060	3-1/2 Ton	15,100	18,700	33,800
1070	4 Ton	15,000	18,900	33,900
1080	5 Ton	18,300	26,600	44,900
1090	6 Ton	20,500	32,200	52,700
1100	7 Ton	23,800	36,300	60,100
1110	8 Ton	24,400	38,900	63,300
1120	10 Ton	29,500	46,800	76,300

D30 HVAC

D3040 Distribution Systems

VAV Terminal   Fan Powered VAV Terminal

System Components	QUANTITY	UNIT	COST EACH MAT.	COST EACH INST.	COST EACH TOTAL
SYSTEM D3040 132 1010					
VAV TERMINAL, COOLING ONLY, WITH ACTUATOR/CONTROLS, 200 CFM					
Mixing box variable volume 300 to 600 CFM, cool only	1.000	Ea.	1,182.50	151.80	1,334.30
Ductwork, 12" x 8" fabricated, galvanized steel, 12 LF	55.000	Lb.	40.70	552.75	593.45
Insulation, ductwork, blanket type, fiberglass, 1" thk, 1-1/2 LB density	40.000	S.F.	220	684	904
Diffusers, aluminum, OB damper, ceiling, perf, 24"x24" panel size, 6"x6"	2.000	Ea.	484	106	590
Ductwork, flexible, fiberglass fabric, insulated, 1"thk, PE jacket, 6" dia	16.000	L.F.	96.80	93.60	190.40
Round volume control damper 6" dia.	2.000	Ea.	400	77	477
VAV box balancing	1.000	Ea.		101	101
Diffuser/register, high, balancing	2.000	Ea.		304	304
TOTAL			2,424	2,070.15	4,494.15

D3040 132	VAV Terminal, Cooling Only	MAT.	INST.	TOTAL
1010	VAV terminal, cooling only, with actuator/controls, 200 CFM	2,425	2,075	4,500
1020	400 CFM	3,075	3,975	7,050
1030	600 CFM	4,200	5,925	10,125
1040	800 CFM	4,525	7,475	12,000
1050	1000 CFM	5,275	8,625	13,900
1060	1250 CFM	6,350	11,200	17,550
1070	1500 CFM	6,900	13,500	20,400
1080	2000 CFM	9,025	19,000	28,025

D3040 134	VAV Terminal, Hot Water Reheat	MAT.	INST.	TOTAL
1010	VAV terminal, cooling, HW reheat, with actuator/controls, 200 CFM	4,400	3,400	7,800
1020	400 CFM	5,075	5,175	10,250
1030	600 CFM	6,175	7,250	13,425
1040	800 CFM	6,550	8,825	15,375
1050	1000 CFM	7,250	9,975	17,225
1060	1250 CFM	8,475	12,700	21,175
1070	1500 CFM	9,550	15,200	24,750
1080	2000 CFM	12,000	20,800	32,800

D3040 136	Fan Powered VAV Terminal, Cooling Only	MAT.	INST.	TOTAL
1010	VAV terminal, cooling, fan powrd, with actuator/controls, 200 CFM	3,300	2,075	5,375
1020	400 CFM	4,425	3,800	8,225

D30 HVAC

D3040 Distribution Systems

D3040 136	Fan Powered VAV Terminal, Cooling Only	COST EACH		
		MAT.	INST.	TOTAL
1030	600 CFM	5,500	5,925	11,425
1040	800 CFM	6,050	7,400	13,450
1050	1000 CFM	6,725	8,525	15,250
1060	1250 CFM	8,000	11,400	19,400
1070	1500 CFM	8,475	13,600	22,075
1080	2000 CFM	10,800	19,400	30,200

D3040 138	Fan Powered VAV Terminal, Hot Water Reheat	COST EACH		
		MAT.	INST.	TOTAL
1010	VAV terminal, cool, HW reht, fan powrd, with actuator/ctrls, 200 CFM	5,850	3,400	9,250
1020	400 CFM	6,575	5,200	11,775
1030	600 CFM	7,675	7,275	14,950
1040	800 CFM	8,200	8,750	16,950
1050	1000 CFM	8,900	9,900	18,800
1060	1250 CFM	10,400	12,700	23,100
1070	1500 CFM	11,500	15,300	26,800
1080	2000 CFM	13,800	21,200	35,000

D30 HVAC

D3040 Distribution Systems

Axial Flow Centrifugal Fan
Belt Drive

Belt Drive Utility Set

Centrifugal Roof Exhaust Fan
Direct Drive

System Components	QUANTITY	UNIT	COST EACH MAT.	COST EACH INST.	COST EACH TOTAL
SYSTEM D3040 220 1010					
FAN SYSTEM, IN-LINE CENTRIFUGAL, 500 CFM					
Fans, in-line centrifugal, supply/exhaust, 500 CFM, 10" dia conn	1.000	Ea.	1,900	640	2,540
Louver, alum., w/screen, damper, mill fin, fxd blade, cont line, stormproof	4.050	S.F.	271.35	121.50	392.85
Motor for louver damper, electric or pneumatic	1.000	Ea.	775	60.50	835.50
Ductwork, 12" x 8" fabricated, galvanized steel, 60 LF	200.000	Lb.	215.80	2,509	2,724.80
Grilles, aluminum, air supply, single deflection, adjustable, 12" x 6"	1.000	Ea.	81	111	192
Fire damper, curtain type, vertical, 12" x 8"	1.000	Ea.	44	38.50	82.50
Duct access door, insulated, 10" x 10"	1.000	Ea.	42	77	119
Duct access door, insulated, 16" x 12"	1.000	Ea.	42	94	136
Pressure controller/switch, air flow controller	1.000	Ea.	490	72	562
Fan control switch and mounting base	1.000	Ea.	196	54	250
Fan balancing	1.000	Ea.		505	505
Diffuser/register balancing	3.000	Ea.		303	303
TOTAL			4,057.15	4,585.50	8,642.65

D3040 220	Centrifugal In Line Fan Systems	MAT.	INST.	TOTAL
1010	Fan system, in-line centrifugal, 500 CFM	4,050	4,575	8,625
1020	1300 CFM	4,950	7,950	12,900
1030	1500 CFM	5,150	9,200	14,350
1040	2500 CFM	7,450	28,000	35,450
1050	3500 CFM	9,125	37,800	46,925
1060	5000 CFM	12,400	56,000	68,400
1070	7500 CFM	14,500	57,500	72,000
1080	10,000 CFM	17,200	67,000	84,200

D3040 230	Utility Set Fan Systems	MAT.	INST.	TOTAL
1010	Utility fan set system, belt drive, 2000 CFM	3,625	14,900	18,525
1020	3500 CFM	5,650	26,300	31,950
1030	5000 CFM	6,925	36,500	43,425
1040	7500 CFM	9,925	42,400	52,325
1050	10,000 CFM	14,200	55,500	69,700
1060	15,000 CFM	15,000	56,500	71,500
1070	20,000 CFM	17,500	64,500	82,000

D30 HVAC

D3040 Distribution Systems

D3040 240	Roof Exhaust Fan Systems	COST EACH		
		MAT.	INST.	TOTAL
1010	Roof vent. system, centrifugal, alum., galv curb, BDD, 500 CFM	1,700	3,000	4,700
1020	800 CFM	2,075	5,825	7,900
1030	1500 CFM	2,725	8,650	11,375
1040	2750 CFM	2,575	19,500	22,075
1050	3500 CFM	4,900	25,100	30,000
1060	5000 CFM	6,450	41,400	47,850
1070	8500 CFM	9,425	53,000	62,425
1080	13,800 CFM	13,200	77,000	90,200

D30 HVAC

D3040 Distribution Systems

Commercial/Industrial Dust Collection System

System Components	QUANTITY	UNIT	COST EACH MAT.	COST EACH INST.	COST EACH TOTAL
SYSTEM D3040 250 1010					
COMMERCIAL/INDUSTRIAL VACUUM DUST COLLECTION SYSTEM, 500 CFM					
Dust collection central vac unit inc. stand, filter & shaker, 500 CFM 2 HP	1.000	Ea.	4,625	800	5,425
Galvanized tubing, 16 ga., 4" OD	80.000	L.F.	640	338.40	978.40
Galvanized tubing, 90° ell, 4" dia.	3.000	Ea.	160.50	91.50	252
Galvanized tubing, 45° ell, 4" dia.	4.000	Ea.	188	122	310
Galvanized tubing, TY slip fit, 4" dia.	4.000	Ea.	680	202	882
Flexible rubber hose, 4" dia.	32.000	L.F.	345.60	135.36	480.96
Galvanized air gate valve, 4" dia.	4.000	Ea.	648	264	912
Galvanized compression coupling, 4" dia.	36.000	Ea.	828	1,656	2,484
Pipe hangers, steel, 4" pipe size	16.000	Ea.	816	224.80	1,040.80
TOTAL			8,931.10	3,834.06	12,765.16

D3040 250	Commercial/Industrial Vacuum Dust Collection	MAT.	INST.	TOTAL
1010	Commercial/industrial, vacuum dust collection system, 500 CFM	8,925	3,825	12,750
1020	1000 CFM	12,500	4,375	16,875
1030	1500 CFM	15,600	4,825	20,425
1040	3000 CFM	28,700	6,750	35,450
1050	5000 CFM	44,700	10,200	54,900

D30 HVAC

D3040 Distribution Systems

Commercial Kitchen Exhaust/Make-up Air Rooftop System

System Components	QUANTITY	UNIT	COST EACH		
			MAT.	INST.	TOTAL
SYSTEM D3040 260 1010					
COMMERCIAL KITCHEN EXHAUST/MAKE-UP AIR SYSTEM, ROOFTOP, GAS, 2000 CFM					
Make-up air rooftop unit, gas, 750 MBH	1.000	Ea.	6,870	185.49	7,055.49
Pipe, black steel, Sch 40, thrded, nipples, W/cplngs/hngrs, 10' OC, 1" dia.	22.000	L.F.	234.30	356.40	590.70
Elbow, 90°, black steel, straight, 3/4" dia.	2.000	Ea.	15.40	123	138.40
Elbow, 90°, black steel, straight, 1" dia.	3.000	Ea.	40.35	198	238.35
Tee, black steel, reducing, 1" dia.	1.000	Ea.	24	107	131
Union, black with brass seat, 1" dia.	1.000	Ea.	45	71.50	116.50
Pipe nipples, black, 3/4" dia	2.000	Ea.	15.50	28.20	43.70
Pipe cap, malleable iron, black, 1" dia.	1.000	Ea.	10.60	28.50	39.10
Gas cock, brass, 1" size	1.000	Ea.	63.50	45	108.50
Ductwork, 20" x 14" fabricated, galv. steel, 30 LF	220.000	Lb.	169.40	2,046	2,215.40
Ductwork, 18" x 10" fabricated, galv. steel, 12 LF	72.000	Lb.	55.44	669.60	725.04
Ductwork, 30" x 10" fabricated, galv. steel, 30 LF	260.000	Lb.	200.20	2,418	2,618.20
Ductwork, 16" x 10" fabricated, galv. steel, 12 LF	70.000	Lb.	53.90	651	704.90
Kitchen ventilation, island style, water wash, Stainless Steel	5.000	L.F.	14,500	1,675	16,175
Control system, Make-up Air Unit/Exhauster	1.000	Ea.	4,600	3,050	7,650
Rooftop unit heat/cool balancing	1.000	Ea.		590	590
Roof fan balancing	1.000	Ea.		340	340
TOTAL			26,897.59	12,582.69	39,480.28

D3040 260	Kitchen Exhaust/Make-Up Air	COST EACH		
		MAT.	INST.	TOTAL
1010	Commercial kitchen exhaust/make-up air system, rooftop, gas, 2000 CFM	26,900	12,600	39,500
1020	3000 CFM	39,200	17,600	56,800
1030	5000 CFM	46,900	20,800	67,700
1040	8000 CFM	68,000	30,700	98,700
1050	12,000 CFM	88,000	36,100	124,100
1060	16,000 CFM	107,500	55,000	162,500

D30 HVAC

D3040 Distribution Systems

Plate Heat Exchanger

Shell and Tube Heat Exchanger

System Components	QUANTITY	UNIT	COST EACH MAT.	COST EACH INST.	COST EACH TOTAL
SYSTEM D3040 620 1010					
SHELL & TUBE HEAT EXCHANGER, 40 GPM					
Heat exchanger, 4 pass, 3/4" O.D. copper tubes, by steam at 10 psi, 40 GPM	1.000	Ea.	7,775	390	8,165
Pipe, black steel, Sch 40, threaded, w/couplings & hangers, 10' OC, 2" dia.	50.500	L.F.	1,136.25	1,212	2,348.25
Elbow, 90°, straight, 2" dia.	16.000	Ea.	800	1,376	2,176
Reducer, black steel, concentric, 2" dia.	2.000	Ea.	85	147	232
Valves, bronze, gate, rising stem, threaded, class 150, 2" size	6.000	Ea.	3,120	468	3,588
Valves, bronze, globe, class 150, rising stem, threaded, 2" size	2.000	Ea.	2,650	156	2,806
Strainers, Y type, bronze body, screwed, 125 lb, 2" pipe size	2.000	Ea.	710	133	843
Valve, electric motor actuated, brass, 2 way, screwed, 1-1/2" pipe size	1.000	Ea.	955	66.50	1,021.50
Union, black with brass seat, 2" dia.	8.000	Ea.	744	728	1,472
Tee, black, straight, 2" dia.	9.000	Ea.	571.50	1,269	1,840.50
Tee, black, reducing run and outlet, 2" dia.	4.000	Ea.	304	564	868
Pipe nipple, black, 2" dia.	2.000	Ea.	11.25	12	23.25
Thermometers, stem type, 9" case, 8" stem, 3/4" NPT	2.000	Ea.	422	62	484
Gauges, pressure or vacuum, 3-1/2" diameter dial	2.000	Ea.	72	54	126
Insulation, fiberglass pipe covering, 1" wall, 2" IPS	40.000	L.F.	121.20	288	409.20
Heat exchanger control system	1.000	Ea.	4,475	2,750	7,225
Coil balancing	1.000	Ea.		160	160
TOTAL			23,952.20	9,835.50	33,787.70

D3040 610	Heat Exchanger, Plate Type	MAT.	INST.	TOTAL
1010	Plate heat exchanger, 400 GPM	81,000	19,800	100,800
1020	800 GPM	129,500	25,300	154,800
1030	1200 GPM	193,500	34,200	227,700
1040	1800 GPM	263,500	42,500	306,000

D3040 620	Heat Exchanger, Shell & Tube	MAT.	INST.	TOTAL
1010	Shell & tube heat exchanger, 40 GPM	24,000	9,825	33,825
1020	96 GPM	81,000	17,400	98,400
1030	240 GPM	180,000	23,600	203,600
1040	600 GPM	132,500	33,200	165,700

D30 HVAC

D3050 Terminal & Package Units

Cabinet Unit Heater   Gas Unit Heater   Hydronic Unit Heater

System Components	QUANTITY	UNIT	COST EACH		
			MAT.	INST.	TOTAL
SYSTEM D3050 120 1010					
SPACE HEATER, SUSPENDED, GAS FIRED, PROPELLER FAN, 20 MBH					
Space heater, propeller fan, 20 MBH output	1.000	Ea.	830	183	1,013
Pipe, black steel, Sch 40, threaded, w/coupling & hangers, 10' OC, 3/4" dia	21.000	L.F.	162.75	296.10	458.85
Elbow, 90°, black steel, straight, 1/2" dia.	3.000	Ea.	19.20	172.50	191.70
Elbow, 90°, black steel, straight, 3/4" dia.	3.000	Ea.	23.10	184.50	207.60
Tee, black steel, reducing, 3/4" dia.	1.000	Ea.	19	95.50	114.50
Union, black with brass seat, 3/4" dia.	1.000	Ea.	34.50	66	100.50
Pipe nipples, black, 1/2" dia	2.000	Ea.	12.30	27.30	39.60
Pipe nipples, black, 3/4" dia	2.000	Ea.	7.75	14.10	21.85
Pipe cap, black, 3/4" dia.	1.000	Ea.	8.75	27	35.75
Gas cock, brass, 3/4" size	1.000	Ea.	41	39	80
Thermostat, 1 set back, electric, timed	1.000	Ea.	111	108	219
Wiring, thermostat hook-up, 25' of #18-3	1.000	Ea.	15.40	33.50	48.90
Vent chimney, prefab metal, U.L. listed, gas, double wall, galv. st, 4" dia	12.000	L.F.	178.20	270	448.20
Vent chimney, gas, double wall, galv. steel, elbow 90°, 4" dia.	2.000	Ea.	84	90	174
Vent chimney, gas, double wall, galv. steel, Tee, 4" dia.	1.000	Ea.	59.50	58.50	118
Vent chimney, gas, double wall, galv. steel, T cap, 4" dia.	1.000	Ea.	3.97	36	39.97
Vent chimney, gas, double wall, galv. steel, roof flashing, 4" dia.	1.000	Ea.	14.40	45	59.40
Vent chimney, gas, double wall, galv. steel, top, 4" dia.	1.000	Ea.	29.50	34.50	64
TOTAL			1,654.32	1,780.50	3,434.82

D3050 120	Unit Heaters, Gas	COST EACH		
		MAT.	INST.	TOTAL
1010	Space heater, suspended, gas fired, propeller fan, 20 MBH	1,650	1,775	3,425
1020	60 MBH	2,875	1,850	4,725
1030	100 MBH	2,250	1,950	4,200
1040	160 MBH	2,625	2,150	4,775
1050	200 MBH	3,350	2,375	5,725
1060	280 MBH	5,525	2,550	8,075
1070	320 MBH	5,725	2,875	8,600

D3050 130	Unit Heaters, Hydronic	COST EACH		
		MAT.	INST.	TOTAL
1010	Space heater, suspended, horiz. mount, HW, prop. fan, 20 MBH	3,275	1,900	5,175
1020	60 MBH	5,000	2,125	7,125

D30 HVAC

D3050 Terminal & Package Units

D3050 130		Unit Heaters, Hydronic	COST EACH		
			MAT.	INST.	TOTAL
1030		100 MBH	5,725	2,325	8,050
1040		150 MBH	6,075	2,575	8,650
1050		200 MBH	7,000	2,875	9,875
1060		300 MBH	6,575	3,400	9,975

D3050 140	Cabinet Unit Heaters, Hydronic		COST EACH		
			MAT.	INST.	TOTAL
1010	Unit heater, cabinet type, horizontal blower, hot water, 20 MBH		4,675	1,850	6,525
1020	60 MBH		6,025	2,050	8,075
1030	100 MBH		7,825	2,250	10,075
1040	120 MBH		6,100	2,325	8,425

D30 HVAC

D3050 Terminal & Package Units

System Description: Rooftop single zone units are electric cooling and gas heat. Duct systems are low velocity, galvanized steel supply and return. Price variations between sizes are due to several factors. Jumps in the cost of the rooftop unit occur when the manufacturer shifts from the largest capacity unit on a small frame to the smallest capacity on the next larger frame, or changes from one compressor to two. As the unit capacity increases for larger areas the duct distribution grows in proportion. For most applications there is a tradeoff point where it is less expensive and more efficient to utilize smaller units with short simple distribution systems. Larger units also require larger initial supply and return ducts which can create a space problem. Supplemental heat may be desired in colder locations. The table below is based on one unit supplying the area listed. The 10,000 S.F. unit for bars and taverns is not listed because a nominal 110 ton unit would be required and this is above the normal single zone rooftop capacity.

System Components	QUANTITY	UNIT	COST EACH		
			MAT.	INST.	TOTAL
SYSTEM D3050 150 1280		S.F.			
ROOFTOP, SINGLE ZONE, AIR CONDITIONER					
APARTMENT CORRIDORS, 500 S.F., .92 TON					
Rooftop air conditioner, 1 zone, electric cool, standard controls, curb	1.000	Ea.	931.50	1,023.50	1,955
Ductwork package for rooftop single zone units	1.000	System	386.40	1,449	1,835.40
TOTAL			1,317.90	2,472.50	3,790.40
COST PER S.F.			2.64	4.95	7.59

*Size would suggest multiple units.

D3050 150	Rooftop Single Zone Unit Systems		COST PER S.F.		
			MAT.	INST.	TOTAL
1260	Rooftop, single zone, air conditioner				
1280	Apartment corridors, 500 S.F., .92 ton		2.65	4.95	7.60
1320	1,000 S.F., 1.83 ton	R236000	2.62	4.92	7.54
1360	1,500 S.F., 2.75 ton	-20	2.52	4.06	6.58
1400	3,000 S.F., 5.50 ton		2.49	3.91	6.40
1440	5,000 S.F., 9.17 ton		2.39	3.55	5.94
1480	10,000 S.F., 18.33 ton		2.36	3.34	5.70
1560	Banks or libraries, 500 S.F., 2.08 ton		5.95	11.20	17.15
1600	1,000 S.F., 4.17 ton		5.75	9.25	15
1640	1,500 S.F., 6.25 ton		5.65	8.90	14.55
1680	3,000 S.F., 12.50 ton		5.45	8.05	13.50
1720	5,000 S.F., 20.80 ton		5.35	7.60	12.95
1760	10,000 S.F., 41.67 ton		6.95	7.55	14.50
1840	Bars and taverns, 500 S.F., 5.54 ton		12.75	14.85	27.60
1880	1,000 S.F., 11.08 ton		12.15	12.75	24.90
1920	1,500 S.F., 16.62 ton		12.20	11.85	24.05
1960	3,000 S.F., 33.25 ton		17.45	11.35	28.80
2000	5,000 S.F., 55.42 ton		14.95	11.30	26.25
2040	10,000 S.F., 110.83 ton*				
2080	Bowling alleys, 500 S.F., 2.83 ton		7.80	12.55	20.35
2120	1,000 S.F., 5.67 ton		7.70	12.05	19.75
2160	1,500 S.F., 8.50 ton		7.40	11	18.40
2200	3,000 S.F., 17.00 ton		7.45	10.55	18
2240	5,000 S.F., 28.33 ton		10.10	10.25	20.35
2280	10,000 S.F., 56.67 ton		8.85	10.25	19.10
2360	Department stores, 500 S.F., 1.46 ton		4.18	7.85	12.03

D30 HVAC

D3050 Terminal & Package Units

D3050 150	Rooftop Single Zone Unit Systems	COST PER S.F.		
		MAT.	INST.	TOTAL
2400	1,000 S.F., 2.92 ton	4.01	6.50	10.51
2440	1,500 S.F., 4.37 ton	3.97	6.20	10.17
2480	3,000 S.F., 8.75 ton	3.81	5.65	9.46
2520	5,000 S.F., 14.58 ton	3.83	5.40	9.23
2560	10,000 S.F., 29.17 ton	5.20	5.30	10.50
2640	Drug stores, 500 S.F., 3.33 ton	9.15	14.80	23.95
2680	1,000 S.F., 6.67 ton	9.05	14.20	23.25
2720	1,500 S.F., 10.00 ton	8.70	12.90	21.60
2760	3,000 S.F., 20.00 ton	8.55	12.15	20.70
2800	5,000 S.F., 33.33 ton	11.90	12.05	23.95
2840	10,000 S.F., 66.67 ton	10.40	12.05	22.45
2920	Factories, 500 S.F., 1.67 ton	4.76	8.95	13.71
2960	1,000 S.F., 3.33 ton	4.58	7.40	11.98
3000	1,500 S.F., 5.00 ton	4.53	7.10	11.63
3040	3,000 S.F., 10.00 ton	4.35	6.45	10.80
3080	5,000 S.F., 16.67 ton	4.38	6.20	10.58
3120	10,000 S.F., 33.33 ton	5.95	6.05	12
3200	Food supermarkets, 500 S.F., 1.42 ton	4.06	7.60	11.66
3240	1,000 S.F., 2.83 ton	3.87	6.25	10.12
3280	1,500 S.F., 4.25 ton	3.85	6.05	9.90
3320	3,000 S.F., 8.50 ton	3.70	5.50	9.20
3360	5,000 S.F., 14.17 ton	3.72	5.25	8.97
3400	10,000 S.F., 28.33 ton	5.05	5.15	10.20
3480	Medical centers, 500 S.F., 1.17 ton	3.34	6.30	9.64
3520	1,000 S.F., 2.33 ton	3.34	6.25	9.59
3560	1,500 S.F., 3.50 ton	3.21	5.20	8.41
3600	3,000 S.F., 7.00 ton	3.17	4.97	8.14
3640	5,000 S.F., 11.67 ton	3.04	4.52	7.56
3680	10,000 S.F., 23.33 ton	3	4.25	7.25
3760	Offices, 500 S.F., 1.58 ton	4.53	8.50	13.03
3800	1,000 S.F., 3.17 ton	4.36	7.05	11.41
3840	1,500 S.F., 4.75 ton	4.31	6.75	11.06
3880	3,000 S.F., 9.50 ton	4.13	6.15	10.28
3920	5,000 S.F., 15.83 ton	4.16	5.90	10.06
3960	10,000 S.F., 31.67 ton	5.65	5.75	11.40
4000	Restaurants, 500 S.F., 2.50 ton	7.15	13.45	20.60
4040	1,000 S.F., 5.00 ton	6.80	10.65	17.45
4080	1,500 S.F., 7.50 ton	6.55	9.70	16.25
4120	3,000 S.F., 15.00 ton	6.55	9.30	15.85
4160	5,000 S.F., 25.00 ton	6.45	9.10	15.55
4200	10,000 S.F., 50.00 ton	7.80	9.05	16.85
4240	Schools and colleges, 500 S.F., 1.92 ton	5.50	10.30	15.80
4280	1,000 S.F., 3.83 ton	5.25	8.50	13.75
4320	1,500 S.F., 5.75 ton	5.20	8.15	13.35
4360	3,000 S.F., 11.50 ton	5	7.45	12.45
4400	5,000 S.F., 19.17 ton	4.93	7	11.93
4440	10,000 S.F., 38.33 ton	6.40	6.95	13.35
5000				
9000	Components of ductwork packages for above systems, per ton of cooling:			
9010	Ductwork; galvanized steel, 120 pounds			
9020	Insulation; fiberglass 2" thick, FRK faced, 52 S.F.			
9030	Diffusers; aluminum, 24" x 12", one			
9040	Registers; aluminum, return with dampers, one			

D30 HVAC

D3050 Terminal & Package Units

System Description: Rooftop units are multizone with up to 12 zones, and include electric cooling, gas heat, thermostats, filters, supply and return fans complete. Duct systems are low velocity, galvanized steel supply and return with insulated supplies.

Multizone units cost more per ton of cooling than single zone. However, they offer flexibility where load conditions are varied due to heat generating areas or exposure to radiational heating. For example, perimeter offices on the "sunny side" may require cooling at the same time "shady side" or central offices may require heating. It is possible to accomplish similar results using duct heaters in branches of the single zone unit. However, heater location could be a problem and total system operating energy efficiency could be lower.

System Components	QUANTITY	UNIT	COST EACH		
			MAT.	INST.	TOTAL
SYSTEM D3050 155 1280					
ROOFTOP, MULTIZONE, AIR CONDITIONER					
APARTMENT CORRIDORS, 3,000 S.F., 5.50 TON					
Rooftop multizone unit, standard controls, curb	1.000	Ea.	34,320	2,376	36,696
Ductwork package for rooftop multizone units	1.000	System	3,300	16,775	20,075
TOTAL			37,620	19,151	56,771
COST PER S.F.			11.29	5.75	17.04

Note A: Small single zone unit recommended.
Note B: A combination of multizone units recommended.

D3050 155	Rooftop Multizone Unit Systems		COST PER S.F.		
			MAT.	INST.	TOTAL
1240	Rooftop, multizone, air conditioner				
1260	Apartment corridors, 1,500 S.F., 2.75 ton. See Note A.				
1280	3,000 S.F., 5.50 ton	R236000	11.28	5.76	17.04
1320	10,000 S.F., 18.30 ton	-20	7.55	6.15	13.70
1360	15,000 S.F., 27.50 ton		7.30	6.10	13.40
1400	20,000 S.F., 36.70 ton		7.65	6.15	13.80
1440	25,000 S.F., 45.80 ton		7.15	6.15	13.30
1520	Banks or libraries, 1,500 S.F., 6.25 ton		28.50	14.50	43
1560	3,000 S.F., 12.50 ton		24	14.20	38.20
1600	10,000 S.F., 41.67 ton		16.30	14.05	30.35
1640	15,000 S.F., 62.50 ton		12.40	13.95	26.35
1680	20,000 S.F., 83.33 ton		12.40	13.95	26.35
1720	25,000 S.F., 104.00 ton		12.40	13.90	26.30
1800	Bars and taverns, 1,500 S.F., 16.62 ton		61	21	82
1840	3,000 S.F., 33.24 ton		43	20	63
1880	10,000 S.F., 110.83 ton		30	20	50
1920	15,000 S.F., 165 ton, See Note B.				
1960	20,000 S.F., 220 ton, See Note B.				
2000	25,000 S.F., 275 ton, See Note B.				
2080	Bowling alleys, 1,500 S.F., 8.50 ton		39	19.75	58.75
2120	3,000 S.F., 17.00 ton		33	19.30	52.30
2160	10,000 S.F., 56.70 ton		22	19.10	41.10
2200	15,000 S.F., 85.00 ton		16.85	18.95	35.80
2240	20,000 S.F., 113.00 ton		16.85	18.85	35.70
2280	25,000 S.F., 140.00 ton see Note B.				
2360	Department stores, 1,500 S.F., 4.37 ton, See Note A.				

D30 HVAC

D3050 Terminal & Package Units

D3050 155 Rooftop Multizone Unit Systems

		COST PER S.F.		
		MAT.	INST.	TOTAL
2400	3,000 S.F., 8.75 ton	19.95	10.15	30.10
2440	10,000 S.F., 29.17 ton	12.15	9.75	21.90
2480	15,000 S.F., 43.75 ton	11.40	9.80	21.20
2520	20,000 S.F., 58.33 ton	8.70	9.75	18.45
2560	25,000 S.F., 72.92 ton	8.65	9.75	18.40
2640	Drug stores, 1,500 S.F., 10.00 ton	45.50	23	68.50
2680	3,000 S.F., 20.00 ton	27.50	22.50	50
2720	10,000 S.F., 66.66 ton	19.85	22.50	42.35
2760	15,000 S.F., 100.00 ton	19.90	22	41.90
2800	20,000 S.F., 135 ton, See Note B.			
2840	25,000 S.F., 165 ton, See Note B.			
2920	Factories, 1,500 S.F., 5 ton, See Note A.			
2960	3,000 S.F., 10.00 ton	23	11.60	34.60
3000	10,000 S.F., 33.33 ton	13.90	11.15	25.05
3040	15,000 S.F., 50.00 ton	13.05	11.20	24.25
3080	20,000 S.F., 66.66 ton	9.95	11.15	21.10
3120	25,000 S.F., 83.33 ton	9.90	11.15	21.05
3200	Food supermarkets, 1,500 S.F., 4.25 ton, See Note A.			
3240	3,000 S.F., 8.50 ton	19.40	9.85	29.25
3280	10,000 S.F., 28.33 ton	11.30	9.45	20.75
3320	15,000 S.F., 42.50 ton	11.10	9.55	20.65
3360	20,000 S.F., 56.67 ton	8.45	9.45	17.90
3400	25,000 S.F., 70.83 ton	8.45	9.45	17.90
3480	Medical centers, 1,500 S.F., 3.5 ton, See Note A.			
3520	3,000 S.F., 7.00 ton	15.95	8.10	24.05
3560	10,000 S.F., 23.33 ton	9.30	7.80	17.10
3600	15,000 S.F., 35.00 ton	9.70	7.80	17.50
3640	20,000 S.F., 46.66 ton	9.10	7.85	16.95
3680	25,000 S.F., 58.33 ton	6.95	7.80	14.75
3760	Offices, 1,500 S.F., 4.75 ton, See Note A.			
3800	3,000 S.F., 9.50 ton	21.50	11.05	32.55
3840	10,000 S.F., 31.66 ton	13.20	10.60	23.80
3880	15,000 S.F., 47.50 ton	12.40	10.65	23.05
3920	20,000 S.F., 63.33 ton	9.45	10.60	20.05
3960	25,000 S.F., 79.16 ton	9.40	10.60	20
4000	Restaurants, 1,500 S.F., 7.50 ton	34	17.40	51.40
4040	3,000 S.F., 15.00 ton	29	17.05	46.05
4080	10,000 S.F., 50.00 ton	19.55	16.85	36.40
4120	15,000 S.F., 75.00 ton	14.90	16.70	31.60
4160	20,000 S.F., 100.00 ton	14.90	16.70	31.60
4200	25,000 S.F., 125 ton, See Note B.			
4240	Schools and colleges, 1,500 S.F., 5.75 ton	26	13.35	39.35
4280	3,000 S.F., 11.50 ton	22	13.05	35.05
4320	10,000 S.F., 38.33 ton	15	12.90	27.90
4360	15,000 S.F., 57.50 ton	11.40	12.80	24.20
4400	20,000 S.F., 76.66 ton	11.40	12.80	24.20
4440	25,000 S.F., 95.83 ton	11.90	12.80	24.70
4450				
9000	Components of ductwork packages for above systems, per ton of cooling:			
9010	Ductwork; galvanized steel, 240 pounds			
9020	Insulation; fiberglass, 2" thick, FRK faced, 104 S.F.			
9030	Diffusers; aluminum, 24" x 12", two			
9040	Registers; aluminum, return with dampers, one			

D30 HVAC

D3050 Terminal & Package Units

System Description: Self-contained, single package water cooled units include cooling tower, pump, piping allowance. Systems for 1000 S.F. and up include duct and diffusers to provide for even distribution of air. Smaller units distribute air through a supply air plenum, which is integral with the unit.

Returns are not ducted and supplies are not insulated.

Hot water or steam heating coils are included but piping to boiler and the boiler itself is not included.

Where local codes or conditions permit single pass cooling for the smaller units, deduct 10%.

System Components	QUANTITY	UNIT	COST EACH MAT.	COST EACH INST.	COST EACH TOTAL
SYSTEM D3050 160 1300 SELF-CONTAINED, WATER COOLED UNIT APARTMENT CORRIDORS, 500 S.F., .92 TON					
Self-contained, water cooled, single package air conditioner unit	1.000	Ea.	1,461.60	814.80	2,276.40
Ductwork package for water or air cooled packaged units	1.000	System	81.88	1,104	1,185.88
Cooling tower, draw thru single flow, belt drive	1.000	Ea.	231.84	24.84	256.68
Cooling tower pumps & piping	1.000	System	115.92	58.88	174.80
TOTAL			1,891.24	2,002.52	3,893.76
COST PER S.F.			3.78	4.01	7.79

D3050 160	Self-contained, Water Cooled Unit Systems	COST PER S.F. MAT.	COST PER S.F. INST.	COST PER S.F. TOTAL
1280	Self-contained, water cooled unit	3.78	4.01	7.79
1300	Apartment corridors, 500 S.F., .92 ton	3.80	4	7.80
1320	1,000 S.F., 1.83 ton	3.77	3.99	7.76
1360	3,000 S.F., 5.50 ton	3.16	3.34	6.50
1400	5,000 S.F., 9.17 ton	2.89	3.10	5.99
1440	10,000 S.F., 18.33 ton	3.99	2.78	6.77
1520	Banks or libraries, 500 S.F., 2.08 ton	8.20	4.07	12.27
1560	1,000 S.F., 4.17 ton	7.15	7.60	14.75
1600	3,000 S.F., 12.50 ton	6.60	7.05	13.65
1640	5,000 S.F., 20.80 ton	9.05	6.30	15.35
1680	10,000 S.F., 41.66 ton	7.65	6.30	13.95
1760	Bars and taverns, 500 S.F., 5.54 ton	18	6.90	24.90
1800	1,000 S.F., 11.08 ton	16.90	12.05	28.95
1840	3,000 S.F., 33.25 ton	21.50	9.55	31.05
1880	5,000 S.F., 55.42 ton	18	9.95	27.95
1920	10,000 S.F., 110.00 ton	17.40	9.80	27.20
2000	Bowling alleys, 500 S.F., 2.83 ton	11.15	5.55	16.70
2040	1,000 S.F., 5.66 ton	9.75	10.35	20.10
2080	3,000 S.F., 17.00 ton	12.35	8.60	20.95
2120	5,000 S.F., 28.33 ton	11.20	8.30	19.50
2160	10,000 S.F., 56.66 ton	9.45	8.50	17.95
2200	Department stores, 500 S.F., 1.46 ton	5.75	2.86	8.61
2240	1,000 S.F., 2.92 ton	5	5.30	10.30
2280	3,000 S.F., 8.75 ton	4.60	4.94	9.54
2320	5,000 S.F., 14.58 ton	6.35	4.43	10.78
2360	10,000 S.F., 29.17 ton	5.75	4.27	10.02

R236000-20

D30 HVAC

D3050 Terminal & Package Units

D3050 160	Self-contained, Water Cooled Unit Systems	COST PER S.F.		
		MAT.	INST.	TOTAL
2440	Drug stores, 500 S.F., 3.33 ton	13.15	6.55	19.70
2480	1,000 S.F., 6.66 ton	11.45	12.15	23.60
2520	3,000 S.F., 20.00 ton	14.50	10.10	24.60
2560	5,000 S.F., 33.33 ton	15.20	10	25.20
2600	10,000 S.F., 66.66 ton	11.10	10	21.10
2680	Factories, 500 S.F., 1.66 ton	6.55	3.26	9.81
2720	1,000 S.F., 3.37 ton	5.80	6.15	11.95
2760	3,000 S.F., 10.00 ton	5.25	5.65	10.90
2800	5,000 S.F., 16.66 ton	7.25	5.05	12.30
2840	10,000 S.F., 33.33 ton	6.60	4.88	11.48
2920	Food supermarkets, 500 S.F., 1.42 ton	5.60	2.77	8.37
2960	1,000 S.F., 2.83 ton	5.85	6.15	12
3000	3,000 S.F., 8.50 ton	4.88	5.15	10.03
3040	5,000 S.F., 14.17 ton	4.47	4.80	9.27
3080	10,000 S.F., 28.33 ton	5.60	4.15	9.75
3160	Medical centers, 500 S.F., 1.17 ton	4.60	2.28	6.88
3200	1,000 S.F., 2.33 ton	4.81	5.10	9.91
3240	3,000 S.F., 7.00 ton	4.02	4.26	8.28
3280	5,000 S.F., 11.66 ton	3.68	3.95	7.63
3320	10,000 S.F., 23.33 ton	5.10	3.54	8.64
3400	Offices, 500 S.F., 1.58 ton	6.25	3.10	9.35
3440	1,000 S.F., 3.17 ton	6.50	6.90	13.40
3480	3,000 S.F., 9.50 ton	5	5.35	10.35
3520	5,000 S.F., 15.83 ton	6.90	4.81	11.71
3560	10,000 S.F., 31.67 ton	6.25	4.63	10.88
3640	Restaurants, 500 S.F., 2.50 ton	9.85	4.90	14.75
3680	1,000 S.F., 5.00 ton	8.60	9.10	17.70
3720	3,000 S.F., 15.00 ton	7.90	8.45	16.35
3760	5,000 S.F., 25.00 ton	10.90	7.60	18.50
3800	10,000 S.F., 50.00 ton	6.85	6.95	13.80
3880	Schools and colleges, 500 S.F., 1.92 ton	7.55	3.75	11.30
3920	1,000 S.F., 3.83 ton	6.60	7	13.60
3960	3,000 S.F., 11.50 ton	6.05	6.50	12.55
4000	5,000 S.F., 19.17 ton	8.35	5.80	14.15
4040	10,000 S.F., 38.33 ton	7.05	5.80	12.85
4050				
9000	Components of ductwork packages for above systems, per ton of cooling:			
9010	Ductwork; galvanized steel, 108 pounds			
9020	Diffusers, aluminum, 24" x 12", two			

D30 HVAC

D3050 Terminal & Package Units

System Description: Self-contained air cooled units with remote air cooled condenser and interconnecting tubing. Systems for 1000 S.F. and up include duct and diffusers. Smaller units distribute air directly.

Returns are not ducted and supplies are not insulated.

Potential savings may be realized by using a single zone rooftop system or through-the-wall unit, especially in the smaller capacities, if the application permits.

Hot water or steam heating coils are included but piping to boiler and the boiler itself is not included.

Condenserless models are available for 15% less where remote refrigerant source is available.

System Components	QUANTITY	UNIT	COST EACH MAT.	COST EACH INST.	COST EACH TOTAL
SYSTEM D3050 165 1320					
SELF-CONTAINED, AIR COOLED UNIT					
APARTMENT CORRIDORS, 500 S.F., .92 TON					
Air cooled, package unit	1.000	Ea.	1,598	527	2,125
Ductwork package for water or air cooled packaged units	1.000	System	81.88	1,104	1,185.88
Refrigerant piping	1.000	System	487.60	717.60	1,205.20
Air cooled condenser, direct drive, propeller fan	1.000	Ea.	953.25	201.50	1,154.75
TOTAL			3,120.73	2,550.10	5,670.83
COST PER S.F.			6.24	5.10	11.34

D3050 165	Self-contained, Air Cooled Unit Systems		COST PER S.F. MAT.	COST PER S.F. INST.	COST PER S.F. TOTAL
1300	Self-contained, air cooled unit				
1320	Apartment corridors, 500 S.F., .92 ton		6.25	5.10	11.35
1360	1,000 S.F., 1.83 ton		6.15	5.05	11.20
1400	3,000 S.F., 5.50 ton	R236000 -20	5.40	4.73	10.13
1440	5,000 S.F., 9.17 ton		4.68	4.50	9.18
1480	10,000 S.F., 18.33 ton		3.94	4.13	8.07
1560	Banks or libraries, 500 S.F., 2.08 ton		13.55	6.50	20.05
1600	1,000 S.F., 4.17 ton		12.25	10.75	23
1640	3,000 S.F., 12.50 ton		10.65	10.25	20.90
1680	5,000 S.F., 20.80 ton		9.05	9.40	18.45
1720	10,000 S.F., 41.66 ton		10	9.20	19.20
1800	Bars and taverns, 500 S.F., 5.54 ton		30	14.15	44.15
1840	1,000 S.F., 11.08 ton		28	20.50	48.50
1880	3,000 S.F., 33.25 ton		26.50	17.80	44.30
1920	5,000 S.F., 55.42 ton		26.50	17.80	44.30
1960	10,000 S.F., 110.00 ton		27	17.65	44.65
2040	Bowling alleys, 500 S.F., 2.83 ton		18.55	8.85	27.40
2080	1,000 S.F., 5.66 ton		16.75	14.65	31.40
2120	3,000 S.F., 17.00 ton		12.20	12.80	25
2160	5,000 S.F., 28.33 ton		13.75	12.50	26.25
2200	10,000 S.F., 56.66 ton		13.80	12.50	26.30
2240	Department stores, 500 S.F., 1.46 ton		9.55	4.56	14.11
2280	1,000 S.F., 2.92 ton		8.60	7.55	16.15
2320	3,000 S.F., 8.75 ton		7.45	7.15	14.60

D30 HVAC

D3050 Terminal & Package Units

D3050 165	Self-contained, Air Cooled Unit Systems	COST PER S.F.		
		MAT.	INST.	TOTAL
2360	5,000 S.F., 14.58 ton	7.45	7.15	14.60
2400	10,000 S.F., 29.17 ton	7.10	6.45	13.55
2480	Drug stores, 500 S.F., 3.33 ton	22	10.45	32.45
2520	1,000 S.F., 6.66 ton	19.65	17.20	36.85
2560	3,000 S.F., 20.00 ton	14.55	15.05	29.60
2600	5,000 S.F., 33.33 ton	16.20	14.70	30.90
2640	10,000 S.F., 66.66 ton	16.40	14.70	31.10
2720	Factories, 500 S.F., 1.66 ton	11.05	5.25	16.30
2760	1,000 S.F., 3.33 ton	9.90	8.60	18.50
2800	3,000 S.F., 10.00 ton	8.50	8.20	16.70
2840	5,000 S.F., 16.66 ton	7.15	7.50	14.65
2880	10,000 S.F., 33.33 ton	8.10	7.35	15.45
2960	Food supermarkets, 500 S.F., 1.42 ton	9.30	4.43	13.73
3000	1,000 S.F., 2.83 ton	9.50	7.80	17.30
3040	3,000 S.F., 8.50 ton	8.35	7.30	15.65
3080	5,000 S.F., 14.17 ton	7.25	6.95	14.20
3120	10,000 S.F., 28.33 ton	6.90	6.25	13.15
3200	Medical centers, 500 S.F., 1.17 ton	7.70	3.66	11.36
3240	1,000 S.F., 2.33 ton	7.90	6.45	14.35
3280	3,000 S.F., 7.00 ton	6.90	6	12.90
3320	5,000 S.F., 16.66 ton	6	5.75	11.75
3360	10,000 S.F., 23.33 ton	5	5.25	10.25
3440	Offices, 500 S.F., 1.58 ton	10.40	4.96	15.36
3480	1,000 S.F., 3.16 ton	10.70	8.75	19.45
3520	3,000 S.F., 9.50 ton	8.10	7.80	15.90
3560	5,000 S.F., 15.83 ton	6.90	7.15	14.05
3600	10,000 S.F., 31.66 ton	7.70	7	14.70
3680	Restaurants, 500 S.F., 2.50 ton	16.30	7.80	24.10
3720	1,000 S.F., 5.00 ton	14.75	12.90	27.65
3760	3,000 S.F., 15.00 ton	12.75	12.30	25.05
3800	5,000 S.F., 25.00 ton	12.10	11	23.10
3840	10,000 S.F., 50.00 ton	12.70	11	23.70
3920	Schools and colleges, 500 S.F., 1.92 ton	12.55	6	18.55
3960	1,000 S.F., 3.83 ton	11.40	9.90	21.30
4000	3,000 S.F., 11.50 ton	9.80	9.40	19.20
4040	5,000 S.F., 19.17 ton	8.25	8.65	16.90
4080	10,000 S.F., 38.33 ton	9.20	8.45	17.65
4090				
9000	Components of ductwork packages for above systems, per ton of cooling:			
9010	Ductwork; galvanized steel, 102 pounds			
9020	Diffusers; aluminum, 24" x 12", two			

D30 HVAC

D3050 Terminal & Package Units

General: Split systems offer several important advantages which should be evaluated when a selection is to be made. They provide a greater degree of flexibility in component selection which permits an accurate match-up of the proper equipment size and type with the particular needs of the building. This allows for maximum use of modern energy saving concepts in heating and cooling. Outdoor installation of the air cooled condensing unit allows space savings in the building and also isolates the equipment operating sounds from building occupants.

Design Assumptions: The systems below are comprised of a direct expansion air handling unit and air cooled condensing unit with interconnecting copper tubing. Ducts and diffusers are also included for distribution of air. Systems are priced for cooling only. Heat can be added as desired either by putting hot water/steam coils into the air unit or into the duct supplying the particular area of need. Gas fired duct furnaces are also available. Refrigerant liquid line is insulated.

System Components	QUANTITY	UNIT	COST EACH		
			MAT.	INST.	TOTAL
SYSTEM D3050 170 1280					
SPLIT SYSTEM, AIR COOLED CONDENSING UNIT					
APARTMENT CORRIDORS, 1,000 S.F., 1.80 TON					
Fan coil AC unit, cabinet mntd & filters direct expansion air cool	1.000	Ea.	567.30	190.32	757.62
Ductwork package, for split system, remote condensing unit	1.000	System	76.86	1,052.25	1,129.11
Refrigeration piping	1.000	System	360.51	1,189.50	1,550.01
Condensing unit, air cooled, incls compressor & standard controls	1.000	Ea.	1,799.50	762.50	2,562
TOTAL			2,804.17	3,194.57	5,998.74
COST PER S.F.			2.80	3.19	5.99

*Cooling requirements would lead to choosing a water cooled unit.

D3050 170	Split Systems With Air Cooled Condensing Units		COST PER S.F.		
			MAT.	INST.	TOTAL
1260	Split system, air cooled condensing unit				
1280	Apartment corridors, 1,000 S.F., 1.83 ton		2.80	3.20	6
1320	2,000 S.F., 3.66 ton	R236000	2.03	3.22	5.25
1360	5,000 S.F., 9.17 ton	-20	1.72	4.04	5.76
1400	10,000 S.F., 18.33 ton		2.09	4.41	6.50
1440	20,000 S.F., 36.66 ton		2.66	4.48	7.14
1520	Banks and libraries, 1,000 S.F., 4.17 ton		4.63	7.35	11.98
1560	2,000 S.F., 8.33 ton		3.91	9.20	13.11
1600	5,000 S.F., 20.80 ton		4.74	10	14.74
1640	10,000 S.F., 41.66 ton		6.05	10.20	16.25
1680	20,000 S.F., 83.32 ton		6.95	10.55	17.50
1760	Bars and taverns, 1,000 S.F., 11.08 ton		8.85	14.45	23.30
1800	2,000 S.F., 22.16 ton		13.05	17.30	30.35
1840	5,000 S.F., 55.42 ton		13.35	16.20	29.55
1880	10,000 S.F., 110.84 ton		14.85	16.85	31.70
1920	20,000 S.F., 220 ton*				
2000	Bowling alleys, 1,000 S.F., 5.66 ton		6.30	13.75	20.05
2040	2,000 S.F., 11.33 ton		5.30	12.50	17.80
2080	5,000 S.F., 28.33 ton		6.45	13.65	20.10
2120	10,000 S.F., 56.66 ton		8.25	13.85	22.10
2160	20,000 S.F., 113.32 ton		9.85	15	24.85
2320	Department stores, 1,000 S.F., 2.92 ton		3.37	5.05	8.42
2360	2,000 S.F., 5.83 ton		3.26	7.05	10.31
2400	5,000 S.F., 14.58 ton		2.74	6.45	9.19

D30 HVAC

D3050 Terminal & Package Units

D3050 170	Split Systems With Air Cooled Condensing Units	COST PER S.F.		
		MAT.	INST.	TOTAL
2440	10,000 S.F., 29.17 ton	3.33	7	10.33
2480	20,000 S.F., 58.33 ton	4.24	7.15	11.39
2560	Drug stores, 1,000 S.F., 6.66 ton	7.45	16.15	23.60
2600	2,000 S.F., 13.32 ton	6.25	14.70	20.95
2640	5,000 S.F., 33.33 ton	9.70	16.30	26
2680	10,000 S.F., 66.66 ton	8.70	16.95	25.65
2720	20,000 S.F., 133.32 ton*			
2800	Factories, 1,000 S.F., 3.33 ton	3.85	5.75	9.60
2840	2,000 S.F., 6.66 ton	3.72	8.05	11.77
2880	5,000 S.F., 16.66 ton	3.80	8	11.80
2920	10,000 S.F., 33.33 ton	4.84	8.15	12.99
2960	20,000 S.F., 66.66 ton	4.35	8.50	12.85
3040	Food supermarkets, 1,000 S.F., 2.83 ton	3.28	4.90	8.18
3080	2,000 S.F., 5.66 ton	3.16	6.85	10.01
3120	5,000 S.F., 14.66 ton	2.66	6.25	8.91
3160	10,000 S.F., 28.33 ton	3.23	6.80	10.03
3200	20,000 S.F., 56.66 ton	4.12	6.95	11.07
3280	Medical centers, 1,000 S.F., 2.33 ton	2.80	3.95	6.75
3320	2,000 S.F., 4.66 ton	2.60	5.65	8.25
3360	5,000 S.F., 11.66 ton	2.19	5.15	7.34
3400	10,000 S.F., 23.33 ton	2.66	5.60	8.26
3440	20,000 S.F., 46.66 ton	3.39	5.70	9.09
3520	Offices, 1,000 S.F., 3.17 ton	3.66	5.45	9.11
3560	2,000 S.F., 6.33 ton	3.53	7.65	11.18
3600	5,000 S.F., 15.83 ton	2.97	7	9.97
3601	Self contained heating and air conditioning, offices, 7,500 S.F., 30 ton	20.50	1.65	22.15
3640	10,000 S.F., 31.66 ton	3.61	7.60	11.21
3680	20,000 S.F., 63.32 ton	4.13	8.05	12.18
3760	Restaurants, 1,000 S.F., 5.00 ton	5.60	12.10	17.70
3800	2,000 S.F., 10.00 ton	4.69	11.05	15.74
3840	5,000 S.F., 25.00 ton	5.70	12.05	17.75
3880	10,000 S.F., 50.00 ton	7.25	12.25	19.50
3920	20,000 S.F., 100.00 ton	8.70	13.25	21.95
4000	Schools and colleges, 1,000 S.F., 3.83 ton	4.26	6.75	11.01
4040	2,000 S.F., 7.66 ton	3.60	8.45	12.05
4080	5,000 S.F., 19.17 ton	4.37	9.20	13.57
4120	10,000 S.F., 38.33 ton	5.55	9.35	14.90
4160	20,000 S.F., 76.66 ton	5	9.70	14.70
5000				
8012	Fan coil A.C., DX w/air cooled condensing unit, 20 ton cooling	19,400	5,000	24,400
9000	Components of ductwork packages for above systems, per ton of cooling:			
9010	Ductwork; galvanized steel, 102 pounds			
9020	Diffusers; aluminum, 24" x 12", two			

D30 HVAC

D3050 Terminal & Package Units

Rooftop Air Conditioner Unit

System Components	QUANTITY	UNIT	COST EACH		
			MAT.	INST.	TOTAL
SYSTEM D3050 175 1010					
A/C, ROOFTOP, DX COOL, GAS HEAT, CURB, ECONOMIZER, FILTERS., 5 TON					
Roof top A/C, curb, economizer, sgl zone, elec cool, gas ht, 5 ton, 112 MBH	1.000	Ea.	4,700	2,775	7,475
Pipe, black steel, Sch 40, threaded, w/cplgs & hangers, 10' OC, 1" dia	21.000	L.F.	223.65	340.20	563.85
Elbow, 90°, black, straight, 3/4" dia.	3.000	Ea.	23.10	184.50	207.60
Elbow, 90°, black, straight, 1" dia.	3.000	Ea.	40.35	198	238.35
Tee, black, reducing, 1" dia.	1.000	Ea.	24	107	131
Union, black with brass seat, 1" dia.	1.000	Ea.	45	71.50	116.50
Pipe nipple, black, 3/4" dia	2.000	Ea.	15.50	28.20	43.70
Pipe nipple, black, 1" dia	2.000	Ea.	10.65	16.20	26.85
Cap, black, 1" dia.	1.000	Ea.	10.60	28.50	39.10
Gas cock, brass, 1" size	1.000	Ea.	63.50	45	108.50
Control system, pneumatic, Rooftop A/C unit	1.000	Ea.	4,600	3,050	7,650
Rooftop unit heat/cool balancing	1.000	Ea.		590	590
TOTAL			9,756.35	7,434.10	17,190.45

D3050 175	Rooftop Air Conditioner, Const. Volume	COST EACH		
		MAT.	INST.	TOTAL
1010	A/C, rooftop, DX cool, gas heat, curb, economizer, fltrs, 5 Ton	9,750	7,425	17,175
1020	7-1/2 Ton	12,200	7,750	19,950
1030	12-1/2 Ton	15,200	8,500	23,700
1040	18 Ton	19,700	9,300	29,000
1050	25 Ton	45,800	10,600	56,400
1060	40 Ton	55,500	14,200	69,700

D3050 180	Rooftop Air Conditioner, Variable Air Volume	COST EACH		
		MAT.	INST.	TOTAL
1010	A/C, rooftop, DX cool, gas heat, curb, ecmizr, fltrs, VAV, 12-1/2 Ton	18,100	9,100	27,200
1020	18 Ton	23,400	10,000	33,400
1030	25 Ton	50,500	11,500	62,000
1040	40 Ton	63,500	15,600	79,100
1050	60 Ton	88,500	21,200	109,700
1060	80 Ton	112,500	26,500	139,000

D30 HVAC

D3050 Terminal & Package Units

Computer rooms impose special requirements on air conditioning systems. A prime requirement is reliability, due to the potential monetary loss that could be incurred by a system failure. A second basic requirement is the tolerance of control with which temperature and humidity are regulated, and dust eliminated. As the air conditioning system reliability is so vital, the additional cost of reserve capacity and redundant components is often justified.

System Descriptions: Computer areas may be environmentally controlled by one of three methods as follows:

1. Self-contained Units
These are units built to higher standards of performance and reliability. They usually contain alarms and controls to indicate component operation failure, filter change, etc. It should be remembered that these units in the room will occupy space that is relatively expensive to build and that all alterations and service of the equipment will also have to be accomplished within the computer area.

2. Decentralized Air Handling Units In operation these are similar to the self-contained units except that their cooling capability comes from remotely located refrigeration equipment as refrigerant or chilled water. As no compressors or refrigerating equipment are required in the air units, they are smaller and require less service than self-contained units. An added plus for this type of system occurs if some of the computer components themselves also require chilled water for cooling.

3. Central System Supply Cooling is obtained from a central source which, since it is not located within the computer room, may have excess capacity and permit greater flexibility without interfering with the computer components. System performance criteria must still be met.

Note: The costs shown below do not include an allowance for ductwork or piping.

D3050 185		Computer Room Cooling Units	COST EACH		
			MAT.	INST.	TOTAL
0560	Computer room unit, air cooled, includes remote condenser				
0580		3 ton	34,300	3,125	37,425
0600		5 ton	36,700	3,450	40,150
0620		8 ton	68,500	5,775	74,275
0640		10 ton	71,500	6,225	77,725
0660		15 ton	79,000	7,075	86,075
0680		20 ton	95,500	10,100	105,600
0700		23 ton	117,500	11,500	129,000
0800	Chilled water, for connection to existing chiller system				
0820		5 ton	24,900	2,100	27,000
0840		8 ton	25,100	3,125	28,225
0860		10 ton	25,300	3,175	28,475
0880		15 ton	28,200	3,250	31,450
0900		20 ton	29,900	3,375	33,275
0920		23 ton	31,900	3,850	35,750
1000	Glycol system, complete except for interconnecting tubing				
1020		3 ton	43,100	3,900	47,000
1040		5 ton	47,200	4,100	51,300
1060		8 ton	75,500	6,775	82,275
1080		10 ton	80,500	7,425	87,925
1100		15 ton	100,000	9,325	109,325
1120		20 ton	109,500	10,100	119,600
1140		23 ton	115,500	10,500	126,000
1240	Water cooled, not including condenser water supply or cooling tower				
1260		3 ton	35,000	2,525	37,525
1280		5 ton	39,400	2,875	42,275
1300		8 ton	62,500	4,725	67,225
1320		15 ton	75,500	5,775	81,275
1340		20 ton	81,000	6,375	87,375
1360		23 ton	85,000	6,925	91,925

D3050 201		Packaged A/C, Elec. Ht., Const. Volume	COST EACH		
			MAT.	INST.	TOTAL
1010	A/C packaged, DX, air cooled, electric heat, constant vol., 5 Ton		11,200	7,250	18,450
1020		10 Ton	18,200	9,800	28,000
1030		20 Ton	27,800	13,000	40,800
1040		30 Ton	51,000	14,400	65,400

D30 HVAC

D3050 Terminal & Package Units

D3050 201 Packaged A/C, Elec. Ht., Const. Volume

		\multicolumn{3}{c}{COST EACH}		
		MAT.	INST.	TOTAL
1050	40 Ton	66,500	16,300	82,800
1060	50 Ton	88,500	18,100	106,600

D3050 202 Packaged Air Conditioner, Elect. Heat, VAV

		MAT.	INST.	TOTAL
1010	A/C packaged, DX, air cooled, electric heat, VAV, 10 Ton	20,500	9,175	29,675
1020	20 Ton	31,800	12,100	43,900
1030	30 Ton	57,000	13,200	70,200
1040	40 Ton	73,500	15,100	88,600
1050	50 Ton	98,500	16,900	115,400
1060	60 Ton	109,500	19,600	129,100

D3050 203 Packaged A/C, Hot Wtr. Heat, Const. Volume

		MAT.	INST.	TOTAL
1010	A/C packaged, DX, air cooled, H/W heat, constant vol., 5 Ton	10,100	9,800	19,900
1020	10 Ton	15,300	12,800	28,100
1030	20 Ton	23,600	16,300	39,900
1040	30 Ton	42,200	20,900	63,100
1050	40 Ton	58,000	23,300	81,300
1060	50 Ton	76,000	25,300	101,300

D3050 204 Packaged A/C, Hot Wtr. Heat, VAV

		MAT.	INST.	TOTAL
1010	A/C packaged, DX, air cooled, H/W heat, VAV, 10 Ton	17,500	11,900	29,400
1020	20 Ton	28,200	15,700	43,900
1030	30 Ton	48,200	19,400	67,600
1040	40 Ton	65,500	21,000	86,500
1050	50 Ton	85,500	24,400	109,900
1060	60 Ton	100,000	27,300	127,300

D30 HVAC

D3050 Terminal & Package Units

Condenser Supply Water Piping | Condenser Return Water Piping

Self-Contained Air Conditioner Unit, Water Cooled

System Components	QUANTITY	UNIT	COST EACH MAT.	COST EACH INST.	COST EACH TOTAL
SYSTEM D3050 210 1010					
A/C, SELF CONTAINED, SINGLE PKG., WATER COOLED, ELECT. HEAT, 5 TON					
Self-contained, water cooled, elect. heat, not inc tower, 5 ton, const vol	1.000	Ea.	10,400	2,025	12,425
Pipe, black steel, Sch 40, threaded, w/cplg & hangers, 10' OC, 1-1/4" dia.	21.500	L.F.	303.15	374.10	677.25
Elbow, 90°, black, straight, 1-1/4" dia.	6.000	Ea.	132	423	555
Tee, black, straight, 1-1/4" dia.	2.000	Ea.	68	222	290
Tee, black, reducing, 1-1/4" dia.	2.000	Ea.	83	222	305
Thermometers, stem type, 9" case, 8" stem, 3/4" NPT	2.000	Ea.	422	62	484
Union, black with brass seat, 1-1/4" dia.	2.000	Ea.	128	147	275
Pipe nipple, black, 1-1/4" dia	3.000	Ea.	21.15	26.10	47.25
Valves, bronze, gate, N.R.S., threaded, class 150, 1-1/4" size	2.000	Ea.	640	115	755
Circuit setter, bal valve, bronze body, threaded, 1-1/4" pipe size	1.000	Ea.	233	57.50	290.50
Insulation, fiberglass pipe covering, 1" wall, 1-1/4" IPS	20.000	L.F.	52	137	189
Control system, pneumatic, A/C Unit with heat	1.000	Ea.	4,600	3,050	7,650
Re-heat coil balancing	1.000	Ea.		160	160
Rooftop unit heat/cool balancing	1.000	Ea.		590	590
TOTAL			17,082.30	7,610.70	24,693

D3050 210		AC Unit, Package, Elec. Ht., Water Cooled	COST EACH MAT.	COST EACH INST.	COST EACH TOTAL
1010	A/C, self contained, single pkg., water cooled, elect. heat, 5 Ton		17,100	7,600	24,700
1020		10 Ton	25,400	9,375	34,775
1030		20 Ton	32,800	11,900	44,700
1040		30 Ton	57,000	12,900	69,900
1050		40 Ton	73,000	14,300	87,300
1060		50 Ton	95,500	17,100	112,600

D3050 215		AC Unit, Package, Elec. Ht., Water Cooled, VAV	COST EACH MAT.	COST EACH INST.	COST EACH TOTAL
1010	A/C, self contained, single pkg., water cooled, elect. ht, VAV, 10 Ton		28,000	9,375	37,375
1020		20 Ton	37,500	11,900	49,400
1030		30 Ton	64,000	12,900	76,900
1040		40 Ton	80,500	14,300	94,800
1050		50 Ton	106,000	17,100	123,100
1060		60 Ton	119,500	20,700	140,200

D30 HVAC

D3050 Terminal & Package Units

D3050 220	AC Unit, Package, Hot Water Coil, Water Cooled	COST EACH		
		MAT.	INST.	TOTAL
1010	A/C, self contn'd, single pkg., water cool, H/W ht, const. vol, 5 Ton	15,900	10,600	26,500
1020	10 Ton	21,700	12,600	34,300
1030	20 Ton	47,100	15,700	62,800
1040	30 Ton	59,500	19,900	79,400
1050	40 Ton	70,000	24,100	94,100
1060	50 Ton	81,500	29,700	111,200

D3050 225	AC Unit, Package, HW Coil, Water Cooled, VAV	COST EACH		
		MAT.	INST.	TOTAL
1010	A/C, self contn'd, single pkg., water cool, H/W ht, VAV, 10 Ton	24,400	11,800	36,200
1020	20 Ton	33,700	15,300	49,000
1030	30 Ton	56,000	19,000	75,000
1040	40 Ton	73,000	20,700	93,700
1050	50 Ton	94,500	24,500	119,000
1060	60 Ton	109,000	26,500	135,500

D30 HVAC

D3050 Terminal & Package Units

Note: Water source units do not include an allowance for any type of water source or piping to it.

Heat Pump, Air/Air, Rooftop w/Economizer

System Components	QUANTITY	UNIT	COST EACH		
			MAT.	INST.	TOTAL
SYSTEM D3050 245 1010					
HEAT PUMP, ROOFTOP, AIR/AIR, CURB., ECONOMIZER., SUP. ELECT. HEAT, 10 TON					
Heat pump, air to air, rooftop, curb, economizer, elect ht, 10 ton cooling	1.000	Ea.	81,000	6,050	87,050
Ductwork, 32" x 12" fabricated, galvanized steel, 16 LF	176.000	Lb.	130.24	1,768.80	1,899.04
Insulation, ductwork, blanket type, fiberglass, 1" thk, 1-1/2 LB density	117.000	S.F.	643.50	2,000.70	2,644.20
Rooftop unit heat/cool balancing	1.000	Ea.		590	590
TOTAL			81,773.74	10,409.50	92,183.24

D3050 230	Heat Pump, Water Source, Central Station	COST EACH		
		MAT.	INST.	TOTAL
1010	Heat pump, central station, water source, constant vol., 5 Ton	6,000	4,250	10,250
1020	10 Ton	11,800	5,975	17,775
1030	20 Ton	22,200	11,100	33,300
1040	30 Ton	32,100	16,000	48,100
1050	40 Ton	43,800	17,500	61,300
1060	50 Ton	49,600	23,700	73,300

D3050 235	Heat Pump, Water Source, Console	COST EACH		
		MAT.	INST.	TOTAL
1020	Heat pump, console, water source, 1 Ton	3,600	2,325	5,925
1030	1-1/2 Ton	3,425	2,425	5,850
1040	2 Ton	4,750	2,850	7,600
1050	3 Ton	9,675	3,075	12,750
1060	3-1/2 Ton	5,325	3,150	8,475

D3050 240	Heat Pump, Horizontal, Duct Mounted	COST EACH		
		MAT.	INST.	TOTAL
1020	Heat pump, horizontal, ducted, water source, 1 Ton	4,675	5,000	9,675
1030	1-1/2 Ton	4,950	6,275	11,225
1040	2 Ton	6,350	7,525	13,875
1050	3 Ton	11,800	9,850	21,650
1060	3-1/2 Ton	7,475	10,200	17,675

D30 HVAC

D3050 Terminal & Package Units

D3050 245	Heat Pump, Rooftop, Air/Air	COST EACH		
		MAT.	INST.	TOTAL
1010	Heat pump, rooftop, air/air, curb, economizer, sup. elect heat, 10 Ton	82,000	10,400	92,400
1020	20 Ton	112,000	16,900	128,900
1030	30 Ton	157,000	23,300	180,300
1040	40 Ton	157,500	27,100	184,600
1050	50 Ton	203,500	30,400	233,900
1060	60 Ton	215,000	34,200	249,200

D30 HVAC

D3050 Terminal & Package Units

Thru–Wall Heat Pump

Thru–Wall Air Conditioner

System Components	QUANTITY	UNIT	COST EACH		
			MAT.	INST.	TOTAL
SYSTEM D3050 255 1010					
A/C UNIT, THRU-THE-WALL, SUPPLEMENTAL ELECT. HEAT, CABINET, LOUVER, 1/2 TON					
A/C unit, thru-wall, electric heat., cabinet, louver, 1/2 ton	1.000	Ea.	1,300	260	1,560
TOTAL			1,300	260	1,560

D3050 255	Thru-Wall A/C Unit	COST EACH		
		MAT.	INST.	TOTAL
1010	A/C unit, thru-the-wall, supplemental elect. heat, cabinet, louver, 1/2 Ton	1,300	260	1,560
1020	3/4 Ton	3,825	310	4,135
1030	1 Ton	4,175	390	4,565
1040	1-1/2 Ton	5,175	650	5,825
1050	2 Ton	5,200	820	6,020

D3050 260	Thru-Wall Heat Pump	COST EACH		
		MAT.	INST.	TOTAL
1010	Heat pump, thru-the-wall, cabinet, louver, 1/2 Ton	3,225	195	3,420
1020	3/4 Ton	3,400	260	3,660
1030	1 Ton	4,400	390	4,790
1040	Supplemental. elect. heat, 1-1/2 Ton	3,850	1,000	4,850
1050	2 Ton	3,900	1,050	4,950

D30 HVAC

D3090 Other HVAC Systems/Equip

System Components	QUANTITY	UNIT	COST EACH		
			MAT.	INST.	TOTAL
SYSTEM D3090 310 1010					
FUME HOOD EXHAUST SYSTEM, 3' LONG, 1000 CFM					
Fume hood	3.000	L.F.	37,500	1,740	39,240
Ductwork, plastic, FM approved for acid fume & smoke, straight, 10" dia	60.000	L.F.	318	1,074	1,392
Ductwork, plastic, FM approved for acid fume & smoke, elbow 90°, 10" dia	3.000	Ea.	372	585	957
Fan, corrosive fume resistant plastic, 1,630 CFM, 1/2 HP	1.000	Ea.	8,925	480	9,405
Fan control switch & mounting base	1.000	Ea.	196	54	250
Roof fan balancing	1.000	Ea.		340	340
TOTAL			47,311	4,273	51,584

D3090 310	Fume Hood Exhaust Systems	COST EACH		
		MAT.	INST.	TOTAL
1010	Fume hood exhaust system, 3' long, 1000 CFM	47,300	4,275	51,575
1020	4' long, 2000 CFM	60,500	5,400	65,900
1030	6' long, 3500 CFM	88,000	8,050	96,050
1040	6' long, 5000 CFM	101,000	9,500	110,500
1050	10' long, 8000 CFM	154,000	13,000	167,000

D30 HVAC

D3090 Other HVAC Systems/Equip

Cast Iron Garage Exhaust System

Dual Exhaust System

System Components	QUANTITY	UNIT	COST EACH MAT.	COST EACH INST.	COST EACH TOTAL
SYSTEM D3090 320 1040					
GARAGE, EXHAUST, SINGLE 3" EXHAUST OUTLET, CARS & LIGHT TRUCKS					
A Outlet top assy, for engine exhaust system with adapters and ftngs, 3" diam	1.000	Ea.	340	53	393
F Bullnose (guide) for engine exhaust system, 3" diam	1.000	Ea.	39.50		39.50
G Galvanized flexible tubing for engine exhaust system, 3" diam	8.000	L.F.	106.80		106.80
H Adapter for metal tubing end of engine exhaust system, 3" tail pipe	1.000	Ea.	66		66
J Pipe, sewer, cast iron, push-on joint, 8" diam.	18.000	L.F.	1,071	954	2,025
Excavating utility trench, chain trencher, 8" wide, 24" deep	18.000	L.F.		48.06	48.06
Backfill utility trench by hand, incl. compaction, 8" wide 24" deep	18.000	L.F.		59.22	59.22
Stand for blower, concrete over polystyrene core, 6" high	1.000	Ea.	6.25	26.50	32.75
AC&V duct spiral reducer 10"x8"	1.000	Ea.	66	47.50	113.50
AC&V duct spiral reducer 12"x10"	1.000	Ea.	77.50	63.50	141
AC&V duct spiral preformed 45° elbow, 8" diam	1.000	Ea.	41	54.50	95.50
AC&V utility fan, belt drive, 3 phase, 2000 CFM, 1 HP	2.000	Ea.	3,450	840	4,290
Safety switch, heavy duty fused, 240V, 3 pole, 30 amp	1.000	Ea.	153	250	403
TOTAL			5,417.05	2,396.28	7,813.33

D3090 320	Garage Exhaust Systems	COST PER BAY MAT.	COST PER BAY INST.	COST PER BAY TOTAL
1040	Garage, single 3" exhaust outlet, cars & light trucks, one bay	5,425	2,400	7,825
1060	Additional bays up to seven bays	1,150	645	1,795
1500	4" outlet, trucks, one bay	5,450	2,400	7,850
1520	Additional bays up to six bays	1,175	645	1,820
1600	5" outlet, diesel trucks, one bay	5,800	2,400	8,200
1650	Additional single bays up to six bays	1,650	760	2,410
1700	Two adjoining bays	5,800	2,400	8,200
2000	Dual exhaust, 3" outlets, pair of adjoining bays	6,550	2,975	9,525
2100	Additional pairs of adjoining bays	1,800	760	2,560

D30 HVAC

D3090 Other HVAC Systems/Equip

System Components	QUANTITY	UNIT	COST EACH		
			MAT.	INST.	TOTAL
SYSTEM D3090 750 1000					
SEISMIC PAD FOR 20-38 SELF-CONTAINED UNIT					
Form equipment pad	28.000	L.F.	77.56	145.60	223.16
Reinforcing in hold down pad, #3 to #7	60.000	Lb.	46.80	43.80	90.60
Concrete 3000 PSI	.866	C.Y.	147.22		147.22
Place concrete pad	.866	C.Y.		38.54	38.54
Finish concrete equipment pad	47.000	S.F.		47	47
Drill for 3/8 inch slab anchors	10.000	Ea.	.30	111	111.30
Exisiting slab anchors 3/8 inch	10.000	Ea.	8.90	49.90	58.80
Equipment anchors 3/8 inch for plate/foot	8.000	Ea.	21.84	42.80	64.64
TOTAL			302.62	478.64	781.26

D3090 750	Seismic Concrete Equipment Pads	COST PER EACH		
		MAT.	INST.	TOTAL
1000	Seismic pad for 20-38 tons self-contained AC unit without economizer .25g	305	480	785
1010	0.5 g seismic acceleration	305	480	785
1020	0.75 g seismic acceleration	305	480	785
1030	1.0 g seismic acceleration	305	480	785
1040	1.5 g seismic acceleration	305	545	850
1050	2.0 g seismic acceleration	325	745	1,070
1060	2.5 g seismic acceleration	335	940	1,275
1100	Seismic pad for 40-80 tons self contained AC unit without economizer .25g	460	695	1,155
1110	0.5 g seismic acceleration	460	695	1,155
1120	0.75 g seismic acceleration	460	695	1,155
1130	1.0 g seismic acceleration	460	695	1,155
1140	1.5 g seismic acceleration	490	990	1,480
1150	2.0 g seismic acceleration	555	1,525	2,080
1160	2.5 g seismic acceleration	620	2,200	2,820

D30 HVAC

D3090 Other HVAC Systems/Equip

D3090 750	Seismic Concrete Equipment Pads	COST PER EACH		
		MAT.	INST.	TOTAL
1200	Seismic pad for 80-110 tons self contained AC unit without economizer .25g	510	750	1,260
1210	0.5 g seismic acceleration	510	750	1,260
1220	0.75 g seismic acceleration	510	750	1,260
1230	1.0 g seismic acceleration	510	750	1,260
1240	1.5 g seismic acceleration	540	1,075	1,615
1250	2.0 g seismic acceleration	605	1,675	2,280
1260	2.5 g seismic acceleration	680	2,375	3,055
1990	Seismic pad for self-contained AC units for isolator/snubber bolts			
2000	Seismic pad for 20-38 tons self contained AC unit without economizer .25g	325	520	845
2010	0.5 g seismic acceleration	325	520	845
2020	0.75 g seismic acceleration	325	520	845
2030	1.0 g seismic acceleration	325	520	845
2040	1.5 g seismic acceleration	330	585	915
2050	2.0 g seismic acceleration	350	800	1,150
2060	2.5 g seismic acceleration	360	995	1,355
2100	Seismic pad for 40-80 tons self contained AC unit without economizer .25g	490	750	1,240
2110	0.5 g seismic acceleration	490	750	1,240
2120	0.75 g seismic acceleration	490	750	1,240
2130	1.0 g seismic acceleration	490	750	1,240
2140	1.5 g seismic acceleration	520	1,050	1,570
2150	2.0 g seismic acceleration	590	1,600	2,190
2160	2.5 g seismic acceleration	665	2,275	2,940
2200	Seismic pad for 80-110 tons self contained AC unit without economizer .25g	535	805	1,340
2210	0.5 g seismic acceleration	535	805	1,340
2220	0.75 g seismic acceleration	535	805	1,340
2230	1.0 g seismic acceleration	535	805	1,340
2240	1.5 g seismic acceleration	565	1,125	1,690
2250	2.0 g seismic acceleration	645	1,750	2,395
2260	2.5 g seismic acceleration	725	2,450	3,175
2990	Seismic pad for self-contained AC economizer units for plate/foot attachment			
3000	Seismic pad for 20-38 tons self contained AC unit economizer .25 g-2.0 g	198	278	476
3010	2.5 g seismic acceleration	208	370	578
3100	Seismic pad for 40-80 tons self contained AC unit economizer .25-1.5 g	262	370	632
3110	2.0 g seismic acceleration	268	430	698
3120	2.5 g seismic acceleration	275	505	780
3190	Seismic pad for self-contained AC unit economizer for isolator/snubber bolts			
3200	Seismic pad for 20-38 tons self contained AC unit economizer .25 g-2.0 g	207	294	501
3210	2.5 g seismic acceleration	222	395	617
3300	Seismic pad for 40-80 tons self contained AC unit economizer .25-1.5 g	278	400	678
3310	2.0 g seismic acceleration	284	460	744
3320	2.5 g seismic acceleration	292	540	832

Same Data. Simplified.

Enjoy the convenience and efficiency of accessing your costs anywhere:
- **Skip the multiplier** by setting your location
- **Quickly search,** edit, favorite and share costs
- **Stay on top of price changes** with automatic updates

Discover more at rsmeans.com/online

No part of this cost data may be reproduced, stored in a retrieval system, or transmitted in any form or by any means without prior written permission of Gordian.

G Building Sitework

G10 Site Preparation

G1030 Site Earthwork

Trenching Systems are shown on a cost per linear foot basis. The systems include: excavation; backfill and removal of spoil; and compaction for various depths and trench bottom widths. The backfill has been reduced to accommodate a pipe of suitable diameter and bedding.

The slope for trench sides varies from none to 1:1.

The Expanded System Listing shows Trenching Systems that range from 2' to 12' in width. Depths range from 2' to 25'.

System Components			COST PER L.F.		
	QUANTITY	UNIT	EQUIP.	LABOR	TOTAL
SYSTEM G1030 805 1310 TRENCHING, COMMON EARTH, NO SLOPE, 2' WIDE, 2' DP, 3/8 C.Y. BUCKET					
Excavation, trench, hyd. backhoe, track mtd., 3/8 C.Y. bucket	.148	C.Y.	.30	1.30	1.60
Backfill and load spoil, from stockpile	.153	L.C.Y.	.17	.39	.56
Compaction by vibrating plate, 6" lifts, 4 passes	.118	C.Y.	.13	.47	.60
Remove excess spoil, 8 C.Y. dump truck, 2 mile roundtrip	.040	L.C.Y.	.15	.22	.37
TOTAL			.75	2.38	3.13

G1030 805	Trenching Common Earth	COST PER L.F.		
		EQUIP.	LABOR	TOTAL
1310	Trenching, common earth, no slope, 2' wide, 2' deep, 3/8 C.Y. bucket	.75	2.38	3.14
1320	3' deep, 3/8 C.Y. bucket	1.09	3.58	4.67
1330	4' deep, 3/8 C.Y. bucket	1.43	4.77	6.20
1340	6' deep, 3/8 C.Y. bucket	2.08	6.20	8.25
1350	8' deep, 1/2 C.Y. bucket	2.80	8.20	11
1360	10' deep, 1 C.Y. bucket	5.25	9.80	15.05
1400	4' wide, 2' deep, 3/8 C.Y. bucket	1.64	4.75	6.40
1410	3' deep, 3/8 C.Y. bucket	2.31	7.15	9.45
1420	4' deep, 1/2 C.Y. bucket	3.11	7.95	11.05
1430	6' deep, 1/2 C.Y. bucket	4.22	12.80	17
1440	8' deep, 1/2 C.Y. bucket	8.50	16.60	25
1450	10' deep, 1 C.Y. bucket	10.15	20.50	30.50
1460	12' deep, 1 C.Y. bucket	13.20	26	39.50
1470	15' deep, 1-1/2 C.Y. bucket	10.55	23.50	34
1480	18' deep, 2-1/2 C.Y. bucket	15.20	32.50	48
1520	6' wide, 6' deep, 5/8 C.Y. bucket w/trench box	10.95	19.20	30
1530	8' deep, 3/4 C.Y. bucket	14.75	25	40
1540	10' deep, 1 C.Y. bucket	13.55	26	39.50
1550	12' deep, 1-1/2 C.Y. bucket	14.10	28	42
1560	16' deep, 2-1/2 C.Y. bucket	18.35	35	53
1570	20' deep, 3-1/2 C.Y. bucket	23	41.50	64.50
1580	24' deep, 3-1/2 C.Y. bucket	27.50	50	77.50
1640	8' wide, 12' deep, 1-1/2 C.Y. bucket w/trench box	19.45	35.50	55
1650	15' deep, 1-1/2 C.Y. bucket	25.50	46.50	72
1660	18' deep, 2-1/2 C.Y. bucket	26	46.50	72.50
1680	24' deep, 3-1/2 C.Y. bucket	37	64.50	101
1730	10' wide, 20' deep, 3-1/2 C.Y. bucket w/trench box	30	61.50	91.50
1740	24' deep, 3-1/2 C.Y. bucket	43.50	74	118
1780	12' wide, 20' deep, 3-1/2 C.Y. bucket w/trench box	46.50	78	125
1790	25' deep, bucket	58	99.50	157
1800	1/2 to 1 slope, 2' wide, 2' deep, 3/8 C.Y. bucket	1.09	3.58	4.67
1810	3' deep, 3/8 C.Y. bucket	1.86	6.25	8.15
1820	4' deep, 3/8 C.Y. bucket	2.79	9.55	12.35
1840	6' deep, 3/8 C.Y. bucket	5.10	15.45	20.50

G10 Site Preparation

G1030 Site Earthwork

G1030 805	Trenching Common Earth	COST PER L.F.		
		EQUIP.	LABOR	TOTAL
1860	8' deep, 1/2 C.Y. bucket	8.15	24.50	33
1880	10' deep, 1 C.Y. bucket	18.25	34.50	53
2300	4' wide, 2' deep, 3/8 C.Y. bucket	1.98	5.95	7.90
2310	3' deep, 3/8 C.Y. bucket	3.08	9.85	12.90
2320	4' deep, 1/2 C.Y. bucket	4.46	12.10	16.55
2340	6' deep, 1/2 C.Y. bucket	7.05	22.50	29.50
2360	8' deep, 1/2 C.Y. bucket	16.40	33.50	50
2380	10' deep, 1 C.Y. bucket	22.50	47	69.50
2400	12' deep, 1 C.Y. bucket	28.50	63.50	92
2430	15' deep, 1-1/2 C.Y. bucket	30	68	98
2460	18' deep, 2-1/2 C.Y. bucket	50	106	156
2840	6' wide, 6' deep, 5/8 C.Y. bucket w/trench box	16.45	28.50	45
2860	8' deep, 3/4 C.Y. bucket	24	42.50	66.50
2880	10' deep, 1 C.Y. bucket	21	43	64.50
2900	12' deep, 1-1/2 C.Y. bucket	27	56.50	83.50
2940	16' deep, 2-1/2 C.Y. bucket	42	83	125
2980	20' deep, 3-1/2 C.Y. bucket	57.50	112	169
3020	24' deep, 3-1/2 C.Y. bucket	81.50	153	234
3100	8' wide, 12' deep, 1-1/2 C.Y. bucket w/trench box	33	64.50	97.50
3120	15' deep, 1-1/2 C.Y. bucket	48.50	93.50	142
3140	18' deep, 2-1/2 C.Y. bucket	57.50	111	169
3180	24' deep, 3-1/2 C.Y. bucket	91	167	258
3270	10' wide, 20' deep, 3-1/2 C.Y. bucket w/trench box	59	129	187
3280	24' deep, 3-1/2 C.Y. bucket	100	183	283
3370	12' wide, 20' deep, 3-1/2 C.Y. bucket w/trench box	84	149	234
3380	25' deep, 3-1/2 C.Y. bucket	117	213	330
3500	1 to 1 slope, 2' wide, 2' deep, 3/8 C.Y. bucket	1.43	4.78	6.20
3520	3' deep, 3/8 C.Y. bucket	4	10.95	14.95
3540	4' deep, 3/8 C.Y. bucket	4.15	14.35	18.50
3560	6' deep, 1/2 C.Y. bucket	5.10	15.45	20.50
3580	8' deep, 1/2 C.Y. bucket	10.15	31	41
3600	10' deep, 1 C.Y. bucket	31.50	59.50	90.50
3800	4' wide, 2' deep, 3/8 C.Y. bucket	2.32	7.15	9.45
3820	3' deep, 3/8 C.Y. bucket	3.84	12.50	16.35
3840	4' deep, 1/2 C.Y. bucket	5.80	16.20	22
3860	6' deep, 1/2 C.Y. bucket	9.85	32.50	42.50
3880	8' deep, 1/2 C.Y. bucket	24.50	50.50	75
3900	10' deep, 1 C.Y. bucket	35.	73.50	109
3920	12' deep, 1 C.Y. bucket	52	106	158
3940	15' deep, 1-1/2 C.Y. bucket	49.50	113	162
3960	18' deep, 2-1/2 C.Y. bucket	68.50	147	215
4030	6' wide, 6' deep, 5/8 C.Y. bucket w/trench box	21.50	38.50	60
4040	8' deep, 3/4 C.Y. bucket	32	52.50	84.50
4050	10' deep, 1 C.Y. bucket	30.50	63.50	94
4060	12' deep, 1-1/2 C.Y. bucket	41.50	86	127
4070	16' deep, 2-1/2 C.Y. bucket	66	131	197
4080	20' deep, 3-1/2 C.Y. bucket	93	182	275
4090	24' deep, 3-1/2 C.Y. bucket	136	256	390
4500	8' wide, 12' deep, 1-1/2 C.Y. bucket w/trench box	46.50	93.50	140
4550	15' deep, 1-1/2 C.Y. bucket	71	140	211
4600	18' deep, 2-1/2 C.Y. bucket	88	172	260
4650	24' deep, 3-1/2 C.Y. bucket	145	270	415
4800	10' wide, 20' deep, 3-1/2 C.Y. bucket w/trench box	87.50	196	283
4850	24' deep, 3-1/2 C.Y. bucket	154	286	440
4950	12' wide, 20' deep, 3-1/2 C.Y. bucket w/trench box	122	220	340
4980	25' deep, 3-1/2 C.Y. bucket	175	325	500

G10 Site Preparation

G1030 Site Earthwork

Trenching Systems are shown on a cost per linear foot basis. The systems include: excavation; backfill and removal of spoil; and compaction for various depths and trench bottom widths. The backfill has been reduced to accommodate a pipe of suitable diameter and bedding.

The slope for trench sides varies from none to 1:1.

The Expanded System Listing shows Trenching Systems that range from 2' to 12' in width. Depths range from 2' to 25'.

System Components			COST PER L.F.		
	QUANTITY	UNIT	EQUIP.	LABOR	TOTAL
SYSTEM G1030 806 1310					
TRENCHING, LOAM & SANDY CLAY, NO SLOPE, 2' WIDE, 2' DP, 3/8 C.Y. BUCKET					
Excavation, trench, hyd. backhoe, track mtd., 3/8 C.Y. bucket	.148	C.Y.	.28	1.20	1.48
Backfill and load spoil, from stockpile	.165	L.C.Y.	.18	.43	.61
Compaction by vibrating plate 18" wide, 6" lifts, 4 passes	.118	C.Y.	.13	.47	.60
Remove excess spoil, 8 C.Y. dump truck, 2 mile roundtrip	.042	L.C.Y.	.16	.23	.39
TOTAL			.75	2.33	3.08

G1030 806	Trenching Loam & Sandy Clay	COST PER L.F.		
		EQUIP.	LABOR	TOTAL
1310	Trenching, loam & sandy clay, no slope, 2' wide, 2' deep, 3/8 C.Y. bucket	.75	2.33	3.08
1320	3' deep, 3/8 C.Y. bucket	1.16	3.83	4.98
1330	4' deep, 3/8 C.Y. bucket	1.42	4.66	6.10
1340	6' deep, 3/8 C.Y. bucket	2.70	5.55	8.25
1350	8' deep, 1/2 C.Y. bucket	3.62	7.35	10.95
1360	10' deep, 1 C.Y. bucket	3.88	7.85	11.75
1400	4' wide, 2' deep, 3/8 C.Y. bucket	1.66	4.66	6.30
1410	3' deep, 3/8 C.Y. bucket	2.33	7	9.30
1420	4' deep, 1/2 C.Y. bucket	3.13	7.85	11
1430	6' deep, 1/2 C.Y. bucket	5.50	11.55	17
1440	8' deep, 1/2 C.Y. bucket	8.25	16.35	24.50
1450	10' deep, 1 C.Y. bucket	7.45	16.70	24
1460	12' deep, 1 C.Y. bucket	9.40	21	30
1470	15' deep, 1-1/2 C.Y. bucket	11.05	24	35
1480	18' deep, 2-1/2 C.Y. bucket	12.40	26.50	39
1520	6' wide, 6' deep, 5/8 C.Y. bucket w/trench box	10.50	18.85	29.50
1530	8' deep, 3/4 C.Y. bucket	14.15	24.50	39
1540	10' deep, 1 C.Y. bucket	12.40	25	37.50
1550	12' deep, 1-1/2 C.Y. bucket	13.75	28	41.50
1560	16' deep, 2-1/2 C.Y. bucket	18	35	53
1570	20' deep, 3-1/2 C.Y. bucket	21.50	41.50	63
1580	24' deep, 3-1/2 C.Y. bucket	26.50	50.50	77.50
1640	8' wide, 12' deep, 1-1/4 C.Y. bucket w/trench box	19.10	35.50	54.50
1650	15' deep, 1-1/2 C.Y. bucket	23.50	45	68.50
1660	18' deep, 2-1/2 C.Y. bucket	27	50.50	78
1680	24' deep, 3-1/2 C.Y. bucket	36	65.50	102
1730	10' wide, 20' deep, 3-1/2 C.Y. bucket w/trench box	36	66	102
1740	24' deep, 3-1/2 C.Y. bucket	45.50	81.50	127
1780	12' wide, 20' deep, 3-1/2 C.Y. bucket w/trench box	43.50	78.50	122
1790	25' deep, 3-1/2 C.Y. bucket	56.50	101	158
1800	1/2:1 slope, 2' wide, 2' deep, 3/8 C.Y. bucket	1.09	3.50	4.58
1810	3' deep, 3/8 C.Y. bucket	1.85	6.10	7.95
1820	4' deep, 3/8 C.Y. bucket	2.77	9.30	12.10
1840	6' deep, 3/8 C.Y. bucket	6.65	13.90	20.50

G10 Site Preparation

G1030 Site Earthwork

G1030 806	Trenching Loam & Sandy Clay	COST PER L.F.		
		EQUIP.	LABOR	TOTAL
1860	8' deep, 1/2 C.Y. bucket	10.60	22	33
1880	10' deep, 1 C.Y. bucket	13.45	28	41
2300	4' wide, 2' deep, 3/8 C.Y. bucket	1.99	5.85	7.85
2310	3' deep, 3/8 C.Y. bucket	3.08	9.60	12.70
2320	4' deep, 1/2 C.Y. bucket	4.45	11.90	16.35
2340	6' deep, 1/2 C.Y. bucket	9.20	20.50	29.50
2360	8' deep, 1/2 C.Y. bucket	15.90	33	49
2380	10' deep, 1 C.Y. bucket	16.45	38.50	54.50
2400	12' deep, 1 C.Y. bucket	27.50	63.50	91
2430	15' deep, 1-1/2 C.Y. bucket	31.50	70.50	102
2460	18' deep, 2-1/2 C.Y. bucket	49	108	157
2840	6' wide, 6' deep, 5/8 C.Y. bucket w/trench box	15.40	28.50	44
2860	8' deep, 3/4 C.Y. bucket	23	41.50	64.50
2880	10' deep, 1 C.Y. bucket	22.50	47	69
2900	12' deep, 1-1/2 C.Y. bucket	27	57	84
2940	16' deep, 2-1/2 C.Y. bucket	41.50	84	125
2980	20' deep, 3-1/2 C.Y. bucket	56	113	169
3020	24' deep, 3-1/2 C.Y. bucket	79.50	155	234
3100	8' wide, 12' deep, 1-1/2 C.Y. bucket w/trench box	32.50	64.50	97
3120	15' deep, 1-1/2 C.Y. bucket	44	91	135
3140	18' deep, 2-1/2 C.Y. bucket	56.50	112	169
3180	24' deep, 3-1/2 C.Y. bucket	88.50	170	259
3270	10' wide, 20' deep, 3-1/2 C.Y. bucket w/trench box	71	138	209
3280	24' deep, 3-1/2 C.Y. bucket	98	186	284
3320	12' wide, 20' deep, 3-1/2 C.Y. bucket w/trench box	78.50	150	228
3380	25' deep, 3-1/2 C.Y. bucket w/trench box	107	201	310
3500	1:1 slope, 2' wide, 2' deep, 3/8 C.Y. bucket	1.43	4.66	6.10
3520	3' deep, 3/8 C.Y. bucket	2.60	8.75	11.35
3540	4' deep, 3/8 C.Y. bucket	4.11	14	18.10
3560	6' deep, 1/2 C.Y. bucket	6.65	13.90	20.50
3580	8' deep, 1/2 C.Y. bucket	17.60	37	54.50
3600	10' deep, 1 C.Y. bucket	23	47.50	70.50
3800	4' wide, 2' deep, 3/8 C.Y. bucket	2.33	7	9.35
3820	3' deep, 1/2 C.Y. bucket	3.84	12.25	16.10
3840	4' deep, 1/2 C.Y. bucket	5.80	16	22
3860	6' deep, 1/2 C.Y. bucket	12.95	29.50	42.50
3880	8' deep, 1/2 C.Y. bucket	23.50	49.50	73.50
3900	10' deep, 1 C.Y. bucket	25.50	60	85.50
3920	12' deep, 1 C.Y. bucket	37	85	122
3940	15' deep, 1-1/2 C.Y. bucket	51.50	117	169
3960	18' deep, 2-1/2 C.Y. bucket	67.50	148	216
4030	6' wide, 6' deep, 5/8 C.Y. bucket w/trench box	20.50	38	58.50
4040	8' deep, 3/4 C.Y. bucket	31.50	58.50	90
4050	10' deep, 1 C.Y. bucket	32	69	101
4060	12' deep, 1-1/2 C.Y. bucket	40	86.50	127
4070	16' deep, 2-1/2 C.Y. bucket	64.50	132	197
4080	20' deep, 3-1/2 C.Y. bucket	91	185	276
4090	24' deep, 3-1/2 C.Y. bucket	132	259	390
4500	8' wide, 12' deep, 1-1/4 C.Y. bucket w/trench box	45.50	94	140
4550	15' deep, 1-1/2 C.Y. bucket	65	137	202
4600	18' deep, 2-1/2 C.Y. bucket	86	174	260
4650	24' deep, 3-1/2 C.Y. bucket	141	274	415
4800	10' wide, 20' deep, 3-1/2 C.Y. bucket w/trench box	106	209	315
4850	24' deep, 3-1/2 C.Y. bucket	151	290	440
4950	12' wide, 20' deep, 3-1/2 C.Y. bucket w/trench box	113	222	335
4980	25' deep, 3-1/2 C.Y. bucket	171	325	500

G10 Site Preparation

G1030 Site Earthwork

Trenching Systems are shown on a cost per linear foot basis. The systems include: excavation; backfill and removal of spoil; and compaction for various depths and trench bottom widths. The backfill has been reduced to accommodate a pipe of suitable diameter and bedding.

The slope for trench sides varies from none to 1:1.

The Expanded System Listing shows Trenching Systems that range from 2' to 12' in width. Depths range from 2' to 25'.

System Components	QUANTITY	UNIT	COST PER L.F.		
			EQUIP.	LABOR	TOTAL
SYSTEM G1030 807 1310					
TRENCHING, SAND & GRAVEL, NO SLOPE, 2' WIDE, 2' DEEP, 3/8 C.Y. BUCKET					
Excavation, trench, hyd. backhoe, track mtd., 3/8 C.Y. bucket	.148	C.Y.	.27	1.18	1.45
Backfill and load spoil, from stockpile	.140	L.C.Y.	.15	.36	.51
Compaction by vibrating plate 18" wide, 6" lifts, 4 passes	.118	C.Y.	.13	.47	.60
Remove excess spoil, 8 C.Y. dump truck, 2 mile roundtrip	.035	L.C.Y.	.14	.19	.33
TOTAL			.69	2.20	2.89

G1030 807	Trenching Sand & Gravel	COST PER L.F.		
		EQUIP.	LABOR	TOTAL
1310	Trenching, sand & gravel, no slope, 2' wide, 2' deep, 3/8 C.Y. bucket	.70	2.21	2.90
1320	3' deep, 3/8 C.Y. bucket	1.09	3.68	4.77
1330	4' deep, 3/8 C.Y. bucket	1.33	4.43	5.75
1340	6' deep, 3/8 C.Y. bucket	2.58	5.30	7.90
1350	8' deep, 1/2 C.Y. bucket	3.46	7	10.50
1360	10' deep, 1 C.Y. bucket	3.66	7.40	11.05
1400	4' wide, 2' deep, 3/8 C.Y. bucket	1.51	4.38	5.90
1410	3' deep, 3/8 C.Y. bucket	2.14	6.60	8.75
1420	4' deep, 1/2 C.Y. bucket	2.88	7.40	10.30
1430	6' deep, 1/2 C.Y. bucket	5.20	11.05	16.20
1440	8' deep, 1/2 C.Y. bucket	7.75	15.50	23.50
1450	10' deep, 1 C.Y. bucket	6.95	15.75	22.50
1460	12' deep, 1 C.Y. bucket	8.80	19.65	28.50
1470	15' deep, 1-1/2 C.Y. bucket	10.35	23	33
1480	18' deep, 2-1/2 C.Y. bucket	11.65	25	36.50
1520	6' wide, 6' deep, 5/8 C.Y. bucket w/trench box	9.95	17.85	28
1530	8' deep, 3/4 C.Y. bucket	13.40	23.50	37
1540	10' deep, 1 C.Y. bucket	11.65	23.50	35
1550	12' deep, 1-1/2 C.Y. bucket	12.90	26.50	39.50
1560	16' deep, 2 C.Y. bucket	17.05	33	50.50
1570	20' deep, 3-1/2 C.Y. bucket	19.95	39	59
1580	24' deep, 3-1/2 C.Y. bucket	25	47.50	72.50
1640	8' wide, 12' deep, 1-1/2 C.Y. bucket w/trench box	17.95	33.50	51.50
1650	15' deep, 1-1/2 C.Y. bucket	22	42.50	64.50
1660	18' deep, 2-1/2 C.Y. bucket	25.50	47.50	73
1680	24' deep, 3-1/2 C.Y. bucket	33.50	61.50	95
1730	10' wide, 20' deep, 3-1/2 C.Y. bucket w/trench box	34	61.50	95.50
1740	24' deep, 3-1/2 C.Y. bucket	42.50	76	118
1780	12' wide, 20' deep, 3-1/2 C.Y. bucket w/trench box	40.50	73	114
1790	25' deep, 3-1/2 C.Y. bucket	53	94.50	147
1800	1/2:1 slope, 2' wide, 2' deep, 3/8 C.Y. bucket	1.01	3.32	4.33
1810	3' deep, 3/8 C.Y. bucket	1.72	5.80	7.55
1820	4' deep, 3/8 C.Y. bucket	2.59	8.90	11.45
1840	6' deep, 3/8 C.Y. bucket	6.35	13.30	19.65

G10 Site Preparation

G1030 Site Earthwork

G1030 807	Trenching Sand & Gravel	COST PER L.F.		
		EQUIP.	LABOR	TOTAL
1860	8' deep, 1/2 C.Y. bucket	10.15	21	31.50
1880	10' deep, 1 C.Y. bucket	12.70	26	39
2300	4' wide, 2' deep, 3/8 C.Y. bucket	1.82	5.50	7.30
2310	3' deep, 3/8 C.Y. bucket	2.85	9.10	11.95
2320	4' deep, 1/2 C.Y. bucket	4.12	11.25	15.35
2340	6' deep, 1/2 C.Y. bucket	8.75	19.60	28.50
2360	8' deep, 1/2 C.Y. bucket	15.05	31.50	46.50
2380	10' deep, 1 C.Y. bucket	15.45	36	51.50
2400	12' deep, 1 C.Y. bucket	26	60	86
2430	15' deep, 1-1/2 C.Y. bucket	29.50	66.50	96
2460	18' deep, 2-1/2 C.Y. bucket	46	101	148
2840	6' wide, 6' deep, 5/8 C.Y. bucket w/trench box	14.60	27	41.50
2860	8' deep, 3/4 C.Y. bucket	21.50	39.50	61.50
2880	10' deep, 1 C.Y. bucket	21	44.50	65.50
2900	12' deep, 1-1/2 C.Y. bucket	25.50	54	79.50
2940	16' deep, 2 C.Y. bucket	39	79	118
2980	20' deep, 3-1/2 C.Y. bucket	52.50	106	159
3020	24' deep, 3-1/2 C.Y. bucket	74.50	146	220
3100	8' wide, 12' deep, 1-1/4 C.Y. bucket w/trench box	30.50	61	91.50
3120	15' deep, 1-1/2 C.Y. bucket	41.50	85.50	127
3140	18' deep, 2-1/2 C.Y. bucket	53.50	106	159
3180	24' deep, 3-1/2 C.Y. bucket	83.50	159	243
3270	10' wide, 20' deep, 3-1/2 C.Y. bucket w/trench box	66.50	129	195
3280	24' deep, 3-1/2 C.Y. bucket	92	174	266
3370	12' wide, 20' deep, 3-1/2 C.Y. bucket w/trench box	74.50	143	218
3380	25' deep, 3-1/2 C.Y. bucket	107	201	310
3500	1:1 slope, 2' wide, 2' deep, 3/8 C.Y. bucket	2.23	5.60	7.80
3520	3' deep, 3/8 C.Y. bucket	2.43	8.30	10.75
3540	4' deep, 3/8 C.Y. bucket	3.86	13.35	17.20
3560	6' deep, 3/8 C.Y. bucket	6.35	13.30	19.65
3580	8' deep, 1/2 C.Y. bucket	16.90	35.50	52.50
3600	10' deep, 1 C.Y. bucket	22	45	66.50
3800	4' wide, 2' deep, 3/8 C.Y. bucket	2.14	6.60	8.75
3820	3' deep, 3/8 C.Y. bucket	3.56	11.60	15.15
3840	4' deep, 1/2 C.Y. bucket	5.35	15.10	20.50
3860	6' deep, 1/2 C.Y. bucket	12.35	28	40.50
3880	8' deep, 1/2 C.Y. bucket	22.50	47.50	69.50
3900	10' deep, 1 C.Y. bucket	24	56.50	80.50
3920	12' deep, 1 C.Y. bucket	34.50	80.50	115
3940	15' deep, 1-1/2 C.Y. bucket	48.50	110	159
3960	18' deep, 2-1/2 C.Y. bucket	63.50	140	203
4030	6' wide, 6' deep, 5/8 C.Y. bucket w/trench box	19.30	36	55.50
4040	8' deep, 3/4 C.Y. bucket	30	56	86
4050	10' deep, 1 C.Y. bucket	30.50	65	95.50
4060	12' deep, 1-1/2 C.Y. bucket	38	81.50	119
4070	16' deep, 2 C.Y. bucket	61.50	125	186
4080	20' deep, 3-1/2 C.Y. bucket	85.50	173	259
4090	24' deep, 3-1/2 C.Y. bucket	124	244	370
4500	8' wide, 12' deep, 1-1/2 C.Y. bucket w/trench box	43	89	132
4550	15' deep, 1-1/2 C.Y. bucket	61	129	190
4600	18' deep, 2-1/2 C.Y. bucket	81	164	245
4650	24' deep, 3-1/2 C.Y. bucket	133	257	390
4800	10' wide, 20' deep, 3-1/2 C.Y. bucket w/trench box	99.50	196	295
4850	24' deep, 3-1/2 C.Y. bucket	141	272	415
4950	12' wide, 20' deep, 3-1/2 C.Y. bucket w/trench box	106	207	315
4980	25' deep, 3-1/2 C.Y. bucket	161	305	470

G10 Site Preparation

G1030 Site Earthwork

The Pipe Bedding System is shown for various pipe diameters. Compacted bank sand is used for pipe bedding and to fill 12" over the pipe. No backfill is included. Various side slopes are shown to accommodate different soil conditions. Pipe sizes vary from 6" to 84" diameter.

System Components	QUANTITY	UNIT	COST PER L.F.		
			MAT.	INST.	TOTAL
SYSTEM G1030 815 1440					
PIPE BEDDING, SIDE SLOPE 0 TO 1, 1' WIDE, PIPE SIZE 6" DIAMETER					
Borrow, bank sand, 2 mile haul, machine spread	.086	C.Y.	1.30	.81	2.11
Compaction, vibrating plate	.086	C.Y.		.31	.31
TOTAL			1.30	1.12	2.42

G1030 815	Pipe Bedding	COST PER L.F.		
		MAT.	INST.	TOTAL
1440	Pipe bedding, side slope 0 to 1, 1' wide, pipe size 6" diameter	1.30	1.11	2.41
1460	2' wide, pipe size 8" diameter	2.81	2.40	5.21
1480	Pipe size 10" diameter	2.87	2.45	5.32
1500	Pipe size 12" diameter	2.93	2.51	5.44
1520	3' wide, pipe size 14" diameter	4.76	4.06	8.82
1540	Pipe size 15" diameter	4.80	4.10	8.90
1560	Pipe size 16" diameter	4.85	4.14	8.99
1580	Pipe size 18" diameter	4.94	4.22	9.16
1600	4' wide, pipe size 20" diameter	7	6	13
1620	Pipe size 21" diameter	7.10	6.05	13.15
1640	Pipe size 24" diameter	7.25	6.20	13.45
1660	Pipe size 30" diameter	7.35	6.30	13.65
1680	6' wide, pipe size 32" diameter	12.60	10.75	23.35
1700	Pipe size 36" diameter	12.90	11	23.90
1720	7' wide, pipe size 48" diameter	20.50	17.50	38
1740	8' wide, pipe size 60" diameter	25	21.50	46.50
1760	10' wide, pipe size 72" diameter	35	29.50	64.50
1780	12' wide, pipe size 84" diameter	46	39	85
2140	Side slope 1/2 to 1, 1' wide, pipe size 6" diameter	2.42	2.07	4.49
2160	2' wide, pipe size 8" diameter	4.12	3.52	7.64
2180	Pipe size 10" diameter	4.42	3.78	8.20
2200	Pipe size 12" diameter	4.68	4	8.68
2220	3' wide, pipe size 14" diameter	6.75	5.80	12.55
2240	Pipe size 15" diameter	6.90	5.90	12.80
2260	Pipe size 16" diameter	7.10	6.05	13.15
2280	Pipe size 18" diameter	7.45	6.35	13.80
2300	4' wide, pipe size 20" diameter	9.85	8.40	18.25
2320	Pipe size 21" diameter	10.05	8.60	18.65
2340	Pipe size 24" diameter	10.70	9.15	19.85
2360	Pipe size 30" diameter	11.85	10.15	22
2380	6' wide, pipe size 32" diameter	17.50	14.95	32.45
2400	Pipe size 36" diameter	18.60	15.90	34.50
2420	7' wide, pipe size 48" diameter	29	25	54
2440	8' wide, pipe size 60" diameter	37	31.50	68.50
2460	10' wide, pipe size 72" diameter	50.50	43	93.50
2480	12' wide, pipe size 84" diameter	66	56.50	122.50
2620	Side slope 1 to 1, 1' wide, pipe size 6" diameter	3.55	3.03	6.58
2640	2' wide, pipe size 8" diameter	5.45	4.67	10.12

G10 Site Preparation

G1030 Site Earthwork

G1030 815	Pipe Bedding	COST PER L.F.		
		MAT.	INST.	TOTAL
2660	Pipe size 10" diameter	5.95	5.10	11.05
2680	Pipe size 12" diameter	6.50	5.55	12.05
2700	3' wide, pipe size 14" diameter	8.75	7.50	16.25
2720	Pipe size 15" diameter	9.05	7.70	16.75
2740	Pipe size 16" diameter	9.35	8	17.35
2760	Pipe size 18" diameter	10	8.55	18.55
2780	4' wide, pipe size 20" diameter	12.70	10.85	23.55
2800	Pipe size 21" diameter	13.05	11.15	24.20
2820	Pipe size 24" diameter	14.15	12.05	26.20
2840	Pipe size 30" diameter	16.35	13.95	30.30
2860	6' wide, pipe size 32" diameter	22.50	19.15	41.65
2880	Pipe size 36" diameter	24.50	21	45.50
2900	7' wide, pipe size 48" diameter	37.50	32	69.50
2920	8' wide, pipe size 60" diameter	49	41.50	90.50
2940	10' wide, pipe size 72" diameter	66.50	56.50	123
2960	12' wide, pipe size 84" diameter	86.50	74	160.50

G30 Site Mechanical Utilities

G3010 Water Supply

G3010 110	Water Distribution Piping	COST PER L.F.		
		MAT.	INST.	TOTAL
2000	Piping, excav. & backfill excl., ductile iron class 250, mech. joint			
2130	4" diameter	111	12.45	123.45
2150	6" diameter	132	15.60	147.60
2160	8" diameter	185	18.70	203.70
2170	10" diameter	242	22	264
2180	12" diameter	299	23.50	322.50
2210	16" diameter	158	34.50	192.50
2220	18" diameter	211	36	247
3000	Tyton joint			
3130	4" diameter	26.50	6.25	32.75
3150	6" diameter	26	7.50	33.50
3160	8" diameter	36.50	12.45	48.95
3170	10" diameter	56.50	13.70	70.20
3180	12" diameter	59.50	15.60	75.10
3210	16" diameter	63	22	85
3220	18" diameter	70	25	95
3230	20" diameter	73	28	101
3250	24" diameter	102	32.50	134.50
4000	Copper tubing, type K			
4050	3/4" diameter	4.85	3.87	8.72
4060	1" diameter	6.30	4.84	11.14
4080	1-1/2" diameter	10.20	5.85	16.05
4090	2" diameter	15.45	6.75	22.20
4110	3" diameter	31.50	11.55	43.05
4130	4" diameter	55	16.30	71.30
4150	6" diameter	112	30	142
5000	Polyvinyl chloride class 160, S.D.R. 26			
5130	1-1/2" diameter	1.57	1.44	3.01
5150	2" diameter	1.54	1.57	3.11
5160	4" diameter	5.70	4.96	10.66
5170	6" diameter	8.25	5.95	14.20
5180	8" diameter	10.55	9.45	20
6000	Polyethylene 160 psi, S.D.R. 7			
6050	3/4" diameter	.76	2.06	2.82
6060	1" diameter	.77	2.23	3
6080	1-1/2" diameter	2.04	2.40	4.44
6090	2" diameter	2.61	2.96	5.57

G30 Site Mechanical Utilities

G3020 Sanitary Sewer

G3020 110	Drainage & Sewage Piping	COST PER L.F.		
		MAT.	INST.	TOTAL
2000	Piping, excavation & backfill excluded, PVC, plain			
2130	4" diameter	3.78	5.05	8.83
2150	6" diameter	8.95	5.40	14.35
2160	8" diameter	10.85	5.65	16.50
2900	Box culvert, precast, 8' long			
3000	6' x 3'	340	47.50	387.50
3020	6' x 7'	530	53.50	583.50
3040	8' x 3'	455	58.50	513.50
3060	8' x 8'	630	66.50	696.50
3080	10' x 3'	630	60.50	690.50
3100	10' x 8'	900	83	983
3120	12' x 3'	1,475	66.50	1,541.50
3140	12' x 8'	1,125	99.50	1,224.50
4000	Concrete, nonreinforced			
4150	6" diameter	13.15	14.55	27.70
4160	8" diameter	14.45	17.20	31.65
4170	10" diameter	16	17.85	33.85
4180	12" diameter	16.70	19.25	35.95
4200	15" diameter	24	21.50	45.50
4220	18" diameter	30	26.50	56.50
4250	24" diameter	36.50	38.50	75
4400	Reinforced, no gasket			
4580	12" diameter	24.50	25.50	50
4600	15" diameter	29	25.50	54.50
4620	18" diameter	33.50	29.50	63
4650	24" diameter	48.50	38.50	87
4670	30" diameter	67	77.50	144.50
4680	36" diameter	114	94	208
4690	42" diameter	162	103	265
4700	48" diameter	217	110	327
4720	60" diameter	260	146	406
4730	72" diameter	375	175	550
4740	84" diameter	605	219	824
4800	With gasket			
4980	12" diameter	26.50	14.80	41.30
5000	15" diameter	32	15.60	47.60
5020	18" diameter	37	16.40	53.40
5050	24" diameter	59.50	18.30	77.80
5070	30" diameter	80	77.50	157.50
5080	36" diameter	130	94	224
5090	42" diameter	191	87.50	278.50
5100	48" diameter	239	110	349
5120	60" diameter	300	140	440
5130	72" diameter	405	175	580
5140	84" diameter	730	292	1,022
5700	Corrugated metal, alum. or galv. bit. coated			
5760	8" diameter	9.25	11.65	20.90
5770	10" diameter	9.60	14.80	24.40
5780	12" diameter	15.30	18.35	33.65
5800	15" diameter	16.15	19.25	35.40
5820	18" diameter	24	20.50	44.50
5850	24" diameter	26.50	24	50.50
5870	30" diameter	33.50	57	90.50
5880	36" diameter	37.50	57	94.50
5900	48" diameter	50.50	68	118.50
5920	60" diameter	89	93.50	182.50
5930	72" diameter	92.50	156	248.50
6000	Plain			

G30 Site Mechanical Utilities

G3020 Sanitary Sewer

G3020 110	Drainage & Sewage Piping	COST PER L.F.		
		MAT.	INST.	TOTAL
6060	8" diameter	10.40	10.85	21.25
6070	10" diameter	10.35	13.75	24.10
6080	12" diameter	34.50	17.55	52.05
6100	15" diameter	33	17.55	50.55
6120	18" diameter	39	18.80	57.80
6140	24" diameter	44	22	66
6170	30" diameter	35.50	52.50	88
6180	36" diameter	40.50	52.50	93
6200	48" diameter	60	61.50	121.50
6220	60" diameter	99	89.50	188.50
6230	72" diameter	199	179	378
6300	Steel or alum. oval arch, coated & paved invert			
6400	15" equivalent diameter	15.65	19.25	34.90
6420	18" equivalent diameter	16	25.50	41.50
6450	24" equivalent diameter	24.50	31	55.50
6470	30" equivalent diameter	30	38.50	68.50
6480	36" equivalent diameter	28	68	96
6490	42" equivalent diameter	36	76	112
6500	48" equivalent diameter	47.50	91	138.50
6600	Plain			
6700	15" equivalent diameter	25	17.10	42.10
6720	18" equivalent diameter	41.50	22	63.50
6750	24" equivalent diameter	18.65	25.50	44.15
6770	30" equivalent diameter	24	63	87
6780	36" equivalent diameter	43	63	106
6790	42" equivalent diameter	52	73.50	125.50
6800	48" equivalent diameter	52	91	143
8000	Polyvinyl chloride SDR 35			
8130	4" diameter	3.78	5.05	8.83
8150	6" diameter	8.95	5.40	14.35
8160	8" diameter	10.85	5.65	16.50
8170	10" diameter	13.25	7.55	20.80
8180	12" diameter	18.65	7.75	26.40
8200	15" diameter	62.50	10.40	72.90

G30 Site Mechanical Utilities

G3030 Storm Sewer

Manhole   Catch Basin

The Manhole and Catch Basin System includes: excavation with a backhoe; a formed concrete footing; frame and cover; cast iron steps and compacted backfill.

The Expanded System Listing shows manholes that have a 4', 5' and 6' inside diameter riser. Depths range from 4' to 14'. Construction material shown is either concrete, concrete block, precast concrete, or brick.

System Components	QUANTITY	UNIT	MAT.	INST.	TOTAL
SYSTEM G3030 210 1920					
MANHOLE/CATCH BASIN, BRICK, 4' I.D. RISER, 4' DEEP					
Excavation, hydraulic backhoe, 3/8 C.Y. bucket	14.815	C.Y.		155.26	155.26
Trim sides and bottom of excavation	64.000	S.F.		80	80
Forms in place, manhole base, 4 uses	20.000	SFCA	41.80	128	169.80
Reinforcing in place footings, #4 to #7	.019	Ton	29.93	28.03	57.96
Concrete, 3000 psi	.925	C.Y.	157.25		157.25
Place and vibrate concrete, footing, direct chute	.925	C.Y.		59.84	59.84
Catch basin or MH, brick, 4' ID, 4' deep	1.000	Ea.	1,625	1,250	2,875
Catch basin or MH steps; heavy galvanized cast iron	1.000	Ea.	23	17.25	40.25
Catch basin or MH frame and cover	1.000	Ea.	1,050	274	1,324
Fill, granular	12.954	L.C.Y.	369.19		369.19
Backfill, spread with wheeled front end loader	12.954	L.C.Y.		36.79	36.79
Backfill compaction, 12" lifts, air tamp	12.954	C.Y.		144.56	144.56
TOTAL			3,296.17	2,173.73	5,469.90

G3030 210	Manholes & Catch Basins	MAT.	INST.	TOTAL
1920	Manhole/catch basin, brick, 4' I.D. riser, 4' deep	3,300	2,175	5,475
1940	6' deep	4,400	3,025	7,425
1960	8' deep	5,625	4,150	9,775
1980	10' deep	6,750	5,150	11,900
3000	12' deep	8,225	5,575	13,800
3020	14' deep	9,850	7,875	17,725
3200	Block, 4' I.D. riser, 4' deep	2,200	1,750	3,950
3220	6' deep	2,725	2,500	5,225
3240	8' deep	3,350	3,425	6,775
3260	10' deep	3,825	4,250	8,075
3280	12' deep	4,650	5,400	10,050
3300	14' deep	5,625	6,625	12,250
4620	Concrete, cast-in-place, 4' I.D. riser, 4' deep	2,525	3,000	5,525
4640	6' deep	3,275	4,000	7,275
4660	8' deep	4,300	5,775	10,075
4680	10' deep	5,050	7,175	12,225
4700	12' deep	6,150	8,925	15,075
4720	14' deep	7,400	10,700	18,100
5820	Concrete, precast, 4' I.D. riser, 4' deep	3,000	1,600	4,600
5840	6' deep	3,650	2,175	5,825

G30 Site Mechanical Utilities

G3030 Storm Sewer

G3030 210	Manholes & Catch Basins	COST PER EACH		
		MAT.	INST.	TOTAL
5860	8' deep	4,575	3,050	7,625
5880	10' deep	5,250	3,775	9,025
5900	12' deep	6,275	4,550	10,825
5920	14' deep	7,450	5,950	13,400
6000	5' I.D. riser, 4' deep	4,325	1,750	6,075
6020	6' deep	5,275	2,475	7,750
6040	8' deep	6,375	3,275	9,650
6060	10' deep	7,750	4,175	11,925
6080	12' deep	9,250	5,350	14,600
6100	14' deep	10,900	6,550	17,450
6200	6' I.D. riser, 4' deep	6,500	2,300	8,800
6220	6' deep	6,925	3,050	9,975
6240	8' deep	8,275	4,275	12,550
6260	10' deep	9,950	5,425	15,375
6280	12' deep	11,800	6,850	18,650
6300	14' deep	13,800	8,325	22,125

For customer support on your Mechanical Costs with RSMeans data, call 800.448.8182.

G30 Site Mechanical Utilities

G3060 Fuel Distribution

G3060 110	Gas Service Piping	COST PER L.F.		
		MAT.	INST.	TOTAL
2000	Piping, excavation & backfill excluded, polyethylene			
2070	1-1/4" diam, SDR 10	3.05	4.96	8.01
2090	2" diam, SDR 11	5.15	5.55	10.70
2110	3" diam, SDR 11.5	11.20	6.60	17.80
2130	4" diam, SDR 11	11.90	11.90	23.80
2150	6" diam, SDR 21	57.50	12.80	70.30
2160	8" diam, SDR 21	96.50	15.40	111.90
3000	Steel, schedule 40, plain end, tarred & wrapped			
3060	1" diameter	3.77	11.15	14.92
3090	2" diameter	5.90	11.95	17.85
3110	3" diameter	9.80	12.85	22.65
3130	4" diameter	12.75	24.50	37.25
3140	5" diameter	18.50	28	46.50
3150	6" diameter	22.50	34.50	57
3160	8" diameter	36	44	80

G30 Site Mechanical Utilities

G3060 Fuel Distribution

Fiberglass Underground Fuel Storage Tank, Double Wall

System Components	QUANTITY	UNIT	COST EACH MAT.	COST EACH INST.	COST EACH TOTAL
SYSTEM G3060 310 1010					
STORAGE TANK, FUEL, UNDERGROUND, DOUBLE WALL FIBERGLASS, 600 GAL.					
Excavating trench, no sheeting or dewatering, 6'-10 ' D, 3/4 CY hyd backhoe	18.000	Ea.		188.64	188.64
Corrosion resistance wrap & coat, small diam. pipe, 1" diam., add	120.000	Ea.	156		156
Fiberglass-reinforced elbows 90 & 45 degree, 2 inch	7.000	Ea.	304.50	707	1,011.50
Fiberglass-reinforced threaded adapters, 2 inch	2.000	Ea.	38.90	230	268.90
Remote tank gauging system, 30', 5" pointer travel	1.000	Ea.	7,875	435	8,310
Corrosion resistance wrap & coat, small diam. pipe. 4 " diam. add	30.000	Ea.	132.60		132.60
Pea gravel	9.000	Ea.	1,242	549	1,791
Reinforcing in hold down pad, #3 to #7	120.000	Ea.	93.60	87.60	181.20
Tank leak detector system, 8 channel, external monitoring	1.000	Ea.	2,325		2,325
Tubbing copper, type L, 3/4" diam.	120.000	Ea.	846	1,356	2,202
Elbow 90 degree ,wrought cu x cu 3/4 " diam.	4.000	Ea.	28.60	180	208.60
Pipe, black steel welded, sch 40, 3" diam.	30.000	Ea.	1,350	1,129.20	2,479.20
Elbow 90 degree, steel welded butt joint, 3 " diam.	3.000	Ea.	181.50	693.30	874.80
Fiberglass-reinforced plastic pipe, 2 inch	156.000	Ea.	1,123.20	889.20	2,012.40
Fiberglass-reinforced plastic pipe, 3 inch	36.000	Ea.	1,278	232.20	1,510.20
Fiberglass-reinforced elbows 90 & 45 degree, 3 inch	3.000	Ea.	453	405	858
Tank leak detection system, probes, well monitoring, liquid phase detection	2.000	Ea.	1,860		1,860
Double wall fiberglass annular space	1.000	Ea.	580		580
Flange, weld neck, 150 lb, 3 " pipe size	1.000	Ea.	39.50	116.05	155.55
Vent protector/breather, 2" diam.	1.000	Ea.	73.50	27	100.50
Corrosion resistance wrap & coat, small diam. pipe, 2" diam., add	36.000	Ea.	83.88		83.88
Concrete hold down pad, 6' x 5' x 8" thick	30.000	Ea.	135	55.80	190.80
600 gallon capacity, underground storage tank, double wall fiberglass	1.000	Ea.	12,600	645	13,245
Tank, for hold-downs 500-4,000 gal., add	1.000	Ea.	615	206	821
Foot valve, single poppet, 3/4" diam.	1.000	Ea.	85.50	48	133.50
Fuel fill box, locking inner cover, 3" diam.	1.000	Ea.	59	173	232
Fuel oil specialties, valve,ball chk, globe type fusible, 3/4" diam.	2.000	Ea.	402	87	489
TOTAL			33,961.28	8,439.99	42,401.27

G3060 310	Fiberglass Fuel Tank, Double Wall	COST EACH MAT.	COST EACH INST.	COST EACH TOTAL
1010	Storage tank, fuel, underground, double wall fiberglass, 600 Gal.	34,000	8,450	42,450
1020	2500 Gal.	51,000	11,600	62,600
1030	4000 Gal.	61,000	14,400	75,400
1040	6000 Gal.	70,000	16,200	86,200

G30 Site Mechanical Utilities

G3060 Fuel Distribution

G3060 310		Fiberglass Fuel Tank, Double Wall	COST EACH		
			MAT.	INST.	TOTAL
1050		8000 Gal.	86,000	19,600	105,600
1060		10,000 Gal.	100,000	22,600	122,600
1070		15,000 Gal.	150,000	26,000	176,000
1080		20,000 Gal.	172,000	31,500	203,500
1090		25,000 Gal.	197,000	36,600	233,600
1100		30,000 Gal.	225,500	38,800	264,300

G30 Site Mechanical Utilities

G3060 Fuel Distribution

Steel Underground Fuel Storage Tank, Double Wall

System Components	QUANTITY	UNIT	COST EACH MAT.	COST EACH INST.	COST EACH TOTAL
SYSTEM G3060 320 1010					
STORAGE TANK, FUEL, UNDERGROUND, DOUBLE WALL STEEL, 500 GAL.					
Fiberglass-reinforced plastic pipe, 2 inch	156.000	Ea.	1,123.20	889.20	2,012.40
Fiberglass-reinforced plastic pipe, 3 inch	36.000	Ea.	1,278	232.20	1,510.20
Fiberglass-reinforced elbows 90 & 45 degree, 3 inch	3.000	Ea.	453	405	858
Tank leak detection system, probes, well monitoring, liquid phase detection	2.000	Ea.	1,860		1,860
Flange, weld neck, 150 lb, 3" pipe size	1.000	Ea.	39.50	116.05	155.55
Vent protector/breather, 2" diam.	1.000	Ea.	73.50	27	100.50
Concrete hold down pad, 6' x 5' x 8" thick	30.000	Ea.	135	55.80	190.80
Tanks, for hold-downs, 500-2,000 gal, add	1.000	Ea.	292	206	498
Double wall steel tank annular space	1.000	Ea.	350		350
Foot valve, single poppet, 3/4" diam.	1.000	Ea.	85.50	48	133.50
Fuel fill box, locking inner cover, 3" diam.	1.000	Ea.	59	173	232
Fuel oil specialties, valve, ball chk, globe type fusible, 3/4" diam.	2.000	Ea.	402	87	489
Pea gravel	9.000	Ea.	1,242	549	1,791
Reinforcing in hold down pad, #3 to #7	120.000	Ea.	93.60	87.60	181.20
Tank, for manways, add	1.000	Ea.	1,625		1,625
Tank leak detector system, 8 channel, external monitoring	1.000	Ea.	2,325		2,325
Tubbing copper, type L, 3/4" diam.	120.000	Ea.	846	1,356	2,202
Elbow 90 degree, wrought cu x cu 3/4" diam.	8.000	Ea.	57.20	360	417.20
Pipe, black steel welded, sch 40, 3" diam.	30.000	Ea.	1,350	1,129.20	2,479.20
Elbow 90 degree, steel welded butt joint, 3" diam.	3.000	Ea.	181.50	693.30	874.80
Excavating trench, no sheeting or dewatering, 6'-10' D, 3/4 CY hyd backhoe	18.000	Ea.		188.64	188.64
Fiberglass-reinforced elbows 90 & 45 degree, 2 inch	7.000	Ea.	304.50	707	1,011.50
Fiberglass-reinforced threaded adapters, 2 inch	2.000	Ea.	38.90	230	268.90
500 gallon capacity, underground storage tank, double wall steel	1.000	Ea.	4,825	650	5,475
Remote tank gauging system, 30', 5" pointer travel	1.000	Ea.	7,875	435	8,310
TOTAL			26,914.40	8,624.99	35,539.39

G3060 320	Steel Fuel Tank, Double Wall	COST EACH MAT.	COST EACH INST.	COST EACH TOTAL
1010	Storage tank, fuel, underground, double wall steel, 500 Gal.	26,900	8,625	35,525
1020	2000 Gal.	33,600	11,300	44,900
1030	4000 Gal.	45,700	14,600	60,300
1040	6000 Gal.	52,000	16,100	68,100
1050	8000 Gal.	58,500	19,900	78,400
1060	10,000 Gal.	67,000	22,900	89,900

G30 Site Mechanical Utilities

G3060 Fuel Distribution

G3060 320	Steel Fuel Tank, Double Wall	COST EACH		
		MAT.	INST.	TOTAL
1070	15,000 Gal.	81,500	26,600	108,100
1080	20,000 Gal.	115,500	31,900	147,400
1090	25,000 Gal.	131,500	36,500	168,000
1100	30,000 Gal.	131,000	39,000	170,000
1110	40,000 Gal.	274,000	49,000	323,000
1120	50,000 Gal.	331,000	58,500	389,500

G3060 325	Steel Tank, Above Ground, Single Wall	COST EACH		
		MAT.	INST.	TOTAL
1010	Storage tank, fuel, above ground, single wall steel, 550 Gal.	22,700	6,025	28,725
1020	2000 Gal.	34,300	6,175	40,475
1030	5000 Gal.	47,100	9,475	56,575
1040	10,000 Gal.	61,500	10,100	71,600
1050	15,000 Gal.	76,500	10,400	86,900
1060	20,000 Gal.	88,500	10,700	99,200
1070	25,000 Gal.	146,500	11,000	157,500
1080	30,000 Gal.	114,000	11,400	125,400

G3060 330	Steel Tank, Above Ground, Double Wall	COST EACH		
		MAT.	INST.	TOTAL
1010	Storage tank, fuel, above ground, double wall steel, 500 Gal.	21,800	6,100	27,900
1020	2000 Gal.	25,100	6,250	31,350
1030	4000 Gal.	34,000	6,375	40,375
1040	6000 Gal.	67,000	9,825	76,825
1050	8000 Gal.	75,000	10,100	85,100
1060	10,000 Gal.	84,500	10,300	94,800
1070	15,000 Gal.	108,500	10,600	119,100
1080	20,000 Gal.	126,500	11,000	137,500
1090	25,000 Gal.	121,000	11,300	132,300
1100	30,000 Gal.	156,500	11,700	168,200

Reference Section

All the reference information is in one section, making it easy to find what you need to know and easy to use the data set on a daily basis. This section is visually identified by a vertical black bar on the page edges.

In this Reference Section, we've included Equipment Rental Costs, a listing of rental and operating costs; Crew Listings, a full listing of all crews and equipment and their costs; Historical Cost Indexes for cost comparisons over time; City Cost Indexes and Location Factors for adjusting costs to the region you are in; Reference Tables, where you will find explanations, estimating information and procedures, and technical data; Change Orders, information on pricing changes to contract documents; and an explanation of all the Abbreviations in the data set.

Table of Contents

Construction Equipment Rental Costs	609
Crew Listings	621
Historical Cost Indexes	658
City Cost Indexes	659
Location Factors	702
Reference Tables	708
R01 General Requirements	708
R02 Existing Conditions	722
R07 Thermal & Moisture Protection	723
R09 Finishes	724
R22 Plumbing	724
R23 Heating, Ventilating & Air Conditioning	730
R26 Electrical	741
R31 Earthwork	742
R33 Utilities	744
Change Orders	745
Project Costs	749
Abbreviations	754

Equipment Rental Costs

Estimating Tips
- This section contains the average costs to rent and operate hundreds of pieces of construction equipment. This is useful information when one is estimating the time and material requirements of any particular operation in order to establish a unit or total cost. Bare equipment costs shown on a unit cost line include, not only rental, but also operating costs for equipment under normal use.

Rental Costs
- Equipment rental rates are obtained from the following industry sources throughout North America: contractors, suppliers, dealers, manufacturers, and distributors.
- Rental rates vary throughout the country, with larger cities generally having lower rates. Lease plans for new equipment are available for periods in excess of six months, with a percentage of payments applying toward purchase.
- Monthly rental rates vary from 2% to 5% of the purchase price of the equipment depending on the anticipated life of the equipment and its wearing parts.
- Rental rates can also be treated as reimbursement costs for contractor-owned equipment. Owned equipment costs include depreciation, loan payments, interest, taxes, insurance, storage, and major repairs.

Operating Costs
- The operating costs include parts and labor for routine servicing, such as the repair and replacement of pumps, filters, and worn lines. Normal operating expendables, such as fuel, lubricants, tires, and electricity (where applicable), are also included.
- Extraordinary operating expendables with highly variable wear patterns, such as diamond bits and blades, are excluded. These costs can be found as material costs in the Unit Price section.
- The hourly operating costs listed do not include the operator's wages.

Equipment Cost/Day
- Any power equipment required by a crew is shown in the Crew Listings with a daily cost.
- This daily cost of equipment needed by a crew includes both the rental cost and the operating cost and is based on dividing the weekly rental rate by 5 (the number of working days in the week), then adding the hourly operating cost multiplied by 8 (the number of hours in a day). This "Equipment Cost/Day" is shown in the far right column of the Equipment Rental section.
- If equipment is needed for only one or two days, it is best to develop your own cost by including components for daily rent and hourly operating costs. This is important when the listed Crew for a task does not contain the equipment needed, such as a crane for lifting mechanical heating/cooling equipment up onto a roof.
- If the quantity of work is less than the crew's Daily Output shown for a Unit Price line item that includes a bare unit equipment cost, the recommendation is to estimate one day's rental cost and operating cost for equipment shown in the Crew Listing for that line item.
- Please note, in some cases the equipment description in the crew is followed by a time period in parenthesis. For example: (daily) or (monthly). In these cases the equipment cost/day is calculated by adding the rental cost per time period to the hourly operating cost multiplied by 8.

Mobilization, Demobilization Costs
- The cost to move construction equipment from an equipment yard or rental company to the job site and back again is not included in equipment rental costs listed in the Reference Section. It is also not included in the bare equipment cost of any Unit Price line item or in any equipment costs shown in the Crew Listings.
- Mobilization (to the site) and demobilization (from the site) costs can be found in the Unit Price section.
- If a piece of equipment is already at the job site, it is not appropriate to utilize mobilization or demobilization costs again in an estimate. ■

Same Data. Simplified.

Enjoy the convenience and efficiency of accessing your costs anywhere:
- **Skip the multiplier** by setting your location
- **Quickly search,** edit, favorite and share costs
- **Stay on top of price changes** with automatic updates

Discover more at rsmeans.com/online

No part of this cost data may be reproduced, stored in a retrieval system, or transmitted in any form or by any means without prior written permission of Gordian.

01 54 | Construction Aids

01 54 33 | Equipment Rental

			UNIT	HOURLY OPER. COST	RENT PER DAY	RENT PER WEEK	RENT PER MONTH	EQUIPMENT COST/DAY	
10	0010	**CONCRETE EQUIPMENT RENTAL** without operators							10
	0200	Bucket, concrete lightweight, 1/2 C.Y.	Ea.	.83	58.58	175.73	527.18	41.75	
	0300	1 C.Y.		1.08	70.61	211.82	635.46	50.97	
	0400	1-1/2 C.Y.		1.40	92.10	276.31	828.93	66.47	
	0500	2 C.Y.		1.52	107.25	321.76	965.28	76.52	
	0580	8 C.Y.		7.61	134.90	404.70	1,214.10	141.86	
	0600	Cart, concrete, self-propelled, operator walking, 10 C.F.		3.13	208.12	624.35	1,873.05	149.92	
	0700	Operator riding, 18 C.F.		5.27	145	402.71	965.71	122.73	
	0800	Conveyer for concrete, portable, gas, 16" wide, 26' long		11.64	114	342	1,026	161.50	
	0900	46' long		12.05	155	465	1,395	189.41	
	1000	56' long		12.23	161.53	484.58	1,453.73	194.76	
	1100	Core drill, electric, 2-1/2 H.P., 1" to 8" bit diameter		1.72	75	238.33	568.33	61.41	
	1150	11 H.P., 8" to 18" cores		5.92	131.80	354	895	118.14	
	1200	Finisher, concrete floor, gas, riding trowel, 96" wide		10.59	241	703	1,843.10	225.34	
	1300	Gas, walk-behind, 3 blade, 36" trowel		2.23	107.57	334.08	969.15	84.69	
	1400	4 blade, 48" trowel		3.37	110	293.33	710	85.62	
	1500	Float, hand-operated (Bull float) 48" wide		.09	13.85	43.07	124.61	9.33	
	1570	Curb builder, 14 H.P., gas, single screw		15.36	160	480	1,440	218.85	
	1590	Double screw		13.58	350	1,050	3,150	318.63	
	1600	Floor grinder, concrete and terrazzo, electric, 22" path		3.33	140.63	416.25	1,013.13	109.91	
	1700	Edger, concrete, electric, 7" path		1.30	77	211.25	513.13	52.63	
	1750	Vacuum pick-up system for floor grinders, wet/dry		1.78	98.78	296.67	832.78	73.53	
	1800	Mixer, powered, mortar and concrete, gas, 6 C.F., 18 H.P.		8.13	84.29	255.71	707.14	116.18	
	1900	10 C.F., 25 H.P.		9.86	122.17	354.29	859.35	149.77	
	2000	16 C.F.		10.26	112.50	310	812.50	144.05	
	2100	Concrete, stationary, tilt drum, 2 C.Y.		8.67	84	249.38	686.25	119.22	
	2120	Pump, concrete, truck mounted, 4" line, 80' boom		33.94	926.67	2,780	8,340	827.49	
	2140	5" line, 110' boom		43.44	1,203.33	3,610	10,830	1,069.53	
	2160	Mud jack, 50 C.F. per hr.		7.06	170	510	1,530	158.45	
	2180	225 C.F. per hr.		9.35	201.67	605	1,815	195.81	
	2190	Shotcrete pump rig, 12 C.Y./hr.		18.17	843	2,529	7,587	651.19	
	2200	35 C.Y./hr.		17.28	1,098.33	3,295	9,885	797.28	
	2600	Saw, concrete, manual, gas, 18 H.P.		6.07	107.67	320.83	832.50	112.72	
	2650	Self-propelled, gas, 30 H.P.		8.65	193.33	533.89	1,411.11	176	
	2675	V-groove crack chaser, manual, gas, 6 H.P.		1.80	138.92	361.15	1,022.75	86.61	
	2700	Vibrators, concrete, electric, 60 cycle, 2 H.P.		.51	41	144	425	32.92	
	2800	3 H.P.		.62	73.33	198.67	461.67	44.66	
	2900	Gas engine, 5 H.P.		1.69	18.16	56.56	164.01	24.85	
	3000	8 H.P.		2.28	18.37	57.14	165.08	29.68	
	3050	Vibrating screed, gas engine, 8 H.P.		3.08	128.75	330.13	781.25	90.64	
	3120	Concrete transit mixer, 6 x 4, 250 H.P., 8 C.Y., rear discharge		55.49	167	501	1,503	544.13	
	3200	Front discharge		64.42	102.55	307.64	922.92	576.87	
	3300	6 x 6, 285 H.P., 12 C.Y., rear discharge		63.61	333.33	1,000	3,000	708.92	
	3400	Front discharge		66.28	283.33	850	2,550	700.26	
20	0010	**EARTHWORK EQUIPMENT RENTAL** without operators							20
	0040	Aggregate spreader, push type, 8' to 12' wide	Ea.	2.84	74.55	223.65	670.95	67.49	
	0045	Tailgate type, 8' wide		2.79	56.09	168.27	504.81	55.94	
	0055	Earth auger, truck mounted, for fence & sign posts, utility poles		15.16	66.30	163.60	464.30	153.97	
	0060	For borings and monitoring wells		46.66	122.70	368.09	1,104.27	446.91	
	0070	Portable, trailer mounted		2.52	119.75	314.25	746.25	83.02	
	0075	Truck mounted, for caissons, water wells		93.42	181.47	544.40	1,633.20	856.23	
	0080	Horizontal boring machine, 12" to 36" diameter, 45 H.P.		24.91	231.67	695	2,085	338.28	
	0090	12" to 48" diameter, 65 H.P.		34.19	273.33	820	2,460	437.50	
	0095	Auger, for fence posts, gas engine, hand held		.49	77.79	241.44	578.16	52.21	
	0100	Excavator, diesel hydraulic, crawler mounted, 1/2 C.Y. cap.		23.81	977.86	2,872.14	5,938.57	764.88	
	0120	5/8 C.Y. capacity		31.83	1,052.44	2,792.78	6,226.11	813.17	
	0140	3/4 C.Y. capacity		35.80	1,195.25	3,144.88	7,524.38	915.34	
	0150	1 C.Y. capacity		45.17	1,160.22	3,126	7,463.89	986.56	

01 54 | Construction Aids

01 54 33 | Equipment Rental

		UNIT	HOURLY OPER. COST	RENT PER DAY	RENT PER WEEK	RENT PER MONTH	EQUIPMENT COST/DAY
0200	1-1/2 C.Y. capacity	Ea.	53.25	1,479	3,796	9,465	1,185.24
0300	2 C.Y. capacity		62.02	1,000	3,000	9,000	1,096.14
0320	2-1/2 C.Y. capacity		90.57	1,868.60	4,795.50	12,022.50	1,683.69
0325	3-1/2 C.Y. capacity		131.66	2,156.63	6,705.94	19,383	2,394.44
0330	4-1/2 C.Y. capacity		166.19	3,940.50	12,294.23	35,571	3,788.37
0335	6 C.Y. capacity		210.86	3,461.25	10,785.39	31,204.50	3,843.97
0340	7 C.Y. capacity		192.03	4,450	13,350	40,050	4,206.21
0342	Excavator attachments, bucket thumbs		3.73	277.97	865.74	2,502.75	202.95
0345	Grapples		3.44	239.63	744.53	2,156.63	176.44
0346	Hydraulic hammer for boom mounting, 4000 ft lb.		14.77	958.50	2,984.15	8,626.50	715.03
0347	5000 ft lb.		17.48	1,022.40	3,185.33	9,212.25	776.94
0348	8000 ft lb.		25.80	1,304.63	4,023.57	11,608.50	1,011.13
0349	12,000 ft lb.		29.67	1,500.32	4,627.11	13,349.78	1,162.80
0350	Gradall type, truck mounted, 3 ton @ 15' radius, 5/8 C.Y.		47.61	833.33	2,500	7,500	880.91
0370	1 C.Y. capacity		65.11	1,666.67	5,000	15,000	1,520.84
0400	Backhoe-loader, 40 to 45 H.P., 5/8 C.Y. capacity		13.04	211.38	589.63	1,520.13	222.27
0450	45 H.P. to 60 H.P., 3/4 C.Y. capacity		19.75	214.56	595.78	1,565.67	277.19
0460	80 H.P., 1-1/4 C.Y. capacity		22.31	325	896	2,266.44	357.71
0470	112 H.P., 1-1/2 C.Y. capacity		36.15	660.30	2,048.91	5,937.38	699
0482	Backhoe-loader attachment, compactor, 20,000 lb.		7.06	397	1,009	2,993	258.25
0485	Hydraulic hammer, 750 ft lb.		4.03	115.02	357.84	1,033.05	103.85
0486	Hydraulic hammer, 1200 ft lb.		7.18	220.46	686.82	1,996.88	194.78
0500	Brush chipper, gas engine, 6" cutter head, 35 H.P.		10.05	276.50	920.13	2,218.13	264.41
0550	Diesel engine, 12" cutter head, 130 H.P.		25.95	512.33	1,552.78	4,121	518.12
0600	15" cutter head, 165 H.P.		29.14	548.48	1,706.31	4,925.63	574.37
0750	Bucket, clamshell, general purpose, 3/8 C.Y.		1.53	40	120	360	36.25
0800	1/2 C.Y.		1.66	40	120	360	37.28
0850	3/4 C.Y.		1.80	43.67	131	393	40.58
0900	1 C.Y.		1.86	53.33	160	480	46.89
0950	1-1/2 C.Y.		3.05	49.17	147.50	442.50	53.92
1000	2 C.Y.		3.20	168.33	505	1,515	126.58
1010	Bucket, dragline, medium duty, 1/2 C.Y.		.90	35	105	315	28.17
1020	3/4 C.Y.		.85	37.83	113.50	340.50	29.54
1030	1 C.Y.		.87	43.17	129.50	388.50	32.89
1040	1-1/2 C.Y.		1.38	43.83	131.50	394.50	37.32
1050	2 C.Y.		1.70	43.20	129.60	388.80	39.49
1070	3 C.Y.		2.28	55.83	167.50	502.50	51.71
1200	Compactor, manually guided 2-drum vibratory smooth roller, 7.5 H.P.		7.91	182.38	471	1,302.56	157.50
1250	Rammer/tamper, gas, 8"		2.42	108.50	272.50	807.50	73.84
1260	15"		2.88	104.37	324.83	755.09	88.02
1300	Vibratory plate, gas, 18" plate, 3000 lb. blow		2.33	213.97	625.83	1,586.50	143.82
1350	21" plate, 5000 lb. blow		2.87	244.63	615.88	1,715.88	146.12
1370	Curb builder/extruder, 14 H.P., gas, single screw		13.58	1,065	3,195	9,585	747.63
1390	Double screw		16.29	1,278	3,834	11,502	897.16
1500	Disc harrow attachment, for tractor		.52	372.75	1,171.50	3,514.50	238.45
1810	Feller buncher, shearing & accumulating trees, 100 H.P.		47.53	1,236.67	3,710	11,130	1,122.21
1860	Grader, self-propelled, 25,000 lb.		36.55	1,058.33	3,175	9,525	927.41
1910	30,000 lb.		46.71	1,195.83	3,587.50	10,762.50	1,091.19
1920	40,000 lb.		56.87	1,333.33	4,000	12,000	1,254.97
1930	55,000 lb.		73.36	1,666.67	5,000	15,000	1,586.87
1950	Hammer, pavement breaker, self-propelled, diesel, 1000 to 1250 lb.		31.13	600	1,800	5,400	609.02
2000	1300 to 1500 lb.		46.91	600	1,800	5,400	735.29
2050	Pile driving hammer, steam or air, 4150 ft lb. @ 225 bpm		13.32	537.83	1,676.49	4,845.75	441.85
2100	8750 ft lb. @ 145 bpm		15.72	756.15	2,347.08	6,789.38	595.21
2150	15,000 ft lb. @ 60 bpm		16.08	899.93	2,794.14	8,094	687.50
2200	24,450 ft lb. @ 111 bpm		17.19	1,043.70	3,241.21	9,372	785.80
2250	Leads, 60' high for pile driving hammers up to 20,000 ft lb.		4.02	324.83	1,005.89	2,902.13	233.36
2300	90' high for hammers over 20,000 ft lb.		5.97	580.43	1,810.61	5,245.13	409.90

01 54 | Construction Aids

01 54 33 | Equipment Rental

		UNIT	HOURLY OPER. COST	RENT PER DAY	RENT PER WEEK	RENT PER MONTH	EQUIPMENT COST/DAY
2350	Diesel type hammer, 22,400 ft lb.	Ea.	19.53	527.18	1,644.90	4,765.88	485.21
2400	41,300 ft lb.		28.15	665.63	2,077.77	6,017.25	640.74
2450	141,000 ft lb.		45.30	1,059.68	3,289.81	9,505.13	1,020.34
2500	Vib. elec. hammer/extractor, 200 kW diesel generator, 34 H.P.		45.34	772.13	2,395.21	6,922.50	841.80
2550	80 H.P.		80.04	1,118.25	3,462.95	10,011	1,332.90
2600	150 H.P.		148.12	2,130	6,666.18	19,276.50	2,518.21
2700	Hydro Excavator w/EXT boom 12 C.Y., 1200 gallons		41.44	1,730.63	5,364.76	15,549	1,404.51
2800	Log chipper, up to 22" diameter, 600 H.P.		48.88	492.50	1,477.50	4,432.50	686.57
2850	Logger, for skidding & stacking logs, 150 H.P.		47.62	141.67	425	1,275	465.97
2860	Mulcher, diesel powered, trailer mounted		21.79	765.50	2,296.50	6,889.50	633.63
2900	Rake, spring tooth, with tractor		16.13	58.20	162.50	410.60	161.55
3000	Roller, vibratory, tandem, smooth drum, 20 H.P.		8.56	380.83	1,095	2,632.50	287.45
3050	35 H.P.		11.11	496.88	1,451.88	3,263.13	379.22
3100	Towed type vibratory compactor, smooth drum, 50 H.P.		27.70	766.67	2,300	6,900	681.59
3150	Sheepsfoot, 50 H.P.		28.10	366.67	1,100	3,300	444.83
3170	Landfill compactor, 220 H.P.		76.59	1,798.33	5,395	16,185	1,691.72
3200	Pneumatic tire roller, 80 H.P.		14.16	436.65	1,356.32	3,913.88	384.55
3250	120 H.P.		21.25	566.67	1,700	5,100	510
3300	Sheepsfoot vibratory roller, 240 H.P.		68.18	366.67	1,100	3,300	765.47
3320	340 H.P.		91.87	1,500	4,500	13,500	1,635
3350	Smooth drum vibratory roller, 75 H.P.		25.58	268.33	711.67	2,012.22	346.96
3400	125 H.P.		30.27	479.25	1,437.75	4,206.75	529.68
3410	Rotary mower, brush, 60", with tractor		20.59	133	370.50	944	238.84
3420	Rototiller, walk-behind, gas, 5 H.P.		2.34	125	260	645	70.72
3422	8 H.P.		3.08	130	325	706	89.64
3440	Scrapers, towed type, 7 C.Y. capacity		7.06	137.39	427.10	1,224.75	141.88
3450	10 C.Y. capacity		7.90	183.18	571.38	1,650.75	177.45
3500	15 C.Y. capacity		8.11	211.94	657.96	1,890.38	196.46
3525	Self-propelled, single engine, 14 C.Y. capacity		146.09	1,666.67	5,000	15,000	2,168.71
3550	Dual engine, 21 C.Y. capacity		154.95	1,666.67	5,000	15,000	2,239.60
3600	31 C.Y. capacity		205.89	2,208.33	6,625	19,875	2,972.09
3640	44 C.Y. capacity		255.02	2,333.33	7,000	21,000	3,440.19
3650	Elevating type, single engine, 11 C.Y. capacity		67.81	800	2,400	7,200	1,022.46
3700	22 C.Y. capacity		125.63	1,666.67	5,000	15,000	2,005.03
3710	Screening plant, 110 H.P. w/5' x 10' screen		23.16	692.25	2,156.42	6,230.25	616.57
3720	5' x 16' screen		29.24	1,222.22	3,666.67	11,000	967.25
3850	Shovel, crawler-mounted, front-loading, 7 C.Y. capacity		239.65	4,233.38	13,159.21	38,020.50	4,549.05
3855	12 C.Y. capacity		369.25	5,857.50	18,238.21	52,717.50	6,601.66
3860	Shovel/backhoe bucket, 1/2 C.Y.		2.95	78.81	244.72	708.23	72.55
3870	3/4 C.Y.		2.92	88.40	274.73	793.43	78.31
3880	1 C.Y.		3.02	59.13	175	488.75	59.18
3890	1-1/2 C.Y.		3.24	115.02	357.84	1,033.05	97.47
3910	3 C.Y.		3.77	155.49	484.81	1,411.13	127.10
3950	Stump chipper, 18" deep, 30 H.P.		7.55	329.43	1,017.29	2,480.14	263.85
4110	Dozer, crawler, torque converter, diesel 80 H.P.		27.68	692.50	1,852	4,464	591.82
4150	105 H.P.		37.63	644.33	2,008.05	5,804.25	702.68
4200	140 H.P.		45.24	660	1,980	5,940	757.89
4260	200 H.P.		69.22	1,381	4,143	12,429	1,382.36
4310	300 H.P.		88.48	1,611.11	4,833.33	14,500	1,674.53
4360	410 H.P.		117.00	2,666.67	8,000	24,000	2,535.96
4370	500 H.P.		146.19	2,333.33	7,000	21,000	2,569.55
4380	700 H.P.		252.27	3,466.67	10,400	31,200	4,098.16
4400	Loader, crawler, torque conv., diesel, 1-1/2 C.Y., 80 H.P.		32.38	591.08	1,841.82	5,325	627.38
4450	1-1/2 to 1-3/4 C.Y., 95 H.P.		33.18	750.83	2,341.34	6,762.75	733.70
4510	1-3/4 to 2-1/4 C.Y., 130 H.P.		52.34	900	2,700	8,100	958.76
4530	2-1/2 to 3-1/4 C.Y., 190 H.P.		63.34	1,198.13	3,754.98	10,863	1,257.68
4560	3-1/2 to 5 C.Y., 275 H.P.		78.26	1,466.67	4,400	13,200	1,506.11
4610	Front end loader, 4WD, articulated frame, diesel, 1 to 1-1/4 C.Y., 70 H.P.		18.22	495.20	1,245.10	3,126	394.79

01 54 | Construction Aids

01 54 33 | Equipment Rental

			UNIT	HOURLY OPER. COST	RENT PER DAY	RENT PER WEEK	RENT PER MONTH	EQUIPMENT COST/DAY	
20	4620	1-1/2 to 1-3/4 C.Y., 95 H.P.	Ea.	21.92	466.67	1,400	4,200	455.32	20
	4650	1-3/4 to 2 C.Y., 130 H.P.		23.09	497.14	1,455.50	4,235.40	475.82	
	4710	2-1/2 to 3-1/2 C.Y., 145 H.P.		32.36	666.67	2,000	6,000	658.89	
	4730	3 to 4-1/2 C.Y., 185 H.P.		35.17	879.10	2,543	5,789.50	789.98	
	4760	5-1/4 to 5-3/4 C.Y., 270 H.P.		58.30	1,200	3,600	10,800	1,186.42	
	4810	7 to 9 C.Y., 475 H.P.		99.93	2,000	6,000	18,000	1,999.44	
	4870	9 to 11 C.Y., 620 H.P.		144.59	3,470	8,530	21,500	2,862.71	
	4880	Skid-steer loader, wheeled, 10 C.F., 30 H.P. gas		10.49	295	885.40	1,880.40	260.99	
	4890	1 C.Y., 78 H.P., diesel		20.21	438.75	1,341.25	3,095	429.91	
	4892	Skid-steer attachment, auger		.82	135.67	341.11	875	74.76	
	4893	Backhoe		.81	100.29	262.86	759.29	59.06	
	4894	Broom		.78	184.60	429.20	969.60	92.04	
	4895	Forks		.17	44.63	117.75	310	24.90	
	4896	Grapple		.79	86.53	235.63	652.85	53.47	
	4897	Concrete hammer		1.15	209.29	588.57	1,515	126.94	
	4898	Tree spade		.66	335.48	1,006.43	2,415.42	206.55	
	4899	Trencher		.72	152.78	415.56	1,068.89	88.83	
	4900	Trencher, chain, boom type, gas, operator walking, 12 H.P.		4.58	277.13	829.25	2,053.88	202.47	
	4910	Operator riding, 40 H.P.		18.29	453	1,201	2,779	386.50	
	5000	Wheel type, diesel, 4' deep, 12" wide		75.31	1,038.38	3,232.08	9,345.38	1,248.89	
	5100	6' deep, 20" wide		95.99	1,268.75	2,852.50	6,592.50	1,338.44	
	5150	Chain type, diesel, 5' deep, 8" wide		17.87	388.73	1,212.03	3,514.50	385.33	
	5200	Diesel, 8' deep, 16" wide		98.27	2,076.75	6,464.18	18,744	2,079.03	
	5202	Rock trencher, wheel type, 6" wide x 18" deep		51.55	1,268.75	2,900	6,592.50	992.44	
	5206	Chain type, 18" wide x 7' deep		114.54	271.67	815	2,445	1,079.31	
	5210	Tree spade, self-propelled		14.98	415	1,245	3,735	368.85	
	5250	Truck, dump, 2-axle, 12 ton, 8 C.Y. payload, 220 H.P.		26.25	366.85	1,037.44	2,773.47	417.49	
	5300	Three axle dump, 16 ton, 12 C.Y. payload, 400 H.P.		48.92	666.67	2,000	6,000	791.36	
	5310	Four axle dump, 25 ton, 18 C.Y. payload, 450 H.P.		54.80	583.33	1,750	5,250	788.42	
	5350	Dump trailer only, rear dump, 16-1/2 C.Y.		6.30	162.95	507.90	1,464.38	151.94	
	5400	20 C.Y.		6.80	183.18	571.38	1,650.75	168.66	
	5450	Flatbed, single axle, 1-1/2 ton rating		20.88	271.58	974.48	2,556	361.95	
	5500	3 ton rating		28.19	275.83	827.50	2,482.50	391.02	
	5550	Off highway rear dump, 25 ton capacity		68.89	1,533.33	4,600	13,800	1,471.16	
	5600	35 ton capacity		73.55	1,533.33	4,600	13,800	1,508.36	
	5610	50 ton capacity		92.20	2,166.67	6,500	19,500	2,037.60	
	5620	65 ton capacity		98.46	2,156.63	6,695.04	19,383	2,126.70	
	5630	100 ton capacity		133.29	3,168.38	9,869.41	28,542	3,040.18	
	6000	Vibratory plow, 25 H.P., walking	▼	7.43	344.35	1,033.05	3,099.15	266.08	
40	0010	**GENERAL EQUIPMENT RENTAL** without operators	R015433-10						40
	0020	Aerial lift, scissor type, to 20' high, 1200 lb. capacity, electric	Ea.	3.83	195.84	399.97	744.90	110.61	
	0030	To 30' high, 1200 lb. capacity		4.15	350	815	1,975	196.19	
	0040	Over 30' high, 1500 lb. capacity		5.64	410	861.25	1,817.50	217.41	
	0070	Articulating boom, to 45' high, 500 lb. capacity, diesel	R015433-15	13.51	561.06	1,309.50	2,950.56	369.98	
	0075	To 60' high, 500 lb. capacity		15.02	623.40	1,455	3,278.40	411.13	
	0080	To 80' high, 500 lb. capacity		17.65	918.44	2,459.44	6,057	633.06	
	0085	To 125' high, 500 lb. capacity		20.17	1,986.67	4,695	11,533.89	1,100.34	
	0100	Telescoping boom to 40' high, 500 lb. capacity, diesel		12.35	540	1,233.75	2,615	345.57	
	0105	To 45' high, 500 lb. capacity		13.75	520	1,209	2,582	351.80	
	0110	To 60' high, 500 lb. capacity		17.98	520	1,209	2,582	385.68	
	0115	To 80' high, 500 lb. capacity		23.38	1,112	2,615	5,357	710.06	
	0120	To 100' high, 500 lb. capacity		31.57	918.44	2,459.44	6,057	744.42	
	0125	To 120' high, 500 lb. capacity		32.06	1,818.33	4,756.11	11,001.67	1,207.69	
	0195	Air compressor, portable, 6.5 CFM, electric		.99	46.05	121.75	353	32.29	
	0196	Gasoline		.72	50.74	144	387.43	34.53	
	0200	Towed type, gas engine, 60 CFM		10.37	150.25	451.25	984.38	173.21	
	0300	160 CFM	▼	11.51	250	760	1,810	244.12	

01 54 | Construction Aids

01 54 33 | Equipment Rental

		UNIT	HOURLY OPER. COST	RENT PER DAY	RENT PER WEEK	RENT PER MONTH	EQUIPMENT COST/DAY
0400	Diesel engine, rotary screw, 250 CFM	Ea.	13.29	137.50	450	1,155	196.28
0500	365 CFM		17.59	474.29	1,246.43	3,123.57	389.99
0550	450 CFM		21.93	357.78	966.67	2,764.44	368.76
0600	600 CFM		37.49	267.32	831.10	2,396.25	466.11
0700	750 CFM		38.06	690	1,757	4,224	655.87
0915	Air purifier		.77	10.53	24.89	69.11	11.12
0917	Air scrubber, 500 - 700 CFM, 110 V		.76	86.80	270.58	782.78	60.20
0919	200 - 1200 CFM, 110 V		.76	102.77	320.28	926.55	70.14
0930	Air tools, breaker, pavement, 60 lb.		.62	52	147.50	381.67	34.47
0940	80 lb.		.62	49.80	154	389	35.75
0950	Drills, hand (jackhammer), 65 lb.		.74	66	184.29	465	42.75
0960	Track or wagon, swing boom, 4" drifter		67.89	1,080	3,240	9,720	1,191.15
0970	5" drifter		67.89	1,080	3,240	9,720	1,191.15
0975	Track mounted quarry drill, 6" diameter drill		111.83	798.33	2,395	7,185	1,373.61
0980	Dust control per drill		1.14	10.67	32	96	15.54
0990	Hammer, chipping, 12 lb.		.66	39	109.50	270	27.16
1000	Hose, air with couplings, 50' long, 3/4" diameter		.07	14.40	37.83	95.83	8.16
1100	1" diameter		.09	17.18	43.13	127.25	9.31
1200	1-1/2" diameter		.24	43.87	108.33	304.44	23.60
1300	2" diameter		.26	61.50	151.25	419.38	32.35
1400	2-1/2" diameter		.39	65.78	183.56	534.56	39.86
1410	3" diameter		.46	83	215.50	636	46.76
1450	Drill, steel, 7/8" x 2'		.09	14.47	35	104.22	7.74
1460	7/8" x 6'		.13	21.14	65.80	190.64	14.17
1520	Moil points		.03	8.98	20.88	61.13	4.42
1525	Pneumatic nailer w/accessories		.52	25	75	150	19.20
1530	Sheeting driver for 60 lb. breaker		.05	8.36	25.98	75.08	5.58
1540	For 90 lb. breaker		.14	11.34	35.21	101.71	8.19
1550	Spade, 25 lb.		.55	7.99	24.81	71.89	9.37
1560	Tamper, single, 35 lb.		.65	96	259.20	701.70	57.02
1570	Triple, 140 lb.		.97	56.43	155	402.86	38.79
1580	Wrenches, impact, air powered, up to 3/4" bolt		.47	41.82	110.22	305.89	25.78
1590	Up to 1-1/4" bolt		.63	79.33	206.11	581.11	46.28
1600	Barricades, barrels, reflectorized, 1 to 99 barrels		.04	4.70	11.80	35	2.64
1610	100 to 200 barrels		.03	5.33	12.67	40.11	2.75
1620	Barrels with flashers, 1 to 99 barrels		.04	5.33	12.67	40.11	2.84
1630	100 to 200 barrels		.03	5.33	12.67	40.11	2.78
1640	Barrels with steady burn type C lights		.05	5.33	12.67	40.11	2.94
1650	Illuminated board, trailer mounted, with generator		3.60	91	288.57	734.14	86.53
1670	Portable barricade, stock, with flashers, 1 to 6 units		.04	4.29	12.14	39	2.73
1680	25 to 50 units		.04	4.29	12.14	39	2.72
1685	Butt fusion machine, wheeled, 1.5 HP electric, 2" - 8" diameter pipe		2.89	429	1,287	3,861	280.48
1690	Tracked, 20 HP diesel, 4"-12" diameter pipe		10.91	408.33	1,225	3,675	332.25
1695	83 HP diesel, 8" - 24" diameter pipe		56.31	561.67	1,685	5,055	787.50
1700	Carts, brick, gas engine, 1000 lb. capacity		3.23	32.22	84.52	215.66	42.77
1800	1500 lb., 7-1/2' lift		3.21	74.55	232.47	670.95	72.14
1822	Dehumidifier, medium, 6 lb./hr., 150 CFM		1.31	45.86	159.86	487.43	42.42
1824	Large, 18 lb./hr., 600 CFM		2.41	257.50	1,795	5,382.50	378.29
1830	Distributor, asphalt, trailer mounted, 2000 gal., 38 H.P. diesel		12.09	378.08	1,183.17	3,434.63	333.32
1840	3000 gal., 38 H.P. diesel		14.14	410.03	1,269.75	3,674.25	367.10
1850	Drill, rotary hammer, electric		1.22	36	126	378	34.98
1860	Carbide bit, 1-1/2" diameter, add to electric rotary hammer		.03	51.98	131.70	385.50	26.61
1865	Rotary, crawler, 250 H.P.		149.26	2,458.33	7,375	22,125	2,669.07
1870	Emulsion sprayer, 65 gal., 5 H.P. gas engine		3.04	115.02	357.84	1,033.05	95.90
1880	200 gal., 5 H.P. engine		7.94	192.77	600.24	1,730.63	183.58
1900	Floor auto-scrubbing machine, walk-behind, 28" path		6.18	222.67	728.67	1,475	195.20
1930	Floodlight, mercury vapor, or quartz, on tripod, 1000 watt		.50	43.10	108.70	293.30	25.76
1940	2000 watt		.65	45.60	124.50	343	30.09

01 54 | Construction Aids

01 54 33 | Equipment Rental

			UNIT	HOURLY OPER. COST	RENT PER DAY	RENT PER WEEK	RENT PER MONTH	EQUIPMENT COST/DAY
40	1950	Floodlights, trailer mounted with generator, 1 - 300 watt light	Ea.	3.90	185	413.33	916.67	113.84
	1960	2 - 1000 watt lights		4.93	185	413.33	916.67	122.12
	2000	4 - 300 watt lights		4.67	185	413.33	916.67	119.99
	2005	Foam spray rig, incl. box trailer, compressor, generator, proportioner		27.99	575.10	1,789.19	5,165.25	581.75
	2015	Forklift, pneumatic tire, rough terr, straight mast, 5000 lb, 12' lift, gas		20.44	535.67	1,292.78	2,935.11	422.09
	2025	8000 lb, 12' lift		24.93	687.78	1,678.33	3,556.11	535.15
	2030	5000 lb, 12' lift, diesel		16.94	427.33	1,069	2,580.17	349.30
	2035	8000 lb, 12' lift, diesel		18.36	687.78	1,678.33	3,556.11	482.54
	2045	All terrain, telescoping boom, diesel, 5000 lb, 10' reach, 19' lift		18.91	535.67	1,292.78	2,935.11	409.81
	2055	6600 lb, 29' reach, 42' lift		23.13	593.75	1,432.50	3,192.50	471.51
	2065	10,000 lb, 31' reach, 45' lift		25.31	957.50	2,353.75	4,978.75	673.26
	2070	Cushion tire, smooth floor, gas, 5000 lb capacity		9.04	381.11	938.89	2,223.33	260.12
	2075	8000 lb capacity		12.46	435	1,057	2,638	311.06
	2085	Diesel, 5000 lb capacity		8.49	327.50	823	2,002.50	232.55
	2090	12,000 lb capacity		13.21	680.63	1,817.64	4,240.39	469.19
	2095	20,000 lb capacity		18.91	866.79	2,460.30	6,396.21	643.35
	2100	Generator, electric, gas engine, 1.5 kW to 3 kW		2.82	59.25	167.50	408.75	56.08
	2200	5 kW		3.53	84.83	238.33	585.83	75.88
	2300	10 kW		6.50	129.17	340.83	949.17	120.15
	2400	25 kW		8.12	370.50	958.50	2,186.50	256.64
	2500	Diesel engine, 20 kW		10.09	288.50	733.50	1,665	227.44
	2600	50 kW		17.48	388.33	1,125	2,645	364.82
	2700	100 kW		31.34	626	1,586.50	3,968	568.06
	2800	250 kW		59.57	1,019.50	2,677.50	6,297.50	1,012.10
	2850	Hammer, hydraulic, for mounting on boom, to 500 ft lb.		3.18	100.64	312.82	905.25	88
	2860	1000 ft lb.		5.05	150.17	467.50	1,357.88	133.88
	2900	Heaters, space, oil or electric, 50 MBH		1.60	93.20	284	750	69.63
	3000	100 MBH		2.98	135.63	352.50	861.25	94.34
	3100	300 MBH		8.69	678.50	1,928	5,358	455.08
	3150	500 MBH		14.42	267.06	609.69	1,686.25	237.32
	3200	Hose, water, suction with coupling, 20' long, 2" diameter		.02	8.33	21	60	4.37
	3210	3" diameter		.03	15.88	43.50	124.38	8.96
	3220	4" diameter		.03	30.35	93.88	271.58	19.04
	3230	6" diameter		.12	43.67	135.80	394.05	28.12
	3240	8" diameter		.30	57.51	178.82	516.53	38.13
	3250	Discharge hose with coupling, 50' long, 2" diameter		.01	7.20	20	55.60	4.09
	3260	3" diameter		.01	9.10	23.95	74.55	4.88
	3270	4" diameter		.02	22.37	69.85	202.35	14.15
	3280	6" diameter		.07	31.42	97.23	281.16	19.99
	3290	8" diameter		.26	40.47	125.73	362.10	27.24
	3295	Insulation blower		.91	125.67	390.45	1,118.25	85.38
	3300	Ladders, extension type, 16' to 36' long		.20	44.05	122	347.25	25.99
	3400	40' to 60' long		.70	119.03	333.67	989.67	72.33
	3405	Lance for cutting concrete		2.42	103.33	310	930	81.33
	3407	Lawn mower, rotary, 22", 5 H.P.		1.16	25	140	400	37.25
	3408	48" self-propelled		3.18	161.20	429	1,186	111.21
	3410	Level, electronic, automatic, with tripod and leveling rod		1.15	47.37	121.83	344.50	33.60
	3430	Laser type, for pipe and sewer line and grade		2.38	144.37	365.14	1,111.86	92.11
	3440	Rotating beam for interior control		.99	83.28	214	622.80	50.71
	3460	Builder's optical transit, with tripod and rod		.11	47.37	121.83	344.50	25.23
	3500	Light towers, towable, with diesel generator, 2000 watt		4.68	185	413.33	916.67	120.08
	3600	4000 watt		4.95	185	413.33	916.67	122.23
	3700	Mixer, powered, plaster and mortar, 6 C.F., 7 H.P.		2.26	89.29	257.86	648.57	69.62
	3800	10 C.F., 9 H.P.		2.46	111	328	956	85.26
	3850	Nailer, pneumatic		.53	25	75	150	19.21
	3900	Paint sprayers complete, 8 CFM		.96	93.16	222.09	619.25	52.14
	4000	17 CFM		1.75	169.38	403.80	1,125.90	94.79
	4020	Pavers, bituminous, rubber tires, 8' wide, 50 H.P., diesel		35.10	612.38	1,904.62	5,511.38	661.71

01 54 | Construction Aids

01 54 33 | Equipment Rental

		UNIT	HOURLY OPER. COST	RENT PER DAY	RENT PER WEEK	RENT PER MONTH	EQUIPMENT COST/DAY
4030	10' wide, 150 H.P.	Ea.	105.12	2,103.38	6,521.89	18,850.50	2,145.33
4050	Crawler, 8' wide, 100 H.P., diesel		96.29	1,200	3,560	9,240	1,482.34
4060	10' wide, 150 H.P.		114.29	1,425	4,225	10,975	1,759.34
4070	Concrete paver, 12' to 24' wide, 250 H.P.		96.32	1,810.50	5,656.15	16,401	1,901.82
4080	Placer-spreader-trimmer, 24' wide, 300 H.P.		129.19	2,742.38	8,570.80	24,814.50	2,747.64
4100	Pump, centrifugal gas pump, 1-1/2" diam., 65 GPM		4.31	58.04	181.23	521.85	70.74
4200	2" diameter, 130 GPM		5.47	44.44	140	368.80	71.79
4300	3" diameter, 250 GPM		5.62	62.94	187	521	82.39
4400	6" diameter, 1500 GPM		24.40	366.90	956.30	2,400.30	386.48
4500	Submersible electric pump, 1-1/4" diameter, 55 GPM		.44	47.70	125.17	331.50	28.54
4600	1-1/2" diameter, 83 GPM		.49	59.23	160.43	428.57	35.99
4700	2" diameter, 120 GPM		1.81	58.58	182.23	527.18	50.89
4800	3" diameter, 300 GPM		3.33	132.11	347.80	976.83	96.23
4900	4" diameter, 560 GPM		16.19	80.76	242.29	726.86	177.96
5000	6" diameter, 1590 GPM		24.22	225.43	676.28	2,028.83	329.05
5100	Diaphragm pump, gas, single, 1-1/2" diameter		1.24	40	120	360	33.88
5200	2" diameter		4.37	45	135	405	61.92
5300	3" diameter		4.44	79.40	243.40	614.20	84.23
5400	Double, 4" diameter		6.62	218.19	488.77	1,246.91	150.72
5450	Pressure washer 5 GPM, 3000 psi		4.25	109.50	351	838	104.23
5460	7 GPM, 3000 psi		5.43	112	350	847	113.42
5470	High Pressure Water Jet 10 KSI		43.48	777.45	2,414.14	6,975.75	830.66
5480	40 KSI		30.65	1,054.35	3,285.92	9,505.13	902.38
5500	Trash pump, self-priming, gas, 2" diameter		4.19	82.50	247.50	742.50	83
5600	Diesel, 4" diameter		7.33	275	717.22	1,955.56	202.06
5650	Diesel, 6" diameter		18.49	366.90	956.30	2,400.30	339.17
5655	Grout Pump		20.55	302.46	940.77	2,715.75	352.58
5700	Salamanders, L.P. gas fired, 100,000 Btu		3.17	60.10	169.40	451.90	59.23
5705	50,000 Btu		1.83	28.20	72.30	192	29.07
5720	Sandblaster, portable, open top, 3 C.F. capacity		.66	131.67	395	1,185	84.26
5730	6 C.F. capacity		1.10	263.33	790	2,370	166.82
5740	Accessories for above		.15	25.56	79.65	230.04	17.14
5750	Sander, floor		.84	75.68	215	521.49	49.75
5760	Edger		.57	33	109	319	26.35
5800	Saw, chain, gas engine, 18" long		1.93	46.25	160.88	426.25	47.58
5900	Hydraulic powered, 36" long		.86	77.92	233.77	701.30	53.61
5950	60" long		.86	86.98	260.93	782.78	59.04
6000	Masonry, table mounted, 14" diameter, 5 H.P.		1.45	86.87	297.65	723.88	71.14
6050	Portable cut-off, 8 H.P.		1.99	81.25	262.50	590	68.42
6100	Circular, hand held, electric, 7-1/4" diameter		.25	23	50	125	11.99
6200	12" diameter		.26	48.14	126.43	331.43	27.37
6250	Wall saw, w/hydraulic power, 10 H.P.		3.61	137.74	413.22	1,239.66	111.53
6275	Shot blaster, walk-behind, 20" wide		5.20	302.46	940.77	2,715.75	229.79
6280	Sidewalk broom, walk-behind		2.46	88.93	277.04	804.08	75.10
6300	Steam cleaner, 100 gallons per hour		3.67	88.93	277.04	804.08	84.77
6310	200 gallons per hour		4.76	107.57	334.75	969.15	105.05
6340	Tar Kettle/Pot, 400 gallons		18.08	126.67	380	1,140	220.65
6350	Torch, cutting, acetylene-oxygen, 150' hose, excludes gases		.50	16.51	51.36	149.10	14.24
6360	Hourly operating cost includes tips and gas		23.00	7.56	23.45	67.63	188.67
6410	Toilet, portable chemical		.14	25.03	77.34	223.65	16.63
6420	Recycle flush type		.18	30.89	95.81	276.90	20.58
6430	Toilet, fresh water flush, garden hose,		.21	36.74	114.27	330.15	24.56
6440	Hoisted, non-flush, for high rise		.17	29.82	93.50	270.51	20.08
6465	Tractor, farm with attachment		19.09	342.50	984	2,422	349.52
6480	Trailers, platform, flush deck, 2 axle, 3 ton capacity		1.86	102.24	317.41	915.90	78.34
6500	25 ton capacity		6.85	154.43	479.04	1,384.50	150.61
6600	40 ton capacity		8.84	219.39	681.05	1,970.25	206.92
6700	3 axle, 50 ton capacity		9.59	433.33	1,300	3,900	336.69

01 54 | Construction Aids

01 54 33 | Equipment Rental

			UNIT	HOURLY OPER. COST	RENT PER DAY	RENT PER WEEK	RENT PER MONTH	EQUIPMENT COST/DAY	
40	6800	75 ton capacity	Ea.	12.18	324.83	1,002.39	2,902.13	297.90	40
	6810	Trailer mounted cable reel for high voltage line work		6.46	252.67	758	2,274	203.26	
	6820	Trailer mounted cable tensioning rig		12.81	83.33	250	750	152.47	
	6830	Cable pulling rig		80.95	156.67	470	1,410	741.56	
	6850	Portable cable/wire puller, 8000 lb max pulling capacity		4.06	170.69	428.86	1,132.86	118.26	
	6900	Water tank trailer, engine driven discharge, 5000 gallons		7.87	170.40	530.99	1,544.25	169.14	
	6925	10,000 gallons		10.72	232.17	721.45	2,076.75	230.04	
	6950	Water truck, off highway, 6000 gallons		78.88	1,333.33	4,000	12,000	1,431.03	
	7010	Tram car for high voltage line work, powered, 2 conductor		7.55	31.33	94	282	79.21	
	7020	Transit (builder's level) with tripod		.11	47.37	121.83	344.50	25.23	
	7030	Trench box, 3000 lb., 6' x 8'		.61	103.84	323.76	937.20	69.67	
	7040	7200 lb., 6' x 20'		.79	201.29	625.89	1,810.50	131.49	
	7050	8000 lb., 8' x 16'		1.18	218.33	679.21	1,970.25	145.31	
	7060	9500 lb., 8' x 20'		1.32	250.28	779.16	2,263.13	166.41	
	7065	11,000 lb., 8' x 24'		1.39	235.37	732.99	2,130	157.70	
	7070	12,000 lb., 10' x 20'		1.64	284.36	883.06	2,556	189.71	
	7100	Truck, pickup, 3/4 ton, 2 wheel drive		10.15	66.56	206.62	596.40	122.56	
	7200	4 wheel drive		10.42	185.73	541.70	1,602.98	191.73	
	7250	Crew carrier, 9 passenger		13.91	116.09	362.57	1,049.03	183.83	
	7290	Flat bed truck, 20,000 lb. GVW		16.78	142.71	444.41	1,278	223.10	
	7300	Tractor, 4 x 2, 220 H.P.		24.46	232.17	721.45	2,076.75	339.98	
	7410	330 H.P.		35.54	317.37	986.95	2,848.88	481.71	
	7500	6 x 4, 380 H.P.		39.68	367.43	1,142.78	3,301.50	545.98	
	7600	450 H.P.		48.63	447.30	1,385.18	4,020.38	666.04	
	7610	Tractor, with A frame, boom and winch, 225 H.P.		27.20	315.24	979.34	2,822.25	413.43	
	7620	Vacuum truck, hazardous material, 2500 gallons		14.06	335.48	1,038.89	3,008.63	320.26	
	7625	5,000 gallons		14.32	473.93	1,471.76	4,260	408.90	
	7650	Vacuum, HEPA, 16 gallon, wet/dry		.93	126	362	959.50	79.88	
	7655	55 gallon, wet/dry		.93	126	362	959	79.84	
	7660	Water tank, portable		.80	156.99	453.41	1,153.82	97.09	
	7690	Sewer/catch basin vacuum, 14 C.Y., 1500 gallons		19.03	713.55	2,222.06	6,416.63	596.69	
	7700	Welder, electric, 200 amp		4.19	35.40	81.80	236.50	49.91	
	7800	300 amp		6.10	29.96	76.90	198.50	64.17	
	7900	Gas engine, 200 amp		9.83	107.10	290.20	681.10	136.72	
	8000	300 amp		11.13	107.10	290.20	681.10	147.09	
	8100	Wheelbarrow, any size		.07	12	32	93	6.97	
	8200	Wrecking ball, 4000 lb.	▼	2.75	68.33	205	615	62.98	
50	0010	**HIGHWAY EQUIPMENT RENTAL** without operators	R015433-10						50
	0050	Asphalt batch plant, portable drum mixer, 100 ton/hr.	Ea.	97.19	1,650.75	5,165.57	14,910	1,810.63	
	0060	200 ton/hr.		112.12	1,783.88	5,511.86	15,975	1,999.31	
	0070	300 ton/hr.		131.76	2,076.75	6,464.18	18,744	2,346.93	
	0100	Backhoe attachment, long stick, up to 185 H.P., 10.5' long		.41	27.69	85.42	247.08	20.33	
	0140	Up to 250 H.P., 12' long		.45	30.89	95.81	276.90	22.78	
	0180	Over 250 H.P., 15' long		.62	42.07	130.44	378.08	31.05	
	0200	Special dipper arm, up to 100 H.P., 32' long		1.27	85.73	266.64	772.13	63.50	
	0240	Over 100 H.P., 33' long		1.59	107.57	334.75	969.15	79.65	
	0280	Catch basin/sewer cleaning truck, 3 ton, 9 C.Y., 1000 gal.		38.90	452.63	1,414.04	4,100.25	594.04	
	0300	Concrete batch plant, portable, electric, 200 C.Y./hr.		26.59	601.73	1,875.76	5,431.50	587.85	
	0520	Grader/dozer attachment, ripper/scarifier, rear mounted, up to 135 H.P.		3.46	68.16	212.39	612.38	70.18	
	0540	Up to 180 H.P.		4.55	103.31	320.90	926.55	100.54	
	0580	Up to 250 H.P.		6.43	165.08	513.67	1,491	154.19	
	0700	Pvmt. removal bucket, for hyd. excavator, up to 90 H.P.		2.37	62.84	195.08	564.45	58	
	0740	Up to 200 H.P.		2.53	80.41	249.33	718.88	70.14	
	0780	Over 200 H.P.		2.77	98.51	305.89	883.95	83.32	
	0900	Aggregate spreader, self-propelled, 187 H.P.		55.63	798.75	2,481.78	7,188.75	941.36	
	1000	Chemical spreader, 3 C.Y.		3.48	99.67	299	897	87.61	
	1900	Hammermill, traveling, 250 H.P.	▼	73.90	358.67	1,076	3,228	806.43	

For customer support on your Mechanical Costs with RSMeans data, call 800.448.8182.

01 54 | Construction Aids

01 54 33 | Equipment Rental

			UNIT	HOURLY OPER. COST	RENT PER DAY	RENT PER WEEK	RENT PER MONTH	EQUIPMENT COST/DAY	
50	2000	Horizontal borer, 3" diameter, 13 H.P. gas driven	Ea.	5.94	111.67	335	1,005	114.54	50
	2150	Horizontal directional drill, 20,000 lb. thrust, 78 H.P. diesel		30.26	738.67	2,216	6,648	685.30	
	2160	30,000 lb. thrust, 115 H.P.		37.20	738.67	2,216	6,648	740.76	
	2170	50,000 lb. thrust, 170 H.P.		53.33	738.67	2,216	6,648	869.81	
	2190	Mud trailer for HDD, 1500 gallons, 175 H.P., gas		27.98	787.17	2,361.50	7,084.50	696.17	
	2200	Hydromulcher, diesel, 3000 gallon, for truck mounting		19.13	986.90	2,960.70	8,882.10	745.16	
	2300	Gas, 600 gallon		8.22	281.67	845	2,535	234.78	
	2400	Joint & crack cleaner, walk behind, 25 H.P.		3.47	232.67	698	2,094	167.33	
	2500	Filler, trailer mounted, 400 gallons, 20 H.P.		9.16	213.33	640	1,920	201.26	
	3000	Paint striper, self-propelled, 40 gallon, 22 H.P.		7.42	24	72	216	73.74	
	3100	120 gallon, 120 H.P.		19.36	155	465	1,395	247.91	
	3200	Post drivers, 6" I-Beam frame, for truck mounting		13.62	125	375	1,125	183.96	
	3400	Road sweeper, self-propelled, 8' wide, 90 H.P.		39.47	397.01	1,111.15	2,832.90	538.01	
	3450	Road sweeper, vacuum assisted, 4 C.Y., 220 gallons		64.07	3,232.28	6,938.48	13,360.43	1,900.22	
	4000	Road mixer, self-propelled, 130 H.P.		50.83	889.28	2,770.36	8,014.13	960.69	
	4100	310 H.P.		82.46	2,316.38	7,243.34	20,980.50	2,108.32	
	4220	Cold mix paver, incl. pug mill and bitumen tank, 165 H.P.		104.40	716.67	2,150	6,450	1,265.22	
	4240	Pavement brush, towed		3.77	107.57	334.75	969.15	97.08	
	4250	Paver, asphalt, wheel or crawler, 130 H.P., diesel		103.60	2,449.50	7,618.49	22,045.50	2,352.46	
	4300	Paver, road widener, gas, 1' to 6', 67 H.P.		51.29	1,049.03	3,260.94	9,425.25	1,062.55	
	4400	Diesel, 2' to 14', 88 H.P.		61.98	1,251.38	3,866.96	11,182.50	1,269.25	
	4600	Slipform pavers, curb and gutter, 2 track, 75 H.P.		63.58	910.58	2,828.08	8,173.88	1,074.23	
	4700	4 track, 165 H.P.		39.23	1,357.88	4,213.26	12,141	1,156.49	
	4800	Median barrier, 215 H.P.		64.23	1,437.75	4,501.84	12,993	1,414.24	
	4901	Trailer, low bed, 75 ton capacity		11.77	304.59	946.54	2,742.38	283.47	
	5000	Road planer, walk behind, 10" cutting width, 10 H.P.		2.69	421	1,089	2,635	239.34	
	5100	Self-propelled, 12" cutting width, 64 H.P.		9.06	347.31	934.84	2,587.95	259.43	
	5120	Traffic line remover, metal ball blaster, truck mounted, 115 H.P.		51.09	2,066.67	6,200	18,600	1,648.72	
	5140	Grinder, truck mounted, 115 H.P.		55.84	2,066.67	6,200	18,600	1,686.74	
	5160	Walk-behind, 11 H.P.		3.90	305.30	915.90	2,747.70	214.39	
	5200	Pavement profiler, 4' to 6' wide, 450 H.P.		237.65	1,125	3,375	10,125	2,576.21	
	5300	8' to 10' wide, 750 H.P.		363.84	1,283.33	3,850	11,550	3,680.74	
	5400	Roadway plate, steel, 1" x 8' x 20'		.09	65.50	203.97	591.08	41.55	
	5600	Stabilizer, self-propelled, 150 H.P.		45.14	251.67	755	2,265	512.10	
	5700	310 H.P.		83.59	313.33	940	2,820	856.73	
	5800	Striper, truck mounted, 120 gallon paint, 460 H.P.		53.49	410	1,230	3,690	673.88	
	5900	Thermal paint heating kettle, 115 gallons		8.46	170	510	1,530	169.64	
	6000	Tar kettle, 330 gallon, trailer mounted		13.47	153	459	1,377	199.54	
	7000	Tunnel locomotive, diesel, 8 to 12 ton		32.71	665.63	2,077.77	6,017.25	677.26	
	7005	Electric, 10 ton		32.15	761.48	2,366.34	6,842.63	730.48	
	7010	Muck cars, 1/2 C.Y. capacity		2.53	28.76	89.46	258.80	38.10	
	7020	1 C.Y. capacity		2.76	37.28	116.59	335.48	45.41	
	7030	2 C.Y. capacity		2.92	42.07	130.44	378.08	49.44	
	7040	Side dump, 2 C.Y. capacity		3.16	52.19	161.60	468.60	57.56	
	7050	3 C.Y. capacity		4.24	56.98	177.77	516.53	69.44	
	7060	5 C.Y. capacity		6.18	74.02	229.71	665.63	95.40	
	7100	Ventilating blower for tunnel, 7-1/2 H.P.		2.35	56.98	176.61	511.20	54.12	
	7110	10 H.P.		2.66	59.11	184.69	532.50	58.22	
	7120	20 H.P.		3.89	77.21	240.09	692.25	79.16	
	7140	40 H.P.		6.75	102.24	317.43	915.90	117.47	
	7160	60 H.P.		9.55	109.70	340.52	985.13	144.52	
	7175	75 H.P.		11.40	170.40	530.99	1,544.25	197.38	
	7180	200 H.P.		22.85	335.48	1,044.66	3,035.25	391.71	
	7800	Windrow loader, elevating		59.19	1,666.67	5,000	15,000	1,473.50	
60	0010	**LIFTING AND HOISTING EQUIPMENT RENTAL** without operators							60
	0150	Crane, flatbed mounted, 3 ton capacity	Ea.	15.84	815	2,348.50	5,692	596.44	
	0200	Crane, climbing, 106' jib, 6000 lb. capacity, 410 fpm		43.59	3,006.59	9,019.77	27,059.32	2,152.66	
	0300	101' jib, 10,250 lb. capacity, 270 fpm		50.95	3,165.64	9,496.92	28,490.76	2,306.99	

Reference notes: R015433-10, R312316-45

01 54 | Construction Aids

01 54 33 | Equipment Rental

		UNIT	HOURLY OPER. COST	RENT PER DAY	RENT PER WEEK	RENT PER MONTH	EQUIPMENT COST/DAY
0500	Tower, static, 130' high, 106' jib, 6200 lb. capacity at 400 fpm	Ea.	49.55	2,588.20	7,764.59	23,293.78	1,949.33
0520	Mini crawler spider crane, up to 24" wide, 1990 lb. lifting capacity		13.74	591.08	1,846.91	5,351.63	479.34
0525	Up to 30" wide, 6450 lb. lifting capacity		15.97	702.90	2,193.20	6,336.75	566.37
0530	Up to 52" wide, 6680 lb. lifting capacity		25.40	862.65	2,683.79	7,774.50	739.94
0535	Up to 55" wide, 8920 lb. lifting capacity		28.36	953.18	2,972.36	8,599.88	821.33
0540	Up to 66" wide, 13,350 lb. lifting capacity		38.39	1,491	4,617.26	13,312.50	1,230.57
0600	Crawler mounted, lattice boom, 1/2 C.Y., 15 tons at 12' radius		40.56	957.29	2,871.87	8,615.60	898.84
0700	3/4 C.Y., 20 tons at 12' radius		59.44	1,075.55	3,226.64	9,679.92	1,120.87
0800	1 C.Y., 25 tons at 12' radius		73.98	1,136.92	3,410.76	10,232.29	1,274
0900	1-1/2 C.Y., 40 tons at 12' radius		72.77	1,300.84	3,902.51	11,707.52	1,362.63
1000	2 C.Y., 50 tons at 12' radius		97.40	1,541.84	4,625.52	13,876.57	1,704.33
1100	3 C.Y., 75 tons at 12' radius		71.32	2,698.22	8,094.67	24,284	2,189.46
1200	100 ton capacity, 60' boom		94.27	1,330	3,990	11,970	1,552.12
1300	165 ton capacity, 60' boom		116.43	1,593.33	4,780	14,340	1,887.41
1400	200 ton capacity, 70' boom		151.66	1,775	5,325	15,975	2,278.25
1500	350 ton capacity, 80' boom		199.92	3,725	11,175	33,525	3,834.39
1600	Truck mounted, lattice boom, 6 x 4, 20 tons at 10' radius		43.62	1,026.25	2,595.54	7,663.02	868.10
1700	25 tons at 10' radius		46.88	2,698.11	8,094.34	24,283.02	1,993.94
1800	8 x 4, 30 tons at 10' radius		59.43	2,891.04	8,673.13	26,019.39	2,210.08
1900	40 tons at 12' radius		59.43	3,160.64	9,481.91	28,445.73	2,371.83
2000	60 tons at 15' radius		58.91	3,315.05	9,945.16	29,835.48	2,460.30
2050	82 tons at 15' radius		65.21	3,411.34	10,234.01	30,702.03	2,568.46
2100	90 tons at 15' radius		72.85	3,511.25	10,533.76	31,601.28	2,689.54
2200	115 tons at 15' radius		82.18	3,615.53	10,846.59	32,539.77	2,826.79
2300	150 tons at 18' radius		88.98	3,122.12	9,366.37	28,099.11	2,585.11
2350	165 tons at 18' radius		95.50	3,180.26	9,540.77	28,622.31	2,672.17
2400	Truck mounted, hydraulic, 12 ton capacity		32.37	3,152.78	9,458.34	28,375.03	2,150.65
2500	25 ton capacity		39.89	3,256.95	9,770.86	29,312.57	2,273.31
2550	33 ton capacity		59.43	3,256.95	9,770.86	29,312.57	2,429.62
2560	40 ton capacity		59.43	3,285.77	9,857.31	29,571.92	2,446.91
2600	55 ton capacity		59.01	3,314.96	9,944.88	29,834.63	2,461.06
2700	80 ton capacity		77.27	3,372.59	10,117.77	30,353.32	2,641.70
2720	100 ton capacity		82.25	3,517.04	10,551.13	31,653.40	2,768.24
2740	120 ton capacity		115.52	3,565.70	10,697.09	32,091.26	3,063.55
2760	150 ton capacity		123.62	3,791.37	11,374.11	34,122.32	3,263.79
2800	Self-propelled, 4 x 4, with telescoping boom, 5 ton		16.61	421.67	1,265	3,795	385.89
2900	12-1/2 ton capacity		23.50	750	2,250	6,750	637.99
3000	15 ton capacity		37.77	855	2,565	7,695	815.14
3050	20 ton capacity		24.50	941.67	2,825	8,475	760.97
3100	25 ton capacity		40.26	1,008.33	3,025	9,075	927.07
3150	40 ton capacity		49.27	1,241.67	3,725	11,175	1,139.14
3200	Derricks, guy, 20 ton capacity, 60' boom, 75' mast		24.96	1,638.39	4,915.18	14,745.54	1,182.69
3300	100' boom, 115' mast		39.55	2,312.76	6,938.29	20,814.86	1,704.04
3400	Stiffleg, 20 ton capacity, 70' boom, 37' mast		27.88	713.29	2,139.87	6,419.60	650.99
3500	100' boom, 47' mast		43.14	770.92	2,312.76	6,938.29	807.69
3550	Helicopter, small, lift to 1250 lb. maximum, w/pilot		108.79	8,233.33	24,700	74,100	5,810.29
3600	Hoists, chain type, overhead, manual, 3/4 ton		.16	15.98	40.47	79.88	9.37
3900	10 ton		.86	124	310	620	68.92
4000	Hoist and tower, 5000 lb. cap., portable electric, 40' high		5.24	163.91	491.74	1,475.23	140.24
4100	For each added 10' section, add		.13	36.67	110.02	330.07	23.02
4200	Hoist and single tubular tower, 5000 lb. electric, 100' high		7.63	121.63	364.88	1,094.63	134.03
4300	For each added 6'-6" section, add		.23	44.16	132.48	397.44	28.31
4400	Hoist and double tubular tower, 5000 lb., 100' high		8.31	139.88	419.65	1,258.95	150.40
4500	For each added 6'-6" section, add		.25	44.33	132.98	398.94	28.58
4550	Hoist and tower, mast type, 6000 lb., 100' high		10.12	519.22	1,557.67	4,673.01	392.53
4570	For each added 10' section, add		.14	36.67	110.02	330.07	23.16
4600	Hoist and tower, personnel, electric, 2000 lb., 100' @ 125 fpm		19.20	576.32	1,728.96	5,186.87	499.39
4700	3000 lb., 100' @ 200 fpm		21.97	605.14	1,815.41	5,446.22	538.83

01 54 | Construction Aids

01 54 33 | Equipment Rental

			UNIT	HOURLY OPER. COST	RENT PER DAY	RENT PER WEEK	RENT PER MONTH	EQUIPMENT COST/DAY	
60	4800	3000 lb., 150' @ 300 fpm	Ea.	24.38	817.33	2,451.98	7,355.93	685.43	60
	4900	4000 lb., 100' @ 300 fpm		25.22	845.77	2,537.30	7,611.91	709.22	
	5000	6000 lb., 100' @ 275 fpm		27.10	874.96	2,624.87	7,874.62	741.81	
	5100	For added heights up to 500', add	L.F.	.01	3.74	11.23	33.68	2.33	
	5200	Jacks, hydraulic, 20 ton	Ea.	.05	35	80	175	16.44	
	5500	100 ton		.44	27.75	68.91	142.16	17.29	
	6100	Jacks, hydraulic, climbing w/50' jackrods, control console, 30 ton cap.		2.38	35.93	107.78	323.34	40.57	
	6150	For each added 10' jackrod section, add		.05	5.61	16.84	50.52	3.81	
	6300	50 ton capacity		3.82	38.55	115.64	346.91	53.69	
	6350	For each added 10' jackrod section, add		.07	5.61	16.84	50.52	3.89	
	6500	125 ton capacity		9.99	38.55	115.64	346.91	103.05	
	6550	For each added 10' jackrod section, add		.68	5.61	16.84	50.52	8.77	
	6600	Cable jack, 10 ton capacity with 200' cable		1.74	41.17	123.50	370.49	38.60	
	6650	For each added 50' of cable, add		.24	17.21	51.64	154.93	12.27	
70	0010	**WELLPOINT EQUIPMENT RENTAL** without operators	R015433 -10						70
	0020	Based on 2 months rental							
	0100	Combination jetting & wellpoint pump, 60 H.P. diesel	Ea.	17.20	345.04	1,035.13	3,105.39	344.59	
	0200	High pressure gas jet pump, 200 H.P., 300 psi	"	37.12	192	576	1,728	412.18	
	0300	Discharge pipe, 8" diameter	L.F.	.01	53.25	159.75	479.25	32.03	
	0350	12" diameter		.01	56.80	170.40	511.20	34.19	
	0400	Header pipe, flows up to 150 GPM, 4" diameter		.01	31.33	94	282	18.87	
	0500	400 GPM, 6" diameter		.01	41.33	124	372	24.88	
	0600	800 GPM, 8" diameter		.01	45.67	137	411	27.51	
	0700	1500 GPM, 10" diameter		.01	57.51	172.53	517.59	34.62	
	0800	2500 GPM, 12" diameter		.03	65.32	195.96	587.88	39.41	
	0900	4500 GPM, 16" diameter		.04	55.67	167	501	33.68	
	0950	For quick coupling aluminum and plastic pipe, add		.04	10.55	31.64	94.91	6.62	
	1100	Wellpoint, 25' long, with fittings & riser pipe, 1-1/2" or 2" diameter	Ea.	.07	82.27	246.81	740.44	49.95	
	1200	Wellpoint pump, diesel powered, 4" suction, 20 H.P.		7.68	161.67	485	1,455	158.46	
	1300	6" suction, 30 H.P.		10.31	296.67	890	2,670	260.45	
	1400	8" suction, 40 H.P.		13.96	258.33	775	2,325	266.71	
	1500	10" suction, 75 H.P.		20.37	290.67	872	2,616	337.35	
	1600	12" suction, 100 H.P.		29.89	298.33	895	2,685	418.09	
	1700	12" suction, 175 H.P.		42.77	306.67	920	2,760	526.15	
80	0010	**MARINE EQUIPMENT RENTAL** without operators	R015433 -10						80
	0200	Barge, 400 Ton, 30' wide x 90' long	Ea.	19.38	1,278	4,011.25	11,608.50	957.33	
	0240	800 Ton, 45' wide x 90' long		24.34	1,597.50	4,934.71	14,271	1,181.66	
	2000	Tugboat, diesel, 100 H.P.		32.51	255.60	796.48	2,316.38	419.35	
	2040	250 H.P.		63.11	463.28	1,442.89	4,180.13	793.50	
	2080	380 H.P.		137.40	1,384.50	4,328.69	12,567	1,964.96	
	3000	Small work boat, gas, 16-foot, 50 H.P.		12.47	51.65	160.15	463.28	131.82	
	4000	Large, diesel, 48-foot, 200 H.P.		82.09	1,464.38	4,588.41	13,312.50	1,574.43	

Crews - Standard

Crew No.	Bare Costs		Incl. Subs O&P		Cost Per Labor-Hour	
Crew A-1	Hr.	Daily	Hr.	Daily	Bare Costs	Incl. O&P
1 Building Laborer	$47.25	$378.00	$70.35	$562.80	$47.25	$70.35
1 Concrete Saw, Gas Manual		112.72		123.99	14.09	15.50
8 L.H., Daily Totals		$490.72		$686.79	$61.34	$85.85
Crew A-1A	Hr.	Daily	Hr.	Daily	Bare Costs	Incl. O&P
1 Skilled Worker	$61.25	$490.00	$92.00	$736.00	$61.25	$92.00
1 Shot Blaster, 20"		229.79		252.77	28.72	31.60
8 L.H., Daily Totals		$719.79		$988.77	$89.97	$123.60
Crew A-1B	Hr.	Daily	Hr.	Daily	Bare Costs	Incl. O&P
1 Building Laborer	$47.25	$378.00	$70.35	$562.80	$47.25	$70.35
1 Concrete Saw		176.00		193.60	22.00	24.20
8 L.H., Daily Totals		$554.00		$756.40	$69.25	$94.55
Crew A-1C	Hr.	Daily	Hr.	Daily	Bare Costs	Incl. O&P
1 Building Laborer	$47.25	$378.00	$70.35	$562.80	$47.25	$70.35
1 Chain Saw, Gas, 18"		47.58		52.34	5.95	6.54
8 L.H., Daily Totals		$425.58		$615.14	$53.20	$76.89
Crew A-1D	Hr.	Daily	Hr.	Daily	Bare Costs	Incl. O&P
1 Building Laborer	$47.25	$378.00	$70.35	$562.80	$47.25	$70.35
1 Vibrating Plate, Gas, 18"		143.82		158.20	17.98	19.78
8 L.H., Daily Totals		$521.82		$721.00	$65.23	$90.13
Crew A-1E	Hr.	Daily	Hr.	Daily	Bare Costs	Incl. O&P
1 Building Laborer	$47.25	$378.00	$70.35	$562.80	$47.25	$70.35
1 Vibrating Plate, Gas, 21"		146.12		160.73	18.27	20.09
8 L.H., Daily Totals		$524.12		$723.53	$65.52	$90.44
Crew A-1F	Hr.	Daily	Hr.	Daily	Bare Costs	Incl. O&P
1 Building Laborer	$47.25	$378.00	$70.35	$562.80	$47.25	$70.35
1 Rammer/Tamper, Gas, 8"		73.84		81.22	9.23	10.15
8 L.H., Daily Totals		$451.84		$644.02	$56.48	$80.50
Crew A-1G	Hr.	Daily	Hr.	Daily	Bare Costs	Incl. O&P
1 Building Laborer	$47.25	$378.00	$70.35	$562.80	$47.25	$70.35
1 Rammer/Tamper, Gas, 15"		88.02		96.82	11.00	12.10
8 L.H., Daily Totals		$466.02		$659.62	$58.25	$82.45
Crew A-1H	Hr.	Daily	Hr.	Daily	Bare Costs	Incl. O&P
1 Building Laborer	$47.25	$378.00	$70.35	$562.80	$47.25	$70.35
1 Exterior Steam Cleaner		84.77		93.25	10.60	11.66
8 L.H., Daily Totals		$462.77		$656.05	$57.85	$82.01
Crew A-1J	Hr.	Daily	Hr.	Daily	Bare Costs	Incl. O&P
1 Building Laborer	$47.25	$378.00	$70.35	$562.80	$47.25	$70.35
1 Cultivator, Walk-Behind, 5 H.P.		70.72		77.79	8.84	9.72
8 L.H., Daily Totals		$448.72		$640.59	$56.09	$80.07
Crew A-1K	Hr.	Daily	Hr.	Daily	Bare Costs	Incl. O&P
1 Building Laborer	$47.25	$378.00	$70.35	$562.80	$47.25	$70.35
1 Cultivator, Walk-Behind, 8 H.P.		89.64		98.60	11.21	12.33
8 L.H., Daily Totals		$467.64		$661.40	$58.45	$82.68
Crew A-1M	Hr.	Daily	Hr.	Daily	Bare Costs	Incl. O&P
1 Building Laborer	$47.25	$378.00	$70.35	$562.80	$47.25	$70.35
1 Snow Blower, Walk-Behind		75.10		82.61	9.39	10.33
8 L.H., Daily Totals		$453.10		$645.41	$56.64	$80.68

Crew No.	Bare Costs		Incl. Subs O&P		Cost Per Labor-Hour	
Crew A-2	Hr.	Daily	Hr.	Daily	Bare Costs	Incl. O&P
2 Laborers	$47.25	$756.00	$70.35	$1125.60	$49.13	$73.23
1 Truck Driver (light)	52.90	423.20	79.00	632.00		
1 Flatbed Truck, Gas, 1.5 Ton		361.95		398.14	15.08	16.59
24 L.H., Daily Totals		$1541.15		$2155.74	$64.21	$89.82
Crew A-2A	Hr.	Daily	Hr.	Daily	Bare Costs	Incl. O&P
2 Laborers	$47.25	$756.00	$70.35	$1125.60	$49.13	$73.23
1 Truck Driver (light)	52.90	423.20	79.00	632.00		
1 Flatbed Truck, Gas, 1.5 Ton		361.95		398.14		
1 Concrete Saw		176.00		193.60	22.41	24.66
24 L.H., Daily Totals		$1717.15		$2349.34	$71.55	$97.89
Crew A-2B	Hr.	Daily	Hr.	Daily	Bare Costs	Incl. O&P
1 Truck Driver (light)	$52.90	$423.20	$79.00	$632.00	$52.90	$79.00
1 Flatbed Truck, Gas, 1.5 Ton		361.95		398.14	45.24	49.77
8 L.H., Daily Totals		$785.15		$1030.15	$98.14	$128.77
Crew A-3A	Hr.	Daily	Hr.	Daily	Bare Costs	Incl. O&P
1 Equip. Oper. (light)	$59.70	$477.60	$88.85	$710.80	$59.70	$88.85
1 Pickup Truck, 4x4, 3/4 Ton		191.73		210.90	23.97	26.36
8 L.H., Daily Totals		$669.33		$921.70	$83.67	$115.21
Crew A-3B	Hr.	Daily	Hr.	Daily	Bare Costs	Incl. O&P
1 Equip. Oper. (medium)	$63.05	$504.40	$93.80	$750.40	$59.25	$88.33
1 Truck Driver (heavy)	55.45	443.60	82.85	662.80		
1 Dump Truck, 12 C.Y., 400 H.P.		791.36		870.50		
1 F.E. Loader, W.M., 2.5 C.Y.		658.89		724.78	90.64	99.70
16 L.H., Daily Totals		$2398.25		$3008.47	$149.89	$188.03
Crew A-3C	Hr.	Daily	Hr.	Daily	Bare Costs	Incl. O&P
1 Equip. Oper. (light)	$59.70	$477.60	$88.85	$710.80	$59.70	$88.85
1 Loader, Skid Steer, 78 H.P.		429.91		472.90	53.74	59.11
8 L.H., Daily Totals		$907.51		$1183.70	$113.44	$147.96
Crew A-3D	Hr.	Daily	Hr.	Daily	Bare Costs	Incl. O&P
1 Truck Driver (light)	$52.90	$423.20	$79.00	$632.00	$52.90	$79.00
1 Pickup Truck, 4x4, 3/4 Ton		191.73		210.90		
1 Flatbed Trailer, 25 Ton		150.61		165.67	42.79	47.07
8 L.H., Daily Totals		$765.54		$1008.57	$95.69	$126.07
Crew A-3E	Hr.	Daily	Hr.	Daily	Bare Costs	Incl. O&P
1 Equip. Oper. (crane)	$66.30	$530.40	$98.65	$789.20	$60.88	$90.75
1 Truck Driver (heavy)	55.45	443.60	82.85	662.80		
1 Pickup Truck, 4x4, 3/4 Ton		191.73		210.90	11.98	13.18
16 L.H., Daily Totals		$1165.73		$1662.90	$72.86	$103.93
Crew A-3F	Hr.	Daily	Hr.	Daily	Bare Costs	Incl. O&P
1 Equip. Oper. (crane)	$66.30	$530.40	$98.65	$789.20	$60.88	$90.75
1 Truck Driver (heavy)	55.45	443.60	82.85	662.80		
1 Pickup Truck, 4x4, 3/4 Ton		191.73		210.90		
1 Truck Tractor, 6x4, 380 H.P.		545.98		600.58		
1 Lowbed Trailer, 75 Ton		283.47		311.82	63.82	70.21
16 L.H., Daily Totals		$1995.18		$2575.30	$124.70	$160.96

Crews - Standard

Crew No.	Bare Costs		Incl. Subs O&P		Cost Per Labor-Hour		Crew No.	Bare Costs		Incl. Subs O&P		Cost Per Labor-Hour	
Crew A-3G	Hr.	Daily	Hr.	Daily	Bare Costs	Incl. O&P	**Crew A-3R**	Hr.	Daily	Hr.	Daily	Bare Costs	Incl. O&P
1 Equip. Oper. (crane)	$66.30	$530.40	$98.65	$789.20	$60.88	$90.75	1 Equip. Oper. (light)	$59.70	$477.60	$88.85	$710.80	$59.70	$88.85
1 Truck Driver (heavy)	55.45	443.60	82.85	662.80			1 Forklift, Smooth Floor, 8,000 Lb.		311.06		342.17	38.88	42.77
1 Pickup Truck, 4x4, 3/4 Ton		191.73		210.90			8 L.H., Daily Totals		$788.66		$1052.97	$98.58	$131.62
1 Truck Tractor, 6x4, 450 H.P.		666.04		732.64			**Crew A-4**	Hr.	Daily	Hr.	Daily	Bare Costs	Incl. O&P
1 Lowbed Trailer, 75 Ton		283.47		311.82	71.33	78.46	2 Carpenters	$58.60	$937.60	$87.25	$1396.00	$55.62	$82.68
16 L.H., Daily Totals		$2115.24		$2707.36	$132.20	$169.21	1 Painter, Ordinary	49.65	397.20	73.55	588.40		
Crew A-3H	Hr.	Daily	Hr.	Daily	Bare Costs	Incl. O&P	24 L.H., Daily Totals		$1334.80		$1984.40	$55.62	$82.68
1 Equip. Oper. (crane)	$66.30	$530.40	$98.65	$789.20	$66.30	$98.65	**Crew A-5**	Hr.	Daily	Hr.	Daily	Bare Costs	Incl. O&P
1 Hyd. Crane, 12 Ton (Daily)		2150.65		2365.72	268.83	295.71	2 Laborers	$47.25	$756.00	$70.35	$1125.60	$47.88	$71.31
8 L.H., Daily Totals		$2681.05		$3154.92	$335.13	$394.36	.25 Truck Driver (light)	52.90	105.80	79.00	158.00		
Crew A-3I	Hr.	Daily	Hr.	Daily	Bare Costs	Incl. O&P	.25 Flatbed Truck, Gas, 1.5 Ton		90.49		99.54	5.03	5.53
1 Equip. Oper. (crane)	$66.30	$530.40	$98.65	$789.20	$66.30	$98.65	18 L.H., Daily Totals		$952.29		$1383.14	$52.90	$76.84
1 Hyd. Crane, 25 Ton (Daily)		2273.31		2500.64	284.16	312.58	**Crew A-6**	Hr.	Daily	Hr.	Daily	Bare Costs	Incl. O&P
8 L.H., Daily Totals		$2803.71		$3289.84	$350.46	$411.23	1 Instrument Man	$61.25	$490.00	$92.00	$736.00	$58.65	$87.65
Crew A-3J	Hr.	Daily	Hr.	Daily	Bare Costs	Incl. O&P	1 Rodman/Chainman	56.05	448.40	83.30	666.40		
1 Equip. Oper. (crane)	$66.30	$530.40	$98.65	$789.20	$66.30	$98.65	1 Level, Electronic		33.60		36.96	2.10	2.31
1 Hyd. Crane, 40 Ton (Daily)		2446.91		2691.60	305.86	336.45	16 L.H., Daily Totals		$972.00		$1439.36	$60.75	$89.96
8 L.H., Daily Totals		$2977.31		$3480.80	$372.16	$435.10	**Crew A-7**	Hr.	Daily	Hr.	Daily	Bare Costs	Incl. O&P
Crew A-3K	Hr.	Daily	Hr.	Daily	Bare Costs	Incl. O&P	1 Chief of Party	$71.80	$574.40	$107.20	$857.60	$63.03	$94.17
1 Equip. Oper. (crane)	$66.30	$530.40	$98.65	$789.20	$61.35	$91.28	1 Instrument Man	61.25	490.00	92.00	736.00		
1 Equip. Oper. (oiler)	56.40	451.20	83.90	671.20			1 Rodman/Chainman	56.05	448.40	83.30	666.40		
1 Hyd. Crane, 55 Ton (Daily)		2461.06		2707.17			1 Level, Electronic		33.60		36.96	1.40	1.54
1 P/U Truck, 3/4 Ton (Daily)		157.41		173.15	163.65	180.02	24 L.H., Daily Totals		$1546.40		$2296.96	$64.43	$95.71
16 L.H., Daily Totals		$3600.07		$4340.72	$225.00	$271.29	**Crew A-8**	Hr.	Daily	Hr.	Daily	Bare Costs	Incl. O&P
Crew A-3L	Hr.	Daily	Hr.	Daily	Bare Costs	Incl. O&P	1 Chief of Party	$71.80	$574.40	$107.20	$857.60	$61.29	$91.45
1 Equip. Oper. (crane)	$66.30	$530.40	$98.65	$789.20	$61.35	$91.28	1 Instrument Man	61.25	490.00	92.00	736.00		
1 Equip. Oper. (oiler)	56.40	451.20	83.90	671.20			2 Rodmen/Chainmen	56.05	896.80	83.30	1332.80		
1 Hyd. Crane, 80 Ton (Daily)		2641.70		2905.87			1 Level, Electronic		33.60		36.96	1.05	1.16
1 P/U Truck, 3/4 Ton (Daily)		157.41		173.15	174.94	192.44	32 L.H., Daily Totals		$1994.80		$2963.36	$62.34	$92.61
16 L.H., Daily Totals		$3780.71		$4539.42	$236.29	$283.71	**Crew A-9**	Hr.	Daily	Hr.	Daily	Bare Costs	Incl. O&P
Crew A-3M	Hr.	Daily	Hr.	Daily	Bare Costs	Incl. O&P	1 Asbestos Foreman	$65.75	$526.00	$100.60	$804.80	$65.31	$99.90
1 Equip. Oper. (crane)	$66.30	$530.40	$98.65	$789.20	$61.35	$91.28	7 Asbestos Workers	65.25	3654.00	99.80	5588.80		
1 Equip. Oper. (oiler)	56.40	451.20	83.90	671.20			64 L.H., Daily Totals		$4180.00		$6393.60	$65.31	$99.90
1 Hyd. Crane, 100 Ton (Daily)		2768.24		3045.06			**Crew A-10A**	Hr.	Daily	Hr.	Daily	Bare Costs	Incl. O&P
1 P/U Truck, 3/4 Ton (Daily)		157.41		173.15	182.85	201.14	1 Asbestos Foreman	$65.75	$526.00	$100.60	$804.80	$65.42	$100.07
16 L.H., Daily Totals		$3907.25		$4678.61	$244.20	$292.41	2 Asbestos Workers	65.25	1044.00	99.80	1596.80		
Crew A-3N	Hr.	Daily	Hr.	Daily	Bare Costs	Incl. O&P	24 L.H., Daily Totals		$1570.00		$2401.60	$65.42	$100.07
1 Equip. Oper. (crane)	$66.30	$530.40	$98.65	$789.20	$66.30	$98.65	**Crew A-10B**	Hr.	Daily	Hr.	Daily	Bare Costs	Incl. O&P
1 Tower Crane (monthly)		1891.47		2080.62	236.43	260.08	1 Asbestos Foreman	$65.75	$526.00	$100.60	$804.80	$65.38	$100.00
8 L.H., Daily Totals		$2421.87		$2869.82	$302.73	$358.73	3 Asbestos Workers	65.25	1566.00	99.80	2395.20		
Crew A-3P	Hr.	Daily	Hr.	Daily	Bare Costs	Incl. O&P	32 L.H., Daily Totals		$2092.00		$3200.00	$65.38	$100.00
1 Equip. Oper. (light)	$59.70	$477.60	$88.85	$710.80	$59.70	$88.85	**Crew A-10C**	Hr.	Daily	Hr.	Daily	Bare Costs	Incl. O&P
1 A.T. Forklift, 31' reach, 45' lift		673.26		740.59	84.16	92.57	3 Asbestos Workers	$65.25	$1566.00	$99.80	$2395.20	$65.25	$99.80
8 L.H., Daily Totals		$1150.86		$1451.39	$143.86	$181.42	1 Flatbed Truck, Gas, 1.5 Ton		361.95		398.14	15.08	16.59
Crew A-3Q	Hr.	Daily	Hr.	Daily	Bare Costs	Incl. O&P	24 L.H., Daily Totals		$1927.95		$2793.34	$80.33	$116.39
1 Equip. Oper. (light)	$59.70	$477.60	$88.85	$710.80	$59.70	$88.85							
1 Pickup Truck, 4x4, 3/4 Ton		191.73		210.90									
1 Flatbed Trailer, 3 Ton		78.34		86.17	33.76	37.13							
8 L.H., Daily Totals		$747.67		$1007.88	$93.46	$125.98							

Crews - Standard

Crew No.		Bare Costs		Incl. Subs O&P		Cost Per Labor-Hour	
Crew A-10D	Hr.	Daily	Hr.	Daily	Bare Costs	Incl. O&P
2 Asbestos Workers	$65.25	$1044.00	$99.80	$1596.80	$63.30	$95.54
1 Equip. Oper. (crane)	66.30	530.40	98.65	789.20		
1 Equip. Oper. (oiler)	56.40	451.20	83.90	671.20		
1 Hydraulic Crane, 33 Ton		2429.62		2672.58	75.93	83.52
32 L.H., Daily Totals		$4455.22		$5729.78	$139.23	$179.06
Crew A-11	Hr.	Daily	Hr.	Daily	Bare Costs	Incl. O&P
1 Asbestos Foreman	$65.75	$526.00	$100.60	$804.80	$65.31	$99.90
7 Asbestos Workers	65.25	3654.00	99.80	5588.80		
2 Chip. Hammers, 12 Lb., Elec.		54.32		59.75	.85	.93
64 L.H., Daily Totals		$4234.32		$6453.35	$66.16	$100.83
Crew A-12	Hr.	Daily	Hr.	Daily	Bare Costs	Incl. O&P
1 Asbestos Foreman	$65.75	$526.00	$100.60	$804.80	$65.31	$99.90
7 Asbestos Workers	65.25	3654.00	99.80	5588.80		
1 Trk-Mtd Vac, 14 CY, 1500 Gal.		596.69		656.36		
1 Flatbed Truck, 20,000 GVW		223.10		245.41	12.81	14.09
64 L.H., Daily Totals		$4999.79		$7295.37	$78.12	$113.99
Crew A-13	Hr.	Daily	Hr.	Daily	Bare Costs	Incl. O&P
1 Equip. Oper. (light)	$59.70	$477.60	$88.85	$710.80	$59.70	$88.85
1 Trk-Mtd Vac, 14 CY, 1500 Gal.		596.69		656.36		
1 Flatbed Truck, 20,000 GVW		223.10		245.41	102.47	112.72
8 L.H., Daily Totals		$1297.39		$1612.57	$162.17	$201.57
Crew B-1	Hr.	Daily	Hr.	Daily	Bare Costs	Incl. O&P
1 Labor Foreman (outside)	$49.25	$394.00	$73.30	$586.40	$47.92	$71.33
2 Laborers	47.25	756.00	70.35	1125.60		
24 L.H., Daily Totals		$1150.00		$1712.00	$47.92	$71.33
Crew B-1A	Hr.	Daily	Hr.	Daily	Bare Costs	Incl. O&P
1 Labor Foreman (outside)	$49.25	$394.00	$73.30	$586.40	$47.92	$71.33
2 Laborers	47.25	756.00	70.35	1125.60		
2 Cutting Torches		28.48		31.33		
2 Sets of Gases		377.34		415.07	16.91	18.60
24 L.H., Daily Totals		$1555.82		$2158.40	$64.83	$89.93
Crew B-1B	Hr.	Daily	Hr.	Daily	Bare Costs	Incl. O&P
1 Labor Foreman (outside)	$49.25	$394.00	$73.30	$586.40	$52.51	$78.16
2 Laborers	47.25	756.00	70.35	1125.60		
1 Equip. Oper. (crane)	66.30	530.40	98.65	789.20		
2 Cutting Torches		28.48		31.33		
2 Sets of Gases		377.34		415.07		
1 Hyd. Crane, 12 Ton		2150.65		2365.72	79.89	87.88
32 L.H., Daily Totals		$4236.87		$5313.32	$132.40	$166.04
Crew B-1C	Hr.	Daily	Hr.	Daily	Bare Costs	Incl. O&P
1 Labor Foreman (outside)	$49.25	$394.00	$73.30	$586.40	$47.92	$71.33
2 Laborers	47.25	756.00	70.35	1125.60		
1 Telescoping Boom Lift, to 60'		385.68		424.25	16.07	17.68
24 L.H., Daily Totals		$1535.68		$2136.25	$63.99	$89.01
Crew B-1D	Hr.	Daily	Hr.	Daily	Bare Costs	Incl. O&P
2 Laborers	$47.25	$756.00	$70.35	$1125.60	$47.25	$70.35
1 Small Work Boat, Gas, 50 H.P.		131.82		145.00		
1 Pressure Washer, 7 GPM		113.42		124.76	15.33	16.86
16 L.H., Daily Totals		$1001.24		$1395.36	$62.58	$87.21
Crew B-1E	Hr.	Daily	Hr.	Daily	Bare Costs	Incl. O&P
1 Labor Foreman (outside)	$49.25	$394.00	$73.30	$586.40	$47.75	$71.09
3 Laborers	47.25	1134.00	70.35	1688.40		
1 Work Boat, Diesel, 200 H.P.		1574.43		1731.87		
2 Pressure Washers, 7 GPM		226.84		249.52	56.29	61.92
32 L.H., Daily Totals		$3329.27		$4256.20	$104.04	$133.01
Crew B-1F	Hr.	Daily	Hr.	Daily	Bare Costs	Incl. O&P
2 Skilled Workers	$61.25	$980.00	$92.00	$1472.00	$56.58	$84.78
1 Laborer	47.25	378.00	70.35	562.80		
1 Small Work Boat, Gas, 50 H.P.		131.82		145.00		
1 Pressure Washer, 7 GPM		113.42		124.76	10.22	11.24
24 L.H., Daily Totals		$1603.24		$2304.56	$66.80	$96.02
Crew B-1G	Hr.	Daily	Hr.	Daily	Bare Costs	Incl. O&P
2 Laborers	$47.25	$756.00	$70.35	$1125.60	$47.25	$70.35
1 Small Work Boat, Gas, 50 H.P.		131.82		145.00	8.24	9.06
16 L.H., Daily Totals		$887.82		$1270.60	$55.49	$79.41
Crew B-1H	Hr.	Daily	Hr.	Daily	Bare Costs	Incl. O&P
2 Skilled Workers	$61.25	$980.00	$92.00	$1472.00	$56.58	$84.78
1 Laborer	47.25	378.00	70.35	562.80		
1 Small Work Boat, Gas, 50 H.P.		131.82		145.00	5.49	6.04
24 L.H., Daily Totals		$1489.82		$2179.80	$62.08	$90.83
Crew B-1J	Hr.	Daily	Hr.	Daily	Bare Costs	Incl. O&P
1 Labor Foreman (inside)	$47.75	$382.00	$71.10	$568.80	$47.50	$70.72
1 Laborer	47.25	378.00	70.35	562.80		
16 L.H., Daily Totals		$760.00		$1131.60	$47.50	$70.72
Crew B-1K	Hr.	Daily	Hr.	Daily	Bare Costs	Incl. O&P
1 Carpenter Foreman (inside)	$59.10	$472.80	$88.00	$704.00	$58.85	$87.63
1 Carpenter	58.60	468.80	87.25	698.00		
16 L.H., Daily Totals		$941.60		$1402.00	$58.85	$87.63
Crew B-2	Hr.	Daily	Hr.	Daily	Bare Costs	Incl. O&P
1 Labor Foreman (outside)	$49.25	$394.00	$73.30	$586.40	$47.65	$70.94
4 Laborers	47.25	1512.00	70.35	2251.20		
40 L.H., Daily Totals		$1906.00		$2837.60	$47.65	$70.94
Crew B-2A	Hr.	Daily	Hr.	Daily	Bare Costs	Incl. O&P
1 Labor Foreman (outside)	$49.25	$394.00	$73.30	$586.40	$47.92	$71.33
2 Laborers	47.25	756.00	70.35	1125.60		
1 Telescoping Boom Lift, to 60'		385.68		424.25	16.07	17.68
24 L.H., Daily Totals		$1535.68		$2136.25	$63.99	$89.01
Crew B-3	Hr.	Daily	Hr.	Daily	Bare Costs	Incl. O&P
1 Labor Foreman (outside)	$49.25	$394.00	$73.30	$586.40	$52.95	$78.92
2 Laborers	47.25	756.00	70.35	1125.60		
1 Equip. Oper. (medium)	63.05	504.40	93.80	750.40		
2 Truck Drivers (heavy)	55.45	887.20	82.85	1325.60		
1 Crawler Loader, 3 C.Y.		1257.68		1383.45		
2 Dump Trucks, 12 C.Y., 400 H.P.		1582.72		1740.99	59.17	65.09
48 L.H., Daily Totals		$5382.00		$6912.44	$112.13	$144.01
Crew B-3A	Hr.	Daily	Hr.	Daily	Bare Costs	Incl. O&P
4 Laborers	$47.25	$1512.00	$70.35	$2251.20	$50.41	$75.04
1 Equip. Oper. (medium)	63.05	504.40	93.80	750.40		
1 Hyd. Excavator, 1.5 C.Y.		1185.24		1303.76	29.63	32.59
40 L.H., Daily Totals		$3201.64		$4305.36	$80.04	$107.63

Crews - Standard

Crew No.		Bare Costs		Incl. Subs O&P		Cost Per Labor-Hour	
Crew B-3B	Hr.	Daily	Hr.	Daily	Bare Costs	Incl. O&P
2 Laborers	$47.25	$756.00	$70.35	$1125.60	$53.25	$79.34
1 Equip. Oper. (medium)	63.05	504.40	93.80	750.40		
1 Truck Driver (heavy)	55.45	443.60	82.85	662.80		
1 Backhoe Loader, 80 H.P.		357.71		393.48		
1 Dump Truck, 12 C.Y., 400 H.P.		791.36		870.50	35.91	39.50
32 L.H., Daily Totals		$2853.07		$3802.78	$89.16	$118.84
Crew B-3C	Hr.	Daily	Hr.	Daily	Bare Costs	Incl. O&P
3 Laborers	$47.25	$1134.00	$70.35	$1688.40	$51.20	$76.21
1 Equip. Oper. (medium)	63.05	504.40	93.80	750.40		
1 Crawler Loader, 4 C.Y.		1506.11		1656.72	47.07	51.77
32 L.H., Daily Totals		$3144.51		$4095.52	$98.27	$127.99
Crew B-4	Hr.	Daily	Hr.	Daily	Bare Costs	Incl. O&P
1 Labor Foreman (outside)	$49.25	$394.00	$73.30	$586.40	$48.95	$72.92
4 Laborers	47.25	1512.00	70.35	2251.20		
1 Truck Driver (heavy)	55.45	443.60	82.85	662.80		
1 Truck Tractor, 220 H.P.		339.98		373.98		
1 Flatbed Trailer, 40 Ton		206.92		227.61	11.39	12.53
48 L.H., Daily Totals		$2896.50		$4101.99	$60.34	$85.46
Crew B-5	Hr.	Daily	Hr.	Daily	Bare Costs	Incl. O&P
1 Labor Foreman (outside)	$49.25	$394.00	$73.30	$586.40	$52.05	$77.47
4 Laborers	47.25	1512.00	70.35	2251.20		
2 Equip. Oper. (medium)	63.05	1008.80	93.80	1500.80		
1 Air Compressor, 250 cfm		196.28		215.91		
2 Breakers, Pavement, 60 lb.		68.94		75.83		
2 -50' Air Hoses, 1.5"		47.20		51.92		
1 Crawler Loader, 3 C.Y.		1257.68		1383.45	28.04	30.84
56 L.H., Daily Totals		$4484.90		$6065.51	$80.09	$108.31
Crew B-5A	Hr.	Daily	Hr.	Daily	Bare Costs	Incl. O&P
1 Labor Foreman (outside)	$49.25	$394.00	$73.30	$586.40	$52.45	$78.13
6 Laborers	47.25	2268.00	70.35	3376.80		
2 Equip. Oper. (medium)	63.05	1008.80	93.80	1500.80		
1 Equip. Oper. (light)	59.70	477.60	88.85	710.80		
2 Truck Drivers (heavy)	55.45	887.20	82.85	1325.60		
1 Air Compressor, 365 cfm		389.99		428.99		
2 Breakers, Pavement, 60 lb.		68.94		75.83		
8 -50' Air Hoses, 1"		74.48		81.93		
2 Dump Trucks, 8 C.Y., 220 H.P.		834.98		918.48	14.25	15.68
96 L.H., Daily Totals		$6403.99		$9005.63	$66.71	$93.81
Crew B-5B	Hr.	Daily	Hr.	Daily	Bare Costs	Incl. O&P
1 Powderman	$61.25	$490.00	$92.00	$736.00	$58.95	$88.03
2 Equip. Oper. (medium)	63.05	1008.80	93.80	1500.80		
3 Truck Drivers (heavy)	55.45	1330.80	82.85	1988.40		
1 F.E. Loader, W.M., 2.5 C.Y.		658.89		724.78		
3 Dump Trucks, 12 C.Y., 400 H.P.		2374.08		2611.49		
1 Air Compressor, 365 cfm		389.99		428.99	71.31	78.44
48 L.H., Daily Totals		$6252.56		$7990.46	$130.26	$166.47

Crew No.		Bare Costs		Incl. Subs O&P		Cost Per Labor-Hour	
Crew B-5C	Hr.	Daily	Hr.	Daily	Bare Costs	Incl. O&P
3 Laborers	$47.25	$1134.00	$70.35	$1688.40	$54.80	$81.64
1 Equip. Oper. (medium)	63.05	504.40	93.80	750.40		
2 Truck Drivers (heavy)	55.45	887.20	82.85	1325.60		
1 Equip. Oper. (crane)	66.30	530.40	98.65	789.20		
1 Equip. Oper. (oiler)	56.40	451.20	83.90	671.20		
2 Dump Trucks, 12 C.Y., 400 H.P.		1582.72		1740.99		
1 Crawler Loader, 4 C.Y.		1506.11		1656.72		
1 S.P. Crane, 4x4, 25 Ton		927.07		1019.78	62.75	69.02
64 L.H., Daily Totals		$7523.10		$9642.29	$117.55	$150.66
Crew B-5D	Hr.	Daily	Hr.	Daily	Bare Costs	Incl. O&P
1 Labor Foreman (outside)	$49.25	$394.00	$73.30	$586.40	$52.48	$78.14
4 Laborers	47.25	1512.00	70.35	2251.20		
2 Equip. Oper. (medium)	63.05	1008.80	93.80	1500.80		
1 Truck Driver (heavy)	55.45	443.60	82.85	662.80		
1 Air Compressor, 250 cfm		196.28		215.91		
2 Breakers, Pavement, 60 lb.		68.94		75.83		
2 -50' Air Hoses, 1.5"		47.20		51.92		
1 Crawler Loader, 3 C.Y.		1257.68		1383.45		
1 Dump Truck, 12 C.Y., 400 H.P.		791.36		870.50	36.90	40.59
64 L.H., Daily Totals		$5719.86		$7598.81	$89.37	$118.73
Crew B-5E	Hr.	Daily	Hr.	Daily	Bare Costs	Incl. O&P
1 Labor Foreman (outside)	$49.25	$394.00	$73.30	$586.40	$52.48	$78.14
4 Laborers	47.25	1512.00	70.35	2251.20		
2 Equip. Oper. (medium)	63.05	1008.80	93.80	1500.80		
1 Truck Driver (heavy)	55.45	443.60	82.85	662.80		
1 Water Tank Trailer, 5000 Gal.		169.14		186.05		
1 High Pressure Water Jet 40 KSI		902.38		992.62		
2 -50' Air Hoses, 1.5"		47.20		51.92		
1 Crawler Loader, 3 C.Y.		1257.68		1383.45		
1 Dump Truck, 12 C.Y., 400 H.P.		791.36		870.50	49.50	54.45
64 L.H., Daily Totals		$6526.16		$8485.74	$101.97	$132.59
Crew B-6	Hr.	Daily	Hr.	Daily	Bare Costs	Incl. O&P
2 Laborers	$47.25	$756.00	$70.35	$1125.60	$51.40	$76.52
1 Equip. Oper. (light)	59.70	477.60	88.85	710.80		
1 Backhoe Loader, 48 H.P.		277.19		304.91	11.55	12.70
24 L.H., Daily Totals		$1510.79		$2141.31	$62.95	$89.22
Crew B-6A	Hr.	Daily	Hr.	Daily	Bare Costs	Incl. O&P
.5 Labor Foreman (outside)	$49.25	$197.00	$73.30	$293.20	$53.97	$80.32
1 Laborer	47.25	378.00	70.35	562.80		
1 Equip. Oper. (medium)	63.05	504.40	93.80	750.40		
1 Vacuum Truck, 5000 Gal.		408.90		449.79	20.45	22.49
20 L.H., Daily Totals		$1488.30		$2056.19	$74.42	$102.81
Crew B-6B	Hr.	Daily	Hr.	Daily	Bare Costs	Incl. O&P
2 Labor Foremen (outside)	$49.25	$788.00	$73.30	$1172.80	$47.92	$71.33
4 Laborers	47.25	1512.00	70.35	2251.20		
1 S.P. Crane, 4x4, 5 Ton		385.89		424.48		
1 Flatbed Truck, Gas, 1.5 Ton		361.95		398.14		
1 Butt Fusion Mach., 4"-12" diam.		332.25		365.48	22.50	24.75
48 L.H., Daily Totals		$3380.09		$4612.10	$70.42	$96.09

Crews - Standard

Crew No.	Bare Costs		Incl. Subs O&P		Cost Per Labor-Hour	
Crew B-6C	Hr.	Daily	Hr.	Daily	Bare Costs	Incl. O&P
2 Labor Foremen (outside)	$49.25	$788.00	$73.30	$1172.80	$47.92	$71.33
4 Laborers	47.25	1512.00	70.35	2251.20		
1 S.P. Crane, 4x4, 12 Ton		637.99		701.79		
1 Flatbed Truck, Gas, 3 Ton		391.02		430.12		
1 Butt Fusion Mach., 8"-24" diam.		787.50		866.25	37.84	41.63
48 L.H., Daily Totals		$4116.51		$5422.16	$85.76	$112.96
Crew B-6D	Hr.	Daily	Hr.	Daily	Bare Costs	Incl. O&P
.5 Labor Foreman (outside)	$49.25	$197.00	$73.30	$293.20	$53.97	$80.32
1 Laborer	47.25	378.00	70.35	562.80		
1 Equip. Oper. (medium)	63.05	504.40	93.80	750.40		
1 Hydro Excavator, 12 C.Y.		1404.51		1544.96	70.23	77.25
20 L.H., Daily Totals		$2483.91		$3151.36	$124.20	$157.57
Crew B-7	Hr.	Daily	Hr.	Daily	Bare Costs	Incl. O&P
1 Labor Foreman (outside)	$49.25	$394.00	$73.30	$586.40	$50.22	$74.75
4 Laborers	47.25	1512.00	70.35	2251.20		
1 Equip. Oper. (medium)	63.05	504.40	93.80	750.40		
1 Brush Chipper, 12", 130 H.P.		518.12		569.93		
1 Crawler Loader, 3 C.Y.		1257.68		1383.45		
2 Chain Saws, Gas, 36" Long		107.22		117.94	39.23	43.15
48 L.H., Daily Totals		$4293.42		$5659.32	$89.45	$117.90
Crew B-7A	Hr.	Daily	Hr.	Daily	Bare Costs	Incl. O&P
2 Laborers	$47.25	$756.00	$70.35	$1125.60	$51.40	$76.52
1 Equip. Oper. (light)	59.70	477.60	88.85	710.80		
1 Rake w/Tractor		161.55		177.71		
2 Chain Saws, Gas, 18"		95.16		104.68	10.70	11.77
24 L.H., Daily Totals		$1490.31		$2118.78	$62.10	$88.28
Crew B-7B	Hr.	Daily	Hr.	Daily	Bare Costs	Incl. O&P
1 Labor Foreman (outside)	$49.25	$394.00	$73.30	$586.40	$50.96	$75.91
4 Laborers	47.25	1512.00	70.35	2251.20		
1 Equip. Oper. (medium)	63.05	504.40	93.80	750.40		
1 Truck Driver (heavy)	55.45	443.60	82.85	662.80		
1 Brush Chipper, 12", 130 H.P.		518.12		569.93		
1 Crawler Loader, 3 C.Y.		1257.68		1383.45		
2 Chain Saws, Gas, 36" Long		107.22		117.94		
1 Dump Truck, 8 C.Y., 220 H.P.		417.49		459.24	41.08	45.19
56 L.H., Daily Totals		$5154.51		$6781.36	$92.04	$121.10
Crew B-7C	Hr.	Daily	Hr.	Daily	Bare Costs	Incl. O&P
1 Labor Foreman (outside)	$49.25	$394.00	$73.30	$586.40	$50.96	$75.91
4 Laborers	47.25	1512.00	70.35	2251.20		
1 Equip. Oper. (medium)	63.05	504.40	93.80	750.40		
1 Truck Driver (heavy)	55.45	443.60	82.85	662.80		
1 Brush Chipper, 12", 130 H.P.		518.12		569.93		
1 Crawler Loader, 3 C.Y.		1257.68		1383.45		
2 Chain Saws, Gas, 36" Long		107.22		117.94		
1 Dump Truck, 12 C.Y., 400 H.P.		791.36		870.50	47.76	52.53
56 L.H., Daily Totals		$5528.38		$7192.62	$98.72	$128.44

Crew No.	Bare Costs		Incl. Subs O&P		Cost Per Labor-Hour	
Crew B-8	Hr.	Daily	Hr.	Daily	Bare Costs	Incl. O&P
1 Labor Foreman (outside)	$49.25	$394.00	$73.30	$586.40	$54.64	$81.40
2 Laborers	47.25	756.00	70.35	1125.60		
2 Equip. Oper. (medium)	63.05	1008.80	93.80	1500.80		
1 Equip. Oper. (oiler)	56.40	451.20	83.90	671.20		
2 Truck Drivers (heavy)	55.45	887.20	82.85	1325.60		
1 Hyd. Crane, 25 Ton		2273.31		2500.64		
1 Crawler Loader, 3 C.Y.		1257.68		1383.45		
2 Dump Trucks, 12 C.Y., 400 H.P.		1582.72		1740.99	79.90	87.89
64 L.H., Daily Totals		$8610.91		$10834.68	$134.55	$169.29
Crew B-9	Hr.	Daily	Hr.	Daily	Bare Costs	Incl. O&P
1 Labor Foreman (outside)	$49.25	$394.00	$73.30	$586.40	$47.65	$70.94
4 Laborers	47.25	1512.00	70.35	2251.20		
1 Air Compressor, 250 cfm		196.28		215.91		
2 Breakers, Pavement, 60 lb.		68.94		75.83		
2 -50' Air Hoses, 1.5"		47.20		51.92	7.81	8.59
40 L.H., Daily Totals		$2218.42		$3181.26	$55.46	$79.53
Crew B-9A	Hr.	Daily	Hr.	Daily	Bare Costs	Incl. O&P
2 Laborers	$47.25	$756.00	$70.35	$1125.60	$49.98	$74.52
1 Truck Driver (heavy)	55.45	443.60	82.85	662.80		
1 Water Tank Trailer, 5000 Gal.		169.14		186.05		
1 Truck Tractor, 220 H.P.		339.98		373.98		
2 -50' Discharge Hoses, 3"		9.76		10.74	21.62	23.78
24 L.H., Daily Totals		$1718.48		$2359.17	$71.60	$98.30
Crew B-9B	Hr.	Daily	Hr.	Daily	Bare Costs	Incl. O&P
2 Laborers	$47.25	$756.00	$70.35	$1125.60	$49.98	$74.52
1 Truck Driver (heavy)	55.45	443.60	82.85	662.80		
2 -50' Discharge Hoses, 3"		9.76		10.74		
1 Water Tank Trailer, 5000 Gal.		169.14		186.05		
1 Truck Tractor, 220 H.P.		339.98		373.98		
1 Pressure Washer		104.23		114.65	25.96	28.56
24 L.H., Daily Totals		$1822.71		$2473.82	$75.95	$103.08
Crew B-9D	Hr.	Daily	Hr.	Daily	Bare Costs	Incl. O&P
1 Labor Foreman (outside)	$49.25	$394.00	$73.30	$586.40	$47.65	$70.94
4 Common Laborers	47.25	1512.00	70.35	2251.20		
1 Air Compressor, 250 cfm		196.28		215.91		
2 -50' Air Hoses, 1.5"		47.20		51.92		
2 Air Powered Tampers		114.04		125.44	8.94	9.83
40 L.H., Daily Totals		$2263.52		$3230.87	$56.59	$80.77
Crew B-9E	Hr.	Daily	Hr.	Daily	Bare Costs	Incl. O&P
1 Cement Finisher	$55.00	$440.00	$80.45	$643.60	$51.13	$75.40
1 Laborer	47.25	378.00	70.35	562.80		
1 Chip. Hammers, 12 Lb., Elec.		27.16		29.88	1.70	1.87
16 L.H., Daily Totals		$845.16		$1236.28	$52.82	$77.27
Crew B-10	Hr.	Daily	Hr.	Daily	Bare Costs	Incl. O&P
1 Equip. Oper. (medium)	$63.05	$504.40	$93.80	$750.40	$57.78	$85.98
.5 Laborer	47.25	189.00	70.35	281.40		
12 L.H., Daily Totals		$693.40		$1031.80	$57.78	$85.98
Crew B-10A	Hr.	Daily	Hr.	Daily	Bare Costs	Incl. O&P
1 Equip. Oper. (medium)	$63.05	$504.40	$93.80	$750.40	$57.78	$85.98
.5 Laborer	47.25	189.00	70.35	281.40		
1 Roller, 2-Drum, W.B., 7.5 H.P.		157.50		173.25	13.13	14.44
12 L.H., Daily Totals		$850.90		$1205.05	$70.91	$100.42

Crews - Standard

Crew No.		Bare Costs		Incl. Subs O&P		Cost Per Labor-Hour	
Crew B-10B	Hr.	Daily	Hr.	Daily	Bare Costs	Incl. O&P
1 Equip. Oper. (medium)	$63.05	$504.40	$93.80	$750.40	$57.78	$85.98
.5 Laborer	47.25	189.00	70.35	281.40		
1 Dozer, 200 H.P.		1382.36		1520.60	115.20	126.72
12 L.H., Daily Totals		$2075.76		$2552.40	$172.98	$212.70

Crew B-10C	Hr.	Daily	Hr.	Daily	Bare Costs	Incl. O&P
1 Equip. Oper. (medium)	$63.05	$504.40	$93.80	$750.40	$57.78	$85.98
.5 Laborer	47.25	189.00	70.35	281.40		
1 Dozer, 200 H.P.		1382.36		1520.60		
1 Vibratory Roller, Towed, 23 Ton		681.59		749.75	172.00	189.20
12 L.H., Daily Totals		$2757.35		$3302.15	$229.78	$275.18

Crew B-10D	Hr.	Daily	Hr.	Daily	Bare Costs	Incl. O&P
1 Equip. Oper. (medium)	$63.05	$504.40	$93.80	$750.40	$57.78	$85.98
.5 Laborer	47.25	189.00	70.35	281.40		
1 Dozer, 200 H.P.		1382.36		1520.60		
1 Sheepsft. Roller, Towed		444.83		489.31	152.27	167.49
12 L.H., Daily Totals		$2520.59		$3041.71	$210.05	$253.48

Crew B-10E	Hr.	Daily	Hr.	Daily	Bare Costs	Incl. O&P
1 Equip. Oper. (medium)	$63.05	$504.40	$93.80	$750.40	$57.78	$85.98
.5 Laborer	47.25	189.00	70.35	281.40		
1 Tandem Roller, 5 Ton		287.45		316.19	23.95	26.35
12 L.H., Daily Totals		$980.85		$1347.99	$81.74	$112.33

Crew B-10F	Hr.	Daily	Hr.	Daily	Bare Costs	Incl. O&P
1 Equip. Oper. (medium)	$63.05	$504.40	$93.80	$750.40	$57.78	$85.98
.5 Laborer	47.25	189.00	70.35	281.40		
1 Tandem Roller, 10 Ton		379.22		417.14	31.60	34.76
12 L.H., Daily Totals		$1072.62		$1448.94	$89.39	$120.75

Crew B-10G	Hr.	Daily	Hr.	Daily	Bare Costs	Incl. O&P
1 Equip. Oper. (medium)	$63.05	$504.40	$93.80	$750.40	$57.78	$85.98
.5 Laborer	47.25	189.00	70.35	281.40		
1 Sheepsfoot Roller, 240 H.P.		765.47		842.02	63.79	70.17
12 L.H., Daily Totals		$1458.87		$1873.82	$121.57	$156.15

Crew B-10H	Hr.	Daily	Hr.	Daily	Bare Costs	Incl. O&P
1 Equip. Oper. (medium)	$63.05	$504.40	$93.80	$750.40	$57.78	$85.98
.5 Laborer	47.25	189.00	70.35	281.40		
1 Diaphragm Water Pump, 2"		61.92		68.11		
1 -20' Suction Hose, 2"		4.37		4.81		
2 -50' Discharge Hoses, 2"		8.18		9.00	6.21	6.83
12 L.H., Daily Totals		$767.87		$1113.72	$63.99	$92.81

Crew B-10I	Hr.	Daily	Hr.	Daily	Bare Costs	Incl. O&P
1 Equip. Oper. (medium)	$63.05	$504.40	$93.80	$750.40	$57.78	$85.98
.5 Laborer	47.25	189.00	70.35	281.40		
1 Diaphragm Water Pump, 4"		150.72		165.79		
1 -20' Suction Hose, 4"		19.04		20.94		
2 -50' Discharge Hoses, 4"		28.30		31.13	16.50	18.16
12 L.H., Daily Totals		$891.46		$1249.67	$74.29	$104.14

Crew B-10J	Hr.	Daily	Hr.	Daily	Bare Costs	Incl. O&P
1 Equip. Oper. (medium)	$63.05	$504.40	$93.80	$750.40	$57.78	$85.98
.5 Laborer	47.25	189.00	70.35	281.40		
1 Centrifugal Water Pump, 3"		82.39		90.63		
1 -20' Suction Hose, 3"		8.96		9.86		
2 -50' Discharge Hoses, 3"		9.76		10.74	8.43	9.27
12 L.H., Daily Totals		$794.51		$1143.02	$66.21	$95.25

Crew B-10K	Hr.	Daily	Hr.	Daily	Bare Costs	Incl. O&P
1 Equip. Oper. (medium)	$63.05	$504.40	$93.80	$750.40	$57.78	$85.98
.5 Laborer	47.25	189.00	70.35	281.40		
1 Centr. Water Pump, 6"		386.48		425.13		
1 -20' Suction Hose, 6"		28.12		30.93		
2 -50' Discharge Hoses, 6"		39.98		43.98	37.88	41.67
12 L.H., Daily Totals		$1147.98		$1531.84	$95.67	$127.65

Crew B-10L	Hr.	Daily	Hr.	Daily	Bare Costs	Incl. O&P
1 Equip. Oper. (medium)	$63.05	$504.40	$93.80	$750.40	$57.78	$85.98
.5 Laborer	47.25	189.00	70.35	281.40		
1 Dozer, 80 H.P.		591.82		651.00	49.32	54.25
12 L.H., Daily Totals		$1285.22		$1682.80	$107.10	$140.23

Crew B-10M	Hr.	Daily	Hr.	Daily	Bare Costs	Incl. O&P
1 Equip. Oper. (medium)	$63.05	$504.40	$93.80	$750.40	$57.78	$85.98
.5 Laborer	47.25	189.00	70.35	281.40		
1 Dozer, 300 H.P.		1674.53		1841.98	139.54	153.50
12 L.H., Daily Totals		$2367.93		$2873.78	$197.33	$239.48

Crew B-10N	Hr.	Daily	Hr.	Daily	Bare Costs	Incl. O&P
1 Equip. Oper. (medium)	$63.05	$504.40	$93.80	$750.40	$57.78	$85.98
.5 Laborer	47.25	189.00	70.35	281.40		
1 F.E. Loader, T.M., 1.5 C.Y.		627.38		690.12	52.28	57.51
12 L.H., Daily Totals		$1320.78		$1721.92	$110.07	$143.49

Crew B-10O	Hr.	Daily	Hr.	Daily	Bare Costs	Incl. O&P
1 Equip. Oper. (medium)	$63.05	$504.40	$93.80	$750.40	$57.78	$85.98
.5 Laborer	47.25	189.00	70.35	281.40		
1 F.E. Loader, T.M., 2.25 C.Y.		958.76		1054.64	79.90	87.89
12 L.H., Daily Totals		$1652.16		$2086.44	$137.68	$173.87

Crew B-10P	Hr.	Daily	Hr.	Daily	Bare Costs	Incl. O&P
1 Equip. Oper. (medium)	$63.05	$504.40	$93.80	$750.40	$57.78	$85.98
.5 Laborer	47.25	189.00	70.35	281.40		
1 Crawler Loader, 3 C.Y.		1257.68		1383.45	104.81	115.29
12 L.H., Daily Totals		$1951.08		$2415.25	$162.59	$201.27

Crew B-10Q	Hr.	Daily	Hr.	Daily	Bare Costs	Incl. O&P
1 Equip. Oper. (medium)	$63.05	$504.40	$93.80	$750.40	$57.78	$85.98
.5 Laborer	47.25	189.00	70.35	281.40		
1 Crawler Loader, 4 C.Y.		1506.11		1656.72	125.51	138.06
12 L.H., Daily Totals		$2199.51		$2688.52	$183.29	$224.04

Crew B-10R	Hr.	Daily	Hr.	Daily	Bare Costs	Incl. O&P
1 Equip. Oper. (medium)	$63.05	$504.40	$93.80	$750.40	$57.78	$85.98
.5 Laborer	47.25	189.00	70.35	281.40		
1 F.E. Loader, W.M., 1 C.Y.		394.79		434.27	32.90	36.19
12 L.H., Daily Totals		$1088.19		$1466.07	$90.68	$122.17

Crew B-10S	Hr.	Daily	Hr.	Daily	Bare Costs	Incl. O&P
1 Equip. Oper. (medium)	$63.05	$504.40	$93.80	$750.40	$57.78	$85.98
.5 Laborer	47.25	189.00	70.35	281.40		
1 F.E. Loader, W.M., 1.5 C.Y.		455.32		500.85	37.94	41.74
12 L.H., Daily Totals		$1148.72		$1532.65	$95.73	$127.72

Crew B-10T	Hr.	Daily	Hr.	Daily	Bare Costs	Incl. O&P
1 Equip. Oper. (medium)	$63.05	$504.40	$93.80	$750.40	$57.78	$85.98
.5 Laborer	47.25	189.00	70.35	281.40		
1 F.E. Loader, W.M., 2.5 C.Y.		658.89		724.78	54.91	60.40
12 L.H., Daily Totals		$1352.29		$1756.58	$112.69	$146.38

Crews - Standard

Crew No.	Bare Costs		Incl. Subs O&P		Cost Per Labor-Hour	
Crew B-10U	Hr.	Daily	Hr.	Daily	Bare Costs	Incl. O&P
1 Equip. Oper. (medium)	$63.05	$504.40	$93.80	$750.40	$57.78	$85.98
.5 Laborer	47.25	189.00	70.35	281.40		
1 F.E. Loader, W.M., 5.5 C.Y.		1186.42		1305.06	98.87	108.76
12 L.H., Daily Totals		$1879.82		$2336.86	$156.65	$194.74
Crew B-10V	Hr.	Daily	Hr.	Daily	Bare Costs	Incl. O&P
1 Equip. Oper. (medium)	$63.05	$504.40	$93.80	$750.40	$57.78	$85.98
.5 Laborer	47.25	189.00	70.35	281.40		
1 Dozer, 700 H.P.		4098.16		4507.98	341.51	375.66
12 L.H., Daily Totals		$4791.56		$5539.78	$399.30	$461.65
Crew B-10W	Hr.	Daily	Hr.	Daily	Bare Costs	Incl. O&P
1 Equip. Oper. (medium)	$63.05	$504.40	$93.80	$750.40	$57.78	$85.98
.5 Laborer	47.25	189.00	70.35	281.40		
1 Dozer, 105 H.P.		702.68		772.95	58.56	64.41
12 L.H., Daily Totals		$1396.08		$1804.75	$116.34	$150.40
Crew B-10X	Hr.	Daily	Hr.	Daily	Bare Costs	Incl. O&P
1 Equip. Oper. (medium)	$63.05	$504.40	$93.80	$750.40	$57.78	$85.98
.5 Laborer	47.25	189.00	70.35	281.40		
1 Dozer, 410 H.P.		2535.96		2789.56	211.33	232.46
12 L.H., Daily Totals		$3229.36		$3821.36	$269.11	$318.45
Crew B-10Y	Hr.	Daily	Hr.	Daily	Bare Costs	Incl. O&P
1 Equip. Oper. (medium)	$63.05	$504.40	$93.80	$750.40	$57.78	$85.98
.5 Laborer	47.25	189.00	70.35	281.40		
1 Vibr. Roller, Towed, 12 Ton		346.96		381.66	28.91	31.80
12 L.H., Daily Totals		$1040.36		$1413.46	$86.70	$117.79
Crew B-11A	Hr.	Daily	Hr.	Daily	Bare Costs	Incl. O&P
1 Equipment Oper. (med.)	$63.05	$504.40	$93.80	$750.40	$55.15	$82.08
1 Laborer	47.25	378.00	70.35	562.80		
1 Dozer, 200 H.P.		1382.36		1520.60	86.40	95.04
16 L.H., Daily Totals		$2264.76		$2833.80	$141.55	$177.11
Crew B-11B	Hr.	Daily	Hr.	Daily	Bare Costs	Incl. O&P
1 Equipment Oper. (light)	$59.70	$477.60	$88.85	$710.80	$53.48	$79.60
1 Laborer	47.25	378.00	70.35	562.80		
1 Air Powered Tamper		57.02		62.72		
1 Air Compressor, 365 cfm		389.99		428.99		
2 -50' Air Hoses, 1.5"		47.20		51.92	30.89	33.98
16 L.H., Daily Totals		$1349.81		$1817.23	$84.36	$113.58
Crew B-11C	Hr.	Daily	Hr.	Daily	Bare Costs	Incl. O&P
1 Equipment Oper. (med.)	$63.05	$504.40	$93.80	$750.40	$55.15	$82.08
1 Laborer	47.25	378.00	70.35	562.80		
1 Backhoe Loader, 48 H.P.		277.19		304.91	17.32	19.06
16 L.H., Daily Totals		$1159.59		$1618.11	$72.47	$101.13
Crew B-11J	Hr.	Daily	Hr.	Daily	Bare Costs	Incl. O&P
1 Equipment Oper. (med.)	$63.05	$504.40	$93.80	$750.40	$55.15	$82.08
1 Laborer	47.25	378.00	70.35	562.80		
1 Grader, 30,000 Lbs.		1091.19		1200.31		
1 Ripper, Beam & 1 Shank		100.54		110.59	74.48	81.93
16 L.H., Daily Totals		$2074.13		$2624.10	$129.63	$164.01

Crew No.	Bare Costs		Incl. Subs O&P		Cost Per Labor-Hour	
Crew B-11K	Hr.	Daily	Hr.	Daily	Bare Costs	Incl. O&P
1 Equipment Oper. (med.)	$63.05	$504.40	$93.80	$750.40	$55.15	$82.08
1 Laborer	47.25	378.00	70.35	562.80		
1 Trencher, Chain Type, 8' D		2079.03		2286.93	129.94	142.93
16 L.H., Daily Totals		$2961.43		$3600.13	$185.09	$225.01
Crew B-11L	Hr.	Daily	Hr.	Daily	Bare Costs	Incl. O&P
1 Equipment Oper. (med.)	$63.05	$504.40	$93.80	$750.40	$55.15	$82.08
1 Laborer	47.25	378.00	70.35	562.80		
1 Grader, 30,000 Lbs.		1091.19		1200.31	68.20	75.02
16 L.H., Daily Totals		$1973.59		$2513.51	$123.35	$157.09
Crew B-11M	Hr.	Daily	Hr.	Daily	Bare Costs	Incl. O&P
1 Equipment Oper. (med.)	$63.05	$504.40	$93.80	$750.40	$55.15	$82.08
1 Laborer	47.25	378.00	70.35	562.80		
1 Backhoe Loader, 80 H.P.		357.71		393.48	22.36	24.59
16 L.H., Daily Totals		$1240.11		$1706.68	$77.51	$106.67
Crew B-11N	Hr.	Daily	Hr.	Daily	Bare Costs	Incl. O&P
1 Labor Foreman (outside)	$49.25	$394.00	$73.30	$586.40	$56.45	$84.22
2 Equipment Operators (med.)	63.05	1008.80	93.80	1500.80		
6 Truck Drivers (heavy)	55.45	2661.60	82.85	3976.80		
1 F.E. Loader, W.M., 5.5 C.Y.		1186.42		1305.06		
1 Dozer, 410 H.P.		2535.96		2789.56		
6 Dump Trucks, Off Hwy., 50 Ton		12225.60		13448.16	221.50	243.65
72 L.H., Daily Totals		$20012.38		$23606.78	$277.95	$327.87
Crew B-11Q	Hr.	Daily	Hr.	Daily	Bare Costs	Incl. O&P
1 Equipment Operator (med.)	$63.05	$504.40	$93.80	$750.40	$57.78	$85.98
.5 Laborer	47.25	189.00	70.35	281.40		
1 Dozer, 140 H.P.		757.89		833.68	63.16	69.47
12 L.H., Daily Totals		$1451.29		$1865.48	$120.94	$155.46
Crew B-11R	Hr.	Daily	Hr.	Daily	Bare Costs	Incl. O&P
1 Equipment Operator (med.)	$63.05	$504.40	$93.80	$750.40	$57.78	$85.98
.5 Laborer	47.25	189.00	70.35	281.40		
1 Dozer, 200 H.P.		1382.36		1520.60	115.20	126.72
12 L.H., Daily Totals		$2075.76		$2552.40	$172.98	$212.70
Crew B-11S	Hr.	Daily	Hr.	Daily	Bare Costs	Incl. O&P
1 Equipment Operator (med.)	$63.05	$504.40	$93.80	$750.40	$57.78	$85.98
.5 Laborer	47.25	189.00	70.35	281.40		
1 Dozer, 300 H.P.		1674.53		1841.98		
1 Ripper, Beam & 1 Shank		100.54		110.59	147.92	162.71
12 L.H., Daily Totals		$2468.47		$2984.38	$205.71	$248.70
Crew B-11T	Hr.	Daily	Hr.	Daily	Bare Costs	Incl. O&P
1 Equipment Operator (med.)	$63.05	$504.40	$93.80	$750.40	$57.78	$85.98
.5 Laborer	47.25	189.00	70.35	281.40		
1 Dozer, 410 H.P.		2535.96		2789.56		
1 Ripper, Beam & 2 Shanks		154.19		169.61	224.18	246.60
12 L.H., Daily Totals		$3383.55		$3990.97	$281.96	$332.58
Crew B-11U	Hr.	Daily	Hr.	Daily	Bare Costs	Incl. O&P
1 Equipment Operator (med.)	$63.05	$504.40	$93.80	$750.40	$57.78	$85.98
.5 Laborer	47.25	189.00	70.35	281.40		
1 Dozer, 520 H.P.		2569.55		2826.51	214.13	235.54
12 L.H., Daily Totals		$3262.95		$3858.30	$271.91	$321.53

Crews - Standard

Crew No.	Bare Costs Hr.	Bare Costs Daily	Incl. Subs O&P Hr.	Incl. Subs O&P Daily	Cost Per Labor-Hour Bare Costs	Cost Per Labor-Hour Incl. O&P
Crew B-11V						
3 Laborers	$47.25	$1134.00	$70.35	$1688.40	$47.25	$70.35
1 Roller, 2-Drum, W.B., 7.5 H.P.		157.50		173.25	6.56	7.22
24 L.H., Daily Totals		$1291.50		$1861.65	$53.81	$77.57
Crew B-11W						
1 Equipment Operator (med.)	$63.05	$504.40	$93.80	$750.40	$55.40	$82.72
1 Common Laborer	47.25	378.00	70.35	562.80		
10 Truck Drivers (heavy)	55.45	4436.00	82.85	6628.00		
1 Dozer, 200 H.P.		1382.36		1520.60		
1 Vibratory Roller, Towed, 23 Ton		681.59		749.75		
10 Dump Trucks, 8 C.Y., 220 H.P.		4174.90		4592.39	64.99	71.49
96 L.H., Daily Totals		$11557.25		$14803.93	$120.39	$154.21
Crew B-11Y						
1 Labor Foreman (outside)	$49.25	$394.00	$73.30	$586.40	$52.74	$78.49
5 Common Laborers	47.25	1890.00	70.35	2814.00		
3 Equipment Operators (med.)	63.05	1513.20	93.80	2251.20		
1 Dozer, 80 H.P.		591.82		651.00		
2 Rollers, 2-Drum, W.B., 7.5 H.P.		315.00		346.50		
4 Vibrating Plates, Gas, 21"		584.48		642.93	20.71	22.78
72 L.H., Daily Totals		$5288.50		$7292.03	$73.45	$101.28
Crew B-12A						
1 Equip. Oper. (crane)	$66.30	$530.40	$98.65	$789.20	$56.77	$84.50
1 Laborer	47.25	378.00	70.35	562.80		
1 Hyd. Excavator, 1 C.Y.		986.56		1085.22	61.66	67.83
16 L.H., Daily Totals		$1894.96		$2437.22	$118.44	$152.33
Crew B-12B						
1 Equip. Oper. (crane)	$66.30	$530.40	$98.65	$789.20	$56.77	$84.50
1 Laborer	47.25	378.00	70.35	562.80		
1 Hyd. Excavator, 1.5 C.Y.		1185.24		1303.76	74.08	81.49
16 L.H., Daily Totals		$2093.64		$2655.76	$130.85	$165.99
Crew B-12C						
1 Equip. Oper. (crane)	$66.30	$530.40	$98.65	$789.20	$56.77	$84.50
1 Laborer	47.25	378.00	70.35	562.80		
1 Hyd. Excavator, 2 C.Y.		1096.14		1205.75	68.51	75.36
16 L.H., Daily Totals		$2004.54		$2557.75	$125.28	$159.86
Crew B-12D						
1 Equip. Oper. (crane)	$66.30	$530.40	$98.65	$789.20	$56.77	$84.50
1 Laborer	47.25	378.00	70.35	562.80		
1 Hyd. Excavator, 3.5 C.Y.		2394.44		2633.88	149.65	164.62
16 L.H., Daily Totals		$3302.84		$3985.88	$206.43	$249.12
Crew B-12E						
1 Equip. Oper. (crane)	$66.30	$530.40	$98.65	$789.20	$56.77	$84.50
1 Laborer	47.25	378.00	70.35	562.80		
1 Hyd. Excavator, .5 C.Y.		764.88		841.37	47.81	52.59
16 L.H., Daily Totals		$1673.28		$2193.37	$104.58	$137.09
Crew B-12F						
1 Equip. Oper. (crane)	$66.30	$530.40	$98.65	$789.20	$56.77	$84.50
1 Laborer	47.25	378.00	70.35	562.80		
1 Hyd. Excavator, .75 C.Y.		915.34		1006.87	57.21	62.93
16 L.H., Daily Totals		$1823.74		$2358.87	$113.98	$147.43
Crew B-12G						
1 Equip. Oper. (crane)	$66.30	$530.40	$98.65	$789.20	$56.77	$84.50
1 Laborer	47.25	378.00	70.35	562.80		
1 Crawler Crane, 15 Ton		898.84		988.72		
1 Clamshell Bucket, .5 C.Y.		37.28		41.01	58.51	64.36
16 L.H., Daily Totals		$1844.52		$2381.73	$115.28	$148.86
Crew B-12H						
1 Equip. Oper. (crane)	$66.30	$530.40	$98.65	$789.20	$56.77	$84.50
1 Laborer	47.25	378.00	70.35	562.80		
1 Crawler Crane, 25 Ton		1274.00		1401.40		
1 Clamshell Bucket, 1 C.Y.		46.89		51.58	82.56	90.81
16 L.H., Daily Totals		$2229.29		$2804.98	$139.33	$175.31
Crew B-12I						
1 Equip. Oper. (crane)	$66.30	$530.40	$98.65	$789.20	$56.77	$84.50
1 Laborer	47.25	378.00	70.35	562.80		
1 Crawler Crane, 20 Ton		1120.87		1232.96		
1 Dragline Bucket, .75 C.Y.		29.54		32.49	71.90	79.09
16 L.H., Daily Totals		$2058.81		$2617.45	$128.68	$163.59
Crew B-12J						
1 Equip. Oper. (crane)	$66.30	$530.40	$98.65	$789.20	$56.77	$84.50
1 Laborer	47.25	378.00	70.35	562.80		
1 Gradall, 5/8 C.Y.		880.91		969.00	55.06	60.56
16 L.H., Daily Totals		$1789.31		$2321.00	$111.83	$145.06
Crew B-12K						
1 Equip. Oper. (crane)	$66.30	$530.40	$98.65	$789.20	$56.77	$84.50
1 Laborer	47.25	378.00	70.35	562.80		
1 Gradall, 3 Ton, 1 C.Y.		1520.84		1672.92	95.05	104.56
16 L.H., Daily Totals		$2429.24		$3024.92	$151.83	$189.06
Crew B-12L						
1 Equip. Oper. (crane)	$66.30	$530.40	$98.65	$789.20	$56.77	$84.50
1 Laborer	47.25	378.00	70.35	562.80		
1 Crawler Crane, 15 Ton		898.84		988.72		
1 F.E. Attachment, .5 C.Y.		72.55		79.81	60.71	66.78
16 L.H., Daily Totals		$1879.79		$2420.53	$117.49	$151.28
Crew B-12M						
1 Equip. Oper. (crane)	$66.30	$530.40	$98.65	$789.20	$56.77	$84.50
1 Laborer	47.25	378.00	70.35	562.80		
1 Crawler Crane, 20 Ton		1120.87		1232.96		
1 F.E. Attachment, .75 C.Y.		78.31		86.14	74.95	82.44
16 L.H., Daily Totals		$2107.58		$2671.10	$131.72	$166.94
Crew B-12N						
1 Equip. Oper. (crane)	$66.30	$530.40	$98.65	$789.20	$56.77	$84.50
1 Laborer	47.25	378.00	70.35	562.80		
1 Crawler Crane, 25 Ton		1274.00		1401.40		
1 F.E. Attachment, 1 C.Y.		59.18		65.10	83.32	91.66
16 L.H., Daily Totals		$2241.58		$2818.50	$140.10	$176.16
Crew B-12O						
1 Equip. Oper. (crane)	$66.30	$530.40	$98.65	$789.20	$56.77	$84.50
1 Laborer	47.25	378.00	70.35	562.80		
1 Crawler Crane, 40 Ton		1362.63		1498.89		
1 F.E. Attachment, 1.5 C.Y.		97.47		107.22	91.26	100.38
16 L.H., Daily Totals		$2368.50		$2958.11	$148.03	$184.88

Crews - Standard

Crew No.	Bare Costs		Incl. Subs O&P		Cost Per Labor-Hour	
Crew B-12P	Hr.	Daily	Hr.	Daily	Bare Costs	Incl. O&P
1 Equip. Oper. (crane)	$66.30	$530.40	$98.65	$789.20	$56.77	$84.50
1 Laborer	47.25	378.00	70.35	562.80		
1 Crawler Crane, 40 Ton		1362.63		1498.89		
1 Dragline Bucket, 1.5 C.Y.		37.32		41.05	87.50	96.25
16 L.H., Daily Totals		$2308.35		$2891.95	$144.27	$180.75
Crew B-12Q	Hr.	Daily	Hr.	Daily	Bare Costs	Incl. O&P
1 Equip. Oper. (crane)	$66.30	$530.40	$98.65	$789.20	$56.77	$84.50
1 Laborer	47.25	378.00	70.35	562.80		
1 Hyd. Excavator, 5/8 C.Y.		813.17		894.49	50.82	55.91
16 L.H., Daily Totals		$1721.57		$2246.49	$107.60	$140.41
Crew B-12S	Hr.	Daily	Hr.	Daily	Bare Costs	Incl. O&P
1 Equip. Oper. (crane)	$66.30	$530.40	$98.65	$789.20	$56.77	$84.50
1 Laborer	47.25	378.00	70.35	562.80		
1 Hyd. Excavator, 2.5 C.Y.		1683.69		1852.06	105.23	115.75
16 L.H., Daily Totals		$2592.09		$3204.06	$162.01	$200.25
Crew B-12T	Hr.	Daily	Hr.	Daily	Bare Costs	Incl. O&P
1 Equip. Oper. (crane)	$66.30	$530.40	$98.65	$789.20	$56.77	$84.50
1 Laborer	47.25	378.00	70.35	562.80		
1 Crawler Crane, 75 Ton		2189.46		2408.41		
1 F.E. Attachment, 3 C.Y.		127.10		139.81	144.79	159.26
16 L.H., Daily Totals		$3224.96		$3900.22	$201.56	$243.76
Crew B-12V	Hr.	Daily	Hr.	Daily	Bare Costs	Incl. O&P
1 Equip. Oper. (crane)	$66.30	$530.40	$98.65	$789.20	$56.77	$84.50
1 Laborer	47.25	378.00	70.35	562.80		
1 Crawler Crane, 75 Ton		2189.46		2408.41		
1 Dragline Bucket, 3 C.Y.		51.71		56.88	140.07	154.08
16 L.H., Daily Totals		$3149.57		$3817.29	$196.85	$238.58
Crew B-12Y	Hr.	Daily	Hr.	Daily	Bare Costs	Incl. O&P
1 Equip. Oper. (crane)	$66.30	$530.40	$98.65	$789.20	$53.60	$79.78
2 Laborers	47.25	756.00	70.35	1125.60		
1 Hyd. Excavator, 3.5 C.Y.		2394.44		2633.88	99.77	109.75
24 L.H., Daily Totals		$3680.84		$4548.68	$153.37	$189.53
Crew B-12Z	Hr.	Daily	Hr.	Daily	Bare Costs	Incl. O&P
1 Equip. Oper. (crane)	$66.30	$530.40	$98.65	$789.20	$53.60	$79.78
2 Laborers	47.25	756.00	70.35	1125.60		
1 Hyd. Excavator, 2.5 C.Y.		1683.69		1852.06	70.15	77.17
24 L.H., Daily Totals		$2970.09		$3766.86	$123.75	$156.95
Crew B-13	Hr.	Daily	Hr.	Daily	Bare Costs	Incl. O&P
1 Labor Foreman (outside)	$49.25	$394.00	$73.30	$586.40	$51.56	$76.75
4 Laborers	47.25	1512.00	70.35	2251.20		
1 Equip. Oper. (crane)	66.30	530.40	98.65	789.20		
1 Equip. Oper. (oiler)	56.40	451.20	83.90	671.20		
1 Hyd. Crane, 25 Ton		2273.31		2500.64	40.59	44.65
56 L.H., Daily Totals		$5160.91		$6798.64	$92.16	$121.40

Crew No.	Bare Costs		Incl. Subs O&P		Cost Per Labor-Hour	
Crew B-13A	Hr.	Daily	Hr.	Daily	Bare Costs	Incl. O&P
1 Labor Foreman (outside)	$49.25	$394.00	$73.30	$586.40	$54.39	$81.04
2 Laborers	47.25	756.00	70.35	1125.60		
2 Equipment Operators (med.)	63.05	1008.80	93.80	1500.80		
2 Truck Drivers (heavy)	55.45	887.20	82.85	1325.60		
1 Crawler Crane, 75 Ton		2189.46		2408.41		
1 Crawler Loader, 4 C.Y.		1506.11		1656.72		
2 Dump Trucks, 8 C.Y., 220 H.P.		834.98		918.48	80.90	88.99
56 L.H., Daily Totals		$7576.55		$9522.00	$135.30	$170.04
Crew B-13B	Hr.	Daily	Hr.	Daily	Bare Costs	Incl. O&P
1 Labor Foreman (outside)	$49.25	$394.00	$73.30	$586.40	$51.56	$76.75
4 Laborers	47.25	1512.00	70.35	2251.20		
1 Equip. Oper. (crane)	66.30	530.40	98.65	789.20		
1 Equip. Oper. (oiler)	56.40	451.20	83.90	671.20		
1 Hyd. Crane, 55 Ton		2461.06		2707.17	43.95	48.34
56 L.H., Daily Totals		$5348.66		$7005.17	$95.51	$125.09
Crew B-13C	Hr.	Daily	Hr.	Daily	Bare Costs	Incl. O&P
1 Labor Foreman (outside)	$49.25	$394.00	$73.30	$586.40	$51.56	$76.75
4 Laborers	47.25	1512.00	70.35	2251.20		
1 Equip. Oper. (crane)	66.30	530.40	98.65	789.20		
1 Equip. Oper. (oiler)	56.40	451.20	83.90	671.20		
1 Crawler Crane, 100 Ton		1552.12		1707.33	27.72	30.49
56 L.H., Daily Totals		$4439.72		$6005.33	$79.28	$107.24
Crew B-13D	Hr.	Daily	Hr.	Daily	Bare Costs	Incl. O&P
1 Laborer	$47.25	$378.00	$70.35	$562.80	$56.77	$84.50
1 Equip. Oper. (crane)	66.30	530.40	98.65	789.20		
1 Hyd. Excavator, 1 C.Y.		986.56		1085.22		
1 Trench Box		131.49		144.64	69.88	76.87
16 L.H., Daily Totals		$2026.45		$2581.86	$126.65	$161.37
Crew B-13E	Hr.	Daily	Hr.	Daily	Bare Costs	Incl. O&P
1 Laborer	$47.25	$378.00	$70.35	$562.80	$56.77	$84.50
1 Equip. Oper. (crane)	66.30	530.40	98.65	789.20		
1 Hyd. Excavator, 1.5 C.Y.		1185.24		1303.76		
1 Trench Box		131.49		144.64	82.30	90.53
16 L.H., Daily Totals		$2225.13		$2800.40	$139.07	$175.03
Crew B-13F	Hr.	Daily	Hr.	Daily	Bare Costs	Incl. O&P
1 Laborer	$47.25	$378.00	$70.35	$562.80	$56.77	$84.50
1 Equip. Oper. (crane)	66.30	530.40	98.65	789.20		
1 Hyd. Excavator, 3.5 C.Y.		2394.44		2633.88		
1 Trench Box		131.49		144.64	157.87	173.66
16 L.H., Daily Totals		$3434.33		$4130.52	$214.65	$258.16
Crew B-13G	Hr.	Daily	Hr.	Daily	Bare Costs	Incl. O&P
1 Laborer	$47.25	$378.00	$70.35	$562.80	$56.77	$84.50
1 Equip. Oper. (crane)	66.30	530.40	98.65	789.20		
1 Hyd. Excavator, .75 C.Y.		915.34		1006.87		
1 Trench Box		131.49		144.64	65.43	71.97
16 L.H., Daily Totals		$1955.23		$2503.51	$122.20	$156.47
Crew B-13H	Hr.	Daily	Hr.	Daily	Bare Costs	Incl. O&P
1 Laborer	$47.25	$378.00	$70.35	$562.80	$56.77	$84.50
1 Equip. Oper. (crane)	66.30	530.40	98.65	789.20		
1 Gradall, 5/8 C.Y.		880.91		969.00		
1 Trench Box		131.49		144.64	63.27	69.60
16 L.H., Daily Totals		$1920.80		$2465.64	$120.05	$154.10

Crews - Standard

Crew No.		Bare Costs		Incl. Subs O&P		Cost Per Labor-Hour	
Crew B-13I	Hr.	Daily	Hr.	Daily	Bare Costs	Incl. O&P
1 Laborer	$47.25	$378.00	$70.35	$562.80	$56.77	$84.50
1 Equip. Oper. (crane)	66.30	530.40	98.65	789.20		
1 Gradall, 3 Ton, 1 C.Y.		1520.84		1672.92		
1 Trench Box		131.49		144.64	103.27	113.60
16 L.H., Daily Totals		$2560.73		$3169.56	$160.05	$198.10

Crew B-13J	Hr.	Daily	Hr.	Daily	Bare Costs	Incl. O&P
1 Laborer	$47.25	$378.00	$70.35	$562.80	$56.77	$84.50
1 Equip. Oper. (crane)	66.30	530.40	98.65	789.20		
1 Hyd. Excavator, 2.5 C.Y.		1683.69		1852.06		
1 Trench Box		131.49		144.64	113.45	124.79
16 L.H., Daily Totals		$2723.58		$3348.70	$170.22	$209.29

Crew B-13K	Hr.	Daily	Hr.	Daily	Bare Costs	Incl. O&P
2 Equip. Opers. (crane)	$66.30	$1060.80	$98.65	$1578.40	$66.30	$98.65
1 Hyd. Excavator, .75 C.Y.		915.34		1006.87		
1 Hyd. Hammer, 4000 ft-lb		715.03		786.53		
1 Hyd. Excavator, .75 C.Y.		915.34		1006.87	159.11	175.02
16 L.H., Daily Totals		$3606.51		$4378.68	$225.41	$273.67

Crew B-13L	Hr.	Daily	Hr.	Daily	Bare Costs	Incl. O&P
2 Equip. Opers. (crane)	$66.30	$1060.80	$98.65	$1578.40	$66.30	$98.65
1 Hyd. Excavator, 1.5 C.Y.		1185.24		1303.76		
1 Hyd. Hammer, 5000 ft-lb		776.94		854.63		
1 Hyd. Excavator, .75 C.Y.		915.34		1006.87	179.85	197.83
16 L.H., Daily Totals		$3938.32		$4743.67	$246.15	$296.48

Crew B-13M	Hr.	Daily	Hr.	Daily	Bare Costs	Incl. O&P
2 Equip. Opers. (crane)	$66.30	$1060.80	$98.65	$1578.40	$66.30	$98.65
1 Hyd. Excavator, 2.5 C.Y.		1683.69		1852.06		
1 Hyd. Hammer, 8000 ft-lb		1011.13		1112.24		
1 Hyd. Excavator, 1.5 C.Y.		1185.24		1303.76	242.50	266.75
16 L.H., Daily Totals		$4940.86		$5846.47	$308.80	$365.40

Crew B-13N	Hr.	Daily	Hr.	Daily	Bare Costs	Incl. O&P
2 Equip. Opers. (crane)	$66.30	$1060.80	$98.65	$1578.40	$66.30	$98.65
1 Hyd. Excavator, 3.5 C.Y.		2394.44		2633.88		
1 Hyd. Hammer, 12,000 ft-lb		1162.80		1279.08		
1 Hyd. Excavator, 1.5 C.Y.		1185.24		1303.76	296.40	326.05
16 L.H., Daily Totals		$5803.28		$6795.13	$362.70	$424.70

Crew B-14	Hr.	Daily	Hr.	Daily	Bare Costs	Incl. O&P
1 Labor Foreman (outside)	$49.25	$394.00	$73.30	$586.40	$49.66	$73.92
4 Laborers	47.25	1512.00	70.35	2251.20		
1 Equip. Oper. (light)	59.70	477.60	88.85	710.80		
1 Backhoe Loader, 48 H.P.		277.19		304.91	5.77	6.35
48 L.H., Daily Totals		$2660.79		$3853.31	$55.43	$80.28

Crew B-14A	Hr.	Daily	Hr.	Daily	Bare Costs	Incl. O&P
1 Equip. Oper. (crane)	$66.30	$530.40	$98.65	$789.20	$59.95	$89.22
.5 Laborer	47.25	189.00	70.35	281.40		
1 Hyd. Excavator, 4.5 C.Y.		3788.37		4167.21	315.70	347.27
12 L.H., Daily Totals		$4507.77		$5237.81	$375.65	$436.48

Crew B-14B	Hr.	Daily	Hr.	Daily	Bare Costs	Incl. O&P
1 Equip. Oper. (crane)	$66.30	$530.40	$98.65	$789.20	$59.95	$89.22
.5 Laborer	47.25	189.00	70.35	281.40		
1 Hyd. Excavator, 6 C.Y.		3843.97		4228.37	320.33	352.36
12 L.H., Daily Totals		$4563.37		$5298.97	$380.28	$441.58

Crew B-14C	Hr.	Daily	Hr.	Daily	Bare Costs	Incl. O&P
1 Equip. Oper. (crane)	$66.30	$530.40	$98.65	$789.20	$59.95	$89.22
.5 Laborer	47.25	189.00	70.35	281.40		
1 Hyd. Excavator, 7 C.Y.		4206.21		4626.83	350.52	385.57
12 L.H., Daily Totals		$4925.61		$5697.43	$410.47	$474.79

Crew B-14F	Hr.	Daily	Hr.	Daily	Bare Costs	Incl. O&P
1 Equip. Oper. (crane)	$66.30	$530.40	$98.65	$789.20	$59.95	$89.22
.5 Laborer	47.25	189.00	70.35	281.40		
1 Hyd. Shovel, 7 C.Y.		4549.05		5003.95	379.09	417.00
12 L.H., Daily Totals		$5268.45		$6074.56	$439.04	$506.21

Crew B-14G	Hr.	Daily	Hr.	Daily	Bare Costs	Incl. O&P
1 Equip. Oper. (crane)	$66.30	$530.40	$98.65	$789.20	$59.95	$89.22
.5 Laborer	47.25	189.00	70.35	281.40		
1 Hyd. Shovel, 12 C.Y.		6601.66		7261.83	550.14	605.15
12 L.H., Daily Totals		$7321.06		$8332.43	$610.09	$694.37

Crew B-14J	Hr.	Daily	Hr.	Daily	Bare Costs	Incl. O&P
1 Equip. Oper. (medium)	$63.05	$504.40	$93.80	$750.40	$57.78	$85.98
.5 Laborer	47.25	189.00	70.35	281.40		
1 F.E. Loader, 8 C.Y.		1999.44		2199.38	166.62	183.28
12 L.H., Daily Totals		$2692.84		$3231.18	$224.40	$269.27

Crew B-14K	Hr.	Daily	Hr.	Daily	Bare Costs	Incl. O&P
1 Equip. Oper. (medium)	$63.05	$504.40	$93.80	$750.40	$57.78	$85.98
.5 Laborer	47.25	189.00	70.35	281.40		
1 F.E. Loader, 10 C.Y.		2862.71		3148.98	238.56	262.42
12 L.H., Daily Totals		$3556.11		$4180.78	$296.34	$348.40

Crew B-15	Hr.	Daily	Hr.	Daily	Bare Costs	Incl. O&P
1 Equipment Oper. (med.)	$63.05	$504.40	$93.80	$750.40	$56.45	$84.19
.5 Laborer	47.25	189.00	70.35	281.40		
2 Truck Drivers (heavy)	55.45	887.20	82.85	1325.60		
2 Dump Trucks, 12 C.Y., 400 H.P.		1582.72		1740.99		
1 Dozer, 200 H.P.		1382.36		1520.60	105.90	116.49
28 L.H., Daily Totals		$4545.68		$5618.99	$162.35	$200.68

Crew B-16	Hr.	Daily	Hr.	Daily	Bare Costs	Incl. O&P
1 Labor Foreman (outside)	$49.25	$394.00	$73.30	$586.40	$49.80	$74.21
2 Laborers	47.25	756.00	70.35	1125.60		
1 Truck Driver (heavy)	55.45	443.60	82.85	662.80		
1 Dump Truck, 12 C.Y., 400 H.P.		791.36		870.50	24.73	27.20
32 L.H., Daily Totals		$2384.96		$3245.30	$74.53	$101.42

Crew B-17	Hr.	Daily	Hr.	Daily	Bare Costs	Incl. O&P
2 Laborers	$47.25	$756.00	$70.35	$1125.60	$52.41	$78.10
1 Equip. Oper. (light)	59.70	477.60	88.85	710.80		
1 Truck Driver (heavy)	55.45	443.60	82.85	662.80		
1 Backhoe Loader, 48 H.P.		277.19		304.91		
1 Dump Truck, 8 C.Y., 220 H.P.		417.49		459.24	21.71	23.88
32 L.H., Daily Totals		$2371.88		$3263.35	$74.12	$101.98

Crew B-17A	Hr.	Daily	Hr.	Daily	Bare Costs	Incl. O&P
2 Labor Foremen (outside)	$49.25	$788.00	$73.30	$1172.80	$50.65	$75.57
6 Laborers	47.25	2268.00	70.35	3376.80		
1 Skilled Worker Foreman (out)	63.25	506.00	95.00	760.00		
1 Skilled Worker	61.25	490.00	92.00	736.00		
80 L.H., Daily Totals		$4052.00		$6045.60	$50.65	$75.57

Crews - Standard

Crew No.	Bare Costs		Incl. Subs O&P		Cost Per Labor-Hour	
Crew B-17B	**Hr.**	**Daily**	**Hr.**	**Daily**	**Bare Costs**	**Incl. O&P**
2 Laborers	$47.25	$756.00	$70.35	$1125.60	$52.41	$78.10
1 Equip. Oper. (light)	59.70	477.60	88.85	710.80		
1 Truck Driver (heavy)	55.45	443.60	82.85	662.80		
1 Backhoe Loader, 48 H.P.		277.19		304.91		
1 Dump Truck, 12 C.Y., 400 H.P.		791.36		870.50	33.39	36.73
32 L.H., Daily Totals		$2745.75		$3674.61	$85.80	$114.83
Crew B-17C	**Hr.**	**Daily**	**Hr.**	**Daily**	**Bare Costs**	**Incl. O&P**
1 Labor Foreman (outside)	$49.25	$394.00	$73.30	$586.40	$52.13	$77.64
3 Laborers	47.25	1134.00	70.35	1688.40		
1 Equip. Oper. (heavy)	66.30	530.40	98.65	789.20		
1 Truck Driver (heavy)	55.45	443.60	82.85	662.80		
1 Hyd. Excavator, 2 C.Y.		1096.14		1205.75		
1 Dump Truck, 12 C.Y., 400 H.P.		791.36		870.50		
1 P/U, 3/4 ton, Tool Truck		157.41		173.15	42.60	46.86
48 L.H., Daily Totals		$4546.91		$5976.20	$94.73	$124.50
Crew B-18	**Hr.**	**Daily**	**Hr.**	**Daily**	**Bare Costs**	**Incl. O&P**
1 Labor Foreman (outside)	$49.25	$394.00	$73.30	$586.40	$47.92	$71.33
2 Laborers	47.25	756.00	70.35	1125.60		
1 Vibrating Plate, Gas, 21"		146.12		160.73	6.09	6.70
24 L.H., Daily Totals		$1296.12		$1872.73	$54.01	$78.03
Crew B-19	**Hr.**	**Daily**	**Hr.**	**Daily**	**Bare Costs**	**Incl. O&P**
1 Pile Driver Foreman (outside)	$62.50	$500.00	$96.70	$773.60	$61.69	$94.04
4 Pile Drivers	60.50	1936.00	93.60	2995.20		
2 Equip. Oper. (crane)	66.30	1060.80	98.65	1578.40		
1 Equip. Oper. (oiler)	56.40	451.20	83.90	671.20		
1 Crawler Crane, 40 Ton		1362.63		1498.89		
1 Lead, 90' High		409.90		450.89		
1 Hammer, Diesel, 22k ft-lb		485.21		533.73	35.28	38.80
64 L.H., Daily Totals		$6205.74		$8501.91	$96.96	$132.84
Crew B-19A	**Hr.**	**Daily**	**Hr.**	**Daily**	**Bare Costs**	**Incl. O&P**
1 Pile Driver Foreman (outside)	$62.50	$500.00	$96.70	$773.60	$61.69	$94.04
4 Pile Drivers	60.50	1936.00	93.60	2995.20		
2 Equip. Oper. (crane)	66.30	1060.80	98.65	1578.40		
1 Equip. Oper. (oiler)	56.40	451.20	83.90	671.20		
1 Crawler Crane, 75 Ton		2189.46		2408.41		
1 Lead, 90' High		409.90		450.89		
1 Hammer, Diesel, 41k ft-lb		640.74		704.81	50.63	55.69
64 L.H., Daily Totals		$7188.10		$9582.51	$112.31	$149.73
Crew B-19B	**Hr.**	**Daily**	**Hr.**	**Daily**	**Bare Costs**	**Incl. O&P**
1 Pile Driver Foreman (outside)	$62.50	$500.00	$96.70	$773.60	$61.69	$94.04
4 Pile Drivers	60.50	1936.00	93.60	2995.20		
2 Equip. Oper. (crane)	66.30	1060.80	98.65	1578.40		
1 Equip. Oper. (oiler)	56.40	451.20	83.90	671.20		
1 Crawler Crane, 40 Ton		1362.63		1498.89		
1 Lead, 90' High		409.90		450.89		
1 Hammer, Diesel, 22k ft-lb		485.21		533.73		
1 Barge, 400 Ton		957.33		1053.06	50.24	55.26
64 L.H., Daily Totals		$7163.07		$9554.98	$111.92	$149.30

Crew No.	Bare Costs		Incl. Subs O&P		Cost Per Labor-Hour	
Crew B-19C	**Hr.**	**Daily**	**Hr.**	**Daily**	**Bare Costs**	**Incl. O&P**
1 Pile Driver Foreman (outside)	$62.50	$500.00	$96.70	$773.60	$61.69	$94.04
4 Pile Drivers	60.50	1936.00	93.60	2995.20		
2 Equip. Oper. (crane)	66.30	1060.80	98.65	1578.40		
1 Equip. Oper. (oiler)	56.40	451.20	83.90	671.20		
1 Crawler Crane, 75 Ton		2189.46		2408.41		
1 Lead, 90' High		409.90		450.89		
1 Hammer, Diesel, 41k ft-lb		640.74		704.81		
1 Barge, 400 Ton		957.33		1053.06	65.58	72.14
64 L.H., Daily Totals		$8145.43		$10635.57	$127.27	$166.18
Crew B-20	**Hr.**	**Daily**	**Hr.**	**Daily**	**Bare Costs**	**Incl. O&P**
1 Labor Foreman (outside)	$49.25	$394.00	$73.30	$586.40	$52.58	$78.55
1 Skilled Worker	61.25	490.00	92.00	736.00		
1 Laborer	47.25	378.00	70.35	562.80		
24 L.H., Daily Totals		$1262.00		$1885.20	$52.58	$78.55
Crew B-20A	**Hr.**	**Daily**	**Hr.**	**Daily**	**Bare Costs**	**Incl. O&P**
1 Labor Foreman (outside)	$49.25	$394.00	$73.30	$586.40	$56.55	$84.26
1 Laborer	47.25	378.00	70.35	562.80		
1 Plumber	72.05	576.40	107.45	859.60		
1 Plumber Apprentice	57.65	461.20	85.95	687.60		
32 L.H., Daily Totals		$1809.60		$2696.40	$56.55	$84.26
Crew B-21	**Hr.**	**Daily**	**Hr.**	**Daily**	**Bare Costs**	**Incl. O&P**
1 Labor Foreman (outside)	$49.25	$394.00	$73.30	$586.40	$54.54	$81.42
1 Skilled Worker	61.25	490.00	92.00	736.00		
1 Laborer	47.25	378.00	70.35	562.80		
.5 Equip. Oper. (crane)	66.30	265.20	98.65	394.60		
.5 S.P. Crane, 4x4, 5 Ton		192.94		212.24	6.89	7.58
28 L.H., Daily Totals		$1720.15		$2492.04	$61.43	$89.00
Crew B-21A	**Hr.**	**Daily**	**Hr.**	**Daily**	**Bare Costs**	**Incl. O&P**
1 Labor Foreman (outside)	$49.25	$394.00	$73.30	$586.40	$58.50	$87.14
1 Laborer	47.25	378.00	70.35	562.80		
1 Plumber	72.05	576.40	107.45	859.60		
1 Plumber Apprentice	57.65	461.20	85.95	687.60		
1 Equip. Oper. (crane)	66.30	530.40	98.65	789.20		
1 S.P. Crane, 4x4, 12 Ton		637.99		701.79	15.95	17.54
40 L.H., Daily Totals		$2977.99		$4187.39	$74.45	$104.68
Crew B-21B	**Hr.**	**Daily**	**Hr.**	**Daily**	**Bare Costs**	**Incl. O&P**
1 Labor Foreman (outside)	$49.25	$394.00	$73.30	$586.40	$51.46	$76.60
3 Laborers	47.25	1134.00	70.35	1688.40		
1 Equip. Oper. (crane)	66.30	530.40	98.65	789.20		
1 Hyd. Crane, 12 Ton		2150.65		2365.72	53.77	59.14
40 L.H., Daily Totals		$4209.05		$5429.72	$105.23	$135.74
Crew B-21C	**Hr.**	**Daily**	**Hr.**	**Daily**	**Bare Costs**	**Incl. O&P**
1 Labor Foreman (outside)	$49.25	$394.00	$73.30	$586.40	$51.56	$76.75
4 Laborers	47.25	1512.00	70.35	2251.20		
1 Equip. Oper. (crane)	66.30	530.40	98.65	789.20		
1 Equip. Oper. (oiler)	56.40	451.20	83.90	671.20		
2 Cutting Torches		28.48		31.33		
2 Sets of Gases		377.34		415.07		
1 Lattice Boom Crane, 90 Ton		2689.54		2958.49	55.27	60.80
56 L.H., Daily Totals		$5982.96		$7702.90	$106.84	$137.55

Crews - Standard

Crew No.		Bare Costs		Incl. Subs O&P		Cost Per Labor-Hour	
Crew B-22	Hr.	Daily	Hr.	Daily	Bare Costs	Incl. O&P
1 Labor Foreman (outside)	$49.25	$394.00	$73.30	$586.40	$55.33	$82.57
1 Skilled Worker	61.25	490.00	92.00	736.00		
1 Laborer	47.25	378.00	70.35	562.80		
.75 Equip. Oper. (crane)	66.30	397.80	98.65	591.90		
.75 S.P. Crane, 4x4, 5 Ton		289.42		318.36	9.65	10.61
30 L.H., Daily Totals		$1949.22		$2795.46	$64.97	$93.18
Crew B-22A	Hr.	Daily	Hr.	Daily	Bare Costs	Incl. O&P
1 Labor Foreman (outside)	$49.25	$394.00	$73.30	$586.40	$54.26	$80.93
1 Skilled Worker	61.25	490.00	92.00	736.00		
2 Laborers	47.25	756.00	70.35	1125.60		
1 Equipment Operator, Crane	66.30	530.40	98.65	789.20		
1 S.P. Crane, 4x4, 5 Ton		385.89		424.48		
1 Butt Fusion Mach., 4"-12" diam.		332.25		365.48	17.95	19.75
40 L.H., Daily Totals		$2888.54		$4027.15	$72.21	$100.68
Crew B-22B	Hr.	Daily	Hr.	Daily	Bare Costs	Incl. O&P
1 Labor Foreman (outside)	$49.25	$394.00	$73.30	$586.40	$54.26	$80.93
1 Skilled Worker	61.25	490.00	92.00	736.00		
2 Laborers	47.25	756.00	70.35	1125.60		
1 Equip. Oper. (crane)	66.30	530.40	98.65	789.20		
1 S.P. Crane, 4x4, 5 Ton		385.89		424.48		
1 Butt Fusion Mach., 8"-24" diam.		787.50		866.25	29.33	32.27
40 L.H., Daily Totals		$3343.79		$4527.93	$83.59	$113.20
Crew B-22C	Hr.	Daily	Hr.	Daily	Bare Costs	Incl. O&P
1 Skilled Worker	$61.25	$490.00	$92.00	$736.00	$54.25	$81.17
1 Laborer	47.25	378.00	70.35	562.80		
1 Butt Fusion Mach., 2"-8" diam.		280.48		308.53	17.53	19.28
16 L.H., Daily Totals		$1148.48		$1607.33	$71.78	$100.46
Crew B-23	Hr.	Daily	Hr.	Daily	Bare Costs	Incl. O&P
1 Labor Foreman (outside)	$49.25	$394.00	$73.30	$586.40	$47.65	$70.94
4 Laborers	47.25	1512.00	70.35	2251.20		
1 Drill Rig, Truck-Mounted		856.23		941.85		
1 Flatbed Truck, Gas, 3 Ton		391.02		430.12	31.18	34.30
40 L.H., Daily Totals		$3153.25		$4209.57	$78.83	$105.24
Crew B-23A	Hr.	Daily	Hr.	Daily	Bare Costs	Incl. O&P
1 Labor Foreman (outside)	$49.25	$394.00	$73.30	$586.40	$53.18	$79.15
1 Laborer	47.25	378.00	70.35	562.80		
1 Equip. Oper. (medium)	63.05	504.40	93.80	750.40		
1 Drill Rig, Truck-Mounted		856.23		941.85		
1 Pickup Truck, 3/4 Ton		122.56		134.82	40.78	44.86
24 L.H., Daily Totals		$2255.19		$2976.27	$93.97	$124.01
Crew B-23B	Hr.	Daily	Hr.	Daily	Bare Costs	Incl. O&P
1 Labor Foreman (outside)	$49.25	$394.00	$73.30	$586.40	$53.18	$79.15
1 Laborer	47.25	378.00	70.35	562.80		
1 Equip. Oper. (medium)	63.05	504.40	93.80	750.40		
1 Drill Rig, Truck-Mounted		856.23		941.85		
1 Pickup Truck, 3/4 Ton		122.56		134.82		
1 Centr. Water Pump, 6"		386.48		425.13	56.89	62.57
24 L.H., Daily Totals		$2641.67		$3401.40	$110.07	$141.72
Crew B-24	Hr.	Daily	Hr.	Daily	Bare Costs	Incl. O&P
1 Cement Finisher	$55.00	$440.00	$80.45	$643.60	$53.62	$79.35
1 Laborer	47.25	378.00	70.35	562.80		
1 Carpenter	58.60	468.80	87.25	698.00		
24 L.H., Daily Totals		$1286.80		$1904.40	$53.62	$79.35

Crew No.		Bare Costs		Incl. Subs O&P		Cost Per Labor-Hour	
Crew B-25	Hr.	Daily	Hr.	Daily	Bare Costs	Incl. O&P
1 Labor Foreman (outside)	$49.25	$394.00	$73.30	$586.40	$51.74	$77.01
7 Laborers	47.25	2646.00	70.35	3939.60		
3 Equip. Oper. (medium)	63.05	1513.20	93.80	2251.20		
1 Asphalt Paver, 130 H.P.		2352.46		2587.71		
1 Tandem Roller, 10 Ton		379.22		417.14		
1 Roller, Pneum. Whl., 12 Ton		384.55		423.01	35.41	38.95
88 L.H., Daily Totals		$7669.43		$10205.05	$87.15	$115.97
Crew B-25B	Hr.	Daily	Hr.	Daily	Bare Costs	Incl. O&P
1 Labor Foreman (outside)	$49.25	$394.00	$73.30	$586.40	$52.68	$78.41
7 Laborers	47.25	2646.00	70.35	3939.60		
4 Equip. Oper. (medium)	63.05	2017.60	93.80	3001.60		
1 Asphalt Paver, 130 H.P.		2352.46		2587.71		
2 Tandem Rollers, 10 Ton		758.44		834.28		
1 Roller, Pneum. Whl., 12 Ton		384.55		423.01	36.41	40.05
96 L.H., Daily Totals		$8553.05		$11372.59	$89.09	$118.46
Crew B-25C	Hr.	Daily	Hr.	Daily	Bare Costs	Incl. O&P
1 Labor Foreman (outside)	$49.25	$394.00	$73.30	$586.40	$52.85	$78.66
3 Laborers	47.25	1134.00	70.35	1688.40		
2 Equip. Oper. (medium)	63.05	1008.80	93.80	1500.80		
1 Asphalt Paver, 130 H.P.		2352.46		2587.71		
1 Tandem Roller, 10 Ton		379.22		417.14	56.91	62.60
48 L.H., Daily Totals		$5268.48		$6780.45	$109.76	$141.26
Crew B-25D	Hr.	Daily	Hr.	Daily	Bare Costs	Incl. O&P
1 Labor Foreman (outside)	$49.25	$394.00	$73.30	$586.40	$53.12	$79.06
3 Laborers	47.25	1134.00	70.35	1688.40		
2.130 Equip. Oper. (medium)	63.05	1074.37	93.80	1598.35		
.13 Truck Driver (heavy)	55.45	57.67	82.85	86.16		
.13 Truck Tractor, 6x4, 380 H.P.		70.98		78.08		
.13 Dist. Tanker, 3000 Gallon		47.72		52.50		
1 Asphalt Paver, 130 H.P.		2352.46		2587.71		
1 Tandem Roller, 10 Ton		379.22		417.14	56.92	62.61
50.08 L.H., Daily Totals		$5510.42		$7094.73	$110.03	$141.67
Crew B-25E	Hr.	Daily	Hr.	Daily	Bare Costs	Incl. O&P
1 Labor Foreman (outside)	$49.25	$394.00	$73.30	$586.40	$53.34	$79.40
3 Laborers	47.25	1134.00	70.35	1688.40		
2.250 Equip. Oper. (medium)	63.05	1134.90	93.80	1688.40		
.25 Truck Driver (heavy)	55.45	110.90	82.85	165.70		
.25 Truck Tractor, 6x4, 380 H.P.		136.50		150.14		
.25 Dist. Tanker, 3000 Gallon		91.78		100.95		
1 Asphalt Paver, 130 H.P.		2352.46		2587.71		
1 Tandem Roller, 10 Ton		379.22		417.14	56.92	62.61
52 L.H., Daily Totals		$5733.75		$7384.85	$110.26	$142.02
Crew B-26	Hr.	Daily	Hr.	Daily	Bare Costs	Incl. O&P
1 Labor Foreman (outside)	$49.25	$394.00	$73.30	$586.40	$52.58	$78.17
6 Laborers	47.25	2268.00	70.35	3376.80		
2 Equip. Oper. (medium)	63.05	1008.80	93.80	1500.80		
1 Rodman (reinf.)	64.55	516.40	96.40	771.20		
1 Cement Finisher	55.00	440.00	80.45	643.60		
1 Grader, 30,000 Lbs.		1091.19		1200.31		
1 Paving Mach. & Equip.		2747.64		3022.40	43.62	47.99
88 L.H., Daily Totals		$8466.03		$11101.51	$96.20	$126.15

Crews - Standard

Crew No.	Bare Costs		Incl. Subs O&P		Cost Per Labor-Hour	
Crew B-26A	Hr.	Daily	Hr.	Daily	Bare Costs	Incl. O&P
1 Labor Foreman (outside)	$49.25	$394.00	$73.30	$586.40	$52.58	$78.17
6 Laborers	47.25	2268.00	70.35	3376.80		
2 Equip. Oper. (medium)	63.05	1008.80	93.80	1500.80		
1 Rodman (reinf.)	64.55	516.40	96.40	771.20		
1 Cement Finisher	55.00	440.00	80.45	643.60		
1 Grader, 30,000 Lbs.		1091.19		1200.31		
1 Paving Mach. & Equip.		2747.64		3022.40		
1 Concrete Saw		176.00		193.60	45.62	50.19
88 L.H., Daily Totals		$8642.03		$11295.11	$98.20	$128.35

Crew B-26B	Hr.	Daily	Hr.	Daily	Bare Costs	Incl. O&P
1 Labor Foreman (outside)	$49.25	$394.00	$73.30	$586.40	$53.45	$79.47
6 Laborers	47.25	2268.00	70.35	3376.80		
3 Equip. Oper. (medium)	63.05	1513.20	93.80	2251.20		
1 Rodman (reinf.)	64.55	516.40	96.40	771.20		
1 Cement Finisher	55.00	440.00	80.45	643.60		
1 Grader, 30,000 Lbs.		1091.19		1200.31		
1 Paving Mach. & Equip.		2747.64		3022.40		
1 Concrete Pump, 110' Boom		1069.53		1176.48	51.13	56.24
96 L.H., Daily Totals		$10039.96		$13028.40	$104.58	$135.71

Crew B-26C	Hr.	Daily	Hr.	Daily	Bare Costs	Incl. O&P
1 Labor Foreman (outside)	$49.25	$394.00	$73.30	$586.40	$51.53	$76.61
6 Laborers	47.25	2268.00	70.35	3376.80		
1 Equip. Oper. (medium)	63.05	504.40	93.80	750.40		
1 Rodman (reinf.)	64.55	516.40	96.40	771.20		
1 Cement Finisher	55.00	440.00	80.45	643.60		
1 Paving Mach. & Equip.		2747.64		3022.40		
1 Concrete Saw		176.00		193.60	36.55	40.20
80 L.H., Daily Totals		$7046.44		$9344.40	$88.08	$116.81

Crew B-27	Hr.	Daily	Hr.	Daily	Bare Costs	Incl. O&P
1 Labor Foreman (outside)	$49.25	$394.00	$73.30	$586.40	$47.75	$71.09
3 Laborers	47.25	1134.00	70.35	1688.40		
1 Berm Machine		897.16		986.88	28.04	30.84
32 L.H., Daily Totals		$2425.16		$3261.68	$75.79	$101.93

Crew B-28	Hr.	Daily	Hr.	Daily	Bare Costs	Incl. O&P
2 Carpenters	$58.60	$937.60	$87.25	$1396.00	$54.82	$81.62
1 Laborer	47.25	378.00	70.35	562.80		
24 L.H., Daily Totals		$1315.60		$1958.80	$54.82	$81.62

Crew B-29	Hr.	Daily	Hr.	Daily	Bare Costs	Incl. O&P
1 Labor Foreman (outside)	$49.25	$394.00	$73.30	$586.40	$51.56	$76.75
4 Laborers	47.25	1512.00	70.35	2251.20		
1 Equip. Oper. (crane)	66.30	530.40	98.65	789.20		
1 Equip. Oper. (oiler)	56.40	451.20	83.90	671.20		
1 Gradall, 5/8 C.Y.		880.91		969.00	15.73	17.30
56 L.H., Daily Totals		$3768.51		$5267.00	$67.29	$94.05

Crew B-30	Hr.	Daily	Hr.	Daily	Bare Costs	Incl. O&P
1 Equip. Oper. (medium)	$63.05	$504.40	$93.80	$750.40	$57.98	$86.50
2 Truck Drivers (heavy)	55.45	887.20	82.85	1325.60		
1 Hyd. Excavator, 1.5 C.Y.		1185.24		1303.76		
2 Dump Trucks, 12 C.Y., 400 H.P.		1582.72		1740.99	115.33	126.86
24 L.H., Daily Totals		$4159.56		$5120.76	$173.32	$213.36

Crew B-31	Hr.	Daily	Hr.	Daily	Bare Costs	Incl. O&P
1 Labor Foreman (outside)	$49.25	$394.00	$73.30	$586.40	$49.92	$74.32
3 Laborers	47.25	1134.00	70.35	1688.40		
1 Carpenter	58.60	468.80	87.25	698.00		
1 Air Compressor, 250 cfm		196.28		215.91		
1 Sheeting Driver		8.19		9.01		
2 -50' Air Hoses, 1.5"		47.20		51.92	6.29	6.92
40 L.H., Daily Totals		$2248.47		$3249.64	$56.21	$81.24

Crew B-32	Hr.	Daily	Hr.	Daily	Bare Costs	Incl. O&P
1 Laborer	$47.25	$378.00	$70.35	$562.80	$59.10	$87.94
3 Equip. Oper. (medium)	63.05	1513.20	93.80	2251.20		
1 Grader, 30,000 Lbs.		1091.19		1200.31		
1 Tandem Roller, 10 Ton		379.22		417.14		
1 Dozer, 200 H.P.		1382.36		1520.60	89.15	98.06
32 L.H., Daily Totals		$4743.97		$5952.05	$148.25	$186.00

Crew B-32A	Hr.	Daily	Hr.	Daily	Bare Costs	Incl. O&P
1 Laborer	$47.25	$378.00	$70.35	$562.80	$57.78	$85.98
2 Equip. Oper. (medium)	63.05	1008.80	93.80	1500.80		
1 Grader, 30,000 Lbs.		1091.19		1200.31		
1 Roller, Vibratory, 25 Ton		529.68		582.65	67.54	74.29
24 L.H., Daily Totals		$3007.67		$3846.56	$125.32	$160.27

Crew B-32B	Hr.	Daily	Hr.	Daily	Bare Costs	Incl. O&P
1 Laborer	$47.25	$378.00	$70.35	$562.80	$57.78	$85.98
2 Equip. Oper. (medium)	63.05	1008.80	93.80	1500.80		
1 Dozer, 200 H.P.		1382.36		1520.60		
1 Roller, Vibratory, 25 Ton		529.68		582.65	79.67	87.64
24 L.H., Daily Totals		$3298.84		$4166.84	$137.45	$173.62

Crew B-32C	Hr.	Daily	Hr.	Daily	Bare Costs	Incl. O&P
1 Labor Foreman (outside)	$49.25	$394.00	$73.30	$586.40	$55.48	$82.57
2 Laborers	47.25	756.00	70.35	1125.60		
3 Equip. Oper. (medium)	63.05	1513.20	93.80	2251.20		
1 Grader, 30,000 Lbs.		1091.19		1200.31		
1 Tandem Roller, 10 Ton		379.22		417.14		
1 Dozer, 200 H.P.		1382.36		1520.60	59.43	65.38
48 L.H., Daily Totals		$5515.97		$7101.25	$114.92	$147.94

Crew B-33A	Hr.	Daily	Hr.	Daily	Bare Costs	Incl. O&P
1 Equip. Oper. (medium)	$63.05	$504.40	$93.80	$750.40	$58.54	$87.10
.5 Laborer	47.25	189.00	70.35	281.40		
.25 Equip. Oper. (medium)	63.05	126.10	93.80	187.60		
1 Scraper, Towed, 7 C.Y.		141.88		156.07		
1.25 Dozers, 300 H.P.		2093.16		2302.48	159.65	175.61
14 L.H., Daily Totals		$3054.54		$3677.95	$218.18	$262.71

Crew B-33B	Hr.	Daily	Hr.	Daily	Bare Costs	Incl. O&P
1 Equip. Oper. (medium)	$63.05	$504.40	$93.80	$750.40	$58.54	$87.10
.5 Laborer	47.25	189.00	70.35	281.40		
.25 Equip. Oper. (medium)	63.05	126.10	93.80	187.60		
1 Scraper, Towed, 10 C.Y.		177.45		195.19		
1.25 Dozers, 300 H.P.		2093.16		2302.48	162.19	178.41
14 L.H., Daily Totals		$3090.11		$3717.07	$220.72	$265.51

Crews - Standard

Crew No.		Bare Costs		Incl. Subs O&P		Cost Per Labor-Hour	
Crew B-33C	Hr.	Daily	Hr.	Daily	Bare Costs	Incl. O&P	
1 Equip. Oper. (medium)	$63.05	$504.40	$93.80	$750.40	$58.54	$87.10	
.5 Laborer	47.25	189.00	70.35	281.40			
.25 Equip. Oper. (medium)	63.05	126.10	93.80	187.60			
1 Scraper, Towed, 15 C.Y.		196.46		216.11			
1.25 Dozers, 300 H.P.		2093.16		2302.48	163.54	179.90	
14 L.H., Daily Totals		$3109.12		$3737.98	$222.08	$267.00	
Crew B-33D	Hr.	Daily	Hr.	Daily	Bare Costs	Incl. O&P	
1 Equip. Oper. (medium)	$63.05	$504.40	$93.80	$750.40	$58.54	$87.10	
.5 Laborer	47.25	189.00	70.35	281.40			
.25 Equip. Oper. (medium)	63.05	126.10	93.80	187.60			
1 S.P. Scraper, 14 C.Y.		2168.71		2385.58			
.25 Dozer, 300 H.P.		418.63		460.50	184.81	203.29	
14 L.H., Daily Totals		$3406.84		$4065.48	$243.35	$290.39	
Crew B-33E	Hr.	Daily	Hr.	Daily	Bare Costs	Incl. O&P	
1 Equip. Oper. (medium)	$63.05	$504.40	$93.80	$750.40	$58.54	$87.10	
.5 Laborer	47.25	189.00	70.35	281.40			
.25 Equip. Oper. (medium)	63.05	126.10	93.80	187.60			
1 S.P. Scraper, 21 C.Y.		2239.60		2463.56			
.25 Dozer, 300 H.P.		418.63		460.50	189.87	208.86	
14 L.H., Daily Totals		$3477.73		$4143.46	$248.41	$295.96	
Crew B-33F	Hr.	Daily	Hr.	Daily	Bare Costs	Incl. O&P	
1 Equip. Oper. (medium)	$63.05	$504.40	$93.80	$750.40	$58.54	$87.10	
.5 Laborer	47.25	189.00	70.35	281.40			
.25 Equip. Oper. (medium)	63.05	126.10	93.80	187.60			
1 Elev. Scraper, 11 C.Y.		1022.46		1124.71			
.25 Dozer, 300 H.P.		418.63		460.50	102.94	113.23	
14 L.H., Daily Totals		$2260.59		$2804.60	$161.47	$200.33	
Crew B-33G	Hr.	Daily	Hr.	Daily	Bare Costs	Incl. O&P	
1 Equip. Oper. (medium)	$63.05	$504.40	$93.80	$750.40	$58.54	$87.10	
.5 Laborer	47.25	189.00	70.35	281.40			
.25 Equip. Oper. (medium)	63.05	126.10	93.80	187.60			
1 Elev. Scraper, 22 C.Y.		2005.03		2205.53			
.25 Dozer, 300 H.P.		418.63		460.50	173.12	190.43	
14 L.H., Daily Totals		$3243.16		$3885.43	$231.65	$277.53	
Crew B-33H	Hr.	Daily	Hr.	Daily	Bare Costs	Incl. O&P	
.5 Laborer	$47.25	$189.00	$70.35	$281.40	$58.54	$87.10	
1 Equipment Operator (med.)	63.05	504.40	93.80	750.40			
.25 Equipment Operator (med.)	63.05	126.10	93.80	187.60			
1 S.P. Scraper, 44 C.Y.		3440.19		3784.21			
.25 Dozer, 410 H.P.		633.99		697.39	291.01	320.11	
14 L.H., Daily Totals		$4893.68		$5701.00	$349.55	$407.21	
Crew B-33J	Hr.	Daily	Hr.	Daily	Bare Costs	Incl. O&P	
1 Equipment Operator (med.)	$63.05	$504.40	$93.80	$750.40	$63.05	$93.80	
1 S.P. Scraper, 14 C.Y.		2168.71		2385.58	271.09	298.20	
8 L.H., Daily Totals		$2673.11		$3135.98	$334.14	$392.00	
Crew B-33K	Hr.	Daily	Hr.	Daily	Bare Costs	Incl. O&P	
1 Equipment Operator (med.)	$63.05	$504.40	$93.80	$750.40	$58.54	$87.10	
.25 Equipment Operator (med.)	63.05	126.10	93.80	187.60			
.5 Laborer	47.25	189.00	70.35	281.40			
1 S.P. Scraper, 31 C.Y.		2972.09		3269.30			
.25 Dozer, 410 H.P.		633.99		697.39	257.58	283.33	
14 L.H., Daily Totals		$4425.58		$5186.09	$316.11	$370.43	

Crew No.		Bare Costs		Incl. Subs O&P		Cost Per Labor-Hour	
Crew B-34A	Hr.	Daily	Hr.	Daily	Bare Costs	Incl. O&P	
1 Truck Driver (heavy)	$55.45	$443.60	$82.85	$662.80	$55.45	$82.85	
1 Dump Truck, 8 C.Y., 220 H.P.		417.49		459.24	52.19	57.40	
8 L.H., Daily Totals		$861.09		$1122.04	$107.64	$140.25	
Crew B-34B	Hr.	Daily	Hr.	Daily	Bare Costs	Incl. O&P	
1 Truck Driver (heavy)	$55.45	$443.60	$82.85	$662.80	$55.45	$82.85	
1 Dump Truck, 12 C.Y., 400 H.P.		791.36		870.50	98.92	108.81	
8 L.H., Daily Totals		$1234.96		$1533.30	$154.37	$191.66	
Crew B-34C	Hr.	Daily	Hr.	Daily	Bare Costs	Incl. O&P	
1 Truck Driver (heavy)	$55.45	$443.60	$82.85	$662.80	$55.45	$82.85	
1 Truck Tractor, 6x4, 380 H.P.		545.98		600.58			
1 Dump Trailer, 16.5 C.Y.		151.94		167.13	87.24	95.96	
8 L.H., Daily Totals		$1141.52		$1430.51	$142.69	$178.81	
Crew B-34D	Hr.	Daily	Hr.	Daily	Bare Costs	Incl. O&P	
1 Truck Driver (heavy)	$55.45	$443.60	$82.85	$662.80	$55.45	$82.85	
1 Truck Tractor, 6x4, 380 H.P.		545.98		600.58			
1 Dump Trailer, 20 C.Y.		168.66		185.53	89.33	98.26	
8 L.H., Daily Totals		$1158.24		$1448.90	$144.78	$181.11	
Crew B-34E	Hr.	Daily	Hr.	Daily	Bare Costs	Incl. O&P	
1 Truck Driver (heavy)	$55.45	$443.60	$82.85	$662.80	$55.45	$82.85	
1 Dump Truck, Off Hwy., 25 Ton		1471.16		1618.28	183.90	202.28	
8 L.H., Daily Totals		$1914.76		$2281.08	$239.35	$285.13	
Crew B-34F	Hr.	Daily	Hr.	Daily	Bare Costs	Incl. O&P	
1 Truck Driver (heavy)	$55.45	$443.60	$82.85	$662.80	$55.45	$82.85	
1 Dump Truck, Off Hwy., 35 Ton		1508.36		1659.20	188.54	207.40	
8 L.H., Daily Totals		$1951.96		$2322.00	$244.00	$290.25	
Crew B-34G	Hr.	Daily	Hr.	Daily	Bare Costs	Incl. O&P	
1 Truck Driver (heavy)	$55.45	$443.60	$82.85	$662.80	$55.45	$82.85	
1 Dump Truck, Off Hwy., 50 Ton		2037.60		2241.36	254.70	280.17	
8 L.H., Daily Totals		$2481.20		$2904.16	$310.15	$363.02	
Crew B-34H	Hr.	Daily	Hr.	Daily	Bare Costs	Incl. O&P	
1 Truck Driver (heavy)	$55.45	$443.60	$82.85	$662.80	$55.45	$82.85	
1 Dump Truck, Off Hwy., 65 Ton		2126.70		2339.37	265.84	292.42	
8 L.H., Daily Totals		$2570.30		$3002.17	$321.29	$375.27	
Crew B-34I	Hr.	Daily	Hr.	Daily	Bare Costs	Incl. O&P	
1 Truck Driver (heavy)	$55.45	$443.60	$82.85	$662.80	$55.45	$82.85	
1 Dump Truck, 18 C.Y., 450 H.P.		788.42		867.26	98.55	108.41	
8 L.H., Daily Totals		$1232.02		$1530.06	$154.00	$191.26	
Crew B-34J	Hr.	Daily	Hr.	Daily	Bare Costs	Incl. O&P	
1 Truck Driver (heavy)	$55.45	$443.60	$82.85	$662.80	$55.45	$82.85	
1 Dump Truck, Off Hwy., 100 Ton		3040.18		3344.20	380.02	418.02	
8 L.H., Daily Totals		$3483.78		$4007.00	$435.47	$500.87	
Crew B-34K	Hr.	Daily	Hr.	Daily	Bare Costs	Incl. O&P	
1 Truck Driver (heavy)	$55.45	$443.60	$82.85	$662.80	$55.45	$82.85	
1 Truck Tractor, 6x4, 450 H.P.		666.04		732.64			
1 Lowbed Trailer, 75 Ton		283.47		311.82	118.69	130.56	
8 L.H., Daily Totals		$1393.11		$1707.26	$174.14	$213.41	

Crews - Standard

Crew No.	Bare Costs Hr.	Bare Costs Daily	Incl. Subs O&P Hr.	Incl. Subs O&P Daily	Cost Per Labor-Hour Bare Costs	Cost Per Labor-Hour Incl. O&P
Crew B-34L						
1 Equip. Oper. (light)	$59.70	$477.60	$88.85	$710.80	$59.70	$88.85
1 Flatbed Truck, Gas, 1.5 Ton		361.95		398.14	45.24	49.77
8 L.H., Daily Totals		$839.55		$1108.94	$104.94	$138.62
Crew B-34M						
1 Equip. Oper. (light)	$59.70	$477.60	$88.85	$710.80	$59.70	$88.85
1 Flatbed Truck, Gas, 3 Ton		391.02		430.12	48.88	53.77
8 L.H., Daily Totals		$868.62		$1140.92	$108.58	$142.62
Crew B-34N						
1 Truck Driver (heavy)	$55.45	$443.60	$82.85	$662.80	$59.25	$88.33
1 Equip. Oper. (medium)	63.05	504.40	93.80	750.40		
1 Truck Tractor, 6x4, 380 H.P.		545.98		600.58		
1 Flatbed Trailer, 40 Ton		206.92		227.61	47.06	51.76
16 L.H., Daily Totals		$1700.90		$2241.39	$106.31	$140.09
Crew B-34P						
1 Pipe Fitter	$72.55	$580.40	$108.20	$865.60	$62.83	$93.67
1 Truck Driver (light)	52.90	423.20	79.00	632.00		
1 Equip. Oper. (medium)	63.05	504.40	93.80	750.40		
1 Flatbed Truck, Gas, 3 Ton		391.02		430.12		
1 Backhoe Loader, 48 H.P.		277.19		304.91	27.84	30.63
24 L.H., Daily Totals		$2176.21		$2983.03	$90.68	$124.29
Crew B-34Q						
1 Pipe Fitter	$72.55	$580.40	$108.20	$865.60	$63.92	$95.28
1 Truck Driver (light)	52.90	423.20	79.00	632.00		
1 Equip. Oper. (crane)	66.30	530.40	98.65	789.20		
1 Flatbed Trailer, 25 Ton		150.61		165.67		
1 Dump Truck, 8 C.Y., 220 H.P.		417.49		459.24		
1 Hyd. Crane, 25 Ton		2273.31		2500.64	118.39	130.23
24 L.H., Daily Totals		$4375.41		$5412.35	$182.31	$225.51
Crew B-34R						
1 Pipe Fitter	$72.55	$580.40	$108.20	$865.60	$63.92	$95.28
1 Truck Driver (light)	52.90	423.20	79.00	632.00		
1 Equip. Oper. (crane)	66.30	530.40	98.65	789.20		
1 Flatbed Trailer, 25 Ton		150.61		165.67		
1 Dump Truck, 8 C.Y., 220 H.P.		417.49		459.24		
1 Hyd. Crane, 25 Ton		2273.31		2500.64		
1 Hyd. Excavator, 1 C.Y.		986.56		1085.22	159.50	175.45
24 L.H., Daily Totals		$5361.97		$6497.57	$223.42	$270.73
Crew B-34S						
2 Pipe Fitters	$72.55	$1160.80	$108.20	$1731.20	$66.71	$99.47
1 Truck Driver (heavy)	55.45	443.60	82.85	662.80		
1 Equip. Oper. (crane)	66.30	530.40	98.65	789.20		
1 Flatbed Trailer, 40 Ton		206.92		227.61		
1 Truck Tractor, 6x4, 380 H.P.		545.98		600.58		
1 Hyd. Crane, 80 Ton		2641.70		2905.87		
1 Hyd. Excavator, 2 C.Y.		1096.14		1205.75	140.34	154.37
32 L.H., Daily Totals		$6625.54		$8123.01	$207.05	$253.84
Crew B-34T						
2 Pipe Fitters	$72.55	$1160.80	$108.20	$1731.20	$66.71	$99.47
1 Truck Driver (heavy)	55.45	443.60	82.85	662.80		
1 Equip. Oper. (crane)	66.30	530.40	98.65	789.20		
1 Flatbed Trailer, 40 Ton		206.92		227.61		
1 Truck Tractor, 6x4, 380 H.P.		545.98		600.58		
1 Hyd. Crane, 80 Ton		2641.70		2905.87	106.08	116.69
32 L.H., Daily Totals		$5529.40		$6917.26	$172.79	$216.16

Crew No.	Bare Costs Hr.	Bare Costs Daily	Incl. Subs O&P Hr.	Incl. Subs O&P Daily	Cost Per Labor-Hour Bare Costs	Cost Per Labor-Hour Incl. O&P
Crew B-34U						
1 Truck Driver (heavy)	$55.45	$443.60	$82.85	$662.80	$57.58	$85.85
1 Equip. Oper. (light)	59.70	477.60	88.85	710.80		
1 Truck Tractor, 220 H.P.		339.98		373.98		
1 Flatbed Trailer, 25 Ton		150.61		165.67	30.66	33.73
16 L.H., Daily Totals		$1411.79		$1913.25	$88.24	$119.58
Crew B-34V						
1 Truck Driver (heavy)	$55.45	$443.60	$82.85	$662.80	$60.48	$90.12
1 Equip. Oper. (crane)	66.30	530.40	98.65	789.20		
1 Equip. Oper. (light)	59.70	477.60	88.85	710.80		
1 Truck Tractor, 6x4, 450 H.P.		666.04		732.64		
1 Equipment Trailer, 50 Ton		336.69		370.36		
1 Pickup Truck, 4x4, 3/4 Ton		191.73		210.90	49.77	54.75
24 L.H., Daily Totals		$2646.06		$3476.71	$110.25	$144.86
Crew B-34W						
5 Truck Drivers (heavy)	$55.45	$2218.00	$82.85	$3314.00	$58.17	$86.74
2 Equip. Opers. (crane)	66.30	1060.80	98.65	1578.40		
1 Equip. Oper. (mechanic)	66.40	531.20	98.80	790.40		
1 Laborer	47.25	378.00	70.35	562.80		
4 Truck Tractors, 6x4, 380 H.P.		2183.92		2402.31		
2 Equipment Trailers, 50 Ton		673.38		740.72		
2 Flatbed Trailers, 40 Ton		413.84		455.22		
1 Pickup Truck, 4x4, 3/4 Ton		191.73		210.90		
1 S.P. Crane, 4x4, 20 Ton		760.97		837.07	58.66	64.53
72 L.H., Daily Totals		$8411.84		$10891.82	$116.83	$151.28
Crew B-35						
1 Labor Foreman (outside)	$49.25	$394.00	$73.30	$586.40	$60.65	$90.44
1 Skilled Worker	61.25	490.00	92.00	736.00		
2 Welders	72.05	1152.80	107.45	1719.20		
1 Laborer	47.25	378.00	70.35	562.80		
1 Equip. Oper. (crane)	66.30	530.40	98.65	789.20		
1 Equip. Oper. (oiler)	56.40	451.20	83.90	671.20		
2 Welder, Electric, 300 amp		128.34		141.17		
1 Hyd. Excavator, .75 C.Y.		915.34		1006.87	18.64	20.50
56 L.H., Daily Totals		$4440.08		$6212.85	$79.29	$110.94
Crew B-35A						
1 Labor Foreman (outside)	$49.25	$394.00	$73.30	$586.40	$57.11	$85.14
2 Laborers	47.25	756.00	70.35	1125.60		
1 Skilled Worker	61.25	490.00	92.00	736.00		
1 Welder (plumber)	72.05	576.40	107.45	859.60		
1 Equip. Oper. (crane)	66.30	530.40	98.65	789.20		
1 Equip. Oper. (oiler)	56.40	451.20	83.90	671.20		
1 Welder, Gas Engine, 300 amp		147.09		161.80		
1 Crawler Crane, 75 Ton		2189.46		2408.41	41.72	45.90
56 L.H., Daily Totals		$5534.55		$7338.20	$98.83	$131.04
Crew B-36						
1 Labor Foreman (outside)	$49.25	$394.00	$73.30	$586.40	$53.97	$80.32
2 Laborers	47.25	756.00	70.35	1125.60		
2 Equip. Oper. (medium)	63.05	1008.80	93.80	1500.80		
1 Dozer, 200 H.P.		1382.36		1520.60		
1 Aggregate Spreader		67.49		74.24		
1 Tandem Roller, 10 Ton		379.22		417.14	45.73	50.30
40 L.H., Daily Totals		$3987.87		$5224.78	$99.70	$130.62

Crews - Standard

Crew No.	Bare Costs		Incl. Subs O&P		Cost Per Labor-Hour	
Crew B-36A	Hr.	Daily	Hr.	Daily	Bare Costs	Incl. O&P
1 Labor Foreman (outside)	$49.25	$394.00	$73.30	$586.40	$56.56	$84.17
2 Laborers	47.25	756.00	70.35	1125.60		
4 Equip. Oper. (medium)	63.05	2017.60	93.80	3001.60		
1 Dozer, 200 H.P.		1382.36		1520.60		
1 Aggregate Spreader		67.49		74.24		
1 Tandem Roller, 10 Ton		379.22		417.14		
1 Roller, Pneum. Whl., 12 Ton		384.55		423.01	39.53	43.48
56 L.H., Daily Totals		$5381.22		$7148.58	$96.09	$127.65
Crew B-36B	Hr.	Daily	Hr.	Daily	Bare Costs	Incl. O&P
1 Labor Foreman (outside)	$49.25	$394.00	$73.30	$586.40	$56.42	$84.01
2 Laborers	47.25	756.00	70.35	1125.60		
4 Equip. Oper. (medium)	63.05	2017.60	93.80	3001.60		
1 Truck Driver (heavy)	55.45	443.60	82.85	662.80		
1 Grader, 30,000 Lbs.		1091.19		1200.31		
1 F.E. Loader, Crl, 1.5 C.Y.		733.70		807.07		
1 Dozer, 300 H.P.		1674.53		1841.98		
1 Roller, Vibratory, 25 Ton		529.68		582.65		
1 Truck Tractor, 6x4, 450 H.P.		666.04		732.64		
1 Water Tank Trailer, 5000 Gal.		169.14		186.05	76.00	83.60
64 L.H., Daily Totals		$8475.48		$10727.11	$132.43	$167.61
Crew B-36C	Hr.	Daily	Hr.	Daily	Bare Costs	Incl. O&P
1 Labor Foreman (outside)	$49.25	$394.00	$73.30	$586.40	$58.77	$87.51
3 Equip. Oper. (medium)	63.05	1513.20	93.80	2251.20		
1 Truck Driver (heavy)	55.45	443.60	82.85	662.80		
1 Grader, 30,000 Lbs.		1091.19		1200.31		
1 Dozer, 300 H.P.		1674.53		1841.98		
1 Roller, Vibratory, 25 Ton		529.68		582.65		
1 Truck Tractor, 6x4, 450 H.P.		666.04		732.64		
1 Water Tank Trailer, 5000 Gal.		169.14		186.05	103.26	113.59
40 L.H., Daily Totals		$6481.38		$8044.04	$162.03	$201.10
Crew B-36D	Hr.	Daily	Hr.	Daily	Bare Costs	Incl. O&P
1 Labor Foreman (outside)	$49.25	$394.00	$73.30	$586.40	$59.60	$88.67
3 Equip. Oper. (medium)	63.05	1513.20	93.80	2251.20		
1 Grader, 30,000 Lbs.		1091.19		1200.31		
1 Dozer, 300 H.P.		1674.53		1841.98		
1 Roller, Vibratory, 25 Ton		529.68		582.65	102.98	113.28
32 L.H., Daily Totals		$5202.60		$6462.54	$162.58	$201.95
Crew B-37	Hr.	Daily	Hr.	Daily	Bare Costs	Incl. O&P
1 Labor Foreman (outside)	$49.25	$394.00	$73.30	$586.40	$49.66	$73.92
4 Laborers	47.25	1512.00	70.35	2251.20		
1 Equip. Oper. (light)	59.70	477.60	88.85	710.80		
1 Tandem Roller, 5 Ton		287.45		316.19	5.99	6.59
48 L.H., Daily Totals		$2671.05		$3864.59	$55.65	$80.51
Crew B-37A	Hr.	Daily	Hr.	Daily	Bare Costs	Incl. O&P
2 Laborers	$47.25	$756.00	$70.35	$1125.60	$49.13	$73.23
1 Truck Driver (light)	52.90	423.20	79.00	632.00		
1 Flatbed Truck, Gas, 1.5 Ton		361.95		398.14		
1 Tar Kettle, T.M.		199.54		219.49	23.40	25.73
24 L.H., Daily Totals		$1740.69		$2375.24	$72.53	$98.97
Crew B-37B	Hr.	Daily	Hr.	Daily	Bare Costs	Incl. O&P
3 Laborers	$47.25	$1134.00	$70.35	$1688.40	$48.66	$72.51
1 Truck Driver (light)	52.90	423.20	79.00	632.00		
1 Flatbed Truck, Gas, 1.5 Ton		361.95		398.14		
1 Tar Kettle, T.M.		199.54		219.49	17.55	19.30
32 L.H., Daily Totals		$2118.69		$2938.04	$66.21	$91.81

Crew No.	Bare Costs		Incl. Subs O&P		Cost Per Labor-Hour	
Crew B-37C	Hr.	Daily	Hr.	Daily	Bare Costs	Incl. O&P
2 Laborers	$47.25	$756.00	$70.35	$1125.60	$50.08	$74.67
2 Truck Drivers (light)	52.90	846.40	79.00	1264.00		
2 Flatbed Trucks, Gas, 1.5 Ton		723.90		796.29		
1 Tar Kettle, T.M.		199.54		219.49	28.86	31.74
32 L.H., Daily Totals		$2525.84		$3405.38	$78.93	$106.42
Crew B-37D	Hr.	Daily	Hr.	Daily	Bare Costs	Incl. O&P
1 Laborer	$47.25	$378.00	$70.35	$562.80	$50.08	$74.67
1 Truck Driver (light)	52.90	423.20	79.00	632.00		
1 Pickup Truck, 3/4 Ton		122.56		134.82	7.66	8.43
16 L.H., Daily Totals		$923.76		$1329.62	$57.73	$83.10
Crew B-37E	Hr.	Daily	Hr.	Daily	Bare Costs	Incl. O&P
3 Laborers	$47.25	$1134.00	$70.35	$1688.40	$52.90	$78.81
1 Equip. Oper. (light)	59.70	477.60	88.85	710.80		
1 Equip. Oper. (medium)	63.05	504.40	93.80	750.40		
2 Truck Drivers (light)	52.90	846.40	79.00	1264.00		
4 Barrels w/ Flasher		11.36		12.50		
1 Concrete Saw		176.00		193.60		
1 Rotary Hammer Drill		34.98		38.48		
1 Hammer Drill Bit		26.61		29.27		
1 Loader, Skid Steer, 30 H.P.		260.99		287.09		
1 Conc. Hammer Attach.		126.94		139.63		
1 Vibrating Plate, Gas, 18"		143.82		158.20		
2 Flatbed Trucks, Gas, 1.5 Ton		723.90		796.29	26.87	29.55
56 L.H., Daily Totals		$4467.00		$6068.66	$79.77	$108.37
Crew B-37F	Hr.	Daily	Hr.	Daily	Bare Costs	Incl. O&P
3 Laborers	$47.25	$1134.00	$70.35	$1688.40	$48.66	$72.51
1 Truck Driver (light)	52.90	423.20	79.00	632.00		
4 Barrels w/ Flasher		11.36		12.50		
1 Concrete Mixer, 10 C.F.		149.77		164.75		
1 Air Compressor, 60 cfm		173.21		190.53		
1 -50' Air Hose, 3/4"		8.16		8.98		
1 Spade (Chipper)		9.37		10.31		
1 Flatbed Truck, Gas, 1.5 Ton		361.95		398.14	22.31	24.54
32 L.H., Daily Totals		$2271.02		$3105.60	$70.97	$97.05
Crew B-37G	Hr.	Daily	Hr.	Daily	Bare Costs	Incl. O&P
1 Labor Foreman (outside)	$49.25	$394.00	$73.30	$586.40	$49.66	$73.92
4 Laborers	47.25	1512.00	70.35	2251.20		
1 Equip. Oper. (light)	59.70	477.60	88.85	710.80		
1 Berm Machine		897.16		986.88		
1 Tandem Roller, 5 Ton		287.45		316.19	24.68	27.15
48 L.H., Daily Totals		$3568.21		$4851.47	$74.34	$101.07
Crew B-37H	Hr.	Daily	Hr.	Daily	Bare Costs	Incl. O&P
1 Labor Foreman (outside)	$49.25	$394.00	$73.30	$586.40	$49.66	$73.92
4 Laborers	47.25	1512.00	70.35	2251.20		
1 Equip. Oper. (light)	59.70	477.60	88.85	710.80		
1 Tandem Roller, 5 Ton		287.45		316.19		
1 Flatbed Truck, Gas, 1.5 Ton		361.95		398.14		
1 Tar Kettle, T.M.		199.54		219.49	17.69	19.45
48 L.H., Daily Totals		$3232.54		$4482.23	$67.34	$93.38

Crews - Standard

Crew B-37I

Crew B-37I	Hr.	Daily	Hr.	Daily	Bare Costs	Incl. O&P
3 Laborers	$47.25	$1134.00	$70.35	$1688.40	$52.90	$78.81
1 Equip. Oper. (light)	59.70	477.60	88.85	710.80		
1 Equip. Oper. (medium)	63.05	504.40	93.80	750.40		
2 Truck Drivers (light)	52.90	846.40	79.00	1264.00		
4 Barrels w/ Flasher		11.36		12.50		
1 Concrete Saw		176.00		193.60		
1 Rotary Hammer Drill		34.98		38.48		
1 Hammer Drill Bit		26.61		29.27		
1 Air Compressor, 60 cfm		173.21		190.53		
1 -50' Air Hose, 3/4"		8.16		8.98		
1 Spade (Chipper)		9.37		10.31		
1 Loader, Skid Steer, 30 H.P.		260.99		287.09		
1 Conc. Hammer Attach.		126.94		139.63		
1 Concrete Mixer, 10 C.F.		149.77		164.75		
1 Vibrating Plate, Gas, 18"		143.82		158.20		
2 Flatbed Trucks, Gas, 1.5 Ton		723.90		796.29	32.95	36.24
56 L.H., Daily Totals		$4807.51		$6443.22	$85.85	$115.06

Crew B-37J

Crew B-37J	Hr.	Daily	Hr.	Daily	Bare Costs	Incl. O&P
1 Labor Foreman (outside)	$49.25	$394.00	$73.30	$586.40	$49.66	$73.92
4 Laborers	47.25	1512.00	70.35	2251.20		
1 Equip. Oper. (light)	59.70	477.60	88.85	710.80		
1 Air Compressor, 60 cfm		173.21		190.53		
1 -50' Air Hose, 3/4"		8.16		8.98		
2 Concrete Mixers, 10 C.F.		299.54		329.49		
2 Flatbed Trucks, Gas, 1.5 Ton		723.90		796.29		
1 Shot Blaster, 20"		229.79		252.77	29.89	32.88
48 L.H., Daily Totals		$3818.20		$5126.46	$79.55	$106.80

Crew B-37K

Crew B-37K	Hr.	Daily	Hr.	Daily	Bare Costs	Incl. O&P
1 Labor Foreman (outside)	$49.25	$394.00	$73.30	$586.40	$49.66	$73.92
4 Laborers	47.25	1512.00	70.35	2251.20		
1 Equip. Oper. (light)	59.70	477.60	88.85	710.80		
1 Air Compressor, 60 cfm		173.21		190.53		
1 -50' Air Hose, 3/4"		8.16		8.98		
2 Flatbed Trucks, Gas, 1.5 Ton		723.90		796.29		
1 Shot Blaster, 20"		229.79		252.77	23.65	26.01
48 L.H., Daily Totals		$3518.66		$4796.97	$73.31	$99.94

Crew B-38

Crew B-38	Hr.	Daily	Hr.	Daily	Bare Costs	Incl. O&P
1 Labor Foreman (outside)	$49.25	$394.00	$73.30	$586.40	$53.30	$79.33
2 Laborers	47.25	756.00	70.35	1125.60		
1 Equip. Oper. (light)	59.70	477.60	88.85	710.80		
1 Equip. Oper. (medium)	63.05	504.40	93.80	750.40		
1 Backhoe Loader, 48 H.P.		277.19		304.91		
1 Hyd. Hammer (1200 lb.)		194.78		214.26		
1 F.E. Loader, W.M., 4 C.Y.		789.98		868.98		
1 Pvmt. Rem. Bucket		70.14		77.15	33.30	36.63
40 L.H., Daily Totals		$3464.09		$4638.50	$86.60	$115.96

Crew B-39

Crew B-39	Hr.	Daily	Hr.	Daily	Bare Costs	Incl. O&P
1 Labor Foreman (outside)	$49.25	$394.00	$73.30	$586.40	$49.66	$73.92
4 Laborers	47.25	1512.00	70.35	2251.20		
1 Equip. Oper. (light)	59.70	477.60	88.85	710.80		
1 Air Compressor, 250 cfm		196.28		215.91		
2 Breakers, Pavement, 60 lb.		68.94		75.83		
2 -50' Air Hoses, 1.5"		47.20		51.92	6.51	7.16
48 L.H., Daily Totals		$2696.02		$3892.06	$56.17	$81.08

Crew B-40

Crew B-40	Hr.	Daily	Hr.	Daily	Bare Costs	Incl. O&P
1 Pile Driver Foreman (outside)	$62.50	$500.00	$96.70	$773.60	$61.69	$94.04
4 Pile Drivers	60.50	1936.00	93.60	2995.20		
2 Equip. Oper. (crane)	66.30	1060.80	98.65	1578.40		
1 Equip. Oper. (oiler)	56.40	451.20	83.90	671.20		
1 Crawler Crane, 40 Ton		1362.63		1498.89		
1 Vibratory Hammer & Gen.		2518.21		2770.03	60.64	66.70
64 L.H., Daily Totals		$7828.84		$10287.32	$122.33	$160.74

Crew B-40B

Crew B-40B	Hr.	Daily	Hr.	Daily	Bare Costs	Incl. O&P
1 Labor Foreman (outside)	$49.25	$394.00	$73.30	$586.40	$52.28	$77.82
3 Laborers	47.25	1134.00	70.35	1688.40		
1 Equip. Oper. (crane)	66.30	530.40	98.65	789.20		
1 Equip. Oper. (oiler)	56.40	451.20	83.90	671.20		
1 Lattice Boom Crane, 40 Ton		2371.83		2609.01	49.41	54.35
48 L.H., Daily Totals		$4881.43		$6344.21	$101.70	$132.17

Crew B-41

Crew B-41	Hr.	Daily	Hr.	Daily	Bare Costs	Incl. O&P
1 Labor Foreman (outside)	$49.25	$394.00	$73.30	$586.40	$48.90	$72.79
4 Laborers	47.25	1512.00	70.35	2251.20		
.25 Equip. Oper. (crane)	66.30	132.60	98.65	197.30		
.25 Equip. Oper. (oiler)	56.40	112.80	83.90	167.80		
.25 Crawler Crane, 40 Ton		340.66		374.72	7.74	8.52
44 L.H., Daily Totals		$2492.06		$3577.42	$56.64	$81.31

Crew B-42

Crew B-42	Hr.	Daily	Hr.	Daily	Bare Costs	Incl. O&P
1 Labor Foreman (outside)	$49.25	$394.00	$73.30	$586.40	$53.19	$79.58
4 Laborers	47.25	1512.00	70.35	2251.20		
1 Equip. Oper. (crane)	66.30	530.40	98.65	789.20		
1 Equip. Oper. (oiler)	56.40	451.20	83.90	671.20		
1 Welder	64.55	516.40	99.40	795.20		
1 Hyd. Crane, 25 Ton		2273.31		2500.64		
1 Welder, Gas Engine, 300 amp		147.09		161.80		
1 Horz. Boring Csg. Mch.		437.50		481.25	44.65	49.12
64 L.H., Daily Totals		$6261.90		$8236.89	$97.84	$128.70

Crew B-43

Crew B-43	Hr.	Daily	Hr.	Daily	Bare Costs	Incl. O&P
1 Labor Foreman (outside)	$49.25	$394.00	$73.30	$586.40	$52.28	$77.82
3 Laborers	47.25	1134.00	70.35	1688.40		
1 Equip. Oper. (crane)	66.30	530.40	98.65	789.20		
1 Equip. Oper. (oiler)	56.40	451.20	83.90	671.20		
1 Drill Rig, Truck-Mounted		856.23		941.85	17.84	19.62
48 L.H., Daily Totals		$3365.83		$4677.05	$70.12	$97.44

Crew B-44

Crew B-44	Hr.	Daily	Hr.	Daily	Bare Costs	Incl. O&P
1 Pile Driver Foreman (outside)	$62.50	$500.00	$96.70	$773.60	$60.54	$92.34
4 Pile Drivers	60.50	1936.00	93.60	2995.20		
2 Equip. Oper. (crane)	66.30	1060.80	98.65	1578.40		
1 Laborer	47.25	378.00	70.35	562.80		
1 Crawler Crane, 40 Ton		1362.63		1498.89		
1 Lead, 60' High		233.36		256.70		
1 Hammer, Diesel, 15K ft.-lbs.		687.50		756.25	35.68	39.25
64 L.H., Daily Totals		$6158.29		$8421.84	$96.22	$131.59

Crew B-45

Crew B-45	Hr.	Daily	Hr.	Daily	Bare Costs	Incl. O&P
1 Equip. Oper. (medium)	$63.05	$504.40	$93.80	$750.40	$59.25	$88.33
1 Truck Driver (heavy)	55.45	443.60	82.85	662.80		
1 Dist. Tanker, 3000 Gallon		367.10		403.81		
1 Truck Tractor, 6x4, 380 H.P.		545.98		600.58	57.07	62.77
16 L.H., Daily Totals		$1861.08		$2417.59	$116.32	$151.10

Crews - Standard

Crew No.	Bare Costs		Incl. Subs O&P		Cost Per Labor-Hour	
Crew B-46	Hr.	Daily	Hr.	Daily	Bare Costs	Incl. O&P
1 Pile Driver Foreman (outside)	$62.50	$500.00	$96.70	$773.60	$54.21	$82.49
2 Pile Drivers	60.50	968.00	93.60	1497.60		
3 Laborers	47.25	1134.00	70.35	1688.40		
1 Chain Saw, Gas, 36" Long		53.61		58.97	1.12	1.23
48 L.H., Daily Totals		$2655.61		$4018.57	$55.33	$83.72
Crew B-47	Hr.	Daily	Hr.	Daily	Bare Costs	Incl. O&P
1 Blast Foreman (outside)	$49.25	$394.00	$73.30	$586.40	$52.07	$77.50
1 Driller	47.25	378.00	70.35	562.80		
1 Equip. Oper. (light)	59.70	477.60	88.85	710.80		
1 Air Track Drill, 4"		1191.15		1310.27		
1 Air Compressor, 600 cfm		466.11		512.72		
2 -50' Air Hoses, 3"		93.52		102.87	72.95	80.24
24 L.H., Daily Totals		$3000.38		$3785.86	$125.02	$157.74
Crew B-47A	Hr.	Daily	Hr.	Daily	Bare Costs	Incl. O&P
1 Drilling Foreman (outside)	$49.25	$394.00	$73.30	$586.40	$57.32	$85.28
1 Equip. Oper. (heavy)	66.30	530.40	98.65	789.20		
1 Equip. Oper. (oiler)	56.40	451.20	83.90	671.20		
1 Air Track Drill, 5"		1191.15		1310.27	49.63	54.59
24 L.H., Daily Totals		$2566.75		$3357.07	$106.95	$139.88
Crew B-47C	Hr.	Daily	Hr.	Daily	Bare Costs	Incl. O&P
1 Laborer	$47.25	$378.00	$70.35	$562.80	$53.48	$79.60
1 Equip. Oper. (light)	59.70	477.60	88.85	710.80		
1 Air Compressor, 750 C.F.M.		655.87		721.46		
2 -50' Air Hoses, 3"		93.52		102.87		
1 Air Track Drill, 4"		1191.15		1310.27	121.28	133.41
16 L.H., Daily Totals		$2796.14		$3408.19	$174.76	$213.01
Crew B-47E	Hr.	Daily	Hr.	Daily	Bare Costs	Incl. O&P
1 Labor Foreman (outside)	$49.25	$394.00	$73.30	$586.40	$47.75	$71.09
3 Laborers	47.25	1134.00	70.35	1688.40		
1 Flatbed Truck, Gas, 3 Ton		391.02		430.12	12.22	13.44
32 L.H., Daily Totals		$1919.02		$2704.92	$59.97	$84.53
Crew B-47G	Hr.	Daily	Hr.	Daily	Bare Costs	Incl. O&P
1 Labor Foreman (outside)	$49.25	$394.00	$73.30	$586.40	$50.86	$75.71
2 Laborers	47.25	756.00	70.35	1125.60		
1 Equip. Oper. (light)	59.70	477.60	88.85	710.80		
1 Air Track Drill, 4"		1191.15		1310.27		
1 Air Compressor, 600 cfm		466.11		512.72		
2 -50' Air Hoses, 3"		93.52		102.87		
1 Gunite Pump Rig		352.58		387.84	65.73	72.30
32 L.H., Daily Totals		$3730.96		$4736.50	$116.59	$148.02
Crew B-47H	Hr.	Daily	Hr.	Daily	Bare Costs	Incl. O&P
1 Skilled Worker Foreman (out)	$63.25	$506.00	$95.00	$760.00	$61.75	$92.75
3 Skilled Workers	61.25	1470.00	92.00	2208.00		
1 Flatbed Truck, Gas, 3 Ton		391.02		430.12	12.22	13.44
32 L.H., Daily Totals		$2367.02		$3398.12	$73.97	$106.19

Crew No.	Bare Costs		Incl. Subs O&P		Cost Per Labor-Hour	
Crew B-48	Hr.	Daily	Hr.	Daily	Bare Costs	Incl. O&P
1 Labor Foreman (outside)	$49.25	$394.00	$73.30	$586.40	$53.34	$79.39
3 Laborers	47.25	1134.00	70.35	1688.40		
1 Equip. Oper. (crane)	66.30	530.40	98.65	789.20		
1 Equip. Oper. (oiler)	56.40	451.20	83.90	671.20		
1 Equip. Oper. (light)	59.70	477.60	88.85	710.80		
1 Centr. Water Pump, 6"		386.48		425.13		
1 -20' Suction Hose, 6"		28.12		30.93		
1 -50' Discharge Hose, 6"		19.99		21.99		
1 Drill Rig, Truck-Mounted		856.23		941.85	23.05	25.36
56 L.H., Daily Totals		$4278.02		$5865.90	$76.39	$104.75
Crew B-49	Hr.	Daily	Hr.	Daily	Bare Costs	Incl. O&P
1 Labor Foreman (outside)	$49.25	$394.00	$73.30	$586.40	$56.10	$84.14
3 Laborers	47.25	1134.00	70.35	1688.40		
2 Equip. Oper. (crane)	66.30	1060.80	98.65	1578.40		
2 Equip. Oper. (oilers)	56.40	902.40	83.90	1342.40		
1 Equip. Oper. (light)	59.70	477.60	88.85	710.80		
2 Pile Drivers	60.50	968.00	93.60	1497.60		
1 Hyd. Crane, 25 Ton		2273.31		2500.64		
1 Centr. Water Pump, 6"		386.48		425.13		
1 -20' Suction Hose, 6"		28.12		30.93		
1 -50' Discharge Hose, 6"		19.99		21.99		
1 Drill Rig, Truck-Mounted		856.23		941.85	40.50	44.55
88 L.H., Daily Totals		$8500.93		$11324.54	$96.60	$128.69
Crew B-50	Hr.	Daily	Hr.	Daily	Bare Costs	Incl. O&P
2 Pile Driver Foremen (outside)	$62.50	$1000.00	$96.70	$1547.20	$58.48	$89.09
6 Pile Drivers	60.50	2904.00	93.60	4492.80		
2 Equip. Oper. (crane)	66.30	1060.80	98.65	1578.40		
1 Equip. Oper. (oiler)	56.40	451.20	83.90	671.20		
3 Laborers	47.25	1134.00	70.35	1688.40		
1 Crawler Crane, 40 Ton		1362.63		1498.89		
1 Lead, 60' High		233.36		256.70		
1 Hammer, Diesel, 15K ft.-lbs.		687.50		756.25		
1 Air Compressor, 600 cfm		466.11		512.72		
2 -50' Air Hoses, 3"		93.52		102.87		
1 Chain Saw, Gas, 36" Long		53.61		58.97	25.86	28.45
112 L.H., Daily Totals		$9446.73		$13164.40	$84.35	$117.54
Crew B-51	Hr.	Daily	Hr.	Daily	Bare Costs	Incl. O&P
1 Labor Foreman (outside)	$49.25	$394.00	$73.30	$586.40	$48.52	$72.28
4 Laborers	47.25	1512.00	70.35	2251.20		
1 Truck Driver (light)	52.90	423.20	79.00	632.00		
1 Flatbed Truck, Gas, 1.5 Ton		361.95		398.14	7.54	8.29
48 L.H., Daily Totals		$2691.15		$3867.74	$56.07	$80.58
Crew B-52	Hr.	Daily	Hr.	Daily	Bare Costs	Incl. O&P
1 Carpenter Foreman (outside)	$60.60	$484.80	$90.20	$721.60	$54.25	$80.58
1 Carpenter	58.60	468.80	87.25	698.00		
3 Laborers	47.25	1134.00	70.35	1688.40		
1 Cement Finisher	55.00	440.00	80.45	643.60		
.5 Rodman (reinf.)	64.55	258.20	96.40	385.60		
.5 Equip. Oper. (medium)	63.05	252.20	93.80	375.20		
.5 Crawler Loader, 3 C.Y.		628.84		691.72	11.23	12.35
56 L.H., Daily Totals		$3666.84		$5204.12	$65.48	$92.93
Crew B-53	Hr.	Daily	Hr.	Daily	Bare Costs	Incl. O&P
1 Equip. Oper. (light)	$59.70	$477.60	$88.85	$710.80	$59.70	$88.85
1 Trencher, Chain, 12 H.P.		202.47		222.72	25.31	27.84
8 L.H., Daily Totals		$680.07		$933.52	$85.01	$116.69

Crews - Standard

Crew B-54	Hr.	Daily	Hr.	Daily	Bare Costs	Incl. O&P
1 Equip. Oper. (light)	$59.70	$477.60	$88.85	$710.80	$59.70	$88.85
1 Trencher, Chain, 40 H.P.		386.50		425.15	48.31	53.14
8 L.H., Daily Totals		$864.10		$1135.95	$108.01	$141.99

Crew B-54A	Hr.	Daily	Hr.	Daily	Bare Costs	Incl. O&P
.17 Labor Foreman (outside)	$49.25	$66.98	$73.30	$99.69	$61.04	$90.82
1 Equipment Operator (med.)	63.05	504.40	93.80	750.40		
1 Wheel Trencher, 67 H.P.		1248.89		1373.78	133.43	146.77
9.36 L.H., Daily Totals		$1820.27		$2223.87	$194.47	$237.59

Crew B-54B	Hr.	Daily	Hr.	Daily	Bare Costs	Incl. O&P
.25 Labor Foreman (outside)	$49.25	$98.50	$73.30	$146.60	$60.29	$89.70
1 Equipment Operator (med.)	63.05	504.40	93.80	750.40		
1 Wheel Trencher, 150 H.P.		1338.44		1472.28	133.84	147.23
10 L.H., Daily Totals		$1941.34		$2369.28	$194.13	$236.93

Crew B-54C	Hr.	Daily	Hr.	Daily	Bare Costs	Incl. O&P
1 Laborer	$47.25	$378.00	$70.35	$562.80	$55.15	$82.08
1 Equipment Operator (med.)	63.05	504.40	93.80	750.40		
1 Wheel Trencher, 67 H.P.		1248.89		1373.78	78.06	85.86
16 L.H., Daily Totals		$2131.29		$2686.98	$133.21	$167.94

Crew B-54D	Hr.	Daily	Hr.	Daily	Bare Costs	Incl. O&P
1 Laborer	$47.25	$378.00	$70.35	$562.80	$55.15	$82.08
1 Equipment Operator (med.)	63.05	504.40	93.80	750.40		
1 Rock Trencher, 6" Width		992.44		1091.68	62.03	68.23
16 L.H., Daily Totals		$1874.84		$2404.88	$117.18	$150.31

Crew B-54E	Hr.	Daily	Hr.	Daily	Bare Costs	Incl. O&P
1 Laborer	$47.25	$378.00	$70.35	$562.80	$55.15	$82.08
1 Equipment Operator (med.)	63.05	504.40	93.80	750.40		
1 Rock Trencher, 18" Width		1079.31		1187.24	67.46	74.20
16 L.H., Daily Totals		$1961.71		$2500.44	$122.61	$156.28

Crew B-55	Hr.	Daily	Hr.	Daily	Bare Costs	Incl. O&P
2 Laborers	$47.25	$756.00	$70.35	$1125.60	$49.13	$73.23
1 Truck Driver (light)	52.90	423.20	79.00	632.00		
1 Truck-Mounted Earth Auger		446.91		491.60		
1 Flatbed Truck, Gas, 3 Ton		391.02		430.12	34.91	38.41
24 L.H., Daily Totals		$2017.13		$2679.32	$84.05	$111.64

Crew B-56	Hr.	Daily	Hr.	Daily	Bare Costs	Incl. O&P
1 Laborer	$47.25	$378.00	$70.35	$562.80	$53.48	$79.60
1 Equip. Oper. (light)	59.70	477.60	88.85	710.80		
1 Air Track Drill, 4"		1191.15		1310.27		
1 Air Compressor, 600 cfm		466.11		512.72		
1 -50' Air Hose, 3"		46.76		51.44	106.50	117.15
16 L.H., Daily Totals		$2559.62		$3148.02	$159.98	$196.75

Crew B-57	Hr.	Daily	Hr.	Daily	Bare Costs	Incl. O&P
1 Labor Foreman (outside)	$49.25	$394.00	$73.30	$586.40	$54.36	$80.90
2 Laborers	47.25	756.00	70.35	1125.60		
1 Equip. Oper. (crane)	66.30	530.40	98.65	789.20		
1 Equip. Oper. (light)	59.70	477.60	88.85	710.80		
1 Equip. Oper. (oiler)	56.40	451.20	83.90	671.20		
1 Crawler Crane, 25 Ton		1274.00		1401.40		
1 Clamshell Bucket, 1 C.Y.		46.89		51.58		
1 Centr. Water Pump, 6"		386.48		425.13		
1 -20' Suction Hose, 6"		28.12		30.93		
20 -50' Discharge Hoses, 6"		399.80		439.78	44.49	48.93
48 L.H., Daily Totals		$4744.49		$6232.02	$98.84	$129.83

Crew B-58	Hr.	Daily	Hr.	Daily	Bare Costs	Incl. O&P
2 Laborers	$47.25	$756.00	$70.35	$1125.60	$51.40	$76.52
1 Equip. Oper. (light)	59.70	477.60	88.85	710.80		
1 Backhoe Loader, 48 H.P.		277.19		304.91		
1 Small Helicopter, w/ Pilot		5810.29		6391.32	253.65	279.01
24 L.H., Daily Totals		$7321.08		$8532.63	$305.05	$355.53

Crew B-59	Hr.	Daily	Hr.	Daily	Bare Costs	Incl. O&P
1 Truck Driver (heavy)	$55.45	$443.60	$82.85	$662.80	$55.45	$82.85
1 Truck Tractor, 220 H.P.		339.98		373.98		
1 Water Tank Trailer, 5000 Gal.		169.14		186.05	63.64	70.00
8 L.H., Daily Totals		$952.72		$1222.83	$119.09	$152.85

Crew B-59A	Hr.	Daily	Hr.	Daily	Bare Costs	Incl. O&P
2 Laborers	$47.25	$756.00	$70.35	$1125.60	$49.98	$74.52
1 Truck Driver (heavy)	55.45	443.60	82.85	662.80		
1 Water Tank Trailer, 5000 Gal.		169.14		186.05		
1 Truck Tractor, 220 H.P.		339.98		373.98	21.21	23.33
24 L.H., Daily Totals		$1708.72		$2348.43	$71.20	$97.85

Crew B-60	Hr.	Daily	Hr.	Daily	Bare Costs	Incl. O&P
1 Labor Foreman (outside)	$49.25	$394.00	$73.30	$586.40	$55.12	$82.04
2 Laborers	47.25	756.00	70.35	1125.60		
1 Equip. Oper. (crane)	66.30	530.40	98.65	789.20		
2 Equip. Oper. (light)	59.70	955.20	88.85	1421.60		
1 Equip. Oper. (oiler)	56.40	451.20	83.90	671.20		
1 Crawler Crane, 40 Ton		1362.63		1498.89		
1 Lead, 60' High		233.36		256.70		
1 Hammer, Diesel, 15K ft.-lbs.		687.50		756.25		
1 Backhoe Loader, 48 H.P.		277.19		304.91	45.73	50.30
56 L.H., Daily Totals		$5647.48		$7410.75	$100.85	$132.33

Crew B-61	Hr.	Daily	Hr.	Daily	Bare Costs	Incl. O&P
1 Labor Foreman (outside)	$49.25	$394.00	$73.30	$586.40	$50.14	$74.64
3 Laborers	47.25	1134.00	70.35	1688.40		
1 Equip. Oper. (light)	59.70	477.60	88.85	710.80		
1 Cement Mixer, 2 C.Y.		119.22		131.14		
1 Air Compressor, 160 cfm		244.12		268.53	9.08	9.99
40 L.H., Daily Totals		$2368.94		$3385.27	$59.22	$84.63

Crew B-62	Hr.	Daily	Hr.	Daily	Bare Costs	Incl. O&P
2 Laborers	$47.25	$756.00	$70.35	$1125.60	$51.40	$76.52
1 Equip. Oper. (light)	59.70	477.60	88.85	710.80		
1 Loader, Skid Steer, 30 H.P.		260.99		287.09	10.87	11.96
24 L.H., Daily Totals		$1494.59		$2123.49	$62.27	$88.48

Crews - Standard

Crew No.	Bare Costs		Incl. Subs O&P		Cost Per Labor-Hour	
Crew B-62A	Hr.	Daily	Hr.	Daily	Bare Costs	Incl. O&P
2 Laborers	$47.25	$756.00	$70.35	$1125.60	$51.40	$76.52
1 Equip. Oper. (light)	59.70	477.60	88.85	710.80		
1 Loader, Skid Steer, 30 H.P.		260.99		287.09		
1 Trencher Attachment		88.83		97.71	14.58	16.03
24 L.H., Daily Totals		$1583.42		$2221.20	$65.98	$92.55
Crew B-63	Hr.	Daily	Hr.	Daily	Bare Costs	Incl. O&P
4 Laborers	$47.25	$1512.00	$70.35	$2251.20	$49.74	$74.05
1 Equip. Oper. (light)	59.70	477.60	88.85	710.80		
1 Loader, Skid Steer, 30 H.P.		260.99		287.09	6.52	7.18
40 L.H., Daily Totals		$2250.59		$3249.09	$56.26	$81.23
Crew B-63B	Hr.	Daily	Hr.	Daily	Bare Costs	Incl. O&P
1 Labor Foreman (inside)	$47.75	$382.00	$71.10	$568.80	$50.49	$75.16
2 Laborers	47.25	756.00	70.35	1125.60		
1 Equip. Oper. (light)	59.70	477.60	88.85	710.80		
1 Loader, Skid Steer, 78 H.P.		429.91		472.90	13.43	14.78
32 L.H., Daily Totals		$2045.51		$2878.10	$63.92	$89.94
Crew B-64	Hr.	Daily	Hr.	Daily	Bare Costs	Incl. O&P
1 Laborer	$47.25	$378.00	$70.35	$562.80	$50.08	$74.67
1 Truck Driver (light)	52.90	423.20	79.00	632.00		
1 Power Mulcher (small)		264.41		290.85		
1 Flatbed Truck, Gas, 1.5 Ton		361.95		398.14	39.15	43.06
16 L.H., Daily Totals		$1427.56		$1883.80	$89.22	$117.74
Crew B-65	Hr.	Daily	Hr.	Daily	Bare Costs	Incl. O&P
1 Laborer	$47.25	$378.00	$70.35	$562.80	$50.08	$74.67
1 Truck Driver (light)	52.90	423.20	79.00	632.00		
1 Power Mulcher (Large)		633.63		696.99		
1 Flatbed Truck, Gas, 1.5 Ton		361.95		398.14	62.22	68.45
16 L.H., Daily Totals		$1796.78		$2289.94	$112.30	$143.12
Crew B-66	Hr.	Daily	Hr.	Daily	Bare Costs	Incl. O&P
1 Equip. Oper. (light)	$59.70	$477.60	$88.85	$710.80	$59.70	$88.85
1 Loader-Backhoe, 40 H.P.		222.27		244.50	27.78	30.56
8 L.H., Daily Totals		$699.87		$955.30	$87.48	$119.41
Crew B-67	Hr.	Daily	Hr.	Daily	Bare Costs	Incl. O&P
1 Millwright	$62.85	$502.80	$90.80	$726.40	$61.27	$89.83
1 Equip. Oper. (light)	59.70	477.60	88.85	710.80		
1 R.T. Forklift, 5,000 Lb., diesel		349.30		384.23	21.83	24.01
16 L.H., Daily Totals		$1329.70		$1821.43	$83.11	$113.84
Crew B-67B	Hr.	Daily	Hr.	Daily	Bare Costs	Incl. O&P
1 Millwright Foreman (inside)	$63.35	$506.80	$91.55	$732.40	$63.10	$91.17
1 Millwright	62.85	502.80	90.80	726.40		
16 L.H., Daily Totals		$1009.60		$1458.80	$63.10	$91.17
Crew B-68	Hr.	Daily	Hr.	Daily	Bare Costs	Incl. O&P
2 Millwrights	$62.85	$1005.60	$90.80	$1452.80	$61.80	$90.15
1 Equip. Oper. (light)	59.70	477.60	88.85	710.80		
1 R.T. Forklift, 5,000 Lb., diesel		349.30		384.23	14.55	16.01
24 L.H., Daily Totals		$1832.50		$2547.83	$76.35	$106.16
Crew B-68A	Hr.	Daily	Hr.	Daily	Bare Costs	Incl. O&P
1 Millwright Foreman (inside)	$63.35	$506.80	$91.55	$732.40	$63.02	$91.05
2 Millwrights	62.85	1005.60	90.80	1452.80		
1 Forklift, Smooth Floor, 8,000 Lb.		311.06		342.17	12.96	14.26
24 L.H., Daily Totals		$1823.46		$2527.37	$75.98	$105.31
Crew B-68B	Hr.	Daily	Hr.	Daily	Bare Costs	Incl. O&P
1 Millwright Foreman (inside)	$63.35	$506.80	$91.55	$732.40	$66.84	$98.32
2 Millwrights	62.85	1005.60	90.80	1452.80		
2 Electricians	67.35	1077.60	100.10	1601.60		
2 Plumbers	72.05	1152.80	107.45	1719.20		
1 R.T. Forklift, 5,000 Lb., gas		422.09		464.30	7.54	8.29
56 L.H., Daily Totals		$4164.89		$5970.30	$74.37	$106.61
Crew B-68C	Hr.	Daily	Hr.	Daily	Bare Costs	Incl. O&P
1 Millwright Foreman (inside)	$63.35	$506.80	$91.55	$732.40	$66.40	$97.47
1 Millwright	62.85	502.80	90.80	726.40		
1 Electrician	67.35	538.80	100.10	800.80		
1 Plumber	72.05	576.40	107.45	859.60		
1 R.T. Forklift, 5,000 Lb., gas		422.09		464.30	13.19	14.51
32 L.H., Daily Totals		$2546.89		$3583.50	$79.59	$111.98
Crew B-68D	Hr.	Daily	Hr.	Daily	Bare Costs	Incl. O&P
1 Labor Foreman (inside)	$47.75	$382.00	$71.10	$568.80	$51.57	$76.77
1 Laborer	47.25	378.00	70.35	562.80		
1 Equip. Oper. (light)	59.70	477.60	88.85	710.80		
1 R.T. Forklift, 5,000 Lb., gas		422.09		464.30	17.59	19.35
24 L.H., Daily Totals		$1659.69		$2306.70	$69.15	$96.11
Crew B-68E	Hr.	Daily	Hr.	Daily	Bare Costs	Incl. O&P
1 Struc. Steel Foreman (inside)	$65.05	$520.40	$100.20	$801.60	$64.65	$99.56
3 Struc. Steel Workers	64.55	1549.20	99.40	2385.60		
1 Welder	64.55	516.40	99.40	795.20		
1 Forklift, Smooth Floor, 8,000 Lb.		311.06		342.17	7.78	8.55
40 L.H., Daily Totals		$2897.06		$4324.57	$72.43	$108.11
Crew B-68F	Hr.	Daily	Hr.	Daily	Bare Costs	Incl. O&P
1 Skilled Worker Foreman (out)	$63.25	$506.00	$95.00	$760.00	$61.92	$93.00
2 Skilled Workers	61.25	980.00	92.00	1472.00		
1 R.T. Forklift, 5,000 Lb., gas		422.09		464.30	17.59	19.35
24 L.H., Daily Totals		$1908.09		$2696.30	$79.50	$112.35
Crew B-68G	Hr.	Daily	Hr.	Daily	Bare Costs	Incl. O&P
2 Structural Steel Workers	$64.55	$1032.80	$99.40	$1590.40	$64.55	$99.40
1 R.T. Forklift, 5,000 Lb., gas		422.09		464.30	26.38	29.02
16 L.H., Daily Totals		$1454.89		$2054.70	$90.93	$128.42
Crew B-69	Hr.	Daily	Hr.	Daily	Bare Costs	Incl. O&P
1 Labor Foreman (outside)	$49.25	$394.00	$73.30	$586.40	$52.28	$77.82
3 Laborers	47.25	1134.00	70.35	1688.40		
1 Equip. Oper. (crane)	66.30	530.40	98.65	789.20		
1 Equip. Oper. (oiler)	56.40	451.20	83.90	671.20		
1 Hyd. Crane, 80 Ton		2641.70		2905.87	55.04	60.54
48 L.H., Daily Totals		$5151.30		$6641.07	$107.32	$138.36
Crew B-69A	Hr.	Daily	Hr.	Daily	Bare Costs	Incl. O&P
1 Labor Foreman (outside)	$49.25	$394.00	$73.30	$586.40	$51.51	$76.43
3 Laborers	47.25	1134.00	70.35	1688.40		
1 Equip. Oper. (medium)	63.05	504.40	93.80	750.40		
1 Concrete Finisher	55.00	440.00	80.45	643.60		
1 Curb/Gutter Paver, 2-Track		1074.23		1181.65	22.38	24.62
48 L.H., Daily Totals		$3546.63		$4850.45	$73.89	$101.05

Crews - Standard

Crew No.	Bare Costs		Incl. Subs O&P		Cost Per Labor-Hour	
Crew B-69B	**Hr.**	**Daily**	**Hr.**	**Daily**	**Bare Costs**	**Incl. O&P**
1 Labor Foreman (outside)	$49.25	$394.00	$73.30	$586.40	$51.51	$76.43
3 Laborers	47.25	1134.00	70.35	1688.40		
1 Equip. Oper. (medium)	63.05	504.40	93.80	750.40		
1 Cement Finisher	55.00	440.00	80.45	643.60		
1 Curb/Gutter Paver, 4-Track		1156.49		1272.14	24.09	26.50
48 L.H., Daily Totals		$3628.89		$4940.94	$75.60	$102.94
Crew B-70	**Hr.**	**Daily**	**Hr.**	**Daily**	**Bare Costs**	**Incl. O&P**
1 Labor Foreman (outside)	$49.25	$394.00	$73.30	$586.40	$54.31	$80.82
3 Laborers	47.25	1134.00	70.35	1688.40		
3 Equip. Oper. (medium)	63.05	1513.20	93.80	2251.20		
1 Grader, 30,000 Lbs.		1091.19		1200.31		
1 Ripper, Beam & 1 Shank		100.54		110.59		
1 Road Sweeper, S.P., 8' wide		538.00		591.81		
1 F.E. Loader, W.M., 1.5 C.Y.		455.32		500.85	39.02	42.92
56 L.H., Daily Totals		$5226.26		$6929.57	$93.33	$123.74
Crew B-70A	**Hr.**	**Daily**	**Hr.**	**Daily**	**Bare Costs**	**Incl. O&P**
1 Laborer	$47.25	$378.00	$70.35	$562.80	$59.89	$89.11
4 Equip. Oper. (medium)	63.05	2017.60	93.80	3001.60		
1 Grader, 40,000 Lbs.		1254.97		1380.47		
1 F.E. Loader, W.M., 2.5 C.Y.		658.89		724.78		
1 Dozer, 80 H.P.		591.82		651.00		
1 Roller, Pneum. Whl., 12 Ton		384.55		423.01	72.26	79.48
40 L.H., Daily Totals		$5285.83		$6743.65	$132.15	$168.59
Crew B-71	**Hr.**	**Daily**	**Hr.**	**Daily**	**Bare Costs**	**Incl. O&P**
1 Labor Foreman (outside)	$49.25	$394.00	$73.30	$586.40	$54.31	$80.82
3 Laborers	47.25	1134.00	70.35	1688.40		
3 Equip. Oper. (medium)	63.05	1513.20	93.80	2251.20		
1 Pvmt. Profiler, 750 H.P.		3680.74		4048.81		
1 Road Sweeper, S.P., 8' wide		538.01		591.81		
1 F.E. Loader, W.M., 1.5 C.Y.		455.32		500.85	83.47	91.81
56 L.H., Daily Totals		$7715.27		$9667.48	$137.77	$172.63
Crew B-72	**Hr.**	**Daily**	**Hr.**	**Daily**	**Bare Costs**	**Incl. O&P**
1 Labor Foreman (outside)	$49.25	$394.00	$73.30	$586.40	$55.40	$82.44
3 Laborers	47.25	1134.00	70.35	1688.40		
4 Equip. Oper. (medium)	63.05	2017.60	93.80	3001.60		
1 Pvmt. Profiler, 750 H.P.		3680.74		4048.81		
1 Hammermill, 250 H.P.		806.43		887.07		
1 Windrow Loader		1473.50		1620.85		
1 Mix Paver, 165 H.P.		1265.22		1391.74		
1 Roller, Pneum. Whl., 12 Ton		384.55		423.01	118.91	130.80
64 L.H., Daily Totals		$11156.04		$13647.88	$174.31	$213.25
Crew B-73	**Hr.**	**Daily**	**Hr.**	**Daily**	**Bare Costs**	**Incl. O&P**
1 Labor Foreman (outside)	$49.25	$394.00	$73.30	$586.40	$57.38	$85.38
2 Laborers	47.25	756.00	70.35	1125.60		
5 Equip. Oper. (medium)	63.05	2522.00	93.80	3752.00		
1 Road Mixer, 310 H.P.		2108.32		2319.15		
1 Tandem Roller, 10 Ton		379.22		417.14		
1 Hammermill, 250 H.P.		806.43		887.07		
1 Grader, 30,000 Lbs.		1091.19		1200.31		
.5 F.E. Loader, W.M., 1.5 C.Y.		227.66		250.43		
.5 Truck Tractor, 220 H.P.		169.99		186.99		
.5 Water Tank Trailer, 5000 Gal.		84.57		93.03	76.05	83.66
64 L.H., Daily Totals		$8539.38		$10818.12	$133.43	$169.03

Crew No.	Bare Costs		Incl. Subs O&P		Cost Per Labor-Hour	
Crew B-74	**Hr.**	**Daily**	**Hr.**	**Daily**	**Bare Costs**	**Incl. O&P**
1 Labor Foreman (outside)	$49.25	$394.00	$73.30	$586.40	$57.45	$85.57
1 Laborer	47.25	378.00	70.35	562.80		
4 Equip. Oper. (medium)	63.05	2017.60	93.80	3001.60		
2 Truck Drivers (heavy)	55.45	887.20	82.85	1325.60		
1 Grader, 30,000 Lbs.		1091.19		1200.31		
1 Ripper, Beam & 1 Shank		100.54		110.59		
2 Stabilizers, 310 H.P.		1713.46		1884.81		
1 Flatbed Truck, Gas, 3 Ton		391.02		430.12		
1 Chem. Spreader, Towed		87.61		96.37		
1 Roller, Vibratory, 25 Ton		529.68		582.65		
1 Water Tank Trailer, 5000 Gal.		169.14		186.05		
1 Truck Tractor, 220 H.P.		339.98		373.98	69.10	76.01
64 L.H., Daily Totals		$8099.42		$10341.28	$126.55	$161.58
Crew B-75	**Hr.**	**Daily**	**Hr.**	**Daily**	**Bare Costs**	**Incl. O&P**
1 Labor Foreman (outside)	$49.25	$394.00	$73.30	$586.40	$57.74	$85.96
1 Laborer	47.25	378.00	70.35	562.80		
4 Equip. Oper. (medium)	63.05	2017.60	93.80	3001.60		
1 Truck Driver (heavy)	55.45	443.60	82.85	662.80		
1 Grader, 30,000 Lbs.		1091.19		1200.31		
1 Ripper, Beam & 1 Shank		100.54		110.59		
2 Stabilizers, 310 H.P.		1713.46		1884.81		
1 Dist. Tanker, 3000 Gallon		367.10		403.81		
1 Truck Tractor, 6x4, 380 H.P.		545.98		600.58		
1 Roller, Vibratory, 25 Ton		529.68		582.65	77.64	85.41
56 L.H., Daily Totals		$7581.15		$9596.34	$135.38	$171.36
Crew B-76	**Hr.**	**Daily**	**Hr.**	**Daily**	**Bare Costs**	**Incl. O&P**
1 Dock Builder Foreman (outside)	$62.50	$500.00	$96.70	$773.60	$61.56	$93.99
5 Dock Builders	60.50	2420.00	93.60	3744.00		
2 Equip. Oper. (crane)	66.30	1060.80	98.65	1578.40		
1 Equip. Oper. (oiler)	56.40	451.20	83.90	671.20		
1 Crawler Crane, 50 Ton		1704.33		1874.76		
1 Barge, 400 Ton		957.33		1053.06		
1 Hammer, Diesel, 15K ft.-lbs.		687.50		756.25		
1 Lead, 60' High		233.36		256.70		
1 Air Compressor, 600 cfm		466.11		512.72		
2 -50' Air Hoses, 3"		93.52		102.87	57.53	63.28
72 L.H., Daily Totals		$8574.15		$11323.57	$119.09	$157.27
Crew B-76A	**Hr.**	**Daily**	**Hr.**	**Daily**	**Bare Costs**	**Incl. O&P**
1 Labor Foreman (outside)	$49.25	$394.00	$73.30	$586.40	$51.02	$75.95
5 Laborers	47.25	1890.00	70.35	2814.00		
1 Equip. Oper. (crane)	66.30	530.40	98.65	789.20		
1 Equip. Oper. (oiler)	56.40	451.20	83.90	671.20		
1 Crawler Crane, 50 Ton		1704.33		1874.76		
1 Barge, 400 Ton		957.33		1053.06	41.59	45.75
64 L.H., Daily Totals		$5927.26		$7788.63	$92.61	$121.70
Crew B-77	**Hr.**	**Daily**	**Hr.**	**Daily**	**Bare Costs**	**Incl. O&P**
1 Labor Foreman (outside)	$49.25	$394.00	$73.30	$586.40	$48.78	$72.67
3 Laborers	47.25	1134.00	70.35	1688.40		
1 Truck Driver (light)	52.90	423.20	79.00	632.00		
1 Crack Cleaner, 25 H.P.		167.33		184.06		
1 Crack Filler, Trailer Mtd.		201.26		221.39		
1 Flatbed Truck, Gas, 3 Ton		391.02		430.12	18.99	20.89
40 L.H., Daily Totals		$2710.81		$3742.37	$67.77	$93.56

Crews - Standard

Crew No.	Bare Costs		Incl. Subs O&P		Cost Per Labor-Hour	
Crew B-78	Hr.	Daily	Hr.	Daily	Bare Costs	Incl. O&P
1 Labor Foreman (outside)	$49.25	$394.00	$73.30	$586.40	$48.52	$72.28
4 Laborers	47.25	1512.00	70.35	2251.20		
1 Truck Driver (light)	52.90	423.20	79.00	632.00		
1 Paint Striper, S.P., 40 Gallon		73.74		81.11		
1 Flatbed Truck, Gas, 3 Ton		391.02		430.12		
1 Pickup Truck, 3/4 Ton		122.56		134.82	12.24	13.46
48 L.H., Daily Totals		$2916.52		$4115.65	$60.76	$85.74
Crew B-78A	Hr.	Daily	Hr.	Daily	Bare Costs	Incl. O&P
1 Equip. Oper. (light)	$59.70	$477.60	$88.85	$710.80	$59.70	$88.85
1 Line Rem. (Metal Balls) 115 H.P.		1648.72		1813.59	206.09	226.70
8 L.H., Daily Totals		$2126.32		$2524.39	$265.79	$315.55
Crew B-78B	Hr.	Daily	Hr.	Daily	Bare Costs	Incl. O&P
2 Laborers	$47.25	$756.00	$70.35	$1125.60	$48.63	$72.41
.25 Equip. Oper. (light)	59.70	119.40	88.85	177.70		
1 Pickup Truck, 3/4 Ton		122.56		134.82		
1 Line Rem.,11 H.P.,Walk Behind		214.39		235.83		
.25 Road Sweeper, S.P., 8' wide		134.50		147.95	26.19	28.81
18 L.H., Daily Totals		$1346.85		$1821.90	$74.83	$101.22
Crew B-78C	Hr.	Daily	Hr.	Daily	Bare Costs	Incl. O&P
1 Labor Foreman (outside)	$49.25	$394.00	$73.30	$586.40	$48.52	$72.28
4 Laborers	47.25	1512.00	70.35	2251.20		
1 Truck Driver (light)	52.90	423.20	79.00	632.00		
1 Paint Striper, T.M., 120 Gal.		673.88		741.27		
1 Flatbed Truck, Gas, 3 Ton		391.02		430.12		
1 Pickup Truck, 3/4 Ton		122.56		134.82	24.74	27.21
48 L.H., Daily Totals		$3516.66		$4775.81	$73.26	$99.50
Crew B-78D	Hr.	Daily	Hr.	Daily	Bare Costs	Incl. O&P
2 Labor Foremen (outside)	$49.25	$788.00	$73.30	$1172.80	$48.22	$71.81
7 Laborers	47.25	2646.00	70.35	3939.60		
1 Truck Driver (light)	52.90	423.20	79.00	632.00		
1 Paint Striper, T.M., 120 Gal.		673.88		741.27		
1 Flatbed Truck, Gas, 3 Ton		391.02		430.12		
3 Pickup Trucks, 3/4 Ton		367.68		404.45		
1 Air Compressor, 60 cfm		173.21		190.53		
1 -50' Air Hose, 3/4"		8.16		8.98		
1 Breaker, Pavement, 60 lb.		34.47		37.92	20.61	22.67
80 L.H., Daily Totals		$5505.62		$7557.66	$68.82	$94.47
Crew B-78E	Hr.	Daily	Hr.	Daily	Bare Costs	Incl. O&P
2 Labor Foremen (outside)	$49.25	$788.00	$73.30	$1172.80	$48.05	$71.56
9 Laborers	47.25	3402.00	70.35	5065.20		
1 Truck Driver (light)	52.90	423.20	79.00	632.00		
1 Paint Striper, T.M., 120 Gal.		673.88		741.27		
1 Flatbed Truck, Gas, 3 Ton		391.02		430.12		
4 Pickup Trucks, 3/4 Ton		490.24		539.26		
2 Air Compressors, 60 cfm		346.42		381.06		
2 -50' Air Hoses, 3/4"		16.32		17.95		
2 Breakers, Pavement, 60 lb.		68.94		75.83	20.70	22.77
96 L.H., Daily Totals		$6600.02		$9055.50	$68.75	$94.33

Crew No.	Bare Costs		Incl. Subs O&P		Cost Per Labor-Hour	
Crew B-78F	Hr.	Daily	Hr.	Daily	Bare Costs	Incl. O&P
2 Labor Foremen (outside)	$49.25	$788.00	$73.30	$1172.80	$47.94	$71.39
11 Laborers	47.25	4158.00	70.35	6190.80		
1 Truck Driver (light)	52.90	423.20	79.00	632.00		
1 Paint Striper, T.M., 120 Gal.		673.88		741.27		
1 Flatbed Truck, Gas, 3 Ton		391.02		430.12		
7 Pickup Trucks, 3/4 Ton		857.92		943.71		
3 Air Compressors, 60 cfm		519.63		571.59		
3 -50' Air Hoses, 3/4"		24.48		26.93		
3 Breakers, Pavement, 60 lb.		103.41		113.75	22.95	25.24
112 L.H., Daily Totals		$7939.54		$10822.97	$70.89	$96.63
Crew B-79	Hr.	Daily	Hr.	Daily	Bare Costs	Incl. O&P
1 Labor Foreman (outside)	$49.25	$394.00	$73.30	$586.40	$48.78	$72.67
3 Laborers	47.25	1134.00	70.35	1688.40		
1 Truck Driver (light)	52.90	423.20	79.00	632.00		
1 Paint Striper, T.M., 120 Gal.		673.88		741.27		
1 Heating Kettle, 115 Gallon		169.64		186.60		
1 Flatbed Truck, Gas, 3 Ton		391.02		430.12		
2 Pickup Trucks, 3/4 Ton		245.12		269.63	36.99	40.69
40 L.H., Daily Totals		$3430.86		$4534.43	$85.77	$113.36
Crew B-79A	Hr.	Daily	Hr.	Daily	Bare Costs	Incl. O&P
1.5 Equip. Oper. (light)	$59.70	$716.40	$88.85	$1066.20	$59.70	$88.85
.5 Line Remov. (Grinder) 115 H.P.		843.37		927.71		
1 Line Rem. (Metal Balls) 115 H.P.		1648.72		1813.59	207.67	228.44
12 L.H., Daily Totals		$3208.49		$3807.50	$267.37	$317.29
Crew B-79B	Hr.	Daily	Hr.	Daily	Bare Costs	Incl. O&P
1 Laborer	$47.25	$378.00	$70.35	$562.80	$47.25	$70.35
1 Set of Gases		188.67		207.54	23.58	25.94
8 L.H., Daily Totals		$566.67		$770.34	$70.83	$96.29
Crew B-79C	Hr.	Daily	Hr.	Daily	Bare Costs	Incl. O&P
1 Labor Foreman (outside)	$49.25	$394.00	$73.30	$586.40	$48.34	$72.01
5 Laborers	47.25	1890.00	70.35	2814.00		
1 Truck Driver (light)	52.90	423.20	79.00	632.00		
1 Paint Striper, T.M., 120 Gal.		673.88		741.27		
1 Heating Kettle, 115 Gallon		169.64		186.60		
1 Flatbed Truck, Gas, 3 Ton		391.02		430.12		
3 Pickup Trucks, 3/4 Ton		367.68		404.45		
1 Air Compressor, 60 cfm		173.21		190.53		
1 -50' Air Hose, 3/4"		8.16		8.98		
1 Breaker, Pavement, 60 lb.		34.47		37.92	32.47	35.71
56 L.H., Daily Totals		$4525.26		$6032.27	$80.81	$107.72
Crew B-79D	Hr.	Daily	Hr.	Daily	Bare Costs	Incl. O&P
2 Labor Foremen (outside)	$49.25	$788.00	$73.30	$1172.80	$48.46	$72.17
5 Laborers	47.25	1890.00	70.35	2814.00		
1 Truck Driver (light)	52.90	423.20	79.00	632.00		
1 Paint Striper, T.M., 120 Gal.		673.88		741.27		
1 Heating Kettle, 115 Gallon		169.64		186.60		
1 Flatbed Truck, Gas, 3 Ton		391.02		430.12		
4 Pickup Trucks, 3/4 Ton		490.24		539.26		
1 Air Compressor, 60 cfm		173.21		190.53		
1 -50' Air Hose, 3/4"		8.16		8.98		
1 Breaker, Pavement, 60 lb.		34.47		37.92	30.32	33.35
64 L.H., Daily Totals		$5041.82		$6753.48	$78.78	$105.52

Crews - Standard

Crew No.		Bare Costs		Incl. Subs O&P		Cost Per Labor-Hour	
Crew B-79E	Hr.	Daily	Hr.	Daily	Bare Costs	Incl. O&P
2 Labor Foremen (outside)	$49.25	$788.00	$73.30	$1172.80	$48.22	$71.81
7 Laborers	47.25	2646.00	70.35	3939.60		
1 Truck Driver (light)	52.90	423.20	79.00	632.00		
1 Paint Striper, T.M., 120 Gal.		673.88		741.27		
1 Heating Kettle, 115 Gallon		169.64		186.60		
1 Flatbed Truck, Gas, 3 Ton		391.02		430.12		
5 Pickup Trucks, 3/4 Ton		612.80		674.08		
2 Air Compressors, 60 cfm		346.42		381.06		
2 -50' Air Hoses, 3/4"		16.32		17.95		
2 Breakers, Pavement, 60 lb.		68.94		75.83	28.49	31.34
80 L.H., Daily Totals		$6136.22		$8251.32	$76.70	$103.14
Crew B-80	Hr.	Daily	Hr.	Daily	Bare Costs	Incl. O&P
1 Labor Foreman (outside)	$49.25	$394.00	$73.30	$586.40	$52.27	$77.88
1 Laborer	47.25	378.00	70.35	562.80		
1 Truck Driver (light)	52.90	423.20	79.00	632.00		
1 Equip. Oper. (light)	59.70	477.60	88.85	710.80		
1 Flatbed Truck, Gas, 3 Ton		391.02		430.12		
1 Earth Auger, Truck-Mtd.		153.97		169.37	17.03	18.73
32 L.H., Daily Totals		$2217.79		$3091.49	$69.31	$96.61
Crew B-80A	Hr.	Daily	Hr.	Daily	Bare Costs	Incl. O&P
3 Laborers	$47.25	$1134.00	$70.35	$1688.40	$47.25	$70.35
1 Flatbed Truck, Gas, 3 Ton		391.02		430.12	16.29	17.92
24 L.H., Daily Totals		$1525.02		$2118.52	$63.54	$88.27
Crew B-80B	Hr.	Daily	Hr.	Daily	Bare Costs	Incl. O&P
3 Laborers	$47.25	$1134.00	$70.35	$1688.40	$50.36	$74.97
1 Equip. Oper. (light)	59.70	477.60	88.85	710.80		
1 Crane, Flatbed Mounted, 3 Ton		596.44		656.08	18.64	20.50
32 L.H., Daily Totals		$2208.04		$3055.28	$69.00	$95.48
Crew B-80C	Hr.	Daily	Hr.	Daily	Bare Costs	Incl. O&P
2 Laborers	$47.25	$756.00	$70.35	$1125.60	$49.13	$73.23
1 Truck Driver (light)	52.90	423.20	79.00	632.00		
1 Flatbed Truck, Gas, 1.5 Ton		361.95		398.14		
1 Manual Fence Post Auger, Gas		52.21		57.43	17.26	18.98
24 L.H., Daily Totals		$1593.36		$2213.18	$66.39	$92.22
Crew B-81	Hr.	Daily	Hr.	Daily	Bare Costs	Incl. O&P
1 Laborer	$47.25	$378.00	$70.35	$562.80	$55.25	$82.33
1 Equip. Oper. (medium)	63.05	504.40	93.80	750.40		
1 Truck Driver (heavy)	55.45	443.60	82.85	662.80		
1 Hydromulcher, T.M., 3000 Gal.		745.16		819.68		
1 Truck Tractor, 220 H.P.		339.98		373.98	45.21	49.74
24 L.H., Daily Totals		$2411.14		$3169.65	$100.46	$132.07
Crew B-81A	Hr.	Daily	Hr.	Daily	Bare Costs	Incl. O&P
1 Laborer	$47.25	$378.00	$70.35	$562.80	$50.08	$74.67
1 Truck Driver (light)	52.90	423.20	79.00	632.00		
1 Hydromulcher, T.M., 600 Gal.		234.78		258.26		
1 Flatbed Truck, Gas, 3 Ton		391.02		430.12	39.11	43.02
16 L.H., Daily Totals		$1427.00		$1883.18	$89.19	$117.70
Crew B-82	Hr.	Daily	Hr.	Daily	Bare Costs	Incl. O&P
1 Laborer	$47.25	$378.00	$70.35	$562.80	$53.48	$79.60
1 Equip. Oper. (light)	59.70	477.60	88.85	710.80		
1 Horiz. Borer, 6 H.P.		114.54		125.99	7.16	7.87
16 L.H., Daily Totals		$970.14		$1399.59	$60.63	$87.47

Crew No.		Bare Costs		Incl. Subs O&P		Cost Per Labor-Hour	
Crew B-82A	Hr.	Daily	Hr.	Daily	Bare Costs	Incl. O&P
2 Laborers	$47.25	$756.00	$70.35	$1125.60	$53.48	$79.60
2 Equip. Opers. (light)	59.70	955.20	88.85	1421.60		
2 Dump Truck, 8 C.Y., 220 H.P.		834.98		918.48		
1 Flatbed Trailer, 25 Ton		150.61		165.67		
1 Horiz. Dir. Drill, 20k lb. Thrust		685.30		753.83		
1 Mud Trailer for HDD, 1500 Gal.		696.17		765.79		
1 Pickup Truck, 4x4, 3/4 Ton		191.73		210.90		
1 Flatbed Trailer, 3 Ton		78.34		86.17		
1 Loader, Skid Steer, 78 H.P.		429.91		472.90	95.84	105.43
32 L.H., Daily Totals		$4778.24		$5920.94	$149.32	$185.03
Crew B-82B	Hr.	Daily	Hr.	Daily	Bare Costs	Incl. O&P
2 Laborers	$47.25	$756.00	$70.35	$1125.60	$53.48	$79.60
2 Equip. Opers. (light)	59.70	955.20	88.85	1421.60		
2 Dump Truck, 8 C.Y., 220 H.P.		834.98		918.48		
1 Flatbed Trailer, 25 Ton		150.61		165.67		
1 Horiz. Dir. Drill, 30k lb. Thrust		740.76		814.84		
1 Mud Trailer for HDD, 1500 Gal.		696.17		765.79		
1 Pickup Truck, 4x4, 3/4 Ton		191.73		210.90		
1 Flatbed Trailer, 3 Ton		78.34		86.17		
1 Loader, Skid Steer, 78 H.P.		429.91		472.90	97.58	107.34
32 L.H., Daily Totals		$4833.70		$5981.95	$151.05	$186.94
Crew B-82C	Hr.	Daily	Hr.	Daily	Bare Costs	Incl. O&P
2 Laborers	$47.25	$756.00	$70.35	$1125.60	$53.48	$79.60
2 Equip. Opers. (light)	59.70	955.20	88.85	1421.60		
2 Dump Truck, 8 C.Y., 220 H.P.		834.98		918.48		
1 Flatbed Trailer, 25 Ton		150.61		165.67		
1 Horiz. Dir. Drill, 50k lb. Thrust		869.81		956.79		
1 Mud Trailer for HDD, 1500 Gal.		696.17		765.79		
1 Pickup Truck, 4x4, 3/4 Ton		191.73		210.90		
1 Flatbed Trailer, 3 Ton		78.34		86.17		
1 Loader, Skid Steer, 78 H.P.		429.91		472.90	101.61	111.77
32 L.H., Daily Totals		$4962.75		$6123.90	$155.09	$191.37
Crew B-82D	Hr.	Daily	Hr.	Daily	Bare Costs	Incl. O&P
1 Equip. Oper. (light)	$59.70	$477.60	$88.85	$710.80	$59.70	$88.85
1 Mud Trailer for HDD, 1500 Gal.		696.17		765.79	87.02	95.72
8 L.H., Daily Totals		$1173.77		$1476.59	$146.72	$184.57
Crew B-83	Hr.	Daily	Hr.	Daily	Bare Costs	Incl. O&P
1 Tugboat Captain	$63.05	$504.40	$93.80	$750.40	$55.15	$82.08
1 Tugboat Hand	47.25	378.00	70.35	562.80		
1 Tugboat, 250 H.P.		793.50		872.85	49.59	54.55
16 L.H., Daily Totals		$1675.90		$2186.05	$104.74	$136.63
Crew B-84	Hr.	Daily	Hr.	Daily	Bare Costs	Incl. O&P
1 Equip. Oper. (medium)	$63.05	$504.40	$93.80	$750.40	$63.05	$93.80
1 Rotary Mower/Tractor		238.84		262.72	29.86	32.84
8 L.H., Daily Totals		$743.24		$1013.12	$92.91	$126.64
Crew B-85	Hr.	Daily	Hr.	Daily	Bare Costs	Incl. O&P
3 Laborers	$47.25	$1134.00	$70.35	$1688.40	$52.05	$77.54
1 Equip. Oper. (medium)	63.05	504.40	93.80	750.40		
1 Truck Driver (heavy)	55.45	443.60	82.85	662.80		
1 Telescoping Boom Lift, to 80'		710.06		781.07		
1 Brush Chipper, 12", 130 H.P.		518.12		569.93		
1 Pruning Saw, Rotary		27.37		30.11	31.39	34.53
40 L.H., Daily Totals		$3337.55		$4482.70	$83.44	$112.07

Crews - Standard

Crew No.	Bare Costs		Incl. Subs O&P		Cost Per Labor-Hour	
Crew B-86	Hr.	Daily	Hr.	Daily	Bare Costs	Incl. O&P
1 Equip. Oper. (medium)	$63.05	$504.40	$93.80	$750.40	$63.05	$93.80
1 Stump Chipper, S.P.		263.85		290.24	32.98	36.28
8 L.H., Daily Totals		$768.25		$1040.64	$96.03	$130.08
Crew B-86A	Hr.	Daily	Hr.	Daily	Bare Costs	Incl. O&P
1 Equip. Oper. (medium)	$63.05	$504.40	$93.80	$750.40	$63.05	$93.80
1 Grader, 30,000 Lbs.		1091.19		1200.31	136.40	150.04
8 L.H., Daily Totals		$1595.59		$1950.71	$199.45	$243.84
Crew B-86B	Hr.	Daily	Hr.	Daily	Bare Costs	Incl. O&P
1 Equip. Oper. (medium)	$63.05	$504.40	$93.80	$750.40	$63.05	$93.80
1 Dozer, 200 H.P.		1382.36		1520.60	172.79	190.07
8 L.H., Daily Totals		$1886.76		$2271.00	$235.85	$283.87
Crew B-87	Hr.	Daily	Hr.	Daily	Bare Costs	Incl. O&P
1 Laborer	$47.25	$378.00	$70.35	$562.80	$59.89	$89.11
4 Equip. Oper. (medium)	63.05	2017.60	93.80	3001.60		
2 Feller Bunchers, 100 H.P.		2244.42		2468.86		
1 Log Chipper, 22" Tree		686.57		755.23		
1 Dozer, 105 H.P.		702.68		772.95		
1 Chain Saw, Gas, 36" Long		53.61		58.97	92.18	101.40
40 L.H., Daily Totals		$6082.88		$7620.41	$152.07	$190.51
Crew B-88	Hr.	Daily	Hr.	Daily	Bare Costs	Incl. O&P
1 Laborer	$47.25	$378.00	$70.35	$562.80	$60.79	$90.45
6 Equip. Oper. (medium)	63.05	3026.40	93.80	4502.40		
2 Feller Bunchers, 100 H.P.		2244.42		2468.86		
1 Log Chipper, 22" Tree		686.57		755.23		
2 Log Skidders, 50 H.P.		931.94		1025.13		
1 Dozer, 105 H.P.		702.68		772.95		
1 Chain Saw, Gas, 36" Long		53.61		58.97	82.49	90.73
56 L.H., Daily Totals		$8023.62		$10146.34	$143.28	$181.18
Crew B-89	Hr.	Daily	Hr.	Daily	Bare Costs	Incl. O&P
1 Equip. Oper. (light)	$59.70	$477.60	$88.85	$710.80	$56.30	$83.92
1 Truck Driver (light)	52.90	423.20	79.00	632.00		
1 Flatbed Truck, Gas, 3 Ton		391.02		430.12		
1 Concrete Saw		176.00		193.60		
1 Water Tank, 65 Gal.		97.09		106.80	41.51	45.66
16 L.H., Daily Totals		$1564.91		$2073.32	$97.81	$129.58
Crew B-89A	Hr.	Daily	Hr.	Daily	Bare Costs	Incl. O&P
1 Skilled Worker	$61.25	$490.00	$92.00	$736.00	$54.25	$81.17
1 Laborer	47.25	378.00	70.35	562.80		
1 Core Drill (Large)		118.14		129.95	7.38	8.12
16 L.H., Daily Totals		$986.14		$1428.75	$61.63	$89.30
Crew B-89B	Hr.	Daily	Hr.	Daily	Bare Costs	Incl. O&P
1 Equip. Oper. (light)	$59.70	$477.60	$88.85	$710.80	$56.30	$83.92
1 Truck Driver (light)	52.90	423.20	79.00	632.00		
1 Wall Saw, Hydraulic, 10 H.P.		111.53		122.68		
1 Generator, Diesel, 100 kW		568.06		624.87		
1 Water Tank, 65 Gal.		97.09		106.80		
1 Flatbed Truck, Gas, 3 Ton		391.02		430.12	72.98	80.28
16 L.H., Daily Totals		$2068.50		$2627.27	$129.28	$164.20
Crew B-89C	Hr.	Daily	Hr.	Daily	Bare Costs	Incl. O&P
1 Cement Finisher	$55.00	$440.00	$80.45	$643.60	$55.00	$80.45
1 Masonry cut-off saw, gas		68.42		75.26	8.55	9.41
8 L.H., Daily Totals		$508.42		$718.86	$63.55	$89.86

Crew No.	Bare Costs		Incl. Subs O&P		Cost Per Labor-Hour	
Crew B-90	Hr.	Daily	Hr.	Daily	Bare Costs	Incl. O&P
1 Labor Foreman (outside)	$49.25	$394.00	$73.30	$586.40	$52.66	$78.47
3 Laborers	47.25	1134.00	70.35	1688.40		
2 Equip. Oper. (light)	59.70	955.20	88.85	1421.60		
2 Truck Drivers (heavy)	55.45	887.20	82.85	1325.60		
1 Road Mixer, 310 H.P.		2108.32		2319.15		
1 Dist. Truck, 2000 Gal.		333.32		366.65	38.15	41.97
64 L.H., Daily Totals		$5812.04		$7707.80	$90.81	$120.43
Crew B-90A	Hr.	Daily	Hr.	Daily	Bare Costs	Incl. O&P
1 Labor Foreman (outside)	$49.25	$394.00	$73.30	$586.40	$56.56	$84.17
2 Laborers	47.25	756.00	70.35	1125.60		
4 Equip. Oper. (medium)	63.05	2017.60	93.80	3001.60		
2 Graders, 30,000 Lbs.		2182.38		2400.62		
1 Tandem Roller, 10 Ton		379.22		417.14		
1 Roller, Pneum. Whl., 12 Ton		384.55		423.01	52.61	57.87
56 L.H., Daily Totals		$6113.75		$7954.36	$109.17	$142.04
Crew B-90B	Hr.	Daily	Hr.	Daily	Bare Costs	Incl. O&P
1 Labor Foreman (outside)	$49.25	$394.00	$73.30	$586.40	$55.48	$82.57
2 Laborers	47.25	756.00	70.35	1125.60		
3 Equip. Oper. (medium)	63.05	1513.20	93.80	2251.20		
1 Roller, Pneum. Whl., 12 Ton		384.55		423.01		
1 Road Mixer, 310 H.P.		2108.32		2319.15	51.93	57.13
48 L.H., Daily Totals		$5156.07		$6705.36	$107.42	$139.69
Crew B-90C	Hr.	Daily	Hr.	Daily	Bare Costs	Incl. O&P
1 Labor Foreman (outside)	$49.25	$394.00	$73.30	$586.40	$53.98	$80.42
4 Laborers	47.25	1512.00	70.35	2251.20		
3 Equip. Oper. (medium)	63.05	1513.20	93.80	2251.20		
3 Truck Drivers (heavy)	55.45	1330.80	82.85	1988.40		
3 Road Mixers, 310 H.P.		6324.96		6957.46	71.87	79.06
88 L.H., Daily Totals		$11074.96		$14034.66	$125.85	$159.48
Crew B-90D	Hr.	Daily	Hr.	Daily	Bare Costs	Incl. O&P
1 Labor Foreman (outside)	$49.25	$394.00	$73.30	$586.40	$52.94	$78.87
6 Laborers	47.25	2268.00	70.35	3376.80		
3 Equip. Oper. (medium)	63.05	1513.20	93.80	2251.20		
3 Truck Drivers (heavy)	55.45	1330.80	82.85	1988.40		
3 Road Mixers, 310 H.P.		6324.96		6957.46	60.82	66.90
104 L.H., Daily Totals		$11830.96		$15160.26	$113.76	$145.77
Crew B-90E	Hr.	Daily	Hr.	Daily	Bare Costs	Incl. O&P
1 Labor Foreman (outside)	$49.25	$394.00	$73.30	$586.40	$53.65	$79.88
4 Laborers	47.25	1512.00	70.35	2251.20		
3 Equip. Oper. (medium)	63.05	1513.20	93.80	2251.20		
1 Truck Driver (heavy)	55.45	443.60	82.85	662.80		
1 Road Mixer, 310 H.P.		2108.32		2319.15	29.28	32.21
72 L.H., Daily Totals		$5971.12		$8070.75	$82.93	$112.09
Crew B-91	Hr.	Daily	Hr.	Daily	Bare Costs	Incl. O&P
1 Labor Foreman (outside)	$49.25	$394.00	$73.30	$586.40	$56.42	$84.01
2 Laborers	47.25	756.00	70.35	1125.60		
4 Equip. Oper. (medium)	63.05	2017.60	93.80	3001.60		
1 Truck Driver (heavy)	55.45	443.60	82.85	662.80		
1 Dist. Tanker, 3000 Gallon		367.10		403.81		
1 Truck Tractor, 6x4, 380 H.P.		545.98		600.58		
1 Aggreg. Spreader, S.P.		941.36		1035.50		
1 Roller, Pneum. Whl., 12 Ton		384.55		423.01		
1 Tandem Roller, 10 Ton		379.22		417.14	40.91	45.00
64 L.H., Daily Totals		$6229.41		$8256.43	$97.33	$129.01

Crews - Standard

Crew No.	Bare Costs		Incl. Subs O&P		Cost Per Labor-Hour	
Crew B-91B	Hr.	Daily	Hr.	Daily	Bare Costs	Incl. O&P
1 Laborer	$47.25	$378.00	$70.35	$562.80	$55.15	$82.08
1 Equipment Oper. (med.)	63.05	504.40	93.80	750.40		
1 Road Sweeper, Vac. Assist.		1900.22		2090.24	118.76	130.64
16 L.H., Daily Totals		$2782.62		$3403.44	$173.91	$212.72
Crew B-91C	Hr.	Daily	Hr.	Daily	Bare Costs	Incl. O&P
1 Laborer	$47.25	$378.00	$70.35	$562.80	$50.08	$74.67
1 Truck Driver (light)	52.90	423.20	79.00	632.00		
1 Catch Basin Cleaning Truck		594.04		653.44	37.13	40.84
16 L.H., Daily Totals		$1395.24		$1848.24	$87.20	$115.52
Crew B-91D	Hr.	Daily	Hr.	Daily	Bare Costs	Incl. O&P
1 Labor Foreman (outside)	$49.25	$394.00	$73.30	$586.40	$54.74	$81.52
5 Laborers	47.25	1890.00	70.35	2814.00		
5 Equip. Oper. (medium)	63.05	2522.00	93.80	3752.00		
2 Truck Drivers (heavy)	55.45	887.20	82.85	1325.60		
1 Aggreg. Spreader, S.P.		941.36		1035.50		
2 Truck Tractors, 6x4, 380 H.P.		1091.96		1201.16		
2 Dist. Tankers, 3000 Gallon		734.20		807.62		
2 Pavement Brushes, Towed		194.16		213.58		
2 Rollers Pneum. Whl., 12 Ton		769.10		846.01	35.87	39.46
104 L.H., Daily Totals		$9423.98		$12581.86	$90.62	$120.98
Crew B-92	Hr.	Daily	Hr.	Daily	Bare Costs	Incl. O&P
1 Labor Foreman (outside)	$49.25	$394.00	$73.30	$586.40	$47.75	$71.09
3 Laborers	47.25	1134.00	70.35	1688.40		
1 Crack Cleaner, 25 H.P.		167.33		184.06		
1 Air Compressor, 60 cfm		173.21		190.53		
1 Tar Kettle, T.M.		199.54		219.49		
1 Flatbed Truck, Gas, 3 Ton		391.02		430.12	29.10	32.01
32 L.H., Daily Totals		$2459.10		$3299.01	$76.85	$103.09
Crew B-93	Hr.	Daily	Hr.	Daily	Bare Costs	Incl. O&P
1 Equip. Oper. (medium)	$63.05	$504.40	$93.80	$750.40	$63.05	$93.80
1 Feller Buncher, 100 H.P.		1122.21		1234.43	140.28	154.30
8 L.H., Daily Totals		$1626.61		$1984.83	$203.33	$248.10
Crew B-94A	Hr.	Daily	Hr.	Daily	Bare Costs	Incl. O&P
1 Laborer	$47.25	$378.00	$70.35	$562.80	$47.25	$70.35
1 Diaphragm Water Pump, 2"		61.92		68.11		
1 -20' Suction Hose, 2"		4.37		4.81		
2 -50' Discharge Hoses, 2"		8.18		9.00	9.31	10.24
8 L.H., Daily Totals		$452.47		$644.72	$56.56	$80.59
Crew B-94B	Hr.	Daily	Hr.	Daily	Bare Costs	Incl. O&P
1 Laborer	$47.25	$378.00	$70.35	$562.80	$47.25	$70.35
1 Diaphragm Water Pump, 4"		150.72		165.79		
1 -20' Suction Hose, 4"		19.04		20.94		
2 -50' Discharge Hoses, 4"		28.30		31.13	24.76	27.23
8 L.H., Daily Totals		$576.06		$780.67	$72.01	$97.58
Crew B-94C	Hr.	Daily	Hr.	Daily	Bare Costs	Incl. O&P
1 Laborer	$47.25	$378.00	$70.35	$562.80	$47.25	$70.35
1 Centrifugal Water Pump, 3"		82.39		90.63		
1 -20' Suction Hose, 3"		8.96		9.86		
2 -50' Discharge Hoses, 3"		9.76		10.74	12.64	13.90
8 L.H., Daily Totals		$479.11		$674.02	$59.89	$84.25

Crew No.	Bare Costs		Incl. Subs O&P		Cost Per Labor-Hour	
Crew B-94D	Hr.	Daily	Hr.	Daily	Bare Costs	Incl. O&P
1 Laborer	$47.25	$378.00	$70.35	$562.80	$47.25	$70.35
1 Centr. Water Pump, 6"		386.48		425.13		
1 -20' Suction Hose, 6"		28.12		30.93		
2 -50' Discharge Hoses, 6"		39.98		43.98	56.82	62.50
8 L.H., Daily Totals		$832.58		$1062.84	$104.07	$132.85
Crew C-1	Hr.	Daily	Hr.	Daily	Bare Costs	Incl. O&P
3 Carpenters	$58.60	$1406.40	$87.25	$2094.00	$55.76	$83.03
1 Laborer	47.25	378.00	70.35	562.80		
32 L.H., Daily Totals		$1784.40		$2656.80	$55.76	$83.03
Crew C-2	Hr.	Daily	Hr.	Daily	Bare Costs	Incl. O&P
1 Carpenter Foreman (outside)	$60.60	$484.80	$90.20	$721.60	$57.04	$84.92
4 Carpenters	58.60	1875.20	87.25	2792.00		
1 Laborer	47.25	378.00	70.35	562.80		
48 L.H., Daily Totals		$2738.00		$4076.40	$57.04	$84.92
Crew C-2A	Hr.	Daily	Hr.	Daily	Bare Costs	Incl. O&P
1 Carpenter Foreman (outside)	$60.60	$484.80	$90.20	$721.60	$56.44	$83.79
3 Carpenters	58.60	1406.40	87.25	2094.00		
1 Cement Finisher	55.00	440.00	80.45	643.60		
1 Laborer	47.25	378.00	70.35	562.80		
48 L.H., Daily Totals		$2709.20		$4022.00	$56.44	$83.79
Crew C-3	Hr.	Daily	Hr.	Daily	Bare Costs	Incl. O&P
1 Rodman Foreman (outside)	$66.55	$532.40	$99.40	$795.20	$59.87	$89.32
4 Rodmen (reinf.)	64.55	2065.60	96.40	3084.80		
1 Equip. Oper. (light)	59.70	477.60	88.85	710.80		
2 Laborers	47.25	756.00	70.35	1125.60		
3 Stressing Equipment		51.87		57.06		
.5 Grouting Equipment		97.91		107.70	2.34	2.57
64 L.H., Daily Totals		$3981.38		$5881.15	$62.21	$91.89
Crew C-4	Hr.	Daily	Hr.	Daily	Bare Costs	Incl. O&P
1 Rodman Foreman (outside)	$66.55	$532.40	$99.40	$795.20	$65.05	$97.15
3 Rodmen (reinf.)	64.55	1549.20	96.40	2313.60		
3 Stressing Equipment		51.87		57.06	1.62	1.78
32 L.H., Daily Totals		$2133.47		$3165.86	$66.67	$98.93
Crew C-4A	Hr.	Daily	Hr.	Daily	Bare Costs	Incl. O&P
2 Rodmen (reinf.)	$64.55	$1032.80	$96.40	$1542.40	$64.55	$96.40
4 Stressing Equipment		69.16		76.08	4.32	4.75
16 L.H., Daily Totals		$1101.96		$1618.48	$68.87	$101.15
Crew C-5	Hr.	Daily	Hr.	Daily	Bare Costs	Incl. O&P
1 Rodman Foreman (outside)	$66.55	$532.40	$99.40	$795.20	$63.92	$95.36
4 Rodmen (reinf.)	64.55	2065.60	96.40	3084.80		
1 Equip. Oper. (crane)	66.30	530.40	98.65	789.20		
1 Equip. Oper. (oiler)	56.40	451.20	83.90	671.20		
1 Hyd. Crane, 25 Ton		2273.31		2500.64	40.59	44.65
56 L.H., Daily Totals		$5852.91		$7841.04	$104.52	$140.02
Crew C-6	Hr.	Daily	Hr.	Daily	Bare Costs	Incl. O&P
1 Labor Foreman (outside)	$49.25	$394.00	$73.30	$586.40	$48.88	$72.53
4 Laborers	47.25	1512.00	70.35	2251.20		
1 Cement Finisher	55.00	440.00	80.45	643.60		
2 Gas Engine Vibrators		59.36		65.30	1.24	1.36
48 L.H., Daily Totals		$2405.36		$3546.50	$50.11	$73.89

Crews - Standard

Crew No.	Bare Costs		Incl. Subs O&P		Cost Per Labor-Hour	
Crew C-6A	Hr.	Daily	Hr.	Daily	Bare Costs	Incl. O&P
2 Cement Finishers	$55.00	$880.00	$80.45	$1287.20	$55.00	$80.45
1 Concrete Vibrator, Elec, 2 HP		32.92		36.21	2.06	2.26
16 L.H., Daily Totals		$912.92		$1323.41	$57.06	$82.71
Crew C-7	Hr.	Daily	Hr.	Daily	Bare Costs	Incl. O&P
1 Labor Foreman (outside)	$49.25	$394.00	$73.30	$586.40	$51.11	$75.91
5 Laborers	47.25	1890.00	70.35	2814.00		
1 Cement Finisher	55.00	440.00	80.45	643.60		
1 Equip. Oper. (medium)	63.05	504.40	93.80	750.40		
1 Equip. Oper. (oiler)	56.40	451.20	83.90	671.20		
2 Gas Engine Vibrators		59.36		65.30		
1 Concrete Bucket, 1 C.Y.		50.97		56.07		
1 Hyd. Crane, 55 Ton		2461.06		2707.17	35.71	39.29
72 L.H., Daily Totals		$6250.99		$8294.13	$86.82	$115.20
Crew C-7A	Hr.	Daily	Hr.	Daily	Bare Costs	Incl. O&P
1 Labor Foreman (outside)	$49.25	$394.00	$73.30	$586.40	$49.55	$73.84
5 Laborers	47.25	1890.00	70.35	2814.00		
2 Truck Drivers (heavy)	55.45	887.20	82.85	1325.60		
2 Conc. Transit Mixers		1400.52		1540.57	21.88	24.07
64 L.H., Daily Totals		$4571.72		$6266.57	$71.43	$97.92
Crew C-7B	Hr.	Daily	Hr.	Daily	Bare Costs	Incl. O&P
1 Labor Foreman (outside)	$49.25	$394.00	$73.30	$586.40	$51.02	$75.95
5 Laborers	47.25	1890.00	70.35	2814.00		
1 Equipment Operator, Crane	66.30	530.40	98.65	789.20		
1 Equipment Oiler	56.40	451.20	83.90	671.20		
1 Conc. Bucket, 2 C.Y.		76.52		84.17		
1 Lattice Boom Crane, 165 Ton		2672.17		2939.39	42.95	47.24
64 L.H., Daily Totals		$6014.29		$7884.36	$93.97	$123.19
Crew C-7C	Hr.	Daily	Hr.	Daily	Bare Costs	Incl. O&P
1 Labor Foreman (outside)	$49.25	$394.00	$73.30	$586.40	$51.45	$76.58
5 Laborers	47.25	1890.00	70.35	2814.00		
2 Equipment Operators (med.)	63.05	1008.80	93.80	1500.80		
2 F.E. Loaders, W.M., 4 C.Y.		1579.96		1737.96	24.69	27.16
64 L.H., Daily Totals		$4872.76		$6639.16	$76.14	$103.74
Crew C-7D	Hr.	Daily	Hr.	Daily	Bare Costs	Incl. O&P
1 Labor Foreman (outside)	$49.25	$394.00	$73.30	$586.40	$49.79	$74.12
5 Laborers	47.25	1890.00	70.35	2814.00		
1 Equip. Oper. (medium)	63.05	504.40	93.80	750.40		
1 Concrete Conveyer		194.76		214.24	3.48	3.83
56 L.H., Daily Totals		$2983.16		$4365.04	$53.27	$77.95
Crew C-8	Hr.	Daily	Hr.	Daily	Bare Costs	Incl. O&P
1 Labor Foreman (outside)	$49.25	$394.00	$73.30	$586.40	$52.01	$77.01
3 Laborers	47.25	1134.00	70.35	1688.40		
2 Cement Finishers	55.00	880.00	80.45	1287.20		
1 Equip. Oper. (medium)	63.05	504.40	93.80	750.40		
1 Concrete Pump (Small)		827.49		910.24	14.78	16.25
56 L.H., Daily Totals		$3739.89		$5222.64	$66.78	$93.26
Crew C-8A	Hr.	Daily	Hr.	Daily	Bare Costs	Incl. O&P
1 Labor Foreman (outside)	$49.25	$394.00	$73.30	$586.40	$50.17	$74.21
3 Laborers	47.25	1134.00	70.35	1688.40		
2 Cement Finishers	55.00	880.00	80.45	1287.20		
48 L.H., Daily Totals		$2408.00		$3562.00	$50.17	$74.21

Crew No.	Bare Costs		Incl. Subs O&P		Cost Per Labor-Hour	
Crew C-8B	Hr.	Daily	Hr.	Daily	Bare Costs	Incl. O&P
1 Labor Foreman (outside)	$49.25	$394.00	$73.30	$586.40	$50.81	$75.63
3 Laborers	47.25	1134.00	70.35	1688.40		
1 Equip. Oper. (medium)	63.05	504.40	93.80	750.40		
1 Vibrating Power Screed		90.64		99.70		
1 Roller, Vibratory, 25 Ton		529.68		582.65		
1 Dozer, 200 H.P.		1382.36		1520.60	50.07	55.07
40 L.H., Daily Totals		$4035.08		$5228.15	$100.88	$130.70
Crew C-8C	Hr.	Daily	Hr.	Daily	Bare Costs	Incl. O&P
1 Labor Foreman (outside)	$49.25	$394.00	$73.30	$586.40	$51.51	$76.43
3 Laborers	47.25	1134.00	70.35	1688.40		
1 Cement Finisher	55.00	440.00	80.45	643.60		
1 Equip. Oper. (medium)	63.05	504.40	93.80	750.40		
1 Shotcrete Pump Rig, 12 C.Y./hr		651.19		716.31		
1 Air Compressor, 160 cfm		244.12		268.53		
4 -50' Air Hoses, 1"		37.24		40.96		
4 -50' Air Hoses, 2"		129.40		142.34	22.12	24.34
48 L.H., Daily Totals		$3534.35		$4836.94	$73.63	$100.77
Crew C-8D	Hr.	Daily	Hr.	Daily	Bare Costs	Incl. O&P
1 Labor Foreman (outside)	$49.25	$394.00	$73.30	$586.40	$52.80	$78.24
1 Laborer	47.25	378.00	70.35	562.80		
1 Cement Finisher	55.00	440.00	80.45	643.60		
1 Equipment Oper. (light)	59.70	477.60	88.85	710.80		
1 Air Compressor, 250 cfm		196.28		215.91		
2 -50' Air Hoses, 1"		18.62		20.48	6.72	7.39
32 L.H., Daily Totals		$1904.50		$2739.99	$59.52	$85.62
Crew C-8E	Hr.	Daily	Hr.	Daily	Bare Costs	Incl. O&P
1 Labor Foreman (outside)	$49.25	$394.00	$73.30	$586.40	$50.95	$75.61
3 Laborers	47.25	1134.00	70.35	1688.40		
1 Cement Finisher	55.00	440.00	80.45	643.60		
1 Equipment Oper. (light)	59.70	477.60	88.85	710.80		
1 Shotcrete Rig, 35 C.Y./hr		797.28		877.01		
1 Air Compressor, 250 cfm		196.28		215.91		
4 -50' Air Hoses, 1"		37.24		40.96		
4 -50' Air Hoses, 2"		129.40		142.34	24.17	26.59
48 L.H., Daily Totals		$3605.80		$4905.42	$75.12	$102.20
Crew C-9	Hr.	Daily	Hr.	Daily	Bare Costs	Incl. O&P
1 Cement Finisher	$55.00	$440.00	$80.45	$643.60	$52.30	$77.50
2 Laborers	47.25	756.00	70.35	1125.60		
1 Equipment Oper. (light)	59.70	477.60	88.85	710.80		
1 Grout Pump, 50 C.F./hr.		158.45		174.29		
1 Air Compressor, 160 cfm		244.12		268.53		
2 -50' Air Hoses, 1"		18.62		20.48		
2 -50' Air Hoses, 2"		64.70		71.17	15.18	16.70
32 L.H., Daily Totals		$2159.49		$3014.48	$67.48	$94.20
Crew C-10	Hr.	Daily	Hr.	Daily	Bare Costs	Incl. O&P
1 Laborer	$47.25	$378.00	$70.35	$562.80	$52.42	$77.08
2 Cement Finishers	55.00	880.00	80.45	1287.20		
24 L.H., Daily Totals		$1258.00		$1850.00	$52.42	$77.08
Crew C-10B	Hr.	Daily	Hr.	Daily	Bare Costs	Incl. O&P
3 Laborers	$47.25	$1134.00	$70.35	$1688.40	$50.35	$74.39
2 Cement Finishers	55.00	880.00	80.45	1287.20		
1 Concrete Mixer, 10 C.F.		149.77		164.75		
2 Trowels, 48" Walk-Behind		171.24		188.36	8.03	8.83
40 L.H., Daily Totals		$2335.01		$3328.71	$58.38	$83.22

Crews - Standard

Crew No.	Bare Costs		Incl. Subs O&P		Cost Per Labor-Hour	
Crew C-10C	Hr.	Daily	Hr.	Daily	Bare Costs	Incl. O&P
1 Laborer	$47.25	$378.00	$70.35	$562.80	$52.42	$77.08
2 Cement Finishers	55.00	880.00	80.45	1287.20		
1 Trowel, 48" Walk-Behind		85.62		94.18	3.57	3.92
24 L.H., Daily Totals		$1343.62		$1944.18	$55.98	$81.01
Crew C-10D	Hr.	Daily	Hr.	Daily	Bare Costs	Incl. O&P
1 Laborer	$47.25	$378.00	$70.35	$562.80	$52.42	$77.08
2 Cement Finishers	55.00	880.00	80.45	1287.20		
1 Vibrating Power Screed		90.64		99.70		
1 Trowel, 48" Walk-Behind		85.62		94.18	7.34	8.08
24 L.H., Daily Totals		$1434.26		$2043.89	$59.76	$85.16
Crew C-10E	Hr.	Daily	Hr.	Daily	Bare Costs	Incl. O&P
1 Laborer	$47.25	$378.00	$70.35	$562.80	$52.42	$77.08
2 Cement Finishers	55.00	880.00	80.45	1287.20		
1 Vibrating Power Screed		90.64		99.70		
1 Cement Trowel, 96" Ride-On		225.34		247.87	13.17	14.48
24 L.H., Daily Totals		$1573.98		$2197.58	$65.58	$91.57
Crew C-10F	Hr.	Daily	Hr.	Daily	Bare Costs	Incl. O&P
1 Laborer	$47.25	$378.00	$70.35	$562.80	$52.42	$77.08
2 Cement Finishers	55.00	880.00	80.45	1287.20		
1 Telescoping Boom Lift, to 60'		385.68		424.25	16.07	17.68
24 L.H., Daily Totals		$1643.68		$2274.25	$68.49	$94.76
Crew C-11	Hr.	Daily	Hr.	Daily	Bare Costs	Incl. O&P
1 Struc. Steel Foreman (outside)	$66.55	$532.40	$102.50	$820.00	$64.06	$97.94
6 Struc. Steel Workers	64.55	3098.40	99.40	4771.20		
1 Equip. Oper. (crane)	66.30	530.40	98.65	789.20		
1 Equip. Oper. (oiler)	56.40	451.20	83.90	671.20		
1 Lattice Boom Crane, 150 Ton		2585.11		2843.62	35.90	39.49
72 L.H., Daily Totals		$7197.51		$9895.22	$99.97	$137.43
Crew C-12	Hr.	Daily	Hr.	Daily	Bare Costs	Incl. O&P
1 Carpenter Foreman (outside)	$60.60	$484.80	$90.20	$721.60	$58.33	$86.83
3 Carpenters	58.60	1406.40	87.25	2094.00		
1 Laborer	47.25	378.00	70.35	562.80		
1 Equip. Oper. (crane)	66.30	530.40	98.65	789.20		
1 Hyd. Crane, 12 Ton		2150.65		2365.72	44.81	49.29
48 L.H., Daily Totals		$4950.25		$6533.31	$103.13	$136.11
Crew C-13	Hr.	Daily	Hr.	Daily	Bare Costs	Incl. O&P
1 Struc. Steel Worker	$64.55	$516.40	$99.40	$795.20	$62.57	$95.35
1 Welder	64.55	516.40	99.40	795.20		
1 Carpenter	58.60	468.80	87.25	698.00		
1 Welder, Gas Engine, 300 amp		147.09		161.80	6.13	6.74
24 L.H., Daily Totals		$1648.69		$2450.20	$68.70	$102.09
Crew C-14	Hr.	Daily	Hr.	Daily	Bare Costs	Incl. O&P
1 Carpenter Foreman (outside)	$60.60	$484.80	$90.20	$721.60	$57.42	$85.38
5 Carpenters	58.60	2344.00	87.25	3490.00		
4 Laborers	47.25	1512.00	70.35	2251.20		
4 Rodmen (reinf.)	64.55	2065.60	96.40	3084.80		
2 Cement Finishers	55.00	880.00	80.45	1287.20		
1 Equip. Oper. (crane)	66.30	530.40	98.65	789.20		
1 Equip. Oper. (oiler)	56.40	451.20	83.90	671.20		
1 Hyd. Crane, 80 Ton		2641.70		2905.87	18.35	20.18
144 L.H., Daily Totals		$10909.70		$15201.07	$75.76	$105.56

Crew No.	Bare Costs		Incl. Subs O&P		Cost Per Labor-Hour	
Crew C-14A	Hr.	Daily	Hr.	Daily	Bare Costs	Incl. O&P
1 Carpenter Foreman (outside)	$60.60	$484.80	$90.20	$721.60	$58.76	$87.47
16 Carpenters	58.60	7500.80	87.25	11168.00		
4 Rodmen (reinf.)	64.55	2065.60	96.40	3084.80		
2 Laborers	47.25	756.00	70.35	1125.60		
1 Cement Finisher	55.00	440.00	80.45	643.60		
1 Equip. Oper. (medium)	63.05	504.40	93.80	750.40		
1 Gas Engine Vibrator		29.68		32.65		
1 Concrete Pump (Small)		827.49		910.24	4.29	4.71
200 L.H., Daily Totals		$12608.77		$18436.89	$63.04	$92.18
Crew C-14B	Hr.	Daily	Hr.	Daily	Bare Costs	Incl. O&P
1 Carpenter Foreman (outside)	$60.60	$484.80	$90.20	$721.60	$58.61	$87.20
16 Carpenters	58.60	7500.80	87.25	11168.00		
4 Rodmen (reinf.)	64.55	2065.60	96.40	3084.80		
2 Laborers	47.25	756.00	70.35	1125.60		
2 Cement Finishers	55.00	880.00	80.45	1287.20		
1 Equip. Oper. (medium)	63.05	504.40	93.80	750.40		
1 Gas Engine Vibrator		29.68		32.65		
1 Concrete Pump (Small)		827.49		910.24	4.12	4.53
208 L.H., Daily Totals		$13048.77		$19080.49	$62.73	$91.73
Crew C-14C	Hr.	Daily	Hr.	Daily	Bare Costs	Incl. O&P
1 Carpenter Foreman (outside)	$60.60	$484.80	$90.20	$721.60	$56.09	$83.45
6 Carpenters	58.60	2812.80	87.25	4188.00		
2 Rodmen (reinf.)	64.55	1032.80	96.40	1542.40		
4 Laborers	47.25	1512.00	70.35	2251.20		
1 Cement Finisher	55.00	440.00	80.45	643.60		
1 Gas Engine Vibrator		29.68		32.65	.27	.29
112 L.H., Daily Totals		$6312.08		$9379.45	$56.36	$83.75
Crew C-14D	Hr.	Daily	Hr.	Daily	Bare Costs	Incl. O&P
1 Carpenter Foreman (outside)	$60.60	$484.80	$90.20	$721.60	$58.28	$86.74
18 Carpenters	58.60	8438.40	87.25	12564.00		
2 Rodmen (reinf.)	64.55	1032.80	96.40	1542.40		
2 Laborers	47.25	756.00	70.35	1125.60		
1 Cement Finisher	55.00	440.00	80.45	643.60		
1 Equip. Oper. (medium)	63.05	504.40	93.80	750.40		
1 Gas Engine Vibrator		29.68		32.65		
1 Concrete Pump (Small)		827.49		910.24	4.29	4.71
200 L.H., Daily Totals		$12513.57		$18290.49	$62.57	$91.45
Crew C-14E	Hr.	Daily	Hr.	Daily	Bare Costs	Incl. O&P
1 Carpenter Foreman (outside)	$60.60	$484.80	$90.20	$721.60	$57.52	$85.62
2 Carpenters	58.60	937.60	87.25	1396.00		
4 Rodmen (reinf.)	64.55	2065.60	96.40	3084.80		
3 Laborers	47.25	1134.00	70.35	1688.40		
1 Cement Finisher	55.00	440.00	80.45	643.60		
1 Gas Engine Vibrator		29.68		32.65	.34	.37
88 L.H., Daily Totals		$5091.68		$7567.05	$57.86	$85.99
Crew C-14F	Hr.	Daily	Hr.	Daily	Bare Costs	Incl. O&P
1 Labor Foreman (outside)	$49.25	$394.00	$73.30	$586.40	$52.64	$77.41
2 Laborers	47.25	756.00	70.35	1125.60		
6 Cement Finishers	55.00	2640.00	80.45	3861.60		
1 Gas Engine Vibrator		29.68		32.65	.41	.45
72 L.H., Daily Totals		$3819.68		$5606.25	$53.05	$77.86

Crews - Standard

Crew No.	Bare Costs		Incl. Subs O&P		Cost Per Labor-Hour	
Crew C-14G	Hr.	Daily	Hr.	Daily	Bare Costs	Incl. O&P
1 Labor Foreman (outside)	$49.25	$394.00	$73.30	$586.40	$51.96	$76.54
2 Laborers	47.25	756.00	70.35	1125.60		
4 Cement Finishers	55.00	1760.00	80.45	2574.40		
1 Gas Engine Vibrator		29.68		32.65	.53	.58
56 L.H., Daily Totals		$2939.68		$4319.05	$52.49	$77.13
Crew C-14H	Hr.	Daily	Hr.	Daily	Bare Costs	Incl. O&P
1 Carpenter Foreman (outside)	$60.60	$484.80	$90.20	$721.60	$57.43	$85.32
2 Carpenters	58.60	937.60	87.25	1396.00		
1 Rodman (reinf.)	64.55	516.40	96.40	771.20		
1 Laborer	47.25	378.00	70.35	562.80		
1 Cement Finisher	55.00	440.00	80.45	643.60		
1 Gas Engine Vibrator		29.68		32.65	.62	.68
48 L.H., Daily Totals		$2786.48		$4127.85	$58.05	$86.00
Crew C-14L	Hr.	Daily	Hr.	Daily	Bare Costs	Incl. O&P
1 Carpenter Foreman (outside)	$60.60	$484.80	$90.20	$721.60	$54.68	$81.30
6 Carpenters	58.60	2812.80	87.25	4188.00		
4 Laborers	47.25	1512.00	70.35	2251.20		
1 Cement Finisher	55.00	440.00	80.45	643.60		
1 Gas Engine Vibrator		29.68		32.65	.31	.34
96 L.H., Daily Totals		$5279.28		$7837.05	$54.99	$81.64
Crew C-14M	Hr.	Daily	Hr.	Daily	Bare Costs	Incl. O&P
1 Carpenter Foreman (outside)	$60.60	$484.80	$90.20	$721.60	$56.86	$84.51
2 Carpenters	58.60	937.60	87.25	1396.00		
1 Rodman (reinf.)	64.55	516.40	96.40	771.20		
2 Laborers	47.25	756.00	70.35	1125.60		
1 Cement Finisher	55.00	440.00	80.45	643.60		
1 Equip. Oper. (medium)	63.05	504.40	93.80	750.40		
1 Gas Engine Vibrator		29.68		32.65		
1 Concrete Pump (Small)		827.49		910.24	13.39	14.73
64 L.H., Daily Totals		$4496.37		$6351.29	$70.26	$99.24
Crew C-15	Hr.	Daily	Hr.	Daily	Bare Costs	Incl. O&P
1 Carpenter Foreman (outside)	$60.60	$484.80	$90.20	$721.60	$54.90	$81.45
2 Carpenters	58.60	937.60	87.25	1396.00		
3 Laborers	47.25	1134.00	70.35	1688.40		
2 Cement Finishers	55.00	880.00	80.45	1287.20		
1 Rodman (reinf.)	64.55	516.40	96.40	771.20		
72 L.H., Daily Totals		$3952.80		$5864.40	$54.90	$81.45
Crew C-16	Hr.	Daily	Hr.	Daily	Bare Costs	Incl. O&P
1 Labor Foreman (outside)	$49.25	$394.00	$73.30	$586.40	$52.01	$77.01
3 Laborers	47.25	1134.00	70.35	1688.40		
2 Cement Finishers	55.00	880.00	80.45	1287.20		
1 Equip. Oper. (medium)	63.05	504.40	93.80	750.40		
1 Gunite Pump Rig		352.58		387.84		
2 -50' Air Hoses, 3/4"		16.32		17.95		
2 -50' Air Hoses, 2"		64.70		71.17	7.74	8.52
56 L.H., Daily Totals		$3346.00		$4789.36	$59.75	$85.52
Crew C-16A	Hr.	Daily	Hr.	Daily	Bare Costs	Incl. O&P
1 Laborer	$47.25	$378.00	$70.35	$562.80	$55.08	$81.26
2 Cement Finishers	55.00	880.00	80.45	1287.20		
1 Equip. Oper. (medium)	63.05	504.40	93.80	750.40		
1 Gunite Pump Rig		352.58		387.84		
2 -50' Air Hoses, 3/4"		16.32		17.95		
2 -50' Air Hoses, 2"		64.70		71.17		
1 Telescoping Boom Lift, to 60'		385.68		424.25	25.60	28.16
32 L.H., Daily Totals		$2581.68		$3501.61	$80.68	$109.43

Crew No.	Bare Costs		Incl. Subs O&P		Cost Per Labor-Hour	
Crew C-17	Hr.	Daily	Hr.	Daily	Bare Costs	Incl. O&P
2 Skilled Worker Foremen (out)	$63.25	$1012.00	$95.00	$1520.00	$61.65	$92.60
8 Skilled Workers	61.25	3920.00	92.00	5888.00		
80 L.H., Daily Totals		$4932.00		$7408.00	$61.65	$92.60
Crew C-17A	Hr.	Daily	Hr.	Daily	Bare Costs	Incl. O&P
2 Skilled Worker Foremen (out)	$63.25	$1012.00	$95.00	$1520.00	$61.71	$92.68
8 Skilled Workers	61.25	3920.00	92.00	5888.00		
.13 Equip. Oper. (crane)	66.30	68.95	98.65	102.60		
.13 Hyd. Crane, 80 Ton		343.42		377.76	4.24	4.66
81.04 L.H., Daily Totals		$5344.37		$7888.36	$65.95	$97.34
Crew C-17B	Hr.	Daily	Hr.	Daily	Bare Costs	Incl. O&P
2 Skilled Worker Foremen (out)	$63.25	$1012.00	$95.00	$1520.00	$61.76	$92.75
8 Skilled Workers	61.25	3920.00	92.00	5888.00		
.25 Equip. Oper. (crane)	66.30	132.60	98.65	197.30		
.25 Hyd. Crane, 80 Ton		660.42		726.47		
.25 Trowel, 48" Walk-Behind		21.41		23.55	8.31	9.15
82 L.H., Daily Totals		$5746.43		$8355.31	$70.08	$101.89
Crew C-17C	Hr.	Daily	Hr.	Daily	Bare Costs	Incl. O&P
2 Skilled Worker Foremen (out)	$63.25	$1012.00	$95.00	$1520.00	$61.82	$92.82
8 Skilled Workers	61.25	3920.00	92.00	5888.00		
.38 Equip. Oper. (crane)	66.30	201.55	98.65	299.90		
.38 Hyd. Crane, 80 Ton		1003.85		1104.23	12.09	13.30
83.04 L.H., Daily Totals		$6137.40		$8812.13	$73.91	$106.12
Crew C-17D	Hr.	Daily	Hr.	Daily	Bare Costs	Incl. O&P
2 Skilled Worker Foremen (out)	$63.25	$1012.00	$95.00	$1520.00	$61.87	$92.89
8 Skilled Workers	61.25	3920.00	92.00	5888.00		
.5 Equip. Oper. (crane)	66.30	265.20	98.65	394.60		
.5 Hyd. Crane, 80 Ton		1320.85		1452.93	15.72	17.30
84 L.H., Daily Totals		$6518.05		$9255.53	$77.60	$110.18
Crew C-17E	Hr.	Daily	Hr.	Daily	Bare Costs	Incl. O&P
2 Skilled Worker Foremen (out)	$63.25	$1012.00	$95.00	$1520.00	$61.65	$92.60
8 Skilled Workers	61.25	3920.00	92.00	5888.00		
1 Hyd. Jack with Rods		40.57		44.63	.51	.56
80 L.H., Daily Totals		$4972.57		$7452.63	$62.16	$93.16
Crew C-18	Hr.	Daily	Hr.	Daily	Bare Costs	Incl. O&P
.13 Labor Foreman (outside)	$49.25	$51.22	$73.30	$76.23	$47.48	$70.69
1 Laborer	47.25	378.00	70.35	562.80		
1 Concrete Cart, 10 C.F.		149.92		164.91	16.58	18.24
9.04 L.H., Daily Totals		$579.14		$803.94	$64.06	$88.93
Crew C-19	Hr.	Daily	Hr.	Daily	Bare Costs	Incl. O&P
.13 Labor Foreman (outside)	$49.25	$51.22	$73.30	$76.23	$47.48	$70.69
1 Laborer	47.25	378.00	70.35	562.80		
1 Concrete Cart, 18 C.F.		122.73		135.00	13.58	14.93
9.04 L.H., Daily Totals		$551.95		$774.03	$61.06	$85.62
Crew C-20	Hr.	Daily	Hr.	Daily	Bare Costs	Incl. O&P
1 Labor Foreman (outside)	$49.25	$394.00	$73.30	$586.40	$50.44	$74.91
5 Laborers	47.25	1890.00	70.35	2814.00		
1 Cement Finisher	55.00	440.00	80.45	643.60		
1 Equip. Oper. (medium)	63.05	504.40	93.80	750.40		
2 Gas Engine Vibrators		59.36		65.30		
1 Concrete Pump (Small)		827.49		910.24	13.86	15.24
64 L.H., Daily Totals		$4115.25		$5769.94	$64.30	$90.16

Crews - Standard

Crew No.	Bare Costs		Incl. Subs O&P		Cost Per Labor-Hour	
Crew C-21	**Hr.**	**Daily**	**Hr.**	**Daily**	**Bare Costs**	**Incl. O&P**
1 Labor Foreman (outside)	$49.25	$394.00	$73.30	$586.40	$50.44	$74.91
5 Laborers	47.25	1890.00	70.35	2814.00		
1 Cement Finisher	55.00	440.00	80.45	643.60		
1 Equip. Oper. (medium)	63.05	504.40	93.80	750.40		
2 Gas Engine Vibrators		59.36		65.30		
1 Concrete Conveyer		194.76		214.24	3.97	4.37
64 L.H., Daily Totals		$3482.52		$5073.93	$54.41	$79.28
Crew C-22	**Hr.**	**Daily**	**Hr.**	**Daily**	**Bare Costs**	**Incl. O&P**
1 Rodman Foreman (outside)	$66.55	$532.40	$99.40	$795.20	$64.77	$96.72
4 Rodmen (reinf.)	64.55	2065.60	96.40	3084.80		
.13 Equip. Oper. (crane)	66.30	68.95	98.65	102.60		
.13 Equip. Oper. (oiler)	56.40	58.66	83.90	87.26		
.13 Hyd. Crane, 25 Ton		295.53		325.08	7.02	7.73
42.08 L.H., Daily Totals		$3021.14		$4394.94	$71.80	$104.44
Crew C-23	**Hr.**	**Daily**	**Hr.**	**Daily**	**Bare Costs**	**Incl. O&P**
2 Skilled Worker Foremen (out)	$63.25	$1012.00	$95.00	$1520.00	$61.67	$92.45
6 Skilled Workers	61.25	2940.00	92.00	4416.00		
1 Equip. Oper. (crane)	66.30	530.40	98.65	789.20		
1 Equip. Oper. (oiler)	56.40	451.20	83.90	671.20		
1 Lattice Boom Crane, 90 Ton		2689.54		2958.49	33.62	36.98
80 L.H., Daily Totals		$7623.14		$10354.89	$95.29	$129.44
Crew C-23A	**Hr.**	**Daily**	**Hr.**	**Daily**	**Bare Costs**	**Incl. O&P**
1 Labor Foreman (outside)	$49.25	$394.00	$73.30	$586.40	$53.29	$79.31
2 Laborers	47.25	756.00	70.35	1125.60		
1 Equip. Oper. (crane)	66.30	530.40	98.65	789.20		
1 Equip. Oper. (oiler)	56.40	451.20	83.90	671.20		
1 Crawler Crane, 100 Ton		1552.12		1707.33		
3 Conc. Buckets, 8 C.Y.		425.58		468.14	49.44	54.39
40 L.H., Daily Totals		$4109.30		$5347.87	$102.73	$133.70
Crew C-24	**Hr.**	**Daily**	**Hr.**	**Daily**	**Bare Costs**	**Incl. O&P**
2 Skilled Worker Foremen (out)	$63.25	$1012.00	$95.00	$1520.00	$61.67	$92.45
6 Skilled Workers	61.25	2940.00	92.00	4416.00		
1 Equip. Oper. (crane)	66.30	530.40	98.65	789.20		
1 Equip. Oper. (oiler)	56.40	451.20	83.90	671.20		
1 Lattice Boom Crane, 150 Ton		2585.11		2843.62	32.31	35.55
80 L.H., Daily Totals		$7518.71		$10240.02	$93.98	$128.00
Crew C-25	**Hr.**	**Daily**	**Hr.**	**Daily**	**Bare Costs**	**Incl. O&P**
2 Rodmen (reinf.)	$64.55	$1032.80	$96.40	$1542.40	$51.70	$79.67
2 Rodmen Helpers	38.85	621.60	62.95	1007.20		
32 L.H., Daily Totals		$1654.40		$2549.60	$51.70	$79.67
Crew C-27	**Hr.**	**Daily**	**Hr.**	**Daily**	**Bare Costs**	**Incl. O&P**
2 Cement Finishers	$55.00	$880.00	$80.45	$1287.20	$55.00	$80.45
1 Concrete Saw		176.00		193.60	11.00	12.10
16 L.H., Daily Totals		$1056.00		$1480.80	$66.00	$92.55
Crew C-28	**Hr.**	**Daily**	**Hr.**	**Daily**	**Bare Costs**	**Incl. O&P**
1 Cement Finisher	$55.00	$440.00	$80.45	$643.60	$55.00	$80.45
1 Portable Air Compressor, Gas		34.53		37.98	4.32	4.75
8 L.H., Daily Totals		$474.53		$681.58	$59.32	$85.20
Crew C-29	**Hr.**	**Daily**	**Hr.**	**Daily**	**Bare Costs**	**Incl. O&P**
1 Laborer	$47.25	$378.00	$70.35	$562.80	$47.25	$70.35
1 Pressure Washer		104.23		114.65	13.03	14.33
8 L.H., Daily Totals		$482.23		$677.45	$60.28	$84.68

Crew No.	Bare Costs		Incl. Subs O&P		Cost Per Labor-Hour	
Crew C-30	**Hr.**	**Daily**	**Hr.**	**Daily**	**Bare Costs**	**Incl. O&P**
1 Laborer	$47.25	$378.00	$70.35	$562.80	$47.25	$70.35
1 Concrete Mixer, 10 C.F.		149.77		164.75	18.72	20.59
8 L.H., Daily Totals		$527.77		$727.55	$65.97	$90.94
Crew C-31	**Hr.**	**Daily**	**Hr.**	**Daily**	**Bare Costs**	**Incl. O&P**
1 Cement Finisher	$55.00	$440.00	$80.45	$643.60	$55.00	$80.45
1 Grout Pump		352.58		387.84	44.07	48.48
8 L.H., Daily Totals		$792.58		$1031.44	$99.07	$128.93
Crew C-32	**Hr.**	**Daily**	**Hr.**	**Daily**	**Bare Costs**	**Incl. O&P**
1 Cement Finisher	$55.00	$440.00	$80.45	$643.60	$51.13	$75.40
1 Laborer	47.25	378.00	70.35	562.80		
1 Crack Chaser Saw, Gas, 6 H.P.		86.61		95.27		
1 Vacuum Pick-Up System		73.53		80.88	10.01	11.01
16 L.H., Daily Totals		$978.14		$1382.55	$61.13	$86.41
Crew D-1	**Hr.**	**Daily**	**Hr.**	**Daily**	**Bare Costs**	**Incl. O&P**
1 Bricklayer	$57.50	$460.00	$86.35	$690.80	$52.08	$78.20
1 Bricklayer Helper	46.65	373.20	70.05	560.40		
16 L.H., Daily Totals		$833.20		$1251.20	$52.08	$78.20
Crew D-2	**Hr.**	**Daily**	**Hr.**	**Daily**	**Bare Costs**	**Incl. O&P**
3 Bricklayers	$57.50	$1380.00	$86.35	$2072.40	$53.65	$80.50
2 Bricklayer Helpers	46.65	746.40	70.05	1120.80		
.5 Carpenter	58.60	234.40	87.25	349.00		
44 L.H., Daily Totals		$2360.80		$3542.20	$53.65	$80.50
Crew D-3	**Hr.**	**Daily**	**Hr.**	**Daily**	**Bare Costs**	**Incl. O&P**
3 Bricklayers	$57.50	$1380.00	$86.35	$2072.40	$53.42	$80.18
2 Bricklayer Helpers	46.65	746.40	70.05	1120.80		
.25 Carpenter	58.60	117.20	87.25	174.50		
42 L.H., Daily Totals		$2243.60		$3367.70	$53.42	$80.18
Crew D-4	**Hr.**	**Daily**	**Hr.**	**Daily**	**Bare Costs**	**Incl. O&P**
1 Bricklayer	$57.50	$460.00	$86.35	$690.80	$52.63	$78.83
2 Bricklayer Helpers	46.65	746.40	70.05	1120.80		
1 Equip. Oper. (light)	59.70	477.60	88.85	710.80		
1 Grout Pump, 50 C.F./hr.		158.45		174.29	4.95	5.45
32 L.H., Daily Totals		$1842.45		$2696.70	$57.58	$84.27
Crew D-5	**Hr.**	**Daily**	**Hr.**	**Daily**	**Bare Costs**	**Incl. O&P**
1 Bricklayer	57.50	460.00	86.35	690.80	57.50	86.35
8 L.H., Daily Totals		$460.00		$690.80	$57.50	$86.35
Crew D-6	**Hr.**	**Daily**	**Hr.**	**Daily**	**Bare Costs**	**Incl. O&P**
3 Bricklayers	$57.50	$1380.00	$86.35	$2072.40	$52.34	$78.56
3 Bricklayer Helpers	46.65	1119.60	70.05	1681.20		
.25 Carpenter	58.60	117.20	87.25	174.50		
50 L.H., Daily Totals		$2616.80		$3928.10	$52.34	$78.56
Crew D-7	**Hr.**	**Daily**	**Hr.**	**Daily**	**Bare Costs**	**Incl. O&P**
1 Tile Layer	$55.30	$442.40	$80.80	$646.40	$49.90	$72.90
1 Tile Layer Helper	44.50	356.00	65.00	520.00		
16 L.H., Daily Totals		$798.40		$1166.40	$49.90	$72.90
Crew D-8	**Hr.**	**Daily**	**Hr.**	**Daily**	**Bare Costs**	**Incl. O&P**
3 Bricklayers	$57.50	$1380.00	$86.35	$2072.40	$53.16	$79.83
2 Bricklayer Helpers	46.65	746.40	70.05	1120.80		
40 L.H., Daily Totals		$2126.40		$3193.20	$53.16	$79.83

Crews - Standard

Crew No.	Bare Costs		Incl. Subs O&P		Cost Per Labor-Hour	
Crew D-9	Hr.	Daily	Hr.	Daily	Bare Costs	Incl. O&P
3 Bricklayers	$57.50	$1380.00	$86.35	$2072.40	$52.08	$78.20
3 Bricklayer Helpers	46.65	1119.60	70.05	1681.20		
48 L.H., Daily Totals		$2499.60		$3753.60	$52.08	$78.20
Crew D-10	Hr.	Daily	Hr.	Daily	Bare Costs	Incl. O&P
1 Bricklayer Foreman (outside)	$59.50	$476.00	$89.35	$714.80	$57.49	$86.10
1 Bricklayer	57.50	460.00	86.35	690.80		
1 Bricklayer Helper	46.65	373.20	70.05	560.40		
1 Equip. Oper. (crane)	66.30	530.40	98.65	789.20		
1 S.P. Crane, 4x4, 12 Ton		637.99		701.79	19.94	21.93
32 L.H., Daily Totals		$2477.59		$3456.99	$77.42	$108.03
Crew D-11	Hr.	Daily	Hr.	Daily	Bare Costs	Incl. O&P
1 Bricklayer Foreman (outside)	$59.50	$476.00	$89.35	$714.80	$54.55	$81.92
1 Bricklayer	57.50	460.00	86.35	690.80		
1 Bricklayer Helper	46.65	373.20	70.05	560.40		
24 L.H., Daily Totals		$1309.20		$1966.00	$54.55	$81.92
Crew D-12	Hr.	Daily	Hr.	Daily	Bare Costs	Incl. O&P
1 Bricklayer Foreman (outside)	$59.50	$476.00	$89.35	$714.80	$52.58	$78.95
1 Bricklayer	57.50	460.00	86.35	690.80		
2 Bricklayer Helpers	46.65	746.40	70.05	1120.80		
32 L.H., Daily Totals		$1682.40		$2526.40	$52.58	$78.95
Crew D-13	Hr.	Daily	Hr.	Daily	Bare Costs	Incl. O&P
1 Bricklayer Foreman (outside)	$59.50	$476.00	$89.35	$714.80	$55.87	$83.62
1 Bricklayer	57.50	460.00	86.35	690.80		
2 Bricklayer Helpers	46.65	746.40	70.05	1120.80		
1 Carpenter	58.60	468.80	87.25	698.00		
1 Equip. Oper. (crane)	66.30	530.40	98.65	789.20		
1 S.P. Crane, 4x4, 12 Ton		637.99		701.79	13.29	14.62
48 L.H., Daily Totals		$3319.59		$4715.39	$69.16	$98.24
Crew D-14	Hr.	Daily	Hr.	Daily	Bare Costs	Incl. O&P
3 Bricklayers	$57.50	$1380.00	$86.35	$2072.40	$54.79	$82.28
1 Bricklayer Helper	46.65	373.20	70.05	560.40		
32 L.H., Daily Totals		$1753.20		$2632.80	$54.79	$82.28
Crew E-1	Hr.	Daily	Hr.	Daily	Bare Costs	Incl. O&P
1 Welder Foreman (outside)	$66.55	$532.40	$102.50	$820.00	$63.60	$96.92
1 Welder	64.55	516.40	99.40	795.20		
1 Equip. Oper. (light)	59.70	477.60	88.85	710.80		
1 Welder, Gas Engine, 300 amp		147.09		161.80	6.13	6.74
24 L.H., Daily Totals		$1673.49		$2487.80	$69.73	$103.66
Crew E-2	Hr.	Daily	Hr.	Daily	Bare Costs	Incl. O&P
1 Struc. Steel Foreman (outside)	$66.55	$532.40	$102.50	$820.00	$63.92	$97.52
4 Struc. Steel Workers	64.55	2065.60	99.40	3180.80		
1 Equip. Oper. (crane)	66.30	530.40	98.65	789.20		
1 Equip. Oper. (oiler)	56.40	451.20	83.90	671.20		
1 Lattice Boom Crane, 90 Ton		2689.54		2958.49	48.03	52.83
56 L.H., Daily Totals		$6269.14		$8419.69	$111.95	$150.35
Crew E-3	Hr.	Daily	Hr.	Daily	Bare Costs	Incl. O&P
1 Struc. Steel Foreman (outside)	$66.55	$532.40	$102.50	$820.00	$65.22	$100.43
1 Struc. Steel Worker	64.55	516.40	99.40	795.20		
1 Welder	64.55	516.40	99.40	795.20		
1 Welder, Gas Engine, 300 amp		147.09		161.80	6.13	6.74
24 L.H., Daily Totals		$1712.29		$2572.20	$71.35	$107.17
Crew E-3A	Hr.	Daily	Hr.	Daily	Bare Costs	Incl. O&P
1 Struc. Steel Foreman (outside)	$66.55	$532.40	$102.50	$820.00	$65.22	$100.43
1 Struc. Steel Worker	64.55	516.40	99.40	795.20		
1 Welder	64.55	516.40	99.40	795.20		
1 Welder, Gas Engine, 300 amp		147.09		161.80		
1 Telescoping Boom Lift, to 40'		345.57		380.13	20.53	22.58
24 L.H., Daily Totals		$2057.86		$2952.33	$85.74	$123.01
Crew E-4	Hr.	Daily	Hr.	Daily	Bare Costs	Incl. O&P
1 Struc. Steel Foreman (outside)	$66.55	$532.40	$102.50	$820.00	$65.05	$100.18
3 Struc. Steel Workers	64.55	1549.20	99.40	2385.60		
1 Welder, Gas Engine, 300 amp		147.09		161.80	4.60	5.06
32 L.H., Daily Totals		$2228.69		$3367.40	$69.65	$105.23
Crew E-5	Hr.	Daily	Hr.	Daily	Bare Costs	Incl. O&P
2 Struc. Steel Foremen (outside)	$66.55	$1064.80	$102.50	$1640.00	$64.31	$98.39
5 Struc. Steel Workers	64.55	2582.00	99.40	3976.00		
1 Equip. Oper. (crane)	66.30	530.40	98.65	789.20		
1 Welder	64.55	516.40	99.40	795.20		
1 Equip. Oper. (oiler)	56.40	451.20	83.90	671.20		
1 Lattice Boom Crane, 90 Ton		2689.54		2958.49		
1 Welder, Gas Engine, 300 amp		147.09		161.80	35.46	39.00
80 L.H., Daily Totals		$7981.43		$10991.89	$99.77	$137.40
Crew E-6	Hr.	Daily	Hr.	Daily	Bare Costs	Incl. O&P
3 Struc. Steel Foremen (outside)	$66.55	$1597.20	$102.50	$2460.00	$64.22	$98.31
9 Struc. Steel Workers	64.55	4647.60	99.40	7156.80		
1 Equip. Oper. (crane)	66.30	530.40	98.65	789.20		
1 Welder	64.55	516.40	99.40	795.20		
1 Equip. Oper. (oiler)	56.40	451.20	83.90	671.20		
1 Equip. Oper. (light)	59.70	477.60	88.85	710.80		
1 Lattice Boom Crane, 90 Ton		2689.54		2958.49		
1 Welder, Gas Engine, 300 amp		147.09		161.80		
1 Air Compressor, 160 cfm		244.12		268.53		
2 Impact Wrenches		92.56		101.82	24.79	27.27
128 L.H., Daily Totals		$11393.71		$16073.84	$89.01	$125.58
Crew E-7	Hr.	Daily	Hr.	Daily	Bare Costs	Incl. O&P
1 Struc. Steel Foreman (outside)	$66.55	$532.40	$102.50	$820.00	$64.31	$98.39
4 Struc. Steel Workers	64.55	2065.60	99.40	3180.80		
1 Equip. Oper. (crane)	66.30	530.40	98.65	789.20		
1 Equip. Oper. (oiler)	56.40	451.20	83.90	671.20		
1 Welder Foreman (outside)	66.55	532.40	102.50	820.00		
2 Welders	64.55	1032.80	99.40	1590.40		
1 Lattice Boom Crane, 90 Ton		2689.54		2958.49		
2 Welder, Gas Engine, 300 amp		294.18		323.60	37.30	41.03
80 L.H., Daily Totals		$8128.52		$11153.69	$101.61	$139.42
Crew E-8	Hr.	Daily	Hr.	Daily	Bare Costs	Incl. O&P
1 Struc. Steel Foreman (outside)	$66.55	$532.40	$102.50	$820.00	$63.99	$97.82
4 Struc. Steel Workers	64.55	2065.60	99.40	3180.80		
1 Welder Foreman (outside)	66.55	532.40	102.50	820.00		
4 Welders	64.55	2065.60	99.40	3180.80		
1 Equip. Oper. (crane)	66.30	530.40	98.65	789.20		
1 Equip. Oper. (oiler)	56.40	451.20	83.90	671.20		
1 Equip. Oper. (light)	59.70	477.60	88.85	710.80		
1 Lattice Boom Crane, 90 Ton		2689.54		2958.49		
4 Welder, Gas Engine, 300 amp		588.36		647.20	31.52	34.67
104 L.H., Daily Totals		$9933.10		$13778.49	$95.51	$132.49

Crews - Standard

Crew No.		Bare Costs		Incl. Subs O&P		Cost Per Labor-Hour	
Crew E-9	Hr.	Daily	Hr.	Daily	Bare Costs	Incl. O&P
2 Struc. Steel Foremen (outside)	$66.55	$1064.80	$102.50	$1640.00	$64.22	$98.31
5 Struc. Steel Workers	64.55	2582.00	99.40	3976.00		
1 Welder Foreman (outside)	66.55	532.40	102.50	820.00		
5 Welders	64.55	2582.00	99.40	3976.00		
1 Equip. Oper. (crane)	66.30	530.40	98.65	789.20		
1 Equip. Oper. (oiler)	56.40	451.20	83.90	671.20		
1 Equip. Oper. (light)	59.70	477.60	88.85	710.80		
1 Lattice Boom Crane, 90 Ton		2689.54		2958.49		
5 Welder, Gas Engine, 300 amp		735.45		809.00	26.76	29.43
128 L.H., Daily Totals		$11645.39		$16350.69	$90.98	$127.74
Crew E-10	Hr.	Daily	Hr.	Daily	Bare Costs	Incl. O&P
1 Welder Foreman (outside)	$66.55	$532.40	$102.50	$820.00	$65.55	$100.95
1 Welder	64.55	516.40	99.40	795.20		
1 Welder, Gas Engine, 300 amp		147.09		161.80		
1 Flatbed Truck, Gas, 3 Ton		391.02		430.12	33.63	37.00
16 L.H., Daily Totals		$1586.91		$2207.12	$99.18	$137.95
Crew E-11	Hr.	Daily	Hr.	Daily	Bare Costs	Incl. O&P
2 Painters, Struc. Steel	$51.20	$819.20	$81.75	$1308.00	$52.34	$80.67
1 Building Laborer	47.25	378.00	70.35	562.80		
1 Equip. Oper. (light)	59.70	477.60	88.85	710.80		
1 Air Compressor, 250 cfm		196.28		215.91		
1 Sandblaster, Portable, 3 C.F.		84.26		92.69		
1 Set Sand Blasting Accessories		17.14		18.85	9.30	10.23
32 L.H., Daily Totals		$1972.48		$2909.05	$61.64	$90.91
Crew E-11A	Hr.	Daily	Hr.	Daily	Bare Costs	Incl. O&P
2 Painters, Struc. Steel	$51.20	$819.20	$81.75	$1308.00	$52.34	$80.67
1 Building Laborer	47.25	378.00	70.35	562.80		
1 Equip. Oper. (light)	59.70	477.60	88.85	710.80		
1 Air Compressor, 250 cfm		196.28		215.91		
1 Sandblaster, Portable, 3 C.F.		84.26		92.69		
1 Set Sand Blasting Accessories		17.14		18.85		
1 Telescoping Boom Lift, to 60'		385.68		424.25	21.36	23.49
32 L.H., Daily Totals		$2358.16		$3333.30	$73.69	$104.17
Crew E-11B	Hr.	Daily	Hr.	Daily	Bare Costs	Incl. O&P
2 Painters, Struc. Steel	$51.20	$819.20	$81.75	$1308.00	$49.88	$77.95
1 Building Laborer	47.25	378.00	70.35	562.80		
2 Paint Sprayer, 8 C.F.M.		104.28		114.71		
1 Telescoping Boom Lift, to 60'		385.68		424.25	20.41	22.46
24 L.H., Daily Totals		$1687.16		$2409.76	$70.30	$100.41
Crew E-12	Hr.	Daily	Hr.	Daily	Bare Costs	Incl. O&P
1 Welder Foreman (outside)	$66.55	$532.40	$102.50	$820.00	$63.13	$95.67
1 Equip. Oper. (light)	59.70	477.60	88.85	710.80		
1 Welder, Gas Engine, 300 amp		147.09		161.80	9.19	10.11
16 L.H., Daily Totals		$1157.09		$1692.60	$72.32	$105.79
Crew E-13	Hr.	Daily	Hr.	Daily	Bare Costs	Incl. O&P
1 Welder Foreman (outside)	$66.55	$532.40	$102.50	$820.00	$64.27	$97.95
.5 Equip. Oper. (light)	59.70	238.80	88.85	355.40		
1 Welder, Gas Engine, 300 amp		147.09		161.80	12.26	13.48
12 L.H., Daily Totals		$918.29		$1337.20	$76.52	$111.43
Crew E-14	Hr.	Daily	Hr.	Daily	Bare Costs	Incl. O&P
1 Welder Foreman (outside)	$66.55	$532.40	$102.50	$820.00	$66.55	$102.50
1 Welder, Gas Engine, 300 amp		147.09		161.80	18.39	20.22
8 L.H., Daily Totals		$679.49		$981.80	$84.94	$122.72

Crew No.		Bare Costs		Incl. Subs O&P		Cost Per Labor-Hour	
Crew E-16	Hr.	Daily	Hr.	Daily	Bare Costs	Incl. O&P
1 Welder Foreman (outside)	$66.55	$532.40	$102.50	$820.00	$65.55	$100.95
1 Welder	64.55	516.40	99.40	795.20		
1 Welder, Gas Engine, 300 amp		147.09		161.80	9.19	10.11
16 L.H., Daily Totals		$1195.89		$1777.00	$74.74	$111.06
Crew E-17	Hr.	Daily	Hr.	Daily	Bare Costs	Incl. O&P
1 Struc. Steel Foreman (outside)	$66.55	$532.40	$102.50	$820.00	$65.55	$100.95
1 Structural Steel Worker	64.55	516.40	99.40	795.20		
16 L.H., Daily Totals		$1048.80		$1615.20	$65.55	$100.95
Crew E-18	Hr.	Daily	Hr.	Daily	Bare Costs	Incl. O&P
1 Struc. Steel Foreman (outside)	$66.55	$532.40	$102.50	$820.00	$64.65	$98.90
3 Structural Steel Workers	64.55	1549.20	99.40	2385.60		
1 Equipment Operator (med.)	63.05	504.40	93.80	750.40		
1 Lattice Boom Crane, 20 Ton		868.10		954.91	21.70	23.87
40 L.H., Daily Totals		$3454.10		$4910.91	$86.35	$122.77
Crew E-19	Hr.	Daily	Hr.	Daily	Bare Costs	Incl. O&P
1 Struc. Steel Foreman (outside)	$66.55	$532.40	$102.50	$820.00	$63.60	$96.92
1 Structural Steel Worker	64.55	516.40	99.40	795.20		
1 Equip. Oper. (light)	59.70	477.60	88.85	710.80		
1 Lattice Boom Crane, 20 Ton		868.10		954.91	36.17	39.79
24 L.H., Daily Totals		$2394.50		$3280.91	$99.77	$136.70
Crew E-20	Hr.	Daily	Hr.	Daily	Bare Costs	Incl. O&P
1 Struc. Steel Foreman (outside)	$66.55	$532.40	$102.50	$820.00	$64.00	$97.76
5 Structural Steel Workers	64.55	2582.00	99.40	3976.00		
1 Equip. Oper. (crane)	66.30	530.40	98.65	789.20		
1 Equip. Oper. (oiler)	56.40	451.20	83.90	671.20		
1 Lattice Boom Crane, 40 Ton		2371.83		2609.01	37.06	40.77
64 L.H., Daily Totals		$6467.83		$8865.41	$101.06	$138.52
Crew E-22	Hr.	Daily	Hr.	Daily	Bare Costs	Incl. O&P
1 Skilled Worker Foreman (out)	$63.25	$506.00	$95.00	$760.00	$61.92	$93.00
2 Skilled Workers	61.25	980.00	92.00	1472.00		
24 L.H., Daily Totals		$1486.00		$2232.00	$61.92	$93.00
Crew E-24	Hr.	Daily	Hr.	Daily	Bare Costs	Incl. O&P
3 Structural Steel Workers	$64.55	$1549.20	$99.40	$2385.60	$64.17	$98.00
1 Equipment Operator (med.)	63.05	504.40	93.80	750.40		
1 Hyd. Crane, 25 Ton		2273.31		2500.64	71.04	78.14
32 L.H., Daily Totals		$4326.91		$5636.64	$135.22	$176.15
Crew E-25	Hr.	Daily	Hr.	Daily	Bare Costs	Incl. O&P
1 Welder Foreman (outside)	$66.55	$532.40	$102.50	$820.00	$66.55	$102.50
1 Cutting Torch		14.24		15.66	1.78	1.96
8 L.H., Daily Totals		$546.64		$835.66	$68.33	$104.46
Crew E-26	Hr.	Daily	Hr.	Daily	Bare Costs	Incl. O&P
1 Struc. Steel Foreman (outside)	$66.55	$532.40	$102.50	$820.00	$65.86	$100.91
1 Struc. Steel Worker	64.55	516.40	99.40	795.20		
1 Welder	64.55	516.40	99.40	795.20		
.25 Electrician	67.35	134.70	100.10	200.20		
.25 Plumber	72.05	144.10	107.45	214.90		
1 Welder, Gas Engine, 300 amp		147.09		161.80	5.25	5.78
28 L.H., Daily Totals		$1991.09		$2987.30	$71.11	$106.69

Crews - Standard

Crew No.	Bare Costs		Incl. Subs O&P		Cost Per Labor-Hour	
Crew E-27	**Hr.**	**Daily**	**Hr.**	**Daily**	**Bare Costs**	**Incl. O&P**
1 Struc. Steel Foreman (outside)	$66.55	$532.40	$102.50	$820.00	$64.00	$97.76
5 Struc. Steel Workers	64.55	2582.00	99.40	3976.00		
1 Equip. Oper. (crane)	66.30	530.40	98.65	789.20		
1 Equip. Oper. (oiler)	56.40	451.20	83.90	671.20		
1 Hyd. Crane, 12 Ton		2150.65		2365.72		
1 Hyd. Crane, 80 Ton		2641.70		2905.87	74.88	82.37
64 L.H., Daily Totals		$8888.35		$11527.99	$138.88	$180.12
Crew F-3	**Hr.**	**Daily**	**Hr.**	**Daily**	**Bare Costs**	**Incl. O&P**
4 Carpenters	$58.60	$1875.20	$87.25	$2792.00	$60.14	$89.53
1 Equip. Oper. (crane)	66.30	530.40	98.65	789.20		
1 Hyd. Crane, 12 Ton		2150.65		2365.72	53.77	59.14
40 L.H., Daily Totals		$4556.25		$5946.92	$113.91	$148.67
Crew F-4	**Hr.**	**Daily**	**Hr.**	**Daily**	**Bare Costs**	**Incl. O&P**
4 Carpenters	$58.60	$1875.20	$87.25	$2792.00	$59.52	$88.59
1 Equip. Oper. (crane)	66.30	530.40	98.65	789.20		
1 Equip. Oper. (oiler)	56.40	451.20	83.90	671.20		
1 Hyd. Crane, 55 Ton		2461.06		2707.17	51.27	56.40
48 L.H., Daily Totals		$5317.86		$6959.57	$110.79	$144.99
Crew F-5	**Hr.**	**Daily**	**Hr.**	**Daily**	**Bare Costs**	**Incl. O&P**
1 Carpenter Foreman (outside)	$60.60	$484.80	$90.20	$721.60	$59.10	$87.99
3 Carpenters	58.60	1406.40	87.25	2094.00		
32 L.H., Daily Totals		$1891.20		$2815.60	$59.10	$87.99
Crew F-6	**Hr.**	**Daily**	**Hr.**	**Daily**	**Bare Costs**	**Incl. O&P**
2 Carpenters	$58.60	$937.60	$87.25	$1396.00	$55.60	$82.77
2 Building Laborers	47.25	756.00	70.35	1125.60		
1 Equip. Oper. (crane)	66.30	530.40	98.65	789.20		
1 Hyd. Crane, 12 Ton		2150.65		2365.72	53.77	59.14
40 L.H., Daily Totals		$4374.65		$5676.52	$109.37	$141.91
Crew F-7	**Hr.**	**Daily**	**Hr.**	**Daily**	**Bare Costs**	**Incl. O&P**
2 Carpenters	$58.60	$937.60	$87.25	$1396.00	$52.92	$78.80
2 Building Laborers	47.25	756.00	70.35	1125.60		
32 L.H., Daily Totals		$1693.60		$2521.60	$52.92	$78.80
Crew G-1	**Hr.**	**Daily**	**Hr.**	**Daily**	**Bare Costs**	**Incl. O&P**
1 Roofer Foreman (outside)	$53.80	$430.40	$87.20	$697.60	$48.39	$78.41
4 Roofers Composition	51.80	1657.60	83.95	2686.40		
2 Roofer Helpers	38.85	621.60	62.95	1007.20		
1 Application Equipment		189.41		208.35		
1 Tar Kettle/Pot		220.65		242.72		
1 Crew Truck		183.83		202.21	10.61	11.67
56 L.H., Daily Totals		$3303.49		$5044.48	$58.99	$90.08
Crew G-2	**Hr.**	**Daily**	**Hr.**	**Daily**	**Bare Costs**	**Incl. O&P**
1 Plasterer	$53.35	$426.80	$79.30	$634.40	$49.38	$73.43
1 Plasterer Helper	47.55	380.40	70.65	565.20		
1 Building Laborer	47.25	378.00	70.35	562.80		
1 Grout Pump, 50 C.F./hr.		158.45		174.29	6.60	7.26
24 L.H., Daily Totals		$1343.65		$1936.69	$55.99	$80.70

Crew No.	Bare Costs		Incl. Subs O&P		Cost Per Labor-Hour	
Crew G-2A	**Hr.**	**Daily**	**Hr.**	**Daily**	**Bare Costs**	**Incl. O&P**
1 Roofer Composition	$51.80	$414.40	$83.95	$671.60	$45.97	$72.42
1 Roofer Helper	38.85	310.80	62.95	503.60		
1 Building Laborer	47.25	378.00	70.35	562.80		
1 Foam Spray Rig, Trailer-Mtd.		581.75		639.92		
1 Pickup Truck, 3/4 Ton		122.56		134.82	29.35	32.28
24 L.H., Daily Totals		$1807.51		$2512.74	$75.31	$104.70
Crew G-3	**Hr.**	**Daily**	**Hr.**	**Daily**	**Bare Costs**	**Incl. O&P**
2 Sheet Metal Workers	$70.15	$1122.40	$105.70	$1691.20	$58.70	$88.03
2 Building Laborers	47.25	756.00	70.35	1125.60		
32 L.H., Daily Totals		$1878.40		$2816.80	$58.70	$88.03
Crew G-4	**Hr.**	**Daily**	**Hr.**	**Daily**	**Bare Costs**	**Incl. O&P**
1 Labor Foreman (outside)	$49.25	$394.00	$73.30	$586.40	$47.92	$71.33
2 Building Laborers	47.25	756.00	70.35	1125.60		
1 Flatbed Truck, Gas, 1.5 Ton		361.95		398.14		
1 Air Compressor, 160 cfm		244.12		268.53	25.25	27.78
24 L.H., Daily Totals		$1756.07		$2378.68	$73.17	$99.11
Crew G-5	**Hr.**	**Daily**	**Hr.**	**Daily**	**Bare Costs**	**Incl. O&P**
1 Roofer Foreman (outside)	$53.80	$430.40	$87.20	$697.60	$47.02	$76.20
2 Roofers Composition	51.80	828.80	83.95	1343.20		
2 Roofer Helpers	38.85	621.60	62.95	1007.20		
1 Application Equipment		189.41		208.35	4.74	5.21
40 L.H., Daily Totals		$2070.21		$3256.35	$51.76	$81.41
Crew G-6A	**Hr.**	**Daily**	**Hr.**	**Daily**	**Bare Costs**	**Incl. O&P**
2 Roofers Composition	$51.80	$828.80	$83.95	$1343.20	$51.80	$83.95
1 Small Compressor, Electric		32.29		35.52		
2 Pneumatic Nailers		38.40		42.24	4.42	4.86
16 L.H., Daily Totals		$899.49		$1420.96	$56.22	$88.81
Crew G-7	**Hr.**	**Daily**	**Hr.**	**Daily**	**Bare Costs**	**Incl. O&P**
1 Carpenter	$58.60	$468.80	$87.25	$698.00	$58.60	$87.25
1 Small Compressor, Electric		32.29		35.52		
1 Pneumatic Nailer		19.20		21.12	6.44	7.08
8 L.H., Daily Totals		$520.29		$754.64	$65.04	$94.33
Crew H-1	**Hr.**	**Daily**	**Hr.**	**Daily**	**Bare Costs**	**Incl. O&P**
2 Glaziers	$56.05	$896.80	$83.30	$1332.80	$60.30	$91.35
2 Struc. Steel Workers	64.55	1032.80	99.40	1590.40		
32 L.H., Daily Totals		$1929.60		$2923.20	$60.30	$91.35
Crew H-2	**Hr.**	**Daily**	**Hr.**	**Daily**	**Bare Costs**	**Incl. O&P**
2 Glaziers	$56.05	$896.80	$83.30	$1332.80	$53.12	$78.98
1 Building Laborer	47.25	378.00	70.35	562.80		
24 L.H., Daily Totals		$1274.80		$1895.60	$53.12	$78.98
Crew H-3	**Hr.**	**Daily**	**Hr.**	**Daily**	**Bare Costs**	**Incl. O&P**
1 Glazier	$56.05	$448.40	$83.30	$666.40	$50.50	$75.63
1 Helper	44.95	359.60	67.95	543.60		
16 L.H., Daily Totals		$808.00		$1210.00	$50.50	$75.63
Crew H-4	**Hr.**	**Daily**	**Hr.**	**Daily**	**Bare Costs**	**Incl. O&P**
1 Carpenter	$58.60	$468.80	$87.25	$698.00	$54.89	$82.10
1 Carpenter Helper	44.95	359.60	67.95	543.60		
.5 Electrician	67.35	269.40	100.10	400.40		
20 L.H., Daily Totals		$1097.80		$1642.00	$54.89	$82.10

Crews - Standard

Crew No.		Bare Costs	Incl. Subs O&P		Cost Per Labor-Hour	

Crew J-1	Hr.	Daily	Hr.	Daily	Bare Costs	Incl. O&P
3 Plasterers	$53.35	$1280.40	$79.30	$1903.20	$51.03	$75.84
2 Plasterer Helpers	47.55	760.80	70.65	1130.40		
1 Mixing Machine, 6 C.F.		116.18		127.80	2.90	3.19
40 L.H., Daily Totals		$2157.38		$3161.40	$53.93	$79.03

Crew J-2	Hr.	Daily	Hr.	Daily	Bare Costs	Incl. O&P
3 Plasterers	$53.35	$1280.40	$79.30	$1903.20	$52.27	$77.42
2 Plasterer Helpers	47.55	760.80	70.65	1130.40		
1 Lather	58.45	467.60	85.30	682.40		
1 Mixing Machine, 6 C.F.		116.18		127.80	2.42	2.66
48 L.H., Daily Totals		$2624.98		$3843.80	$54.69	$80.08

Crew J-3	Hr.	Daily	Hr.	Daily	Bare Costs	Incl. O&P
1 Terrazzo Worker	$55.25	$442.00	$80.70	$645.60	$51.02	$74.53
1 Terrazzo Helper	46.80	374.40	68.35	546.80		
1 Floor Grinder, 22" Path		109.91		120.90		
1 Terrazzo Mixer		144.05		158.46	15.87	17.46
16 L.H., Daily Totals		$1070.36		$1471.76	$66.90	$91.98

Crew J-4	Hr.	Daily	Hr.	Daily	Bare Costs	Incl. O&P
2 Cement Finishers	$55.00	$880.00	$80.45	$1287.20	$52.42	$77.08
1 Laborer	47.25	378.00	70.35	562.80		
1 Floor Grinder, 22" Path		109.91		120.90		
1 Floor Edger, 7" Path		52.63		57.89		
1 Vacuum Pick-Up System		73.53		80.88	9.84	10.82
24 L.H., Daily Totals		$1494.07		$2109.68	$62.25	$87.90

Crew J-4A	Hr.	Daily	Hr.	Daily	Bare Costs	Incl. O&P
2 Cement Finishers	$55.00	$880.00	$80.45	$1287.20	$51.13	$75.40
2 Laborers	47.25	756.00	70.35	1125.60		
1 Floor Grinder, 22" Path		109.91		120.90		
1 Floor Edger, 7" Path		52.63		57.89		
1 Vacuum Pick-Up System		73.53		80.88		
1 Floor Auto Scrubber		195.20		214.72	13.48	14.82
32 L.H., Daily Totals		$2067.27		$2887.20	$64.60	$90.22

Crew J-4B	Hr.	Daily	Hr.	Daily	Bare Costs	Incl. O&P
1 Laborer	$47.25	$378.00	$70.35	$562.80	$47.25	$70.35
1 Floor Auto Scrubber		195.20		214.72	24.40	26.84
8 L.H., Daily Totals		$573.20		$777.52	$71.65	$97.19

Crew J-6	Hr.	Daily	Hr.	Daily	Bare Costs	Incl. O&P
2 Painters	$49.65	$794.40	$73.55	$1176.80	$51.56	$76.58
1 Building Laborer	47.25	378.00	70.35	562.80		
1 Equip. Oper. (light)	59.70	477.60	88.85	710.80		
1 Air Compressor, 250 cfm		196.28		215.91		
1 Sandblaster, Portable, 3 C.F.		84.26		92.69		
1 Set Sand Blasting Accessories		17.14		18.85	9.30	10.23
32 L.H., Daily Totals		$1947.68		$2777.85	$60.87	$86.81

Crew J-7	Hr.	Daily	Hr.	Daily	Bare Costs	Incl. O&P
2 Painters	$49.65	$794.40	$73.55	$1176.80	$49.65	$73.55
1 Floor Belt Sander		49.75		54.73		
1 Floor Sanding Edger		26.35		28.98	4.76	5.23
16 L.H., Daily Totals		$870.50		$1260.51	$54.41	$78.78

Crew K-1	Hr.	Daily	Hr.	Daily	Bare Costs	Incl. O&P
1 Carpenter	$58.60	$468.80	$87.25	$698.00	$55.75	$83.13
1 Truck Driver (light)	52.90	423.20	79.00	632.00		
1 Flatbed Truck, Gas, 3 Ton		391.02		430.12	24.44	26.88
16 L.H., Daily Totals		$1283.02		$1760.12	$80.19	$110.01

Crew K-2	Hr.	Daily	Hr.	Daily	Bare Costs	Incl. O&P
1 Struc. Steel Foreman (outside)	$66.55	$532.40	$102.50	$820.00	$61.33	$93.63
1 Struc. Steel Worker	64.55	516.40	99.40	795.20		
1 Truck Driver (light)	52.90	423.20	79.00	632.00		
1 Flatbed Truck, Gas, 3 Ton		391.02		430.12	16.29	17.92
24 L.H., Daily Totals		$1863.02		$2677.32	$77.63	$111.56

Crew L-1	Hr.	Daily	Hr.	Daily	Bare Costs	Incl. O&P
1 Electrician	$67.35	$538.80	$100.10	$800.80	$69.70	$103.78
1 Plumber	72.05	576.40	107.45	859.60		
16 L.H., Daily Totals		$1115.20		$1660.40	$69.70	$103.78

Crew L-2	Hr.	Daily	Hr.	Daily	Bare Costs	Incl. O&P
1 Carpenter	$58.60	$468.80	$87.25	$698.00	$51.77	$77.60
1 Carpenter Helper	44.95	359.60	67.95	543.60		
16 L.H., Daily Totals		$828.40		$1241.60	$51.77	$77.60

Crew L-3	Hr.	Daily	Hr.	Daily	Bare Costs	Incl. O&P
1 Carpenter	$58.60	$468.80	$87.25	$698.00	$63.67	$95.08
.5 Electrician	67.35	269.40	100.10	400.40		
.5 Sheet Metal Worker	70.15	280.60	105.70	422.80		
16 L.H., Daily Totals		$1018.80		$1521.20	$63.67	$95.08

Crew L-3A	Hr.	Daily	Hr.	Daily	Bare Costs	Incl. O&P
1 Carpenter Foreman (outside)	$60.60	$484.80	$90.20	$721.60	$63.78	$95.37
.5 Sheet Metal Worker	70.15	280.60	105.70	422.80		
12 L.H., Daily Totals		$765.40		$1144.40	$63.78	$95.37

Crew L-4	Hr.	Daily	Hr.	Daily	Bare Costs	Incl. O&P
2 Skilled Workers	$61.25	$980.00	$92.00	$1472.00	$55.82	$83.98
1 Helper	44.95	359.60	67.95	543.60		
24 L.H., Daily Totals		$1339.60		$2015.60	$55.82	$83.98

Crew L-5	Hr.	Daily	Hr.	Daily	Bare Costs	Incl. O&P
1 Struc. Steel Foreman (outside)	$66.55	$532.40	$102.50	$820.00	$65.09	$99.74
5 Struc. Steel Workers	64.55	2582.00	99.40	3976.00		
1 Equip. Oper. (crane)	66.30	530.40	98.65	789.20		
1 Hyd. Crane, 25 Ton		2273.31		2500.64	40.59	44.65
56 L.H., Daily Totals		$5918.11		$8085.84	$105.68	$144.39

Crew L-5A	Hr.	Daily	Hr.	Daily	Bare Costs	Incl. O&P
1 Struc. Steel Foreman (outside)	$66.55	$532.40	$102.50	$820.00	$65.49	$99.99
2 Structural Steel Workers	64.55	1032.80	99.40	1590.40		
1 Equip. Oper. (crane)	66.30	530.40	98.65	789.20		
1 S.P. Crane, 4x4, 25 Ton		927.07		1019.78	28.97	31.87
32 L.H., Daily Totals		$3022.67		$4219.38	$94.46	$131.86

Crews - Standard

Crew No.	Bare Costs		Incl. Subs O&P		Cost Per Labor-Hour	
Crew L-5B	**Hr.**	**Daily**	**Hr.**	**Daily**	**Bare Costs**	**Incl. O&P**
1 Struc. Steel Foreman (outside)	$66.55	$532.40	$102.50	$820.00	$66.46	$100.05
2 Structural Steel Workers	64.55	1032.80	99.40	1590.40		
2 Electricians	67.35	1077.60	100.10	1601.60		
2 Steamfitters/Pipefitters	72.55	1160.80	108.20	1731.20		
1 Equip. Oper. (crane)	66.30	530.40	98.65	789.20		
1 Equip. Oper. (oiler)	56.40	451.20	83.90	671.20		
1 Hyd. Crane, 80 Ton		2641.70		2905.87	36.69	40.36
72 L.H., Daily Totals		$7426.90		$10109.47	$103.15	$140.41
Crew L-6	**Hr.**	**Daily**	**Hr.**	**Daily**	**Bare Costs**	**Incl. O&P**
1 Plumber	$72.05	$576.40	$107.45	$859.60	$70.48	$105.00
.5 Electrician	67.35	269.40	100.10	400.40		
12 L.H., Daily Totals		$845.80		$1260.00	$70.48	$105.00
Crew L-7	**Hr.**	**Daily**	**Hr.**	**Daily**	**Bare Costs**	**Incl. O&P**
2 Carpenters	$58.60	$937.60	$87.25	$1396.00	$56.61	$84.26
1 Building Laborer	47.25	378.00	70.35	562.80		
.5 Electrician	67.35	269.40	100.10	400.40		
28 L.H., Daily Totals		$1585.00		$2359.20	$56.61	$84.26
Crew L-8	**Hr.**	**Daily**	**Hr.**	**Daily**	**Bare Costs**	**Incl. O&P**
2 Carpenters	$58.60	$937.60	$87.25	$1396.00	$61.29	$91.29
.5 Plumber	72.05	288.20	107.45	429.80		
20 L.H., Daily Totals		$1225.80		$1825.80	$61.29	$91.29
Crew L-9	**Hr.**	**Daily**	**Hr.**	**Daily**	**Bare Costs**	**Incl. O&P**
1 Labor Foreman (inside)	$47.75	$382.00	$71.10	$568.80	$53.44	$80.28
2 Building Laborers	47.25	756.00	70.35	1125.60		
1 Struc. Steel Worker	64.55	516.40	99.40	795.20		
.5 Electrician	67.35	269.40	100.10	400.40		
36 L.H., Daily Totals		$1923.80		$2890.00	$53.44	$80.28
Crew L-10	**Hr.**	**Daily**	**Hr.**	**Daily**	**Bare Costs**	**Incl. O&P**
1 Struc. Steel Foreman (outside)	$66.55	$532.40	$102.50	$820.00	$65.80	$100.18
1 Structural Steel Worker	64.55	516.40	99.40	795.20		
1 Equip. Oper. (crane)	66.30	530.40	98.65	789.20		
1 Hyd. Crane, 12 Ton		2150.65		2365.72	89.61	98.57
24 L.H., Daily Totals		$3729.85		$4770.11	$155.41	$198.75
Crew L-11	**Hr.**	**Daily**	**Hr.**	**Daily**	**Bare Costs**	**Incl. O&P**
2 Wreckers	$47.25	$756.00	$71.35	$1141.60	$55.13	$82.55
1 Equip. Oper. (crane)	66.30	530.40	98.65	789.20		
1 Equip. Oper. (light)	59.70	477.60	88.85	710.80		
1 Hyd. Excavator, 2.5 C.Y.		1683.69		1852.06		
1 Loader, Skid Steer, 78 H.P.		429.91		472.90	66.05	72.66
32 L.H., Daily Totals		$3877.60		$4966.56	$121.18	$155.21
Crew M-1	**Hr.**	**Daily**	**Hr.**	**Daily**	**Bare Costs**	**Incl. O&P**
3 Elevator Constructors	$96.60	$2318.40	$143.00	$3432.00	$91.78	$135.86
1 Elevator Apprentice	77.30	618.40	114.45	915.60		
5 Hand Tools		344.60		379.06	10.77	11.85
32 L.H., Daily Totals		$3281.40		$4726.66	$102.54	$147.71
Crew M-3	**Hr.**	**Daily**	**Hr.**	**Daily**	**Bare Costs**	**Incl. O&P**
1 Electrician Foreman (outside)	$69.35	$554.80	$103.05	$824.40	$72.06	$106.89
1 Common Laborer	47.25	378.00	70.35	562.80		
.25 Equipment Operator (med.)	63.05	126.10	93.80	187.60		
1 Elevator Constructor	96.60	772.80	143.00	1144.00		
1 Elevator Apprentice	77.30	618.40	114.45	915.60		
.25 S.P. Crane, 4x4, 20 Ton		190.24		209.27	5.60	6.15
34 L.H., Daily Totals		$2640.34		$3843.67	$77.66	$113.05
Crew M-4	**Hr.**	**Daily**	**Hr.**	**Daily**	**Bare Costs**	**Incl. O&P**
1 Electrician Foreman (outside)	$69.35	$554.80	$103.05	$824.40	$71.37	$105.89
1 Common Laborer	47.25	378.00	70.35	562.80		
.25 Equipment Operator, Crane	66.30	132.60	98.65	197.30		
.25 Equip. Oper. (oiler)	56.40	112.80	83.90	167.80		
1 Elevator Constructor	96.60	772.80	143.00	1144.00		
1 Elevator Apprentice	77.30	618.40	114.45	915.60		
.25 S.P. Crane, 4x4, 40 Ton		284.79		313.26	7.91	8.70
36 L.H., Daily Totals		$2854.18		$4125.16	$79.28	$114.59
Crew Q-1	**Hr.**	**Daily**	**Hr.**	**Daily**	**Bare Costs**	**Incl. O&P**
1 Plumber	$72.05	$576.40	$107.45	$859.60	$64.85	$96.70
1 Plumber Apprentice	57.65	461.20	85.95	687.60		
16 L.H., Daily Totals		$1037.60		$1547.20	$64.85	$96.70
Crew Q-1A	**Hr.**	**Daily**	**Hr.**	**Daily**	**Bare Costs**	**Incl. O&P**
.25 Plumber Foreman (outside)	$74.05	$148.10	$110.40	$220.80	$72.45	$108.04
1 Plumber	72.05	576.40	107.45	859.60		
10 L.H., Daily Totals		$724.50		$1080.40	$72.45	$108.04
Crew Q-1C	**Hr.**	**Daily**	**Hr.**	**Daily**	**Bare Costs**	**Incl. O&P**
1 Plumber	$72.05	$576.40	$107.45	$859.60	$64.25	$95.73
1 Plumber Apprentice	57.65	461.20	85.95	687.60		
1 Equip. Oper. (medium)	63.05	504.40	93.80	750.40		
1 Trencher, Chain Type, 8' D		2079.03		2286.93	86.63	95.29
24 L.H., Daily Totals		$3621.03		$4584.53	$150.88	$191.02
Crew Q-2	**Hr.**	**Daily**	**Hr.**	**Daily**	**Bare Costs**	**Incl. O&P**
2 Plumbers	$72.05	$1152.80	$107.45	$1719.20	$67.25	$100.28
1 Plumber Apprentice	57.65	461.20	85.95	687.60		
24 L.H., Daily Totals		$1614.00		$2406.80	$67.25	$100.28
Crew Q-3	**Hr.**	**Daily**	**Hr.**	**Daily**	**Bare Costs**	**Incl. O&P**
1 Plumber Foreman (inside)	$72.55	$580.40	$108.20	$865.60	$68.58	$102.26
2 Plumbers	72.05	1152.80	107.45	1719.20		
1 Plumber Apprentice	57.65	461.20	85.95	687.60		
32 L.H., Daily Totals		$2194.40		$3272.40	$68.58	$102.26
Crew Q-4	**Hr.**	**Daily**	**Hr.**	**Daily**	**Bare Costs**	**Incl. O&P**
1 Plumber Foreman (inside)	$72.55	$580.40	$108.20	$865.60	$68.58	$102.26
1 Plumber	72.05	576.40	107.45	859.60		
1 Welder (plumber)	72.05	576.40	107.45	859.60		
1 Plumber Apprentice	57.65	461.20	85.95	687.60		
1 Welder, Electric, 300 amp		64.17		70.59	2.01	2.21
32 L.H., Daily Totals		$2258.57		$3342.99	$70.58	$104.47
Crew Q-5	**Hr.**	**Daily**	**Hr.**	**Daily**	**Bare Costs**	**Incl. O&P**
1 Steamfitter	$72.55	$580.40	$108.20	$865.60	$65.30	$97.38
1 Steamfitter Apprentice	58.05	464.40	86.55	692.40		
16 L.H., Daily Totals		$1044.80		$1558.00	$65.30	$97.38

Crews - Standard

Crew No.	Bare Costs Hr.	Bare Costs Daily	Incl. Subs O&P Hr.	Incl. Subs O&P Daily	Cost Per Labor-Hour Bare Costs	Cost Per Labor-Hour Incl. O&P
Crew Q-6						
2 Steamfitters	$72.55	$1160.80	$108.20	$1731.20	$67.72	$100.98
1 Steamfitter Apprentice	58.05	464.40	86.55	692.40		
24 L.H., Daily Totals		$1625.20		$2423.60	$67.72	$100.98
Crew Q-7						
1 Steamfitter Foreman (inside)	$73.05	$584.40	$108.95	$871.60	$69.05	$102.97
2 Steamfitters	72.55	1160.80	108.20	1731.20		
1 Steamfitter Apprentice	58.05	464.40	86.55	692.40		
32 L.H., Daily Totals		$2209.60		$3295.20	$69.05	$102.97
Crew Q-8						
1 Steamfitter Foreman (inside)	$73.05	$584.40	$108.95	$871.60	$69.05	$102.97
1 Steamfitter	72.55	580.40	108.20	865.60		
1 Welder (steamfitter)	72.55	580.40	108.20	865.60		
1 Steamfitter Apprentice	58.05	464.40	86.55	692.40		
1 Welder, Electric, 300 amp		64.17		70.59	2.01	2.21
32 L.H., Daily Totals		$2273.77		$3365.79	$71.06	$105.18
Crew Q-9						
1 Sheet Metal Worker	$70.15	$561.20	$105.70	$845.60	$63.13	$95.10
1 Sheet Metal Apprentice	56.10	448.80	84.50	676.00		
16 L.H., Daily Totals		$1010.00		$1521.60	$63.13	$95.10
Crew Q-10						
2 Sheet Metal Workers	$70.15	$1122.40	$105.70	$1691.20	$65.47	$98.63
1 Sheet Metal Apprentice	56.10	448.80	84.50	676.00		
24 L.H., Daily Totals		$1571.20		$2367.20	$65.47	$98.63
Crew Q-11						
1 Sheet Metal Foreman (inside)	$70.65	$565.20	$106.45	$851.60	$66.76	$100.59
2 Sheet Metal Workers	70.15	1122.40	105.70	1691.20		
1 Sheet Metal Apprentice	56.10	448.80	84.50	676.00		
32 L.H., Daily Totals		$2136.40		$3218.80	$66.76	$100.59
Crew Q-12						
1 Sprinkler Installer	$70.80	$566.40	$105.70	$845.60	$63.73	$95.13
1 Sprinkler Apprentice	56.65	453.20	84.55	676.40		
16 L.H., Daily Totals		$1019.60		$1522.00	$63.73	$95.13
Crew Q-13						
1 Sprinkler Foreman (inside)	$71.30	$570.40	$106.45	$851.60	$67.39	$100.60
2 Sprinkler Installers	70.80	1132.80	105.70	1691.20		
1 Sprinkler Apprentice	56.65	453.20	84.55	676.40		
32 L.H., Daily Totals		$2156.40		$3219.20	$67.39	$100.60
Crew Q-14						
1 Asbestos Worker	$65.25	$522.00	$99.80	$798.40	$58.73	$89.83
1 Asbestos Apprentice	52.20	417.60	79.85	638.80		
16 L.H., Daily Totals		$939.60		$1437.20	$58.73	$89.83
Crew Q-15						
1 Plumber	$72.05	$576.40	$107.45	$859.60	$64.85	$96.70
1 Plumber Apprentice	57.65	461.20	85.95	687.60		
1 Welder, Electric, 300 amp		64.17		70.59	4.01	4.41
16 L.H., Daily Totals		$1101.77		$1617.79	$68.86	$101.11
Crew Q-16						
2 Plumbers	$72.05	$1152.80	$107.45	$1719.20	$67.25	$100.28
1 Plumber Apprentice	57.65	461.20	85.95	687.60		
1 Welder, Electric, 300 amp		64.17		70.59	2.67	2.94
24 L.H., Daily Totals		$1678.17		$2477.39	$69.92	$103.22
Crew Q-17						
1 Steamfitter	$72.55	$580.40	$108.20	$865.60	$65.30	$97.38
1 Steamfitter Apprentice	58.05	464.40	86.55	692.40		
1 Welder, Electric, 300 amp		64.17		70.59	4.01	4.41
16 L.H., Daily Totals		$1108.97		$1628.59	$69.31	$101.79
Crew Q-17A						
1 Steamfitter	$72.55	$580.40	$108.20	$865.60	$65.63	$97.80
1 Steamfitter Apprentice	58.05	464.40	86.55	692.40		
1 Equip. Oper. (crane)	66.30	530.40	98.65	789.20		
1 Hyd. Crane, 12 Ton		2150.65		2365.72		
1 Welder, Electric, 300 amp		64.17		70.59	92.28	101.51
24 L.H., Daily Totals		$3790.02		$4783.50	$157.92	$199.31
Crew Q-18						
2 Steamfitters	$72.55	$1160.80	$108.20	$1731.20	$67.72	$100.98
1 Steamfitter Apprentice	58.05	464.40	86.55	692.40		
1 Welder, Electric, 300 amp		64.17		70.59	2.67	2.94
24 L.H., Daily Totals		$1689.37		$2494.19	$70.39	$103.92
Crew Q-19						
1 Steamfitter	$72.55	$580.40	$108.20	$865.60	$65.98	$98.28
1 Steamfitter Apprentice	58.05	464.40	86.55	692.40		
1 Electrician	67.35	538.80	100.10	800.80		
24 L.H., Daily Totals		$1583.60		$2358.80	$65.98	$98.28
Crew Q-20						
1 Sheet Metal Worker	$70.15	$561.20	$105.70	$845.60	$63.97	$96.10
1 Sheet Metal Apprentice	56.10	448.80	84.50	676.00		
.5 Electrician	67.35	269.40	100.10	400.40		
20 L.H., Daily Totals		$1279.40		$1922.00	$63.97	$96.10
Crew Q-21						
2 Steamfitters	$72.55	$1160.80	$108.20	$1731.20	$67.63	$100.76
1 Steamfitter Apprentice	58.05	464.40	86.55	692.40		
1 Electrician	67.35	538.80	100.10	800.80		
32 L.H., Daily Totals		$2164.00		$3224.40	$67.63	$100.76
Crew Q-22						
1 Plumber	$72.05	$576.40	$107.45	$859.60	$64.85	$96.70
1 Plumber Apprentice	57.65	461.20	85.95	687.60		
1 Hyd. Crane, 12 Ton		2150.65		2365.72	134.42	147.86
16 L.H., Daily Totals		$3188.25		$3912.92	$199.27	$244.56
Crew Q-22A						
1 Plumber	$72.05	$576.40	$107.45	$859.60	$60.81	$90.60
1 Plumber Apprentice	57.65	461.20	85.95	687.60		
1 Laborer	47.25	378.00	70.35	562.80		
1 Equip. Oper. (crane)	66.30	530.40	98.65	789.20		
1 Hyd. Crane, 12 Ton		2150.65		2365.72	67.21	73.93
32 L.H., Daily Totals		$4096.65		$5264.92	$128.02	$164.53

Crews - Standard

Crew No.		Bare Costs		Incl. Subs O&P		Cost Per Labor-Hour	
Crew Q-23	Hr.	Daily	Hr.	Daily	Bare Costs	Incl. O&P	
1 Plumber Foreman (outside)	$74.05	$592.40	$110.40	$883.20	$69.72	$103.88	
1 Plumber	72.05	576.40	107.45	859.60			
1 Equip. Oper. (medium)	63.05	504.40	93.80	750.40			
1 Lattice Boom Crane, 20 Ton		868.10		954.91	36.17	39.79	
24 L.H., Daily Totals		$2541.30		$3448.11	$105.89	$143.67	

Crew R-1	Hr.	Daily	Hr.	Daily	Bare Costs	Incl. O&P
1 Electrician Foreman	$67.85	$542.80	$100.85	$806.80	$62.95	$93.56
3 Electricians	67.35	1616.40	100.10	2402.40		
2 Electrician Apprentices	53.90	862.40	80.10	1281.60		
48 L.H., Daily Totals		$3021.60		$4490.80	$62.95	$93.56

Crew R-1A	Hr.	Daily	Hr.	Daily	Bare Costs	Incl. O&P
1 Electrician	$67.35	$538.80	$100.10	$800.80	$60.63	$90.10
1 Electrician Apprentice	53.90	431.20	80.10	640.80		
16 L.H., Daily Totals		$970.00		$1441.60	$60.63	$90.10

Crew R-1B	Hr.	Daily	Hr.	Daily	Bare Costs	Incl. O&P
1 Electrician	$67.35	$538.80	$100.10	$800.80	$58.38	$86.77
2 Electrician Apprentices	53.90	862.40	80.10	1281.60		
24 L.H., Daily Totals		$1401.20		$2082.40	$58.38	$86.77

Crew R-1C	Hr.	Daily	Hr.	Daily	Bare Costs	Incl. O&P
2 Electricians	$67.35	$1077.60	$100.10	$1601.60	$60.63	$90.10
2 Electrician Apprentices	53.90	862.40	80.10	1281.60		
1 Portable cable puller, 8000 lb.		118.26		130.09	3.70	4.07
32 L.H., Daily Totals		$2058.26		$3013.29	$64.32	$94.17

Crew R-2	Hr.	Daily	Hr.	Daily	Bare Costs	Incl. O&P
1 Electrician Foreman	$67.85	$542.80	$100.85	$806.80	$63.43	$94.29
3 Electricians	67.35	1616.40	100.10	2402.40		
2 Electrician Apprentices	53.90	862.40	80.10	1281.60		
1 Equip. Oper. (crane)	66.30	530.40	98.65	789.20		
1 S.P. Crane, 4x4, 5 Ton		385.89		424.48	6.89	7.58
56 L.H., Daily Totals		$3937.89		$5704.48	$70.32	$101.87

Crew R-3	Hr.	Daily	Hr.	Daily	Bare Costs	Incl. O&P
1 Electrician Foreman	$67.85	$542.80	$100.85	$806.80	$67.34	$100.11
1 Electrician	67.35	538.80	100.10	800.80		
.5 Equip. Oper. (crane)	66.30	265.20	98.65	394.60		
.5 S.P. Crane, 4x4, 5 Ton		192.94		212.24	9.65	10.61
20 L.H., Daily Totals		$1539.74		$2214.44	$76.99	$110.72

Crew R-4	Hr.	Daily	Hr.	Daily	Bare Costs	Incl. O&P
1 Struc. Steel Foreman (outside)	$66.55	$532.40	$102.50	$820.00	$65.51	$100.16
3 Struc. Steel Workers	64.55	1549.20	99.40	2385.60		
1 Electrician	67.35	538.80	100.10	800.80		
1 Welder, Gas Engine, 300 amp		147.09		161.80	3.68	4.04
40 L.H., Daily Totals		$2767.49		$4168.20	$69.19	$104.21

Crew R-5	Hr.	Daily	Hr.	Daily	Bare Costs	Incl. O&P
1 Electrician Foreman	$67.85	$542.80	$100.85	$806.80	$59.25	$88.48
4 Electrician Linemen	67.35	2155.20	100.10	3203.20		
2 Electrician Operators	67.35	1077.60	100.10	1601.60		
4 Electrician Groundmen	44.95	1438.40	67.95	2174.40		
1 Crew Truck		183.83		202.21		
1 Flatbed Truck, 20,000 GVW		223.10		245.41		
1 Pickup Truck, 3/4 Ton		122.56		134.82		
.2 Hyd. Crane, 55 Ton		492.21		541.43		
.2 Hyd. Crane, 12 Ton		430.13		473.14		
.2 Earth Auger, Truck-Mtd.		30.79		33.87		
1 Tractor w/Winch		413.43		454.77	21.55	23.70
88 L.H., Daily Totals		$7110.06		$9871.66	$80.80	$112.18

Crew R-6	Hr.	Daily	Hr.	Daily	Bare Costs	Incl. O&P
1 Electrician Foreman	$67.85	$542.80	$100.85	$806.80	$59.25	$88.48
4 Electrician Linemen	67.35	2155.20	100.10	3203.20		
2 Electrician Operators	67.35	1077.60	100.10	1601.60		
4 Electrician Groundmen	44.95	1438.40	67.95	2174.40		
1 Crew Truck		183.83		202.21		
1 Flatbed Truck, 20,000 GVW		223.10		245.41		
1 Pickup Truck, 3/4 Ton		122.56		134.82		
.2 Hyd. Crane, 55 Ton		492.21		541.43		
.2 Hyd. Crane, 12 Ton		430.13		473.14		
.2 Earth Auger, Truck-Mtd.		30.79		33.87		
1 Tractor w/Winch		413.43		454.77		
3 Cable Trailers		609.78		670.76		
.5 Tensioning Rig		76.23		83.86		
.5 Cable Pulling Rig		370.78		407.86	33.56	36.91
88 L.H., Daily Totals		$8166.85		$11034.14	$92.81	$125.39

Crew R-7	Hr.	Daily	Hr.	Daily	Bare Costs	Incl. O&P
1 Electrician Foreman	$67.85	$542.80	$100.85	$806.80	$48.77	$73.43
5 Electrician Groundmen	44.95	1798.00	67.95	2718.00		
1 Crew Truck		183.83		202.21	3.83	4.21
48 L.H., Daily Totals		$2524.63		$3727.01	$52.60	$77.65

Crew R-8	Hr.	Daily	Hr.	Daily	Bare Costs	Incl. O&P
1 Electrician Foreman	$67.85	$542.80	$100.85	$806.80	$59.97	$89.51
3 Electrician Linemen	67.35	1616.40	100.10	2402.40		
2 Electrician Groundmen	44.95	719.20	67.95	1087.20		
1 Pickup Truck, 3/4 Ton		122.56		134.82		
1 Crew Truck		183.83		202.21	6.38	7.02
48 L.H., Daily Totals		$3184.79		$4633.43	$66.35	$96.53

Crew R-9	Hr.	Daily	Hr.	Daily	Bare Costs	Incl. O&P
1 Electrician Foreman	$67.85	$542.80	$100.85	$806.80	$56.21	$84.12
1 Electrician Lineman	67.35	538.80	100.10	800.80		
2 Electrician Operators	67.35	1077.60	100.10	1601.60		
4 Electrician Groundmen	44.95	1438.40	67.95	2174.40		
1 Pickup Truck, 3/4 Ton		122.56		134.82		
1 Crew Truck		183.83		202.21	4.79	5.27
64 L.H., Daily Totals		$3903.99		$5720.63	$61.00	$89.38

Crew R-10	Hr.	Daily	Hr.	Daily	Bare Costs	Incl. O&P
1 Electrician Foreman	$67.85	$542.80	$100.85	$806.80	$63.70	$94.87
4 Electrician Linemen	67.35	2155.20	100.10	3203.20		
1 Electrician Groundman	44.95	359.60	67.95	543.60		
1 Crew Truck		183.83		202.21		
3 Tram Cars		237.63		261.39	8.78	9.66
48 L.H., Daily Totals		$3479.06		$5017.21	$72.48	$104.53

Crews - Standard

Crew No.	Bare Costs		Incl. Subs O&P		Cost Per Labor-Hour	
Crew R-11	**Hr.**	**Daily**	**Hr.**	**Daily**	**Bare Costs**	**Incl. O&P**
1 Electrician Foreman	$67.85	$542.80	$100.85	$806.80	$64.40	$95.75
4 Electricians	67.35	2155.20	100.10	3203.20		
1 Equip. Oper. (crane)	66.30	530.40	98.65	789.20		
1 Common Laborer	47.25	378.00	70.35	562.80		
1 Crew Truck		183.83		202.21		
1 Hyd. Crane, 12 Ton		2150.65		2365.72	41.69	45.86
56 L.H., Daily Totals		$5940.88		$7929.93	$106.09	$141.61
Crew R-12	**Hr.**	**Daily**	**Hr.**	**Daily**	**Bare Costs**	**Incl. O&P**
1 Carpenter Foreman (inside)	$59.10	$472.80	$88.00	$704.00	$55.46	$82.87
4 Carpenters	58.60	1875.20	87.25	2792.00		
4 Common Laborers	47.25	1512.00	70.35	2251.20		
1 Equip. Oper. (medium)	63.05	504.40	93.80	750.40		
1 Steel Worker	64.55	516.40	99.40	795.20		
1 Dozer, 200 H.P.		1382.36		1520.60		
1 Pickup Truck, 3/4 Ton		122.56		134.82	17.10	18.81
88 L.H., Daily Totals		$6385.72		$8948.21	$72.56	$101.68
Crew R-13	**Hr.**	**Daily**	**Hr.**	**Daily**	**Bare Costs**	**Incl. O&P**
1 Electrician Foreman	$67.85	$542.80	$100.85	$806.80	$65.31	$97.09
3 Electricians	67.35	1616.40	100.10	2402.40		
.25 Equip. Oper. (crane)	66.30	132.60	98.65	197.30		
1 Equipment Oiler	56.40	451.20	83.90	671.20		
.25 Hydraulic Crane, 33 Ton		607.40		668.15	14.46	15.91
42 L.H., Daily Totals		$3350.41		$4745.85	$79.77	$113.00
Crew R-15	**Hr.**	**Daily**	**Hr.**	**Daily**	**Bare Costs**	**Incl. O&P**
1 Electrician Foreman	$67.85	$542.80	$100.85	$806.80	$66.16	$98.35
4 Electricians	67.35	2155.20	100.10	3203.20		
1 Equipment Oper. (light)	59.70	477.60	88.85	710.80		
1 Telescoping Boom Lift, to 40'		345.57		380.13	7.20	7.92
48 L.H., Daily Totals		$3521.17		$5100.93	$73.36	$106.27
Crew R-15A	**Hr.**	**Daily**	**Hr.**	**Daily**	**Bare Costs**	**Incl. O&P**
1 Electrician Foreman	$67.85	$542.80	$100.85	$806.80	$59.46	$88.43
2 Electricians	67.35	1077.60	100.10	1601.60		
2 Common Laborers	47.25	756.00	70.35	1125.60		
1 Equip. Oper. (light)	59.70	477.60	88.85	710.80		
1 Telescoping Boom Lift, to 40'		345.57		380.13	7.20	7.92
48 L.H., Daily Totals		$3199.57		$4624.93	$66.66	$96.35
Crew R-18	**Hr.**	**Daily**	**Hr.**	**Daily**	**Bare Costs**	**Incl. O&P**
.25 Electrician Foreman	$67.85	$135.70	$100.85	$201.70	$59.11	$87.85
1 Electrician	67.35	538.80	100.10	800.80		
2 Electrician Apprentices	53.90	862.40	80.10	1281.60		
26 L.H., Daily Totals		$1536.90		$2284.10	$59.11	$87.85
Crew R-19	**Hr.**	**Daily**	**Hr.**	**Daily**	**Bare Costs**	**Incl. O&P**
.5 Electrician Foreman	$67.85	$271.40	$100.85	$403.40	$67.45	$100.25
2 Electricians	67.35	1077.60	100.10	1601.60		
20 L.H., Daily Totals		$1349.00		$2005.00	$67.45	$100.25
Crew R-21	**Hr.**	**Daily**	**Hr.**	**Daily**	**Bare Costs**	**Incl. O&P**
1 Electrician Foreman	$67.85	$542.80	$100.85	$806.80	$67.37	$100.13
3 Electricians	67.35	1616.40	100.10	2402.40		
.1 Equip. Oper. (medium)	63.05	50.44	93.80	75.04		
.1 S.P. Crane, 4x4, 25 Ton		92.71		101.98	2.83	3.11
32.8 L.H., Daily Totals		$2302.35		$3386.22	$70.19	$103.24

Crew No.	Bare Costs		Incl. Subs O&P		Cost Per Labor-Hour	
Crew R-22	**Hr.**	**Daily**	**Hr.**	**Daily**	**Bare Costs**	**Incl. O&P**
.66 Electrician Foreman	$67.85	$358.25	$100.85	$532.49	$61.65	$91.62
2 Electricians	67.35	1077.60	100.10	1601.60		
2 Electrician Apprentices	53.90	862.40	80.10	1281.60		
37.28 L.H., Daily Totals		$2298.25		$3415.69	$61.65	$91.62
Crew R-30	**Hr.**	**Daily**	**Hr.**	**Daily**	**Bare Costs**	**Incl. O&P**
.25 Electrician Foreman (outside)	$69.35	$138.70	$103.05	$206.10	$55.13	$82.02
1 Electrician	67.35	538.80	100.10	800.80		
2 Laborers (Semi-Skilled)	47.25	756.00	70.35	1125.60		
26 L.H., Daily Totals		$1433.50		$2132.50	$55.13	$82.02
Crew R-31	**Hr.**	**Daily**	**Hr.**	**Daily**	**Bare Costs**	**Incl. O&P**
1 Electrician	$67.35	$538.80	$100.10	$800.80	$67.35	$100.10
1 Core Drill, Electric, 2.5 H.P.		61.41		67.55	7.68	8.44
8 L.H., Daily Totals		$600.21		$868.35	$75.03	$108.54
Crew W-41E	**Hr.**	**Daily**	**Hr.**	**Daily**	**Bare Costs**	**Incl. O&P**
.5 Plumber Foreman (outside)	$74.05	$296.20	$110.40	$441.60	$62.53	$93.20
1 Plumber	72.05	576.40	107.45	859.60		
1 Laborer	47.25	378.00	70.35	562.80		
20 L.H., Daily Totals		$1250.60		$1864.00	$62.53	$93.20

Historical Cost Indexes

The table below lists both the RSMeans® historical cost index based on Jan. 1, 1993 = 100 as well as the computed value of an index based on Jan. 1, 2023 costs. Since the Jan. 1, 2023 figure is estimated, space is left to write in the actual index figures as they become available through the quarterly *RSMeans Construction Cost Indexes*.

To compute the actual index based on Jan. 1, 2023 = 100, divide the historical cost index for a particular year by the actual Jan. 1, 2023 construction cost index. Space has been left to advance the index figures as the year progresses.

Year	Historical Cost Index Jan. 1, 1993 = 100		Current Index Based on Jan. 1, 2023 = 100		Year	Historical Cost Index Jan. 1, 1993 = 100	Current Index Based on Jan. 1, 2023 = 100		Year	Historical Cost Index Jan. 1, 1993 = 100	Current Index Based on Jan. 1, 2023 = 100	
	Est.	Actual	Est.	Actual		Actual	Est.	Actual		Actual	Est.	Actual
Oct 2023					July 2006	162.0	50.8		July 1986	84.2	26.4	
July 2023					2005	151.6	47.6		1985	82.6	25.9	
April 2023					2004	143.7	45.1		1984	82.0	25.7	
Jan 2023	318.8		100.0		2003	132.0	41.4		1983	80.2	25.1	
July 2022		297.1	93.2		2002	128.7	40.4		1982	76.1	23.9	
2021		257.5	80.8		2001	125.1	39.2		1981	70.0	22.0	
2020		234.6	73.6		2000	120.9	37.9		1980	62.9	19.7	
2019		232.2	72.8		1999	117.6	36.9		1979	57.8	18.1	
2018		222.9	69.9		1998	115.1	36.1		1978	53.5	16.8	
2017		213.6	67.0		1997	112.8	35.4		1977	49.5	15.5	
2016		207.3	65.0		1996	110.2	34.6		1976	46.9	14.7	
2015		206.2	64.7		1995	107.6	33.8		1975	44.8	14.1	
2014		204.9	64.3		1994	104.4	32.7		1974	41.4	13.0	
2013		201.2	63.1		1993	101.7	31.9		1973	37.7	11.8	
2012		194.6	61.0		1992	99.4	31.2		1972	34.8	10.9	
2011		191.2	60.0		1991	96.8	30.4		1971	32.1	10.1	
2010		183.5	57.6		1990	94.3	29.6					
2009		180.1	56.5		1989	92.1	28.9					
2008		180.4	56.6		1988	89.9	28.2					
2007		169.4	53.1		1987	87.7	27.5					

Adjustments to Costs

The "Historical Cost Index" can be used to convert national average building costs at a particular time to the approximate building costs for some other time.

Example:

Estimate and compare construction costs for different years in the same city.

To estimate the national average construction cost of a building in 1971, knowing that it cost $900,000 in 2023:

INDEX in 1970 = 32.1
INDEX in 2023 = 318.8

Note: The city cost indexes for Canada can be used to convert U.S. national averages to local costs in Canadian dollars.

Time Adjustment Using the Historical Cost Indexes:

$$\frac{\text{Index for Year A}}{\text{Index for Year B}} \times \text{Cost in Year B} = \text{Cost in Year A}$$

$$\frac{\text{INDEX 1971}}{\text{INDEX 2023}} \times \text{Cost 2023} = \text{Cost 1971}$$

$$\frac{32.1}{318.8} \times \$900{,}000 = .100 \times \$900{,}000 = \$90{,}000$$

The construction cost of the building in 1971 was $90,000.

Example:

To estimate and compare the cost of a building in Toronto, ON in 2023 with the known cost of $600,000 (US$) in New York, NY in 2023:

INDEX Toronto = 132.1
INDEX New York = 139.6

$$\frac{\text{INDEX Toronto}}{\text{INDEX New York}} \times \text{Cost New York} = \text{Cost Toronto}$$

$$\frac{132.1}{139.6} \times \$600{,}000 = .947 \times \$600{,}000 = \$568{,}200$$

The construction cost of the building in Toronto is $568,200 (CN$).

*Historical Cost Index updates and other resources are provided on the following website:
rsmeans.com/2023books

City Cost Indexes

How to Use the City Cost Indexes

What you should know before you begin

RSMeans City Cost Indexes (CCI) are an extremely useful tool for when you want to compare costs from city to city and region to region.

This publication contains average construction cost indexes for 731 U.S. and Canadian cities covering over 930 three-digit zip code locations, as listed directly under each city.

Keep in mind that a City Cost Index number is a percentage ratio of a specific city's cost to the national average cost of the same item at a stated time period.

In other words, these index figures represent relative construction factors (or, if you prefer, multipliers) for material and installation costs, as well as the weighted average for Total In Place costs for each CSI MasterFormat division. Installation costs include both labor and equipment rental costs. When estimating equipment rental rates only for a specific location, use 01 54 33 EQUIPMENT RENTAL COSTS in the Reference Section.

The 30 City Average Index is the average of 30 major U.S. cities and serves as a national average. This national average represents the baseline from which all locations are calculated.

Index figures for both material and installation are based on the 30 major city average of 100 and represent the cost relationship as of July 1, 2022. The index for each division is computed from representative material and labor quantities for that division. The weighted average for each city is a weighted total of the components listed above it. It does not include relative productivity between trades or cities.

As changes occur in local material prices, labor rates, and equipment rental rates (including fuel costs), the impact of these changes should be accurately measured by the change in the City Cost Index for each particular city (as compared to the 30 city average).

Therefore, if you know (or have estimated) building costs in one city today, you can easily convert those costs to expected building costs in another city.

In addition, by using the Historical Cost Index, you can easily convert national average building costs at a particular time to the approximate building costs for some other time. The City Cost Indexes can then be applied to calculate the costs for a particular city.

Quick calculations

Location Adjustment Using the City Cost Indexes:

$$\frac{\text{Index for City A}}{\text{Index for City B}} \times \text{Cost in City B} = \text{Cost in City A}$$

Time Adjustment for the National Average Using the Historical Cost Index:

$$\frac{\text{Index for Year A}}{\text{Index for Year B}} \times \text{Cost in Year B} = \text{Cost in Year A}$$

Adjustment from the National Average:

$$\frac{\text{Index for City A}}{100} \times \text{National Average Cost} = \text{Cost in City A}$$

Since each of the other RSMeans data sets contains many different items, any *one* item multiplied by the particular city index may give incorrect results. However, the larger the number of items compiled, the closer the results should be to actual costs for that particular city.

The City Cost Indexes for Canadian cities are calculated using Canadian material and equipment prices and labor rates in Canadian dollars. When compared to the baseline mentioned previously, the resulting index enables the user to convert baseline costs to local costs. Therefore, indexes for Canadian cities can be used to convert U.S. national average prices to local costs in Canadian dollars.

How to use this section

1. Compare costs from city to city.

In using the RSMeans Indexes, remember that an index number is not a fixed number but a ratio: It's a percentage ratio of a building component's cost at any stated time to the national average cost of that same component at the same time period. Put in the form of an equation:

$$\frac{\text{Specific City Cost}}{\text{National Average Cost}} \times 100 = \text{City Index Number}$$

Therefore, when making cost comparisons between cities, do not subtract one city's index number from the index number of another city and read the result as a percentage difference. Instead, divide one city's index number by that of the other city. The resulting number may then be used as a multiplier to calculate cost differences from city to city.

The formula used to find cost differences between cities for the purpose of comparison is as follows:

$$\frac{\text{City A Index}}{\text{City B Index}} \times \text{City B Cost (Known)} = \text{City A Cost (Unknown)}$$

In addition, you can use RSMeans CCI to calculate and compare costs division by division between cities using the same basic formula. (Just be sure that you're comparing similar divisions.)

2. Compare a specific city's construction costs with the national average.

When you're studying construction location feasibility, it's advisable to compare a prospective project's cost index with an index of the national average cost.

For example, divide the weighted average index of construction costs of a specific city by that of the 30 City Average, which = 100.

$$\frac{\text{City Index}}{100} = \% \text{ of National Average}$$

As a result, you get a ratio that indicates the relative cost of construction in that city in comparison with the national average.

3. Convert U.S. national average to actual costs in Canadian City.

$$\frac{\text{Index for Canadian City}}{100} \times \text{National Average Cost} = \text{Cost in Canadian City in \$ CAN}$$

4. Adjust construction cost data based on a national average.
When you use a source of construction cost data which is based on a national average (such as RSMeans cost data), it is necessary to adjust those costs to a specific location.

$$\frac{\text{City Index}}{100} \times \text{Cost Based on National Average Costs} = \text{City Cost (Unknown)}$$

5. When applying the City Cost Indexes to demolition projects, use the appropriate division installation index. For example, for removal of existing doors and windows, use the Division 8 (Openings) index.

What you might like to know about how we developed the Indexes

The information presented in the CCI is organized according to the Construction Specifications Institute (CSI) MasterFormat 2018 classification system.

To create a reliable index, RSMeans researched the building type most often constructed in the United States and Canada. Because it was concluded that no one type of building completely represented the building construction industry, nine different types of buildings were combined to create a composite model.

The exact material, labor, and equipment quantities are based on detailed analyses of these nine building types, and then each quantity is weighted in proportion to expected usage. These various material items, labor hours, and equipment rental rates are thus combined to form a composite building representing as closely as possible the actual usage of materials, labor, and equipment in the North American building construction industry.

The following structures were chosen to make up that composite model:

1. Factory, 1 story
2. Office, 2–4 stories
3. Store, Retail
4. Town Hall, 2–3 stories
5. High School, 2–3 stories
6. Hospital, 4–8 stories
7. Garage, Parking
8. Apartment, 1–3 stories
9. Hotel/Motel, 2–3 stories

For the purposes of ensuring the timeliness of the data, the components of the index for the composite model have been streamlined. They currently consist of:

- specific quantities of 66 commonly used construction materials;
- specific labor-hours for 21 building construction trades; and
- specific days of equipment rental for 6 types of construction equipment (normally used to install the 66 material items by the 21 trades.) Fuel costs and routine maintenance costs are included in the equipment cost.

Material and equipment price quotations are gathered quarterly from cities in the United States and Canada. These prices and the latest negotiated labor wage rates for 21 different building trades are used to compile the quarterly update of the City Cost Index.

The 30 major U.S. cities used to calculate the national average are:

Atlanta, GA
Baltimore, MD
Boston, MA
Buffalo, NY
Chicago, IL
Cincinnati, OH
Cleveland, OH
Columbus, OH
Dallas, TX
Denver, CO
Detroit, MI
Houston, TX
Indianapolis, IN
Kansas City, MO
Los Angeles, CA
Memphis, TN
Milwaukee, WI
Minneapolis, MN
Nashville, TN
New Orleans, LA
New York, NY
Philadelphia, PA
Phoenix, AZ
Pittsburgh, PA
St. Louis, MO
San Antonio, TX
San Diego, CA
San Francisco, CA
Seattle, WA
Washington, DC

What the CCI does not indicate

The weighted average for each city is a total of the divisional components weighted to reflect typical usage. It does not include the productivity variations between trades or cities.

In addition, the CCI does not take into consideration factors such as the following:

- managerial efficiency
- competitive conditions
- automation
- restrictive union practices
- unique local requirements
- regional variations due to specific building codes

City Cost Indexes

DIVISION		UNITED STATES 30 CITY AVERAGE			ANNISTON 362			BIRMINGHAM 350 - 352			BUTLER 369			DECATUR 356			DOTHAN 363		
		MAT.	INST.	TOTAL	MAT.	INST.	TOTAL	MAT.	INST.	TOTAL	MAT.	INST.	TOTAL	MAT.	INST.	TOTAL	MAT.	INST.	TOTAL
015433	CONTRACTOR EQUIPMENT		100.0	100.0		98.3	98.3		102.9	102.9		96.1	96.1		98.3	98.3		96.1	96.1
0241, 31 - 34	SITE & INFRASTRUCTURE, DEMOLITION	100.0	100.0	100.0	104.1	85.5	92.0	99.0	93.6	95.5	111.3	82.0	92.2	91.3	85.1	87.3	108.9	82.2	91.4
0310	Concrete Forming & Accessories	100.0	100.0	100.0	92.5	63.3	69.9	100.0	67.6	74.9	88.2	65.5	70.6	99.3	61.9	70.3	98.4	69.0	75.5
0320	Concrete Reinforcing	100.0	100.0	100.0	88.0	67.9	82.4	98.0	68.1	89.7	92.9	67.4	85.8	91.4	64.4	83.9	92.9	68.2	86.3
0330	Cast-in-Place Concrete	100.0	100.0	100.0	87.9	65.7	80.0	106.6	70.4	93.8	85.7	65.9	78.7	99.0	65.0	86.9	85.7	67.6	79.3
03	CONCRETE	100.0	100.0	100.0	90.5	66.7	81.1	98.4	70.1	87.2	91.5	67.7	82.1	92.2	65.2	81.5	91.5	70.0	83.0
04	MASONRY	100.0	100.0	100.0	81.2	59.8	68.2	86.2	62.3	71.7	82.5	59.8	68.7	81.8	58.8	67.8	84.4	63.1	71.5
05	METALS	100.0	100.0	100.0	104.2	92.5	101.9	104.6	90.3	101.8	103.2	92.9	101.2	105.9	90.6	102.9	103.3	94.0	101.5
06	WOOD, PLASTICS & COMPOSITES	100.0	100.0	100.0	87.0	63.5	76.4	94.5	67.8	82.5	80.8	65.9	74.1	97.8	61.6	81.6	94.5	69.6	83.3
07	THERMAL & MOISTURE PROTECTION	100.0	100.0	100.0	102.7	59.2	87.2	106.7	66.1	92.2	102.7	62.9	88.5	104.1	62.1	89.1	102.8	64.4	89.1
08	OPENINGS	100.0	100.0	100.0	102.9	65.0	94.4	103.0	67.9	95.1	102.9	66.7	94.8	106.5	63.6	96.8	103.0	68.9	95.3
0920	Plaster & Gypsum Board	100.0	100.0	100.0	92.5	63.0	73.8	93.2	67.1	76.7	90.1	65.5	74.5	92.5	61.1	72.6	101.2	69.3	81.0
0950, 0980	Ceilings & Acoustic Treatment	100.0	100.0	100.0	92.1	63.0	75.8	90.1	67.1	77.2	92.1	65.5	77.2	87.9	61.1	72.9	92.1	69.3	79.3
0960	Flooring	100.0	100.0	100.0	68.1	64.2	67.1	106.5	67.5	96.7	71.7	64.2	69.8	100.1	64.2	91.1	75.8	68.8	74.0
0970, 0990	Wall Finishes & Painting/Coating	100.0	100.0	100.0	96.2	50.1	68.7	99.2	51.1	70.5	96.2	42.4	64.1	88.5	56.4	69.4	96.2	82.0	87.7
09	FINISHES	100.0	100.0	100.0	84.6	62.0	73.3	97.9	65.6	81.7	87.4	62.6	75.0	92.8	61.4	77.0	89.9	70.3	80.0
COVERS	DIVS. 10 - 14, 25, 28, 41, 43, 44, 46	100.0	100.0	100.0	100.0	83.4	96.8	100.0	85.0	97.1	100.0	84.5	97.0	100.0	78.9	95.9	100.0	85.2	97.1
21, 22, 23	FIRE SUPPRESSION, PLUMBING & HVAC	100.0	100.0	100.0	105.5	49.6	85.5	100.0	63.5	86.9	95.9	61.3	83.5	100.0	61.3	86.1	95.9	61.8	83.7
26, 27, 3370	ELECTRICAL, COMMUNICATIONS & UTIL.	100.0	100.0	100.0	98.0	53.3	78.6	100.7	64.2	84.9	99.1	53.5	79.3	98.0	60.3	81.6	98.4	73.4	87.6
MF2018	WEIGHTED AVERAGE	100.0	100.0	100.0	99.2	64.0	86.3	100.6	70.5	89.5	97.5	66.7	86.2	99.3	66.7	87.3	97.8	71.5	88.1

DIVISION		ALABAMA																	
		EVERGREEN 364			GADSDEN 359			HUNTSVILLE 357 - 358			JASPER 355			MOBILE 365 - 366			MONTGOMERY 360 - 361		
		MAT.	INST.	TOTAL	MAT.	INST.	TOTAL	MAT.	INST.	TOTAL	MAT.	INST.	TOTAL	MAT.	INST.	TOTAL	MAT.	INST.	TOTAL
015433	CONTRACTOR EQUIPMENT		96.1	96.1		98.3	98.3		98.3	98.3		98.3	98.3		96.1	96.1		103.7	103.7
0241, 31 - 34	SITE & INFRASTRUCTURE, DEMOLITION	111.8	82.0	92.3	101.5	85.5	91.1	91.0	85.5	87.4	101.4	85.5	91.1	105.7	82.0	90.2	104.4	94.8	98.1
0310	Concrete Forming & Accessories	84.7	63.5	68.3	90.5	65.8	71.3	99.3	72.0	78.1	96.3	64.1	71.3	97.4	66.8	73.6	102.8	67.3	75.2
0320	Concrete Reinforcing	92.9	67.4	85.8	96.5	68.0	88.7	91.4	76.0	87.1	91.4	67.9	84.9	91.0	68.8	84.8	99.8	68.1	91.0
0330	Cast-in-Place Concrete	85.7	65.8	78.7	99.0	67.8	87.9	96.4	67.6	86.2	109.8	66.4	94.3	89.9	66.9	81.7	89.8	68.8	82.3
03	CONCRETE	91.6	66.8	81.8	95.6	68.6	84.9	91.1	72.7	83.8	98.5	67.3	86.2	89.0	68.9	81.1	92.2	69.4	83.2
04	MASONRY	82.5	59.8	68.7	80.4	61.8	69.1	82.7	61.5	69.8	77.9	60.8	67.5	83.9	61.3	70.2	81.4	61.4	69.3
05	METALS	103.3	92.7	101.2	102.9	93.2	101.0	105.9	96.1	103.9	102.8	92.9	100.9	106.1	93.5	103.6	105.7	90.3	102.7
06	WOOD, PLASTICS & COMPOSITES	76.4	63.5	70.6	86.2	65.7	77.0	97.8	74.1	87.2	94.5	63.5	80.6	93.3	67.5	81.7	97.9	67.8	84.4
07	THERMAL & MOISTURE PROTECTION	102.7	61.8	88.1	104.2	64.2	90.0	104.1	65.0	90.1	104.3	62.3	89.3	102.5	63.2	88.5	102.5	65.6	89.3
08	OPENINGS	102.9	65.3	94.5	103.0	66.7	94.8	106.2	73.3	98.8	102.9	65.5	94.5	105.9	67.9	97.3	104.2	67.9	96.0
0920	Plaster & Gypsum Board	89.8	63.0	72.8	83.4	65.3	71.9	92.5	73.9	80.7	87.9	63.0	72.1	98.9	67.1	78.8	101.4	67.1	79.6
0950, 0980	Ceilings & Acoustic Treatment	92.1	63.0	75.8	81.1	65.3	72.2	88.9	73.9	80.5	81.1	63.0	70.9	101.3	67.1	82.1	104.0	67.1	83.3
0960	Flooring	70.0	64.2	68.6	97.0	66.8	89.4	100.1	66.8	91.7	98.7	64.2	90.0	75.7	67.5	73.6	75.0	67.5	73.1
0970, 0990	Wall Finishes & Painting/Coating	96.2	42.4	64.1	88.5	50.1	65.6	88.5	58.8	70.8	88.5	50.1	65.6	99.8	42.4	65.6	101.2	50.1	70.7
09	FINISHES	86.9	61.2	74.0	89.3	64.0	76.6	93.1	69.8	81.4	90.3	62.2	76.2	91.6	64.2	77.8	94.1	65.3	79.6
COVERS	DIVS. 10 - 14, 25, 28, 41, 43, 44, 46	100.0	84.2	96.9	100.0	83.9	96.9	100.0	84.7	97.0	100.0	83.7	96.8	100.0	84.7	97.0	100.0	84.7	97.0
21, 22, 23	FIRE SUPPRESSION, PLUMBING & HVAC	95.9	55.4	81.4	107.1	63.7	91.5	100.0	63.4	86.9	107.1	63.3	91.4	100.1	60.2	85.8	100.1	60.3	85.8
26, 27, 3370	ELECTRICAL, COMMUNICATIONS & UTIL.	97.6	53.5	78.5	98.2	64.2	83.5	98.7	65.6	84.4	97.8	53.3	78.5	99.7	58.6	81.9	100.8	71.1	87.9
MF2018	WEIGHTED AVERAGE	97.3	65.0	85.4	100.2	69.5	88.9	99.3	71.6	89.1	100.6	67.2	88.3	99.4	67.8	87.8	99.8	70.6	89.0

DIVISION		ALABAMA									ALASKA								
		PHENIX CITY 368			SELMA 367			TUSCALOOSA 354			ANCHORAGE 995 - 996			FAIRBANKS 997			JUNEAU 998		
		MAT.	INST.	TOTAL	MAT.	INST.	TOTAL	MAT.	INST.	TOTAL	MAT.	INST.	TOTAL	MAT.	INST.	TOTAL	MAT.	INST.	TOTAL
015433	CONTRACTOR EQUIPMENT		96.1	96.1		96.1	96.1		98.3	98.3		104.7	104.7		109.1	109.1		104.7	104.7
0241, 31 - 34	SITE & INFRASTRUCTURE, DEMOLITION	115.8	81.9	93.7	108.4	81.9	91.2	91.5	85.5	87.6	137.2	112.6	121.2	133.5	118.5	123.7	149.0	112.6	125.3
0310	Concrete Forming & Accessories	92.4	65.3	71.3	89.7	63.8	69.6	99.3	66.9	74.1	96.6	113.8	110.0	100.2	113.7	110.7	96.1	113.8	109.9
0320	Concrete Reinforcing	92.8	64.2	84.9	92.9	67.9	86.0	91.4	68.0	84.9	106.6	117.1	109.5	103.7	117.1	107.4	106.5	117.1	109.4
0330	Cast-in-Place Concrete	85.8	66.2	78.8	85.7	65.9	78.7	100.4	67.5	88.7	131.6	112.9	125.0	130.4	111.0	123.5	131.5	112.9	124.9
03	CONCRETE	94.0	67.2	83.4	90.8	67.0	81.4	92.8	69.0	83.4	116.1	113.4	115.0	108.8	112.8	110.4	120.9	113.4	117.9
04	MASONRY	82.5	59.8	68.7	87.3	59.8	70.6	82.1	61.3	69.5	180.4	113.1	139.5	179.4	113.0	139.1	165.4	113.1	133.6
05	METALS	103.2	91.6	100.9	103.2	93.0	101.2	105.0	93.2	102.7	132.1	101.8	126.1	126.8	104.1	122.3	127.1	101.8	122.1
06	WOOD, PLASTICS & COMPOSITES	86.4	65.4	77.0	82.9	63.5	74.2	97.8	67.5	84.2	107.6	111.8	109.5	120.9	111.7	116.8	112.1	111.8	112.0
07	THERMAL & MOISTURE PROTECTION	103.0	63.3	88.9	102.6	62.6	88.3	104.1	64.1	89.9	119.1	111.1	116.3	119.1	109.8	115.8	114.7	111.1	113.4
08	OPENINGS	102.9	65.6	94.5	102.6	65.5	94.5	106.2	67.7	97.5	121.5	113.6	119.7	124.5	112.2	121.7	123.4	113.6	121.2
0920	Plaster & Gypsum Board	94.2	65.0	75.7	92.0	63.0	73.6	92.5	67.1	76.4	129.5	112.1	118.4	154.7	112.1	127.7	142.9	112.1	123.4
0950, 0980	Ceilings & Acoustic Treatment	92.1	65.0	76.9	92.1	63.0	75.8	88.9	67.1	76.7	112.6	112.1	112.3	103.7	112.1	108.4	123.9	112.1	117.3
0960	Flooring	73.2	64.2	70.9	72.0	64.2	70.0	100.1	66.8	91.7	112.5	109.5	111.7	101.7	109.5	103.6	108.1	109.5	108.4
0970, 0990	Wall Finishes & Painting/Coating	96.2	74.4	83.2	96.2	50.1	68.7	88.5	50.1	65.6	105.1	115.5	111.3	101.8	109.7	106.5	105.1	115.5	111.3
09	FINISHES	88.8	65.8	77.3	87.5	62.0	74.7	93.1	64.9	78.9	113.5	113.3	113.4	111.4	112.7	112.0	116.7	113.3	115.0
COVERS	DIVS. 10 - 14, 25, 28, 41, 43, 44, 46	100.0	80.3	96.2	100.0	83.4	96.8	100.0	83.9	96.9	100.0	111.3	102.2	100.0	111.2	102.2	100.0	111.3	102.2
21, 22, 23	FIRE SUPPRESSION, PLUMBING & HVAC	95.9	60.1	83.1	95.9	60.8	83.3	100.0	63.3	86.8	100.0	107.3	102.6	99.8	107.2	102.5	100.0	107.3	102.6
26, 27, 3370	ELECTRICAL, COMMUNICATIONS & UTIL.	98.8	63.0	83.3	98.3	67.7	85.0	98.5	64.2	83.6	102.4	102.2	102.3	117.4	102.2	110.8	102.4	102.2	102.3
MF2018	WEIGHTED AVERAGE	98.0	67.8	86.9	97.5	68.3	86.7	99.3	69.6	88.4	116.6	109.2	113.9	116.2	109.6	113.8	116.1	109.2	113.5

City Cost Indexes

		ALASKA			ARIZONA														
		KETCHIKAN			CHAMBERS			FLAGSTAFF			GLOBE			KINGMAN			MESA/TEMPE		
	DIVISION	999			865			860			855			864			852		
		MAT.	INST.	TOTAL	MAT.	INST.	TOTAL	MAT.	INST.	TOTAL	MAT.	INST.	TOTAL	MAT.	INST.	TOTAL	MAT.	INST.	TOTAL
015433	CONTRACTOR EQUIPMENT		109.1	109.1		87.5	87.5		87.5	87.5		89.5	89.5		87.5	87.5		89.5	89.5
0241, 31 - 34	SITE & INFRASTRUCTURE, DEMOLITION	186.9	118.5	142.3	74.0	87.4	82.7	94.9	87.7	90.2	105.8	88.8	94.7	74.0	87.7	82.9	99.0	89.1	92.6
0310	Concrete Forming & Accessories	92.6	113.8	109.1	98.6	65.6	72.9	104.8	73.1	80.2	93.0	65.8	71.8	96.5	62.0	69.7	96.3	70.6	76.3
0320	Concrete Reinforcing	80.6	117.1	90.7	93.5	73.7	88.0	93.4	73.3	87.9	104.7	73.7	96.1	93.6	73.7	88.1	105.4	73.7	96.6
0330	Cast-in-Place Concrete	264.1	111.7	209.9	80.9	67.0	75.9	80.9	67.4	76.1	78.5	66.9	74.4	80.6	67.3	75.9	79.2	67.3	75.0
03	CONCRETE	175.7	113.1	151.0	89.4	67.6	80.8	104.5	71.2	91.4	95.1	67.8	84.3	89.1	66.2	80.1	89.9	70.1	82.1
04	MASONRY	188.4	113.0	142.6	97.3	65.2	77.8	97.5	58.9	74.0	118.6	65.1	86.1	97.3	65.3	77.9	118.8	65.2	86.3
05	METALS	127.0	104.1	122.5	98.5	72.4	93.4	99.1	73.0	94.0	95.8	73.8	91.4	99.3	73.4	94.2	96.1	74.8	91.9
06	WOOD, PLASTICS & COMPOSITES	110.6	111.7	111.1	104.3	66.3	87.3	112.5	76.2	96.2	91.7	66.5	80.4	98.6	61.2	81.8	96.4	72.7	85.8
07	THERMAL & MOISTURE PROTECTION	131.5	109.5	123.6	91.1	68.9	83.2	92.6	68.6	84.1	90.9	67.7	82.6	91.0	68.8	83.1	90.9	68.8	83.0
08	OPENINGS	120.5	113.6	118.9	100.3	63.8	92.1	100.4	72.9	94.2	90.9	63.9	84.8	100.4	62.5	91.9	91.0	68.2	85.8
0920	Plaster & Gypsum Board	138.2	112.1	121.6	104.2	65.6	79.7	109.1	75.8	88.0	101.5	65.6	78.8	94.4	60.4	72.8	105.6	72.1	84.3
0950, 0980	Ceilings & Acoustic Treatment	100.7	112.1	107.1	110.8	65.6	85.5	111.7	75.8	91.6	99.0	65.6	80.3	111.7	60.4	82.9	99.0	72.1	83.9
0960	Flooring	101.3	109.5	103.4	90.4	57.7	82.2	92.0	62.8	84.7	93.8	57.7	84.8	89.5	57.7	81.5	94.9	61.7	86.6
0970, 0990	Wall Finishes & Painting/Coating	101.8	115.5	110.0	87.5	55.2	68.2	87.5	55.2	68.2	93.3	55.2	70.6	87.5	55.2	68.2	93.3	55.2	70.6
09	FINISHES	112.7	113.3	113.0	97.4	62.6	79.9	100.3	69.4	84.8	98.6	62.8	80.6	96.0	59.7	77.7	98.4	67.3	82.8
COVERS	DIVS. 10 - 14, 25, 28, 41, 43, 44, 46	100.0	111.2	102.2	100.0	83.6	96.8	100.0	84.6	97.0	100.0	84.0	96.9	100.0	83.0	96.7	100.0	84.6	97.0
21, 22, 23	FIRE SUPPRESSION, PLUMBING & HVAC	93.2	107.2	98.2	94.2	74.1	87.0	100.4	76.2	91.7	92.8	74.2	86.1	94.2	76.2	87.8	100.4	74.2	91.0
26, 27, 3370	ELECTRICAL, COMMUNICATIONS & UTIL.	117.4	102.2	110.8	101.9	65.6	86.2	101.4	63.8	85.1	97.7	63.8	83.0	101.9	63.8	85.4	96.1	63.8	82.1
MF2018	WEIGHTED AVERAGE	124.5	109.8	119.1	96.2	70.2	86.6	100.3	71.7	89.8	96.3	70.2	86.7	96.2	69.8	86.5	97.1	71.5	87.7

		ARIZONA												ARKANSAS					
		PHOENIX			PRESCOTT			SHOW LOW			TUCSON			BATESVILLE			CAMDEN		
	DIVISION	850,853			863			859			856 - 857			725			717		
		MAT.	INST.	TOTAL	MAT.	INST.	TOTAL	MAT.	INST.	TOTAL	MAT.	INST.	TOTAL	MAT.	INST.	TOTAL	MAT.	INST.	TOTAL
015433	CONTRACTOR EQUIPMENT		98.6	98.6		87.5	87.5		89.5	89.5		89.5	89.5		87.3	87.3		87.3	87.3
0241, 31 - 34	SITE & INFRASTRUCTURE, DEMOLITION	99.8	97.3	98.2	83.3	87.7	86.2	108.0	88.8	95.5	95.0	89.2	91.2	73.4	82.4	79.3	78.5	82.3	81.0
0310	Concrete Forming & Accessories	101.4	71.6	78.3	100.3	68.7	75.8	100.9	65.8	73.6	97.1	77.7	82.0	86.0	56.9	63.4	83.1	57.1	62.9
0320	Concrete Reinforcing	100.7	71.7	92.6	93.4	73.7	88.0	105.4	73.7	96.6	86.5	73.4	82.8	96.2	63.6	87.2	96.0	64.6	87.3
0330	Cast-in-Place Concrete	83.4	71.7	79.2	80.9	67.4	76.1	78.5	66.9	74.4	81.5	67.3	76.5	61.7	71.7	65.2	67.1	71.2	68.6
03	CONCRETE	91.0	71.9	83.5	93.5	69.3	83.9	97.1	67.8	85.5	85.9	73.3	80.9	73.1	64.1	69.6	75.3	64.2	70.9
04	MASONRY	110.7	65.6	83.3	97.4	65.3	77.9	118.6	65.1	86.1	103.2	58.8	76.2	89.3	58.2	70.4	110.3	58.1	78.6
05	METALS	103.4	76.5	98.1	99.2	73.7	94.1	95.5	73.8	91.2	96.9	74.4	92.5	98.5	74.8	93.8	109.3	75.1	102.5
06	WOOD, PLASTICS & COMPOSITES	104.1	73.1	90.2	106.4	70.2	90.2	102.3	66.5	86.2	96.9	82.4	90.4	82.0	57.7	71.1	81.7	58.2	71.2
07	THERMAL & MOISTURE PROTECTION	91.6	71.0	84.3	91.5	70.5	84.0	91.2	67.7	82.8	91.4	68.1	83.1	106.1	58.8	89.2	100.7	59.1	85.9
08	OPENINGS	100.8	70.3	93.9	100.4	66.4	92.7	90.3	65.4	84.7	87.7	76.3	85.2	103.7	56.0	93.0	97.1	56.5	88.0
0920	Plaster & Gypsum Board	116.1	72.1	88.2	104.8	69.7	82.5	108.5	65.6	81.3	110.6	82.0	92.5	74.9	57.0	63.6	84.7	57.5	67.5
0950, 0980	Ceilings & Acoustic Treatment	115.1	72.1	91.0	109.0	69.7	86.9	99.0	65.6	80.3	101.7	82.0	90.7	98.9	57.0	75.4	103.7	57.5	77.8
0960	Flooring	100.1	66.3	91.7	91.1	61.9	83.7	95.9	57.7	86.3	85.0	62.5	79.3	91.2	66.1	84.9	92.8	67.4	86.5
0970, 0990	Wall Finishes & Painting/Coating	101.2	55.0	73.7	87.5	55.2	68.2	87.5	55.2	68.2	93.5	55.2	70.7	95.8	48.8	67.8	97.1	50.4	69.2
09	FINISHES	106.2	68.9	87.4	97.6	65.8	81.6	100.3	62.8	81.5	96.7	73.1	84.9	87.8	57.5	72.6	92.1	58.0	75.0
COVERS	DIVS. 10 - 14, 25, 28, 41, 43, 44, 46	100.0	86.1	97.3	100.0	84.0	96.9	100.0	84.0	96.9	100.0	85.7	97.2	100.0	78.4	95.8	100.0	78.2	95.8
21, 22, 23	FIRE SUPPRESSION, PLUMBING & HVAC	100.1	77.2	91.9	100.4	74.1	91.0	92.8	74.2	86.1	100.3	76.2	91.7	93.0	49.2	77.3	92.6	54.0	78.8
26, 27, 3370	ELECTRICAL, COMMUNICATIONS & UTIL.	100.1	63.8	84.4	101.2	63.8	85.0	96.3	63.8	82.2	97.3	57.9	80.2	93.8	53.8	76.5	95.6	51.7	76.6
MF2018	WEIGHTED AVERAGE	100.4	73.7	90.6	98.4	70.9	88.3	96.6	70.3	86.9	95.9	72.1	87.1	92.6	60.4	80.7	95.9	61.2	83.1

		ARKANSAS																	
		FAYETTEVILLE			FORT SMITH			HARRISON			HOT SPRINGS			JONESBORO			LITTLE ROCK		
	DIVISION	727			729			726			719			724			720 - 722		
		MAT.	INST.	TOTAL	MAT.	INST.	TOTAL	MAT.	INST.	TOTAL	MAT.	INST.	TOTAL	MAT.	INST.	TOTAL	MAT.	INST.	TOTAL
015433	CONTRACTOR EQUIPMENT		87.3	87.3		87.3	87.3		87.3	87.3		87.3	87.3		107.9	107.9		93.8	93.8
0241, 31 - 34	SITE & INFRASTRUCTURE, DEMOLITION	73.1	82.3	79.1	80.8	82.4	81.8	77.5	82.3	80.6	81.1	82.4	81.9	96.7	97.7	97.3	86.0	92.5	90.2
0310	Concrete Forming & Accessories	80.9	57.1	62.4	103.1	58.1	68.1	91.3	56.9	64.6	79.7	57.4	62.4	89.8	57.6	64.8	102.5	58.7	68.5
0320	Concrete Reinforcing	96.2	61.4	86.6	97.4	63.6	88.1	95.8	64.7	87.2	94.2	64.4	86.0	93.5	65.5	85.8	98.7	66.3	89.7
0330	Cast-in-Place Concrete	61.7	71.2	65.1	70.5	72.5	71.2	68.4	71.2	69.4	68.7	72.0	69.9	67.1	72.9	69.2	68.4	75.1	70.8
03	CONCRETE	72.7	63.7	69.1	79.3	64.9	73.6	77.9	64.1	72.5	77.0	64.6	72.1	75.9	66.1	72.0	81.8	66.5	75.7
04	MASONRY	81.6	58.1	67.3	91.8	59.0	71.9	89.7	58.1	70.5	82.9	57.4	67.4	83.3	59.7	69.0	88.8	61.6	72.3
05	METALS	98.5	74.0	93.6	101.3	74.6	96.0	100.1	74.9	95.2	109.2	74.7	102.4	95.5	89.0	94.2	101.4	74.5	96.1
06	WOOD, PLASTICS & COMPOSITES	77.1	58.2	68.6	103.4	59.3	83.7	89.1	58.2	75.2	78.1	58.2	69.2	85.9	58.5	73.6	98.1	59.6	80.8
07	THERMAL & MOISTURE PROTECTION	106.7	59.1	89.7	107.2	59.4	90.2	106.3	59.1	89.5	100.9	58.4	85.8	111.8	59.7	93.2	100.8	61.6	86.8
08	OPENINGS	103.7	55.7	92.9	105.4	56.8	94.4	104.4	56.4	93.6	97.1	56.0	87.9	109.1	56.9	97.3	98.6	57.3	89.3
0920	Plaster & Gypsum Board	73.4	57.5	63.3	81.5	58.7	67.0	81.1	57.5	66.1	83.5	57.5	67.0	83.1	57.5	66.9	93.2	58.7	71.3
0950, 0980	Ceilings & Acoustic Treatment	98.9	57.5	75.7	101.6	58.7	77.5	101.6	57.5	76.9	103.7	57.5	77.8	100.4	57.5	76.3	109.0	58.7	80.8
0960	Flooring	88.7	67.4	83.4	96.6	74.6	91.1	93.1	67.4	86.6	92.0	63.5	84.9	63.4	74.6	66.2	99.8	80.1	94.9
0970, 0990	Wall Finishes & Painting/Coating	95.8	50.4	68.7	95.8	50.1	68.6	95.8	50.4	68.7	97.1	48.4	68.1	84.3	49.5	63.6	99.1	49.5	69.6
09	FINISHES	87.0	58.0	72.4	91.3	60.4	75.7	90.2	58.0	74.1	92.0	57.4	74.6	83.3	59.9	71.6	100.7	61.6	81.1
COVERS	DIVS. 10 - 14, 25, 28, 41, 43, 44, 46	100.0	78.1	95.8	100.0	78.6	95.8	100.0	78.2	95.8	100.0	78.7	95.9	100.0	79.2	96.0	100.0	79.3	96.0
21, 22, 23	FIRE SUPPRESSION, PLUMBING & HVAC	93.1	58.2	79.0	100.3	47.7	81.7	93.0	46.8	76.4	92.6	47.7	76.5	101.2	48.6	82.4	100.2	50.1	82.2
26, 27, 3370	ELECTRICAL, COMMUNICATIONS & UTIL.	90.9	48.0	72.3	92.5	56.8	77.0	93.1	51.9	75.0	96.6	58.0	79.9	99.9	58.3	81.9	100.8	58.5	82.4
MF2018	WEIGHTED AVERAGE	91.9	61.4	80.6	96.4	61.1	83.4	93.9	59.6	81.3	95.1	60.6	82.4	95.4	64.2	83.9	97.4	63.4	84.9

City Cost Indexes

		ARKANSAS													CALIFORNIA					
DIVISION		PINE BLUFF			RUSSELLVILLE			TEXARKANA			WEST MEMPHIS			ALHAMBRA			ANAHEIM		
		716			728			718			723			917 - 918			928		
		MAT.	INST.	TOTAL	MAT.	INST.	TOTAL	MAT.	INST.	TOTAL	MAT.	INST.	TOTAL	MAT.	INST.	TOTAL	MAT.	INST.	TOTAL
015433	CONTRACTOR EQUIPMENT		87.3	87.3		87.3	87.3		88.4	88.4		107.9	107.9		93.7	93.7		96.6	96.6
0241, 31 - 34	SITE & INFRASTRUCTURE, DEMOLITION	86.2	82.4	83.7	74.7	82.4	79.7	94.7	84.2	87.8	99.1	97.5	98.1	113.1	101.2	105.4	110.8	101.5	104.8
0310	Concrete Forming & Accessories	79.5	57.5	62.4	86.9	57.3	63.9	87.3	57.3	64.0	96.1	57.7	66.3	97.0	138.9	129.6	96.1	139.0	129.5
0320	Concrete Reinforcing	95.9	66.1	87.7	96.9	64.4	87.9	95.4	66.1	87.3	93.5	56.9	83.4	99.5	132.7	108.7	79.8	132.6	94.4
0330	Cast-in-Place Concrete	68.7	71.8	69.8	64.6	72.0	67.2	74.8	71.5	73.7	70.4	73.0	71.3	94.3	126.6	105.8	99.3	129.5	110.0
03	CONCRETE	77.7	64.8	72.6	75.3	64.5	71.1	77.4	64.7	72.4	80.5	64.7	74.3	101.6	132.4	113.7	99.9	133.5	113.1
04	MASONRY	117.5	60.2	82.7	91.1	57.4	70.6	96.6	59.6	74.1	76.2	57.3	64.7	150.7	138.1	143.0	83.0	135.6	114.9
05	METALS	110.0	75.7	103.3	98.5	74.5	93.7	100.8	75.8	95.9	94.5	85.5	92.8	95.9	114.8	99.6	110.8	114.9	111.6
06	WOOD, PLASTICS & COMPOSITES	77.6	58.2	68.9	83.7	58.2	72.3	88.1	58.2	74.7	93.4	58.5	77.7	94.2	137.6	113.6	102.8	137.8	118.5
07	THERMAL & MOISTURE PROTECTION	101.0	60.1	86.4	106.9	58.4	89.6	101.5	59.6	86.6	112.3	58.3	93.0	125.1	129.5	126.7	91.3	131.9	105.8
08	OPENINGS	98.2	56.7	88.8	103.7	56.0	93.0	102.3	56.9	92.0	107.0	54.5	95.1	92.0	136.4	102.0	99.6	136.6	107.9
0920	Plaster & Gypsum Board	83.3	57.5	66.9	74.9	57.5	63.9	87.6	57.5	68.5	85.7	57.5	67.8	140.3	139.1	139.5	120.5	139.1	132.3
0950, 0980	Ceilings & Acoustic Treatment	103.7	57.5	77.8	98.9	57.5	75.7	112.8	57.5	81.8	99.8	57.5	76.1	105.4	139.1	124.3	105.3	139.1	124.2
0960	Flooring	91.9	74.6	87.6	90.7	63.5	83.9	93.4	75.7	89.0	65.4	63.5	64.9	91.7	118.3	98.4	89.6	118.3	96.8
0970, 0990	Wall Finishes & Painting/Coating	97.1	51.1	69.7	95.8	48.4	67.6	97.1	50.4	69.2	84.3	48.4	62.9	95.3	127.1	114.2	87.9	127.1	111.2
09	FINISHES	92.0	59.8	75.8	87.9	57.4	72.6	95.9	59.8	77.8	85.0	57.7	71.2	104.3	133.9	119.1	98.5	134.0	116.3
COVERS	DIVS. 10 - 14, 25, 28, 41, 43, 44, 46	100.0	78.5	95.8	100.0	78.7	95.9	100.0	78.3	95.8	100.0	79.7	96.1	100.0	116.2	103.1	100.0	116.7	103.2
21, 22, 23	FIRE SUPPRESSION, PLUMBING & HVAC	100.3	51.1	82.7	93.1	47.2	76.7	100.3	54.8	84.0	93.7	59.4	81.4	92.5	128.4	105.4	99.8	128.4	110.1
26, 27, 3370	ELECTRICAL, COMMUNICATIONS & UTIL.	95.6	55.4	78.2	92.5	51.2	74.6	96.5	53.3	77.8	100.7	58.1	82.2	101.3	134.5	115.7	84.4	117.1	98.6
MF2018	WEIGHTED AVERAGE	98.5	61.8	85.0	92.9	59.5	80.6	96.7	62.3	84.1	94.0	65.3	83.4	100.4	128.2	110.6	99.9	125.8	109.4

		CALIFORNIA																	
DIVISION		BAKERSFIELD			BERKELEY			EUREKA			FRESNO			INGLEWOOD			LONG BEACH		
		932 - 933			947			955			936 - 938			903 - 905			906 - 908		
		MAT.	INST.	TOTAL	MAT.	INST.	TOTAL	MAT.	INST.	TOTAL	MAT.	INST.	TOTAL	MAT.	INST.	TOTAL	MAT.	INST.	TOTAL
015433	CONTRACTOR EQUIPMENT		99.2	99.2		95.8	95.8		94.7	94.7		94.9	94.9		95.8	95.8		95.8	95.8
0241, 31 - 34	SITE & INFRASTRUCTURE, DEMOLITION	112.0	107.6	109.1	113.5	102.4	106.3	121.2	99.1	106.8	114.5	99.5	104.7	97.7	98.8	98.4	106.0	98.8	101.3
0310	Concrete Forming & Accessories	101.1	138.0	129.8	112.0	168.4	155.9	103.3	155.5	143.9	102.4	155.0	143.2	103.6	139.3	131.3	97.6	139.3	130.0
0320	Concrete Reinforcing	97.9	132.6	107.5	89.1	138.5	102.7	87.9	134.0	100.7	81.1	133.3	95.5	99.7	132.8	108.9	98.9	132.8	108.3
0330	Cast-in-Place Concrete	95.2	130.3	107.7	109.1	133.0	117.6	107.7	129.4	115.4	103.1	129.1	112.4	107.2	129.0	114.9	122.1	129.0	124.5
03	CONCRETE	101.5	133.1	114.0	106.7	148.7	123.3	110.6	141.1	122.6	99.9	140.6	115.9	105.6	133.5	116.6	114.8	133.5	122.2
04	MASONRY	111.1	137.1	126.9	105.8	152.0	133.9	101.1	153.7	133.1	116.5	143.3	132.8	84.1	138.2	117.0	94.3	138.2	121.0
05	METALS	103.9	112.3	105.6	100.2	116.6	103.5	110.4	117.4	111.8	104.8	115.8	106.9	87.4	116.8	93.2	87.3	116.8	93.1
06	WOOD, PLASTICS & COMPOSITES	101.0	136.8	117.1	136.9	174.4	153.7	117.8	159.7	136.6	109.5	159.7	132.0	98.9	137.9	116.4	90.5	137.9	111.7
07	THERMAL & MOISTURE PROTECTION	105.3	126.1	112.7	90.6	155.2	113.6	93.9	149.1	113.6	95.7	134.7	109.6	102.8	131.0	112.9	102.9	131.0	112.9
08	OPENINGS	98.5	134.9	106.7	91.6	163.2	107.8	98.8	144.0	109.0	100.7	147.5	111.2	86.8	136.6	98.0	86.8	136.6	98.0
0920	Plaster & Gypsum Board	110.5	137.9	127.9	123.1	176.3	156.9	127.6	161.6	149.2	104.4	161.6	140.7	119.8	139.1	132.0	113.2	139.1	129.6
0950, 0980	Ceilings & Acoustic Treatment	113.8	137.9	127.3	93.3	176.3	139.9	111.7	161.6	139.7	101.5	161.6	135.2	100.5	139.1	122.1	100.5	139.1	122.1
0960	Flooring	96.0	118.3	101.6	110.5	143.2	118.7	94.5	143.2	106.7	95.2	123.7	102.3	95.0	118.3	100.8	93.1	118.3	99.4
0970, 0990	Wall Finishes & Painting/Coating	99.1	110.3	105.8	98.4	165.8	138.6	90.1	134.0	116.3	105.9	121.6	115.2	99.8	127.1	116.1	99.8	127.1	116.1
09	FINISHES	104.2	131.7	118.0	104.9	165.1	135.1	105.1	152.7	129.0	100.4	148.0	124.3	101.2	134.1	117.7	100.2	134.1	117.3
COVERS	DIVS. 10 - 14, 25, 28, 41, 43, 44, 46	100.0	117.8	103.4	100.0	129.9	105.8	100.0	127.1	105.3	100.0	127.0	105.2	100.0	117.0	103.3	100.0	117.0	103.3
21, 22, 23	FIRE SUPPRESSION, PLUMBING & HVAC	100.0	128.3	110.1	92.7	167.5	119.5	92.3	130.0	105.8	100.0	132.6	111.7	91.7	128.5	104.9	91.7	128.5	104.9
26, 27, 3370	ELECTRICAL, COMMUNICATIONS & UTIL.	98.7	108.0	102.8	99.7	165.2	128.1	91.2	125.7	106.1	87.4	107.6	96.1	100.5	134.5	115.2	100.4	134.5	115.1
MF2018	WEIGHTED AVERAGE	102.0	124.3	110.2	99.5	151.3	118.6	101.7	134.0	113.6	100.7	129.9	111.4	94.6	128.5	107.0	96.1	128.5	108.0

		CALIFORNIA																	
DIVISION		LOS ANGELES			MARYSVILLE			MODESTO			MOJAVE			OAKLAND			OXNARD		
		900 - 902			959			953			935			946			930		
		MAT.	INST.	TOTAL	MAT.	INST.	TOTAL	MAT.	INST.	TOTAL	MAT.	INST.	TOTAL	MAT.	INST.	TOTAL	MAT.	INST.	TOTAL
015433	CONTRACTOR EQUIPMENT		108.2	108.2		94.7	94.7		94.7	94.7		94.9	94.9		95.8	95.8		93.9	93.9
0241, 31 - 34	SITE & INFRASTRUCTURE, DEMOLITION	108.7	112.2	111.0	117.2	99.1	105.4	114.4	99.1	104.4	104.2	99.7	101.2	122.1	102.4	109.2	114.8	98.0	103.9
0310	Concrete Forming & Accessories	101.5	139.7	131.1	93.0	155.5	141.3	88.9	155.2	140.4	110.9	138.0	131.9	99.2	168.4	153.0	102.7	139.1	131.0
0320	Concrete Reinforcing	98.6	134.4	108.5	87.9	133.4	100.5	91.1	133.4	102.8	99.1	132.6	108.4	91.1	138.5	104.2	97.3	132.7	107.1
0330	Cast-in-Place Concrete	110.8	131.4	118.2	120.4	129.2	123.5	107.8	129.2	115.4	89.2	128.7	103.2	103.4	133.0	114.0	103.9	128.9	112.8
03	CONCRETE	112.8	135.0	121.6	111.6	140.8	123.1	103.6	140.7	118.3	95.5	132.7	110.2	107.2	148.7	123.6	102.5	133.3	114.6
04	MASONRY	102.2	138.3	124.2	102.3	144.3	127.8	106.2	144.3	129.4	114.5	137.0	128.1	113.6	152.0	136.9	117.9	137.2	129.6
05	METALS	102.5	120.4	106.1	109.8	116.2	111.1	103.1	116.1	105.6	104.3	114.5	106.3	96.1	116.6	100.1	100.3	114.8	103.1
06	WOOD, PLASTICS & COMPOSITES	102.7	138.3	118.7	102.2	159.7	128.0	96.4	159.7	124.8	110.1	136.7	122.0	120.0	174.4	144.4	103.5	137.9	118.9
07	THERMAL & MOISTURE PROTECTION	99.9	132.8	111.7	93.3	139.5	109.8	93.0	139.8	109.7	101.4	123.2	109.2	89.5	155.2	113.1	103.1	131.5	113.2
08	OPENINGS	101.4	137.2	109.5	98.2	148.4	109.5	97.3	148.4	108.8	95.3	134.8	104.2	91.7	163.2	107.8	98.0	136.6	106.7
0920	Plaster & Gypsum Board	115.4	139.1	130.4	117.6	161.6	145.5	120.5	161.6	146.6	117.1	137.9	130.3	114.3	176.3	153.7	107.9	139.1	127.7
0950, 0980	Ceilings & Acoustic Treatment	112.8	139.1	127.5	110.8	161.6	139.3	105.3	161.6	136.9	107.8	137.9	124.7	94.8	176.3	140.5	104.1	139.1	123.7
0960	Flooring	97.0	118.3	102.4	91.9	130.2	101.5	92.1	133.9	102.6	94.0	118.3	100.1	106.7	143.2	115.8	87.8	118.3	95.4
0970, 0990	Wall Finishes & Painting/Coating	99.1	127.1	115.8	90.1	134.0	116.3	90.1	130.3	114.1	90.4	110.3	102.3	98.4	165.8	138.6	90.4	127.1	112.2
09	FINISHES	105.2	134.4	119.9	102.2	150.5	126.4	100.6	150.7	125.8	101.9	131.6	116.8	103.4	165.1	134.4	98.1	134.1	116.2
COVERS	DIVS. 10 - 14, 25, 28, 41, 43, 44, 46	100.0	117.8	103.5	100.0	127.1	105.2	100.0	127.0	105.2	100.0	123.8	104.6	100.0	129.9	105.8	100.0	116.8	103.3
21, 22, 23	FIRE SUPPRESSION, PLUMBING & HVAC	100.1	128.6	110.3	92.3	130.9	106.1	99.8	132.6	111.6	92.4	128.2	105.2	100.2	167.5	124.3	99.9	128.4	110.1
26, 27, 3370	ELECTRICAL, COMMUNICATIONS & UTIL.	99.5	134.5	114.7	89.6	118.5	102.1	91.1	109.9	99.2	86.0	108.0	95.5	99.2	165.2	127.8	94.4	111.7	101.9
MF2018	WEIGHTED AVERAGE	102.9	130.2	112.9	101.1	131.6	112.3	100.3	130.8	111.5	97.8	123.9	107.4	100.5	151.3	119.2	100.6	124.8	109.5

City Cost Indexes

CALIFORNIA

DIVISION		PALM SPRINGS 922			PALO ALTO 943			PASADENA 910 - 912			REDDING 960			RICHMOND 948			RIVERSIDE 925		
		MAT.	INST.	TOTAL	MAT.	INST.	TOTAL	MAT.	INST.	TOTAL	MAT.	INST.	TOTAL	MAT.	INST.	TOTAL	MAT.	INST.	TOTAL
015433	CONTRACTOR EQUIPMENT		95.6	95.6		95.8	95.8		93.7	93.7		94.7	94.7		95.8	95.8		95.6	95.6
0241, 31 - 34	SITE & INFRASTRUCTURE, DEMOLITION	99.2	99.8	99.6	110.0	102.4	105.0	109.0	101.2	104.0	136.0	99.1	111.9	118.2	102.3	107.9	109.2	99.8	103.1
0310	Concrete Forming & Accessories	92.8	139.0	128.7	97.2	168.6	152.6	90.7	138.9	128.2	86.8	155.2	139.9	115.2	168.1	156.3	96.8	139.1	129.6
0320	Concrete Reinforcing	92.3	132.7	103.5	89.1	138.5	102.8	101.2	132.7	109.9	88.1	133.4	100.7	89.1	138.5	102.7	89.7	132.7	101.6
0330	Cast-in-Place Concrete	94.6	129.5	107.0	92.2	133.1	106.8	89.4	126.6	102.6	131.5	129.2	130.7	106.1	132.9	115.6	102.9	129.5	112.4
03	CONCRETE	96.7	133.5	111.2	97.5	148.8	117.7	98.0	132.4	111.6	116.9	140.7	126.3	109.1	148.4	124.6	101.9	133.5	114.4
04	MASONRY	80.0	137.2	114.8	91.1	152.0	128.1	132.4	138.1	135.9	112.6	144.3	131.9	105.6	152.0	133.8	81.2	137.2	115.2
05	METALS	111.1	115.0	111.8	93.7	116.7	98.3	87.3	114.8	92.8	105.3	116.1	107.4	93.8	116.2	98.2	109.0	115.1	110.2
06	WOOD, PLASTICS & COMPOSITES	96.3	137.8	114.9	116.6	174.4	142.5	84.6	137.8	108.3	100.9	159.7	127.3	141.4	174.4	156.2	102.8	137.8	118.5
07	THERMAL & MOISTURE PROTECTION	90.8	130.6	105.0	89.1	155.2	112.7	111.7	129.5	118.0	97.3	139.5	112.3	89.9	154.3	112.8	91.5	132.4	106.1
08	OPENINGS	95.8	136.6	105.0	91.7	162.3	107.6	87.7	136.4	98.7	103.8	148.4	113.8	91.7	163.2	107.8	98.4	136.6	107.0
0920	Plaster & Gypsum Board	112.3	139.1	129.3	111.9	176.3	152.8	118.0	139.1	131.4	108.5	161.6	142.2	123.7	176.3	157.1	119.1	139.1	131.8
0950, 0980	Ceilings & Acoustic Treatment	100.8	139.1	122.2	93.8	176.3	140.1	98.1	139.1	121.1	120.7	161.6	143.7	93.8	176.3	140.1	105.4	139.1	124.3
0960	Flooring	93.9	118.3	100.0	105.9	143.2	115.3	88.7	118.3	96.1	71.0	119.0	83.0	111.9	143.2	119.8	94.6	118.3	100.6
0970, 0990	Wall Finishes & Painting/Coating	86.9	127.1	110.8	98.4	165.8	138.6	94.7	127.1	114.0	96.3	134.0	118.8	98.4	165.8	138.6	86.9	127.1	110.8
09	FINISHES	96.8	134.0	115.5	101.9	165.1	133.7	97.8	133.9	115.9	99.1	148.5	123.9	106.0	165.1	135.7	99.5	134.0	116.8
COVERS	DIVS. 10 - 14, 25, 28, 41, 43, 44, 46	100.0	116.7	103.2	100.0	130.0	105.8	100.0	116.2	103.1	100.0	127.1	105.2	100.0	129.8	105.8	100.0	117.6	103.4
21, 22, 23	FIRE SUPPRESSION, PLUMBING & HVAC	92.3	128.4	105.2	92.7	168.7	119.9	92.5	128.4	105.4	99.7	130.9	110.9	92.7	157.7	116.0	99.8	128.4	110.1
26, 27, 3370	ELECTRICAL, COMMUNICATIONS & UTIL.	85.8	118.3	99.9	99.2	181.5	134.8	109.1	134.5	120.1	93.3	118.5	104.2	99.4	139.1	116.6	84.2	118.3	99.0
MF2018	WEIGHTED AVERAGE	97.1	125.9	107.7	95.8	153.9	117.2	96.8	128.2	108.4	103.9	131.4	114.0	98.5	145.5	115.8	99.6	126.0	109.3

CALIFORNIA

DIVISION		SACRAMENTO 942,956 - 958			SALINAS 939			SAN BERNARDINO 923 - 924			SAN DIEGO 919 - 921			SAN FRANCISCO 940 - 941			SAN JOSE 951		
		MAT.	INST.	TOTAL	MAT.	INST.	TOTAL	MAT.	INST.	TOTAL	MAT.	INST.	TOTAL	MAT.	INST.	TOTAL	MAT.	INST.	TOTAL
015433	CONTRACTOR EQUIPMENT		94.8	94.8		94.9	94.9		95.6	95.6		105.6	105.6		112.4	112.4		96.2	96.2
0241, 31 - 34	SITE & INFRASTRUCTURE, DEMOLITION	102.9	107.1	105.7	127.0	99.6	109.1	84.4	99.8	94.5	119.7	112.3	114.9	122.3	117.6	119.2	148.4	94.8	113.5
0310	Concrete Forming & Accessories	98.2	157.5	144.3	107.2	158.0	146.6	100.7	139.0	130.5	101.5	137.7	129.6	101.0	168.9	153.8	94.7	168.3	151.9
0320	Concrete Reinforcing	83.5	133.5	97.3	97.9	133.9	107.9	89.7	132.7	101.6	98.6	129.0	107.0	99.3	139.6	110.4	79.7	138.5	96.0
0330	Cast-in-Place Concrete	87.5	130.2	102.6	102.6	129.5	112.2	71.0	129.5	91.8	102.5	128.4	111.7	115.6	134.7	122.4	125.3	132.1	127.7
03	CONCRETE	98.6	141.6	115.5	110.9	142.2	123.2	79.0	133.5	100.5	109.4	131.9	118.3	117.3	150.2	130.3	108.4	148.8	124.3
04	MASONRY	92.0	144.3	123.8	114.6	149.4	135.8	89.7	137.2	118.6	121.4	133.9	129.0	116.2	155.0	139.7	133.9	152.0	144.9
05	METALS	91.7	108.9	95.1	107.4	117.2	109.4	100.9	115.0	110.1	103.7	114.3	105.8	105.9	126.3	109.9	102.5	124.1	106.8
06	WOOD, PLASTICS & COMPOSITES	113.6	162.7	135.6	110.3	162.4	133.7	107.4	137.8	121.0	102.8	137.7	118.5	121.2	174.4	145.0	108.7	174.1	138.0
07	THERMAL & MOISTURE PROTECTION	98.0	141.1	113.4	102.1	145.6	117.6	90.2	132.4	105.3	105.6	121.9	111.4	95.0	157.3	117.2	90.6	155.2	113.6
08	OPENINGS	103.5	150.0	114.0	99.2	155.5	111.9	95.8	136.6	105.0	99.2	132.6	106.7	103.7	163.4	117.1	89.2	163.0	105.8
0920	Plaster & Gypsum Board	108.0	164.4	143.7	110.1	164.4	144.5	121.5	139.1	132.6	113.6	138.6	129.5	111.8	176.3	152.7	113.3	176.3	153.3
0950, 0980	Ceilings & Acoustic Treatment	93.8	164.4	133.4	107.8	164.4	139.5	105.3	139.1	124.2	105.8	138.6	124.1	113.6	176.3	148.8	99.9	176.3	142.8
0960	Flooring	105.4	130.2	111.6	90.1	143.2	103.4	95.9	118.3	101.5	97.3	118.3	102.6	104.0	142.0	113.5	84.4	143.2	99.2
0970, 0990	Wall Finishes & Painting/Coating	95.4	138.5	121.1	91.3	170.3	138.4	86.9	127.1	110.8	95.2	118.9	109.3	99.1	174.0	143.8	89.8	165.8	135.1
09	FINISHES	100.4	152.7	126.7	102.0	158.3	130.3	98.6	134.0	116.4	102.9	132.6	117.8	107.1	165.8	136.6	97.6	164.9	131.4
COVERS	DIVS. 10 - 14, 25, 28, 41, 43, 44, 46	100.0	127.9	105.4	100.0	127.4	105.3	100.0	115.1	102.9	100.0	116.6	103.2	100.0	130.2	105.8	100.0	129.4	105.7
21, 22, 23	FIRE SUPPRESSION, PLUMBING & HVAC	100.1	130.8	111.1	92.4	138.0	108.7	92.3	128.4	105.2	100.1	127.2	109.8	100.1	180.3	128.8	99.8	168.7	124.5
26, 27, 3370	ELECTRICAL, COMMUNICATIONS & UTIL.	94.3	118.4	104.8	86.9	135.3	107.8	85.8	113.5	97.8	101.0	103.0	101.9	99.7	189.6	138.7	95.5	181.5	132.8
MF2018	WEIGHTED AVERAGE	97.6	132.2	110.3	101.3	137.9	114.7	94.8	125.2	106.0	103.7	123.3	110.9	105.4	160.2	125.6	102.2	153.9	121.3

CALIFORNIA

DIVISION		SAN LUIS OBISPO 934			SAN MATEO 944			SAN RAFAEL 949			SANTA ANA 926 - 927			SANTA BARBARA 931			SANTA CRUZ 950		
		MAT.	INST.	TOTAL	MAT.	INST.	TOTAL	MAT.	INST.	TOTAL	MAT.	INST.	TOTAL	MAT.	INST.	TOTAL	MAT.	INST.	TOTAL
015433	CONTRACTOR EQUIPMENT		94.9	94.9		95.8	95.8		95.1	95.1		95.6	95.6		94.9	94.9		96.2	96.2
0241, 31 - 34	SITE & INFRASTRUCTURE, DEMOLITION	118.0	99.7	106.1	116.0	102.4	107.1	112.1	97.1	102.3	97.4	99.8	99.0	114.8	99.7	104.9	148.5	94.7	113.4
0310	Concrete Forming & Accessories	112.9	139.1	133.3	104.2	168.5	154.1	112.3	168.1	155.7	101.1	139.0	130.6	103.1	139.1	131.0	94.7	158.0	143.9
0320	Concrete Reinforcing	99.1	132.6	108.4	89.1	138.7	102.8	89.4	134.3	101.8	92.6	132.7	103.7	97.3	132.6	107.0	99.1	133.9	108.7
0330	Cast-in-Place Concrete	110.3	128.8	116.9	102.7	133.0	113.5	119.6	132.1	124.0	90.8	129.5	104.5	103.5	128.8	112.5	124.4	131.0	126.8
03	CONCRETE	109.8	133.2	119.0	105.8	148.7	122.7	125.9	147.3	134.3	94.7	133.5	110.0	102.3	133.2	114.5	113.1	143.0	124.9
04	MASONRY	116.3	136.2	128.4	105.2	154.8	135.3	86.1	154.8	127.8	77.7	137.5	114.0	114.7	136.2	127.8	138.1	149.6	145.1
05	METALS	105.7	114.7	107.5	93.6	116.8	98.2	96.6	111.6	99.6	109.0	115.0	110.2	101.9	114.7	104.5	109.1	121.1	111.5
06	WOOD, PLASTICS & COMPOSITES	112.9	137.9	124.1	127.3	174.4	148.4	126.4	174.4	147.8	109.6	137.8	122.2	103.5	137.9	118.9	108.7	162.5	132.8
07	THERMAL & MOISTURE PROTECTION	102.2	130.8	112.3	89.6	155.2	113.0	92.6	154.8	114.7	91.1	131.6	105.5	101.6	130.8	112.0	90.3	147.4	110.6
08	OPENINGS	97.3	135.4	105.9	91.6	162.3	107.5	100.9	161.2	114.5	95.1	136.6	104.5	99.1	136.6	107.6	90.0	155.6	104.8
0920	Plaster & Gypsum Board	118.0	139.1	131.4	120.3	176.3	155.9	124.3	176.3	157.3	122.9	139.1	133.2	107.9	139.1	127.7	121.6	164.4	148.7
0950, 0980	Ceilings & Acoustic Treatment	107.8	139.1	125.3	93.8	176.3	140.1	107.4	176.3	146.0	105.3	139.1	124.2	104.1	139.1	123.7	106.7	164.4	139.0
0960	Flooring	94.6	118.3	100.6	108.1	143.2	116.9	117.5	143.2	123.9	96.3	118.3	101.8	89.5	118.3	96.7	88.1	143.2	101.9
0970, 0990	Wall Finishes & Painting/Coating	90.4	114.0	104.5	98.4	165.8	138.6	94.8	170.3	139.8	86.9	127.1	110.8	90.4	127.1	112.2	89.5	165.8	135.0
09	FINISHES	103.4	132.7	118.1	104.2	165.1	134.8	109.5	165.5	137.6	100.1	134.0	117.1	98.8	134.1	116.5	101.6	157.9	129.9
COVERS	DIVS. 10 - 14, 25, 28, 41, 43, 44, 46	100.0	125.6	105.0	100.0	130.0	105.8	100.0	129.3	105.7	100.0	116.6	103.2	100.0	117.7	103.4	100.0	127.7	105.4
21, 22, 23	FIRE SUPPRESSION, PLUMBING & HVAC	92.4	128.4	105.3	92.7	168.3	119.7	92.7	180.1	124.0	92.3	128.4	105.2	99.9	128.4	110.1	99.8	138.0	113.5
26, 27, 3370	ELECTRICAL, COMMUNICATIONS & UTIL.	86.0	109.0	96.0	99.2	174.4	131.8	91.9	125.7	106.5	85.8	117.1	99.4	85.5	107.5	95.1	95.2	135.3	112.6
MF2018	WEIGHTED AVERAGE	100.5	124.5	109.3	97.7	152.4	117.9	100.4	148.3	118.1	96.6	125.8	107.4	100.0	124.3	108.9	104.7	138.0	117.0

City Cost Indexes

DIVISION		CALIFORNIA															COLORADO		
		SANTA ROSA			STOCKTON			SUSANVILLE			VALLEJO			VAN NUYS			ALAMOSA		
		954			952			961			945			913 - 916			811		
		MAT.	INST.	TOTAL	MAT.	INST.	TOTAL	MAT.	INST.	TOTAL	MAT.	INST.	TOTAL	MAT.	INST.	TOTAL	MAT.	INST.	TOTAL
015433	CONTRACTOR EQUIPMENT		95.2	95.2		94.7	94.7		94.7	94.7		95.1	95.1		93.7	93.7		89.2	89.2
0241, 31 - 34	SITE & INFRASTRUCTURE, DEMOLITION	112.3	99.0	103.6	114.1	99.1	104.3	141.5	99.1	113.8	103.5	107.0	105.8	129.5	101.2	111.1	131.3	81.7	98.9
0310	Concrete Forming & Accessories	93.8	167.3	150.9	93.2	157.2	142.9	88.0	155.2	140.2	101.4	167.2	152.5	97.5	138.9	129.7	99.9	68.7	75.6
0320	Concrete Reinforcing	88.6	134.3	101.2	91.1	133.4	102.8	88.1	133.4	100.7	90.5	134.2	102.6	101.2	132.7	109.9	101.8	63.4	91.2
0330	Cast-in-Place Concrete	118.3	130.5	122.6	105.0	129.2	113.6	119.6	129.2	123.0	95.2	131.3	108.0	94.3	126.6	105.8	90.2	69.2	82.7
03	CONCRETE	111.6	146.9	125.5	102.9	141.6	118.2	117.9	140.8	126.9	103.8	146.5	120.7	110.4	132.4	119.1	104.9	68.6	90.6
04	MASONRY	102.2	153.8	133.6	106.1	144.3	129.3	110.8	144.3	131.2	68.6	153.8	120.4	151.3	138.1	143.3	132.0	67.4	92.8
05	METALS	109.4	118.8	111.2	103.7	116.1	106.2	103.1	116.2	105.6	96.5	111.0	99.3	86.4	114.4	92.0	99.1	78.5	95.0
06	WOOD, PLASTICS & COMPOSITES	98.2	173.9	132.2	103.5	162.4	129.9	102.8	159.7	128.3	111.5	174.2	139.6	94.5	137.6	113.8	99.2	71.1	86.6
07	THERMAL & MOISTURE PROTECTION	91.4	153.8	113.6	93.4	137.7	109.2	97.4	139.5	112.4	91.1	154.0	113.5	112.6	129.5	118.6	99.9	66.9	88.2
08	OPENINGS	96.6	161.9	111.3	97.3	150.8	109.4	103.7	149.3	114.0	102.7	161.2	115.9	87.5	136.4	98.6	91.6	68.2	86.3
0920	Plaster & Gypsum Board	115.9	176.3	154.2	120.5	164.4	148.3	108.9	161.6	142.3	115.9	176.3	154.2	122.9	139.1	133.2	89.0	70.3	77.1
0950, 0980	Ceilings & Acoustic Treatment	105.3	176.3	145.1	109.9	164.4	140.4	115.4	161.6	141.3	108.4	176.3	146.5	109.3	139.1	119.5	105.3	70.3	85.7
0960	Flooring	94.2	133.7	104.1	92.1	133.9	102.6	71.2	119.0	83.2	113.9	143.2	121.3	90.6	118.5	97.5	110.5	79.6	102.7
0970, 0990	Wall Finishes & Painting/Coating	86.9	161.3	131.2	90.1	138.5	119.0	96.3	134.0	118.8	95.7	170.3	140.2	94.7	127.1	114.0	100.7	71.0	83.0
09	FINISHES	99.5	162.4	131.1	101.8	153.2	127.6	98.8	148.5	123.8	106.4	165.2	135.9	99.5	133.9	116.8	104.3	71.2	87.7
COVERS	DIVS. 10 - 14, 25, 28, 41, 43, 44, 46	100.0	128.5	105.5	100.0	125.7	105.0	100.0	127.1	105.3	100.0	129.0	105.6	100.0	116.2	103.1	100.0	84.9	97.1
21, 22, 23	FIRE SUPPRESSION, PLUMBING & HVAC	92.3	174.5	121.8	99.8	132.6	111.6	92.1	132.7	106.7	100.2	146.9	116.9	92.5	128.4	105.4	92.5	66.8	83.3
26, 27, 3370	ELECTRICAL, COMMUNICATIONS & UTIL.	85.9	120.9	101.1	91.1	112.2	100.3	93.5	120.8	105.3	89.9	125.0	105.1	109.0	134.5	120.1	92.6	56.3	76.9
MF2018	WEIGHTED AVERAGE	100.0	145.9	116.9	100.5	131.6	111.9	102.0	132.1	113.1	98.1	140.9	113.8	99.5	128.2	110.1	99.5	69.1	88.3

DIVISION		COLORADO																	
		BOULDER			COLORADO SPRINGS			DENVER			DURANGO			FORT COLLINS			FORT MORGAN		
		803			808 - 809			800 - 802			813			805			807		
		MAT.	INST.	TOTAL	MAT.	INST.	TOTAL	MAT.	INST.	TOTAL	MAT.	INST.	TOTAL	MAT.	INST.	TOTAL	MAT.	INST.	TOTAL
015433	CONTRACTOR EQUIPMENT		90.0	90.0		88.2	88.2		94.7	94.7		89.2	89.2		90.0	90.0		90.0	90.0
0241, 31 - 34	SITE & INFRASTRUCTURE, DEMOLITION	92.5	87.8	89.5	97.5	83.4	88.3	101.3	94.4	96.8	125.4	81.7	96.9	105.8	87.4	93.8	94.2	86.8	89.4
0310	Concrete Forming & Accessories	99.9	71.6	77.9	90.3	68.5	73.4	99.3	70.5	75.5	106.5	68.4	76.9	97.8	68.6	75.2	100.4	68.3	75.5
0320	Concrete Reinforcing	97.1	69.1	89.3	96.5	68.8	88.9	100.8	69.0	92.0	101.8	63.4	91.2	97.1	65.8	88.5	97.2	63.4	87.9
0330	Cast-in-Place Concrete	97.8	75.1	89.7	100.4	71.1	90.0	101.7	73.2	91.6	103.7	69.1	91.4	110.4	71.0	96.4	95.9	68.3	86.1
03	CONCRETE	100.1	72.9	89.3	102.4	70.1	89.7	109.1	70.8	94.0	107.0	68.5	91.8	108.6	69.6	93.2	98.9	68.1	86.7
04	MASONRY	94.2	69.3	79.1	97.8	61.2	75.6	103.9	64.0	79.7	119.1	67.4	87.7	108.5	67.5	83.6	107.7	65.5	83.3
05	METALS	89.5	79.2	87.5	92.9	78.8	90.1	102.0	78.1	97.2	99.1	78.2	95.0	90.7	77.9	88.2	89.7	76.7	86.7
06	WOOD, PLASTICS & COMPOSITES	100.5	72.7	88.0	87.3	70.7	79.9	102.4	70.8	88.2	110.4	71.1	92.8	97.2	70.6	85.3	100.5	70.6	87.1
07	THERMAL & MOISTURE PROTECTION	97.9	72.9	89.0	98.7	68.6	88.0	97.4	72.3	88.5	99.9	66.9	88.2	98.1	70.4	88.3	97.9	68.1	87.3
08	OPENINGS	90.0	71.7	85.9	93.8	70.0	88.4	99.3	70.6	92.8	97.7	68.2	91.0	90.0	69.3	85.3	90.0	68.0	85.0
0920	Plaster & Gypsum Board	114.9	72.4	88.0	99.3	70.3	80.9	110.4	70.3	85.0	107.1	70.3	83.8	105.0	70.3	83.0	114.9	70.3	86.6
0950, 0980	Ceilings & Acoustic Treatment	97.6	72.4	83.5	111.7	70.3	88.5	114.5	70.3	89.7	105.3	70.3	85.7	97.6	70.3	82.3	97.6	70.3	82.3
0960	Flooring	119.9	79.6	109.8	110.4	79.6	102.7	116.5	79.6	107.2	114.2	79.6	105.5	116.8	79.6	107.5	120.2	79.6	110.1
0970, 0990	Wall Finishes & Painting/Coating	90.2	75.4	81.4	89.9	78.3	83.0	99.1	73.2	83.6	100.7	71.0	83.0	90.2	71.0	78.8	90.2	71.0	78.8
09	FINISHES	106.0	73.4	89.6	104.8	71.6	88.2	109.5	71.0	90.2	104.1	71.2	87.6	104.1	70.9	87.4	106.0	70.9	88.4
COVERS	DIVS. 10 - 14, 25, 28, 41, 43, 44, 46	100.0	85.3	97.2	100.0	84.1	96.9	100.0	84.1	96.9	100.0	84.9	97.1	100.0	84.0	96.9	100.0	84.0	96.9
21, 22, 23	FIRE SUPPRESSION, PLUMBING & HVAC	92.6	74.6	86.1	100.3	66.7	88.3	100.1	74.2	90.8	92.5	54.4	78.8	100.1	71.7	89.9	92.6	67.7	83.7
26, 27, 3370	ELECTRICAL, COMMUNICATIONS & UTIL.	96.8	79.8	89.4	98.3	70.0	86.1	99.4	80.0	91.0	92.3	49.4	73.7	96.8	76.9	88.2	97.3	69.5	85.3
MF2018	WEIGHTED AVERAGE	94.9	76.0	87.9	98.2	70.9	88.1	102.2	75.1	92.3	99.9	65.5	87.3	98.5	73.7	89.4	95.3	71.3	86.7

DIVISION		COLORADO																	
		GLENWOOD SPRINGS			GOLDEN			GRAND JUNCTION			GREELEY			MONTROSE			PUEBLO		
		816			804			815			806			814			810		
		MAT.	INST.	TOTAL	MAT.	INST.	TOTAL	MAT.	INST.	TOTAL	MAT.	INST.	TOTAL	MAT.	INST.	TOTAL	MAT.	INST.	TOTAL
015433	CONTRACTOR EQUIPMENT		92.0	92.0		90.0	90.0		92.0	92.0		90.0	90.0		90.6	90.6		89.2	89.2
0241, 31 - 34	SITE & INFRASTRUCTURE, DEMOLITION	139.3	88.3	106.1	103.4	87.0	92.7	128.0	88.9	102.5	94.7	87.5	90.0	133.6	85.3	102.1	121.1	82.1	95.7
0310	Concrete Forming & Accessories	96.3	68.2	74.4	92.8	68.1	73.6	105.2	69.2	77.2	95.5	68.7	74.7	95.9	68.3	74.5	102.4	68.8	76.3
0320	Concrete Reinforcing	101.1	63.4	90.6	97.2	63.2	87.8	101.3	65.7	91.4	97.1	65.8	88.4	101.0	63.4	90.6	97.6	69.0	89.7
0330	Cast-in-Place Concrete	90.1	68.1	82.3	96.0	70.4	86.9	99.8	71.6	89.8	92.2	71.0	84.7	90.1	68.6	82.5	89.5	71.6	83.1
03	CONCRETE	108.5	68.0	92.5	106.9	68.7	91.8	104.2	70.1	90.7	96.1	69.6	85.6	101.7	68.3	88.5	95.9	70.5	85.9
04	MASONRY	104.1	67.4	81.8	110.5	64.0	82.2	139.9	65.7	94.8	102.2	67.5	81.1	111.5	67.4	84.7	100.5	63.8	78.2
05	METALS	98.7	77.8	94.6	89.4	76.6	86.9	100.4	78.9	96.2	90.6	78.0	88.1	97.5	78.0	93.7	102.9	80.6	98.5
06	WOOD, PLASTICS & COMPOSITES	93.6	70.8	83.4	90.2	70.6	81.5	108.7	70.8	91.7	93.9	70.6	83.5	94.1	70.9	83.7	102.6	71.1	88.5
07	THERMAL & MOISTURE PROTECTION	99.8	66.9	88.1	98.6	68.5	87.9	99.2	69.0	88.4	97.6	70.4	87.9	99.9	66.9	88.1	98.8	68.1	87.9
08	OPENINGS	96.7	68.1	90.2	90.0	68.0	85.0	97.3	69.3	91.0	90.0	69.3	85.3	97.8	68.2	91.1	90.7	70.2	87.9
0920	Plaster & Gypsum Board	122.4	70.3	89.4	100.4	70.3	81.3	141.0	70.3	96.2	103.1	70.3	82.3	87.8	70.3	76.7	95.5	70.3	79.5
0950, 0980	Ceilings & Acoustic Treatment	104.4	70.3	85.3	97.6	70.3	82.3	104.4	70.3	85.3	97.6	70.3	82.3	105.3	70.3	85.7	115.3	70.3	90.1
0960	Flooring	109.8	79.6	102.3	114.8	79.6	106.0	113.6	79.6	105.1	115.8	79.6	106.7	112.3	79.6	104.1	111.3	79.6	103.4
0970, 0990	Wall Finishes & Painting/Coating	100.7	71.0	83.0	90.2	71.0	78.8	100.7	71.0	83.0	90.2	71.0	78.8	100.7	71.0	83.0	100.7	71.0	83.0
09	FINISHES	108.8	71.0	89.8	103.5	70.6	87.0	110.8	71.4	91.0	103.0	70.9	86.9	104.7	71.1	87.9	106.6	71.1	88.7
COVERS	DIVS. 10 - 14, 25, 28, 41, 43, 44, 46	100.0	84.3	97.0	100.0	83.7	96.9	100.0	84.8	97.1	100.0	84.0	96.9	100.0	84.6	97.0	100.0	84.8	97.0
21, 22, 23	FIRE SUPPRESSION, PLUMBING & HVAC	92.5	54.4	78.8	92.6	67.3	83.5	100.0	71.3	89.7	100.1	71.7	89.9	92.5	54.4	78.8	100.0	67.7	88.4
26, 27, 3370	ELECTRICAL, COMMUNICATIONS & UTIL.	91.0	49.4	73.0	97.3	71.7	86.2	92.2	54.0	75.6	96.8	76.9	88.2	92.2	49.4	73.6	92.6	62.8	79.7
MF2018	WEIGHTED AVERAGE	99.5	65.9	87.1	96.4	71.2	87.1	102.6	70.5	90.8	96.4	73.7	88.0	98.5	65.7	86.5	99.8	70.4	89.0

City Cost Indexes

		COLORADO			CONNECTICUT														
	DIVISION	SALIDA 812			BRIDGEPORT 066			BRISTOL 060			HARTFORD 061			MERIDEN 064			NEW BRITAIN 060		
		MAT.	INST.	TOTAL	MAT.	INST.	TOTAL	MAT.	INST.	TOTAL	MAT.	INST.	TOTAL	MAT.	INST.	TOTAL	MAT.	INST.	TOTAL
015433	CONTRACTOR EQUIPMENT		90.6	90.6		93.0	93.0		93.0	93.0		97.4	97.4		93.3	93.3		93.0	93.0
0241, 31 - 34	SITE & INFRASTRUCTURE, DEMOLITION	125.1	85.0	99.0	100.2	93.5	95.8	99.5	93.5	95.6	96.9	101.1	99.6	94.4	94.1	94.2	99.6	93.5	95.6
0310	Concrete Forming & Accessories	105.2	68.6	76.7	103.5	112.3	110.4	103.5	114.6	112.1	104.5	114.8	112.5	103.1	114.5	112.0	104.1	114.6	112.3
0320	Concrete Reinforcing	100.8	63.4	90.5	103.8	139.9	113.8	103.8	139.9	113.8	99.0	139.9	110.3	103.8	139.9	113.8	103.8	139.9	113.8
0330	Cast-in-Place Concrete	103.3	68.7	91.0	81.6	124.8	97.0	76.5	124.8	93.6	77.9	126.4	95.2	73.6	124.7	91.8	77.7	124.8	94.4
03	CONCRETE	103.1	68.4	89.4	96.6	120.9	106.2	94.5	121.9	105.3	95.0	122.5	105.9	93.2	121.9	104.5	95.0	121.9	105.6
04	MASONRY	140.4	67.4	96.1	121.0	128.9	125.8	112.5	128.9	122.4	116.1	129.0	123.9	112.2	128.9	122.3	114.7	128.9	123.3
05	METALS	97.2	78.3	93.4	98.4	116.0	101.8	98.4	115.9	101.8	101.6	114.1	104.1	95.3	115.8	99.4	94.4	115.9	98.6
06	WOOD, PLASTICS & COMPOSITES	104.3	70.9	89.4	110.5	109.2	109.9	110.5	112.4	111.4	102.0	112.6	106.7	110.5	112.4	111.4	110.5	112.4	111.4
07	THERMAL & MOISTURE PROTECTION	99.2	66.9	87.7	96.7	118.4	104.4	96.8	116.7	103.9	101.6	119.1	107.8	96.8	116.7	103.9	96.8	116.7	103.9
08	OPENINGS	91.6	68.2	86.3	95.8	117.0	100.6	95.8	118.3	100.9	97.6	118.4	102.3	97.7	118.8	102.5	95.8	118.3	100.9
0920	Plaster & Gypsum Board	88.0	70.3	76.8	130.8	109.5	117.3	130.8	112.8	119.3	119.8	112.8	115.3	134.2	112.8	120.6	130.8	112.8	119.3
0950, 0980	Ceilings & Acoustic Treatment	105.3	70.3	85.7	95.0	109.5	103.1	95.0	112.8	104.9	96.3	112.8	105.5	105.4	112.8	109.5	95.0	112.8	104.9
0960	Flooring	116.1	79.6	107.0	94.2	121.9	101.1	94.2	121.9	101.1	102.3	125.0	108.0	94.2	111.5	98.5	94.2	121.9	101.1
0970, 0990	Wall Finishes & Painting/Coating	100.7	71.0	83.0	91.3	126.9	112.6	91.3	126.9	112.6	99.1	126.9	115.7	91.3	126.9	112.6	91.3	126.9	112.6
09	FINISHES	105.0	71.1	88.0	99.0	115.3	107.2	99.1	117.1	108.1	102.3	117.8	110.1	102.3	115.3	108.9	99.1	117.1	108.1
COVERS	DIVS. 10 - 14, 25, 28, 41, 43, 44, 46	100.0	84.6	97.0	100.0	110.9	102.1	100.0	111.3	102.2	100.0	111.7	102.3	100.0	111.2	102.2	100.0	111.3	102.2
21, 22, 23	FIRE SUPPRESSION, PLUMBING & HVAC	92.5	67.8	83.6	100.2	117.5	106.4	100.2	117.5	106.4	100.1	117.5	106.3	92.6	117.5	101.5	100.2	117.5	106.4
26, 27, 3370	ELECTRICAL, COMMUNICATIONS & UTIL.	92.3	56.3	76.7	96.6	101.3	98.6	96.6	103.3	99.5	99.9	105.1	102.1	96.5	94.2	95.5	96.6	103.3	99.5
MF2018	WEIGHTED AVERAGE	99.1	69.5	88.2	99.3	114.2	104.8	98.7	114.9	104.7	100.3	115.8	106.0	96.5	113.4	102.7	98.0	114.9	104.2

		CONNECTICUT																	
	DIVISION	NEW HAVEN 065			NEW LONDON 063			NORWALK 068			STAMFORD 069			WATERBURY 067			WILLIMANTIC 062		
		MAT.	INST.	TOTAL	MAT.	INST.	TOTAL	MAT.	INST.	TOTAL	MAT.	INST.	TOTAL	MAT.	INST.	TOTAL	MAT.	INST.	TOTAL
015433	CONTRACTOR EQUIPMENT		93.3	93.3		93.3	93.3		93.0	93.0		93.0	93.0		93.0	93.0		93.0	93.0
0241, 31 - 34	SITE & INFRASTRUCTURE, DEMOLITION	99.5	94.0	95.9	90.2	94.0	92.6	100.0	93.4	95.7	100.5	93.4	95.8	99.9	93.5	95.7	100.0	93.2	95.6
0310	Concrete Forming & Accessories	103.1	114.5	112.0	103.1	114.4	111.9	103.5	112.3	110.3	103.4	112.3	110.3	103.5	114.6	112.1	103.4	114.3	111.9
0320	Concrete Reinforcing	103.8	139.9	113.8	81.4	139.9	97.6	103.8	139.8	113.8	103.8	139.8	113.8	103.8	139.9	113.8	103.8	139.9	113.8
0330	Cast-in-Place Concrete	79.1	122.1	94.3	67.4	122.0	86.8	80.3	123.2	95.5	81.6	123.2	96.4	81.6	124.8	97.0	76.2	118.5	91.2
03	CONCRETE	106.9	120.9	112.4	82.4	120.8	97.6	96.0	120.3	105.6	96.6	120.3	105.9	96.6	121.9	106.6	94.3	119.6	104.3
04	MASONRY	112.7	128.9	122.5	111.0	128.9	121.8	112.0	127.1	121.2	113.0	127.1	121.5	113.0	128.9	122.6	112.3	128.9	122.4
05	METALS	94.6	115.8	98.8	94.3	115.7	98.5	98.4	115.8	101.8	98.4	115.8	101.8	98.4	115.9	101.8	98.1	115.6	101.6
06	WOOD, PLASTICS & COMPOSITES	110.5	112.4	111.4	110.5	112.4	111.4	110.5	109.2	109.9	110.5	109.2	109.9	110.5	112.4	111.4	110.5	112.4	111.4
07	THERMAL & MOISTURE PROTECTION	96.9	116.3	103.8	96.7	116.4	103.7	96.9	117.7	104.3	96.8	117.7	104.2	96.8	116.7	103.9	97.0	115.6	103.6
08	OPENINGS	95.8	118.8	101.0	98.3	116.5	102.4	95.8	117.0	100.6	95.8	117.0	100.6	95.8	118.8	101.0	98.3	118.8	102.9
0920	Plaster & Gypsum Board	130.8	112.8	119.3	130.8	112.8	119.3	130.8	109.5	117.3	130.8	109.5	117.3	130.8	112.8	119.3	130.8	112.8	119.3
0950, 0980	Ceilings & Acoustic Treatment	95.0	112.8	104.9	94.5	112.8	104.7	95.0	109.5	103.1	95.0	109.5	103.1	95.0	112.8	104.9	94.5	112.8	104.7
0960	Flooring	94.2	121.9	101.1	94.2	113.7	99.1	94.2	121.9	101.1	94.2	121.9	101.1	94.2	121.9	101.1	94.2	108.5	97.8
0970, 0990	Wall Finishes & Painting/Coating	91.3	122.0	109.6	91.3	118.3	107.4	91.3	126.9	112.6	91.3	126.9	112.6	91.3	126.9	112.6	91.3	126.9	112.6
09	FINISHES	99.1	116.6	107.9	98.5	114.8	106.7	99.1	115.3	107.2	99.1	115.3	107.2	99.0	117.1	108.1	99.0	114.8	106.9
COVERS	DIVS. 10 - 14, 25, 28, 41, 43, 44, 46	100.0	111.3	102.2	100.0	111.2	102.2	100.0	110.9	102.1	100.0	110.9	102.1	100.0	111.3	102.2	100.0	111.2	102.2
21, 22, 23	FIRE SUPPRESSION, PLUMBING & HVAC	100.2	117.5	106.4	92.6	117.4	101.5	100.2	117.5	106.4	100.2	117.5	106.4	100.2	117.5	106.4	100.2	117.4	106.3
26, 27, 3370	ELECTRICAL, COMMUNICATIONS & UTIL.	96.5	101.7	98.7	95.0	96.1	95.5	96.6	101.3	98.6	96.6	104.0	99.8	96.3	101.7	98.6	96.6	99.0	97.6
MF2018	WEIGHTED AVERAGE	99.4	114.5	104.9	94.4	113.4	101.4	98.9	113.9	104.4	99.0	114.3	104.6	98.9	114.7	104.7	98.8	113.6	104.3

		D.C.			DELAWARE									FLORIDA					
	DIVISION	WASHINGTON 200 - 205			DOVER 199			NEWARK 197			WILMINGTON 198			DAYTONA BEACH 321			FORT LAUDERDALE 333		
		MAT.	INST.	TOTAL	MAT.	INST.	TOTAL	MAT.	INST.	TOTAL	MAT.	INST.	TOTAL	MAT.	INST.	TOTAL	MAT.	INST.	TOTAL
015433	CONTRACTOR EQUIPMENT		104.8	104.8		113.6	113.6		113.7	113.7		113.8	113.8		96.1	96.1		90.1	90.1
0241, 31 - 34	SITE & INFRASTRUCTURE, DEMOLITION	111.7	99.1	103.5	111.9	103.6	106.5	109.7	103.0	105.3	107.6	104.7	105.7	127.6	81.5	97.5	105.8	71.5	83.4
0310	Concrete Forming & Accessories	99.1	74.2	79.8	104.2	95.1	97.2	99.4	94.8	95.8	104.2	95.4	97.4	99.0	60.8	69.3	94.3	60.1	67.7
0320	Concrete Reinforcing	100.4	89.8	97.5	98.7	114.5	103.1	97.6	114.5	102.3	98.5	114.6	103.0	90.5	58.2	81.5	89.3	60.9	81.5
0330	Cast-in-Place Concrete	129.2	79.9	111.7	119.7	104.9	114.5	99.8	102.5	100.7	116.4	105.0	112.3	90.2	66.2	81.7	92.9	62.7	82.2
03	CONCRETE	105.6	79.7	95.4	102.0	102.9	102.4	93.8	102.1	97.1	100.6	103.1	101.6	89.5	64.0	79.4	90.7	63.0	79.8
04	MASONRY	108.1	87.7	95.7	106.2	100.9	103.0	103.4	100.8	101.8	106.0	100.9	102.9	87.1	61.9	71.8	101.3	56.6	74.1
05	METALS	102.3	95.3	100.9	101.1	119.5	104.7	102.6	122.8	106.6	102.7	119.8	106.1	107.4	86.8	103.4	104.6	88.8	101.5
06	WOOD, PLASTICS & COMPOSITES	97.0	72.6	86.0	101.5	92.2	97.4	97.0	91.9	94.7	101.5	92.2	97.4	96.0	59.0	79.4	82.7	60.2	72.6
07	THERMAL & MOISTURE PROTECTION	101.8	87.4	96.6	103.2	111.7	106.2	102.9	110.0	107.5	102.9	111.7	106.0	92.2	65.9	82.8	94.4	59.1	81.8
08	OPENINGS	104.7	75.6	98.2	98.1	104.1	99.5	95.2	103.9	97.1	98.1	104.1	99.5	93.6	58.0	85.5	96.1	59.3	87.8
0920	Plaster & Gypsum Board	109.8	71.8	85.7	125.6	91.9	104.2	121.9	91.9	102.8	125.6	91.9	104.2	92.7	58.4	70.9	111.6	59.7	78.7
0950, 0980	Ceilings & Acoustic Treatment	96.8	71.8	82.8	110.0	91.9	99.8	108.1	91.9	99.0	110.0	91.9	99.8	73.1	58.4	64.9	88.2	59.7	72.2
0960	Flooring	97.6	74.4	91.8	105.5	109.5	106.5	96.6	109.5	99.8	105.8	109.5	106.8	102.8	57.3	91.4	107.1	61.4	95.6
0970, 0990	Wall Finishes & Painting/Coating	94.9	68.7	79.3	99.1	116.8	109.6	89.0	116.8	105.5	99.1	116.8	109.6	102.0	57.9	75.7	92.6	57.3	71.5
09	FINISHES	99.9	72.6	86.2	108.1	99.0	103.5	100.9	98.7	99.8	108.5	99.0	103.7	93.5	59.2	76.3	99.3	59.5	79.3
COVERS	DIVS. 10 - 14, 25, 28, 41, 43, 44, 46	100.0	95.6	99.2	100.0	94.5	98.9	100.0	93.7	98.8	100.0	107.5	101.5	100.0	82.0	96.5	100.0	82.2	96.5
21, 22, 23	FIRE SUPPRESSION, PLUMBING & HVAC	100.0	93.1	97.5	99.9	117.6	106.3	100.3	117.5	106.5	100.3	117.6	106.5	99.9	75.6	91.2	99.9	67.1	88.1
26, 27, 3370	ELECTRICAL, COMMUNICATIONS & UTIL.	99.9	98.9	99.5	101.3	106.2	103.4	100.3	106.2	102.9	100.1	106.2	102.7	97.2	59.6	80.9	95.4	69.2	84.1
MF2018	WEIGHTED AVERAGE	102.2	88.6	97.2	101.7	107.3	103.7	100.1	107.3	102.8	101.7	107.8	103.9	98.9	68.8	87.9	98.9	67.0	87.1

City Cost Indexes

DIVISION		FLORIDA																	
		FORT MYERS			GAINESVILLE			JACKSONVILLE			LAKELAND			MELBOURNE			MIAMI		
		339,341			326,344			320,322			338			329			330 - 332,340		
		MAT.	INST.	TOTAL	MAT.	INST.	TOTAL	MAT.	INST.	TOTAL	MAT.	INST.	TOTAL	MAT.	INST.	TOTAL	MAT.	INST.	TOTAL
015433	CONTRACTOR EQUIPMENT		96.1	96.1		96.1	96.1		96.1	96.1		96.1	96.1		96.1	96.1		96.3	96.3
0241, 31 - 34	SITE & INFRASTRUCTURE, DEMOLITION	117.1	81.8	94.1	134.0	81.7	99.9	127.6	81.2	97.3	119.0	81.7	94.7	135.3	81.5	100.2	108.1	83.4	92.0
0310	Concrete Forming & Accessories	89.5	61.6	67.8	93.4	62.2	69.2	98.8	63.3	71.2	85.5	63.8	68.7	94.8	63.0	70.5	103.3	62.6	71.7
0320	Concrete Reinforcing	90.3	73.5	85.7	95.9	60.8	86.2	90.5	60.6	82.2	92.6	71.8	86.8	91.5	67.4	84.8	99.7	62.6	88.9
0330	Cast-in-Place Concrete	96.9	65.4	85.7	103.6	65.5	90.1	91.1	64.9	81.8	99.1	65.9	87.3	108.8	66.3	93.7	90.0	69.0	82.5
03	CONCRETE	91.4	66.7	81.7	99.0	64.8	85.5	89.8	65.0	80.0	93.0	67.6	82.9	99.0	66.8	86.3	93.5	66.0	82.6
04	MASONRY	96.9	56.6	72.4	96.7	60.2	74.5	86.8	56.9	68.7	117.3	60.3	82.7	80.2	61.9	69.1	109.5	61.2	80.2
05	METALS	106.3	92.9	103.7	105.9	88.2	102.4	106.1	86.5	102.2	106.1	92.4	103.4	114.9	90.3	110.0	104.6	85.0	100.7
06	WOOD, PLASTICS & COMPOSITES	79.0	60.7	70.8	88.5	61.6	76.4	96.0	63.4	81.4	73.6	64.2	69.4	90.7	62.4	78.0	98.2	60.6	81.3
07	THERMAL & MOISTURE PROTECTION	94.2	61.1	82.4	92.5	62.6	81.8	92.5	62.0	81.6	94.1	62.5	82.8	92.6	64.5	82.6	95.4	63.9	84.2
08	OPENINGS	97.4	62.5	89.5	93.2	60.6	85.7	93.6	61.0	86.2	97.4	64.0	89.8	93.0	62.0	86.0	98.3	59.5	89.5
0920	Plaster & Gypsum Board	105.8	60.1	76.8	89.0	61.0	71.3	92.7	62.9	73.8	102.9	63.8	78.1	89.0	61.9	71.8	102.2	59.7	75.2
0950, 0980	Ceilings & Acoustic Treatment	82.6	60.1	70.0	70.1	61.0	65.0	73.1	62.9	67.4	82.6	63.8	72.1	72.7	61.9	66.6	88.6	59.7	72.4
0960	Flooring	104.9	69.2	96.0	101.1	59.6	90.7	102.8	60.2	92.1	103.6	63.9	93.6	101.3	62.0	91.5	105.7	60.2	94.3
0970, 0990	Wall Finishes & Painting/Coating	97.2	61.7	76.0	102.0	61.1	77.6	102.0	61.1	77.6	97.2	61.7	76.0	102.0	79.8	88.8	99.1	57.3	74.2
09	FINISHES	98.7	62.6	80.6	92.8	61.2	76.9	93.6	62.4	77.9	98.0	63.4	80.6	93.2	64.5	78.8	99.4	60.9	80.1
COVERS	DIVS. 10 - 14, 25, 28, 41, 43, 44, 46	100.0	80.5	96.2	100.0	80.2	96.2	100.0	80.4	96.2	100.0	81.8	96.5	100.0	82.4	96.6	100.0	84.9	97.1
21, 22, 23	FIRE SUPPRESSION, PLUMBING & HVAC	95.8	57.7	82.1	95.6	64.2	84.3	99.9	63.8	87.0	95.8	57.2	81.9	99.9	75.8	91.3	99.9	64.2	87.1
26, 27, 3370	ELECTRICAL, COMMUNICATIONS & UTIL.	96.3	60.1	80.6	97.3	58.2	80.4	97.0	64.4	82.9	95.6	52.1	76.7	98.0	67.9	85.0	98.1	74.9	88.0
MF2018	WEIGHTED AVERAGE	98.6	66.0	86.6	99.2	66.5	87.2	98.7	67.0	87.0	99.4	65.4	86.9	101.6	71.6	90.6	100.2	69.1	88.8

DIVISION		FLORIDA																	
		ORLANDO			PANAMA CITY			PENSACOLA			SARASOTA			ST. PETERSBURG			TALLAHASSEE		
		327 - 328,347			324			325			342			337			323		
		MAT.	INST.	TOTAL	MAT.	INST.	TOTAL	MAT.	INST.	TOTAL	MAT.	INST.	TOTAL	MAT.	INST.	TOTAL	MAT.	INST.	TOTAL
015433	CONTRACTOR EQUIPMENT		103.7	103.7		96.1	96.1		96.1	96.1		96.1	96.1		96.1	96.1		103.7	103.7
0241, 31 - 34	SITE & INFRASTRUCTURE, DEMOLITION	126.6	94.4	105.6	141.2	81.6	102.4	140.8	81.4	102.0	128.0	81.7	97.8	122.4	81.5	95.7	123.0	94.3	104.3
0310	Concrete Forming & Accessories	104.5	64.9	73.8	98.0	64.9	72.2	95.3	68.9	74.8	98.9	63.6	71.5	93.8	59.5	67.4	104.5	64.0	73.0
0320	Concrete Reinforcing	100.4	63.2	90.1	94.5	67.7	87.1	96.8	65.5	88.2	91.5	68.7	85.2	92.6	70.8	86.5	100.6	60.8	89.6
0330	Cast-in-Place Concrete	111.7	68.6	96.4	95.8	66.3	85.3	118.4	64.7	99.3	106.9	65.8	92.3	100.2	63.9	87.3	93.6	68.9	84.8
03	CONCRETE	102.7	67.3	88.8	97.0	67.5	85.4	106.0	68.3	91.2	95.8	66.9	84.4	94.5	64.9	82.8	96.3	66.6	84.6
04	MASONRY	94.0	62.0	74.5	90.3	60.3	72.1	114.0	59.2	80.7	86.6	60.3	70.6	165.0	57.3	99.6	82.5	60.1	68.9
05	METALS	105.3	85.6	101.4	106.6	90.3	103.4	107.7	89.0	104.0	105.1	90.6	102.3	107.0	91.0	103.8	104.4	84.5	100.5
06	WOOD, PLASTICS & COMPOSITES	99.4	64.6	83.8	94.5	64.6	81.1	93.0	71.2	83.3	95.1	64.2	81.3	84.6	59.0	73.1	99.2	63.7	83.3
07	THERMAL & MOISTURE PROTECTION	95.6	68.0	85.8	92.7	62.8	82.0	92.6	62.1	81.8	101.8	62.5	87.8	94.3	58.9	81.7	95.3	64.3	84.2
08	OPENINGS	98.3	62.2	90.2	91.9	63.3	85.5	91.9	66.4	86.1	98.4	62.9	90.4	96.4	60.9	88.4	98.4	61.2	90.0
0920	Plaster & Gypsum Board	103.9	63.8	78.5	91.6	64.2	74.2	105.4	71.0	83.6	97.1	63.8	76.0	108.9	58.4	76.9	104.8	62.9	78.2
0950, 0980	Ceilings & Acoustic Treatment	84.1	63.8	72.7	72.7	64.2	67.9	72.7	71.0	71.7	86.8	63.8	73.9	83.6	58.4	69.5	90.0	62.9	74.8
0960	Flooring	104.5	59.6	93.3	102.6	73.8	95.4	99.7	60.8	89.9	106.9	49.1	92.4	106.3	53.9	93.2	106.1	61.6	90.8
0970, 0990	Wall Finishes & Painting/Coating	99.1	83.4	89.7	102.0	61.1	77.6	102.0	61.1	77.6	101.1	61.7	77.6	96.1	61.1	75.7	101.2	61.1	77.3
09	FINISHES	99.9	65.8	82.8	94.7	65.7	80.1	95.3	66.9	81.0	100.3	60.8	80.5	100.0	58.5	79.2	100.0	63.1	81.4
COVERS	DIVS. 10 - 14, 25, 28, 41, 43, 44, 46	100.0	83.4	96.8	100.0	81.6	96.4	100.0	81.7	96.5	100.0	80.5	96.2	100.0	80.2	96.2	100.0	81.4	96.4
21, 22, 23	FIRE SUPPRESSION, PLUMBING & HVAC	100.1	55.7	84.2	99.9	64.4	87.2	99.9	61.3	86.0	99.6	53.2	83.0	99.9	55.5	84.0	100.0	64.3	87.2
26, 27, 3370	ELECTRICAL, COMMUNICATIONS & UTIL.	100.1	62.3	83.7	96.4	56.9	79.3	98.6	49.8	77.5	97.8	52.1	78.0	95.6	58.9	79.7	100.7	55.8	81.2
MF2018	WEIGHTED AVERAGE	101.7	67.5	89.1	100.0	67.7	88.1	102.5	66.3	89.1	100.4	63.9	87.0	102.8	64.3	88.6	100.2	67.5	88.2

DIVISION		FLORIDA						GEORGIA											
		TAMPA			WEST PALM BEACH			ALBANY			ATHENS			ATLANTA			AUGUSTA		
		335 - 336,346			334,349			317,398			306			300 - 303,399			308 - 309		
		MAT.	INST.	TOTAL	MAT.	INST.	TOTAL	MAT.	INST.	TOTAL	MAT.	INST.	TOTAL	MAT.	INST.	TOTAL	MAT.	INST.	TOTAL
015433	CONTRACTOR EQUIPMENT		96.1	96.1		90.1	90.1		90.9	90.9		89.4	89.4		97.5	97.5		89.4	89.4
0241, 31 - 34	SITE & INFRASTRUCTURE, DEMOLITION	122.8	81.9	96.1	100.7	71.5	81.6	116.4	74.1	88.8	136.8	86.7	104.1	134.8	97.8	110.7	129.0	87.4	101.9
0310	Concrete Forming & Accessories	96.9	64.9	72.1	98.6	59.6	68.3	94.1	68.9	74.4	96.9	39.8	52.5	103.2	75.2	81.4	98.1	71.0	77.0
0320	Concrete Reinforcing	89.3	71.8	84.5	91.8	51.7	80.7	92.3	71.6	86.5	91.9	56.7	82.2	100.3	70.4	92.0	92.1	68.4	85.6
0330	Cast-in-Place Concrete	97.9	67.5	87.1	88.3	62.5	79.2	90.9	67.3	82.5	125.9	66.2	104.7	129.9	71.5	109.2	118.9	69.3	101.3
03	CONCRETE	93.0	68.6	83.4	88.7	61.1	77.8	86.7	70.4	80.3	98.3	53.4	80.6	102.5	73.6	91.1	93.6	70.7	84.5
04	MASONRY	102.2	63.1	78.4	100.8	51.6	70.9	83.5	67.6	73.8	73.8	64.1	67.9	84.5	68.0	74.5	85.7	69.9	76.1
05	METALS	106.4	92.5	103.7	103.0	84.9	99.4	107.4	96.8	105.3	91.9	75.3	88.7	97.8	82.1	94.7	91.7	82.1	89.8
06	WOOD, PLASTICS & COMPOSITES	89.6	64.2	78.2	88.4	60.2	75.8	86.2	69.6	78.8	91.2	32.7	65.0	101.4	78.3	91.0	93.0	72.9	84.0
07	THERMAL & MOISTURE PROTECTION	94.6	63.8	83.6	94.2	58.6	81.5	104.8	66.9	91.3	91.6	61.6	80.9	92.3	72.1	85.1	91.5	70.8	84.1
08	OPENINGS	97.4	64.0	89.8	95.7	57.3	87.1	87.8	71.5	84.1	88.5	46.9	79.1	100.5	75.6	94.9	88.5	72.1	84.8
0920	Plaster & Gypsum Board	112.8	63.8	81.7	116.4	59.7	80.4	95.9	69.4	79.1	93.4	31.2	54.0	99.2	77.9	85.7	94.8	72.7	80.8
0950, 0980	Ceilings & Acoustic Treatment	88.2	63.8	74.5	82.6	59.7	69.8	73.6	69.4	71.3	92.5	31.2	58.1	85.0	77.9	81.0	93.6	72.7	81.8
0960	Flooring	107.1	63.9	96.3	108.3	49.1	93.5	105.8	66.8	96.0	92.2	66.8	85.9	97.6	70.2	90.7	92.3	72.2	87.3
0970, 0990	Wall Finishes & Painting/Coating	97.2	61.7	76.0	92.6	57.0	71.4	96.9	96.8	96.9	94.5	83.5	87.9	101.2	95.6	97.9	94.5	81.7	86.9
09	FINISHES	102.0	64.1	83.0	98.6	57.0	77.7	94.2	71.0	82.5	97.1	47.3	72.1	97.7	76.6	87.1	96.6	72.4	84.4
COVERS	DIVS. 10 - 14, 25, 28, 41, 43, 44, 46	100.0	81.5	96.4	100.0	82.1	96.5	100.0	84.3	97.0	100.0	79.7	96.1	100.0	97.9	99.6	100.0	84.8	97.1
21, 22, 23	FIRE SUPPRESSION, PLUMBING & HVAC	99.9	58.7	85.1	95.8	55.1	81.2	99.9	71.0	89.6	92.6	59.6	80.8	100.1	71.7	89.9	100.1	65.8	87.8
26, 27, 3370	ELECTRICAL, COMMUNICATIONS & UTIL.	94.9	64.4	81.7	96.2	60.0	80.5	97.0	57.4	79.8	99.8	56.9	81.2	100.1	69.6	86.9	100.1	64.6	84.7
MF2018	WEIGHTED AVERAGE	100.3	68.1	88.4	97.3	61.6	84.2	98.0	71.6	88.3	94.8	60.7	82.2	99.8	75.6	90.9	96.1	71.8	87.2

667

City Cost Indexes

GEORGIA

DIVISION		COLUMBUS 318-319			DALTON 307			GAINESVILLE 305			MACON 310-312			SAVANNAH 313-314			STATESBORO 304		
		MAT.	INST.	TOTAL	MAT.	INST.	TOTAL	MAT.	INST.	TOTAL	MAT.	INST.	TOTAL	MAT.	INST.	TOTAL	MAT.	INST.	TOTAL
015433	CONTRACTOR EQUIPMENT		90.9	90.9		102.8	102.8		89.4	89.4		99.4	99.4		98.2	98.2		92.0	92.0
0241, 31 - 34	SITE & INFRASTRUCTURE, DEMOLITION	116.3	74.5	89.0	136.7	91.2	107.1	135.2	86.6	103.5	118.1	87.2	98.0	118.4	86.6	97.7	138.6	74.1	96.6
0310	Concrete Forming & Accessories	94.0	70.0	75.4	87.9	58.6	65.1	101.4	37.8	52.0	93.9	70.0	75.3	101.7	70.4	77.4	82.2	68.6	71.7
0320	Concrete Reinforcing	92.9	71.8	87.1	91.6	54.4	81.3	91.8	56.7	82.1	94.1	71.8	87.9	100.1	68.3	91.3	91.4	63.6	83.7
0330	Cast-in-Place Concrete	90.6	70.0	83.3	122.3	64.8	101.9	132.3	65.8	108.7	89.4	68.2	81.9	91.8	70.6	84.3	125.6	65.5	104.3
03	CONCRETE	86.8	72.0	80.9	96.6	62.0	82.9	100.9	52.4	81.8	86.5	71.4	80.6	88.5	71.5	81.8	97.1	68.4	85.8
04	MASONRY	82.7	70.0	75.0	72.4	62.6	66.5	82.8	63.2	70.9	95.1	69.4	79.5	77.9	68.1	72.0	75.7	64.0	68.6
05	METALS	107.1	98.2	105.3	92.7	88.8	92.0	91.2	75.4	88.1	101.7	98.2	101.0	104.0	92.6	101.7	96.0	93.4	95.5
06	WOOD, PLASTICS & COMPOSITES	86.2	71.1	79.4	74.7	59.2	67.7	96.0	30.3	66.6	90.5	71.8	82.1	98.8	71.9	86.7	66.8	71.6	69.0
07	THERMAL & MOISTURE PROTECTION	104.7	69.1	92.0	93.4	63.1	82.6	91.6	60.9	80.7	103.3	69.7	91.4	101.9	70.3	90.6	92.0	63.5	81.9
08	OPENINGS	87.8	72.2	84.3	90.0	61.0	83.4	88.4	45.6	78.8	87.8	72.3	84.3	97.8	71.6	91.9	90.8	70.2	86.2
0920	Plaster & Gypsum Board	95.9	70.9	80.0	82.9	58.6	67.5	95.8	28.8	53.3	97.0	71.5	80.9	99.6	71.4	81.7	82.8	71.4	75.6
0950, 0980	Ceilings & Acoustic Treatment	73.6	70.9	72.1	101.5	58.6	77.5	92.5	28.8	56.8	70.5	71.5	71.1	90.4	71.4	79.7	99.7	71.4	83.8
0960	Flooring	105.8	72.2	97.4	92.4	66.8	86.0	93.6	66.8	86.8	83.3	66.8	79.1	99.6	69.4	92.1	112.2	66.8	100.8
0970, 0990	Wall Finishes & Painting/Coating	96.9	85.0	89.8	84.1	62.2	71.1	94.5	83.5	87.9	99.2	96.8	97.8	99.1	82.0	88.9	92.7	62.2	74.5
09	FINISHES	94.1	71.7	82.8	104.3	60.2	82.2	97.5	45.7	71.5	83.2	71.9	77.5	97.9	71.3	84.6	108.8	67.8	88.2
COVERS	DIVS. 10 - 14, 25, 28, 41, 43, 44, 46	100.0	84.5	97.0	100.0	76.2	95.4	100.0	79.3	96.0	100.0	84.2	96.9	100.0	85.4	97.2	100.0	83.8	96.9
21, 22, 23	FIRE SUPPRESSION, PLUMBING & HVAC	100.0	66.3	87.9	92.6	54.6	79.0	92.6	59.1	80.6	100.0	68.3	88.6	100.1	66.8	88.1	94.5	62.6	83.1
26, 27, 3370	ELECTRICAL, COMMUNICATIONS & UTIL.	96.8	68.1	84.3	112.5	55.4	87.8	99.8	65.4	84.9	94.3	58.1	78.6	99.1	59.8	82.1	101.2	58.6	82.8
MF2018	WEIGHTED AVERAGE	97.9	72.9	88.7	96.6	64.5	84.8	95.3	61.2	82.8	96.2	72.8	87.6	98.7	72.0	88.9	97.1	66.4	86.5

GEORGIA / HAWAII / IDAHO

DIVISION		VALDOSTA 316			WAYCROSS 315			HILO 967			HONOLULU 968			STATES & POSS., GUAM 969			BOISE 836-837		
		MAT.	INST.	TOTAL	MAT.	INST.	TOTAL	MAT.	INST.	TOTAL	MAT.	INST.	TOTAL	MAT.	INST.	TOTAL	MAT.	INST.	TOTAL
015433	CONTRACTOR EQUIPMENT		90.9	90.9		90.9	90.9		95.8	95.8		101.5	101.5		151.9	151.9		93.2	93.2
0241, 31 - 34	SITE & INFRASTRUCTURE, DEMOLITION	126.9	74.1	92.4	121.4	73.6	90.2	158.4	99.2	119.8	165.4	109.9	129.2	209.0	96.2	135.4	89.8	88.9	89.2
0310	Concrete Forming & Accessories	83.1	70.0	72.9	85.2	68.3	72.1	89.8	119.1	112.6	100.4	119.2	115.0	92.0	59.7	66.9	97.7	81.4	85.1
0320	Concrete Reinforcing	94.6	60.7	85.2	94.6	53.4	83.2	91.7	120.4	99.6	104.7	120.4	109.0	154.3	41.3	123.0	96.4	76.3	90.8
0330	Cast-in-Place Concrete	89.0	67.3	81.3	100.6	65.4	88.1	221.5	120.3	185.6	172.8	121.6	154.6	191.9	99.1	158.9	81.6	99.0	87.8
03	CONCRETE	89.3	69.1	81.3	92.7	66.2	82.3	152.3	119.0	139.1	144.2	119.3	134.4	156.5	71.2	122.8	93.0	86.9	90.6
04	MASONRY	87.6	70.3	77.1	88.5	64.0	73.6	140.7	119.3	127.7	135.1	119.5	125.6	208.8	45.9	109.8	127.7	84.6	101.5
05	METALS	105.7	92.5	103.1	104.8	84.3	100.8	111.0	106.2	110.0	125.4	104.0	121.2	141.4	79.4	129.2	106.0	82.2	101.3
06	WOOD, PLASTICS & COMPOSITES	71.7	71.6	71.6	73.8	71.6	72.8	104.6	119.4	111.2	123.8	119.4	121.8	116.8	59.9	91.3	95.6	79.6	88.4
07	THERMAL & MOISTURE PROTECTION	104.8	69.0	92.1	104.7	63.8	90.1	96.6	114.4	102.9	107.8	116.2	110.8	111.2	65.9	95.1	92.2	85.7	89.9
08	OPENINGS	84.6	69.4	81.2	84.8	65.4	80.5	101.4	118.3	105.2	112.3	118.3	113.7	106.0	49.8	93.4	92.0	74.9	88.1
0920	Plaster & Gypsum Board	86.8	71.4	77.0	86.8	71.4	77.0	110.9	120.0	116.7	142.8	120.0	128.3	239.6	49.7	119.1	99.1	79.2	86.5
0950, 0980	Ceilings & Acoustic Treatment	72.3	71.4	71.8	71.2	71.4	71.3	109.5	120.0	115.3	121.4	120.0	120.6	254.0	49.7	139.5	111.3	79.2	93.3
0960	Flooring	101.5	72.9	94.3	102.4	66.8	93.5	79.0	135.4	93.1	100.8	135.4	109.5	96.5	44.4	83.4	94.2	84.7	91.8
0970, 0990	Wall Finishes & Painting/Coating	96.9	86.9	90.9	96.9	62.2	76.2	91.4	128.8	113.7	104.7	128.8	119.1	96.3	36.9	60.9	92.1	61.4	73.8
09	FINISHES	92.2	72.3	82.2	91.8	67.8	79.7	99.8	123.6	111.7	115.1	123.6	119.4	187.1	54.8	120.7	99.0	79.9	89.4
COVERS	DIVS. 10 - 14, 25, 28, 41, 43, 44, 46	100.0	84.5	97.0	100.0	77.9	95.7	100.0	110.8	102.1	100.0	110.8	102.1	100.0	87.6	97.6	100.0	90.2	98.1
21, 22, 23	FIRE SUPPRESSION, PLUMBING & HVAC	100.0	70.7	89.5	95.5	57.1	81.7	99.7	106.8	102.2	99.7	106.8	102.3	101.7	49.6	83.0	100.2	74.1	90.8
26, 27, 3370	ELECTRICAL, COMMUNICATIONS & UTIL.	95.9	52.5	77.1	97.8	58.6	80.8	101.2	114.9	107.1	102.0	114.9	107.6	142.1	45.5	100.2	100.0	73.1	88.3
MF2018	WEIGHTED AVERAGE	97.7	70.7	87.8	97.1	65.8	85.6	111.8	113.3	112.3	116.5	114.1	115.6	134.9	60.4	107.5	100.3	80.3	93.0

IDAHO / ILLINOIS

DIVISION		COEUR D'ALENE 838			IDAHO FALLS 834			LEWISTON 835			POCATELLO 832			TWIN FALLS 833			BLOOMINGTON 617		
		MAT.	INST.	TOTAL	MAT.	INST.	TOTAL	MAT.	INST.	TOTAL	MAT.	INST.	TOTAL	MAT.	INST.	TOTAL	MAT.	INST.	TOTAL
015433	CONTRACTOR EQUIPMENT		88.7	88.7		93.2	93.2		88.7	88.7		93.2	93.2		93.2	93.2		98.1	98.1
0241, 31 - 34	SITE & INFRASTRUCTURE, DEMOLITION	90.4	85.9	87.5	90.5	89.0	89.5	99.2	84.4	89.6	91.1	88.9	89.7	97.3	88.4	91.5	86.6	91.5	89.8
0310	Concrete Forming & Accessories	99.5	82.0	85.9	90.9	77.2	80.2	105.2	81.7	87.0	97.9	80.8	84.6	99.1	76.7	81.7	85.3	115.5	108.8
0320	Concrete Reinforcing	101.3	97.0	100.1	97.6	74.1	91.1	101.3	96.9	100.1	96.6	76.3	91.0	97.8	73.0	91.0	98.5	102.7	99.6
0330	Cast-in-Place Concrete	88.2	81.3	85.8	77.7	94.6	83.7	91.7	82.8	88.6	83.9	98.8	89.2	86.1	94.0	88.9	88.3	110.9	96.3
03	CONCRETE	98.1	84.5	92.7	86.8	83.1	85.3	101.1	84.9	94.7	92.4	86.5	90.1	98.3	82.5	92.1	89.9	112.5	98.8
04	MASONRY	130.2	84.8	102.6	123.1	86.1	100.6	130.7	83.2	101.9	125.6	86.3	101.7	128.7	79.1	98.5	114.2	109.7	111.5
05	METALS	99.0	89.5	97.1	112.9	81.3	106.7	98.4	89.1	96.6	113.4	81.7	107.1	113.0	80.5	106.6	94.4	122.9	100.0
06	WOOD, PLASTICS & COMPOSITES	93.3	81.0	87.8	87.1	75.2	81.8	100.9	81.0	92.0	95.6	79.6	88.4	96.8	75.2	87.1	77.0	115.3	94.2
07	THERMAL & MOISTURE PROTECTION	136.7	80.9	116.8	91.1	78.3	86.5	137.1	79.8	116.7	91.6	75.5	85.9	92.2	81.3	88.4	101.3	107.3	103.5
08	OPENINGS	107.4	75.9	100.3	94.7	70.3	89.2	101.4	79.5	96.4	92.6	67.9	87.0	95.3	70.9	89.8	88.9	119.5	95.8
0920	Plaster & Gypsum Board	155.5	80.8	108.1	88.3	74.6	79.7	157.7	80.8	108.9	91.2	79.2	83.6	94.1	74.6	81.7	78.0	116.1	102.2
0950, 0980	Ceilings & Acoustic Treatment	131.0	80.8	102.9	107.2	74.6	88.9	131.0	80.8	102.9	115.3	79.2	95.1	110.8	74.6	90.5	89.8	116.1	104.6
0960	Flooring	136.5	90.1	124.8	95.2	76.2	90.4	138.8	74.7	122.7	97.6	74.7	91.9	98.5	79.7	93.8	90.7	124.5	99.2
0970, 0990	Wall Finishes & Painting/Coating	109.4	68.2	84.8	92.2	41.9	62.2	109.4	59.6	79.7	92.0	57.9	71.7	92.2	57.9	71.7	87.9	119.7	106.9
09	FINISHES	156.4	82.0	119.0	96.4	73.0	84.7	157.5	77.8	117.5	100.1	77.5	88.8	100.1	75.3	87.6	88.3	118.1	103.3
COVERS	DIVS. 10 - 14, 25, 28, 41, 43, 44, 46	100.0	97.6	99.5	100.0	97.5	99.5	100.0	90.1	98.1	100.0	88.8	97.8	100.0	105.0	101.0			
21, 22, 23	FIRE SUPPRESSION, PLUMBING & HVAC	96.8	86.6	93.1	103.6	77.2	94.1	101.3	75.1	94.8	100.0	71.9	89.9	100.0	69.0	88.9	92.4	103.0	96.2
26, 27, 3370	ELECTRICAL, COMMUNICATIONS & UTIL.	84.2	78.3	81.7	83.9	67.9	77.0	83.3	81.2	82.4	95.2	67.9	83.4	84.6	70.1	78.3	92.5	95.7	93.9
MF2018	WEIGHTED AVERAGE	103.8	84.3	96.6	99.8	78.5	92.0	104.8	83.3	96.9	101.3	78.3	92.9	101.4	76.5	92.2	93.4	107.8	98.7

City Cost Indexes

		ILLINOIS																	
	DIVISION	CARBONDALE 629			CENTRALIA 628			CHAMPAIGN 618 - 619			CHICAGO 606 - 608			DECATUR 625			EAST ST. LOUIS 620 - 622		
		MAT.	INST.	TOTAL	MAT.	INST.	TOTAL	MAT.	INST.	TOTAL	MAT.	INST.	TOTAL	MAT.	INST.	TOTAL	MAT.	INST.	TOTAL
015433	CONTRACTOR EQUIPMENT		105.5	105.5		105.5	105.5		98.9	98.9		98.7	98.7		98.9	98.9		105.5	105.5
0241, 31 - 34	SITE & INFRASTRUCTURE, DEMOLITION	93.1	92.3	92.5	93.4	93.0	93.1	93.1	93.7	93.5	92.1	103.0	99.2	92.9	92.4	92.6	98.3	93.1	94.9
0310	Concrete Forming & Accessories	97.5	105.8	104.0	99.8	109.3	107.2	92.7	126.9	119.3	100.7	158.5	145.6	101.3	114.9	111.8	94.4	115.5	107.7
0320	Concrete Reinforcing	101.6	93.2	99.3	101.6	93.8	99.5	98.5	98.9	98.6	98.0	150.7	112.6	99.4	98.5	99.1	101.6	104.5	102.4
0330	Cast-in-Place Concrete	86.0	100.7	91.2	86.4	108.7	94.3	102.3	119.6	108.5	107.9	153.7	124.2	93.9	111.1	100.0	87.9	115.4	97.7
03	CONCRETE	85.3	103.3	92.4	85.8	107.8	94.5	99.6	119.9	107.6	101.3	154.8	122.4	92.9	111.4	100.2	86.3	113.1	96.9
04	MASONRY	98.7	110.2	105.7	98.8	116.9	109.8	138.3	133.9	135.6	107.2	163.8	141.6	93.4	119.2	109.1	99.0	120.3	112.0
05	METALS	98.9	123.5	103.7	98.9	126.1	104.3	94.4	120.6	99.6	98.1	145.2	107.4	104.5	119.0	107.4	100.0	131.8	106.3
06	WOOD, PLASTICS & COMPOSITES	97.8	103.5	100.4	101.6	108.3	104.6	86.0	126.3	104.1	98.4	157.7	125.0	102.1	114.1	107.5	93.8	108.3	100.3
07	THERMAL & MOISTURE PROTECTION	93.7	95.7	94.4	93.8	106.8	98.4	102.0	118.1	107.7	105.6	148.6	120.9	98.4	110.2	102.6	93.7	107.8	98.7
08	OPENINGS	87.9	107.9	92.4	87.9	110.5	93.0	89.4	121.9	96.8	99.2	148.1	114.7	98.8	115.2	102.5	88.0	117.3	94.6
0920	Plaster & Gypsum Board	84.2	104.0	96.8	85.6	109.0	100.4	80.0	127.5	110.1	83.7	159.5	131.8	89.2	114.9	105.5	83.0	109.0	99.5
0950, 0980	Ceilings & Acoustic Treatment	94.5	104.0	99.8	94.5	109.0	102.6	89.8	127.5	110.9	92.2	159.5	129.9	105.9	114.9	110.9	94.5	109.0	102.6
0960	Flooring	116.5	110.3	114.9	117.3	102.5	113.6	93.3	125.6	101.4	98.8	160.9	114.4	103.2	120.3	107.5	115.6	102.5	112.4
0970, 0990	Wall Finishes & Painting/Coating	101.3	102.5	102.0	101.3	108.4	105.5	87.9	125.6	110.4	99.1	161.8	136.5	94.2	104.7	100.4	101.3	110.8	107.0
09	FINISHES	96.2	106.3	101.3	96.7	108.1	102.4	89.9	127.6	108.8	94.1	160.1	127.2	97.4	115.4	106.5	95.9	109.6	102.8
COVERS	DIVS. 10 - 14, 25, 28, 41, 43, 44, 46	100.0	104.7	100.9	100.0	104.9	100.9	100.0	109.2	101.8	100.0	126.9	105.2	100.0	105.7	101.1	100.0	109.3	101.8
21, 22, 23	FIRE SUPPRESSION, PLUMBING & HVAC	92.4	99.8	95.1	92.4	88.2	90.9	92.4	106.2	97.3	99.9	134.9	112.4	100.0	95.6	98.4	99.9	95.3	98.3
26, 27, 3370	ELECTRICAL, COMMUNICATIONS & UTIL.	92.3	107.1	98.7	93.0	94.6	93.7	94.1	95.7	94.8	99.2	133.2	113.9	94.4	88.9	92.0	92.8	103.2	97.3
MF2018	WEIGHTED AVERAGE	93.8	105.2	98.0	94.0	103.3	97.4	96.0	113.7	102.6	99.4	143.7	115.7	98.8	105.4	101.2	95.9	108.2	100.5

		ILLINOIS																	
	DIVISION	EFFINGHAM 624			GALESBURG 614			JOLIET 604			KANKAKEE 609			LA SALLE 613			NORTH SUBURBAN 600 - 603		
		MAT.	INST.	TOTAL	MAT.	INST.	TOTAL	MAT.	INST.	TOTAL	MAT.	INST.	TOTAL	MAT.	INST.	TOTAL	MAT.	INST.	TOTAL
015433	CONTRACTOR EQUIPMENT		98.9	98.9		98.1	98.1		90.0	90.0		90.0	90.0		98.1	98.1		90.0	90.0
0241, 31 - 34	SITE & INFRASTRUCTURE, DEMOLITION	92.3	92.2	92.2	88.3	91.6	90.5	88.5	93.6	91.9	81.2	92.1	88.3	88.0	93.0	91.3	88.2	93.0	91.3
0310	Concrete Forming & Accessories	106.5	105.7	105.8	92.6	116.2	110.9	99.0	161.0	147.2	91.9	144.4	132.7	108.6	124.8	121.2	98.2	157.9	144.5
0320	Concrete Reinforcing	102.3	84.2	97.3	98.1	103.1	99.5	108.1	139.2	116.7	108.5	131.4	114.8	98.2	129.7	107.0	108.1	150.6	119.9
0330	Cast-in-Place Concrete	93.6	107.1	98.4	90.9	108.0	97.0	98.1	150.9	116.8	91.4	132.3	105.9	90.8	125.8	103.2	98.1	143.1	114.1
03	CONCRETE	94.1	103.4	97.7	92.4	111.8	100.0	97.7	153.0	119.5	93.0	137.4	110.5	93.7	126.8	106.7	97.7	150.7	118.6
04	MASONRY	102.6	107.8	105.8	114.4	121.9	118.9	106.2	163.1	140.8	102.8	145.4	128.7	114.4	132.7	125.5	103.3	163.5	139.9
05	METALS	101.1	110.6	103.0	94.4	122.8	100.0	90.3	139.3	100.0	90.3	130.8	98.3	94.5	141.2	103.7	91.3	142.2	101.4
06	WOOD, PLASTICS & COMPOSITES	105.5	103.3	104.5	85.8	115.3	99.0	90.6	161.7	122.5	82.0	143.8	109.7	105.8	121.7	112.9	89.6	157.3	120.0
07	THERMAL & MOISTURE PROTECTION	98.0	100.1	98.8	101.5	106.1	103.1	112.1	146.4	124.3	111.4	137.4	120.6	101.9	120.6	108.6	112.6	147.4	125.0
08	OPENINGS	94.5	104.9	96.8	88.9	115.2	94.8	93.4	166.6	109.9	86.9	154.6	102.2	88.9	131.2	98.5	93.5	167.9	110.3
0920	Plaster & Gypsum Board	87.1	103.7	97.7	80.0	116.2	102.9	78.3	164.0	132.7	77.9	145.1	120.8	87.7	122.7	109.9	82.7	159.5	131.4
0950, 0980	Ceilings & Acoustic Treatment	94.5	103.7	99.7	89.8	116.2	104.6	94.8	164.0	133.6	94.8	145.1	123.2	89.8	122.7	108.2	94.8	159.5	131.1
0960	Flooring	104.2	111.6	106.1	93.1	124.5	101.0	97.5	160.9	113.4	95.0	144.4	107.3	98.3	128.8	105.9	98.0	160.9	113.7
0970, 0990	Wall Finishes & Painting/Coating	94.2	106.3	101.4	87.9	95.4	92.3	88.1	161.8	132.0	88.1	129.4	112.7	87.9	129.4	112.6	90.2	161.8	132.9
09	FINISHES	94.4	107.1	100.8	89.4	116.3	102.9	91.8	162.2	127.2	90.7	143.5	117.2	92.0	125.5	108.8	92.6	159.8	126.4
COVERS	DIVS. 10 - 14, 25, 28, 41, 43, 44, 46	100.0	104.0	100.8	100.0	106.2	101.2	100.0	126.2	105.1	100.0	113.0	102.5	100.0	108.2	101.6	100.0	126.0	105.0
21, 22, 23	FIRE SUPPRESSION, PLUMBING & HVAC	92.5	95.9	93.7	92.4	100.6	95.3	99.9	134.3	112.2	92.4	126.9	104.8	92.4	127.6	105.0	99.8	135.1	112.5
26, 27, 3370	ELECTRICAL, COMMUNICATIONS & UTIL.	93.4	107.0	99.3	93.0	92.7	92.9	97.7	134.5	113.6	94.8	133.9	111.8	91.6	133.9	109.9	98.0	133.1	113.2
MF2018	WEIGHTED AVERAGE	96.2	103.0	98.7	93.9	107.6	99.0	96.4	142.3	113.3	92.9	132.1	107.3	94.3	126.4	106.1	96.6	142.0	113.3

		ILLINOIS																	
	DIVISION	PEORIA 615 - 616			QUINCY 623			ROCK ISLAND 612			ROCKFORD 610 - 611			SOUTH SUBURBAN 605			SPRINGFIELD 626 - 627		
		MAT.	INST.	TOTAL	MAT.	INST.	TOTAL	MAT.	INST.	TOTAL	MAT.	INST.	TOTAL	MAT.	INST.	TOTAL	MAT.	INST.	TOTAL
015433	CONTRACTOR EQUIPMENT		98.1	98.1		98.9	98.9		98.1	98.1		98.1	98.1		90.0	90.0		104.6	104.6
0241, 31 - 34	SITE & INFRASTRUCTURE, DEMOLITION	92.4	91.7	92.0	91.2	93.1	92.5	87.0	90.5	89.3	92.0	93.4	92.9	88.2	92.8	91.2	96.3	102.0	100.0
0310	Concrete Forming & Accessories	96.7	117.4	112.8	103.6	111.5	109.7	94.4	102.7	100.9	101.0	133.3	126.1	98.2	157.9	144.6	101.8	115.4	112.4
0320	Concrete Reinforcing	95.7	103.2	97.8	102.1	78.1	95.5	98.1	96.0	97.6	90.1	135.5	102.7	108.1	150.6	119.8	99.1	98.5	98.9
0330	Cast-in-Place Concrete	88.2	115.3	97.8	93.7	116.0	101.6	88.9	100.8	93.1	90.2	131.5	104.9	98.1	150.4	116.7	89.3	109.9	96.6
03	CONCRETE	90.1	114.9	99.9	93.7	108.1	99.4	90.9	101.9	95.2	89.9	133.6	107.1	97.7	153.2	119.6	91.6	111.0	99.3
04	MASONRY	113.3	123.1	119.2	136.3	121.9	127.5	114.2	105.1	108.7	88.7	145.5	123.2	103.3	163.5	139.8	109.1	119.9	115.7
05	METALS	97.5	123.6	102.7	101.1	111.1	103.1	94.5	116.3	98.8	97.5	144.0	106.7	91.3	142.1	101.3	102.0	116.5	104.9
06	WOOD, PLASTICS & COMPOSITES	96.5	115.3	104.9	101.9	108.9	105.1	88.0	101.8	94.2	96.4	130.5	111.7	89.6	157.3	120.0	99.9	114.4	106.4
07	THERMAL & MOISTURE PROTECTION	102.2	111.5	105.5	98.0	105.0	100.5	101.5	95.8	99.5	104.6	132.8	114.7	112.6	147.4	125.0	102.7	112.2	106.1
08	OPENINGS	93.9	119.5	99.7	95.1	105.9	97.5	88.9	105.7	92.7	93.9	140.2	104.3	93.5	167.9	110.3	98.6	115.4	102.4
0920	Plaster & Gypsum Board	86.1	116.2	105.2	85.6	109.6	100.8	80.0	102.2	94.1	86.1	131.8	115.1	82.7	159.5	131.4	90.2	114.9	105.9
0950, 0980	Ceilings & Acoustic Treatment	98.0	116.2	108.2	94.5	109.6	103.0	89.8	102.2	96.8	98.0	131.8	116.9	94.8	159.5	131.1	109.5	114.9	112.5
0960	Flooring	95.9	124.5	103.0	103.2	102.5	103.1	93.9	96.0	94.5	95.9	129.0	104.2	98.0	160.9	113.7	103.0	122.4	107.9
0970, 0990	Wall Finishes & Painting/Coating	87.9	129.4	112.6	94.2	108.4	102.7	87.9	95.4	92.3	87.9	140.0	119.0	90.2	161.8	132.9	99.1	107.5	104.1
09	FINISHES	93.3	120.3	106.8	93.9	109.7	101.8	89.6	100.8	95.2	93.3	133.2	113.3	92.6	159.8	126.4	101.3	116.6	109.0
COVERS	DIVS. 10 - 14, 25, 28, 41, 43, 44, 46	100.0	106.6	101.3	100.0	105.8	101.1	100.0	98.8	99.7	100.0	113.4	102.6	100.0	126.0	105.0	100.0	106.6	101.3
21, 22, 23	FIRE SUPPRESSION, PLUMBING & HVAC	99.9	99.9	99.9	92.5	95.0	93.4	92.4	97.0	94.0	100.1	118.6	106.7	99.8	135.1	112.5	99.7	99.7	99.9
26, 27, 3370	ELECTRICAL, COMMUNICATIONS & UTIL.	93.4	92.2	92.9	92.2	103.2	97.0	89.0	91.6	90.2	93.7	131.0	109.8	98.0	133.1	113.2	101.0	87.4	95.1
MF2018	WEIGHTED AVERAGE	96.9	108.8	101.3	97.3	105.1	100.1	93.3	99.9	95.7	96.0	128.6	108.0	96.6	142.3	113.4	99.8	106.8	102.4

City Cost Indexes

		\multicolumn{18}{c	}{INDIANA}
\multicolumn{2}{	c	}{DIVISION}	\multicolumn{3}{c	}{ANDERSON 460}	\multicolumn{3}{c	}{BLOOMINGTON 474}	\multicolumn{3}{c	}{COLUMBUS 472}	\multicolumn{3}{c	}{EVANSVILLE 476 - 477}	\multicolumn{3}{c	}{FORT WAYNE 467 - 468}	\multicolumn{3}{c	}{GARY 463 - 464}
		MAT.	INST.	TOTAL	MAT.	INST.	TOTAL	MAT.	INST.	TOTAL	MAT.	INST.	TOTAL	MAT.	INST.	TOTAL	MAT.	INST.	TOTAL
015433	CONTRACTOR EQUIPMENT		92.4	92.4		81.1	81.1		81.1	81.1		106.9	106.9		92.4	92.4		92.4	92.4
0241, 31 - 34	SITE & INFRASTRUCTURE, DEMOLITION	93.0	86.1	88.5	80.6	84.7	83.3	74.7	84.3	81.0	84.9	109.7	101.1	94.4	85.6	88.7	93.5	88.8	90.4
0310	Concrete Forming & Accessories	93.1	74.5	78.7	100.8	78.7	83.6	94.5	74.9	79.2	93.6	78.9	82.2	91.5	78.2	81.2	93.2	102.5	100.4
0320	Concrete Reinforcing	100.3	79.3	94.5	91.6	82.1	88.9	92.0	80.0	88.7	100.2	93.9	98.4	100.3	76.8	93.8	100.3	106.0	101.9
0330	Cast-in-Place Concrete	89.4	72.4	83.3	96.9	74.1	88.8	96.5	70.1	87.1	92.6	81.8	88.8	95.0	71.5	86.6	93.4	103.8	97.1
03	CONCRETE	92.6	75.4	85.8	95.3	77.5	88.3	94.6	74.0	86.5	96.2	82.9	91.0	94.8	76.3	87.5	94.2	103.6	98.0
04	MASONRY	92.3	74.5	81.5	92.0	69.7	78.4	91.8	68.7	77.8	87.5	78.1	81.8	98.3	70.3	81.3	93.8	101.4	98.4
05	METALS	97.6	88.5	95.8	97.5	76.2	93.3	97.5	74.2	92.9	91.9	90.2	91.6	97.6	86.7	95.4	97.6	103.1	98.7
06	WOOD, PLASTICS & COMPOSITES	88.6	74.6	82.3	105.7	79.5	94.0	99.1	75.3	88.4	88.4	78.0	83.7	88.5	80.9	85.1	86.5	100.9	93.0
07	THERMAL & MOISTURE PROTECTION	110.5	71.8	96.7	97.3	74.5	89.2	96.8	72.0	87.9	101.4	80.7	94.0	110.3	75.6	97.9	109.3	97.1	105.0
08	OPENINGS	91.5	72.8	87.3	91.4	76.6	91.2	91.9	73.6	87.8	90.2	79.0	87.7	91.5	75.0	87.8	91.5	105.9	94.7
0920	Plaster & Gypsum Board	101.1	74.3	84.1	91.6	79.8	84.1	88.0	75.3	80.0	86.3	77.2	80.5	100.4	80.8	88.0	93.9	101.4	98.6
0950, 0980	Ceilings & Acoustic Treatment	93.8	74.3	82.9	80.9	79.8	80.2	80.9	75.3	77.8	83.4	77.2	79.9	93.8	80.8	86.5	93.8	101.4	98.0
0960	Flooring	98.4	71.3	91.6	99.7	76.8	94.0	95.7	76.8	90.9	94.9	71.3	89.0	98.4	72.1	91.8	98.4	101.0	99.0
0970, 0990	Wall Finishes & Painting/Coating	93.0	69.2	78.8	85.2	76.6	80.1	85.2	74.4	78.7	91.3	82.3	85.9	93.0	68.2	78.2	93.0	109.4	102.8
09	FINISHES	94.4	73.2	83.7	91.2	78.2	84.7	89.5	75.2	82.3	89.8	77.5	83.6	94.2	76.6	85.3	93.3	102.6	98.1
COVERS	DIVS. 10 - 14, 25, 28, 41, 43, 44, 46	100.0	88.7	97.8	100.0	88.8	97.8	100.0	88.1	97.7	100.0	89.4	97.9	100.0	90.0	98.1	100.0	96.7	99.4
21, 22, 23	FIRE SUPPRESSION, PLUMBING & HVAC	99.9	72.4	90.0	99.6	75.1	90.8	92.1	72.6	85.1	100.0	78.3	92.2	99.9	71.2	89.6	99.9	97.3	99.0
26, 27, 3370	ELECTRICAL, COMMUNICATIONS & UTIL.	83.5	78.6	81.3	100.7	82.7	92.9	100.2	80.5	91.7	94.6	80.0	88.3	84.6	79.3	82.3	94.3	99.9	96.7
MF2018	WEIGHTED AVERAGE	95.4	77.1	88.7	97.1	77.7	89.9	94.6	75.5	87.6	94.7	83.1	90.4	96.0	77.2	89.1	96.7	99.9	97.9

		\multicolumn{18}{c	}{INDIANA}
\multicolumn{2}{	c	}{DIVISION}	\multicolumn{3}{c	}{INDIANAPOLIS 461 - 462}	\multicolumn{3}{c	}{KOKOMO 469}	\multicolumn{3}{c	}{LAFAYETTE 479}	\multicolumn{3}{c	}{LAWRENCEBURG 470}	\multicolumn{3}{c	}{MUNCIE 473}	\multicolumn{3}{c	}{NEW ALBANY 471}
		MAT.	INST.	TOTAL	MAT.	INST.	TOTAL	MAT.	INST.	TOTAL	MAT.	INST.	TOTAL	MAT.	INST.	TOTAL	MAT.	INST.	TOTAL
015433	CONTRACTOR EQUIPMENT		91.2	91.2		92.4	92.4		81.1	81.1		98.2	98.2		91.2	91.2		89.3	89.3
0241, 31 - 34	SITE & INFRASTRUCTURE, DEMOLITION	92.9	96.6	95.3	86.7	85.4	85.8	75.0	84.3	81.1	75.9	97.4	89.9	81.2	85.4	83.9	72.5	86.3	81.5
0310	Concrete Forming & Accessories	93.8	84.8	86.8	96.3	72.8	78.0	91.7	77.1	80.3	90.6	73.0	77.0	90.9	74.1	77.9	90.4	71.7	75.9
0320	Concrete Reinforcing	99.9	87.5	96.5	90.7	80.3	87.8	91.6	80.2	88.4	91.2	73.5	86.3	101.3	79.2	95.2	92.2	75.7	87.6
0330	Cast-in-Place Concrete	86.8	87.1	86.9	88.5	77.1	84.4	97.0	74.9	89.1	90.7	69.6	83.2	101.8	71.7	91.1	93.6	69.5	85.1
03	CONCRETE	96.7	85.6	92.3	88.7	76.4	83.9	94.6	76.7	87.5	89.3	72.7	82.8	95.9	75.0	87.6	93.4	72.2	85.0
04	MASONRY	104.8	80.4	90.0	91.8	71.4	79.4	96.6	71.6	81.4	76.3	68.6	71.6	93.9	74.6	82.2	83.1	66.1	72.8
05	METALS	98.7	78.2	94.7	93.2	87.6	92.1	95.3	74.8	91.3	92.8	84.3	91.1	99.3	88.5	97.2	94.3	80.6	91.6
06	WOOD, PLASTICS & COMPOSITES	89.7	85.0	87.6	91.6	72.1	82.9	95.5	78.1	87.7	86.3	73.2	80.4	95.6	74.2	86.0	89.2	72.5	81.7
07	THERMAL & MOISTURE PROTECTION	105.6	81.2	96.9	109.7	71.8	96.2	96.7	74.2	88.7	102.2	71.4	91.2	99.5	73.1	90.1	90.9	68.9	83.1
08	OPENINGS	99.3	81.4	95.2	87.1	71.8	83.7	90.7	75.2	87.2	91.8	71.0	87.1	88.8	72.6	85.2	89.9	68.9	85.1
0920	Plaster & Gypsum Board	87.7	84.5	85.7	105.8	71.7	84.2	84.9	78.3	80.7	71.8	73.1	72.6	86.3	74.3	78.7	83.4	72.3	76.3
0950, 0980	Ceilings & Acoustic Treatment	101.3	84.5	91.9	94.2	71.7	81.6	76.3	78.3	77.4	90.2	73.1	80.6	80.9	74.3	77.2	83.4	72.3	77.2
0960	Flooring	102.3	84.9	97.9	97.7	76.8	91.9	94.7	76.8	90.2	68.9	76.8	70.9	95.5	71.3	89.5	92.5	48.4	81.5
0970, 0990	Wall Finishes & Painting/Coating	97.1	81.3	87.7	93.0	62.7	75.0	85.2	76.7	80.2	85.6	67.0	74.5	85.2	69.2	75.7	91.3	60.1	72.7
09	FINISHES	98.0	84.4	91.2	96.0	73.3	84.6	87.5	77.1	82.3	81.6	73.2	77.4	88.9	72.9	80.9	88.9	66.0	77.4
COVERS	DIVS. 10 - 14, 25, 28, 41, 43, 44, 46	100.0	92.4	98.5	100.0	88.5	97.8	100.0	88.3	97.7	100.0	83.6	96.8	100.0	87.8	97.6	100.0	83.4	96.8
21, 22, 23	FIRE SUPPRESSION, PLUMBING & HVAC	99.9	80.2	92.8	92.4	72.7	85.3	92.1	73.5	85.4	93.3	69.9	84.8	99.6	72.3	89.8	92.4	72.4	85.2
26, 27, 3370	ELECTRICAL, COMMUNICATIONS & UTIL.	98.5	87.6	93.8	85.7	71.6	79.6	100.0	74.3	88.8	92.7	68.4	82.1	90.4	70.0	81.6	94.0	69.2	83.2
MF2018	WEIGHTED AVERAGE	99.0	84.2	93.5	92.1	75.8	86.1	94.0	75.9	87.4	91.3	74.3	85.1	95.8	75.7	88.4	92.3	72.4	85.0

		\multicolumn{9}{c	}{INDIANA}	\multicolumn{9}{c	}{IOWA}
\multicolumn{2}{	c	}{DIVISION}	\multicolumn{3}{c	}{SOUTH BEND 465 - 466}	\multicolumn{3}{c	}{TERRE HAUTE 478}	\multicolumn{3}{c	}{WASHINGTON 475}	\multicolumn{3}{c	}{BURLINGTON 526}	\multicolumn{3}{c	}{CARROLL 514}	\multicolumn{3}{c	}{CEDAR RAPIDS 522 - 524}
		MAT.	INST.	TOTAL	MAT.	INST.	TOTAL	MAT.	INST.	TOTAL	MAT.	INST.	TOTAL	MAT.	INST.	TOTAL	MAT.	INST.	TOTAL
015433	CONTRACTOR EQUIPMENT		108.7	108.7		106.9	106.9		106.9	106.9		95.2	95.2		95.2	95.2		92.4	92.4
0241, 31 - 34	SITE & INFRASTRUCTURE, DEMOLITION	92.8	97.4	95.8	86.0	109.6	101.4	81.6	109.8	100.0	84.6	86.9	86.1	77.3	87.6	84.0	88.9	87.2	87.8
0310	Concrete Forming & Accessories	99.4	73.4	79.2	94.6	74.0	78.6	95.4	76.8	81.0	96.4	85.3	87.7	82.4	76.0	77.4	103.1	80.8	85.7
0320	Concrete Reinforcing	98.9	78.1	93.1	100.2	79.1	94.3	92.7	80.0	89.2	93.4	87.7	91.8	94.0	77.0	89.3	94.0	93.6	93.9
0330	Cast-in-Place Concrete	89.5	77.2	85.1	89.6	75.3	84.5	97.5	81.7	91.9	118.2	50.5	94.1	118.2	75.0	102.8	118.5	80.2	104.8
03	CONCRETE	99.7	77.0	90.7	98.0	75.9	89.3	101.3	79.5	92.7	103.3	74.2	91.8	101.9	76.7	92.0	103.8	83.6	95.8
04	MASONRY	92.1	70.9	79.2	95.2	70.9	80.5	87.6	73.6	79.1	107.6	64.8	81.6	108.8	65.2	82.3	113.3	77.8	91.7
05	METALS	101.3	98.2	100.7	92.5	84.3	90.9	85.6	85.2	85.5	88.0	93.9	89.1	88.0	90.6	88.5	90.8	98.6	92.3
06	WOOD, PLASTICS & COMPOSITES	96.7	72.6	86.0	91.3	73.8	83.4	91.6	76.0	84.6	94.1	89.0	91.8	76.3	80.2	78.0	103.1	80.0	92.7
07	THERMAL & MOISTURE PROTECTION	101.9	75.3	92.4	101.5	75.3	92.2	101.4	77.7	93.0	105.3	69.1	92.4	105.3	70.7	93.0	106.1	76.4	95.6
08	OPENINGS	98.4	72.1	92.5	90.6	72.1	86.5	88.0	75.9	85.3	91.1	86.8	90.2	95.2	76.3	90.9	95.6	82.6	92.6
0920	Plaster & Gypsum Board	91.0	71.8	78.9	86.3	72.8	77.7	86.4	75.2	79.3	100.0	89.1	93.0	95.6	80.0	85.7	106.5	80.3	89.9
0950, 0980	Ceilings & Acoustic Treatment	85.3	71.8	77.7	83.4	72.8	77.5	78.4	75.2	76.6	108.4	89.1	97.6	108.4	80.0	92.5	111.6	80.3	94.1
0960	Flooring	99.9	81.9	95.4	94.9	71.9	89.2	95.6	76.8	90.9	98.5	61.9	89.4	94.1	71.2	88.3	114.7	82.5	106.6
0970, 0990	Wall Finishes & Painting/Coating	99.1	77.8	86.4	91.3	73.8	80.8	91.3	80.7	85.0	93.6	75.2	82.6	93.6	75.2	82.6	95.8	67.4	78.9
09	FINISHES	93.6	75.1	84.3	89.7	73.3	81.5	88.9	77.0	82.9	98.9	80.7	89.9	96.0	75.4	85.7	105.6	79.6	92.5
COVERS	DIVS. 10 - 14, 25, 28, 41, 43, 44, 46	100.0	90.7	98.2	100.0	89.9	98.0	100.0	88.8	97.8	100.0	92.3	98.5	100.0	88.5	97.8	100.0	91.6	98.4
21, 22, 23	FIRE SUPPRESSION, PLUMBING & HVAC	99.8	71.6	89.7	100.0	73.7	90.5	92.4	75.4	86.4	92.5	75.3	86.4	92.5	69.9	84.4	100.1	79.6	92.7
26, 27, 3370	ELECTRICAL, COMMUNICATIONS & UTIL.	99.7	82.1	92.1	93.9	78.9	87.4	94.1	77.5	86.9	96.3	64.3	82.4	96.7	68.5	84.4	95.1	74.1	86.0
MF2018	WEIGHTED AVERAGE	99.1	79.4	91.9	95.4	78.7	89.2	92.0	80.4	87.7	94.9	76.9	88.3	94.6	75.2	87.5	98.4	82.0	92.4

City Cost Indexes

IOWA

DIVISION		COUNCIL BLUFFS 515			CRESTON 508			DAVENPORT 527 - 528			DECORAH 521			DES MOINES 500 - 503,509			DUBUQUE 520		
		MAT.	INST.	TOTAL	MAT.	INST.	TOTAL	MAT.	INST.	TOTAL	MAT.	INST.	TOTAL	MAT.	INST.	TOTAL	MAT.	INST.	TOTAL
015433	CONTRACTOR EQUIPMENT		91.9	91.9		95.2	95.2		95.2	95.2		95.2	95.2		101.2	101.2		91.4	91.4
0241, 31 - 34	SITE & INFRASTRUCTURE, DEMOLITION	89.6	84.6	86.3	81.4	88.5	86.0	88.5	90.4	89.8	83.6	86.7	85.6	88.0	99.2	95.3	87.1	84.8	85.6
0310	Concrete Forming & Accessories	81.5	72.3	74.3	81.0	78.5	79.1	102.4	94.4	96.2	93.6	65.1	71.5	102.1	89.1	92.0	83.2	78.2	79.3
0320	Concrete Reinforcing	95.9	82.4	92.2	89.3	77.1	85.9	94.0	94.1	94.0	93.4	76.5	88.7	98.4	99.0	98.5	92.7	76.1	88.1
0330	Cast-in-Place Concrete	123.2	84.1	109.3	121.3	78.1	106.0	114.1	91.4	106.0	115.0	69.5	98.8	103.4	92.8	99.6	116.0	79.6	103.1
03	CONCRETE	105.3	79.2	95.0	101.8	79.0	92.8	101.9	94.0	98.8	101.4	69.8	88.9	101.7	92.6	98.1	100.1	79.2	91.8
04	MASONRY	113.1	74.1	89.4	112.1	71.9	87.7	108.4	89.4	96.9	129.7	62.3	88.8	98.7	88.4	92.5	114.3	65.8	84.9
05	METALS	94.4	93.9	94.3	93.1	91.1	92.7	90.8	104.0	93.4	88.1	89.5	88.4	99.2	101.3	99.6	89.0	90.6	89.3
06	WOOD, PLASTICS & COMPOSITES	74.6	70.6	72.8	74.5	80.2	77.1	103.1	94.1	99.1	90.2	64.4	78.6	99.4	88.2	94.4	77.0	79.0	77.9
07	THERMAL & MOISTURE PROTECTION	105.4	71.4	93.3	110.0	73.7	97.1	105.7	88.0	99.4	105.4	62.7	90.2	102.4	87.1	96.9	105.6	72.2	93.7
08	OPENINGS	94.8	77.0	90.8	105.5	77.9	99.3	95.6	95.8	95.6	93.9	70.6	88.6	97.3	93.8	96.5	94.8	79.1	91.3
0920	Plaster & Gypsum Board	95.6	70.3	79.5	95.9	80.0	85.8	106.5	94.4	98.8	99.0	63.7	76.6	90.2	88.0	88.8	95.6	79.0	85.1
0950, 0980	Ceilings & Acoustic Treatment	108.4	70.3	87.0	99.7	80.0	88.7	111.6	94.4	101.9	108.4	63.7	83.3	104.2	88.0	95.1	108.4	79.0	91.9
0960	Flooring	93.4	80.1	90.0	90.4	61.9	83.2	100.4	85.0	96.5	98.6	61.9	89.4	102.4	89.8	99.3	107.5	67.0	97.4
0970, 0990	Wall Finishes & Painting/Coating	90.8	57.5	70.9	87.4	75.2	80.1	93.6	86.8	89.6	93.6	75.2	82.6	99.1	82.1	89.0	95.4	74.0	82.6
09	FINISHES	96.6	71.6	84.0	91.9	75.2	83.5	101.2	91.9	96.5	98.8	65.3	82.0	99.2	88.3	93.7	101.0	75.7	88.3
COVERS	DIVS. 10 - 14, 25, 28, 41, 43, 44, 46	100.0	89.5	98.0	100.0	90.7	98.2	100.0	95.6	99.1	100.0	88.1	97.7	100.0	94.8	99.0	100.0	90.6	98.2
21, 22, 23	FIRE SUPPRESSION, PLUMBING & HVAC	100.1	75.6	91.3	92.5	71.7	85.0	100.1	90.1	96.5	92.5	66.9	83.3	99.9	85.0	94.6	100.1	72.0	90.0
26, 27, 3370	ELECTRICAL, COMMUNICATIONS & UTIL.	97.8	81.6	90.8	90.2	68.5	80.8	92.7	81.5	87.8	95.1	42.1	72.1	99.5	89.6	95.2	97.0	71.2	85.8
MF2018	WEIGHTED AVERAGE	98.7	79.0	91.4	96.0	76.8	88.9	97.4	91.3	95.1	95.6	67.4	85.2	99.4	90.8	96.2	97.1	76.4	89.5

IOWA

DIVISION		FORT DODGE 505			MASON CITY 504			OTTUMWA 525			SHENANDOAH 516			SIBLEY 512			SIOUX CITY 510 - 511		
		MAT.	INST.	TOTAL	MAT.	INST.	TOTAL	MAT.	INST.	TOTAL	MAT.	INST.	TOTAL	MAT.	INST.	TOTAL	MAT.	INST.	TOTAL
015433	CONTRACTOR EQUIPMENT		95.2	95.2		95.2	95.2		91.4	91.4		91.9	91.9		95.2	95.2		95.2	95.2
0241, 31 - 34	SITE & INFRASTRUCTURE, DEMOLITION	86.0	85.7	85.8	86.1	86.6	86.4	83.9	82.4	83.0	85.1	84.2	84.5	91.2	86.6	88.2	96.2	88.6	91.3
0310	Concrete Forming & Accessories	81.6	70.7	73.1	86.3	64.7	69.5	91.2	79.0	81.7	83.5	70.0	73.0	84.1	34.5	45.6	103.1	70.9	78.0
0320	Concrete Reinforcing	89.3	76.4	85.7	89.2	76.5	85.6	93.4	87.9	91.8	95.9	77.0	90.7	95.9	76.4	90.5	94.0	92.2	93.5
0330	Cast-in-Place Concrete	113.8	38.9	87.2	113.8	65.2	96.6	118.9	58.8	97.6	119.1	75.6	103.7	116.7	51.1	93.4	117.4	82.8	105.1
03	CONCRETE	97.7	61.7	83.5	98.1	68.1	86.2	102.8	74.4	91.6	103.1	74.3	91.8	102.2	49.6	81.4	102.3	79.8	94.0
04	MASONRY	111.0	46.8	72.0	124.8	61.2	86.2	110.2	49.8	73.5	112.5	67.1	85.0	133.1	47.0	80.8	106.8	64.3	81.0
05	METALS	93.2	89.2	92.5	93.3	89.5	92.5	87.9	95.1	89.3	93.4	91.3	93.0	88.2	88.7	88.3	90.8	97.6	92.1
06	WOOD, PLASTICS & COMPOSITES	75.1	80.2	77.4	80.8	64.4	73.5	86.7	88.8	87.7	77.0	71.2	74.4	78.1	31.2	57.1	103.1	70.1	88.3
07	THERMAL & MOISTURE PROTECTION	109.5	58.5	91.3	109.2	63.3	92.8	105.8	63.0	90.6	104.9	65.8	90.9	105.1	49.6	85.3	105.7	67.2	92.0
08	OPENINGS	99.5	68.8	92.6	91.8	70.6	87.0	95.2	84.1	92.7	87.1	69.3	83.1	92.2	41.8	80.8	95.6	76.1	91.2
0920	Plaster & Gypsum Board	95.9	80.0	85.8	95.9	63.7	75.5	96.1	89.1	91.6	95.6	70.9	80.0	95.6	29.5	53.7	106.5	69.6	83.1
0950, 0980	Ceilings & Acoustic Treatment	99.7	80.0	88.7	99.7	63.7	79.5	108.4	89.1	97.6	108.4	70.9	87.4	108.4	29.5	64.2	111.6	69.6	88.0
0960	Flooring	91.8	61.9	84.3	93.5	61.9	85.6	109.9	61.9	97.9	93.9	66.2	87.0	94.8	61.9	86.5	100.5	67.0	92.1
0970, 0990	Wall Finishes & Painting/Coating	87.4	72.2	78.3	87.4	75.2	80.1	95.4	75.2	83.3	90.8	75.2	81.5	93.6	74.3	82.1	93.6	84.0	87.9
09	FINISHES	93.2	70.4	81.8	93.7	65.0	79.3	101.9	76.5	89.1	96.6	69.6	83.0	98.2	41.9	69.9	102.2	71.0	86.5
COVERS	DIVS. 10 - 14, 25, 28, 41, 43, 44, 46	100.0	84.7	97.0	100.0	87.7	97.6	100.0	86.2	97.3	100.0	87.4	97.6	100.0	79.5	96.0	100.0	89.2	97.9
21, 22, 23	FIRE SUPPRESSION, PLUMBING & HVAC	92.5	64.2	82.3	92.5	69.8	84.3	92.5	65.7	82.9	92.5	75.4	86.4	92.5	64.2	82.4	100.1	74.4	90.9
26, 27, 3370	ELECTRICAL, COMMUNICATIONS & UTIL.	93.3	61.8	79.6	92.9	42.1	70.9	96.2	63.2	81.9	95.1	69.8	84.1	95.1	42.0	72.1	95.1	68.5	83.6
MF2018	WEIGHTED AVERAGE	95.5	67.4	85.1	95.4	67.7	85.2	95.4	71.9	86.8	95.5	74.8	87.9	95.7	57.3	81.6	98.0	76.4	90.1

IOWA / KANSAS

DIVISION		IOWA SPENCER 513			IOWA WATERLOO 506 - 507			KANSAS BELLEVILLE 669			KANSAS COLBY 677			KANSAS DODGE CITY 678			KANSAS EMPORIA 668		
		MAT.	INST.	TOTAL	MAT.	INST.	TOTAL	MAT.	INST.	TOTAL	MAT.	INST.	TOTAL	MAT.	INST.	TOTAL	MAT.	INST.	TOTAL
015433	CONTRACTOR EQUIPMENT		95.2	95.2		95.2	95.2		99.6	99.6		99.6	99.6		99.6	99.6		98.1	98.1
0241, 31 - 34	SITE & INFRASTRUCTURE, DEMOLITION	91.3	85.5	87.5	93.6	88.3	90.1	97.4	87.2	90.7	92.1	87.6	89.2	97.3	87.9	91.2	92.0	85.0	87.4
0310	Concrete Forming & Accessories	91.0	34.2	46.9	99.5	66.0	73.5	97.2	50.1	60.6	103.9	55.7	66.4	95.7	57.3	65.9	87.2	63.6	68.8
0320	Concrete Reinforcing	95.9	76.3	90.5	89.9	76.4	86.2	101.9	93.9	99.7	110.5	93.9	105.9	107.8	93.7	103.9	100.5	94.0	98.7
0330	Cast-in-Place Concrete	116.7	60.1	96.6	122.0	80.5	107.2	106.0	77.3	95.8	101.7	79.5	93.8	103.5	83.6	96.4	102.5	79.6	94.3
03	CONCRETE	102.8	52.5	82.9	103.8	74.1	92.1	103.7	68.8	89.9	103.7	72.1	91.2	103.8	74.2	92.1	97.7	75.7	89.0
04	MASONRY	133.1	47.0	80.8	111.9	71.8	87.6	105.0	54.5	74.3	89.9	58.2	70.6	97.4	56.2	72.4	111.6	59.5	79.9
05	METALS	88.2	88.4	88.2	96.0	91.3	95.1	96.9	94.7	96.4	97.2	95.4	96.8	98.5	95.1	97.9	95.5	95.6	95.5
06	WOOD, PLASTICS & COMPOSITES	86.5	31.2	61.7	98.3	61.9	82.0	90.6	46.6	70.8	95.6	52.2	76.1	95.4	52.9	70.8	79.1	62.5	71.7
07	THERMAL & MOISTURE PROTECTION	105.9	50.1	86.0	109.5	73.0	96.5	99.9	57.3	84.7	104.3	59.4	88.3	104.3	63.1	89.6	98.3	67.6	87.4
08	OPENINGS	102.5	41.8	88.8	92.1	70.1	87.1	89.3	57.1	82.0	95.4	60.1	87.5	95.4	60.6	87.5	87.5	67.8	83.1
0920	Plaster & Gypsum Board	96.1	29.5	53.8	104.5	61.1	77.0	79.9	45.3	57.9	88.5	51.0	64.7	81.8	51.8	62.8	76.3	61.7	67.1
0950, 0980	Ceilings & Acoustic Treatment	108.4	29.5	64.2	102.4	61.1	79.3	87.3	45.3	63.7	83.6	51.0	65.3	83.6	51.8	65.8	87.3	61.7	73.0
0960	Flooring	96.9	61.9	88.1	98.0	75.0	92.3	92.7	61.2	84.8	84.3	61.2	78.5	81.7	62.4	76.9	88.9	61.2	82.0
0970, 0990	Wall Finishes & Painting/Coating	93.6	50.8	68.1	87.4	78.9	82.3	92.7	91.5	92.0	97.3	91.5	93.9	97.3	91.5	93.9	92.7	91.5	92.0
09	FINISHES	98.9	38.3	68.5	97.1	68.0	82.5	88.7	55.2	71.9	86.2	59.3	72.7	84.6	60.5	72.5	86.2	65.4	75.8
COVERS	DIVS. 10 - 14, 25, 28, 41, 43, 44, 46	100.0	79.5	96.0	100.0	89.3	97.9	100.0	75.0	95.2	100.0	76.8	95.5	100.0	80.8	96.2	100.0	76.5	95.5
21, 22, 23	FIRE SUPPRESSION, PLUMBING & HVAC	92.5	62.4	82.4	100.0	76.4	91.5	92.2	64.1	82.2	92.6	63.9	82.3	100.2	72.0	90.1	92.2	66.1	82.8
26, 27, 3370	ELECTRICAL, COMMUNICATIONS & UTIL.	95.9	42.0	72.6	91.2	59.3	77.4	97.0	55.8	79.1	99.0	60.4	82.3	97.5	65.8	83.8	95.5	59.6	79.9
MF2018	WEIGHTED AVERAGE	96.9	57.1	82.3	98.3	74.3	89.5	96.0	65.7	84.9	96.2	68.0	85.9	98.2	71.1	88.2	94.7	70.3	85.7

City Cost Indexes

KANSAS

DIVISION		FORT SCOTT 667			HAYS 676			HUTCHINSON 675			INDEPENDENCE 673			KANSAS CITY 660 - 662			LIBERAL 679		
		MAT.	INST.	TOTAL	MAT.	INST.	TOTAL	MAT.	INST.	TOTAL	MAT.	INST.	TOTAL	MAT.	INST.	TOTAL	MAT.	INST.	TOTAL
015433	CONTRACTOR EQUIPMENT		98.8	98.8		99.6	99.6		99.6	99.6		99.6	99.6		96.7	96.7		99.6	99.6
0241, 31 - 34	SITE & INFRASTRUCTURE, DEMOLITION	89.5	85.1	86.6	95.0	87.5	90.1	80.8	87.8	85.4	94.5	87.8	90.1	89.8	86.5	87.7	94.7	87.4	90.0
0310	Concrete Forming & Accessories	106.7	75.1	82.1	100.9	54.4	64.7	89.1	51.6	60.0	114.0	61.6	73.3	102.7	98.9	99.7	96.1	53.6	63.1
0320	Concrete Reinforcing	99.8	90.4	97.2	107.8	93.9	103.9	107.8	93.9	103.9	107.1	90.4	102.5	96.9	101.2	98.1	109.3	93.6	105.0
0330	Cast-in-Place Concrete	95.0	75.3	88.0	80.2	77.6	79.3	74.3	79.4	76.1	103.9	79.5	95.3	81.4	96.1	86.6	80.2	76.4	78.9
03	CONCRETE	94.9	78.8	88.5	96.4	70.8	86.3	83.9	70.2	78.5	105.4	74.1	93.1	88.2	98.7	92.3	97.7	70.0	86.8
04	MASONRY	115.0	50.6	75.9	96.4	54.7	71.0	90.3	58.1	70.8	87.1	58.1	69.5	113.3	96.8	103.3	95.2	48.3	66.7
05	METALS	96.5	94.1	96.0	96.6	95.4	96.4	96.4	95.0	96.1	96.3	94.2	95.9	106.4	104.4	106.0	97.0	94.7	96.5
06	WOOD, PLASTICS & COMPOSITES	103.9	82.1	94.2	91.9	52.2	74.1	78.6	46.8	64.3	109.0	59.8	87.0	99.2	98.8	99.0	86.0	52.2	70.8
07	THERMAL & MOISTURE PROTECTION	99.3	65.3	87.2	104.6	57.9	88.0	103.2	58.5	87.2	104.5	67.2	91.2	99.0	97.2	98.4	104.7	55.4	87.1
08	OPENINGS	87.5	77.8	85.4	95.4	60.1	87.4	95.4	57.2	86.7	93.5	63.6	86.8	88.3	97.3	90.3	95.4	60.1	87.5
0920	Plaster & Gypsum Board	83.1	81.9	82.3	86.1	51.0	63.9	80.8	45.5	58.4	97.7	58.9	73.1	77.2	99.1	91.1	82.3	51.0	62.4
0950, 0980	Ceilings & Acoustic Treatment	87.3	81.9	84.3	83.6	51.0	65.3	83.6	45.5	62.2	83.6	58.9	69.8	87.3	99.1	93.9	83.6	51.0	65.3
0960	Flooring	102.2	59.9	91.6	83.5	61.2	77.9	79.6	61.2	75.0	87.3	59.9	80.4	80.8	95.6	84.5	81.8	61.2	76.7
0970, 0990	Wall Finishes & Painting/Coating	94.2	68.8	79.1	97.3	91.5	93.9	97.3	91.5	93.9	97.3	91.5	93.9	100.6	105.3	103.4	97.3	91.5	93.9
09	FINISHES	91.3	72.8	82.0	86.0	58.5	72.2	82.7	56.2	69.4	88.4	64.1	76.2	86.2	99.0	92.6	85.2	58.0	71.5
COVERS	DIVS. 10 - 14, 25, 28, 41, 43, 44, 46	100.0	77.5	95.6	100.0	75.6	95.3	100.0	76.2	95.4	100.0	77.6	95.7	100.0	96.1	99.2	100.0	75.0	95.2
21, 22, 23	FIRE SUPPRESSION, PLUMBING & HVAC	92.2	60.6	80.9	92.6	61.6	81.5	92.6	63.9	82.3	92.6	63.3	82.1	99.7	103.5	101.1	92.6	62.3	81.8
26, 27, 3370	ELECTRICAL, COMMUNICATIONS & UTIL.	95.1	60.4	80.1	98.5	60.4	82.0	96.2	54.3	78.0	97.2	64.8	83.2	97.6	92.3	95.3	97.5	60.4	81.5
MF2018	WEIGHTED AVERAGE	95.0	70.2	85.9	95.5	66.9	84.9	92.7	66.3	83.0	96.1	69.8	86.5	97.9	98.0	98.0	95.4	66.1	84.6

DIVISION		KANSAS SALINA 674			TOPEKA 664 - 666			WICHITA 670 - 672			KENTUCKY ASHLAND 411 - 412			BOWLING GREEN 421 - 422			CAMPTON 413 - 414		
		MAT.	INST.	TOTAL	MAT.	INST.	TOTAL	MAT.	INST.	TOTAL	MAT.	INST.	TOTAL	MAT.	INST.	TOTAL	MAT.	INST.	TOTAL
015433	CONTRACTOR EQUIPMENT		99.6	99.6		104.6	104.6		104.7	104.7		95.4	95.4		89.3	89.3		94.8	94.8
0241, 31 - 34	SITE & INFRASTRUCTURE, DEMOLITION	90.5	87.5	88.6	93.0	96.6	95.4	89.7	97.0	94.5	98.5	76.1	83.9	75.8	86.5	82.8	79.5	86.8	84.2
0310	Concrete Forming & Accessories	91.5	58.1	65.6	98.8	64.2	71.9	101.0	55.5	65.7	85.3	81.2	82.1	86.4	77.7	79.6	88.1	73.8	77.0
0320	Concrete Reinforcing	107.1	93.8	103.4	98.5	95.2	97.6	99.5	97.4	98.9	92.9	86.0	91.0	90.8	74.7	86.4	91.7	83.5	89.4
0330	Cast-in-Place Concrete	89.8	80.2	86.4	90.2	85.5	88.5	84.1	76.4	81.3	85.2	86.4	85.6	84.5	65.5	77.8	94.3	62.8	83.1
03	CONCRETE	94.1	73.4	85.9	92.3	78.0	86.7	90.2	71.3	82.8	89.6	85.2	87.8	88.3	73.4	82.5	91.7	72.2	84.0
04	MASONRY	109.5	51.8	74.4	107.6	61.2	79.4	88.0	52.4	66.4	94.2	82.9	87.3	96.2	65.4	77.5	93.0	49.3	66.4
05	METALS	98.3	95.8	97.8	101.0	94.9	99.8	100.8	94.8	99.6	93.7	102.9	95.5	95.0	83.4	92.7	94.3	86.6	92.8
06	WOOD, PLASTICS & COMPOSITES	80.7	57.1	70.1	95.5	62.9	80.9	98.7	52.8	78.1	71.4	79.6	75.1	82.8	80.2	81.7	80.8	80.2	80.5
07	THERMAL & MOISTURE PROTECTION	103.7	58.7	87.7	101.9	79.7	94.0	101.6	60.3	86.9	93.3	80.0	88.6	90.9	73.4	84.6	101.5	60.9	87.0
08	OPENINGS	95.4	63.3	88.1	98.0	70.5	91.8	98.0	62.0	89.9	89.2	81.0	87.3	89.9	75.7	86.7	91.1	79.2	88.4
0920	Plaster & Gypsum Board	80.8	56.2	65.2	89.1	61.7	71.7	87.6	51.3	64.6	59.4	79.4	72.1	78.6	80.2	79.6	78.6	79.4	79.1
0950, 0980	Ceilings & Acoustic Treatment	83.6	56.2	68.2	106.8	61.7	81.5	101.8	51.3	73.5	80.9	79.4	80.0	83.4	80.2	81.6	83.4	79.4	81.2
0960	Flooring	80.6	62.4	76.0	95.1	62.4	86.9	91.2	66.4	85.0	73.1	72.8	73.1	90.8	56.6	82.3	92.9	57.6	84.1
0970, 0990	Wall Finishes & Painting/Coating	97.3	91.5	93.9	99.1	91.5	94.6	99.1	99.6	99.4	92.7	80.3	85.3	91.3	62.4	74.1	91.3	47.9	65.4
09	FINISHES	83.6	61.4	72.4	98.0	65.5	81.7	95.3	60.8	78.0	77.6	79.5	78.6	87.6	72.3	79.9	88.4	68.5	78.4
COVERS	DIVS. 10 - 14, 25, 28, 41, 43, 44, 46	100.0	85.1	97.1	100.0	81.2	96.4	100.0	85.7	97.2	100.0	78.8	95.9	100.0	88.3	97.7	100.0	86.6	97.4
21, 22, 23	FIRE SUPPRESSION, PLUMBING & HVAC	100.2	65.5	87.7	99.9	70.3	89.3	99.9	68.2	88.5	92.1	76.4	86.5	100.0	73.5	90.5	92.5	68.7	83.9
26, 27, 3370	ELECTRICAL, COMMUNICATIONS & UTIL.	97.4	71.6	86.2	99.5	66.5	85.2	99.5	71.6	87.4	91.8	78.6	86.1	94.3	70.7	84.1	93.0	78.5	86.7
MF2018	WEIGHTED AVERAGE	97.2	70.3	87.3	99.0	74.1	89.9	97.7	71.2	88.0	91.5	81.8	87.9	94.0	74.7	86.9	92.9	72.6	85.4

DIVISION		KENTUCKY CORBIN 407 - 409			COVINGTON 410			ELIZABETHTOWN 427			FRANKFORT 406			HAZARD 417 - 418			HENDERSON 424		
		MAT.	INST.	TOTAL	MAT.	INST.	TOTAL	MAT.	INST.	TOTAL	MAT.	INST.	TOTAL	MAT.	INST.	TOTAL	MAT.	INST.	TOTAL
015433	CONTRACTOR EQUIPMENT		94.8	94.8		98.2	98.2		89.3	89.3		99.9	99.9		94.8	94.8		106.9	106.9
0241, 31 - 34	SITE & INFRASTRUCTURE, DEMOLITION	81.6	87.2	85.3	76.9	96.8	89.9	68.3	85.8	79.7	81.9	97.9	92.3	77.7	87.7	84.3	73.8	108.2	96.2
0310	Concrete Forming & Accessories	85.0	68.9	72.5	83.5	64.3	68.6	80.8	65.7	69.1	101.8	71.5	78.2	84.2	74.6	76.8	91.3	69.8	74.6
0320	Concrete Reinforcing	89.5	82.8	87.6	90.8	70.5	85.2	91.3	75.1	86.8	98.1	75.4	91.9	92.2	83.0	89.6	90.9	75.7	86.7
0330	Cast-in-Place Concrete	87.6	66.6	80.2	90.2	74.7	84.7	76.4	62.5	71.5	87.8	71.0	81.9	90.7	64.2	81.3	74.7	77.3	75.6
03	CONCRETE	83.6	71.2	78.7	89.9	70.1	82.1	82.1	67.1	76.2	89.4	72.5	82.8	89.2	73.0	82.8	85.7	74.1	81.1
04	MASONRY	100.0	54.0	72.1	107.0	64.8	81.4	80.2	55.7	65.4	96.8	66.9	78.7	91.4	51.1	66.9	99.3	70.9	82.1
05	METALS	97.7	85.7	95.3	92.8	84.7	91.2	94.2	83.0	92.0	100.8	81.7	97.0	94.3	86.5	92.8	85.3	83.6	95.0
06	WOOD, PLASTICS & COMPOSITES	71.8	70.5	71.2	77.3	62.1	70.5	76.3	67.2	72.2	98.6	70.5	86.0	76.7	80.2	78.3	85.6	68.9	78.1
07	THERMAL & MOISTURE PROTECTION	103.8	62.5	89.1	102.4	65.4	89.2	90.4	61.6	80.1	102.7	69.1	90.7	101.3	62.5	87.5	100.8	74.3	91.4
08	OPENINGS	91.4	63.9	85.2	92.7	66.7	86.8	89.9	66.2	84.5	98.4	72.5	92.6	91.4	79.1	88.6	88.4	71.1	84.5
0920	Plaster & Gypsum Board	88.3	69.4	76.3	67.9	61.6	63.9	76.9	66.8	70.5	96.6	69.4	79.3	76.9	79.4	78.5	81.8	67.8	72.9
0950, 0980	Ceilings & Acoustic Treatment	73.2	69.4	71.1	90.2	61.6	74.2	83.4	66.8	74.1	94.1	69.4	80.2	83.4	79.4	81.2	78.4	67.8	72.4
0960	Flooring	89.0	57.6	81.1	66.9	74.8	68.9	88.7	66.1	83.0	102.2	70.4	94.2	91.5	57.9	83.0	94.2	68.1	87.6
0970, 0990	Wall Finishes & Painting/Coating	87.7	55.1	68.2	85.6	63.2	72.2	91.3	60.5	73.0	99.1	81.5	88.6	91.3	47.9	65.4	91.3	77.1	82.8
09	FINISHES	83.8	65.4	74.6	80.7	65.9	73.1	86.5	64.6	75.5	97.4	72.3	84.8	87.6	69.0	78.3	87.3	70.3	78.7
COVERS	DIVS. 10 - 14, 25, 28, 41, 43, 44, 46	100.0	87.9	97.7	100.0	86.8	97.4	100.0	85.2	97.1	100.0	89.7	98.0	100.0	83.1	96.7	100.0	50.2	90.3
21, 22, 23	FIRE SUPPRESSION, PLUMBING & HVAC	92.8	66.7	83.4	93.3	68.2	84.3	92.7	70.1	84.6	100.1	76.7	90.3	92.5	69.7	84.3	92.7	71.3	85.0
26, 27, 3370	ELECTRICAL, COMMUNICATIONS & UTIL.	93.3	78.5	86.9	94.0	64.5	81.2	92.8	69.3	82.7	100.6	69.3	87.1	93.0	78.5	86.7	94.0	69.3	83.3
MF2018	WEIGHTED AVERAGE	92.7	71.4	84.9	92.6	71.4	84.8	90.3	69.9	82.8	98.2	74.8	89.6	92.4	73.1	85.3	90.2	74.6	84.5

City Cost Indexes

		KENTUCKY																	
		LEXINGTON			LOUISVILLE			OWENSBORO			PADUCAH			PIKEVILLE			SOMERSET		
	DIVISION	403 - 405			400 - 402			423			420			415 - 416			425 - 426		
		MAT.	INST.	TOTAL	MAT.	INST.	TOTAL	MAT.	INST.	TOTAL	MAT.	INST.	TOTAL	MAT.	INST.	TOTAL	MAT.	INST.	TOTAL
015433	CONTRACTOR EQUIPMENT		94.8	94.8		96.9	96.9		106.9	106.9		106.9	106.9		95.4	95.4		94.8	94.8
0241, 31 - 34	SITE & INFRASTRUCTURE, DEMOLITION	86.9	89.7	88.7	80.5	98.5	92.2	84.3	109.7	100.8	75.1	108.4	96.8	105.9	75.4	86.0	72.6	87.2	82.1
0310	Concrete Forming & Accessories	98.4	70.7	76.9	98.9	78.7	83.2	89.5	73.9	77.4	87.3	73.6	76.6	94.9	77.5	81.4	85.3	69.5	73.0
0320	Concrete Reinforcing	98.2	84.9	94.5	97.5	85.0	94.1	90.9	75.2	86.6	91.5	74.0	86.6	93.4	85.9	91.3	91.3	83.0	89.0
0330	Cast-in-Place Concrete	89.7	79.9	86.2	84.4	70.7	79.5	87.1	80.0	84.6	79.6	74.3	77.7	93.7	81.7	89.4	74.7	80.4	76.7
03	CONCRETE	87.8	77.1	83.6	87.6	77.3	83.5	94.8	76.9	87.7	89.1	74.5	83.3	100.0	81.9	92.8	78.8	76.3	77.8
04	MASONRY	98.6	67.4	79.7	96.4	69.4	80.0	91.7	75.2	81.7	94.9	71.3	80.6	91.1	75.0	81.3	86.4	57.0	68.5
05	METALS	100.6	88.0	98.1	101.6	86.0	98.5	86.8	85.5	86.5	83.8	84.0	83.9	93.6	102.7	95.4	94.2	86.3	92.7
06	WOOD, PLASTICS & COMPOSITES	90.1	68.8	80.6	94.6	80.6	88.3	83.0	72.9	78.5	80.1	74.0	77.4	83.8	79.6	81.9	77.4	70.5	74.3
07	THERMAL & MOISTURE PROTECTION	104.2	74.3	93.5	100.4	74.3	91.1	101.4	77.1	92.7	100.9	74.2	91.4	94.1	72.3	86.3	100.8	64.6	87.9
08	OPENINGS	91.5	72.8	87.3	98.2	76.8	93.4	88.4	74.7	85.3	87.7	73.5	84.5	89.8	78.0	87.1	90.6	69.9	85.9
0920	Plaster & Gypsum Board	100.4	67.7	79.7	96.6	80.2	86.2	80.2	71.9	74.9	79.2	73.0	75.3	64.0	79.4	73.8	76.9	69.4	72.2
0950, 0980	Ceilings & Acoustic Treatment	76.4	67.7	71.6	94.1	80.2	86.3	78.4	71.9	74.8	78.4	73.0	75.4	80.9	79.4	80.0	83.4	69.4	75.6
0960	Flooring	93.0	59.9	84.7	93.8	58.2	84.9	93.7	56.5	84.4	92.9	68.1	86.7	76.5	57.6	71.8	91.7	57.6	83.2
0970, 0990	Wall Finishes & Painting/Coating	87.7	75.1	80.2	94.9	66.1	77.8	91.3	84.6	87.3	91.3	65.0	75.6	92.7	81.5	86.0	91.3	60.5	73.0
09	FINISHES	87.6	68.4	78.0	94.3	73.5	83.9	87.3	71.3	79.3	86.7	71.7	79.1	79.9	74.5	77.2	87.2	66.1	76.6
COVERS	DIVS. 10 - 14, 25, 28, 41, 43, 44, 46	100.0	89.5	98.0	100.0	89.5	98.0	100.0	90.4	98.1	100.0	81.4	96.4	100.0	43.4	89.0	100.0	88.1	97.7
21, 22, 23	FIRE SUPPRESSION, PLUMBING & HVAC	100.3	72.6	90.4	100.0	76.7	91.6	100.0	73.5	90.5	92.7	70.3	84.7	92.1	73.9	85.6	92.7	66.5	83.3
26, 27, 3370	ELECTRICAL, COMMUNICATIONS & UTIL.	94.7	70.5	84.2	100.6	73.6	88.9	94.0	68.3	82.9	95.3	68.8	83.8	93.4	78.6	87.0	93.2	78.5	86.8
MF2018	WEIGHTED AVERAGE	96.2	75.2	88.5	97.7	78.2	90.5	93.1	77.7	87.5	90.1	75.8	84.9	93.3	77.8	87.6	90.8	72.8	84.1

		LOUISIANA																	
		ALEXANDRIA			BATON ROUGE			HAMMOND			LAFAYETTE			LAKE CHARLES			MONROE		
	DIVISION	713 - 714			707 - 708			704			705			706			712		
		MAT.	INST.	TOTAL	MAT.	INST.	TOTAL	MAT.	INST.	TOTAL	MAT.	INST.	TOTAL	MAT.	INST.	TOTAL	MAT.	INST.	TOTAL
015433	CONTRACTOR EQUIPMENT		88.4	88.4		95.2	95.2		87.3	87.3		87.3	87.3		86.8	86.8		88.4	88.4
0241, 31 - 34	SITE & INFRASTRUCTURE, DEMOLITION	99.8	84.9	90.1	102.2	96.3	98.3	96.9	84.4	88.8	101.2	84.6	90.4	101.8	84.0	90.2	99.8	84.8	90.0
0310	Concrete Forming & Accessories	81.9	57.8	63.1	99.2	67.6	74.7	78.3	51.6	57.5	96.9	61.9	69.7	97.0	65.2	72.3	81.4	57.3	62.7
0320	Concrete Reinforcing	97.3	50.7	84.4	98.7	50.8	85.5	93.7	48.9	81.3	95.1	48.9	82.3	95.1	50.7	82.8	96.2	50.7	83.6
0330	Cast-in-Place Concrete	78.2	64.5	73.3	87.8	67.7	80.6	83.1	63.3	76.0	82.7	64.9	76.4	87.0	65.8	79.5	78.2	63.8	73.1
03	CONCRETE	80.8	59.8	72.5	88.3	65.4	79.3	83.3	56.2	72.6	85.0	61.5	75.7	86.8	63.6	77.6	80.5	59.4	72.2
04	MASONRY	114.1	60.7	81.6	84.5	58.6	68.8	89.0	58.5	70.5	88.9	61.5	72.3	88.6	62.9	73.0	108.8	59.5	78.8
05	METALS	99.1	70.3	93.4	101.8	72.8	96.1	89.3	68.4	85.2	88.6	68.5	84.6	88.6	69.2	84.8	99.0	70.3	93.3
06	WOOD, PLASTICS & COMPOSITES	82.1	56.6	70.7	94.5	70.6	83.8	73.6	49.4	62.7	97.8	61.8	81.6	95.6	65.4	82.1	81.3	56.6	70.2
07	THERMAL & MOISTURE PROTECTION	101.9	62.2	87.7	97.6	64.7	85.9	96.9	59.9	83.6	97.4	63.1	85.2	97.3	64.1	85.5	101.8	61.7	87.5
08	OPENINGS	103.7	56.1	92.9	98.0	67.7	91.2	94.8	49.8	84.7	98.3	56.4	88.8	98.3	59.5	89.5	103.6	54.6	92.6
0920	Plaster & Gypsum Board	83.9	55.9	66.1	95.2	69.9	79.2	89.6	48.4	63.5	98.9	61.2	75.0	98.9	65.0	77.4	83.7	55.9	66.0
0950, 0980	Ceilings & Acoustic Treatment	105.0	55.9	77.5	95.0	69.9	80.9	92.4	48.4	67.7	88.3	61.2	73.1	88.8	65.0	75.5	105.0	55.9	77.5
0960	Flooring	92.0	63.4	84.8	99.6	63.4	90.6	92.7	63.4	85.4	99.4	63.4	90.4	99.4	63.4	90.4	91.8	63.4	84.7
0970, 0990	Wall Finishes & Painting/Coating	97.1	56.3	72.8	99.1	56.3	73.6	102.9	53.2	73.3	102.9	53.1	73.2	102.9	56.3	75.1	97.1	58.0	73.8
09	FINISHES	93.4	58.3	75.8	98.8	66.0	82.3	95.0	53.1	74.0	97.2	61.2	79.1	97.3	64.0	80.6	93.3	58.2	75.7
COVERS	DIVS. 10 - 14, 25, 28, 41, 43, 44, 46	100.0	77.9	95.7	100.0	84.6	97.0	100.0	81.6	96.4	100.0	83.9	96.9	100.0	84.7	97.0	100.0	77.5	95.6
21, 22, 23	FIRE SUPPRESSION, PLUMBING & HVAC	100.3	59.5	85.7	100.1	58.2	85.1	92.6	56.6	79.7	100.1	57.8	85.0	100.1	60.6	86.0	100.3	58.4	85.3
26, 27, 3370	ELECTRICAL, COMMUNICATIONS & UTIL.	92.8	50.8	74.6	100.7	54.8	80.8	96.3	62.0	81.4	96.9	56.8	79.5	96.6	61.1	81.2	93.7	54.1	76.6
MF2018	WEIGHTED AVERAGE	97.0	61.8	84.1	98.2	65.6	86.2	92.0	60.8	80.5	94.6	63.0	83.0	94.7	65.3	83.9	96.9	61.7	83.9

		LOUISIANA						MAINE											
		NEW ORLEANS			SHREVEPORT			THIBODAUX			AUGUSTA			BANGOR			BATH		
	DIVISION	700 - 701			710 - 711			703			043			044			045		
		MAT.	INST.	TOTAL	MAT.	INST.	TOTAL	MAT.	INST.	TOTAL	MAT.	INST.	TOTAL	MAT.	INST.	TOTAL	MAT.	INST.	TOTAL
015433	CONTRACTOR EQUIPMENT		91.1	91.1		96.9	96.9		87.3	87.3		98.6	98.6		93.0	93.0		93.0	93.0
0241, 31 - 34	SITE & INFRASTRUCTURE, DEMOLITION	101.6	96.5	98.3	102.0	97.6	99.1	99.0	84.4	89.5	89.0	102.1	97.5	90.0	91.3	90.9	84.9	89.7	88.0
0310	Concrete Forming & Accessories	100.7	69.5	76.4	102.3	59.1	68.8	89.3	58.9	65.7	101.8	74.6	80.6	95.7	77.0	81.2	90.8	74.2	77.9
0320	Concrete Reinforcing	99.2	70.8	91.4	98.7	49.9	85.2	93.7	48.9	81.3	99.0	80.5	93.9	84.5	80.7	83.5	83.7	80.3	82.7
0330	Cast-in-Place Concrete	80.3	71.9	77.3	80.9	66.6	75.8	89.3	63.0	79.9	74.4	106.5	85.8	58.8	110.2	77.0	58.8	105.3	75.3
03	CONCRETE	87.9	70.5	81.0	86.4	60.9	76.4	87.4	59.4	76.4	93.4	87.3	91.0	84.0	89.9	86.3	83.7	86.9	84.9
04	MASONRY	92.7	63.4	74.9	96.5	59.9	74.3	111.4	58.1	79.0	113.3	89.3	98.7	126.9	91.7	105.5	134.3	86.9	105.5
05	METALS	99.3	69.9	93.5	101.9	68.2	95.2	89.3	68.4	85.2	105.2	90.8	102.4	91.3	93.6	91.7	89.7	92.4	90.2
06	WOOD, PLASTICS & COMPOSITES	98.4	71.6	86.4	98.7	58.8	80.8	82.2	59.6	72.1	100.8	71.3	87.6	95.1	74.0	85.7	87.5	71.3	80.2
07	THERMAL & MOISTURE PROTECTION	95.1	68.7	85.7	99.4	63.7	86.7	97.1	60.5	84.0	82.4	95.7	87.2	89.5	99.2	93.0	89.4	93.6	90.9
08	OPENINGS	100.0	68.5	92.9	98.1	54.4	88.2	99.0	51.6	88.4	98.2	75.6	93.1	95.2	80.2	91.8	95.2	74.7	90.6
0920	Plaster & Gypsum Board	87.0	70.9	76.8	100.9	57.7	73.5	91.1	58.9	70.7	91.3	70.3	78.0	96.0	73.2	81.5	89.7	70.3	77.4
0950, 0980	Ceilings & Acoustic Treatment	85.5	70.9	77.3	119.0	57.7	84.7	92.4	58.9	73.6	108.2	70.3	87.0	77.3	73.2	75.0	77.3	70.3	73.4
0960	Flooring	102.8	68.6	94.3	99.2	63.4	90.3	97.1	62.9	88.5	107.7	103.1	106.6	99.3	103.1	100.2	97.8	99.1	98.1
0970, 0990	Wall Finishes & Painting/Coating	113.5	59.9	81.5	99.1	58.0	74.6	102.9	53.2	73.3	113.5	83.8	95.8	99.1	93.6	95.8	99.1	79.0	87.1
09	FINISHES	98.8	68.5	83.6	105.1	59.6	82.2	96.7	58.9	77.7	105.3	79.8	92.5	92.0	82.5	87.2	90.7	78.5	84.6
COVERS	DIVS. 10 - 14, 25, 28, 41, 43, 44, 46	100.0	85.3	97.2	100.0	78.7	95.9	100.0	82.5	96.6	100.0	95.0	99.0	100.0	99.9	100.0	100.0	90.9	98.2
21, 22, 23	FIRE SUPPRESSION, PLUMBING & HVAC	99.7	66.5	85.8	100.1	57.1	85.4	92.6	56.3	79.6	99.7	71.6	89.6	100.2	75.4	91.3	92.7	71.6	85.1
26, 27, 3370	ELECTRICAL, COMMUNICATIONS & UTIL.	104.5	67.7	88.5	101.3	60.7	83.7	95.6	62.0	81.0	104.3	72.5	90.5	100.0	65.5	85.1	98.9	72.5	87.5
MF2018	WEIGHTED AVERAGE	98.3	69.5	87.7	99.0	64.1	86.2	93.9	62.2	82.2	100.7	82.4	94.0	95.7	83.1	91.0	93.5	80.9	88.9

City Cost Indexes

		\multicolumn{18}{c}{MAINE}
		\multicolumn{3}{c}{HOULTON}	\multicolumn{3}{c}{KITTERY}	\multicolumn{3}{c}{LEWISTON}	\multicolumn{3}{c}{MACHIAS}	\multicolumn{3}{c}{PORTLAND}	\multicolumn{3}{c}{ROCKLAND}
\multicolumn{2}{c}{DIVISION}	\multicolumn{3}{c}{047}	\multicolumn{3}{c}{039}	\multicolumn{3}{c}{042}	\multicolumn{3}{c}{046}	\multicolumn{3}{c}{040 - 041}	\multicolumn{3}{c}{048}
		MAT.	INST.	TOTAL	MAT.	INST.	TOTAL	MAT.	INST.	TOTAL	MAT.	INST.	TOTAL	MAT.	INST.	TOTAL	MAT.	INST.	TOTAL
015433	CONTRACTOR EQUIPMENT		93.0	93.0		93.0	93.0		93.0	93.0		93.0	93.0		95.9	95.9		93.0	93.0
0241, 31 - 34	SITE & INFRASTRUCTURE, DEMOLITION	86.4	89.7	88.6	75.5	89.7	84.8	88.8	91.3	90.5	85.8	89.7	88.4	89.5	97.7	94.8	83.3	89.7	87.5
0310	Concrete Forming & Accessories	100.3	74.1	80.0	91.8	74.3	78.2	102.2	77.0	82.6	96.7	74.1	79.2	104.7	77.7	83.7	98.0	74.2	79.5
0320	Concrete Reinforcing	84.5	80.3	83.4	84.5	80.3	83.3	103.9	80.7	97.5	84.5	80.3	83.4	97.8	80.9	93.1	84.5	80.3	83.4
0330	Cast-in-Place Concrete	58.8	104.3	74.9	58.9	105.3	75.4	60.0	110.2	77.8	58.8	105.3	75.3	71.1	111.5	85.4	60.0	105.3	76.1
03	CONCRETE	85.0	86.5	85.6	79.4	86.9	82.4	86.9	89.9	88.1	84.4	86.8	85.4	91.9	90.6	91.4	82.1	86.9	84.0
04	MASONRY	106.4	86.9	94.5	122.5	86.9	100.8	107.2	91.7	97.8	106.4	86.9	94.5	108.1	91.8	98.2	100.0	86.9	92.0
05	METALS	90.0	92.3	90.4	85.6	92.5	87.0	95.7	93.6	95.3	90.0	92.3	90.5	100.8	92.2	99.1	89.8	92.4	90.3
06	WOOD, PLASTICS & COMPOSITES	100.3	71.3	87.3	90.1	71.3	81.6	103.0	74.0	90.0	96.4	71.3	85.1	102.6	74.1	89.8	97.7	71.3	85.8
07	THERMAL & MOISTURE PROTECTION	89.6	93.6	91.0	95.3	93.6	94.7	89.4	99.2	92.9	89.6	93.6	91.0	101.2	100.7	101.0	89.3	93.6	90.8
08	OPENINGS	95.2	74.7	90.6	97.7	77.9	93.2	98.0	80.2	94.0	95.2	74.7	90.6	98.6	80.2	94.4	95.2	74.7	90.6
0920	Plaster & Gypsum Board	97.9	70.3	80.4	102.9	70.3	82.2	103.4	73.2	84.2	97.0	70.3	80.1	108.1	73.2	85.9	97.0	70.3	80.1
0950, 0980	Ceilings & Acoustic Treatment	77.3	70.3	73.4	88.2	70.3	78.2	90.9	73.2	81.0	77.3	70.3	73.4	86.8	73.2	79.2	77.3	70.3	73.4
0960	Flooring	100.5	99.1	100.1	97.1	99.1	97.6	101.8	103.1	102.1	99.8	99.1	99.6	102.5	166.4	118.5	100.1	99.1	99.8
0970, 0990	Wall Finishes & Painting/Coating	99.1	79.0	87.1	82.5	90.7	87.4	99.1	93.6	95.8	99.1	79.0	87.1	99.1	93.6	95.8	99.1	79.0	87.1
09	FINISHES	92.6	78.5	85.5	94.8	79.8	87.2	97.1	82.5	89.8	92.3	78.5	85.3	97.4	95.5	96.4	92.1	78.5	85.2
COVERS	DIVS. 10 - 14, 25, 28, 41, 43, 44, 46	100.0	88.0	97.7	100.0	90.9	98.2	100.0	99.9	100.0	100.0	88.1	97.7	100.0	100.0	100.0	100.0	90.9	98.2
21, 22, 23	FIRE SUPPRESSION, PLUMBING & HVAC	92.7	71.6	85.1	92.8	71.6	85.2	100.2	75.4	91.3	92.7	71.6	85.1	100.1	75.5	91.3	92.7	71.6	85.1
26, 27, 3370	ELECTRICAL, COMMUNICATIONS & UTIL.	101.1	72.5	88.7	100.3	72.5	88.3	101.1	74.8	89.7	101.1	72.5	88.7	101.4	74.8	89.9	101.0	72.5	88.7
MF2018	WEIGHTED AVERAGE	93.2	80.7	88.6	92.3	81.2	88.2	97.0	84.4	92.4	93.1	80.8	88.5	99.2	86.6	94.5	92.4	80.9	88.2

		MAINE			\multicolumn{15}{c}{MARYLAND}
		\multicolumn{3}{c}{WATERVILLE}	\multicolumn{3}{c}{ANNAPOLIS}	\multicolumn{3}{c}{BALTIMORE}	\multicolumn{3}{c}{COLLEGE PARK}	\multicolumn{3}{c}{CUMBERLAND}	\multicolumn{3}{c}{EASTON}
\multicolumn{2}{c}{DIVISION}	\multicolumn{3}{c}{049}	\multicolumn{3}{c}{214}	\multicolumn{3}{c}{210 - 212}	\multicolumn{3}{c}{207 - 208}	\multicolumn{3}{c}{215}	\multicolumn{3}{c}{216}
		MAT.	INST.	TOTAL	MAT.	INST.	TOTAL	MAT.	INST.	TOTAL	MAT.	INST.	TOTAL	MAT.	INST.	TOTAL	MAT.	INST.	TOTAL
015433	CONTRACTOR EQUIPMENT		93.0	93.0		107.1	107.1		105.3	105.3		104.4	104.4		100.8	100.8		100.8	100.8
0241, 31 - 34	SITE & INFRASTRUCTURE, DEMOLITION	86.1	89.7	88.5	109.6	97.1	101.4	110.6	98.5	102.7	105.5	89.4	95.0	98.2	87.2	91.1	104.8	85.6	92.3
0310	Concrete Forming & Accessories	90.2	74.1	77.7	103.0	70.3	77.6	102.9	74.9	81.2	82.5	69.4	72.3	93.3	76.3	80.1	91.2	67.3	72.6
0320	Concrete Reinforcing	84.5	80.3	83.4	98.2	88.7	95.6	100.4	90.6	97.7	97.7	97.0	97.6	87.5	84.7	86.7	86.8	78.2	84.4
0330	Cast-in-Place Concrete	58.8	105.3	75.3	103.7	74.5	93.3	111.4	77.8	99.4	136.4	70.3	112.9	86.0	82.0	84.6	95.6	61.0	83.3
03	CONCRETE	85.1	86.8	85.8	95.1	76.3	87.7	101.7	79.6	93.0	106.4	76.2	94.5	83.5	81.1	82.6	89.2	68.6	81.1
04	MASONRY	118.0	86.9	99.1	98.1	68.6	80.2	105.6	73.9	86.3	123.1	67.3	89.2	100.6	84.5	90.8	114.9	53.1	77.4
05	METALS	89.9	92.3	90.4	101.0	101.1	101.0	100.4	97.8	99.9	84.1	108.6	88.9	95.7	102.1	97.0	96.0	98.5	96.5
06	WOOD, PLASTICS & COMPOSITES	86.6	71.3	79.7	99.6	70.6	86.6	100.6	74.6	89.0	70.9	68.7	69.9	85.4	73.6	80.1	82.6	73.5	78.5
07	THERMAL & MOISTURE PROTECTION	89.5	93.6	91.0	107.6	78.8	97.3	102.8	82.4	95.5	101.3	74.5	91.7	101.6	76.8	92.8	101.8	67.4	89.5
08	OPENINGS	95.2	74.7	90.6	98.5	79.7	94.2	99.7	80.3	95.3	92.9	78.6	89.6	93.4	78.3	90.0	91.8	76.3	88.3
0920	Plaster & Gypsum Board	89.7	70.3	77.4	115.1	69.7	86.3	115.1	73.7	88.8	98.6	68.1	79.3	114.5	73.2	88.3	114.5	73.1	88.2
0950, 0980	Ceilings & Acoustic Treatment	77.3	70.3	73.4	96.8	69.7	81.6	96.8	73.7	83.8	98.3	68.1	81.4	101.8	73.2	85.8	101.8	73.1	85.7
0960	Flooring	97.6	99.1	98.0	108.4	71.2	99.1	96.0	75.3	90.8	92.5	70.3	86.9	96.0	88.5	94.1	95.3	67.8	88.4
0970, 0990	Wall Finishes & Painting/Coating	99.1	79.0	87.1	99.1	64.8	78.6	99.1	68.5	80.8	93.9	64.8	76.5	93.6	75.2	82.6	93.6	64.8	76.4
09	FINISHES	90.8	78.5	84.6	104.4	69.1	86.7	100.3	73.7	86.9	96.4	68.3	82.3	102.3	78.3	90.2	102.5	67.3	84.8
COVERS	DIVS. 10 - 14, 25, 28, 41, 43, 44, 46	100.0	87.9	97.7	100.0	87.5	97.6	100.0	89.6	98.0	100.0	77.5	95.6	100.0	90.6	98.2	100.0	79.1	95.9
21, 22, 23	FIRE SUPPRESSION, PLUMBING & HVAC	92.7	71.6	85.1	100.0	78.6	92.3	100.1	84.1	94.3	92.6	78.8	87.6	92.3	67.3	83.3	92.3	65.5	82.7
26, 27, 3370	ELECTRICAL, COMMUNICATIONS & UTIL.	101.1	72.5	88.7	100.0	82.1	92.3	100.0	87.0	94.4	100.3	98.9	99.7	99.5	75.9	89.2	99.2	55.5	80.3
MF2018	WEIGHTED AVERAGE	93.4	80.8	88.7	100.2	80.3	92.9	100.9	83.8	94.6	95.6	82.1	90.6	94.8	79.9	89.3	96.1	69.1	86.2

		\multicolumn{15}{c}{MARYLAND}	\multicolumn{3}{c}{MASSACHUSETTS}
		\multicolumn{3}{c}{ELKTON}	\multicolumn{3}{c}{HAGERSTOWN}	\multicolumn{3}{c}{SALISBURY}	\multicolumn{3}{c}{SILVER SPRING}	\multicolumn{3}{c}{WALDORF}	\multicolumn{3}{c}{BOSTON}
\multicolumn{2}{c}{DIVISION}	\multicolumn{3}{c}{219}	\multicolumn{3}{c}{217}	\multicolumn{3}{c}{218}	\multicolumn{3}{c}{209}	\multicolumn{3}{c}{206}	\multicolumn{3}{c}{020 - 022, 024}
		MAT.	INST.	TOTAL	MAT.	INST.	TOTAL	MAT.	INST.	TOTAL	MAT.	INST.	TOTAL	MAT.	INST.	TOTAL	MAT.	INST.	TOTAL
015433	CONTRACTOR EQUIPMENT		100.8	100.8		100.8	100.8		100.8	100.8		97.2	97.2		97.2	97.2		103.3	103.3
0241, 31 - 34	SITE & INFRASTRUCTURE, DEMOLITION	92.6	86.1	88.3	99.7	87.5	91.8	104.8	85.4	92.1	92.9	82.3	86.0	99.0	82.1	88.0	89.8	103.7	98.8
0310	Concrete Forming & Accessories	97.9	83.8	86.9	92.2	80.7	83.3	107.6	46.1	59.8	90.8	68.7	73.6	98.6	68.6	75.3	106.5	137.3	130.4
0320	Concrete Reinforcing	86.8	105.3	91.9	87.5	84.7	86.7	86.8	58.6	79.0	97.0	97.0	97.0	97.7	96.9	97.5	101.1	149.3	114.4
0330	Cast-in-Place Concrete	77.4	66.9	73.6	82.0	82.1	82.0	95.6	59.1	82.6	139.6	70.6	115.1	156.5	70.4	125.9	80.3	140.6	101.7
03	CONCRETE	78.3	82.8	80.1	80.9	83.2	81.8	90.6	55.0	76.5	106.2	75.8	94.2	115.9	75.7	100.0	96.7	139.9	113.7
04	MASONRY	100.1	60.5	76.0	106.2	84.5	93.0	114.0	50.0	75.1	122.4	67.6	89.1	105.7	67.5	82.5	121.3	144.5	135.4
05	METALS	96.0	109.3	98.6	95.8	102.5	97.1	96.0	90.0	94.8	89.0	104.9	92.2	89.0	104.4	92.1	98.7	132.8	105.4
06	WOOD, PLASTICS & COMPOSITES	91.4	91.9	91.7	84.3	79.1	81.9	105.4	46.9	79.1	78.5	68.1	73.8	86.7	68.1	78.3	104.9	136.7	119.1
07	THERMAL & MOISTURE PROTECTION	101.4	72.9	91.2	101.9	82.3	94.9	102.1	63.1	88.2	104.0	78.8	95.0	104.5	78.8	95.4	96.5	137.7	111.2
08	OPENINGS	91.8	93.6	92.2	91.8	81.3	89.4	92.0	56.2	84.0	84.9	78.2	83.4	85.5	78.2	83.8	98.6	143.4	108.7
0920	Plaster & Gypsum Board	117.9	92.1	101.5	114.5	78.9	91.9	130.2	45.6	76.6	108.2	68.1	82.8	111.1	68.1	83.8	123.5	137.7	132.5
0950, 0980	Ceilings & Acoustic Treatment	101.8	92.1	96.4	103.3	78.9	89.6	101.8	45.6	70.3	107.4	68.1	85.4	107.4	68.1	85.4	101.3	137.7	121.7
0960	Flooring	97.3	67.8	89.9	95.6	88.5	93.8	100.4	67.8	92.2	98.2	70.3	91.2	100.8	70.3	93.2	104.8	159.0	118.4
0970, 0990	Wall Finishes & Painting/Coating	93.6	64.8	76.4	93.6	67.2	77.8	93.6	64.8	76.4	100.6	64.8	79.2	100.6	64.8	79.2	99.1	156.1	133.1
09	FINISHES	102.7	79.9	91.3	102.3	80.6	91.4	106.2	50.8	78.4	98.0	67.7	82.8	99.5	67.8	83.6	104.2	143.9	124.1
COVERS	DIVS. 10 - 14, 25, 28, 41, 43, 44, 46	100.0	51.1	90.5	100.0	91.2	98.3	100.0	75.2	95.2	100.0	76.2	95.4	100.0	74.3	95.0	100.0	116.7	103.2
21, 22, 23	FIRE SUPPRESSION, PLUMBING & HVAC	92.3	70.8	84.6	99.8	83.9	94.1	92.3	63.7	82.0	92.6	79.2	87.8	92.6	79.1	87.8	100.0	133.0	111.9
26, 27, 3370	ELECTRICAL, COMMUNICATIONS & UTIL.	100.1	77.4	90.3	99.4	75.9	89.2	98.6	53.5	79.1	95.9	98.9	97.2	94.6	98.9	96.5	102.6	126.4	112.9
MF2018	WEIGHTED AVERAGE	94.2	78.8	88.5	96.3	84.3	91.9	96.7	62.0	83.9	95.5	81.2	90.2	96.3	81.1	90.7	100.3	133.3	112.5

City Cost Indexes

		MASSACHUSETTS																	
	DIVISION	BROCKTON			BUZZARDS BAY			FALL RIVER			FITCHBURG			FRAMINGHAM			GREENFIELD		
		023			025			027			014			017			013		
		MAT.	INST.	TOTAL	MAT.	INST.	TOTAL	MAT.	INST.	TOTAL	MAT.	INST.	TOTAL	MAT.	INST.	TOTAL	MAT.	INST.	TOTAL
015433	CONTRACTOR EQUIPMENT		96.0	96.0		96.0	96.0		96.8	96.8		93.0	93.0		94.5	94.5		93.0	93.0
0241, 31 - 34	SITE & INFRASTRUCTURE, DEMOLITION	88.1	94.3	92.2	77.1	94.0	88.1	87.4	94.4	92.0	79.1	93.6	88.6	76.7	93.1	87.4	82.3	92.2	88.7
0310	Concrete Forming & Accessories	98.0	115.4	111.5	95.7	114.6	110.4	98.0	115.1	111.3	94.9	108.2	105.2	103.2	115.3	112.6	93.0	111.8	107.6
0320	Concrete Reinforcing	98.5	135.8	108.9	79.0	114.2	88.7	98.5	114.3	102.9	81.3	127.9	94.2	81.3	135.6	96.3	83.5	113.8	91.9
0330	Cast-in-Place Concrete	69.1	125.5	89.2	57.5	125.2	81.5	66.9	125.7	87.8	63.2	125.1	85.2	63.2	125.3	85.3	64.9	111.2	81.4
03	CONCRETE	88.3	122.4	101.7	74.7	118.2	91.8	86.3	118.6	99.0	75.8	117.4	92.2	78.3	122.2	95.6	78.6	111.6	91.7
04	MASONRY	119.6	128.1	124.8	110.6	128.1	121.2	120.0	128.1	124.9	107.1	120.4	115.2	114.0	124.2	120.2	112.5	111.4	111.8
05	METALS	94.4	124.2	100.3	87.7	114.7	93.0	94.4	115.3	98.5	92.2	116.8	97.0	92.2	123.2	98.4	96.2	108.5	98.6
06	WOOD, PLASTICS & COMPOSITES	95.7	114.6	104.2	91.4	114.6	101.8	95.7	114.8	104.3	95.2	105.6	99.9	103.8	114.4	108.5	92.5	114.9	102.5
07	THERMAL & MOISTURE PROTECTION	93.5	119.4	102.7	92.5	116.3	101.0	93.3	116.2	101.5	92.6	112.4	99.7	92.8	117.2	101.5	92.6	103.1	96.4
08	OPENINGS	94.9	122.6	101.2	91.3	112.2	96.0	94.9	113.2	99.0	97.8	115.6	101.8	88.2	122.5	96.0	97.8	113.7	101.4
0920	Plaster & Gypsum Board	109.0	115.0	112.8	99.4	115.0	109.3	109.0	115.0	112.8	108.2	105.7	106.6	113.1	115.0	114.3	110.5	115.3	113.5
0950, 0980	Ceilings & Acoustic Treatment	104.8	115.0	110.5	86.1	115.0	102.3	104.8	115.0	110.5	85.4	105.7	96.8	85.4	115.0	102.0	97.2	115.3	107.4
0960	Flooring	102.9	149.0	114.5	100.5	149.0	112.7	101.5	149.0	113.5	96.7	149.0	109.8	97.6	149.0	110.5	96.0	128.3	104.1
0970, 0990	Wall Finishes & Painting/Coating	87.3	129.5	112.5	87.3	129.5	112.5	87.3	129.5	112.5	89.2	129.5	113.3	90.0	129.5	113.6	89.2	107.2	99.9
09	FINISHES	100.7	123.3	112.0	93.2	123.3	108.3	100.3	123.4	111.9	93.0	118.0	105.6	93.8	123.1	108.5	96.5	115.3	105.9
COVERS	DIVS. 10 - 14, 25, 28, 41, 43, 44, 46	100.0	110.7	102.1	100.0	110.7	102.1	100.0	111.1	102.2	100.0	99.8	100.0	100.0	110.2	102.0	100.0	103.4	100.7
21, 22, 23	FIRE SUPPRESSION, PLUMBING & HVAC	100.6	98.5	99.8	93.1	93.9	93.3	100.6	98.2	99.7	93.0	94.9	93.7	93.0	109.8	99.0	93.0	92.7	92.9
26, 27, 3370	ELECTRICAL, COMMUNICATIONS & UTIL.	101.6	92.3	97.6	100.0	89.2	95.3	101.1	93.6	97.8	100.5	92.7	97.1	98.7	110.7	103.9	100.5	93.9	97.6
MF2018	WEIGHTED AVERAGE	97.5	111.2	102.6	91.1	107.8	97.2	97.2	109.5	101.7	92.7	106.7	97.9	92.4	115.5	100.9	94.4	103.4	97.7

		MASSACHUSETTS																	
	DIVISION	HYANNIS			LAWRENCE			LOWELL			NEW BEDFORD			PITTSFIELD			SPRINGFIELD		
		026			019			018			027			012			010 - 011		
		MAT.	INST.	TOTAL	MAT.	INST.	TOTAL	MAT.	INST.	TOTAL	MAT.	INST.	TOTAL	MAT.	INST.	TOTAL	MAT.	INST.	TOTAL
015433	CONTRACTOR EQUIPMENT		96.0	96.0		95.1	95.1		93.0	93.0		96.8	96.8		93.0	93.0		93.0	93.0
0241, 31 - 34	SITE & INFRASTRUCTURE, DEMOLITION	85.0	94.2	91.0	89.6	93.7	92.3	88.8	94.0	92.2	86.4	94.4	91.6	89.5	92.3	91.3	89.1	92.6	91.4
0310	Concrete Forming & Accessories	89.3	115.0	109.3	104.6	115.8	113.3	100.7	117.6	113.8	98.0	115.2	111.4	100.7	100.1	100.3	101.0	113.0	110.3
0320	Concrete Reinforcing	79.0	114.3	88.8	100.5	133.5	109.7	101.4	133.3	110.2	98.5	114.2	102.9	82.9	110.6	90.6	101.4	113.8	104.5
0330	Cast-in-Place Concrete	63.1	125.4	85.2	73.1	125.5	91.7	66.5	128.2	88.4	58.9	125.8	82.7	72.5	109.5	85.7	69.2	112.9	84.7
03	CONCRETE	78.8	118.4	94.4	91.8	122.1	103.8	85.7	123.7	100.7	84.1	118.7	97.7	83.3	105.3	92.0	86.8	112.8	97.1
04	MASONRY	118.4	128.1	124.3	120.4	130.5	126.5	106.1	131.5	121.6	118.7	126.7	123.6	106.7	106.5	106.6	106.4	114.5	111.3
05	METALS	89.2	115.1	94.3	96.6	123.3	101.9	96.6	120.3	101.3	94.4	115.3	98.5	96.4	106.9	98.4	99.5	108.6	101.3
06	WOOD, PLASTICS & COMPOSITES	83.6	114.6	97.5	105.0	114.6	109.3	103.5	114.6	108.4	95.7	114.8	104.3	103.5	100.4	102.1	103.5	114.9	108.6
07	THERMAL & MOISTURE PROTECTION	92.9	118.6	102.0	93.2	120.1	102.8	93.0	121.1	103.0	93.3	115.6	101.3	93.1	99.7	95.4	93.0	104.5	97.1
08	OPENINGS	91.8	113.4	96.7	91.6	121.9	98.4	98.9	121.9	104.1	94.8	117.3	100.0	98.9	104.9	100.2	98.9	113.7	102.2
0920	Plaster & Gypsum Board	94.4	115.0	107.4	117.5	115.0	115.9	117.5	115.0	115.9	109.0	115.0	112.8	117.5	100.4	106.6	117.5	115.3	116.1
0950, 0980	Ceilings & Acoustic Treatment	91.2	115.0	104.5	97.7	115.0	107.4	97.7	115.0	107.4	104.8	115.0	110.5	97.7	100.4	99.2	97.7	115.3	107.6
0960	Flooring	98.3	149.0	111.0	98.5	149.0	111.2	98.5	149.0	111.2	101.5	149.0	113.5	98.7	123.4	104.9	97.7	128.3	105.5
0970, 0990	Wall Finishes & Painting/Coating	87.3	129.5	112.5	89.3	129.5	113.3	89.2	129.5	113.3	87.3	129.5	112.5	89.2	107.2	99.9	89.9	107.2	100.2
09	FINISHES	93.5	123.3	108.5	98.5	123.3	110.9	98.5	124.5	111.5	100.2	123.4	111.9	98.5	105.3	101.9	98.3	116.1	107.3
COVERS	DIVS. 10 - 14, 25, 28, 41, 43, 44, 46	100.0	110.7	102.1	100.0	110.7	102.1	100.0	112.3	102.4	100.0	111.1	102.2	100.0	101.1	100.2	100.0	104.4	100.9
21, 22, 23	FIRE SUPPRESSION, PLUMBING & HVAC	100.6	102.4	101.3	100.0	113.5	104.8	100.0	119.4	107.0	100.6	98.2	99.7	100.0	89.8	96.4	100.0	94.3	97.9
26, 27, 3370	ELECTRICAL, COMMUNICATIONS & UTIL.	100.8	93.5	97.6	100.0	116.1	107.0	100.2	115.0	106.6	102.5	95.4	99.4	100.2	93.9	97.5	100.3	95.1	98.0
MF2018	WEIGHTED AVERAGE	94.1	110.4	100.1	97.8	117.8	105.2	97.1	119.2	105.2	97.0	109.8	101.7	96.9	99.3	97.7	97.9	104.6	100.4

		MASSACHUSETTS			MICHIGAN														
	DIVISION	WORCESTER			ANN ARBOR			BATTLE CREEK			BAY CITY			DEARBORN			DETROIT		
		015 - 016			481			490			487			481			482		
		MAT.	INST.	TOTAL	MAT.	INST.	TOTAL	MAT.	INST.	TOTAL	MAT.	INST.	TOTAL	MAT.	INST.	TOTAL	MAT.	INST.	TOTAL
015433	CONTRACTOR EQUIPMENT		93.0	93.0		104.6	104.6		94.2	94.2		104.6	104.6		104.6	104.6		95.0	95.0
0241, 31 - 34	SITE & INFRASTRUCTURE, DEMOLITION	89.1	93.6	92.0	82.5	88.4	86.4	86.1	79.0	81.5	77.1	87.1	83.6	82.3	88.5	86.4	94.4	98.7	97.2
0310	Concrete Forming & Accessories	101.3	116.5	113.1	98.0	99.0	98.8	103.1	78.9	84.3	98.1	75.4	80.5	97.9	99.7	99.3	95.6	104.4	102.4
0320	Concrete Reinforcing	101.4	140.0	112.1	97.1	98.7	97.6	94.6	76.8	89.7	97.1	98.0	97.4	97.1	99.9	97.9	100.7	100.4	100.6
0330	Cast-in-Place Concrete	68.8	125.2	88.8	91.2	93.9	92.2	80.8	89.3	83.8	87.3	82.0	85.4	89.2	94.7	91.2	108.6	99.4	105.4
03	CONCRETE	86.7	123.3	101.1	88.9	98.2	92.5	84.9	82.1	83.8	87.2	83.3	85.6	88.0	99.0	92.4	98.8	101.4	99.8
04	MASONRY	106.1	126.7	118.6	104.1	94.0	98.0	100.8	74.0	84.5	103.6	78.6	88.4	103.9	116.0	111.3	108.0	97.3	101.5
05	METALS	99.6	122.5	104.1	95.0	113.9	98.7	101.5	81.9	97.7	95.6	110.1	98.5	95.1	115.7	99.1	95.8	92.5	95.2
06	WOOD, PLASTICS & COMPOSITES	104.1	116.3	109.6	93.3	100.5	96.5	98.6	78.5	89.6	93.3	74.3	84.8	93.3	100.5	96.5	92.3	106.7	98.8
07	THERMAL & MOISTURE PROTECTION	93.0	115.3	101.0	109.4	93.9	103.9	104.1	75.1	93.8	107.2	79.9	97.5	108.0	101.2	105.6	108.2	103.9	106.7
08	OPENINGS	98.9	124.7	104.7	91.3	96.0	92.4	84.5	73.6	82.1	91.3	78.6	88.4	91.3	96.0	92.4	98.6	101.3	99.2
0920	Plaster & Gypsum Board	117.5	116.7	117.0	103.8	100.4	101.5	86.2	75.1	79.1	103.5	73.5	84.5	103.5	100.4	101.5	109.5	107.0	107.9
0950, 0980	Ceilings & Acoustic Treatment	97.7	116.6	108.4	101.1	100.4	100.7	82.2	75.1	78.2	101.6	73.5	85.8	101.1	100.4	100.7	113.1	107.0	109.7
0960	Flooring	98.5	150.2	111.4	92.6	104.0	95.5	101.3	63.3	91.7	92.6	80.2	89.5	91.6	98.5	93.3	97.8	103.4	99.2
0970, 0990	Wall Finishes & Painting/Coating	89.2	129.5	113.3	86.1	93.7	90.6	88.7	67.7	76.2	86.1	76.9	80.6	86.1	92.0	89.6	99.1	95.5	97.0
09	FINISHES	98.5	124.5	111.5	97.3	99.5	98.4	90.7	74.5	82.6	97.1	75.7	86.3	97.0	98.7	97.8	103.8	103.7	103.8
COVERS	DIVS. 10 - 14, 25, 28, 41, 43, 44, 46	100.0	105.4	101.1	100.0	100.0	100.0	100.0	101.1	100.2	100.0	94.4	98.9	100.0	100.4	100.1	100.0	100.6	100.1
21, 22, 23	FIRE SUPPRESSION, PLUMBING & HVAC	100.0	99.2	99.7	100.2	88.7	96.1	99.9	76.2	91.4	100.2	78.6	92.5	100.2	99.1	99.8	100.2	100.2	100.2
26, 27, 3370	ELECTRICAL, COMMUNICATIONS & UTIL.	100.3	98.3	99.4	96.1	97.3	96.6	93.7	69.2	83.1	95.0	73.4	85.7	96.1	92.6	94.6	100.6	100.0	100.3
MF2018	WEIGHTED AVERAGE	97.9	111.9	103.1	96.2	96.4	96.3	95.7	77.0	88.8	95.8	82.2	90.8	96.1	100.1	97.5	99.5	99.9	99.7

City Cost Indexes

MICHIGAN

DIVISION		FLINT 484-485			GAYLORD 497			GRAND RAPIDS 493,495			IRON MOUNTAIN 498-499			JACKSON 492			KALAMAZOO 491		
		MAT.	INST.	TOTAL	MAT.	INST.	TOTAL	MAT.	INST.	TOTAL	MAT.	INST.	TOTAL	MAT.	INST.	TOTAL	MAT.	INST.	TOTAL
015433	CONTRACTOR EQUIPMENT		104.6	104.6		100.9	100.9		99.4	99.4		89.7	89.7		100.9	100.9		94.2	94.2
0241, 31-34	SITE & INFRASTRUCTURE, DEMOLITION	75.3	87.4	83.2	82.8	76.8	78.9	85.1	91.0	89.0	85.2	84.8	84.9	94.4	78.4	84.0	86.3	79.0	81.6
0310	Concrete Forming & Accessories	101.4	83.8	87.7	101.6	67.3	74.9	100.7	75.0	80.8	95.1	71.4	76.7	97.9	74.8	80.0	103.1	79.2	84.5
0320	Concrete Reinforcing	97.1	98.3	97.5	88.4	83.4	87.0	98.7	76.8	92.7	87.6	76.3	84.4	85.8	97.9	89.1	94.6	75.5	89.4
0330	Cast-in-Place Concrete	91.8	84.7	89.3	80.6	72.0	77.5	84.9	86.4	85.5	95.4	62.3	83.7	80.5	85.5	82.2	82.4	89.4	84.9
03	CONCRETE	89.4	88.0	88.8	81.7	73.5	78.5	91.4	79.3	86.6	88.1	70.0	81.0	77.9	84.0	80.3	87.1	82.1	85.1
04	MASONRY	104.1	87.0	93.7	111.9	65.5	83.7	97.9	72.2	82.3	96.3	71.8	81.4	90.1	78.2	82.9	99.1	80.4	87.7
05	METALS	95.1	110.7	98.2	103.0	105.5	103.5	97.9	80.5	94.5	102.2	87.4	99.3	103.3	108.6	104.4	101.5	82.0	97.7
06	WOOD, PLASTICS & COMPOSITES	98.0	83.6	91.5	92.0	66.7	80.7	97.8	74.0	87.1	92.0	71.7	82.9	90.6	72.5	82.4	98.6	78.5	89.6
07	THERMAL & MOISTURE PROTECTION	107.5	85.1	99.5	102.7	67.1	90.0	105.7	69.8	92.9	106.0	67.1	92.2	102.1	79.6	94.1	104.1	77.1	94.5
08	OPENINGS	91.3	83.0	89.4	83.6	71.4	80.8	98.8	72.8	93.0	89.5	63.3	83.6	82.8	78.8	81.9	84.5	74.7	82.3
0920	Plaster & Gypsum Board	105.9	83.0	91.4	85.5	65.0	72.5	93.9	70.9	79.3	55.4	71.5	65.7	84.1	70.9	75.7	86.2	75.1	79.1
0950, 0980	Ceilings & Acoustic Treatment	101.1	83.0	91.0	79.9	65.0	71.6	90.9	70.9	79.7	80.6	71.5	75.5	79.9	70.9	74.9	82.2	75.1	78.2
0960	Flooring	92.6	85.2	90.8	93.2	76.7	89.1	103.9	82.6	98.6	117.8	81.5	108.7	92.2	70.4	86.8	101.3	70.7	93.7
0970, 0990	Wall Finishes & Painting/Coating	86.1	75.6	79.8	84.4	72.5	77.3	99.1	72.5	83.3	103.1	61.9	78.5	84.4	83.3	83.8	88.7	73.4	79.6
09	FINISHES	96.9	82.8	89.8	89.3	68.8	79.0	97.0	75.8	86.3	93.5	72.2	82.8	89.8	73.9	81.8	90.7	76.6	83.6
COVERS	DIVS. 10-14, 25, 28, 41, 43, 44, 46	100.0	96.6	99.3	100.0	93.5	98.7	100.0	99.2	99.8	100.0	91.9	98.4	100.0	96.3	99.3	100.0	101.1	100.2
21, 22, 23	FIRE SUPPRESSION, PLUMBING & HVAC	100.2	83.6	94.2	92.8	71.0	85.0	99.9	80.7	93.0	92.6	75.4	86.4	92.9	77.2	87.2	99.9	77.8	92.0
26, 27, 3370	ELECTRICAL, COMMUNICATIONS & UTIL.	96.1	88.9	93.0	92.9	67.9	82.1	99.3	79.9	90.9	96.9	71.8	86.0	94.9	91.7	93.5	93.4	76.6	86.1
MF2018	WEIGHTED AVERAGE	96.1	88.4	93.3	94.0	74.3	86.7	97.8	79.6	91.1	95.3	75.0	87.8	93.3	83.5	89.7	95.8	79.9	89.8

MICHIGAN / MINNESOTA

DIVISION		LANSING 488-489			MUSKEGON 494			ROYAL OAK 480,483			SAGINAW 486			TRAVERSE CITY 496			BEMIDJI 566		
		MAT.	INST.	TOTAL	MAT.	INST.	TOTAL	MAT.	INST.	TOTAL	MAT.	INST.	TOTAL	MAT.	INST.	TOTAL	MAT.	INST.	TOTAL
015433	CONTRACTOR EQUIPMENT		109.0	109.0		94.2	94.2		87.3	87.3		104.6	104.6		89.7	89.7		94.2	94.2
0241, 31-34	SITE & INFRASTRUCTURE, DEMOLITION	89.5	99.0	95.6	84.7	79.0	81.0	80.5	87.1	84.8	78.0	87.1	84.0	74.8	83.9	80.7	82.0	91.0	87.9
0310	Concrete Forming & Accessories	100.6	78.6	83.5	103.6	78.1	83.8	93.6	97.9	96.9	98.0	79.8	83.9	95.1	65.8	72.3	86.7	88.6	88.1
0320	Concrete Reinforcing	99.6	98.1	99.2	95.5	77.2	90.4	88.0	94.0	89.7	97.1	98.0	97.4	88.9	72.0	84.3	95.9	103.8	98.1
0330	Cast-in-Place Concrete	100.6	84.5	94.9	80.5	88.1	83.2	79.8	88.7	83.0	90.1	82.0	87.2	74.4	73.5	74.1	112.1	96.0	106.4
03	CONCRETE	94.3	84.0	90.7	84.1	81.4	83.0	77.8	93.5	84.0	88.4	85.2	87.1	75.8	70.6	73.8	99.0	95.1	97.5
04	MASONRY	99.6	85.4	91.0	98.2	78.9	86.5	97.9	89.7	92.9	105.9	78.6	89.3	94.4	67.4	78.0	106.4	104.8	105.4
05	METALS	97.3	106.4	99.1	100.2	82.5	96.7	97.6	87.6	95.6	95.1	110.0	98.0	102.1	85.4	98.8	91.1	119.6	96.7
06	WOOD, PLASTICS & COMPOSITES	97.8	76.8	88.4	97.3	77.0	88.2	88.8	100.5	94.0	90.9	80.4	86.2	92.0	65.4	80.1	70.5	84.7	76.9
07	THERMAL & MOISTURE PROTECTION	105.2	82.9	97.3	103.2	71.7	92.0	105.8	90.9	100.5	108.1	80.5	98.3	105.2	66.9	91.5	107.1	91.1	101.4
08	OPENINGS	98.7	79.4	94.4	83.7	74.5	81.6	91.1	93.9	91.7	89.7	82.0	88.0	89.5	59.4	82.7	95.8	106.6	98.2
0920	Plaster & Gypsum Board	89.5	76.1	81.0	68.9	73.5	71.8	100.2	100.4	100.3	103.5	79.8	88.4	55.4	65.0	61.5	94.4	84.9	88.3
0950, 0980	Ceilings & Acoustic Treatment	102.2	76.1	87.6	82.2	73.5	77.3	100.3	100.4	100.3	101.1	79.8	89.2	80.6	65.0	71.9	119.3	84.9	100.0
0960	Flooring	93.9	82.6	91.1	100.2	82.6	95.8	90.4	95.5	91.7	92.6	80.2	89.5	117.8	76.7	107.5	96.3	107.4	99.0
0970, 0990	Wall Finishes & Painting/Coating	99.1	73.9	84.1	87.0	73.7	79.1	87.8	83.3	85.2	86.1	76.9	80.6	103.1	35.0	62.5	90.8	94.2	92.8
09	FINISHES	97.2	78.2	87.6	87.4	78.2	82.8	96.1	96.2	96.2	97.0	79.2	88.1	92.7	64.1	78.3	100.1	92.2	96.1
COVERS	DIVS. 10-14, 25, 28, 41, 43, 44, 46	100.0	95.8	99.2	100.0	100.9	100.2	100.0	99.6	99.9	100.0	95.1	99.1	100.0	90.7	98.2	100.0	98.8	99.8
21, 22, 23	FIRE SUPPRESSION, PLUMBING & HVAC	99.9	85.1	94.6	99.8	81.7	93.3	93.1	91.1	92.4	100.2	78.2	92.3	92.6	70.9	84.8	92.8	85.0	90.0
26, 27, 3370	ELECTRICAL, COMMUNICATIONS & UTIL.	99.3	87.4	94.1	94.0	73.1	84.9	97.2	91.8	94.9	95.0	80.8	88.8	94.5	67.9	82.9	100.4	79.8	91.4
MF2018	WEIGHTED AVERAGE	98.2	87.6	94.3	94.8	79.6	89.2	93.5	91.9	92.9	95.8	84.1	91.5	93.2	71.6	85.2	95.8	93.7	95.0

MINNESOTA

DIVISION		BRAINERD 564			DETROIT LAKES 565			DULUTH 556-558			MANKATO 560			MINNEAPOLIS 553-555			ROCHESTER 559		
		MAT.	INST.	TOTAL	MAT.	INST.	TOTAL	MAT.	INST.	TOTAL	MAT.	INST.	TOTAL	MAT.	INST.	TOTAL	MAT.	INST.	TOTAL
015433	CONTRACTOR EQUIPMENT		96.5	96.5		94.2	94.2		102.3	102.3		96.5	96.5		102.8	102.8		96.9	96.9
0241, 31-34	SITE & INFRASTRUCTURE, DEMOLITION	84.9	95.4	91.8	80.7	90.6	87.2	92.6	102.0	98.8	82.4	94.7	90.4	88.3	102.1	97.3	90.7	93.8	92.7
0310	Concrete Forming & Accessories	86.6	91.3	90.3	83.1	76.6	78.1	101.4	104.4	103.8	95.8	101.1	99.9	101.7	120.8	116.6	101.8	104.7	104.0
0320	Concrete Reinforcing	95.2	103.9	97.6	95.9	103.5	98.0	99.0	104.5	100.6	95.1	107.0	98.4	99.3	107.9	101.7	95.5	107.5	98.9
0330	Cast-in-Place Concrete	122.0	100.5	114.4	108.9	97.0	104.7	141.0	107.1	129.0	112.3	101.1	108.3	124.8	119.7	123.0	134.6	102.1	123.0
03	CONCRETE	102.7	97.9	100.8	96.7	90.0	94.1	120.3	106.2	114.7	98.9	103.1	100.6	114.5	118.5	116.1	110.3	105.3	108.3
04	MASONRY	133.3	113.0	121.0	131.9	102.3	113.9	112.8	118.3	116.1	120.9	107.8	113.0	109.4	123.6	118.0	109.2	115.3	112.9
05	METALS	91.9	119.6	97.4	91.0	118.2	96.4	98.4	120.2	102.7	91.8	121.2	97.6	96.9	123.8	102.2	95.9	124.0	101.4
06	WOOD, PLASTICS & COMPOSITES	82.8	84.6	83.6	66.8	67.6	67.1	98.8	102.4	100.4	94.8	99.9	97.1	99.8	119.6	108.1	100.6	103.4	101.8
07	THERMAL & MOISTURE PROTECTION	104.7	98.7	102.6	106.9	94.5	102.5	105.2	106.8	105.8	105.2	93.1	100.9	106.6	121.0	111.7	111.3	100.3	107.4
08	OPENINGS	83.2	106.5	88.5	95.7	97.1	96.0	98.4	113.2	101.7	87.6	115.2	93.8	98.9	127.9	105.5	95.3	117.9	100.4
0920	Plaster & Gypsum Board	79.1	84.9	82.8	93.9	67.2	76.9	91.2	102.8	98.6	83.5	100.6	94.4	88.2	120.3	108.6	94.6	104.1	100.6
0950, 0980	Ceilings & Acoustic Treatment	63.9	84.9	75.6	119.3	67.2	90.1	110.4	102.8	106.1	63.9	100.6	84.5	100.9	120.3	111.8	99.9	104.1	102.3
0960	Flooring	95.3	107.0	98.2	95.2	76.6	90.6	100.6	107.0	102.2	96.2	94.0	95.7	95.5	125.3	103.0	95.5	95.9	95.6
0970, 0990	Wall Finishes & Painting/Coating	84.8	94.2	90.4	90.4	94.2	92.8	99.1	114.7	108.4	96.6	98.4	97.7	99.1	129.3	117.1	89.3	103.3	97.6
09	FINISHES	82.5	93.8	88.2	99.6	77.4	88.5	101.2	106.1	103.7	83.9	100.1	92.0	96.7	122.5	109.7	94.9	103.2	99.1
COVERS	DIVS. 10-14, 25, 28, 41, 43, 44, 46	100.0	99.4	99.9	100.0	97.8	99.6	100.0	101.3	100.2	100.0	101.3	100.2	100.0	107.6	101.5	100.0	102.1	100.4
21, 22, 23	FIRE SUPPRESSION, PLUMBING & HVAC	91.8	87.7	90.7	92.8	86.4	90.5	99.9	98.3	99.3	91.8	90.3	91.3	100.0	116.6	105.9	100.0	100.0	100.0
26, 27, 3370	ELECTRICAL, COMMUNICATIONS & UTIL.	99.5	100.9	100.1	100.2	77.9	90.5	99.7	100.9	100.2	102.9	96.1	99.9	99.5	118.1	107.6	98.8	96.1	97.6
MF2018	WEIGHTED AVERAGE	94.9	99.5	96.9	96.3	90.2	94.1	102.4	106.1	103.8	94.8	100.6	97.0	100.9	118.4	107.4	99.9	104.7	101.7

City Cost Indexes

		MINNESOTA																	MISSISSIPPI		
		SAINT PAUL			ST. CLOUD			THIEF RIVER FALLS			WILLMAR			WINDOM			BILOXI		
DIVISION		550 - 551			563			567			562			561			395		
		MAT.	INST.	TOTAL	MAT.	INST.	TOTAL	MAT.	INST.	TOTAL	MAT.	INST.	TOTAL	MAT.	INST.	TOTAL	MAT.	INST.	TOTAL
015433	CONTRACTOR EQUIPMENT		102.2	102.2		96.5	96.5		94.2	94.2		96.5	96.5		96.5	96.5		96.7	96.7
0241, 31 - 34	SITE & INFRASTRUCTURE, DEMOLITION	90.7	102.8	98.6	84.8	96.1	92.2	81.4	90.6	87.4	80.9	95.0	90.1	76.4	93.9	87.8	111.8	82.8	92.9
0310	Concrete Forming & Accessories	96.8	118.9	113.9	83.6	115.4	108.3	87.5	88.2	88.1	83.3	97.0	93.9	88.1	76.6	79.2	101.2	65.3	73.3
0320	Concrete Reinforcing	99.8	107.8	102.0	95.2	107.5	98.6	96.1	103.5	98.1	94.9	107.3	98.4	94.9	105.8	98.0	87.4	60.9	80.1
0330	Cast-in-Place Concrete	141.5	119.7	133.8	107.5	115.1	110.2	111.2	89.3	103.4	109.2	110.2	109.6	94.5	78.8	88.9	128.8	65.8	106.4
03	CONCRETE	120.1	117.7	119.1	94.8	114.5	102.6	98.0	92.5	95.8	94.9	104.5	98.7	87.0	84.0	85.8	100.8	66.4	87.2
04	MASONRY	110.6	124.9	119.3	116.1	118.3	117.4	106.4	99.9	102.5	119.1	114.9	116.6	131.5	83.7	102.5	76.9	60.7	67.0
05	METALS	98.3	122.9	103.2	92.6	122.9	98.5	91.2	118.1	96.5	91.7	122.0	97.7	91.6	117.8	96.8	92.3	88.8	91.6
06	WOOD, PLASTICS & COMPOSITES	93.5	116.2	103.7	79.0	113.7	94.5	72.1	84.7	77.8	78.6	91.6	84.4	84.6	72.5	79.2	97.1	65.7	83.0
07	THERMAL & MOISTURE PROTECTION	105.1	119.7	110.3	104.8	113.2	107.8	107.9	91.2	102.0	104.7	104.4	104.6	104.7	76.5	94.6	102.1	61.2	87.5
08	OPENINGS	98.3	125.0	104.3	87.9	123.7	96.0	95.8	106.6	98.2	85.1	111.4	91.0	88.4	96.1	90.1	96.2	60.3	88.1
0920	Plaster & Gypsum Board	88.3	117.0	106.5	79.1	114.9	101.8	94.4	84.9	88.3	79.1	92.1	87.4	79.1	72.4	74.9	109.6	65.3	81.5
0950, 0980	Ceilings & Acoustic Treatment	102.4	117.0	110.6	63.9	114.9	92.5	119.3	84.9	100.0	63.9	92.1	79.7	63.9	72.4	68.7	85.0	65.3	74.0
0960	Flooring	100.9	120.8	105.9	92.3	88.1	91.3	95.9	76.6	91.1	93.9	90.2	93.0	95.9	76.6	91.1	101.7	60.4	91.3
0970, 0990	Wall Finishes & Painting/Coating	98.4	127.2	115.6	96.6	126.7	114.5	90.8	94.2	92.8	90.8	94.2	92.8	90.8	98.4	95.3	91.9	46.0	64.5
09	FINISHES	98.7	120.1	109.4	82.0	112.1	97.1	99.9	86.9	93.4	82.2	95.0	88.6	82.4	78.3	80.3	95.7	62.4	79.0
COVERS	DIVS. 10 - 14, 25, 28, 41, 43, 44, 46	100.0	107.5	101.5	100.0	105.2	101.0	100.0	98.8	99.8	100.0	101.6	100.3	100.0	95.6	99.2	100.0	82.1	96.5
21, 22, 23	FIRE SUPPRESSION, PLUMBING & HVAC	99.9	116.7	105.9	99.3	113.3	104.3	92.8	85.2	90.1	91.8	105.6	96.7	91.8	78.8	87.1	100.0	53.7	83.4
26, 27, 3370	ELECTRICAL, COMMUNICATIONS & UTIL.	99.5	118.1	107.6	99.5	118.1	107.6	99.1	77.9	89.9	99.5	92.8	96.6	102.9	96.1	99.9	98.8	51.9	78.5
MF2018	WEIGHTED AVERAGE	102.0	117.9	107.9	95.4	114.2	102.3	95.6	91.8	94.2	93.4	103.8	97.2	93.5	88.3	91.6	97.1	64.0	84.9

		MISSISSIPPI																	
		CLARKSDALE			COLUMBUS			GREENVILLE			GREENWOOD			JACKSON			LAUREL		
DIVISION		386			397			387			389			390 - 392			394		
		MAT.	INST.	TOTAL	MAT.	INST.	TOTAL	MAT.	INST.	TOTAL	MAT.	INST.	TOTAL	MAT.	INST.	TOTAL	MAT.	INST.	TOTAL
015433	CONTRACTOR EQUIPMENT		96.7	96.7		96.7	96.7		96.7	96.7		96.7	96.7		101.6	101.6		96.7	96.7
0241, 31 - 34	SITE & INFRASTRUCTURE, DEMOLITION	108.1	80.9	90.4	108.7	81.6	91.0	116.5	82.8	94.5	111.6	80.7	91.4	107.7	91.4	97.1	114.2	81.0	92.5
0310	Concrete Forming & Accessories	86.4	40.2	50.5	87.4	42.3	52.3	82.7	59.2	64.4	97.2	40.4	53.1	103.9	67.3	75.5	87.6	54.3	61.8
0320	Concrete Reinforcing	98.6	59.8	87.9	93.5	59.9	84.2	99.2	60.0	88.4	98.6	59.8	87.9	98.6	65.0	89.3	94.1	29.5	76.2
0330	Cast-in-Place Concrete	105.9	55.1	87.9	131.4	57.1	105.0	109.1	64.3	93.2	113.9	54.9	92.9	111.0	70.3	96.5	128.4	56.3	102.8
03	CONCRETE	95.3	51.0	77.8	102.5	52.7	82.8	99.2	63.0	84.9	100.9	51.0	81.2	98.6	69.4	87.1	103.6	52.6	83.3
04	MASONRY	87.0	47.0	62.7	96.2	49.5	67.9	126.1	61.2	86.7	87.7	46.9	63.0	82.0	64.2	71.2	92.9	49.5	66.5
05	METALS	95.5	84.1	93.2	88.6	86.4	88.2	96.5	88.4	94.9	95.5	83.9	93.2	98.1	87.7	96.1	88.7	73.7	85.8
06	WOOD, PLASTICS & COMPOSITES	78.3	40.4	61.3	77.9	41.2	61.4	73.7	57.1	66.3	93.6	40.4	69.8	101.9	67.6	86.5	79.5	58.6	70.1
07	THERMAL & MOISTURE PROTECTION	99.7	47.2	81.0	101.9	50.3	83.5	100.0	60.6	86.0	100.1	49.2	82.0	99.8	64.6	87.2	102.0	52.3	84.3
08	OPENINGS	95.6	43.7	83.9	95.9	44.1	84.2	95.4	53.4	85.9	95.6	43.7	83.9	98.3	60.3	89.7	93.6	47.0	83.1
0920	Plaster & Gypsum Board	88.8	39.3	57.4	96.9	40.0	60.8	87.9	56.4	67.9	101.4	39.3	62.0	94.9	66.9	77.1	96.9	58.0	72.2
0950, 0980	Ceilings & Acoustic Treatment	85.0	39.3	59.4	78.6	40.0	57.0	86.0	56.4	69.4	85.0	39.3	59.4	89.1	66.9	76.6	78.6	58.0	67.0
0960	Flooring	102.7	60.4	92.1	97.5	60.4	88.2	101.4	60.4	91.1	106.9	60.4	95.2	98.8	65.3	90.4	96.6	60.4	87.5
0970, 0990	Wall Finishes & Painting/Coating	96.5	41.7	63.8	91.9	41.7	61.9	96.5	54.5	71.5	96.5	41.7	63.8	99.1	54.5	72.5	91.9	41.7	61.9
09	FINISHES	94.6	43.8	69.1	91.1	44.8	67.9	95.0	58.5	76.6	97.9	43.8	70.7	96.2	65.7	80.9	91.4	55.1	73.1
COVERS	DIVS. 10 - 14, 25, 28, 41, 43, 44, 46	100.0	43.2	89.0	100.0	44.1	89.2	100.0	81.4	96.4	100.0	43.2	89.0	100.0	83.3	96.8	100.0	31.0	86.6
21, 22, 23	FIRE SUPPRESSION, PLUMBING & HVAC	96.3	46.1	78.3	95.8	47.9	78.6	100.1	54.1	83.6	96.3	46.5	78.5	100.1	59.7	85.6	95.9	42.8	76.9
26, 27, 3370	ELECTRICAL, COMMUNICATIONS & UTIL.	98.0	37.0	71.6	97.5	49.0	76.5	98.0	56.1	79.8	98.0	34.7	70.6	101.3	56.1	81.7	98.3	51.6	78.0
MF2018	WEIGHTED AVERAGE	96.2	51.3	79.7	95.6	54.4	80.4	99.4	63.3	86.1	97.3	51.0	80.3	98.7	67.8	87.3	95.7	53.7	80.2

		MISSISSIPPI										MISSOURI							
		MCCOMB			MERIDIAN			TUPELO			BOWLING GREEN			CAPE GIRARDEAU			CHILLICOTHE		
DIVISION		396			393			388			633			637			646		
		MAT.	INST.	TOTAL	MAT.	INST.	TOTAL	MAT.	INST.	TOTAL	MAT.	INST.	TOTAL	MAT.	INST.	TOTAL	MAT.	INST.	TOTAL
015433	CONTRACTOR EQUIPMENT		96.7	96.7		96.7	96.7		96.7	96.7		103.2	103.2		103.2	103.2		97.8	97.8
0241, 31 - 34	SITE & INFRASTRUCTURE, DEMOLITION	101.2	80.8	87.9	107.2	82.8	91.3	106.2	80.8	89.7	83.6	85.6	84.9	88.0	85.7	86.5	98.1	84.0	88.9
0310	Concrete Forming & Accessories	87.5	41.5	51.7	84.2	66.1	70.1	83.2	41.7	51.0	96.6	85.3	87.8	88.6	76.7	79.3	86.7	86.8	86.8
0320	Concrete Reinforcing	94.7	30.9	77.0	93.5	64.8	85.6	96.5	59.7	86.3	102.9	86.6	98.4	104.2	80.0	97.5	101.5	92.1	98.9
0330	Cast-in-Place Concrete	114.0	54.7	92.9	122.0	66.0	102.1	105.9	55.9	88.1	79.5	87.1	82.2	78.7	80.8	79.4	93.4	78.6	88.1
03	CONCRETE	93.6	46.4	75.0	97.2	67.5	85.5	94.5	51.9	77.7	90.0	87.8	89.1	89.2	80.6	85.8	95.5	85.9	91.7
04	MASONRY	96.4	46.5	66.1	76.4	60.9	67.0	115.4	48.0	74.4	106.6	88.2	95.4	104.1	75.3	86.6	101.7	83.0	90.4
05	METALS	88.9	72.8	85.7	89.7	90.4	89.9	95.3	83.7	93.0	85.8	111.3	90.8	86.8	107.8	91.0	81.2	104.8	85.9
06	WOOD, PLASTICS & COMPOSITES	77.9	42.6	62.1	74.1	66.3	70.6	74.5	41.2	59.5	95.4	85.7	91.0	85.3	74.9	80.6	84.7	88.0	86.2
07	THERMAL & MOISTURE PROTECTION	101.5	49.2	82.9	101.6	61.7	87.4	99.7	47.5	81.1	101.4	88.9	97.0	100.8	78.0	92.7	99.4	83.1	93.6
08	OPENINGS	96.0	37.5	82.8	95.7	62.6	88.2	95.6	46.6	84.6	93.1	89.0	92.2	93.1	73.4	88.7	85.6	87.1	85.9
0920	Plaster & Gypsum Board	96.9	41.5	61.7	96.9	66.0	77.3	87.9	40.0	57.5	79.1	85.8	83.3	78.7	74.6	76.1	74.0	87.8	82.8
0950, 0980	Ceilings & Acoustic Treatment	78.6	41.5	57.8	79.1	66.0	71.7	85.0	40.0	59.8	90.5	85.8	87.9	90.5	74.6	81.6	87.9	87.8	87.8
0960	Flooring	97.5	60.4	88.2	96.6	60.4	87.5	101.6	60.4	91.3	100.4	86.8	97.0	97.5	79.4	93.0	104.7	89.3	100.8
0970, 0990	Wall Finishes & Painting/Coating	91.9	41.7	61.9	91.9	53.5	69.0	96.5	40.2	62.9	95.0	94.4	94.7	95.0	71.6	81.0	93.0	91.7	92.2
09	FINISHES	90.5	45.0	67.6	90.7	63.7	77.1	94.2	44.6	69.3	93.9	86.3	90.1	92.9	75.9	84.4	94.8	88.0	91.4
COVERS	DIVS. 10 - 14, 25, 28, 41, 43, 44, 46	100.0	45.7	89.5	100.0	82.2	96.6	100.0	44.1	89.2	100.0	95.5	99.1	100.0	94.4	98.9	100.0	95.2	99.1
21, 22, 23	FIRE SUPPRESSION, PLUMBING & HVAC	95.8	45.6	77.8	100.0	58.0	84.9	96.5	47.4	78.9	92.4	89.4	91.3	99.9	92.7	97.3	92.5	89.8	91.5
26, 27, 3370	ELECTRICAL, COMMUNICATIONS & UTIL.	96.7	49.8	76.4	98.3	53.7	79.0	97.9	49.0	76.7	95.5	68.4	83.8	95.5	87.7	92.1	93.7	67.5	82.3
MF2018	WEIGHTED AVERAGE	94.2	51.3	78.4	95.3	65.8	84.4	97.0	53.7	81.1	92.4	87.5	90.6	94.0	85.9	91.0	91.3	86.0	89.4

City Cost Indexes

		MISSOURI																
DIVISION		COLUMBIA 652			FLAT RIVER 636			HANNIBAL 634			HARRISONVILLE 647			JEFFERSON CITY 650 - 651			JOPLIN 648		
		MAT.	INST.	TOTAL	MAT.	INST.	TOTAL	MAT.	INST.	TOTAL	MAT.	INST.	TOTAL	MAT.	INST.	TOTAL	MAT.	INST.	TOTAL
015433	CONTRACTOR EQUIPMENT		105.5	105.5		103.2	103.2		103.2	103.2		97.8	97.8		112.0	112.0		100.8	100.8
0241, 31 - 34	SITE & INFRASTRUCTURE, DEMOLITION	88.2	90.1	89.4	85.6	85.3	85.4	81.7	85.4	84.1	91.2	85.0	87.1	89.0	101.2	97.0	102.7	88.4	93.4
0310	Concrete Forming & Accessories	84.6	83.3	83.6	104.1	80.0	85.4	94.9	75.0	79.4	83.6	89.8	88.4	101.5	80.3	85.0	98.7	71.4	77.5
0320	Concrete Reinforcing	94.9	99.7	96.2	104.2	92.3	100.9	102.3	86.6	98.0	101.3	99.5	100.8	99.1	96.4	98.4	104.9	96.6	102.6
0330	Cast-in-Place Concrete	78.2	83.4	80.1	82.1	82.6	82.3	75.3	85.3	78.8	95.6	90.8	93.9	83.0	86.2	84.2	101.1	71.4	90.6
03	CONCRETE	80.7	87.9	83.6	92.7	84.8	89.6	87.0	82.5	85.2	92.9	92.8	92.9	88.3	86.7	87.7	96.8	77.0	89.0
04	MASONRY	126.2	86.8	102.3	104.2	68.8	82.7	98.4	85.2	90.4	95.8	89.6	92.0	88.3	87.0	87.5	95.2	79.2	85.5
05	METALS	97.2	117.9	101.3	85.7	112.4	90.9	85.8	110.9	90.7	81.6	108.9	87.0	97.2	113.3	100.3	83.6	103.2	87.5
06	WOOD, PLASTICS & COMPOSITES	76.4	81.5	78.7	105.8	81.3	94.8	93.0	73.7	84.3	80.7	89.5	84.7	99.0	77.2	89.2	98.5	70.7	86.0
07	THERMAL & MOISTURE PROTECTION	95.3	85.3	91.7	101.6	81.6	94.5	101.2	83.8	95.0	98.8	90.3	95.8	100.6	86.7	95.6	98.8	76.8	91.0
08	OPENINGS	97.9	85.1	95.0	93.1	88.3	92.0	93.1	75.9	89.2	85.5	93.5	87.3	97.6	81.9	94.1	86.5	73.8	83.6
0920	Plaster & Gypsum Board	75.0	81.3	79.0	85.7	81.2	82.9	78.9	73.4	75.4	72.4	89.4	83.2	84.2	76.4	79.3	80.9	69.9	73.9
0950, 0980	Ceilings & Acoustic Treatment	88.6	81.3	84.5	90.5	81.2	85.3	90.5	73.4	80.9	87.9	89.4	88.7	95.4	76.4	84.8	89.2	69.9	78.4
0960	Flooring	96.5	99.0	97.2	103.3	75.7	96.4	99.8	86.8	96.5	99.1	90.2	96.9	100.4	96.1	99.3	133.8	67.1	117.1
0970, 0990	Wall Finishes & Painting/Coating	98.3	81.1	88.1	95.0	63.7	76.4	95.0	83.6	88.2	97.5	95.8	96.5	99.1	81.1	88.4	92.7	67.4	77.6
09	FINISHES	87.8	85.4	86.6	95.7	76.8	86.2	93.5	77.0	85.2	92.6	90.3	91.4	95.4	82.3	88.8	103.6	70.2	86.8
COVERS	DIVS. 10 - 14, 25, 28, 41, 43, 44, 46	100.0	94.7	99.0	100.0	89.2	97.9	100.0	93.3	98.7	100.0	96.5	99.3	100.0	96.6	99.3	100.0	92.2	98.5
21, 22, 23	FIRE SUPPRESSION, PLUMBING & HVAC	99.9	94.2	97.8	92.4	87.0	90.4	92.4	87.8	90.7	92.5	90.6	91.8	99.9	97.8	99.2	100.1	66.0	87.8
26, 27, 3370	ELECTRICAL, COMMUNICATIONS & UTIL.	92.9	80.9	87.7	97.9	87.7	93.4	94.9	68.4	83.4	97.0	90.1	94.0	97.9	80.9	90.5	92.5	69.1	82.4
MF2018	WEIGHTED AVERAGE	95.6	90.7	93.8	93.1	85.8	90.4	91.5	84.0	88.8	90.8	92.2	91.3	96.5	91.3	94.6	94.2	76.5	87.7

		MISSOURI																
DIVISION		KANSAS CITY 640 - 641			KIRKSVILLE 635			POPLAR BLUFF 639			ROLLA 654 - 655			SEDALIA 653			SIKESTON 638		
		MAT.	INST.	TOTAL	MAT.	INST.	TOTAL	MAT.	INST.	TOTAL	MAT.	INST.	TOTAL	MAT.	INST.	TOTAL	MAT.	INST.	TOTAL
015433	CONTRACTOR EQUIPMENT		103.4	103.4		94.5	94.5		96.5	96.5		105.5	105.5		96.7	96.7		96.5	96.5
0241, 31 - 34	SITE & INFRASTRUCTURE, DEMOLITION	96.1	97.8	97.2	83.4	81.0	81.8	73.4	84.2	80.5	84.0	89.5	87.6	83.2	84.7	84.2	76.1	84.8	81.8
0310	Concrete Forming & Accessories	99.0	101.5	100.9	86.7	71.2	74.7	86.9	71.9	75.3	93.3	92.2	92.4	91.4	71.0	75.5	87.7	71.9	75.5
0320	Concrete Reinforcing	99.7	107.7	101.9	102.5	74.8	94.8	105.7	68.2	95.3	95.4	95.3	95.4	93.6	98.9	95.1	105.0	68.2	94.8
0330	Cast-in-Place Concrete	99.2	100.9	99.7	82.0	75.2	79.6	63.1	76.3	67.8	80.1	91.9	84.3	83.6	74.3	80.3	67.5	76.3	70.6
03	CONCRETE	96.6	102.6	99.0	100.4	74.7	90.2	82.4	74.2	79.2	82.5	94.1	87.1	91.4	78.4	86.3	85.1	74.2	80.8
04	MASONRY	101.4	98.6	99.7	110.3	76.4	89.7	102.3	66.7	80.7	102.6	83.4	90.9	108.4	73.5	87.2	102.0	66.7	80.6
05	METALS	97.0	109.7	99.5	86.2	96.1	88.2	86.7	93.0	87.9	96.5	115.4	100.2	97.5	106.6	99.3	87.6	93.0	88.6
06	WOOD, PLASTICS & COMPOSITES	96.7	102.0	99.0	79.2	69.5	74.8	77.9	72.2	75.5	86.2	94.0	89.7	81.0	69.7	75.9	79.9	72.6	76.6
07	THERMAL & MOISTURE PROTECTION	100.2	103.6	101.4	106.6	81.4	97.7	105.1	74.5	94.2	95.6	89.7	93.5	100.3	78.7	92.6	105.2	73.7	94.0
08	OPENINGS	100.6	101.5	100.8	98.1	71.5	92.1	99.0	68.2	92.0	97.9	90.7	96.2	103.8	78.8	98.2	99.0	68.2	92.0
0920	Plaster & Gypsum Board	82.0	102.0	94.7	73.0	69.1	70.5	73.6	72.3	72.8	76.4	94.2	87.7	71.8	69.1	70.1	76.0	72.3	73.7
0950, 0980	Ceilings & Acoustic Treatment	94.1	102.0	98.5	88.7	69.1	77.7	90.5	72.3	80.3	88.6	94.2	91.7	88.6	69.1	77.7	90.5	72.3	80.3
0960	Flooring	103.3	99.3	102.3	75.8	86.4	78.4	91.6	75.7	87.6	99.1	90.6	97.0	74.2	65.3	71.9	92.1	75.7	88.0
0970, 0990	Wall Finishes & Painting/Coating	99.1	109.2	105.1	90.6	69.6	78.1	89.9	59.6	71.8	98.3	87.2	91.7	98.3	91.7	94.4	89.9	59.6	71.8
09	FINISHES	96.5	102.0	99.3	89.9	73.2	81.5	91.6	70.7	81.1	88.8	91.3	90.1	84.7	71.3	78.0	92.2	71.0	81.6
COVERS	DIVS. 10 - 14, 25, 28, 41, 43, 44, 46	100.0	99.5	99.9	100.0	92.8	98.6	100.0	92.0	98.4	100.0	97.0	99.4	100.0	90.9	98.2	100.0	87.6	97.6
21, 22, 23	FIRE SUPPRESSION, PLUMBING & HVAC	99.8	101.3	100.4	92.4	87.3	90.6	92.4	85.3	89.9	92.3	95.5	93.5	92.3	85.3	89.8	92.4	85.3	89.9
26, 27, 3370	ELECTRICAL, COMMUNICATIONS & UTIL.	99.4	97.3	98.5	93.9	68.3	82.8	94.5	87.6	91.5	92.2	76.2	85.3	91.9	90.1	91.1	94.1	87.6	91.3
MF2018	WEIGHTED AVERAGE	98.6	101.2	99.6	93.8	79.5	88.5	91.4	80.1	87.2	93.1	91.8	92.6	94.8	83.5	90.7	92.0	80.0	87.6

		MISSOURI									MONTANA							
DIVISION		SPRINGFIELD 656 - 658			ST. JOSEPH 644 - 645			ST. LOUIS 630 - 631			BILLINGS 590 - 591			BUTTE 597			GREAT FALLS 594		
		MAT.	INST.	TOTAL	MAT.	INST.	TOTAL	MAT.	INST.	TOTAL	MAT.	INST.	TOTAL	MAT.	INST.	TOTAL	MAT.	INST.	TOTAL
015433	CONTRACTOR EQUIPMENT		98.8	98.8		97.8	97.8		107.6	107.6		94.4	94.4		94.2	94.2		94.2	94.2
0241, 31 - 34	SITE & INFRASTRUCTURE, DEMOLITION	88.1	88.8	88.6	97.8	83.6	88.5	93.6	99.1	97.2	85.5	89.4	88.0	88.0	88.6	88.4	91.0	88.9	89.6
0310	Concrete Forming & Accessories	100.5	77.4	82.6	97.5	89.9	91.6	101.4	102.6	102.4	100.9	68.0	75.4	86.2	65.3	69.9	101.0	65.4	73.4
0320	Concrete Reinforcing	90.9	99.3	93.3	98.3	102.4	99.4	100.1	103.8	101.1	91.0	80.3	88.1	98.9	79.6	93.6	91.2	80.0	88.1
0330	Cast-in-Place Concrete	85.0	76.5	82.0	93.9	95.0	94.3	88.9	103.6	94.1	126.3	71.2	106.7	139.1	67.2	113.5	147.0	68.9	119.2
03	CONCRETE	88.9	82.0	86.2	92.3	94.8	93.3	93.2	104.1	97.5	103.8	72.2	91.4	108.2	69.5	92.9	112.2	70.2	95.6
04	MASONRY	82.9	84.7	84.0	96.4	87.7	91.1	84.0	105.4	97.0	146.7	84.3	108.8	142.4	71.7	99.4	147.9	76.5	104.6
05	METALS	104.4	105.0	104.5	88.5	110.5	92.8	97.5	116.7	101.3	104.6	89.5	101.6	98.4	88.1	96.4	101.7	89.0	99.2
06	WOOD, PLASTICS & COMPOSITES	90.3	75.1	83.5	98.5	90.3	94.8	100.3	101.6	100.9	99.2	64.1	83.5	82.2	62.6	73.4	100.9	62.6	83.7
07	THERMAL & MOISTURE PROTECTION	99.0	77.9	91.5	99.2	87.8	95.1	101.1	103.3	101.9	101.8	72.9	91.5	101.5	65.6	88.7	102.1	68.5	90.1
08	OPENINGS	105.9	87.4	101.7	89.8	95.8	91.2	99.1	105.7	100.6	101.7	64.9	93.4	100.0	63.4	91.8	102.9	67.6	94.9
0920	Plaster & Gypsum Board	77.6	74.7	75.7	83.4	90.2	87.7	81.7	102.0	94.5	121.4	63.6	84.7	114.4	62.0	81.2	127.7	62.0	86.0
0950, 0980	Ceilings & Acoustic Treatment	88.6	74.7	80.8	96.9	90.2	93.2	87.2	102.0	95.5	108.1	63.6	83.2	111.4	62.0	83.7	113.7	62.0	84.7
0960	Flooring	96.0	73.4	90.3	108.7	93.7	104.9	102.0	96.8	100.7	95.5	77.5	91.0	94.9	74.6	89.8	99.9	72.3	93.0
0970, 0990	Wall Finishes & Painting/Coating	92.2	101.4	97.7	93.0	106.7	101.2	99.1	105.6	103.0	92.2	86.5	88.8	90.5	60.2	72.4	90.5	85.0	87.2
09	FINISHES	90.1	79.3	84.7	99.1	92.5	95.8	94.3	101.5	97.9	99.8	70.9	85.3	99.4	65.9	82.5	103.4	67.9	85.6
COVERS	DIVS. 10 - 14, 25, 28, 41, 43, 44, 46	100.0	94.1	98.8	100.0	96.1	99.2	100.0	99.4	99.9	100.0	94.4	98.9	100.0	93.3	98.7	100.0	93.0	98.7
21, 22, 23	FIRE SUPPRESSION, PLUMBING & HVAC	99.9	72.5	90.1	100.1	85.6	94.9	99.9	104.4	101.5	99.9	75.5	91.2	99.9	64.6	87.3	99.9	71.0	89.6
26, 27, 3370	ELECTRICAL, COMMUNICATIONS & UTIL.	94.2	67.8	82.8	97.1	74.0	87.1	99.2	102.8	100.8	95.1	72.9	85.5	98.3	65.2	83.9	94.6	67.8	83.0
MF2018	WEIGHTED AVERAGE	97.7	81.0	91.6	95.1	89.3	93.0	97.3	104.5	99.9	102.5	77.4	93.3	101.6	71.1	90.4	103.4	74.1	92.6

City Cost Indexes

DIVISION		MONTANA																	
		HAVRE 595			HELENA 596			KALISPELL 599			MILES CITY 593			MISSOULA 598			WOLF POINT 592		
		MAT.	INST.	TOTAL	MAT.	INST.	TOTAL	MAT.	INST.	TOTAL	MAT.	INST.	TOTAL	MAT.	INST.	TOTAL	MAT.	INST.	TOTAL
015433	CONTRACTOR EQUIPMENT		94.2	94.2		101.0	101.0		94.2	94.2		94.2	94.2		94.2	94.2		94.2	94.2
0241, 31 - 34	SITE & INFRASTRUCTURE, DEMOLITION	89.4	88.0	88.5	83.2	99.3	93.7	77.5	88.2	84.5	81.8	88.1	85.9	75.8	88.2	83.9	93.0	88.1	89.8
0310	Concrete Forming & Accessories	78.2	63.8	67.0	103.5	65.0	73.6	90.0	64.8	70.4	99.0	64.0	71.8	90.0	65.2	70.7	90.5	64.0	69.9
0320	Concrete Reinforcing	99.7	80.3	94.3	101.3	80.2	95.4	101.5	81.9	96.1	99.1	80.4	93.9	100.6	81.7	95.3	100.5	80.4	95.0
0330	Cast-in-Place Concrete	149.8	65.2	119.7	107.1	68.5	93.4	120.7	66.3	101.4	132.2	65.3	108.4	102.4	66.9	89.8	148.1	64.3	118.3
03	CONCRETE	115.0	68.2	96.5	103.8	69.7	90.3	99.5	69.3	87.6	105.9	68.3	91.0	89.3	69.6	81.5	118.1	68.0	98.3
04	MASONRY	143.6	72.6	100.5	128.9	70.6	93.5	141.1	74.4	100.6	150.1	72.6	103.0	172.0	71.4	110.9	151.6	72.6	103.6
05	METALS	94.6	87.3	93.2	100.0	84.9	97.0	94.5	88.0	93.2	93.9	87.4	92.6	95.0	87.8	93.6	94.0	87.4	92.7
06	WOOD, PLASTICS & COMPOSITES	71.2	62.6	67.4	104.9	62.9	86.0	86.8	62.6	76.0	96.8	62.6	81.5	86.8	62.6	76.0	85.4	62.6	75.2
07	THERMAL & MOISTURE PROTECTION	101.7	59.9	86.8	103.0	66.7	90.1	101.2	66.5	88.8	101.5	61.1	87.1	100.9	67.6	89.0	102.2	61.0	87.5
08	OPENINGS	100.5	63.5	92.2	99.4	63.7	91.3	100.5	63.8	92.2	100.0	63.5	91.8	100.1	63.8	91.9	100.0	63.5	91.8
0920	Plaster & Gypsum Board	108.9	62.0	79.2	117.5	62.0	82.3	114.5	62.0	81.2	125.3	62.0	85.1	114.5	62.0	81.2	117.3	62.0	82.2
0950, 0980	Ceilings & Acoustic Treatment	111.4	62.0	83.7	115.4	62.0	85.5	111.4	62.0	83.7	106.0	62.0	81.3	111.4	62.0	83.7	106.0	62.0	81.3
0960	Flooring	93.3	81.4	90.3	106.4	74.6	98.4	96.3	81.4	92.5	99.9	81.4	95.2	96.3	74.6	90.8	97.2	81.4	93.3
0970, 0990	Wall Finishes & Painting/Coating	90.5	60.2	72.4	99.1	53.4	71.8	90.5	80.9	84.7	90.5	60.2	72.4	90.5	80.9	84.7	90.5	60.2	72.4
09	FINISHES	98.6	66.6	82.5	107.3	65.1	86.1	99.3	69.3	84.3	100.7	66.6	83.6	98.9	68.1	83.5	99.9	66.6	83.2
COVERS	DIVS. 10 - 14, 25, 28, 41, 43, 44, 46	100.0	79.7	96.1	100.0	87.1	97.5	100.0	80.3	96.2	100.0	79.7	96.1	100.0	86.7	97.4	100.0	79.7	96.1
21, 22, 23	FIRE SUPPRESSION, PLUMBING & HVAC	92.4	62.0	81.5	100.1	64.2	87.2	92.4	62.4	81.6	92.4	67.7	83.6	99.9	64.5	87.2	92.4	67.7	83.6
26, 27, 3370	ELECTRICAL, COMMUNICATIONS & UTIL.	94.6	61.6	80.3	101.2	65.5	85.7	96.7	60.6	81.1	94.6	66.3	82.3	97.2	63.9	82.8	94.6	66.3	82.3
MF2018	WEIGHTED AVERAGE	99.5	69.4	88.4	101.9	71.3	90.6	97.6	70.3	87.6	98.7	71.3	88.6	99.3	71.0	88.9	100.4	71.3	89.6

DIVISION		NEBRASKA																	
		ALLIANCE 693			COLUMBUS 686			GRAND ISLAND 688			HASTINGS 689			LINCOLN 683 - 685			MCCOOK 690		
		MAT.	INST.	TOTAL	MAT.	INST.	TOTAL	MAT.	INST.	TOTAL	MAT.	INST.	TOTAL	MAT.	INST.	TOTAL	MAT.	INST.	TOTAL
015433	CONTRACTOR EQUIPMENT		92.1	92.1		98.1	98.1		98.1	98.1		98.1	98.1		104.1	104.1		98.1	98.1
0241, 31 - 34	SITE & INFRASTRUCTURE, DEMOLITION	92.5	90.8	91.4	91.9	85.8	87.9	98.8	86.7	90.9	94.5	85.8	88.8	91.0	97.0	94.9	91.4	85.8	87.8
0310	Concrete Forming & Accessories	89.6	50.3	59.1	101.0	68.1	75.4	100.5	77.8	82.9	104.5	65.5	74.5	100.3	70.2	76.9	95.3	50.8	60.7
0320	Concrete Reinforcing	110.9	78.4	101.9	100.5	77.1	94.0	99.9	78.4	94.0	99.9	68.3	91.2	98.6	78.7	93.1	106.2	68.5	95.8
0330	Cast-in-Place Concrete	97.4	74.7	89.4	97.8	74.7	89.6	103.5	73.1	92.7	103.5	67.8	90.8	81.9	79.3	81.0	105.3	67.7	91.9
03	CONCRETE	108.2	64.7	91.0	97.3	73.3	87.8	100.8	77.4	91.5	101.1	68.3	88.2	91.0	75.9	85.0	101.0	61.5	85.4
04	MASONRY	109.3	69.8	85.3	104.4	69.7	83.3	97.8	69.4	80.6	104.6	66.6	81.6	88.5	73.5	79.4	104.2	69.7	83.3
05	METALS	97.9	81.5	94.6	92.9	93.1	93.0	94.7	94.7	94.7	95.2	89.2	94.0	102.6	92.2	100.5	92.9	89.2	92.2
06	WOOD, PLASTICS & COMPOSITES	81.1	44.4	64.6	93.9	68.0	82.3	93.0	78.6	86.5	97.9	65.4	83.3	97.0	68.3	84.1	89.3	45.2	69.6
07	THERMAL & MOISTURE PROTECTION	105.6	68.0	92.2	105.5	72.1	93.6	105.7	75.7	95.0	105.7	69.6	92.9	101.1	75.3	91.9	101.9	68.2	89.9
08	OPENINGS	88.4	52.7	80.3	88.4	66.8	83.5	88.4	76.9	85.8	88.4	63.3	82.7	98.1	65.0	90.7	88.9	50.6	80.3
0920	Plaster & Gypsum Board	73.3	43.0	54.1	91.3	67.3	76.1	90.5	78.3	82.8	92.2	64.7	74.8	103.9	67.3	80.7	80.0	43.9	57.1
0950, 0980	Ceilings & Acoustic Treatment	92.0	43.0	64.6	88.8	67.3	76.8	88.8	78.3	82.9	88.8	64.7	75.3	115.4	67.3	88.5	89.8	43.9	64.1
0960	Flooring	97.2	78.2	92.4	87.3	78.2	85.0	87.1	70.7	83.0	88.1	72.8	84.2	100.1	77.5	94.4	93.8	78.2	89.9
0970, 0990	Wall Finishes & Painting/Coating	158.6	45.9	91.4	74.2	53.4	61.8	74.2	73.3	73.6	74.2	53.4	61.8	99.1	70.5	82.0	87.9	40.0	59.3
09	FINISHES	93.3	53.5	73.3	87.9	68.2	78.0	87.9	76.0	81.9	88.5	65.6	77.0	104.1	71.1	87.5	90.1	53.3	71.6
COVERS	DIVS. 10 - 14, 25, 28, 41, 43, 44, 46	100.0	84.2	96.9	100.0	86.9	97.5	100.0	89.3	97.9	100.0	86.6	97.4	100.0	88.9	97.8	100.0	84.4	97.0
21, 22, 23	FIRE SUPPRESSION, PLUMBING & HVAC	93.8	67.4	84.3	92.6	67.7	83.7	100.2	77.9	92.2	92.6	67.0	83.5	99.9	78.0	92.1	92.4	67.7	83.5
26, 27, 3370	ELECTRICAL, COMMUNICATIONS & UTIL.	90.2	58.4	76.4	91.3	72.5	83.1	90.6	61.1	77.8	90.3	70.7	81.8	99.7	61.1	82.9	91.2	58.5	77.0
MF2018	WEIGHTED AVERAGE	96.8	67.0	85.9	93.8	73.9	86.5	96.1	76.9	89.0	94.8	71.5	86.2	98.9	76.4	90.6	94.2	66.9	84.2

DIVISION		NEBRASKA												NEVADA					
		NORFOLK 687			NORTH PLATTE 691			OMAHA 680 - 681			VALENTINE 692			CARSON CITY 897			ELKO 898		
		MAT.	INST.	TOTAL	MAT.	INST.	TOTAL	MAT.	INST.	TOTAL	MAT.	INST.	TOTAL	MAT.	INST.	TOTAL	MAT.	INST.	TOTAL
015433	CONTRACTOR EQUIPMENT		88.9	88.9		98.1	98.1		96.2	96.2		91.9	91.9		98.2	98.2		93.2	93.2
0241, 31 - 34	SITE & INFRASTRUCTURE, DEMOLITION	76.6	85.0	82.1	95.8	85.7	89.2	86.7	97.1	93.5	79.4	89.9	86.3	85.6	97.0	93.1	71.1	87.5	81.8
0310	Concrete Forming & Accessories	86.4	67.2	71.5	98.3	69.0	75.6	101.0	76.5	82.0	86.1	48.6	56.9	102.0	79.6	84.6	105.8	87.0	91.2
0320	Concrete Reinforcing	100.6	59.7	89.3	105.7	73.3	96.7	100.0	79.1	94.2	106.3	59.6	93.3	101.9	110.9	104.4	102.9	85.0	97.9
0330	Cast-in-Place Concrete	98.4	65.2	86.6	105.3	63.1	90.3	80.9	81.8	81.2	92.9	50.0	77.7	88.8	80.8	86.0	83.2	66.5	77.3
03	CONCRETE	95.7	66.0	84.0	101.1	69.0	88.4	91.0	79.2	86.3	98.1	52.3	80.0	102.0	85.5	95.5	93.1	79.6	87.8
04	MASONRY	109.2	69.7	85.2	93.3	69.2	78.7	89.5	80.5	84.0	104.3	69.2	83.0	131.3	63.2	89.9	141.6	61.0	92.6
05	METALS	96.2	77.0	92.4	92.5	91.4	92.2	103.1	85.1	99.5	103.5	76.4	98.2	103.3	92.4	101.2	107.5	83.7	102.8
06	WOOD, PLASTICS & COMPOSITES	78.2	67.6	73.4	92.1	69.8	82.1	98.6	76.1	88.5	77.1	43.2	61.9	102.1	80.4	92.4	114.4	92.8	104.7
07	THERMAL & MOISTURE PROTECTION	104.4	70.2	92.2	101.8	71.9	91.1	104.0	81.8	96.1	101.3	66.3	88.9	97.6	77.7	90.5	94.2	66.1	84.2
08	OPENINGS	89.1	62.2	83.1	88.3	70.0	84.2	98.1	77.5	93.5	89.8	48.5	80.4	97.8	78.8	93.5	98.5	80.1	94.3
0920	Plaster & Gypsum Board	92.0	67.3	76.3	80.0	69.2	73.2	99.2	75.8	84.3	82.7	42.2	57.0	117.4	79.8	93.6	129.8	92.8	106.4
0950, 0980	Ceilings & Acoustic Treatment	102.0	67.3	82.6	89.8	69.2	78.3	103.3	75.8	87.9	105.0	42.2	69.8	108.8	79.8	92.5	103.7	92.8	97.6
0960	Flooring	113.5	78.2	104.6	94.7	70.7	88.7	100.1	90.0	97.5	124.7	78.2	113.0	101.0	60.1	90.7	98.5	60.1	88.9
0970, 0990	Wall Finishes & Painting/Coating	133.8	53.4	85.8	87.9	69.1	76.7	99.1	58.6	74.9	157.4	54.2	95.9	99.1	79.4	87.4	94.5	70.5	80.2
09	FINISHES	106.5	67.8	87.1	90.4	69.2	79.8	99.9	76.9	88.3	111.7	53.3	82.5	103.9	75.6	89.7	100.6	81.6	91.0
COVERS	DIVS. 10 - 14, 25, 28, 41, 43, 44, 46	100.0	86.0	97.3	100.0	86.9	97.5	100.0	89.0	97.9	100.0	83.1	96.7	100.0	99.8	100.0	100.0	81.3	96.4
21, 22, 23	FIRE SUPPRESSION, PLUMBING & HVAC	92.2	66.8	83.1	99.9	69.6	89.0	99.9	76.5	91.6	91.8	66.1	82.6	100.1	76.8	91.7	96.1	69.0	86.4
26, 27, 3370	ELECTRICAL, COMMUNICATIONS & UTIL.	90.6	72.4	82.7	90.4	61.1	77.7	99.5	82.6	92.2	88.7	58.5	75.6	99.9	85.1	93.5	95.8	78.6	88.3
MF2018	WEIGHTED AVERAGE	95.2	70.8	86.2	95.4	72.1	86.8	98.7	81.2	92.3	97.0	64.2	85.0	101.9	81.5	94.4	100.3	76.4	91.5

City Cost Indexes

		NEVADA								NEW HAMPSHIRE								
		ELY			LAS VEGAS			RENO			CHARLESTON			CLAREMONT			CONCORD		
DIVISION		893			889 - 891			894 - 895			036			037			032 - 033		
		MAT.	INST.	TOTAL	MAT.	INST.	TOTAL	MAT.	INST.	TOTAL	MAT.	INST.	TOTAL	MAT.	INST.	TOTAL	MAT.	INST.	TOTAL
015433	CONTRACTOR EQUIPMENT		93.2	93.2		93.2	93.2		93.2	93.2		93.0	93.0		93.0	93.0		97.1	97.1
0241, 31 - 34	SITE & INFRASTRUCTURE, DEMOLITION	76.1	88.5	84.2	80.5	92.9	88.6	77.8	89.2	85.2	77.0	91.2	86.2	72.6	91.2	84.7	88.1	101.3	96.7
0310	Concrete Forming & Accessories	97.4	91.7	93.0	98.7	108.4	106.2	94.0	79.6	82.8	89.0	78.1	80.5	96.1	78.1	82.1	104.6	91.5	94.4
0320	Concrete Reinforcing	101.7	85.2	97.1	94.1	125.2	102.7	96.2	123.1	103.6	84.5	86.6	85.1	84.5	86.6	85.1	97.6	87.1	94.7
0330	Cast-in-Place Concrete	89.3	86.8	88.4	86.5	109.4	94.6	94.5	78.6	88.8	70.4	105.6	82.9	64.7	105.6	79.2	85.7	113.3	95.5
03	CONCRETE	99.2	88.9	95.1	94.5	111.2	101.1	97.9	86.9	93.6	85.5	89.6	87.1	80.1	89.6	83.8	97.9	98.3	98.1
04	MASONRY	147.1	67.4	98.7	130.9	107.0	116.4	139.9	63.1	93.2	99.2	89.6	93.4	100.5	89.6	93.9	111.2	100.2	104.5
05	METALS	107.4	86.4	103.3	116.7	106.7	114.7	109.3	98.4	107.1	91.3	90.8	91.2	91.3	90.8	91.2	98.6	90.2	96.9
06	WOOD, PLASTICS & COMPOSITES	101.1	94.7	98.3	99.7	105.6	102.3	94.0	80.2	87.8	87.5	75.7	82.2	96.2	75.7	87.0	102.6	90.2	97.0
07	THERMAL & MOISTURE PROTECTION	94.5	82.7	90.3	103.5	102.2	103.1	94.1	75.4	87.4	94.9	96.8	95.6	94.8	96.8	95.5	97.8	107.1	101.1
08	OPENINGS	98.4	81.2	94.5	97.5	112.1	100.8	96.4	81.4	93.0	97.7	76.8	93.0	98.7	76.8	93.8	97.9	88.0	95.7
0920	Plaster & Gypsum Board	122.6	94.8	105.0	113.3	106.0	108.6	107.2	79.8	89.8	102.9	74.9	85.1	103.9	74.9	85.5	102.1	89.9	94.4
0950, 0980	Ceilings & Acoustic Treatment	103.7	94.8	98.7	111.8	106.0	108.5	107.7	79.8	92.1	88.2	74.9	80.7	88.2	74.9	80.7	82.7	89.9	86.8
0960	Flooring	96.9	60.1	87.7	88.7	104.7	92.7	94.8	60.1	86.1	95.8	101.3	97.2	98.0	101.3	98.8	103.1	105.4	103.7
0970, 0990	Wall Finishes & Painting/Coating	94.5	99.5	97.5	97.3	120.9	111.3	94.5	79.4	85.5	82.5	80.0	81.0	82.5	80.0	81.0	99.1	97.2	98.0
09	FINISHES	99.6	87.5	93.5	98.2	108.8	103.5	97.8	75.4	86.6	93.7	81.9	87.8	94.1	81.9	88.0	95.9	94.2	95.1
COVERS	DIVS. 10 - 14, 25, 28, 41, 43, 44, 46	100.0	63.4	92.9	100.0	106.1	101.2	100.0	99.3	99.9	100.0	79.4	96.0	100.0	79.4	96.0	100.0	106.3	101.2
21, 22, 23	FIRE SUPPRESSION, PLUMBING & HVAC	96.1	86.2	92.6	100.2	105.4	102.1	100.1	76.8	91.7	92.8	73.9	86.1	92.8	74.0	86.1	100.2	87.7	95.7
26, 27, 3370	ELECTRICAL, COMMUNICATIONS & UTIL.	96.1	82.8	90.3	101.9	107.8	104.5	96.1	85.1	91.3	101.0	67.0	86.3	101.0	67.0	86.3	101.6	74.7	90.0
MF2018	WEIGHTED AVERAGE	101.1	83.6	94.7	103.7	106.4	104.7	101.7	81.6	94.3	93.4	81.5	89.0	92.9	81.5	88.7	99.3	91.9	96.5

		NEW HAMPSHIRE														NEW JERSEY		
		KEENE			LITTLETON			MANCHESTER			NASHUA			PORTSMOUTH			ATLANTIC CITY		
DIVISION		034			035			031			030			038			082,084		
		MAT.	INST.	TOTAL	MAT.	INST.	TOTAL	MAT.	INST.	TOTAL	MAT.	INST.	TOTAL	MAT.	INST.	TOTAL	MAT.	INST.	TOTAL
015433	CONTRACTOR EQUIPMENT		93.0	93.0		93.0	93.0		97.4	97.4		93.0	93.0		93.0	93.0		90.8	90.8
0241, 31 - 34	SITE & INFRASTRUCTURE, DEMOLITION	82.4	91.2	88.1	72.8	90.3	84.2	85.6	101.3	95.8	87.6	92.0	90.5	82.2	92.6	89.0	87.6	95.5	92.7
0310	Concrete Forming & Accessories	94.4	78.3	81.9	108.4	72.8	80.8	104.6	91.9	94.8	104.2	91.7	94.5	90.7	90.3	90.4	115.4	140.6	135.0
0320	Concrete Reinforcing	84.5	86.6	85.1	85.2	86.6	85.6	99.5	87.2	96.1	105.5	87.1	100.4	84.5	87.1	85.2	76.5	134.6	92.6
0330	Cast-in-Place Concrete	70.7	105.7	83.1	63.5	97.8	75.7	80.8	115.6	93.2	67.0	114.4	83.8	63.5	113.5	81.3	65.4	132.9	89.4
03	CONCRETE	85.4	89.7	87.1	80.3	84.5	81.9	96.4	99.3	97.5	89.3	98.9	93.1	79.5	98.0	86.8	83.2	135.6	103.9
04	MASONRY	101.5	89.6	94.3	114.4	75.7	90.9	111.0	100.2	104.4	106.0	100.1	102.4	100.7	97.3	98.6	108.1	137.2	125.8
05	METALS	92.0	91.2	91.9	92.1	90.8	91.8	100.1	91.2	98.3	99.5	92.6	98.1	93.6	94.1	93.7	96.2	114.5	99.8
06	WOOD, PLASTICS & COMPOSITES	94.1	75.7	85.9	109.2	75.7	94.2	102.6	90.3	97.1	107.6	90.3	99.9	89.4	90.3	89.8	124.3	141.6	132.0
07	THERMAL & MOISTURE PROTECTION	95.5	96.9	96.0	95.0	90.6	93.4	100.6	107.3	103.0	95.9	105.8	99.4	95.3	101.5	97.5	99.9	132.8	111.6
08	OPENINGS	96.4	80.0	92.7	99.6	76.8	94.5	97.6	90.8	96.1	100.6	87.5	97.6	101.1	79.0	96.1	97.8	137.6	106.8
0920	Plaster & Gypsum Board	103.4	74.9	85.3	125.1	74.9	93.2	107.8	89.9	96.4	118.0	89.9	100.2	102.9	89.9	94.7	131.5	142.8	138.7
0950, 0980	Ceilings & Acoustic Treatment	88.2	74.9	80.7	88.2	74.9	80.7	100.9	89.9	94.7	101.5	89.9	95.0	88.8	89.9	89.4	102.3	142.8	125.0
0960	Flooring	97.7	101.3	98.6	107.3	101.3	105.8	103.1	110.7	105.0	101.0	103.3	101.6	96.0	103.3	97.8	104.3	152.0	116.3
0970, 0990	Wall Finishes & Painting/Coating	82.5	91.8	88.1	82.5	80.0	81.0	99.1	113.4	107.6	82.5	110.1	98.9	82.5	90.8	87.5	82.6	143.0	118.6
09	FINISHES	95.3	83.2	89.2	99.7	78.4	89.0	101.4	97.2	99.3	101.8	95.3	98.5	94.4	92.4	93.4	102.4	144.2	123.4
COVERS	DIVS. 10 - 14, 25, 28, 41, 43, 44, 46	100.0	84.9	97.1	100.0	85.7	97.2	100.0	106.5	101.3	100.0	106.5	101.3	100.0	105.5	101.1	100.0	114.9	102.9
21, 22, 23	FIRE SUPPRESSION, PLUMBING & HVAC	92.8	74.0	86.1	92.8	66.7	83.5	100.2	87.7	95.7	100.4	87.8	95.8	100.4	86.0	95.2	99.3	132.7	111.3
26, 27, 3370	ELECTRICAL, COMMUNICATIONS & UTIL.	101.0	67.0	86.3	101.5	43.8	76.5	101.6	76.6	90.8	102.2	76.6	91.1	101.2	71.7	88.4	93.1	134.1	110.9
MF2018	WEIGHTED AVERAGE	93.8	82.1	89.5	94.3	74.1	86.9	99.8	92.9	97.3	99.0	91.8	96.3	95.4	89.6	93.3	96.5	130.3	108.9

		NEW JERSEY																
		CAMDEN			DOVER			ELIZABETH			HACKENSACK			JERSEY CITY			LONG BRANCH		
DIVISION		081			078			072			076			073			077		
		MAT.	INST.	TOTAL	MAT.	INST.	TOTAL	MAT.	INST.	TOTAL	MAT.	INST.	TOTAL	MAT.	INST.	TOTAL	MAT.	INST.	TOTAL
015433	CONTRACTOR EQUIPMENT		90.8	90.8		93.0	93.0		93.0	93.0		93.0	93.0		90.8	90.8		90.5	90.5
0241, 31 - 34	SITE & INFRASTRUCTURE, DEMOLITION	89.1	95.8	93.5	100.3	96.8	98.0	104.4	96.8	99.5	101.3	96.8	98.4	93.8	96.8	95.7	96.5	96.5	96.5
0310	Concrete Forming & Accessories	104.8	140.6	132.7	94.2	141.9	131.2	106.4	142.0	134.1	94.2	141.8	131.2	98.6	142.1	132.4	99.3	141.0	131.7
0320	Concrete Reinforcing	100.5	134.6	109.9	73.9	148.3	94.5	73.9	148.3	94.5	73.9	148.3	94.5	95.9	148.3	110.4	73.9	148.2	94.5
0330	Cast-in-Place Concrete	63.4	133.0	88.1	67.6	134.5	91.4	58.1	134.2	85.2	66.1	134.1	90.3	52.8	134.6	81.8	58.7	132.8	85.0
03	CONCRETE	86.9	135.6	106.2	80.9	139.0	103.9	79.4	139.1	103.0	79.7	139.0	103.1	80.9	139.1	103.8	80.5	138.0	103.2
04	MASONRY	97.2	137.2	121.5	95.2	139.0	121.8	111.7	139.0	128.3	99.3	139.0	123.4	89.1	139.0	119.4	104.2	137.2	124.2
05	METALS	104.0	114.6	106.1	94.2	122.6	99.8	95.7	122.7	101.0	94.3	122.5	99.9	102.1	120.0	105.6	94.3	119.6	99.3
06	WOOD, PLASTICS & COMPOSITES	109.1	141.6	123.7	91.2	141.6	113.8	108.0	141.6	123.0	91.2	141.6	113.8	92.4	141.6	114.5	93.6	141.6	115.1
07	THERMAL & MOISTURE PROTECTION	99.7	133.5	113.7	97.8	134.3	110.8	98.1	137.4	112.1	97.6	132.5	110.0	97.4	137.4	111.6	97.5	131.3	109.6
08	OPENINGS	99.6	137.6	108.2	100.4	139.3	109.2	98.8	139.3	107.9	98.1	139.3	107.4	96.4	139.3	106.1	92.9	139.3	103.4
0920	Plaster & Gypsum Board	128.0	142.8	137.4	119.7	142.8	134.4	129.6	142.8	138.0	119.7	142.8	134.4	126.0	142.8	136.7	122.2	142.8	135.3
0950, 0980	Ceilings & Acoustic Treatment	120.1	142.8	132.8	97.7	142.8	123.0	98.2	142.8	123.2	97.7	142.8	123.0	113.6	142.8	130.0	97.7	142.8	123.0
0960	Flooring	101.5	152.0	114.2	86.4	176.5	108.9	90.8	176.5	112.3	86.4	176.5	108.9	87.2	176.5	109.6	87.5	176.5	109.8
0970, 0990	Wall Finishes & Painting/Coating	82.6	143.0	118.6	81.8	140.9	117.0	81.8	140.9	117.0	81.8	140.9	117.0	81.9	140.9	117.1	81.9	143.0	118.3
09	FINISHES	105.8	144.2	125.1	95.7	148.2	122.1	99.0	148.8	124.0	95.6	148.2	122.0	100.9	148.9	125.0	96.6	148.4	122.6
COVERS	DIVS. 10 - 14, 25, 28, 41, 43, 44, 46	100.0	114.9	102.9	100.0	127.4	105.3	100.0	127.4	105.3	100.0	127.4	105.3	100.0	127.4	105.3	100.0	114.8	102.9
21, 22, 23	FIRE SUPPRESSION, PLUMBING & HVAC	99.9	132.9	111.7	99.3	134.8	112.0	99.9	133.9	112.1	99.3	134.8	112.0	99.9	134.9	112.4	99.3	132.8	111.3
26, 27, 3370	ELECTRICAL, COMMUNICATIONS & UTIL.	95.5	134.1	112.2	92.4	136.6	111.5	92.7	136.6	111.7	92.4	136.0	111.3	94.8	136.0	112.7	92.3	131.3	109.2
MF2018	WEIGHTED AVERAGE	98.9	130.4	110.5	94.9	133.7	109.1	96.2	133.6	110.0	94.7	133.5	109.0	96.6	133.5	110.2	94.5	131.4	108.1

City Cost Indexes

DIVISION		NEW JERSEY																	
		NEW BRUNSWICK 088 - 089			NEWARK 070 - 071			PATERSON 074 - 075			POINT PLEASANT 087			SUMMIT 079			TRENTON 085 - 086		
		MAT.	INST.	TOTAL	MAT.	INST.	TOTAL	MAT.	INST.	TOTAL	MAT.	INST.	TOTAL	MAT.	INST.	TOTAL	MAT.	INST.	TOTAL
015433	CONTRACTOR EQUIPMENT		90.5	90.5		98.0	98.0		93.0	93.0		90.5	90.5		93.0	93.0		96.1	96.1
0241, 31 - 34	SITE & INFRASTRUCTURE, DEMOLITION	97.4	96.7	96.9	107.4	104.5	105.5	103.4	96.8	99.1	98.5	96.1	96.9	102.2	96.8	98.7	88.5	105.5	99.6
0310	Concrete Forming & Accessories	108.5	142.0	134.5	99.0	142.3	132.7	96.2	142.0	131.7	101.8	126.7	121.1	96.9	141.8	131.8	103.6	140.9	132.6
0320	Concrete Reinforcing	77.4	148.3	97.0	99.7	148.3	113.1	95.9	148.3	110.4	77.4	147.6	96.8	73.9	148.3	94.5	100.0	134.7	109.6
0330	Cast-in-Place Concrete	80.8	133.9	99.7	76.5	136.3	97.7	67.2	134.2	91.0	80.8	123.7	96.1	56.2	134.1	83.9	77.4	133.9	97.5
03	CONCRETE	95.7	138.8	112.7	92.7	139.9	111.3	86.6	139.1	107.3	95.1	128.3	108.2	76.9	139.0	101.4	93.6	136.0	110.3
04	MASONRY	105.6	139.0	125.9	99.9	139.1	123.7	96.0	139.0	122.1	93.8	122.1	111.0	98.2	139.0	122.9	104.5	137.3	124.4
05	METALS	96.3	119.9	100.9	103.1	121.1	106.7	98.1	122.7	102.9	96.3	118.4	100.7	94.2	122.5	99.8	103.2	114.0	105.3
06	WOOD, PLASTICS & COMPOSITES	115.8	141.6	127.3	94.8	141.9	115.9	94.1	141.6	115.4	105.7	126.2	114.9	95.4	141.6	116.1	100.8	141.6	119.1
07	THERMAL & MOISTURE PROTECTION	100.1	136.6	113.1	100.4	138.9	114.1	97.9	132.5	110.2	100.1	121.8	107.8	98.1	137.4	112.1	101.2	134.8	113.2
08	OPENINGS	92.9	139.3	103.4	98.7	139.4	107.9	103.0	139.3	111.2	94.7	132.3	103.2	104.7	139.3	112.5	97.8	136.1	106.4
0920	Plaster & Gypsum Board	128.8	142.8	137.7	117.7	142.8	133.6	126.0	142.8	136.7	121.1	127.0	124.9	122.2	142.8	135.3	120.1	142.8	134.5
0950, 0980	Ceilings & Acoustic Treatment	102.3	142.8	125.0	114.0	142.8	130.2	113.6	142.8	130.0	102.3	127.0	116.1	97.7	142.8	123.0	113.5	142.8	130.0
0960	Flooring	102.6	176.5	121.1	104.1	176.5	122.2	87.2	176.5	109.6	100.6	152.0	113.5	87.5	176.5	109.8	106.4	176.5	124.0
0970, 0990	Wall Finishes & Painting/Coating	82.6	140.9	117.4	94.9	140.9	122.4	81.8	140.9	117.0	82.6	143.0	118.6	81.8	140.9	117.0	99.1	143.0	125.3
09	FINISHES	102.5	148.8	125.8	107.0	149.1	128.1	101.0	148.9	125.1	100.9	133.5	117.3	96.7	148.2	122.5	107.7	148.5	128.2
COVERS	DIVS. 10 - 14, 25, 28, 41, 43, 44, 46	100.0	127.3	105.3	100.0	128.1	105.4	100.0	127.4	105.3	100.0	99.5	99.9	100.0	127.4	105.3	100.0	114.9	102.9
21, 22, 23	FIRE SUPPRESSION, PLUMBING & HVAC	99.3	133.7	111.7	99.9	134.9	112.5	99.9	134.9	112.4	99.3	129.1	110.0	99.4	130.1	110.4	99.9	132.7	111.7
26, 27, 3370	ELECTRICAL, COMMUNICATIONS & UTIL.	93.5	134.1	111.1	100.3	136.0	115.8	94.8	136.6	112.9	93.1	131.3	109.7	92.7	136.6	111.7	100.2	126.7	111.7
MF2018	WEIGHTED AVERAGE	97.7	120.1	110.7	100.4	134.5	112.9	97.5	133.7	110.8	97.1	124.5	107.2	95.1	132.7	108.9	100.2	130.6	111.4

DIVISION		NEW JERSEY			NEW MEXICO														
		VINELAND 080,083			ALBUQUERQUE 870 - 872			CARRIZOZO 883			CLOVIS 881			FARMINGTON 874			GALLUP 873		
		MAT.	INST.	TOTAL	MAT.	INST.	TOTAL	MAT.	INST.	TOTAL	MAT.	INST.	TOTAL	MAT.	INST.	TOTAL	MAT.	INST.	TOTAL
015433	CONTRACTOR EQUIPMENT		90.8	90.8		104.7	104.7		104.7	104.7		104.7	104.7		104.7	104.7		104.7	104.7
0241, 31 - 34	SITE & INFRASTRUCTURE, DEMOLITION	90.9	95.8	94.1	93.8	94.0	93.9	107.4	94.0	98.6	95.8	94.0	94.6	98.9	94.0	95.7	105.1	94.0	97.9
0310	Concrete Forming & Accessories	98.4	140.7	131.3	99.7	68.7	75.6	96.1	68.7	74.8	96.1	68.5	74.7	99.8	68.7	75.6	99.8	68.7	75.6
0320	Concrete Reinforcing	76.5	134.6	92.6	94.2	68.8	87.2	103.8	68.8	94.1	105.0	68.7	94.9	103.0	68.8	93.5	98.6	68.8	90.3
0330	Cast-in-Place Concrete	70.5	132.9	92.7	82.6	69.5	78.0	85.4	69.5	79.7	85.3	69.4	79.7	83.4	69.5	78.5	78.5	69.5	75.3
03	CONCRETE	85.9	135.6	105.5	90.2	70.3	82.4	107.9	70.3	93.0	99.2	70.2	87.7	94.3	70.3	84.8	98.2	70.3	87.2
04	MASONRY	96.1	137.2	121.1	101.6	60.1	76.4	109.6	60.1	79.6	109.6	60.1	79.6	107.1	60.1	78.6	99.0	60.1	75.4
05	METALS	96.1	114.5	99.8	105.8	91.0	102.9	101.2	91.0	99.2	100.8	90.9	98.9	102.5	91.0	100.2	101.6	91.0	99.6
06	WOOD, PLASTICS & COMPOSITES	101.4	141.6	119.4	102.2	70.0	87.8	95.6	70.0	84.1	95.6	70.0	84.1	102.4	70.0	87.9	102.4	70.0	87.9
07	THERMAL & MOISTURE PROTECTION	99.6	132.8	111.4	100.9	70.7	90.1	95.5	70.7	86.6	94.5	70.7	86.0	101.1	70.7	90.3	102.0	70.7	90.9
08	OPENINGS	94.3	137.6	104.0	97.9	67.8	91.1	91.6	67.8	86.3	91.8	67.8	86.4	100.2	67.8	92.9	100.2	67.8	92.9
0920	Plaster & Gypsum Board	118.5	142.8	133.9	99.4	69.1	80.2	88.0	69.1	76.0	88.0	69.1	76.0	90.1	69.1	76.8	90.1	69.1	76.8
0950, 0980	Ceilings & Acoustic Treatment	102.3	142.8	125.0	122.6	69.1	92.6	105.3	69.1	85.0	105.3	69.1	85.0	114.6	69.1	89.1	114.6	69.1	89.1
0960	Flooring	100.1	152.0	113.1	94.1	66.7	87.2	99.0	66.7	90.9	99.0	66.7	90.9	95.6	66.7	88.4	95.6	66.7	88.4
0970, 0990	Wall Finishes & Painting/Coating	82.6	143.0	118.6	94.1	51.0	68.4	92.2	51.0	67.6	92.2	51.0	67.6	88.2	51.0	66.0	88.2	51.0	66.0
09	FINISHES	99.7	144.2	122.1	101.6	66.5	83.9	98.9	66.5	82.6	97.8	66.5	82.1	98.6	66.5	82.4	99.7	66.5	83.0
COVERS	DIVS. 10 - 14, 25, 28, 41, 43, 44, 46	100.0	114.9	102.9	100.0	86.7	97.4	100.0	86.7	97.4	100.0	86.7	97.4	100.0	86.7	97.4	100.0	86.7	97.4
21, 22, 23	FIRE SUPPRESSION, PLUMBING & HVAC	99.3	132.7	111.3	100.3	67.8	88.6	95.4	67.8	85.5	95.4	67.5	85.4	100.2	67.8	88.6	95.5	67.8	85.6
26, 27, 3370	ELECTRICAL, COMMUNICATIONS & UTIL.	93.1	134.1	110.9	83.3	69.0	77.1	85.6	69.0	78.4	84.4	69.0	77.7	82.1	69.0	76.4	81.7	69.0	76.2
MF2018	WEIGHTED AVERAGE	95.7	130.4	108.5	98.2	72.3	88.7	98.3	72.3	88.7	96.6	72.2	87.6	98.2	72.3	88.6	97.4	72.3	88.1

DIVISION		NEW MEXICO																	
		LAS CRUCES 880			LAS VEGAS 877			ROSWELL 882			SANTA FE 875			SOCORRO 878			TRUTH/CONSEQUENCES 879		
		MAT.	INST.	TOTAL	MAT.	INST.	TOTAL	MAT.	INST.	TOTAL	MAT.	INST.	TOTAL	MAT.	INST.	TOTAL	MAT.	INST.	TOTAL
015433	CONTRACTOR EQUIPMENT		83.2	83.2		104.7	104.7		104.7	104.7		108.5	108.5		104.7	104.7		83.3	83.3
0241, 31 - 34	SITE & INFRASTRUCTURE, DEMOLITION	98.4	76.0	83.8	95.8	94.0	94.6	99.9	94.0	96.0	99.7	100.4	100.2	93.0	94.0	93.7	108.3	76.0	87.3
0310	Concrete Forming & Accessories	92.8	67.7	73.3	99.8	68.7	75.6	96.1	68.7	74.8	100.4	68.9	75.9	99.8	68.7	75.6	97.8	67.7	74.4
0320	Concrete Reinforcing	102.9	68.5	93.4	100.3	68.8	91.6	105.0	68.8	94.9	100.3	68.8	91.6	102.2	68.8	93.0	97.8	68.6	89.7
0330	Cast-in-Place Concrete	80.6	63.2	74.4	81.1	69.5	77.0	85.3	69.5	79.7	86.2	71.8	81.1	79.5	69.5	75.9	87.1	63.2	78.6
03	CONCRETE	82.7	67.3	76.6	92.0	70.3	83.4	99.8	70.3	88.2	97.0	71.0	86.8	91.5	70.3	83.1	86.3	67.3	78.8
04	MASONRY	105.0	57.8	76.3	99.3	60.1	75.5	121.0	60.1	84.0	95.8	60.3	74.2	99.2	60.1	75.5	95.4	59.9	73.8
05	METALS	99.1	83.9	96.1	101.3	91.0	99.3	102.1	91.0	99.9	100.0	88.5	97.7	101.7	91.0	99.6	100.6	84.1	97.3
06	WOOD, PLASTICS & COMPOSITES	86.3	69.1	78.6	102.4	70.0	87.9	95.6	70.0	84.1	98.7	70.3	85.9	102.4	70.0	87.9	95.6	69.1	83.8
07	THERMAL & MOISTURE PROTECTION	86.3	66.0	79.1	100.8	70.7	90.1	94.6	70.7	86.1	103.7	73.0	92.8	100.8	70.7	90.1	91.7	66.6	82.7
08	OPENINGS	87.2	67.3	82.7	97.0	67.8	90.4	91.6	67.8	86.2	98.4	67.9	91.5	96.8	67.8	90.3	90.1	67.3	84.9
0920	Plaster & Gypsum Board	86.8	69.1	75.6	90.1	69.1	76.8	88.0	69.1	76.0	95.3	69.1	78.7	90.1	69.1	76.8	93.1	69.1	77.9
0950, 0980	Ceilings & Acoustic Treatment	101.6	69.1	83.4	114.6	69.1	89.1	105.3	69.1	85.0	112.8	69.1	88.3	114.6	69.1	89.1	113.4	69.1	88.6
0960	Flooring	129.2	66.7	113.6	95.6	66.7	88.4	99.0	66.7	90.9	105.3	66.7	95.6	95.6	66.7	88.4	123.4	66.7	109.2
0970, 0990	Wall Finishes & Painting/Coating	80.6	51.0	62.9	88.2	51.0	66.0	92.2	51.0	67.6	99.1	51.0	70.4	88.2	51.0	66.0	80.6	51.0	62.9
09	FINISHES	109.2	65.6	87.3	98.4	66.5	82.4	97.9	66.5	82.1	104.0	66.5	85.2	98.4	66.5	82.3	111.8	65.8	88.7
COVERS	DIVS. 10 - 14, 25, 28, 41, 43, 44, 46	100.0	84.6	97.0	100.0	86.7	97.4	100.0	86.7	97.4	100.0	87.2	97.5	100.0	86.7	97.4	100.0	84.5	97.0
21, 22, 23	FIRE SUPPRESSION, PLUMBING & HVAC	100.7	67.6	88.8	95.5	67.8	85.6	100.0	67.8	88.5	100.1	67.9	88.6	95.5	67.8	85.6	94.4	67.6	84.8
26, 27, 3370	ELECTRICAL, COMMUNICATIONS & UTIL.	88.0	74.6	82.2	82.8	69.0	76.8	85.1	69.0	78.1	100.8	69.0	87.0	81.9	69.0	76.3	85.9	69.0	78.6
MF2018	WEIGHTED AVERAGE	95.8	70.0	86.3	96.0	72.3	87.3	98.6	72.3	88.9	99.8	72.8	89.9	95.9	72.3	87.2	95.5	69.4	85.9

City Cost Indexes

		NEW MEXICO			NEW YORK													
		TUCUMCARI			ALBANY			BINGHAMTON			BRONX			BROOKLYN			BUFFALO		
DIVISION		884			120 - 122			137 - 139			104			112			140 - 142		
		MAT.	INST.	TOTAL	MAT.	INST.	TOTAL	MAT.	INST.	TOTAL	MAT.	INST.	TOTAL	MAT.	INST.	TOTAL	MAT.	INST.	TOTAL
015433	CONTRACTOR EQUIPMENT		104.7	104.7		111.6	111.6		112.7	112.7		100.4	100.4		105.3	105.3		96.9	96.9
0241, 31 - 34	SITE & INFRASTRUCTURE, DEMOLITION	95.4	94.0	94.5	78.6	103.0	94.5	91.8	86.1	88.1	93.3	104.2	100.4	109.7	114.3	112.7	90.5	97.5	95.1
0310	Concrete Forming & Accessories	96.1	68.5	74.7	104.7	102.5	103.0	100.4	88.6	91.3	90.9	177.7	158.3	106.4	174.2	159.1	105.1	109.7	108.7
0320	Concrete Reinforcing	102.9	68.7	93.4	99.2	110.4	102.3	95.6	106.0	98.5	91.8	163.7	111.7	96.0	238.8	135.5	99.6	109.0	102.2
0330	Cast-in-Place Concrete	85.3	69.4	79.7	76.3	114.3	89.8	105.5	101.0	103.9	69.6	159.4	101.5	107.4	158.2	125.4	126.3	117.2	123.0
03	CONCRETE	98.3	70.2	87.2	92.9	108.9	99.2	95.4	98.2	96.5	76.7	168.4	112.9	104.1	178.3	133.4	121.3	111.9	117.6
04	MASONRY	121.0	60.1	84.0	115.4	115.2	115.3	109.4	99.5	103.4	86.5	181.9	144.5	121.5	181.9	158.2	117.1	119.3	118.5
05	METALS	100.8	90.9	98.9	99.2	120.3	103.4	91.3	131.6	99.2	83.8	164.7	99.8	97.4	173.2	112.4	97.0	103.8	98.3
06	WOOD, PLASTICS & COMPOSITES	95.6	70.0	84.1	103.2	98.4	101.0	103.5	85.3	95.3	103.1	175.8	135.7	107.7	170.5	135.8	102.6	108.0	105.0
07	THERMAL & MOISTURE PROTECTION	94.5	70.7	86.0	97.6	107.3	101.1	106.3	90.5	100.7	97.2	160.1	119.6	105.1	159.0	124.3	99.8	106.9	102.3
08	OPENINGS	91.6	67.8	86.2	97.9	100.6	98.5	91.0	91.2	91.0	94.7	184.5	115.0	88.7	186.7	110.8	100.1	104.5	101.1
0920	Plaster & Gypsum Board	88.0	69.1	76.0	104.0	98.2	100.3	122.7	84.8	98.7	98.7	178.2	149.1	115.9	173.0	152.1	111.6	108.2	109.5
0950, 0980	Ceilings & Acoustic Treatment	105.3	69.1	85.0	95.4	98.2	97.0	104.8	84.8	93.6	77.0	178.2	134.1	97.1	173.0	139.7	95.4	108.2	102.6
0960	Flooring	99.0	66.7	90.9	100.6	104.5	101.6	109.9	95.7	106.3	96.3	180.0	117.3	117.0	180.0	132.8	99.3	115.4	103.3
0970, 0990	Wall Finishes & Painting/Coating	92.2	51.0	67.6	99.1	98.7	98.9	87.1	96.3	92.6	100.0	161.9	136.9	113.0	161.9	142.2	99.1	108.7	104.8
09	FINISHES	97.8	66.5	82.0	98.4	101.8	100.1	101.9	89.9	95.8	93.2	177.0	135.3	111.5	173.9	142.8	98.7	111.0	104.9
COVERS	DIVS. 10 - 14, 25, 28, 41, 43, 44, 46	100.0	86.7	97.4	100.0	101.2	100.2	100.0	97.2	99.5	100.0	139.3	107.6	100.0	138.1	107.4	100.0	105.8	101.1
21, 22, 23	FIRE SUPPRESSION, PLUMBING & HVAC	95.4	67.5	85.4	100.2	107.1	102.7	100.9	95.5	98.9	100.2	169.2	124.9	99.8	169.4	124.7	100.2	98.5	99.6
26, 27, 3370	ELECTRICAL, COMMUNICATIONS & UTIL.	85.6	69.0	78.4	100.6	105.1	102.5	100.3	96.1	98.5	98.0	171.2	129.7	103.1	171.2	132.6	100.9	99.3	100.2
MF2018	WEIGHTED AVERAGE	97.0	72.2	87.9	98.8	107.5	102.0	97.5	97.8	97.6	91.8	165.6	119.0	101.4	168.1	126.0	102.4	105.4	103.5

		NEW YORK																
		ELMIRA			FAR ROCKAWAY			FLUSHING			GLENS FALLS			HICKSVILLE			JAMAICA		
DIVISION		148 - 149			116			113			128			115, 117, 118			114		
		MAT.	INST.	TOTAL	MAT.	INST.	TOTAL	MAT.	INST.	TOTAL	MAT.	INST.	TOTAL	MAT.	INST.	TOTAL	MAT.	INST.	TOTAL
015433	CONTRACTOR EQUIPMENT		115.1	115.1		105.3	105.3		105.3	105.3		108.2	108.2		105.3	105.3		105.3	105.3
0241, 31 - 34	SITE & INFRASTRUCTURE, DEMOLITION	86.3	87.0	86.8	108.9	114.3	112.4	108.9	114.3	112.4	68.8	94.3	85.4	104.4	112.6	109.7	104.4	114.3	110.9
0310	Concrete Forming & Accessories	82.4	91.3	89.3	91.7	178.0	158.7	95.9	178.0	159.7	85.1	90.6	89.4	87.8	146.4	133.3	95.9	178.0	159.7
0320	Concrete Reinforcing	99.4	105.0	100.9	96.0	238.8	135.5	97.7	238.8	136.8	96.3	101.5	97.7	96.0	165.0	115.1	96.0	238.8	135.5
0330	Cast-in-Place Concrete	111.0	100.5	107.3	116.2	158.2	131.1	116.2	158.2	131.1	73.5	107.4	85.5	98.6	147.4	116.0	107.4	158.2	125.5
03	CONCRETE	104.1	99.2	102.2	119.4	180.0	137.3	119.4	180.0	137.3	81.7	99.8	88.8	96.8	149.3	117.5	103.2	180.0	133.5
04	MASONRY	109.4	100.2	103.8	124.6	181.9	159.4	118.0	181.9	156.8	120.5	107.8	112.8	114.5	164.6	144.9	124.0	181.9	159.2
05	METALS	90.7	133.4	99.1	97.5	173.2	112.4	97.5	173.2	112.4	93.3	118.0	98.1	98.9	143.0	107.6	97.5	173.2	112.4
06	WOOD, PLASTICS & COMPOSITES	76.2	89.3	82.0	87.0	175.6	126.7	93.0	175.6	130.0	84.4	87.2	85.7	82.7	143.7	110.1	93.0	175.6	130.0
07	THERMAL & MOISTURE PROTECTION	99.1	90.6	96.1	104.9	159.9	124.5	105.0	159.9	124.6	91.4	98.5	94.0	104.6	147.6	119.9	104.8	159.9	124.5
08	OPENINGS	93.6	93.1	93.5	87.5	189.5	110.5	87.5	189.5	110.5	92.0	89.7	91.5	87.8	153.9	102.7	87.5	189.5	110.5
0920	Plaster & Gypsum Board	107.7	89.1	95.9	97.1	178.2	148.6	101.5	178.2	150.2	86.5	87.0	86.8	96.6	145.4	127.6	101.5	178.2	150.2
0950, 0980	Ceilings & Acoustic Treatment	99.4	89.1	93.6	80.3	178.2	135.2	80.3	178.2	135.2	85.0	87.0	86.1	79.8	145.4	116.6	80.3	178.2	135.2
0960	Flooring	95.5	95.7	95.6	112.7	180.0	129.6	113.9	180.0	130.5	90.3	96.5	91.8	111.8	172.4	127.0	113.9	180.0	130.5
0970, 0990	Wall Finishes & Painting/Coating	94.3	86.9	89.9	113.0	161.9	142.2	113.0	161.9	142.2	89.8	101.7	96.9	113.0	161.9	142.2	113.0	161.9	142.2
09	FINISHES	96.1	91.1	93.6	103.6	176.8	140.4	104.5	176.8	140.8	88.8	92.1	90.5	102.4	152.4	127.5	104.2	176.8	140.7
COVERS	DIVS. 10 - 14, 25, 28, 41, 43, 44, 46	100.0	96.1	99.2	100.0	138.7	107.5	100.0	138.7	107.5	100.0	86.4	97.4	100.0	123.8	104.6	100.0	138.7	107.5
21, 22, 23	FIRE SUPPRESSION, PLUMBING & HVAC	92.8	91.3	92.3	92.0	169.4	119.7	92.0	169.4	119.7	92.7	101.0	95.7	99.8	149.6	117.7	92.0	169.4	119.7
26, 27, 3370	ELECTRICAL, COMMUNICATIONS & UTIL.	97.8	99.7	98.6	106.6	171.2	134.6	106.6	171.2	134.6	95.0	93.5	94.3	102.5	134.8	116.5	101.9	171.2	131.9
MF2018	WEIGHTED AVERAGE	95.6	98.2	96.5	99.8	169.0	125.3	99.8	169.0	125.3	92.3	99.2	94.9	99.4	145.1	116.2	98.6	169.0	124.5

		NEW YORK																
		JAMESTOWN			KINGSTON			LONG ISLAND CITY			MONTICELLO			MOUNT VERNON			NEW ROCHELLE		
DIVISION		147			124			111			127			105			108		
		MAT.	INST.	TOTAL	MAT.	INST.	TOTAL	MAT.	INST.	TOTAL	MAT.	INST.	TOTAL	MAT.	INST.	TOTAL	MAT.	INST.	TOTAL
015433	CONTRACTOR EQUIPMENT		88.8	88.8		105.3	105.3		105.3	105.3		105.3	105.3		100.4	100.4		100.4	100.4
0241, 31 - 34	SITE & INFRASTRUCTURE, DEMOLITION	87.6	85.7	86.4	121.9	108.8	113.4	110.8	114.3	113.1	118.4	108.8	112.1	94.4	99.9	98.0	93.8	99.9	97.8
0310	Concrete Forming & Accessories	82.4	81.6	81.8	86.5	118.3	111.2	100.7	178.0	160.7	95.2	118.3	113.1	81.8	127.2	117.1	95.8	124.1	117.8
0320	Concrete Reinforcing	99.5	99.8	99.6	96.9	143.8	109.9	96.0	238.8	135.5	96.0	143.9	109.3	91.7	163.9	111.7	91.8	163.8	111.7
0330	Cast-in-Place Concrete	115.2	95.8	108.3	99.2	132.5	111.0	110.8	158.2	127.7	92.9	132.5	107.0	77.7	140.1	99.9	77.7	139.8	99.8
03	CONCRETE	107.1	90.1	100.3	98.4	127.6	109.9	105.9	180.0	135.2	94.7	127.6	107.7	82.1	138.9	104.5	82.4	137.4	104.1
04	MASONRY	118.6	94.2	103.8	139.4	139.9	139.7	118.3	181.9	156.9	132.2	139.9	136.9	91.9	146.7	125.2	91.9	146.7	125.2
05	METALS	88.7	97.0	90.3	99.5	127.7	105.0	97.4	173.2	112.4	99.4	127.9	105.0	83.6	163.0	99.2	83.9	162.3	99.3
06	WOOD, PLASTICS & COMPOSITES	74.9	78.2	76.4	86.0	112.4	97.8	100.4	175.6	134.1	96.2	112.4	103.5	93.0	120.0	105.1	111.1	116.6	113.6
07	THERMAL & MOISTURE PROTECTION	98.6	85.5	93.0	108.4	131.4	116.6	105.0	159.9	124.6	108.2	131.4	116.5	97.8	136.4	111.6	98.0	134.2	110.9
08	OPENINGS	93.4	84.3	91.4	94.6	131.8	103.0	87.5	189.5	110.5	90.7	131.8	100.0	94.7	157.7	108.9	94.8	155.8	108.6
0920	Plaster & Gypsum Board	92.5	77.7	83.1	85.0	113.1	102.8	108.5	178.2	152.7	85.7	113.1	103.1	92.7	120.7	110.4	110.1	117.1	114.6
0950, 0980	Ceilings & Acoustic Treatment	94.9	77.7	85.3	70.0	113.1	94.2	80.3	178.2	135.2	70.0	113.1	94.2	75.0	120.7	100.6	75.0	117.1	98.6
0960	Flooring	98.8	91.8	97.0	108.8	143.8	117.5	115.4	180.0	131.6	110.5	143.8	118.9	88.1	160.9	106.4	95.0	146.9	108.0
0970, 0990	Wall Finishes & Painting/Coating	96.0	89.4	92.1	117.2	116.3	116.6	113.0	161.9	142.2	117.2	109.6	112.7	98.3	161.9	136.2	98.3	161.9	136.2
09	FINISHES	94.0	83.5	88.7	99.3	122.0	110.7	105.7	176.8	141.4	99.7	121.2	110.5	89.8	135.6	112.8	94.0	130.8	112.5
COVERS	DIVS. 10 - 14, 25, 28, 41, 43, 44, 46	100.0	94.9	98.0	100.0	108.0	101.5	100.0	138.7	107.5	100.0	108.0	101.5	100.0	116.1	103.1	100.0	101.8	100.3
21, 22, 23	FIRE SUPPRESSION, PLUMBING & HVAC	92.6	84.1	89.6	92.4	120.9	102.7	99.8	169.4	124.7	92.4	124.8	104.0	92.5	142.2	110.3	92.5	141.9	110.3
26, 27, 3370	ELECTRICAL, COMMUNICATIONS & UTIL.	96.5	84.5	91.3	96.6	103.5	99.6	102.2	171.2	132.1	96.6	103.5	99.6	94.9	151.8	119.6	94.9	126.1	108.5
MF2018	WEIGHTED AVERAGE	95.5	87.5	92.6	99.3	121.3	107.4	100.8	169.0	125.9	98.3	122.0	107.0	90.3	140.7	108.9	90.9	135.5	107.3

City Cost Indexes

		NEW YORK																	
	DIVISION	NEW YORK 100 - 102			NIAGARA FALLS 143			PLATTSBURGH 129			POUGHKEEPSIE 125 - 126			QUEENS 110			RIVERHEAD 119		
		MAT.	INST.	TOTAL	MAT.	INST.	TOTAL	MAT.	INST.	TOTAL	MAT.	INST.	TOTAL	MAT.	INST.	TOTAL	MAT.	INST.	TOTAL
015433	CONTRACTOR EQUIPMENT		102.4	102.4		88.8	88.8		92.0	92.0		105.3	105.3		105.3	105.3		105.3	105.3
0241, 31 - 34	SITE & INFRASTRUCTURE, DEMOLITION	101.6	107.8	105.6	89.1	86.6	87.5	101.5	91.7	95.1	119.3	108.0	111.9	106.7	114.3	111.7	105.0	112.6	110.0
0310	Concrete Forming & Accessories	99.4	177.9	160.4	82.4	102.4	97.9	91.9	82.7	84.7	86.5	151.7	137.1	88.0	178.0	157.9	92.9	147.0	135.0
0320	Concrete Reinforcing	100.8	165.3	118.7	98.1	100.5	98.8	99.2	100.5	99.6	96.9	144.0	109.9	97.7	238.8	136.8	97.9	230.0	134.4
0330	Cast-in-Place Concrete	80.6	161.7	109.4	119.2	112.7	116.9	89.8	91.6	90.4	96.1	122.9	105.6	102.0	158.2	122.0	100.3	147.8	117.2
03	CONCRETE	87.4	169.6	119.8	109.1	105.5	107.7	92.6	89.0	91.2	96.2	139.4	113.3	99.7	180.0	131.4	97.9	160.8	122.7
04	MASONRY	101.3	182.0	150.3	125.6	112.7	117.8	114.6	87.7	98.2	130.4	133.0	132.0	112.6	181.9	154.7	120.0	164.6	147.1
05	METALS	101.6	166.2	114.4	90.9	97.5	92.2	95.8	94.4	95.5	99.5	128.6	105.2	97.4	173.2	112.4	99.6	166.6	112.8
06	WOOD, PLASTICS & COMPOSITES	112.0	176.1	140.7	74.8	98.2	85.3	92.8	80.0	87.1	86.0	162.4	120.2	82.9	175.6	124.4	89.1	143.7	113.6
07	THERMAL & MOISTURE PROTECTION	101.5	162.6	123.2	98.7	98.6	98.7	104.6	87.1	98.4	108.3	132.6	117.0	104.6	159.9	124.3	106.0	149.0	121.3
08	OPENINGS	102.7	188.2	122.0	93.4	94.8	93.7	99.2	85.8	96.2	94.6	154.3	108.1	87.5	189.5	110.5	87.8	169.8	106.3
0920	Plaster & Gypsum Board	110.6	178.2	153.5	92.5	98.2	96.1	112.4	79.2	91.3	85.0	164.6	135.5	96.6	178.2	148.4	98.4	145.4	128.2
0950, 0980	Ceilings & Acoustic Treatment	101.5	178.2	144.5	94.9	98.2	96.8	97.7	79.2	87.3	70.0	164.6	123.1	80.3	178.2	135.2	80.7	145.4	117.0
0960	Flooring	96.5	177.3	116.8	98.8	100.4	99.2	116.5	94.1	110.9	108.8	142.9	117.1	111.8	180.0	128.9	112.7	172.4	127.7
0970, 0990	Wall Finishes & Painting/Coating	99.1	161.9	136.6	96.0	108.7	103.6	112.9	84.5	96.0	117.2	109.6	112.7	113.0	161.9	142.2	113.0	161.9	142.2
09	FINISHES	101.7	176.7	139.4	94.1	102.8	98.5	101.8	84.4	93.1	99.2	147.9	123.6	102.7	176.8	139.9	103.1	152.4	127.9
COVERS	DIVS. 10 - 14, 25, 28, 41, 43, 44, 46	100.0	139.6	107.7	100.0	101.7	100.3	100.0	82.8	96.7	100.0	117.9	103.5	100.0	138.7	107.5	100.0	123.8	104.6
21, 22, 23	FIRE SUPPRESSION, PLUMBING & HVAC	100.1	169.4	124.9	92.6	94.5	93.3	92.6	90.1	91.7	92.4	108.1	98.1	99.8	169.4	124.7	100.1	150.4	118.1
26, 27, 3370	ELECTRICAL, COMMUNICATIONS & UTIL.	101.2	176.5	133.8	95.8	88.0	92.4	88.8	81.7	85.7	96.6	107.9	101.5	102.5	171.2	132.2	103.3	135.0	117.1
MF2018	WEIGHTED AVERAGE	99.6	167.2	124.5	96.5	98.0	97.1	96.1	87.7	93.0	98.7	125.3	108.5	99.4	169.0	125.0	100.2	149.7	118.4

		NEW YORK																	
	DIVISION	ROCHESTER 144 - 146			SCHENECTADY 123			STATEN ISLAND 103			SUFFERN 109			SYRACUSE 130 - 132			UTICA 133 - 135		
		MAT.	INST.	TOTAL	MAT.	INST.	TOTAL	MAT.	INST.	TOTAL	MAT.	INST.	TOTAL	MAT.	INST.	TOTAL	MAT.	INST.	TOTAL
015433	CONTRACTOR EQUIPMENT		111.6	111.6		108.2	108.2		100.4	100.4		100.4	100.4		108.2	108.2		108.2	108.2
0241, 31 - 34	SITE & INFRASTRUCTURE, DEMOLITION	83.7	100.0	94.3	80.1	95.9	90.4	101.3	104.2	103.2	91.6	97.6	95.5	90.6	94.8	93.4	74.0	94.5	87.4
0310	Concrete Forming & Accessories	101.1	96.3	97.4	105.1	102.3	102.9	81.2	174.1	153.4	89.5	127.3	118.9	99.7	90.8	92.8	100.4	89.9	92.2
0320	Concrete Reinforcing	99.6	105.1	101.1	95.3	110.4	99.4	91.8	194.2	120.1	91.8	136.3	104.1	96.6	106.2	99.2	96.6	105.1	98.9
0330	Cast-in-Place Concrete	106.6	104.2	105.7	88.7	112.2	97.1	77.7	159.4	106.8	75.4	125.7	93.3	97.9	105.0	100.4	89.5	104.8	94.9
03	CONCRETE	112.0	101.7	108.0	93.1	108.3	99.1	83.0	171.5	117.9	80.4	127.9	99.2	97.1	99.8	98.2	95.1	99.1	96.7
04	MASONRY	104.3	103.7	103.9	117.6	115.1	116.1	98.6	181.9	149.2	92.0	128.0	113.9	102.4	105.5	104.4	92.8	105.7	100.7
05	METALS	101.7	117.9	104.9	98.5	123.6	103.5	82.3	164.9	98.6	82.3	123.8	90.5	95.9	119.6	100.6	94.0	119.1	98.9
06	WOOD, PLASTICS & COMPOSITES	96.7	94.0	95.5	111.0	98.1	105.2	91.6	170.8	127.1	102.8	129.1	114.5	100.6	86.9	94.5	100.6	85.2	93.7
07	THERMAL & MOISTURE PROTECTION	98.6	98.8	98.6	92.9	105.6	97.4	97.4	159.6	119.6	97.8	127.7	108.5	101.4	96.2	99.6	92.3	96.2	93.7
08	OPENINGS	98.0	96.0	97.6	97.0	99.4	97.5	94.7	181.8	114.3	94.8	139.2	104.8	92.8	90.4	92.3	95.6	89.2	94.1
0920	Plaster & Gypsum Board	112.7	93.8	100.7	101.9	98.2	99.6	93.4	173.0	143.9	97.3	130.0	118.1	111.5	86.6	95.7	111.5	84.9	94.6
0950, 0980	Ceilings & Acoustic Treatment	95.4	93.8	94.5	97.2	98.2	97.8	77.7	173.0	131.1	75.0	130.0	105.8	104.8	86.6	94.6	104.8	84.9	93.6
0960	Flooring	103.1	103.0	103.1	95.7	104.5	97.9	92.2	180.0	114.2	91.3	153.7	106.9	96.1	95.4	95.9	93.6	95.5	94.1
0970, 0990	Wall Finishes & Painting/Coating	94.9	97.7	96.6	89.8	98.7	95.1	100.0	161.9	136.9	98.3	112.8	106.9	89.9	98.8	95.2	83.6	98.8	92.6
09	FINISHES	99.6	97.4	98.5	96.3	101.6	99.0	92.2	174.1	133.3	91.0	131.3	111.3	99.3	91.7	95.4	97.6	90.9	94.3
COVERS	DIVS. 10 - 14, 25, 28, 41, 43, 44, 46	100.0	101.4	100.3	100.0	100.7	100.1	100.0	138.8	107.5	100.0	102.1	100.4	100.0	98.0	99.6	100.0	94.3	98.9
21, 22, 23	FIRE SUPPRESSION, PLUMBING & HVAC	100.1	90.4	96.6	100.2	107.0	102.6	100.2	169.3	124.9	92.5	111.1	99.2	100.4	92.8	97.7	100.4	99.0	99.9
26, 27, 3370	ELECTRICAL, COMMUNICATIONS & UTIL.	100.6	92.3	97.0	97.3	105.1	100.7	98.0	171.2	129.7	98.5	102.0	100.0	100.0	102.5	101.1	96.9	102.5	99.3
MF2018	WEIGHTED AVERAGE	101.4	98.6	100.4	98.2	107.0	101.4	92.7	165.2	119.5	90.3	118.0	100.5	98.1	99.0	98.4	96.2	99.9	97.5

		NEW YORK									NORTH CAROLINA								
	DIVISION	WATERTOWN 136			WHITE PLAINS 106			YONKERS 107			ASHEVILLE 287 - 288			CHARLOTTE 281 - 282			DURHAM 277		
		MAT.	INST.	TOTAL	MAT.	INST.	TOTAL	MAT.	INST.	TOTAL	MAT.	INST.	TOTAL	MAT.	INST.	TOTAL	MAT.	INST.	TOTAL
015433	CONTRACTOR EQUIPMENT		108.2	108.2		100.4	100.4		100.4	100.4		97.1	97.1		102.2	102.2		101.7	101.7
0241, 31 - 34	SITE & INFRASTRUCTURE, DEMOLITION	80.2	94.5	89.5	93.0	100.0	97.5	99.9	100.0	99.9	102.2	76.7	85.6	104.4	87.1	93.1	107.0	84.4	92.3
0310	Concrete Forming & Accessories	83.8	91.7	90.0	94.4	137.0	127.9	94.7	138.3	128.6	95.9	59.4	67.6	102.0	62.8	71.6	102.0	59.9	69.3
0320	Concrete Reinforcing	97.2	106.1	99.7	91.8	164.0	111.8	95.4	164.0	114.4	97.3	59.4	86.8	99.7	65.7	90.3	98.4	60.1	87.8
0330	Cast-in-Place Concrete	104.3	105.3	104.6	69.1	140.2	94.3	77.2	140.3	99.7	111.5	69.2	96.4	113.7	72.6	99.1	126.0	69.2	105.9
03	CONCRETE	104.7	100.3	103.0	76.7	143.7	103.1	83.1	144.1	107.1	92.8	64.6	81.7	95.2	68.2	84.5	101.0	64.9	86.7
04	MASONRY	94.2	106.8	101.8	91.6	146.7	125.1	95.2	146.7	126.5	79.6	61.3	68.5	81.3	63.6	70.5	82.6	61.3	69.7
05	METALS	94.0	119.3	99.0	83.8	163.4	99.5	93.7	163.7	107.5	99.7	87.7	97.3	101.0	87.3	98.3	115.1	88.0	109.7
06	WOOD, PLASTICS & COMPOSITES	78.4	87.6	82.5	108.8	133.5	119.9	108.7	134.2	120.1	96.9	57.4	79.2	98.8	60.8	81.7	101.5	57.9	82.0
07	THERMAL & MOISTURE PROTECTION	92.5	96.9	94.0	97.7	139.4	112.6	98.0	140.1	113.0	110.0	59.3	91.9	102.6	64.8	89.1	106.7	59.4	89.9
08	OPENINGS	95.6	92.3	94.8	94.8	165.2	110.7	98.0	165.6	113.2	88.7	56.3	81.4	98.7	61.4	90.3	96.7	56.8	87.7
0920	Plaster & Gypsum Board	98.5	87.4	91.4	102.2	134.6	122.7	111.0	135.1	126.4	107.8	56.1	75.0	102.3	59.5	75.1	102.8	56.7	73.6
0950, 0980	Ceilings & Acoustic Treatment	104.8	87.4	95.0	75.0	134.6	108.4	104.0	135.3	121.6	102.0	56.1	76.3	104.1	59.5	79.1	91.7	56.7	72.1
0960	Flooring	88.1	94.6	89.7	93.5	172.4	113.2	92.9	180.0	114.7	100.0	59.8	89.9	103.4	65.5	93.9	111.4	59.8	98.5
0970, 0990	Wall Finishes & Painting/Coating	83.6	96.7	91.4	98.3	161.9	136.2	98.3	161.9	136.2	103.1	50.7	71.9	99.1	64.4	78.4	102.8	50.7	71.8
09	FINISHES	94.7	92.2	93.4	91.9	146.0	119.1	101.3	147.9	124.7	102.0	58.2	80.0	102.8	63.1	82.8	100.7	58.5	79.5
COVERS	DIVS. 10 - 14, 25, 28, 41, 43, 44, 46	100.0	98.6	99.7	100.0	120.1	103.9	100.0	128.5	105.5	100.0	84.0	96.9	100.0	85.1	97.1	100.0	84.0	96.9
21, 22, 23	FIRE SUPPRESSION, PLUMBING & HVAC	100.4	87.0	95.6	100.3	142.4	115.4	100.3	142.5	115.4	100.9	60.2	86.3	100.1	62.7	86.7	101.0	60.2	86.4
26, 27, 3370	ELECTRICAL, COMMUNICATIONS & UTIL.	100.0	87.3	94.5	94.9	153.7	120.4	98.6	158.9	124.7	99.8	51.5	78.9	100.6	81.2	92.2	94.4	51.1	75.6
MF2018	WEIGHTED AVERAGE	97.5	95.9	96.9	91.7	143.7	110.8	96.3	145.1	114.2	98.0	63.8	85.4	99.3	71.1	88.9	102.5	64.5	88.5

City Cost Indexes

DIVISION		NORTH CAROLINA																
		ELIZABETH CITY 279			FAYETTEVILLE 283			GASTONIA 280			GREENSBORO 270,272 - 274			HICKORY 286			KINSTON 285		
		MAT.	INST.	TOTAL	MAT.	INST.	TOTAL	MAT.	INST.	TOTAL	MAT.	INST.	TOTAL	MAT.	INST.	TOTAL	MAT.	INST.	TOTAL
015433	CONTRACTOR EQUIPMENT		105.2	105.2		101.7	101.7		97.1	97.1		101.7	101.7		101.7	101.7		101.7	101.7
0241, 31 - 34	SITE & INFRASTRUCTURE, DEMOLITION	107.8	85.6	93.3	101.6	84.1	90.2	102.1	76.7	85.5	106.9	84.4	92.2	98.0	84.1	89.0	96.8	84.1	88.5
0310	Concrete Forming & Accessories	85.3	58.2	64.2	95.4	58.1	66.5	103.1	60.1	69.7	101.7	59.9	69.2	91.4	59.9	67.0	87.2	58.1	64.6
0320	Concrete Reinforcing	96.8	62.8	87.4	100.6	60.1	89.4	97.7	60.1	87.3	97.7	60.1	87.3	97.3	60.1	87.0	96.8	60.1	86.6
0330	Cast-in-Place Concrete	126.3	68.8	105.8	116.9	66.7	99.0	108.9	69.3	94.9	125.1	69.2	105.2	111.4	69.0	96.4	107.6	66.7	93.0
03	CONCRETE	99.8	64.5	85.9	95.4	63.3	82.7	92.1	65.1	81.5	100.4	64.9	86.4	92.4	64.9	81.5	89.9	63.3	79.4
04	MASONRY	92.9	56.7	70.9	83.7	56.8	67.3	84.8	61.3	70.6	81.9	61.3	69.4	70.1	61.2	64.7	76.0	56.8	64.3
05	METALS	100.7	89.9	98.6	118.8	88.0	112.7	100.6	88.2	98.2	106.3	88.0	102.7	99.8	87.4	97.3	98.7	88.0	96.6
06	WOOD, PLASTICS & COMPOSITES	79.9	57.7	70.0	95.1	57.9	78.5	107.3	57.9	85.2	101.2	57.9	81.8	89.7	57.9	75.4	85.2	57.9	73.0
07	THERMAL & MOISTURE PROTECTION	105.6	57.1	88.3	109.3	57.3	90.7	110.2	59.4	92.1	106.2	59.4	89.5	110.2	59.4	92.1	110.1	57.3	91.3
08	OPENINGS	94.0	57.2	85.7	88.8	56.8	81.6	91.9	56.8	84.0	96.7	56.8	87.7	88.8	56.8	81.6	88.9	56.8	81.6
0920	Plaster & Gypsum Board	94.2	55.9	69.9	111.5	56.7	76.7	116.4	56.7	78.5	103.4	56.7	73.8	107.8	56.7	75.4	108.4	56.7	75.6
0950, 0980	Ceilings & Acoustic Treatment	91.7	55.9	71.6	106.5	56.7	78.6	110.2	56.7	80.2	91.7	56.7	72.1	102.0	56.7	76.6	110.2	56.7	80.2
0960	Flooring	104.4	59.8	93.2	100.1	59.8	90.0	102.8	59.8	92.0	111.4	59.8	98.5	99.9	59.8	89.9	97.4	59.8	88.0
0970, 0990	Wall Finishes & Painting/Coating	102.8	50.7	71.8	103.1	50.7	71.9	103.1	50.7	71.9	102.8	50.7	71.8	103.1	50.7	71.9	103.1	50.7	71.9
09	FINISHES	97.8	57.3	77.5	103.7	57.4	80.4	106.1	58.5	82.2	100.8	58.5	79.6	102.1	58.5	80.2	103.5	57.4	80.3
COVERS	DIVS. 10 - 14, 25, 28, 41, 43, 44, 46	100.0	83.9	96.9	100.0	82.5	96.6	100.0	84.2	96.9	100.0	84.0	96.9	100.0	84.2	96.9	100.0	82.5	96.6
21, 22, 23	FIRE SUPPRESSION, PLUMBING & HVAC	93.3	58.0	80.7	100.7	57.8	85.3	100.9	60.2	86.3	100.8	60.2	86.3	93.4	60.2	81.5	93.4	57.8	80.6
26, 27, 3370	ELECTRICAL, COMMUNICATIONS & UTIL.	93.7	61.6	79.8	102.1	51.1	80.0	99.5	81.5	91.7	93.7	51.5	75.4	98.6	81.5	91.2	98.5	49.7	77.4
MF2018	WEIGHTED AVERAGE	97.2	65.0	85.4	102.9	63.0	88.2	98.9	68.2	87.6	100.4	64.5	87.2	95.7	68.7	85.7	95.4	62.8	83.4

DIVISION		NORTH CAROLINA															NORTH DAKOTA		
		MURPHY 289			RALEIGH 275 - 276			ROCKY MOUNT 278			WILMINGTON 284			WINSTON-SALEM 271			BISMARCK 585		
		MAT.	INST.	TOTAL	MAT.	INST.	TOTAL	MAT.	INST.	TOTAL	MAT.	INST.	TOTAL	MAT.	INST.	TOTAL	MAT.	INST.	TOTAL
015433	CONTRACTOR EQUIPMENT		97.1	97.1		107.8	107.8		101.7	101.7		97.1	97.1		101.7	101.7		100.3	100.3
0241, 31 - 34	SITE & INFRASTRUCTURE, DEMOLITION	100.1	76.4	84.7	106.0	96.3	99.7	105.9	84.1	91.7	103.1	76.4	85.7	107.2	84.4	92.4	89.2	99.1	95.7
0310	Concrete Forming & Accessories	103.8	54.9	65.8	101.7	59.6	69.0	92.7	59.3	66.8	97.3	58.1	66.9	103.7	59.9	69.6	101.7	75.7	81.5
0320	Concrete Reinforcing	96.8	57.9	86.0	98.9	60.1	88.2	96.8	60.1	86.7	98.1	60.1	87.6	97.7	60.1	87.3	98.8	97.4	98.4
0330	Cast-in-Place Concrete	115.3	66.6	98.0	129.7	70.3	108.6	123.5	68.3	103.9	111.0	66.7	95.3	128.2	69.2	107.3	111.8	91.0	104.4
03	CONCRETE	95.3	61.4	81.9	101.6	65.0	87.1	100.0	64.3	85.9	92.9	63.3	81.2	101.8	64.9	87.3	106.1	85.3	97.9
04	MASONRY	72.5	56.8	62.9	83.1	60.3	69.3	73.4	60.1	65.3	70.8	56.8	62.3	82.2	61.3	69.5	103.4	82.6	90.7
05	METALS	97.7	87.2	95.6	99.8	84.8	96.9	99.8	87.2	97.3	99.4	88.0	97.2	103.8	88.0	100.7	102.1	92.3	100.2
06	WOOD, PLASTICS & COMPOSITES	108.3	53.6	83.8	97.8	58.1	80.0	89.6	57.9	75.4	98.9	57.9	80.5	101.2	57.9	81.8	102.1	70.9	88.1
07	THERMAL & MOISTURE PROTECTION	110.2	56.6	91.1	101.4	60.5	86.8	106.1	58.9	89.3	110.0	57.3	91.2	106.2	59.4	89.5	105.8	84.5	98.2
08	OPENINGS	88.7	53.9	80.9	98.7	56.9	89.2	93.4	56.8	85.1	88.9	56.8	81.6	96.7	56.8	87.7	98.2	80.9	94.3
0920	Plaster & Gypsum Board	113.8	52.2	74.8	98.9	56.7	72.1	95.4	56.7	70.9	109.9	56.7	76.2	103.4	56.7	73.8	108.6	70.2	84.3
0950, 0980	Ceilings & Acoustic Treatment	102.0	52.2	74.1	88.2	56.7	70.5	88.5	56.7	70.7	106.5	56.7	78.6	91.7	56.7	72.1	113.8	70.2	89.4
0960	Flooring	103.1	59.8	92.2	102.4	59.8	91.7	107.5	59.8	95.5	100.5	59.8	90.3	111.4	59.8	98.5	100.2	51.6	88.0
0970, 0990	Wall Finishes & Painting/Coating	103.1	50.7	71.9	99.1	50.7	70.3	102.8	50.7	71.8	103.1	50.7	71.9	102.8	50.7	71.8	98.4	58.6	74.7
09	FINISHES	103.9	54.8	79.3	98.0	58.4	78.1	98.2	58.2	78.1	103.6	57.4	80.4	100.8	58.5	79.6	104.1	69.8	86.9
COVERS	DIVS. 10 - 14, 25, 28, 41, 43, 44, 46	100.0	82.1	96.5	100.0	84.0	96.9	100.0	83.7	96.8	100.0	82.5	96.6	100.0	84.0	96.9	100.0	91.9	98.4
21, 22, 23	FIRE SUPPRESSION, PLUMBING & HVAC	93.4	57.8	80.6	100.1	59.6	85.6	93.3	59.6	81.2	100.0	57.8	85.5	100.8	60.2	86.3	100.0	76.6	91.6
26, 27, 3370	ELECTRICAL, COMMUNICATIONS & UTIL.	100.3	49.7	78.4	99.9	50.1	78.3	94.7	51.1	75.8	100.4	49.7	78.4	93.7	51.5	75.4	99.8	86.1	93.8
MF2018	WEIGHTED AVERAGE	96.2	61.4	83.4	99.4	64.8	86.7	96.4	64.0	84.5	97.8	62.2	84.7	100.0	64.5	87.0	101.4	82.9	94.6

DIVISION		NORTH DAKOTA																	
		DEVILS LAKE 583			DICKINSON 586			FARGO 580 - 581			GRAND FORKS 582			JAMESTOWN 584			MINOT 587		
		MAT.	INST.	TOTAL	MAT.	INST.	TOTAL	MAT.	INST.	TOTAL	MAT.	INST.	TOTAL	MAT.	INST.	TOTAL	MAT.	INST.	TOTAL
015433	CONTRACTOR EQUIPMENT		94.2	94.2		94.2	94.2		100.6	100.6		94.2	94.2		94.2	94.2		94.2	94.2
0241, 31 - 34	SITE & INFRASTRUCTURE, DEMOLITION	89.1	88.6	88.8	93.4	88.5	90.2	89.2	99.2	95.7	94.4	89.2	91.0	88.3	88.6	88.5	92.9	89.3	90.5
0310	Concrete Forming & Accessories	105.5	65.2	74.2	93.1	65.1	71.4	101.7	66.0	73.9	97.8	71.7	77.5	95.0	65.4	71.8	92.6	65.4	71.5
0320	Concrete Reinforcing	102.1	97.3	100.8	103.1	97.2	101.5	99.0	97.9	98.7	100.5	97.4	99.7	102.7	97.8	101.3	104.1	97.2	102.2
0330	Cast-in-Place Concrete	131.2	74.6	111.1	118.7	74.5	103.0	108.6	81.6	99.0	118.7	80.6	105.1	129.6	74.6	110.1	118.7	74.9	103.1
03	CONCRETE	111.2	74.9	96.9	109.2	74.8	95.7	107.5	77.7	95.7	107.0	80.0	96.3	109.6	75.0	95.9	106.3	75.2	94.0
04	MASONRY	111.1	77.5	90.7	113.0	75.9	90.4	92.4	85.8	88.4	105.6	80.4	90.3	123.1	85.6	100.3	103.4	74.4	85.8
05	METALS	98.5	92.6	96.7	98.4	92.6	97.2	102.1	92.5	100.2	98.4	93.7	97.5	98.4	93.5	97.4	98.7	93.7	97.7
06	WOOD, PLASTICS & COMPOSITES	103.1	61.3	84.4	87.1	61.3	75.5	98.8	61.7	82.2	93.2	68.2	82.0	89.7	61.3	77.0	86.7	61.3	75.3
07	THERMAL & MOISTURE PROTECTION	105.7	76.0	95.1	106.0	77.5	95.8	101.4	81.2	94.2	105.8	79.0	96.2	105.4	78.7	95.8	105.5	77.7	95.6
08	OPENINGS	96.1	75.6	91.4	96.0	75.6	91.4	96.9	75.8	92.1	94.9	79.4	91.4	96.0	75.6	91.4	95.0	75.6	90.6
0920	Plaster & Gypsum Board	110.9	60.7	79.1	100.0	60.7	75.1	93.8	60.7	72.8	101.7	67.8	80.2	101.2	60.7	75.5	100.0	60.7	75.1
0950, 0980	Ceilings & Acoustic Treatment	105.8	60.7	80.5	105.8	60.7	80.5	113.6	60.7	83.9	105.8	67.8	84.5	105.8	60.7	80.5	105.8	60.7	80.5
0960	Flooring	101.1	51.6	88.6	96.2	51.6	85.0	100.6	51.6	88.3	97.5	51.6	86.0	96.7	51.6	85.4	96.0	51.6	84.8
0970, 0990	Wall Finishes & Painting/Coating	89.9	50.1	66.1	89.9	50.1	66.1	99.1	59.8	75.7	89.9	58.7	71.3	89.9	50.1	66.1	89.9	51.1	66.7
09	FINISHES	99.4	61.3	80.3	97.1	61.3	79.1	102.4	62.7	82.4	97.4	67.0	82.1	96.8	61.3	79.0	96.5	61.4	78.9
COVERS	DIVS. 10 - 14, 25, 28, 41, 43, 44, 46	100.0	77.9	95.7	100.0	77.9	95.7	100.0	88.6	97.8	100.0	85.3	97.2	100.0	77.8	95.7	100.0	87.8	97.6
21, 22, 23	FIRE SUPPRESSION, PLUMBING & HVAC	92.5	70.6	84.7	92.5	65.9	83.0	99.9	66.7	88.0	100.1	73.6	90.6	92.5	65.0	82.7	100.1	64.9	87.5
26, 27, 3370	ELECTRICAL, COMMUNICATIONS & UTIL.	93.3	64.8	80.9	97.7	64.5	83.3	99.6	61.8	83.2	95.1	64.8	81.9	93.3	60.8	79.2	96.7	65.2	83.1
MF2018	WEIGHTED AVERAGE	98.6	73.8	89.5	98.7	72.6	89.1	100.7	75.3	91.3	99.5	76.9	91.2	98.5	73.0	89.2	99.5	72.9	89.7

City Cost Indexes

DIVISION		NORTH DAKOTA WILLISTON 588			OHIO															
					AKRON 442 - 443			ATHENS 457			CANTON 446 - 447			CHILLICOTHE 456			CINCINNATI 451 - 452		
		MAT.	INST.	TOTAL	MAT.	INST.	TOTAL	MAT.	INST.	TOTAL	MAT.	INST.	TOTAL	MAT.	INST.	TOTAL	MAT.	INST.	TOTAL
015433	CONTRACTOR EQUIPMENT		94.2	94.2		88.0	88.0		84.2	84.2		88.0	88.0		93.6	93.6		97.6	97.6
0241, 31 - 34	SITE & INFRASTRUCTURE, DEMOLITION	89.5	89.3	89.4	86.2	90.8	89.2	87.8	82.4	84.3	86.3	90.7	89.2	82.0	90.6	87.6	84.8	99.4	94.3
0310	Concrete Forming & Accessories	99.8	71.7	78.0	98.6	82.4	86.0	88.2	83.2	84.3	98.6	74.4	79.8	90.8	74.1	77.8	94.4	73.1	77.9
0320	Concrete Reinforcing	105.0	97.2	102.8	102.1	90.5	98.9	97.1	80.1	92.4	102.1	73.2	94.1	95.5	79.7	91.1	99.2	79.4	93.7
0330	Cast-in-Place Concrete	118.7	80.6	105.1	100.9	85.7	95.5	111.6	88.6	103.5	101.9	84.3	95.6	101.3	84.5	95.3	96.8	79.9	90.8
03	CONCRETE	107.7	80.0	96.8	96.6	84.7	91.9	103.4	84.4	95.9	97.0	77.6	89.3	98.5	79.3	91.0	97.4	76.9	89.3
04	MASONRY	99.1	77.2	85.8	96.4	88.9	91.8	60.0	89.5	77.9	97.0	81.0	87.3	65.2	81.5	75.1	69.1	81.9	76.9
05	METALS	98.6	93.5	97.6	91.4	82.3	89.6	95.8	78.7	92.4	91.4	75.3	88.2	89.2	86.9	88.7	97.6	82.5	94.6
06	WOOD, PLASTICS & COMPOSITES	95.4	68.2	83.2	98.9	81.3	91.0	77.0	81.2	78.9	99.4	72.5	87.3	87.2	70.8	79.9	91.4	70.9	82.2
07	THERMAL & MOISTURE PROTECTION	105.7	79.0	96.2	101.7	88.3	96.9	98.3	87.3	94.4	102.6	84.8	96.2	100.8	80.1	93.4	99.8	81.2	93.1
08	OPENINGS	96.1	79.4	92.3	101.5	82.2	97.1	93.5	76.7	89.7	95.7	69.6	89.8	84.9	70.7	81.7	90.9	71.5	92.8
0920	Plaster & Gypsum Board	101.7	67.8	80.2	85.8	80.8	82.7	84.4	80.7	82.1	87.5	71.7	77.5	87.7	70.5	76.8	84.8	70.2	75.5
0950, 0980	Ceilings & Acoustic Treatment	105.8	67.8	84.5	95.1	80.8	87.1	114.2	80.7	95.4	95.1	71.7	82.0	108.2	70.5	87.1	97.2	70.2	82.1
0960	Flooring	98.2	51.6	86.5	89.3	75.1	85.8	111.2	74.4	102.0	89.6	68.0	84.2	90.0	67.4	84.4	93.8	77.8	89.8
0970, 0990	Wall Finishes & Painting/Coating	89.9	56.4	69.9	95.0	86.6	90.0	102.6	82.9	90.9	95.0	72.1	81.4	99.7	79.2	87.5	99.1	71.6	82.7
09	FINISHES	97.5	66.9	82.1	92.2	81.5	86.8	99.9	81.3	90.6	92.5	72.2	82.3	96.6	72.5	84.5	94.0	73.3	83.6
COVERS	DIVS. 10 - 14, 25, 28, 41, 43, 44, 46	100.0	87.4	97.6	100.0	92.1	98.5	100.0	91.3	98.3	100.0	90.5	98.2	100.0	88.1	97.7	100.0	88.2	97.7
21, 22, 23	FIRE SUPPRESSION, PLUMBING & HVAC	92.5	70.5	84.6	100.0	86.4	95.1	92.6	79.2	87.8	100.0	76.3	91.5	93.3	83.1	89.6	100.0	77.0	91.8
26, 27, 3370	ELECTRICAL, COMMUNICATIONS & UTIL.	95.3	65.2	82.3	99.3	80.8	91.3	102.5	87.5	96.0	99.0	80.7	91.1	99.1	79.9	90.8	99.4	75.8	89.2
MF2018	WEIGHTED AVERAGE	97.8	76.0	89.8	96.8	85.0	92.4	95.5	83.1	90.9	96.4	78.5	89.8	92.5	81.0	88.3	96.9	79.3	90.4

DIVISION		OHIO																	
		CLEVELAND 441			COLUMBUS 430 - 432			DAYTON 453 - 454			HAMILTON 450			LIMA 458			LORAIN 440		
		MAT.	INST.	TOTAL	MAT.	INST.	TOTAL	MAT.	INST.	TOTAL	MAT.	INST.	TOTAL	MAT.	INST.	TOTAL	MAT.	INST.	TOTAL
015433	CONTRACTOR EQUIPMENT		93.9	93.9		97.1	97.1		87.7	87.7		93.6	93.6		87.1	87.1		88.0	88.0
0241, 31 - 34	SITE & INFRASTRUCTURE, DEMOLITION	85.8	97.8	93.6	83.6	97.6	92.7	82.8	90.6	87.9	82.9	90.3	87.7	83.8	81.7	82.4	85.6	90.7	88.9
0310	Concrete Forming & Accessories	98.5	88.7	90.9	93.5	85.4	87.2	92.7	77.1	80.6	92.8	70.5	75.4	88.1	69.6	73.7	98.7	76.4	81.4
0320	Concrete Reinforcing	100.5	91.7	98.1	100.8	80.1	95.1	101.2	78.0	94.8	101.2	69.3	92.4	97.1	77.8	91.8	102.1	90.5	98.9
0330	Cast-in-Place Concrete	100.6	97.2	99.4	99.4	90.9	96.4	86.8	81.5	84.9	93.0	76.0	86.9	102.5	82.1	95.3	96.0	88.4	93.3
03	CONCRETE	95.8	91.8	94.2	94.5	86.3	91.3	92.2	78.9	86.9	94.8	73.0	86.2	97.4	75.8	88.9	94.6	82.9	90.0
04	MASONRY	100.8	98.2	99.2	76.0	89.0	83.9	64.4	77.3	72.2	64.6	73.2	69.8	77.4	70.4	73.2	93.3	87.9	90.0
05	METALS	97.6	85.0	95.1	97.6	81.8	94.5	91.4	78.2	88.6	91.0	83.0	89.4	95.8	80.4	92.8	92.0	82.2	90.1
06	WOOD, PLASTICS & COMPOSITES	96.3	86.3	91.8	90.7	85.0	88.1	90.7	77.2	84.7	89.9	70.1	81.0	76.9	68.2	73.0	98.9	74.4	87.9
07	THERMAL & MOISTURE PROTECTION	100.5	96.4	99.0	102.0	87.9	97.0	104.3	78.0	95.0	100.9	74.4	91.4	97.9	79.4	91.4	102.5	85.0	96.3
08	OPENINGS	98.9	85.2	95.8	98.6	78.8	94.1	91.9	74.6	88.0	89.6	69.3	85.1	93.5	68.4	87.8	95.7	78.4	91.8
0920	Plaster & Gypsum Board	85.6	85.9	85.8	87.8	84.4	85.6	88.9	77.1	81.4	88.9	69.7	76.7	84.4	67.3	73.6	85.8	73.7	78.2
0950, 0980	Ceilings & Acoustic Treatment	93.6	85.9	89.3	95.4	84.4	89.2	108.2	77.1	90.8	108.2	69.7	86.6	114.2	67.3	87.9	95.1	73.7	83.1
0960	Flooring	93.8	96.6	94.3	91.2	76.6	87.6	93.4	71.4	87.9	91.0	70.3	85.8	110.7	69.1	100.3	89.6	83.8	88.1
0970, 0990	Wall Finishes & Painting/Coating	99.1	86.6	91.6	94.9	78.0	84.8	99.7	68.5	81.1	99.7	63.4	78.0	102.6	68.0	81.9	95.0	84.9	89.0
09	FINISHES	93.2	89.5	91.4	92.8	82.9	87.9	97.6	75.0	86.2	96.8	69.4	83.1	99.5	68.6	83.9	92.3	78.2	85.2
COVERS	DIVS. 10 - 14, 25, 28, 41, 43, 44, 46	100.0	96.9	99.4	100.0	91.4	98.3	100.0	87.6	97.6	100.0	86.0	97.3	100.0	90.0	98.1	100.0	92.9	98.6
21, 22, 23	FIRE SUPPRESSION, PLUMBING & HVAC	100.0	91.5	97.0	100.0	90.8	96.7	101.0	78.6	93.0	100.8	67.4	88.8	92.6	82.5	89.0	100.0	76.7	91.6
26, 27, 3370	ELECTRICAL, COMMUNICATIONS & UTIL.	99.6	88.6	94.8	99.2	83.0	92.2	97.6	75.4	88.0	97.9	67.2	84.6	102.8	67.4	87.4	99.1	73.9	88.2
MF2018	WEIGHTED AVERAGE	98.0	91.4	95.6	96.8	87.0	93.2	94.5	78.6	88.6	94.4	73.1	86.6	95.3	75.6	88.1	96.0	80.9	90.5

DIVISION		OHIO																	
		MANSFIELD 448 - 449			MARION 433			SPRINGFIELD 455			STEUBENVILLE 439			TOLEDO 434 - 436			YOUNGSTOWN 444 - 445		
		MAT.	INST.	TOTAL	MAT.	INST.	TOTAL	MAT.	INST.	TOTAL	MAT.	INST.	TOTAL	MAT.	INST.	TOTAL	MAT.	INST.	TOTAL
015433	CONTRACTOR EQUIPMENT		88.0	88.0		89.0	89.0		87.7	87.7		92.2	92.2		92.3	92.3		88.0	88.0
0241, 31 - 34	SITE & INFRASTRUCTURE, DEMOLITION	79.8	90.2	86.6	75.7	87.6	83.5	83.1	90.5	88.0	98.5	94.7	96.0	81.3	88.4	86.0	86.1	90.4	88.9
0310	Concrete Forming & Accessories	87.4	74.9	77.7	91.1	72.2	76.4	92.7	75.8	79.6	91.0	72.0	76.2	94.8	88.4	89.8	98.6	75.3	80.5
0320	Concrete Reinforcing	93.0	71.0	86.9	97.2	70.9	89.9	101.2	78.0	94.8	95.4	91.8	94.4	105.4	86.2	100.1	102.1	81.1	96.3
0330	Cast-in-Place Concrete	93.4	80.7	88.9	86.0	80.9	84.2	89.1	81.7	86.5	93.4	82.3	89.5	94.2	89.9	92.7	99.9	84.4	94.4
03	CONCRETE	88.6	76.2	83.7	84.7	75.3	81.0	93.1	78.3	87.3	87.7	79.0	84.3	92.1	88.6	90.8	96.2	79.4	89.6
04	MASONRY	95.3	80.1	86.1	79.0	80.9	80.2	64.4	77.7	72.4	70.8	82.1	77.7	83.8	90.1	87.6	96.6	83.6	88.7
05	METALS	92.6	74.7	89.0	92.9	77.1	89.8	91.1	78.1	88.6	90.4	82.7	88.9	93.4	88.4	92.4	91.5	78.3	88.9
06	WOOD, PLASTICS & COMPOSITES	83.6	74.4	79.5	84.0	70.5	78.0	91.6	75.3	84.3	79.1	69.5	74.8	88.6	89.4	89.0	98.9	73.6	87.5
07	THERMAL & MOISTURE PROTECTION	101.0	83.1	94.6	97.9	80.6	91.7	104.2	78.0	94.9	109.3	79.2	98.5	98.0	89.8	95.1	102.7	85.6	96.6
08	OPENINGS	96.5	70.3	90.6	87.5	68.1	83.1	90.1	73.7	86.4	87.5	72.9	84.2	89.9	84.2	88.6	95.7	78.4	91.8
0920	Plaster & Gypsum Board	78.3	73.7	75.4	87.1	69.8	76.1	88.9	75.1	80.1	83.5	68.3	73.8	89.0	89.3	89.2	85.8	72.9	77.6
0950, 0980	Ceilings & Acoustic Treatment	96.4	73.7	83.7	100.6	69.8	83.3	108.2	75.1	89.7	99.1	68.3	81.8	100.6	89.3	94.3	95.1	72.9	82.6
0960	Flooring	85.1	87.4	85.7	87.9	87.4	87.8	93.4	71.4	87.9	115.3	85.2	107.8	88.3	92.4	89.3	89.6	86.1	88.7
0970, 0990	Wall Finishes & Painting/Coating	95.0	69.1	79.6	96.8	69.1	80.3	99.7	68.5	81.1	110.3	77.4	90.7	96.8	82.0	87.9	95.0	75.3	83.2
09	FINISHES	90.1	76.3	83.2	93.7	74.3	83.9	97.6	73.9	85.7	109.1	74.1	91.5	94.3	88.6	91.4	92.4	76.7	84.5
COVERS	DIVS. 10 - 14, 25, 28, 41, 43, 44, 46	100.0	89.8	98.0	100.0	87.4	97.6	100.0	87.4	97.6	100.0	86.5	97.4	100.0	93.9	98.8	100.0	90.3	98.1
21, 22, 23	FIRE SUPPRESSION, PLUMBING & HVAC	92.5	75.2	86.3	92.5	83.7	89.3	101.0	76.5	92.2	93.2	82.2	89.3	100.0	91.7	97.0	100.0	79.8	92.8
26, 27, 3370	ELECTRICAL, COMMUNICATIONS & UTIL.	97.9	80.8	90.5	97.3	80.8	90.2	97.6	77.4	88.8	90.1	94.8	92.1	100.8	92.5	97.2	99.1	80.7	91.1
MF2018	WEIGHTED AVERAGE	93.3	78.4	87.8	91.6	79.6	87.2	94.5	78.2	88.5	92.4	83.1	89.0	95.2	90.0	93.3	96.3	80.9	90.6

For customer support on your Mechanical Costs with RSMeans data, call 800.448.8182.

City Cost Indexes

DIVISION		OHIO ZANESVILLE 437 - 438			OKLAHOMA ARDMORE 734			OKLAHOMA CLINTON 736			OKLAHOMA DURANT 747			OKLAHOMA ENID 737			OKLAHOMA GUYMON 739		
		MAT.	INST.	TOTAL	MAT.	INST.	TOTAL	MAT.	INST.	TOTAL	MAT.	INST.	TOTAL	MAT.	INST.	TOTAL	MAT.	INST.	TOTAL
015433	CONTRACTOR EQUIPMENT		89.0	89.0		79.3	79.3		78.5	78.5		78.5	78.5		78.5	78.5		78.5	78.5
0241, 31 - 34	SITE & INFRASTRUCTURE, DEMOLITION	77.5	87.5	84.0	93.2	88.5	90.1	94.4	87.2	89.7	91.8	86.9	88.6	99.2	87.2	91.4	98.2	86.4	90.5
0310	Concrete Forming & Accessories	88.2	71.2	75.0	89.2	52.3	60.5	87.6	52.3	60.2	84.4	50.5	58.1	91.6	52.6	61.3	94.8	50.4	60.3
0320	Concrete Reinforcing	96.6	83.1	92.9	88.3	65.1	81.9	88.8	65.1	82.2	96.0	57.2	85.3	88.3	65.1	81.9	88.8	56.8	80.0
0330	Cast-in-Place Concrete	90.6	79.5	86.7	83.7	70.2	78.9	80.9	70.2	77.1	81.1	67.8	76.4	80.9	73.7	78.3	80.9	67.2	76.0
03	CONCRETE	87.3	76.5	83.0	82.3	61.0	73.9	81.8	61.0	73.6	83.0	58.0	73.1	82.2	62.3	74.3	84.2	57.6	73.7
04	MASONRY	76.9	78.0	77.6	94.0	60.6	73.7	118.4	60.6	83.3	87.2	56.0	68.3	100.7	60.6	76.3	95.6	49.9	67.9
05	METALS	94.1	84.2	92.2	97.0	63.0	90.3	97.1	63.0	90.4	91.6	60.0	85.3	98.5	63.3	91.6	97.7	58.1	89.9
06	WOOD, PLASTICS & COMPOSITES	78.8	70.5	75.1	90.9	49.5	72.4	89.9	49.5	71.8	81.1	49.5	66.9	94.0	49.5	74.1	98.4	49.5	76.5
07	THERMAL & MOISTURE PROTECTION	97.9	77.2	90.5	103.5	62.3	88.8	103.6	62.3	88.9	97.9	60.1	84.4	103.7	62.3	89.0	104.0	56.1	87.0
08	OPENINGS	87.5	73.2	84.3	102.2	50.8	90.6	102.2	50.8	90.6	93.2	49.0	83.2	103.2	52.4	91.8	102.3	49.0	90.3
0920	Plaster & Gypsum Board	81.8	69.8	74.2	90.9	48.7	64.1	90.7	48.7	64.0	73.2	48.7	57.6	91.9	48.7	64.5	91.9	48.7	64.5
0950, 0980	Ceilings & Acoustic Treatment	100.6	69.8	83.3	101.9	48.7	72.1	101.9	48.7	72.1	83.6	48.7	64.0	101.9	48.7	72.1	101.9	48.7	72.1
0960	Flooring	86.7	67.4	81.9	94.7	51.3	83.8	93.9	51.3	83.2	96.0	46.3	83.6	95.1	69.2	88.6	96.3	51.3	85.0
0970, 0990	Wall Finishes & Painting/Coating	96.8	79.2	86.3	92.9	42.3	62.7	92.9	42.3	62.7	96.4	42.3	64.1	92.9	42.3	62.7	92.9	37.5	59.9
09	FINISHES	92.7	70.6	81.6	95.5	49.6	72.5	95.5	49.6	72.4	87.9	47.6	67.7	96.0	53.3	74.6	96.8	49.2	72.9
COVERS	DIVS. 10 - 14, 25, 28, 41, 43, 44, 46	100.0	86.5	97.4	100.0	78.2	95.8	100.0	78.2	95.8	100.0	76.8	95.5	100.0	78.2	95.8	100.0	76.8	95.5
21, 22, 23	FIRE SUPPRESSION, PLUMBING & HVAC	92.5	80.8	88.3	92.7	66.2	83.2	92.7	66.2	83.2	92.6	63.9	82.3	100.2	66.2	88.0	92.7	61.8	81.6
26, 27, 3370	ELECTRICAL, COMMUNICATIONS & UTIL.	97.7	79.9	90.0	92.8	70.8	83.3	93.4	70.8	83.6	96.3	61.6	81.3	93.4	70.8	83.6	94.2	58.4	78.7
MF2018	WEIGHTED AVERAGE	92.0	79.0	87.2	94.3	64.4	83.3	95.3	64.3	83.9	91.7	60.9	80.4	96.9	65.0	85.2	95.2	59.2	82.0

DIVISION		OKLAHOMA LAWTON 735			OKLAHOMA MCALESTER 745			OKLAHOMA MIAMI 743			OKLAHOMA MUSKOGEE 744			OKLAHOMA OKLAHOMA CITY 730 - 731			OKLAHOMA PONCA CITY 746		
		MAT.	INST.	TOTAL	MAT.	INST.	TOTAL	MAT.	INST.	TOTAL	MAT.	INST.	TOTAL	MAT.	INST.	TOTAL	MAT.	INST.	TOTAL
015433	CONTRACTOR EQUIPMENT		79.3	79.3		78.5	78.5		88.4	88.4		88.4	88.4		90.9	90.9		78.5	78.5
0241, 31 - 34	SITE & INFRASTRUCTURE, DEMOLITION	95.9	88.6	91.1	86.0	87.1	86.7	86.7	84.4	85.2	90.5	84.3	86.5	95.8	101.6	99.6	92.4	86.9	88.8
0310	Concrete Forming & Accessories	94.6	56.2	64.8	82.4	55.1	61.2	96.7	50.5	60.8	101.7	54.1	64.7	98.4	62.0	70.1	91.7	50.6	59.7
0320	Concrete Reinforcing	88.5	65.1	82.0	95.7	68.1	88.1	94.2	65.0	86.1	95.1	62.7	86.2	99.7	65.2	90.1	95.1	65.0	86.8
0330	Cast-in-Place Concrete	78.2	73.8	76.6	71.1	70.5	70.9	74.5	68.7	72.4	75.4	69.2	73.2	82.2	72.1	78.6	83.3	67.9	77.8
03	CONCRETE	79.8	64.0	73.6	76.2	62.8	71.0	79.8	60.5	72.2	81.4	61.9	73.7	87.7	66.1	79.2	84.7	59.4	74.7
04	MASONRY	95.6	60.6	74.3	103.4	57.9	75.8	90.0	56.5	69.6	103.7	57.7	75.7	94.7	58.0	72.4	81.9	56.4	66.4
05	METALS	103.1	63.3	95.2	91.5	64.2	86.1	91.5	76.5	88.5	92.9	75.6	89.5	97.2	65.5	91.0	91.5	62.9	85.8
06	WOOD, PLASTICS & COMPOSITES	97.2	54.4	78.0	78.3	54.5	67.6	96.5	49.6	75.5	102.2	53.5	80.4	94.7	63.5	80.7	90.7	49.5	72.2
07	THERMAL & MOISTURE PROTECTION	103.6	63.0	89.1	97.6	61.7	84.8	98.1	61.0	84.8	98.4	60.2	84.8	95.4	64.3	84.3	98.1	60.4	84.7
08	OPENINGS	104.5	55.1	93.3	93.2	55.4	84.7	93.2	50.9	83.6	94.2	52.5	84.8	98.0	60.1	89.4	93.2	50.8	83.6
0920	Plaster & Gypsum Board	97.0	53.7	69.6	73.0	53.8	60.8	79.5	48.7	59.9	84.5	52.7	64.3	96.7	62.7	75.2	78.0	48.7	59.4
0950, 0980	Ceilings & Acoustic Treatment	118.3	53.7	82.1	83.6	53.8	66.9	83.6	48.7	64.0	99.5	52.7	73.2	106.8	62.7	82.1	83.6	48.7	64.0
0960	Flooring	96.4	69.2	89.6	95.3	65.6	87.9	100.5	46.3	86.9	102.3	60.9	91.9	99.9	69.2	92.2	98.4	51.3	86.6
0970, 0990	Wall Finishes & Painting/Coating	92.9	42.3	62.7	96.4	46.2	66.4	96.4	37.5	61.3	96.4	37.5	61.3	99.1	42.3	65.2	96.4	42.3	64.1
09	FINISHES	101.0	56.2	78.5	87.1	55.3	71.1	89.4	47.1	68.2	95.0	52.7	73.7	101.5	60.9	81.1	89.4	49.5	69.3
COVERS	DIVS. 10 - 14, 25, 28, 41, 43, 44, 46	100.0	78.8	95.9	100.0	77.9	95.7	100.0	77.2	95.6	100.0	78.0	95.7	100.0	79.6	96.1	100.0	76.8	95.5
21, 22, 23	FIRE SUPPRESSION, PLUMBING & HVAC	100.2	66.2	88.0	92.6	60.8	81.2	92.6	57.3	79.9	100.1	60.6	86.0	100.1	64.9	87.5	92.6	57.3	79.9
26, 27, 3370	ELECTRICAL, COMMUNICATIONS & UTIL.	94.2	70.8	84.1	95.4	67.7	83.4	96.2	67.8	83.9	95.2	82.6	89.7	99.9	70.9	87.3	95.2	58.4	79.3
MF2018	WEIGHTED AVERAGE	97.9	65.9	86.1	91.2	63.7	81.1	91.5	62.1	80.7	94.8	65.9	84.2	97.4	67.9	86.5	91.8	59.8	80.0

DIVISION		OKLAHOMA POTEAU 749			OKLAHOMA SHAWNEE 748			OKLAHOMA TULSA 740 - 741			OKLAHOMA WOODWARD 738			OREGON BEND 977			OREGON EUGENE 974		
		MAT.	INST.	TOTAL	MAT.	INST.	TOTAL	MAT.	INST.	TOTAL	MAT.	INST.	TOTAL	MAT.	INST.	TOTAL	MAT.	INST.	TOTAL
015433	CONTRACTOR EQUIPMENT		87.3	87.3		78.5	78.5		88.4	88.4		78.5	78.5		94.9	94.9		94.9	94.9
0241, 31 - 34	SITE & INFRASTRUCTURE, DEMOLITION	75.7	82.6	80.2	94.8	87.0	89.7	95.8	84.5	88.5	94.8	87.2	89.9	122.1	94.6	104.1	114.0	94.6	101.3
0310	Concrete Forming & Accessories	89.4	50.6	59.2	84.3	50.6	58.1	101.6	55.1	65.5	87.8	56.7	63.6	100.0	99.3	99.5	96.3	99.5	98.8
0320	Concrete Reinforcing	96.2	65.1	87.6	95.1	59.1	85.1	95.3	65.1	87.0	88.3	65.1	81.9	88.4	112.6	95.1	91.8	112.6	97.5
0330	Cast-in-Place Concrete	74.5	68.7	72.5	85.9	67.9	79.5	82.1	71.4	78.3	80.9	71.2	77.4	133.1	100.6	121.6	128.9	100.7	118.9
03	CONCRETE	81.3	60.5	73.1	85.6	58.4	74.9	85.2	63.6	76.6	81.9	63.3	74.5	116.8	101.6	110.8	109.4	101.8	106.4
04	MASONRY	90.3	56.5	69.7	104.7	56.4	75.4	91.0	57.3	70.8	89.7	60.6	72.0	114.9	102.9	107.6	111.2	102.9	106.1
05	METALS	91.5	76.5	88.6	91.4	60.8	85.4	97.2	77.0	93.2	97.2	63.3	90.5	110.2	96.9	107.6	110.9	97.2	108.2
06	WOOD, PLASTICS & COMPOSITES	86.7	49.6	70.1	80.9	49.5	66.8	101.2	54.6	80.3	90.0	55.2	74.4	107.3	99.5	103.8	101.9	99.5	100.8
07	THERMAL & MOISTURE PROTECTION	98.1	60.9	84.9	98.1	58.7	84.0	98.4	63.4	85.9	103.7	63.1	89.2	95.3	99.9	97.0	94.6	101.7	97.2
08	OPENINGS	93.2	50.9	83.6	93.2	49.4	83.3	95.5	55.1	86.4	102.3	55.1	91.6	92.2	102.6	94.5	92.4	102.6	94.7
0920	Plaster & Gypsum Board	76.3	48.7	58.8	73.2	48.7	57.6	84.5	53.8	65.0	90.7	54.5	67.7	123.3	99.5	108.2	120.1	99.5	107.0
0950, 0980	Ceilings & Acoustic Treatment	83.6	48.7	64.0	83.6	48.7	64.0	99.5	53.8	73.9	101.9	54.5	75.3	94.5	99.5	97.3	94.5	99.5	97.3
0960	Flooring	97.9	46.3	84.9	96.0	51.3	84.8	101.4	60.1	91.1	93.6	65.9	86.9	106.9	101.7	105.6	105.8	101.7	104.8
0970, 0990	Wall Finishes & Painting/Coating	96.4	42.3	64.1	96.4	37.5	61.3	96.4	56.0	72.3	92.9	42.3	62.7	97.7	74.2	83.7	97.7	62.2	76.5
09	FINISHES	87.5	47.7	67.5	88.2	48.1	68.0	94.9	55.2	75.0	95.5	55.9	75.6	106.3	97.0	101.6	104.3	95.7	100.0
COVERS	DIVS. 10 - 14, 25, 28, 41, 43, 44, 46	100.0	77.1	95.6	100.0	76.9	95.5	100.0	78.2	95.8	100.0	78.8	95.9	100.0	101.9	100.4	100.0	101.9	100.4
21, 22, 23	FIRE SUPPRESSION, PLUMBING & HVAC	92.6	57.3	79.9	92.6	63.9	82.3	100.1	60.7	86.0	92.7	66.2	83.2	92.6	97.6	94.4	100.1	108.7	103.2
26, 27, 3370	ELECTRICAL, COMMUNICATIONS & UTIL.	95.3	67.8	83.4	96.3	70.8	85.3	96.3	64.7	82.6	94.1	70.8	84.0	93.5	91.5	92.6	92.8	91.5	92.2
MF2018	WEIGHTED AVERAGE	91.1	62.0	80.4	92.8	62.4	81.6	96.0	64.4	84.4	94.3	65.9	83.8	102.7	97.9	100.9	103.1	100.1	102.0

City Cost Indexes

OREGON

DIVISION		KLAMATH FALLS 976			MEDFORD 975			PENDLETON 978			PORTLAND 970 - 972			SALEM 973			VALE 979		
		MAT.	INST.	TOTAL	MAT.	INST.	TOTAL	MAT.	INST.	TOTAL	MAT.	INST.	TOTAL	MAT.	INST.	TOTAL	MAT.	INST.	TOTAL
015433	CONTRACTOR EQUIPMENT		94.9	94.9		94.9	94.9		92.7	92.7		94.9	94.9		99.4	99.4		92.7	92.7
0241, 31 - 34	SITE & INFRASTRUCTURE, DEMOLITION	126.7	94.5	105.7	122.6	94.5	104.3	121.0	88.7	99.9	116.3	94.6	102.1	109.3	101.7	104.3	107.2	88.6	95.1
0310	Concrete Forming & Accessories	92.6	99.0	97.5	91.5	99.1	97.4	94.8	99.1	98.2	97.7	99.7	99.2	96.0	99.7	98.9	101.8	97.9	98.8
0320	Concrete Reinforcing	88.4	112.5	95.1	89.9	112.5	96.2	88.8	112.5	95.4	92.3	112.6	98.1	98.6	112.6	102.5	86.6	112.3	93.7
0330	Cast-in-Place Concrete	133.1	92.1	118.5	133.1	100.5	121.5	134.0	92.5	119.3	132.5	100.8	121.2	121.8	102.7	115.0	105.4	92.7	100.9
03	CONCRETE	118.8	98.5	110.8	114.5	101.5	109.4	103.6	98.7	101.7	111.2	101.9	107.5	109.7	102.4	106.8	88.3	98.2	92.2
04	MASONRY	129.2	102.9	113.2	107.3	102.9	104.6	118.7	103.0	109.1	113.4	102.9	107.0	114.9	103.0	107.7	116.1	103.0	108.1
05	METALS	110.2	96.6	107.5	110.5	96.7	107.7	117.8	97.1	113.7	112.8	97.3	109.7	118.8	95.3	114.2	117.5	95.8	113.2
06	WOOD, PLASTICS & COMPOSITES	95.6	99.5	97.3	94.3	99.5	96.6	99.3	99.6	99.4	103.4	99.5	101.7	95.5	99.7	97.3	109.9	99.6	105.5
07	THERMAL & MOISTURE PROTECTION	95.4	95.1	95.3	95.1	94.5	94.9	90.8	92.0	91.2	94.6	100.5	96.7	91.3	101.8	95.0	90.4	88.4	89.7
08	OPENINGS	92.2	102.6	94.5	94.8	102.6	96.5	89.1	102.7	92.1	90.5	102.6	93.2	97.5	102.7	98.7	89.0	89.8	89.2
0920	Plaster & Gypsum Board	115.6	99.5	105.4	114.9	99.5	105.1	102.6	99.5	100.6	118.3	99.5	106.4	117.6	99.5	106.1	111.8	99.5	104.0
0950, 0980	Ceilings & Acoustic Treatment	105.4	99.5	102.1	108.4	99.5	103.4	72.5	99.5	87.6	96.5	99.5	98.2	115.0	99.5	106.3	72.5	99.5	87.6
0960	Flooring	104.8	101.7	104.0	104.4	101.7	103.7	71.1	101.7	78.8	103.0	101.7	102.7	105.8	101.7	104.8	72.6	101.7	79.9
0970, 0990	Wall Finishes & Painting/Coating	97.7	71.7	82.2	97.7	71.7	82.2	89.0	77.7	82.3	97.2	77.7	85.6	99.1	69.5	81.4	89.0	74.2	80.2
09	FINISHES	108.0	96.7	102.3	107.7	96.7	102.2	76.2	97.5	86.9	103.8	97.4	100.6	108.1	96.6	102.3	76.9	97.1	87.0
COVERS	DIVS. 10 - 14, 25, 28, 41, 43, 44, 46	100.0	101.8	100.4	100.0	101.8	100.4	100.0	99.9	100.0	100.0	102.0	100.4	100.0	102.4	100.5	100.0	102.0	100.4
21, 22, 23	FIRE SUPPRESSION, PLUMBING & HVAC	92.6	97.5	94.3	100.1	103.0	101.1	99.9	103.6	101.2	100.1	108.8	103.2	100.1	108.8	103.2	99.9	66.9	88.0
26, 27, 3370	ELECTRICAL, COMMUNICATIONS & UTIL.	92.9	79.5	87.1	94.5	79.5	88.0	86.5	86.2	86.4	93.5	115.4	103.0	100.9	91.5	96.8	86.5	60.6	75.3
MF2018	WEIGHTED AVERAGE	103.6	95.5	100.6	104.2	97.1	101.6	101.1	97.4	99.7	103.7	103.8	103.7	106.3	100.8	104.3	98.9	85.1	93.9

PENNSYLVANIA

DIVISION		ALLENTOWN 181			ALTOONA 166			BEDFORD 155			BRADFORD 167			BUTLER 160			CHAMBERSBURG 172		
		MAT.	INST.	TOTAL	MAT.	INST.	TOTAL	MAT.	INST.	TOTAL	MAT.	INST.	TOTAL	MAT.	INST.	TOTAL	MAT.	INST.	TOTAL
015433	CONTRACTOR EQUIPMENT		108.2	108.2		108.2	108.2		106.9	106.9		108.2	108.2		108.2	108.2		107.5	107.5
0241, 31 - 34	SITE & INFRASTRUCTURE, DEMOLITION	89.4	93.6	92.1	91.3	93.4	92.6	89.9	90.3	90.1	84.9	91.0	88.9	81.1	93.0	88.9	85.0	90.4	88.5
0310	Concrete Forming & Accessories	99.0	104.7	103.4	82.4	83.9	83.6	80.9	73.9	75.4	85.0	87.6	87.0	83.8	87.8	86.9	85.6	69.7	73.2
0320	Concrete Reinforcing	96.6	108.3	99.8	93.6	99.1	95.1	95.5	94.9	95.3	95.6	94.9	95.4	94.2	114.1	99.7	94.3	100.7	96.0
0330	Cast-in-Place Concrete	88.7	100.4	92.8	98.8	88.4	95.1	101.9	78.6	93.6	94.4	82.8	90.3	87.2	93.9	89.6	94.0	85.5	91.0
03	CONCRETE	92.6	104.8	97.4	88.9	89.5	89.1	98.7	80.7	91.6	93.6	88.4	91.5	82.5	95.8	87.7	95.7	82.4	90.5
04	MASONRY	97.3	95.0	95.9	100.0	86.9	92.0	97.9	72.3	82.3	97.7	73.8	83.2	101.9	89.7	94.5	100.5	71.3	82.8
05	METALS	95.1	119.3	99.9	90.2	112.3	94.5	92.4	107.7	95.4	92.5	107.3	95.4	89.9	117.9	95.4	92.8	112.1	96.6
06	WOOD, PLASTICS & COMPOSITES	99.8	105.6	102.4	75.3	82.3	78.4	71.4	74.2	72.7	81.2	91.8	86.0	77.1	85.3	80.8	79.5	68.7	74.6
07	THERMAL & MOISTURE PROTECTION	101.4	109.2	104.2	99.4	91.5	96.6	102.6	79.9	94.5	101.1	81.1	94.0	99.0	90.7	96.0	98.6	74.5	90.0
08	OPENINGS	92.8	104.4	95.4	86.6	85.4	86.3	91.2	80.0	88.6	93.0	88.8	92.0	86.6	94.6	88.4	87.2	73.8	84.2
0920	Plaster & Gypsum Board	107.7	105.9	106.5	96.0	81.9	87.1	108.8	73.6	86.5	96.8	91.7	93.6	96.0	85.0	89.0	102.5	67.8	80.5
0950, 0980	Ceilings & Acoustic Treatment	92.5	105.5	100.0	96.6	81.9	88.4	108.0	73.6	88.7	96.7	91.7	93.9	97.1	85.0	90.4	88.8	67.8	77.1
0960	Flooring	96.1	93.6	95.5	89.6	100.2	92.3	96.1	92.9	95.3	91.5	92.9	91.8	90.0	94.3	91.4	99.1	69.8	91.8
0970, 0990	Wall Finishes & Painting/Coating	89.9	109.8	101.8	85.6	107.1	98.4	92.3	93.9	93.2	89.9	93.9	92.2	85.6	94.3	90.8	91.6	89.5	90.3
09	FINISHES	95.4	103.1	99.2	93.2	88.7	90.9	101.0	78.8	89.9	93.7	89.6	91.6	93.1	89.1	91.1	93.9	71.1	82.4
COVERS	DIVS. 10 - 14, 25, 28, 41, 43, 44, 46	100.0	102.3	100.4	100.0	97.6	99.5	100.0	93.8	98.8	100.0	96.3	99.3	100.0	99.9	99.9	100.0	91.5	98.3
21, 22, 23	FIRE SUPPRESSION, PLUMBING & HVAC	100.4	113.6	105.2	99.8	85.4	94.6	92.8	76.0	86.7	92.9	81.4	88.8	92.2	89.0	91.1	92.8	80.6	88.5
26, 27, 3370	ELECTRICAL, COMMUNICATIONS & UTIL.	99.3	94.2	97.1	91.2	107.9	98.4	100.1	107.8	103.5	96.0	107.8	101.1	91.5	95.9	93.4	93.5	76.4	86.1
MF2018	WEIGHTED AVERAGE	96.8	104.4	99.6	93.5	93.3	93.4	95.4	86.0	92.0	94.0	90.4	92.6	90.8	94.5	92.2	93.6	81.5	89.1

PENNSYLVANIA

DIVISION		DOYLESTOWN 189			DUBOIS 158			ERIE 164 - 165			GREENSBURG 156			HARRISBURG 170 - 171			HAZLETON 182		
		MAT.	INST.	TOTAL	MAT.	INST.	TOTAL	MAT.	INST.	TOTAL	MAT.	INST.	TOTAL	MAT.	INST.	TOTAL	MAT.	INST.	TOTAL
015433	CONTRACTOR EQUIPMENT		89.3	89.3		106.9	106.9		108.2	108.2		106.9	106.9		111.3	111.3		108.2	108.2
0241, 31 - 34	SITE & INFRASTRUCTURE, DEMOLITION	96.8	81.9	87.1	93.2	90.6	91.5	89.0	93.1	91.7	86.8	92.3	90.4	90.3	100.3	96.8	80.8	91.9	88.1
0310	Concrete Forming & Accessories	81.6	114.7	107.3	80.4	76.2	77.2	98.0	88.4	90.5	87.6	83.0	84.0	98.9	90.9	92.7	79.2	80.5	80.2
0320	Concrete Reinforcing	93.2	135.3	104.9	94.8	107.1	98.2	95.6	107.8	98.9	94.8	113.9	100.1	98.2	114.6	102.7	93.7	101.4	95.9
0330	Cast-in-Place Concrete	83.7	117.6	95.8	98.2	88.8	94.9	97.1	89.8	94.5	94.5	93.6	94.2	92.7	101.8	95.9	83.7	87.2	84.9
03	CONCRETE	87.7	118.9	100.0	99.9	87.4	95.0	89.1	93.5	90.8	94.9	93.3	94.3	92.6	99.9	95.5	85.7	88.0	86.6
04	MASONRY	100.2	121.5	113.1	98.2	84.1	89.6	90.3	91.8	91.2	107.2	86.2	94.4	96.5	96.1	96.3	109.1	80.6	91.8
05	METALS	93.0	116.8	97.7	92.4	112.8	96.4	90.6	115.2	95.4	92.4	116.4	97.1	99.8	117.6	103.3	94.8	113.0	98.4
06	WOOD, PLASTICS & COMPOSITES	76.2	114.0	93.1	70.3	74.2	72.0	96.7	87.4	92.5	78.8	79.1	78.9	95.7	87.6	92.0	74.3	79.0	76.4
07	THERMAL & MOISTURE PROTECTION	98.2	117.9	105.2	102.9	86.6	97.1	99.9	91.7	97.0	102.6	82.7	95.5	102.3	109.3	104.8	100.6	90.3	96.9
08	OPENINGS	95.0	120.6	100.8	91.2	82.8	89.3	86.7	90.9	87.6	91.1	91.2	91.1	98.4	89.9	96.3	93.3	84.5	91.4
0920	Plaster & Gypsum Board	94.2	114.6	107.1	107.4	73.6	85.9	107.7	87.1	94.6	109.5	78.6	89.9	111.6	87.1	96.1	94.7	78.5	84.4
0950, 0980	Ceilings & Acoustic Treatment	91.7	114.6	104.5	108.0	73.6	88.7	92.5	87.1	89.5	108.0	78.6	91.5	96.8	87.1	91.4	93.0	78.5	84.9
0960	Flooring	80.8	124.8	91.8	95.9	92.9	95.2	92.6	101.4	94.8	98.9	69.8	91.6	107.7	95.6	104.7	89.1	80.0	86.8
0970, 0990	Wall Finishes & Painting/Coating	89.9	127.7	112.4	92.3	109.8	102.7	95.9	90.3	92.6	92.3	94.3	93.5	98.4	91.2	94.1	89.9	92.5	91.4
09	FINISHES	86.8	117.6	102.2	101.1	81.8	91.4	95.1	90.6	92.8	101.7	80.9	91.3	101.8	91.1	96.4	91.3	81.4	86.3
COVERS	DIVS. 10 - 14, 25, 28, 41, 43, 44, 46	100.0	112.8	102.5	100.0	95.5	99.1	100.0	98.7	99.8	100.0	98.6	99.7	100.0	98.9	99.8	100.0	97.0	99.4
21, 22, 23	FIRE SUPPRESSION, PLUMBING & HVAC	92.2	119.1	101.9	92.8	78.7	87.7	99.8	94.1	97.7	92.8	81.7	88.8	100.2	98.1	99.5	92.9	85.9	90.4
26, 27, 3370	ELECTRICAL, COMMUNICATIONS & UTIL.	94.8	117.8	104.8	100.4	107.8	103.6	92.3	88.9	90.8	100.4	107.9	103.6	100.3	91.0	96.3	96.4	80.1	89.4
MF2018	WEIGHTED AVERAGE	93.0	115.6	101.3	95.7	89.9	93.6	93.6	94.3	93.9	95.4	92.4	94.3	98.8	98.0	98.5	93.7	87.5	91.4

City Cost Indexes

		PENNSYLVANIA																	
	DIVISION	INDIANA			JOHNSTOWN			KITTANNING			LANCASTER			LEHIGH VALLEY			MONTROSE		
		157			159			162			175 - 176			180			188		
		MAT.	INST.	TOTAL	MAT.	INST.	TOTAL	MAT.	INST.	TOTAL	MAT.	INST.	TOTAL	MAT.	INST.	TOTAL	MAT.	INST.	TOTAL
015433	CONTRACTOR EQUIPMENT		106.9	106.9		106.9	106.9		108.2	108.2		107.5	107.5		108.2	108.2		108.2	108.2
0241, 31 - 34	SITE & INFRASTRUCTURE, DEMOLITION	85.5	91.6	89.5	90.3	92.6	91.8	83.0	93.4	89.8	78.5	93.3	88.1	83.9	92.3	89.4	82.5	92.1	88.7
0310	Concrete Forming & Accessories	81.6	87.5	86.2	80.4	83.4	82.7	83.8	84.7	84.5	87.5	89.8	89.3	91.8	99.9	98.1	80.1	81.0	80.8
0320	Concrete Reinforcing	94.1	114.2	99.7	95.5	114.1	100.6	94.2	114.0	99.7	93.9	106.1	97.3	93.7	96.9	94.6	98.2	104.3	99.9
0330	Cast-in-Place Concrete	92.6	93.4	92.9	102.8	87.5	97.3	90.7	93.6	91.7	79.9	98.4	86.5	90.7	90.4	90.6	88.9	84.8	87.5
03	CONCRETE	92.6	95.4	93.7	99.5	91.4	96.3	84.6	94.2	88.4	86.2	97.1	90.5	91.3	97.1	93.6	90.4	87.8	89.4
04	MASONRY	95.6	91.9	93.3	96.5	83.8	88.8	104.5	87.6	94.3	107.0	90.0	96.7	97.3	86.9	91.0	97.2	82.4	88.2
05	METALS	92.5	116.3	97.2	92.5	116.5	97.2	90.0	116.9	95.3	92.8	119.2	98.0	94.7	112.4	98.2	92.6	113.7	96.7
06	WOOD, PLASTICS & COMPOSITES	72.3	85.3	78.1	70.3	82.3	75.7	77.1	81.1	78.9	83.0	87.3	85.0	89.3	102.1	95.0	75.2	79.0	76.9
07	THERMAL & MOISTURE PROTECTION	102.4	91.3	98.5	102.6	87.4	97.2	99.1	89.7	95.7	98.1	107.2	101.3	101.1	100.3	100.8	100.7	81.6	93.9
08	OPENINGS	91.2	90.6	91.0	91.2	88.9	90.6	86.6	92.3	87.9	87.2	87.1	87.2	93.3	96.6	94.1	90.3	83.2	88.7
0920	Plaster & Gypsum Board	109.1	85.0	93.8	107.4	81.9	91.2	96.0	80.6	86.2	106.8	87.1	94.3	97.3	102.3	100.5	95.8	78.5	84.8
0950, 0980	Ceilings & Acoustic Treatment	108.0	85.0	95.1	108.0	81.9	93.4	97.1	80.6	87.9	88.8	87.1	87.9	93.0	102.3	98.2	96.7	78.5	86.5
0960	Flooring	96.5	92.9	95.6	95.9	97.3	96.3	90.4	92.9	91.0	100.0	95.6	98.9	93.7	84.3	91.3	89.7	92.9	90.5
0970, 0990	Wall Finishes & Painting/Coating	92.3	109.8	102.7	92.3	107.1	101.1	85.6	109.8	100.0	91.6	83.5	86.8	89.9	89.7	89.8	89.9	92.5	91.4
09	FINISHES	100.9	90.3	95.5	100.8	87.8	94.2	93.2	87.8	90.5	94.2	89.5	91.8	93.3	96.0	94.7	92.8	83.6	88.2
COVERS	DIVS. 10 - 14, 25, 28, 41, 43, 44, 46	100.0	99.2	99.9	100.0	97.0	99.4	100.0	98.9	99.8	100.0	97.5	99.5	100.0	101.0	100.2	100.0	97.7	99.5
21, 22, 23	FIRE SUPPRESSION, PLUMBING & HVAC	92.8	80.7	88.5	92.8	84.8	89.9	92.2	85.7	89.9	92.8	96.9	94.3	92.9	105.6	97.4	92.9	85.2	90.1
26, 27, 3370	ELECTRICAL, COMMUNICATIONS & UTIL.	100.4	107.8	103.6	100.4	107.9	103.6	91.2	107.8	98.4	94.3	89.2	92.1	96.4	115.2	104.6	96.0	84.8	91.1
MF2018	WEIGHTED AVERAGE	94.6	94.4	94.5	95.5	93.4	94.7	91.2	94.7	92.5	92.6	95.7	93.8	94.2	101.6	96.9	93.2	88.3	91.4

		PENNSYLVANIA																	
	DIVISION	NEW CASTLE			NORRISTOWN			OIL CITY			PHILADELPHIA			PITTSBURGH			POTTSVILLE		
		161			194			163			190 - 191			150 - 152			179		
		MAT.	INST.	TOTAL	MAT.	INST.	TOTAL	MAT.	INST.	TOTAL	MAT.	INST.	TOTAL	MAT.	INST.	TOTAL	MAT.	INST.	TOTAL
015433	CONTRACTOR EQUIPMENT		108.2	108.2		94.4	94.4		108.2	108.2		101.1	101.1		98.4	98.4		107.5	107.5
0241, 31 - 34	SITE & INFRASTRUCTURE, DEMOLITION	81.4	93.7	89.4	99.8	90.0	93.4	80.3	91.3	87.4	105.3	103.9	104.4	94.0	95.7	95.1	80.9	90.9	87.4
0310	Concrete Forming & Accessories	83.8	91.6	89.9	83.7	119.0	111.1	83.8	84.2	84.1	99.8	136.4	128.2	99.7	98.5	98.8	79.0	79.6	79.5
0320	Concrete Reinforcing	93.1	95.4	93.8	96.3	135.3	107.1	94.2	85.2	91.7	101.0	152.1	115.1	100.4	122.8	106.6	93.2	102.4	95.7
0330	Cast-in-Place Concrete	88.1	93.8	90.1	94.2	115.5	101.8	85.5	86.1	85.7	105.7	133.5	115.6	101.4	100.6	101.1	85.2	95.1	88.7
03	CONCRETE	82.6	94.3	87.2	88.6	122.0	101.1	81.5	86.6	83.5	99.3	137.0	114.2	101.1	103.3	102.0	88.7	90.5	89.4
04	MASONRY	101.5	92.5	96.1	110.3	118.1	115.1	101.0	79.9	88.2	96.9	134.1	119.5	90.5	100.4	96.5	100.7	78.9	87.4
05	METALS	90.0	111.4	94.2	97.5	116.8	101.3	90.0	109.1	93.8	100.9	123.8	105.4	100.8	107.6	102.1	93.1	113.8	97.1
06	WOOD, PLASTICS & COMPOSITES	77.1	90.5	83.1	77.4	121.6	97.2	77.1	85.3	80.8	97.0	136.2	114.6	96.6	98.5	97.6	71.4	77.3	74.0
07	THERMAL & MOISTURE PROTECTION	99.0	90.9	96.1	105.1	117.3	109.5	98.9	83.1	93.3	101.2	137.2	114.0	104.8	100.3	103.2	98.1	90.4	95.4
08	OPENINGS	86.6	93.6	88.1	90.1	124.8	97.9	86.6	87.2	86.7	99.0	139.9	108.2	99.1	104.6	100.3	87.2	84.3	86.6
0920	Plaster & Gypsum Board	96.0	90.3	92.4	104.2	122.5	115.8	96.0	85.0	89.0	121.1	137.2	131.3	114.7	98.4	104.3	98.6	76.7	84.7
0950, 0980	Ceilings & Acoustic Treatment	97.1	90.3	93.3	100.9	122.5	113.0	97.1	85.0	90.4	106.8	137.2	123.9	102.2	98.4	100.1	88.8	76.7	82.0
0960	Flooring	90.4	97.0	92.1	93.7	124.8	102.5	90.4	92.9	91.0	101.7	147.9	113.3	101.9	106.8	103.1	96.5	92.9	95.6
0970, 0990	Wall Finishes & Painting/Coating	85.6	101.9	95.3	90.0	127.7	112.5	85.6	109.8	100.0	98.4	188.7	152.2	98.4	109.8	105.2	91.6	92.5	92.1
09	FINISHES	93.1	93.5	93.3	95.4	121.2	108.3	93.0	88.4	90.7	105.4	144.0	124.8	102.2	100.7	101.4	92.2	82.3	87.3
COVERS	DIVS. 10 - 14, 25, 28, 41, 43, 44, 46	100.0	99.9	100.0	100.0	112.3	102.4	100.0	96.7	99.4	100.0	118.5	103.6	100.0	103.4	100.7	100.0	96.9	99.4
21, 22, 23	FIRE SUPPRESSION, PLUMBING & HVAC	92.2	92.4	92.3	92.6	117.3	101.4	92.2	84.7	89.5	100.2	141.7	115.0	100.2	99.5	100.0	92.8	86.1	90.4
26, 27, 3370	ELECTRICAL, COMMUNICATIONS & UTIL.	91.5	93.2	92.2	97.9	126.4	110.2	92.6	95.9	94.0	100.6	160.7	126.6	100.8	114.6	106.8	93.3	81.3	88.1
MF2018	WEIGHTED AVERAGE	90.9	95.0	92.4	95.4	117.6	103.6	90.8	89.7	90.4	100.5	137.6	114.2	100.1	103.2	101.3	92.4	88.0	90.8

		PENNSYLVANIA																	
	DIVISION	READING			SCRANTON			STATE COLLEGE			STROUDSBURG			SUNBURY			UNIONTOWN		
		195 - 196			184 - 185			168			183			178			154		
		MAT.	INST.	TOTAL	MAT.	INST.	TOTAL	MAT.	INST.	TOTAL	MAT.	INST.	TOTAL	MAT.	INST.	TOTAL	MAT.	INST.	TOTAL
015433	CONTRACTOR EQUIPMENT		113.7	113.7		108.2	108.2		107.5	107.5		108.2	108.2		108.2	108.2		106.9	106.9
0241, 31 - 34	SITE & INFRASTRUCTURE, DEMOLITION	106.9	102.6	104.1	89.8	93.0	91.9	78.7	92.2	87.5	82.1	92.2	88.7	90.1	91.6	91.1	85.8	92.2	90.0
0310	Concrete Forming & Accessories	101.5	85.8	89.3	99.2	86.5	89.4	85.3	84.3	84.5	85.8	82.1	82.9	89.2	76.8	79.6	74.6	87.8	84.8
0320	Concrete Reinforcing	97.6	108.2	100.5	96.6	108.0	99.7	94.9	99.3	96.1	96.9	104.4	99.0	95.8	100.7	97.2	94.8	114.2	100.2
0330	Cast-in-Place Concrete	84.4	94.0	87.8	92.6	90.5	91.8	89.3	89.1	89.2	87.2	86.2	86.9	93.1	86.5	90.8	92.6	93.5	93.0
03	CONCRETE	87.6	94.0	90.2	94.2	93.1	93.7	93.3	90.0	92.0	89.4	88.8	89.2	92.6	86.0	90.0	92.2	95.5	93.5
04	MASONRY	100.0	88.4	93.0	97.7	90.1	93.1	102.3	88.8	94.1	94.5	86.7	89.8	100.1	72.9	83.6	108.6	91.9	98.4
05	METALS	97.9	119.1	102.1	97.1	117.3	101.1	92.3	112.9	96.3	94.8	114.1	98.6	92.7	112.7	96.7	92.2	116.8	97.1
06	WOOD, PLASTICS & COMPOSITES	100.5	82.8	92.6	99.8	84.8	93.1	83.4	82.3	82.9	82.2	79.0	80.8	80.6	77.3	79.1	62.9	85.3	72.9
07	THERMAL & MOISTURE PROTECTION	106.1	104.1	105.4	101.3	89.2	97.0	100.4	101.5	100.8	100.9	81.9	94.1	99.2	83.1	93.5	102.3	91.3	98.4
08	OPENINGS	94.9	91.8	94.2	92.8	88.9	91.9	90.2	85.4	89.1	93.4	85.7	91.6	87.3	81.5	86.0	91.1	91.6	91.2
0920	Plaster & Gypsum Board	115.7	82.5	94.7	111.5	84.4	94.3	97.2	81.9	87.5	95.4	78.5	84.7	97.3	76.7	84.3	103.5	85.0	91.8
0950, 0980	Ceilings & Acoustic Treatment	88.1	82.5	85.0	104.8	84.4	93.4	92.6	81.9	86.6	91.7	78.5	84.3	84.7	76.7	80.3	108.0	85.0	95.1
0960	Flooring	96.6	90.5	95.1	96.1	98.0	96.6	94.2	92.4	93.7	91.9	84.3	90.0	97.0	92.9	96.0	93.5	103.4	96.0
0970, 0990	Wall Finishes & Painting/Coating	89.0	103.5	97.6	89.9	103.5	98.0	89.9	107.1	100.1	89.9	92.5	91.4	91.6	92.5	92.1	92.3	101.9	98.0
09	FINISHES	94.6	87.2	90.9	99.1	89.9	94.5	92.7	87.6	90.1	92.0	82.8	87.4	92.2	80.8	86.5	99.2	91.2	95.2
COVERS	DIVS. 10 - 14, 25, 28, 41, 43, 44, 46	100.0	98.0	99.6	100.0	98.7	99.7	100.0	95.8	99.2	100.0	98.6	99.7	100.0	92.9	98.6	100.0	99.3	99.9
21, 22, 23	FIRE SUPPRESSION, PLUMBING & HVAC	100.4	111.2	104.3	100.4	94.8	98.4	92.9	94.8	93.6	92.9	88.0	91.1	92.8	78.5	87.7	92.9	85.7	90.2
26, 27, 3370	ELECTRICAL, COMMUNICATIONS & UTIL.	101.9	93.3	98.2	99.3	89.8	95.2	95.1	107.7	100.6	96.4	126.2	109.3	94.0	81.8	88.7	98.8	107.9	102.7
MF2018	WEIGHTED AVERAGE	97.9	99.3	98.4	97.7	94.3	96.5	93.5	95.6	94.3	93.7	95.4	94.4	93.2	84.6	90.0	94.6	95.7	95.0

City Cost Indexes

		PENNSYLVANIA																	
	DIVISION	WASHINGTON			WELLSBORO			WESTCHESTER			WILKES-BARRE			WILLIAMSPORT			YORK		
		153			169			193			186 - 187			177			173 - 174		
		MAT.	INST.	TOTAL	MAT.	INST.	TOTAL	MAT.	INST.	TOTAL	MAT.	INST.	TOTAL	MAT.	INST.	TOTAL	MAT.	INST.	TOTAL
015433	CONTRACTOR EQUIPMENT		106.9	106.9		108.2	108.2		94.4	94.4		108.2	108.2		108.2	108.2		107.5	107.5
0241, 31 - 34	SITE & INFRASTRUCTURE, DEMOLITION	85.9	93.0	90.5	87.5	91.6	90.2	105.7	90.9	96.1	80.1	92.7	88.3	82.7	92.8	89.3	85.0	93.3	90.4
0310	Concrete Forming & Accessories	81.8	93.7	91.0	84.3	76.3	78.0	91.0	114.5	109.2	88.9	84.9	85.8	85.9	82.2	83.0	82.4	86.4	85.5
0320	Concrete Reinforcing	94.8	114.5	100.2	94.9	104.2	97.4	95.5	135.3	106.5	95.6	110.3	99.6	95.1	110.1	99.2	95.8	110.1	99.8
0330	Cast-in-Place Concrete	92.6	94.1	93.2	93.6	80.5	88.9	104.4	117.4	109.0	83.7	88.8	85.5	78.8	87.5	81.9	85.6	98.4	90.1
03	CONCRETE	92.8	98.5	95.1	95.1	84.2	90.8	95.1	118.7	104.4	87.0	92.0	89.0	82.7	90.4	85.8	90.1	96.1	92.5
04	MASONRY	96.2	94.3	95.0	104.3	73.3	85.5	104.5	121.5	114.8	109.4	92.9	99.4	92.2	87.2	89.2	101.0	90.0	94.3
05	METALS	92.2	118.0	97.3	92.4	112.9	96.4	97.5	116.8	101.3	92.5	117.9	97.5	92.8	118.6	97.9	94.4	119.1	99.3
06	WOOD, PLASTICS & COMPOSITES	72.3	92.8	81.5	80.5	76.6	78.7	86.2	113.9	98.6	85.3	83.1	84.3	76.7	80.9	78.6	75.2	82.9	78.6
07	THERMAL & MOISTURE PROTECTION	102.4	93.4	99.2	101.4	77.1	92.7	105.6	113.8	108.5	100.7	90.0	96.9	98.6	87.6	94.7	98.2	104.5	100.4
08	OPENINGS	91.1	98.7	92.8	93.0	81.5	90.4	90.1	120.5	97.0	90.3	88.1	89.8	87.3	86.9	87.2	87.2	85.4	86.8
0920	Plaster & Gypsum Board	109.1	92.7	98.7	95.5	76.0	83.2	104.7	114.6	111.0	97.0	82.7	87.9	98.6	80.5	87.1	98.6	82.5	88.4
0950, 0980	Ceilings & Acoustic Treatment	108.0	92.7	99.4	92.6	76.0	83.3	100.9	114.6	108.6	96.7	82.7	88.8	88.8	80.5	84.2	87.8	82.5	84.8
0960	Flooring	96.6	103.4	98.3	91.2	92.9	91.6	96.0	124.8	103.2	92.6	98.0	93.9	96.1	88.6	94.2	97.7	95.6	97.2
0970, 0990	Wall Finishes & Painting/Coating	92.3	101.9	98.0	89.9	92.5	91.4	90.0	127.7	112.5	89.9	106.2	99.6	91.6	106.2	100.3	91.6	86.7	88.7
09	FINISHES	100.9	95.9	98.4	92.6	80.8	86.7	96.6	117.5	107.1	93.6	88.9	91.3	92.6	85.3	88.9	92.3	87.2	89.8
COVERS	DIVS. 10 - 14, 25, 28, 41, 43, 44, 46	100.0	100.1	100.0	100.0	92.9	98.6	100.0	112.6	102.4	100.0	98.1	99.6	100.0	94.9	99.0	100.0	97.0	99.4
21, 22, 23	FIRE SUPPRESSION, PLUMBING & HVAC	92.8	89.0	91.4	92.9	78.5	87.7	92.6	119.1	102.1	92.9	94.4	93.4	92.8	93.6	93.1	100.3	96.9	99.1
26, 27, 3370	ELECTRICAL, COMMUNICATIONS & UTIL.	100.1	107.9	103.5	96.0	84.8	91.1	97.8	117.8	106.5	96.4	85.1	91.5	94.2	78.7	87.5	94.3	79.2	87.7
MF2018	WEIGHTED AVERAGE	94.5	98.3	95.9	94.4	84.6	90.8	96.3	116.1	103.6	93.4	93.5	93.4	91.6	91.0	91.4	94.8	93.7	94.4

		PUERTO RICO			RHODE ISLAND						SOUTH CAROLINA								
	DIVISION	SAN JUAN			NEWPORT			PROVIDENCE			AIKEN			BEAUFORT			CHARLESTON		
		009			028			029			298			299			294		
		MAT.	INST.	TOTAL	MAT.	INST.	TOTAL	MAT.	INST.	TOTAL	MAT.	INST.	TOTAL	MAT.	INST.	TOTAL	MAT.	INST.	TOTAL
015433	CONTRACTOR EQUIPMENT		91.1	91.1		95.8	95.8		100.9	100.9		101.3	101.3		101.3	101.3		101.3	101.3
0241, 31 - 34	SITE & INFRASTRUCTURE, DEMOLITION	125.9	88.5	101.5	84.4	93.9	90.6	87.6	103.4	97.9	131.9	83.3	100.2	127.3	83.3	98.6	115.8	83.7	94.9
0310	Concrete Forming & Accessories	77.0	20.5	33.1	97.9	116.4	112.2	95.3	116.5	111.8	95.5	59.0	67.2	94.4	61.3	68.7	93.4	62.4	69.3
0320	Concrete Reinforcing	107.9	17.3	82.8	98.5	115.1	103.1	98.7	115.1	103.3	98.3	54.2	86.1	97.4	59.7	86.9	97.2	64.1	88.0
0330	Cast-in-Place Concrete	90.5	32.5	69.9	56.3	112.1	76.1	77.2	113.5	90.1	97.4	64.2	85.6	97.4	64.3	85.6	114.4	66.6	97.4
03	CONCRETE	97.7	25.5	69.2	83.0	114.5	95.4	93.9	114.9	102.2	95.8	61.8	82.4	94.1	63.8	82.1	95.1	65.9	83.6
04	MASONRY	121.2	22.1	61.0	112.4	118.9	116.4	124.6	119.0	121.2	82.6	53.9	65.2	98.1	53.9	71.3	99.8	64.8	78.6
05	METALS	104.0	43.2	92.0	94.4	112.6	98.0	99.2	110.4	101.4	98.0	85.7	95.6	98.0	87.7	96.0	100.4	91.3	98.6
06	WOOD, PLASTICS & COMPOSITES	81.2	19.6	53.5	95.6	115.4	104.5	93.5	115.5	103.4	93.1	60.8	78.6	91.2	63.7	78.9	89.6	63.7	78.0
07	THERMAL & MOISTURE PROTECTION	143.0	26.1	101.4	93.0	113.3	100.2	97.7	114.7	103.8	108.3	56.9	90.0	108.0	57.9	90.1	107.1	63.5	91.5
08	OPENINGS	159.8	18.0	127.8	94.9	116.2	99.7	97.4	116.3	101.7	92.7	56.7	84.6	92.7	59.5	85.2	96.1	61.9	88.4
0920	Plaster & Gypsum Board	156.5	17.2	68.1	106.5	115.8	112.4	120.0	115.8	117.3	101.5	59.6	74.9	109.0	62.6	79.6	109.2	62.6	79.6
0950, 0980	Ceilings & Acoustic Treatment	227.8	17.2	109.7	91.6	115.8	105.1	113.1	115.8	114.6	96.0	59.6	75.6	106.9	62.6	82.1	106.9	62.6	82.1
0960	Flooring	194.8	26.6	152.6	101.5	126.3	107.8	108.2	126.3	112.7	107.7	80.4	100.8	109.0	67.9	98.7	108.7	79.7	101.4
0970, 0990	Wall Finishes & Painting/Coating	200.1	20.6	93.1	87.3	114.6	103.6	98.4	114.6	108.1	94.3	58.7	73.1	94.3	50.5	68.2	94.3	66.0	77.4
09	FINISHES	197.7	21.5	109.2	96.4	118.4	107.5	107.9	118.5	113.2	103.5	62.9	83.1	107.4	61.6	84.4	105.2	66.0	85.5
COVERS	DIVS. 10 - 14, 25, 28, 41, 43, 44, 46	100.0	24.9	85.4	100.0	106.1	101.2	100.0	106.4	101.2	100.0	82.5	96.6	100.0	75.5	95.3	100.0	83.3	96.8
21, 22, 23	FIRE SUPPRESSION, PLUMBING & HVAC	117.6	17.3	81.6	100.6	110.9	104.3	100.2	110.9	104.0	93.0	49.8	77.5	93.0	54.9	79.4	100.5	57.7	85.2
26, 27, 3370	ELECTRICAL, COMMUNICATIONS & UTIL.	120.3	22.3	77.9	102.5	94.8	99.2	101.1	94.8	98.3	94.0	55.1	77.1	95.9	59.1	79.9	95.1	61.6	80.6
MF2018	WEIGHTED AVERAGE	121.3	28.7	87.2	96.3	109.9	101.3	100.1	110.6	104.0	96.8	61.8	84.0	97.6	63.7	85.1	99.6	67.5	87.8

		SOUTH CAROLINA																SOUTH DAKOTA		
	DIVISION	COLUMBIA			FLORENCE			GREENVILLE			ROCK HILL			SPARTANBURG			ABERDEEN		
		290 - 292			295			296			297			293			574		
		MAT.	INST.	TOTAL	MAT.	INST.	TOTAL	MAT.	INST.	TOTAL	MAT.	INST.	TOTAL	MAT.	INST.	TOTAL	MAT.	INST.	TOTAL
015433	CONTRACTOR EQUIPMENT		106.4	106.4		101.3	101.3		101.3	101.3		101.3	101.3		101.3	101.3		94.2	94.2
0241, 31 - 34	SITE & INFRASTRUCTURE, DEMOLITION	115.4	96.0	102.7	124.8	83.2	97.7	120.1	83.5	96.3	114.4	83.2	94.1	119.9	83.5	96.2	89.1	88.8	88.9
0310	Concrete Forming & Accessories	97.1	57.3	66.2	80.6	57.2	62.5	93.0	57.4	65.3	91.0	58.8	66.0	96.0	57.4	66.0	96.9	64.0	71.4
0320	Concrete Reinforcing	99.9	63.9	90.0	96.7	64.0	87.7	96.7	58.1	86.0	97.5	58.9	86.8	96.7	60.6	86.7	97.7	70.0	90.1
0330	Cast-in-Place Concrete	115.8	66.3	98.2	97.4	66.1	86.3	97.4	66.6	86.4	97.4	63.8	85.4	97.4	66.6	86.4	125.0	75.6	107.5
03	CONCRETE	95.7	63.2	82.9	90.5	63.3	79.7	90.4	62.6	79.5	89.5	62.3	78.8	90.7	63.0	79.8	108.1	70.1	93.1
04	MASONRY	92.4	63.2	74.7	82.8	64.7	71.8	80.9	64.8	71.1	104.6	53.2	73.4	82.7	64.8	71.9	125.1	70.6	92.0
05	METALS	98.2	87.1	96.0	98.8	89.7	97.0	98.8	89.3	96.9	98.0	87.3	95.9	98.8	89.7	97.0	95.6	82.4	93.0
06	WOOD, PLASTICS & COMPOSITES	94.3	57.0	77.6	73.9	57.1	66.3	89.4	57.1	74.9	87.6	60.8	75.6	94.0	57.1	77.5	95.9	59.0	79.3
07	THERMAL & MOISTURE PROTECTION	103.4	63.4	89.2	107.3	62.8	91.5	107.3	62.8	91.5	107.2	52.4	87.7	107.4	62.8	91.5	103.6	71.1	92.0
08	OPENINGS	98.3	58.3	89.3	92.8	58.3	85.0	92.7	57.3	84.7	92.7	57.8	84.8	92.7	57.5	84.8	92.8	70.4	87.7
0920	Plaster & Gypsum Board	108.4	55.8	75.1	94.9	55.8	70.1	99.6	55.8	71.8	99.1	59.6	74.1	102.5	55.8	72.9	109.7	58.3	77.1
0950, 0980	Ceilings & Acoustic Treatment	108.6	55.8	79.0	98.8	55.8	74.7	96.0	55.8	73.5	96.0	59.6	75.6	96.0	55.8	73.5	104.3	58.3	78.5
0960	Flooring	102.4	75.1	95.6	101.2	75.1	94.7	106.7	75.1	98.8	105.8	67.9	96.3	107.9	75.1	99.7	93.1	65.0	86.0
0970, 0990	Wall Finishes & Painting/Coating	94.9	66.0	77.7	94.3	66.0	77.4	94.3	66.0	77.4	94.3	58.7	73.1	94.3	66.0	77.4	85.1	72.9	77.8
09	FINISHES	104.9	61.2	82.9	100.1	61.4	80.7	101.2	61.4	81.2	100.6	60.6	80.5	102.0	61.4	81.6	95.8	65.3	80.5
COVERS	DIVS. 10 - 14, 25, 28, 41, 43, 44, 46	100.0	82.5	96.6	100.0	82.6	96.6	100.0	82.7	96.6	100.0	82.4	96.6	100.0	82.7	96.6	100.0	80.9	96.3
21, 22, 23	FIRE SUPPRESSION, PLUMBING & HVAC	100.0	54.1	83.6	100.5	54.1	83.9	100.5	53.2	83.6	93.0	49.4	77.4	100.5	53.2	83.6	100.1	77.1	91.9
26, 27, 3370	ELECTRICAL, COMMUNICATIONS & UTIL.	100.2	55.9	81.0	94.0	55.9	77.5	95.1	78.7	88.0	95.1	80.7	88.9	95.1	78.7	88.0	92.9	67.2	81.8
MF2018	WEIGHTED AVERAGE	99.5	65.1	86.8	97.4	64.5	85.3	97.5	67.4	86.5	96.3	65.2	84.8	97.7	67.5	86.6	99.1	73.5	89.7

City Cost Indexes

		SOUTH DAKOTA																	
	DIVISION	MITCHELL 573			MOBRIDGE 576			PIERRE 575			RAPID CITY 577			SIOUX FALLS 570 - 571			WATERTOWN 572		
		MAT.	INST.	TOTAL	MAT.	INST.	TOTAL	MAT.	INST.	TOTAL	MAT.	INST.	TOTAL	MAT.	INST.	TOTAL	MAT.	INST.	TOTAL
015433	CONTRACTOR EQUIPMENT		94.2	94.2		94.2	94.2		100.3	100.3		94.2	94.2		100.3	100.3		94.2	94.2
0241, 31 - 34	SITE & INFRASTRUCTURE, DEMOLITION	83.3	88.2	86.5	83.3	88.2	86.5	89.3	98.0	95.0	88.1	88.5	88.4	84.3	98.9	93.8	83.2	88.2	86.4
0310	Concrete Forming & Accessories	95.8	41.2	53.4	85.5	41.7	51.5	99.0	79.6	83.9	104.7	52.5	64.2	97.3	80.1	84.0	81.7	68.2	71.2
0320	Concrete Reinforcing	97.2	69.9	89.6	99.7	69.8	91.4	100.0	72.2	92.3	91.3	71.9	85.9	100.3	95.9	99.1	94.5	69.7	87.6
0330	Cast-in-Place Concrete	121.5	48.6	95.6	121.5	74.2	104.7	126.9	78.3	109.6	120.5	74.8	104.3	99.8	80.3	92.9	121.5	73.9	104.6
03	CONCRETE	105.8	50.4	83.9	105.6	59.5	87.4	112.0	78.2	98.6	104.7	64.9	89.0	100.7	83.3	93.8	103.9	71.3	91.1
04	MASONRY	110.9	69.8	85.9	119.4	65.6	86.7	111.9	74.3	89.1	118.5	68.3	88.0	113.9	75.5	90.6	147.9	66.4	98.4
05	METALS	94.6	81.2	92.0	94.7	81.6	92.1	99.5	79.8	95.6	97.9	81.3	94.6	98.8	90.4	97.2	94.6	81.0	91.9
06	WOOD, PLASTICS & COMPOSITES	94.6	30.7	66.0	80.5	30.5	58.1	100.0	79.2	90.6	101.8	43.7	75.7	94.3	79.0	87.4	75.5	67.4	71.9
07	THERMAL & MOISTURE PROTECTION	103.5	65.9	90.1	103.4	68.9	91.1	104.1	79.4	95.3	104.0	72.5	92.8	104.5	81.8	96.4	103.2	70.3	91.4
08	OPENINGS	91.9	54.8	83.0	94.3	54.7	85.4	97.0	82.5	93.7	96.1	62.9	88.6	97.6	87.4	95.3	91.9	57.2	84.1
0920	Plaster & Gypsum Board	107.7	29.2	57.9	101.2	29.0	55.4	108.2	78.7	89.5	109.8	42.5	67.1	99.2	78.5	86.1	98.3	67.0	78.4
0950, 0980	Ceilings & Acoustic Treatment	99.8	29.2	60.2	104.3	29.0	62.1	111.9	78.7	93.3	107.1	42.5	70.9	110.4	78.5	92.5	99.8	67.0	81.4
0960	Flooring	92.8	70.3	87.1	89.4	41.6	77.4	102.4	69.6	94.2	92.5	65.0	85.6	99.9	74.2	93.4	88.3	39.2	76.0
0970, 0990	Wall Finishes & Painting/Coating	85.1	72.9	77.8	85.1	72.9	77.8	99.1	114.6	108.4	85.1	114.6	102.7	94.9	114.6	106.7	85.1	72.9	77.8
09	FINISHES	94.1	48.0	71.0	93.5	44.0	68.6	103.9	82.8	93.3	96.3	60.8	78.5	101.2	82.6	91.8	91.5	65.2	78.3
COVERS	DIVS. 10 - 14, 25, 28, 41, 43, 44, 46	100.0	73.3	94.8	100.0	73.1	94.8	100.0	88.1	97.7	100.0	83.0	96.7	100.0	88.2	97.7	100.0	76.6	95.5
21, 22, 23	FIRE SUPPRESSION, PLUMBING & HVAC	92.6	44.2	75.2	92.6	68.4	83.9	100.1	70.3	89.4	100.1	69.4	89.1	100.0	70.6	89.5	92.6	47.0	76.2
26, 27, 3370	ELECTRICAL, COMMUNICATIONS & UTIL.	92.1	67.2	81.3	92.9	35.4	68.0	99.5	42.5	74.8	91.2	42.5	70.1	99.6	67.2	85.6	91.6	67.2	81.0
MF2018	WEIGHTED AVERAGE	96.0	60.0	82.8	96.4	61.1	83.4	101.6	73.9	91.4	99.1	66.3	87.1	99.9	79.6	92.4	96.8	66.0	85.5

		TENNESSEE																	
	DIVISION	CHATTANOOGA 373 - 374			COLUMBIA 384			COOKEVILLE 385			JACKSON 383			JOHNSON CITY 376			KNOXVILLE 377 - 379		
		MAT.	INST.	TOTAL	MAT.	INST.	TOTAL	MAT.	INST.	TOTAL	MAT.	INST.	TOTAL	MAT.	INST.	TOTAL	MAT.	INST.	TOTAL
015433	CONTRACTOR EQUIPMENT		101.0	101.0		96.1	96.1		96.1	96.1		101.5	101.5		95.7	95.7		95.7	95.7
0241, 31 - 34	SITE & INFRASTRUCTURE, DEMOLITION	102.4	90.0	94.3	97.2	81.1	86.7	103.4	80.3	88.3	109.9	90.6	97.3	107.4	80.4	89.8	91.3	81.2	84.7
0310	Concrete Forming & Accessories	100.6	58.5	67.9	82.9	56.9	62.7	83.0	30.0	41.8	90.9	66.6	72.0	85.2	56.5	62.9	99.2	63.3	71.3
0320	Concrete Reinforcing	93.1	64.4	85.1	86.0	58.4	78.3	86.0	58.1	78.3	86.0	65.3	80.2	93.5	60.6	84.4	93.1	66.8	85.8
0330	Cast-in-Place Concrete	94.9	61.1	82.9	94.4	60.5	82.3	107.0	54.1	88.2	104.5	63.6	90.0	76.3	55.8	69.0	89.2	64.1	80.2
03	CONCRETE	94.8	62.2	81.9	94.7	60.2	78.8	97.8	45.8	77.9	92.7	66.9	82.5	100.8	58.8	84.2	92.6	65.8	82.0
04	MASONRY	96.3	53.5	70.3	104.9	50.0	71.5	101.1	35.5	61.3	105.5	55.6	75.2	108.2	41.3	67.5	74.7	55.5	63.1
05	METALS	96.3	88.1	94.7	95.5	85.0	93.4	95.6	84.3	93.4	99.2	87.9	96.9	92.1	86.3	91.0	96.3	88.9	94.8
06	WOOD, PLASTICS & COMPOSITES	99.9	59.0	81.5	68.0	57.6	63.4	68.3	26.9	49.8	82.5	67.7	75.9	73.1	61.4	67.9	91.1	64.1	79.0
07	THERMAL & MOISTURE PROTECTION	107.9	59.0	90.5	98.0	56.7	83.3	98.4	47.5	80.3	99.9	62.0	86.4	103.6	53.8	85.9	101.9	62.6	87.9
08	OPENINGS	98.4	57.8	89.2	91.7	48.4	81.9	91.7	32.3	78.3	98.1	61.7	89.9	95.3	58.5	87.0	92.8	57.6	84.9
0920	Plaster & Gypsum Board	77.4	58.4	65.3	84.1	57.0	66.9	84.1	25.4	46.9	87.5	67.4	74.7	84.6	60.9	69.6	93.3	63.6	74.4
0950, 0980	Ceilings & Acoustic Treatment	98.0	58.4	75.8	75.4	57.0	65.1	75.4	25.4	47.4	80.5	67.4	73.1	94.1	60.9	75.5	95.9	63.6	77.8
0960	Flooring	102.4	57.7	91.2	87.8	48.3	77.9	87.8	44.8	77.0	83.9	52.7	76.1	102.4	52.7	90.0	106.5	56.8	94.1
0970, 0990	Wall Finishes & Painting/Coating	95.2	52.9	70.0	86.7	50.2	64.9	86.7	50.2	64.9	89.4	56.5	69.8	92.0	52.9	68.7	92.0	54.5	69.6
09	FINISHES	96.2	57.4	76.7	88.9	54.3	71.5	89.4	32.8	61.0	88.0	63.1	75.5	99.9	55.4	77.2	93.9	61.0	77.3
COVERS	DIVS. 10 - 14, 25, 28, 41, 43, 44, 46	100.0	80.4	96.2	100.0	80.1	96.2	100.0	73.2	94.8	100.0	82.9	96.7	100.0	77.5	95.6	100.0	81.7	96.5
21, 22, 23	FIRE SUPPRESSION, PLUMBING & HVAC	100.2	53.6	83.5	94.4	66.2	84.3	94.4	60.4	82.2	100.1	63.0	86.8	100.0	50.1	82.1	100.0	62.7	86.6
26, 27, 3370	ELECTRICAL, COMMUNICATIONS & UTIL.	103.8	73.8	90.8	96.0	45.0	73.9	96.8	54.6	78.5	103.7	58.5	84.1	93.6	46.7	73.3	96.7	57.0	79.5
MF2018	WEIGHTED AVERAGE	98.8	65.4	86.5	94.5	61.5	82.3	95.7	53.8	80.3	98.6	67.2	87.1	97.6	57.8	82.9	95.7	65.6	84.6

		TENNESSEE						TEXAS											
	DIVISION	MCKENZIE 382			MEMPHIS 375,380 - 381			NASHVILLE 370 - 372			ABILENE 795 - 796			AMARILLO 790 - 791			AUSTIN 786 - 787		
		MAT.	INST.	TOTAL	MAT.	INST.	TOTAL	MAT.	INST.	TOTAL	MAT.	INST.	TOTAL	MAT.	INST.	TOTAL	MAT.	INST.	TOTAL
015433	CONTRACTOR EQUIPMENT		96.1	96.1		97.2	97.2		103.4	103.4		88.4	88.4		95.3	95.3		95.6	95.6
0241, 31 - 34	SITE & INFRASTRUCTURE, DEMOLITION	102.9	80.5	88.3	90.3	90.1	90.2	100.2	97.6	98.5	95.4	84.5	88.3	95.5	94.8	95.0	90.8	94.2	93.0
0310	Concrete Forming & Accessories	92.1	32.0	45.4	100.2	67.6	74.9	101.2	71.0	77.7	100.8	58.5	67.9	102.4	53.3	64.2	97.6	53.3	63.2
0320	Concrete Reinforcing	86.1	58.9	78.6	100.1	70.0	91.7	101.0	68.3	92.0	98.9	49.7	85.3	99.2	48.5	85.1	99.6	47.7	85.2
0330	Cast-in-Place Concrete	104.7	55.1	87.1	92.0	69.1	83.8	86.9	70.4	81.0	77.3	64.2	72.6	75.5	70.2	73.6	83.8	66.5	77.7
03	CONCRETE	98.1	47.2	78.0	97.9	69.5	86.7	97.3	71.3	87.0	84.5	59.9	74.8	88.8	59.3	77.2	88.3	57.8	76.3
04	MASONRY	104.1	40.6	65.6	81.7	57.7	67.1	97.0	63.5	76.6	94.3	59.6	73.2	88.0	61.9	72.2	91.0	60.7	72.6
05	METALS	95.6	84.9	93.5	100.4	82.0	96.8	100.4	84.0	97.2	108.8	71.0	101.4	104.5	68.8	97.4	101.5	67.7	94.8
06	WOOD, PLASTICS & COMPOSITES	79.7	29.7	57.0	95.8	67.2	83.0	90.8	71.6	86.1	101.1	60.3	82.8	98.7	51.3	77.4	94.7	52.8	76.0
07	THERMAL & MOISTURE PROTECTION	98.5	48.4	80.6	106.1	66.4	91.9	105.3	69.2	92.5	96.5	61.6	84.1	93.1	63.7	82.6	90.9	64.3	81.4
08	OPENINGS	91.7	33.8	78.6	100.3	63.5	92.0	99.2	68.1	92.2	100.8	56.0	90.7	98.9	51.0	88.1	98.4	50.7	87.6
0920	Plaster & Gypsum Board	88.2	27.5	49.7	87.8	66.4	74.2	81.2	70.8	74.6	91.3	59.7	71.2	104.4	50.0	69.9	92.0	51.6	66.4
0950, 0980	Ceilings & Acoustic Treatment	75.4	27.5	48.5	111.8	66.4	86.3	86.8	70.8	77.8	105.1	59.7	79.6	101.4	50.0	72.6	98.2	51.6	72.1
0960	Flooring	89.9	48.3	79.5	103.1	55.3	91.1	108.4	64.1	97.3	96.3	66.9	88.9	98.6	64.9	90.2	103.9	64.3	94.0
0970, 0990	Wall Finishes & Painting/Coating	86.7	39.2	58.4	95.5	74.1	82.7	98.7	65.9	79.2	98.8	53.2	71.6	104.7	51.7	73.1	104.7	43.4	68.1
09	FINISHES	90.5	34.0	62.1	101.8	65.7	83.7	97.8	69.2	83.4	95.5	59.5	77.4	101.2	54.6	77.8	99.2	54.0	76.5
COVERS	DIVS. 10 - 14, 25, 28, 41, 43, 44, 46	100.0	73.9	94.9	100.0	84.3	97.0	100.0	84.9	97.1	100.0	79.1	95.9	100.0	80.1	96.1	100.0	80.4	96.2
21, 22, 23	FIRE SUPPRESSION, PLUMBING & HVAC	94.4	52.7	79.5	100.1	73.5	90.5	100.1	73.0	90.4	100.1	49.4	81.9	100.0	53.2	83.2	99.7	58.5	84.9
26, 27, 3370	ELECTRICAL, COMMUNICATIONS & UTIL.	96.7	49.3	76.1	99.2	63.9	83.9	104.0	64.2	86.8	97.4	51.0	77.3	100.8	58.3	82.3	98.4	56.0	80.1
MF2018	WEIGHTED AVERAGE	95.8	52.5	79.9	99.1	70.7	88.7	100.0	73.1	90.1	99.1	59.8	84.7	98.9	61.6	85.2	97.6	61.9	84.4

City Cost Indexes

TEXAS

DIVISION		BEAUMONT 776-777			BROWNWOOD 768			BRYAN 778			CHILDRESS 792			CORPUS CHRISTI 783-784			DALLAS 752-753		
		MAT.	INST.	TOTAL	MAT.	INST.	TOTAL	MAT.	INST.	TOTAL	MAT.	INST.	TOTAL	MAT.	INST.	TOTAL	MAT.	INST.	TOTAL
015433	CONTRACTOR EQUIPMENT		91.2	91.2		88.4	88.4		91.2	91.2		88.4	88.4		97.6	97.6		108.2	108.2
0241, 31 - 34	SITE & INFRASTRUCTURE, DEMOLITION	92.5	87.3	89.1	100.0	84.4	89.8	81.0	87.0	84.9	101.7	84.4	90.4	123.8	80.1	95.3	111.7	100.4	104.3
0310	Concrete Forming & Accessories	104.4	54.9	65.9	97.4	55.4	64.8	82.9	53.0	59.7	99.0	55.5	65.2	102.5	51.7	63.0	97.7	61.6	69.6
0320	Concrete Reinforcing	100.0	70.5	91.8	89.8	46.0	77.6	101.4	46.0	86.1	99.0	46.0	84.3	87.9	48.8	77.0	100.3	50.7	86.6
0330	Cast-in-Place Concrete	72.0	66.7	70.1	96.7	54.6	81.7	57.7	54.6	56.6	79.3	54.7	70.5	102.0	64.3	88.6	101.8	69.1	90.2
03	CONCRETE	85.4	62.7	76.4	90.4	54.5	76.3	74.2	53.5	66.0	90.4	54.6	76.3	91.9	57.6	78.4	95.9	63.7	83.2
04	MASONRY	94.9	60.8	74.2	116.2	54.8	78.9	126.2	54.6	82.7	97.4	54.4	71.2	81.1	57.9	67.0	112.3	57.9	79.3
05	METALS	93.4	79.1	90.6	100.0	68.9	93.8	92.8	69.0	88.1	105.4	69.0	98.3	95.8	83.5	93.4	101.2	79.7	96.9
06	WOOD, PLASTICS & COMPOSITES	106.5	54.0	82.9	101.2	57.4	81.6	72.9	53.9	64.4	100.3	57.4	81.1	113.1	51.5	85.5	95.3	63.4	81.0
07	THERMAL & MOISTURE PROTECTION	96.1	64.6	84.9	91.7	58.0	79.7	89.4	58.4	78.3	97.1	57.9	83.1	97.4	60.1	84.1	91.8	65.3	82.3
08	OPENINGS	86.5	58.5	80.2	98.5	52.5	88.1	87.4	50.7	79.1	96.0	52.5	86.2	96.0	49.4	85.5	98.1	59.1	89.3
0920	Plaster & Gypsum Board	97.0	53.3	69.3	81.5	56.7	65.7	81.7	53.2	63.6	89.4	56.7	68.6	95.1	50.5	66.8	93.9	62.1	73.7
0950, 0980	Ceilings & Acoustic Treatment	107.0	53.3	76.9	84.9	56.7	69.1	96.3	53.2	72.1	99.2	56.7	75.4	100.8	50.5	72.6	103.2	62.1	80.1
0960	Flooring	109.9	72.4	100.5	82.3	48.9	73.9	85.5	60.0	79.1	95.0	48.9	83.5	114.6	70.6	103.6	103.1	67.5	94.2
0970, 0990	Wall Finishes & Painting/Coating	94.2	55.5	71.1	91.8	45.9	64.4	91.5	51.0	67.4	98.8	45.9	67.3	112.4	42.5	70.7	104.7	52.2	73.4
09	FINISHES	97.6	57.5	77.4	84.0	53.1	68.5	84.9	53.6	69.2	94.6	53.1	73.7	103.7	53.7	78.6	102.2	61.6	81.8
COVERS	DIVS. 10 - 14, 25, 28, 41, 43, 44, 46	100.0	75.9	95.3	100.0	78.4	95.8	100.0	75.1	95.2	100.0	78.4	95.8	100.0	77.5	95.6	100.0	81.3	96.4
21, 22, 23	FIRE SUPPRESSION, PLUMBING & HVAC	99.7	63.6	86.8	92.2	44.8	75.2	92.2	59.2	80.3	92.6	48.8	76.9	99.8	57.0	84.4	100.0	60.2	85.7
26, 27, 3370	ELECTRICAL, COMMUNICATIONS & UTIL.	96.6	65.1	83.0	95.0	41.1	71.7	97.5	56.4	79.7	97.4	49.7	76.7	97.2	61.1	81.5	93.4	60.5	79.1
MF2018	WEIGHTED AVERAGE	94.6	66.0	84.1	95.7	54.9	80.7	91.2	60.0	79.7	97.3	56.9	82.4	97.6	61.9	84.5	99.5	66.4	87.3

TEXAS

DIVISION		DEL RIO 788			DENTON 762			EASTLAND 764			EL PASO 798-799,885			FORT WORTH 760-761			GALVESTON 775		
		MAT.	INST.	TOTAL	MAT.	INST.	TOTAL	MAT.	INST.	TOTAL	MAT.	INST.	TOTAL	MAT.	INST.	TOTAL	MAT.	INST.	TOTAL
015433	CONTRACTOR EQUIPMENT		88.2	88.2		96.7	96.7		88.4	88.4		95.4	95.4		96.9	96.9		102.5	102.5
0241, 31 - 34	SITE & INFRASTRUCTURE, DEMOLITION	105.5	82.7	90.6	100.2	79.3	86.6	102.3	84.4	90.6	91.4	94.7	93.6	98.9	97.2	97.8	106.1	85.8	92.9
0310	Concrete Forming & Accessories	98.7	46.7	58.3	105.7	55.7	66.9	98.4	55.4	65.0	103.1	58.4	68.4	98.0	59.3	67.9	92.3	50.8	60.1
0320	Concrete Reinforcing	88.2	42.7	75.6	90.6	46.4	78.4	89.9	46.0	77.8	100.7	49.9	86.6	99.6	49.7	85.8	101.1	53.6	87.9
0330	Cast-in-Place Concrete	109.8	54.0	90.0	74.8	55.6	68.0	102.2	54.6	85.3	68.4	66.6	67.7	87.0	66.1	79.5	76.6	55.5	69.1
03	CONCRETE	106.4	49.7	84.0	75.7	56.0	67.9	94.0	54.6	78.4	87.1	60.6	76.7	88.4	60.8	77.5	85.9	55.1	73.7
04	MASONRY	93.6	54.5	69.9	122.9	60.2	84.8	90.5	54.8	68.8	93.4	63.7	75.4	90.6	61.6	73.0	90.4	54.7	68.7
05	METALS	94.3	65.6	88.7	99.3	83.3	96.1	99.7	69.0	93.7	105.0	69.7	98.0	102.5	69.7	96.0	94.5	86.6	93.0
06	WOOD, PLASTICS & COMPOSITES	96.5	45.9	73.8	115.3	57.5	89.4	107.5	57.4	85.1	98.7	58.9	80.9	95.5	60.7	79.9	87.1	50.8	70.8
07	THERMAL & MOISTURE PROTECTION	94.8	56.9	81.3	89.8	60.3	79.3	92.0	58.0	79.9	98.3	64.9	86.4	88.8	65.5	80.5	88.8	58.7	78.1
08	OPENINGS	91.9	43.4	81.0	116.5	52.2	102.0	67.3	52.5	64.0	98.8	53.7	88.6	98.2	56.2	88.7	90.8	50.8	81.8
0920	Plaster & Gypsum Board	90.3	44.8	61.5	86.9	56.7	67.7	81.5	56.7	65.7	87.6	57.8	68.7	90.4	59.7	70.9	89.6	49.8	64.4
0950, 0980	Ceilings & Acoustic Treatment	95.2	44.8	67.0	89.9	56.7	71.3	84.9	56.7	69.1	105.8	57.8	78.9	98.2	59.7	76.6	102.2	49.8	72.9
0960	Flooring	96.4	48.9	84.5	77.3	48.9	70.2	104.9	48.9	90.9	98.6	75.6	92.9	104.1	69.0	95.3	98.8	60.0	89.1
0970, 0990	Wall Finishes & Painting/Coating	101.1	37.8	63.4	102.0	43.4	67.1	93.3	45.9	65.1	104.7	48.7	71.3	104.7	50.8	72.6	103.5	47.7	70.2
09	FINISHES	94.9	45.5	70.1	82.8	52.9	67.8	91.2	53.1	72.1	99.8	60.3	80.0	100.0	60.1	79.9	95.1	51.4	73.2
COVERS	DIVS. 10 - 14, 25, 28, 41, 43, 44, 46	100.0	72.8	94.7	100.0	78.7	95.9	100.0	78.4	95.8	100.0	81.2	96.4	100.0	80.1	96.1	100.0	75.1	95.2
21, 22, 23	FIRE SUPPRESSION, PLUMBING & HVAC	92.2	53.6	78.4	92.2	50.4	77.2	92.2	44.8	75.2	99.9	61.8	86.2	99.7	58.0	84.8	92.1	59.3	80.4
26, 27, 3370	ELECTRICAL, COMMUNICATIONS & UTIL.	98.3	53.3	78.8	97.9	52.2	78.1	94.9	52.2	76.4	100.0	47.5	77.2	94.8	55.3	77.7	97.9	56.5	80.0
MF2018	WEIGHTED AVERAGE	96.3	55.7	81.3	95.8	59.4	82.4	93.1	56.5	79.6	98.9	63.3	85.8	97.6	63.7	85.1	93.4	61.5	81.6

TEXAS

DIVISION		GIDDINGS 789			GREENVILLE 754			HOUSTON 770-772			HUNTSVILLE 773			LAREDO 780			LONGVIEW 756		
		MAT.	INST.	TOTAL	MAT.	INST.	TOTAL	MAT.	INST.	TOTAL	MAT.	INST.	TOTAL	MAT.	INST.	TOTAL	MAT.	INST.	TOTAL
015433	CONTRACTOR EQUIPMENT		88.2	88.2		97.2	97.2		100.9	100.9		91.2	91.2		88.2	88.2		89.4	89.4
0241, 31 - 34	SITE & INFRASTRUCTURE, DEMOLITION	94.0	83.0	86.8	98.8	81.8	87.7	108.7	94.0	99.1	94.0	87.0	89.5	92.5	83.3	86.5	96.1	87.2	90.3
0310	Concrete Forming & Accessories	96.4	46.9	57.9	87.3	52.6	60.3	98.2	59.9	68.3	90.8	49.4	58.6	98.8	52.1	62.5	82.9	55.6	61.7
0320	Concrete Reinforcing	88.6	43.5	76.1	101.0	46.4	85.8	99.7	52.1	86.5	101.6	45.9	86.2	88.2	48.8	77.3	100.6	45.7	85.4
0330	Cast-in-Place Concrete	93.0	54.3	79.3	104.2	55.6	87.0	71.3	69.8	70.7	79.3	54.6	70.5	78.6	65.0	73.8	121.3	54.6	97.6
03	CONCRETE	89.4	50.1	73.9	93.8	54.5	78.3	84.0	62.9	75.7	90.2	51.8	75.1	85.0	57.1	74.0	106.2	54.5	85.8
04	MASONRY	99.0	54.6	72.1	178.5	60.1	106.6	89.1	64.4	74.1	125.9	54.6	82.6	87.8	59.9	70.8	173.6	53.5	100.6
05	METALS	93.7	66.6	88.4	94.2	82.0	91.8	101.2	75.1	96.0	92.7	68.9	88.0	97.3	69.8	91.9	87.2	67.9	83.4
06	WOOD, PLASTICS & COMPOSITES	95.9	45.9	73.5	79.3	53.2	67.6	95.5	59.5	79.4	83.7	49.1	68.2	96.5	51.4	76.3	72.2	57.5	65.6
07	THERMAL & MOISTURE PROTECTION	95.1	57.5	81.7	90.9	59.3	79.6	90.2	69.1	82.7	90.3	57.9	78.8	94.1	62.6	82.9	92.2	57.2	79.7
08	OPENINGS	91.1	44.2	80.5	89.8	50.2	80.9	98.8	56.7	89.3	87.4	47.6	78.4	91.9	49.2	82.2	81.1	52.1	74.5
0920	Plaster & Gypsum Board	89.4	44.8	61.1	79.3	52.1	62.0	90.4	58.3	70.0	85.3	48.2	61.8	92.5	50.5	65.8	76.6	56.7	63.9
0950, 0980	Ceilings & Acoustic Treatment	95.2	44.8	67.0	95.8	52.1	71.3	98.2	58.3	75.8	96.3	48.2	69.4	102.0	50.5	73.1	87.2	56.7	70.1
0960	Flooring	97.8	48.9	85.5	94.7	48.9	83.2	103.1	74.9	96.0	88.2	48.9	78.4	96.2	64.3	88.2	100.0	48.9	87.2
0970, 0990	Wall Finishes & Painting/Coating	101.1	39.3	64.2	94.5	45.9	65.5	104.7	57.4	76.5	91.5	51.0	67.4	101.1	43.8	66.9	86.7	43.4	60.9
09	FINISHES	94.3	45.6	69.8	94.5	50.7	72.5	100.7	62.0	81.3	87.2	48.8	67.9	95.6	52.8	74.1	97.5	52.9	75.1
COVERS	DIVS. 10 - 14, 25, 28, 41, 43, 44, 46	100.0	78.3	95.8	100.0	78.4	95.8	100.0	82.5	96.6	100.0	74.6	95.1	100.0	77.7	95.7	100.0	78.6	95.8
21, 22, 23	FIRE SUPPRESSION, PLUMBING & HVAC	92.3	58.4	80.1	92.5	52.4	78.1	99.7	62.6	86.4	92.2	59.2	80.3	99.7	59.3	85.2	92.5	52.0	77.9
26, 27, 3370	ELECTRICAL, COMMUNICATIONS & UTIL.	96.4	49.5	76.1	91.7	52.2	74.6	99.4	64.2	84.1	97.5	52.6	78.0	98.4	55.7	79.9	90.6	45.3	71.0
MF2018	WEIGHTED AVERAGE	93.7	56.6	80.1	96.7	59.2	82.9	97.6	67.2	86.4	93.7	58.4	80.7	95.5	60.7	82.7	95.8	57.0	81.5

691

City Cost Indexes

TEXAS

DIVISION		LUBBOCK 793-794			LUFKIN 759			MCALLEN 785			MCKINNEY 750			MIDLAND 797			ODESSA 797		
		MAT.	INST.	TOTAL	MAT.	INST.	TOTAL	MAT.	INST.	TOTAL	MAT.	INST.	TOTAL	MAT.	INST.	TOTAL	MAT.	INST.	TOTAL
015433	CONTRACTOR EQUIPMENT		99.1	99.1		89.4	89.4		97.8	97.8		97.2	97.2		99.1	99.1		88.4	88.4
0241, 31-34	SITE & INFRASTRUCTURE, DEMOLITION	118.1	83.7	95.6	91.3	86.5	88.2	123.9	80.3	95.4	95.5	81.8	86.6	117.4	83.6	95.3	95.7	84.6	88.5
0310	Concrete Forming & Accessories	100.8	54.0	64.4	86.1	49.5	57.7	102.6	47.5	59.8	86.4	52.6	60.1	105.2	60.7	70.6	100.7	60.4	69.4
0320	Concrete Reinforcing	99.7	49.7	85.9	102.4	59.9	90.6	87.9	48.7	77.1	101.0	46.6	85.8	100.3	49.8	86.3	98.9	49.7	85.3
0330	Cast-in-Place Concrete	77.4	67.9	74.1	108.4	53.9	89.1	110.8	56.2	91.4	97.7	55.6	82.8	82.3	68.1	77.3	77.3	64.1	72.6
03	CONCRETE	83.8	60.1	74.5	99.9	53.8	81.7	97.7	52.8	80.0	89.8	54.5	75.9	87.2	63.2	77.7	84.5	60.7	75.1
04	MASONRY	93.9	62.6	74.9	132.3	54.5	85.0	92.9	59.1	72.4	192.1	60.1	112.0	108.8	60.9	79.7	94.3	60.8	74.0
05	METALS	112.4	84.8	107.0	94.4	71.0	89.8	94.2	82.9	91.9	94.1	82.0	91.7	110.6	85.0	105.5	108.0	71.0	100.7
06	WOOD, PLASTICS & COMPOSITES	103.2	52.3	80.4	78.8	49.3	65.6	111.1	46.0	81.9	78.0	53.2	66.9	109.0	62.1	88.0	101.1	62.0	83.6
07	THERMAL & MOISTURE PROTECTION	87.4	63.1	78.8	92.0	56.7	79.4	97.4	59.9	84.0	90.7	59.3	79.5	87.7	63.3	79.0	96.5	62.5	84.4
08	OPENINGS	108.6	52.9	96.0	61.0	51.3	58.8	95.3	44.8	83.9	89.8	50.2	80.9	109.9	57.7	98.1	100.8	57.6	91.1
0920	Plaster & Gypsum Board	91.7	51.4	66.1	74.3	48.2	57.8	96.3	44.8	63.7	79.3	52.1	62.0	91.6	61.4	72.5	91.3	61.4	72.3
0950, 0980	Ceilings & Acoustic Treatment	106.5	51.4	75.6	79.9	48.2	62.2	102.0	44.8	70.0	95.8	52.1	71.3	101.5	61.4	79.0	105.1	61.4	80.6
0960	Flooring	91.3	67.5	85.4	134.3	48.9	112.9	114.3	70.6	103.3	94.3	48.9	82.9	92.1	66.8	85.8	96.3	62.5	87.8
0970, 0990	Wall Finishes & Painting/Coating	109.9	51.7	75.2	86.7	45.9	62.4	112.4	37.8	67.9	94.5	45.9	65.5	109.9	52.7	75.8	98.8	52.7	71.3
09	FINISHES	98.5	55.7	77.0	105.2	48.7	76.8	104.4	50.3	77.3	94.1	50.7	72.3	97.8	61.0	79.3	95.5	60.0	77.7
COVERS	DIVS. 10-14, 25, 28, 41, 43, 44, 46	100.0	79.6	96.0	100.0	75.0	95.1	100.0	77.3	95.6	100.0	78.4	95.8	100.0	80.1	96.1	100.0	79.8	96.1
21, 22, 23	FIRE SUPPRESSION, PLUMBING & HVAC	99.5	50.2	81.8	92.5	52.4	78.1	92.3	44.8	75.2	92.5	54.4	78.8	92.0	53.5	78.2	100.1	48.5	81.6
26, 27, 3370	ELECTRICAL, COMMUNICATIONS & UTIL.	96.1	50.5	76.4	91.4	54.6	75.4	97.0	28.2	67.2	91.8	52.2	74.6	96.1	58.4	79.8	97.6	58.4	80.6
MF2018	WEIGHTED AVERAGE	100.7	60.8	86.0	93.9	57.8	80.6	96.7	53.4	80.8	96.6	59.6	83.0	99.7	63.9	86.5	99.0	61.1	85.0

TEXAS

DIVISION		PALESTINE 758			SAN ANGELO 769			SAN ANTONIO 781-782			TEMPLE 765			TEXARKANA 755			TYLER 757		
		MAT.	INST.	TOTAL	MAT.	INST.	TOTAL	MAT.	INST.	TOTAL	MAT.	INST.	TOTAL	MAT.	INST.	TOTAL	MAT.	INST.	TOTAL
015433	CONTRACTOR EQUIPMENT		89.4	89.4		88.4	88.4		94.9	94.9		88.4	88.4		89.4	89.4		89.4	89.4
0241, 31-34	SITE & INFRASTRUCTURE, DEMOLITION	96.1	87.2	90.3	96.8	84.4	88.7	90.7	94.5	93.2	87.2	83.8	85.0	86.7	87.4	87.1	95.3	87.3	90.1
0310	Concrete Forming & Accessories	76.9	55.5	60.3	97.8	47.5	58.7	97.7	55.8	65.1	101.5	46.8	59.0	94.1	59.2	67.0	87.9	56.2	63.3
0320	Concrete Reinforcing	99.9	45.9	84.9	89.7	50.9	79.0	101.5	50.3	87.3	89.8	45.7	77.6	99.7	49.5	85.8	100.6	49.2	86.3
0330	Cast-in-Place Concrete	99.1	54.6	83.3	91.2	65.6	82.1	74.9	70.3	73.2	74.7	54.0	67.4	99.8	64.1	87.1	119.1	55.4	96.5
03	CONCRETE	98.7	54.5	81.3	87.1	54.5	74.7	85.9	60.6	75.9	77.2	50.3	66.6	94.0	60.1	80.6	105.8	55.7	86.0
04	MASONRY	126.1	53.5	82.0	113.2	78.9	92.4	93.9	63.0	75.1	121.8	54.6	81.0	196.5	58.6	112.9	185.0	54.8	105.9
05	METALS	94.2	68.0	89.0	100.2	72.4	94.7	101.3	66.9	94.5	99.8	67.1	93.3	87.0	70.1	83.7	94.0	69.4	89.1
06	WOOD, PLASTICS & COMPOSITES	67.8	57.5	63.2	101.6	45.9	76.6	95.3	54.8	77.2	111.1	45.9	81.9	87.3	60.8	75.4	81.0	57.5	70.4
07	THERMAL & MOISTURE PROTECTION	92.4	56.9	79.7	91.5	64.7	81.9	90.9	67.1	82.4	91.1	56.6	78.8	91.9	62.2	81.3	92.3	59.3	80.5
08	OPENINGS	60.9	52.5	59.0	98.5	47.0	86.9	98.8	52.1	88.2	63.9	46.1	59.9	81.0	56.5	75.5	60.9	54.7	59.5
0920	Plaster & Gypsum Board	74.1	56.7	63.0	81.5	44.8	58.2	93.4	53.5	68.1	81.5	44.8	58.2	82.6	60.1	68.4	74.3	56.7	63.1
0950, 0980	Ceilings & Acoustic Treatment	79.9	56.7	66.9	84.9	44.8	62.5	91.4	53.5	70.2	84.9	44.8	62.5	87.2	60.1	72.0	79.9	56.7	66.9
0960	Flooring	128.2	48.9	108.3	82.4	48.9	74.0	103.1	73.6	95.7	106.1	48.9	91.7	105.6	64.0	95.1	135.9	48.9	114.1
0970, 0990	Wall Finishes & Painting/Coating	86.7	45.9	62.4	91.8	45.9	64.4	104.7	45.1	69.2	93.3	39.3	61.1	86.7	51.7	65.8	86.7	51.7	65.8
09	FINISHES	104.0	53.2	78.5	83.8	46.4	65.0	97.5	57.5	77.4	90.3	45.6	67.9	99.3	59.2	79.2	106.0	54.1	80.0
COVERS	DIVS. 10-14, 25, 28, 41, 43, 44, 46	100.0	78.6	95.8	100.0	78.3	95.8	100.0	79.8	96.1	100.0	77.2	95.6	100.0	79.4	96.0	100.0	79.0	95.9
21, 22, 23	FIRE SUPPRESSION, PLUMBING & HVAC	92.5	51.2	77.7	92.2	48.8	76.7	99.7	62.6	86.4	92.2	48.0	76.4	92.5	54.1	78.7	92.5	53.2	78.4
26, 27, 3370	ELECTRICAL, COMMUNICATIONS & UTIL.	89.1	43.1	69.2	97.4	48.6	76.3	99.7	59.7	82.4	95.7	46.3	74.3	91.3	54.7	75.4	90.6	47.9	72.1
MF2018	WEIGHTED AVERAGE	93.2	56.5	79.7	95.4	58.7	81.9	97.4	64.4	85.3	91.7	54.1	77.8	95.3	61.4	82.8	96.7	58.4	82.6

TEXAS / UTAH

DIVISION		VICTORIA 779			WACO 766-767			WAXAHACHIE 751			WHARTON 774			WICHITA FALLS 763			UTAH LOGAN 843		
		MAT.	INST.	TOTAL	MAT.	INST.	TOTAL	MAT.	INST.	TOTAL	MAT.	INST.	TOTAL	MAT.	INST.	TOTAL	MAT.	INST.	TOTAL
015433	CONTRACTOR EQUIPMENT		101.4	101.4		88.4	88.4		97.2	97.2		102.5	102.5		88.4	88.4		92.5	92.5
0241, 31-34	SITE & INFRASTRUCTURE, DEMOLITION	110.3	83.7	93.0	97.6	84.1	88.8	97.3	82.2	87.4	115.2	85.6	95.9	98.3	84.5	89.3	101.3	86.7	91.8
0310	Concrete Forming & Accessories	91.8	46.9	57.0	100.0	59.6	68.6	86.4	62.7	67.9	86.5	48.8	56.9	99.9	58.7	67.9	99.9	68.9	75.8
0320	Concrete Reinforcing	97.1	45.7	82.9	89.6	49.7	78.6	101.0	53.2	87.7	101.0	45.7	85.7	89.6	49.7	78.5	96.6	82.6	92.7
0330	Cast-in-Place Concrete	85.9	55.5	75.1	80.9	64.1	74.9	103.1	64.6	89.4	88.3	54.6	76.3	86.4	68.3	80.0	77.8	73.2	76.2
03	CONCRETE	90.4	52.0	75.2	81.8	60.3	73.3	92.9	63.4	81.3	93.6	52.3	77.3	84.1	61.1	75.1	98.3	73.4	88.5
04	MASONRY	105.4	54.7	74.6	88.7	59.9	71.2	179.2	62.8	108.5	91.4	54.6	69.0	89.2	58.4	70.5	110.9	60.9	80.5
05	METALS	92.9	83.5	91.0	102.9	70.0	96.4	94.2	85.4	92.4	94.5	83.0	92.3	102.8	71.1	96.6	104.5	83.6	100.4
06	WOOD, PLASTICS & COMPOSITES	89.9	45.9	70.2	108.8	61.4	87.5	78.0	64.5	71.9	79.2	47.9	65.2	108.7	60.3	87.0	90.0	69.1	80.6
07	THERMAL & MOISTURE PROTECTION	91.8	56.0	79.1	91.8	62.6	81.4	90.8	64.0	81.3	89.1	58.3	78.1	91.8	61.3	81.0	93.0	67.1	83.8
08	OPENINGS	90.7	46.3	80.7	74.6	57.6	70.8	89.8	60.5	83.2	90.8	47.4	81.0	74.6	56.0	70.4	87.6	70.5	83.7
0920	Plaster & Gypsum Board	85.5	44.8	59.7	81.8	60.9	68.5	80.1	63.8	69.8	84.8	46.9	60.7	81.8	59.7	67.7	88.6	68.4	75.8
0950, 0980	Ceilings & Acoustic Treatment	104.5	44.8	71.1	85.8	60.9	71.8	98.6	63.8	79.1	102.2	46.9	71.2	85.8	59.7	71.2	107.2	68.4	85.4
0960	Flooring	99.6	48.9	86.9	105.6	67.3	96.0	94.3	61.9	86.2	97.0	59.6	87.7	106.1	69.7	97.0	99.0	62.1	89.8
0970, 0990	Wall Finishes & Painting/Coating	103.7	51.0	72.3	93.3	54.8	70.4	94.5	56.5	71.8	103.5	49.5	71.3	95.1	50.7	68.6	92.2	60.2	73.1
09	FINISHES	94.1	47.0	70.4	90.9	60.5	75.6	95.2	61.8	78.4	94.7	49.8	72.2	91.2	59.8	75.4	98.9	66.4	82.6
COVERS	DIVS. 10-14, 25, 28, 41, 43, 44, 46	100.0	74.5	95.0	100.0	79.3	96.0	100.0	80.5	96.2	100.0	74.7	95.1	100.0	79.1	95.9	100.0	85.3	97.1
21, 22, 23	FIRE SUPPRESSION, PLUMBING & HVAC	92.2	59.2	80.4	99.9	59.4	85.3	92.5	63.1	82.0	92.1	55.8	79.1	99.7	54.7	83.6	100.0	56.9	90.0
26, 27, 3370	ELECTRICAL, COMMUNICATIONS & UTIL.	101.4	48.1	78.3	97.6	54.0	78.7	91.8	62.3	79.0	100.1	52.7	79.5	100.3	51.8	79.3	93.0	70.9	83.5
MF2018	WEIGHTED AVERAGE	94.6	58.5	81.3	94.7	62.5	82.9	96.6	66.9	85.7	94.7	59.1	81.6	95.3	61.2	82.7	99.1	72.6	89.3

City Cost Indexes

UTAH / VERMONT

DIVISION		OGDEN 842,844			PRICE 845			PROVO 846-847			SALT LAKE CITY 840-841			BELLOWS FALLS 051			BENNINGTON 052		
		MAT.	INST.	TOTAL	MAT.	INST.	TOTAL	MAT.	INST.	TOTAL	MAT.	INST.	TOTAL	MAT.	INST.	TOTAL	MAT.	INST.	TOTAL
015433	CONTRACTOR EQUIPMENT		92.5	92.5		91.7	91.7		91.7	91.7		92.5	92.5		93.0	93.0		93.0	93.0
0241, 31 - 34	SITE & INFRASTRUCTURE, DEMOLITION	90.3	86.7	87.9	97.0	84.3	88.7	97.8	85.3	89.7	90.0	86.6	87.8	82.7	91.5	88.4	82.2	91.5	88.2
0310	Concrete Forming & Accessories	99.9	68.9	75.8	102.7	59.8	69.4	101.9	68.9	76.2	102.2	68.9	76.3	101.7	92.8	94.8	98.6	92.6	94.0
0320	Concrete Reinforcing	96.4	82.6	92.6	103.7	80.4	97.3	104.6	82.5	98.5	98.8	82.5	94.3	80.2	78.2	79.6	80.2	78.2	79.6
0330	Cast-in-Place Concrete	79.0	73.2	77.0	77.9	68.0	74.4	77.9	73.2	76.2	86.3	73.2	81.7	71.1	110.7	85.1	71.1	110.6	85.1
03	CONCRETE	90.5	73.4	83.7	100.5	67.0	87.3	99.4	73.3	89.1	105.6	73.3	92.9	82.6	96.6	88.2	82.4	96.5	88.0
04	MASONRY	105.2	60.9	78.3	116.7	62.3	83.7	116.8	60.9	82.8	119.4	60.9	83.8	103.5	89.4	94.9	115.1	89.4	99.5
05	METALS	105.0	83.6	100.8	101.4	81.6	97.5	102.3	83.5	98.6	109.1	83.6	104.1	91.1	89.5	90.8	91.0	89.4	90.7
06	WOOD, PLASTICS & COMPOSITES	90.0	69.1	80.6	94.2	58.2	78.1	92.0	69.1	81.8	92.5	69.1	82.1	107.6	96.8	102.8	103.9	96.8	100.7
07	THERMAL & MOISTURE PROTECTION	92.1	67.1	83.2	94.3	63.0	83.2	94.4	67.1	84.7	98.6	67.1	87.4	90.1	83.8	87.9	90.0	83.8	87.8
08	OPENINGS	87.6	70.5	83.7	91.1	70.3	86.4	91.1	70.5	86.5	89.1	70.5	84.9	95.6	88.4	93.9	95.6	88.4	93.9
0920	Plaster & Gypsum Board	88.6	68.4	75.8	92.9	57.2	70.3	89.6	68.4	76.2	96.5	68.4	78.7	99.9	96.6	97.8	98.7	96.6	97.4
0950, 0980	Ceilings & Acoustic Treatment	107.2	68.4	85.4	107.2	57.2	79.1	107.2	68.4	85.4	103.1	68.4	83.7	72.8	96.6	86.2	72.8	96.6	86.2
0960	Flooring	96.5	62.1	87.9	99.8	50.2	87.3	99.7	62.1	90.2	100.3	62.1	90.7	91.2	109.2	95.7	90.5	109.2	95.2
0970, 0990	Wall Finishes & Painting/Coating	92.2	60.2	73.1	92.2	53.9	69.4	92.2	58.5	72.1	95.3	59.1	73.7	89.3	90.2	89.8	89.3	90.2	89.8
09	FINISHES	97.0	66.4	81.7	100.0	56.7	78.3	99.5	66.2	82.8	98.7	66.3	82.4	85.7	96.0	90.9	85.4	96.0	90.7
COVERS	DIVS. 10 - 14, 25, 28, 41, 43, 44, 46	100.0	85.3	97.1	100.0	83.8	96.9	100.0	85.2	97.1	100.0	85.3	97.1	100.0	98.9	99.8	100.0	98.8	99.8
21, 22, 23	FIRE SUPPRESSION, PLUMBING & HVAC	100.0	72.0	90.0	95.9	58.7	82.6	100.0	72.0	90.0	100.2	72.0	90.1	92.6	78.9	87.7	92.6	78.9	87.7
26, 27, 3370	ELECTRICAL, COMMUNICATIONS & UTIL.	93.6	70.9	83.8	95.6	61.2	80.7	93.2	66.2	81.5	96.5	68.7	84.5	101.6	70.8	88.2	101.6	48.5	78.6
MF2018	WEIGHTED AVERAGE	97.7	72.6	88.4	98.6	65.8	86.5	99.3	71.8	89.2	101.7	72.3	90.9	92.6	86.7	90.4	92.9	83.5	89.5

VERMONT

DIVISION		BRATTLEBORO 053			BURLINGTON 054			GUILDHALL 059			MONTPELIER 056			RUTLAND 057			ST. JOHNSBURY 058		
		MAT.	INST.	TOTAL	MAT.	INST.	TOTAL	MAT.	INST.	TOTAL	MAT.	INST.	TOTAL	MAT.	INST.	TOTAL	MAT.	INST.	TOTAL
015433	CONTRACTOR EQUIPMENT		93.0	93.0		97.6	97.6		93.0	93.0		97.6	97.6		93.0	93.0		93.0	93.0
0241, 31 - 34	SITE & INFRASTRUCTURE, DEMOLITION	83.3	91.5	88.6	90.6	101.7	97.9	82.1	91.1	88.0	86.0	100.9	95.7	89.2	92.5	91.4	82.2	90.6	87.7
0310	Concrete Forming & Accessories	102.0	92.8	94.8	103.7	83.2	87.8	98.5	87.5	90.0	103.7	94.5	96.5	102.3	83.2	87.5	96.0	87.5	89.4
0320	Concrete Reinforcing	79.3	78.2	79.0	98.7	82.1	94.1	80.9	78.2	80.1	97.9	82.1	93.5	100.2	82.1	95.2	79.3	78.2	79.0
0330	Cast-in-Place Concrete	73.3	110.7	86.6	88.1	114.2	97.4	68.9	103.2	81.1	81.7	114.2	93.3	69.6	113.1	85.1	68.9	103.1	81.1
03	CONCRETE	84.0	96.6	89.0	99.2	94.1	97.2	80.7	91.6	85.0	96.4	99.1	97.5	88.0	93.8	90.3	80.1	91.6	84.6
04	MASONRY	114.9	89.4	99.4	117.0	94.0	103.0	115.3	76.2	91.6	113.3	94.0	101.6	94.2	93.9	94.0	145.4	76.2	103.4
05	METALS	91.0	89.5	90.7	99.8	88.8	97.6	91.1	89.2	90.7	97.8	88.7	96.0	98.6	90.9	97.1	91.1	89.2	90.7
06	WOOD, PLASTICS & COMPOSITES	108.1	96.8	103.0	102.5	81.5	93.1	101.8	96.8	99.6	102.5	96.8	99.9	108.3	81.5	96.3	94.7	96.8	95.6
07	THERMAL & MOISTURE PROTECTION	90.2	83.8	87.9	95.2	95.9	95.5	89.9	77.9	85.6	94.8	97.6	95.8	90.3	94.4	91.7	89.7	77.9	85.5
08	OPENINGS	95.6	88.6	94.0	97.8	82.0	94.2	95.6	89.6	94.2	98.0	90.5	96.3	98.2	82.0	94.6	95.6	89.6	94.2
0920	Plaster & Gypsum Board	99.9	96.6	97.8	107.9	80.9	90.8	110.0	96.6	101.5	107.9	96.6	100.8	100.5	80.9	88.0	113.4	96.6	102.8
0950, 0980	Ceilings & Acoustic Treatment	72.8	96.6	86.2	81.2	80.9	81.0	72.8	96.6	86.2	80.7	96.6	89.6	78.2	80.9	79.7	72.8	96.6	86.2
0960	Flooring	91.4	109.2	95.8	99.2	109.2	101.7	93.5	109.2	97.4	99.2	109.2	101.7	91.2	109.2	95.7	96.0	109.2	99.3
0970, 0990	Wall Finishes & Painting/Coating	89.3	90.2	89.8	104.7	97.6	100.5	89.3	97.6	94.2	104.7	97.6	100.5	89.3	97.6	94.2	89.3	97.6	94.2
09	FINISHES	85.9	96.0	91.0	95.1	89.0	92.0	87.7	93.5	90.6	95.0	97.9	96.5	87.4	89.0	88.2	88.9	93.5	91.2
COVERS	DIVS. 10 - 14, 25, 28, 41, 43, 44, 46	100.0	98.9	99.8	100.0	98.7	99.8	100.0	94.4	98.9	100.0	100.4	100.1	100.0	98.7	99.7	100.0	94.4	98.9
21, 22, 23	FIRE SUPPRESSION, PLUMBING & HVAC	92.6	78.9	87.7	99.9	66.5	87.9	92.6	57.2	79.9	92.5	66.5	83.2	100.1	66.5	88.1	92.6	57.2	79.9
26, 27, 3370	ELECTRICAL, COMMUNICATIONS & UTIL.	101.6	70.8	88.2	101.0	51.9	79.7	101.6	48.5	78.6	101.1	51.9	79.8	101.6	51.9	80.1	101.6	48.5	78.6
MF2018	WEIGHTED AVERAGE	93.2	86.7	90.8	99.7	81.3	92.9	92.9	76.4	86.8	97.1	83.7	92.1	96.7	80.7	90.8	94.0	76.3	87.5

VERMONT / VIRGINIA

DIVISION		WHITE RIVER JCT. 050			ALEXANDRIA 223			ARLINGTON 222			BRISTOL 242			CHARLOTTESVILLE 229			CULPEPER 227		
		MAT.	INST.	TOTAL	MAT.	INST.	TOTAL	MAT.	INST.	TOTAL	MAT.	INST.	TOTAL	MAT.	INST.	TOTAL	MAT.	INST.	TOTAL
015433	CONTRACTOR EQUIPMENT		93.0	93.0		102.8	102.8		101.7	101.7		101.7	101.7		105.3	105.3		101.7	101.7
0241, 31 - 34	SITE & INFRASTRUCTURE, DEMOLITION	85.1	90.7	88.7	120.0	85.7	97.6	129.5	83.7	99.8	112.6	83.8	93.8	116.5	85.5	96.3	114.8	83.3	94.3
0310	Concrete Forming & Accessories	95.5	87.9	89.6	94.2	68.8	74.4	92.2	59.1	66.5	87.6	56.2	63.2	85.8	57.9	64.1	82.4	64.9	68.8
0320	Concrete Reinforcing	80.2	78.2	79.6	82.6	88.0	84.1	93.2	85.4	91.0	93.4	66.3	85.9	92.8	67.7	85.8	93.2	87.8	91.7
0330	Cast-in-Place Concrete	73.3	103.8	84.1	116.7	73.4	101.3	113.5	73.5	99.3	113.1	48.3	90.1	117.7	71.0	101.1	116.2	71.4	100.3
03	CONCRETE	85.3	92.0	88.0	95.8	75.2	87.7	99.6	70.5	88.1	97.3	57.1	81.4	98.2	66.1	85.5	96.2	72.7	86.9
04	MASONRY	129.5	77.5	97.9	89.1	71.4	78.4	99.6	71.0	82.2	90.6	52.4	67.4	114.1	53.4	77.2	104.1	66.1	81.1
05	METALS	91.1	89.2	90.7	102.4	101.2	102.2	100.4	100.4	100.4	99.2	91.4	97.6	99.5	94.1	98.4	99.6	100.0	99.6
06	WOOD, PLASTICS & COMPOSITES	99.5	96.8	98.3	94.9	67.5	82.6	90.7	54.5	74.5	81.1	54.4	69.1	79.1	54.9	68.3	77.3	63.8	71.2
07	THERMAL & MOISTURE PROTECTION	90.2	78.4	86.0	103.4	75.9	93.6	105.1	74.5	94.2	104.5	58.5	88.1	104.1	66.1	90.6	104.2	73.0	93.1
08	OPENINGS	95.6	89.6	94.2	94.7	72.6	89.7	93.0	65.3	86.8	95.8	61.0	87.9	94.1	61.6	86.8	94.4	70.6	89.0
0920	Plaster & Gypsum Board	97.0	96.6	96.8	109.7	66.5	82.3	105.1	53.2	72.2	99.8	53.0	70.1	99.8	53.0	70.1	100.0	62.7	76.4
0950, 0980	Ceilings & Acoustic Treatment	72.8	96.6	86.2	102.0	66.5	82.1	98.8	53.2	73.2	97.9	53.0	72.8	97.9	53.0	72.8	98.8	62.7	78.6
0960	Flooring	89.8	109.2	94.7	105.7	70.7	96.9	104.4	73.4	96.6	101.5	51.7	89.0	100.2	51.7	88.1	100.2	66.7	91.8
0970, 0990	Wall Finishes & Painting/Coating	89.3	97.6	94.2	116.2	65.4	85.9	116.2	68.1	87.5	102.1	69.9	82.9	102.1	56.0	74.6	116.2	65.2	85.8
09	FINISHES	85.2	93.8	89.5	104.7	67.9	86.3	104.1	61.2	82.6	100.8	56.5	78.6	100.5	55.3	77.8	101.1	64.3	82.6
COVERS	DIVS. 10 - 14, 25, 28, 41, 43, 44, 46	100.0	94.8	99.0	100.0	87.8	97.6	100.0	86.3	97.3	100.0	81.6	96.4	100.0	82.9	96.7	100.0	86.6	97.4
21, 22, 23	FIRE SUPPRESSION, PLUMBING & HVAC	92.6	57.9	80.2	100.4	81.4	93.6	100.4	83.3	94.3	92.9	47.3	76.5	96.8	63.8	83.5	92.9	78.6	87.8
26, 27, 3370	ELECTRICAL, COMMUNICATIONS & UTIL.	101.6	48.4	78.5	96.2	93.2	94.9	94.6	97.3	95.8	95.7	32.4	68.2	95.7	68.5	83.9	96.9	90.0	93.9
MF2018	WEIGHTED AVERAGE	93.9	76.7	87.5	99.7	81.2	92.9	100.1	79.9	92.6	97.1	57.2	82.4	98.1	68.2	87.1	97.6	78.3	90.5

City Cost Indexes

DIVISION		VIRGINIA																	
		FAIRFAX 220 - 221			FARMVILLE 239			FREDERICKSBURG 224 - 225			GRUNDY 246			HARRISONBURG 228			LYNCHBURG 245		
		MAT.	INST.	TOTAL	MAT.	INST.	TOTAL	MAT.	INST.	TOTAL	MAT.	INST.	TOTAL	MAT.	INST.	TOTAL	MAT.	INST.	TOTAL
015433	CONTRACTOR EQUIPMENT		101.7	101.7		105.3	105.3		101.7	101.7		101.7	101.7		101.7	101.7		101.7	101.7
0241, 31 - 34	SITE & INFRASTRUCTURE, DEMOLITION	125.5	83.8	98.3	113.2	84.4	94.4	114.4	83.2	94.1	110.5	82.4	92.2	122.4	83.6	97.1	111.1	84.0	93.4
0310	Concrete Forming & Accessories	85.9	61.6	67.0	102.9	57.0	67.3	85.9	59.7	65.5	91.3	55.3	63.3	81.3	58.2	63.3	87.6	57.5	64.2
0320	Concrete Reinforcing	93.2	88.1	91.8	90.1	61.2	82.1	93.9	72.9	88.1	92.1	39.8	77.6	93.2	75.9	88.4	92.8	66.6	85.5
0330	Cast-in-Place Concrete	113.5	74.5	99.6	117.4	80.3	104.2	115.3	69.5	99.0	113.1	48.4	90.1	113.5	72.7	99.0	113.1	71.7	98.4
03	CONCRETE	99.0	72.4	88.5	99.4	67.7	86.9	96.1	67.2	84.7	96.5	51.9	78.9	97.5	68.1	85.9	96.3	66.0	84.3
04	MASONRY	99.4	72.7	83.2	92.7	53.5	68.8	102.9	76.7	87.0	94.9	53.4	69.7	99.2	67.7	80.1	107.2	53.4	74.5
05	METALS	99.7	101.4	100.0	95.9	87.8	94.3	99.6	95.4	98.8	99.2	73.7	94.2	99.5	96.5	98.9	99.4	92.9	98.1
06	WOOD, PLASTICS & COMPOSITES	81.1	57.0	70.3	100.1	54.9	79.8	81.1	58.8	71.1	85.0	54.4	71.3	76.0	54.5	66.4	81.1	54.5	69.2
07	THERMAL & MOISTURE PROTECTION	104.8	76.6	94.7	99.6	65.9	87.6	104.3	74.7	93.7	104.5	56.0	87.2	104.6	75.0	94.0	104.3	65.9	90.6
08	OPENINGS	93.0	67.2	87.2	94.4	50.2	84.4	94.1	63.6	87.2	95.8	42.0	83.6	94.4	63.1	87.3	94.4	61.1	86.9
0920	Plaster & Gypsum Board	100.0	55.7	71.9	114.5	53.0	75.5	100.0	57.6	73.1	99.8	53.0	70.1	99.8	53.2	70.2	99.8	53.2	70.2
0950, 0980	Ceilings & Acoustic Treatment	98.8	55.7	74.6	99.7	53.0	73.6	98.8	57.6	75.7	97.9	53.0	72.8	97.9	53.2	72.8	97.9	53.2	72.8
0960	Flooring	101.7	75.8	95.2	103.4	51.7	90.4	101.7	64.8	92.5	102.6	51.7	89.8	100.0	72.2	93.0	101.5	51.7	89.0
0970, 0990	Wall Finishes & Painting/Coating	116.2	68.1	87.5	103.0	50.8	71.9	116.2	50.6	77.1	102.1	27.8	57.8	116.2	54.9	79.7	102.1	69.9	82.9
09	FINISHES	102.7	63.4	83.0	103.1	54.8	78.9	101.5	58.8	80.0	100.9	51.9	76.3	101.4	59.1	80.2	100.6	56.5	78.5
COVERS	DIVS. 10 - 14, 25, 28, 41, 43, 44, 46	100.0	87.1	97.5	100.0	79.2	96.0	100.0	70.2	94.2	100.0	77.9	95.7	100.0	81.8	96.5	100.0	81.6	96.4
21, 22, 23	FIRE SUPPRESSION, PLUMBING & HVAC	92.9	84.2	89.8	92.7	50.3	77.5	92.9	71.8	85.3	92.9	59.5	81.1	92.9	71.2	85.1	92.9	66.8	83.5
26, 27, 3370	ELECTRICAL, COMMUNICATIONS & UTIL.	96.2	95.9	96.1	92.0	64.6	80.1	94.7	97.3	95.8	95.7	64.6	82.2	95.8	72.4	85.6	96.2	60.3	80.7
MF2018	WEIGHTED AVERAGE	98.0	80.9	91.7	96.4	63.1	84.1	97.4	76.2	89.6	97.1	60.5	83.7	97.7	72.3	88.3	97.5	66.9	86.3

DIVISION		VIRGINIA																	
		NEWPORT NEWS 236			NORFOLK 233 - 235			PETERSBURG 238			PORTSMOUTH 237			PULASKI 243			RICHMOND 230 - 232		
		MAT.	INST.	TOTAL	MAT.	INST.	TOTAL	MAT.	INST.	TOTAL	MAT.	INST.	TOTAL	MAT.	INST.	TOTAL	MAT.	INST.	TOTAL
015433	CONTRACTOR EQUIPMENT		105.3	105.3		105.3	105.3		105.3	105.3		105.2	105.2		101.7	101.7		105.3	105.3
0241, 31 - 34	SITE & INFRASTRUCTURE, DEMOLITION	115.4	85.6	96.0	115.3	90.5	99.1	115.7	85.6	96.1	114.1	85.1	95.2	109.9	82.7	92.1	107.9	90.5	96.6
0310	Concrete Forming & Accessories	101.9	60.5	69.7	102.1	60.2	69.5	94.2	58.0	66.1	89.2	57.2	64.3	91.3	55.7	63.7	102.2	60.6	69.9
0320	Concrete Reinforcing	89.9	63.8	82.7	98.8	63.7	89.1	89.5	67.8	83.5	89.5	63.0	82.2	92.1	75.4	87.5	98.7	67.8	90.2
0330	Cast-in-Place Concrete	114.1	73.7	99.7	126.7	75.4	108.5	121.2	73.9	104.4	113.0	62.7	95.1	113.1	76.7	100.2	96.5	75.6	89.1
03	CONCRETE	97.2	67.7	85.5	104.6	67.7	90.1	101.0	67.1	87.6	95.5	62.0	82.3	96.5	68.2	85.3	92.1	68.7	82.9
04	MASONRY	90.2	54.0	68.2	90.4	54.1	68.3	99.2	55.2	72.4	94.3	52.6	69.0	86.5	50.3	64.5	90.5	55.3	69.1
05	METALS	98.8	92.5	97.6	100.1	88.6	97.8	96.0	94.3	95.6	97.7	91.5	96.5	99.2	92.6	97.9	100.3	90.5	98.4
06	WOOD, PLASTICS & COMPOSITES	98.4	58.8	80.6	98.8	58.5	80.7	87.2	54.9	72.8	82.3	54.9	70.1	85.0	54.4	71.3	98.8	58.5	80.7
07	THERMAL & MOISTURE PROTECTION	99.5	64.9	87.2	98.1	68.1	87.4	99.5	67.0	87.9	99.5	63.0	86.5	104.5	64.6	90.2	97.2	69.1	87.2
08	OPENINGS	94.6	62.3	87.3	98.5	62.6	90.4	94.1	61.6	86.8	94.7	60.0	86.9	95.8	52.8	86.1	98.3	63.5	90.5
0920	Plaster & Gypsum Board	117.2	57.0	79.0	111.8	57.0	77.0	106.8	53.0	72.7	108.8	53.0	73.4	99.8	53.0	70.1	108.6	57.0	75.9
0950, 0980	Ceilings & Acoustic Treatment	108.4	57.0	79.6	102.5	57.0	77.0	102.0	53.0	74.6	108.4	53.0	77.3	97.9	53.0	72.8	103.0	57.0	77.2
0960	Flooring	103.4	52.7	90.7	100.6	52.7	92.6	99.9	54.8	88.6	97.4	51.7	85.9	102.6	51.7	89.8	101.2	54.8	89.6
0970, 0990	Wall Finishes & Painting/Coating	103.0	54.1	73.8	104.7	54.9	75.0	103.0	56.0	75.0	103.0	54.9	74.3	102.1	42.9	66.8	104.7	56.0	75.7
09	FINISHES	105.6	57.5	81.5	105.0	57.5	81.1	101.9	55.9	78.8	102.7	55.0	78.8	100.9	52.7	76.7	103.3	58.0	80.5
COVERS	DIVS. 10 - 14, 25, 28, 41, 43, 44, 46	100.0	83.3	96.8	100.0	83.3	96.8	100.0	82.9	96.7	100.0	83.1	96.7	100.0	80.8	96.3	100.0	82.8	96.7
21, 22, 23	FIRE SUPPRESSION, PLUMBING & HVAC	100.2	62.6	86.7	99.7	62.1	86.2	92.7	66.2	83.4	100.2	62.2	86.6	92.9	60.3	81.2	99.7	66.8	87.9
26, 27, 3370	ELECTRICAL, COMMUNICATIONS & UTIL.	93.5	64.4	80.9	100.0	61.8	83.5	93.5	68.5	82.7	92.6	61.8	79.2	95.7	74.2	86.4	99.3	68.4	85.9
MF2018	WEIGHTED AVERAGE	98.7	67.2	87.1	100.7	66.9	88.3	96.8	68.7	86.5	97.9	65.2	85.9	96.8	66.5	85.7	98.8	69.4	88.0

DIVISION		VIRGINIA									WASHINGTON								
		ROANOKE 240 - 241			STAUNTON 244			WINCHESTER 226			CLARKSTON 994			EVERETT 982			OLYMPIA 985		
		MAT.	INST.	TOTAL	MAT.	INST.	TOTAL	MAT.	INST.	TOTAL	MAT.	INST.	TOTAL	MAT.	INST.	TOTAL	MAT.	INST.	TOTAL
015433	CONTRACTOR EQUIPMENT		101.7	101.7		105.3	105.3		101.7	101.7		88.6	88.6		96.9	96.9		99.6	99.6
0241, 31 - 34	SITE & INFRASTRUCTURE, DEMOLITION	113.5	84.0	94.3	113.3	84.2	94.3	121.2	83.3	96.5	108.8	82.8	91.9	107.9	101.4	103.7	109.4	105.0	106.5
0310	Concrete Forming & Accessories	98.7	57.8	66.9	90.9	57.0	64.6	84.0	60.3	65.6	83.6	58.5	64.1	116.4	103.9	106.7	100.4	103.1	102.5
0320	Concrete Reinforcing	93.1	66.7	85.8	92.8	65.3	85.2	92.6	72.0	86.9	77.0	96.2	82.3	93.3	114.3	99.1	100.0	113.8	103.8
0330	Cast-in-Place Concrete	128.5	80.4	111.4	117.7	80.2	104.4	113.5	59.0	94.2	97.8	76.1	90.1	111.7	110.2	111.2	98.4	111.0	102.9
03	CONCRETE	102.1	69.1	89.1	98.1	68.3	86.3	97.3	63.6	84.0	90.8	71.8	83.3	101.1	107.5	103.6	100.7	107.1	103.2
04	MASONRY	96.5	54.4	70.9	104.2	53.4	73.4	96.8	62.8	76.2	94.7	82.6	87.3	119.1	105.5	110.8	141.2	96.2	113.9
05	METALS	102.3	93.0	100.5	99.5	88.9	97.4	99.6	93.8	98.5	100.6	86.6	97.9	107.1	100.2	105.7	109.1	97.1	106.7
06	WOOD, PLASTICS & COMPOSITES	96.1	54.5	77.5	85.0	54.9	71.5	79.1	59.0	70.1	97.3	53.3	77.6	130.8	102.5	118.1	103.8	102.7	103.3
07	THERMAL & MOISTURE PROTECTION	104.3	67.6	91.2	104.1	65.9	90.5	104.7	69.8	92.2	84.3	74.4	80.8	99.8	106.7	102.3	96.9	105.4	99.9
08	OPENINGS	94.7	61.1	87.1	94.4	51.0	84.6	95.8	62.0	88.2	108.2	61.2	97.6	97.9	107.3	100.0	98.2	106.2	100.0
0920	Plaster & Gypsum Board	109.7	53.2	73.9	99.8	53.0	70.1	100.0	57.8	73.2	130.2	51.9	80.5	127.5	102.8	111.8	117.6	102.8	108.2
0950, 0980	Ceilings & Acoustic Treatment	102.0	53.2	74.6	97.9	53.0	72.8	98.8	57.8	75.8	86.6	51.9	67.1	98.7	102.8	101.0	106.2	102.8	104.3
0960	Flooring	105.7	53.2	92.6	102.1	51.7	89.5	101.2	66.7	92.6	82.7	69.4	79.4	99.8	101.6	100.2	100.3	86.0	96.7
0970, 0990	Wall Finishes & Painting/Coating	102.1	69.9	82.9	102.1	27.3	57.5	116.2	68.9	88.0	82.6	64.1	71.6	96.3	95.5	95.8	104.7	90.9	96.5
09	FINISHES	103.8	56.9	80.3	100.8	52.2	76.4	102.0	61.7	81.8	94.4	59.4	76.8	104.7	101.9	103.3	104.8	98.0	101.4
COVERS	DIVS. 10 - 14, 25, 28, 41, 43, 44, 46	100.0	81.8	96.5	100.0	79.2	96.0	100.0	74.0	95.0	100.0	92.5	98.5	100.0	102.2	100.4	100.0	102.2	100.4
21, 22, 23	FIRE SUPPRESSION, PLUMBING & HVAC	100.4	63.8	87.3	92.9	54.0	79.0	92.9	73.2	85.8	92.1	72.5	85.1	100.1	108.1	103.0	100.1	108.5	103.0
26, 27, 3370	ELECTRICAL, COMMUNICATIONS & UTIL.	95.7	55.2	78.1	95.1	74.9	86.4	95.0	81.7	89.2	83.3	85.1	84.2	104.1	103.5	103.8	100.9	101.3	101.1
MF2018	WEIGHTED AVERAGE	100.5	66.2	87.9	97.6	65.2	85.7	97.6	72.6	88.4	95.3	75.6	88.1	103.5	104.7	104.0	104.1	102.9	103.7

City Cost Indexes

		WASHINGTON																	
DIVISION		RICHLAND			SEATTLE			SPOKANE			TACOMA			VANCOUVER			WENATCHEE		
		993			980 - 981,987			990 - 992			983 - 984			986			988		
		MAT.	INST.	TOTAL	MAT.	INST.	TOTAL	MAT.	INST.	TOTAL	MAT.	INST.	TOTAL	MAT.	INST.	TOTAL	MAT.	INST.	TOTAL
015433	CONTRACTOR EQUIPMENT		88.6	88.6		99.2	99.2		88.6	88.6		96.9	96.9		93.7	93.7		96.9	96.9
0241, 31 - 34	SITE & INFRASTRUCTURE, DEMOLITION	113.9	83.9	94.4	113.0	103.0	106.5	113.7	83.9	94.2	111.3	101.1	104.7	122.7	89.8	101.3	118.6	98.6	105.6
0310	Concrete Forming & Accessories	83.7	82.7	82.9	104.7	108.4	107.5	89.2	82.3	83.9	105.5	103.1	103.6	105.3	95.7	97.9	107.1	74.9	82.0
0320	Concrete Reinforcing	73.8	96.3	80.1	99.5	119.4	105.0	74.3	96.9	80.6	92.6	114.3	98.6	93.1	114.2	98.9	93.1	86.2	91.2
0330	Cast-in-Place Concrete	98.0	84.3	93.1	117.8	112.0	115.8	101.9	84.1	95.6	114.9	109.1	112.8	128.3	99.9	118.2	117.3	84.1	105.5
03	CONCRETE	90.2	85.6	88.4	110.8	111.0	110.6	92.4	85.5	89.7	102.4	106.7	104.1	111.5	100.3	107.0	109.1	80.5	97.8
04	MASONRY	95.8	85.6	89.6	104.2	105.6	105.0	96.5	96.4	96.5	122.7	103.8	111.2	121.5	104.2	111.0	127.1	85.1	101.6
05	METALS	101.0	88.5	98.5	105.5	103.3	105.1	102.2	88.8	99.5	109.5	99.7	107.6	109.4	100.3	107.6	106.3	87.2	102.5
06	WOOD, PLASTICS & COMPOSITES	97.5	81.7	90.4	122.8	107.6	116.0	107.0	81.7	95.6	116.4	102.5	110.1	109.9	94.7	103.1	118.6	73.3	98.3
07	THERMAL & MOISTURE PROTECTION	92.6	84.2	89.6	99.7	110.0	103.4	91.3	84.8	89.0	99.7	106.9	102.3	99.9	100.7	100.2	99.3	79.9	92.4
08	OPENINGS	106.4	78.2	100.0	103.6	111.2	105.3	107.0	77.0	100.2	98.5	106.1	100.2	93.5	101.0	95.2	98.1	69.8	91.7
0920	Plaster & Gypsum Board	130.2	81.1	99.1	116.2	108.0	111.0	127.0	81.1	97.9	119.4	108.0	108.9	115.8	95.1	102.7	124.5	72.7	91.7
0950, 0980	Ceilings & Acoustic Treatment	89.6	81.1	84.9	100.7	108.0	104.8	87.6	81.1	84.0	103.2	102.8	103.0	95.8	95.1	95.4	94.0	72.7	82.1
0960	Flooring	82.8	77.1	81.4	92.2	103.4	95.0	81.0	93.9	84.3	95.1	95.2	95.1	100.3	98.7	99.9	97.0	69.4	90.1
0970, 0990	Wall Finishes & Painting/Coating	82.6	62.7	70.8	104.7	95.5	99.2	83.0	73.8	77.5	96.3	90.9	93.1	97.8	80.9	87.7	96.3	94.0	95.0
09	FINISHES	95.4	78.8	87.1	101.0	105.3	103.2	94.0	83.4	88.7	103.6	99.7	101.7	100.4	94.2	97.3	103.5	74.9	89.2
COVERS	DIVS. 10 - 14, 25, 28, 41, 43, 44, 46	100.0	97.3	99.5	100.0	103.2	100.6	100.0	97.2	99.5	100.0	101.7	100.3	100.0	95.4	99.1	100.0	94.8	99.0
21, 22, 23	FIRE SUPPRESSION, PLUMBING & HVAC	99.9	106.2	102.2	100.1	122.3	108.0	99.9	81.8	93.4	100.2	108.5	103.2	100.2	108.1	103.0	92.7	82.7	89.1
26, 27, 3370	ELECTRICAL, COMMUNICATIONS & UTIL.	79.7	97.9	87.6	100.9	126.4	112.0	81.0	80.1	80.6	104.0	101.3	102.9	113.5	100.9	108.1	104.5	84.1	95.7
MF2018	WEIGHTED AVERAGE	97.0	91.0	94.8	103.6	112.6	106.9	97.6	84.9	93.0	104.3	103.8	104.1	105.9	100.6	103.9	103.1	83.2	95.8

		WASHINGTON			WEST VIRGINIA													
DIVISION		YAKIMA			BECKLEY			BLUEFIELD			BUCKHANNON			CHARLESTON			CLARKSBURG		
		989			258 - 259			247 - 248			262			250 - 253			263 - 264		
		MAT.	INST.	TOTAL	MAT.	INST.	TOTAL	MAT.	INST.	TOTAL	MAT.	INST.	TOTAL	MAT.	INST.	TOTAL	MAT.	INST.	TOTAL
015433	CONTRACTOR EQUIPMENT		96.9	96.9		101.7	101.7		101.7	101.7		101.7	101.7		104.3	104.3		101.7	101.7
0241, 31 - 34	SITE & INFRASTRUCTURE, DEMOLITION	113.9	100.6	105.2	104.8	84.4	91.5	104.7	84.4	91.4	110.5	84.7	93.7	106.2	92.6	97.3	111.2	84.7	93.9
0310	Concrete Forming & Accessories	105.8	78.1	84.3	87.3	79.5	81.2	87.6	79.2	81.1	86.9	79.7	81.3	103.0	86.0	89.8	84.1	79.9	80.8
0320	Concrete Reinforcing	92.9	97.1	94.0	93.6	81.7	90.3	91.8	74.1	86.9	92.4	81.6	89.4	99.1	82.1	94.4	92.4	92.5	92.4
0330	Cast-in-Place Concrete	122.7	85.9	109.7	109.1	85.1	100.5	110.6	85.0	101.5	110.3	87.7	102.3	105.6	88.0	99.3	120.9	83.9	107.8
03	CONCRETE	106.8	84.4	97.9	92.2	83.1	88.6	93.4	81.7	88.8	95.1	84.2	90.8	94.2	86.9	91.3	99.1	84.7	93.4
04	MASONRY	115.3	96.8	104.1	85.2	80.3	82.2	87.7	80.3	83.2	97.9	86.0	90.7	83.3	86.2	85.1	100.9	86.0	91.9
05	METALS	107.0	92.7	104.1	99.2	100.9	99.5	99.5	98.1	99.2	99.7	101.2	100.0	97.9	98.6	98.1	99.7	105.0	100.7
06	WOOD, PLASTICS & COMPOSITES	116.9	73.3	97.4	84.8	79.4	82.4	83.3	79.4	81.5	82.3	77.0	79.9	99.4	86.2	93.5	78.1	77.0	77.6
07	THERMAL & MOISTURE PROTECTION	99.8	87.4	95.4	104.9	78.9	95.6	104.2	78.9	95.2	104.5	82.7	96.7	101.5	85.0	95.6	104.4	82.4	96.6
08	OPENINGS	98.1	84.0	94.9	97.7	76.6	92.9	96.2	74.8	91.4	96.2	75.2	91.5	97.9	80.3	93.9	96.2	79.9	92.6
0920	Plaster & Gypsum Board	118.7	72.7	89.6	90.2	78.8	83.0	97.8	78.8	85.7	99.0	76.4	84.7	102.3	85.7	91.8	96.4	76.4	83.7
0950, 0980	Ceilings & Acoustic Treatment	95.0	72.7	82.5	74.0	78.8	76.7	93.8	78.8	85.4	97.9	76.4	85.8	85.5	85.7	85.6	97.9	76.4	85.8
0960	Flooring	95.6	93.9	95.2	104.6	95.1	102.2	99.5	95.1	98.4	99.2	90.7	97.1	106.2	95.1	103.4	98.4	90.7	96.4
0970, 0990	Wall Finishes & Painting/Coating	96.3	73.8	82.9	101.9	81.9	89.9	102.1	79.8	88.8	102.1	85.5	92.2	104.7	87.9	94.7	102.1	85.5	92.2
09	FINISHES	101.7	78.8	90.2	92.5	82.7	87.6	98.2	82.5	90.3	99.9	82.0	90.9	99.1	87.9	93.5	99.1	82.7	90.6
COVERS	DIVS. 10 - 14, 25, 28, 41, 43, 44, 46	100.0	96.3	99.3	100.0	86.3	97.3	100.0	90.4	98.1	100.0	91.7	98.4	100.0	92.1	98.5	100.0	91.7	98.4
21, 22, 23	FIRE SUPPRESSION, PLUMBING & HVAC	100.2	107.3	102.7	92.7	87.1	90.7	92.9	75.6	86.7	92.9	89.7	91.7	99.7	88.9	95.8	92.9	89.9	91.8
26, 27, 3370	ELECTRICAL, COMMUNICATIONS & UTIL.	105.6	102.5	104.3	93.8	74.9	85.6	95.1	74.9	86.4	95.9	88.9	92.8	100.8	83.5	93.3	95.9	88.9	92.8
MF2018	WEIGHTED AVERAGE	104.0	94.7	100.6	95.4	83.9	91.2	96.2	81.0	90.6	97.2	87.2	93.5	98.2	88.3	94.5	97.7	87.9	94.1

		WEST VIRGINIA																	
DIVISION		GASSAWAY			HUNTINGTON			LEWISBURG			MARTINSBURG			MORGANTOWN			PARKERSBURG		
		266			255 - 257			249			254			265			261		
		MAT.	INST.	TOTAL	MAT.	INST.	TOTAL	MAT.	INST.	TOTAL	MAT.	INST.	TOTAL	MAT.	INST.	TOTAL	MAT.	INST.	TOTAL
015433	CONTRACTOR EQUIPMENT		101.7	101.7		101.7	101.7		101.7	101.7		101.7	101.7		101.7	101.7		101.7	101.7
0241, 31 - 34	SITE & INFRASTRUCTURE, DEMOLITION	108.1	84.7	92.8	112.3	85.6	94.9	119.7	84.4	96.7	108.4	84.6	92.9	105.5	85.8	92.7	116.6	85.8	96.5
0310	Concrete Forming & Accessories	86.3	80.4	81.7	101.2	83.3	87.1	84.5	79.3	80.5	87.4	72.2	75.6	84.5	80.3	81.2	89.3	86.3	87.0
0320	Concrete Reinforcing	92.4	82.3	89.6	94.9	85.1	92.2	92.4	74.1	87.3	93.6	85.4	91.3	92.4	92.5	92.4	91.8	81.5	88.9
0330	Cast-in-Place Concrete	115.5	87.6	105.6	118.9	89.8	108.6	110.7	85.0	101.6	114.3	80.9	102.4	110.3	92.7	104.0	112.7	88.1	104.0
03	CONCRETE	96.3	84.5	91.6	97.8	87.0	93.5	98.8	81.8	92.1	95.0	78.9	88.7	93.2	88.0	91.1	96.7	87.3	93.0
04	MASONRY	101.8	84.9	91.5	87.5	86.7	87.0	94.3	80.3	85.8	87.5	75.6	80.3	118.9	86.0	98.9	79.7	78.4	78.9
05	METALS	99.6	101.1	99.9	102.3	102.7	102.4	99.6	98.2	99.3	99.6	99.8	99.6	99.7	105.4	100.9	100.3	101.3	100.5
06	WOOD, PLASTICS & COMPOSITES	81.2	78.3	79.9	99.4	82.1	91.6	78.5	79.4	78.9	84.8	71.4	78.8	78.5	77.0	77.8	82.9	87.9	85.2
07	THERMAL & MOISTURE PROTECTION	104.2	83.0	96.7	105.2	82.5	97.1	105.0	78.9	95.7	105.1	72.5	93.5	104.2	83.7	96.9	104.5	81.7	96.4
08	OPENINGS	94.5	76.1	90.4	96.8	78.7	92.7	96.2	74.8	91.4	99.5	67.0	92.2	97.4	79.9	93.4	95.7	80.9	92.0
0920	Plaster & Gypsum Board	97.8	77.7	85.0	98.2	81.6	87.6	96.4	78.8	85.2	90.2	70.7	77.8	96.4	76.4	83.7	99.8	87.6	92.1
0950, 0980	Ceilings & Acoustic Treatment	97.9	77.7	86.6	74.0	81.6	78.2	97.9	78.8	87.2	74.0	70.6	72.1	97.9	76.4	85.8	97.9	87.6	92.1
0960	Flooring	99.1	95.1	98.1	111.2	94.3	106.9	98.5	95.1	97.7	104.6	88.6	100.6	98.5	90.7	96.6	101.8	94.2	99.9
0970, 0990	Wall Finishes & Painting/Coating	102.1	87.9	93.7	101.9	83.2	90.7	102.1	57.3	75.4	101.9	74.4	85.5	102.1	85.5	92.2	102.1	87.2	93.2
09	FINISHES	99.4	83.9	91.6	95.5	85.1	90.2	100.4	80.0	90.2	92.7	74.9	83.8	98.8	82.0	90.3	100.9	88.2	94.5
COVERS	DIVS. 10 - 14, 25, 28, 41, 43, 44, 46	100.0	91.8	98.4	100.0	91.8	98.4	100.0	90.4	98.1	100.0	89.0	97.9	100.0	91.7	98.4	100.0	91.4	98.3
21, 22, 23	FIRE SUPPRESSION, PLUMBING & HVAC	92.9	77.9	87.5	100.2	86.4	95.3	92.9	87.0	90.8	92.7	72.8	85.6	92.9	90.2	91.9	100.4	85.5	95.0
26, 27, 3370	ELECTRICAL, COMMUNICATIONS & UTIL.	95.9	83.5	90.5	95.9	83.0	90.3	93.8	74.9	85.6	97.0	68.4	84.6	96.0	88.9	92.9	95.9	84.4	90.9
MF2018	WEIGHTED AVERAGE	97.2	84.2	92.4	99.2	87.0	94.7	97.5	83.1	92.2	96.6	77.2	89.4	97.6	88.6	94.3	98.6	86.6	94.2

City Cost Indexes

DIVISION		WEST VIRGINIA									WISCONSIN								
		PETERSBURG 268			ROMNEY 267			WHEELING 260			BELOIT 535			EAU CLAIRE 547			GREEN BAY 541 - 543		
		MAT.	INST.	TOTAL	MAT.	INST.	TOTAL	MAT.	INST.	TOTAL	MAT.	INST.	TOTAL	MAT.	INST.	TOTAL	MAT.	INST.	TOTAL
015433	CONTRACTOR EQUIPMENT		101.7	101.7		101.7	101.7		101.7	101.7		95.4	95.4		96.2	96.2		94.2	94.2
0241, 31 - 34	SITE & INFRASTRUCTURE, DEMOLITION	104.9	85.5	92.3	107.7	85.5	93.2	117.2	85.6	96.6	85.3	96.0	92.3	86.2	95.3	92.1	88.6	91.7	90.6
0310	Concrete Forming & Accessories	88.1	81.1	82.7	83.6	81.0	81.6	91.4	79.4	82.1	95.4	87.7	89.4	98.2	92.8	94.0	110.6	102.7	104.5
0320	Concrete Reinforcing	91.8	82.3	89.2	92.4	85.7	90.5	91.2	92.4	91.6	100.2	138.6	110.8	91.8	109.2	96.6	90.7	106.2	95.0
0330	Cast-in-Place Concrete	110.3	87.6	102.2	115.5	80.0	102.9	112.7	89.8	104.6	89.9	91.6	90.5	110.0	99.3	106.2	113.8	99.0	108.5
03	CONCRETE	93.3	84.9	90.0	96.0	82.7	90.8	96.7	86.6	92.7	95.9	98.1	96.7	100.2	98.3	99.5	103.5	102.1	102.9
04	MASONRY	94.0	86.0	89.2	94.7	84.9	88.8	100.4	83.4	90.1	99.9	103.2	101.9	97.5	104.4	101.7	128.8	98.4	110.4
05	METALS	99.8	101.1	100.1	99.9	102.0	100.3	100.5	105.1	101.4	92.7	113.1	96.7	91.5	105.1	94.2	96.2	104.2	97.8
06	WOOD, PLASTICS & COMPOSITES	83.6	79.4	81.7	77.4	79.4	78.3	85.0	77.0	81.4	93.0	85.4	89.6	101.3	90.5	96.5	115.6	103.8	110.3
07	THERMAL & MOISTURE PROTECTION	104.3	78.1	95.0	104.4	77.7	94.9	104.7	81.1	96.3	102.0	87.8	96.9	104.7	99.9	103.0	107.0	99.3	104.3
08	OPENINGS	97.4	75.8	92.5	97.3	76.6	92.6	95.9	79.9	92.3	93.9	101.5	95.6	99.8	92.4	98.2	95.4	103.3	97.2
0920	Plaster & Gypsum Board	99.0	78.8	86.2	97.9	78.8	85.1	99.8	76.4	84.9	82.0	85.6	84.3	97.2	90.8	93.2	95.5	104.5	101.2
0950, 0980	Ceilings & Acoustic Treatment	97.9	78.8	87.2	97.9	78.8	87.2	97.9	76.4	85.8	89.9	85.6	87.5	93.9	90.8	92.2	87.8	104.5	97.1
0960	Flooring	100.0	90.7	97.6	98.3	88.6	95.9	102.6	90.7	99.6	96.3	106.1	98.8	83.8	115.1	91.7	100.3	116.7	104.4
0970, 0990	Wall Finishes & Painting/Coating	102.1	85.5	92.2	102.1	85.5	92.2	102.1	85.5	92.2	97.2	92.0	94.1	85.4	79.5	81.9	92.9	117.9	107.8
09	FINISHES	99.6	83.3	91.4	98.9	82.9	90.9	101.1	81.6	91.3	92.0	90.8	91.4	89.5	95.1	92.3	93.4	107.3	100.4
COVERS	DIVS. 10 - 14, 25, 28, 41, 43, 44, 46	100.0	89.8	98.0	100.0	91.9	98.4	100.0	86.4	97.4	100.0	96.7	99.4	100.0	93.3	98.7	100.0	97.6	99.5
21, 22, 23	FIRE SUPPRESSION, PLUMBING & HVAC	92.9	78.4	87.7	92.9	78.1	87.6	100.4	89.1	96.3	99.7	86.2	94.7	100.0	85.9	94.9	100.3	92.6	97.6
26, 27, 3370	ELECTRICAL, COMMUNICATIONS & UTIL.	97.6	68.5	85.0	97.2	68.4	84.7	94.5	88.9	92.1	98.9	75.0	88.6	97.6	98.3	97.9	95.4	100.3	97.5
MF2018	WEIGHTED AVERAGE	96.9	82.2	91.5	97.2	81.8	91.6	99.4	87.6	95.0	96.3	92.8	95.0	96.9	95.8	96.5	99.5	99.3	99.4

DIVISION		WISCONSIN																	
		KENOSHA 531			LA CROSSE 546			LANCASTER 538			MADISON 537			MILWAUKEE 530,532			NEW RICHMOND 540		
		MAT.	INST.	TOTAL	MAT.	INST.	TOTAL	MAT.	INST.	TOTAL	MAT.	INST.	TOTAL	MAT.	INST.	TOTAL	MAT.	INST.	TOTAL
015433	CONTRACTOR EQUIPMENT		93.7	93.7		96.2	96.2		95.4	95.4		99.4	99.4		88.6	88.6		96.5	96.5
0241, 31 - 34	SITE & INFRASTRUCTURE, DEMOLITION	88.8	94.6	92.6	81.6	95.3	90.5	80.9	95.5	90.4	85.1	103.1	96.8	82.1	93.8	89.8	83.0	94.2	90.3
0310	Concrete Forming & Accessories	106.8	107.7	107.5	83.0	92.9	90.7	94.7	86.5	88.4	100.1	102.3	101.8	100.5	116.0	112.6	92.0	83.8	85.7
0320	Concrete Reinforcing	100.1	109.7	102.7	91.6	105.0	95.3	100.9	96.1	99.6	98.7	105.2	100.5	98.7	116.4	103.6	90.2	103.3	93.8
0330	Cast-in-Place Concrete	97.8	103.0	99.6	98.9	99.4	99.1	89.3	91.1	90.0	82.8	104.9	90.6	83.3	113.1	93.9	114.5	93.7	107.1
03	CONCRETE	100.0	106.2	102.5	92.0	97.6	94.2	95.6	90.2	93.5	96.4	103.5	99.2	96.7	114.1	103.5	98.4	91.3	95.6
04	MASONRY	97.9	108.9	104.6	96.4	99.0	98.0	100.0	103.2	101.9	114.4	103.0	107.5	88.6	119.7	107.5	123.0	103.3	111.0
05	METALS	94.7	103.9	96.5	91.4	103.5	93.8	89.3	97.1	90.9	97.4	99.6	97.9	96.9	98.8	97.3	93.4	101.6	95.0
06	WOOD, PLASTICS & COMPOSITES	106.2	107.8	106.9	81.6	90.5	85.6	91.9	85.4	89.0	98.9	101.7	100.1	98.9	114.2	105.7	88.7	81.8	85.6
07	THERMAL & MOISTURE PROTECTION	102.9	104.1	103.3	104.1	97.8	101.9	101.8	87.5	96.7	99.5	102.7	100.6	101.3	115.1	106.2	104.9	93.8	101.0
08	OPENINGS	88.2	107.0	92.5	99.8	90.5	97.7	90.2	83.3	88.6	98.7	102.4	99.6	100.1	113.4	103.1	85.4	81.8	84.6
0920	Plaster & Gypsum Board	74.3	108.7	96.1	92.1	90.8	91.3	79.6	85.6	83.4	86.4	102.1	96.3	86.4	114.8	104.4	79.2	82.0	81.0
0950, 0980	Ceilings & Acoustic Treatment	89.9	108.7	100.5	92.1	90.8	91.4	82.2	85.6	84.1	94.8	102.1	98.9	99.9	114.8	108.2	62.5	82.0	73.4
0960	Flooring	115.7	111.0	114.6	79.4	116.6	88.7	96.0	99.4	96.9	103.1	114.8	106.0	95.4	121.9	102.1	94.9	102.6	96.8
0970, 0990	Wall Finishes & Painting/Coating	107.2	114.2	111.4	83.4	117.5	104.5	97.2	86.8	91.0	104.7	97.7	100.5	104.7	124.7	116.6	96.6	72.6	82.3
09	FINISHES	97.4	109.5	103.5	86.7	99.6	93.2	89.5	88.7	89.1	96.5	104.4	100.5	95.9	118.3	107.1	82.6	85.8	84.2
COVERS	DIVS. 10 - 14, 25, 28, 41, 43, 44, 46	100.0	99.5	99.9	100.0	98.6	99.7	100.0	96.7	99.4	100.0	101.2	100.2	100.0	103.8	100.7	100.0	84.8	97.1
21, 22, 23	FIRE SUPPRESSION, PLUMBING & HVAC	99.9	96.5	98.7	100.0	85.8	94.9	92.2	80.2	87.9	99.7	95.2	98.1	99.7	109.6	103.2	91.8	79.9	87.5
26, 27, 3370	ELECTRICAL, COMMUNICATIONS & UTIL.	99.0	95.2	97.4	97.8	100.3	98.9	98.5	75.5	88.6	98.4	98.3	98.3	98.3	102.8	100.3	96.9	75.6	87.7
MF2018	WEIGHTED AVERAGE	97.4	101.9	99.0	95.3	95.9	95.5	93.2	88.0	91.3	98.6	100.5	99.3	97.6	109.3	101.9	94.2	87.7	91.8

DIVISION		WISCONSIN																	
		OSHKOSH 549			PORTAGE 539			RACINE 534			RHINELANDER 545			SUPERIOR 548			WAUSAU 544		
		MAT.	INST.	TOTAL	MAT.	INST.	TOTAL	MAT.	INST.	TOTAL	MAT.	INST.	TOTAL	MAT.	INST.	TOTAL	MAT.	INST.	TOTAL
015433	CONTRACTOR EQUIPMENT		94.2	94.2		95.4	95.4		95.4	95.4		94.2	94.2		96.5	96.5		94.2	94.2
0241, 31 - 34	SITE & INFRASTRUCTURE, DEMOLITION	79.1	86.7	86.6	75.0	96.3	88.9	85.2	97.8	93.4	87.3	90.3	89.2	80.6	93.9	89.3	76.2	91.3	86.0
0310	Concrete Forming & Accessories	91.2	87.1	88.0	86.3	87.2	87.0	95.8	107.7	105.0	88.5	86.0	86.6	89.7	80.5	82.7	90.6	88.7	89.1
0320	Concrete Reinforcing	90.8	99.4	93.2	101.0	96.3	99.7	100.2	109.7	102.8	90.9	96.4	92.4	90.2	112.5	96.4	90.9	105.2	94.9
0330	Cast-in-Place Concrete	105.5	90.7	100.2	76.8	89.9	81.4	88.2	102.7	93.3	119.6	89.5	108.9	107.9	89.9	101.5	98.3	84.7	93.5
03	CONCRETE	94.1	91.0	92.9	85.7	90.3	87.5	95.2	106.2	99.5	104.5	89.6	98.6	93.6	90.1	92.2	89.7	90.6	90.1
04	MASONRY	111.3	104.6	107.2	98.9	103.2	101.5	99.9	108.9	105.4	132.4	102.6	114.3	122.1	101.1	109.4	110.7	102.6	105.8
05	METALS	93.7	100.5	95.0	90.1	100.9	92.2	94.3	104.0	96.2	93.1	99.2	94.3	94.5	105.4	96.7	93.0	102.9	95.0
06	WOOD, PLASTICS & COMPOSITES	89.7	85.5	87.8	80.4	85.4	82.6	93.3	107.8	99.8	86.2	85.5	85.9	86.6	77.8	82.7	88.9	88.1	88.6
07	THERMAL & MOISTURE PROTECTION	106.1	89.1	100.1	101.3	93.3	98.5	102.1	104.3	102.9	106.7	78.5	96.7	104.6	88.9	99.0	105.9	89.3	100.0
08	OPENINGS	92.2	87.2	91.0	90.3	90.3	90.3	93.9	107.0	96.8	92.2	83.3	90.2	84.7	90.0	85.9	92.3	90.1	91.8
0920	Plaster & Gypsum Board	81.5	85.6	84.1	73.5	85.6	81.2	82.0	108.7	99.0	81.5	85.6	84.1	79.6	77.9	78.5	81.5	88.4	85.9
0950, 0980	Ceilings & Acoustic Treatment	87.8	85.6	86.6	87.7	85.6	86.5	89.9	108.7	100.5	87.8	85.6	86.6	63.9	77.9	71.7	87.8	88.4	88.1
0960	Flooring	93.9	102.8	96.2	93.1	102.6	95.4	96.3	111.0	100.0	93.5	102.6	95.8	96.3	110.2	99.8	93.9	102.6	96.1
0970, 0990	Wall Finishes & Painting/Coating	90.8	99.1	95.8	97.2	86.8	91.0	97.2	116.4	108.6	90.8	71.1	79.0	84.8	94.0	90.3	90.8	74.0	80.7
09	FINISHES	89.1	91.3	90.2	88.9	89.6	89.2	92.0	109.7	100.9	89.7	87.7	88.7	82.5	86.9	84.7	88.9	89.6	89.2
COVERS	DIVS. 10 - 14, 25, 28, 41, 43, 44, 46	100.0	95.2	99.1	100.0	96.8	99.4	100.0	99.5	99.9	100.0	94.5	98.9	100.0	83.7	96.8	100.0	94.8	99.0
21, 22, 23	FIRE SUPPRESSION, PLUMBING & HVAC	92.8	79.6	88.1	92.2	86.1	90.0	99.7	96.5	98.6	92.8	79.7	88.1	91.8	82.1	88.3	92.8	80.2	88.3
26, 27, 3370	ELECTRICAL, COMMUNICATIONS & UTIL.	97.2	75.0	87.6	100.9	83.7	93.4	99.0	92.3	96.1	96.8	69.5	85.0	99.4	87.5	94.4	97.8	69.5	85.5
MF2018	WEIGHTED AVERAGE	94.6	88.2	92.2	92.1	91.4	91.8	96.5	101.8	98.5	96.7	86.2	92.8	94.0	90.1	92.6	93.9	87.7	91.6

City Cost Indexes

DIVISION		WYOMING																	
		CASPER			CHEYENNE			NEWCASTLE			RAWLINS			RIVERTON			ROCK SPRINGS		
		826			820			827			823			825			829 - 831		
		MAT.	INST.	TOTAL	MAT.	INST.	TOTAL	MAT.	INST.	TOTAL	MAT.	INST.	TOTAL	MAT.	INST.	TOTAL	MAT.	INST.	TOTAL
015433	CONTRACTOR EQUIPMENT		99.7	99.7		93.2	93.2		93.2	93.2		93.2	93.2		93.2	93.2		93.2	93.2
0241, 31 - 34	SITE & INFRASTRUCTURE, DEMOLITION	102.3	98.5	99.8	96.7	87.2	90.5	87.2	86.9	87.0	100.0	86.9	91.4	94.3	86.9	89.4	91.9	86.9	88.7
0310	Concrete Forming & Accessories	103.3	62.8	71.8	105.9	62.5	72.2	94.4	60.8	68.3	99.3	60.8	69.4	93.1	60.6	67.9	101.6	62.7	71.4
0320	Concrete Reinforcing	101.2	82.3	96.0	92.5	82.6	89.7	99.8	82.4	95.0	99.5	82.4	94.8	100.4	82.4	95.4	100.4	79.0	94.5
0330	Cast-in-Place Concrete	95.9	78.8	89.8	90.4	77.3	85.7	91.3	75.8	85.8	91.4	75.8	85.8	91.3	75.7	85.8	91.3	76.3	86.0
03	CONCRETE	102.3	72.3	90.4	96.1	71.8	86.5	96.9	70.5	86.5	107.8	70.5	93.0	103.4	70.4	90.4	97.7	71.0	87.1
04	MASONRY	91.2	64.4	75.0	93.0	68.3	78.0	90.2	64.0	74.2	90.1	64.0	74.2	90.2	64.0	74.3	142.3	59.1	91.8
05	METALS	105.3	79.7	100.2	107.3	82.2	102.3	103.3	81.8	99.1	103.4	81.8	99.1	103.5	81.6	99.2	104.2	80.3	99.5
06	WOOD, PLASTICS & COMPOSITES	102.9	59.7	83.5	104.1	59.1	83.9	90.1	58.3	75.8	95.7	58.3	78.9	88.5	58.3	75.0	101.1	60.6	82.9
07	THERMAL & MOISTURE PROTECTION	97.5	67.7	86.9	93.4	67.6	84.2	94.1	63.9	83.3	95.3	63.9	84.1	94.8	66.9	84.8	94.2	66.7	84.4
08	OPENINGS	97.9	65.6	90.6	76.3	62.9	89.0	99.4	62.9	91.2	99.2	62.9	91.0	99.3	62.9	91.1	99.7	64.6	91.8
0920	Plaster & Gypsum Board	111.2	58.4	77.7	98.6	58.0	72.9	95.8	57.3	71.4	95.8	57.3	71.4	95.8	57.3	71.4	112.0	59.6	78.7
0950, 0980	Ceilings & Acoustic Treatment	99.1	58.4	76.3	84.4	58.0	69.6	85.4	57.3	69.6	85.4	57.3	69.6	85.4	57.3	69.6	85.4	59.6	70.9
0960	Flooring	103.1	75.3	96.1	101.8	75.3	95.2	96.4	63.5	88.1	98.5	63.5	89.7	95.9	63.5	87.8	100.2	55.8	89.1
0970, 0990	Wall Finishes & Painting/Coating	104.7	56.4	75.9	103.7	56.4	75.5	99.9	69.6	81.9	99.9	69.6	81.9	99.9	53.7	72.4	99.9	71.0	82.7
09	FINISHES	102.4	63.8	83.0	96.8	63.4	80.0	92.4	61.3	76.8	94.2	61.3	77.7	93.0	59.6	76.2	95.7	61.5	78.6
COVERS	DIVS. 10 - 14, 25, 28, 41, 43, 44, 46	100.0	84.4	97.0	100.0	88.0	97.7	100.0	92.6	98.6	100.0	92.6	98.6	100.0	82.2	96.6	100.0	86.8	97.4
21, 22, 23	FIRE SUPPRESSION, PLUMBING & HVAC	99.9	71.9	89.9	100.2	77.8	92.2	96.0	74.5	88.3	96.0	74.5	88.3	96.0	74.4	88.3	100.1	75.0	91.1
26, 27, 3370	ELECTRICAL, COMMUNICATIONS & UTIL.	97.7	59.3	81.1	95.2	65.1	82.2	93.4	55.5	77.0	93.4	55.5	77.0	93.4	59.4	78.7	92.5	62.4	79.5
MF2018	WEIGHTED AVERAGE	100.8	71.1	89.9	99.6	72.8	89.7	97.2	69.8	87.1	99.0	69.8	88.3	98.2	69.8	87.8	100.0	70.3	89.6

DIVISION		WYOMING												CANADA					
		SHERIDAN			WHEATLAND			WORLAND			YELLOWSTONE NAT'L PA			BARRIE, ONTARIO			BATHURST, NEW BRUNSWICK		
		828			822			824			821								
		MAT.	INST.	TOTAL	MAT.	INST.	TOTAL	MAT.	INST.	TOTAL	MAT.	INST.	TOTAL	MAT.	INST.	TOTAL	MAT.	INST.	TOTAL
015433	CONTRACTOR EQUIPMENT		93.2	93.2		93.2	93.2		93.2	93.2		93.2	93.2		97.9	97.9		98.6	98.6
0241, 31 - 34	SITE & INFRASTRUCTURE, DEMOLITION	94.5	87.2	89.7	91.1	86.9	88.3	88.5	86.9	87.4	88.6	86.9	87.5	122.1	90.8	101.7	116.5	87.8	97.8
0310	Concrete Forming & Accessories	103.7	61.7	71.1	96.6	60.5	68.6	96.7	60.8	68.7	96.7	60.7	68.7	124.9	77.5	88.1	91.1	54.6	62.8
0320	Concrete Reinforcing	100.4	82.4	95.4	99.8	81.7	94.8	100.4	82.4	95.4	102.1	79.4	95.8	151.8	81.2	132.3	70.2	53.8	65.6
0330	Cast-in-Place Concrete	94.4	77.2	88.3	95.3	75.7	88.3	91.3	75.8	85.8	91.3	75.7	85.8	165.1	77.7	134.1	115.6	53.8	93.6
03	CONCRETE	104.0	71.4	91.1	101.0	70.2	88.8	97.3	70.5	86.7	97.7	69.9	86.7	150.7	78.9	122.4	104.1	55.4	84.9
04	MASONRY	90.5	66.5	75.9	90.5	52.9	67.7	90.2	64.0	74.3	90.2	64.0	74.3	171.6	83.8	118.3	156.6	53.9	94.2
05	METALS	107.3	81.7	102.2	103.3	80.7	98.8	103.5	81.8	99.2	104.2	80.7	99.5	114.3	89.5	109.4	128.6	73.0	117.6
06	WOOD, PLASTICS & COMPOSITES	106.1	58.3	84.7	92.8	58.3	77.3	92.9	58.3	77.4	92.9	58.3	77.4	117.3	76.4	99.0	91.3	54.8	74.9
07	THERMAL & MOISTURE PROTECTION	95.4	67.0	85.3	94.3	60.8	82.4	94.1	63.9	83.3	93.8	63.9	83.1	113.9	80.1	101.9	118.3	54.4	95.6
08	OPENINGS	100.0	62.9	91.6	98.3	62.9	90.3	99.6	62.9	91.3	93.8	62.2	86.7	89.2	76.4	86.3	84.8	48.4	76.6
0920	Plaster & Gypsum Board	118.7	57.3	79.7	95.8	57.3	71.4	95.8	57.3	71.4	96.1	57.3	71.5	153.8	75.9	104.4	119.8	53.5	77.8
0950, 0980	Ceilings & Acoustic Treatment	87.4	57.3	70.5	85.4	57.3	69.6	85.4	57.3	69.6	86.3	57.3	70.0	92.9	75.9	83.3	91.7	53.5	70.3
0960	Flooring	100.6	54.0	88.9	97.4	63.5	88.9	97.4	63.5	88.9	97.4	63.5	88.9	120.7	81.5	110.9	95.7	38.7	81.4
0970, 0990	Wall Finishes & Painting/Coating	102.6	56.4	75.1	99.9	51.9	71.3	99.9	69.6	81.9	99.9	53.7	72.4	106.8	77.6	89.4	112.3	44.4	71.8
09	FINISHES	99.8	59.3	79.4	93.0	59.4	76.1	92.7	61.3	77.0	93.0	59.6	76.2	112.4	78.5	95.4	98.0	50.7	74.2
COVERS	DIVS. 10 - 14, 25, 28, 41, 43, 44, 46	100.0	83.7	96.9	100.0	82.9	96.7	100.0	92.7	98.6	100.0	92.7	98.6	139.3	60.6	124.0	131.1	54.1	116.2
21, 22, 23	FIRE SUPPRESSION, PLUMBING & HVAC	96.0	75.9	88.8	96.0	74.4	88.3	96.0	74.5	88.3	96.0	74.4	88.3	110.3	87.6	102.2	110.6	60.7	92.7
26, 27, 3370	ELECTRICAL, COMMUNICATIONS & UTIL.	95.3	59.4	79.7	93.4	56.9	78.7	93.4	59.4	78.7	92.9	59.4	78.4	124.9	76.9	104.1	137.5	51.8	100.4
MF2018	WEIGHTED AVERAGE	100.1	70.6	89.2	97.8	68.4	87.0	97.4	70.3	87.4	97.1	69.9	87.1	121.0	82.1	106.7	117.1	59.1	95.7

DIVISION		CANADA																	
		BRANDON, MANITOBA			BRANTFORD, ONTARIO			BRIDGEWATER, NOVA SCOTIA			CALGARY, ALBERTA			CAP-DE-LA-MADELEINE, QUEBEC			CHARLESBOURG, QUEBEC		
		MAT.	INST.	TOTAL	MAT.	INST.	TOTAL	MAT.	INST.	TOTAL	MAT.	INST.	TOTAL	MAT.	INST.	TOTAL	MAT.	INST.	TOTAL
015433	CONTRACTOR EQUIPMENT		97.2	97.2		97.8	97.8		98.1	98.1		119.7	119.7		99.0	99.0		99.0	99.0
0241, 31 - 34	SITE & INFRASTRUCTURE, DEMOLITION	126.4	87.8	101.2	126.1	91.0	103.2	110.6	89.3	96.6	118.5	108.8	112.2	106.2	90.6	96.0	106.2	90.6	96.0
0310	Concrete Forming & Accessories	129.6	62.2	77.3	112.0	84.0	90.2	84.9	64.1	68.7	119.6	87.1	94.3	117.3	74.7	84.2	117.3	74.7	84.2
0320	Concrete Reinforcing	87.1	51.0	77.1	84.1	80.0	83.0	72.3	44.6	64.6	75.3	74.9	75.2	72.3	67.7	71.0	72.3	67.7	71.0
0330	Cast-in-Place Concrete	124.7	66.2	103.9	149.0	96.1	130.2	153.2	63.7	121.4	145.8	93.5	127.2	120.2	82.9	107.0	120.2	82.9	107.0
03	CONCRETE	131.8	62.8	104.5	134.4	88.1	116.1	132.5	61.7	104.6	183.8	88.1	146.0	119.9	77.1	103.0	119.9	77.1	103.0
04	MASONRY	219.9	56.9	120.9	172.2	87.6	120.8	167.4	61.5	103.1	230.3	80.8	139.5	167.6	71.6	109.3	167.6	71.6	109.3
05	METALS	143.1	75.9	129.9	128.1	90.0	120.6	126.9	75.1	116.7	154.9	95.9	143.2	125.4	83.8	117.2	125.4	83.8	117.2
06	WOOD, PLASTICS & COMPOSITES	135.6	63.1	103.1	114.0	82.9	100.1	82.0	63.8	73.9	103.2	87.2	96.0	125.8	74.8	102.9	125.8	74.8	102.9
07	THERMAL & MOISTURE PROTECTION	133.6	63.8	108.7	126.8	85.1	111.9	121.7	63.0	100.8	147.2	89.3	126.5	120.7	78.4	105.6	120.7	78.4	105.6
08	OPENINGS	100.3	56.5	90.4	88.0	81.8	86.6	83.7	57.9	77.9	91.0	77.1	87.9	89.6	68.3	84.8	89.6	68.3	84.8
0920	Plaster & Gypsum Board	100.6	61.9	76.1	117.8	82.6	95.5	114.7	62.8	81.8	120.5	86.0	98.6	146.5	74.0	100.5	146.5	74.0	100.5
0950, 0980	Ceilings & Acoustic Treatment	94.0	61.9	76.0	78.3	82.6	80.7	78.3	62.8	69.6	105.8	86.0	94.7	78.3	74.0	75.9	78.3	74.0	75.9
0960	Flooring	123.0	57.8	106.7	107.9	81.5	101.3	94.1	55.0	84.3	126.8	77.8	114.5	107.9	80.2	100.9	107.9	80.2	100.9
0970, 0990	Wall Finishes & Painting/Coating	118.1	50.1	77.5	110.9	85.2	95.6	110.9	54.9	77.5	111.0	94.5	101.2	110.9	77.4	90.9	110.9	77.4	90.9
09	FINISHES	109.7	60.4	84.9	99.3	83.9	91.6	94.3	61.7	77.9	119.9	86.7	103.3	102.6	76.3	89.4	102.6	76.3	89.4
COVERS	DIVS. 10 - 14, 25, 28, 41, 43, 44, 46	131.1	55.8	116.5	131.1	62.3	117.8	131.1	56.8	116.7	131.1	84.5	122.1	131.1	70.4	119.4	131.1	70.4	119.4
21, 22, 23	FIRE SUPPRESSION, PLUMBING & HVAC	117.2	73.8	101.7	110.5	90.2	103.2	110.5	74.5	97.6	109.8	81.1	99.5	110.2	78.9	99.0	110.2	78.9	99.0
26, 27, 3370	ELECTRICAL, COMMUNICATIONS & UTIL.	130.8	68.5	99.5	134.6	76.5	109.4	135.4	54.4	100.3	134.7	83.6	112.5	129.3	60.5	99.5	129.3	60.5	99.5
MF2018	WEIGHTED AVERAGE	130.0	66.3	106.6	122.0	85.5	108.5	119.8	66.5	100.2	137.9	86.9	119.1	118.6	75.6	102.8	118.6	75.6	102.8

City Cost Indexes

CANADA

		CHARLOTTETOWN, PRINCE EDWARD ISLAND			CHICOUTIMI, QUEBEC			CORNER BROOK, NEWFOUNDLAND			CORNWALL, ONTARIO			DALHOUSIE, NEW BRUNSWICK			DARTMOUTH, NOVA SCOTIA		
	DIVISION	MAT.	INST.	TOTAL	MAT.	INST.	TOTAL	MAT.	INST.	TOTAL	MAT.	INST.	TOTAL	MAT.	INST.	TOTAL	MAT.	INST.	TOTAL
015433	CONTRACTOR EQUIPMENT		122.2	122.2		99.2	99.2		96.8	96.8		97.8	97.8		97.9	97.9		95.3	95.3
0241, 31 - 34	SITE & INFRASTRUCTURE, DEMOLITION	145.2	107.9	120.9	113.2	91.0	98.7	131.7	86.3	102.1	124.2	90.6	102.3	109.2	87.3	94.9	123.0	87.3	99.7
0310	Concrete Forming & Accessories	112.5	50.5	64.4	117.8	86.2	93.3	105.9	71.0	78.8	109.8	77.7	84.8	90.6	54.8	62.8	95.8	63.9	71.0
0320	Concrete Reinforcing	60.5	43.6	55.9	52.9	90.0	63.2	80.2	45.6	70.6	84.1	79.7	82.9	75.6	53.8	69.6	83.6	44.6	72.8
0330	Cast-in-Place Concrete	136.8	57.4	108.6	108.8	91.3	102.6	145.2	60.2	115.0	134.0	87.7	117.6	129.4	53.7	102.5	140.1	63.1	112.8
03	CONCRETE	121.8	53.6	94.9	96.4	89.0	93.4	169.1	63.7	127.5	128.0	82.2	109.9	138.6	55.4	105.8	147.6	61.4	113.6
04	MASONRY	167.4	50.1	97.1	158.1	85.9	114.2	215.3	69.6	126.8	170.9	80.3	115.9	172.1	53.9	100.3	229.0	61.5	127.3
05	METALS	147.7	78.4	134.0	128.5	91.5	121.2	143.6	73.4	129.8	127.9	88.8	120.2	119.3	72.8	110.1	144.0	73.7	130.2
06	WOOD, PLASTICS & COMPOSITES	110.2	50.1	83.3	125.4	86.9	108.2	113.8	76.7	97.2	112.2	77.1	96.5	94.1	54.8	76.5	102.1	63.7	84.9
07	THERMAL & MOISTURE PROTECTION	146.1	54.9	113.6	118.8	91.4	109.0	136.8	61.3	109.9	126.4	80.2	109.9	124.2	54.4	99.3	134.7	62.9	109.1
08	OPENINGS	92.5	43.5	81.4	88.2	73.3	84.9	105.7	62.7	96.0	89.6	76.1	86.5	88.5	48.4	79.5	92.5	57.8	84.7
0920	Plaster & Gypsum Board	154.2	47.7	86.7	147.0	86.6	108.7	129.8	76.1	95.8	171.2	76.6	111.2	125.7	53.5	79.9	126.8	62.8	86.2
0950, 0980	Ceilings & Acoustic Treatment	107.0	47.7	73.8	90.8	86.6	88.4	94.0	76.1	84.0	81.5	76.6	78.7	78.4	53.5	64.5	100.8	62.8	79.5
0960	Flooring	123.1	51.6	105.2	107.9	80.2	101.0	108.9	46.2	93.2	107.9	80.3	101.0	102.9	59.2	92.0	105.0	55.0	92.5
0970, 0990	Wall Finishes & Painting/Coating	112.9	36.9	67.6	112.3	98.3	104.0	117.9	52.3	78.8	110.9	79.3	92.1	114.6	44.4	72.7	117.9	54.9	80.4
09	FINISHES	125.3	49.6	87.3	104.8	87.4	96.0	109.6	65.8	87.6	107.2	78.5	92.8	101.0	54.8	77.8	108.8	61.6	85.1
COVERS	DIVS. 10 - 14, 25, 28, 41, 43, 44, 46	131.1	55.4	116.5	131.1	75.3	120.3	131.1	56.3	116.6	131.1	60.2	117.4	131.1	54.0	116.2	131.1	56.5	116.7
21, 22, 23	FIRE SUPPRESSION, PLUMBING & HVAC	117.1	55.4	94.9	110.6	77.3	98.7	117.2	61.7	97.3	110.2	88.5	102.4	111.1	60.7	93.0	117.2	74.4	101.9
26, 27, 3370	ELECTRICAL, COMMUNICATIONS & UTIL.	148.2	44.1	103.1	130.8	79.5	108.6	125.0	47.8	91.6	132.4	77.4	108.5	134.6	49.0	97.5	127.7	54.4	96.0
MF2018	WEIGHTED AVERAGE	130.7	58.1	104.0	116.5	84.0	104.6	134.3	64.4	108.5	121.4	82.3	107.1	120.2	59.1	97.7	131.0	66.1	107.2

CANADA

		EDMONTON, ALBERTA			FORT MCMURRAY, ALBERTA			FREDERICTON, NEW BRUNSWICK			GATINEAU, QUEBEC			GRANBY, QUEBEC			HALIFAX, NOVA SCOTIA		
	DIVISION	MAT.	INST.	TOTAL	MAT.	INST.	TOTAL	MAT.	INST.	TOTAL	MAT.	INST.	TOTAL	MAT.	INST.	TOTAL	MAT.	INST.	TOTAL
015433	CONTRACTOR EQUIPMENT		120.6	120.6		99.4	99.4		121.9	121.9		99.0	99.0		99.0	99.0		119.5	119.5
0241, 31 - 34	SITE & INFRASTRUCTURE, DEMOLITION	124.6	110.3	115.3	129.8	91.5	104.8	150.0	108.6	123.0	106.0	90.6	95.9	106.4	90.6	96.1	114.2	108.2	110.3
0310	Concrete Forming & Accessories	112.2	86.5	92.2	110.4	82.3	88.5	112.5	55.9	68.5	117.3	74.6	84.1	117.3	74.5	84.1	112.5	81.3	88.2
0320	Concrete Reinforcing	73.3	74.9	73.7	78.2	74.8	77.2	58.7	54.1	57.4	76.2	67.7	73.8	76.2	67.7	73.8	60.7	73.2	64.2
0330	Cast-in-Place Concrete	163.8	93.5	138.8	198.0	87.4	158.7	155.3	58.0	120.7	118.6	82.9	105.9	122.5	82.9	108.4	143.9	76.4	119.9
03	CONCRETE	190.1	87.8	149.7	152.9	83.3	125.5	129.0	58.0	101.0	120.2	77.1	103.2	121.9	77.0	104.2	124.8	79.3	106.9
04	MASONRY	227.7	80.8	138.4	213.4	78.8	131.6	179.7	55.3	104.1	167.5	71.6	109.2	167.7	71.6	109.4	176.9	79.4	117.7
05	METALS	148.5	96.0	138.1	159.2	87.8	145.2	144.6	83.1	132.5	125.4	83.7	117.2	125.7	83.6	117.4	147.4	96.5	137.4
06	WOOD, PLASTICS & COMPOSITES	102.1	86.4	95.1	107.8	81.9	96.2	101.3	55.7	80.9	125.8	74.8	102.9	125.8	74.8	102.9	101.3	81.6	92.5
07	THERMAL & MOISTURE PROTECTION	147.0	89.2	126.4	135.0	84.4	117.0	146.1	56.7	114.3	120.7	78.4	105.6	120.9	77.0	105.3	149.6	82.2	125.6
08	OPENINGS	91.4	76.7	88.1	89.6	74.2	86.1	92.0	47.9	82.1	89.6	64.2	83.9	89.6	64.2	83.9	91.8	73.8	87.7
0920	Plaster & Gypsum Board	157.4	85.2	111.6	115.4	81.3	93.8	123.8	53.5	79.2	121.2	74.0	91.2	121.2	74.0	91.2	123.7	80.3	96.2
0950, 0980	Ceilings & Acoustic Treatment	100.3	85.2	91.8	85.1	81.3	83.0	99.4	53.5	73.7	78.3	74.0	75.9	78.3	74.0	75.9	100.9	80.3	89.4
0960	Flooring	127.5	77.8	115.0	107.9	77.8	100.3	121.5	61.8	106.6	107.9	80.2	100.9	107.9	80.2	100.9	116.3	74.8	105.9
0970, 0990	Wall Finishes & Painting/Coating	113.8	94.5	102.3	111.0	81.8	93.6	113.7	56.5	79.6	110.9	77.4	90.9	110.9	77.4	90.9	113.4	82.6	95.0
09	FINISHES	123.8	86.2	104.9	101.9	81.7	91.7	113.5	57.3	85.3	99.2	76.3	87.7	99.2	76.3	87.7	109.5	80.7	95.1
COVERS	DIVS. 10 - 14, 25, 28, 41, 43, 44, 46	131.1	85.5	122.3	131.1	82.9	121.8	131.1	55.9	116.6	131.1	70.4	119.4	131.1	70.4	119.4	131.1	63.9	118.1
21, 22, 23	FIRE SUPPRESSION, PLUMBING & HVAC	109.8	81.1	99.5	110.9	87.2	102.4	117.1	69.2	99.9	110.2	78.8	99.0	110.5	78.8	99.1	110.7	75.2	97.9
26, 27, 3370	ELECTRICAL, COMMUNICATIONS & UTIL.	134.8	83.6	112.6	125.1	71.9	102.0	148.5	64.7	112.1	129.3	60.5	99.5	130.9	60.5	100.4	114.4	81.0	99.9
MF2018	WEIGHTED AVERAGE	137.6	86.9	118.9	132.2	82.5	113.9	130.6	66.7	107.0	118.4	75.4	102.6	118.9	75.3	102.9	124.4	82.1	108.8

CANADA

		HAMILTON, ONTARIO			HULL, QUEBEC			JOLIETTE, QUEBEC			KAMLOOPS, BRITISH COLUMBIA			KINGSTON, ONTARIO			KITCHENER, ONTARIO		
	DIVISION	MAT.	INST.	TOTAL	MAT.	INST.	TOTAL	MAT.	INST.	TOTAL	MAT.	INST.	TOTAL	MAT.	INST.	TOTAL	MAT.	INST.	TOTAL
015433	CONTRACTOR EQUIPMENT		118.0	118.0		99.0	99.0		99.0	99.0		101.6	101.6		99.7	99.7		100.9	100.9
0241, 31 - 34	SITE & INFRASTRUCTURE, DEMOLITION	118.6	107.9	111.6	105.9	90.6	95.9	106.5	90.6	96.1	127.3	93.9	105.3	124.2	93.9	104.4	106.6	96.8	100.2
0310	Concrete Forming & Accessories	118.8	89.0	95.7	117.3	74.6	84.1	117.3	74.7	84.2	105.7	77.5	83.8	110.0	77.7	84.9	103.5	84.7	88.9
0320	Concrete Reinforcing	73.8	96.8	80.2	76.2	67.7	73.8	72.3	67.7	71.0	56.4	70.9	60.4	84.1	79.7	82.9	50.7	96.6	63.4
0330	Cast-in-Place Concrete	151.6	100.5	133.5	118.6	82.9	105.9	123.5	82.9	109.1	106.9	86.8	99.8	134.0	87.7	117.6	141.2	93.6	124.3
03	CONCRETE	136.1	95.2	119.9	120.2	77.1	103.2	121.3	77.1	103.8	133.6	80.3	112.6	130.4	82.2	111.4	108.7	90.3	101.5
04	MASONRY	183.4	96.7	130.7	167.4	71.6	109.2	167.8	71.6	109.4	174.2	78.8	116.3	177.7	80.4	118.6	152.4	94.2	117.1
05	METALS	153.6	105.3	144.1	125.7	83.7	117.4	125.7	83.8	117.4	129.2	85.7	120.6	130.3	88.8	122.1	145.0	97.4	135.6
06	WOOD, PLASTICS & COMPOSITES	104.0	87.7	96.7	125.8	74.8	102.9	125.8	74.8	102.9	95.1	76.3	86.7	112.2	77.2	96.5	95.5	83.0	89.9
07	THERMAL & MOISTURE PROTECTION	146.8	97.7	129.3	120.9	78.4	105.7	120.9	78.4	105.7	136.7	76.1	115.1	126.4	81.3	110.3	127.2	93.8	115.3
08	OPENINGS	87.4	87.1	87.3	89.6	64.2	83.9	89.6	68.3	84.8	86.9	74.1	84.0	89.6	75.8	86.5	78.4	83.0	79.4
0920	Plaster & Gypsum Board	125.1	86.5	100.6	121.2	74.0	91.2	146.5	74.0	100.5	99.4	75.3	84.1	174.4	76.7	112.5	108.2	82.6	91.9
0950, 0980	Ceilings & Acoustic Treatment	106.9	86.5	95.5	78.3	74.0	75.9	78.3	74.0	75.9	78.3	75.3	76.6	91.8	76.7	83.4	82.5	82.6	82.5
0960	Flooring	121.0	87.1	112.5	107.9	80.2	100.9	107.9	80.2	100.9	108.5	45.9	92.8	107.9	80.3	101.0	95.2	87.2	93.2
0970, 0990	Wall Finishes & Painting/Coating	110.4	97.6	102.7	107.9	77.4	90.9	107.9	77.4	90.9	110.9	70.8	87.0	110.9	73.3	88.5	105.3	88.3	95.2
09	FINISHES	113.4	89.3	101.3	99.2	76.3	87.7	102.6	76.3	89.4	98.5	71.2	84.8	110.5	77.9	94.1	93.0	85.0	89.0
COVERS	DIVS. 10 - 14, 25, 28, 41, 43, 44, 46	131.1	85.8	122.4	131.1	70.4	119.4	131.1	70.4	119.4	131.1	78.5	120.9	131.1	60.2	117.4	131.1	82.8	121.8
21, 22, 23	FIRE SUPPRESSION, PLUMBING & HVAC	109.9	88.5	102.2	110.5	78.8	99.1	110.5	78.8	99.1	110.2	82.0	100.2	110.2	88.4	102.4	109.1	88.1	101.6
26, 27, 3370	ELECTRICAL, COMMUNICATIONS & UTIL.	135.2	98.2	119.2	134.0	60.5	102.1	130.9	60.5	100.4	136.4	68.8	107.1	132.4	76.2	108.1	136.2	96.1	118.8
MF2018	WEIGHTED AVERAGE	129.4	94.9	116.7	119.0	75.4	103.0	119.1	75.6	103.1	122.4	78.8	106.3	122.7	82.4	107.9	119.8	91.0	109.2

698

City Cost Indexes

CANADA

DIVISION		LAVAL, QUEBEC			LETHBRIDGE, ALBERTA			LLOYDMINSTER, ALBERTA			LONDON, ONTARIO			MEDICINE HAT, ALBERTA			MONCTON, NEW BRUNSWICK		
		MAT.	INST.	TOTAL	MAT.	INST.	TOTAL	MAT.	INST.	TOTAL	MAT.	INST.	TOTAL	MAT.	INST.	TOTAL	MAT.	INST.	TOTAL
015433	CONTRACTOR EQUIPMENT		99.0	99.0		99.4	99.4		99.4	99.4		118.6	118.6		99.4	99.4		98.6	98.6
0241, 31 - 34	SITE & INFRASTRUCTURE, DEMOLITION	106.4	90.6	96.1	122.7	92.0	102.7	122.4	91.5	102.2	120.2	107.4	111.8	121.3	91.5	101.9	116.0	90.0	99.1
0310	Concrete Forming & Accessories	117.5	75.2	84.6	111.3	82.3	88.8	109.6	73.6	81.6	119.2	85.3	92.9	111.3	73.6	82.0	91.1	61.7	68.3
0320	Concrete Reinforcing	76.2	68.4	74.0	78.2	74.8	77.2	78.2	74.7	77.2	73.4	95.7	79.6	78.2	74.7	77.2	70.2	65.4	68.8
0330	Cast-in-Place Concrete	122.5	83.5	108.7	148.4	87.4	126.7	137.7	84.1	118.6	151.7	98.7	132.9	137.7	84.1	118.6	111.3	65.4	95.0
03	CONCRETE	121.9	77.7	104.4	132.6	83.4	113.1	128.0	78.3	108.4	136.1	92.7	119.0	128.1	78.2	108.4	102.3	64.9	87.6
04	MASONRY	167.8	72.3	109.8	186.0	78.8	120.9	167.7	73.0	110.2	190.8	95.1	132.7	167.6	73.0	110.1	156.2	71.3	104.6
05	METALS	125.5	84.0	117.3	149.9	87.9	137.6	129.1	87.7	120.9	152.0	105.9	142.9	129.3	87.7	121.1	128.6	85.8	120.1
06	WOOD, PLASTICS & COMPOSITES	125.8	75.4	98.2	111.4	81.9	98.2	107.8	73.2	92.3	104.0	83.3	94.7	111.4	73.2	94.3	91.3	59.2	76.9
07	THERMAL & MOISTURE PROTECTION	122.5	78.8	106.9	132.8	84.4	115.6	129.7	80.4	112.1	147.1	95.4	128.7	135.2	80.4	115.6	121.9	68.1	102.7
08	OPENINGS	89.6	64.8	84.0	89.6	74.2	86.1	89.6	69.4	85.0	88.0	83.7	87.0	89.6	69.4	85.0	84.8	56.9	78.5
0920	Plaster & Gypsum Board	121.2	74.7	91.7	108.8	81.3	91.3	103.8	72.3	83.8	125.1	82.0	97.8	106.7	72.3	84.9	119.8	58.0	80.6
0950, 0980	Ceilings & Acoustic Treatment	78.3	74.7	76.3	85.1	81.3	83.0	78.3	72.3	74.9	106.9	82.0	92.9	78.3	72.3	74.9	91.7	58.0	72.8
0960	Flooring	107.9	81.1	101.1	107.9	77.8	100.3	107.9	77.8	100.3	100.9	87.2	97.5	107.9	77.8	100.3	95.7	60.5	86.9
0970, 0990	Wall Finishes & Painting/Coating	110.9	78.1	91.3	110.8	89.3	98.0	111.0	69.5	86.3	113.0	94.6	102.0	110.8	69.5	86.2	112.3	74.2	89.6
09	FINISHES	99.2	76.9	88.0	100.2	82.5	91.3	98.7	73.8	85.8	107.7	86.2	96.9	98.1	73.8	85.9	98.0	62.3	80.0
COVERS	DIVS. 10 - 14, 25, 28, 41, 43, 44, 46	131.1	71.0	119.5	131.1	81.8	121.6	131.1	80.1	121.3	131.1	85.0	122.2	131.1	79.0	121.0	131.1	57.1	116.8
21, 22, 23	FIRE SUPPRESSION, PLUMBING & HVAC	109.3	79.6	98.7	110.7	84.2	101.2	110.2	84.2	100.9	110.9	86.6	101.5	110.5	81.2	100.0	110.6	75.3	97.9
26, 27, 3370	ELECTRICAL, COMMUNICATIONS & UTIL.	131.1	61.0	100.7	129.0	71.9	104.3	124.0	71.9	101.4	134.9	95.9	118.0	124.0	71.9	101.4	138.9	85.2	115.6
MF2018	WEIGHTED AVERAGE	118.7	75.9	103.0	126.7	82.0	110.3	120.0	79.1	104.9	128.9	93.0	115.7	120.3	78.4	104.9	117.1	73.6	101.1

CANADA

DIVISION		MONTREAL, QUEBEC			MOOSE JAW, SASKATCHEWAN			NEW GLASGOW, NOVA SCOTIA			NEWCASTLE, NEW BRUNSWICK			NORTH BAY, ONTARIO			OSHAWA, ONTARIO		
		MAT.	INST.	TOTAL	MAT.	INST.	TOTAL	MAT.	INST.	TOTAL	MAT.	INST.	TOTAL	MAT.	INST.	TOTAL	MAT.	INST.	TOTAL
015433	CONTRACTOR EQUIPMENT		120.6	120.6		96.5	96.5		95.3	95.3		98.6	98.6		95.2	95.2		100.9	100.9
0241, 31 - 34	SITE & INFRASTRUCTURE, DEMOLITION	129.1	107.0	114.7	122.1	86.6	98.9	115.6	87.3	97.1	116.5	87.8	97.8	128.3	88.5	102.3	116.5	96.9	103.7
0310	Concrete Forming & Accessories	113.1	87.2	93.0	94.7	51.5	61.2	95.7	63.9	71.0	91.1	54.8	62.9	130.3	75.3	87.6	108.5	87.7	92.4
0320	Concrete Reinforcing	61.6	90.2	69.5	55.2	57.4	55.8	80.2	44.6	70.3	70.2	53.8	65.5	94.2	79.3	90.0	80.3	98.9	85.4
0330	Cast-in-Place Concrete	117.7	96.2	110.0	133.6	60.6	107.6	140.1	63.1	112.8	115.6	53.9	93.6	135.0	75.5	113.8	163.4	102.7	141.8
03	CONCRETE	111.2	91.7	103.5	111.6	56.9	90.0	146.7	61.4	113.0	104.1	55.5	84.9	148.7	76.7	120.3	132.2	95.3	117.6
04	MASONRY	173.4	86.1	120.4	165.8	52.9	97.2	214.9	61.5	121.7	156.6	53.9	94.2	221.5	76.8	133.6	156.4	97.4	120.6
05	METALS	164.9	101.5	152.4	124.2	73.9	114.3	140.6	73.7	127.4	128.6	73.2	117.6	141.9	87.2	131.1	134.1	98.6	127.1
06	WOOD, PLASTICS & COMPOSITES	99.5	87.8	94.3	92.2	50.4	73.4	102.1	63.7	84.9	91.3	54.8	74.9	138.3	75.8	110.3	102.7	86.4	95.4
07	THERMAL & MOISTURE PROTECTION	144.5	93.6	126.4	120.0	55.9	97.2	134.7	62.9	109.1	121.9	54.4	97.9	140.4	76.9	117.8	127.9	98.3	117.4
08	OPENINGS	88.6	75.6	85.6	86.1	48.5	77.6	92.5	57.8	84.7	84.8	48.4	76.6	98.4	73.8	92.9	82.5	86.4	83.4
0920	Plaster & Gypsum Board	122.8	86.6	99.8	97.6	49.0	66.8	124.7	62.8	85.4	119.8	53.5	77.8	122.4	75.3	92.6	112.7	86.1	95.9
0950, 0980	Ceilings & Acoustic Treatment	113.2	86.6	98.3	78.3	49.0	61.9	94.0	62.8	76.5	91.7	53.5	70.3	94.0	75.3	83.5	79.3	86.1	83.1
0960	Flooring	103.2	83.0	98.2	100.2	50.1	87.7	105.0	55.0	92.5	95.7	59.2	86.6	123.0	80.3	112.3	97.4	89.2	95.3
0970, 0990	Wall Finishes & Painting/Coating	119.3	98.3	106.8	110.9	56.5	78.5	117.9	54.9	80.4	112.3	44.4	71.8	117.9	78.7	94.6	105.3	101.3	102.9
09	FINISHES	110.2	88.5	99.3	94.6	51.5	73.0	106.6	61.6	84.0	98.0	54.8	76.3	112.3	76.9	94.6	93.8	89.1	91.5
COVERS	DIVS. 10 - 14, 25, 28, 41, 43, 44, 46	131.1	77.4	120.7	131.1	53.6	116.1	131.1	56.5	116.7	131.1	54.1	116.2	131.1	58.8	117.1	131.1	83.5	121.9
21, 22, 23	FIRE SUPPRESSION, PLUMBING & HVAC	109.2	77.6	97.9	110.2	65.9	94.3	117.2	74.4	101.9	110.6	60.7	92.7	117.2	86.5	106.2	109.1	84.4	100.3
26, 27, 3370	ELECTRICAL, COMMUNICATIONS & UTIL.	148.0	79.5	118.3	136.4	52.3	99.9	125.8	54.4	94.9	137.2	51.8	100.2	130.0	77.3	107.1	136.6	97.3	119.5
MF2018	WEIGHTED AVERAGE	129.7	87.0	114.0	117.3	60.4	96.3	129.1	66.1	105.9	117.2	59.6	96.0	132.0	80.1	112.9	121.1	92.4	110.6

CANADA

DIVISION		OTTAWA, ONTARIO			OWEN SOUND, ONTARIO			PETERBOROUGH, ONTARIO			PORTAGE LA PRAIRIE, MANITOBA			PRINCE ALBERT, SASKATCHEWAN			PRINCE GEORGE, BRITISH COLUMBIA		
		MAT.	INST.	TOTAL	MAT.	INST.	TOTAL	MAT.	INST.	TOTAL	MAT.	INST.	TOTAL	MAT.	INST.	TOTAL	MAT.	INST.	TOTAL
015433	CONTRACTOR EQUIPMENT		120.2	120.2		97.9	97.9		97.8	97.8		99.8	99.8		96.5	96.5		101.6	101.6
0241, 31 - 34	SITE & INFRASTRUCTURE, DEMOLITION	119.6	108.0	112.0	122.1	90.7	101.6	126.1	90.5	102.9	123.0	89.5	101.2	118.6	86.7	97.8	130.6	93.6	106.5
0310	Concrete Forming & Accessories	113.1	89.6	94.8	124.9	74.2	85.5	112.0	76.4	84.3	111.5	62.0	73.0	94.7	51.4	61.0	100.4	73.1	79.2
0320	Concrete Reinforcing	65.6	95.7	73.9	151.8	81.2	132.3	84.1	79.8	82.9	78.2	51.0	70.7	57.6	57.4	57.6	56.4	70.9	60.4
0330	Cast-in-Place Concrete	137.9	101.9	125.1	165.1	72.6	132.2	149.0	77.4	123.6	137.7	66.2	112.3	121.0	60.5	99.5	134.0	86.9	117.3
03	CONCRETE	127.8	95.9	115.2	150.7	75.6	121.0	134.4	78.0	112.2	120.4	62.7	97.7	107.1	56.8	87.2	144.4	78.3	118.3
04	MASONRY	189.2	96.0	132.6	171.6	81.7	117.0	172.2	82.6	117.8	170.7	56.1	101.0	164.8	52.9	96.9	176.7	78.8	117.2
05	METALS	153.6	107.3	144.5	114.3	89.3	109.3	128.1	89.0	120.4	129.3	77.2	119.0	124.2	73.8	114.3	129.2	85.8	120.6
06	WOOD, PLASTICS & COMPOSITES	93.8	88.8	91.6	117.3	73.1	97.5	114.0	74.7	96.4	111.4	63.2	89.8	92.2	50.4	73.4	95.1	70.1	83.9
07	THERMAL & MOISTURE PROTECTION	147.2	97.2	129.4	113.9	77.7	101.0	126.8	82.0	110.8	120.7	63.5	100.3	119.9	54.9	96.8	131.8	75.4	111.7
08	OPENINGS	87.8	86.7	87.5	89.2	73.3	85.6	88.0	75.5	85.2	89.6	56.6	82.2	85.2	48.5	76.9	86.9	70.7	83.3
0920	Plaster & Gypsum Board	125.1	87.5	101.3	153.8	72.4	102.2	117.8	74.2	90.1	106.4	61.9	78.2	97.6	49.0	66.8	99.4	69.0	80.1
0950, 0980	Ceilings & Acoustic Treatment	106.9	87.5	96.1	92.9	72.4	81.4	78.3	74.2	76.0	78.3	61.9	69.1	78.3	49.0	61.9	78.3	69.0	73.1
0960	Flooring	100.9	83.1	96.4	120.7	81.5	110.9	107.9	80.3	101.0	107.9	57.8	95.3	100.2	50.1	87.7	104.3	62.9	94.0
0970, 0990	Wall Finishes & Painting/Coating	113.5	89.8	99.3	106.8	77.6	89.4	110.9	80.7	92.9	111.0	50.1	74.7	110.8	48.2	73.5	110.9	70.8	87.0
09	FINISHES	107.8	88.3	98.0	112.4	76.0	94.1	99.3	77.6	88.4	98.0	60.3	79.1	94.6	50.6	72.5	97.3	70.5	83.8
COVERS	DIVS. 10 - 14, 25, 28, 41, 43, 44, 46	131.1	84.1	122.0	139.3	59.5	123.8	131.1	60.4	117.4	131.1	55.8	116.5	131.1	53.6	116.1	131.1	77.8	120.8
21, 22, 23	FIRE SUPPRESSION, PLUMBING & HVAC	109.9	87.3	101.8	110.3	86.9	101.8	110.5	89.7	103.0	110.5	73.4	97.2	110.5	59.3	92.0	110.5	82.0	100.3
26, 27, 3370	ELECTRICAL, COMMUNICATIONS & UTIL.	135.2	96.5	118.5	127.1	76.3	105.1	134.6	76.9	109.6	135.7	50.5	98.8	136.4	52.3	99.9	134.2	68.8	105.9
MF2018	WEIGHTED AVERAGE	128.2	94.4	115.7	121.3	80.5	106.3	122.0	82.1	107.3	120.4	65.3	100.1	116.5	58.9	95.3	123.4	78.2	106.7

City Cost Indexes

CANADA

DIVISION		QUEBEC CITY, QUEBEC			RED DEER, ALBERTA			REGINA, SASKATCHEWAN			RIMOUSKI, QUEBEC			ROUYN-NORANDA, QUEBEC			SAINT HYACINTHE, QUEBEC		
		MAT.	INST.	TOTAL	MAT.	INST.	TOTAL	MAT.	INST.	TOTAL	MAT.	INST.	TOTAL	MAT.	INST.	TOTAL	MAT.	INST.	TOTAL
015433	CONTRACTOR EQUIPMENT		122.1	122.1		99.4	99.4		127.3	127.3		99.0	99.0		99.0	99.0		99.0	99.0
0241, 31 - 34	SITE & INFRASTRUCTURE, DEMOLITION	129.6	107.3	115.1	121.3	91.5	101.9	138.5	118.0	125.1	106.1	90.8	96.2	105.9	90.6	95.9	106.4	90.6	96.1
0310	Concrete Forming & Accessories	113.0	87.4	93.1	119.0	73.6	83.7	120.1	83.4	91.6	117.3	86.2	93.2	117.3	74.6	84.1	117.3	74.6	84.1
0320	Concrete Reinforcing	62.6	90.2	70.3	78.2	74.7	77.2	71.7	79.8	73.9	54.5	90.0	64.3	76.2	67.7	73.8	76.2	67.7	73.8
0330	Cast-in-Place Concrete	117.6	96.4	110.1	137.7	84.1	118.6	176.1	92.3	146.3	124.8	91.2	112.8	118.6	82.9	105.9	122.5	82.9	108.5
03	CONCRETE	111.5	92.0	103.8	128.8	78.2	108.8	180.3	86.9	143.5	117.2	89.0	106.0	120.2	77.1	103.2	121.9	77.1	104.2
04	MASONRY	183.9	86.1	124.5	167.6	73.0	110.1	220.1	78.6	134.1	166.8	85.9	117.7	167.4	71.6	109.2	167.7	71.6	109.3
05	METALS	164.9	103.3	152.8	129.3	87.7	121.1	153.7	98.3	142.8	125.2	91.4	118.5	125.7	83.7	117.4	125.7	83.7	117.4
06	WOOD, PLASTICS & COMPOSITES	100.2	87.8	94.7	111.4	73.2	94.3	122.3	83.9	105.1	125.8	86.9	108.4	125.8	74.8	102.9	125.8	74.8	102.9
07	THERMAL & MOISTURE PROTECTION	143.5	93.7	125.7	143.0	80.4	120.7	147.2	79.3	123.0	120.9	91.3	110.4	120.9	78.4	105.7	122.5	78.4	106.8
08	OPENINGS	89.5	82.4	87.9	89.6	69.4	85.0	93.0	72.8	88.4	89.1	73.3	85.6	89.6	64.2	83.9	89.6	64.2	83.9
0920	Plaster & Gypsum Board	118.5	86.6	98.2	106.7	72.3	84.9	134.9	82.6	101.7	146.4	86.6	108.4	121.0	74.0	91.2	121.0	74.0	91.2
0950, 0980	Ceilings & Acoustic Treatment	107.5	86.6	95.8	78.3	72.3	74.9	113.8	82.6	96.3	77.8	86.6	82.7	77.8	74.0	75.7	77.8	74.0	75.7
0960	Flooring	102.9	83.0	97.9	111.0	77.8	102.7	122.7	87.2	113.8	109.0	80.2	101.8	107.9	80.2	100.9	107.9	80.2	100.9
0970, 0990	Wall Finishes & Painting/Coating	120.3	98.3	107.2	110.8	69.5	86.2	113.5	79.1	93.0	114.1	98.3	104.7	110.9	77.4	90.9	110.9	77.4	90.9
09	FINISHES	108.1	88.5	98.3	99.0	73.8	86.4	118.4	84.4	101.3	103.0	87.4	95.1	99.0	76.3	87.6	99.0	76.3	87.6
COVERS	DIVS. 10 - 14, 25, 28, 41, 43, 44, 46	131.1	77.4	120.7	131.1	79.0	121.0	131.1	65.0	118.3	131.1	75.3	120.3	131.1	70.4	119.4	131.1	70.4	119.4
21, 22, 23	FIRE SUPPRESSION, PLUMBING & HVAC	108.9	77.6	97.7	110.5	81.2	100.0	109.8	78.2	98.5	110.5	77.3	98.6	110.5	78.8	99.1	106.2	78.8	96.4
26, 27, 3370	ELECTRICAL, COMMUNICATIONS & UTIL.	148.0	79.6	118.3	124.0	71.9	101.4	134.4	81.5	111.5	130.9	79.5	108.6	130.9	60.5	100.4	131.4	60.5	100.7
MF2018	WEIGHTED AVERAGE	130.0	87.5	114.4	120.7	78.4	105.1	137.5	85.1	118.2	118.5	84.0	105.8	118.7	75.4	102.8	118.1	75.4	102.4

CANADA

DIVISION		SAINT JOHN, NEW BRUNSWICK			SARNIA, ONTARIO			SASKATOON, SASKATCHEWAN			SAULT STE MARIE, ONTARIO			SHERBROOKE, QUEBEC			SOREL, QUEBEC		
		MAT.	INST.	TOTAL	MAT.	INST.	TOTAL	MAT.	INST.	TOTAL	MAT.	INST.	TOTAL	MAT.	INST.	TOTAL	MAT.	INST.	TOTAL
015433	CONTRACTOR EQUIPMENT		98.6	98.6		97.8	97.8		96.1	96.1		97.8	97.8		99.0	99.0		99.0	99.0
0241, 31 - 34	SITE & INFRASTRUCTURE, DEMOLITION	116.6	90.0	99.3	124.6	90.6	102.4	119.3	89.4	99.8	115.2	90.2	98.9	106.5	90.6	96.1	106.5	90.6	96.1
0310	Concrete Forming & Accessories	109.8	65.7	75.5	110.7	82.6	88.9	94.6	82.3	85.0	100.2	82.6	86.5	117.3	74.6	84.1	117.3	74.7	84.2
0320	Concrete Reinforcing	70.2	65.4	68.8	61.2	81.1	66.7	60.1	79.6	65.5	54.0	80.1	61.2	76.2	67.7	73.8	72.3	67.7	71.0
0330	Cast-in-Place Concrete	113.9	65.4	96.6	137.5	89.0	120.3	132.9	86.1	116.3	123.5	76.3	106.7	122.5	82.9	108.5	123.5	82.9	109.1
03	CONCRETE	105.1	66.7	90.0	123.6	85.1	108.4	121.5	83.6	106.5	107.6	80.6	97.0	121.9	77.1	104.2	121.3	77.1	103.8
04	MASONRY	175.6	71.3	112.2	183.2	85.0	123.5	180.4	78.3	118.4	167.9	87.8	119.3	167.8	71.6	109.4	167.8	71.6	109.4
05	METALS	128.5	85.8	120.0	128.1	89.3	120.4	120.4	86.6	113.7	127.3	92.9	120.5	125.4	83.7	117.2	125.7	83.8	117.4
06	WOOD, PLASTICS & COMPOSITES	114.4	64.6	92.1	113.0	82.0	99.1	94.7	82.9	89.4	99.7	84.7	93.0	125.8	74.8	102.9	125.8	74.8	102.9
07	THERMAL & MOISTURE PROTECTION	122.3	68.3	103.1	126.8	85.2	112.0	122.2	76.0	105.8	125.8	82.4	110.4	120.7	78.4	105.6	120.9	78.4	105.7
08	OPENINGS	84.8	58.9	78.9	91.1	78.9	88.3	88.3	72.2	84.6	83.1	81.9	82.8	89.6	64.2	83.9	89.6	68.3	84.8
0920	Plaster & Gypsum Board	138.8	63.6	91.1	140.0	81.6	103.0	115.1	82.6	94.5	107.6	84.5	92.9	121.0	74.0	91.2	146.4	74.0	100.5
0950, 0980	Ceilings & Acoustic Treatment	95.4	63.6	77.6	82.8	81.6	82.2	92.9	82.6	87.1	78.3	84.5	81.7	77.8	74.0	75.7	77.8	74.0	75.7
0960	Flooring	104.7	60.5	93.6	107.9	87.8	102.8	106.5	87.2	101.7	102.4	84.9	98.1	107.9	80.2	100.9	107.9	80.2	100.9
0970, 0990	Wall Finishes & Painting/Coating	112.3	74.2	89.6	110.9	91.2	99.2	114.6	79.1	93.4	110.9	84.6	95.2	110.9	77.4	90.9	110.9	77.4	90.9
09	FINISHES	104.2	65.4	84.7	103.5	84.8	94.1	105.1	83.6	94.3	95.7	83.7	89.7	99.0	76.3	87.6	102.4	76.3	89.3
COVERS	DIVS. 10 - 14, 25, 28, 41, 43, 44, 46	131.1	58.0	117.0	131.1	61.6	117.7	131.1	63.0	117.9	131.1	80.8	121.4	131.1	70.4	119.4	131.1	70.4	119.4
21, 22, 23	FIRE SUPPRESSION, PLUMBING & HVAC	110.6	75.3	97.9	110.5	95.1	104.9	109.5	77.9	98.2	110.5	85.2	101.4	110.2	78.8	99.0	110.5	78.9	99.1
26, 27, 3370	ELECTRICAL, COMMUNICATIONS & UTIL.	140.2	85.2	116.4	141.8	78.8	114.5	135.8	81.4	112.2	138.6	77.3	112.0	130.9	60.5	100.4	130.9	60.5	100.4
MF2018	WEIGHTED AVERAGE	119.0	74.5	102.6	122.4	86.0	109.0	118.9	81.0	105.0	117.7	84.3	105.4	118.8	75.4	102.8	119.1	75.6	103.1

CANADA

DIVISION		ST CATHARINES, ONTARIO			ST JEROME, QUEBEC			ST JOHN'S, NEWFOUNDLAND			SUDBURY, ONTARIO			SUMMERSIDE, PRINCE EDWARD ISLAND			SYDNEY, NOVA SCOTIA		
		MAT.	INST.	TOTAL	MAT.	INST.	TOTAL	MAT.	INST.	TOTAL	MAT.	INST.	TOTAL	MAT.	INST.	TOTAL	MAT.	INST.	TOTAL
015433	CONTRACTOR EQUIPMENT		99.1	99.1		99.0	99.0		122.4	122.4		99.1	99.1		95.3	95.3		95.3	95.3
0241, 31 - 34	SITE & INFRASTRUCTURE, DEMOLITION	106.2	93.8	98.1	105.9	90.6	95.9	116.2	112.3	113.7	106.3	93.5	97.9	124.1	84.9	98.6	111.6	87.3	95.7
0310	Concrete Forming & Accessories	101.5	89.7	92.3	117.3	74.6	84.1	112.3	79.5	86.8	97.5	85.9	88.2	96.0	49.2	59.9	95.7	63.9	71.0
0320	Concrete Reinforcing	51.1	96.6	63.7	76.2	67.7	73.8	120.0	77.6	108.2	51.5	93.3	63.1	79.0	43.4	69.1	80.2	44.6	70.3
0330	Cast-in-Place Concrete	134.9	95.1	120.7	118.6	82.9	105.9	136.7	94.9	121.8	136.0	92.0	120.4	133.0	51.8	104.2	108.1	63.1	92.1
03	CONCRETE	106.0	93.1	101.0	120.2	77.1	103.2	141.0	85.7	119.1	106.3	89.6	99.7	157.6	50.5	115.3	133.5	61.4	105.0
04	MASONRY	151.8	96.4	118.1	167.4	71.6	109.2	195.1	85.1	128.3	151.8	93.2	116.2	213.9	51.5	115.3	212.0	61.5	120.6
05	METALS	134.0	97.4	126.8	125.7	83.7	117.4	142.4	96.0	133.2	133.5	96.2	126.1	140.6	67.5	126.2	140.6	73.7	127.4
06	WOOD, PLASTICS & COMPOSITES	93.1	89.3	91.4	125.8	74.8	102.9	102.0	77.6	91.0	88.8	84.8	87.0	102.7	49.1	78.7	102.1	63.7	84.9
07	THERMAL & MOISTURE PROTECTION	127.2	96.7	116.4	120.9	78.4	105.7	146.2	88.8	125.7	125.3	92.2	113.5	134.2	53.2	105.3	134.7	62.9	109.1
08	OPENINGS	77.7	86.8	79.8	89.6	64.2	83.9	91.7	69.4	86.7	78.3	82.3	79.2	102.2	42.9	88.8	92.5	57.8	84.7
0920	Plaster & Gypsum Board	102.6	89.1	94.0	121.0	74.0	91.2	146.5	76.1	101.8	100.7	84.5	90.4	125.9	47.7	76.3	124.7	62.8	85.4
0950, 0980	Ceilings & Acoustic Treatment	79.3	89.1	84.8	77.8	74.0	75.7	111.3	76.1	91.6	75.2	84.5	80.4	94.0	47.7	68.1	94.0	62.8	76.5
0960	Flooring	94.3	84.3	91.8	107.9	80.2	100.9	119.5	47.9	101.6	92.9	84.9	90.9	105.0	51.6	91.6	105.0	55.0	92.5
0970, 0990	Wall Finishes & Painting/Coating	105.3	97.6	100.7	110.9	77.4	90.9	116.4	76.1	101.2	105.3	89.2	95.7	117.9	36.9	69.6	117.9	54.9	80.4
09	FINISHES	91.1	89.6	90.3	99.0	76.3	87.6	116.8	74.7	95.7	89.3	85.5	87.4	107.6	48.8	78.1	106.6	61.6	84.0
COVERS	DIVS. 10 - 14, 25, 28, 41, 43, 44, 46	131.1	64.7	118.3	131.1	70.4	119.4	131.1	63.6	118.0	131.1	82.7	121.8	131.1	53.0	116.0	131.1	56.5	116.7
21, 22, 23	FIRE SUPPRESSION, PLUMBING & HVAC	109.1	87.3	101.3	110.5	78.8	99.1	109.5	78.1	98.3	109.2	85.1	100.6	117.2	55.1	95.0	117.2	74.4	101.9
26, 27, 3370	ELECTRICAL, COMMUNICATIONS & UTIL.	140.3	96.8	121.4	132.4	60.5	101.2	150.1	72.4	116.4	135.9	96.9	119.0	123.6	44.0	89.1	125.8	54.4	94.9
MF2018	WEIGHTED AVERAGE	117.3	91.6	107.8	118.9	75.4	102.9	130.0	82.4	112.5	116.6	90.0	106.8	131.2	54.5	103.0	127.3	66.1	104.8

City Cost Indexes

CANADA

DIVISION		THUNDER BAY, ONTARIO			TIMMINS, ONTARIO			TORONTO, ONTARIO			TROIS RIVIERES, QUEBEC			TRURO, NOVA SCOTIA			VANCOUVER, BRITISH COLUMBIA		
		MAT.	INST.	TOTAL	MAT.	INST.	TOTAL	MAT.	INST.	TOTAL	MAT.	INST.	TOTAL	MAT.	INST.	TOTAL	MAT.	INST.	TOTAL
015433	CONTRACTOR EQUIPMENT		99.1	99.1		97.8	97.8		118.9	118.9		96.2	96.2		98.1	98.1		135.4	135.4
0241, 31 - 34	SITE & INFRASTRUCTURE, DEMOLITION	110.9	93.6	99.6	126.1	90.2	102.7	117.7	108.1	111.4	111.6	88.7	96.6	110.8	89.1	96.7	122.0	122.1	122.1
0310	Concrete Forming & Accessories	108.5	87.7	92.3	112.0	75.4	83.6	112.7	98.6	101.8	137.2	74.5	88.5	84.9	64.1	68.7	118.1	85.6	92.8
0320	Concrete Reinforcing	45.7	96.2	59.7	84.1	79.3	82.8	65.5	99.2	74.8	80.2	67.7	76.7	72.3	44.6	64.6	71.9	89.3	76.7
0330	Cast-in-Place Concrete	148.5	94.5	129.3	149.0	76.0	123.1	137.8	111.6	128.5	111.9	82.3	101.4	154.8	63.7	122.4	142.1	96.9	126.1
03	CONCRETE	114.2	91.9	105.4	134.4	77.0	111.8	127.7	103.9	118.3	136.1	76.8	112.7	133.2	61.8	105.0	135.7	91.5	118.3
04	MASONRY	152.6	94.7	117.4	172.2	76.9	114.3	185.6	104.2	136.2	216.0	71.6	128.3	167.6	61.5	103.1	183.7	89.2	126.3
05	METALS	134.0	96.5	122.6	128.1	88.5	120.3	149.5	108.4	141.4	139.3	82.3	128.1	126.9	75.2	116.7	151.5	108.9	143.1
06	WOOD, PLASTICS & COMPOSITES	102.7	87.1	95.7	114.0	75.9	96.9	93.8	97.0	95.2	152.2	74.6	117.4	82.0	63.8	73.9	120.1	84.7	104.2
07	THERMAL & MOISTURE PROTECTION	127.5	93.7	115.4	126.8	77.0	109.0	147.1	105.5	132.3	133.8	78.2	114.0	121.7	63.0	100.8	147.4	87.4	126.0
08	OPENINGS	77.1	85.1	78.9	88.0	73.9	84.8	87.1	94.6	88.7	100.3	68.2	93.1	83.7	57.9	77.9	93.1	82.6	90.8
0920	Plaster & Gypsum Board	127.3	86.9	101.7	117.8	75.3	90.9	126.9	96.1	107.4	150.6	74.0	102.0	114.7	62.8	81.8	133.3	83.1	101.4
0950, 0980	Ceilings & Acoustic Treatment	75.2	86.9	81.8	78.3	75.3	76.6	113.8	96.1	103.9	92.6	74.0	82.2	78.3	62.8	69.6	113.8	83.1	96.6
0960	Flooring	97.4	90.3	95.6	107.9	80.3	101.0	120.8	92.5	113.7	123.0	80.2	112.3	94.1	55.0	84.3	112.5	81.2	104.7
0970, 0990	Wall Finishes & Painting/Coating	105.3	90.1	96.3	110.9	78.7	91.7	109.7	101.3	104.7	117.9	77.4	93.8	110.9	54.9	77.5	109.2	91.8	98.8
09	FINISHES	94.5	88.3	91.4	99.3	77.0	88.1	115.3	97.7	106.5	115.1	76.2	95.5	94.3	61.7	77.9	114.5	85.2	99.8
COVERS	DIVS. 10 - 14, 25, 28, 41, 43, 44, 46	131.1	64.2	118.2	131.1	59.1	117.2	131.1	88.7	122.9	131.1	70.1	119.3	131.1	56.8	116.7	131.1	83.6	121.9
21, 22, 23	FIRE SUPPRESSION, PLUMBING & HVAC	109.1	86.5	101.0	110.5	86.5	101.9	109.9	97.6	105.5	117.2	78.8	103.4	110.5	74.5	97.6	109.9	84.1	100.6
26, 27, 3370	ELECTRICAL, COMMUNICATIONS & UTIL.	136.2	96.0	118.8	138.6	77.3	112.0	134.9	98.4	119.1	126.5	60.5	97.9	130.0	54.4	97.3	135.1	75.4	109.3
MF2018	WEIGHTED AVERAGE	118.2	90.6	108.1	122.4	80.4	106.9	127.5	100.9	117.7	129.3	75.2	109.4	119.3	66.5	99.9	129.7	89.8	115.0

CANADA

DIVISION		VICTORIA, BRITISH COLUMBIA			WHITEHORSE, YUKON			WINDSOR, ONTARIO			WINNIPEG, MANITOBA			YARMOUTH, NOVA SCOTIA			YELLOWKNIFE, NWT		
		MAT.	INST.	TOTAL	MAT.	INST.	TOTAL	MAT.	INST.	TOTAL	MAT.	INST.	TOTAL	MAT.	INST.	TOTAL	MAT.	INST.	TOTAL
015433	CONTRACTOR EQUIPMENT		103.8	103.8		130.8	130.8		99.1	99.1		125.6	125.6		95.3	95.3		123.8	123.8
0241, 31 - 34	SITE & INFRASTRUCTURE, DEMOLITION	129.7	97.9	109.0	134.3	117.0	123.0	103.6	93.8	97.2	125.5	114.3	118.2	115.4	87.3	97.1	147.3	113.1	125.0
0310	Concrete Forming & Accessories	100.0	82.7	86.6	115.3	53.7	67.5	108.6	86.1	91.1	112.6	60.9	72.5	95.7	63.9	71.0	121.5	71.7	82.8
0320	Concrete Reinforcing	58.8	89.1	67.2	84.8	59.2	77.7	50.1	95.5	62.6	69.0	56.1	65.4	80.2	44.6	70.3	74.7	61.6	71.0
0330	Cast-in-Place Concrete	137.7	91.2	121.2	178.6	69.2	139.8	138.2	96.0	123.2	172.0	69.3	135.5	138.7	63.1	111.8	199.5	84.5	158.6
03	CONCRETE	163.9	87.2	133.6	178.8	62.0	132.7	107.7	91.6	101.4	149.4	64.6	115.9	146.1	61.4	112.7	171.7	75.7	133.8
04	MASONRY	183.3	89.0	126.0	260.7	54.6	135.5	152.0	95.7	117.8	211.8	60.3	119.7	214.7	61.5	121.7	246.4	64.8	136.1
05	METALS	122.9	92.0	116.8	152.6	87.3	139.7	134.0	96.9	126.7	153.3	85.3	139.9	140.6	73.7	127.4	154.5	89.1	141.6
06	WOOD, PLASTICS & COMPOSITES	99.0	82.6	91.4	110.2	52.6	84.4	102.7	84.6	94.6	109.9	61.7	88.3	102.1	63.7	84.9	117.1	73.1	97.4
07	THERMAL & MOISTURE PROTECTION	132.4	82.7	114.7	150.0	60.6	118.1	127.3	94.0	115.4	147.6	65.9	118.5	134.7	62.9	109.1	152.0	75.0	124.6
08	OPENINGS	89.6	77.4	86.8	103.1	50.2	91.2	77.0	84.1	78.6	94.0	55.6	85.3	92.5	57.8	84.7	94.6	62.1	87.2
0920	Plaster & Gypsum Board	108.3	81.2	91.1	159.5	50.1	90.1	113.0	84.3	94.8	134.9	59.6	87.1	124.7	62.8	85.4	162.8	71.3	104.8
0950, 0980	Ceilings & Acoustic Treatment	78.0	81.2	79.8	131.2	50.1	85.7	75.2	84.3	80.3	113.8	59.6	83.4	94.0	62.8	76.5	129.0	71.3	96.7
0960	Flooring	110.7	62.9	98.7	125.5	51.5	107.0	97.4	87.9	95.0	140.4	62.8	120.9	105.0	55.0	92.5	120.8	77.4	109.9
0970, 0990	Wall Finishes & Painting/Coating	114.6	91.8	101.0	121.1	49.2	78.2	105.3	91.0	96.8	109.4	48.6	73.2	117.9	54.9	80.4	125.1	70.4	92.4
09	FINISHES	102.7	80.2	91.4	135.5	52.6	93.9	92.3	86.7	89.5	123.2	60.3	91.6	106.6	61.6	84.0	132.6	72.1	102.2
COVERS	DIVS. 10 - 14, 25, 28, 41, 43, 44, 46	131.1	60.8	117.5	131.1	56.9	116.8	131.1	64.2	118.2	131.1	59.1	117.2	131.1	56.5	116.7	131.1	59.9	117.3
21, 22, 23	FIRE SUPPRESSION, PLUMBING & HVAC	111.1	81.7	100.6	117.7	67.1	99.6	109.1	88.0	101.6	110.0	59.5	91.9	117.2	74.4	101.9	118.2	83.0	105.6
26, 27, 3370	ELECTRICAL, COMMUNICATIONS & UTIL.	133.4	76.1	108.6	166.0	53.0	117.0	147.7	96.7	125.6	135.2	58.1	101.8	125.8	54.4	94.9	157.1	71.9	120.2
MF2018	WEIGHTED AVERAGE	125.3	83.6	110.0	145.7	65.7	116.3	118.3	90.8	108.2	133.5	66.9	109.0	129.0	66.1	105.9	143.4	78.2	119.4

Location Factors - Commercial

Costs shown in RSMeans cost data publications are based on national averages for materials and installation. To adjust these costs to a specific location, simply multiply the base cost by the factor and divide by 100 for that city. The data is arranged alphabetically by state and postal zip code numbers. For a city not listed, use the factor for a nearby city with similar economic characteristics.

STATE/ZIP	CITY	MAT.	INST.	TOTAL
ALABAMA				
350-352	Birmingham	100.6	70.5	89.5
354	Tuscaloosa	99.3	69.6	88.4
355	Jasper	100.6	67.2	88.3
356	Decatur	99.3	66.7	87.3
357-358	Huntsville	99.3	71.6	89.1
359	Gadsden	100.2	69.5	88.9
360-361	Montgomery	99.8	70.6	89.0
362	Anniston	99.2	64.0	86.3
363	Dothan	97.8	71.5	88.1
364	Evergreen	97.3	65.0	85.4
365-366	Mobile	99.4	67.8	87.8
367	Selma	97.5	68.3	86.7
368	Phenix City	98.0	67.8	86.9
369	Butler	97.5	66.7	86.2
ALASKA				
995-996	Anchorage	116.6	109.2	113.9
997	Fairbanks	116.2	109.6	113.8
998	Juneau	116.1	109.2	113.5
999	Ketchikan	124.5	109.8	119.1
ARIZONA				
850,853	Phoenix	100.4	73.7	90.6
851,852	Mesa/Tempe	97.1	71.5	87.7
855	Globe	96.3	70.2	86.7
856-857	Tucson	95.9	72.1	87.1
859	Show Low	96.6	70.3	86.9
860	Flagstaff	100.3	71.7	89.8
863	Prescott	98.4	70.9	88.3
864	Kingman	96.2	69.8	86.5
865	Chambers	96.2	70.2	86.6
ARKANSAS				
716	Pine Bluff	98.5	61.8	85.0
717	Camden	95.9	61.2	83.1
718	Texarkana	96.7	62.3	84.1
719	Hot Springs	95.1	60.6	82.4
720-722	Little Rock	97.4	63.4	84.9
723	West Memphis	94.0	65.3	83.4
724	Jonesboro	95.4	64.2	83.9
725	Batesville	92.6	60.4	80.7
726	Harrison	93.9	59.6	81.3
727	Fayetteville	91.9	61.4	80.6
728	Russellville	92.9	59.5	80.6
729	Fort Smith	96.4	61.1	83.4
CALIFORNIA				
900-902	Los Angeles	102.9	130.2	112.9
903-905	Inglewood	94.6	128.5	107.0
906-908	Long Beach	96.1	128.5	108.0
910-912	Pasadena	96.8	128.2	108.4
913-916	Van Nuys	99.5	128.2	110.1
917-918	Alhambra	100.4	128.2	110.6
919-921	San Diego	103.7	123.3	110.9
922	Palm Springs	97.1	125.9	107.7
923-924	San Bernardino	94.8	125.2	106.0
925	Riverside	99.6	126.0	109.3
926-927	Santa Ana	96.6	125.8	107.4
928	Anaheim	99.9	125.8	109.4
930	Oxnard	100.6	124.8	109.5
931	Santa Barbara	100.0	124.3	108.9
932-933	Bakersfield	102.0	124.3	110.2
934	San Luis Obispo	100.5	124.5	109.3
935	Mojave	97.8	123.9	107.4
936-938	Fresno	100.7	129.9	111.4
939	Salinas	101.3	137.9	114.7
940-941	San Francisco	105.4	160.2	125.6
942,956-958	Sacramento	97.6	132.2	110.3
943	Palo Alto	95.8	153.9	117.2
944	San Mateo	97.7	152.4	117.9
945	Vallejo	98.1	140.9	113.8
946	Oakland	100.5	151.3	119.2
947	Berkeley	99.5	151.3	118.6
948	Richmond	98.5	145.5	115.8
949	San Rafael	100.4	148.3	118.1
950	Santa Cruz	104.7	138.0	117.0

STATE/ZIP	CITY	MAT.	INST.	TOTAL
CALIFORNIA (CONT'D)				
951	San Jose	102.2	153.9	121.3
952	Stockton	100.5	131.6	111.9
953	Modesto	100.3	130.8	111.5
954	Santa Rosa	100.0	145.9	116.9
955	Eureka	101.7	134.0	113.6
959	Marysville	101.1	131.6	112.3
960	Redding	103.9	131.4	114.0
961	Susanville	102.0	132.1	113.1
COLORADO				
800-802	Denver	102.2	75.1	92.3
803	Boulder	94.9	76.0	87.9
804	Golden	96.4	71.2	87.1
805	Fort Collins	98.5	73.7	89.4
806	Greeley	96.4	73.7	88.0
807	Fort Morgan	95.3	71.3	86.5
808-809	Colorado Springs	98.2	70.9	88.1
810	Pueblo	99.8	70.4	89.0
811	Alamosa	99.5	69.1	88.3
812	Salida	99.1	69.5	88.2
813	Durango	99.9	65.5	87.3
814	Montrose	98.5	65.7	86.5
815	Grand Junction	102.6	70.5	90.8
816	Glenwood Springs	99.5	65.9	87.1
CONNECTICUT				
060	New Britain	98.0	114.9	104.2
061	Hartford	100.3	115.8	106.0
062	Willimantic	98.8	113.6	104.3
063	New London	94.4	113.4	101.4
064	Meriden	96.5	113.4	102.7
065	New Haven	99.4	114.5	104.9
066	Bridgeport	99.3	114.2	104.8
067	Waterbury	98.9	114.7	104.7
068	Norwalk	98.9	113.9	104.4
069	Stamford	99.0	114.3	104.6
D.C.				
200-205	Washington	102.2	88.6	97.2
DELAWARE				
197	Newark	100.1	107.3	102.8
198	Wilmington	101.7	107.8	103.9
199	Dover	101.7	107.3	103.7
FLORIDA				
320,322	Jacksonville	98.7	67.0	87.0
321	Daytona Beach	98.9	68.8	87.9
323	Tallahassee	100.2	67.5	88.2
324	Panama City	100.0	67.7	88.1
325	Pensacola	102.5	66.3	89.1
326,344	Gainesville	99.2	66.5	87.2
327-328,347	Orlando	101.7	67.5	89.1
329	Melbourne	101.6	71.6	90.6
330-332,340	Miami	100.2	69.1	88.8
333	Fort Lauderdale	98.9	67.0	87.1
334,349	West Palm Beach	97.3	61.6	84.2
335-336,346	Tampa	100.3	68.1	88.4
337	St. Petersburg	102.8	64.3	88.6
338	Lakeland	99.4	65.4	86.9
339,341	Fort Myers	98.6	66.0	86.6
342	Sarasota	100.4	63.9	87.0
GEORGIA				
300-303,399	Atlanta	99.8	75.6	90.9
304	Statesboro	97.1	68.5	86.5
305	Gainesville	95.3	61.2	82.8
306	Athens	94.8	60.7	82.2
307	Dalton	96.6	64.5	84.8
308-309	Augusta	96.1	71.8	87.2
310-312	Macon	96.2	72.8	87.6
313-314	Savannah	98.7	72.0	88.9
315	Waycross	97.1	65.8	85.6
316	Valdosta	97.7	70.7	87.8
317,398	Albany	98.0	71.6	88.3
318-319	Columbus	97.9	72.9	88.7

Location Factors - Commercial

STATE/ZIP	CITY	MAT.	INST.	TOTAL
HAWAII				
967	Hilo	111.8	113.3	112.3
968	Honolulu	116.5	114.1	115.6
STATES & POSS.				
969	Guam	134.9	60.4	107.5
IDAHO				
832	Pocatello	101.3	78.3	92.9
833	Twin Falls	101.4	76.5	92.2
834	Idaho Falls	99.8	78.5	92.0
835	Lewiston	104.8	83.3	96.9
836-837	Boise	100.3	80.3	93.0
838	Coeur d'Alene	103.8	84.3	96.6
ILLINOIS				
600-603	North Suburban	96.6	142.0	113.3
604	Joliet	96.4	142.3	113.3
605	South Suburban	96.6	142.3	113.4
606-608	Chicago	99.4	143.7	115.7
609	Kankakee	92.9	132.1	107.3
610-611	Rockford	96.0	128.6	108.0
612	Rock Island	93.3	99.9	95.7
613	La Salle	94.3	126.4	106.1
614	Galesburg	93.9	107.6	99.0
615-616	Peoria	96.9	108.8	101.3
617	Bloomington	93.4	107.8	98.7
618-619	Champaign	96.0	113.7	102.6
620-622	East St. Louis	95.9	108.2	100.5
623	Quincy	97.3	105.1	100.1
624	Effingham	96.2	103.0	98.7
625	Decatur	98.8	105.4	101.2
626-627	Springfield	99.8	106.8	102.4
628	Centralia	94.0	103.3	97.4
629	Carbondale	93.8	105.2	98.0
INDIANA				
460	Anderson	95.4	77.1	88.7
461-462	Indianapolis	99.0	84.2	93.5
463-464	Gary	96.7	99.9	97.9
465-466	South Bend	99.1	79.4	91.9
467-468	Fort Wayne	96.0	77.2	89.1
469	Kokomo	92.1	75.8	86.1
470	Lawrenceburg	91.3	74.3	85.1
471	New Albany	92.3	72.4	85.0
472	Columbus	94.6	75.5	87.6
473	Muncie	95.8	75.7	88.4
474	Bloomington	97.1	77.7	89.9
475	Washington	92.0	80.4	87.7
476-477	Evansville	94.7	83.1	90.4
478	Terre Haute	95.4	78.7	89.2
479	Lafayette	94.0	75.9	87.4
IOWA				
500-503,509	Des Moines	99.4	90.8	96.2
504	Mason City	95.4	67.7	85.2
505	Fort Dodge	95.5	67.4	85.1
506-507	Waterloo	98.3	74.3	89.5
508	Creston	96.0	76.8	88.9
510-511	Sioux City	98.0	76.4	90.1
512	Sibley	95.7	57.3	81.6
513	Spencer	96.9	57.1	82.3
514	Carroll	94.6	75.2	87.5
515	Council Bluffs	98.7	79.0	91.4
516	Shenandoah	95.5	74.8	87.9
520	Dubuque	97.1	76.4	89.5
521	Decorah	95.6	67.4	85.2
522-524	Cedar Rapids	98.4	82.0	92.4
525	Ottumwa	95.4	71.9	86.8
526	Burlington	94.9	76.9	88.3
527-528	Davenport	97.4	91.3	95.1
KANSAS				
660-662	Kansas City	97.9	98.0	98.0
664-666	Topeka	99.0	74.1	89.9
667	Fort Scott	95.0	70.2	85.9
668	Emporia	94.7	70.3	85.7
669	Belleville	96.0	65.7	84.9
670-672	Wichita	97.7	71.2	88.0
673	Independence	96.1	69.8	86.5
674	Salina	97.2	70.3	87.3
675	Hutchinson	92.7	66.3	83.0
676	Hays	95.5	66.9	84.9
677	Colby	96.2	68.1	85.9

STATE/ZIP	CITY	MAT.	INST.	TOTAL
KANSAS (CONT'D)				
678	Dodge City	98.2	71.1	88.2
679	Liberal	95.4	66.1	84.6
KENTUCKY				
400-402	Louisville	97.7	78.2	90.5
403-405	Lexington	96.2	75.2	88.5
406	Frankfort	98.2	74.8	89.6
407-409	Corbin	92.7	71.4	84.9
410	Covington	92.6	71.4	84.8
411-412	Ashland	91.5	81.8	87.9
413-414	Campton	92.9	72.6	85.4
415-416	Pikeville	93.3	77.8	87.6
417-418	Hazard	92.4	73.1	85.3
420	Paducah	90.1	75.8	84.9
421-422	Bowling Green	94.0	74.7	86.9
423	Owensboro	93.1	77.7	87.5
424	Henderson	90.2	74.6	84.5
425-426	Somerset	90.8	72.8	84.1
427	Elizabethtown	90.3	69.9	82.8
LOUISIANA				
700-701	New Orleans	98.3	69.5	87.7
703	Thibodaux	93.9	62.2	82.2
704	Hammond	92.0	60.8	80.5
705	Lafayette	94.6	63.0	83.0
706	Lake Charles	94.7	65.3	83.9
707-708	Baton Rouge	98.2	65.6	86.2
710-711	Shreveport	99.0	64.1	86.2
712	Monroe	96.9	61.7	83.9
713-714	Alexandria	97.0	61.8	84.1
MAINE				
039	Kittery	92.3	81.2	88.2
040-041	Portland	99.2	86.6	94.5
042	Lewiston	97.0	84.4	92.4
043	Augusta	100.7	82.4	94.0
044	Bangor	95.7	83.1	91.0
045	Bath	93.5	80.9	88.9
046	Machias	93.1	80.8	88.5
047	Houlton	93.2	80.7	88.6
048	Rockland	92.4	80.9	88.2
049	Waterville	93.4	80.8	88.7
MARYLAND				
206	Waldorf	96.3	81.1	90.7
207-208	College Park	95.6	82.1	90.6
209	Silver Spring	95.5	81.2	90.2
210-212	Baltimore	100.9	83.8	94.6
214	Annapolis	100.2	80.3	92.9
215	Cumberland	94.8	79.8	89.3
216	Easton	96.1	69.1	86.2
217	Hagerstown	96.3	84.3	91.9
218	Salisbury	96.7	62.0	83.9
219	Elkton	94.2	78.8	88.5
MASSACHUSETTS				
010-011	Springfield	97.9	104.6	100.4
012	Pittsfield	96.9	99.3	97.7
013	Greenfield	94.4	103.4	97.7
014	Fitchburg	92.7	106.7	97.9
015-016	Worcester	97.9	111.9	103.1
017	Framingham	92.4	115.5	100.9
018	Lowell	97.1	119.2	105.2
019	Lawrence	97.8	117.8	105.2
020-022, 024	Boston	100.3	133.3	112.5
023	Brockton	97.5	111.2	102.6
025	Buzzards Bay	91.1	107.8	97.2
026	Hyannis	94.1	110.4	100.1
027	New Bedford	97.0	109.8	101.7
MICHIGAN				
480,483	Royal Oak	93.5	91.9	92.9
481	Ann Arbor	96.2	96.4	96.3
482	Detroit	99.5	99.9	99.7
484-485	Flint	96.1	88.4	93.3
486	Saginaw	95.8	84.1	91.5
487	Bay City	95.8	82.2	90.8
488-489	Lansing	98.2	87.6	94.3
490	Battle Creek	95.7	77.0	88.8
491	Kalamazoo	95.8	79.4	89.8
492	Jackson	93.3	83.5	89.7
493,495	Grand Rapids	97.8	79.6	91.1
494	Muskegon	94.8	79.6	89.2

Location Factors - Commercial

STATE/ZIP	CITY	MAT.	INST.	TOTAL
MICHIGAN (CONT'D)				
496	Traverse City	93.2	71.6	85.2
497	Gaylord	94.0	74.3	86.7
498-499	Iron Mountain	95.3	75.0	87.8
MINNESOTA				
550-551	Saint Paul	102.0	117.9	107.9
553-555	Minneapolis	100.9	118.4	107.4
556-558	Duluth	102.4	106.1	103.8
559	Rochester	99.9	104.7	101.7
560	Mankato	94.8	100.6	97.0
561	Windom	93.5	88.3	91.6
562	Willmar	93.4	103.8	97.2
563	St. Cloud	95.4	114.2	102.3
564	Brainerd	94.9	99.5	96.6
565	Detroit Lakes	96.3	90.2	94.1
566	Bemidji	95.8	93.7	95.0
567	Thief River Falls	95.6	91.8	94.2
MISSISSIPPI				
386	Clarksdale	96.2	51.3	79.7
387	Greenville	99.4	63.3	86.1
388	Tupelo	97.0	53.7	81.1
389	Greenwood	97.3	51.0	80.3
390-392	Jackson	98.7	67.8	87.3
393	Meridian	95.3	65.8	84.4
394	Laurel	95.7	53.7	80.2
395	Biloxi	97.1	64.0	84.9
396	McComb	94.2	51.3	78.4
397	Columbus	95.6	54.4	80.4
MISSOURI				
630-631	St. Louis	97.3	104.5	99.9
633	Bowling Green	92.4	87.5	90.6
634	Hannibal	91.5	84.0	88.8
635	Kirksville	93.8	79.5	88.5
636	Flat River	93.1	85.8	90.4
637	Cape Girardeau	94.0	85.9	91.0
638	Sikeston	92.0	80.0	87.6
639	Poplar Bluff	91.4	80.1	87.2
640-641	Kansas City	98.6	101.2	99.6
644-645	St. Joseph	95.1	89.3	93.0
646	Chillicothe	91.3	86.0	89.4
647	Harrisonville	90.8	92.2	91.3
648	Joplin	94.2	76.5	87.7
650-651	Jefferson City	96.5	91.3	94.6
652	Columbia	95.6	90.7	93.8
653	Sedalia	94.8	83.5	90.7
654-655	Rolla	93.1	91.8	92.6
656-658	Springfield	97.7	81.0	91.6
MONTANA				
590-591	Billings	102.5	77.4	93.3
592	Wolf Point	100.4	71.3	89.6
593	Miles City	98.7	71.3	88.6
594	Great Falls	103.4	74.1	92.6
595	Havre	99.5	69.4	88.4
596	Helena	101.9	71.3	90.6
597	Butte	101.6	71.1	90.4
598	Missoula	99.3	71.0	88.9
599	Kalispell	97.6	70.3	87.6
NEBRASKA				
680-681	Omaha	98.7	81.2	92.3
683-685	Lincoln	98.9	76.4	90.6
686	Columbus	93.8	73.9	86.5
687	Norfolk	95.2	70.8	86.2
688	Grand Island	96.1	76.9	89.0
689	Hastings	94.8	71.5	86.2
690	McCook	94.2	66.9	84.2
691	North Platte	95.4	72.1	86.8
692	Valentine	97.0	64.2	85.0
693	Alliance	96.8	67.0	85.9
NEVADA				
889-891	Las Vegas	103.7	106.4	104.7
893	Ely	101.1	83.6	94.7
894-895	Reno	101.7	81.6	94.3
897	Carson City	101.9	81.5	94.4
898	Elko	100.3	76.4	91.5
NEW HAMPSHIRE				
030	Nashua	99.0	91.8	96.3
031	Manchester	99.8	92.9	97.3

STATE/ZIP	CITY	MAT.	INST.	TOTAL
NEW HAMPSHIRE (CONT'D)				
032-033	Concord	99.3	91.9	96.5
034	Keene	93.8	82.1	89.5
035	Littleton	94.3	74.1	86.9
036	Charleston	93.4	81.5	89.0
037	Claremont	92.9	81.5	88.7
038	Portsmouth	95.4	89.6	93.3
NEW JERSEY				
070-071	Newark	100.4	134.5	112.9
072	Elizabeth	96.2	133.6	110.0
073	Jersey City	96.6	133.5	110.2
074-075	Paterson	97.5	133.7	110.8
076	Hackensack	94.7	133.5	109.0
077	Long Branch	94.5	131.4	108.1
078	Dover	94.9	133.7	109.1
079	Summit	95.1	132.7	108.9
080,083	Vineland	95.7	130.4	108.5
081	Camden	98.9	130.4	110.5
082,084	Atlantic City	96.5	130.3	108.9
085-086	Trenton	100.2	130.6	111.4
087	Point Pleasant	97.1	124.5	107.2
088-089	New Brunswick	97.7	132.9	110.7
NEW MEXICO				
870-872	Albuquerque	98.2	72.3	88.7
873	Gallup	97.4	72.3	88.1
874	Farmington	98.2	72.3	88.6
875	Santa Fe	99.8	72.8	89.9
877	Las Vegas	96.0	72.3	87.3
878	Socorro	95.9	72.3	87.2
879	Truth/Consequences	95.5	69.4	85.9
880	Las Cruces	95.8	70.0	86.3
881	Clovis	96.6	72.2	87.6
882	Roswell	98.6	72.3	88.9
883	Carrizozo	98.3	72.3	88.7
884	Tucumcari	97.0	72.2	87.9
NEW YORK				
100-102	New York	99.6	167.2	124.5
103	Staten Island	92.7	165.5	119.5
104	Bronx	91.8	165.6	119.0
105	Mount Vernon	90.3	140.7	108.9
106	White Plains	91.7	143.7	110.8
107	Yonkers	96.3	145.1	114.2
108	New Rochelle	90.9	135.5	107.3
109	Suffern	90.3	118.0	100.5
110	Queens	99.4	169.0	125.0
111	Long Island City	100.8	169.0	125.9
112	Brooklyn	101.4	168.1	126.0
113	Flushing	99.8	169.0	125.3
114	Jamaica	98.6	169.0	124.5
115,117,118	Hicksville	99.4	145.1	116.2
116	Far Rockaway	99.8	169.0	125.3
119	Riverhead	100.2	149.7	118.4
120-122	Albany	98.8	107.5	102.0
123	Schenectady	98.2	107.0	101.4
124	Kingston	99.3	121.3	107.4
125-126	Poughkeepsie	98.7	125.3	108.5
127	Monticello	98.3	122.0	107.0
128	Glens Falls	92.3	99.2	94.9
129	Plattsburgh	96.1	87.7	93.0
130-132	Syracuse	98.1	99.0	98.4
133-135	Utica	96.2	99.9	97.5
136	Watertown	97.5	95.9	96.9
137-139	Binghamton	97.5	97.8	97.6
140-142	Buffalo	102.4	105.4	103.5
143	Niagara Falls	96.5	98.0	97.1
144-146	Rochester	101.4	98.6	100.4
147	Jamestown	95.5	87.5	92.6
148-149	Elmira	95.6	98.2	96.5
NORTH CAROLINA				
270,272-274	Greensboro	100.4	64.5	87.2
271	Winston-Salem	100.0	64.5	87.0
275-276	Raleigh	99.4	64.8	86.7
277	Durham	102.5	64.5	88.5
278	Rocky Mount	96.4	64.0	84.5
279	Elizabeth City	97.2	65.0	85.4
280	Gastonia	98.9	68.2	87.6
281-282	Charlotte	99.3	71.1	88.9
283	Fayetteville	102.9	63.0	88.2
284	Wilmington	97.8	62.2	84.7
285	Kinston	95.4	62.8	83.4

Location Factors - Commercial

STATE/ZIP	CITY	MAT.	INST.	TOTAL
NORTH CAROLINA (CONT'D)				
286	Hickory	95.7	68.7	85.7
287-288	Asheville	98.0	63.8	85.4
289	Murphy	96.2	61.4	83.4
NORTH DAKOTA				
580-581	Fargo	100.7	75.3	91.3
582	Grand Forks	99.5	76.9	91.2
583	Devils Lake	98.6	73.8	89.5
584	Jamestown	98.5	73.0	89.2
585	Bismarck	101.4	82.9	94.6
586	Dickinson	98.7	72.6	89.1
587	Minot	99.5	72.9	89.7
588	Williston	97.8	76.0	89.8
OHIO				
430-432	Columbus	96.8	87.0	93.2
433	Marion	91.6	79.6	87.2
434-436	Toledo	95.2	90.0	93.3
437-438	Zanesville	92.0	79.0	87.2
439	Steubenville	92.4	83.1	89.0
440	Lorain	96.0	80.9	90.5
441	Cleveland	98.0	91.4	95.6
442-443	Akron	96.8	85.0	92.4
444-445	Youngstown	96.3	80.9	90.6
446-447	Canton	96.4	78.5	89.8
448-449	Mansfield	93.3	78.4	87.8
450	Hamilton	94.4	73.1	86.6
451-452	Cincinnati	96.9	79.3	90.4
453-454	Dayton	94.5	78.6	88.6
455	Springfield	94.5	78.2	88.5
456	Chillicothe	92.5	81.0	88.3
457	Athens	95.5	83.1	90.9
458	Lima	95.3	75.6	88.1
OKLAHOMA				
730-731	Oklahoma City	97.4	67.9	86.5
734	Ardmore	94.3	64.4	83.3
735	Lawton	97.9	65.9	86.1
736	Clinton	95.3	64.3	83.9
737	Enid	96.9	65.0	85.2
738	Woodward	94.3	65.7	83.8
739	Guymon	95.2	59.2	82.0
740-741	Tulsa	96.0	64.4	84.4
743	Miami	91.5	62.1	80.7
744	Muskogee	94.8	65.9	84.2
745	McAlester	91.2	63.7	81.1
746	Ponca City	91.8	59.8	80.0
747	Durant	91.7	60.9	80.4
748	Shawnee	92.8	62.4	81.6
749	Poteau	91.1	62.0	80.4
OREGON				
970-972	Portland	103.7	103.8	103.7
973	Salem	106.3	100.8	104.3
974	Eugene	103.1	100.1	102.0
975	Medford	104.2	97.1	101.6
976	Klamath Falls	103.6	95.5	100.6
977	Bend	102.7	97.9	100.9
978	Pendleton	101.1	97.4	99.7
979	Vale	98.9	85.1	93.9
PENNSYLVANIA				
150-152	Pittsburgh	100.1	103.2	101.3
153	Washington	94.5	98.3	95.9
154	Uniontown	94.6	95.7	95.0
155	Bedford	95.4	86.0	92.0
156	Greensburg	95.4	92.4	94.3
157	Indiana	94.6	94.4	94.5
158	Dubois	95.7	89.9	93.6
159	Johnstown	95.5	93.4	94.7
160	Butler	90.8	94.5	92.2
161	New Castle	90.9	95.0	92.4
162	Kittanning	91.2	94.7	92.5
163	Oil City	90.8	89.7	90.4
164-165	Erie	93.6	94.3	93.9
166	Altoona	93.5	93.3	93.4
167	Bradford	94.0	90.4	92.6
168	State College	93.5	95.6	94.3
169	Wellsboro	94.4	84.6	90.8
170-171	Harrisburg	98.8	98.0	98.5
172	Chambersburg	93.6	81.5	89.1
173-174	York	94.8	93.7	94.4
175-176	Lancaster	92.6	95.7	93.8

STATE/ZIP	CITY	MAT.	INST.	TOTAL
PENNSYLVANIA (CONT'D)				
177	Williamsport	91.6	91.0	91.4
178	Sunbury	93.2	84.6	90.0
179	Pottsville	92.4	88.0	90.8
180	Lehigh Valley	94.2	101.6	96.9
181	Allentown	96.8	104.4	99.6
182	Hazleton	93.7	87.5	91.4
183	Stroudsburg	93.7	95.4	94.4
184-185	Scranton	97.7	94.3	96.5
186-187	Wilkes-Barre	93.4	93.5	93.4
188	Montrose	93.2	88.3	91.4
189	Doylestown	93.0	115.6	101.3
190-191	Philadelphia	100.5	137.6	114.2
193	Westchester	96.3	116.1	103.6
194	Norristown	95.4	117.6	103.6
195-196	Reading	97.9	99.3	98.4
PUERTO RICO				
009	San Juan	121.3	28.7	87.2
RHODE ISLAND				
028	Newport	96.3	109.9	101.3
029	Providence	100.1	110.6	104.0
SOUTH CAROLINA				
290-292	Columbia	99.5	65.1	86.8
293	Spartanburg	97.7	67.5	86.6
294	Charleston	99.6	67.5	87.8
295	Florence	97.4	64.5	85.3
296	Greenville	97.5	67.4	86.5
297	Rock Hill	96.3	65.2	84.8
298	Aiken	96.8	61.8	84.0
299	Beaufort	97.6	63.7	85.1
SOUTH DAKOTA				
570-571	Sioux Falls	99.9	79.6	92.4
572	Watertown	96.8	66.0	85.5
573	Mitchell	96.0	60.0	82.8
574	Aberdeen	99.1	73.5	89.7
575	Pierre	101.6	73.9	91.4
576	Mobridge	96.4	61.1	83.4
577	Rapid City	99.1	66.3	87.1
TENNESSEE				
370-372	Nashville	100.0	73.1	90.1
373-374	Chattanooga	98.8	65.4	86.5
375,380-381	Memphis	99.1	70.7	88.7
376	Johnson City	97.6	57.8	82.9
377-379	Knoxville	95.7	65.6	84.6
382	McKenzie	95.8	52.5	79.9
383	Jackson	98.6	67.2	87.1
384	Columbia	94.5	61.5	82.3
385	Cookeville	95.7	53.8	80.3
TEXAS				
750	McKinney	96.6	59.6	83.0
751	Waxahachie	96.6	66.9	85.7
752-753	Dallas	99.5	66.4	87.3
754	Greenville	96.7	59.2	82.9
755	Texarkana	95.3	61.4	82.8
756	Longview	95.8	57.0	81.5
757	Tyler	96.7	58.4	82.6
758	Palestine	93.2	56.5	79.7
759	Lufkin	93.9	57.8	80.6
760-761	Fort Worth	97.6	63.7	85.1
762	Denton	95.8	59.4	82.4
763	Wichita Falls	95.3	61.2	82.7
764	Eastland	93.1	56.5	79.6
765	Temple	91.7	54.1	77.8
766-767	Waco	94.7	62.5	82.9
768	Brownwood	95.7	54.9	80.7
769	San Angelo	95.4	58.7	81.9
770-772	Houston	97.6	67.2	86.4
773	Huntsville	93.7	58.4	80.7
774	Wharton	94.7	59.1	81.6
775	Galveston	93.4	61.5	81.6
776-777	Beaumont	94.6	66.0	84.1
778	Bryan	91.2	60.0	79.7
779	Victoria	94.6	58.5	81.3
780	Laredo	95.5	60.7	82.7
781-782	San Antonio	97.4	64.4	85.3
783-784	Corpus Christi	97.6	61.9	84.5
785	McAllen	96.7	53.4	80.8
786-787	Austin	97.6	61.9	84.4

Location Factors - Commercial

STATE/ZIP	CITY	MAT.	INST.	TOTAL	STATE/ZIP	CITY	MAT.	INST.	TOTAL
TEXAS (CONT'D)					**WISCONSIN (CONT'D)**				
788	Del Rio	96.3	55.7	81.3	538	Lancaster	93.2	88.0	91.3
789	Giddings	93.7	56.6	80.1	539	Portage	92.1	91.4	91.8
790-791	Amarillo	98.9	61.6	85.2	540	New Richmond	94.2	87.7	91.8
792	Childress	97.3	56.9	82.4	541-543	Green Bay	99.5	99.3	99.4
793-794	Lubbock	100.7	60.8	86.0	544	Wausau	93.9	87.7	91.6
795-796	Abilene	99.1	59.8	84.7	545	Rhinelander	96.7	86.2	92.8
797	Midland	99.7	63.9	86.5	546	La Crosse	95.3	95.9	95.5
798-799,885	El Paso	98.9	63.3	85.8	547	Eau Claire	96.9	95.8	96.5
UTAH					548	Superior	94.0	90.1	92.6
840-841	Salt Lake City	101.7	72.3	90.9	549	Oshkosh	94.6	88.2	92.2
842,844	Ogden	97.7	72.6	88.4	**WYOMING**				
843	Logan	99.1	72.6	89.3	820	Cheyenne	99.6	72.8	89.7
845	Price	98.6	65.8	86.5	821	Yellowstone Nat'l Park	97.1	69.9	87.1
846-847	Provo	99.3	71.8	89.2	822	Wheatland	97.8	68.4	87.0
VERMONT					823	Rawlins	99.0	69.8	88.3
050	White River Jct.	93.9	76.7	87.5	824	Worland	97.4	70.3	87.4
051	Bellows Falls	92.6	86.7	90.4	825	Riverton	98.2	69.8	87.8
052	Bennington	92.9	83.5	89.5	826	Casper	100.8	71.1	89.9
053	Brattleboro	93.2	86.7	90.8	827	Newcastle	97.2	69.8	87.1
054	Burlington	99.7	81.3	92.9	828	Sheridan	100.1	70.6	89.2
056	Montpelier	97.1	83.7	92.1	829-831	Rock Springs	100.8	70.3	89.6
057	Rutland	96.7	80.7	90.8	**CANADIAN FACTORS (reflect Canadian currency)**				
058	St. Johnsbury	94.0	76.3	87.5	**ALBERTA**				
059	Guildhall	92.9	76.4	86.8		Calgary	137.9	86.9	119.1
VIRGINIA						Edmonton	137.6	86.9	118.9
220-221	Fairfax	98.0	80.9	91.7		Fort McMurray	132.2	82.5	113.9
222	Arlington	100.1	79.9	92.6		Lethbridge	126.7	82.0	110.3
223	Alexandria	99.7	81.2	92.9		Lloydminster	120.0	79.1	104.9
224-225	Fredericksburg	97.4	76.2	89.6		Medicine Hat	120.3	78.4	104.9
226	Winchester	97.6	72.6	88.4		Red Deer	120.7	78.4	105.1
227	Culpeper	97.6	78.3	90.5	**BRITISH COLUMBIA**				
228	Harrisonburg	97.7	72.3	88.3		Kamloops	122.4	78.8	106.1
229	Charlottesville	98.1	68.2	87.1		Prince George	123.4	78.2	106.7
230-232	Richmond	98.8	69.4	88.0		Vancouver	129.7	89.8	115.0
233-235	Norfolk	100.7	66.9	88.3		Victoria	125.3	83.6	110.0
236	Newport News	98.7	67.2	87.1	**MANITOBA**				
237	Portsmouth	97.9	65.2	85.9		Brandon	130.0	66.3	106.6
238	Petersburg	96.8	68.7	86.5		Portage la Prairie	120.4	65.3	100.1
239	Farmville	96.4	63.1	84.1		Winnipeg	133.5	66.9	109.0
240-241	Roanoke	100.5	66.2	87.9	**NEW BRUNSWICK**				
242	Bristol	97.1	57.2	82.4		Bathurst	117.1	59.1	95.7
243	Pulaski	96.8	66.5	85.7		Dalhousie	120.2	59.1	97.7
244	Staunton	97.6	65.2	85.7		Fredericton	130.6	66.7	107.0
245	Lynchburg	97.5	66.9	86.3		Moncton	117.1	73.6	101.1
246	Grundy	97.1	60.5	83.7		Newcastle	117.2	59.6	96.0
WASHINGTON						St. John	119.0	74.5	102.6
980-981,987	Seattle	103.6	112.6	106.9	**NEWFOUNDLAND**				
982	Everett	103.5	104.7	104.0		Corner Brook	134.3	64.4	108.5
983-984	Tacoma	104.3	103.8	104.1		St. Johns	130.0	82.4	112.5
985	Olympia	104.1	102.9	103.7	**NORTHWEST TERRITORIES**				
986	Vancouver	105.9	100.6	103.9		Yellowknife	143.4	78.2	119.4
988	Wenatchee	103.1	83.2	95.8	**NOVA SCOTIA**				
989	Yakima	104.0	94.7	100.6		Bridgewater	119.8	66.5	100.2
990-992	Spokane	97.6	84.9	93.0		Dartmouth	131.0	66.1	107.2
993	Richland	97.0	91.0	94.8		Halifax	124.4	82.1	108.8
994	Clarkston	95.3	75.6	88.1		New Glasgow	129.1	66.1	105.9
WEST VIRGINIA						Sydney	127.3	66.1	104.8
247-248	Bluefield	96.2	81.0	90.6		Truro	119.3	66.5	99.9
249	Lewisburg	97.5	83.1	92.2		Yarmouth	129.0	66.1	105.9
250-253	Charleston	98.2	88.3	94.5	**ONTARIO**				
254	Martinsburg	96.6	77.2	89.4		Barrie	121.0	82.1	106.7
255-257	Huntington	99.2	87.0	94.7		Brantford	122.0	85.5	108.5
258-259	Beckley	95.4	83.9	91.2		Cornwall	121.4	82.3	107.1
260	Wheeling	99.4	87.6	95.0		Hamilton	129.4	94.9	116.7
261	Parkersburg	98.6	86.6	94.2		Kingston	122.7	82.4	107.9
262	Buckhannon	97.2	87.2	93.5		Kitchener	119.8	91.0	109.2
263-264	Clarksburg	97.7	87.9	94.1		London	128.9	93.0	115.7
265	Morgantown	97.6	88.6	94.3		North Bay	132.0	80.1	112.9
266	Gassaway	97.2	84.2	92.4		Oshawa	121.1	92.4	110.6
267	Romney	97.2	81.8	91.6		Ottawa	128.2	94.4	115.7
268	Petersburg	96.9	82.2	91.5		Owen Sound	121.3	80.5	106.3
WISCONSIN						Peterborough	122.0	82.1	107.3
530,532	Milwaukee	97.6	109.3	101.9		Sarnia	122.4	86.0	109.0
531	Kenosha	97.4	101.9	99.0					
534	Racine	96.5	101.8	98.5					
535	Beloit	96.3	92.8	95.0					
537	Madison	98.6	100.5	99.3					

Location Factors - Commercial

STATE/ZIP	CITY	MAT.	INST.	TOTAL
ONTARIO (CONT'D)				
	Sault Ste. Marie	117.7	84.3	105.4
	St. Catharines	117.3	91.6	107.8
	Sudbury	116.6	90.0	106.8
	Thunder Bay	118.2	90.6	108.1
	Timmins	122.4	80.4	106.9
	Toronto	127.5	100.9	117.7
	Windsor	118.3	90.8	108.2
PRINCE EDWARD ISLAND				
	Charlottetown	130.7	58.1	104.0
	Summerside	131.2	54.5	103.0
QUEBEC				
	Cap-de-la-Madeleine	118.6	75.6	102.8
	Charlesbourg	118.6	75.6	102.8
	Chicoutimi	116.5	84.0	104.6
	Gatineau	118.4	75.4	102.6
	Granby	118.9	75.3	102.9
	Hull	119.0	75.4	103.0
	Joliette	119.1	75.6	103.1
	Laval	118.7	75.9	103.0
	Montreal	129.7	87.0	114.0
	Quebec City	130.0	87.5	114.4
	Rimouski	118.5	84.0	105.8
	Rouyn-Noranda	118.7	75.4	102.8
	Saint-Hyacinthe	118.1	75.4	102.4
	Sherbrooke	118.8	75.4	102.8
	Sorel	119.1	75.6	103.1
	Saint-Jerome	118.9	75.4	102.9
	Trois-Rivieres	129.3	75.2	109.4
SASKATCHEWAN				
	Moose Jaw	117.3	60.4	96.3
	Prince Albert	116.5	58.9	95.3
	Regina	137.5	85.1	118.2
	Saskatoon	118.9	81.0	105.0
YUKON				
	Whitehorse	145.7	65.7	116.3

General Requirements — R0111 Summary of Work

R011105-05 Tips for Accurate Estimating

1. Use computer applications or pre-printed forms for orderly sequence of dimensions and locations. Keep track of phone conversations by recording (with permission) or note taking on computer applications or pre-printed forms.
2. Use only the front side if pre-printed forms are necessary. Label all pre-printed forms with the same convention.
3. Be consistent in listing dimensions: For example, length x width x height. This helps in rechecking to ensure that, the total length of partitions is appropriate for the building area.
4. Use printed (rather than measured) dimensions where given.
5. Add up multiple printed dimensions for a single entry where possible.
6. Measure all other dimensions carefully.
7. Use each set of dimensions to calculate multiple related quantities.
8. Convert foot and inch measurements to decimal feet when listing. Memorize decimal equivalents to .01 parts of a foot (1/8" equals approximately .01').
9. Do not "round off" quantities until the final summary.
10. Mark drawings with different colors as items are taken off.
11. Keep similar items together, different items separate.
12. Identify location and drawing numbers to aid in future checking for completeness.
13. Measure or list everything on the drawings or mentioned in the specifications.
14. It may be necessary to list items not called for to make the job complete.
15. Be alert for: Notes on plans such as N.T.S. (not to scale); changes in scale throughout the drawings; reduced size drawings; discrepancies between the specifications and the drawings.
16. Develop a consistent pattern of performing an estimate. For example:
    a. Start the quantity takeoff at the lower floor and move to the next higher floor.
    b. Proceed from the main section of the building to the wings.
    c. Proceed from south to north or vice versa, clockwise or counterclockwise.
    d. Take off floor plan quantities first, elevations next, then detail drawings.
17. List all gross dimensions that can be either used again for different quantities, or used as a rough check of other quantities for verification (exterior perimeter, gross floor area, individual floor areas, etc.).
18. Utilize design symmetry or repetition (repetitive floors, repetitive wings, symmetrical design around a center line, similar room layouts, etc.). Note: Extreme caution is needed here so as not to omit or duplicate an area.
19. Do not convert units until the final total is obtained. For instance, when estimating concrete work, keep all units to the nearest cubic foot, then summarize and convert to cubic yards.
20. When figuring alternatives, it is best to total all items involved in the basic system, then total all items involved in the alternates. Therefore you work with positive numbers in all cases. When adds and deducts are used, it is often confusing whether to add or subtract a portion of an item; especially on a complicated or involved alternate.

R011105-10 Unit Gross Area Requirements

The figures in the table below indicate typical ranges in square feet as a function of the "occupant" unit. This table is best used in the preliminary design stages to help determine the probable size requirement for the total project.

Building Type	Unit	Gross Area in S.F.		
		1/4	Median	3/4
Apartments	Unit	660	860	1,100
Auditorium & Play Theaters	Seat	18	25	38
Bowling Alleys	Lane		940	
Churches & Synagogues	Seat	20	28	39
Dormitories	Bed	200	230	275
Fraternity & Sorority Houses	Bed	220	315	370
Garages, Parking	Car	325	355	385
Hospitals	Bed	685	850	1,075
Hotels	Rental Unit	475	600	710
Housing for the elderly	Unit	515	635	755
Housing, Public	Unit	700	875	1,030
Ice Skating Rinks	Total	27,000	30,000	36,000
Motels	Rental Unit	360	465	620
Nursing Homes	Bed	290	350	450
Restaurants	Seat	23	29	39
Schools, Elementary	Pupil	65	77	90
Junior High & Middle	↓	85	110	129
Senior High		102	130	145
Vocational		110	135	195
Shooting Ranges	Point		450	
Theaters & Movies	Seat		15	

General Requirements R0111 Summary of Work

R011105-20 Floor Area Ratios

Table below lists commonly used gross to net area and net to gross area ratios expressed in % for various building types.

Building Type	Gross to Net Ratio	Net to Gross Ratio	Building Type	Gross to Net Ratio	Net to Gross Ratio
Apartment	156	64	School Buildings (campus type)		
Bank	140	72	Administrative	150	67
Church	142	70	Auditorium	142	70
Courthouse	162	61	Biology	161	62
Department Store	123	81	Chemistry	170	59
Garage	118	85	Classroom	152	66
Hospital	183	55	Dining Hall	138	72
Hotel	158	63	Dormitory	154	65
Laboratory	171	58	Engineering	164	61
Library	132	76	Fraternity	160	63
Office	135	75	Gymnasium	142	70
Restaurant	141	70	Science	167	60
Warehouse	108	93	Service	120	83
			Student Union	172	59

The gross area of a building is the total floor area based on outside dimensions.

The net area of a building is the usable floor area for the function intended and excludes such items as stairways, corridors and mechanical rooms. In the case of a commercial building, it might be considered as the "leasable area."

General Requirements — R0111 Summary of Work

R011105-30 Occupancy Determinations

Function of Space	SF/Person Required
Accessory storage areas, mechanical equipment rooms	300
Agriculture Building	300
Aircraft Hangars	500
Airport Terminal	
Baggage claim	20
Baggage handling	300
Concourse	100
Waiting areas	15
Assembly	
Gaming floors (keno, slots, etc.)	11
Exhibit Gallery and Museum	30
Assembly w/ fixed seats	load determined by seat number
Assembly w/o fixed seats	
Concentrated (chairs only-not fixed)	7
Standing space	5
Unconcentrated (tables and chairs)	15
Bowling centers, allow 5 persons for each lane including 15 feet of runway, and for additional areas	7
Business areas	100
Courtrooms-other than fixed seating areas	40
Day care	35
Dormitories	50
Educational	
Classroom areas	20
Shops and other vocational room areas	50
Exercise rooms	50
Fabrication and Manufacturing areas where hazardous materials are used	200
Industrial areas	100
Institutional areas	
Inpatient treatment areas	240
Outpatient areas	100
Sleeping areas	120
Kitchens commercial	200
Library	
Reading rooms	50
Stack area	100
Mercantile	
Areas on other floors	60
Basement and grade floor areas	30
Storage, stock, shipping areas	300
Parking garages	200
Residential	200
Skating rinks, swimming pools	
Rink and pool	50
Decks	15
Stages and platforms	15
Warehouses	500

Excerpted from the 2012 *International Building Code*, Copyright 2011. Washington, D.C.: International Code Council. Reproduced with permission. All rights reserved. www.ICCSAFE.org

General Requirements — R0111 Summary of Work

R011105-50 Metric Conversion Factors

Description: This table is primarily for converting customary U.S. units in the left hand column to SI metric units in the right hand column. In addition, conversion factors for some commonly encountered Canadian and non-SI metric units are included.

	If You Know		Multiply By		To Find
Length	Inches	x	25.4[a]	=	Millimeters
	Feet	x	0.3048[a]	=	Meters
	Yards	x	0.9144[a]	=	Meters
	Miles (statute)	x	1.609	=	Kilometers
Area	Square inches	x	645.2	=	Square millimeters
	Square feet	x	0.0929	=	Square meters
	Square yards	x	0.8361	=	Square meters
Volume (Capacity)	Cubic inches	x	16,387	=	Cubic millimeters
	Cubic feet	x	0.02832	=	Cubic meters
	Cubic yards	x	0.7646	=	Cubic meters
	Gallons (U.S. liquids)[b]	x	0.003785	=	Cubic meters[c]
	Gallons (Canadian liquid)[b]	x	0.004546	=	Cubic meters[c]
	Ounces (U.S. liquid)[b]	x	29.57	=	Milliliters[c,d]
	Quarts (U.S. liquid)[b]	x	0.9464	=	Liters[c,d]
	Gallons (U.S. liquid)[b]	x	3.785	=	Liters[c,d]
Force	Kilograms force[d]	x	9.807	=	Newtons
	Pounds force	x	4.448	=	Newtons
	Pounds force	x	0.4536	=	Kilograms force[d]
	Kips	x	4448	=	Newtons
	Kips	x	453.6	=	Kilograms force[d]
Pressure, Stress, Strength (Force per unit area)	Kilograms force per square centimeter[d]	x	0.09807	=	Megapascals
	Pounds force per square inch (psi)	x	0.006895	=	Megapascals
	Kips per square inch	x	6.895	=	Megapascals
	Pounds force per square inch (psi)	x	0.07031	=	Kilograms force per square centimeter[d]
	Pounds force per square foot	x	47.88	=	Pascals
	Pounds force per square foot	x	4.882	=	Kilograms force per square meter[d]
Flow	Cubic feet per minute	x	0.4719	=	Liters per second
	Gallons per minute	x	0.0631	=	Liters per second
	Gallons per hour	x	1.05	=	Milliliters per second
Bending Moment Or Torque	Inch-pounds force	x	0.01152	=	Meter-kilograms force[d]
	Inch-pounds force	x	0.1130	=	Newton-meters
	Foot-pounds force	x	0.1383	=	Meter-kilograms force[d]
	Foot-pounds force	x	1.356	=	Newton-meters
	Meter-kilograms force[d]	x	9.807	=	Newton-meters
Mass	Ounces (avoirdupois)	x	28.35	=	Grams
	Pounds (avoirdupois)	x	0.4536	=	Kilograms
	Tons (metric)	x	1000	=	Kilograms
	Tons, short (2000 pounds)	x	907.2	=	Kilograms
	Tons, short (2000 pounds)	x	0.9072	=	Megagrams[e]
Mass per Unit Volume	Pounds mass per cubic foot	x	16.02	=	Kilograms per cubic meter
	Pounds mass per cubic yard	x	0.5933	=	Kilograms per cubic meter
	Pounds mass per gallon (U.S. liquid)[b]	x	119.8	=	Kilograms per cubic meter
	Pounds mass per gallon (Canadian liquid)[b]	x	99.78	=	Kilograms per cubic meter
Temperature	Degrees Fahrenheit	(F-32)/1.8		=	Degrees Celsius
	Degrees Fahrenheit	(F+459.67)/1.8		=	Degrees Kelvin
	Degrees Celsius	C+273.15		=	Degrees Kelvin

[a] The factor given is exact
[b] One U.S. gallon = 0.8327 Canadian gallon
[c] 1 liter = 1000 milliliters = 1000 cubic centimeters
   1 cubic decimeter = 0.001 cubic meter
[d] Metric but not SI unit
[e] Called "tonne" in England and "metric ton" in other metric countries

General Requirements — R0111 Summary of Work

R011105-60 Weights and Measures

Measures of Length
1 Mile = 1760 Yards = 5280 Feet
1 Yard = 3 Feet = 36 inches
1 Foot = 12 Inches
1 Mil = 0.001 Inch
1 Fathom = 2 Yards = 6 Feet
1 Rod = 5.5 Yards = 16.5 Feet
1 Hand = 4 Inches
1 Span = 9 Inches
1 Micro-inch = One Millionth Inch or 0.000001 Inch
1 Micron = One Millionth Meter + 0.00003937 Inch

Surveyor's Measure
1 Mile = 8 Furlongs = 80 Chains
1 Furlong = 10 Chains = 220 Yards
1 Chain = 4 Rods = 22 Yards = 66 Feet = 100 Links
1 Link = 7.92 Inches

Square Measure
1 Square Mile = 640 Acres = 6400 Square Chains
1 Acre = 10 Square Chains = 4840 Square Yards = 43,560 Sq. Ft.
1 Square Chain = 16 Square Rods = 484 Square Yards = 4356 Sq. Ft.
1 Square Rod = 30.25 Square Yards = 272.25 Square Feet = 625 Square Lines
1 Square Yard = 9 Square Feet
1 Square Foot = 144 Square Inches
An Acre equals a Square 208.7 Feet per Side

Cubic Measure
1 Cubic Yard = 27 Cubic Feet
1 Cubic Foot = 1728 Cubic Inches
1 Cord of Wood = 4 x 4 x 8 Feet = 128 Cubic Feet
1 Perch of Masonry = 16½ x 1½ x 1 Foot = 24.75 Cubic Feet

Avoirdupois or Commercial Weight
1 Gross or Long Ton = 2240 Pounds
1 Net or Short Ton = 2000 Pounds
1 Pound = 16 Ounces = 7000 Grains
1 Ounce = 16 Drachms = 437.5 Grains
1 Stone = 14 Pounds

Power
1 British Thermal Unit per Hour = 0.2931 Watts
1 Ton (Refrigeration) = 3.517 Kilowatts
1 Horsepower (Boiler) = 9.81 Kilowatts
1 Horsepower (550 ft-lb/s) = 0.746 Kilowatts

Shipping Measure
For Measuring Internal Capacity of a Vessel:
1 Register Ton = 100 Cubic Feet

For Measurement of Cargo:
Approximately 40 Cubic Feet of Merchandise is considered a Shipping Ton, unless that bulk would weigh more than 2000 Pounds, in which case Freight Charge may be based upon weight.

40 Cubic Feet = 32.143 U.S. Bushels = 31.16 Imp. Bushels

Liquid Measure
1 Imperial Gallon = 1.2009 U.S. Gallon = 277.42 Cu. In.
1 Cubic Foot = 7.48 U.S. Gallons

General Requirements — R0111 Summary of Work

R011110-10 Architectural Fees

Tabulated below are typical percentage fees by project size, for good professional architectural service. Fees may vary from those listed depending upon degree of design difficulty and economic conditions in any particular area.

Rates can be interpolated horizontally and vertically. Various portions of the same project requiring different rates should be adjusted proportionately. For alterations, add 50% to the fee for the first $500,000 of project cost and add 25% to the fee for project cost over $500,000.

Architectural fees tabulated below include Structural, Mechanical and Electrical Engineering Fees. They do not include the fees for special consultants such as kitchen planning, security, acoustical, interior design, etc.

Civil Engineering fees are included in the Architectural fee for project sites requiring minimal design such as city sites. However, separate Civil Engineering fees must be added when utility connections require design, drainage calculations are needed, stepped foundations are required, or provisions are required to protect adjacent wetlands.

Building Types	Total Project Size in Thousands of Dollars						
	100	250	500	1,000	5,000	10,000	50,000
Factories, garages, warehouses, repetitive housing	9.0%	8.0%	7.0%	6.2%	5.3%	4.9%	4.5%
Apartments, banks, schools, libraries, offices, municipal buildings	12.2	12.3	9.2	8.0	7.0	6.6	6.2
Churches, hospitals, homes, laboratories, museums, research	15.0	13.6	12.7	11.9	9.5	8.8	8.0
Memorials, monumental work, decorative furnishings	—	16.0	14.5	13.1	10.0	9.0	8.3

R011110-30 Engineering Fees

Typical **Structural Engineering Fees** based on type of construction and total project size. These fees are included in Architectural Fees.

Type of Construction	Total Project Size (in thousands of dollars)			
	$500	$500-$1,000	$1,000-$5,000	Over $5000
Industrial buildings, factories & warehouses	Technical payroll times 2.0 to 2.5	1.60%	1.25%	1.00%
Hotels, apartments, offices, dormitories, hospitals, public buildings, food stores		2.00%	1.70%	1.20%
Museums, banks, churches and cathedrals		2.00%	1.75%	1.25%
Thin shells, prestressed concrete, earthquake resistive		2.00%	1.75%	1.50%
Parking ramps, auditoriums, stadiums, convention halls, hangars & boiler houses		2.50%	2.00%	1.75%
Special buildings, major alterations, underpinning & future expansion	↓	Add to above 0.5%	Add to above 0.5%	Add to above 0.5%

For complex reinforced concrete or unusually complicated structures, add 20% to 50%.

Typical **Mechanical and Electrical Engineering Fees** are based on the size of the subcontract. The fee structure for both is shown below. These fees are included in Architectural Fees.

Type of Construction	Subcontract Size							
	$25,000	$50,000	$100,000	$225,000	$350,000	$500,000	$750,000	$1,000,000
Simple structures	6.4%	5.7%	4.8%	4.5%	4.4%	4.3%	4.2%	4.1%
Intermediate structures	8.0	7.3	6.5	5.6	5.1	5.0	4.9	4.8
Complex structures	10.1	9.0	9.0	8.0	7.5	7.5	7.0	7.0

For renovations, add 15% to 25% to applicable fee.

General Requirements   R0121 Allowances

R012153-10   Repair and Remodeling

Cost figures are based on new construction utilizing the most cost-effective combination of labor, equipment and material with the work scheduled in proper sequence to allow the various trades to accomplish their work in an efficient manner.

The costs for repair and remodeling work must be modified due to the following factors that may be present in any given repair and remodeling project.

1. Equipment usage curtailment due to the physical limitations of the project, with only hand-operated equipment being used.
2. Increased requirement for shoring and bracing to hold up the building while structural changes are being made and to allow for temporary storage of construction materials on above-grade floors.
3. Material handling becomes more costly due to having to move within the confines of an enclosed building. For multi-story construction, low capacity elevators and stairwells may be the only access to the upper floors.
4. Large amount of cutting and patching and attempting to match the existing construction is required. It is often more economical to remove entire walls rather than create many new door and window openings. This sort of trade-off has to be carefully analyzed.
5. Cost of protection of completed work is increased since the usual sequence of construction usually cannot be accomplished.
6. Economies of scale usually associated with new construction may not be present. If small quantities of components must be custom fabricated due to job requirements, unit costs will naturally increase. Also, if only small work areas are available at a given time, job scheduling between trades becomes difficult and subcontractor quotations may reflect the excessive start-up and shut-down phases of the job.
7. Work may have to be done on other than normal shifts and may have to be done around an existing production facility which has to stay in production during the course of the repair and remodeling.
8. Dust and noise protection of adjoining non-construction areas can involve substantial special protection and alter usual construction methods.
9. Job may be delayed due to unexpected conditions discovered during demolition or removal. These delays ultimately increase construction costs.
10. Piping and ductwork runs may not be as simple as for new construction. Wiring may have to be snaked through walls and floors.
11. Matching "existing construction" may be impossible because materials may no longer be manufactured. Substitutions may be expensive.
12. Weather protection of existing structure requires additional temporary structures to protect building at openings.
13. On small projects, because of local conditions, it may be necessary to pay a tradesman for a minimum of four hours for a task that is completed in one hour.

All of the above areas can contribute to increased costs for a repair and remodeling project. Each of the above factors should be considered in the planning, bidding and construction stage in order to minimize the increased costs associated with repair and remodeling jobs.

R012153-60   Security Factors

Contractors entering, working in, and exiting secure facilities often lose productive time during a normal workday. The recommended allowances in this section are intended to provide for the loss of productivity by increasing labor costs. Note that different costs are associated with searches upon entry only and searches upon entry and exit. Time spent in a queue is unpredictable and not part of these allowances. Contractors should plan ahead for this situation.

Security checkpoints are designed to reflect the level of security required to gain access or egress. An extreme example is when contractors, along with any materials, tools, equipment, and vehicles, must be physically searched and have all materials, tools, equipment, and vehicles inventoried and documented prior to both entry and exit.

Physical searches without going through the documentation process represent the next level and take up less time.

Electronic searches—passing through a detector or x-ray machine with no documentation of materials, tools, equipment, and vehicles—take less time than physical searches.

Visual searches of materials, tools, equipment, and vehicles represent the next level of security.

Finally, access by means of an ID card or displayed sticker takes the least amount of time.

Another consideration is if the searches described above are performed each and every day, or if they are performed only on the first day with access granted by ID card or displayed sticker for the remainder of the project. The figures for this situation have been calculated to represent the initial check-in as described and subsequent entry by ID card or displayed sticker for up to 20 days on site. For the situation described above, where the time period is beyond 20 days, the impact on labor cost is negligible.

There are situations where tradespeople must be accompanied by an escort and observed during the work day. The loss of freedom of movement will slow down productivity for the tradesperson. Costs for the observer have not been included. Those costs are normally born by the owner.

R012153-65   Infectious Disease Precautions

Contractors entering and working on job sites may be required to take precautions to prevent the spread of infectious diseases. Those precautions will reduce the amount of productive time during a normal workday. The recommended allowances in this section are intended to provide for the loss of productive time by increasing labor costs.

The estimator should be aware that one, many or none of these precautions apply to the line items in an estimate. Job site requirements and sound judgement must be applied.

Labor cost implications are based upon:

Temperature checks	Once per day
Donning/doffing masks and gloves	Four times per day (2 times each)
Washing hands (additional over normal)	Eight times per day
Informational meetings	Once per day
Maintaining social distance	Throughout the day
Disinfecting tools or equipment	Throughout the day

General Requirements — R0129 Payment Procedures

R012909-80 Sales Tax by State

State sales tax on materials is tabulated below (5 states have no sales tax). Many states allow local jurisdictions, such as a county or city, to levy additional sales tax.

Some projects may be sales tax exempt, particularly those constructed with public funds.

State	Tax (%)	State	Tax (%)	State	Tax (%)	State	Tax (%)
Alabama	4	Illinois	6.25	Montana	0	Rhode Island	7
Alaska	0	Indiana	7	Nebraska	5.5	South Carolina	6
Arizona	5.6	Iowa	6	Nevada	6.85	South Dakota	4.5
Arkansas	6.5	Kansas	6.5	New Hampshire	0	Tennessee	7
California	7.25	Kentucky	6	New Jersey	6.625	Texas	6.25
Colorado	2.9	Louisiana	4.45	New Mexico	5.125	Utah	6.10
Connecticut	6.35	Maine	5.5	New York	4	Vermont	6
Delaware	0	Maryland	6	North Carolina	4.75	Virginia	5.3
District of Columbia	6	Massachusetts	6.25	North Dakota	5	Washington	6.5
Florida	6	Michigan	6	Ohio	5.75	West Virginia	6
Georgia	4	Minnesota	6.875	Oklahoma	4.5	Wisconsin	5
Hawaii	4	Mississippi	7	Oregon	0	Wyoming	4
Idaho	6	Missouri	4.225	Pennsylvania	6	Average	5.11 %

Sales Tax by Province (Canada)

GST - a value-added tax, which the government imposes on most goods and services provided in or imported into Canada. PST - a retail sales tax, which five of the provinces impose on the prices of most goods and some services. QST - a value-added tax, similar to the federal GST, which Quebec imposes. HST - Three provinces have combined their retail sales taxes with the federal GST into one harmonized tax.

Province	PST (%)	QST (%)	GST (%)	HST (%)
Alberta	0	0	5	0
British Columbia	7	0	5	0
Manitoba	7	0	5	0
New Brunswick	0	0	0	15
Newfoundland	0	0	0	15
Northwest Territories	0	0	5	0
Nova Scotia	0	0	0	15
Ontario	0	0	0	13
Prince Edward Island	0	0	0	15
Quebec	9.975	0	5	0
Saskatchewan	6	0	5	0
Yukon	0	0	5	0

General Requirements — R0129 Payment Procedures

R012909-85 Unemployment Taxes and Social Security Taxes

State unemployment tax rates vary not only from state to state, but also with the experience rating of the contractor. The federal unemployment tax rate is 6.2% of the first $7,000 of wages. This is reduced by a credit of up to 5.4% for timely payment to the state. The minimum federal unemployment tax is 0.6% after all credits.

Social security (FICA) for 2023 is estimated at time of publication to be 7.65% of wages up to $147,000.

R012909-86 Unemployment Tax by State

Information is from the U.S. Department of Labor, state unemployment tax rates.

State	Tax (%)	State	Tax (%)	State	Tax (%)	State	Tax (%)
Alabama	6.10	Illinois	7.625	Montana	6.30	Rhode Island	9.80
Alaska	5.4	Indiana	7.4	Nebraska	5.4	South Carolina	5.46
Arizona	20.93	Iowa	7.5	Nevada	5.4	South Dakota	9.3
Arkansas	14.2	Kansas	7.6	New Hampshire	8.5	Tennessee	10.0
California	6.2	Kentucky	9.5	New Jersey	5.8	Texas	6.3
Colorado	10.39	Louisiana	6.2	New Mexico	6.4	Utah	7.3
Connecticut	6.8	Maine	6.16	New York	9.9	Vermont	6.5
Delaware	8.20	Maryland	10.50	North Carolina	5.76	Virginia	6.43
District of Columbia	7.6	Massachusetts	14.37	North Dakota	9.69	Washington	6.02
Florida	5.4	Michigan	10.3	Ohio	10.2	West Virginia	8.5
Georgia	8.1	Minnesota	9.5	Oklahoma	7.5	Wisconsin	8.5
Hawaii	5.8	Mississippi	5.6	Oregon	5.4	Wyoming	8.5
Idaho	5.4	Missouri	6.75	Pennsylvania	9.93	Median	7.50%

R012909-90 Overtime

One way to improve the completion date of a project or eliminate negative float from a schedule is to compress activity duration times. This can be achieved by increasing the crew size or working overtime with the proposed crew.

To determine the costs of working overtime to compress activity duration times, consider the following examples. Below is an overtime efficiency and cost chart based on a five, six, or seven day week with an eight through twelve hour day. Payroll percentage increases for time and one half and double times are shown for the various working days.

Days per Week	Hours per Day	Production Efficiency					Payroll Cost Factors	
		1st Week	2nd Week	3rd Week	4th Week	Average 4 Weeks	@ 1-1/2 Times	@ 2 Times
5	8	100%	100%	100%	100%	100%	1.000	1.000
	9	100	100	95	90	96	1.056	1.111
	10	100	95	90	85	93	1.100	1.200
	11	95	90	75	65	81	1.136	1.273
	12	90	85	70	60	76	1.167	1.333
6	8	100	100	95	90	96	1.083	1.167
	9	100	95	90	85	93	1.130	1.259
	10	95	90	85	80	88	1.167	1.333
	11	95	85	70	65	79	1.197	1.394
	12	90	80	65	60	74	1.222	1.444
7	8	100	95	85	75	89	1.143	1.286
	9	95	90	80	70	84	1.183	1.365
	10	90	85	75	65	79	1.214	1.429
	11	85	80	65	60	73	1.240	1.481
	12	85	75	60	55	69	1.262	1.524

General Requirements R0131 Project Management & Coordination

R013113-40 Builder's Risk Insurance

Builder's risk insurance is insurance on a building during construction. Premiums are paid by the owner or the contractor. Blasting, collapse and underground insurance would raise total insurance costs.

R013113-50 General Contractor's Overhead

There are two distinct types of overhead on a construction project: Project overhead and main office overhead. Project overhead includes those costs at a construction site not directly associated with the installation of construction materials. Examples of project overhead costs include the following:

1. Superintendent
2. Construction office and storage trailers
3. Temporary sanitary facilities
4. Temporary utilities
5. Security fencing
6. Photographs
7. Cleanup
8. Performance and payment bonds

The above project overhead items are also referred to as general requirements and therefore are estimated in Division 1. Division 1 is the first division listed in the CSI MasterFormat but it is usually the last division estimated. The sum of the costs in Divisions 1 through 49 is referred to as the sum of the direct costs.

All construction projects also include indirect costs. The primary components of indirect costs are the contractor's main office overhead and profit. The amount of the main office overhead expense varies depending on the following:

1. Owner's compensation
2. Project managers' and estimators' wages
3. Clerical support wages
4. Office rent and utilities
5. Corporate legal and accounting costs
6. Advertising
7. Automobile expenses
8. Association dues
9. Travel and entertainment expenses

These costs are usually calculated as a percentage of annual sales volume. This percentage can range from 35% for a small contractor doing less than $500,000 to 5% for a large contractor with sales in excess of $100 million.

R013113-55 Installing Contractor's Overhead

Installing contractors (subcontractors) also incur costs for general requirements and main office overhead.

Included within the total incl. overhead and profit costs is a percent mark-up for overhead that includes:

1. Compensation and benefits for office staff and project managers
2. Office rent, utilities, business equipment, and maintenance
3. Corporate legal and accounting costs
4. Advertising
5. Vehicle expenses (for office staff and project managers)
6. Association dues
7. Travel, entertainment
8. Insurance
9. Small tools and equipment

General Requirements — R0131 Project Management & Coordination

R013113-60 Workers' Compensation Insurance Rates by Trade

The table below tabulates the national averages for Workers' Compensation insurance rates by trade and type of building. The average "Insurance Rate" is multiplied by the "% of Building Cost" for each trade. This produces the "Workers' Compensation Cost" by % of total labor cost, to be added for each trade by building type to determine the weighted average Workers' Compensation rate for the building types analyzed.

Trade	Insurance Rate (% Labor Cost) Range			Insurance Rate Average	% of Building Cost Office Bldgs.	Schools & Apts.	Mfg.	Workers' Compensation Office Bldgs.	Schools & Apts.	Mfg.
Excavation, Grading, etc.	1.9 %	to	14.7%	8.3%	4.8%	4.9%	4.5%	0.40%	0.41%	0.37%
Piles & Foundations	2.1	to	32.0	17.0	7.1	5.2	8.7	1.21	0.88	1.48
Concrete	2.6	to	26.5	14.5	5.0	14.8	3.7	0.73	2.15	0.54
Masonry	2.9	to	48.0	25.5	6.9	7.5	1.9	1.76	1.91	0.48
Structural Steel	2.3	to	30.9	16.6	10.7	3.9	17.6	1.78	0.65	2.92
Miscellaneous & Ornamental Metals	2.2	to	22.6	12.4	2.8	4.0	3.6	0.35	0.50	0.45
Carpentry & Millwork	2.7	to	25.2	14.0	3.7	4.0	0.5	0.52	0.56	0.07
Metal or Composition Siding	3.2	to	129.7	66.4	2.3	0.3	4.3	1.53	0.20	2.86
Roofing	4.0	to	101.9	52.9	2.3	2.6	3.1	1.22	1.38	1.64
Doors & Hardware	2.5	to	26.3	14.4	0.9	1.4	0.4	0.13	0.20	0.06
Sash & Glazing	3.1	to	18.1	10.6	3.5	4.0	1.0	0.37	0.42	0.11
Lath & Plaster	1.2	to	32.4	16.8	3.3	6.9	0.8	0.55	1.16	0.13
Tile, Marble & Floors	1.7	to	19.5	10.6	2.6	3.0	0.5	0.28	0.32	0.05
Acoustical Ceilings	1.4	to	18.3	9.9	2.4	0.2	0.3	0.24	0.02	0.03
Painting	2.1	to	35.8	18.9	1.5	1.6	1.6	0.28	0.30	0.30
Interior Partitions	2.7	to	26.8	14.7	3.9	4.3	4.4	0.57	0.63	0.65
Miscellaneous Items	1.3	to	97.7	49.5	5.2	3.7	9.7	2.57	1.83	4.80
Elevators	1.2	to	8.3	4.8	2.1	1.1	2.2	0.10	0.05	0.11
Sprinklers	1.5	to	13.2	7.3	0.5	—	2.0	0.04	—	0.15
Plumbing	1.3	to	12.6	6.9	4.9	7.2	5.2	0.34	0.50	0.36
Heat., Vent., Air Conditioning	2.1	to	14.7	8.4	13.5	11.0	12.9	1.13	0.92	1.08
Electrical	1.4	to	9.5	5.5	10.1	8.4	11.1	0.56	0.46	0.61
Total	1.2 %	to	129.7%	65.4	100.0%	100.0%	100.0%	16.66%	15.45%	19.25%
				Overall Weighted Average	17.12%					

Workers' Compensation Insurance Rates by States

The table below lists the weighted average Workers' Compensation base rate for each state with a factor comparing this with the national average of 8.4%.

State	Weighted Average	Factor	State	Weighted Average	Factor	State	Weighted Average	Factor
Alabama	21.1%	251	Kentucky	21.0%	250	North Dakota	7.6%	90
Alaska	13.3	158	Louisiana	31.3	373	Ohio	7.8	93
Arizona	11.6	138	Maine	14.9	177	Oklahoma	14.3	170
Arkansas	8.4	100	Maryland	15.8	188	Oregon	12.5	149
California	35.8	426	Massachusetts	16.1	192	Pennsylvania	34.9	415
Colorado	7.2	86	Michigan	9.0	107	Rhode Island	14.7	175
Connecticut	23.9	285	Minnesota	22.7	270	South Carolina	31.6	376
Delaware	15.9	189	Mississippi	15.1	180	South Dakota	13.3	158
District of Columbia	12.8	152	Missouri	23.1	275	Tennessee	9.6	114
Florida	13.4	160	Montana	14.6	174	Texas	5.7	68
Georgia	55.3	658	Nebraska	18.1	215	Utah	7.9	94
Hawaii	16.8	200	Nevada	13.5	161	Vermont	15.6	186
Idaho	14.2	169	New Hampshire	14.9	177	Virginia	10.4	124
Illinois	34.5	411	New Jersey	23.2	276	Washington	11.8	140
Indiana	5.8	69	New Mexico	23.7	282	West Virginia	6.6	79
Iowa	17.2	205	New York	28.2	336	Wisconsin	17.1	204
Kansas	10.3	123	North Carolina	20.8	248	Wyoming	8.4	100
			Weighted Average for U.S. is	17.1% of payroll = 100%				

The weighted average skilled worker rate for 35 trades is 17.12%. For bidding purposes, apply the full value of Workers' Compensation directly to total labor costs, or if labor is 38%, materials 42% and overhead and profit 20% of total cost, carry 38/80 x 17.12% = 8.13% of cost (before overhead and profit) into overhead. Rates vary not only from state to state but also with the experience rating of the contractor.

Rates are the most current available at the time of publication.

General Requirements — R0131 Project Management & Coordination

R013113-80   Performance Bond

This table shows the cost of a Performance Bond for a construction job scheduled to be completed in 12 months. Add 1% of the premium cost per month for jobs requiring more than 12 months to complete. The rates are "standard" rates offered to contractors that the bonding company considers financially sound and capable of doing the work. Preferred rates are offered by some bonding companies based upon financial strength of the contractor. Actual rates vary from contractor to contractor and from bonding company to bonding company. Contractors should prequalify through a bonding agency before submitting a bid on a contract that requires a bond.

Contract Amount	Building Construction Class B Projects			Highways & Bridges Class A New Construction			Class A-1 Highway Resurfacing		
First $ 100,000 bid	$25.00 per M			$15.00 per M			$9.40 per M		
Next 400,000 bid	$ 2,500	plus $15.00	per M	$ 1,500	plus $10.00	per M	$ 940	plus $7.20	per M
Next 2,000,000 bid	8,500	plus 10.00	per M	5,500	plus 7.00	per M	3,820	plus 5.00	per M
Next 2,500,000 bid	28,500	plus 7.50	per M	19,500	plus 5.50	per M	15,820	plus 4.50	per M
Next 2,500,000 bid	47,250	plus 7.00	per M	33,250	plus 5.00	per M	28,320	plus 4.50	per M
Over 7,500,000 bid	64,750	plus 6.00	per M	45,750	plus 4.50	per M	39,570	plus 4.00	per M

General Requirements — R0154 Construction Aids

R015423-10   Steel Tubular Scaffolding

On new construction, tubular scaffolding is efficient up to 60' high or five stories. Above this it is usually better to use a hung scaffolding if construction permits. Swing scaffolding operations may interfere with tenants. In this case, the tubular is more practical at all heights.

In repairing or cleaning the front of an existing building the cost of tubular scaffolding per S.F. of building front increases as the height increases above the first tier. The first tier cost is relatively high due to leveling and alignment.

The minimum efficient crew for erecting and dismantling is three workers. They can set up and remove 18 frame sections per day up to 5 stories high. For 6 to 12 stories high, a crew of four is most efficient. Use two or more on top and two on the bottom for handing up or hoisting. They can also set up and remove 18 frame sections per day. At 7' horizontal spacing, this will run about 800 S.F. per day of erecting and dismantling. Time for placing and removing planks must be added to the above. A crew of three can place and remove 72 planks per day up to 5 stories. For over 5 stories, a crew of four can place and remove 80 planks per day.

The table below shows the number of pieces required to erect tubular steel scaffolding for 1000 S.F. of building frontage. This area is made up of a scaffolding system that is 12 frames (11 bays) long by 2 frames high.

For jobs under twenty-five frames, add 50% to rental cost. Rental rates will be lower for jobs over three months duration. Large quantities for long periods can reduce rental rates by 20%.

Description of Component	Number of Pieces for 1000 S.F. of Building Front	Unit
5' Wide Standard Frame, 6'-4" High	24	Ea.
Leveling Jack & Plate	24	
Cross Brace	44	
Side Arm Bracket, 21"	12	
Guardrail Post	12	
Guardrail, 7' section	22	
Stairway Section	2	
Stairway Starter Bar	1	
Stairway Inside Handrail	2	
Stairway Outside Handrail	2	
Walk-Thru Frame Guardrail	2	

Scaffolding is often used as falsework over 15' high during construction of cast-in-place concrete beams and slabs. Two foot wide scaffolding is generally used for heavy beam construction. The span between frames depends upon the load to be carried with a maximum span of 5'.

Heavy duty shoring frames with a capacity of 10,000#/leg can be spaced up to 10' O.C. depending upon form support design and loading.

Scaffolding used as horizontal shoring requires less than half the material required with conventional shoring.

On new construction, erection is done by carpenters.

Rolling towers supporting horizontal shores can reduce labor and speed the job. For maintenance work, catwalks with spans up to 70' can be supported by the rolling towers.

General Requirements R0154 Construction Aids

R015433-10 Contractor Equipment

Rental Rates shown elsewhere in the data set pertain to late model high quality machines in excellent working condition, rented from equipment dealers. Rental rates from contractors may be substantially lower than the rental rates from equipment dealers depending upon economic conditions; for older, less productive machines, reduce rates by a maximum of 15%. Any overtime must be added to the base rates. For shift work, rates are lower. Usual rule of thumb is 150% of one shift rate for two shifts; 200% for three shifts.

For periods of less than one week, operated equipment is usually more economical to rent than renting bare equipment and hiring an operator.

Costs to move equipment to a job site (mobilization) or from a job site (demobilization) are not included in rental rates, nor in any Equipment costs on any Unit Price line items or crew listings. These costs can be found elsewhere. If a piece of equipment is already at a job site, it is not appropriate to utilize mob/demob costs in an estimate again.

Rental rates vary throughout the country with larger cities generally having lower rates. Lease plans for new equipment are available for periods in excess of six months with a percentage of payments applying toward purchase.

Rental rates can also be treated as reimbursement costs for contractor-owned equipment. Owned equipment costs include depreciation, loan payments, interest, taxes, insurance, storage, and major repairs.

Monthly rental rates vary from 2% to 5% of the cost of the equipment depending on the anticipated life of the equipment and its wearing parts. Weekly rates are about 1/3 the monthly rates and daily rental rates are about 1/3 the weekly rates.

The hourly operating costs for each piece of equipment include costs to the user such as fuel, oil, lubrication, normal expendables for the equipment, and a percentage of the mechanic's wages chargeable to maintenance. The hourly operating costs listed do not include the operator's wages.

The daily cost for equipment used in the standard crews is figured by dividing the weekly rate by five, then adding eight times the hourly operating cost to give the total daily equipment cost, not including the operator. This figure is in the right hand column of the Equipment listings under Equipment Cost/Day.

Pile Driving rates shown for the pile hammer and extractor do not include leads, cranes, boilers or compressors. Vibratory pile driving requires an added field specialist during set-up and pile driving operation for the electric model. The hydraulic model requires a field specialist for set-up only. Up to 125 reuses of sheet piling are possible using vibratory drivers. For normal conditions, crane capacity for hammer type and size is as follows.

Crane Capacity	Hammer Type and Size		
	Air or Steam	Diesel	Vibratory
25 ton	to 8,750 ft.-lb.		70 H.P.
40 ton	15,000 ft.-lb.	to 32,000 ft.-lb.	170 H.P.
60 ton	25,000 ft.-lb.		300 H.P.
100 ton		112,000 ft.-lb.	

Cranes should be specified for the job by size, building and site characteristics, availability, performance characteristics, and duration of time required.

Backhoes & Shovels rent for about the same as equivalent size cranes but maintenance and operating expenses are higher. The crane operator's rate must be adjusted for high boom heights. Average adjustments: for 150' boom add 2% per hour; over 185', add 4% per hour; over 210', add 6% per hour; over 250', add 8% per hour and over 295', add 12% per hour.

Tower Cranes of the climbing or static type have jibs from 50' to 200' and capacities at maximum reach range from 4,000 to 14,000 pounds. Lifting capacities increase up to maximum load as the hook radius decreases.

Typical rental rates, based on purchase price, are about 2% to 3% per month.

Erection and dismantling run between 500 and 2000 labor hours. Climbing operation takes 10 labor hours per 20' climb. Crane dead time is about 5 hours per 40' climb. If crane is bolted to side of the building add cost of ties and extra mast sections. Climbing cranes have from 80' to 180' of mast while static cranes have 80' to 800' of mast.

Truck Cranes can be converted to tower cranes by using tower attachments. Mast heights over 400' have been used.

A single 100' high material **Hoist and Tower** can be erected and dismantled in about 400 labor hours; a double 100' high hoist and tower in about 600 labor hours. Erection times for additional heights are 3 and 4 labor hours per vertical foot respectively up to 150', and 4 to 5 labor hours per vertical foot over 150' high. A 40' high portable Buck hoist takes about 160 labor hours to erect and dismantle. Additional heights take 2 labor hours per vertical foot to 80' and 3 labor hours per vertical foot for the next 100'. Most material hoists do not meet local code requirements for carrying personnel.

A 150' high **Personnel Hoist** requires about 500 to 800 labor hours to erect and dismantle. Budget erection time at 5 labor hours per vertical foot for all trades. Local code requirements or labor scarcity requiring overtime can add up to 50% to any of the above erection costs.

Earthmoving Equipment: The selection of earthmoving equipment depends upon the type and quantity of material, moisture content, haul distance, haul road, time available, and equipment available. Short haul cut and fill operations may require dozers only, while another operation may require excavators, a fleet of trucks, and spreading and compaction equipment. Stockpiled material and granular material are easily excavated with front end loaders. Scrapers are most economically used with hauls between 300' and 1-1/2 miles if adequate haul roads can be maintained. Shovels are often used for blasted rock and any material where a vertical face of 8' or more can be excavated. Special conditions may dictate the use of draglines, clamshells, or backhoes. Spreading and compaction equipment must be matched to the soil characteristics, the compaction required and the rate the fill is being supplied.

R015433-15 Heavy Lifting

Hydraulic Climbing Jacks

The use of hydraulic heavy lift systems is an alternative to conventional type crane equipment. The lifting, lowering, pushing, or pulling mechanism is a hydraulic climbing jack moving on a square steel jackrod from 1-5/8" to 4" square, or a steel cable. The jackrod or cable can be vertical or horizontal, stationary or movable, depending on the individual application. When the jackrod is stationary, the climbing jack will climb the rod and push or pull the load along with itself. When the climbing jack is stationary, the jackrod is movable with the load attached to the end and the climbing jack will lift or lower the jackrod with the attached load. The heavy lift system is normally operated by a single control lever located at the hydraulic pump.

The system is flexible in that one or more climbing jacks can be applied wherever a load support point is required, and the rate of lift synchronized.

Economic benefits have been demonstrated on projects such as: erection of ground assembled roofs and floors, complete bridge spans, girders and trusses, towers, chimney liners and steel vessels, storage tanks, and heavy machinery. Other uses are raising and lowering offshore work platforms, caissons, tunnel sections and pipelines.

General Requirements | R0154 Construction Aids

R015436-50 Mobilization

Costs to move rented construction equipment to a job site from an equipment dealer's or contractor's yard (mobilization) or off the job site (demobilization) are not included in the rental or operating rates, nor in the equipment cost on a unit price line or in a crew listing. These costs can be found consolidated in the Mobilization section of the data and elsewhere in particular site work sections. If a piece of equipment is already on the job site, it is not appropriate to include mob/demob costs in a new estimate that requires use of that equipment. The following table identifies approximate sizes of rented construction equipment that would be hauled on a towed trailer. Because this listing is not all-encompassing, the user can infer as to what size trailer might be required for a piece of equipment not listed.

3-ton Trailer	20-ton Trailer	40-ton Trailer	50-ton Trailer
20 H.P. Excavator	110 H.P. Excavator	200 H.P. Excavator	270 H.P. Excavator
50 H.P. Skid Steer	165 H.P. Dozer	300 H.P. Dozer	Small Crawler Crane
35 H.P. Roller	150 H.P. Roller	400 H.P. Scraper	500 H.P. Scraper
40 H.P. Trencher	Backhoe	450 H.P. Art. Dump Truck	500 H.P. Art. Dump Truck

Existing Conditions — R0241 Demolition

R024119-10 Demolition Defined

Whole Building Demolition - Demolition of the whole building with no concern for any particular building element, component, or material type being demolished. This type of demolition is accomplished with large pieces of construction equipment that break up the structure, load it into trucks and haul it to a disposal site, but disposal or dump fees are not included. Demolition of below-grade foundation elements, such as footings, foundation walls, grade beams, slabs on grade, etc., is not included. Certain mechanical equipment containing flammable liquids or ozone-depleting refrigerants, electric lighting elements, communication equipment components, and other building elements may contain hazardous waste, and must be removed, either selectively or carefully, as hazardous waste before the building can be demolished.

Foundation Demolition - Demolition of below-grade foundation footings, foundation walls, grade beams, and slabs on grade. This type of demolition is accomplished by hand or pneumatic hand tools, and does not include saw cutting, or handling, loading, hauling, or disposal of the debris.

Gutting - Removal of building interior finishes and electrical/mechanical systems down to the load-bearing and sub-floor elements of the rough building frame, with no concern for any particular building element, component, or material type being demolished. This type of demolition is accomplished by hand or pneumatic hand tools, and includes loading into trucks, but not hauling, disposal or dump fees, scaffolding, or shoring. Certain mechanical equipment containing flammable liquids or ozone-depleting refrigerants, electric lighting elements, communication equipment components, and other building elements may contain hazardous waste, and must be removed, either selectively or carefully, as hazardous waste, before the building is gutted.

Selective Demolition - Demolition of a selected building element, component, or finish, with some concern for surrounding or adjacent elements, components, or finishes (see the first Subdivision (s) at the beginning of appropriate Divisions). This type of demolition is accomplished by hand or pneumatic hand tools, and does not include handling, loading, storing, hauling, or disposal of the debris, scaffolding, or shoring. "Gutting" methods may be used in order to save time, but damage that is caused to surrounding or adjacent elements, components, or finishes may have to be repaired at a later time.

Careful Removal - Removal of a piece of service equipment, building element or component, or material type, with great concern for both the removed item and surrounding or adjacent elements, components or finishes. The purpose of careful removal may be to protect the removed item for later re-use, preserve a higher salvage value of the removed item, or replace an item while taking care to protect surrounding or adjacent elements, components, connections, or finishes from cosmetic and/or structural damage. An approximation of the time required to perform this type of removal is 1/3 to 1/2 the time it would take to install a new item of like kind (see Reference Number R220105-10). This type of removal is accomplished by hand or pneumatic hand tools, and does not include loading, hauling, or storing the removed item, scaffolding, shoring, or lifting equipment.

Cutout Demolition - Demolition of a small quantity of floor, wall, roof, or other assembly, with concern for the appearance and structural integrity of the surrounding materials. This type of demolition is accomplished by hand or pneumatic hand tools, and does not include saw cutting, handling, loading, hauling, or disposal of debris, scaffolding, or shoring.

Rubbish Handling - Work activities that involve handling, loading or hauling of debris. Generally, the cost of rubbish handling must be added to the cost of all types of demolition, with the exception of whole building demolition.

Minor Site Demolition - Demolition of site elements outside the footprint of a building. This type of demolition is accomplished by hand or pneumatic hand tools, or with larger pieces of construction equipment, and may include loading a removed item onto a truck (check the Crew for equipment used). It does not include saw cutting, hauling or disposal of debris, and, sometimes, handling or loading.

R024119-20 Dumpsters

Dumpster rental costs on construction sites are presented in two ways.

The cost per week rental includes the delivery of the dumpster; its pulling or emptying once per week, and its final removal. The assumption is made that the dumpster contractor could choose to empty a dumpster by simply bringing in an empty unit and removing the full one. These costs also include the disposal of the materials in the dumpster.

The Alternate Pricing can be used when actual planned conditions are not approximated by the weekly numbers. For example, these lines can be used when a dumpster is needed for 4 weeks and will need to be emptied 2 or 3 times per week. Conversely the Alternate Pricing lines can be used when a dumpster will be rented for several weeks or months but needs to be emptied only a few times over this period.

Existing Conditions — R0265 Underground Storage Tank Removal

R026510-20 Underground Storage Tank Removal

Underground Storage Tank Removal can be divided into two categories: Non-Leaking and Leaking. Prior to removing an underground storage tank, tests should be made, with the proper authorities present, to determine whether a tank has been leaking or the surrounding soil has been contaminated.

To safely remove Liquid Underground Storage Tanks:
1. Excavate to the top of the tank.
2. Disconnect all piping.
3. Open all tank vents and access ports.
4. Remove all liquids and/or sludge.
5. Purge the tank with an inert gas.
6. Provide access to the inside of the tank and clean out the interior using proper personal protective equipment (PPE).
7. Excavate soil surrounding the tank using proper PPE for on-site personnel.
8. Pull and properly dispose of the tank.
9. Clean up the site of all contaminated material.
10. Install new tanks or close the excavation.

Existing Conditions — R0282 Asbestos Remediation

R028213-20 Asbestos Removal Process

Asbestos removal is accomplished by a specialty contractor who understands the federal and state regulations regarding the handling and disposal of the material. The process of asbestos removal is divided into many individual steps. An accurate estimate can be calculated only after all the steps have been priced.

The steps are generally as follows:
1. Obtain an asbestos abatement plan from an industrial hygienist.
2. Monitor the air quality in and around the removal area and along the path of travel between the removal area and transport area. This establishes the background contamination.
3. Construct a two part decontamination chamber at entrance to removal area.
4. Install a HEPA filter to create a negative pressure in the removal area.
5. Install wall, floor and ceiling protection as required by the plan, usually 2 layers of fireproof 6 mil polyethylene.
6. Industrial hygienist visually inspects work area to verify compliance with plan.
7. Provide temporary supports for conduit and piping affected by the removal process.
8. Proceed with asbestos removal and bagging process. Monitor air quality as described in Step #2. Discontinue operations when contaminate levels exceed applicable standards.
9. Document the legal disposal of materials in accordance with EPA standards.
10. Thoroughly clean removal area including all ledges, crevices and surfaces.
11. Post abatement inspection by industrial hygienist to verify plan compliance.
12. Provide a certificate from a licensed industrial hygienist attesting that contaminate levels are within acceptable standards before returning area to regular use.

Thermal & Moist. Protec. — R0784 Firestopping

R078413-30 Firestopping

Firestopping is the sealing of structural, mechanical, electrical and other penetrations through fire-rated assemblies. The basic components of firestop systems are safing insulation and firestop sealant on both sides of wall penetrations and the top side of floor penetrations.

Pipe penetrations are assumed to be through concrete, grout, or joint compound and can be sleeved or unsleeved. Costs for the penetrations and sleeves are not included. An annular space of 1″ is assumed. Escutcheons are not included.

A metallic pipe is assumed to be copper, aluminum, cast iron or similar metallic material. An insulated metallic pipe is assumed to be covered with a thermal insulating jacket of varying thickness and materials.

A non-metallic pipe is assumed to be PVC, CPVC, FR Polypropylene or similar plastic piping material. Intumescent firestop sealants or wrap strips are included. Collars on both sides of wall penetrations and a sheet metal plate on the underside of floor penetrations are included.

Ductwork is assumed to be sheet metal, stainless steel or similar metallic material. Duct penetrations are assumed to be through concrete, grout or joint compound. Costs for penetrations and sleeves are not included. An annular space of 1/2″ is assumed.

Multi-trade openings include costs for sheet metal forms, firestop mortar, wrap strips, collars and sealants as necessary.

Structural penetrations joints are assumed to be 1/2″ or less. CMU walls are assumed to be within 1-1/2″ of the metal deck. Drywall walls are assumed to be tight to the underside of metal decking.

Metal panel, glass or curtain wall systems include a spandrel area of 5′ filled with mineral wool foil-faced insulation. Fasteners and stiffeners are included.

Finishes — R0991 Painting

R099100-10 Painting Estimating Techniques

Proper estimating methodology is needed to obtain an accurate painting estimate. There is no known reliable shortcut or square foot method. The following steps should be followed:

- List all surfaces to be painted, with an accurate quantity (area) of each. Items having similar surface condition, finish, application method and accessibility may be grouped together.
- List all the tasks required for each surface to be painted, including surface preparation, masking, and protection of adjacent surfaces. Surface preparation may include minor repairs, washing, sanding and puttying.
- Select the proper Means line for each task. Review and consider all adjustments to labor and materials for type of paint and location of work. Apply the height adjustment carefully. For instance, when applying the adjustment for work over 8' high to a wall that is 12' high, apply the adjustment only to the area between 8' and 12' high, and not to the entire wall.

When applying more than one percent (%) adjustment, apply each to the base cost of the data, rather than applying one percentage adjustment on top of the other.

When estimating the cost of painting walls and ceilings remember to add the brushwork for all cut-ins at inside corners and around windows and doors as a LF measure. One linear foot of cut-in with a brush equals one square foot of painting.

All items for spray painting include the labor for roll-back.

Deduct for openings greater than 100 SF or openings that extend from floor to ceiling and are greater than 5' wide. Do not deduct small openings.

The cost of brushes, rollers, ladders and spray equipment are considered part of a painting contractor's overhead, and should not be added to the estimate. The cost of rented equipment such as scaffolding and swing staging should be added to the estimate.

Plumbing — R2201 Operation & Maintenance of Plumbing

R220102-20 Labor Adjustment Factors

Labor Adjustment Factors are provided for Divisions 21, 22, and 23 to assist the mechanical estimator account for the various complexities and special conditions of any particular project. While a single percentage has been entered on each line of Division 22 01 02.20, it should be understood that these are just suggested midpoints of ranges of values commonly used by mechanical estimators. They may be increased or decreased depending on the severity of the special conditions.

The group for "existing occupied buildings" has been the subject of requests for explanation. Actually there are two stages to this group: buildings that are existing and "finished" but unoccupied, and those that also are occupied. Buildings that are "finished" may result in higher labor costs due to the workers having to be more careful not to damage finished walls, ceilings, floors, etc. and may necessitate special protective coverings and barriers. Also corridor bends and doorways may not accommodate long pieces of pipe or larger pieces of equipment. Work above an already hung ceiling can be very time consuming. The addition of occupants may force the work to be done on premium time (nights and/or weekends), eliminate the possible use of some preferred tools such as pneumatic drivers, powder charged drivers, etc. The estimator should evaluate the access to the work area and just how the work is going to be accomplished to arrive at an increase in labor costs over "normal" new construction productivity.

Plumbing — R2201 Operation & Maintenance of Plumbing

R220105-10 Demolition (Selective vs. Removal for Replacement)

Demolition can be divided into two basic categories.

One type of demolition involves the removal of material with no concern for its replacement. The labor-hours to estimate this work are found under "Selective Demolition" in the Fire Protection, Plumbing and HVAC Divisions. It is selective in that individual items or all the material installed as a system or trade grouping such as plumbing or heating systems are removed. This may be accomplished by the easiest way possible, such as sawing, torch cutting, or sledge hammering as well as simple unbolting.

The second type of demolition is the removal of some items for repair or replacement. This removal may involve careful draining, opening of unions, disconnecting and tagging electrical connections, capping pipes/ducts to prevent entry of debris or leakage of the material contained as well as transporting the item away from its in-place location to a truck/dumpster. An approximation of the time required to accomplish this type of demolition is to use half of the time indicated as necessary to install a new unit. For example: installation of a new pump might be listed as requiring 6 labor-hours so if we had to estimate the removal of the old pump we would allow an additional 3 hours for a total of 9 hours. That is, the complete replacement of a defective pump with a new pump would be estimated to take 9 labor-hours.

Plumbing — R2205 Common Work Results for Plumbing

R220523-80 Valve Materials

VALVE MATERIALS

Bronze:
Bronze is one of the oldest materials used to make valves. It is most commonly used in hot and cold water systems and other non-corrosive services. It is often used as a seating surface in larger iron body valves to ensure tight closure.

Carbon Steel:
Carbon steel is a high strength material. Therefore, valves made from this metal are used in higher pressure services, such as steam lines up to 600 psi at 850° F. Many steel valves are available with butt-weld ends for economy and are generally used in high pressure steam service as well as other higher pressure non-corrosive services.

Forged Steel:
Valves from tough carbon steel are used in service up to 2000 psi and temperatures up to 1000° F in Gate, Globe and Check valves.

Iron:
Valves are normally used in medium to large pipe lines to control non-corrosive fluid and gases, where pressures do not exceed 250 psi at 450° F or 500 psi cold water, oil or gas.

Stainless Steel:
Developed steel alloys can be used in over 90% corrosive services.

Plastic PVC:
This is used in a great variety of valves generally in high corrosive service with lower temperatures and pressures.

VALVE SERVICE PRESSURES

Pressure ratings on valves provide an indication of the safe operating pressure for a valve at some elevated temperature. This temperature is dependent upon the materials used and the fabrication of the valve. When specific data is not available, a good "rule-of-thumb" to follow is the temperature of saturated steam on the primary rating indicated on the valve body. Example: The valve has the number 150S printed on the side indicating 150 psi and hence, a maximum operating temperature of 367° F (temperature of saturated steam and 150 psi).

DEFINITIONS

1. "WOG" – Water, oil, gas (cold working pressures).
2. "SWP" – Steam working pressure.
3. 100% area (full port) – means the area through the valve is equal to or greater than the area of standard pipe.
4. "Standard Opening" – means that the area through the valve is less than the area of standard pipe and therefore these valves should be used only where restriction of flow is unimportant.
5. "Round Port" – means the valve has a full round opening through the plug and body, of the same size and area as standard pipe.
6. "Rectangular Port" – valves have rectangular shaped ports through the plug body. The area of the port is either equal to 100% of the area of standard pipe, or restricted (standard opening). In either case it is clearly marked.
7. "ANSI" – American National Standards Institute.

R220523-90 Valve Selection Considerations

INTRODUCTION: In any piping application, valve performance is critical. Valves should be selected to give the best performance at the lowest cost.

The following is a list of performance characteristics generally expected of valves.

1. Stopping flow or starting it.
2. Throttling flow (Modulation).
3. Flow direction changing.
4. Checking backflow (Permitting flow in only one direction).
5. Relieving or regulating pressure.

In order to properly select the right valve, some facts must be determined.

A. What liquid or gas will flow through the valve?
B. Does the fluid contain suspended particles?
C. Does the fluid remain in liquid form at all times?
D. Which metals does fluid corrode?
E. What are the pressure and temperature limits? (As temperature and pressure rise, so will the price of the valve.)
F. Is there constant line pressure?
G. Is the valve merely an on-off valve?
H. Will checking of backflow be required?
I. Will the valve operate frequently or infrequently?

Valves are classified by design type into such classifications as Gate, Globe, Angle, Check, Ball, Butterfly and Plug. They are also classified by end connection, stem, pressure restrictions and material such as bronze, cast iron, etc. Each valve has a specific use. A quality valve used correctly will provide a lifetime of trouble-free service, but a high quality valve installed in the wrong service may require frequent attention.

Plumbing
R2205 Common Work Results for Plumbing

STEM TYPES
(OS & Y)—Rising Stem-Outside Screw and Yoke
Offers a visual indication of whether the valve is open or closed. Recommended where high temperatures, corrosives, and solids in the line might cause damage to inside-valve stem threads. The stem threads are engaged by the yoke bushing so the stem rises through the hand wheel as it is turned.

(R.S.)—Rising Stem-Inside Screw
Adequate clearance for operation must be provided because both the hand wheel and the stem rise.
The valve wedge position is indicated by the position of the stem and hand wheel.

(N.R.S.)—Non-Rising Stem-Inside Screw
A minimum clearance is required for operating this type of valve. Excessive wear or damage to stem threads inside the valve may be caused by heat, corrosion, and solids. Because the hand wheel and stem do not rise, wedge position cannot be visually determined.

VALVE TYPES
Gate Valves
Provide full flow, minute pressure drop, minimum turbulence and minimum fluid trapped in the line.
They are normally used where operation is infrequent.

Globe Valves
Globe valves are designed for throttling and/or frequent operation with positive shut-off. Particular attention must be paid to the several types of seating materials available to avoid unnecessary wear. The seats must be compatible with the fluid in service and may be composition or metal. The configuration of the Globe valve opening causes turbulence which results in increased resistance. Most bronze Globe valves are rising stem-inside screw, but they are also available on O.S. & Y.

Angle Valves
The fundamental difference between the Angle valve and the Globe valve is the fluid flow through the Angle valve. It makes a 90° turn and offers less resistance to flow than the Globe valve while replacing an elbow. An Angle valve thus reduces the number of joints and installation time.

Plumbing
R2205 Common Work Results for Plumbing

Check Valves

Check valves are designed to prevent backflow by automatically seating when the direction of fluid is reversed.

Swing Check valves are generally installed with Gate-valves, as they provide comparable full flow. Usually recommended for lines where flow velocities are low and should not be used on lines with pulsating flow. Recommended for horizontal installation, or in vertical lines only where flow is upward.

Lift Check Valves

These are commonly used with Globe and Angle valves since they have similar diaphragm seating arrangements and are recommended for preventing backflow of steam, air, gas and water, and on vapor lines with high flow velocities. For horizontal lines, horizontal lift checks should be used and vertical lift checks for vertical lines.

Ball Valves

Ball valves are light and easily installed, yet because of modern elastomeric seats, provide tight closure. Flow is controlled by rotating up to 90° a drilled ball which fits tightly against resilient seals. This ball seats with flow in either direction, and valve handle indicates the degree of opening. Recommended for frequent operation readily adaptable to automation, ideal for installation where space is limited.

Butterfly Valves

Butterfly valves provide bubble-tight closure with excellent throttling characteristics. They can be used for full-open, closed and for throttling applications.

The Butterfly valve consists of a disc within the valve body which is controlled by a shaft. In its closed position, the valve disc seals against a resilient seat. The disc position throughout the full 90° rotation is visually indicated by the position of the operator.

A Butterfly valve is only a fraction of the weight of a Gate valve and requires no gaskets between flanges in most cases. Recommended for frequent operation and adaptable to automation where space is limited.

Wafer and Lug type bodies when installed between two pipe flanges, can be easily removed from the line. The pressure of the bolted flanges holds the valve in place.
Locating lugs makes installation easier.

Plug Valves

Lubricated plug valves, because of the wide range of service to which they are adapted, may be classified as all purpose valves. They can be safely used at all pressure and vacuums, and at all temperatures up to the limits of available lubricants. They are the most satisfactory valves for the handling of gritty suspensions and many other destructive, erosive, corrosive and chemical solutions.

Plumbing — R2211 Facility Water Distribution

R221113-50 Pipe Material Considerations

1. Malleable fittings should be used for gas service.
2. Malleable fittings are used where there are stresses/strains due to expansion and vibration.
3. Cast fittings may be broken as an aid to disassembling heating lines frozen by long use, temperature and minerals.
4. A cast iron pipe is extensively used for underground and submerged service.
5. Type M (light wall) copper tubing is available in hard temper only and is used for nonpressure and less severe applications than K and L.
6. Type L (medium wall) copper tubing, available hard or soft for interior service.
7. Type K (heavy wall) copper tubing, available in hard or soft temper for use where conditions are severe. For underground and interior service.
8. Hard drawn tubing requires fewer hangers or supports but should not be bent. Silver brazed fittings are recommended, but soft solder is normally used.
9. Type DMV (very light wall) copper tubing designed for drainage, waste and vent plus other non-critical pressure services.

Domestic/Imported Pipe and Fittings Costs

The prices shown in this publication for steel/cast iron pipe and steel, cast iron, and malleable iron fittings are based on domestic production sold at the normal trade discounts. The above listed items of foreign manufacture may be available at prices 1/3 to 1/2 of those shown. Some imported items after minor machining or finishing operations are being sold as domestic to further complicate the system.

Caution: Most pipe prices in this data set also include a coupling and pipe hangers which for the larger sizes can add significantly to the per foot cost and should be taken into account when comparing "book cost" with the quoted supplier's cost.

Plumbing R2211 Facility Water Distribution

R221113-70 Piping to 10' High

When taking off pipe, it is important to identify the different material types and joining procedures, as well as distances between supports and components required for proper support.

During the takeoff, measure through all fittings. Do not subtract the lengths of the fittings, valves, or strainers, etc. This added length plus the final rounding of the totals will compensate for nipples and waste.

When rounding off totals always increase the actual amount to correspond with manufacturer's shipping lengths.

A. Both red brass and yellow brass pipe are normally furnished in 12' lengths, plain end. The Unit Price section includes in the linear foot costs two field threads and one coupling per 10' length. A carbon steel clevis type hanger assembly every 10' is also prorated into the linear foot costs, including both material and labor.

B. Cast iron soil pipe is furnished in either 5' or 10' lengths. For pricing purposes, the Unit Price section features 10' lengths with a joint and a carbon steel clevis hanger assembly every 5' prorated into the per foot costs of both material and labor.

Three methods of joining are considered: lead and oakum poured joints or push-on gasket type joints for the bell and spigot pipe and a joint clamp for the no-hub soil pipe. The labor and material costs for each of these individual joining procedures are also prorated into the linear costs per foot.

C. Copper tubing covers types K, L, M, and DWV which are furnished in 20' lengths. Means pricing data is based on a tubing cut each length and a coupling and two soft soldered joints every 10'. A carbon steel, clevis type hanger assembly every 10' is also prorated into the per foot costs. The prices for refrigeration tubing are for materials only. Labor for full lengths may be based on the type L labor but short cut measures in tight areas can increase the installation labor-hours from 20 to 40%.

D. Corrosion-resistant piping does not lend itself to one particular standard of hanging or support assembly due to its diversity of application and placement. The several varieties of corrosion-resistant piping do not include any material or labor costs for hanger assemblies (See the Unit Price section for appropriate selection).

E. Glass pipe is furnished in standard lengths either 5' or 10' long, beaded on one end. Special orders for diverse lengths beaded on both ends are also available. For pricing purposes, R.S. Means features 10' lengths with a coupling and a carbon steel band hanger assembly every 10' prorated into the per foot linear costs.

Glass pipe is also available with conical ends and standard lengths ranging from 6" through 3' in 6" increments, then up to 10' in 12" increments. Special lengths can be customized for particular installation requirements.

For pricing purposes, Means has based the labor and material pricing on 10' lengths. Included in these costs per linear foot are the prorated costs for a flanged assembly every 10' consisting of two flanges, a gasket, two insertable seals, and the required number of bolts and nuts. A carbon steel band hanger assembly based on 10' center lines has also been prorated into the costs per foot for labor and materials.

F. Plastic pipe of several compositions and joining methods are considered. Fiberglass reinforced pipe (FRP) is priced, based on 10' lengths (20' lengths are also available), with coupling and epoxy joints every 10'. FRP is furnished in both "General Service" and "High Strength." A carbon steel clevis hanger assembly, 3 for every 10', is built into the prorated labor and material costs on a per foot basis.

The PVC and CPVC pipe schedules 40, 80 and 120, plus SDR ratings are all based on 20' lengths with a coupling installed every 10', as well as a carbon steel clevis hanger assembly every 3'. The PVC and ABS type DWV piping is based on 10' lengths with solvent weld couplings every 10', and with carbon steel clevis hanger assemblies, 3 for every 10'. The rest of the plastic piping in this section is based on flexible 100' coils and does not include any coupling or supports.

This section ends with PVC drain and sewer piping based on 10' lengths with bell and spigot ends and O-ring type, push-on joints.

G. Stainless steel piping includes both weld end and threaded piping, both in the type 304 and 316 specification and in the following schedules, 5, 10, 40, 80, and 160. Although this piping is usually furnished in 20' lengths, this cost grouping has a joint (either heli-arc butt-welded or threads and coupling) every 10'. A carbon steel clevis type hanger assembly is also included at 10' intervals and prorated into the linear foot costs.

H. Carbon steel pipe includes both black and galvanized. This section encompasses schedules 40 (standard) and 80 (extra heavy).

Several common methods of joining steel pipe — such as thread and coupled, butt welded, and flanged (150 lb. weld neck flanges) are also included.

For estimating purposes, it is assumed that the piping is purchased in 20' lengths and that a compatible joint is made up every 10'. These joints are prorated into the labor and material costs per linear foot. The following hanger and support assemblies every 10' are also included: carbon steel clevis for the T & C pipe, and single rod roll type for both the welded and flanged piping. All of these hangers are oversized to accommodate pipe insulation 3/4" thick through 5" pipe size and 1-1/2" thick from 6" through 12" pipe size.

I. Grooved joint steel pipe is priced both black and galvanized, in schedules 10, 40, and 80, furnished in 20' lengths. This section describes two joining methods: cut groove and roll groove. The schedule 10 piping is roll-grooved, while the heavier schedules are cut-grooved. The labor and material costs are prorated into per linear foot prices, including a coupled joint every 10', as well as a carbon steel clevis hanger assembly.

Notes:

The pipe hanger assemblies mentioned in the preceding paragraphs include the described hanger; appropriately sized steel, box-type insert and nut; plus 18" of threaded hanger rod.

C clamps are used when the pipe is to be supported from steel shapes rather than anchored in the slab. C clamps are slightly less costly than inserts. However, to save time in estimating, it is advisable to use the given line number cost, rather than substituting a C clamp for the insert.

Add to piping labor for elevated installation:

10' to 14.5' high	10%	30' to 34.5' high	40%
15' to 19.5' high	20%	35' to 39.5' high	50%
20' to 24.5' high	25%	Over 40' and higher	55%
25' to 29.5' high	35%		

When using the percentage adds for elevated piping installations as shown above, bear in mind that the given heights are for the pipe supports, even though the insert, anchor, or clamp may be several feet higher than the pipe itself.

An allowance has been included in the piping installation time for testing and minor tightening of leaking joints, fittings, stuffing boxes, packing glands, etc. For extraordinary test requirements such as x-rays, prolonged pressure or demonstration tests, a percentage of the piping labor, based on the estimator's experience, must be added to the labor total. A testing service specializing in weld x-rays should be consulted for pricing if it is an estimate requirement. Equipment installation time includes start-up with associated adjustments.

Heating, Ventilating & A.C. R2305 Common Work Results for HVAC

R230500-10 Subcontractors

On the unit cost section of the R.S. Means Cost Data, the last column is entitled "Total Incl. O&P". This is normally the cost of the installing contractor. In the HVAC Division, this is the cost of the mechanical contractor. If the particular work being estimated is to be performed by a sub to the mechanical contractor, the mechanical's profit and handling charge (usually 10%) is added to the total of the last column.

Heating, Ventilating & A.C. R2331 HVAC Ducts & Casings

R233100-30 Duct Fabrication/Installation

The labor cost for fabricated sheet metal duct includes both the cost of fabrication and installation of the duct. The split is approximately 40% for fabrication, 60% for installation. It is for this reason that the percentage add for elevated installation of fabricated duct is less than the percentage add for prefabricated/preformed duct.

Example: assume a piece of duct cost $100 installed (labor only)

$$\text{Sheet Metal Fabrication} = 40\% = \$40$$
$$\text{Installation} = 60\% = \$60$$

The add for elevated installation is:

$$\frac{\text{Based on total labor}}{\text{(fabrication \& installation)}} = \$100 \times 6\% = \$6.00$$

$$\frac{\text{Based on installation cost only}}{\text{(Material purchased prefabricated)}} = \$60 \times 10\% = \$6.00$$

The $6.00 markup (10' to 15' high) is the same.

Heating, Ventilating & A.C.   R2331 HVAC Ducts & Casings

R233100-40   Steel Sheet Metal Calculator (Weight in Lb./Ft. of Length)

Gauge	26	24	22	20	18	16	Gauge	26	24	22	20	18	16
Wt.-Lb./S.F.	.906	1.156	1.406	1.656	2.156	2.656	Wt.-Lb./S.F.	.906	1.156	1.406	1.656	2.156	2.656
SMACNA Max. Dimension – Long Side	*	30″	54″	84″	85″ Up	*	SMACNA Max. Dimension – Long Side	*	30″	54″	84″	85″ Up	*
Sum-2 sides							Sum-2 Sides						
2	.3	.40	.50	.60	.80	.90	56	9.3	12.0	14.0	16.2	21.3	25.2
3	.5	.65	.80	.90	1.1	1.4	57	9.5	12.3	14.3	16.5	21.7	25.7
4	.7	.85	1.0	1.2	1.5	1.8	58	9.7	12.5	14.5	16.8	22.0	26.1
5	.8	1.1	1.3	1.5	1.9	2.3	59	9.8	12.7	14.8	17.1	22.4	26.6
6	1.0	1.3	1.5	1.7	2.3	2.7	60	10.0	12.9	15.0	17.4	22.8	27.0
7	1.2	1.5	1.8	2.0	2.7	3.2	61	10.2	13.1	15.3	17.7	23.2	27.5
8	1.3	1.7	2.0	2.3	3.0	3.6	62	10.3	13.3	15.5	18.0	23.6	27.9
9	1.5	1.9	2.3	2.6	3.4	4.1	63	10.5	13.5	15.8	18.3	24.0	28.4
10	1.7	2.2	2.5	2.9	3.8	4.5	64	10.7	13.7	16.0	18.6	24.3	28.8
11	1.8	2.4	2.8	3.2	4.2	5.0	65	10.8	13.9	16.3	18.9	24.7	29.3
12	2.0	2.6	3.0	3.5	4.6	5.4	66	11.0	14.1	16.5	19.1	25.1	29.7
13	2.2	2.8	3.3	3.8	4.9	5.9	67	11.2	14.3	16.8	19.4	25.5	30.2
14	2.3	3.0	3.5	4.1	5.3	6.3	68	11.3	14.6	17.0	19.7	25.8	30.6
15	2.5	3.2	3.8	4.4	5.7	6.8	69	11.5	14.8	17.3	20.0	26.2	31.1
16	2.7	3.4	4.0	4.6	6.1	7.2	70	11.7	15.0	17.5	20.3	26.6	31.5
17	2.8	3.7	4.3	4.9	6.5	7.7	71	11.8	15.2	17.8	20.6	27.0	32.0
18	3.0	3.9	4.5	5.2	6.8	8.1	72	12.0	15.4	18.0	20.9	27.4	32.4
19	3.2	4.1	4.8	5.5	7.2	8.6	73	12.2	15.6	18.3	21.2	27.7	32.9
20	3.3	4.3	5.0	5.8	7.6	9.0	74	12.3	15.8	18.5	21.5	28.1	33.3
21	3.5	4.5	5.3	6.1	8.0	9.5	75	12.5	16.1	18.8	21.8	28.5	33.8
22	3.7	4.7	5.5	6.4	8.4	9.9	76	12.7	16.3	19.0	22.0	28.9	34.2
23	3.8	5.0	5.8	6.7	8.7	10.4	77	12.8	16.5	19.3	22.3	29.3	34.7
24	4.0	5.2	6.0	7.0	9.1	10.8	78	13.0	16.7	19.5	22.6	29.6	35.1
25	4.2	5.4	6.3	7.3	9.5	11.3	79	13.2	16.9	19.8	22.9	30.0	35.6
26	4.3	5.6	6.5	7.5	9.9	11.7	80	13.3	17.1	20.0	23.2	30.4	36.0
27	4.5	5.8	6.8	7.8	10.3	12.2	81	13.5	17.3	20.3	23.5	30.8	36.5
28	4.7	6.0	7.0	8.1	10.6	12.6	82	13.7	17.5	20.5	23.8	31.2	36.9
29	4.8	6.2	7.3	8.4	11.1	13.1	83	13.8	17.8	20.8	24.1	31.5	37.4
30	5.0	6.5	7.5	8.7	11.4	13.5	84	14.0	18.0	21.0	24.4	31.9	37.8
31	5.2	6.7	7.8	9.0	11.8	14.0	85	14.2	18.2	21.3	24.7	32.3	38.3
32	5.3	6.9	8.0	9.3	12.2	14.4	86	14.3	18.4	21.5	24.9	32.7	38.7
33	5.5	7.1	8.3	9.6	12.5	14.9	87	14.5	18.6	21.8	25.2	33.1	39.2
34	5.7	7.3	8.5	9.9	12.9	15.3	88	14.7	18.8	22.0	25.5	33.4	39.6
35	5.8	7.5	8.8	10.2	13.3	15.8	89	14.8	19.0	22.3	25.8	33.8	40.1
36	6.0	7.8	9.0	10.4	13.7	16.2	90	15.0	19.3	22.5	26.1	34.2	40.5
37	6.2	8.0	9.3	10.7	14.1	16.7	91	15.2	19.5	22.8	26.4	34.6	41.0
38	6.3	8.2	9.5	11.0	14.4	17.1	92	15.3	19.7	23.0	26.7	35.0	41.4
39	6.5	8.4	9.8	11.3	14.8	17.6	93	15.5	19.9	23.3	27.0	35.3	41.9
40	6.7	8.6	10.0	11.6	15.2	18.0	94	15.7	20.1	23.5	27.3	35.7	42.3
41	6.8	8.8	10.3	11.9	15.6	18.5	95	15.8	20.3	23.8	27.6	36.1	42.8
42	7.0	9.0	10.5	12.2	16.0	18.9	96	16.0	20.5	24.0	27.8	36.5	43.2
43	7.2	9.2	10.8	12.5	16.3	19.4	97	16.2	20.8	24.3	28.1	36.9	43.7
44	7.3	9.5	11.0	12.8	16.7	19.8	98	16.3	21.0	24.5	28.4	37.2	44.1
45	7.5	9.7	11.3	13.1	17.1	20.3	99	16.5	21.2	24.8	28.7	37.6	44.6
46	7.7	9.9	11.5	13.3	17.5	20.7	100	16.7	21.4	25.0	29.0	38.0	45.0
47	7.8	10.1	11.8	13.6	17.9	21.2	101	16.8	21.6	25.3	29.3	38.4	45.5
48	8.0	10.3	12.0	13.9	18.2	21.6	102	17.0	21.8	25.5	29.6	38.8	45.9
49	8.2	10.5	12.3	14.2	18.6	22.1	103	17.2	22.0	25.8	29.9	39.1	46.4
50	8.3	10.7	12.5	14.5	19.0	22.5	104	17.3	22.3	26.0	30.2	39.5	46.8
51	8.5	11.0	12.8	14.8	19.4	23.0	105	17.5	22.5	26.3	30.5	39.9	47.3
52	8.7	11.2	13.0	15.1	19.8	23.4	106	17.7	22.7	26.5	30.7	40.3	47.7
53	8.8	11.4	13.3	15.4	20.1	23.9	107	17.8	22.9	26.8	31.0	40.7	48.2
54	9.0	11.6	13.5	15.7	20.5	24.3	108	18.0	23.1	27.0	31.3	41.0	48.6
55	9.2	11.8	13.8	16.0	20.9	24.8	109	18.2	23.3	27.3	31.6	41.4	49.1
							110	18.3	23.5	27.5	31.9	41.8	49.5

Example: If duct is 34″ x 20″ x 15′ long, 34″ is greater than 30″ maximum, for 24 ga. so must be 22 ga. 34″ + 20″ = 54″ going across from 54″ find 13.5 lb. per foot. 13.5 x 15′ = 202.5 lbs. For S.F. of surface area 202.5 ÷ 1.406 = 144 S.F.

Note: Figures include an allowance for scrap.
***Do Not** use unless engineer specified. 26GA is very light and sometimes used for toilet exhaust. 16 GA is heavy plate and mostly specified for plenums and hoods.

Heating, Ventilating & A.C. R2331 HVAC Ducts & Casings

R233100-50 Ductwork Packages (per Ton of Cooling)

System	Sheet Metal	Insulation	Diffusers	Return Register
Roof Top Unit Single Zone	120 Lbs.	52 S.F.	1	1
Roof Top Unit Multizone	240 Lbs.	104 S.F.	2	1
Self-contained Air or Water Cooled	108 Lbs.	—	2	—
Split System Air Cooled	102 Lbs.	—	2	—

Systems reflect most common usage.
Refer to system graphics for duct layout.

Heating, Ventilating & A.C. R2337 Air Outlets & Inlets

R233700-60 Diffuser Evaluation

CFM = V × An × K where V = Outlet velocity in feet per minute. An = Neck area in square feet and K = Diffuser delivery factor. An undersized diffuser for a desired CFM will produce a high velocity and noise level. When air moves past people at a velocity in excess of 25 FPM, an annoying draft is felt. An oversized diffuser will result in low velocity with poor mixing. Consideration must be given to avoid vertical stratification or horizontal areas of stagnation.

Heating, Ventilating & A.C. R2350 Central Heating Equipment

R235000-10 Heating Systems

Heating Systems

The basic function of a heating system is to bring an enclosed volume up to a desired temperature and then maintain that temperature within a reasonable range. To accomplish this, the selected system must have sufficient capacity to offset transmission losses resulting from the temperature difference on the interior and exterior of the enclosing walls in addition to losses due to cold air infiltration through cracks, crevices and around doors and windows. The amount of heat to be furnished is dependent upon the building size, construction, temperature difference, air leakage, use, shape, orientation and exposure. Air circulation is also an important consideration. Circulation will prevent stratification which could result in heat losses through uneven temperatures at various levels. For example, the most efficient use of unit heaters can usually be achieved by circulating the space volume through the total number of units once every 20 minutes or 3 times an hour. This general rule must, of course, be adapted for special cases such as large buildings with low ratios of heat transmitting surface to cubical volume. The type of occupancy of a building will have considerable bearing on the number of heat transmitting units and the location selected. It is axiomatic, however, that the basis of any successful heating system is to provide the maximum amount of heat at the points of maximum heat loss such as exposed walls, windows, and doors. Large roof areas, wind direction, and wide doorways create problems of excessive heat loss and require special consideration and treatment.

Heat Transmission

Heat transfer is an important parameter to be considered during selection of the exterior wall style, material and window area. A high rate of transfer will permit greater heat loss during the wintertime with the resultant increase in heating energy costs and a greater rate of heat gain in the summer with proportionally greater cooling cost. Several terms are used to describe various aspects of heat transfer. However, for general estimating purposes this data set lists U values for systems of construction materials. U is the "overall heat transfer coefficient." It is defined as the heat flow per hour through one square foot when the temperature difference in the air on either side of the structure wall, roof, ceiling or floor is one degree Fahrenheit. The structural segment may be a single homogeneous material or a composite.

Total heat transfer is found using the following equation:

$Q = AU(T_2 - T_1)$ where
Q = Heat flow, BTU per hour
A = Area, square feet
U = Overall heat transfer coefficient
$(T_2 - T_1)$ = Difference in temperature of air on each side of the construction component. (Also abbreviated TD)

Note that heat can flow through all surfaces of any building and this flow is in addition to heat gain or loss due to ventilation, infiltration and generation (appliances, machinery, people).

R235000-20 Heating Approximations for Quick Estimating

Oil Piping & Boiler Room Piping
   Small System .... 20 to 30% of Boiler
   Complex System
   with Pumps, Headers, Etc. .... 80 to 110% of Boiler

Breeching With Insulation:
   Small .... 10 to 15% of Boiler
   Large .... 15 to 25% of Boiler

Coils: .... 15 to 30% of Containing Unit

Balancing (Independent) .... 1/2% of H.V.A.C. Estimate

Quality/Complexity Adjustment: For all heating installations add these adjustments to the estimate to more closely allow for the equipment and conditions of the particular job under consideration.
   Economy installation, add .... 0 to 5% of System
   Good quality, medium complexity, add .... 5 to 15% of System
   Above average quality and complexity, add .... 15 to 25% of System

Heating, Ventilating & A.C. R2350 Central Heating Equipment

R235000-30 The Basics of a Heating System

The function of a heating system is to achieve and maintain a desired temperature in a room or building by replacing the amount of heat being dissipated. There are four kinds of heating systems: hot-water, steam, warm-air and electric resistance. Each has certain essential and similar elements with the exception of electric resistance heating.

The basic elements of a heating system are:

A. A **combustion chamber** in which fuel is burned and heat transferred to a conveying medium.

B. The **"fluid"** used for conveying the heat (water, steam or air).

C. **Conductors** or pipes for transporting the fluid to specific desired locations.

D. A means of disseminating the heat, sometimes called **terminal units**.

A. The **combustion chamber** in a furnace heats air which is then distributed. This is called a warm-air system.

The combustion chamber in a boiler heats water which is either distributed as hot water or steam and this is termed a hydronic system.

The maximum allowable working pressures are limited by ASME "Code for Heating Boilers" to 15 PSI for steam and 160 PSI for hot water heating boilers, with a maximum temperature limitation of 250° F. Hot water boilers are generally rated for a working pressure of 30 PSI. High pressure boilers are governed by the ASME "Code for Power Boilers" which is used almost universally for boilers operating over 15 PSIG. High pressure boilers used for a combination of heating/process loads are usually designed for 150 PSIG.

Boiler ratings are usually indicated as either Gross or Net Output. The Gross Load is equal to the Net Load plus a piping and pickup allowance. When this allowance cannot be determined, divide the gross output rating by 1.25 for a value equal to or greater than the net heat loss requirement of the building.

B. Of the three **fluids** used, steam carries the greatest amount of heat per unit volume. This is due to the fact that it gives up its latent heat of vaporization at a temperature considerably above room temperature. Another advantage is that the pressure to produce a positive circulation is readily available. Piping conducts the steam to terminal units and returns condensate to the boiler.

The **steam system** is well adapted to large buildings because of its positive circulation, its comparatively economical installation and its ability to deliver large quantities of heat. Nearly all large office buildings, stores, hotels, and industrial buildings are so heated, in addition to many residences.

Hot water, when used as the heat carrying fluid, gives up a portion of its sensible heat and then returns to the boiler or heating apparatus for reheating. As the heat conveyed by each pound of water is about one-fiftieth of the heat conveyed by a pound of steam, it is necessary to circulate about fifty times as much water as steam by weight (although only one-thirtieth as much by volume). The hot water system is usually, although not necessarily, designed to operate at temperatures below that of the ordinary steam system and so the amount of heat transfer surface must be correspondingly greater. A temperature of 190° F to 200° F is normally the maximum. Circulation in small buildings may depend on the difference in density between hot water and the cool water returning to the boiler; circulating pumps are normally used to maintain a desired rate of flow. Pumps permit a greater degree of flexibility and better control.

In **warm-air** furnace systems, cool air is taken from one or more points in the building, passed over the combustion chamber and flue gas passages and then distributed through a duct system. A disadvantage of this system is that the ducts take up much more building volume than steam or hot water pipes. Advantages of this system are the relative ease with which humidification can be accomplished by the evaporation of water as the air circulates through the heater, and the lack of need for expensive disseminating units as the warm air simply becomes part of the interior atmosphere of the building.

C. **Conductors** (pipes and ducts) have been lightly treated in the discussion of conveying fluids. For more detailed information such as sizing and distribution methods, the reader is referred to technical publications such as the American Society of Heating, Refrigerating and Air-Conditioning Engineers "Handbook of Fundamentals."

D. **Terminal units** come in an almost infinite variety of sizes and styles, but the basic principles of operation are very limited. As previously mentioned, warm-air systems require only a simple register or diffuser to mix heated air with that present in the room. Special application items such as radiant coils and infrared heaters are available to meet particular conditions but are not usually considered for general heating needs. Most heating is accomplished by having air flow over coils or pipes containing the heat transporting medium (steam, hot-water, electricity). These units, while varied, may be separated into two general types, (1) radiator/convectors and (2) unit heaters.

Radiator/convectors may be cast, fin-tube or pipe assemblies. They may be direct, indirect, exposed, concealed or mounted within a cabinet enclosure, upright or baseboard style. These units are often collectively referred to as "radiatiors" or "radiation" although none gives off heat either entirely by radiation or by convection but rather a combination of both. The air flows over the units as a gravity "current." It is necessary to have one or more heat-emitting units in each room. The most efficient placement is low along an outside wall or under a window to counteract the cold coming into the room and achieve an even distribution.

In contrast to radiator/convectors which operate most effectively against the walls of smaller rooms, **unit heaters** utilize a fan to move air over heating coils and are very effective in locations of relatively large volume. Unit heaters, while usually suspended overhead, may be floor mounted. They also may take in fresh outside air for ventilation. The heat distributed by unit heaters may be from a remote source and conveyed by a fluid or it may be from the combustion of fuel in each individual heater. In the latter case the only piping required would be for fuel, however, a vent for the products of combustion would be necessary.

The following list gives may of the advantages of unit heaters for applications other than office or residential:

a. Large capacity so smaller number of units are required, **b.** Piping system simplified, **c.** Space saved where they are located overhead out of the way, **d.** Rapid heating directed where needed with effective wide distribution, **e.** Difference between floor and ceiling temperature reduced, **f.** Circulation of air obtained, and ventilation with introduction of fresh air possible, **g.** Heat output flexible and easily controlled.

Heating, Ventilating & A.C. R2356 Solar Energy Heating Equipment

R235616-60 Solar Heating (Space and Hot Water)

Collectors should face as close to due South as possible, but variations of up to 20 degrees on either side of true South are acceptable. Local climate and collector type may influence the choice between east or west deviations. Obviously they should be located so they are not shaded from the sun's rays. Incline collectors at a slope of latitude minus 5 degrees for domestic hot water and latitude plus 15 degrees for space heating.

Flat plate collectors consist of a number of components as follows: Insulation to reduce heat loss through the bottom and sides of the collector. The enclosure which contains all the components in this assembly is usually weatherproof and prevents dust, wind and water from coming in contact with the absorber plate. The cover plate usually consists of one or more layers of a variety of glass or plastic and reduces the reradiation by creating an air space which traps the heat between the cover and the absorber plates.

The absorber plate must have a good thermal bond with the fluid passages. The absorber plate is usually metallic and treated with a surface coating which improves absorptivity. Black or dark paints or selective coatings are used for this purpose, and the design of this passage and plate combination helps determine a solar system's effectiveness.

Heat transfer fluid passage tubes are attached above and below or integral with an absorber plate for the purpose of transferring thermal energy from the absorber plate to a heat transfer medium. The heat exchanger is a device for transferring thermal energy from one fluid to another.

Piping and storage tanks should be well insulated to minimize heat losses.

Size domestic water heating storage tanks to hold 20 gallons of water per user, minimum, plus 10 gallons per dishwasher or washing machine. For domestic water heating an optimum collector size is approximately 3/4 square foot of area per gallon of water storage. For space heating of residences and small commercial applications the collector is commonly sized between 30% and 50% of the internal floor area. For space heating of large commercial applications, collector areas less than 30% of the internal floor area can still provide significant heat reductions.

A supplementary heat source is recommended for Northern states for December through February.

The solar energy transmission per square foot of collector surface varies greatly with the material used. Initial cost, heat transmittance and useful life are obviously interrelated.

Heating, Ventilating & A.C. R2360 Central Cooling Equipment

R236000-10 Air Conditioning

General: The purpose of air conditioning is to control the environment of a space so that comfort is provided for the occupants and/or conditions are suitable for the processes or equipment contained therein. The several items which should be evaluated to define system objectives are:

Temperature Control
Humidity Control
Cleanliness
Odor, smoke and fumes
Ventilation

Efforts to control the above parameters must also include consideration of the degree or tolerance of variation, the noise level introduced, the velocity of air motion and the energy requirements to accomplish the desired results.

The variation in **temperature** and **humidity** is a function of the sensor and the controller. The controller reacts to a signal from the sensor and produces the appropriate suitable response in either the terminal unit, the conductor of the transporting medium (air, steam, chilled water, etc.), or the source (boiler, evaporating coils, etc.).

The **noise level** is a by-product of the energy supplied to moving components of the system. Those items which usually contribute the most noise are pumps, blowers, fans, compressors and diffusers. The level of noise can be partially controlled through use of vibration pads, isolators, proper sizing, shields, baffles and sound absorbing liners.

Some **air motion** is necessary to prevent stagnation and stratification. The maximum acceptable velocity varies with the degree of heating or cooling which is taking place. Most people feel air moving past them at velocities in excess of 25 FPM as an annoying draft. However, velocities up to 45 FPM may be acceptable in certain cases. Ventilation, expressed as air changes per hour and percentage of fresh air, is usually an item regulated by local codes.

Selection of the system to be used for a particular application is usually a trade-off. In some cases the building size, style, or room available for mechanical use limits the range of possibilities. Prime factors influencing the decision are first cost and total life (operating, maintenance and replacement costs). The accuracy with which each parameter is determined will be an important measure of the reliability of the decision and subsequent satisfactory operation of the installed system.

Heat delivery may be desired from an air conditioning system. Heating capability usually is added as follows: A gas fired burner or hot water/steam/electric coils may be added to the air handling unit directly and heat all air equally. For limited or localized heat requirements the water/steam/electric coils may be inserted into the duct branch supplying the cold areas. Gas fired duct furnaces are also available.

Note: When water or steam coils are used the cost of the piping and boiler must also be added. For a rough estimate use the cost per square foot of the appropriate sized hydronic system with unit heaters. This will provide a cost for the boiler and piping, and the unit heaters of the system would equate to the approximate cost of the heating coils.

Heating, Ventilating & A.C. R2360 Central Cooling Equipment

R236000-20 Air Conditioning Requirements

BTUs per hour per S.F. of floor area and S.F. per ton of air conditioning.

Type of Building	BTU/Hr per S.F.	S.F. per Ton	Type of Building	BTU/Hr per S.F.	S.F. per Ton	Type of Building	BTU/Hr per S.F.	S.F. per Ton
Apartments, Individual	26	450	Dormitory, Rooms	40	300	Libraries	50	240
Corridors	22	550	Corridors	30	400	Low Rise Office, Exterior	38	320
Auditoriums & Theaters	40	300/18*	Dress Shops	43	280	Interior	33	360
Banks	50	240	Drug Stores	80	150	Medical Centers	28	425
Barber Shops	48	250	Factories	40	300	Motels	28	425
Bars & Taverns	133	90	High Rise Office—Ext. Rms.	46	263	Office (small suite)	43	280
Beauty Parlors	66	180	Interior Rooms	37	325	Post Office, Individual Office	42	285
Bowling Alleys	68	175	Hospitals, Core	43	280	Central Area	46	260
Churches	36	330/20*	Perimeter	46	260	Residences	20	600
Cocktail Lounges	68	175	Hotel, Guest Rooms	44	275	Restaurants	60	200
Computer Rooms	141	85	Corridors	30	400	Schools & Colleges	46	260
Dental Offices	52	230	Public Spaces	55	220	Shoe Stores	55	220
Dept. Stores, Basement	34	350	Industrial Plants, Offices	38	320	Shop'g. Ctrs., Supermarkets	34	350
Main Floor	40	300	General Offices	34	350	Retail Stores	48	250
Upper Floor	30	400	Plant Areas	40	300	Specialty	60	200

*Persons per ton
12,000 BTU = 1 ton of air conditioning

Heating, Ventilating & A.C. R2360 Central Cooling Equipment

R236000-30 Psychrometric Table

Dewpoint or Saturation Temperature (F)

Relative humidity (%)

	32	35	40	45	50	55	60	65	70	75	80	85	90	95	100
100	32	35	40	45	50	55	60	65	70	75	80	85	90	95	100
90	30	33	37	42	47	52	57	62	67	72	77	82	87	92	97
80	27	30	34	39	44	49	54	58	64	68	73	78	83	88	93
70	24	27	31	36	40	45	50	55	60	64	69	74	79	84	88
60	20	24	28	32	36	41	46	51	55	60	65	69	74	79	83
50	16	20	24	28	33	36	41	46	50	55	60	64	69	73	78
40	12	15	18	23	27	31	35	40	45	49	53	58	62	67	71
30	8	10	14	18	21	25	29	33	37	42	46	50	54	59	62
20	6	7	8	9	13	16	20	24	28	31	35	40	43	48	52
10	4	4	5	5	6	8	9	10	13	17	20	24	27	30	34

Dry bulb temperature (F)

This table shows the relationship between RELATIVE HUMIDITY, DRY BULB TEMPERATURE AND DEWPOINT.

As an example, assume that the thermometer in a room reads 75° F, and we know that the relative humidity is 50%. The chart shows the dewpoint temperature to be 55° F. That is, any surface colder than 55° F will "sweat" or collect condensing moisture. This surface could be the outside of an uninsulated chilled water pipe in the summertime, or the inside surface of a wall or deck in the wintertime. After determining the extreme ambient parameters, the table at the left is useful in determining which surfaces need insulation or vapor barrier protection.

TEMPERATURE DEGREES FAHRENHEIT
TOTAL PRESSURE = 14.696 LB. PER SQ. IN. ABS.

Psychrometric chart showing different variables based on one pound of dry air. Space marked A B C D is temperature-humidity range which is most comfortable for majority of people.

Heating, Ventilating & A.C. R2360 Central Cooling Equipment

R236000-90 Quality/Complexity Adjustment for Air Conditioning Systems

Economy installation, add	0 to 5%
Good quality, medium complexity, add	5 to 15%
Above average quality and complexity, add	15 to 25%

Add the above adjustments to the estimate to more closely allow for the equipment and conditions of the particular job under consideration.

Heating, Ventilating & A.C. R2383 Radiant Heating Units

Fig. R238313-11

R238313-10 Heat Trace Systems

Before you can determine the cost of a HEAT TRACE installation, the method of attachment must be established. There are (4) common methods:

1. Cable is simply attached to the pipe with polyester tape every 12'.
2. Cable is attached with a continuous cover of 2" wide aluminum tape.
3. Cable is attached with factory extruded heat transfer cement and covered with metallic raceway with clips every 10'.
4. Cable is attached between layers of pipe insulation using either clips or polyester tape.

Example: Components for method 3 must include:
  A. Heat trace cable by voltage and watts per linear foot.
  B. Heat transfer cement, 1 gallon per 60 linear feet of cover.
  C. Metallic raceway by size and type.
  D. Raceway clips by size of pipe.

When taking off linear foot lengths of cable add the following for each valve in the system. (E)

In all of the above methods each component of the system must be priced individually.

SCREWED OR WELDED VALVE:			FLANGED VALVE:			BUTTERFLY VALVES:		
1/2"	=	6"	1/2"	=	1'-0"	1/2"	=	0'
3/4"	=	9"	3/4"	=	1'-6"	3/4"	=	0'
1"	=	1'-0"	1"	=	2'-0"	1"	=	1'-0"
1-1/2"	=	1'-6"	1-1/2"	=	2'-6"	1-1/2"	=	1'-6"
2"	=	2'	2"	=	2'-6"	2"	=	2'-0"
2-1/2"	=	2'-6"	2-1/2"	=	3'-0"	2-1/2"	=	2'-0"
3"	=	2'-6"	3"	=	3'-6"	3"	=	2'-6"
4"	=	4'-0"	4"	=	4'-0"	4"	=	3'-0"
6"	=	7'-0"	6"	=	8'-0"	6"	=	3'-6"
8"	=	9'-6"	8"	=	11'-0"	8"	=	4'-0"
10"	=	12'-6"	10"	=	14'-0"	10"	=	4'-0"
12"	=	15'-0"	12"	=	16'-6"	12"	=	5'-0"
14"	=	18'-0"	14"	=	19'-6"	14"	=	5'-6"
16"	=	21'-6"	16"	=	23'-0"	16"	=	6'-0"
18"	=	25'-6"	18"	=	27'-0"	18"	=	6'-6"
20"	=	28'-6"	20"	=	30'-0"	20"	=	7'-0"
24"	=	34'-0"	24"	=	36'-0"	24"	=	8'-0"
30"	=	40'-0"	30"	=	42'-0"	30"	=	10'-0"

Heating, Ventilating & A.C. R2383 Radiant Heating Units

R238313-10 Heat Trace Systems (cont.)

Add the following quantities of heat transfer cement to linear foot totals for each valve:

Nominal Valve Size	Gallons of Cement per Valve
1/2"	0.14
3/4"	0.21
1"	0.29
1-1/2"	0.36
2"	0.43
2-1/2"	0.70
3"	0.71
4"	1.00
6"	1.43
8"	1.48
10"	1.50
12"	1.60
14"	1.75
16"	2.00
18"	2.25
20"	2.50
24"	3.00
30"	3.75

The following must be added to the list of components to accurately price HEAT TRACE systems:
1. Expediter fitting and clamp fasteners (F)
2. Junction box and nipple connected to expediter fitting (G)
3. Field installed terminal blocks within junction box
4. Ground lugs
5. Piping from power source to expediter fitting
6. Controls
7. Thermostats
8. Branch wiring
9. Cable splices
10. End of cable terminations
11. Branch piping fittings and boxes

Deduct the following percentages from labor if cable lengths in the same area exceed:

150' to 250' 10%   351' to 500' 20%
251' to 350' 15%   Over 500'   25%

Add the following percentages to labor for elevated installations:

15' to 20' high 10%   31' to 35' high 40%
21' to 25' high 20%   36' to 40' high 50%
26' to 30' high 30%   Over 40' high   60%

R238313-20 Spiral-Wrapped Heat Trace Cable (Pitch Table)

In order to increase the amount of heat, occasionally heat trace cable is wrapped in a spiral fashion around a pipe; increasing the number of feet of heater cable per linear foot of pipe.

Engineers first determine the heat loss per foot of pipe (based on the insulating material, its thickness, and the temperature differential across it). A ratio is then calculated by the formula:

$$\text{Feet of Heat Trace per Foot of Pipe} = \frac{\text{Watts/Foot of Heat Loss}}{\text{Watts/Foot of the Cable}}$$

The linear distance between wraps (pitch) is then taken from a chart or table. Generally, the pitch is listed on a drawing leaving the estimator to calculate the total length of heat tape required. An approximation may be taken from this table.

Feet of Heat Trace Per Foot of Pipe

Pitch In Inches	Nominal Pipe Size in Inches														
	1	1¼	1½	2	2½	3	4	6	8	10	12	14	16	18	20	24
3.5	1.80															
4	1.65															
5	1.46	1.60	1.80													
6	1.34	1.45	1.55	1.75												
7	1.25	1.35	1.43	1.57	1.75											
8	1.20	1.28	1.34	1.45	1.60	1.80										
9	1.16	1.23	1.28	1.37	1.51	1.68	1.82									
10	1.13	1.19	1.24	1.32	1.44	1.57	1.78									
15	1.06	1.08	1.10	1.15	1.21	1.29	1.42	1.49	1.73							
20	1.04	1.05	1.06	1.08	1.13	1.17	1.25	1.33	1.51	1.72						
25		1.04	1.04	1.06	1.08	1.11	1.17	1.24	1.37	1.54	1.70	1.80				
30				1.04	1.06	1.08	1.12	1.17	1.28	1.42	1.54	1.64	1.78			
35						1.06	1.09	1.14	1.22	1.33	1.44	1.52	1.64	1.75		
40						1.05	1.07	1.09	1.15	1.22	1.29	1.35	1.44	1.53	1.64	1.83
50							1.05	1.06	1.11	1.16	1.21	1.25	1.31	1.39	1.46	1.62
60								1.05	1.08	1.12	1.17	1.19	1.24	1.30	1.35	1.47
70									1.06	1.09	1.13	1.15	1.19	1.24	1.28	1.38
80									1.04	1.06	1.10	1.13	1.16	1.19	1.23	1.32
90																
100										1.05	1.08	1.10	1.13	1.15	1.19	1.23

Note: Common practice would normally limit the lower end of the table to 5% of additional heat and above 80% an engineer would likely opt for two (2) parallel cables.

Electrical — R2605 Common Work Results for Electrical

R260519-90 Wire

Wire quantities are taken off by either measuring each cable run or by extending the conduit and raceway quantities times the number of conductors in the raceway. Ten percent should be added for waste and tie-ins. Keep in mind that the unit of measure of wire is C.L.F. not L.F. as in raceways so the formula would read:

$$\frac{(\text{L.F. Raceway} \times \text{No. of Conductors}) \times 1.10}{100} = \text{C.L.F.}$$

Price per C.L.F. of wire includes:
1. Setting up wire coils or spools on racks
2. Attaching wire to pull in means
3. Measuring and cutting wire
4. Pulling wire into a raceway
5. Identifying and tagging

Price does not include:
1. Connections to breakers, panelboards, or equipment
2. Splices

Job Conditions: Productivity is based on new construction to a height of 15′ using rolling staging in an unobstructed area. Material staging is assumed to be within 100′ of work being performed.

Economy of Scale: If more than three wires at a time are being pulled, deduct the following percentages from the labor of that grouping:

4-5 wires	25%
6-10 wires	30%
11-15 wires	35%
over 15	40%

If a wire pull is less than 100′ in length and is interrupted several times by boxes, lighting outlets, etc., it may be necessary to add the following lengths to each wire being pulled:

Junction box to junction box	2 L.F.
Lighting panel to junction box	6 L.F.
Distribution panel to sub panel	8 L.F.
Switchboard to distribution panel	12 L.F.
Switchboard to motor control center	20 L.F.
Switchboard to cable tray	40 L.F.

Measure of Drops and Riser: It is important when taking off wire quantities to include the wire for drops to electrical equipment. If heights of electrical equipment are not clearly stated, use the following guide:

	Bottom A.F.F.	Top A.F.F.	Inside Cabinet
Safety switch to 100A	5′	6′	2′
Safety switch 400 to 600A	4′	6′	3′
100A panel 12 to 30 circuit	4′	6′	3′
42 circuit panel	3′	6′	4′
Switch box	3′	3′6″	1′
Switchgear	0′	8′	8′
Motor control centers	0′	8′	8′
Transformers - wall mount	4′	8′	2′
Transformers - floor mount	0′	12′	4′

Earthwork

R3123 Excavation & Fill

R312316-45 Excavating Equipment

The table below lists theoretical hourly production in C.Y./hr. bank measure for some typical excavation equipment. Figures assume 50 minute hours, 83% job efficiency, 100% operator efficiency, 90° swing and properly sized hauling units, which must be modified for adverse digging and loading conditions. Actual production costs in the front of the data set average about 50% of the theoretical values listed here.

Equipment	Soil Type	B.C.Y. Weight	% Swell	1 C.Y.	1-1/2 C.Y.	2 C.Y.	2-1/2 C.Y.	3 C.Y.	3-1/2 C.Y.	4 C.Y.
Hydraulic Excavator "Backhoe" 15' Deep Cut	Moist loam, sandy clay	3400 lb.	40%	165	195	200	275	330	385	440
	Sand and gravel	3100	18	140	170	225	240	285	330	380
	Common earth	2800	30	150	180	230	250	300	350	400
	Clay, hard, dense	3000	33	120	140	190	200	240	260	320
Power Shovel Optimum Cut (Ft.)	Moist loam, sandy clay	3400	40	170 (6.0)	245 (7.0)	295 (7.8)	335 (8.4)	385 (8.8)	435 (9.1)	475 (9.4)
	Sand and gravel	3100	18	165 (6.0)	225 (7.0)	275 (7.8)	325 (8.4)	375 (8.8)	420 (9.1)	460 (9.4)
	Common earth	2800	30	145 (7.8)	200 (9.2)	250 (10.2)	295 (11.2)	335 (12.1)	375 (13.0)	425 (13.8)
	Clay, hard, dense	3000	33	120 (9.0)	175 (10.7)	220 (12.2)	255 (13.3)	300 (14.2)	335 (15.1)	375 (16.0)
Drag Line Optimum Cut (Ft.)	Moist loam, sandy clay	3400	40	130 (6.6)	180 (7.4)	220 (8.0)	250 (8.5)	290 (9.0)	325 (9.5)	385 (10.0)
	Sand and gravel	3100	18	130 (6.6)	175 (7.4)	210 (8.0)	245 (8.5)	280 (9.0)	315 (9.5)	375 (10.0)
	Common earth	2800	30	110 (8.0)	160 (9.0)	190 (9.9)	220 (10.5)	250 (11.0)	280 (11.5)	310 (12.0)
	Clay, hard, dense	3000	33	90 (9.3)	130 (10.7)	160 (11.8)	190 (12.3)	225 (12.8)	250 (13.3)	280 (12.0)

Equipment	Soil Type	B.C.Y. Weight	% Swell	Wheel Loaders				Track Loaders		
				3 C.Y.	4 C.Y.	6 C.Y.	8 C.Y.	2-1/4 C.Y.	3 C.Y.	4 C.Y.
Loading Tractors	Moist loam, sandy clay	3400	40	260	340	510	690	135	180	250
	Sand and gravel	3100	18	245	320	480	650	130	170	235
	Common earth	2800	30	230	300	460	620	120	155	220
	Clay, hard, dense	3000	33	200	270	415	560	110	145	200
	Rock, well-blasted	4000	50	180	245	380	520	100	130	180

Earthwork — R3123 Excavation & Fill

R312319-90 Wellpoints

A single stage wellpoint system is usually limited to dewatering an average 15' depth below normal ground water level. Multi-stage systems are employed for greater depth with the pumping equipment installed only at the lowest header level. Ejectors with unlimited lift capacity can be economical when two or more stages of wellpoints can be replaced or when horizontal clearance is restricted, such as in deep trenches or tunneling projects, and where low water flows are expected. Wellpoints are usually spaced on 2-1/2' to 10' centers along a header pipe. Wellpoint spacing, header size, and pump size are all determined by the expected flow as dictated by soil conditions.

In almost all soils encountered in wellpoint dewatering, the wellpoints may be jetted into place. Cemented soils and stiff clays may require sand wicks about 12" in diameter around each wellpoint to increase efficiency and eliminate weeping into the excavation. These sand wicks require 1/2 to 3 C.Y. of washed filter sand and are installed by using a 12" diameter steel casing and hole puncher jetted into the ground 2' deeper than the wellpoint. Rock may require predrilled holes.

Labor required for the complete installation and removal of a single stage wellpoint system is in the range of 3/4 to 2 labor-hours per linear foot of header, depending upon jetting conditions, wellpoint spacing, etc.

Continuous pumping is necessary except in some free draining soil where temporary flooding is permissible (as in trenches which are backfilled after each day's work). Good practice requires provision of a stand-by pump during the continuous pumping operation.

Systems for continuous trenching below the water table should be installed three to four times the length of expected daily progress to ensure uninterrupted digging, and header pipe size should not be changed during the job.

For pervious free draining soils, deep wells in place of wellpoints may be economical because of lower installation and maintenance costs. Daily production ranges between two to three wells per day, for 25' to 40' depths, to one well per day for depths over 50'.

Detailed analysis and estimating for any dewatering problem is available at no cost from wellpoint manufacturers. Major firms will quote "sufficient equipment" quotes or their affiliates will offer lump sum proposals to cover complete dewatering responsibility.

	Description for 200' System with 8" Header	Quantities
Equipment & Material	Wellpoints 25' long, 2" diameter @ 5' O.C.	40 Each
	Header pipe, 8" diameter	200 L.F.
	Discharge pipe, 8" diameter	100 L.F.
	8" valves	3 Each
	Combination jetting & wellpoint pump (standby)	1 Each
	Wellpoint pump, 8" diameter	1 Each
	Transportation to and from site	1 Day
	Fuel for 30 days x 60 gal./day	1800 Gallons
	Lubricants for 30 days x 16 lbs./day	480 Lbs.
	Sand for points	40 C.Y.
Labor	Technician to supervise installation	1 Week
	Labor for installation and removal of system	300 Labor-hours
	4 Operators straight time 40 hrs./wk. for 4.33 wks.	693 Hrs.
	4 Operators overtime 2 hrs./wk. for 4.33 wks.	35 Hrs.

Earthwork

R3141 Shoring

R314116-40 Wood Sheet Piling

Wood sheet piling may be used for depths to 20' where there is no ground water. If moderate ground water is encountered Tongue & Groove sheeting will help to keep it out. When considerable ground water is present, steel sheeting must be used.

For estimating purposes on trench excavation, sizes are as follows:

Depth	Sheeting	Wales	Braces	B.F. per S.F.
To 8'	3 x 12's	6 x 8's, 2 line	6 x 8's, @ 10'	4.0 @ 8'
8' x 12'	3 x 12's	10 x 10's, 2 line	10 x 10's, @ 9'	5.0 average
12' to 20'	3 x 12's	12 x 12's, 3 line	12 x 12's, @ 8'	7.0 average

Sheeting to be toed in at least 2' depending upon soil conditions. A five person crew with an air compressor and sheeting driver can drive and brace 440 SF/day at 8' deep, 360 SF/day at 12' deep, and 320 SF/day at 16' deep.

For normal soils, piling can be pulled in 1/3 the time to install. Pulling difficulty increases with the time in the ground. Production can be increased by high pressure jetting.

R314116-45 Steel Sheet Piling

Limiting weights are 22 to 38#/S.F. of wall surface with 27#/S.F. average for usual types and sizes. (Weights of piles themselves are from 30.7#/L.F. to 57#/L.F. but they are 15" to 21" wide.) Lightweight sections 12" to 28" wide from 3 ga. to 12 ga. thick are also available for shallow excavations. Piles may be driven two at a time with an impact or vibratory hammer (use vibratory to pull) hung from a crane without leads. A reasonable estimate of the life of steel sheet piling is 10 uses with up to 125 uses possible if a vibratory hammer is used. Used piling costs from 50% to 80% of new piling depending on location and market conditions. Sheet piling and H piles can be rented for about 30% of the delivered mill price for the first month and 5% per month thereafter. Allow 1 labor-hour per pile for cleaning and trimming after driving. These costs increase with depth and hydrostatic head. Vibratory drivers are faster in wet granular soils and are excellent for pile extraction. Pulling difficulty increases with the time in the ground and may cost more than driving. It is often economical to abandon the sheet piling, especially if it can be used as the outer wall form. Allow about 1/3 additional length or more for toeing into ground. Add bracing, waler and strut costs. Waler costs can equal the cost per ton of sheeting.

Utilities

R3311 Water Utility Distribution Piping

R331113-80 Piping Designations

There are several systems currently in use to describe pipe and fittings. The following paragraphs will help to identify and clarify classifications of piping systems used for water distribution.

Piping may be classified by schedule. Piping schedules include 5S, 10S, 10, 20, 30, Standard, 40, 60, Extra Strong, 80, 100, 120, 140, 160 and Double Extra Strong. These schedules are dependent upon the pipe wall thickness. The wall thickness of a particular schedule may vary with pipe size.

Ductile iron pipe for water distribution is classified by Pressure Classes such as Class 150, 200, 250, 300 and 350. These classes are actually the rated water working pressure of the pipe in pounds per square inch (psi). The pipe in these pressure classes is designed to withstand the rated water working pressure plus a surge allowance of 100 psi.

The American Water Works Association (AWWA) provides standards for various types of **plastic pipe**. C-900 is the specification for polyvinyl chloride (PVC) piping used for water distribution in sizes ranging from 4" through 12". C-901 is the specification for polyethylene (PE) pressure pipe, tubing and fittings used for water distribution in sizes ranging from 1/2" through 3". C-905 is the specification for PVC piping sizes 14" and greater.

PVC pressure-rated pipe is identified using the standard dimensional ratio (SDR) method. This method is defined by the American Society for Testing and Materials (ASTM) Standard D 2241. This pipe is available in SDR numbers 64, 41, 32.5, 26, 21, 17, and 13.5. A pipe with an SDR of 64 will have the thinnest wall while a pipe with an SDR of 13.5 will have the thickest wall. When the pressure rating (PR) of a pipe is given in psi, it is based on a line supplying water at 73 degrees F.

The National Sanitation Foundation (NSF) seal of approval is applied to products that can be used with potable water. These products have been tested to ANSI/NSF Standard 14.

Valves and strainers are classified by American National Standards Institute (ANSI) Classes. These Classes are 125, 150, 200, 250, 300, 400, 600, 900, 1500 and 2500. Within each class there is an operating pressure range dependent upon temperature. Design parameters should be compared to the appropriate material dependent, pressure-temperature rating chart for accurate valve selection.

Change Orders

Change Order Considerations

A change order is a written document usually prepared by the design professional and signed by the owner, the architect/engineer, and the contractor. A change order states the agreement of the parties to: an addition, deletion, or revision in the work; an adjustment in the contract sum, if any; or an adjustment in the contract time, if any. Change orders, or "extras", in the construction process occur after execution of the construction contract and impact architects/ engineers, contractors, and owners.

Change orders that are properly recognized and managed can ensure orderly, professional, and profitable progress for everyone involved in the project. There are many causes for change orders and change order requests. In all cases, change orders or change order requests should be addressed promptly and in a precise and prescribed manner. The following paragraphs include information regarding change order pricing and procedures.

The Causes of Change Orders

Reasons for issuing change orders include:

- Unforeseen field conditions that require a change in the work
- Correction of design discrepancies, errors, or omissions in the contract documents
- Owner-requested changes, either by design criteria, scope of work, or project objectives
- Completion date changes for reasons unrelated to the construction process
- Changes in building code interpretations, or other public authority requirements that require a change in the work
- Changes in availability of existing or new materials and products

Procedures

Properly written contract documents must include the correct change order procedures for all parties—owners, design professionals, and contractors—to follow in order to avoid costly delays and litigation.

Being "in the right" is not always a sufficient or acceptable defense. The contract provisions requiring notification and documentation must be adhered to within a defined or reasonable time frame.

The appropriate method of handling change orders is by a written proposal and acceptance by all parties involved. Prior to starting work on a project, all parties should identify their authorized agents who may sign and accept change orders, as well as any limits placed on their authority.

Time may be a critical factor when the need for a change arises. For such cases, the contractor might be directed to proceed on a "time and materials" basis, rather than wait for all paperwork to be processed—a delay that could impede progress. In this situation, the contractor must still follow the prescribed change order procedures including, but not limited to, notification and documentation.

Lack of documentation can be very costly, especially if legal judgments are to be made, and if certain field personnel are no longer available. For time and material change orders, the contractor should keep accurate daily records of all labor and material allocated to the change.

Owners or awarding authorities who do considerable and continual building construction (such as the federal government) realize the inevitability of change orders for numerous reasons, both predictable and unpredictable. As a result, the federal government, the American Institute of Architects (AIA), the Engineers Joint Contract Documents Committee (EJCDC), and other contractor, legal, and technical organizations have developed standards and procedures to be followed by all parties to achieve contract continuance and timely completion, while being financially fair to all concerned.

Pricing Change Orders

When pricing change orders, regardless of their cause, the most significant factor is when the change occurs. The need for a change may be perceived in the field or requested by the architect/engineer *before* any of the actual installation has begun, or may evolve or appear *during* construction when the item of work in question is partially installed. In the latter cases, the original sequence of construction is disrupted, along with all contiguous and supporting systems. Change orders cause the greatest impact when they occur *after* the installation has been completed and must be uncovered, or even replaced. Post-completion changes may be caused by necessary design changes, product failure, or changes in the owner's requirements that are not discovered until the building or the systems begin to function.

Specified procedures of notification and record keeping must be adhered to and enforced regardless of the stage of construction: *before*, *during*, or *after* installation. Some bidding documents anticipate change orders by requiring that unit prices including overhead and profit percentages—for additional as well as deductible changes—be listed. Generally these unit prices do not fully take into account the ripple effect, or impact on other trades, and should be used for general guidance only.

When pricing change orders, it is important to classify the time frame in which the change occurs. There are two basic time frames for change orders: *pre-installation change orders*, which occur before the start of construction, and *post-installation change orders*, which involve reworking after the original installation. Change orders that occur between these stages may be priced according to the extent of work completed using a combination of techniques developed for pricing *pre-* and *post-installation* changes.

Factors To Consider When Pricing Change Orders

As an estimator begins to prepare a change order, the following questions should be reviewed to determine their impact on the final price.

General

- *Is the change order work* pre-installation *or* post-installation?

  Change order work costs vary according to how much of the installation has been completed. Once workers have the project scoped in their minds, even though they have not started, it can be difficult to refocus. Consequently they may spend more than the normal amount of time understanding the change. Also, modifications to work in place, such as trimming or refitting, usually take more time than was initially estimated. The greater the amount of work in place, the more reluctant workers are to change it. Psychologically they may resent the change and as a result the rework takes longer than normal. Post-installation change order estimates must include demolition of existing work as required to accomplish the change. If the work is performed at a later time, additional obstacles, such as building finishes, may be present which must be protected. Regardless of whether the change occurs pre-installation or post-installation, attempt to isolate the identifiable factors and price them separately. For example, add shipping costs that may be required pre-installation or any demolition required post-installation. Then analyze the potential impact on productivity of psychological and/or learning curve factors and adjust the output rates accordingly. One approach is to break down the typical workday into segments and quantify the impact on each segment.

Change Order Installation Efficiency

The labor-hours expressed (for new construction) are based on average installation time, using an efficiency level. For change order situations, adjustments to this efficiency level should reflect the daily labor-hour allocation for that particular occurrence.

- *Will the change substantially delay the original completion date?*

A significant change in the project may cause the original completion date to be extended. The extended schedule may subject the contractor to new wage rates dictated by relevant labor contracts. Project supervision and other project overhead must also be extended beyond the original completion date. The schedule extension may also put installation into a new weather season. For example, underground piping scheduled for October installation was delayed until January. As a result, frost penetrated the trench area, thereby changing the degree of difficulty of the task. Changes and delays may have a ripple effect throughout the project. This effect must be analyzed and negotiated with the owner.

- *What is the net effect of a deduct change order?*

In most cases, change orders resulting in a deduction or credit reflect only bare costs. The contractor may retain the overhead and profit based on the original bid.

Materials

- *Will you have to pay more or less for the new material, required by the change order, than you paid for the original purchase?*

The same material prices or discounts will usually apply to materials purchased for change orders as new construction. In some instances, however, the contractor may forfeit the advantages of competitive pricing for change orders. Consider the following example:

A contractor purchased over $20,000 worth of fan coil units for an installation and obtained the maximum discount. Some time later it was determined the project required an additional matching unit. The contractor has to purchase this unit from the original supplier to ensure a match. The supplier at this time may not discount the unit because of the small quantity, and he is no longer in a competitive situation. The impact of quantity on purchase can add between 0% and 25% to material prices and/or subcontractor quotes.

- *If materials have been ordered or delivered to the job site, will they be subject to a cancellation charge or restocking fee?*

Check with the supplier to determine if ordered materials are subject to a cancellation charge. Delivered materials not used as a result of a change order may be subject to a restocking fee if returned to the supplier. Common restocking charges run between 20% and 40%. Also, delivery charges to return the goods to the supplier must be added.

Labor

- *How efficient is the existing crew at the actual installation?*

Is the same crew that performed the initial work going to do the change order? Possibly the change consists of the installation of a unit identical to one already installed; therefore, the change should take less time. Be sure to consider this potential productivity increase and modify the productivity rates accordingly.

- *If the crew size is increased, what impact will that have on supervision requirements?*

Under most bargaining agreements or management practices, there is a point at which a working foreperson is replaced by a nonworking foreperson. This replacement increases project overhead by adding a nonproductive worker. If additional workers are added to accelerate the project or to perform changes while maintaining the schedule, be sure to add additional supervision time if warranted. Calculate the hours involved and the additional cost directly if possible.

- *What are the other impacts of increased crew size?*

The larger the crew, the greater the potential for productivity to decrease. Some of the factors that cause this productivity loss are: overcrowding (producing restrictive conditions in the working space) and possibly a shortage of any special tools and equipment required. Such factors affect not only the crew working on the elements directly involved in the change order, but other crews whose movements may also be hampered. As the crew increases, check its basic composition for changes by the addition or deletion of apprentices or nonworking foreperson, and quantify the potential effects of equipment shortages or other logistical factors.

- *As new crews, unfamiliar with the project, are brought onto the site, how long will it take them to become oriented to the project requirements?*

The orientation time for a new crew to become 100% effective varies with the site and type of project. Orientation is easiest at a new construction site and most difficult at existing, very restrictive renovation sites. The type of work also affects orientation time. When all elements of the work are exposed, such as concrete or masonry work, orientation is decreased. When the work is concealed or less visible, such as existing electrical systems, orientation takes longer. Usually orientation can be accomplished in one day or less. Costs for added orientation should be itemized and added to the total estimated cost.

- *How much actual production can be gained by working overtime?*

Short term overtime can be used effectively to accomplish more work in a day. However, as overtime is scheduled to run beyond several weeks, studies have shown marked decreases in output. The following chart shows the effect of long term overtime on worker efficiency. If the anticipated change requires extended overtime to keep the job on schedule, these factors can be used as a guide to predict the impact on time and cost. Add project overhead, particularly supervision, that may also be incurred.

Days per Week	Hours per Day	Production Efficiency					Payroll Cost Factors	
		1st Week	2nd Week	3rd Week	4th Week	Average 4 Weeks	@ 1-1/2 Times	@ 2 Times
5	8	100%	100%	100%	100%	100%	100%	100%
	9	100	100	95	90	96	1.056	1.111
	10	100	95	90	85	93	1.100	1.200
	11	95	90	75	65	81	1.136	1.273
	12	90	85	70	60	76	1.167	1.333
6	8	100	100	95	90	96	1.083	1.167
	9	100	95	90	85	93	1.130	1.259
	10	95	90	85	80	88	1.167	1.333
	11	95	85	70	65	79	1.197	1.394
	12	90	80	65	60	74	1.222	1.444
7	8	100	95	85	75	89	1.143	1.286
	9	95	90	80	70	84	1.183	1.365
	10	90	85	75	65	79	1.214	1.429
	11	85	80	65	60	73	1.240	1.481
	12	85	75	60	55	69	1.262	1.524

Effects of Overtime

Caution: Under many labor agreements, Sundays and holidays are paid at a higher premium than the normal overtime rate.

The use of long-term overtime is counterproductive on almost any construction job; that is, the longer the period of overtime, the lower the actual production rate. Numerous studies have been conducted, and while they have resulted in slightly different numbers, all reach the same conclusion. The figure above tabulates the effects of overtime work on efficiency.

As illustrated, there can be a difference between the *actual* payroll cost per hour and the *effective* cost per hour for overtime work. This is due to the reduced production efficiency with the increase in weekly hours beyond 40. This difference between actual and effective cost results from overtime work over a prolonged period. Short-term overtime work does not result in as great a reduction in efficiency and, in such cases, effective cost may not vary significantly from the actual payroll cost. As the total hours per week are increased on a regular basis, more time is lost due to fatigue, lowered morale, and an increased accident rate.

As an example, assume a project where workers are working 6 days a week, 10 hours per day. From the figure above (based on productivity studies), the average effective productive hours over a 4-week period are:

$$0.875 \times 60 = 52.5$$

Depending upon the locale and day of week, overtime hours may be paid at time and a half or double time. For time and a half, the overall (average) *actual* payroll cost (including regular and overtime hours) is determined as follows:

$$\frac{40 \text{ reg. hrs.} + (20 \text{ overtime hrs.} \times 1.5)}{60 \text{ hrs.}} = 1.167$$

Based on 60 hours, the payroll cost per hour will be 116.7% of the normal rate at 40 hours per week. However, because the effective production (efficiency) for 60 hours is reduced to the equivalent of 52.5 hours, the effective cost of overtime is calculated as follows:

For time and a half:

$$\frac{40 \text{ reg. hrs.} + (20 \text{ overtime hrs.} \times 1.5)}{52.5 \text{ hrs.}} = 1.33$$

The installed cost will be 133% of the normal rate (for labor).

Thus, when figuring overtime, the actual cost per unit of work will be higher than the apparent overtime payroll dollar increase, due to the reduced productivity of the longer work week. These efficiency calculations are true only for those cost factors determined by hours worked. Costs that are applied weekly or monthly, such as equipment rentals, will not be similarly affected.

Equipment

- *What equipment is required to complete the change order?*

Change orders may require extending the rental period of equipment already on the job site, or the addition of special equipment brought in to accomplish the change work. In either case, the additional rental charges and operator labor charges must be added.

Summary

The preceding considerations and others you deem appropriate should be analyzed and applied to a change order estimate. The impact of each should be quantified and listed on the estimate to form an audit trail.

Change orders that are properly identified, documented, and managed help to ensure the orderly, professional, and profitable progress of the work. They also minimize potential claims or disputes at the end of the project.

Project Costs

Back by customer demand!

You asked and we listened. For customer convenience and estimating ease, we have made the 2023 Project Costs available for download at **RSMeans.com/2023books**. You will also find sample estimates, an RSMeans data overview video, and a book registration form to receive quarterly data updates throughout 2023.

Estimating Tips

- The cost figures available in the download were derived from hundreds of projects contained in the RSMeans database of completed construction projects. They include the contractor's overhead and profit. The figures have been adjusted to January of the current year.
- These projects were located throughout the U.S. and reflect a tremendous variation in square foot (S.F.) costs. This is due to differences, not only in labor and material costs, but also in individual owners' requirements. For instance, a bank in a large city would have different features than one in a rural area. This is true of all the different types of buildings analyzed. Therefore, caution should be exercised when using these Project Costs. For example, for courthouses, costs in the database are local courthouse costs and will not apply to the larger, more elaborate federal courthouses.
- None of the figures "go with" any others. All individual cost items were computed and tabulated separately. Thus, the sum of the median figures for plumbing, HVAC, and electrical will not normally total up to the total mechanical and electrical costs arrived at by separate analysis and tabulation of the projects.
- Each building was analyzed as to total and component costs and percentages. The figures were arranged in ascending order with the results tabulated as shown. The 1/4 column shows that 25% of the projects had lower costs and 75% had higher. The 3/4 column shows that 75% of the projects had lower costs and 25% had higher. The median column shows that 50% of the projects had lower costs and 50% had higher.
- Project Costs are useful in the conceptual stage when no details are available. As soon as details become available in the project design, the square foot approach should be discontinued and the project should be priced as to its particular components. When more precision is required, or for estimating the replacement cost of specific buildings, the current edition of *Square Foot Costs with RSMeans data* should be used.
- In using the figures in this section, it is recommended that the median column be used for preliminary figures if no additional information is available. The median figures, when multiplied by the total city construction cost index figures (see City Cost Indexes) and then multiplied by the project size modifier at the end of this section, should present a fairly accurate base figure, which would then have to be adjusted in view of the estimator's experience, local economic conditions, code requirements, and the owner's particular requirements. There is no need to factor in the percentage figures, as these should remain constant from city to city.
- The editors of this data would greatly appreciate receiving cost figures on one or more of your recent projects, which would then be included in the averages for next year. All cost figures received will be kept confidential, except that they will be averaged with other similar projects to arrive at square foot cost figures for next year.

See the website above for details and the discount available for submitting one or more of your projects.

Same Data. Simplified.

Enjoy the convenience and efficiency of accessing your costs anywhere:

- **Skip the multiplier** by setting your location
- **Quickly search,** edit, favorite and share costs
- **Stay on top of price changes** with automatic updates

Discover more at rsmeans.com/online

No part of this cost data may be reproduced, stored in a retrieval system, or transmitted in any form or by any means without prior written permission of Gordian.

50 17 | Project Costs

50 17 00 | Project Costs

			UNIT	UNIT COSTS			% OF TOTAL		
				1/4	MEDIAN	3/4	1/4	MEDIAN	3/4
01	0000	**Auto Sales with Repair**	S.F.						
	0100	Architectural		146	163	176	58%	64%	67%
	0200	Plumbing		12.20	12.75	17.05	4.84%	5.20%	6.80%
	0300	Mechanical		16.30	22	24	6.40%	8.70%	10.15%
	0400	Electrical		25	31	39	9.05%	11.70%	15.90%
	0500	Total Project Costs		244	255	262			
02	0000	**Banking Institutions**	S.F.						
	0100	Architectural		220	270	330	59%	65%	69%
	0200	Plumbing		8.85	12.35	17.15	2.12%	3.39%	4.19%
	0300	Mechanical		17.60	24.50	28.50	4.41%	5.10%	10.75%
	0400	Electrical		43	52	80	10.45%	13.05%	15.90%
	0500	Total Project Costs		365	410	505			
03	0000	**Courthouse**	S.F.						
	0100	Architectural		116	228	320	54.50%	58.50%	61%
	0200	Plumbing		4.38	16.30	16.30	2.07%	3.13%	3.13%
	0300	Mechanical		27.50	32.50	32.50	6.25%	12.95%	12.95%
	0400	Electrical		35	40	40	7.65%	16.60%	16.60%
	0500	Total Project Costs		211	390	520			
04	0000	**Data Centers**	S.F.						
	0100	Architectural		262	262	262	68%	68%	68%
	0200	Plumbing		14.35	14.35	14.35	3.71%	3.71%	3.71%
	0300	Mechanical		36.50	36.50	36.50	9.45%	9.45%	9.45%
	0400	Electrical		34.50	34.50	34.50	9%	9%	9%
	0500	Total Project Costs		385	385	385			
05	0000	**Detention Centers**	S.F.						
	0100	Architectural		243	256	272	52%	53%	60.50%
	0200	Plumbing		25.50	31	37.50	5.15%	7.10%	7.25%
	0300	Mechanical		32.50	46.50	55.50	7.55%	9.50%	13.80%
	0400	Electrical		53.50	63	82	10.90%	14.85%	17.95%
	0500	Total Project Costs		410	435	510			
06	0000	**Fire Stations**	S.F.						
	0100	Architectural		141	180	284	46%	54.50%	61.50%
	0200	Plumbing		14.75	19.70	25.50	4.67%	5.60%	6.35%
	0300	Mechanical		22	31	42	6.10%	8.25%	10.20%
	0400	Electrical		33.50	41	57.50	10.75%	12.55%	14.95%
	0500	Total Project Costs		292	350	465			
07	0000	**Gymnasium**	S.F.						
	0100	Architectural		121	160	160	57%	64.50%	64.50%
	0200	Plumbing		2.97	9.75	9.75	1.58%	3.48%	3.48%
	0300	Mechanical		4.56	41	41	2.42%	14.65%	14.65%
	0400	Electrical		14.95	29	29	7.95%	10.35%	10.35%
	0500	Total Project Costs		189	280	280			
08	0000	**Hospitals**	S.F.						
	0100	Architectural		147	242	263	41.50%	47.50%	48%
	0200	Plumbing		10.80	44.50	53	6%	7.65%	10.35%
	0300	Mechanical		65	80.50	105	12.55%	17.95%	23.50%
	0400	Electrical		32.50	73.50	84.50	10.95%	14.10%	16.85%
	0500	Total Project Costs		345	520	555			
09	0000	**Industrial Buildings**	S.F.						
	0100	Architectural		80.50	158	320	52%	56%	82%
	0200	Plumbing		2.32	6.30	18.20	1.57%	2.11%	6.30%
	0300	Mechanical		6.60	12.55	60	4.77%	5.55%	14.80%
	0400	Electrical		10.10	11.50	96	7.85%	13.55%	16.20%
	0500	Total Project Costs		119	181	595			
10	0000	**Medical Clinics & Offices**	S.F.						
	0100	Architectural		134	166	218	48.50%	54%	62%
	0200	Plumbing		12.30	18.55	30.50	4.50%	6.65%	8.75%
	0300	Mechanical		19.90	30.50	54.50	7.80%	10.85%	15.75%
	0400	Electrical		27	33.50	51	8.90%	11.20%	13.85%
	0500	Total Project Costs		231	305	400			

50 17 | Project Costs

50 17 00 | Project Costs

			UNIT	UNIT COSTS 1/4	UNIT COSTS MEDIAN	UNIT COSTS 3/4	% OF TOTAL 1/4	% OF TOTAL MEDIAN	% OF TOTAL 3/4
11	0000	**Mixed Use**	S.F.						
	0100	Architectural		151	209	285	45.50%	52.50%	61.50%
	0200	Plumbing		8.55	15.55	16.55	3.31%	3.47%	4.18%
	0300	Mechanical		22.50	49	65	6.10%	13.60%	17.05%
	0400	Electrical		30	50.50	72.50	8.60%	11.65%	15.65%
	0500	Total Project Costs		264	460	470			
12	0000	**Multi-Family Housing**	S.F.						
	0100	Architectural		105	143	233	54.50%	62%	69%
	0200	Plumbing		9.40	15.15	20.50	5.25%	6.65%	8%
	0300	Mechanical		9.65	13	37	4.41%	6.05%	10.25%
	0400	Electrical		12.70	21.50	31	5.65%	7.90%	10.25%
	0500	Total Project Costs		174	286	370			
13	0000	**Nursing Home & Assisted Living**	S.F.						
	0100	Architectural		99	143	162	51.50%	55.50%	63.50%
	0200	Plumbing		10.60	15.95	19	6.25%	7.40%	9.20%
	0300	Mechanical		8.70	12.85	25	4.04%	6.70%	9.55%
	0400	Electrical		14.60	25.50	33.50	7.25%	11%	13.10%
	0500	Total Project Costs		174	224	296			
14	0000	**Office Buildings**	S.F.						
	0100	Architectural		130	177	244	54.50%	61%	69%
	0200	Plumbing		7	11	20.50	2.70%	3.78%	5.20%
	0300	Mechanical		13.70	23.50	36	5.55%	8.15%	11.10%
	0400	Electrical		18.35	30	48	7.80%	10.10%	12.90%
	0500	Total Project Costs		221	292	400			
15	0000	**Parking Garage**	S.F.						
	0100	Architectural		43.50	53	55.50	70%	79%	88%
	0200	Plumbing		1.43	1.50	2.80	2.05%	2.70%	2.83%
	0300	Mechanical		1.11	1.71	6.50	2.11%	3.62%	3.81%
	0400	Electrical		3.81	4.19	8.75	5.30%	6.35%	7.95%
	0500	Total Project Costs		53	64.50	70			
16	0000	**Parking Garage/Mixed Use**	S.F.						
	0100	Architectural		141	154	157	61%	62%	65.50%
	0200	Plumbing		4.52	5.95	9.10	2.47%	2.72%	3.66%
	0300	Mechanical		19.35	22	31.50	7.80%	13.10%	13.60%
	0400	Electrical		20.50	29	30	8.20%	12.65%	18.15%
	0500	Total Project Costs		230	240	248			
17	0000	**Police Stations**	S.F.						
	0100	Architectural		159	225	277	49%	61%	61.50%
	0200	Plumbing		21	25.50	25.50	5.05%	5.55%	7.70%
	0300	Mechanical		47.50	66.50	69	12.35%	14.55%	16.55%
	0400	Electrical		36	41.50	61.50	9.15%	12.10%	14%
	0500	Total Project Costs		298	415	455			
18	0000	**Police/Fire**	S.F.						
	0100	Architectural		155	155	475	55.50%	66%	68%
	0200	Plumbing		12.40	12.85	47.50	5.45%	5.50%	5.55%
	0300	Mechanical		19	30	109	8.35%	12.70%	12.80%
	0400	Electrical		21.50	27.50	124	9.50%	11.75%	14.55%
	0500	Total Project Costs		228	235	855			
19	0000	**Public Assembly Buildings**	S.F.						
	0100	Architectural		158	206	320	56.50%	61%	64%
	0200	Plumbing		8.35	12.25	18.10	2.63%	3.36%	4.39%
	0300	Mechanical		17.60	30.50	48.50	6.45%	8.75%	12.45%
	0400	Electrical		26	35	56	8.60%	10.70%	12.80%
	0500	Total Project Costs		254	340	505			
20	0000	**Recreational**	S.F.						
	0100	Architectural		152	230	325	49.50%	59%	64.50%
	0200	Plumbing		11.35	18.30	30	3.08%	4.67%	7.40%
	0300	Mechanical		18.10	27.50	41	5.15%	6.65%	11.35%
	0400	Electrical		22	37.50	54.50	7.10%	8.95%	10.80%
	0500	Total Project Costs		270	390	610			

For customer support on your Mechanical Costs with RSMeans data, call 800.448.8182.

50 17 | Project Costs

		50 17 00	Project Costs	UNIT	UNIT COSTS			% OF TOTAL			
					1/4	MEDIAN	3/4	1/4	MEDIAN	3/4	
21	0000	Restaurants		S.F.							21
	0100		Architectural		172	270	340	57.50%	60%	63.50%	
	0200		Plumbing		18.95	38	50	7.35%	7.70%	8.75%	
	0300		Mechanical		20.50	27	51	6.50%	8.15%	11.15%	
	0400		Electrical		20.50	33	66	6.75%	10.30%	11.60%	
	0500		Total Project Costs		285	470	570				
22	0000	Retail		S.F.							22
	0100		Architectural		77	120	248	54.50%	60%	64.50%	
	0200		Plumbing		9.60	13.40	16.65	4.18%	5.45%	8.45%	
	0300		Mechanical		9	12.75	23.50	4.98%	6.15%	7.05%	
	0400		Electrical		14.30	29	43	7.90%	11.25%	12.45%	
	0500		Total Project Costs		117	208	400				
23	0000	Schools		S.F.							23
	0100		Architectural		133	169	226	50.50%	55.50%	60.50%	
	0200		Plumbing		10.60	14.55	21	3.66%	4.57%	6.95%	
	0300		Mechanical		25	36	52.50	8.90%	11.95%	14.55%	
	0400		Electrical		25	34.50	44.50	9.45%	11.25%	13.30%	
	0500		Total Project Costs		242	310	415				
24	0000	University, College & Private School Classroom & Admin Buildings		S.F.							24
	0100		Architectural		172	224	272	50%	53.50%	58.50%	
	0200		Plumbing		11.75	16.10	29.50	3.04%	4.30%	6.35%	
	0300		Mechanical		34	51.50	66	9.20%	11.40%	14.40%	
	0400		Electrical		28.50	41	53.50	7.70%	9.95%	12.55%	
	0500		Total Project Costs		297	415	540				
25	0000	University, College & Private School Dormitories		S.F.							25
	0100		Architectural		111	195	207	53%	61.50%	68%	
	0200		Plumbing		14.65	21	24	6.35%	6.65%	8.95%	
	0300		Mechanical		6.60	28	44.50	4.13%	9%	11.80%	
	0400		Electrical		7.80	27	41.50	4.75%	7.35%	10.60%	
	0500		Total Project Costs		164	310	370				
26	0000	University, College & Private School Science, Eng. & Lab Buildings		S.F.							26
	0100		Architectural		191	226	335	48%	54.50%	58%	
	0200		Plumbing		13.15	19.90	33.50	3.29%	3.77%	5%	
	0300		Mechanical		50.50	94	96.50	11.70%	19.40%	23.50%	
	0400		Electrical		39.50	51.50	53	9%	12.05%	13.15%	
	0500		Total Project Costs		400	430	585				
27	0000	University, College & Private School Student Union Buildings		S.F.							27
	0100		Architectural		151	395	395	54.50%	54.50%	59.50%	
	0200		Plumbing		23	23	34	3.13%	4.27%	11.45%	
	0300		Mechanical		43.50	70	70	9.60%	9.60%	14.55%	
	0400		Electrical		38	66	66	9.05%	12.80%	13.15%	
	0500		Total Project Costs		297	730	730				
28	0000	Warehouses		S.F.							28
	0100		Architectural		65	98.50	180	60.50%	67%	71.50%	
	0200		Plumbing		3.37	7.20	13.90	2.82%	3.72%	5%	
	0300		Mechanical		3.99	22.50	35.50	4.56%	8.15%	10.70%	
	0400		Electrical		8.40	27	45.50	7.75%	10.10%	18.30%	
	0500		Total Project Costs		96.50	154	310				

Square Foot Project Size Modifier

One factor that affects the S.F. cost of a particular building is the size. In general, for buildings built to the same specifications in the same locality, the larger building will have the lower S.F. cost. This is due mainly to the decreasing contribution of the exterior walls plus the economy of scale usually achievable in larger buildings. The Area Conversion Scale shown below will give a factor to convert costs for the typical size building to an adjusted cost for the particular project.

The Square Foot Base Size lists the median costs, most typical project size in our accumulated data, and the range in size of the projects.

The Size Factor for your project is determined by dividing your project area in S.F. by the typical project size for the particular Building Type. With this factor, enter the Area Conversion Scale at the appropriate Size Factor and determine the appropriate Cost Multiplier for your building size.

Example: Determine the cost per S.F. for a 107,200 S.F. Multi-family housing.

$$\frac{\text{Proposed building area} = 107{,}200 \text{ S.F.}}{\text{Typical size from below} = 53{,}600 \text{ S.F.}} = 2.00$$

Enter Area Conversion Scale at 2.0, intersect curve, read horizontally the appropriate cost multiplier of .94. Size adjusted cost becomes .94 x $286.00 = $268.84 based on national average costs.

Note: For Size Factors less than .50, the Cost Multiplier is 1.1
For Size Factors greater than 3.5, the Cost Multiplier is .90

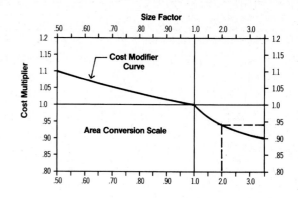

System	Median Cost (Total Project Costs)	Typical Size Gross S.F. (Median of Projects)	Typical Range (Low – High) (Projects)
Auto Sales with Repair	$255.00	24,900	4,700 – 29,300
Banking Institutions	410.00	9,300	3,300 – 38,100
Courthouse	390.00	56,000	24,700 – 70,500
Data Centers	385.00	14,400	14,400 – 14,400
Detention Centers	435.00	37,800	12,300 – 183,330
Fire Stations	350.00	12,400	6,300 – 49,600
Gymnasium	280.00	52,400	22,800 – 82,000
Hospitals	520.00	73,300	12,700 – 410,300
Industrial Buildings	181.00	21,100	5,100 – 200,600
Medical Clinics & Offices	305.00	24,200	2,300 – 327,000
Mixed Use	460.00	31,800	7,200 – 188,900
Multi-Family Housing	286.00	53,600	2,500 – 1,161,500
Nursing Home & Assisted Living	224.00	38,700	1,500 – 242,600
Office Buildings	292.00	21,000	1,100 – 930,000
Parking Garage	64.50	151,800	99,900 – 287,000
Parking Garage/Mixed Use	240.00	254,200	5,300 – 318,000
Police Stations	415.00	25,200	12,700 – 88,600
Police/Fire	235.00	44,300	8,600 – 50,300
Public Assembly Buildings	340.00	20,800	2,200 – 235,300
Recreational	390.00	27,700	1,000 – 223,800
Restaurants	470.00	5,900	2,100 – 42,000
Retail	208.00	26,000	4,000 – 84,300
Schools	310.00	69,400	1,300 – 410,800
University, College & Private School Classroom & Admin Buildings	415.00	48,300	2,400 – 196,200
University, College & Private School Dormitories	310.00	39,200	1,500 – 126,900
University, College & Private School Science, Eng. & Lab Buildings	430.00	60,000	5,300 – 117,600
University, College & Private School Student Union Buildings	730.00	48,700	42,100 – 50,000
Warehouses	154.00	10,900	600 – 303,800

Abbreviations

A	Area Square Feet; Ampere	Brk., brk	Brick	Csc	Cosecant
AAFES	Army and Air Force Exchange Service	brkt	Bracket	C.S.F.	Hundred Square Feet
ABS	Acrylonitrile Butadiene Stryrene; Asbestos Bonded Steel	Brs.	Brass	CSI	Construction Specifications Institute
A.C., AC	Alternating Current; Air-Conditioning; Asbestos Cement; Plywood Grade A & C	Brz.	Bronze	CT	Current Transformer
		Bsn.	Basin	CTS	Copper Tube Size
		Btr.	Better	Cu	Copper, Cubic
		BTU	British Thermal Unit	Cu. Ft.	Cubic Foot
		BTUH	BTU per Hour	cw	Continuous Wave
ACI	American Concrete Institute	Bu.	Bushels	C.W.	Cool White; Cold Water
ACR	Air Conditioning Refrigeration	BUR	Built-up Roofing	Cwt.	100 Pounds
ADA	Americans with Disabilities Act	BX	Interlocked Armored Cable	C.W.X.	Cool White Deluxe
AD	Plywood, Grade A & D	°C	Degree Centigrade	C.Y.	Cubic Yard (27 cubic feet)
Addit.	Additional	c	Conductivity, Copper Sweat	C.Y./Hr.	Cubic Yard per Hour
Adh.	Adhesive	C	Hundred; Centigrade	Cyl.	Cylinder
Adj.	Adjustable	C/C	Center to Center, Cedar on Cedar	d	Penny (nail size)
af	Audio-frequency	C-C	Center to Center	D	Deep; Depth; Discharge
AFFF	Aqueous Film Forming Foam	Cab	Cabinet	Dis., Disch.	Discharge
AFUE	Annual Fuel Utilization Efficiency	Cair.	Air Tool Laborer	Db	Decibel
AGA	American Gas Association	Cal.	Caliper	Dbl.	Double
Agg.	Aggregate	Calc	Calculated	DC	Direct Current
A.H., Ah	Ampere Hours	Cap.	Capacity	DDC	Direct Digital Control
A hr.	Ampere-hour	Carp.	Carpenter	Demob.	Demobilization
A.H.U., AHU	Air Handling Unit	C.B.	Circuit Breaker	d.f.t.	Dry Film Thickness
A.I.A.	American Institute of Architects	C.C.A.	Chromate Copper Arsenate	d.f.u.	Drainage Fixture Units
AIC	Ampere Interrupting Capacity	C.C.F.	Hundred Cubic Feet	D.H.	Double Hung
Allow.	Allowance	cd	Candela	DHW	Domestic Hot Water
alt., alt	Alternate	cd/sf	Candela per Square Foot	DI	Ductile Iron
Alum.	Aluminum	CD	Grade of Plywood Face & Back	Diag.	Diagonal
a.m.	Ante Meridiem	CDX	Plywood, Grade C & D, exterior glue	Diam., Dia	Diameter
Amp.	Ampere	Cefi.	Cement Finisher	Distrib.	Distribution
Anod.	Anodized	Cem.	Cement	Div.	Division
ANSI	American National Standards Institute	CF	Hundred Feet	Dk.	Deck
		C.F.	Cubic Feet	D.L.	Dead Load; Diesel
APA	American Plywood Association	CFM	Cubic Feet per Minute	DLH	Deep Long Span Bar Joist
Approx.	Approximate	CFRP	Carbon Fiber Reinforced Plastic	dlx	Deluxe
Apt.	Apartment	c.g.	Center of Gravity	Do.	Ditto
Asb.	Asbestos	CHW	Chilled Water; Commercial Hot Water	DOP	Dioctyl Phthalate Penetration Test (Air Filters)
A.S.B.C.	American Standard Building Code				
Asbe.	Asbestos Worker	C.I., CI	Cast Iron	Dp., dp	Depth
ASCE	American Society of Civil Engineers	C.I.P., CIP	Cast in Place	D.P.S.T.	Double Pole, Single Throw
A.S.H.R.A.E.	American Society of Heating, Refrig. & AC Engineers	Circ.	Circuit	Dr.	Drive
		C.L.	Carload Lot	DR	Dimension Ratio
ASME	American Society of Mechanical Engineers	CL	Chain Link	Drink.	Drinking
		Clab.	Common Laborer	D.S.	Double Strength
ASTM	American Society for Testing and Materials	Clam	Common Maintenance Laborer	D.S.A.	Double Strength A Grade
		C.L.F.	Hundred Linear Feet	D.S.B.	Double Strength B Grade
Attchmt.	Attachment	CLF	Current Limiting Fuse	Dty.	Duty
Avg., Ave.	Average	CLP	Cross Linked Polyethylene	DWV	Drain Waste Vent
AWG	American Wire Gauge	cm	Centimeter	DX	Deluxe White, Direct Expansion
AWWA	American Water Works Assoc.	CMP	Corr. Metal Pipe	dyn	Dyne
Bbl.	Barrel	CMU	Concrete Masonry Unit	e	Eccentricity
B&B, BB	Grade B and Better; Balled & Burlapped	CN	Change Notice	E	Equipment Only; East; Emissivity
		Col.	Column	Ea.	Each
B&S	Bell and Spigot	CO_2	Carbon Dioxide	EB	Encased Burial
B.&W.	Black and White	Comb.	Combination	Econ.	Economy
b.c.c.	Body-centered Cubic	comm.	Commercial, Communication	E.C.Y	Embankment Cubic Yards
B.C.Y.	Bank Cubic Yards	Compr.	Compressor	EDP	Electronic Data Processing
BE	Bevel End	Conc.	Concrete	EIFS	Exterior Insulation Finish System
B.F.	Board Feet	Cont., cont	Continuous; Continued, Container	E.D.R.	Equiv. Direct Radiation
Bg. cem.	Bag of Cement	Corkbd.	Cork Board	Eq.	Equation
BHP	Boiler Horsepower; Brake Horsepower	Corr.	Corrugated	EL	Elevation
		Cos	Cosine	Elec.	Electrician; Electrical
B.I.	Black Iron	Cot	Cotangent	Elev.	Elevator; Elevating
bidir.	bidirectional	Cov.	Cover	EMT	Electrical Metallic Conduit; Thin Wall Conduit
Bit., Bitum.	Bituminous	C/P	Cedar on Paneling		
Bit., Conc.	Bituminous Concrete	CPA	Control Point Adjustment	Eng.	Engine, Engineered
Bk.	Backed	Cplg.	Coupling	EPDM	Ethylene Propylene Diene Monomer
Bkrs.	Breakers	CPM	Critical Path Method		
Bldg., bldg	Building	CPVC	Chlorinated Polyvinyl Chloride	EPS	Expanded Polystyrene
Blk.	Block	C.Pr.	Hundred Pair	Eqhv.	Equip. Oper., Heavy
Bm.	Beam	CRC	Cold Rolled Channel	Eqlt.	Equip. Oper., Light
Boil.	Boilermaker	Creos.	Creosote	Eqmd.	Equip. Oper., Medium
bpm	Blows per Minute	Crpt.	Carpet & Linoleum Layer	Eqmm.	Equip. Oper., Master Mechanic
BR	Bedroom	CRT	Cathode-ray Tube	Eqol.	Equip. Oper., Oilers
Brg., brng.	Bearing	CS	Carbon Steel, Constant Shear Bar Joist	Equip.	Equipment
Brhe.	Bricklayer Helper			ERW	Electric Resistance Welded
Bric.	Bricklayer				

Abbreviations

E.S.	Energy Saver	H	High Henry	Lath.	Lather
Est.	Estimated	HC	High Capacity	Lav.	Lavatory
esu	Electrostatic Units	H.D., HD	Heavy Duty; High Density	lb.; #	Pound
E.W.	Each Way	H.D.O.	High Density Overlaid	L.B., LB	Load Bearing; L Conduit Body
EWT	Entering Water Temperature	HDPE	High Density Polyethylene Plastic	L. & E.	Labor & Equipment
Excav.	Excavation	Hdr.	Header	lb./hr.	Pounds per Hour
excl	Excluding	Hdwe.	Hardware	lb./L.F.	Pounds per Linear Foot
Exp., exp	Expansion, Exposure	H.I.D., HID	High Intensity Discharge	lbf/sq.in.	Pound-force per Square Inch
Ext., ext	Exterior; Extension	Help.	Helper Average	L.C.L.	Less than Carload Lot
Extru.	Extrusion	HEPA	High Efficiency Particulate Air Filter	L.C.Y.	Loose Cubic Yard
f.	Fiber Stress			Ld.	Load
F	Fahrenheit; Female; Fill	Hg	Mercury	LE	Lead Equivalent
Fab., fab	Fabricated; Fabric	HIC	High Interrupting Capacity	LED	Light Emitting Diode
FBGS	Fiberglass	HM	Hollow Metal	L.F.	Linear Foot
F.C.	Footcandles	HMWPE	High Molecular Weight Polyethylene	L.F. Hdr	Linear Feet of Header
f.c.c.	Face-centered Cubic			L.F. Nose	Linear Foot of Stair Nosing
f'c.	Compressive Stress in Concrete; Extreme Compressive Stress	HO	High Output	L.F. Rsr	Linear Foot of Stair Riser
		Horiz.	Horizontal	Lg.	Long; Length; Large
F.E.	Front End	H.P., HP	Horsepower; High Pressure	L & H	Light and Heat
FEP	Fluorinated Ethylene Propylene (Teflon)	H.P.F.	High Power Factor	LH	Long Span Bar Joist
		Hr.	Hour	L.H.	Labor Hours
F.G.	Flat Grain	Hrs./Day	Hours per Day	L.L., LL	Live Load
F.H.A.	Federal Housing Administration	HSC	High Short Circuit	L.L.D.	Lamp Lumen Depreciation
Fig.	Figure	Ht.	Height	lm	Lumen
Fin.	Finished	Htg.	Heating	lm/sf	Lumen per Square Foot
FIPS	Female Iron Pipe Size	Htrs.	Heaters	lm/W	Lumen per Watt
Fixt.	Fixture	HVAC	Heating, Ventilation & Air-Conditioning	LOA	Length Over All
FJP	Finger jointed and primed			log	Logarithm
Fl. Oz.	Fluid Ounces	Hvy.	Heavy	L-O-L	Lateralolet
Flr.	Floor	HW	Hot Water	long.	Longitude
Flrs.	Floors	Hyd.; Hydr.	Hydraulic	L.P., LP	Liquefied Petroleum; Low Pressure
FM	Frequency Modulation; Factory Mutual	Hz	Hertz (cycles)	L.P.F.	Low Power Factor
		I.	Moment of Inertia	LR	Long Radius
Fmg.	Framing	IBC	International Building Code	L.S.	Lump Sum
FM/UL	Factory Mutual/Underwriters Labs	I.C.	Interrupting Capacity	Lt.	Light
Fdn.	Foundation	ID	Inside Diameter	Lt. Ga.	Light Gauge
FNPT	Female National Pipe Thread	I.D.	Inside Dimension; Identification	L.T.L.	Less than Truckload Lot
Fori.	Foreman, Inside	I.F.	Inside Frosted	Lt. Wt.	Lightweight
Foro.	Foreman, Outside	I.M.C.	Intermediate Metal Conduit	L.V.	Low Voltage
Fount.	Fountain	In.	Inch	M	Thousand; Material; Male; Light Wall Copper Tubing
fpm	Feet per Minute	Incan.	Incandescent		
FPT	Female Pipe Thread	Incl.	Included; Including	M²CA	Meters Squared Contact Area
Fr	Frame	Int.	Interior	m/hr.; M.H.	Man-hour
F.R.	Fire Rating	Inst.	Installation	mA	Milliampere
FRK	Foil Reinforced Kraft	Insul., insul	Insulation/Insulated	Mach.	Machine
FSK	Foil/Scrim/Kraft	I.P.	Iron Pipe	Mag. Str.	Magnetic Starter
FRP	Fiberglass Reinforced Plastic	I.P.S., IPS	Iron Pipe Size	Maint.	Maintenance
FS	Forged Steel	IPT	Iron Pipe Threaded	Marb.	Marble Setter
FSC	Cast Body; Cast Switch Box	I.W.	Indirect Waste	Mat; Mat'l.	Material
Ft., ft	Foot; Feet	J	Joule	Max.	Maximum
Ftng.	Fitting	J.I.C.	Joint Industrial Council	MBF	Thousand Board Feet
Ftg.	Footing	K	Thousand; Thousand Pounds; Heavy Wall Copper Tubing; Kelvin	MBH	Thousand BTU's per hr.
Ft lb.	Foot Pound			MC	Metal Clad Cable
Furn.	Furniture	K.A.H.	Thousand Amp. Hours	MCC	Motor Control Center
FVNR	Full Voltage Non-Reversing	kcmil	Thousand Circular Mils	M.C.F.	Thousand Cubic Feet
FVR	Full Voltage Reversing	KD	Knock Down	MCFM	Thousand Cubic Feet per Minute
FXM	Female by Male	K.D.A.T.	Kiln Dried After Treatment	M.C.M.	Thousand Circular Mils
Fy.	Minimum Yield Stress of Steel	kg	Kilogram	MCP	Motor Circuit Protector
g	Gram	kG	Kilogauss	MD	Medium Duty
G	Gauss	kgf	Kilogram Force	MDF	Medium-density fibreboard
Ga.	Gauge	kHz	Kilohertz	M.D.O.	Medium Density Overlaid
Gal., gal.	Gallon	Kip	1000 Pounds	Med.	Medium
Galv., galv	Galvanized	KJ	Kilojoule	MF	Thousand Feet
GC/MS	Gas Chromatograph/Mass Spectrometer	K.L.	Effective Length Factor	M.F.B.M.	Thousand Feet Board Measure
		K.L.F.	Kips per Linear Foot	Mfg.	Manufacturing
Gen.	General	Km	Kilometer	Mfrs.	Manufacturers
GFI	Ground Fault Interrupter	KO	Knock Out	mg	Milligram
GFRC	Glass Fiber Reinforced Concrete	K.S.F.	Kips per Square Foot	MGD	Million Gallons per Day
Glaz.	Glazier	K.S.I.	Kips per Square Inch	MGPH	Million Gallons per Hour
GPD	Gallons per Day	kV	Kilovolt	MH, M.H.	Manhole; Metal Halide; Man-Hour
gpf	Gallon per Flush	kVA	Kilovolt Ampere	MHz	Megahertz
GPH	Gallons per Hour	kVAR	Kilovar (Reactance)	Mi.	Mile
gpm, GPM	Gallons per Minute	KW	Kilowatt	MI	Malleable Iron; Mineral Insulated
GR	Grade	KWh	Kilowatt-hour	MIPS	Male Iron Pipe Size
Gran.	Granular	L	Labor Only; Length; Long; Medium Wall Copper Tubing	mj	Mechanical Joint
Grnd.	Ground			m	Meter
GVW	Gross Vehicle Weight	Lab.	Labor	mm	Millimeter
GWB	Gypsum Wall Board	lat	Latitude	Mill.	Millwright
				Min., min.	Minimum, Minute

Abbreviations

Misc.	Miscellaneous	PCM	Phase Contrast Microscopy	SBS	Styrene Butadiere Styrene
ml	Milliliter, Mainline	PDCA	Painting and Decorating	SC	Screw Cover
M.L.F.	Thousand Linear Feet		Contractors of America	SCFM	Standard Cubic Feet per Minute
Mo.	Month	P.E., PE	Professional Engineer;	Scaf.	Scaffold
Mobil.	Mobilization		Porcelain Enamel;	Sch., Sched.	Schedule
Mog.	Mogul Base		Polyethylene; Plain End	S.C.R.	Modular Brick
MPH	Miles per Hour	P.E.C.I.	Porcelain Enamel on Cast Iron	S.D.	Sound Deadening
MPT	Male Pipe Thread	Perf.	Perforated	SDR	Standard Dimension Ratio
MRGWB	Moisture Resistant Gypsum	PEX	Cross Linked Polyethylene	S.E.	Surfaced Edge
	Wallboard	Ph.	Phase	Sel.	Select
MRT	Mile Round Trip	P.I.	Pressure Injected	SER, SEU	Service Entrance Cable
ms	Millisecond	Pile.	Pile Driver	S.F.	Square Foot
M.S.F.	Thousand Square Feet	Pkg.	Package	S.F.C.A.	Square Foot Contact Area
Mstz.	Mosaic & Terrazzo Worker	Pl.	Plate	S.F. Flr.	Square Foot of Floor
M.S.Y.	Thousand Square Yards	Plah.	Plasterer Helper	S.F.G.	Square Foot of Ground
Mtd., mtd., mtd	Mounted	Plas.	Plasterer	S.F. Hor.	Square Foot Horizontal
Mthe.	Mosaic & Terrazzo Helper	plf	Pounds Per Linear Foot	SFR	Square Feet of Radiation
Mtng.	Mounting	Pluh.	Plumber Helper	S.F. Shlf.	Square Foot of Shelf
Mult.	Multi; Multiply	Plum.	Plumber	S4S	Surface 4 Sides
MUTCD	Manual on Uniform Traffic Control	Ply.	Plywood	Shee.	Sheet Metal Worker
	Devices	p.m.	Post Meridiem	Sin.	Sine
M.V.A.	Million Volt Amperes	Pntd.	Painted	Skwk.	Skilled Worker
M.V.A.R.	Million Volt Amperes Reactance	Pord.	Painter, Ordinary	SL	Saran Lined
MV	Megavolt	pp	Pages	S.L.	Slimline
MW	Megawatt	PP, PPL	Polypropylene	Sldr.	Solder
MXM	Male by Male	P.P.M.	Parts per Million	SLH	Super Long Span Bar Joist
MYD	Thousand Yards	Pr.	Pair	S.N.	Solid Neutral
N	Natural; North	P.E.S.B.	Pre-engineered Steel Building	SO	Stranded with oil resistant inside
nA	Nanoampere	Prefab.	Prefabricated		insulation
NA	Not Available; Not Applicable	Prefin.	Prefinished	S-O-L	Socketolet
N.B.C.	National Building Code	Prop.	Propelled	sp	Standpipe
NC	Normally Closed	PSF, psf	Pounds per Square Foot	S.P.	Static Pressure; Single Pole; Self-
NEMA	National Electrical Manufacturers	PSI, psi	Pounds per Square Inch		Propelled
	Assoc.	PSIG	Pounds per Square Inch Gauge	Spri.	Sprinkler Installer
NEHB	Bolted Circuit Breaker to 600V.	PSP	Plastic Sewer Pipe	spwg	Static Pressure Water Gauge
NFPA	National Fire Protection Association	Pspr.	Painter, Spray	S.P.D.T.	Single Pole, Double Throw
NLB	Non-Load-Bearing	Psst.	Painter, Structural Steel	SPF	Spruce Pine Fir; Sprayed
NM	Non-Metallic Cable	P.T.	Potential Transformer		Polyurethane Foam
nm	Nanometer	P. & T.	Pressure & Temperature	S.P.S.T.	Single Pole, Single Throw
No.	Number	Ptd.	Painted	SPT	Standard Pipe Thread
NO	Normally Open	Ptns.	Partitions	Sq.	Square; 100 Square Feet
N.O.C.	Not Otherwise Classified	Pu	Ultimate Load	Sq. Hd.	Square Head
Nose.	Nosing	PVC	Polyvinyl Chloride	Sq. In.	Square Inch
NPT	National Pipe Thread	Pvmt.	Pavement	S.S.	Single Strength; Stainless Steel
NQOD	Combination Plug-on/Bolt on	PRV	Pressure Relief Valve	S.S.B.	Single Strength B Grade
	Circuit Breaker to 240V.	Pwr.	Power	sst, ss	Stainless Steel
N.R.C., NRC	Noise Reduction Coefficient/	Q	Quantity Heat Flow	Sswk.	Structural Steel Worker
	Nuclear Regulator Commission	Qt.	Quart	Sswl.	Structural Steel Welder
N.R.S.	Non Rising Stem	Quan., Qty.	Quantity	St.; Stl.	Steel
ns	Nanosecond	Q.C.	Quick Coupling	STC	Sound Transmission Coefficient
NTP	Notice to Proceed	r	Radius of Gyration	Std.	Standard
nW	Nanowatt	R	Resistance	Stg.	Staging
OB	Opposing Blade	R.C.P.	Reinforced Concrete Pipe	STK	Select Tight Knot
OC	On Center	Rect.	Rectangle	STP	Standard Temperature & Pressure
OD	Outside Diameter	recpt.	Receptacle	Stpi.	Steamfitter, Pipefitter
O.D.	Outside Dimension	Reg.	Regular	Str.	Strength; Starter; Straight
ODS	Overhead Distribution System	Reinf.	Reinforced	Strd.	Stranded
O.G.	Ogee	Req'd.	Required	Struct.	Structural
O.H.	Overhead	Res.	Resistant	Sty.	Story
O&P	Overhead and Profit	Resi.	Residential	Subj.	Subject
Oper.	Operator	RF	Radio Frequency	Subs.	Subcontractors
Opng.	Opening	RFID	Radio-frequency Identification	Surf.	Surface
Orna.	Ornamental	Rgh.	Rough	Sw.	Switch
OSB	Oriented Strand Board	RGS	Rigid Galvanized Steel	Swbd.	Switchboard
OS&Y	Outside Screw and Yoke	RHW	Rubber, Heat & Water Resistant;	S.Y.	Square Yard
OSHA	Occupational Safety and Health		Residential Hot Water	Syn.	Synthetic
	Act	rms	Root Mean Square	S.Y.P.	Southern Yellow Pine
Ovhd.	Overhead	Rnd.	Round	Sys.	System
OWG	Oil, Water or Gas	Rodm.	Rodman	t.	Thickness
Oz.	Ounce	Rofc.	Roofer, Composition	T	Temperature; Ton
P.	Pole; Applied Load; Projection	Rofp.	Roofer, Precast	Tan	Tangent
p.	Page	Rohe.	Roofer Helpers (Composition)	T.C.	Terra Cotta
Pape.	Paperhanger	Rots.	Roofer, Tile & Slate	T & C	Threaded and Coupled
P.A.P.R.	Powered Air Purifying Respirator	R.O.W.	Right of Way	T.D.	Temperature Difference
PAR	Parabolic Reflector	RPM	Revolutions per Minute	TDD	Telecommunications Device for
P.B., PB	Push Button	R.S.	Rapid Start		the Deaf
Pc., Pcs.	Piece, Pieces	Rsr	Riser	T.E.M.	Transmission Electron Microscopy
P.C.	Portland Cement; Power Connector	RT	Round Trip	temp	Temperature, Tempered, Temporary
P.C.F.	Pounds per Cubic Foot	S.	Suction; Single Entrance; South	TFFN	Nylon Jacketed Wire

Abbreviations

TFE	Tetrafluoroethylene (Teflon)	U.L., UL	Underwriters Laboratory	w/	With
T. & G.	Tongue & Groove; Tar & Gravel	Uld.	Unloading	W.C., WC	Water Column; Water Closet
		Unfin.	Unfinished	W.F.	Wide Flange
Th., Thk.	Thick	UPS	Uninterruptible Power Supply	W.G.	Water Gauge
Thn.	Thin	URD	Underground Residential Distribution	Wldg.	Welding
Thrded	Threaded			W. Mile	Wire Mile
Tilf.	Tile Layer, Floor	US	United States	W-O-L	Weldolet
Tilh.	Tile Layer, Helper	USGBC	U.S. Green Building Council	W.R.	Water Resistant
THHN	Nylon Jacketed Wire	USP	United States Primed	Wrck.	Wrecker
THW.	Insulated Strand Wire	UTMCD	Uniform Traffic Manual For Control Devices	WSFU	Water Supply Fixture Unit
THWN	Nylon Jacketed Wire			W.S.P.	Water, Steam, Petroleum
T.L., TL	Truckload	UTP	Unshielded Twisted Pair	WT., Wt.	Weight
T.M.	Track Mounted	V	Volt	WWF	Welded Wire Fabric
Tot.	Total	VA	Volt Amperes	XFER	Transfer
T-O-L	Threadolet	VAT	Vinyl Asbestos Tile	XFMR	Transformer
tmpd	Tempered	V.C.T.	Vinyl Composition Tile	XHD	Extra Heavy Duty
TPO	Thermoplastic Polyolefin	VAV	Variable Air Volume	XHHW	Cross-Linked Polyethylene Wire
T.S.	Trigger Start	VC	Veneer Core	XLPE	Insulation
Tr.	Trade	VDC	Volts Direct Current	XLP	Cross-linked Polyethylene
Transf.	Transformer	Vent.	Ventilation	Xport	Transport
Trhv.	Truck Driver, Heavy	Vert.	Vertical	Y	Wye
Trlr	Trailer	V.F.	Vinyl Faced	yd	Yard
Trlt.	Truck Driver, Light	V.G.	Vertical Grain	yr	Year
TTY	Teletypewriter	VHF	Very High Frequency	Δ	Delta
TV	Television	VHO	Very High Output	%	Percent
T.W.	Thermoplastic Water Resistant Wire	Vib.	Vibrating	~	Approximately
		VLF	Vertical Linear Foot	Ø	Phase; diameter
UCI	Uniform Construction Index	VOC	Volatile Organic Compound	@	At
UF	Underground Feeder	Vol.	Volume	#	Pound; Number
UGND	Underground Feeder	VRP	Vinyl Reinforced Polyester	<	Less Than
UHF	Ultra High Frequency	W	Wire; Watt; Wide; West	>	Greater Than
U.I.	United Inch			Z	Zone

Index

A

Abandon catch basin	22
Abatement asbestos	25
equipment asbestos	25
Aboveground storage tank concrete	284
ABS DWV pipe	200
Absorber shock	235
vibration	105
Absorption chiller	545
chiller water cool steam	545
chiller water cooled gas	545
water chiller	383
A/C coil furnace	372
fan coil horizontal	554
fan coil system	553, 554
packaged DX	575, 576
packaged DXVAV	576
packaged terminal	396
refrigerant	305
removal fan-coil	253
removal rooftop	254
removal thru-the-wall	254
removal window	254
rooftop const volume	574
rooftop DX	574
rooftop DXVAV	574
rooftop VAV	574
self contained	577, 578
self contained VAV	577, 578
unit elec ht/water cooled	577
unit elec ht/water cooled VAV	577
unit hot water coil water cool	578
unit hw coil water cooled VAV	578
Access control video camera	436
door duct	327
floor	64
flooring	64
road and parking area	16
Accessory compressor	245
duct	321
fuel oil	278
masonry	42
polypropylene	216
Accumulator refrigerant	303
Acoustical aluminum duct	329
sealant	57
ACR tubing copper	130
Adapter fill	278
polybutylene	215
Adjustable frequency drive	432
Adjustment factor labor	86, 422
Aerator	248
Aggregate spreader	610, 617
AHU built up	547
built up VAV	548
ceiling concealed	410
ceiling mounted	410
central station	549
central station VAV	550
field fabricated	547
floor standing unit	410
floor standing unit concealed	410
packaged indoor	390
rooftop	551
rooftop VAV	552
wall mounted	410
Air & dirt eliminator	285
automatic vent	286
balancing	264
barrier curtain	336
circulator hvls	334
circulator large diameter	334
cleaner electronic	353
cock	287
compressor	246, 613
compressor control system	271
compressor package	246
compressor portable	613
compressor removal	87
condition and ventilation	730, 738
conditioner cooling & heating	396
conditioner direct expansion	408
conditioner fan coil	408
conditioner fan coil VRV	400, 409, 410
conditioner gas heat	391
conditioner general	252
conditioner maintenance	19
conditioner packaged term.	396
conditioner portable	396
conditioner receptacle	428
conditioner removal	252
conditioner rooftop	391, 392
conditioner self-contained	397
conditioner thru-wall	396
conditioner ventilating	306
conditioner window	396
conditioner wiring	430
conditioning	730, 732, 735, 736
conditioning and vent.	731, 732
conditioning computer	398
conditioning computer room	399
conditioning fan	330
conditioning pump	304
conditioning ventilating	271, 306, 309, 322, 324, 333, 336, 342, 345, 350, 385, 388, 390, 394, 396, 397
control	284
cooled belt drive condenser	381
cooled condensing unit	381, 572, 573
cooled direct drive condenser	382
curtain	336
curtain removal	252
deaerator	285
eliminator	285
filter	351, 353
filter mechanical media	351
filter permanent washable	351
filter regulator lubricator	245
filter removal	252
filter roll type	351
filter washable	351
filtration	25
filtration charcoal type	353
fitting boiler	285
fitting compression tank	286
gap fitting	235
handler heater	373
handler modular	373
hose	614
line coupler	245
make-up unit	390
purging scoop	286
quality	72
register	345
return grille	343
sampling	25
scoop	286
Air scrubber	614
Air separator	284
spade	614
supply grille	343
supply pneumatic control	271
supply register	345
terminal unit	340
tube system	84
turning vane	327
unit make-up	390
unit removal make-up	253
vent automatic	286
vent convector or baseboard	411
Air-conditioner air cooled	542, 570-573, 575
chilled water	539-541, 575
direct expansion	565, 565, 567-573
fan coil	539, 540, 542, 573
multizone	393, 567
penthouse	393
self-contained	568-571
single zone	564, 565
split system	572, 573
water cooled	568, 569, 575
Air-conditioning air cooled	539
computer	575
drug store	567
Airfoil fan centrifugal	332
Air-handling unit	389, 391, 408
unit packaged indoor	390
unit packaged outdoor	391
Airless sprayer	25
Air-source heat pump	400
Alarm device	438
panel and device	438
residential	429
system medical	249
vent	279
All fuel chimney	357, 360
service jacket insulation	107, 113
Aluminum corrugated pipe	598
diffuser	341
diffuser perforated	341
downspout	53
duct acoustical	329
duct silencer	329
duct silencer flexible	329
ductwork	306
flashing	52, 241
flex duct	328
grille	343
handrail	64
insulation jacketing	121
louver	61, 348
louver commercial grade	61
operating louver	348
pipe	478, 479
register	345
rivet	46
Anchor bolt	33
chemical	39, 44
epoxy	39, 44
expansion	44
hollow wall	44
lead screw	44
machinery	35
pipe conduit casing	485
plastic screw	45
screw	44
toggle bolt	44
wedge	45
Angle valve bronze	88
valve plastic	93
Anti-freeze inhibited	305
Anti-siphon device	235
Appliance	71
residential	71, 430
Approach ramp	64
Aquastat	271
Arch culvert oval	480
Architectural fee	713
Area clean-up	27
Articulating boom lift	613
Asbestos abatement	25
abatement equipment	25
area decontamination	27
demolition	27
disposal	28
encapsulation	28
remediation plan/method	25
removal	26
removal process	723
Ash conveyor	76
Asphalt concrete	440
distributor	614
paver	616
paving	458
plant portable	617
Asphaltic binder	458
concrete	458
concrete paving	458
pavement	458
wearing course	458
Aspirator dental	75
Assembly duct	393
package ductwork	393
Atomizer water	25
Attachment ripper	617
Attachments skidsteer	613
Attic ventilation fan	335
Auger earth	610
Automatic timed thermostat	273
washing machine	71
Automotive equipment	70
exhaust system	583
spray painting booth	70
Autopsy equipment	75
Autoscrub machine	614

B

Backer rod	56
Backfill	444
trench	442
Backflow preventer	234
preventer removal	87
preventer solar	378
Backhoe	611
bucket	612
extension	617
trenching	588, 590, 592
Bag disposable	25, 30
glove	26
Balance valve circuit setter	287
Balancing air	264
hydronic	299
water	265
Baler	76
Ball check valve	94
check valve plastic	94
joint weld end	300
valve	261
valve brass	254
valve bronze	88, 89
valve grooved joint	180
valve plastic	93
valve polypropylene	93
wrecking	617
Bank air-conditioning	539, 541, 564, 566, 568, 570, 572
Barge construction	620
Barometric damper	354
Barrels flasher	614
reflectorized	614
Barricade	17
flasher	614
tape	17
Barrier and enclosure	16
dust	16

Index

separation	26, 28, 29
slipform paver	618
Base stabilizer	618
Baseboard diffuser	342
expansion coupling	289
heat	411
heat electric	415
heater electric	415
register	346
removal hydronic	253
Baseplate scaffold	14
shoring	14
Basket type strainer	296
Bath steam	81
whirlpool	75
Bathroom exhaust fan	335
heater & fan	335
Bead board insulation	80
Beam attachment welded	95
clamp	96
flange clip	105
soldier	455
Bedding pipe	444
Bell mouth collar	315
signal	438
Bellow expansion joint	289
Belt driven fan	332
Bibb hose	287
Binder asphaltic	458
Bituminous coating	462
paver	615
Blade louver movable	60
Blanket insulation	266
Blaster shot	616
Blasting	442
Blind flange	163
structural bolt	47
Block manhole	467
manhole/catch basin	599
Blowdown boiler	369
removal boiler	252
Blower HVAC fan	331
insulation	615
pneumatic tube	84
Board insulation	267
mineral wool	267
Boat work	620
Boiler	361
air fitting	285
blowdown	369
blowdown removal	252
coal-fired hydronic	533
condensing	362
control system	271
cut off low water	268
demolition	252
drain	287
electric	361, 362, 531
electric hot water	534
electric steam	361, 535
fire tube	367
fossil fuel	364, 365, 368
fossil fuel hydronic	533
gas fired	363
gas pulse	363
gas/oil combination	364
general	86
hot water	362, 363, 365, 366
hot-water electric	531
hydronic fossil fuel	533
insulation	267
oil-fired	365, 366
oil-fired hydronic	533
packaged water tube	366
removal	252
Scotch marine	367

solid fuel	366
steam	363-365, 367
steam electric	530
stoker fired	366
water gauge	268
water tube	366
Bolt & gasket set	162
anchor	33
blind structural	47
Bond performance	11, 719
Boom lift articulating	613
lift telescoping	613
Booster coil	404
fan	332
system water pressure	239
Booth painting	70
Borer horizontal	618
Boring horizontal	466
machine horizontal	610
service	466
Bowling alley air-conditioning	539, 541, 564, 566, 568, 570, 572
Box buffalo	468
culvert precast	597
mixing	340
storage	13
trench	617
VAV	340
vent	42
Brace cross	47
Bracing shoring	14
Bracket pipe	95
scaffold	14
Braided bronze hose	228
steel hose	228
Brass pipe	126
pipe fitting	127
valve	88
Break glass station	438
Breaker air gap vacuum	235
pavement	614
vacuum	235
Breather cap fuel	279
Breeching draft inducer	353
insulation	268
Brick cart	614
catch basin	467
chimney simulated	68
manhole	467
vent	348
vent box	42
Bridge sidewalk	15
Bronze angle valve	88
ball valve	89
body strainer	298
butterfly valve	89
globe valve	90
swing check valve	89
valve	88
Bronze/brass valve	254
Broom finish concrete	38
sidewalk	616
Brush chipper	611
cutter	611, 612
Bucket backhoe	612
clamshell	611
concrete	610
dragline	611
excavator	617
pavement	617
Buffalo box	468
Buggy concrete	610
Builder's risk insurance	717
Building air conditioning	539
air-conditioning	539-539, 566-573, 575

demolition selective	22
permit	12
portable	13
temporary	13
Built-in range	71
Bulldozer	444, 612
Bull float concrete	610
Buncher feller	611
Bunk house trailer	13
Burner gas conversion	369
gas/oil	369
gun type	369
industrial	369
oil	369
residential	369
Butt fusion machine	614
Butterfly valve	255, 475
valve bronze	89
valve grooved joint	180
Butyl caulking	57
rubber	56

C

Cabinet convector heater	417
heater electric	417
unit heater	412, 417, 563
Cable hanger	104
jack	620
pulling	617
tensioning	617
trailer	617
Cable/wire puller	617
Calcium silicate insulated system	485
silicate insulation	268, 485
silicate pipe covering	110
Cap HDPE piping	473
vent	279
Car tram	617
Carbon monoxide detector	271, 437
Carousel compactor	76
Carpet computer room	64
Carrier pipe	96, 100
Cart brick	614
concrete	610
Case refrigerated	72
Cased evaporator coil	372
Casing anchor pipe conduit	485
Cast in place concrete	36, 37
iron fitting	161
iron manhole cover	481
iron pipe fitting	150
iron radiator	411
iron trap	240
Caster scaffold	14
Catch basin	481
basin and manhole	600
basin brick	467
basin cleaner	617
basin precast	467
basin removal	22
basin vacuum	617
basin/manhole	599
Cathodic protection	81
Catwalk scaffold	15
Caulking	57
polyurethane	57
sealant	56
Ceiling concealed AHU	410
diffuser	341
fan	331
heater	72
mounted AHU	410
polystyrene	79
register	345

Cellular glass insulation	108
Cement plaster	79
underlayment self-leveling	39
Central station AHU removal	252
station air-handling unit	390
station heat pump	579
vacuum	76
vacuum unit	490
Centrifugal airfoil fan	332
chiller	544
chiller water cooled	544
compressor	379
fan system	557
in line fan system	557
in-line motor	238
liquid chiller	384
pump	237, 616
refrigerant compressor	379
type HVAC fan	332
Chain fall hoist	619
link fence	18
saw	616
trencher	441, 613
Chair dental	75
hydraulic	75
pipe support	100
Chamber decontamination	26, 28
Channel steel	99
Charcoal type air filter	353
Charge disposal	28
powder	46
Chart recorder	274
Check lift valve	89
swing valve	89
valve	476
valve ball	94
valve flanged cast iron	475
valve grooved joint	180
valve silent	92, 257, 260, 264
valve stainless steel	263
valve steel	259
valve wafer	92, 258, 264
Chemical anchor	39, 44
feeder shot	369
spreader	617
toilet	616
Chilled water cooling tower system	541, 542
water pipe underground	483
Chiller centrifugal type water	384
direct expansion water	386
reciprocating	543
removal water	254
water	383
Chimney	42
accessory	68
all fuel	357, 360
all fuel vent	360
brick	42
cap rotating	349
cap ventilator	349
draft inducer	353
fireplace	68
foundation	36
metal	68
positive pressure	357, 360
prefabricated metal	357
rain cap	350
simulated brick	68
vent	354
vent fitting	360
vent oval	356
Chipper brush	611
log	612
stump	612
Chipping hammer	614

Index

Chloride accelerator concrete 37
Chlorination system 248
Chute 84
   linen 84
   package 84
   refuse 84
Circuit sensor 286
   setter 287
Circular saw 616
Circulating pump 301
   pump double suction 538
   pump end suction 538
Clamp beam 96
   pipe 95, 462
   pipe repair 463
   riser 96
Clamshell bucket 611
Classroom heating & cooling ... 409
Clean control joint 33
   ductwork 19
   room 79
   tank 24
Cleaner catch basin 617
   crack 618
   steam 616
Cleaning & disposal equipment . 73
   duct 19
   internal pipe 465
   up 18
Cleanouts 467
Clean-up area 27
Clevis pipe hanger 98
Climbing crane 618
   hydraulic jack 620
Clock timer 429
Closed circuit cooling-tower 388
Clothes dryer commercial 70
Coating bituminous 462
   epoxy 462
   polyethylene 462
Cock air 287
   drain and specialty 287
   gas 88
   gauge 288
   pet 287
   steam 287
Cofferdam 455
Coil booster 404
   condenser 402, 403
   cooling 402
   flanged 402
   water 402
Cold mix paver 618
   storage door 60
   storage room 79
Collar spin-in duct 315
Collection sewage/drainage 479
   system dust 490
Collector solar energy system ... 376
Combination ball valve 254
   device 427
Comfort station 81
Commercial air-conditioner 539
   air-conditioning . 540, 541, 564-572,
                                575
   dishwasher 73
   fin tube 411
   fin-tube heating 521
   heater electric 415
   kitchen exhaust 560
   refrigeration 72, 79
   unit-heater heating 522
Commissioning 19
Compact fill 444
Compaction soil 444
Compactor 76

earth 611
landfill 612
waste 76
Companion flange 163
Compensation workers 10
Component control 270, 271
   furnace 372
   pneumatic 275
Component/DDC sys. control ... 269
Compressed air equipment
   automotive 70
Compression joint fitting 135
   seal 55
   tank 290
Compressor accessory 245
   air 246, 613
   air package 246
   centrifugal 379
   centrifugal refrigerant 379
   reciprocating 246
   reciprocating hermetic 246
   refrigerant 379, 380
   removal air 87
   removal refrigerant 254
   rotary 380
   rotary hermetic 379
   scroll 380
   tank mounted 271
Computer air conditioning 398
   floor 64
   room carpet 64
   room unit removal 252
Concrete asphalt 440
   asphaltic 458
   broom finish 38
   bucket 610
   buggy 610
   bull float 610
   cart 610
   cast in place 36, 37
   catch basin 467
   chloride accelerator 37
   conveyer 610
   core drilling 39
   demo 22
   direct chute 38
   drill 423
   drilling 40
   equipment rental 610
   fiber reinforcing 38
   float finish 38
   floor edger 610
   floor grinder 610
   floor patching 32
   hand trowel finish 38
   hole cutting 424
   hole drilling 423
   impact drilling 40
   insert hanger 97
   lance 615
   machine trowel finish 38
   manhole 467
   mixer 610
   non-chloride accelerator 37
   paver 616
   pipe 479
   placement footing 38
   placing 38
   pump 610
   ready mix 37
   reinforcing 36
   removal 22
   retarder 37
   saw 610
   short load 38
   spreader 616

tank 477
tank aboveground storage 284
trowel 610
truck 610
truck holding 38
vibrator 610
wall patching 32
water reducer 37
water storage tank 477
winter 37
Condensate meter rem. steam ... 254
   pan drip-drain 303
   pump 302
   removal pump 302
   return pump 302
   steam meter 302
Condenser 381
   air cooled belt drive 381
   air cooled direct drive 382
   chilled water air cooled .. 539, 540
   coil 402, 403
   evaporative 382
   removal 252
Condensing boiler 362
   furnace 371
   unit air cooled 381
   unit removal 252
   unit water-cooled 381
Conditioner general air 252
   maintenance air 19
   portable air 396
   rooftop air 392
Cond. computer room air 399
   ventilating air .. 309, 342, 343, 345,
                390, 394, 396, 397
Conduit & fitting flexible 425
   fitting pipe 484
   pipe prefabricated 486
   prefabricated pipe 483, 485
   preinsulated pipe 483
Connection motor 425
   split system tubing 399
   utility 467
Connector flexible 227
   gas 227
   water copper tubing 228
Console heat pump 579
Construction barge 620
   management fee 8
   photography 12
   sump hole 443
   temporary 16
   time 714
Contained pipe 223
Containment unit dust 17, 29
Contaminated soil 24
Contingency 8
Contractor overhead 18
Control & motor starter 431
   air 284
   component 270, 271
   component electronic 277
   component relay 272
   component sensor 272
   component transmitter 274
   component/DDC system 269
   damper volume 322
   DDC 269
   DDC system 270
   draft 354
   flow check 291
   hand/off/automatic 432
   joint 33
   joint clean 33
   joint sawn 33
   joint sealant 33

pneumatic 272
radiator supply 291
station 432
station stop-start 432
system 269
system air compressor 271
system boiler 271
system cooling 270
system pneumatic 270
system split system 270
system VAV box 271
system ventilator 270
valve heating 274, 291
water feeder 268
water level 268
Control-component 274
Controller pneumatic 276
Convector cabinet heater 417
   hydronic heating 411
Conveyor ash 76
   door 336
Cooking equipment 73
   range 71
Cooler 80
   beverage 73
   evaporative 394
   evaporator 394
   removal evaporative 253
   swamp 394
Cooling coil 402
   computer 575
   control system 270
   tower 387
   tower fiberglass 388
   tower forced-draft 387
   tower louver 348
   tower removal 252
   tower stainless 388
   tower stainless steel 546
Cooling-tower closed circuit ... 388
   liquid cooler 388
Copper ACR tubing 130
   drum trap 240
   DWV tubing 129
   fitting 131
   flashing 52, 241
   grooved joint 139
   pipe 128
   rivet 46
   tube 128
   tube fitting 131
   tubing oxygen class 129
Core drill 610
   drilling concrete 39
Cork insulation 80
Corridor air-conditioning ... 539, 541,
           564, 566, 568, 570, 572
Corrosion resistance 462
   resistant tank 290
Corrosive fume resistant duct ... 315,
                                317-320
Corrugated metal pipe 478, 479
   pipe 478
   steel pipe 478
Cost mark-up 11
Coupler air line 245
Coupling expansion 289
   mechanical 173
   plastic 212
   polypropylene 216
Course wearing 458
Cover manhole 481
   stair tread 18
Covering calcium silicate pipe ... 110
   protection saddle 101
CPVC pipe 201

Index

valve 93
Crack cleaner 618
   filler 618
Crane climbing 618
   crawler 619
   crew daily 13
   hydraulic 619
   tower 13, 619
   truck mounted 619
Crawler crane 619
   drill rotary 614
   shovel 612
Crematory 75
Crew daily crane 13
   forklift 13
Cross 473
   brace 47
Crossflow fuel heater 279
Culvert box precast 597
   end 480
   pipe 480
   reinforced 479
Curb builder 610
   extruder 611
   prefabricated 420
   slipform paver 618
Curtain air 336
   air barrier 336
   damper fire 323
   removal air 252
Cut in sleeve 474
   in valve 474
   off low water boiler 268
   pipe groove 181
Cutoff feeder combination 268
Cutter brush 611, 612
Cutting and drilling 423
   steel pipe labor 148
   torch 616

D

Daily crane crew 13
Dairy case 72
Damper 321, 324
   actuator 275
   assembly splitter 325
   barometric 354
   fire curtain 323
   fire round 324
   fire/smoke 324
   foundation vent 42
   multi-blade 321
   relief 325
   round 323
   vent 354
   volume-control 321
Darkroom equipment 70
Dasher hockey 79
   ice rink 79
DDC control 269
Deaerator 284
   air 285
Deck roof 50
Decontamination asbestos area ... 27
   chamber 26, 28
   enclosure 26-28
   equipment 25
Decorator device 426
   switch 426
Dehumidifier 614
   removal 252
   selfcontained 420
Delicatessen case 72
Delivery charge 15

Demo concrete 22
   hydronic convector & radiator . 253
Demolish remove pavement
and curb 22
Demolition 722
   asbestos 27
   boiler 252
   furnace 253
   hammer 611
   HVAC 252
   mold contaminated area ... 28
   pavement 22
   plumbing 87
   selective building 22
   site 22
   torch cutting 23
Dental chair 75
   equipment 75
   office equipment 75
Department store
air-conditioning 542, 565
Derrick crane guyed 619
   crane stiffleg 619
Detection intrusion 436
   leak 437
   probe leak 437
   system 436
Detector carbon monoxide . 271, 437
   check valve 476
   explosive 436
   metal 436
   meter water supply .. 233
   smoke 437
   temperature rise ... 437
Detour sign 17
Device alarm 438
   anti-siphon 235
   combination 427
   decorator 426
   GFI 428
   receptacle 427
   residential 426
Dewater 443
   pumping 443
Dewatering 443, 743
   equipment 620
Diaphragm pump 616
Dielectric union 288
Diesel hammer 612
   tugboat 620
Diffuser aluminum 341
   baseboard 342
   ceiling 341
   floor 342
   linear 341
   opposed blade damper 341
   perforated aluminum 341
   pump suction 299
   rectangular 341
   sidewall 342
   steel 343
   suction 299
   supply/return combination . 342
   T-bar mount 342
Dimmer switch 426
Direct chute concrete 38
   expansion A/C 408
   expansion water chiller . 386
Direct-fired water chiller 383
Directional drill horizontal 618
Disc harrow 611
Discharge hose 615
Disease infectious ... 9
Dishwasher commercial . 73
   residential 71
Disposable bag 25, 30

Disposal asbestos 28
   charge 28
   garbage 71
   waste 76
Distiller water 74
Distribution pipe water 469, 471
Distributor asphalt 614
Ditching 443
Diving stand 78
Domestic hot water temp maint . 105
   water booster system 239
Door bell residential 429
   cold storage 60
   conveyor 336
   duct access 327
   fire 438
   grille 344
   refrigerator 60
   steel louver 345
Double wall pipe 219, 482
Downspout 53
   aluminum 53
   steel 53
Dozer 612
Draft control 354
   damper vent 354
   inducer breeching 353
   inducer chimney 353
Draft-induction fan 353
Dragline bucket 611
Drain boiler 287
   pipe 443
Drainage pipe 477, 479
   site 494
   trap 240
Draindown valve 378
Drainer liquid 292
Drill concrete 423
   core 610
   main 473
   quarry 614
   rock 442
   steel 614
   tap main 473
   track 614
Drilling and blasting rock .. 442
   concrete 40
   concrete impact 40
   horizontal 466
   plaster 64
   rig 610
   steel 45
Drip pan elbow 240
Driver post 618
   sheeting 614
Driveway removal 22
Drug store air-conditioning . 540, 542,
               565, 569, 571, 573
Drum trap copper 240
Dryer commercial clothes ... 70
   industrial 70
   receptacle 428
   residential 71
   vent 71
Duck tarpaulin 16
Duct access door 327
   accessory 321
   acoustical aluminum .. 329
   assembly 393
   assembly residential .. 393
   cleaning 19
   collar spin-in 315
   connection fabric flexible . 315
   corrosive fume
      resistant 315, 317-320
   fiberglass 315-318

fiberglass-reinforced plastic ... 315
fibrous-glass 315
fire rated blanket 266
fitting plastic 319
fitting round 308
fitting spiral 307
flexible 327
flexible insulated 327
flexible noninsulated 327
furnace 373
grille 64
heater electric 406
humidifier 419
HVAC 306
insulation 266
liner 330
liner non-fibrous 321, 330
mechanical 306
mixing box 340
plastic 321
polypropylene 320
polypropylene fitting 320
preformed spiral 307
PVC 319
rigid fiberglass 316
rigid plastic 319, 320
round 307
round and flat-oval spiral ... 307
silencer 326
smoke exhaust 315
sound trap 326
spin-in collar 315
thermal insulation 266
Ducted evaporative cooler 394
Ductile iron fitting 470
   iron fitting mech joint 470
   iron grooved joint 175, 180
   iron pipe 469
Ductless removal split 254
   split system 399
Ductwork 306, 308, 328, 329
   aluminum 306
   assembly package 393
   clean 19
   fabric coated flexible 327
   fabricated 306, 307
   fiberglass 315
   flexible 328
   galvanized 306
   metal 306
   rectangular 306, 307
   rigid 306
Dump charge 23
   truck 613
Dumpster 22
Dumpsters 722
Dump truck off highway 613
Duplex style strainer 297
Dust barrier 16
   collection system 490
   containment unit 17, 29
DWV pipe ABS 200
   PVC pipe 201, 477
   tubing copper 129
DX coil evaporator 394

E

Earth auger 610
   compactor 611
   scraper 612
   vibrator 440, 444
Earthquake shutoff gas 369
   valve gas 369
Earthwork equipment 444

Index

equipment rental 610
Edger concrete floor 610
Eggcrate framed grille 344
   grille lay-in 344
   T-bar grille 345
Ejector pump 243
Elbow drip pan 240
   HDPE piping 472
   pipe 175
Electric baseboard heater 415
   boiler 361, 362, 530
   boiler large hydronic 531
   boiler small hydronic 530
   cabinet heater 417
   duct heater 406
   fuel oil heater 279
   furnace 370
   generator 615
   heater 72
   heater removal 253
   heating 362, 415
   hot air heater 417
   log 68
   pool heater 367
   unit heater 416
Electrical fee 8
   installation drilling 423
   knockout 425
   laboratory 74
Electricity temporary 12
Electronic air cleaner 353
   control component 277
Electrostatic precipitator 491
Elevated installation add 86
   pipe add 86
   water storage tank 476
   water tank 476
Elevator fee 8
   sump pump 244
Eliminator air 285
   air & dirt 285
Emergency equipment laboratory . 74
Employer liability 10
Emulsion sprayer 614
Encapsulation asbestos 28
   pipe 28
Enclosure decontamination 26-28
End culvert 480
Energy circulator air solar 376
   distribution pipe steam 485
   recovery wheel 389
   system air purger solar 378
   system air vent solar 378
   system balancing valve solar .. 378
   system control valve solar 378
   system controller solar 377
   system expansion tank solar ... 378
   system gauge pressure solar .. 378
   system heat exchanger solar .. 377
   system storage tank solar 377
   system vacuum relief solar ... 378
Engine exhaust elimination 337
Engineering fee 8, 713
Enthalpy control 272
   recovery wheel 389
Entrainment eliminator 242
Epoxy anchor 39, 44
   coating 462
   resin fitting 204
   welded wire 36
Equipment 70, 610
   automotive 70
   cleaning & disposal 73
   darkroom 70
   dental 75
   dental office 75

earthwork 444
feedwater 369
foundation formwork 32
hospital 74
ice skating 79
insulation 267
insurance 10
laboratory emergency 74
laundry 70
lubrication 70
medical 74, 75
medical sterilizing 74
pad 36
refrigerated storage 73
refrigeration 79
rental 610, 720, 721
rental concrete 610
rental earthwork 610
rental general 613
rental highway 617
rental lifting 618
rental marine 620
rental wellpoint 620
roof support 103
swimming pool 78
waste handling 76
Escutcheon 233
Estimate electrical heating 415
Estimating 708
Ethylene glycol 305
Evap/condes unit line set 399
Evaporative condenser 382
   cooler 394
   cooler ducted 394
   cooler removal 253
Evaporator coil cased 372
   cooler 394
   DX coil 394
   freezer 395
   removal 253
Excavating equipment 742
   trench 440
   utility trench 441
Excavation 440
   hand 440, 442, 444
   machine 444
   structural 442
   tractor 440
   trench 440, 442, 588-590, 592
Excavator bucket 617
   hydraulic 610
Excavator hydro 612
Exchanger heat 378
   removal heat 253
Exhaust elimination engine 337
   elimination garage 337
   fume hood 582
   granular fan 333
   hood 71, 73
   hood kitchen 351
   register 348
   system 338
   system removal 253
   vent 349
   vent damper 325
Exhauster industrial 333
   roof 333
Expansion anchor 44
   coupling 289
   coupling baseboard 289
   coupling hydronic 289
   joint 289
   joint bellow 289
   joint grooved joint 180
   shield 44
   tank 290

tank steel 290
water chiller direct 386
Explosive detection equipment .. 436
   detector 436
Extension backhoe 617
   ladder 615
Extra work 11
Extractor fitting 278
Extruder curb 611

F

Fabric pillow water tank 477
Fabricated ductwork 306, 307
Factor 8
   security 8
Factory air-conditioning .. 540, 542,
                     565, 567, 571, 573
Fan 332
   air conditioning 330
   attic ventilation 335
   bathroom exhaust 335
   belt driven 332
   blower HVAC 331
   booster 332
   ceiling 331
   centrifugal type HVAC 332
   coil air conditioning 408
   draft-induction 353
   exhaust granular 333
   house ventilation 336
   HVAC axial flow 330
   induced draft 353
   in-line 332
   kitchen exhaust 335
   paddle 430
   propeller exhaust 334
   removal 253
   residential 334, 430
   roof 333
   utility set 331, 332
   vaneaxial 331
   ventilation 430
   wall 334
   wall exhaust 333
   wiring 430
Fan-coil A/C removal 253
Faucet & fitting 247
F&C plate 233
Fee engineering 8
Feeder control water 268
   cut-off combination 268
Feedwater equipment 369
Feller buncher 611
Fence chain link 18
   plywood 18
   temporary 18
   wire 18
Fiber reinforcing concrete 38
Fiberglass cooling tower ... 388, 546
   duct 315-318
   ductwork 315
   fuel tank double wall ... 602, 603
   panel 16
   pipe covering 112
   rainwater storage tank 244
   reinforced ceiling 79
   storage tank 602
   tank 282
   underground storage tank .. 239
Fibrous-glass duct 315
Field office 13
   office expense 13
   personnel 10, 11
Fill 444

adapter 278
   box fuel 278
   by borrow & utility bedding .. 444
   cap fuel 278
   gravel 444
Filler crack 618
   joint 56
Fillet welding 46
Film equipment 70
Filter air 353
   dryer refrigerant 303
   grille 344
   HEPA 352
   mechanical media 351
   oil 278
   rainwater 494
   removal air 252
   swimming pool 248
Filtration air 25
   equipment 78
Fin tube commercial 411
   tube radiation 411
Finish refrigeration 79
Finishing floor concrete 38
Fin-tube radiation
   apartment bldg 520
   radiation commercial bldg 521
Fire call pullbox 438
   damper curtain type 323
   damper round 324
   door 438
   horn 438
   hydrant remove 22
   rated blanket duct 266
   tube boiler 367
Fireplace chimney 68
   free standing 68
   prefabricated 68
Fire/smoke damper 324
Firestopping 54, 723
Fitting adapter pipe 133
   cast iron 161
   cast iron pipe 150
   compression joint 135
   compression tank air 286
   copper 131
   copper pipe 131, 141
   drainage special pipe 240
   ductile iron 470
   DWV pipe 209
   epoxy resin 204
   extractor 278
   flanged 162
   flanged cast iron pipe 161
   flare joint 137
   flexible gas pipe 280
   forged steel pipe 168
   gas vent 354
   grooved joint 140, 174
   grooved joint pipe 175
   grooved unit 139, 177
   HDPE 220
   insert pipe 215
   malleable iron 154
   malleable iron pipe ... 155, 171
   mechanical joint pipe 171
   monoflow 294
   pipe 161, 483, 485
   pipe conduit 484
   plastic 209
   polybutylene pipe 215
   polypropylene 216
   PVC 207, 471
   PVC pipe 216
   refrigeration 137
   removal piping 87

762

Index

round duct 308
   stainless steel 189
   stainless steel pipe 189
   steel 150, 161
   steel carbon pipe 164
   steel pipe 164
   tube 183
   vent chimney 354, 360
   weld 167
   weld joint pipe 168
   welded steel pipe 172
Fixed blade louver 348
Fixture plumbing 247, 301, 469
   residential 429
Flange blind 163
   clip beam 105
   companion 163
   gasket 162
   grooved joint 179
   PVC 214
   slip on escutcheon 233
   stainless steel 194
   steel 170, 179
   steel weld-on 170
   threaded 163
Flanged coil 402
   fitting 162
   pipe 145
Flare joint fitting 137
Flasher barrels 614
   barricade 614
Flashing 52
   aluminum 52, 241
   copper 52, 241
   galvanized 242
   laminated sheet 52
   lead 242
   masonry 52
   neoprene 242
   plastic sheet 52
   PVC 52
   sheet metal 52
   stainless 52
   vent 241
   vent chimney 355, 361
Flatbed truck 613, 617
   truck crane 618
Flex duct aluminum 328
Flexible aluminum duct silencer . 329
   conduit & fitting 425
   connector 227
   duct 327
   duct connection fabric 315
   ductwork 328
   ductwork fabric coated 327
   gas pipe fitting 280
   insulated duct 327
   metal hose 228
   noninsulated duct 327
Float finish concrete 38
   valve 291
Floater equipment 10
Floodlight trailer 615
   tripod 614
Floor access 64
   cleaning 18
   concrete finishing 38
   diffuser 342
   heating radiant 413
   heating removal radiant 253
   pedestal 64
   refrigeration 80
   register 346
   sander 616
   standing unit AHU 410
   standing unit concealed AHU . 410

Flow check control 291
   fitting hydronic 294
   meter 300
   meter circuit sensor 286
Flue chimney metal 354
   liner 42
   prefab metal 354
   shutter damper removal 253
Fluid heat transfer 377
Foam core DWV ABS pipe 200
   core DWV PVC pipe 201
   pipe covering 115
   rubber pipe covering 115
   spray rig 615
Food service equipment 73
Foot valve 94, 278
   valve oil 278
Footing concrete placement 38
   formwork continuous 32
   formwork spread 32
   reinforcing 36
   spread 36
Forced-draft cooling tower 387
Forged valve 261
Forklift 615
   crew 13
Formwork continuous footing . . . 32
   equipment foundation 32
   slab edge 32
   slab haunch 37
   slab on grade 32
   slab thickened edge 37
   slab trench 32
   slab turndown 37
   sleeve 32
   spread footing 32
Fossil fuel boiler 364, 365, 368
   fuel hydronic heating . . . 532, 533
Foundation chimney 36
   mat 37
   mat concrete placement 38
   vent 42
Fountain lighting 248
   pump 248
   water pump 248
Frame scaffold 14
Framing lightweight 47
   lightweight angle 47
   lightweight channel 47
   pipe support 47
   slotted channel 47
Freezer 72, 73, 80
   evaporator 395
Freezestat 272
Frequency drive adjustable 432
   drive variable 432
Fuel breather cap 279
   fill box 278
   fill cap 278
   furnace solid 371
   heater crossflow 279
   heater steam 279
   oil gauge 278
   oil heater 279
   oil heater electric 279
   oil pump 281
   oil pump & motor set 281
   oil specialty 278
   oil valve 278
   spill container 278
   system component 278
   tank 282
Fume elimination welding 339
   hood 73
   hood removal weld 253
Furnace A/C coil 372

   component 372
   condensing 371
   demolition 253
   duct 373
   electric 370
   gas 373
   gas fired 370
   hot air 370
   oil fired 371
   type humidifier 419
   wall 370, 375
   wood 371
Fused pipe 472
Fusible oil valve 278
Fusion machine butt 614

G

Gage stick wood 278
Galvanized cooling tower 546
   ductwork 306
   flashing 242
   welded wire 36
Gap fitting air 235
Garage exhaust elimination 337
   exhaust system 583
   ventilation 337
Garbage disposal 71
Gas boiler cast iron hot water . . . 536,
                                          537
   boiler cast iron steam 537
   boiler hot water 536
   boiler steam 537
   cock 88
   connector 227
   conversion burner 369
   earthquake valve 369
   fired boiler 363
   fired furnace 370
   fired infrared heater 374
   fired space heater 375
   furnace 373
   furnace wood 372
   heat air conditioner 391
   incinerator 76
   log 68
   meter 279
   meter residential 279
   pipe 483
   piping flexible (CSST) 279
   piping medical 249
   pressure regulator 230
   pulse combustion 363
   regulator 230
   safety valve 369
   space heater 562
   station tank 282
   stop valve 88
   tubing (CSST) 279
   vent 354
   vent fitting 354
Gas-fired duct heater 373
   heating 364, 374, 375
Gasket & bolt set 162
   flange 162
   joint 55
   neoprene 55
Gas/oil boiler cast iron
hot water 537
   boiler cast iron steam 537
   boiler hot water 537
   boiler steam 537
   burner 369
   combination boiler 364
Gasoline piping 482

Gas-service polyethylene pipe . . . 601
Gate box 474
   valve 256, 260, 263, 475, 476
   valve grooved joint 180
   valve soldered 90
Gauge cock 288
   fuel oil 278
   pressure 272
   pressure/vacuum 272
   vacuum 272
   water 268
General air conditioner 252
   boiler 86
   contractor's overhead 717
   equipment rental 613
   fill 444
   maintenance 19
Generator electric 615
   steam 74
GFI receptacle 428
Gland seal pipe conduit 483
Glass insulation cellular 108
   lined water heater 71
Glassware sterilizer 74
   washer 74
Globe valve 256, 260, 263
   valve bronze 90
Glove bag 26
Glycol ethylene 305
   propylene 305
Gradall 611
Grader motorized 611
Grading 450
Gravel fill 444
   pack well 468
Gravity syphon ventilator 349
Grease duct round 311
Grille air return 343
   aluminum 343
   door 344
   duct 64
   eggcrate framed 344
   filter 344
   lay-in T-bar 344
   painting 65
   plastic 345
   transfer 344
Grinder concrete floor 610
   system pump 242
Grit removal and handling
equipment 494
Groove cut labor steel 181
   roll labor steel 181
Grooved joint check valve 180
   joint copper 139
   joint ductile iron 175, 180
   joint fitting 140, 174
   joint flange 179
   joint pipe 174
   joint plug valve 180
   joint reducer 140
   joint strainer 179
   joint suction diffuser 179
   reducer 177
   unit fitting 139, 177
Ground box hydrant 236
   post hydrant 237
Grout pump 616
   topping 39
Guard house 81
   snow 53
Guardrail scaffold 14
   temporary 17
Guide pipe 97
Gun type burner 369
Guyed derrick crane 619

Index

H

Entry	Page
Hammer chipping	614
demolition	611
diesel	612
drill rotary	614
hydraulic	611, 615
pile	611
vibratory	612
Hammermill	617
Hand excavation	440, 442, 444
trowel finish concrete	38
Handling material	18
waste	76
Hand/off/automatic control	432
Handrail aluminum	64
Hanger & support pipe	95
assembly pipe	100
cable	104
clevis	98
pipe	95
plastic pipe	104
rod coupling	100
rod pipe	99
rod socket	102
roll	100
split ring	98
trapeze	100
U-bolt pipe	103
U-hook	103
vibration absorbing	105
Hanger/support removal pipe	87
Hanging lintel	47
Harrow disc	611
Hauling	445
cycle	445
Haunch slab	37
Hazardous waste cleanup	24
waste disposal	24
waste handling	76
HDPE fitting	220
pipe	219
pipe dual wall	223
pipe liner	466
piping	472
piping cap	473
piping elbow	472
piping tee	473
Header pipe wellpoint	620
Heat baseboard	411
coil steam	405
electric baseboard	415
exchanger	378
exchanger plate-type	379
exchanger removal	253
exchanger shell-type	379
pipe	389
pump	400
pump air-source	400
pump central station	579
pump console	579
pump gas driven	400
pump horizontal duct mounted	579
pump removal	253
pump residential	431
pump rooftop air/air	580
pump water heater	400
pump water source console	579
pump water source station	579
pump water-source	401
recovery	76
recovery air to air	389
recovery package	389
recovery package removal	253
recovery wheel	389
steam	406
trace system	415
transfer fluid	377
transfer package	247
Heater & fan bathroom	335
air handler	373
cabinet convector	417
ceiling mount unit	418
electric	72
electric commercial	415
electric hot air	417
floor mounted space	375
fuel oil	279
gas fired infrared	374
gas-fired duct	373
infrared	374
infrared quartz	416
oil fired space	374
quartz	416
removal electric	253
removal space	254
sauna	80
space	615
swimming pool	367
swimming pool solar	527
terminal	374, 412
terminal unit comm bldg	522
tubular infrared	374
unit	375, 401, 409
valance	401
vertical discharge	417
wall mounted	417
warm air	373
water	71, 430
Heating	278, 734
& cooling classroom	409
& ventilating unit removal	253
coal hydronic	532
commercial bldg	522
control valve	291
electric	362, 415
estimate electrical	415
fin-tube	533
fin-tube residential	520
gas-fired	364, 374, 375
hot air	370, 373, 401, 409, 412
hot water solar	509
hydronic	361, 364-366, 401, 411
hydronic fossil fuel	532, 533
industrial	361
insulation	107, 111, 112, 267
kettle	618
oil hydronic	532, 533
panel radiant	416
solar	376
solar-energy	517, 527
steam-to-water	378
subsoil	79
systems	733
terminal unit-heater	532
Heavy duty shoring	14
lifting	720
Helicopter	619
HEPA filter	352
High impact pipe	198
Highway equipment rental	617
Hockey dasher	79
Hoist chain fall	619
personnel	619
tower	619
Hole cutting electrical	424
drilling electrical	423
Hollow wall anchor	44
Hood and ventilation equip.	350
exhaust	71, 73
fire protection	351
fume	73
range	71
Hook type pipe outlet	173
Hopper refuse	84
Horizontal borer	618
boring	466
boring machine	610
directional drill	618
drilling	466
heat pump	579
Horn fire	438
Hose adapter vapor	278
air	614
bibb	287
bibb sillcock	247
braided bronze	228
braided stainless steel	228
braided steel	228
discharge	615
metal flexible	228
suction	615
water	615
Hospital equipment	74
Hot air furnace	370
air heater electric	417
air heating	370, 373, 401, 409, 412
water boiler	362, 363, 365, 366
water coil	404
water heating	362, 411
water temp maint domestic	105
water-steam exchange	247, 378
water-water exchange	379
Hot-water heating forced	520
solar-energy	507, 509, 511, 513, 515, 519, 525
House fan whole	334
guard	81
ventilation fan	336
Humidifier	72, 419
duct	419
furnace type	419
removal	253
room	419
HVAC axial flow fan	330
demolition	252
duct	306
equipment insulation	268
louver	348
piping specialty	228, 230, 242, 268, 289, 296, 298
power circulator & ventilator	334
HVLS air circulator	334
Hydrant ground box	236
ground post	237
removal	22
remove fire	22
wall	236
water	236
Hydraulic chair	75
crane	619
excavator	610
hammer	611, 615
jack	620
jack climbing	620
jacking	720
pressure test	265
Hydro excavator	612
Hydrocumulator	239
Hydromulcher	618
Hydronic balancing	299
baseboard removal	253
cabinet unit heater	563
convector & radiator demo	253
energy underground	485
expansion coupling	289
flow fitting	294
heating	361, 364-366, 401, 411
heating control valve	291
heating convector	411
space heater	562, 563
unit heater removal	253

I

Entry	Page
Ice machine	73
rink dasher	79
skating equipment	79
Icemaker	71, 73
Impact wrench	614
Incinerator gas	76
waste	76
Indicator thermoflo	299
Indirect-fired make-up air unit	391
water chiller	383
Indoor AHU packaged	390
AHU VRV	409
water storage tank	240
Induced draft fan	353
draft fan removal	253
Industrial burner	369
dryer	70
exhauster	333
heating	361
Inert gas	24
Infectious disease	9
disease precautions	714
Infrared heater	374
heater gas fired	374
heater tubular	374
quartz heater	416
In-line fan	332
Insert fitting PVC	216
hanger concrete	97
Inspection internal pipe	465
Installation add elevated	86
Insulated protector ADA	107
Insulation	112
all service jacket	107, 113
blanket	266
blower	615
board	267
boiler	267
breeching	268
calcium silicate	268
duct	266
duct thermal	266
equipment	267
heating	107, 111, 112, 267
HVAC equipment	268
jacket stainless-steel	125
jacketing	117
jacketing aluminum	121
jacketing protective	117
pipe	107
polyethylene	115, 267
polyolefin	116
polystyrene	80
refrigeration	80
removal	26
subsoil	79
vaporproof	108, 116
water heater	116
Insurance	10, 717
builder risk	10
equipment	10
public liability	10
Intake-exhaust louver	348
vent	350
Internal cleaning pipe	465
Interval timer	426
Intrusion detection	436

Index

system 436
Invert manhole 481
Inverted bucket steam trap 294
Iron body valve 255
Irrigation system sprinkler 459

J

J hook clamp w/nail 104
Jack cable 620
   hydraulic 620
Jacketing insulation 117
Jackhammer 614
Jacking 466
Jet water system 469
Job condition 9
Joint control 33
   expansion 289
   filler 56
   gasket 55
   grooved joint expansion 180
   push-on 470
   restraint 470, 472
   sealer 55, 56
   weld end ball 300

K

Kettle 73
   heating 618
   tar 616, 618
Kitchen equipment 73
   equipment fee 8
   exhaust fan 335
   exhaust hood 351
   smoke control 491
   unit commercial 72
   ventilation 351
Knockout electrical 425

L

Label pipe & valve 106
Labor adjustment factor 86, 422
   modifier 86
   pipe cutting steel 148
   pipe groove roll 181
   pipe threading st steel 187
   pipe threading steel 148
   pipe weld stainless steel 188
   pipe weld steel 149
Laboratory safety equipment 74
   sink 73, 74
Ladder extension 615
   rolling 15
Lag screw 46
   screw shield 44
Lagging 455
Laminated sheet flashing 52
Lance concrete 615
Landfill compactor 612
Laser level 615
Latex caulking 56
Laundry equipment 70
Lawn mower 615
Lead flashing 52, 242
   screw anchor 44
Leads pile 611
Leak detection 437
   detection probe 437
   detection tank 437
Level laser 615
Leveling jack shoring 14

Liability employer 10
   insurance 717
Library air-cond. . 539, 541, 564, 568, 570
Lift scissor 613
Lifting equipment rental 618
Light dental 75
   stand 25
   temporary 12
   tower 615
   underwater 78
Lighting fountain 248
   outlet 429
   residential 429
   temporary 12
Lightning suppressor 426
Lightweight angle framing 47
   channel framing 47
   framing 47
Line remover traffic 618
   set 399
   set refrigerant 304
Linear diffuser 341
Linen chute 84
   collector 84
Liner duct 330
   flue 42
   non-fibrous duct 321, 330
Link seal pipe 232
Lintel hanging 47
Liquid chiller centrifugal 384
   chiller screw 386
   cooler cooling-tower 388
   cooler tower 388
   drainer 292
Loader skidsteer 613
   tractor 612
   vacuum 25
   wheeled 612
   windrow 618
Locking receptacle 428
Locomotive tunnel 618
Log chipper 612
   electric 68
   gas 68
   skidder 612
Louver 61
   aluminum 61, 348
   aluminum operating 348
   coating 348
   commercial grade aluminum . . . 61
   cooling tower 348
   door steel 345
   fixed blade 348
   galvanized steel 61
   HVAC 348
   intake-exhaust 348
   midget 61
   mullion type 348
   operable 60
   PVC 61
   stainless 349
   stainless steel 349
   wall 62
Low bed trailer 618
Lubricated plug valve 259
Lubricating oil 382
Lubrication equipment 70
Lubricator air filter regulator . . . 245

M

Machine autoscrub 614
   excavation 444
   screw 46

trowel finish concrete 38
welding 617
X-ray 436
Machinery anchor 35
Magnetic motor starter 431
   particle test 12
Maintenance cable temperature . 105
   general 19
   mechanical 19
Make-up air unit 390
   air unit removal 253
   air unit rooftop 391
Malleable iron fitting 154
   iron pipe fitting 154
Management fee construction . . . 8
Manhole 467
   brick 467
   concrete 467
   cover 481
   frame and cover 481
   invert 481
   raise 481
   removal 22
   step 467
Marine equipment rental 620
Marker pipe 106
Mark-up cost 11
Mason scaffold 14
Masonry accessory 42
   brick 42
   flashing 52
   manhole 467
   saw 616
   ventilator 42
Mat concrete placement
   foundation 38
   foundation 37
Material handling 18
Meat case 72
Mechanical 724, 725
   coupling 173
   duct 306
   equipment demolition 253
   fee 8
   maintenance 19
   media filter 351
   roof support 103
Medical alarm system 249
   center air-conditioner 573
   center air-conditioning . . . 540, 542, 565, 567, 569, 571
   clean copper tubing 128
   equipment 74, 75
   gas piping 249
   nitrogen or oxygen 249
   sterilizer 74
   sterilizing equipment 74
   vacuum pump 248
   vacuum system 248
Metal chimney 68
   detector 436
   ductwork 306
   flexible hose 228
   flue chimney 354
   pipe 479
   pipe removal 87
   support assembly 64
   valve removal 87
Meter 279
   flow 300
   gas 279
   steam condensate 302
   venturi flow 300
   water supply 233
   water supply detector 233
   water supply domestic 233

Metric conversion factors 711
Microtunneling 466
Mineral wool board 267
   wool pipe covering 107
Minor site demolition 22
Miscellaneous painting 65
   pump 238
Mixed bituminous
   concrete plant 440
Mixer concrete 610
   mortar 610, 615
   plaster 615
   road 618
Mixing box 340
   box constant volume 340
   box duct 340
   box VAV 340
   valve 229
Mobilization or demobilization . . . 15
Modification to cost 9
Modifier labor 86
Modular air handler 373
Modulating damper motorized . . 322
Moil point 614
Mold abatement work area 28
   contaminated area demolition . . 28
Monoflow fitting 294
   tee fitting 294
Monoxide detector carbon 271
Mortar mixer 610, 615
Mortuary equipment 75
   refrigeration 75
Motor actuated valve 274
   centrifugal in-line 238
   connection 425
   controlled valve 274
   starter 431
   starter & control 431
   starter enclosed & heated . . . 431
   starter magnetic 431
   starter w/circuit protector 431
   starter w/fused switch 431
Motorized grader 611
   modulating damper 322
   zone valve 274
Mount vibration absorbing 105
Mounting board plywood 50
Mouth collar bell 315
Movable blade louver 60
   louver PVC 60
Mower lawn 615
Muck car tunnel 618
Mud pump 610
   trailer 618
Mulcher power 612
Mullion type louver 348
Multi-blade damper 321
Multipurpose valve 258
Multizone air conditioner
   rooftop 392
   air-conditioner 393
Mushroom ventilator stationary . 350
Mylar tarpaulin 16

N

Nailer pneumatic 614, 615
Needle valve 94
Neoprene flashing 242
   gasket 55
Nipple pipe 154
Nitrogen or oxygen medical . . . 249
Non-chloride accelerator conc. . . 37
Nondestructive pipe testing 265
Non-destructive testing 12

Index

Nonfusible oil valve 278
Nut threaded 99

O

Observation well 468
Occupancy determinations 710
Off highway dump truck 613
Office & storage space 13
   air-conditioner 573
   air-conditioning 540, 542, 565,
                         567, 569, 571
   field 13
   floor 64
   trailer 13
Oil 382
   burner 369
   filter 278
   fired boiler 365
   fired furnace 371
   fired heating 365
   fired space heater 374
   furnace wood 371
   lubricating 382
   refrigeration 382
   shut-off valve 278
   specialty fuel 278
   valve fuel 278
Oil-fired boiler 366
Oil/water separator 494
Omitted work 11
Opening roof frame 47
Operable louver 60
OSHA testing 27
Outdoor air-handling
   unit packaged 391
       unit VRV 400
Outlet lighting 429
Oval arch culvert 480
   chimney vent 356
Oven 71, 73
Overhaul 23
Overhead & profit 11
   contractor 18, 717
Overtime 10, 11
Oxygen lance cutting 23

P

P trap 240
   trap refrigeration 304
Package chute 84
Packaged A/C elec heat
const volume 575, 576
   A/C elec heat VAV 576
   A/C hot wtr. heat VAV 576
   A/C hw heat const volume ... 576
   outdoor air-handling unit 391
   terminal A/C removal 254
   terminal air conditioner 396
   water tube boiler 366
Packaging waste 28
Pad equipment 36
   prefabricated 420
   vibration absorbing 106
Paddle blade air circulator ... 334, 337
   fan 430
Paint & coating 65
   interior miscellaneous 65
   sprayer 615
   striper 618
Painting 724
   booth 70
   grille 65

miscellaneous 65
pipe 65
swimming pool 78
Pan drip-drain condensate 303
Panel and device alarm 438
   board residential 426
   fiberglass 16
   fiberglass refrigeration 79
   radiant heat 416
Parking lot paving 458
Partition refrigeration 80
Patching asphalt 440
   concrete floor 32
   concrete wall 32
Patient care equipment 75
Pavement asphaltic 458
   breaker 614
   bucket 617
   demolition 22
   planer 618
   profiler 618
   replacement 458
   widener 618
Paver asphalt 616
   bituminous 615
   cold mix 618
   concrete 616
   roof 53
   shoulder 618
Paving asphalt 458
   asphaltic concrete 458
   parking lot 458
Pedestal floor 64
Penthouse air-conditioner 393
   roof louver 348
Perforated aluminum pipe 478
   HDPE pipe 504
   pipe 478
   PVC pipe 478
Performance bond 11, 719
Permit building 12
Personal respirator 25
Personnel field 10, 11
   hoist 619
Pet cock 287
Pete's plug 232
PEX pipe 203
   tubing 203, 413
   tubing fitting 414
Photography 12
   construction 12
   time lapse 12
Pickup truck 617
Pick-up vacuum 610
Pier brick 42
Pigtail steam syphon 288
Pile driving 720, 721
   H 455
   hammer 611
   leads 611
   steel sheet 454
   wood sheet 454
Piling sheet 454, 744
Pillow tank 477
Pin powder 46
Pipe & fitting 95
   & fitting backflow preventer .. 234
   & fitting brass 88, 128
   & fitting bronze 91
   & fitting carbon steel 164
   & fitting copper .. 128, 129, 131, 141
   & fitting DWV 209
   & fitting grooved joint 174
   & fitting hydrant 236
   & fitting iron body 257
   & fitting malleable iron 155

& fitting polypropylene 93
& fitting PVC 199
& fitting semi-steel 259
& fitting stainless steel ... 184, 189,
                              263
& fitting steel 144, 260
& fitting steel cast iron 152
& fitting trap 241
& fitting turbine water meter .. 233
& valve label 106
add elevated 86
aluminum 478, 479
and fittings 728
bedding 444, 594, 595
bedding trench 442
bituminous coated metal 597
bituminous fiber perforated ... 504
bracket 95
brass 126
bursting 466
carrier 96, 100
clamp 95, 462
clamp plastic 104
cleaning internal 465
concrete 479
concrete nonreinforced 597
concrete porous wall 504
concrete reinforced 597
conduit gland seal 483
conduit prefabricated 483, 485
conduit preinsulated 483
conduit system 483, 486
contained 223
copper 128
copper in trench 596
corrugated 478
corrugated metal 478, 479
corrugated metal coated 597
corrugated metal plain 597
corrugated oval arch coated .. 598
corrugated oval arch plain ... 598
covering 107
covering calcium silicate 110
covering fiberglass 112
covering foam 115
covering mineral wool 107
CPVC 201
culvert 480
cutting steel labor 148
double wall 219, 482
drain 443
drainage 477, 479
dual wall HDPE 223
ductile iron 469
ductile iron in trench 596
DWV PVC 201, 477
elbow 175
encapsulation 28
fitting 161, 483, 485
fitting adapter 133
fitting brass 127
fitting cast iron 150
fitting copper 131, 141
fitting drainage special 240
fitting DWV 209
fitting flanged cast iron 161
fitting forged steel 168
fitting grooved joint 175
fitting insert 215
fitting malleable iron ... 155, 171
fitting mechanical joint 171
fitting plastic 204, 212, 213
fitting polybutylene 215
fitting polypropylene 217
fitting PVC 216
fitting stainless steel 189

fitting steel 150, 164
fitting steel carbon 164
fitting weld joint 168
fitting weld steel 164
fitting welded steel 172
flanged 145
foam core DWV ABS 200
foam core DWV PVC 201
freezing 463
fused 472
gas 483
groove cut 181
groove roll labor 181
grooved joint 174
guide 97
hanger 95
hanger & support 95
hanger assembly 100
hanger clevis 98
hanger plastic 104
hanger rod 99
hanger strap 103
hanger U-bolt 103
hanger/support removal 87
HDPE 219
heat 389
high impact 198
in trench 504, 596-598, 601
inspection internal 465
insulation 107
insulation removal 26
internal cleaning 465
iron ductile mech joint 596
iron ductile Tyton joint 596
liner HDPE 466
lining 466
link seal 232
marker 106
metal 479
metal perforated coated 504
nipple 154
nipple steel 154
painting 65
perforated aluminum 478
PEX 203
plastic 198, 201
plastic FRP 198
polyethylene 483
polyethylene gas-service 601
polyethylene in trench 596
polypropylene 203
polyvinyl chloride 598
prefabricated 483, 485
preinsulated 483, 485
pressed joint 140
PVC 199, 471, 477, 597
PVC in trench 596
PVC pressure 200
reinforced concrete 479
relay 443
removal metal 87
removal plastic 87
repair 462
repair clamp 463
ring hanger 97
rodding 465
roll single 100
roof support 103
seal 232
sewage 477, 479
sewage collection PVC 477
shock absorber 235
sleeve 232
sleeve plastic 32
sleeve sheet metal 32
sleeve steel 32

Index

stainless steel 183
steam 487
steel 143, 479
steel gas-service 601
steel tarred & wrapped 601
subdrainage 478
subdrainage plastic 478
supply register spiral 347
support 95
support chair 100
support framing 47
support saddle 101
tee 176
testing 265
testing nondestructive ... 265
threading st steel labor . 187
threading steel labor 148
water 469
weld joint 144, 183
weld stainless steel labor 188
weld steel labor 149
wrapping 462
X-ray 266
Pipe bursting 466
Piping designations 744
Piping drainage & sewage 597
   excavation 588, 590, 592
   fitting removal 87
   flexible (CSST) gas 279
   gas service polyethylene . 483
   gasoline 482
   gas-service 601
   HDPE 472
   specialty 268
   specialty HVAC ... 228, 230, 242,
                268, 289, 296, 298
   storm drainage 479
   to 10' high 729
   water distribution 596
Pit excavation 442
   sump 443
Pitch pocket 53
Placing concrete 38
Plan remediation 25
Planer pavement 618
Plank scaffolding 14
Plant mixed bituminous conc. 440
   screening 612
Plant-mix asphalt paving 458
Plaster cement 79
   drilling 64
   mixer 615
Plastic angle valve 93
   ball check valve 94
   ball valve 93
   coupling 212
   duct 321
   duct fiberglass-reinforced 315
   duct fitting 319
   fitting 209
   FRP pipe 198
   grille 345
   pipe 198, 201
   pipe clamp 104
   pipe fitting ... 204, 212, 213
   pipe hanger 104
   pipe polyethylene 219
   pipe removal 87
   pipe weld 222
   screw anchor 45
   sheet flashing 52
   trap 241
   valve 93
   valve removal 87
Plate F&C 233
   heat exchanger 561

roadway 618
Plate-type heat exchanger .. 379
Platform trailer 616
Plow vibrator 613
Plug Pete's 232
   pressure/temperature safety 232
   p/t 232
   p/t probe 232
   valve 259
   valve grooved joint 180
Plumbing 234
   demolition 87
   fixture 247, 301, 469
   laboratory 74
Plywood fence 18
   mounting board 50
   sheathing roof & wall 50
   sidewalk 18
Pneumatic air operated valve 275
   component 275
   control 272
   control system 270
   controller 276
   nailer 614, 615
   thermostat 273
   tube 276
   tube fitting 276
   tube system 84
Pocket pitch 53
Point moil 614
Polybutylene adapter 215
Polyethylene coating 462
   insulation 115, 267
   pipe 483
   plastic pipe 219
   tarpaulin 16
Polyolefin insulation 116
Polypropylene accessory 216
   coupling 216
   duct 320
   fitting 216
   fitting duct 320
   pipe 203
   pipe fitting 217
   tool 218
   trap 241
   tubing 203
   valve 93
Polystyrene ceiling 79
   insulation 80
Polysulfide caulking 57
Polyurethane caulking 57
Polyvinyl tarpaulin 16
Pool filtration swimming ... 248
   heater electric 367
   heater swimming 367
   swimming 78
Portable air compressor 613
   asphalt plant 617
   building 13
Positive pressure chimney 357, 360
Post driver 618
Potable-water storage 240
   storage tank 239
Powder actuated tool 46
   charge 46
   pin 46
Power mulcher 612
   roof vent 558
   temporary 12
   trowel 610
Powerfoil 337
Precast catch basin 467
Precipitator electrostatic . 491
Prefab metal flue 354
Prefabricated comfort station 81

fireplace 68
metal chimney 357
pad 420
pipe 483, 485
Preinsulated pipe 483, 485
Pressed joint pipe 140
Pressure & temperature
   measurement 232
   booster package water ... 239
   booster pump 239
   booster system water 239
   gauge 272
   pipe 200
   pipe PVC 200
   reducing valve steam 230
   reducing valve water 91
   regulator 230
   regulator gas 230
   regulator oil 230
   regulator steam 231
   relief valve 91
   switch well water 469
   test 265
   test hydraulic 265
   valve relief 91
   washer 616
Pressure/temperature
   safety plug 232
Pressure/vacuum gauge 272
Preventer backflow 234
   removal backflow 87
Probe plug p/t 232
Produce case 72
Product piping 482
Profiler pavement 618
Project overhead 11
   sign 18
Propeller exhaust fan 334
   unit heater 412
Propylene glycol 305
Protection winter 16
   worker 25
Protective insulation jacketing 117
Protector ADA insulated 107
Psychrometric table 737
P/t plug 232
P&T relief valve 91
PTAC unit 396
Pulse boiler gas 363
   combustion gas 363
Pump 301, 468
   air conditioning 304
   and motor set 281
   centrifugal 237, 616
   circulating 301
   concrete 610
   condensate 302
   condensate removal 302
   condensate return 302
   contractor 443
   diaphragm 616
   double suction 538
   end suction 538
   fountain 248
   fuel oil 281
   gas driven heat 400
   general utility 237
   grinder system 242
   grout 616
   heat 400
   in-line centrifugal 301
   medical vacuum 248
   miscellaneous 238
   mud 610
   operator 443
   pressure booster 239

removal 87
removal heat 253
rotary 238
sewage ejector 243
shallow well 469
shotcrete 610
submersible 244, 468, 616
sump 71, 244
trash 616
turbine 238
vacuum 248, 304
water 301, 468, 616
water supply well 469
wellpoint 620
Pumping 443
   dewater 443
Push-on joint 470
Putlog scaffold 15
PVC duct 319
   fitting 207, 471
   flange 214
   flashing 52
   insert fitting 216
   louver 61
   movable louver 60
   pipe 199, 471, 477
   pipe perforated 478
   SDR35 pipe 598
   trap 241
   union 214
   valve 93
   well casing 468

Q

Quarry drill 614
Quartz heater 416

R

Raceway 423, 424
Radiant floor heating 413
   floor heating removal ... 253
   heating panel 416
Radiation fin tube 411
Radiator air vent 286
   cast iron 411
   supply control 291
   supply valve 291
   thermostat control system 271
   valve 292
Radiography test 12
Rain cap chimney 350
Rainwater filter 494
   storage tank fiberglass . 244
Raise manhole 481
   manhole frame 481
Raised floor 64
Rake tractor 612
Rammer/tamper 611
Ramp approach 64
   temporary 16
Range cooking 71
   hood 71
   receptacle 428
Reach-in cooler evaporator . 394
Ready mix concrete 37, 714
Receptacle air conditioner . 428
   device 427
   dryer 428
   GFI 428
   locking 428
   range 428
   telephone 429

Index

television 429
 weatherproof 428
Reciprocating chiller 543
 chiller air cooled 543
 chiller water cooled 543
 compressor 246
 hermetic compressor 246
 water chiller 384
Recorder chart 274
Recovery heat 76
 package heat 389
 package removal heat 253
 wheel energy 389
 wheel enthalpy 389
Rectangular diffuser 341
 ductwork 306, 307
Reducer grooved 177
 grooved joint 140
Reducing tee 151
Reflectorized barrels 614
Refrigerant A/C 305
 accumulator 303
 compressor 379, 380
 compressor removal 254
 filter dryer 303
 line set 304
 removal 254
Refrigerated case 72
 storage equipment 73
Refrigeration 79
 commercial 72
 equipment 79
 fitting 137
 floor 80
 insulation 80
 mortuary 75
 oil 382
 P trap 304
 panel fiberglass 79
 partition 80
 sightglass 304
 specialty 303
 tubing 130
 valve 303
 walk-in 80
Refrigerator door 60
Refuse chute 84
 hopper 84
Register air supply 345
 baseboard 346
 exhaust 348
 return 347
 steel 346
 wall 347
Regulator gas 230
 lubricator air filter 245
 oil pressure 230
 pressure 230
 steam pressure 231
Reinforced concrete pipe 479
 culvert 479
Reinforcing concrete 36
 footing 36
Relay control component 272
 pipe 443
Relief damper 325
 valve P&T 91
 valve self-closing 91
 valve temperature 91
 vent removal 254
 vent ventilator 350
Remediation plan 25
 plan/method asbestos 25
Remote oil gauge 278
Removal air conditioner 252
 asbestos 26

boiler 252
catch basin 22
concrete 22
condenser 252
dehumidifier 252
driveway 22
evaporator 253
fan 253
heating & ventilating unit 253
humidifier 253
hydrant 22
insulation 26
pipe insulation 26
pump 87
refrigerant 254
sidewalk 22
tank 24
utility line 22
ventilator 254
water softener 88
Rental equipment 610
Repair pipe 462
Replacement pavement 458
Residential alarm 429
 appliance 71, 430
 application 425
 burner 369
 device 426
 dishwasher 71
 door bell 429
 dryer 71
 duct assembly 393
 fan 334, 430
 fin-tube heating 520
 fixture 429
 gas meter 279
 heat pump 430
 lighting 429
 panel board 426
 roof jack 335
 service 426
 smoke detector 429
 switch 426
 transition 335
 wall cap 335
 washer 71
 water heater 71, 430
 wiring 426, 429
Resistance corrosion 462
Respirator 25
 personal 25
Restaurant air-conditioner 573
 air-conditioning 540, 542, 565,
         567, 569, 571
Retarder concrete 37
Return register 347
Ridge vent 53
Rigid fiberglass duct 316
 joint sealant 57
 plastic duct 319, 320
Ring hanger pipe 97
Ripper attachment 617
Riser clamp 96
 pipe wellpoint 620
Rivet 46
 aluminum 46
 copper 46
 steel 46
 tool 46
Road mixer 618
 sweeper 618
 temporary 16
Roadway plate 618
Rock drill 442
 trencher 613
Rod backer 56

coupling hanger 100
pipe hanger 99
socket 102
threaded 99
tie 47
Roll hanger 100
 type air filter 351
Roller compaction 444
 sheepsfoot 444, 612
 tandem 612
 vibratory 612
Rolling ladder 15
 tower scaffold 15
Roof exhaust fan system 558
 exhauster 333
 fan 333
 flashing vent chimney 361
 frame opening 47
 jack residential 335
 paver 53
 paver and support 53
 sheathing 50
 specialty prefab 53
 support equipment 103
 support mechanical 103
 support pipe 103
Rooftop A/C removal 254
 air conditioner 391, 564-567
 heat pump 580
 make-up air unit 391
 multizone 566, 567
 multizone air conditioner .. 392
 multizone unit 566, 567
 single zone 565
 single zone unit 564, 565
 space heater 375
 variable air volume 393
Room clean 79
 humidifier 419
 unit removal computer 252
Rotary compressor 380
 crawler drill 614
 hammer drill 614
 hermetic compressor 379
 pump 238
Rotating chimney cap 349
Rototiller 612
Round damper 323
 damper fire 324
 diffuser 341
 duct 307
 duct fitting 308
 fire damper 324
 grease duct 311
 volume damper 323
Rubber pipe insulation 115
Rubbish handling 22

S

Saddle covering protection ... 101
 pipe support 101
 tap spiral 309
Safety equipment laboratory . 74
 plug pressure/temperature . 232
 valve gas 369
Salamander 616
Sales tax 10, 715, 716
Sampling air 25
Sand backfill 594
Sandblasting equipment 616
Sander floor 616
Sauna 80
Saw chain 616
 circular 616

concrete 610
 masonry 616
Sawn control joint 33
Scaffold baseplate 14
 bracket 14
 caster 14
 catwalk 15
 frame 14
 guardrail 14
 mason 14
 putlog 15
 rolling tower 15
 specialty 15
 stairway 14
 wood plank 14
Scaffolding 719
 plank 14
 tubular 14
School air-conditioner 573
 air-conditioning 540, 542, 565,
        567, 569, 571
Scissor lift 613
Scoop air 286
 air purging 286
Scotch marine boiler 367
Scraper earth 612
Screed, gas engine,
 8HP vibrating 610
Screening plant 612
Screw anchor 44
 lag 46
 liquid chiller 386
 machine 46
 water chiller 386
Scroll compressor 380
 water chiller 385
Scrubber air 614
Seal compression 55
 pipe 232
Sealant acoustical 57
 caulking 56
 control joint 33
 rigid joint 57
 tape 57
Sealer joint 55, 56
Security factor 8
 X-ray equipment 436
Sediment strainer Y valve 95
Seismic equipment pad 584
Self-closing relief valve 91
Self-contained air conditioner . 397
 air cooled unit 570, 571
Self contained dehumidifier .. 420
Self-contained single
 pkg A/C rmvl 254
 water cooled unit 568, 569
Semi-steel valve 259
Sensor circuit 286
 control component 272
Separation barrier 26, 28, 29
Separator 242
 air 284
 oil/water 494
Service boring 466
 residential 426
 station equipment 70
Setter circuit 287
Sewage collection PVC pipe .. 477
 collection vent 478
 ejector pump 243
 pipe 477, 479
 piping 597
Sewage/drainage collection .. 479
Sheathing 50
 roof 50
 roof & wall plywood 50

Index

wall 50
Sheepsfoot roller 444, 612
Sheet metal flashing 52
   metal transition 329
   piling 454, 744
Sheeting 454
   driver 614
   open 455
   tie back 455
   wale 454
   wood 443, 454, 744
Shell/tube heat exchanger 561
Shell-type heat exchanger 379
Shelving refrigeration 80
Shield expansion 44
   lag screw 44
Shift work 10
Shock absorber 235
   absorber pipe 235
Shoring baseplate 14
   bracing 14
   heavy duty 14
   leveling jack 14
   slab 15
   temporary 454
Short load concrete 38
Shot blaster 616
   chemical feeder 369
Shotcrete pump 610
Shoulder paver 618
Shovel crawler 612
Shredder compactor 76
Shutoff gas earthquake 369
Shut-off valve oil 278
Shutter damper removal flue 253
Sidewalk bridge 15
   broom 616
   removal 22
   temporary 18
Sidewall diffuser 342
Sightglass refrigeration 304
Sign 18
   detour 17
   project 18
Signal bell 438
Silencer aluminum duct 329
   duct 326
Silent check valve . . 92, 257, 260, 264
Silicone 56
   caulking 57
Sillcock hose bibb 247
Simplex style strainer 296
Single pipe roll 100
   pkg A/C mvl self-contained . . 254
   zone rooftop unit 391
Sink laboratory 73, 74
Site demolition 22
   drainage 494
   improvement 459
   utility 594
Sitework manhole 599
Skidder log 612
Skidsteer attachments 613
   loader 613
Slab edge formwork 32
   haunch 37
   haunch formwork 37
   on grade 37
   on grade formwork 32
   shoring 15
   thickened edge 37
   thickened edge formwork 37
   trench formwork 32
   turndown 37
   turndown formwork 37
Sleeve 232, 474

and tap 471
   cut in 474
   formwork 32
   pipe 232
   plastic pipe 32
   sheet metal pipe 32
   steel pipe 32
   wall 232
Slip on escutcheon flange 233
Slipform paver barrier 618
   paver curb 618
Slotted channel framing 47
   pipe 480
Smoke control kitchen 491
   detector 437
   exhaust duct 315
   vent chimney 354
Snow guard 53
Snubber valve 288
Socket hanger rod 102
Socket-o-let 170
Softener water 247
Soil compaction 444
   decontamination 24
   tamping 444
Solar air to water heat exchange . 529
   backflow preventer 378
   closed loop add-on hot water . 507
   closed loop hot water system . 519
   closed loop space/hot water . . 525
   drain back hot water 508
   draindown hot-water 511
   energy 377
   energy circulator air 376
   energy system . 507, 513, 515, 519,
      525
   energy system air purger 378
   energy system air vent 378
   energy sys. balancing valve . . . 378
   energy system collector 376
   energy system control valve . . 378
   energy system controller 377
   energy system expansion tank . 378
   energy sys. gauge pressure . . . 378
   energy sys. heat exchanger . . . 377
   energy system storage tank . . 377
   energy system thermometer . . 378
   energy system vacuum relief . 378
   heating 376, 735
   heating system 376
   hot water 517
   recirculation hot water 513
   swimming pool heater 527
   system solenoid valve 378
Solar-energy pool heater 527
   water-heater 517
Solder 128
Soldier beam 455
Solid fuel boiler 366
   fuel furnace 371
Sound trap duct 326
Source heat pump water 401
Space heater 615
   heater floor mounted 375
   heater removal 254
   heater rooftop 375
   heater suspended 375
   office & storage 13
Spade air 614
   tree 613
Specialty piping 268
   piping HVAC . . 228, 242, 289, 296,
      298
   refrigeration 303
   scaffold 15
Spill container fuel 278

Spin-in collar duct 315
   duct collar 315
Spinner ventilator 349
Spiral duct fitting 307
   duct preformed 307
   duct steel 307
   duct tap 309
   pipe supply register 347
   saddle tap 309
Split ductless removal 254
   ring hanger 98
   system control system 270
   system ductless 399
Splitter damper assembly 325
Spotter 450
Spray painting booth automotive . 70
   rig foam 615
   substrate 27
Sprayer airless 25
   emulsion 614
   paint 615
Spread footing 36
   footing formwork 32
Spreader aggregate 610, 617
   chemical 617
   concrete 616
Sprinkler irrigation system 459
   underground 459
Stabilizer base 618
Stainless cooling tower . . . 388, 546
   duct 306
   flashing 52
   louver 349
   steel fitting 189
   steel flange 194
   steel globe valve 264
   steel louver 349
   steel movable louver 60
   steel pipe 183
   steel tubing 182, 183
   steel valve 263
Stainless-steel insulation jacket . . 125
Stair temporary protection 18
Stairway scaffold 14
Stand heat pump 420
Standpipe steel 477
Starter board & switch 432
   motor 431
Station AHU removal central . . . 252
   control 432
Stationary ventilator 349
   ventilator mushroom 350
Steam bath 81
   bath residential 81
   boiler 363-365, 367
   boiler electric 361
   cleaner 616
   cock 287
   condensate meter 302
   condensate meter removal . . . 254
   energy distribution pipe 485
   fuel heater 279
   heat 406
   heat coil 405
   heating commercial 521
   humidifier 419
   jacketed kettle 73
   pipe 487
   pipe underground 483
   pressure reducing valve 230
   pressure valve 291
   radiator valve 292
   regulator pressure 231
   syphon pigtail 288
   trap 294
Steam-to-water heating 378

Steel channel 99
   cooling tower 546
   diffuser 343
   downspout 53
   drill 614
   drilling 45
   expansion tank 290
   fitting 150, 161
   flange 170, 179
   fuel tank double wall . . . 604, 605
   louver galvanized 61
   movable louver stainless 60
   oval arch corrugated pipe . . . 598
   pipe 143, 479
   pipe corrugated 478
   pipe fitting 150, 164
   pipe labor cutting 148
   pipe nipple 154
   register 346
   rivet 46
   sheet pile 454
   spiral duct 307
   standpipe 477
   storage tank 604, 605
   tank 290
   tank aboveground 284
   tank aboveground
      double wall 605
   tank aboveground
      single wall 605
   underground stor. tank . . 281, 282
   valve 259
   water storage tank 476
   water tank ground level 476
   well screen 468
Step manhole 467
Sterilizer dental 75
   glassware 74
   medical 74
Stiffleg derrick crane 619
Stoker fired boiler 366
Stop valve 247
Stop-start control station 432
Storage box 13
   potable-water 240
   room cold 79
   tank 282, 477
   tank concrete aboveground . . 284
   tank fiberglass rainwater 244
   tank fiberglass underground . . 239
   tank potable-water 239
   tank steel underground 281
   tank underground 282
Store air-conditioning . 539, 567, 568,
      570, 572
Storm drainage manhole frame . . 467
   drainage piping 479
Stove 68
   woodburning 68
Strainer 296
   basket type 296
   bronze body 298
   duplex style 297
   grooved joint 179
   simplex style 296
   Y type bronze body 298
   Y type iron body 298
Strap pipe hanger 103
Strapless outlet 173
Strap-on T outlet 178
Strip footing 37
Striper paint 618
Structural excavation 442
   welding 45
Stump chipper 612
Subcontractor O&P 11

Index

Subcontractors 730
Subdrainage pipe 478
   piping 504
   plastic pipe 478
   system 478
Submersible pump 244, 468, 616
   sump pump 244
Subsoil heating 79
Suction diffuser 299
   diffuser grooved joint 179
   diffuser pump 299
   hose 615
Sump hole construction 443
   pit 443
   pump 71, 244
   pump elevator 244
   pump submersible 244
Supermarket air-conditioning ... 540, 542, 565, 567, 569, 571, 573
Supply ductile iron pipe water ... 469
   HDPE water 472
Supply/return combination diffuser 342
Support framing pipe 47
   pipe 95
Suppressor lightning 426
Surfactant 27
Suspended space heater 375, 562
Suspension mounted heater 375
Swamp cooler 394
Sweeper road 618
Swimming pool 78
   pool equipment 78
   pool filter 248
   pool filtration 248
   pool heater 367
   pool painting 78
Swing check steel valve 259
   check valve 89, 257
   check valve bronze 89
Switch decorator 426
   dimmer 426
   residential 426
   well water pressure 469
Switchboard electric 432
System boiler hot-water 531
   boiler oil fired 533
   boiler steam 530
   component fuel 278
   control 269, 270
   exhaust 338
   fin-tube radiation 533
   grinder pump 242
   heat trace 415
   heating hydronic 533
   hydronic fossil fuel 532, 533
   pipe conduit 483, 486
   removal exhaust 253
   sitework catch basin 599
   sitework trenching ... 588, 590, 592
   solar-energy 513, 527
   solenoid valve solar 378
   subdrainage 478
   tube 84
   VAV box control 271

T

T outlet strap-on 178
Tag valve 106
Tamper 440, 614
Tamping soil 444
Tandem roller 612
Tank aboveground steel 284
   aboveground storage conc. ... 284
   clean 24
   compression 290
   corrosion resistant 290
   darkroom 70
   disposal 24
   expansion 290
   fiberglass 282
   fiberglass rainwater storage ... 244
   fiberglass underground storage 239
   horizontal above ground 284
   leak detection 437
   pillow 477
   potable-water storage 239
   removal 24
   steel 290
   steel underground storage ... 281
   storage 282, 477
   water 282, 477, 617
   water heater storage 240
   water htr liquid container 87
   water storage solar 378
Tank/wtr htr liquid ctnr removal .. 87
Tap and sleeve 471
   spiral duct 309
Tape barricade 17
   sealant 57
   underground 467
Tapping cross and sleeve 473
   main 473
   valve 474
Tar kettle 616, 618
Tarpaulin 16
   duck 16
   Mylar 16
   polyethylene 16
   polyvinyl 16
Tavern air-cond. ... 539, 541, 564, 566, 568, 570, 572
Tax 10
   sales 10
   Social Security 10
   unemployment 10
Taxes 716
T-bar grille eggcrate 345
   grille lay-in 344
   mount diffuser 342
Tee fitting monoflow 294
   HDPE piping 473
   pipe 176
   reducing 151
Telephone receptacle 429
Telescoping boom lift 613
Television receptacle 429
Temperature maintenance cable . 105
   relief valve 91
   rise detector 437
Tempering valve 92
   valve water 92, 229
Temporary barricade 17
   building 13
   construction 12, 16
   electricity 12
   facility 17
   fence 18
   guardrail 17
   light 12
   lighting 12
   power 12
   ramp 16
   road 16
   shoring 454
   toilet 616
   utility 12
Terminal A/C packaged 396
   A/C removal packaged 254
   air conditioner packaged 396
   heater 374, 412
Terne coated flashing 52
Test pressure 265
   ultrasonic 12
   well 468
Testing 12
   OSHA 27
   pipe 265
Thermoflo indicator 299
Thermometer 273
   solar energy system 378
   well 173
Thermostat 273
   automatic timed 273
   contactor combination 416
   control system radiator 271
   integral 415
   pneumatic 273
   wire 431
Thermosyphon hot-water 515
Thickened edge slab 37
Threaded flange 163
   nut 99
   rod 99
Threading labor st steel 187
   labor steel 148
Thread-o-let 169
Thru-the-wall A/C 581
   A/C removal 254
   heat pump 581
Thru-wall air conditioner 396
Tie back sheeting 455
   rod 47
Time lapse photography 12
Timer clock 429
   interval 426
   switch ventilator 336
Toggle-bolt anchor 44
Toilet chemical 616
   temporary 616
Tool polypropylene 218
   powder actuated 46
   rivet 46
Topping grout 39
Torch cutting 616
   cutting demolition 23
Tower cooling 387
   crane 13, 619, 720, 721
   hoist 619
   light 619
   liquid cooler 388
   removal cooling 252
Track drill 614
Tractor 444
   loader 612
   rake 612
   truck 617
Traffic line remover 618
Trailer bunk house 13
   floodlight 615
   low bed 618
   mud 618
   office 13
   platform 616
   truck 616
   water 617
Tram car 617
Transfer grille 344
Transition residential 335
   sheet metal 329
Transmitter control component .. 274
Trap cast iron 240
   drainage 240
   inverted bucket steam 294
   plastic 241
   polypropylene 241
   PVC 241
   steam 294
Trapeze hanger 100
Trash pump 616
Tree spade 613
Trench backfill 442, 594, 595
   box 617
   excavating 440
   excavation 440, 442
   utility 441
Trencher chain 441, 613
   rock 613
   wheel 613
Trenching 443, 589
   common earth 588, 589
   loam & sandy clay 590, 591
   sand & gravel 592, 593
Triple duty valve 258
Tripod floodlight 614
Trowel concrete 610
   power 610
Truck concrete 610
   crane flatbed 618
   dump 613
   flatbed 613, 617
   holding concrete 38
   mounted crane 619
   pickup 617
   tractor 617
   trailer 616
   vacuum 617
   winch 617
Tube and wire kit 399
   copper 128
   fitting 183
   fitting copper 131
   fitting pneumatic 276
   pneumatic 276
   system 84
   system air 84
   system pneumatic 84
Tubing connection split system .. 399
   copper 128
   copper type K 596
   (CSST) gas 279
   fitting PEX 414
   oxygen class copper 129
   PEX 203, 413
   polypropylene 203
   refrigeration 130
   stainless steel 182, 183
Tubular scaffolding 14
Tugboat diesel 620
Tunnel locomotive 618
   muck car 618
   ventilator 618
Turbine pump 238
   ventilator 349
   water meter 233
Turnbuckle 99
Turndown slab 37
Turning vane 327
TV inspection sewer pipeline ... 465

U

U-bolt pipe hanger 103
U-hook hanger 103
Ultrasonic test 12
Underdrain 467
Undereave vent 62
Underground chilled water pipe . 483
   hydronic energy 485
   piping 594

Index

sprinkler 459
steam pipe 483
storage tank 282
storage tank fiberglass 239
storage tank removal 722
storage tank steel 281, 282
tape 467
Underlayment self-leveling
   cement 39
Underwater light 78
Unemployment tax 10
Union dielectric 288
   PVC 214
Unit air-handling 389, 391, 408
   commercial kitchen 72
   gross area requirements 708
   heater 375, 401, 409
   heater cabinet 412, 417
   heater electric 416
   heater propeller 412
   heater removal hydronic 253
   line set evap/condes 399
   packaged indoor air-handling 390
   pkgd. outdoor air-handling 391
   removal condensing 252
   removal valance 253
Urethane insulation 80
Utensil washer medical 74
   washer-sanitizer 74
Utility accessory 467
   connection 467
   excavation 588, 590, 592
   fan system 557
   line removal 22
   set fan 331, 332
   structure 599
   temporary 12
   trench 441
   trench excavating 441

V

Vacuum breaker 235
   breaker air gap 235
   catch basin 617
   central 76
   cleaning 76
   dust collection 559
   gauge 272
   loader 25
   pick-up 610
   pump 248, 304
   pump medical 248
   system medical 248
   truck 617
   unit central 490
   wet/dry 617
Valance heater 401
   unit removal 253
Valve 254, 476
   balancing & shut-off 292
   ball 261
   ball check 94
   box 474
   brass 88
   brass ball 254
   bronze 88
   bronze angle 88
   bronze butterfly 89
   bronze/brass 254
   butterfly 255, 475
   check 476
   check lift 89
   circuit setter balance 287
   control solar energy system 378

CPVC 93
cut in 474
draindown 378
float 291
foot 94, 278
foot oil 278
forged 261
fusible oil 278
gas stop 88
gate 256, 260, 263, 475, 476
globe 256, 260, 263
grooved joint butterfly 180
grooved joint gate 180
heating control 291
hot water radiator 291
iron body 255
lubricated plug 259
materials 725-727
mixing 229
motor actuated 274
motor controlled 274
motorized zone 274
multipurpose 258
needle 94
nonfusible oil 278
oil shut-off 278
plastic 93
plastic angle 93
plug 259
pneumatic air operated 275
polypropylene 93
polypropylene ball 93
PVC 93
radiator 292
radiator supply 291
refrigeration 303
relief pressure 91
removal metal 87
removal plastic 87
selection considerations 725
semi-steel 259
snubber 288
soldered gate 90
stainless steel 263
stainless steel globe 264
steam pressure 291
steam radiator 292
steel 259
stop 247
swing check 89, 257
swing check steel 259
tag 106
tapping 474
tempering 92
triple duty 258
water pressure 91
water tempering 229
water utility distribution 475
Y sediment strainer 95
Y-check 95
zone 300
Vane air turning 327
turning 327
Vaneaxial fan 331
Vapor barrier 80
   hose adapter 278
   proof insulation 108
Vaporproof insulation 116
Variable air volume 393
   air volume rooftop 393
   frequency drive 432
   volume damper 322
VAV box 340
   mixing box 340
   terminal 555, 556
   terminal cooling only 555

terminal fan powered 555, 556
terminal hot water reheat 555
Vent air automatic 286
   alarm 279
   automatic air 286
   box 42
   brick 348
   cap 279
   chimney 354
   chimney all fuel 360
   chimney fitting 354, 360
   chimney flashing 355, 361
   chimney prefabricated rem. 254
   convector or baseboard air 411
   damper 354
   damper exhaust 325
   draft damper 354
   dryer 71
   exhaust 349
   flashing 241
   flashing and cap removal 87
   foundation 42
   gas 354
   intake-exhaust 350
   metal chimney 354
   radiator air 286
   removal relief 254
   ridge 53
   ridge strip 62
   sewage collection 478
Ventilating air cond. 271, 306, 322,
   324, 331, 333, 336, 350, 385, 388, 397
Ventilation equip. and hood 350
   fan 430
   garage 337
   kitchen 351
Ventilator chimney cap 349
   control system 270
   gravity syphon 349
   masonry 42
   mushroom stationary 350
   relief vent 350
   removal 254
   spinner 349
   stationary mushroom 350
   timer switch 336
   tunnel 618
   turbine 349
Venturi flow meter 300
Vertical discharge heater 417
Vibrating screed,
gas engine, 8HP 610
Vibration absorber 105
   absorbing hanger 105
   absorbing mount 105
   absorbing pad 106
Vibrator concrete 610
   earth 440, 444
   plate 444
   plow 613
Vibratory hammer 612
   roller 612
Video surveillance 436
Volume control damper 322
   damper round 323
Volume-control damper 321
VRV indoor AHU 409
   outdoor unit 400

W

Wafer check valve 92, 258, 264
Wale 454
   sheeting 454
Walk-in cooler evaporator 394

refrigeration 80
Wall cap residential 335
   exhaust fan 333
   fan 334
   furnace 370, 375
   heater 72
   hydrant 236
   louver 62
   mounted AHU 410
   register 347
   sheathing 50
   sleeve 232
Warm air heater 373
Washable air filter 351
   air filter permanent 351
Washer 99
   and extractor 70
   commercial 70
   pressure 616
   residential 71
Washer-sanitizer utensil 74
Washing machine automatic 71
Waste cleanup hazardous 24
   compactor 76
   disposal 76
   disposal hazardous 24
   handling 76
   handling equipment 76
   incinerator 76
   packaging 28
Water atomizer 25
   balancing 265
   booster system domestic 239
   chiller 383
   chiller absorption 383
   chiller centrifugal type 384
   chiller direct expansion 386
   chiller direct-fired 383
   chiller indirect-fired 383
   chiller reciprocating 384
   chiller removal 254
   chiller screw 386
   chiller scroll 385
   coil 402
   coil hot 404
   copper tubing connector 228
   distiller 74
   distribution pipe 469, 471
   filter commercial removal 87
   gauge 268
   gauge boiler 268
   hammer arrester 235
   heater 71, 430
   heater heat pump 400
   heater insulation 107
   heater residential 71, 430
   heater storage tank 240
   heater wrap kit 107
   heating hot 362, 411
   hose 615
   hydrant 236
   level control 268
   meter turbine 233
   pipe 469
   piping polyethylene 596
   pressure booster package 239
   pressure booster system 239
   pressure reducing valve 91
   pressure relief valve 91
   pressure switch well 469
   pressure valve 91
   pump 301, 468, 616
   pump fountain 248
   pumping 443
   reducer concrete 37
   softener 247

Index

softener removal 88
source heat pump 401
storage solar tank 378
storage tank indoor 240
supply detector meter 233
supply domestic meter 233
supply ductile iron pipe 469
supply HDPE 472
supply meter 233
supply PVC pipe 471
supply well pump 469
tank 282, 477, 617
tank elevated 476
tank ground level steel 476
tempering valve 92, 229
trailer 617
tube boiler 366
utility distribution valve ... 475
well 468
Water-cooled condensing unit ... 381
Water-heater solar-energy .. 509, 511, 513, 515, 519, 525
Water-source heat pump 401
Water-water exchange hot 379
Wearing course 458
Weatherproof receptacle 428
Wedge anchor 45
Weights and measures 712
Weld fitting 167
 fume hood removal 253
 joint pipe 144, 183
plastic pipe 222
X-ray 266
Welded beam attachment 95
 wire epoxy 36
 wire fabric 36
 wire galvanized 36
Welding fillet 46
 fume elimination 339
 labor stainless-steel 188
 labor steel 149
 machine 617
 structural 45
Weld-O-Let 169
Weld-on flange steel 170
Well 443
 & accessory 468
 casing PVC 468
 gravel pack 468
 pump 468
 pump shallow 469
 screen steel 468
 thermometer 173
 water 468
 water pressure switch 469
Wellpoint 443
 discharge pipe 620
 equipment rental 620
 header pipe 620
 pump 620
 riser pipe 620
Wellpoints 743
Wet/dry vacuum 617
Wheel trencher 613
Wheelbarrow 617
Wheeled loader 612
Whirlpool bath 75
Whole house fan 334
Widener pavement 618
Winch truck 617
Window A/C removal 254
 air conditioner 396
Windrow loader 618
Winter concrete 37
 protection 16
Wire 741
 fence 18
 thermostat 431
Wiring air conditioner 430
 fan 430
 residential 426, 429
Wood furnace 371
 gage stick 278
 gas furnace 372
 oil furnace 371
 plank scaffold 14
 sheet piling 744
 sheeting 443, 454, 744
Woodburning stove 68
Work boat 620
 extra 11
Worker protection 25
Workers' compensation 10, 718
Wrapping pipe 462
Wrecking ball 617
Wrench impact 614

X

X-ray equipment 436
 equipment security 436
 machine 436
 pipe 266
 weld 266

Y

Y sediment strainer valve 95
 type bronze body strainer 298
 type iron body strainer 298
Y-check valve 95

Z

Zone valve 300

Notes

Notes

Notes

Notes

Notes

Notes

Division Notes

		CREW	DAILY OUTPUT	LABOR-HOURS	UNIT	BARE COSTS				TOTAL INCL O&P
						MAT.	LABOR	EQUIP.	TOTAL	

Division Notes

Division Notes

		CREW	DAILY OUTPUT	LABOR-HOURS	UNIT	BARE COSTS				TOTAL INCL O&P
						MAT.	LABOR	EQUIP.	TOTAL	

Division Notes

		CREW	DAILY OUTPUT	LABOR-HOURS	UNIT	BARE COSTS				TOTAL INCL O&P
						MAT.	LABOR	EQUIP.	TOTAL	

Division Notes

		CREW	DAILY OUTPUT	LABOR-HOURS	UNIT	BARE COSTS				TOTAL INCL O&P
						MAT.	LABOR	EQUIP.	TOTAL	

Division Notes

		CREW	DAILY OUTPUT	LABOR-HOURS	UNIT	BARE COSTS				TOTAL INCL O&P
						MAT.	LABOR	EQUIP.	TOTAL	

Division Notes

	CREW	DAILY OUTPUT	LABOR-HOURS	UNIT	BARE COSTS				TOTAL INCL O&P
					MAT.	LABOR	EQUIP.	TOTAL	

Division Notes

	CREW	DAILY OUTPUT	LABOR-HOURS	UNIT	BARE COSTS				TOTAL INCL O&P
					MAT.	LABOR	EQUIP.	TOTAL	

2023 Training Class Options
A tradition of excellence in construction cost information and services since 1942

Virtual classes offered monthly. Call for the schedule. ☏ 877.620.6245

Gordian offers training classes in a variety of formats—eLearning training modules, instructor-led classes, on-site training, and virtual training classes, as well as custom solutions. Please visit our website at rsmeans.com/products/training/seminars for our current schedule of class offerings.

Training classes that are offered in one or more of our formats are: Building Systems and the Construction Process; Construction Cost Estimating: Concepts & Practice; Introduction to Estimating; Scope of Work for Facilities Estimating; Facilities Construction Estimating; Fundamentals to Construction Cost Estimating; Maintenance & Repair Estimating for Facilities; Mechanical & Electrical Estimating; RSMeans CostWorks CD; and RSMeans Data Online Training.

Registration Information

How to register
By Phone
Register by phone at 877.620.6245

Online
Register online at rsmeans.com/products/services/training

Note: Purchase orders or credits cards are required to register.

Instructor-led Government Pricing
All federal government employees save off the regular seminar price. Other promotional discounts cannot be combined with the government discount. Call 781.422.5115 for government pricing.

If you have any questions or you would like to register for any class or purchase a training module, call us at 877.620.6245.

Construction Cost Estimating: Concepts and Practice

This one- or two-day introductory course to improve estimating skills and effectiveness starts with the details of interpreting bid documents and ends with the summary of the estimate and bid submission.

Topics include:
- Using the plans and specifications to create estimates
- The takeoff process — deriving all tasks with correct quantities
- Summarizing the estimate to arrive at the final number
- Formulas for area and cubic measure, adding waste and adjusting productivity to specific projects
- Evaluating subcontractors' proposals and prices
- Adding insurance and bonds
- Understanding how labor costs are calculated
- Submitting bids and proposals

Who should attend: project managers, architects, engineers, owners' representatives, contractors, and anyone responsible for budgeting or estimating construction projects.

Fundamentals to Construction Cost Estimating

This self-paced course focuses on unit price estimating for facilities renovation, repair, and remodeling. Combining hands-on skill building with a discussion of best estimating practices and real-life problems, this informative online course will boost your estimating skills, bring you up to date with key concepts, and provide tips and guidelines that can save you time and help you avoid costly estimating oversights and errors.

Topics include:
- The three phases of estimating
- Bid document review
- How to perform quantity takeoffs
- How to price the work

Who should attend: facilities professionals and anyone involved in facilities planning, design, and construction.

For novice estimators, this course can serve as a primer to Facilities Construction Estimating Self-Paced Training or the following live training courses: Facilities Construction Estimating, Mechanical & Electrical Estimating, Assessing Scope of Work for Facilities Estimating, or Maintenance & Repair Estimating.

Visit rsmeans.com for more details.

Mechanical & Electrical Estimating

This two-day course teaches attendees how to prepare more accurate and complete mechanical/electrical estimates, avoid the pitfalls of omission and double-counting, and understand the composition and rationale within the RSMeans data mechanical/electrical database.

Topics include:
- The unique way mechanical and electrical systems are interrelated
- M&E estimates — conceptual, planning, budgeting, and bidding stages
- Order of magnitude, square foot, assemblies, and unit price estimating
- Comparative cost analysis of equipment and design alternatives

Who should attend: architects, engineers, facilities managers, mechanical and electrical contractors, and others who need a highly reliable method for developing, understanding, and evaluating mechanical and electrical contracts.

Facilities Construction Estimating

In this two-day course, professionals working in facilities management can get help with their daily challenges to establish budgets for all phases of a project.

Topics include:
- Determining the full scope of a project
- Understanding of RSMeans data and what is included in prices
- Identifying appropriate factors to be included in your estimate
- Creative solutions to estimating issues
- Organizing estimates for presentation and discussion
- Special estimating techniques for repair/remodel and maintenance projects
- Appropriate use of contingency, city cost indexes, and reference notes
- Techniques to get to the correct estimate quickly

Who should attend: facility managers, engineers, contractors, facility tradespeople, planners, and project managers.

Assessing Scope of Work for Facilities Construction Estimating

This two-day practical training program addresses the vital importance of understanding the scope of projects in order to produce accurate cost estimates for facilities repair and remodeling.

Topics include:
- Discussions of site visits, plans/specs, record drawings of facilities, and site-specific lists
- Review of CSI divisions, including means, methods, materials, and the challenges of scoping each topic
- Exercises in scope identification and scope writing for accurate estimating of projects
- Hands-on exercises that require scope, takeoff, and pricing

Who should attend: corporate and government estimators, planners, facility managers, and others who need to produce accurate project estimates.

CostWorks CD Self-Paced Training Course

This self-paced course helps users become more familiar with the functionality of the CD. Each menu, icon, screen, and function found in the program is explained in depth. Time is devoted to hands-on estimating exercises.

Topics include:
- Searching the database using all navigation methods
- Exporting RSMeans data to your preferred spreadsheet format
- Viewing crews, assembly components, and much more
- Automatically regionalizing the database

This training session requires users to bring a laptop computer to class and to follow along using a purchased copy of RSMeans data CostWorks CD.

When you register for this course you will receive an outline for your laptop requirements.

Maintenance & Repair Estimating for Facilities

This two-day course teaches attendees how to plan, budget, and estimate the cost of ongoing and preventive maintenance and repair for existing buildings and grounds.

Topics include:
- The most financially favorable maintenance, repair, and replacement scheduling and estimating
- Preventive planning and facilities upgrading
- Determining both in-house and contract-out service costs
- Annual, asset-protecting M&R plan

Who should attend: facility managers, maintenance supervisors, buildings and grounds superintendents, plant managers, planners, estimators, and others involved in facilities planning and budgeting.

RSMeans Data Online Training

Construction estimating is vital to the decision-making process at each state of every project. Our online solution works the way you do. It's systematic, flexible, and intuitive. In this self-paced course you will see how you can estimate any phase of any project faster and better.

Topics include:
- Customizing our online estimating solution
- Making the most of RSMeans data "Circle Reference" numbers
- How to integrate your cost data
- Generating reports, exporting estimates to MS Excel, sharing, collaborating, and more

Also offered as a self-paced or on-site training program!

Visit rsmeans.com for more details.

RSMeans data Training Cancellation Policy

Virtual Training (Individual)
If you are unable to attend a training class, a colleague may substitute at any time before the session starts by notifying the training registrar at 781.422.5115 or your sales representative. Gordian is not responsible for sending duplicate materials to the substitute colleague.

If you are unable to find a substitute and cancel fewer than ten (10) business days prior to the training class, you will either forfeit the registration fee or be allowed to apply your registration fee to the same class only once within the same calendar year. No-shows will forfeit their registration fees and no rescheduling is permitted. In the unfortunate circumstance that Gordian must cancel your event, Gordian will work with you to reschedule your attendance in the same training class at a later date or will fully refund your registration fee.

Any on-demand (self-paced) training modules are not eligible for cancellation, substitution, transfer, return, or refund.

Virtual Training (Private Group)
If you provide notice more than ten (10) business days prior to the training class, Gordian will work to reschedule your event. If you cancel your event fewer than ten (10) business days prior to the training class, you are responsible for paying for the trainer's time for the cancelled training, as well as the full cost of materials and shipping. In the unfortunate circumstance that Gordian must cancel your event, Gordian will work with you to reschedule your attendance in the same training class at a later date or will fully refund your registration fee.

Public Training Events (Individual)
If you are unable to attend a training conference, a colleague may substitute no fewer than ten (10) business days before the session starts by notifying the training registrar at 781.422.5115 or your sales representative. Gordian is not responsible for sending duplicate materials to the substitute colleague.

If you are unable to find a substitute and cancel fewer than ten (10) business days prior to the conference, you will forfeit the registration fee. No-shows will forfeit their registration fees and no rescheduling is permitted. In the unfortunate circumstance that Gordian must cancel your event, Gordian will fully refund your registration fee.

On-Site Training (Private Group)
If you provide notice more than ten (10) business days prior to the training class, Gordian will work with you to reschedule your event, but you are responsible for rescheduling fees associated with the trainer's time, airfare, and lodging. If you cancel fewer than ten (10) business days before your event, you are responsible for the full cost of the event. In the unfortunate event that Gordian must cancel your event, Gordian will work with you to reschedule your attendance at a later date or will fully refund your registration fee.

AACE Approved Courses
The AACE recognizes .1 CEUs per hour of training attended for all of Gordian's virtual training courses.

AIA Continuing Education
We are registered with the AIA Continuing Education System (AIA/CES) and are committed to developing quality learning activities in accordance with the CES criteria. Many seminars meet the AIA/CES criteria for Quality Level 2. AIA members may receive 14 learning units (LUs) for each two-day course.

Daily Course Schedule
The first day of each seminar session begins at 8:30 a.m. and ends at 4:30 p.m. The second day begins at 8:00 a.m. and ends at 4:00 p.m. Participants are urged to bring a hand-held calculator since many actual problems will be worked out in each session.

Continental Breakfast
Your registration includes the cost of a continental breakfast and a morning and afternoon refreshment break. These informal segments allow you to discuss topics of mutual interest with other seminar attendees. You are free to make your own lunch and dinner arrangements.

Hotel/Transportation Arrangements
We arrange to hold a block of rooms at most host hotels. To take advantage of special group rates when making your reservation, be sure to mention that you are attending the Gordian RSMeans data seminar. You are, of course, free to stay at the lodging place of your choice. Hotel reservations and transportation arrangements should be made directly by seminar attendees.

Important
Class sizes are limited, so please register as soon as possible.